Fundamentals of Mathematics

Integral Calculus

Sanjay Mishra

B.Tech.
Indian Institute of Technology, Varanasi

G K Publications (P) Ltd

Title : Fundamentals of Mathematics Integral Calculus

Language : English

Author : Sanjay Mishra

Typeset & Published by :

Career Launcher Infrastructure (P) Ltd.

A-45, Mohan Cooperative Industrial Area, Near Mohan Estate Metro Station, New Delhi - 110044

Marketed by :

G.K. Publications (P) Ltd.

Plot No. 63, Sector-27A, Near Sector - 28 Metro Station, Faridabad, Haryana-121003

ISBN : **978-81-93975-91-6**

Printer's Details : Printed in India, New Delhi.

For product information :

Visit ***www.gkpublications.com*** or email to ***gkp@gkpublications.com***

Preface

Two classical problems from geometry inspired the two biggest ideas in calculus. The problem of tangent line led us to the origin of differential calculus, whereas the problem of area motivated the advent of integral calculus. The origin of integral calculus can be sought back to the early period of development of mathematics and can be related to the method of exhaustion developed by ancient Greek mathematicians in an attempt to find area of plane figures, surface areas, and volumes of solid bodies. The development of above-method reached at its apex during the era of Eudoxus (440 BC) and Archimedes (300 BC). In 1665 AD, Newton proposed theory of fluxion in which he introduced the concept of anti-derivative as an inverse method of tangents to find tangent and radius of curvature of a function at any point. During the same period, Leibnitz (1684–86) published an article titled *Calculas sumatorius* which was about the summation of infinite number of small areas. Through this article, he was the first to propose the symbol $\int$. Later, he changed the name of article to *Calculus integrali* following the suggestion of J. Bernauli.

Both Newton and Leibnitz adopted quite an independent line of approach which was radically different from each other but finally concluded identical results. Although the theory of integral calculus and its connection with differential calculus were conclusively developed in the later works of Sir Isaac Newton, P. De Fermat, and G. Leibnitz at the dawn of the 17th century. Interestingly, rigorous analysis and justification, to establish above proposed theory, was given only after the concept of limit developed by A. L. Cauchy in 19th century.

This book has been written with the objective of providing a text book as well as an exercise book, focusing on problem solving in integral calculus. I feel that this will not only fulfill the need of a beginner (i.e., 10+2 students) but also meet the requirements of advance-level students who are preparing for various entrance examinations like IIT-JEE MAINS/ADVANCED, BIT-SAT, and other state engineering entrance examinations. This book develops a deep insight of topics, like 'indefinite integral', 'definite integral', 'area enclosed between curves' and 'differential equations' in detail. When I was studying Engineering, which was followed by an intensive teaching career, I realized that the topics of integral calculus find huge application in applied mathematics. Probably that is the reason why all competitive exams focus over these topics a lot. As far as applicability in competitive exams is concerned, all the topics of this book are highly scoring topics of Mathematics. Although the solving problems of indefinite integrals is very intuitive in nature whereas those of definite integrals is highly conceptual. One of the reasons for the phobia in the students mind against these topics is non-availability of good books that lay down these concepts in lucid manner. The well-arranged content list will help both students and teachers to access the topics conveniently. Each chapter is divided into several topics and subtopics. Each topic contains its theory and sometimes subtopics with sufficient number of worked out illustrative problems. This is followed by a textual exercise of both objective and subjective problems, as per the requirement. At the end of the theory, in each chapter, a large set of solved examples of both objective and subjective type is given. This will involve application of all the concepts learnt in the chapter so that students can develop expertise over the chapter. The tutorial exercise given at the end contains a large number of multiple-choice questions of single- and multiple-correct options and comprehension passage, the column matching problems, numerical integer-type questions to facilitate the students to do the thorough revision of entire chapter and to raise their level of understanding of these topics. For teachers, this text book will also be quite helpful as it will provide a set of well-graded problems, arranged topic and subtopic wise, that can be used as home assignment for their students.

All suggestions for improvement are welcome and shall be gratefully acknowledged.

Sanjay Mishra

Acknowledgements

I am really grateful to GK Publications for providing me an opportunity to transform my vast experience of teaching and knowledge into the present text book, *Fundamentals of Mathematics_Integral Calculus*. I would like to thank all my friends and teachers for their valuable criticism, support and advice that was really helpful to carve out this work. My interactions with students gave me the inspiration for writing this text book. Regular interaction with student made me strongly feel that I have learnt more than what I could have ever taught them. I wish to thank my parents and all my family members for their patience and support in bringing out this book and allocating their valuable share of time for such cause. I extend my special thanks to Rakesh Gupta, Sanket Sinha, Raj and other team members at MIIT Edu. Services Pvt. Ltd, for their hard work and dedication in completing this task.

Sanjay Mishra

Contents

Indefinite Integration

CHAPTER 1

■ INTRODUCTION

The name "integral" has its origin in the Greek word "summa" and its symbol $\int$ was proposed by G.W. Leibnitz (it is an abbreviated form of *S*). The integral is the "process of summation" and the word "to integrate" literally means "to find the summation of" but afterwards it was seen that the subject of integration can also be viewed as the inverse process of differentiation, i.e., to obtain a single variable function whose derivative function and an output of the function is known.

Each step in mathematics basically involves operating upon quantities/functions by various operators. For example, addition (+), subtraction (–), multiplication (×) and division (÷) are all operators. We have already learnt the operation of differentiation (i.e., of operate differential operator denoted by d/dx or D). Differentiable operator is an operator with which we operate the given function say $f(x)$ to obtain a function $f'(x)$ which represents the instantaneous rate of change of $f(x)$.

Let us understand that in mathematics, for every operator the possible existence of a reverse operator (that up-to the first) is explorable so that we arrive at the original quantity/function, for example if x is multiplied by 3 to yield $3x$, then $3x$ is divided (reverse operated) by 3 to yield the original quantity, i.e., x. Similarly, if $ex = y$, then we know that $\log ey = x$, i.e., taking $\log e(x)$ is a reverse operation of the operation of exponentiation. Therefore, addition and subtraction; multiplication and division; exponentiation and taking roots; logarithm and antilogarithm are pairs of inverse operations. Knowing that differentiation is essentially an operation, a natural question therefore arises: "does the reverse operation of differentiation exist?"

Let us ask more specific question. If we know the position of an object at different times, we can find the velocity of the object but knowing the velocity of the object, can we find its position at different times? The answer is almost yes. The question arises, "why is it not a strict yes?" More important question is, "how we can find this almost yes?" Other important questions are, can we always carry out this reverse process of differentiation on any given function? what are the different techniques of doing so? and most importantly, if this is how integral is defined, then why do we call it Indefinite Integral?

The answer to these and other related questions have been attempted in the next few pages. Here we will only say that each question of Integration is an experience. Each substitution is a tool and many such tools can be possible for same integral. The mastery over this chapter depends upon the ability to identify the most useful tool in a given situation. Remember, "where a needle is required, a sword is useless".

■ DEFINITION OF INTEGRAL

Integration is the process of finding limit of a sum of certain number of elements where, as the number of elements tends to infinity each element tends to become infinitesimally small". It originated in an attempt of finding general method to determine the area of a region with straight/curved boundaries, by dividing the region into an infinite number of infinitesimal area elements and getting the limit of their summation.

Once the method of such continuous sum was developed, then it was applied to various field, e.g., in Geometry; (to find length of arc, area, volume etc.), in Physics; (to find work done, current/heat flow, electric and magnetic field and potential), in Chemistry (to study radioactivity, chemical kinetics), in Engineering and Technology (to study pressure of fluids, centroid, moment of inertia of various object), in Geophysics and Geography etc.

Integral as Inverse Operation of Differentiation

In previous chapters we studied to find out a function $f(x)$ which is called as derivative of a given function $F(x)$ and we have defined such function as $f(x) = F'(x)$. Now we are going to consider the reverse problem that is given a function $f(x)$ and to find out a function $F(x)$ such that $F'(x) = f(x)$. So if $f(x)$ is derivative of $F(x)$ then $F(x)$ is called as anti-derivative of the function $f(x)$, and we can also define subject of integration as reverse operation of differentiation i.e., "Integration is a process of finding out the original function (primitive/indefinite integral or anti-derivative) from the derivative or differential expression".

$$\underbrace{f(x)}_{\text{primitive or antiderivative}} \underset{\int dx}{\overset{\frac{d}{dx}}{\rightleftarrows}} f'(x)$$

Anti-derivative of a Function

A function $F(x)$ is called an anti-derivative of the function $f(x)$ on the interval I, say $[x_1, x_2]$; iff at all the points of the interval I, $F'(x) = f(x)$, if x is terminal point of the interval i.e., x_1 or x_2, then $F'(x)$ shall be only one-sided derivative, e.g., $F'(x_1^+)$ at x_1 and $F'(x_2^-)$ at $x = x_2$. The use of an anti-derivative in place of "the anti-derivative" is deliberate. You will soon learn the reason for this.

For example, to find an antiderivative of the function $f(x) = 5x^4$ on the interval $x \in \mathbb{R}$, we seek a function F satisfying the condition $F'(x) = 5x^4 \ \forall\, x \in \mathbb{R}$. By our knowledge of differentiation we know that $F(x) = x^5$ is one such function, and a little thinking suggests many other solutions as well. For example, $F(x) = x^5 + 2, x^5 + 5, \ldots$ etc. In fact $F(x) = x^5 + C$, where C is an arbitrary constant is a set of all anti-derivatives of $f(x)$. (Think! is it really true? soon we will come back to it).

Anti-derivative via Concept of Differential

With regard to differential calculus we have taken $\frac{dy}{dx}$ as a compositive symbol for derivative function $F'(x)$ of $y = f(x)$ whose component parts dy and dx had no meaning by themselves.

Now it is the appropriate time to modify this point of view and attach meaning to dy and dx so that here-after we can treat $\frac{dy}{dx}$ as though it were a fraction (as we have derived in the topic differentiability) .

For a function of single variable $y = f(x)$ differential of y denoted by dy is a producte of derivative of y (w.r.t. x) and differential of x denoted by dx, i.e., $dy = f'(x)\, dx$.

For example, if $y = x^4$, then $dy = 4x^3dx$, i.e., $dx^4 = 4x^3dx$
Similarly $d(\sin x) = \cos x\, dx$, and $dy^2 = 2y\, dy$;
$d(\tan\theta) = \sec^2\theta\, d\theta$, $de^x = e^x dx$, ... etc.

$$\because \frac{d}{dx} f(x) = f'(x) \qquad \Rightarrow d(f(x)) = f'(x)dx$$

$$\Rightarrow \int f'(x)dx = \int df(x) \qquad \Rightarrow \int f'(x)dx = f(x) + c$$

ILLUSTRATION 1: Find the differential of the following functions:

(a) $x \sin x$ (b) $\ln\left(x + \sqrt{x^2+1}\right)$

(c) $\left(x - \frac{1}{x}\right)$ (d) $\sin\left(\frac{\log x}{x}\right)$

SOLUTION: For the function $y = f(x)$ the differential of y; $dy = f'(x)\, dx$ therefore

(a) $y = f(x) = x \sin x, \ \Rightarrow dy = df(x) = f'(x)\, dx \ \Rightarrow dy = (x \cos x + \sin x)dx$

(b) $y = \ln\left(x + \sqrt{x^2+1}\right) = f(x)$

$$\Rightarrow dy = f'(x)dx = \frac{1 + \frac{x}{\sqrt{x^2+1}}}{x + \sqrt{x^2+1}}dx \qquad \Rightarrow dy = \frac{dx}{\sqrt{x^2+1}}$$

(c) $y = x - \frac{1}{x}$ $\qquad \Rightarrow \frac{dy}{dx} = f'(x)$

$$\Rightarrow dy = f'(x)dx \qquad \Rightarrow dy = \left(1 + \frac{1}{x^2}\right)dx$$

(d) $y = \sin\left(\frac{\log x}{x}\right)$ $\Rightarrow dy = f'(x)dx$

$\Rightarrow dy = \cos\left(\frac{\log x}{x}\right).\left(\frac{1-\log x}{x^2}\right)dx$

ILLUSTRATION 2: Find $f(x)$ if $d(f(x))$ is given as

(a) $\sec x \tan x\, dx$ (b) $\left(1-\frac{1}{x^2}\right)dx$

(c) $\frac{2\log x}{x}dx$ (d) $e^x\left(x^2+2x\right)dx$

SOLUTION: (a) Given $df(x) = \sec x \tan x\, dx$

$\Rightarrow \int d\left(f(x)\right) = \int\left(\sec x \tan x\right)dx$

As we know that $\sec x \tan x$ is derivative of $\sec x$

i.e., $\frac{d}{dx}(\sec x) = \sec x \tan x$, thus, $\sec x \tan x\, dx = d(\sec x)$

$\Rightarrow f(x) = \int d\left(\sec x\right)$ $\Rightarrow f(x) = \sec x + C$

(b) Given $df(x) = 1-\frac{1}{x^2}dx$

$\Rightarrow \int d\left(f(x)\right) = \int\left(1-\frac{1}{x^2}\right)dx$ $\Rightarrow f(x) = x+\frac{1}{x}+C$

$\because$ Derivative of $x+\frac{1}{x}$ with respect to x is $1-\frac{1}{x^2}$

(c) $df(x) = \frac{2\log x}{x}dx$

$\int d\left(f(x)\right) = \int\frac{2\log x}{x}dx$

$\because$ $\frac{2\log x}{x}$ is derivative of $(\log x)^2$ $\Rightarrow \frac{d}{dx}(\log x)^2 = \frac{2\log x}{x}$

$\Rightarrow d\left(\log x\right)^2 = \frac{2\log x}{x}dx$ $\Rightarrow \int d\left(f(x)\right) = \int d(\log x)^2$

$\Rightarrow f(x) = (\log x)^2 + C$

(d) Differential coefficient of the function x^2e^x with respect to x is $e^x(x^2+2x)$

$\Rightarrow \frac{d}{dx}\left(x^2e^x\right) = e^x(x^2+2x)$

$\Rightarrow d\left(x^2e^x\right) = e^x(x^2+2x)dx$, taking anti-derivative, we get

$\Rightarrow \int e^x(x^2+2x)dx = \int d(x^2e^x)dx = x^2e^x + C$

ILLUSTRATION 3: Find the anti-derivative of following functions

(a) $3x^2+2$ (b) $\text{cosec } x.\cot x$

(c) $1/x$

SOLUTION: (a) Let $F'(x) = 3x^2 + 2$

$\therefore$ anti-derivative of $f'(x) = F'(x) = x^3 + 2x + c$

$\{$since $\frac{d}{dx}(x^3 + 2x + c) = 3x^2 + 2\}$

(b) $F'(x) = \text{cosec}x.\cot x$

$\therefore$ anti-derivative of $f'(x) = F'(x) = -\text{cosec } x + c$

$\{\because \frac{d}{dx}(\text{cosec } x + c) = \text{cosec } x.\cot x\}$

(c) $F'(x) = 1/x$

$\therefore$ anti-derivative of $F'(x) = F(x) = \ln x + c$ $\{\because \frac{d}{dx}(\ln x + c) = 1/x\}$.

Properties

(a) If for a given function $f(x)$ an anti-derivative $F(x)$ exist then it is never an unique function. Any two anti-derivatives of any function $f(x)$ differ only by a constant (also known as constant Difference Theorem).

Proof: If $F_1(x)$ and $F_2(x)$ are two anti-derivatives of a function $f(x)$ on an interval $[x_1, x_2]$, then applying the definition of anti-derivatives we have

$$\left.\begin{aligned} F'_1(x) = f(x) \\ F'_2(x) = f(x) \end{aligned}\right\} \qquad \ldots\text{(i)}$$

For any value of x on the interval $[x_1, x_2]$, if possible let us assume $F_1(x) - F_2(x)$ be a function $g(x)$ which is not constant. Then, we have $g(x) = F_1(x) - F_2(x)$

$\Rightarrow g'(x) = F'_1(x) - F'_2(x) = f(x) - f(x) = 0$

or $g'(x) = 0$

for each and every x on the interval $[x_1, x_2]$. Consequently we find that $g(x)$ is a constant. Applying is Lagrange's theorem to the function $g(x)$, which obviously continuous and differentiable on the interval $[x_1, x]$ for any arbitrary x on the interval $[x_1, x_2]$, we may conclude that there always exist atleast one c in the interval $[x_1, x]$, such that $g(x) - g(x_1) = (x - x_1)\, g'(c)$ and as a matter of fact $g'(c) = 0$, thus,

$$g(x) - g(x_1) = 0 \text{ or } g(x) = g(x_1) \qquad \ldots\text{(ii)}$$

Thus, the function $g(x)$ retains its value $g(x_1)$ at any point x of the interval $[x_1, x_2]$. Therefore, we conclude that the function $F_1(x) - F_2(x)$ is constant on $[x_1, x_2]$, Denoting this constant by C, we get from (i) and (ii),

$$F_1(x) - F_2(x) = C.$$

Hence, we can say that if two functions $F_1(x)$ and $F_2(x)$ have same derivative in the interval $[x_1, x_2]$, then there exists a number C such that $F_1(x) = F_2(x) + C$ $\forall x \in [x_1, x_2]$. For instance $\sec^2 x$ and $\tan^2 x$ in the interval $\left(-\frac{\pi}{2}, \frac{\pi}{2}\right)$ also $\sin^2 x$ and $-\cos^2 x$ on set of real numbers.

(b) Generally if $F(x)$ is anti-derivative of $f(\mathbf{x})$, then $F(x) + C$ (where C is arbitrary constant) is also an anti-derivative of $f(x)$. Therefore, anti-derivative of a function is not unique; existence of an anti-derivative means existence of infinitely many of these.

Indeed one can conclude from the discussion in the property (b) that, if for a given function $f(x)$ one anti-derivative $F(x)$ is obtained, then other anti-derivatives of the function $f(x)$ can be expressed in the form $F(x) + C$, where C is an arbitrary constant known as constant of integration. (Now your query must have been answered.)

ILLUSTRATION 4: Find the anti-derivatives of the following functions, and therefore, obtain one of them $F'(x) = 4x^3 + 6x^2$; passing through origin $(-2, 1)$.

SOLUTION: If $F'(x) = 4x^3 + 6x^2$, then one of the anti-derivative of the function is $F(x) = x^4 + 2x^3$

Therefore, the set of all anti-derivatives of $f(x)$ can be written as $F(x) + C$ i.e., $x^4 + 2x^3 + C$, where C is some constant parameter. These are family of parallel curves that can be obtained by translating $F(x) = x^4 + 2x^3$ continuously vertically. Hence, it is very obvious that for some suitable value of C one of the member of this family of curve can pass through any chosen point in xy plane. For instance the one passing through $(-2, 1)$ must satisfy $y = x^4 + 2x^3 + C$, thus, obtaining the value of C as 1. There are no other anti-derivatives of $4x^3 + 6x^2$ other than $y = x^4 + 2x^3 + 1$ that satisfies the given condition.

The equation $F'(x) = 4x^3 + 6x^2$ is called as a differential equation, and the condition $F(-2) = 1$ is known to be a boundary condition of F.

Conclusion

Given the differential expression $F'(x)$ and a boundary condition on F, one can find an unique anti-derivative $F(x)$ of $F'(x)$ satisfying the given boundary condition. This function $F(x)$ obtained is also known as particular solution/integral/primitive of the given differential equation.

(c) For anti-derivative of a function $f(x)$ to exist over an interval $[x_1, x_2]$ it is necessary that the function is continuous in that interval.

The anti-derivative of every function do not exist, For instance, let us consider a function $f(x)$ piecewise defined over the interval $[-1, 3]$, discontinuous at $x = 0$, as given in Fig. 1.1

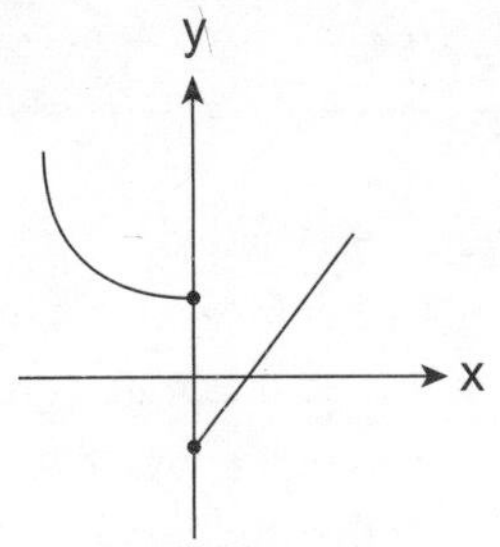

FIGURE 1.1

$F'(x) = f(x) = \begin{cases} 3x^2+2; & -1 \le x < 0 \\ 2x-1; & 0 \le x \le 3 \end{cases}$. Finding anti-derivative of $f(x)$ for both definitions, we observe

$$F(x) = \begin{cases} x^3+2x+C; & -1 \le x < 0 \\ x^2-x+C'; & 0 \le x \le 3 \end{cases}.$$

Clearly $F(x)$ to be anti-derivative of $f(x)$ $\forall x \in [-1,3]$ by definition, $F'(x) = f(x)$ $\forall x \in [-1,3]$.

Consequently $F'(0) = f(0) = -1$ should hold good.

$F'(x)$ to be defined first we make $F(x)$ continuous by choosing C and C' suitably such that: $F(a^-) = F(a^+)$

$\Rightarrow C = C'$

Now $F(x) = \begin{cases} x^3+2x+C; & -1 \le x < 0 \\ x^2-x+C; & 0 \le x \le 3 \end{cases}$

$\because$ $F'(x) = f(x)$ at $x = 0$

$\Rightarrow F'(0^+) = F'(0^-) = -1$ $\Rightarrow -1 = 2$ which is false.

Whereas if we consider a continuous function say $f(x)$ over an interval $[0, 3]$

E.g., $f(x) = \begin{cases} 3-2x; & 0 \le x \le 1 \\ 6x^2-5; & 1 < x \le 3 \end{cases}$

its anti-derivative is

$$F(x) = \begin{cases} 3x-x^2+C_1; & 0 \le x \le 1 \\ 2x^3-5x+C_2; & 1 < x \le 3 \end{cases}$$

Making $F(x)$ continuous on $[0, 3]$

$F(1^-) = F(1^+)$, we get $3 - 1 + C_1 = 2 - 5 + C_2$

$\Rightarrow C_2 = C_1 + 5$

The continuous anti-derivative thus obtained, is

$$F(x) = \begin{cases} 3x-x^2+C; & \text{if } x \in [0,1] \\ 2x^3-5x+5+C; & \text{if } x \in (1,3] \end{cases}$$

Indeed we observe that $F'(x) = f(x)$ $\forall x \in [0,3]$

$\because$ $F'(1^-) = F'(1^+) = f(1) = 1$

Hence, without any rigorous proof we conclude here that if a function $f(x)$ is continuous on an interval $[x_1, x_2]$, then its anti-derivative exist over that interval (Rigorous proof is beyond the scope of this book).

(d) Although, if a function $f(x)$ is continuous in $[x_1, x_2]$, then its anti-derivative exist, but it is not necessary that it can be expressed in terms of elementary functions. The process of finding derivative is definite in nature, and derivative of a function is always expressed in terms of elementary functions, whereas the anti-derivative of an elementary function is not necessarily expressible as combination of finitely many elementary functions (although it exists). Such elementary functions are called non-elementary integrals. These will be elaborated at the end of this topic. The process of finding indefinite integral is very intuitive in nature, that is why some-times it appears to be a guess work, inspite the methods are available to carry out the operation over the vast range of integrand functions. The present topic is basically dedicated to learn these methods that facilitate the so-called guess work to judge the correct anti-derivative of the given integrand function.

ILLUSTRATION 5: Find $f(x)$, given $f''(x) + \sin x = 0$, $f'(\pi) = a$ and $f(0) = 1$.

SOLUTION: $f''(x) + \sin x = 0$ $\Rightarrow f''(x) = -\sin x$

$\int d(f'(x)) = -\int \sin x\, dx$

$\Rightarrow f'(x) = \cos x + C$ $\Rightarrow a = f'(\pi) = -1 + C$

$\Rightarrow C = a + 1$ $\Rightarrow f'(x) = \cos x + a + 1$

$\Rightarrow \int d(f(x)) = \int (\cos x + a + 1)\, dx$ $\qquad \Rightarrow f(x) = \sin x + ax + x + C$

Also $f(0) = 1$ (given) $\Rightarrow \quad C = 0$ $\qquad \Rightarrow f(x) = \sin x + (a + 1)x$.

ILLUSTRATION 6: A curve $y = f(x)$ is such that $f''(x) = 6x$ at each point (x, y) on it and crosses the x-axis at $(-1, 0)$ at an angle of 135°. Find the value of $f(1)$.

SOLUTION: $f''(x) = 6x$

$\Rightarrow \int d(f'(x)) = \int 6x\, dx$ $\qquad \Rightarrow f'(x) = 3x^2 + C$.

Also $f'(-1) = -1$ ($\because$ angle subtended by tangent at $x = -1$ is 135°)

$\Rightarrow -1 = 3 + C$ $\qquad \Rightarrow C = -4$

$\Rightarrow f'(x) = 3x^2 - 4$ $\qquad \Rightarrow \int d(f(x)) = \int (3x^2 - 4)\, dx$

$\Rightarrow f(x) = x^3 - 4x + C$. Also $f(-1) = 0$

$\Rightarrow 0 = -1 + 4 + C$ i.e., $C = -3$

$\Rightarrow f(x) = x^3 - 4x - 3$ $\qquad \Rightarrow f(1) = -6$.

INDEFINITE INTEGRAL (DEFINITION)

If the function $F(x)$ is an anti-derivative of $f(x)$, then the expression $F(x) + C$ is the indefinite integral of the function $f(x)$ and is denoted by the symbol $\int f(x)\, dx$. It is the set of all anti-derivatives of $f(x)$ thus, by definition $\int f(x)\, dx = F(x) + C$ if $F'(x) = f(x)$

Here, the function $f(x)$ is called the integrand, $f(x)dx$ is the element of integration (the expression under the integral sign), the variable x the variable of integration, and $\int$ is the integral sign. The symbol $\int$ for the integral was introduced by Leibnitz. This elongated S stood for a "sum" in his notation.

$$\underbrace{\int}_{\text{symbol of integration}} \underbrace{f'(x)}_{\text{integrand}} \overbrace{dx}^{\text{integral element}} = \underbrace{f(x)}_{\text{antiderivative}} + \underbrace{C}_{\text{cosntant of integration}}$$

REMARK

The above process is known as indefinite integration due to the presence of constant of integration. Also the result becomes an indefinite function.

Geometric Significance

Therefore, geometrically an indefinite integral $\int f(x)\, dx$ is a family of curves $y = F(x) + C$, each of whose members is obtained by translating any one of the curves parallel to itself vertically upwards or downwards (that is, along the y-axis).

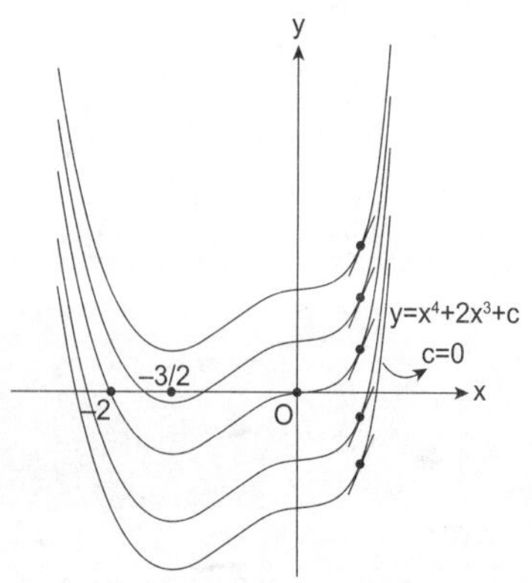

FIGURE 1.2

The members of this family of curves are known as integral curves of the function $y = f(x)$. It is evident from the above discussion that each and every integral curve has same slope at the points having common abscissa (say x_0), given by $f'(x_0)$, i.e., y tangent to the integral curves at such points are parallel.

Algebra of Integration:

If $f(x)$ and $g(x)$ are two integrable functions whose anti-derivative exist then the following results hold good.

- ❑ **Constant Rule:** $\int c dx = c \int x^0 dx = cx + b$

Proof: $\frac{d}{dx}(cx + b) = c$; for all c independent of x

$\Rightarrow d(cx + b) = c\, dx$

$\Rightarrow \int c\, dx = cx + b$

- **Constant Multiple Rule:** $\int kf(x)dx = k\int f(x)dx$

Proof: It is only required to prove that the derivative of $k\int f(x)dx$ is $k.f(x)$.

Consider the R.H.S. function and differentiate with respect to x.

$$\frac{d}{dx}\left(k\int f(x)dx\right) = k\frac{d}{dx}\left(\int f(x)dx\right) = kf(x)$$

- **Addition Rule:**

$$\int\{f(x)\pm g(x)\}dx = \int f(x)dx \pm \int g(x)dx$$

Proof: To prove the above it is sufficient to show that the derivative of $\int f(x)dx \pm \int g(x)dx$ is $f(x) \pm g(x)$

Therefore, consider $\frac{d}{dx}\left(\int f(x)dx \pm \int g(x)dx\right)$

∵ We know that derivative operation distributes over sum and difference, thus,

$$= \frac{d}{dx}\left(\int f(x)dx\right) \pm \frac{d}{dx}\left(\int g(x)dx\right) = f(x) \pm g(x)$$

The above rule can be extended to any finite number of functions. For instance,

$$\int\{(u(x))\pm v(x)\pm w(x)\}\,dx$$
$$= \int u(x)dx \pm \int v(x)dx \pm \int w(x)\,dx$$

- **Product Rule:**

$$\int f(x).g(x)dx = \int u.v\,dx = u\int v dx - \int\left(u'\int v dx\right)dx\,;$$

$u = f(x)$; $v = g(x)$

Proof: It suffices to prove that derivative of RHS is $u\,.\,v$, i.e., $f(x)\,.\,g(x)$

Consider the R.H.S. expression, i.e.,

$$u\int v\,dx - \int\left(\frac{du}{dx}\int v\,dx\right)dx$$

Differentiating with respect to x; applying algebra of differentiates

$$\frac{d}{dx}\left(u\int v\,dx\right) - \frac{d}{dx}\int\left(\frac{du}{dx}\int v\,dx\right)dx$$

$$= u\left(\frac{d}{dx}\int v\,dx\right) + \left(\int v\,dx\right)\frac{du}{dx} - \frac{du}{dx}\int v\,dx$$
$$= u.v = f(x).g(x)$$

Note: (i) Note the following representations:

(a) $\frac{d}{dx}\left(\int f(x)\,dx\right) = f(x)$ or $d\left(\int f(x)\,dx\right) = f(x)$

(b) $\int f'(x)\,dx = \int df(x) = f(x) + C$

Proof: Since

$$\int f'(x)\,dx = \int\frac{d}{dx}f(x)\,dx = \int df(x) = f(x) + C$$

- **Power Rule:** If r is any rational number except -1, then $\int x^r dx = \frac{x^{r+1}}{r+1} + C$

Proof: To establish any result of the form $\int f(x)\,dx = F(x) + C$, it is sufficient to show that $\frac{d}{dx}[F(x)+C] = f(x)$. In our case,

$$\frac{d}{dx}\left[\frac{x^{r+1}}{r+1} + C\right] = \frac{1}{r+1}(r+1)x^r = x^r$$

We make two comments about above rule . First, it is meant to include the case $r = 0$, that is $\int 1.dx = x + C$. Second, since no interval I is specified, the conclusion is understood to be valid only on intervals on which x^r is defined. In particular, we must exclude any interval containing the origin if $r < 0$.

- **Generalized Rule:** Let f be a differentiable function and n a rational number different from -1.

Then $\int[f(x)]^n f'(x)dx = \frac{[f(x)]^{n+1}}{n+1} + C$

Proof: Let $y = \frac{(f(x))^{n+1}}{n+1} + C$; $\frac{dy}{dx} = (f(x))^n.f'(x)$

$\Rightarrow dy = (f(x))^n.f'(x)dx$

$\Rightarrow \int(f(x))^n.f'(x)\,dx = \int dy$

$\Rightarrow \int f^n(x).f'(x)\,dx = \frac{(f(x))^{n+1}}{n+1} + C.$

ILLUSTRATION 7: Find (a) $\int(x^4+3x)^{30}(4x^3+3)dx$ and (b) $\int\sin^{10}x\cos x\,dx$

SOLUTION: (a) $\int(x^4+3x)^{30}(4x^3+3)dx$, then $g'(x) = 4x^3 + 3$, $g(x) = x^4 + 3x$.

Thus, $I = \int g(x)^{30}g'(x)dx = \frac{[g(x)]^{31}}{31} + C$ (by using last generalized rule)

$$\therefore \int(x^4+3x)^{30}(4x^3+3)dx = \frac{[g(x)]^{31}}{31} + C = \frac{(x^4+3x)^{31}}{31} + C$$

(b) Let g(x) = sinx, then $g'(x) = \cos x$

$\therefore \int \sin^{10} x \cos x \, dx = \int [g(x)]^{10} g'(x) \, dx = \frac{\sin^{11} x}{11} + C$

Now we can see why Leibniz used the differential dx in his notation $\int (g(x)^r g'(x) \, dx$.

If we let $u = g(x)$, then $g'(x)dx = du$. The conclusion of last generalized result is therefore, $\int u^r du = \frac{u^{r+1}}{r+1} + C$, $r \neq -1$

which is the ordinary power rule with u as variable. Thus, the generalized power rule is just the ordinary power rule applied to function. But in applying it, we must always make sure that we have to go with u'. The following examples illustrate what we mean.

Note: $\int x^n dt = tx^n + c$ and $\int e^x da = ae^x + c$

Proof: Since x^n with respect to t is a constant, therefore, applying constant multiple rule, we can take out x^n outside the integral symbol. Thus, $\int x^n \, dt = x^n \int t^0 \, dt = x^n t + C$

❑ **Theorem:** If $f(x)$ and $g(x)$ are two continuous functions such that $\int f(x)dx = g(x) + C$, then integral of $f(ax + b)$ with respect to x is given by $\frac{1}{a}(g(ax+b)) + C$

Proof: $\int f(ax+b)dx = \int f(ax+b).\frac{d(ax+b)}{d(ax+b)} dx$

$$= \int \frac{f(ax+b).d(ax+b)}{\frac{d}{dx}(ax+b)}$$

$$= \frac{1}{a} \int f(ax+b).d(ax+b)$$

$$= \frac{1}{a}(g(ax+b)) + C$$

ILLUSTRATION 8: Find the primitive of function $f(x)$ with respect to variable $(x - 1)$. Given f is a polynomial function defined by $f(x^2 - 2) = x^4 - 3x^2 + 4 \ \forall x \in \mathbb{R}$

SOLUTION: Let $x^2 - 2 = z$ $\Rightarrow x^2 = 2 + z$

$\Rightarrow f(z) = (2 + z)^2 - 3(2 + z) + 4$ $\Rightarrow f(z) = z^2 + z + 2$

$\Rightarrow \int f(x) \, d(x-1) = \int (x^2 + x + 2) \, d(x-1) = \int (x^2 + x + 2) \, dx = \frac{x^3}{3} + \frac{x^2}{2} + 2x + C$

Ans. $\frac{x^3}{3} + \frac{x^2}{2} + 2x + C$

ILLUSTRATION 9: Prove that $\int \frac{t^{2m} - 1}{t^2 - 1} dt = t + \frac{1}{3}t^3 + \frac{1}{5}t^5 + ... + \frac{1}{2m-1}t^{2m-1}$.

SOLUTION: As we know from summation of GP that $1 + t^2 + t^4 + t^6 + ... + t^{2m-2} = \frac{t^{2m} - 1}{t^2 - 1}$

$\Rightarrow \sum_{k=0}^{m-1} t^{2k} = \frac{t^{2m} - 1}{t^2 - 1}$

Integrating both sides w.r.t. x we get $\int \sum_{k=0}^{m-1} t^{2k} dt = \int \frac{t^{2m} - 1}{t^2 - 1} dt$

As integral distribute over sum of function (by property), so, we get

$\int \frac{t^{2m} - 1}{t^2 - 1} dt = \sum_{k=0}^{m-1} \int t^{2k} dt = \sum_{k=0}^{m-1} \frac{t^{2k+1}}{2k+1} = t + \frac{t^3}{3} + \frac{t^5}{5} + \frac{t^7}{7} + ... + \frac{t^{2m-1}}{2m-1}$. Hence proved.

TEXTUAL EXERCISE-1: (SUBJECTIVE)

1. Find an anti-derivative of the function:

   (i) $f(x) = 2x + 6x^2 - 12x^3$

   (ii) $f(x)=\dfrac{1}{2\sqrt{x}}+x^2\sqrt{x}-2x+1$

   (iii) $f(x)=\sqrt[3]{x+1}$

   (iv) $f(x)=\left(\dfrac{1}{4}x+1\right)^3$

2. Explain that the indefinite integral of any integrable function represents the family of parallel curves and find the integral curves for the following equations and represent them geometrically.

   (a) $a\,dy = bx\,dx;\ a, b > 0$

   (b) $dy = \cos x\ dx$

   (c) $a^{-x/2}dy = a^{x/2}dx$, $a > 0$ and $\neq 1$

3. Prove that the following pair of functions differ by constant, by showing that they are anti-derivatives of the same function and find that constant.

   (a) $f(x)=3-\cos 2x$ & $g(x)=\sin^2 x-\cos^2 x$

   (b) $f(x)=x^2-3x+4$ & $g(x)=\left(x-\dfrac{3}{2}\right)^2-\dfrac{1}{4}$

4. Given f and g be two non-uniformly defined functions as $f(x)=\begin{cases}x^2-1\ ; & x\neq 0\\ 0\ ; & x=0\end{cases}$ and

   $g(x)=\begin{cases}x^2+2; & x\geq 0\\ -3+x^2; & x<0\end{cases}$

   Verify the truth of the following statements.

   S_1: f and g have the same derivative.

   S_2: $f(x)\neq g(x)+C$ for any value of the constant C.

   S_3: Do the statements S_1 and S_2 violate the constant difference theorem? Explain.

5. Prove that the function $f(x)$ given below do not have an anti-derivative on any interval which contains 1.

   (i) $f(x)=\begin{cases}x^2-4; & x<1\\ x^2+2; & x\geq 1\end{cases}$

   (ii) $f(x)=\begin{cases}3+2x^2; & x\neq 0\\ 3; & x=0\end{cases}$

6. Find the function satisfying the given equation and the boundary conditions.

   (i) $f'(x)=2(x-1)^5,\ f(2)=4$

   (ii) $f''(x)=6, f'(0)=2, f(1)=4$

7. Prove that

   $$\int\frac{x^{3m}-1}{x^3-1}dx = x+\frac{x^4}{4}+\frac{x^7}{7}+\frac{x^{10}}{10}+\ldots+\frac{x^{3m-2}}{3m-2}.$$

8. Find the function $y = f(x)$ satisfying the following conditions:

   (a) $\dfrac{dy}{dx}+\dfrac{x}{y}=0;\ y=2$ at $x=0$

   (b) $\dfrac{dy}{dx}=y^3(x^3-x);\ y=4$ at $x=0$

   (c) $\dfrac{dy}{dx}=(2x+1)^4;\ y=6$ at $x=0$

   (d) $\dfrac{dy}{dx}=-y^2x(x^2+2)^4;\ y=1$ at $x=0$

9. In each case, find a function f satisfying the given conditions.

   (a) $f'(x^2)=\dfrac{1}{x}\ \forall x>0,\ f(1)=1$

   (b) $f'(\sin^2 x)=\cos^2 x\ \forall\ x,\ f(1)=1$

   (c) $f'(\sin x)=\cos^2 x\ \forall\ x,\ f(1)=1$

   (d) $f'(\ln x)=\begin{cases}1; & 0<x\leq 1\\ x; & x>1\end{cases},\ f(0)=0$

10. A function g, defined for all positive real numbers, satisfies the following two conditions:

    $g(1) = 1$ and $g'(x^2) = x^3$ for all $x > 0$. Compute $g(4)$.

Answer Keys

1. (i) $x^2 + 2x^3 - 3x^4$ (ii) $\sqrt{x}+\dfrac{2}{5}x^{5/2}-x^2+x$ (iii) $\dfrac{3}{4}(x+1)^{4/3}$ (iv) $\left(\dfrac{x+4}{4}\right)^4$

2. (a) $y=\dfrac{b}{2a}x^2+C$ (b) $y=\sin x+C$ (c) $y=\dfrac{a^x}{\ln a}+C$

3. (a) 3 (b) 2

6. (i) $\dfrac{1}{3}\left((x-1)^6+11\right)$ (ii) $3x^2+2x-1$

8. (a) $y=\sqrt{4-x^2}$ (b) $y=\dfrac{4}{\sqrt{1+16x^2-8x^4}}$ (c) $y=\dfrac{(2x+1)^5}{10}+\dfrac{59}{10}$ (d) $y=\dfrac{10}{(x^2+2)^5-22}$

9. (a) $f(t)=2\sqrt{t}-1$ if $t>0$ (b) $f(t)=t-\frac{1}{2}t^2+\frac{1}{2}$ if $0\le t\le 1$

(c) $f(t)=t-\frac{1}{3}t^3+\frac{1}{3}$ if $|t|\le 1$ (d) $f(t)=t$ if $t\le 0$; $f(t)=e^t-1$ if $t>0$ **10.** 67/5

TEXTUAL EXERCISE–1: (OBJECTIVE)

1. Given $f''(x)=2$, $f'(0)=-1$ and $f(2)=1$, then which of the following is/are true about $f(x)$.
(a) $f(-1)=1$
(b) $f(x)$ is a parabolic curve
(c) $f(x)$ increases for all x greater than 1
(d) None of these

2. Given a function f such that $f(0)=3$, $f(1)=2$, and $f''(x)=0$ for all x. Then the number of functions satisfying the above condition is/are
(a) one (b) two
(c) three (d) infinitely many

3. Which of the following statements is/are true?
(a) Anti-derivative of an even function is always an odd function.
(b) Anti-derivative of an odd function is always an even function.
(c) Anti-derivative of periodic function is always periodic.
(d) None of these.

Hints. ($f(x)=1+\cos x$ is a periodic function and $F(x)=\int(1+\cos x)\,dx=x+\sin x+C$ is a non-periodic function)

4. The anti-derivatives of the function $f(x)=3x-2$ whose graphs touch the curve $y=\frac{1}{3}x^3$ are
(a) $\frac{3}{2}x^2-2x+\frac{5}{6}$ (b) $\frac{3}{2}x^2+2x+\frac{2}{3}$
(c) $\frac{3}{2}x^2+2x+\frac{5}{6}$ (d) $\frac{3}{2}x^2-2x+\frac{2}{3}$

5. Given $f''(x)=3\cos 2x-1$ and $f(0)=0$ and $|f(0)|=1$, then the function $4f(x)$ is/are
(a) $7+2x^2-3\cos 2x$ (b) $7-2x^2-3\cos 2x$
(c) $3\cos 2x+2x^2-1$ (d) $3\cos 2x+2x^2+1$

6. A polynomial $f(x)$ of degree ≤ 4 satisfying the condition $f(0)=1$, $f(1)=-4$, $f'(0)=0$; $f''(0)=-40$; $f'(1)=5$ is.
(a) $15x^3-20x^2+1$ (b) $15x^2-12x+1$
(c) $15x^4-12x^3+1$ (d) None of these.

7. Find a function f such that $f''(x)=x+\cos x$ and such that $f(0)=4$ and $f'(0)=2$.
(a) $\frac{x^3}{6}-\cos x+2x+5$
(b) $\frac{x^3}{3}-\cos x+3x+5$
(c) $\frac{x^3}{3}-\cos 2x+3x+5$
(d) None of these

8. Find the xy-equation of the curve through (1, 2) whose slope at any point is three times its x-coordinate.
(a) $y=3x^2-1$ (b) $2y=3x^2+1$
(c) $y=x^2+1$ (d) None of these

9. Find the xy-equation of the curve through (–4, 1) whose slope at any point is one third the square of its y-coordinate.
(a) $x^2y+y-17=0$ (b) $xy+3y+1=0$
(c) $xy+y+3=0$ (d) None of these

Answer Keys

1. (a, b, c) **2.** (a) **3.** (b) **4.** (a, d) **5.** (b, d) **6.** (a) **7.** (a) **8.** (b) **9.** (c)

INTEGRAL OF SOME STANDARD FUNCTIONS

As we have already experienced that in order to prove $\int f(x)dx = F(x)+C$, it is sufficient to show that $F'(x) = f(x)$, therefore from our experience of differentiation we can derive a list of standard functions and their integrals as illustrated below. The proofs of these results are trivial, hence, they are left to the students as an exercise.

(a) Algebraic and Exponential Functions:

f(x)	$\int f(x)dx$	f(ax + b)	$\int f(ax+b)dx$
$x^n; n \neq -1$	$\frac{x^{n+1}}{n+1}+C$	$(ax+b)^n; n \neq -1$	$\frac{(ax+b)^{n+1}}{(n+1)a}+C$
$\frac{1}{x}$	$\ln\|x\| + C$	$\frac{1}{ax+b}$	$\frac{\ln(ax+b)}{a}+C$
$a^x; a>0; a \neq 1$	$\frac{a^x}{\ln a}+C$	$a^{bx+c}; a>0; a\neq 1; b \neq 0$	$\frac{1}{b}\left(\frac{a^{bx+c}}{\ln a}\right)+C$
e^x	$e^x + C$	$e^{ax+b}; a \neq 0$	$\frac{1}{a}e^{ax+b}+C$

ILLUSTRATION 10: Find the following integrals:

(a) $\int \frac{1}{\sqrt{5x+2}}dx$ (b) $\int e^{\ln\left(\sqrt{2x+3}\right)}dx$

(c) $\int e^{2\ln x + 4\ln 2}dx$

SOLUTION: (a) Consider integral $I = \int \frac{1}{\sqrt{5x+2}}dx = \int (5x+2)^{-1/2}dx$.

Now applying the standard form, we get

$$\Rightarrow I = \frac{1}{5}\left[\frac{(5x+2)^{-\frac{1}{2}+1}}{-\frac{1}{2}+1}\right]+C = \frac{2}{5}(5x+2)^{1/2}+C.$$

(b) Given integral $I = \int e^{\ln(2x+3)^{1/2}}dx$

Since $e^{\ln x} = x$ as e^x and $\ln x$ are inverse functions of each other, therefore,

$$\Rightarrow I = \int (2x+3)^{1/2}dx = \frac{1}{2}\frac{(2x+3)^{\frac{1}{2}+1}}{\frac{1}{2}+1}+C = \frac{1}{3}(2x+3)^{\frac{3}{2}}+C$$

(c) $\int e^{\ln x^2 + \ln 16}dx = \int e^{\ln(16x^2)}dx = 16\int x^2 dx = \frac{16x^3}{3}+C$

ILLUSTRATION 11: Find the following integrals:

(a) $\int \frac{x}{3-2x}dx$ (b) $\int \frac{x}{x^2+4x+4}dx$

(c) $\int \frac{x^2+2x}{x^2+3x+2}dx$

SOLUTION: (a) $I = \left(-\frac{1}{2}\right)\int \frac{(-2x)}{3-2x}dx = \left(\frac{-1}{2}\right)\int \frac{3-2x-3}{(3-2x)}dx$

$$= \frac{-1}{2}\int\left(\frac{3-2x}{3-2x} - \frac{3}{(3-2x)}\right)dx = -\frac{1}{2}\int\left(1 - \frac{3}{3-2x}\right)dx$$

$$= \frac{-1}{2}\left[x - 3\left(\frac{-1}{2}\right)\ln(3-2x)\right] + C = \frac{-1}{2}\left[x + \frac{3}{2}\ln(3-2x)\right] + C$$

(b) Given integral $I = \int \frac{x}{x^2+4x+4}dx$

Observe the perfect square expression in the denominator of the integrand function, and thus, adding and subtracting 2 in the numerator, we get

$$I = \int \frac{x}{(x+2)^2}dx = \int \frac{x+2-2}{(x+2)^2}dx$$

$$I = \int \frac{1}{x+2}dx - 2\int \frac{1}{(x+2)^2}dx = \left[\int \frac{1}{(x+2)}dx - 2\int (x+2)^{-2}dx\right]$$

Applying the standard results, we get

$$I = \left[\ln|x+2| + \frac{2}{(x+2)}\right] + C$$

(c) It is always suggestible to simplify the integrand function as much as is possible before carrying out the process of integration.

Consider $I = \int \frac{x^2+2x}{x^2+3x+2}dx$

Factorizing the numerator as well as denominator, we get

$\int \frac{x(x+2)}{(x+1)(x+2)}dx = \int \frac{x}{x+1}dx$. Adding and subtracting 1 in numerator, we get

$$I = \int \frac{x+1-1}{x+1}dx = \int 1.dx - \int \frac{1}{x+1}dx = x - \ln|x+1| + C.$$

ILLUSTRATION 12: Find the following integrals

(a) $\int\left(x^3 + 5x^2 - 4 + \frac{7}{x} + \frac{2}{\sqrt{x}}\right)dx$ (b) $\int \frac{(x+1)^3}{\sqrt{x}}dx$

SOLUTION: (a) Consider $\int\left(x^3 + 5x^2 - 4 + \frac{7}{x} + \frac{2}{\sqrt{x}}\right)dx$

As integral operator distributes on summation, therefore, we get

$$= \int x^3\,dx + \int 5x^2\,dx - \int 4dx + \int \frac{7}{x}dx + \int \frac{2}{\sqrt{x}}dx$$

Moving the constant factors past the integral sign, we get

$$= \int x^3\,dx + 5.\int x^2\,dx - 4.\int 1.\,dx + 7.\int \frac{1}{x}dx + 2.\int x^{-1/2}dx.$$

Applying the standard results, we get

$$= \frac{x^4}{4} + 5.\frac{x^3}{3} - 4x + 7\ln|x| + 2\left(\frac{x^{1/2}}{1/2}\right) + C = \frac{x^4}{4} + \frac{5}{3}x^3 - 4x + 7\ln|x| + 4\sqrt{x} + C$$

(b) $$\int \frac{(x+1)^3}{\sqrt{x}} dx = \int \frac{x^3+3x^2+3x+1}{\sqrt{x}} dx = \int (x^{5/2}+3x^{3/2}+3x^{1/2}+x^{-1/2})dx$$

$$= \int x^{5/2}dx + 3\int x^{3/2}dx + 3\int x^{1/2}dx + \int x^{-1/2}dx = \frac{x^{7/2}}{7/2} + 3\frac{x^{5/2}}{5/2} + 3\frac{x^{3/2}}{3/2} + \frac{x^{1/2}}{1/2} + C$$

$$= \frac{2}{7}x^{7/2} + \frac{6}{5}x^{5/2} + 2x^{3/2} + 2x^{1/2} + C$$

ILLUSTRATION 13: Find the following integrals:

(a) $\int e^{x\log a} + e^{a\log x} + e^{a\log a}\, dx$ (b) $\int (e^{2x}).2^x\, dx$

SOLUTION: (a) We have, $\int e^{x\log a} + e^{a\log x} + e^{a\log a}\, dx$

$$= \int \left(e^{\log a^x} + e^{\log x^a} + e^{\log a^a}\right)dx = \int (a^x + x^a + a^a)\,dx$$

$$= \int a^x\, dx + \int x^a\, dx + \int a^a\, dx = \frac{a^x}{\ln a} + \frac{x^{a+1}}{a+1} + a^a.x + C$$

(b) $\int (e^2)^x.2^x\, dx = \int (2e^2)^x\, dx$

$$\Rightarrow \frac{(2e^2)^x}{\ln(2e^2)} + C.$$

ILLUSTRATION 14: Find: $\int \frac{2^x+3^x}{5^x}\, dx$

SOLUTION: Consider $\int \frac{2^x+3^x}{5^x}\, dx = \int \left(\frac{2^x}{5^x} + \frac{3^x}{5^x}\right) dx = \int \left[\left(\frac{2}{5}\right)^x + \left(\frac{3}{5}\right)^x\right] dx = \frac{(2/5)^x}{\ln(2/5)} + \frac{(3/5)^x}{\ln(3/5)} + C$

ILLUSTRATION 15: Find the following integrals:

(a) $\int \frac{\sqrt{x^2+x^{-2}+2}}{x} dx$ (b) $\int \frac{(1)dx}{\sqrt{x+2}-\sqrt{x+4}}$

(c) $\int \frac{x+x^{-3}+2x^{-1}}{\left(x^2+x^{-2}+2\right)^{1/2}} dx$

SOLUTION: (a) $$\int \frac{\sqrt{x^4+1+2x^2}}{x^2} dx = \int \frac{\sqrt{(x^2+1)^2}}{x^2} dx = \int \frac{x^2+1}{x^2} dx = x + \left[\frac{x^{-2+1}}{-2+1}\right] + C = x - \frac{1}{x} + C$$

(b) $$\int \frac{\sqrt{x+2}+\sqrt{x+4}}{(x+2)-(x+4)} dx = -\frac{1}{2}\int \sqrt{x+2}dx - \frac{1}{2}\int \sqrt{x+4}\, dx$$

$$= -\frac{1}{2}\int \left(\frac{(x+2)^{1+\frac{1}{2}}}{(1+1/2)}\right) dx - \frac{1}{2}\int \left(\frac{(x+4)^{\frac{1}{2}+1}}{1+\frac{1}{2}}\right) + C = -\frac{1}{2}\frac{(x+2)^{3/2}}{3/2} - \frac{1}{2}\frac{(x+4)^{3/2}}{3/2} + C$$

$$= -\frac{1}{3}(x+2)^{3/2} - \frac{1}{3}(x+4)^{3/2} + C$$

(c) Simplifying the integrand function $\dfrac{x+x^{-3}+2x^{-1}}{\left(x^2+x^{-2}+2\right)^{1/2}}$

$$\Rightarrow\ I=\int\frac{x^4+2x^2+1}{x^3\left(x^2+x^{-2}+2\right)^{1/2}}dx=\int\frac{x^2+2+x^{-2}}{x\left(x^2+x^{-2}+2\right)^{1/2}}dx$$

(Dividing numerator and denominator by x^2)

$$\Rightarrow\ I=\int\frac{\left(x^2+x^{-2}+2\right)^{1/2}}{x}dx \qquad \Rightarrow\ I=\int\frac{\left((x^2+1)^2\right)^{1/2}}{x^2}dx=\int\frac{\left(x^2+1\right)}{x^2}dx$$

$$\Rightarrow\ I=\int 1+\frac{1}{x^2}dx = x-\frac{1}{x}+C$$

(b) Trigonometric functions:

f(x)	$\int f(x)dx$	f(ax + b)	$\int f(ax+b)dx$
$\sin x$	$-\cos x + C$	$\sin(ax + b)$	$-\frac{1}{a}\cos(ax+b)+C$
$\cos x$	$\sin x + C$	$\cos(ax + b)$	$\frac{1}{a}\sin(ax+b)+C$
$\tan x$	$\ln\lvert\sec x\rvert + C$	$\tan(ax + b)$	$\frac{1}{a}\ln\lvert\sec(ax+b)\rvert+C$
$\cot x$	$\ln\lvert\sin x\rvert + C$	$\cot(ax + b)$	$\frac{1}{a}\ln\lvert\sin(ax+b)\rvert+C$
$\sec x$	$\ln\lvert\sec x + \tan x\rvert + C$ or $-\ln\left\lvert\tan\left(\frac{\pi}{4}-\frac{x}{2}\right)\right\rvert+C$	$\sec(ax + b)$	$\frac{1}{a}\ln\lvert\sec(ax+b)+\tan(ax+b)\rvert+C$ or $-\frac{1}{a}\ln\left\lvert\tan\left(\frac{\pi}{4}-\frac{(ax+b)}{2}\right)\right\rvert+C$
$\operatorname{cosec} x$	$\ln\lvert\operatorname{cosec} x - \cot x\rvert + C$ or $\ln\left\lvert\tan\left(\frac{x}{2}\right)\right\rvert+C$	$\operatorname{cosec}(ax + b)$	$\frac{1}{a}\ln\lvert\operatorname{cosec}(ax+b)-\cot(ax+b)\rvert+C$ or $\frac{1}{a}\ln\left\lvert\tan\left(\frac{ax+b}{2}\right)\right\rvert+C$
$\sec^2 x$	$\tan x + C$	$\sec^2(ax + b)$	$\frac{1}{a}\tan(ax+b)+C$
$\operatorname{cosec}^2 x$	$-\cot x + C$	$\operatorname{cosec}^2(ax + b)$	$-\frac{1}{a}\cot(ax+b)+C$
$\sec x.\ \tan x$	$\sec x + C$	$\sec(ax + b)\tan(ax+ b)$	$\frac{1}{a}\sec(ax+b)+C$
$\operatorname{cosec} x \cot x$	$-\operatorname{cosec} x + C$	$\operatorname{cosec}(ax+b)\cot(ax+b)$	$-\frac{1}{a}\operatorname{cosec}(ax+b)+C$

ILLUSTRATION 16: Find the following integrals:

(a) $\int\left(e^{\ln \sin x}+\cos x\right)\sin x\, dx$ (b) $\int\left(e^{x}+\frac{2}{x}+\cos x+\sec^{2} x\right)dx$

SOLUTION: (a) $I=\int(\sin x+\cos x)\sin x\, dx = \int\left(\sin^{2} x+\cos x \sin x\right)dx$

$\therefore\ I=\int \sin^{2} x\, dx+\frac{1}{2}\int \sin 2x\, dx=\int\left(\frac{1-\operatorname{cosn} 2x}{2}\right)dx+\frac{1}{2}\int \sin 2x\, dx$

$=\frac{1}{2}\left[x-\frac{\sin 2x}{2}\right]+\frac{1}{2}\frac{(-\cos 2x)}{2}+C = \frac{1}{2}\left[x-\frac{1}{2}(\sin 2x)\right]-\frac{\cos 2x}{4}+C$

(b) $\int\left(e^{x}+\frac{2}{x}+\cos x+\sec^{2} x\right)dx = e^{x}+2\ln|x|+\sin x+\tan x+C$

ILLUSTRATION 17: Find the following integrals:

(a) $\int\sqrt{1+\sin\frac{x}{2}}\, dx$ (b) $\int\sqrt{1+\cos 2x}\, dx$

SOLUTION: (a) $\int\sqrt{1+2\sin\frac{x}{4}\cos\frac{x}{4}}\, dx = \int\sqrt{\sin^{2}\frac{x}{4}+\cos^{2}\frac{x}{4}+2\sin\frac{x}{4}\cos\frac{x}{4}}\, dx$

$=\int\sqrt{\left(\sin\frac{x}{4}+\cos\frac{x}{4}\right)^{2}}\, dx = \int\left(\sin\frac{x}{4}+\cos\frac{x}{4}\right)dx=(4)\left(-\cos\frac{x}{4}\right)+(4)\left(\sin\frac{x}{4}\right)+C$

(b) $\int\sqrt{1+\cos 2x}\, dx = \int\sqrt{2\cos^{2} x}\, dx = \sqrt{2}\int \cos x\, dx = \sqrt{2}\sin x+C$

Note: We know that $\sqrt{x^{2}}=|x|$, hence, $\sqrt{(\cos x)^{2}}=|\cos x|$, but conventionally we have taken here $\sqrt{(\cos x)^{2}}=\cos x$. Although we have to follow $\sqrt{\cos^{2} x}=|\cos x|$

ILLUSTRATION 18: Find the following integrals:

(a) $\int\cos(ax+b)^{\circ}dx$ (b) $\int\sin^{2}(px+q)dx$

(c) $\int\left(\cos^{3}(ax+b)+3\sin mx\right)dx$

SOLUTION: (a) Given integral $I=\int\cos(ax+b)^{0}dx$

Converting the argument angle of integrand functions to radians, the integral reduces to

$I=\int\cos\frac{\pi(ax+b)}{180}dx$

$=\frac{180}{a\pi}\sin\frac{\pi(ax+b)}{180}+C$ $\left(\because\int\cos(px+q)dx=\frac{1}{p}\sin(px+q)+C\right)$

$=\frac{180}{a\pi}\sin(ax+b)^{\circ}+C$

(b) Given integral $I=\int\sin^{2}(px+q)dx$

Converting into linear function of cosine using the formula $\cos 2\theta = 1-2\sin^{2}\theta$ the integral reduce to $I=\frac{1}{2}\int 1-\cos 2(px+q)dx$

$\Rightarrow\ I=\frac{1}{2}\int 1\, dx-\frac{1}{2}\int\cos 2(px+q)dx$ $\Rightarrow\ I=\frac{1}{2}\left(x-\frac{1}{2p}\sin 2(px+q)\right)+C$

(c) Given integral $I = \int\left(\cos^3(ax+b)+3\sin mx\right)dx = \int\cos^3(ax+b)dx + \int 3\sin mx\ dx$

Transforming into linear function of cosine using the formula $\cos 3\theta = 4\cos^3\theta - 3\cos\theta$, the integral reduce to

$$I = \frac{1}{4}\int\left(\cos 3(ax+b)+3\cos(ax+b)\right)dx + 3\int \sin mx\ dx$$

$$= \frac{1}{12a}\sin 3(ax+b) + \frac{3}{4a}\sin(ax+b) - \frac{3}{m}\cos mx + C$$

ILLUSTRATION 19: Find the following integrals:

(a) $\int \tan^2(2x+1)\ dx$

(b) $\int \frac{1+\cos 2x}{1-\cos 2x}dx$

(c) $\int \frac{dx}{\cos^2 x\sin^2 x}$

SOLUTION: (a) Consider $\int \tan^2(2x+1)\ dx$

Indeed the knowledge of trigonometric identities help a lot in evaluation of elementary trigonometric integral for instance the given integral I can be written as

$$\int \sec^2(2x+1)dx - \int 1.dx = \frac{1}{2}\tan(2x+1) - x + C$$

(b) Consider $I = \int \frac{1+\cos 2x}{1-\cos 2x}dx$

Simplifying the integrand by substituting $1 + \cos 2x = 2\cos^2 x$ and $1 - \cos 2x = 2\sin^2 x$, we get

$$I = \int \cot^2 x dx = \int\left(\operatorname{cosec}^2 x - 1\right)dx = -\cot x - x + C.$$

Aliter: Multiplying and dividing the integrand by $(1 + \cos 2x)$, we get

$$I = \int \frac{(1+\cos 2x)^2}{\sin^2 2x}dx = \int\left(\operatorname{cosec}^2 2x + \cot^2 x + 2\operatorname{cosec} 2x\cot 2x\right)dx$$

$$= 2\int \operatorname{cosec}^2 2x\ dx - \int 1.dx + 2\int \operatorname{cosec} 2x\cot 2x\,dx = 2\left(\frac{-\cot 2x}{2}\right) - x - 2\left(\frac{\operatorname{cosec} 2x}{2}\right) + C$$

$$= -(\operatorname{cosec} 2x + \cot 2x) - x + C$$

Indeed the form of anti-derivative changes by changing the method of integration but all the anti-derivatives differ by a constant. Students are advised to do the conversion themselves.

(c) $\int \frac{dx}{\cos^2 x\sin^2 x} = \int \frac{\cos^2 x+\sin^2 x}{\cos^2 x\sin^2 x}dx = \int (\operatorname{cosec}^2 x + \sec^2 x)\,dx = -\cot x + \tan x + c$

ILLUSTRATION 20: Find the following integrals:

(a) $\int \frac{1}{1+\sin x}dx$

(b) $\int \frac{1}{1-\cos x}dx$

SOLUTION: (a) Given integral $I = \int \frac{1}{1+\sin x}dx$

Method 1: Multiplying the numerator and denominator both by $(1 - \sin x)$, integral reduces to

$$\int \frac{1}{1+\sin x}dx = \int \sec^2 x\,dx - \int \sec x\tan x\ dx = \tan x - \sec x + C.$$

Method 2: $I = \int \frac{dx}{\left(\sin\frac{x}{2}+\cos\frac{x}{2}\right)^2} = \int \frac{dx}{2\left(\frac{1}{\sqrt{2}}\cos\frac{x}{2}+\frac{1}{\sqrt{2}}\sin\frac{x}{2}\right)^2} = \frac{1}{2}\int \frac{dx}{\cos^2\left(\frac{x}{2}-\frac{\pi}{4}\right)}$

$$=\frac{1}{2}\int \sec^2\left(\frac{x}{2}-\frac{\pi}{4}\right)dx \text{ applying standard result}$$

$$=\frac{\frac{1}{2}.\tan\left(\frac{x}{2}-\frac{\pi}{4}\right)}{\frac{1}{2}}+C=\tan\left(\frac{x}{2}-\frac{\pi}{4}\right)+C$$

Method 3: Let us think about the integrand in another manner

$$I=\int\frac{1}{1+\frac{2\tan\frac{x}{2}}{1+\tan^2\left(\frac{x}{2}\right)}}dx \qquad \left[\because \sin x=\frac{2\tan\frac{x}{2}}{1+\tan^2\frac{x}{2}}\right]$$

$$=2\int\frac{\frac{1}{2}\sec^2\frac{x}{2}\,dx}{\left(\tan\frac{x}{2}+1\right)^2}=2\int\frac{d\left(\tan\frac{x}{2}+1\right)}{\left(1+\tan\frac{x}{2}\right)^2}dx \qquad \because\ d\left(1+\tan\frac{x}{2}\right)=\frac{1}{2}\sec^2\frac{x}{2}dx$$

$$=2\int\frac{du}{u^2}=\frac{-2}{1+\tan\frac{x}{2}}+C$$

(b) Given the integral $I=\int\frac{1}{1-\cos x}dx$

Method 1: Multiplying the numerator and denominator both by $(1+\cos x)$, integral reduces to

$$I=\int\frac{(1+\cos x)}{\sin^2 x}dx \qquad \Rightarrow I=\int\frac{(1+\cos x)}{\sin^2 x}dx$$

$$=\int \text{cosec}^2 x\,dx+\int \cot x\,\text{cosec}\,x\,dx=-\cot x+(-\text{cosec}\,x)+C$$

$\Rightarrow$ $-\cot x-\text{cosec}\,x+C$.

Method 2: $\int\frac{1}{2\sin^2\frac{x}{2}}dx=\int\frac{1}{2}\text{cosec}^2\frac{x}{2}dx=\frac{\frac{1}{2}\left(-\cot\frac{x}{2}\right)}{\frac{1}{2}}+C=-\cot\frac{x}{2}+C$

Method 3: Integrand can also be simplified to standard form by converting $\cos x=\frac{1-\tan^2\frac{x}{2}}{1+\tan^2\frac{x}{2}}$

as $I=\int\frac{\sec^2\frac{x}{2}dx}{1-\left(\frac{1-\tan^2\frac{x}{2}}{1+\tan^2\frac{x}{2}}\right)^2}=\int\frac{\sec^2\frac{x}{2}}{2\tan^2\frac{x}{2}}dx=\int\frac{\frac{1}{2}\sec^2\frac{x}{2}}{\tan^2\frac{x}{2}}dx=\int\frac{d\left(\tan\frac{x}{2}\right)}{\tan^2\frac{x}{2}}$

$$=\int\frac{dt}{t^2}=-\frac{1}{t}+C=-\frac{1}{\tan\frac{x}{2}}+C$$

ILLUSTRATION 21: Find the following integrals:

(a) $\int \sin^3 x \cos^3 x\, dx$ (b) $\int \cos x \cos 2x\, dx$

(c) $\int \dfrac{\cos 2x - \cos 2\alpha}{\sin x - \sin \alpha} dx$

SOLUTION: (a) $= \frac{1}{8}\int (2\sin x \cos x)^3 dx = \frac{1}{8}\int \sin^3 2x\, dx$

$$= \frac{1}{8}\int \frac{3\sin 2x - \sin 6x}{4} dx = \frac{1}{32}\int (3\sin 2x - \sin 6x)\, dx = \frac{1}{32}\left[-\frac{3}{2}\cos 2x + \frac{1}{6}\cos 6x\right] + C$$

(b) Consider $\int \cos x \cos 2x\, dx$

$$= \frac{1}{2}\int 2\cos x \cos 2x\, dx = \frac{1}{2}\int (\cos 3x + \cos x)\, dx = \frac{1}{2}\left(\frac{\sin 3x}{3} + \frac{\sin x}{1}\right) + C$$

(c) $\int \dfrac{\cos 2x - \cos 2\alpha}{\sin x - \sin \alpha} dx = \int \dfrac{(1 - 2\sin^2 x) - (1 - 2\sin^2 \alpha)}{\sin x - \sin \alpha} dx$

$$= -2\int \frac{(\sin x - \sin\alpha)(\sin\alpha + \sin x)}{\sin x - \sin\alpha} dx$$

$$= -2\int (\sin\alpha + \sin x)\, dx = -2\left[\sin\alpha \int dx + \int \sin x\, dx\right] = -2x\sin\alpha + 2\cos x + C.$$

ILLUSTRATION 22: Find the following integrals:

(a) $\int \dfrac{1}{\cos 2x - \cos^2 x} dx$ (b) $\int \dfrac{\cos x - \cos 2x}{1 - \cos x} dx$

SOLUTION: (a) $I = \int \dfrac{1}{2\cos^2 x - 1 - \cos^2 x} dx \quad \Rightarrow I = \int \dfrac{1}{\cos^2 x - 1} dx$

$\Rightarrow \quad I = -\int \text{cosec}^2 x\, dx = \cot x + C$

(b) Simplify this to convert it into standard form

$I = \int \dfrac{(\cos x - 1) + (1 - \cos 2x)}{1 - \cos x} dx \quad \Rightarrow \int \left(\dfrac{-(1 - \cos x)}{(1 + \cos x)} + \dfrac{(1 - \cos 2x)}{(1 - \cos x)}\right) dx$

$\Rightarrow I = \int (-1)\, dx + \int \dfrac{2\sin^2 x}{2\sin^2 (x/2)} dx \quad \Rightarrow I = -x + \int \dfrac{4\sin^2 \frac{x}{2}\cos^2 \frac{x}{2}}{\sin^2 \frac{x}{2}} dx$

$\Rightarrow I = -x + 2\int (\cos x + 1)\, dx \quad \Rightarrow I = -x + 2\sin x + 2x + C$

$\Rightarrow I = 2\sin x + x + C.$

ILLUSTRATION 23: Find the following integrals:

(a) $\int \cos ec^4 x \tan^2 x\, dx$ (b) $\int \sin 2x \cos 4x\, dx$

SOLUTION: (a) $I = \int \dfrac{1}{\sin^4 x} \cdot \dfrac{\sin^2 x}{\cos^2 x} dx$

$\Rightarrow I = \int \dfrac{1}{\sin^2 x \cos^2 x} dx = \int \dfrac{\sin^2 x + \cos^2 x}{\sin^2 x \cos^2 x} dx$

$$= \int \frac{1}{\cos^2 x} dx + \int \frac{1}{\sin^2 x} dx = \int \sec^2 x dx + \int \text{cosec}^2 x\, dx = \tan x - \cot x + C$$

(b) $I=\frac{1}{2}\int(2\sin 2x\cos 4x)dx$ $\Rightarrow I=\frac{1}{2}\left[\int(\sin(4x+2x)+\sin(4x-2x))dx\right]$

$\Rightarrow I=\frac{1}{2}\left[\int\sin 6x\,dx+\int\sin 2x\,dx\right]$ $\Rightarrow I=\frac{-1}{2}\left[\frac{\cos 6x}{6}+\frac{\cos 2x}{2}\right]+C$

ILLUSTRATION 24: Find the following integrals:

(a) $\int\frac{x^5+x^4\cos\theta+4x^3+4x^2\cos\theta}{x^3+x^2\cos\theta}dx$ (b) $\int\frac{(\cos 10x-\cos 5x)}{1+2\cos 5x}dx$

SOLUTION: (a) $I=\int\frac{x^3(x^2+4)+x^2\cos\theta(x^2+4)}{x^3+x^2\cos\theta}dx=\int\frac{(x^3+x^2\cos\theta)(x^2+4)}{(x^3+x^2\cos\theta)}dx=\frac{x^3}{3}+4x+C$

(b) $I=\int\frac{\cos 10x-\cos 5x}{1+2\cos 5x}dx=\int\frac{-2\sin\frac{15x}{2}\sin\frac{5x}{2}}{1+2\cos 5x}dx$

Multiplying both numerator and denominator by $\sin\frac{5x}{2}$, we get

$$=\int\frac{-\left(2\sin\frac{15x}{2}\sin\frac{5x}{2}\right)\left(\sin\frac{5x}{2}\right)}{\sin\frac{5x}{2}+2\cos 5x\sin\frac{5x}{2}}dx=\int\frac{-2\sin\frac{15x}{2}\sin^2\frac{5x}{2}}{\left(\sin\frac{5x}{2}+\sin\frac{15}{2}x-\sin\frac{5x}{2}\right)}dx=\int-2\sin^2\frac{5x}{2}dx$$

$$\Rightarrow I=\int\left(-2\sin^2\frac{5x}{2}\right)dx=\int(-1+\cos 5x)dx \quad\Rightarrow -x+\frac{\sin 5x}{5}+C$$

ILLUSTRATION 25: Find the following integrals:

(a) $\int\tan x\,dx$ (b) $\int\cot x\,dx$

SOLUTION: (a) Consider the integral

$$I=\int\tan x\,dx=\int\frac{\sin x}{\cos x}dx=-\int\frac{-\sin x}{\cos x}dx=-\ln||\cos x|+C=\ln|\sec x|+C$$

(b) $I=\int\cot x\,dx=\int\frac{\cos x}{\sin x}dx=\ln|\sin x|+C=-\ln|\operatorname{cosec} x|+C.$

(c) Rational and Irrational Functions:

$f(x)$	$\int f(x)dx$	$f(ax+b)$	$\int f(ax+b)dx$
$\frac{1}{\sqrt{1-x^2}}$	$\sin^{-1}x+C$ or $-\cos^{-1}x+C$	$\frac{1}{\sqrt{a^2-x^2}}$	$\sin^{-1}\left(\frac{x}{a}\right)+C$
$\frac{1}{\sqrt{x^2-1}}$	$\ln\|x+\sqrt{x^2-1}\|+C$	$\frac{1}{\sqrt{x^2-a^2}}$	$\ln\|x+\sqrt{x^2-a^2}\|+C$
$\frac{1}{\sqrt{x^2+1}}$	$\ln\|x+\sqrt{x^2+1}\|+C$	$\frac{1}{\sqrt{x^2+a^2}}$	$\ln\|x+\sqrt{x^2+a^2}\|+C$

$\frac{1}{1-x^2}$	$\frac{1}{2}\ln\left\|\frac{1+x}{1-x}\right\|+C$	$\frac{1}{a^2-x^2}$	$\frac{1}{2}\ln\left\|\frac{a+x}{a-x}\right\|+C$
$\frac{1}{x^2-1}$	$\frac{1}{2}\ln\left\|\frac{x-1}{x+1}\right\|+C$	$\frac{1}{x^2-a^2}$	$\frac{1}{2a}\ln\left\|\frac{x-a}{x+a}\right\|+C$
$\frac{1}{x^2+1}$	$\tan^{-1}x + C$ or $-\cot^{-1}x + C$	$\frac{1}{x^2+a^2}$	$\frac{1}{a}\tan^{-1}\left(\frac{x}{a}\right)+C$ or $-\frac{1}{a}\cot^{-1}\left(\frac{x}{a}\right)+C$
$\sqrt{1-x^2}$	$\frac{x\sqrt{1-x^2}}{2}+\frac{1}{2}\sin^{-1}x+C$	$\sqrt{a^2-x^2}$	$\frac{x\sqrt{a^2-x^2}}{2}+\frac{a^2}{2}\sin^{-1}\left(\frac{x}{a}\right)+C$
$\sqrt{x^2-1}$	$\frac{x\sqrt{x^2-1}}{2}-\frac{1}{2}\ln\left\|x+\sqrt{x^2-1}\right\|+C$	$\sqrt{x^2-a^2}$	$\frac{x\sqrt{x^2-a^2}}{2}-\frac{a^2}{2}\ln\left\|x+\sqrt{x^2-a^2}\right\|+C$
$\sqrt{1+x^2}$	$\frac{x\sqrt{1+x^2}}{2}+\frac{1}{2}\ln\left\|x+\sqrt{x^2+1}\right\|+C$	$\sqrt{a^2+x^2}$	$\frac{x\sqrt{a^2-x^2}}{2}+\frac{a^2}{2}\ln\left\|x+\sqrt{a^2+x^2}\right\|+C$
$\frac{1}{x\sqrt{x^2-1}}$	$\sec^{-1}x+C$ or $-\text{cosec}^{-1}x+C$	$\frac{1}{x\sqrt{x^2-a^2}}$	$\frac{1}{a}\sec^{-1}\frac{x}{a}+C$ or $-\frac{1}{a}\text{cosec}^{-1}\left(\frac{x}{a}\right)+C$

ILLUSTRATION 26: Let $F'(x) = x+\frac{1}{1+x^2}$ and $f(0) = 0$, then find $f(x)$.

SOLUTION: $f(x) = \int f'(x)\,dx = \int\left(x+\frac{1}{1+x^2}\right)dx = \frac{x^2}{2}+\tan^{-1}x+C$

Putting $x = 0$, we get $f(0) = 0 + \tan^{-1} 0 + C$

$\Rightarrow C = f(0) = 0$ $\quad\therefore f(x) = \frac{x^2}{2}+\tan^{-1}x$

ILLUSTRATION 27: Find the following integrals:

(a) $\int\frac{dx}{\sqrt{a^2-x^2}}$ (b) $\int\frac{dx}{x\sqrt{x^2-a^2}}$

(c) $\int\frac{dx}{x^2-a^2}$ (d) $\int\frac{dx}{x^2+a^2}$

SOLUTION: (a) Consider the integral, $I = \int\frac{dx}{\sqrt{a^2-x^2}} = \frac{1}{a}\int\frac{dx}{\sqrt{1-\left(\frac{x}{a}\right)^2}} = \frac{1}{a}\left(\frac{\sin^{-1}(x/a)}{1/a}\right) = \sin^{-1}\frac{x}{a}+C$

(b) Consider the integral, $I = \int\frac{dx}{x\sqrt{x^2-a^2}}$

(Dividing numerator and denominator both by a^2)

Simplifying the integral, $I = \frac{1}{a^2}\int\frac{dx}{\frac{x}{a}\sqrt{\left(\frac{x}{a}\right)^2-1}}$

Applying the standard result, we get

$$I = \frac{1}{a^2}\left(\frac{\sec^{-1}(x/a)}{1/a}\right)+C = \frac{1}{a}\sec^{-1}\frac{x}{a}+C.$$

(c) Consider the integral, $I = \int \frac{dx}{x^2-a^2}$

Factorizing the denominator of integrand function, and thus, simplifying the integrand, we get

$$I = \frac{1}{2a}\int \frac{2a}{(x-a)(x+a)}dx = \frac{1}{2a}\int \frac{(x+a)-(x-a)}{(x-a)(x+a)}dx$$

Indeed the integrand breaks up into sum of two standard functions as shown below:

$$I = \frac{1}{2a}\left(\int \frac{1}{x-a}dx - \int \frac{1}{x+a}dx\right) = \frac{1}{2a}(\ln|x-a| - \ln|x+a|)+C = \frac{1}{2a}\ln\left|\frac{x-a}{x+a}\right|+C$$

It is from now onwards would be regarded as standard result.

(d) Consider the integral $\qquad I = \int \frac{dx}{x^2+a^2}$

Taking a^2 common factor denominator integrand reduces to standard form

$$I = \frac{1}{a^2}\int \frac{1}{1+\left(\frac{x}{a}\right)^2}dx = \frac{1}{a^2}\left(\frac{\tan^{-1}(x/a)}{1/a}\right)+C = \frac{1}{a}\tan^{-1}\left(\frac{x}{a}\right)+C$$

From now onwards it would be regarded as standard result.

ILLUSTRATION 28: Find the following integral:

(a) $\int \frac{dx}{9x^2+12x+8}$ $\qquad$ (b) $\int \frac{dx}{bx^2-a}$

(c) $\int \frac{dx}{(x+1)\sqrt{x^2+2x}}$

SOLUTION: (a) Consider the integral, $I = \int \frac{dx}{9x^2+12x+8}$

Completing the square, $I = \int \frac{dx}{(3x+2)^2+4}$

Applying the standard result $\int \frac{dx}{a^2+x^2} = \tan^{-1}\frac{x}{a}+C$, we get

$$I = \frac{1}{2}\left(\frac{\tan^{-1}\frac{3x+2}{2}}{3}\right)+C = \frac{1}{6}\tan^{-1}\left(\frac{3}{2}x+1\right)+C$$

Note that in above illustration in place of x, we have $(ax + b)$, in this case we divide the integral of standard result by a.

(b) Consider the integral, $I = \int \frac{dx}{bx^2-a}$

$$\therefore\quad I = \int \frac{1}{(x\sqrt{b})^2-(\sqrt{a})^2}dx \qquad \left(\because \int \frac{1}{x^2-a^2}dx = \frac{1}{2a}\ln\left|\frac{x-a}{x+a}\right|+C\right)$$

$$\therefore\quad I = \frac{1}{2\sqrt{a}}\cdot\frac{1}{\sqrt{b}}\ln\left|\frac{x\sqrt{b}-\sqrt{a}}{x\sqrt{b}+\sqrt{a}}\right|+C = \frac{1}{2\sqrt{ab}}\ln\left|\frac{x\sqrt{b}-\sqrt{a}}{x\sqrt{b}+\sqrt{a}}\right|+C$$

(c) Consider the integral, $I = \int \frac{dx}{(x+1)\sqrt{x^2+2x}}$

Completing the square of quadratic expression $I = \int \frac{dx}{(x+1)\sqrt{(x+1)^2-1}}$

Applying standard result, we get $\sec^{-1}(x+1) + C$.

ILLUSTRATION 29: Find the following integrals:

(a) $\int \frac{dx}{\sqrt{1-9x^2}}$ (b) $\int \frac{dx}{x\sqrt{2x^2-1}}$

(c) $\int \frac{dx}{4x^2-9}$

SOLUTION: (a) Consider the integral, $I = \int \frac{dx}{\sqrt{1-9x^2}} = \int \frac{1}{\sqrt{1-(3x)^2}}dx$.

Applying the standard result, we get $I = \frac{1}{3}\sin^{-1}3x + C$.

(b) Consider the integral $I = \int \frac{dx}{x\sqrt{2x^2-1}} = \int \frac{1}{x\sqrt{(\sqrt{2}x)^2-1}}dx = \int \frac{\sqrt{2}\,dx}{\sqrt{2}\,x\sqrt{(\sqrt{2}x)^2-1}}$

or $I = \int \frac{d(\sqrt{2}\,x)}{(\sqrt{2}x)(\sqrt{2}x)^2-1}dx$

Applying the standard result, we get $I = \sec^{-1}(\sqrt{2}\,x) + C$.

(c) Consider the integral $I = \int \frac{dx}{4x^2-9} = \frac{1}{4}\int \frac{dx}{x^2-\left(\frac{3}{2}\right)^2}$

Applying the standard result, we get

$$I = \frac{1}{4}\left(\frac{1}{2(3/2)}\ln\left(\frac{x-3/2}{x+3/2}\right)\right) + C = \frac{1}{4\times 3}\ln\left|\frac{2x-3}{2x+3}\right| + C$$

ILLUSTRATION 30: Find the anti-derivatives of the function $y = x + 1$ which touch the curve $y = x^2$.

SOLUTION: Let $f(x)$ be the antiderivative of function $y = x + 1$

$\Rightarrow f(x) = \int (x+1)\,dx$ ...(i)

$\therefore$ $f(x)$ touches the curve $y = x^2$ $\Rightarrow f'(x) = 2x$ at the point of contact.

$\Rightarrow 2x = x + 1$ $\Rightarrow x = 1$

$\therefore$ Point of contact is (1, 1)

$\therefore f(x) = \int (x+1)\,dx = \frac{x^2}{2} + x + C$ $\Rightarrow f(x) = \frac{x^2}{2} + x + C$ passes through (1, 1)

$\Rightarrow 1 = \frac{1}{2} + 1 + C$ $\Rightarrow C = -\frac{1}{2}$

$\Rightarrow f(x) = \frac{1}{2}\left(x^2 + 2x - 1\right)$.

ILLUSTRATION 31: Deduce the expansion for $\ln(1+x)$ and $\tan^{-1}x$ using the suitable infinite geometric progression from $\frac{1}{1+x^2} = 1 - x^2 + x^4 - x^6 + \ldots$; when $x \in (-1,1)$

SOLUTION: As we know that $\forall x \in (-1,1)$

$$\frac{1}{1+x} = 1 - x + x^2 - x^3 + x^4 - x^5 + \ldots\infty$$

Integrating both sides with respect to x, we get

$$\int \frac{1}{1+x}dx = \int \sum_{r=0}^{\infty}(-1)^r . x^r dx$$

As integral operation distributes over sum and difference, therefore

$$\ln|1+x| = \sum_{r=0}^{\infty}(-1)^r \int x^r dx = \sum_{r=0}^{\infty}(-1)^r \frac{x^{r+1}}{r+1}+C$$

$$\ln|1+x| = C + x - \frac{x^2}{2} + \frac{x^3}{3} - \frac{x^4}{4} + \frac{x^5}{5} - \ldots\infty$$

Substituting $x = 0$, we get $C = 0$

Consequently, $\ln|1+x| = x - \frac{x^2}{2} + \frac{x^3}{3} - \frac{x^4}{4} + \ldots\infty$

Also $\int \frac{1}{1+x^2}dx = \tan^{-1}x + C$ $\quad\Rightarrow \tan^{-1}x + C = \int\left(1-x^2+x^4-x^6+\ldots\right)dx$

$\Rightarrow \tan^{-1}x + C = x - \frac{x^3}{3} + \frac{x^5}{5} - \ldots$

But $\tan^{-1}(0) = 0$ $\quad\Rightarrow C = 0$

$\Rightarrow \tan^{-1}x = x - \frac{x^3}{3} + \frac{x^5}{5} + \ldots.$

ILLUSTRATION 32: Find the following integral

(a) $\int \frac{3x^2}{1+3x^2}dx$ (b) $\int \frac{(2x+1)^2}{x(1+4x^2)}dx$

SOLUTION: (a) Consider the integral, $I = \int \frac{3x^2}{1+3x^2}dx$

Simplifying, we get $I = \int \frac{3x^2+1-1}{1+3x^2}dx$

$\Rightarrow I = \int 1.dx - \int \frac{1}{1+(\sqrt{3}x)^2}dx = x - \frac{1}{\sqrt{3}}\tan^{-1}\sqrt{3}x + C$

(b) Consider the integral $I = \int \frac{4x^2+1+4x}{x(1+4x^2)}dx = \int \frac{4x^2+1}{x(1+4x^2)}dx + \int \frac{4x}{x(1+4x^2)}dx$

Applying the standard result, we get

$$I = \int \frac{1}{x} + \int \frac{4}{(1+4x^2)}dx = \ln|x| + 4\left(\frac{1}{2}\tan^{-1}2x\right) + C = \ln|x| + \tan^{-1}2x + C.$$

ILLUSTRATION 33: Find the integral, $I = \int\left(\frac{(x^2+\cos^2 x)}{1+x^2}\right)\operatorname{cosec}^2 x dx$

SOLUTION: $I = \int\left(\frac{x^2+1-\sin^2 x}{1+x^2}\right)\operatorname{cosec}^2 x dx = \int\left(\left(1-\frac{\sin^2 x}{1+x^2}\right)\frac{1}{\sin^2 x}\right)dx$

$= \int\left(\frac{1}{\sin^2 x} - \frac{1}{1+x^2}\right)dx = \int \operatorname{cosec}^2 x dx - \int \frac{1}{1+x^2}dx = -\cot x - \tan^{-1}x + C.$

TEXTUAL EXERCISE-2: (SUBJECTIVE)

1. Find the following integrals using standard results and algebra of integration.

(a) $\int \frac{\sqrt{x}-x^3e^x+x^2}{x^3}dx$ (b) $\int \frac{(1+\sqrt{x})^3}{\sqrt[3]{x}}dx$

(c) $\int \frac{\sqrt[3]{x^2}-\sqrt[4]{x}}{\sqrt{x}}dx$

2. Find the following integrals:

(a) $\int \frac{x^7+3x^6+x+3}{x^2+1}dx$ (b) $\int \frac{x}{x^2+2x+1}dx$

3. Find the following integrals:

(a) $\int \frac{\sqrt{x^4+x^{-4}+2}}{x^3}dx$ (b) $\int \frac{dx}{\sqrt{2x+3}-\sqrt{2x-1}}$

(c) $\int \sqrt{\frac{x^4+x^{-4}+2}{x^3}}dx$

4. Integrate the following:

(a) $\int \frac{e^{5\ln x}-e^{4\ln x}}{e^{3\ln x}-e^{2\ln x}}dx$

(b) $\int \left(1+x+\frac{x^2}{2!}+\frac{x^3}{3!}+......\infty\right)dx$, and hence, show that $\int e^x dx = e^x + C$

5. Find the following integrals:

(a) $\int \frac{e^{3x}+e^{5x}}{e^x+e^{-x}}dx$ (b) $\int \frac{e^{2x}-1}{e^x}dx$

(c) $\int \frac{2^{x+1}-5^{x-1}}{10^x}dx$

6. Find the following integrals:

(a) $\int \cos(3x+2)dx$ (b) $\int \sec^2(ax+b)dx$

(c) $\int \cot^2(mx+n)\,dx$ (d) $\int \frac{1-\cos x}{1+\cos x}dx$

(e) $\int \cos^2(2x+1)dx$ (f) $\int \left(\cos^3(x+1)+3\cos 2x\right)dx$

7. Find the following integrals:

(a) $\int \frac{\sin^3 x+\cos^3 x}{\sin x+\cos x}dx$

(b) $\int \frac{\cos ecx+\tan^2 x-\sin^2 x}{\sin x}dx$

8. Integrate the following integrals:

(a) $\int \frac{\cos 2x}{\sin^2 x\cos^2 x}dx$

(b) $\int \cos x\cos 2x\cos 3x\,dx$

(c) $\int \frac{\sin^6 x+\cos^6 x}{\sin^2 x.\cos^2 x}dx$

(d) $\int \frac{1+\tan^2 x}{1+\cot^2 x}dx$

(e) $\int (3\sin x\cos^2 x-\sin^3 x)\,dx$

(f) $\int \frac{\sin 2x+\sin 5x-\sin 3x}{\cos x+1-2\sin^2 2x}dx$

(g) $\int \sin x\cos x\cos 2x\cos 4x\,dx$

9. Find the following integrals:

(a) $\int \frac{\sin x}{\cos^3 x}dx$

(b) $\int \frac{dx}{\sqrt{3}\cos x+\sin x}$

(c) $\int \left(\frac{1}{x^{3/4}}+\frac{1-x^4}{1-x}+\sec x\tan x\right)dx$

(d) $\int \left(\frac{x^2+\cos^2 x}{1+x^2}\right)\cos ec^2 x\,dx$

(e) $\int \frac{\cos\left(1-\frac{x}{2}\right)}{\sin^2\left(1-\frac{x}{2}\right)}dx$

10. Find the following integrals:

(a) $\int \frac{\cos 5x+\cos 4x}{1-2\cos 3x}dx$

(b) $\int \tan^2 x\sin^2 x\,dx$

(c) $\int \frac{dx}{\tan x+\cot x+\sec x+\operatorname{cosec} x}$

11 Find the following integrals:

(a) $\int \frac{3-2\cot^2 x}{\cos^2 x}dx$ (b) $\int \frac{\cos 2x}{\cos x-\sin x}dx$

(c) $\int (\sin 5x-\sin 5\alpha)dx$

12. Find the following integrals:

(a) $\int \frac{dx}{x\sqrt{3x^2-1}}$ (b) $\int \frac{dx}{\sqrt{1-4x^2}}$

(c) $\int \frac{dx}{x\sqrt{25x^2-2}}$

(d) $\int \frac{dx}{(2x+1)\sqrt{x^2+x}}$

(e) $\int \frac{dx}{(2x-1)\sqrt{(2x-1)^2-4}}$

(f) $\int \frac{1}{\sqrt{\left(3-\frac{x^2}{4}\right)}}dx$

(g) $\int \frac{1}{3+(2-3x)^2}dx$

13. Integrate the following integrals:

(a) $\int \frac{1+2x^2}{x^2\left(1+x^2\right)}dx$ (b) $\int \frac{x^4+x^2+1}{2\left(1+x^2\right)}dx$

(c) $\int \frac{3dx}{\sqrt{4-4x^2}}$

14. Find the following integrals:

(a) $\int \frac{x^2}{1+x^2}dx$ (b) $\int \frac{(x+1)^2}{x\left(1+x^2\right)}dx$

(c) $\int \frac{x^2}{x^2-1}dx$ (d) $\int \frac{x^4}{1+x^2}dx$

(e) $\int \frac{5(x-3)^2}{x\sqrt{x}}dx$ (f) $\int \frac{x^2+3}{x^6(x^2+1)}dx$

15. Find the following integrals:

(a) $\int \frac{dx}{4x^2+25}$

(b) $\int \frac{dx}{\sqrt{5-x^2-4x}}$

(c) $\int \frac{dx}{4-x^2-4x}$

(d) $\int \frac{2+3x^2}{x^2(1+x^2)}dx$

(e) $\int \frac{\sqrt{1-x^2}+\sqrt{1+x^2}}{\sqrt{1-x^4}}dx$

(f) $\int \sqrt[5]{(8-3x)^6}\,dx$

Answer Keys

1. (a) $C-\frac{2}{3x\sqrt{x}}-e^x+\ln|x|$ (b) $\frac{3}{2}\sqrt[3]{x^2}+\frac{18}{7}x\sqrt[6]{x}+\frac{9}{5}x\sqrt[3]{x^2}+\frac{6}{13}x^2\sqrt[6]{6}+C$ (c) $\frac{6}{7}\sqrt[6]{x^7}-\frac{4}{3}x\sqrt[4]{x^3}+C$

2. (a) $\frac{x^6}{6}+\frac{3x^5}{5}-\frac{x^4}{4}-x^3+\frac{x^2}{2}+3x+C$ (b) $\ln|x+1|+\frac{1}{x+1}+C$

3. (a) $\ln|x|-\frac{1}{4x^4}+C$ (b) $\frac{1}{12}(2x+3)^{3/2}-(2x-1)+C$ (c) $\frac{2}{3}\left(\frac{x^3-1}{x\sqrt{x}}\right)+C$

4. (a) $\frac{x^3}{3}+C$ (b) $\left(x+\frac{x^2}{2!}+\frac{x^3}{3!}+\frac{x^4}{4!}+......\infty\right)+C$

5. (a) $\frac{e^{4x}}{4}+C$ (b) $e^x+e^{-x}+C$ (c) $-\frac{2}{\ln 5}5^{-x}+\frac{1}{5\ln 2}2^{-x}+C$

6. (a) $\frac{60}{\pi}\sin(3x+2)°+C$ (b) $\frac{1}{a}\tan(ax+b)+C$ (c) $-\frac{1}{m}\cot(mx+n)-x+C$ (d) $2\tan\frac{x}{2}-x+C$

(e) $\frac{1}{2}x+\frac{1}{8}\sin(4x+2)+C$ (f) $\frac{1}{12}\sin 3(x+1)+\frac{3}{4}\sin(x+1)+\frac{3}{2}\sin 2x+C$

7. (a) $x+\frac{1}{4}\cos 2x+C$ (b) $-\cot x+\sec x+\cos x+C$

8. (a) $\tan x-\cot x+C$ (b) $(x+b)\cos b-\sin b\ln|\sin(x+b)|+C$ (c) $\tan x-\cot x-3x+C$

(d) $\tan x-x+C$ (e) $-\frac{\cos 3x}{3}+C$ (f) $-2\cos x+C$ (g) $-\frac{1}{64}\cos 8x+C$

9. (a) $\frac{1}{2}\tan^2 x+C$ (b) $\frac{1}{2}\ln\left|\sec\left(x-\frac{\pi}{6}\right)+\tan\left(x-\frac{\pi}{6}\right)\right|+C$

(c) $4x^{1/4}+x+\frac{x^2}{2}+\frac{x^3}{3}+\frac{x^4}{4}+\sec x+C$ (d) $-\cot x-\tan^{-1}x+C$ (e) $2\operatorname{cosec}\left(1-\frac{x}{2}\right)+C$

10. (a) $-\left(\frac{1}{2}\sin 2x+\sin x\right)+C$ (b) $\tan x-\frac{3x}{2}+\frac{1}{4}\sin 2x+C$ (c) $\frac{\sin x}{2}-\frac{\cos x}{2}-\frac{x}{2}+C$

11. (a) $\frac{1}{2}\text{arc tan}\frac{x-3}{2}+C$ (b) $\sin x - \cos x + C$ (c) $-0.2\cos 5x - x\sin 5\alpha + C$

12. (a) $\sec^{-1}(\sqrt{3}\,x) + C$ (b) $\frac{1}{2}\sin^{-1}(2x)+C$ (c) $\frac{1}{\sqrt{2}}\sec^{-1}\left(\frac{5x}{\sqrt{2}}\right)+C$

(d) $\sec^{-1}(2x+1)+C$ (e) $\frac{1}{4}\sec^{-1}\left(\frac{2x-1}{2}\right)+C$ (f) $2\sin^{-1}\left(\frac{x}{2\sqrt{3}}\right)+C$

(g) $-\frac{1}{3\sqrt{3}}\tan^{-1}\left(\frac{2-3x}{\sqrt{3}}\right)+C$

13. (a) $-\frac{1}{x}+\tan^{-1}x+C$ (b) $\frac{1}{2}\left[\frac{x^3}{3}+\tan^{-1}x\right]+C$ (c) $\frac{3}{2}\sin^{-1}x+C$

14. (a) $x-\tan^{-1}x+C$ (b) $\ln|x|+2\tan^{-1}x+C$ (c) $\frac{x^3}{3}-x+\tan^{-1}x+C$

(d) $x+\frac{1}{2}\ln\left|\frac{x-1}{x+1}\right|+C$ (e) $5\left[\frac{2}{3}x\sqrt{x}-12\sqrt{x}-\frac{18}{\sqrt{x}}\right]+C$ (f) $\frac{-3}{5x^5}+\frac{2}{3x^3}-\frac{2}{x}-2\tan^{-1}x+C$

15. (a) $I=\frac{1}{10}\text{arc tan}\frac{2x}{5}+C$ (b) $\text{arc sin}\frac{3x}{2}+C$ (c) $\frac{1}{4\sqrt{2}}\ln\left|\frac{2\sqrt{2}+x+2}{2\sqrt{2}-(x+2)}\right|+C$

(d) $-\frac{2}{x}+\text{arc tan}\,x+C$ (e) $\ln\left(x+\sqrt{1+x^2}\right)+\text{arc sin}\,x+C$ (f) $C-\frac{5}{33}(8-3x)^{11/5}$

INTEGRATION BY METHODS OF SUBSTITUTION

Now we have realized that integration is an intuitive process of obtaining the anti-derivative of the given integrand function and while doing so usually we have to change variable by substituting some function involved in the integrand as a new variable to simplify the integrand such that its anti-derivative can be judged. At times there may be many possible substitutions to reduce the integrand to an integrable form but to find out the most suitable one is really an art and an integration is nothing but to acquiring that skill by practicing. In practice it is very possible to make a wrong substitution, if it does not work, abandon it and guess another substitution.

This method has evolved from the generalized power rule and afterward grown up so vast that it governs the entire process of indefinite integration.

Given integral $I=\int f(x)\,dx$ if we wish to substitute $x = g(t)$, anticipating that it will reduce the integral to standard form, then

Since $\frac{dI}{dx}=f(x)$ and $\frac{dx}{dt}=g'(t)$.

Now applying chain rule of differentiation,

we get $\frac{dI}{dt}=\frac{dI}{dx}\cdot\frac{dx}{dt}$

$\Rightarrow \frac{dI}{dt}=f(x).g'(t)$

$\Rightarrow dI=f\left(g(t)\right).g'(t)\,dt$

Therefore, integrating both sides we conclude $I=\int dI=\int f\left(g(t)\right).g'(t)\,dt$

ILLUSTRATION 34: Find the following integrals:

(a) $\int \frac{dx}{1+\sqrt{x+1}}$ (b) $\int \frac{4x+3}{(x-2)^3}dx$

(c) $\int \frac{dx}{1+\sqrt{x}}$ (d) $\int \frac{\sqrt{x}}{x+4}dx$

SOLUTION: (a) Consider the integral $I=\int \frac{dx}{1+\sqrt{x+1}}$, to rationalize the integral part, put $\sqrt{x+1}=t$

i.e., $x + 1 = t^2$, thus, integral reduces to

$$I=\int \frac{2t\,dt}{1+t}=2\int \frac{t+1-1}{1+t}dt=2\int 1.dt-2\int \frac{1}{1+t}dt=2t-2\ln|1+t|+C$$

Re-substituting $t=\sqrt{x+1}$, we get

$$I=2\sqrt{x+1}-2\ln\left(1+\sqrt{x+1}\right)+C$$

(b) Given integral $I=\int \frac{4x+3}{(x-2)^3}dx$

For simplifying the integrand without reducing it into partial fractions, put $x - 2 = t$

$\Rightarrow dx = dt,$

$$\therefore \quad I=\int \frac{4(2+t)+3}{t^3}dt=\int\left(\frac{11}{t^3}+\frac{4}{t^2}\right)dt=11\left(\frac{t^{-2}}{-2}\right)+4\left(\frac{t^{-1}}{-1}\right)+C=-\frac{11}{2t^2}-\frac{4}{t}+C$$

(c) Consider the integral, $I=\int \frac{dx}{1+\sqrt{x}}$; let $x = t^2$, thus, $dx = 2t\,dt$

$$\Rightarrow \quad I=\int \frac{2t\,dt}{1+t}=2\int \frac{t+1-1}{1+t}dt=2\int 1.dt-2\int \frac{dt}{1+t}$$

$$=2t-2\ln|1+t|+C=2\sqrt{x}-2\ln|1+\sqrt{x}|+C$$

(d) Consider the integral, $I=\int \frac{\sqrt{x}}{x+4}dx$, to rationalize the integrand expression put $x = t^2$

$\Rightarrow dx = 2t\,dt$, thus

$$\Rightarrow \quad I=\int \frac{2t^2dt}{4+t^2}=2\int \frac{t^2+4-4}{4+t^2}dt$$

$$=2\int 1.dt-8\int \frac{dt}{4+t^2}=2(t)-\frac{8}{2}\left(\tan^{-1}\frac{t}{2}\right)+C=2\left(\sqrt{x}\right)-4\tan^{-1}\left(\frac{\sqrt{x}}{2}\right)+C$$

THE METHOD OF SUBSTITUTION

If the integrand is of the type $f\left(g(x)\right).g'(x)$; where g be a differentiable function with range set R_g and $f(x)$ is continuous over interval R_g. Suppose F is an anti-derivative of f over the interval R_g, then to find the integral, we substitute $t = g(x)$ and proceed as below

$$\because \; g(x)=t \;\Rightarrow g'(x)=\frac{dt}{dx}$$

$$\Rightarrow g'(x)dx=dt$$

$$\therefore \quad \int f\left(g(x)\right)g'(x)dx=\int f(t)dt$$

$$= F(t) + C = F(g(x)) + C$$

Proof: It is enough to show that the derivative of the right member is the integrand of the left member. But that is a simple application of the Chain rule combined with the fact that $F' = f$.

$$\frac{d}{dx}\left[F(g(x))+C\right] = F'(g(x))g'(x) = f(g(x))g'(x)$$

Algorithm for substitution: To carry out this process follow the steps given below.

Step I: Choose some input of composite function $g(x) = t$ whose differential occurs in the integrand as a factor.

Step II: Change the differential to new variable. i.e., $g'(x)dx = dt$

Step III: Reconstruct the integrand in terms of new variable t and find the resulting integral in terms of 't'.

Step 4: Now replace t by $g(x)$ to generate anti-derivative in terms of x.

ILLUSTRATION 35: Find the integrals given below

(a) $\int (x^3+6x)^5(6x^2+12)\,dx$ (b) $\int (x^2+4)^{10} x\,dx$

(c) $\int \left(\frac{x^2}{2}+3\right)^2 x^2 dx$

SOLUTION: (a) Let $u = x^3 + 6x$; then $du = (3x^2 + 6)dx$. Thus, $(6x^2 + 12)dx = 2(3x^2 + 6)dx = 2du$,

and so $\int (x^3+6x)^5(6x^2+12)dx = \int u^5 2\,du = 2\int u^5\,du = 2\left[\frac{u^6}{6}+C\right]$

$$= \frac{u^6}{3}+2C = \frac{(x^3+6x)^6}{3}+K.$$

Two things should be noted about our solution. First, the fact that $(6x^2 + 12)dx$ is $2\,du$ instead of du caused no trouble; the factor 2 could be moved in front of the integral sign by linearity. Second, we wind up with an arbitrary constant of $2C$. This is still an arbitrary constant; we called it K.

(b) Let $u = x^2 + 4$; then $du = 2x\,dx$.

Thus, $\int (x^2+4)^{10} xdx = \int (x^2+4)^{10} \cdot \frac{1}{2} \cdot 2xdx$

$$= \frac{1}{2}\int u^{10}\,du = \frac{1}{2}\left(\frac{u^{11}}{11}+C\right) = \frac{(x^2+4)^{11}}{22}+K$$

(c) Let $u = x^2/2 + 3$; then $du = x\,dx$. The method illustrated in (a) and (b) fails because $x^2\,dx = x(x\,dx) = x\,du$, and the x cannot be passed in front of the integral sign (that can be done only with a constant factor). However, we can expand the integrand by ordinary algebra and then use the power rule.

$$\int\left(\frac{x^2}{2}+3\right)^2 x^2 dx = \int\left(\frac{x^4}{4}+3x^2+9\right)x^2 dx$$

$$= \int\left(\frac{x^6}{4}+3x^4+9x^2\right)dx = \frac{x^7}{28}+\frac{3x^5}{5}+3x^3+C$$

ILLUSTRATION 36: Find the integral $\int (2x+3)\cos(x^2+3x)dx$.

SOLUTION: If we let $u = x^2 + 3x$ so that $du = (2x + 3)dx$, the integral above transforms to $\int \cos u\,du$ which you will note is not the integral of a power function. However, formally, $\int (2x+3)\cos(x^2+3x)dx = \int \cos u\,du = \sin u + C = \sin(x^2 + 3x) + C$

In this example, we can easily check our answer by differentiating the result. But will the method of substitution always work? Yes, provided we can prove the substitution rule for indefinite integrals. This rule plays the same role for integrals that the Chain rule plays for derivatives. Both deal with composite functions.

ILLUSTRATION 37: Find the integrals

(a) $\int \frac{\sin\sqrt{x}}{\sqrt{x}}dx$ (b) $\int x\sin^3(x^2)\cos(x^2)\,dx$

SOLUTION: (a) Let $u = \sqrt{x}$. So $du = \frac{1}{2}x^{-1/2}dx$

$$\int \frac{\sin\sqrt{x}}{\sqrt{x}}dx = 2\int \sin\sqrt{x}\left(\frac{1}{2}x^{-1/2}dx\right)$$

$$= 2\int \sin u\; du = -2\cos u + C = -2\cos\sqrt{x} + C$$

(b) Let $u = \sin(x^2)$, so $du = 2x\cos(x^2)\,dx$. Then

$$\int x\sin^3(x^2)\cos(x^2)dx = \frac{1}{2}\int \sin^3(x^2)\cos(x^2)2x\,dx$$

$$= \frac{1}{2}\int u^3 du = \frac{1}{2}\frac{u^4}{4} + C \;= \frac{1}{8}\sin^4(x^2) + C$$

ILLUSTRATION 38: Find the following integrals by substitution method:

(a) $\int e^x(x+1)\cos(xe^x)\,dx$ (b) $\int \frac{x^2}{1+x^6}dx$

SOLUTION: (a) Substitute here $f(x) = \cos(xe^x)$, now put $t = g(x) = xe^x$

$\Rightarrow (g'(x)) = (x+1)e^x = \frac{dt}{dx}$

$\Rightarrow e^x(x+1)dx = dt$

$\Rightarrow \int \cos t\; dt = \sin t + C = \sin(xe^x) + C$

(b) Substitute $x^3 = t \Rightarrow 3x^2 dx = dt \Rightarrow x^2 dx = \frac{dt}{3}$

$$\therefore\; I = \frac{1}{3}\int \frac{dt}{1+t^2} = \frac{1}{3}\tan^{-1}t + C = \frac{1}{3}\tan^{-1}x^3 + C$$

ILLUSTRATION 39: Find the integrals by substitution method : $\int \frac{1}{x(4x^2+1)}dx$

SOLUTION: Now, we will make the numerator the derivative of denominator.

Method 1: $I = \frac{1}{2}\int \frac{2x\,dx}{x^2(4x^2+1)}$ (by dividing both numerator and denominator by $2x$),

put $t = x^2$.

$$\therefore\; I = \frac{1}{2}\int \frac{dt}{t(4t+1)} = \frac{1}{2}\int \frac{4t+1-4t}{t(4t+1)}dt = \frac{1}{2}\int\left(\frac{dt}{t}\right) - \frac{1}{2}\int \frac{4t}{(4t+1)}dt$$

$$= \frac{1}{2}\ln|t| - 2\ln|4t+1| + C = \frac{1}{2}\ln\left|x^2\right| - 2\ln\left|4x^2+1\right| + C$$

Method 2: Let $I = \int \frac{1}{x^3\left(4+\frac{1}{x^2}\right)}dx$ $0 = \left(-\frac{1}{2}\right)\int \frac{(-2)x^{-3}}{\left(4+\frac{1}{x^2}\right)}dx$

Substitute $m = 4+\frac{1}{x^2} \Rightarrow \frac{dm}{dx} = 0+\frac{(-2)}{x^3}$ $\Rightarrow -2x^3\,dx = dm$

$$\Rightarrow I = \left(\frac{-1}{2}\right)\int \frac{1}{m}dm = \left(\frac{-1}{2}\right)\ln|m|+C = \left(\frac{-1}{2}\right)\ln\left|4+\frac{1}{x^2}\right|+C$$

$$= -\frac{1}{2}\left[\ln|4x^2+1|-\ln|x^2|\right]+C = \frac{1}{2}\left[\ln x^2-\ln(4x^2+1)\right]+C$$

ILLUSTRATION 40: Find the integral: $\int \sec x dx$ by substitution method.

SOLUTION: Since we have secant function, so we will convert it into tangent function so that it reduces to $\int f(g(x))g'(x)\,dx$

$$\Rightarrow \int \frac{1}{\cos x}dx = \int \frac{1}{\frac{1-\tan^2 x/2}{1+\tan^2 x/2}}dx = \int \frac{1+\tan^2 x/2}{1-\tan^2 x/2}dx = \int \frac{\sec^2\frac{x}{2}}{1-\tan^2\frac{x}{2}}dx;$$

Let, $m = \tan\frac{x}{2} \Rightarrow \frac{dm}{dx} = \left(\sec^2\frac{x}{2}\right)\left(\frac{1}{2}\right)$

$$\Rightarrow dx = \frac{2(dm)}{\sec^2\frac{x}{2}}$$

$$\Rightarrow I = \int \frac{\sec^2\frac{x}{2}}{1-m^2}\frac{2dm}{\sec^2\frac{x}{2}} = 2\int \frac{1}{1-m^2}dm = (-2)\int \frac{1}{m^2-1}dm = (-2)\left[\frac{1}{2(1)}\ln\left|\frac{m-1}{m+1}\right|\right]+C$$

$$= -\ln\left|\frac{m-1}{m+1}\right|+C = \ln\left|\frac{1+\tan\frac{x}{2}}{1-\tan\frac{x}{2}}\right|+C$$

ILLUSTRATION 41: If $\int \operatorname{cosec} x\,dx = k\ln|\operatorname{cosec} x-\cot x|+C$. Then find the value of k, by using substitution method.

SOLUTION: $I = \int \frac{1}{\sin x}dx = \int \frac{1+\tan^2\left(\frac{x}{2}\right)}{2\tan\left(\frac{x}{2}\right)}dx$ put $m = \tan\frac{x}{2} \Rightarrow \frac{dm}{dx} = \frac{1}{2}\left(\sec^2\frac{x}{2}\right)$

$$\Rightarrow dx = 2dm\left(\frac{1}{\sec^2\frac{x}{2}}\right)$$

$$\Rightarrow I = \int \frac{\sec^2\frac{x}{2}}{2m}\frac{2dm}{\sec^2\frac{x}{2}} \Rightarrow \ln|m|+C = \ln\left|\tan\frac{x}{2}\right|+C = \ln\left|\frac{\sin\frac{x}{2}}{\cos\frac{x}{2}}\right|+C = \ln\left|\frac{2\sin^2\frac{x}{2}}{2\sin\frac{x}{2}\cos\frac{x}{2}}\right|+C$$

$$= \ln\left|\frac{1-\cos x}{\sin x}\right|+C = \ln|\operatorname{cosec} x-\cot x|+C$$

$\therefore$ value of $k = 1$.

ILLUSTRATION 42: Find the integrals by substitution method: $\int e^{4x^2+2}d\left(x^2-2\right)$

SOLUTION: Put $x^2-2=t$,

Here we have to integrate w.r.t. (x^2-2). So, for convenience we are converting it into single variable, so we can put $x^2-2=t$.

$\Rightarrow x^2=t+2 \qquad \Rightarrow I=\int e^{4(2+t)+2}\,dt$

$$=\int e^{8+4t+2}\,dt = e^{10}\int e^{4t}\,dt = \frac{e^{4\left(x^2-2\right)+10}}{4}+C = \frac{e^{4x^2+2}}{4}+C$$

ILLUSTRATION 43: Find the integrals by substitution method: $\int \sin\left(x^2+x+1\right)d\left(x^2+x\right)$

SOLUTION: Put $x^2+x=t$; we get $I=\int \sin(t+1)\,dt$

$$\Rightarrow I=\int(\sin t.\cos 1+\cos t.\sin 1)\,dt = (\cos 1)\int \sin t\,dt+(\sin 1)\int \cos t\,dt$$

$$=(\cos 1)(-\cos t)+(\sin 1)(\sin t)+C = -\left[\cos(t+1)\right]+C = -\left[\cos\left(x^2+x+1\right)\right]+C$$

ILLUSTRATION 44: Find the integrals by substitution method: $\int\left(\tan^n\{x\}+\tan^{n-2}\{x\}\right)d\left(x-[x]\right)$

SOLUTION: Let $x-[x]=y$ (Since this represents fractional part) So, here we replace the $x-[x]$, i.e., $\{x\}$ by y,

$$\Rightarrow I=\int\left(\tan^n y+\tan^{n-2} y\right)dy \text{ and } \left[\because \{x\}=x-[x]=y\right] = \int\left(\tan^n y+\frac{\tan^n y}{\tan^2 y}\right)dy$$

$$\Rightarrow \int \tan^n y\left(\frac{\sec^2 y}{\tan^2 y}\right)dy = \int \tan^{n-2} y\sec^2 y\,dy$$

Let $m=\tan y \Rightarrow \dfrac{dm}{dy}=\sec^2 y \qquad \Rightarrow \sec^2 y\,dy=dm$

$$\Rightarrow I=\int m^{n-2}\,dm=\frac{m^{n-2+1}}{n-2+1}+C$$

$$\Rightarrow I=\frac{m^{n-1}}{n-1}+C=\frac{(\tan y)^{n-1}}{n-1}+C=\frac{\left(\tan\left[x-[x]\right]\right)^{n-1}}{n-1}+C$$

ILLUSTRATION 45: Find the following integrals:

(a) $\int e^{\left(e^{e^{e^x}}+e^{e^x}+e^x+x\right)}dx$ (b) $\int\dfrac{\left(x^3+4x\right)\sqrt{4-x^2}}{16-x^4}dx$

(c) $\int\dfrac{3-2\cot^{n-2}x}{3\tan x+2\cot x\cot^{n-2}x}dx$

SOLUTION: (a) Let $m=e^{e^{e^{e^x}}}$; $\dfrac{dm}{dx}=e^{e^{e^{e^x}}}.e^{e^{e^x}}.e^{e^x}.e^x$; $I=\int e^{e^{e^{e^x}}}.e^{e^{e^x}}.e^{e^x}.e^x\,dx$

$\Rightarrow I=\int dm=m+C \qquad \Rightarrow I=e^{e^{e^{e^x}}}+C$ Ans.

(b) $I=\int\dfrac{x\left(x^2+4\right)\sqrt{4-x^2}}{\left(4-x^2\right)\left(4+x^2\right)}dx \qquad \Rightarrow I=\int\dfrac{x\sqrt{4-x^2}}{\left(4-x^2\right)}dx \Rightarrow \int\dfrac{x}{\sqrt{4-x^2}}dx$

Now put $x = 2\sin\theta$ $\Rightarrow dx = 2\cos\theta\, d\theta$

$$\Rightarrow I = \int \frac{2\sin\theta}{2\cos\theta} 2\cos\theta\, d\theta = 2\int \sin\theta\, d\theta = 2(-\cos\theta) + C = -2\left(\sqrt{1-\frac{x^2}{4}}\right) + C$$

$$= \frac{-2}{2}\sqrt{4-x^2} + C = -\sqrt{4-x^2} + C.$$

Method 2: $I = \int \frac{x(x^2+4)\sqrt{4-x^2}}{(4-x^2)(4+x^2)}dx \Rightarrow I = \int \frac{x\sqrt{4-x^2}}{(4-x^2)}dx = \int \frac{x}{\sqrt{4-x^2}}dx$

Put $4 - x^2 = p$ $\Rightarrow \frac{dp}{dx} = -2x \Rightarrow dx = \frac{dp}{-2x}$

$$\Rightarrow xdx = \frac{dp}{-2}$$

$$\Rightarrow I = -\frac{1}{2}\int \frac{1}{\sqrt{p}}dp = -\frac{1}{2}\left(\frac{(p)^{1/2}}{1/2}\right) + C = -\sqrt{4-x^2} + C$$

(c) Let $I = \int \frac{3 - 2\cot^{n-2} x}{3\tan x + 2\cot x \cot^{n-2} x}dx \Rightarrow I = \int \frac{3\tan x - 2\tan x \cot^{n-2} x}{3\tan^2 x + 2\cot^{n-2} x}dx$

$$\Rightarrow I = \int \frac{\tan x(3 - 2\cot^{n-2} x)}{3\tan^2 x + 2\cot^{n-2} x}dx \Rightarrow I = \int \frac{(\tan x)(\cot^2 x)(3 - 2\cot^{n-2} x)}{3\tan^2 x \cot^2 x + 2\cot^n x}dx$$

$$\Rightarrow I = \int \frac{3\cot x - 2\cot^{n-1} x}{3 + 2\cot^n x}dx$$

$I = \int \frac{3\cos x(\sin^{n-1} x) - 2(\cos^{n-1} x)(\sin x)}{3\sin^n x + 2\cos^n x}dx$; put $m = 3\sin^n x + 2\cos^n x$

$$\Rightarrow \frac{dm}{dx} = 3(n)\sin^{n-1} x(\cos x) + 2n\cos^{n-1} x(-\sin x)$$

$$\Rightarrow dx = \frac{dm}{3n\sin^{n-1} x(\cos x) - 2n\sin x\cos^{n-1} x}$$

$$\Rightarrow I = \frac{1}{n}\int \frac{1}{m}dm = \frac{1}{n}\ln|m| + C = \frac{1}{n}\ln\left|3\sin^n x + 2\cos^n x\right| + C$$

■ LIST OF SOME STANDARD SUBSTITUTIONS

Integrand	Standard Substitutions	Mutation of Differential
$f(e^x)$	$e^x = t$	$\Rightarrow dx = t^{-1}\, dt$
$f(\log x)$	$\log x = t$	$\Rightarrow dx = e^t\, dt$
$f(\tan x)$	$\tan x = t$	$\Rightarrow dx = \frac{dt}{1+t^2}$
$f(\cot x)$	$\cot x = t$	$\Rightarrow dx = -\frac{dt}{1+t^2}$
$f(x^x)(1 + \ln x)$	$x^x = t$	$\Rightarrow (1 + \ln x)\, dx = t^{-1}\, dt$

ILLUSTRATION 46 Find $\int \frac{2\log x}{x} \sec^2 \left\{1+(\log x)^2\right\} dx$

SOLUTION: Put $m = 1+(\log x)^2 \Rightarrow \frac{dm}{dx} = 0+2(\log x)\left(\frac{1}{x}\right) \Rightarrow \frac{2\log x}{x} dx = dm$

$\Rightarrow I = \int \sec^2 m \, dm = \tan m + C = \tan\{1+(\log x)^2\} + C.$

ILLUSTRATION 47: Find the integrals by substitution method: $\int \frac{dx}{x\log\left(\frac{x}{2}\right)\sqrt{\left(\log\frac{x}{2}\right)^2 - 1}}$

SOLUTION: Let $I = \int \frac{dx}{(x)\log\left(\frac{x}{2}\right)\sqrt{\left(\log\frac{x}{2}\right)^2 - 1}}$ and put, $m = \log\frac{x}{2} \Rightarrow \frac{dm}{dx} = \frac{1}{(x/2)}.\left(\frac{1}{2}\right)$

$\Rightarrow \frac{dm}{dx} = \frac{1}{x} \qquad \Rightarrow \frac{dx}{x} = dm$

$\Rightarrow I = \int \frac{dm}{m\sqrt{m^2-1}} = \frac{1}{1}\sec^{-1}\frac{m}{1} + C = \sec^{-1}\left(\ln\frac{x}{2}\right) + C$

ILLUSTRATION 48: Find $\int \frac{(1+\ln x)}{x^x(x^x+1)} dx$ by substitution method:

SOLUTION: Let $t = x^x \Rightarrow \ln t = x \ln x \Rightarrow \frac{1}{t}\frac{dt}{dx} = (\ln x + 1)$

$\Rightarrow (1+\ln x)dx = \frac{1}{t}dt \qquad \Rightarrow I = \int \frac{1}{t^2(t+1)} dt$

$\Rightarrow I = (-1)\int \frac{t^2-1-t^2}{t^2(t+1)} dt$

$\Rightarrow I = (-1)\left[\int \frac{t-1}{t^2} dt - \int \frac{1}{1+t} dt\right] \qquad \Rightarrow I = (-1)\left[\int\left(\frac{1}{t} - \frac{1}{t^2}\right)dt - \ln(1+t)\right] + C$

$\Rightarrow (-1)\left[\ln t + \frac{1}{t} - \ln(1+t)\right] + C \qquad \Rightarrow (-1)\left[\ln\left|\frac{t}{1+t}\right| + \frac{1}{t}\right] + C$

$\Rightarrow -\frac{1}{x^x} + \ln\left|\frac{x^x+1}{x^x}\right| + C = \ln\left|\frac{x^x+1}{x^x}\right| - \frac{1}{x^x} + C.$

ILLUSTRATION 49: Find the integrals by substitution method: $\int \sin(4x^2).\, e^{\tan^2 x^2} dx^2$

SOLUTION: Put $x^2 = t$

$\Rightarrow I = \int \sin(4t)\, e^{\tan^2 t} dt = \int 2\sin 2t \cos 2t\, e^{\tan^2 t} dt = \int 2(2\sin t \cos t)\cos 2t\, e^{\tan^2 t} dt$

$= \int 4\sin t \cos t(\cos^2 t - \sin^2 t) e^{\tan^2 t} dt = \int 4\sin t \cos^3 t(1-\tan^2 t)\, e^{\tan^2 t} dt$

$= \int \frac{4\sin t}{\sec^3 t}(1-\tan^2 t) e^{\tan^2 t} dt$

$\Rightarrow$ Putting $m = \tan^2 t$

$\Rightarrow \frac{dm}{dt} = 2\tan t \sec^2 t \qquad \Rightarrow dt = \frac{dm}{2\tan t \sec^2 t}$

$$\Rightarrow \mathrm{I} = \int \frac{4\sin t}{\sec^3 t}(1-m)e^m \frac{dm}{2\tan t \sec^2 t} = \frac{1}{2}\int \frac{4\sin t \cos t}{\sec^3 t \sec^2 t}\frac{(1-m)e^m}{\sin t}dm$$

$$= \int \frac{2}{(\sec^3 t)^2}(1-m)e^m dm = \int \frac{2(1-m)e^m}{(1+m)^3}dm = 2\left(\int \frac{2-(1+m)}{(1+m)^3}\right)e^m dm$$

$$\Rightarrow 2\int e^m\left(\frac{2}{(1+m)^3} - \frac{1}{(1+m)^2}\right)dm \qquad \left[\because \int e^x\left(f(x)+f'(x)\right)dx = e^x f(x) + C\right]$$

$$\Rightarrow I = \frac{2}{(1+m)^2}e^m + C = \frac{2}{(1+\tan^2 x^2)^2}e^{\tan^2 x^2} + C$$

LIST OF SOME STANDARD SUBSTITUTIONS

Integrand	Standard Substitutions	Mutation of Differential
$f\left(x+\sqrt{x^2+1}\right)$	$x+\sqrt{x^2+1}=t$	$\Rightarrow dx = \frac{(1+t^2)}{2t^2}dt;\ x = \frac{1}{2}\left(t-\frac{1}{t}\right)$ & $\sqrt{x^2+1} = \frac{t^2+1}{2t}$
$f\left(x+\frac{1}{x}\right)\left(1-\frac{1}{x^2}\right)$	$x+\frac{1}{x}=t$	$\Rightarrow \left(1-\frac{1}{x^2}\right)dx = dt$
$f\left(x-\frac{1}{x}\right)\left(1+\frac{1}{x^2}\right)$	$x-\frac{1}{x}=t$	$\Rightarrow \left(1+\frac{1}{x^2}\right)dx = dt$
$e^x\left(f(x)+f'(x)\right)$	$e^x f(x) = t$	$\Rightarrow e^x (f(x) + f'(x))dx = dt$
$\left(f(x)+xf'(x)\right)$	$xf(x) = t$	$\Rightarrow (f(x) + xf'(x))\, dx = dt$

ILLUSTRATION 50: Find the integral $\int \frac{x^2-1}{x^4+1}dx$ by using proper substitution procedure.

SOLUTION: Let $I = \int \frac{x^2-1}{x^4+1}dx$. Dividing both numerator and denominator by x^2, we get

$$I = \int \frac{\left(1-\frac{1}{x^2}\right)}{\left(x^2+\frac{1}{x^2}\right)}dx = \int \frac{\left(1-\frac{1}{x^2}\right)}{x^2+\frac{1}{x^2}+2-2}dx = \int \frac{\left(1-\frac{1}{x^2}\right)}{\left(x+\frac{1}{x}\right)^2-\left(\sqrt{2}\right)^2}dx$$

$\Rightarrow$ Let $m = x + 1/x$

$$\Rightarrow \frac{dm}{dx} = 1-\frac{1}{x^2} \qquad \Rightarrow dx = \frac{dm}{\left(1-\frac{1}{x^2}\right)}$$

$$\Rightarrow I = \int \frac{1}{m^2-\left(\sqrt{2}\right)^2}dm = \frac{1}{2\left(\sqrt{2}\right)}\ln\left|\frac{m-\sqrt{2}}{m+\sqrt{2}}\right| + C$$

ILLUSTRATION 51: Find the integrals $\int \frac{x^2+1}{x^4+1}dx$ by using proper substitution procedure.

SOLUTION: Let $I = \int \frac{x^2+1}{x^4+1}dx$. Dividing numerator and denominator both by x^2 we get,

$$I = \int \frac{1+\frac{1}{x^2}}{x^2+\frac{1}{x^2}}dx \qquad \Rightarrow I = \int \frac{1+\frac{1}{x^2}}{\left(x-\frac{1}{x}\right)^2+\left(\sqrt{2}\right)^2}dx$$

Let $m = x - \frac{1}{x}$ $\qquad \Rightarrow \frac{dm}{dx} = 1+\frac{1}{x^2}$

$$\Rightarrow dx = \frac{1}{\left(1+\frac{1}{x^2}\right)}dm$$

$$\Rightarrow I = \int \frac{1}{m^2+\left(\sqrt{2}\right)^2}dm = \frac{1}{\sqrt{2}}\tan^{-1}\frac{m}{\sqrt{2}}+C = \frac{1}{\sqrt{2}}\tan^{-1}\left(\frac{x^2-1}{\sqrt{2}\,x}\right)+C$$

ILLUSTRATION 52: Find $I(x) = \int \frac{\left(x^2-1\right)}{\left(x^4+3x^2+1\right)\tan^{-1}\left(\frac{x^2+1}{x}\right)}dx$

SOLUTION: Let $I = \int \frac{\left(x^2-1\right)}{\left(x^4+3x^2+1\right)\tan^{-1}\left(\frac{x^2+6x+1}{x}\right)}dx$

Now, take $m = \tan^{-1}\left(\frac{x^2+1}{x}\right)$

$$\Rightarrow \frac{dm}{dx} = \frac{1}{1+\left(\frac{x^2+1}{x}\right)^2}\frac{d}{dx}\left(\frac{x^2+1}{x}\right) = \left(\frac{x^2}{x^2+\left(x^2+1\right)^2}\right)\times\left(\frac{x(2x)-\left(x^2+1\right)(1)}{x^2}\right)$$

$$= \left(\frac{x^2}{(x^4+3x^2+1)}\right)\times\left(\frac{2x^2-x^2-1}{x^2}\right) = \frac{x^2-1}{(x^4+3x^2+1)}$$

$$\Rightarrow \frac{x^2-1}{x^4+3x^2+1}dx = dm$$

$$\Rightarrow I = \int \frac{1}{m}dm = \ln|m|+c = \ln\left|\tan^{-1}\left(\frac{x^2+1}{x}\right)\right|+C$$

ILLUSTRATION 53: Find the following integral by using proper substitution procedure.
$\int e^x\left(x^3+3x^2+1\right)dx$

SOLUTION: For changing this integral functions into some of two functions one of which is $f(x)$ and other is its derivatives $f'(x)$; $\int e^x\left(\left(x^3+1\right)+3x^2\right)dx = \int e^x\left(f(x)+f'(x)\right)dx$; $f(x) = x^3+1, f'(x) = 3x^2$

$\therefore\ I = \int e^x\left(f(x)+f'(x)\right)dx = e^x f(x) + C$ (by using properties of integration)

$= e^x(x^3+1) + C.$

ILLUSTRATION 54: Find the following integral by using proper substitution procedure $\int \left(x\cot x - x\operatorname{cosec}^2 x + \cot x\right)e^x dx$

SOLUTION: Let $f(x) = x\cot x \Rightarrow \dfrac{d\left(f(x)\right)}{dx} = -x\operatorname{cosec}^2 x + \cot x$

$\therefore\ I = \int e^x\left[f(x)+f'(x)\right]dx = e^x f(x) + C$

$\Rightarrow x\cot x + C$ $\qquad\Rightarrow x\cot x + C$.

ILLUSTRATION 55: Find the following integral by using proper substitution procedure $\int e^x\left(x^4+3x^3+6x^2-5x+1\right)dx$

SOLUTION: Let $I = \int e^x\left(x^4+4x^3-x^3-3x^2+9x^2+18x-18x-5x+1\right)dx$

$\Rightarrow \int e^x\left[\left(x^4-x^3+9x^2-23x+24\right)+\left(4x^3-3x^2+18x-23\right)\right]dx$

In the above step we put x^4 in first bracket, its derivative $4x^3$ in second bracket, but we have $3x^3$ integrand, so for compensation take $-x^3$ in first bracket, its derivative $-3x^2$ in second bracket, but in integrand we have $6x^2$, so for compensation take $9x^2$ in first bracket and so on.

$= \int e^x\left[f(x)+f'(x)\right]dx$; $f(x) = x^4 - x^3 + 9x^2 - 23x + 24$.

$\therefore\ I = e^x\left[x^4-x^3+9x^2-23x+24\right]+C$

ILLUSTRATION 56: Find the integrals $\int e^x\left(x(\sin x+\cos x)+\sin x\right)dx$ by using proper substitution procedure.

SOLUTION: Let $f(x) = x\sin x \Rightarrow f'(x) = x\cos x + \sin x$

$\therefore\ \int e^x\left[f(x)+f'(x)\right] = e^x f(x) + C = e^x\left(x\sin x\right)+C$

ILLUSTRATION 57: Find the following integral by using proper substitution procedure $\int \dfrac{1}{1+x^4}dx$

SOLUTION: Let $I = \int \dfrac{1}{x^4+1}dx = \dfrac{1}{2}\int\dfrac{2}{x^4+1}dx = \dfrac{1}{2}\int\dfrac{(x^2+1)-(x^2-1)}{x^4+1}dx = \dfrac{1}{2}\int\dfrac{x^2+1}{x^4+1}dx - \dfrac{1}{2}\int\dfrac{x^2-1}{x^4+1}dx$

Dividing both numerator and denominator by x^2, we get

$$I = \frac{1}{2}\int\frac{\left(1+\frac{1}{x^2}\right)}{x^2+\frac{1}{x^2}}dx = -\frac{1}{2}\int\frac{\left(1-\frac{1}{x^2}\right)}{x^2+\frac{1}{x^2}}dx$$

. In first integral put $x - \dfrac{1}{x} = m$.

In second integral put $x + \dfrac{1}{x} = n$

$$\Rightarrow \left(1+\frac{1}{x^2}\right)dx = dm \text{ and } \left(1-\frac{1}{x^2}\right)dx = dn$$

$$\Rightarrow I = \frac{1}{2}\int\frac{dm}{m^2+2} - \frac{1}{2}\int\frac{dn}{n^2-2} = \frac{1}{2}\int\frac{1}{m^2+\left(\sqrt{2}\right)^2}dm - \frac{1}{2}\int\frac{1}{n^2-\left(\sqrt{2}\right)^2}dn$$

$$= \frac{1}{2\sqrt{2}}\tan^{-1}\left(\frac{m}{\sqrt{2}}\right) - \frac{1}{2}\cdot\frac{1}{2\sqrt{2}}\ln\left|\frac{n+\sqrt{2}}{n-\sqrt{2}}\right| + C$$

$$= \frac{1}{2\sqrt{2}}\tan^{-1}\left(\frac{x-\frac{1}{x}}{\sqrt{2}}\right) - \frac{1}{4\sqrt{2}}\ln\left|\frac{x+\frac{1}{x}+\sqrt{2}}{x+\frac{1}{x}-\sqrt{2}}\right| + C$$

$$= \frac{1}{2\sqrt{2}}\tan^{-1}\left(\frac{x^2-1}{\sqrt{2}x}\right) - \frac{1}{4\sqrt{2}}\ln\left|\frac{x^2+\sqrt{2}x+1}{x^2-\sqrt{2}x+1}\right| + C$$

ILLUSTRATION 58: Find the integral $\int\sqrt{\tan\theta}\,d\theta$

SOLUTION: Put $m=\sqrt{\tan\theta}$ $m^2=\tan\theta$

$\Rightarrow m^4 = \sec^2\theta - 1$ $\qquad\qquad \Rightarrow 2m\frac{dm}{d\theta} = \sec^2\theta$

$\Rightarrow m^4 = \sec^2\theta - 1$ $\qquad\qquad \Rightarrow m^4 + 1 = \sec^2\theta$

$$\Rightarrow \left(d\theta = \frac{2m}{m^4+1}dm\right)$$

$$\Rightarrow \int m\left(\frac{2m}{m^4+1}\right)dm = \int\frac{2m^2}{m^4+1}dm = 2\int\frac{m^2}{m^4+1}(dm) = 2\int\frac{1}{m^2+\frac{1}{m^2}}dm$$

$$= \int\left(\frac{1+\frac{1}{m^2}+1-\frac{1}{m^2}}{m^2+\frac{1}{m^2}}\right)dm = \int\frac{1+\frac{1}{m^2}+1-\frac{1}{m^2}}{m^2+\frac{1}{m^2}+2-2}dm$$

$$= \int\frac{\left(1+\frac{1}{m^2}\right)}{\left(m-\frac{1}{m}\right)^2+\left(\sqrt{2}\right)^2}dm + \int\frac{\left(1-\frac{1}{m^2}\right)}{\left(m+\frac{1}{m}\right)^2-\left(\sqrt{2}\right)^2}dm$$

Let $u = m-\frac{1}{m}$ and $v = m+\frac{1}{m}$

$$\therefore\ I = \int\frac{1}{u^2+\left(\sqrt{2}\right)^2}du + \int\frac{1}{v^2-\left(\sqrt{2}\right)^2}dv = \frac{1}{\sqrt{2}}\left(\tan^{-1}\left(\frac{u}{\sqrt{2}}\right)\right) + \frac{1}{2\sqrt{2}}\ln\left|\frac{v-\sqrt{2}}{v+\sqrt{2}}\right| + C$$

$$= \frac{1}{\sqrt{2}}\tan^{-1}\left(\frac{m-\frac{1}{m}}{\sqrt{2}}\right) + \left(\frac{1}{2\sqrt{2}}\right)\ln\left|\frac{m+\frac{1}{m}-\sqrt{2}}{m+\frac{1}{m}+\sqrt{2}}\right| + C$$

$$= \frac{1}{\sqrt{2}}\tan^{-1}\left(\frac{m^2-1}{\sqrt{2}m}\right) + \frac{1}{2\sqrt{2}}\ln\left|\frac{m^2-\sqrt{2}m+1}{m^2+\sqrt{2}m+1}\right| + C$$

$$= \frac{1}{\sqrt{2}}\tan^{-1}\left(\frac{\tan\theta-1}{\sqrt{2\tan\theta}}\right) + \frac{1}{2\sqrt{2}}\ln\left|\frac{\tan\theta-\sqrt{2\tan\theta}+1}{\tan\theta+\sqrt{2\tan\theta}+1}\right| + C$$

ILLUSTRATION 59: Find the following integrals:

(a) $\int\frac{x^5}{x^4+1}dx$ $\qquad\qquad$ (b) $\int\frac{1}{x^4+3x^2+1}dx$

SOLUTION: (a) Put $x^2 = m;\ \frac{dm}{dx} = 2x \quad \Rightarrow \quad dx = \frac{dm}{2x}$

$$\Rightarrow \frac{1}{2}\left[\int 1.dm - \int\frac{1}{m^2+1}dm\right] = \frac{1}{2}\left[m-\tan^{-1}m\right]+C = \frac{1}{2}\left[x^2-\tan^{-1}x^2\right]+C$$

(b) $I=\frac{1}{2}\int\frac{2}{x^4+3x^2+1}dx \quad \Rightarrow \quad I=\frac{1}{2}\left[\int\frac{x^2\left(1+\frac{1}{x^2}\right)-\left(1-\frac{1}{x^2}\right)x^2}{x^4+3x^2+1}dx\right]$

$$\Rightarrow \quad I=\frac{1}{2}\left[\int\frac{x^2\left(1+\frac{1}{x^2}\right)}{x^2\left(x^2+3+\frac{1}{x^2}\right)}dx-\int\frac{x^2\left(1-\frac{1}{x^2}\right)dx}{x^2\left(x^2+3+\frac{1}{x^2}\right)}\right]$$

$$=\frac{1}{2}\left[\int\frac{1+\frac{1}{x^2}}{\left(x^2+\frac{1}{x^2}+2-2\right)+3}dx-\int\frac{1-\frac{1}{x^2}}{\left(x^2+\frac{1}{x^2}+2-2\right)+3}dx\right]$$

$$=\frac{1}{2}\left[\int\frac{\left(1+\frac{1}{x^2}\right)}{\left(x-\frac{1}{x}\right)^2+\left(\sqrt{5}\right)^2}dx-\int\frac{\left(1-\frac{1}{x^2}\right)}{\left(x+\frac{1}{x}\right)^2+(1)^2}dx\right]$$

Put $m=x-\frac{1}{x}$ & $n=x+\frac{1}{x}$ in first and second integrals, respectively

$$\therefore \quad I=\frac{1}{2}\frac{1}{\sqrt{5}}\tan^{-1}\frac{m}{\sqrt{5}}-\frac{1}{2(1)}\tan^{-1}n+C$$

$$\therefore \quad I=\frac{1}{2\sqrt{5}}\tan^{-1}\left(\frac{x^2-1}{\sqrt{5}\,x}\right)-\frac{1}{2}\tan^{-1}\left(\frac{x^2+1}{x}\right)+C.$$

ILLUSTRATION 60: Find the intégral $\int\frac{2}{\sin^4 x+\cos^4 x}dx$

SOLUTION: Let $I=2\int\frac{1}{\sin^4 x+\cos^4 x}dx=2\int\frac{\sec^4 x}{\tan^4 x+1}dx=2\int\left(\frac{\sec^4 x}{\tan^4 x+1}\right)dx$

Put $m=\tan x \quad \Rightarrow \quad \frac{dm}{dx}=\sec^2 x$

$$\Rightarrow \quad dx=\frac{dm}{\sec^2 x}$$

$$\Rightarrow \quad I=2\int\left[\left(\frac{1+m^2}{1+m^4}\right)dm\right]=2\int\frac{1+m^2}{1+m^4}dm=2\int\left(\frac{1+\frac{1}{m^2}}{\frac{1}{m^2}+m^2}\right)dm=2\int\frac{1+\frac{1}{m^2}}{\frac{1}{m^2}+m^2+2-2}dm$$

$$=2\int\frac{\left(1+\frac{1}{m^2}\right)dm}{\left(m-\frac{1}{m}\right)^2+\left(\sqrt{2}\right)^2}=2\frac{1}{\left(\sqrt{2}\right)}\tan^{-1}\left(\frac{m-\frac{1}{m}}{\sqrt{2}}\right)+C=\sqrt{2}\tan^{-1}\left(\frac{\tan^2 x-1}{\sqrt{2}\tan x}\right)+C.$$

ILLUSTRATION 61: Find the integral $\int\frac{e^x\left(x^2+5x+7\right)}{(x+3)^2}dx$

SOLUTION: Let $I = \int e^x\left[\frac{x^2+5x+6}{(x+3)^2}+\frac{1}{(x+3)^2}\right]dx = \int e^x\left[\frac{(x+3)(x+2)}{(x+3)^2}+\frac{1}{(x+3)^2}\right]dx$

$$= \int\left(e^x\left[\frac{(x+2)}{(x+3)}+\frac{1}{(x+3)^2}\right]dx\right)$$

Substitute $m = \frac{x+2}{x+3} \Rightarrow \frac{dm}{dx} = \frac{x+3-x-2}{(x+3)^2} = \frac{1}{(x+3)^2}$

$$\Rightarrow I = \int e^x\left(f(x)+f'(x)\right)dx = e^x f(x)+C = e^x\left(\frac{x+2}{x+3}\right)+C$$

ILLUSTRATION 62: Find the following integrals:

(a) $\int e^x\left(\frac{2+\sin 2x}{1+\cos 2x}\right)dx$ (b) $\int e^{\tan^{-1}x}\left(\frac{1+x+x^2}{1+x^2}\right)dx$

SOLUTION: (a) Let $I = \int e^x\left(\frac{2+\sin 2x}{1+\cos 2x}\right)dx = \int e^x\left(\frac{2+2\cos x\sin x}{2\cos^2 x}\right)dx$

$$= \int e^x\left(\frac{1}{\cos^2 x}+\tan x\right)dx = \int e^x\left(\sec^2 x+\tan x\right)dx = \int e^x\left(f(x)+f'(x)\right)dx$$

$$= e^x f(x)+C = e^x \tan x+C.$$

(b) Let $I = \int e^{\tan^{-1}x}\left(\frac{1+x^2+x}{1+x^2}\right)dx$

Substitute $m = \tan^{-1} x$ $\Rightarrow x - \tan m$

$\therefore \frac{dm}{dx} = \frac{1}{1+x^2}$ $\Rightarrow dx = \left(1+x^2\right)dm$

$$\Rightarrow I = \int e^m\left(1+\tan^2 m+\tan m\right)dm$$

$$\Rightarrow I = \int e^m\left(\sec^2 m+\tan m\right)dm \qquad \left(\because \int e^x\left(f(x)+f'(x)\right)dx = e^x f(x)+C\right)$$

$$\Rightarrow e^m \tan m+C = xe^{\tan^{-1}x}+C.$$

ILLUSTRATION 63: Find the following intégral

(a) $\int \frac{e^x\left(1+nx^{n-1}-x^{2n}\right)}{\left(1-x^n\right)\sqrt{1-x^{2n}}}dx$ (b) $\int \frac{\left(x^4-1\right)}{x^2\left(x^4+x^2+1\right)^{1/2}}dx$

SOLUTION: (a) Consider $e^x\left(\frac{\left(1-x^{2n}\right)+\left(nx^{n-1}\right)}{\left(1-x^n\right)\sqrt{1-x^{2n}}}\right) = e^x\left(\frac{1+x^n}{\sqrt{1-x^{2n}}}+\frac{nx^{n-1}}{\left(1-x^n\right)\left(\sqrt{1-x^{2n}}\right)}\right)$

If $f(x) = \frac{1+x^n}{\sqrt{1-x^{2n}}}$ then $f'(x) = \frac{nx^{n-1}\sqrt{1-x^{2n}}-\left(1+x^n\right)\left(\frac{-n(x)^{2n-1}}{2\sqrt{1-x^{2n}}}\right)}{1-x^{2n}}$

$$= \frac{nx^{n-1}\left(1-x^{2n}\right)+\left(1+x^n\right)nx^{2n-1}}{\left(1-x^{2n}\right)\sqrt{1-x^{2n}}} = \frac{nx^{n-1}\left(1-x^{2n}\right)+\left(1+x^n\right)nx^{2n-1}}{\left(1-x^{2n}\right)\left(1-x^{2n}\right)^{1/2}}$$

$$= \frac{nx^{n-1}+nx^{2n-1}}{\left(1-x^{2n}\right)\sqrt{1-x^{2n}}} = \frac{nx^{n-1}}{\left(1-x^n\right)\sqrt{1-x^{2n}}}$$

$$\therefore \quad I = \int e^x [f(x) + f'(x)]dx = e^x f(x) + C = e^x\left(\frac{1+x^n}{\sqrt{1-x^{2n}}}\right) + C$$

ILLUSTRATION 64: Find $\int \frac{(x^4-1)}{x^2(x^4+x^2+1)^{1/2}}dx$

SOLUTION: Let $I = \int \frac{x^4-1}{x^3\left(x^2+1+\frac{1}{x^2}\right)^{1/2}}dx = \int \frac{x^4-1}{x^3\left(x^2+\frac{1}{x^2}+1\right)^{1/2}}dx = \int \frac{x-\frac{1}{x^3}}{\left(x^2+\frac{1}{x^2}+1\right)^{1/2}}dx$

Let us substitute $x^2 + \frac{1}{x^2} = t$

$\Rightarrow \frac{dt}{dx} = \left(2x - \frac{2}{x^3}\right) \qquad \Rightarrow \left(x - \frac{1}{x^3}\right)dx = \frac{dt}{2}$

$\Rightarrow I = \frac{1}{2}\int \frac{dt}{(t+1)^{1/2}} = \frac{1}{2}\left[\frac{(t+1)^{-\frac{1}{2}+1}}{-\frac{1}{2}}\right] + C = (t+1)^{1/2} + C$

$= \left[\left(x^2+\frac{1}{x^2}+1\right)^{1/2} + C\right] = \frac{(x^4+x^2+1)^{1/2}}{x} + C.$

LIST OF SOME STANDARD SUBSTITUTIONS, FOR INTEGRAND FUNCTION INVOLVING $\sqrt{a^2-x^2}$, $\sqrt{x^2-a^2}$, $\sqrt{a^2+x^2}$; $\sqrt{\frac{a-x}{a+x}}$

Integrand	Standard Substitutions	Mutation of Differential
$f\left(\sqrt{a^2-x^2}\right)$	$x = \begin{cases} a\sin\theta \\ a\cos\theta \end{cases}$	$\Rightarrow dx = a\cos\theta\, d\theta$ or $-a\sin\theta\, d\theta$
$f\left(\sqrt{a^2+x^2}\right)$	$x = \begin{cases} a\tan\theta \\ a\cot\theta \end{cases}$	$\Rightarrow dx = a\sec^2\theta\, d\theta$ or $-a\,\text{cosec}^2\theta\, d\theta$ or $-a\,\text{cosec}\theta\cot\theta\, d\theta$
$f\left(\sqrt{x^2-a^2}\right)$	$x = \begin{cases} a\sec\theta \\ a\,\text{cosec}\theta \end{cases}$	$\Rightarrow dx = a\sec\theta\tan\theta\, d\theta$ or $-a\,\text{cosec}\theta \,.\, \cot\theta$
$f\left(\sqrt{\frac{a-x}{a+x}}\right)$	$x = \begin{cases} a\cos\theta \\ a\sin\theta \end{cases}$	$\Rightarrow dx = -a\sin\theta\, d\theta$ or $a\cos\theta\, d\theta$

ILLUSTRATION 65: Find the integral $\int\sqrt{a^2-x^2}\,dx$ by using proper substitution.

SOLUTION: Put $x = a(\sin\theta)$

$\Rightarrow \frac{dx}{d\theta} = a\cos\theta \qquad \Rightarrow dx = a\cos\theta d\theta$

$$\Rightarrow I=\int\sqrt{a^2-a^2\sin^2\theta}\,(a\cos\theta)d\theta=\int(a\cos\theta)^2\,d\theta=a^2\int\cos^2\theta\,d\theta$$

$$=\left(\frac{1}{2}a^2\right)\int\left(2\cos^2\theta\right)d\theta=\left(\frac{a^2}{2}\right)\left[\int(1+\cos 2\theta)d\theta\right]=\frac{a^2}{2}\left[\theta+\frac{\sin 2\theta}{2}\right]+C$$

$$=\frac{a^2}{2}\left[\sin^{-1}\left(\frac{x}{a}\right)+\frac{1}{2}(\sin 2\theta)\right]+C=\frac{a^2}{2}\left[\sin^{-1}\left(\frac{x}{a}\right)+(\sin\theta\cos\theta)\right]+C$$

$$=\frac{a^2}{2}\left[\sin^{-1}\left(\frac{x}{a}\right)+\left(\frac{x}{a}\right)\sqrt{1-\frac{x^2}{a^2}}\right]+C=\frac{a^2}{2}\sin^{-1}\left(\frac{x}{a}\right)+\frac{ax}{2}\sqrt{1-\frac{x^2}{a^2}}+C.$$

ILLUSTRATION 66: Find $\int\frac{1}{\sqrt{a^2+x^2}}dx$ by using proper substitution.

SOLUTION: Put $x = a\tan\theta$ $\qquad \Rightarrow \sec^2\theta=\frac{x^2+a^2}{a^2}$

$$\Rightarrow \frac{dx}{d\theta}=a\left(\sec^2\theta\right) \qquad \Rightarrow dx=(a\sec^2\theta)d\theta$$

$$\Rightarrow I=\int\frac{1}{\sec\theta}\left(\sec^2\theta\right)d\theta=\int\sec\theta\,d\theta=\ln\left|\sec\theta+\tan\theta\right|+C$$

$$=\ln\left|\frac{\sqrt{x^2+a^2}}{a}+\frac{x}{a}\right|+C=\ln\left|x+\sqrt{x^2+a^2}\right|+C.$$

ILLUSTRATION 67: Find the integral $\int\sqrt{\frac{a-x}{a+x}}\,dx$ by using proper substitution.

SOLUTION: Put $x = a\sin\theta$ $\qquad \Rightarrow dx = a\cos\theta\,d\theta$

$$\Rightarrow I=\int\sqrt{\frac{a(1-\sin\theta)}{a(1+\sin\theta)}}\,a\cos\theta d\theta=\int\sqrt{\left(\frac{\cos\frac{\theta}{2}-\sin\frac{\theta}{2}}{\cos\frac{\theta}{2}+\sin\frac{\theta}{2}}\right)^2}\,a\cos\theta d\theta$$

$$=\int\frac{\left(1-\tan\frac{\theta}{2}\right)}{\left(1+\tan\frac{\theta}{2}\right)}\frac{a\left(1-\tan^2\frac{\theta}{2}\right)}{\left(1+\tan^2\frac{\theta}{2}\right)}d\theta$$

$$\Rightarrow a\int\frac{\left(1-\tan\frac{\theta}{2}\right)^2}{\left(1+\tan^2\frac{\theta}{2}\right)}d\theta=a\left[\int\frac{\left(1+\tan^2\frac{\theta}{2}-2\tan\frac{\theta}{2}\right)}{\left(1+\tan^2\frac{\theta}{2}\right)}d\theta\right]$$

$$\Rightarrow a\left[\int 1.\,d\theta-\int\frac{2\tan\frac{\theta}{2}}{1+\tan^2\frac{\theta}{2}}d\theta\right]$$

$$\Rightarrow a\left[\theta-\int\sin\theta\,d\theta\right] \qquad \Rightarrow a\left[\theta+\cos\theta\right]+C$$

$$\Rightarrow a\left[\sin^{-1}\frac{x}{a}+\frac{1}{a}\sqrt{a^2-x^2}\right]+C$$

ILLUSTRATION 68: Find the integral $\int \cos\left(2\cot^{-1}\sqrt{\frac{a-x}{a+x}}\right)dx$ by using proper substitution.

SOLUTION: Put $x = a\cos 2\theta$

$\Rightarrow dx = 2a(-\sin 2\theta)d\theta$

$\Rightarrow I = \int \cos\left(2\cot^{-1}\sqrt{\frac{1-\cos 2x}{1+\cos 2x}}\right)2a(-\sin 2\theta)\,d\theta$

$\Rightarrow I = \int \cos\left(2\cot^{-1}(\tan\theta)\right)(-2a\sin 2\theta)\,d\theta$

$\Rightarrow \text{I} = \int \cos\left[2\left(\frac{\pi}{2}-\theta\right)(-2a\sin 2\theta)\right]d\theta = \int \cos(\pi-2\theta)(-2a\sin 2\theta)\,d\theta$

$= \int(-\cos 2\theta)(-2a\sin 2\theta)\,d\theta = a\int \sin 4\theta\,d\theta = a\left[-\frac{\cos 4\theta}{4}\right]+C$ ...(1)

Now, $x = a\cos 2\theta$

$\Rightarrow \frac{x}{a} = \cos 2\theta \Rightarrow \sin 2\theta = \sqrt{\frac{a^2-x^2}{a^2}}$

$\Rightarrow \sin 2\theta = \sqrt{1-\frac{x^2}{a^2}}$ and $\cos 4\theta = \cos^2 2\theta - \sin^2 2\theta = \frac{x^2}{a^2}-1+\frac{x^2}{a^2} = \frac{2x^2-a^2}{a^2}$

$\therefore \cos 4\theta = \frac{2x^2-a^2}{a^2}$; from (1)

$\therefore I = \frac{-a}{4}\left(\frac{2x^2-a^2}{a^2}\right)+C = \left(\frac{a^2-2x^2}{4a}\right)+C.$

ILLUSTRATION 69: Find the integral $\int \frac{dx}{\sin x\cos^2 x}$

SOLUTION: Let $I = \int \frac{1}{\sin x\cos^2 x}dx = \int \frac{\sin^2 x+\cos^2 x}{\sin x\cos^2 x}dx.$

$= \int\left(\frac{\sin x}{\cos^2 x}+\frac{1}{\sin x}\right)dx = \int(\tan x\sec x+\operatorname{cosec} x)\,dx$

$= \int(\tan x\sec x)dx + \int \operatorname{cosec} dx = \sec x + \ln|\operatorname{cosec} x - \cot x| + C.$

ILLUSTRATION 70: Find the integral $\int \frac{1}{1+4\sin^2 x}dx$ by using proper substitution.

SOLUTION: Dividing both numerator and denominator by $\cos^2 x$, we get

$I = \int \frac{\sec^2 x}{\sec^2 x+4\tan^2 x}dx = \int \frac{\sec^2 x}{1+5\tan^2 x}dx$

Let $m = \tan x$ $\Rightarrow \frac{dm}{dx} = \sec^2 x$

$\Rightarrow dx = \frac{dm}{\sec^2 x}$ $\Rightarrow I = \int \frac{1}{1+5m^2}dm = \frac{1}{5}\int \frac{1}{m^2+\left(\frac{1}{\sqrt{5}}\right)^2}dm$

$= \frac{1}{5}\left[\frac{1}{1/\sqrt{5}}\tan^{-1}\left(\frac{m}{1/\sqrt{5}}\right)\right]+C = \frac{1}{\sqrt{5}}\tan^{-1}(\sqrt{5}\tan x)+C$

ILLUSTRATION 71: Find the integral $\int \sqrt{1+\sec x}\, dx$

SOLUTION: Given $I = \int \sqrt{\dfrac{1+\cos x}{\cos x}}\,dx = \int \sqrt{\dfrac{2\cos^2(x/2)}{\cos^2(x/2)-\sin^2(x/2)}}\,dx = \sqrt{2}\int \dfrac{\cos\frac{x}{2}}{\sqrt{1-2\sin^2\frac{x}{2}}}\,dx$

Let $m = \sin\dfrac{x}{2}$

$\Rightarrow \quad dm = \dfrac{1}{2}\left(\cos\dfrac{x}{2}\right)dx \qquad\qquad \Rightarrow \quad dx = \dfrac{dm}{\frac{1}{2}\cos\frac{x}{2}}$

$\Rightarrow \quad I = 2\sqrt{2}\int \dfrac{dm}{\sqrt{1-2m^2}} = (2\sqrt{2})\int \dfrac{1}{\sqrt{1-(\sqrt{2}m)^2}}\,dm$

$= = \dfrac{(2\sqrt{2})}{\sqrt{2}}\int \dfrac{1}{\sqrt{\left(\frac{1}{\sqrt{2}}\right)^2 - m^2}}\,dm = 2\sin^{-1}\left(\dfrac{m}{\frac{1}{\sqrt{2}}}\right)+C$

$= 2\sin^{-1}\left(\sqrt{2}m\right)+C = 2\sin^{-1}\left(\sqrt{2}\sin\dfrac{x}{2}\right)+C$

ILLUSTRATION 72: Find the integral $\int \dfrac{\sqrt{(4-x^2)^3}}{x^6}\,dx$ by using proper substitution.

SOLUTION: ***Method 1:*** Put $x = 2\sin\theta \qquad \Rightarrow \quad dx = 2\cos\theta\, d\theta$

$\Rightarrow \quad I = \int \dfrac{\sqrt{(4-4\sin^2\theta)^3}}{2^6\sin^6\theta}2\cos\theta\, d\theta = \int \dfrac{4^{3/2}(\cos^2\theta)^{3/2}}{2^6\sin^6\theta}2\cos\theta\, d\theta$

$= \dfrac{1}{4}\int \dfrac{\cos^4\theta}{\sin^6\theta}d\theta = \dfrac{1}{4}\int \dfrac{\cos^4\theta}{\sin^4\theta}.\dfrac{1}{\sin^2\theta}d\theta = \dfrac{1}{4}\int\left(\dfrac{\cos^4\theta}{\sin^4\theta}.\operatorname{cosec}^2\theta\right)d\theta;$

Substitute $m = \cot\theta \qquad\qquad \Rightarrow \quad \dfrac{dm}{d\theta} = -\operatorname{cosec}^2\theta$

$\Rightarrow \quad d\theta = -\dfrac{dm}{\operatorname{cosec}^2\theta}$

$\Rightarrow \quad I = \dfrac{1}{4}\int\left(-m^4\,dm\right) = -\left(\dfrac{1}{4}\right)\left[\dfrac{m^5}{5}\right]+C = -\dfrac{m^5}{20}+C = -\dfrac{(\cot\theta)^5}{20}+C$

$\because \quad x = 2\sin\theta \qquad\qquad \Rightarrow \quad \left(\dfrac{x}{2}\right)^2 = 1-\cos^2\theta$

$\Rightarrow \quad \cos^2\theta = 1-\left(\dfrac{x}{2}\right)^2 \qquad\qquad \Rightarrow \quad \cos\theta = \left(\dfrac{4-x^2}{4}\right)^{1/2}$

$\Rightarrow \quad \cot\theta = \dfrac{\cos\theta}{\sin\theta} = \left(\dfrac{4-x^2}{4}\right)^{1/2}\times\dfrac{2}{x} = \dfrac{(4-x^2)^{1/2}}{x}$

$\therefore \quad I = -\dfrac{1}{20}\left(\dfrac{(4-x^2)^{5/2}}{x^5}\right)+C.$

Method 2: Let $I = \int \frac{\sqrt{x^6\left(\frac{4}{x^2}-1\right)^3}}{x^6}dx = \int \frac{\sqrt{\left(\frac{4}{x^2}-1\right)^3}}{x^3}dx$;

Now, Put $m = \frac{4}{x^2}-1 \quad \Rightarrow \quad \frac{dm}{dx} = \frac{-8}{x^3}$

$\Rightarrow -\frac{1}{8}dm = \frac{dx}{x^3} \quad \Rightarrow \quad I = -\frac{1}{8}\int m^{3/2}dm = \frac{-1}{8}\left[\frac{m^{\frac{3}{2}+1}}{\frac{3}{2}+1}\right]+C = \frac{-1}{8}\left[\frac{m^{\frac{5}{2}}}{\frac{5}{2}}\right]+C$

$\Rightarrow I = \frac{-1}{20}(m)^{\frac{5}{2}}+C = \frac{-1}{20}\left(\frac{4-x^2}{x^2}\right)^{\frac{5}{2}}+C = \frac{-1}{20x^5}(4-x^2)^{5/2}+C$

ILLUSTRATION 73: Find the integral $\int \frac{x^2}{\sqrt{a^6-x^6}}dx$

SOLUTION: Put $x^3 = a^3\sin\theta \quad \Rightarrow \quad x = (a^3\sin\theta)^{1/3} = a(\sin\theta)^{1/3}$ and $dx = \frac{1}{3}a(\sin\theta)^{-\frac{2}{3}}\cos\theta\, d\theta$

Also, $x^2 = (a^3\sin\theta)^{2/3}$ and $x^6 = (x^3)^2 = (a^3\sin\theta)^2 = a^6\sin^2\theta$

$\Rightarrow I = \int \frac{(a^3\sin\theta)^{2/3}}{\sqrt{a^6-a^6\sin^2\theta}}\left(\frac{1}{3}a\cos\theta\right)(\sin\theta)^{-\frac{2}{3}}d\theta = a^2\int \frac{(\sin\theta)^{2/3}}{a^3\cos\theta}\frac{a}{3}(\cos\theta)(\sin\theta)^{-2/3}d\theta$

$= \frac{1}{3}\int 1.\, d\theta = \frac{1}{3}(\theta)+C = \frac{1}{3}\sin^{-1}\left(\frac{x^3}{a^3}\right)+C$

ILLUSTRATION 74: Find the integral $\int \frac{\sqrt{\cot x}}{\sin x\cos x}dx$

SOLUTION: Put $\cot x = m$

$\Rightarrow \frac{dm}{dx} = -\operatorname{cosec}^2 x \Rightarrow dx = \frac{-dm}{\operatorname{cosec}^2 x}$

$\Rightarrow I = \int \frac{\sqrt{\cot x}}{\sin x\cos x}\frac{(-dm)}{\operatorname{cosec}^2 x} = -\int \frac{\sqrt{\cot x}}{\cot x}dm = -\int(\cot x)^{-\frac{1}{2}}dm$

$= -\int (m)^{-\frac{1}{2}}dm = \frac{(-1)(m)^{\frac{1}{2}}}{1-\frac{1}{2}}+C = \frac{-m^{1/2}}{1/2}+C = -2m^{1/2}+C = -2(\cot x)^{1/2}+C.$

ILLUSTRATION 75: Find the integral $\int \frac{\sin^{-4}\theta}{1+\sin^{-3}\theta}d\theta$ by using proper substitution procedure.

SOLUTION: Let $I = \int \frac{\sin^{-4}\theta}{1+\sin^{-3}\theta}d\theta$ and put $m = 1+\sin^{-3}\theta$

$\Rightarrow \frac{dm}{d\theta} = 0+(-3)\sin^{-4}\theta \quad \Rightarrow \quad d\theta = \frac{-dm}{3\sin^{-4}\theta}$

$\Rightarrow I = \frac{-1}{3}\int \frac{1}{m}dm = -\frac{1}{3}\ln|m|+C = \frac{-1}{3}\ln\left|1+\sin^{-3}\theta\right|+C = \frac{-1}{3}\ln\left|\frac{1+\sin^3\theta}{\sin^3\theta}\right|+C.$

LIST OF SOME STANDARD SUBSTITUTIONS FOR INTEGRAND HAVING FUNCTION OF $\sqrt{(x-a)\div \text{or} \times (b \pm x)}$; $\left(\frac{x+a}{x+b}\right)^{\frac{1}{n}-1}$

Integrand	Standard Substitutions	Mutation of Differential
$f\left(\sqrt{(x-a)(b-x)}\right)$ or $f\left(\sqrt{\frac{x-a}{b-x}}\right)$	$x = a\cos^2\theta + b\sin^2\theta$	$\Rightarrow dx = 2(b-a)\sin\theta\cos\theta\, d\theta$
$f\left(\sqrt{(x-a)(b+x)}\right)$ or $f\left(\sqrt{\frac{x-a}{b+x}}\right)$	$x = a\sec^2\theta + b\tan^2\theta$	$\Rightarrow dx = 2(a+b)\sec^2\theta\tan\theta\, d\theta$
$\left((x+a)^{\frac{1}{n}-1}(x+b)^{-1-\frac{1}{n}}\right)$	$\frac{x+a}{x+b} = t$	$dt = \frac{(b-a)}{(x+b)^2}dx$ or $dt = \frac{(a-b)}{(x+a)^2}dx$

ILLUSTRATION 76: Find the following integrals by using proper substitution procedure.

(a) $\int \sqrt{(4-x)(x-3)}\, dx$ (b) $\int \sqrt{\frac{x-6}{x+3}}\, dx$

SOLUTION: (a) Substitute $x = 4\cos^2\theta + 3\sin^2\theta$

$\Rightarrow \frac{dx}{d\theta} = 4\times 2\cos\theta(-\sin\theta) + 3\times 2\sin\theta(\cos\theta)$

Also $x = 4(1-\sin^2\theta) + 3\sin^2\theta = 4 - \sin^2\theta$

$\Rightarrow \sin^2\theta = 4 - x.$ $\Rightarrow \sin\theta = (4-x)^{1/2}$

$\Rightarrow \theta = \sin^{-1}(4-x)^{1/2}$ and $dx = (-2\cos\theta\sin\theta)\, d\theta$

$$\therefore I = \int \sqrt{\left(4-4\cos^2\theta - 3\sin\theta^2\right)\left(4cos^2\theta + 3\sin^2\theta - 3\right)}\left(-2\cos\theta\sin\theta\, d\theta\right)$$

$$= \int \sqrt{\left(4\sin^2\theta - 3\sin^2\theta\right)\left(4\cos^2\theta - 3\cos^2\theta\right)}\left(-\sin 2\theta\, d\theta\right)$$

$$= \int \sqrt{\sin^2\theta\cos^2\theta}\left(-\sin 2\theta\right)d\theta = \frac{1}{2}\int \sqrt{\left(2\sin\theta\cos\theta\right)^2}\left\{-\left(\sin 2\theta\right)\right\}d\theta$$

$$= \frac{1}{2}\left[\int \sin 2\theta\left(-\sin 2\theta\right)d\theta\right] = \frac{1}{4}\left[\int\left(-2\sin^2 2\theta\right)d\theta\right] = \frac{1}{4}\left\{\int\left(\cos 4\theta - 1\right)\right\}d\theta$$

$$= \frac{1}{4}\left[-\theta + \frac{\sin 4\theta}{4}\right] + C \quad \text{...(1)}$$

Also $x = 4\cos^2\theta + 3\sin^2\theta$

$\Rightarrow x = 2(2\cos^2\theta) + \frac{3}{2}(2\sin^2\theta) = 2(1 + \cos 2\theta) + \frac{3}{2}(1 - \cos 2\theta)$

$\Rightarrow x = 2 + \frac{3}{2} + \left(2 - \frac{3}{2}\right)\cos 2\theta$ $\Rightarrow x = \left(\frac{7}{2}\right) + \left(\frac{1}{2}\right)\cos 2\theta$

$\Rightarrow 2x - 7 = \cos 2\theta$ ...(2)

Similarly, $\sin 2\theta = \sqrt{1-(2x-7)^2} = 2\sqrt{-x^2+7x-12}$

$\because$ Sin $4\theta = 2\sin 2\theta\cos 2\theta$ $\Rightarrow 4\sqrt{-x^2+7x-12}\,(2x-7)$

$\therefore$ From (1); $I = \frac{1}{4}\left[-\sin^{-1}(4-x)^{1/2} + (2x-7)\sqrt{-x^2-7x-12}\right] + C$

(b) Given $I = \int \sqrt{\frac{x-6}{x+3}}\, dx$

Put $x = 6\sec^2\theta + 3\tan^2\theta$; $x + 3 = 9\sec^2\theta$; $x - 6 = 9\tan^2\theta$

$\Rightarrow dx = 18\sec^2\theta \tan\theta\, d\theta$

$$\Rightarrow I = \int \sqrt{\frac{9(\tan^2\theta)}{9\sec^2\theta}}\left(18\sec^2\theta\tan\theta\right)d\theta = \int\left(\frac{\tan\theta}{\sec\theta}\right)\left(18\sec^2\theta\tan\theta\right)d\theta = 18\int \sec\theta\tan^2\theta\, d\theta$$

$= 18\int(\sec\theta\tan\theta)\sqrt{(\sec\theta)^2 - 1}\, d\theta$; put $m = \sec\theta$

$\Rightarrow \frac{dm}{d\theta} = \sec\theta\tan\theta \qquad \Rightarrow d\theta = \frac{dm}{\sec\theta\tan\theta}$

$$\Rightarrow I = 18\int\sqrt{m^2-1}\, dm = 18\left(\frac{1}{2}m\sqrt{m^2-1} - \frac{1}{2}\ln\left|m + \sqrt{m^2-1}\right|\right) + C$$

$$= 18\left[\frac{1}{2}(\sec\theta)(\tan\theta) - \frac{1}{2}\ln|\sec\theta + \tan\theta|\right] + C$$

$$= 18\left[\frac{1}{2}\frac{1}{9}((x+3)(x-6))^{\frac{1}{2}} - \frac{1}{2}\ln\left|\frac{\sqrt{x+3}+\sqrt{x-6}}{3}\right|\right] + C$$

$$= 18\left[\frac{1}{18}((x+3)(x-6))^{\frac{1}{2}} - \frac{1}{2}\ln\left|\frac{\sqrt{x+3}+\sqrt{x-6}}{3}\right|\right] + C$$

ILLUSTRATION 77: Find the following integrals:

(a) $\int \frac{1}{\sqrt[4]{(x-2)^5(x+1)^3}}\, dx$ (b) $\int e^x \frac{(1+2x-x^4)}{(1-x^2)\sqrt{1-x^4}}\, dx$ \

(c) $\int \left(\frac{x}{4-x}\right)^{1/2} dx$

SOLUTION: (a) Let $I = \int \frac{1}{\sqrt[4]{(x-2)^5(x+1)^3}}\, dx \qquad \Rightarrow I = \int\left(\frac{(x-2)^5}{(x+1)^5}(x+1)^5(x+1)^3\right)^{-\frac{1}{4}} dx$

$I = \int\left(\left(\frac{x-2}{x+1}\right)^5(x+1)^8\right)^{-\frac{1}{4}} dx$; Let $m = \frac{x-2}{x+1} \Rightarrow \frac{dm}{dx} = \frac{(x+1)(1)-(x-2)(1)}{(x+1)^2}$

$\Rightarrow \frac{dm}{dx} = \frac{3}{(x+1)^2} \qquad \Rightarrow dx = \frac{1}{3}(dm)(x+1)^2$

$$\Rightarrow I = \int\left((m^5)^{-1/4}(x+1)^{-2}.\frac{1}{3}dm(x+1)^2\right) = \frac{1}{3}\int(m)^{-5/4}\, dm$$

$$= \frac{1}{3}\frac{(m)^{-\frac{5}{4}+1}}{\frac{-5}{4}+1} + C = \frac{-4}{3}\frac{1}{\left(\frac{x-2}{x+1}\right)^{1/4}} + C = \frac{-4}{3}\left(\frac{x+1}{x-2}\right)^{1/4} + C$$

(b) Given $I = \int e^x\left(\frac{1-x^4}{(1-x^2)\sqrt{1-x^4}} + \frac{2x}{(1-x^2)\sqrt{1-x^4}}\right)dx$.

Put $f(x)=\dfrac{1-x^4}{\left(1-x^2\right)\sqrt{1-x^4}}$ $\Rightarrow$ $f(x)=\dfrac{1+x^2}{\sqrt{1-x^4}}$

$$\Rightarrow\ f'(x)=\frac{\sqrt{1-x^4}\,(2x)-\left(1+x^2\right)\dfrac{1}{2}\dfrac{\left(-4x^3\right)}{\sqrt{1-x^4}}}{\left(1-x^4\right)}=\frac{2x\left(1-x^4\right)+2x^3\left(1+x^2\right)}{\left(1-x^4\right)\sqrt{1-x^4}}$$

$$\Rightarrow\ \frac{2x-2x^5+2x^3+2x^5}{\left(1-x^4\right)\sqrt{1-x^4}}=\frac{2x(1+x^2)}{\left(1-x^4\right)\sqrt{1-x^4}}=\frac{2x}{\left(1-x^2\right)\sqrt{1-x^4}}$$

Now, $f'(x)=\dfrac{2x}{\left(1-x^2\right)\sqrt{1-x^4}}$

$$\Rightarrow\ I=\int e^x\left(f(x)+f'(x)\right)dx=e^x f(x)+C=\frac{e^x\left(1-x^4\right)}{\left(1-x^2\right)\sqrt{1-x^4}}+C=\frac{e^x\left(1+x^2\right)}{\sqrt{1-x^4}}+C$$

(c) Put $x = 4\sin^2\theta$; $\dfrac{dx}{d\theta}=4(2\sin\theta)(\cos\theta)$ $\Rightarrow I=2\int(\tan\theta)(8\sin\theta\cos\theta)d\theta$

$$=16\int\sin^2\theta\ \ d\theta=8\int 2\sin^2\theta\,d\theta=8\int(1-\cos 2\theta)\,d\theta=8\left[\theta-\frac{\sin 2\theta}{2}\right]+C \qquad \ldots(1)$$

Also $\sin\theta=\dfrac{\sqrt{x}}{2}$. $\Rightarrow$ $\cos^2\theta=1-\sin^2\theta=1-\dfrac{x}{4}=\dfrac{4-x}{4}$

$\Rightarrow$ $\cos\theta=\dfrac{\sqrt{4-x}}{2}$ $\Rightarrow$ $2\sin\theta\,.\,\cos\theta=\dfrac{\sqrt{x(4-x)}}{2}$

$\Rightarrow$ $\sin 2\theta=\dfrac{\sqrt{x(4-x)}}{2}$ $\Rightarrow I=8\left[\sin^{-1}\left(\dfrac{\sqrt{x}}{2}\right)-\dfrac{1}{4}\sqrt{x(4-x)}\right]+C$ (from (1))

ILLUSTRATION 78: Find the following integrals:

(a) $\displaystyle\int\left(\frac{1}{\left(2+3\sqrt{x}\right)\sqrt{4x-9x^2}}dx\right)$ (b) $\displaystyle\int\frac{1}{(p+4)^{8/7}(p-3)^{6/7}}dp$

SOLUTION: (a) Let $I=\displaystyle\int\frac{1}{\left(2+3\sqrt{x}\right)\left(\sqrt{4x-9x^2}\right)}dx=\int\frac{1}{\left(2+3\sqrt{x}\right)\sqrt{x}\sqrt{4-9x}}dx$

Put $\sqrt{x}=t\Rightarrow\dfrac{dt}{dx}=\dfrac{1}{2}x^{-1/2}$ $\Rightarrow$ $dx=2\,dt\left(\sqrt{x}\right)$

$$\Rightarrow\ I=\int\frac{2\sqrt{x}\,dt}{(2+3t)\sqrt{x}\sqrt{4-9x}}=(2)\int\frac{dt}{(2+3t)\left(\sqrt{4-9t^2}\right)}$$

Put $2+3t=\dfrac{1}{u}$ $\Rightarrow$ $\left(\dfrac{1}{u}-2\right)\dfrac{1}{3}=t$

$\Rightarrow$ $t=\dfrac{1}{3}\left(\dfrac{1-2u}{u}\right)$ $\Rightarrow$ $3t=\dfrac{1}{u}-2$

$\Rightarrow$ $3\dfrac{dt}{du}=\dfrac{-1}{u^2}-0$ $\Rightarrow$ $dt=-\dfrac{1}{3u^2}(du)$

$$\Rightarrow I=(2)\int\frac{-(du)/3u^3}{\frac{1}{u}\sqrt{(2-3t)(2+3t)}}=(-2)\int\frac{(du)/3u^3}{\frac{1}{u}\sqrt{\frac{(4u-1)}{u}\left(\frac{1}{u}\right)}}=-2\int\frac{du/3u^2}{\frac{1}{u^2}\sqrt{4u-1}}=-\frac{2}{3}\int\frac{du}{\sqrt{4u-1}}$$

$$=-\frac{2}{3}\int(4u-1)^{-\frac{1}{2}}du=-\frac{2}{3}\left[\frac{(4u-1)^{-1/2+1}}{1/2}\right]+C=\frac{1}{3}[4u-1]^{1/2}+C=\frac{1}{3}\left(\frac{2-3t}{2+3t}\right)^{1/2}+C$$

$$=\frac{1}{3}\left(\frac{2-3\sqrt{x}}{2+3\sqrt{x}}\right)^{1/2}+C.$$

(b) Given $I=\int\frac{1}{(p+4)^{\frac{8}{7}}.(p+4)^{\frac{6}{7}}\left(\frac{p-3}{p+4}\right)^{\frac{6}{7}}}dp=\int\frac{1}{(p+4)^2\left(\frac{p-3}{p+4}\right)^{6/7}}dp$

Put $m=\frac{p-3}{p+4}$ $\qquad\Rightarrow\frac{dm}{dp}=\frac{(p+4)(1)-(p-3)(1)}{(p+4)^2}$

$\Rightarrow\frac{dm}{dp}=\frac{4+3}{(p+4)^2}$ $\qquad\Rightarrow dp=\frac{(p+4)^2}{7}dm$

$$\Rightarrow I=\int\frac{dm}{7m^{6/7}}=\frac{1}{7}\frac{m^{\left(\frac{-6}{7}+1\right)}}{\left(-\frac{6}{7}+1\right)}+C=m^{1/7}+C=7\left(\frac{p-3}{p+4}\right)^{\frac{1}{7}}+C.$$

Substitution after Taking x^n Common

Many integrals can be evaluated by taking x^n common from some bracketed expression and then using substitution. Some of the suggested forms are given below.

(i) $\int\frac{dx}{x(x^n+1)}$; $n\in\mathbb{N}$. Take x^n common and put $1+x^{-n}=t$.

(ii) $\int\frac{dx}{x^2(x^n+1)^{(n-1)/n}}$; $n\in\mathbb{N}$. Take x^n common and put $1+x^{-n}=t^n$

(iii) $\int\frac{dx}{x^n(1+x^n)^{1/n}}$. Take x^n common and put $1+x^{-n}=t$.

ILLUSTRATION 79: Find the integral $\int\frac{dx}{x^4(x^3+1)^2}$

SOLUTION: Given $I=\int\frac{dx}{x^4(x^3+1)^2}=\int\frac{dx}{x^{10}\left(1+\frac{1}{x^3}\right)^2}$

Put $1+\frac{1}{x^3}=t$ $\qquad\Rightarrow-\frac{3}{x^4}dx=dt$

$\Rightarrow\frac{1}{x^6}=(t-1)^2$ $\qquad\Rightarrow I=\frac{-1}{3}\int\frac{(t-1)^2}{t^2}dt=\frac{-1}{3}\int\frac{t^2+1-2t}{t^2}dt$

$$=\frac{-1}{3}\int\left(1+\frac{1}{t^2}-\frac{2}{t}\right)dt=\frac{-1}{3}\left[t-\frac{1}{t}-2\ln|t|\right]+C;\text{ where }t=1+\frac{1}{x^3}.$$

ILLUSTRATION 80: Find the integral $\int \frac{5x^4+4x^5}{(x^5+x+1)^2}dx$

SOLUTION: Given $I=\int \frac{5x^4+4x^5}{(x^5+x+1)^2}dx=\int \frac{x^4(5+4x)}{x^{10}\left(1+\frac{1}{x^4}+\frac{1}{x^5}\right)^2}dx=\int \frac{5/x^6+4/x^5}{\left(1+\frac{1}{x^4}+\frac{1}{x^5}\right)^2}dx$

Put $1+\frac{1}{x^4}+\frac{1}{x^5}=t \quad \Rightarrow \left(-\frac{4}{x^5}-\frac{5}{x^6}\right)dx=dt$

$\Rightarrow \; I=\int -\frac{dt}{t^2}=\frac{1}{t}+C=\frac{1}{\left(1+\frac{1}{x^4}+\frac{1}{x^5}\right)}+C=\frac{x^5}{x^5+x+1}+C.$

ILLUSTRATION 81: Find the integral $\int \frac{dx}{x^{22}\left(2x^7-7\right)}$

SOLUTION: Given $I=\int \frac{1}{x^{22}\left(2x^7-7\right)}$. Now, $\int \frac{1}{(x)^{22}\left(\frac{2x^7-7}{2x^7}\right)2x^7}dx=\frac{1}{2}\int \frac{1}{(x)^{29}\left(\frac{2x^7-7}{2x^7}\right)}dx$

Let $m=\frac{2x^7-7}{2x^7}=1-\frac{7x^{-7}}{2} \quad \Rightarrow \frac{7x^{-7}}{2}=1-m$

$\Rightarrow \; \frac{7x^{-7}}{2}=1-m$

$\Rightarrow \; \frac{dm}{dx}=0-\frac{7}{2}(-7)x^{-8}=\frac{49}{2x^8} \quad \Rightarrow dx=\frac{2x^8dm}{49}$

$\Rightarrow \; I=\frac{1}{2}\int \frac{2x^8dm}{x^{29}49m}=\frac{1}{49}\int \frac{1}{x^{21}m}dm=\left(\frac{1}{49}\right)\int \frac{1}{(x^7)^3m}dm=\frac{1}{49}\int \frac{(x^{-7})^3}{m}dm$

$=\frac{8}{343\times 49}\int \frac{(1-m)^3}{m}dm=\frac{1}{49}\times\frac{8}{343}\int \frac{(1-m)^3}{m}dm$

$=\frac{8}{343\times 49}\left[\int\left(\frac{1}{m}-m^2-3+3m\right)dm\right]=\frac{8}{343\times 49}\left[\ln m-\frac{m^3}{3}-3m+\frac{3m^2}{2}\right]+C$

$=\frac{8}{16807}\left[ln\left(\frac{2x^7-7}{2x^7}\right)-\frac{1}{3}\left(\frac{2x^7-7}{2x^7}\right)^3-3\left(\frac{2x^7-7}{2x^7}\right)+\frac{3}{2}\left(\frac{2x^7-7}{2x^7}\right)^2\right]+C$

Deduction I:

$\int \frac{f'(x)}{f(x)}dx=\ln|f(x)|+C$

We prove this as follows:

Put $f(x)=z$

$\because \; f'(x)dx=dz$

$\therefore \; I=\int \frac{dz}{z}=\ln|z|=\ln|f(x)|+C$

Hence, if the integrand be a fraction such that its numerator is the differential coefficient of the denominator, then the integral is equal to ln |(denominator)| + *C*.

ILLUSTRATION 82: Find $\int \frac{dx}{1+e^x}$

SOLUTION: We write the integrand as follows:

$$\frac{1}{1+e^x} = \frac{e^{-x}}{e^{-x}}\left(\frac{1}{1+e^x}\right) = \frac{e^{-x}}{e^{-x}+1} \text{ put } u = e^{-x} + 1,$$

$\Rightarrow du = -e^{-x}\, dx$

$$\therefore\ I = \int \frac{dx}{1+e^x} = \int \frac{e^{-x}dx}{e^{-x}+1} = \int \frac{-du}{u} = \ln u + C = -\ln(e^{-x} + 1) + C$$

Remeber, $e^{-x} + 1 > 0$ for all x, so $\ln|e^{-x} + 1| = \ln(e^{-x} + 1)$.

(i) $\int \tan x dx = \ln|\sec x| + C$

Proof: Put $\cos x = z$, then $-\sin x\, dx = dz$

$$\therefore\ I = \int \frac{\sin x}{\cos x} dx = \int -\frac{dz}{z} = -\ln|z| + C = -\ln|\cos x| + C = \ln|\sec x| + C$$

Alternative: $\int \tan x dx = \int \frac{\sec x \tan x}{\sec x} dx = \ln|\sec x| + C$

(ii) $\int \cot x dx = \ln|\sin x| + C$

Proof: By substituting $\sin x = z$, the result follows, as given below

$$\int \cot x dx = \int \frac{\cos x}{\sin x} dx = \ln|\sin x| + C$$

(iii) $\int \operatorname{cosec} x dx = \ln\left|\tan\frac{x}{2}\right| + C$

Proof: $\int \operatorname{cosec} x dx = \int \frac{dx}{\sin x} = \int \frac{dx}{2\sin\frac{1}{2}x\cos\frac{1}{2}x}$

We multiply the numerator and denominator by $\sec^2\frac{1}{2}x$ to get numerator as the differential coefficient of the denominator.

$$= \int \frac{\frac{1}{2}\sec^2\frac{1}{2}x}{\tan\frac{1}{2}x} = \ln\left|\tan\frac{x}{2}\right| + C$$

***Alternative* 1:** $\int \operatorname{cosec} x dx = \int \frac{\operatorname{cosec} x(\operatorname{cosec} x - \cot x)}{\operatorname{cosec} x - \cot x} dx = \ln|(\operatorname{cosec} x - \cot x)| + C$

***Alternative* 2:** $\int \operatorname{cosec} x dx = \int \frac{dx}{\sin x} = \int \frac{\sin x}{\sin^2 x} dx$

$$= -\int \frac{d(\cos x)}{1-\cos^2 x} = \int \frac{dz}{1-z^2}, \text{ where } z = \cos x$$

$$= \frac{1}{2}\ln\frac{z-1}{z+1} = \frac{1}{2}\ln\left|\frac{1-\cos x}{1+\cos x}\right| + C = \frac{1}{2}\ln\left|\tan^2\frac{x}{2}\right| + C = \ln\left|\tan\frac{x}{2}\right| + C$$

It should be noted that the different forms in which the integral of cosec x is obtained by different methods can be easily shown to be identical by elementary trigonometry.

(iv) $\int \sec x dx = \ln\left|\tan\left(\frac{\pi}{2}+\frac{x}{2}\right)\right| + C = \ln\left|(\sec x + \tan x)\right| + C$

Proof: $\int \sec x dx = \int \frac{dx}{\cos x} = \int \frac{dx}{\sin\left(\frac{1}{2}\pi + x\right)} = \int \frac{dx}{2\sin\left(\frac{\pi}{4}+\frac{x}{2}\right)\cos\left(\frac{\pi}{4}+\frac{x}{2}\right)}$

$$= \int \frac{\frac{1}{2}\sec^2\left(\frac{\pi}{4}+\frac{x}{2}\right)dx}{\tan\left(\frac{\pi}{4}+\frac{x}{2}\right)} = \ln\left|\tan\left(\frac{\pi}{4}+\frac{x}{2}\right)\right| + C$$

Alternative 1: $\int \sec x dx = \int \frac{\sec x(\sec x + \tan x)}{\sec x + \tan x} dx = \ln|(\sec x + \tan x)| + C$

Since the numerator is the derivative of the denominator.

While this is the shortest method, it does seem artificial. The next method may seem a little less contrived.

Alternative 2: $\int \sec x dx = \int \frac{\cos x}{\cos^2 x} dx = \int \frac{\cos x}{1-\sin^2 x} dx$

The substitution $z = \sin x$ and $dz = \cos x dx$ transforms this last integral into the integral of a rational function.

$$I = \int \frac{dz}{1-z^2} = \frac{1}{2}\int\left(\frac{1}{1+z}+\frac{1}{1-z}\right)dz = \frac{1}{2}[\ln|1+z| - \ln|1-z|] + C = \frac{1}{2}\ln\left|\frac{1+z}{1-z}\right| + C$$

Since $z = \sin x$; $I = \frac{1}{2}\ln\left|\frac{1+z}{1-z}\right| = \frac{1}{2}\ln\left|\frac{1+\sin x}{1-\sin x}\right| + C$

The reader may check that this equals $\ln|\sec x + \tan x|$ by showing that

$\frac{1+\sin x}{1-\sin x} = (\sec x + \tan x)^2$.

Neither method gives $\ln\left|\tan\left(\frac{x}{2}+\frac{\pi}{4}\right)\right|$.

However, we can show that $\tan\left(\frac{x}{2}+\frac{\pi}{4}\right) = \sec x + \tan x$.

ILLUSTRATION 83: Find $\int \cos x\sqrt{(4-\sin^2 x)}\ dx = dt$

SOLUTION: Put $\sin x = t$ so that $\cos x dx = dt$, then the given integral, becomes

$$I = \int\sqrt{(4-t^2)}\,dt = \int\sqrt{(2^2-t^2)}\,dt$$

$$= \frac{1}{2}t\sqrt{(2^2-t^2)} + \frac{2^2}{2}\sin^{-1}\left(\frac{t}{2}\right) + C$$

$$= \frac{1}{2}\sin x.\sqrt{(4-\sin^2 x)} + 2\sin^{-1}\left(\frac{1}{2}\sin x\right) + C$$

ILLUSTRATION 84: Find $\int\sqrt{2+\sqrt{4+\sqrt{x}}}\,dx$

SOLUTION: Let $I=\int\sqrt{2+\sqrt{4+\sqrt{x}}}\,dx$ and put $\sqrt{2\sqrt{4+\sqrt{x}}}=u$

$\Rightarrow \sqrt{4+\sqrt{x}}=u^2-2$ $\Rightarrow 4+\sqrt{x}=\left(u^2-2\right)^2$

$\Rightarrow \sqrt{x}=\left(u^2-2\right)^2-4$ $\Rightarrow x=[(u^2-2)^2-4]^2$

$\Rightarrow dx=2[(u^2-2)^2-4]\,.\,2(u^2-2)\,.\,2u\,du$

$=8u(u^2-2)\,(u^4-4u^2)\,du$

$=8(u^3-2u)\,(u^4-4u^2)\,du=8(u^7-4u^5-2u^5+8u^3)$

$\therefore\ I=8\int u\left(u^7-6u^5+8u^3\right)du$

$=\int\left(u^8-6u^6+8u^4\right)du\ =8\left[\frac{u^9}{9}-\frac{6u^7}{7}+\frac{8u^5}{5}\right]+C;$

where $u=\sqrt{2+\sqrt{4+\sqrt{x}}}$.

ILLUSTRATION 85: Find $\int\frac{\sec x dx}{\sqrt{\cos(2x+a)+\cos a}}$

SOLUTION: Let $I=\frac{1}{\sqrt{2}}\int\frac{\sec x\ dx}{\sqrt{(\cos x\cos a-\sin x\sin a)\cos x}}$

$=\frac{1}{\sqrt{2}}\int\frac{\sec^2 x dx}{\sqrt{\cos a-\tan x\sin a}}=\frac{1}{\sqrt{2\sin a}}\int\frac{\sec^2 x dx}{\sqrt{\cot a-\tan x}}$

Put $\cot a-\tan x=t^2$

$\Rightarrow -\sec^2 x\ dx=2t\ dt$

$\therefore\ I=\frac{1}{\sqrt{2\sin a}}\int\frac{-2t\ dt}{t}=\frac{-2}{\sqrt{2\sin a}}\int dt$

$=-\frac{\sqrt{2}}{\sqrt{\sin a}}\sqrt{\cot a-\tan x}+C\ =C-\sqrt{\frac{2(\cot a-\tan x)}{\sin a}}$

ILLUSTRATION 86: Find $\int\frac{\sin^3 x\ dx}{\left(\cos^4 x+3\cos^2 x+1\right)\tan^{-1}\left(\sec x+\cos x\right)}$

SOLUTION: Let $I=\int\frac{\sin^3 x\ dx}{\left(\cos^4 x+3\cos^2 x+1\right)\tan^{-1}\left(\sec x+\cos x\right)}$

Put $\tan^{-1}(\sec x+\cos x)=t$

$\Rightarrow \frac{1}{1+(\sec x+\cos x)^2}(\sec x\tan x-\sin x)\,dx=dt$

$\Rightarrow \frac{\sin^3 x\ dx}{\cos^4 x+3\cos^2 x+1}=dt$

$\Rightarrow I=\int\frac{dt}{t}=\ln|t|+C\ =\ln|\tan^{-1}(\sec x+\cos x)|+C$

ILLUSTRATION 87: Find $\int \frac{\cos x - \sin x - x + 1}{e^x + \sin x + x} dx$ = ln |$f(x)$| + $g(x)$ + C; where C is constant of integration and $f(x)$, $x + \sin x$ are positive, then find $f(x) + g(x)$.

SOLUTION: Let $I = \int \frac{\left(e^x + \cos x + 1\right) - \left(e^x + \sin x + x\right)}{e^x + \sin x + x} dx = \ln |e^x + \sin x + x| - x + C$

$\therefore\ f(x) = \pm\,(e^x + \sin x + x)$ and $g(x) = -x$

$\Rightarrow\ f(x) = e^x + \sin x + x$ or $-e^x - \sin x - x$

But $x + \sin x$ and $f(x)$ are positive

$\Rightarrow\ f(x) = e^x + \sin x + x$ and $g(x) = -x$ $\Rightarrow\ f(x) + g(x) = e^x + \sin x$

ILLUSTRATION 88: Find $\int \frac{x + e^x\left(\sin x + \cos x\right) + \sin x \cos x}{\left(x^2 + 2e^x \sin x - \cos^2 x\right)^2} dx$

SOLUTION: Let $I = \int \frac{x + e^x\left(\sin x + \cos x\right) + \sin x \cos x}{\left(x^2 + 2e^x \sin x - \cos^2 x\right)^2} dx$

Put $x^2 + 2e^x \sin x - \cos^2 x = t$

$\Rightarrow\ [2x + 2(e^x \cos x + e^x \sin x) + 2\sin x \cos x]\, dx = dt$

$\Rightarrow\ [2x + 2e^x (\cos x + \sin x) + 2\sin x \cos x]\, dx = dt$

$\Rightarrow\ I = \frac{1}{2}\int \frac{dt}{t^2} = C - \frac{1}{2}.\frac{1}{t} = C - \frac{1}{2\left(x^2 + 2e^x \sin x - \cos^2 x\right)}$

ILLUSTRATION 89: Find $\int \frac{e^{2x} - e^x + 1}{\left(e^x \sin x + \cos x\right)\left(e^x \cos x - \sin x\right)} dx$

SOLUTION: Let $f(x) = e^x \sin x + \cos x = f'(x) = e^x \cos x + \sin x\, e^x - \sin x$ and $g(x) = e^x \cos x - \sin x$

$\Rightarrow\ g'(x) = \cos x\,.\,e^x - e^x \sin x - \cos x$

Now $f(x).g'(x) = (e^x \sin x + \cos x)(\cos x\,.\,e^x - e^x \sin x - \cos x)$

$= (e^{2x} \sin x \cos x - e^{2x} \sin^2 x - e^x \sin x \cos x) + e^x \cos^2 x - e^x \sin x \cos x - \cos^2 x$ ...(i)

And $g(x).f'(x)$

$= (e^x \cos x - \sin x)(e^x \cos x + \sin x\, e^x - \sin x)$

$= e^{2x} \cos^2 x + e^{2x} \sin x \cos x - e^x \sin x \cos x$

$-e^x \sin x \cos x - e^x \sin^2 x + \sin^2 x$ ...(ii)

$\therefore\ g(x).f'(x) - f(x).g'(x) = e^{2x} - e^x + 1$

$I = \int \frac{g(x)f'(x) - f(x)g'(x)}{f(x)g(x)} dx = \ln\left|\frac{f(x)}{g(x)}\right| + C = \ln\left|\frac{e^x \sin x + \cos x}{e^x \cos x - \sin x}\right| + C$

ILLUSTRATION 90: Find $\int \frac{10x^9 + 10^x \ln 10}{10^x + x^{10}} dx$

SOLUTION: Put $10^x + x^{10} = t$

$\Rightarrow\ (10^x \ln 10 + 10\, x^9)dx = dt$

$\therefore\ I = \int \frac{1}{t} dt = \ln|t| + C = \ln|10^x + x^{10}| + C$

TEXTUAL EXERCISE–3: (SUBJECTIVE)

1. Find the following integrals using method of substitution:

(a) $\int \frac{x^3 dx}{\sqrt{x-1}}$ (b) $\int \frac{x+1}{x\sqrt{x-2}} dx$

(c) $\int \frac{dx}{1+\sqrt[3]{x+1}}$

2. Find the following integrals using method of substitution:

(a) $\int \frac{\sqrt{x}}{x+1} dx$ (b) $\int \frac{\sqrt{x}\, dx}{\sqrt{x}-\sqrt[3]{x}}$

(c) $\int \frac{dx}{\sqrt[3]{x}\left(\sqrt[3]{x}-1\right)}$ (d) $\int \frac{dx}{\sqrt{x}+\sqrt[4]{x}}$

(e) $\int \frac{\sqrt{x}}{\sqrt[3]{x^2}-\sqrt[4]{x}} dx$

3. Find the following integrals using method of substitution:

(a) $\int \frac{e^{2x} dx}{\sqrt[4]{e^x+1}}$ (b) $\int \frac{dx}{e^x\sqrt{1-e^{-2x}}}$

(c) $\int e^{2x^2+\ln x} dx$ (d) $\int \frac{dx}{e^x(3+e^{-x})}$

4. Find the following integrals using method of substitution:

(a) $\int \sqrt{1+\cos^2 x}\, \sin 2x.\cos 2x dx$

(b) $\int \frac{\ln(\tan x)}{\sin x.\cos x} dx$

(c) $\int \frac{\sin x}{e^{\cos x}} dx$

(d) $\int x \cos x^2\, dx$

(e) $\int \frac{\sin^4 x\, dx}{\cos^6 x}$

(f) $\int \left(\sqrt{\sin x}+\cos x\right)^2 dx$

5. Find the following integrals using method of substitution:

(a) $\int \frac{dx}{x^2\sqrt{x^2+a^2}}$ (b) $\int \frac{x^2 dx}{\sqrt{x^2-a^2}}$

(c) $\int \frac{dx}{x\sqrt{x^2-a^2}}$

6. Find the following integrals using method of substitution:

(a) $\int \frac{x^5 dx}{\sqrt{a^3-x^3}}$ (b) $\int \frac{x^5 dx}{\left(x^2-4\right)^2}$

(c) $\int \frac{(x+1)dx}{x(1+xe^x)}$

7. Find the following integrals using method of substitution:

(a) $\int \frac{\sqrt{1+x^2}}{x^4} dx$ (b) $\int \frac{dx}{\sqrt{(a^2+x^2)^3}}$

(c) $\int \frac{\sqrt{(9-x^2)^3}}{x^6} dx$ (d) $\int \frac{dx}{x^2\sqrt{x^2-9}}$

8. Find the following integrals using method of substitution:

(a) $\int \frac{\sqrt{1-x^2}}{x^2} dx$ (b) $\int \frac{dx}{\sqrt{(x^2-a^2)^3}}$

(c) $\int \frac{dx}{x\sqrt{1+x^2}}$

9. Find the following integrals:

(a) $\int \frac{dx}{x^4+1}$ (b) $\int \frac{x}{x^4+1} dx$

(c) $\int \frac{x^2}{x^4+1} dx$ (d) $\int \frac{x^3}{x^4+1} dx$

(e) $\int \frac{x^4}{x^4+1} dx$ (f) $\int \frac{x^5}{x^4+1} dx$

10. Find the following integrals using method of substitution:

(a) $\int \frac{\sin x \cos x}{(a\cos^2 x+b\sin^2 x)} dx$

(b) $\int \sec\theta\sqrt{\cos 2\theta}\; d\theta$

(c) $\int \frac{\sin^{-1}\sqrt{x}-\cos^{-1}\sqrt{x}}{\sin^{-1}\sqrt{x}+\cos^{-1}\sqrt{x}} dx$

11. Find the following integrals using method of substitution:

(a) $\int \frac{m}{\sqrt[3]{(a+bx)^2}} dx$

(b) $\int \frac{ax^{a-1}+a^x \ln a+2}{(a^x+x^a+2x)^n} dx$

(c) $\int \frac{dx}{\sqrt[4]{(x-1)^3(x+2)^5}}$

(d) $\int \frac{1}{x^2-6x-9}\sqrt{x^2-6x+4}\,dx$

(e) $\int \frac{1}{x-\sqrt{(x^2-1)}}dx$

12. Find the following integrals using method of substitution:

(a) $\int \frac{(1+\ln x)^m}{x}dx$ (b) $\int \frac{\sin x\cos x}{(a\cos^2 x+b\sin^2 x)}dx$

(c) $\int \sqrt{\left(\frac{x-a}{b-x}\right)}\,dx$

13. Solve the following integrals:

(a) $\int \frac{dx}{\sin x(2\cos^2 x-1)}$

(b) $\int \frac{t}{\sqrt{1-t^2}}d(\sin^{-1} t)$

(c) $\int \left(x+\frac{1}{x}\right)^{n+5}\left(\frac{x^2-1}{x^2}\right)dx$

(d) $\int \frac{1}{\sqrt{\tan^2\theta+2}}d\left(\sqrt{\tan^2\theta-1}\right)$

14. Find the following integrals:

(a) $\int \frac{\sqrt{1-\sin x}}{1+\cos x}.e^{-x/2}\,dx$

(b) $\int \left[\ln(\ln x)+\frac{1}{(\ln x)^2}\right]dx$

15. Show that the following integrals can be solved by the substitution/s given for them.

(a) $\int \frac{dx}{x^2\sqrt{x^2+a^2}}$

(i) $x = \frac{1}{z}$

(ii) $x = a\tan z$

(b) $\int \frac{x^2dx}{\sqrt{x^2-a^2}}$

(i) $x = a\sin z$, $x = a\cos z$

(ii) $x = \frac{1}{z}$

(c) $\int \frac{dx}{x\sqrt{x^2-a^2}}$

(i) $x = \frac{1}{z}$

(ii) $x = \frac{a}{\cos z}$

(iii) $x = a\cos h\, z$

16. Show that the integral $\int\left((x^2-1)(x+1)\right)^{-2/3}dx$, can be solved with any of the following substitutions.

(a) $u = \frac{1}{(x+1)}$

(b) $u = \left(\frac{(x-1)}{(x+1)}\right)^k$ for $k = 1, 1/2, 1/3, -1/3, -2/3$ and -1.

(c) $u = \tan^{-1}x$

(d) $u = \tan^{-1}\sqrt{x}$

(e) $u = \cos^{-1}x$

Answer Keys

1. (a) $\frac{2\sqrt{x-1}}{35}\left(5x^3+6x^2+8x+16\right)+C$ (b) $2\sqrt{x-2}+\sqrt{2}\,\text{arc}\tan\sqrt{\frac{x-2}{2}}+C$

(c) $\frac{3}{2}(x+1)^{2/3}-3(x+1)^{1/3}+3\ln\left|1+\sqrt[3]{x+1}\right|+C$

2. (a) $2\left(\sqrt{x}-\text{arc}\tan\sqrt{x}\right)+C$ (b) $x+\frac{6\sqrt[6]{x^5}}{5}+\frac{3\sqrt[3]{x^2}}{2}+2\sqrt{x}+3\sqrt[3]{x}+6\sqrt[6]{x}+6\ln|\sqrt[6]{x}-1|+C$

Hint: (apply the substitution $x = z^6$)

(c) $3\sqrt[3]{x}+3\ln\left|\sqrt[3]{x}-1\right|+C$ (d) $2\sqrt{x}-4\sqrt[4]{x}+4\ln\left(1+\sqrt[4]{x}\right)+C$ (e) $\frac{6}{5}\left[\sqrt[6]{x^5}+2\sqrt[12]{x^5}+2\ln\left|\sqrt[12]{x^5}-1\right|\right]+C$

3. (a) $\frac{4}{21}\left(3e^x-4\right)\sqrt[4]{(e^x+1)^3}+C$ **Hint:** (apply substitution $e^x+1=z^4$)

(b) $C-\arcsin e^{-x}$ (c) $\frac{1}{4}e^{2x^2}+C$ (d) $C-\ln(3+e^{-x})$

4. (a) $0.4\sqrt{(1+\cos^2 x)^3}\left(3-2\cos^2 x\right)+C$ (b) $\frac{1}{2}\ln^2(\tan x)+C$

(d) $\frac{1}{2}\sin x^2+C$ (e) $\frac{1}{5}\tan^5 x+C$ (f) $\frac{x}{2}+\frac{1}{4}\sin 2x+\frac{4}{3}\sqrt{\sin^3 x}-\cos x+C$

5. (a) $C-\frac{\sqrt{x^2+a^2}}{a^2x}$ **Hint:** (apply the substitution $x=\frac{1}{z}$ or $x = a\tan z$)

(b) $\frac{a^2}{2}\text{arc sin}\frac{x}{a}-\frac{x}{2}\sqrt{a^2-x^2}+C$ **Hint:** (apply the substitution $x = a\sin z$)

(c) $C-\frac{1}{a}\arcsin\frac{a}{|x|}$ **Hint:** (apply the substitution $x=\frac{1}{z}$ or, $x=\frac{a}{\cos z}$)

6. (a) $C-\frac{2}{9}\sqrt{a^3-x^3}\left(2a^3+x^3\right)$ (b) $\frac{x^2-4}{2}+\frac{8}{x^2-4}+4\ln|x^2-4|+C$ (c) $\ln\left|\frac{xe^x}{1+xe^x}\right|+C$

Hint: (Multiply both the numerator and denominator by e^x and put $xe^x = z$)

7. (a) $C-\frac{\sqrt{(1+x^2)^3}}{3x^3}$ (b) $C-\frac{\sqrt{1-x^2}}{x}-\arcsin x$

(c) $C-\frac{\sqrt{(9-x^2)^5}}{45x^5}$ (d) $\frac{\sqrt{x^2-9}}{9x}+C$

8. (a) $\frac{x}{a^2\sqrt{x^2+a^2}}+C$ (b) $C-\frac{x}{a^2\sqrt{x^2-a^2}}$ (c) $\ln\frac{|x|}{1+\sqrt{x^2+1}}+C$

9. (a) $\frac{1}{2\sqrt{2}}\left[\tan^{-1}\left(\frac{x^2-1}{\sqrt{2}x}\right)-\frac{1}{2}\ln\left|\frac{x^2-\sqrt{2}x+1}{x^2+\sqrt{2}x+1}\right|\right]+C$ (b) $\frac{1}{2}\tan^{-1}x^2+C$

(c) $\frac{1}{2\sqrt{2}}\left[\tan^{-1}\left(\frac{x^2-1}{\sqrt{2}x}\right)+\frac{1}{2}\ln\left|\frac{x^2-\sqrt{2}x+1}{x^2+\sqrt{2}x+1}\right|\right]+C$ (d) $\frac{1}{4}\ln(x^4+1)+C$

(e) $x-\frac{1}{2\sqrt{2}}\tan^{-1}\left(\frac{x^2-1}{\sqrt{2}x}\right)+\frac{1}{4\sqrt{2}}\ln\left|\frac{x^2-\sqrt{2}x+1}{x^2+\sqrt{2}x+1}\right|+C$ (f) $\frac{1}{2}\left[x^2-\tan^{-1}x^2\right]+C$

10. (a) $\frac{1}{2(b-a)}\ln|a\cos^2 x+b\sin^2 x|+C$ (b) $\frac{1}{\sqrt{2}}\sin^{-1}(\sqrt{2}\sec\theta)-\tan\theta+c$

(c) $x+\frac{1}{\pi}\left|-2\cos^{-1}\sqrt{x}(2x-1)+\frac{1}{4}\sqrt{2-4x-4x^2}\right|+C$

11. (a) $\frac{3m}{b}\sqrt[3]{a+x^2}+C$ (b) $\frac{(a^x+x^a+2x)^{1-n}}{1-n}+C$ if $n\neq 1$ or $\ln|ax+x^a+2x|+c$ if $n+1$

(c) $\frac{4}{3}\left(\frac{x-1}{x+2}\right)^{1/4}+C$ (d) $\sqrt{x^2-6x+4}+\frac{1}{2\sqrt{3}}+\ln\left|\frac{\sqrt{x^2-6x+4}-\sqrt{13}}{\sqrt{x^2-6x+4}+\sqrt{13}}\right|+C$

(e) $\frac{x^2}{2}+\frac{1}{2}(\sqrt{x^2-1}-\ln|x+\sqrt{x^2-1}|)+C$

12. (a) $\begin{cases}\frac{t^{m+1}}{m+1}+C=\frac{(1+\log x)^{m+1}}{m+1}+C & \text{if } m\neq -1\\ \log|t|+C=\log|1+\log x|+C & \text{if } m=-1\end{cases}$ (b) $\frac{1}{2(b-a)}\ln|a\cos^2 x+b\sin^2 x|+C$

(c) $(b-a)\left|\tan^{-1}\sqrt{\frac{x-a}{b-x}}-\frac{\sqrt{(x-a)(b-x)}}{(b-a)}\right|+C$

13. (a) $\frac{1}{\sqrt{2}}\ln\left|\frac{1+\sqrt{2}\cos x}{1-\sqrt{2}\cos x}\right|-\frac{1}{2}\ln\left|\frac{1+\cos x}{1-\cos x}\right|+C$ (b) $-\ln\sqrt{1-t^2}+C$

(c) $\frac{(x+1/x)^{n+6}}{n+6}+C$ (d) $\ln\left|x+\sqrt{x^2+3}\right|+C$

14. (a) $-e^{-x/2}\sec\left(\frac{x}{2}\right)+C$ (b) $x\left(\ln(\ln x)-\frac{1}{\ln x}\right)+C$

15. (a) $C-\frac{\sqrt{x^2+a^2}}{a^2x}$ (b) $\frac{a^2}{2}\arcsin\frac{x}{a}-\frac{x}{2}\sqrt{a^2-x^2}+C$

(c) $C-\frac{1}{a}\text{arc}\sin\frac{a}{|x|}$

TEXTUAL EXERCISE–3: (OBJECTIVE)

1. The integral $\int 3x^2\sec^5 x^3\tan x^3 dx$ equals

(a) $\frac{1}{5}\sec^4 x^3+C$ (b) $\frac{1}{5}\sec^5 x^3+C$

(c) $\frac{1}{5}\sec^3 x^3\tan^2 x^3+C$ (d) $\frac{1}{5}\tan x^3\sec^4 x^3+C$

2. The integral $\int \cos x.e^{\cos 2x}d(\cos x)$ equals

(a) $\frac{1}{4}e^{\cos 2x}+C$ (b) $\frac{1}{2}e^{\cos 2x}+C$

(c) $\frac{1}{4}e^{\sin 2x}+C$ (d) $\frac{1}{2}e^{\sin 2x}+C$

3. The integral $\int \frac{1+\log x}{\sqrt{(x^x)^2-1}}dx$ equals

(a) $x\tan^{-1}(x^x)+C$ (b) $x\sec^{-1}(x^x)+C$

(c) $\sec^{-1}(x^x)+C$ (d) $\tan^{-1}(x^x)+C$

4. The integral $\int \frac{f(x)\phi'(x)+\phi(x)f'(x)}{(f(x)\phi(x)+1)\sqrt{f(x)\phi(x)-1}}dx$ equals

(a) $\sqrt{2}\tan^{-1}\left(\frac{\sqrt{f(x)\varphi(x)+1}}{\sqrt{2}}\right)+C$

(b) $\sqrt{2}\tan^{-1}\left(\frac{\sqrt{f(x)\varphi(x)-1}}{\sqrt{2}}\right)+C$

(c) $\frac{1}{\sqrt{2}}\tan^{-1}\left(\frac{\sqrt{f(x)\varphi(x)-1}}{\sqrt{2}}\right)+C$

(d) $\frac{1}{\sqrt{2}}\tan^{-1}\left(\frac{\sqrt{f(x)\varphi(x)+1}}{\sqrt{2}}\right)+C$

5. The integral $\int\left[\ln(\ln x)+\frac{1}{(\ln x)^2}\right]dx$ equals

(a) $x\left(\ln(\ln x)-\frac{1}{\ln x}\right)+C$

(b) $x\left(\ln(\ln x)+\frac{1}{\ln x}\right)+C$

(c) $x\left(\frac{1}{\ln x}-\ln(\ln x)\right)+C$

(d) None of these

6. The integral $\int \frac{1}{x+\sqrt{(x^2+2)}}dx$ equals

(a) $-\frac{x^2}{4}+\frac{1}{4}(x\sqrt{x^2+2}+2\ln|x+\sqrt{x^2+2}|)+C$

(b) $-\frac{x^2}{4}+\frac{1}{4}(x\sqrt{x^2+2}-\ln|x+\sqrt{x^2+2}|)+C$

(c) $-\frac{x^2}{4}+\frac{1}{2}(x\sqrt{x^2+2}-2\ln|x+\sqrt{x^2+2}|)+C$

(d) $-\frac{x^2}{4}+\frac{1}{4}(x\sqrt{x^2+2}-2\ln|x+\sqrt{x^2+2}|)+C$

7. The integral $\int \frac{dx}{1+\tan x+\tan^2 x}$ equals

(a) $\ln\left|\frac{\tan(x/2)+1/2-\sqrt{3}/2}{\tan(x/2)+1/2+\sqrt{3}/2}\right|+\frac{1}{2}\ln|2+\sin 2x|+C$

(b) $\ln\left|\frac{\tan(x/2)+1/2-\sqrt{3}/2}{\tan(x/2)+1/2+\sqrt{3}/2}\right|-\frac{1}{2}\ln|2+\sin 2x|+C$

(c) $\ln\left|\frac{\tan(x/2)+1/2+\sqrt{3}/2}{\tan(x/2)+1/2-\sqrt{3}/2}\right|+\frac{1}{2}\ln|2+\sin 2x|+C$

(d) $\ln\left|\frac{\tan(x/2)-1/2+\sqrt{3}/2}{\tan(x/2)+1/2+\sqrt{3}/2}\right|+\frac{1}{2}\ln|2+\sin 2x|+C$

8. The integral $\int \frac{(x^2-2)}{(x^4+5x^2+4)\tan^{-1}((x^2+2)/x)}dx$ equals

(a) $\ln\left|\tan^{-1}\left(x-\frac{2}{x}\right)\right|+C$

(b) $\frac{1}{2}\ln\left|\tan^{-1}\left(x+\frac{2}{x}\right)\right|+C$

(c) $\ln\left|\tan^{-1}\left(x+\frac{2}{x}\right)\right|+C$

(d) $\ln\left|\frac{1}{2}\tan^{-1}\left(x+\frac{2}{x}\right)\right|+C$

9. The integral $\int \frac{x\cos x\log x-\sin x}{x(\log x)^2}dx$ equals

(a) $\frac{\cos x}{\ln x}+C$ (b) $\frac{\sin x}{\ln x}+C$

(c) $-\frac{\sin x}{\ln x}+C$ (d) $-\frac{\cos x}{\ln x}+C$

Answer Keys

1. (b) **2.** (a) **3.** (c) **4.** (b) **5.** (a) **6.** (d) **7.** (a) **8.** (c) **9.** (b)

■ INTEGRATION BY PARTS

Integration by parts is a method to solve the integrals having integrand as a product of two functions.

For example, $\int u(x).v(x)\,dx$ using a double substitution method. It is directly derived from the product rule of differentiation. It can be stated as below.

Theorem

If u and v are two functions of x, then $\int u.v\,dx = u.\int v dx-\int\left(\frac{du}{dx}.\int v\,dx\right)dx$ known as product rule ($u-v$ rule)

Proof: Let $y = u(x)$ and $y = v(x)$ be two differentiable functions

$$\because \frac{d}{dx}\left(u(x).v(x)\right)= u(x).v'(x)+ v(x).u'(x)$$

$$\Rightarrow d\left(u(x).v(x)\right)=u(x).v'(x)\,dx+ v(x).u'(x)\,dx$$

integrating both sides, we get

$$\Rightarrow \int d(u(x).v(x)) = \int u(x).v'(x)dx+\int v(x).u'(x)dx$$

$$\Rightarrow u(x).v(x) = \int u(x)v'(x)dx+\int v(x)u'(x)dx,$$

After rearranging the terms, we get

$$\int u(x).v'(x)dx = u(x).v(x) - \int u'(x).v(x)dx \quad \ldots(1)$$

The result can be concluded and presented in two ways

$\because v'(x)dx = d\left(v(x)\right)$ & $u'(x)dx = d\left(u(x)\right)$,

therefore, equation (1) becomes

$$\int u(x)dv(x) = u(x)v(x)-\int v(x)\,du(x)$$

$$\Rightarrow \int udv = uv-\int v\,du \quad \ldots(2)$$

or substituting $u(x) = f(x)$; $v'(x) = g(x)$

$$\Rightarrow dv(x) = g(x)\,dx$$

$$\Rightarrow \int dv(x) = \int g(x)dx$$

$$\Rightarrow v(x) = \int g(x)dx$$

Now equation (1) becomes

$$\int f(x).g(x)dx = f(x).\int g(x)dx-\int\left(\frac{d}{dx}f(x).\int g(x)dx\right)dx \quad \ldots(3)$$

REMARK

1. *The integral of product of two functions = (1st function) × (integral of 2nd function) – integral of (differential of 1st function × integral of 2nd function).*
2. *Integration by parts of indefinite integrals is* $\int udv = uv-\int vdu$.

The corresponding formula for definite integrals is

$$\int_a^b u(x)v'(x)dx = [u(x)v(x)]_a^b - \int_a^b v(x)u'(x)dx$$

$$\int_a^b udv = [uv]_a^b - \int_a^b vdu$$

3. *When determining the function v from its derivative, we can take any arbitrary constant, since it does not enter into the final result. This can be seen by adding the arbitrary constant C in the formula of integration by parts. It is however convenient to consider this constant equal to zero.*

$$\int u.v\,dx = u\left(\int v\,dx + C_1\right) - \int\left[\frac{du}{dx}\left(\int vdx + C_1\right)\right]dx$$

$$= u\int v\,dx + uC_1 - \int\left[\frac{du}{dx}.\int v\,dx\right]dx - uC_1 = u\int v\,dx - \int\left[\frac{du}{dx}.\int v\,dx\right]dx$$

We see that the constant C_1 cancels out, thus, giving the same solution obtained by omitting C_1, thereby justifying the omission of the constant of integration when calculating v in integration by parts.

Also note that $\int v\,dx$ should be taken as same in both terms.

4. *Sometimes a constant can be used to simplify calculations.*

If the integrand consists of only one function, e.g., $\int f(x)\,dx$, then consider one (1) as 1st function and apply integration by part.

i.e. $\int \underbrace{1}_{2^{nd}\ f^n}\ \underbrace{f(x)}_{1^{st}\ f^n}\,dx$

Example:

(1) $\int \ln x\,dx = \int \underbrace{\ln x}_{I}.\underbrace{1}_{II}\,dx = x\ln x - \int \frac{1}{x}.x\,dx = x\ln x - x + C$

(2) $\int \ln(1+x)dx = \int 1.\ln(1+x)dx = x\ln(1+x) - \int \frac{1.x}{1+x}dx = x\ln(1+x) - \int 1 - \frac{1}{(1+x)}dx$

$= x\ln(1+x) - x + \ln(1+x) + C = (x+1)\ln(1+x) - x + C.$

Thus, we have simplified the computation of the second term by introducing a constant of integration 1.

Very often an integral involving a single logarithmic function or a single inverse circular function can be evaluated by the application of the rule for integration by parts, by considering the integral as the product of the given function and unity, and taking the given function as the first function and unity as the second.

5. $\int f(x)\,dx$ *: f(x) is not directly integrable, then multiply and divide by f'(x) and integrate by part.*

i.e. $\int \underbrace{f(x).f'(x)}_{2^{nd}\ f^n}\ \underbrace{\frac{1}{f'(x)}}_{1^{st}\ f^n}\,dx$

6. *The method sometimes fails because it leads back to the original integral, e.g., let us try to integrate $\int x^{-1}dx$ by parts.*

$$\int x^{-1}dx = \int 1.x^{-1}dx = \frac{1}{x}.x - \int\left(-\frac{1}{x^2}\right)x\,dx$$

$$\Rightarrow \int x^{-1}dx = 1 + \int x^{-1}\,dx + C$$

And we are back from where we started.

This example is often used to illustration the importance of paying attention to the arbitrary constant C, If (1) is written without C, it leads to the equation $\int x^{-1}dx = -1 + \int x^{-1}\,dx$, which is false.

Geometric Interpretation of Integration by Part

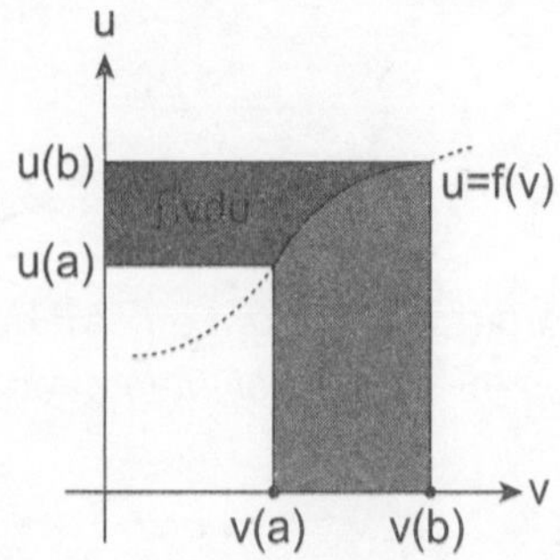

FIGURE 1.3

These formulae allow us to shift the problem of integrating $u\ dv$ to that of integrating v du. Success depends on the proper choice of u and dv, which comes with practice.

ILLUSTRATION 91: Find the integral $\int x \cos x\, dx$

SOLUTION: We wish to write $x \cos x\, dx$ as $u\ dv$. One possibility is to let $u = x$ and $dv = \cos x\, dx$. Then $du = dx$ and $v = \int \cos x\, dx = \sin x$ (we can omit the arbitrary constant at this stage).

Here is a summary of this double substitution in a convenient format.

$u = x;\ dv = \cos x\ dx$

$\Rightarrow\ du = dx;\ v = \sin x$

The integration by parts formula gives

$$\int \underbrace{x}_{u} \underbrace{\cos x dx}_{dv} = \underbrace{x}_{u} \underbrace{\sin x}_{v} - \int \underbrace{\sin x}_{v} \underbrace{dx}_{du} = x \sin x + \cos x + C \text{ (using (2))}$$

We were successful on our first try. Another substitution would be $u = \cos x$; $dv = x\ dx$

$$\Rightarrow\ du = -\sin x\ dx;\ v = \frac{x^2}{2}$$

The integration by parts formula gives

$$\int \underbrace{\cos x}_{u} \underbrace{dx}_{dv} = \underbrace{(\cos x)}_{u} \underbrace{\frac{x^2}{2}}_{v} - \int \underbrace{\frac{x^2}{2}}_{v} \underbrace{(-\sin x\, dx)}_{du}$$

This is correct but not helpful. The new integral on the right hand side is more complicated than the original one. Thus, we see the importance of a wise choice for u and dv. The function which is selected as 2nd function ($v(x)$) must be such that it is integrable in standard form. and its integral multiplied with derivative of 1st function i.e., $u'(x).\int v(x)\, dx$ is further integrable. Thus, choice if 1st and 2nd function is not arbitrary.

Order of Preference for Choice of 1st Function

Thus, the choice of 1st and 2nd function is not arbitrary.

ILATE Rule: Following order of preference is suggested for selection of 1st function.

I: Inverse

L: Logarithmic

A: Algebraic

T: Trigonometric

E: Exponential

ILLUSTRATION 92: Find the integral $\int e^x \sin x\,dx$

SOLUTION: Take $u = e^x$ and $dv = \sin x\,dx$. Then $du = e^x\,dx$ and $v = -\cos x$.

Thus, $\int e^x \sin x\,dx = -e^x \cos x + \int e^x \cos x\,dx$

which does not seem to have improved things. But do not give up; let us integrate by parts again. In the right integral, let $u = e^x$ and $dv = \cos x\,dx$,

so $du = e^x\,dx$ and $v = \sin x$, then $\int e^x \cos x\,dx = e^x \sin x - \int e^x \sin x\,dx$

When we substitute this in our first result, we get

$\int e^x \sin x\,dx = -e^x \cos x + e^x \sin x\,dx - \int e^x \sin x\,dx$

By transposing the last term to the left side and combining terms, we obtain

$2\int e^x \sin x\,dx = e^x(\sin x - \cos x) + C$

from which $\int e^x \sin x\,dx = \frac{1}{2}e^x(\sin x - \cos x) + K$

The fact that the integral we wanted to find is repeated on the right side, is what made the illustration to work.

ILLUSTRATION 93: Find the following integrals:

(i) $\int x\sec^2 x\,dx$ (ii) $\int \tan^{-1} dx$

(iii) $\int xe^x dx$

SOLUTION: (i) $\int x\sec^2 x\,dx = x\tan x - \int \tan x\,dx = x\tan x - \ln|\sec x| + C$

(ii) $\int \tan^{-1} x\,dx = \int \tan^{-1} x.1\,dx$

$= x\tan^{-1} x - \int \frac{1}{1+x^2} x\,dx = x\tan^{-1} x - \frac{1}{2}\ln|1+x^2| + C$

(iii) $\int xe^x dx = xe^x - \int 1.e^x dx = xe^x - e^x + C$

ILLUSTRATION 94: Solve the integral $\int e^x(f(x) + f'(x))\,dx$ by parts.

SOLUTION: $\int e^x(f(x) + f'(x))\,dx = \int e^x f(x)\,dx + \int \underbrace{e^x}_{u} \underbrace{f'(x)dx}_{dv}$,

Let $u = ex$, $dv = f'(x)\,dx$

$\Rightarrow du = e^x\,dx$, $v = f(x)$

$= \int e^x f(x)\,dx + e^x f(x) - \int e^x f(x)\,dx + C = e^x f(x) + C$

ILLUSTRATION 95: Find the following integrals $\int x\sec^2 x\,dx$

SOLUTION: Consider $\int \underbrace{x}_{I^{st} f^n} \underbrace{\sec^2 x}_{2^{nd} f^n} dx$ according to ILATE rule, algebraic equation is given first preference

and trigonometric is given second preference so now $x\int \sec^2 x dx - \int\left(\frac{dx}{dx}\int \sec^2 x dx\right)dx$.

$= x\tan x - \int \tan x\,dx = x\tan x - \ln|\sec x| + C$

ILLUSTRATION 96: Solve the following integrals, using by parts.

(a) $\int \sin^{-1} x\, dx$ (b) $\int \cos^{-1} x\, dx$

(c) $\int \sec^{-1} \frac{x}{2}\, dx$

SOLUTION: (a) Here we have to break it in a pattern in described manner

i.e., $\int f(x).g(x)\, dx$

Since in this no other function is given so we will choose 1 as the 2nd function.

$\Rightarrow I = \int \underset{IIst}{1} . \underset{Ist}{\sin^{-1} x}\, dx$ (By ILATE Rule)

$= \sin^{-1} x \int 1.dx - \int \left\{ \frac{d}{dx}(\sin^{-1} x) \int 1.dx \right\} dx = \sin^{-1}(x) - \int \frac{x}{\sqrt{1-x^2}} dx$

Now, let us take $1 - x^2 = t$ $\Rightarrow -2x = \frac{dt}{dx}$

$\Rightarrow dx = -\left(\frac{dt}{2x}\right)$

$\Rightarrow I = x(\sin^{-1}x) - \int \frac{x}{\sqrt{t}}\left(\frac{-dt}{2x}\right) = x(\sin^{-1} x) + \frac{1}{2}\frac{(t)^{1/2}}{(1/2)} + C = x(\sin^{-1} x) + (1-x^2)^{1/2} + C$

(b) By procedure described above $I = \int \underset{IInd}{1} . \underset{Ist}{\cos^{-1} x}\, dx$ (BY ILATE Rule)

Now, let us take: Ist function = $\cos^{-1}x$ and 2nd function = 1

$\Rightarrow I = (\cos^{-1} x)\int 1.dx - \int \left\{ \frac{d}{dx}(\cos^{-1} x) \int 1.dx \right\} dx = (\cos^{-1}x)(x) - \int \left\{ \frac{-1(x)}{\sqrt{1-x^2}} \right\} dx$

$= (\cos^{-1}x)(x) + \int \frac{(x)}{\sqrt{1-x^2}} dx$ let $t = 1 - x^2$

$\Rightarrow \frac{dt}{dx} = 0 - 2x \Rightarrow dx = -\left(\frac{dt}{2x}\right)$

$\Rightarrow dx = -\frac{1}{2}\frac{dt}{x}$

$\Rightarrow I = x(\cos^{-1}x) - (1 - x^2)^{1/2} + C = x(\cos^{-1} x) - (1 - x^2)^{1/2} + C.$

(c) Here $I = \int \underset{IInd}{1} . \underset{Ist}{\sec^{-1}} \frac{x}{2}\, dx$

Let's put $x/2 = m$ $\Rightarrow dx = 2dm$

$\Rightarrow I = \int 1.\sec^{-1} m(2dm) = 2\int 1.\sec^{-1} m\, dm$

Taking Ist function = $\sec^{-1} m$ and 2nd function = 1

$\Rightarrow I = 2(\sec^{-1} m)(m) - 2\int \left(\frac{d}{dm}(\sec^{-1} m) \int 1.dm \right) dm = 2m\,(\sec^{-1}m) - 2\int \frac{1}{\sqrt{m^2-1}} dm$

$= 2m\,(\sec^{-1}m) - 2\int \frac{1}{\sqrt{m^2-1}} dm$

$= 2m \sec^{-1}(m) - I_1$; where $I_1 = 2\int \frac{1}{\sqrt{m^2-1}} dm$

$$\Rightarrow \frac{I_1}{2} = \int \frac{1}{\sqrt{m^2-1}} dm$$

Now, put $m = \sec\theta$ $\Rightarrow dm = \sec\theta \tan\theta \, d\theta$

$$\Rightarrow \frac{I_1}{2} = \int \frac{1}{\tan\theta}(\sec\theta\tan\theta)d\theta = \ln|\sec\theta + \tan\theta| + C$$

$$= \ln|m+\sqrt{m^2-1}| + C = \ln\left|\frac{x}{2}+\sqrt{\frac{x^2}{4}-1}\right| + C$$

$$\Rightarrow I_1 = 2\ln\left|\frac{x}{2}+\sqrt{\frac{x^2}{4}-1}\right| + C$$

$$\therefore \ I = \int \sec^{-1}\frac{x}{2}dx = x\sec^{-1}\frac{x}{2} - 2\ln\left|\frac{x}{2}+\sqrt{\frac{x^2}{4}-1}\right| + C$$

ILLUSTRATION 97: Solve the following integrals by part:

(a) $\int x^2 \ln x \, dx$ (b) $\int \sin(\ln x)dx$

(c) $\int \left(\underbrace{\ln(x+1)}_{I}\right)\underbrace{\left(\frac{1}{(x+2)^2}\right)}_{II}dx$

SOLUTION: (a) As according to rule of ILATE 'log' function is 1st function 'x^2' function is 2nd function.

$$\Rightarrow I = \int \underbrace{(x^2)}_{2^{nd}\text{ function}} \cdot \underbrace{(\ln x)}_{1^{st}\text{ function}} dx = \ln x\int x^2 dx - \int\left\{\frac{d}{dx}(\ln x)\int x^2 dx\right\}dx$$

$$= (\ln x)\left(\frac{x^3}{3}\right) - \int\left\{\frac{1}{x}.\frac{x^3}{3}\right\}dx = \left(\frac{x^3}{3}\right)(\ln x) - \frac{1}{3}\frac{x^3}{3} + C = \frac{x^3(\ln x)}{3} - \frac{x^3}{9} + C$$

(b) ***Method 1:*** $I = \int 1.\sin(\ln x)dx$

$$\therefore \ I = \sin(\ln x)\int 1.dx - \int\left\{\cos(\ln x).\frac{1}{x}\int 1.dx\right\}dx = \sin(\ln x)(x) - \int\left\{\cos(\ln x).\frac{1}{x}x\right\}dx$$

$$= x\sin(\ln x) - \int \cos(\ln x)dx = x\sin(\ln x) - \int \underset{II}{1}\left(\underset{I}{\cos}(\ln x)dx\right)$$

$$\Rightarrow I = x\sin(\ln x) - (\cos(\ln x))(x) + \int -\sin(\ln x)\frac{1}{x}x\,dx$$

$$\Rightarrow I = x\sin(\ln x) - x\cos(\ln x) - \int \sin(\ln x)dx$$

$$\Rightarrow 2I = x\sin(\ln x) - x\cos(\ln x)$$

$$\Rightarrow I = \frac{x}{2}[\sin(\ln x) - \cos(\ln x)] + C$$

(c) $$I = \ln(x+1)\int\frac{1}{(x+2)^2}dx - \int\left\{\frac{1}{x+1}\int\frac{1}{(x+2)^2}dx\right\}dx$$

$$= \ln(x+1)\int(x+2)^{-2}dx - \int\left\{\frac{1}{(x+1)}\int(x+2)^{-2}dx\right\}dx$$

$$= \ln(x+1)\left[\frac{(x+2)^{-2+1}}{-2+1}\right] - \int\frac{1}{(x+1)}.\frac{(x+2)^{-2+1}}{(-2+1)}dx$$

$$= \frac{-\ln(x+1)}{(x+2)} - \int \frac{1}{(x+1)} \cdot \frac{-1}{(x+2)} dx = \frac{-\ln(x+1)}{(x+2)} + \int \frac{1}{(x+2)(x+1)} dx$$

$$= \frac{-\ln(x+1)}{(x+2)} + \int \left(\frac{1}{x+1} - \frac{1}{x+2} \right) dx$$

$$\frac{-\ln(x+1)}{(x+2)} + \ln|1+x| - \ln|x+2| + C = \frac{-\ln(x+1)}{(x+2)} + \ln\left|\frac{1+x}{2+x}\right| + C.$$

ILLUSTRATION 98: Solve the following integral $\int \frac{dx}{(x^3-1)^2}$ by parts.

SOLUTION: Here $f(x) = x^3 - 1$ and $f'(x) = 3x^2$; Multiply and dividing by $3x^2$, we get

$$\therefore\ I = \int \frac{1}{(x^3-1)^2} \cdot \frac{3x^2}{3x^2} . dx = \int \underbrace{\frac{3x^2}{(x^3-1)^2}}_{II} \cdot \underbrace{\frac{1}{3x^2}}_{I} dx = \frac{1}{3x^2} \int \frac{3x^2}{(x^3-1)^2} dx - \frac{1}{3} \int \frac{-2}{x^3} \left(\frac{-1}{x^3-1} \right) dx$$

$$= \frac{1}{3x^2} \left(\frac{-1}{x^3-1} \right) - \frac{2}{3} \int \left(\frac{1}{x^3} - \frac{1}{x^3-1} \right) dx$$

$$= \frac{-1}{3x^2(x^3-1)} + \frac{1}{3x^2} + \frac{2}{3} \int \frac{dx}{(x-1)(x^2+x+1)} \qquad \ldots(1)$$

Now integrate by breaking into partial fractions.

Consider $\frac{1}{(x-1)(x^2+x+1)} = \frac{A}{x-1} + \frac{Bx+C}{x^2+x+1}$

Clearly $A = \frac{1}{3}$, we get $B = -\frac{1}{3}$ & $C = -\frac{2}{3}$

$$\therefore\ \int \frac{dx}{(x-1)(x^2+x+1)} = \frac{1}{3} \int \frac{dx}{x-1} - \frac{1}{3} \int \frac{x+2}{x^2+x+1} = \frac{1}{3} \ln|x-1| - \frac{1}{6} \int \frac{2x+1+3}{x^2+x+1} dx$$

$$= \frac{1}{3} \ln|x-1| - \frac{1}{6} \ln(x^2+x+1) - \frac{1}{2} \int \frac{dx}{(x+1/2)^2 + 3/4}$$

$$= \frac{1}{3} \ln\left(\frac{|x-1|}{\sqrt{x^2+x+1}} \right) - \frac{1}{\sqrt{3}} \tan^{-1}\left(\frac{2x+1}{\sqrt{3}} \right) + C$$

ILLUSTRATION 99: Solve $\int 1 . \frac{1}{(x^4-1)^2} dx$

SOLUTION: Consider $\int \underbrace{\frac{4x^3}{(x^4-1)^2}}_{II^{nd}} \cdot \underbrace{\frac{1}{4x^3}}_{I^{st}} dx = \frac{1}{4x^3} \int \frac{4x^3}{(x^4-1)^2} dx - \int \left\{ \frac{d}{dx} \left(\frac{1}{4x^3} \right) \int \frac{4x^3}{(x^4-1)^2} \right\} dx$

Put $x^4 - 1 = t$ $\qquad \Rightarrow \frac{dt}{dx} = 4x^3 \Rightarrow dx = \frac{dt}{4x^3}$

$$\Rightarrow \mathrm{I} = \frac{1}{4x^3} \int \frac{1}{t^2} dt - \int \left\{ \frac{1}{4} \frac{(-3)}{x^4} \int \frac{1}{t^2} dt \right\} dx = \frac{1}{4x^3} \left(\frac{t^{-2+1}}{-2+1} \right) + \frac{3}{4} \int \left(\frac{1}{x^4} \left(\frac{t^{-2+1}}{-2+1} \right) \right) dx$$

$$= \frac{-1}{4x^3} \left(\frac{1}{t} \right) - \frac{3}{4} \int \frac{1}{x^4} \frac{1}{(x^4-1)} dx = -\frac{1}{4x^3} \left(\frac{1}{x^4-1} \right) - \frac{3}{4} \left[\int \left(\frac{-1}{x^4} + \frac{1}{x^4-1} \right) dx \right]$$

$$= \frac{-1}{4x^3}\left(\frac{1}{x^4-1}\right) - \frac{3}{4}\left[-\int \frac{1}{x^4}dx + \int \frac{1}{x^4-1}dx\right] = \frac{-1}{4x^3}\left(\frac{1}{x^4-1}\right) - \frac{3}{4}\left[(-1)\frac{x^{-4+1}}{-4+1} + \int \frac{1}{x^4-1}dx\right]$$

$$= \frac{-1}{4x^3(x^4-1)} - \frac{1}{4x^3} - \frac{3}{4}\int \frac{1}{x^4-1}dx = \frac{-1}{4x^3(x^4-1)} - \frac{1}{4x^3} - \frac{3}{8}\int \frac{1}{x^4-1}dx$$

$$= \frac{-1}{4x^3(x^4-1)} - \frac{1}{4x^3} - \frac{3}{8}\int\left(\frac{1}{x^2-1} - \frac{1}{x^2+1}\right)dx$$

$$= \frac{-1}{4x^3(x^4-1)} - \frac{1}{4x^3} + \frac{3}{8}\left[\int\left(\frac{1}{(1-x^2)} + \frac{1}{(x^2+1)}\right)dx\right]$$

$$= \frac{1}{4x^3(1-x^4)} - \frac{1}{4x^3} + \frac{3}{4}\left[\ln\left|\frac{1+x}{1-x}\right| + \tan^{-1}x\right] + C$$

■ INTEGRATING INVERSES OF FUNCTIONS

Integration by parts leads to a rule for integrating inverse that usually gives good results:

Let $I = \int f^{-1}(x)dx$ to be evaluated

Let $y = f^{-1}(x)$,

$\Rightarrow\ x = f(y)$

$\Rightarrow\ dx = f'(y)\, dy$

$\Rightarrow\ I = \int y f'(y) dy$

$= yf(y) - \int f(y)dy = xf^{-1}(x) - \int f(y)dy$

The idea is to take the most complicated part of the integral, in this case $f^{-1}(x)$, and simplify it first. For the integral of $\ln x$, i.e., $\int \ln x\, dx$

Let $y = \ln x$,

$\Rightarrow\ x = e^y,\ dx = e^y\, dy$

$\Rightarrow\ \int \ln x\, dx = \int ye^y\, dy$

$= ye^y - e^y + C = x\ln x - x + C$

For the integral of $\cos^{-1}x$, we get

$\int \cos^{-1} x dx = y\cos y - \int \cos y\, dy$;

where $y = \cos^{-1}x$, x

$= \cos y = x\cos^{-1} x - \int \cos y\, dy$

$= x\cos^{-1} x - \sin y + C$

$= x\cos^{-1} x - \sin(\cos^{-1} x) + C$

Generally, we can integrate $f^{-1}(x)$, the inverse function of $f(x)$, if we can integrate $f(x)$.

ILLUSTRATION 100: Find the following integrals:

(a) $\int \frac{\sin^{-1} x}{x^3} dx$ (b) $\int \sin^{-1}\frac{1}{x} dx$

(c) $\int \frac{\cos^{-1} x}{(1-x^2)^{3/2}} dx$

SOLUTION: (a) Put $\theta = \sin^{-1} x \Rightarrow x = \sin\theta$

$\Rightarrow\ \frac{dx}{d\theta} = \cos\theta \Rightarrow \cos\theta\, d\theta = dx$

$$I = \int \frac{\theta\cos\theta\, d\theta}{\sin^3\theta} = \int \underbrace{(\theta)}_{I}\underbrace{(\cot\theta\,\mathrm{cosec}^2\theta)}_{II} d\theta$$

$$= \theta\int \cot\theta\,\mathrm{cosec}^2\theta\, d\theta - \int\left\{\frac{d\theta}{d\theta}\int \cot\theta\,\mathrm{cosec}^2\theta\, d\theta\right\}d\theta = -\theta\left(\frac{(\cot\theta)^2}{2}\right) - \int -\frac{(\cot\theta)^2}{2}d\theta$$

$$= -\frac{1}{2}\theta(\cot\theta)^2 + \frac{1}{2}\int(\operatorname{cosec}^2\theta - 1)d\theta = -\frac{1}{2}\theta(\cot\theta)^2 + \frac{1}{2}\left[\int \operatorname{cosec}^2\theta\, d\theta - \int d\theta\right]$$

$$= -\frac{1}{2}\theta(\cot\theta)^2 + \frac{1}{2}[-\cot\theta - \theta] + C$$

$$= -\frac{1}{2}(\sin^{-1}x)\left(\cot(\sin^{-1}x)\right)^2 - \frac{1}{2}\left[\sin^{-1}x + \cot(\sin^{-1}x)\right] + C$$

(b) Given integral $= \int \underbrace{1}_{2^{nd}\text{ function}} .\underbrace{\sin^{-1}\frac{1}{x}}_{1^{st}\text{ function}} dx = \sin^{-1}\frac{1}{x}\int 1.dx - \int\left\{\frac{1}{\sqrt{1-\frac{1}{x^2}}}.\left(\frac{-1}{x^2}\right)\int dx\right\}dx$

$$= x\sin^{-1}\frac{1}{x} - \int\left\{\frac{x}{\sqrt{x^2-1}}\left(\frac{-1}{x^2}\right).x\,dx\right\} = x\sin^{-1}\left(\frac{1}{x}\right) + \int\frac{1}{\sqrt{x^2-1}}dx$$

$$= x\sin^{-1}\left(\frac{1}{x}\right) + \ln\left|x + \sqrt{x^2-1}\right| + C$$

(c) Put $\theta = \cos^{-1}x \Rightarrow x = \cos\theta \Rightarrow \frac{dx}{d\theta} = -\sin\theta \Rightarrow dx = -\sin\theta\, d\theta$

$$\Rightarrow \mathrm{I} = \int\frac{\theta(-\sin\theta)d\theta}{\sin^3\theta} = -\int\underset{I}{\theta}\,\underset{II}{\operatorname{cosec}^2\theta}\,d\theta = -\left[\theta\int\operatorname{cosec}^2\theta\, d\theta - \int\frac{d\theta}{d\theta}\int\{\operatorname{cosec}^2\theta\}d\theta\right]$$

$$= -\left[\theta.(-\cot\theta) - \int(-\cot\theta)d\theta\right] = -\left[-\theta\cot\theta + \ln|\sin\theta|\right] + C$$

$= \theta\cot\theta - \ln|\sin\theta| + C = (\cos^{-1}x)\cot(\cos^{-1}x) - \ln|\sin(\cos^{-1}x)| + C.$

INTEGRATION OF A COMPLEX FUNCTION OF A REAL VARIABLE

We can define a complex function of a real variable 'x' as $f(x) = u(x) + iv(x)$; and also its derivative $f'(x) = u'(x) + iv'(x)$.

A function $F(x) = U(x) + iV(x)$ is called an antiderivative of $f(x)$ if

$F'(x) = f(x)$ ...(1)

if $U'(x) + iV'(x) = u(x) + iv(x)$ ...(2)

i.e., from (2) it follows that $U'(x) = u(x)$, $V'(x) = v(x)$, that is, antiderivative of $v(x)$.

It follows, from this definition, that if $F(x) = U(x) + iV(x)$ is an antiderivative of the function $f(x)$, then any antiderivative of $f(x)$ is of the form $F(x) + C$, where C is an arbitrary complex constant. We will call the expression $F(x) + C$ the indefinite integral of a complex function of a real variable and we will write

$$\int f(x)dx = \int u(x)dx + i\int v(x)dx = F(x) + C$$

The definite integral of a complex function of a real variable, $f(x) = u(x) + iv(x)$, is defined as follows:

$$\int_a^b f(x)dx = \int_a^b u(x)dx + i\int_a^b v(x)dx$$

Now this provides an alternative method to find the integrals $\int e^{ax}\cos bx\,dx$ and $\int e^{ax}\sin bx\,dx$ as given below.

Let $P = \int e^{ax}\cos bx\,dx$ and $Q = \int e^{ax}\sin bx\,dx$

$$\therefore\quad P + iQ = \int e^{ax}(\cos bx + i\sin bx)dx$$

$$= \int e^{ax}e^{ibx}dx = \int e^{(a+ib)x}dx$$

$$= \frac{e^{(a+ib)x}}{a+ib} + C + iD = \frac{a-ib}{a^2+b^2}e^{ax}e^{ibx} + C + iD$$

$$= \frac{e^{ax}}{a^2+b^2}(a-ib)(\cos bx + i\sin bx) + C + iD$$

$$= \frac{\left(ae^{ax}\cos bx + be^{ax}\sin bx\right) + i\left(ae^{ax}\sin bx - be^{ax}\cos bx\right)}{a^2+b^2} + C + iD$$

Equating real and imaginary parts, we get the values of P and Q as before.

$$P = \frac{e^{ax}(a\cos bx + b\sin bx)}{a^2+b^2} + C$$

$Q=\frac{e^{ax}(a\sin bx-b\cos bx)}{a^2+b^2}+D$; where C and D are constants of integration.

MULTIPLE INTEGRATION BY PARTS

While calculating several integrals we are to use integration by parts number of times successively. The same calculation work can be done more rapidly and conveniently by using the so called generalized formula for multiple integration by parts.

Let u and v be two differentiable functions of x (differentiable n times), and let us denote $u'(x)$ by u'; $u''(x)$ by u'' and so on and $\int v\,dx$ by v'; $\int v'\,dx$ by v'' and so on

Now, $\int uv\,dx = uv_1 - \int u'v_1 dx$, ...(1)

(by integrating by parts)

Again, $\int u'v_1\,dx = u'v_2 - \int u''v_2 dx$; ...(2)

$\int u''v_2 dx = u''v_3 - \int u'''v_3 dx$; ...(3)

$\int u'''v_3 dx = u'''v_4 - \int u^{iv}v_4 dx$ ...(4)

Combining (1), (2) and (3) and (4), we get

$$\int uv\,dx = uv_1 - u'v_2 + u''v_3 - u'''v_4 + (-1)^4\int u^{(iv)}v_4\,dx \quad ...(5)$$

And generally,

$$\int uv\,dx = uv_1 - u'v_2 + u''v_3 - u'''v_4 + ... + (-1)^{n-1}u^{n-1}v_n + (-1)^n\int u^n v_n\,dx \quad ...(6)$$

where $u^{(n)}$ denotes n^{th} order derivative of u.

REMARK

The above generalized formula for integration by parts has its advantage while calculating the integrals of the form $\int P_n(x)\phi(x)dx$; where $P_n(x)$ is a polynomial of degree n, and the factor $\phi(x)$ is integrable successively (n + 1) times.

E.g., $I=\int x^4\cos x\,dx = x^4\sin x - 4x^3(-\cos x) + 12x^2(-\sin x) - 24x(\cos x) + 24\sin x + C$

$= x^4\sin x + 4x^3\cos x - 12x^2\sin x - 24x\cos x + 24\sin x + C$

ILLUSTRATION 101: Find the integral $\int(x^2+x+1)e^{2x}dx$

SOLUTION: According to ILATE rule choose $e^{2x}\to$ IInd function $(x^2+x+1)\to$ 1st function

$$\therefore\ I = (x^2+x+1)\int e^{2x}dx - \int\left\{\frac{d}{dx}(x^2+x+1)\int e^{2x}dx\right\}dx$$

$$=\frac{e^{2x}(x^2+x+1)}{2} - \int\left\{\frac{(2x+1).e^{2x}}{2}\right\}dx = \frac{(x^2+x+1)e^{2x}}{2} - \frac{1}{2}\left[\int(2x+1)e^{2x}dx\right]$$

$$=\frac{(x^2+x+1)e^{2x}}{2} - \frac{1}{2}\left[(2x+1)\frac{e^{2x}}{2} - \int 2.\frac{e^{2x}}{2}dx\right]+C$$

[Since according to ILATE rule. $e^{2x}\to$ IInd function; $(2x+1)\to$ Ist function]

$$=\frac{(x^2+x+1)}{2}e^{2x} - \frac{1}{4}(2x+1)e^{2x} + \frac{e^{2x}}{4} + C$$

$$=e^{2x}\left[\frac{x^2+x+1}{2} - \frac{x}{2} - \frac{1}{4} + \frac{1}{4}\right]+C = e^{2x}\left[\frac{x^2+1}{2}\right]+C$$

ILLUSTRATION 102: Find the following integrals:

(a) $\int e^{-x}(1-x)\ln(xe^{-x})dx$

(b) $\int\ln\left(x+\sqrt{x^2+4}\right)dx$

(c) $\int(\log x^2)^2 dx$

SOLUTION: (a) let $m = xe^{-x}$

$$\frac{dm}{dx} = x\left(-e^{-x}\right) + e^{-x} = e^{-x}(1-x) \qquad \Rightarrow \; dm = e^{-x}(1-x)\,dx$$

$$\Rightarrow \; I = \int \ln(m)dm \qquad \Rightarrow \; I = \int \underbrace{\ln(m)}_{I}.\underbrace{(1)}_{II}\,dm$$

$$= \ln(m)\int 1.\,dm - \left(\int \frac{d}{dn}(\ln m).\int 1.dm\right)dm = m\ln m - \int \frac{1}{m}.m\,dm + C$$

$= m \ln m - m + C = xe^{-x} \ln (xe^{-x}) - xe^{-x} + C.$

(b) Consider $\int \underbrace{1}_{II}.\underbrace{\ln\left(x+\sqrt{x^2+4}\right)}_{I}dx$

To use integration by parts assign first function according to ILATE rule here $1x^{\circ}$ is an algebraic function 2nd function and $\ln\left[x+\sqrt{x^2+4}\right]$ being logarithmic is a 1st function

$$\Rightarrow \; I = \ln\left(x+\sqrt{x^2+4}\right)\int 1.dx - \int\left(\left\{\frac{d\ln\left(x+\sqrt{x^2+4}\right)}{dx}\right\}\int 1.dx\right)dx$$

$$= x\ln\left(x+\sqrt{x^2+4}\right) - \int\left\{\frac{1}{x+\sqrt{x^2+4}}\left(1+\frac{2x}{2\sqrt{x^2+4}}\right)x\right\}dx$$

$$= x\ln\left(x+\sqrt{x^2+4}\right) - \int\left\{\frac{x}{\left(x+\sqrt{x^2+4}\right)}\frac{\left(x+\sqrt{x^2+4}\right)}{\sqrt{x^2+4}}\right\}dx$$

$$= x\ln\left(x+\sqrt{x^2+4}\right) - \frac{1}{2}\int\frac{(2x)}{\sqrt{x^2+4}}dx;$$

Now, put $m = x^2 + 4$

$$\Rightarrow \; 2x\,dx = dm = x\ln\left(x+\sqrt{x^2+4}\right) - \frac{1}{2}\int (m)^{-1/2}\,dm$$

$$= x\ln\left(x+\sqrt{x^2+4}\right) - \frac{1}{2}\frac{(m)^{-1/2+1}}{\left(1-\frac{1}{2}\right)} + C = x\ln\left(x+\sqrt{x^2+4}\right) - \sqrt{m} + C$$

$$= x\ln\left(x+\sqrt{x^2+4}\right) - \sqrt{x^2+4} + C.$$

(c) Consider $I = \int \underbrace{1}_{2^{nd}\text{ function}}\underbrace{\left(\ln x^2\right)^2}_{1^{st}\text{ function}}dx$

Since here no second function is specified so,

we will assign 2nd function = 1; 1st function = $(\ln x^2)^2$

$$\Rightarrow \; I = \left(\ln x^2\right)^2\int 1.dx - \int\left\{2\left(\ln x^2\right)\frac{1}{x^2}(2x).x\right\}dx = x\left(\ln x^2\right)^2 - 4\left[\int 1.\left(\ln x^2\right)dx\right]$$

$$= x\left(\ln x^2\right)^2 - 4\left[\left(\ln x^2\right)\int 1.dx - \int\left\{\frac{1}{x^2}(2x).x\right\}dx\right]$$

$$= x\left(\ln x^2\right)^2 - 4\left[\left(\ln x^2\right)x - 2x\right] + C = x\left(\ln x^2\right)^2 - 4x\left(\ln x^2\right) + 8x + C.$$

ILLUSTRATION 103: Find the following integrals:

(a) $\int \sqrt{x^2 - a^2}\, dx$ (b) $\int \sqrt{a^2 - x^2}\, dx$

(c) $\int \sqrt{x^2 + a^2}\, dx$

SOLUTION: (a) Consider $I = \int \underbrace{1}_{II} . \underbrace{\sqrt{x^2 - a^2}}_{I}\, dx$ (Taking 1 as 2nd function and $\sqrt{x^2 - a^2}$ as 1st function)

$$\Rightarrow \quad I = x\sqrt{x^2 - a^2} - \int \frac{\left(x^2 - a^2\right)^{-1/2}}{2}(2x).x\,dx$$

$$= x\sqrt{x^2 - a^2} - \int \frac{x^2}{\sqrt{x^2 - a^2}}dx = x\sqrt{x^2 - a^2} - \int \frac{\left(x^2 - a^2 + a^2\right)}{\sqrt{x^2 - a^2}}dx$$

$$= x\sqrt{x^2 - a^2} - \int\left(\sqrt{x^2 - a^2} + \frac{a^2}{\sqrt{x^2 - a^2}}\right)dx = x\sqrt{x^2 - a^2} - \int \sqrt{x^2 - a^2}\,dx - a^2\int \frac{1}{\sqrt{x^2 - a^2}}dx$$

$$= x\sqrt{x^2 - a^2} - I - a^2\left[\ln\left(x + \sqrt{x^2 - a^2}\right)\right] \qquad \left(\because \int \frac{1}{\sqrt{x^2 - a^2}}dx = \ln\left(x + \sqrt{x^2 - a^2}\right)\right)$$

$$\Rightarrow \quad 2I = x\sqrt{x^2 - a^2} - a^2 \ln\left(x + \sqrt{x^2 - a^2}\right)$$

$$\Rightarrow \quad I = \frac{x\sqrt{x^2 - a^2}}{2} - \frac{a^2}{2}\ln\left(x + \sqrt{x^2 - a^2}\right) + C$$

Aliter: put $x = a$ secc θ $\Rightarrow dx = a \sec\theta \tan\theta\, d\theta$

$$\Rightarrow \quad I = \sqrt{a^2\cos^2\theta - a^2}.a\sec\theta\tan\theta\,d\theta = a^2\int \sec\theta\tan^2\theta\,d\theta$$

$$= a^2\int \underbrace{\left(\sec\theta\tan^2\theta\right)}_{II}\underbrace{\left(\tan\theta\right)}_{I}d\theta$$

$$= a^2\left[\tan\theta.\sec\theta - \int \sec^3 d\theta\right] \qquad \ldots(i)$$

Consider $I_1 = \int \sec^3\theta d\theta = \int \sec^2\theta.\sec\theta\,d\theta = \sec\theta\tan\theta - \int \sec\theta.\tan^2\theta\,d\theta$

$$= \sec\theta\tan\theta - \int \sec\theta(\sec^2\theta - 1)\,d\theta$$

$$\Rightarrow \quad I_1 = \sec\theta\tan\theta - \int \sec^3\theta + \ln|\sec\theta + \tan\theta|$$

$$\Rightarrow \quad 2I_1 = \sec\theta\tan\theta + \ln|\sec\theta + \tan\theta|$$

$$\Rightarrow \quad I_1 = \frac{1}{2} = \sec\theta\tan\theta + \frac{1}{2}\ln|\sec\theta + \tan\theta|$$

∴ From (i)

$$I = a^2\sec\theta\tan\theta - a^2\left[\frac{1}{2}\sec\theta\tan\theta + \frac{1}{2}\ln|\sec\theta + \tan\theta|\right] + C$$

$$\Rightarrow \quad I = \frac{a^2}{2}\sec\theta\tan\theta - \frac{a^2}{2}\ln|\sec\theta + \tan\theta| + C$$

$$\Rightarrow \quad I = \frac{a^2}{2}.\frac{x}{a}\frac{\sqrt{x^2 - a^2}}{a} - \frac{a^2}{2}\ln\left|\frac{x}{a} + \frac{\sqrt{x^2 - a^2}}{a}\right| + C$$

or $I = \dfrac{x\sqrt{x^2 - a^2}}{2} - \dfrac{a^2}{2}\ln\left|x + \sqrt{x^2 - a^2}\right| + C'$ (Replacing $C + \dfrac{a^2}{2}\ln a$ by C')

(b) Consider $\int \underbrace{1}_{2^{nd}\text{ function}} . \underbrace{\sqrt{a^2-x^2}}_{1^{st}\text{ function}}\, dx = \sqrt{a^2-x^2}\int 1.dx - \int\left\{\frac{1(-2x)}{2\sqrt{a^2-x^2}}.x\,dx\right\}$

$= x\sqrt{a^2-x^2} + \int \frac{x^2}{\sqrt{a^2-x^2}}dx = x\sqrt{a^2-x^2} + \int \frac{x^2+a^2-a^2}{\sqrt{a^2-x^2}}dx$

$= x\sqrt{a^2-x^2} - \int\sqrt{(a^2-x^2)}dx + a^2\int\frac{1}{\sqrt{a^2-x^2}}dx$

$\Rightarrow \quad 2I = x\sqrt{a^2-x^2} + a^2\sin^{-1}\frac{x}{a} + C \qquad \Rightarrow \quad I = \frac{x}{2}\sqrt{a^2-x^2} + \frac{a^2}{2}\sin^{-1}\frac{x}{a} + C.$

Aliter: $I = \int\sqrt{a^2-x^2}\,dx$

Put $x = a\sin\theta$ $\qquad \Rightarrow \quad dx = a\cos\theta\, d\theta$

$\therefore \quad I = \int\sqrt{a^2-a^2\sin^2\theta}.a\cos\theta\, d\theta = a^2\int\cos^2\theta\, d\theta$

$= a^2\int\frac{1+\cos 2\theta}{2}d\theta = \frac{a^2}{2}\left[\theta + \frac{1}{2}(\sin 2\theta)\right] + C = \frac{a^2}{2}\theta + \frac{a^2}{4}(2\sin\theta\cos\theta) + C$

$= \frac{a^2}{2}\theta + \frac{a^2}{2}\sin\theta\cos\theta + C$

$= \frac{a^2}{2}\sin^{-1}\left(\frac{x}{a}\right) + \frac{a^2}{2}\left(\frac{x}{a}\right)\sqrt{1-\frac{x^2}{a^2}} + C = \frac{a^2}{2}\sin^{-1}\left(\frac{x}{a}\right) + \frac{x}{2}\sqrt{a^2-x^2} + C$

$\therefore \quad \int\sqrt{a^2-x^2}\,dx = \frac{x}{2}\sqrt{a^2-x^2} + \frac{a^2}{2}\sin^{-1}\left(\frac{x}{a}\right) + C$

(c) Consider $\int \underbrace{\sqrt{x^2+a^2}}_{1^{st}\text{ function}} . \underbrace{1.dx}_{2^{nd}\text{ function}} = \left(\sqrt{x^2+a^2}\right)(x) - \int\frac{1}{2\sqrt{x^2+a^2}}(2x)x\,dx$

$= x\sqrt{x^2+a^2} - \int\frac{x^2}{\sqrt{x^2+a^2}}dx = x\sqrt{x^2+a^2} - \int\frac{x^2+a^2-a^2}{\sqrt{x^2+a^2}}dx$

$= x\sqrt{x^2+a^2} - \int\sqrt{x^2+a^2}\,dx + a^2\int\frac{1}{\sqrt{x^2+a^2}}dx$

$\Rightarrow \quad 2\int\sqrt{x^2+a^2}\,dx = x\sqrt{x^2+a^2} + a^2\ln\left|x+\sqrt{x^2+a^2}\right| + C$

$\Rightarrow \quad \int\sqrt{x^2+a^2}\,dx = \frac{x}{2}\sqrt{x^2+a^2} + \frac{a^2}{2}\ln\left|x+\sqrt{x^2+a^2}\right| + C$

Aliter: $I = \int\sqrt{a^2+x^2}\,dx$

Put $x = a\tan\theta$ $\qquad \Rightarrow \quad dx = a\sec^2\theta\, d\theta$

$\Rightarrow \quad I = \int\sqrt{a^2+a^2\tan^2\theta}.a\sec^2\theta\, d\theta$

$\Rightarrow \quad I = \int a^2\sec^3\theta\, d\theta = a^2\left[\frac{1}{2}\sec\theta\tan\theta + \frac{1}{2}\ln|\sec\theta+\tan\theta|\right] + C$ $\qquad$ ($\therefore$ From part (a))

$= \frac{a^2}{2}\sec\theta\tan\theta + \frac{a^2}{4}\ln|\sec\theta+\tan\theta| + C = \frac{a^2}{2}\frac{\sqrt{x^2+a^2}}{a}.\frac{x}{a} + \frac{a^2}{2}\ln\left|\frac{\sqrt{x^2+a^2}}{a}+\frac{x}{a}\right| + C$

$= \frac{x\sqrt{x^2+a^2}}{2} + \frac{a^2}{2}\ln\left|x+\sqrt{x^2+a^2}\right| + C$

ILLUSTRATION 104: Find the following integrals:

(a) $\int x^2 \sin x \cos^2 x\, dx$ (b) $\int x \sec^2 x(1+\tan x)\, dx$

SOLUTION: (a) Consider $\int \underbrace{x^2}_{I} \underbrace{(\sin x \cos^2 x)}_{II} dx$

$$= x^2 \int \sin x \cos^2 x\, dx - \int \left\{ \frac{d}{dx}(x^2) \int \sin x \cos^2 x\, dx \right\} dx = -x^2 \frac{(\cos x)^3}{3} + \frac{2}{3}\int x(\cos x)^3\, dx$$

$$\left[\because \cos 3x = 4\cos^3 x - 3\cos x \Rightarrow \cos^3 x = \frac{3}{4}\cos x + \frac{1}{4}\cos 3x \right]$$

$$= -\frac{1}{3}x^2 \cos^3 x + \frac{2}{3}\int \left(\frac{3}{4} x\cos x + \frac{1}{4} x\cos 3x \right) dx$$

$$= -\frac{1}{3}x^2 \cos^3 x + \frac{1}{2}\int x\cos x\, dx + \frac{1}{6}\int x\cos 3x\, dx$$

$$= -\frac{1}{3}x^2 \cos^3 x + \frac{1}{2}\left[x\sin x - \int (1)\sin x\, dx \right] + \frac{1}{6}\left[\frac{x\sin 3x}{3} - \int \frac{\sin 3x}{3} dx \right]$$

$$= -\frac{1}{3}x^2 \cos^3 x + \frac{1}{2}x\sin x + \frac{1}{2}\cos x + \frac{1}{18}x\sin x3x + \frac{1}{54}\cos 3x + C$$

(b) Consider $\int x\sec^2 x.dx + \int x\sec^2 x\tan x.dx$

$$= x\int \sec^2 xdx - \int \left\{ \frac{dx}{dx} \int \sec^2 xdx \right\} dx \;+\; x\int (\sec^2 x\tan x)dx - \int \left\{ \frac{dx}{dx} \int \sec^2 x\tan x\, dx \right\} dx$$

$$= x(\tan x) - \int \tan x\, dx + x\left(\frac{\tan^2 x}{2} \right) - \int \frac{1}{2}(\tan^2 x)dx$$

$$= x\left(\tan x + \frac{\tan^2 x}{2} \right) - \ln|\sec x| - \frac{1}{2}\int (\sec^2 x - 1)dx$$

$$= x\left(\tan x + \frac{\tan^2 x}{2} \right) - \ln|\sec x| - \frac{1}{2}[\tan x - x] + C$$

$$= x\left(\tan x + \frac{1}{2}\tan^2 x + \frac{1}{2} \right) - \ln|\sec x| - \frac{1}{2}\tan x + C$$

ILLUSTRATION 105: Find $\int \frac{x-1}{1+\sin x} dx$

SOLUTION: Given integral, $I = \int \frac{x}{1+\sin x} dx - \int \frac{1}{1+\sin x} dx$

$$= \int \frac{x(1-\sin x)}{1-\sin^2 x} dx - \int \frac{(1-\sin x)}{1-\sin^2 x} dx = \int \frac{x(1-\sin x)}{\cos^2 x} dx - \int \frac{(1-\sin x)}{\cos^2 x} dx$$

$$= \int x(\sec^2 x - \tan x\sec x)dx - \int (\sec^2 x - \tan x\sec x)dx$$

$$= \int \underset{I}{x} \underbrace{\sec^2 x}_{II} dx - \int x\sec x\tan x\, dx - \int \sec^2 dx + \int \tan x\sec x\, dx$$

$$= (x\tan x) - \log|\sec x| - \left[x\sec x - \ln|\sec x + \tan x| \right] - \tan x + \sec x + C$$

$$= (x-1)\tan x + (1-x)\sec x + \ln\left| \frac{\sec x + \tan x}{\sec x} \right| + C$$

TEXTUAL EXCERISE 4: (SUBJECTIVE)

1. Prove that $\int f(x).g(x)\,dx = f(x).\int g(x)dx - \int\left(f'(x)\int g(x)dx\right)dx$ and using this result, find the following integrals:
   (a) $\int x^3 \ln x\, dx$ (b) $\int \frac{\ln x}{x^2}\, dx$
   (c) $\int (3x^3 - 17)e^{2x}\, dx$ (d) $\int x \sin^{-1} x\, dx$
   (e) $\int x^3 e^x\, dx$ (f) $\int x^3 \sin x\, dx$
   (g) $\int x^2 \cos^2 x\, dx$
2. Integrate the following by parts:
   (a) $\int \frac{dx}{(x^4-1)^2}$ (b) $\int x\ln(1+x^2)dx$
3. Prove that
   $$\int e^{f(x)}\left[xf'(x)+\frac{f''(x)}{(f'(x))^2}\right]dx = e^{f(x)}\left(x-\frac{1}{f'(x)}\right)+C$$
4. Integrate the following by parts:
   (a) $\int x\tan^2 x\, dx$ (b) $\int x\cos^2 x\, dx$
   (c) $\int \frac{\ln x}{x^3} dx$ (d) $\int \ln(x^2+1)dx$
5. Integrate the following by parts:
   (a) $\int (\text{arc}\sin x)^2\, dx$
   (b) $\int (\text{arc}\tan x)^2\, x dx$
   (c) $\int e^{3x}(\sin 2x - \cos 2x)\, dx$
6. Integrate the following by parts:
   (a) $\int \frac{x^3 dx}{\sqrt{1+x^2}}$ (b) $\int \frac{x^2\, dx}{\sqrt{1-x^2}}$
   (c) $\int \frac{x^2 dx}{(1+x^2)^2}$
7. Integrate the following Integrals by parts:
   (a) $\int x^n \ln x\, dx\ (n \neq -1)$ (b) $\int \frac{\log x}{x^3} dx$
   (c) $\int \frac{\ln^3 x}{x^2}\, dx$
8. Integrate the following by parts:
   (a) $\int \text{arc}\tan\sqrt{x}\, dx$ (b) $\int \frac{\text{arc}\sin x}{\sqrt{x+1}} dx$
   (c) $\int \frac{x\,\text{arc}\tan x}{\sqrt{1+x^2}} dx$
9. Integrate the following by parts:
   (a) $\int \ln(x^2+1)\, dx$ (b) $\int \cos(\ln x)\, dx$
   (c) $\int x^2 \ln(1+x)\, dx$

Answer Keys

1. (a) $\frac{x^4}{4}\ln x - \frac{1}{16}x^4 + C$ (b) $-\frac{1}{x}(\ln x + 1) + C$ (c) $\left(\frac{3x^3}{2} - \frac{9}{4}x^2 + \frac{9}{4}x - \frac{77}{8}\right)e^{2x} + C$
   (d) $\frac{1}{4}\left[x\sqrt{1-x^2} + (2x^2-1)\sin^{-1} x\right] + C$ (e) $e^x(x^3 - 3x^2 + 6x - 6) + C$
   (f) $C - x^3 \cos x + 3x^2 \sin x + 6x \cos x - 6 \sin x$ (g) $\frac{1}{6}x^3 + \frac{1}{4}x^2 \sin 2x + \frac{1}{4}x\cos 2x - \frac{1}{8}\sin 2x + C$
2. (a) $\frac{1}{4}x^3 - \frac{3}{16}\ln\left|\frac{x-1}{x+1}\right| + \frac{3}{8}\tan^{-1} x + C$ (b) $\frac{1}{2}[x^2 \log(1+x^2) - x^2 + \ln|x^2+1|] + C$
4. (a) $x\tan x - \frac{x^2}{2} + \ln|\cos x| + C$ (b) $\frac{x^2}{4} + \frac{1}{4}x\sin 2x + \frac{1}{8}\cos 2x + C$
   (c) $C - \frac{1}{2x^2}\ln(x\sqrt{e})$ (d) $x\ln(x^2+1) - 2x + 2\,\text{arc}\tan x + C$
5. (a) $x(\text{arc}\sin x)^2 + 2\text{arc}\sin x.\sqrt{1-x^2} - 2x + C$ (b) $\frac{x^2+1}{2}(\text{arc}\tan x)^2 - x\,\text{arc}\tan x + \frac{1}{2}\ln(1+x^2) + C$
   (c) $\frac{e^{3x}}{13}(\sin 2x - 5\cos 2x) + C$
6. (a) $C - \frac{x}{2(1+x^2)} + \frac{1}{2}\text{arc}\tan x$ (b) $x^2\sqrt{1+x^2} - \frac{2}{3}\sqrt{(1+x^2)^3} + C$ (c) $\frac{1}{2}\tan^{-1} x - \frac{1}{2}\frac{x}{(1+x^2)} + C$

7. (a) $\frac{x^{n+1}}{n+1}\left(\ln x-\frac{1}{n+1}\right)+C$ (b) $C-\frac{1}{2x^2}\ln\left(x\sqrt{e}\right)$ (c) $C-\frac{1}{x}\left(\ln^3 x+3\ln^2 x+6\ln x+6\right)$

8. (a) $x\arctan\sqrt{x}-\sqrt{x}+\arctan\sqrt{x}+C$ (b) $2\sqrt{x+1}\arcsin x+4\sqrt{1-x}+C$

(c) $\sqrt{1+x^2}\arcsin x-\ln\left(x+\sqrt{1+x^2}\right)+C$

9. (a) $x\ln(x^2+1)-2x+2\arctan x+C$ (b) $\frac{x}{2}\left(\cos\ln x+\sin\ln x\right)+C$ (c) $\frac{(x^3+1)\ln(1+x)}{2}-\frac{x^3}{9}+\frac{x^2}{6}-\frac{x}{3}+C$

TEXTUAL EXCERISE 4: (OBJECTIVE)

1. The integral $\int\frac{\ln^2 x}{\sqrt{x^5}}dx$ given by

(a) $C-\frac{8}{27\sqrt{x^3}}\left(\frac{9}{4}\ln^2 x+3\ln x+2\right)$

(b) $\frac{8}{27\sqrt{x^3}}\left(\frac{9}{4}\ln x-3\ln x+2\right)+C$

(c) $C-\frac{8}{27\sqrt{x^3}}\left(\frac{9}{4}\ln^2 x-3\ln x-2\right)$

(d) $C+\frac{8}{27\sqrt{x^3}}\left(\frac{9}{5}\ln^2 x+3\ln x-2\right)$

2. The integral $\int\frac{\arcsin\sqrt{x}}{\sqrt{1-x}}dx$ is given by

(a) $2\left(\sqrt{x}+\sqrt{1-x}\arccos\sqrt{x}\right)+C$

(b) $\left(\sqrt{x}-\sqrt{1-x}\arccos\sqrt{x}\right)+C$

(c) $2\left(\sqrt{x}-\sqrt{1-x}\arcsin\sqrt{x}\right)+C$

(d) None of these

3. The integral $\int\left(\arcsin x\right)^2 dx$ is given by

(a) $x(\arccos x)^2+2\arcsin\sqrt{1-x^2}+C$

(b) $x(\arcsin x)+2\arcsin x\sqrt{1+x^2}+2x+C$

(c) $x(\arccos x)+2\arccos\sqrt{1-x^2}+C$

(d) $x(\arcsin x)^2+2\arcsin x\sqrt{1-x^2}-2x+C$

4. The integral $\int\frac{x^2e^x dx}{(x+2)^2}$ is given by

(a) $\frac{x-2}{x+2}e^x+C$ (b) $\frac{x+2}{x-2}e^x+C$

(c) $\frac{x-2}{x+2}e^{-x}+C$ (d) $\frac{x+1}{x-2}e^x+C$

5. The integral $\int\left(\arctan x\right)^2 x\,dx$ is given by

(a) $\frac{x^2-1}{2}(\arctan x)-x\,\mathrm{arc}(\tan x)+\frac{1}{3}\ln(1+x^2)+C$

(b) $\frac{x^2+1}{2}(\arctan x)^2+\frac{1}{2}\ln(1+x^2)+C$

(c) $\frac{x^2+1}{2}(\mathrm{arccot}\,x)^2-x\,\mathrm{arc}(\cot x)+\frac{1}{2}\ln(1+x^2)+C$

(d) $\frac{x^2+1}{2}(\arctan x)^2-x\arctan x+\frac{1}{2}\ln(1+x^2)+C$

6. The integral $\int x^2e^x\sin x\,dx$ is given by

(a) $\frac{1}{2}\left[(x^2-1)\sin x-(x-1)^2\cos x\right]e^x+C$

(b) $\frac{1}{2}\left[(x^2+1)\cos x-(x-1)^2\sin x\right]e^x+C$

(c) $\frac{1}{2}\left[(x^2-1)\cos x-(x+1)^2\sin x\right]e^x+C$

(d) None of these

7. The integral $\int\sin(\ln x)$ is given by

(a) $\frac{x}{2}(\sin\ln x+\cos\ln x)+C$

(b) $\frac{x}{2}(\sin\ln x-\cos\ln x)+C$

(c) $x(\sin\ln x+\cos\ln x)+C$

(d) None of these

Answer Keys

1. (a) **2.** (c) **3.** (d) **4.** (a) **5.** (d) **6.** (a) **7.** (b) **8.** (b)

■ INTEGRATION OF RATIONAL AND IRRATIONAL EXPRESSIONS

Type (i): Integration of rational expressions of the type: $\frac{1}{ax^2+bx+c}dx$; where $b^2 - 4ac < 0$, i.e., quadratic in denominator is irreducible.

4Let $I = \int \frac{1}{ax^2+bx+c}dx = \frac{1}{a}\int \frac{1}{x^2+\frac{b}{a}x+\frac{c}{a}}dx$

Completing the square in denominator we get

$$I = \frac{1}{a}\int \frac{dx}{x^2+\frac{b}{a}x+\frac{b^2}{4a^2}+\frac{c}{a}-\frac{b^2}{4a^2}}$$

$$= \frac{1}{a}\int \frac{dx}{\left(x+\frac{b}{2a}\right)^2+\frac{(4ac-b^2)}{4a^2}}$$

$$= \frac{1}{a}\int \frac{dx}{\left(x+\frac{b}{2a}\right)^2+\left(\frac{\sqrt{4ac-b^2}}{2a}\right)^2}$$

Since $b^2 - 4ac < 0$

$\Rightarrow\ 4ac - b^2 > 0$

$$\therefore\ I = \int \frac{dx}{\left(x+\frac{b}{2a}\right)^2+\left(\frac{\sqrt{-D}}{2a}\right)^2}$$

$$= \frac{2a}{\sqrt{-D}}\tan^{-1}\left(\frac{2ax+b}{\sqrt{-D}}\right)+C$$

ILLUSTRATION 106: Find $\int \frac{1}{2x^2+3x+5}dx$

SOLUTION: $\int \frac{1}{2x^2+3x+5}dx$; Here a = 2, $b = 3$, $c = 5$

$\therefore\ b^2 - 4ac = 9 - 40 = -31 < 0$ $\quad\therefore$ Quadratic in the denominator is irreducible

$$\therefore\ I = \int \frac{dx}{2\left(x^2+\frac{3}{2}x+\frac{5}{2}\right)} = \frac{1}{2}\int \frac{dx}{\left(x^2+\frac{3}{2}x+\frac{9}{16}+\frac{5}{2}-\frac{9}{16}\right)} = \frac{1}{2}\int \frac{dx}{\left(x+\frac{3}{4}\right)^2+\left(\frac{\sqrt{31}}{4}\right)^2}$$

$$= \frac{1}{2}\times\frac{4}{\sqrt{31}}\tan^{-1}\left(\frac{4x+3}{\sqrt{31}}\right)+C = \frac{2}{\sqrt{31}}\tan^{-1}\left(\frac{4x+3}{\sqrt{31}}\right)+C.$$

Type (ii): Integration of rational expression of the type: $\int \frac{1}{ax^2+bx+c}dx$; where $b^2 - 4ac = 0$, i.e., denominator has repeated roots.

Let $ax^2 + bx + c = a(x - \alpha)^2$, then

$$\int \frac{1}{ax^2+bx+c}dx = \int \frac{1}{a(x-\alpha)^2}dx$$

$$\frac{1}{a}\int (x-\alpha)^{-2}dx = \frac{1}{a}\frac{(x-\alpha)^{-2+1}}{(-2+1)}+C = -\frac{1}{a}.\frac{1}{(x-\alpha)}+C$$

ILLUSTRATION 107: Find $\int \frac{dx}{4x^2-12x+9}$

SOLUTION: Here $a = 4$, $b = -12$, $c = 9$

$D = b^2 - 4ac = 144 - 144 = 0$

$\therefore$ Denominator has repeated roots.

Now $4x^2 - 12x + 9 = (2x - 3)^2$

$$\therefore\ I = \int \frac{dx}{(2x-3)^2} = \int (2x-3)^{-2}dx = \frac{(2x-3)^{-2+1}}{2(-2+1)}+C = -\frac{1}{2(2x-3)}+C$$

Type (iii): Integration of rational expression of type: $\int \frac{1}{ax^2+bx+c}dx$; where $b^2 - 4ac > 0$, i.e., denominator contains a reducible quadratic factors.

Method 1: Let $ax^2 + bx + c = 4(x - \alpha)(x - \beta)$, then

$$I = \int \frac{dx}{a(x-\alpha)(x-\beta)} = \frac{1}{a}\int \frac{dx}{\frac{(x-\alpha)}{(x-\beta)}(x-\beta)^2} \quad \text{...(i)}$$

Let $\frac{x-\alpha}{x-\beta} = t$

$$\Rightarrow \frac{(x-\beta)-(x-\alpha)}{(x-\beta)^2}dx = dt$$

$$\Rightarrow \frac{(x-\beta)}{(x-\beta)^2}dx = dt \Rightarrow \frac{dx}{(x-\beta)^2}\frac{dt}{(x-\beta)} \quad \text{...(ii)}$$

Using (ii) in (i), we get

$$I = \frac{1}{a}\int \frac{dt}{(t)(\alpha-\beta)} = \frac{1}{a(\alpha-\beta)}\ln|t| + C$$

$$\therefore \quad I = \frac{1}{a(\alpha-\beta)}\ln\left|\frac{x-\alpha}{x-\beta}\right| + C$$

Method 2: (By using partial fractions, will be discussed soon)

$$\text{Let } I = \int \frac{dx}{ax^2+bx+c} = \int \frac{dx}{a(x-\alpha)(x-\beta)} \quad \text{...(i)}$$

$$\text{Let } \frac{1}{(x-\alpha)(x-\beta)} = \frac{A}{x-\alpha} + \frac{B}{x-\beta} \quad \text{...(ii)}$$

$$\Rightarrow 1 = A(x-\beta) + B(x-\alpha) \quad \text{...(iii)}$$

Putting $x = \alpha$ in (iii), we get

$$A = \frac{1}{\alpha-\beta}$$

Putting $x = B$ in (ii), we get $B = \frac{1}{\beta-\alpha}$

Using the values of A and B in (ii) and from (i), we have

$$I = \frac{1}{a}\int \frac{1}{(\alpha-\beta)(x-\alpha)}dx - \frac{1}{a}\int \frac{dx}{(\alpha-\beta)(x-\beta)}$$

$$= \frac{1}{a(\alpha-\beta)}[\ln|x-\alpha| - \ln|x-\beta|] + C$$

$$= \frac{1}{a(\alpha-\beta)}\ln\left|\frac{x-\alpha}{x-\beta}\right| + C$$

ILLUSTRATION 108: Find $\int \frac{dx}{(x^2-3x+2)}$

SOLUTION: Let $I = \int \frac{dx}{x^2-3x+2} = \int \frac{dx}{(x-1)(x-2)}$

Method I: $I = \int \frac{dx}{\frac{(x-1)}{(x-2)}(x-2)^2}$ ...(i)

Putting $\frac{x-1}{x-2} = t$ $\quad \Rightarrow \frac{(x-2)-(x-1)}{(x-2)^2}dx = dt$

$\Rightarrow \frac{-1}{(x-2)^2}dx = dt$ $\quad \Rightarrow \frac{dx}{(x-2)^2} = -dt$

$\therefore$ From (i)

$$I = \int \frac{-dt}{t} = -\ln|t| + C = -\ln\left|\frac{x-1}{x-2}\right| + C$$

Method 2: Let $\frac{1}{(x-1)(x-2)} = \frac{A}{(x-1)} + \frac{B}{(x-2)}$

$\Rightarrow 1 = A(x-2) + B(x-1)$

Putting $x = 1$ and $x = 2$ successively, we get $A = -1, B = 1$

$$\therefore \quad I = \int\left(\frac{-1}{x-1} + \frac{1}{(x-2)}\right)dx = -\ln|x-1| + \ln|x-2| + C = -\ln\left|\frac{x-1}{x-2}\right| + C$$

Type (iv): Integration of irrational expression of type $\int \sqrt{ax^2+bx+c}\, dx$:

$I = \int \sqrt{ax^2+bx+c}\, dx$

Completing square inside the root we have

$$= \int \sqrt{a\left(x^2+\frac{b}{a}x+\frac{c}{a}+\frac{b^2}{4a^2}-\frac{b^2}{4a^2}\right)}\, dx$$

$$= \int \sqrt{a\left[\left(x+\frac{b}{2a}\right)^2+\frac{4ac-b^2}{4a^2}\right]}\, dx$$

$$= \int \sqrt{a\left[\left(x+\frac{b}{2a}\right)^2-\frac{D}{(2a)^2}\right]}\, dx$$

Case (i): When $a, D > 0$, then $I = \sqrt{a}\int\sqrt{t^2-\left(\frac{\sqrt{D}}{2a}\right)^2}\, dt$; where $t = \left(x+\frac{b}{2a}\right)$

$$= \sqrt{a}\left[\frac{t\sqrt{t^2-\left(\frac{\sqrt{D}}{2a}\right)^2}}{2}-\frac{D}{8a^2}\ln\left|t+\sqrt{t^2-\left(\frac{\sqrt{D}}{2a}\right)^2}\right|\right]+C$$

Case (ii): When $a > 0, D < 0$ then

$$I = \sqrt{a}\int\sqrt{t^2+\left(\frac{\sqrt{-D}}{2a}\right)^2}\, dt \text{ ; where } t = \left(x+\frac{b}{2a}\right)$$

$$= \sqrt{a}\left[\frac{t\sqrt{t^2+\left(\frac{\sqrt{-D}}{2a}\right)^2}}{2}-\frac{D}{8a^2}\ln\left|t+\sqrt{t^2-\left(\frac{\sqrt{-D}}{2a}\right)^2}\right|\right]+C;$$

$$t = x+\frac{b}{2a}$$

Case (iii): When $a < 0, D > 0$

$$I = \int\sqrt{-(-a)\left[\left(x+\frac{b}{2a}\right)^2-\left(\frac{\sqrt{D}}{2a}\right)^2\right]}\, dx$$

$$= \int\sqrt{(-a)\left[\left(\frac{\sqrt{D}}{2a}\right)^2-\left(x+\frac{b}{2a}\right)^2\right]}\, dx$$

$$= \sqrt{-a}\int\sqrt{\left(\frac{\sqrt{D}}{2a}\right)^2-t^2}\, dt \text{ where } t = \left(x+\frac{b}{2a}\right).$$

$$= \sqrt{-a}\left[\frac{t\sqrt{\left(\frac{\sqrt{D}}{2a}\right)^2-t^2}}{2}+\frac{D}{8a^2}\sin^{-1}\left(\frac{2at}{\sqrt{D}}\right)\right]+C$$

Case (iv): When $a < 0, D < 0$, integration is impossible as the integrand becomes imaginary.

ILLUSTRATION 109: Evaluate the $\int\sqrt{4x-3-x^2}\, dx$

SOLUTION: $\int\sqrt{-\left(x^2-4x+3\right)}\, dx$

Once again by comparing it with $ax^2 + bx + c$

$a = 1, b = -4, c = 3$

$$ax^2+bx+c = \left(x+\frac{b}{2a}\right)^2-\frac{D}{4a^2} = \left(x+\frac{b}{2a}\right)^2-\frac{\left(b^2-4ac\right)}{4a^2}$$

$D = b^2 - 4ac = (-4)^2 - 4\,(1)\,(3) = 16 - 12 = 4$

$\therefore\ D > 0$

$$\therefore\ \left(x+\frac{b}{2a}\right)^2-\frac{D}{4a^2} = +\left(t^2-k^2\right)$$

$$\Rightarrow I = \int\sqrt{-\left(\left(x+\frac{(-4)}{2(1)}\right)^2-\frac{4}{4}\right)}\, dx = \int\sqrt{-\left((x-2)^2-1\right)}\, dx = \int\sqrt{1-(x-2)^2}\, dx$$

$\Rightarrow$ Put $x-2=t$ $\Rightarrow dt=dx$

$$\Rightarrow I=\int\sqrt{1-t^2}\,dt=\frac{t}{2}\left(\sqrt{1-t^2}\right)+\frac{1}{2}\sin^{-1}\frac{t}{1}+C=\frac{1}{2}(x-2)\sqrt{1-(x-2)^2}+\frac{1}{2}\sin^{-1}(x-2)+C$$

$$=\frac{1}{2}(x-2)\sqrt{4x-3-x^2}+\frac{1}{2}\sin^{-1}(x-2)+C$$

Type (v): Integration of irrational expression of type $\int\frac{1}{\sqrt{ax^2+bx+c}}dx$

Case (i): When $a>0, D>0$

$$I=\int\frac{1}{\sqrt{a\left[\left(x+\frac{b}{2a}\right)^2-\frac{D}{4a^2}\right]}}dx$$

$$=\frac{1}{\sqrt{a}}\int\frac{1}{\sqrt{\left(x+\frac{b}{2a}\right)^2-\left(\frac{\sqrt{D}}{2a}\right)^2}}dx$$

$$=\frac{1}{\sqrt{a}}\ln\left|t+\sqrt{t^2-\left(\frac{\sqrt{D}}{2a}\right)^2}\right|+C\text{ ; where } t=\left(x+\frac{b}{2a}\right)$$

Case (ii): When $a>0, D<0$

$$I=\int\frac{1}{\sqrt{a}}\frac{1}{\sqrt{\left(x+\frac{b}{2a}\right)^2+\left(\frac{\sqrt{-D}}{2a}\right)^2}}dx$$

$$=\frac{1}{\sqrt{a}}\int\frac{1}{\sqrt{t^2+\left(\frac{\sqrt{-D}}{2a}\right)^2}}dt\ ;\ t=x+\frac{b}{2a}$$

$$=\frac{1}{\sqrt{a}}\ln\left|t+\sqrt{t^2+\left(\frac{\sqrt{-D}}{2a}\right)^2}\right|+C\text{ where } t=\left(x+\frac{b}{2a}\right)$$

Case (iii): When $a<0, D>0$

$$I=\int\frac{1}{\sqrt{-(-a)\left[\left(x+\frac{b}{2a}\right)^2-\frac{D}{4a^2}\right]}}dx$$

$$=\int\frac{1}{\sqrt{-a}\sqrt{\left(\frac{\sqrt{D}}{2a^2}\right)-\left(x+\frac{b}{2a}\right)^2}}dx$$

$$=\frac{1}{\sqrt{-a}}\int\frac{1}{\sqrt{\left(\frac{\sqrt{D}}{2a}\right)^2-t^2}}dt\ ;$$

$$t=x+\frac{b}{2a}$$

$$=\frac{1}{\sqrt{-a}}\sin^{-1}\left(\frac{t}{\sqrt{D}/2a}\right)+C\text{ where } t=\left(x+\frac{b}{2a}\right)$$

Case (iv): When $a<0, D<0$ integration is impossible as the integrand becomes imaginary.

ILLUSTRATION 110: Evaluate $\int\frac{1}{\sqrt{x^2+4x+3}}dx$

SOLUTION: Comparing this with equation ax^2+bx+c

$\Rightarrow a=1, b=4, c=3$

$$\left(ax^2+bx+c\right)=\left(x+\frac{b}{2a}\right)^2-\frac{D}{4a^2} \quad \text{...(1)}$$

$D=b^2-4ac=(4)^2-4(3)(1)=16-12=4$

$\Rightarrow D>0$

$\therefore$ Equation (1) becomes $\left(x+\frac{4}{2}\right)^2-\frac{4}{4}=(x+2)^2-1$

$$\Rightarrow I=\int\frac{1}{\sqrt{(x+2)^2-1}}dx$$

Now, put $x+2=t$

$\Rightarrow dt=dx$

$$\Rightarrow I=\int\frac{1}{\sqrt{(t)^2-1}}dt=\ln\left|t+\sqrt{t^2-1}\right|+C=\ln\left|(x+2)+\sqrt{(x+2)^2-1}\right|+C$$

$$=\ln\left|(x+2)+\sqrt{x^2+4x+3}\right|+C$$

Type (vi): Integration of rational and irrational expressions of the type:

(a) $\int\frac{px+q}{ax^2+bx+c}dx$

(b) $\int\frac{px+q}{\sqrt{ax^2+bx+c}}dx$

(c) $\int(px+q)\sqrt{ax^2+bx+c}\ dx$

Algorithm: Let $px+q=A\frac{d}{dx}(ax^2+bx+c)+B\ px$

$=A(2ax+b)+B$

$$\Rightarrow A=\frac{p}{2a}\text{ and }B=q-\frac{pc}{2a}$$

$$\Rightarrow \int\frac{px+q}{ax^2+bx+c}dx$$

$$=A\underbrace{\int\frac{2ax+b}{ax^2+bx+c}dx}_{\text{put }ax^2+bx+c=t}+B\underbrace{\int\frac{dx}{ax^2+bx+c}}_{\text{solve as discussed earlier}};$$

$$\int\frac{px+q}{\sqrt{ax^2+bx+c}}dx$$

$$=A\underbrace{\int\frac{2ax+b}{\sqrt{ax^2+bx+c}}dx}_{\text{put }ax^2+bx+c=t}+B\underbrace{\int\frac{dx}{\sqrt{ax^2+bx+c}}}_{\text{solve as discussed earlier}}\text{ and}$$

$$\int(px+q)\sqrt{ax^2+bx+c}\,dx$$

$$=A\underbrace{\int(2ax+b)\sqrt{ax^2+bx+c}\ dx}_{\text{put }ax^2+bx+c=t}+B\underbrace{\int\sqrt{ax^2+bx+c}}_{\text{solve as disccused earlier}}$$

ILLUSTRATION 111: Evaluate $\int\frac{3x+1}{\sqrt{x^2+4x+1}}dx$

SOLUTION: Proceeding as explained above let $3x+1=A\frac{d}{dx}\left(x^2+4x+1\right)+B$

$\Rightarrow 3x+1=A(2x+4)+B$

$\Rightarrow A=\frac{3}{2}$ and $B=1-4A=1-6=-5$

$$\therefore\int\frac{3x+1}{\sqrt{x^2+4x+1}}dx=\int\frac{\frac{3}{2}(2x+4)+(-5)}{\sqrt{x^2+4x+1}}dx=\frac{3}{2}\int\frac{2x+4}{\sqrt{x^2+4x+1}}dx-5\int\frac{1}{\sqrt{x^2+4x+1}}dx$$

$=I_1+I_2$ (say) ...(1)

Now, Put $x^2+4x+1=t$

$$\Rightarrow \frac{dt}{dx}=2x+4\Rightarrow dx=\frac{dt}{2x+4}\qquad\Rightarrow I_1=\frac{3}{2}\int\frac{(2x+4)}{\sqrt{t}}\frac{dt}{(2x+4)}=\frac{3}{2}\int t^{-1/2}dt$$

$$=\frac{3}{2}\left[\frac{(t)^{1/2}}{1/2}\right]+C_1=3(x^2+4x+1)^{1/2}+C_1\qquad\text{...(2)}$$

Now, $I_2 = -5\int \frac{1}{\sqrt{x^2+4x+1}}dx$, Comparing $x^2 + 4x + 1$ with $ax^2 + bx + c$

$\Rightarrow$ $a = 1, b = 4, c = 1$

Now $ax^2 + bx + c = \left(x+\frac{b}{2a}\right)^2 - \frac{D}{4a^2}$ ...(3)

Now, $D = b^2 - 4ac = 4^2 - 4(1)(1) = 16 - 4 = 12$

$D > 0$

$\therefore$ Equation (2) becomes $\left(x+\frac{b}{2a}\right)^2 - \frac{D}{4a^2} = (t^2 - k^2)$

Here $t = x + \frac{b}{2a} = x + \frac{4}{2} = x + 2$; and $k^2 = \frac{D}{4a} = \frac{(12)}{4(1)^2} = 3$

$I_2 = -5\int \frac{1}{\sqrt{(x+2)^2 - (\sqrt{3})^2}}dx$; put $t = x + 2$

$\Rightarrow$ $dt = dx$

$\Rightarrow$ $I_2 = -5\int \frac{1}{\sqrt{t^2-(\sqrt{3})^2}}dt = -5\ln\left|t+\sqrt{t^2-(\sqrt{3})^2}\right| + C_2 = -5\ln\left|(x+2)+\sqrt{(x+2)^2-3}\right| + C_2$

$= -5\ln\left|(x+2)+\sqrt{x^2+4x+1}\right| + C_2$ ...(4)

Now, substituting the values of I_1 and I_2 from (2) and (4) in (1), we get

$I = \frac{3}{2}\int \frac{2x+4}{\left(\sqrt{x^2+4x+1}\right)} - 5\int \frac{1}{\sqrt{x^2+4x+1}}dx$

$= 3\left(x^2+4x+1\right)^{1/2} - 5\ln\left|(x+2)+\sqrt{x^2+4x+1}\right| + C$; where $C = C_1 + C_2$

ILLUSTRATION 112 Evaluate $\int (2x+5)\sqrt{4x-3-x^2}\,dx$

SOLUTION: $\int (2x+5)\sqrt{4x-3-x^2}\,dx = \int (2x+5)\sqrt{-(x^2-4x+3)}\,dx$

Now, let $(2x + 5) = A\frac{d}{dx}\left(-\left(x^2-4x+3\right)\right) + B = A(-(2x-4)) + B$

$\Rightarrow$ $2x + 5 = -2Ax + 4A + B$ $\Rightarrow$ $-2A = 2; 4A + B = 5$

$\Rightarrow$ $A = -1; 4(-1) + B = 5$ $\Rightarrow$ $B = 9$

Now, $(2x + 5) = (-1)(4 - 2x) + 9$

$\Rightarrow$ $I = \int ((-1)(4-2x)+9)\sqrt{4x-3-x^2}\,dx$

$= \underbrace{\int (-1)(4-2x)\left(\sqrt{4x-3-x^2}\right)dx}_{I_1} + \underbrace{\int 9\sqrt{4x-3-x^2}\,dx}_{I_2}$ ...(1)

Now, $I_1 = \int -(4-2x)\sqrt{4x-3-x^2}\,dx$

Put $4x - 3 - x^2 = t$ $\Rightarrow$ $\frac{dt}{dx} = 4 - 2x$

$\Rightarrow$ $dx = \frac{dt}{4-2x}$

$I_1 = \int -(4-2x)\sqrt{t}\frac{dt}{4-2x}$

$\Rightarrow \ -\int \sqrt{t}\, dt = -\dfrac{(t)^{3/2}}{3/2} + C_1 = \dfrac{-2}{3}(t)^{3/2} + C_1$ ....(2)

$= -\dfrac{2}{3}(4x-3-x^2)^{3/2} + C_1$

Now, $I_2 = 9\int \sqrt{4x-3-x^2}\, dx = 9\int \sqrt{-(x^2-4x+3)}\, dx$

Comparing with $ax^2 + bx + c$, we have $a = 1$; $b = -4$; $c = 3$

$\therefore \ ax^2 + bx + c = \left(x + \dfrac{b}{2a}\right)^2 - \dfrac{D}{4a^2} = \left(x - \dfrac{(4)}{2}\right)^2 - \dfrac{\left((-4)^2 - 4(1)(3)\right)}{4(1)^2}$

$= (x-2)^2 - \dfrac{(16-12)}{4} = (x-2)^2 - 1$

$\therefore \ \int \sqrt{-\left((x-2)^2 - 1\right)}\, dx \qquad \Rightarrow \int \sqrt{1-(x-2)^2}\, dx$

Now, put $x - 2 = t \qquad \Rightarrow \dfrac{dt}{dx} = 1$

$\Rightarrow \ dx = dt$

$\Rightarrow \ I_2 = 9\int \sqrt{1-t^2}\, dt = \dfrac{9}{2}(t)\sqrt{1-t^2} + \left(\dfrac{9}{2}\right)\sin^{-1} t + C_2$

$= \dfrac{9}{2}(x-2)\sqrt{1-(x-2)^2} + \dfrac{9}{2}\sin^{-1}(x-2) + C_2$

$= \dfrac{9}{2}(x-2)\sqrt{4x-3-x^2} + \dfrac{9}{2}\sin^{-1}(x-2) + C_2$ ...(3)

Now putting the values of I_1 and I_2 from (2) and (3) in (1), we get

$I = \dfrac{-2}{3}\left(4x-3-x^2\right)^{3/2} + 9\left(\dfrac{1}{2}(x-2)\sqrt{4x-3-x^2} + \dfrac{9}{2}\sin^{-1}(x-2)\right) + C;$

where $C = C_1 + C_2$.

ILLUSTRATION 113: Evaluate $\int \dfrac{3x-4}{x^2+4x+3}\, dx$

SOLUTION: Let $3x - 4 = A\dfrac{d}{dx}\left(x^2+4x+3\right) + B \qquad \Rightarrow 3x - 4 = A(2x+4) + B$

$\Rightarrow \ 2A = 3 \qquad A = 3/2$ and $4A + B = -4$

$\Rightarrow \ 4(3/2) + B = -4 \qquad \Rightarrow B = -4 - 6 = -10$

$(3x-4) = \dfrac{3}{2}(2x+4) - 10$

$\Rightarrow \ I = \int \dfrac{\frac{3}{2}(2x+4) - 10}{x^2+4x+3}\, dx = \dfrac{3}{2}\underbrace{\int \dfrac{(2x+4)}{x^2+4x+3}(dx)}_{I_1} - 10\underbrace{\int \dfrac{1}{x^2+4x+3}\, dx}_{I_2}$ ...(1)

Now, $I_1 = \dfrac{3}{2}\int \dfrac{2x+4}{x^2+4x+3}\, dx$

Put $t = x^2 + 4x + 3 \qquad \Rightarrow \dfrac{dt}{dx} = 2x + 4$

$\Rightarrow \ dx = \dfrac{dt}{2x+4}$

$\Rightarrow \ I_1 = \dfrac{3}{2}\int \dfrac{2x+4}{t}\dfrac{dt}{(2x+4)} = \dfrac{3}{2}\int \dfrac{1}{t}\, dt = \ln|t| + C_1$

$$\therefore\ I_1 = \left(\frac{3}{2}\ln|x^2+4x+3|\right)+C_1 \qquad \ldots(2)$$

Now, $I_2 = 10\int\frac{1}{x^2+4x+3}dx$

Now, comparing this with $ax^2 + bx + C$, we have $a = 1, b = 4, c = 3$

$$\therefore\ ax^2 + bx + c = a\left[\left(x+\frac{b}{2a}\right)^2 - \frac{D}{4a^2}\right]$$

$D = b^2 - 4ac = (4)^2 - 4(1)(3) = 16 - 12 = 4$

Now, $\left[\left(x+\frac{4}{2}\right)^2 - \frac{4}{4}\right] = (x+2)^2 - 1 \qquad \therefore\ I_2 = 10\int\frac{1}{(x+2)^2-1}dx$

Put $t = x + 2 \Rightarrow \frac{dt}{dx} = 1 \Rightarrow dx = dt$

$$I_2 = 10\int\frac{1}{t^2-1}dt = 10\,\frac{-1}{2(1)}\ln\left|\frac{1+t}{1-t}\right| + C_2 = -5\ln\left|\frac{1+(x+2)}{1-(x+2)}\right| + C_2 = -5\ln\left|\frac{x+3}{1+x}\right| + C_2 \qquad \ldots(3)$$

Substituting the values of I_1 and I_2 from (2) and (3) in (1), we get

$$I = \frac{3}{2}\int\frac{(2x+4)}{x^2+4x+3}dx - 10\int\frac{1}{x^2+4x+3}dx = \frac{3}{2}\ln|x^2+4x+3| - 5\ln\left|\frac{x+3}{1+x}\right| + C_2;\ \text{where } C = C_1 + C_2$$

Type (vii): Integration of rational expression of type $\int\frac{1}{ax^4+bx^2+c}dx$:

$$I = \int\frac{1}{ax^4+bx^2+c}dx$$

Here $ax^4 + bx^2 + c$ is a quadratic in x^2 with discriminant $D = b^2 - 4ac$.

Case I: $D > 0$

For $D > 0$, bi-quadratic $ax^4 + bx^2 + c$ can be factorized as $a(x^2 - \alpha)(x^2 - \beta)$.

$$\therefore\quad I = \frac{1}{a}\int\frac{dx}{(x^2-\alpha)(x^2-\beta)}$$

$$= \frac{1}{a(\alpha-\beta)}\int\left(\frac{1}{x^2-\alpha} - \frac{1}{x^2-\beta}\right)dx,$$

which can be further solved by using the standard integral $\int\frac{1}{x^2-a^2}dx = \frac{1}{2a}\ln\left|\frac{x-a}{x+a}\right| + C$.

Case II: $D < 0$

The bi-quadratic $ax^4 + bx^2 + C$ cannot be further factorized as above. So we proceed as follows:

$$I = \int\frac{dx}{x^2\left(ax^2+\frac{c}{x^2}+b\right)} \qquad \ldots(1)$$

Now depending upon the nature of 'a', three arise two sub cases.

Sub Case (i): $a > 0 \qquad (\because b^2 - 4ac < 0;\ a < 0 \Rightarrow c > 0)$

$$I = \int\frac{dx}{x^2\left[\left(\sqrt{a}x\right)^2 + \left(\frac{\sqrt{c}}{x}\right)^2 + 2\sqrt{a}\sqrt{c} - 2\sqrt{a}\sqrt{c} + b\right]}$$

$$= \int\frac{dx}{x^2\left[\left(\sqrt{a}x \pm \frac{\sqrt{c}}{x}\right)^2 + b \mp 2\sqrt{a}\sqrt{c}\right]} \qquad \ldots(2)$$

Now putting $\sqrt{a}x \pm \frac{\sqrt{c}}{x} = t \qquad \ldots(3)$

$$\Rightarrow\quad \left(\sqrt{a} \mp \frac{\sqrt{c}}{x^2}\right)dx = dt \qquad \ldots(4)$$

Now from (2),

$$I = \frac{1}{2\sqrt{c}}\int\frac{2\sqrt{c}\,dx}{x^2\left[\left(\sqrt{a}x \pm \frac{\sqrt{c}}{x}\right)^2 + b \mp 2\sqrt{a}\sqrt{c}\right]}$$

$$= \frac{1}{2\sqrt{c}}\int\frac{\left(\sqrt{a}x^2+\sqrt{c}\right) - \left(\sqrt{a}x^2-\sqrt{c}\right)dx}{x^2\left[\left(\sqrt{a}x \pm \frac{\sqrt{c}}{x}\right)^2 + b \mp 2\sqrt{a}\sqrt{c}\right]}$$

$$= \frac{1}{2\sqrt{c}}\int \frac{\left(\sqrt{a}+\frac{\sqrt{c}}{x^2}\right)dx}{\left[\left(\sqrt{ax}-\frac{\sqrt{c}}{x}\right)^2+b+2\sqrt{a}\sqrt{c}\right]} - \frac{1}{2\sqrt{c}}$$

$$\int \frac{\left(\sqrt{a}-\frac{\sqrt{c}}{x^2}\right)dx}{\left[\left(\sqrt{ax}+\frac{\sqrt{c}}{x}\right)^2+b-2\sqrt{a}\sqrt{c}\right]}$$

using (3) and (4), we get

$$I = \frac{1}{2\sqrt{c}}\int \frac{dt}{t^2+b+2\sqrt{a}\sqrt{c}} - \frac{1}{2\sqrt{c}}\int \frac{dt}{t^2+b-2\sqrt{a}\sqrt{c}} \quad ....(5)$$

where $t = \sqrt{ax}-\frac{\sqrt{c}}{x}$ in first integral and $t = \sqrt{ax}+\frac{\sqrt{c}}{x}$ in 2nd integral.

Now (5) can be solved by using the standard integral

$$\int \frac{dx}{x^2+a^2} = \frac{1}{a}\tan^{-1}\left(\frac{x}{a}\right)+C$$

or $\int \frac{dx}{x^2-a^2} = \frac{1}{2a}\ln\left|\frac{x-a}{x+a}\right|+C$.

Sub Case (ii): $a < 0$ $\quad (\because b^2-4ac<0;\ a<0 \Rightarrow c<0)$

$$\therefore\ I = \int \frac{dx}{-x^2\left((-a)x^2+\frac{(-c)}{x^2}+b\right)}$$

$$= -\int \frac{dx}{x^2\left[Ax^2+\frac{C}{x^2}+B\right]}$$

where $-a = A > 0$

and $-c = C > 0$ and $b = B$

$\therefore$ from sub case (i) we have

$$I = -\frac{1}{2\sqrt{C}}\int \frac{dt}{t^2+B+2\sqrt{AC}} + \frac{1}{2\sqrt{C}}\int \frac{dt}{t^2+B-2\sqrt{AC}};$$

where $t = \sqrt{Ax}-\frac{\sqrt{C}}{x}$ in 1st integral and $t = \sqrt{Ax}+\frac{\sqrt{C}}{x}$ in 2nd integral; and $A = -a$, $C = -c$, $B = b$.

ILLUSTRATION 114: Find $\int \frac{dx}{9x^4-6x^2-8}$

SOLUTION: $I = \int \frac{dx}{9x^4-6x^2-8}$; Here $a = 9$, $b = -6$, $c = -8$

$\therefore$ Discriminant $= (-6)^2 - 4(9)(-8) = 36 + 288 > 0$

$\therefore$ $9x^4 - 6x^2 - 8$ can be factorized and $9x^4 - 6x^2 - 8 = 9x^4 - 12x^2 + 6x^2 - 8$

$= 3x^2(3x^2-4) + 2(3x^2-4) = (3x^2+2)(3x^2-4)$

$$\therefore\ I = \int \frac{dx}{(3x^2+2)(3x^2-4)} = \frac{1}{6}\int \frac{(3x^2+2)-(3x^2-4)}{(3x^2+2)(3x^2-4)}dx$$

$$= \frac{1}{6}\int \frac{1}{3x^2-4}dx - \frac{1}{6}\int \frac{1}{3x^2+2}dx = \frac{1}{18}\int \frac{1}{x^2-\frac{4}{3}}dx - \frac{1}{18}\int \frac{1}{x^2+\frac{2}{3}}dx$$

$$= \frac{1}{18}\int \frac{dx}{x^2-\left(\frac{2}{\sqrt{3}}\right)^2} - \frac{1}{18}\int \frac{dx}{x^2+\left(\sqrt{\frac{2}{3}}\right)^2}$$

$$= \frac{1}{18}\times\frac{1}{2\left(\frac{2}{\sqrt{3}}\right)}\ln\left|\frac{x-2/\sqrt{3}}{x+2/\sqrt{3}}\right| - \frac{1}{18}.\sqrt{\frac{3}{2}}\tan^{-1}\left(\frac{\sqrt{3}x}{\sqrt{2}}\right)+C$$

$$= \frac{\sqrt{3}}{72}\ln\left|\frac{\sqrt{3}x-2}{\sqrt{3}x+2}\right| - \frac{\sqrt{3}}{\sqrt{2}(18)}\tan^{-1}\left(\frac{\sqrt{3}x}{\sqrt{2}}\right)+C$$

$$= \frac{1}{24\sqrt{3}} \ln\left|\frac{\sqrt{3}x-2}{\sqrt{3}x+2}\right| - \frac{1}{6\sqrt{6}} \tan^{-1}\left(\frac{\sqrt{3}x}{\sqrt{2}}\right) + C.$$

ILLUSTRATION 115: Evaluate $\int \frac{1}{7x^4+x^2+1} dx$

SOLUTION: Comparing $7x^4 + x^2 + 1$ with equation $ax^4 + bx^2 + c$ we have $a = 7$; $b = 1$; $c = 1$.

$D = b^2 - 4ac = 1 - 4(7)(1) = 1 - 28 = -27 < 0$

So, we will proceed as per algorithm of case II as below:

Hence, $I = \int \frac{1}{x^2\left(7x^2+\frac{1}{x^2}+1\right)} dx = \int \frac{1}{x^2} \frac{1}{\left(\left(x\sqrt{7} \pm \frac{\sqrt{1}}{x}\right)^2 + 1 \mp 2\sqrt{7}\right)} dx$ ...(1)

Now Put $\sqrt{7}x \pm \frac{1}{x} = t$

$$\Rightarrow \frac{dt}{dx} = \left(\sqrt{7} \pm \left(-\frac{1}{x^2}\right)\right) = \frac{\sqrt{7}x^2 \mp 1}{x^2} \qquad \Rightarrow dx = \frac{x^2}{\left(\sqrt{7}x^2 \mp 1\right)} dt$$

$$\Rightarrow \frac{1}{2\sqrt{1}} \int \frac{1}{x^2} \frac{2}{\left(\left(x\sqrt{7} \pm \frac{1}{x}\right)^2 + 1 \mp 2\sqrt{7}\right)} dx = \frac{1}{2} \int \frac{1}{x^2} \cdot \frac{\left(\sqrt{7}x^2+1\right) - \left(\sqrt{7}x^2-1\right)}{\left(\left(x\sqrt{7} \pm \frac{1}{x}\right)^2 + 1 \mp 2\sqrt{7}\right)} dx$$

$$= \frac{1}{2}\left(\int \frac{\sqrt{7}+(1/x^2)}{\left(\left(\sqrt{7}x-\frac{1}{x}\right)^2+1+2\sqrt{7}\right)} dx - \int \frac{\sqrt{7}-(1/x^2)}{\left(\left(x\sqrt{7}+\frac{1}{x}\right)+1-2\sqrt{7}\right)} dx\right)$$

Put $\sqrt{7}x - \frac{1}{x} = t$ and $\sqrt{7}x + \frac{1}{x} = t$ in first and second integral, respectively, to get

$$I = \frac{1}{2}\left(\int \frac{1}{t^2+\left(1+2\sqrt{7}\right)} dt + \int \frac{1}{t^2+\left(1-2\sqrt{7}\right)} dt\right)$$

$$= \frac{1}{2}\left(\int \frac{1}{t^2+\left(\sqrt{1+2\sqrt{7}}\right)^2} dt + \int \frac{1}{t^2+\left(2\sqrt{7}-1\right)} dt\right)$$

$$\Rightarrow \frac{1}{2}\left(\frac{1}{\sqrt{1+2\sqrt{7}}} \tan^{-1}\left(\frac{t}{\sqrt{1+2\sqrt{7}}}\right) + \int \frac{1}{t^2-\left(\sqrt{2\sqrt{7}-1}\right)^2} dt\right) + C$$

$$\Rightarrow \frac{1}{2}\left(\frac{1}{\sqrt{1+2\sqrt{7}}} \tan^{-1}\left(\frac{t}{\sqrt{1+2\sqrt{7}}}\right) + \frac{1}{2\sqrt{2\sqrt{7}-1}} \ln\left|\frac{t-\sqrt{2\sqrt{7}-1}}{t+\sqrt{2\sqrt{7}-1}}\right|\right) + C$$

$$= \frac{1}{2}\left[\frac{1}{\sqrt{1+2\sqrt{7}}} \tan^{-1}\left(\frac{\sqrt{7}x^2-1}{x\sqrt{1+2\sqrt{7}}}\right) + \frac{1}{2\sqrt{2\sqrt{7}-1}} \ln\left|\frac{\sqrt{7}x^2+1-\sqrt{2\sqrt{7}-1}}{\sqrt{7}x^2+1+\sqrt{2\sqrt{7}-1}}\right|\right] + C$$

Type (viii): Integration of the of type $\int \frac{ax^2+bx+c}{px^2+qx+r}dx$, $\int \frac{ax^2+bx+c}{\sqrt{px^2+qx+r}}dx$, $\int (ax^2+bx+c)\sqrt{px^2+qx+r}\,dx$

(a) For integrals of the form $\int \frac{ax^2+bx+c}{px^2+qx+r}dx$ and $\int \frac{ax^2+bx+c}{\sqrt{px^2+qx+r}}dx$

Put $(ax^2 + bx + c) = A(px^2 + qx + r) + B\frac{d}{dx}(px^2 + qx + r) + C$

i.e., $(ax^2 + bx + c) = A(px^2 + qx + r) + B(2px + q) + C$

By comparing the coefficients of like terms on both sides we obtain the values of constant A, B and C.

$$\therefore \int \frac{ax^2+bx+c}{px^2+qx+r}dx = A\int \frac{px^2+qx+r}{px^2+qx+r}dx + B\int \frac{2px+q}{px^2+qx+r}dx + C\int \frac{1}{px^2+qx+r}dx$$

$$= Ax + B\ln(px^2 + qx + r) + C\int \frac{1}{px^2+qx+r}dx$$

which can be further solved by using the method of solving the integral of the type $\int \frac{1}{ax^2+bx+c}dx$ as discussed earlier.

Similarly, $\int \frac{ax^2+bx+c}{\sqrt{px^2+qx+r}}dx = A\int \frac{(px^2+qx+r)}{\sqrt{px^2+qx+r}}dx + B\int \frac{2px+q}{\sqrt{px^2+qx+r}}dx + C\int \frac{dx}{\sqrt{px^2+qx+r}}$

$$= A\int \sqrt{px^2+qx+r}\,dx + B\int (2px+q)(px^2+qx+r)^{-1/2}dx + C\int \frac{dx}{\sqrt{px^2+qx+r}}$$

$$= A\int \sqrt{px^2+qx+r}\,dx + B\int (2px+q)(px^2+qx+r)^{-1/2}dx + C\int \frac{1}{\sqrt{px^2+qx+r}}dx$$

$$= A\int \sqrt{px^2+qx+r}\,dx + 2B\int \sqrt{px^2+qx+r} + C\int \frac{1}{\sqrt{px^2+qx+r}}dx$$

which can be further solved by using the method of solving integrals of the form

$\int \sqrt{ax^2+bx+c}\,dx$ and $\int \frac{1}{\sqrt{ax^2+bx+c}}dx$ as discussed earlier.

ILLUSTRATION 116: Find $\int \frac{5x^2+2x+4}{3x^2+2x+8}dx$

SOLUTION: Let $I = \int \frac{5x^2+2x+4}{3x^2+2x+8}dx$ ...(1)

Consider $5x^2 + 2x + 4 = A(3x^2 + 2x + 8) + B\frac{d}{dx}(3x^2 + 2x + 8) + C$

$\Rightarrow 5x^2 + 2x + 4 = A(3x^2 + 2x + 8) + B(6x + 2) + C$ ...(2)

$\Rightarrow 3A = 5;\ 2A + 6B = 2;\ 8A + 2B + C = 4$

$\Rightarrow A = \frac{5}{3};\ B = \frac{1-A}{3} = \frac{1-5/3}{3} = \frac{-2}{9};$

$C = 4 - 8A - 2B = \frac{-80}{9}.$

Using the values of A, B and C in (2) and from (1) we have

$$I = \int \frac{\frac{5}{3}(3x^2+2x+8) - \frac{2}{9}(6x+2) - \frac{80}{9}}{3x^2+2x+8}dx$$

$$= \frac{5}{3}\int 1\, dx - \frac{2}{9}\int \frac{6x+2}{3x^2+2x+8}dx - \frac{80}{9}\int \frac{1}{3x^2+2x+8}dx$$

$$= \frac{5}{3}x - \frac{2}{9}\ln|3x^2+2x+8| - \frac{80}{27}\int \frac{1}{x^2+\frac{2}{3}x+\frac{8}{9}}dx$$

$$= \frac{5}{3}x - \frac{2}{9}\ln|3x^2+2x+8| - \frac{80}{27}\int \frac{dx}{x^2+\frac{2}{3}x+\frac{1}{9}+\frac{23}{9}}$$

$$= \frac{5}{3}x - \frac{2}{9}\ln|3x^2+2x+8| - \frac{80}{27}\int \frac{dx}{\left(x+\frac{1}{3}\right)^2+\left(\frac{\sqrt{23}}{3}\right)^2}$$

$$= \frac{5}{3}x - \frac{2}{9}\ln|3x^2+2x+8| - \frac{80}{9\sqrt{23}}\tan^{-1}\left(\frac{3x+1}{\sqrt{23}}\right)+C$$

ILLUSTRATION 117: Find $\int \frac{2x^2+3x-5}{\sqrt{4x^2-7x+2}}dx$

SOLUTION: Let $I = \int \frac{2x^2+3x-5}{\sqrt{4x^2-7x+2}}dx$ ...(1)

Consider $2x^2 + 3x - 5 = A(4x^2 - 7x + 2) + B\frac{d}{dx}(4x^2 - 7x + 2) + C$

$\Rightarrow$ $2x^2 + 3x - 5 = A(4x^2 - 7x + 2) + B(8x - 7) + C$ ...(2)

$\Rightarrow$ $4A = 2; -7A + 8B = 3; 2A - 7B + C = -5$

$\Rightarrow$ $A = \frac{1}{2};\ B = \frac{13}{16},\ C = \frac{-5}{16}$

Using these values of A, B and C in (2), and hence, from (1) we have

$$I = \int \frac{\frac{1}{2}(4x^2-7x+2)}{\sqrt{4x^2-7x+2}}dx + \frac{13}{16}\int \frac{8x-7}{\sqrt{4x^2-7x+2}}dx - \frac{5}{16}\int \frac{1}{\sqrt{4x^2-7x+2}}dx$$

$$= \frac{1}{2}\int \sqrt{4x^2-7x+2}\, dx + \frac{13}{16}\int (8x-7)\left(4x^2-7x+2\right)^{-1/2} dx - \frac{5}{16}\int \frac{dx}{2\sqrt{x^2-\frac{7}{4}x+\frac{1}{2}}}$$

$$= \int \sqrt{x^2-\frac{7}{4}x+\frac{1}{2}}\, dx + \frac{13}{16}\frac{(4x^2-7x+2)^{1/2}}{1/2} - \frac{5}{32}\int \frac{dx}{\sqrt{x^2-\frac{7}{4}x+\frac{49}{64}-\frac{17}{64}}}$$

$$= \int \sqrt{\left(x-\frac{7}{8}\right)^2-\left(\frac{\sqrt{17}}{8}\right)^2}\, dx + \frac{13}{8}\sqrt{4x^2-7x+2} - \frac{5}{32}\int \frac{dx}{\sqrt{\left(x-\frac{7}{8}\right)^2-\left(\frac{\sqrt{17}}{8}\right)^2}}$$

$$= \frac{\left(x-\frac{7}{8}\right)\sqrt{\left(x-\frac{7}{8}\right)^2-\left(\frac{\sqrt{17}}{8}\right)^2}}{2} - \frac{17}{128}\ln\left|\left(x-\frac{7}{8}\right)+\sqrt{\left(x-\frac{7}{8}\right)^2-\left(\frac{\sqrt{17}}{8}\right)^2}\right|$$

$$+\frac{13}{8}\sqrt{4x^2-7x+2}-\frac{5}{32}\ln\left|\left(x-\frac{7}{8}\right)+\sqrt{\left(x-\frac{7}{8}\right)^2-\left(\frac{\sqrt{17}}{8}\right)^2}\right|+C$$

$$=\frac{(8x-7).\frac{1}{2}\sqrt{4x^2-7x+2}}{2}-\frac{17}{128}\ln\left|\frac{8x-7}{8}+\frac{1}{2}\sqrt{4x^2-7x+2}\right|$$

$$+\frac{13}{8}\sqrt{4x^2-7x+2}-\frac{5}{32}\ln\left|\frac{(8x-7)}{8}+\frac{1}{2}\sqrt{4x^2-7x+2}\right|+C$$

$$=\frac{(8x-7).\sqrt{4x^2-7x+2}}{4}-\frac{17}{128}\ln\left|\frac{8x-7+4\sqrt{4x^2-7x+2}}{8}\right|$$

$$+\frac{13}{8}\sqrt{4x^2-7x+2}-\frac{5}{32}\ln\left|\frac{(8x-7)+4\sqrt{4x^2-7x+2}}{8}\right|+C$$

$$=\frac{1}{4}(8x-7)\sqrt{4x^2-7x+2}+\frac{13}{8}\sqrt{4x^2-7x+2}-\frac{37}{128}\ln\left|(8x-7)+4\sqrt{4x^2-7x+2}\right|+C$$

$$=\frac{1}{8}(16x-1)\sqrt{4x^2-7x+2}-\frac{13}{128}\ln\left|(8x-7)+4\sqrt{4x^2-7x+2}\right|+C.$$

Type (ix): **Integration of the type**

$$\int\frac{f(x)}{\sqrt{ax^4+bx^3+cx^2\pm bx+a}}dx$$

where $f(x)$ is a rational function of x and is expressible in the form $\left(x-\frac{1}{x}\right)g\left(x+\frac{1}{x}\right)$ or $\left(x+\frac{1}{x}\right)g\left(x-\frac{1}{x}\right)$.

Algorithm: Given integral is

$$I=\int\frac{f(x)}{\sqrt{ax^2+bx^3+cx^2\pm bx+a}}dx$$

$$=\int\frac{f(x)\,dx}{x\sqrt{a\left(x^2+\frac{1}{x^2}\right)+b\left(x\pm\frac{1}{x}\right)+c}}$$

These a arise two cases.

Case (i): If $I=\int\frac{\left(x-\frac{1}{x}\right)g\left(x+\frac{1}{x}\right)dx}{x\sqrt{a\left(x^2+\frac{1}{x^2}\right)+b\left(x+\frac{1}{x}\right)+c}}$

$$=\int\frac{\left(1-\frac{1}{x^2}\right)g\left(x+\frac{1}{x}\right)dx}{\sqrt{a\left(x^2+\frac{1}{x^2}\right)+b\left(x+\frac{1}{x}\right)+c}}$$

Putting $x+\frac{1}{x}=t$ and $\left(1-\frac{1}{x^2}\right)dx=dt$, we have

$$I=\int\frac{g(t)\,dt}{\sqrt{a\left(t^2-2\right)+bt+c}}=\int\frac{g(t)\,dt}{\sqrt{at^2+bt+(c-2a)}}$$

which can be solved further by one of the methods discussed earlier.

Case (ii): If $I=\int\frac{\left(x+\frac{1}{x}\right)g\left(x-\frac{1}{x}\right)dx}{x\sqrt{a\left(x^2+\frac{1}{x^2}\right)+b\left(x-\frac{1}{x}\right)+c}}$

Putting $\left(x-\frac{1}{x}\right)=t$ and

$\left(1+\frac{1}{x^2}\right)dx=dt$, we have

$$I=\int\frac{g(t)\,dt}{\sqrt{a\left(t^2+2\right)+bt+c}}=\int\frac{g(t)\,dt}{\sqrt{at^2+bt+(2a+c)}}$$

which can be solved further by one of the methods discussed earlier.

ILLUSTRATION 118: Find $\int \frac{\left(x^3+3x+\frac{3}{x}+\frac{1}{x^3}\right)dx}{\sqrt{2x^4+3x^3-8x^2-3x+2}}$

SOLUTION: Let $I = \int \frac{\left\{\left(x^3+\frac{1}{x^3}\right)+3\left(x+\frac{1}{x}\right)\right\}dx}{\sqrt{2(x^4+1)+3(x^3-x)-8x^2}} = \int \frac{\left(x+\frac{1}{x}\right)\left(x^2+\frac{1}{x^2}-1\right)+3\left(x+\frac{1}{x}\right)dx}{x\sqrt{2\left(x^2+\frac{1}{x^2}\right)+3\left(x-\frac{1}{x}\right)-8}}$

$$= \int \frac{\left(x+\frac{1}{x}\right)\left[x^2+\frac{1}{x^2}+2\right]dx}{x\sqrt{2\left(x^2+\frac{1}{x^2}\right)+3\left(x-\frac{1}{x}\right)-8}} = \int \frac{\left(1+\frac{1}{x^2}\right)\left[\left(x-\frac{1}{x}\right)^2+4\right]dx}{\sqrt{2\left(x^2+\frac{1}{x^2}\right)+3\left(x-\frac{1}{x}\right)-8}}$$

Now put $x-\frac{1}{x}=t$ and $\left(1+\frac{1}{x^2}\right)dx = dt$ $\quad \therefore\ I = \int \frac{(t^2+4)\,dt}{\sqrt{2(t^2+2)+3t-8}} = \int \frac{(t^2+4)\,dt}{\sqrt{2t^2+3t-4}}$

Now put $(t^2+4) = A(2t^2+3t-4) + B\frac{d}{dx}(2t^2+3t-4) + C$

$\Rightarrow\ 2A = 1;\ 3A+4B = 0;\ -4A+3B+C = 4$

$\Rightarrow\ A = \frac{1}{2};\ B = -\frac{3}{8};\ C = \frac{57}{8}$

$$\therefore\ I = \int \frac{\frac{1}{2}(2t^2+3t-4)-\frac{3}{8}(4t+3)+\frac{57}{8}}{\sqrt{2}\sqrt{t^2+\frac{3}{2}t-2}}\,dt$$

$$= \frac{\sqrt{2}}{2}\int\sqrt{t^2+\frac{3}{2}t-2}\;dt - \frac{3}{8}\int\frac{4t+3}{\sqrt{2t^2+3t-4}}\,dt + \frac{57}{8\sqrt{2}}\int\frac{1}{\sqrt{t^2+\frac{3}{2}t-2}}\,dt$$

$$= \frac{1}{\sqrt{2}}\int\sqrt{\left(t+\frac{3}{4}\right)^2-\left(\frac{\sqrt{41}}{4}\right)^2}\,dt - \frac{3}{8}\frac{\sqrt{2t^2+3t-4}}{1/2} + \frac{57}{8\sqrt{2}}\int\frac{dt}{\sqrt{\left(t+\frac{3}{4}\right)^2-\left(\frac{\sqrt{41}}{4}\right)^2}}$$

$$= \frac{1}{\sqrt{2}}\int\sqrt{\left(t+\frac{3}{4}\right)^2-\left(\frac{\sqrt{41}}{4}\right)^2}\,dt - \frac{3}{4}\sqrt{2t^2+3t-4} + \frac{57}{8\sqrt{2}}\int\frac{dt}{\sqrt{\left(t+\frac{3}{4}\right)^2-\left(\frac{\sqrt{41}}{4}\right)^2}}$$

$$= \frac{1}{\sqrt{2}}\frac{z\sqrt{z^2-41/16}}{2} - \frac{41}{32}\ln\left|z+\sqrt{z^2-41/16}\right| -$$
$$\frac{3}{4}\sqrt{2t^2+3t-4} + \frac{57}{8\sqrt{2}}\ln\left|z+\sqrt{z^2-41/16}\right| + C;$$

where $z = t+\frac{3}{4}$.

ILLUSTRATION 119: Find $\int \frac{(x^2+1)}{x\sqrt{x^4+x^2+1}}dx$

SOLUTION: Let $I = \int \frac{\left(x+\frac{1}{x}\right)}{x\sqrt{x^2+\frac{1}{x^2}+1}}dx = \int \frac{\left(1+\frac{1}{x^2}\right)}{\sqrt{\left(x-\frac{1}{x}\right)^2+3}}dx$

Putting $x - \frac{1}{x} = t$, we have $\left(1+\frac{1}{x^2}\right)dx = dt$

$\Rightarrow \; I = \int \frac{dt}{\sqrt{t^2+3}} = \ln\left|t+\sqrt{t^2+3}\right|+C = \ln\left|\left(x-\frac{1}{x}\right)+\sqrt{\left(x-\frac{1}{x}\right)^2+3}\right|+C$

$= \ln\left|\left(\frac{x^2-1}{x}\right)+\frac{\sqrt{x^4+x^2+1}}{x}\right|+C$

ILLUSTRATION 120: Find $\int \frac{(x^2-1)}{x\sqrt{x^4+3x^2+1}}dx$

SOLUTION: Let $I = \int \frac{\left(x-\frac{1}{x}\right)dx}{x\sqrt{x^2+\frac{1}{x^2}+3}} = \int \frac{\left(1-\frac{1}{x^2}\right)dx}{\sqrt{\left(x+\frac{1}{x}\right)^2+1}}$

Putting $x + \frac{1}{x} = t$, and $\left(1-\frac{1}{x^2}\right)dx = dt$

$\therefore \; I = \int \frac{dt}{\sqrt{t^2+1}} = \ln\left|t+\sqrt{t^2+1}\right|+C$

$= \ln\left|\left(x+\frac{1}{x}\right)+\sqrt{\left(x+\frac{1}{x}\right)^2+1}\right|+C = \ln\left|\left(\frac{x^2+1}{x}\right)+\sqrt{\frac{x^4+3x^2+1}{x}}\right|+C$

Type (x): **Integration of the type** $\int \frac{P_m(x)}{\sqrt{px^2+qx+r}}dx$

where $P_m(x)$ is a polynomial of degree (m).

Algorithm: Consider

$$\int \frac{P_m(x)\,dx}{\sqrt{px^2+qx+r}} = P_{m-1}(x)\sqrt{px^2+qx+r}+K\int \frac{dx}{\sqrt{px^2+qx+r}} \quad \text{....(1)}$$

where $P_{m-1}(x)$ is a polynomial of degree $(m-1)$.

Differentiating both sides of (1) w.r.t. x, we get

$$\frac{P_m(x)}{\sqrt{px^2+qx+r}} = \frac{P_{m-1}(x).(2px+q)}{2\sqrt{px^2+qx+r}} + \left(\sqrt{px^2+qx+r}\right)P'_{m-1}(x)+\frac{K}{\sqrt{px^2+qx+r}}$$

$\Rightarrow \; 2P_m(x) = P_{m-1}(x)(2px+q) + 2(px^2+qx+r)P'_{m-1}(x) + 2K \quad \text{...(2)}$

Comparing the coefficients of like terms on both sides of (2), we get the coefficients of polynomial $P_{m-1}(x)$ and K, and further the integral can be solved.

ILLUSTRATION 121: Find $\int \frac{9x^3 - 3x^2 + 2}{\sqrt{3x^2 - 2x + 1}} dx$

SOLUTION: Consider $I = \int \frac{9x^3 - 3x^2 + 2}{\sqrt{3x^2 - 2x + 1}} dx$

$$= (Ax^2 + Bx + C)\sqrt{3x^2 - 2x + 1} + k\int \frac{1}{\sqrt{3x^2 - 2x + 1}} dx \quad \ldots(1)$$

Differentiating both sides w.r.t. x, we get

$$= \int \frac{9x^3 - 3x^2 + 2}{\sqrt{3x^2 - 2x + 1}} = (2Ax + B)\sqrt{3x^2 - 2x + 1} + (Ax^2 + Bx + C).\frac{(6x-2)}{2\sqrt{3x^2 - 2x + 1}} + \frac{K}{\sqrt{3x^2 - 2x + 1}}$$

$\Rightarrow$ $(9x^3 - 3x^2 + 2) = (2Ax + B)(3x^2 - 2x + 1) + (Ax^2 + Bx + C)(3x - 1) + K$

$\Rightarrow$ $(9x^3 - 3x^2 + 2) = x^3(6A + 3A) + x^2(3B - 4A - A + 3B) +$
$x(2A - 2B - B + 3C) + (B - C + k)$

$\Rightarrow$ $9A = 9;\ 6B - 5A = -3;\ 2A - 3B + 3C = 0;\ B - C + K = 2.$

$\Rightarrow$ $A = 1;\ B = \frac{1}{3};\ C = -\frac{1}{3};\ K = \frac{4}{3}$

$\therefore$ from (1)

$$\int \frac{9x^3 - 3x^2 + 2}{\sqrt{3x^2 - 2x + 1}} dx = \left(x^2 + \frac{1}{3}x - \frac{1}{3}\right)\sqrt{3x^2 - 2x + 1} + \frac{4}{3}\int \frac{1}{\sqrt{3x^2 - 2x + 1}} dx$$

$$= \frac{1}{3}(3x^2 + x - 1)\sqrt{3x^2 - 2x + 1} + \frac{4}{3\sqrt{3}}\int \frac{1}{\sqrt{x^2 - \frac{2}{3}x + \frac{1}{3}}} dx$$

$$= \frac{1}{3}(3x^2 + x - 1)\sqrt{3x^2 - 2x + 1} + \frac{4}{3\sqrt{3}}\int \frac{1}{\sqrt{\left(x - \frac{1}{3}\right)^2 + \frac{2}{9}}} dx$$

$$= \frac{1}{3}(3x^2 + x - 1)\sqrt{3x^2 - 2x + 1} + \frac{4}{3\sqrt{3}} \ln\left|\left(x - \frac{1}{3}\right) + \frac{\sqrt{3x^2 - 2x + 1}}{\sqrt{3}}\right| + C$$

TEXTUAL EXERCISE–5: (SUBJECTIVE)

1. Evaluate the following integrals:

(a) $\int \frac{dx}{x^2 + 2x + 3}$ (b) $\int \frac{dz}{z^2 - z + 1}$

(c) $\int \frac{2x - 3}{x^2 + x + 1} dx$ (d) $\int \sqrt{x^2 + 5x + 1}\, dx$

(e) $\int \frac{x^2 - x + 1}{2x^2 + x + 2} dx$

2. Integrate the following:

(a) $\int \frac{3x + 5}{x^2 + 2x - 3} dx$ (b) $\int \frac{2x - 1}{\sqrt{3 + 2x - x^2}} dx$

(c) $\int \frac{x\, dx}{\sqrt{x^2 + x + 1}}$ (d) $\int (x - 1)\sqrt{x^2 + x + 1}\, dx$

3. Find $\int \frac{2x^2 + 3x + 4}{x^2 + 6x + 10} dx$

4. Find $\int \frac{x^2 - 3x + 1}{\sqrt{1 - x^2}} dx$

5. Find $\int \frac{x^2 + 4x + 7}{\sqrt{x^2 + x + 1}} dx$

6. Find $\int \frac{x^2-3x+1}{\sqrt{-2x^2+4x-1}}dx$

7. Find $\int \frac{x^4+x^3+2x+1}{x^2+x+1}dx$

8. Find $\int \frac{x^3+3}{\sqrt{x^2+1}}dx$

9. Find $\int \frac{x^4-1}{x^2\sqrt{x^4+x^2+1}}dx$

10. Find

(i) $\int (3x+5)\sqrt{x^2+2x-3}\,dx$

(ii) $\int (x+2)\sqrt{2x^2+2x+1}\,dx$

11. Find $\int \frac{\ln x\,dx}{x\sqrt{-\ln^2 x-4\ln x+1}}$

12. Find $\int \frac{dx}{x^4+8x^2+9}$

13. Find $\int \frac{x}{x^4+x^2+1}dx$

14. Find $\int \frac{x^4+1}{x^6+1}dx$

15. Find $\int \frac{dx}{x\sqrt{x^4+3x^2+1}}$

16. Find $\int \frac{x^3-x-1}{\sqrt{x^2+2x+2}}dx$

Answer Keys

1. (a) $\frac{1}{\sqrt{2}}\tan^{-1}\left(\frac{x+1}{\sqrt{2}}\right)+C$ (b) $\frac{2}{\sqrt{3}}\tan^{-1}\left(\frac{2z-1}{\sqrt{3}}\right)+C$ (c) $\log(x^2+x+1)-\frac{8}{\sqrt{3}}\tan^{-1}\left(\frac{2x+1}{\sqrt{3}}\right)+C$

(d) $\frac{2x+5}{4}\sqrt{x^2+5x+1}-\frac{21}{8}\log|x+5/2+\sqrt{x^2+5x+1}|+C$

(e) $\frac{x}{2}-\frac{3}{8}\log|2x^2+x+2|+\frac{3}{4\sqrt{15}}\tan^{-1}\left(\frac{4x+1}{\sqrt{15}}\right)+C$

2. (a) $\frac{3}{2}\log(x^2+2x-3)+\frac{1}{2}\log\left|\frac{x-1}{x+3}\right|+C$ (b) $-2\sqrt{3+2x-x^2}+3\sin^{-1}\left(\frac{x-1}{2}\right)+C$

(c) $\sqrt{x^2+x+1}-\frac{1}{2}\log\left(x+1/2+\sqrt{x^2+x+1}\right)+C$

3. $2x-\frac{9}{2}\ln|x^2+6x+10|+11\tan^{-1}(x+3)+C$

4. $\frac{6-x}{2}\sqrt{1-x^2}+\frac{3}{2}\sin^{-1}x+C$

5. $\left(\frac{2x+13}{4}\right)\sqrt{x^2+x+1}+\frac{39}{8}\ln\left|x+\frac{1}{2}+\sqrt{x^2+x+1}\right|+C$

6. $-\frac{1}{4}(x-3)\sqrt{-2x^2+4x-1}-\frac{3}{4\sqrt{2}}\sin^{-1}\sqrt{2}(x-1)+C$

7. $\frac{x}{3}-x+\frac{3}{2}\ln(x^2+x+1)+\frac{1}{\sqrt{3}}\tan^{1}\left(\frac{2x\ \ 1}{\sqrt{3}}\right)+C$

8. $\frac{1}{3}(x^2+1)^{3/2}-\sqrt{x^2+1}+3\ln\left|x+\sqrt{x^2+1}\right|+C$

9. $\frac{\sqrt{x^4+x^2+1}}{x}+C$

10. (i) $(x^2+2x-3)^{3/2}+(x+1)(x^2+3x-2)-4+\ln\left|x+1+\sqrt{x^2+2x-3}\right|+C$

(ii) $\frac{1}{6}(2x^2+2x+1)^{3/2}+\frac{3}{8}(2x+1)\sqrt{2x^2+2x+1}+\frac{3}{8\sqrt{2}}\ln\left\{(2x+1)+\sqrt{2(2x^2+2x+1)}\right\}+C$

11. $-\sqrt{-\ln^2 x-4\ln x+1}-2\sin^{-1}\left(\dfrac{2+\ln x}{\sqrt{5}}\right)+C$

12. $\dfrac{1}{6\sqrt{14}}\tan^{-1}\left(\dfrac{x^2-3}{\sqrt{14}\,x}\right)-\dfrac{1}{6\sqrt{2}}\tan^{-1}\left(\dfrac{x^2+3}{\sqrt{2}\,x}\right)+C$

13. $\dfrac{1}{\sqrt{3}}\tan^{-1}\left(\dfrac{2x^2+1}{\sqrt{3}}\right)+C$

14. $\tan^{-1}\left(\dfrac{x^2-1}{x}\right)-\dfrac{2}{3}\tan^{-1}x^3+C$

15. $\dfrac{1}{2}\ln\left(\dfrac{x^2-1}{x}+\dfrac{\sqrt{x^4+3x^2+1}}{x}\right)-\dfrac{1}{2}\ln\left(\dfrac{x^2+1}{x}+\dfrac{\sqrt{x^4+3x^2+1}}{x}\right)+C$

16. $\left(\dfrac{1}{3}x^2-\dfrac{5}{6}x+\dfrac{1}{6}\right)\sqrt{x^2+2x+2}+\dfrac{1}{2}\ln\left|(x+1)+\sqrt{x^2+2x+2}\right|+C$

TEXTUAL EXERCISE–5: (OBJECTIVE)

1. $\int\dfrac{1}{4x^2+4x+5}dx$ is

(a) $\dfrac{1}{4}\tan^{-1}\left(x+\dfrac{1}{2}\right)+C$

(b) $\dfrac{1}{4}\tan^{-1}(2x+1)+C$

(c) $\tan^{-1}\left(x+\dfrac{1}{2}\right)+C$

(d) None of these

2. $\int\dfrac{1}{x^2+4x-5}dx$ is

(a) In|x + 5| + *In* |x – 1| + C

(b) In|x + 5| – 3*In* |x – 1| + C

(c) $\dfrac{1}{6}In\dfrac{x-1}{x+5}+C$

(d) None of these

3. $\int\dfrac{3x+2}{4x^2+4x+5}dx$ is l ln $(x^2 + 4x + 5) + m\tan^{-1}$ $(x + 1/2) + C$. Then l and m are

(a) $\dfrac{3}{2},\dfrac{1}{2}$ (b) $\dfrac{1}{2},\dfrac{3}{2}$

(c) $\dfrac{3}{8},\dfrac{1}{8}$ (d) None of these

4. If $\int\dfrac{(x+3)\,dx}{\sqrt{4x^2+4x-3}}=A\sqrt{4x^2+4x-3}+B$ $\ln\left|2x+1+\sqrt{4x^2+4x-3}\right|+C,$

then B/A equals

(a) 2 (b) 3

(c) 4 (d) 5

5. If $\int\dfrac{5x+4}{\sqrt{x^2+2x+5}}dx=A\sqrt{x^2+2x+5}-B$ $\ln\left(x+1+\sqrt{x^2+2x+5}\right),$

then $A + B$ equals

(a) 4 (b) 5

(c) 6 (d) None of these

6. $\int\left(\dfrac{x^2+1}{x^4-x^2+1}\right)dx$ is

(a) $x-\tan^{-1}\left(x+\dfrac{1}{x}\right)-C$

(b) $x-\tan^{-1}\left(x-\dfrac{1}{x}\right)+C$

(c) $\tan^{-1}\left(x-\dfrac{1}{x}\right)+C$

(d) None of these

7. If $\int\dfrac{(x^2-1)}{x\sqrt{x^4+3x^2+1}}$ is $m\ln$ $\left[\dfrac{\left\{(x^2+1)+\sqrt{(x^4+3x^2+1)}\right\}}{x}\right]+C$. Then m is

(a) 1 (b) 2

(c) 1/3 (d) None of these

8. If $\int\sqrt{4x^2-4x+3}\,dx=\left(\dfrac{x}{2}-\dfrac{1}{4}\right)\sqrt{4x^2-4x+3}+\dfrac{1}{2}$ $g(x)+C$, then $g(x)$ equals

(a) $\ln\left((2x-1)-\sqrt{4x^2-4x+3}\right)+C$

(b) $\ln\left((2x-1)+\sqrt{4x^2-4x+3}\right)+C$

(c) $\ln\left(\dfrac{2x-1}{\sqrt{4x^2-4x+3}}\right)+C$

(d) None of these

9. If $\int \dfrac{x^3-6x^2+11x-6}{\sqrt{x^2+4x+3}}\,dx = \dfrac{1}{3}(x^2-14x+111)$ $\sqrt{x^2+4x+3}-66g(x)+C,$ then $g(x)$ equals

(a) $\ln\left|(x+3)+\sqrt{x^2+4x+3}\right|+C$

(b) $\ln\left|(x-2)+\sqrt{x^2+4x+3}\right|+C$

(c) $\ln\left|(x+2)+\sqrt{x^2+4x+3}\right|+C$

(d) $\ln\left|\dfrac{(x+2)}{\sqrt{x^2+4x+3}}\right|+C$

10. If $\int \dfrac{3x^3+5x^2-7x+9}{\sqrt{2x^2+5x+7}}\,dx = \dfrac{1}{2A}(Ax^2-20x-373)$ $\sqrt{2x^2+5x+7}+\dfrac{3297}{4A\sqrt{B}}.\ln\left|(4x+5)+2\sqrt{4x^2+10x+14}\right|$ $+C$, then $(A-B)$ equals

(a) 30 (b) 32

(c) 34 (d) None of these

Answer Keys

1. (a)	**2.** (c)	**3.** (c)	**4.** (d)	**5.** (c)	**6.** (c)	**7.** (a)	**8.** (b)	**9.** (c)	**10.** (a)

INTEGRATION OF RATIONAL FUNCTIONS BY PARTIAL FRACTION

Polynomial of degree n: An expression of the type $P(x) = a_0x^n + a_1x^{n-1} + ... + a_{n-1}x + a_n$ where $a_0, a_1, a_2, ..., a_n$ are real numbers, $a_0 \neq 0$ and n is non-negative integer is called a **polynomial of degree *n*.**

Rational Function: A function of the form $P(x)/Q(x)$; where $P(x)$ and $Q(x)$ are polynomials ($Q(x) \neq 0$) is called a **rational function.**

Types of Rational Functions: Rational functions are of two types as described below.

(i) **Proper Fraction:** A rational function is called a proper fraction, if the degree of $P(x)$ (numerator) is less than that of $Q(x)$ (denominator).

E.g., $\dfrac{x^2+x+2}{x^3+4x^2-7x+1}$ is a proper fraction.

(ii) **Improper Fraction:** A rational function is called an improper fraction, if the degree of $P(x)$ (numerator) is greater than or equal to that of $Q(x)$ (denominator).

E.g., (1) $\dfrac{x^4-9x^2-10x+7}{x^2+4x+5}$ is an improper fraction.

(2) $\dfrac{x^3-1}{x^3+5x+4}$ is also an improper fraction.

REMARK

Any rational improper fraction can be expressed as sum of a polynomial and a proper fraction.

Let $\dfrac{f(x)}{g(x)}$ *be improper fraction, then by division algorithm* $f(x) = g(x)\,.\,q(x) + r(x)$ *such that degree of* $r(x) <$ *degree of* $g(x)$

$$\Rightarrow \underbrace{\frac{f(x)}{g(x)}}_{\text{improper fraction}} = \underbrace{q(x)}_{\text{polynomial}} + \underbrace{\frac{r(x)}{g(x)}}_{\text{proper fraction}}$$

E.g., (1) $\dfrac{x^4-9x^2-10x+7}{x^2+4x+5} = \left\{(x^2-4x+2)+\dfrac{2x-3}{x^2+4x+5}\right\}$

E.g., (2) $\dfrac{x^3-1}{x^3+5x+4} = \left\{1-\dfrac{5(x+1)}{x^3+5x+4}\right\}$

Partial Fraction: If a fraction $\dfrac{f(x)}{g(x)}$ is expressed as sum of simple proper fractions with denominator that cannot be factorized further, then these simple proper fractions are called partial fractions of $\dfrac{f(x)}{g(x)}$.

i.e., $$\frac{f(x)}{g(x)}=\underbrace{\frac{f_1(x)}{g_1(x)}+\frac{f_2(x)}{g_2(x)}+\frac{f_3(x)}{g_3(x)}+\ldots}_{\text{partial fractions}}$$

E.g., (1) $$\frac{x+7}{(2x-3)(3x+4)}=\frac{1}{2x-3}-\frac{1}{3x+4}$$

E.g.,(2) $$\frac{x+1}{(x-1)(x^2-4)}=\frac{-2}{3(x-1)}+\frac{3}{4(x-2)}-\frac{1}{12(x+2)}$$

■ INTEGRATION BY PARTIAL FRACTION

Let us now study the technique of integration of rational functions by using partial fractions. To form a partial fraction of rational function $\dfrac{P(x)}{Q(x)}$ (integrand) we use the following steps:

Step I: If f is improper, that is deg(P) ≥ deg(Q), then we must take the preliminary step of dividing Q into P (by division) until a remainder $R(x)$ is obtained such that deg. $R(x)$ < deg. $Q(x)$.

i.e., $\dfrac{P(x)}{Q(x)}=S(x)+\dfrac{R(x)}{Q(x)}$; where $S(x)$ and $R(x)$ are also polynomials.

E.g., $$\frac{x^4-2x^3+5x^2+2x+7}{x^2+4}=\left(x^2-2x+1\right)\left(x^2+4\right)+\frac{10x+3}{x^2+4}$$

Then, apply the following steps to the remainder, which is a proper fraction.

Step II: Factor $Q(x)$ completely into factors of the form $(ax + b)^m$ or $(cx^2 + dx + e)^n$, where $cx^2 + dx + e$ is irreducible and m and n are integers. Express the polynomial $Q(x)$ as a product of linear factors of the form $(ax + b)$ and irreducible quadratic factors of the form $(ax^2 + bx + c)$, where $b^2 - 4ac < 0$. For instance, if $Q(x) = x^4 - 16$, we could factor it as $Q(x) = (x^2 - 4)(x^2 + 4) = (x - 2)(x + 2)(x^2 + 4)$. Thus, at this stage the integrand converts into one of the following four forms:

(i) $\dfrac{f(x)}{(x-\alpha)(x-\beta)}$

(ii) $\dfrac{f(x)}{(x-\alpha)(x-\beta)^k}$ (k a positive integer ≥ 2),

(iii) $\dfrac{f(x)}{x^2+px+q}$ (the roots of the denominator are imaginary, that is $p^2 - 4q < 0$, the denominator may also contain one or more linear factors (repeated or non-repeated).

(iv) $\dfrac{f(x)}{(x^2+px+q)^k}$ (k a positive integer ≥ 2; the roots of the denominator are imaginary). The denominator may also contain one or more linear factors (repeated or non-repeated).

> **NOTE**
>
> *If the equation Q(x) = 0 cannot be solved algebraically, then the method of partial fractions naturally fails and recourse must be had to other methods.*

Step III: (i) For each distinct linear factor $(ax + b)$, the decomposition must include the term $\dfrac{A}{ax+b}$.

(ii) For each repeated linear factor $(ax + b)^m$, the decomposition must include the term

$$\frac{A_1}{ax+b}+\frac{A_2}{(ax+b)^2}+\ldots.+\frac{A_3}{(ax+b)^m}$$

(iii) For each distinct quadratic factor $(cx^2 + dx + e)$, the decomposition must include the term $\dfrac{Bx+C}{cx^2+dx+e}$

(iv) For each repeated quadratic factor $(cx^2 + dx + e)^n$, the decomposition must include the term

$$\frac{B_1x+C_1}{cx^2+dx+e}+\frac{B_2x+C_2}{(cx^2+dx+e)^2}+\ldots.+\frac{B_nx+C_n}{(cx^2+dx+e)^n}$$

Step 4: Use techniques to solve for the constants in the numerators of the decomposition. These techniques are explained below.

Method 1: **(Method of Comparison of Coefficients):**

Let the integrand be

$$\frac{x^2+5x+2}{(x-1)(x+1)(x+2)}=\frac{A}{x-1}+\frac{B}{x+1}+\frac{C}{x+2} \quad ...(1)$$

To determine the values of A, B and C, we multiply both sides of this equation by the product of the denominators, i.e., $(x-1)(x+1)(x+2)$ getting

$$x^2+5x+2=A(x+1)(x+2)+B(x-1)(x+2)+C(x+1)(x-1) \quad ...(2)$$

$$\Rightarrow x^2+5x+2=(A+B+C)x^2+(3A+B)x+(2A-2B-C) \quad ...(3)$$

The polynomials in equation (3) are identical, so their coefficients must be equal. The coefficient of x^2 on the right side, $A+B+C$, must be equal to the coefficient of x^2 on the left side i.e., 1.

Similarly, the coefficients of x must be equal and also the constant terms must be equal.

This gives the following system of equations for A, B and C.

$$A+B+C=1 \quad ...(4)$$

$$3A+B=5 \quad ...(5)$$

$$2A-2B-C=2 \quad ...(6)$$

Solving, we get $A=\frac{4}{3}$, $B=1$, and $C=-\frac{4}{3}$,

So $\int\frac{x^2+5x+2}{(x-1)(x+1)(x+2)}dx$

$$=\int\frac{4/3}{x-1}dx+\int\frac{1}{x+1}dx+\int\frac{-4/3}{x+1}dx$$

$$=\frac{4}{3}\ln|x-1|+\ln|x+1|-\frac{4}{3}\ln|x+2|+C$$

Method (2): **Method of particular values:** In this method we substitute as many different values of x as is the number of unknown constants getting equal number of equations, solving which we get the values of constants of partial fractions.

For example, to integrate $\int\frac{x^2+2}{(x-1)(x-2)(x-3)}dx$

Let $$\frac{x^2+2}{(x-1)(x-2)(x-3)}=\frac{A}{(x-1)}+\frac{B}{(x-2)}+\frac{C}{(x-3)} \quad ...(1)$$

$$\Rightarrow (x^2+2)=A(x-2)(x-3)+B(x-1)(x-3)+C(x-1)(x-2) \quad ...(2)$$

Putting $x=1$ in (2), we get

$$3=A(-1)(-2)\Rightarrow A=3/2$$

Putting $x=2$ in (2), we get

$$6=B(1)(-1)\Rightarrow B=-6$$

Putting $x=3$ in (2), we get

$$11=C(2)(1)\Rightarrow C=11/2$$

∴ (1) becomes

$$\frac{x^2+2}{(x-1)(x-2)(x-3)}=\frac{3}{2(x-1)}+\frac{(-6)}{(x-2)}+\frac{11}{2(x-3)}$$

$$\Rightarrow \int\frac{x^2+2}{(x-1)(x-2)(x-3)}dx$$

$$=\frac{3}{2}\ln|x-1|-6\ln|x-2|+\frac{11}{2}\ln|x-3|+C$$

Method (3): **Heaviside Cover-up Method for Linear Factors:**

When the degree of the polynomial $P(x)$ is less than the degree of $Q(x)$, and $Q(x)$ is a product of n distinct linear factors, each raised to the first power, there is a quick way to express $\frac{P(x)}{Q(x)}$ into partial fractions.

Let the integrand be

$$\frac{P(x)}{Q(x)}=\frac{2x^2+3}{(x-2)(x-3)(x-4)}$$

$$=\frac{A}{(x-2)}+\frac{B}{(x-3)}+\frac{C}{(x-4)} \quad ...(1)$$

If we multiply both sides of equation (1) by $(x-2)$, we get $\frac{2x^2+3}{(x-3)(x-4)}=A+\frac{B(x-2)}{(x-3)}+\frac{C(x-2)}{(x-4)}$ and by substituting $x=2$, the resulting equation gives the value of A:

i.e., $$A=\frac{2(2)^2+3}{(2-3)(2-4)}=\frac{11}{(-1)}=\frac{11}{2}$$

Thus, the value of A is the number we would have obtained if we had covered the factor $(x-2)$ in the denominator of the original fraction $\frac{2x^3+3}{(x-2)(x-3)(x-4)}$ and evaluate the rest at $x=1$.

i.e., $$\frac{2(2)^2+3}{(2-3)(2-4)}=A+0+0$$

$$\Rightarrow A=11/2$$

Similarly, we find the value of B and C in (1) covering the factor $(x-3)$ and $(x-4)$, respectively, and evaluate the rest at $x=3$ and $x=4$ in the original fraction.

The Heaviside cover-up method can be applied to integrand having repeated linear factors in denominator as illustrated below.

Let $\frac{P(x)}{Q(x)} = \frac{3x+4}{(x-2)(x-3)^2} = \frac{3x+4}{(x-3)(x-2)(x-3)}$

$$= \frac{1}{(x-3)}\left[\frac{(3x+4)}{(x-2)(x-3)}\right]$$

$$= \frac{1}{(x-3)}\left[\frac{A}{(x-2)} + \frac{B}{(x-3)}\right] \quad \ldots(i)$$

By Haviside cover-up method applied square bracket of (1), we get $A = -10$ and $B = 13$

∴ (1) becomes

$$\frac{P(x)}{Q(x)} = \frac{1}{(x-3)}\left[\frac{-10}{(x-2)} + \frac{13}{(x-3)}\right]$$

$$= \frac{-10}{(x-2)(x-3)} + \frac{13}{(x-3)^2}$$

$$= \left[\frac{C}{(x-2)} + \frac{D}{x-3}\right] + \frac{13}{(x-3)^2} \quad \ldots.(ii)$$

Again by applying Heaviside cover-up method equation (2), we get $C = 10$; $D = -10$

∴ (2) becomes $\frac{P(x)}{Q(x)} = \frac{10}{(x-2)} - \frac{10}{(x-3)} + \frac{13}{(x-3)^2}$.

Method (4): **Application of Limit:**

Let the integrand be

$$\frac{P(x)}{Q(x)} = \frac{P(x)}{(x-a)(x-b)^r}$$

$$= \frac{A_0}{(x-a)} + \frac{A_1}{(x-b)} + \frac{A_2}{(x-b)^2} + \ldots. + \frac{A_r}{(x-b)^r} \quad \ldots.(i)$$

Now in order to obtain $A_0, A_1, A_2, \ldots., A_r$, the following steps are taken:

(i) To obtain the constant of the partial fraction corresponding to $(x-a)$, i.e., A_0 multiply both sides of the identity (1) by $(x-a)$ and then put $x = a$.

(ii) To obtain the constant of partial fraction corresponding to $(x-b)$ i.e., A_1 multiply both sides of the given equation (1) by $(x-b)$ and then take limit $x \to \infty$.

(iii) To obtain the constant of the partial fraction containing $(x-b)^r$ in the denominator put $x = b$ in the given fraction except for $(x-b)^r$ present in the denominator, this gives $A_r = \frac{P(b)}{(b-a)}$.

(iv) To obtain the other constants, we can multiply both sides of the identity again and again by $(x-a)$ and then let $x \to \infty$, or put some particular values of x (say 0, ±1, ±2 etc.) except the roots of denominator in the identity, thus forming a system of linear equations and solving it.

E.g., Let $\int \frac{x^3+3}{(x+1)(x+2)^3}dx$ be the integral

Let $$\frac{x^3+3}{(x+1)(x+2)^3} = \frac{A}{x+1} + \frac{B}{x+2} + \frac{C}{(x+2)^2} + \frac{D}{(x+2)^3} \quad \ldots(1)$$

Multiplying both sides of (1) by $(x+1)$, we get

$$\frac{x^3+3}{(x+2)^3} = A + \frac{B(x+1)}{(x+2)} + \frac{C(x+1)}{(x+2)^2} + \frac{D(x+1)}{(x+2)^3}$$

Putting $x = -1$ in above equation, we get $A = 2$

$$\therefore \quad \frac{x^3+3}{(x+2)^3(x+1)} = \frac{2}{(x+1)} + \frac{B}{(x+2)} + \frac{C}{(x+2)^2} + \frac{D}{(x+2)^3} \quad \ldots(2)$$

Now to evaluate B multiply both sides of (2) by $(x+2)$ and taking limit $x \to \infty$, we get

$$\lim_{x\to\infty}\frac{x^3+3}{(x+2)^3(x+1)} = \lim_{x\to\infty}\frac{2(x+2)}{(x+1)} + B + \lim_{x\to\infty}\frac{C}{(x+2)} + \lim_{x\to\infty}\frac{D}{(x+2)^2}$$

$\Rightarrow\ 1 = 2 + B$

$\Rightarrow\ B = -1$

Thus, equation (2) becomes

$$\frac{x^3+3}{(x+1)(x+2)^3} = \frac{2}{(x+1)} + \frac{-1}{(x+2)} + \frac{C}{(x+2)^2} + \frac{D}{(x+2)^3} \quad \ldots.(3)$$

Now to evaluate D, multiply both sides of (3) by $(x+2)3$ and put $x = -2$

i.e., $$\frac{(x^3+3)}{(x+1)} = \frac{2(x+2)^3}{(x+1)} - (x+2)^2 + C(x+2) + D$$

$\Rightarrow\ D = 5$

$$\therefore \quad \frac{x^3+3}{(x+1)(x+2)^3} = \frac{2}{(x+1)} + \frac{(-1)}{(x+2)} + \frac{C}{(x+2)^2} + \frac{5}{(x+2)^3} \quad \ldots.(4)$$

Putting $x = 0$ in (4), we get $\frac{3}{8} = 2 - \frac{1}{2} + \frac{C}{4} + \frac{5}{8}$

$\Rightarrow\ \frac{-1}{4} + \frac{1}{2} - 2 = \frac{C}{4}$

$\Rightarrow\ C = -7$

$$\therefore\quad I=\int\frac{x^3+3}{(x+1)(x+2)^3}dx=\int\frac{2}{x+1}dx-\int\frac{1}{(x+2)}dx$$

$$-7\int\frac{1}{(x+2)^2}dx+5\int\frac{1}{(x+2)^3}dx$$

$$=2\ell n|x+1|-\ell n|x+2|+\frac{7}{(x+2)}-\frac{5}{2}\frac{1}{(x+2)^2}+C$$

Method (5): **Application of differentiation:**

Let the integrand be

$$\frac{P(x)}{(x-a)^r}=\frac{A_1}{(x-a)}+\frac{A_2}{(x-a)^2}+\frac{A_3}{(x-a)^3}+\ldots\frac{A_r}{(x-a)^r}$$

$\Rightarrow P(x) = A_1(x-a)^{r-1} + A_2(x-a)^{r-2} + A_3(x-a)^{r-3} + \ldots + A_{r-1}(x-a) + A_r$ ...(1)

Putting $x = a$, we get $A_r = P(a)$

Differentiating equation (1) we get

$P'(x) = A_1(r-1)(x-a)^{r-2} + A_2(r-2)(x-a)^{r-3} + A_3(r-3)(x-a)^{r-4} + \ldots + 2A_{r-2}(x-a) + A_{r-1}$

Putting $x = a$ we get $P'(a) = A_{r-1}$

Continuing differentiating both sides with respect to x successively and substituting $x = a$, we get

$A_{r-2}, A_{r-3}, \ldots A_3, A_2, A_1$.

For example: To solve the integral $\int\frac{x+1}{(x-2)^3}dx$

Let $\frac{x+1}{(x-2)^3}=\frac{A}{(x-2)}+\frac{B}{(x-2)^2}+\frac{C}{(x-2)^3}$

$\Rightarrow (x+1) = A(x-2)^2 + B(x-2) + C$ ...(1)

Substituting $x = 2$ in (1) with respect to x,

we get $3 = C$

Differentiating (1) again with respect to x, we get

$1 = 2A(x-2) + B$

Substituting $(x = 2)$ we get $1 = B$

$\therefore\ 1 = 2A(x-2) + B$ ...(2)

Differentiating (2) again with respect to x, we get $0 = 2A$

$\Rightarrow A = 0$

$$\therefore\quad I=\int\frac{1}{(x-2)^2}dx+\int\frac{3}{(x-2)^3}dx$$

$$\Rightarrow\quad I=\frac{-1}{(x-2)}-\frac{3}{2(x-2)^2}+C$$

Four Cases of Partial Fraction—Explanation

Let us now study the four possible cases depending upon the nature of integrand:

Case I: When denominator contains non-repeated linear factors. Let the integrand be $\frac{f(x)}{(x-\alpha)(x-\beta)}$

Algorithm:

Let $\frac{f(x)}{(x-\alpha)(x-\beta)}=\frac{A}{x-\alpha}+\frac{B}{x-\beta}$ ...(1)

where A and B are constants to be determined.

$\Rightarrow\ \frac{f(x)}{x-\beta}=A+\left(\frac{B}{x-\beta}\right)(x-\alpha)$ ...(2)

Taking $\lim\limits_{x\to\alpha}$ on both sides of (1) we have,

$A=\lim\limits_{x\to\alpha}\frac{f(x)}{(x-\beta)}=\frac{f(\alpha)}{(\alpha-\beta)}$ ...(3)

Similarly $B=\lim\limits_{x\to\beta}\frac{f(x)}{(x-\alpha)}=\frac{f(\beta)}{(\beta-\alpha)}$ ....(4)

Using (3) and (4) in (1), we get

$$\frac{f(x)}{(x-\alpha)(x-\beta)}=\frac{f(\alpha)}{(\alpha-\beta)(x-\alpha)}+\frac{f(\beta)}{(\beta-\alpha)(x-\beta)}$$

$$\Rightarrow\ \int\frac{f(x)}{(x-\alpha)(x-\beta)}dx=\frac{f(\alpha)}{(\alpha-\beta)}\int\frac{dx}{(x-\alpha)}+\frac{f(\beta)}{(\beta-\alpha)}\int\frac{dx}{(x-\beta)}$$

$$=\frac{f(\alpha)}{(\alpha-\beta)}\ln|x-\alpha|+\frac{f(\beta)}{(\beta-\alpha)}\ln|x-\beta|+C$$

REMARK

If above integrand is an improper fraction, then first we divide the numerator by denominator and convert it into a proper fraction, i.e., $\frac{f(x)}{(x-\alpha)(x-\beta)}=g(x)+\frac{A'}{x-\alpha}+\frac{\beta}{x-\beta}$; *where g(x) is the quotient obtained by dividing f(x) by (x – α) (x – β).*

Thus, $\int\frac{f(x)}{(x-\alpha)(x-\beta)}dx=\int g(x)\,dx+A\int\frac{1}{(x-\alpha)}dx+B\int\frac{1}{(x-\beta)}dx$

ILLUSTRATION 122: Evaluate the integral $\int \frac{2x-1}{(x+1)(x^2-9)}dx$ by breaking the integrand into partial fractions.

SOLUTION: $\frac{2x-1}{(x+1)(x^2-9)} = \frac{2x-1}{(x+1)(x-3)(x+3)} = \frac{A}{x+1} + \frac{B}{x-3} + \frac{C}{x+3}$ (say) ...(1)

where A, B, and C are constants to be determined.

$$\Rightarrow \quad A = \lim_{x\to -1}\left(\frac{2x-1}{x^2-9}\right) = \frac{3}{8},\ B = \lim_{x\to 3}\frac{2x-1}{(x+1)(x+3)} = \frac{5}{24}$$

and $C = \lim_{x\to -3}\frac{2x-1}{(x+1)(x-3)} = -\frac{7}{12}$

Using the values of A, B and C in (1), we get

$$\Rightarrow \quad \frac{2x-1}{(x+1)(x^2-9)} = \frac{3}{8(x+1)} + \frac{5}{24(x-3)} - \frac{7}{12(x+3)}$$

$$\Rightarrow \quad \int \frac{2x-1}{(x+1)(x^2-9)}dx = \frac{3}{8}\int\frac{dx}{(x+1)} + \frac{5}{24}\int\frac{dx}{x-3} - \frac{7}{12}\int\frac{dx}{x+3}$$

$$= \frac{3}{8}\ln|x+1| + \frac{5}{24}\ln|x-3| - \frac{7}{12}\ln|x+3| + C.$$

ILLUSTRATION 123: Evaluate $\int \frac{2x^3-x^2-6x+6}{2x^2-5x+3}dx$ by using partial fractions.

SOLUTION: Since in integrand the degree of numerator is greater than the degree of denominator, so it is an improper fraction. Therefore, by division, we have

$$\frac{2x^3-x^2-6x+6}{2x^2-5x+3} = (x+2) + \frac{x}{2x^2-5x+3}$$

$$= (x+2) + \frac{x}{(2x-3)(x-1)} = (x+2) + \frac{A}{x-1} + \frac{B}{2x-3} \quad ...(1)$$

$$\Rightarrow \quad A = \lim_{x\to 1}\left\{(x+2)(x-1) + \frac{x}{(2x-3)}\right\} = -1;\ B = \lim_{x\to 3/2}\left\{(x+2)(2x-3) + \frac{x}{(x-1)}\right\} = 3$$

Using the value of A and B in (1), we have the given

$$\text{Integral} = \int\left[x+2-\frac{1}{x-1}+\frac{3}{2x-3}\right]dx = \frac{x^2}{2} + 2x - \ln|x-1| + \frac{3}{2}\ln|2x-3| + C$$

ILLUSTRATION 124: Evaluate $\int \frac{4x^2+12x-81}{(x-1)(x+3)(x-4)}dx$ by using partial fraction.

SOLUTION: By breaking the integrand into partial fractions we have

$$\frac{4x^2+12x-81}{(x-1)(x+3)(x-4)} = \left(\frac{A}{(x+1)} + \frac{B}{(x+3)} + \frac{C}{(x-4)}\right) \quad ....(1)$$

$\Rightarrow$ $4x^2 + 12x - 81 = A(x+3)(x-4) + B(x+1)(x-4) + C(x+1)(x+3)$ ...(2)

Putting $x = 4$ in (2), we get

$C(4+1)(4+3) = 4(4)^2 + 12(4) - 81$

$C(5 \times 7) = 64 + 48 - 81$

$\Rightarrow$ $C = \frac{31}{35}$

Putting $x = -3$ in (2), we get $4(-3)^2 + 12(-3) - 81 = A(0) + B(-3+1)(-3-4) + 1(0)$

$\Rightarrow$ $36 - 36 - 81 = B(-2)(-7)$

$\Rightarrow$ $B = -\dfrac{81}{14}$

Putting $x = -1$ in (2) we get $4(-1)^2 + 12(-1) - 81 = A(-1+3)(-1-4) + B(0) + C(0)$

$\Rightarrow$ $4 - 12 - 81 = A(2)(-5) = -10A$

$\Rightarrow$ $A = \dfrac{89}{10}$

Put the values of A, B and C in (1), we get

$$I = \frac{89}{10}\int \frac{1}{(x+1)}dx - \frac{81}{14}\int \frac{1}{(x+3)}dx + \frac{31}{35}\int \frac{1}{(x-4)}dx$$

$$= \frac{89}{10}\ln|x+1| - \frac{81}{14}\ln|x+3| + \frac{31}{35}\ln|x-4| + C$$

ILLUSTRATION 125: Evaluate $\displaystyle\int \frac{x^3+1}{4x^3-x}dx$

SOLUTION: Let $I = \displaystyle\int \frac{x^3+1}{x(4x^2-1)}dx = \int \frac{x^3+1}{x(2x-1)(2x+1)}dx$

$$\Rightarrow \int\left(\frac{x^2}{(2x-1)(2x+1)} + \frac{1}{x(2x-1)(2x+1)}\right)dx$$

$$\Rightarrow \int\left(\frac{x^2}{4x^2-1} + \frac{1}{x(2x-1)(2x+1)}\right)dx = \int \frac{x^2}{4x^2-1}dx + \int \frac{1}{x(2x-1)(2x+1)}dx$$

$$\Rightarrow \frac{1}{4}\int \frac{4x^2}{4x^2-1}dx + \int \frac{1}{x(2x-1)(2x+1)}dx = \frac{1}{4}\left[\int \frac{4x^2+1-1}{4x^2-1}dx + \int \frac{1}{x(2x-1)(2x+1)}dx\right]$$

$$\Rightarrow \frac{1}{4}\left[\int \frac{4x^2-1}{4x^2-1}dx + \int \frac{1}{4x^2-1}dx + \int \frac{1}{x(2x-1)(2x+1)}dx\right] \quad \text{...(i)}$$

Now, let $\dfrac{1}{x(2x-1)(2x+1)} = \dfrac{A}{x} + \dfrac{B}{(2x-1)} + \dfrac{C}{(2x+1)}$ ...(ii)

$\Rightarrow$ $1 = A(4x^2 - 1) + Bx(2x + 1) + Cx(2x - 1)$ ...(iii)

Putting $x = 0$ in (iii), we get $A = \dfrac{1}{(-1)} = -1$

Putting $x = 1/2$ in (iii), we get $B = \dfrac{1}{(1/2)(2)} = 1$

Putting $x = -1/2$ in (iii), we get $C = \dfrac{1}{\left(-\frac{1}{2}\right)(-1-1)} = 1$

Using the values of A, B and C in (ii), we get $\dfrac{1}{x(2x-1)(2x+1)} = \dfrac{-1}{x} + \dfrac{1}{(2x-1)} + \dfrac{1}{(2x+1)}$

$$\Rightarrow \int \frac{dx}{x(2x-1)(2x+1)}$$

$$= -\int \frac{1}{x}dx + \int \frac{1dx}{2x-1} + \int \frac{1dx}{2x+1} = -\ln|x| + \frac{1}{2}\ln|2x-1| + \frac{1}{2}\ln|2x+1| + C. \quad \text{...(iv)}$$

Putting (iv) in (i), we get

$$I = \frac{1}{4}\int 1.dx + \frac{1}{4}\int \frac{1}{4x^2-1}dx - \ln|x| + \frac{1}{2}\ln|2x-1| + \frac{1}{2}\ln|2x+1| + C$$

$$= \frac{1}{4}x + \frac{1}{16}\ln\left|\frac{2x-1}{2x+1}\right| - \ln|x| + \frac{1}{2}\ln|2x-1| + \frac{1}{2}\ln|2x+1| + C$$

ILLUSTRATION 126: Evaluate $\int \frac{1}{(\cos x)(3\sin x+2)}dx$

SOLUTION: Let $I = \int \frac{1}{(\cos x)(3\sin x+2)}dx$ ...(1)

Put $\sin x = t$

$\Rightarrow \frac{dt}{dx} = \cos x \qquad \Rightarrow dx = \frac{dt}{\cos x}$

$\Rightarrow I = \int \frac{dt}{\cos^2 x(3\sin x+2)}$; $t = \sin x$

$\Rightarrow I = \int \frac{1}{(1-t^2)(3t+2)}dt = \int \frac{1}{(1-t)(1+t)(3t+2)}dt$ ...(2)

Let $\frac{1}{(1-t)(1+t)(3t+2)} = \frac{A}{1-t} + \frac{B}{1+t} + \frac{C}{3t+2}$ ...(3)

$\Rightarrow 1 = A(1+t)(3t+2) + B(1-t)(3t+2) + C(1-t^2)$ ...(4)

Now, putting $t = 1$ in (4), we get $A = \frac{1}{2\times 5} = \frac{1}{10}$

Putting $t = -1$ in (4), we get $B = \frac{1}{(2)(-1)} = -\frac{1}{2}$

Putting $t = -2/3$ in (4), we get $C = \frac{1}{\left(1+\frac{2}{3}\right)\left(1-\frac{2}{3}\right)} = \frac{9}{5\times(1)} = \frac{9}{5}$

Using the values of A, B and C in (3) we get

$$\frac{1}{(1-t)(1+t)(3t+2)} = \frac{1}{10(1-t)} - \frac{1}{2(1+t)} + \frac{9}{5(3t+2)}$$

$$\Rightarrow \int \frac{1}{(1-t)(1+t)(3t+2)}dt = \frac{1}{10}\int \frac{1}{1-t}dt + \left(\frac{-1}{2}\right)\int \frac{1}{1+t}dt + \frac{9}{5}\int \frac{1}{3t+2}dt$$

$$= \frac{1}{10}\ln|1-t|(-1) + \left(-\frac{1}{2}\right)\ln|1+t| + \frac{9}{5}.\frac{1}{3}\ln|3t+2| + C$$

$$= -\frac{1}{10}\ln|1-t| - \frac{1}{2}\ln|1+t| + \frac{3}{5}\ln|3t+2| + C$$

$$= -\frac{1}{10}\ln|1-\sin x| - \frac{1}{2}\ln|1+\sin x| + \frac{3}{5}\ln|3\sin x+2| + C$$

ILLUSTRATION 127: Evaluate $\int \frac{1}{4\sin 2x - \cos x}dx$

SOLUTION: Let $I = \int \frac{1}{4\sin 2x-\cos x}dx = \int \frac{1}{4(2\sin x\cos x)-\cos x}dx = \int \frac{1}{\cos x(8\sin x-1)}dx$

$$= \int \frac{1.\cos x}{\cos^2 x(8\sin x - 1)} dx = \int \frac{\cos x}{(1-\sin^2 x)(8\sin x - 1)} dx$$

Put $m = \sin x$ $\Rightarrow \frac{dm}{dx} = \cos x$

$\Rightarrow dx = \frac{dm}{\cos x}$ $\Rightarrow I = \int \frac{1}{(1-m^2)(8m-1)} dm$ ...(1)

Let $\frac{1}{(1+m)(1-m)(8m-1)} = \frac{A}{1+m} + \frac{B}{1-m} + \frac{C}{8m-1}$ ...(2)

$\Rightarrow 1 = A(1-m)(8m-1) + B(1+m)(8m-1) + C(1+m)(1-m)$ ...(3)

Putting $m = -1$ in (3) we get $A = \frac{1}{(2)(-9)} = \frac{-1}{18}$

Putting $m = 1$ in (3) we get $B = \frac{1}{(2)(8-1)} = \frac{1}{2(7)} = \frac{1}{14}$

Putting $m = \frac{1}{8}$ in (3) we get $C = \frac{1}{\left(1+\frac{1}{8}\right)\left(1-\frac{1}{8}\right)} = \frac{8\times 8}{9\times 7} = \frac{64}{63}$

Using the values of A, B and C in (3) we get

$$\frac{1}{(1+m)(1-m)(8m-1)} = \frac{-1/18}{1+m} + \frac{1/14}{1-m} + \frac{64/63}{8m-1}$$

$$\Rightarrow \int \frac{1}{(1+m)(1-m)(8m-1)} dm = \left(\frac{-1}{18}\right)\int \frac{1}{1+m} dm + \left(\frac{1}{14}\right)\int \frac{1}{1-m} dm + \frac{64}{63}\int \frac{1}{8m-1} dm$$

$$= -\frac{1}{18}\ln|1+m| + \frac{1}{14}(-1)\ln|1-m| + \frac{64}{63}.\frac{1}{8}\ln|8m-1| + C$$

$$= -\frac{1}{18}\ln|1+\sin x| - \frac{1}{14}\ln|1-\sin x| + \frac{8}{63}\ln|8\sin x - 1| + C$$

Case II: When denominator contains repeated linear factors as well i.e., denominator may contain different linear factors along with repeated linear factors. Let the given integrand be $\frac{f(x)}{(x-\alpha)(x-\beta)^n}$; $n \in \mathbb{N}, n \geq 2$.

Algorithm:

$$\frac{f(x)}{(x-\alpha)(x-\beta)^n} = \frac{A_0}{x-\alpha} + \frac{A_1}{x-\beta} + \frac{A_2}{(x-\beta)^2} + \ldots + \frac{A_n}{(x-\beta)^n} \quad \ldots(1)$$

$$\Rightarrow A = \lim_{x\to\alpha}\left(\frac{f(x)}{(x-\beta)^n}\right) = \frac{f(\alpha)}{(\alpha-\beta)^n} \text{ and}$$

$$A_n = \lim_{x\to\beta}\frac{f(x)}{(x-\alpha)} = \frac{f(\beta)}{(\beta-\alpha)}$$

For the remaining $(n-1)$ unknowns $A_1, A_2, A_3, \ldots, A_{n-1}$, we substitute $(n-1)$ convenient values for x (except for α and β) getting $(n-1)$ equations, and hence, can be solved to obtained $A_1, A_2, A_3, \ldots, A_{n-1}$.

For example, if $n = 2$, then substituting $x = 0$ in (1), we get

$$\frac{f(0)}{-\alpha\beta^2} = -\frac{A_0}{\alpha} - \frac{A_1}{\beta} + \frac{A_2}{\beta^2}$$

$$\Rightarrow \frac{A_1}{\beta} = \frac{f(0)}{\alpha\beta^2} - \frac{A_0}{\alpha} + \frac{A_2}{\beta^2}$$

$$\Rightarrow A_1 = \frac{f(0)}{\alpha\beta} - \frac{\beta}{\alpha}A_0 + \frac{A_2}{\beta}$$

ILLUSTRATION 128: Evaluate the integral $\int \frac{2x-3}{(x-1)^2(x+2)}dx$ by breaking the integrand into partial fractions.

SOLUTION: $\frac{2x-3}{(x-1)^2(x+2)}$, here as per the algorithm explained above $f(x) = 2x - 3$;

Now denominator contains repeated linear factors as well. So using procedure explained above

$$\frac{f(x)}{(x+2)(x-1)^2} = \frac{A}{x+2} + \frac{B}{x-1} + \frac{C}{(x-1)^2} \qquad \text{...(1)}$$

Here; $A = \lim_{x \to -2}\left(\frac{2x-3}{(x-1)^2}\right) = \frac{-7}{9}$ and $C = \lim_{x \to 1}\frac{2x-3}{(x+2)} = \frac{-1}{3}$

Now for B put suitable value of x, $x = 0$ (say) in (1) we get

$$\Rightarrow \frac{2(0)-3}{(-1)^2(2)} = \frac{A}{(2)} + \frac{B}{(-1)} + \frac{C}{(-1)^2} \qquad \Rightarrow B = \frac{A}{2} + C + \frac{3}{2} = \frac{7}{9}$$

$$\therefore \; I = \int \frac{-7}{9}\frac{1}{(x+2)}dx + \int \frac{7}{9}\left(\frac{1}{(x-1)}\right)dx - \int \frac{1}{3}\left(\frac{1}{x-1}\right)^2 dx$$

$$= -\frac{7}{9}\ln|x+2| + \frac{7}{9}\ln|x-1| + \frac{1}{3}\frac{1}{(x-1)} + C$$

ILLUSTRATION 129: Evaluate $\int \frac{x^2-8x^2+4}{x^2(x-4)^2}dx$

SOLUTION: Here the integral contains repeated linear factors in its denominator.

$$\therefore \; \text{Let } \frac{x^3-8x^2+4}{x^2(x-4)^2} = \frac{A}{(x-4)} + \frac{B}{(x-4)^2} + \frac{Cx+D}{x^2} \qquad \text{...(1)}$$

$$\frac{x^3-8x^2+4}{x^2(x-4)^2} = \frac{A}{(x-4)} + \frac{B}{(x-4)^2} + Cx + D$$

$$\Rightarrow x^3 - 8x^2 + 4 = Ax^2(x-4) + Bx^2 + (Cx+D)(x-4)^2 \qquad \text{...(2)}$$

Putting $x = 4$ in (2) we get

$4^3 - 8(4)^2 + 4 = 0 + B(4)^2 + 0$

$$\frac{64-(8\times16)+4}{16} = B$$

$$\Rightarrow B = \frac{68-128}{16} = \frac{-60}{16} = \frac{-15}{4}$$

Putting $x = 0$ in (2) we get $4 = D(-4)^2$

$\Rightarrow D = 1/4.$

Putting $x = 1$ in (2) we get

$1 - 8 + 4 = A(1-4) + B + (C+D)(1-4)^2$

$\Rightarrow -3 = A(-3) + B + 9(C+D)$

$$\Rightarrow -3 = A - \frac{15}{4} + 9\left(C + \frac{1}{4}\right)$$

$$\Rightarrow A - 3C = 1/2 \qquad \text{....(3)}$$

Now, putting $x = 2$ in (2) we get

$(2)^3 - 8(2)^2 + 4 = A(2)^2(2-4) + B(2)^2 + (2C+D)(2-4)^2$

$\Rightarrow A - C = 3/4$ ...(4)

Also $3C - A = -1/2$ [from (3)]

Solving (3) and (4), we get

$\Rightarrow C = \frac{1}{8}$ and $A = \frac{7}{8}$

Now, substituting the values of A, B and C in (1) we get

$$\frac{x^3 - 8x^2 + 4}{x^2(x-4)^2} = \frac{7}{8(x-4)} - \frac{15}{4(x-4)^2} + \frac{\frac{1}{8}x + \frac{1}{4}}{x^2}$$

$$\Rightarrow \int \frac{x^3 - 8x^2 + 4}{x^2(x-4)^2}dx = \int \frac{7}{8}.\frac{1}{(x-4)}dx + \int\left(-\frac{15}{4}\right).\frac{1.dx}{(x-4)^2} + \int \frac{\left(\frac{1}{8}x + \frac{1}{4}\right)}{x^2}dx$$

$$= \frac{7}{8}\int \frac{1}{(x-4)}dx - \frac{15}{4}\int \frac{1}{(x-4)^2}dx + \frac{1}{8}\int \frac{1}{x}dx + \frac{1}{4}\int \frac{1}{x^2}dx$$

$$\Rightarrow \frac{7}{8}ln|x-4| - \frac{15}{4}\frac{(x-4)^{-2+1}}{(-2+1)} + \frac{1}{8}\ln|x| + \frac{1}{4}\left(\frac{x^{-2+1}}{-2+1}\right) + C$$

$$= \frac{7}{8}ln|x-4| + \frac{15}{4}\frac{1}{(x-4)} + \frac{1}{8}\ln|x| - \frac{1}{4}\left(\frac{1}{x}\right) + C$$

ILLUSTRATION 130: Solve $\int \frac{1}{x^3(1-x^2)^2}dx$ by using partial fractions.

SOLUTION: For more simplified integral divide both numerator and denominator by x and put $x^2 = m$, we get $I = \int \frac{dm}{m^2(1-m)^2}$ ...(1)

$$\frac{1}{m^2(1-m)^2} = \frac{A}{m} + \frac{B}{m^2} + \frac{C}{(1-m)} + \frac{D}{(1-m)^2}$$ ...(2)

Now, $\frac{1}{m^2(1-m)^2} = \frac{Am(1-m)^2 + B(1-m)^2 + C(m^2)(1-m) + Dm^2}{m^2(1-m)^2}$

$\Rightarrow 1 = Am(1-m)^2 + B(1-m)^2 + C(m^2)(1-m) + D(m)^2$ ...(3)

Putting $m = 0$ in (3) we get

$1 = B + 0 + 0 + 0$ $\quad\Rightarrow B = 1$

Putting $m = 1$ in (3) we get

$1 = A(0) + B(0) + C(0) + D(1)$ $\quad\Rightarrow D = 1$

Putting $m = -1$ in (3) we get

$\Rightarrow 1 = -A(-2)^2 + B(+2)^2 + C(-1)^2(2) + D(-1)^2$

$\Rightarrow 1 = -4A + 4B + 2C + D$

$\Rightarrow 1 = -4A + 4 + 2C + 1$

$\Rightarrow 4A - 2C = 4$

$\Rightarrow 2A - C = 2$ ...(4)

Now, putting $m = 2$ (3) we get

$1 = A(2) + B(1) + C(4)(-1) + D(4)$

$1 = 2A + B - 4C + 4D = 2A + 1 - 4C + 4$

$\Rightarrow A-2C=-2.$ ...(5)

Solving (4) and (5) we get

$\Rightarrow C=2$ $\qquad\Rightarrow A=2$

using the values of A, B, C and D in (2) we get

$$\Rightarrow \int\frac{1}{m^2(1-m)^2}dx=\int\frac{2}{m}dx+\int\frac{1}{m^2}dx+\int\frac{2}{(1-m)}dx+\int\frac{1}{(1-m)^2}dx$$

$$\Rightarrow \int\frac{1}{m^2(1-m)^2}dx=2\ln|m|+\frac{m^{-n+1}}{-2+1}+\frac{2\ln|1-m|}{-1}+\frac{(1-m)^{-2+1}}{(-2+1)(-1)}+C$$

$$=2\ln|m|-\frac{1}{m}-2\ln|1-m|+\frac{1}{(m-1)}+C$$

$$=2\ln x^2-\frac{1}{x^2}-2\ln|1-x^2|+\frac{1}{1-x^2}+C$$

Case III: When denominator contains non-destructible quadratic factor, i.e., denominator may contain linear factors (repeated/non-repeated) along with irreducible quadratic factors.

Algorithm: Let the given integrand the $\dfrac{f(x)}{(x^2+\alpha)(x-\beta)};\alpha>0.$

Take $\dfrac{f(x)}{(x^2+\alpha)(x-\beta)}=\dfrac{Ax+B}{x^2+\alpha}+\dfrac{C}{x-\beta}$ ...(1)

$\Rightarrow f(x) = (Ax + B)(x - \beta) + C(x^2 + \alpha)$ ...(2)

Multiplying (1) by $(x - \beta)$ both sides, and taking $\lim\limits_{x\to\beta}$ on both sides we have,

$$C=\lim_{x\to\beta}\frac{f(x)}{(x^2+\alpha)}=\frac{f(\beta)}{(\beta^2+\alpha)}$$

For the values of A and B we substitute suitable values of x in the identity (1) and solve two linear equations obtained in A and B. For finding the values of A and B we can also equate the coefficients of like terms on both sides of (2).

ILLUSTRATION 131: Evaluate $\displaystyle\int\frac{x}{(x-1)(x^2+1)}dx$ by breaking the integrand into partial fractions.

SOLUTION: Decompose the fraction under the integral sign into partial fractions as given below

Let $\dfrac{x}{(x^2+1)(x-1)}=\dfrac{Ax+B}{x^2+1}+\dfrac{C}{x-1}$ ...(1)

Consequently, $x = (Ax + B)(x - 1) + C(x^2 + 1)$ ...(2)

Setting $x = 1$ we get $1 = 2C$ $\qquad\Rightarrow C = 1/2;$

setting $x = 0$, we get $0 = -B + C$ $\qquad B = 1/2$

Equating the coefficients of x^2 in (2) we get $0 = A + C$,

$\Rightarrow A = -1/2.$

$$\text{Thus, } \int\frac{x\,dx}{(x^2+1)(x-1)}=-\frac{1}{2}\int\frac{x-1}{x^2+1}dx+\frac{1}{2}\int\frac{dx}{x-1}$$

$$=-\frac{1}{2}\int\frac{x}{x^2+1}dx+\frac{1}{2}\int\frac{dx}{x^2+1}+\frac{1}{2}\int\frac{dx}{x-1}=-\frac{1}{4}\ln|x^2+1|+\frac{1}{2}\tan^{-1}x+\frac{1}{2}\ln|x-1|+C$$

ILLUSTRATION 132: Evaluate $\int \frac{1}{1+x^3}dx$ by partial fraction.

SOLUTION: Since $(a^3 + b^3) = (a + b)(a^2 - ab + b^2)$

$$\Rightarrow I = \int \frac{1}{(1+x)(1-x+x^2)}dx$$

Now, this fraction can be broken into simpler fractions as given below.

$$\frac{1}{(1+x)(1-x+x^2)} = \frac{A}{(1+x)} + \frac{Bx+C}{(1-x+x^2)} \quad \text{...(1)}$$

$$\Rightarrow 1 = A(1 - x + x^2) + (Bx + C)(1 + x) \quad \text{...(2)}$$

Putting $x = -1$ in (2) we get

$1 = A(1 + 1 + 1)$ $\Rightarrow A = 1/3$

Putting $x = 0$ in (2) we get

$1 = A(1) + C(1)$ $\Rightarrow C = 1 - A = 1 - 1/3 = 2/3$

Putting $x = 1$ in (2) we get

$1 = A(1) + (B + C)(2)$ $\Rightarrow 1 = A + 2B + 2C$

$\Rightarrow 1 = 1/3 + 2B + 2(2/3)$

$\Rightarrow 1 - \frac{1}{3} - \frac{4}{3} = 2B$ $\Rightarrow \frac{3-1-4}{3} = 2B$ $\Rightarrow B = \frac{1}{2}\left(\frac{-2}{3}\right) = \frac{-1}{3}.$

Substituting the values of A, B and C in (1) we get

$$\frac{1}{(1+x)(1-x+x^2)} = \frac{1}{3}\left(\frac{1}{x+1}\right) - \frac{1}{3}\frac{(x-2)}{(x^2+1-x)}$$

$$\Rightarrow \int \frac{1}{(1+x)(1-x+x^2)}dx = \int \frac{1}{3}\left(\frac{1}{1+x}\right)dx - \frac{1}{3}$$

$$\int \frac{\left(x-\frac{1}{2}\right)}{\left(x-\frac{1}{2}\right)^2 + \left(\frac{\sqrt{3}}{2}\right)^2}dx + \frac{1}{2}\int \frac{1}{\left(x-\frac{1}{2}\right)^2 + \left(\frac{\sqrt{3}}{2}\right)^2}dx$$

$$= \frac{1}{3}\ln|x+1| - \frac{1}{3}.\frac{1}{2}\ln\left|\left(x-\frac{1}{2}\right)^2 + \left(\frac{\sqrt{3}}{2}\right)^2\right| + \frac{1}{2}\frac{2}{\sqrt{3}}\tan^{-1}\left(\frac{x-\frac{1}{2}}{\frac{\sqrt{3}}{2}}\right) + C$$

$$= \frac{1}{3}\ln|x+1| - \frac{1}{6}\ln|x^2 - x + 1| + \frac{1}{\sqrt{3}}\tan^{-1}\left(\frac{2x-1}{\sqrt{3}}\right) + C$$

ILLUSTRATION 133: Find the following integrals:

(a) $\int \frac{x}{x^6+1}dx$ (b) $\int \frac{x^2}{x^6+1}dx$

(c) $\int \frac{x^3}{x^6+1}dx$ (d) $\int \frac{x^4}{x^6+1}dx$

(e) $\int \frac{x^5}{x^6+1}dx$

SOLUTION: (a) Let $I = \int \frac{x}{x^6+1}dx = \int \frac{x}{(x^2)^3+1}dx$

Put $t = x^2$ $\Rightarrow \frac{dt}{dx} = 2x$ in I

$$\therefore \quad I = \frac{1}{2}\int \frac{1}{t^3+1}dt = \frac{1}{2}\int \frac{1}{(t+1)(t^2-t+1)}dt \qquad ...(1)$$

Now, breaking this fraction into partial fractions, we have

$$\frac{1}{(t+1)(t^2-t+1)} = \frac{A}{(t+1)} + \frac{Bt+C}{(t^2-t+1)}$$

$\Rightarrow$ $1 = A(t^2 - t + 1) + (Bt + C)(t + 1)$

Put $= t = -1$

$\Rightarrow$ $1 = A(1 + 1 + 1) + (0)$ $\Rightarrow A = 1/3$

Put $t = 0$

$\Rightarrow$ $1 = A(1) + C(1)$ $\Rightarrow C = 1 - \frac{1}{3} = \frac{2}{3}$

Put $t = 1$

$\Rightarrow$ $1 = A(1) + (B + C)(2)$

$\Rightarrow$ $1 = \frac{1}{3} + \left(\frac{2}{3} + B\right)(2)$

$\Rightarrow$ $B = \frac{-1}{3}$

Using the values of A, B and C, we have

$$\Rightarrow \quad \frac{1}{(t+1)(t^2-t+1)} = \frac{1}{3}\cdot\frac{1}{(t+1)} + \frac{\left(-\frac{1}{3}t + \frac{2}{3}\right)}{(t^2-t+1)} \qquad ...(2)$$

by substituting (2) in (1) we get

$$I = \frac{1}{2}\left[\int \frac{1}{3}\frac{1}{(t+1)}dt + \frac{1}{3}\int \frac{(-t+2)}{(t^2-t+1)}dt\right] = \frac{1}{2}\left[\frac{1}{3}\ln|t+1| - \frac{1}{3}\underbrace{\int \frac{(t-2)}{(t^2-t+1)}dt}_{I_2\ (say)}\right] \qquad ...(3)$$

where $I_2 = \int \frac{(t-2)}{t^2-t+1}dt$ which is of type $\int \frac{px+q}{ax^2+bx+c}dx$, so according to algorithm of above type let $(t-2) = A\frac{d}{dt}(t^2-t+1) + B$

$\Rightarrow$ $t - 2 = A(2t - 1) + B$ $\Rightarrow t - 2 = 2(A)t + (B - A)$

$\Rightarrow$ $2A = 1$

$\Rightarrow$ $A = 1/2$ and $B - A = -2$ $\Rightarrow B = -2 + A$

$\Rightarrow$ $B = -2 + 1/2 = -3/2.$

$$\therefore \quad I_2 = \int \frac{\frac{1}{2}(2t-1) - \frac{3}{2}}{t^2 - t + 1} dt = \frac{1}{2}\ln|t^2 - t + 1| - \frac{3}{2}\int \frac{1}{t^2 - t + 1} dt$$

$$= \frac{1}{2}\ln|t^2 - t + 1| - \frac{3}{2}\int \frac{1}{\left(\left(t + \frac{(-1)}{2}\right)^2 - \frac{(-3)}{4}\right)} dt = \frac{1}{2}\ln|t^2 - t + 1| - \frac{3}{2}\int \frac{1}{\left(t - \frac{1}{2}\right)^2 + \frac{3}{4}} dt$$

$$= \frac{1}{2}\ln|t^2 - t + 1| - \frac{3}{2}\int \frac{1}{\left(t - \frac{1}{2}\right)^2 + \left(\frac{\sqrt{3}}{2}\right)^2} dt$$

$$= \frac{1}{2}\ln|t^2 - t + 1| - \frac{3}{2}\left[\frac{1}{\left(\sqrt{3}/2\right)} \tan^{-1}\left(\frac{2t-1}{\sqrt{3}}\right)\right] + C$$

$$= \frac{1}{2}\ln|t^2 - t + 1| - \sqrt{3}\tan^{-1}\left(\frac{2t-1}{\sqrt{3}}\right) + C$$

Now substituting back $t = x^2$, we have

$$I_2 = \frac{1}{2}\ln|x^4 - x^2 + 1| - \sqrt{3}\tan^{-1}\left(\frac{2x^2-1}{\sqrt{3}}\right) + C \qquad \text{...(4)}$$

Now putting (4) in (3) we have

$$= \frac{1}{2}\left[\frac{1}{3}\ln|x^2 + 1| - \frac{1}{3}\left(\frac{1}{2}\ln|x^4 - x^2 + 1|\right) + \frac{\sqrt{3}}{3}\tan^{-1}\left(\frac{2x^2-1}{\sqrt{3}}\right)\right] + C$$

$$= \frac{1}{6}\ln|x^2 + 1| - \frac{1}{2}\ln|x^4 - x^2 + 1| + \frac{1}{2\sqrt{3}}\tan^{-1}\left(\frac{2x^2-1}{\sqrt{3}}\right) + C.$$

(b) $\int \frac{x^2}{x^6 + 1} dx$

Now this can be solved by simple substitution method putting $x^3 = t$ in denominator

$$\Rightarrow \quad \frac{dt}{dx} = 3x^2$$

$$\Rightarrow \quad dx = \frac{dt}{3x^2} = \int \frac{x^2}{(t)^2 + 1}.\frac{dt}{3x^2} = \frac{1}{3}\int \frac{1}{t^2 + 1} dt$$

$$= \frac{1}{3}\tan^{-1} t + C = \frac{1}{3}\tan^{-1} x^3 + C$$

(c) $\int \frac{x^3}{x^6 + 1} dx = \int \frac{x^2 . x\, dx}{(x^2)^3 + 1}$

Put $x^2 = t \qquad \Rightarrow 2x\, dx = dt$

$$= \frac{1}{2}\int \frac{t(dt)}{t^3 + 1} \qquad \text{...(1)}$$

$$\text{Let } \frac{t}{t^3 + 1} = \frac{A}{t+1} + \frac{Bt + C}{t^2 - t + 1} \qquad \text{...(2)}$$

$\Rightarrow t = A(t^2 - t + 1) + (t + 1)(Bt + C)$

$\Rightarrow\ t = t^2(A + B) + t(-A + B + C) + (A + C)$ ...(3)

Comparing the coefficient on both sides we get

$A + B = 0$

$-A + B + C = 1$

$A + C = 0$

$\Rightarrow\ B = -A = C$ and $C + C + C = 1$

$\Rightarrow\ C = \frac{1}{3}$

$\Rightarrow\ A = -\frac{1}{3},\ B = \frac{1}{3},\ C = \frac{1}{3}$

$\therefore$ from (1) and (2) we have

$$I = \frac{1}{2}\int \frac{-1/3}{t+1}dt + \frac{1}{6}\int \frac{t+1}{t^2-t+1}dt$$

$$= -\frac{1}{6}\ln|t+1| + \frac{1}{12}\int \frac{2t+2}{t^2-t+1}dt \ = -\frac{1}{6}\ln|t+1| + \frac{1}{12}\ln|t^2-t+1| + \frac{1}{4}\int \frac{dt}{t^2-t+\frac{1}{4}+\frac{3}{4}}$$

$$= -\frac{1}{6}\ln|t+1| + \frac{1}{12}\ln|t^2-t+1| + \frac{1}{4}\int \frac{dt}{\left(t-\frac{1}{2}\right)^2 + \left(\frac{\sqrt{3}}{2}\right)^2}$$

$$= -\frac{1}{6}\ln|t+1| + \frac{1}{12}\ln|t^2-t+1| + \frac{1}{2\sqrt{3}}\left(\frac{2t-1}{\sqrt{3}}\right) + C$$

$$= -\frac{1}{6}\ln|x^2+1| + \frac{1}{12}\ln|x^4-x^2+1| + \frac{1}{2\sqrt{3}}\tan^{-1}\left(\frac{2x^2-1}{\sqrt{3}}\right) + C$$

(d) $\int \frac{x^4}{x^6+1}dx = \frac{1}{2}\int \frac{2x^4}{x^6+1}dx = \frac{1}{2}\int \frac{\left(x^4+1+x^4-1\right)}{x^6+1}dx$

$$= \frac{1}{2}\left[\int \frac{x^4+1}{x^6+1}dx + \int \frac{(x-1)\left(x^2+1\right)(x+1)}{\left(x^2+1\right)\left(x^4+1-x^2\right)}dx\right]$$

$$= \frac{1}{2}\left[\int \frac{x^4+1-x^2}{\left(x^6+1\right)}dx + \int \frac{x^2-1}{x^4+1-x^2}dx\right] = \frac{1}{2}\left[\int \frac{x^4-x^2+1}{x^6+1}dx + \int \frac{x^2-1}{x^4+1-x^2}dx\right]$$

$$= \frac{1}{2}\left[\int \frac{x^4-x^2+1}{\left(x^2+1\right)\left(x^4-x^2+1\right)}dx + \int \frac{1-\frac{1}{x^2}}{x^2+\frac{1}{x^2}-1}dx\right] = \frac{1}{2}\left[\int \frac{1}{x^2+1}dx + \int \frac{1-\frac{1}{x^2}}{x^2+\frac{1}{x^2}+2-3}dx\right]$$

$$= \frac{1}{2}\left[\tan^{-1}x + \int \frac{1-\frac{1}{x^2}}{\left(x+\frac{1}{x}\right)^2-3}dx\right]$$

Put $m = x + \frac{1}{x}$

$$\Rightarrow \frac{dm}{dx} = 1 - \frac{1}{x^2} \Rightarrow dx = \frac{dm}{\left(1-\frac{1}{x^2}\right)}$$

$$\Rightarrow I = \frac{1}{2}\left[\tan^{-1}(x) + \int \frac{dm}{m^2 - (\sqrt{3})^2}\right]$$

$$= \frac{1}{2}\left[\tan^{-1}(x) + \frac{1}{2\sqrt{3}}\ln\left|\frac{m-\sqrt{3}}{m+\sqrt{3}}\right|\right] + C = \frac{1}{2}\left[\tan^{-1}(x) + \frac{1}{2\sqrt{3}}\ln\left|\frac{-\sqrt{3}x + x^2 + 1}{\sqrt{3}x + x^2 + 1}\right|\right] + C.$$

(e) $\int \frac{x^5}{x^6+1} dx$

Put $x^6 + 1 = t$

$\Rightarrow 6x^5\, dx = dt$

$$\therefore I = \int \frac{dt}{6(t)} = \frac{1}{6}\ln|t| + C = \frac{1}{6}\ln|x^6+1| + C$$

ILLUSTRATION 134: Find the following integrals:

(i) $\int \frac{x^4+1}{x^6+1} dx$ (ii) $\int \frac{1}{x^6+1} dx$

SOLUTION: (i) Let $I = \int \frac{x^4+1}{x^6+1} dx = \int \frac{x^4+x^2+1-x^2}{x^6+1} dx = \int \frac{x^4-x^2+1}{x^6+1} dx + \int \frac{x^2}{x^6+1} dx$

$$= \int \frac{x^4-x^2+1}{(x^2+1)(x^4-x^2+1)} dx + \int \frac{x^2}{x^6+1} dx = \int \frac{1}{1+x^2} dx + \frac{1}{3}\int \frac{3x^2}{(x^3)^2+1} dx$$

$$= \tan^{-1} x + \frac{1}{3}\tan^{-1}(x^3) + C$$

(ii) Let $I = \int \frac{1}{x^6+1} dx = \frac{1}{2}\int \frac{2}{x^6+1} dx = \frac{1}{2}\int \frac{(x^4+1)-(x^4-1)}{x^6+1} dx$

$$= \frac{1}{2}\int \frac{x^4+1}{x^6+1} dx - \frac{1}{2}\int \frac{x^4-1}{x^6+1} dx$$

$$= \frac{1}{2}\int \frac{x^4-x^2+1+x^2}{x^6+1} dx - \frac{1}{2}\int \frac{(x^2+1)(x^2-1)}{(x^2+1)(x^4-x^2+1)} dx$$

$$= \frac{1}{2}\int \frac{x^4-x^2+1}{x^6+1} dx + \frac{1}{2}\int \frac{x^2}{x^6+1} dx - \frac{1}{2}\int \frac{x^2-1}{x^4-x^2+1} dx$$

$$= \frac{1}{2}\int \frac{1}{x^2+1} dx + \frac{1}{6}\int \frac{3x^2}{(x^3)^2+1} dx - \frac{1}{2}\int \frac{1-\frac{1}{x^2}}{x^2+\frac{1}{x^2}-1} dx$$

$$= \frac{1}{2}\tan^{-1} x + \frac{1}{6}\tan^{-1}(x^3) - \frac{1}{2}\int \frac{dt}{(t)^2-3}; \text{ where } t = x + \frac{1}{x}$$

$$= \frac{1}{2}\tan^{-1} x + \frac{1}{6}\tan^{-1} x^3 - \frac{1}{2}\int \frac{dt}{t^2-(\sqrt{3})^2}$$

$$= \frac{1}{2}\tan^{-1} x + \frac{1}{6}\tan^{-1} x^3 - \frac{1}{4\sqrt{3}}\ln\left|\frac{t-\sqrt{3}}{t+\sqrt{3}}\right| + C$$

$$= \frac{1}{2}\tan^{-1} x + \frac{1}{6}\tan^{-1} x^3 - \frac{1}{4\sqrt{3}}\ln\left|\frac{x^2-\sqrt{3}x+1}{x^2+\sqrt{3}x+1}\right| + C.$$

ILLUSTRATION 135: Find $\int \frac{(x+1)^2}{x^4+x^2+1}dx$

SOLUTION: Let $I = \int \frac{x^2+2x+1}{x^4+x^2+1}dx = \int \frac{x^2+1}{x^4+x^2+1}dx + \int \frac{2x\,dx}{x^4+x^2+1}$

$$= \int \frac{1+\frac{1}{x^2}}{x^2+1+\frac{1}{x^2}}dx + \int \frac{2x}{(x^2)^2+x^2+1}dx$$

$$= I_1 + I_2 \text{ (say)} \qquad \ldots(1)$$

Now $I_1 = \int \frac{1+\frac{1}{x^2}}{x^2+\frac{1}{x^2}-2+3}dx = \int \frac{1+\frac{1}{x^2}}{\left(x-\frac{1}{x}\right)^2+(\sqrt{3})^2}dx$

Put $x - \frac{1}{x} = t$

$\Rightarrow \left(1+\frac{1}{x^2}\right)dx = dt$

$\Rightarrow I_1 = \int \frac{dt}{t^2+\left(\sqrt{3}\right)^2} = \frac{1}{2\sqrt{3}}\tan^{-1}\left(\frac{t}{\sqrt{3}}\right)$

$$= \frac{1}{2\sqrt{3}}\tan^{-1}\left(\frac{x^2-1}{\sqrt{3}x}\right) + C_1 \qquad \ldots(2)$$

Now $I_2 = \int \frac{2x}{(x^2)^2+x^2+1}dx$

Put $x^2 = t$ $\Rightarrow 2x\,dx = dt$

$\therefore\ I_2 = \int \frac{dt}{t^2+t+1} = \int \frac{dt}{\left(t^2+t+\frac{1}{4}+\frac{3}{4}\right)} = \int \frac{dt}{\left(t+\frac{1}{2}\right)^2+\left(\frac{\sqrt{3}}{2}\right)^2}$

$$= \frac{2}{\sqrt{3}}\tan^{-1}\left(\frac{2t+1}{\sqrt{3}}\right) + C_2 = \frac{2}{\sqrt{3}}\tan^{-1}\left(\frac{2x^2+1}{\sqrt{3}}\right) + C_2 \qquad \ldots(3)$$

$\therefore$ Using the values of I_1 and I_2 from (2) and (3) in (1) we have

$$I = \frac{1}{2\sqrt{3}}\tan^{-1}\left(\frac{x^2-1}{\sqrt{3}x}\right) + \frac{2}{\sqrt{3}}\tan^{-1}\left(\frac{2x^2+1}{\sqrt{3}}\right) + C\text{; where } C = C_1 + C_2.$$

Case (IV): If the denominator contains repeated non-reducible quadratic factors, i.e., denominator may contain linear factors along with it.

i.e., $\dfrac{P(x)}{Q(x)} = \dfrac{P(x)}{(x-\alpha)(ax^2+bx+c)^r}$; where $b^2 - 4ac < 0$,

then we take

$$\frac{P(x)}{Q(x)} = \frac{A_0}{(x-\alpha)} + \frac{A_1x+B_1}{(ax^2+bx+c)} + \frac{A_2x+B_2}{(ax^2+bx+c)^2} +$$

$$\frac{A_3x+B_3}{(ax^2+bx+c)^3} + ... + \frac{A_rx+B_r}{(ax^2+bx+c)^r} \quad ...(i)$$

Now by evaluating the values of constants of partial fractions *Ai's* and *Bi's*,

we integrate $\dfrac{P(x)}{Q(x)}$ w.r.t. x by using the formulae

$$\int \frac{f'(x)}{[f(x)]^r}dx = \frac{(f(x))^{-r+1}}{(-r+1)} + C$$

or $\displaystyle\int \frac{dx}{(ax^2+bx+c)} = \frac{1}{a}\int \frac{dx}{\left(x^2+\frac{b}{a}x+\frac{c}{a}\right)}$

$$= \frac{1}{a}\int \frac{dx}{x^2+\frac{b}{a}x+\frac{b^2}{4a^2}+\left(\frac{c}{a}-\frac{b^2}{4a^2}\right)}$$

$$= \frac{1}{a}\int \frac{dx}{\left(x+\frac{b}{2a}\right)^2+\left(\frac{4ac-b^2}{4a^2}\right)}$$

$$= \frac{1}{a}\int \frac{dx}{\left(x+\frac{b}{2a}\right)^2+\left(\frac{\sqrt{-D}}{2a}\right)^2}$$

$$= \frac{1}{a}.\frac{2a}{\sqrt{-D}}\tan^{-1}\left(\frac{2ax+b}{\sqrt{-D}}\right)+C$$

$$= \frac{2}{\sqrt{-D}}\tan^{-1}\left(\frac{2ax+b}{\sqrt{-D}}\right)+C$$

For integrals of the form $\displaystyle\int \frac{dx}{(ax^2+bx+c)^r}$; $r \geq 2$

Use techniques of substitutions as discussed in the coming illustrations.

ILLUSTRATION 136: Find $\displaystyle\int \frac{3x^2+5}{(x^2+1)^2}dx$

SOLUTION: Let $\dfrac{3x^2+5}{(x^2+1)^2} = \dfrac{Ax+B}{(x^2+1)} + \dfrac{Cx+D}{(x^2+1)^2}$ ...(1)

$\Rightarrow$ $(3x^2 + 5) = (Ax + B)(x^2 + 1) + (Cx + D)$

$\Rightarrow$ $3x^2 + 5 = Ax^3 + (B)x^2 + (A + C)x + (B + D)$ ...(2)

Comparing the coefficients of x^3, x^2, x and constant terms on both sides of (2) we get

$A = 0; B = 3, A + C = 0, B + D = 5$

$\Rightarrow$ $A = 0, B = 3, C = 0, D = 2$

$\therefore$ From (1) $\dfrac{3x^2+5}{(x^2+1)^2} = \dfrac{3}{(x^2+1)} + \dfrac{2}{(x^2+1)^2}$

$\Rightarrow$ $\displaystyle\int \frac{3x^2+5}{(x^2+1)^2}dx = 3\int \frac{1}{(x+1)}dx + 2\int \frac{1}{(x^2+1)^2}dx$

$= 3I_1 + 2I_2$ ...(3)

Hence, $I_1 = \displaystyle\int \frac{1}{x^2+1}dx = \tan^{-1}x + C_1$ and $I_2 = \displaystyle\int \frac{1}{(x^2+1)^2}dx$

Put $x = \tan\theta$ $\Rightarrow$ $dx = \sec^2\theta\, d\theta$

$\therefore$ $I_2 = \displaystyle\int \frac{\sec^2\theta\, d\theta}{(\tan^2\theta+1)^2} = \int \frac{\sec^2\theta}{\sec^4\theta}d\theta = \int \cos^2\theta\, d\theta = \int \frac{(1+\cos 2\theta)}{2}d\theta$

$$= \frac{1}{2}\theta + \frac{1}{4}\sin 2\theta + C_2 = \frac{1}{2}\tan^{-1} x + \frac{1}{4}\left(\frac{2\tan\theta}{1+\tan^2\theta}\right) + C_2$$

$$= \frac{1}{2}\tan^{-1} x + \frac{1}{2}\left(\frac{x}{1+x^2}\right) + C_2$$

Using the values of I_1 and I_2 in (3), we get

$$\int \frac{3x^2+5}{(x^2+1)^2}dx = 3\tan^{-1} x + \tan^{-1} x + \frac{x}{1+x^2} + C$$

$$= 4\tan^{-1} x + \frac{x}{1+x^2} + C$$

ILLUSTRATION 137: Find $\int \frac{x+2}{(x^2+3x+5)^2}dx$

SOLUTION: Let $\frac{x+2}{(x^2+3x+5)^2} = \frac{Ax+B}{(x^2+3x+5)} + \frac{Cx+D}{(x^2+3x+5)^2}$ ...(*i*)

$\Rightarrow$ $(x+2) = (Ax+B)(x^2+3x+5) + (Cx+D)$

$\Rightarrow$ $(x+2) = Ax^3 + (3A+B)x^2 + (5A+3B+C)x + (5B+D)$

Comparing the coefficients on both sides, we get

$A = 0;\ 3A + B = 0;\ 5A + 3B + C = 1;\ 5B + D = 2$

$\Rightarrow$ $A = 0;\ B = 0;\ C = 1;\ D = 2$

$\therefore$ $\frac{x+2}{(x^2+3x+5)^2}$ cannot be represented as the sum of partial fractions. In fact every integrand of type $\frac{\text{linear}}{(\text{irreducible quadratic})^r}$ cannot be further reduced to partial fractions.

So let us use another approach of making the numerator an exact derivative of given quadratic as given below.

$$\int \frac{x+2}{(x^2+3x+5)^2}dx = \frac{1}{2}\int \frac{2x+4}{(x^2+3x+5)^2}dx = \frac{1}{2}\int \frac{(2x+3)+1}{(x^2+3x+5)^2}dx$$

$$= \frac{1}{2}\int \frac{(2x+3)}{(x^2+3x+5)^2}dx + \frac{1}{2}\int \frac{1}{(x^2+3x+5)^2}dx$$

$$= \frac{1}{2}\left(\frac{(x^2+3x+5)^{-2+1}}{-2+1}\right) + \frac{1}{2}\int \frac{1}{\left(x^2+3x+\frac{9}{4}+5-\frac{9}{4}\right)^2}dx$$

$$= \frac{-1}{2(x^2+3x+5)} + \frac{1}{2}\int \frac{1}{\left[\left(x+\frac{3}{2}\right)^2 + \frac{11}{4}\right]^2}dx$$

In second integral put $\left(x+\frac{3}{2}\right) = t$

$\Rightarrow$ $dx = dt$ $\qquad \therefore\ I = \frac{-1}{2(x^2+3x+5)} + \frac{1}{2}\int \frac{dt}{\left(t^2+\frac{11}{4}\right)^2}$

Put $t = \frac{\sqrt{11}}{2}\tan\theta \qquad \Rightarrow t^2 = \frac{11}{2}\tan^2\theta$

And $dt = \frac{\sqrt{11}}{2}\sec^2\theta\, d\theta$

$$\therefore \quad I = \frac{-1}{2(x^2+3x+5)} + \frac{1}{2}\int \frac{\frac{\sqrt{11}}{2}\sec^2\theta\, d\theta}{\left(\frac{121}{16}\right)\sec^4\theta}$$

$$= \frac{-1}{2(x^2+3x+5)} + \frac{1}{2}.\frac{\sqrt{11}}{2}\times\frac{16}{121}\int\cos^2\theta\, d\theta$$

$$= \frac{-1}{2(x^2+3x+5)} + \frac{4}{11\sqrt{11}}\int\frac{1+\cos 2\theta}{2}\, d\theta$$

$$= \frac{-1}{2(x^2+3x+5)} + \frac{2}{11\sqrt{11}}\left(\theta + \frac{1}{2}\sin 2\theta\right) + C$$

$$= \frac{-1}{2(x^2+3x+5)} + \frac{2}{11\sqrt{11}}\theta + \frac{1}{11\sqrt{11}}\sin 2\theta + C$$

$$= \frac{-1}{2(x^2+3x+5)} + \frac{2}{11\sqrt{11}}\tan^{-1}\left(\frac{2t}{\sqrt{11}}\right)\left[\frac{2\left(\frac{2t}{\sqrt{11}}\right)}{1+\frac{4t^2}{11}}\right] + C$$

$$= \frac{-1}{2(x^2+3x+5)} + \frac{2}{11\sqrt{11}}\tan^{-1}\left(\frac{2x+3}{\sqrt{11}}\right)\left[\frac{4\sqrt{11}\,t}{11+4t^2}\right] + C$$

$$= \frac{-1}{2(x^2+3x+5)} + \frac{8t}{11}\times\left(\frac{1}{11+4t^2}\right)\tan^{-1}\left(\frac{2x+3}{\sqrt{11}}\right) + C$$

$$= \frac{-1}{2(x^2+3x+5)} + \frac{8x+12}{121+11(2x+3)^2}\tan^{-1}\left(\frac{2x+3}{\sqrt{11}}\right) + C$$

$$= \frac{-1}{2(x^2+3x+5)} + \frac{(8x+12)}{11(11+4x^2+9+12x)}\tan^{-1}\left(\frac{2x+3}{\sqrt{11}}\right) + C$$

$$= \frac{-1}{2(x^2+3x+5)} + \frac{8x+12}{11(4x^2+12x+20)}\tan^{-1}\left(\frac{2x+3}{\sqrt{11}}\right) + C$$

$$= \frac{-1}{2(x^2+3x+5)} + \frac{2x+3}{11(x^2+3x+5)}\tan^{-1}\left(\frac{2x+3}{\sqrt{11}}\right) + C$$

ILLUSTRATION 138: Find $\int \frac{x^3+3x^2-2x+3}{(1+x^2)^2}dx$

SOLUTION: Let $\frac{x^3+3x^2-2x+3}{(x^2+1)^2} = \frac{Ax+B}{(x^2+1)} + \frac{Cx+D}{(x^2+1)^2}$ ...(1)

$\Rightarrow (x^3+3x^2-2x+3) = (Ax+B)(x^2+1) + (Cx+D)$

$\Rightarrow x^3+3x^2-2x+3 = Ax^3 + (B)x^2 + (A+C)x + (B+D)$

Comparing the coefficients we have

$\Rightarrow$ $A = 1; B = 3, A + C = -2, B + D = 3$

$\Rightarrow$ $A = 1; B = 3, C = -3, D = 0$

$\therefore$ (1) becomes

$$\frac{x^3+3x^2-2x+3}{(x^2+1)^2} = \frac{x+3}{(x^2+1)} + \frac{-3x}{(x^2+1)^2}$$

$$\therefore \int \frac{x^3+3x^2-2x+3}{(x^2+1)^2}dx = \int \frac{x+3}{(x^2+1)}dx - 3\int \frac{x}{(x^2+1)^2}dx$$

$$= \frac{1}{2}\int \frac{2x+6}{(x^2+1)}dx - \frac{3}{2}\int \frac{2x}{(x^2+1)^2}dx = \frac{1}{2}\int \frac{2x}{(x^2+1)}dx + 3\int \frac{1}{x^2+1}dx - \frac{3}{2}\int \frac{2x}{(x^2+1)^2}dx$$

$$= \frac{1}{2}\ln(x^2+1) + 3\tan^{-1}x - \frac{3}{2}\left(\frac{-1}{(x^2+1)}\right) + C = \frac{1}{2}\ln(x^2+1) + 3\tan^{-1}x + \frac{3}{2(x^2+1)} + C$$

INTEGRATION OF RATIONAL FUNCTIONS BY USING OSTROGRADSKY METHOD

Let $\int \frac{P(x)}{Q(x)}dx$ be the integral to be found where $Q(x)$ has repeated roots, then we get

$$\int \frac{P(x)}{Q(x)}dx = \frac{G_0(x)}{G_1(x)} + \int \frac{H_0(x)}{Q(x)/G_1(x)}dx \quad \ldots(1)$$

where $G_1(x)$ = greatest common divisor of $Q(x)$ and $Q'(x)$ (derivative of $Q(x)$).

$G_0(x)$ = polynomial of degree 1 less than that of $G_1(x)$.

$H_0(x)$ = polynomial of degree 1 less than that of $Q(x)/G_1(x)$.

The unknown coefficients of $G_0(x)$ and $H_0(x)$ are obtained by differentiating the identity (1) w.r.t. (x).

ILLUSTRATION 139: Find $\int \frac{1}{(x^3+1)^2}dx$

SOLUTION: Here $\frac{P(x)}{Q(x)} = \frac{1}{(x^3+1)^2}$

$\Rightarrow$ $Q(x) = (x^3 + 1)^2$ and $Q'(x) = 2(x^3 + 1)(3x^2)$

$\therefore$ $G_1(x)$ = Greatest common divisor of $Q(x)$ and $Q'(x) = (x^3 + 1)$

and $\frac{Q(x)}{G_1(x)} = \frac{(x^3+1)^2}{(x^3+1)} = (x^3+1)$

$\therefore$ Let $G_0(x) = Ax^2 + Bx + C$ and $H_0(x) = Dx^2 + Ex + F$

$$\therefore \int \frac{P(x)}{Q(x)}dx = \frac{Ax^2+Bx+C}{(x^3+1)} + \int \frac{Dx^2+Ex+F}{(x^3+1)}dx \quad \ldots(i)$$

Differentiating both sides of (i) w.r.t. x we get

$$\frac{P(x)}{Q(x)} = \frac{1}{(x^3+1)^2} = \frac{(2Ax+B)(x^3+1)-(Ax^2+Bx+C)(3x^2)}{(x^3+1)^2} + \frac{Dx^2+Ex+F}{(x^3+1)}$$

$\Rightarrow\ 1 = (2Ax + B)(x^3 + 1) - (Ax^2 + Bx + C)(3x^2) + (x^3 + 1)(Dx^2 + Ex + F)$

$\Rightarrow\ 1 = Dx^5 + x^4(2A - 3A + E) + x^3(B - 3B + F) + x^2(-3C + D) + x(2A + E) + (B + F)$

$\Rightarrow\ D = 0; -3C + D = 0; -2B + F = 0; B + F = 1; -A + E = 0; 2A + E = 0.$

$\Rightarrow\ D = 0; C = 0; B = \frac{1}{3}; F = \frac{2}{3}; A = 0, E = 0$

$\therefore$ From (i)

$$\int \frac{1}{(x^3+1)^2}dx = \frac{\frac{1}{3}x}{(x^3+1)} + \int \frac{\frac{2}{3}}{(x^3+1)}dx$$

$$= \frac{x}{3(x^3+1)} + \frac{2}{3}\int \frac{1}{(x+1)(x^2-x+1)}dx \qquad \ldots\text{(ii)}$$

Let $\frac{1}{(x+1)(x^2-x+1)} = \frac{L}{(x+1)} + \frac{Mx+N}{(x^2-x+1)}$ ...(iii)

$\Rightarrow\ 1 = L(x^2 - x + 1) + (Mx + N)(x + 1)$

$\Rightarrow\ 1 = x^2(L + M) + x(-L + M + N) + (L + N)$

Comparing the coefficients on both sides, we get

$L + M = 0; -L + M + N = 0; L + N = 1$

$\Rightarrow\ 2M + N = 0$ and $-M + N = 1$

$\Rightarrow\ M = -\frac{1}{3}; N = \frac{2}{3}; L = \frac{1}{3}$

$\therefore$ Using the values of L, M and N in (iii) and from (ii), we have

$$\int \frac{1}{(x^3+1)^2}dx = \frac{x}{3(x^3+1)} + \frac{2}{3}\int \frac{\frac{1}{3}}{(x+1)}dx + \int \frac{-\frac{1}{3}x+\frac{2}{3}}{x^2-x+1}dx$$

$$= \frac{x}{3(x^3+1)} + \frac{2}{9}\ln|x+1| - \frac{1}{3}\int \frac{x-2}{x^2-x+1}dx$$

$$= \frac{x}{3(x^3+1)} + \frac{2}{9}\ln|x+1| - \frac{1}{6}\int \frac{2x-1-3}{(x^2-x+1)}dx$$

$$= \frac{x}{3(x^3+1)} + \frac{2}{9}\ln|x+1| - \frac{1}{6}\ln|x^2-x+1| + \frac{1}{2}\int \frac{dx}{x^2-x+1} \qquad \ldots\text{(iv)}$$

Now, $\int \frac{dx}{x^2-x+1} = \int \frac{dx}{\left(x^2-x+\frac{1}{4}+\frac{3}{4}\right)} = \int \frac{dx}{\left(x-\frac{1}{2}\right)^2+\left(\frac{\sqrt{3}}{2}\right)^2}$

$$= \frac{2}{\sqrt{3}}\tan^{-1}\left(\frac{2x-1}{\sqrt{3}}\right) + C \qquad \ldots\text{(v)}$$

$\therefore$ using (v) in (iv) we get

$$\int \frac{1}{\left(x^3+1\right)^2}dx = \frac{x}{3(x^3+1)} + \frac{2}{9}\ln|x+1| - \frac{1}{6}\ln|x^2-x+1| + \frac{1}{\sqrt{3}}\tan^{-1}\left(\frac{2x-1}{\sqrt{3}}\right) + C.$$

TEXTUAL EXERCISE–6: (SUBJECTIVE)

1. Evaluate the following integrals using partial fraction:

(a) $\int \frac{x^3}{x^6+1}dx$

(b) $\int \frac{dx}{x^3(x^3-1)}$

(c) $\int \frac{dx}{x^4(x^3-1)}$

2. Evaluate the following integrals using partial fraction:

(a) $\int \frac{dx}{(x^2-1)(x^2-4)}$

(b) $\int \frac{f'(x)dx}{\{f(x)+a\}\{f(x)+b\}}$

(c) $\int \frac{x\,dx}{(x+1)(1+x^2)}$

3. Evaluate the following integrals using partial fraction:

(a) $\int \frac{2x^2+1}{(x^2+1)(x^2+3)}dx$

(b) $\int \frac{x^3+2}{(x-1)(x-2)^3}dx$

(c) $\int \frac{dx}{(x-1)(x+1)^6}$

(d) $\int \frac{1}{\cos^4 x \sin^2 x}dx$

(e) $\int \frac{dx}{(x^2+2)^3}$

4. Evaluate the following integrals using partial fraction:

(a) $\int \frac{1-2x}{(3+2x-x^2)}dx$

(b) $\int \frac{x^4-x^2+1}{x^2(x^2+1)^2}dx$

(c) $\int \frac{x^4-x^3+5x^2+x+3}{(x+1)(x^2-x+1)^2}dx$

5. Evaluate the following integrals using partial fraction:

(i) $\int \frac{15x^2-4x-81}{(x-3)(x+4)(x-1)}dx$

(ii) $\int \frac{x^4-3x^2-3x-2}{x^3-x^2-2x}dx$

(iii) $\int \frac{2x^2-3x+3}{x^3-2x^2+x}dx$

(iv) $\int \frac{x\,dx}{(x^3+1)}$

(v) $\int \frac{dx}{(x^2+1)(x^2+4)}$

(vi) $\int \frac{x^4+4x^3+11x^2+12x+8}{(x^2+2x+3)^2(x+1)}dx$

(vii) $\int \frac{5x^3+9x^2-22x-8}{x^3-4x}dx$

(viii) $\int \frac{dx}{(x^2-4x+4)(x^2-4x+5)}$

(ix) $\int \frac{dx}{(x+1)(x^2+1)(x^3+1)}$

(x) $\int \frac{x^3+3}{(x+1)(x^2+1)}$

Answer Keys

1. (a) $\frac{1}{12}\log\left|\frac{x^4-x^2+1}{x^4+2x^2+1}\right|+\frac{1}{2\sqrt{3}}\tan^{-1}\left(\frac{2x^2-1}{\sqrt{3}}\right)+C$ (b) $\frac{1}{3}\ln\left|\frac{x-1}{\sqrt{x^2+x+1}}\right|+\left(-\frac{1}{2x^2}\right)-\frac{1}{\sqrt{3}}\tan^{-1}\left(\frac{2x+1}{\sqrt{3}}\right)+C$

(c) $\frac{1}{3}\ln\left|\frac{x^3-1}{x^3}\right|+\frac{1}{3x^3}+C$

2. (a) $\frac{1}{6}\left[\ln\left|\frac{x-2}{x+2}\right|^{1/2}\cdot\left|\frac{x+1}{x-1}\right|\right]+C$ (b) $\log\left|\frac{f(x)+a}{f(x)+b}\right|+C$ (c) $-\frac{1}{2}\log|1+x|+\frac{1}{4}\log(1+x^2)+\frac{1}{2}\tan^{-1}x+C$

3. (a) $\frac{1}{2}\left[-\tan^{-1}+\frac{5}{\sqrt{3}}\tan^{-1}\left(\frac{x}{\sqrt{3}}\right)\right]+C$ (b) $-\log|x-1|+4\log|x-2|-\frac{2}{x-2}-\frac{5}{(x-2)^2}+C$

(c) $\frac{1}{32}\ln\left|\frac{x-1}{x+1}\right|+\frac{1}{16(x+1)}+\frac{1}{16(x+1)^2}+\frac{1}{24(x+1)^3}+C$ (d) $\tan x+\frac{\tan^3 x}{3}-\cot x-\tan x+C$

(e) $\frac{x}{8(x^2+2)^2}+\frac{3x}{32(x^2+2)}+\frac{3}{32\sqrt{2}}\tan^{-1}\left(\frac{x}{\sqrt{2}}\right)+C$

4. (a) $\frac{5}{4}\ln|3-x|+\frac{3}{4}\ln|1+x|+C$ (b) $\frac{1}{x}-\frac{3x}{2(1+x^2)}-\frac{3}{2}\tan^{-1}x+C$

(c) $\ln|x+1|+\frac{14}{3\sqrt{3}}\tan^{-1}\left(\frac{2x-1}{\sqrt{3}}\right)+\frac{(4x-5)}{3(x^2-x+1)}+C$

5. (i) $3\ln|x-3|+5\ln|x+4|+7\ln|x-1|+C$ or $\ln|(x-3)^2(x+4)^5(x-1)^7|+C$

(ii) $\frac{x^2}{2}+x+\ln|x|-\frac{2}{3}|x-2|-\frac{1}{3}\ln|x+1|+C$

(iii) $3\ln|x|-\frac{2}{(x-1)}-\ln|x-1|+C$ (iv) $-\frac{1}{3}\ln|x+1|+\frac{1}{6}(x^2-x+1)+\frac{1}{\sqrt{3}}\tan^{-1}\left(\frac{2x-1}{\sqrt{3}}\right)+C$

(v) $\frac{1}{3}\tan^{-1}x-\frac{1}{6}\tan^{-1}\left(\frac{x}{2}\right)+C$ (vi) $\ln|x+1|-\frac{(x+2)}{2(x^2+2x+3)}-\frac{1}{2\sqrt{2}}\tan^{-1}\left(\frac{x+1}{\sqrt{2}}\right)+C$

(vii) $5x+\ln(x^2+(x+2)^4)|x-2|^3+C$ (viii) $-\frac{1}{(x-2)}-\tan^{-1}(x-2)+C$

(ix) $-\frac{1}{6(x+1)}+\frac{1}{6}\ln\frac{(1+x)^2}{x^2-x+1}+\frac{1}{2}\tan^{-1}x-\frac{1}{3\sqrt{3}}\tan^{-1}\left(\frac{2x-1}{\sqrt{3}}\right)+C$

(x) $\frac{x+2}{2(x^2+1)}+2\tan^{-1}x+\ln\left(\frac{\sqrt{x+1}}{\sqrt[4]{x^2+1}}\right)+C$

TEXTUAL EXERCISE–6: (OBJECTIVE)

1. If $\int\frac{x\,dx}{(x^2+1)(x-1)}=\ln\left((x^2+1)^a|x-1|^b\right)+\frac{1}{2}\tan^{-1}x+$ C, then $4|b-a|$ equals

(a) 2 (b) 3
(c) 4 (d) None of these

2. If $\int\frac{x^2+2}{(x+1)^2(x-2)}dx=\int\frac{A}{(x+1)^3}dx+\int\frac{B}{(x+1)^2}dx+$ $\int\frac{C}{(x+1)}dx+\int\frac{D}{(x-2)}dx$, then A, B, C, D are respectively

(a) $\frac{1}{3},-1,\frac{2}{9},-\frac{2}{9}$

(b) $-1,\frac{2}{9},-1,-\frac{2}{9}$

(c) $-1,\frac{1}{3},-\frac{2}{9},\frac{2}{9}$

(d) None of these

3. If $\int\frac{x^4+4x^3+11x^2+12x+8}{(x^2+2x+3)^2(x+1)}dx=$

$=-\frac{(x+2)}{2(x^2+2x+3)}-\frac{\sqrt{2}}{4}g(x)+h(x)+C$, then

(a) $g(x)=\tan^{-1}\left(\frac{x+1}{\sqrt{2}}\right)$; $h(x)=\ln|x+1|$

(b) $g(x)=\ln\frac{x+1}{\sqrt{2}}$; $h(x)=\ln\left|(x+1)+\sqrt{(x+1)^2+1}\right|+C$

(c) $g(x)=\ln|x+1|$; $h(x)=\ln\left|(x+1)+\sqrt{(x+1)^2+1}\right|+C$

(d) None of these

4. If $\int \frac{x^3+3}{x^3-3x}dx$ equals

(a) $x-\ln x+\frac{(\sqrt{3}+1)}{2}\ln|x-\sqrt{3}|+\frac{(1-\sqrt{3})}{2}\ln|x+\sqrt{3}|+C$

(b) $2x+\ln x-\frac{(\sqrt{3}+1)}{2}\ln|x+\sqrt{3}|-\frac{(1-\sqrt{3})}{2}\ln|x-\sqrt{3}|+C$

(c) $\ln x+\frac{1}{2}\ln|x+\sqrt{3}|-\frac{1}{2}\ln|x-\sqrt{3}|+C$

(d) None of these

5. If $\int \frac{(x^2+1)}{(x^2-1)(x^2-4)}dx$ equals

(a) $\frac{1}{12}\ln\left|\frac{x-2}{x+2}\right|+\frac{1}{3}\ln\left|\frac{x-1}{x+1}\right|+C$

(b) $\frac{5}{12}\ln\left|\frac{x-2}{x+2}\right|-\frac{1}{3}\ln\left|\frac{x-1}{x+1}\right|+C$

(c) $\frac{1}{6}\ln\left|\frac{x-1}{x+1}\right|+\frac{1}{3}\ln\left|\frac{x-2}{x+2}\right|+C$

(d) None of these

6. $\int \frac{x^5\,dx}{x^3-2x^2-5x+6}$ equals

(a) $\frac{1}{3}x^3+x^2+9x-\frac{1}{6}\ln|x-1|-\frac{82}{15}\ln|x+2|+\frac{248}{10}\ln|x-3|+C$

(b) $\frac{1}{2}x^3-\frac{1}{3}x^2+6x+\frac{1}{6}\ln|x-1|-\frac{82}{15}\ln|x+2|+\frac{240}{10}\ln|x-3|+C$

(c) $\frac{1}{3}x^3+x^2+9x-\frac{1}{6}\ln|x-1|-\frac{92}{15}\ln|x+2|+\frac{248}{10}\ln|x-3|+C$

(d) None of these

7. If $\int \frac{1}{x^3(x-1)^2(x+1)}dx$ equals

(a) $\ln x^2+\frac{2}{x}-\frac{3}{2x^2}-\frac{7}{4}\ln|x-1|+\frac{1}{2(x-1)}+\frac{1}{4}\ln|x+1|+C$

(b) $2\ln x-\frac{1}{x}-\frac{1}{2x^2}+\frac{7}{4}\ln|x-1|+\frac{1}{3(x-1)}+\frac{1}{4}\ln|x+1|+C$

(c) $2\ln|x|-\frac{1}{x}-\frac{1}{2x^2}-\frac{7}{4}\ln|x-1|-\frac{1}{2(x-1)}-\frac{1}{4}\ln|x+1|+C$

(d) None of these

8. If $\int \frac{dx}{(x-1)^2(x-2)(x^2+4)}=-\frac{3}{A}\ln|x-1|+\frac{1}{B|x-1|}+\frac{1}{8}\ln|x-2|-\frac{1}{C}\ln(x^2+4)+\frac{7}{D}\tan^{-1}\left(\frac{x}{2}\right)+K$, then $(A+B+C+D)$ equals

(a) 625 (b) 630

(c) 635 (d) None of these

9. If $\int \frac{x^2+6x-25}{(x^2+4x)^2-25}dx=\frac{1}{2}\ln|x+5|+\frac{3}{A}\ln|x-1|-\frac{1}{B}\ln(x^2+4x+5)+\frac{17}{C}\tan^{-1}(x+2)+K$, then the value of $(A+B+C)$ equals

(a) 5 (b) 25

(c) 15 (d) None of these

10. $\int \frac{(x^2-3x+2)}{x(x^2+2x+1)}dx$ is

(a) $\ln\left|\frac{x^2}{x+1}\right|+\frac{6}{x+1}+C$

(b) $\ln\left|\frac{x^2}{x+1}\right|+\frac{6}{x+1}+C$

(c) $\left|\frac{x^2}{x-1}\right|+\frac{6}{x+1}+C$

(d) None of these

Answer Keys

1. (b) **2.** (c) **3.** (a) **4.** (a) **5.** (b) **6.** (c) **7.** (c) **8.** (b) **9.** (a) **10.** (a)

INTEGRATION OF TRIGONOMETRIC FUNCTIONS

Integral of Type I: $\int \frac{dx}{a\sin^2 x + b\cos^2 x + c}$,

Algorithm:

Step I: Multiply numerator and denominator by $\sec^2 x$.

Step II: Put $\tan x = t$ and $\sec^2 x\, dx = dt$.

Step III: Integral is reduced to the form $\int \frac{dt}{At^2 + Bt + C}$ which can be solved as discussed in earlier topics.

ILLUSTRATION 140: Find the integral $\int \frac{dx}{5 + 4\sin^2 x}$

SOLUTION: Now according to algorithm

Step I: $\int \frac{\sec^2 x}{5\sec^2 x + 4\tan^2 x} dx = \int \frac{\sec^2 x}{5(1+\tan^2 x) + 4\tan^2 x} dx$

Step II: Put $\tan x = t$, $dt = (dx)(\sec^2 x)$

$\Rightarrow I = \int \frac{1}{5(1+t^2) + 4t^2} dt$

Step III: $I = \int \frac{1}{9t^2+1} dt = \frac{1}{9}\int \frac{1}{t^2 + \left(\frac{1}{3}\right)^2} dt = \frac{1}{9} \times \frac{1}{1/3} \tan^{-1}\left(\frac{t}{1/3}\right) + C$

$= \frac{1}{3}\tan^{-1}(3t) + C = \frac{1}{3}\tan^{-1}(3\tan x) + C$.

ILLUSTRATION 141: Find the integral $\int \frac{dx}{\sin^2 x + 2\cos^2 x + 3\sin x \cos x}$.

SOLUTION: ***Step I:*** Multiply both numerator and denominator by $\sec^2 x$, we get

$I = \int \frac{\sec^2 x}{\tan^2 x + 2 + 3\tan x} dx$

Step II: Put $t = \tan x$

$\Rightarrow \frac{dt}{dx} = \sec^2 x \qquad \Rightarrow dx = \frac{dt}{\sec^2 x}$

Step III: $I = \int \frac{1}{t^2 + 3t + 2} dt = \int \frac{1}{(t+2)(t+1)} dt$

$\Rightarrow \int \left(\frac{-1}{(t+2)} + \frac{1}{(t+1)}\right) dt \Rightarrow -\int \frac{1}{t+2} dt + \int \frac{1}{t+1} dt$

$\Rightarrow -\ln|t+2| + \ln|t+1| + C$

$= \ln\left|\frac{t+1}{t+2}\right| + C = \ln\left|\frac{\tan x + 1}{\tan x + 2}\right| + C$.

Integral of Type II: $\int \frac{dx}{a+b\sin x}$, $\int \frac{dx}{a+b\cos x}$, $\int \frac{dx}{a\sin x+b\cos x}$, $\int \frac{\cos x\, dx}{a+b\cos x}$, $\int \frac{\sin x\, dx}{a+b\sin x}$.

Algorithm Step I Put $\tan\frac{x}{2}=t$ and $\frac{1}{2}\sec^2\frac{x}{2}\,dx = dt$ and $dx = \frac{2dt}{1+t^2}$

Step II: Take $\sin x = \frac{2\tan(x/2)}{1+\tan^2(x/2)} = \frac{2t}{1+t^2}$ and $\cos x = \frac{1-\tan^2(x/2)}{1+\tan^2(x/2)} = \frac{1-t^2}{1+t^2}$.

Step III: The integral is reduced to the form $\int \frac{f(t)dt}{At^2+Bt+C}$. where $f(t)$ is a polynomial in t.

ILLUSTRATION 142: Evaluate the integral $\int \frac{dx}{5+4\cos x}$.

SOLUTION: ***Step I:*** Put $\tan\frac{x}{2}=t \Rightarrow dt = \frac{1}{2}\times\sec^2\frac{x}{2}dx \Rightarrow dx = \frac{2dt}{1+t^2}$

Step II: $I = \int \frac{1}{\left\{5+4\left(\frac{1-\tan^2(x/2)}{1+\tan^2(x/2)}\right)\right\}}\frac{2dt}{1+t^2}$

Step III: $I = \int \frac{1}{\left\{5+4\frac{(1-t^2)}{(1+t^2)}\right\}}\frac{2dt}{(1+t^2)}$

$$\Rightarrow I = 2\int\frac{dt}{9+t^2} = 2\int\frac{1}{t^2+3^2}dt = 2\times\frac{1}{3}\tan^{-1}\left(\frac{t}{3}\right)+C = \frac{2}{3}\tan^{-1}\left(\frac{\tan\frac{x}{2}}{3}\right)+C.$$

ILLUSTRATION 143: Evaluate the integral $\int \frac{1}{5\sin x+4\cos x}dx$

SOLUTION: ***Step I:*** Put $\tan x/2 = t$ and $\frac{1}{2}\sec^2 x\, dx = dt$

$\Rightarrow dx = \frac{2dt}{1+t^2}$

Step II: Put $\sin x = \frac{2\tan(x/2)}{1+\tan^2(x/2)} = \frac{2t}{1+t^2}$ and $\cos x = \frac{1-\tan^2(x/2)}{1+\tan^2(x/2)} = \frac{1-t^2}{1+t^2}$

Step III: $\int \frac{1}{\left\{5\left(\frac{2t}{1+t^2}\right)+4\left(\frac{1-t^2}{1+t^2}\right)\right\}}\cdot\frac{2dt}{1+t^2} = \int\frac{(1+t^2)}{(10t+4-4t^2)}\frac{2dt}{(1+t^2)}$

$$= \int\frac{1}{-2t^2+2+5t}dt = \int\frac{1}{-2t^2+5t+2}dt = \frac{-1}{2}\int\frac{1}{t^2-\frac{5t}{2}-1}dt \quad \ldots(1)$$

$$\text{Now } t^2-\frac{5t}{2}-1 = \left(t-\frac{5}{4}\right)^2-\frac{41}{16} \quad \ldots(2)$$

Putting (2) in (1), we get $I = -\frac{1}{2}\int \frac{1}{\left(t-\frac{5}{4}\right)^2 - \frac{41}{16}} dt$

Put $t - \frac{5}{4} = m$ $\Rightarrow dm = dt$

$$\Rightarrow I = -\frac{1}{2}\int \frac{1}{m^2 - \frac{41}{16}} dm = -\frac{1}{\sqrt{41}} \ln\left|\frac{m - \frac{\sqrt{41}}{4}}{m + \frac{\sqrt{41}}{4}}\right| + C$$

$$= \frac{1}{\sqrt{41}} \ln\left|\frac{4m+\sqrt{41}}{4m-\sqrt{41}}\right| + C = \frac{1}{\sqrt{41}} \ln\left|\frac{4t-5+\sqrt{41}}{4t-5-\sqrt{41}}\right| + C$$

ILLUSTRATION 144: Evaluate the integral $\int \frac{\cos x}{5 - 3\cos x} dx$

SOLUTION: ***Step I:*** Put $t = \tan \frac{x}{2}$

$\Rightarrow dt = \frac{1}{2}\sec^2 \frac{x}{2} dx$ $\Rightarrow dx = \frac{2\,dt}{1+t^2}$

Step II: $I = \int \frac{\left(1-\tan^2(x/2)\right)/\left(1+\tan^2 x/2\right)}{5 - 3\left(\frac{1-\tan^2 x/2}{1+\tan^2 x/2}\right)} dx = \int \frac{\left(1-\tan^2 x/2\right)}{5\left(1+\tan^2 x/2\right) - 3\left(1-\tan^2 x/2\right)} dx$

$$= \int \frac{1-t^2}{\left(2+8t^2\right)} \frac{2dt}{\left(1+t^2\right)} = \frac{1}{2}\int \frac{1-t^2}{\left(1+4t^2\right)} \frac{2dt}{\left(1+t^2\right)} = \frac{1}{2}\int \left\{ \frac{\left(\frac{3}{2}+t^2\right)}{\left(1+4t^2\right)} - \frac{\frac{1}{2}\left(1+4t^2\right)}{\left(1+t^2\right)} \right\} dt$$

(By using partial fractions)

$$= \frac{1}{2}\int \frac{\left(\frac{3}{2}\right)dt}{\left(1+4t^2\right)} + \frac{1}{8}\int \frac{4t^2+1-1}{4t^2+1} dt - \frac{1}{4}\int \frac{1}{1+t^2} dt - \int \frac{t^2+1-1}{1+t^2} dt$$

$$= \frac{3}{4} \times \frac{1}{2} \tan^{-1}(2t) + \frac{1}{8}t - \frac{1}{8} \times \frac{1}{2} \tan^{-1}(2t) - \frac{1}{4}\tan^{-1} t - t + \tan^{-1} t + C$$

$$= \frac{5}{16}\tan^{-1}(2t) - \frac{7}{8}t + \frac{3}{4}\tan^{-1} t + C = \frac{5}{16}\tan^{-1}\left(2\tan\frac{x}{2}\right) - \frac{7}{8}\left(\tan\frac{x}{2}\right) + \frac{3}{8}x + C.$$

Integral of type III: $I = \int \frac{\overbrace{a\sin x + b\cos x}^{N^r}}{\underbrace{c\sin x + d\cos x}_{D^r}} dx$

Algorithm:

Step I: Express the numerator $N^r = A\left(\frac{d}{dx} D^r\right) + B\left(D^r\right)$

Step II: Obtain the constants A and B which reduces the integral to the sum of two integrals.

Step III: Solve the above integrals as $I = A(\ln |D^r| + Bx + C)$.

ILLUSTRATION 145: Evaluate the integral $\int \frac{11\cos x - 16\sin x}{2\cos x + 5\sin x}dx$

SOLUTION: ***Step I:*** Express the numerator

$11\cos x - 16\sin x = A\left(\frac{d}{dx}(2\cos x + 5\sin x)\right) + B(2\cos x + \sin x)$

$\Rightarrow$ $11\cos x - 16\sin x = A(-2\sin x + 5\cos x) + B(2\cos x + 5\sin x)$

$\Rightarrow$ $11\cos x - 16\sin x = (-2A + 5B)\sin x + (5A + 2B)\cos x$

$\Rightarrow$ $-2A + 5B = -16$ and $5A + 2B = 11$ $\quad\Rightarrow 2A - 5B = 16$ ...(1)

and $5A + 2B = 11$ ....(2)

Solving (1) and (2), we get $A = 3, B = -2$

$\therefore\ I = \int \frac{3(-2\sin x + 5\cos x) + (-2)(2\cos x + 5\sin x)}{2\cos x + 5\sin x}dx$

$= \int \frac{3(-2\sin x + 5\cos x)}{2\cos x + 5\sin x}dx - 2\int 1.dx = 3\int \frac{dm}{m} - 2x + C$

$= 3\ln|2\cos x + 5\sin x| - 2x + C$ Ans.

Integral of type IV: $\int \frac{a\sin x + b\cos x + c}{p\sin x + q\cos x + r}dx$

Algorithm:

Step I: Express the numerator in the form $\ell\left(\frac{d}{dx}(Dr)\right) + m(Dr) + n$

Step II: $a\sin x + b\cos x + c = l(p\cos x - q\sin x) + m(p\sin x + q\cos x + r) + n$ where l, m and n are constants. Comparing the coefficients of $\sin x$, $\cos x$ and constant terms on both sides and determine l, m, n.

Step III: We have $I = l\ln(\text{denominator}) + mx + n \int \frac{dx}{p\sin x + q\cos x + r} + C$

ILLUSTRATION 146: Evaluate the integral $\int \frac{6 + 3\sin x + 14\cos x}{3 + 4\sin x + 5\cos x}dx$

SOLUTION: ***Algorithm:***

Step I: $6 + 3\sin x + 14\cos x = l\left(\frac{d}{dx}(3 + 4\sin x + 5\cos x)\right) + m(3 + 4\sin x + 5\cos x) + n$

$\Rightarrow$ $6 + 3\sin x + 14\cos x = \ln(0 + 4\cos x - 5\sin x) + m(3 + 4\sin x + 5\cos x) + n$

$l(0 + 4\cos x - 5\sin x) + m(3 + 4\sin x + 5\cos x) + n$

Step II: Equating the coefficients we have $3 = (-5l) + (4m)$; $14 = 4l + 5m$;
Solving these two equations $m = 2$; $l = 1$ and $6 = n + 3m \Rightarrow n = 0$.

Step III: $I = \int \frac{6 + 3\sin x + 14\cos x}{3 + 4\sin x + 5\cos x}dx = \int \frac{(0 + 4\cos x - 5\sin x) + 2(3 + 4\sin x + 5\cos x)}{(3 + 4\sin x + 5\cos x)}dx$

$= \int \frac{(4\cos x - 5\sin x)}{3 + 4\sin x + 5\cos x}dx + 2\int 1.\,dx = \int \frac{dt}{t} + 2x + C$; where $t = 3 + 4\sin x + \cos x$

$= \ln|3 + 4\sin x + 5\cos x| + 2x + C.$

Integral of type v: $\int(\sin^m x \cdot \cos^n x)\, dx$; $m, n \in \mathbb{Z}$,

Depending upon the nature of m and n (odd or even) we have following four cases.

Case I: If one of m and n is odd positive integer and other is an even positive integer.

Case II: If both m and n are odd positive integers.

Case III: If m and n are integers such that $(m + n)$ is a negative even integer.

Case IV: If both m and n are even positive integers.

Let us discuss algorithm of solving integrals of each case with their applications.

Case (i) If one of m and n is odd positive integer and other is an even positive integer. Let n is even and m is odd then,

$$I = \int \cos^n x.\sin^{m-1} x.\sin x\, dx$$

put $\cos x = t$ and $\sin x\, dx = -dt$

$$\therefore \quad I = \int t^n.(1-t^2)^{\frac{m-1}{2}}(-dt)$$

Expand binomially and integrate term-by-term.

Now let n to odd and m to even, then $\int \sin^m x \cos^{n-1} x \cos x\, dx$ put $\sin x = t$

$\Rightarrow \cos x\, dx = dt$

$\therefore \quad I = \int t^m\left(1-t^2\right)^{(n-1)/2} dt$ expand binomially and integrate term-by-term.

i.e., put the trigonometric ratio with even power equal to 't'.

ILLUSTRATION 147: Evaluate the following integral $\int \sin^5 x \cos^4 x\, dx$

SOLUTION: Here $m = 5$ (odd) and $n = 4$ (even)

Put $t = \cos x \quad \Rightarrow dt = -\sin x\, dx$

$$\Rightarrow I = \int \sin^4 x \cos^4 x \sin x dx = -\int\left(1-\cos^2 x\right)^2 t^4\, dt$$

$$= -\int\left(1-t^2\right)^2 t^4\, dt = -\int\left(1+t^4-2t^2\right)t^4 dt$$

$$= -\int\left(t^4+t^8-2t^6\right)dt = -\left[\frac{t^5}{5}+\frac{t^9}{9}-\frac{2t^7}{7}\right]+C$$

$$= -\left[\frac{(\cos x)^5}{5}+\frac{(\cos x)^9}{9}-\frac{2}{7}(\cos x)^7\right]+C$$

ILLUSTRATION 148: Evaluate the integral $\int \sin^4 x \cos^3 x\, dx$

SOLUTION: Here m is even and n is odd

$\therefore$ put $t = \sin x \quad \Rightarrow dx = \dfrac{dt}{\cos x}$

$$\Rightarrow I = \int t^4 \cos^2 x\, dt = \int t^4\left(1-t^2\right)dt$$

$$= \int\left(t^4-t^6\right)dt = \frac{t^5}{5}-\frac{t^7}{7}+C = \frac{(\sin x)^5}{5}-\frac{(\sin x)^7}{7}+C.$$

Case (ii): If m and n both are odd, then

if $m > n$, put $\sin x = t$;

and if $m < n$, put $\cos x = t$;

if $m = n$, put $\sin x = t$;

or $\cos x = t$

i.e., put the trigonometric ratio with greater degree equal to 't'.

$$\therefore \quad I = \int \cos^n x.\sin^{m-1} x.\sin x dx = \int t^n.(1-t^2)^{\frac{m-1}{2}}(-dt)$$

for $m > n$; $t = \cos x$

and $I = \int \sin^m x.\cos^{n-1} x.\cos x\, dx$

$= \int t^m(1-t^2)^{\frac{n-1}{2}} dt$ for $m > n$; $t = \sin x$,

then, expand binomially and integrate term-by-term.

ILLUSTRATION 149: Evaluate the following integral $\int \sin^5 x \cos^7 x\, dx$

SOLUTION: As here both m and n are odd and $m < n$, so put $\cos x = t$, $dx = \frac{-dt}{\sin x}$

$$= \int \sin^5 x\, t^7 \frac{(-dt)}{\sin x} \Rightarrow -\int \left(1-\cos^2 x\right)^2 t^7 dl$$

$$= -\int \left(1-t^2\right)^2 t^7 dt = -\int \left(1+t^4-2t^2\right) t^7 dt$$

$$= -\int (t^7+t^{11}-2t^9)dt = -\frac{t^8}{8} - \frac{t^{12}}{12} + \frac{2t^{10}}{10} + C$$

$$= \frac{-(\cos x)^8}{8} - \frac{(\cos x)^{12}}{12} + \frac{(\cos x)^{10}}{5} + C$$

Case (iii): If $m + n$ is even and $(m + n)$ is a negative integer, then convert the given integrand in terms of tan x and sec x.

$$I = \int \sin^m x.\cos^n x\, dx = \int \frac{\sin^m x}{\cos^m x}.\cos^{m+n} x\, dx$$

then put $\tan x = t$ $= \int \frac{\sin^m x}{\cos^m x}.\cos^{m+n+2} x.\sec^2 x\, dx$

$$= \int t^m.(1+t^2)^{\frac{-m-n-2}{2}}.dt$$

Now expand binomially and integrate term-by-term.

ILLUSTRATION 150: Evaluate the following integral $\int \sin^9 x \cos^{-11} x\, dx$

SOLUTION: $m + n = 9 - 11 = -2$ is even and belong to $\mathbb{Z}$, proceeding according to algorithm,

$$I = \int \frac{\sin^9 x}{\cos^9 x} \cos^9 x \cos^{-11} x\, dx = \int \tan^9 x \cos^{-2} x\, dx = \int \tan^9 x \sec^2 x\, dx$$

Put $t = \tan x$ $\Rightarrow \frac{dt}{\sec^2 x} = dx$

$$\therefore\ I = \int t^9\, dt = \frac{t^{10}}{10} + C = \frac{(\tan x)^{10}}{10} + C$$

Case (iv): If m and n are even, then convert the given integrand in terms of multiple angles by using the formulae; $2 \cos x \cos y = \cos(x + y) + \cos(x - y)$; $2 \sin x \cos x = \sin 2x$ etc.

ILLUSTRATION 151: Find the integral $\int \sin^4 x \cos^6 x\, dx$

SOLUTION: Let $I = \int \sin^4 x \cos^6 x\, dx = \frac{1}{2}.\frac{1}{2^4}\int \left(2^4 \sin^4 x \cos^4 x\right)\left(2\cos^2 x\right) dx$

$$= \frac{1}{32}\int \left(16\sin^4 x \cos^4 x\right)\left(2\cos^2 x\right) dx = \frac{1}{32}\int \left(\sin^2 2x\right)^2 \left(2\cos^2 x\right) dx$$

$$= \frac{1}{32} \times \frac{1}{4} \int (1-\cos 4x)^2 (1+\cos 2x)\, dx$$

$$= \frac{1}{128}\int\left(1+\cos^2 4x-2\cos 4x\right)\left(1+\cos 2x\right)dx$$

$$= \frac{1}{128}\int\left\{\left(1+\cos^2 4x\right)\left(1+\cos 2x\right)-2\cos 4x\left(1+\cos 2x\right)\right\}dx$$

$$= \frac{1}{128}\int\left\{\left(1+\cos 2x+\cos^2 4x+\cos 2x\cos^2 4x\right)-2\cos 4x\left(1+\cos 2x\right)\right\}dx$$

$$= \frac{1}{128}\int\left(1+\cos 2x+\frac{1}{2}\left(1+\cos 8x\right)+\frac{1}{2}\cos 2x\left(1+\cos 8x\right)-2\cos 4x-2\cos 4x\cos 2x\right)dx$$

$$= \frac{1}{128}\int\begin{pmatrix}1+\cos 2x+\frac{1}{2}+\frac{\cos 8x}{2}+\frac{1}{2}\cos 2x+\frac{1}{2}\cos 2x\cos 8x- \\ 2\cos 4x-\cos(4x-2x)-\cos(4x+2x)\end{pmatrix}dx$$

$$= \frac{1}{128}\int\begin{pmatrix}\frac{3}{2}+\cos 2x+\frac{1}{2}\cos 8x+\frac{1}{2}\cos 2x+\frac{1}{4}\left(\cos\left(8x-2x\right)\right)+ \\ \frac{1}{4}\cos\left(8x+2x\right)-2\cos 4x-\cos 2x-\cos 6x\end{pmatrix}dx$$

$$= \frac{1}{128}\int\begin{pmatrix}\frac{3}{2}+\cos 2x+\frac{1}{2}\cos 8x+\frac{1}{2}\cos 2x+\frac{1}{4}\cos 2x+ \\ \frac{1}{4}\cos 6x+\frac{1}{4}\cos 10x-2\cos 4x-\cos 2x-\cos 6x\end{pmatrix}dx$$

$$= \frac{1}{128}\int\left(\frac{3}{2}+\frac{1}{2}\cos 2x-2\cos 4x-\frac{3}{4}\cos 6x+\frac{1}{2}\cos 8x+\frac{1}{4}\cos 10x\right)dx$$

$$= \frac{1}{128}\int\left(\frac{3}{2}x+\frac{1}{4}\sin 2x-\frac{1}{2}\sin 4x-\frac{3}{24}\cos 6x+\frac{1}{16}\sin 8x+\frac{1}{40}\sin 10x\right)dx$$

Integral of type V: (a) $\int(\tan^n x.\sec^m x)\,dx$

If m is even and $\in \mathbb{Z}^+$

substitute $\tan x = z$, $\sec^2 x\, dx = dz$

If n is odd and $\in \mathbb{Z}^+$

substitute $\sec x = z$; $\sec x \tan x\, dx = dz$

(b) $\int(\cot^n x.\operatorname{cosec}^m x)\,dx$

If m is even and $\in \mathbb{Z}^+$,

substitute $\cot x = z$, $\operatorname{cosec}^2 x\, dx = -dz$

If n is odd and $\in \mathbb{Z}^+$,

substitute $\operatorname{cosec} x = z$, $\operatorname{cosec} x \cot x\, dx = -dz$

ILLUSTRATION 152: Find the integral $\int \tan^4 x.\sec^6 x\, dx$

SOLUTION: Comparing the given integral with $\int \tan^n x.\sec^m x\, dx$ we have $n = 4$, $m = 6$.

Since m is even, put $t = \tan x$

$$\Rightarrow\quad dx = \frac{dt}{\sec^2 x} \qquad\qquad \Rightarrow I = \int t^4.\sec^4 x\, dt$$

$$= \int t^4\left(1+\tan^2 x\right)^2 dt = \int t^4\left(1+t^2\right)^2 dt = \int t^4\left(1+t^4+2t^2\right)dt$$

$$= \int\left(t^4+t^8+2t^6\right)dt = \frac{t^5}{5}+\frac{t^9}{9}+\frac{2t^7}{7}+C = \frac{(\tan x)^5}{5}+\frac{(\tan x)^9}{9}+2\frac{(\tan x)^7}{7}+C$$

ILLUSTRATION 153: Find the integral $\int \tan^5 x.sec^6 x\, dx$

SOLUTION: Since, here n is odd, then put $z = \sec x$ and $\frac{dz}{dx} = (\sec x)(\tan x)$

$\Rightarrow$ sec tan $x\, dx = dz$ $\qquad I = \int \tan^4 x \sec^5 x\, dz$

$$= \int (\sec^2 x - 1)^2 . z^5\, dz = \int (z^2 - 1)^2 . z^5 dz = \int (z^4 + 1 - 2z^2) z^5\, dz$$

$$= \int (z^9 + z^5 - 2z^7) dz = \left[\frac{z^{10}}{10} + \frac{z^6}{6} - \frac{2z^8}{8}\right] + C = \left[\frac{(\sec x)^{10}}{10} + \frac{(\sec x)^6}{6} - \frac{1}{4}(\sec x)^8\right] + C$$

ILLUSTRATION 154: Find the integral $\int \cot^4 x \operatorname{cosec}^6 x\, dx$

SOLUTION: On comparing the given integral with $\int (\cot^n x.\operatorname{cosec}^m x) dx$

We have $n = 4$, $m = 6$ (even). Let us substitute $\cot x = z$ and $\frac{dz}{dx} = -\operatorname{cosec}^2 x$

$$\Rightarrow I = -\int z^4 (\operatorname{cosec}^4 x) dx$$

$$= -\int z^4 (1 + \cot^2 x)^2\, dz = -\int z^4 (1 + z^2)^2\, dz \Rightarrow -\int z^4 (1 + z^4 + 2z^2) dz$$

$$= -\int (z^4 + z^8 + 2z^6) dz \qquad \Rightarrow -\left[\frac{z^5}{5} + \frac{7^9}{9} + \frac{2z^7}{7}\right] + C$$

$$= -\left[\frac{(\cot x)^5}{5} + \frac{(\cot x)^9}{9} + \frac{2}{7}(\cot x)^7\right] + C \text{ Ans.}$$

Integral of type (VI): $\int R(\sin x.\cos x, \sin x \pm \cos x)\, dx$

Algorithm: Substitute $\sin x \pm \cos x = t$ and $(\cos x \pm \sin x)dx = dt$

$\Rightarrow$ $1 \pm 2\sin x.\cos x = t^2$,

$$\int R\left(\frac{t^2 - 1}{\pm 2}, t, \sqrt{t^2 \pm 2(t^2 - 1)}\right)$$

ILLUSTRATION 155: Find the following integral $\int \frac{\sin x - \cos x}{(\sin x + \cos x)\sqrt{2\sin^2 x.\cos^2 x - \sin x.\cos x}} dx$

SOLUTION: $\int \frac{\sin x - \cos x}{(\sin x + \cos x)\sqrt{2\sin^2 x.\cos^2 x - \sin x.\cos x}} dx$

Put $\sin x + \cos x = t$; $dt = (\cos x - \sin x)\, dx$

$$\Rightarrow dx = \frac{dt}{-(\sin x - \cos x)}$$

$\Rightarrow$ $\sin^2 x + \cos^2 x + 2 \sin x \cos x = t^2$

$\Rightarrow$ $2 \sin x \cos x = t^2 - 1$

or $\sin x \cos x = \frac{(t^2 - 1)}{2}$

$$\therefore\ I=\int\frac{-1}{t\sqrt{2\left(\frac{(t^2-1)}{2}\right)^2-\frac{(t^2-1)}{2}}}dt=\int\frac{-\sqrt{2}}{t\sqrt{(t^2-1)^2-(t^2-1)}}dt=\int\frac{-\sqrt{2}}{t\sqrt{t^4+t^2-2t^2-t^2+1}}dt$$

$$=\int\frac{-\sqrt{2}}{t\sqrt{t^4-2t^2+1}}dt=\int\frac{-\sqrt{2}}{t\sqrt{(t^2-1)^2}}dt=\int\frac{-\sqrt{2}}{t\,|t^2+1|}dt$$

Case (i) $t^2>1$ then $|t^2-1|=t^2-1$

$$\therefore\ I=\int\frac{-\sqrt{2}}{t(t^2-1)}dt=-\sqrt{2}\int\frac{1}{t^3(1-t^{-2})}dt=-\sqrt{2}\int\frac{t^{-3}}{(1-t^{-2})}dt$$

put $1-t^{-2}=z$ $\Rightarrow 2t^{-3}\,dt=dz$ $\Rightarrow t^{-3}dt=\frac{dz}{2}$

$$\therefore\ \frac{-\sqrt{2}}{2}\int\frac{dz}{z}=\frac{-1}{\sqrt{2}}\ln|z|+C=\frac{-1}{\sqrt{2}}\ln|1-t^2|+C=\frac{-1}{\sqrt{2}}\ln\left|\frac{t^2-1}{t^2}\right|+C\ \text{ as } t^2>1$$

Case (ii): $t^2<1$ $\Rightarrow |t^2-1|=-(1-t^2)$

$$\therefore\ I=\int\frac{-\sqrt{2}\,dt}{-t(1-t^2)}=\int\frac{\sqrt{2}\,dt}{t^3(t^{-2}-1)}=\int\frac{\sqrt{2}\,t^{-3}\,dt}{(t^{-2}-1)}$$

Put $t^{-2}-1=z\Rightarrow -2t^{-3}\,dt=dz$ $\Rightarrow t^{-3}dt=-\frac{1}{2}dz$

$$\therefore\ I=\int\frac{\sqrt{2}\left(-\frac{1}{2}\right)dz}{z}=-\frac{1}{\sqrt{2}}\int\frac{dz}{z}=-\frac{1}{\sqrt{2}}\ln|z|+C$$

$$=-\frac{1}{\sqrt{2}}\ln|t^2-1|+C=-\frac{1}{\sqrt{2}}\ln\left|\frac{1-t^2}{t^2}\right|+C=-\frac{1}{\sqrt{2}}\ln\left(\frac{1-t^2}{t^2}\right)+C\ \text{ as } 1-t^2>0$$

$\therefore$ from case (i) and case (ii) we see that

$$I=-\frac{1}{\sqrt{2}}\ln\left|\frac{t^2-1}{t^2}\right|+C=-\frac{1}{\sqrt{2}}\ln\left|\frac{2\sin x\cos x}{1+2\sin x\cos x}\right|+C.$$

ILLUSTRATION 156: Find the integral $\int\frac{dx}{(6\sin x-8\cos x)^2}$

SOLUTION: ***Step I:*** Multiplying numerator and denominator by $\sec^2 x$, we have

$$I=\int\frac{\sec^2 x}{(6\sin x-8\cos x)^2\sec^2 x}dx=\int\frac{\sec^2 x}{(6\sin x\sec x-8\cos x\sec x)^2}dx=\int\frac{\sec^2 x}{(6\tan x-8)^2}dx,$$

Now put $t=\tan x$ and $\frac{dt}{dx}=\sec^2 x$ $\Rightarrow dx=\frac{dt}{\sec^2 x}$

$$I=\int\frac{1}{(6t-8)^2}dt=\frac{1}{(6)^2}\int(t-4/3)^{-2}dt=\frac{1}{36}\left[\frac{(t-4/3)^{-2+1}}{-2+1}\right]+C$$

$$=\frac{-1}{36}\left[\frac{1}{(t-4/3)}\right]+C=\frac{-1}{36}\left[\frac{3}{3\tan x-4}\right]=\frac{-1}{12}\left(\frac{1}{3\tan x-4}\right)+C$$

ILLUSTRATION 157: Find the integral $\int \frac{1}{9-\cos^2 x} dx$

SOLUTION: Multiplying numerator and denominator by $\sec^2 x$, we have

$$I = \int \frac{\sec^2 x}{9\sec^2 x - \cos^2 x \sec^2 x} dx = \int \frac{\sec^2 x}{9\sec^2 x - 1} dx = \int \frac{\sec^2 x}{8+9\tan^2 x} dx$$

Put $\tan x = t$

$$\Rightarrow \frac{dt}{dx} = \sec^2 x, I = \int \frac{1}{8+9t^2} dt = \frac{1}{9}\int \frac{1}{t^2+\frac{8}{9}} dt$$

$$= \frac{1}{9}\int \frac{1}{t^2+\left(\frac{2\sqrt{2}}{3}\right)^2} dt = \frac{1}{3} \times \frac{1}{2\sqrt{2}} . \tan^{-1}\left(\frac{3t}{2\sqrt{2}}\right) + C = \frac{1}{6\sqrt{2}} \tan^{-1}\left(\frac{3\tan x}{2\sqrt{2}}\right) + C.$$

ILLUSTRATION 158: Find the integral $\int \frac{\sin 2x}{(2+3\cos x)^2} dx$

SOLUTION: Since, $\sin 2x = 2 \sin x \cos x$. So, we can substitute, $2 + 3\cos x = t$

$$\Rightarrow \cos x = \frac{(t-2)}{3} \text{ and } \frac{dt}{dx} = 0 - 3\sin x \quad \Rightarrow \left(dx = \frac{-dt}{3\sin x}\right)$$

Now, on substituting to integrand function we get $I = \frac{2}{3}\int \frac{\cos x}{t^2}(-dt)$

$$= \frac{-2}{3}\int \frac{(t-2)}{3t^2} dt = \frac{-2}{9}\int \frac{(t-2)}{t^2} dt = \frac{2}{9}\int \left(-\frac{1}{t}+\frac{2}{t^2}\right) dt = \frac{2}{9}\left[-\ln|t| - \frac{2}{t}\right] + C$$

$$= \frac{-2}{9}\left[\ln t + \frac{2}{t}\right] + C = \frac{-2}{9}\left[\ln|2+3\cos x| + \frac{2}{(2+3\cos x)}\right] + C$$

ILLUSTRATION 159: Find the integral $\int \frac{1}{\sin^4 x + \cos^4 x} dx$

SOLUTION: $I = \int \frac{1}{\sin^4 x+\cos^4 x} dx$; multiplying numerator and denominator by $\sec^4 x$, we get

$I = \int \frac{\sec^4 x}{\tan^4 x + 1} dx$. Now, put $\tan x = t$; $\frac{dt}{dx} = \sec^2 x$

$$\Rightarrow dx = \frac{dt}{\sec^2 x}$$

$$\Rightarrow I = \int \frac{\sec^2 x}{t^4+1} dt = \int \frac{1+\tan^2 x}{t^4+1} dt = \int \frac{1+t^2}{t^4+1} dt$$

Now, dividing both numerator and denominator by (t^2) we have

$$\Rightarrow I = \int \frac{\left(\frac{1}{t^2}+1\right) dt}{t^2+\frac{1}{t^2}+2-2} = \int \frac{1+\frac{1}{t^2}}{\left(t-\frac{1}{t}\right)^2+2} dt = \int \frac{1}{m^2+\left(\sqrt{2}\right)^2} dm \text{ where } m = t - \frac{1}{t}$$

$$\Rightarrow I = \frac{1}{\sqrt{2}}\tan^{-1}\left(\frac{m}{\sqrt{2}}\right)+C = \frac{1}{\sqrt{2}}\tan^{-1}\left(\frac{t^2-1}{\sqrt{2}t}\right)+C$$

$$= \frac{1}{\sqrt{2}}\tan^{-1}\left(\frac{\tan^2 x-1}{\sqrt{2}\tan x}\right)+C.$$

ILLUSTRATION 160: Find the integral $\int \frac{\sin\left(\frac{x}{2}\right)-\cos\left(\frac{x}{2}\right)}{3+2\sin\left(\frac{x}{2}\right)\cos\left(\frac{x}{2}\right)}dx$

SOLUTION: Consider $I = \int \frac{\sin\left(\frac{x}{2}\right)-\cos\left(\frac{x}{2}\right)}{3+\sin x}dx = \int \frac{\sin\left(\frac{x}{2}\right)-\cos\left(\frac{x}{2}\right)}{2+\left(\sin\frac{x}{2}+\cos\frac{x}{2}\right)^2}dx$

Put $t = \left(\sin\frac{x}{2}+\cos\frac{x}{2}\right)$

$$\Rightarrow \frac{dt}{dx} = \frac{1}{2}\left(\cos\frac{x}{2}-\sin\frac{x}{2}\right) \qquad \Rightarrow dx = \frac{2\,dt}{\left(\cos\frac{x}{2}-\sin\frac{x}{2}\right)}$$

$$\Rightarrow I = -\int\frac{2dt}{t^2+2} = -2\int\frac{dt}{t^2+\left(\sqrt{2}\right)^2} = \frac{-2}{\sqrt{2}}.\tan^{-1}\left(\frac{t}{\sqrt{2}}\right)+C$$

$$= -\sqrt{2}\tan^{-1}\left(\frac{1}{\sqrt{2}}\left(\sin\frac{x}{2}+\cos\frac{x}{2}\right)\right)+C.$$

ILLUSTRATION 161: Find the integral $\int \frac{\cos 4x}{10+\sin 8x}dx$

SOLUTION: Consider $I = \int \frac{\cos 4x}{10+\sin 8x}dx$

$$= \frac{1}{2}\int\frac{2\cos 4x}{10+\sin 8x}dx = \frac{1}{2}\int\frac{\cos 4x+\sin 4x+\cos 4x-\sin 4x}{10+\sin 8x}dx$$

$$= \frac{1}{2}\int\frac{(\cos 4x+\sin 4x)}{10+\sin 8x}dx+\frac{1}{2}\int\frac{(\cos 4x-\sin 4x)}{10+\sin 8x}dx$$

$$= \frac{1}{2}\int\frac{\cos 4x+\sin 4x}{10+1-1+\sin 8x}+\frac{1}{2}\int\frac{\cos 4x-\sin 4x}{10-1+1+\sin 8x}dx$$

$$\therefore\; I = \frac{1}{2}\underbrace{\int\frac{(\cos 4x+\sin 4x)dx}{11-\left(\sin^2 4x+\cos^2 4x-2\sin 4x\cos 4x\right)}}_{I_1}$$

$$+\frac{1}{2}\underbrace{\int\frac{(\cos 4x-\sin 4x)dx}{9+(\sin^2 4x+\cos^2 4x+2\sin 4x\cos 4x)}}_{I_2} = \frac{1}{2}I_1+\frac{1}{2}I_2 \qquad \ldots(1)$$

Put $t_1 = \sin 4x - \cos 4x$ in I_1 $\qquad \Rightarrow \frac{dt_1}{dx} = 4(\cos 4x+\sin 4x)$

$$\Rightarrow\ I_1=\int\frac{dt_1}{4(11-t_1^2)}=\frac{1}{4}\times\frac{1}{2\sqrt{11}}\left|\frac{\sqrt{11}+t_1}{\sqrt{11}-t_1}\right|+C_1=\frac{1}{8\sqrt{11}}\ln\left|\frac{\sqrt{11}+t_1}{\sqrt{11}-t_1}\right|+C_1$$

Now put $t_2 = \sin 4x + \cos 4x$ in I_2.

$$\Rightarrow\ I_2=\frac{dt_2}{dx}=4(\cos 4x-\sin 4x)$$

$$\therefore\ I_2=\int\frac{dt_2}{4(9+t^2)}=\frac{1}{4}\int\frac{dt_2}{3^2+t_2^2}=\frac{1}{4}\times\frac{1}{3}\tan^{-1}\frac{t_2}{3}+C_2=\frac{1}{12}\tan^{-1}\frac{t_2}{3}+C_2$$

$\therefore$ from (1)

$$I=\frac{1}{16\sqrt{11}}\ln\left|\frac{\sqrt{11}+\sin 4x-\cos 4x}{\sqrt{11}-\sin 4x+\cos 4x}\right|+\frac{1}{12}\tan^{-1}\left[\frac{1}{3}(\sin 4x+\cos 4x)\right]+C;$$

where $C = C_1 + C_2$.

ILLUSTRATION 162: Find the integral $\int\frac{dx}{\left(\operatorname{cosec}\left(\frac{x}{2}\right)-\sec\left(\frac{x}{2}\right)\right)}$

SOLUTION: Put $\frac{x}{2}=t$; $\frac{dt}{dx}=\frac{1}{2}\ \Rightarrow\ dx = 2dt$

$$\Rightarrow\ I=\int\frac{(2dt)}{\operatorname{cosec}t-\sec t}=2\int\frac{dt}{\operatorname{cosec}t-\sec t}=2\int\frac{(\sin t\cos t)dt}{\cos t-\sin t}=\int\frac{(2\sin t\cos t)}{\cos t-\sin t}dt$$

$$=\int\frac{1-(\cos t-\sin t)^2}{\cos t-\sin t}dt=\underbrace{\int\frac{1}{\cos t-\sin t}dt}_{I_1}-\underbrace{\int\frac{(\cos t-\sin t)^2}{(\cos t-\sin t)}dt}_{I_2}=I_1-I_2 \quad \text{...(1)}$$

$$I_1=\int\frac{1}{(-\sin t+\cos t)}(dt)$$

Now, Put $u=\tan\frac{t}{2}$ $\qquad\Rightarrow\ dt=\frac{(2du)}{1+u^2}$;

$$\sin t=\frac{2\tan(t/2)}{1+\tan^2(t/2)}=\frac{2u}{1+u^2}\ \text{ and }\ \cos t=\frac{1-\tan^2(t/2)}{1+\tan^2(t/2)}=\frac{1-u^2}{1+u^2}$$

$$\therefore\ I=\int\frac{(1+u^2)}{(-2u+(1-u^2))}\frac{2du}{(1+u^2)}=(-1)\int\frac{(2du)}{u^2+2u-1}$$

$$=(-2)\int\frac{du}{u^2+2u-1}=(-2)\int\frac{du}{u^2+2u-1+1-1}$$

$$=(-2)\int\frac{du}{(u+1)^2-2}=(-2)\int\frac{du}{(u+1)^2-(\sqrt{2})^2}$$

Put $u + 1 = m$ and $du = dm$

$$\Rightarrow\ I_1=(-2)\int\frac{dm}{m^2-(\sqrt{2})^2}=\frac{1}{\sqrt{2}}\ln\left|\frac{\sqrt{2}+m}{\sqrt{2}-m}\right|+C$$

Now, put $m = u + 1 = \tan\frac{t}{2}+1$ & $t = \frac{x}{2}$; $m = \tan\frac{x}{4}+1$

$$\Rightarrow I_1 = \frac{1}{\sqrt{2}}\ln\left|\frac{\sqrt{2}+1+\tan\frac{x}{4}}{\sqrt{2}-1-\tan\frac{x}{4}}\right|+C_1 \qquad ...(2)$$

Now $I_2 = \int\frac{(\cos t-\sin t)^2}{(\cos t-\sin t)}dt$

$$\Rightarrow I_2 = \int(\cos t-\sin t)dt = \sin t+\cos t+C_2 = \sin\frac{x}{2}+\cos\frac{x}{2}+C_2 \qquad ...(3)$$

Using (2) and (3) in (1) we get,

$$I = \frac{1}{\sqrt{2}}\ln\left|\frac{\sqrt{2}+1+\tan\frac{x}{4}}{\sqrt{2}-1-\tan\frac{x}{4}}\right|+\sin\frac{x}{2}+\cos\frac{x}{2}+C;\text{ where } C = C_1 + C_2.$$

ILLUSTRATION 163: Find the integral $\int\frac{1}{(1+3\sin 2x)}dx$

SOLUTION: Substitute $\sin 2x = \frac{2\tan x}{1+\tan^2 x}$ in $I = \int\frac{1}{(1+3\sin x)}dx$

$$\Rightarrow I = \int\frac{(1+\tan^2 x)}{(1+\tan^2 x+6\tan x)}dx = \int\frac{\sec^2 x}{(\tan^2 x+6\tan x+1)}dx$$

Put $\tan x = t$ $\qquad \Rightarrow \frac{dt}{dx} = \sec^2 x$

$\Rightarrow dx = \frac{dt}{\sec^2 x}$ $\qquad \Rightarrow I = \int\frac{1}{(t^2+6t+1)}dt$

Now, $t^2 + 6t + 1 = \left[\left(t+\frac{6}{2}\right)^2-\frac{32}{4}\right]$

$\Rightarrow \left[(t+3)^2-8\right]$

$$\Rightarrow I = \int\frac{1}{(t+3)^2-8}dt = \int\frac{1}{(t+3)^2-(2\sqrt{2})^2}dt$$

Put $u = t + 3$

$\Rightarrow dt = du$

$$\Rightarrow \int\frac{1}{u^2-(2\sqrt{2})^2}du = \frac{1}{4\sqrt{2}}\ln\left|\frac{4-2\sqrt{2}}{4+2\sqrt{2}}\right|+C = \frac{1}{4\sqrt{2}}\ln\left|\frac{t+3-2\sqrt{2}}{t+3+2\sqrt{2}}\right|+C$$

$$= \frac{1}{4\sqrt{2}}\ln\left|\frac{\tan x+-2\sqrt{2}}{\tan+3+2\sqrt{2}}\right|+C$$

TEXTUAL EXERCISE–7: (SUBJECTIVE)

1. Find $\int \frac{\sin^3 x}{3+\cos x} dx$

2. Find $\int \frac{3\tan x - 4\cot x}{\cos 2x} dx$

3. Find $\int \frac{\sin^4 x}{\cos^8 x} dx$

4. Find $\int \frac{\cos 7x - \cos 8x}{1+2\cos 5x} dx$

5. Find $\int \frac{dx}{\sin x(2+\cos x - 2\sin x)}$

6. Find $\int \frac{\sin^2 x \cos x}{\sin x + \cos x} dx$

7. Find $\int \frac{dx}{\cos^4 x \sin^2 x}$

8. Find $\int \frac{dx}{\sqrt[3]{\sin^{11} x \cos x}}$

9. Find the following integrals:
   (i) $\int \tan^9 \theta \, d\theta$ (ii) $\int \tan^{10} \theta \, d\theta$

10. Find $\int \sqrt[3]{\tan \theta} \, d\theta$

11. Find $\int \sqrt{\tan \theta} \, d\theta$

12. Find $\int \sqrt{\frac{\sin x - \sin^3 x}{(1-\sin^3 x)}} dx$

13. Find $\int \frac{\sqrt{\tan x} - \sqrt{\cot x}}{(2+11\sin 2x)} dx$

14. Find $\int \frac{x\sin 2x}{(4\cos^2 x + 9\sin^2 x)} dx$

15. Find $\int \frac{dx}{(a+bx^2)\sqrt{b-ax^2}}$ using the substitution $ax^2 = b\sin^2\theta$.

16. Find $\int \frac{\sin x + \sin 2x}{\sqrt{\cos x + \cos 2x}} dx$

Answer Keys

1. $\frac{\cos^2 x}{2} - 3\cos x + 8\ln x\,|\cos x + 3| + C$

2. $\frac{1}{2}\ln\left|\frac{1+\tan x}{1-\tan x}\right| - 4\ln|\tan x| + C$

3. $\frac{1}{5}\tan^5 x + \frac{1}{7}\tan^7 x + C$

4. $\frac{1}{2}\sin x - \frac{1}{3}\sin 3x + C$

5. $\frac{1}{3}\ln\left|\tan\frac{x}{2}\right| + \frac{5}{3}\ln\left|\tan\frac{x}{2} - 3\right| - \ln\left|\tan\frac{x}{2} - 1\right| + C$

6. $\frac{1}{4}\ln|\sin x + \cos x| - \frac{1}{4}\cos x(\sin x + \cos x) + C$

7. $\frac{1}{3}\tan^3 x + 2\tan x - \cot x + C$

8. $\frac{-3}{8}\frac{(1+4\tan^2 x)}{\tan^2 x \cdot \sqrt[3]{\tan^2 x}} + C$

9. (i) $\frac{1}{8}\tan^8\theta - \frac{1}{6}\tan^6\theta + \frac{1}{4}\tan^4\theta - \frac{1}{2}\tan^2\theta + \ln|\sec\theta| + C$

   (ii) $\frac{1}{9}\tan^9\theta - \frac{1}{7}\tan^7\theta + \frac{1}{5}\tan^5\theta - \frac{1}{3}\tan^3\theta + \tan\theta - \theta + C$

10. $\frac{\sqrt{3}}{2}\tan^{-1}\left(\frac{2z-1}{\sqrt{3}}\right) - \frac{1}{2}\ln|z^3+1| + \frac{3}{4}\ln|z^2 - z + 1| + C$ where $C = (\tan\theta)^{2/3}$.

11. $\frac{1}{\sqrt{2}}\tan^{-1}\left(\frac{y^2-1}{\sqrt{2}y}\right) + \frac{1}{2\sqrt{2}}\ln\left|\frac{y^2-\sqrt{2}y+1}{y^2+\sqrt{2}y+1}\right| + C$ where $y = \sqrt{\tan\theta}$

12. $\frac{2}{3}\sin^{-1}\left(\sin^{3/2} x\right) + C$

13. $\frac{1}{3}\tan^{-1}\left(\frac{\sqrt{\cot x}+\sqrt{\tan x}}{3}\right)+C$

14. $\frac{1}{5}\left[\frac{1}{6}\tan^{-1}\left(\frac{3}{2}\tan x\right)-\frac{x}{(4\cos^2 x+9\sin^2 x)}\right]+C$

15. $\frac{1}{\sqrt{a(a^2+b^2)}}\cdot\tan^{-1}\left(\frac{x\sqrt{a^2+b^2}}{\sqrt{a(b-ax^2)}}\right)+C$

16. $-\sqrt{\cos x+\cos 2x}-\frac{1}{2\sqrt{2}}\ln\left|\frac{4\cos x+1}{4}+\frac{\sqrt{\cos x+\cos 2x}}{\sqrt{2}}\right|+C$

TEXTUAL EXERCISE–7: (OBJECTIVE)

1. $\int\frac{dx}{a^2\sin^2 x+b^2\cos^2 x}$ is

(a) $\tan^{-1}\left(\frac{a}{b}\tan x\right)+C$

(b) $\frac{1}{ab}\tan^{-1}(\tan x)+C$

(c) $\frac{1}{ab}\tan^{-1}\left(\frac{a}{b}\tan x\right)+C$

(d) None of these

2. $\int\left(\frac{dx}{\sin x+\sec x}\right)$ is

(a) $\frac{1}{2\sqrt{3}}\ln\left|\frac{\tan x+\sqrt{3}}{\tan x-\sqrt{3}}\right|$ + $\tan^{-1}$ (sin$x$ + cos x) + C

(b) $\frac{1}{2\sqrt{3}}\ln\left|\frac{\sin x-\cos x+\sqrt{3}}{\sin x-\cos x-\sqrt{3}}\right|$ + $\tan^{-1}$ (sin$x$ + cos$x$) + C

(c) $\frac{1}{2\sqrt{3}}\ln\left|\frac{\tan x+\sqrt{3}}{\tan x-\sqrt{3}}\right|$ + $\tan^{-1}$ (sin x – cos x) + C

(d) None of these

3. $\int\frac{dx}{(\tan x-\cot x)}$ is

(a) $\ln|\cos 2x|+C$ (b) $\frac{1}{2}\ln|\cos 2x|+C$

(c) $\frac{1}{4}\ln|\cos 2x|+C$ (d) None of these

4. $\int\frac{\cos^3 x}{\sqrt{\sin^7 x}}dx$ is

(a) $\frac{2}{5}\text{cosec}^{7/2}x+2\sqrt{\text{cosec } x}+C$

(b) $-\frac{2}{5}\sin^{5/2}x+2\sqrt{\text{cosec } x}+C$

(c) $\frac{2}{5}\text{cosec}^{-5/2}x+2\sqrt{\text{cosec } x}+C$

(d) None of these

5. $\int\sec^{7/3}x.\ \text{cosec}^{5/3}x\ dx$ is

(a) $\frac{-3}{2}\cot^{2/3}x+\frac{3}{4}\tan^{4/3}x+C$

(b) $\frac{3}{2}\cot^{2/3}x+\frac{3}{4}\tan^{4/3}x+C$

(c) $\frac{-3}{2}\cot^{2/3}x-\frac{3}{4}\tan^{4/3}x+C$

(d) None of these

6. $\int\frac{dx}{\sin x(2\cos^2 x-1)}$ is

(a) $\frac{1}{4}\ln\left|\frac{\sqrt{2}+\cos x}{\sqrt{2}-\cos x}\right|+\frac{1}{2}\ln\left|\tan^2\frac{x}{2}\right|+C$

(b) $\frac{1}{4}\ln\left|\frac{1+\sqrt{2}\cos x}{1-\sqrt{2}\cos x}\right|+\frac{1}{2}\ln\left|\tan^2\frac{x}{2}\right|+C$

(c) $\frac{1}{4}\ln\left|\frac{1+\sqrt{2}\cos x}{1-\sqrt{2}\cos x}\right|+\ln\left|\tan^2\frac{x}{2}\right|+C$

(d) None of these

7. $\int\frac{2\tan x+3}{\sin^2 x+2\cos^2 x}dx$ is

(a) $\ln(\tan^2 x+2)+\tan^{-1}\left(\frac{\tan x}{\sqrt{2}}\right)+C$

(b) $\ln(\tan^2 x+2)+C$

(c) $\ln(\tan^2 x+2)+\frac{3}{\sqrt{2}}\tan^{-1}\left(\frac{\tan(x/2)}{\sqrt{2}}\right)+C$

(d) None of these

8. $I=\int\frac{\sin x}{\sin 3x}dx$ is

(a) $\frac{1}{2\sqrt{3}}\ln\left|\frac{\sqrt{3}+\tan x}{\sqrt{3}-\tan x}\right|+C$

(b) $\frac{1}{\sqrt{3}}\ln\left|\frac{\sqrt{3}+\tan x}{\sqrt{3}-\tan x}\right|+C$

(c) $\frac{1}{2\sqrt{3}}\ln\left|\frac{\sqrt{2}+\tan x}{\sqrt{2}-\tan x}\right|+C$

(d) None of these

9. $\int\frac{dx}{4\sin^2 x+4\sin x\cos x+5\cos^2 x}$ is

(a) $\frac{1}{4}\tan^{-1}(2\tan x+1)+C$

(b) $\frac{1}{4}\tan^{-1}\left(\tan x+\frac{1}{2}\right)+C$

(c) $\frac{1}{2}\tan^{-1}(2\tan x+1)+C$

(d) None of these

10. $\int\sin^6 x.\cos^4 x\,dx$ is

(a) $\frac{1}{16}\left[\frac{3}{8}x-\frac{1}{8}\sin 4x\right]-\frac{\sin^5 2x}{320}+C$

(b) $\frac{1}{16}\left[\frac{3}{8}x+\frac{1}{8}\sin 4x\right]-\frac{\sin^5 2x}{320}+C$

(c) $\frac{1}{32}\left[\frac{3}{8}x+\frac{1}{8}\sin 4x\right]-\frac{\sin^5 2x}{320}+C$

(d) None of these

11. If the value of $\int\sin^2 x\cos^5 x\,dx$ is $\frac{\sin^3 x}{3}-\frac{2}{5}\sin^5 x-l\frac{\sin^7 x}{7}+C$. Then the value of l is.

(a) 2 (b) –2

(c) –1 (d) None of these

12. $\int\frac{\cos x\,dx}{(1+\sin x)(2+\sin x)}$ is

(a) $2\ln\left(\frac{1+\sin x}{2+\sin x}\right)+C$ (b) $\ln\left(\frac{1-\sin x}{2-\sin x}\right)+C$

(c) $\ln\left(\frac{1+\sin x}{2+\sin x}\right)+C$ (d) None of these

13. $\int\frac{\sin x\,dx}{(1-\cos x)^2}$ is

(a) $\ln\left(\frac{1}{\cos x-1}\right)+C$

(b) $\frac{1}{\cos x-1}+C$

(c) $\tan^{-1}\left(\frac{1}{\cos x-1}\right)+C$

(d) None of these

14. $\int\frac{dx}{(\sin x+\cos x)^2}$ is

(a) $C-\left(\frac{1}{1+\tan x}\right)$ (b) $\frac{1}{1+\tan x}+C$

(c) $\left(\frac{1}{1+\tan x}\right)^2+C$ (d) None of these

15. $\int\frac{dx}{\tan x.\cos 2x}$ is

(a) $\ln\frac{|C\sin x|}{\sqrt{\cos 2x}}$ (b) $\ln\frac{|C\cos x|}{\sqrt{\cos 2x}}$

(c) $\ln\frac{|C\sin x|}{\sqrt{1-4\sin^2 x}}$ (d) None of these

16. $\int\frac{dx}{\sin^2 x+\tan^2 x}$ is

(a) $C-\frac{1}{2}\left[\frac{x}{2}+\frac{1}{\sqrt{2}}\tan^{-1}\left(\frac{\tan x}{\sqrt{2}}\right)\right]$

(b) $C-\frac{1}{2}\left[\cot x+\frac{1}{\sqrt{2}}\tan^{-1}\left(\frac{\tan x}{\sqrt{2}}\right)\right]$

(c) $C-\frac{1}{2}\left[\cot x-\frac{1}{\sqrt{2}}\tan^{-1}\left(\frac{\tan x}{\sqrt{2}}\right)\right]$

(d) None of these

17. $\int\frac{\sqrt{\tan x}}{\sin x.\cos x}dx$ is

(a) $\sqrt{\tan x}+C$

(b) $2\sqrt{\tan x}+C$

(c) $\tan^{-1}x+C$

(d) $2\tan^{-1}x+C$

18. $\int\frac{1}{2+\sin x+\cos x}dx$ is

(a) $2\tan^{-1}\frac{\left(\tan\frac{x}{2}+1\right)}{\sqrt{2}}+C$

(b) $\sqrt{2}\tan^{-1}\frac{\left(\tan\frac{x}{2}+1\right)}{2}+C$

(c) $\sqrt{2}\tan^{-1}\frac{\left(\tan\frac{x}{2}+1\right)}{\sqrt{2}}+C$

(d) None of these

Answer Keys

1. (c)	**2.** (b)	**3.** (c)	**4.** (b)	**5.** (a)	**6.** (b)	**7.** (b)	**8.** (a)	**9.** (b)	**10.** (d)
11. (c)	**12.** (b)	**13.** (b)	**14.** (a)	**15.** (a)	**16.** (b)	**17.** (b)	18. (c)		

INTEGRAL OF IRRATIONAL FUNCTIONS

Integral of type: $\int \frac{dx}{\text{linear}\sqrt{\text{linear}}}$, $\int \frac{dx}{(\text{linear})^n\sqrt{\text{linear}}}$

E.g., $\int \frac{dx}{(ax+b)\sqrt{cx+d}}$

Algorithm: Put $cx + d = t^2$

$\Rightarrow\ x = \frac{t^2-d}{c}$ and $dx = \frac{2t\,dt}{c}$

$$\Rightarrow ax+b = a\left(\frac{t^2-d}{c}\right)+b,$$

$$I = \frac{1}{c}\int \frac{2t\,dt\,c}{t(at^2+bc-ad)}$$

$$= 2\int \frac{dt}{at^2+bc-ad} = \frac{2}{a}\int \frac{dt}{t^2+\frac{bc-ad}{a}}$$

which can be solved further by using the standard integrals $\int \frac{1}{t^2+a^2}dt$, $\int \frac{1}{t^2-a^2}dt$; $\int \frac{dt}{a^2-t^2}$.

ILLUSTRATION 164: Find the integral $\int \frac{dx}{(2x+1)\cdot\sqrt{4x+3}}$.

SOLUTION: Let $4x + 3 = t^2$

$$\Rightarrow\ x = \frac{t^2-3}{4} \text{ and } dx = \frac{2t.dt}{4} = \frac{t\,dt}{2}$$

Now, $2x + 1 = 2\left(\frac{t^2-3}{4}\right)+1 = \frac{1}{2}(t^2-1)$.

$$\therefore\ I = \int \frac{t(dt)2}{2(t^2-1)t} = \int \frac{1}{t^2-1}dt$$

$$= \frac{1}{2}\ln\left|\frac{t-1}{t+1}\right|+C = \frac{1}{2}\ln\left|\frac{\sqrt{4x+3}-1}{\sqrt{4x+3}+1}\right|+C.$$

Integral of type: $\int \frac{dx}{\text{linear}\sqrt{\text{quadratic}}}$ and

$\int \frac{dx}{(\text{linear})^n\sqrt{\text{quadratic}}}$

E.g., $\int \frac{dx}{(ax+b)\sqrt{cx^2+d}}$

Algorithm: Put $ax + b = \frac{1}{t}$

$\Rightarrow\ x = \left(\frac{1-bt}{at}\right)$ and $dx = -\frac{1}{at^2}dt$

$$\Rightarrow\ I = \frac{1}{a}\int \frac{-dt/t^2}{\frac{1}{t}\sqrt{c\left(\frac{1-bt}{at}\right)^2+d}}$$

$$= -\int \frac{dt}{\sqrt{(b^2c+a^2d)t^2-2bct+c}};$$

which can be integrated by using the method of solving integrals of the type $\int \frac{dt}{\sqrt{at^2+bt+c}}$.

ILLUSTRATION 165: Find the integral $\int \frac{dx}{(2x-1)\cdot\sqrt{x^2+4}}$

SOLUTION: Put $2x - 1 = \frac{1}{u}$ $\Rightarrow$ $2x = \frac{1+u}{u}$.

$$\Rightarrow x = \frac{1+u}{2u} \qquad \Rightarrow x = \frac{1}{2u} + \frac{1}{2}$$

$$\Rightarrow \frac{dx}{du} = \frac{1}{2}\frac{(-1)}{u^2} + 0 \qquad \Rightarrow dx = \frac{-1}{2u^2}du$$

Now $x^2 + 4 = \frac{(1+u)^2}{(2u)^2} + 4 = \frac{(1+u)^2 + 16u^2}{4u^2}$

$$\therefore \; I = \int \frac{\frac{-du}{2u^2}}{\left(\frac{1}{u}\right)\sqrt{\frac{(1+u)^2+16u^2}{4u^2}}} = -\int \frac{du}{\sqrt{17u^2+2u+1}}$$

$$= -\frac{1}{\sqrt{17}}\int \frac{du}{\sqrt{u^2+\frac{2}{17}u+\frac{1}{17}}} = \frac{-1}{\sqrt{17}}\int \frac{du}{\sqrt{u^2+\frac{2u}{17}+\frac{1}{(17)^2}-\frac{1}{(17)^2}+\frac{1}{17}}}$$

$$= \frac{-1}{\sqrt{17}}\int \frac{du}{\sqrt{\left(u+\frac{1}{17}\right)^2+\frac{1}{17}\left(\frac{16}{17}\right)}} = \frac{-1}{\sqrt{17}}\int \frac{du}{\sqrt{\left(u+\frac{1}{17}\right)^2+\left(\frac{4}{17}\right)^2}}$$

$$= \frac{-1}{\sqrt{17}}\ln\left|\left(u+\frac{1}{17}\right)+\sqrt{\left(u+\frac{1}{17}\right)^2+\left(\frac{4}{17}\right)^2}\right| + C = \frac{-1}{\sqrt{17}}\ln\left|\left(u+\frac{1}{17}\right)+\sqrt{\frac{17u^2+2u+1}{17}}\right| + C$$

$$= \frac{-1}{\sqrt{17}}\ln\left|\frac{2x+16}{17(2x-1)}+\frac{1}{\sqrt{17}}\sqrt{17u^2+2u+1}\right| + C$$

$$= \frac{-1}{\sqrt{17}}\ln\left|\frac{2x+16}{17(2x-1)}+\frac{1}{\sqrt{17}}\sqrt{17\left(\frac{1}{2x-1}\right)^2+\frac{2}{2x-1}+1}\right| + C$$

$$= \frac{-1}{\sqrt{17}}\ln\left|\frac{2x+16}{17(2x-1)}+\frac{2}{\sqrt{17}}\frac{\sqrt{x^2+4}}{(2x-1)}\right| + C$$

ILLUSTRATION 166: Find the integral $\int \frac{x-1}{x^2\sqrt{4x^2-4x+1}}dx$

SOLUTION: $I = \underbrace{\int \frac{x}{x^2\sqrt{4x^2-4x+1}}dx}_{I_1} - \underbrace{\int \frac{1}{x^2\sqrt{4x^2-4x+1}}dx}_{I_2}$ ...(1)

Now consider $I_1 = \int \frac{1}{x\sqrt{4x^2-4x+1}}dx$

Here put $x = \frac{1}{t}$ $\qquad \Rightarrow dx = -\frac{1}{t^2}dt$

$$\Rightarrow I_1 = \int \frac{1}{\left(\frac{1}{t}\right)\sqrt{4\frac{1}{t^2} - 4\frac{1}{t} + 1}} \left(\frac{-1}{t^2}\right) dt = \int \frac{1}{\sqrt{4 - 4t + t^2}} dt = \int \frac{1}{\sqrt{(t-2)^2}} dt$$

$$= \int \frac{1}{t-2} dt = \ln|t-2| + C = \ln\left|\frac{1-2x}{x}\right| + C_1 \qquad \ldots(2)$$

Now, $I_2 = \int \frac{1}{x^2\sqrt{4x^2 - 4x + 1}} dx = \int \frac{1}{P\sqrt{Q}} dx$

Put $x = \frac{1}{t}$

⇒ [Since both P and Q are quadratic]

$dx = -\frac{1}{t^2}(dt)$; $\qquad \Rightarrow I_2 = \int \frac{1}{\frac{1}{t^2}\sqrt{\frac{4}{t^2} - \frac{4}{t} + 1}} \left(\frac{-1}{t^2}\right) dt$

$$= -\int \frac{-t}{\sqrt{t^2 + 4 - 4t}} dt = \int \frac{-t}{\sqrt{(t-2)^2}} dt = \int \frac{-t}{t-2} dt$$

$$= -\int \frac{t+2-2}{t-2} dt = [(-t)] - 2\ln|t-2| + C_2 = -\frac{1}{x} - 2\ln\left|\frac{1-2x}{x}\right| + C_2 \qquad \ldots(3)$$

using (2) and (3) in (1) we get

$$\Rightarrow I = \frac{1}{x} + 3\ln\left|\frac{1-2x}{x}\right| + C \text{ ; where } C = C_1 - C_2.$$

Integral of type $\int \frac{dx}{\text{quadratic}\sqrt{\text{linear}}}$

Algorithm: Let $I = \int \frac{dx}{(ax^2 + bx + c)\sqrt{px + q}}$; put $px + q = t^2$;

$$\Rightarrow x = \frac{t^2 - q}{p} \text{ and } dx = \frac{2tdt}{p}$$

$$\Rightarrow I = \frac{2}{p}\int \frac{dt}{a\left(\frac{t^2 - q}{p}\right)^2 + b\left(\frac{t^2 - q}{p}\right) + c}$$

$$= 2p\int \frac{dt}{at^4 + (bp - 2aq)t^2 + aq^2 + cp^2 - bpq}$$

which can be integrated by using the method of solving $\int \frac{dx}{\sqrt{ax^4 + bx^2 + c}}$.

ILLUSTRATION 167: Find the integral $\int \frac{dx}{(x^2 + 5x + 2)\sqrt{x-2}}$

SOLUTION: Let $x - 2 = t^2$

$\Rightarrow x = t^2 + 2 \qquad \Rightarrow dx = 2t\,dt$

and $x^2 + 5x + 2 = (t^2 + 2)^2 + 5t^2 + 10 + 2 = t^4 + 9t^2 + 16$

$$\therefore I = \int \frac{2\,dt}{(t^4 + 9t^2 + 16)} = 2\int \frac{dt}{(t^4 + 9t^2 + 16)} = 2\int \frac{dt}{(t^4 + 9t^2 + 16)} dt$$

$$= 2\int \frac{1}{t^2\left(t^2+9+\frac{16}{t^2}\right)}dt = 2\int \frac{1}{t^2\left(t^2+\frac{16}{t^2}+9\right)}(dt) = 2\int \frac{1}{t^2\left[\left(t^2+\left(\frac{4}{t}\right)^2+2(4)-8+9\right)\right]}(dt)$$

$$= \frac{1}{4}\int \frac{8}{t^2\left(t^2+\left(\frac{4}{t}\right)^2+2(4)-2(4)+9\right)}dt = \frac{1}{4}\int \frac{t^2+4+4-t^2}{t^2\left(t^2+\left(\frac{4}{t}\right)^2+2(4)-2(4)+9\right)}dt$$

$$= \frac{1}{4}\int \frac{t^2+4}{t^2\left(\left(t-\frac{4}{t}\right)^2+17\right)} + \frac{1}{4}\int \frac{-(t^2-4)}{t^2\left(\left(t+\frac{4}{t}\right)^2+1\right)}dt$$

$$= \frac{1}{4}\int \left(\frac{t^2+4}{t^2}\right)\frac{1}{\left(t-\frac{4}{t}\right)^2+(\sqrt{17})^2}dt - \frac{1}{4}\int \frac{t^2-4}{t^2\left(\left(t+\frac{4}{t}\right)^2+(1)^2\right)}dt$$

$$= I_1 - I_2 \qquad \ldots(1)$$

In I_1, put $t-\frac{4}{t}=m_1$ $\qquad \Rightarrow dm_1 = dt\left(\frac{t^2+4}{t^2}\right)$

$$\Rightarrow I_1 = \frac{1}{4}\int \frac{dm_1}{m_1^2+\left(\sqrt{17}\right)^2} = \frac{1}{4}\left(\frac{1}{\sqrt{17}}\right)\tan^{-1}\left(\frac{m}{\sqrt{17}}\right)+C_1 = \frac{1}{4\sqrt{17}}\tan^{-1}\left(\frac{t^2-4}{\sqrt{17}t}\right)+C_1 \qquad \ldots(2)$$

In I_2 put $t+\frac{4}{t}=m_2$ $\qquad \Rightarrow dm_2 = dt\left(\frac{t^2-4}{t^2}\right)$

$$\Rightarrow I_2 = \frac{1}{4}\int \frac{dm_2}{m_2^2+(1)^2} = \frac{1}{4}\tan^{-1}(m_2)+C_2 \qquad \ldots(3)$$

Using (2) and (3) we have

$$I = \frac{1}{4\sqrt{17}}\tan^{-1}\left(\frac{t^2-4}{\sqrt{17}t}\right) - \frac{1}{4}\tan^{-1}\left(\frac{t^2+4}{t}\right)+C$$

Integral of type: $\int \frac{dx}{\text{quadratic}\sqrt{\text{quadratic}}}$

i.e., $\int \frac{dx}{(ax^2+bx+c)\sqrt{px^2+qx+r}}$

Case I: When $(ax^2 + bx + c)$ breaks up into two linear factors, say $a(x-\alpha)(x-\beta)$

So let $\int \frac{1}{(ax^2+bx+c)}\frac{dx}{\sqrt{px^2+qx+r}}$

$$= \frac{1}{a}\int \left(\frac{A}{(x-\alpha)}+\frac{B}{(x-\beta)}\right)\times\frac{1}{\sqrt{px^2+qx+r}}dx$$

$$\Rightarrow I = \frac{A}{a}\underbrace{\int \frac{dx}{(x-\alpha)\sqrt{px^2+qx+r}}}_{\text{put } (x-\alpha)=\frac{1}{t}} + \frac{B}{a}\underbrace{\int \frac{dx}{(x-\beta)\sqrt{px^2+qx+r}}}_{\text{put } (x-\beta)=\frac{1}{t}}$$

which can be further be solved by using the method of solving integral of the form $\int \frac{dx}{\text{linear}\sqrt{\text{quadratic}}}$.

ILLUSTRATION 168: Find the integral $\int \frac{dx}{(x^2-x-2)\sqrt{x^2+x+1}}$.

SOLUTION: Now, for $x^2 - x - 2$

$\therefore\ (x-2)(x+1)$

$$\Rightarrow I = \int \frac{1}{(x-2)(x+1)}\frac{1}{\sqrt{x^2+x+1}}dx$$

$$= \int\left(\frac{A}{x-2}+\frac{B}{x+1}\right)\frac{1}{\sqrt{x^2+x+1}}dx \text{ [by breaking into partial fraction] (say)}$$

$$= \int \frac{A}{(x-2)\sqrt{x^2+x+1}}dx + \int \frac{B}{(x+1)\sqrt{x^2+x+1}}dx \quad \ldots(1)$$

Now, $\frac{1}{(x-2)(x+1)} = \frac{A}{(x-2)} + \frac{B}{(x+1)}$

(using partial fraction concept, $A = 1/3$ and $B = -1/3$)

$$= \frac{1}{3}\int \frac{1}{(x-2)\sqrt{x^2+x+1}}dx + \left(\frac{-1}{3}\right)\int \frac{1}{(x+1)\sqrt{x^2+x+1}}dx = I_1 - I_2 \text{ (say)} \quad \ldots(2)$$

In I_1, put $x - 2 = \frac{1}{t}$ $\qquad \Rightarrow\ dx = \frac{(-1)dt}{t^2}$

$$\Rightarrow I_1 = \frac{1}{3}\int \frac{(-1)dt}{\left(\frac{1}{t}\right)\sqrt{\left(\frac{1}{t}+2\right)^2+\left(2+\frac{1}{t}\right)+1}}\frac{1}{t^2} = \frac{1}{3}\int \frac{(-1)\frac{dt}{t}}{\sqrt{\frac{(1+2t)^2}{t^2}+\frac{(2t+1)}{t}+1}}$$

$$= \frac{1}{3}\int \frac{(-1)\frac{dt}{t}}{\left(\frac{1}{t}\right)\sqrt{(1+2t)^2+(2t+1)t+t^2}} = \frac{-1}{3}\int \frac{dt}{\sqrt{7t^2+5t+1}} = \frac{-1}{3\sqrt{7}}\int \frac{dt}{\sqrt{t^2+\frac{5}{7}t+\frac{1}{7}}}$$

$$= \frac{-1}{3\sqrt{7}}\int \frac{dt}{\sqrt{t^2+\frac{5}{7}t+\left(\frac{5}{14}\right)^2-\left(\frac{5}{14}\right)^2+\frac{1}{7}}} = \frac{-1}{3\sqrt{7}}\int \frac{dt}{\sqrt{\left(t+\frac{5}{14}\right)^2+\frac{1}{7}-\frac{25}{196}}}$$

$$= \frac{-1}{3\sqrt{7}}\int \frac{dt}{\sqrt{\left(t+\frac{5}{14}\right)^2+\left(\frac{\sqrt{3}}{14}\right)^2}} = \frac{-1}{3\sqrt{7}}\ln\left|t+\frac{5}{14}+\sqrt{t^2+\frac{5}{7}t+\frac{1}{7}}\right|+C_1$$

Now putting back $x - 2 = \frac{1}{t}$ or $t = \frac{1}{x-2}$ we have

$$I_1 = \frac{-1}{3\sqrt{7}}\ln\left|\frac{1}{x-2}+\frac{5}{14}+\frac{\sqrt{7t^2+5t+1}}{\sqrt{7}}\right|+C_1$$

$$\Rightarrow \frac{-1}{3\sqrt{7}}\ln\left|\left(\frac{1}{x-2}+\frac{5}{14}\right)+\frac{1}{\sqrt{7}}\sqrt{7\left(\frac{1}{x-2}\right)^2+5\left(\frac{1}{x-2}\right)+1}\right|+C_1$$

$$= \frac{-1}{3\sqrt{17}}\ln\left|\frac{5x+4}{14(x-2)}+\frac{1}{\sqrt{7}(x-2)}\sqrt{(x-2)^2+5(x-2)+7}\right|$$

$$= \frac{-1}{3\sqrt{17}}\ln\left|\frac{5x+4}{14}+\frac{1}{\sqrt{7}}\sqrt{x^2+x+1}\right|+\frac{1}{3\sqrt{17}}\ln|x-2|+C_1 \qquad \ldots(3)$$

Now, put $x + 1 = \frac{1}{t}$ in I_2 and

$$\Rightarrow\ dx = \frac{(-1)}{t^2}dt,\ I_2 = \frac{1}{3}\int\frac{\frac{(-1)}{t^2}dt}{\left(\frac{1}{t}\right)\sqrt{\left(\frac{1}{t}-1\right)^2+\left(\frac{1}{t}-1\right)+1}} = -\frac{1}{3}\int\frac{dt/t}{\left(\frac{1}{t}\right)\sqrt{(1-t)^2+(1-t)t+t^2}}$$

$$= -\frac{1}{3}\int\frac{dt}{\sqrt{1+t^2-2t+t-t^2+t^2}} = -\frac{1}{3}\int\frac{dt}{\sqrt{t^2-t+1}} = -\frac{1}{3}\int\frac{dt}{\sqrt{t^2-t+1+\left(\frac{1}{2}\right)^2-\left(\frac{1}{2}\right)^2}}$$

$$= -\frac{1}{3}\int\frac{dt}{\sqrt{\left(t-\frac{1}{2}\right)^2+\left(\frac{\sqrt{3}}{2}\right)^2}} = -\frac{1}{3}\ln\left|\left(t-\frac{1}{2}\right)+\sqrt{t^2-t+1}\right|+C_2$$

Now substituting back $t = \frac{1}{x+1}$ in the above equation we have,

$$I_2 = -\frac{1}{3}\ln\left|\frac{2-x-1}{2(x+1)}+\sqrt{\frac{1-(x+1)+(x+1)^2}{(x+1)^2}}\right|+C_2$$

$$= -\frac{1}{3}\ln\left|\frac{1-x}{2(x+1)}+\frac{1}{(x+1)}\sqrt{(x+1)^2-(x+1)+1}\right|+C_2$$

$$= -\frac{1}{3}\ln\left|\frac{1-x}{2(x+1)}+\frac{1}{(x+1)}\sqrt{x^2+x+1}\right|+C_2$$

$$= -\frac{1}{3}\ln\left|\frac{(1-x)}{2}+\sqrt{x^2+x+1}\right|+\frac{1}{3}\ln|x+1|+C_2 \qquad \ldots(4)$$

Putting the values of (3) and (4) in (2) we get

$$I = \frac{1}{3}\ln\left|\frac{(1-x)}{2}+\sqrt{x^2+x+1}\right|-\frac{1}{3\sqrt{7}}\ln\left|\frac{(5x+4)}{14}+\frac{\sqrt{x^2+x+1}}{\sqrt{7}}\right|$$

$$-\frac{1}{3}\ln|x+1|+\frac{1}{3\sqrt{7}}\ln|x-2|+C;\ \text{where } C = C_1 - C_2.$$

Case II: If $ax^2 + bx + c$ is a perfect square say $(lx + m)^2$.

$$I = \int\frac{dx}{(lx+m^2)\sqrt{px^2+qx+r}}$$

put $lx + m = \frac{1}{t}$

$$\Rightarrow\ x = \frac{\left(\frac{1}{t}-m\right)}{l}$$

$$\Rightarrow\ ldx = -\frac{1}{t^2}dt$$

$$\therefore\ I=\int\frac{-\frac{1}{t^2}dt}{\frac{1}{t^2}\sqrt{p\left(\frac{1-tm}{lt}\right)^2+q\left(\frac{1-tm}{lt}\right)+r}}$$

$$=\int\frac{-dt}{\sqrt{p\left(\frac{1-tm}{lt}\right)^2+q\left(\frac{1-tm}{lt}\right)+r}}$$

$$=\int\frac{-lt\ dt}{\sqrt{p(1-tm)^2+qlt(1-tm)+rl^2t^2}};$$

which can be solved further by using the integral of type $\int\frac{\text{linear}}{\sqrt{\text{quadratic}}}dx$.

Case III: If $b=0$; $q=0$.

E.g., $I=\int\frac{dx}{(ax^2+c)\sqrt{px^2+r}}$, then put $x=\frac{1}{t}$

$$\Rightarrow\ dx=-\frac{1}{t^2}dt$$

$$\Rightarrow\ I=\int\frac{-dt/t^2}{\left(\frac{ct^2+a}{t^2}\right)\sqrt{\frac{p+rt^2}{t^2}}}=\int\frac{-tdt}{(ct^2+a)\sqrt{rt^2+p}}$$

put $rt^2+p=z^2$

$$\Rightarrow\ tdt=\frac{zdz}{r}$$

$$\therefore\ I=-\int\frac{zdz}{\left(c\left(\frac{z^2-p}{r}\right)+a\right)z}=-\int\frac{dz}{(cz^2+ar-cp)};$$

which is a standard form.

ILLUSTRATION 169: $\int\frac{dx}{(x^2+2)\sqrt{4x^2-1}}$

SOLUTION: Let $I=\int\frac{dx}{(x^2+2)\sqrt{4x^2-1}}$; Put $x=\frac{1}{t}$

$$\Rightarrow\ dx=\frac{(-1)}{t^2}dt \qquad \Rightarrow\ I=\int\frac{-t\,dt}{(1+2t^2)\sqrt{4-t^2}}$$

Put $4-t^2=z^2$ $\qquad\Rightarrow\ -2t\ dt=2z\,dz$

$$\Rightarrow\ I=\int\frac{z\ dz}{(1+2(4-z^2))\sqrt{z^2}}=\int\frac{z\ dz}{(9-2z^2)z}=\frac{-1}{2}\int\frac{dz}{z^2-\frac{9}{2}}=\frac{-1}{2}\int\frac{dz}{z^2-\left(\frac{3}{\sqrt{2}}\right)^2}$$

$$=\frac{1}{2}\int\frac{1}{\left(\frac{3}{\sqrt{2}}\right)^2-z^2}=\frac{1}{2}\frac{1}{2\left(\frac{3}{\sqrt{2}}\right)}\ln\left|\frac{\frac{3}{\sqrt{2}}+z}{\frac{3}{\sqrt{2}}-z}\right|+C$$

$$=\frac{1}{6\sqrt{2}}\ln\left|\frac{3+\sqrt{2}z}{3-z\sqrt{2}}\right|+C=\frac{1}{6\sqrt{2}}\ln\left|\frac{3+(4-t^2)^{1/2}\sqrt{2}}{3-(4-t^2)^{1/2}\sqrt{2}}\right|+C$$

$$=\frac{1}{6\sqrt{2}}\ln\left|\frac{3+\left(4-\frac{1}{x^2}\right)^{1/2}\sqrt{2}}{3-\left(4-\frac{1}{x^2}\right)^{1/2}\sqrt{2}}\right|+C=\frac{1}{6\sqrt{2}}\ln\left|\frac{3x+(4x^2-1)^{1/2}\sqrt{2}}{3x-(4x^2-1)^{1/2}\sqrt{2}}\right|+C$$

Integral of type: $\int R\left(x^{m/n}, x^{p/q}, x^{r/s}....\right)dx$; where $p, q, r, s, m, n..... \in \mathbb{Z}$ and $R(x)$ is a rational algebraic function of x. Put $x = t^k$ such that k = L.C.M. $(n, q, s,...)$ and integrand reduced to rational function of t.

ILLUSTRATION 170: Find the integral $\int \frac{x^{1/2}+x^{1/3}}{1+x}dx$

SOLUTION: Let $I = \int \frac{x^{1/2}+x^{1/3}}{1+x}dx$

Put $x = t^6$ $\Rightarrow dx = 6t^5\,dt$

$$\Rightarrow I = \int\left(\frac{t^3+t^2}{1+t^6}\right)6t^5\,dt = 6\int\frac{t^8+t^7}{1+t^6}dt$$

$$= 6\int\frac{(t^6+1)(t^2+t)}{1+t^6}dt - 6\int\frac{t^2+t}{1+t^6}dt = 6\int(t^2+t)dt - 6\int\frac{t^2}{1+t^6}dt - 6\int\frac{t}{1+t^6}dt$$

$$= 2t^3+3t^2-2\tan^{-1}(t^3) - 3\int\frac{d(t^2)}{1+(t^2)^3}; \text{ where } t = x^{1/6} \quad ......(1)$$

Now consider $\int\frac{dt^2}{1+(t^2)^3} = \int\frac{dz}{1+z^3}$; where $z = t^2$ (say)

$$= -\int\frac{z^2-1-z^2}{1+z^3}dz = -\int\frac{z-1}{z^2-z+1}dz + \frac{1}{3}\int\frac{3z^2}{z^3+1}dz$$

$$= -\frac{1}{2}\int\frac{2z-1-1}{z^2-z+1}dz + \frac{1}{3}\ln|z^3+1|$$

$$= -\frac{1}{2}\ln|z^2-z+1| + \frac{1}{2}\int\frac{dz}{\left(z-\frac{1}{2}\right)^2+\left(\frac{\sqrt{3}}{2}\right)^2}dz - \frac{1}{3}\ln|z^3+1|$$

$$= -\frac{1}{2}\ln|z^2-z+1| + \frac{1}{2}\times\frac{2}{\sqrt{3}}\tan^{-1}\left(\frac{2z-1}{\sqrt{3}}\right) + \frac{1}{3}\ln|z^3+1|$$

$$= -\frac{1}{2}\ln|t^4-t^2+1| + \frac{1}{\sqrt{3}}\tan^{-1}\left(\frac{2t^2-1}{\sqrt{3}}\right) + \frac{1}{3}\ln|1+t^6| + C \quad ...(2)$$

$\therefore$ from (1) and (2) we have

$$I = 2t^3+3t^2-2\tan^{-1}(t^3) + \frac{3}{2}\ln|t^4-t^2+1| - \sqrt{3}\tan^{-1}\left(\frac{2t^2-1}{\sqrt{3}}\right) - \ln|1+t^6| + C$$

$$= 3\sqrt{x}+3\sqrt[3]{x}-2\tan^{-1}\left(\sqrt{x}\right) + \frac{3}{2}\ln|x^{2/3}-x^{1/3}-1| - \sqrt{3}\tan^{-1}\left(\frac{2x^{1/3}-1}{\sqrt{3}}\right) - \ln|1+x| + C$$

Integral of type: $\int x^m\left(a+bx^n\right)^p dx$ where m, n, p are rationals.

Case I: If $p \in \mathbb{Z}$ expand binomially and integrate term-by-term

i.e., $I = \int x^m \sum_{r=0}^{p} {}^pC_r\, a^{p-r}(bx^n)^r\,dx$

$$= \sum_{r=0}^{p}\left({}^pC_r\, a^{p-r}\, b^r\,\frac{x^{nr+m+1}}{nr+m+1}\right) + C$$

ILLUSTRATION 171: Find the integral $\int x^{1/4}(1+x^{3/2})^4\,dx$

SOLUTION: Since $p = 4 \in \mathbb{N}$, we can use binomial theorem.

$$\therefore\ I=\int x^{\frac{1}{4}}\left(\sum_{\gamma=0}^{4}(1)^{4-\gamma}\left(x^{\frac{3}{2}}\right)^{\gamma}\right)dx=\int x^{\frac{1}{4}}\left(1+(x)^{\frac{3}{2}}+x^{3}+x^{\frac{9}{2}}+x^{6}\right)dx$$

$$=\int\left(x^{\frac{1}{4}}+(x)^{\frac{1}{4}+\frac{3}{2}}+x^{3+\frac{1}{4}}+x^{\frac{1}{4}+\frac{9}{2}}+x^{\frac{1}{4}+6}\right)dx=\int\left(x^{\frac{1}{4}}+(x)^{\frac{7}{4}}+x^{\frac{13}{4}}+x^{\frac{19}{4}}+x^{\frac{25}{4}}\right)dx$$

$$\Rightarrow\ \left[\frac{4}{5}(x)^{\frac{5}{4}}+\frac{4}{11}x^{\frac{11}{4}}+\frac{4}{17}x^{\frac{17}{4}}+\frac{4}{23}x^{\frac{23}{4}}+\frac{4}{29}(x)^{\frac{29}{4}}\right]+C$$

Case II: If $p\in\mathbb{Z}^-$; i.e., $I=\int x^m\left(a+bx^n\right)^p\,dx$ then put $x = t^k$; where k = L.C.M of denominator of m and n.

ILLUSTRATION 172: Find the integral $\int x^{\frac{5}{2}}\left(1+x^{\frac{3}{2}}\right)^{-2}dx$

SOLUTION: Let $I=\int x^{\frac{5}{2}}\left(1+x^{\frac{3}{2}}\right)^{-2}dx$. Here $m=\frac{5}{2}$ and $n=\frac{3}{2}$

L.C.M. of (2, 2) = 2 = k (say)

$\therefore$ put $x = t^2$ $\qquad\Rightarrow dx = 2t\,dt$

$$\Rightarrow\ I=\int t^5\left(1+t^3\right)^{-2}2t\,dt=2\int t^6\left(1+t^3\right)^{-2}dt=2\int\frac{t^6}{\left(1+t^3\right)^2}dt$$

$$=2\int\frac{t^6-1+1}{\left(1+t^3\right)^2}dt=2\int\frac{\left(t^3-1\right)\left(t^3+1\right)}{\left(1+t^3\right)^2}dt+2\int\frac{1}{\left(1+t^3\right)^2}dt$$

$$=2\int\frac{t^3-1}{t^3+1}dt+2\int\frac{1}{\left(t^3+1\right)^2}dt=2\int\frac{t^3-1}{t^3+1}dt+2\int\frac{1}{\left(t^3+1\right)^2}dt$$

$$=2\int\frac{t^3+1-2}{\left(t^3+1\right)}dt+2\int\frac{1}{\left(t^3+1\right)^2}dt=2\int dt-4\int\frac{dt}{\left(t^3+1\right)}+2\int\frac{1}{\left(t^3+1\right)^2}dt$$

$$=2t-4\left(-\frac{1}{2}\ln|t^2-t+1|+\frac{1}{\sqrt{3}}\tan^{-1}\left(\frac{2t-1}{\sqrt{3}}\right)+\frac{1}{3}\ln|t^3+1|+C_1\right)+2\int\frac{1}{(t^3+1)^2}dt$$

(By Illustration 166)

$$=2t+2\ln|t^2-t+1|-\frac{4}{\sqrt{3}}\tan^{-1}\left(\frac{2t-1}{\sqrt{3}}\right)-\frac{4}{3}\ln|t^3+1|$$

$$-8\left[\frac{t}{3(t^3+1)}+\frac{2}{9}\ln|t+1|-\frac{1}{6}\ln|t^2-t+1|+\frac{1}{\sqrt{3}}\tan^{-1}\left(\frac{2t-1}{\sqrt{3}}\right)\right]+C\ \text{(By Illustration }(M))$$

$$=2x^{\frac{1}{2}}+2\ln\left|x-x^{\frac{1}{2}}+1\right|-\frac{4}{\sqrt{3}}\tan^{-1}\left(\frac{2x^{\frac{1}{2}}-1}{\sqrt{3}}\right)-\frac{4}{\sqrt{3}}\ln\left|x^{\frac{3}{2}}+1\right|-\frac{8}{3}\left(\frac{x^{\frac{1}{2}}}{1+x^{\frac{3}{2}}}\right)$$

$$-\frac{16}{9}\ln\left|1+x^{\frac{1}{2}}\right|+\frac{4}{3}\ln\left|x-x^{\frac{1}{2}}+1\right|-\frac{8}{\sqrt{3}}\tan^{-1}\left(\frac{2x^{\frac{1}{2}}-1}{\sqrt{3}}\right)+C$$

Case (III): If $p \in \mathbb{Q}; I = \int x^m (a+bx^n)^p\, dx$; where $p = \frac{r}{s}$.

Case (a): $\frac{m+1}{n} \in \mathbb{Z}$ The substitution $a + bx^n = t^s$ reduces the integral into integrable form.

$$\therefore \quad x = \left(\frac{t^s - a}{b}\right)^{1/n} \quad \Rightarrow x^m = \left(\frac{t^s - a}{b}\right)^{m/n}$$

$$\because \quad bx^n = t^s - a \quad \Rightarrow nbx^{n-1}dx = st^{s-1}dt$$

$$\Rightarrow \quad dx = \frac{st^{s-1}dt}{nbx^{n-1}}$$

$$\Rightarrow \quad I = \int\left(\frac{t^s - a}{b}\right)^{m/n} t^r . \frac{st^{s-1}dt}{nb.\left(\frac{t^s-a}{b}\right)^{\frac{n-1}{n}}}$$

$$= \frac{s}{nb}\int\left(\frac{t^s - a}{b}\right)^{\frac{m-n+1}{n}} t^{s+r-1}dt$$

$$= \frac{s}{nb}\int\left(\frac{t^s - a}{b}\right)^{\frac{m+1}{n}-1} t^{r+s-1}\, dt$$

ILLUSTRATION 173: Find the integral $\int x^{3/2}\sqrt{1+x^{5/2}}\, dx$

SOLUTION: Now, comparing this with $\int x^m (a+bx^n)^p\, dx$; we have

$$p = \frac{r}{s}$$

$$\Rightarrow r = 1, s = 2; a = 1; b = 1; m = \frac{3}{2}; n = \frac{5}{2}.$$

$$\text{Now } \frac{m+1}{n} = 1 \in \mathbb{Z}.$$

$$\Rightarrow \quad 1 + x^{\frac{5}{2}} = t^2 \qquad\qquad \Rightarrow \quad x = (t^2 - 1)^{\frac{2}{5}}$$

$$\Rightarrow \quad \frac{5}{2}x^{\frac{3}{2}}\, dx = 2t\, dt \qquad\qquad \Rightarrow \quad dx = \left(\frac{4\, t\, dt}{5\, x^{\frac{3}{2}}}\right)$$

$$I = \int x^{\frac{3}{2}}\, t\, \frac{4\, t\, dt}{5\, x^{3/2}} = \frac{4}{5}\int t^2 dt = \frac{4}{5}\left(\frac{t^3}{3}\right) + C = \frac{4}{15}t^3 + C = \frac{4}{15}\left(1 + x^{\frac{5}{2}}\right)^{\frac{3}{2}} + C$$

Case (b): If $I = \int x^m (a+bx^n)^p\, dx$; where $p = \frac{r}{s}$ and $\frac{m+1}{n} \notin \mathbb{Z}$ and $\frac{m+1}{n} + p \in \mathbb{Z}$.

The substitution $a + bx^n = t^s x^n$ reduces the integral into integrable form.

$$\Rightarrow \quad \frac{a}{x^n} = t^s - b$$

$$\Rightarrow \quad -\frac{na}{x^{n+1}}dx = st^{s-1}dt \text{ and } x^n = \frac{a}{t^s - b}$$

$$\Rightarrow \quad I = -\int x^m (x^n t^s)^{\frac{r}{s}} \frac{x^{n+1}}{na} st^{s-1}dt$$

$$= -\frac{s}{na}\int x^{m+np+n+1} t^{r+s-1}dt$$

$$= -\frac{s}{na}\int\left(\frac{a}{t^s - b}\right)^{\frac{m+np+n+1}{n}} t^{r+s-1}dt$$

ILLUSTRATION 174: Find the integral $\int \frac{dx}{x^{1/2}(1+x^2)^{5/4}}\, dx$

SOLUTION: After rearranging, given integral becomes, $I = \int x^{-\frac{1}{2}}(1+x^2)^{-\frac{5}{4}}\, dx$

Comparing the given integral with $\int x^m (a+bx^n)^p\, dx$, we have, $m = -\frac{1}{2}, n = 2, p = -\frac{5}{4}$

Here $\frac{m+1}{n} = \frac{\frac{-1}{2}+1}{2} = \frac{1}{4} \notin \mathbb{Z}$ and $\frac{1}{4}+\left(\frac{-5}{4}\right) = -1 \in \mathbb{Z}$

∴ all requisite conditions are satisfied

∴ above mentioned algorithm can be used

So let $1 + x^2 = t^4x^2$

$\Rightarrow \frac{1}{x^2} = t^4 - 1 \qquad \Rightarrow t = \left(\frac{1+x^2}{x^2}\right)^{1/4}$

$\Rightarrow (-2)\,x^{-3}\,dx = 4t^3\,dt$

$\Rightarrow dx = -2(t^3\,dt)\,x^3$

$\Rightarrow I = \int x^{-\frac{1}{2}}\left(t^4x^2\right)^{-\frac{5}{4}}\left(-2t^3dt\,x^3\right) = -2\int x^{\frac{1}{2}}t^{-5}x^{-\frac{5}{2}}t^3\,dt$

$= (-2)\int t^{-2}dt = (+2)\left(\frac{1}{t}\right) + C = 2\left(\frac{x^2}{1+x^2}\right)^{1/4} + C$

Euler's Substitution

If the integrand is of the form $R\left(x, \sqrt{ax^2+bx+c}\right)$, i.e., to evaluate $\int R\left(x, \sqrt{ax^2+bx+c}\right)dx$

Case (i): If $D = b^2 - 4ac > 0$; then put $\underbrace{\sqrt{ax^2+bx+c} = t(x-\alpha)}_{\text{Where } \alpha \text{ is a root of } ax^2+bx+c=0}$

Case (ii): If $D = b^2 - 4ac < 0$

$\Rightarrow ax^2 + bx + c > 0\ \forall\ x \in \mathbb{R}$

iff $a, c > 0$; put $\sqrt{ax^2+bx+c} = \begin{cases} t \pm x\sqrt{a} \\ xt \pm \sqrt{c} \end{cases}$

Or try to carry out the trigonometric substitutions as given below.

1. Substitute $x + \frac{b}{2a} = \begin{cases} \frac{\sqrt{D}}{2a}\sin t \\ \frac{\sqrt{D}}{2a}\cos t \end{cases}$ if $a < 0, D > 0$

2. Substitute $x + \frac{b}{2a} = \begin{cases} \frac{\sqrt{-D}}{2a}\tan t \\ \frac{\sqrt{-D}}{2a}\cot t \end{cases}$ if $a > 0, D < 0$

3. Substitute $x + \frac{b}{2a} = \begin{cases} \frac{\sqrt{D}}{2a}\sec t \\ \frac{\sqrt{D}}{2a}\operatorname{cosec} t \end{cases}$ if $a > 0, D > 0$

ILLUSTRATION 175: Evaluate the integral $\int \frac{x\,dx}{\sqrt{(7x-10-x^2)^3}}dx$

SOLUTION: $a < 0, c < 0$ and $D > 0$. Also the roots are 2 and 5.

$\Rightarrow$ put $\sqrt{7x-10-x^2} = \sqrt{(x-2)(5-x)} = (x-2)t$

$\Rightarrow (5-x) = (x-2)t^2$

$\Rightarrow dx = \frac{-6t}{(1+t^2)^2}dt$

$$\Rightarrow I=\int\frac{\left(\frac{5+2t^2}{1+t^2}\right)\frac{-6t}{(1+t^2)^2}}{\left(\frac{3t}{1+t^2}\right)^3}dt=-\frac{6}{27}\int\left(\frac{5}{t^2}+2\right)dt$$

$$=\frac{10}{9}\left(\frac{-1}{t}\right)-\frac{4}{9}t+C=\frac{10}{9t}-\frac{4}{9}t+C=\frac{10(x-2)}{9\sqrt{(x-2)(5-x)}}-\frac{4}{9}\times\frac{\sqrt{(x-2)(5-x)}}{(x-2)}+C$$

ILLUSTRATION 176: Evaluate the integral $\int\frac{dx}{x+\sqrt{x^2-x+1}}$

SOLUTION: Now, as per above mentioned rule $a = 1 > 0$ and $c = 1 > 0$.

$\therefore$ Let $\sqrt{x^2-x+1} = tx - \sqrt{1}$.

$\Rightarrow$ Now, on squaring both sides $x^2 - x + 1 = (tx - 1)^2$

$x^2 - x + 1 = t^2x^2 + 1 - 2tx$

$\Rightarrow x^2(1 - t^2) = (1 - 2t)x$

$\Rightarrow x=\frac{1-2t}{1-t^2}$ $\qquad\qquad \Rightarrow dx=\left(\frac{-2t^2+2t-2}{(1-t^2)^2}\right)dt$

Now, evaluating $x+\sqrt{x^2-x+1}$ in terms of 't'

$$\sqrt{x^2-x+1}=t\left(\frac{2t-1}{t^2-1}\right)-1=\frac{t(2t-1)-(t^2-1)}{(t^2-1)}=\frac{t^2-t+1}{t^2-1}$$

Now, $x+\sqrt{x^2-x+1}=\left(\frac{2t-1}{t^2-1}\right)+\frac{(t^2-t+1)}{t^2-1}=\frac{t^2+t}{t^2-1}=\frac{t}{t-1}$

$$\Rightarrow I=\int\frac{1}{\frac{t}{(t-1)}}\cdot\left(\frac{-2t^2+2t-2}{(t^2-1)^2}\right)dt=\int\frac{(-2t^2+2t-2)}{t(t+1)^2(t-1)}dt$$

$$=\frac{-2t^2+2t-2}{t(t+1)^2(t-1)}=\frac{A}{t}+\frac{B}{(t+1)}+\frac{C}{(t+1)^2}+\frac{D}{(t-1)}$$

On solving the previous equation we get the values of $A = 2$, $B=-\frac{3}{2}$, $C = -3$, $D=-\frac{1}{2}$

$$\int\frac{\left(-2t^2+2t-2\right)dt}{t(t+1)^2(t-1)}=\int\frac{2}{t}dt-\int\frac{3}{2}\frac{1dt}{(t+1)}-3\int\frac{1}{(t+1)^2}dt-\frac{1}{2}\int\frac{1}{(t-1)}dt$$

$$=2\ln t-\frac{3}{2}\ln|t+1|+3\frac{1}{(t+1)}-\frac{1}{2}\ln|t-1|+C\text{; where } t=\frac{\sqrt{x^2-x+1}+1}{x}$$

ILLUSTRATION 177: Find $\int\frac{dx}{x-\sqrt{x^2+2x+4}}$

SOLUTION: Put $x-\sqrt{x^2+2x+4}=t$

$\Rightarrow \sqrt{x^2+2x+4}=x-t$ $\qquad\qquad \Rightarrow x^2 + 2x + 4 = x^2 + t^2 - 2xt$

$\Rightarrow 2x + 4 = t^2 - 2xt$ $\qquad\qquad \Rightarrow 2x(1 + t) = t^2 - 4$

$\Rightarrow x=\frac{1}{2}\frac{\left(t^2-4\right)}{(t+1)}$

$$\Rightarrow\ dx=\frac{1}{2}\left[\frac{(t+1)(2t)-(t^2-4)}{(t+1)^2}\right]dt\ =\frac{1}{2}\left[\frac{2t^2+2t-t^2+4}{(t+1)^2}\right]dt=\frac{1}{2}\left[\frac{t^2+2t+4}{(t+1)^2}\right]$$

$$\therefore\quad I=\int\frac{1}{2}\times\frac{(t^2+2t+4)}{(t+1)^2}\times\frac{1}{t}dt\ =\frac{1}{2}\int\frac{\left[(t+1)^2+2\right]}{t(t+1)^2}dt\ =\frac{1}{2}\int\left[\frac{1}{t}+\frac{2}{t(t+1)^2}\right]dt$$

$$=\frac{1}{2}\int\left(\frac{1}{t}+\frac{2\left[(t+1)-t\right]}{t(t+1)^2}\right)dt\ =\frac{1}{2}\int\left(\frac{1}{t}+\frac{2}{t(t+1)}-\frac{2}{(t+1)^2}\right)dt$$

$$=\frac{1}{2}\int\left(\frac{1}{t}+\frac{2\left[(t+1)-t\right]}{t(t+1)}-\frac{2}{(t+1)^2}\right)dt\ =\frac{3}{2}\ln|t|-\ln|t+1|+\frac{1}{(t+1)}+C$$

$$=\frac{3}{2}\ln\left|x-\sqrt{x^2+2x+4}\right|+\ln\left|x-\sqrt{x^2+2x+4}+1\right|+\frac{1}{\left(x-\sqrt{x^2+2x+4}+1\right)}+C$$

ILLUSTRATION 178: Find $\int\frac{\left(x+\sqrt{1+x^2}\right)^{15}}{\sqrt{1+x^2}}dx$

SOLUTION: Put $x+\sqrt{1+x^2}=t$

$\Rightarrow\ \sqrt{1+x^2}=t-x$ $\qquad\Rightarrow\ 1+x^2=t^2+x^2-2xt$

$\Rightarrow\ 1=t^2-2xt$ $\qquad\Rightarrow\ 2xt=t^2-1$

$$\Rightarrow\ x=\frac{t^2-1}{2t}$$

$$\Rightarrow\ dx=\frac{1}{2}\left[\frac{t(2t)-(t^2-1)}{t^2}\right]dt\ =\frac{1}{2}\left[\frac{t^2+1}{t^2}\right]dt$$

Also $\sqrt{1+x^2}=t-x=t-\left(\frac{t^2-1}{2t}\right)=\frac{2t^2-t^2+1}{2t}$

$$\Rightarrow\ \sqrt{1+x^2}=\frac{t^2+1}{2t}$$

$$\therefore\quad I=\int\frac{t^{15}(2t)}{(t^2+1)}\cdot\frac{(t^2+1)}{2t^2}dt\ =\int t^{14}dt=\frac{t^{15}}{15}+C\ =\frac{1}{15}\left(x+\sqrt{1+x^2}\right)^{15}+C$$

ILLUSTRATION 179: Find the integral $\int\frac{dx}{\sqrt{(2x-x^2)^3}}$

SOLUTION: $I=\int\frac{dx}{\left(\sqrt{-x(x-2)}\right)^3}$

Put $=\sqrt{-x(x-2)}=(x-2)t$ $\qquad\Rightarrow\ -x(x-2)=(x-2)^2t^2$

$\Rightarrow\ -x=(x-2)t^2$ $\qquad\Rightarrow\ -x=xt^2-2t^2$

$\Rightarrow\ x(1+t^2)=2t^2$ $\qquad\Rightarrow\ x=\frac{2t^2}{t^2+1}$

$$\Rightarrow dx = \frac{(t^2+1)(4t)-(2t^2)(2t)}{(t^2+1)^2}dt \qquad \Rightarrow dx = \frac{4t^3+4t-4t^3}{(t^2+1)^2}dt = \frac{4t}{(t^2+1)^2}dt$$

$$\therefore \quad I = \int \frac{4t}{(t^2+1)^2}\cdot\frac{1}{[(x-2)t]^3}dt = \int \frac{4}{(t^2+1)^2\left[\frac{2t^2}{t^2+1}-2\right]^3 t^2}dt$$

$$= \int \frac{4(t^2+1)^3}{(t^2+1)^2(-8)t^2}dt = -\frac{1}{2}\int\frac{(t^2+1)}{t^2}dt = -\frac{1}{2}\int(1+t^{-2})\,dt$$

$$= -\frac{1}{2}t + \frac{1}{2t} + C = -\frac{1}{2t} + C = \frac{-1}{2}\frac{\sqrt{2x-x^2}}{(x-2)} + \frac{(x-2)}{2\sqrt{2x-x^2}} + C$$

$$= \frac{1}{2}\left[\frac{(x-2)}{\sqrt{2x-x^2}} - \frac{\sqrt{2x-x^2}}{(x-2)}\right] + C = \frac{1}{2}\left[\frac{x^2+4-4x-2x+x^2}{(x-2)\sqrt{2x-x^2}}\right]+C$$

$$= \frac{1}{2}\left[\frac{2x^2-6x+4}{(x-2)\sqrt{2x-x^2}}\right]+C = \left[\frac{x^2-3x+2}{(x-2)\sqrt{2x-x^2}}\right]+C = \left[\frac{(x-2)(x-1)}{(x-2)\sqrt{2x-x^2}}\right]+C$$

$$= \frac{(x-1)}{\sqrt{2x-x^2}} + C \text{ Ans}$$

TEXTUAL EXERCISE–8: (SUBJECTIVE)

1. Evaluate the following integrals:

(a) $\int \frac{dx}{(x-1)^3\sqrt{x^2-3x+2}}$

(b) $\int \frac{dx}{(2x+1)\sqrt{x-1}}$

(c) $\int \frac{dx}{(x-1)\sqrt{2x^2+1}}$

(d) $\int \frac{dx}{(2x^2+3)\sqrt{x^2-1}}$

(e) $\int \frac{(x-1)\,dx}{(x+1)\sqrt{x^3+x^2+x}}$

(f) $\int \frac{dx}{(x-a)^{3/2}(x+a)^{1/2}}$

2. Evaluate the integrals of the following irrational functions:

(a) $\int \frac{x+\sqrt[3]{x^2}+\sqrt[6]{x}}{x(1+\sqrt[3]{x})}dx$

(b) $\int \frac{1}{(1+x)^{1/2}-(1+x)^{1/3}}dx$

(c) $\int \frac{x^{1/2}}{x^{1/2}-x^{1/3}}dx$

(d) $\int \frac{x+x^{2/3}+2x^{1/6}}{x(1+x^{1/3})}dx$

(e) $\int \frac{1+x^{1/2}-x^{2/3}}{1+x^{1/3}}dx$

(f) $\int \frac{\sqrt[4]{x}}{\sqrt{x}-1}dx$

(g) $\int \frac{1}{x+\sqrt[3]{x}}dx$

(h) $\int \frac{1}{\sqrt{(x+1)}-\sqrt[4]{(x+1)}}dx$

(i) $\int \sqrt{\left(\frac{e^x+a}{e^x-a}\right)}dx$

(j) $\int \frac{\sqrt[3]{1+\sqrt[4]{x}}}{\sqrt{x}}dx$

(k) $\int \frac{(x^{-7/6}-x^{5/6})\,dx}{x^{1/3}(x^2+x+1)^{1/2}-x^{1/2}(x^2+x+1)^{1/3}}$

(l) $\int \frac{(x+\sqrt{1+x^2})^{15}}{\sqrt{1+x^2}}dx$

3. Prove that $x^{-m}(a+bx)^{-n}$ is directly integrable when $(m+n)$ is a positive integer greater than unity.

4. Integrate the following irrational functions:

(a) $\int x^{3/2}(a+bx^3)^5\,dx$

(b) $\int x^{1/2}(1+x^{3/2})^{-2}\,dx$

(c) $\int x^{3/2}\sqrt{1+x^{5/2}}\,dx$

(d) $\int \dfrac{dx}{x^{1/2}(1+x^2)^{5/4}}$

(e) $\int x^{-11}(1+x^4)^{-1/2}\,dx$

(f) $\int x^{-8}(1+x^7)^{1/3}\,dx$

(g) $\int \sqrt[3]{x}\sqrt[7]{(1+\sqrt[3]{x^4})}\,dx$

(h) $\int \sin^{3/2}x.\cos^{5/2}x\,dx$

(i) $\int x^{13/2}\sqrt{1+x^{5/2}}\,dx$

5. Find $\dfrac{dx}{x\sqrt{x^2+x+2}}$

6. Find $\int \dfrac{x.dx}{\left(5-4x-x^2\right)^{3/2}}$

7. Find $\int \dfrac{dx}{\left(x+\sqrt{x^2-4}\right)^{5/3}}$

Answer Keys

1. (a) $\frac{2}{5}\left(\frac{x-2}{x-1}\right)^{5/2}+2\sqrt{\frac{x-2}{x-1}}-\frac{4}{3}\left(\frac{x-2}{x-1}\right)^{3/2}+C$

(b) $\sqrt{\frac{2}{3}}\tan^{-1}\left(\sqrt{x-1}\sqrt{\frac{2}{3}}\right)+C$

(c) $-\ln\left|t+\frac{2}{3}+\sqrt{t^2+\frac{4t}{3}+\frac{2}{3}}\right|+C\ ;\ t=\frac{1}{x-1}$

(d) $\frac{1}{2\sqrt{15}}\left|\frac{\sqrt{5}+\sqrt{3}(\sqrt{x^2-1})}{\sqrt{5}-\sqrt{3}(\sqrt{x^2-1})}\right|+C$

(e) $2\tan^{-1}\sqrt{\frac{x^2+x+1}{x}}+C$

(f) $-\frac{1}{a}\sqrt{\left(\frac{x+a}{x-a}\right)}+C$

2. (a) $\frac{x^{2/3}}{4}+\tan^{-1}x^{1/6}+C$

(b) $2(1+x)^{1/2}+3(1+x)^{1/3}+6(1+x)^{1/6}+6\ln|(1+x)^{1/6}-1|+C$

(c) $6\left[\frac{t^6}{6}+\frac{t^5}{5}+\frac{t^4}{4}+\frac{t^3}{3}+\frac{t^2}{2}+t+\ln|t-1|\right]+C\ ;\ t=x^{1/6}$

(d) $\frac{3}{2}x^{2/3}+12\tan^{-1}x^{1/6}+C$

(e) $-\frac{3}{4}x^{4/3}+\frac{6}{7}x^{7/6}+x-\frac{6}{5}x^{5/6}+2x^{1/2}-6x^{1/6}+6\tan^{-1}(x^{1/6})+C$

(f) $\frac{4}{3}x^{3/4}+4x^{1/4}+2\ln\left|\frac{x^{1/4}-1}{x^{1/4}+1}\right|+C$

(g) $\frac{3}{2}\ln|x^{2/3}+1|+C$

(h) $2(x+1)^{1/2}+4(x+1)^{1/4}+4\ln|(x+1)^{1/4}-1|+C$

(i) $\ln(e^x+\sqrt{(e^{2x}-e^2)})+\sec^{-1}\left(\frac{e^x}{a}\right)+C$

(j) $\frac{12(1+x^{1/4})^{7/3}}{7}-\frac{12x(1+x^{1/4})^{4/3}}{4}+C$

(k) $-6\left[\frac{t^4}{4}+\frac{t^3}{3}+\frac{t^2}{2}+t\right]-6\ln|t-1|+C$, where $t=\left(\frac{x^2+x+1}{x}\right)^{1/6}$

(l) $\frac{\left(x+\sqrt{1+x^2}\right)^{15}}{15}+C$

4. (a) $\frac{b^5}{35/2}x^{35/2}+\frac{45b^4}{29/2}x^{29/2}+\frac{1620b^3}{23/2}x^{23/2}+\frac{9^3\times 5b^2}{13/2}x^{13/2}+\frac{9^5}{5/2}x^{5/2}+C$

(b) $\frac{-2}{3(1+x^{3/2})}+C$

(c) $\frac{4}{15}(1+x^{5/2})^{3/2}+C$

(d) $2\left(\frac{x^2}{1+x^2}\right)^{1/4}+C$

(e) $-\frac{1}{4(t-1)}-\frac{1}{4(t+1)}-\frac{1}{4}\ln\left|\frac{t-1}{t+1}\right|+C$, where $t=\frac{\sqrt{x^4+1}}{x^2}$

(f) $\frac{1}{7}\left\{-\frac{t}{t^3-1}+\frac{1}{3}\ln|t-1|-\frac{1}{6}\ln|t^2+t+1|-\frac{1}{\sqrt{3}}\tan^{-1}\left(\frac{2t+1}{\sqrt{3}}\right)\right\}+C$; where $t = (1 + x^7)^{1/3}$

(i) $\frac{4}{5}\left[\frac{(1+x^{5/2})^{7/2}}{7}-\frac{(1+x^{5/2})^2}{2}+\frac{(1+x^{5/2})^{3/2}}{3}\right]+C$

5. $\frac{1}{\sqrt{2}}\ln\left|\frac{2\sqrt{2}\sqrt{x^2+x+2}-4-x}{x}\right|+C$

6. $-\frac{1}{18}\left(t+\frac{5}{t}\right)$; where $t = \frac{\sqrt{5-4x-x^2}}{(x-1)}$

7. $\frac{3}{4}(1-t^2)t^{-8/3}+C$; where $t = x+\sqrt{x^2-4}$

TEXTUAL EXERCISE–8: (OBJECTIVE)

1. $\int\frac{\sqrt{x}+\sqrt[3]{x}}{\sqrt[4]{x^5}-\sqrt[6]{x^7}}dx$ equals

(a) $4\sqrt[4]{x}+6\sqrt[6]{x}+\sqrt[12]{x}+\ln|\sqrt[12]{x}+1|+C$

(b) $\sqrt[4]{x}+\sqrt[6]{x}+24\sqrt[12]{x}+24\ln|\sqrt[12]{x}-1|+C$

(c) $4\sqrt[4]{x}+6\sqrt[6]{x}+24\sqrt[12]{x}+24\ln|\sqrt[12]{x}-1|+C$

(d) None of these

2. $\int\frac{(2x-3)^{1/2}\,dx}{(2x-3)^{1/3}+1}$ equals

(a) $3\left[\frac{1}{7}(2x-3)^{1/3}-\frac{1}{5}(2x-3)^{1/6}+\frac{1}{3}(2x-3)^{1/2}-(2x-3)^{7/6}+\tan^{-1}(2x-3)^{1/6}\right]+C$

(b) $3\left[\frac{1}{7}(2x-3)^{7/6}-\frac{1}{5}(2x-3)^{5/6}+\frac{1}{3}(2x-3)^{1/2}-(2x-3)^{1/6}+\tan^{-1}(2x-3)^{1/6}\right]+C$

(c) $\left[\frac{1}{7}(2x-3)^{7/6}+\frac{2}{5}(2x-3)^{5/6}-\frac{5}{3}(2x-3)^{1/3}-(2x-3)^{1/6}+\ln(2x-3)^{1/6}\right]+C$

(d) None of these

3. $\int\frac{2}{(2-x)^2}\sqrt[3]{\frac{2-x}{2+x}}dx$ equals

(a) $\frac{3}{4}\sqrt[3]{\left(\frac{2+x}{2-x}\right)^2}+C$ (b) $\frac{4}{3}\sqrt[3]{\left(\frac{2-x}{2+x}\right)^2}+C$

(c) $\frac{1}{3}\sqrt[3]{\left(\frac{2+x}{2-x}\right)^5}+C$ (d) None of these

4. $\int\frac{dx}{x\left(2+\sqrt[3]{\frac{x-1}{x}}\right)}$ equals

(a) $\frac{2}{\sqrt{3}}\tan^{-1}\left(\frac{2t+1}{\sqrt{3}}\right)-\ln\left|\sqrt[3]{(t+2)^4}+\sqrt{t^2+t+1}\right|+C$

(b) $\tan^{-1}\left(\frac{2t+1}{\sqrt{3}}\right)+\ln\left|(t-1)+\sqrt{t^2+t+1}\right|+C$

(c) $\frac{1}{\sqrt{3}}\tan^{-1}\left(\frac{2t-1}{\sqrt{3}}\right)+\ln\left|\frac{\sqrt[3]{(t+2)^4}}{\sqrt[3]{t+1}.\sqrt{t^2+t+1}}\right|+C$; $t=\sqrt[3]{\frac{x-1}{x}}$

(d) $-\frac{1}{\sqrt{3}}\tan^{-1}\left(\frac{2t+1}{\sqrt{3}}\right)+\ln\left|\frac{\sqrt[3]{(t+2)^4}}{\sqrt[3]{t-1}.\sqrt{t^2+t+1}}\right|+C$; $t=\sqrt[3]{\frac{x-1}{x}}$

5. $\int\frac{dx}{\sqrt[3]{(x+1)^2(x-1)^4}}$ equals

(a) $\sqrt[3]{\frac{1+x}{1-x}}+C$ (b) $\frac{3}{2}\sqrt[3]{\frac{1+x}{1-x}}+C$

(c) $\sqrt[3]{\frac{1-x}{1+x}}+C$ (d) None of these

6. $\int(x-2)\sqrt{\frac{1+x}{1-x}}dx$ equals

(a) $\left(\frac{x-1}{2}\right)\sqrt{x^2-1}-\sin^{-1}x+C$

(b) $\left(\frac{x-2}{2}\right)\sqrt{1-x^2}+\cos^{-1}x+C$

(c) $\left(\frac{2-x}{2}\right)\sqrt{1-x^2}-\frac{3}{2}\sin^{-1}x+C$

(d) None of these

7. $\int\frac{dx}{(1-x)^{3/2}\sqrt{(1+x)}}$ equals

(a) $\sqrt{\frac{1+x}{1-x}}+2(1-x)^{1/2}+C$

(b) $\sqrt{\frac{1-x}{1+x}}+\sqrt{1-x}+C$

(c) $\sqrt{\frac{1+x}{1-x}}+C$

(d) None of these

8. $\int\frac{dx}{\sqrt{x^2+2x+2}+1}$ equals

(a) $\ln|t+1|+\frac{2}{t+2}+C;\ t=x+\sqrt{x^2+2x+2}$

(b) $-\frac{2}{t}-\ln|1-t|+C;\ t=\sqrt{x^2+2x+2}-x$

(c) $-\frac{2}{t}+\ln|1-t|+C;\ t=x+\sqrt{x^2+2x+2}$

(d) $-\ln|t+1|+\frac{2}{t+2}+C;\ t=\sqrt{x^2+2x+2}-x$

9. $\int\frac{(x+3)\,dx}{\sqrt{4x^2+4x-3}}$ equals

(a) $\sqrt{4x^2+4x-3}-5\ln\left|2x+1+\sqrt{4x^2+4x-3}\right|+C$

(b) $\frac{1}{4}\sqrt{4x^2+4x-3}+\frac{5}{4}\ln\left|2x+1+\sqrt{4x^2+4x-3}\right|+C$

(c) $\sqrt{4x^2+4x-3}-\frac{5}{4}\ln\left|(2x+1)-\sqrt{4x^2+4x-3}\right|+C$

(d) None of these

10. $\int\frac{x\,dx}{(x^2-3x+2)\sqrt{x^2-4x+3}}$ equals

(a) $-\frac{\sqrt{x^2-4x+3}}{(x-1)}-2\sin^{-1}\left(\frac{1}{x-2}\right)+C$

(b) $\frac{\sqrt{x^2-4x+3}}{(x-1)}+2\sin^{-1}\left(\frac{1}{x-2}\right)+C$

(c) $\sqrt{x^2-4x+3}-2\sin^{-1}(x-2)+C$

(d) None of these

11. $\int x^{-\frac{2}{3}}\left(1+x^{\frac{2}{3}}\right)^{-1}dx$ equals

(a) $3\tan^{-1}(x)^{-2/3}+C$ (b) $3\tan^{-1}(x)^{1/3}+C$

(c) $\tan^{-1}(x)^{2/3}+C$ (d) None of these

12. $\int x^{1/3}\left(2+\sqrt{x}\right)^2dx$ equals

(a) $\frac{3}{7}x^{-\frac{7}{3}}+24x^{-\frac{11}{6}}+3x^{\frac{4}{3}}+C$

(b) $3x^{\frac{7}{3}}-24x^{\frac{11}{6}}+3x^{\frac{4}{3}}+C$

(c) $\frac{3}{7}x^{\frac{7}{3}}+\frac{24}{11}x^{\frac{11}{6}}+3x^{\frac{4}{3}}+C$

(d) None of these

13. $\int\frac{\sqrt{1+\sqrt[3]{x}}}{\sqrt[3]{x^2}}dx$ equals

(a) $\left(1-x^{1/3}\right)^{3/2}+C$

(b) $\left(1+x^{2/3}\right)^{3/2}+C$

(c) $2\left(1+x^{2/3}\right)^{3/2}+C$

(d) $2\left(1+x^{1/3}\right)^{3/2}+C$

14. $\int\frac{dx}{x\left(1+\sqrt[3]{x}\right)^2}$ equals

(a) $2\ln\left(\frac{\sqrt[3]{x}}{1+\sqrt[3]{x}}\right)-\left(\frac{1}{1+\sqrt[3]{x}}\right)+C$

(b) $3\ln\frac{\sqrt[3]{x}}{1+\sqrt[3]{x}}+\left(\frac{3}{1+\sqrt[3]{x}}\right)+C$

(c) $\ln\left(\frac{\sqrt[3]{x}}{1+\sqrt[3]{x}}\right)+\left(\frac{1}{1+\sqrt[3]{x}}\right)+C$

(d) None of these

15. $\int\frac{dx}{x^3\sqrt[5]{1+\frac{1}{x}}}$ equals

(a) $\frac{-5}{11}\left(1+\frac{1}{x}\right)^{11/5}+\frac{5}{6}\left(1+\frac{1}{x}\right)^{6/5}+C$

(b) $\frac{-2}{15}\sqrt{\frac{x+2}{x+1}}-\frac{8x^2+12x+7}{(x+1)^2}+C$

(c) $-\frac{2}{15}\sqrt{\frac{x+2}{x+1}}+\frac{8x^2+12x+7}{(x+1)^2}+C$

(d) None of these

Answer Keys

1. (c)	**2.** (b)	**3.** (a)	**4.** (d)	**5.** (b)	**6.** (c)	**7.** (c)	**8.** (a, b)	**9.** (b)	**10.** (a)
11. (b)	**12.** (c)	**13.** (d)	**14.** (b)	**15.** (a)					

REDUCTION FORMULA

Let a general integral $I_n = \int (f(x))^n g(x)\, dx$; $n \in \mathbb{N}$ to be found. A relation $R(I_n, I_{n-1}, I_{n-2} \dots) = 0$, by which an integral with higher index is reduced to integral having lower index is called a reduction formula.

E.g., $I_n = \int (\ln x)^n\, dx = (\ln x)^n \,.\, x - n\int (\ln x)^{n-1} dx$

$\Rightarrow$ $I_n = x(\ln x)^x - nI_{n-1}$ is the reduction formula.

ILLUSTRATION 180: Evaluate the integral $I_6 = \int (\ln x)^6\, dx$

SOLUTION: $I_6 = x(\ln x)^6 - 6I_5 = x(\ln x)^6 - 6\left(x(\ln x)^5 - 5I_4\right)$

$= x(\ln x)^6 - 6x(\ln x)^5 + 30I_4 = x(\ln x)^6 - 6x (\ln x)^5 + 30I_4 = x(\ln x)^6 - 6x (\ln x)^5$
$+ 30(x(\ln x)^4 - 4I_3)$

$= x(\ln x)^6 - 6x(\ln x)^5 + 30x(\ln x)^4 - 120 (x \ln^3 x - 3I_2)$

$= x(\ln x)^6 - 6x(\ln x)^5 + 30x(\ln x)^4 - 120\, x \ln^3 x + 360 (x \ln^2 x - 2I_1)$

$= x(\ln x)^6 - 6x(\ln x)^5 + 30x\ln^4 x - 120\, x \ln^3 x + 360\, x\ln^2 x - 720 (x \ln x - x) + C$

$= x(\ln x)^6 - 6x(\ln x)^5 + 30x (\ln x)^4 - 120\, x(\ln x)^3 + 360\, x(\ln x)^2 - 720\, x \ln x + 720\, x + C.$

Reduction formula for $\int \sin^n x\, dx$ and $\int \cos^n x\, dx$ and Walli's Formulae:

(a) $I_n = \int \sin^n x\, dx$

$\Rightarrow I_n = -\cos x \sin^{n-1} x + (n-1)\int \sin^{n-2} x.\cos^2 x\, dx$

$\Rightarrow I_n = -\cos x \sin^{n-1} + (n-1)\int \sin^{n-2} x.\left(1-\sin^2 x\right) dx$

$\Rightarrow I_n = -\cos x \sin^{n-1} + (n-1)\,.\, I_{n-2} - (n-1)I_n$

$\Rightarrow I_n = -\dfrac{\cos x \sin^{n-1} x}{n} + \dfrac{(n-1)}{n} I_{n-2}$

Let us evaluate $\int_0^{\pi/2} \sin^n x dx$ = ln (say)

$\therefore\ I_n = \left[-\dfrac{\cos x \sin^{n-1} x}{n}\right]_0^{\pi/2} + \left(\dfrac{n-1}{n}\right) I_{n-2}$

$= \left(\dfrac{n-1}{n}\right) \cdot \dfrac{(n-3)}{n-2} . I_{n-4}; = \left(\dfrac{n-1}{n}\right)\cdot\left(\dfrac{n-3}{n-2}\right)\cdot\left(\dfrac{n-5}{n-4}\right) . I_{n-6}$

and so on.

Case (i): If n is even then $I_n = \dfrac{n-1}{n} \cdot \dfrac{n-3}{n-2} \cdot \dfrac{n-5}{n-4} \dots \dfrac{1}{2} .. I_0$

$= \left(\dfrac{n-1}{n}\right)\cdot\left(\dfrac{n-3}{n-2}\right)\cdot\left(\dfrac{n-5}{n-4}\right)\dots\dfrac{1}{2}\int_0^{\pi/2} 1\, dx$

$= \left(\left(\dfrac{n-1}{n}\right)\cdot\left(\dfrac{n-3}{n-2}\right)\cdot\left(\dfrac{n-5}{n-4}\right)\dots\dfrac{1}{2}\right)\dfrac{\pi}{2}$

Case (ii): If n is odd, then

$I_n = \left(\dfrac{n-1}{n}\right)\cdot\left(\dfrac{n-3}{n-2}\right)\cdot\left(\dfrac{n-5}{n-4}\right)\dots\dfrac{2}{3} .. I_1$

$= \left(\dfrac{n-1}{n}\right)\cdot\left(\dfrac{n-3}{n-2}\right)\cdot\left(\dfrac{n-5}{n-4}\right)\dots\dfrac{2}{3}\int_0^{\pi/2} \sin x\, dx$

$= \left(\dfrac{n-1}{n}\right)\cdot\left(\dfrac{n-3}{n-2}\right)\cdot\left(\dfrac{n-5}{n-4}\right)\dots\dfrac{2}{3}$

$$\Rightarrow I_n = \begin{cases} \left(\dfrac{n-1}{n} \cdot \dfrac{n-3}{n-2} \dots \dfrac{1}{2}\right)\dfrac{\pi}{2} & \text{if } n \text{ even} \\ \left(\dfrac{n-1}{n} \cdot \dfrac{n-3}{n-2} \dots \dfrac{2}{3}\right) & \text{if } n \text{ odd} \end{cases}$$

Thus, $\int_0^{\pi/2} \sin^n x\, dx = \dfrac{(n-1).(n-3).(n-5)\dots}{(n).(n-2).(n-4)\dots} \times \dfrac{\pi}{2}$; where $\dfrac{\pi}{2}$ stands for multiplication by $\dfrac{\pi}{2}$ iff n is even otherwise not.

i.e., $I_n = \dfrac{(n-1) \times \text{go on diminishing by } 2}{n \times \text{go on diminishing by } 2} \times \dfrac{\pi}{2}$.

ILLUSTRATION 181: Evaluate the following integral $I_5 = \int \sin^5 x\, dx$

SOLUTION: Consider $I_5 = \int \underbrace{\sin^4 x}_{(\text{II}^{\text{nd}}\text{ function})} . \underbrace{\sin x\, dx}_{(\text{I}^{\text{st}}\text{ function})} = (sin^4 x)\int \sin x\, dx - \int\left\{\frac{d}{dx}(\sin^4 x)\int \sin x\, dx\right\}dx$

$= (\sin^4 x)(-\cos x) - \int(4\sin^3 x.\cos x(-\cos x))\,dx = -\sin^4 x \cos x + \int(4\sin^3 x\cos^2 x)\,dx$

$= -\sin^4 x\cos x + \int(4\sin^3 x(1-\sin^2 x))\,dx = -(\cos x)\sin^4 x + 4\int \sin^3 x dx - 4\int \sin^5 dx$

$\Rightarrow\ 5I_5 = -\cos x \sin^4 x + 4\int \underbrace{\sin x}_{II}\underbrace{\sin^2 x\, dx}_{I}$

$= -\cos x \sin^4 x + 4\left[\sin^2 x\int \sin x\, dx - \int\left\{\frac{d}{dx}(\sin^2 x)\int \sin x\, dx\right\}dx\right]$

$= -\cos x \sin^4 x + 4\left[\sin^2 x(-\cos x) + \int 2\sin x\cos^2 x\, dx\right]$

$= -\cos x . \sin^4 x - 4\sin^2 x\cos x + 8\left(\frac{-\cos^3 x}{3}\right) + C_1$

$\Rightarrow\ I_5 = -\frac{1}{5}\cos x\sin^4 x - \frac{4}{5}\sin^2 x\cos x - \frac{8}{15}\cos^3 x + C$

ILLUSTRATION 182: Evaluate (i) $\int_0^{\pi/2} \sin^7 x dx$ (ii) $\int_0^{\pi/2} \sin^8 x dx$

SOLUTION: (i) $\int_0^{\pi/2} \sin^7 x dx = \frac{6}{7}.\frac{4}{5}.\frac{2}{3} = \frac{16}{35}$

(ii) $\int_0^{\pi/2} \sin^8 x dx = \frac{7}{8}.\frac{5}{6}.\frac{3}{4}.\frac{1}{2}.\frac{\pi}{2} = \frac{35\pi}{256}$

(b) Let $I_n = \int \cos^n x\, dx$

$\therefore\ I_n = \int \cos^n x\, dx = \int \underbrace{\cos x}_{II}.\underbrace{\cos^{n-1} x}_{I}\, dx$

$\therefore\ I_n = \sin x\cos^{n-1} x + (n-1)\int \cos^{n-2} x(1-\cos^2 x)\, dx$

$\Rightarrow I_n = \sin x \cos (n-1) I_{n-2} - (n-1) I_n$

$I_n = \frac{\sin x\cos^{n-1} x}{n} + \frac{(n-1)}{n} I_{n-2}$

and if we let $I_n = \int_0^{\pi/2} \cos^n x\, dx$

$= \left[\frac{\sin x\cos^{n-1} x}{n}\right]_0^{\pi/2} + \frac{(n-1)}{n} I_{n-2}$

$= \frac{(n-1)}{n}.\frac{(n-3)}{(n-2)} I_{n-4}$

$= \frac{(n-1)}{n}.\frac{(n-3)}{(n-2)}.\frac{(n-5)}{(n-4)} I_{n-6}$

Proceeding as in (case (i)), we have

$I_n = \left\{\frac{(n-1)\times\text{go on diminishing by 2}}{n\times\text{go on diminishing by 2}}\right\}\times\frac{\pi}{2}$ where multiplication by $\frac{\pi}{2}$ stands iff n is even otherwise no multiplication by $\frac{\pi}{2}$ is needed.

ILLUSTRATION 183: Evaluate the integral $\int \cos^6 x\, dx$

SOLUTION: Consider $I_6 = \frac{\sin x\cos^5 x}{6} + \frac{5}{6} I_4$

$= \frac{\sin x\cos^5 x}{6} + \frac{5}{6}\left(\frac{\sin x\cos^3 x}{4} + \frac{3}{4} I_2\right) = \frac{1}{6}\sin x\cos^5 x + \frac{5}{29}\sin x\cos^3 x + \frac{5}{8} I_2$

But $I_2 = \int \cos^2 x\, dx = \frac{\sin x \cos x}{2} + \frac{1}{2}x$

$\therefore \quad I_6 = \frac{1}{6}\sin x \cos^5 x + \frac{5}{24}\sin x \cos^3 x + \frac{5}{32}\sin 2x + \frac{5}{16}x + C.$

ILLUSTRATION 184: Evaluate: (i) $\int_0^{\pi/2} \cos^{12} x dx$ (ii) $\int_0^{\pi/2} \cos^9 x dx$

SOLUTION: (i) $\int_0^{\pi/2} \cos^{12} x dx = \frac{11}{12}.\frac{9}{10}.\frac{7}{8}.\frac{5}{6}.\frac{3}{4}.\frac{1}{2}.\frac{\pi}{2} = \frac{231\pi}{2048}$

(ii) $\int_0^{\pi/2} \cos^9 x dx = \frac{8}{9}.\frac{6}{7}.\frac{4}{5}.\frac{2}{3} = \frac{128}{315}$

Reduction formula for tan^{n}x: Given $I_n = \int \tan^n x\, dx$

$\Rightarrow I_n = \int \tan^{n-2} x.(\tan^2 x)\, dx$

$\Rightarrow I_n = \int \tan^{n-2} x.(\sec^2 x - 1)\, dx$

$\Rightarrow I_n = \int \tan^{n-2} x.\sec^2 x\, dx - \int \tan^{n-2} x\, dx$

$\Rightarrow I_n = \int \tan^{n-2} x\, d(\tan x) - \int \tan^{n-2} x\, dx$

$\Rightarrow I_n = \frac{\tan^{n-1} x}{n-1} - I_{n-2}$

ILLUSTRATION 185: Evaluate the integral $\int \tan^7 x dx$

SOLUTION: Given $I_n = \int \tan^7 x\, dx \quad \Rightarrow I_7 = \int \tan^{7-2} x.(\tan^2 x)\, dx$

$\Rightarrow I_7 = \int \tan^{7-2} x.(\sec^2 x - 1)\, dx \quad \Rightarrow I_7 = \int \tan^{7-2} x.\sec^2 x\, dx - \int \tan^{7-2} x\, dx$

$\Rightarrow I_7 = \int \tan^{7-2} x\, d(\tan x) - \int \tan^{7-2} x\, dx$

$\Rightarrow I_7 = \frac{\tan^{7-1} x}{7-1} - I_5$ ...(1)

$\Rightarrow I_5 = \frac{\tan^{5-1} x}{5-1} - I_3$ ...(2)

and $I_3 = \frac{\tan^{3-1} x}{3-1} - I_1 = \frac{\tan^2 x}{2} - \ln|\sec x| + C$ ...(3)

$\therefore$ from (1), (2) and (3)

$I_7 = \frac{1}{6}\tan^6 x - \frac{1}{4}\tan^4 x + \frac{\tan^2 x}{2} - \ln|\sec x| + C.$

Reduction formula for sec^{n}x: Given $I_n = \int \sec^n x\, dx$

$\Rightarrow I_n = \int \underbrace{\sec^{n-2} x}_{I} \underbrace{\sec^2 x}_{II}\, dx$

$\Rightarrow \sec^{n-2} x \tan x - \int (n-2)\sec^{n-3} x \sec x \tan^2 x\, dx$

$\Rightarrow \sec^{n-2} x \tan x - (n-2) \int \sec^{n-3} x\left(\sec^3 x - \sec x\right) dx$

$\Rightarrow I_n = \sec^{n-2} x \tan x - (n-2)I_n + (n-2)I_{n-2}$

$\Rightarrow I_n = \frac{\sec^{n-2} x \tan x}{n-1} + \frac{(n-2)}{n-1} I_{n-2}$

ILLUSTRATION 186: Evaluate the integral $\int \sec^5 x dx$

SOLUTION: According to the above derived equation $I_5 = \dfrac{\sec^{5-2} x \tan x}{5-1} + \dfrac{(5-2)}{5-1} I_{5-2}$ ...(1)

Now, $I_3 = \dfrac{\sec^{3-2} x \tan x}{3-1} + \dfrac{(3-2)}{3-1} I_{3-2}$ ...(2)

and $I_1 = \int \sec x\, dx = \ln|\sec x + \tan x| + C$ ...(3)

now after combining all the above equations (1), (2) and (3), we have

$I_3 = \dfrac{\sec x.\tan x}{2} + \dfrac{1}{2}(\ln|\sec x + \tan x|) + C$;

and $I_5 = \dfrac{\sec^3 x.\tan x}{4} + \dfrac{3}{8}(\sec x.\tan x + \ln|\sec x + \tan x|) + C$

ILLUSTRATION 187: Obtain a reduction formula for $I_{m,n} = \int x^m (\ln x)^n dx$, hence, evaluate $\int_0^1 x^2 (\ln x)^1 dx$

SOLUTION: Consider $I_{m,n} = \int x^m (\ln x)^n dx$

(Integrate by parts, taking $(\ln x)^n$ as the first function),

$$I_{m,n} = (\ln x)^n.\frac{x^{m+1}}{m+1} - \int n(\ln x)^{n-1}.\frac{1}{x}.\frac{x^{m+1}}{m+1} dx = \frac{x^{m+1}}{m+1}(\ln x)^n - \frac{n}{m+1}\int x^m (\ln x)^{n-1} dx \quad ...(1)$$

$$= \frac{x^{m+1}}{m+1}(\ln x)^n - \frac{n}{m+1} I_{m,n-1}.$$

which is the required reduction formula, hence, $I_{2,1} = \dfrac{x^{2+1}}{2+1}(\ln x)^1 - \dfrac{1}{2+1}\int x^2 (\ln x)^0 dx$

$$= \frac{x^3}{3}(\ln x) - \frac{1}{3}\int x^2 (\ln x)^0 dx = \frac{x^3}{3}(\ln x) - \frac{1}{3} \times \frac{x^3}{3} + C$$

$$\therefore \int_0^1 x^2 (\ln x) dx = \left[\frac{x^3}{3}(\log x) - \frac{x^3}{9}\right]_0^1 = -\frac{1}{9}.$$

ILLUSTRATION 188: Derive reduction formulae for $I_{(n,m)} = \int \dfrac{\sin^n x}{\cos^m x} dx$, hence, evaluate $\int_{\pi/3}^{\pi} \dfrac{\sin^3 x}{\cos^2 x} dx$

SOLUTION: Using integration by parts for $I_{(n,m)}$, we get $I_{(n,m)} = \int \sin^{n-1} x \dfrac{\sin x}{\cos^m x} dx$

$$= \sin^{n-1} x.\frac{(\cos x)^{-m+1}}{(m-1)} - \int (n-1)\sin^{n-2} x.\cos x.\frac{(\cos x)^{-m+1}}{(m-1)} dx$$

$$= \frac{1}{m-1}.\frac{\sin^{n-1} x}{\cos^{m-1} x} - \frac{n-1}{m-1}.\int \frac{\sin^{n-2} x}{\cos^{m-2} x} dx$$

$$\therefore I_{(n,m)} = \frac{1}{m-1}.\frac{\sin^{n-1} x}{\cos^{m-1} x} - \frac{n-1}{m-1}.I_{(n-2,m-2)}$$

Hence, $\displaystyle\int_{\pi/3}^{\pi} \frac{\sin^3 x}{\cos^2 x} dx = \left[\frac{1}{(2-1)}\frac{\sin^{3-1} x}{\cos^{2-1} x}\right]_{\pi/3}^{\pi} - \frac{(3-1)}{(2-1)}\int_{\pi/3}^{\pi} \cos x dx$

$$= \left[-\frac{\sin^2 \frac{\pi}{3}}{\cos\frac{\pi}{3}}\right] - 2[\sin x]_{\pi/3}^{\pi} = -\left[\frac{3}{4} \times \frac{2}{1}\right] - 2\left[0 - \frac{\sqrt{3}}{2}\right] = -\frac{3}{2} + \sqrt{3}.$$

LLUSTRATION 189: Obtain the reduction formula for the integral $I_n = \int \frac{dx}{(x^2+a^2)^n}$

SOLUTION: Let $I_n = \int \underset{II}{1} \underbrace{\frac{dx}{(x^2+a^2)^n}}_{I} = \frac{x}{(x^2+a^2)^n} - \int \frac{-n.2x}{(x^2+a^2)^{n+1}} x\, dx$

$$\Rightarrow I_n = \frac{x}{(x^2+a^2)^n} + 2n\int \frac{x^2+a^2-a^2}{(x^2+a^2)^{n+1}}\, dx = I_n = \frac{x}{(x^2+a^2)^n} + 2n\, I_n - 2na^2 I_{n+1}$$

$$\Rightarrow 2na^2 I_{n+1} = \frac{x}{(x^2+a^2)^n} - (2n-1)I_n.$$ Replacing n by $(n-1)$ we get

$$\Rightarrow 2(n-1)a^2 I_n = \frac{x}{(x^2+a^2)^{n-1}} - (2n-3)I_{n-1}.$$

TEXTUAL EXERCISE–9: (SUBJECTIVE)

1. Evaluate the following integrals:

(a) $\int \tan^2 x \sec^4 x\, dx$ (b) $\int \tan^3 x \sec^6 x\, dx$

(c) $\int \tan^3 x \sec^5 x\, dx$ (d) $\int \tan^{-5} x \sec^6 x dx$

(e) $\int \frac{(2\tan x+3)\sec^2 x\, dx}{(\tan^2 x - 2\tan x + 5)}$

(f) $\int \text{cosec}^5 x\, dx$

2. Obtain the reduction formula for the following functions $\sin^n x$, $\cos^n x$, $\tan^n x$, $\cot^n x$, $\sec^n x$, $\text{cosec}^n x$, and hence, or otherwise evaluate the following integrals:

(a) $\int \sin^4 x\, dx$ (b) $\int \cos^5 x\, dx$

(c) $\int \tan^5 x\, dx$ (d) $\int \cot^4 x\, dx$

(e) $\int \sec^5 x\, dx$ (f) $\int \sec^4 x\, dx$

(g) $\int (\ln x)^n dx$ (h) $\int \frac{dx}{(x-1)(x+1)^n}$

3. (a) If $I_n = \int \frac{dx}{(x^2+a^2)^n}$, then show that $2(n-1)a^2 I_n = (2n-3)\, I_{n-1} + \frac{x}{(x^2+a^2)^{n-1}}$

(b) If $I_{mn} = \int \cos^m x \cos nx\, dx$, then prove that $\frac{\cos^m x \sin nx}{m+n} + \frac{m}{m+n} I_{m-1,n-1}$

(c) If $I_n = \int e^{ax} \cos^n x dx$, then prove that $\frac{a\cos x + n\sin x}{a^2+n^2} e^{ax}.\cos^{n-1} x + \frac{n(n-1)}{a^2+n^2} I_{n-2}$

(d) If $I_n = \int \frac{x^n}{\sqrt{ax^2+bx+c}}\, dx$, then prove that $\frac{\left(\sqrt{ax^2+bx+c}\right)x^{n-1}}{an} - \frac{b(2n-1)}{2an} I_{n-1} - \frac{c(n-1)}{an} I_{n-2} = I_n$

Answer Keys

1. (a) $\frac{\tan^3 x}{3} + \frac{\tan^5 x}{5} + C$ (b) $\frac{\tan^4 x}{4} + \frac{\tan^6 x}{3} + \frac{\tan^8 x}{8} + C$ (c) $\frac{\sec^7 x}{7} - \frac{\sec^5 x}{5} + C$

(d) $-\frac{1}{4}\cot^4 x - \cot^2 x + \ln|\tan x| + C$ (e) $\ln|\tan^2 x - 2\tan x + 5| + \frac{5}{2}\tan^{-1}\left(\frac{\tan x - 1}{2}\right) + C$

(f) $-\frac{1}{4}\text{cosec}^3 x \cot x - \frac{3}{8}\text{cosec}\, x \cot x + \frac{3}{8}\ln\left|\tan\frac{x}{2}\right| + C$

2. (a) $\frac{3x}{6} + \frac{\sin x}{4} - \sin 2x + C$ (b) $\frac{\sin^5 x}{5} + \frac{2}{3}\sin^3 + \sin x + C$ (c) $\frac{\tan^4 x}{4} - \frac{\tan^2 x}{2} + \ln|\sec x| + C$

(d) $-\frac{\cot^3 x}{3} + \cot x + x + C$ (e) $\frac{\tan x \sec^3 x}{4} + \frac{3\sec x \tan x}{8} + \frac{3}{8}\ln|\sec x + \tan x| + C$ (f) $\frac{\tan x \sec^2 x}{3} + \frac{2}{3}\tan x + C$

TEXTUAL EXERCISE-9: (OBJECTIVE)

1. If $\int \cos^8 x\, dx = f(x)$, then $f(\pi/2)$ equals

(a) $\frac{35\pi}{64}$ (b) $\frac{35\pi}{256}$

(c) $\frac{105\pi}{256}$ (d) None of these

2. If $\int \sin^9 x\, dx = f(x)$, then $f(\pi/2) - f(0)$ equals

(a) $\frac{128\pi}{315}$ (b) $\frac{64\pi}{315}$

(c) $\frac{128}{315}$ (d) None of these

3. If $\int \cos^8 x \sin^6 x\, dx = f(x)$, then $f(\pi/2) - f(0)$ equals

(a) $\frac{15\pi}{256}$ (b) $\frac{5}{256}$

(c) $\frac{5\pi}{512}$ (d) None of these

4. If $\int \cos^7 x \sin^6 x\, dx = f(x)$, then $f(\pi/2) - f(0)$ equals

(a) $\frac{16}{3003}$ (b) $\frac{16}{3003}\pi$

(c) $\frac{32\pi}{3003}$ (d) None of these

5. If $I_n = \int (\ln x)^n\, dx = x(\ln x)^n - nI_{n-1}; n \in \mathbb{N}$, then $\int (\ln x)^4 dx$ equals ($t = \ln x$)

(a) $x(t^4 + 4t^3 + 12t^2 + 24) + C$

(b) $x(t^4 - 4t^3 + 12t^2 - 24t + 24)$

(c) $x(t^4 + 12t^2 + 24) + C$

(d) None of these

6. If $I_n = \int \cos^n x\, dx$, then I_5 equals

(a) $\frac{\sin x}{15}(3\cos^3 x + 4\cos x + 8) + C$

(b) $\frac{\sin x}{15}(3\cos^4 x + 4\cos^2 x + 8) + C$

(c) $\frac{1}{15}(3\cos^5 x + 4\cos^3 x + 8\cos x + 12) + C$

(d) None of these

7. If $I_n = \int \tan^n x\, dx = \frac{\tan^{n-1} x}{(n-1)} - I_{n-2}$, then $\int \tan^6 x\, dx$ equals ($t = \tan x$)

(a) $\frac{t^5}{5} - \frac{t^3}{3} + t - x + C$

(b) $\frac{t^5}{5} + \frac{t^3}{3} + t + x + C$

(c) $\frac{t^6}{6} - \frac{t^4}{4} + \frac{t^2}{2} + C$

(d) None of these

8. If $I_n = \int \sec^n x\, dx = \frac{\sec^{n-2} x \tan x}{n-1} + \frac{(n-2)}{(n-1)} I_{n-2}$, then $\int \sec^4 x\, dx$ equals

(a) $\frac{\tan x}{3}(2 + \sec^2 x) + C$

(b) $\frac{\tan x}{2}(2 - \sec^2 x) + C$

(c) $\frac{\tan x}{3}(3 + \tan^2 x) + C$

(d) None of these

9. If $I_{(m,n)} = \int x^m (\ln x)^n x\, dx = \frac{x^{n+1}}{m+1}(\ln x)^n - \frac{n}{m+1} I_{(m,n-1)}$, then $\int x^4 (\ln x)^3\, dx$ equals ($t = \ln x$)

(a) $\frac{x^4}{625}\left[125t^3 + 30t - 6\right] + C$

(b) $\frac{x^5}{625}\left[125t^3 - 75t^2 + 30t - 6\right] + C$

(c) $\frac{x^5}{125}\left[25t^3 - 125t^2 + 5t - 6\right] + C$

(d) None of these

10. If $I_{(m,n)} = \int \frac{\sin^m x}{\cos^n x} dx = \frac{1}{(n-1)} \cdot \frac{\sin^{m-1} x}{\cos^{n-1} x} - \frac{(m-1)}{(n-1)} I_{(m-2,n-2)}$, then $\int \frac{\sin^2 x}{\cos^n x} dx$ equals.

(a) $\frac{1}{2}\sin x - \frac{1}{2}\ln|\sec x + \tan x| + C$

(b) $\frac{1}{2} six \sec^2 x + \frac{1}{2}\ln|\sec x + \tan x| + C$

(c) $\frac{1}{2}\cos x\, \text{cosec}^2 x + \frac{1}{2}\ln|\sec x + \tan x| + C$

(d) $\frac{1}{2}\sin x \sec^2 x - \frac{1}{2}\ln|\sec x + \tan x| + C$

11. If $I_n = \int x^n e^{1/e} dx; n \in \mathbb{N} = \frac{e^{1/x} x^{n+1}}{(n+1)} + \frac{I_{n-1}}{(n+1)}$, then I_4 equals.

(a) $\frac{1}{4!}\left[e^{1/x}\sum_{k=1}^{4} x^k (k+1)! + I_0\right]$

(b) $\left[e^{1/x}\sum_{k=1}^{5} x^k (k+1)!\right] + I_0$

(c) $\frac{1}{5!}e^{1/x}\left[\sum_{k=2}^{5} x^k (k-1)! + I_0\right]$

(d) $\frac{1}{5!}\left[e^{1/x}\sum_{k=2}^{5} x^k (k-1)! + I_0\right]$

12. If $I_n = \int (\sin x + \cos x)^n dx = \frac{(\sin x + \cos x)^{n-1}}{n}(\sin x - \cos x) + 2\frac{(n-1)}{n} I_{n-2}$, then I_5 equals (t = (sin$x$ + cos$x$))

(a) $\frac{(\sin x - \cos x)}{15}\left[t^5 - 3t^3 + 8t - 32\right] + C$

(b) $\frac{(\sin x - \cos x)}{15}\left[t^5 + 3t^4 + 8t^3 + 32t + 1\right] + C$

(c) $\frac{(\sin x - \cos x)}{15}\left[3t^4 + 8t^2 + 32\right] + C$

(d) None of these

13. If $I_{(m,n)} = \int \cos^m x \cos nx\, dx = \frac{\cos^m x \sin nx}{(m+n)} + \frac{m}{(m+n)} I_{(m-1,n-1)}$, then $I_{(3,4)}$ equals

(a) $\frac{1}{7}$[5 cos^3x sin 4x – 2cos^2x sin3x + 3cos$x$ sin 2x – 2 sin x] + C

(b) $\frac{1}{35}$[5 cos^3x sin 4x + 3cos^2x sin3x + 2cos$x$ sin 2x + 2 sin$x$] + C

(c) $\frac{1}{35}$[5 cos^3x sin 4x – 3cos^2x sin3x + 2cos$x$ sin 2x – 2 sin$x$] + C

(d) None of these

14. If

$$I_n = \int x^n \sqrt{a^2 - x^2}\, dx = -\frac{x^{n-1}(a^2 - x^2)^{3/2}}{(n+2)} + \frac{(n-1)a^2}{(n+2)} I_{n-2},$$

then I_4 equals

(a) $-\frac{x^3}{6}(a^2 - x^2)^{3/2} - \frac{1}{8}a^2 x(a^2 - x^2)^{3/2} + \frac{1}{16}a^4 x(a^2 - x^2)^{1/2} + \frac{a^6}{16}\sin^{-1}\left(\frac{x}{a}\right) + C$

(b) $-\frac{x^3}{6}(a^2 - x^2)^{3/2} - \frac{a^2 x}{8}(a^2 - x^2)^{3/2} - \frac{1}{16}a^4 x(a^2 - x^2)^{1/2} + \frac{a^6}{16}\sin^{-1}\left(\frac{x}{a}\right) + C$

(c) $\frac{x^3}{6}(a^2 - x^2)^{3/2} + \frac{1}{4}a^2 x(a^2 - x^2)^{3/2} - \frac{1}{8}a^4 x(a^2 - x^2)^{1/2} - \frac{a^6}{16}\sin^{-1}\left(\frac{x}{a}\right) + C$

(d) None of these

15. If $I_n = \int \frac{\cos nx}{\sin x} dx = \frac{2\cos(n-1)x}{(n-1)} + I_{n-2}$, then $\int \frac{\cos 5x}{\sin x} dx$ equals

(a) $\frac{1}{4}\cos 4x - \frac{1}{2}\cos 2x + \ln|\sin x| + C$

(b) $\frac{1}{2}\cos 4x - \cos 2x + \ln|\sin x| + C$

(c) $\frac{1}{2}\cos 4x + \cos 2x + \ln|\sin x| + C$

(d) None of these

Answer Keys

1. (b)	**2.** (c)	**3.** (d)	**4.** (a)	**5.** (b)	**6.** (b)	**7.** (a)	**8.** (c)	**9.** (b)	**10.** (d)
11. (d)	**12.** (c)	**13.** (b)	**14.** (a)	**15.** (c)					

MULTIPLE CHOICE QUESTIONS

SECTION–I

OBJECTIVE-TYPE SOLVED EXAMPLES

1. $\int \frac{dx}{\sqrt{(x-a)(b-x)}}$ equals

(a) $\sin^{-1}\sqrt{\left(\frac{x+a}{b-a}\right)}+c$ (b) $2\cos^{-1}\sqrt{\left(\frac{x-a}{b-a}\right)}+c$

(c) $2\sin^{-1}\sqrt{\left(\frac{x-a}{b-a}\right)}+c$ (d) None of these

Solution: (c) Put $x = a\cos^2\theta + b\sin^2\theta$, the given integral becomes

$$I=\int \frac{2(b-a)\sin\theta\cos\theta d\theta}{\{(a\cos^2\theta+b\sin^2\theta-a)(b-a\cos^2\theta-b\sin^2\theta)\}^{\frac{1}{2}}}$$

$$=\int \frac{2(b-a)\sin\theta\cos\theta d\theta}{(b-a)\sin\theta\cos\theta}$$

$$=\left(\frac{b-a}{b-a}\right)\int 2d\theta = 2\theta + C = 2\sin^{-1}\sqrt{\left(\frac{x-a}{b-a}\right)}+C$$

2. $\int \frac{\sin x+\cos x}{9+16\sin 2x}dx$ equals

(a) $\frac{1}{10}\ln\left|\frac{5-4(\sin x-\cos x)}{5+4(\sin x-\cos x)}\right|+c$

(b) $\frac{1}{40}\ln\left|\frac{5-4(\sin x-\cos x)}{5+4(\sin x-\cos x)}\right|+c$

(c) $\frac{1}{40}\ln\left|\frac{5+4(\sin x-\cos x)}{5-4(\sin x+\cos x)}\right|+c$

(d) None of these

Solution: (b) $I=\int \frac{\sin x+\cos x}{25-16(\sin x-\cos x)^2}dx$

Put $t = \sin x - \cos x \Rightarrow dt = (\cos x + \sin x)dx$

$$\Rightarrow I=\int \frac{dt}{25-16t^2} = \frac{1}{40}\ln\left|\frac{5-4t}{5+4t}\right|+C$$

$$=\frac{1}{40}\ln\left|\frac{5-4(\sin x-\cos x)}{5+4(\sin x-\cos x)}\right|+C$$

3. $\int \frac{ax^2-b}{x\sqrt{c^2x^2-(ax^2+b)^2}}dx$ equals

(a) $\sin^{-1}\left(\frac{ax+b/x}{c}\right)+k$

(b) $\cos^{-1}\left(\frac{ax+b/x}{c}\right)+k$

(c) $\sin^{-1}\left(\frac{ax-b/x}{c}\right)+k$

(d) None of these

Solution: (a) Here, $I=\int \frac{(ax^2-b)\,dx}{x\sqrt{c^2x^2-(ax^2+b)^2}}$

$$=\int \frac{\{a-(b/x^2)\}\,dx}{\sqrt{c^2-(ax+b/x)^2}}$$

Now put $ax+\frac{b}{x}=t$

$$\Rightarrow \left(a-\frac{b}{x^2}\right)dx = dt$$

$$\therefore\ I=\int \frac{dt}{\sqrt{c^2-t^2}} = \sin^{-1}\left(\frac{t}{c}\right) = \sin^{-1}\left(\frac{ax+b/x}{c}\right)+k$$

4. Let $\int \frac{x^{1/2}}{\sqrt{1-x^3}}dx = \frac{2}{3}gof(x)+C$, then

(a) $f(x)=\sqrt{x}$ and $g(x)=\sin^{-1}x$

(b) $f(x)=x^{3/2}$ and $g(x)=\sin^{-1}x$

(c) $f(x)=x^{2/3}$ and $g(x)=\cos^{-1}x$

(d) $g(x)=\sin^{-1}x$ and $f(x)=x^2$

Solution: (b) Putting $x^{3/2} = t$,

we have $\sqrt{x}\,dx = \frac{2\,dt}{3}$

So, $\int \frac{x^{1/2}}{\sqrt{1-x^3}}dx = \frac{2}{3}\int \frac{dt}{\sqrt{1-t^2}}$

$$=\frac{2}{3}\sin^{-1}t+C = \frac{2}{3}\sin^{-1}x^{3/2}+C$$

Thus, $f(x) = x^{3/2}$ and $g(x) = \sin^{-1}x$

5. $\int \frac{1}{(\sin^3 x \cos^5 x)^{1/4}} dx$

(a) $(\tan x)^{3/4} + c$ (b) $4(\tan x)^{1/4} + c$
(c) $(\tan x)^{1/4} + c$ (d) None of these

Solution: (b)

$$I = \int \frac{1}{\left(\frac{\sin^4 x}{\sin x}\cos^5 x\right)^{1/4}} dx = \int \frac{1}{\left(\frac{\sin^4 x}{\sin x}\cos^4 x . \cos x\right)^{1/4}} dx$$

$$= \int \frac{1}{(\sin x . \cos x)(\cot x)^{1/4}} dx = \int \frac{(\sec^2 x)(\tan x)^{1/4}}{(\tan x)} dx$$

$$= \frac{(\tan x)^{1/4}}{1/4} + C = 4(\tan x)^{1/4} + C.$$

6. The function f whose graph passes through the point (0, 7/3) and having its derivative whose $x\sqrt{1-x^2}$ is given by
(a) $f(x) = (-1/3)\,[(1 - x^2)^{3/2} - 8]$
(b) $f(x) = (1/3)\,[(1 - x^2)^{3/2} + 8]$
(c) $f(x) = (-1/3)\,[\sin^{-1} x + 7]$
(d) None of these

Solution: (a)

$$f(x) = \int x\sqrt{1-x^2}\, dx = -\frac{1}{2}\int(-2x)\sqrt{1-x^2}\, dx$$

$= (-1/3)\,(1 - x^2)^{3/2} + C$ (Putting $1 - x^2 = t$)

So $7/3 = (-1/3) + C \Rightarrow C = 8/3$

($\because$ graph passa through the point 0, 7/3)

Therefore, $f(x) = (-1/3)\,[(1 - x^2)^{3/2} - 8]$

7. If $I = \int \sec^2 x \operatorname{cosec}^4 x\, dx = K \cot^3 x + L \tan x + M \cot x + C$, then
(a) $K = -1/3$ (b) $L = 2$
(c) $M = -2$ (d) None of these

Solution: (a, c) Put $\tan x = t$

$$\Rightarrow I = \int (1+t^2)\frac{(1+t^2)^2}{t^4}\frac{dt}{1+t^2}$$

$$= \int \frac{1+t^4+2t^2}{t^4} dt = \int \frac{dt}{t^4} + \int \frac{2}{t^2} dt + \int dt$$

$$= -\frac{1}{3}(\tan x)^{-3} - 2(\tan x)^{-1} + \tan x + C$$

$$= -\frac{1}{3}\cot^3 x + \tan x - 2\cot x + C$$

Therefore, $K = -\frac{1}{3}$ 1/3, $L = -1$, $M = -2$

8. If $I = \int \frac{\sin x + \sin^3 x}{\cos 2x} dx = A \cos x + B \ln|f(x)| + C$, then which of the following is/are possible

(a) $A = \frac{1}{2}, B = \frac{3}{4\sqrt{2}}$ (b) $A = \frac{1}{2}, B = -\frac{3}{4\sqrt{2}}$

(c) $A = -\frac{1}{2}, B = \frac{3}{\sqrt{2}}$ (d) $A = \frac{1}{2}, B = \frac{3}{\sqrt{2}}$

Solution: (a, b) Since the integral is odd w.r.t $\sin x$, we put $\cos x = t$,
So $\cos 2x = 2t^2 - 1$ and $dt = -\sin x\, dx$, Thus,

$$I = \int \frac{t^2-2}{2t^2-1} dt = \frac{1}{2}\int \frac{2t^2-4}{2t^2-1} dt$$

$$= \frac{1}{2}\int dt - \frac{3}{2}\int \frac{dt}{2t^2-1}$$

$$= \frac{1}{2}t - \frac{3}{2\sqrt{2}}\frac{1}{2}\ln\left|\frac{\sqrt{2}t-1}{\sqrt{2}t+1}\right| + C$$

$$= \frac{1}{2}\cos x - \frac{3}{4\sqrt{2}}\ln\left|\frac{\sqrt{2}\cos x - 1}{\sqrt{2}\cos x + 1}\right| + C$$

So $A = \frac{1}{2}, B = -\frac{3}{4\sqrt{2}}, f(x) = \frac{\sqrt{2}\cos x - 1}{\sqrt{2}\cos x + 1}$

or $A = \frac{1}{2}, B = \frac{3}{4\sqrt{2}}, f(x) = \frac{\sqrt{2}\cos x + 1}{\sqrt{2}\cos x - 1}$

9. The value of $\int \frac{\cos^3 x + \cos^5 x}{\sin^2 x + \sin^4 x} dx$ is

(a) $\sin x - 6 \tan^{-1}(\sin x) + C$
(b) $\sin x - 2(\sin x)^{-1} + C$
(c) $\sin x - 2(\sin x)^{-1} + 5 \tan^{-1}(\sin x) + C$
(d) None of these

Solution: (d) We substitute $\sin x = t$, so that $\cos x\, dx = dt$.

$$\int \frac{\cos^3 x + \cos^5 x}{\sin^2 x + \sin^4 x} dx$$

$$= \int \frac{[(1-\sin^2 x) + (1-\sin^2 x)^2]\cos x}{(\sin^2 x + \sin^4 x)} dx$$

$$= \int \frac{[(1-t^2)+(1-t^2)^2]}{(t^2+t^4)} dt = \int \frac{(1-t^2)\times(2-t^2)}{t^2+t^4} dt$$

$$= \int \left(1 + \frac{2}{t^2} - \frac{6}{1+t^2}\right) dt = t - \frac{2}{t} - 6\tan^{-1} t + C$$

$= \sin x - 2(\sin x)^{-1} - 6 \tan^{-1}(\sin x) + C$

10. The value of $\int \frac{dx}{(x-a)^{3/2}(b-x)^{1/2}}$ is

(a) $\frac{1}{b-a}\left[\frac{b-x}{x-a}\right]^{1/2} + C$

(b) $\frac{1}{4(b-a)}\left[\frac{b-x}{x-a}\right]^{1/2} + C$

(c) $\frac{1}{b-a}\left[\frac{x-a}{b-a}\right]^{1/2}+C$

(d) None of these

Solution: (d) Putting $x-a=\frac{1}{t}$,

we have $dx=-\frac{1}{t^2}dt$ and the given integral can be

written as $I=\int\frac{-\frac{1}{t^2}dt}{(1/t)^{3/2}(b-a-1/t)^{1/2}}$

$=-\int\frac{dt}{\sqrt{(b-a)t-1}}=-2\frac{\sqrt{(b-a)t-1}}{b-a}+C$

$=\frac{-2}{b-a}\sqrt{\frac{b-a-(x-a)}{x-a}}+C=\frac{-2}{b-a}\sqrt{\frac{b-x}{x-a}}+C$

11. If $\int\frac{(x^2-1)dx}{(x^4+3x^2+1)\tan^{-1}\frac{x^2+1}{x}}=\ell n\,|\tan^{-1}f(x)|+C,$

then

(a) $f(x)=x^2+1$ (b) $f(x)=\frac{x^2+1}{2x}$

(c) $f(x)=(x^2+1)/x^2$ (d) $f(x)=\frac{x^2+1}{x}$

Solution: (d) $I=\int\frac{(1-1/x^2)dx}{\left[(x+1/x)^2+1\right]\tan^{-1}(x+1/x)}$

Let $(x+1/x)=t$. differentiating

we get $(1-1/x^2)\,dx=dt$; Hence, $I=\int\frac{dt}{(t^2+1)\tan^{-1}t}$

Now make one more substitution $\tan^{-1}t=u$.

Then $\frac{dt}{(t^2+1)}=du$ and $I=\int\frac{du}{u}=\ell n\,|u|+c$

Returning to t, and then to x, we have

$I=\ell n\,|\tan^{-1}t|+C=\ell n\,|\tan^{-1}(x+1/x)|+C$

Thus, $f(x)=x+\frac{1}{x}=\frac{x^2+1}{x}$

12. $\int\cos\left\{2\tan^{-1}\sqrt{\frac{1-x}{1+x}}\right\}dx$; $x\in(-1,0)$ equals

(a) $\frac{1}{8}(x^2-1)+C$ (b) x^2+C

(c) $x+C$ (d) None of these

Solution: (d) Let $\cos^{-1}x=2\theta$; As $x\in(-1,0)$,

$2\theta\in\left(\frac{\pi}{2},\pi\right)$

$\Rightarrow\theta\in\left(\frac{\pi}{4},\frac{\pi}{2}\right)$

$\therefore\ I=\int\cos\{2\tan^{-1}|\tan\theta|\}(-2\sin 2\theta)d\theta$

$=\int\cos\{2\tan^{-1}(\tan\theta)\,(-2\sin 2\theta)\}d\theta$

$=-\int\sin 4\theta\,d\theta=\frac{1}{4}\cos 4\theta+C$

$=\frac{1}{4}(2x^2-1)+C=\frac{x^2}{2}+C'$ (where $C'=C-\frac{1}{4}$)

13. $\int\cos^2x\sin 2x.\ln\cos x\,dx$ is equal to

(a) $\cos^2x\left(\frac{1}{2}+\ell n\cos x\right)+C$

(b) $\cos^2x\ \ell n\cos x+C$

(c) $\cos^2x\left(\frac{1}{2}-\ell n\cos x\right)+C$

(d) None of these

Solution: (c) $I=\int\cos^2x\sin 2x.\ell n\cos x\,dx$.

Putting $\ell n\cos x=z$

$\therefore\ \frac{1}{\sin x}(-\cos x)dx=dz$

$\Rightarrow -\cos x dx=\sin x dz$

$\Rightarrow -\cos^2x dx=\sin x\cos x dz$

$\Rightarrow -2\cos^2x dx=\sin^2x dz$

14. $\int\frac{dx}{\cot\frac{x}{2}.\cot\frac{x}{3}.\cot\frac{x}{6}}$ equals

(a) $\ell n\left|\sec\frac{x}{2}\sec\frac{x}{3}\sec\frac{x}{6}\right|+C$

(b) $\ell n\left|\sec^2\frac{x}{2}\sec^3\frac{x}{3}\sec^6\frac{x}{6}\right|+C$

(c) $\ell n\left|\sec^2\frac{x}{2}.\cos^3\frac{x}{3}\cos^6\frac{x}{6}\right|+C$

(d) None of these

Solution: (c) Let $I=\int\frac{dx}{\cot\frac{x}{2}.\cot\frac{x}{3}.\cot\frac{x}{6}}$

$=\int\tan\frac{x}{2}.\tan\frac{x}{3}.\tan\frac{x}{6}\,dx$

$\because\ \frac{x}{2}-\frac{x}{3}=\frac{x}{6}\quad\Rightarrow\tan\left(\frac{x}{2}-\frac{x}{3}\right)=\tan\frac{x}{6}$

$\Rightarrow\frac{\tan\frac{x}{2}-\tan\frac{x}{3}}{1+\tan\frac{x}{2}\tan\frac{x}{3}}=\tan\frac{x}{6}$

$\Rightarrow\tan\frac{x}{2}-\tan\frac{x}{3}-\tan\frac{x}{6}=\tan\frac{x}{2}\tan\frac{x}{3}\tan\frac{x}{6}$

$$\Rightarrow I = \int\left(\tan\frac{x}{2} - \tan\frac{x}{3} - \tan\frac{x}{6}\right)dx$$

$$= \frac{\ell n\left(\sec\frac{x}{2}\right)}{\frac{1}{2}} - \frac{\ell n\left(\sec\frac{x}{3}\right)}{\frac{1}{3}} - \frac{\ell n\left(\sec\frac{x}{6}\right)}{\frac{1}{6}} + C$$

$$\Rightarrow I = 2\ell n\left(\sec\frac{x}{2}\right) - 3\ell n\left(\sec\frac{x}{3}\right) - 6\ell n\left(\sec\frac{x}{6}\right) + C$$

$$\Rightarrow I = \ell n\left|\sec^2\frac{x}{2}.\cos^3\frac{x}{3}\cos^6\frac{x}{6}\right| + C$$

15. $\int\sqrt{\frac{\sin(x-a)}{\sin(x+a)}}dx = -\cos a.\sin^{-1}\left(\frac{\cos x}{\cos a}\right) - \sin x\ ln$ $|g(x)| + C$, then g(x) equals

(a) $\cos x + \sqrt{\cos^2 x - \cos^2 a}$

(b) $\sin x + \sqrt{\sin^2 x - \sin^2 a}$

(c) $\sin x + \sqrt{\cos^2 x - \sin^2 a}$

(d) None of these

Solution: (b) $I = \int\sqrt{\frac{\sin(x-a)}{\sin(x+a)}}dx$

$$= \int\sqrt{\frac{\sin(x-a)\times\sin(x-a)}{\sin(x+a)\sin(x-a)}}dx = \int\frac{\sin(x-a)}{\sqrt{\sin^2 x - \sin^2 a}}dx$$

$$= \int\frac{\sin x\cos a}{\sqrt{1-\cos^2 x - \sin^2 a}}dx - \int\frac{\cos x\sin a}{\sqrt{\sin^2 x - \sin^2 a}}dx$$

$$= \int\frac{\sin x\cos a}{\sqrt{(1-\sin^2 a) - \cos^2 x}}dx - \int\frac{\cos x\sin a}{\sqrt{\sin^2 x - \sin^2 a}}dx$$

$$\Rightarrow I = I_1 - I_2 \quad \text{.... (1)}$$

where $I_1 = \int\frac{\sin x\cos a}{\sqrt{\cos^2 a - \cos^2 x}}dx$

put $\cos x = u - \sin x\,dx = du = -\cos a\int\frac{du}{\sqrt{\cos^2 a - u^2}}$

$$= -\cos a.\sin^{-1}\left(\frac{u}{\cos a}\right) = -\cos a\sin^{-1}\left(\frac{\cos x}{\cos a}\right) + C_1 \quad \text{.... (2)}$$

$I_2 = \int\frac{\cos x\sin a}{\sqrt{\sin^2 x - \sin^2 a}}dx$ put $\sin x = v\ \cos x dx = dv$

$$\therefore I_2 = \int\frac{\sin a\ dv}{\sqrt{v^2 - \sin^2 a}} = -\cos a\ \sin^{-1}\left(\frac{\cos x}{\cos a}\right)$$

$$= \sin a\ \ell n\left|\sin x + \sqrt{\sin^2 x - \sin^2 a}\right|$$

$$= \sin a.\ell n\left|\sin x + \sqrt{\sin^2 x - \sin^2 a}\right| + C_2 \quad \text{...(3)}$$

Using (2) and (3) in (1) we get

$$I = -\cos a\sin^{-1}\left(\frac{\cos x}{\cos a}\right) - \sin a.\ell n\left|\sin x + \sqrt{\sin^2 x - \sin^2 a}\right| + C$$

Clearly $g(x) = \sin x + \sqrt{\sin^2 x - \sin^2 a}$

Now $I = -\cos a\ \sin^{-1}\left(\frac{\cos x}{\cos a}\right) - \sin a\ \ell n\left|\sin x + \sqrt{\sin^2 x - \sin^2 a}\right| + C$

$$= -\cos a\left[\frac{\pi}{2} - \cos^{-1}\left(\frac{\cos x}{\cos a}\right)\right] - \sin a\ \ell n\left|\sin x + \sqrt{\sin^2 x - \sin^2 a}\right| + C$$

$$= -(\cos a).\frac{\pi}{2} + \cos a.\cos^{-1}\left(\frac{\cos x}{\cos a}\right) - \sin a\ \ell n\left|\sin x + \sqrt{\sin^2 x - \sin^2 a}\right| + C$$

$$= \cos a\ \cos^{-1}\left(\frac{\cos x}{\cos a}\right) - \sin a.\ell n\left|\sin x + \sqrt{\sin^2 x - |\sin^2 a|}\right| + C$$

16. $\int\frac{\tan(\ell n x)\tan\left(\ell n\frac{x}{2}\right)\tan(\ell n 2)}{x}dx$ equals

(a) $\ell n\left|\frac{\sec(\ell n)}{x^{\tan(\ell n2)}.\sec\left(\ell n\frac{x}{2}\right)}\right| + C$

(b) $\ell n\left|\frac{\sec(\ell n x)}{x^{\tan(\ell n2)}.\cos\left(\ell n\frac{x}{2}\right)}\right| + C$

(c) $\ell n\left|\sec(\ell n x)\sec\left(\ell n\frac{x}{2}\right).x^{\tan(\ell n2)}\right| + C$

(d) None of these

Solution: (a) $I = \int\frac{\tan(\ell nx)\tan\left(\ell n\frac{x}{2}\right)\tan(\ell n2)}{x}dx$

put $\ell nx = t \quad \Rightarrow \frac{1}{x}dx = dt$

$$\therefore I = \int\tan t.\tan(t - \ell n2)\tan(\ell n2)\,dt$$

$$I = \int(\tan t - \tan(\ell n2) - \tan(t - \ell n2))dt$$

$= \ell n\sec t - t\tan(\ell n2) - \ell n\sec(t - \ell n2) + C$

$= \ell n(\sec(\ell nx)) - \ell n(x).$

$\tan(\ell n2) - \ell n\left(\sec\left(\ell n\frac{x}{2}\right)\right) + C$

17. $\int \frac{3x^2+1}{(x^2-1)^3}dx$ equals

(a) $-\frac{x}{(x-1)^2}+C$ (b) $\frac{x}{(x^2-1)^2}+C$

(c) $\frac{2x}{(x^2-1)^2}+C$ (d) $-\frac{x}{(x^2-1)^2}+C$

Solution: (d) $I = \int \frac{3x^2+1}{(x^2-1)^3}dx$

$= \int \frac{3x^2+1-x^2+x^2}{(x^2-1)^3}dx = \int \frac{-(x^2-1)}{(x^2-1)^3}dx + \int \frac{4x^2}{(x^2-1)^3}dx$

$= \int \left[\frac{-1}{(x^2-1)^2} + x.\frac{4x}{(x^2-1)^3}\right]dx$

This is the integral form of $\int [f(x)+xf'(x)]dx = xf(x)+C = x\left(\frac{-1}{(x^2-1)^2}\right)+C$

$\Rightarrow I = -\frac{x}{(x^2-1)^2}+C$

18. $\int \frac{dx}{(x+\sqrt{x(1+x)})^2}$ equals

(a) $-2\ell n\left(1+\sqrt{1+\frac{1}{x}}\right)+\frac{1}{1+\sqrt{1+\frac{1}{x}}}+C$

(b) $2\ell n\left(1+\sqrt{1+\frac{1}{x}}\right)+\frac{1}{1+\sqrt{1+\frac{1}{x}}}+C$

(c) $-2\ell n\left(1+\sqrt{1+\frac{1}{x}}\right)+\frac{2}{1+\sqrt{1+\frac{1}{x}}}+C$

(d) None of these

Solution: (c) $I = \int \frac{dx}{(x+\sqrt{x(1+x)})^2}$ dx

$= \int \frac{1}{x^2\left(1+\sqrt{1+\frac{1}{x}}\right)^2}dx$ put $1+\frac{1}{x} = t^2$

$\Rightarrow -\frac{1}{x^2}dx = 2tdt$ or $I = \int \frac{-2t\,dt}{(1+t)^2} = -\int \frac{2t}{t^2+2t+1}dt$

$= -\left[\int \frac{2t+2}{t^2+2t+1}dt - \int \frac{2}{t^2+2t+1}dt\right]$

$= -\ell n\,(t+1)^2 - 2\int \frac{1}{(t+1)^2}dt$

$= -2\ell n\,(t+1) + \frac{2}{t+1}+C$

or $I = -2\ell n\left(1+\sqrt{1+\frac{1}{x}}\right)+\frac{2}{1+\sqrt{1+\frac{1}{x}}}+C$

19. Integration of $\frac{1}{2}f(x)$ w.r.t. x^4; where $f(x) = \tan^{-1}x + \ell n\sqrt{1+x} - \ell n\sqrt{1-x}$ is

(a) $\ell n|1-x^2|+C$

(b) $\ell n|1-x^4|+C$

(c) $\ell n\left|\frac{1}{\sqrt{1+x}}+\frac{1}{\sqrt{1-x}}\right|+C$

(d) $\ell n\left|\frac{1}{1-x^4}\right|+C$

Solution: (d)

$f'(x) = \frac{1}{1+x^2}+\frac{1}{2\left(\sqrt{1+x}\right)^2}+\frac{1}{2\left(\sqrt{1-x}\right)^2}$

$= \frac{1}{1+x^2}+\frac{1}{2}\left(\frac{2}{1-x^2}\right) = \frac{1-x^2+1+x^2}{1-x^4}$ $f'(x) = \frac{2}{1-x^4}$

$\int \frac{1}{2}f'(x)d\left(x^4\right) = \int \frac{1}{1-x^4}d\left(x^4\right)$

Let $x^4 = t$

$d(x^4) = dt = \int \frac{dt}{1-t} = -\ln|-t|+C$

$= -\ln|1-x^4| + C = \ell n\left|\frac{1}{1-x^4}\right|+C$

20. $\int \frac{\cos^2 x}{1+\tan x}dx$ equals

(a) $\frac{1}{8}g(2x)+\frac{1}{4}\ell n|g(x)|+\frac{x}{2}+C$; $g(x) = \sin x + \cos x$

(b) $g(2x) + \ln|g(x)| + \frac{x}{2} + C$; $g(x) = \sin x + \cos x$

(c) $\frac{1}{4}\{g(2x)+\ell n|g(x)|+2x\}+C$; $g(x) = \sin x + \cos x$

(d) None of these

Solution: (a) $I = \int \frac{\cos^2 x}{1+\tan x}dx = \frac{1}{2}\int \frac{2\cos^3 x}{\sin x+\cos x}dx$

$= \frac{1}{2}\int \frac{\cos^3 x-\sin^3 x+\cos^3 x+\sin^3 x}{(\sin x+\cos x)}dx$

$= \frac{1}{2}\int \frac{(\cos x-\sin x)\,(1+\sin x\cos x)}{\sin x+\cos x}dx +$

$\frac{1}{2}\int \frac{(\cos x+\sin x)}{(\cos x+\sin x)}(1-\sin x\cos x)dx$

$= $ put $\sin x + \cos x = t$; $(\cos x - \sin x)dx = dt$

$$= \frac{1}{2}\int \frac{\left[1+\frac{1}{2}(t^2-1)\right]}{t}dt + \frac{1}{2}\int\left(1-\frac{1}{2}\sin 2x\right)dx$$

$$= \frac{1}{2}[\ell n t] + \frac{1}{4}\left[\frac{t^2}{2}-\ell n t\right] + \frac{1}{2}x - \frac{1}{4}\frac{(-\cos 2x)}{2} + C$$

$$= \frac{(\sin x+\cos x)^2}{8} + \frac{1}{4}\ell n(\sin x+\cos x)$$

$$+\frac{x}{2}+\frac{1}{8}\cos 2x + C$$

$$= \frac{1}{8}+\frac{\sin 2x}{8}+\frac{1}{4}\ell n(\sin x+\cos x)+\frac{x}{2}+\frac{\cos 2x}{8}+C$$

or $I = \dfrac{(\sin 2x+\cos 2x)}{8}+\dfrac{1}{4}\ell n|\sin x+\cos x|+\dfrac{x}{2}+C$

21. $\displaystyle\int \frac{\cos x-\sin x}{7-9\sin 2x}dx$ equals

(a) $\dfrac{1}{24}\ell n\left|\dfrac{4+5g(x)}{4-5g(x)}\right|+C$; $g(x) = \sin x + \cos x$

(b) $\dfrac{1}{24}\ell n\left|\dfrac{4-3g(x)}{4+3g(x)}\right|+C$; $g(x) = \sin x + \cos x$

(c) $\dfrac{1}{36}\ell n\left|\dfrac{4+g(x)}{4-g(x)}\right|+C$; $g(x) = \sin x + \cos x$

(d) $\dfrac{1}{24}\ell n\left|\dfrac{4+3g(x)}{4-3g(x)}\right|+C$; $g(x) = (\sin x + \cos x)$

Solution: (d) $I = \displaystyle\int \frac{\cos x-\sin x}{7-9\sin 2x}dx$

or $I = \displaystyle\int \frac{dt}{7-9(t^2-1)}$; Let $\sin x + \cos x = t$

$\Rightarrow$ $(\cos x - \sin x)dx = dt = \displaystyle\int \frac{dt}{4^2-(3t)^2}$

$\because$ $\sin^2 x + \cos^2 x + 2\sin x\cos x = t^2$

or $\sin^2 x + \cos^2 x + 2\sin x\cos x = t^2 = \displaystyle\int \frac{dt}{4^2-(3t)^2}$

or $1 + \sin 2x = t^2$ or $\sin 2x = t^2 - 1$

$$= \frac{1}{2.4}.\frac{1}{3}\ell n\left|\frac{4+3t}{4-3t}\right|+C$$

or $I = \dfrac{1}{24}\ell n\left|\dfrac{4+3(\sin x+\cos x)}{4-3(\sin x+\cos x)}\right|+C$

22. $\displaystyle\int \frac{\sqrt{\cot x}-\sqrt{\tan x}}{1+3\sin 2x}dx$ equals

(a) $\tan^{-1}\left(\dfrac{\sin 2x}{|\sin x+\cos x|}\right)+C$

(b) $\tan^{-1}\left(\dfrac{\sqrt{\sin 2x}}{|\sin x+\cos x|}\right)+C$

(c) $\tan^{-1}\left(\dfrac{\sqrt{2\sin 2x}}{|\sin x+\cos x|}\right)+C$

(d) None of these

Solution: (c) $I = \displaystyle\int \frac{\sqrt{\cot x}-\sqrt{\tan x}}{1+3\sin 2x}dx$

$$= \int \frac{(\cos x-\sin x)}{\sqrt{\sin x\cos x}(1+3\sin 2x)}dx$$

$= \displaystyle\int \frac{1}{\sqrt{\frac{t^2-1}{2}}(3t^2-2)}dt$; put $\sin x + \cos x = t$

and $(\cos x - \sin x)\,dx = dt$, we get

$I = \sqrt{2}\displaystyle\int \frac{1}{(3t^2-2)\sqrt{t^2-1}}dt$ and $1 + \sin 2x = t^2$

$\Rightarrow$ $\sin 2x = t^2 - 1$ put $t = \dfrac{1}{u}$ $\Rightarrow dt = -\dfrac{1}{u^2}du$

$\therefore$ $I = \sqrt{2}\displaystyle\int \frac{-du}{u^2\left(\frac{3}{u^2}-2\right)\sqrt{\frac{1}{u^2}-1}}$

$$= -\sqrt{2}\int \frac{u\,du}{(3-2u^2)\sqrt{1-u^2}}$$

Now put $\sqrt{1-u^2} = z$

$\Rightarrow$ $\dfrac{1(-2u)\,du}{2\sqrt{1-u^2}} = dz$ $\Rightarrow$ $\dfrac{-u\,du}{\sqrt{1-u^2}} = dz$

$\therefore$ $I = \sqrt{2}\displaystyle\int \frac{dz}{3-2(1-z^2)} = \sqrt{2}\int\frac{dz}{1+2z^2} = \frac{\sqrt{2}}{2}\int\frac{dz}{z^2+(1/2)}$

$$= \frac{1}{\sqrt{2}}\times\frac{1}{1/\sqrt{2}}\tan^{-1}\left(\frac{z}{1/\sqrt{2}}\right)+C$$

$$= \tan^{-1}\left(\sqrt{2}z\right)+C = \tan^{-1}\left(\sqrt{2}\sqrt{1-u^2}\right)+C$$

$$= \tan^{-1}\left(\sqrt{2}\frac{\sqrt{t^2-1}}{|t|}\right)+C$$

$$= \tan^{-1}\left(\sqrt{2}\frac{\sqrt{\sin 2x}}{|\sin x+\cos x|}\right)+C$$

23. $\displaystyle\int \frac{dx}{\cos^3 x-\sin^3 x}$ equals; ($g(x) = \sin x + \cos x$)

(a) $\dfrac{2}{3}\tan^{-1}g(x)+\dfrac{1}{3\sqrt{2}}\ell n\left|\dfrac{\sqrt{2}+g(x)}{\sqrt{2}-g(x)}\right|+C$

(b) $\dfrac{1}{3}\tan^{-1}g(x)-\dfrac{1}{3\sqrt{2}}\ell n\left|\dfrac{\sqrt{2}+g(x)}{\sqrt{2}-g(x)}\right|+C$

(c) $\dfrac{1}{9}\tan^{-1}g(x)-\dfrac{1}{3\sqrt{2}}\ell n\left|\dfrac{\sqrt{2}+g(x)}{\sqrt{2}-g(x)}\right|+C$

(d) None of these

Solution: (a) $I = \int \frac{dx}{\cos^3 x - \sin^3 x}$

$$= \int \frac{1}{(\cos x - \sin x)\left(1 + \frac{\sin 2x}{2}\right)} dx$$

$$= \int \frac{(\cos x - \sin x)}{(\cos x - \sin x)^2\left(1 + \frac{\sin 2x}{2}\right)} dx$$

$$= \int \frac{(\cos x - \sin x)}{(1 - \sin 2x)\left(1 + \frac{\sin 2x}{2}\right)} dx$$

$$= 2\int \frac{(\cos x - \sin x)}{[2 - (\sin x + \cos x)^2][1 + (\sin x + \cos x)^2]} dx$$

Put $\sin x + \cos x = t \Rightarrow (\cos x - \sin x)dx = dt$

$$= 2\int \frac{dt}{(2 - t^2)(1 + t^2)} = \frac{2}{3}\int\left(\frac{1}{1 + t^2} + \frac{1}{2 - t^2}\right)dt$$

$$= \frac{2}{3}\int \frac{1}{1 + t^2}dt + \frac{2}{3}\int \frac{1}{2 - t^2}dt$$

$$= \frac{2}{3}\tan^{-1} t + \frac{2}{3}\cdot\frac{1}{2\sqrt{2}}\ell n\left|\frac{\sqrt{2} + t}{\sqrt{2} - t}\right| + C$$

or $I = \frac{2}{3}\tan^{-1}(\sin x + \cos x) +$

$$\frac{1}{3\sqrt{2}}\ell n\left|\frac{\sqrt{2} + (\sin x + \cos x)}{\sqrt{2} - (\sin x + \cos x)}\right| + C$$

24. $\int \frac{dx}{(x - \alpha)\sqrt{(x - \alpha)(x - \beta)}}$ equals

(a) $\frac{2}{(\alpha - \beta)}\sqrt{\frac{(x - \alpha)}{(x - \beta)}} + C$

(b) $-\frac{2}{(\alpha - \beta)}\sqrt{\frac{(x - \beta)}{(x - \alpha)}} + C$

(c) $\frac{2}{(\alpha + \beta)}\sqrt{\frac{(x - \beta)}{(x - \alpha)}} + C$

(d) None of these

Solution: (b) ***Method 1***

$$I = \int \frac{dx}{(x - \alpha)\sqrt{(x - \alpha)(x - \beta)}} = \int \frac{dx}{(x - \alpha)^2\sqrt{\left(\frac{x - \beta}{x - \alpha}\right)}}$$

Put $\left(\frac{x - \beta}{x - \alpha}\right) = t^2 \quad \frac{(\beta - \alpha)}{(x - \alpha)^2}dx = 2t\, dt$

$$\frac{dx}{(x - \alpha)^2} = \frac{-2}{(\alpha - \beta)}t\, dt$$

$$\therefore\ I = \frac{-2}{(\alpha - \beta)}\int \frac{t\, dt}{t} = \frac{-2}{\alpha - \beta}(t) + C$$

$$= \frac{-2}{(\alpha - \beta)}\sqrt{\frac{x - \beta}{x - \alpha}} + C$$

Method 2: Put $x - \alpha = \frac{1}{t} \quad \Rightarrow dx = -\frac{1}{t^2}dt$

$$\Rightarrow I = \int \frac{-\frac{1}{t^2}dt}{\frac{1}{t}\sqrt{\frac{1}{t}\left[\frac{1}{t} + \alpha - \beta\right]}} = -\int \frac{dt}{\sqrt{1 + (\alpha - \beta)t}}$$

$= -\int \frac{1}{u}\cdot\frac{2u\, du}{(\alpha - \beta)}$; By substituting $1 + (\alpha - \beta)t = u^2$

$\Rightarrow (\alpha - \beta)dt = 2udu \quad \Rightarrow dt = \frac{2u}{(\alpha - \beta)}du$

$$\therefore\ I = -\frac{2}{(\alpha - \beta)}.u + C = -\frac{2}{(\alpha - \beta)}\sqrt{1 + (\alpha - \beta)t} + C$$

or $I = -\frac{2}{(\alpha - \beta)}\sqrt{1 + \frac{(\alpha - \beta)}{(x - \alpha)}} + C$

or $I = -\frac{2}{(\alpha - \beta)}\sqrt{\frac{(x - \beta)}{(x - \alpha)}} + C$

25. $\int \frac{\ell n\left(\ell n\left(\frac{1 + x}{1 - x}\right)\right)}{1 - x^2}dx$; $g(x) = \ell n\left(\frac{1 + x}{1 - x}\right)$; equals

(a) $\frac{1}{2}g(x)\{\ell n(g(x)) + 1\} + C$

(b) $g(x)\{\ell n(g(x)) + 1\} + C$

(c) $g(x)\{\ell n(g(x)) - 1\} + C$

(d) $\frac{1}{2}g(x)\{\ell n(g(x)) - 1\} + C$

Solution: (d) $\int \frac{\ell n\left(\ell n\left(\frac{1 + x}{1 - x}\right)\right)}{1 - x^2}dx$

put $\ell n\left(\frac{1 + x}{1 - x}\right) = t$

and $\left(\frac{1 - x}{1 + x}\right) \times \frac{(1 - x) - (1 + x)(-1)}{(1 - x)^2}dx = dt$

or $\frac{2}{(1 - x^2)}dx = dt$ or $I = \int \ell n(t).\frac{dt}{2}$

$$= \frac{1}{2}\int \underset{II}{1}.\underset{I}{\ell n(t)}\, dt = \frac{1}{2}t(\ell n\, t - 1)$$

$$\Rightarrow\ I = \frac{1}{2}\ell n\left(\frac{1 + x}{1 - x}\right)\left[\ell n\left\{\ell n\left(\frac{1 + x}{1 - x}\right)\right\} - 1\right] + C$$

26. $\int\left[\left(\frac{x}{e}\right)^x + \left(\frac{e}{x}\right)^x\right]\ell nx\, dx$ equals

(a) $\left(\frac{x}{e}\right)^x + \left(\frac{e}{x}\right)^x + C$ (b) $\left(\frac{e}{x}\right)^x - \left(\frac{x}{e}\right)^x + C$

(c) $\left(\frac{x}{e}\right)^x - \left(\frac{e}{x}\right)^x + C$ (d) None of these

Solution: (c) Let $I = \int \left[\left(\frac{x}{e}\right)^x + \left(\frac{e}{x}\right)^x\right] \ell nx\, dx$

Put $\left(\frac{x}{e}\right)^x = t$ or $x\,\ell n\left(\frac{x}{e}\right) = \ell nt$

$\Rightarrow \left(x.\frac{1}{x/e}.\frac{1}{e} + \ell n\left(\frac{x}{e}\right)\right)dx = \frac{1}{t}dt$

$\Rightarrow (1 + \ell nx - \ell ne)\, dx = \frac{1}{t}\, dt$

$\Rightarrow (\ell ne + \ell nx - \ell ne)\, dx = \frac{1}{t}\, dt$

$\Rightarrow (\ell nx)dx = \frac{1}{t}\, dt$

$\therefore\ I = \int\left(t+\frac{1}{t}\right)\frac{1}{t}\, dt = \int 1.dt + \int \frac{1}{t^2}dt = t - \frac{1}{t} + C$

or $I = \left(\frac{x}{e}\right)^x - \left(\frac{e}{x}\right)^x + C$

27. $\int (\sqrt{x^2+1})\left[\frac{\ell n(x^2+1) - 2\ell nx}{x^4}\right] dx$; $g(x) = \left(1+\frac{1}{x^2}\right)$; equals

(a) $\frac{1}{3}(g(x))^{1/2}\,\ell n(g(x)) + \frac{2}{9}(g(x)) + C$

(b) $-\frac{1}{3}(g(x))^{3/2}\,\ell n(g(x)) + \frac{2}{9}(g(x))^{3/2} + C$

(c) $\frac{1}{3}(g(x))^{3/2}\,\ell n(g(x)) - \frac{2}{9}(g(x)) + C$

(d) None of these

Solution: (b)

$$I = \int x\left(\sqrt{1+\frac{1}{x^2}}\right)\frac{\left[\ell n x^2 + \ell n\left(1+\frac{1}{x^2}\right) - \ell n x^2\right]^2}{x^4}$$

$$= \int\left[x\sqrt{1+\frac{1}{x^2}}\left[\frac{\ell nx^2 + \ell n\left(1+\frac{1}{x^2}\right) - 2\ell nx}{x^4}\right]\right]dx$$

$$= \int\left\{\frac{1}{x^3}\sqrt{1+\frac{1}{x^2}}\left[\ell n\left(1+\frac{1}{x^2}\right)\right]\right\}dx$$

Put $1 + \frac{1}{x^2} = t$; $\frac{-2}{x^3}dx = dt$

$\Rightarrow I = \left(\frac{-1}{2}\right)\int \sqrt{t}\,\ell nt\, dt = \left(\frac{-1}{2}\right)\left[\int t^{1/2}.\ell nt\, dt\right]$

$= -\frac{1}{2}\int \underset{II}{t^{1/2}}.\underset{I}{\ell nt}\, dt$ (using by parts)

$= -\frac{1}{2}\left[\ell nt\int t^{1/2}dt - \int\frac{1}{t}\left(\int t^{1/2}dt\right)dt\right]$

$= -\frac{1}{2}\left[(\ell nt)\frac{t^{3/2}}{3/2} - \int\frac{t^{1/2}}{(3/2)}\, dt\right]$

$= -\frac{1}{3}t^{3/2}\,\ell nt + \frac{1}{3}\frac{t^{3/2}}{3/2} + C$

$\therefore\ I = -\frac{1}{3}\left(1+\frac{1}{x^2}\right)^{3/2}\ell n\left(1+\frac{1}{x^2}\right) + \frac{2}{9}\left(1+\frac{1}{x^2}\right)^{3/2} + C$

28. $\int\frac{\tan 2\theta}{\sqrt{\cos^6\theta + \sin^6\theta}}\, d\theta$; $g(\theta) = \left[\frac{1}{(1-\tan^2\theta)} - \frac{1}{2}\right]$; equals

(a) $\ell n\left|\left(g(\theta) + \sqrt{[g(\theta)]^2 + \frac{3}{4}}\right)\right| + C$

(b) $\ell n\left|\left(g(\theta) + \sqrt{(g(\theta))^2 + 1}\right)\right| + C$

(c) $\ell n\left|\left(g(\theta) - \sqrt{(g(\theta))^2 + 3}\right)\right| + C$

(d) $\ell n\left|\left(g(\theta) + \sqrt{(g(\theta))^2 + 4}\right)\right| + C$

Solution: (a) $I = \int\frac{\tan 2\theta}{\sqrt{\cos^6\theta + \sin^6\theta}}\, d\theta$

$$= \int\frac{\tan 2\theta}{\sqrt{\cos^4\theta(1-\sin^2\theta) + \sin^4\theta(1-\cos^2\theta)}}d\theta$$

$$= \int\frac{\tan 2\theta}{\sqrt{\cos^4\theta + \sin^4\theta - \sin^2\theta\cos^2\theta(\cos^2\theta + \sin^2\theta)}}d\theta$$

$$= \int\frac{2\tan\theta.\sec^2\theta}{(1-\tan^2\theta)\sec^2\theta.\sqrt{\cos^4\theta + \sin^4\theta - \sin^2\theta\cos^2\theta}}d\theta$$

$= \int\frac{dt}{(1-t)\sqrt{t^2 - t + 1}}$ put $\tan^2\theta = t$

Put $1 - t = \frac{1}{u}$; $2\tan\theta\sec^2\theta\, d\theta = dt$

or $I = \int\frac{du}{u^2.\frac{1}{u}\sqrt{\left(1-\frac{1}{u}\right)^2 - \left(1-\frac{1}{u}\right) + 1}}$

$= \int\frac{du}{\frac{u}{u}\sqrt{u^2+1-u}} = \int\frac{du}{\sqrt{\left(u-\frac{1}{2}\right)^2 + \left(\frac{\sqrt{3}}{2}\right)^2}}$

$= \ell n\left[\left(u - \frac{1}{2}\right) + \sqrt{\left(u-\frac{1}{2}\right)^2 + \left(\frac{\sqrt{3}}{2}\right)^2}\right]$

$= \ell n\left[\left(\frac{1}{1-t} - \frac{1}{2}\right) + \sqrt{\left(\frac{1}{1-t} - \frac{1}{2}\right)^2 + \frac{3}{4}}\right]$

$$= \ell n\left[\left(\frac{1}{1-\tan^2\theta}-\frac{1}{2}\right)+\sqrt{\left(\frac{1}{1-\tan^2\theta}-\frac{1}{2}\right)^2+\frac{3}{4}}+C\right]$$

29. $\int \frac{e^{\cos x}(x\sin^3 x+\cos x)}{\sin^3 x}dx$; equals

(a) $e^{\cos x}(x-\text{cosec}\,x)+C$

(b) $-e^{\cos x}(x+\text{cosec}\,x)+C$

(c) $e^{\cos x}(x-\sec x)+C$

(d) None of these

Solution: (b) ***Method 1:*** Put $\cos x = t$;

$\sin x\, dx = -\,dt$

$$\Rightarrow I = -\int e^t \cos^{-1} t + \frac{1}{\left(\sqrt{1-t^2}\right)^3}dx$$

$$= e^t\left(\cos^{-1} t - \frac{1}{\sqrt{1-t^2}} + \frac{1}{\sqrt{1-t^2}} + \frac{1}{\left(\sqrt{1-t^2}\right)^3}\right)$$

Method 2: $I = \int \frac{e^{\cos x}(x\sin^3 x+\cos x)}{\sin^2 x}dx$

$= \int e^{\cos x}(x\sin x+\cot x\,\text{cosec}\,x)\,dx$

or $I = \int \underbrace{x.e^{\cos x}}_{I}\underbrace{\sin x}_{II}\,dx + \int \underbrace{e^{\cos x}}_{I}\underbrace{\text{cosec}\,x\cot x}_{II}\,dx$

$\therefore\ I = I_1 + I_2$ .... (1)

Now, $I_1 = \int x e^{\cos x}.\sin x\,dx$

$= x\int e^{\cos x}\sin x dx - \int 1.\left(\int e^{\cos x}\sin x\,dx\right)dx$

$= -xe^{\cos x} + \int 1.e^{\cos x}dx + C$

$I_2 = \int \underbrace{e^{\cos x}}_{I}.\underbrace{\text{cosec}\ x\ \cot x}_{II}\ dx$

$= e^{\cos x}\int \text{cosec}\,x\cot x\ dx -$

$\int (e^{\cos x}(-\sin x)\int \text{cosec}\,x\ \cot x\,dx)\,dx$

$= e^{\cos x}(-\text{cosec}\,x) + \int e^{\cos x}.\sin x(-\text{cosec}\,x)dx$

$= -\,e^{\cos x}\ \text{cosec}\ x - \int e^{\cos x}dx + C$

$\therefore\ I = I_1 + I_2$

$= -\,xe^{\cos x} + \int e^{\cos x}dx - e^{\cos x}\text{cosec}\,x - \int e^{\cos x}dx + C$

$= -\,e^{\cos x}(x + \text{cosec}\ x) + C$

30. $\int \frac{5x^4+4x^5}{(x^5+x+1)^2}dx$; equals

(a) $\frac{x+4}{(x^5+x+1)^2}+C$ (b) $\frac{x-1}{(x^5+x+1)^2}+C$

(c) $\frac{-(x+1)}{(x^5+x+1)^2}+C$ (d) None of these

Solution: (c) $I = \int \frac{5x^4+4x^5}{(x^5+x+1)^2}dx$

$= \int \frac{5x^4+1}{(x^5+x+1)^2}dx + \int \frac{4x^5-1}{(x^5+x+1)^2}dx$

$\therefore\ I = I_1 + I_2$ .... (1)

Now, $I_1 = \int \frac{du}{(u)^2} = \frac{-1}{u} + C_1 = \frac{-1}{(x^5+x+1)} + C_1$

and $I_2 = \int \frac{4x^3 - \frac{1}{x^2}}{\left(x^4+1+\frac{1}{x}\right)^2}dx$

$\Rightarrow I_2 = \int \frac{1}{t^2}dt$ (on substituting $x^4 + \frac{1}{x} + 1 = t$)

$= -\frac{1}{t} + C_2 = -\frac{x}{x^5+x+1} + C_2$

or $I = I_1 + I_2 = -\frac{1}{(x^5+x+1)} - \frac{x}{(x^5+x+1)} + C;$

where $C = C_1 + C_2$ or $I = -\frac{(x+1)}{x^5+x+1} + C$

31. $\int \frac{x^3+x+1}{x^4+x^2+1}dx$; equals

(a) $\frac{1}{2}\ell n(x^2+x+1)+\frac{1}{\sqrt{3}}\tan^{-1}\left(\frac{2x-1}{\sqrt{3}}\right)+C$

(b) $\ell n(x^2+x+1)+\frac{2}{\sqrt{3}}\tan^{-1}\left(\frac{2x-1}{\sqrt{3}}\right)+C$

(c) $\ell n(x^2+x+1)-\frac{2}{\sqrt{3}}\tan^{-1}\left(\frac{2x-1}{\sqrt{3}}\right)+C$

(d) None of these

Solution: (a) $I = \int \frac{x^3+x+1}{x^4+x^2+1}dx$

$= \int \frac{x^3+x+1}{x^4+x^2+1+x^2-x^2}dx = \int \frac{x^3+x+1}{(x^2+1)^2-x^2}dx$

or $I = \int \frac{x^3+x+1}{(x^2+x+1)\,(x^2-x+1)}dx$

Now $\frac{x^3+x+1}{(x^2+1-x)\,(x^2+1+x)} = \frac{Ax+B}{(x^2+1-x)} + \frac{Cx+D}{x^2+1+x}$

on comparing, $A = 0$, $B = \frac{1}{2}$, $C = 1$, $D = \frac{1}{2}$;

$I = \frac{x+\frac{1}{2}}{x^2+1+x} + \frac{\frac{1}{2}}{x^2+1-x}$

or $I = \int \frac{2x+1}{x^2+x+1}\,dx + \frac{1}{2}\int \frac{1}{x^2-x+1+\frac{1}{4}-\frac{1}{4}}\,dx$

$= \frac{1}{2}\ell n(x^2+x+1) + \frac{1}{2}\int \frac{dx}{\left(x-\frac{1}{2}\right)^2+\left(\frac{\sqrt{3}}{2}\right)^2}$

or $I = \frac{1}{2}\ell n(x^2+x+1) + \frac{1}{2}\cdot\frac{1}{\sqrt{3}/2}\tan^{-1}\left(\frac{x-\frac{1}{2}}{\frac{\sqrt{3}}{2}}\right)+C$

$\Rightarrow I = \frac{1}{2}\ell n(x^2+x+1) + \frac{1}{\sqrt{3}}\tan^{-1}\left(\frac{2x-1}{\sqrt{3}}\right)+C$

32. $\int \frac{1}{\sqrt{\sin^3 x\sin(x+\alpha)}}\,dx$; equals

(a) $\frac{2}{\sin\alpha}\sqrt{\frac{\sin(x-\alpha)}{\sin x}}+C$

(b) $\frac{2}{\cos\alpha}\sqrt{\frac{\sin(x-\alpha)}{\sin x}}+C$

(c) $-\frac{2}{\cos\alpha}\sqrt{\frac{\sin(x+\alpha)}{\sin x}}+C$

(d) $-\frac{2}{\sin\alpha}\sqrt{\frac{\sin(x+\alpha)}{\sin x}}+C$

Solution: (d) $I = \int \frac{dx}{\sqrt{\sin^3 x\sin(x+\alpha)}}\,dx$

$= \int \frac{1}{\sqrt{\sin^3 x[\sin x\cos\alpha+\cos x\sin\alpha]}}\,dx$

$= \int \frac{1}{\sqrt{\sin^4 x[\cos\alpha+\cot x\sin\alpha]}}\,dx$

$= \int \frac{\cos ec^2 x}{\sqrt{\cot x.\sin\alpha+\cos\alpha}}\,dx$

Put sinα. cot*x* + cosα = t^2

$\Rightarrow$ – sinα cosec²*x dx* = 2*t dt*

or $I = \int \frac{-1}{\sin\alpha}\frac{2t}{t}\,dt = -\frac{2}{\sin\alpha}.\int 1.dt = -\frac{2}{\sin\alpha}t+C$

$\Rightarrow I = -\frac{2}{\sin\alpha}\sqrt{\frac{\sin(x+\alpha)}{\sin x}}+C$

33. $\int \frac{x}{(7x-10-x^2)^{3/2}}\,dx$; $g(x) = 9-(2x-7)^2$; equals

(a) $\frac{3}{g(x)}+\frac{14}{3\sqrt{g(x)}}\left[\frac{-g'(x)}{4\sqrt{g(x)}}+1\right]+C$

(b) $\frac{3}{g(x)}+\frac{14}{3\sqrt{g(x)}}\left[\frac{-g'(x)}{4\sqrt{g(x)}}-1\right]+C$

(c) $\frac{3}{g(x)}-\frac{14}{3\sqrt{g(x)}}\left[\frac{g'(x)}{\sqrt{g(x)}}+1\right]+C$

(d) None of these

Solution: (b) $I = \int \frac{x}{(7x-10-x^2)^{3/2}}\,dx$

$= \int \frac{x}{\left(\sqrt{\frac{1}{4}[9-(2x-7)^2]}\right)^3}\,dx$

Put $2x-7 = 3\sin\theta \quad \Rightarrow 2dx = 3\cos\theta\, d\theta$

$= \frac{3}{4}\int \frac{3\sin\theta+7}{\left(\sqrt{\frac{1}{4}(9-9\sin^2\theta)}\right)^3}\,d\theta$; $\sin\theta = \frac{2x-7}{3}$

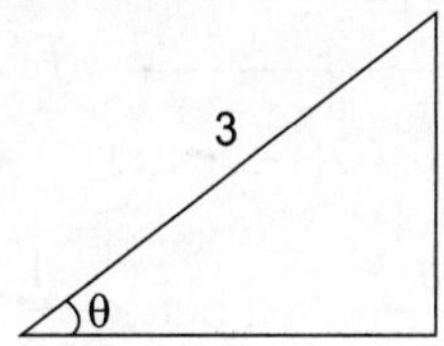

$= \frac{3}{4}\int \frac{3\sin\theta+7}{\left(\frac{3}{2}\cos\theta\right)^3}\,d\theta$; $\cos\theta = \frac{\sqrt{9-(2x-7)^2}}{3}$

$= \frac{3}{4}\times\frac{8}{27}\int \frac{3\sin\theta+7}{\cos^3\theta}\,d\theta$; $\tan\theta = \frac{2x-7}{\sqrt{9-(2x-7)^2}}$

$= \frac{2}{9}\int \frac{3\sin\theta}{\cos^3\theta}\,d\theta + \frac{2}{9}\int \frac{7}{\cos^3\theta}\,d\theta$

$= \frac{2}{3}\int \frac{\sin\theta}{\cos^3\theta}\,d\theta + \frac{14}{9}\int \sec^3\theta\, d\theta$; Put cosθ = *t*

$\Rightarrow$ – sin θ dθ = *dt* (using by part method)

$\therefore I = -\frac{2}{3}\int t^{-3}dt + \frac{14}{9}\sec\theta(\tan\theta-1)$

$= \frac{1}{3}.\frac{1}{t^2}+\frac{14}{9}.\frac{3}{\sqrt{9-(2x-7)^2}}\left(\frac{2x-7}{\sqrt{9-(2x-7)^2}}-1\right)$

$= \frac{3}{9-(2x-7)^2}$

$+\frac{14}{3\sqrt{9-(2x-7)^2}}\left(\frac{(2x-7)}{\sqrt{9-(2x-7)^2}}-1\right)+C$

34. $\int \frac{(1+x^2)dx}{1-2x^2\cos\alpha+x^4}$; $\alpha\in(0,\pi)$ equals

(a) $\frac{1}{2}\left(\text{cosec}\frac{\alpha}{2}\right)\tan^{-1}\left(\frac{x+\frac{1}{x}}{\sin\frac{\alpha}{2}}\right)+C$

(b) $\frac{1}{2}(\sin\alpha)\tan^{-1}\left(\frac{x+\frac{1}{x}}{\sin\frac{\alpha}{2}}\right)+C$

(c) $\frac{1}{2}\left(\text{cosec}\frac{\alpha}{2}\right)\tan^{-1}\sqrt{\left(\frac{x-\frac{1}{x}}{2\sin\frac{\alpha}{2}}\right)}+C$

(d) None of these

Solution: (c) $I=\int\frac{x^2+1}{x^4-2x^2\cos\alpha+1}dx$

On dividing numerator and denominator by x^2 we have,

$$=\int\frac{\left(1+\frac{1}{x^2}\right)}{x^2+\frac{1}{x^2}-2\cos\alpha+2-2}dx$$

$$=\int\frac{1+\frac{1}{x^2}}{\left(x-\frac{1}{x}\right)^2+2(1-\cos\alpha)}dx$$

$$=\int\frac{dt}{t^2+\left(2\sin\frac{\alpha}{2}\right)^2};\ \text{put } x-\frac{1}{x}=t$$

$$\Rightarrow \left(1+\frac{1}{x^2}\right)dx=dt$$

or $I=\frac{1}{2}\left(\text{cosec}\frac{\alpha}{2}\right)\tan^{-1}\left(\frac{x-\frac{1}{x}}{2\sin\frac{\alpha}{2}}\right)+C$

35. $\int\frac{x^2}{(x\cos x-\sin x)(x\sin x+\cos x)}dx$ equals

(a) $\ell n\left|\frac{x\sin x+\cos x}{x\cos x-\sin x}\right|+C$

(b) $\ell n\left|\frac{x\sin x+\cos x}{x\cos x+\sin x}\right|+C$

(c) $\ell n\left|\frac{x\sin x-\cos x}{x\cos x+\sin x}\right|+C$

(d) None of these

Solution: (a)

$$I=\int\frac{x^2}{(x\cos x-\sin x)(x\sin x+\cos x)}dx$$

$$\Rightarrow I=\int\left[\frac{x\cos x}{(x\sin x+\cos x)}+\frac{x\sin x}{x\cos x-\sin x}\right]dx$$

$$=\underbrace{\int\frac{x\cos x}{x\sin x+\cos x}dx}_{I_1}+\underbrace{\int\frac{x\sin x}{x\cos x-\sin x}dx}_{I_2}$$

Put $x\sin x+\cos x=t$ in I_1 and put $x\cos x-\sin x=t$ in I_2, we have

$(x\cos x+\sin x-\sin x)\,dx=dt$

and $(-x\sin x+\cos x-\cos x)\,dx=dt$

$\Rightarrow x\cos x\,dx=dt$ and $-x\sin x\,dx=dt$

$\Rightarrow I_1=\int\frac{1}{t}dt$ and $I_2=-\int\frac{1}{t}dt$

$\Rightarrow I_1=\ell n|x\sin x+\cos x|+C_1$ and

$I_2=-\ell n|x\cos x-\sin x|+C_2$

or $I=I_1+I_2 \quad\Rightarrow\quad I=\ell n\left|\frac{x\sin x+\cos x}{x\cos x-\sin x}\right|+C$

36. $\int\frac{x^{3/2}+x^{5/2}+x}{x^2+2x^{1/2}+x+1}dx$ equals

(a) $\frac{2}{3}(x)^{3/2}+x-\tan^{-1}(x)^{1/4}+C$

(b) $\frac{2}{5}(x)^{5/2}-x+\tan^{-1}(x)^{1/2}+C$

(c) $\frac{2}{3}(x)^{1/2}-x-\tan^{-1}(x)^{1/4}+C$

(d) $\frac{2}{3}(x)^{3/2}-x+\tan^{-1}(x)^{1/4}+C$

Solution: (d) $I=\frac{x\left(x^{1/2}+x^{3/2}+1\right)}{x^2+x^{1/2}+x+x^{1/2}+1+x^{3/2}}$

$$=\frac{x\left(x^{1/2}+x^{3/2}+1\right)}{x^{1/2}\left(x^{3/2}+x^{1/2}+1\right)+1\left(x^{3/2}+x^{1/2}+1\right)}$$

$$=\frac{x\left(x^{3/2}+x^{1/2}+1\right)}{\left(x^{1/2}+1\right)\left(x^{3/2}+x^{1/2}+1\right)}$$

$$\Rightarrow \frac{x-1+1}{\sqrt{x}+1}=\frac{(\sqrt{x})^2-(1)^2}{\sqrt{x}+1}+\frac{1}{\sqrt{x}+1}$$

$$\Rightarrow \left(\sqrt{x}-1\right)+\frac{1}{\sqrt{x}+1}$$

$$\Rightarrow \int\left(\sqrt{x}-1\right)dx+\int\frac{1}{\sqrt{x}+1}dx$$

$$\Rightarrow \frac{x^{3/2}}{3/2}-x+\int\frac{1}{\left(x^{1/4}\right)^2+(1)^2}dx$$

$$=\frac{2x^{3/2}}{3}-x+\tan^{-1}\frac{x^{1/4}}{1}+C.$$

SECTION–II

SUBJECTIVE-TYPE SOLVED EXAMPLES

1. Find $\int \frac{dx}{2\sin x + \sec x}$

Solution: $I = \int \frac{dx}{2\sin x+\sec x} = \int \frac{\cos x\,dx}{\sin 2x+1}$

$= \frac{1}{2}\int \frac{\cos x+\sin x+\cos x-\sin x}{\sin 2x+1}dx$

$= \frac{1}{2}\int \frac{\cos x+\sin x}{1+\sin 2x}dx + \frac{1}{2}\int \frac{\cos x-\sin x}{1+\sin 2x}dx$

$= \frac{1}{2}\int \frac{\cos x+\sin x}{1+1-(\sin x-\cos x)^2}dx + \frac{1}{2}\int \frac{\cos x-\sin x}{(\sin x+\cos x)^2}dx$

Let $u = \sin x - \cos x$

and $v = \sin x + \cos x$

Then

$I = \frac{1}{2}\int \frac{du}{2-u^2} + \frac{1}{2}\int \frac{dv}{v^2} = \frac{1}{4\sqrt{2}}\ln\left|\frac{\sqrt{2}+u}{\sqrt{2}-u}\right| - \frac{1}{2v} + C$

$= \frac{1}{4\sqrt{2}}\ln\left|\frac{\sqrt{2}+\sin x-\cos x}{\sqrt{2}-\sin x+\cos x}\right| - \frac{1}{2(\sin x+\cos x)} + C$

2. Find $\int \ln\left(\sqrt{1-x}+\sqrt{1+x}\right)dx$

Solution: Here we have only one function. If we take $u = ln\left(\sqrt{1-x}+\sqrt{1+x}\right)$ as the first function and $v = 1$ as the second function, then

$I = \ell n\left(\sqrt{1-x}+\sqrt{1+x}\right)\int 1dx$

$- \int\left(\frac{d}{dx}\left(\ln\left(\sqrt{1-x}+\sqrt{1+x}\right)\right)\int 1dx\right)dx$

$= x\,\ell n\left(\sqrt{1-x}+\sqrt{1+x}\right) -$

$\int \frac{1}{\left(\sqrt{1-x}+\sqrt{1+x}\right)}\left(-\frac{1}{2\sqrt{1-x}}+\frac{1}{2\sqrt{1+x}}\right)xdx$

$= x\,\ell n\left(\sqrt{1-x}+\sqrt{1+x}\right) - \frac{1}{2}\int x\frac{\sqrt{1-x^2}-1}{x\sqrt{1-x^2}}dx$

$= x\ell n\left(\sqrt{1-x}+\sqrt{1+x}\right) - \frac{1}{2}\int dx + \frac{1}{2}\int \frac{1}{\sqrt{1-x^2}}dx$

$= x\,\ell n\left(\sqrt{1-x}+\sqrt{1+x}\right) - \frac{x}{2} + \frac{1}{2}\sin^{-1}x + C$

3. Find $\int \frac{dx}{(x-b)^3(x-a)^2}$

Solution: Put $x - b = t(x - a)$

$\Rightarrow x = \frac{\text{at}-b}{t-1}$ $\Rightarrow dx = \frac{b-a}{(t-1)^2}dt$;

Also $x - a = \frac{a-b}{t-1} \Rightarrow x - b = \frac{(a-b)t}{t-1}$

Hence, $I = \int \frac{(t-1)^3(t-1)^2}{(a-b)^3t^3(a-b)^2}\cdot\frac{b-a}{(t-1)^2}dt$

$= -\frac{1}{(a-b)^4}\int \frac{t^3-3t^2+3t-1}{t^3}dt$

$= -\frac{1}{(a-b)^4}\int\left(1-\frac{3}{t}+\frac{3}{t^2}-\frac{1}{t^3}\right)dt$

$= -\frac{1}{(a-b)^4}\left[t-3\ln|t|-\frac{3}{t}+\frac{1}{2t^2}\right]$; where $t = \frac{x-b}{x-a}$

4. Find $\int \frac{(2x^2+5x+9)}{(x+1)\sqrt{x^2+x+1}}dx$

Solution: Let $2x^2 + 5x + 9 = A(x + 1)(2x + 1) + B(x + 1) + C = x^2.2A + x(3A + B) + A + B + C$

$\Rightarrow 2A = 2, 3A + B = 5, A + B + C = 9$

$\Rightarrow A = 1, B = 2, C = 6$

Thus, $\int \frac{(2x^2+5x+9)}{(x+1)\sqrt{x^2+x+1}}dx$

$= \int \frac{(2x+1)\,dx}{\sqrt{x^2+x+1}} + 2\int \frac{dx}{\sqrt{x^2+x+1}} + 6\int \frac{dx}{(x+1)\sqrt{x^2+x+1}}$ ...(1)

Let $I_1 = 6\int \frac{dx}{(x+1)\sqrt{x^2+x+1}}$

Put $x + 1 = \frac{1}{t}$ $\Rightarrow dx = -\frac{1}{t^2}dt$

$\Rightarrow I_1 = -6\int \frac{dt}{\sqrt{t^2-t+1}} = -6\int \frac{dt}{\sqrt{(t-1/2)^2+3/4}}$

$= -6\ln\left(t-1/2+\sqrt{(t+1/2)^2+3/4}\right) + C$

$= -6\ln\left(\frac{1-x+2\sqrt{x^2+x+1}}{x+1}\right) + C$

$\therefore I = 2\sqrt{x^2+x+1} + 2\ell n\left(1+2x+\sqrt{x^2+x+1}\right) -$

$6\ell n\left(\frac{1-x+2\sqrt{x^2+x+1}}{x+1}\right) + C$

5. Find $\int x^{-11}(1+x^4)^{-1/2}dx$

Solution: Here $\left(\frac{m+1}{n}+p\right) = \left(\frac{-11+1}{4}-\frac{1}{2}\right) = -3$

If we substitute $(1 + x^4) = R^2x^4$, then $\left(1+\frac{1}{x^4}\right) = R^2$

and $\frac{-4}{x^5}dx = 2RdR$; Now $I = \int \frac{dx}{x^{13}\left(1+\frac{1}{x^4}\right)^{1/2}}$

$$= \frac{-1}{4}\int \frac{2RdR}{x^8 R} = \frac{-1}{2}\int (R^2-1)^2 dR$$

$$= \frac{-1}{2}\int (R^4 - 2R^2 + 1)\, dR = \frac{-R^5}{10} + \frac{R^3}{3} - \frac{R}{2} + C$$

where $R = \sqrt{1+\frac{1}{x^4}}$.

6. Find $\int \sin^2 x \cos^4 x\, dx$

Solution: $\int \left(\frac{1-\cos 2x}{2}\right)\left(\frac{\cos 2x+1}{2}\right)^2 dx$

$$= \frac{1}{8}\int (1-\cos 2x)(\cos^2 2x + 2\cos 2x + 1)\, dx$$

$$= \frac{1}{8}\int \left(\frac{\cos 4x+1}{2}\right)dx + \int \frac{2\cos 2x dx}{8}dx + \int \frac{dx}{8}$$

$$-\frac{1}{8}\int \cos^3 2x\, dx - \frac{1}{4}\int \cos^2 2x\, dx - \frac{1}{8}\int \cos 2x\, dx$$

$$= \frac{1}{16}\frac{\sin 4x}{4} + \frac{x}{16} + \frac{\sin 2x}{8} + \frac{x}{8}$$

$$-\frac{1}{8}\int \frac{\cos 6x + 3\cos 2x}{4}dx - \frac{1}{8}\int (\cos 4x + 1)dx - \frac{1}{16}\sin 2x$$

$$= \frac{1}{64}\sin 4x + \frac{1}{8}\sin 2x + \frac{3x}{16} - \frac{1}{32}\left[\frac{\sin 6x}{6} + \frac{3\sin 2x}{2}\right] -$$

$$\frac{1}{32}\sin 4x - \frac{x}{8} - \frac{1}{16}\sin 2x$$

$$= -\frac{\sin 6x}{192} - \frac{\sin 4x}{64} + \frac{1}{64}\sin 2x + \frac{x}{16} + C$$

7. Find $\int \frac{1}{(\sin x + 2\cos x)(\cos x + 2\sin x)}dx$

Solution: $I = \int \frac{1}{(\sin x + 2\cos x)(\cos x + 2\sin x)}dx$

$$= \int \frac{\sec^2 x dx}{(2+\tan x)(1+2\tan x)} = \int \frac{dp}{(2+p)(1+2p)}$$

(if $\tan x = p$)

$$= -\frac{1}{3}\int \frac{dp}{(2+p)} + \frac{2}{3}\int \frac{dp}{(1+2p)} \text{ (by partial fraction)}$$

$$= -\frac{1}{3}\ell n|(2+p)| + \frac{1}{3}\ell n|(1+2p)|$$

$$= \frac{1}{3}\ell n\left|\frac{1+2p}{2+p}\right| = \frac{1}{3}\ell n\left|\frac{1+2\tan x}{2+\tan x}\right| + C$$

8. Prove that

$$\int \frac{x+2}{(x^2+3x+3)\sqrt{x+1}}dx = \frac{2}{\sqrt{3}}\tan^{-1}\left(\frac{\sqrt{3}\sqrt{x+1}}{-x}\right) + C$$

Solution: Let $f(x) = \int \frac{x+2}{(x^2+3x+3)\sqrt{x+1}}dx$

Substituting $x + 1 = p^2$, $dx = 2p\, dp$,

we get $f(x) = \int \frac{(p^2+1)2p\, dp}{p\{(p^2-1)^2 + 3(p)^2\}}$

$$= 2\int \frac{(p^2+1)dp}{p^4+1-2p^2+3p^2} = 2\int \frac{(p^2+1)dp}{(p^4+p^2+1)}$$

$$= 2\int \frac{(p^2+1)dp}{(p^2+p+1)(p^2-p+1)} = \int \frac{dp}{p^2+p+1} + \int \frac{dp}{p^2-p+1}$$

$$= \int \frac{dp}{(p+1/2)^2 + (\sqrt{3}/2)^2} + \int \frac{dp}{(p-1/2)^2 + (\sqrt{3}/2)^2}$$

$$= \frac{2}{\sqrt{3}}\left(\tan^{-1}\frac{2p+1}{\sqrt{3}} + \tan^{-1}\frac{2p-1}{\sqrt{3}}\right) + C$$

$$= \frac{2}{\sqrt{3}}\tan^{-1}\frac{2\sqrt{x+1}+1}{\sqrt{3}} + \frac{2}{\sqrt{3}}\tan^{-1}\frac{2\sqrt{x+1}-1}{\sqrt{3}} + C$$

$$= \frac{2}{\sqrt{3}}\left[\tan^{-1}\left\{\frac{\frac{4\sqrt{x+1}}{\sqrt{3}}}{\frac{3-(4x+4-1)}{3}}\right\}\right] + C$$

$$= \frac{2}{\sqrt{3}}\tan^{-1}\left(\frac{-\sqrt{3}\sqrt{x+1}}{x}\right) + C$$

9. Evaluate $\int \sin^{-1}\sqrt{\frac{x}{a+x}}dx$

Solution: Let $I = \int \sin^{-1}\sqrt{\frac{x}{a+x}}dx$

Let $x = a\tan^2\theta \quad \Rightarrow dx = 2a\tan\theta\sec^2\theta d\theta$

$$I = \int \sin^{-1}\sqrt{\frac{a\tan^2\theta}{a\sec^2\theta}}\; 2a\tan\theta\sec^2\theta d\theta$$

$$= 2a\int \theta\tan\theta\sec^2\theta d\theta = 2a\left[\frac{\theta\tan^2\theta}{2} - \int \frac{\tan^2\theta}{2}d\theta\right]$$

$$= a\theta\tan^2\theta - a\tan\theta + a\theta + C;$$

Writing θ in terms of x

We get $I = x\tan^{-1}\sqrt{\frac{x}{a}} - \sqrt{ax} + a\tan^{-1}\sqrt{\frac{x}{a}} + C$

10. Find $\int \frac{\cos^4 x\, dx}{\sin^3 x(\sin^5 x + \cos^5 x)^{3/5}}$

Solution: $I = \int \frac{\cos^4 x\, dx}{\sin^3 x(\sin^5 x + \cos^5 x)^{3/5}}$

$$= \int \frac{\cos^4 x\, dx}{\sin^6 x(1+\cot^5 x)^{3/5}} = \int \frac{\sec^2 x\, dx}{\tan^6 x\left(1+\frac{1}{\tan^5 x}\right)^{3/5}}$$

Let $\tan x = p$, then $\sec^2 x dx = dp$

$\therefore\ I = \int \frac{dp}{p^6\left(1+\frac{1}{p^5}\right)^{3/5}}$; Let $\left(1+\frac{1}{p^5}\right) = k$

$\Rightarrow -5\frac{1}{p^6}dp = dk$

$\Rightarrow I = \int \frac{dk}{-5k^{3/5}} = -\frac{1}{5}(k^{2/5})\left(\frac{5}{2}\right)+C$

$\Rightarrow -\frac{1}{2}\left[\frac{p^5+1}{p^5}\right]^{2/5}+C = -\frac{1}{2}\left[\frac{\tan^5 x+1}{\tan^5 x}\right]^{2/5}+C$

$= -\frac{1}{2}\left(1+\cot^5 x\right)^{2/5}+C$

11. Evaluate $\int \{1+\tan x.\tan(x+A)\}dx$

Solution: Let $I = \int \{1+\tan x.\tan(x+A)\}dx$

$= \int\left[1+\frac{\sin x\sin(x+A)}{\cos x\cos(x+A)}\right]dx = \int\frac{\cos(x+A-x)}{\cos x\cos(x+A)}dx$

$= \frac{\cos A}{\sin A}\int\frac{\sin(x+A-x)}{\cos x\cos(x+A)}dx$

$= \cot A\int\frac{\sin(x+A)\cos x-\sin x\cos(x+A)}{\cos x\cos(x+A)}dx$

$= \cot A \int \tan(x+A)\,dx - \cot A\int \tan x dx$

$= \cot A\,[\ln|\sec(x+A)| - \ln|\sec x|]$

$= \cot A\,\ln\left|\frac{\sec(x+A)}{\sec A}\right|+C$

12. Evaluate $\int\sqrt{\frac{1+x^{2n}}{x^{2n}}}\frac{\{\ln(1+x^{2n})-2n\ln x\}}{x^{2n+1}}dx$

Solution: Let $I = \int\sqrt{\frac{1+x^{2n}}{x^{2n}}}\frac{\{\ln(1+x^{2n})-2n\ln x\}}{x^{2n+1}}dx$

$= \frac{-1}{2n}\int p\ln p^2(2p)dp$

$\left[\text{for}\left(\frac{1}{x^{2n}}+1\right)=p^2, \frac{-2n}{x^{2n+1}}dx = 2p\,dp\right]$

$= -\frac{1}{n}\int p^2\ln p^2 dp = -\frac{1}{n}\left[\ln p^2.\frac{p^3}{3}-\int\frac{2p}{p^2}.\frac{p^3}{3}dp\right]$

$= -\frac{1}{n}\left[\frac{p^3}{3}\ln p^2-\frac{2}{9}p^3\right]+C = -\frac{p^3}{3n}\left(\ln p^2-\frac{2}{3}\right)+C$

13. Evaluate

$\int\left(\frac{1}{1-x^8}\right)\left[\cos^{-1}\left(\frac{2x}{1+x^2}\right)+\tan^{-1}\left(\frac{2x}{1-x^2}\right)\right]dx$

Solution: Let

$I = \int\left(\frac{1}{1-x^8}\right)\left[\cos^{-1}\left(\frac{2x}{1+x^2}\right)+\tan^{-1}\left(\frac{2x}{1-x^2}\right)\right]dx$

$= \int\left(\frac{1}{1-x^8}\right)\left[\frac{\pi}{2}-\sin^{-1}\frac{2x}{1+x^2}+\tan^{-1}\frac{2x}{1-x^2}\right]dx$

$= \frac{\pi}{8}\int\left(\frac{1}{1+x^2}+\frac{1}{1-x^2}\right)dx+\frac{\pi}{4}\int\frac{dx}{x^4+1}$

$= \frac{\pi}{8}\left(\tan^{-1}x+\frac{1}{2}\ell n\left|\frac{1+x}{1-x}\right|\right)+\frac{\pi}{8}\int\left[\frac{x^2+1}{x^4+1}-\frac{x^2-1}{x^4+1}\right]dx$

$= \frac{\pi}{8}\left[\tan^{-1}x+\frac{1}{2}\ell n\left|\frac{1+x}{1-x}\right|+\frac{1}{\sqrt{2}}\tan^{-1}\frac{x^2-1}{x\sqrt{2}}\right.$

$\left.-\frac{1}{2\sqrt{2}}\ell n\left|\frac{x^2-x\sqrt{2}+1}{x^2+x\sqrt{2}+1}\right|\right]+C$

14. Evaluate $\int\frac{(x^3+5)dx}{(x-5)^3(x-1)}$

Solution: Put $x - 5 = t \Rightarrow dx = dt$

The given integral becomes $\int\frac{[(t+5)^3+5]}{t^3(t+4)}dt$.

Breaking the intgrand into partial fractions, we get

$\frac{[(t+5)^3+5]}{t^3(t+4)} = \frac{A}{t}+\frac{B}{t^2}+\frac{C}{t^3}+\frac{D}{(t+4)}$

Solving , we get $A + D = 1 \Rightarrow 4A + B = 15$

or $4B + C = 75$ or $4C = 130$

So, $A = 35/32$, $B = 85/8$, $C = 65/2$, $D = -3/32$

$\therefore$ Given integral $= A\,\ell n\,|t| - B/t - C/2t^2 + D\ell n\,|t+4| + k$

$= \frac{35}{32}\ell n|x-5|-\frac{85}{8}\frac{1}{(x-5)}-\frac{65}{4}\frac{1}{(x-5)^2}-\frac{3}{32}\ell n$

$|x-1| + k$; where k is any arbitrary constant.

15. Find $\int\sin 4x.e^{\tan^2 x}dx$

Solution: $I = \int 4\sin x.\cos x.\cos 2x.e^{\tan^2 x}dx = 4$

$\int\tan x.\cos^2 x(\cos^2 x-\sin^2 x).e^{\tan^2 x}dx$

$= 4\int\tan x.\cos^4 x(1-\tan^2 x).e^{\tan^2 x}dx$

$= 4\int\frac{\tan x}{(\sec^4 x)}(1-\tan^2 x).e^{\tan^2 x}dx$; Put, $\tan^2 x = t$

$\Rightarrow 2\tan x\,.\,\sec^2 x\,dx = dt$

$\therefore\ I = 4\int\frac{(1-t)e^t}{(1+t)^3}\frac{dt}{2} = 2\int\frac{(1-t)e^t}{(1+t)^3}dt$

$= 2\left\{\int\frac{2e^t-(1+t)e^t}{(1+t)^3}dt\right\}$

$= 2\int e^t\left\{\frac{2}{(1+t)^3}-\frac{1}{(1+t)^2}\right\}dt = -2\frac{1}{(1+t)^2}e^t+C$

{using, $\int e^x(f(x)+f'(x))dx = e^x.f(x) + C$}

$\therefore\ I = -\frac{2e^{\tan^2 x}}{(1+\tan^2 x)^2}+C = -2\cos^4 x.e^{\tan^2 x}+C$

16. Find $\int \left(x+\frac{1}{x}\right)^{n+5}\left(\frac{x^2-1}{x^2}\right)dx$

Solution: Let, $I = \int \left(x+\frac{1}{x}\right)^{n+5}\left(\frac{x^2-1}{x^2}\right)dx$

$I = \int \left(x+\frac{1}{x}\right)^{n+5}\left(1-\frac{1}{x^2}\right)dx$ put $\left(x+\frac{1}{x}\right) = t$

$\Rightarrow \left(1-\frac{1}{x^2}\right) dx = dt \quad \therefore \; I = \int t^{n+5}\, dt$

$\Rightarrow I = \frac{t^{n+6}}{n+6}+C = \frac{(x+1/x)^{n+6}}{n+6}+C$

17. Find $\int \frac{(1-\cot^{n-2}x)\,dx}{\tan x+\cot x.\cot^{n-2}x}$

Solution: Here, $I = \int \frac{(1-\cot^{n-2}x)\,dx}{\tan x+\cot x.\cot^{n-2}x}$

$= \int \frac{(\sin^{n-2}x-\cos^{n-2}x)\,dx}{(\sin^{n-2}x.\tan x+\cos^{n-2}x.\cot x)}$

$\therefore \; I = \int \frac{\sin x\cos x(\sin^{n-2}x-\cos^{n-2}x)\,dx}{(\sin^n x+\cos^n x)}$;

put $\sin^n x + \cos^n x = t$

$\Rightarrow n(\sin^{n-1}x.\cos x - \cos^{n-1}x.\sin x)dx = dt$

$\therefore \; I = \frac{1}{n}\int \frac{dt}{t} = \frac{1}{n}\, ln|\,t\,| + C$

$= \frac{1}{n}\, ln|\,\sin^n x + \cos^n x\,| + C$

18. Prove that $\int (\cos x)^{2n+1}dx =$

$\left\{\sin x - {}^nC_1\frac{\sin^3 x}{3}+{}^nC_2\frac{\sin^5 x}{5}+...+(-1)^n\frac{\sin^{2n+1}x}{2n+1}\right\}+C$

Solution: Here, $I = \int (\cos x)^{2n+1}dx$ could be written as;

$= \int (\cos x)^{2n}.\cos x\,dx = \int (\cos^2 x)^n.\cos x\,dx$

$= \int (1-\sin^2 x)^n.\cos x\,dx$; $\left\{\begin{array}{l}\text{put } \sin x = t\\ \Rightarrow \cos x\,dx = dt\end{array}\right.$

$= \int (1-t^2)^n dt$

Using binomial expansion for $(1-t^2)^n$, we get

$= \int\{1-{}^nC_1t^2+{}^nC_2t^4+....+(-1)^nt^{2n}\}dt$

$= t-{}^nC_1\frac{t^3}{3}+{}^nC_2\frac{t^5}{5}+...+(-1)^n\frac{t^{2n+1}}{(2n+1)}+C$

$\therefore \int (\cos x)^{2n+1}dx = \sin x-{}^nC_1\frac{\sin^3 x}{3}+{}^nC_2\frac{\sin^5 x}{5}$

$+...+\frac{(-1)^n\sin^{2n+1}x}{(2n+1)}+C$

19. Find $\int \frac{\sec x\,dx}{\sqrt{\sin(2x+A)+\sin A}}$

Solution: Let $I = \int \frac{\sec x\,dx}{\sqrt{\sin(2x+A)+\sin A}}$

$= \int \frac{\sec^2 x\,dx}{\sqrt{\frac{2\sin(x+A)}{\cos x}}} = \frac{1}{\sqrt{2}}\int \frac{\sec^2 x\,dx}{\sqrt{\tan x.\cos A+\sin A}}$

Put, $(\tan x\,.\,\cos A + \sin A) = t^2$

$\Rightarrow \cos A\,.\,\sec^2 x\,dx = 2t\,dt$

$\therefore \; I = \frac{1}{\sqrt{2}}\int \frac{1}{t}.\frac{2t\,dt}{\cos A} = \sqrt{2}\sec A\int 1\,dt$

$\Rightarrow I = \sqrt{2}\sec A.\,(t) + C$

$= \sqrt{2}\sec A\sqrt{\tan x.\cos A+\sin A}+C$

20. Find $\int\left(\frac{1}{\sqrt[3]{x}+\sqrt[4]{x}}+\frac{\ell n(1+\sqrt[6]{x})}{\sqrt[3]{x}+\sqrt{x}}\right)dx$

Solution: Let,

$I = \int\left(\frac{1}{\sqrt[3]{x}+\sqrt[4]{x}}\right)dx + \int\frac{\ell n(1+\sqrt[6]{x})}{\sqrt[3]{x}+\sqrt{x}}dx = I_1 + I_2$ (say)

$\therefore \; I = I_1 + I_2$ ...(i)

Here, $I_1 = \int \frac{dx}{\sqrt[3]{x}+\sqrt[4]{x}}$ put $x = t^{12}$, $dx = 12\,t^{11}\,dt$

$\therefore \; I_1 = \int \frac{12t^{11}dt}{(t^4+t^3)} = 12\int\frac{t^8dt}{(t+1)}$

$= 12\int\left\{t^7-t^6+t^5-t^4+t^3-t^2+t-1+\left(\frac{1}{t+1}\right)\right\}dt$

$=12\left\{\frac{t^8}{8}-\frac{t^7}{7}+\frac{t^6}{6}-\frac{t^5}{5}+\frac{t^4}{4}-\frac{t^3}{3}+\frac{t^2}{2}-t+\ell n(t+1)\right\}+C$

...(ii)

Again $I_2 = \int\frac{\ell n(1+\sqrt[6]{x})}{\sqrt[3]{x}+\sqrt{x}}dx$; put $x = z^6$

$\Rightarrow dx = 6z^5\,dz$

$\therefore \; I_2 = \int\frac{\ell n(1+z)}{z^2+z^3}6z^5dz = 6\int\frac{\ell n(1+z)}{1+z}z^3dz$

Again let, $ln(1 + z) = \theta \Rightarrow 1 + z = e^\theta$

$\Rightarrow dz = e^\theta\, d\theta$

$\therefore \; I_2 = 6\int\frac{\theta.(e^\theta-1)^3}{e^\theta}e^\theta d\theta = 6\int \theta.(e^\theta-1)^3d\theta$

$\Rightarrow I_2 = 6\int \theta.(e^{3\theta}-3e^{2\theta}+3e^\theta-1)d\theta$

$= 6\left[\begin{array}{l}\theta\left(\frac{e^{3\theta}}{3}-\frac{3e^{2\theta}}{2}+\frac{3e^\theta}{1}-\theta\right)-\\ \int\left(1.\frac{e^{3\theta}}{3}-\frac{3e^{2\theta}}{2}+\frac{3e^\theta}{1}-\theta\right)d\theta\end{array}\right]$

$$= 6\begin{bmatrix} \theta\left(\frac{e^{3\theta}}{3}-\frac{3e^{2\theta}}{2}+3e^{\theta}-\theta\right)- \\ \left(\frac{e^{3\theta}}{9}-\frac{3e^{2\theta}}{4}+3e^{\theta}-\frac{\theta^2}{2}\right)\end{bmatrix}+C \quad \text{...(iii)}$$

$$\therefore\ I=12\left\{\frac{t^8}{8}-\frac{t^7}{7}+\frac{t^6}{6}-\frac{t^5}{5}+\frac{t^4}{4}-\frac{t^3}{3}+\frac{t^2}{2}-t+\ell n(t+1)\right\}$$

$$+\ 6\begin{bmatrix} \theta\left(\frac{e^{3\theta}}{3}-\frac{3e^{2\theta}}{2}+3e^{\theta}-\theta\right)- \\ \left(\frac{e^{3\theta}}{9}-\frac{3e^{2\theta}}{4}+3e^{\theta}-\frac{\theta^2}{2}\right)\end{bmatrix}+C;$$

where $t = x^{1/12}$ and $\theta = ln(1 + z)$.

21. Find $\int\frac{1+x^{2/3}}{1+x}dx$

Solution: Let, $I = \int\frac{1+x^{2/3}}{1+x}dx$; putting $x = t^3$ and $dx = 3t^2\,dt$

$$\therefore\ I = \int\frac{1+t^2}{1+t^3}3t^2\,dt = 3\int\left(\frac{t^4+t^2}{t^3+1}\right)dt$$

$$=3\int\left(t+\frac{t^2-t}{t^3+1}\right)dt = 3\left\{\frac{t^2}{2}+\int\frac{t^2-t}{(t+1)(t^2-t+1)}dt\right\}$$

Applying partial fractions.

$$\frac{t^2-t}{(t+1)(t^2-t+1)} = \frac{A}{t+1}+\frac{Bt+C}{(t^2-t+1)}$$

$$\Rightarrow A = \frac{2}{3},\ B = \frac{1}{3},\ C = -\frac{2}{3}$$

$$\therefore\ I = 3\left\{\frac{t^2}{2}+\int\frac{2\,dt}{3(t+1)}+\frac{1}{3}\int\frac{t-2}{t^2-t+1}dt\right\}$$

$$= 3\left\{\frac{t^2}{2}+\frac{2}{3}\ell n|t+1|+\frac{1}{3(2)}\int\frac{(2t-1)-3}{t^2-t+1}dt\right\}$$

$$= 3\left\{\frac{t^2}{2}+\frac{2}{3}\ell n|t+1|+\frac{1}{6}\int\frac{2t-1}{t^2-t+1}dt-\frac{1}{2}\int\frac{1}{t^2-t+1}dt\right\}$$

$$= 3\begin{Bmatrix}\frac{t^2}{2}+\frac{2}{3}\ell n|t+1|+\frac{1}{6}\ell n|t^2-t+1|- \\ \frac{1}{2}\int\frac{dt}{(t-1/2)^2+(\sqrt{3}/2)^2}\end{Bmatrix}$$

$$= \frac{3t^2}{2}+2\ell n|t+1|+\frac{1}{2}\ell n|t^2-t+1|-$$

$$\frac{3}{2}.\frac{1}{\sqrt{3}/2}\tan^{-1}\left(\frac{t-1/2}{\sqrt{3}/2}\right)+C$$

$$= \frac{3}{2}x^{2/3}+2\ell n|1+x^{1/3}|+\frac{1}{2}\ell n|x^{2/3}-x^{1/3}+1|$$

$$-\sqrt{3}\tan^{-1}\left(\frac{2x^{1/3}-1}{\sqrt{3}}\right)+C$$

22. Find $\int\frac{dx}{\sec x+\operatorname{cosec} x}$

Solution: Let, $I = \int\frac{dx}{\sec x+\cos ecx}$

$$= \frac{1}{2}\int\frac{2(\sin x\cos x)\,dx}{\cos x+\sin x} = \frac{1}{2}\int\frac{(2\sin x\cos x+1-1)\,dx}{\sin x+\cos x}$$

$$= \frac{1}{2}\int\frac{(\sin x+\cos x)^2-1)}{(\sin x+\cos x)}dx$$

$$= \frac{1}{2}\left(\int(\sin x+\cos x)\,dx-\int\frac{dx}{\sin x+\cos x}\right)$$

$$= \frac{1}{2}\left\{(-\cos x+\sin x)-\int\frac{\sec^2 x/2}{2\tan x/2+1-\tan^2 x/2}dx\right\}$$

Putting $\tan x/2 = t = t$ and using

$\sin x = \frac{2\tan x/2}{1+\tan^2 x/2}$ and $\cos x = \frac{1-\tan^2 x/2}{1+\tan^2 x/2}$ we have

$$= \frac{1}{2}\left\{-\cos x+\sin x-\int\frac{2\,dt}{-t^2+2t+1}\right\}$$

$$= \frac{1}{2}\left\{-\cos x+\sin x+2\int\frac{dt}{(t-1)^2-2}\right\}$$

$$= \frac{1}{2}\left\{-\cos x+\sin x+\frac{2}{2\sqrt{2}}\ell n\left|\frac{t-1-\sqrt{2}}{t-1+\sqrt{2}}\right|\right\}+C$$

$$= \frac{1}{2}\left\{\sin x-\cos x+\frac{1}{\sqrt{2}}\ell n\left|\frac{\tan\frac{x}{2}-1-\sqrt{2}}{\tan\frac{x}{2}-1+\sqrt{2}}\right|\right\}+C$$

23. Evaluate $\int e^{(x\sin x+\cos x)}.\left(\frac{x^4\cos^3 x-x\sin x+\cos x}{x^2\cos^2 x}\right)dx$

Solution: Let, $I = \int\left(e^{(x\sin x+\cos x)}.x^2\cos x\right)dx -$

$$\int e^{(x\sin x+\cos x)}.\left(\frac{x\sin x-\cos x}{x^2\cos^2 x}\right)dx$$

$$= \int\underbrace{x}_{I}\underbrace{\left(e^{(x\sin x+\cos x)}.x\cos x\right)}_{II}dx -$$

$$\int\left(\underbrace{e^{(x\sin x+\cos x)}}_{I}.\underbrace{\frac{d}{dx}\left(\frac{1}{x\cos x}\right)}_{II}\right)dx$$

$$= x\int\left(e^{(x\sin x+\cos x)}.x\cos x\right)dx-\int 1\left(\int e^{(x\sin x+\cos x)}.x\cos x\,dx\right)dx$$

$$-\left[e^{(x\sin x+\cos x)}\frac{1}{x\cos x}-\int e^{(x\sin x+\cos x)}.[x\cos x].\frac{1}{x\cos x}dx\right]$$

$$= xe^{(x\sin x+\cos x)}-\int e^{(x\sin x+\cos x)}dx-\frac{e^{(x\sin x+\cos x)}}{x\cos x}+$$

$$\int e^{(x\sin x+\cos x)}dx+C$$

$$= \left(x-\frac{1}{x\cos x}\right)e^{(x\sin x+\cos x)}+C$$

24. Find $\int (x+\sqrt{1+x^2})^n dx$

Solution: Let, $I = \int (x+\sqrt{1+x^2})^n dx$;

put $x+\sqrt{1+x^2} = t$ ...(i)

$\Rightarrow \left(1+\frac{1}{2\sqrt{1+x^2}}.2x\right)dx = dt$

$\Rightarrow \left(\frac{\sqrt{1+x^2}+x}{\sqrt{1+x^2}}\right)dx = dt$ ...(ii)

We know $t = x+\sqrt{1+x^2}$

$= x+\sqrt{1+x^2}\ .\ x\frac{x-\sqrt{1+x^2}}{x-\sqrt{1+x^2}}$; $\quad t = \frac{-1}{x-\sqrt{1+x^2}}$

$\Rightarrow -\frac{1}{t} = x - \sqrt{1+x^2}$ ...(iii)

Subtracting (iii) from (ii) we get, $2\sqrt{1+x^2} = t + 1/t$

or $\frac{1}{\sqrt{1+x^2}} = \frac{2t}{t^2+1}$ ...(iv)

from (i), (ii) and (iii) we get; $dx = \frac{t^2+1}{2t^2}dt$

$\therefore\ I = \int t^n.\frac{t^2+1}{(2t^2)}dt = \frac{1}{2}\int (t^n + t^{n-2})\,dt$

$= \frac{1}{2}\left[\frac{t^{n+1}}{n+1}+\frac{t^{n-1}}{n-1}\right]+C$

$\Rightarrow I = \frac{1}{2(n+1)}[x+\sqrt{(1+x^2)}]^{n+1} + \frac{1}{2(n-1)}$

$[x+\sqrt{(1+x^2)}]^{n-1} + C$

25. Find $\int \frac{dx}{\tan x+\cot x+\sec x+\operatorname{cosec} x}$

Solution: Here, $I = \int \frac{dx}{\tan x+\cot x+\sec x+\operatorname{cosec} x}$

$= \int \frac{(\sin x\ \cos x)dx}{1+\sin x+\cos x} = \int \frac{\sin x\, dx}{\sec x+\tan x+1}$

Multiplying and dividing by (1 + tan$x$ – sec$x$), we get

$= \int \frac{\sin x(1+\tan x-\sec x)}{(1+\tan x)^2-\sec^2 x}dx$

$= \int \frac{\sin x(1+\tan x-\sec x)}{2\tan x}dx$

$= \frac{1}{2}\int \cos x(1+\tan x-\sec x)\,dx$

$= \frac{1}{2}\int (\cos x+\sin x-1)\,dx = \frac{1}{2}\{\sin x - \cos x - x\} + C$

Thus, $\int \frac{dx}{\tan x+\cot x+\sec x+\operatorname{cosec} x}$

$= \frac{1}{2}\{\sin x - \cos x - x\} + C$

26. Find $\int x^2 \ell n(1-x^2)\,dx$, and hence prove that $\frac{1}{1.5}+\frac{1}{2.7}+\frac{1}{3.9}+..... = \frac{8}{9}-\frac{2}{3}\ell n 2$.

Solution: We know,

$ln(1-x) = -\left\{x+\frac{x^2}{2}+\frac{x^3}{3}+\frac{x^4}{4}+.....\infty\right\}$

put x^2 instead of x in the above identity,

$\Rightarrow ln(1-x^2) = -\left\{x^2+\frac{x^4}{2}+\frac{x^6}{3}+\frac{x^8}{4}+.....\infty\right\}$

$\Rightarrow x^2 ln(1-x^2) = -\left\{x^4+\frac{x^6}{2}+\frac{x^8}{3}+\frac{x^{10}}{4}+......\infty\right\}$

Integrating both sides, we get

$\int x^2\ell n(1-x^2)\,dx = -\left\{\frac{x^5}{1.5}+\frac{x^7}{2.7}+\frac{x^9}{3.9}+......\infty\right\}+C$

Now to find constant of integration, put $x = 0$

$\Rightarrow 0 = 0 + C \qquad \Rightarrow C = 0$

$\therefore\ \int x^2\ell n(1-x^2)dx = -\left\{\frac{x^5}{1.5}+\frac{x^7}{2.7}+\frac{x^9}{3.9}+...\infty\right\}$ ...(i)

Applying integration by parts, and taking limit 0 to 1 for L.H.S., we get

$\Rightarrow \int_0^1 x^2\ell n(1-x^2)\,dx$

$= \left(\frac{x^3}{3}\ell n(1-x^2)\right)_0^1 - \int_0^1 \frac{x^3}{3}.\frac{1(-2x)}{1-x^2}dx$

L.H.S. of (i)

$= \left(\frac{x^3}{3}\log(1-x^2)\right)_0^1 + \frac{2}{3}\left(-\frac{x^3}{3}-x+\frac{1}{2}\ell n\frac{1+x}{1-x}\right)_0^1$

$= = \frac{1}{3}\ell n2+\frac{2}{3}\left[-\frac{1}{3}-1+\frac{1}{2}\ell n2\right]$

$= \frac{1}{3}\ell n2+\frac{2}{3}\left[-\frac{4}{3}+\frac{1}{2}\ell n2\right]$

$= \frac{1}{3}\ell n2-\frac{8}{9}+\frac{1}{3}\ell n2 = \frac{2}{3}\ell n2-\frac{8}{9}$ ...(ii)

$\left[\begin{array}{l}\text{Taking } \ln(1-x^2) = \ln(1+x)+\ln(1-x)\\ \text{and } \ln\left(\frac{1+x}{1-x}\right) = \ln(1+x)-\ln(1-x)\end{array}\right]$

and applying limit as x varies from 0 to 1 to R.H.S. of (i) we have,

$\therefore$ from (i) and (ii)

$\Rightarrow \frac{2}{3}\ell n2-\frac{8}{9} = \frac{1}{1.5}+\frac{1}{2.7}+\frac{1}{3.9}+...\infty$.

27. Find the integral $\int \frac{1}{\sin 2x + \tan 2x} dx$

Solution: Let $\int \frac{\cos 2x}{\sin 2x \cos 2x + \sin 2x}$

$= \int \frac{\cos 2x}{\sin 2x (1+\cos 2x)} dx$

Multiply both Numerator and denominator by sin2*x*,

we have, $I = \int \frac{(\sin 2x)(\cos 2x)}{\sin^2(2x)(1+\cos 2x)} dx$

Now, Put $t = \cos 2x$

$\Rightarrow \frac{dt}{dx} = -2\sin 2x \quad \Rightarrow dx = \left(\frac{-dt}{2\sin 2x}\right)$

$\Rightarrow I = \frac{1}{2}\int \frac{t}{(1-t^2)(1+t)}(-dt) = \frac{1}{2}\int \frac{t}{(t^2-1)(1+t)} dt$

$= \frac{1}{2}\int \frac{t}{(t+1)^2(t-1)} dt$

Now, applying partial fraction method, we have

$\frac{t}{(t+1)^2(t-1)} = \frac{A}{(t+1)^2} + \frac{B}{(t+1)} + \frac{C}{(t-1)}$

$\frac{A(t-1)+B(t+1)(t-1)+C(t+1)^2}{(t+1)^2(t-1)}$

$\Rightarrow t = A(t-1) + B(t+1)(t-1) + C(t+1)^2$

Put $t = 1$

$1 = 0 + 0 + C(2)^2 \Rightarrow C = \frac{1}{4}$

Put $t = -1$

$-1 = A(-2) \qquad \Rightarrow A = \frac{1}{2}$

Put $t = 0 \qquad 0 = -A - B + C$

$\Rightarrow B = C - A = \frac{1}{4} - \frac{1}{2} = -\frac{1}{4}$; Now,

$\int \frac{t}{(t+1)^2(t-1)} dt$

$= \int \frac{1}{2}\frac{1}{(t+1)^2} dt + \left(\frac{-1}{4}\right)\int \left(\frac{1}{t+1}\right) dt + \int \frac{1}{4}\left(\frac{1}{t-1}\right) dt$

$\therefore \int \frac{t}{(t+1)^2(t-1)} dt$

$= \frac{-1}{2(t+1)} - \frac{1}{4}\ell n|t+1| + \frac{1}{4}\ell n|t-1| + C$

$\Rightarrow \frac{-1}{2(\cos 2x+1)} + \frac{1}{4}\ell n\left|\frac{\cos 2x-1}{\cos 2x+1}\right| + C.$

28. Find $\int \frac{x^2}{(x\cos x - \sin x)^2} dx$

Solution: Now, multiplying both numerator and denominator by (–sin *x*)

$\Rightarrow \int \underbrace{\frac{x(-\sin x)}{(x\cos x-\sin x)^2}}_{f(x)} \underbrace{\frac{x}{(-\sin x)}}_{g(x)} dx$ [∵ g(*x*) is easy to differentiate and *f*(*x*) is easy to integrate]

So *f*(*x*) = IInd function and g(*x*) = *I*[st] function

∴ Now using integration by parts, we have

$\Rightarrow I = \frac{x}{(-\sin x)}\int \frac{-(x\sin x)}{(x\cos x-\sin x)^2} dx -$

$\int\left\{\frac{d}{dx}\left(\frac{-x}{\sin x}\right)\int \frac{-(x\sin x)}{(x\cos x-\sin x)^2} dx\right\} dx$

$\Rightarrow$ Now, $t = x\cos x - \sin x$ and $\frac{dt}{dx} = x(-\sin x)$

$\Rightarrow I = \left(\frac{-x}{\sin x}\right)\int \frac{dt}{t^2} - \int\left\{\operatorname{cosec} x(x\cot x - 1)\int \frac{1}{t^2} dt\right\} dx$

$= \left(\frac{-x}{\sin x}\right)\left(\frac{(-1)}{t}\right) - \int\left\{\frac{\operatorname{cosec} x(x\cos x - \sin x)}{\sin x}\left(\frac{-1}{t}\right)\right\} dx$

$= \frac{x}{\sin x(x\cos x - \sin x)} - \int -\operatorname{cosec}^2 x\, dx$

$\Rightarrow \frac{x}{\sin x(x\cos x-\sin x)} - \cot x + C$

29. $\int \frac{(2x^2-3)}{x\sqrt{4x^2-(2x^2+3)^2}} dx$

Solution: Let $I = \int \frac{2x^2-3}{x\sqrt{4x^2-(2x^2+3)^2}} dx$

Dividing both numerator and denominator by x^2,

we have $I = \int \frac{\left(2-\frac{3}{x^2}\right)}{\sqrt{4-\left(2x+\frac{3}{x}\right)^2}} dx$; Now, put $t = 2x + \frac{3}{x}$

$\Rightarrow \frac{dt}{dx} = 2 - \frac{3}{x^2} \qquad \Rightarrow \left(x - \frac{3}{x^2}\right) dx = dt$

$\Rightarrow I = \int \frac{1}{\sqrt{4-t^2}} dt = \int \frac{1}{\sqrt{2^2-t^2}} dt$

$= \sin^{-1}\left(\frac{t}{2}\right) + C = \sin^{-1}\left(\frac{2x+\frac{3}{x}}{2}\right) + C$

$= \sin^{-1}\left(\frac{2x^2+3}{2x}\right) + C.$

30. Evaluate $\int \frac{1}{\tan^8 x} dx$

Solution: Let $I = \int \frac{\sec^2 x - \tan^2 x}{\tan^8 x} dx$

$$= \int \frac{\sec^2 x}{\tan^8 x} dx - \int \frac{1}{\tan^6 x} dx$$

$$= \int \frac{\sec^2 x}{\tan^8 x} dx - \int \frac{(\sec^2 x - \tan^2 x)}{\tan^6 x} dx$$

$$= \int \frac{\sec^2 x}{\tan^8 x} dx - \int \frac{\sec^2 x}{\tan^6 x} dx + \int \frac{1}{\tan^4 x} dx$$

$$= \int \frac{\sec^2 x}{\tan^8 x} dx - \int \frac{\sec^2 x}{\tan^6 x} dx + \int \frac{(\sec^2 x - \tan^2 x)}{\tan^4 x} dx$$

$$= \int \frac{\sec^2 x}{\tan^8 x} dx - \int \frac{\sec^2 x}{\tan^6 x} dx + \int \frac{\sec^2 x}{\tan^4 x} dx - \int \frac{1}{\tan^2 x} dx$$

$$= \int \frac{\sec^2 x}{\tan^8 x} dx - \int \frac{\sec^2 x}{\tan^6 x} dx + \int \frac{\sec^2 x}{\tan^4 x} dx -$$

$$\int \frac{\sec^2 x}{\tan^2 x} dx + \int 1.dx$$

Now, putting $t = \tan x$

$$\Rightarrow \frac{dt}{\sec^2 x} = dx$$

$$= \int \frac{1}{t^8} dt - \int \frac{1}{t^6} dt + \int \frac{1}{t^4} dt - \int \frac{1}{t^2} dt + x + C$$

$$= -\frac{1}{7}\frac{1}{(\tan x)^7} + \frac{1}{5}.\frac{1}{(\tan x)^5} - \frac{1}{3}.\frac{1}{(\tan x)^3} + \frac{1}{(\tan x)} + x + C$$

31. Evaluate $\int \frac{\cos x}{\sin 4x} dx$

Solution: $I = \int \frac{\cos x}{\sin 4x} dx = \int \frac{\cos x}{2 \sin 2x \cos 2x} dx$

$$\Rightarrow \int \frac{\cos x}{2(2 \sin x \cos x)(\cos 2x)} dx = \int \frac{1}{4 \sin x \cos 2x} dx$$

$$\Rightarrow I = \int \frac{1}{4 \sin x \cos 2x} dx$$

$$= \int \frac{\sin x}{4 \sin^2 x . \cos 2x} dx = \int \frac{\sin x}{4(1 - \cos^2 x)(2\cos^2 x - 1)} dx$$

Put $\cos x = t$

$$\Rightarrow \frac{dt}{dx} = -\sin x$$

$\Rightarrow \sin x \, dx = -dt$

$$\Rightarrow I = \frac{1}{4} \int \frac{-1}{(1-t)(1+t)(\sqrt{2}t+1)(\sqrt{2}t-1)} dt \quad \text{...(1)}$$

Let $\frac{1}{(t-1)(t+1)(\sqrt{2}t+1)(\sqrt{2}t-1)}$

$$= \frac{A}{t-1} + \frac{B}{t+1} + \frac{C}{(\sqrt{2}t+1)} + \frac{D}{(\sqrt{2}t-1)} \quad \text{...(2)}$$

$\Rightarrow 1 = A(t + 1)(2t^2 - 1) + B(t - 1)(2t^2 - 1) + C(t^2 - 1)(\sqrt{2}t - 1) + D(t^2 - 1)(\sqrt{2}t + 1)$ .... (3)

$$\Rightarrow A = \frac{1}{2(2-1)} = \frac{1}{2};\ B = \frac{-1}{2(2-1)} = -\frac{1}{2};$$

$C = 1; D = -1$

Using the values of A, B, C and D in (2) we get

$$\frac{1}{(t-1)(t+1)(\sqrt{2}t+1)(\sqrt{2}t-1)}$$

$$= \frac{1/2}{t-1} + \frac{-1/2}{t+1} + \frac{(-1)}{(\sqrt{2}t+1)} + \frac{(-1)}{(\sqrt{2}t-1)}.$$

$$\Rightarrow I = \left(\frac{1}{4}\right)\left[\frac{1}{2}\int \frac{1}{t-1} dt - \frac{1}{2}\int \frac{1}{1+t} dt + \int \frac{1}{(\sqrt{2}t+1)} dt - \int \frac{1}{(\sqrt{2}t-1)} dt\right] + C$$

$$= \frac{1}{4}\left(\frac{1}{2}\ln|\cos x - 1| - \frac{1}{2}\ln|1 + \cos x| + \frac{1}{\sqrt{2}}\ln|\sqrt{2}\cos x + 1| - \frac{1}{\sqrt{2}}\ln|\sqrt{2}\cos x - 1|\right) + C$$

$$= \frac{1}{4}\left[\frac{1}{2}\ln\left|\frac{1-\cos x}{1+\cos x}\right| + \frac{1}{\sqrt{2}}\ln\left|\frac{\sqrt{2}\cos x + 1}{\sqrt{2}\cos x - 1}\right|\right] + C$$

$$= \frac{2}{8}\ln\left|\tan\frac{x}{2}\right| + \frac{1}{4\sqrt{2}}\left|\frac{\sqrt{2}\cos x + 1}{\sqrt{2}\cos x - 1}\right| + C$$

$$= \frac{1}{4}\ln\left|\tan\frac{x}{2}\right| + \frac{1}{4\sqrt{2}}\left|\frac{\sqrt{2}\cos x + 1}{\sqrt{2}\cos x - 1}\right| + C$$

32. Evaluate $\int \frac{1}{(x - \sqrt{1+x^2})x} dx$

Solution: Let $I = \int \frac{1}{x(x - \sqrt{1+x^2})} \times \frac{(x + \sqrt{1+x^2})}{(x + \sqrt{1+x^2})} dx$

$$\Rightarrow \int \frac{\left(x + \sqrt{1+x^2}\right)dx}{x\left(x^2 - (1+x^2)\right)} = \int \frac{\left(x + \sqrt{1+x^2}\right)dx}{(-1)x}$$

$$= \int \frac{-x - \sqrt{1+x^2}}{x} dx = \int -dx - \int \frac{\sqrt{1+x^2}}{x} dx$$

$$\Rightarrow -x - \int \frac{\sqrt{1+x^2}}{x} dx \quad \text{...(i)}$$

Putting $x^2 + 1 = m^2$

$$\Rightarrow 2m\frac{dm}{dx} = 2x \quad \Rightarrow dx = \frac{mdm}{x}$$

we get, $I = -x - \int \frac{m}{x}.\frac{mdm}{x} = -x - \int \frac{m^2}{x^2} dm$

$$= -x - \int \frac{m^2}{m^2-1}dm = -x - \int \frac{m^2-1+1}{m^2-1}dm$$

$$= -x - \int 1dm - \int \frac{1}{m^2-1}dm$$

$$= -x - m - \frac{1}{2}\ln\left|\frac{m-1}{m+1}\right| + C$$

$$= -x - \sqrt{x^2+1} - \frac{1}{2}\ln\left|\frac{\sqrt{x^2+1}-1}{\sqrt{x^2+1}+1}\right| + C$$

33. Find the integral $\int \frac{(x-1)}{(x+1)\sqrt{x^3+x^2+x}}dx$

Solution: Let $I = \int \frac{(x-1)}{(x+1)\sqrt{x}\sqrt{x^2+x+1}}dx$

Put $x = t^2$ $\Rightarrow dx = 2t\ dt$

$$\Rightarrow I = 2\int \frac{(t^2-1)}{(t^2+1)\sqrt{t^4+t^2+1}}dt$$

$$= 2\int \frac{(t^2-1)}{(t^2+1)\sqrt{t^4+t^2+1}}dt$$

Now taking t^2 common we get

$$I = 2\int \frac{\left(1-\frac{1}{t^2}\right)}{\left(t+\frac{1}{t}\right)\sqrt{t^2+1+\frac{1}{t^2}}}dt$$

$$= 2\int \frac{\left(1-\frac{1}{t^2}\right)}{\left(t+\frac{1}{t}\right)\sqrt{t^2+\frac{1}{t^2}+1+1-1}}dt$$

$$= 2\int \frac{\left(1-\frac{1}{t^2}\right)}{\left(t+\frac{1}{t}\right)\sqrt{\left(t+\frac{1}{t}\right)^2-1^2}}dt$$

Put $m = t + \frac{1}{t}$, $dm = \left(1-\frac{1}{t^2}\right)dt$

$$\Rightarrow I = 2\int \frac{1}{m\sqrt{m^2-1}}dm = 2\sec^{-1} m + C$$

$$\Rightarrow 2\sec^{-1}\left(\frac{t^2+1}{t}\right) + C = 2\sec^{-1}\left(\frac{x+1}{\sqrt{x}}\right) + C$$

34. $\int \frac{\sqrt{\cos 2x}}{\sin x}dx$

Solution: Let $I = \int \frac{\sqrt{\cos 2x}}{\sin x}dx$

$$= \int \sqrt{\frac{\cos^2 x - \sin^2 x}{\sin^2 x}}dx = \int \sqrt{\cot^2 x - 1}\,dx$$

Putting $\cot x = \sec\theta$

$\Rightarrow -\operatorname{cosec}^2 x\ dx = \sec\theta\tan\theta\ d\theta$

or $I = \int \sqrt{\sec^2\theta - 1} \times \frac{\sec\theta\tan\theta}{-\operatorname{cosec}^2 x}d\theta$ and $\cot x = \sec\theta$

$\Rightarrow 1 + \cot^2 x = 1 + \sec^2\theta \Rightarrow \operatorname{cosec}^2 x = 1 + \sec^2\theta$

$$= -\int \frac{\sec\theta\tan^2\theta}{1+\sec^2\theta}d\theta = \int \frac{\sin^2\theta}{\cos\theta + \cos^3\theta}d\theta$$

$$= -\int \frac{1-\cos^2\theta}{\cos\theta(1+\cos^2\theta)}d\theta$$

$$= -\int \sec\theta\, d\theta + 2\int \frac{\cos\theta}{1+\cos^2\theta}d\theta$$

$$= -\int \sec\theta\, d\theta + 2\int \frac{\cos\theta}{2-\sin^2\theta}d\theta \quad \text{put } \sin\theta = t$$

$\Rightarrow \cos\theta\ d\theta = dt$

$$\therefore\ I = -ln|\sec\theta + \tan\theta| + 2 \times \frac{1}{2\sqrt{2}}\ell n\left|\frac{\sqrt{2}+\sin\theta}{\sqrt{2}-\sin\theta}\right| + C$$

$$= -ln|\sec\theta + \tan\theta| + \frac{1}{\sqrt{2}}\ell n\left|\frac{\sqrt{2}+\sqrt{1-\cos^2\theta}}{\sqrt{2}-\sqrt{1-\cos^2\theta}}\right| + C$$

or $I = -\ell n\left|\cot x + \sqrt{\cot^2 x - 1}\right| +$

$$\frac{1}{\sqrt{2}}\ell n\left|\frac{\sqrt{2}+\sqrt{1-\tan^2 x}}{\sqrt{2}-\sqrt{1-\tan^2 x}}\right| + C$$

35. $\int \frac{\sqrt{\sin^4 x + \cos^4 x}}{\sin^3 x \cos x}dx, x \in \left(0, \frac{\pi}{2}\right)$

Solution: $I = \int \frac{\sqrt{\sin^4 x + \cos^4 x}}{\sin^3 x \cos x}d\tilde{x}$

$$= \int \frac{\sin^2 x\sqrt{1+\cot^4 x}}{\sin x.\sin^3 x.\frac{\cos x}{\sin x}}dx = \int \frac{\sqrt{1+(\cot^2 x)^2}}{\sin^2 x.\cot x}dx$$

put $\cot^2 x = t$ $\Rightarrow 2\cot x.(-\operatorname{cosec}^2 x)\,dx = dt$

$$= \int \frac{-\sqrt{1+t^2}}{2\cot x.\cot x}dt = -\frac{1}{2}\int \frac{\sqrt{1+t^2}}{t}dt$$

$$= -\frac{1}{2}\int \frac{(1+t^2)}{t\sqrt{1+t^2}}dt = -\frac{1}{2}\left[\int \frac{1}{t\sqrt{1+t^2}}dt + \int \frac{t}{\sqrt{1+t^2}}dt\right]$$

$$= -\frac{1}{2}[I_1 + I_2] \text{ (say)}$$

put $t = \frac{1}{u}$ in I_1 and put $1 + t^2 = v^2$ in I_2, we have

$$I=-\frac{1}{2}\left[\int\frac{-1}{\sqrt{1+u^2}}du+\int\frac{v\,dv}{v}\right]$$

$$=-\frac{1}{2}\left[-\int\frac{1}{\sqrt{1+u^2}}du+v\right]$$

$$=-\frac{1}{2}\left[-\ell n(u+\sqrt{u^2+1})+\sqrt{1+t^2}\right]$$

$$=\left(\frac{1}{2}\ell n(u+\sqrt{u^2+1})-\frac{\sqrt{1+t^2}}{2}\right)+C$$

$$=-\frac{1}{2}\ell n(\tan^2x+\sqrt{1+\tan^4x})-\frac{1}{2}\sqrt{1+\cot^4x}+C$$

36. $\int\cos 2\theta.\ln\left(\frac{\cos\theta+\sin\theta}{\cos\theta-\sin\theta}\right)d\theta$

Solution: $I=\int\cos 2\theta.\ln\left(\frac{\cos\theta+\sin\theta}{\cos\theta-\sin\theta}\right)d\theta$

$$=\frac{1}{2}\int\cos 2\theta\ln\left(\frac{\cos\theta+\sin\theta}{\cos\theta-\sin\theta}\right)^2d\theta$$

$$=\frac{1}{2}\int\cos 2\theta\ln\left(\frac{1+\sin 2\theta}{1-\sin 2\theta}\right)d\theta$$

$$=\frac{1}{4}\int\ln\left(\frac{1+\sin 2\theta}{1-\sin 2\theta}\right).2\cos 2\theta\,d\theta \quad \text{put } \sin 2\theta=t$$

$\Rightarrow$ $2\cos 2\theta\, d\theta = dt$

$$\therefore\ I=\frac{1}{4}\int\ln\left(\frac{1+t}{1-t}\right)dt=\frac{1}{4}\left[\int\ln(1+t)dt-\int\ln(1-t)dt\right]$$

$$=\frac{1}{4}[t\,ln(1+t)-t+ln(1+t)-t\,ln(1-t)+t+ln(1-t)]+C$$

$$=\frac{1}{4}\left[t\ln\left(\frac{1+t}{1-t}\right)+\ln(1-t^2)\right]+C$$

$$=\frac{1}{4}\left[\sin 2\theta\ln\left(\frac{1+\sin 2\theta}{1-\sin 2\theta}\right)-\frac{1}{2}\ln(\sec^2 2\theta)+C\right]$$

or $I=\frac{1}{2}(\sin 2\theta)\ln\left(\frac{\cos\theta+\sin\theta}{\cos\theta-\sin\theta}\right)-\frac{1}{4}\ln(\sec 2\theta)+C$

Solved Assertion And Reason

37. A: If $I_n=\int\tan^n x dx$, then $5(I_4+I_6)=\tan^5 x$

R: If $I_n=\int\tan^n x dx$, then

$$\frac{\tan^{n-1}x}{n-1}=I_n+I_{n-2} \text{ where } n\in N$$

Solution: (a) $I_n=\int\tan^n x dx$

$\Rightarrow I_n=\int\left(\tan^{n-2}x\sec^2x-\tan^{n-2}x\right)dx$

$\Rightarrow I_n=\frac{\tan^{n-1}(x)}{n-1}-I_{n-2}\Rightarrow I_n+I_{n-2}=\frac{\tan^{n-1}x}{n-1}$

$\Rightarrow$ $(n-1)(I_n+I_{n-2})=\tan^{n-1}x$; Put $n=6$,

$\Rightarrow$ $5(I_6+I_4)=\tan^5 x$. *A* is true, *R* is true.

38 A: $P(x)$ and $Q(x)$ are two polynomials, then $\frac{P(x)}{Q(x)}$ is always integrable if $Q(x)$ has all distinct real roots.

R: Denominator gets factorized into linear factors thereafter the expression reduces to basic integrals with help of partial fraction.

Solution: (a) An algebraic function $\frac{P(x)}{Q(x)}$ which may be represented as,

$$\frac{P(x)}{Q(x)}=\frac{a_0+a_1x+a_2x^2+....+a_mx^m}{b_0+b_1x+b_2x^2+....+b_nx^n}.$$

If degree of Numerator is lower than that of the Denominator, then fraction is called proper otherwise improper. An improper fraction can be reduced to proper fraction as $\frac{P(x)}{Q(x)}=f(x)+\frac{R(x)}{Q(x)}$.

Where $f(x)$ is quotient, $R(x)$ is remainder and $Q(x)$ can be factorized in linear, non-linear and quadratic repeated and non-repeated.

39. A: $\int f(x)dx=k\int g(x)dx;\ k\in\mathbb{R}\ \Rightarrow\ f(x)=kg(x)$

R: $\int(f(x)-kg(x))dx=0\Rightarrow(f(x)-kg(x))=0$

Solution: (a) We have

(i) $\frac{d}{dx}(f(x)+g(x))=\frac{d}{dx}f(x)+\frac{d}{dx}g(x)$

and $\int[f(x)+g(x)]dx=\int f(x)dx+\int g(x)dx$

(ii) $\frac{d}{dx}kf(x)=k\frac{d}{dx}f(x),\int kf(x)dx=k\int f(x)dx$

$\Rightarrow\int f(x)dx=k\int g(x)dx$

$\Rightarrow$ diff. w.r.t. x in both sides

$\Rightarrow f(x)=k.g(x)$ $\qquad\Rightarrow$ Assertion is true.

Reason: $\int(f(x)-kg(x))dx=0$

$\Rightarrow\int f(x)-k\int g(x)dx=0$

$\Rightarrow$ Diff. $\Rightarrow\ \frac{d}{dx}\left(\int f(x)dx\right)-k\frac{d}{dx}\left(\int g(x)dx\right)=0$

$\Rightarrow f(x)-kg(x)=0$ $\qquad\Rightarrow f(x)=kg(x)$ is true.

40. A: If $a>0$ and $b^2-4ac<0$, then the value of the integral $\int\frac{dx}{ax^2+bx+c}$ will be of the type $\mu\tan^{-1}\left(\frac{x+A}{B}\right)+C$; where A, B, C, μ are constants.

R: If $a > 0$, $b^2 - 4ac < 0$, then $ax^2 + bx + c$ can be written as sum of two squares.

Solution: (a) If $a > 0$ and $b^2 - 4ac < 0$, then

$$ax^2 + bx + c = a\left(x+\frac{b}{2a}\right)^2 + \frac{4ac-b^2}{4a}$$

$$\Rightarrow \int\frac{dx}{ax^2+bx+c} = \int\frac{dx}{a\left(x+\frac{b}{2a}\right)+k^2}$$

where $k^2 = \dfrac{4ac-b^2}{4a} > 0$

which will of the type $\dfrac{1}{a}.\dfrac{1}{k/\sqrt{a}}\tan^{-1}\dfrac{x+\frac{b}{2a}}{k/\sqrt{a}}+C$

or $\mu\tan^{-1}\left(\dfrac{x+A}{B}\right)+C$

41. A: If y is a function of x such that $y(x-y)^2 = x$, then $\displaystyle\int\frac{dx}{x-3y} = \frac{1}{2}\left[\ln(x-y)^2-1\right]$

R: $\displaystyle\int\frac{dx}{x-3y} = \ln(x-3y)+C$

Solution: (c) The reason R is false since in writing $\displaystyle\int\frac{dx}{x-3y}$ = *ln*(*x* – 3*y*) + *C*, we are assuming that *y* is a constant. We will now prove the assertion.

Give integral to be prved is $\displaystyle\int\frac{dx}{x-3y} = \frac{1}{2}[\ln(x-y)^2-1]$ ...(1)

From the given relation,

and $(x-y)^2 = \dfrac{x}{y}$ and $2\ln(x-y) = \ln x - \ln y$ ...(2)

Also $\dfrac{dy}{dx} = \left(-\dfrac{y}{x}\right).\dfrac{x+y}{x-3y}$.

To prove the integral relation it is succficient to show that $\dfrac{d}{dx}$ RHS of (1) $= \dfrac{1}{x-3y}$.

Now RHS of (1) $= \dfrac{1}{2}\ln\left[\dfrac{x}{y}-1\right]$ $\quad\left(\because (x-y)^2 = \dfrac{x}{y}\right)$

$$= \frac{1}{2}[\ln(x-y)-\ln y] = \frac{1}{2}\left[\frac{\ln x-\ln y}{2}-\ln y\right]$$

$$= \frac{1}{4}[\ln x - 3\ln y]$$

$$\Rightarrow \frac{d}{dx}\text{RHS of (1)} = \frac{1}{4}\left[\frac{1}{x}-\frac{3}{y}\frac{dy}{dx}\right]$$

$$= \frac{1}{4}\left[\frac{1}{x}-\frac{3}{y}\left(-\frac{y}{x}\right)\frac{x+y}{x-3y}\right] = \frac{1}{x-3y}$$

$\Rightarrow$ Assertion A is true.

42. A: $\displaystyle\int 5^x\left(\sec^2 x + \tan x\ln 5\right)dx = 5^x\tan x + C$

R: If $a > 0$, then

$$\int a^x\left(f(x)+f'(x)\log_e a\right)dx = a^x f(x)+C$$

Solution: (c)

$$\because \frac{d}{dx}\left(a^x f(x)\right) = a^x f'(x) + f(x).a^x\log_e a$$

$$\Rightarrow \int a^x\left(f'(x)+f(x)\log_e a\right)dx = a^x f(x)+C$$

$\therefore$ Reason is incorrect. $\therefore$ By given reason

$$\int 5^x\left(\sec^2 x+\tan x\ln 5\right)dx = 5^x\tan x + C$$

$\therefore$ Assertion is correct.

43. A: $\displaystyle\int(\sin x.\cos x.\cos 2x.\cos 4x.\cos 8x.\cos 16x)\,dx = \frac{-\cos 32x}{1024}+C$

R: $\displaystyle\int\sin(2)^n x\,dx = -\frac{\cos(2)^n x}{(2)^{2n}}+C$

Solution: (c) $\displaystyle\int\sin(2)^n x\,dx = -\frac{\cos(2)^n x}{(2)^n}+C$

$\Rightarrow$ Reason is incorrect.

Now

$$\int(\sin x.\cos x.\cos 2x.\cos 4x.\cos 8x.\cos 16x)\,dx$$

$$= \frac{1}{2}\int(\sin 2x.\cos 2x.\cos 4x.\cos 8x.\cos 16x)\,dx$$

$$= \frac{1}{(2)^2}\int(\sin 4x.\cos 4x.\cos 8x.\cos 16x)\,dx$$

$$= \frac{1}{(2)^3}\int\sin 8x.\cos 8x.\cos 16x\,dx$$

$$= \frac{1}{(2)^5}\int\sin 32x\,dx = -\frac{1}{(2)^5}\frac{\cos 32x}{(32)}+C$$

$= -\dfrac{1}{1024}\cos 32x + C$ $\quad\therefore$ Assertion is correct.

44. A: $\displaystyle\int\frac{\tan(\ln x)\tan\left(\ln\frac{x}{2}\right)\tan(\ln 2)}{x}dx$

$$= \ln\left|\frac{\sec(\ln x)}{\sec\left(\ln\frac{x}{2}\right)x^{\tan(\ln 2)}}\right|+C$$

R: $\tan(A+B)\tan A.\tan B = \tan(A+B) - \tan A - \tan B$

and $\displaystyle\int\frac{\tan(\ln x)}{x}dx = \ln\sec|\ln x|+C$.

Solution: (a) $\tan(\ln x) = \tan\left(\ln\left(\dfrac{x}{2}.2\right)\right)$

$$= \tan\left[\ln\frac{x}{2} + \ln 2\right] = \frac{\tan\left(\ln\frac{x}{2}\right) + \tan(\ln 2)}{1 - \tan\left(\ln\frac{x}{2}\right).\tan(\ln 2)}$$

$$\Rightarrow \tan(\ln x) - \tan(\ln x).\tan\left(\ln\frac{x}{2}\right).\tan(\ln 2)$$

$$= \tan\left(\ln\frac{x}{2}\right) + \tan(\ln 2)$$

$$\Rightarrow \tan(\ln x).\tan\left(\ln\frac{x}{2}\right).\tan(\ln 2)$$

$$= \tan(\ln x) - \tan\left(\ln\frac{x}{2}\right) - \tan(\ln 2)$$

$$\therefore \int \frac{\tan(\ln x).\tan\left(\ln\frac{x}{2}\right).\tan(\ln 2)}{x}dx = \int\frac{\tan(\ln x)}{x}dx$$

$$-\int\frac{\tan\left(\ln\frac{x}{2}\right)}{x}dx - \int\frac{\tan(\ln 2)}{x}dx$$

$$= \ln|\sec(\ln x)| - \ln\left|\sec\left(\ln\frac{x}{2}\right)\right| - \tan(\ln 2)\ln|x| + C$$

$$= \ln\left|\frac{\sec(\ln x)}{\sec\left(\ln\frac{x}{2}\right)x^{\tan(\ln 2)}}\right| + C$$

∴ Assertion and reason both are correct.

45. A: For $2 < a < 5$, $\int\frac{dx}{x^2+2(a-3)x+(a-1)}$ $= A\ ln|g(x)| + C$; where A and C are constants, $g(x) = \left|\frac{(x+a-3)-f(a)}{(x+a-3)+f(a)}\right|$ and $f(a) = \sqrt{a^2-7a+10}$

R: For $2 < a < 5$, $\frac{1}{x^2+2(a-3)x+(a-1)}$ is a continuous function.

Solution: (d) $f(x) = \frac{1}{x^2+2(a-3)x+(a-1)}$ is continuous for disc. < 0

$\Rightarrow 4(a-3)^2 - 4(a-1) < 0$

$\Rightarrow a^2 - 6a + 9 - a + 1 < 0$

$\Rightarrow a^2 - 7a + 10 < 0 \quad \Rightarrow (a-2)(a-5) < 0$

$\Rightarrow a \in (2, 5)$

∴ for $2 < a < 5$, $\frac{1}{x^2+2(a-3)x+(a-1)}$ is continuous, and hence integrable

$$I = \int\frac{dx}{x^2+2(a-3)x+(a-1)}$$

$$= \int\frac{dx}{x^2+2(a-3)x+(a-3)^2+(a-1)-(a-3)^2}$$

$$= \int\frac{dx}{[x+(a-3)]^2-[(a-3)^2-(a-1)]}$$

$$= \int\frac{dx}{[x+a-3]^2-[a^2+10-7a]}$$

for $a \in (2, 5)$, $a^2 - 7a + 10 < 0$

$$= \int\frac{dx}{(x+a-3)^2+(-a^2+7a-10)}$$

$$= \int\frac{dx}{(x+a-3)^2+\left(\sqrt{-a^2+7a-10}\right)^2}$$

As $-a^2 + 7a - 10 > 0$ for $a \in (2, 5)$

$$= \frac{1}{\sqrt{-a^2+7a-10}}\tan^{-1}\left[\frac{x+a-3}{\sqrt{-a^2+7a-10}}\right] + C$$

∴ Assertion is wrong and Reason is correct.

46. A: If the primitive of $f(x) = \pi \sin \pi x + 2x - 4$, has the value 3 for $x = 1$, then there are exactly two values of x for which the primitive of $f(x)$ vanishes.

R: $\cos \pi x$ has period 2.

Solution: (d) Primitive of $f(x) = \int f(x)dx$

$= \int(\pi\sin\pi x + 2x - 4)dx$

Let $F(x) = \frac{-\pi\cos\pi x}{\pi} + x^2 - 4x + C$

Given, $F(1) = 3 \quad \Rightarrow 3 = 1 + (-3) + C$

$\Rightarrow C = 5$

∴ $F(x) = -\cos \pi x + x^2 - 4x + 5$, when primitive vanishes, $F(x) = 0$

$\Rightarrow x^2 - 4x + 5 = \cos \pi x$ .... (i)

Now $x^2 - 4x + 5 = (x^2 - 4x + 4) + 1 = (x - 2)^2 + 1 \geq 1$; $\cos \pi x \in [-1, 1]$

and clearly at $x = 2$, (i) holds good. Also $\cos \pi x$ being periodic with period 2 oscillates in between -1 and 1 and would never meet the graph of $x^2 - 4x + 5$ again, as shown below.

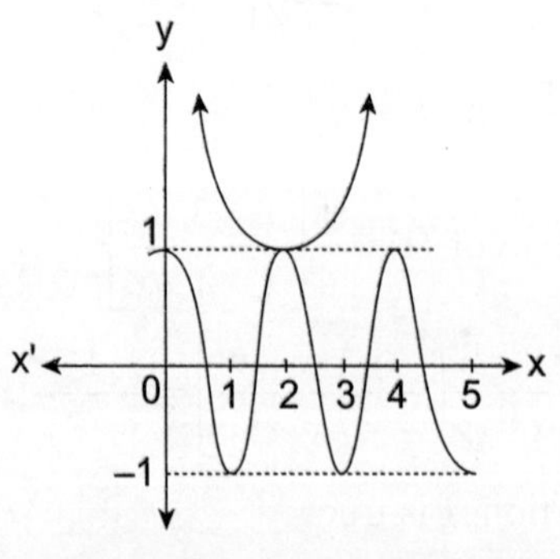

Thus, primitive gets vanished only once.

Thus, assertion is incorrect but reason is correct.

Comprehension-Type Questions

A: If the integrand is a rational function of x and fractional powers of a linear fractional function of the form $\frac{ax+b}{cx+d}$, then rationalization of the integral is affected by the substitution $\left(\frac{ax+b}{cx+d}\right)^m = t$, where m is g.c.d. of fractional powers of $\frac{ax+b}{cx+d}$. On the basis of above information answer the following questions.

47. If $I = \int \frac{(2x-3)^{1/2}}{(2x-3)^{1/3}+1}dx = 3\left[\frac{1}{7}(2x-3)^{7/6} - \frac{1}{5}(2x-3)^{5/6} + \frac{1}{3}(2x-3)^{1/2} - (2x-3)^{1/6} + 3g(x)\right] + C$, then $g(x)$ is equal to

(a) $\tan^{-1}(2x-3)^{1/6}$ (b) $(2x-3)^{1/2}$

(c) $3\tan^{-1}(2x-3)^{1/6}$ (d) $4(2x-3)^{1/6}$

48. If $I = \int \frac{dx}{\sqrt[4]{(x-1)^3(x+2)^5}} = A\left(\sqrt[4]{\frac{x-1}{x+2}}\right) + C$, then A is equal to

(a) 1/3 (b) 2/3

(c) 3/4 (d) 4/3

49. If $\int \frac{dx}{(1-x)\sqrt{1-x^2}} = k\sqrt{\frac{1+x}{1-x}} + C$, then k is equal to

(a) 1/2 (b) 1

(c) 1/3 (d) 2/3

Ans. 47. (a) **48.** (d) **49.** (b)

Solutions:

47. $\int \frac{(2x-3)^{1/2}}{(2x-3)^{1/3}+1}dx$; Put $(2x-3)^{1/6} = t$

$\Rightarrow (2x-3) = t^6$ $\left[\because \frac{1}{6} \text{ is g.c.d. of } \frac{1}{2}, \frac{1}{3}\right]$

$\Rightarrow I = \int \frac{t^3}{t^2+1} 3t^5 dt$ $\left[\because \frac{dx}{dt} = 3t^5\right]$

$$\Rightarrow I = \int \frac{3t^8}{t^2+1}dt = 3\int \frac{t^8}{t^2+1}dt$$

$$= 3\int \frac{t^8-1+1}{t^2+1}dt = 3\int \frac{t^8-1}{t^2+1}dt + 3\int \frac{1}{t^2+1}dt$$

$$= 3\int \frac{(t^4-1)(t^4+1)}{t^2+1}dt + 3\int \frac{1}{t^2+1}dt$$

$$= 3\int (t^2-1)(t^4+1)dt + 3\int \frac{1}{1+t^2}dt$$

$$= 3\int (t^6+t^2-t^4-1)dt + 3\int \frac{1}{1+t^2}dt$$

$$= 3\left[\frac{t^7}{7} + \frac{t^3}{3} - \frac{t^5}{5} - t + 3\tan^{-1} t\right] + C$$

$$= 3\left[\frac{1}{7}(2x-3)^{7/6} + \frac{1}{3}(2x-3)^{1/2} - \frac{1}{5}(2x-3)^{5/6} - (2x-3)^{1/6} + 3\tan^{-1}(2x-3)^{1/6}\right] + C$$

$\therefore$ $g(x) = \tan^{-1}(2x-3)^{1/6}$.

48. If $I = \int \frac{dx}{\sqrt[4]{(x-1)^3(x+2)^5}} = A\sqrt[4]{\frac{x-1}{x+2}} + C$; Put $\frac{x+2}{x-1} = t$

$\Rightarrow (x+2) = t(x-1)$ $\Rightarrow I = \int \frac{dx}{\sqrt[4]{(x-1)^3 t^5 (x-1)^5}}$.

Now $\frac{dt}{dx} = \frac{(x-1)(1)-(x+2)(1)}{(x-1)^2} = \frac{-3}{(x-1)^2}$

$$\Rightarrow dx = \frac{-(x-1)^2}{3}dt$$

$$\therefore I = -\frac{1}{3}\int \frac{(x-1)^2}{(x-1)^2 . t^{5/4}}dt = \frac{-1}{3}\int t^{-\frac{5}{4}}dt$$

$$\Rightarrow -\frac{1}{3}\left[\frac{t^{-\frac{5}{4}+1}}{-\frac{5}{4}+1}\right] + C = \frac{4}{3}\left[\frac{1}{t^{1/4}}\right] + C$$

$$= \frac{4}{3}\left(\frac{x-1}{x+2}\right)^{1/4} + C = \frac{4}{3}\sqrt[4]{\frac{x-1}{x+2}} + C$$

49. $\int \frac{dx}{(1-x)\sqrt{1-x^2}} = k\sqrt{\frac{1+x}{1-x}} + C$

Let $I = \int \frac{dx}{(1-x)\sqrt{1-x^2}}$

$$\Rightarrow I = \int \frac{dx}{(1-x)\sqrt{\frac{(1-x)^2(1+x)}{(1-x)}}} = \int \frac{dx}{(1-x)^2\sqrt{\frac{1+x}{1-x}}};$$

Now put $\frac{1+x}{1-x} = t^2$, and hence,

$$2t\frac{dt}{dx} = \frac{(1-x)(1)-(x+1)(-1)}{(1-x)^2} = \frac{1-x+x+1}{(1-x)^2}$$

$$\Rightarrow 2t\frac{dt}{dx} = \frac{2}{(1-x)^2} \quad \Rightarrow (1-x)^2 t\, dt = dx$$

$$\Rightarrow I = \int \frac{(1-x)^2 t\, dt}{(1-x)^2 t} = t + C = \sqrt{\frac{1+x}{1-x}} + C$$

$\Rightarrow k = 1.$

B: In calculating a number of integrals we had to use the method of integration by parts several times in succession. The result could be obtained more rapidly and in a more concise form by using the so-called generalized formula for integration by parts $\int u(x)\, v(x)\, dx = u(x)\, v_1(x) - u'(x)\, v_2(x) + u''(x)\, v_3(x) + \ldots\ldots + (-1)^{n-1} u^{n-1}(x)\, v_n(x) + (-1)^n \int u^n(x)\, v_n(x)\, dx$; where $v_1(x) = \int v(x)\, dx$, $v_2(x) = \int v_1(x)\, dx$ ..., $v_n(x) = \int v_{n-1}(x)\, dx$.

Of course, we assume that all derivatives and integrals appearing in this formula exist. The use of the generalized formula for integration by parts is especially useful when calculating $Q(x)dx$, where $P_n(x)$ is polynomial of degree n and the factor $Q(x)$ is such that it can be integrated successively $(n + 1)$ times. On the basis of above information answer the following questions.

50. If $\int\left(x^3-2x^2+3x-1\right)\cos 2x\, dx$

$=\dfrac{\sin 2x}{4}u(x)+\dfrac{\cos 2x}{8}v(x)+C$, then:

(a) $u(x) = x^3 - 4x^2 + 3x$

(b) $u(x) = 2x^3 - 4x^2 + 3x$

(c) $v(x) = 3x^2 - 4x + 3$

(d) $v(x) = 6x^2 - 8x$

51. If $\int\left(3x^2+x-2\right)\sin^2(3x+1)\, dx=-\dfrac{u(x)}{72}\sin(6x+2)$

$+\dfrac{v(x)}{72}\cos(6x+2)+\dfrac{1}{2}x^3+\dfrac{1}{4}x^2-x+C$

(a) $u(x) = 3x^2 - 6x + 13$

(b) $u(x) = 18x^2 + 2x - 13$

(c) $v(x) = 3x + 1$

(d) $v(x) = -(6x + 1)$

Ans. **50.** (b) **51.** (d)

Solutions:

50. The given integral is $\int\left(x^3-2x^2+3x-1\right)\cos 2x\, dx$

$= (x^3 - 2x^2 + 3x - 1)\dfrac{\sin 2x}{2} - (3x^2 - 4x + 3)$

$\left(-\dfrac{\cos 2x}{4}\right)+(6x-4)\left(-\dfrac{\sin 2x}{8}\right)-6\dfrac{\cos 2x}{16}+C$

$=\dfrac{\sin 2x}{4}\left[2x^3-4x^2+3x\right]+\dfrac{\cos 2x}{8}[6x^2-8x+3)+C$

51. First write the given integral as $\dfrac{1}{2}\int\left(3x^2+x-2\right)\left(1-\cos(6x+2)\right)dx$. Now applying the formula in comprehension, the last integral can be written as $\dfrac{1}{2}\left[x^3+\dfrac{x^2}{2}-2x\right]$

$-\dfrac{1}{2}\left[\left(3x^2+x-2\right)\dfrac{\sin(6x+2)}{6}+\right.$

$\left.(6x+1)\dfrac{\cos(6x+2)}{36}-6\dfrac{\sin(6x+2)}{6\times 36}\right]+C$

$=\dfrac{1}{2}\left[x^3+\dfrac{x^2}{2}-2x\right]-\dfrac{18x^2+6x-13}{72}\sin(6x+2)$

$-\dfrac{1}{72}(6x+1)\cos(6x+2)+C$.

C: In a certain problem of differentiation, a student has to use differentiation of product $f(x) . g(x)$ and by mistake he used $\dfrac{d}{dx}[f(x).g(x)]=\dfrac{df}{dx}.\dfrac{dg}{dx}$, but get the correct result if $f(x) = x^3$ and for certain function $g(x)$ such that $g(4) = 9, g(2) = -9$ and $g(0)=-\dfrac{1}{3}$. On the basis of above information answer the following questions.

52. The function $g(x)$ is

(a) $\dfrac{1}{(x-3)^3}$ (b) $\dfrac{2}{(x-3)^3}$

(c) $\dfrac{9}{(x-3)^3}$ (d) $\dfrac{-9}{(x-3)^3}$

53. The derivative of $f(x - 3) . g(x)$ with respect to x at $x = 200$ is

(a) 1 (b) 0

(c) –1 (d) 2

54. $\lim\limits_{x\to\infty}\dfrac{f(x).g(x)}{[1+g(x)]}$ equals

(a) 9 (b) 0

(c) 1/9 (d) None of these

Ans. **52.** (c) **53.** (b) **54.** (a)

Solutions:

The result used by student $\dfrac{d}{dx}[f(x).g(x)]=\dfrac{df}{dx}.\dfrac{dg}{dx}$ ...(1)

Given that the result (1) is correct for $f(x) = x^3$; $g(x) =?$; $g(4) = 9$; $g(2) = -9$; $g(0)=-\dfrac{1}{3}$

52. $\dfrac{d}{dx}[f(x).g(x)]=\dfrac{df}{dx}.\dfrac{dg}{dx}$

$\Rightarrow \dfrac{d}{dx}\left[x^3.g(x)\right]=\left(3x^2\right).\dfrac{dg}{dx}$

$\Rightarrow x^3 g'(x) + g(x) . 3x^2 = 3x^2 g'(x)$

$\Rightarrow (x^3 - 3x^2) g'(x) = - 3x^2 g(x)$

$\Rightarrow (x - 3) g'(x) = - 3g(x)$

$\Rightarrow \dfrac{g'(x)}{g(x)}=\dfrac{-3}{(x-3)}$

$\Rightarrow ln|g(x)| = -3ln|x-3| + lnC$

$\Rightarrow |g(x)| = \dfrac{C}{|x-3|^3} \quad \Rightarrow g(x) = \pm\dfrac{C}{|x-3|^3}$

$\Rightarrow g(x) = \dfrac{C}{(x-3)^3}$. But $g(0) = -\dfrac{1}{3}$; $g(2) = -9$; $g(4) = 9$

$\Rightarrow C = 9 \quad \Rightarrow g(x) = \dfrac{9}{(x-3)^3}$

53. $\dfrac{d}{dx}[f(x-3).g(x)] = \dfrac{d}{dx}\left[(x-3)^3.\dfrac{9}{(x-3)^3}\right] = \dfrac{d}{dx}(9) = 0$

$\Rightarrow \left[\dfrac{d}{dx}(9)\right]_{x=200} = 0$

54. $\lim\limits_{x\to\infty}\dfrac{f(x).g(x)}{[1+g(x)]} = \lim\limits_{x\to\infty}\dfrac{x^3\dfrac{9}{(x-3)^3}}{\left[1+\dfrac{9}{(x-3)^3}\right]} = \lim\limits_{x\to\infty}\dfrac{9x^3}{\left[(x-3)^3+9\right]}$

$= \lim\limits_{x\to\infty}\dfrac{9}{\left[\left(1-\dfrac{3}{x}\right)^3+\dfrac{9}{x^3}\right]} = \dfrac{9}{[(1-0)+0]} = 9$

D: If A is a square matrix defined by $A = \begin{bmatrix} x & x \\ x & x\end{bmatrix}$; $x \in \mathbb{R}$ such that $e^A = I + A + \dfrac{A^2}{2!} + \dfrac{A^3}{3!} + \ldots = \begin{bmatrix} \dfrac{f(x)}{2} & \dfrac{g(x)}{2} \\ \dfrac{g(x)}{2} & \dfrac{f(x)}{2}\end{bmatrix}$ and $0 < x < 1$, I being the identity matrix of order 2. On the basis of above information answer the following questions.

55. $\displaystyle\int\frac{g(x)}{f(x)}dx$ equals

(a) $ln(e^x + e^{-x}) + C$ (b) $ln(e^x - e^{-x}) + C$
(c) $ln(e^{2x} + 1) + C$ (d) None of these

56. $\displaystyle\int(g(x)+1)\sin x dx$ equals

(a) $\dfrac{e^x}{5}(\sin x - \cos x) + C$

(b) $\dfrac{e^{2x}}{5}(2\sin x - \cos x) + C$

(c) $\dfrac{e^{2x}}{5}(2\sin x + \cos x) + C$

(d) $\dfrac{e^x}{5}(\sin 2x - \cos 2x) + C$

57. $\displaystyle\int\frac{1}{\sqrt{g(x)}}dx$ equals

(a) $\text{cosec}^{-1}(e^x) + C$ (b) $\sin^{-1}(e^x) + C$
(c) $\sec^{-1}(e^x) + C$ (d) None of these

Ans. 55. (a) **56.** (b) **57.** (c)

Solution:

$A = \begin{bmatrix} x & x \\ x & x\end{bmatrix}$; $A^2 = \begin{bmatrix} 2x^2 & 2x^2 \\ 2x^2 & 2x^2\end{bmatrix}$; $A^3 = \begin{bmatrix} 4x^3 & 4x^3 \\ 4x^3 & 4x^3\end{bmatrix}$;

$A^4 = \begin{bmatrix} 8x^4 & 8x^4 \\ 8x^4 & 8x^4\end{bmatrix}$

$\therefore e^A = \begin{bmatrix} 1 & 0 \\ 0 & 1\end{bmatrix} + \begin{bmatrix} x & x \\ x & x\end{bmatrix} + \dfrac{1}{2!}\begin{bmatrix} 2x^2 & 2x^2 \\ 2x^2 & 2x^2\end{bmatrix} + \dfrac{1}{3!}\begin{bmatrix} 4x^3 & 4x^3 \\ 4x^3 & 4x^3\end{bmatrix} + \dfrac{1}{4!}\begin{bmatrix} 8x^4 & 8x^4 \\ 8x^4 & 8x^4\end{bmatrix} + \ldots$

$= \begin{bmatrix} \dfrac{f(x)}{2} & \dfrac{g(x)}{2} \\ \dfrac{g(x)}{2} & \dfrac{f(x)}{2}\end{bmatrix}$

$\Rightarrow \begin{bmatrix} 1+\dfrac{1}{2}\sum\limits_{r=0}^{\infty}\dfrac{(2x)^{r+1}}{(r+1)!} & \dfrac{1}{2}\sum\limits_{r=0}^{\infty}\dfrac{(2x)^{r+1}}{(r+1)!} \\ \dfrac{1}{2}\sum\limits_{r=0}^{\infty}\dfrac{(2x)^{r+1}}{(r+1)!} & 1+\dfrac{1}{2}\sum\limits_{r=0}^{\infty}\dfrac{(2x)^{r+1}}{(r+1)!}\end{bmatrix} = \begin{bmatrix} \dfrac{f(x)}{2} & \dfrac{g(x)}{2} \\ \dfrac{g(x)}{2} & \dfrac{f(x)}{2}\end{bmatrix}$

$\Rightarrow \begin{bmatrix} \dfrac{1}{2}+\dfrac{1}{2}e^{2x} & \dfrac{1}{2}e^{2x}-\dfrac{1}{2} \\ \dfrac{1}{2}e^{2x}-\dfrac{1}{2} & \dfrac{1}{2}+\dfrac{1}{2}e^{2x}\end{bmatrix} = \begin{bmatrix} \dfrac{f(x)}{2} & \dfrac{g(x)}{2} \\ \dfrac{g(x)}{2} & \dfrac{f(x)}{2}\end{bmatrix}$

$\Rightarrow f(x) = e^{2x} + 1$; $g(x) = e^{2x} - 1$

55. $\displaystyle\int\frac{g(x)}{f(x)}dx = \int\frac{e^{2x}-1}{e^{2x}+1}dx = \int\frac{e^x - e^{-x}}{e^x + e^{-x}}dx$

$= ln(e^x + e^{-x}) + C$

56. $\displaystyle\int(g(x)+1)\sin x dx$

$= \displaystyle\int(e^{2x}-1+1)\sin x\, dx = \int e^{2x}\sin x\, dx$

$= \text{Im}\displaystyle\int e^{2x}(\cos x + i\sin x)dx$

$= \text{Im}.\displaystyle\int e^{2x}.e^{ix}\, dx = \text{Im}.\int e^{(2+i)x}\, dx = \text{Im}.\left[\frac{e^{(2+i)x}}{2+i}\right] + C$

$= \text{Im}.\left[\dfrac{(2-i)}{5}\left(e^{2x}(\cos x + i\sin x)\right)\right] + C$

$= \text{Im}.\left[\dfrac{e^{2x}}{5}\{(2\cos x + \sin x) + i(2\sin x - \cos x)\}\right] + C$

$= \dfrac{e^{2x}}{5}[2\sin x - \cos x] + C$

57. $\displaystyle\int\frac{1}{\sqrt{g(x)}}dx =$

$\displaystyle\int\frac{1}{\sqrt{e^{2x}-1}}dx = \int\frac{e^x}{e^x\sqrt{e^{2x}-1}}dx = \int\frac{dt}{t\sqrt{t^2-1}}$; $t = e^x$

$\Rightarrow \sec^{-1}(t) + C = \sec^{-1}(e^x) + C$

E: If $\int \frac{\ln\left(x+\sqrt{1+x^2}\right)}{\sqrt{1+x^2}}dx = fog(x)+C$; where f and g are same functions of x and C is an arbitrary constant. On the basis of above information answer the following questions.

58. The function $h(x) = f(x) + (g(x))^2$ is

(a) odd function

(b) even function

(c) neither even nor odd

(d) one-one function

59. If $\int f(x) \cdot g(x)\, dx = ax^3 g(x) + b(1 + x^2)^{3/2} + c(1 + x^2)^{1/2} + d$; then $a + c - 12b$ equals

(a) 2 (b) −1

(c) 1 (d) None of these

60. $\int e^{g(x)}\, dx = ax.e^{g(x)} + a.g(x) + C$; then '$a$' equals

(a) $\frac{1}{4}$ (b) $\frac{1}{3}$

(c) 2 (d) $\frac{1}{2}$

Ans. 58. (b) **59.** (c) **60.** (d)

Solution:

Let $I = \int \frac{\ln\left(x+\sqrt{1+x^2}\right)}{\sqrt{1+x^2}}dx$

Put $\ln\left(x+\sqrt{1+x^2}\right) = t$

$\Rightarrow \frac{1}{x+\sqrt{1+x^2}} \times \left(1+\frac{1}{2\sqrt{1+x^2}}.2x\right)dx = dt$

$\Rightarrow \frac{1}{\sqrt{1+x^2}}dx = dt$

$\therefore\ I = \int t\, dt = \frac{t^2}{2} + C = \frac{1}{2}\left[\ln\left(x+\sqrt{1+x^2}\right)\right]^2 + C$

$= fog(x) + C = f(g(x)) + C$

$\Rightarrow f(x) = \frac{1}{2}x^2$ and $g(x) = \ln\left(x+\sqrt{1+x^2}\right)$.

58. $y = f(x) + (g(x))^2$

Let $y = h(x) = \frac{1}{2}x^2 + \left[\ln\left(x+\sqrt{1+x^2}\right)\right]^2$

$\therefore\ h(-x) = \frac{1}{2}x^2 + \left[\ln\left(-x+\sqrt{1+x^2}\right)\right]^2$

$= \frac{1}{2}x^2 + \left[\ln\left(x+\sqrt{1+x^2}\right)^{-1}\right]^2$ (By rationalization)

$= \frac{1}{2}x^2 + \left[\ln\left(x+\sqrt{1+x^2}\right)\right]^2 = h(x)$

$\Rightarrow f(x) + (g(x))^2$ is even function, and hence can't be one-one

59. $\int f(x).g(x)\,dx = \int \frac{1}{2}x^2 \ln\left(x+\sqrt{1+x^2}\right)dx$

$= \frac{1}{2}\left[\ln\left(x+\sqrt{1+x^2}\right)\frac{x^3}{3} - \int \frac{1}{\sqrt{1+x^2}}.\frac{x^3}{3}dx\right]$

$= \frac{1}{2}\left[\frac{1}{3}x^3 \ln\left(x+\sqrt{1+x^2}\right) - \frac{1}{3}\int \frac{x^2.x}{\sqrt{1+x^2}}dx\right]$

Put $\sqrt{1+x^2} = t \quad \Rightarrow \quad \frac{1}{2\sqrt{1+x^2}}(2x)\,dx = dt$

$\Rightarrow I = \frac{1}{6}x^3 \ln\left(x+\sqrt{1+x^2}\right) - \frac{1}{6}\int (t^2-1)dt$

$= \frac{1}{6}x^3 \ln\left[x+\sqrt{1+x^2}\right] - \frac{t^3}{18} + \frac{1}{6}t + d$

$= \frac{1}{6}x^3 g(x) - \frac{1}{18}(1+x^2)^{3/2} + \frac{1}{6}(1+x^2)^{1/2} + d$

$= ax^3 g(x) + b(1+x^2)^{3/2} + c(1+x^2)^{1/2} + d$

$\Rightarrow a = \frac{1}{6};\ b = -\frac{1}{18};\ c = \frac{1}{6}$

$\therefore\ a + c - 12b = \frac{1}{6} + \frac{1}{6} + \frac{12}{18} = 1$

60. $\int e^{g(x)}\,dx = \int e^{\ln\left(x+\sqrt{1+x^2}\right)}dx = \int \left(x+\sqrt{1+x^2}\right)dx$

$= \frac{x^2}{2} + \left(\frac{x\sqrt{1+x^2}}{2} + \frac{1}{2}\ln\left(x+\sqrt{1+x^2}\right)\right) + C$

$= \frac{x}{2}\left(x+\sqrt{1+x^2}\right) + \frac{1}{2}g(x) + C$

$= \frac{1}{2}(x)\left(x+\sqrt{1+x^2}\right) + \frac{1}{2}g(x) + C$

$= \frac{1}{2}xe^{g(x)} + \frac{1}{2}g(x) + C = ax\, e^{g(x)} + ag(x) + C$ (given)

$\Rightarrow a = \frac{1}{2}$.

Solved Matrix Matching

61. The anti-derivatives of functions given in column I are given in column II, match them;

Column I

(i) $f(x) = \frac{1}{(a^2+b^2)-(a^2-b^2)\cos x}$

(ii) $\frac{e^x(2-x^2)}{(1-x)\sqrt{1-x^2}}$

(iii) $\frac{x+1}{x(1+xe^x)^2}$

(iv) $f(x) = \frac{1}{x+x^{1/3}}$

Column II

(a) $\frac{3}{2}\ln\left(1+x^{2/3}\right)+C$

(b) $ln\left|\frac{xe^x}{1+xe^x}\right|+\frac{1}{1+xe^x}+C$

(c) $\frac{1}{ab}\tan^{-1}\left(\frac{a}{b}\tan\frac{x}{2}\right)+C$

(d) $e^x\sqrt{\frac{1+x}{1-x}}$

Ans. (i) → (c); (ii) → (d); (iii) → (b); (iv) → (a);

Solution: (i) $\int\frac{dx}{\left(a^2+b^2\right)-\left(a^2-b^2\right)\cos x}$

$$=2\int\frac{dt}{\left(a^2+b^2\right)\left(1+t^2\right)-\left(a^2-b^2\right)\left(1-t^2\right)}\quad (\tan x/2=t)$$

$$=\int\frac{dt}{a^2t^2+b^2}=\frac{1}{ab}\tan^{-1}\frac{a}{b}t+C$$

$$=\frac{1}{ab}\tan^{-1}\left(\frac{a}{b}\tan(x/2)\right)+C$$

(ii) The integrand can be written as

$$e^x\frac{1+\left(1-x^2\right)}{(1-x)\sqrt{1-x^2}}=e^x\left[\frac{1}{(1-x)\sqrt{1-x^2}}+\sqrt{\frac{1+x}{1-x}}\right]$$

Now $\frac{d}{dx}\left(\sqrt{\frac{1+x}{1-x}}\right)=\frac{1}{(1-x)\sqrt{1-x^2}}$

Thus, $\int e^x\frac{\left(2-x^2\right)}{(1-x)\sqrt{1-x^2}}dx=e^x\sqrt{\frac{1+x}{1-x}}+C$

taking $\int e^x\left(f(x)+f'(x)\right)dx=e^x f(x)+C$

(iii) The given integral can be written as

$$\int\frac{(x+1)e^x}{xe^x\left(1+xe^x\right)^2}dx=\int\frac{dt}{(t-1)t^2}$$

$(t = 1 + xe^x,\ dt = (x + 1)\, e^x\, dx)$

$$=\int\left[\frac{1}{t-1}-\frac{1}{t}\right]\frac{1}{t}\,dt=\int\left(\frac{1}{t(t-1)}-\frac{1}{t^2}\right)dt$$

$$=\int\left(\frac{1}{t-1}-\frac{1}{t}-\frac{1}{t^2}\right)dt$$

$$=ln\,|t-1|-ln\,|t|+\frac{1}{t}+C$$

$$=ln\left|\frac{xe^x}{1+xe^x}\right|+\frac{1}{1+xe^x}+C$$

(iv) $\int\frac{dx}{x+x^{1/3}}=3\int\frac{t^2}{t^3+t}dt\left(t^3=x\right)=\frac{3}{2}\int\frac{2t\,dt}{t^2+1}$

$$=\frac{3}{2}\ell n\left(t^2+1\right)+C=\frac{3}{2}\ell n\left(1+x^{2/3}\right)+C$$

62. Match the Column:

Column I

(i) $\int\frac{x^4-1}{x^2\sqrt{x^4+x^2+1}}dx$

(ii) $\int\frac{x^2-1}{x\sqrt{1+x^4}}dx$

(iii) $\int\frac{1+x^2}{(1-x^2)\sqrt{1+x^4}}dx$

(iv) $\int\frac{1}{(1+x^4)\sqrt{\sqrt{1+x^4}-x^2}}$

Column II

(a) $\ell n\left(\frac{(x^2+1)+\sqrt{x^4+1}}{x}\right)+C$

(b) $C-\frac{1}{\sqrt{2}}\ell n\left(\frac{\sqrt{x^4+1}-\sqrt{2}x}{(x^2-1)}\right)$

(c) $C-\tan^{-1}\left(\sqrt{\sqrt{1+\frac{1}{x^4}}-1}\right)$

(d) $\frac{\sqrt{x^4+x^2+1}}{x}+C$

Ans. (i) → (d); (ii) → (a); (iii) → (b); (iv) → (c);

Solution: (i) $I=\int\frac{x^4-1}{x^2\sqrt{x^4+x^2+1}}dx$

$$=\int\frac{x^4-1}{x^3\sqrt{x^2+1+\frac{1}{x^2}}}dx=\int\frac{x-\frac{1}{x^3}}{\sqrt{x^2+1+\frac{1}{x^2}}}$$

On substituting $x^2+1+\frac{1}{x^2}=t$;

$$\left(2x-\frac{2}{x^3}\right)dx=dt\,;\ \left(x-\frac{1}{x^3}\right)dx=\frac{dt}{2}$$

or $I=\frac{1}{2}\int\frac{dt}{\sqrt{t}}=\frac{1}{2}\frac{t^{1/2}}{\frac{1}{2}}+C$

$$\therefore\quad I=\frac{\sqrt{x^4+x^2+1}}{x}+C$$

(ii) $I = \int \frac{x^2-1}{x\sqrt{1+x^4}}dx = \int \frac{1-\frac{1}{x^2}}{\sqrt{x^2+\frac{1}{x^2}+2-2}}dx$

$= \int \frac{\left(1-\frac{1}{x^2}\right)}{\sqrt{\left(x+\frac{1}{x}\right)^2-(\sqrt{2})^2}}dx$; Put $x+\frac{1}{x}=t$

$\Rightarrow \left(1-\frac{1}{x^2}\right)dx = dt$; $I = \int \frac{dt}{\sqrt{t^2-(\sqrt{2})^2}}$

$= ln[t+\sqrt{t^2-(\sqrt{2})^2}] = \ell n\left[\left(x+\frac{1}{x}\right)+\sqrt{x^2+\frac{1}{x^2}}\right]$

or $I = \ell n\left[\frac{(x^2+1)+\sqrt{x^4+1}}{x}\right]+C$

(iii) $I = \int \frac{1+x^2}{(1-x^2)\sqrt{1+x^4}}dx$

$= \int \frac{1+\frac{1}{x^2}dx}{\left(\frac{1}{x}-x\right)\sqrt{\frac{1}{x^2}+x^2+2-2}}$

or $I = -\int \frac{\left(1+\frac{1}{x^2}\right)}{\left(x-\frac{1}{x}\right)\sqrt{\left(x-\frac{1}{x}\right)^2+(\sqrt{2})^2}}dx$

put $x-\frac{1}{x}=t \quad \Rightarrow \left(1+\frac{1}{x^2}\right)dx = dt$

or $I = -\int \frac{dt}{t\sqrt{t^2+(\sqrt{2})^2}}$, put $t = \frac{1}{z}$

$\Rightarrow dt = -\frac{1}{z^2}dz \quad$ or $I = \int \frac{\frac{1}{z^2}dz}{\frac{1}{z}\sqrt{\frac{1}{z^2}+(\sqrt{2})^2}}$

$= \int \frac{\frac{1}{z^2}dz}{\frac{1}{z^2}\sqrt{1+2z^2}} = \int \frac{1}{\sqrt{1+(\sqrt{2}z)^2}}dz$

$= \frac{1}{\sqrt{2}}\ell n\left[\sqrt{2}z+\sqrt{1+(\sqrt{2}z)^2}\right]+C$

$= \frac{1}{\sqrt{2}}\ell n\left(\frac{\sqrt{2}}{t}+\sqrt{1+\frac{2}{t^2}}\right)+C$

$= \frac{1}{\sqrt{2}}\ell n\left[\sqrt{2}\left(\frac{x}{x^2-1}\right)+\frac{\sqrt{x^4+1}}{(x^2-1)}\right]+C$

$= \frac{1}{\sqrt{2}}\ell n\left[\frac{\sqrt{2}x+\sqrt{x^4+1}}{(x^2-1)}\right]+C$

$= -\frac{1}{\sqrt{2}}\ell n\left[\frac{\sqrt{x^4+1}-\sqrt{2}x}{(x^2-1)}\right]+C$

(iv) $I = \int \frac{1}{(1+x^4)\sqrt{\sqrt{1+x^4}-x^2}}dx$

$= \int \frac{1}{(1+x^4)x\sqrt{\sqrt{1+\frac{1}{x^4}}-1}}dx$

$\Rightarrow I = \int \frac{\frac{1}{x^5}}{\left(1+\frac{1}{x^4}\right)\sqrt{\sqrt{1+\frac{1}{x^4}}-1}}dx$ put $1+\frac{1}{x^4}=t^2$

$\Rightarrow I = -\frac{1}{2}\int \frac{t}{t^2\sqrt{t-1}}dt = -\frac{1}{2}\int \frac{dt}{t\sqrt{t-1}}$ put $t-1=z^2$

$\Rightarrow dt = 2zdz$

$\Rightarrow I = -\frac{1}{2}\int \frac{2zdz}{(z^2+1)z} = -\int \frac{1dz}{z^2+1} = -\tan^{-1}z + C$

$= -\tan^{-1}(\sqrt{t-1})+C$

$= -\tan^{-1}\left(\sqrt{\sqrt{1+\frac{1}{x^4}}-1}\right)+C$

63. Let $I_1 = \int \tan x\tan(ax+b)dx$ and

$I_2 = \int \cot x\cot(ax+b)dx$

Column I

(i) value of I_1 for $a = 1$ is

(ii) value of I_2 for $a = 1$ is

(iii) value of I_1 for $a = -1$ is

(iv) value of I_2 for $a = -1$ is

Column II

(a) $x - \cot b\ \ell n\left|\frac{\cos(x-b)}{\cos x}\right|+C$

(b) $\cot b\ \ell n\left|\frac{\sin x}{\sin(x+b)}\right|-x+C$

(c) $\cot b\ \ell n\left|\frac{\cos x}{\cos(x+b)}\right|-x+C$

(d) $x + \cot b\ \ell n\left|\frac{\sin x}{\sin(b-x)}\right|+C$

Ans. (i) → (c); (ii) → (b); (iii) → (a); (iv) → (d)

Solution: $I_1 = \int \tan x \tan(ax+b)dx$

(i) For $a = 1$, $I_1 = \int \tan x \tan(x+b)dx$

$\tan b = \tan[(x+b)-(x)] = \dfrac{\tan(x+b)-\tan x}{1+\tan(x+b)\tan x}$

or $\tan(x+b)\tan x = \dfrac{\tan(x+b)-\tan x-\tan b}{\tan b}$

or $I_1 = \dfrac{1}{\tan b}\int(\tan(x+b)-\tan x-\tan b)dx$

$= \dfrac{1}{\tan b}[-\log\cos(x+b)+\log\cos x - x\tan b]+C$

or $I_1 = \cot b\,\ell n\left|\dfrac{\cos x}{\cos(x+b)}\right| - x + C$;

(ii) $I_2 = \int \cot x\cot(ax+b)dx$; for $a = 1$,

$I_2 = \int \cot x\cot(x+b)\,dx$

Now, $\cot b = \cot((x+b)-x)$

$\Rightarrow \cot b = \dfrac{\cot(x+b)\cot x+1}{\cot x-\cot(x+b)}$

or $\cot(x+b)\cot x = \cot b\cot x - \cot b\cot(x+b) - 1$

or $I_2 = \int(\cot b\cot x - \cot b\cot(x+b)-1)\,dx$

$= \cot b\int\cot x dx - \cot b\int\cot(x+b)dx - \int 1.dx$

$= \cot b\, ln|\sin x| - \cot b\, ln|\sin(x+b)| - x + C$

$= \cot b\;\ell n\left|\dfrac{\sin x}{\sin(x+b)}\right| - x + C$

(iii) For $a = -1$; $I_1 = \int \tan x\tan(b-x)dx$; Now,

$\tan b = \tan(x+(b-x)) = \dfrac{\tan x+\tan(b-x)}{1-\tan x\tan(b-x)}$

$\tan x\tan(b-x) = \dfrac{\tan b-\tan x-\tan(b-x)}{\tan b}$

or $I_1 = \dfrac{1}{\tan b}\int(\tan b-\tan x-\tan(b-x))dx$

$= \dfrac{1}{\tan b}[x\tan b + \ell n|\cos x| - \ell n|\cos(b-x)|]+C$

$= x + \cot b\,\ell n\left|\dfrac{\cos x}{\cos(b-x)}\right| + C$

$= x - \cot b\ln\left|\dfrac{\cos(b-x)}{\cos x}\right| + C$

(iv) $I_2 = \int\cot x\cot(ax+b)dx$

for $a = -1$; $I_2 = \int\cot x\cot(b-ax)\,dx$

Now, $\cot b = \cot(x+(b-x)) = \dfrac{\cot x\cot(b-x)-1}{\cot x+\cot(b-x)}$

or $\cot x\cot(b-x) = \cot b(\cot x + \cot(b-x)) + 1$

or $I_2 = \int[\cot b(\cot x+\cot(b-x))+1]dx$

$= \cot b\,\ell n\left|\dfrac{\sin x}{\sin(b-x)}\right| + x + C$

64. **Column I**

(i) If $\int\dfrac{2^x}{\sqrt{1-4^x}}dx = \lambda\sin^{-1}g(x)+C$, then λ ≥

(ii) If $\int\dfrac{\left(\sqrt{x}\right)^5}{\left(\sqrt{x}\right)^7+x^6}dx = \mu\ln\left|\dfrac{x^\lambda}{x^\lambda+1}\right|+C$, then μλ ≤

(iii) $\int\dfrac{x^4+1}{x(x^2+1)^2}dx = \lambda\ln|x| + \dfrac{\mu}{1+x^2}+C$; then λμ ≥

(iv) $\int\dfrac{dx}{5+4\cos x} = \lambda\tan^{-1}\left(\mu\tan\dfrac{x}{2}\right)+C$; then $\dfrac{2\lambda}{\mu} \geq$

Column II

(a) 0

(b) 1

(c) 3

(d) 4

Ans. (i) → (a), (b); (ii) → (b), (c), (d); (iii) → (a), (b); (iv) → (a), (b), (c), (d)

Solutions:

(i) $I = \int\dfrac{2^x}{\sqrt{1-4^x}}dx$; Put $2^x = t$

$\Rightarrow 2^x\, ln\,2\,dx = dt \quad \Rightarrow 2^x dx = \dfrac{1}{\ln 2}dt$

$\therefore\; I = \int\dfrac{dt}{(\ln 2)\sqrt{1-t^2}} = \dfrac{1}{\ln 2}\sin^{-1}(t)+C$

$= (\log_2 e)(\sin^{-1}(t)) + C = \lambda\sin^{-1}(2^x) + C$

$\because\; e \approx 2.7183 \qquad \therefore\; \lambda = \log_2 e > 1 > 0$

(ii) $I = \int\dfrac{\left(\sqrt{x}\right)^5}{\left(\sqrt{x}\right)^7+x^6}dx = \int\dfrac{(x)^{5/2}}{(x)^{7/2}+x^6}dx$

Dividing numerator and denominator by x^6;

we get $I = \int\dfrac{x^{-7/2}}{x^{-5/2}+1}dx$

Now $\dfrac{d}{dx}\left(x^{-5/2}+1\right) = -\dfrac{5}{2}(x)^{-7/2}$

$\Rightarrow I = -\dfrac{2}{5}\int\dfrac{-\frac{5}{2}x^{-7/2}}{(1+x^{-5/2})}dx = -\dfrac{2}{5}\ln\left|1+x^{-5/2}\right|+C$

$= -\dfrac{2}{5}\ln\left|\dfrac{x^{5/2}+1}{x^{5/2}}\right|+C = \dfrac{2}{5}\ln\left|\dfrac{x^{5/2}}{x^{5/2}+1}\right|+C$

$$= \mu \ln\left|\frac{x^{\lambda}}{x^{\lambda}+1}\right| + C \Rightarrow \mu = \frac{2}{5}, \lambda = \frac{5}{2}.$$

$\therefore$ $\mu\lambda = 1 < 3 < 4$

(iii) $\int \frac{x^4+1}{x(x^2+1)^2}dx = \int \frac{x^4+2x^2+1-2x^2}{x(x^2+1)^2}dx$

$$= \int \frac{(x^2+1)^2-2x^2}{x(x^2+1)^2}dx = \int \frac{1}{x}dx - \int \frac{2x}{(x^2+1)^2}dx$$

$$= \ln|x| + (x^2+1)^{-1} + C = \ln|x| + \frac{1}{1+x^2} + C$$

$\Rightarrow \lambda = 1, \mu = 1 \qquad \Rightarrow \lambda\mu = 1$

(iv) $\int \frac{dx}{5+4\cos x} = \int \frac{\left(1+\tan^2\frac{x}{2}\right)}{5\left(1+\tan^2\frac{x}{2}\right)+4\left(1-\tan^2\frac{x}{2}\right)}dx$

$$= \int \frac{\sec^2\frac{x}{2}}{\tan^2\frac{x}{2}+9}dx$$

Put $\tan\frac{x}{2} = t \qquad \Rightarrow \frac{1}{2}\sec^2\frac{x}{2}dx = dt$

$\Rightarrow \sec^2\frac{x}{2}dx = 2dt$

$$\therefore I = \int \frac{2dt}{t^2+9} = \frac{2}{3}\tan^{-1}\left(\frac{t}{3}\right) + C$$

$$= \frac{2}{3}\tan^{-1}\left(\frac{\tan\frac{x}{2}}{3}\right) + C$$

$\Rightarrow \lambda = \frac{2}{3}; \mu = \frac{1}{3} \quad \Rightarrow \frac{\lambda}{\mu} = 2 \quad \Rightarrow \frac{2\lambda}{\mu} = 4$

65. **Column-I**

(i) Let $f(x) = \int x^{\sin x}(1+\cos x(\ln x)+\sin x)dx$ and $f\left(\frac{\pi}{2}\right) = \frac{\pi^2}{4}$, then $f(\pi)$ is

(ii) Let $g(x) = \int \frac{1+2\cos x}{(2+\cos x)^2}dx$; $g(0) = 0$; then $g(\pi/2)$ is

(iii) Let $x, y \in \mathbb{R}$ and such that $(x+5)^2 + (y-12)^2 = (14)^2$, then the least value of $\sqrt{x^2+y^2}$ is

(iv) Let $g(x) = \int \frac{(x^2+1)}{\sqrt[3]{x^3+3x+6}}$ and $g(-1) = \frac{1}{\sqrt[3]{2}}$; then $g(-2)$ is

Column-II

(a) Rational number
(b) Irrational number
(c) Integer number
(d) Prime number

Ans. (i) → (b); (ii) → (a); (iii) → (a), (c); (iv) → (a), (c), (d)

Solution:

(i) $f(x) = \int x^{\sin x}(1+x\cos x(\ln x)+\sin x)dx$

$$= \int x^{\sin x}dx + \int x^{\sin x}(x\cos x.\ln x+\sin x)dx \quad \text{.... (1)}$$

Let $x^{\sin x} = t \qquad \Rightarrow \sin x \ln x = \ln t$

$\Rightarrow \left[\sin x.\frac{1}{x} + (\ln x)\cos x\right]dx = \frac{1}{t}dt$

$\Rightarrow \frac{t}{x}[\sin x + x(\ln x).\cos x]dx = dt$

$\Rightarrow x^{(\sin x-1)}[\sin x + x(\ln x).\cos x]dx = dt$

$\therefore$ from (1)

$$I = \int x^{\sin x}dx + \int \underset{I}{x}\,\underbrace{x^{(\sin x-1)}(x\cos x.\ln x+\sin x)dx}_{II}$$

(Integrating the second integral by parts)

$$= \int x^{\sin x}dx + x.t - \int 1.t\,dt$$

$$= \int x^{\sin x}dx + x.x^{\sin x} - \int x^{\sin x}dx = x^{(\sin x+1)} + C$$

$\therefore f(x) = x^{(\sin x+1)} + C$

$$\therefore f\left(\frac{\pi}{2}\right) = \left(\frac{\pi}{2}\right)^{\left(\sin\frac{\pi}{2}+1\right)} + C = \left(\frac{\pi}{2}\right)^2 + C = \frac{\pi^2}{4}\text{(given)}$$

$\Rightarrow C = 0 \qquad \therefore f(x) = x^{(\sin x+1)}$

$\therefore f(\pi) = (\pi)^{(\sin\pi+1)} = (\pi)^1 = \pi$; which is an irrational number.

$\therefore$ (i) → (b)

(ii) $g(x) = \int \frac{1+2\cos x}{(2+\cos x)^2}dx$; If we let $\frac{\sin x}{(\cos x+2)} = t$

$$\Rightarrow \frac{(\cos x+2)\cos x - \sin x(-\sin x)}{(\cos x+2)^2}dx = dt$$

$$\Rightarrow \frac{1+2\cos x}{(\cos x+2)^2}dx = dt$$

$\therefore g(x) = \int dt = t = \frac{\sin x}{(\cos x+2)} + C$; Now $g(0) = 0$

$\Rightarrow C = 0 \qquad \Rightarrow g(x) = \frac{\sin x}{(\cos x+2)}$

$\therefore g\left(\frac{\pi}{2}\right) = \frac{1}{2}$ which is a rational number.

$\therefore$ (ii) → (a)

(iii) $(x+5)^2 + (y-12)^2 = (14)^2$; least value of $\sqrt{x^2+y^2} = ?$

The point (x, y) lies on the circle with centre at $(-5, 12)$ and radius 14 units.

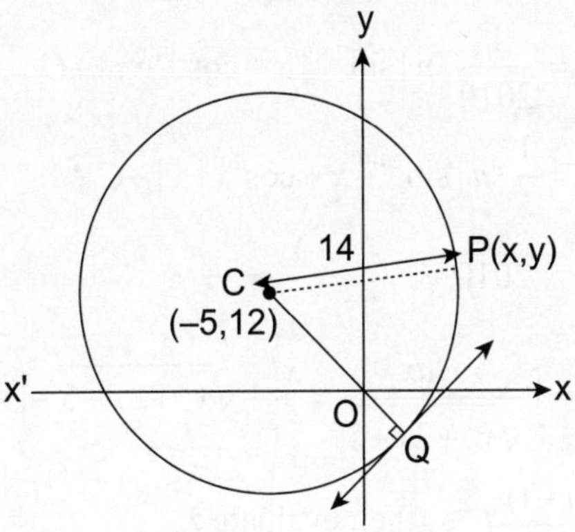

We are to find least value of $\sqrt{x^2+y^2}$

i.e., least distance of point on circle from origin.

$= OQ = CQ - OC = r - \sqrt{(12-0)^2+(-5-0)^2}$

$= 14 - 13 = 1$ units

$\therefore$ Least value of $\sqrt{x^2+y^2}$ is rational and an integer number

$\therefore$ (iii) → (a), (c)

(iv) $g(x) = \int \frac{(x^2+1)}{\sqrt[3]{x^3+3x+6}}dx$; $g(-1) = \frac{1}{\sqrt[3]{2}}$; $g(-2) = ?$

$g(x) = \frac{1}{3}\int (3x^2+3)(x^3+3x+6)^{-1/3}dx$

$= \frac{1}{3}\frac{(x^3+3x+6)^{2/3}}{2/3} + C = \frac{1}{2}(x^3+3x+6)^{2/3} + C$

$\therefore\ g(-1) = \frac{1}{2}(-1-3+6)^{2/3} + C = \frac{1}{\sqrt[3]{2}} + C$

$\Rightarrow C = 0$ ($\because k(-1) = \frac{1}{\sqrt[3]{2}}$ (given))

$\therefore\ g(x) = \frac{1}{2}(x^3+3x+6)^{2/3}$

$\therefore\ g(-2) = \frac{1}{2}(-8-6+6)^{2/3} = 2$

which is rational, prime and an integer number

$\therefore$ (iv) → (a), (c), (d)

Solved Integer Type

66. $\int \frac{(5x^2-12)dx}{(x^2-6x+13)^2} = \frac{k(13x-159)}{8(x^2-6x+13)} + \frac{53}{L}\tan^{-1}\left(\frac{x-3}{2}\right) + C$,

then evaluate $(k + L)$.

Solution: Let $5x^2 - 12 = l(x^2 - 6x + 13) + m(2x - 6) + n$

Equating the coefficients on both sides, we get

$l = 5;\ m = 15;\ n = 13$

$\Rightarrow\ I = \int \frac{5\,dx}{(x-3)^2+4} + \int \frac{15(2x-6)}{(x^2-6x+13)^2}dx +$

$13\int \frac{dx}{\left((x-3)^2+4\right)^2} = I_1 + I_2 + I_3$ (say)

Now, $I_1 = \frac{5}{2}\tan^{-1}\frac{x-3}{2}$; $I_2 = -\frac{15}{x^2-6x+13}$

and $I_3 = 13\int \frac{2\sec^2\theta}{16\sec^4\theta}d\theta$

where $(x - 3) = 2\tan\theta$;

$I_3 = \frac{13}{16}\int (1+\cos 2\theta)\,d\theta = \frac{13}{16}\left[\theta + \frac{1}{2}\sin 2\theta\right]$

$= \frac{13}{16}\left[\tan^{-1}\frac{x-3}{2}\right] + \frac{13}{32}\cdot\frac{x-3}{1+\left(\frac{x-3}{2}\right)^2}$

$= \frac{13}{16}\tan^{-1}\frac{x-3}{2} + \frac{13}{8}\cdot\frac{x-3}{x^2-6x+13}$

$\Rightarrow\ I = I_1 + I_2 + I_3 = \frac{5}{2}\tan^{-1}\left(\frac{x-3}{2}\right) - \frac{15}{(x^2-6x+13)} +$

$\frac{13}{16}\tan^{-1}\left(\frac{x-3}{2}\right) + \frac{13}{8}\left(\frac{x-3}{x^2-6x+13}\right)$

$= \frac{53}{16}\tan^{-1}\left(\frac{x-3}{2}\right) + \frac{1}{8}\cdot\frac{(13x-159)}{(x^2-6x+13)}$

$\Rightarrow k = 1, L = 16 \qquad \Rightarrow k + L = 17.$

67. If the graph of the antiderivative $F(x)$ of $f(x) = ln(ln\,x) + (ln\,x)^{-2}$ passes through $(e, 1998 - e)$, then find the term independent of x in $F(x)$.

Solution: An antiderivative of $f(x) = F(x)$

$= \int \left(\ell n(\ell nx) + (\ell nx)^{-2}\right)dx + C$

$= x\,ln\,(ln\,x) - x\,(ln\,x)^{-1} + C$

Putting $x = e$, we have $1998 - e = e.0 - e + C$. Thus, $C = 1998$.

68. If $\int \frac{\cos^2 x + \sin 2x}{(2\cos x - \sin x)^2}dx = \frac{-Ax}{1725} - \frac{2}{5}\ell n|2\cos x - \sin x|$

$+ \frac{1}{2-\tan x} + C$, then evaluate A.

Solution: Dividing the numerator and denominator by $\cos^2 x$, the given integral can be written as

$I = \int \frac{1+2\tan x}{(2-\tan x)^2}dx = \int \frac{\sec^2 x - \tan^2 x + 2\tan x}{(2-\tan x)^2}dx$

$$= \int \frac{\sec^2 x - \tan x(\tan x - 2)}{(2-\tan x)^2} dx$$

$$= \int \frac{\sec^2 x}{(2-\tan x)^2} dx + \int \frac{\tan x}{2-\tan x} dx = I_1 + I_2 \text{ (say)}$$

where $I_1 = \int \frac{dt}{(2-t)^2}$ $[t = \tan x]$

$= \frac{1}{2-t} = \frac{1}{2-\tan x}$ and

$$I_2 = \int \frac{\tan x}{2-\tan x} dx = \int \frac{\sin x}{2\cos x - \sin x} dx$$

Putting $\sin x = a(2 \cos x - \sin x) + b(-2 \sin x - \cos x)$
Equating coefficients of $\sin x$ and $\cos x$,
we get $0 = 2a - b$ and $1 = -a - 2b$.
Solving we get $a = -1/5$ and $b = -2/5$.

$$\therefore\ I_2 = -\frac{1}{5}\int \frac{2\cos x - \sin x}{2\cos x - \sin x} dx - \frac{2}{5}\int \frac{-2\sin x - \cos x}{2\cos x - \sin x} dx$$

$$= -\frac{1}{5}x - \frac{2}{5}\ \ell n|2\cos x - \sin x| + C$$

$$\text{Thus, } I = \frac{1}{2-\tan x} - \frac{1}{5}x - \frac{2}{5}\ \ell n|2\cos x - \sin x| + C$$

so that $\frac{-A}{1725} = \frac{-1}{5}$ i.e., $A = 345$.

69. If $\int \frac{1-(\cot x)^{2008}}{\tan x + (\cot x)^{2009}} dx = \frac{1}{k}\ell n|\sin^k x + \cos^k x| + C$,

then find k.

Solution:

$$I = \int \frac{1-(\cot x)^{2008}}{\tan x + (\cot x)^{2009}} dx = \frac{1}{k}\ln|\sin^k x + \cos^k x| + C$$

$$I = \int \frac{1 - \left(\frac{\cos x}{\sin x}\right)^{2008}}{\frac{\sin x}{\cos x} + \left(\frac{\cos x}{\sin x}\right)^{2009}} dx$$

$$= \int \frac{\sin^{2008} x - \cos^{2008} x}{\sin^{2008} x \frac{(\sin^{2010} x + \cos^{2010} x)}{\sin^{2009} x \cos x}} dx$$

$$= \int \frac{(\sin^{2008} x - \cos^{2008} x)\sin x \cos x}{\sin^{2010} x + \cos^{2010} x} dx$$

put $\sin^{2010} x + \cos^{2010} x = t$

$\Rightarrow$ $[(2010)\sin^{2009} x.\cos x + 2010\cos^{2009} x(-\sin x)]\,dx = dt$

$\Rightarrow$ $(2010)\sin x.\cos x[\sin^{2008} x - \cos^{2008} x]dx = dt$

$$\therefore\ I = \frac{1}{2010}\int \frac{1}{t} dt = \frac{1}{2010}\ell n|t| + C$$

$$= \frac{1}{2010}\ell n|\sin^{2010} x + \cos^{2010} x| + C$$

$$= \frac{1}{k}\ell n|\sin^{2010} x + \cos^{2010} x| + C$$

$\Rightarrow k = 2010.$

70. If $I_n = \int \frac{x^n dx}{\sqrt{x^2+2x+5}} = \frac{x^{n-1}}{n}\sqrt{x^2+2x+5} - \left(\frac{2n-1}{n}\right) I_{n-1}$

$-\frac{\lambda(n-1)}{n} I_{n-2}$, then evaluate λ.

Solution:

$$I_n = \int \frac{x^{n-1}.x\,dx}{\sqrt{x^2+2x+5}} = \frac{1}{2}\int \frac{x^{n-1}(2x+2-2)\,dx}{\sqrt{x^2+2x+5}}$$

$$= \frac{1}{2}\int \frac{x^{n-1}(2x+2)}{\sqrt{x^2+2x+5}} dx - \int \frac{x^{n-1}}{\sqrt{x^2+2x+5}} dx$$

$$= \frac{1}{2}\left[\begin{array}{l} 2x^{n-1}\sqrt{(x^2+2x+5)} - 2 \\ \int (n-1)x^{n-2}\sqrt{x^2+2x+5}\,dx \end{array}\right] - I_{n-1}$$

$$= x^{n-1}\sqrt{x^2+2x+5} - (n-1)\int x^{n-2}\sqrt{x^2+2x+5}\,dx - I_{n-1}$$

$$= x^{(n-1)}\sqrt{x^2+2x+5} - (n-1)\int \frac{x^{(n-2)}(x^2+2x+5)}{\sqrt{x^2+2x+5}} dx - I_{n-1}$$

$$= x^{(n-1)}\sqrt{x^2+2x+5} - (n-1)\int \frac{x^n + 2x^{n-1} + 5x^{n-2}}{\sqrt{x^2+2x+5}} dx - I_{n-1}$$

$\Rightarrow I_n = x^{(n-1)}\sqrt{x^2+2x+5} - (n-1)I_n - 2(n-1)$
$I_{n-1} - 5(n-1)I_{n-2} - I_{n-1}$

$\Rightarrow nI_n = x^{(n-1)}\sqrt{x^2+2x+5} - (2n-1)I_{n-1} - 5(n-1)I_{n-2}$

$$\Rightarrow I_n = \frac{x^{n-1}\sqrt{x^2+2x+5}}{n} - \frac{(2n-1)}{n} I_{n-1} - 5\frac{(n-1)}{n} I_{n-2}$$

$\Rightarrow \lambda = 5$

71. If $\int \frac{\sin^8 x}{\cos x} dx = -\frac{\sin^7 x}{a} + \frac{\sin^5 x}{b} - \frac{\sin^3 x}{c} + \frac{\sin x}{d} + \ln$

$\left|\tan\left(\frac{\pi}{4} + \frac{x}{2}\right)\right| + C$, then evaluate $(a + b + c + d)$.

Solution:

$$I = \int \frac{\sin^8 x}{\cos x} dx = \int \frac{\sin^8 x.\cos x}{\cos^2 x} dx = \int \frac{\sin^8 x}{(1-\sin^2 x)}.\cos x\,dx$$

Put $\sin x = t$, $\cos x dx = dt$

$\therefore \quad I=\int \frac{t^8}{1-t^2}dt=\int \frac{t^8-1+1}{1-t^2}dt$

$=\int \frac{(t^2-1)(t^2+1)(t^4+1)}{1-t^2}dt+\int \frac{1}{1-t^2}dt$

$=\int (t^2+1)(-1-t^4)dt+\int \frac{1}{1-t^2}dt$

$=\int \left(-t^6-t^4-t^2-1\right)dt+\int \frac{1}{1-t^2}dt$

$=\frac{-t^7}{7}-\frac{t^5}{5}-\frac{t^3}{3}-t+\frac{1}{2}\ln\left|\frac{1+t}{1-t}\right|+C$

$=\frac{-\sin^7 x}{7}-\frac{\sin^5 x}{5}-\frac{\sin^3 x}{3}-\sin x+\frac{1}{2}\ln\left|\frac{1+\sin x}{1-\sin x}\right|+C$ ...(1)

Now

$\ln\left|\frac{\left(\sin\frac{x}{2}+\cos\frac{x}{2}\right)^2}{\left(\cos\frac{x}{2}-\sin\frac{x}{2}\right)^2}\right|=2\ln\left|\frac{1+\tan x/2}{1-\tan x/2}\right|=2\ln\left|\tan\left(\frac{\pi}{4}+\frac{x}{2}\right)\right|$ ...(2)

$\therefore$ From (1) and (2)

$\therefore \quad I=\frac{-\sin^7 x}{7}-\frac{\sin^5 x}{5}-\frac{\sin^3 x}{3}-\sin x+\ln\left|\tan\left(\frac{\pi}{4}+\frac{x}{2}\right)\right|+C$

$=\frac{-\sin^7 x}{a}+\frac{\sin^5 x}{b}-\frac{\sin^3 x}{c}+\frac{\sin x}{d}+\ln\left|\tan\left(\frac{\pi}{4}+\frac{x}{2}\right)\right|+C$ (given)

$\Rightarrow a=7, b=-5, c=3, d=-1$

$\Rightarrow (a+b+c+d)=(7-5+3-1)=4$

72. Let $f(x)$ be a function such that $f(xy)=f(x)\,.\,f(x)\ \forall\ x, y\in\mathbb{R}$. If $f(1+x)=1+x(1+g(x))$ where $\lim_{x\to 0} g(x)=0$. Further if $\int \frac{f(x)}{f'(x)}dx=\frac{x^k}{k}+C$, the evaluate the numerical quantity k.

Solution: $f'(x)=\lim_{h\to 0}\frac{f(x+h)-f(x)}{h}$

$=\lim_{h\to 0}\frac{f\left(x\left(1+\frac{h}{x}\right)\right)-f(x)}{h}$

$=\lim_{h\to 0}\frac{f(x).f\left(1+\frac{h}{x}\right)-f(x)}{h}$

$(\because f(xy)=f(x)\,.\,f(y)\ \forall\ x,y\in\mathbb{R})$

$=f(x)\lim_{h\to 0}\frac{f\left(1+\frac{h}{x}\right)-1}{h}$

$=f(x)\left\{\lim_{h\to 0}\frac{1+\frac{h}{x}\left(1+g\left(\frac{h}{x}\right)\right)-1}{h}\right\}$

$=f(x).\left\{\lim_{h\to 0}\frac{1}{x}\left(1+g\left(\frac{h}{x}\right)\right)\right\}$

As $h\to 0;\ \frac{h}{x}\to 0$

$\Rightarrow g\left(\frac{h}{x}\right)\to 0$ as $\lim_{x\to 0}g(x)=0$ (given)

$\therefore \quad f'(x)=f(x).\frac{1}{x} \quad \Rightarrow \quad \frac{f(x)}{f'(x)}=x$

$\Rightarrow \int \frac{f(x)}{f'(x)}dx=\frac{x^2}{2}+C \quad \Rightarrow \quad k=2$

73. If $\int \frac{\cos 6x+\cos 9x}{1-2\cos 5x}dx=-\frac{\sin kx}{m}-\sin x+C$, then evaluate $(k+m)$

Solution:

$\int \frac{\cos 6x+\cos 9x}{1-2\cos 5x}dx=\int \frac{2\cos\left(\frac{15}{2}x\right)\cos\left(\frac{3}{2}x\right)}{1-2\left(2\cos^2\frac{5x}{2}-1\right)}dx$

$=\int \frac{2\cos\frac{15}{2}x.\cos\frac{3}{2}x}{\left(3-4\cos^2\frac{5x}{2}\right)}dx$

$=2\int \frac{\left(4\cos^3\frac{5}{2}x-3\cos\frac{5}{2}x\right)\cos\frac{3}{2}x}{\left(3-4\cos^2\frac{5x}{2}\right)}dx$

$=2\int \left(-\cos\frac{5}{2}x\right)\left(\cos\frac{3}{2}x\right)dx=-\int 2\cos\frac{5}{2}x\cos\frac{3}{2}x\,dx$

$=-\int (\cos 4x+\cos x)\,dx=-\frac{\sin 4x}{4}-\sin x+C$

$=-\frac{\sin kx}{m}-\sin x+C$ (given)

$\Rightarrow k=m=4 \qquad \Rightarrow (k+m)=8$

74. If $\int (\sin 3x+\sin x)e^{\sin x}\cos x\,dx=(A\sin^3 x-B\cos^2 x+C\sin x+D\cos x+E)e^{\sin x}+k$, then evaluate B.

Solution: $I = \int\left(3\sin x - 4\sin^3 x + \sin x\right)e^{\sin x}\cos x\, dx$

$= \int\left(4\sin x - 4\sin^3 x\right)e^{\sin x}\cos x\, dx$

Put $\sin x = t$ $\Rightarrow I = \int\left(4t - 4t^3\right)e^t\, dt$

$= \left(At^3 - B(1-t^2) + Ct + D\sqrt{1-t^2} + E\right)e^t + k$

$= \left[At^3 + Bt^3 + Ct + (E-B) + D\sqrt{1-t^2}\right]e^t + k$

Differentating on both sides, we get $(4t - 4t^3)e^t$

$= \left(At^3 + Bt^3 + Ct + (E-B) + D\sqrt{1-t^2}\right)e^t + \left[3At^2 + 2Bt + C + \frac{D(-t)}{\sqrt{1-t^2}}\right]e^t$

$= \begin{bmatrix} At^3 + (B+3A)t^2 + (C+2B)t + \\ (E-B+C) + \left(\sqrt{1-t^2} - \frac{t}{\sqrt{1-t^2}}\right)D \end{bmatrix} e^t$

$= \begin{bmatrix} At^3 + (3A+B)t^2 + (2B+C)t + \\ (E-B+C) + \left(\frac{1-t^2-t}{\sqrt{1-t^2}}\right)D \end{bmatrix} e^t$

$\therefore$ L.H.S. is a (polynomial)e^t

$\Rightarrow D = 0; A = -4; 3A + B = 0$

$\Rightarrow B = -3A = 12$

75. If $\int \frac{\cos 4x + 1}{\cot x - \tan x}dx = -\frac{1}{k}\cos 4x + C$, then evaluate k.

Solution:

$I = \int \frac{\cos 4x + 1}{\frac{\cos x}{\sin x} - \frac{\sin x}{\cos x}}dx = \int \frac{(\sin x\cos x)(\cos 4x + 1)}{(\cos^2 x - \sin^2 x)}dx$

$\frac{1}{2}\int \frac{(\sin 2x)(\cos 4x + 1)}{\cos 2x}dx = \frac{1}{2}\int \frac{\sin 2x\cos 4x + \sin 2x}{\cos 2x}dx$

$= \frac{1}{4}\int \frac{2\cos 4x\sin 2x + 2\sin 2x}{\cos 2x}dx$

$= \frac{1}{4}\int \frac{\sin 6x - \sin 2x + 2\sin 2x}{\cos 2x}dx$

$= \frac{1}{4}\int \frac{\sin 6x + \sin 2x}{\cos 2x}dx = \frac{1}{4}\int \frac{2\sin 4x\cos 2x}{\cos 2x}dx$

$= \frac{1}{2}\int \sin 4x\, dx = -\frac{1}{8}\cos 4x + C$

$\Rightarrow k = 8$

76. If $\int \frac{4e^x + 6e^{-x}}{9e^x - 4e^{-x}}dx = -\frac{3}{2}x + \frac{7\lambda}{6(\lambda+1)}\ln\left(9e^{2x} - 4\right) + C$;

then find λ.

Solution: Let $4e^x + 6e^{-x} = A(9e^x - 4e^{-x}) + B\frac{d}{dx}\left(9e^x - 4e^{-x}\right)$

$\Rightarrow 4e^x + 6e^{-x} = A(9e^x - 4e^{-x}) + B\left(9e^x + 4e^{-x}\right)$

$\Rightarrow 9A + 9B = 4; -4A + 4B = 6$

$\Rightarrow A = \frac{-19}{36}, B = \frac{35}{36}$

$\therefore \int \frac{4e^x + 6e^{-x}}{9e^x - 4e^{-x}}dx = \int -\frac{19}{36}dx + \frac{35}{36}\int \frac{9e^x + 4e^{-x}}{9e^x - 4e^{-x}}dx$

$= -\frac{19}{36}x + \frac{35}{36}\ln\left|9e^x - 4e^{-x}\right| + C$

$= -\frac{19}{36}x + \frac{35}{36}\ln\left|\frac{9e^{2x} - 4}{e^x}\right| + C$

$= -\frac{19}{36}x - \frac{35}{36}x + \frac{35}{36}\ln\left|9e^{2x} - 4\right| + C$

$= -\frac{3}{2}x + \frac{35}{36}\ln\left|9e^{2x} - 4\right| + C$

$= -\frac{3}{2}x + \frac{7(5)}{6(5+1)}\ln\left|9e^{2x} - 4\right| + C \Rightarrow \lambda = 5$

77. If $\int \frac{bx\cos 4x - \sin 4x}{x^2}dx = \frac{\sin 4x}{x}$, then find b.

Solution:

$\int \frac{bx\cos 4x - \sin 4x}{x^2}dx = \int (bx\cos 4x - \sin 4x).x^{-2}\, dx$

$= (bx\cos 4x - \sin 4x).$

$\left(\frac{-1}{x}\right) - \int\left(-4bx\sin 4x + b\cos 4x - 4\cos 4x\right).\left(\frac{-1}{x}\right)dx$

$= -\frac{(bx\cos 4x - \sin 4x)}{x} +$

$\int\left\{-4b\sin 4x + (b-4)\frac{\cos 4x}{x}\right\}dx$

$= -\frac{(bx\cos 4x - \sin 4x)}{x} + \frac{4b\cos 4x}{4} + \int (b-4)\frac{\cos 4x}{x}dx$

$= -b\cos 4x + \frac{\sin 4x}{x} + b\cos 4x + (b-4)\int \frac{\cos 4x}{x}dx$

$= \frac{\sin 4x}{x} + (b-4)\int \frac{\cos 4x}{x}dx$

But it is given to be $\frac{\sin 4x}{x}$

$\Rightarrow b - 4 = 0$

$\Rightarrow b = 4.$

TUTORIAL EXERCISE

SECTION–III

ONLY ONE CORRECT ANSWER

1. $I_1 = \int \sin^{-1} x dx$ and $I_2 = \int \sin^{-1} \sqrt{1-x^2}\, dx$, then

(a) $I_1 = I_2$ (b) $I_2 = \pi/2I_1$
(c) $I_1 + I_2 = \pi x/2$ (d) $I_1 - I_2 = \pi x/2$

2. $\int 5^{\ell nx} .dx$ is

(a) $\frac{x^{\ell n5+1}}{\ell n5+1}+C$ (b) $5^{lnx} + C$
(c) $\frac{5^{\ell nx+1}}{\ell nx+1}+C$ (d) None of these

3. $\int \cos^3 x\, e^{\ell n(\sin x)}\, dx$ is equal to

(a) $-\frac{\sin^4 x}{4}+C$ (b) $-\frac{\cos^4 x}{4}+C$
(c) $\frac{e^{\sin x}}{4}+C$ (d) None of these

4. $\int \frac{x^{9/2}}{\sqrt{1+x^{11}}}\, dx$ is

(a) $\frac{2}{11}\ell n\left(x^{11/2}+\sqrt{x^{11}+1}\right)+C$
(b) $\frac{1}{2}\ell n\frac{x^{11}+1}{x^{11}-1} + C$
(c) $2\sqrt{1+x^{11}} + C$
(d) None of these

5. $\int \cos x.\, \sqrt[5]{1+3\sin x}\, dx$

(a) $\frac{5}{8}(1+3\sin x)^{6/5}+C$
(b) $\frac{5}{6}(1+3\sin x)^{6/5}+C$
(c) $\frac{5}{18}(1+3\sin x)^{5/6}+C$
(d) None of these

6. The value of $\int \frac{dx}{x^{13}\left(x^6-1\right)}$ is

(a) $ln\left(\left|\frac{x^6-1}{x^6}\right|\right) + x^{-6} + x^{-12} + C$
(b) $\frac{1}{6}\ell n\left(\left|\frac{x^6-1}{x^6}\right|\right)+\frac{1}{6}x^{-6}+\frac{1}{4}x^{-12}+C$
(c) $\frac{1}{6}\left|\ell n\left(\left|\frac{x^6-1}{x^6}\right|\right)+x^{-6}+\frac{1}{2}x^{-12}\right|+C$
(d) None of these

7. $\int \sqrt{\frac{x-1}{x+1}}.\frac{dx}{x^2}$ is

(a) $\cos^{-1}\left(\frac{1}{|x|}\right)+\sqrt{\frac{x^2-1}{x^2}}+C$
(b) $\cos^{-1}\left(\frac{1}{|x|}\right)-\sqrt{\frac{x^2-1}{x^2}}+C$
(c) $\sin^{-1}\left(\frac{1}{|x|}\right)-\sqrt{\frac{x^2-1}{x^2}}+C$
(d) None of these

8. $\int \frac{(x^4-x)^{1/4}}{x^5}\, dx$ is equal to

(a) $\frac{4}{15}\left(1-\frac{1}{x^3}\right)^{5/4}+C$ (b) $\frac{4}{5}\left(1-\frac{1}{x^3}\right)^{5/4}+C$
(c) $\frac{4}{15}\left(1+\frac{1}{x^3}\right)^{5/4}+C$ (d) None of these

9. If $\int e^x(\tan x - \ell n\cos x)\, dx = f(x)\ ln\ \sec x$ (say $F(x)$), with $F(0) = 0$, then range of $f(x)$ is

(a) $(-\infty,\infty)$ (b) R^+
(c) $R - \{1\}$ (d) None of these

10. If $\int f(x)dx = f(x)$, then $\int [f(x)]^2 dx$ is

(a) $\frac{1}{2}[f(x)]^2$ (b) $[f(x)]^3$
(c) $\frac{[f(x)]^3}{3}$ (d) $[f(x)]^2$

11. $\int e^x\left(\frac{1+\sin x\cos x}{\cos^2 x}\right)dx$ is

(a) $e^x \sec^2 x + C$ (b) $e^x \tan x + C$
(c) $e^x.\, ln \sec x + C$ (d) None of these

12. If $\int f(x)dx = g(x)$, then $\int f^{-1}(x)$ is equal to

(a) $g^{-1}(x)$ (b) $xf^{-1}(x) - g(f^{-1}(x))$
(c) $xf^{-1}(x) - g^{-1}(x)$ (d) $f^{-1}(x)$

13. $\int \tan^{-1}\frac{2x}{1-x^2}dx$ is equal to

(a) $x\tan^{-1}x + C$
(b) $x\tan^{-1}x - ln(1+x^2) + C$
(c) $2x\tan^{-1}x + ln(1+x^2) + C$
(d) $2x\tan^{-1}x - ln(1+x^2) + C$

14. If $\int \frac{(x^2-1)}{x\sqrt{x^4+3x^2+1}}dx$ is

$m\ell n\left[\frac{\left\{(x^2+1)+\sqrt{(x^4+3x^2+1)}\right\}}{x}\right]$ + C. Then m is

(a) 1 (b) 2
(c) 1/3 (d) None of these

15. $\int x.\sin 2x.\cos 3x\, dx$ is.

(a) $-\frac{x\cos 5x}{10}+\frac{\sin 5x}{50}+C$

(b) $-\frac{x\cos 5x}{10}+\frac{\sin 5x}{50}+\frac{x\cos x}{2}-\frac{\sin x}{2}+C$

(c) $-\frac{x\cos 5x}{10}+\frac{\sin 5x}{50}-\frac{x\cos x}{2}+\frac{\sin x}{2}+C$

(d) None of these

16. Let $\int e^x\{f(x)-f'(x)\}dx = \phi(x)$, then $\int e^x f(x)dx$ is.

(a) $\phi(x) + e^x f(x) + C$
(b) $\phi(x) - e^x f(x) + C$
(c) $\frac{1}{2}\{\phi(x) + e^x f(x)\} + C$
(d) $\frac{1}{2}\{\phi(x) + e^x f'(x)\} + C$

17. $\int \frac{dx}{1+x+x^2+x^3}$ is equal to

(a) $\ell n\sqrt{1+x}-\frac{1}{2}\ell n\sqrt{1+x^2}+\frac{1}{2}\tan^{-1}x+C$

(b) $\ell n\sqrt{1+x}-\ell n\sqrt{1+x^2}+\tan^{-1}x+C$

(c) $\ell n\sqrt{1+x^2}-\ell n\sqrt{1+x}+\frac{1}{2}\tan^{-1}x+C$

(d) $\ell n\sqrt{1+x}+\tan^{-1}x+\ell n\sqrt{1+x^2}+C$

18. $\int \frac{1}{(x^2+a^2)(x^2+b^2)}dx =$

(a) $\frac{1}{(a^2-b^2)}\left[\frac{1}{b}\tan^{-1}\left(\frac{x}{b}\right)-\frac{1}{a}\tan^{-1}\left(\frac{x}{a}\right)\right]+C$

(b) $\frac{1}{(b^2-a^2)}\left[\frac{1}{b}\tan^{-1}\left(\frac{x}{b}\right)-\frac{1}{a}\tan^{-1}\left(\frac{x}{a}\right)\right]+C$

(c) $\left[\frac{1}{b}\tan^{-1}\left(\frac{x}{b}\right)-\frac{1}{a}\tan^{-1}\left(\frac{x}{a}\right)\right]+C$

(d) $\left[\frac{1}{a}\tan^{-1}\left(\frac{x}{a}\right)-\frac{1}{a}\tan^{-1}\left(\frac{x}{b}\right)\right]+C$

19. $\int\left(\frac{dx}{\sin x+\sec x}\right)$ is

(a) $\frac{1}{2\sqrt{3}}\ln\left|\frac{\tan x+\sqrt{3}}{\tan x-\sqrt{3}}\right| + \tan^{-1}(\sin x + \cos x) + C$

(b) $\frac{1}{2\sqrt{3}}\ln\left|\frac{\sin x-\cos x+\sqrt{3}}{-\sin x+\cos x+\sqrt{3}}\right| + \tan^{-1}(\sin x+\cos x) + C$

(c) $\frac{1}{2\sqrt{3}}\ln\left|\frac{\tan x+\sqrt{3}}{\tan x-\sqrt{3}}\right| + \tan^{-1}(\sin x-\cos x) + C$

(d) None of these

20. $\int \frac{\cos^3 x}{\sqrt{\sin^7 x}}dx$ is

(a) $\frac{2}{5}\mathrm{cosec}^{7/2}x+2\sqrt{\mathrm{cosec}\ x}+C$

(b) $-\frac{2}{5}\sin^{-5/2}x+2\sqrt{\mathrm{cosec}\,x}+C$

(c) $\frac{2}{5}\mathrm{cosec}^{-5/2}x+2\sqrt{\mathrm{cosec}\,x}+C$

(d) None of these

21. $\int \sec^{7/3}x.\,\mathrm{cosec}^{5/3}x\,dx$

(a) $\frac{-3}{2}\cot^{2/3}x+\frac{3}{4}\tan^{4/3}x+C$

(b) $\frac{3}{2}\cot^{2/3}x+\frac{3}{4}\tan^{4/3}x+C$

(c) $\frac{-3}{2}\cot^{2/3}x-\frac{3}{4}\tan^{4/3}x+C$

(d) None of these

22. $\int \frac{dx}{4\sin^2 x+4\sin x\cos x+5\cos^2 x}$ is

(a) $\frac{1}{4}\tan^{-1}(2\tan x+1)+C$

(b) $\frac{1}{4}\tan^{-1}\left(\tan x+\frac{1}{2}\right)+C$

(c) $\frac{1}{2}\tan^{-1}(2\tan x+1)+C$

(d) None of these

23. If $\int \sin^2 x\cos^5 x dx$ is $\frac{\sin^3 x}{3}+l\left(\frac{2}{5}\sin^5 x-\frac{\sin^7 x}{7}\right)+C.$

Then the value of l is.

(a) 2 (b) –2

(c) –1 (d) None of these

24. $\int \frac{dx}{\tan x.\cos 2x}$ is

(a) $ln\frac{|C\sin x|}{\sqrt{\cos 2x}}$ (b) $ln\frac{|C\cos x|}{\sqrt{\cos 2x}}$

(c) $ln\frac{|C\sin x|}{\sqrt{1-4\sin^2 x}}$ (d) None of these

25. $\int \frac{dx}{\sin^2 x+\tan^2 x}$ is

(a) $C-\frac{1}{2}\left[\frac{x}{2}+\frac{1}{\sqrt{2}}+\tan^{-1}\left(\frac{\tan x}{\sqrt{2}}\right)\right]$

(b) $C-\frac{1}{2}\left[\cot x+\frac{1}{\sqrt{2}}\tan^{-1}\left(\frac{\tan x}{\sqrt{2}}\right)\right]$

(c) $C-\frac{1}{2}\left[\cot x-\frac{1}{\sqrt{2}}\tan^{-1}\left(\frac{\tan x}{\sqrt{2}}\right)\right]$

(d) None of these

26. $\int \frac{dx}{\sqrt{x}.(x^{1/4}+1)^{10}}$ is

(a) $-\frac{4}{8}\left(\frac{1}{(\sqrt[4]{x}+1)^8}\right)+\frac{4}{9}x+C$

(b) $-\frac{4}{8}\frac{1}{(\sqrt[4]{x}+1)^9}+\frac{4}{9(\sqrt[4]{x}+1)^8}+C$

(c) $\frac{4}{9(4\sqrt{x}+1)^9}+C$

(d) None of these

27. $\int \frac{dx}{\sqrt[4]{(x-1)^3(x+2)^5}}$ is

(a) $\frac{3}{4}\left(\frac{x-1}{x+2}\right)^{1/4}+C$ (b) $\frac{4}{3}\left(\frac{x-1}{x+2}\right)^{1/4}+C$

(c) $\frac{4}{3}\left(\frac{x-1}{x+2}\right)^{-1/4}+C$ (d) None of these

28. The function f whose graph passes through the point (0, 7/3) and whose derivative is $x\sqrt{1-x^2}$ given by

(a) $f(x) = (-1/3)\,[(1-x^2)^{3/2}-8]$

(b) $f(x) = (1/3)\,[(1-x^2)^{3/2}+8]$

(c) $f(x) = (-1/3)\,[\sin^{-1} x + 7]$

(d) None of these

29. The value of $\int \frac{\cos^3 x+\cos^5 x}{\sin^2 x+\sin^4 x}dx$ is

(a) $\sin x - 6\tan^{-1}(\sin x) + C$

(b) $\sin x - 2(\sin x)^{-1} + C$

(c) $\sin x - 2(\sin x)^{-1} + 6\tan^{-1}(\sin x) + C$

(d) None of these

30. The integral $\int \frac{\sin^2 x}{\cos^4 x}dx$ is

(a) polynomial of degree 5 in $\sin x$

(b) polynomial of degree 4 in $\tan x$

(c) polynomial of degree 3 in $\tan x$

(d) polynomial of degree 5 in $\cos x$

31. The integral of $\int \frac{dx}{(x-a)^{3/2}(b-x)^{1/2}}$ is

(a) $\frac{-2}{b-a}\left[\frac{b-x}{x-a}\right]^{1/2}+C$

(b) $\frac{1}{4(b-a)}\left[\frac{b-x}{x-a}\right]^{1/2}+C$

(c) $\frac{1}{b-a}\left[\frac{x-a}{b-a}\right]^{1/2}+C$

(d) None of these

32. The integral of $\int \frac{\cos x}{\sin x+\cos x}dx$ is

(a) $\frac{x^2}{2} + ln\,(\sin x + \cos x) + C$

(b) $\frac{1}{2}(x + ln\,(\sin x + \cos x)) + C$

(c) $2ln\,(\sin x + \cos x) + C$

(d) None of these

33. If $\int \frac{(x^2-1)dx}{(x^4+3x^2+1)\tan^{-1}\frac{x^2+1}{x}} = ln\,|\tan^{-1} f(x)| + C$, then

(a) $f(x) = x^2 + 1$ (b) $f(x) = \frac{x^2+1}{2x}$

(c) $f(x)=\frac{1}{2}(x^2+1)$ (d) $f(x) = \frac{x^2+1}{x}$

34. $\int \frac{8x^7 + 8^x \ell n8}{x^8 + 8^x} dx$ is equal to

(a) $x^8 - 8^x + C$ (b) $x^8 + 8^x + C$

(c) $8\ lnx + xln8 + C$ (d) $ln|x^8 + 8^x| + C$

35. $\int \frac{dx}{e^x - 1}$ is equal to

(a) $ln\ |e^x - 1| + C$ (b) $ln\ |\ e^x + 1| + C$

(c) $x - ln\ |\ e^x - 1|$ (d) $ln|e^x - 1| - x + C$

36. $\int \frac{1+\sin x}{1+\cos x} e^x\, dx$ is equal to

(a) $e^x \tan (x/2) + C$ (b) $e^x \tan x + C$

(c) $(1/2)\ e^x \tan x/2 + C$ (d) $e^x \sec^2 (x/2) + C$

37. If $\int \frac{(1-\sin x)^{1/2}}{1+\cos x} .e^{-x/2}\, dx = k_1 e^{k_2 x} + C$, then

(a) $k_1 = \sec (x/2),\ k_2 = -1/2$

(b) $k_1 = -\sec(x/2),\ k_2 = 1/2$

(c) $k_1 = \cos (x/2),\ k_2 = 0$

(d) None of these

38. $\int x^x (1 + \ell n)\, dx$ is equal to

(a) $x^x\ ln\ x + C$ (b) $e^{x^x} + C$

(c) $x^x + C$ (d) None of these

39. $\int \frac{\ell n(\ell n(\ell nx))}{x \ell n(\ell nx) \ell nx} dx$ is equal to

(a) $\left(\frac{1}{2}\right)\{\ell n(\ell n(\ell n(x)))\}^2 + C$

(b) $\frac{1}{2}\{\ell n(\ell nx)\}^2 + C$

(c) $\left(\frac{1}{2}\right)^2 \{\ell n(\ell nx).\ell nx\}^2 + C$

(d) None of these

40. $\int \frac{e^{(x)^{1/2}} \cos e^{(x)^{1/2}}}{(x)^{1/2}} dx$ is equal to

(a) $2\cos\ e^{(x)^{1/2}} + C$ (b) $2\ (\cos e^x)^{1/2} + C$

(c) $2\sin\ e^{(x)^{1/2}} + C$ (d) None of these

41. $\int \frac{dx}{\cos^2 x(1-\tan x)^2} dx$ is equal to

(a) $\frac{1}{1+\tan x} + C$ (b) $\frac{1}{1-\tan x} + C$

(c) $(1 + \tan x) + C$ (d) None of these

42. $I = \int xe^x \cos x dx = f(x) + C$, then $f(x)$ is

(a) $\frac{e^x}{2}\{(1-x)\sin x - x\cos x\} + C$

(b) $\frac{e^x}{2}\{(x-1)\sin x + x\cos x\} + C$

(c) $\frac{e^x}{2}\{(1+x)\sin x - x\cos x\} + C$

(d) None of these

43. $\int \frac{e^x(1+x)dx}{\sin^2(xe^x)}$ is equal to

(a) $\cot (x\ e^x) + C$ (b) $\tan (\ x\ e^x) + C$

(c) $-\cot (x\ e^x) + C$ (d) $-\tan (\ x\ e^x) + C$

44. $\int \frac{\sin x + \cos x}{\sqrt{1+\sin 2x}} dx$ is equal to

(a) $ln|(\sin x + \cos x)| + C$

(b) $-x + C$ for all x

(c) $\begin{Bmatrix} x + C, & if\ \sin x + \cos x > 0 \\ -x + C, & if\ \sin x + \cos x < 0 \end{Bmatrix}$

(d) $x + C$ for all x

45. If $\frac{3\pi}{4} < x < \frac{7\pi}{4}$, then $\int \frac{\sin x + \cos x}{\sqrt{1+\sin 2x}} dx$ is equal to

(a) $-x + C$

(b) $x + C$

(c) $ln\ |(\sin x + \cos x\ )\ | + C$

(d) None of these

46. If $l^r(x)$ means $ln\ ln\ ln$ ..... x, the log being repeated r times, then $\int \{x.l(x)\, l^2(x)\, l^3(x)......l^r(x)\}^{-1} dx$ is

(a) $l^{r+1}(x) + C$ (b) $\frac{l^{r+1}(x)}{r+1} + C$

(c) $l^r(x) + C$ (d) None of these

47. $\int \frac{\sin x + \cos x}{9 + 16\sin 2x} dx$ is equal to

(a) $\frac{1}{20} \ell n \left|\frac{5 + 4(\sin x - \cos x)}{5 - 4(\sin x - \cos x)}\right| + C$

(b) $\frac{1}{40} \ell n \left|\frac{5 + 4(\sin x - \cos x)}{5 - 4(\sin x - \cos x)}\right| + C$

(c) $\frac{1}{20} \tan^{-1} \frac{4(\sin x - \cos x)}{5} + C$

(d) None of these

48. $\int e^x(\sec x + \log|\sec x + \tan x|)\, dx$ is

(a) $e^x \sec x + C$ (b) $e^x\ ln\ |\sec x + \tan x| + C$

(c) $ln\ |\sec x + \tan x| + C$ (d) None of these

49. $\int \frac{dx}{x(x^4+1)}$ is equal to

(a) $ln\, x^4\,(x^4+1) + C$ (b) $\frac{1}{4}\, lnx^4\,(x^4+1) + C$

(c) $\frac{1}{4}\ell n\frac{x^4+1}{x^4}+C$ (d) $\frac{1}{4}\ell n\frac{x^4}{x^4+1}+C$

50. $\int \cos\sqrt{x}\, dx$ is equal to

(a) $2\sqrt{x}\,(\sin\sqrt{x}+\cos\sqrt{x})+C$

(b) $2\,(\sqrt{x}\sin\sqrt{x}-\cos\sqrt{x})+C$

(c) $\sqrt{x}\sin\sqrt{x}-\cos\sqrt{x}+C$

(d) $2\,(\sqrt{x}\sin\sqrt{x}+\cos\sqrt{x})+C$

51. $\int \frac{x-\sin x}{1+\cos x}\, dx$ is equal to

(a) $\int x\tan\frac{x}{2}+C$

(b) $\int x\cot\frac{x}{2}+C$

(c) $x\tan\frac{x}{2}-2\ell n\left|\sec\frac{x}{2}\right|+C$

(d) $x\tan\frac{x}{2}-4\ell n\left|\sec\frac{x}{2}\right|+C$

52. If $\frac{-\pi}{4}<x<\frac{\pi}{4}$, then $\int\frac{\tan x dx}{\sqrt{1-\tan^2 x}}$ is.

(a) $-\frac{1}{\sqrt{2}}\ell n\left|\sqrt{2}\cos x+\sqrt{2\cos^2 x-1}\right|+C$

(b) $\frac{1}{\sqrt{2}}\ell n\left|\sqrt{2}\cos x+\sqrt{2\cos^2 x-1}\right|+C$

(c) $\sqrt{2}\ell n\left|\sqrt{2}\cos x+\sqrt{2\cos^2 x-1}\right|+C$

(d) $-\sqrt{2}\ell n\left|\sqrt{2}\cos x+\sqrt{2\cos^2 x-1}\right|+C$

53. $\int e^x\frac{x-1}{(x+1)^3}dx$ is equal to

(a) $\frac{e^x}{(x+1)^2}+C$ (b) $\frac{e^x}{x+1}+C$

(c) $-\frac{e^x}{x+1}+C$ (d) $-\frac{e^x}{(x+1)^2}+C$

54. If $x>0$, $\int\frac{a^{\sqrt[n]{x}}}{\sqrt[n]{x^{n-1}}}dx$ is equal to

(a) $na^{\sqrt[n]{x}}\,\ell na+C$ (b) $-na^{\sqrt{\ }}\quad nae+C$

(c) $na^{\sqrt[n]{x}}\,\ell n_{10}a+C$ (d) None of these

55. $\int\left(\sqrt{\tan x}+\sqrt{\cot x}\right)dx$

(a) $-\sqrt{2}\cot^{-1}\frac{\sqrt{\tan x}-\sqrt{\cot x}}{\sqrt{2}}+C$

(b) $\sqrt{2}\tan^{-1}\frac{\sqrt{\tan x}+\sqrt{\cot x}}{\sqrt{2}}+C$

(c) $\sqrt{2}\cot^{-1}\frac{\sqrt{\tan x}+\sqrt{\cot x}}{\sqrt{2}}+C$

(d) None of these

56. $\int\sec x\log|\sec x-\tan x|\,dx$ is

(a) $\ell n^2\left|\frac{\sec x-\tan x}{2}\right|+C$

(b) $\frac{\ell n^2|\sec x+\tan x|}{2}+C$

(c) $-\ell n^2|\sec x-\tan x|+C$

(d) $-\frac{\ell n^2|\sec x-\tan x|}{2}+C$

57. Let $f(x)$ a function such that, $f(0)=f'(0)=0$ and $f''(x)=\sec^4 x+4$, then the function is

(a) $ln\log(\sin x)+1/3\tan^3 x+xb$

(b) $2/3\, ln\log(\sec x)+1/6\tan^2 x+2x^2$

(c) $ln\log\cos x+1/6\cos^2 x+x^2/5$

(d) None of these

58. If $x>1$, $\int\sin^{-1}\frac{2x}{1+x^2}dx$ is equal to

(a) $2x\tan^{-1}x-\ell n(1+x^2)+C$

(b) $2x\tan^{-1}x+\ell n(1+x^2)+C$

(c) $\pi x-2x\tan^{-1}x+\ell n(1+x^2)+C$

(d) None of these

59. Let the equation of the curve passing through the point (0, 1) be given by $y=\int x^2.\,e^{x^3}dx$ and if equation of the curve is written in form $x=f(y)$, then $f(y)$ is

(a) $[\log_e(3y-1)]^{1/2}$ (b) $(\log_e(3y-2))^{1/3}$

(c) $[\log_e(2-3y)]^{1/3}$ (d) None of these

60. $\int\frac{dx}{x^{1/5}(1+x^{4/5})^{1/2}}$ is equal to

(a) $5\,(1+x^{4/5})^{1/2}+C$ (b) $(1/2)(1+x^{4/5})^{1/2}+C$

(c) $x^{4/5}(1+x^{4/5})^{1/2}+C$ (d) None of these

61. $\int\frac{10x^9+10^x\,\ell ne10}{10^x+x^{10}}$ dx is equal to

(a) $\frac{5}{2}\ell n\,(10^x+x^{10})+C$

(b) $ln_e(10^{10}x^x)+C$

(c) $\frac{1}{2}\ell n_e(10^x x^{10})+C$

(d) None of these

62. $\int \cos\left\{2\tan^{-1}\sqrt{\frac{1-x}{1+x}}\right\} dx$ is equal to

(a) $(1/8)(x^2-1)+C$ (b) $(x^2/2)+C$

(c) $(1/2)x+C$ (d) None of these

63. The integral $\int \frac{dx}{x(1-x^3)^{1/2}}$ is equal to

(a) $\frac{1}{3}\ell n\left|\frac{(1-x^3)^{1/2}+1}{(1-x^3)^{1/2}-1}\right|+C$

(b) $\frac{1}{3}\ell n\left|\frac{(1-x^3)^{1/2}-1}{(1-x^3)^{1/2}+1}\right|+C$

(c) $\frac{2}{3}\ell n\left|\frac{1}{(1-x^3)^{1/2}}\right|+C$

(d) $\frac{1}{3}\ell n\,|1-x^3|+C$

64. $\int \frac{2^{x+1}-3^{x-1}}{6^x}dx$ is equal to

(a) $\left(-\frac{2}{3^x}+\frac{1}{3.2^x}\right)+C$ (b) $\left(\frac{3}{2^x}-\frac{2}{3^x}\right)+C$

(c) $\frac{3}{2^x}+\frac{1}{2(3^x)}+C$ (d) None of these

65. $\int e^x\{f(x)-f'(x)\}dx=\phi(x)$, then $\int e^x f(x)dx$ is equal to

(a) $f(x)+e^x f(x)$ (b) $f(x)-e^x f(x)$

(c) $\frac{1}{2}\{\phi(x)+e^x f(x)\}$ (d) $\frac{1}{2}\{\phi(x)+e^x f(x)\}$

66. $\int \left(x+\frac{1}{x}\right)^{n+5}\left(\frac{x^2-1}{x^2}\right)dx$ is equal to

(a) $\frac{(x+1/x)^{n+6}}{n+6}+C$

(b) $\left(\frac{x^2+1}{x^2}\right)^{n+6}(n+6)+C$

(c) $\left(\frac{x}{x^2+1}\right)^{n+6}(n+6)+C$

(d) None of these

67. If $f(x)=\lim_{n\to\infty}\frac{x^n-x^{-n}}{x^n+x^{-n}}$, $0<x<1$, $n\in N$, then $f(x)$ is equal to

(a) $-\left[x\sin^{-1}x+\sqrt{1-x^2}\right]+C$

(b) $\left[x\sin^{-1}x+\sqrt{1-x^2}\right]+C$

(c) constant

(d) None of these

68. $\int \frac{\cos^4 x}{\sin^3 x(\sin^5 x+\cos^5 x)^{3/5}}dx=$

(a) $-\frac{1}{2}\left(\frac{\tan^5 x+1}{\tan^5 x}\right)^{2/5}+C$

(b) $-\frac{1}{5}\left(\frac{\tan^5 x+1}{\tan^5 x}\right)^{2/5}+C$

(c) $-\frac{1}{2}\left(\frac{\tan^{3/5} x+1}{\tan^5 x}\right)^{5/3}+C$

(d) None of these

69. Let $f(x)$ be a polynomial satisfying $f(0)=2$, $f'(0)=3$ and $f''(x)=f(x)$. Then, $f(4)$ is equal to

(a) $\frac{5(e^8-1)}{2e^4}$ (b) $\frac{5(e^8+1)}{2e^4}$

(c) $\frac{2e^4}{5(e^8+1)}$ (d) $\frac{2e^4}{5(e^8-1)}$

70. Let $x^2 \neq n\pi-1$, $n\in \mathbb{N}$. The value of $\int x\sqrt{\frac{2\sin(x^2+1)-\sin 2(x^2+1)}{2\sin(x^2+1)+\sin 2(x^2+1)}}dx=$

(a) $\ell n\left|\sec\left(\frac{x^2+1}{2}\right)\right|+C$

(b) $\ell n\left|\frac{1}{2}\sec(x^2+1)\right|+C$

(c) $ln|(\sec(x^2+1)|+C$

(d) None of these

71. $\int x\{f(x^2)\,g''(x^2)-f''(x^2)g(x^2)\}dx$ is equal to

(a) $f(x^2)\,g'(x^2)-g(x^2)\,f'(x^2)+C$

(b) $\frac{1}{2}\{f(x^2)\,g(x^2)f'(x^2)\}+C$

(c) $\frac{1}{2}\{f(x^2)g'(x^2)-g(x^2)f'(x^2)\}+C$

(d) None of these

72. $\int \frac{\cos 5x+\cos 4x}{1-2\cos 3x}dx = k\sin x(1+\cos x)+C$, where k is equal to

(a) 2 (b) -2

(c) 1 (d) -1

SECTION-IV

MORE THAN ONE CORRECT ANSWER

1. Which of the following statements is/are true?

(a) $\int f(x)d(g(x)) = f(x)g(x) - \int g(x)d(f(x))$

(b) $\int f'(g(x)).g'(x)dx = f(g(x))$

(c) $\int e^x\{f(x)+f'(x)\}dx = e^x f(x) + C$

(d) None of these

2. Let $\int x^{1/2}/(1-x^3)^{1/2}\, dx = (2/3)\, gof(x) + C$, then

(a) $f(x) = (x)^{1/2}$ (b) $f(x) = x^{3/2}$

(c) $f(x) = x^{2/3}$ (d) $g(x) = \sin^{-1} x$

3. $\int \frac{dx}{5+4\cos x} = k\tan^{-1}\left(m\tan\frac{x}{2}\right) + C$, then

(a) $k = 2$ (b) $k = 2/3$

(c) $m = 1/3$ (d) $m = 3$

4. If $\int \frac{4e^x + 6e^{-x}}{9e^x - 4e^{-x}}dx$ is equal to $Ax + B\log_e(9e^{2x} - 4) + c$ then

(a) $A = -3/2$ (b) $B = 35/36$

(c) C is indefinite (d) $A + B = -19/36$

5. If $I = \int \sec^2 x \,\mathrm{cosec}^4 x\, dx = K\cot^3 x + L\tan x + M\cot x + C$, then

(a) $K = -1/3$ (b) $L = 2$

(c) $M = -2$ (d) None of these

6. $\int \frac{dx}{(1+\sqrt{x})^8} = \frac{-1}{3(1+\sqrt{x})^{k_1}} + \frac{2}{7(1+\sqrt{x})^{k_2}} + C$, where

(a) $k_1 = 6$ (b) $k_2 = 7$

(c) $k_1 = -6$ (d) $k_2 = -7$

7. If $\int f(x)\sin 2x\, dx = \frac{\ln|f(x)|}{b^2 - a^2} + C$, then $f(x)$ is equal to

(a) $\frac{1}{a^2\sin^2 x + b^2\cos^2 x}$

(b) $\frac{1}{a^2\sin^2 x - b^2\cos^2 x}$

(c) $\frac{1}{a^2\cos^2 x - b^2\sin^2 x}$

(d) $\frac{1}{a^2\cos^2 x + b^2\sin^2 x}$

8. If $\int \frac{(\sqrt{x})^5}{(\sqrt{x})^7 + x^6}dx = a\,\ell n\left(\frac{x^k}{1+x^k}\right) + C$, then

(a) $a = \frac{2}{5}$ (b) $a = -\frac{2}{5}$

(c) $k = \frac{5}{2}$ (d) $k = -\frac{5}{2}$

9. Let $f(x) = \frac{x+2}{2x+3}$, if $\int\left(\frac{f(x)}{x^2}\right)^{1/2}dx = \frac{1}{\sqrt{2}}g\left(\frac{1+\sqrt{2f(x)}}{1-\sqrt{2f(x)}}\right) - \sqrt{\frac{2}{3}}h\left(\frac{\sqrt{3f(x)}+\sqrt{2}}{\sqrt{3f(x)}-\sqrt{2}}\right) + C$, then

(a) $g(x) = \ln|x|$ (b) $h(x) = \ln|x|$

(c) $g(x) = \tan^{-1} x$ (d) $h(x) = \tan^{-1} x$

10. If $f(x) = \lim_{n\to\infty} e^{x\tan\left(\frac{1}{n}\right)\log\left(\frac{1}{n}\right)}$ and $\int \frac{f(x)}{\sqrt[3]{\sin^{11} x\cos x}}dx = g(x) + C$, then

(a) $g\left(\frac{\pi}{4}\right) = \frac{15}{8}$

(b) $g(x)$ is continuous for all x

(c) $g\left(\frac{\pi}{4}\right) = -\frac{15}{8}$

(d) $g(x)$ is not differentiable at infinitely many points

11. If for all x [–1, 0), $\int(\cos^{-1} x + \cos^{-1}\sqrt{1-x^2})dx = Ax + f(x)\sin^{-1} x - 2 + C$, then

(a) $A = \pi/4$ (b) $A = \pi/4$

(c) $f(x) = x$ (d) $f(x) = -2x$

SECTION-V

ASSERTION AND REASON TYPE QUESTIONS

1. A: $\int \frac{\sec x}{\ell n|\sec x - \tan x|}dx = -\ell n|\ell n|\sec x - \tan||+C$

R: $\int f(x)dx = g(x) + C$

$\Rightarrow \int f(ax+b)dx = \frac{g(ax+b)}{a} + C$

2. A: $\int(\sin x)^5\cos x\, dx = \frac{\sin^6 x}{6} + C$

R: $\int (f(x))^n f'(x)dx = \frac{(f(x))^{n+1}}{n+1}, n \in \mathbb{Z}$

3. **A:** If $x > 0, x \neq 1$ then $\int (\log_x e - (\log_x e))^2 dx = x \log_x e + C$

R: $\int e^x (f(x) + f'(x))dx = e^x f(x) + C$ and $e^t = x$ ff $t = \ell\, nx$

4. **A:** $\int e^{(x\sin x + \cos x)} \left(\dfrac{x^2 \cos^2 x - x\sin x - \cos x}{x^2} \right) dx$

$= e^{(x\sin x + \cos x)} . \dfrac{\cos x}{x} + C$

R: $\int e^{g(x)} \{f(x)g'(x) + f'(x)\}dx = e^{g(x)} f(x)$

5. **A:** $\int \sqrt{2 + \tan^2 x}\, dx = \tan^{-1}\left(\dfrac{\tan x}{\sqrt{2 + \tan^2 x}} \right) + \dfrac{1}{2} \ln \left| \dfrac{\tan^2 x + \tan x + 2}{\tan^2 x - \tan x + 2} \right|$

R: $\int \dfrac{2}{(1 - x^2)(1 + x^2)} dx = \tan^{-1} x + \dfrac{1}{2} \ln \left| \dfrac{x+1}{x-1} \right|$.

SECTION–VI

COMPREHENSION-TYPE QUESTIONS

A: Integrals of the form $\int \dfrac{p_m(x)}{\sqrt{ax^2 + bx + c}} dx$, where $p_m(x)$ is a polynomial of degree m are calculated by the reduction formula $\int \dfrac{p_m(x)}{\sqrt{ax^2 + bx + c}} dx = p_{m-1}(x)$, $\sqrt{ax^2 + bx + c} + \lambda \int \dfrac{dx}{\sqrt{ax^2 + bx + c}}$ where $p_{m-1}(x)$ is a polynomial of degree $m - 1$ and λ is some constant number.

E.g., if $I = \int \dfrac{x^3 - x - 1}{\sqrt{x^2 + 2x + 2}} dx$, then applying the above formula, we can write $\int \dfrac{x^3 - x - 1}{\sqrt{x^2 + 2x + 2}} dx$ = $(Ax^2 + Bx + C)$.

$\sqrt{x^2 + 2x + 2} + \lambda \int \dfrac{dx}{\sqrt{x^2 + 2x + 2}}$; Now, differentiating both sides, we get $\dfrac{x^3 - x - 1}{\sqrt{x^2 + 2x + 2}} = (Ax^2 + Bx + C)$

$\dfrac{2(x+1)}{2\sqrt{x^2 + 2x + 2}} + (2Ax + B)\sqrt{x^2 + 2x + 2}$

$+ \lambda \left[\dfrac{1}{\sqrt{x^2 + 2x + 2}} \right]$.

$= (Ax^2 + Bx + C)(x + 1) + (2Ax + B)(x^2 + 2x + 2) + \lambda$.

On comparing coefficients of like powers of x we obtain the values of A, B, C and λ .

1. If $\int \dfrac{x^3 - 6x^2 + 11x - 6}{\sqrt{x^2 + 4x + 3}} dx = (Ax^2 + Bx + C)$ $\sqrt{x^2 + 4x + 3} + \lambda \int \dfrac{dx}{\sqrt{x^2 + 4x + 3}}$ then value of 'A' is

(a) 1/3 (b) 1
(c) 3 (d) –1/3

2. In Q. NO. 1 value of 'C" is
(a) – 37 (b) –14/3
(c) 14/3 (d) 37

3. In Q. No 1 value of 'λ' is
(a) 66 (b) –66
(c) 37/3 (d) –37/3

B: By using formula $\int e^x (f(x) + f'(x))dx = e^x . f(x) + C$. Integration $\int e^x (f(x) - f''(x))dx$ can be solved $e^x (f(x) - f''(x))dx = e^x [(f(x) + f'(x)) - f'(x) + f''(x)]$ $dx = e^x (f(x) - f'(x)) + C$

4. $\int e^x \left(\ell n|x| + \dfrac{2}{x^3} \right) dx$ is equal to

(a) $e^x \ell n|x| + C$
(b) $e^x \left(\ln|x| - \dfrac{1}{x^2} \right)$
(c) $e^x \left(\ell n|x| - \dfrac{1}{x} - \dfrac{1}{x^2} \right) + C$
(d) None of these

5. $\int e^x f(x) - (-1)^x f^n(x) dx$, where $f^n(x) = \dfrac{d^n}{(dx)^n} f(x)$ equals

(a) $e^x \sum_{r=0}^{n-1} (-1)^r f^r(x)$ (b) $e^x \sum_{r=0}^{n-1} (-1)^{\,r}{}^{r+1}(x)$
(c) $e^x \sum_{r=0}^{n-1} (-1)^r f^{r+1}(x)$ (d) None of these

6. $\int e^x [f(x)g(x) + g'(x).f(x) + f'(x)g(x)]dx$ equals

(a) $e^x f(x)g(x) + C$
(b) $e^x (f(x) + g(x)) + C$
(c) $e^x + (f(x) - g(x)) + C$
(d) $e^x f(x).\, g'(x) + C$

C: Let $I_{n,m} = \int \sin^n x \cos^n x.dx$, then we can relate $I_{n,m}$ with each of the following

(i) $I_{n-2,m}$ (ii) $I_{n+2,m}$
(iii) $I_{n,m-2}$ (iv) $I_{n,m+2}$
(v) $I_{n-2,m+2}$ (vi) $I_{n+2,m-2}$

Suppose we want to establish a relation between $I_{n,m}$ and $I_{n,m-2}$, then we get

$P(x) = \sin^{n+1} x \cos^{m-1}x$ ...(i)

In $I_{n,m}$ and $I_{n,m-2}$ the exponent of cos*x* is *m* and $m-2$ respectively, the minimum of the two is $m-2$, adding 1 to the minimum we get $m-2+1 = m-1$. Now choose the exponent $m-1$ to cos*x* in *P*(*x*). Similarly choose the exponent of sin *x* for *P*(*x*). Now differentiating both sides of (i), we get

$P'(x) = (n+1)\sin^n x \cos^m x - (m-1)\sin^{n+2}x \cos^{m-2}x$
$= (n+1)\sin^n x\cos^m x - (m-1)\sin^n x(1-\cos^2 x)\cos^{m-2}x$
$= (n+1)\sin^n x\cos^m x - (m-1)\sin^n x\cos^{m-2}x + (m-1)\sin^n x\cos^m x$
$= (n+m)\sin^n x\cos^m x - (m-1)\sin^n x\cos^{m-2}x.$

Now, integrating both sides we get $\sin^{n+1}x\cos^{m-1}x = (n+m)I_{n,m} - (m-1)I_{n,m-2}$.

7. The relation between $I_{4,2}$ and $I_{2,2}$ is

(a) $I_{4,2} = \frac{1}{6}(-\sin^3 x\cos^3 x + 3I_{2,2})$

(b) $I_{4,2} = \frac{1}{6}(\sin^3 x\cos^3 x + 3I_{2,2})$

(c) $I_{4,2} = \frac{1}{6}(\sin^3 x\cos^3 x - 3I_{2,2})$

(d) $I_{4,2} = \frac{1}{4}(-\sin^3 x\cos^3 x + 2I_{2,2})$

8. The relation between $I_{4,2}$ and $I_{6,2}$ is

(a) $I_{4,2} = \frac{1}{5}(\sin^5 x\cos^3 x + 8I_{6,2})$

(b) $I_{4,2} = \frac{1}{5}(-\sin^5 x\cos^3 x + 8I_{6,2})$

(c) $I_{4,2} = \frac{1}{5}(\sin^5 x\cos^3 x - 8I_{6,2})$

(d) $I_{4,2} = \frac{1}{6}(\sin^5 x\cos^3 x + 8I_{6,2})$

9. The relation between $I_{4,2}$ and $I_{4,4}$ is

(a) $I_{4,2} = \frac{1}{3}(\sin^5 x\cos^3 x + 8I_{4,4})$

(b) $I_{4,2} = \frac{1}{3}(-\sin^5 x\cos^3 x + 8I_{4,4})$

(c) $I_{4,2} = \frac{1}{3}(\sin^5 x\cos^3 x - 8I_{4,4})$

(d) $I_{4,2} = \frac{1}{3}(\sin^5 x\cos^3 x + 6I_{4,4})$

D: It is known that

$$\sqrt{\tan x} + \sqrt{\cot x} = \begin{cases} \frac{\sqrt{\sin x}}{\sqrt{\cos x}} + \frac{\sqrt{\cos x}}{\sqrt{\sin x}} & if \quad 0 < x < \frac{\pi}{2} \\ \frac{\sqrt{-\sin x}}{\sqrt{-\cos x}} + \frac{\sqrt{-\cos x}}{\sqrt{-\sin x}} & if \quad \pi < x < \frac{3\pi}{2} \end{cases}$$

$\frac{d}{dx}(\sqrt{\tan x} - \sqrt{\cot}) = \frac{1}{2}(\sqrt{\tan x} + \sqrt{\cot x})$

$(\tan x + \cot x), \forall x \in \left(0, \frac{\pi}{2}\right) \cup \left(\pi, \frac{3\pi}{2}\right)$ and

$\frac{d}{dx}(\sqrt{\tan x} + \sqrt{\cot x}) = \frac{1}{2}(\sqrt{\tan x} - \sqrt{\cot x})$

$(\tan x + \cot x), \forall x \in \left(0, \frac{\pi}{2}\right) \cup \left(\pi, \frac{3\pi}{2}\right)$.

Now answer each of the following

10. Value of integral $I = \int(\sqrt{\tan x} + \sqrt{\cot x})dx$, where $x \in \left(0, \frac{\pi}{2}\right) \cup \left(\pi, \frac{3\pi}{2}\right)$ is

(a) $\sqrt{2}\tan^{-1}\left(\frac{\sqrt{\tan x} - \sqrt{\cot x}}{\sqrt{2}}\right) + C$

(b) $\sqrt{2}\tan^{-1}\left(\frac{\sqrt{\tan x} + \sqrt{\cot x}}{\sqrt{2}}\right) + C$

(c) $-\sqrt{2}\tan^{-1}\left(\frac{\sqrt{\tan x} - \sqrt{\cot x}}{\sqrt{2}}\right) + C$

(d) $-\sqrt{2}\tan^{-1}\left(\frac{\sqrt{\tan x} + \sqrt{\cot x}}{\sqrt{2}}\right) + C$

11. Value of the integral $I = \int(\sqrt{\tan x} + \sqrt{\cot x})dx$, where $x \in \left(0, \frac{\pi}{2}\right)$ is

(a) $\sqrt{2}\sin^{-1}(\cos x - \sin x) + C$
(b) $\sqrt{2}\sin^{-1}(\sin x - \cos x) + C$
(c) $\sqrt{2}\sin^{-1}(\sin x + \cos x) + C$
(d) $-\sqrt{2}\sin^{-1}(\sin x + \cos x) + C$

12. Value of the integral $I = \int(\sqrt{\tan x} + \sqrt{\cot x})dx$, where $x \in \left(\pi, \frac{3\pi}{2}\right)$ is

(a) $\sqrt{2}\sin^{-1}(\cos x - \sin x) + C$
(b) $\sqrt{2}\sin^{-1}(\sin x - \cos x) + C$
(c) $\sqrt{2}\sin^{-1}(\sin x + \cos x) + C$
(d) $-\sqrt{2}\sin^{-1}(\sin x + \cos x) + C$

E: The integral of the form $\int x^m(a+bx^n)^p\,dx$, where m, n, p are rational numbers, is expressed through elementary functions only in the following cases:

I: p is a positive integer
In this case, $(a + bx^n)^p$ can be expanded by the binomial theorem and the integrand can be expressed as a sum of rational powers of x^n in the form $a_0 = a_1 x^n + \ldots + a_p x^{np}$, which can be integrated easily.

II: p is a negative integer. Put $x = z^k$, where k is the common denominator of the fractions m and n.

III: $\dfrac{m+1}{n}$ is an integer. Put $a + bx^n = z^k$, where k is the denominator of the fraction p.

IV: $\dfrac{m+1}{n}+p$ is an integer. Put $a + bx^n = x^n z^k$, where k is the denominator of the fraction p.

13. $\int x^{1/3}(2+x^{2/3})^{1/4}\,dx$ is equal to

(a) $\frac{2}{3}(2+x^{2/3})^{9/4}+\frac{12}{5}(2+x^{2/3})^{5/4}+C$

(b) $\frac{2}{3}(2+x^{2/3})^{9/4}-\frac{12}{5}(2+x^{2/3})^{5/4}+C$

(c) $\frac{1}{3}(2+x^{2/3})^{9/4}-\frac{12}{5}(2+x^{2/3})^{5/4}+C$

(d) None of these

14. $\int\sqrt{\frac{1+\sqrt{x}}{x}}\,dx$ is equal to

(a) $2\sqrt{1+\sqrt{x}}-2\ell n\left(\frac{\sqrt{1+\sqrt{x}}-1}{\sqrt{1+\sqrt{x}}+1}\right)+C$

(b) $4\sqrt{1+\sqrt{x}}+2\ell n\left(\frac{\sqrt{1+\sqrt{x}}+1}{\sqrt{1+\sqrt{x}}-1}\right)+C$

(c) $\frac{4}{3}\left(1+\sqrt{x}\right)^{\frac{3}{2}}+C$

(d) None of these

15. $\int\frac{\sqrt[3]{1+\sqrt[4]{x}}}{\sqrt{x}}$ dx is equal to

(a) $12\left(\frac{(1+\sqrt[4]{x})^{7/3}}{7}+\frac{(1+\sqrt[4]{x})^{4/3}}{4}\right)+C$

(b) $12\left(\frac{(1+\sqrt[4]{x})^{7/3}}{7}-\frac{(1+\sqrt[4]{x})^{4/3}}{4}\right)+C$

(c) $6\left(\frac{(1+\sqrt[4]{x})^{7/3}}{7}-\frac{(1+\sqrt[4]{x})^{4/3}}{4}\right)+C$

(d) None of these

16. $\int\sqrt[3]{x}\sqrt[7]{1+\sqrt[3]{x^4}}$ dx is equal to

(a) $\frac{21}{32}\left(1+\sqrt[3]{x^4}\right)^{8/7}+C$ (b) $\frac{32}{21}\left(1+\sqrt[3]{x^4}\right)^{8/7}+C$

(c) $\frac{7}{32}(1+\sqrt[3]{x^4})^{8/7}+C$ (d) None of these

F: If the integrand is a rational function of fractional powers of an independent variable x

i.e., $f\left\{(ax+b),(ax+b)^{\frac{p_1}{q_1}},(ax+b)^{\frac{p_2}{q_2}}\ldots.(ax+b)^{\frac{pk}{qk}}\right\}$,

where $p_i, q_i \in \mathbb{Z}$ $q_i \neq 0 \forall\ 1 \le I \le k$, we take the L.C.M. of all denominators of radicals, i.e., q_is and then substitute $x = t^{(\text{LCM of all } q_i\text{'s})}\ \forall 1\le i\le k$.

The above integration reduces the fractional powers of x to integral powers of t, thereby transforming the integrand into a rational function of t.

17. $\int\frac{x+\sqrt[3]{x^2}+\sqrt[6]{x}}{x(1+\sqrt[3]{x})}dx$ is equal to

(a) $\frac{3}{2}x^{2/3}+6\tan^{-1}x^{1/6}+C$

(b) $\frac{3}{2}x^{2/3}-6\tan^{-1}x^{1/6}+C$

(c) $-\frac{3}{2}x^{2/3}+6\tan^{-1}x^{1/6}+C$

(d) None of these

18. $\int\frac{dx}{x(1+\sqrt[3]{x})^2}$ is equal to

(a) $2\left(\ell n\frac{x^{1/3}}{1+x^{1/3}}+\frac{1}{1+\sqrt[3]{x}}\right)+C$

(b) $3\left(\ell n\frac{1+\sqrt[3]{x}}{\sqrt[3]{x}}+\frac{1}{1+\sqrt[3]{x}}\right)+C$

(c) $3\left(\ell n\frac{1+\sqrt[3]{x}}{\sqrt[3]{x}}-\frac{1}{1+\sqrt[3]{x}}\right)+C$

(d) None of these

19. $\int\frac{\sqrt{x}+\sqrt[3]{x}}{\sqrt[4]{x^5}-\sqrt[6]{x^7}}dx=$

(a) $4x^{1/4}-6x^{1/6}+24^{1/12}+2\,ln\,|x^{1/12}-1|+C$

(b) $4x^{1/4}-6x^{1/6}-24x^{1/12}+2ln\,|x^{1/12}-1|+C$

(c) $4x^{1/4}+6x^{1/6}+24x^{1/12}+2ln\,|\,x^{1/12}-1|+C$

(d) None of these

20. $\int \frac{x^{1/2}}{x^{3/4}+1}dx =$

(a) $\frac{4}{3}x^{3/4} - \frac{4}{3}\ln|x^{3/4}+1| + C$

(b) $\frac{4}{3}x^{3/4} + \frac{4}{3}\ln|x^{3/4}+1| + C$

(c) $\frac{4}{3}x^{3/4} - \frac{1}{3}\ln|x^{3/4}+1| + C$

(d) None of these

SECTION–VII

MATRIX MATCHING-TYPE QUESTIONS

1. **Column I**

(i) $\int \frac{\sin x - \cos x}{|\sin x - \cos x|}dx$; where $\frac{\pi}{4} < x < \frac{3\pi}{8}$

(ii) $\int \frac{x^2}{(x^3+1)(x^3+2)}dx = \frac{1}{3}f\left(\frac{x^3+1}{x^3+2}\right) + C$ then $f(x)$ is

(iii) $\int \sin^{-1} x.\cos^{-1} x\ dx = f^{-1}(x)$,

$\left[\frac{\pi}{2}x - xf^{-1}(x) - 2\sqrt{1-x^2}\right] + 2x + C$, then $f(x) =$

(iv) $\int \frac{dx}{xf(x)} = f(f(x)) + C$, then $f(x)$ is equal to

Column II

(a) $\sin x$

(b) $x + C$

(c) $\ell n|x|$

(d) $\sin^{-1}x$

2. Match the column:

Column I

(i) $\int \frac{\cos x}{2+\cos x}dx + \int \frac{\sin^2 x}{(2+\cos x)^2}dx$ equals

(ii) $\int \frac{1}{x+x^{7/2}}dx = a\ell n\left(\frac{x^k}{1+x^k}\right) + C$, then $a + k =$

(iii) $2\int \frac{(\tan x - \cot x)(\tan^2 x + \cot^2 x + \tan x \cot x)}{\sec^2 x + \operatorname{cosec}^2 x}dx$ equals

(iv) $\int \frac{1}{\sin^2 x + \sin 2x}dx$ equals

Column II

(a) $\frac{29}{10}$

(b) $\ell n\,|2 + \tan^2 x + \cot^2 x| + C_2$

(c) $\frac{\sin x}{2+\cos x} + C_1$

(d) $\ell n + C_3$

3. **Column I**

(i) If $f(x) = \int \frac{x+\sin x}{1+\cos x}dx$ and $F(0) = 0$, then $f(\pi/2)=$

(ii) Let $F(x) = \int e^{\sin^{-1}x}\left(1 - \frac{x}{\sqrt{1-x^2}}\right)dx$ and $F(0) = 1$

If $F(1/2) = \frac{k\sqrt{3}e^{\pi/6}}{\pi}$, then k equals

(iii) Let $F(x) = \int \frac{dx}{(x^2+1)(x^2+9)}$ and $F(0) = 0$,

If $F(\sqrt{3}) = \frac{5}{36}k$, then k equals

(iv) Let $F(x) = \int \frac{\sqrt{\tan x}}{\sin x \cos x}$ dx and F(0) = 0; if $F(\pi/4) = \frac{2k}{\pi}$, then k equals

Column II

(a) $\pi/2$

(b) $\pi/3$

(c) $\pi/4$

(d) π

4. Column A contains the irrational function in the integrand and column *B* contains the corresponding substitutions. Match the columns correctly.

Column I

(i) $\sqrt{\frac{x}{a+x}}$ or $\sqrt{\frac{a+x}{x}}$

(ii) $\sqrt{\left(\frac{x-a}{b-x}\right)}$ or $\sqrt{(x-a)(b-x)}$

(iii) $\sqrt{\left(\frac{x-a}{x-b}\right)}$ or $\sqrt{(x-a)(x-b)}$

(iv) $\frac{1}{\sqrt{(x-a)(b-x)}}$

Column II

(a) $a\tan^2\theta$, $a\cot^2\theta$

(b) $x = a\cos^2\theta + a\sin^2\theta$

(c) $x = a\sec^2\theta + b\tan^2\theta$

(d) $x - a = t^2$ or $x - b = t^2$

5. Column A contains the given function in the integrand and column B contains the corresponding substitutions. Match the columns correctly.

Column I

(i) $f\left\{\left(x\pm\sqrt{a^2+x^2}\right)^n\right\}$

(ii) $\dfrac{1}{x^m(a+bx)^p}$; $m+p\in\mathbb{N}, m+p>1$

(iii) $\dfrac{1}{\{L_1(x)\}^m\{L_2(x)\}^n}$

(iv) $x^\beta(a+bx^\gamma)^\alpha$

Column II

(a) $x\pm\sqrt{a^2+b^2}=t$

(b) $a + bx = tx$

(c) i: $n>m$; $\dfrac{L_1x}{L_2x}=t$, ii : $n<m$; $\dfrac{L_2x}{L_1x}=t$

ii: If $\dfrac{\beta+1}{\lambda}=s\in\mathbb{Z}$ substitute $a + bx^\gamma = t^{sm}$

iii: If $\dfrac{\beta+1}{\lambda}+\alpha\in\mathbb{Z}$ substitute $ax^{-\gamma} + b = t^s$ where s is denominator of rational number α

(d) I If $\alpha\in\mathbb{Z}$, substitute $x = t^s$ where s is L.C.M. of the denominator of β and γ

6. **Column I**

(i) $\displaystyle\int\frac{\sin^8x-\cos^8x}{1-2\sin^2x\cos^2x}dx$

(ii) $\displaystyle\int\frac{\cos5x+\cos4x}{1-2\cos3x}dx$

(iii) $\displaystyle\int\sqrt{\frac{\cos x-\cos^3x}{1-\cos^3x}}dx$

(iv) $\displaystyle\int\frac{dx}{\sin^6+\cos^6x}$

Column II

(a) $-\frac{2}{3}\sin^{-1}(\cos^{3/2}x)+C$

(b) $-\frac{1}{2}\sin2x+C$

(c) $\tan^{-1}(\tan x - \cot x) + C$

(d) $-\dfrac{\sin2x}{2}-\sin x+C$

SECTION–VIII

INTEGER-TYPE QUESTIONS

1. If $I=\displaystyle\int\frac{dx}{1+\sqrt{(x+1)^2+1}}=\frac{\lambda}{3}\ln\left|x+1+\sqrt{(x+1)^2+1}\right|-\frac{\sqrt{(x+1)^2+1}-1}{x+1}+C$, then find λ.

2. $\displaystyle\int\frac{\cos^3x}{(\sin^4x+3\sin^2x+1)\tan^{-1}(\sin x+\operatorname{cosec}x)}dx=-\frac{4}{\lambda}$ $\ln|\tan^{-1}(\sin x+\operatorname{cosec}x)|+C$ then evaluate λ.

3. If $\displaystyle\int\frac{\sin x(\cos x)^{-5/2}}{\sqrt{\sin x+3\cos x}+\sqrt{\sin x+4\cos x}}dx$ $=\dfrac{\lambda}{740}\left((\tan x+4)^{5/2}-(\tan x+3)^{3/2}\right)$ $-\dfrac{\mu}{3}\left[4(\tan x+4)^{3/2}-3(\tan x+3)^{3/2}\right]+C$, then evaluate $\dfrac{\lambda}{\mu}$.

4. If $\displaystyle\int\frac{x^3}{x^{16}+4}dx=\frac{1}{\lambda}\tan^{-1}\frac{z}{\sqrt2}-\frac{1}{\mu}\ln\left|\frac{u-\sqrt2}{u+\sqrt2}\right|+C$ where $u=y+\dfrac{1}{y}$ and $z=y-\dfrac{1}{y}$, $y=\dfrac{x^4}{\sqrt2}$, then evaluate $\lambda+\mu$.

5. If $\displaystyle\int\frac{\cos^2x\sin x}{\sin x-\cos x}dx=\frac{\lambda}{4}\ln|\sin x-\cos x|+\frac{\mu}{64}$ (sin2x + cos2x) + C, then evaluate $\mu-\lambda$.

6. Let $F(x)$ be anti-derivative of $f(x)=\dfrac{1}{(3+5\sin x+3\cos x)}$ whose graph passes through the point (0, 0). Then $F\left(\dfrac{\pi}{2}\right)-\dfrac{1}{5}\ln\dfrac{8}{3}+2013$.

Answer Keys

SECTION–III

1. (c) **2.** (a) **3.** (b) **4.** (a) **5.** (d) **6.** (c) **7.** (b) **8.** (a) **9.** (b) **10.** (a)
11. (b) **12.** (b) **13.** (d) **14.** (a) **15.** (b) **16.** (c) **17.** (a) **18.** (a) **19.** (b) **20.** (b)
21. (a) **22.** (b) **23.** (c) **24.** (a) **25.** (b) **26.** (b) **27.** (b) **28.** (a) **29.** (c) **30.** (c)
31. (a) **32.** (b) **33.** (d) **34.** (d) **35.** (d) **36.** (a) **37.** (a) **38.** (c) **39.** (a) **40.** (c)
41. (b) **42.** (b) **43.** (c) **44.** (c) **45.** (a) **46.** (a) **47.** (b) **48.** (b) **49.** (d) **50.** (d)
51. (d) **52.** (a) **53.** (a) **54.** (a) **55.** (a) **56.** (d) **57.** (b) **58.** (c) **59.** (b) **60.** (a)
61. (a) **62.** (b) **63.** (b) **64.** (a) **65.** (d) **66.** (a) **67.** (a) **68.** (a) **69.** (a) **70.** (a)
71. (c) **72.** (d)

SECTION–IV

1. (a,b,c) **2.** (b,d) **3.** (b,c) **4.** (a,b,c) **5.** (a,c) **6.** (a,b) **7.** (a,d) **8.** (a,c) **9.** (a,b)
10. (c,d) **11.** (b,d)

SECTION–V

1. (b) **2.** (a) **3.** (a) **4.** (d) **5.** (d)

SECTION–VI

1. (a) **2.** (d) **3.** (b) **4.** (c) **5.** (a) **6.** (a) **7.** (a) **8.** (a) **9.** (b) **10.** (a)
11. (b) **12.** (a) **13.** (b) **14.** (c) **15.** (b) **16.** (a) **17.** (a) **18.** (a) **19.** (c) **20.** (a)

SECTION–VII

1. (i) → (b) (ii) → (c) (iii) → (a) (iv) → (c)
2. (i) → (c) (ii) → (a) (iii) → (b) (iv) → (d)
3. (i) → (a) (ii) → (a) (iii) → (c) (iv) → (d)
4. (i) → (a) (ii) → (b) (iii) → (c) (iv) → (d)
5. (i) → (c) (ii) → (a) (iii) → (d) (iv) → (b)
6. (i) → (a) (ii) → (c) (iii) → (d) (iv) → (b)

SECTION–VIII

1. 3 **2.** 4 **3.** 148 **4.** 96 **5.** 7 **6.** 2013

HINTS AND SOLUTIONS

TEXTUAL EXERCISE–1: (SUBJECTIVE)

1. (i) $f(x) = 2x + 6x^2 - 12x^3$

$\int f(x)dx = \int(2x + 6x^2 - 12x^3)\,dx$

$= \int 2x\,dx + \int 6x^2 dx - \int 12x^3\,dx$

$= x^2 + 2x^3 - 3x^4 + C$

(ii) $f(x) = \dfrac{1}{2\sqrt{x}} + x^2\sqrt{x} - 2x + 1$

$f(x) = \dfrac{1}{2}x^{-\frac{1}{2}} + x^{\frac{5}{2}} - 2x + 1$

$\int f(x)dx = \int\left(\dfrac{1}{2}x^{-\frac{1}{2}} + x^{\frac{5}{2}} - 2x + 1\right)dx$

$= \int\dfrac{1}{2}x^{-\frac{1}{2}}dx + \int x^{\frac{5}{2}}dx - \int 2x\,dx + \int dx$

$= \sqrt{x} + \dfrac{2}{7}x^{\frac{7}{2}} - x^2 + x + C$

(iii) $f(x) = \sqrt[3]{x+1}$

$\int f(x)dx = \int (x+1)^{\frac{1}{3}}dx$

$= \int (x+1)^{\frac{1}{3}}\dfrac{d(x+1)}{d(x+1)}dx = \dfrac{\int (x+1)^{\frac{1}{3}}d(x+1)}{\dfrac{d(x+1)}{dx}}$

$= \dfrac{3}{4}(x+1)^{\frac{4}{3}} + C$

(iv) $f(x) = \left(\dfrac{1}{4}x + 1\right)^3$

$\int f(x)dx = \int\left(\dfrac{x+4}{4}\right)^3 dx = \int\left(\dfrac{x+4}{4}\right)^3 \dfrac{d\left(\dfrac{x+4}{4}\right)}{d\left(\dfrac{x+4}{4}\right)}dx$

$= \dfrac{\int\left(\dfrac{x+4}{4}\right)^3 d\left(\dfrac{x+4}{4}\right)}{\dfrac{d\left(\dfrac{x+4}{4}\right)}{dx}} = \left(\dfrac{x+4}{4}\right)^4 + C$

2. (a) $a\,dy = bx\,dx;\ a, b > 0$

$dy = \dfrac{b}{a}x\,dx;\ \int dy = \dfrac{b}{a}\int x dx;\ y = \dfrac{b}{a}\dfrac{x^2}{2} + C$

(b) $dy = \cos x\,dx$

$\int dy = \int \cos x\,dx$

$y = \sin x + C$

(c) $a^{-\frac{x}{2}}dy = a^{\frac{x}{2}}dx, a > 0;\ a \neq 1$

$dy = \dfrac{a^{\frac{x}{2}}}{a^{-\frac{x}{2}}}dx;\ dy = ax\,dx$

$\int dy = \int ax\,dx$

$y = \dfrac{a^x}{\ln a} + c$

3. (a) $f(x) = 3 - \cos 2x;\ g(x) = \sin^2 x - \cos^2 x$

$f'(x) = \dfrac{d}{dx}f(x) = 2\sin 2x$

$g'(x) = \dfrac{d}{dx}g(x) = 2\sin x\cos x + 2\sin x\cos x = 2\sin 2x$

$\therefore\ f(x) = g'(x) \Rightarrow f'(x) - g'(x) = 0'$

Integrating, $f(x) - g(x) =$ constant

$f(x) - g(x) = 3 - \cos 2x - \sin^2 x + \cos^2 x$

$= 3 - (\cos^2 x - \sin^2 x) - \sin^2 x + \cos^2 x = 3$

(b) $f(x) = x^2 - 3x + 4$

$g(x) = \left(x - \dfrac{3}{2}\right)^2 - \dfrac{1}{4}$

$f'(x) = 2x - 3;\qquad g'(x) = 2\left(x - \dfrac{3}{2}\right) = 2x - 3$

$\therefore\ f'(x) = g'(x)\qquad \Rightarrow f'(x) - g'(x) = 0$

Integrating, $f(x) - g(x) =$ constant

$f(x) - g(x) = x^2 - 3x + 4 - \left(x - \dfrac{3}{2}\right)^2 + \dfrac{1}{4}$

$= x^2 - 3x + 4 - x^2 - \dfrac{9}{4} + 3x + \dfrac{1}{4} = 2$

4. $f(x) = \begin{cases} x^2 - 1; & x \neq 0 \\ 0; & x = 0 \end{cases}$ and $g(x) = \begin{cases} x^2 + 2; & x \geq 0 \\ -3 + x^2; & x < 0 \end{cases}$

$\Rightarrow$ $f'(x)$ does not exist at $x = 0$ due to discontinuity at $x = 0$, however $f'(x) = 2x\ \forall\ x \neq 0$

Also $g'(x)$ does not exist at $x = 0$ due to discontinuity at $x = 0$, however $g'(x) = 2x\ \forall\ x \neq 0$

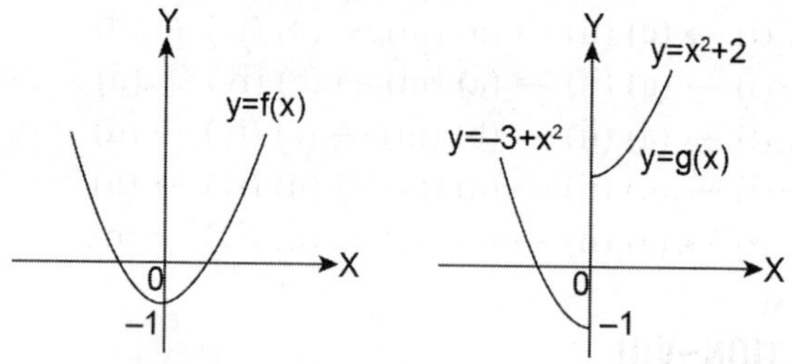

$\therefore$ S_1 is false as f and g do not have same derivatives $\forall\ x \notin \mathbb{R}$, but they have same derivative $\forall\ x \notin \mathbb{R} - \{0\}$

For $x > 0$, $f(x) - g(x) = (x^2 - 1) - (x^2 + 2) = -3$

$\Rightarrow f(x) = g(x) + (-3)\ \forall\ x > 0$

$\therefore$ $S_2 : f(x) \neq g(x) + C$ for any value of constant C is false

For $x < 0$, $f(x) - g(x) = (x^2 - 1) - (-3 + x^2) = 2$

For $x = 0$, $f(x) - g(x) = 0 - (2) = -2$

$\therefore\ f(x) - g(x) = -3\ \forall\ x > 0$ and $f'(x) = 2x$, $g'(x) = 2x\ \forall\ x \neq 0$

$\Rightarrow\ \int(2x)dx = f(x) + C_1;\ \int(2x)dx = g(x) + C_2$

$= (x^2 - 1) + C_1;\qquad = \begin{cases} x^2 + 2 + C_2; & x > 0 \\ -3 + x^2 + C_2; & x < 0 \end{cases}$

$= x^2 + (C_1 - 1);\ = \begin{cases} x^2 + (C_2 + 2); & x > 0 \\ x^2 + (C_2 - 3); & x < 0 \end{cases}$

Thus, anti-derivative of '$2x$' are $x^2 + k$;
k = constant of parameter i.e., they differ by constant
$\Rightarrow$ S_3 is false.

5. **(i)** $f(x)=\begin{cases}x^2-4; & x<1\\ x^2+2; & x\geq 1\end{cases}$

$\therefore$ $f(1^-) = -3$ and $f(1^+) = 3$
$\Rightarrow$ $f'(1)$ does not exist and $f'(x) = 2x\ \forall\ x \notin \mathbb{R} - \{1\}$
$\Rightarrow$ $f(x)$ do not have anti-derivative in any interval containing $x = 1$.

(ii) $f(x)=\begin{cases}3+2x^2; & x\neq 1\\ 3; & x=1\end{cases}$

$\Rightarrow$ $f(1^-) = f(1^+) = 5$ and $f(1) = 3$
$\Rightarrow$ $f(x)$ is discontinuous at $x = 1$
$\Rightarrow$ $f'(x)$ does not exist at $x = 1$
$\Rightarrow$ $f(x)$ do not have anti-derivative in any interval containing $x = 1$.

6. **(i)** $f'(x) = 2(x-1)^5$; $f(2) = 4$

$f(x) = \int f'(x)\,dx = \int 2(x-1)^5\,dx$

$$f(x)=\frac{(x-1)^6}{3}+C$$

$$\left(\text{using}\int[f(x)]^n f'(x)dx=\frac{[f(x)]^{n+1}}{n+1}+c\right)$$

$$f(2)=4=\frac{(2-1)^6}{3}+C \quad \therefore \quad C=4-\frac{1}{3}=\frac{11}{3}$$

$$\Rightarrow f(x)=\frac{(x-1)^6+11}{3}$$

(ii) $f''(x) = 6$; $f'(0) = 2$; $f(1) = 4$

$f'(x) = \int f''(x)\,dx$
$f'(x) = \int 6dx = 6x + C_1$
$f'(0) = 6(0) + C_1 = 2$
$\therefore$ $C_1 = 2$
$\Rightarrow$ $f'(x) = 6x + 2$ $\quad\Rightarrow$ $f(x) = \int f'(x)\,dx = \int(6x + 2)\,dx$
$\Rightarrow$ $f(x) = 3x^2 + 2x + C_2$ $\quad\Rightarrow$ $f(1) = 3 + 2 + C_2 = 4$
$\therefore$ $C_2 = -1$ $\quad\Rightarrow$ $f(x) = 3x^2 + 2x - 1$

7. We know that summation of G.P.

$$1+x^3+x^6+.....+x^{3(m-1)}=\frac{x^{3m}-1}{x^3-1}$$

$$\Rightarrow \int\sum_{k=0}^{m-1}x^{3k}=\int\frac{x^{3m}-1}{x^3-1}$$

Integrating both sides w.r.t. x, $\int\sum_{k=0}^{m-1}x^{3k}dx=\int\frac{x^{3m}-1}{x^3-1}dx$

We get, $\int\frac{x^{3m}-1}{x^3-1}dx=\int\sum_{k=0}^{m-1}x^{3k}dx=\sum_{k=0}^{m-1}\frac{x^{3k+1}}{3k+1}$

$$=x+\frac{x^4}{4}+\frac{x^7}{7}+....+\frac{x^{3m-2}}{3m-2}$$

8. **(a)** $\frac{dy}{dx}+\frac{x}{y}=0$; $y = 2$ at $x = 0$

$$\frac{dy}{dx}=-\frac{x}{y}$$

$\Rightarrow$ $y\,dy = -x\,dx$

Integrating both sides, we get $\int y\,dy = -\int x\,dx$

$$\frac{y^2}{2}=-\frac{x^2}{2}+C$$

$y = 2$ at $x = 0$

$$\therefore \quad \frac{2^2}{2}=-\frac{(0)^2}{2}+C$$

$\therefore$ $C = 2$
$\Rightarrow$ $y^2 = -x^2 + 4$

$$y=\sqrt{4-x^2}=f(x)$$

(b) $\frac{dy}{dx}=y^3(x^3-x)$; $y = 4$ at $x = 0$

$$\frac{dy}{y^3}=(x^3-x)dx$$

Integrating both sides, we get $\int\frac{dy}{y^3}=\int(x^3-x)dx$

$$\frac{y^{-3+1}}{-3+1}=\frac{x^4}{4}-\frac{x^2}{2}+C \quad -\frac{1}{2y^2}=\frac{x^4}{4}-\frac{x^2}{2}+C$$

$y = 4$ at $x = 0$

$$\therefore \quad -\frac{1}{2(4)^2}=0-0+C$$

$$\therefore \quad C=-\frac{1}{32}$$

$$-\frac{1}{2y^2}=\frac{x^4}{4}-\frac{x^2}{2}-\frac{1}{32}$$

$$\frac{16}{y^2}=1-8x^4+16x^2$$

$$y^2=\frac{16}{1-8x^4-16x^2}$$

$$\Rightarrow \quad y=\frac{4}{\sqrt{1-8x^4+16x^2}}=f(x)$$

(c) $\frac{dy}{dx}=(2x+1)^4$; $y = 6$ at $x = 0$

$dy = (2x + 1)^4\,dx$

Integrating both sides, we get $\int dy = \int(2x + 1)^4\,dx$

$$\Rightarrow \quad y=\frac{(2x+1)^5}{5}.\frac{1}{2}+C$$

$y = 6$ at $x = 0$ $\quad\therefore\quad 6=\frac{1}{10}+C$

$$\Rightarrow \quad C=\frac{59}{10} \qquad \Rightarrow \quad y=\frac{(2x+1)+59}{10}$$

(d) $\frac{dy}{dx}=-y^2x(x^2+2)^4$; $y = 1$ at $x = 0$

$$-\frac{dy}{y^2}=x(x^2+2)^4dx$$

Integrating both sides, we get $\int-\frac{dy}{y^2}=\int x(x^2+2)^4dx$

$$\frac{1}{y}=\frac{1}{2}\int 2x(x^2+2)^4dx$$

$$\frac{1}{y}=\frac{1}{2}\frac{(x^2+2)^5}{5}+C$$

$\because \quad \int f'(x)(f(x))^n dx = \frac{f(x)^{n+1}}{n+1} + C$

$y = 1$ at $x = 0$

$\therefore \quad 1 = \frac{16}{5} + C \quad \Rightarrow \quad C = 1 - \frac{16}{5} = -\frac{11}{5}$

$\therefore \quad y = \frac{1}{\frac{(x^2+2)^5}{10} - \frac{11}{5}} \quad \Rightarrow \quad y = \frac{10}{(x^2+2)^5 - 22}$

9. (a) $f'(x^2) = \frac{1}{x} \forall x > 0, f(1) = 1$

Let $x^2 = t \ \forall \ x > 0$

$\therefore \quad t > 0$

$x = \sqrt{t}$

$\therefore \quad f'(t) = \frac{1}{\sqrt{t}} = \frac{d}{dt} f(t)$

$df(t) = \frac{dt}{\sqrt{t}}$

Integrating both sides, we get $f(t) = 2\sqrt{t} + C$

$f(1) = 1 = 2 + C$

$\Rightarrow \quad C = -1$

$\therefore \quad f(t) = 2\sqrt{t} - 1$

(b) $f'(\sin^2 x) = \cos^2 x \ \forall \ x, f(1) = 1$

Let $\sin^2 x = t$

$\therefore \quad 0 \le t \le 1$

$\therefore \quad \cos^2 x = 1 - \sin^2 x = 1 - t$

$\Rightarrow \quad f'(t) = 1 - t = \frac{df(t)}{dt}$

$df(t) = (1 - t)dt$

Integrating both sides, we get $\int df(t) = \int (1 - t)dt$

$f(t) = t - \frac{t^2}{2} + C$

$f(1) = 1 = 1 - \frac{1}{2} + C$

$\therefore \quad C = \frac{1}{2}$

$f(t) = t - \frac{t^2}{2} + \frac{1}{2}$

(c) $f'(\sin x) = \cos^2 x \ \forall \ x; f(1) = 1$

Let $\sin x = t \quad \Rightarrow \quad -1 \le t \le 1$ or $|t| \le 1$

$\text{Cos}^2 x = 1 - \sin^2 x = 1 - t^2$

$\therefore \quad f'(t) = 1 - t^2 = \frac{d}{dt} f(t)$

$df(t) = (1 - t^2)\, dt$

Integrating both sides, we get $\int df(t) = \int (1 - t^2)dt$

$f(t) = t - \frac{t^3}{3} + C$

$f(1) = 1 = 1 - \frac{1}{3} + C$

$\therefore \quad C = \frac{1}{3}$

$f(t) = t - \frac{t^3}{3} + \frac{1}{3}$

(d) $f'(\ln x) = \begin{cases} 1; & 0 < x \le 1 \\ x; & x > 1 \end{cases}; f(0) = 0$

Let $\ln x = t \qquad \therefore \quad 0 < x \le 1$

$\Rightarrow \quad t \le 0$

$x = e^t \ \forall \ x > 1 \qquad \Rightarrow \quad t > 0$

$\therefore f'(t) = \frac{d f(t)}{dt} = \begin{cases} 1; & t \le 0 \\ e^t; & t > 0 \end{cases}$

Integrating both sides

for $t \le 0$

$\int df(t) = \int dt$

$f(t) = t + C$

$f(0) = 0 = 0 + C$

$\Rightarrow \quad C = 0$

$\therefore \quad f(t) = t$ for $t \le 0$

for $t > 0$

$\int df(t) = \int e^t\, dt$

$f(t) = e^t + C$

For $f'(t)$ to exist, $f(t)$ should be continuous at $t = 0$

$\therefore \quad f(0) = 0 = e^0 + C$

$\Rightarrow \quad C = -1$

$\therefore \quad f(t) = e^t - 1$ for $t > 0$

10. $g(1) = 1, g'(x^2) = x^3 \ \forall \ x > 0$

Let $x^2 = t \qquad \Rightarrow \quad x = t^{1/2}$

$\Rightarrow \quad x^3 = t^{3/2} \ \forall \ t > 0$

$\therefore \quad g'(t) = t^{3/2} = \frac{d}{dt} g(t)$

$dg(t) = t^{3/2}\, dt$

Integrating both sides, we get $\int dg(t) = \int t^{3/2}\, dt$

$g(t) = \frac{2}{5} t^{5/2} + C$

$g(1) = 1 = \frac{2}{5} + C$

$\therefore \quad C = \frac{3}{5}$

$g(t) = \frac{2t^{5/2} + 3}{5}$

$g(4) = \frac{2(4)^{5/2} + 3}{5} = \frac{2(32) + 3}{5}$

$g(4) = \frac{67}{5}$

TEXTUAL EXERCISE–1: (OBJECTIVE)

1. (a), (b), (c)

$f''(x) = 2, f'(0) = -1, f(2) = 1$

$f''(x) = 2$

Integrating both sides, we get $f'(x) = 2x + C$

$f'(0) = 2(0) + C = -1$

$\therefore \quad C = -1$

$\therefore \quad f'(x) = 2x - 1$

Integrating both sides, we get $f(x) = x^2 - x + C$

$f(2) = 2^2 - 2 + C = 1$

$\therefore \quad C = -1$

$\Rightarrow \quad f(x) = x^2 - x - 1$

(a) $f(-1) = (-1)^2 + 1 - 1 = 1$
Hence true.

(b) $f(x) = x^2 - x - 1$ (A quadratic equation has a parabolic curve)
Hence true.

(c) $f'(x) = 2x - 1$
for $x > 1$
$f'(x) > 0$
Since slope ($f'(x)$) is positive, so $f(x)$ increases for $x > 1$.
Hence true.

2. (a) $f(0) = 3, f(1) = 2, f''(x) = 0 \ \forall\ x$
$f''(x) = 0$
Integrating both sides, we get $f'(x) = C_1$
Again integrating both side, we get $f(x) = C_1 x + C_2$
$f(0) = C_1(0) + C_2 = 3$
$\therefore\ C_2 = 3$
$f(x) = C_1 x + 3$
$f(1) = C_1 + 3 = 2$
$\therefore\ C_1 = -1$
$\therefore\ f(x) = -x + 3$
So given the boundary conditions only one such function exists.

3. (b) (a) Let $f(x)$ be an even function, such that $g(x)$ is its anti-derivative.
$\therefore\ g'(x) = f(x)$
$\Rightarrow\ \frac{d}{dx}g(x) = f(x)$
$g(x) = \int f(x)\,dx + C_1$
$g(-x) = -\int f(-x)dx + C_1 = -\int f(x)\,dx + C_1 = -g(x) + C$
($\because f(x)$ is even)
$\therefore$ $g(x)$ is odd only when the constant term is 0.
Hence false.

(b) Let $f(x)$ be an odd function, such that $g(x)$ is its anti-derivative.
$\therefore\ g'(x) = f(x)$
$\Rightarrow\ \frac{dg(x)}{dx} = f(x)$
Integrating, $g(x) = \int f(x)\,dx + C_1$
$g(-x) = -\int f(-x)\,dx + C_1$
$= \int f(x)\,dx + C_1$ ($\because f(x)$ is odd)
$= g(x)$
$\therefore$ $g(x)$ is always even.
Hence true.

(c) Lets take example of $f(x) = 1 + \cos x$
This is a periodic function since $\cos x$ is a periodic function.
Let $g(x)$ be anti derivative of $f(x)$
$\therefore\ g'(x) = f(x) = 1 + \cos x$
$g(x) = \int(1 + \cos x)dx + C = \int dx + \int \cos\,dx + C$
$\Rightarrow\ g(x) = x + \sin x + C$
which is a non-periodic function.
Hence false.

4. (a), (d) $f(x) = 3x - 2$
Let $g(x)$ be its anti-derivative.
$\therefore\ g'(x) = 3x - 2$
$g(x) = \int f(x)\,dx = \int(3x - 2)\,dx + C$
$g(x) = \frac{3x^2}{2} - 2x + C$
Now for $g(x)$ to touch the curve $y = \frac{1}{3}x^3 = h(x)$
$g'(x) = h'(x)$ i.e., their slopes would be equal at such points and $g(x) = h(x)$ i.e., their value shall also be equal.
$g'(x) = 3x - 2$
$h'(x) = \frac{d}{dx}\left(\frac{1}{3}x^3\right) = x^2$
$g'(x) = h'(x) \qquad \Rightarrow\ 3x - 2 = x^2$
$x^2 - 3x + 2 = 0 \qquad \therefore\ x = 1, 2$
For $x = 1,\ y = \frac{(1)^3}{3} = \frac{1}{3}$
$g(1) = h(1) = \frac{1}{3} = \frac{3}{2}(1)^2 - 2(1) + C$
$C = \frac{1}{3} + \frac{1}{2} = \frac{5}{6}$
$\therefore\ g(x) = \frac{3}{2}x^2 - 2x + \frac{5}{6}$
For $x = 2,\ y = \frac{(2)^3}{3} = \frac{8}{3}$
$g(2) = h(2) = \frac{8}{2} = \frac{3}{2}(2)^2 - 2(2) + C$
$C = \frac{8}{3} - 2 = \frac{2}{3}$
$\therefore\ g(x) = \frac{3}{2}x^2 - 2x + \frac{2}{3}$
Hence, (a) and (d) are the two anti-derivatives of $f(x)$.

5. (b), (d) $f''(x) = 3\cos 2x - 1, f'(0) = 0, |f(0)| = 1$
$f''(x) = 3\cos 2x - 1$
Integrating, $f'(x) = \frac{3}{2}\sin 2x - x + C$
$f'(0) = 0 - 0 + C = 0$
$\therefore\ C = 0$
$\therefore\ f'(x) = \frac{3}{2}\sin 2x - x$
Integrating, $f(x) = -\frac{3}{4}\cos 2x - \frac{x^2}{2} + C$
$\therefore\ f(0) = -\frac{3}{4}\cos 0 - 0 + C$
$\Rightarrow\ f(0) = C - \frac{3}{4}$
Given $|f(0)| = 1$
$\Rightarrow f(0) = +1$ or -1 and for $f(0) = 1$
$\Rightarrow\ 1 = C - \frac{3}{4} \qquad \Rightarrow\ C = \frac{7}{4}$
For $f(0) = -1$
$-1 = C - \frac{3}{4} \qquad \Rightarrow\ C = -\frac{1}{4}$
$\therefore\ f(x) = -\frac{3}{4}\cos 2x - \frac{x^2}{2} + \frac{7}{4}$ or
$f(x) = -\frac{3}{4}\cos 2x - \frac{x^2}{2} - \frac{1}{4}$
$\therefore\ 4f(x) = -3\cos 2x - 2x^2 + 7$ or $4f(x) = -3\cos 2x - 2x^2 - 1$

6. (a) Let the polynomial be $f(x) = ax^4 + bx^3 + cx^2 + dx + e$

$f(0) = e = 1$

$\therefore\ f(x) = ax^4 + bx^3 + cx^2 + dx + 1$

$f'(x) = 4ax^3 + 3bx^2 + 2cx + d$

$f'(0) = d = 0$

$\therefore\ f(x) = ax^4 + bx^3 + cx^2 + 1$

$f''(x) = 12ax^2 + 6bx + 2c$

$f''(0) = 2c = -40$

$\therefore\ c = -20$

$\therefore\ f(x) = ax^4 + bx^3 - 20x^2 + 1$

$f'(1) = 4a + 3b - 40 = 5$

$\therefore\ 4a + 3b = 45$

$f(1) = a + b - 19 = -4$

$a + b = 15$

$4a + 4b = 60$

$\therefore\ b = 15$

$\therefore\ a = 0$

$f(x) = 15x^3 - 20x^2 + 1$

7. (a) $f''(x) = x + \cos x,\ f(0) = 4,\ f'(0) = 2$

Integrating, $f'(x) = \dfrac{x^2}{2} + \sin x + C$

$f'(0) = C = 2$

$\therefore\ f'(x) = \dfrac{x^2}{2} + \sin x + 2$

Integrating, $f(x) = \dfrac{x^3}{6} - \cos x + 2x + C$

$f(0) = -1 + C = 4$

$\Rightarrow\ C = 5$

$\therefore\ f(x) = \dfrac{x^3}{6} - \cos x + 2x + 5$

8. (b) Let the curve be $f(x) = y$

Slope at any point $= f'(x) = \dfrac{dy}{dx} = 3x$

$\Rightarrow\ dy = 3x\,dx$

Integrating $y = \dfrac{3x^2}{2} + C$

Since it passes through (1, 2)

$\therefore\ 2 = \dfrac{3}{2} + C$

$\Rightarrow\ C = \dfrac{1}{2}$

$\therefore\ y = \dfrac{3x^2 + 1}{2}$

9. (c) Let the curve be $f(x) = y$

$\therefore$ Slope at any point $f'(x) = \dfrac{dy}{dx} = y^{\frac{2}{3}}$

$\dfrac{dy}{y^{\frac{2}{3}}} = dx$

Integrating $3y^{1/3} = x + C$

Since it passes through (–4, 1)

$\therefore\ 3(1)^{1/3} = -4 + C$

$\Rightarrow\ C = 7$

$\therefore\ 3y^{1/3} = x + 7$

TEXTUAL EXERCISE–2: (SUBJECTIVE)

1. (a) $\displaystyle\int \frac{\sqrt{x} - x^3e^x + x^2}{x^3}dx$

$= \displaystyle\int x^{\frac{1}{2}-3}dx - \int e^x dx + \int \frac{1}{x}dx$

$= \displaystyle\int x^{-\frac{5}{2}}dx - \int e^x dx + \int \frac{1}{x}dx$

$= -\dfrac{2}{3}x^{-\frac{3}{2}} - e^x + \ln|x| + C$

(b) $\displaystyle\int \frac{(1+\sqrt{x})^3}{\sqrt[3]{x}}dx = \int \frac{(1 + 3\sqrt{x} + 3x + x^{\frac{3}{2}})}{x^{\frac{1}{3}}}dx$

$= \displaystyle\int x^{-\frac{1}{3}}dx + 3\int x^{\frac{1}{2}-\frac{1}{3}}dx + 3\int x^{1-\frac{1}{3}}dx + \int x^{\frac{3}{2}-\frac{1}{3}}dx$

$= \dfrac{3}{2}x^{\frac{2}{3}} + \dfrac{18}{7}x^{\frac{7}{6}} + \dfrac{9}{5}x^{\frac{5}{3}} + \dfrac{6}{13}x^{\frac{13}{6}} + C$

(c) $\displaystyle\int \frac{\sqrt[3]{x^2} - \sqrt[4]{x}}{\sqrt{x}}dx$

$= \displaystyle\int x^{\frac{2}{3}-\frac{1}{2}}dx - \int x^{\frac{1}{4}-\frac{1}{2}}dx = \frac{6}{7}x^{\frac{7}{6}} - \frac{4}{3}x^{\frac{3}{4}} + C$

2. (a) $\displaystyle\int \frac{x^7 + 3x^6 + x + 3}{x^2 + 1}dx$

$= \displaystyle\int \frac{(x+3)(x^6+1)}{(x^2+1)}dx = \int \frac{(x+3)[(x^2)^3 + 1^3]}{x^2+1}dx$

$= \displaystyle\int \frac{(x+3)(x^2+1)(x^4 - x^2 + 1)}{(x^2+1)}dx$

($\because\ a^3 + b^3 = (a + b)(a^2 - ab + b^2)$)

$= \int(x + 3)(x^4 - x^2 + 1)dx = \int(x^5 - x^3 + x + 3x^4 - 3x^2 + 3)dx$

$= \dfrac{x^6}{6} - \dfrac{x^4}{4} + \dfrac{x^2}{2} + \dfrac{3}{5}x^5 - x^3 + 3x + C$

(b) $\displaystyle\int \frac{x}{(x^2 + 2x + 1)}dx$

$= \displaystyle\int \frac{x + 1 - 1}{(x+1)^2}dx = \int \frac{x+1}{(x+1)^2}dx - \int \frac{1}{(x+1)^2}dx$

$= \ln|x+1| + \dfrac{1}{(x+1)} + C$

3. (a) $\displaystyle\int \frac{\sqrt{x^4 + x^{-4} + 2}}{x^3}dx = \int \frac{\sqrt{\left(x^2 + \frac{1}{x^2}\right)^2}}{x^3}dx$

$= \displaystyle\int \frac{\left(x^2 + \frac{1}{x^2}\right)}{x^3}dx = \int \frac{1}{x}dx + \int x^{-5}dx = \ln|x| - \frac{1}{4}x^{-4} + C$

(b) $\displaystyle\int \frac{dx}{\sqrt{2x+3} - \sqrt{2x-1}}$

Multiplying numerator and denominator by

$(\sqrt{2x+3} + \sqrt{2x-1})$

$$= \int \frac{\sqrt{2x+3}+\sqrt{2x-1}}{(\sqrt{2x+3}-\sqrt{2x-1})(\sqrt{2x+3}+\sqrt{2x-1})}dx$$

$$= \int \frac{\sqrt{2x+3}+\sqrt{2x-1}}{2x+3-2x+1}dx$$

$$= \frac{1}{4}\left(\int \sqrt{2x+3}\,dx + \int \sqrt{2x-1}\,dx\right)$$

$$= \frac{1}{4}\left(\frac{1}{2}\cdot\frac{2}{3}(2x+3)^{\frac{3}{2}} + \frac{1}{2}\cdot\frac{2}{3}(2x-1)^{\frac{3}{2}} + C\right)$$

$$= \frac{1}{12}[(2x+3)^{\frac{3}{2}} + (2x-1)^{\frac{3}{2}} + C]$$

(c) $\int \sqrt{\frac{x^4+x^{-4}+2}{x^3}}dx = \int \sqrt{\frac{\left(x^2+\frac{1}{x^2}\right)^2}{x^3}}dx = \int \frac{x^2+\frac{1}{x^2}}{x^{\frac{3}{2}}}dx$

$$= \int x^{2-\frac{3}{2}}dx + \int x^{-2-\frac{3}{2}}dx = \frac{2}{3}x^{\frac{3}{2}} - \frac{2}{5}x^{-\frac{5}{2}} + C$$

4. (a) $\int \frac{e^{5\ln x}-e^{4\ln x}}{e^{3\ln x}-e^{2\ln x}}dx$

$$= \int \frac{x^5-x^4}{x^3-x^2}dx \qquad (\because e^{\ln x^a} = x^a)$$

$$= \int \frac{x^2(x^3-x^2)}{x^2(x-1)}dx = \int \frac{x^2(x-1)}{(x-1)}dx$$

$$= \int x^2\,dx = \frac{x^3}{3} + C$$

(b) $\int \left(1+x+\frac{x^2}{2!}+\frac{x^3}{3!}+\ldots\infty\right)dx$

$$= \left(\frac{x}{1}+\frac{x^2}{2}+\frac{x^3}{3(2!)}+\frac{x^4}{4(3!)}+\ldots.+\infty\right)+C$$

$$= \left(1+x+\frac{x^2}{2!}+\frac{x^3}{3!}+\frac{x^4}{4!}+\ldots+\infty\right)+(C-1)$$

$$= 1+x+\frac{x^2}{2!}+\frac{x^3}{3!}+\frac{x^4}{4!}+\ldots+\infty+C_1;\text{ where } C_1 = C-1$$

$= ex + C_1$

Aliter: $I = \int e^x dx = ex + C$

5. (a) $\int \frac{e^{3x}+e^{5x}}{e^x+e^{-x}}dx = \int \frac{e^{3x}(e^{2x}+1)}{\frac{e^{2x}+1}{e^x}}dx = \int e^{4x}dx = \frac{1}{4}e^{4x}+C$

(b) $\int \frac{e^{2x}-1}{e^x}dx = \int ex\,dx - \int e^-x\,dx = ex + e^-x + C$

(c) $\int \frac{2^{x+1}-5^{x-1}}{10^x}dx = \int \frac{2^{x+1}-5^{x-1}}{2^x5^x}dx = \int \frac{2^{x+1}}{2^x5^x}dx - \int \frac{5^{x-1}}{2^x5^x}dx$

$$= 2\int 5^{-x}dx - \frac{1}{5}\int 2^{-x}dx = \frac{-2(5^{-x})}{\ln 5} + \frac{1}{5}\frac{2^{-x}}{\ln 2} + C$$

6. (a) $\int \cos(3x+2)^\circ\,dx = \int \cos\left\{(3x+2)\frac{\pi}{180}\right\}dx$

$(\because 1^\circ = \frac{\pi}{180}$ radius)

$$= \frac{180}{3\pi}\sin\left\{(3x+2)\frac{\pi}{180}\right\}+C = \frac{60}{\pi}\sin(3x+2)^\circ + C$$

(b) $\int \sec^2(ax+b)\,dx = \frac{1}{a}\tan(ax+b)+C$

(c) $\int \cot^2(mx+n)\,dx = \int[\text{cosec}^2(mx+n)-1]dx$

$(\because 1+\cot^2\theta = \text{cosec}^2\theta)$

$$= \int \text{cosec}^2(mx+n)dx - \int dx = -\frac{1}{m}\cot(mx+n) - x + C$$

(d) $\int \frac{1-\cos x}{1+\cos x}dx = \int \frac{1-\left(1-2\sin^2\left(\frac{x}{2}\right)\right)}{1+\left(2\cos^2\left(\frac{x}{2}\right)-1\right)}dx$

$$\left(\because \cos\theta = 2\cos^2\frac{\theta}{2}-1 = 1-2\sin^2\frac{\theta}{2}\right)$$

$$= \int \frac{2\sin^2\left(\frac{x}{2}\right)}{2\cos^2\left(\frac{x}{2}\right)}dx = \int \tan^2\left(\frac{x}{2}\right)dx = \int\left(\sec^2\left(\frac{x}{2}\right)-1\right)dx$$

$$= \int \sec^2\left(\frac{x}{2}\right)dx - \int dx = 2\tan\left(\frac{x}{2}\right) - x + C$$

(e) $\int \cos^2(2x+1)\,dx \qquad (\because \cos 2x = 2\cos^2 x - 1)$

$$= \int \frac{1+\cos 2(2x+1)}{2}dx = \int \frac{1}{2}dx + \int \frac{\cos 2(2x+1)}{2}dx$$

$$= \frac{x}{2} + \frac{1}{8}\sin(4x+2) + C$$

(f) $\int(\cos^3(x+1) + 3\cos 2x)\,dx$

$(\because \cos 3x = 4\cos^3 x - 3\cos x)$

$$= \int \frac{\cos 3(x+1)+3\cos(x+1)}{4}dx + 3\int \cos 2x\,dx$$

$$= \frac{1}{12}\sin 3(x+1) + \frac{3}{4}\sin(x+1) + \frac{3}{2}\sin 2x + C$$

7. (a) $\int \frac{\sin^3 x+\cos^3 x}{\sin x+\cos x}dx$

$$= \int \frac{(\sin x+\cos x)(\sin^2 x - \sin x\cos x + \cos^2 x)}{(\sin x+\cos x)}dx$$

$(\because a^3 + b^3 = (a+b)(a^2 - ab + b^2))$

$$= \int(1-\sin x\cos x)\,dx = \int dx - \frac{1}{2}\int \sin 2x\,dx$$

$$= x + \frac{1}{4}\cos 2x + C$$

(b) $\int \frac{\text{cosec}\,x + \tan^2 x - \sin^2 x}{\sin x}dx = \int \text{cosec}^2 x\,dx + \int \tan x\sec$ $dx - \int \sin x\,dx = -\cot x + \sec x + \cos x + C$

8. (a) $\int \frac{\cos 2x}{\sin^2 x\cos^2 x}dx = \int \frac{\cos^2 x - \sin^2 x}{\sin^2 x\cos^2 x}dx = \int \text{cosec}^2 x\,dx$ $- \int \sec^2 x\,dx = -\cot x + \tan x + C$

(b) $\int \cos x\cos 2x\cos 3x\,dx = \frac{1}{2}\int \cos 2x\,2\cos x\cos 3x\,dx$

$(\because 2\cos A\cos B = \cos(A+B) + \cos(A-B))$

$$= \frac{1}{2}\int \cos 2x(\cos 4x + \cos 2x)dx$$

$$= \frac{1}{2}\int \cos 2x \cos 4x dx + \frac{1}{2}\int \cos^2 2x\, dx$$

$$= \frac{1}{4}\int 2\cos 2x \cos 4x\, dx + \frac{1}{2}\int \frac{1+\cos 4x}{2} dx$$

$$= \frac{1}{4}\int (\cos 6x + \cos 2x)dx + \frac{1}{4}\int dx + \frac{1}{4}\int \cos 4x\, dx$$

$$= \frac{1}{4}\int \cos 6x\, dx + \frac{1}{4}\int \cos 2x\, dx + \frac{1}{4}\int dx + \frac{1}{4}\int \cos 4x\, dx$$

$$= \frac{1}{4}\left(\frac{\sin 6x}{6} + \frac{\sin 2x}{2} + x + \frac{\sin 4x}{4}\right) + C$$

(c) $\int \frac{(\sin^6 x + \cos^6 x)}{\sin^2 x \cos^2 x} dx = \int \frac{(\sin^2 x)^3 + (\cos^2 x)^3}{\sin^2 x \cos^2 x} dx$

$$= \int \frac{(\sin^2 x + \cos^2 x)(\sin^4 x - \sin^2 x \cos^2 x + \cos^4 x)}{\sin^2 x \cos^2 x} dx$$

$= \int \frac{\sin^4 x}{\sin^2 x \cos^2 x} dx - \int dx + \int \frac{\cos^4 x}{\sin^2 x \cos^2 x} dx = \int \tan^2 x\, dx - x + \int \cot^2 x\, dx$

$= \int(\sec^2 x - 1)\, dx - x + \int(\text{cosec}^2 x - 1)\, dx = \tan x - 3x - \cot x + C$

(d) $\int \frac{1+\tan^2 x}{1+\cot^2 x} dx = \int \frac{1+\tan^2 x}{1+\frac{1}{\tan^2 x}} dx = \int \tan^2 dx = \int(\sec^2 x - 1)\, dx = \tan x - x + C$

(e) $\int(3\sin x \cos^2 x - \sin^3 x)dx = \int \sin x\,(3\cos^2 x - \sin^2 x)\, dx$

$= \int \sin x\,(4\cos^2 x - 1)\, dx = 4\int \sin x \cos^2 x\, dx - \int \sin x\, dx$

$$= -4\frac{\cos^3 x}{3} + \cos x + C$$

$$\left(\because \quad \int f'(x) f^n(x) dx = \frac{f(x)^{n+1}}{n+1}\right)$$

$$= \frac{3\cos x - 4\cos^3 x}{3} + C \quad (\because \cos 3x = 4\cos^3 x - 3\cos x)$$

$$= -\frac{\cos 3x}{3} + C$$

(f) $\int \frac{\sin 2x + \sin 5x - \sin 3x}{\cos x + 1 - 2\sin^2 2x} dx$

$$= \int \frac{\sin 2x + 2\cos 4x \sin x}{\cos x + \cos^2 2x + \sin^2 2x - 2\sin^2 2x} dx$$

$$= \int \frac{2\sin x \cos x + 2\sin x \cos 4x}{\cos x + \cos^2 2x - \sin^2 2x} dx$$

$$= \int \frac{2\sin x(\cos x + \cos 4x)}{\cos x + \cos 4x} dx$$

$$(\because \cos 4x = \cos^2 2x - \sin^2 2x)$$

$= \int 2\sin x\, dx = -2\cos x + C$

(g) $\int \sin x \cos x \cos 2x \cos 4x\, dx = \frac{1}{2}\int \sin 2x \cos 2x \cos 4x dx$

$$= \frac{1}{4}\int \sin 4x \cos 4x\, dx = \frac{1}{8}\int \sin 8x\, dx = -\frac{1}{64}\cos 8x + C$$

9. (a) $\int \frac{\sin x}{\cos^3 x} dx$ Let $y = \cos x \Rightarrow dy = -\sin x\, dx$

$\therefore \int \frac{\sin x}{\cos^3 x} dx = -\int \frac{dy}{y^3} = \frac{1}{2}\frac{1}{\cos^2 x} + C$

(b) $\int \frac{dx}{\sqrt{3}\cos x + \sin x} = \frac{1}{2}\int \frac{dx}{\frac{\sqrt{3}}{2}\cos x + \frac{1}{2}\sin x}$

$$= \frac{1}{2}\int \frac{dx}{\cos\frac{\pi}{6}\cos x + \sin\left(\frac{\pi}{6}\right)\sin x} = \frac{1}{2}\int \frac{dy}{\cos\left(x - \frac{\pi}{6}\right)}$$

$$= \frac{1}{2}\int \sec\left(x - \frac{\pi}{6}\right) dx$$

$$= \frac{1}{2}\ln\left|\sec\left(x - \frac{\pi}{6}\right) + \tan\left(x - \frac{\pi}{6}\right)\right| + C$$

(c) $\int\left(\frac{1}{x^{3/4}} + \frac{1-x^4}{1-x} + \sec x \tan x\right) dx$

$$= \int x^{-3/4} dx + \int \frac{(1+x^2)(1+x)(1-x)}{(1-x)} dx + \int \sec x \tan x\, dx$$

$= 4x^{1/4} + \int(1 + x^2 + x + x^3)\, dx + \sec x$

$$= 4x^{1/4} + x + \frac{x^3}{3} + \frac{x^2}{2} + \frac{x^4}{4} + \sec x + C$$

(d) $\int\left(\frac{x^2 + \cos^2 x}{1+x^2}\right)\text{cosec}^2 x\, dx$

$$= \int\left(\frac{x^2 + 1 - \sin^2 x}{1+x^2}\right)\text{cosec}^2 x\, dx$$

$$= \int \text{cosec}^2 x\, dx - \int \frac{1}{1+x^2} dx = -\cot x - \tan^{-1} x + C$$

(e) $\int \frac{\cos\left(1-\frac{x}{2}\right)}{\sin^2\left(1-\frac{x}{2}\right)} dx = \int \text{cosec}\left(1-\frac{x}{2}\right)\cot\left(1-\frac{x}{2}\right) dx$

$$= -\frac{\text{cosec}\left(1-\frac{x}{2}\right)}{-\frac{1}{2}} + C = 2\,\text{cosec}\left(1-\frac{x}{2}\right) + C$$

10. (a) $\int \frac{\cos 5x + \cos 4x}{1 - 2\cos 3x} dx = \int \frac{\left(2\cos\frac{9x}{2}\cos\frac{x}{2}\right)\sin 3x}{(\sin 3x - 2\cos 3x \sin 3x)} dx$

$$= \int \frac{2\cos\frac{9x}{2}\cos\frac{x}{2}\sin 3x}{(\sin 3x - \sin 6x)} dx$$

$$= \int \frac{2\cos\frac{9x}{2}\cos\frac{x}{2}\sin 3x}{-2\cos\frac{9x}{2}\sin\frac{3x}{2}} dx$$

$= -\int 2\cos\frac{x}{2}\cos\frac{3x}{2} dx = -\int(\cos 2x + \cos x)\, dx$

$$= -\frac{\sin 2x}{2} - \sin x + C$$

(b) $\int \tan^2 x \sin^2 x\, dx = \int \tan^2 x(1-\cos^2 x)\, dx = \int \tan^2 x\, dx - \int \sin^2 x\, dx$

$= \int (\sec^2 x - 1)dx - \int \frac{1-\cos 2x}{2} dx$

$= \int \sec^2 x\, dx - \int dx - \frac{1}{2}\int dx + \int \frac{\cos 2x}{2} dx$

$= \tan x - \frac{3}{2}x + \frac{\sin 2x}{4} + C$

(c) $\int \frac{dx}{\tan x + \cot x + \sec x + \text{cosec}\, x}$

$= \int \frac{dx}{\frac{\sin x}{\cos x} + \frac{\cos x}{\sin x} + \frac{1}{\cos x} + \frac{1}{\sin x}}$

$= \int \frac{\sin x \cos x\, dx}{\sin^2 x + \cos^2 x + \sin x + \cos x}$

$= \int \frac{\sin x \cos x\, dx}{1 + \sin x + \cos x} = \frac{1}{2}\int \frac{(\sin x + \cos x)^2 - 1}{1 + \sin x + \cos x} dx$

($\because$ $(\sin x + \cos x)^2 = 1 + 2 \sin x \cos x$)

$= \frac{1}{2}\int \frac{(\sin x + \cos x + 1)(\sin x + \cos x - 1)}{1 + \sin x + \cos x} dx$

($\because$ $\sin x \cos x = \frac{(\sin x + \cos x)^2 - 1}{2}$)

$= \frac{1}{2}\left[\int \sin x\, dx + \int \cos x\, dx - \int dx\right]$

$= \frac{1}{2}(-\cos x + \sin x - x) + C$

11. (a) $\int \frac{3 - 2\cot^2 x}{\cos^2 x} dx = 3\int \sec^2 x\, dx - 2\int \text{cosec}^2 x\, dx = 3 \tan x + 2 \cot x + C$

(b) $\int \frac{\cos 2x}{\cos x - \sin x} dx$

Multiplying numerator and Denominator by $\cos x + \sin x$

$= \int \frac{\cos 2x(\cos x + \sin x)}{(\cos x - \sin x)(\cos x + \sin x)} dx$

$= \int \frac{\cos 2x(\cos x + \sin x)}{\cos^2 x - \sin^2 x} dx = \int \frac{\cos 2x}{\cos 2x}(\cos x + \sin x)dx$

($\because \cos 2x = \cos^2 x - \sin^2 x$)

$= \int \cos x\, dx + \int \sin x\, dx = \sin x - \cos x + C$

(c) $\int(\sin 5x - \sin 5\alpha)dx = \int \sin 5x\, dx - \sin 5\alpha \int dx$

$= -\frac{1}{5}\cos 5x - x \sin 5\alpha + C$

12. (a) $\int \frac{dx}{x\sqrt{3x^2 - 1}} = \sqrt{3}\int \frac{dx}{(\sqrt{3}x)\sqrt{(\sqrt{3}x)^2 - 1}}$

$= \sqrt{3}\frac{\sec^{-1}(\sqrt{3}x)}{\sqrt{3}} + C = \sec^{-1}(\sqrt{3}x) + C$

(b) $\int \frac{dx}{\sqrt{1-4x^2}} dx = \int \frac{dx}{\sqrt{1-(2x)^2}} = \frac{1}{2}\sin^{-1}(2x) + C$

(c) $\int \frac{dx}{x\sqrt{25x^2 - 2}} = 5\int \frac{dx}{5x\sqrt{(5x)^2 - (\sqrt{2})^2}}$

$= \frac{1}{\sqrt{2}}\sec^{-1}\left(\frac{5x}{\sqrt{2}}\right) + C$

$\because \int \frac{dx}{x\sqrt{x^2 - a^2}} = \frac{1}{a}\sec^{-1}\left(\frac{x}{a}\right) + C$

(d) $\int \frac{dx}{(2x+1)\sqrt{x^2 + x}} = \int \frac{dx}{(2x+1)\sqrt{\left(x + \frac{1}{2}\right)^2 - \frac{1}{4}}}$

$= 2\int \frac{dx}{(2x+1)\sqrt{(2x+1)^2 - 1}} = \sec^{-1}(2x + 1) + C$

(e) $\int \frac{dx}{(2x-1)\sqrt{(2x-1)^2 - 4}} = \int \frac{dx}{(2x-1)\sqrt{(2x-1)^2 - (2)^2}}$

$= \frac{1}{4}\sec^{-1}\frac{2x-1}{2} + C \quad \because \int \frac{dx}{x\sqrt{x^2 - a^2}}$

$= \frac{1}{a}\sec^{-1}\frac{x}{a} + C$

(f) $\int \frac{1}{\sqrt{3 - \frac{x^2}{4}}} dx = \int \frac{1}{\sqrt{(\sqrt{3})^2 - \left(\frac{x}{2}\right)^2}} = 2\sin^{-1}\frac{x}{2\sqrt{3}} + C$

$= 2\sin^{-1}\left(\frac{x}{2\sqrt{3}}\right) + C$

(g) $\int \frac{1}{3 + (2-3x)^2} dx = \int \frac{1}{(\sqrt{3})^2 + (2-3x)^2} dx$

$= -\frac{1}{3\sqrt{3}}\tan^{-1}\left(\frac{2-3x}{\sqrt{3}}\right) + C$

$\left(\because \int \frac{1}{a^2 + x^2} dx = \frac{1}{a}\tan^{-1}\frac{x}{a} + C\right)$

13. (a) $\int \frac{1 + 2x^2}{x^2(1+x^2)} dx = \int \frac{(x^2) + (1+x^2)}{x^2(1+x^2)} dx$

$= \int \frac{dx}{1+x^2} + \int \frac{1}{x^2} dx = \tan^{-1} x - \frac{1}{x} + C$

$\left(\because \int \frac{dx}{1+x^2} = \tan^{-1} x + C\right)$

(b) $\int \frac{x^4 + x^2 + 1}{2(1+x^2)} dx = \int \frac{x^2(x^2+1) + 1}{2(1+x^2)} dx$

$= \int \frac{x^2 dx}{2} + \int \frac{1}{2(1+x^2)} dx = \frac{x^3}{6} + \frac{\tan^{-1} x}{2} + C$

(c) $\int \frac{3dx}{\sqrt{4 - 4x^2}} = \int \frac{3dx}{\sqrt{(2)^2 - (2x)^2}} = \frac{3}{2}\sin^{-1}\left(\frac{2x}{2}\right) + C$

$= \frac{3}{2}\sin^{-1} x + C$

14. (a) $\int \frac{x^2}{1+x^2}dx = \int \frac{x^2+1-1}{1+x^2}dx = \int dx - \int \frac{dx}{1+x^2}$
$= x - \tan^{-1} x + C$

(b) $\int \frac{(x+1)^2}{x(1+x^2)}dx = \int \frac{(x^2+1)+2x}{x(1+x^2)}dx = \int \frac{1}{x}dx + \int \frac{2dx}{1+x^2}$
$= \ln |x| + 2\tan^{-1} x + C$

(c) $\int \frac{x^2}{x^2-1}dx = \int \frac{x^2-1+1}{x^2-1}dx = \int dx + \int \frac{dx}{x^2-1}$
$= x + \frac{1}{2}\ln\left|\frac{x-1}{x+1}\right| + C$

(d) $\int \frac{x^4}{1+x^2}dx = \int \frac{x^4+1-1}{(1+x^2)}dx$
$= \int \frac{dx}{1+x^2} + \int \frac{(x^2+1)(x^2-1)}{(x^2+1)}dx$
$= \tan^{-1} x + \int x^2\,dx - \int dx = \tan^{-1} x + \frac{x^3}{3} - x + C$

(e) $\int \frac{5(x-3)^2}{x\sqrt{x}}dx = \int 5\left(\frac{x^2+9-6x}{x^{\frac{3}{2}}}\right)dx$
$= 5\left[\int x^{2-\frac{3}{2}}dx + 9\int x^{-\frac{3}{2}}dx - 6\int x^{1-\frac{3}{2}}dx\right]$
$= 5\left(\frac{2}{3}x^{\frac{3}{2}} - 18x^{-\frac{1}{2}} - 12x^{\frac{1}{2}}\right) + C$

(f) $\int \frac{x^2+3}{x^6(x^2+1)}dx = \int \frac{x^2+1+2}{x^6(x^2+1)}dx$
$= \int \frac{1}{x^6}dx + 2\int \frac{1}{x^6(x^2+1)}dx = \frac{x^{-5}}{-5} + 2\int \frac{\sec^2\theta\, d\theta}{\tan^6\theta \sec^2\theta}$
(Put $x = \tan\theta$, $dx = \sec^2\theta\, d\theta$)
$= -\frac{1}{5x^5} + 2\int \cot^6\theta\, d\theta$
$= -\frac{1}{5x^5} + 2\int \cot^4\theta(\text{cosec}^2\theta - 1)\, d\theta$
$= -\frac{1}{5x^5} + 2\int \cot^4\theta.\text{cosec}^2\theta\, d\theta - 2\int \cot^2\theta.(\text{cosec}^2\theta - 1)\, d\theta$
$= -\frac{1}{5x^5} + 2\left(\frac{-(\cot\theta)^5}{5}\right) + 2\left(\frac{\cot^3\theta}{3}\right) + 2\int(\text{cosec}^2\theta - 1)\, d\theta$
$= -\frac{1}{5x^5} - \frac{2}{5}(\cot\theta)^5 + \frac{2}{3}(\cot\theta)^3 + 2(-\cot\theta) - 2\theta + C$
$= -\frac{1}{5x^5} - \frac{2}{5x^5} + \frac{2}{3x^3} - \frac{2}{x} - 2\tan^{-1}(x) + C$
$= -\frac{3}{5x^5} + \frac{2}{3x^3} - \frac{2}{x} - 2\tan^{-1} x + C$

15. (a) $\int \frac{dx}{4x^2+25} = \frac{1}{4}\int \frac{dx}{x^2+\left(\frac{5}{2}\right)^2} = \frac{1}{10}\tan^{-1}\frac{2x}{5} + C$

(b) $\int \frac{dx}{\sqrt{5-x^2-4x}} = \int \frac{dx}{\sqrt{9-(x+2)^2}} = \frac{1}{3}\sin^{-1}\frac{x+2}{3} + C$

(c) $\int \frac{dx}{4-x^2-4x} = \int \frac{dx}{(2\sqrt{2})^2-(x+2)^2}$
$= \frac{1}{4\sqrt{2}}\ln\left|\frac{2\sqrt{2}+(x+2)}{2\sqrt{2}-(x+2)}\right| + C$

(d) $\int \frac{2+3x^2}{x^2(1+x^2)}dx = \int \frac{2(1+x^2)+x^2}{x^2(1+x^2)}dx$
$= \int \frac{2}{x^2}dx + \int \frac{dx}{1+x^2} = -\frac{2}{x} + \tan^{-1} x + C$

(e) $\int \frac{\sqrt{1-x^2}+\sqrt{1+x^2}}{\sqrt{1-x^4}}dx = \int \frac{\sqrt{1-x^2}+\sqrt{1+x^2}}{\sqrt{(1-x^2)(1+x^2)}}dx$
$= \int \frac{dx}{\sqrt{1+x^2}} + \int \frac{dx}{\sqrt{1-x^2}}$
$= \ln|x+\sqrt{1+x^2}| + \sin^{-1} x + C$
$\left(\because \int \frac{dx}{\sqrt{1+x^2}} = \ln|x+\sqrt{x^2+1}| + C\right)$

(f) $\int \sqrt[5]{(8-3x)^6}dx = \int (8-3x)^{\frac{6}{5}}dx = -\frac{1}{3}\frac{(8-3x)^{\frac{6}{5}+1}}{\frac{6}{5}+1} + C$
$= -\frac{5}{33}(8-3x)^{\frac{11}{5}} + C$

TEXTUAL EXERCISE–3: (SUBJECTIVE)

1. (a) $\int \frac{x^3 dx}{\sqrt{x-1}} = I$

Let $x - 1 = t^2$ $\Rightarrow$ $dx = 2t\, dt$ and $x = t^2 + 1$

$\therefore$ $I = \int \frac{(t^2+1)^3 2t\, dt}{t} = 2\int(t^6 + 1 + 3t^4 + 3t^2)\, dt$
$= 2\left(\frac{t^7}{7} + t + \frac{3t^5}{5} + t^3\right) + C$
$= \frac{2t}{35}(5t^6 + 35 + 21t^4 + 35t^2) + C$
$= \frac{2}{35}\sqrt{x-1}\,[5(x-1)^3 + 35 + 21(x-1)^2 + 35(x-1)] + C$
$= \frac{2}{35}\sqrt{x-1}\,[5x^3 - 5 - 15x^2 + 15x + 35 + 21x^2 + 21 - 42x + 35x - 35] + C$
$= \frac{2}{35}\sqrt{x-1}(5x^3 + 6x^2 + 8x + 16) + C$

(b) $\int \frac{x+1}{x\sqrt{x-2}}dx = I$

Let $\sqrt{x-2} = t$ $\Rightarrow$ $\frac{1}{2\sqrt{x-2}}dx = dt$

$\Rightarrow$ $\frac{dx}{\sqrt{x-2}} = 2dt$

$x = t^2 + 2$

$\therefore \quad I = \int 2\left(\frac{t^2+3}{t^2+2}\right)dt = 2\left[\int dt + \int \frac{dt}{t^2+(\sqrt{2})^2}\right]$

$= 2t + \frac{2}{\sqrt{2}}\tan^{-1}\frac{t}{\sqrt{2}} + C$

$= 2\sqrt{x-2} + \sqrt{2}\tan^{-1}\sqrt{\frac{x-2}{2}} + C$

(c) $\int \frac{dx}{1+\sqrt[3]{x+1}} = I$

Let $x + 1 = t^3 \quad \Rightarrow \quad dx = 3t^2\, dt$

$\therefore \quad I = \int \frac{3t^2 dt}{1+t} = 3\int \frac{t^2-1+1}{1+t}dt = 3\int (t-1)dt + 3\int \frac{dt}{1+t}$

$= \frac{3t^2}{2} - 3t + 3\ln|1+t| + C$

$= \frac{3}{2}(x+1)^{\frac{2}{3}} - 3(x+1)^{\frac{1}{3}} + 3\ln|1+(x+1)^{\frac{1}{3}}| + C$

2. (a) $\int \frac{\sqrt{x}}{x+1}dx = I$

Let $x = t^2 \quad \Rightarrow \quad dx = 2t\, dt$

$\therefore \quad I = \int \frac{t(2t)}{t^2+1}dt = 2\int \frac{t^2}{t^2+1}dt$

$= 2\int \frac{t^2+1-1}{t^2+1}dt = 2\int dt - 2\int \frac{dt}{t^2+1}$

$= 2(t - \tan^{-1} t) + C = 2(\sqrt{x} - \tan^{-1}\sqrt{x}) + C$

(b) $\int \frac{\sqrt{x}dx}{\sqrt{x}-\sqrt[3]{x}} = I$

Let $x = z^6 \quad \Rightarrow \quad dx = 6z^5\, dz$

$\Rightarrow \quad I = \int \frac{z^3}{z^3-z^2}6z^5\, dz = 6\int \frac{z^6}{z-1}dz$

$= 6\left[\int \frac{z^6-1}{z-1}dz + \int \frac{dz}{z-1}\right]$

$= 6\left[\int \frac{(z^2-1)(z^4+1+z^2)}{z-1}dz + \int \frac{dz}{z-1}\right]$

$= 6\left[(z+1)(z^4+z^2+1)dz + \int \frac{dz}{z-1}\right]$

$= 6\left[\int (z^5+z^3+z+z^4+z^2+1)dz + \int \frac{dz}{z-1}\right]$

$= 6\left[\frac{z^6}{6} + \frac{z^4}{4} + \frac{z^2}{2} + \frac{z^5}{5} + \frac{z^3}{3} + z + \ln|z-1|\right] + C$

$= x + \frac{6}{5}x^{\frac{5}{6}} + \frac{3}{2}x^{\frac{2}{3}} + 2\sqrt{x} + 3x^{\frac{1}{3}} + 6x^{\frac{1}{6}} + 6\ln|x^{\frac{1}{6}} - 1| + C$

(c) $\int \frac{dx}{\sqrt[3]{x}(\sqrt[3]{x}-1)} = I$

Let $x = z^3 \quad \Rightarrow \quad dx = 3z^2\, dz$

$I = \int \frac{3z^2\, dz}{z(z-1)} = \int \frac{3z}{z-1}dz = 3\int \frac{z-1+1}{z-1}dz$

$= 3\int dz + 3\int \frac{dz}{z-1} = 3z + 3\ln|z-1| + C$

$= 3x^{\frac{1}{3}} + 3\ln|x^{\frac{1}{3}} - 1| + C$

(d) $\int \frac{dx}{\sqrt{x}+\sqrt[4]{x}} = I$

Let $x = z^4 \quad \therefore \quad dx = 4z^3\, dz$

$\therefore \quad I = \int \frac{4z^3 dz}{z^2+z} = 4\int \frac{z^2}{z+1}dz = 4\int \frac{z^2-1+1}{z+1}dz$

$= 4\int (z-1)dz + 4\int \frac{dz}{z+1}$

$= 2z^2 - 4z + 4\ln|z+1| + C$

$= 2\sqrt{x} - 4x^{\frac{1}{4}} + 4\ln|x^{\frac{1}{4}} + 1| + C$

(e) $\int \frac{\sqrt{x}}{\sqrt[3]{x^2}-\sqrt[4]{x}}dx$

Let $x = z^{12} \quad \therefore \quad dx = 12z^{11}\, dz$

$\therefore \quad I = \int \frac{z^6}{z^8-z^3}12z^{11}\, dz = 12\int \frac{z^{14}}{z^5-1}dz$

Let $z^5 = t \quad \therefore \quad 5z^4\, dz = dt$

$\Rightarrow \quad z^4\, dz = \frac{dt}{5}$

$\therefore \quad I = \frac{12}{5}\int \frac{t^2}{t-1}dt = \frac{12}{5}\int \frac{t^2-1+1}{t-1}dt$

$= \frac{12}{5}\left[\int (t+1)dt + \int \frac{dt}{t-1}\right]$

$= \frac{6}{5}t^2 + \frac{12}{5}t + \frac{12}{5}\ln|t-1| + C$

($\because t = z^5$ and $z = x^{1/12} \Rightarrow t = x^{5/12}$)

$= \frac{6}{5}x^{\frac{5}{6}} + \frac{12}{5}x^{\frac{5}{12}} + \frac{12}{5}\ln|x^{\frac{5}{12}} - 1| + C$

3. (a) $I = \int \frac{e^{2x}dx}{\sqrt[4]{e^x+1}}$

Let $ex + 1 = t^4 \quad \therefore \quad ex\, dx = 4t^3 dt$

$I = \int \frac{(t^4-1)4t^3 dt}{t} = 4[\int (t^6 - t^2)dt]$

$= 4\left[\frac{t^7}{7} - \frac{t^3}{3}\right] + C = \frac{4}{7}(e^x+1)^{\frac{7}{4}} - \frac{4}{3}(e^x+1)^{\frac{3}{4}} + C$

$= 4(e^x+1)^{\frac{3}{4}}\left[\frac{e^x+1}{7} - \frac{1}{3}\right] + C$

$= \frac{4}{21}\sqrt[4]{(e^x+1)^3}(3e^x - 4) + C$

(b) $I = \int \frac{dx}{e^x\sqrt{1-e^{-2x}}}$

Let $e^-x = t \quad \therefore \quad -e^-x\, dx = dt$

$\therefore \quad I = -\int \frac{dt}{\sqrt{1-t^2}} = -\sin^{-1} t + C = -\sin^{-1}(e^{-x}) + C$

(c) $I=\int e^{2x^2+\ln x}dx = \int e^{2x^2}\cdot x\,dx$

Let $x^2 = t$ $\quad\therefore\quad 2x\,dx = dt$

$I=\int \frac{e^{2t}}{2}dt = \frac{e^{2t}}{4}+C = \frac{e^{2x^2}}{4}+C$

(d) $I=\int \frac{dx}{e^x(3+e^{-x})}$

Let $e^{-x} = t$ $\quad\therefore\quad -e^{-x}\,dx = dt$

$\therefore\quad I=-\int\frac{dt}{3+t} = -\ln|3+t|+C = -\ln|3+e^{-x}|+C$

4. (a) $I=\int\sqrt{1+\cos^2 x}\sin 2x\cos 2x\,dx$

Let $\sqrt{1+\cos^2 x}=t$ $\quad\therefore\quad \frac{-2\cos x\sin x\,dx}{2\sqrt{1+\cos^2 x}}=dt$

$\Rightarrow \sin 2x\,dx = -2t\,dt \quad\therefore\quad I=\int(t)(\cos 2x)(-2t)\,dt$

$\cos^2 x = t^2-1=\frac{1+\cos 2x}{2}$

$\Rightarrow \cos 2x = 2t^2-3$

$=-2\int t^2(2t^2-3)\,dt = -4\frac{t^5}{5}+2t^3+C = \frac{2}{5}t^3(5-2t^2)+C$

$= 4(1+\cos^2 x)^{3/2}(3-2\cos^2 x)+C$

(b) $I=\int\frac{\ln(\tan x)}{\sin x.\cos x}dx$

Let $\ln(\tan x)=t$ $\quad\Rightarrow\quad \frac{1}{\tan x}\sec^2 x\,dx = dt$

$\Rightarrow \frac{1}{\sin x\cos x}dx = dt$

$\therefore\quad I=\int t\,dt = \frac{t^2}{2}+C = \frac{1}{2}\ln^2(\tan x)+C$

(c) $I=\int\frac{\sin x}{e^{\cos x}}dx$

Let $e^{-\cos}x = t$ $\quad\therefore\quad -e^{-\cos}x(-\sin x)\,dx = dt$

$\therefore\quad I=\int dt = t+C = e^{-\cos}x+C$

(d) $I=\int x\cos x^2\,dx$

Let $x^2 = t$ $\quad\therefore\quad 2x\,dx = dt$

$I=\frac{1}{2}\int\cos t\,dt = \frac{\sin t}{2}+C = \frac{\sin x^2}{2}+C$

(e) $I=\int\frac{\sin^4 x}{\cos^6 x}dx = \int\tan^4 x\sec^2 x\,dx$

Let $\tan x = t$

$\therefore\quad \sec^2 x\,dx = dt$

$\therefore\quad I=\int t^4 dt = \frac{t^5}{5}+C = \frac{(\tan x)^5}{5}+C$

(f) $\int\left(\sqrt{\sin x}+\cos x\right)^2dx$

$=\int\left(\sin x+\cos^2 x+2\sqrt{\sin x}\cos x\right)dx$

$=-\cos x+\int\frac{1+\cos 2x}{2}dx+\int 2\sqrt{\sin x}\cos x\,dx$

$=-\cos x+\frac{1}{2}x+\frac{\sin 2x}{4}+\int 2\sqrt{t}\,dt$

$=-\cos x+\frac{1}{2}x+\frac{1}{4}\sin 2x+\frac{4}{3}\int\sqrt{(\sin x)^3}+C$

5. (a) $I=\int\frac{dt}{x^2\sqrt{x^2+a^2}}$

Let $x = a\tan\theta$

$\Rightarrow dx = a\sec^2\theta\,d\theta$

$\therefore\quad I=\int\frac{a\sec^2\theta\,d\theta}{a^2\tan^2\theta.a\sec\theta} = \int\frac{\sec\theta\,d\theta}{a^2\tan^2\theta}$

$=\frac{1}{a^2}\int\frac{\cos\theta\,d\theta}{\sin^2\theta} = -\frac{1}{a^2\sin\theta}+C = -\frac{\sqrt{x^2+a^2}}{a^2x}+C$

(b) $I=\int\frac{x^2}{\sqrt{a^2-x^2}}dx$

Let $x = a\sin\theta$ $\quad\therefore\quad dx = a\cos\theta\,d\theta$

$\therefore\quad I=\int\frac{a^2\sin^2\theta\,a\cos\theta}{a\cos\theta}d\theta = a^2\int\sin^2\theta\,d\theta$

$=a^2\int\frac{1-\cos 2\theta}{2}d\theta = \frac{a^2}{2}\int d\theta-\frac{a^2}{2}\int\cos 2\theta\,d\theta$

$=\frac{a^2}{2}\theta-\frac{a^2}{4}\sin 2\theta+C = \frac{a^2}{2}\sin^{-1}\frac{x}{a}-\frac{x}{2}\sqrt{a^2-x^2}+C$

(c) $I=\int\frac{dx}{x\sqrt{x^2-a^2}}$

Let $x = a\sec\theta$ $\quad\therefore\quad dx = a\sec\theta\tan\theta\,d\theta$

$I=\int\frac{a\sec\theta\tan\theta\,d\theta}{a\sec\theta\,a\tan\theta} = \frac{\theta}{a}+C$

$=\frac{1}{a}\sec^{-1}\left(\frac{x}{a}\right)+C = \frac{1}{a}\cos^{-1}\left(\frac{a}{x}\right)+C$

$=\frac{1}{a}\left[\frac{\pi}{2}-\sin^{-1}\left(\frac{a}{x}\right)\right]+C = -\frac{1}{a}\sin^{-1}\left(\frac{a}{x}\right)+C'$

6. (a) $I=\int\frac{x^5dx}{\sqrt{a^3-x^3}}$

Let $x = a\sin^{2/3}\theta$ $\quad\Rightarrow\quad dx = \frac{2}{3}a\sin^{-\frac{1}{3}}\theta\cos\theta\,d\theta$

$\therefore\quad I=\int\frac{a^5\sin^{\frac{10}{3}}\theta\frac{2}{3}a\sin^{-\frac{1}{3}}\theta\cos\theta\,d\theta}{a^{\frac{3}{2}}\cos\theta} = \frac{2}{3}a^{\frac{9}{2}}\int\sin^3\theta\,d\theta$

$\left(\because\ \sin^3\theta=\frac{3\sin\theta-\sin 3\theta}{4}\right)$

$=\frac{1}{6}a^{\frac{9}{2}}[3\int\sin\theta\,d\theta-\int\sin 3\theta\,d\theta]$

$=\frac{a^{\frac{9}{2}}}{6}\left[-3\cos\theta+\frac{\cos 3\theta}{3}\right]+C$

$=\frac{a^{\frac{9}{2}}}{6}\left[\frac{4}{3}\cos^3\theta-4\cos\theta\right]+C$

$=\frac{2}{9}a^{\frac{9}{2}}\cos\theta[\cos^2\theta-3]+C$

$$\left[\because \sin\theta = \left(\frac{x}{a}\right)^{\frac{3}{2}} \Rightarrow \cos\theta = \sqrt{1-\frac{x^3}{a^3}}\right]$$

$$= \frac{2}{9}a^3\sqrt{a^3-x^3}\left[1-\frac{x^3}{a^3}-3\right]+C$$

$$= -\frac{2}{9}\sqrt{a^3-x^3}(2a^3+x^3)+C$$

(b) $I = \int \frac{x^5 dx}{(x^2-4)^2} = \int \frac{x\,dx}{\left(1-\frac{4}{x^2}\right)^2}$

Let $1-\frac{4}{x^2}=t$

$\Rightarrow \frac{8}{x^3}dx = dt$

$\Rightarrow x^2 = \frac{4}{1-t}$

$$\therefore \quad I = \int \frac{\frac{1}{8}\left(\frac{4}{1-t}\right)^2}{t^2}dt$$

$$= 2\int \frac{1}{t^2(1-t)^2}dt = 2\int \frac{(1-t^2)+t^2}{t^2(1-t)^2}dt$$

$$= 2\left[\int \frac{(1+t)dt}{(1-t)t^2} + \int \frac{dt}{(1-t)^2}\right]$$

$$= 2\left[\int \frac{dt}{t^2(1-t)} + \int \frac{dt}{t(1-t)} + \int \frac{dt}{(1-t)^2}\right]$$

$$= 2\left[\int \frac{dt}{t^2} + \int \frac{2dt}{t(1-t)} + \int \frac{dt}{(1-t)^2}\right]$$

$$= 2\left[\int \frac{dt}{t^2} + 2\int \frac{dt}{t} + 2\int \frac{dt}{1-t} + \int \frac{dt}{(1-t)^2}\right]$$

$$= 2\left[-\frac{1}{t} + 2\ln[t/(1-t)] + \frac{1}{(1-t)}\right]$$

$$= \frac{2x^2}{4-x^2} + 4\ln\frac{(x^2-4)}{4} + \frac{x^2}{2}$$

(c) $I = \int \frac{(x+1)}{x(1+xe^x)}dx$

Multiply numerator and denominator by e^x, we get

$$I = \int \frac{e^x(x+1)dx}{xe^x(1+xe^x)}$$

Let $xex = t$

$\Rightarrow$ ex $(x+1)\,dx = dt$

$$I = \int \frac{dt}{t(1+t)} = \int \frac{(1-t)-(t)}{t(1+t)}dt = \int \frac{dt}{t} - \int \frac{dt}{1+t}$$

$$= \ln\left|\frac{t}{1+t}\right| + C = \ln\left|\frac{xe^x}{1+xe^x}\right| + C$$

7. (a) $I = \int \frac{\sqrt{1+x^2}}{x^4}dx = \int \frac{\sqrt{1+\frac{1}{x^2}}}{x^3}dx$

Let $1+\frac{1}{x^2}=t \qquad \therefore \quad -\frac{2}{x^3}dx = dt$

$$I = -\frac{1}{2}\int \sqrt{t}dt = -\frac{1}{3}t^{\frac{3}{2}} + C = C - \frac{\sqrt{(1+x^2)^3}}{3x^3}$$

(b) $I = \int \frac{dx}{\sqrt{(a^2+x^2)^3}} = \int \frac{dx}{x^3\sqrt{\left(1+\frac{a^2}{x^2}\right)^3}}$

Let $1+\frac{a^2}{x^2}=t \qquad \therefore \quad -\frac{2a^2}{x^3}dx = dt$

$$I = \frac{-1}{2a^2}\int \frac{dt}{t^{\frac{3}{2}}} = \frac{-1}{2a^2}\frac{t^{-\frac{1}{2}}}{-\frac{1}{2}} + C = \frac{x}{a^2\sqrt{x^2+a^2}} + C$$

(c) $I = \int \frac{\sqrt{(9-x^2)^3}}{x^6}dx = \int \frac{\sqrt{\left(\frac{9}{x^2}-1\right)^3}}{x^3}dx$

Let $\frac{9}{x^2}-1=t \qquad \therefore \quad -\frac{18}{x^3}dx = dt$

$$\therefore \quad I = -\frac{1}{18}\int t^{\frac{3}{2}}dt = -\frac{1}{45}t^{\frac{5}{2}} + C = C - \frac{\sqrt{(9-x^2)^5}}{45x^5}$$

(d) $I = \int \frac{dx}{x^2\sqrt{x^2-9}} = \int \frac{dx}{x^3\sqrt{1-\frac{9}{x^2}}}$

Let $1-\frac{9}{x^2}=t$

$$\Rightarrow \frac{18}{x^3}dx = dt = \frac{1}{18}\int \frac{dt}{t^{\frac{1}{2}}} = \frac{1}{9}t^{\frac{1}{2}} + C = \frac{\sqrt{x^2-9}}{9x} + C$$

8. (a) $I = \int \frac{\sqrt{1-x^2}}{x^2}dx$

Let $x = \sin\theta \qquad \therefore \quad dx = \cos\theta\, d\theta$

$$I = \int \frac{\cos\theta}{\sin^2\theta}\cos\theta\, d\theta = \int \cot^2\theta\, d\theta = \int (\text{cosec}^2\theta - 1)d\theta$$

$$= -\cot\theta - \theta + C = C - \frac{\sqrt{1-x^2}}{x} - \sin^{-1}x$$

(b) $I = \int \frac{dx}{\sqrt{(x^2-a^2)^3}}$

$x = a\sec\theta \qquad \Rightarrow \quad dx = a\sec\theta\tan\theta\, d\theta$

$$I = \int \frac{a\sec\theta\tan\theta}{a^3\tan^3\theta}d\theta = \frac{1}{a^2}\int \frac{\cos\theta\, d\theta}{\sin^2\theta}$$

$$= -\frac{1}{a^2}\frac{1}{\sin\theta} + C = -\frac{1}{a^2}\frac{1}{\sqrt{1-\frac{a^2}{x^2}}} + C = C - \frac{x}{a^2\sqrt{x^2-a^2}}$$

(c) $I = \int \frac{dx}{x\sqrt{1+x^2}}$

Let $x = \tan\theta \qquad \Rightarrow \quad dx = \sec^2\theta\, d\theta$

$$I = \int \frac{\sec^2\theta\, d\theta}{\tan\theta \sec\theta} = \int \operatorname{cosec}\theta\, d\theta$$

$$= \ln|\operatorname{cosec}\theta - \cot\theta| + C = \ln\left|\frac{\sqrt{1+x^2}}{x} - \frac{1}{x}\right| + C$$

9. (a) $I = \int \frac{dx}{x^4+1} = \frac{1}{2}\int \frac{2}{x^4+1}dx = \frac{1}{2}\int \frac{(x^2+1)-(x^2-1)}{x^4+1}dx$

$$= \frac{1}{2}\int \frac{x^2+1}{x^4+1}dx - \frac{1}{2}\int \frac{x^2-1}{x^4+1}dx$$

$$= \frac{1}{2}\int \frac{\left(1+\frac{1}{x^2}\right)}{\left(x^2+\frac{1}{x^2}\right)}dx - \frac{1}{2}\int \frac{\left(1-\frac{1}{x^2}\right)}{x^2+\frac{1}{x^2}}dx$$

$$= \frac{1}{2}\int \frac{\left(1+\frac{1}{x^2}\right)}{\left(x-\frac{1}{x}\right)^2+2}dx - \frac{1}{2}\int \frac{\left(1-\frac{1}{x^2}\right)dx}{\left(x+\frac{1}{x}\right)^2-2}$$

$= I_1 - I_2$ ...(i)

Here, $I_1 = \frac{1}{2}\int \frac{\left(1+\frac{1}{x^2}\right)}{\left(x-\frac{1}{x}\right)^2+2}dx$ and

$$I_2 = \frac{1}{2}\int \frac{1-\frac{1}{x^2}}{\left(x+\frac{1}{x}\right)^2-2}dx$$

Put $x - \frac{1}{x} = m$ and $x + \frac{1}{x} = n$

$\left(1+\frac{1}{x^2}\right)dx = dm$; $\left(1-\frac{1}{x^2}\right)dx = dn$

$\Rightarrow I_1 = \frac{1}{2}\int \frac{dm}{m^2+2}$ and $I_2 = \frac{1}{2}\int \frac{dn}{n^2-2}$

$\Rightarrow I_1 = \frac{1}{2\sqrt{2}}\tan^{-1}\left(\frac{m}{\sqrt{2}}\right)$ and $I_2 = \frac{1}{4\sqrt{2}}\ln\left|\frac{n-\sqrt{2}}{n+\sqrt{2}}\right|$

$\Rightarrow I_1 = \frac{1}{2\sqrt{2}}\tan^{-1}\left(\frac{x^2-1}{\sqrt{2}x}\right)$ and $I_2 = \frac{1}{4\sqrt{2}}\ln\left|\frac{x^2-\sqrt{2}x+1}{x^2+\sqrt{2}x+1}\right|$

$\therefore\ I = I_1 - I_2$ (from (1))

$\Rightarrow I = \frac{1}{2\sqrt{2}}\left[\tan^{-1}\left(\frac{x^2-1}{\sqrt{2}x}\right) - \frac{1}{2}\ln\left|\frac{x^2-\sqrt{2}x+1}{x^2+\sqrt{2}x+1}\right|\right] + C$

(b) $I = \int \frac{x}{x^4+1}dx$

$x^2 = m$ $\quad 2x\,dx = dm$

$I = \frac{1}{2}\int \frac{dm}{m^2+1} = \frac{1}{2}\tan^{-1} m + C = \frac{1}{2}\tan^{-1} x^2 + C$

(c) $I = \int \frac{x^2}{x^4+1}dx = \frac{1}{2}\int \frac{2x^2}{x^4+1}dx = \frac{1}{2}\int \frac{(x^2+1)+(x^2-1)}{x^4+1}dx$

$$= \frac{1}{2}\int \frac{x^2+1}{x^4+1}dx + \frac{1}{2}\int \frac{x^2-1}{x^4+1}dx$$

$= I_1 + I_2$ ...(i)

Where $I_1 = \frac{1}{2}\int \frac{1+\frac{1}{x^2}}{x^2+\frac{1}{x^2}}dx$ and $I_2 = \frac{1}{2}\int \frac{1-\frac{1}{x^2}}{x^2+\frac{1}{x^2}}dx$

$\Rightarrow I_1 = \frac{1}{2}\int \frac{1+\frac{1}{x^2}}{\left(x-\frac{1}{x}\right)^2+2}dx$ and $I_2 = \frac{1}{2}\int \frac{1-\frac{1}{x^2}}{\left(x+\frac{1}{x}\right)^2-2}dx$

Put $x - \frac{1}{x} = m$ and $x + \frac{1}{x} = n$

$\Rightarrow \left(1+\frac{1}{x^2}\right)dx = dm$ and $\left(1-\frac{1}{x^2}\right)dx = dn$

$\Rightarrow I_1 = \frac{1}{2}\int \frac{dm}{m^2+2}$ and $I_2 = \frac{1}{2}\int \frac{dn}{m^2-2}$

$\Rightarrow I_1 = \frac{1}{2\sqrt{2}}\tan^{-1}\left(\frac{m}{\sqrt{2}}\right)$ and $I_2 = \frac{1}{4\sqrt{2}}\ln\left|\frac{n-\sqrt{2}}{n+\sqrt{2}}\right|$

$\Rightarrow I_1 = \frac{1}{2\sqrt{2}}\tan^{-1}\left(\frac{x^2-1}{\sqrt{2}x}\right)$ and $I_2 = \frac{1}{4\sqrt{2}}\ln\left|\frac{x^2-\sqrt{2}x+1}{x^2+\sqrt{2}x+1}\right|$

$\Rightarrow I = I_1 + I_2$

$$= \frac{1}{2\sqrt{2}}\left[\tan^{-1}\left(\frac{x^2-1}{\sqrt{2}x}\right) + \frac{1}{2}\ln\left|\frac{x^2-\sqrt{2}x+1}{x^2+\sqrt{2}x+1}\right|\right] + C$$

(d) $I = \int \frac{x^3}{x^4+1}dx$

$x^4 = m$

$4x^3\,dx = dm$

$I = \frac{1}{4}\int \frac{dm}{m+1} = \frac{1}{4}\ln|m+1| + C = \frac{1}{4}\ln(x^4+1) + C$

(e) $I = \int \frac{x^4}{x^4+1}dx = \int \frac{x^4+1-1}{x^4+1}dx = \int dx - \int \frac{dx}{x^4+1}$

$$= x - \frac{1}{2\sqrt{2}}\tan^{-1}\left(\frac{x^2-1}{\sqrt{2}x}\right) + \frac{1}{4\sqrt{2}}\ln\left|\frac{x^2-\sqrt{2}x+1}{x^2+\sqrt{2}x+1}\right| + C$$

(from 9(a) we know $\int \frac{dx}{x^4+1}$)

(f) $I = \int \frac{x^5}{x^4+1}dx = \int \frac{x(x^4+1-1)}{x^4+1}dx$

$= \int x\,dx - \int \frac{x\,dx}{x^4+1}$ (from 9(b) we know $\int \frac{x}{x^4+1}dx$)

$$= \frac{x^2}{2} - \frac{1}{2}\tan^{-1} x^2 + C$$

10. (a) $I = \int \frac{\sin x\cos x}{a\cos^2 x + b\sin^2 x}dx = \int \frac{\sin x \cos x}{a+(b-a)\sin^2 x}dx$

Let $\sin^2 x = m$

$\therefore\ 2\sin x\cos x\,dx = dm$

$\therefore\ I = \frac{1}{2}\int \frac{dm}{a+(b-a)m} = \frac{1}{2(b-a)}\ln|(b-a)m + a| + C$

$$= \frac{1}{2(b-a)}\ln|(b-a)\sin^2 x + a| + C$$

$$= \frac{1}{2(b-a)}\ln|a\cos^2 x + b\sin^2 x| + C$$

(b) $\int \sec\theta\sqrt{\cos 2\theta}\, d\theta = \int \sec\theta.\sqrt{2\cos^2\theta - 1}\, d\theta$

$$= \int\sqrt{\frac{2\cos^2\theta}{\sec^2\theta} - \frac{1}{\sec^2\theta}}.\sec^2\theta\, d\theta$$

$$= \int\sqrt{2\cos^4\theta - \cos^2\theta}.\sec^2\theta\, d\theta$$

$$= \int\sqrt{\frac{2}{\sin^4\theta} - \frac{1}{\sec^2\theta}}.\sec^2\theta\, d\theta$$

$$= \int\sqrt{\frac{2-\sec^2\theta}{\sec^4\theta}}.\sec^2\theta\, d\theta$$

$$= \int\sqrt{\frac{2-(1+\tan^2\theta)}{(1+\tan^2\theta)^2}}.\sec^2\theta\, d\theta$$

$$= \int\sqrt{\frac{1-\tan^2\theta}{(1+\tan^2\theta)^2}}.\sec^2\theta\, d\theta = \int\sqrt{\frac{1-x^2}{(1+x^2)^2}}.dx\ ;$$

where $x = \tan\theta$

$$= \int\sqrt{\frac{(1-x^2)}{(1+x^2)}}\, dx = \int\sqrt{\frac{(1-x^2)}{(1+x^2)\sqrt{1-x^2}}}\, dx$$

$$= \int\sqrt{\frac{1}{(1+x^2)\sqrt{1-x^2}}}\, dx - \int\sqrt{\frac{(x^2+1-1)}{(1+x^2)\sqrt{1-x^2}}}\, dx$$

$$= \int\sqrt{\frac{2}{(1+x^2)\sqrt{1-x^2}}}\, dx - \int\sqrt{\frac{1}{\sqrt{1-x^2}}}\, dx$$

$= I_1 - \sin^{-1}x + C_1$ (say) ...(1)

Now, $I_1 = 2\int\frac{1}{(1+x^2)\sqrt{1-x^2}}\, dx$

Put $x = 1/t$ $\Rightarrow$ $dx = -\frac{1}{t^2}dt$

$$\therefore\quad I_1 = 2\int\frac{-\frac{1}{t^2}dt}{\left(1+\frac{1}{t^2}\right)\sqrt{1-\frac{1}{t^2}}}$$

$$\therefore\quad I_1 = -2\int\frac{t\,dt}{(t^2+1)\sqrt{t^2-1}}$$

Put $\sqrt{t\ -\ } = z$

$$\Rightarrow\quad \frac{1}{2\sqrt{t^2-1}}(2t)dt = dz \Rightarrow \frac{t\,dt}{\sqrt{t^2+1}} = dz$$

$$\therefore\quad I_1 = -2\int\frac{dz}{(z^2+2)} = -2\frac{1}{\sqrt{2}}\tan^{-1}\left(\frac{z}{\sqrt{2}}\right) + C_2 \qquad ...(2)$$

Using (2) in equation (1) we get,

$$I = -\sqrt{2}\tan^{-1}\left(\frac{\sqrt{t^2-1}}{\sqrt{2}}\right) - \sin^{-1}x + C$$

$$\Rightarrow\quad I = -\sqrt{2}\tan^{-1}\left(\frac{\sqrt{1-x^2}}{\sqrt{2}x}\right) - \sin^{-1}x + C$$

$$\Rightarrow\quad I = -\sqrt{2}\tan^{-1}\left(\frac{\sqrt{1-\tan^2\theta}}{\sqrt{2}\tan\theta}\right) - \sin^{-1}(\tan\theta) + C$$

$$\Rightarrow\quad I = -\sqrt{2}\tan^{-1}\left(\frac{\sqrt{\cot^2\theta-1}}{\sqrt{2}}\right) - \sin^{-1}(\tan\theta) + C$$

(c) $\int\left(\frac{\sin^{-1}\sqrt{x} - \cos^{-1}\sqrt{x}}{\sin^{-1}\sqrt{x} + \cos^{-1}\sqrt{x}}\right)dx$

$$= \frac{2}{\pi}\int\left(\sin^{-1}\sqrt{x} - \left(\frac{\pi}{2} - \sin^{-1}\sqrt{x}\right)\right)dx$$

$$= \frac{2}{\pi}\int 2\sin^{-1}\sqrt{x}\, dx - \int 1\, dx = \frac{4}{\pi}\int\sin^{-1}\sqrt{x}\, dx - x + C_1$$

Let $\sin^{-1}\sqrt{x} = \theta \notin \left[0, \frac{\pi}{2}\right]$; $0 \le x \le 1$

$\Rightarrow$ $\sqrt{x} = \sin\theta$

$\Rightarrow$ $\frac{1}{2\sqrt{x}}dx = \cos\theta d\theta$ $\Rightarrow$ $dx = \sin 2q\ d\theta$

$$\therefore\quad I = \frac{4}{\pi}\int\sin^{-1}(\sin\theta)\sin 2\theta d\theta - x + C_1$$

$$= \frac{4}{\pi}\int\theta.\sin 2\theta d\theta - x + C_1$$

$$= \frac{4}{\pi}\left[\theta.\left(\frac{-\cos 2\theta}{2}\right) - \int 1.\left(\frac{-\cos 2\theta}{2}\right)d\theta\right] - x + C_1$$

$$= -\frac{2}{\pi}\theta\cos 2\theta + \frac{2}{\pi}\int\cos 2\theta d\theta - x + C_1$$

$$= -\frac{2}{\pi}\theta\cos 2\theta + \frac{2}{\pi}\left[\frac{\sin 2\theta}{2}\right] - x + C_2$$

$$= -\frac{2}{\pi}\left(\sin^{-1}\sqrt{x}\right)(1-2x) + \frac{2}{\pi}\sqrt{x}\sqrt{1-x} - x + C_2$$

$$= -\frac{2}{\pi}\left[\frac{\pi}{2} - \cos^{-1}\sqrt{x}\right](1-2x) + \frac{2}{\pi}\sqrt{x(1-x)} - x + C_2$$

$$= \left(-1 + \frac{2}{\pi}\cos^{-1}\sqrt{x}\right)(1-2x) + \frac{2}{\pi}\sqrt{x(1-x)} - x + C_2$$

$$= -1 + 2x + \frac{2}{\pi}(1-2x)\cos^{-1}\sqrt{x} + \frac{2}{\pi}\sqrt{x(1-x)} - x + C_2$$

$$= x + \frac{1}{\pi}\left[-2(2x-1)\cos^{-1}\sqrt{x} + 2\sqrt{x(1-x)}\right] + C$$

11. (a) $I = \int\frac{m}{\sqrt[3]{(a+bx)^2}}dx$

$a + bx = t$

$bdx = dt$

$$I = \int\frac{m}{b}\frac{dt}{t^{2/3}} = \frac{3m}{b}t^{\frac{1}{3}} + C = \frac{3m}{b}(a+bx)^{\frac{1}{3}} + C$$

(b) $I=\int \frac{ax^{a-1}+a^x \ln a+2}{(a^x+x^a+2x)^n}dx$

Put $ax+x^a+2x=t$

$\Rightarrow$ $(ax \ln a+ax^{a-1}+2)dx=dt$

$\Rightarrow$ $I=\int \frac{dt}{t^n}=\frac{t^{-n+1}}{-n+1}+C$

$=\frac{(a^x \ln a+ax^{a-1}+2)^{-n+1}}{n+1}+C$ if $n\neq 1$

For $n=1$

$I=\int \frac{dt}{t}=\ln|t|+C=\ln|ax+x^a+2x|+C$

(c) $I=\int \frac{dx}{\sqrt[4]{(x-1)^3(x+2)^5}}=\int \frac{1}{(x+2)^2}\sqrt[4]{\frac{(x+2)^3}{(x-1)^3}}dx$

Let $x=2\tan^2\theta+\sec^2\theta=3\tan^2\theta+1=3\sec^2\theta-2$

$dx=(4\tan\theta\sec^2\theta+2\sec^2\theta\tan\theta)\,d\theta=6\sec^2\theta\tan\theta\,d\theta$

$\therefore$ $I=\int \frac{1}{(3\sec^2\theta+2-2)^2}\sqrt[4]{\left(\frac{3\sec^2\theta-2+2}{3\tan^2\theta+1-1}\right)^3}$

$6\sec^2\theta\tan\theta\,d\theta$

$=\int \frac{6\sec^2\theta\tan\theta\sec^{6/4}\theta}{9\sec^4\theta\tan^{6/4}\theta}d\theta=\int \frac{2}{3}\frac{d\theta}{\sec\theta^{1/2}\tan^{1/2}\theta}$

$=\int \frac{2}{3}\frac{\cos\theta}{\sqrt{\sin\theta}}d\theta$

Put $\sin\theta=m$ $\Rightarrow$ $\cos\theta\,d\theta=dm$

$\Rightarrow$ $I=\frac{2}{3}\int \frac{dm}{m^{1/2}}=\frac{4}{3}m^{1/2}+C=\frac{4}{3}(\sin\theta)^{1/2}+C$

$=\frac{4}{3}\left(\frac{x-1}{x+2}\right)^{1/4}+C$

(d) $\int \frac{1}{(x^2-6x-9)}\sqrt{x^2-6x+4}\,dx$

$=\int \frac{1}{(x^2-6x+9-18)}\sqrt{x^2-6x+9-5}\,dx$

$=\int \frac{1}{[(x-3)^2-18]}\sqrt{(x-3)^2-5}\,dx$

Put $x-3=t$ $\Rightarrow$ $dx=dt$

$\therefore$ $I=\int \frac{\sqrt{t^2-5}}{(t^2-18)}dt=\int \frac{(t^2-5)}{(t^2-18)\sqrt{t^2-5}}dt$

$=\int \frac{t^2-18+13}{(t^2-18)\sqrt{t^2-5}}dt$

$=\int \frac{1}{\sqrt{t^2-5}}dt+13\int \frac{1}{(t^2-18)\sqrt{(t^2-5)}}dt$ ...(1)

Let $I_1=\int \frac{1}{(t^2-18)\sqrt{t^2-5}}dt$

Put $t=\frac{1}{z}$ $\Rightarrow$ $dt=-\frac{1}{z^2}dz=dt$

$\Rightarrow$ $I_1=\int \frac{-\frac{1}{z^2}dz}{\left(\frac{1}{z^2}-18\right)\sqrt{\frac{1}{z^2}-5}}dt=\int \frac{z\,dz}{(18z^2-1)\sqrt{1-5z^2}}$

Put $z^2=u$ $\Rightarrow$ $2z\,dz=du$

$\Rightarrow$ $I_1=\frac{1}{2}\int \frac{du}{(18u-1)\sqrt{1-5u}}$

Put $\sqrt{1-5u}=v$

$\Rightarrow$ $\frac{1}{2\sqrt{1-5u}}(-5)du=dv$

$\Rightarrow$ $\frac{1}{2\sqrt{1-5u}}du=\frac{-1}{5}dv$

$\therefore$ $I_1=\int \frac{\frac{-1}{5}dv}{\left[18\left(\frac{1-v^2}{5}\right)-1\right]}=-\int \frac{dv}{(13-18v^2)}$

$=\int \frac{dv}{(18v^2-13)}=\frac{1}{\sqrt{18}(2)\sqrt{13}}\ln\left|\frac{\sqrt{18}v-\sqrt{13}}{\sqrt{18}v+\sqrt{13}}\right|+C$

$=\frac{1}{6\sqrt{26}}\ln\left|\frac{\sqrt{18(1-5u)}-\sqrt{13}}{\sqrt{18(1-5u)}+\sqrt{13}}\right|+C$

$=\frac{1}{6\sqrt{26}}\ln\left|\frac{\sqrt{18-90u}-\sqrt{13}}{\sqrt{18-90u}+\sqrt{13}}\right|+C$

$=\frac{1}{6\sqrt{26}}\ln\left|\frac{\sqrt{18-90\left(\frac{1}{t^2}\right)}-\sqrt{13}}{\sqrt{18-\frac{90}{t^2}}+\sqrt{13}}\right|+C$

$=\frac{1}{6\sqrt{26}}\ln\left|\frac{3\sqrt{2}\sqrt{t^2-5}-\sqrt{13}t}{3\sqrt{2}\sqrt{t^2-5}+\sqrt{13}t}\right|+C$

$=\frac{1}{6\sqrt{26}}\ln\left|\frac{3\sqrt{2}\sqrt{x^2-6x+4}-\sqrt{13}(x-3)}{3\sqrt{2}\sqrt{x^2-6x+4}+\sqrt{13}(x-3)}\right|+C$

$\therefore$ From (1); $I=\ln\left|t+\sqrt{t^2-5}\right|+I_1$

or $I=\ln\left|(x-3)+\sqrt{x^2-6x+4}\right|$

$+\frac{1}{6\sqrt{26}}\left|\frac{3\sqrt{2}\sqrt{x^2-6x+4}-\sqrt{13}(x-3)}{3\sqrt{2}\sqrt{x^2-6x+4}+\sqrt{13}(x-3)}\right|+C$

(e) $I=\int \frac{1}{x-\sqrt{x^2-1}}dx=\int \frac{1}{x\left(1-\sqrt{1-\frac{1}{x^2}}\right)}dx$

$=\int \frac{x^2dx}{x^3\left(1-\sqrt{1-\frac{1}{x^2}}\right)}$

Let $\frac{1}{x^2}=t$ $\Rightarrow$ $-\frac{2}{x^3}dx=dt$

$$\Rightarrow \quad I=-\frac{1}{2}\int\frac{dt}{t(1-\sqrt{1-t})}$$

Let $1-t=m^2 \quad \Rightarrow \quad -dt=2m\,dm$

$$\Rightarrow \quad I=\int\frac{m\,dm}{(1-m^2)(1-m)}=-\frac{1}{2}\int\frac{(1-m)-(1+m)}{(1-m^2)(1-m)}dm$$

$$=-\frac{1}{2}\left[\int\frac{dm}{1-m^2}-\int\frac{dm}{(1-m)^2}\right]$$

$$=-\frac{1}{2}\left[\frac{1}{2}\ln\left(\frac{1+m}{1-m}\right)-\frac{1}{1-m}\right]+C$$

$$=-\frac{1}{4}\ln\left(\frac{x+\sqrt{x^2-1}}{x-\sqrt{x^2-1}}\right)+\frac{x}{2(x-\sqrt{x^2-1})}+C$$

$$=-\frac{1}{4}\ln\left[\left(\frac{x+\sqrt{x^2-1}}{x-\sqrt{x^2-1}}\right)\left(\frac{x+\sqrt{x^2-1}}{x+\sqrt{x^2-1}}\right)\right]$$

$$+\frac{x(x+\sqrt{x^2-1})}{2(x-\sqrt{x^2-1})(x+\sqrt{x^2-1})}+C$$

$$=-\frac{1}{2}\ln(x+\sqrt{x^2-1})+\frac{x^2}{2}+\frac{x(x+\sqrt{x^2-1})}{2}+C$$

12. (a) $I=\int\frac{(1+\ln x)^m}{x}dx$

$\ln x=t$

$\frac{1}{x}dx=dt$

$$I=\int(1+t)^m\,dt=\frac{(1+t)^{m+1}}{m+1}+C$$

$$=\frac{(1+\ln x)^{m+1}}{m+1}+C;\ \forall m\neq -1$$

for $m=-1$

$I=\int(1+t)^{-1}\,dt$

$=ln\,(1+t)+C=ln\,|(1+ln\,|x|)|+C$

(b) $I=\int\sqrt{\left(\frac{x-a}{b-x}\right)}dx$

Let $x=a\cos^2\theta+b\sin^2\theta$

$\Rightarrow \quad (x-b)=(a-b)\cos^2\theta$

$$\Rightarrow \quad \cos\theta=\sqrt{\frac{x-b}{a-b}}\ ;\ \sin\theta=\sqrt{\frac{a-x}{a-b}}\ ;\ \tan\theta=\sqrt{\frac{a-x}{x-b}}$$

$\therefore \quad dx=2\sin\theta\cos\theta\,(b-a)d\theta$

$$I=\int\sqrt{\frac{(b-a)\sin^2\theta}{(b-a)\cos^2\theta}}2\sin\theta\cos\theta\,(b-a)d\theta$$

$$=2(b-a)\int\sin^2\theta\,d\theta=2(b-a)\int\left(\frac{1-\cos 2\theta}{2}\right)d\theta$$

$$=(b-a)\left[\theta-\frac{\sin 2\theta}{2}\right]+C$$

$$=(b-a)\left[\tan^{-1}\left(\sqrt{\frac{x-a}{b-x}}\right)-\frac{\sqrt{(x-a)(b-x)}}{(b-a)}\right]+C$$

13. (a) $I=\int\frac{dx}{\sin x(2\cos^2 x-1)}$

Let $2\cos^2 x-1=t=1-2\sin^2 x$

$\therefore \quad -4\cos x\sin x\,dx=dt$

$$\Rightarrow \quad I=\int\frac{-4\cos x\sin x\,dx}{-4\cos x\sin^2 x(2\cos^2 x-1)}$$

$$=-\frac{1}{4}\int\frac{dt}{\sqrt{\frac{t+1}{2}}\left(\frac{1-t}{2}\right)(t)}=-\frac{1}{\sqrt{2}}\int\frac{dt}{t(1-t)\sqrt{(t+1)}}$$

Let $t+1=m^2$

$\therefore \quad dt=2m\,dm$

$$I=-\sqrt{2}\int\frac{mdm}{(m^2-1)(2-m^2)m}$$

$$=-\sqrt{2}\int\frac{(m^2-1)+(2-m^2)}{(m^2-1)(2-m^2)}dm$$

$$=-\sqrt{2}\left[\int\frac{dm}{2-m^2}+\int\frac{dm}{m^2-1}\right]$$

$$=-\sqrt{2}\left[\frac{1}{2\sqrt{2}}\ln\left|\frac{\sqrt{2}+m}{\sqrt{2}-m}\right|+\frac{1}{2}\ln\left|\frac{m-1}{m+1}\right|\right]+C$$

$$=-\frac{1}{2}\ln\left|\frac{\sqrt{2}+m}{\sqrt{2}-m}\right|+\frac{1}{\sqrt{2}}\ln\left|\frac{m+1}{m-1}\right|+C$$

$$=-\frac{1}{2}\ln\left|\frac{1+\cos x}{1-\cos x}\right|+\frac{1}{\sqrt{2}}\ln\left(\left|\frac{1+\sqrt{2}\cos x}{1-\sqrt{2}\cos x}\right|\right)+C$$

$(\because\ m=\sqrt{t+1}=\sqrt{2}\cos x)$

(b) $I=\int\frac{t}{\sqrt{1-t^2}}d(\sin^{-1}t)$

$$=\int\frac{t}{\sqrt{1-t^2}}\frac{d}{dt}(\sin^{-1}t)dt=\int\frac{t}{\sqrt{1-t^2}}.\frac{1}{\sqrt{1-t^2}}dt$$

$$=\int\frac{t}{1-t^2}dt=\frac{1}{2}\int\frac{(1+t)-(1-t)}{(1+t)(1-t)}dt$$

$$=\frac{1}{2}\left[\int\frac{dt}{1-t}-\int\frac{dt}{1+t}\right]=-\frac{1}{2}[\ln|1-t|+\ln|1+t|]+C$$

$$=-\ln\sqrt{1-t^2}+C$$

(c) $I=\int\left(x+\frac{1}{x}\right)^{n+5}\left(\frac{x^2-1}{x^2}\right)dx$

Put $x+\frac{1}{x}=t$

$\Rightarrow \quad \frac{x^2-1}{x^2}dx=dt$

$\Rightarrow \quad I=\int t^{n+5}\,dt$

$\Rightarrow \quad I=\frac{t^{n+6}}{n+6}+C$ for $n\neq -6$

$$\Rightarrow \quad I=\frac{1}{(n+6)}\left(x+\frac{1}{x}\right)^{n+6}+C$$

(d) $I = \int \frac{1}{\sqrt{\tan^2\theta + 2}} d(\sqrt{\tan^2\theta - 1})$

Let $\tan^2\theta - 1 = x$

$\Rightarrow \; I = \int \frac{1}{\sqrt{x+3}} \frac{d\sqrt{x}}{dx} dx$

$\Rightarrow \; I = \int \frac{1}{2\sqrt{x}\sqrt{x+3}} dx$

Let $x + 3 = m^2$

$dx = 2m\, dm$

$\Rightarrow \; I = \int \frac{2m\, dm}{2\sqrt{m^2-3}(m)}$

$= \int \frac{dm}{\sqrt{m^2-3}} = \ln|m + \sqrt{m^2-3}| + C$

$= \ln|\sqrt{x} + \sqrt{x+3}| + C$

$= \ln|\sqrt{\tan^2\theta - 1} + \sqrt{\tan^2\theta + 2}| + C$

14. (a) $I = \int \frac{\sqrt{1-\sin x}}{1+\cos x} e^{-\frac{x}{2}} dx$

$= \int \frac{\sqrt{\cos^2\frac{x}{2} + \sin^2\frac{x}{2} - 2\sin\frac{x}{2}\cos\frac{x}{2}}}{1 + 2\cos^2\frac{x}{2} - 1} e^{-\frac{x}{2}} dx$

$= -\frac{1}{2}\int \frac{\sin\frac{x}{2} - \cos\frac{x}{2}}{\cos^2\frac{x}{2}} e^{-\frac{x}{2}} dx$

$= -\frac{1}{2}\left[\int e^{-\frac{x}{2}}\left(-\sec\frac{x}{2} + \tan\frac{x}{2}\sec\frac{x}{2}\right) dx\right]$

$= -e^{-\frac{x}{2}} \sec\frac{x}{2} + C$

(b) $I = \int \left[\ln(\ln x) + \frac{1}{(\ln x)^2}\right] dx$

Put $\ln x = t$

$\frac{1}{x} dx = dt \qquad \Rightarrow \; dx = e^t\, dt$

$\Rightarrow \; I = \int e^t\left(\ln(t) + \frac{1}{t^2}\right) dt = \int e^t\left[\left(\ln t - \frac{1}{t}\right) + \left(\frac{1}{t} + \frac{1}{t^2}\right)\right] dt$

$= e^t\left(\ln t - \frac{1}{t}\right) + C = x\left(\ln(\ln x) - \frac{1}{\ln x}\right) + C$

15. (a) (i) $I = \int \frac{dx}{x^2\sqrt{x^2+a^2}}$

Let $x = \frac{1}{z}$

$\Rightarrow \; dx = -\frac{1}{z^2} dz$

$\Rightarrow \; I = \int \frac{-\frac{1}{z^2} dz}{\frac{1}{z^2}\sqrt{\frac{1}{z^2} + a^2}} = -\int \frac{z dz}{\sqrt{1 + a^2 z^2}}$

Let $1 + a^2 z^2 = m^2$

$\Rightarrow \; 2 z a^2\, dz = 2m\, dm$

$\Rightarrow \; I = -\frac{1}{a^2}\int \frac{m\, dm}{m} = -\frac{m}{a^2} + C$

$= -\frac{\sqrt{1+a^2z^2}}{a^2} + C = -\frac{\sqrt{x^2+a^2}}{a^2 x} + C$

(ii) $I = \int \frac{dx}{x^2\sqrt{x^2+a^2}}$

Let $x = a\tan z$

$\Rightarrow \; \sin z = \frac{x}{\sqrt{x^2+a^2}}$

$\Rightarrow \; dx = a\sec^2 z\, dz$

$\Rightarrow \; I = \int \frac{a\sec^2 z\, dz}{a^2\tan^2 z\, a\sec z} = \frac{1}{a^2}\int \frac{\cos z\, dz}{\sin^2 z}$

Let $\sin z = t$

$\Rightarrow \; \cos z\, dz = dt$

$\Rightarrow \; I = \frac{1}{a^2}\int \frac{dt}{t^2} = -\frac{1}{a^2}\frac{1}{t} + C = -\frac{1}{a^2}\frac{1}{\sin z} + C$

$= -\frac{\sqrt{x^2+a^2}}{a^2 x} + C$

(b) (i) $I = \int \frac{x^2 dx}{\sqrt{a^2-x^2}}$

Let $x = a\sin z$

$dx = a\cos z\, dz$

$\Rightarrow \; I = \int \frac{a^2\sin^2 z\, a\cos z}{a\cos z} dz$

$\Rightarrow \; I = a^2\int \sin^2 z\, dz = a^2\int \frac{1-\cos 2z}{2} dz$

$= a^2\frac{z}{2} - \frac{a^2}{4}\sin 2z + C = \frac{a^2 z}{2} - \frac{a^2\sin 2z}{4} + C$

$= \frac{a^2}{2}\sin^{-1}\frac{x}{a} - \frac{a^2}{4}\cdot 2\cdot\frac{x}{a}\frac{\sqrt{a^2-x^2}}{a} + C$

$= \frac{a^2}{2}\sin^{-1}\frac{x}{a} - \frac{x}{2}\sqrt{a^2-x^2} + C$

Aliter: Let $x = a\cos z$

$dx = -a\sin z\, dz$

$\Rightarrow \; I = \int \frac{a^2\cos^2 z(-a)\sin z\, dz}{a\sin z}$

$= -a^2\int \cos^2 z\, dz = -a^2\int \frac{1+\cos 2z}{2} dz$

$$= -\frac{a^2 z}{2} - \frac{a^2}{4}\sin 2z + C$$

$$= -\frac{a^2}{2}\cos^{-1}\frac{x}{a} - \frac{a^2}{4}\cdot 2\cdot\frac{x}{a}\cdot\frac{\sqrt{a^2-x^2}}{a} + C$$

$$= -\frac{a^2}{2}\left(\frac{\pi}{2} - \sin^{-1}\frac{\pi}{a}\right) - \frac{x}{2}\sqrt{a^2-x^2} + C$$

$$= \frac{a^2}{2}\sin^{-1}\frac{x}{a} - \frac{x}{2}\sqrt{a^2-x^2} + C_1$$

(ii) $I = \int \frac{x^2 dx}{\sqrt{a^2-x^2}}$

Let $x = \frac{1}{z}$

$\Rightarrow \quad dx = -\frac{1}{z^2}dz$

$$\Rightarrow \quad I = \int \frac{1}{z^2}\left(-\frac{1}{z^2}\right)\frac{dz}{\sqrt{a^2-\frac{1}{z^2}}}$$

$$= -\int \frac{1}{z^4}\frac{dz}{\sqrt{a^2-\frac{1}{z^2}}}$$

Let $a^2 - \frac{1}{z^2} = m^2$

$\Rightarrow \quad z = \frac{1}{\sqrt{a^2-m^2}}$

$\Rightarrow \quad \frac{dz}{z^3} = m\,dm$

$$\Rightarrow \quad I = -\int \frac{m\,dm}{\frac{1}{\sqrt{a^2-m^2}}m} = -\int \sqrt{a^2-m^2}\,dm$$

$$= -\frac{m\sqrt{a^2-m^2}}{2} - \frac{a^2}{2}\sin^{-1}\left(\frac{m}{a}\right) + C$$

$$= -\frac{x}{2}\sqrt{a^2-x^2} - \frac{a^2}{2}\sin^{-1}\left(\frac{\sqrt{a^2-x^2}}{a}\right) + C$$

$$= -\frac{x}{2}\sqrt{a^2-x^2} - \frac{a^2}{2}\cos^{-1}\frac{x}{a} + C$$

$$= -\frac{x}{a}\sqrt{a^2-x^2} - \frac{a^2}{2}\left(\frac{\pi}{2} - \sin^{-1}\frac{x}{a}\right) + C$$

$$= \frac{a^2}{2}\sin^{-1}\frac{x}{a} - \frac{x}{a}\sqrt{a^2-x^2} + C$$

(c) (i) $I = \int \frac{dx}{x\sqrt{x^2-a^2}}$

Let $x = \frac{1}{z}$

$\Rightarrow \quad dx = -\frac{1}{z^2}dz$

$$I = \int\left(-\frac{1}{z^2}\right)\frac{dz}{\left(\frac{1}{z}\right)\sqrt{\frac{1}{z^2}-a^2}}$$

$$= -\int \frac{1}{z}\frac{dz}{\sqrt{\frac{1}{z^2}-a^2}} = -\int \frac{dz}{\sqrt{1-a^2z^2}}$$

$$= -\frac{1}{a}\int \frac{dz}{\sqrt{\frac{1}{a^2}-z^2}} = -\frac{1}{a}\sin^{-1}(az) + C$$

$$= -\frac{1}{a}\sin^{-1}\left(\frac{a}{x}\right) + C$$

(ii) $I = \int \frac{dx}{x\sqrt{x^2-a^2}}$

Let $x = \frac{a}{\cos z}$

$\Rightarrow \quad dx = \frac{a}{(\cos z)^2}\sin z\,dz$

$$\Rightarrow \quad I = \int \frac{a}{(\cos z)^2}\frac{\sin z\,dz}{\frac{a}{\cos z}\sqrt{\frac{a^2}{\cos^2 z}-a^2}} = \int \frac{\sin z\,dz}{a\sin z} = \frac{z}{a} + C$$

$$= \frac{1}{a}\cos^{-1}\frac{a}{x} + C = \frac{1}{a}\left(\frac{\pi}{2} - \sin^{-1}\frac{a}{x}\right) + C$$

$$= -\frac{1}{a}\sin^{-1}\frac{a}{x} + C_1$$

16. (a) $I = \int[(x^2-1)(x+1)]^{-2/3}\,dx$

Let $u = \frac{1}{x+1}$

$\Rightarrow \quad x = \frac{1}{u} - 1$

$\Rightarrow \quad dx = -\frac{1}{u^2}dt$

$\Rightarrow \quad I = \int[(x-1)(x+1)^2]^{-2/3}\,dx$

$$= \int\left[\left(\frac{1}{u}-2\right)\frac{1}{u^2}\right]^{-\frac{2}{3}} - \frac{1}{u^2}du = -\int(1-2u)^{-2/3}\,\text{du}$$

$$= -\int \frac{du}{\sqrt[3]{(1-2u)^2}} = -\frac{1}{4^{1/3}}\int \frac{du}{\sqrt[3]{\left(\frac{1}{2}-u\right)^2}}$$

Let $\frac{1}{2} - u = m^3$

$\Rightarrow du = -3m^2\,dm$

$$\Rightarrow \quad I = -\frac{1}{4^{1/3}}\int \frac{-3m^2\,dm}{m^2} = \frac{3}{4^{1/3}}\int dm = \frac{3}{4^{1/3}}m + C$$

$$= \frac{3}{4^{1/3}}\left(\frac{1}{2}-u\right)^{1/3} + C$$

$$= \frac{3}{4^{1/3}}\left(\frac{1}{2}-\frac{1}{x+1}\right)^{1/3} + C = \frac{3}{2}\left(\frac{x-1}{x+1}\right)^{1/3} + C$$

(b) $I = \int[(x^2-1)(x+1)]^{-2/3}\,dx$

Let $u = \left(\frac{x-1}{x+1}\right)^k \Rightarrow u^{1/k} = \frac{x-1}{x+1}$

$\Rightarrow x = \frac{1+u^{1/k}}{1-u^{1/k}}$

$\Rightarrow dx = \frac{\left(1-u^{\frac{1}{k}}\right)\cdot\frac{1}{k}\cdot u^{\left(\frac{1}{k}-1\right)} + \left(1+u^{\frac{1}{k}}\right)\cdot\frac{1}{k}\cdot u^{\left(\frac{1}{k}-1\right)}}{\left(1-u^{\frac{1}{k}}\right)^2}du$

$= \frac{2}{k}\frac{u^{\left(\frac{1}{k}-1\right)}}{(1-u^{\frac{1}{k}})^2}du$

$\Rightarrow I = \int[(x-1)(x+1)^2]^{-2/3}\,dx$

$\Rightarrow (x-1)(x+1)^2 = \left(\frac{1+u^{\frac{1}{k}}}{1-u^{\frac{1}{k}}}-1\right)\left(\frac{1+u^{\frac{1}{k}}}{1-u^{\frac{1}{k}}}+1\right)^2$

$= \left(\frac{2u^{\frac{1}{k}}}{1-u^{\frac{1}{k}}}\right)\left(\frac{2}{1-u^{1/k}}\right)^2 = \frac{8u^{\frac{1}{k}}}{(1-u^{\frac{1}{k}})^3}$

$\therefore\ I = \int\left[\frac{8u^{\frac{1}{k}}}{(1-u^{\frac{1}{k}})^3}\right]^{-\frac{2}{3}}\frac{2}{k}\frac{u^{\frac{1}{k}-1}}{(1-u^{\frac{1}{k}})^2}du$

$= \frac{1}{2k}\int u^{\left(\frac{1}{3k}-1\right)}du = \frac{3k}{2k}u^{\frac{1}{3k}} + C$

$= \frac{3}{2}u^{\frac{1}{3k}} + C\ ;\ u = \left(\frac{x-1}{x+1}\right)^k$

$\therefore\ I = \frac{3}{2}\left(\frac{x-1}{x+1}\right)^{\frac{1}{3}} + C$

$\therefore$ It is independent of value of k.

(c) $I = \int\left((x^2-1)(x+1)\right)^{-2/3}dx\ ;\ u = \tan^{-1}x$

Put $u = \tan^{-1}x$ or $\tan u = x$

$\Rightarrow du = \frac{1}{(1+x^2)}dx$

$\Rightarrow I = \int\left((\tan^2 u-1)(\tan u+1)\right)^{-2/3}.\left(1+\tan^2 u\right)du$

$= \int(\tan u+1)^{-4/3}(\tan u-1)^{-2/3}\left(1+\tan^2 u\right)du$

$= \int\frac{(\sin u+\cos u)^{-4/3}}{(\cos u)^{-4/3}}\frac{(\sin u-\cos u)^{-2/3}}{(\cos u)^{-2/3}}\left(\frac{1}{\cos^2 u}\right)du$

$= \int(\sin u+\cos u)^{-4/3}(\sin u-\cos u)^{-2/3}du$

$= \int\frac{1}{(\sin u+\cos u)^{4/3}(\sin u-\cos u)^{2/3}}du$

$= \int\frac{(\sin u+\cos u)^{2/3}}{(\sin u+\cos u)^2(\sin u-\cos u)^{2/3}}du$

$= \int\frac{\left(\frac{\sin u-\cos u}{\sin u+\cos u}\right)^{-2/3}}{(\sin u+\cos u)^2}du$

Put $\frac{\sin u-\cos u}{\sin u+\cos u} = t$

$\Rightarrow \frac{(\sin u+\cos u)(\cos u+\sin u)-(\sin u-\cos u)(\cos u-\sin u)}{(\sin u+\cos u)^2}du = dt$

$\Rightarrow \frac{(\sin u+\cos u)^2+(\cos u-\sin u)^2}{(\sin u+\cos u)^2}du = dt$

$\Rightarrow \frac{2}{(\sin u+\cos u)^2}du = dt$

$\Rightarrow I = \int\frac{1}{2}(t)^{-2/3}dt = \frac{1}{2}\frac{(t)^{1/3}}{1/3}+C = \frac{3}{2}t^{1/3}+C$

$= \frac{3}{2}\left(\frac{\sin u-\cos u}{\sin u+\cos u}\right)^{1/3}+C$

$\Rightarrow I = \frac{3}{2}\left(\frac{\tan u-1}{\tan u+1}\right)^{1/3}+C = \frac{3}{2}\left(\frac{x-1}{x+1}\right)^{1/3}+C$

(d) $\int\left((x^2-1)(x+1)\right)^{-2/3}dx$

Put $u = \tan^{-1}\sqrt{x} \Rightarrow du = \frac{1}{1+x}.\frac{1}{2\sqrt{x}}dx$

$\Rightarrow \int(\tan^4 u-1)(\tan^2 u+1)^{-2/3}(1+\tan^2 u)(2\tan u)du$

$= \int(\tan^2 u+1)^{4/3}(\tan^2 u-1)(2\tan u)du$

$= \int 2(\tan^3 u-\tan u).(\tan^2 u+1)^{1/3}.\sec^2 u\,du$

Put $\tan u = z \Rightarrow \sec^2 u\,du = dz$

$= \int 2(z^3-z)(1+z^2)^{1/3}dz = 2\int z(z^2-1)(1+z^2)^{1/3}dz$

Put $1+z^2 = t^3 \Rightarrow 2z\,dz = 3t^2\,dt$

$\therefore\ I = \int(t^3-2)(t)(3t^2\,dt) = \int(3t^6-6t^3)dt$

$= \frac{3t^7}{7}-\frac{6t^4}{4}+C = \frac{3}{7}(1+z^2)^{7/3}-\frac{3}{2}(1+z^2)^{4/3}+C$

$= \frac{3}{7}(\sec^2 u)^{7/3}-\frac{3}{2}(\sec^2 u)^{4/3}+C$

$= \frac{3}{7}(1+x)^{7/3}-\frac{3}{2}(1+x)^{4/3}+C$

(e) $I = \int\left((x^2-1)(x+1)\right)^{-2/3}dx$

Put $u = \cos^{-1}x \Rightarrow \cos u = x$

$\Rightarrow -\sin u\,du = dx$

$\therefore\ I = \int\left(\cos^2 u-1\right)\left(\cos u+1\right)^{-2/3}.(-\sin u\,du)$

$= \int\sin^3 u\left(1+\cos u\right)^{-2/3}du$

$= \int(1-\cos^2 u)(1+\cos u)^{-2/3}.\sin u\,du$

$= \int(1-\cos u)(1+\cos u)^{1/3}\sin u\,du$

$= \int(1+\cos u)^{1/3}\sin u\,du - \int\cos u(1+\cos u)^{1/3}\sin u\,du$

$= \int(1+\cos u)^{1/3}\sin u\,du$

$$-\int(1+\cos u-1)(1+\cos u)^{1/3}\sin u\,du$$

$$=2\int(1+\cos u)^{1/3}\sin u\,du-\int(1+\cos u)^{4/3}\sin u\,du$$

$$=2\left[-\frac{(1+\cos u)^{4/3}}{4/3}\right]-\left[-\frac{(1+\cos u)^{7/3}}{7/3}\right]+C$$

$$=-\frac{3}{2}(1+\cos u)^{4/3}+\frac{3}{7}(1+\cos u)^{7/3}+C$$

$$=-\frac{3}{2}(1+x)^{4/3}+\frac{3}{7}(1+x)^{7/3}+C$$

TEXTUAL EXERCISE–3: (OBJECTIVE)

1. (b) $I=\int 3x^2\sec^5 x^3\tan x^3\,dx$

Let $\sec x^3=t$

$\therefore\ \sec x^3\tan x^3\,3x^2\,dx=dt$

$\therefore\ I=\int(\sec^4 x^3)(3x^2\sec x^3\tan x^3\,dx)$

$$=\int t^4dt=\frac{t^5}{5}+C=\frac{\sec^5 x^3}{5}+C$$

2. (a) $I=\int\cos x\,e^{\cos 2x}\frac{d\cos x}{dx}dx$

$=-\int\sin x\cos x\,e^{\cos 2x}\,dx$

$$=-\frac{1}{2}\int\sin 2x\,e^{(\cos 2x)}dx$$

$\cos 2x=t$ –(sin 2x) (2) $dx=dt$

$$=-\frac{1}{4}\int e^{(t)}dt=\frac{e^t}{4}+C=\frac{e^{\cos 2x}}{4}+C$$

3. (c) $I=\int\frac{1+\log x}{\sqrt{(x^x)^2-1}}dx$

Let $xx=t$

$\Rightarrow\ xx(1+\log x)\,dx=dt$

$$\Rightarrow\ I=\int\frac{dt}{t\sqrt{t^2-1}}=\sec^{-1}t+C=\sec^{-1}(x^x)+C$$

4. (b) $I=\int\frac{f(x)\phi'(x)+\phi(x)f'(x)}{(f(x)\phi(x)+1)\sqrt{f(x)\phi(x)-1}}dx$

Put $f(x)\,f(x)=t$

$\Rightarrow\ [f(x)\,f'(x)+f(x)\,f'(x)]\,dx=dt$

$\Rightarrow\ I=\int\frac{dt}{(t+1)\sqrt{(t-1)}}$; Let $(t-1)=m^2$

$\Rightarrow\ dt=2m\,dm$

$$\Rightarrow\ I=\int\frac{2m\,dm}{(m^2+2)m}=2\int\frac{dm}{m^2+2}=\sqrt{2}\tan^{-1}\left(\frac{m}{\sqrt{2}}\right)+C$$

$$\Rightarrow\ I=\sqrt{2}\tan^{-1}\left[\frac{\sqrt{(f(x)\phi(x)-1)}}{\sqrt{2}}\right]+C$$

5. (a) $I=\int\left[\ln(\ln x)+\frac{1}{(\ln x)^2}\right]dx$

Put $\ln x=t$ $\Rightarrow$ $\frac{1}{x}dx=dt$

$\Rightarrow\ dx=e^t\,dt$

$$\Rightarrow\ I=\int e^t\left(\ln t+\frac{1}{t^2}\right)dt=\int e^t\left[\left(\ln t-\frac{1}{t}\right)+\left(\frac{1}{t}+\frac{1}{t^2}\right)\right]dt$$

$$=e^t\ln t-\frac{e^t}{t}+C=e^t\left(\ln t-\frac{1}{t}\right)+C$$

$$=x\left(\ln(\ln x)-\frac{1}{\ln x}\right)+C$$

6. (a) $I=\int\frac{1}{x+\sqrt{x^2+2}}dx$

Let $x+\sqrt{x^2+2}=t$

$\Rightarrow\ x^2+2=(t-x)^2=t^2+x^2-2tx$

$$x=\frac{t^2-2}{2t}\quad\Rightarrow\quad dx=\left(\frac{1}{2}+\frac{1}{t^2}\right)dt=\frac{t^2+2}{2t^2}dt$$

$$\Rightarrow\ I=\int\frac{1}{t}\cdot\frac{(t^2+2)}{(2t^2)}dt=\frac{1}{2}\left[\int\frac{dt}{t}+2\int\frac{dt}{t^3}\right]$$

$$=\frac{1}{2}\ln t-\frac{1}{2t^2}+C$$

$$=\frac{1}{2}\ln|x+\sqrt{x^2+2}|-\frac{1}{2}\left(\frac{1}{x+\sqrt{x^2+2}}\right)^2+C$$

$$\text{Now, }\left(\frac{1}{x+\sqrt{x^2+2}}\cdot\frac{x-\sqrt{x^2+2}}{x-\sqrt{x^2+2}}\right)^2$$

$$=\frac{1}{4}(x^2+x^2+2-2x\sqrt{x^2+2})=\frac{1}{2}(x^2+1-x\sqrt{x^2+2})$$

$$\therefore\ I=\frac{1}{2}\ln|x+\sqrt{x^2+2}|-\frac{1}{4}(x^2+1-x\sqrt{x^2+2})+C$$

$$=-\frac{x^2}{4}+\frac{1}{4}(x\sqrt{x^2+2}+2\ln|x+\sqrt{x^2+2}|)+C$$

7. (a) $I=\int\frac{1}{1+\tan x+\tan^2 x}dx$

$$=\int\frac{\cos^2 x}{1+\sin x\cos x}dx=\frac{1}{2}\int\frac{1+\cos 2x}{1+\frac{1}{2}\sin 2x}dx$$

$$=\int\frac{1}{2+\sin 2x}dx+\int\frac{\cos 2x}{2+\sin 2x}dx$$

$$=\int\frac{1}{2+\frac{2\tan x}{1+\tan^2 x}}dx+\frac{1}{2}\ln(2+\sin 2x)+C$$

$$=\int\frac{\sec^2 x}{2(1+\tan x+\tan^2 x)}dx+\frac{1}{2}\ln(2+\sin 2x)+C$$

Let $\tan x=t$ $\Rightarrow$ $\sec^2 x\,dx=dt$

$$I=\frac{1}{2}\int\frac{dt}{1+t+t^2}+\frac{1}{2}\ln(2+\sin 2x)+C$$

$$I_1=\int\frac{dt}{1+t+t^2}=\int\frac{dt}{\left(t+\frac{1}{2}\right)^2+\left(\frac{\sqrt{3}}{2}\right)^2}$$

$$=\frac{2}{\sqrt{3}}\tan^{-1}\left(\frac{2t+1}{\sqrt{3}}\right)$$

$\therefore \quad I=\frac{1}{\sqrt{3}}\tan^{-1}\left(\frac{2\tan x+1}{\sqrt{3}}\right)+\frac{1}{2}\ln(2+\sin 2x)+C$

8. (c) $I=\int\frac{x^2-2\,dx}{(x^4+5x^2+4)\tan^{-1}\left(\frac{x^2+2}{x}\right)}$

Let $\tan^{-1}\left(\frac{x^2+2}{x}\right)=t$

$\therefore \quad \frac{1-\frac{2}{x^2}}{1+\left(\frac{x^2+2}{x}\right)^2}dx=dt$

$\Rightarrow \quad \frac{x^2-2}{x^2+5x^2+4}dx=dt$

$\Rightarrow \quad I=\int\frac{dt}{t}=\ln|t|+C=\ln\left|\tan^{-1}\left(\frac{x^2+2}{x}\right)\right|+C$

9. (b) $I=\int\frac{x\cos x\log x-\sin x}{x(\log x)^2}dx$

Let $\frac{\sin x}{\log x}=t \quad \Rightarrow \quad \left[\frac{\cos x}{\log x}-\frac{\sin x}{x(\log x)^2}\right]dx=dt$

$\Rightarrow \quad \frac{x\cos x\log x-\sin x}{x(\log x)^2}dx=dt$

$\therefore \quad I=\int dt=t+C=\frac{\sin x}{\log x}+C$

TEXTUAL EXERCISE–4: (SUBJECTIVE)

1. (a) $I=\int\underbrace{x^3}_{II}\underbrace{\ln x}_{I}dx=\ln x\int x^3dx-\int\frac{1}{x}\left(\int x^3dx\right)dx$

$=(\ln x)\frac{x^4}{4}-\int\frac{x^3}{4}dx=\frac{x^4}{4}\left(\ln x-\frac{1}{4}\right)+C$

(b) $I=\int\underbrace{\ln x}_{I}\underbrace{\frac{1}{x^2}}_{II}dx=\ln x\int\frac{1}{x^2}dx-\int\frac{1}{x}\left(\int\frac{1}{x^2}dx\right)dx$

$=-\frac{\ln x}{x}+\int\frac{1}{x^2}dx=-\frac{1}{x}(\ln x+1)+C$

(c) $I=\int\underbrace{(3x^3-17)}_{I}\underbrace{e^{2x}}_{II}dx$

$=(3x^3-17)\int e^2x\,dx-\int(9x^2)\left(\int e^2x\,dx\right)dx$

$=(3x^3-17)\frac{e^{2x}}{2}-\int\underbrace{\frac{9}{2}x^2}_{I}.\underbrace{e^{2x}}_{II}dx$

$=(3x^2-17)\frac{e^{2x}}{2}-\frac{9}{2}\left[x^2\int e^{2x}dx-\int(2x)\frac{e^{2x}}{2}dx\right]$

$=(3x^3-17)\frac{e^{2x}}{2}-\frac{9}{4}x^2e^{2x}+\frac{9}{2}\int\underbrace{x}_{I}\underbrace{e^{2x}}_{II}dx$

$=(3x^3-17)\frac{e^{2x}}{2}-\frac{9}{4}x^2e^{2x}+\frac{9}{2}\left[\frac{xe^{2x}}{2}-\frac{e^{2x}}{4}\right]+C$

$=e^{2x}\left(\frac{3x^3}{2}-\frac{9}{4}x^2+\frac{9}{4}x-\frac{77}{8}\right)+C$

(d) $I=\int\underbrace{x}_{I}.\underbrace{\sin^{-1}x}_{II}dx=\frac{x^2}{2}\sin^{-1}x-\frac{1}{2}\underbrace{\int\frac{x^2}{\sqrt{1-x^2}}dx}_{I_1}$

$I_1=\int\frac{x^2}{\sqrt{1-x^2}}dx=\int\frac{dx}{\sqrt{1-x^2}}-\int\underbrace{\sqrt{1-x^2}}_{I}dx$

$=\sin^{-1}x-\left[\sqrt{1-x^2}.x+\int\frac{x^2}{\sqrt{1-x^2}}dx\right]$

$=\sin^{-1}x-x\sqrt{1-x^2}-I_1$

$2I_1=\sin^{-1}x-x\sqrt{1-x^2}$

$I_1=\frac{1}{2}\sin^{-1}x-\frac{x}{2}\sqrt{1-x^2}$

$I=\frac{x^2}{2}\sin^{-1}x-\frac{1}{4}\sin^{-1}x+\frac{x}{4}\sqrt{1-x^2}+C$

$=\frac{1}{4}[x\sqrt{1-x^2}+(2x^2-1)\sin^{-1}x]+C$

(e) $I=\int\underbrace{x^3}_{I}\underbrace{e^x}_{II}dx=x^3e^x-3\int\underbrace{x^2}_{I}.\underbrace{e^x}_{II}dx$

$=x^3e^x-3[x^2e^x-2\int\underbrace{x}_{I}.\underbrace{e^x}_{II}dx]$

$=x^3\,ex-3x^2\,ex+6\,[xex-e^x]+C$

$=ex\,[x^3-3x^2+6x-6]+C$

(f) $I=\int\underbrace{x^3}_{I}.\underbrace{\sin x}_{II}dx$

$=-x^3\cos x-\int 3x^3(-\cos x)\,dx=-x^3\cos x+3\int\underbrace{x^2}_{I}.\underbrace{\cos x}_{II}dx$

$=-x^3\cos x+3\left[x^2\sin x-\int\underbrace{2x}_{I}.\underbrace{\sin x}_{II}dx\right]$

$=-x^3\cos x+3x^2\sin x-6[-x\cos x-\int-\cos x\,dx]$

$=-x^3\cos x+3x^2\sin x+6x\cos x-6\sin x+C$

(g) $I=\int x^2\cos^2x\,dx=\frac{1}{2}\int x^2(1+\cos 2x)dx$

$=\int\frac{x^2}{2}dx+\frac{1}{2}\int\underbrace{x^2}_{I}.\underbrace{\cos 2x}_{II}dx$

$=\frac{x^3}{6}+\frac{1}{2}\left[\frac{x^2\sin 2x}{2}-\int\underbrace{2x}_{I}.\underbrace{\frac{\sin 2x}{2}}_{II}dx\right]$

$=\frac{x^3}{6}+\frac{x^2}{4}\sin 2x-\frac{1}{2}\left[\frac{x(-\cos 2x)}{2}-\int\frac{(-\cos 2x)}{2}dx\right]$

$=\frac{x^3}{6}+\frac{x^2}{4}\sin 2x+\frac{x}{4}\cos 2x-\frac{\sin 2x}{8}+C$

2. (a) $I=\int\frac{dx}{(x^4-1)^2}$

Let take $I_1=\int\frac{dx}{x^4-1}=\frac{1}{x^4-1}x-\int\frac{(-1)4x^3}{(x^4-1)^2}x\,dx$

$$I_1=\frac{x}{x^4-1}+4\int\frac{x^4-1+1}{(x^4-1)}dx$$

$$=\frac{x}{x^4-1}+4\int\frac{dx}{(x^4-1)}+4\int\frac{dx}{(x^4-1)^2}$$

$$I_1=\frac{x}{x^4-1}+4I_1+4I$$

$$4I=\frac{-x}{x^4-1}-3I_1$$

Also $I_1=\int\frac{dx}{x^4-1}=\int\frac{dx}{(x^2+1)(x^2-1)}$

$$=\frac{1}{2}\int\frac{(x^2+1)-(x^2-1)}{(x^2+1)(x^2-1)}dx$$

$$=\frac{1}{2}\int\frac{dx}{x^2-1}-\frac{1}{2}\int\frac{dx}{x^2+1}=\frac{1}{4}\ln\left(\frac{x-1}{x+1}\right)-\frac{1}{2}\tan^{-1}x+C$$

$$\therefore\quad I=-\frac{1}{4}\left(\frac{x}{x^4-1}\right)-\frac{3}{16}\ln\left(\frac{x-1}{x+1}\right)+\frac{3}{8}\tan^{-1}x+C$$

(b) $I=\int x\ln(1+x^2)dx$

Let $x^2=t \quad\Rightarrow\quad 2x\,dx=dt$

$$\Rightarrow\quad I=\frac{1}{2}\int\underset{I}{\ln(1+t)}\,dt=\frac{1}{2}\left[t\ln(1+t)-\int\frac{t}{1+t}dt\right]$$

$$=\frac{1}{2}t\ln(1+t)-\frac{1}{2}\int\frac{t+1-1}{1+t}dt$$

$$=\frac{1}{2}t\ln(1+t)-\frac{t}{2}+\frac{1}{2}\ln(1+t)+C$$

$$=\frac{1}{2}[[\ln(1+t)](t+1)-t]+C$$

$$=\frac{1}{2}[(1+x^2)\ln(1+x^2)-x^2]+C$$

3. $I=\int e^{f(x)}\left[xf'(x)+\frac{f''(x)}{(f'(x))^2}\right]dx$

$$=\int\underbrace{xe^{f(x)}}_{I}.\underbrace{f'(x)}_{II}dx+\int\frac{e^{f(x)}f''(x)dx}{(f'(x))^2}dx$$

$$=x\,e^{f(x)}-\int e^{f(x)}\,dx+e^{f(x)}\int\frac{f''(x)}{f'(x)^2}dx$$

$$-\int e^{f(x)}f'(x)\left[\int\frac{f''(x)}{(f'(x))^2}dx\right]dx$$

$$=xe^{f(x)}-\int e^{f(x)}dx-\frac{e^{f(x)}}{f'(x)}+\int e^{f(x)}\frac{f'(x)}{f'(x)}dx+C$$

$$=e^{f(x)}\left(x-\frac{1}{f'(x)}\right)+C=\text{RHS}$$

4. (a) $I=\int x\tan^2x\,dx=\int x(\sec^2x-1)\,dx=\int\underset{I}{x}.\underbrace{\sec xdx}_{II}\quad\int x\,dx$

$$=x\tan x-\int\tan x\,dx-\frac{x^2}{2}=x\tan x-\ln|\sec x|-\frac{x^2}{2}+C$$

$$=x\tan x+\ln|\cos x|-\frac{x^2}{2}+C$$

(b) $I=\int x\cos^2x\,dx=\frac{1}{2}\int x(1+\cos 2x)dx$

$$=\int\frac{x}{2}dx+\int\frac{x\cos 2x}{2}dx=\frac{x^2}{4}+\frac{1}{2}\left[x\frac{\sin 2x}{2}-\int(1)\frac{\sin 2x}{2}dx\right]$$

$$=\frac{x^2}{4}+\frac{x}{4}\sin 2x+\frac{1}{8}\cos 2x+C$$

(c) $I=\int\frac{\ln x}{x^3}dx=\int\underset{I}{\ln x}.\underset{II}{\frac{1}{x^3}}dx$

$$=\ln x\left(-\frac{1}{2x^2}\right)-\int\frac{1}{x}\left(-\frac{1}{2x^2}\right)dx$$

$$=-\frac{1}{2x^2}\ln x+\frac{1}{2}\int\frac{dx}{x^3}=-\frac{1}{2x^2}\ln x-\frac{1}{4x^2}+C$$

$$=-\frac{1}{4x^2}(2\ln x+1)+C$$

$$=-\frac{1}{4x^2}(\ln x+2)+C=-\frac{2}{x^2}\ln(xe^2)+C$$

$$=-\frac{1}{4x^2}(\ln x^2e)+C$$

(d) $I=\int\underset{I}{\ln(x^2+1)}dx=\ln(x^2+1)x-\int\frac{2x^2}{x^2+1}dx$

$$=\ln(x^2+1)-2\left[\int dx-\int\frac{dx}{x^2+1}\right]$$

$$=x\ln(x^2+1)-2x+2\tan^{-1}x+C$$

5. (a) $I=\int(\sin^{-1}x)^2dx=x(\sin^{-1}x)^2-\int\frac{2x\sin^{-1}x}{\sqrt{1-x^2}}dx$

$$\Rightarrow\quad I_1=\int x\frac{\sin^{-1}x}{\sqrt{1-x^2}}dx=-\int\underset{I}{\sin^{-1}x}.\underbrace{\frac{(-x)}{\sqrt{1-x^2}}}_{II}dx$$

$$=-\left[(\sin^{-1}x)\sqrt{1-x^2}-\int\frac{1}{\sqrt{1-x^2}}\sqrt{1-x^2}\,dx\right]$$

$$=-(\sin^{-1}x)\sqrt{1-x^2}+x+C$$

$$\Rightarrow\quad I=x(\sin^{-1}x)^2+2\sqrt{1-x^2}\sin^{-1}x-2x+C$$

(b) $I=\int\underbrace{(\tan^{-1}x)^2}_{I}.\underset{II}{x}dx=(\tan^{-1}x)^2\frac{x^2}{2}-\int\frac{2\tan^{-1}x}{1+x^2}\frac{x^2}{2}dx$

Let $I_1 = \int \underbrace{\frac{x^2}{1+x^2}}_{I} . \underbrace{\tan^{-1} x}_{II} dx$

$= \tan^{-1} x(x - \tan^{-1} x) - \int \frac{(x - \tan^{-1} x)}{x^2+1} dx$

$= x\tan^{-1} x - (\tan^{-1} x)^2 - \frac{1}{2}\ln(x^2+1) + \int \frac{\tan^{-1} x}{x^2+1} dx$

$= x\tan^{-1} x - (\tan^{-1} x)^2 - \frac{1}{2}\ln(x^2+1) + \frac{(\tan^{-1} x)^2}{2} + C$

$I = (\tan^{-1} x)^2 \frac{x^2}{2} - x\tan^{-1} x + (\tan^{-1} x)^2$

$+ \frac{1}{2}\ln(x^2+1) - \frac{(\tan^{-1} x)^2}{2} + C$

$= (\tan^{-1} x)^2 \frac{x^2+1}{2} - x\tan^{-1} x + \frac{1}{2}\ln(1+x^2) + C$

(c) $I = \int e^3x\,(\sin 2x - \cos 2x)\,dx$

$= \int \underbrace{e^{3x}}_{II} . \underbrace{\sin 2x}_{I} dx - \int \underbrace{e^{3x}}_{II} . \underbrace{\cos 2x}_{II} dx$

$= \sin 2x \frac{e^{3x}}{3} - 2\int \cos 2x \frac{e^{3x}}{3} dx$

$-\left[\cos 2x \frac{e^{3x}}{3} + 2\int \sin 2x \frac{e^{3x}}{3} dx\right]$

$= (\sin 2x - \cos 2x)\frac{e^{3x}}{3}$

$-\frac{2}{3}[\int \underbrace{\cos 2x}_{I} . \underbrace{e^{3x}}_{II} dx + \int \underbrace{\sin 2x}_{I} . \underbrace{e^{3x}}_{II} dx]$

$= (\sin 2x - \cos 2x)\frac{e^{3x}}{3} -$

$\frac{2}{3}\left[\cos 2x \frac{e^{3x}}{3} + \frac{2}{3}\int \sin 2x e^{3x} dx + \right.$

$\left. \sin 2x \frac{e^{3x}}{3} - \frac{2}{3}\int \cos 2x e^{3x} dx\right]$

$= \frac{e^{3x}}{3}(\sin 2x - \cos 2x) - \frac{2}{9}e^{3x}(\sin 2x + \cos 2x) - \frac{4}{9}I$

$\frac{13}{9}I = \frac{e^{3x}}{9}(3\sin 2x - 3\cos 2x - 2\sin 2x - 2\cos 2x) + C$

$\Rightarrow \quad I = \frac{e^{3x}}{13}(\sin 2x - 5\cos 2x) + C$

6. (a) $I = \int \frac{x^3}{\sqrt{1+x^2}} dx = \int \underbrace{x^2}_{I} . \underbrace{\frac{x}{\sqrt{1+x^2}}}_{II} dx$

$= x^2\sqrt{1+x^2} - \int 2x\sqrt{1+x^2}\,dx$

$= x^2\sqrt{1+x^2} - \frac{2}{3}(1+x^2)^{\frac{3}{2}} + C$

$= \sqrt{1+x^2}\left(x^2 - \frac{2}{3}(1+x^2)\right) + C = \sqrt{1+x^2}\,\frac{(x^2-2)}{3} + C$

(b) $I = \int \frac{x^2}{\sqrt{1-x^2}} dx = \int \underbrace{(-x)}_{I} . \underbrace{\left(\frac{-x}{\sqrt{1-x^2}}\right)}_{II} dx$

$= (-x)\sqrt{1-x^2} - \int (-1)\sqrt{1-x^2}\,dx$

$= -x\sqrt{1-x^2} + \frac{x\sqrt{1-x^2}}{2} + \frac{1}{2}\sin^{-1} x + C$

$= -\frac{x}{2}\sqrt{1-x^2} + \frac{1}{2}\sin^{-1} x + C$

(c) $I = \int \frac{x^2}{(1+x^2)^2} dx = \int \underbrace{\frac{(-x)}{2}}_{I} . \underbrace{\left(-\frac{2x}{(1+x^2)^2}\right)}_{II} dx$

$= -\left(\frac{x}{2}\right)\left(\frac{1}{1+x^2}\right) - \int \left(-\frac{1}{2}\right)\frac{1}{1+x^2} dx$

$= -\frac{x}{2(1+x^2)} + \frac{1}{2}\tan^{-1} x + C$

7. (a) $I = \int \underbrace{x^n}_{II} . \underbrace{\ln x}_{I} dx (n \neq -1) = (\ln x)\frac{x^{n+1}}{n+1} - \int \frac{1}{x}\frac{x^{n+1}}{n+1} dx$

$= (\ln x)\frac{x^{n+1}}{n+1} - \frac{x^{n+1}}{(n+1)^2} + C = \frac{x^{n+1}}{n+1}\left(\ln x - \frac{1}{n+1}\right) + C$

(b) $I = \int \frac{\log x}{x^3} dx = \int \underbrace{\log x}_{I} . \underbrace{\frac{1}{x^3}}_{II} dx$

$= \frac{\log x}{(-2)}(x^{-2}) - \int \frac{1}{x(-2x^2)} dx = \frac{\log x}{-2x^2} + \frac{1}{2}\int \frac{1}{x^3} dx$

$= -\frac{1}{2}\frac{\log x}{x^2} - \frac{1}{4x^2} + C = -\frac{1}{2x^2}\left(\log x + \frac{1}{2}\right) + C$

$= -\frac{1}{2x^2}\log(x\sqrt{e}) + C$

(c) $I = \int \frac{\ln^3 x}{x^2} dx = \int \underbrace{(\ln^3 x)}_{I} . \underbrace{\frac{1}{x^2}}_{II} dx$

$= \ln^3 x\left(-\frac{1}{x}\right) - \int \frac{3\ln^2 x}{x}\left(-\frac{1}{x}\right) dx$

$= -\frac{\ln^3 x}{x} + 3\int \underbrace{\ln^2 x}_{I} . \underbrace{\frac{1}{x^2}}_{II} dx$

$= -\frac{\ln^3 x}{x} + 3\left[\ln^2 x\left(-\frac{1}{x}\right) - \int 2\frac{\ln x}{x}\left(-\frac{1}{x}\right) dx\right]$

$= -\frac{\ln^3 x}{x} - 3\frac{\ln^2 x}{x} + 6\int \underbrace{\ln x}_{I} . \underbrace{\frac{1}{x^2}}_{II} dx$

$= -\frac{\ln^3 x}{x} - 3\frac{\ln^2 x}{x} + 6\left[\ln x\left(-\frac{1}{x}\right) - \int \frac{1}{x}\left(-\frac{1}{x}\right) dx\right]$

$= -\frac{\ln^3 x}{x} - 3\frac{\ln^2 x}{x} - \frac{6}{x}\ln x - \frac{6}{x} + C$

$= C - \frac{1}{x}(\ln^3 x + 3\ln^2 x + 6\ln x + 6)$

8. (a) $I=\int \underbrace{(l)}_{II}.\underbrace{\tan^{-1}\sqrt{x}}_{I}dx = \tan^{-1}\sqrt{x}(x)-\int \frac{x}{(1+x)2\sqrt{x}}dx$

$= x\tan^{-1}\sqrt{x}-\left[\int \frac{1+x-1}{2(1+x)\sqrt{x}}dx\right]$

$= x\tan^{-1}\sqrt{x}-\int \frac{dx}{2\sqrt{x}}+\int \frac{1}{(1+x)2\sqrt{x}}dx$

$= x\tan^{-1}\sqrt{x}-\sqrt{x}+\tan^{-1}\sqrt{x}+C$

(b) $I=\int \frac{\sin^{-1}x}{\sqrt{x+1}}dx=\sin^{-1}x\int \frac{dx}{\sqrt{x+1}}$

$-\int \frac{1}{\sqrt{1-x^2}}\left(\int \frac{1}{\sqrt{x+1}}dx\right)dx$

$= 2(\sin^{-1}x)\sqrt{x+1}-\int \frac{2\sqrt{x+1}}{\sqrt{1-x^2}}dx$

$= 2(\sin^{-1}x)\sqrt{x+1}-2\int \frac{dx}{\sqrt{1-x}}$

$= 2(\sin^{-1}x)\sqrt{x+1}+4\sqrt{1-x}+C$

(c) $I=\int \frac{x\tan^{-1}x}{\sqrt{1+x^2}}dx = \int \underbrace{\tan^{-1}x}_{I}.\underbrace{\frac{x}{\sqrt{1+x^2}}}_{II}dx$

$= (\tan^{-1}x)\sqrt{1+x^2}-\int \frac{1}{1+x^2}\sqrt{1+x^2}dx$

$= \sqrt{1+x^2}(\tan^{-1}x)-\int \frac{dx}{\sqrt{1+x^2}}$

$= (\sqrt{1+x^2})(\tan^{-1}x)-\ln\left|x+\sqrt{1+x^2}\right|+C$

9. (a) $I=\int \ln(x^2+1)=x\ln(x^2+1)-\int \frac{2x^2}{x^2+1}dx$

$= x\ln(x^2+1)-2\left[\int dx-\int \frac{dx}{x^2+1}\right]$

$= x\ln(x^2+1)-2x+2\tan^{-1}x+C$

(b) $I=\int \cos(\ln x)dx = [\cos(\ln x)x]-\int \frac{-\sin(\ln x)}{x}x\,dx$

$= x\cos(\ln x)+\int \sin(\ln x)dx$

$= x\cos(\ln x)+x\sin(\ln x)-\int \frac{\cos(\ln x)}{x}x\,dx$

$= x[\cos(\ln x)+\sin(\ln x)]-I$

$I=\frac{x}{2}[\cos(\ln x)+\sin(\ln x)]+C$

(c) $I=\int \underbrace{x^2}_{II}.\underbrace{\ln(1+x)}_{I}dx = \frac{x^3}{3}\ln(1+x)-\int \frac{1}{1+x}\frac{x^3}{3}dx$

$= \frac{x^3}{3}\ln(1+x)-\frac{1}{3}\int \frac{x^3+1-1}{1+x}dx$

$= \frac{x^3}{3}\ln(1+x)-\frac{1}{3}\left[\int (x^2+1-x)dx-\int \frac{dx}{1+x}\right]$

$= \frac{x^3}{3}\ln(1+x)-\frac{x^3}{9}-\frac{x}{3}+\frac{x^2}{6}+\frac{1}{3}\ln(1+x)+C$

$= \frac{(x^3+1)}{3}\ln(1+x)-\frac{x^3}{9}+\frac{x^2}{6}-\frac{x}{3}+C$

TEXTUAL EXERCISE–4: (OBJECTIVE)

1. (a) $I=\int \frac{\ln^2 x}{\sqrt{x^5}}dx = \ln^2 x\int x^{-\frac{5}{2}}dx-\int 2\frac{\ln x}{x}\int x^{-\frac{5}{2}}dx$

$= -\frac{2}{3}(\ln^2 x)(x^{-\frac{3}{2}})+\frac{4}{3}\int \underbrace{\ln x}_{I}.\underbrace{x^{-\frac{5}{2}}}_{II}dx$

$= -\frac{2}{3}x^{-\frac{3}{2}}\ln^2 x+\frac{4}{3}\left[-\frac{2}{3}(\ln x)(x)^{-\frac{3}{2}}+\frac{2}{3}\int \frac{1}{x}x^{-\frac{3}{2}}dx\right]$

$= -\frac{2}{3}x^{-\frac{3}{2}}\ln^2 x-\frac{8}{9}(\ln x)x^{-\frac{3}{2}}+\frac{8}{9}\left(-\frac{2}{3}\right)x^{-\frac{3}{2}}+C$

$= C-\frac{8}{27\sqrt{x^3}}\left(\frac{9}{4}\ln^2 x+3\ln x+2\right)$

2. (c) $I=\int \underbrace{\sin^{-1}\sqrt{x}}_{I}.\frac{1}{\sqrt{1-x}}dx$

$= \sin^{-1}\sqrt{x}(-2\sqrt{1-x}) -\int \frac{1}{\sqrt{1-x}}\frac{(-2\sqrt{1-x})}{2\sqrt{x}}dx$

$= 2(\sqrt{x}-\sqrt{1-x}\sin^{-1}\sqrt{x})+C$

3. (d) $I=\int (\sin^{-1}x)^2dx = (\sin^{-1}x)^2x-\int \frac{2\sin^{-1}x}{\sqrt{1-x^2}}(x)dx$

$= (\sin^{-1}x)^2x-2\left[\sin^{-1}x(-\sqrt{1-x^2})-\int \frac{-\sqrt{1-x^2}}{\sqrt{1-x^2}}dx\right]$

$= x(\sin^{-1}x)^2+2\sqrt{1-x^2}\sin^{-1}x-2x+C$

4. (a) $I=\int \frac{x^2e^xdx}{(x+2)^2} = \frac{(x+2-2)^2e^x}{(x+2)^2}dx$

$= \int \frac{(x+2)^2+4-4(x+2)}{(x+2)^2}e^x dx$

$= \int e^xdx+4\int \frac{e^x}{(x+2)^2}dx-4\int \frac{e^x}{(x+2)}dx$

$= e^x+4\left[-\frac{e^x}{(x+2)}+\int \frac{e^x}{(x+2)}dx-\int \frac{e^x}{x+2}dx\right]+C$

$= \left(\frac{x-2}{x+2}\right)e^x+C$

5. (d) $I=\int \underbrace{(\tan^{-1}x)^2}_{I}.\underbrace{x}_{II}dx$

$= (\tan^{-1}x)^2\frac{x^2}{2}-\int \frac{2(\tan^{-1}x)}{1+x^2}\frac{x^2}{2}dx$

$= \frac{x^2}{2}(\tan^{-1}x)^2-\int \tan^{-1}x\,dx+\int \frac{\tan^{-1}x}{1+x^2}dx$

$= \frac{x^2}{2}(\tan^{-1}x)^2-\left[x\tan^{-1}x-\int \frac{1x}{1+x^2}dx\right]+\frac{(\tan^{-1}x)^2}{2}$

$= \frac{(x^2+1)}{2}(\tan^{-1}x)^2-x\tan^{-1}x+\frac{1}{2}\ln(1+x^2)+C$

6. (a) $I = \int \underset{u}{x^2} \underset{v}{e^x} \sin x\, dx$

$= x^2 \int e^x \sin x\, dx - \int \left(2x \int e^x \sin x dx\right) dx$

$= x^2 . \frac{e^x}{2}[\sin x - \cos x] \;\; -2\int x . \frac{e^x}{2}[\sin x - \cos x] dx$

$= \frac{x^2}{2} e^x (\sin x - \cos x) \;\; - \int x e^x \sin x + \int x e^x \cos x\, dx$

$= \frac{x^2}{2} e^x (\sin x - \cos x)$

$-\left[x \frac{e^x}{2}(\sin x - \cos x) - \int \frac{e^x}{2}(\sin x - \cos x) \right] +$

$\left\{ x \frac{e^x}{2}[\cos x + \sin x] - \int \frac{e^x}{2}[\cos x + \sin x] dx \right\}$

$= \frac{x^2}{2} e^x (\sin x - \cos x) - \frac{xe^x}{2}(\sin x - \cos x)$

$+ \frac{xe^x}{2}(\cos x + \sin x)$

$\int x^2$ ex sin x dx = x^2 $\frac{1}{2}$ ex (sin x – cos x) + ex cos x – $\frac{1}{2}$ ex (sin x + cos x) + C

$= \frac{e^x}{2}$ [(sin x) (x^2 – 1) – (cos x) (x^2 – 2x + 1)] + C

$= \frac{e^x}{2}$ [(sin x) (x^2 – 1) – (cos x) $(x - 1)^2$] + C

7. (b) $I = \int \underset{I}{\sin(\ln x)} dx \; = \; x\sin(\ln x) - \int \frac{\cos(\ln x)}{x} x\, dx$

$= x\sin(\ln x) - \int \cos(\ln x) dx$

$= x\sin(\ln x) - \left[x\cos(\ln x) + \int \frac{\sin(\ln x)}{x} x\, dx \right]$

$2I = x \sin(\ln x) - x \cos(\ln x) + C$

$I = \frac{x}{2}(\sin(\ln x) - \cos(\ln x)) + C$

TEXTUAL EXERCISE–5: (SUBJECTIVE)

1. (a) $I = \int \frac{dx}{x^2 + 2x + 3} \; = \int \frac{dx}{(x+1)^2 + (\sqrt{2})^2}$

$= \frac{1}{\sqrt{2}} \tan^{-1}\left(\frac{x+1}{\sqrt{2}}\right) + C$

(b) $I = \int \frac{dx}{z^2 - z + 1} \; = \int \frac{dz}{\left(z - \frac{1}{z}\right)^2 + \left(\frac{\sqrt{3}}{2}\right)^2}$

$= \frac{2}{\sqrt{3}} \tan^{-1}\left(\frac{2z-1}{\sqrt{3}}\right) + C$

(c) $I = \int \frac{2x - 3}{x^2 + x + 1} dx$

Put $x^2 + x + 1 = t \quad \Rightarrow \quad (2x + 1)\, dx = dt$

$\therefore \quad I = \int \frac{(2x + 1 - 4)}{x^2 + x + 1} dx$

$= \int \frac{(2x+1)}{x^2 + x + 1} dx - 4\int \frac{dx}{\left(x + \frac{1}{2}\right)^2 + \left(\frac{\sqrt{3}}{2}\right)^2}$

$= \ln|x^2 + x + 1| - \frac{8}{\sqrt{3}} \tan^{-1}\left(\frac{2x+1}{\sqrt{3}}\right) + C$

(d) $I = \int \sqrt{x^2 + 5x + 1}\, dx \; = \int \sqrt{\left(x + \frac{5}{2}\right)^2 - \left(\frac{\sqrt{21}}{2}\right)^2} dx$

$= \frac{\left(x + \frac{5}{2}\right)}{2} \sqrt{\left(x + \frac{5}{2}\right)^2 - \left(\frac{\sqrt{21}}{2}\right)^2} \; -$

$\frac{\left(\sqrt{21}/2\right)^2}{2} \ln\left| x + \frac{5}{2} + \sqrt{\left(x + \frac{5}{2}\right)^2 - \left(\frac{\sqrt{21}}{2}\right)^2} \right| + C$

$= \frac{2x+5}{4}\sqrt{x^2 + 5x + 1} - \frac{21}{8} \ln\left| x + \frac{5}{2} + \sqrt{x^2 + 5x + 1} \right| + C$

(e) $I = \int \frac{x^2 - x + 1}{2x^2 + x + 2} dx$

Put $x^2 - x + 1 = A\,(2x^2 + x + 2) + B\frac{d}{dx}(2x^2 + x + 2) + C$

$\Rightarrow \; x^2 - x + 1 = A\,(2x^2 + x + 2) + B\,(4x + 1) + C$

$= x^2\,(2A) - x\,(-A - 4B) + (2A + B + C)$

$\therefore \quad 2A = 1 \qquad \Rightarrow \quad A = \frac{1}{2}$

$-A - 4B = 1 \qquad \Rightarrow \quad B = -\frac{3}{8}$

$2A + B + C = 1 \quad \Rightarrow \quad C = \frac{3}{8}$

$\therefore \quad I = \frac{1}{2}\int dx - \frac{3}{8}\int \frac{4x+1}{2x^2 + x + 2} dx + \frac{3}{8}\int \frac{dx}{2x^2 + x + 2}$

$= \frac{x}{2} - \frac{3}{8} \ln|2x^2 + x + 2| + \frac{3}{16}\int \frac{dx}{x^2 + \frac{x}{2} + 1}$

$= \frac{x}{2} - \frac{3}{8} \ln|2x^2 + x + 2| + \frac{3}{16}\int \frac{dx}{\left(x + \frac{1}{4}\right)^2 + \left(\frac{\sqrt{15}}{4}\right)^2}$

$= \frac{x}{2} - \frac{3}{8} \ln|2x^2 + x + 2| + \frac{3}{4\sqrt{15}} \tan^{-1}\left(\frac{4x+1}{\sqrt{15}}\right) + C$

2. (a) $I = \int \frac{3x+5}{x^2 + 2x - 3} dx$

Put $3x + 5 = A\,(2x + 2) + B$

$= 2Ax + 2A + B$

$2A = 3 \qquad \Rightarrow \quad A = \frac{3}{2}$ and $2A + B = 5$

$\Rightarrow \; B = 2$

$\therefore \quad I=\frac{3}{2}\int\frac{2x+2}{x^2+2x-3}dx+2\int\frac{dx}{(x+1)^2-(2)^2}$

$= \frac{3}{2}\ln|x^2+2x-3|+\frac{1}{2}\ln\left(\frac{x-1}{x+3}\right)+C$

(b) $I=\int\frac{2x-1}{\sqrt{3+2x-x^2}}dx$

Put $2x-1=A(2-2x)+B=-2Ax+2A+B$

$\Rightarrow A=-1 \qquad \Rightarrow B=1$

$\therefore \quad I=-\int\frac{2-2x}{\sqrt{3+2x-x^2}}dx+\int\frac{dx}{\sqrt{2^2-(x-1)^2}}$

$= -2\sqrt{3+2x-x^2}+\sin^{-1}\left(\frac{x-1}{2}\right)+C$

(c) $I=\int\frac{x\,dx}{\sqrt{x^2+x+1}}$

$x=A(2x+1)+B$

$=2Ax+A+B$

$A=\frac{1}{2} \qquad \Rightarrow B=-\frac{1}{2}$

$\therefore \quad I=\frac{1}{2}\int\frac{(2x+1)}{\sqrt{x^2+x+1}}dx-\frac{1}{2}\int\frac{dx}{\sqrt{x^2+x+1}}$

$= \sqrt{x^2+x+1}-\frac{1}{2}\int\frac{dx}{\sqrt{\left(x+\frac{1}{2}\right)^2+\left(\frac{\sqrt{3}}{2}\right)^2}}$

$= \sqrt{x^2+x+1}-\frac{1}{2}\ln\left|\left(x+\frac{1}{2}\right)+\sqrt{x^2+x+1}\right|+C$

(d) $I=\int(x-1)\sqrt{x^2+x+1}\,dx$

Put $(x-1)=A(2x+1)+B=2Ax+A+B$

$A=\frac{1}{2}, B=-\frac{3}{2}$

$I=\frac{1}{2}\int(2x+1)\sqrt{x^2+x+1}\,dx$

$-\frac{3}{2}\int\sqrt{\left(x+\frac{1}{2}\right)^2+\left(\frac{\sqrt{3}}{2}\right)^2}\,dx$

$=\frac{1}{3}(x^2+x+1)^{\frac{3}{2}}-\frac{3}{2}$

$\left[\frac{\left(x+\frac{1}{2}\right)}{2}\sqrt{x^2+x+1}+\frac{\left(\frac{\sqrt{3}}{2}\right)^2}{2}\ln\left|x+\frac{1}{2}+\sqrt{x^2+x+1}\right|\right]+C$

$\frac{1}{3}(x^2+x+1)^{\frac{3}{2}}-\frac{3}{4}$

$\left[\left(x+\frac{1}{2}\right)\sqrt{x^2+x+1}+\frac{3}{4}\ln\left|x+\frac{1}{2}+\sqrt{x^2+x+1}\right|\right]+C$

3. $I=\int\frac{2x^2+3x+4}{x^2+6x+10}dx$

$2x^2+3x+4=A(x^2+6x+10)+B(2x+6)+C$

$=Ax^2+x(6A+2B)+(10A+6B+C)$

$A=2$

$6A+2B=3 \qquad \Rightarrow B=-\frac{9}{2}$

$10A+6B+C=4 \qquad \Rightarrow C=11$

$\therefore \quad I=2\int dx-\frac{9}{2}\int\frac{2x+6}{x^2+6x+10}dx+11\int\frac{dx}{(x+3)^2+1^2}$

$= 2x-\frac{9}{2}\ln|x^2+6x+10|+11\tan^{-1}(x+3)+C$

4. $I=\int\frac{x^2-3x+1}{\sqrt{1-x^2}}dx$

Put $x^2-3x+1=A(1+x^2)+B(-2x)+C$

$=-Ax^2-2Bx+(A+C)$

$A=-1,\ B=\frac{3}{2},\ C=2$

$\therefore \quad I=-\int\sqrt{1-x^2}\,dx+\frac{3}{2}\int-\frac{2x}{\sqrt{1-x^2}}dx+2\int\frac{dx}{\sqrt{1-x^2}}$

$= -\frac{x\sqrt{1-x^2}}{2}-\frac{1}{2}\sin^{-1}x+3\sqrt{1-x^2}+2\sin^{-1}x+C$

$= (\sqrt{1-x^2})\frac{(6-x)}{2}+\frac{3}{2}\sin^{-1}x+C$

5. $I=\int\frac{x^2+4x+7}{\sqrt{x^2+x+1}}dx$

$x^2+4x+7=A(x^2+x+1)+B(2x+1)+C$

$=Ax^2+x(A+2B)+(A+B+C)$

$A=1, B=\frac{3}{2}, C=\frac{9}{2}$

$I=\int\sqrt{x^2+x+1}\,dx+\frac{3}{2}\int\frac{2x+1}{\sqrt{x^2+x+1}}dx+\frac{9}{2}\int\frac{dx}{\sqrt{x^2+x+1}}$

$=\int\sqrt{\left(x+\frac{1}{2}\right)^2+\left(\frac{\sqrt{3}}{2}\right)^2}\,dx+3\sqrt{x^2+x+1}$

$+\frac{9}{2}\int\frac{dx}{\sqrt{\left(x+\frac{1}{2}\right)^2+\left(\frac{\sqrt{3}}{2}\right)^2}}$

$=\frac{\left(x+\frac{1}{2}\right)}{2}\sqrt{x^2+x+1}+\frac{\left(\frac{\sqrt{3}}{2}\right)^2}{2}\ln\left|x+\frac{1}{2}+\sqrt{x^2+x+1}\right|$

$+3\sqrt{x^2+x+1}+\frac{9}{2}\ln\left|x+\frac{1}{2}+\sqrt{x^2+x+1}\right|+C$

$=(\sqrt{x^2+x+1})\left(\frac{2x+13}{4}\right)+\frac{39}{8}\ln\left|x+\frac{1}{2}+\sqrt{x^2+x+1}\right|+C$

6. $I=\int \frac{x^2-3x+1}{\sqrt{-2x^2+4x-1}}dx$

Put $x^2 - 3x + 1 = A(-2x^2 + 4x - 1) + B(-4x + 4) + C$
$= -2Ax^2 + x(4A - 4B) - A + 4B + C$

$A=-\frac{1}{2}, B=\frac{1}{4}, C=-\frac{1}{2}$

$\therefore \quad I=-\frac{1}{2}\int\sqrt{-2x^2+4x-1}\,dx + \frac{1}{4}\int\frac{-4x+4}{\sqrt{-2x^2+4x-1}}dx$
$-\frac{1}{2}\int\frac{dx}{\sqrt{-2x^2+4x-1}}$

$=-\frac{1}{\sqrt{2}}\int\sqrt{\left(\frac{1}{\sqrt{2}}\right)^2-(x-1)^2}\,dx + \frac{1}{2}\sqrt{-2x^2+4x-1}$
$-\frac{1}{2\sqrt{2}}\int\frac{dx}{\sqrt{\left(\frac{1}{\sqrt{2}}\right)^2-(x-1)^2}}$

$=-\frac{1}{\sqrt{2}}\left[\frac{x-1}{2}\sqrt{-x^2+2x-\frac{1}{2}}+\frac{\left(\frac{1}{\sqrt{2}}\right)^2}{2}\sin^{-1}\left(\frac{x-1}{\frac{1}{\sqrt{2}}}\right)\right]$
$+\frac{1}{2}\sqrt{-2x^2+4x-1}-\frac{1}{2\sqrt{2}}\sin^{-1}[(x-1)\sqrt{2}]+C$

$=\sqrt{-2x^2+4x-1}\left(\frac{1-x}{4}+\frac{1}{2}\right) - \frac{3}{4\sqrt{2}}\sin^{-1}\sqrt{2}(x-1)+C$

$=-\left(\frac{x-3}{4}\right)\sqrt{-2x^2+4x-1} - \frac{3}{4\sqrt{2}}\sin^{-1}\sqrt{2}(x-1)+C$

7. $I=\int\frac{x^4+x^3+2x+1}{x^2+x+1}dx = \int\frac{x^2(x^2+x+1)-x^2+2x+1}{x^2+x+1}dx$

Put $-x^2 + 2x + 1 = A(x^2 + x + 1) + B(2x + 1) + C$
$= Ax^2 + x(A + 2B) + A + B + C$

$A=-1, B=\frac{3}{2}, C=\frac{1}{2}$

$\therefore \quad I=\int x^2\,dx-\int dx+\frac{3}{2}\int\frac{(2x+1)}{x^2+x+1}$
$+\frac{1}{2}\int\frac{dx}{\left(x+\frac{1}{2}\right)^2+\left(\frac{\sqrt{3}}{2}\right)^2}$

$=\frac{x^3}{3}-x+\frac{3}{2}\ln(x^2+x+1)+\frac{1}{\sqrt{3}}\tan^{-1}\left(\frac{2x+1}{\sqrt{3}}\right)+C$

8. $I=\int\frac{x^3+3}{\sqrt{x^2+1}}dx = (Ax^2+Bx+C)\sqrt{x^2+1}+K\int\frac{dx}{\sqrt{x^2+1}}$

Differentiating both sides w.r.t. x, we get

$\frac{x^3+3}{\sqrt{x^2+1}}=(2Ax+B)\sqrt{x^2+1}$

$+(Ax^2+Bx+C)\frac{x}{\sqrt{x^2+1}}+\frac{K}{\sqrt{x^2+1}}$

$(x^3 + 3) = (2Ax + B)(x^2 + 1) + (Ax^2 + Bx + C)x + K$
$x^3 + 3 = x^3(2A + A) + x^2(B + B) + x(2A + C) + B + K$

$\Rightarrow \quad A=\frac{1}{3}, B=0, C=-\frac{2}{3}, K=3$

$\therefore \quad I=\left(\frac{x^2}{3}-\frac{2}{3}\right)\sqrt{x^2+1}+3\int\frac{dx}{\sqrt{x^2+1}}$

$=\frac{1}{3}(x^2+1-3)\sqrt{x^2+1}+3\ln|x+\sqrt{x^2+1}|+C$

$=\frac{1}{3}(x^2+1)^{\frac{3}{2}}-\sqrt{x^2+1}+3\ln|x+\sqrt{x^2+1}|+C$

9. $I=\int\frac{x^4-1}{x^2\sqrt{x^4+x^2+1}}dx$

$=\int\frac{x^2-\frac{1}{x^2}}{x\sqrt{x^2+1+\frac{1}{x^2}}}dx=\int\frac{\left(x+\frac{1}{x}\right)\left(1-\frac{1}{x^2}\right)}{\sqrt{\left(x+\frac{1}{x}\right)^2-1}}dx$

Put $x+\frac{1}{x}=t \quad \Rightarrow \quad \left(1-\frac{1}{x^2}\right)dx=dt$

$\Rightarrow \quad I=\int\frac{t\,dt}{\sqrt{t^2-1}}$

Let $t^2 = m \quad \Rightarrow \quad 2t\,dt = dm$

$\Rightarrow \quad I=\frac{1}{2}\int\frac{dm}{(m-1)^{1/2}}=(m-1)^{1/2}+C = (t^2-1)^{1/2}+C$

$=\left[\left(x+\frac{1}{x}\right)^2-1\right]^{\frac{1}{2}}+C = \sqrt{x^2+\frac{1}{x^2}+1}+C$

$=\frac{\sqrt{x^4+x^2+1}}{x}+C$

10. (i) $I=\int(3x+5)\sqrt{x^2+2x-3}\,dx$

Put $3x + 5 = A(2x + 2) + B = 2Ax + 2A + B$

$\Rightarrow \quad A=\frac{3}{2}, B=2$

$\Rightarrow \quad I=\frac{3}{2}\int(2x+2)\sqrt{x^2+2x-3}\,dx + 2\int\sqrt{(x+1)^2-(2)^2}\,dx$

$=(x^2+2x-3)^{\frac{3}{2}}+(x+1)\sqrt{x^2+2x-3}\,-$
$4\ln|(x+1)+\sqrt{x^2+2x-3}|+C$

(ii) $I=\int(x+2)\sqrt{2x^2+2x+1}\,dx$

Put $x + 2 = A(4x + 2) + B = 4Ax + 2A + B$

$\Rightarrow \quad A=\frac{1}{4}, B=\frac{3}{2}$

$\therefore \quad I=\frac{1}{4}\int(4x+2)\sqrt{2x^2+2x+1}\,dx$

$+\frac{3}{2}\sqrt{2}\int\sqrt{\left(x+\frac{1}{2}\right)^2+\left(\frac{1}{2}\right)^2}\,dx$

$$= \frac{1}{6}(2x^2+2x+1)^{\frac{3}{2}} + \frac{3}{\sqrt{2}}\left[\frac{x+\frac{1}{2}}{2}\sqrt{x^2+x+\frac{1}{2}}\right.$$

$$\left.+\left[\frac{1}{8}\ln\left|x+\frac{1}{2}+\sqrt{x^2+x+\frac{1}{2}}\right|\right]\right]+C$$

$$= \frac{1}{6}(2x^2+2x+1)^{\frac{3}{2}} + \frac{3}{8}(2x+1)\sqrt{2x^2+2x+1}$$

$$+\frac{3}{8\sqrt{2}}\ln|2x+1+\sqrt{4x^2+4x+2}|+C$$

11. $I = \int \frac{\ln x\, dx}{x\sqrt{-\ln^2 x - 4\ln x + 1}}$

Put $\ln x = t \Rightarrow \frac{dx}{x} = dt$

$\Rightarrow I = \int \frac{t\,dt}{\sqrt{-t^2-4t+1}}$

Put $t = A(-2t-4) + B = -2At - 4A + B$

$\Rightarrow A = -\frac{1}{2}, B = -2$

$$\Rightarrow I = -\frac{1}{2}\int \frac{(-2t-4)}{\sqrt{-t^2-4t+1}}dt - 2\int \frac{dt}{\sqrt{(\sqrt{5})^2-(t+2)^2}}$$

$$= -\sqrt{-t^2-4t+1} - 2\sin^{-1}\left(\frac{t+2}{\sqrt{5}}\right)+C$$

$$= -\sqrt{-\ln^2 x - 4\ln x + 1} - 2\sin^{-1}\left(\frac{\ln x + 2}{\sqrt{5}}\right)+C$$

12. $I = \int \frac{dx}{x^4+8x^2+9} \Rightarrow x^2 = -\frac{8\pm\sqrt{64-36}}{2} = -4\pm\sqrt{7}$

$$I = \int \frac{dx}{(x^2+4-\sqrt{7})(x^2+4+\sqrt{7})}$$

$$= \frac{1}{2\sqrt{7}}\int \frac{(x^2+4+\sqrt{7})-(x^2+4-\sqrt{7})}{(x^2+4-\sqrt{7})(x^2+4+\sqrt{7})}dx$$

$$= \frac{1}{2\sqrt{7}}\int \frac{dx}{x^2+4-\sqrt{7}} - \frac{1}{2\sqrt{7}}\int \frac{dx}{x^2+4+\sqrt{7}}$$

$$= \frac{1}{2\sqrt{7}.\sqrt{4-\sqrt{7}}}\tan^{-1}\left(\frac{x}{\sqrt{4-\sqrt{7}}}\right)$$

$$-\frac{1}{2\sqrt{7}\sqrt{4+\sqrt{7}}}\tan^{-1}\left(\frac{x}{\sqrt{4+\sqrt{7}}}\right)+C$$

$$= \frac{\sqrt{4+\sqrt{7}}}{6\sqrt{7}}\tan^{-1}\left(\frac{x\sqrt{4+\sqrt{7}}}{3}\right)$$

$$-\frac{\sqrt{4-\sqrt{7}}}{6\sqrt{7}}\tan^{-1}\left(\frac{x\sqrt{4-\sqrt{7}}}{3}\right)+C$$

13. $I = \int \frac{x}{x^4+x^2+1}dx$

Let $x^2 = t \Rightarrow 2x\,dx = dt$

$$I = \frac{1}{2}\int \frac{dt}{t^2+t+1} = \frac{1}{2}\int \frac{dt}{\left(t+\frac{1}{2}\right)^2+\left(\frac{\sqrt{3}}{2}\right)^2}$$

$$= \frac{1}{\sqrt{3}}\tan^{-1}\left(\frac{2t+1}{\sqrt{3}}\right)+C = \frac{1}{\sqrt{3}}\left(\tan^{-1}\left(\frac{2x^2+1}{\sqrt{3}}\right)\right)+C$$

14. $I = \int \frac{x^4+1}{x^6+1}dx = \int \frac{x^4+1}{(x^2+1)(x^4+1-x^2)}dx$

$$= \int \frac{x^4+1-x^2+x^2}{(x^2+1)(x^4+1-x^2)}dx$$

$$= \int \frac{dx}{x^2+1} + \int \frac{x^2}{(x^2+1)(x^4+1-x^2)}dx$$

$$= \tan^{-1}x + \underbrace{\int \frac{x^2}{x^6+1}dx}_{I_1}$$

$$I_1 = \int \frac{x^2 dx}{x^6+1}$$

Let $x^3 = t \Rightarrow 3x^2\,dx = dt$

$$I_1 = \frac{1}{3}\int \frac{dt}{t^2+1} = \frac{1}{3}\tan^{-1}t + C = \frac{1}{3}\tan^{-1}x^3 + C$$

15. $I = \int \frac{x^3-x-1}{\sqrt{x^2+2x+2}}dx$

$$= (Ax^2+Bx+C)\sqrt{x^2+2x+2} + K\int \frac{dx}{\sqrt{x^2+2x+2}}$$

Differentiating both sides w.r.t. x, we get

$$\frac{x^3-x-1}{\sqrt{x^2+2x+2}} = (2Ax+B)\sqrt{x^2+2x+2} +$$

$$\frac{(Ax^2+Bx+C)(x+1)}{\sqrt{x^2+2x+2}} + \frac{K}{\sqrt{x^2+2x+2}}$$

$x^3 - x - 1 = (2Ax + B)(x^2 + 2x + 2) + (Ax^2 + Bx + C)(x + 1) + K$

$= x^3(2A + A) + x^2(B + 4A + A + B) + x(4A + 2B + B + C) + (2B + C + K)$

$A = \frac{1}{3}, B = -\frac{5}{6}$

$4A + 3B + C = -1$

$\Rightarrow \frac{4}{3} - \frac{5}{2} + C = -1 \Rightarrow C = \frac{1}{6}$

$2B + C + K = -1$

$\Rightarrow -\frac{10}{6} + \frac{1}{6} + K = -1 \Rightarrow K = \frac{1}{2}$

$$\therefore I = \left(\frac{x^2}{3} - \frac{5x}{6} + \frac{1}{6}\right)\sqrt{x^2+2x+2} + \frac{1}{2}\int \frac{dx}{(x+1)^2+1^2}$$

$$= \frac{1}{6}(2x^2 - 5x + 1)\sqrt{x^2 + 2x + 2}$$

$$+ \frac{1}{2}\ln\left|(x+1) + \sqrt{x^2 + 2x + 2}\right| + C$$

TEXTUAL EXERCISE–5: (OBJECTIVE)

1. (a) $I = \int \frac{dx}{4x^2 + 4x + 5} = \frac{1}{4}\int \frac{dx}{x^2 + x + \frac{5}{4}} = \frac{1}{4}\int \frac{dx}{\left(x + \frac{1}{2}\right)^2 + 1^2}$

$$= \frac{1}{4}\tan^{-1}\left(x + \frac{1}{2}\right) + C$$

2. (c) $I = \int \frac{dx}{x^2 + 4x - 5} = \int \frac{dx}{(x+2)^2 - 3^2} = \frac{1}{6}\ln\left|\frac{x-1}{x+5}\right| + C$

3. (c) $I = \int \frac{3x+2}{4x^2 + 4x + 5}dx = \ell\,(\ln(4x^2 + 4x + 5)) +$

$m\tan^{-1}\left(x + \frac{1}{2}\right) + C$

Differentiating both side w.r.t. x, we get $\frac{3x+2}{4x^2+4x+5}$

$$= \frac{\ell(8x+4)}{4x^2+4x+5} + \frac{m}{\left(x+\frac{1}{2}\right)^2 + 1^2}$$

$$\frac{3x+2}{4x^2+4x+5} = \frac{\ell(8x+4)}{4x^2+4x+5} + \frac{4m}{4x^2+4x+5}$$

$\therefore\quad 3x + 2 = 8\ell x + 4\ell + 4m$

$$\ell = \frac{3}{8},\ 4\ell + 4m = 2$$

$$\frac{3}{2} + 4m = 2 \quad\Rightarrow\quad m = \frac{1}{8}$$

4. (d) $I = \int \frac{(x+3)}{\sqrt{4x^2+4x-3}}dx$

$$= A.\sqrt{4x^2+4x-3} + B\ln\left|2x + 1 + \sqrt{4x^2+4x-3}\right| + C$$

Differentiating both sides w.r.t. x, we get $\frac{(x+3)}{\sqrt{4x^2+4x-3}}$

$$= \frac{A(4x+2)}{\sqrt{4x^2+4x-3}} + \frac{B\left(2 + \frac{4x+2}{\sqrt{4x^2+4x-3}}\right)}{(2x+1)+\sqrt{4x^2+4x-3}}$$

$(x + 3) = (4x + 2)A + 2B$

$$\Rightarrow\quad A = \frac{1}{4},\ B = \frac{5}{4} \quad\Rightarrow\quad \frac{B}{A} = 5$$

5. (c) $I = \int \frac{5x+4}{\sqrt{x^2+2x+5}}dx$

$$= A\sqrt{x^2+2x+5} - B\ln(x + 1 + \sqrt{x^2+2x+5})$$

Differentiating both side w.r.t. x, we get $\frac{5x+4}{\sqrt{x^2+2x+5}}$

$$= \frac{A(x+1)}{\sqrt{x^2+2x+5}} - \frac{B\left(1 + \frac{x+1}{\sqrt{x^2+2x+5}}\right)}{[(x+1)+\sqrt{x^2+2x+5}]}$$

$5x + 4 = Ax + A - B \;\Rightarrow\; A = 5, B = 1$

$\Rightarrow\; A + B = 6$

6. (c) $I = \int \frac{x^2+1}{x^4 - x^2 + 1} = \int \frac{1 + \frac{1}{x^2}}{x^2 - 1 + \frac{1}{x^2}}dx = \int \frac{1 + \frac{1}{x^2}dx}{\left(x - \frac{1}{x}\right)^2 + 1^2}$

Put $x - \frac{1}{x} = t \quad\Rightarrow\quad \left(1 + \frac{1}{x^2}\right)dx = dt$

$$I = \int \frac{dt}{t^2+1} = \tan^{-1}t + C = \tan^{-1}\left(x - \frac{1}{x}\right) + C$$

7. (a) $I = \int \frac{x^2-1}{x\sqrt{x^4+3x^2+1}}dx$

$$= m\ln\left[\frac{(x^2+1)+\sqrt{x^4+3x^2+1}}{x}\right] + C$$

Differentiating both sides w.r.t. x, we get

$$\frac{x^2-1}{x\sqrt{x^4+3x^2+1}} = \frac{mx\left[1 - \frac{1}{x^2} + \frac{2x - \frac{2}{x^3}}{2\sqrt{x^2+3+\frac{1}{x^2}}}\right]}{(x^2+1)+\sqrt{x^4+3x^2+1}}$$

$$\Rightarrow\quad \frac{x^2-1}{x\sqrt{x^4+3x^2+1}} = \frac{mx\left[1 - \frac{1}{x^2} + \frac{x^2 - \frac{1}{x^2}}{\sqrt{x^4+3x^2+1}}\right]}{(x^2+1)+\sqrt{x^4+3x^2+1}}$$

$$\Rightarrow\quad \frac{x^2-1}{x\sqrt{x^4+3x^2+1}} = \frac{mx\left(1 - \frac{1}{x^2} + \frac{x^2 - \frac{1}{x^2}}{\sqrt{x^4+3x^2+1}}\right)}{(x^2+1)+\sqrt{x^4+3x^2+1}}$$

$$= \frac{mx((x^2-1)\sqrt{x^4+3x^2+1} + (x^2-1)(x^2+1))}{[(x^2+1)+\sqrt{x^4+3x^3+1}]x^2\sqrt{x^4+3x^2+1}}$$

$$= \frac{m(x^2-1)[x^2+1+\sqrt{x^2+3x^2+1}]}{x\sqrt{x^4+3x^2+1}[(x^2+1)+\sqrt{x^4+3x^2+1}]}$$

$\therefore\quad m = 1$

8. (b) $I = \int \sqrt{4x^2 - 4x + 3}\,dx$

$$= \left(\frac{x}{2} - \frac{1}{4}\right)\sqrt{4x^2-4x+3} + \frac{1}{2}g(x) + C$$

Differentiating both side w.r.t. x, we get $\sqrt{4x^2-4x+3}$

$$= \frac{1}{2}\sqrt{4x^2-4x+3} + \left(\frac{x}{2} - \frac{1}{4}\right)\frac{(4x-2)}{\sqrt{4x^2-4x+3}} + \frac{1}{2}g'(x)$$

$$\Rightarrow \frac{4x^2-4x+3}{\sqrt{4x^2-4x+3}}$$

$$= \frac{\frac{1}{2}(4x^2-4x+3)+\frac{1}{2}(2x-1)^2+\frac{1}{2}g'(x)\sqrt{4x^2-4x+3}}{\sqrt{4x^2-4x+3}}$$

$$\Rightarrow 4x^2-4x+3 = 2x^2-2x+\frac{3}{2}+2x^2-2x$$

$$+\frac{1}{2}+\frac{1}{2}g'(x)\sqrt{4x^2-4x+3}$$

$$\Rightarrow g'(x)=\frac{2}{\sqrt{4x^2-4x+3}}$$

$$\Rightarrow g(x)=\int\frac{2dx}{\sqrt{4x^2-4x+3}}$$

$$=\int\frac{dx}{\sqrt{x^2-x+\frac{3}{4}}}=\int\frac{dx}{\sqrt{\left(x-\frac{1}{2}\right)^2+\left(\frac{1}{\sqrt{2}}\right)^2}}$$

$$\Rightarrow g(x)=\ln\left|\left(x-\frac{1}{2}\right)+\frac{\sqrt{4x^2-4x+3}}{2}\right|+C$$

$$=\ln|2x-1+\sqrt{4x^2-4x+3}|+C$$

9. (c) $I=\int\frac{x^3-6x^2+11x-6}{\sqrt{x^2+4x+3}}dx$

$$=\frac{1}{3}(x^2-14x+111)\sqrt{x^2+4x+3}-66g(x)+C$$

Differentiating both side w.r.t. x, we get

$$\frac{x^3-6x^2+11x-6}{\sqrt{x^2+4x+3}}$$

$$=\frac{1}{3}(2x-14)\sqrt{x^2+4x+3}$$

$$+\frac{1}{3}\frac{(x^2-14x+111)(x+2)}{\sqrt{x^2+4x+3}}-66g'(x)$$

$$= x^3-6x^2+11x-6=\frac{1}{3}(2x-14)(x^2+4x+3)$$

$$+\frac{1}{3}(x^2-14x+111)(x+2)\;-\;66g'(x)\sqrt{x^2+4x+3}$$

$$=x^3\left(\frac{2}{3}+\frac{1}{3}\right)+x^2\left(-\frac{14}{3}+\frac{8}{3}+\frac{2}{3}-\frac{14}{3}\right)$$

$$+\;x\left(2-\frac{56}{3}-\frac{28}{3}+\frac{111}{3}\right)-66g'(x)\sqrt{x^2+4x+3}$$

$$-\;14+\frac{222}{3}$$

$$= x^3-6x^2+11x+60-\;66g'(x)\sqrt{x^2+4x+3}$$

$$g'(x)=\frac{1}{\sqrt{x^2+4x+3}}$$

$$g(x)=\int\frac{dx}{\sqrt{x^2+4x+3}}=\int\frac{dx}{\sqrt{(x+2)^2-1^2}}$$

$$=\ln\left|x+2+\sqrt{x^2+4x+3}\right|+C$$

10. (a) $I=\int\frac{3x^3+5x^2-7x+9}{\sqrt{2x^2+5x+7}}dx$

$$=\frac{1}{2A}(Ax^2-20x-373)(\sqrt{2x^2+5x+7})$$

$$+\;\frac{3297}{4A\sqrt{B}}\ln\left|4x+5+2\sqrt{4x^2+10x+14}\right|$$

Differentiating both sides w.r.t. x, we get

$$\frac{3x^3+5x^2-7x+9}{\sqrt{2x^2+5x+7}}$$

$$=\frac{1}{2A}(2Ax-20)(\sqrt{2x^2+5x+7})$$

$$+\;\frac{1}{2A}(Ax^2-20x-373)\frac{(4x+5)}{2\sqrt{2x^2+5x+7}}$$

$$+\;\frac{3297}{4A\sqrt{B}}\frac{\left(4+\frac{8x+10}{\sqrt{4x^2+10x+14}}\right)}{4x+5+2\sqrt{4x^2+10x+14}}$$

$$= 3x^3+5x^2-7x+9=\frac{1}{A}(Ax-10)(2x^2+5x+7)$$

$$+\;\frac{1}{4A}(Ax^2-20x-373)(4x+5)\;+\;\frac{3297}{2A\sqrt{B}}$$

$$= x^3(2+1)+x^2\left(-\frac{20}{A}+5+\frac{5}{4}-\frac{20}{A}\right)$$

$$+\;x\left(7-\frac{50}{A}-\frac{373}{A}-\frac{25}{A}\right)-\frac{70}{A}-\frac{1865}{A}+\frac{3297}{2A\sqrt{B}}$$

$$= 3x^3+x^2\left(\frac{25}{4}-\frac{40}{A}\right)+x\left(7-\frac{448}{A}\right)\;-\frac{2145}{4A}+\frac{3297}{2A\sqrt{B}}$$

$$\Rightarrow A=32,\;-\frac{2145}{4A}+\frac{6594}{4A\sqrt{B}}=9$$

$$\Rightarrow -2145+\frac{6594}{\sqrt{B}}=1152$$

$\Rightarrow \sqrt{B}=2 \qquad \Rightarrow B=4$

$\Rightarrow A-B=28$

TEXTUAL EXERCISE-6: (SUBJECTIVE)

1. (a) $I=\int\frac{x^3}{x^6+1}dx$

$$\frac{x^3}{x^6+1}=\frac{x^3}{(x^2+1)(x^4+1-x^2)}$$

$$=\frac{Ax+B}{x^2+1}+\frac{Cx^3+Dx^2+Ex+F}{x^4+1-x^2}$$

$x^3=(Ax+B)(x^4+1-x^2)+(Cx^3+Dx^2+Ex+F)(x^2+1)$
$= x^5(A+C)+x^4(B+D)+x^3(-A+C+E)+x^2(-B+D+F)+x(A+E)+B+F$

$A+C=0, B+D=0, -A+C+E=1, -B+D+F=0,$
$A+E=0, B+F=0$
$B=D=F=0$

$C=+\frac{1}{3}, A=-\frac{1}{3}, E=\frac{1}{3}$

$$I=\int\frac{-\frac{1}{3}x}{x^2+1}dx+\int\frac{\frac{1}{3}x^3+\frac{1}{3}x}{x^4+1-x^2}dx$$

$$=-\frac{1}{6}\int\frac{2x}{x^2+1}dx+\frac{1}{6}\int\frac{2x^3+2x}{x^4+1-x^2}dx$$

$$=-\frac{1}{6}\ln|x^2+1|+\underbrace{\frac{1}{6}\int\frac{(x^2+1)2x}{x^4+1-x^2}}_{I_1} \quad \ldots\text{(i)}$$

Let $I_1=\frac{1}{6}\int\frac{(x^2+1)2x}{x^4+1-x^2}dx$

Let $x^2=t \Rightarrow 2x\,dx=dt$

$$\Rightarrow I_1=\frac{1}{6}\int\frac{(t+1)}{t^2-t+1}dt$$

$$=\frac{1}{12}\left[\int\frac{2t-1}{t^2-t+1}dt+3\int\frac{dt}{\left(t-\frac{1}{2}\right)^2+\left(\frac{\sqrt{3}}{2}\right)^2}\right]$$

$$=\frac{1}{12}\ln|t^2-t+1|+\frac{1}{2\sqrt{3}}\tan^{1}\left(\frac{2t-1}{\sqrt{3}}\right)+C$$

$$\therefore I=-\frac{1}{6}\ln|x^2+1|+\frac{1}{12}\ln|x^4-x^2+1|$$
$$+\frac{1}{2\sqrt{3}}\tan^{-1}\left(\frac{2x^2-1}{\sqrt{3}}\right)+C$$

$$=-\frac{1}{12}\ln|x^4+2x^2+1|+\frac{1}{12}\ln|x^4-x^2+1|$$
$$+\frac{1}{2\sqrt{3}}\tan^{-1}\left(\frac{2x^2-1}{\sqrt{3}}\right)+C$$

$$=\frac{1}{12}\ln\left|\frac{x^4-x^2+1}{x^4+2x^2+1}\right|+\frac{1}{2\sqrt{3}}\tan^{-1}\left(\frac{2x^2-1}{\sqrt{3}}\right)+C$$

(b) $I=\int\frac{dx}{x^3(x^3-1)}=\int\frac{dx}{(x^3-1)}-\int\frac{dx}{x^3}$

$$=\underbrace{\int\frac{dx}{(x-1)(x^2+1+x)}}_{I_1}+\frac{1}{2x^2}+C$$

$$=\frac{1}{(x-1)(x^2+1+x)}=\frac{A}{x-1}+\frac{Bx+C}{x^2+x+1}$$

$1=A(x^2+x+1)+(Bx+C)(x-1)$
$=x^2(A+B)+x(A+C-B)+A-C$
$A+B=0, A+C-B=0$ and $A-C=1$

$\Rightarrow A=\frac{1}{3}, C=-\frac{2}{3}, B=-\frac{1}{3}$

$$\Rightarrow I_1=\frac{1}{3}\int\frac{dx}{x-1}-\frac{1}{3}\int\frac{x+2}{x^2+x+1}dx$$

$$=\frac{1}{3}\ln|x-1|-\frac{1}{6}\left[\int\frac{2x+1}{x^2+x+1}dx+3\int\frac{dx}{\left(x+\frac{1}{2}\right)^2+\left(\frac{\sqrt{3}}{2}\right)^2}\right]$$

$$=\frac{1}{3}\ln|x-1|-\frac{1}{6}\ln|x^2+x+1|$$
$$-\frac{1}{\sqrt{3}}\tan^{-1}\left(\frac{2x+1}{\sqrt{3}}\right)+C$$

$$=\frac{1}{3}\ln\left|\frac{x-1}{\sqrt{x^2+x+1}}\right|-\frac{1}{\sqrt{3}}\tan^{-1}\left(\frac{2x+1}{\sqrt{3}}\right)+C$$

$$\Rightarrow I=\frac{1}{3}\ln\left|\frac{x-1}{\sqrt{x^2+x+1}}\right|+\frac{1}{2x^2}-\frac{1}{\sqrt{3}}\tan^{-1}\left(\frac{2x+1}{\sqrt{3}}\right)+C$$

(c) $I=\int\frac{dx}{x^4(x^3-1)}=\frac{1}{3}\int\frac{3x^2}{x^6(x^3-1)}dx$

Let $x^3=t \Rightarrow 3x^2\,dx=dt$

$$\Rightarrow I=\frac{1}{3}\int\frac{dt}{t^2(t-1)}$$

Let $\frac{1}{t^2(t-1)}=\frac{A}{t-1}+\frac{Bt+C}{t^2}$

$\Rightarrow 1=At^2+(Bt+C)(t-1)$
$\Rightarrow 1=t^2(A+B)+t(C-B)-C$
$\Rightarrow B=C=-1, A=1$

$$\Rightarrow I=\frac{1}{3}\left[\int\frac{dt}{t-1}-\int\frac{t+1}{t^2}dt\right]=\frac{1}{3}\ln|t-1|-\frac{1}{3}\int\frac{dt}{t}-\frac{1}{3}\int\frac{dt}{t^2}$$

$$=\frac{1}{3}\ln|t-1|-\frac{1}{3}\ln t+\frac{1}{3t}+C=\frac{1}{3}\ln\left|\frac{t-1}{t^3}\right|+\frac{1}{3t}+C$$

$$=\frac{1}{3}\ln\left|\frac{x^3-1}{x^3}\right|+\frac{1}{3x^3}+C$$

2. (a) $I=\int\frac{dx}{(x^2-1)(x^2-4)}=\frac{1}{3}\int\frac{(x^2-1)-(x^2-4)}{(x^2-1)(x^2-4)}dx$

$$=\frac{1}{3}\left[\int\frac{dx}{x^4-4}-\int\frac{dx}{x^2-1}\right]$$

$$=\frac{1}{3}\left[\frac{1}{4}\ln\left|\frac{x-2}{x+2}\right|-\frac{1}{2}\ln\left|\frac{x-1}{x+1}\right|\right]+C$$

$$=\frac{1}{6}\ln\left[\left|\frac{x-2}{x+2}\right|^{\frac{1}{2}}\left(\frac{x+1}{x-1}\right)\right]+C$$

(b) $I=\int\frac{f'(x)}{(f(x)+a)(f(x)+b)}dx$

$$=\frac{1}{b-a}\int\frac{([f(x)+b]-[f(x)+a])}{(f(x)+a)(f(x)+b)}f'(x)dx$$

$$=\frac{1}{b-a}\left[\int\frac{f'(x)}{f(x)+a}dx-\int\frac{f'(x)}{f(x)+b}dx\right]$$

$$=\frac{1}{b-a}\ln\left|\frac{f(x)+a}{f(x)+b}\right|+C$$

(c) $I=\int\frac{x}{(x+1)(1+x^2)}dx$

Let $\frac{x}{(x+1)(x^2+1)}=\frac{A}{x+1}+\frac{Bx+C}{(x^2+1)}$

$\Rightarrow x = A(x^2+1)+(Bx+C)(x+1)$

$\Rightarrow x = x^2(A+B)+x(B+C)+A+C$

$\Rightarrow A+B=0,\ B+C=1$ and $A+C=0$

$\Rightarrow A=-\frac{1}{2},\ B=\frac{1}{2},\ C=\frac{1}{2}$

$\Rightarrow I=-\frac{1}{2}\int\frac{dx}{x+1}+\frac{1}{2}\int\frac{x+1}{x^2+1}dx$

$=-\frac{1}{2}\ln|x+1|+\frac{1}{4}\int\frac{2x\,dx}{x^2+1}+\frac{1}{2}\int\frac{dx}{x^2+1}+C$

$=-\frac{1}{2}\ln|x+1|+\frac{1}{4}\ln|x^2+1|+\frac{1}{2}\tan^{-1}x+C$

3. (a) $I=\int\frac{2x^2+1}{(x^2+1)(x^2+3)}dx$

$=\int\frac{2x^2+4}{(x^2+1)(x^2+3)}dx-3\int\frac{dx}{(x^2+1)(x^2+3)}$

$=\int\frac{(x^2+1)+(x^2+3)}{(x^2+1)(x^2+3)}dx-\frac{3}{2}\int\frac{(x^2+3)-(x^2+1)}{(x^2+1)(x^2+3)}dx$

$=\int\frac{dx}{x^2+3}+\int\frac{dx}{x^2+1}-\frac{3}{2}\int\frac{dx}{x^2+1}+\frac{3}{2}\int\frac{dx}{x^2+3}$

$=\frac{5}{2}\int\frac{dx}{x^2+3}-\frac{1}{2}\int\frac{dx}{x^2+1}$

$=\frac{5}{2\sqrt{3}}\tan^{-1}\left(\frac{x}{\sqrt{3}}\right)-\frac{1}{2}\tan^{-1}x+C$

(b) $I=\int\frac{x^3+2}{(x+1)(x-2)^3}dx$

$\Rightarrow \frac{x^3+2}{(x-1)(x-2)^3}=\frac{A}{x-1}+\frac{B}{x-2}+\frac{C}{(x-2)^2}+\frac{D}{(x-2)^3}$

$\Rightarrow (x^3+2)=A(x-2)^3+B(x-1)(x-2)^2+C(x-1)(x-2)+D(x-1)$

Put $x=1$

$\Rightarrow A=-3$

Put $x=2$

$\Rightarrow D=10$

$A+B=\lim_{x\to\infty}\frac{x^3+2}{(x-2)^3}=1$

$\Rightarrow B=4$

Put $x=0$

$2=-8A-4B+2C-D$

$2=+24-16+2C-10$

$\Rightarrow C=2$

$\Rightarrow I=-3\int\frac{dx}{x-1}+4\int\frac{dx}{x-2}+2\int\frac{dx}{(x-2)^2}+10\int\frac{dx}{(x-2)^3}$

$=-3\ln|x-1|+4\ln|x-2|-\frac{2}{(x-2)}-5\frac{1}{(x-2)^2}+C$

(c) $\frac{1}{(x-1)(x+1)^6}=\frac{(x+1)-(x-1)}{2(x-1)(x+1)^6}$

$=\frac{1}{2}\left[\frac{1}{(x-1)(x+1)^5}-\frac{1}{(x+1)^6}\right]$

$=\frac{1}{2}\left[\frac{1}{2}\left[\frac{(x+1)-(x-1)}{(x-1)(x+1)^5}\right]-\frac{1}{(x+1)^6}\right]$

$=\frac{1}{2}\left[\frac{1}{2(x-1)(x+1)^4}-\frac{1}{2(x+1)^5}-\frac{1}{(x+1)^6}\right]$

$=\frac{1}{2}\left[\frac{1}{2}\left\{\frac{(x+1)-(x-1)}{2(x-1)(x+1)^4}\right\}-\frac{1}{2(x+1)^5}-\frac{1}{(x+1)^6}\right]$

$=\frac{1}{2}\left[\frac{1}{4(x-1)(x+1)^3}-\frac{1}{4(x+1)^5}-\frac{1}{(x+1)^6}\right]$

$=\frac{1}{2}\left[\frac{1}{8}\left(\frac{1}{(x-1)(x+1)^2}-\frac{1}{(x+1)^3}\right)\right.$

$\left.-\frac{1}{4(x+1)^4}-\frac{1}{2(x+1)^5}-\frac{1}{(x+1)^6}\right]$

$=\frac{1}{2}\left[\frac{1}{16}\left[\frac{(x+1)-(x-1)}{(x-1)(x+1)^2}\right]-\frac{1}{8(x+1)^3}\right.$

$\left.-\frac{1}{4(x+1)^4}-\frac{1}{2(x+1)^5}-\frac{1}{(x+1)^6}\right]$

$=\frac{1}{32}\cdot\frac{1}{(x^2-1)}-\frac{1}{32}\cdot\frac{1}{(x+1)^2}-\frac{1}{16}\cdot\frac{1}{(x+1)^3}$

$-\frac{1}{8(x+1)^4}-\frac{1}{4(x+1)^5}-\frac{1}{2(x+1)^6}$

$\Rightarrow I=\frac{1}{64}\ln\left|\frac{x-1}{x+1}\right|+\frac{1}{32(x+1)}+\frac{1}{32(x+1)^2}+\frac{1}{24(x+1)^3}$

$+\frac{1}{16(x+1)^4}+\frac{1}{10(x+1)^5}+C$

(d) $I=\int\frac{dx}{\cos^4x\sin^2x}=\int\frac{dx}{\cos^6x\tan^2x}=\int\frac{\sec^4x\sec^2x}{\tan^2x}dx$

$=\int\frac{(1+\tan^2x)^2\sec^2x}{\tan^2x}dx$

Let $\tan x=t \quad \Rightarrow \sec^2x\,dx=dt$

$\Rightarrow I=\int\frac{(1+t^2)^2}{t^2}dt=\int\frac{1+2t^2+t^4}{t^2}dt$

$=\int\frac{1}{t^2}dt+2\int dt+\int t^2dt=-\frac{1}{t}+2t+\frac{t^3}{3}+C$

$=-\cot x+2\tan x+\frac{\tan^3x}{3}+C$

(e) $I=\int\frac{dx}{(x^2+2)^3}$

Using Ostrogradsky Method, we get $\frac{P(x)}{Q(x)}=\frac{1}{(x^2+2)^3}$

$\Rightarrow Q(x)=(x^2+2)^3 \quad \Rightarrow Q'(x)=3(x^2+2)^2(2x)$

$\therefore G_1(x)=(x^2+2)^2 \quad \Rightarrow \frac{Q(x)}{G_1(x)}=x^2+2$

Let $G_0(x) = Ax^3 + Bx^2 + Cx + D$

$H_0(x) = Ex + F$

$$\therefore \int \frac{P(x)}{Q(x)}dx = \frac{G_0(x)}{G_1(x)} + \int \frac{H_0(x)}{\frac{Q(x)}{G_1(x)}}dx$$

$$\int \frac{1}{(x^2+2)^3}dx = \frac{Ax^3+Bx^2+Cx+D}{(x^2+2)^2} + \int \frac{Ex+F}{x^2+2}dx$$

Differentiating both side w.r.t. x, we get $\frac{1}{(x^2+2)^3}$

$$= \frac{(x^2+2)^2(3Ax^2+2Bx+C)-(4x)(x^2+2)(Ax^3+Bx^2+Cx+D)}{(x^2+2)^4} + \frac{Ex+F}{x^2+2}$$

$\Rightarrow$ $1 = (x^2 + 2)(3Ax^2 + 2Bx + C) - 4x(Ax^3 + Bx^2 + Cx + D) + (Ex + F)(x^2 + 2)^2$

$\Rightarrow$ $1 = Ex^5 + x^4(-A + F) + x^3(2B - 4B + 4E) + x^2(C + 6A - 4C + 4F) + x(4B - 4D + 4E) + 2C + 4F$

$\Rightarrow$ $E = 0, A = F, B = 0, 2A = C = 2F, D = 0,$

$$F = A = \frac{3}{32}, C = \frac{5}{16}$$

$$\therefore \quad I = \int \frac{dx}{(x^2+2)^3} = \frac{\frac{3}{32}x^3 + \frac{5x}{16}}{(x^2+2)^2} + \frac{3}{16}\int \frac{dx}{x^2+2}$$

$$= \frac{1}{32}x\left(\frac{3x^2+10}{(x^2+2)^2}\right) + \frac{3}{16\sqrt{2}}\tan^{-1}\left(\frac{x}{\sqrt{2}}\right) + C$$

4. (a) $I = \int \frac{1-2x}{(3+2x-x^2)}dx = \int \frac{2-2x}{3+2x-x^2}dx - \int \frac{dx}{3+2x-x^2}$

$$= \ln(3+2x-x^2) - \int \frac{dx}{2^2-(x-1)^2}$$

$$= \ln(3+2x-x^2) + \frac{1}{4}\ln\left|\frac{x-3}{x+1}\right| + C$$

$$= \ln(3-x)(x+1) + \frac{1}{4}\ln\left|\frac{x-3}{x+1}\right| + C$$

$$= \frac{5}{4}\ln|3+x| + \frac{3}{4}\ln|1+x| + C$$

(b) $I = \int \frac{x^4-x^2+1}{x^2(x^2+1)^2}dx$

$$\Rightarrow \frac{x^4-x^2+1}{x^2(x^2+1)^2} = \frac{Ax+B}{x^2} + \frac{Cx+D}{x^2+1} + \frac{Ex+F}{(x^2+1)^2}$$

$\Rightarrow$ $x^4 - x^2 + 1 = (Ax + B)(x^4 + 2x^2 + 1) + (Cx + D)(x^4 + x^2) + (Ex + F)x^2$

$\Rightarrow$ $x^5(A + C) + x^4(B + D) + x^3(2A + C + E) + x^2(2B + D + F) + x(A) + B$

$\Rightarrow$ $A = C = 0, B = 1, D = 0, E = 0, F = -3$

$$\Rightarrow \quad I = \int \frac{dx}{x^2} - 3\int \frac{dx}{(x^2+1)^2} = -\frac{1}{x} - 3I_1;$$

Where, $I_1 = \int \frac{dx}{(x^2+1)^2}$

Let $x = \tan\theta \quad \Rightarrow dx = \sec^2\theta\, d\theta$

$$\Rightarrow \quad I_1 = \int \frac{\sec^2\theta\, d\theta}{\sec^4\theta} = \int \cos^2\theta\, d\theta = \int \frac{(1+\cos 2\theta)}{2}d\theta$$

$$= \frac{1}{2}\theta + \frac{\sin 2\theta}{4} + C = \frac{1}{2}\tan^{-1}x + \frac{1}{2}\left(\frac{x}{1+x^2}\right) + C$$

$$\left(\because \quad \sin 2\theta = \frac{2\tan\theta}{1+\tan^2\theta} = \frac{2x}{1+x^2}\right)$$

$$\therefore \quad I = -\frac{1}{x} - \frac{3}{2}\tan^{-1}x - \frac{3}{2}\left(\frac{x}{1+x^2}\right) + C$$

(c) $I = \int \frac{x^4-x^3+5x^2+x+3}{(x+1)(x^2-x+1)^2}dx$

$$\Rightarrow \frac{x^4-x^3+5x^2+x+3}{(x+1)(x^2-x+1)^2} = \frac{A}{x+1} + \frac{Bx+C}{(x^2-x+1)} + \frac{Dx+E}{(x^2-x+1)^2}$$

$x^4 - x^3 + 5x^2 + x + 3 = A(x^4 + x^2 - 2x + 1 - 2x^3 + 2x^2) + (Bx + C)(x^3 - x^2 + x + x^2 - x + 1) + (Dx + E)(x + 1)$

$= A(x^4 - 2x^3 + 3x^2 - 2x + 1) + (Bx + C)(x^3 + 1) + (Dx + E)(x + 1)$

$= x^4(A + B) + x^3(-2A + C) + x^2(3A + D) + x(-2A + B + E + D) + A + C + E$

$A + B = 1, -2A + C = -1, 3A + D = 5, -2A + B + E + D = 1, A + C + E = 3$

$\therefore$ $A = C = E = 1, B = 0, D = 2$

$$\therefore \quad I = \int \frac{dx}{x+1} + \int \frac{dx}{\left(x-\frac{1}{2}\right)^2 + \left(\frac{\sqrt{3}}{2}\right)^2} + \int \frac{2x+1}{(x^2-x+1)^2}dx$$

$$= \ln|x+1| + \frac{2}{\sqrt{3}}\tan^{-1}\left(\frac{2x-1}{\sqrt{3}}\right) + \int \frac{2x-1}{(x^2-x+1)^2}dx + 2\int \frac{dx}{(x^2-x+1)^2}$$

$$= \ln|x+1| + \frac{2}{\sqrt{3}}\tan^{-1}\left(\frac{2x-1}{\sqrt{3}}\right) - \frac{1}{(x^2-x+1)} + 2I_1$$

Where, $I_1 = \int \frac{dx}{(x^2-x+1)^2} = \int \frac{dx}{\left[\left(x-\frac{1}{2}\right)^2 + \left(\frac{\sqrt{3}}{2}\right)^2\right]^2}$

Let $x = \frac{\sqrt{3}}{2}\tan\theta + \frac{1}{2}$

$$\Rightarrow \quad dx = \frac{\sqrt{3}}{2}\sec^2\theta\, d\theta$$

$$\Rightarrow \quad I_1 = \int \frac{\frac{\sqrt{3}}{2}\sec^2\theta\, d\theta}{\frac{9}{16}\sec^4\theta} = \frac{8}{3\sqrt{3}}\int \cos^2\theta\, d\theta$$

$$= \frac{4}{3\sqrt{3}}\int (1+\cos 2\theta)d\theta = \frac{4}{3\sqrt{3}}\left(\theta + \frac{\sin 2\theta}{2}\right) + C$$

$$= \frac{4}{3\sqrt{3}}\left(\tan^{-1}\left(\frac{2x-1}{\sqrt{3}}\right) + \frac{\sqrt{3}}{4}\frac{2x-1}{x^2-x+1}\right)$$

$\therefore \quad I = \ln|x+1| + \frac{14}{3\sqrt{3}}\tan^{-1}\left(\frac{2x-1}{\sqrt{3}}\right)$

$- \frac{1}{x^2-x+1} + \frac{2}{3}\frac{2x-1}{x^2-x+1} + C$

$= \ln|x+1| + \frac{14}{3\sqrt{3}}\tan^{-1}\left(\frac{2x-1}{\sqrt{3}}\right) + \frac{4x-5}{3(x^2-x+1)} + C$

5. (i) $I = \int \frac{15x^2-4x-81}{(x-3)(x+4)(x-1)}dx$

Let $\frac{15x^2-4x-81}{(x-3)(x+4)(x-1)} = \frac{A}{x-3} + \frac{B}{x+4} + \frac{C}{x-1}$

$C = \frac{15x^2-4x-81}{(x-3)(x+4)}$ for $x = 1$

$\therefore \quad C = \frac{15-4-81}{(-2)(5)} = 7$

$B = \frac{15x^2-4x-81}{(x-3)(x-1)}$ for $x = -4$

$\therefore \quad B = \frac{240+16-81}{(-7)(-5)} = 5$

$A = \frac{15x^2-4x-81}{(x+4)(x-1)}$ for $x = 3$

$\therefore \quad A = \frac{135-12-81}{(7)(2)} = 3$

$\therefore \quad I = 3\int\frac{dx}{x-3} + 5\int\frac{dx}{x+4} + 7\int\frac{dx}{x-1}$

$= 3ln\,|x-3| + 5ln\,|x+4| + 7ln\,|x-1| + C$

(ii) $I = \int \frac{x^4-3x^2-3x-2}{x^3-x^2-2x}dx = \frac{x^4-3x^2-3x-2}{x^3-x^2-2x}$

$= (x+1) - \frac{x+2}{x(x-2)(x+1)}$

Let $\frac{x+2}{x(x-2)(x+1)} = \frac{A}{x} + \frac{B}{x-2} + \frac{C}{x+1}$

$\Rightarrow \quad A = \frac{x+2}{(x-2)(x+1)}$ for $x = 0$

$\therefore \quad A = -1$

$B = \frac{(x+2)}{x(x+1)}$ for $x = 2$

$\therefore \quad B = \frac{2}{3}$

$C = \frac{(x+2)}{x(x-2)}$ for $x = -1$

$\therefore \quad C = \frac{1}{3}$

$\therefore \quad I = \int(x+1)dx + \int\frac{dx}{x} - \frac{2}{3}\int\frac{dx}{x-2} - \frac{1}{3}\int\frac{dx}{x+1}$

$= \frac{x^2}{2} + x + \ln|x| - \frac{2}{3}\ln|x-2| - \frac{1}{3}\ln|x+1| + C$

(iii) $I = \int\frac{2x^2-3x+3}{x^3-2x^2+x}dx = \int\frac{2x^2-3x+3}{x(x-1)^2}dx$

$$\frac{2x^2-3x+3}{x(x-1)^2} = \frac{A}{x} + \frac{B}{x-1} + \frac{C}{(x-1)^2} \quad \ldots(1)$$

$\Rightarrow \quad A = \frac{2x^2-3x+3}{(x-1)^2}$ for $x = 0$

$\therefore \quad A = 3$

$C = \frac{2x^2-3x+3}{x}$ for $x = 1$

$\therefore \quad C = 2$

For B put $x = -1$ in (1)

$\frac{2+3+3}{-4} = -3 - \frac{B}{2} + \frac{1}{2}$

$\therefore \quad B = -1$

$\therefore \quad I = 3\int\frac{dx}{x} - \int\frac{dx}{x-1} + 2\int\frac{dx}{(x-1)^2}$

$= 3\ln|x| - \ln|x-1| - \frac{2}{(x-1)} + C$

(iv) $I = \int\frac{x\,dx}{x^3+1}$

$\frac{x}{x^3+1} = \frac{x}{(x+1)(x^2-x+1)} = \frac{A}{x+1} + \frac{Bx+C}{x^2-x+1}$

$x = A(x^2-x+1) + (Bx+C)(x+1)$

$= x^2(A+B) + x(-A+B+C) + A + C$

$\Rightarrow \quad A + B = 0, -A + B + C = 1, A + C = 0$

$A = -\frac{1}{3}, B = C = \frac{1}{3}$

$\Rightarrow \quad I = -\frac{1}{3}\int\frac{dx}{x+1} + \frac{1}{3}\int\frac{x+1}{x^2-x+1}dx$

$= -\frac{1}{3}\ln|x+1| + \frac{1}{6}\int\frac{2x-1}{x^2-x+1} + \frac{1}{2}\int\frac{dx}{\left(x-\frac{1}{2}\right)^2 + \left(\frac{\sqrt{3}}{2}\right)^2}$

$= -\frac{1}{3}\ln|x+1| + \frac{1}{6}\ln|x^2-x+1|$

$+ \frac{1}{\sqrt{3}}\tan^{-1}\left(\frac{2x-1}{\sqrt{3}}\right) + C$

(v) $I = \int\frac{dx}{(x^2+1)(x^2+4)} = \frac{1}{3}\int\frac{(x^2+4)-(x^2+1)}{(x^2+1)(x^2+4)}dx$

$= \frac{1}{3}\int\frac{dx}{x^2+1} - \frac{1}{3}\int\frac{dx}{x^2+4} = \frac{1}{3}\tan^{-1}x - \frac{1}{6}\tan^{-1}\frac{x}{2} + C$

(vi) $I = \int\frac{x^4+4x^3+11x^2+12x+8}{(x^2+2x+3)^2(x+1)}dx$

Let $\frac{x^4+4x^3+11x^2+12x+8}{(x+1)(x^2+2x+3)^2}$

$= \frac{A}{x+1} + \frac{Bx+C}{x^2+2x+3} + \frac{Dx+E}{(x^2+2x+3)^2}$

$x^4 + 4x^3 + 11x^2 + 12x + 8 = A(x^4 + 4x^3 + 10x^2 + 12x + 9) + (Bx + C)(x^3 + 2x^2 + 3x + x^2 + 2x + 3) + (Dx + E)(x + 1)$
$= A(x^4 + 4x^3 + 10x^2 + 12x + 9) + (Bx + C)(x^3 + 3x^2 + 5x + 3) + (Dx + E)(x + 1)$
$= x^4(A + B) + x^3(4A + C + 3B) + x^2(10A + 3C + 5B + D) + x(12A + 3B + D + E) + 9A + 3C + E$

$\Rightarrow A + B = 1,\ 4A + C + 3B = 4,\ 10A + 3C + 5B + D = 11,\ 12A + 3B + D + E = 12,\ 9A + 3C + E = 8$

$\Rightarrow A = \dfrac{x^4 + 4x^3 + 11x^2 + 12x + 8}{(x^2 + 2x + 3)^2}$ for $x = -1$

$\therefore A = \dfrac{1 - 4 + 11 - 12 + 8}{(1 - 2 + 3)^2} = \dfrac{4}{4} = 1$

$\Rightarrow A = 1, B = 0, C = 0, D = 1, E = -1$

$\therefore I = \int \dfrac{dx}{x+1} + \int \dfrac{x-1}{(x^2 + 2x + 3)^2}$

$= \ln|x+1| + \dfrac{1}{2}\int \dfrac{2x+2}{(x^2 + 2x + 3)^2}dx - 2\int \dfrac{dx}{(x^2 + 2x + 3)^2}$

$I = \ln|x+1| - \dfrac{1}{2}\dfrac{1}{(x^2 + 2x + 3)} - 2I_1$ ...(i)

$I_1 = \int \dfrac{dx}{((x+1)^2 + (\sqrt{2})^2)^2}$

Let $x = \sqrt{2}\tan\theta - 1 \Rightarrow dx = \sqrt{2}\sec^2\theta\, d\theta$

$\therefore I_1 = \int \dfrac{\sqrt{2}\sec^2\theta\, d\theta}{4\sec^4\theta} = \dfrac{1}{2\sqrt{2}}\int \cos^2\theta\, d\theta$

$= \dfrac{1}{4\sqrt{2}}\int (1 + \cos 2\theta)d\theta = \dfrac{\theta}{4\sqrt{2}} + \dfrac{\sin 2\theta}{8\sqrt{2}} + C$

$= \dfrac{1}{4\sqrt{2}}\tan^{-1}\left(\dfrac{x+1}{\sqrt{2}}\right) + \dfrac{1}{4}\left(\dfrac{x+1}{x^2 + 2x + 3}\right) + C$

$\Rightarrow I = \ln|x+1| - \dfrac{1}{2\sqrt{2}}\tan^{-1}\left(\dfrac{x+1}{\sqrt{2}}\right) - \dfrac{1}{2}\left(\dfrac{x+2}{x^2 + 2x + 3}\right) + C$

(vii) $I = \int \dfrac{5x^3 + 9x^2 - 22x - 8}{x^3 - 4x}dx = \int 5dx + \int \dfrac{9x^2 - 2x - 8}{x^3 - 4x}dx$

Let $\dfrac{9x^2 - 2x - 8}{x(x+2)(x-2)} = \dfrac{A}{x} + \dfrac{B}{x+2} + \dfrac{C}{x-2}$

$\Rightarrow A = \dfrac{9x^2 - 2x - 8}{(x+2)(x-2)}$ for x = 0

$\therefore A = 2$

$B = \dfrac{9x^2 - 2x - 8}{x(x-2)}$ for $x = -2$

$\therefore B = 4$

$C = \dfrac{9x^2 - 2x - 8}{x(x+2)}$ for $x = 2$

$\therefore C = 3$

$\therefore I = 5x + 2\int \dfrac{dx}{x} + 4\int \dfrac{dx}{x+2} + 3\int \dfrac{dx}{x-2} = 5x + 2\ln|x| + 4\ln|x+2| + 3\ln|x-2| + C$
$= 5x + \ln(x^2(x+2)^4|x-2|^3) + C$

(viii) $I = \int \dfrac{dx}{(x^2 - 4x + 4)(x^2 - 4x + 5)} = \int \dfrac{dx}{(x-2)^2(x - 4x + 5)}$

$\Rightarrow \dfrac{1}{(x-2)^2(x^2 - 4x + 5)} = \dfrac{A}{x-2} + \dfrac{B}{(x-2)^2} + \dfrac{Cx + D}{(x^2 - 4x + 5)}$

$\Rightarrow I = A(x-2)(x^2 - 4x + 5) + B(x^2 - 4x + 5) + (Cx + D)(x^2 - 4x + 4)$
$= x^3(A + C) + x^2(-2A - 4A + B + D - 4C) + x(5A + 8A - 4B + 4C - 4D) - 10A + 5B + 4D$

$\Rightarrow A + C = 0, -6A + B - 4C + D = 0, 13A - 4B + 4C - 4D = 0, -10A + 5B + 4D = 1$

$\left.\begin{matrix} -2A + B + D = 0 \\ 9A - 4B - 4D = 0 \end{matrix}\right] \Rightarrow A = C = 0$

$\left.\begin{matrix} B + D = 0 \\ 5B + 4D = 1 \end{matrix}\right] \Rightarrow B = 1, D = -1$

$\therefore I = \int \dfrac{dx}{(x-2)^2} - \int \dfrac{dx}{(x-2)^2 + 1^2}$

$= -\dfrac{1}{(x-2)} - \tan^{-1}(x-2) + C$

(ix) $I = \int \dfrac{dx}{(x+1)(x^2+1)(x^3+1)}$

$= \int \dfrac{dx}{(x+1)^2(x^2+1)(x^2 - x + 1)}$

Let $\dfrac{1}{(x+1)^2(x^2+1)(x^2 - x + 1)}$

$= \dfrac{A}{x+1} + \dfrac{B}{(x+1)^2} + \dfrac{Cx + D}{x^2 + 1} + \dfrac{Ex + F}{x^2 - x + 1}$

$1 = A(x+1)(x^4 - x^3 + 2x^2 - x + 1) + B(x^4 - x^3 + 2x^2 - x + 1) + (Cx + D)(x^2 + 2x + 1)(x^2 - x + 1) + (Ex + F)(x^2 + 2x + 1)(x^2 + 1)$
$= A(x^5 + x^3 + x^2 + 1) + B(x^4 - x^3 + 2x^2 - x + 1) + (Cx + D)(x^4 + x^3 + x + 1) + (Ex + F)(x^4 + 2x^3 + 2x^2 + 2x + 1)$
$= x^5(A + C + E) + x^4(B + D + C + 2E + F) + x^3(A - B + D + 2E + 2F) + x^2(A + 2B + C + 2F + 2E) + x(-B + C + D + E + 2F) + A + B + D + F$

$A + C + E = 0, B + C + D + 2E + F = 0, A - B + D + 2E + 2F = 0, A + 2B + C + 2F + 2E = 0$
$-B + C + D + E + 2F = 0, A + B + D + F = 1$

$B = \dfrac{1}{(x^2+1)(x^2 - x + 1)}$ for $x = -1$

$\Rightarrow B = \dfrac{1}{6}$. Solving for A, C, D, E and F, we get $F = 0$, $D = \dfrac{1}{2}, A = \dfrac{1}{3}, E = -\dfrac{1}{3}, C = 0$

$\therefore I = \dfrac{1}{3}\int \dfrac{dx}{x+1} + \dfrac{1}{6}\int \dfrac{dx}{(x+1)^2} + \dfrac{1}{2}\int \dfrac{dx}{x^2+1} - \dfrac{1}{3}\int \dfrac{x}{x^2 - x + 1}dx$

$= \dfrac{1}{3}\ln|x+1| - \dfrac{1}{6(x+1)} + \dfrac{1}{2}\tan^{-1}x - \dfrac{1}{6}\int \dfrac{2x-1}{x^2 - x + 1}dx - \dfrac{1}{6}\int \dfrac{dx}{\left(x - \dfrac{1}{2}\right)^2 + \left(\dfrac{\sqrt{3}}{2}\right)^2}$

$$= \frac{1}{3}\ln|x+1| - \frac{1}{6(x+1)} + \frac{1}{2}\tan^{-1}x$$

$$- \frac{1}{6}\ln|x^2-x+1| - \frac{1}{3\sqrt{3}}\tan^{-1}\left(\frac{2x-1}{\sqrt{3}}\right) + C$$

$$= -\frac{1}{6(x+1)} + \frac{1}{6}\ln\frac{(1+x)^2}{(x^2-x+1)}$$

$$+\frac{1}{2}\tan^{-1}x - \frac{1}{3\sqrt{3}}\tan^{-1}\left(\frac{2x-1}{\sqrt{3}}\right) + C$$

(x) $I = \int \frac{x^3+3}{(x+1)(x^2+1)} = \int \frac{x^3+3}{x^3+x^2+x+1}dx$

$$= \int dx - \int \frac{x^2+x-2}{x^3+x^2+x+1}dx = \int 1dx - \int \frac{x^2+x-2}{(x^2+1)(x+1)}dx$$

Let $\frac{x^2+x-2}{(x+1)(x^2+1)} = \frac{A}{x+1} + \frac{Bx+C}{x^2+1}$

$A = \frac{x^2+x-2}{x^2+1}$ for $x = -1$

$\therefore$ $A = -1$

Put $x = 0$, we get $-2 = -1 + C$

$\Rightarrow$ C = –1

Put $x = 1$, we get $0 = -\frac{1}{2} + \frac{B-1}{2}$

$\Rightarrow$ $B = 2$

$\therefore$ $I = \int dx + \int \frac{dx}{x+1} - \int \frac{2x-1}{x^2+1}dx$

$$= x + \ln|x+1| - \int \frac{2x}{x^2+1}dx + \int \frac{dx}{x^2+1}$$

$$= x + \ln|x+1| - \ln|x^2+1| + \tan^{-1}x + C$$

TEXTUAL EXERCISE–6: (OBJECTIVE)

1. (b) $I = \int \frac{x}{(x^2+1)(x-1)}dx$

$$= \ln((x^2+1)^a|x-1|^b) + \frac{1}{2}\tan^{-1}x + C$$

Differetiating w.r.t. x, we get

$$\frac{x}{(x^2+1)(x-1)}$$

$$= \frac{2xa(x^2+1)^{a-1}|x-1|^b + b(x-1)^{b-1}(x^2+1)^a}{(x^2+1)^a(x-1)^b} + \frac{1}{2(x^2+1)}$$

$$= \frac{2ax(x-1)+b(x^2+1)}{(x^2+1)(x-1)} + \frac{1}{2(x^2+1)}$$

$$= \frac{4ax(x-1)+2b(x^2+1)+x-1}{2(x^2+1)(x-1)}$$

$$= \frac{x^2(4a+2b)+x(-4a+1)+2b-1}{2(x^2+1)(x-1)}$$

Comparing both sides $\frac{-4a+1}{2} = 1$

$\Rightarrow$ $a = -\frac{1}{4}$, $b = \frac{1}{2}$

$\therefore$ $4|b-a| = 3$

2. (c) $I = \int \frac{x^2+2}{(x+1)^3(x-2)}dx = \int \frac{x^2-4+6}{(x+1)^3(x-2)}dx$

$$= \int \frac{(x+2)}{(x+1)^3}dx + 6\int \frac{dx}{(x+1)^3(x+2)}$$

$$= \int \frac{1}{(x+1)^2}dx + \int \frac{1}{(x+1)^3}dx + \frac{6}{3}\int \frac{\{(x+1)-(x-2)\}}{(x+1)^3(x-2)}dx$$

$$= \int (x+1)^{-2}dx + \int (x+1)^{-3}dx$$

$$+2\int \frac{1}{(x+1)^2(x-2)}dx - 2\int (x+1)^{-3}dx$$

$$= \frac{-1}{(x+1)} + \frac{1}{2(x+1)^2} + \frac{2}{3} + \int \frac{(x+1)-(x-2)}{(x+1)^2(x-2)}dx$$

$$= \frac{-1}{(x+1)} + \frac{1}{2(x+1)^2} + \frac{2}{3}\int \frac{1}{(x+1)(x-2)}dx + \frac{2}{3}\frac{1}{(x+1)}$$

$$= \frac{-1}{3(x+1)} + \frac{1}{2(x+1)^2} + \frac{2}{(3\times 3)}\int \frac{1}{(x+1)(x-2)}dx + \frac{2}{3}\frac{1}{(x+1)}$$

$$= \frac{-1}{3(x+1)} + \frac{1}{2(x+1)^2} + \frac{2}{(3\times 3)}\int \frac{(x-1)-(x-2)}{(x+1)(x-2)}dx$$

$$= \frac{-1}{3(x+1)} + \frac{1}{2(x+1)^2} + \frac{2}{9}\ln|x-2| - \frac{2}{9}\ln|x+1| + C$$

$$= \frac{-1}{3(x+1)} + \frac{1}{2(x+1)^2} + \frac{2}{9}\ln\left|\frac{x-2}{x+1}\right| + C$$

3. (a) $I = \int \frac{x^3+3}{x^3-3x}dx = \int dx + \int \frac{3x+3}{x^3-3x}dx$

$$= x + 3\underbrace{\int \frac{x+1}{x(x+\sqrt{3})(x-\sqrt{3})}dx}_{I_1}$$

Let, $\frac{x+1}{x(x+\sqrt{3})(x-\sqrt{3})} = \frac{A}{x} + \frac{B}{x+\sqrt{3}} + \frac{C}{x-\sqrt{3}}$

$\Rightarrow$ $A = \frac{x+1}{x^2-(\sqrt{3})^2}$ for $x = 0$

$\Rightarrow$ $A = -\frac{1}{3}$

$B = \frac{x+1}{x(x-\sqrt{3})}$ for $x = -\sqrt{3}$

$\Rightarrow$ $B = \frac{1-\sqrt{3}}{6}$

$C = \frac{x+1}{x(x+\sqrt{3})}$ for $x = \sqrt{3}$

$\therefore$ $C = \frac{1+\sqrt{3}}{6}$

$\therefore$ $I_1 = -\frac{1}{3}\int \frac{dx}{x} + \frac{1-\sqrt{3}}{6}\int \frac{dx}{x+\sqrt{3}} + \frac{1+\sqrt{3}}{6}\int \frac{dx}{x-\sqrt{3}}$

$$= -\frac{1}{3}\ln x + \frac{1-\sqrt{3}}{6}\ln|x+\sqrt{3}| + \frac{1+\sqrt{3}}{6}\ln|x-\sqrt{3}| + C$$

$$I = x - \ln x + \frac{1-\sqrt{3}}{2}\ln|x+\sqrt{3}| + \frac{1+\sqrt{3}}{2}\ln|x-\sqrt{3}| + C$$

4. (b) $I = \int \frac{x^2+1}{(x^2-1)(x^2-4)}dx$

$$= \int \frac{x^2+1}{(x+1)(x-1)(x+2)(x-2)}dx$$

$$\frac{x^2+1}{(x+1)(x-1)(x+2)(x-2)} = \frac{A}{x+1} + \frac{B}{x-1} + \frac{C}{x+2} + \frac{D}{x-2}$$

$\Rightarrow A = \frac{x^2+1}{(x-1)(x+2)(x-2)}$ for $x = -1$

$\Rightarrow A = \frac{1}{3}$

$B = \frac{x^2+1}{(x+1)(x+2)(x-2)}$ for $x = 1$

$\Rightarrow B = -\frac{1}{3}$

$C = \frac{x^2+1}{(x+1)(x-1)(x-2)}$ for $x = -2$

$\Rightarrow C = -\frac{5}{12}$

$D = \frac{x^2+1}{(x+1)(x-1)(x+2)}$ for x = 2

$\Rightarrow D = \frac{5}{12}$

$$\therefore \quad I = \frac{1}{3}\int\frac{dx}{x+1} - \frac{1}{3}\int\frac{dx}{x-1} - \frac{5}{12}\int\frac{dx}{x+2} + \frac{5}{12}\int\frac{dx}{x-2}$$

$$= \frac{1}{3}\ln\left|\frac{x+1}{x-1}\right| + \frac{5}{12}\ln\left|\frac{x-2}{x+2}\right| + C$$

$$= \frac{5}{12}\ln\left|\frac{x-2}{x+2}\right| - \frac{1}{3}\ln\left|\frac{x-1}{x+1}\right| + C$$

5. (c) $I = \int \frac{x^5}{x^3-2x^2-5x+6}dx$

$$= \int (x^2+2x+9)dx + \int \frac{22x^2+33x-54}{x^3-2x^2-5x+6}$$

Let $\frac{22x^2+33x-54}{x^3-2x^2-5x+6} = \frac{22x^2+33x-54}{(x-1)(x+2)(x-3)}$

$$= \frac{A}{x-1} + \frac{B}{x+2} + \frac{C}{x-3}$$

$A = \frac{22x^2+33x-54}{(x+2)(x-3)}$ for $x = 1$

$\Rightarrow A = -\frac{1}{6}$

$B = \frac{22x^2+33x-54}{(x-1)(x-3)}$ for $x = -2$

$\Rightarrow B = -\frac{32}{15}$

$C = \frac{22x^2+33x-54}{(x+2)(x-1)}$ for $x = 3$

$\Rightarrow C = \frac{243}{10}$

$$I = \frac{x^3}{3} + x^2 + 9x - \frac{1}{6}\int\frac{dx}{x-1} - \frac{32}{15}\ln\int\frac{dx}{x+2} + \frac{243}{10}\int\frac{dx}{x-3}$$

$$= \frac{x^3}{3} + x^2 + 9x - \frac{\ln|x-1|}{6} - \frac{32}{15}\ln|x+2| + \frac{243}{10}\ln|x-3| + C$$

6. (c) $I = \int \frac{dx}{x^3(x-1)^2(x+1)}$

Let $\frac{1}{x^3(x-1)^2(x+1)}$

$$= \frac{A}{(x-1)} + \frac{B}{(x-1)^2} + \frac{C}{x+1} + \frac{Dx^2+Ex+F}{x^3}$$

$B = \frac{1}{(x^3)(x+1)}$ for $x = 1$

$\Rightarrow B = \frac{1}{2}$

$F = \frac{1}{(x-1)^2(x+1)}$ for $x = 0$

$\Rightarrow F = 1$

$C = \frac{1}{x^3(x-1)^2}$ for $x = -1$

$\Rightarrow C = -\frac{1}{4}$

Put $x = 2$

$$\frac{1}{24} = A + \frac{1}{2} - \frac{1}{12} + \frac{D}{2} + \frac{E}{4} + \frac{1}{8}$$

$$-12 = 24A + 12D + 6E$$

$$-2 = 4A + 2D + E \quad \text{...(i)}$$

Put $x = 3$

$$\frac{1}{432} = \frac{A}{2} + \frac{1}{8} - \frac{1}{16} + \frac{D}{3} + \frac{E}{9} + \frac{1}{27}$$

$$-\frac{42}{432} = -\frac{7}{72} = \frac{A}{2} + \frac{D}{3} + \frac{E}{9}$$

$$\Rightarrow -7 = 36A + 24D + 8E \quad \text{...(ii)}$$

Put $x = -3$

$$\frac{1}{864} = -\frac{A}{4} + \frac{1}{32} + \frac{1}{8} - \frac{D}{3} + \frac{E}{9} - \frac{1}{27}$$

$$-\frac{102}{864} = -\frac{17}{144} = -\frac{A}{4} - \frac{D}{3} + \frac{E}{9}$$

$$\Rightarrow -17 = -36A - 48D + 16E \quad \text{...(iii)}$$

(i) × 9 + (iii)

$$-35 = -30D + 25E \Rightarrow -7 = 5E - 6D \quad \text{...(iv)}$$

(ii) – 9 × (i)

$11 = 6D = E$ ...(v)

$\therefore\ E = 1, D = 2,\ A = -\frac{7}{4}$

$$I = -\frac{7}{4}\int\frac{dx}{x-1} + \frac{1}{2}\int\frac{dx}{(x-1)^2}$$

$$-\frac{1}{4}\int\frac{dx}{x+1} + 2\int\frac{dx}{x} + \int\frac{dx}{x^2} + \int\frac{dx}{x^3}$$

$$= 2\ln|x| - \frac{1}{x} - \frac{1}{2x^2} - \frac{7}{4}\ln|x-1|$$

$$-\frac{1}{2(x-1)} - \frac{1}{4}\ln|x+1| + C$$

7. (b) $I = \int\frac{dx}{(x-1)^2(x-2)(x^2+4)}$

$$\frac{1}{(x-1)^2(x-2)(x^2+4)}$$

$$= \frac{A}{x-1} + \frac{B}{(x-1)^2} + \frac{C}{x-2} + \frac{Dx+E}{x^2+4}$$

$B = \frac{1}{(x-2)(x^2+4)}$ for $x = 1$

$\therefore\ B = -\frac{1}{5}$

$C = \frac{1}{(x-1)^2(x^2+4)}$ for $x = 2$

$\therefore\ C = \frac{1}{8}$

Put $x = 0$ $\ -\frac{1}{8} = -A - \frac{1}{5} - \frac{1}{16} + \frac{E}{4}$

$\Rightarrow\ 11 = -80A + 20E$ ...(i)

Put $x = -1$

$$-\frac{1}{60} = -\frac{A}{2} - \frac{1}{20} - \frac{1}{24} - \frac{D}{5} + \frac{E}{5}$$

$\Rightarrow\ 3 = -20A - 8D + 8E$ ...(ii)

Put $x = -2$

$$-\frac{1}{288} = -\frac{A}{3} - \frac{1}{45} - \frac{1}{32} - \frac{D}{4} + \frac{E}{8}$$

$$\frac{72}{1440} = \frac{1}{20} = -\frac{A}{3} - \frac{D}{4} + \frac{E}{8}$$

$\Rightarrow\ 6 = -40A - 30D + 15E$ ...(iii)

(ii) × 15 – (iii) × 4

$21 = -140A + 60E$ ...(iv)

3 × (i) – (iv)

$12 = -100A \quad \Rightarrow\ A = -\frac{3}{25}$

From (i) $\quad \Rightarrow\ E = \frac{7}{100}$

From (ii) $\quad \Rightarrow\ D = -\frac{1}{200}$

$$I = -\frac{3}{25}\int\frac{dx}{x-1} - \frac{1}{5}\int\frac{dx}{(x-1)^2}$$

$$+\frac{1}{8}\int\frac{dx}{x-2} - \frac{1}{200}\int\frac{x-14}{x^2+4}dx$$

$$= -\frac{3}{25}\ln|x-1| + \frac{1}{5(x-1)}$$

$$+\frac{1}{8}\ln|x-2| - \frac{1}{400}\ln|x^2+4| + \frac{7}{200}\tan^{-1}\frac{x}{2} + k$$

Comparing $A = 25, B = 5, C = 400, D = 200$

$\Rightarrow\ A + B + C + D = 630$

8. (a) $I = \int\frac{x^2+6x-25}{(x^2+4x-5)(x^2+4x+5)}$

$$= \int\frac{x^2+6x-25}{(x+5)(x-1)(x^2+4x+5)}dx$$

$$\frac{x^2+6x-25}{(x+5)(x-1)(x^2+4x+5)} = \frac{A}{x+5} + \frac{B}{x-1} + \frac{Cx+D}{x^2+4x+5}$$

$A = \frac{x^2+6x-25}{(x-1)(x^2+4x+5)}$ for x = –5

$\therefore\ A = \frac{1}{2}$

$B = \frac{x^2+6x-25}{(x+5)(x^2+4x+5)}$ for x = 1

$\therefore\ B = -\frac{18}{6\times10} = -\frac{3}{10}$

Put x = 0

$$\frac{-25}{-25} = 1 = \frac{1}{10} + \frac{3}{10} + \frac{D}{5}$$

$\Rightarrow$ D = 3

Put x = –1

$$\frac{-30}{-16} = \frac{15}{8} = \frac{1}{8} + \frac{3}{20} - \frac{C}{2} + \frac{3}{2}$$

$\Rightarrow\ C = -\frac{1}{5}$

$$I = \frac{1}{2}\int\frac{dx}{x+5} - \frac{3}{10}\int\frac{dx}{x-1}$$

$$-\frac{1}{5}\int\frac{x}{x^2+4x+5}dx + 3\int\frac{dx}{(x+2)^2+1^2}$$

$$= \frac{1}{2}\ln|x+5| - \frac{3}{10}\ln|x-1|$$

$$-\frac{1}{10}\int\frac{2x+4}{x^2+4x+5}dx + \frac{17}{5}\int\frac{dx}{(x+2)^2+1^2}$$

$$= \frac{1}{2}\ln|x+5| - \frac{3}{10}\ln|x-1|$$

$$-\frac{1}{10}\ln|x^2+4x+5| + \frac{17}{5}\tan^{-1}(x+2) + C$$

Comparing, $A = -10, B = 10, C = 5$

$\therefore\ A + B + C = 5$

9. (a) $I = \int\frac{x^2-3x+2}{x(x^2+2x+1)}dx = \frac{x^2-3x+2}{x(x^2+2x+1)}$

$$= \frac{A}{x} + \frac{Bx+C}{x^2+2x+1}$$

$A = \frac{x^2-3x+2}{x^2+2x+1}$ for $x = 0$

$\therefore\ A = 2$

$(x^2 - 3x + 2) = 2(x^2 + 2x + 1) + (Bx + C)\,x$

$= x^2(2 + B) + x(4 + C) + 2$

$\therefore\ 2 + B = 1,\ 4 + C = -3$

$B = -1,\ C = -7$

$$I = 2\int\frac{dx}{x} - \int\frac{x+7}{x^2+2x+1}dx = 2\ln|x| - \frac{1}{2}\int\frac{2x+2}{x^2+2x+1}$$

$$-6\int\frac{dx}{(x+1)^2}$$

$$= 2\ln|x| - \frac{1}{2}\ln(x+1)^2 + \frac{6}{x+1} + C$$

$$= \ln\left|\frac{x^2}{x+1}\right| + \frac{6}{x+1} + C$$

TEXTUAL EXERCISE–7: (SUBJECTIVE)

1. $I = \int\frac{\sin^3 x}{3+\cos x}dx = \int\frac{\sin^2 x\sin x}{3+\cos x}dx$

Let $\cos x = t \quad \Rightarrow \quad -\sin x\, dx = dt$

$$I = -\int\frac{(1-t^2)}{3+t}dt = \int\frac{t^2-1}{3+t}dt$$

$$= \int\frac{t(3+t)}{3+t}dt - \int\frac{(3t+1)}{3+t}dt$$

$$= \frac{t^2}{2} - 3\int\frac{t+3}{t+3}dt + 8\int\frac{dt}{3+t} = \frac{t^2}{2} - 3t + 8\ln|3+t| + C$$

$$= \frac{\cos^2 x}{2} - 3\cos x + 8\ln|\cos x + 3| + C$$

2. $I = \int\frac{3\tan x - 4\cot x}{\cos 2x}dx$

$$= \int\frac{3\tan^2 x - 4}{(\tan x)\left(\frac{1-\tan^2 x}{1+\tan^2 x}\right)} = \int\frac{(3\tan^2 x - 4)}{\tan x(1-\tan^2 x)}\sec^2 x\,dx$$

Let $\tan x = t \quad \Rightarrow \quad \sec^2 x\,dx = dt$

$$\Rightarrow\ I = \int\frac{3t^2-4}{t(1-t^2)}dt = \int\frac{3(t^2-1)}{t(1-t^2)}dt - \int\frac{dt}{t(1-t^2)} = -3\ln|t| - I_1$$

Let $\frac{1}{t(1-t)(1+t)} = \frac{A}{t} + \frac{B}{1-t} + \frac{C}{1+t}$

$\Rightarrow\ A = 1, B = \frac{1}{2}, C = -\frac{1}{2}$

$$I_1 = \int\frac{dt}{t} + \frac{1}{2}\int\frac{dt}{1-t} - \frac{1}{2}\int\frac{dt}{1+t} = \ln|t| - \frac{1}{2}\ln|1-t^2| + C$$

$$I = -4\ln|t| + \frac{1}{2}\ln|1-t^2| + C$$

$$= -4\ln|\tan x| + \frac{1}{2}\ln|1-\tan^2 x| + C$$

3. $I = \int\frac{\sin^4 x}{\cos^8 x}dx = \int\tan^4 x\sec^2 x\sec^2 x\,dx$

Let $\tan x = t \quad \Rightarrow \quad \sec^2 x\,dx = dt$

$$I = \int t^4(1+t^2)\,dt$$

$$= \int t^4\,dt + \int t^6\,dt = \frac{t^5}{5} + \frac{t^7}{7} + C = \frac{\tan^5 x}{5} + \frac{\tan^7 x}{7} + C$$

4. $I = \int\frac{dx}{\sin x(2+\cos x - 2\sin x)}$

$\tan\frac{x}{2} = t \Rightarrow \frac{1}{2}\sec^2\frac{x}{2}dx = dt$

$dx = \frac{2dt}{1+t^2}$

Put $\sin x = \frac{2t}{1+t^2},\ \cos x = \frac{1-t^2}{1+t^2}$

$$\therefore\ I = \int\frac{1}{\frac{2t}{1+t^2}\left(2+\frac{1-t^2}{1+t^2}-\frac{4t}{1+t^2}\right)}\frac{2dt}{(1+t^2)}$$

$$= \int\frac{(1+t^2)dt}{t(t^2-4t+3)} = \int\frac{(1+t^2)dt}{t(t-3)(t-1)}$$

Let $\frac{1+t^2}{t(t-3)(t-1)} = \frac{A}{t} + \frac{B}{t-3} + \frac{C}{t-1}$

$\Rightarrow\ A = \frac{1}{3}, B = \frac{5}{3}, C = -1$

$$\Rightarrow\ I = \frac{1}{3}\int\frac{dt}{t} + \frac{5}{3}\int\frac{dt}{t-3} - \int\frac{dt}{t-1}$$

$$= \frac{1}{3}\ln|t| + \frac{5}{3}\ln|t-3| - \ln|t-1| + C$$

$$= \frac{1}{3}\ln\left|\tan\frac{x}{2}\right| + \frac{5}{3}\ln\left|\tan\frac{x}{2}-3\right| - \ln\left|\tan\frac{x}{2}-1\right| + C$$

5. $I = \int\frac{dx}{\cos^4 x\sin^2 x} = \int\frac{\sin^2 x + \cos^2 x}{\cos^4 x\sin^2 x}dx$

$$= \int\sec\ x\,dx + \int\frac{dx}{\sin^2 x\cos^2 x} = \int(1+\tan^2 x)\sec^2 x\,dx$$

$$+\int\frac{\sin^2 x + \cos^2 x}{\sin^2 x\cos^2 x}dx$$

$$= \int(1+\tan^2 x)(\sec^2 x)dx + \int\sec^2 x\,dx + \int\text{cosec}^2 x\,dx$$

$$\Rightarrow\ I_1 = \int(1+\tan^2 x)\sec^2 x\,dx$$

$\tan x = t$

$$= \int(1+t^2)dt = t + \frac{t^3}{3} + C$$

$$\Rightarrow\ I = \tan x + \frac{1}{3}\tan^3 x + \tan x - \cot x + C$$

$$= = \frac{1}{3}\tan^3 x + 2\tan x - \cot x + C$$

6. $I = \int\frac{dx}{\sqrt[3]{\sin^{11} x\cos x}} = \int\frac{\sec^4 x}{\sqrt[3]{\sin^{11} x\cos x\sec^{12} x}}dx$

$$= \int\frac{(1+\tan^2 x)\sec^2 x}{\sqrt[3]{\tan^{11} x}}dx$$

Let $\tan x = t \Rightarrow \sec^2 x\, dx = dt$

$$= \int \frac{(1+t^2)}{t^{\frac{11}{3}}} dt = \int \frac{dt}{t^{\frac{11}{3}}} + \int \frac{dt}{t^{\frac{5}{3}}} = \frac{-3}{8} \frac{1}{t^{\frac{8}{3}}} - \frac{3}{2} \frac{1}{t^{\frac{2}{3}}} + C$$

$$= \frac{-3}{8}\left(\frac{1}{t^{\frac{8}{3}}} + \frac{4t^2}{t^{\frac{2}{3}}}\right) + C = \frac{-3}{8}\left(\frac{1+4\tan^2 x}{\tan^2 x \sqrt[3]{\tan^2 x}}\right) + C$$

7. (i) $I = \int \tan^9 \theta\, d\theta$

Let $\tan\theta = t, \sec^2\theta\, d\theta = dt \Rightarrow d\theta = \dfrac{dt}{1+t^2}$

$\therefore \quad I = \int \dfrac{t^9}{1+t^2} dt$

Put $t^2 = m \Rightarrow 2t\, dt = dm$

$$\Rightarrow \quad I = \frac{1}{2}\int \frac{t^8 2t}{1+t^2} dt = \frac{1}{2}\int \frac{m^4}{1+m} dm$$

$$= \frac{1}{2}\int \frac{m^4 - 1 + 1}{1+m} dm$$

$$= \frac{1}{2}\left[\int \frac{(m^2+1)(m+1)(m-1)}{(m+1)} dm + \int \frac{dm}{1+m}\right]$$

$$= \frac{1}{2}\left[\int (m^3 - m^2 + m - 1)\, dm + \ln|1+m|\right]$$

$$= \frac{1}{8}m^4 - \frac{1}{6}m^3 + \frac{1}{4}m^2 - \frac{m}{2} + \frac{1}{2}\ln|1+m| + C$$

$$= \frac{1}{8}\tan^8\theta - \frac{1}{6}\tan^6\theta + \frac{1}{4}\tan^4\theta$$

$$- \frac{\tan^2\theta}{2} + \ln|\sec\theta| + C$$

(ii) $I = \int \tan^{10}\theta\, d\theta$

Put $\tan\theta = t \Rightarrow \sec^2\theta\, d\theta = dt$

$$\Rightarrow \quad d\theta = \frac{dt}{1+t^2}$$

$$\Rightarrow \quad I = \int \frac{t^{10}}{1+t^2} dt = \int \left\{(t^8 - t^6 + t^4 - t^2 + 1) - \frac{1}{1+t^2}\right\} dt$$

$$= \frac{t^9}{9} - \frac{t^7}{7} + \frac{t^5}{5} - \frac{t^3}{3} + t - \tan^{-1}(t) + C$$

$$= \frac{(\tan\theta)^9}{9} - \frac{(\tan\theta)^7}{7} + \frac{(\tan\theta)^5}{5}$$

$$- \frac{(\tan\theta)^3}{3} + \tan\theta - \theta + C$$

8. $I = \int \sqrt[3]{\tan\theta}\, d\theta$

Let $\tan\theta = z^{\frac{3}{2}} \quad \Rightarrow \quad \sec^2\theta\, d\theta = \dfrac{3}{2} z^{\frac{1}{2}} dz$

$$\Rightarrow \quad d\theta = \frac{3}{2} \cdot \frac{z^{\frac{1}{2}}}{1+z^3} dz$$

$$\Rightarrow \quad I = \int \frac{z^{\frac{1}{2}} \frac{3}{2} z^{\frac{1}{2}} dz}{1+z^3} = \frac{3}{2}\int \frac{z}{1+z^3} dz = \frac{3}{2}\int \frac{z\, dz}{(1+z)(z^2-z+1)}$$

Let $\dfrac{z}{(1+z)(z^2-z+1)} = \dfrac{A}{z+1} + \dfrac{Bz+C}{z^2-z+1}$

$$\Rightarrow \quad A = \frac{z}{z^2-z+1} \text{ for } z = -1$$

$$\therefore \quad A = -\frac{1}{3}$$

Put z = 0 $\quad \Rightarrow \quad C = \dfrac{1}{3}$

Put z = 1 $\quad \Rightarrow \quad \dfrac{1}{2} = -\dfrac{1}{6} + \dfrac{1}{3} + B$

$$\Rightarrow \quad B = \frac{1}{3}$$

$$\Rightarrow \quad I = \frac{3}{2}\left[-\frac{1}{3}\int \frac{dz}{z+1} + \frac{1}{3}\int \frac{z+1}{z^2-z+1} dz\right]$$

$$= -\frac{1}{2}\ln|z+1| + \frac{1}{2}\int \frac{z+1}{z^2-z+1} dz$$

$$\Rightarrow \quad I_1 = \int \frac{z+1}{z^2-z+1} dz = \frac{1}{2}\int \frac{2z-1}{z^2-z+1} dz$$

$$+ \frac{3}{2}\int \frac{dz}{\left(z-\frac{1}{2}\right)^2 + \left(\frac{\sqrt{3}}{2}\right)^2}$$

$$\Rightarrow \quad \frac{1}{2}\ln|z^2-z+1| + \sqrt{3}\tan^{-1}\left(\frac{2z-1}{\sqrt{3}}\right) + C$$

$$\therefore \quad I = -\frac{1}{2}\ln|z+1| + \frac{1}{4}\ln|z^2-z+1|$$

$$+ \frac{\sqrt{3}}{2}\tan^{-1}\left(\frac{2z-1}{\sqrt{3}}\right) + C \text{ where, } z = \tan^{\frac{2}{3}}\theta$$

9. $I = \int \sqrt{\tan\theta}\, d\theta$

Let $y = (\tan\theta)^{\frac{1}{2}}$

$$\Rightarrow \quad dy = \frac{1}{2\sqrt{\tan\theta}} \sec^2\theta\, d\theta = \frac{(1+y^4)}{2y} d\theta$$

$$\Rightarrow \quad d\theta = \frac{2y}{1+y^4} dy$$

$$\therefore \quad I = \int \frac{2y^2}{1+y^4} dy = \int \frac{y^2+1}{y^4+1} dy + \int \frac{y^2-1}{y^4+1} dy$$

$$= \int \frac{1+\frac{1}{y^2}}{\left(y^2+\frac{1}{y^2}\right)} dy + \int \frac{1+\frac{1}{y^2}}{y^2+\frac{1}{y^2}} dy$$

Put $y = y - 1/y = t,\ y + 1/y = u = \int \dfrac{dt}{t^2+2} + \int \dfrac{du}{u^2-2}$

$$= \frac{1}{\sqrt{2}}\tan^{-1}\left(\frac{t}{\sqrt{2}}\right) + \frac{1}{2\sqrt{2}}\ln\left|\frac{u-\sqrt{2}}{y+\sqrt{2}}\right|$$

$$= \frac{1}{\sqrt{2}}\tan^{-1}\left(\frac{y^2-1}{\sqrt{2}y}\right) + \frac{1}{2\sqrt{2}}\ln\left|\frac{y^2-\sqrt{2}y+1}{y^2+\sqrt{2}y+1}\right| + C;$$

where $y=\sqrt{\tan\theta}$

10. $I=\int\sqrt{\frac{\sin x-\sin^3 x}{1-\sin^3 x}}dx = \int\sqrt{\frac{\sin x(1-\sin^2 x)}{1-\sin^3 x}}dx$

$$= \int\sqrt{\frac{\sin x}{1-\sin^3 x}}\cos x\,dx$$

Let $\sin x = t \quad \Rightarrow \quad \cos x\,dx = dt$

$\therefore \quad I=\int\frac{t^{\frac{1}{2}}}{(1-t^3)^{\frac{1}{2}}}dt\ ;\ t=m^{\frac{2}{3}}$

$\Rightarrow \quad dt=\frac{2}{3}m^{-\frac{1}{3}}dm = \int\frac{m^{\frac{1}{3}}\frac{2}{3}m^{-\frac{1}{3}}dm}{\sqrt{1-m^2}} = \frac{2}{3}\int\frac{dm}{\sqrt{1-m^2}} =$

$\frac{2}{3}\sin^{-1}m + C$

$$= \frac{2}{3}\sin^{-1}\left(t^{\frac{3}{2}}\right)+C = \frac{2}{3}\sin^{-1}\left(\sin^{\frac{3}{2}}x\right)+C$$

11. $I=\int\frac{\sqrt{\tan x}-\sqrt{\cot x}}{2+11\sin 2x}dx = \int\frac{\sqrt{\tan x}-\sqrt{\cot x}}{2+22\frac{\tan x}{1+\tan^2 x}}dx$

Let $\tan x = t^2 \Rightarrow \sec^2 x\,dx = 2t\,dt \Rightarrow dx=\frac{2t\,dt}{1+t^4}$

$\therefore \quad \int\frac{t-\frac{1}{t}}{22t^2+2t^4+2}2t\,dt = \int\frac{t^2-1}{t^4+11t^2+1}dt = \int\frac{1-\frac{1}{t^2}dt}{t^2+\frac{1}{t^2}+11}$

$$= \int\frac{1-\frac{1}{t^2}}{\left(t+\frac{1}{t}\right)^2+3^2}dt$$

Let $t+\frac{1}{t}=z \quad \Rightarrow \quad \left(1-\frac{1}{t^2}\right)dt = dz$

$\therefore \quad I=\int\frac{dz}{z^2+3^2}=\frac{1}{3}\tan^{-1}\left(\frac{z}{3}\right)+C = \frac{1}{3}\tan^{-1}\left(\frac{t+\frac{1}{t}}{3}\right)+C$

$$= \frac{1}{3}\tan^{-1}\left(\frac{\sqrt{\tan x}+\sqrt{\cot x}}{3}\right)+C$$

12. $I=\int\frac{dx}{(a+bx^2)\sqrt{b-ax^2}}$

Let $ax^2 = b\sin^2\theta,\ x=\sqrt{\frac{b}{a}}\sin\theta,\ \ dx=\sqrt{\frac{b}{a}}\cos\theta\,d\theta$

$\therefore \quad I=\int\frac{\sqrt{\frac{b}{a}}\cos\theta\,d\theta}{\left(a+\frac{b^2}{a}\sin^2\theta\right)\sqrt{b-b\sin^2\theta}} = \int\frac{\sqrt{a}\,d\theta}{(a^2+b^2\sin^2\theta)}$

$\Rightarrow \quad \cos^2\theta = 1-\frac{ax^2}{b}=\frac{b-ax^2}{b}$

$\Rightarrow \quad \tan\theta=\sqrt{\frac{ax^2}{b-ax^2}}$

$$= \int\frac{\sqrt{a}\sec^2\theta\,d\theta}{a^2\sec^2\theta+b^2\tan^2\theta} = \int\frac{\sqrt{a}\sec^2\theta\,d\theta}{a^2+(a^2+b^2)\tan^2\theta}$$

Let $\tan\theta = t \Rightarrow \sec^2\theta\,d\theta = dt$

$$= \int\frac{\sqrt{a}\,dt}{a^2+(a^2+b^2)t^2} = \frac{\sqrt{a}}{a^2+b^2}\int\frac{dt}{t^2+\frac{a^2}{a^2+b^2}}$$

$$= \frac{1}{\sqrt{a}\sqrt{a^2+b^2}}\tan^{-1}\left(\frac{t\sqrt{a^2+b^2}}{a}\right)+C$$

$$= \frac{1}{\sqrt{a(a^2+b^2)}}\tan^{-1}\left(\frac{x\sqrt{a^2+b^2}}{\sqrt{a(b-ax^2)}}\right)+C$$

13. $I=\int\frac{\sin x+\sin 2x}{\sqrt{\cos x+\cos 2x}}dx = -\int\frac{-\sin x-2\sin 2x}{\sqrt{\cos x+\cos 2x}}$

$-\int\frac{\sin 2x}{\sqrt{\cos x+\cos 2x}}dx = -2\sqrt{\cos x+\cos 2x}-I_1$

$I_1=\int\frac{\sin 2x}{\sqrt{\cos x+\cos 2x}}dx = -2\int\frac{\cos x(-\sin x)dx}{\sqrt{2\cos^2 x+\cos x-1}}$

Let $\cos x = t \Rightarrow -\sin x\,dx = dt$

$\therefore \quad I_1=-2\int\frac{t\,dt}{\sqrt{2t^2+t-1}}$

$$= -\frac{2}{4}\int\frac{4t+1}{\sqrt{2t^2+t-1}}dt+\frac{1}{2}\int\frac{dt}{\sqrt{2t^2+t-1}}$$

$$= -\sqrt{2t^2+t-1}+\frac{1}{2\sqrt{2}}\int\frac{dt}{\sqrt{\left(t+\frac{1}{4}\right)^2-\left(\frac{3}{4}\right)^2}}$$

$$= -\sqrt{2t^2+t-1}+\frac{1}{2\sqrt{2}}\ln\left|\left(t+\frac{1}{4}\right)+\sqrt{t^2+\frac{t}{2}-\frac{1}{2}}\right|+C$$

$$= -\sqrt{2\cos^2 x+\cos x-1}+\frac{1}{2\sqrt{2}}\ln$$

$$\left|\left(\frac{4\cos x+1}{4}\right)+\frac{\sqrt{2\cos^2 x+\cos x-1}}{\sqrt{2}}\right|+C$$

$\therefore \quad I = -\sqrt{\cos x+\cos 2x}-\frac{1}{2\sqrt{2}}\ln$

$$\left|\frac{4\cos x+1}{4}+\frac{\sqrt{\cos x+\cos 2x}}{\sqrt{2}}\right|+C$$

TEXTUAL EXERCISE–7: (OBJECTIVE)

1. (c) $I=\int\frac{dx}{a^2\sin^2x+b^2\cos^2x}=\int\frac{\sec^2x}{a^2\tan^2x+b^2}dx$

Put $\tan x=t \Rightarrow \sec^2x\,dx=dt$

$\Rightarrow I=\int\frac{dt}{a^2t^2+b^2}=\frac{1}{a^2}\int\frac{dt}{t^2+\frac{b^2}{a^2}}=\frac{1}{ab}\tan^{-1}\left(\frac{at}{b}\right)+C$

$=\frac{1}{ab}\tan^{-1}\left(\frac{a}{b}\tan x\right)+C$

2. (b) $I=\int\frac{dx}{\sin x+\sec x}=\int\frac{\cos x}{1+\sin x\cos x}dx$

$=\frac{1}{2}\int\frac{2\cos x}{1+\sin x\cos x}dx$

$=\frac{1}{2}\int\frac{(\sin x+\cos x)+(\cos x-\sin x)}{1+\sin x\cos x}dx$

$=\int\frac{\sin x+\cos x}{2+2\sin x\cos x}dx+\int\frac{\cos x-\sin x}{2+2\sin x\cos x}dx$

$=-\underbrace{\int\frac{\sin x+\cos x}{(\sin x-\cos x)^2-3}dx}_{I_1}+\underbrace{\int\frac{\cos x-\sin x}{(\sin x+\cos x)^2+1}dx}_{I_2}$

In I_1 put $\sin x-\cos x=t$, In I_2 put $\sin x+\cos x=z$

$\Rightarrow (\sin x+\cos x)\,dx=dt$ and $(\cos x-\sin x)\,dx=dz$

$\Rightarrow I_1=-\int\frac{dt}{t^2-(\sqrt{3})^2};\quad I_2=\int\frac{dz}{z^2+1}$

$\Rightarrow I_1=\frac{1}{2\sqrt{3}}\ln\left|\frac{t+\sqrt{3}}{t-\sqrt{3}}\right|+C_1;\ I_2=\tan^{-1}z+C_2$

$\therefore\ I=\frac{1}{2\sqrt{3}}\ln\left|\frac{\sin x-\cos x+\sqrt{3}}{\sin x-\cos x-\sqrt{3}}\right|+\tan^{-1}(\sin x+\cos x)+C$

3. (c) $I=\int\frac{dx}{\tan x-\cot x}=\int\frac{\tan x}{\tan^2x-1}dx=-\frac{1}{2}\int\frac{2\tan x}{1-\tan^2x}dx$

$=-\frac{1}{2}\int\tan 2x\,dx=\frac{1}{4}\ln|\cos 2x|+C$

4. (b) $I=\int\frac{\cos^3x}{\sqrt{\sin^7x}}dx=\int\frac{\cos^2x\cos x}{\sqrt{\sin^7x}}dx$

Let $\sin x=t \Rightarrow \cos x\,dx=dt$

$\Rightarrow I=\int\frac{(1-t^2)}{t^{7/2}}dt=\int\frac{dt}{t^{7/2}}-\int\frac{dt}{t^{3/2}}$

$=-\frac{2}{5}(\sin x)^{-\frac{5}{2}}+2\sqrt{\operatorname{cosec}x}+C$

5. (a) $I=\int\sec^{\frac{7}{3}}x.\operatorname{cosec}^{\frac{5}{3}}x\,dx=\int\frac{\sin^2x}{\cos^{\frac{7}{3}}x\sin^{\frac{5}{3}}x}\operatorname{cosec}^2x\,dx$

$=\int\frac{\sin^{\frac{1}{3}}x}{\cos^{\frac{7}{3}}x}\operatorname{cosec}^2x\,dx=\int\frac{\operatorname{cosec}^2x}{\cot^{\frac{7}{3}}x}\operatorname{cosec}^2x\,dx$

Let $\cot x=t \Rightarrow -\operatorname{cosec}^2x\,dx=dt$

$I=-\int\frac{(1+t^2)}{t^{7/3}}dt=-\int\frac{dt}{t^{7/3}}-\int\frac{dt}{t^{1/3}}=\frac{3}{4}t^{-\frac{4}{3}}-\frac{3}{2}t^{\frac{2}{3}}+C$

$=-\frac{3}{2}\cot^{\frac{2}{3}}x+\frac{3}{4}\tan^{\frac{4}{3}}x+C$

6. (b) $I=\int\frac{dx}{\sin x(2\cos^2x-1)}=\int\frac{\sin^2x+\cos^2x}{\sin x(2\cos^2x-1)}dx$

$=\int\frac{\sin x}{(2\cos^2x-1)}dx+\int\frac{\cos^2x}{\sin x(2\cos^2x-1)}dx$

$I_1=-\int\frac{dt}{(2t^2-1)}=-\frac{1}{2}\int\frac{dt}{t^2-\left(\frac{1}{\sqrt{2}}\right)^2}$

$=-\frac{1}{2\sqrt{2}}\ln\left|\frac{t-\frac{1}{\sqrt{2}}}{t+\frac{1}{\sqrt{2}}}\right|+C_1$; t = cosx

And $I_2=\int\frac{\cos^2x}{\sin x(2\cos^2x-1)}dx$

$=\frac{1}{2}\int\frac{2\cos^2x-1}{\sin x(2\cos^2x-1)}dx+\frac{1}{2}\int\frac{dx}{\sin x(2\cos^2x-1)}$

$=\frac{1}{2}\int\operatorname{cosec}x\,dx+I_3=\frac{1}{2}\ln\left|\tan\frac{x}{2}\right|+I_3$

$I_3=\frac{1}{2}\int\frac{\sin x}{(1-\cos^2x)(2\cos^2x-1)}dx$

$=\frac{1}{2}\int\frac{dt}{(t^2-1)(2t^2-1)}=\frac{1}{2}\left[\int\frac{1}{t^2-1}dt-\int\frac{2dt}{2t^2-1}\right]$

$=\frac{1}{4}\ln\left|\frac{t-1}{t+1}\right|-\frac{1}{2\sqrt{2}}\ln\left|\frac{t-\frac{1}{\sqrt{2}}}{t+\frac{1}{\sqrt{2}}}\right|$

$I=-\frac{1}{\sqrt{2}}\ln\left|\frac{\sqrt{2}\cos x-1}{\sqrt{2}\cos x+1}\right|+\frac{1}{2}\ln\left|\tan\frac{x}{2}\right|+\frac{1}{4}\ln\left|\frac{\cos x-1}{\cos x+1}\right|$

$=\frac{1}{\sqrt{2}}\ln\left|\frac{1+\sqrt{2}\cos x}{1-\sqrt{2}\cos x}\right|+\frac{1}{2}\ln\left|\tan^2\frac{x}{2}\right|+C$

7. (b) $I=\int\frac{2\tan x+3}{\sin^2x+2\cos^2x}dx=\int\frac{(2\tan x+3)\sec^2x}{\tan^2x+2}dx$

Put $\tan x=t \Rightarrow \sec^2x\,dx=dt$

$=\int\frac{2t+3}{t^2+2}dt=\int\frac{2t}{t^2+2}dt+3\int\frac{dt}{t^2+(\sqrt{2})^2}$

$=\ln|t^2+2|+\frac{3}{\sqrt{2}}\tan^{-1}\left(\frac{t}{\sqrt{2}}\right)+C$

$=\ln|\tan^2x+2|+\frac{3}{\sqrt{2}}\tan^{-1}\left(\frac{\tan x}{\sqrt{2}}\right)+C$

8. (a) $I=\int\frac{\sin x}{\sin 3x}dx=\int\frac{\sin x}{3\sin x-4\sin^3 x}dx=\int\frac{dt}{3-4\sin^2 x}$

$=\int\frac{\sec^2 x}{3-\tan^2 x}dx$

Put $\tan x=t \Rightarrow \sec^2 x\,dx=dt$

$=\int\frac{dt}{3-t^2}=\frac{1}{2\sqrt{3}}\ln\left|\frac{\sqrt{3}+t}{\sqrt{3}-t}\right|+C=\frac{1}{2\sqrt{3}}\ln\left|\frac{\sqrt{3}+\tan x}{\sqrt{3}-\tan x}\right|+C$

9. (b) $I=\int\frac{dx}{4\sin^2 x+4\sin x\cos x+5\cos^2 x}$

$=\int\frac{\sec^2 x}{4\tan^2 x+4\tan x+5}dx$

Put $\tan x=t \Rightarrow \sec^2 dx=dt$

$=\int\frac{dt}{4t^2+4t+5}=\frac{1}{4}\int\frac{dt}{t^2+t+\frac{5}{4}}=\frac{1}{4}\int\frac{dt}{\left(t+\frac{1}{2}\right)^2+1}$

$=\frac{1}{4}\tan^{-1}\left(t+\frac{1}{2}\right)+C=\frac{1}{4}\tan^{-1}\left(\tan x+\frac{1}{2}\right)+C$

10. (d) $I=\int\sin^6 x\cos^4 x\,dx$

$=\frac{1}{2}\cdot\frac{1}{2^4}\int 2^4\sin^4 x\cos^4 x\,2\sin^2 x\,dx$

$=\frac{1}{2^5}\int\sin^4 2x(1-\cos 2x)dx$

$=\frac{1}{32}\underbrace{\int\sin^4 2x\,dx}_{I_1}-\frac{1}{32}\underbrace{\int\sin^4 2x\cos 2x\,dx}_{I_2}$

$\Rightarrow I=\frac{1}{32}(I_1-I_2)$

$I_2=\int\sin^4 2x\cos 2x\,dx$; $\sin 2x=t$

$\Rightarrow 2\cos 2x\,dx=dt$

$=\frac{1}{2}\int t^4dt=\frac{t^5}{10}+C=\frac{\sin^5 2x}{10}+C$

$I_1=\int\sin^4 2x\,dx=\frac{1}{4}\int(2\sin^2 2x)^2dx$

$=\frac{1}{4}\int(1-\cos 4x)^2dx=\frac{1}{4}\int[1+\cos^2 4x-2\cos 4x]dx$

$=\frac{x}{4}+\frac{1}{8}\int(1+\cos 8x)dx-\frac{1}{2}\sin 4x$

$=\frac{3x}{8}+\frac{1}{64}\sin 8x-\frac{1}{2}\sin 4x$

$I=\frac{1}{32}\left[\frac{3x}{8}+\frac{1}{64}\sin 8x-\frac{1}{2}\sin 4x\right]-\frac{\sin^5 2x}{320}+C$

11. (c) $I=\int\sin^2 x\cos^4 x\cos x\,dx$

Let $\sin x=t \Rightarrow \cos x\,dx=dt$

$\Rightarrow I=\int t^2(1-t^2)^2dt=\int t^2(t^4-2t^2+1)dt$

$=\int(t^6-2t^4+t^2)dt=\frac{t^7}{7}-\frac{2t^5}{5}+\frac{t^3}{3}+C$

$=\frac{\sin^7 x}{7}-\frac{2\sin^5 x}{5}+\frac{\sin^3 x}{3}+C$

12. (b) $I=\int\frac{\cos x}{(1+\sin x)(2+\sin x)}dx$

Let $\sin x=t \Rightarrow \cos x\,dx=dt$

$I=\int\frac{dt}{(t+1)(t+2)}=\int\frac{dt}{t+1}-\int\frac{dt}{t+2}$

$=\ln\left|\frac{t+1}{t+2}\right|+C=\ln\left|\frac{\sin x+1}{\sin x+2}\right|+C$

13. (b) $I=\int\frac{\sin x}{(1-\cos x)^2}dx$

$\cos x=t \Rightarrow -\sin x\,dx=dt$

$I=\int-\frac{dt}{(1-t)^2}=-\frac{1}{1-t}+C=\frac{1}{t-1}+C=\frac{1}{\cos x-1}+C$

14. (a) $I=\int\frac{dx}{(\sin x+\cos x)^2}=\int\frac{\sec^2 x}{(\tan x+1)^2}dx$

Put $t=\tan x\Rightarrow dt=\sec^2 x\,dx$

$=\int\frac{dt}{(t+1)^2}=-\frac{1}{(t+1)}+C=-\frac{1}{\tan x+1}+C$

15. (a) $I=\int\frac{dx}{\tan x\cos 2x}=\int\frac{\sec^2 x}{\tan x(1-\tan^2 x)}dx=\int\frac{dt}{t(1-t^2)}$

$=\left(\frac{1}{t}+\frac{t}{1-t^2}\right)dt$; t = tan x

$=\ln|t|-\frac{1}{2}\ln|1-t^2|+C$

$=\ln\left(\frac{t}{\sqrt{1-t^2}}\right)+C=\ln\left|\frac{\tan x}{\sqrt{1-\tan^2 x}}\right|+C=\ln\left|\frac{C\sin x}{\sqrt{\cos 2x}}\right|$

16. (b) $I=\int\frac{dx}{(\sin^2 x+\tan^2 x)}=\int\frac{\sec^2 x}{\tan^2 x+\tan^2 x\sec^2 x}dx$

$=\int\frac{\sec^2 x}{\tan^2 x(2+\tan^2 x)}dx=\int\frac{dt}{t^2(2+t^2)}$; t = tan x

$=\frac{1}{2}\int\left(\frac{1}{t^2}-\frac{1}{t^2+2}\right)dt=-\frac{1}{2t}-\frac{1}{2\sqrt{2}}\tan^{-1}\left(\frac{t}{\sqrt{2}}\right)+C$

$=-\frac{1}{2}\left[\cot x+\frac{1}{\sqrt{2}}\tan^{-1}\left(\frac{\tan x}{\sqrt{2}}\right)\right]+C$

17. (b) $I=\int\frac{\sqrt{\tan x}}{\sin x\cos x}dx=\int\frac{\sqrt{\tan x}}{\tan x}\sec^2 x\,dx$

$=\int t^{-1/2}dt$; $\tan x=t$

$=2\sqrt{t}+C=2\sqrt{\tan x}+C$

18. (c) $I=\int\frac{1}{2+\sin x+\cos x}dx$

$\Rightarrow I=\int\frac{1}{2+\frac{2\tan\frac{x}{2}}{1+\tan^2\frac{x}{2}}+\frac{1-\tan^2\frac{x}{2}}{1+\tan^2\frac{x}{2}}}dx$;

Put $\tan\frac{x}{2}=t\Rightarrow\frac{1}{2}\sec^2\frac{x}{2}dx=dt\Rightarrow dx=\frac{2dt}{1+t^2}$

$$I=\int\frac{1}{2+\frac{2t}{1+t^2}+\frac{1-t^2}{1+t^2}}\frac{2dt}{1+t^2}=\int\frac{2dt}{2+2t^2+2t+1-t^2}$$

$$=\int\frac{2dt}{t^2+2t+3}$$

$$=2\int\frac{dt}{(t+1)^2+(\sqrt{2})^2}=\sqrt{2}\tan^{-1}\left(\frac{t+1}{\sqrt{2}}\right)+C$$

$$=\sqrt{2}\tan^{-1}\left(\frac{\tan\frac{x}{2}+1}{\sqrt{2}}\right)+C$$

TEXTUAL EXERCISE-8: (SUBJECTIVE)

1. (a) $I=\int\frac{dx}{(x-1)^3\sqrt{x^2-3x+2}}$

Let $x-1=\frac{1}{t}\Rightarrow x=\frac{t+1}{t}\Rightarrow dx=-\frac{1}{t^2}dt$

$$=\int\frac{-\frac{1}{t^2}dt}{\frac{1}{t^3}\sqrt{\left(\frac{1}{t}\right)\left(\frac{1-t}{t}\right)}}=\int\frac{-t^2dt}{\sqrt{1-t}}$$

Let $1-t=m^2; -dt=2m\,dm$

$$\therefore\quad I=\int\frac{(1-m^2)^2\,2m\,dm}{m}=2\int(m^4-2m^2+1)dm$$

$$=\frac{2}{5}m^5-\frac{4}{3}m^3+2m+C;$$

$$m=\sqrt{1-t}=\sqrt{1-\frac{1}{x-1}}=\sqrt{\frac{x-2}{x-1}}$$

$$=\frac{2}{5}\left(\frac{x-2}{x-1}\right)^{\frac{5}{2}}-\frac{4}{3}\left(\frac{x-2}{x-1}\right)^{\frac{3}{2}}+2\left(\frac{x-2}{x-1}\right)^{\frac{1}{2}}+C$$

(b) $I=\int\frac{dx}{(2x+1)\sqrt{x-1}}$

Let $x-1=t^2;\ dx=2t\,dt$

$\Rightarrow\ x=t^2+1$

$$\Rightarrow\ I=\int\frac{2t\,dt}{(2t^2+3)t}=2\int\frac{dt}{2t^2+3}=\int\frac{dt}{t^2+\left(\sqrt{\frac{3}{2}}\right)^2}$$

$$=\sqrt{\frac{2}{3}}\tan^{-1}\left(t\sqrt{\frac{2}{3}}\right)+C=\sqrt{\frac{2}{3}}\tan^{-1}\left(\sqrt{x-1}\sqrt{\frac{2}{3}}\right)+C$$

(c) $I=\int\frac{dx}{(x-1)\sqrt{2x^2+1}}$

Put $x-1=\frac{1}{t}\Rightarrow x=\frac{1+t}{t};dx=-\frac{1}{t^2}dt$

$$\Rightarrow\ I=\int\frac{-\frac{1}{t^2}dt}{\frac{1}{t}\sqrt{2\left(\frac{1+t}{t}\right)^2+1}}=-\int\frac{dt}{\sqrt{3t^2+4t+2}}$$

$$=-\frac{1}{\sqrt{3}}\int\frac{dt}{\sqrt{t^2+\frac{4}{3}t+\frac{2}{3}}}=-\frac{1}{\sqrt{3}}\int\frac{dt}{\sqrt{\left(t+\frac{2}{3}\right)^2+\left(\frac{\sqrt{2}}{3}\right)^2}}$$

$$=-\frac{1}{\sqrt{3}}\ln\left|t+\frac{2}{3}+\sqrt{t^2+\frac{4}{3}t+\frac{2}{3}}\right|\text{ where } t=\frac{1}{x-1}$$

(d) $I=\int\frac{dx}{(2x^2+3)\sqrt{x^2-1}}$

Put $x=\frac{1}{t}\Rightarrow dx=-\frac{1}{t^2}dt$

$$\Rightarrow\ I=\int\frac{-\frac{1}{t^2}dt}{\frac{2+3t^2}{t^2}\frac{\sqrt{1-t^2}}{t}}=-\int\frac{t\,dt}{(2+3t^2)\left(\sqrt{1-t^2}\right)}$$

Let $1-t^2=z^2\Rightarrow -t\,dt=z\,dz; t^2=1-z^2$

$$\Rightarrow\ I=\int\frac{z\,dz}{(5-3z^2)z}=\frac{1}{3}\int\frac{dz}{\left(\sqrt{\frac{5}{3}}\right)^2-z^2}$$

$$=\frac{1}{3}\cdot\frac{1}{2}\sqrt{\frac{3}{5}}\ln\left|\frac{\frac{\sqrt{5}}{3}+z}{\frac{\sqrt{5}}{3}-z}\right|+C$$

$$\Rightarrow\ I=\frac{1}{2\sqrt{15}}\ln\left|\frac{x\sqrt{5}+\sqrt{3}\sqrt{x^2-1}}{x\sqrt{5}-\sqrt{3}\sqrt{x^2-1}}\right|+C$$

(e) $I=\int\frac{(x-1)dx}{(x+1)\sqrt{x^3+x^2+x}}$; $I=\int\frac{(x-1)dx}{(x+1)\sqrt{x}\sqrt{x^2+x+1}}$

Let $x=t^2\quad\Rightarrow dx=2t\,dt$

$$=2\int\frac{(t^2-1)dt}{(t^2+1)\sqrt{t^4+t^2+1}}=2\int\frac{\left(1-\frac{1}{t^2}\right)dt}{\left(t+\frac{1}{t}\right)\sqrt{\left(t+\frac{1}{t}\right)^2-1}}$$

Let $t+\frac{1}{t}=m\Rightarrow 1-\frac{1}{t^2}dt=dm$

$$=2\int\frac{dm}{m\sqrt{m^2-1}}=2\sec^{-1}m=2\sec^{-1}\left(x^{\frac{1}{2}}+\frac{1}{x^{\frac{1}{2}}}\right)+C$$

$$=2\tan^{-1}\sqrt{\frac{x^2+x+1}{x}}+C$$

(f) $\int\frac{dx}{(x-a)^{3/2}(x+a)^{1/2}}=\int\frac{dx}{\left(\frac{x-a}{x+a}\right)^{3/2}(x+a)^2}$

Put $\left(\dfrac{x-a}{x+a}\right)=t$

$\Rightarrow \quad \dfrac{(x+a)-(x-a)}{(x+a)^2}dx = dt$

$\Rightarrow \quad \dfrac{dx}{(x+a)^2} = \dfrac{dt}{2a}$

$\therefore \quad I = \int \dfrac{dt}{2a(t)^{3/2}} = \dfrac{1}{2a}\dfrac{(t)^{-1/2}}{-1/2} + C = -\dfrac{1}{a\sqrt{t}} + C$

$= -\dfrac{1}{a}\sqrt{\dfrac{x+a}{x-a}} + C$

2. (a) $\int \dfrac{x+\sqrt[3]{x^2}+\sqrt[6]{x}}{x\left(1+\sqrt[3]{x}\right)}dx$

Put $x = t^6 \quad \Rightarrow \quad dx = 6t^5\,dt$

$\therefore \quad \int \dfrac{t^6+t^4+t}{t^6(1+t^2)}.6t^5 dt = 6\int \dfrac{(t^5+t^3+1)}{(t^2+1)}dt$

$= 6\int\left((t^3)+\dfrac{1}{t^2+1}\right)dt$

$= \dfrac{6t^4}{4} + 6\tan^{-1}(t) + C = \dfrac{3}{2}t^4 + 6\tan^{-1}(t) + C$

$= \dfrac{3}{2}(x^{2/3}) + 6\tan^{-1}(x^{1/6}) + C$

$\therefore \quad \dfrac{3}{2}x^{2/3} + 6\tan^{-1}(x^{1/6}) + C$

(b) $\int \dfrac{1}{(1+x)^{1/2}-(1+x)^{1/3}}dx$

Put $(1+x) = t^6 \quad \Rightarrow \quad dx = 6t^5\,dt$

$\therefore \quad I = \int \dfrac{6t^5}{t^3-t^2}dt = \int \dfrac{6t^3}{t-1}dt = 6\int\left(t^2+t+\dfrac{t}{t-1}\right)dt$

$= \dfrac{6t^3}{3} + \dfrac{6t^2}{2} + 6\int\left(1+\dfrac{t}{t-1}\right)dt$

$= 2t^3 + 3t^2 + 6t + 6ln\,|t-1| + C$

$= 2(1+x)^{1/2} + 3(1+x)^{1/3} + 6(1+x)^{1/6} + 6ln|(1+x)^{1/6} - 1| + C$

(c) $\int \dfrac{x^{1/2}}{x^{1/2}-x^{1/3}}dx$;

Put $x = t^6 \quad \Rightarrow \quad dx = 6t^5\,dt$

$\therefore \quad I = \int \dfrac{t^3.(6t^5\,dt)}{(t^3-t^2)} = \int \dfrac{6t^6\,dt}{(t-1)} = 6\int \dfrac{t^6-1+1}{(t-1)}dt$

$= 6\int\left\{(t^5+t^4+t^3+t^2+t+1)+\dfrac{1}{t-1}\right\}dt$

$= t^6 + \dfrac{6}{5}t^5 + \dfrac{3}{2}t^4 + 2t^3 + 3t^2 + 6t + \ln|t-1| + C$

$= x + \dfrac{6}{5}(x)^{5/6} + \dfrac{3}{2}x^{2/3} + 2x^{1/2} + 3x^{1/3}$
$+ 6x^{1/6} + \ln|x^{1/6}-1| + C$

(d) $\int \dfrac{1+x^{1/2}-x^{2/3}}{1+x^{1/3}}dx$

Put $x = t^6 \quad \Rightarrow \quad dx = 6t^5\,dt$

$\therefore \quad I = \int \dfrac{1+t^3-t^4}{1+t^2}(6t^5)dt = 6\int \dfrac{-t^9+t^8+t^5}{t^2+1}dt$

$= 6\int\left(-t^7+t^6+t^5-t^4+t^2-1+\dfrac{1}{t^2+1}\right)dt$

$= -\dfrac{6}{8}t^8 + \dfrac{6}{7}t^7 + \dfrac{6}{6}t^6 - \dfrac{6}{5}t^5 + \dfrac{6}{3}t^3 - 6t + 6\tan^{-1}t + C$

$= -\dfrac{3}{4}x^{4/3} + \dfrac{6}{7}x^{7/6} + x - \dfrac{6}{5}x^{5/6}$
$+ 2x^{1/2} - 6x^{1/6} + 6\tan^{-1}(x^{1/6}) + C$

(e) $I = \int \dfrac{x^{\frac{1}{4}}}{x^{\frac{1}{2}}-1}dx$

Put $x = t^4 \Rightarrow dx = 4t^3 dt$

$\Rightarrow \quad I = \int \dfrac{t}{t^2-1}4t^3 dt = 4\int \dfrac{t^4-1+1}{t^2-1}dt$

$= 4\int(t^2+1)dt + 4\int \dfrac{dt}{t^2-1} = \dfrac{4}{3}t^3 + 4t + 2\ln\left|\dfrac{t-1}{t+1}\right| + C$

$= = \dfrac{4}{3}x^{\frac{3}{4}} + 4x^{\frac{1}{4}} + 2\ln\left|\dfrac{x^{\frac{1}{4}}-1}{x^{\frac{1}{4}}+1}\right| + C$

(f) $I = \int \dfrac{1}{x+x^{\frac{1}{3}}}dx$

Let $x = t^3 \Rightarrow dx = 3t^2 dt$

$\Rightarrow \quad I = \int \dfrac{3t^2 dt}{t^3+t} = 3\int \dfrac{t\,dt}{t^2+1} = \dfrac{3}{2}\int \dfrac{2t}{t^2+1}dt = \dfrac{3}{2}\ln|t^2+1| + C$

$= \dfrac{3}{2}\ln\left|x^{\frac{2}{3}}+1\right| + C$

(g) $I = \int \dfrac{1}{(x+1)^{\frac{1}{2}}-(x+1)^{\frac{1}{4}}}dx$

Put $x+1 = t^4 \Rightarrow dx = 4t^3 dt$

$\therefore \quad I = \int \dfrac{4t^3 dt}{t^2-t} = 4\int \dfrac{t^2 dt}{t-1} = 4\int \dfrac{t^2-1}{t-1}dt + 4\int \dfrac{dt}{t-1}$

$= 4\int(t+1)dt + 4\int \dfrac{dt}{t-1} = 2t^2 + 4t + 4\ln|t-1| + C$

$= 2(x+1)^{\frac{1}{2}} + 4(x+1)^{\frac{1}{4}} + 4\ln\left|(x+1)^{\frac{1}{4}}-1\right| + C$

(h) $I = \int \sqrt{\left(\dfrac{e^x+a}{e^x-a}\right)}dx$

Put $x = \ln t \quad \Rightarrow \quad dx = \dfrac{1}{t}dt$

$= \int \sqrt{\dfrac{t+a}{t-a}}\dfrac{1}{t}dt = \int \dfrac{(t+a)}{t\sqrt{t^2-a^2}}dt$

$$= \int \frac{dt}{\sqrt{t^2 - a^2}} + \int \frac{a\,dt}{t\sqrt{t^2 - a^2}}$$

$$= \ln\left|t + \sqrt{t^2 - a^2}\right| + \sec^{-1}\left(\frac{t}{a}\right) + C$$

$$= \ln\left|e^x + \left(e^{2x} - a^2\right)^{\frac{1}{2}}\right| + \sec^{-1}\left(\frac{e^x}{a}\right) + C$$

(i) $I = \int \frac{\sqrt[3]{1+\sqrt[4]{x}}}{\sqrt{x}}dx$

Let $x = (t-1)^4 \Rightarrow dx = 4(t-1)^3\,dt$

$$\Rightarrow \quad I = \int \frac{(t)^{\frac{1}{3}}4(t-1)^3}{(t-1)^2}dt = 4\int t^{\frac{1}{3}}(t-1)\,dt$$

$$= 4\int t^{\frac{4}{3}}dt - 4\int t^{\frac{1}{3}}dt = \frac{12}{7}t^{\frac{7}{3}} - 3t^{\frac{4}{3}} + C$$

$$= \frac{12}{7}\left(x^{\frac{1}{4}} + 1\right)^{\frac{7}{3}} - 3\left(x^{\frac{1}{4}} + 1\right)^{\frac{4}{3}} + C$$

(j) $I = \int \frac{\left(x + \sqrt{1+x^2}\right)^{15}}{\sqrt{1+x^2}}dx$

Let $x + \sqrt{1+x^2} = t$

$$\Rightarrow \quad \left(1+x^2\right) = (t-x)^2 = x^2 - 2tx + t^2$$

$$\Rightarrow \quad x = \frac{t^2-1}{2t}$$

$$\Rightarrow \quad dx = \frac{1}{2}\left[\frac{t(2t) - \left(t^2-1\right)}{t^2}\right]dt = \frac{\left(t^2+1\right)}{2t^2}dt \text{ and}$$

$$\sqrt{1+x^2} = t - x = t - \frac{t^2-1}{2t} = \frac{t^2+1}{2t}$$

$$\Rightarrow \quad I = \int \frac{\left(\frac{t^2-1}{2t} + \frac{t^2+1}{2t}\right)^{15}}{\frac{t^2+1}{2t}}.\frac{\left(t^2+1\right)}{2t^2}dt$$

$$\Rightarrow \quad I = \int t^{14}dt = \frac{t^{15}}{15} + C = \frac{\left(x + \sqrt{1+x^2}\right)^{15}}{15} + C$$

3. (a) $I = \int x^{\frac{3}{2}}\left(a + bx^3\right)^5 dx = \int x^{\frac{3}{2}}\left(\sum_{r=0}^{5} a^{5-r}b^r x^{3r\,5}c_r\right)dx$

$$= \int x^{\frac{3}{2}}\left(a^5 + 5a^4bx^3 + 10a^3b^2x^6\right)$$

$$+\left(10a^2b^3x^9 + 5ab^4x^{12} + b^5x^{15}\right)dx$$

$$= \frac{2}{35}b^5x^{\frac{35}{2}} + \frac{10}{29}ab^4x^{\frac{29}{2}} + \frac{20}{23}a^2b^3x^{\frac{23}{2}}$$

$$+ \frac{20}{17}a^3b^2x^{\frac{17}{2}} + \frac{10}{11}a^4bx^{\frac{11}{2}} + \frac{2}{5}a^5x^{\frac{5}{2}}$$

(b) $I = \int x^{\frac{1}{2}}\left(1 + x^{\frac{3}{2}}\right)^{-2}dx$

Let $x = t^2 \Rightarrow dx = 2t\,dt$

$$\Rightarrow \quad I = \int t\left(1+t^3\right)^{-2}2t\,dt = \frac{2}{3}\int \frac{3t^2}{\left(1+t^3\right)^2}dt$$

Let $t^3 = z \Rightarrow 3t^2dt = dz$

$$\Rightarrow \quad I = \frac{2}{3}\int \frac{dz}{(1+z)^2} = \frac{-2}{3(1+z)} + C = \frac{-2}{3\left(1 + x^{\frac{3}{2}}\right)} + C$$

(c) $I = \int x^{\frac{3}{2}}\sqrt{1 + x^{\frac{5}{2}}}dx$

Let $m = \frac{3}{2},\ n = \frac{5}{2} \Rightarrow \frac{m+1}{n} = 1 \in \mathbb{Z}$

Let $1 + x^{\frac{5}{2}} = t^2 \Rightarrow \frac{5}{2}x^{\frac{3}{2}}dx = 2t\,dt$

$$\Rightarrow \quad I = \int t\frac{4}{5}t\,dt = \frac{4}{5}\int t^2dt = \frac{4}{15}t^3 + C = \frac{4}{15}\left(1 + x^{\frac{5}{2}}\right)^{\frac{3}{2}} + C$$

(d) $I = \int \frac{dx}{x^{\frac{1}{2}}\left(1+x^2\right)^{\frac{5}{4}}} = \int x^{-\frac{1}{2}}\left(1+x^2\right)^{-\frac{5}{4}}dx$

Let $m = -\frac{1}{2}, n = 2, p = -\frac{5}{4}$

$$\Rightarrow \quad \frac{m+1}{n} + p = -1 \in \mathbb{Z}$$

Let $\left(1+x^2\right) = t^4x^2 \quad \Rightarrow \quad \frac{1}{x^2} = t^4 - 1$

$$\Rightarrow \quad \frac{-2}{x^3}dx = 4t^3dt, t = \left(\frac{1+x^2}{x^2}\right)^{\frac{1}{4}}$$

$$\Rightarrow \quad I = \int -x^{-\frac{1}{2}}t^{-5}x^{-\frac{5}{2}}2t^3x^3dt = -2\int \frac{1}{t^2}dt = \frac{2}{t} + C$$

$$= 2\left(\frac{x^2}{1+x^2}\right)^{\frac{1}{4}} + C$$

(e) $I = \int x^{-11}\left(1+x^4\right)^{-\frac{1}{2}}dx$

Let $m = -11, n = 4, p = -\frac{1}{2}$

$$\frac{m+1}{n} + p = -3 \in \mathbb{Z}$$

Put $1 + x^4 = t^2x^4 \quad \Rightarrow \quad \frac{1}{x^4} = t^2 - 1$

$$\Rightarrow \quad \frac{-4}{x^5}dx = 2t\,dt$$

$$\Rightarrow \quad I = \int -x^{-11}t^{-1}x^{-2}\frac{1}{2}tx^5dt\ ;\ t = \left(\frac{1+x^4}{x^4}\right)^{\frac{1}{2}}$$

$$= -\frac{1}{2}\int \frac{1}{x^8}dt = -\frac{1}{2}\int \left(t^2-1\right)^2dt = -\frac{1}{2}\int \left(t^4 - 2t^2 + 1\right)dt$$

$$= -\frac{1}{2}\left(\frac{t^5}{5} - \frac{2t^3}{3} + t\right) + C\text{; where } t = \left(\frac{1+x^4}{x^4}\right)^{\frac{1}{2}}$$

(f) $I=\int x^{-8}\left(1+x^{7}\right)^{\frac{1}{3}}dx$

Let $m=-8, n=7 \quad \Rightarrow \quad \dfrac{m+1}{n}=-1 \in \mathbb{Z}$

$\therefore \quad 1+x^{7}=t^{3} \Rightarrow 7x^{6}dx=3t^{2}dt$

$$\therefore \quad I=\int x^{-8}t\frac{3t^{2}}{7x^{6}}dt=\frac{3}{7}\int\frac{t^{3}}{x^{14}}dt=\frac{3}{7}\int\frac{t^{3}-1+1}{\left(t^{3}-1\right)^{2}}dt$$

$$=\frac{3}{7}\int\frac{dt}{t^{3}-1}+\frac{3}{7}\int\frac{dt}{\left(t^{3}-1\right)^{2}}=\frac{3}{7}\left(I_{1}+I_{2}\right)$$

$$\Rightarrow \quad I_{1}=\int\frac{dt}{t^{3}-1}=\frac{1}{(t-1)\left(t^{2}+t+1\right)}=\frac{A}{t-1}+\frac{Bt+C}{t^{2}+t+1}$$

$$\Rightarrow \quad A=\frac{1}{3}, C=-\frac{2}{3}, B=-\frac{1}{3}$$

$$\therefore \quad I_{1}=\frac{1}{3}\int\frac{dt}{t-1}-\frac{1}{3}\int\frac{t+2}{t^{2}+t+1}dt$$

$$=\frac{1}{3}\ln|t-1|-\frac{1}{6}\int\frac{2t+1}{t^{2}+t+1}dt-\frac{1}{2}\int\frac{dt}{\left(t+\frac{1}{2}\right)^{2}+\left(\frac{\sqrt{3}}{2}\right)^{2}}$$

$$=\frac{1}{3}\ln|t-1|-\frac{1}{6}\ln\left|t^{2}+t+1\right|-\frac{1}{\sqrt{3}}\tan^{-1}\left(\frac{2t+1}{\sqrt{3}}\right)+C$$

$$\therefore \quad I_{2}=\int\frac{dt}{\left(t^{3}-1\right)^{2}}\frac{1}{(t-1)^{2}\left(t^{2}+t+1\right)^{2}}$$

$$=\frac{A}{t-1}+\frac{B}{(t-1)^{2}}+\frac{Ct+D}{t^{2}+t+1}+\frac{Et+F}{\left(t^{2}+t+1\right)^{2}};\ B=\frac{1}{9}$$

$I=A(t-1)\left(t^{4}+2t^{3}+3t^{2}+2t+1\right)$

$+B\left(t^{4}+2t^{3}+3t^{2}+2t+1\right)$

$+(Ct+D)\left(t^{2}-2t+1\right)\left(t^{2}+t+1\right)+(Et+F)\left(t^{2}-2t+1\right)$

$=A\left(t^{5}+2t^{4}+3t^{3}+2t^{2}+t-t^{4}-2t^{3}-3t^{2}-2t-1\right)$

$+B\left(t^{4}+2t^{3}+3t^{2}+2t+1\right)+(Ct+D)\left(t^{4}-t^{3}-t+1\right)$

$+E\left(t^{3}-2t^{2}+t\right)+F\left(t^{2}-2t+1\right)$

$=A\left(t^{5}+t^{4}+t^{3}-t^{2}-t-1\right)+B\left(t^{4}+2t^{3}+3t^{2}+2t+1\right)$

$+C\left(t^{5}-t^{4}-t^{2}+t\right)+D\left(t^{4}-t^{3}-t+1\right)+E\left(t^{3}-2t^{2}+t\right)$

$+F\left(t^{2}-2t+1\right)$

$=t^{5}(A+C)+t^{4}(A+B-C+D)+t^{3}(A+2B-D+E)$

$+t^{2}(-A+3B-C-2E+F)$

$+t(-A+2B+C-D+E-2F)$

$-A+B+D+F$

On solving, $A=-\dfrac{2}{9}, B=\dfrac{1}{9}, C=\dfrac{2}{9}, \quad D=\dfrac{1}{3}, E=\dfrac{1}{3}, F=\dfrac{1}{3}$

$$\therefore \quad I_{2}=-\frac{2}{9}\int\frac{dt}{t-1}+\frac{1}{9}\int\frac{dt}{(t-1)^{2}}$$

$$+\frac{1}{9}\int\frac{2t+3}{t^{2}+t+1}dt+\frac{1}{3}\int\frac{t+1}{\left(t^{2}+t+1\right)^{2}}dt$$

$$=-\frac{2}{9}\ln|t-1|-\frac{1}{9}\frac{1}{(t-1)}+\frac{1}{9}\ln\left|t^{2}+t+1\right|$$

$$+\frac{2}{9}\int\frac{dt}{\left(t+\frac{1}{2}\right)^{2}+\left(\frac{\sqrt{3}}{2}\right)^{2}}-\frac{1}{6}\frac{1}{\left(t^{2}+t+1\right)}+\frac{1}{6}\int\frac{dt}{\left(t^{2}+t+1\right)^{2}}$$

$$=-\frac{2}{9}\ln|t-1|-\frac{1}{9}\frac{1}{(t-1)}+\frac{1}{9}\ln\left|t^{2}+t+1\right|$$

$$+\frac{4}{9\sqrt{3}}\tan^{-1}\left(\frac{2t+1}{\sqrt{3}}\right)-\frac{1}{6}\frac{1}{\left(t^{2}+t+1\right)}+\frac{1}{6}I_{3}$$

$$\therefore \quad I_{3}=\int\frac{dt}{\left(\left(t+\frac{1}{2}\right)^{2}+\frac{3}{4}\right)^{2}}$$

Let $t=\dfrac{\sqrt{3}}{2}\tan\theta-\dfrac{1}{2}\Rightarrow dt=\dfrac{\sqrt{3}}{2}Sec^{2}\theta\, d\theta$

$$\therefore \quad I_{3}=\int\frac{\frac{\sqrt{3}}{2}Sec^{2}\theta\, d\theta}{\left(\frac{3}{4}Sec^{2}\theta\right)^{2}}=\frac{8}{3\sqrt{3}}\int\cos^{2}\theta\, d\theta$$

$$=\frac{4}{3\sqrt{3}}\int(1+\cos 2\theta)d\theta=\frac{4}{3\sqrt{3}}\left(\theta+\frac{\sin 2\theta}{2}\right)+C$$

$$=\frac{4}{3\sqrt{3}}\left(\tan^{-1}\left(\frac{2t+1}{\sqrt{3}}\right)+\frac{\tan\theta}{1-\tan^{2}\theta}\right)+C$$

$$=\frac{4}{3\sqrt{3}}\tan^{-1}\left(\frac{2t+1}{\sqrt{3}}\right)-\frac{2}{3}\frac{(2t+1)}{2t^{2}+2t-1}+C$$

$$\therefore \quad I_{2}=-\frac{2}{9}\ln|t-1|-\frac{1}{9}\frac{1}{(t-1)}+$$

$$\frac{1}{9}\ln\left|t^{2}+t+1\right|+\frac{2}{3\sqrt{3}}\tan^{-1}\left(\frac{2t+1}{\sqrt{3}}\right)$$

$$-\frac{1}{6}\frac{1}{\left(t^{2}+t+1\right)}-\frac{1}{9}\frac{(2t+1)}{2t^{2}+2t-1}+C$$

$$\therefore \quad I=\frac{3}{7}\left(\frac{1}{9}\ln|t-1|-\frac{1}{9}\frac{1}{(t-1)}-\frac{1}{18}\ln\left|t^{2}+t+1\right|\right.$$

$$\left.-\left(\frac{1}{3\sqrt{3}}\tan^{-1}\left(\frac{2t+1}{\sqrt{3}}\right)\right)-\frac{1}{6}\frac{1}{\left(t^{2}+t+1\right)}-\frac{1}{9}\frac{(2t+1)}{2t^{2}+2t-1}\right)+C$$

(g) $I=\int x^{\frac{1}{3}}\left(1+x^{\frac{4}{3}}\right)^{\frac{1}{7}}dx;\ m=\dfrac{1}{3}, n=\dfrac{4}{3}, \dfrac{m+1}{n}=1\in\mathbb{Z}$

$\therefore \quad 1+x^{\frac{4}{3}}=t^{7} \quad \Rightarrow \quad \dfrac{4}{3}x^{\frac{1}{3}}dx=7t^{6}dt$

$$\therefore \quad I=\int\frac{3}{4}(t)(7)\left(t^{6}\right)dt=\frac{21}{4}\int t^{7}dt=\frac{21}{32}t^{8}+C$$

$$=\frac{21}{32}\left(1+x^{\frac{4}{3}}\right)^{\frac{8}{7}}+C$$

(h) $I=\int \sin^{\frac{3}{2}} x\cos^{\frac{5}{2}} x\,dx = \int \sin^{\frac{3}{2}} x\cos^{\frac{3}{2}} x\cos x\,dx$

Let $\sin x = t \Rightarrow \cos x\,dx = dt$

$$I=\int t^{\frac{3}{2}}\left(1-t^2\right)^{\frac{3}{4}} dt\ ;\ m=\frac{3}{2}, n=2, p=\frac{3}{4}$$

$$\frac{m+1}{n}+p=2\in\mathbb{Z}$$

Put $1-t^2=t^2z^4 \Rightarrow \frac{1}{t^2}=z^4+1 \Rightarrow -\frac{2}{t^3}dt=4z^3\,dz$

$$\therefore I=\int -t^{\frac{3}{2}}\left(t^2z^4\right)^{\frac{3}{4}} 2t^3z^3 d\,z$$

$$=-2\int t^6z^6dz=-2\int\frac{z^6}{\left(z^4+1\right)^3}dz$$

Put $z^4+1=u$

$\Rightarrow$ $4z^3\,dz=du$

$\Rightarrow$ $z^3\,dz=1/4\,du$

$$\therefore\quad I=-2\int\frac{(u-1)^{3/4}\frac{1}{4}}{u^3}du=-\frac{1}{2}\int u^3(u-1)^{3/4}du$$

(i) $I=\int x^{\frac{13}{2}}\left(1+x^{\frac{5}{2}}\right)^{\frac{1}{2}}dx$

$$\Rightarrow\quad m=\frac{13}{2}, n=\frac{5}{2}\Rightarrow\frac{m+1}{n}=3\ \in\mathbb{Z}$$

Let $1+x^{\frac{5}{2}}=t^2 \Rightarrow \frac{5}{2}x^{\frac{3}{2}}dx=2t\,dt \Rightarrow dx=\frac{4}{5}\frac{t\,dt}{x^{\frac{3}{2}}}$

$$\therefore\quad I=\int x^{\frac{13}{2}}t\frac{4}{5}\frac{t}{x^{\frac{3}{2}}}dt=\frac{4}{5}\int x^5t^2dt$$

$$=\frac{4}{5}\int\left(t^2-1\right)^2t^2dt=\frac{4}{5}\int\left(t^6-2t^4+t^2\right)dt$$

$$=\frac{4}{5}\left(\frac{t^7}{7}-\frac{2}{5}t^5+\frac{t^3}{3}\right)+C$$

$$=\frac{4}{5}\left[\frac{\left(1+x^{\frac{5}{2}}\right)^{7/2}}{7}-\frac{2}{5}\left(1+x^{\frac{5}{2}}\right)^{\frac{5}{2}}+\frac{1}{3}\left(1+x^{\frac{5}{2}}\right)^{\frac{3}{2}}\right]+C$$

4. $I=\int\frac{dx}{x\sqrt{x^2+x+2}}$

Let $\sqrt{x^2+x+2}=t+x \quad\Rightarrow\quad x^2+x+2=x^2+t^2+2tx$

$$\Rightarrow\quad x=\frac{2-t^2}{2t-1}$$

$$\Rightarrow\quad dx=\frac{(-2)\left(t^2-t+2\right)}{(2t-1)^2}$$

$$\therefore\quad \sqrt{x^2+x+2}=t+x=t+\frac{2-t^2}{2t-1}=\frac{t^2-t+2}{2t-1}$$

$$\Rightarrow\quad I=\int\frac{(2t-1)}{\left(2-t^2\right)}\frac{(2t-1)}{\left(t^2-t+2\right)}\frac{(-2)\left(t^2-t+2\right)}{(2t-1)^2}dt$$

$$=2\int\frac{dt}{t^2-2}=\frac{1}{\sqrt{2}}\ln\left|\frac{t-\sqrt{2}}{t+\sqrt{2}}\right|+C\text{, where}$$

$$t=\left(\sqrt{x^2+x+2}\right)-x$$

5. $I=\int\frac{x\,dx}{\left(5-4x-x^2\right)^{\frac{3}{2}}}$

$\sqrt{5-4x-x^2}=\sqrt{(x+5)(1-x)}=(x+5)t$ (say)

Squaring, $(1-x)=(x+5)t^2$

$$\Rightarrow\quad\frac{1-x}{x+5}=t^2\qquad\Rightarrow\quad\frac{6}{x+5}=t^2+1$$

$$\Rightarrow\quad x=\frac{6}{t^2+1}-5=\frac{1-5t^2}{t^2+1}$$

$$\Rightarrow\quad dx=\frac{\left(t^2+1\right)(-10t)-\left(1-5t^2\right)(2t)}{\left(t^2+1\right)^2}$$

$$=\frac{-10t^3-10t-2t+10t^3}{\left(t^2+1\right)^2}=\frac{-12t}{\left(t^2+1\right)^2}dt$$

$$\Rightarrow\quad I=\int\frac{\left(\frac{1-5t^2}{t^2+1}\right)\frac{(-12t)}{\left(t^2+1\right)^2}dt}{\left(\frac{6t}{t^2+1}\right)^3}=\frac{-12}{216}\int\frac{t\left(1-5t^2\right)}{t^3}dt$$

$$=\frac{-1}{18}\left[\int\frac{dt}{t^2}-5\int dt\right]=\frac{1}{18}\left(\frac{1}{t}+5t\right)+C\text{ where}$$

$$t=\frac{\sqrt{5-4x-x^2}}{(x+5)}$$

6. $I=\int\frac{dx}{\left(x+\sqrt{x^2-4}\right)^{\frac{5}{3}}}$

Let $x+\sqrt{x^2-4}=t$

$\Rightarrow$ $\left(x^2-4\right)=(t-x)^2=t^2+x^2-2xt$

$\Rightarrow$ $2xt=t^2+4\Rightarrow x=\frac{t^2+4}{2t}$

$$\Rightarrow\quad dx=\frac{1}{2}\left[1-\frac{4}{t^2}\right]dt=\frac{\left(t^2-4\right)}{2t^2}dt$$

$$\Rightarrow\quad I=\int\frac{\frac{\left(t^2-4\right)}{2t^2}dt}{t^{\frac{5}{3}}}=\frac{1}{2}\int\frac{\left(t^2-4\right)}{t^{\frac{11}{3}}}dt=\frac{1}{2}\int t^{-\frac{5}{3}}dt-2\int t^{-\frac{11}{3}}dt$$

$$=-\frac{3}{4}t^{-\frac{2}{3}}+\frac{3}{4}t^{-\frac{8}{3}}+C=\frac{3}{4}\left(1-t^2\right)t^{-\frac{8}{3}}+C\text{ Where}$$

$$t=x+\sqrt{x^2-4}$$

TEXTUAL EXERCISE–8: (OBJECTIVE)

1. (c) $I=\int \frac{x^{\frac{1}{2}}+x^{\frac{1}{3}}}{x^{\frac{5}{4}}-x^{\frac{7}{6}}}dx$

Let $x=t^{12} \Rightarrow dx=12t^{11}dt$

$$I=\int \frac{t^6+t^4}{t^{15}-t^{14}}12t^{11}dt=12\int \frac{(t^2+1)t^{15}}{t^{14}(t-1)}dt$$

$$=12\int \frac{(t^2+1).t}{t-1}dt=12\left[\int (t^2+1)dt+\int \frac{t^2+1}{t-1}dt\right]$$

$$=12\left[\frac{t^3}{3}+t+\int (t+1)dt+2\int \frac{dt}{t-1}\right]$$

$$=12\left[\frac{t^3}{3}+\frac{t^2}{2}+2t+2\ln|t-1|\right]$$

$$=4x^{\frac{1}{4}}+6x^{\frac{1}{6}}+24x^{\frac{1}{12}}+24\ln\left|x^{\frac{1}{12}}-1\right|+C$$

2. (b) $I=\int \frac{(2x-3)^{\frac{1}{2}}}{(2x-3)^{\frac{1}{3}}+1}dx$

Let $(2x-3)=t^6 \Rightarrow 2dx=6t^5dt \Rightarrow dx=3t^5dt$

$$I=\int \frac{t^3(3)(t^5)dt}{t^2+1}=3\int \frac{t^8}{t^2+1}dt$$

$$=3\left[\int (t^6-t^4+t^2-1)dt+\int \frac{dt}{(t^2+1)}\right]$$

$$=3\left[\frac{t^7}{7}-\frac{t^5}{5}+\frac{t^3}{3}-t+\tan^{-1}t\right]+C$$

3. (a) $I=\int \frac{2}{(2-x)^2}\left(\frac{2-x}{2+x}\right)^{\frac{1}{3}}dx$

Let $\frac{2-x}{2+x}=t^3 \Rightarrow x=\frac{2-2t^3}{t^3+1}$

$\Rightarrow \frac{dx}{dt}=\frac{-12t^2}{(t^3+1)^2}$ and $2-x=\frac{4t^3}{t^3+1}$

$$\therefore \quad I=\int \frac{2}{16t^6}(t^3+1)^2 t\frac{(-12)t^2}{(t^3+1)^2}dt=-\frac{3}{2}\int \frac{dt}{t^3}$$

$$=\frac{3}{4}\frac{1}{t^2}+C=\frac{3}{4}\sqrt[3]{\left(\frac{x+2}{2-x}\right)^2}+C$$

4. (d) $\mathrm{I}=\int \frac{\mathrm{dx}}{\mathrm{x}\left(2+\left(\frac{\mathrm{x}-1}{\mathrm{x}}\right)^{\frac{1}{3}}\right)}$

Let $\left(\frac{x-1}{x}\right)=t^3 \Rightarrow x=\frac{1}{1-t^3}$

$$\Rightarrow dx=\frac{3t^2}{(1-t^3)^2}dt$$

$$\therefore \quad I=\int \frac{1-t^3}{2+t}\frac{3t^2}{(1-t^3)^2}dt$$

$$=3\int \frac{t^2}{(2+t)(1-t)(t^2+t+1)}dt \qquad \frac{t^2}{(2+t)(1-t)(t^2+t+1)}$$

$$=\frac{A}{2+t}+\frac{B}{1-t}+\frac{Ct+D}{t^2+t+1}$$

$A=\frac{t^2}{(1-t)(t^2+t+1)}$ for $t=-2$

$\therefore \quad A=\frac{4}{9}$

$B=\frac{t^2}{(2+t)(t^2+t+1)}$ For $t=1$

$\therefore \quad B=\frac{1}{9}$

Put $t=0 \Rightarrow 0=\frac{2}{9}+\frac{1}{9}+D \Rightarrow D=-\frac{1}{3}$

Put $t=-1$, we get $\frac{1}{2}=\frac{4}{9}+\frac{1}{18}-C-\frac{1}{3} \Rightarrow C=-\frac{1}{3}$

$$I=3\left[\frac{4}{9}\int \frac{dt}{2+t}+\frac{1}{9}\int \frac{dt}{1-t}-\frac{1}{3}\int \frac{t+1}{t^2+t+1}dt\right]$$

$=\frac{4}{3}\ln|t+2|-\frac{1}{3}\ln|t-1|-I_1$, where

$$I_1=\int \frac{t+1}{t^2+t+1}dt=\frac{1}{2}\int \frac{2t+1}{t^2+t+1}dt+\frac{1}{2}\int \frac{dt}{\left(t+\frac{1}{2}\right)^2+\left(\frac{\sqrt{3}}{2}\right)^2}$$

$$=\frac{1}{2}\ln|t^2+t+1|+\frac{1}{\sqrt{3}}\tan^{-1}\left(\frac{2t+1}{\sqrt{3}}\right)$$

$$I=\ln\left|(t+2)^{\frac{4}{3}}\right|-\ln\left|(t-1)^{\frac{1}{3}}\right|$$

$$-\ln\left|(t^2+t+1)^{\frac{1}{2}}\right|-\frac{1}{\sqrt{3}}\tan^{-1}\left(\frac{2t+1}{\sqrt{3}}\right)$$

$$=-\frac{1}{\sqrt{3}}\tan^{-1}\left(\frac{2t+1}{\sqrt{3}}\right)+\ln\left|\frac{\sqrt[3]{(t+2)^4}}{\sqrt[3]{t-1}\sqrt{t^2+t+1}}\right|+C \text{ where}$$

$$t=\sqrt[3]{\frac{x-1}{x}}$$

5. (b) $I=\int \frac{dx}{\sqrt[3]{(x+1)^2(x-1)^4}}$

Let $\frac{1+x}{1-x}=t^3 \Rightarrow x=\frac{t^3-1}{t^3+1}$

$$\Rightarrow \qquad dx=\frac{6t^2}{(t^3+1)^2}dt$$

$$\Rightarrow \qquad (x+1)=\frac{2t^3}{t^3+1},(x-1)=\frac{-2}{(t^3+1)}$$

$$\therefore \quad I=\int \frac{\dfrac{6t^2}{(t^3+1)^2}dt}{\left[\dfrac{4t^6}{(t^3+1)^2}\dfrac{16}{(t^3+1)^4}\right]^{\frac{1}{3}}}=\frac{3}{2}\int dt=\frac{3}{2}t+C$$

$$=\frac{3}{2}\left(\frac{1+x}{1-x}\right)^{\frac{1}{3}}+C$$

6. (c) $I=\int (x-2)\sqrt{\frac{1+x}{1-x}}dx$

Let $\frac{1+x}{1-x}=t^2 \Rightarrow x=\frac{t^2-1}{t^2+1} \Rightarrow \quad dx=\frac{4t}{(t^2+1)^2}dt$;

$$x-2=-\frac{t^2+3}{t^2+1}$$

$$I=\int -\left(\frac{t^2+3}{t^2+1}\right)\frac{t\,4t}{(t^2+1)^2}dt=-4\int \frac{t^2(t^2+3)}{(t^2+1)^3}dt$$

$$=-4\left[\int \frac{t^2}{(t^2+1)^2}dt+2\int \frac{t^2}{(t^2+1)^3}dt\right]$$

$$=-4\left[\int \frac{dt}{t^2+1}-\int \frac{dt}{(t^2+1)^2}+2\int \frac{dt}{(t^2+1)^2}-2\int \frac{dt}{(t^2+1)^3}\right]$$

$$=-4\left[\int \frac{dt}{t^2+1}+\int \frac{dt}{(t^2+1)^2}-2\int \frac{dt}{(t^2+1)^3}\right]$$

$$I_1=\int \frac{dt}{(t^2+1)^2};t=\tan\theta,\ dt=\sec^2\theta\, d\theta$$

$$I_1=\int \cos^2\theta\, d\theta=\frac{1}{2}\int (1+\cos 2\theta)d\theta=\frac{1}{2}\left(\theta+\frac{\sin 2\theta}{2}\right)+C$$

$$=\frac{1}{2}\left(\tan^{-1}t+\frac{t}{1+t^2}\right)+C$$

$$I_2=\int \frac{dt}{(t^2+1)^3}$$

Put $t=\tan\theta \Rightarrow dt=\sec^2\theta\, d\theta$

$$I_2=\int \cos^4\theta\, d\theta=\frac{1}{4}\int (1+\cos 2\theta)^2\, d\theta$$

$$=\frac{1}{4}\int (\cos^2 2\theta+2\cos 2\theta+1)\, d\theta=\frac{1}{8}\int (1+\cos 4\theta)d\theta$$

$$+\frac{1}{2}\int \cos 2\theta\, d\theta+\frac{1}{4}\int d\theta$$

$$=\frac{\theta}{8}+\frac{\sin 4\theta}{32}+\frac{\sin 2\theta}{4}+\frac{\theta}{4}=\frac{3\theta}{8}+\frac{\sin 2\theta}{4}+\frac{\sin 4\theta}{32}$$

$$=\frac{3}{8}\tan^{-1}t+\frac{1}{2}\frac{t}{1+t^2}+\frac{1}{8}\frac{t(1-t^2)}{(1+t^2)^2}$$

$$=\frac{3}{8}\tan^{-1}t+\frac{1}{8}\frac{t(4+4t^2+1-t^2)}{(1+t^2)^2}$$

$$=\frac{3}{8}\tan^{-1}t+\frac{t}{8}\frac{(5+3t^2)}{(1+t^2)^2}+C_2$$

$$\therefore \quad I=-4\tan^{-1}t-2\tan^{-1}t-\frac{2t}{1+t^2}$$

$$+3\tan^{-1}t+\frac{t(5+3t^2)}{(1+t^2)^2}+C$$

$$=-3\tan^{-1}t+\frac{t(5+3t^2-2-2t^2)}{(1+t^2)^2}$$

$$=-3\tan^{-1}t+\frac{t(3+t^2)}{(1+t^2)^2}+C$$

$$=-3\tan^{-1}\sqrt{\frac{1+x}{1-x}}+\sqrt{\frac{1+x}{1-x}}\frac{\left(3+\dfrac{1+x}{1-x}\right)}{\left(1+\dfrac{1+x}{1-x}\right)^2}$$

$$=-3\tan^{-1}\sqrt{\frac{1+x}{1-x}}+\left(\sqrt{\frac{1+x}{1-x}}\right)\frac{\left(\dfrac{4-2x}{1-x}\right)}{\left(\dfrac{2}{1-x}\right)^2}+C$$

$$=-3\tan^{-1}\sqrt{\frac{1+x}{1-x}}+\sqrt{\frac{1+x}{1-x}}\frac{(1-x)}{2}(2-x)+C$$

$$=-3\tan^{-1}\sqrt{\frac{1+x}{1-x}}+\frac{2-x}{2}\sqrt{1-x^2}+C$$

7. (c) $I=\int \frac{dx}{(1-x)^{\frac{3}{2}}\sqrt{1+x}}=\int \frac{dx}{(1-x)\sqrt{1-x^2}}$

Let $(1-x)=\frac{1}{t}\Rightarrow dx=\frac{1}{t^2}dt$

$$x=\frac{t-1}{t},\sqrt{1-x^2}=\sqrt{1-\frac{(t^2-2t+1)}{t^2}}$$

$$=\sqrt{\frac{t^2-t^2+2t-1}{t^2}}=\frac{\sqrt{2t-1}}{t}$$

$$\therefore \quad I=\int \frac{1}{\frac{1}{t}\frac{\sqrt{2t-1}}{t}}\frac{1}{t^2}dt=\int \frac{dt}{(2t-1)^{\frac{1}{2}}}$$

$$=\sqrt{2t-1}+C=\sqrt{\frac{2}{1-x}-1}=\sqrt{\frac{1+x}{1-x}}+C$$

8. (a), (b) $I=\int \frac{dx}{\sqrt{x^2+2x+2}+1}$

Let $\sqrt{x^2+2x+2}=t-x$

$$\Rightarrow x^2+2x+2=x^2-2xt+t^2$$

$$\Rightarrow \quad x(2t+2)=t^2-2$$

$$\Rightarrow \quad x=\frac{1}{2}\frac{t^2-2}{(t+1)}$$

$$\Rightarrow \quad dx = \frac{2(t+1)(2t)-(t^2-2)(2)}{4(t+1)^2}dt$$

$$= \frac{4t^2+4t-2t^2+4}{4(t+1)^2}dt = \frac{2(t^2+2t+2)}{4(t+1)^2}dt$$

$$\Rightarrow \quad t-x = t-\frac{t^2-2}{2t+2} = \frac{2t^2+2t-t^2+2}{2(t+1)} = \frac{t^2+2t+2}{2(t+1)}$$

$$\Rightarrow \quad I = \int \frac{\frac{t^2+2t+2}{2(t+1)^2}dt}{\frac{t^2+2t+2}{2(t+1)}+1} = \int \frac{(t^2+2t+2)}{(t^2+4t+4)(t+1)}dt$$

Let $\frac{t^2+2t+2}{(t+1)(t+2)^2} = \frac{A}{t+1}+\frac{B}{(t+2)}+\frac{C}{(t+2)^2}$

$$\Rightarrow \quad A=1, C=-2, B=0$$

$\Rightarrow \quad I = \int \frac{dt}{t+1} - 2\int \frac{dt}{(t+2)^2} = \ln|t+1| + \frac{2}{t+2}+C$; where $t = x+\sqrt{x^2+2x+2}$

9. (b) $I = \int \frac{(x+3)}{\sqrt{4x^2+4x-3}}dx$

$$= \frac{1}{8}\int \frac{8x+4}{\sqrt{4x^2+4x-3}}dx + \frac{5}{2}\int \frac{dx}{\sqrt{4x^2+4x-3}}$$

$$= \frac{1}{4}\sqrt{4x^2+4x-3} + \frac{5}{2}\int \frac{dx}{\sqrt{(2x+1)^2-2^2}}$$

$$= \frac{1}{4}\sqrt{4x^2+4x-3} + \frac{5}{4}\ln\left|2x+1+\sqrt{4x^2+4x-3}\right| + C$$

10. (a) $I = \int \frac{x\,dx}{(x^2-3x+2)\sqrt{x^2-4x+3}}$

$$= \int \frac{x\,dx}{(x-2)(x-1)\sqrt{x^2-4x+3}}$$

Put $\sqrt{x^2-4x+3} = t-x$

$$\Rightarrow x^2-4x+3 = x^2-2tx+t^2$$

$$\Rightarrow \quad x(2t-4) = t^2-3 \Rightarrow x = \frac{t^2-3}{2(t-2)}$$

$$\Rightarrow \quad dx = \frac{2(t-2)(2t)-(t^2-3)(2)}{4(t-2)^2} = \frac{4t^2-8t-2t^2+6}{4(t-2)^2}dt$$

$\Rightarrow \quad x-2 = \frac{t^2-3}{2(t-2)}-2 = \frac{t^2-3-4t+8}{2(t-2)} = \frac{t^2-4t+8}{2(t-2)}$ and

$$dx = \frac{t^2-4t+3}{2(t-2)^2}dt$$

$$\Rightarrow \quad (x-1) = \frac{t^2-3}{2(t-2)}-1 = \frac{t^2-3-2t+4}{2(t-2)} = \frac{t^2-2t+1}{2(t-2)}$$

$$\Rightarrow \quad t-x = t-\frac{t^2-3}{2(t-2)} = \frac{2t^2-4t-t^2+3}{2(t-2)} = \frac{t^2-4t+3}{2(t-2)}$$

$$\Rightarrow \quad I = \int \frac{\frac{t^2-3}{2(t-2)}\frac{(t-3)(t-1)}{2(t-2)^2}dt}{\frac{(t^2-4t+8)}{2(t-2)}\frac{(t-1)^2}{2(t-2)}\frac{(t^2-4t+3)}{2(t-2)}}$$

$$= 2\int \frac{t^2-3}{(t^2-4t+8)(t-1)^2}dt$$

$$\Rightarrow \quad \frac{t^2-3}{(t^2-4t+8)(t-1)^2} = \frac{A}{t-1}+\frac{B}{(t-1)^2}+\frac{Ct+D}{t^2-4t+8}$$

$$\Rightarrow \quad (t^2-3) = A(t^3-4t^2+8t-t^2+4t-8)$$
$$+B(t^2-4t+8)+(Ct+D)(t^2-2t+1)$$
$$= A(t^3-5t^2+12t-8)+B(t^2-4t+8)$$
$$+C(t^3-2t^2+t)+D(t^2-2t+1)$$
$$= (C+A)t^3+t^2(-5A+B-2C+D)$$
$$+t(12A-4B+C-2D)-8A+8B+C+D$$

$A+C=0, -5A+B-2C+D=1,$

$12A-4B+C-2D=0,\ -8A+8B+C+D=-3$

$\Rightarrow \quad B = \frac{t^2-3}{t^2-4t+8}$ for $t=1$

$$\Rightarrow \quad B = -\frac{2}{5},\ A = \frac{6}{25},\ C = -\frac{6}{25},\ D = \frac{53}{25}$$

$$\Rightarrow \quad I = \frac{12}{25}\int \frac{dt}{t-1} - \frac{4}{5}\int \frac{dt}{(t-1)^2} - \frac{2}{25}\int \frac{6t-53}{t^2-4t+8}$$

$$= \frac{12}{25}\ln|t-1| + \frac{4}{5}\frac{1}{(t-1)} - \frac{6}{25}$$

$$\int \frac{2t-4}{t^2-4t+8}dt + \frac{82}{25}\int \frac{dt}{(t-2)^2+2^2}$$

$$= \frac{12}{25}\ln|t-1| + \frac{4}{5(t-1)} - \frac{6}{25}\ln\left|t^2-4t+8\right|$$

$+\frac{41}{25}\tan^{-1}\left(\frac{t-2}{2}\right)+C$; Where $t = x+\sqrt{x^2-4x+3}$

11. (b) $I = \int x^{-\frac{2}{3}}\left(1+x^{\frac{2}{3}}\right)^{-1}dx$

Let $x = t^3 \quad \Rightarrow dx = 3t^2dt$

$$\Rightarrow \quad I = \int t^{-2}(1+t^2)^{-1}3t^2dt = 3\int \frac{dt}{1+t^2} = 3\tan^{-1}t + C$$

$$= 3\tan^{-1}x^{\frac{1}{3}} + C$$

12. (c) $I=\int x^{\frac{1}{3}}\left(2+x^{\frac{1}{2}}\right)^2 dx=\int x^{\frac{1}{3}}\left(x+4x^{\frac{1}{2}}+4\right)dx$

$=\int x^{\frac{4}{3}}dx+4\int x^{\frac{5}{6}}dx+4\int x^{\frac{1}{3}}dx=\frac{3}{7}x^{\frac{7}{3}}+\frac{24}{11}x^{\frac{11}{6}}+3x^{\frac{4}{3}}+C$

13. (d) $I=\int x^{-\frac{2}{3}}\left(1+x^{\frac{1}{3}}\right)^{\frac{1}{2}}dx$

$m=-\frac{2}{3},\ n=\frac{1}{3},\ \frac{m+1}{n}=1\in\mathbb{Z}$

$\therefore\ 1+x^{\frac{1}{3}}=t^2\Rightarrow\frac{1}{3}x^{-\frac{2}{3}}dx=2t\,dt\Rightarrow x^{-\frac{2}{3}}dx=6t\,dt$

$\therefore\quad I=\int 6t^2dt=2t^3+C=2\left(1+x^{\frac{1}{3}}\right)^{\frac{3}{2}}+C$

14. (b) $I=\int\frac{dx}{x\left(1+x^{\frac{1}{3}}\right)^2}$

Let $x=t^3\Rightarrow dx=3t^2dt$

$\therefore\quad I=\int\frac{3t^2dt}{t^3(1+t)^2}=3\int\frac{dt}{t(1+t)^2}$

$\Rightarrow\quad\frac{1}{t(1+t)^2}=\frac{A}{t}+\frac{B}{1+t}+\frac{C}{(1+t)^2}$

$\Rightarrow\quad A=1,\ C=-1,\ B=-1$

$\Rightarrow\quad I=3\int\frac{dt}{t}-3\int\frac{dt}{1+t}-3$

$\int\frac{dt}{(1+t)^2}=3\ln\left(\frac{t}{1+t}\right)+\frac{3}{1+t}+C$

$=3\ln\left(\frac{x^{\frac{1}{3}}}{1+x^{\frac{1}{3}}}\right)+\frac{3}{1+x^{\frac{1}{3}}}+C$

15. (a) $I=\int\frac{dx}{x^3\left(1+\frac{1}{x}\right)^{\frac{1}{5}}}=\int x^{-3}\left(1+x^{-1}\right)^{-\frac{1}{5}}dx$

$\frac{m+1}{n}=2\in\mathbb{Z}$

$\therefore\quad 1+\frac{1}{x}=t^5\Rightarrow-\frac{1}{x^2}dx=5t^4dt$

$\Rightarrow\quad x=\frac{1}{t^5-1}$

$\Rightarrow\quad I=-\int\frac{1}{x}\frac{1}{t}5t^4dt=\int 5\left(1-t^5\right)t^3dt=5\int\left(t^3-t^8\right)dt$

$=\frac{5t^4}{4}-\frac{5t^9}{9}+C$

$=\int 5t^8-5t^3dt=\frac{5}{9}t^9-\frac{5}{4}t^4+C$

$=-\frac{5}{9}\left(1+\frac{1}{x}\right)^{\frac{9}{5}}+\frac{5}{4}\left(1+\frac{1}{x}\right)^{\frac{4}{5}}+C$

TEXTUAL EXERCIS– 9: (SUBJECTIVE)

1. (a) $I=\int\tan^2x\sec^4x\,dx=\int\tan^2x\left(\tan^2x+1\right)\sec^2x\,dx$

$I=\int t^2\left(t^2+1\right)dt$; $t=\tan x\Rightarrow dt=\sec^2x\,dx$

$=\frac{t^5}{5}+\frac{t^3}{3}+C=\frac{\tan^5x}{5}+\frac{\tan^3x}{3}+C$

(b) $I=\int\tan^3x\sec^6x\,dx=\int\tan^3x\left(1+\tan^2x\right)^2\sec^2x\,dx$

$=\int t^3\left(1+t^2\right)^2dt; t=\tan x\Rightarrow dt=\sec^2x\,dx$

$=\int t^3\left(t^4+2t^2+1\right)dt$

$=\frac{t^8}{8}+\frac{t^6}{3}+\frac{t^4}{4}+C=\frac{\tan^8x}{8}+\frac{\tan^6x}{3}+\frac{\tan^4x}{4}+C$

(c) $I=\int\tan^3x\sec^5x\,dx$

$=\int\left(\sec^2x-1\right)\sec^4x\ \sec x\tan x\,dx$

$=\int\left(t^2-1\right)t^4dt; t=\sec x$

$\Rightarrow\qquad dt=\sec x\ \tan x\,dx$

$=\frac{t^7}{7}-\frac{t^5}{5}+C=\frac{\sec^7x}{7}-\frac{\sec^5x}{5}+C$

(d) $I=\int\tan^{-5}x\ \sec^6x\,dx$

$=\int\frac{\left(1+\tan^2x\right)^2}{\tan^5x}\sec^2x\,dx;\ t=\tan x$

$\Rightarrow dt=\sec^2x\,dx$

$=\int\frac{\left(1+t^2\right)^2}{t^5}dt=\int\frac{t^4+2t^2+1}{t^5}dt=\int\frac{dt}{t}+2\int\frac{dt}{t^3}+\int\frac{dt}{t^5}$

$=\ln|t|-\frac{1}{t^2}-\frac{1}{4}\frac{1}{t^4}+C=\ln|\tan x|-\cot^2x-\frac{\cot^4x}{4}+C$

(e) $I=\int\frac{(2\tan x+3)\sec^2x}{\left(\tan^2x-2\tan x+5\right)}dx$

Put $t=\tan x\qquad\Rightarrow\quad dt=\sec^2x\,dx$

$=\int\frac{2t+3}{t^2-2t+5}dt$

$=\int\frac{2t-2}{t^2-2t+5}dt+5\int\frac{dt}{(t-1)^2+2^2}$

$=\ln\left|t^2-2t+5\right|+\frac{5}{2}\tan^{-1}\left(\frac{t-1}{2}\right)+C$

$=\ln\left|\tan^2x-2\tan x+5\right|+\frac{5}{2}\tan^{-1}\left(\frac{\tan x-1}{2}\right)+C$

(f) Let $I_n=\int(\text{cosec}x)^2dx=\int(\text{cosec}x)^{n-2}.\text{cosec}^2x\,dx$

$=(\text{cosec}x)^{n-2}.(\cot x)-$

$\int(n-2)(\text{cosec})^{n-3}(-\text{cosec}x\cot x)(-\cot x)\,dx$

$=-(\text{cosec}\ x)^{n-2}\cot x-(n-2)$

$$\int (\text{cosec})^{n-2}(-\text{cosec}^2x-1)\,dx$$
$$= -(\text{cosec } x)^{n-2} \cot x + (n-2) I^n_{-2} - (n-2) I_n$$
$$\Rightarrow \ln(n-1) = -(\text{cosec } x)^{n-2}.\cot x + (n-2) I_{n-2}.$$
$$\Rightarrow I_n = \frac{-(\text{cosec}x)^{n-2}\cot x}{(n-1)} + \frac{(n-2)}{(n-1)} I_{n-2}$$
$$\therefore \quad I_5 = \frac{-(\text{cosec}x)^3 \cot x}{4} + \frac{3}{4} I_3$$
$$= -\frac{(\text{cosec}x)^3\cot x}{4} + \frac{3}{4}\left[\frac{-(\text{cosec}x)\cot x}{2} + \frac{1}{2} I_n\right]$$
$$= -\frac{\text{cosec}^3 x\cot x}{4} - \frac{3}{8}\text{cosec}x\cot x + \frac{3}{8}\int \text{cosec}x\,dx$$
$$= -\frac{\text{cosec}^3 x\cot x}{4} - \frac{3}{8}\text{cosec}x\cot x + \frac{3}{8}\ln\left|\tan\frac{x}{2}\right| + C$$

2. (a) $I_n = \int \sin^n x\,dx = \int \underbrace{\sin^{n-1} x}_{I}\ \underbrace{\sin x}_{II}\,dx$

$$= -\sin^{n-1} x\cos x + (n-1)\int \sin^{n-2} x\cos^2 x\,dx$$
$$= -\sin^{n-1} x\cos x + (n-1)\int \sin^{n-2} x(1-\sin^2 x)\,dx$$
$$= -\sin^{n-1} x\cos x - (n-1)\int \sin^n x\,dx + (n-1)\int \sin^{n-2} x\,dx$$
$$nI_n = -\sin^{n-1} x\cos\ x + (n-1)I_{n-2}$$
$$\Rightarrow I_n = -\frac{\sin^{n-1} x\cos x}{n} + \frac{(n-1)}{n} I_{n-2}$$
$$\Rightarrow I_4 = \int \sin^4 x\,dx = -\frac{\sin^3 x\cos x}{4} + \frac{3}{4} I_2$$
$$\text{and } I_2 = -\frac{\sin x\cos x}{2} + \frac{x}{2} = -\frac{\sin 2x}{4} + \frac{x}{2}$$
$$\therefore \quad I_4 = -\frac{\sin^3 x\cos x}{4} - \frac{3}{16}\sin 2x + \frac{3}{8}x + C$$

(b) $I_n = \int \cos^n x\,dx = \int \underbrace{\cos^{n-1} x}_{I}.\underbrace{\cos x}_{II}\,dx$

$$= \cos^{n-1} x\sin x + \int (n-1)\cos^{n-2} x\sin^2 x\,dx$$
$$= \cos^{n-1} x\sin x + (n-1)\int \cos^{n-2} x(1-\cos^2 x)\,dx$$
$$= \cos^{n-1} x\sin x + (n-1)I_{n-2} - (n-1)I_n$$
$$I_n = \frac{\cos^{n-1} x\sin x}{n} + \frac{n-1}{n} I_{n-2}$$
$$\Rightarrow I_5 = \int \cos^5 x\,dx = \frac{\cos^4 x\sin x}{5} + \frac{4}{5} I_3 \text{ and}$$
$$I_3 = \frac{\cos^2 x\sin x}{3} + \frac{2}{3} I_1 \text{ and } I_1 = \int \cos x\,dx = \sin x$$
$$\Rightarrow I_3 = \frac{\cos^2 x\sin x}{3} + \frac{2}{3}\sin x + C$$
$$\Rightarrow I_5 = \frac{\cos^4 x\sin x}{5} + \frac{4}{15}\cos^2 x\sin x + \frac{8}{15}\sin x + C$$

(c) $I_n = \int \tan^n x\,dx = \int \tan^{n-2} x\tan^2 x\,dx$

$$= \int \tan^{n-2} x(\sec^2 x - 1)\,dx = \int \tan^{n-2} x\sec^2 x\,dx - I_{n-2}$$
$$\Rightarrow I_n = \frac{\tan^{n-1} x}{n-1} - I_{n-2}$$
$$\Rightarrow I_5 = \int \tan^5 x\,dx = \frac{\tan^4 x}{4} - I_3 = \frac{\tan^4 x}{4} - \left(\frac{\tan^2 x}{2} - I_1\right)$$
$$\text{and } I_1 = \int \tan x\,dx = \ln|\sec x| + C$$
$$\Rightarrow I_5 = \frac{\tan^4 x}{4} - \frac{\tan^2 x}{2} + \ln|\sec x| + C$$

(d) $I_n = \int \cot^n x\,dx = \int \cot^{n-2} x\cot^2 x\,dx$

$$= \int \cot^{n-2} x(\text{cosec}^2 x - 1)\,dx$$
$$= \int \cot^{n-2} x\,\text{cosec}^2 x - I_{n-2}$$
$$= I_n = -\frac{\cot^{n-1} x}{n-1} - I_{n-2}$$
$$\Rightarrow I_4 = \int \cot^4 x\,dx = -\frac{\cot^3 x}{3} - I_2$$
$$= -\frac{\cot^3 x}{3} - \left(-\frac{\cot x}{1} - I_0\right) = -\frac{\cot^3 x}{3} + \cot x + x + C$$

(e) $I_n = \int \sec^n x\,dx = \int \underbrace{\sec^{n-2} x}_{I}.\underbrace{\sec^2 x}_{II}\,dx$

$$= \sec^{n-2} x\tan x - \int (n-2)\sec^{n-3} x\sec x\tan^2 x\,dx$$
$$= \sec^{n-2} x\tan x - (n-2)\int \sec^{n-2} x(\sec^2 x - 1)\,dx$$
$$= \sec^{n-2} x\tan x - (n-2)I_n + (n-2)I_{n-2}$$
$$I_n = \frac{\sec^{n-2} x\tan x}{n-1} + \frac{n-2}{n-1} I_{n-2}$$
$$\Rightarrow I_5 = \int \sec^5 x\,dx = \frac{\sec^3 x\tan x}{4} + \frac{3}{4} I_3$$
$$= \frac{\sec^3 x\tan x}{4} + \frac{3}{4}\left(\frac{\sec x\tan x}{2} + \frac{1}{2} I_1\right)$$
$$\Rightarrow I_1 = \int \sec x\,dx = \ln|\sec x + \tan x| + C$$
$$\Rightarrow I_5 = \frac{\sec^3 x\tan x}{4} + \frac{3}{8}\sec x\tan x + \frac{3}{8}\ln|\sec x + \tan x| + C$$

(f) $I_n = \int \sec^n x\,dx = \dfrac{\sec^{n-2} x\tan x}{n-1} + \dfrac{(n-2)}{n-1} I_{n-2}$

$$\Rightarrow I_4 = \int \sec^4 x\,dx = \frac{\sec^2 x\tan x}{3} + \frac{2}{3} I_2$$
$$\Rightarrow \frac{\sec^2 x\tan x}{3} + \frac{2}{3}\tan x + C$$

(g) $I_n = \int (\ln x)^n dx = (\ln x)^n x - \int n(\ln x)^{n-1}\dfrac{1}{x}x\,dx$

$$\Rightarrow I_n = x(\ln x)^n - nI_{n-1}$$

(h) $I_n = \int \dfrac{dx}{(x-1)(x+1)^n} = \dfrac{1}{2}\int \dfrac{(x+1)-(x-1)}{(x-1)(x+1)^n}dx$

$$= \frac{1}{2}\int \frac{dx}{(x-1)(x+1)^{n-1}} - \frac{1}{2}\int \frac{dx}{(x+1)^n}$$
$$= \frac{1}{2(x+1)^{n-1}(n-1)} + \frac{1}{2} I_{n-1}$$

3. (a) $I_n = \int \frac{dx}{(x^2+a^2)^n} = \frac{x}{(x^2+a^2)^n} - \int \frac{-n2x}{(x^2+a^2)^{n+1}} x\,dx$

$= \frac{x}{(x^2+a^2)^n} + 2n\int \frac{x^2+a^2-a^2}{(x^2+a^2)^{n+1}}dx$

$= \frac{x}{(x^2+a^2)^n} + 2nI_n - 2na^2 I_{n+1}$

$\Rightarrow \quad 2na^2 I_{n+1} = \frac{x}{(x^2+a^2)^n} + (2n-1)I_n$

Replacing n by $(n-1)$, we get $2(n-1)a^2 I_n$

$= \frac{x}{(x^2+a^2)^{n-1}} + (2n-3)I_{n-1}$

(b) $I_{m,n} = \int \cos^m x \cos nx\,dx$

$= \frac{\cos^m x \sin nx}{n} + \frac{m}{n}\int \cos^{m-1} x \sin x \sin nx\,dx$

$= \frac{\cos^m x \sin nx}{n} + \frac{m}{2n}$

$\int \cos^{m-1} x[\cos(n-1)x - \cos(n+1)x]dx$

$= \frac{\cos^m x \sin nx}{n} + \frac{m}{2n} I_{m-1,n-1}$

$-\frac{m}{2n}\int \cos^{m-1} x \cos(n+1)x\,dx \quad \ldots(i)$

Also, $I_{m,n} = \int \frac{\cos^{m-1} x}{2} 2\cos x \cos nx\,dx$

$2I_{m,n} = \int \cos^{m-1} x[\cos(n+1)x + \cos(n-1)x]dx$

$= \int \cos^{m-1} x \cos(n+1)x\,dx + I_{m-1,n-1}$

$\therefore \quad \int \cos^{m-1} x \cos(n+1)x\,dx = 2I_{m,n} - I_{m-1,n-1}$

Putting back in (1), we get

$I_{m,n} = \frac{\cos^m x \sin nx}{n} + \frac{m}{2n} I_{m-1,n-1} - \frac{m}{2n}(2I_{m,n} - I_{m-1,n-1})$

$I_{m,n}\left(1+\frac{m}{n}\right) = \frac{\cos^m x \sin nx}{n} + \frac{m}{n} I_{m-1,n-1}$

$I_{m,n} = \frac{\cos^m x \sin nx}{m+n} + \frac{m}{m+n} I_{m-1,n-1}$

(c) $I_n = \int \underset{II}{e^{ax}} \underset{I}{\cos^n x}\,dx = \frac{\cos^n x e^{ax}}{a} + \frac{n}{a}\int e^{ax}\cos^{n-1} x \sin x\,dx$

$= \frac{\cos^n x e^{ax}}{a} + \frac{n}{a}\left[\frac{\cos^{n-1} x \sin x e^{ax}}{a} - \frac{1}{a}\right]$

$dx. \int \left[e^{ax}\left(\cos^n x - (n-1)\cos^{n-2} x \sin^2 x\right)\right]dx$

$= \frac{\cos^n x e^{ax}}{a} + \frac{n}{a^2}\cos^{n-1} x \sin x e^{ax}$

$-\frac{n}{a^2}\int e^{ax}\cos^n x + \frac{n(n-1)}{a^2}$

$\int e^{ax}\cos^{n-2} x - \frac{n(n-1)}{a^2}\int e^{ax}\cos^n x$

$= \frac{(a\cos x + n\sin x)}{a^2}\cos^{n-1} x e^{ax}$

$-\frac{n}{a^2}I_n + \frac{n(n-1)}{a^2}\int e^{ax}\cos^{n-2} x\,dx - \frac{n(n-1)}{a^2}I_n$

$I_n\left(1+\frac{n^2}{a^2}\right) = \frac{(a\cos x + n\sin x)}{a^2}\cos^{n-1} x e^{ax}$

$+\frac{n(n-1)}{a^2}\int e^{ax}\cos^{n-2} x\,dx$

$I_n = \left(\frac{a\cos x + n\sin x}{a^2+n^2}\right)\cos^{n-1} x e^{ax} + \frac{n(n-1)}{(a^2+n^2)}I_{n-2}$

(d) $I_n = \int \frac{x^n}{\sqrt{ax^2+bx+c}}dx = \int x^{n-1}.(x(ax^2+bx+c)^{-1/2})dx$

$= \int \frac{x^{n-1}}{2a}(2ax+b-b)(ax^2+bx+c)^{-1/2}dx$

$= \frac{1}{2a}\int \underbrace{x^{n-1}}_{I}.\underbrace{(2ax+b)(ax^2+bx+c)^{-1/2}}_{II}dx$

$-\frac{b}{2a}\int x^{n-1}(ax^2+bx+c)^{-1/2}dx$

$= \frac{1}{2a}\left[2x^{n-1}.(ax^2+bx+c)^{1/2} - \right.$

$\left.\int \frac{(n-1)x^{n-2}.(ax^2+bx+c)^{1/2}}{1/2}dx\right] - \frac{b}{2a}I$

$= \frac{1}{2a}\left[2x^{n-1}\sqrt{ax^2+bx+c} - 2(n-1)\right.$

$\left.\int \frac{x^{n-2}(ax^2+bx+c)dx}{\sqrt{ax^2+bx+c}}\right] - \frac{b}{2a}I_{n-1}$

$= \frac{1}{a}x^{n-1}\sqrt{ax^2+bx+c} - \frac{(n-1)}{a}$

$\int \frac{ax^n+bx^{n-1}+cx^{n-2}}{\sqrt{ax^2+bx+c}}dx - \frac{b}{2a}I_{n-1}$

$= I_n = \frac{1}{a}x^{n-1}\sqrt{ax^2+bx+c} - (n-1)I_n - \frac{b(n-1)}{a}I_{n-1}$

$-\frac{c}{a}(n-1)I_{n-2} - \frac{b}{2a}I_{n-1}$

$= I_n = \frac{1}{na}x^{n-1}\sqrt{ax^2+bx+c}$

$-\frac{(2n-1)}{n}\frac{b}{a}I_{n-1} - \frac{c}{a}\frac{(n-1)}{n}I_{n-2}$

TEXTUAL EXERCISE–9: (OBJECTIVE)

1. (b) $f(x) = \int \cos^8 x\,dx$

$f\left(\frac{\pi}{2}\right) = \int_0^{\frac{\pi}{2}} \cos^8 x\,dx$

$= \frac{7}{8}\frac{5}{6}\frac{3}{4}\frac{1}{2}\frac{\pi}{2} = \frac{35\pi}{256}$

2. (c) $f(x)=\int \sin^9 x\,dx$

$$f\left(\frac{\pi}{2}\right)-f(0)=\int_0^{\frac{\pi}{2}}\sin^9 x\,dx=\frac{8\,6\,4\,2}{9\,7\,5\,3}=\frac{128}{315}$$

3. (d) $I_{m,n}=\int_0^{\pi/2}\cos^m x\sin^n x=\int_0^{\pi/2}\underbrace{\cos^{m-1}x}_{I}.\underbrace{\sin^n x\cos x\,dx}_{II}$

$$=\left|\cos^{m-1}x\frac{\sin^{n+1}x}{n+1}\right|_0^{\pi/2}$$

$$+\int_0^{\pi/2}(m-1)\cos^{m-2}x\frac{\sin x\sin^{n+1}x}{n+1}dx$$

$$=\left|\frac{\cos^{m-1}x\sin^{n+1}x}{n+1}\right|_0^{\pi/2}+\frac{m-1}{n+1}\int_0^{\pi/2}\cos^{m-2}x\sin^{n+2}x\,dx$$

$$\therefore\quad I_{m,n}=\left[\frac{\cos^{m-1}x\sin^{n+1}x}{n+1}\right]_0^{\frac{\pi}{2}}+\frac{m-1}{n+1}\frac{m-3}{n+3}.....$$

For m = odd: $m\left(I_{m,n}\right)=\frac{m-1}{n+1}\frac{m-3}{n+3}......$

$$\frac{2}{n+m-2}\int_0^{\frac{\pi}{2}}\sin^{n+m-1}x\cos x\,dx$$

$$=\frac{m-1}{n+1}\frac{m-3}{n+3}.....\frac{2}{n+m-2}\left(\frac{1}{n+m}\right)$$

For m = even: $m\left(I_{m,n}\right)=\frac{m-1}{n+1}\frac{m-3}{n+3}......$

$$\frac{1}{n+m-1}\int_0^{\frac{\pi}{2}}\sin^{n+m}x\,dx$$

$$\Rightarrow\quad I_{8,6}=\frac{7}{7}.\frac{5}{9}.\frac{3}{11}.\frac{1}{13}\int_0^{\frac{\pi}{2}}\sin^{14}dx$$

$$\left(\because\quad\int_0^{\frac{\pi}{2}}\sin^{14}dx=\frac{13}{14}.\frac{11}{12}.\frac{9}{10}.\frac{7}{8}.\frac{5}{6}.\frac{3}{4}.\frac{1}{2}\frac{\pi}{2}\right)$$

$$\therefore\quad I_{8,6}=\frac{5\pi}{4096}$$

4. (a) $I_{7,6}=\int_0^{\frac{\pi}{2}}\cos^7 x\sin^6 x=\frac{(6\times4\times2)\times(5\times3\times1)}{13\times11\times9\times7\times5\times3\times1}=\frac{16}{3003}$

5. (b) $I_n=\int(\ln x)^n dx=x(\ln x)^n-nI_{n-1}$

$$\therefore\quad I_4=\int(\ln x)^4dx=x(\ln x)^4-4I_3$$

$$=x(\ln x)^4-4\left[x(\ln x)^3-3I_2\right]$$

$$=xt^4-4xt^3+12\left(xt^2-2I_1\right),\text{ where } t=\ln x$$

$$=xt^4-4xt^3+12xt^2-24(xt-x)$$

$$=x\left(t^4-4t^3+12t^2-24t+24\right)$$

6. (b) $I_5=\int\cos^5 x\,dx$

$$I_n=\int\cos^n x\,dx=\frac{\sin x\cos^{n-1}x}{n}+\frac{n-1}{n}I_{n-2}$$

$$\therefore\quad I_5=\frac{\sin x\cos^4 x}{5}+\frac{4}{5}I_3$$

$$=\frac{\sin x\cos^4 x}{5}+\frac{4}{5}\left(\frac{\sin x\cos^2 x}{3}+\frac{2}{3}I_1\right);\ I_1=\sin x$$

$$\Rightarrow\quad I_5=\frac{\sin x}{15}\left(3\cos^4 x+4\cos^2 x+8\right)+C$$

7. (a) $I_n=\int\tan^n x\,dx=\frac{\tan^{n-1}x}{n-1}-I_{n-2}$

$$\Rightarrow\quad I_6=\frac{t^5}{5}-I_4;\text{where } t=\tan x$$

Similarly, $I_4=\frac{\tan^3 x}{3}-I_2=\frac{\tan^3 x}{3}-\int\tan^2 x\,dx$

$$=\frac{\tan^3 x}{3}-\int(\sec^2 x-1)dx=\frac{\tan^3 x}{3}-\tan x+x+C_1$$

$$\therefore\quad I_6=\frac{t^5}{5}-\left(\frac{t^3}{3}-I_2\right)=\frac{t^5}{5}-\frac{t^3}{3}+t-x+C;t=\tan x$$

8. (a), (c) $I_n=\int\sec^n x\,dx=\frac{\sec^{n-2}x}{n-1}\tan x+\frac{n-2}{n-1}I_{n-2}$

$$I_4=\frac{\sec^2 x\tan x}{3}+\frac{2}{3}I_2=\frac{\sec^2 x\tan x}{3}+\frac{2}{3}(\tan x)+C$$

$$=\frac{\tan x}{3}\left(\sec^2 x+2\right)+C$$

9. (b) $I_{m,n}=\int x^m(\ln x)^n dx=\frac{x^{m+1}}{m+1}(\ln x)^n-\frac{n}{m+1}I_{m,n-1}$

$$\Rightarrow\quad I_{4,3}=\int x^4(\ln x)^3dx=\frac{x^5}{5}t^3-\frac{3}{5}I_{4,2}$$

$$=\frac{x^5}{5}t^3-\frac{3}{5}\left(\frac{x^5}{5}(t)^2-\frac{2}{5}I_{4,1}\right)$$

$$=\frac{x^5}{5}t^3-\frac{3}{25}x^5t^2+\frac{6}{25}\left(\frac{x^5}{5}(t)-\frac{1}{5}I_{4,0}\right)$$

$$\Rightarrow\quad I_{4,0}=\int x^4dx=\frac{x^5}{5}+C$$

$$\Rightarrow\quad I_{4,3}=\frac{x^5}{5}t^3-\frac{3}{25}x^5t^2+\frac{6}{125}\left(\frac{x^5}{5}\right)+C$$

$$=\frac{x^5}{625}\left(125t^3-75t^2+30t-6\right)+C$$

10. (d) $I_{m,n}=\int\frac{\sin^m x}{\cos^n x}=\frac{1}{n-1}\frac{\sin^{m-1}x}{\cos^{n-1}x}-\frac{(m-1)}{(n-1)}I_{m-2,n-2}$

$$\Rightarrow\quad I_{2,3}=\int\frac{\sin^2 x}{\cos^3 x}dx=\frac{1}{2}\frac{\sin x}{\cos^2 x}-\frac{1}{2}I_{0,1}$$

$$\Rightarrow\quad I_{0,1}=\int\sec x=\ln|\sec x+\tan x|+C$$

$$\Rightarrow\quad I_{2,3}=\frac{1}{2}\sin x\sec^2 x-\frac{1}{2}\ln|\sec x+\tan x|+C$$

11. (d) $I_n = \int x^n e^{\frac{1}{x}}\,dx = \dfrac{e^{\frac{1}{x}} x^{n+1}}{n+1} + \dfrac{1}{n+1} . I_{n-1}$

$$\Rightarrow I_4 = \frac{e^{\frac{1}{x}} x^5}{5} + \frac{I_3}{5} = \frac{e^{\frac{1}{x}}}{5} x^5 + \frac{1}{5}\left(\frac{e^{\frac{1}{x}} x^4}{4} + \frac{I_2}{4}\right)$$

$$= \frac{e^{\frac{1}{x}} x^5}{5} + \frac{e^{\frac{1}{x}} x^4}{20} + \frac{1}{20}\left(\frac{e^{\frac{1}{x}} x^3}{3} + \frac{I_1}{3}\right)$$

$$= \frac{e^{\frac{1}{x}} x^5}{5} + \frac{e^{\frac{1}{x}} x^4}{20} + \frac{e^{\frac{1}{x}} x^3}{60} + \frac{1}{60}\left(\frac{e^{\frac{1}{x}} x^2}{2} + \frac{I_0}{2}\right)$$

$$= \frac{e^{\frac{1}{x}} x^5}{5} + \frac{e^{\frac{1}{x}} x^4}{20} + \frac{e^{\frac{1}{x}} x^3}{60} + \frac{e^{\frac{1}{x}} x^2}{120} + \frac{I_0}{120}$$

$$= \frac{1}{120} e^{\frac{1}{x}}\left(4!x^5 + 3!x^4 + 2!x^3 + x^2\right) + \frac{I_0}{120}$$

$$= \frac{1}{5!}\left[e^{\frac{1}{x}} \sum_{k=2}^{5} x^k (k-1)! + I_0\right]$$

12. (c) $I_n = \int (\sin x + \cos x)^n dx$

$$= \frac{(\sin x + \cos x)^{n-1}}{n}(\sin x - \cos x) + \frac{2(n-1)}{n} I_{n-2}$$

$$\Rightarrow I_5 = \frac{t^4}{5}(\sin x - \cos x) + \frac{8}{5} I_3 = \frac{t^4}{5}(\sin x - \cos x)$$

$$+ \frac{8}{5}\left(\frac{t^2}{3}(\sin x - \cos x) + \frac{4}{3} I_1\right)$$

$$= \frac{t^4}{5}(\sin x - \cos x) + \frac{8}{15} t^2 (\sin x - \cos x)$$

$$+ \frac{32}{15}(\sin x - \cos x) + C$$

$$= \frac{(\sin x - \cos x)}{15}\left(3t^4 + 8t^2 + 32\right) + C;$$

where $t = (\sin x + \cos x)$

13. (b) $I_{m,n} = \int \cos^m x \cos nx\,dx = \dfrac{\cos^m x \sin nx}{(m+n)} + \dfrac{m}{m+n} I_{m-1,n-1}$

$$\Rightarrow I_{3,4} = \int \cos^3 x \cos 4x\,dx = \frac{\cos^3 x \sin 4x}{7} + \frac{3}{7} I_{2,3}$$

$$= \frac{\cos^3 x \sin 4x}{7} + \frac{3}{7}\left(\frac{\cos^2 x \sin 3x}{5} + \frac{2}{5} I_{1,2}\right)$$

$$= \frac{\cos^3 x \sin 4x}{7} + \frac{3}{35}\cos^2 x \sin 3x$$

$$+ \frac{6}{35}\left(\frac{\cos x \sin 2x}{3} + \frac{1}{3} I_{0,1}\right)$$

$$= \frac{1}{35}\left(5\cos^3 x \sin 4x + 3\cos^2 x \sin 3x + \right.$$

$$\left. 2\cos x \sin 2x + 2\sin x\right) + C$$

14. (a) $I_n = \int x^n \sqrt{a^2 - x^2}\,dx = -\dfrac{x^{n-1}\left(a^2 - x^2\right)^{\frac{3}{2}}}{n+2} + \dfrac{(n-1)}{(n+2)} a^2 I_{n-2}$

$\Rightarrow I_4 = \int x^4 \sqrt{a^2 - x^2}\,dx = -\dfrac{x^3}{6}\left(a^2 - x^2\right)^{\frac{3}{2}} + \dfrac{1}{2} a^2 I_2$ and

$$I_2 = \frac{-x(a^2 - x^2)^{3/4}}{4} + \frac{1}{4} a^2 I_0$$

$$= -\frac{x^3}{6}\left(a^2 - x^2\right)^{\frac{3}{2}} + \frac{1}{2} a^2$$

$$\left(-\frac{x\left(a^2 - x^2\right)^{\frac{3}{2}}}{4} + \frac{1}{4} a^2 \int \sqrt{a^2 - x^2}\,dx\right)$$

$$= -\frac{x^3}{6}\left(a^2 - x^2\right)^{\frac{3}{2}} - \frac{1}{8} a^2 x \left(a^2 - x^2\right)^{\frac{3}{2}}$$

$$+ \frac{1}{8} a^4 \left(\frac{x}{2}\sqrt{a^2 - x^2} + \frac{a^2}{2}\sin^{-1}\left(\frac{x}{a}\right)\right) + C$$

$$= -\frac{x^3}{6}\left(a^2 - x^2\right)^{\frac{3}{2}} - \frac{1}{8} a^2 x \left(a^2 - x^2\right)^{\frac{3}{2}}$$

$$+ \frac{1}{16} a^4 x \left(a^2 - x^2\right)^{\frac{1}{2}} + \frac{a^6}{16}\sin^{-1}\left(\frac{x}{a}\right) + C$$

15. (c) $I_n = \int \dfrac{\cos nx}{\sin x} dx = \dfrac{2\cos(n-1)}{n-1} + I_{n-2}$

$$I_5 = \int \frac{\cos 5x}{\sin x} dx = \frac{2\cos 4x}{4} + I_3$$

$$= \frac{2\cos 4x}{4} + \frac{2\cos 2x}{2} + I_1$$

$$= \frac{1}{2}\cos 4x + \cos 2x + \ln|\sin x| + C$$

SECTION–III (TUTORIAL EXERCISE)

1. (c) $I_1 = \int \sin^{-1} x\,dx$ and $I_2 = \int \sin^{-1}\sqrt{1 - x^2}\,dx$

$$I_2 = \int \cos^{-1} x\,dx = \int\left(\frac{\pi}{2} - \sin^{-1} x\right)dx = \frac{\pi}{2} x - I_1$$

$$\therefore\ I_1 + I_2 = \frac{\pi}{2} x$$

2. (a) $I = \int 5^{\ln x} dx$

Let $\ln x = t \Rightarrow x = e^t \Rightarrow dx = e^t dt$

$$I = \int 5^t e^t dt = \int (5e)^t dt = \frac{(5e)^t}{\ln(5e)} + C = \frac{5^{\ln x} e^{\ln x}}{\ln 5 + 1} + C$$

$$= \frac{x^{\ln 5} . x}{\ln 5 + 1} + C$$

3. (b) $I = \int \cos^3 x e^{\ln(\sin x)} dx = -\int (\cos^3 x)(-\sin x\,dx)$

$$= -\frac{\cos^4 x}{4} + C$$

4. (a) $I=\int \frac{x^{\frac{9}{2}}}{\sqrt{1+x^{11}}}dx$

Let $1+x^{11}=t^2 \Rightarrow 11x^{10}dx = 2t\,dt \Rightarrow dx=\frac{2\,t\,dt}{11\,x^{10}}$

$\therefore\ I=\int \frac{x^{\frac{9}{2}}}{t}\frac{2\ t}{11\,x^{10}}dt = \frac{2}{11}\int\frac{1}{\sqrt{t^2-1}}dt$

$=\frac{2}{11}\ln\left|t+\sqrt{t^2-1}\right|+C = \frac{2}{11}\ln\left|x^{\frac{11}{2}}+\sqrt{x^{11}+1}\right|+C$

5. (d) $I=\int(1+3\sin x)^{\frac{1}{5}}\cos dx$

$=\int(1+3t)^{\frac{1}{5}}dt;\ \sin x = t \Rightarrow \cos x\,dx = dt$

$=\frac{1}{3}(1+3t)^{\frac{6}{5}}.\frac{5}{6} = \frac{5}{18}(1+3t)^{\frac{6}{5}}+C$

$=\frac{5}{18}(1+3\sin x)^{\frac{6}{5}}+C$

6. (c) $I=\int\frac{dx}{x^{13}\left(x^6-1\right)} = \int\frac{dx}{x^{12}.x^7\left(1-\frac{1}{x^6}\right)}$

Let $1-\frac{1}{x^6}=t \Rightarrow \frac{6}{x^7}dx = dt \Rightarrow dx = \frac{x^7}{6}dt$

$\therefore\quad I=\frac{1}{6}\int\frac{(1-t)^2}{t}dt = \frac{1}{6}\int\left(t-2+\frac{1}{t}\right)dt$

$=\frac{1}{6}\left[\frac{t^2}{2}-2t+\ln|t|\right]+C$

$=\frac{1}{6}\left[\ln\left|\frac{x^6-1}{x^6}\right|+\frac{1}{2}\left(1+\frac{1}{x^{12}}-\frac{2}{x^6}\right)-2+\frac{2}{x^6}\right]+C_1$

$=\frac{1}{6}\left[\ln\left|\frac{x^6-1}{x^6}\right|+\frac{1}{2x^{12}}+\frac{1}{x^6}-\frac{3}{2}\right]+C_1$ or

$=\frac{1}{6}\left[\ln\left|\frac{x^6-1}{x^6}\right|+\frac{1}{2x^{12}}+\frac{1}{x^6}\right]+C$

7. (b) $I=\int\sqrt{\frac{x-1}{x+1}}\frac{1}{x^2}dx$

Let $x=\sec\theta \Rightarrow dx = \sec\theta\tan\theta\,d\theta$

$=\int\sqrt{\frac{\sec\theta-1}{\sec\theta+1}}\cos^2\theta\sec\theta\tan\theta\,d\theta$

$=\int\sqrt{\frac{1-\cos\theta}{1+\cos\theta}}\sin\theta\,d\theta = \int\tan\frac{\theta}{2}\frac{2\tan\frac{\theta}{2}}{1+\tan^2\frac{\theta}{2}}d\theta$

Let $\tan\frac{\theta}{2}=t \Rightarrow \frac{1}{2}\sec^2\frac{\theta}{2}d\theta = dt$, $d\theta=\frac{2dt}{1+t^2}$

$=\int\frac{2t^2}{\left(1+t^2\right)}\frac{2dt}{\left(1+t^2\right)} = 4\int\frac{t^2+1-1}{\left(t^2+1\right)^2}dt$

$=4\left[\int\frac{dt}{t^2+1}-\int\frac{dt}{\left(t^2+1\right)^2}\right] = 4\tan^{-1}t-4I_1$

Now, $I_1=\int\frac{dt}{\left(t^2+1\right)^2}$, Let $t=\tan\theta \Rightarrow dt=\sec^2\theta\,d\theta$

$=\int\frac{\sec^2\theta\,d\theta}{\sec^4\theta}=\int\cos^2\theta\,d\theta$

$=\int\frac{1+\cos 2\theta}{2}d\theta = \frac{\theta}{2}+\frac{\sin 2\theta}{4}+C$

and $\left(\sin 2\theta = \frac{2t}{1+t^2}\right)$

$=\frac{1}{2}\tan^{-1}t+\frac{t}{2(1+t^2)}+C$

$\therefore\quad I=4\tan^{-1}t-2\tan^{-1}t-\frac{2t}{1+t^2}+C$

$=2\tan^{-1}t-\frac{2t}{1+t^2}+C$

$=\theta-\sin\theta+C = \sec^{-1}x-\frac{\sqrt{x^2-1}}{x}+C$

$=\cos^{-1}\left(\frac{1}{x}\right)-\sqrt{\frac{x^2-1}{x^2}}+C$

8. (a) $I=\int\frac{\left(x^4-x\right)^{\frac{1}{4}}}{x^5}dx = \int\frac{x\left(1-\frac{1}{x^3}\right)^{\frac{1}{4}}}{x^5}dx$

Let $1-\frac{1}{x^3}=t \Rightarrow \frac{3}{x^4}dx = dt$

$\Rightarrow\ I=\frac{1}{3}\int t^{\frac{1}{4}}dt = \frac{4}{15}t^{\frac{5}{4}}+C = \frac{4}{15}\left(1-\frac{1}{x^3}\right)^{\frac{5}{4}}+C$

9. (b) $F(x)=\int e^x\left(\tan x-\ln\cos x\right)dx$

Let $-\ln(\cos x)=t \Rightarrow \tan x\,dx = dt$

We know $\int e^x\left(g(x)+g'(x)\right)dx = e^x g(x)$

$\therefore\ F(x)=-e^x\ln\cos x+C$

$=e^x\ln\sec x+C$

Comparing, $f(x)=e^x$ range of which is $\mathbb{R}^+$

10. (a) $\int f(x)dx = f(x)=\int f'(x)dx$

$\therefore\quad f'(x)=f(x)$

$\Rightarrow\quad \frac{f'(x)}{f(x)}=1 \Rightarrow \int\frac{f'(x)}{f(x)}dx=\int dx$

$\Rightarrow\ \ln f(x)=x \qquad \Rightarrow\ f(x)=e^x$

Now, $\int f(x)^2dx = \int e^{2x}dx = \frac{e^{2x}}{2}=\frac{f^2(x)}{2}$

11. (b) $I=\int e^x\left(\frac{1+\sin x\cos x}{\cos^2 x}\right)dx = \int e^x\left(\tan x+\sec^2 x\right)dx$

$=e^x\tan x+C$

12. (b) $\int f(x)dx = g(x)$

Let $f(x)=t \Rightarrow x=f^{-1}(t) \Rightarrow dx=\frac{d}{dt}f^{-1}(t)dt$

$\Rightarrow \int t\frac{d}{dt}f^{-1}(t)dt = g\,f^{-1}(t)$

Replacing t by x, we have $\int \underset{I}{x}.\underbrace{\frac{d}{dx}f^{-}(x)}_{II}\,dx = g(f^{-1}(x))$

$\Rightarrow x\int\frac{d}{dx}f^{-1}(x)dx - \int\frac{dx}{dx}\left(\int\frac{d}{dx}f^{-1}(x)dx\right)dx = g\,f^{-1}(x)$

$\Rightarrow x\,f^{-1}(x) - \int f^{-1}(x)dx = g(f^{-1}(x))$

$\Rightarrow \int f^{-1}(x)dx = x\,f^{-1}(x) - g\,f^{-1}(x)$

13. (d) $I = \int \tan^{-1}\frac{2x}{1-x^2}dx = \int \sin^{-1}\frac{2x}{x^2+1}dx$

Let $x = \tan\phi \Rightarrow dx = \sec^2\phi\, d\phi$

$\Rightarrow I = \int \sin^{-1}\left(\frac{2\tan\phi}{\tan^2\phi+1}\right)\sec^2\phi\, d\phi$

$= \int \sin^{-1}\sin 2\phi \sec^2\phi\, d\phi$

$= \int 2\phi\sec^2\phi\, d\phi = 2\left[\phi\tan\phi - \int\tan\phi\, d\phi\right]$

$= 2\phi\tan\phi + 2\ln\cos\phi + C$

$= 2x\tan^{-1}x - \ln(1+x^2) + C$

14. (a) $I = \int\frac{x^2-1}{x\sqrt{x^4+3x^2+1}}dx = \int\frac{\left(1-\frac{1}{x^2}\right)}{\sqrt{\left(x+\frac{1}{x}\right)^2+1^2}}dx$

Let $x+\frac{1}{x} = t \Rightarrow 1-\frac{1}{x^2}dx = dt$

$\Rightarrow I = \int\frac{dt}{\sqrt{t^2+1}} = \ln\left|t+\sqrt{t^2+1}\right| + C$

$= \ln\left|x+\frac{1}{x}+\frac{\sqrt{x^4+3x^2+1}}{x}\right| + C$

Comparing, $m = 1$

15. (b) $I = \int x\sin 2x\cos 3x\, dx$

$= \frac{1}{2}\int x(2\cos 3x\sin 2x)dx = \frac{1}{2}\int x(\sin 5x - \sin x)dx$

$= = \frac{1}{2}\int x\sin 5x - \frac{1}{2}\int x\sin x\, dx$

$= \frac{1}{2}\left[-\frac{x\cos 5x}{5} + \int\frac{\cos 5x}{5}dx\right] - \frac{1}{2}\left[-x\cos x + \int\cos x\, dx\right]$

$= \frac{-x}{10}\cos 5x + \frac{\sin 5x}{50} + \frac{x}{2}\cos x - \frac{1}{2}\sin x + C$

16. (c) $\int e^x(f(x) - f'(x))dx = \phi(x)$

$\Rightarrow \int e^x(f(x)+f'(x))dx - 2\int e^x f'(x)dx = \phi(x)$

$\Rightarrow e^x f(x) - \phi(x) = 2\int e^x f'(x)dx$

$= 2\left[e^x f(x) - \int e^x f(x)dx\right]$

$\Rightarrow \int e^x f(x)dx = \frac{1}{2}\left[e^x f(x) + \phi(x)\right] + C$

17. (a) $I = \int\frac{dx}{1+x+x^2+x^3} = \int\frac{dx}{(1+x)(1+x^2)}$

Let $\frac{1}{(1+x)(1+x^2)} = \frac{A}{1+x} + \frac{Bx+C}{1+x^2}$

$\Rightarrow A = \frac{1}{2}, C = \frac{1}{2}, B = -\frac{1}{2}$

$\Rightarrow I = \frac{1}{2}\int\frac{dx}{1+x} - \frac{1}{2}\int\frac{x-1}{1+x^2}dx$

$= \frac{1}{2}\ln|1+x| - \frac{1}{4}\int\frac{2x}{1+x^2}dx + \frac{1}{2}\int\frac{dx}{1+x^2}$

$= \frac{1}{2}\ln|1+x| - \frac{1}{4}\ln\left|1+x^2\right| + \frac{1}{2}\tan^{-1}x + C$

18. (a) $I = \int\frac{dx}{(x^2+a^2)(x^2+b^2)}$

$= \frac{1}{b^2-a^2}\int\frac{(x^2+b^2)-(x^2+a^2)}{(x^2+a^2)(x^2+b^2)}dx$

$= \frac{1}{b^2-a^2}\left[\int\frac{dx}{x^2+a^2} - \int\frac{dx}{x^2+b^2}\right]$

$= \frac{1}{b^2-a^2}\left[\frac{1}{a}\tan^{-1}\frac{x}{a} - \frac{1}{b}\tan^{-1}\frac{x}{b}\right] + C$

$= \frac{1}{a^2-b^2}\left[\frac{1}{b}\tan^{-1}\frac{x}{b} - \frac{1}{a}\tan^{-1}\frac{x}{a}\right] + C$

19. (b) $I = \int\frac{dx}{\sin x + \sec x} = \frac{1}{2}\int\frac{2\cos x}{1+\sin x\cos x}dx$

$= \frac{1}{2}\int\frac{(\cos x+\sin x)+(\cos x-\sin x)}{1+(\sin x\cos x)}$

$= \frac{1}{2}\int\frac{(\cos x+\sin x)}{1+(\sin x\cos x)} + \int\frac{(\cos x-\sin x)}{1+(\sin x\cos x)}dx$

$= \frac{1}{2}I_1 + \frac{1}{2}I_2\text{(say)}$

Here $I_1 = \int\frac{\cos x+\sin x}{1+\sin x\cos x}dx$

Put $\sin x - \cos x \quad \Rightarrow 1 - 2\sin x\cos x = t^2$

$\Rightarrow \frac{1-t^2}{2} = \sin x\cos x$

$\Rightarrow I_1 = \int\frac{2dt}{3-t^2} = \frac{1}{\sqrt{3}}\ln\left|\frac{\sqrt{3}+t}{\sqrt{3}-t}\right| + C_1$ and

$I_2 = \int\frac{\cos x-\sin x}{1+\sin x\cos x}dx$

Put $\sin x + \cos x = t \quad \Rightarrow 1 + 2\sin x\cos x = t^2$

$\Rightarrow \sin x\cos x = \frac{t^2-1}{2}$

$\therefore\ I_2 = \int\frac{2dt}{2\sqrt{3}} = 2\tan^{-1}(t) + C_2$

$\therefore\ I = \frac{1}{2\sqrt{3}}\ln\left|\frac{\sqrt{3}+\sin x-\cos x}{\sqrt{3}-\sin x+\cos x}\right| + \tan^{-1}(\sin^x + \cos x) + C$

20. (b) $I=\int\frac{\cos^3 x}{\sin^{\frac{7}{2}}x}dx=\int\frac{(1-\sin^2 x)\cos x}{\sin^{\frac{7}{2}}x}dx$

Let $\sin x=t\Rightarrow \cos x\,dx=dt$

$\Rightarrow\ I=\int\frac{1-t^2}{t^{\frac{7}{2}}}dt=\int\frac{dt}{t^{\frac{7}{2}}}-\int\frac{dt}{t^{\frac{3}{2}}}=-\frac{2}{5}t^{-\frac{5}{2}}+2t^{-\frac{1}{2}}+C$

$=-\frac{2}{5}\sin^{-\frac{5}{2}}x+2\sqrt{\operatorname{cosec} x}+C$

21. (a) $I=\int\sec^{\frac{7}{3}}x\operatorname{cosec}^{\frac{5}{3}}x\,dx=\int\frac{1}{\cos^2 x\cos^{\frac{1}{3}}x}\frac{1}{\sin x\sin^{\frac{2}{3}}x}dx$

$=\int\frac{1}{\cos^4 x\tan^{\frac{5}{3}}x}dx=\int\frac{(1+\tan^2 x)}{\tan^{\frac{5}{3}}x}\sec^2 x\,dx$

Let $\tan x=t\Rightarrow\sec^2 x\,dx=dt$

$\Rightarrow\ I=\int\frac{1+t^2}{t^{\frac{5}{3}}}dt=\int\frac{dt}{t^{\frac{5}{3}}}+\int\frac{dt}{t^{-\frac{1}{3}}}=-\frac{3}{2}t^{-\frac{2}{3}}+\frac{3}{4}t^{\frac{4}{3}}+C$

$=-\frac{3}{2}\cot^{\frac{2}{3}}x+\frac{3}{4}\tan^{\frac{4}{3}}x+C$

22. (b) $I=\int\frac{dx}{4\sin^2 x+4\sin x\ \cos x+5\cos^2 x}$

$=\int\frac{\sec^2 x}{4\tan^2 x+4\tan x+5}dx$

Let $\tan x=t\Rightarrow\sec^2 x\,dx=dt$

$\Rightarrow\ I=\int\frac{dt}{4t^2+4t+5}=\frac{1}{4}\int\frac{dt}{t^2+t+\frac{5}{4}}=\frac{1}{4}\int\frac{dt}{\left(t+\frac{1}{2}\right)^2+1}$

$=\frac{1}{4}\tan^{-1}\left(t+\frac{1}{2}\right)+C=\frac{1}{4}\tan^{-1}\left(\tan x+\frac{1}{2}\right)+C$

23. (c) $I=\int\sin^2 x\cos^5 x\,dx=\int\sin^2 x(1-\sin^2 x)^2\cos x\,dx$

Let $\sin x=t\Rightarrow\cos x\,dx=dt$

$=\int t^2(1-t^2)^2dt=\int t^2(t^4-2t^2+1)dt$

$=\int(t^6-2t^4+t^2)dt$

$=\frac{t^7}{7}-\frac{2}{5}t^5+\frac{t^3}{3}+C$

$=\frac{\sin^7 x}{7}-\frac{2}{5}\sin^5 x+\frac{\sin^3 x}{3}+C$

Comparing, $\ell=-1$

24. (a) $I=\int\frac{dx}{\tan x\cos 2x}=\int\frac{dx}{(\tan x)\left(\frac{1-\tan^2 x}{1+\tan^2 x}\right)}$

$=\int\frac{\sec^2 x\,dx}{(\tan x)(1-\tan^2 x)}$

$=\int\frac{dt}{t(1-t^2)}$; $\tan x=t\Rightarrow\sec^2 x\,dx=dt$

Let $\frac{1}{t(1+t)(1-t)}=\frac{A}{t}+\frac{B}{1+t}+\frac{C}{1-t}$

$\therefore\ A=1,B=-\frac{1}{2},C=\frac{1}{2}$

$\therefore\ I=\int\frac{dt}{t}-\frac{1}{2}\int\frac{dt}{1+t}+\frac{1}{2}\int\frac{dt}{1-t}$

$=\ln|t|-\frac{1}{2}\ln|1+t|-\frac{1}{2}\ln|1-t|+C$

$=\ln\left|\frac{t}{\sqrt{1-t^2}}\right|+C=\ln\left|\frac{\sin x}{\sqrt{\cos 2x}}\right|+C$

25. (b) $I=\int\frac{dx}{\sin^2 x+\tan^2 x}=\int\frac{\sec^2 x\,dx}{\tan^2 x+\tan^2 x\sec^2 x}$

Put $\tan x=t\Rightarrow\sec^2 x\,dx=dt$

$\Rightarrow\ I=\int\frac{dt}{t^2+t^2(1+t^2)}=\int\frac{dt}{t^2(2+t^2)}=\frac{1}{2}\left[\int\frac{dt}{t^2}-\int\frac{dt}{t^2+2}\right]$

$=-\frac{1}{2t}-\frac{1}{2\sqrt{2}}\tan^{-1}\frac{t}{\sqrt{2}}+C$

$=C-\frac{1}{2}\left[\cot x+\frac{1}{\sqrt{2}}\tan^{-1}\left(\frac{\tan x}{\sqrt{2}}\right)\right]$

26. (b) $I=\int\frac{dx}{\sqrt{x}\left(x^{\frac{1}{4}}+1\right)^{10}}$

Let $1+x^{\frac{1}{4}}=t$

$\Rightarrow\ x=(t-1)^4\Rightarrow dx=4(t-1)^3dt$

$\Rightarrow\ I=\int\frac{4(t-1)^3dt}{(t-1)^2t^{10}}=4\int\frac{t-1}{t^{10}}dt=-\frac{4}{8}t^{-8}+\frac{4}{9}t^{-9}+C$

$=-\frac{1}{2}\left(x^{\frac{1}{4}}+1\right)^{-8}+\frac{4}{9}\left(x^{\frac{1}{4}}+1\right)^{-9}+C$

27. (b) $I=\int\frac{dx}{\sqrt[4]{(x-1)^3(x+2)^5}}=\int\frac{dx}{(x+2)(x-1)\sqrt[4]{\frac{x+2}{x-1}}}$

Put $\frac{x+2}{x-1}=t\Rightarrow\frac{dt}{dx}=\frac{-3}{(x-1)^2}\Rightarrow dx=-\frac{(x-1)^2}{3}dt$

$\Rightarrow\ I=\int-\frac{1}{3}\frac{(x-1)^2}{(x-1)^2t^{\frac{5}{4}}}dt=-\frac{1}{3}\int t^{-\frac{5}{4}}dt=\frac{4}{3}t^{-\frac{1}{4}}+C$

$=\frac{4}{3}\left(\frac{x-1}{x+2}\right)^{\frac{1}{4}}+C$

28. (a) $I=\int x\sqrt{1-x^2}dx=f(x)$

Let $x=\sin\theta\Rightarrow dx=\cos\theta\,d\theta$

$\Rightarrow\ I=\int\cos^2\theta\sin\theta\,d\theta=-\frac{\cos^3\theta}{3}+C$

$=-\frac{(1-x^2)^{\frac{3}{2}}}{3}+C=f(x)$

$\Rightarrow \; f(0)=\frac{7}{3}=-\frac{1}{3}+C \Rightarrow C=\frac{8}{3}$

$\therefore \; f(x)=-\frac{1}{3}\left(\left(1-x^2\right)^{\frac{3}{2}}-8\right)$

29. (c) $I=\int \frac{\cos^3 x+\cos^5 x}{\sin^2 x+\sin^4 x}dx=\int \frac{\cos^3 x\left(1+\cos^2 x\right)}{\sin^2 x\left(1+\sin^2 x\right)}dx$

$=\int \frac{\left(1-\sin^2 x\right)\left(2-\sin^2 x\right)}{\left(\sin^2 x\right)\left(1+\sin^2 x\right)}\cos x\,dx$

Let $\sin x=t, \cos x\,dx=dt$

$\Rightarrow \; I=\int \frac{\left(1-t^2\right)\left(2-t^2\right)}{t^2\left(1+t^2\right)}dt=\int dt+\int \frac{2-4t^2}{t^2\left(1+t^2\right)}$

$=t+2\left[\int \frac{dt}{t^2}-\int \frac{dt}{1+t^2}\right]-4\int \frac{dt}{1+t^2}$

$\Rightarrow \; t-\frac{2}{t}-2\tan^{-1}t-4\tan^{-1}t+C$

$=\sin x-2\left(\sin x\right)^{-1}-6\tan^{-1}\left(\sin x\right)+C$

30. (c) $I=\int \frac{\sin^2 x}{\cos^4 x}dx=\int \tan^2 x\sec^2 x\,dx=\frac{\tan^3 x}{3}+C$

31. (a) $I=\int \frac{dx}{(x-a)^{\frac{3}{2}}(b-x)^{\frac{1}{2}}}=\int \frac{dx}{(x-a)\sqrt{(x-a)(b-x)}}$

$=\sqrt{(x-a)(b-x)}=(x-a)t$

$=(b-x)=(x-a)t^2 \Rightarrow t=\sqrt{\frac{b-x}{x-a}}$

$=x=\frac{at^2+b}{t^2+1} \Rightarrow dx=\frac{2(a-b)t}{\left(t^2+1\right)^2}dt$

$=I=\int \frac{\frac{2(a-b)t}{\left(t^2+1\right)^2}}{\frac{(b-a)^2}{\left(t^2+1\right)^2}t}dt=\frac{2}{a-b}t+C$

$=\frac{2}{a-b}\left(\frac{b-x}{x-a}\right)^{\frac{1}{2}}+C$

32. (b) $I=\int \frac{\cos x}{\sin x+\cos x}dx$

$\Rightarrow \; I=\frac{1}{2}\int \frac{2\cos x}{\sin x+\cos x}dx$

$=\frac{1}{2}\left[\int \frac{(\cos x+\sin x)+(\cos x-\sin x)}{\sin x+\cos x}dx\right]$

$=\frac{1}{2}\int dx+\frac{1}{2}\int \frac{d(\sin x+\cos x)}{\sin x+\cos x}$

$=\frac{x}{2}+\frac{1}{2}\ln\left|\sin x+\cos x\right|+C$

33. (d) $I=\int \frac{\left(x^2-1\right)dx}{\left(x^4+3x^2+1\right)\tan^{-1}\left(\frac{x^2+1}{x}\right)}$

$=\int \frac{\left(1-\frac{1}{x^2}\right)dx}{\left(x^2+\frac{1}{x^2}\right)+3\tan^{-1}\left(x+\frac{1}{x}\right)}$

$=\int \frac{1-\frac{1}{x^2}}{\left[\left(x+\frac{1}{x}\right)^2+1\right]\tan^{-1}\left(x+\frac{1}{x}\right)}dx$

Let $x+\frac{1}{x}=t \Rightarrow 1-\frac{1}{x^2}dx=dt$

$\Rightarrow \; I=\int \frac{dt}{\left(t^2+1\right)\tan^{-1}t}$

Let $\tan^{-1}t=m \Rightarrow dm=\frac{1}{1+t^2}dt$

$\therefore \; I=\int \frac{dm}{m}=\ln|m|+C=\ln\left|\tan^{-1}t\right|+C$

$=\ln\left|\tan^{-1}\left(\frac{x^2+1}{x}\right)\right|+C$

Comparing, $f(x)=\frac{x^2+1}{x}$

34. (d) $I=\int \frac{8x^7+8^x\ln 8}{x^8+8^x}dx$

Let $x^8+8^x=t \Rightarrow 8x^7+8^x\ln 8\,dx=dt$

$I=\int \frac{dt}{t}=\ln|t|+C=\ln\left|x^8+8^x\right|+C$

35. (d) $I=\int \frac{dx}{e^x-1}$

Let $x=\ln t \Rightarrow dx=\frac{dt}{t}$

$\Rightarrow \; I=\int \frac{dt}{t(t-1)}=\int \frac{dt}{t-1}-\int \frac{dt}{t}=\ln|t-1|-\ln|t|+C$

$=\ln\left|e^x-1\right|-x+C$

36. (a) $I=\int \frac{1+\sin x}{1+\cos x}e^x dx=\int \frac{1+\frac{2\tan\frac{x}{2}}{1+\tan^2\frac{x}{2}}}{1+\frac{1-\tan^2\frac{x}{2}}{1+\tan^2\frac{x}{2}}}e^x dx$

$=\frac{1}{2}\int\left(\sec^2\frac{x}{2}+2\tan\frac{x}{2}\right)e^x dx$

$=\frac{1}{2}\left(2\tan\frac{x}{2}e^x\right)+C$

$=e^x\tan\frac{x}{2}+C$

37. (a) $I=\int \frac{(1-\sin x)^{\frac{1}{2}}}{1+\cos x} e^{-\frac{x}{2}} dx$

$$=\int \frac{\left(\sin^2\frac{x}{2}+\cos^2\frac{x}{2}-2\sin\frac{x}{2}\cos\frac{x}{2}\right)^{\frac{1}{2}}}{1+2\cos^2\frac{x}{2}-1} e^{-\frac{x}{2}} dx$$

$$=\int \frac{\left(\sin\frac{x}{2}-\cos\frac{x}{2}\right)}{2\cos^2\frac{x}{2}} e^{-\frac{x}{2}} dx$$

Let $-\frac{x}{2}=t \Rightarrow -\frac{1}{2}dx=dt$

$$=-\int \frac{\sin(-t)-\cos(-t)}{\cos^2(-t)} e^t dt = \int \frac{\sin t+\cos t}{\cos^2 t} e^t dt$$

$$=\int(\sec t+\sec t\tan t)e^t dt = \sec t e^t + C$$

$$=\sec\frac{x}{2} e^{-\frac{x}{2}} + C$$

38. (c) $I=\int x^x(1+\ln x)dx$

Let $x^x=t \Rightarrow x^x(1+\ln x)=dt$

$\Rightarrow \quad I=\int dt = t+C = x^x+C$

39. (a) $I=\int \frac{\ln(\ln(\ln x))}{x\ln(\ln x)\ln x}dx$

Let $\ln(\ln(\ln x))=t$

$\Rightarrow \quad \frac{1}{\ln(\ln x)}\frac{1}{\ln x}\frac{1}{x}dx=dt$

$\Rightarrow \quad I=\int t\,dt=\frac{t^2}{2}+C=\frac{(\ln(\ln(\ln x)))^2}{2}+C$

40. (c) $I=\int \frac{e^{x^{\frac{1}{2}}}\cos e^{x^{\frac{1}{2}}}}{x^{\frac{1}{2}}}dx$

Let $e^{x^{\frac{1}{2}}}=t \Rightarrow e^{x^{\frac{1}{2}}}\frac{1}{2x^{\frac{1}{2}}}dx=dt$

$\Rightarrow \quad I=2\int \cos t\,dt = 2\sin t + C = 2\sin e^{x^{\frac{1}{2}}}+C$

41. (b) $I=\int \frac{dx}{\cos^2 x(1-\tan x)^2}$

Let $\tan x = t \Rightarrow \sec^2 x\,dx = dt$

$\Rightarrow \quad I=\int \frac{dt}{(1-t)^2}=\frac{1}{1-t}+C=\frac{1}{1-\tan x}+C$

42. (b) $I=\int xe^x\cos x\,dx = \int \underbrace{x\cos x}_{I}.\underbrace{e^x}_{II}dx$

$$=x\cos xe^x-\int(\cos x - x\sin x)e^x dx$$

$$=x\cos xe^x-\int \cos xe^x dx+\int \underbrace{x\sin x}_{I}.\underbrace{e^x}_{II}dx$$

Let $I_1=\int \underbrace{\cos x}_{I}\underbrace{e^x}_{II}dx = \cos xe^x+\int \underbrace{\sin x}_{I}.\underbrace{e^x}_{II}dx$

$$=\cos xe^x+\sin xe^x-\int \cos xe^x dx$$

$\therefore \quad I_1=\frac{e^x}{2}(\sin x+\cos x)$

$\therefore \quad I=x\cos xe^x-\frac{e^x}{2}(\sin x+\cos x)$

$+x\sin xe^x-\int(\sin x+x\cos x)e^x dx$

$I_2=\int \sin xe^x dx=\sin xe^x-\int \cos xe^x dx$

$=\sin xe^x-\cos xe^x-\int \sin xe^x dx$

$I_2=\frac{e^x}{2}(\sin x-\cos x)$

$I=x\cos xe^x-\frac{e^x}{2}(\sin x+\cos x)$

$+x\sin xe^x-\frac{e^x}{2}(\sin x-\cos x)-I+C$

$$I=\frac{e^x}{2}\left(x\cos x-\frac{\sin x}{2}-\frac{\cos x}{2}+x\sin x-\frac{\sin x}{2}+\frac{\cos x}{2}\right)+C$$

$$=\frac{e^x}{2}((x-1)\sin x+x\cos x)+C$$

43. (c) $I=\int \frac{e^x(1+x)}{\sin^2(xe^x)}dx$

Let $xe^x=t \Rightarrow e^x(1+x)dx=dt$

$\therefore I=\int \operatorname{cosec}^2 t\,dt = -\cot(t)+C=-\cot(xe^x)+C$

44. (c) $I=\int \frac{\sin x+\cos x}{\sqrt{1+\sin 2x}}dx=\int \frac{(\sin x+\cos x)dx}{\sqrt{\sin^2 x+\cos^2 x+2\sin x\cos x}}$

$$=\int \frac{\sin x+\cos x}{\sqrt{(\sin x+\cos x)^2}}dx=\int \frac{\sin x+\cos x}{|\sin x+\cos x|}dx$$

If $\sin x+\cos x>0 \Rightarrow |\sin x+\cos x|=\sin x+\cos x$

$\Rightarrow I=\int dx = x+C$

If $\sin x+\cos x<0 \Rightarrow |\sin x+\cos x|=-(\sin x+\cos x)$

$\Rightarrow I=-\int dx=-x+C$

45. (a) $I=\int \frac{\sin x+\cos x}{\sqrt{1+\sin^2 x}}dx=\int \frac{\sin x+\cos x}{|\sin x+\cos x|}$

$\Rightarrow \quad \sin x+\cos x=\sqrt{2}\left(\frac{1}{\sqrt{2}}\sin x+\frac{1}{\sqrt{2}}\cos x\right)$

$$=\sqrt{2}\left(\sin\frac{\pi}{4}\sin x+\cos\frac{\pi}{4}\cos x\right)=\sqrt{2}\sin\left(x+\frac{\pi}{4}\right)$$

Now, $\frac{3\pi}{4}<x<\frac{7\pi}{4} \Rightarrow \pi<x+\frac{\pi}{4}<2\pi$

In this domain $\sin\theta$ is –ve.

$\therefore$ For $\frac{3\pi}{4}<x<\frac{7\pi}{4}$; $\sin x+\cos x<0$

$\Rightarrow \quad |\sin x+\cos x| = -(\sin x+\cos x)$

$\Rightarrow \quad I = -\int dx = -x + C$

46. (a) Let $\ell^{r+1}(x) = t \Rightarrow \dfrac{d\ell^{r+1}x}{d\ell^r x}\dfrac{d\ell^r x}{d\ell^{r-1}x}....\dfrac{d\log(x)}{dx}dx = dt$

$\Rightarrow \quad \dfrac{1}{\ell^r x}.\dfrac{1}{\ell^{r-1}x}.\dfrac{1}{\ell^{r-2}x}.....\dfrac{1}{x}; dx = dt$

$\therefore \quad I = \int dt = t + C = \ell^{r+1}(x) + C$

47. (b) $I = \int \dfrac{\sin x+\cos x}{9+16\sin 2x} = \int \dfrac{\sin x+\cos x}{25-(16-16\sin 2x)}dx$

$= \int \dfrac{\sin x+\cos x}{25-16(\sin x-\cos x)^2}dx$

Let $\sin x - \cos x = t \quad \Rightarrow (\sin x+\cos x)dx = dt$

$\Rightarrow \quad I = \int \dfrac{dt}{5^2-(4t)^2} = \dfrac{1}{4}\dfrac{1}{2.5}\ln\left|\dfrac{5+4t}{5-4t}\right| + C$

$= \dfrac{1}{40}\ln\left|\dfrac{5+4(\sin x-\cos x)}{5-4(\sin x-\cos x)}\right| + C$

48. (b) $I = \int e^x(\sec x + \log|\sec x+\tan x|)dx$

Let $\log|\sec x + \tan x| = t$

$\Rightarrow \quad \dfrac{(\sec x\tan x+\sec^2 x)}{(\sec x+\tan x)}dx = dt$

$\Rightarrow \quad \sec x\,dx = dt$

$\therefore \quad I = \int e^x\left(\log|\sec x+\tan x| + \dfrac{d}{dx}\log|\sec x+\tan x|\right)dx$

$= e^x\log|\sec x+\tan x| + C$

49. (d) $I = \int \dfrac{dx}{x(x^4+1)} = \int \dfrac{dx}{x^5\left(1+\dfrac{1}{x^4}\right)}$

Let $1+\dfrac{1}{x^4} = t \Rightarrow -\dfrac{4}{x^5}dx = dt$

$\therefore \quad I = -\dfrac{1}{4}\int\dfrac{dt}{t} = -\dfrac{1}{4}\ln|t| + C = -\dfrac{1}{4}\ln\left|\dfrac{x^4+1}{x^4}\right| + C$

50. (d) $I = \int \cos\sqrt{x}dx$

Let $\sqrt{x} = t \Rightarrow dx = 2t\,dt$

$\Rightarrow \quad I = 2\int t\cos t\,dt = 2\left[t\sin t - \int \sin t\,dt\right]$

$= 2[t\sin t + \cos t] + C = 2\left[\sqrt{x}\sin\sqrt{x} + \cos\sqrt{x}\right] + C$

51. (d) $I = \int \dfrac{x-\sin x}{1+\cos x}dx = \int \dfrac{x}{2\cos^2\dfrac{x}{2}}dx - \int \dfrac{2\sin\dfrac{x}{2}\cos\dfrac{x}{2}}{2\cos^2\dfrac{x}{2}}dx$

$= \dfrac{1}{2}\int x\sec^2\dfrac{x}{2}dx - \int \tan\dfrac{x}{2}dx$

$= \dfrac{1}{2}\left[2x\tan\dfrac{x}{2} - 2\int\tan\dfrac{x}{2}dx\right] - 2\ln\left|\sec\dfrac{x}{2}\right|$

$= x\tan\dfrac{x}{2} - 4\ln\left|\sec\dfrac{x}{2}\right| + C$

52. (a) $I = \int \dfrac{\tan x\,dx}{\sqrt{1-\tan^2 x}} = \int \dfrac{\tan x|\cos x|}{\sqrt{2\cos^2 x-1}}dx$ for

$x \in \left(-\dfrac{\pi}{4}, \dfrac{\pi}{4}\right)\cos x > 0 \Rightarrow |\cos x| = \cos x$

$\therefore \quad I = \int \dfrac{\sin x\,dx}{\sqrt{2\cos^2 x-1}}$

Let $\cos x = t \Rightarrow -\sin x\,dx = dt$

$\therefore \quad I = -\int \dfrac{dt}{\sqrt{2t^2-1}} = \dfrac{-1}{\sqrt{2}}\int \dfrac{dt}{\sqrt{t^2-\left(\dfrac{1}{\sqrt{2}}\right)^2}}$

$= \dfrac{-1}{\sqrt{2}}\ln\left|t + \sqrt{t^2-\left(\dfrac{1}{\sqrt{2}}\right)^2}\right| + C$

$= -\dfrac{1}{\sqrt{2}}\ln\left|\sqrt{2}t + \sqrt{2t^2-1}\right| + C$

$= -\dfrac{1}{\sqrt{2}}\ln\left|\sqrt{2}\cos x + \sqrt{2\cos^2 x-1}\right| + C$

53. (a) $I = \int e^x\dfrac{x-1}{(x+1)^3}dx = \int e^x\dfrac{x+1-2}{(x+1)^3}dx$

$= \int e^x\left(\dfrac{1}{(x+1)^2} - \dfrac{2}{(x+1)^3}\right)dx$

$= \int e^x\left(\dfrac{1}{(x+1)^2} + \dfrac{d}{dx}\left(\dfrac{1}{(x+1)^2}\right)\right)dx = e^x\dfrac{1}{(x+1)^2} + C$

54. (a) $I = \int \dfrac{a^{x^{\frac{1}{n}}}}{x^{1-\frac{1}{n}}}dx$

Put $x^{\frac{1}{n}} = t \quad \Rightarrow \quad \dfrac{1}{n}x^{\frac{1}{n}-1}dx = dt$

$\Rightarrow \quad I = n\int a^t dt = na^t\ln a + C = na^{x^{\frac{1}{n}}}\ln a + C$

55. (a) $I = \int\left(\sqrt{\tan x} + \sqrt{\cot x}\right)dx$

$= \int \dfrac{\tan x+1}{\sqrt{\tan x}(1+\tan^2 x)}\sec^2 x\,dx$

Let $\sqrt{\tan x} = t \Rightarrow \dfrac{1}{2\sqrt{\tan x}}\sec^2 x\,dx = dt$

$\therefore \quad I = 2\int\dfrac{t^2+1}{t^4+1}dt = 2\int\dfrac{1+\dfrac{1}{t^2}}{t^2+\dfrac{1}{t^2}}dt = 2\int\dfrac{1+\dfrac{1}{t^2}}{\left(t-\dfrac{1}{t}\right)^2+\left(\sqrt{2}\right)^2}dt$

Let $t - \dfrac{1}{t} = m \Rightarrow \left(1+\dfrac{1}{t^2}\right)dt = dm$

$\Rightarrow \quad I = 2\int \frac{dm}{m^2 + \left(\sqrt{2}\right)^2} = \sqrt{2}\tan^{-1}\left(\frac{m}{\sqrt{2}}\right) + C$

$= \sqrt{2}\tan^{-1}\left(\frac{\sqrt{\tan x} - \sqrt{\cot x}}{\sqrt{2}}\right) + C$

$= -\sqrt{2}\cot^{-1}\left(\frac{\sqrt{\tan x} - \sqrt{\cot x}}{\sqrt{2}}\right) + C$

56. (d) $I = \int \sec x \log|\sec x - \tan x| dx$

Let $\log|\sec x - \tan x| = t$

$\Rightarrow \quad \frac{\sec x \tan x - \sec^2 x}{\sec x - \tan x} dx = dt \Rightarrow \sec x\, dx = -dt$

$I = -\int t\, dt = -\frac{t^2}{2} + C = -\frac{\ln^2|\sec x - \tan x|}{2} + C$

57. (b) $f''(x) = \sec^4 x + 4$

$\Rightarrow \quad f'(x) = \int f''(x)dx = \int(\sec^4 x + 4)dx$

$= \int(1 + \tan^2 x)\sec^2 x\, dx + 4\int dx$

$\Rightarrow \quad f'(x) = \tan x + \frac{\tan^3 x}{3} + 4x + C$

$\Rightarrow \quad f'(0) = 0 = 0 + 0 + 0 + C \Rightarrow C = 0$

$\therefore \quad f(x) = \int f'(x)dx = \int(\tan x)dx + \int \frac{\tan^3 x}{3}dx + 4\int x\, dx$

$= \ln|\sec x| + I_1 + 2x^2 + C$

Where, $I_1 = \int \frac{\tan^3 x}{3}dx = \int \frac{\tan^3 x}{1 + \tan^2 x}\sec^2 x\, dx$, Put

$\tan x = t \Rightarrow \sec^2 x\, dx = dt$

$\Rightarrow \quad I_1 = \int \frac{t^3}{1+t^2}dt = \frac{1}{2}\int \frac{m}{1+m}dm$; where

$t^2 = m \Rightarrow 2t\, dt = dm$

$= \frac{1}{2}\left[\int dm - \int \frac{dm}{1+m}\right] = \frac{1}{2}(m - \ln|1+m|)$

$= \frac{1}{2}(\tan^2 x - \ln \sec^2 x)$

$\Rightarrow \quad f(x) = \ln|\sec x| + \frac{\tan^2 x}{2} - \ln|\sec x| + C + 2x^2$

$\Rightarrow \quad f(x) = \frac{\tan^2 x}{2} + C + 2x^2$

Now, $f(0) = 0 = C \Rightarrow f(x) = \frac{\tan^2 x}{2} + 2x^2$

58. (c) $I = \int \sin^{-1}\frac{2x}{1+x^2}dx$

Put $x = \tan\theta \Rightarrow dx = \sec^2\theta\, d\theta$

$\therefore \quad I = \int \sin^{-1}\left(\frac{2\tan\theta}{1+\tan^2\theta}\right)\sec^2\theta\, d\theta$

$= \int \sin^{-1}(\sin 2\theta)\sec^2\theta\, d\theta = 2\int \theta\sec^2\theta\, d\theta$

$= 2\left[\theta\tan\theta - \int \tan\theta\, d\theta\right]$

$= 2x\tan^{-1}x + 2\ln\cos\theta + C$ and $\cos\theta = \frac{1}{\sqrt{1+x^2}}$

$= 2x\tan^{-1}x - \ln(1+x^2) + C$

59. (b) $y = \int x^2 e^{x^3} dx$

Put $x^3 = t \Rightarrow 3x^2 dx = dt$

$\Rightarrow \quad y = \frac{1}{3}\int e^t dt = \frac{e^t}{3} + C \Rightarrow y = \frac{e^{x^3}}{3} + C$

$y = 1$ at $x = 0 \Rightarrow 1 = \frac{e^0}{3} + C \Rightarrow C = \frac{2}{3}$

$\therefore \quad y = \frac{e^{x^3}}{3} + \frac{2}{3}$

$\Rightarrow \quad e^{x^3} = 3y - 2 \qquad \Rightarrow \quad x^3 = \ln(3y-2)$

$\Rightarrow \quad x = \ln^{\frac{1}{3}}(3y-2)$

60. (a) $I = \int \frac{dx}{x^{\frac{1}{5}}\left(1 + x^{\frac{4}{5}}\right)^{\frac{1}{2}}}$

Put $m = \frac{-1}{5}, n = \frac{4}{5}, p = -\frac{1}{2}$

$\Rightarrow \quad \frac{m+1}{n} = 1 \in t \qquad \therefore \quad 1 + x^{\frac{4}{5}} = t^2$

$\Rightarrow \quad \frac{4}{5}x^{-\frac{1}{5}}dx = 2t\, dt \qquad \Rightarrow \quad x^{-\frac{1}{5}}dx = \frac{5}{2}t\, dt$

$\therefore \quad I = \frac{5}{2}\int \frac{t\, dt}{t} = \frac{5}{2}t + C = \frac{5}{2}\left(1 + x^{\frac{4}{5}}\right)^{\frac{1}{2}} + C$

61. (a) $I = \int \frac{10x^9 + 10^x \ln 10}{10^x + x^{10}}dx$

Let $10^x + x^{10} = t$

$\Rightarrow \quad (10^x \ln 10 + 10x^9)dx = dt$

$\Rightarrow \quad I = \int \frac{dt}{t} = \ln|t| + C = \ln(10^x + x^{10}) + C$

62. (b) $I = \int \cos\left[2\tan^{-1}\sqrt{\frac{1-x}{1+x}}\right]dx$

Let $\tan^{-1}\sqrt{\frac{1-x}{1+x}} = \cos^{-1}\frac{\sqrt{1+x}}{\sqrt{2}}$

$= \int\left[2\cos^2\left(\tan^{-1}\sqrt{\frac{1-x}{1+x}}\right) - 1\right]dx$

$= \int\left[2\cos^2\left(\cos^{-1}\sqrt{\frac{1+x}{2}}\right) - 1\right]dx = \int\left[2\left(\frac{1+x}{2}\right) - 1\right]dx$

$= \frac{x^2}{2} + C$

63. **(b)** $I=\int\frac{dx}{x\sqrt{1-x^3}}$

Let $1-x^3=t^2 \Rightarrow -3x^2dx=2t\,dt$

$\Rightarrow x^2dx=-\frac{2t}{3}dt$

$\Rightarrow I=-\frac{2}{3}\int\frac{t\,dt}{x^3\sqrt{1-x^3}}=-\frac{2}{3}\int\frac{t\,dt}{(1-t^2)(t)}=\frac{2}{3}\int\frac{dt}{t^2-1}$

$=\frac{1}{3}\ln\left|\frac{t-1}{t+1}\right|+C=\frac{1}{3}\ln\left|\frac{(1-x^3)^{\frac{1}{2}}-1}{(1-x^3)^{\frac{1}{2}}+1}\right|+C$

64. **(a)** $I=\int\frac{2^{x+1}-3^{x-1}}{6^x}dx=2\int\left(\frac{1}{3}\right)^x dx-\frac{1}{3}\int\left(\frac{1}{2}\right)^x dx$

$=-\frac{2}{3^x\ln 3}+\frac{1}{32^x\ln 2}+C$

65. **(d)** $\phi(x)=\int e^x(f(x)-f'(x))dx$

$=\int e^x(f(x)+f'(x))dx-2\int \underbrace{e^x}_{I}.\underbrace{f'(x)}_{II}dx$

$=e^xf(x)-2\left[e^xf(x)-\int e^xf(x)dx\right]$

$=-e^xf(x)+2\int e^xf(x)dx$

$=\int e^xf(x)dx=\frac{1}{2}(\phi(x)+e^xf(x))$

66. **(a)** $I=\int\left(x+\frac{1}{x}\right)^{n+5}\left(1-\frac{1}{x^2}\right)dx$

Put $x+\frac{1}{x}=t\Rightarrow\left(1-\frac{1}{x^2}\right)dx=dt$

$\Rightarrow I=\int t^{n+5}dt=\frac{t^{n+6}}{n+6}+C=\frac{\left(x+\frac{1}{x}\right)^{n+6}}{n+6}+C$

67. **(a)** $I=\int\frac{\cos^4x\,dx}{\sin^3x(\sin^5x+\cos^5x)^{\frac{3}{5}}}=\int\frac{\cos^4x\sec^6x\,dx}{\tan^3x(\tan^5x+1)^{\frac{3}{5}}}$

$=\int\frac{\sec^2x\,dx}{\tan^3x(\tan^5x+1)^{\frac{3}{5}}}=\int\frac{dt}{t^3(t^5+1)^{\frac{3}{5}}};$

Put $\tan x=t\Rightarrow\sec^2x\,dx=dt$

$\Rightarrow \int\frac{dt}{t^6\left(1+\frac{1}{t^5}\right)^{\frac{3}{5}}}$; Put $1+\frac{1}{t^5}=m\Rightarrow\frac{-5}{t^6}dt=dm$

$\Rightarrow I=-\frac{1}{5}\int\frac{dm}{m^{\frac{3}{5}}}=-\frac{1}{2}m^{\frac{2}{5}}+C=-\frac{1}{2}\left(\frac{\tan^5x+1}{\tan^5x}\right)^{\frac{2}{5}}+C$

68. **(a)** $I=\int x\sqrt{\frac{2\sin(x^2+1)-\sin2(x^2+1)}{2\sin(x^2+1)+\sin2(x^2+1)}}dx$

$=\int x\sqrt{\frac{2\sin(x^2+1)(1-\cos(x^2+1))}{2\sin(x^2+1)(1+\cos(x^2+1))}}dx$

$=\int x\sqrt{\frac{2\sin^2\frac{x^2+1}{2}}{2\cos^2\frac{x^2+1}{2}}}dx=\int x\tan\frac{x^2+1}{2}dx$

Let $\frac{x^2+1}{2}=t\Rightarrow x\,dx=dt=\int\tan t\,dt=\ln|\sec t|+C$

$=\ln\left|\sec\frac{x^2+1}{2}\right|+C$

69. **(c)** $I=\int x\left\{f(x^2)g''(x^2)-f''(x^2)g(x^2)\right\}dx$

$=\frac{1}{2}\int\underbrace{f(x^2)}_{I}\underbrace{2xg''(x^2)}_{II}dx-\frac{1}{2}\int\underbrace{g(x^2)}_{I}\underbrace{2xf''(x^2)}_{II}dx$

$=\frac{1}{2}\left[f(x^2)g'(x^2)-\int f'(x^2)2xg'(x^2)dx\right]$

$-\frac{1}{2}\left[g(x^2)f'(x^2)-\int g'(x^2)2xf'(x^2)dx\right]$

$=\frac{1}{2}\left[f(x^2)g'(x^2)-g(x^2)f'(x^2)\right]$

$-\frac{1}{2}\int f'(x^2)2xg'(x^2)dx$

$+\frac{1}{2}\int f'(x^2)2xg'(x^2)dx+C$

$=\frac{1}{2}\left[f(x^2)g'(x^2)-g(x^2)f'(x^2)\right]+C$

70. **(d)** $I=\int\frac{\cos5x+\cos4x}{1-2\cos3x}dx=\int\frac{2\cos\frac{9}{2}x\cos\frac{x}{2}}{3-4\cos^2\frac{3x}{2}}dx$

$=2\int\frac{\left(4\cos^3\frac{3x}{2}-3\cos\frac{3x}{2}\right)\cos\frac{x}{2}}{3-4\cos^2\frac{3x}{2}}dx$

$=-2\int\cos\frac{3x}{2}\cos\frac{x}{2}dx=-\int(\cos2x+\cos x)dx$

$=-\frac{\sin2x}{2}-\sin x+C$

$=-\sin x(1+\cos x)+C$

Comparing, $k=-1$

SECTION–IV (MORE THANE ONE ARE CORRECT)

1. **(a), (b), (c)**

(a) $I=\int\underbrace{f(x)}_{I}d\underbrace{g(x)}_{II}=f(x)g(x)-\int g(x)d\,f(x)$

= R.H.S

(b) $I=\int f'g(x))g'(x)dx$

From chain rule we know $\frac{d}{dx}f(g(x))=f'(g(x))g'(x)$

$\int d\,f(g(x))=\int f'(g(x))g'(x)dx=f(g(x))$

(c) We know that $\int e^x(f(x)+f'(x))dx=e^xf(x)+C$

2. (b), (d) $I=\int x^{\frac{1}{2}}\left(1-x^3\right)^{-\frac{1}{2}}dx$

Let $\left(1-x^3\right)=x^3t^2 \Rightarrow \frac{1}{x^3}-1=t^2-\frac{3}{x^4}dx=2t\,dt$

$\therefore \quad I=\int x^{\frac{1}{2}}x^{-\frac{3}{2}}t^{-1}\left(-\frac{2}{3}\right)t\,x^4dt$

$=-\frac{2}{3}\int x^3dt=-\frac{2}{3}\int\frac{dt}{t^2+1}=-\frac{2}{3}\tan^{-1}t+C$

$=\frac{2}{3}\tan^{-1}\frac{\sqrt{x^3}}{\sqrt{1-x^3}}+C=\frac{2}{3}\sin^{-1}\sqrt{x^3}+C$

3. (b), (c) $I=\int\frac{dx}{5+4\cos x}=\int\frac{dx}{5+4\left(\dfrac{1-\tan^2\frac{x}{2}}{1+\tan^2\frac{x}{2}}\right)}$

$=2\int\frac{\frac{1}{2}\sec^2\frac{x}{2}dx}{9+\tan^2\frac{x}{2}}$

Let $\tan\frac{x}{2}=t\Rightarrow\frac{1}{2}\sec^2\frac{x}{2}dx=dt$

$\Rightarrow \quad I=2\int\frac{dt}{3^2+t^2}=\frac{2}{3}\tan^{-1}\frac{t}{3}+C=\frac{2}{3}\tan^{-1}\left(\frac{1}{3}\tan\frac{x}{2}\right)+C$

Comparing, $k=\frac{2}{3}, m=\frac{1}{3}$

4. (a), (b), (c), (d)

$I=\int\frac{4e^x+6e^{-x}}{9e^x-4e^{-x}}dx=\int\frac{4e^{2x}+6}{9e^{2x}-4}dx$

Let $4e^{2x}+6=A\left(9e^{2x}-4\right)+B\left(18e^{2x}\right)$

$=e^{2x}\left(9A+18B\right)-4A$

$\Rightarrow \quad A=-\frac{3}{2}, B=\frac{35}{36}$

$\therefore \quad I=-\frac{3}{2}\int dx+\frac{35}{36}\int\frac{18e^{2x}}{9e^{2x}-4}dx$

$=-\frac{3}{2}x+\frac{35}{36}\ln\left(9e^{2x}-4\right)+C$

$\Rightarrow \quad A=-\frac{3}{2}, B=\frac{35}{36}, A+B=-\frac{19}{36}$

5. (a), (c) $I=\int\sec^2x\,\mathrm{cosec}^4x\,dx=\int\left(1+\cot^2x\right)^2\sec^2x\,dx$

Let $\tan x=t\Rightarrow\sec^2x\,dx=dt$

$\Rightarrow \quad I=\int\left(1+\frac{1}{t^2}\right)^2dt=\int\left(1+\frac{1}{t^4}+\frac{2}{t^2}\right)dt$

$\Rightarrow \quad t-\frac{1}{3t^3}-\frac{2}{t}+C=\tan x-\frac{1}{3}\cot^3x-2\cot x+C$

Comparing, $L=1, K=-\frac{1}{3}, M=-2$

6. (a), (b) $I=\int\frac{dx}{\left(1+\sqrt{x}\right)^8}=2\int\frac{\sqrt{x}+1-1}{2\sqrt{x}\left(1+\sqrt{x}\right)^8}dx$

$=2\left[\int\frac{dx}{2\sqrt{x}\left(1+\sqrt{x}\right)^7}-\int\frac{dx}{2\sqrt{x}\left(1+\sqrt{x}\right)^8}\right]$

Let $1+\sqrt{x}=t;\frac{1}{2\sqrt{x}}dx=dt$

$\therefore \quad I=2\left[\int\frac{dt}{t^7}-\int\frac{dt}{t^8}\right]=-\frac{2}{6}\frac{1}{t^6}+\frac{2}{7t^7}+C$

$=-\frac{1}{3\left(1+\sqrt{x}\right)^6}+\frac{2}{7\left(1+\sqrt{x}\right)^7}+C$

Comparing, $k_1=6, k_2=7$

7. (a), (d) $I=\int f(x)\sin 2x\,dx=\frac{\ln|f(x)|}{b^2-a^2}+C$

Differentiating both sides w.r.t. x, we get

$f(x)\sin 2x=\frac{1}{b^2-a^2}\frac{1}{f(x)}f'(x)$ (if $f(x)>0$)

$\Rightarrow \quad \left(b^2-a^2\right)\sin 2x=\frac{f'(x)}{f^2(x)}$

Integrating both sides w.r.t x, we get $-\left(b^2-a^2\right)\frac{\cos 2x}{2}$

$=-\frac{1}{f(x)}+C_1$

$\Rightarrow \quad \frac{1}{f(x)}=\frac{\left(b^2-a^2\right)}{2}\left(2\sin^2x-1\right)+C_1$

$\Rightarrow \quad \frac{1}{f(x)}=\left(b^2-a^2\right)\sin^2x+C_1$

$=b^2\sin^2x-a^2\left(1-\cos^2x\right)+C_1$

$\Rightarrow \quad \frac{1}{f(x)}=a^2\cos^2x+b^2\sin^2x+C_2$

$\Rightarrow \quad f(x)=\frac{1}{a^2\cos^2x+b^2\sin^2x+C_2}$

If $f(x)<0$

$\Rightarrow \quad \int f(x)\sin 2x dx=\frac{\ln(-f(x))}{b^2-a^2}+C$

Differentiating Integrating w.r.t. x,

$f(x)\sin 2x=-\frac{1}{f(x)}\cdot\frac{f'(x)}{(b^2-a^2)}$

$\Rightarrow \quad (a^2-b^2)\sin 2x=\frac{f'(x)}{f^2(x)}$

Integrating w.r.t. x, $-\left(a^2-b^2\right)\frac{\cos 2x}{2}=-\frac{1}{f(x)}+C_3$

$\Rightarrow \quad \frac{1}{f(x)}=\left(a^2-b^2\right)\sin^2x+C_4=a^2\sin^2x+b^2\cos^2x+C_5$

$\Rightarrow \quad f(x)=\frac{1}{a^2\sin^2x+b^2\cos^2x+C_5}$

8. **(a), (c)** $I=\int \frac{x^{\frac{5}{2}}}{x^{\frac{7}{2}}+x^{6}}dx$

Let $x=t^2 \Rightarrow 2t\,dt=dx$

$\therefore\quad I=2\int \frac{t^6\,dt}{t^7+t^{12}}=2\int \frac{1}{t^6\left(1+\frac{1}{t^5}\right)}dt$

Put $1+\frac{1}{t^5}=m \Rightarrow \frac{-5}{t^6}dt=dm$

$\Rightarrow\ I=-\frac{2}{5}\int \frac{dm}{m}=-\frac{2}{5}\ln|m|+C=-\frac{2}{5}\ln\left|\frac{t^5+1}{t^5}\right|+C$

$=-\frac{2}{5}\ln\left|\frac{x^{\frac{5}{2}}+1}{x^{\frac{5}{2}}}\right|+C=\frac{2}{5}\ln\left|\frac{x^{\frac{5}{2}}}{1+x^{\frac{5}{2}}}\right|+C$

Comparing, $a=\frac{2}{5}, k=\frac{5}{2}$

9. **(a), (b)** $f(x)=\frac{x+2}{2x+3}$

$\Rightarrow\ I=\int\left(\frac{f(x)}{x^2}\right)^{\frac{1}{2}}dx=\int \frac{1}{x}\sqrt{\frac{x+2}{2x+3}}dx$

Put $\frac{x+2}{2x+3}=t^2 \Rightarrow x=\frac{2-3t^2}{2t^2-1}, dx=\frac{-2t}{\left(2t^2-1\right)^2}dt$

$\therefore\quad I=\int \frac{2t^2-1}{2-3t^2}(t)\frac{(-2t)}{\left(2t^2-1\right)^2}dt=2\int \frac{t^2}{\left(3t^2-2\right)\left(2t^2-1\right)}dt$

$=\int \frac{dt}{3t^2-2}+\int \frac{dt}{\left(3t^2-2\right)\left(2t^2-1\right)}$

$=\int \frac{dt}{3t^2-2}-2\left[\int \frac{dt}{2t^2-1}-\frac{3}{2}\int \frac{dt}{3t^2-2}\right]$

$=4\int \frac{dt}{3t^2-2}-2\int \frac{dt}{2t^2-1}$

$=-\sqrt{\frac{2}{3}}\ln\left|\frac{\sqrt{3}t+\sqrt{2}}{\sqrt{3}t-\sqrt{2}}\right|+\frac{1}{\sqrt{2}}\ln\left|\frac{\sqrt{2}t+1}{\sqrt{2}t-1}\right|+C$

$=\frac{1}{\sqrt{2}}\ln\left|\frac{\sqrt{2f(x)}+1}{1-\sqrt{2f(x)}}\right|-\sqrt{\frac{2}{3}}\ln\left|\frac{\sqrt{3f(x)}+\sqrt{2}}{\sqrt{3f(x)}-\sqrt{2}}\right|+C$

Hence, $g(x)=\ln|x|, h(x)=\ln|x|$

10. **(c), (d)** $f(x)=\lim\limits_{n\to\infty} e^{x\tan\left(\frac{1}{n}\right)\log\left(\frac{1}{n}\right)}=\lim\limits_{n\to\infty} e^{-x\frac{\tan\left(\frac{1}{n}\right)}{\frac{1}{n}}\frac{\log n}{n}}$

$=e^{-x(0)}=1$

$\Rightarrow\ I=\int \frac{dx}{\sin^{\frac{11}{3}}x\cos^{\frac{1}{3}}x}=\int \frac{\sec^4 x}{\tan^{\frac{11}{3}}x}dx$

$=\int \frac{\left(1+\tan^2 x\right)}{\tan^{\frac{11}{3}}x}\sec^2 x\,dx=\int \frac{\left(1+t^2\right)}{t^{\frac{11}{3}}}dt$

$=-\frac{3}{8}t^{-\frac{8}{3}}-\frac{3}{2}t^{-\frac{2}{3}}+C$

$=-\frac{3}{2}t^{-\frac{2}{3}}\left(\frac{t^{-2}}{4}+1\right)=-\frac{3}{2}\frac{1}{\tan^{\frac{2}{3}}x}\left(\frac{1}{4\tan^2 x}+1\right)+C$

$\therefore\quad g(x)=\frac{-3}{2\tan^{\frac{2}{3}}x}\left(\frac{1}{4\tan^2 x}+1\right)$

$\Rightarrow\ g\left(\frac{\pi}{4}\right)=\frac{-3}{2}\left(\frac{1}{4}+1\right)=\frac{-15}{8}$, also $g(x)$ is not continuous for $x=n\pi$

11. **(b), (d)** $I=\int\left(\cos^{-1}x+\cos^{-1}\sqrt{1-x^2}\right)dx$; $x\in[-1, 0)$

Let $\theta=\cos^{-1}\sqrt{1-x^2}\in\left(0,\frac{\pi}{2}\right]$

$\Rightarrow\ \cos\theta=\cos\left(\cos^{-1}\sqrt{1-x^2}\right)$

$\Rightarrow\ \cos\theta=\sqrt{1-x^2}\qquad\Rightarrow\ \sin\theta=\sqrt{1-(1-x^2)}$

$\left(\because \theta\in\left(0,\frac{\pi}{2}\right]\right)$

$\Rightarrow\ \sin\theta=|x|=-x\qquad(\because x\in[-1, 0))$

$\Rightarrow\ \sin^{-1}(\sin\theta)=\sin^{-1}(x)$

$\Rightarrow\ \theta=-\sin^{-1}x\qquad\left(\because \theta\in\left(0,\frac{\pi}{2}\right]\right)$

$\Rightarrow\ I=\int\left[\cos^{-1}x+\left(-\sin^{-1}x\right)\right]dx=\int\left(\frac{\pi}{2}-2\sin^{-1}x\right)dx$

$=\frac{\pi}{2}x-2\int \sin^{-1}x\,dx$

$=\frac{\pi}{2}x-2\left[\left(\sin^{-1}x\right).x-\int \frac{1}{\sqrt{1-x^2}}(x)dx\right]$

$=\frac{\pi}{2}x-2x\sin^{-1}x+\int(2x)(1-x^2)^{-1/2}dx$

$=\frac{\pi}{2}x-2x\sin^{-1}x-\frac{(1-x^2)^{1/2}}{1/2}+C$

$=\frac{\pi}{2}x-2x\sin^{-1}x-2\sqrt{1-x^2}+C$

$=Ax+f(x)\sin^{-1}x-2\sqrt{1-x^2}+C$ (given)

$\Rightarrow\ A=\frac{\pi}{2}$ and $f(x)=-2x$

SECTION–V: (ASSERTION AND REASON)

1. **(b)** Reason is correct and also assertion is correct as

$I=\int \frac{\sec x}{\ln|\sec x-\tan x|}dx$

Put $\ln|\sec x-\tan x|=t$

$\Rightarrow\ \frac{1}{|\sec x-\tan x|}\times\frac{\sec x-\tan x}{|\sec x-\tan x|}\times\left(\sec x\tan x-\sec^2 x\right)dx=dt$

$\Rightarrow \dfrac{1}{(\sec x - \tan x)}.-\sec x(\sec x - \tan x)dx = dt$

$\Rightarrow$ $\sec x\, dx = -dt$

$\therefore$ $I = \int \frac{-dt}{t} = -\ln|t| + C = -\ln|\ln|\sec x - \tan x|| + C$

But reason is not the correct explanation of assertion.

2. (c) $\int (\sin x)^5 \cos x\, dx = \frac{\sin^6 x}{6} + C$ is true as

$$\int (f(x))^n f'(x)dx = \frac{(f(x))^{n+1}}{n+1} + C \text{ for } n \neq -1$$

$\Rightarrow$ Assertion is correct, but reason is incorrect

3. (a) Given $x > 0, x \neq 1$

$$I = \int\left(\frac{1}{\ln x} - \frac{1}{(\ln x)^2}\right)dx$$

Put $\ln x = t$ $\Rightarrow \frac{1}{x}dx = dt$

$\Rightarrow dx = et\, dt$

$\therefore$ $I = \int\left(\frac{1}{t} - \frac{1}{t^2}\right).e^t\, dt = e^t.\frac{1}{t} + C = \frac{x}{\ln x} + C = x \log_x e + C$

$\Rightarrow$ Assertion and reason both are correct and reason is the correct, explanation of assertion.

4. (a) $\int e^{g(x)}\{f(x).g'(x) + f'(x)\}dx = \int \underbrace{e^{g(x)}.g'(x)}_{II}.\underbrace{f(x)}_{I}dx + \int e^{g(x)}.f'(x)dx$

$= f(x).e^{g(x)} - \int f'(x).e^{g(x)}dx + \int e^{g(x)}.f'(x)dx + C$

$= f(x).e^{g(x)} + C$

Now, if $g(x) = x \sin x + \cos x$ and $f(x) = \frac{\cos x}{x}$

$\Rightarrow g'(x) = x \cos x$ and $f'(x) = \frac{-x\sin x - \cos x}{x^2}$

$\therefore$ $\int e^{g(x)}\{f(x).g'(x) + f'(x)\}dx$

$= \int e^{(x\sin x + \cos x)}\left\{\frac{\cos x}{x}(x\cos x) + \left(\frac{-x\sin x - \cos x}{x^2}\right)\right\}dx$

$= \int e^{(x\sin x + \cos x)}\left\{\frac{x^2\cos^2 x - x\sin x - \cos x}{x^2}\right\}dx$

$= \frac{\cos x}{x}e^{(x\sin x + \cos x)} + C$

$\Rightarrow$ Assertion is correct and reason is the correct explanation of assertion.

SECTION-VI: (PASSAGE)

Passage A:

$$\int \frac{x^3 - 6x^2 + 11x - 6}{\sqrt{x^2 + 4x + 3}}dx = (Ax^2 + Bx + C)\sqrt{x^2 + 4x + 3} + \lambda\int\frac{dx}{\sqrt{x^2 + 4x + 3}}$$

Differentiating both sides, we get $\frac{x^3 - 6x^2 + 11x - 6}{\sqrt{x^2 + 4x + 3}}$

$= \frac{(Ax^2 + Bx + C)(x+2)}{\sqrt{x^2 + 4x + 3}} + \left(\sqrt{x^2 + 4x + 3}\right)(2A + B) + \frac{\lambda}{\sqrt{x^2 + 4x + 3}}$

$\Rightarrow (x^3 - 6x^2 + 11x - 6) = (x + 2)(Ax^2 + Bx + C) + (x^2 + 4x + 3)(2Ax + B) + \lambda$

$\Rightarrow (x^3 - 6x^2 + 11x - 6) = x^3(3A) + x^2(B + 2A + B + 8A) + (C + 2B + 4B + 6A)x + (2C + 3B + \lambda)$

$\Rightarrow 3A = 1,\ 10A + 2B = -6,\ 6A + 6B + C = 11,\ 3B + 2C + \lambda = -6$

$\Rightarrow A = 1/3,\ B = -14/3,\ C = 37,\ \lambda = -66$

1. (a)

2. (d)

3. (b)

Passage B:

4. (c) $I = \int e^x\left(\ln|x| + \frac{2}{x^3}\right)dx$

$= \int e^x\left(\ln|x| + \frac{1}{x} - \frac{1}{x} + \frac{1}{x^2} - \frac{1}{x^2} + \frac{2}{x^3}\right)dx$

$= \int e^x\left(\ln|x| + \frac{1}{x}\right)dx + \int e^x\left(-\frac{1}{x} + \frac{1}{x^2}\right)dx + \int e^x\left(-\frac{1}{x^2} + \frac{2}{x^3}\right)dx$

$= e^x\left(\ln|x| - \frac{1}{x} - \frac{1}{x^2}\right) + C$

5. (a) $I = \int e^x\left[f(x) - (-1)^n f^n(x)\right]dx$,

where $f^n(x) = \frac{d^n}{(dx)^n}f(x)$

$= \int e^x\left[f(x) + f'(x) - f''(x) + f'''(x) + \ldots\ldots + (-1)^{n+1}f^n(x)\right]$

$= e^x\left(f(x) - f'(x) + f''(x) \ldots.(-1)^{n-1}f^{n-1}(x)\right) + C$

$= \left(e^x\sum_{r=0}^{n-1}(-1)^r f^r(x)\right) + C$

6. (a) $I = \int e^x\left(f(x)g(x) + g'(x)f(x) + f'(x)g(x)\right)dx$

$= \int e^x\left(f(x)g(x) + d\left(f(x)g(x)\right)\right)dx = e^x f(x)g(x) + C$

Passage C:

7. (a) For Relation between $I_{n,m}$ and $I_{n+2,m}$

$P(x) = \sin^{n+1}x\cos^{m+1}x$

Here $n = m = 2$

$\therefore$ $P(x) = \sin^3 x\cos^3 x$

Differentiating both sides, we get

$P'(x) = 3\sin^2 x\cos^4 x - 3\cos^2 x\sin^4 x$

$= 3\sin^2 x\cos^2 x(1 - 2\sin^2 x)$

$= 3\sin^2 x\cos^2 x - 6\sin^4 x\cos^2 x$

Integrating both sides $P(x) = \sin^3 x\cos^3 x$

$= 3I_{n,m} - 6I_{n+2,m} = 3I_{2,2} - 6I_{4,2}$

$\Rightarrow I_{4,2} = \frac{1}{6}(3I_{2,2} - \sin^3 x\cos^3 x)$

8. (a) $I_{n,m} = I_{4,2}$

$\Rightarrow I_{n+2,m} = I_{6,2}$

$\Rightarrow P(x) = \sin^{n+1} x\cos^{m+1} x = \sin^5 x\cos^3 x$

Differentiating, we get $P'(x) = 5\sin^4 x\cos^4 x - 3\cos^2 x\sin^6 x$

$= \sin^4 x\cos^2 x(5\cos^2 x - 3\sin^2 x)$

$= \sin^4 x\cos^2 x(5 - 8\sin^2 x) = 5\sin^4 x\cos^2 x - 8\sin^6 x\cos^2 x$

Integrating both sides $P(x) = \sin^5 x\cos^3 x = 5I_{4,2} - 8I_{6,2}$

$\Rightarrow I_{4,2} = \frac{1}{5}(\sin^5 x\cos^3 x + 8I_{6,2})$

9. (b) $I_{n,m} = I_{4,2}$

Put $I_{n,m+2} = I_{4,4}$

$\Rightarrow P(x) = \sin^{n+1} x\cos^{m+1} x = \sin^5 x\cos^3 x$

Differentiating, we get $P'(x) = 5\sin^4 x\cos^4 x - 3\cos^2 x\sin^6 x$

$= \sin^4 x\cos^2 x(5\cos^2 x - 3\sin^2 x)$

$= \sin^4 x\cos^2 x(8\cos^2 x - 3) = 8\sin^4 x\cos^4 x - 3\sin^4 x\cos^2 x$

Integrating, $P(x) = \sin^5 x\cos^3 x = 8I_{4,4} - 3I_{4,2}$

$\Rightarrow I_{4,2} = \frac{1}{3}(-\sin^5 x\cos^3 x + 8I_{4,4})$

Passage D:

10. (a) If $\int(\sqrt{\tan x} + \sqrt{\cot x})dx$

$\Rightarrow \frac{1}{2}(\sqrt{\tan x} - \sqrt{\cot x})$ (tan x + cot x) = dx = dt

$\Rightarrow \frac{1}{2}(\sqrt{t^2 - 4})(t^2 - 2)dx = dt$

$\therefore$ I = $\int \frac{t.2dt}{\sqrt{t^2-4}(t^2-2)}$

Put $t^2 = z$ $\Rightarrow 2t\,dt = dz$

$\therefore \int \frac{dz}{\sqrt{z-4}(z-2)} = \int \frac{dz}{(z-2)\sqrt{z-4}}$

Put $\sqrt{z-4} = u$ $\Rightarrow \frac{1}{2\sqrt{z-4}}dz = du$

$\Rightarrow \frac{dz}{\sqrt{z-4}} = 2du$

$\therefore I = \int \frac{2du}{(u^2+4-2)} = 2\int \frac{du}{u^2+(\sqrt{2})^2}$

$= 2.\frac{1}{\sqrt{2}}\tan^{-1}\left(\frac{u}{\sqrt{2}}\right) + C = \sqrt{2}\tan^{-1}\left(\frac{\sqrt{z-4}}{\sqrt{2}}\right) + C$

$= \sqrt{2}\tan^{-1}\left(\frac{\sqrt{t^2-4}}{\sqrt{2}}\right) + C$

$= \sqrt{2}\tan^{-1}\left(\frac{\sqrt{\tan x} - \sqrt{\cot x}}{\sqrt{2}}\right) + C$

11. (b) I = $\int(\sqrt{\tan x} + \sqrt{\cot x})dx = \sqrt{2}\tan^{-1}\left(\frac{\sqrt{\tan x} - \sqrt{\cot x}}{\sqrt{2}}\right)$

$$= \begin{cases} -\sqrt{2}\tan^{-1}\left(\frac{\sqrt{\cot x} - \sqrt{\tan x}}{\sqrt{2}}\right); & \text{for } x \in \left(0, \frac{\pi}{4}\right) \\ \sqrt{2}\tan^{-1}\left(\frac{\sqrt{\tan x} - \sqrt{\cot x}}{\sqrt{2}}\right); & \text{for } x \in \left(\frac{\pi}{4}, \frac{\pi}{2}\right) \end{cases}$$

If $x > 0$, then $\theta = \tan^{-1}x$

$\Rightarrow \theta = \sin^{-1}\left(\frac{x}{\sqrt{x^2+1}}\right)$

$\Rightarrow I = -\sqrt{2}\sin^{-1}\left(\frac{\sqrt{\cot x} - \sqrt{\tan x}}{\sqrt{2}} \times \frac{\sqrt{2}}{\sqrt{\tan x + \cot x}}\right)$

$\forall\, x \in \left(0, \frac{\pi}{2}\right)$

$\Rightarrow -\sqrt{2}\sin^{-1}(\cos x - \sin x)$

$\Rightarrow \sqrt{2}\sin^{-1}(\sin x - \cos x) + C$

12. (b) $I = \int(\sqrt{\tan x} + \sqrt{\cot x})dx$

$= \sqrt{2}\tan^{-1}\left(\frac{\sqrt{\tan x} - \sqrt{\cot x}}{\sqrt{2}}\right) + C$

For $x \in \left(0, \frac{\pi}{2}\right) \cup \left(\pi, \frac{3\pi}{2}\right)$

$$= \begin{cases} -\sqrt{2}\tan^{-1}\left(\frac{\sqrt{\cot x} - \sqrt{\tan x}}{\sqrt{2}}\right) + C; & \text{for } x \in \left(\pi, \frac{5\pi}{4}\right) \\ \sqrt{2}\tan^{-1}\left(\frac{\sqrt{\tan x} - \sqrt{\cot x}}{\sqrt{2}}\right) + C & \text{for } x \in \left(\frac{5\pi}{4}, \frac{3\pi}{2}\right) \end{cases}$$

$$= \begin{cases} -\sqrt{2}\sin^{-1}\left(\frac{\sqrt{\cot x} - \sqrt{\tan x}}{\sqrt{2}} \times \frac{\sqrt{2}}{\sqrt{\tan x + \sqrt{\cot x}}}\right) + C; & \text{for } x \in \left(\pi, \frac{5\pi}{4}\right) \\ \sqrt{2}\tan^{-1}\left(\frac{\sqrt{\tan x} - \sqrt{\cot x}}{\sqrt{2}} \times \frac{\sqrt{2}}{\sqrt{\tan x + \sqrt{\cot x}}}\right) + C & \text{for } x \in \left(\frac{5\pi}{4}, \frac{3\pi}{2}\right) \end{cases}$$

$\Rightarrow I = -\sqrt{2}\sin^{-1}(\cos x - \sin x) + C$ for $x \in \left(\pi, \frac{3\pi}{2}\right)$

$\Rightarrow$ I = $\sqrt{2}\sin^{-1}(\sin x - \cos x) + C$ for $x \in \left(\pi, \frac{3\pi}{2}\right)$

Passage E:

13. (b) $I=\int x^{\frac{1}{3}}\left(2+x^{\frac{2}{3}}\right)^{\frac{1}{4}}dx$

Put $m=\frac{1}{3}, n=\frac{2}{3} \Rightarrow \frac{m+1}{n}=2\in\mathbb{Z}$

$\therefore$ Let $2+x^{\frac{2}{3}}=t^4 \Rightarrow \frac{2}{3}x^{-\frac{1}{3}}dx=4t^3dt$

$\Rightarrow\ I=\int(t^4-2)t\,6t^3dt=6\int(t^8-2t^4)dt$

$=\frac{2}{3}t^9-\frac{12}{5}t^5+C=\frac{2}{3}\left(2+x^{\frac{2}{3}}\right)^{\frac{9}{4}}-\frac{12}{5}\left(2+x^{\frac{2}{3}}\right)^{\frac{5}{4}}+C$

14. (c) $I=\int\sqrt{\frac{1+\sqrt{x}}{x}}\,dx=\int x^{-\frac{1}{2}}\left(1+x^{\frac{1}{2}}\right)^{\frac{1}{2}}dx$

$m=-\frac{1}{2}, n=\frac{1}{2}\Rightarrow\frac{m+1}{n}=1\in\mathbb{Z}$

Let $1+x^{\frac{1}{2}}=t^2 \Rightarrow \frac{1}{2}x^{-\frac{1}{2}}dx=2t\,dt$

$\therefore\ I=\int 4t^2dt=\frac{4}{3}t^3+C=\frac{4}{3}\left(1+x^{\frac{1}{2}}\right)^{\frac{3}{2}}+C$

15. (b) $I=\int x^{-\frac{1}{2}}\left(1+x^{\frac{1}{4}}\right)^{\frac{1}{3}}dx$

Put $m=-\frac{1}{2}, n=\frac{1}{4}\Rightarrow\frac{m+1}{n}=2\in\mathbb{Z}$

$\therefore$ Let $1+x^{\frac{1}{4}}=t^3 \quad\Rightarrow\ \frac{1}{4}x^{-\frac{3}{4}}dx=3t^2dt$

$\Rightarrow\ I=12\int(t^3-1)t^3dt=\frac{12}{7}t^7-3t^4+C$

$=\frac{12}{7}\left(1+x^{\frac{1}{4}}\right)^{\frac{7}{3}}-3\left(1+x^{\frac{1}{4}}\right)^{\frac{4}{3}}+C$

$=12\left[\frac{\left(1+x^{\frac{1}{4}}\right)^{\frac{7}{3}}}{7}-\frac{\left(1+x^{\frac{1}{4}}\right)^{\frac{4}{3}}}{4}\right]+C$

16. (a) $I=\int x^{\frac{1}{3}}\left(1+x^{\frac{4}{3}}\right)^{\frac{1}{7}}dx$

Put $m=\frac{1}{3}, n=\frac{4}{3}\Rightarrow\frac{m+1}{n}=1\in\mathbb{Z}$

$\therefore$ Let $\left(1+x^{\frac{4}{3}}\right)=t^7$

$\Rightarrow\ \frac{4}{3}x^{\frac{1}{3}}dx=7t^6dt$

$\therefore\ I=\frac{21}{4}\int t^7dt=\frac{21}{32}t^8+C=\frac{21}{32}\left(1+x^{\frac{4}{3}}\right)^{\frac{8}{7}}+C$

Passage F:

17. (a) $I=\int\frac{x+x^{\frac{2}{3}}+x^{\frac{1}{6}}}{x\left(1+x^{\frac{1}{3}}\right)}dx$

Let $x=t^6\Rightarrow dx=6t^5dt$

$\Rightarrow\ I=\int\frac{t^6+t^4+t}{t^6(1+t^2)}6t^5dt=6\int\frac{t^5+t^3+1}{t^2+1}dt$

$=6\left[\int t^3dt+\int\frac{dt}{t^2+1}\right]=\frac{3}{2}t^4+6\tan^{-1}t+C$

$=\frac{3}{2}x^{\frac{2}{3}}+6\tan^{-1}\left(x^{\frac{1}{6}}\right)+C$

18. (a) $I=\int\frac{dx}{x\left(1+x^{\frac{1}{3}}\right)^2}$

Let $x=t^3\Rightarrow dx=3t^2dt$

$\Rightarrow\ I=\int\frac{3t^2dt}{t^3(1+t)^2}=3\int\frac{dt}{t(1+t)^2}=3\left[\int\frac{dt}{t(1+t)}-\int\frac{dt}{(1+t)^2}\right]$

$=3\left[\int\frac{dt}{t}-\int\frac{dt}{1+t}-\int\frac{dt}{(1+t)^2}\right]$

$=3\left[\ln\left(\frac{t}{1+t}\right)+\frac{1}{1+t}\right]+C$

$=3\left[\ln\left(\frac{x^{\frac{1}{3}}}{1+x^{\frac{1}{3}}}\right)+\frac{1}{1+x^{\frac{1}{3}}}\right]+C$

19. (c) $I=\int\frac{x^{\frac{1}{2}}+x^{\frac{1}{3}}}{x^{\frac{5}{4}}-x^{\frac{7}{6}}}dx$

Let $x=t^{12}, dx=12t^{11}dt$

$\therefore\ I=\int\frac{t^6+t^4}{t^{15}-t^{14}}12t^{11}dt=12\int\frac{t^{15}(t^2+1)}{t^{14}(t-1)}dt$

$=12\int\frac{(t^3+t)}{t-1}dt=12\left[\int(t^2+t+2)dt+2\int\frac{dt}{t-1}\right]$

$=4t^3+6t^2+24t+24\ln|t-1|+C$

$=4x^{\frac{1}{4}}+6x^{\frac{1}{6}}+24x^{\frac{1}{12}}+24\ln\left|x^{\frac{1}{12}}-1\right|+C$

20. (a) $I=\int\frac{x^{\frac{1}{2}}}{x^{\frac{3}{4}}+1}dx$

Let $x=t^4, dx=4t^3dt$

$\Rightarrow\ I=\int\frac{t^2}{t^3+1}4t^3dt=4\int\frac{t^5}{t^3+1}dt=4\left[\int t^2dt-\int\frac{t^2}{t^3+1}dt\right]$

$=\frac{4}{3}t^3-\frac{4}{3}\ln|t^3+1|+C=\frac{4}{3}x^{\frac{3}{4}}-\frac{4}{3}\ln\left|x^{\frac{3}{4}}+1\right|+C$

SECTION–VII: (COLUMN MATCHING)

1. (i) →(b); (ii) →(c); (iii) →(a); (iv) →(c)

(i) $I=\int\frac{\sin x-\cos x}{|\sin x-\cos x|}dx=\int\frac{\frac{1}{\sqrt{2}}\sin x-\frac{1}{\sqrt{2}}\cos x}{\left|\frac{1}{\sqrt{2}}\sin x-\frac{1}{\sqrt{2}}\cos x\right|}dx$

$=\int\frac{\sin\left(x-\frac{\pi}{4}\right)}{\left|\sin\left(x-\frac{\pi}{4}\right)\right|}dx$

For $\frac{\pi}{4}<x<\frac{3\pi}{8}\Rightarrow 0<x-\frac{\pi}{4}<\frac{\pi}{4}$

$\Rightarrow\sin\left(x-\frac{\pi}{4}\right)>0$

$\Rightarrow\left|\sin\left(x-\frac{\pi}{4}\right)\right|=\sin\left(x-\frac{\pi}{4}\right)$

$\Rightarrow I=\int dx=x+C\ \therefore$ (i) → (b)

(ii) $I=\int\frac{x^2dx}{(x^3+1)(x^3+2)}$

Let $x^3=t, 3x^2dx=dt$

$\Rightarrow I=\frac{1}{3}\int\frac{dt}{(t+1)(t+2)}=\frac{1}{3}\left[\int\frac{dt}{t+1}-\int\frac{dt}{t+2}\right]$

$=\frac{1}{3}\ln\left(\frac{t+1}{t+2}\right)+C=\frac{1}{3}\ln\left|\frac{x^3+1}{x^3+2}\right|+C$

Hence, $f(x)=\ln|x|\ \therefore$ (ii) →(c)

(iii) $I=\int\underbrace{\sin^{-1}x}_{I}.\underbrace{\cos^{-1}x}_{II}dx=\sin^{-1}x\int\cos^{-1}x\,dx$

$-\int\frac{1}{\sqrt{1-x^2}}\left(\int\cos^{-1}x\,dx\right)dx$

$I_1=\int\underbrace{\cos^{-1}x}_{I}dx=x\cos^{-1}x+\int\frac{x}{\sqrt{1-x^2}}dx$

$=x\cos^{-1}x-\sqrt{1-x^2}$

$\Rightarrow I=\sin^{-1}x\left(x\cos^{-1}x-\sqrt{1-x^2}\right)$

$-\int\underbrace{\frac{x}{\sqrt{1-x^2}}}_{I}.\underbrace{\cos^{-1}x}_{II}+\int dx$

$=\sin^{-1}x\left[x\left(\frac{\pi}{2}-\sin^{-1}x\right)-\sqrt{1-x^2}\right]$

$-\left[\cos^{-1}x\left(-\sqrt{1-x^2}\right)-\int\frac{-1}{\sqrt{1-x^2}}\left(-\sqrt{1-x^2}\right)dx\right]+x+C$

$=\sin^{-1}x\left(\frac{x\pi}{2}-x\sin^{-1}x-\sqrt{1-x^2}\right)$

$+\left(\cos^{-1}x\right)\sqrt{1-x^2}+2x+C$

$=\sin^{-1}x\left(\frac{\pi}{2}x-x\sin^{-1}x-2\sqrt{1-x^2}\right)$

$+\frac{\pi}{2}\sqrt{1-x^2}+2x+C$

Comparing, $f^{-1}(x)=\sin^{-1}(x), f(x)=\sin x$

$\therefore$ (iii) →(a)

(iv) $I=\int\frac{dx}{x\,f(x)}=f(f(x))+C$

$\Rightarrow f(x)=\ln|x|$

$\therefore$ (iv) →(c)

2. (i) →(c); (ii) →(a); (iii) →(b); (iv) →(d)

(i) $I=\int\frac{\cos x}{2+\cos x}dx+\int\frac{\sin^2 x}{(2+\cos x)^2}dx$

$\Rightarrow I_1=\int\frac{\sin^2 x}{(2+\cos x)^2}dx=\int -\sin x\frac{-\sin x}{(2+\cos x)^2}dx$

$=-\sin x\left(\frac{-1}{2+\cos x}\right)-\int(-\cos x)\left(\frac{-1}{2+\cos x}\right)dx$

$=\frac{\sin x}{2+\cos x}-\int\frac{\cos x}{2+\cos x}dx+C$

$\therefore\ I=\frac{\sin x}{2+\cos x}+C\ \therefore$ (i) →(c)

(ii) $I=\int\frac{1}{x+x^{\frac{7}{2}}}dx$

Let $x=t^2\Rightarrow dx=2t\,dt$

$\Rightarrow I=\int\frac{2t\,dt}{t^2+t^7}=2\int\frac{dt}{t^6\left(1+\frac{1}{t^5}\right)}$

Let $1+\frac{1}{t^5}=m\Rightarrow\frac{-5}{t^6}dt=dm$

$=-\frac{2}{5}\int\frac{dm}{m}=-\frac{2}{5}\ln|m|+C=-\frac{2}{5}\ln\left|1+\frac{1}{x^{\frac{5}{2}}}\right|+C$

$=\frac{2}{5}\ln\left|\frac{x^{\frac{5}{2}}}{x^{\frac{5}{2}}+1}\right|+C$

$\Rightarrow a=\frac{2}{5},k=\frac{5}{2},a+k=\frac{29}{10}\ \therefore$ (ii) →(a)

(iii) $I=2\int\frac{(\tan x-\cot x)(\tan^2 x+\cot^2 x+2\tan x\cot x)}{\sec^2 x+\operatorname{cosec}^2 x}dx$

$=2\int\frac{(\tan x-\cot x)(\tan^2 x+\cot^2 x+2\tan x\cot x)}{2+\tan^2 x+\cot^2 x}dx$

Let $2+\tan^2 x+\cot^2 x=t$

$\Rightarrow dt=2\left(\tan x\sec^2 x-\cot x\operatorname{cosec}^2 x\right)dx$

$=2\left(\tan x+\tan^3 x-\cot x-\cot^3 x\right)dx$

$$= 2\left[\frac{(\tan x - \cot x) + (\tan x - \cot x)}{(\tan^2 x + \cot^2 x + \tan x \cot x)}\right]dx$$

$$= 2(\tan x - \cot x)(\tan^2 x + \cot^2 x + 2\tan x \cot x)dx$$

$$\therefore \quad I = \int \frac{dt}{t} = \ln|t| + C = \ln|2 + \tan^2 x + \cot^2 x| + C$$

$\therefore$ (iii) →(b)

(iv) $I = \int \frac{dx}{\sin^2 x + \sin 2x} = \int \frac{\sec^2 x\,dx}{\tan^2 x + 2\tan x} = \int \frac{dt}{t(t+2)}$

$$= \frac{1}{2}\left[\int \frac{dt}{t} - \int \frac{dt}{t+2}\right]$$

Let $t = \tan x \quad dt = \sec^2 x\,dx$

$$\therefore \quad I = \frac{1}{2}\ln\left|\frac{t}{t+2}\right| + C = \frac{1}{2}\ln\left|\frac{\tan x}{\tan x + 2}\right| + C$$ $\therefore$ (iv) →(d)

3. (i) →(a); (ii) →(a); (iii) →(c); (iv) →(d)

(i) $I = f(x) = \int \frac{x + \sin x}{1 + \cos x}dx$

$$= \frac{1}{2}\int x\sec^2\frac{x}{2}dx + \frac{1}{2}\int \sin x \sec^2\frac{x}{2}dx$$

$$= x\tan\frac{x}{2} - \int \tan\frac{x}{2}dx + \int \tan\frac{x}{2}dx + C$$

$$= x\tan\frac{x}{2} + C; f(0) = C = 0$$

$$\therefore \quad f(x) = x\tan\frac{x}{2} \quad \Rightarrow \quad f\left(\frac{\pi}{2}\right) = \frac{\pi}{2}\tan\frac{\pi}{4} = \frac{\pi}{2}$$

$\therefore$ (i) →(a)

(ii) $F(x) = \int e^{\sin^{-1}x}\left(1 - \frac{x}{\sqrt{1-x^2}}\right)dx$

$$= \int \underbrace{e^{\sin^{-1}x}}_{I}dx - \int \underbrace{e^{\sin^{-1}x}}_{I}.\frac{x}{\sqrt{1-x^2}}dx$$

$$\Rightarrow \quad I_1 = \int e^{\sin^{-1}x}dx = e^{\sin^{-1}x}(x) - \int \underbrace{e^{\sin^{-1}x}}_{I}\underbrace{\frac{x}{\sqrt{1-x^2}}}_{II}dx$$

$$= xe^{\sin^{-1}x} - \left[e^{\sin^{-1}x}\left(-\sqrt{1-x^2}\right) - \int e^{\sin^{-1}x}\frac{1}{\sqrt{1-x^2}}\left(-\sqrt{1-x^2}\right)dx\right]$$

$$\Rightarrow \quad I_1 = xe^{\sin^{-1}x} + \sqrt{1-x^2}e^{\sin^{-1}x} - I_1$$

$$\Rightarrow \quad I_1 = \frac{1}{2}e^{\sin^{-1}x}\left(x + \sqrt{1-x^2}\right)$$

$$\Rightarrow \quad I_2 = \int \underbrace{e^{\sin^{-1}x}}_{I}.\underbrace{\frac{x}{\sqrt{1-x^2}}}_{II}dx = e^{\sin} \quad \left(-\sqrt{\quad -x^2}\right)$$

$$-\int e^{\sin^{-1}x}\frac{1}{\sqrt{1-x^2}}\left(-\sqrt{1-x^2}\right)dx$$

$$\Rightarrow \quad I_2 = -\sqrt{1-x^2}e^{\sin^{-1}x} + I_1$$

$$\therefore \quad I = I_1 - I_2 = \sqrt{1-x^2}e^{\sin^{-1}x} + C$$

$$\Rightarrow \quad F\left(\frac{1}{2}\right) = \frac{\sqrt{3}}{2}e^{\sin^{-1}\frac{1}{2}} = \frac{\sqrt{3}}{2}e^{\frac{\pi}{6}}, \text{ Comparing } k = \frac{\pi}{2}$$

$\therefore$ (ii) →(a)

(iii) $F(x) = \int \frac{dx}{(x^2+1)(x^2+9)} = \frac{1}{8}\left[\int \frac{dx}{x^2+1} - \int \frac{dx}{x^2+9}\right]$

$$= \frac{1}{8}\tan^{-1}x - \frac{1}{24}\tan^{-1}\left(\frac{x}{3}\right) + C$$

$$\Rightarrow \quad F\left(\sqrt{3}\right) = \frac{\pi}{24} - \frac{\pi}{144} = \frac{5\pi}{144}, \text{ Comparing, } k = \frac{\pi}{4}$$

$\therefore$ (iii) →(c)

(iv) $F(x) = \int \frac{\sqrt{\tan x}}{\sin x \cos x}dx,\ F(0) = 0$

$$= \int \frac{\sqrt{\tan x}}{\tan x}\sec^2 x\,dx = \int t^{-\frac{1}{2}}dt;\ t = \tan x$$

$$\Rightarrow dt = \sec^2 x\,dx$$

$$2t^{\frac{1}{2}} + C = 2\sqrt{\tan x} + C;\ f(0) = C = 0$$

$$\therefore F(x) = 2\sqrt{\tan x}$$

$$F\left(\frac{\pi}{4}\right) = 2 \text{ Hence, } k = \pi$$

$\therefore$ (iv) →(d)

4. (i) →(a); (ii) →(b); (iii) →(c); (iv) →(d)

(i) $I = \int \sqrt{\frac{x}{a+x}}dx$

Let $x = a\tan^2\theta;\ dx = 2a\tan\theta\sec^2\theta\,d\theta$

$$= \int \frac{\tan\theta\, 2a.\tan\theta\sec^2\theta\,d\theta}{\sqrt{1+\tan^2\theta}} = \int \frac{2at^2}{\sqrt{1+t^2}}dt; t = \tan\theta,$$

$$dt = \sec^2\theta\,d\theta$$

$$2a\left[\int \sqrt{1+t^2}dt - \int \frac{dt}{\sqrt{t^2+1}}\right]$$

$$= 2a\left[\frac{t\sqrt{t^2+1}}{2} + \frac{1}{2}\ln\left|t + \sqrt{t^2+1}\right| - \ln\left|t + \sqrt{t^2+1}\right|\right]$$

$\therefore$ (i) →(a)

(ii) $I = \int \sqrt{\frac{x-a}{b-x}}dx$

Let $x = a\cos^2\theta + b\sin^2\theta \Rightarrow dx = 2\sin\theta\cos\theta(b-a)d\theta$

$$= \int \sqrt{\frac{(b-a)\sin^2\theta}{(b-a)\cos^2\theta}}2\sin\theta\cos\theta(b-a)d\theta$$

$$= 2(b-a)\int \sin^2\theta\,d\theta = (b-a)\int (1-\cos 2\theta)d\theta$$

$$= (b-a)\left[\theta - \frac{\sin 2\theta}{2}\right] + C;\ \theta = \sin^{-1}\sqrt{\frac{x-a}{b-a}}$$

$\therefore$ (ii) →(b)

(iii) $I=\int\sqrt{\frac{x-a}{x-b}}\,dx$

Let $x=a\sec^2\theta+b\tan^2\theta$

$\Rightarrow\ dx=2\sec^2\theta\tan\theta(a+b)d\theta$

$\Rightarrow\ I=\int\sqrt{\frac{(a+b)\tan^2\theta}{(a+b)\tan^2\theta+(a-b)}}\,2\sec^2\theta\tan\theta(a+b)d\theta$

$=2(a+b)\int\frac{t^2}{\sqrt{t^2+\frac{a-b}{a+b}}}dt$

$\Rightarrow\ t=\tan\theta\Rightarrow dt=\sec^2\theta\,d\theta$

$\Rightarrow\ 2(a+b)\left[\int\sqrt{t^2+\frac{a-b}{a+b}}\,dt-\frac{a-b}{a+b}\int\frac{dt}{\sqrt{t^2+\frac{a-b}{a+b}}}\right]$

$\Rightarrow\ 2(a+b)\left[\frac{t}{2}\sqrt{t^2+\frac{a-b}{a+b}}+\ln\left|t+\sqrt{t^2+\frac{a-b}{a+b}}\right|\right.$

$\left.-\frac{a-b}{a+b}\ln\left|t+\sqrt{t^2+\frac{a-b}{a+b}}\right|\right]+C;$

$t=\tan\theta=\sqrt{\frac{x-a}{a+b}}$

$\therefore$ (iii) $\to$(c)

(iv) $\mathrm{I}=\int\frac{1}{\sqrt{(\mathrm{x}-\mathrm{a})(\mathrm{b}-\mathrm{x})}}\mathrm{dt}$

Let $x-a=t^2, b-x=b-a-t^2$

$dx=2t\,dt,$

$\Rightarrow\ I=\int\frac{2t\,dt}{t\sqrt{b-a-t^2}}=2\int\frac{dt}{\sqrt{b-a-t^2}}$

$=\frac{2}{\sqrt{b-a}}\sin^{-1}\left(\frac{t}{\sqrt{b-a}}\right)+C$

$=\frac{2}{\sqrt{b-a}}\sin^{-1}\sqrt{\frac{x-a}{b-a}}+C$

$\therefore$ (iv) $\to$(d)

5. (i) →(b); (ii) →(d); (iii) →(a); (iv) →(c)

(i) $I=\int\frac{\sin^8x-\cos^8x}{1-2\sin^2x\cos^2x}dx$

$=\int\frac{(\sin^4x+\cos^4x)(\sin^2x-\cos^2x)}{1-2\sin^2x\cos^2x}dx$

$=\int\frac{\left[(\sin^2x+\cos^2x)^2-2\sin^2x\cos^2x\right](\sin^2x-\cos^2x)}{(\sin^2x+\cos^2x)^2-2\sin^2x\cos^2x}dx$

$=-\int\cos2x\,dx=\frac{-\sin2x}{2}+C$

$\therefore$ (i) $\to$(b)

(ii) $I=\int\frac{\cos5x+\cos4x}{1-2\cos3x}dx=\int\frac{2\cos\frac{9}{2}x\cos\frac{x}{2}}{3-4\cos^2\frac{3}{2}x}dx$

$=2\int\frac{\left(4\cos^3\frac{3x}{2}-3\cos\frac{3x}{2}\right)\cos\frac{x}{2}}{3-4\cos^2\frac{3x}{2}}dx$

$=-2\int\cos\frac{3x}{2}\cos\frac{x}{2}dx=-\int(\cos2x+\cos x)dx$

$=-\frac{\sin2x}{2}-\sin x+C$

$\therefore$ (ii) $\to$(d)

(iii) $I=\int\sqrt{\frac{\cos x-\cos^3x}{1-\cos^3x}}dx=\int\sqrt{\frac{\cos x}{1-\cos^3x}}\sin x\,dx$

$=-\int\sqrt{\frac{t}{1-t^3}}dt; t=\cos x$

$\Rightarrow dt=-\sin x\,dx$

Let $t=m^{\frac{2}{3}}\Rightarrow dt=\frac{2}{3}m^{-\frac{1}{3}}dm$

$\Rightarrow\ I=-\frac{2}{3}\int\frac{m^{\frac{1}{3}}m^{-\frac{1}{3}}}{\sqrt{1-m^2}}dm=-\frac{2}{3}\sin^{-1}m+C$

$=-\frac{2}{3}\sin^{-1}\left(\cos^{\frac{3}{2}}x\right)+C$

$\therefore$ (iii) $\to$(a)

(iv) $I=\int\frac{dx}{\sin^6x+\cos^6x}$

$=\int\frac{dx}{(\sin^2x)^3+(\cos^2x)^3}$

$=\int\frac{dx}{(\sin^2x+\cos^2x)(\sin^4x+\cos^4x-\sin^2x\cos^2x)}$

$=\int\frac{dx}{1-3\sin^2x\cos^2x}=\int\frac{\sec^4x}{\sec^4x-3\tan^2x}dx$

$=\int\frac{(1+\tan^2x)\sec^2x}{1+\tan^4x-\tan^2x}dx=\int\frac{1+t^2}{1+t^4-t^2}dt$

$=\int\frac{\left(1+\frac{1}{t^2}\right)dt}{\left(t-\frac{1}{t}\right)^2+1}=\int\frac{dm}{m^2+1}=\tan^{-1}m+C$

$=\tan^{-1}\left(t-\frac{1}{t}\right)+C=\tan^{-1}(\tan x-\cot x)+C$

$\therefore$ (iv) $\to$(c)

SECTION–VIII: (INTEGER TYPE)

1. $I = \int \frac{dx}{1+\sqrt{(x+1)^2+1}}$

Put $1+\sqrt{(x+1)^2+1} = t - x$

$\Rightarrow (x+1) + \sqrt{(x+1)^2+1} = t$

$\Rightarrow \left[1+\frac{1}{2\sqrt{(x+1)^2+1}} \times 2(x+1)\right] dx = dt$

$\Rightarrow \left[1+\frac{(x+1)}{\sqrt{(x+1)^2+1}}\right] dx = dt$

$\Rightarrow \frac{1}{\sqrt{(x+1)^2+1}} dx = dt$

$\therefore\ I = \int \frac{\sqrt{(x+1)^2+1}}{t\left(1+\sqrt{(x+1)^2+1}\right)} dt$

Also $\sqrt{(x+1)^2+1} = t-(x+1)$

$\Rightarrow (x+1)^2 + 1 = t^2 + (x+1)^2 - 2t(x+1)$

$\Rightarrow 2t(x+1) = t^2 - 1$

$\Rightarrow (x+1) = \frac{t^2-1}{2t}$

$\therefore\ I = \int \frac{\sqrt{\left(\frac{t^2-1}{2t}\right)^2+1}}{t\left(1+\sqrt{\left(\frac{t^2-1}{2t}\right)^2+1}\right)} dt$

$\Rightarrow I = \int \frac{(t^2+1)\,dt}{t(2t+t^2+1)} = \int \frac{(t^2+1)\,dt}{t(t+1)}$

Let $\frac{t^2+1}{t(t+1)^2} = \frac{A}{t} + \frac{B}{(t+1)} + \frac{C}{(t+1)^2}$

$\Rightarrow t^2 + 1 = A(t+1)^2 + Bt(t+1) + Ct$

At, $t = 0$

$1 = A;$

At, $t = -1;$

$2 = -C \qquad \Rightarrow C = -2$

At $t = 1;\qquad 2 = 4A + 2B + C$

$\Rightarrow 2 = 4 + 2B - 2 \qquad \Rightarrow B = 0$

$\therefore\ I = \int\left[\frac{1}{t} + \frac{-2}{(t+1)^2}\right] dt = \ln|t| - 2\left(\frac{-1}{(t+1)}\right) + C$

$= \ln\left|(x+1)+\sqrt{(x+1)^2+1}\right| +$

$2\left[\frac{1}{(x+2)+\sqrt{(x+1)^2+1}}\right] + C$

$= \ln\left|(x+1)+\sqrt{(x+1)^2+1}\right| + C$

$+\ 2\left[\frac{(x+2)-\sqrt{(x+1)^2+1}}{x^2+4x+4-x^2-2x-2}\right] + C$

$= \ln\left|(x+1)+\sqrt{(x+1)^2+1}\right| + C$

$+\left[\frac{(x+2)-\sqrt{(x+1)^2+1}}{(x+1)}\right] + C$

$= \ln\left|(x+1)+\sqrt{(x+1)^2+1}\right|$

$-\left[\frac{\sqrt{(x+1)^2+1}-1}{(x+1)}\right] + (C+1)$

$\Rightarrow \lambda = 3$

2. $I = \int \frac{\cos^3 x}{(\sin^4 x + 3\sin^2 x + 1).\tan^{-1}(\sin x + \operatorname{cosec} x)} dx$

Put $\tan^{-1}(\sin x + \operatorname{cosec} x) = t$

$\Rightarrow \frac{1}{1+(\sin x + \operatorname{cosec} x)^2}.(\cos x - \operatorname{cosec} x \cot x)dx$

$\Rightarrow \left[\left(\frac{1}{3+\sin^2 x + \frac{1}{\sin^2 x}}\right)\left(\cos\left(1-\frac{1}{\sin^2 x}\right)\right) dx = dt\right]$

$\Rightarrow \frac{-\cos^3 x}{(\sin^4 x + 3\sin^2 x + 1)} = dt$

$\therefore\ I = \int \frac{-dt}{t} = -\ln|t| + C = -\ln|\tan^{-1}(\sin x + \operatorname{cosec} x)| + C$

$\Rightarrow \lambda = 4$

3. $I = \int \frac{(\sin x)(\cos x)^{-5/2}}{\sqrt{\sin x + 3\cos x} + \sqrt{\sin x + 4\cos x}} dx$

$= \int \frac{\frac{\sin x}{\sqrt{\cos x}}.\frac{1}{\cos^2 x}}{\sqrt{\sin x + 3\cos x} + \sqrt{\sin x + 4\cos x}} dx$

$= \int \frac{\sqrt{\tan x}\sec^2 x}{\sqrt{1+3\cot x} + \sqrt{1+4\cot x}} dx$

Put $\sqrt{\tan x} = t \qquad \Rightarrow \frac{1}{2\sqrt{\tan x}}\sec^2 x\,dx = dt$

$\Rightarrow \sec^2 x\,dx = 2\sqrt{\tan x}\,dt = 2t\,dt$

$\therefore\ I = \int \frac{(t)(2t)}{\sqrt{1+(3/t^2)} + \sqrt{1+(4/t^2)}} dt$

Put $t^2 = z \qquad \Rightarrow 2t\,dt = dz$

$\therefore\ I = \int \frac{z\,dz}{\sqrt{z+3} + \sqrt{t^2+4}} = \int \frac{z\left(\sqrt{z+3}-\sqrt{z+4}\right)}{-1} dz$

$= \int z\left(\sqrt{z+4} - \sqrt{z+3}\right) dz$

$= \int z\sqrt{z+4}\,dz - \int z\sqrt{z+3}\,dz$

$$= \int\left((z+4)^{3/2} - 4\sqrt{z+4}\right)dz$$
$$- \int\left((z+3)^{3/2} - 3\sqrt{z+3}\right)dz$$
$$= 2(z+4)^{5/2} - 4\left(\frac{2}{3}\right)(z+4)^{3/2} + C$$
$$= \frac{2}{5}\left[\left(\tan x+4\right)^{5/2} - \left(\tan x+3\right)^{5/2}\right]$$
$$-\frac{2}{3}\left[4\left(\tan x+4\right)^{3/2} - 3\left(\tan x+3\right)^{3/2}\right] + C$$

$\Rightarrow \dfrac{\lambda}{740} = \dfrac{2}{5}$; $\mu = 2$ $\quad\Rightarrow \lambda = 296, \mu = 2$

$\Rightarrow \dfrac{\lambda}{u} = 148$

4. $I = \int \dfrac{x^3}{x^{16}+4}dx$

Put $x^4 = \sqrt{2}\, t$

$\Rightarrow x^3\, dx = \dfrac{\sqrt{2}}{4}dt$

$$\therefore \quad I = \int \frac{\sqrt{2}/4}{4t^4+4}dt = \frac{\sqrt{2}}{16}\int\frac{dt}{t^4+1}dt = \frac{\sqrt{2}}{16}\times\frac{1}{2}\int\frac{2\,dt}{t^4+1}$$
$$= \frac{1}{16\sqrt{2}}\int\frac{(t^2+1)-(t^2-1)}{t^4+1}dt$$
$$= \frac{1}{16\sqrt{2}}\int\frac{(t^2+1)}{t^4+1}dt - \frac{1}{16\sqrt{2}}\int\frac{(t^2-1)}{t^4+1}dt$$
$$= \frac{1}{16\sqrt{2}}\int\frac{1+\frac{1}{t^2}}{t^2+\frac{1}{t^2}}dt - \frac{1}{16\sqrt{2}}\int\frac{1-\frac{1}{t^2}}{t^2+\frac{1}{t^2}}dt$$

In first integral put $t - 1/t = z$ and $t + 1/t = u$ in second integral.

$\Rightarrow \left(1+\dfrac{1}{t^2}\right)dt = dz$ and $\left(1-\dfrac{1}{t^2}\right)dt - du$

$$\Rightarrow \quad I = \frac{1}{16\sqrt{2}}\int\frac{dz}{u^2-2} - \frac{1}{16\sqrt{2}}\int\frac{du}{z^2+2}$$
$$\Rightarrow \quad I = \frac{1}{16\sqrt{2}}\times\frac{1}{2\sqrt{z}}\ln\left|\frac{u-\sqrt{2}}{u+\sqrt{2}}\right| - \frac{1}{16\sqrt{2}}\times\frac{1}{2}\tan^{-1}\left(\frac{z}{\sqrt{2}}\right) + C$$
$$\Rightarrow \quad I = \frac{1}{64}\ln\left|\frac{u-\sqrt{2}}{u+\sqrt{2}}\right| - \frac{1}{32}\tan^{-1}\left(\frac{z}{\sqrt{2}}\right) + C$$
$$\Rightarrow \quad I = \frac{1}{(-32)}\tan^{-1}\left(\frac{z}{\sqrt{2}}\right) - \frac{1}{(-64)}\ln\left|\frac{u-\sqrt{2}}{u+\sqrt{2}}\right| + C$$

$\Rightarrow \lambda = -32, \mu = -64$

$\Rightarrow \lambda + \mu = -96$

5. $I = \int \dfrac{\cos^2 x \sin x}{\sin x - \cos x}dx$

$$\Rightarrow \quad I = \frac{1}{2}\int\frac{(1+\cos 2x)\sin x}{(\sin x - \cos x)}dx$$
$$= \frac{1}{2}\int\frac{\sin x}{\sin x - \cos x}dx + \frac{1}{2}\int\frac{\cos 2x \sin x}{\sin x - \cos x}dx$$
$$= \frac{1}{2}\int\frac{\sin x + \cos x - \cos x}{\sin x - \cos x}dx + \frac{1}{2}\int\frac{(\cos^2 x \sin^2 x)}{(\sin x - \cos x)}dx$$
$$= \frac{1}{2}\ln|\sin x - \cos x| + \frac{1}{2}\int\frac{\cos x}{\cos x - \sin x}dx$$
$$- \frac{1}{2}\int(\cos x + \sin x).\sin x\, dx$$
$$= \frac{1}{2}\ln|\sin x - \cos x| - \frac{1}{4}\int\sin 2x\, dx$$
$$- \frac{1}{4}\int 2\sin^2 x\, dx + \frac{1}{2}\int\frac{\cos x}{\cos x - \sin x}dx$$
$$= \frac{1}{2}\ln|\sin x - \cos x| + \frac{1}{8}\cos 2x - \frac{1}{4}\int(1-\cos 2x)dx$$
$$+ \frac{1}{2}\int\frac{\cos x}{\cos x - \sin x}dx$$

Put $\cos x = A(\cos x + \sin x) + B(\cos x - \sin x)$

$\Rightarrow I = A + B;\ O = A - B;\ \Rightarrow A = B = 1/2$

$$\therefore \quad I = \frac{1}{2}\ln|\sin x - \cos x| + \frac{1}{8}\cos 2x - \frac{1}{4}x + \frac{1}{8}\sin 2x$$
$$+ \frac{1}{4}\int\frac{\cos x + \sin x}{\cos x - \sin x}dx + \frac{1}{4}\int 1.dx$$

$\Rightarrow$ $1/2 \ln|\sin x - \cos x| + 1/8 \cos 2x + 1/8 \sin 2x - 1/4 \ln|\sin x - \cos x| + C$

$= 1/4 \ln|\sin x - \cos x| + 1/8 (\sin 2x + \cos 2x) + C$

$\Rightarrow \lambda = 1, \mu = 8 \qquad \Rightarrow \mu - \lambda = 7$

6. $F(x) = \int \dfrac{1}{3+5\sin x+3\cos x}dx$;

$$F(0) = 0 = \int\frac{dx}{3+5\left(\frac{2\tan(x/2)}{1+\tan^2(x/2)}\right)+3\left(\frac{1-\tan^2(x/2)}{1+\tan^2(x/2)}\right)}$$
$$I = \int\frac{\sec^2 x/2}{10\left(\tan\frac{x}{2}\right)+6}dx = \int\frac{\frac{1}{2}\sec^2\frac{x}{2}}{\left(5\tan\frac{x}{2}+3\right)}dx$$

Put $\tan x/2 = t \qquad \Rightarrow \dfrac{1}{2}\sec^2\dfrac{x}{2}dx = dt$

$$\Rightarrow \quad F(x) = \int\frac{dt}{5t+3}$$
$$\Rightarrow \quad F(x) = \frac{1}{5}\ln|5t+3| + C = \frac{1}{5}\ln\left|5\tan\frac{x}{2}+3\right| + C$$

As $F(0) = 0$

$\Rightarrow 0 = \dfrac{1}{5}\ln|3| + C \qquad \Rightarrow C = -\dfrac{1}{5}\ln 3$

$$\therefore \quad F(x) = \frac{1}{5}\ln\left|\frac{5\tan\frac{x}{2}+3}{3}\right|$$
$$\therefore \quad F\left(\frac{\pi}{2}\right) = \frac{1}{5}\ln\left|\frac{8}{3}\right| \qquad \Rightarrow F\left(\frac{\pi}{2}\right) - \frac{1}{5}\ln\left(\frac{8}{3}\right) = 0$$
$$\Rightarrow \quad F\left(\frac{\pi}{2}\right) - \frac{1}{5}\ln\left(\frac{8}{3}\right) + 2013 = 2013$$

CHAPTER 2

Definite Integration

INTRODUCTION

So far we have integrated the given functions to find their integrals. The integral we find is also a function of the same independent variable.

Now, because the independent variable can take different values with different units, the given function and its integral also have different values and units. Thus, if the given function represents a quantity, its integral also represents a quantity.

Let us be more specific. Say a function $s(t)$ represents position, where t is an independent variable . $\frac{ds}{dt}$ is represented by $v(t)$ being a function of t, v can be integrated $\int v(t)\,dt$. This represents the position with respect to time. If we know position at two different values of t, we can find the change in position between the two values.

Thus, we have found a definite quantity with definite unit by integrating a function between two definite values of the independent variable. The integral $\int_{t=t_1}^{t=t_2} f(t)\,dt$, therefore yields a definite value and is called a definite integral.

Now some questions arise; will every indefinite integral give a definite quantity if two specific values of the independent variable are taken? If the concept of definite integral only involves finding value of integral at two different points, then why a complete chapter is devoted to this?

Note that while finding the indefinite integral we always add a constant with the answer. This constant was the reason for non-definiteness of the answer. But while finding the definite integral, this constant gets eliminated. That is why we get a definite answer. The art of eliminating this constant involves many techniques. In this chapter we will learn these techniques of finding the definite integral. Further, the absence of this constant gives rise to many properties of definite integrals. These properties, if intelligently applied, helps us to solve many difficult difinite integerals.

AREA AS AN ANTI-DERIVATIVE

Given a continuous function $f: f(x) > 0\ \forall\ x \in [a, b]$, the area enclosed by the curve $y = f(x)$ and x-axis between the ordinate $x = a$ to $x = t$ is an anti-derivative of $f(t)$ on $[a, b]$.

To prove that $A'(t) = f(t)$

Proof: Define an area function, $A(t)$ as region enclosed by $y = f(x)$ and the x-axis between $x = a$ to $x = t$ for $a \le t \le b$ as shown in the diagram (of moving certain area).

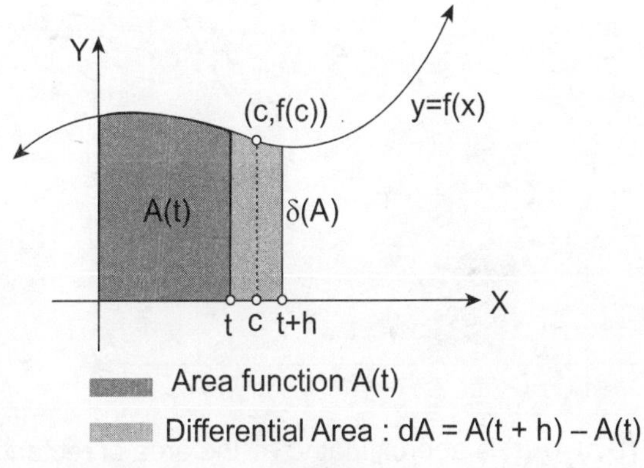

FIGURE 2.1

By mean value theorem of continuous function, there exist $c \in [t, t + h] : f(c) \cdot h = A(t + h) - A(t)$ and $f(c).h$ is the Area of rectangle $MNRS$

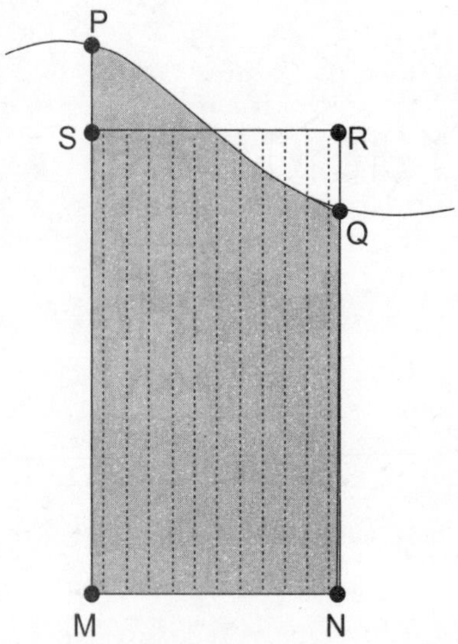

FIGURE 2.2

$\because$ $A(t+h) - A(t) = f(c).h$ = area in enclosed by curve in the interval $[t, t+h]$

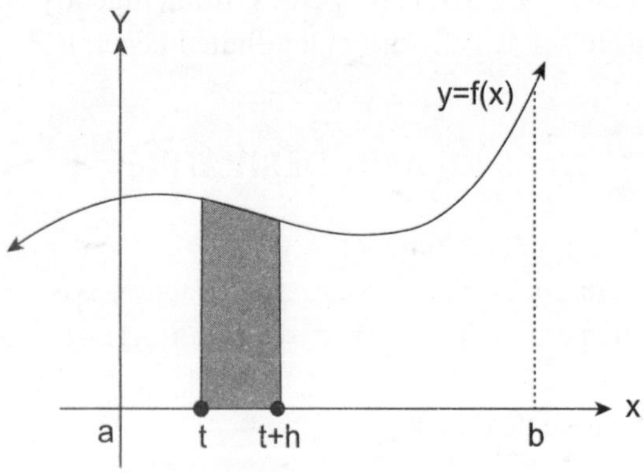

(a). A(t+h) –A(t) is the area over [t,t+h]

FIGURE 2.3

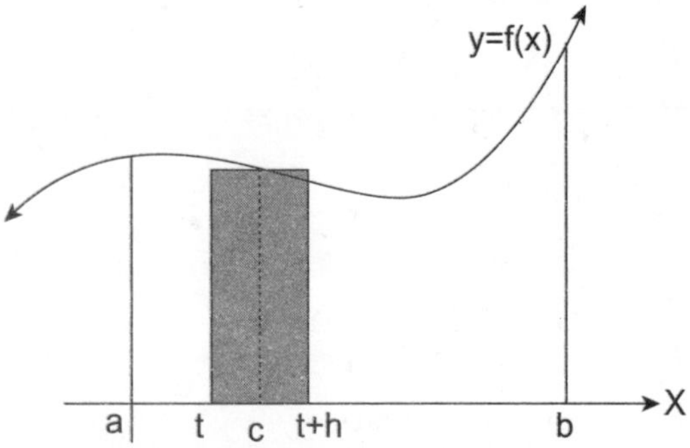

(b) A(t+h) –A(t) is approximated by the area of rectangle

FIGURE 2.4

$$\Rightarrow \quad \frac{A(t+h) - A(t)}{h} \simeq f(c)$$

Taking limit $h \to 0$, we get

$$\lim_{h \to 0} \frac{A(t+h) - A(t)}{h} = \lim_{h \to 0} \frac{h.f(c)}{h}$$

So, $A(t)$ is an anti-derivative of $f(t)$. Clearly, L.H.S is $A'(t)$ where as on R.H.S. since $f(x)$ is continuous and c is a point in $[t, t+h]$; as $h \to 0$, $c \to t$.

$\therefore \quad A'(t) = f(c) = f(t).$

$$\Rightarrow \quad A(t) = \int_a^t f(t)\, dt$$

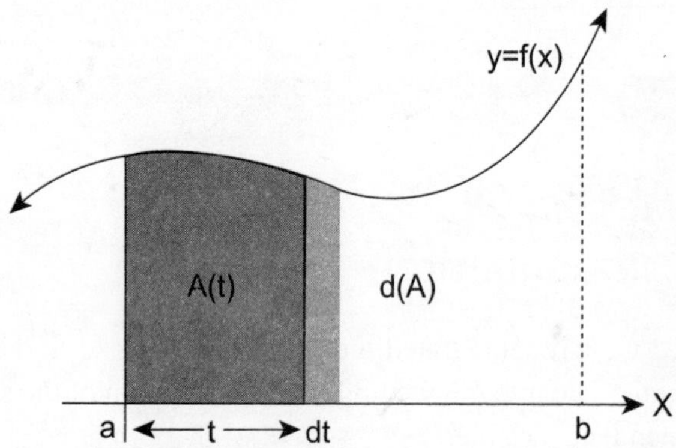

Area function ,A(t)
dA = f(t)dt
If t = a; Area = 0
& t = t; Area = A

FIGURE 2.5

Conclusion: $A = \int_0^A dA = \int_a^b f(t)dt$

Geometric Significance: $\int_a^b f(x)\, dx$; represents algebraic summation of area enclosed by $f(x)$ and x-axis between ordinate $x = a$ to $x = b$.

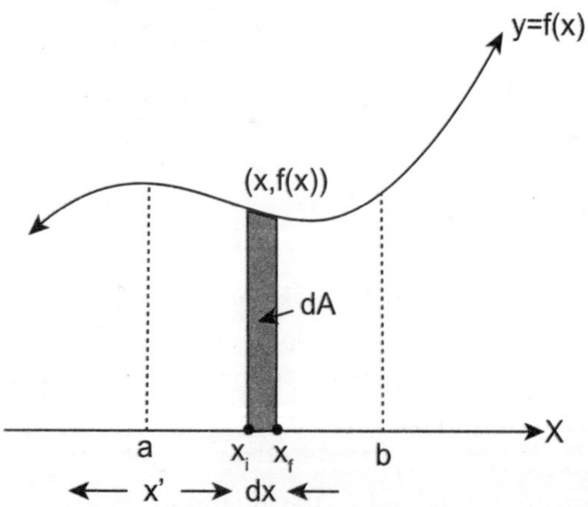

FIGURE 2.6

$\Rightarrow \quad dA = f(x) \cdot dx$

Since $dx = x_f - x_i$ (when $x_f \to x_i$)

$\Rightarrow$ sign of $dx = \begin{cases} +ve & \text{if } a < b \\ -ve & \text{if } a > b \end{cases}$

$\because$ When we move from b to a, $x_f < x_i$

$\Rightarrow$ $x_f - x_i = dx$ (–ve)

$$\Rightarrow \quad dA = \begin{cases} +\text{ve if} \begin{cases} f(x) > 0 & \text{and } a < b \\ f(x) < 0 & \text{and } a > b \end{cases} \\ -\text{ve if} \begin{cases} f(x) > 0 & \text{and } a > b \\ f(x) < 0 & \text{and } a < b \end{cases} \end{cases}$$

$\Rightarrow$ In order to obtain actual area enclosed by function and x-axis between $x = a$ and $x = b$.

$$A = \int_a^b |f(x)|\, dx \quad if \;\; a < b$$

$$= -\int_a^b |f(x)|\, dx \quad if \;\; a > b$$

$$\Rightarrow \quad A = \left| \int_a^b |f(x)|\, dx \right|$$

ILLUSTRATION 1: Evaluate $\left| \int_{-2}^{2} |2x+3|\, dx \right|$ by using the concept of area as an anti-derivative.

SOLUTION: We know that $\left| \int_a^b |f(x)|\, dx \right|$ represents the area enclosed by the function $f(x)$ with x-axis from ordinate $x = a$ to $x = b$ or the area enclosed by $|f(x)|$ x-axis and between ordinates $x = a$ and $x = b$.

Thus, $\left| \int_{-2}^{2} |2x+3|\, dx \right|$ is the area enclosed by the straight line $y = 2x + 3$ with x-axis from ordinate $x = -2$ to $x = 2$ as shown below by shaded portion.

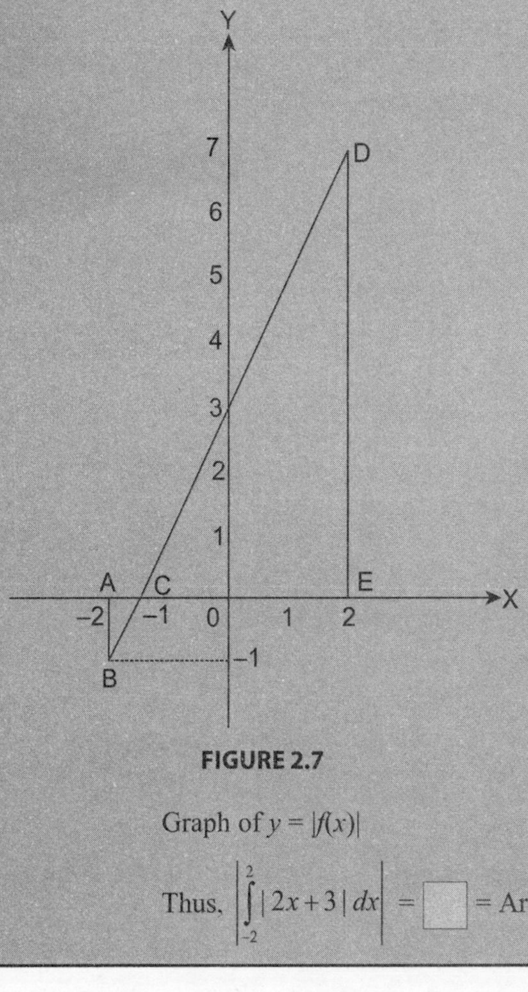

FIGURE 2.7

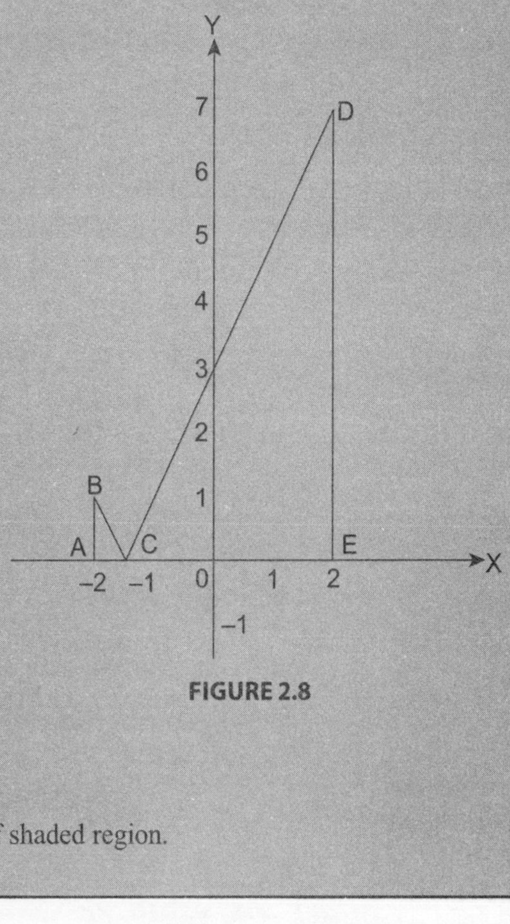

FIGURE 2.8

Graph of $y = |f(x)|$

Thus, $\left| \int_{-2}^{2} |2x+3|\, dx \right| = \square$ = Area of shaded region.

$= \text{Area of } \Delta ABC + \text{Area of } \Delta CED = \frac{1}{2}(AC)\times(AB) + \frac{1}{2}(CE)\times(DE) = \frac{1}{2}\left(\frac{1}{2}\right)\times(1) + \frac{1}{2}\left(\frac{7}{2}\right)\times(7)$

$= \frac{1}{4} + \frac{49}{4} = \frac{50}{4} = \frac{25}{2}$ square units.

ILLUSTRATION 2: Evaluate $\left|\int_{-2}^{\sqrt{2}} \sqrt{4-x^2}\,dx\right|$ by using the concept of area as an anti-derivative.

SOLUTION: Here $4 - x^2 \geq 0$ for $x \in [-2, 2]$, so $\sqrt{4-x^2}$ is defined $\forall\, x \in [-2, \sqrt{2}]$

Now $y = \sqrt{4-x^2} = f(x) = |f(x)|$

$\Rightarrow$ $x^2 + y^2 = 4$ which is a circle with radius 2 and having its centre at origin.

At $x = -2$, $y = 0$ and at $x = \sqrt{2}$, $y = \sqrt{2}$

Thus, $\left|\int_{-2}^{\sqrt{2}} \sqrt{4-x^2}\,dx\right|$ is the area bounded by circle $x^2 + y^2 = 4$, between the ordinates $x = -2$ and $x = \sqrt{2}$ and above x-axis as shown below by shaded region.

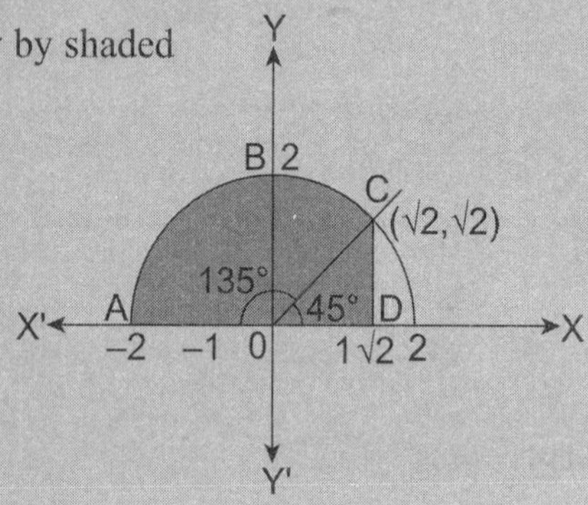

FIGURE 2.9

Thus, $\left|\int_{-2}^{\sqrt{2}} \sqrt{4-x^2}\,dx\right| = \left|\int_{-2}^{\sqrt{2}} |\sqrt{4-x^2}|\,dx\right| =$ ▇

= Area of sector $OABCO$ + area of ΔODC

$= \frac{\left(\frac{3\pi}{4}\right)}{2\pi}\left(\pi(2)^2\right) + \frac{1}{2}(OD)\times CD$

$= \frac{3\pi}{2} + \frac{1}{2}\left(\sqrt{2}\right)\left(\sqrt{2}\right) = \left(\frac{3\pi}{2} + 1\right)$ square units.

ILLUSTRATION 3: A function $f(x)$ is defined as $f(x) = \begin{cases} x+1; & -2 \leq x \leq 1 \\ 2; & 1 \leq x \leq 3 \\ 2-\sqrt{1-(x-4)^2}; & 3 \leq x \leq 5 \\ -2x+12; & 5 \leq x \leq 6 \end{cases}$. Evaluate $\left|\int_{-2}^{6} |f(x)|\,dx\right|$ by using the concept of area as an anti-derivative.

SOLUTION: Let us draw the graph of $f(x)$ between the ordinate $x = -2$ and $x = 6$ as shown below

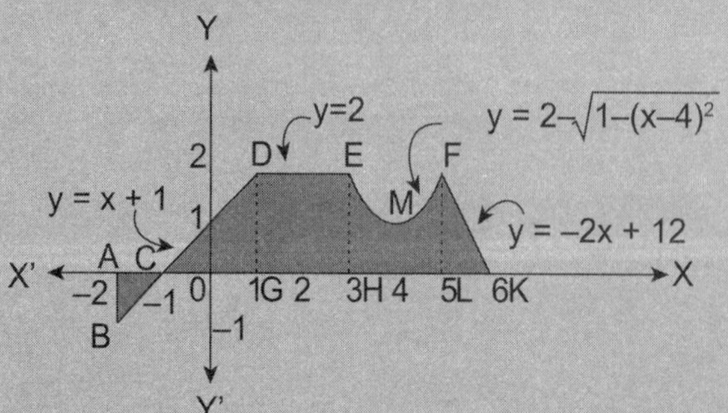

FIGURE 2.10

or

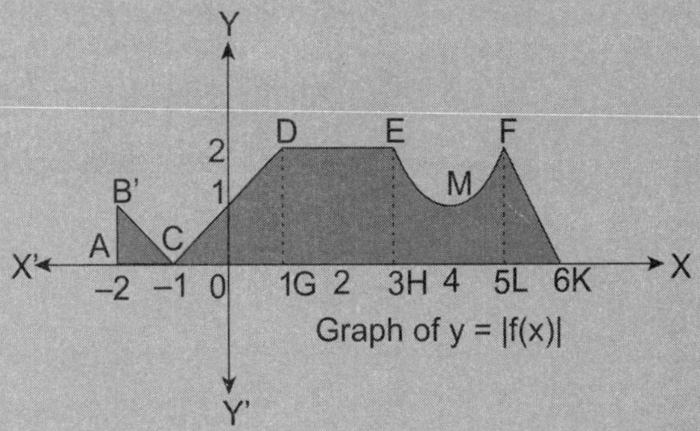

FIGURE 2.11

Clearly $\left|\int_{-2}^{6}|f(x)|dx\right|$ =Area of shaded region

= (Area of ΔABC) + (Area of ΔCGD) + (area rectangle $GHED$) + (area region $HEMFL$) + (Area of ΔLKF)

$$= \frac{1}{2}(AB') \times AC + \frac{1}{2}(CG) \times GD + (GH \times GD) + (HL \times HE - \frac{1}{2}\pi(1)^2) + \frac{1}{2}(LK)(LF)$$

$$= \frac{1}{2}(1)\times(1)+\frac{1}{2}(2)\times(2)+(2)\times 2 + \left(2\times 2-\frac{\pi}{2}\right)+\frac{1}{2}(1)(2)= \frac{(23-\pi)}{2} \text{ square units.}$$

To evaluate area bounded by a given function, *x*-axis and ordinates *x* = *a*, *x* = *b*

Since ancient times, computing of area of different geometrical figures has been a problem of theoretical and practical interest. Computing the areas of some special geometrical figures is easy by using formulae, e.g., circle, rectangle, square, trapezium, etc. But it is not so easy for most of the figures as their shapes are irregular and we have no formulae for computing their areas. Some irregular figures can be sub-divided into finite number of regions and by calculating area of each sub-region and adding these areas we can find the area of given irregular figure. For example, consider the given Fig. 2.12.

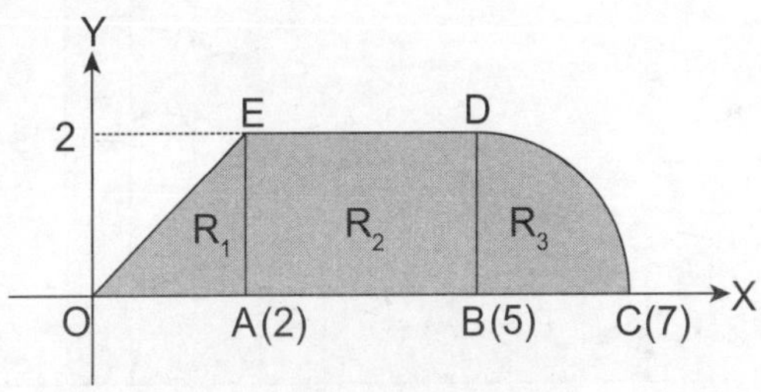

FIGURE 2.12

If we want to find the area of given Fig. 2.12, we need to divide it into three sub-regions, i.e., R_1, R_2 and R_3.

Now clearly R_1 is a right angled triangle, R_2 is a rectangle and R_3 is a quarter circle.

Thus, area of given geometrical figure

= (shaded) = (Area of region R_1) + (Area of region R_2) + (Area of region R_3)

$$= \frac{1}{2}(OA)\times AE + AB \times AE + \frac{1}{4}\pi(BC)^2$$

$$= \frac{1}{2}(2)\times(2)+(3)\times 2+\frac{1}{4}\pi(2)^2$$

$= 2 + 6 + \pi = (8 + \pi)$ square units.

However, how would you find the area bounded by parabola $y = x^2$, x-axis on the interval [0, 2]? Similarly, same problem would arise if we are to find the area bounded by cubic curve $y = x^3$, x-axis on the interval $[-a, a]$; $a > 0$.

We can sort out these problems upto some extend with the help of the following procedure.

(i) To evaluate definite integral using limit of infinite sum (*ab*-into method)

(ii) To evaluate area by using definite integral.

Consider the graph of a continuous function $y = f(x)$ having non-negative values on the interval $[a, b]$ as shown below

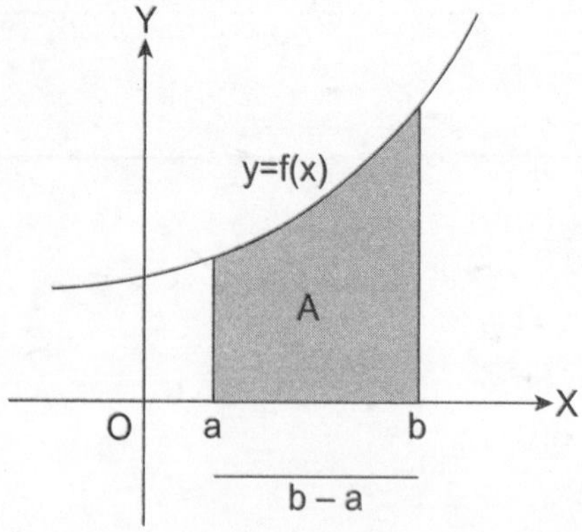

FIGURE 2.13

Suppose we want find the area bounded by $y = f(x)$, x-axis and from the ordinate $x = a$ to $x = b$ as shown by shaded region as shown in Fig. 2.13.

Since $f(x) > 0\ \forall\ x \in [a, b]$ and also $f(x)$ is continuous on $[a, b]$ by concept of area as an anti-derivative we have

$$A = \blacksquare = \int_a^b f(x)\,dx \qquad \ldots(1)$$

If $f(x)$ is defined and continuous in $[a, b]$. Let this interval be divided among n sub-interval and i^{th} interval be $[x_i, x_{i+1}]$ such that $\Delta x_i = x_{i+1} - x_i$, and for any $\xi_i \in [x_i, x_{i+1}]$, i.e., $m_i \le f(\xi_i) \le M_i$.

So we define lower limit sum as (s_n), upper limit sum as (S_n) and integral sum as $s = \sum_{i=0}^{n-1} m_i \Delta x_i$, $S = \sum_{i=0}^{n-1} M_i \Delta x_i$ and

$I = \sum_{i=0}^{n-1} f(\xi_i)\Delta x_i$ respectively.

Clearly, $s \le I \le S$, from here we can also say that $m(b - a) \le I \le M(b - a)$. When largest interval go to zero, then

$$(n \to \infty)\ ;\ I = \int_a^b f(x)dx = \lim_{n\to\infty} \sum_{i=0}^{n-1} f(\xi_i)\Delta x_i\ .$$

If interval be divided into n equal part of width h, then $h = \dfrac{b-a}{n}$ when $n \to \infty$; $h \to 0$,

$$\int_a^b f(x)dx = \lim_{n\to\infty} \sum_{r=1}^{n} hf(a+rh) = \lim_{h\to 0} \sum_{r=0}^{n-1} hf(a+rh)$$

$$= \lim_{n\to\infty} \frac{b-a}{n} \sum_{r=1}^{n} f\left[a + r\left(\frac{b-a}{n}\right)\right].$$

The method to evaluate the integral as limit of the sum of an infinite series is also known as integration by first principle or *ab*-initio method.

Let us explain it more clearly

Divide the interval length $(b - a)$ into n-sub intervals each having equal length $h = \dfrac{b-a}{4}$

If $n = 4$, then the sub-division is as shown below

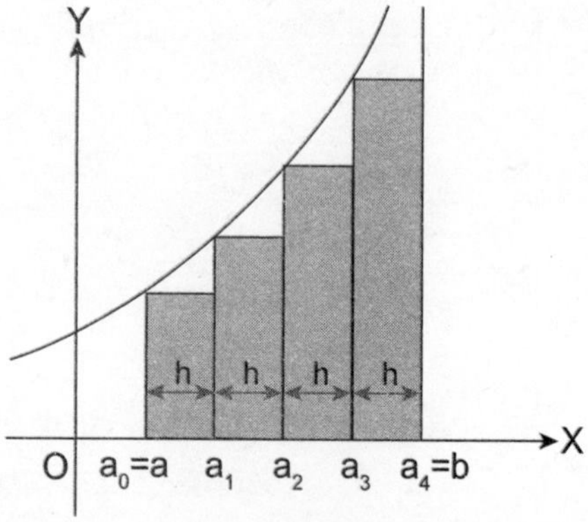

FIGURE 2.14

$$h = \frac{b-a}{4}$$

Now area of first rectangle $= f(a)h$

Area of second rectangle $= f(a_1)h$

Area of third rectangle $= f(a_2)h$

Area of fourth rectangle $= f(a_3)h$

we can observe that

$A > [hf(a) + hf(a_1) + hf(a_2) + hf(a_3)]$

or $A > [hf(a) + hf(a + h) + hf(a + 2h) + hf(a + 3h)]$

If $n = 10$, then the sub-division is as shown below

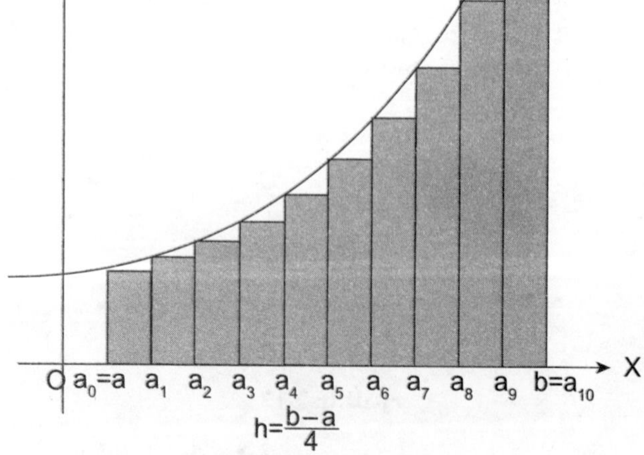

FIGURE 2.15

Now, we can observe that still $A > h[f(a) + f(a + h) + f(a + 2h) + f(a + 3h) + ... + f(a + 9h)]$

but the sum of areas of 10 rectangles is closer to A as compared to the sum of 4 rectangles ($n = 4$).

Next, if $n = 20$, then the sub-division is as shown below.

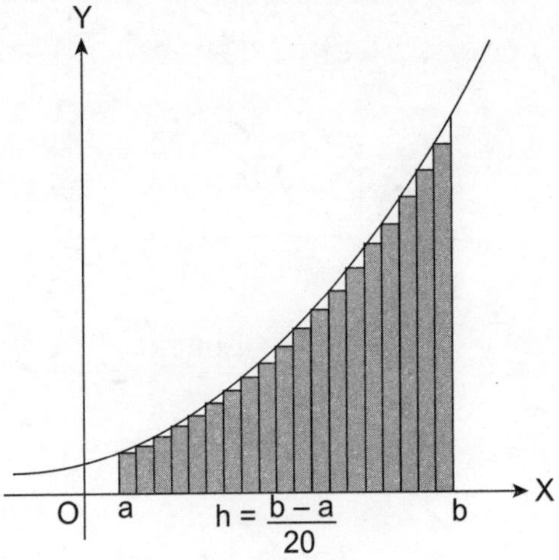

FIGURE 2.16

Now we can observe that required area is much closer to the sum of areas of 20 rectangles. Thus, as we go on increasing the number of sub-intervals, the length of each sub- interval goes on decreasing and tending to zero as n tends to ∞. Further the sum of areas of infinitely many rectangles of extremely small thickness converges to the required area.

Thus, $A \simeq h[f(a) + f(a + h) + f(a + 2h) + ... + f(a + (n - 1)h]$ as $n \to \infty$ equivalently

$$A \simeq \lim_{\substack{n\to\infty \\ h\to 0}}\left[f(a)h + f(a+h).h + f(a+2h).h + ... + f(a+\overline{n-1})h\right]$$

and we write $\int_a^b f(x)\,dx = \lim_{\substack{n\to\infty \\ h\to 0}}[f(a)h + f(a+h).h + f(a+2h).h + ... + f(a+\overline{n-1}).h]$

or $$\int_a^b f(x)\,dx = \lim_{\substack{n\to\infty \\ h\to 0}}\sum_{r=1}^{n} h.f(a+(r-1)h)$$

$$= \underbrace{\lim_{n\to\infty}\sum_{r=1}^{n}\frac{b-a}{n} f\left(a+(r-1)\frac{b-a}{n}\right)}_{\text{Evaluate this limit to get the value of } \int_a^b f(x)dx.}$$

Note that while calculating area A as a limit of infinite sum of areas of rectangles, we draw the rectangles under the curve of function $y = f(x)$ approximating the required area just less but converging to required area.

The above process require to have left top end point of rectangle on the curve $y = f(x)$. We can also draw the rectangles with their right top end point on the curve $y = f(x)$ approximating the area just greater than but converging to required area as shown below.

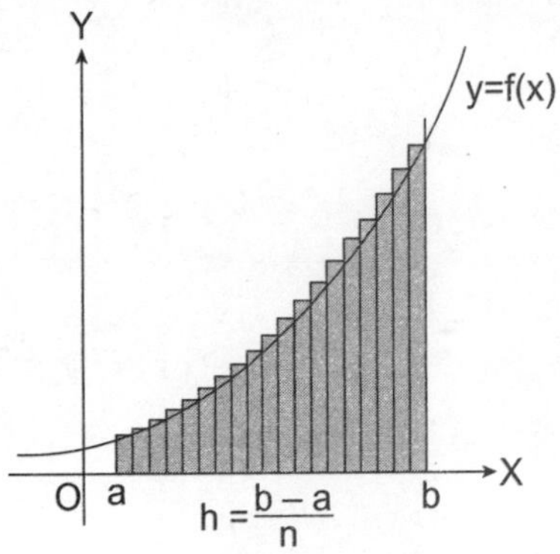

FIGURE 2.17

Thus, $A \simeq [hf(a + h) + hf(a + 2h) + hf(a + 3h) + ... + hf(a + nh)]$ as $n \to \infty$ or we write $A = \lim_{\substack{n\to\infty \\ h\to 0}}\sum_{r=1}^{n} hf(a+rh)$

$$= \lim_{n\to\infty}\sum_{r=1}^{n}\left(\frac{b-a}{n}\right) f\left(a + r\left(\frac{b-a}{n}\right)\right)$$

Thus, $$A = \int_a^b f(x)\,dx = \lim_{\substack{n\to\infty \\ h\to 0}}\sum_{r=1}^{n} hf(a+(r-1)h)$$

$$= \lim_{\substack{n\to\infty \\ h\to 0}}\sum_{r=1}^{n} hf(a+rh) \text{ where } h = \frac{b-a}{n}$$

Here, $\lim_{\substack{n\to\infty \\ h\to 0}}\sum_{r=1}^{n} hf(a+(r-1)h)$ is called left-end estimation of $\int_a^b f(x)\,dx$, whereas

$\lim_{\substack{n\to\infty \\ h\to 0}}\sum_{r=1}^{n} hf(a+rh)$ is called right-end estimation of area $\int_a^b f(x)\,dx$

ILLUSTRATION 4: Evaluate $\int_{-2}^{3}(x+3)\,dx$

SOLUTION: Partition the interval $[-2, 3]$ into n equal sub-intervals, i.e., $\{x_0 = -2, x_1, x_2, x_3, \ldots, x_n\}$, each of length $h = 5/n$. Here P is a regular partition. In each sub-interval $[x_{i-1}, x_i]$ use $\bar{x}_i = x_i$ as the sample point and $\Delta_r = h$.

We have, $x_0 = -2$

$$x_1 = -2 + h = -2 + \frac{5}{n},\ x_2 = -2 + 2h = -2 + 2\left(\frac{5}{n}\right),$$

$$x_r = -2 + rh = -2 + r\left(\frac{5}{n}\right);$$

$$x_n = -2 + nh = -2 + n\left(\frac{5}{n}\right) = 3,$$

Thus, $f(x_r) = x_r + 3 = 1 + r(5/n)$, for $r \in \{1, 2, 3, \ldots\ldots n\}$

Thus, $\int_{-2}^{3}(x+3)dx = \sum_{r=1}^{n} f(\bar{x}_r)\Delta_r = \sum_{r=1}^{n} f(x_r)h$

$$= \sum_{r=1}^{n}\left[1 + r\left(\frac{5}{n}\right)\right]\frac{5}{n} = \frac{5}{n}\sum_{r=1}^{n}1 + \frac{25}{n^2}\sum_{r=1}^{n}r$$

$$= \frac{5}{n}(n) + \frac{25}{n^2}\left[\frac{n(n+1)}{2}\right] \qquad \left(\because \sum_{r=1}^{n} r = \frac{n(n+1)}{2}\right)$$

$$= 5 + \frac{25}{2}\left(1 + \frac{1}{n}\right)$$

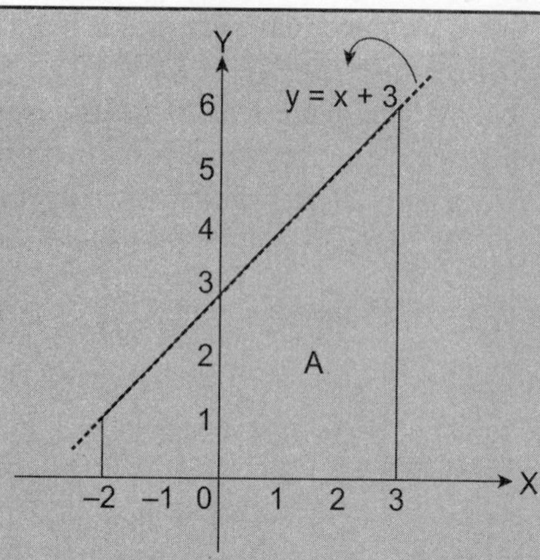

FIGURE 2.18

Since P is a regular partition, $|P| \to 0$ is equivalent to $n \to \infty$.

We conclude that $\int_{-2}^{3}(x+3)\,dx = \lim_{|P|\to 0}\sum_{i=1}^{n} f(\bar{x}_r)\Delta_r = \lim_{n\to\infty}\left[5 + \frac{25}{2}\left(1 + \frac{1}{n}\right)\right] = \frac{35}{2}$

We can easily check our answer. Since the required integral gives the area of the trapezoid as shown in Fig. 2.18. The familiar trapezoidal area formula $A = \frac{1}{2}(a+b)h$ gives $\frac{1}{2}(1+6)5 = \frac{35}{2}$.

ILLUSTRATION 5: Evaluate $\int_{-1}^{3}(2x^2 - 8)\,dx$

SOLUTION: Here no formula read during our school time will help us, though the integral does correspond to $-A_1 + A_2$; where A_1 and A_2 are the areas of the regions below and above the x-axis as shown in Fig. 2.19.

Let P be a regular partition of $[-1, 3]$ into n equal sub-intervals, each of length $\Delta_i = 4/n$. In each sub-interval $[x_{i-1}, x_i]$, chose $\bar{x}_i$ to be the right endpoint, so $\bar{x}_i = x_i$. Then

$$x_i = -1 + i\Delta_i = -1 + i\left(\frac{4}{n}\right) \text{ and}$$

$$f(x_i) = 2x_i^2 - 8 = 2\left[-1 + i\left(\frac{4}{n}\right)\right]^2 - 8$$

$$= -6 - \frac{16i}{n} + \frac{32i^2}{n^2}$$

Consequently, $\sum_{i=1}^{n} f(\bar{x}_i)\Delta x_i = \sum_{i=1}^{n} f(x_i)\left(\frac{4}{n}\right)$

$$= \sum_{i=1}^{n}\left[-6 - \frac{16}{n}i + \frac{32}{n^2}i^2\right]\frac{4}{n}$$

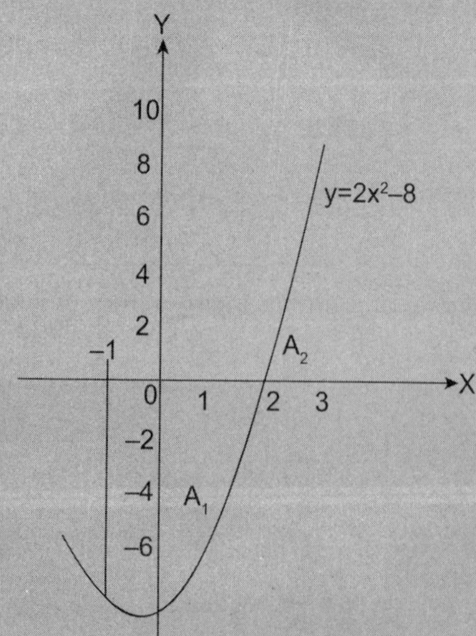

FIGURE 2.19

$$= -\frac{24}{n}\sum_{i=1}^{n}1-\frac{64}{n^2}\sum_{i=1}^{n}i+\frac{128}{n^3}\sum_{i=1}^{n}i^2 = -\frac{24}{n}(n)-\frac{64}{n^2}\frac{n(n+1)}{2}+\frac{128}{n^3}\frac{n(n+1)(2n+1)}{6}$$

$$= -24-32\left(1+\frac{1}{n}\right)+\frac{128}{6}\left(2+\frac{3}{n}+\frac{1}{n^2}\right)$$

We conclude that

$$\int_{-1}^{3}(2x^2-8)dx = \lim_{|P|\to 0}\sum_{i=1}^{n}f(\bar{x}_i)\Delta_i = \lim_{n\to\infty}\left[-24-32\left(1+\frac{1}{n}\right)+\frac{128}{6}\left(2+\frac{3}{n}+\frac{1}{n^2}\right)\right]$$

$$= -24-32+\frac{128}{3}=\frac{-40}{3}$$

The answer is negative is not surprising, since the region below the x-axis is larger than the one above the x-axis in the above figure. Our answer is close to the estimate given in common sense. This reassures us that our answer is correct.

ILLUSTRATION 6: Evaluate $\int_2^3 x^3 dx$

SOLUTION: Here $h=\frac{3-2}{n}=\frac{1}{n}$ and $f(x) = x^3$; $a = 2$; $b = 3$

$$\Rightarrow \int_2^3 x^3dx=\lim_{\substack{n\to\infty\\ h\to o}}\sum_{r=1}^{n}h.f\left(a+(r-1)h\right) = \int_2^3 x^3dx=\lim_{n\to\infty}\sum_{r=1}^{n}\frac{1}{n}\left(2+\frac{(r-1)}{n}\right)^3$$

$$= \lim_{n\to\infty}\sum_{r=1}^{n}\frac{(2n-1+r)^3}{n^4} = \lim_{n\to\infty}\frac{1}{n^4}\sum_{r=1}^{n}(2n-1)^3+r^3+3(2n-1)r(2n-1+r)$$

$$= \lim_{n\to\infty}\frac{1}{n^4}\left\{n(2n-1)^3+\frac{n^2(n+1)^2}{4}+3(2n-1)^2\frac{n(n+1)}{2}+\frac{3(2n-1)}{6}.n(n+1).(2n+1)\right\}$$

$$= \lim_{n\to\infty}\left\{\left(2-\frac{1}{n}\right)^3+\frac{1}{4}\left(1+\frac{1}{n}\right)^2+\frac{3}{2}\left(2-\frac{1}{n}\right)^2\left(1+\frac{1}{n}\right)+\frac{1}{2}\left(2-\frac{1}{n}\right)\left(1+\frac{1}{n}\right)\left(2+\frac{1}{n}\right)\right\}$$

$$= 8+\frac{1}{4}+6+2=\frac{65}{4}$$

ILLUSTRATION 7: Evaluate $\int_2^4\left(x^3+5x^2+6x-5\right)dx$ by using limit of an infinite sum.

SOLUTION: Here $f(x) = x^3 + 5x^2 + 6x - 5$, $a = 2$, $b = 4$, $h=\frac{b-a}{n}=\frac{2}{n}$

$$\text{Now }\int_a^b f(x)dx = \lim_{\substack{h\to 0\\ n\to\infty}}\sum_{r=1}^{n}hf\left(a+(r-1)h\right)$$

$$= \lim_{n\to\infty}\sum_{r=1}^{n}\frac{2}{n}f\left(2+(r-1)\frac{2}{n}\right) = \lim_{n\to\infty}\left[\frac{2}{n}\sum_{r=1}^{n}f\left(\frac{2n+2r-2}{n}\right)\right]$$

$$= \lim_{n\to\infty}\left[\frac{2}{n}\sum_{r=1}^{n}\left\{f\left(\frac{2n-2+2r}{n}\right)^3+5\left(\frac{2n-2+2r}{n}\right)^2+6\left(\frac{2n-2+2r}{n}\right)-5\right\}\right]$$

$$= \lim_{n\to\infty}\frac{2}{n}\left[\begin{array}{l}\sum_{r=1}^{n}\frac{8}{n^3}\left[(n-1)^3+r^3+3(n-1)^2r+3(n-1)r^2\right]\\ +\sum_{r=1}^{n}\frac{20}{n^2}\left[(n-1)^2+r^2+2r(n-1)\right]+\frac{12}{n}n(n-1)+\frac{12}{n}\sum_{r=1}^{n}r-5n\end{array}\right]$$

$$= \lim_{n\to\infty}\frac{2}{n}\left[\begin{array}{l}\frac{8}{n^3}n(n-1)^3+\frac{8}{n^3}\sum_{r=1}^{n}r^3+\frac{24}{n^3}(n-1)^2\sum_{r=1}^{n}r+\frac{24}{n^3}(n-1)\sum_{r=1}^{n}r^2\\ +\frac{20}{n^2}(n)(n-1)^2+\frac{20}{n^2}\sum_{r=1}^{n}r^2+\frac{40}{n^2}(n-1)\sum_{r=1}^{n}r+12(n-1)+6+n\end{array}\right]$$

$$= \lim_{n\to\infty}\frac{2}{n}\left[\begin{array}{l}\frac{8(n-1)^3}{n^2}+\frac{8}{n^3}\cdot\left(\frac{n(n+1)}{2}\right)^2+\frac{24}{n^3}(n-1)^2\frac{n(n+1)}{2}\\ +\frac{24}{n^3}\frac{(n-1)n(n+1)(2n+1)}{6}+\frac{20}{n}(n-1)^2\\ +\frac{20}{n^2}\frac{n(n+1)(2n+1)}{6}+\frac{40}{n^2}(n-1)\frac{n(n+1)}{2}+12(n-1)+6+n\end{array}\right]$$

$$= \lim_{n\to\infty}\left[\begin{array}{l}16\left(1-\frac{1}{n}\right)^3+4\left[1+\frac{1}{n^2}+\frac{2}{n}\right]+24\left[\left(1+\frac{1}{n^2}-\frac{2}{n}\right)\left(1+\frac{1}{n}\right)\right]+8\left(1-\frac{1}{n}\right)\left(1+\frac{1}{n}\right)\left(2+\frac{1}{n}\right)\\ +40\left(1+\frac{1}{n^2}-\frac{2}{n}\right)+\frac{20}{3}\left(1+\frac{1}{n}\right)\left(2+\frac{1}{n}\right)+40\left(1-\frac{1}{n}\right)\left(1+\frac{1}{n}\right)+24\left(1-\frac{1}{n}\right)+\frac{12}{n}+2\end{array}\right]$$

$$= 16+4+24+16+40+\frac{40}{3}+40+24+2 = 166+\frac{40}{3}=\frac{498+40}{3}=\frac{538}{3}$$

ILLUSTRATION 8: Evaluate $\int_a^b \frac{1}{\sqrt{x}}dx$ by using definite integral as limit of an infinite sum.

SOLUTION: Given $f(x)=\frac{1}{\sqrt{x}}$, $h=\frac{b-a}{n}$

Now $\int_a^b \frac{1}{\sqrt{x}}dx = \lim_{n\to\infty} h\sum_{r=1}^{n} f\left(a+\overline{r-1}h\right)$

$$= \lim_{n\to\infty} h\left[\frac{1}{\sqrt{a+0h}}+\frac{1}{\sqrt{a+h}}+\frac{1}{\sqrt{a+2h}}+\ldots+\frac{1}{\sqrt{a+(n-1)h}}\right]$$

$$= \lim_{\to\infty}\left[\frac{h}{\sqrt{a}}+\frac{h}{\sqrt{a+h}}+\frac{h}{\sqrt{a+2h}}+\ldots+\frac{h}{\sqrt{a+(n-1)h}}\right] \qquad \ldots(1)$$

For calculating limit (1), we shall use sandwitch theorem, using the inequality

$\sqrt{r}+\sqrt{r-h}<2\sqrt{r}<\sqrt{r}+\sqrt{r+h}$

For sufficiently small $h>0$

$$\Rightarrow \frac{1}{\sqrt{r}+\sqrt{r-h}}>\frac{1}{2\sqrt{r}}>\frac{1}{\sqrt{r}+\sqrt{r+h}}$$

$$\Rightarrow \frac{\sqrt{r}-\sqrt{r-h}}{h}>\frac{1}{2\sqrt{r}}>\frac{\sqrt{r}-\sqrt{r+h}}{-h}$$

$$\Rightarrow 2\left(\sqrt{r}-\sqrt{r-h}\right)>\frac{h}{\sqrt{r}}>2\left(\sqrt{r+h}-\sqrt{r}\right) \qquad \ldots(2)$$

Substituting $r = a, a+h, a+2h, \ldots. a+(n-1)h$ in (2), we have

$$2\left(\sqrt{a}-\sqrt{a-h}\right)>\frac{h}{\sqrt{a}}>2\left(\sqrt{a+h}-\sqrt{a}\right);$$

$$2\left(\sqrt{a+h}-\sqrt{a}\right)>\frac{h}{\sqrt{a+h}}>2\left(\sqrt{a+2h}-\sqrt{a+h}\right)$$

$$2\left(\sqrt{a+2h}-\sqrt{a+h}\right)>\frac{h}{\sqrt{a+2h}}>2\left(\sqrt{a+3h}-\sqrt{a+2h}\right);$$

$$2\left(\sqrt{a+(n-1)h}-\sqrt{a+(n-2)h}\right)>\frac{h}{\sqrt{a+(n-1)h}}>2\left(\sqrt{a+nh}-\sqrt{a+(n-1)h}\right)$$

Adding above n-inequalities vertically, we get

$$2\left[\sqrt{a+(n-1)h}-\sqrt{a-h}\right]>\sum_{r=1}^{n}\frac{h}{\sqrt{a+(r-1)h}}>2\left[\sqrt{a+nh}-\sqrt{a}\right] \quad \ldots(3)$$

$$\text{Now } \lim_{\substack{h\to 0\\ n\to\infty}} 2\left[\sqrt{a+(n-1)h}-\sqrt{a-h}\right]=\lim_{\substack{h\to 0\\ n\to\infty}} 2\left[\sqrt{b-h}-\sqrt{a-h}\right]=2\left(\sqrt{b}-\sqrt{a}\right) \quad \ldots(4)$$

$$\text{and } \lim_{\substack{h\to 0\\ n\to\infty}} 2\left[\sqrt{a+nh}-\sqrt{a}\right]=\lim_{\substack{h\to 0\\ n\to\infty}} 2\left[\sqrt{b}-\sqrt{a}\right]=2\left(\sqrt{b}-\sqrt{a}\right) \quad \ldots(5)$$

∴ from (3), (4) and (5) by sandwich theorem, we must have

$$\lim_{\substack{n\to\infty\\ h\to 0}}\sum_{r=1}^{n}\frac{h}{\sqrt{a+(r-1)h}}=2\left(\sqrt{b}-\sqrt{a}\right) \quad \ldots(6)$$

∴ from (1) and (2), we get $\int_a^b \frac{1}{\sqrt{x}}dx=2\left(\sqrt{b}-\sqrt{a}\right)$

ILLUSTRATION 9: Find $\int_a^b e^{(cx+d)}dx$ by using definite integral as limit of an infinite sum.

SOLUTION: Given $f(x)=e^{(cx+d)}$, $h=\frac{b-a}{n}$

$$\text{Now } \int_a^b f(x)dx=\lim_{\substack{n\to\infty\\ h\to 0}} h\sum_{r=1}^{n} f\left(a+(r-1)h\right)=\lim_{\substack{n\to\infty\\ h\to 0}} h\sum_{r=1}^{n} e^{c\left(a+\overline{r-1}h\right)+d}$$

$$=\lim_{\substack{n\to\infty\\ h\to 0}} h.e^{(ac+d)}\sum_{r=1}^{n} e^{c(r-1)h}=e^{(ac+d)}\lim_{\substack{n\to\infty\\ h\to 0}} h\left[1+e^{ch}+e^{2ch}+\ldots+e^{c(n-1)h}\right]$$

$$=e^{(ac+d)}\lim_{\substack{n\to\infty\\ h\to 0}} h\left[\frac{\left(e^{ch}\right)^n-1}{e^{ch}-1}\right]=e^{(ac+d)}\lim_{\substack{n\to\infty\\ h\to 0}} h\left[\frac{e^{cnh}-1}{e^{ch}-1}\right]=\frac{e^{(ac+d)}}{c}\lim_{\substack{n\to\infty\\ h\to 0}}\left(\frac{ch}{e^{ch}-1}\right)\left(e^{c(b-a)}-1\right)$$

$$=\frac{e^{(ac+d)}}{c}\left[e^{c(b-a)}-1\right]\lim_{h\to 0}\left(\frac{ch}{e^{ch}-1}\right)=\frac{e^{(ac+d)}}{c}\left(e^{c(b-a)}-1\right) \quad \ldots(1)$$

$$=\frac{1}{c}\left[e^{bc+d}-e^{ac+d}\right] \qquad \left[\because \lim_{x\to 0}\frac{e^x-1}{x}=1\right]$$

ILLUSTRATION 10: Evaluate the integral $\int_2^3 \frac{1}{x}dx$ by using definite integral as limit of an infinite sum.

SOLUTION: Given $f(x)=\frac{1}{x}$, $a=2, b=3$

Let us divide the interval [2, 3] into n-sub-interval such that their end points form a G.P. with first term 2 and common ratio R.

i.e., $a_0=2$, $a_1=2(R)$, $a_2=2(R)^2$, $a_3=2(R)^3$, … , $a_n=2(R)^n=3$

$\Rightarrow R=\left(\frac{3}{2}\right)^{1/n}$,

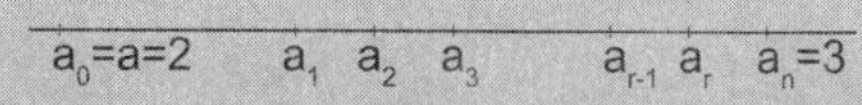

FIGURE 2.20

Now length of rth sub-interval $= \Delta_r = a_r - a_{r-1}; r \geq 1$

$= 2(R)^r - 2(R)^{r-1} = 2(R)^{r-1}(R-1) \to 0$ as $n \to \infty$ as $R = \left(\frac{3}{2}\right)^{1/n} \to 1$ for $n \to \infty$

Graphically:

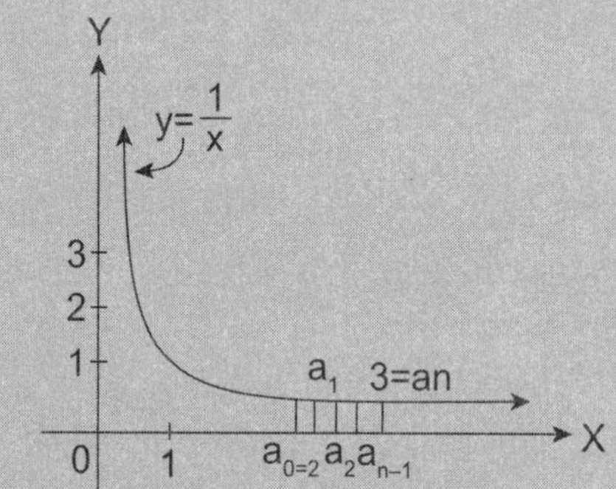

FIGURE 2.21

$$\therefore \quad \int_2^3 \frac{1}{x}dx = \lim_{n\to\infty}\sum_{r=1}^{n} f(a_r)\Delta_r$$

$$\therefore \quad \lim_{n\to\infty}\left[f(a_1)\Delta_1 + f(a_2)\Delta_2 + ... + f(a_{n-1})\Delta_{n-1} + f(a_n)\Delta_n\right]$$

$$= \lim_{n\to\infty}\left[\frac{1}{a_1}\left(2R^0(R-1)\right) + \frac{1}{a_2}\left(2R^1(R-1)\right) + \frac{1}{a_3}\left(2R^2(R-1)\right) + ... + \frac{1}{a_n}\left(2R^{n-1}(R-1)\right)\right]$$

$$= \lim_{n\to\infty} 2(R-1)\left[\frac{1}{2R} + \frac{R}{2R^2} + \frac{R^2}{2R^3} + ... + \frac{R^{n-1}}{2R^n}\right]$$

$$= \lim_{n\to\infty}(R-1)\left[\frac{1}{R} + \frac{1}{R} + \frac{1}{R} + ... + \frac{1}{R}\right] \text{ (}n\text{-times)}$$

$$= \lim_{n\to\infty}(R-1)\frac{n}{R} = \lim_{n\to\infty} n\left[\frac{R-1}{R}\right] = \lim_{n\to\infty} n\left[\frac{(3/2)^{1/n}-1}{(3/2)^{1/n}}\right]$$

$$= \lim_{n\to\infty}\frac{1}{(3/2)^{1/n}} \cdot \lim_{n\to\infty}\left[\frac{(3/2)^{1/n}-1}{1/n}\right] = \frac{1}{(1)} \times \ln\left(\frac{3}{2}\right) = \ln\left(\frac{3}{2}\right)$$

ILLUSTRATION 11: Evaluate $\int_a^b \frac{dx}{x^2}$; $(a < b)$ by using definite integral as limit of an infinite sum

SOLUTION: Here $f(x) = \frac{1}{x^2}$, $h = \frac{b-a}{n}$

$$\text{Now } \int_a^b \frac{dx}{x^2} = \lim_{\substack{n\to\infty \\ h\to 0}} h\sum_{r=1}^{n} f\left(a+(r-1)h\right)$$

$$= \lim_{\substack{n\to\infty \\ h\to 0}} h\sum_{r=1}^{n}\frac{1}{[a+(r-1)h]^2} \quad ...(1)$$

Now, $(a + (r - 2)h)(a + (r - 1)h) < [a + (r - 1)h]^2 < [a + (r - 1)][a + rh]$

$$\Rightarrow \frac{h}{(a+(r-1)h)(a+rh)} < \frac{h}{[a+(r-1)h]^2} < \frac{h}{[a+(r-2)h][a+(r-1)h]} \quad \ldots(2)$$

Substituting $r = 1, 2, 3, \ldots. n$ in (2) and adding, we get

$$\Rightarrow \frac{h}{(a)(a+h)} + \frac{h}{(a+h)(a+2h)} + \frac{h}{(a+2h)(a+3h)} + \ldots. +$$

$$\frac{n}{[a+(h-1)h][a+nh]} < \sum_{r=1}^{n} \frac{h}{[a+(r-1)h]^2}$$

$$< \frac{h}{(a-h).a} + \frac{h}{a(a+h)} + \frac{h}{(a+h)(a+2h)} + \ldots. + \frac{h}{[a+(n-2)h][a+(n-1)h]}$$

$$\Rightarrow \left[\frac{1}{a} - \frac{1}{a+h}\right] + \left[\frac{1}{a+h} - \frac{1}{a+2h}\right] + \ldots + \left[\frac{1}{a+(n-1)h} - \frac{1}{a+nh}\right] < \sum_{r=1}^{n} \frac{h}{[a+(r-1)h]^2}$$

$$< \left[\frac{1}{a-h} - \frac{1}{a}\right] + \left[\frac{1}{a} - \frac{1}{a+h}\right] + \left[\frac{1}{a+h} - \frac{1}{a+2h}\right] + \ldots. + \left[\frac{1}{a+(n-2)h} - \frac{1}{a+(n-1)h}\right]$$

$$\Rightarrow \frac{1}{a} - \frac{1}{a+nh} < \sum_{r=1}^{n} \frac{h}{[a+(r-1)h]^2} < \frac{1}{a-h} - \frac{1}{(a+nh-h)}$$

$$\Rightarrow \frac{1}{a} - \frac{1}{b} < \sum_{r=1}^{n} \frac{h}{[a+(r-1)h]^2} < \frac{1}{a-h} - \frac{1}{b-h}$$

Left and right inequality tends to $\frac{1}{a} - \frac{1}{b}$ as $h \to 0$, thus, by sandwitch theorem

$$\lim_{\substack{h\to 0 \\ n\to\infty}} \sum_{r=1}^{n} \frac{h}{[a+(r-1)h]^2} = \frac{1}{a} - \frac{1}{b}$$

$$\Rightarrow \int_a^b \frac{1}{x^2} dx = \frac{1}{a} - \frac{1}{b}$$

ILLUSTRATION 12: Find $\int_a^b \sin x \, dx$ by using definite integral as limit of an infinite sum.

SOLUTION: Here $f(x) = \sin x$, $h = \frac{b-a}{n}$

$$\text{Now } \int_a^b \sin x \, dx = \lim_{\substack{h\to 0 \\ n\to\infty}} h \sum_{r=1}^{n} f\left(a+(r-1)h\right)$$

$$= \lim_{\substack{h\to 0 \\ n\to\infty}} h \sum_{r=1}^{n} \sin\left(a+(r-1)h\right) \quad \ldots(1)$$

Let us first convert the sum $\sum_{r=1}^{n} \sin\left(a+(r-1)h\right)$ into product of trigonometric ratios.

Let $S = \sin a + \sin(a + h) + \sin(a + 2h) + \ldots. + \sin\left(a+\overline{n-1}h\right)$

$$\Rightarrow 2\sin\frac{h}{2}(S) = 2\sin\frac{h}{2}\sin a + 2\sin\frac{h}{2}\sin(a+h) + 2\sin\frac{h}{2}\sin(a+2h) + \ldots +$$

$$2\sin\frac{h}{2}\sin\left(a+\overline{n-1}h\right)$$

$$= \left[\cos\left(a-\frac{h}{2}\right)-\cos\left(a+\frac{h}{2}\right)\right]+\left[\cos\left(a+\frac{h}{2}\right)-\cos\left(a+\frac{3}{2}h\right)\right]^2$$

$$+\left[\cos\left(a+\frac{3}{2}h\right)-\cos\left(a+\frac{5}{2}h\right)\right]+\ldots+\left[\cos\left(a+\left(n-\frac{3}{2}\right)h\right)-\cos\left(a+\left(n-\frac{1}{2}\right)h\right)\right]$$

$$= \cos\left(a-\frac{h}{2}\right)-\cos\left(a+\left(n-\frac{1}{2}\right)h\right)$$

$$= -2\sin\left[\frac{2a+(n-1)h}{2}\right]\sin\left[\frac{-nh}{2}\right] = 2\sin\left[\frac{a+a+(n-1)h}{2}\right]\sin\left(\frac{nh}{2}\right)$$

$$\Rightarrow \quad S = \frac{\sin\left[\frac{a+a+(n-1)h}{2}\right]\sin\left(\frac{nh}{2}\right)}{\sin\left(\frac{h}{2}\right)} \qquad \ldots(2)$$

$\therefore$ from (1) and (2), we have,

$$\int_a^b \sin x\,dx = \lim_{\substack{h\to 0\\ n\to\infty}} \frac{h\sin\left[\frac{a+a+(n-1)h}{2}\right]\sin\frac{nh}{2}}{\left(\sin\frac{h}{2}\right)} = 2\sin\left(\frac{a+b}{2}\right)\sin\left(\frac{b-a}{2}\right)$$

$$= \cos\left[\frac{a+b-b+a}{2}\right]-\cos\left[\frac{a+b+b-a}{2}\right] = \cos(a)-\cos(b)$$

ILLUSTRATION 13: Find $\int_a^b \cos^2 x\,dx$ by using definite integral as limit of an infinite sum.

SOLUTION: Here $f(x) = \cos^2 x$, $h = \frac{b-a}{n}$

Now $\int_a^b \cos^2 x\,dx = \lim_{\substack{n\to\infty\\ h\to 0}} h\sum_{r=1}^{n} f(a+(r-1)h)$

$$= \lim_{\substack{n\to\infty\\ h\to 0}} h\sum_{r=1}^{n}\cos^2(a+(r-1)h) \qquad \ldots(1)$$

$$= \lim_{\substack{n\to\infty\\ h\to 0}} h\sum_{r=1}^{n}\frac{1+\cos(2a+2(r-1)h)}{2} \qquad \left(\because \cos^2\theta = \frac{1+\cos 2\theta}{2}\right)$$

$$= \lim_{n\to\infty} h\sum_{r=1}^{n}\frac{1}{2}+\frac{1}{2}\lim_{\substack{n\to\infty\\ h\to 0}} h\sum_{r=1}^{n}\cos(2a+2(r-1)h)$$

$$= \lim_{n\to\infty}\frac{h}{2}(n)+\frac{1}{2}\lim_{\substack{n\to\infty\\ h\to 0}} h\sum_{r=1}^{n}\cos[2a+2(r-1)h] \qquad \ldots(2)$$

Similar to last illustration, we can show that $\cos(a) + \cos(a + h) + \cos(a + 2h) + \ldots + \cos(a+(n-1)h)$

$$= \frac{\cos\left(\frac{a+a+(n-1)h}{2}\right).\sin\left(\frac{nh}{2}\right)}{\sin\left(\frac{h}{2}\right)}$$

$$\therefore \sum_{r=1}^{n}\cos\left[2a+(r-1)(2h)\right] = \frac{\left[\cos\left(\frac{2a+2a+(n-1)2h}{2}\right)\right]\sin\left(\frac{n(2h)}{2}\right)}{\sin\left(\frac{2h}{2}\right)} \quad \ldots(3)$$

$$= \frac{\cos\left[a+\left(a+(n-1)h\right)\right]\sin(nh)}{\sinh} = \frac{\cos[a+(b-h)]\sin nh}{\sinh}$$

$\therefore$ From (2) and (3)

$$\therefore \int_a^b \cos^2 x\,dx = \frac{1}{2}(b-a)+\frac{1}{2}\lim_{\substack{n\to\infty \\ h\to 0}}\frac{h}{\sinh}\cos(a+b-h)\sin(b-a)$$

$$= \frac{1}{2}(b-a)+\frac{1}{2}\times\frac{1}{2}\times\lim_{h\to 0}[\sin(a+b-h+b-a)-\sin(a+b-h-b+a)]$$

$$= \frac{1}{2}(b-a)+\frac{1}{4}(\sin 2b-\sin 2a)$$

DISTANCE

The distance traveled by an object with continuous velocity $\upsilon(t)$ along a straight line from time $t = a$ to $t = b$ is $S = \int_a^b |\upsilon(t)|\,dt$

NOTES

There is a difference between the total distance travelled by an object over a given time interval [a, b], and the displacement of the object over the same interval, which is defined as the difference between the object's final and initial positions. It is easy to see that displacement is given by $D = \int_a^b \upsilon(t)\,dt$

Thus, an object that moves forward by 2 units and backward by 3 units on a given time interval has moved a total distance of 5 units, but its displacement is –1 because it ends up 1 unit to the left of its initial position.

ILLUSTRATION 14: An object moves along a straight line with velocity $\upsilon(t) = t^2$ for $t > 0$. How far does the object travel between times $t = 1$ and $t = 2$?

SOLUTION: We have $a = 1$, $b = 2$ and $\Delta t = \frac{2-1}{n} = \frac{1}{n}$; therefore, the required distance is

$$S = \int_{t=1}^{t=2} |\upsilon(t)|\,dt = \lim_{n\to+\infty} \sum_{k=1}^{n} \left|\upsilon\left[1+(k-1)\left(\frac{1}{n}\right)\right]\right|\left(\frac{1}{n}\right)$$

$$= \lim_{n\to\infty} \sum_{k=1}^{n} \left|\upsilon\left(\frac{n+k-1}{n}\right)\right|\left(\frac{1}{n}\right) = \lim_{n\to\infty} \sum_{k=1}^{n} \frac{(n+k-1)^2}{n^2}\left(\frac{1}{n}\right)$$

$$= \lim_{n\to\infty} \frac{1}{n^3} \sum_{k=1}^{n} \left[\left(n^2-2n+1\right)+k^2+2(n-1)k\right]$$

$$= \lim_{n\to\infty} \frac{1}{n^3}\left[(n^2-2n+1)\sum_{k=1}^{n} 1 + \sum_{k=1}^{n} k^2 + 2(n-1)\sum_{k=1}^{n} k\right]$$

$$= \lim_{n\to\infty} \frac{1}{n^3}\left[(n^2-2n+1)n + \frac{n(n+1)(2n+1)}{6} + 2(n-1)\frac{n(n+1)}{2}\right]$$

$$= \lim_{n\to\infty} \frac{14n^3-9n^2+n}{6n^3} = \frac{14}{6} = \frac{7}{3}$$

Thus, we expect the object to travel $\frac{7}{3}$ units during the time interval [1, 2].

By considering the distance as an integral, we see that zero or negative values of a definite integral can also be interpreted geometrically. When $\upsilon(t) > 0$ on a time interval $[a, b]$, then the total distance S travled by the object between times $t = a$ and $t = b$ is the same as the area under the graph of $\upsilon(t)$ on $[a, b]$.

When $\upsilon(t) > 0$, the object moves forward, but when $\upsilon(t) < 0$, it reverses direction and move backward (to the left). In the general case, when $\upsilon(t)$ changes sign on the time interval $[a, b]$, the integral. $\int_a^b \upsilon(t)\,dt$ measures the net displacement of the object, taking into account both forward and backward motion.

For example, for the velocity function $\upsilon(t)$ as shown in Fig. 2.22, the net displacement is 0 because the area above the t-axis is the same as the area below, but in Fig. 2.23, there is more area below the t-axis, which means the net displacement is negative, and the object ends up 'behind' to the left of its starting position.

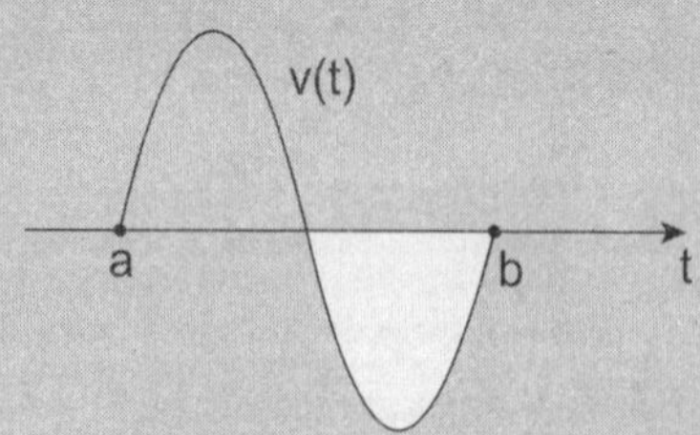

FIGURE 2.22

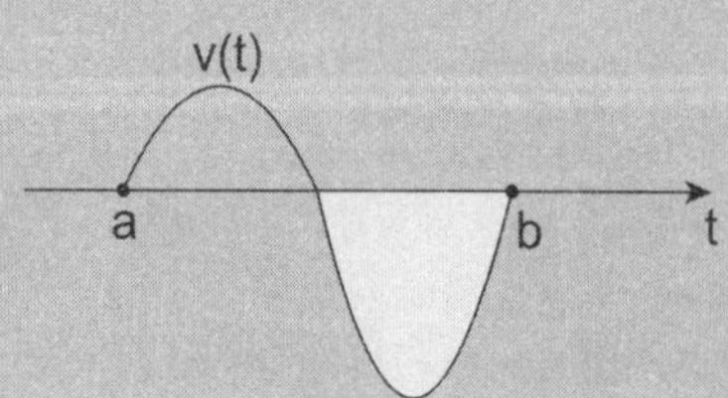

FIGURE 2.23

TEXTUAL EXERCISE–1: (SUBJECTIVE)

1. The graph of function $f(x)$ is as shown below

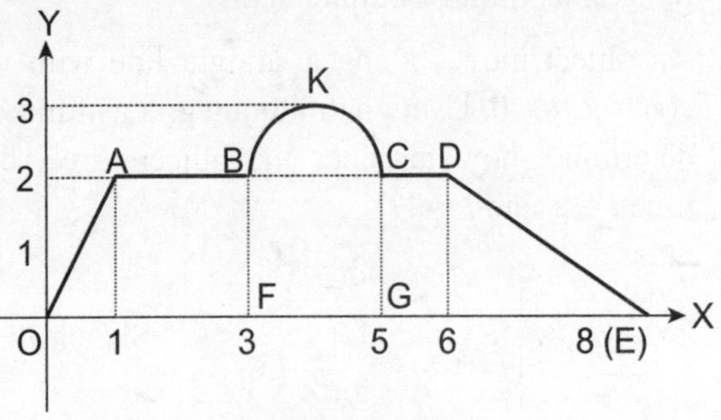

FIGURE 2.24

Given that BC is a circular arc, then evaluate $\int_0^8 f(x)\,dx$ without actually integrating.

2. The graph of the function $f(x)$ is as shown below

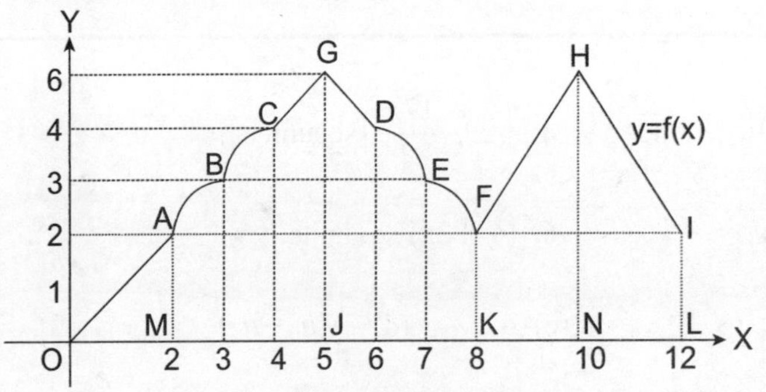

FIGURE 2.25

Given that AB, BC, DE, EF are circular arcs, then evaluate $\int_0^{12} f(x)\,dx$ without actually integrating the function $f(x)$.

3. The graph of function $f(x)$ is as shown below

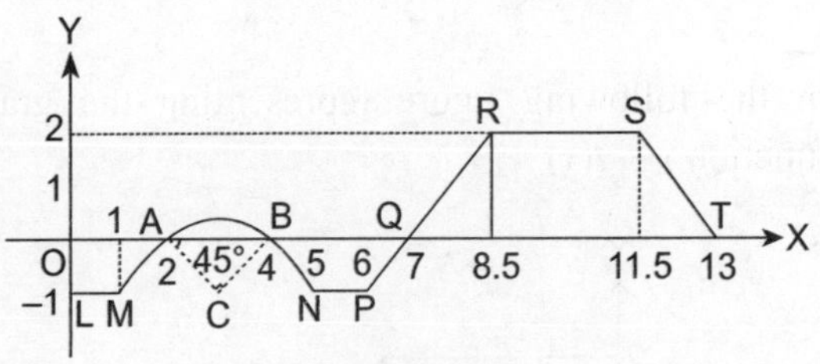

FIGURE 2.26

Given that AB is a circular arc with centre at C, ($\angle ACB = 90°$; $\angle CAB = 45°$) then evaluate $\left|\int_0^{13} |f(x)|\,dx\right|$ without integrating the function $f(x)$.

4. Evaluate $\int_0^6 |f(x)|\,dx + \int_0^{13} |g(x)|\,dx$ without actually integrating the functions $|f(x)|$ for $f(x)$ and $g(x)$ having their graph as shown below.

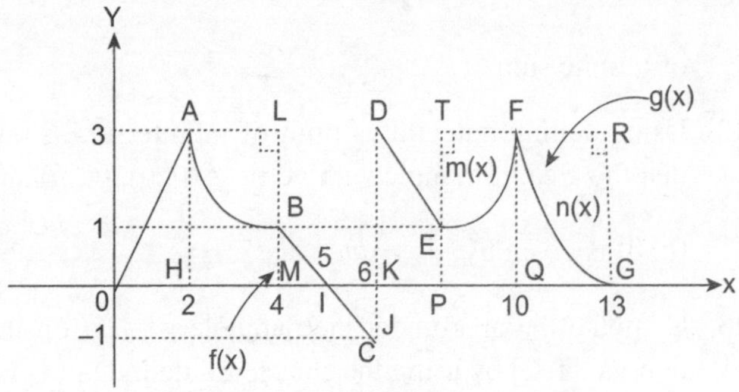

FIGURE 2.27

5. Give the geometrical significance of $\int_a^b f(x)dx$ and hence evaluate the following integrals without actually integrating them:

(a) $\int_{-1}^{1} \{x\}\,dx$ (b) $\int_0^2 |x-1|\,dx$

(c) $\int_0^a \sqrt{a^2-x^2}\,dx$

6. Evaluate $\int_{-2}^{2} \left(1+\sqrt{4-x^2}\right)dx$ without actually integrating.

7. Evaluate $\int_0^4 \sqrt{4-(x-2)^2}\,dx + \int_4^6 \big||x-5|-1\big|\,dx$ without actually integrating.

8. Evaluate the following definite integrals by using limit of infinite sum:

(a) $\int_0^3 (x^2+1)\,dx$ (b) $\int_0^4 (2x^3+5)\,dx$

(c) $\int_0^2 (2x+1)\,dx$ (d) $\int_a^b x^2\,dx$

9. Evaluate the following definite integrals by using limit of infinite sum:

(a) $\int_1^2 e^{-x}\,dx$ (b) $\int_3^5 e^{(3x+4)}\,dx$

(c) $\int_1^2 e^{-2x+4}\,dx$ (d) $\int_0^1 \left(x+e^{2x}\right)dx$

10. Evaluate the following definite integrals by using limit of infinite sum:

(a) $\int_a^b \cos x\, dx$ (b) $\int_a^b \sin^2 x\, dx$

(c) $\int_a^b \sin^3 x\, dx$

11. Evaluate the definite integrals $\int_a^b \sqrt{x}\, dx$ by using limit of infinite sum:

12. Using definite integral as limit of infinite sum, show that the area of triangle with vertices (0, 0), (0, h) and (b, 0) is given by $A = \frac{1}{2}bh$

13. Compute the area under the parabola $y = 2x^2$ on the interval [1, 2] by using the concept of definite integral as limit of infinite sum.

14. Show that the region under the curve $y = \sqrt{1-x^2}$ on the interval [–1, 1] has area $A = \frac{\pi}{2}$ by using definite integral as limit of infinite sum.

15. An object moves along a straight line with velocity $v(t) = t^3$, $t > 0$. Using definite integral as limit of sum, determine, how far does the object travel between time $t = 1$ and $t = 2$?

16. Let $f(x) = \begin{cases} 2; & \text{for } -1 \le x \le 1 \\ 3-x; & \text{for } 1 < x < 4 \\ 2x-9; & \text{for } 4 \le x \le 5 \end{cases}$. Sketch the graph of function $f(x)$, and hence evaluate $\int_{-1}^{5} f(x)\, dx$ without actually integrating.

Answer Keys

1. $\left(13+\frac{\pi}{2}\right)$ sq. units **2.** $(38 + \pi)$ sq. units **3.** $\frac{23+\pi}{2}$ sq. units **4.** $\left(29-\frac{17\pi}{4}\right)$ sq. units

5. (a) 1 sq. units (b) 1 sq. units (c) $\frac{1}{4}\pi a^2$ **6.** $(4 + 2\pi)$ sq. units

7. $(2\pi + 1)$ sq. units **8.** (a) 12 (b) 148 (c) 6 (d) $\frac{1}{3}(b^3 - a^3)$

9. (a) $\frac{1}{e} - \frac{1}{e^2}$ (b) $\frac{1}{3}(e^{19} - e^{13})$ (c) $\frac{1}{2}(e^2 - 1)$ (d) $\frac{1}{2}e^2$

10. (a) $\sin b - \sin a$ (b) $\frac{1}{2}(b-a) - \frac{1}{2}\cos(b+a)\sin(b-a)$ (c) $-\frac{3}{4}(\cos b - \cos a) + \frac{1}{12}(\cos 3b - \cos 3a)$

11. $\frac{2}{3}[b\sqrt{b} - a\sqrt{a}]$ **13.** 14/3 **15.** $\frac{15}{4}$ units **16.** $\frac{11}{2}$

TEXTUAL EXERCISE–1: (OBJECTIVE)

1. If $f(x)$ is continuous function on $[a, b]$, then $\int_a^b f(x)\, dx$ represents

(a) Area bounded by the function $f(x)$, above x-axis from ordinate $x = a$ to $x = b$

(b) Area bounded by the function $f(x)$, x-axis from ordinate $x = a$ to $x = b$

(c) Algebraic sum, of areas bounded by the function $f(x)$, x-axis from ordinate $x = a$ to $x = b$

(d) Area bounded by the function $f(x)$, x-axis from ordinate $x = a$ to $x = b$ if $f(x) \ge 0$

2. In the following figure representing the graph of function $y = f(x)$

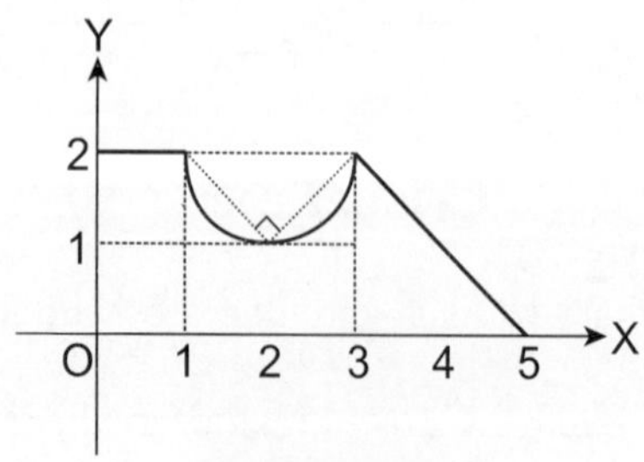

FIGURE 2.28

$\int_0^5 f(x)\,dx$ is equal to

(a) $(4 + \pi)$ sq. units (b) $(8 - \pi/2)$ sq. units
(c) $4(1 + \pi)$ sq. units (d) None of these

3. In the following figure representing the graph of function $y = f(x)$; (AB is a circular arc)

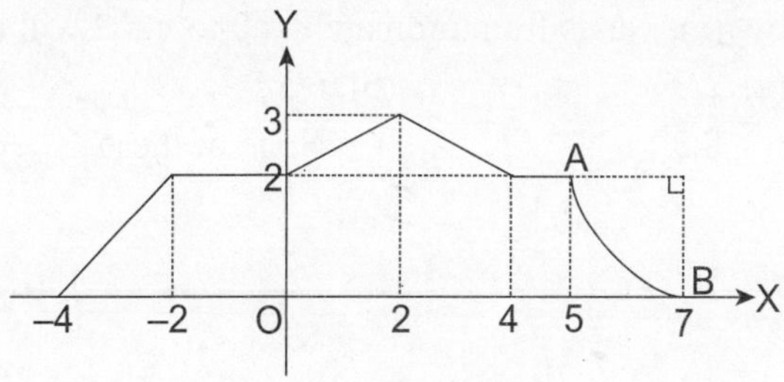

FIGURE 2.29

$\int_{-4}^{7} f(x)\,dx$ is equal to

(a) $(18 - \pi)$ (b) $(18 + \pi)$
(c) $(22 - \pi)$ (d) None of these

4. In the following figure representing the graph of function $y = f(x)$ (OA, BC being circular arcs)

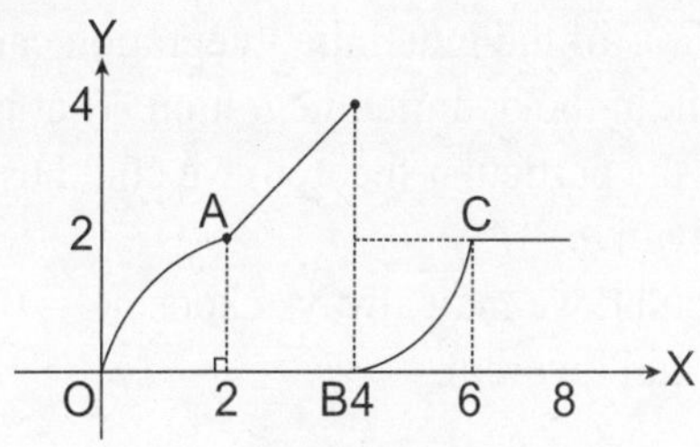

FIGURE 2.30

then $\int_0^4 f(x)\,dx + \int_4^8 f(x)\,dx$ is equal to

(a) 14 (b) $14 + \pi$
(c) $14 - 2\pi$ (d) none of these

5. In the following figure representing the graph of function $y = f(x)$, (each part of function being circular),

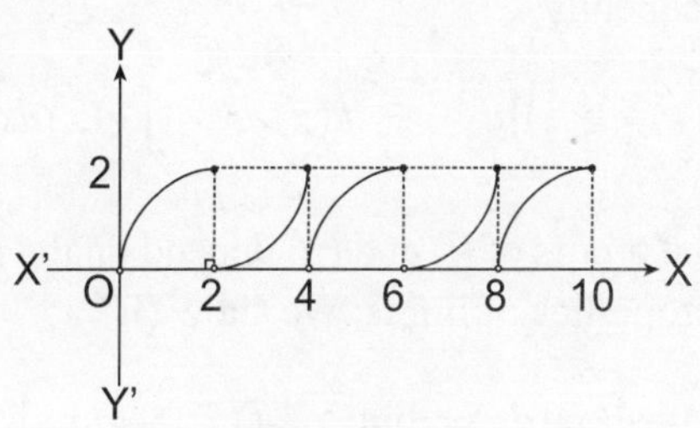

FIGURE 2.31

then $\int_0^2 f(x)\,dx + \int_2^4 f(x)\,dx + \ldots + \int_8^{10} f(x)\,dx$ is equal to

(a) $20 + \pi$ (b) $8 + \pi$
(c) 12 (d) None of these

6. If $f(x)$ is a continuous function on $[a, b]$ and $f(x) \geq 0$, then $\int_a^b f(x)\,dx$ converges to

(a) $\lim_{\substack{h\to 0\\ n\to\infty}} \sum_{r=1}^{n} hf\left(a+\overline{r-1}h\right); h = \dfrac{b-a}{n}$

(b) $\lim_{\substack{h\to 0\\ n\to\infty}} \sum_{r=1}^{n} hf\left(a+rh\right); h = \dfrac{b-a}{n}$

(c) $\lim_{\substack{h\to 0\\ n\to\infty}} \sum_{r=0}^{n} f\left(a+\overline{r-1}h\right); h = \dfrac{b-a}{n}$

(d) None of these

7. If $f(x)$ is a continuous non-decreasing and non constant function on $[a, b]$ and $f(x) \geq 0$, then $\int_a^b f(x)\,dx$ is equal to

(a) $= \lim_{\substack{n\to\infty\\ h\to 0}} \sum_{r=1}^{n} hf\left(a+\overline{r-1}h\right)$

(b) $> \lim_{\substack{n\to\infty\\ h\to 0}} \sum_{r=1}^{n} hf\left(a+\overline{r-1}h\right)$

(c) $< \lim_{\substack{n\to\infty\\ h\to 0}} \sum_{r=1}^{n} hf\left(a+rh\right)$

(d) None of these

8. If an object is moving with velocity $v(t)$ having its graph as shown below (OA, BC being circular arcs),

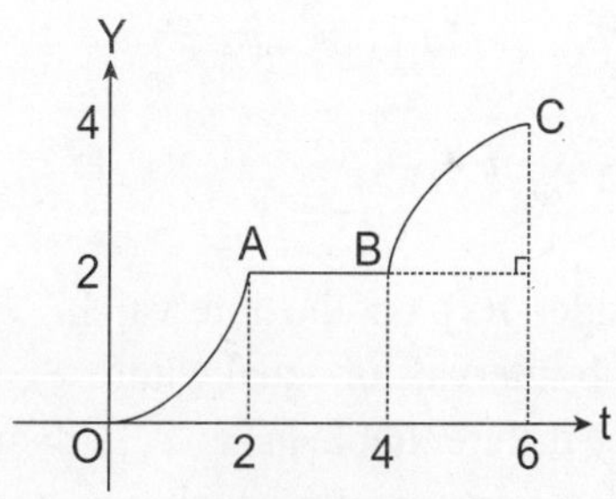

FIGURE 2.32

then the displacement of object in the interval $t = 0$ to $t = 6$ is equal to

(a) $16 - \pi$ (b) 12
(c) $12 + \pi$ (d) None of these

9. In the following figure representing the graph of function $y = f(x)$; (AB and BC circular arcs),

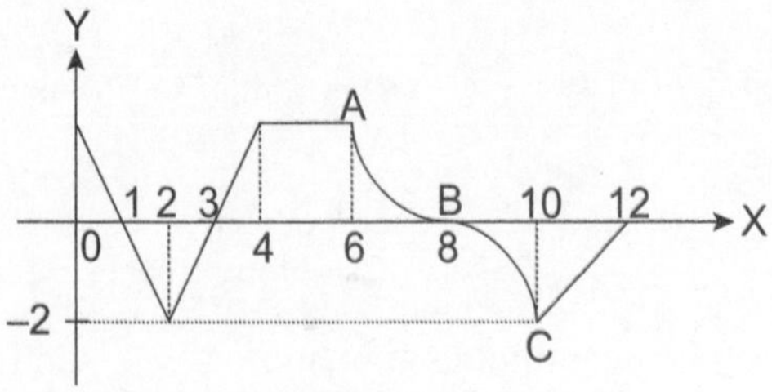

FIGURE 2.33

then $\int_0^{12} |f(x)|dx$ equals

(a) $19 - 2\pi$
(b) $18 - 2\pi$
(c) $20 - 2\pi$
(d) None of these

10. If for a continuous and non-negative function $f(x)$, $\sum_{r=1}^{n}\left(\frac{2}{n}\right)f\left((r).\frac{2}{n}\right) = \frac{8}{n^3}\sum_{r=1}^{n} r^2$, then the area bounded by $f(x)$, x-axis from ordinate $x = 0$ to $x = 2$ will be
(a) 2/3 (b) 6/5
(c) 8/3 (d) None of these

Answer Keys

1. (c, d) **2.** (b) **3.** (c) **4.** (a) **5.** (b) **6.** (a, b) **7.** (b, c) **8.** (c) **9.** (b) **10.** (c)

SECOND FUNDAMENTAL THEOREM OF INTEGRAL CALCULUS

If $f(x)$ is a continuous function $\forall\, x \in [a, b]$ such that its anti-derivative exist and is given as $F(x)$.

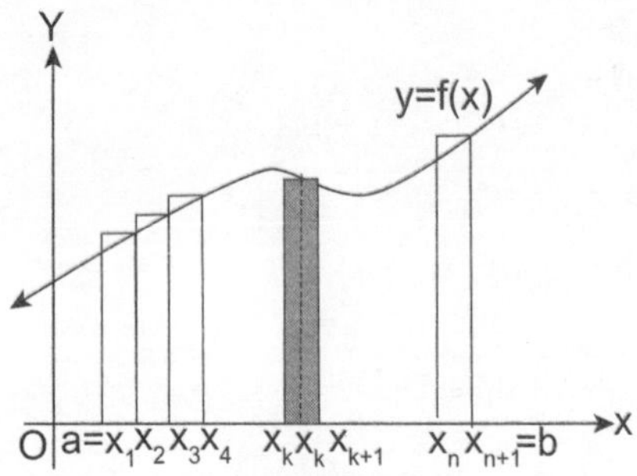

FIGURE 2.34

i.e., $\int f(x)\,dx = F(x)$ or $F'(x) = f(x)$, then $\int_a^b f(x)\,dx = F(b) - F(a)$

Proof: Consider $f(x)$ on the interval $[a, b]$ and divide $[a, b]$ into n sub-intervals of equal width.

Let $F(x)$ be differentiable in $[x_k, x_{k+1}]$, then by L.M.V.T., there exists atleast one point x_k^* such that,

$$F'(x_k^*) = \frac{F(x_{k+1}) - F(x_k)}{x_{k+1} - x_k} \text{ but } F'(x_k^*) = f(x_k^*)$$

$f(x_k^*)\,\Delta x = F(x_{k+1}) - F(x_k)$ and

$$x_{k+1} - x_k = \Delta x = \frac{(b-a)}{n}\ \forall\, k \in 1, 2, ..., n$$

$f(x_k^*)\,\Delta x = F(x_{k+1}) - F(x_k)$

$$\Rightarrow \int_a^b f(x)\,dx = \lim_{n\to\infty}\sum_{k=1}^{n} f(x_k^*)\,\Delta x$$

$$= \lim_{n\to\infty}\sum_{k=1}^{n}\left(F(x_{k+1}) - F(x_k)\right)$$

$= F(x_2) - F(x_1) + F(x_3) - F(x_2) + F(x_4) - F(x_3) + \ldots + F(x_n) - F(x_{n-1}) + F(x_{n+1}) - F(x_n) = F(x_{n+1}) - F(x_1) = F(b) - F(a)$

Note that C of the indefinite integration cancels out, as it always will, in the definite integration. That is why in the statement of the particular theorem we could use the phrase any anti-derivative.

In particular, we may always choose $C = 0$ in applying the fundamental theorem.

LINEARITY OF THE DEFINITE INTEGRAL

Suppose that f and g are integrable on $[a, b]$ and that k is a constant. Then kf and $f + g$ are integrable and:

(i) $\int_a^b kf(x)\,dx = k\int_a^b f(x)\,dx$;

(ii) $\int_a^b [f(x) + g(x)]\,dx = \int_a^b f(x)\,dx + \int_a^b g(x)\,dx$; and

consequently

(iii) $\int_a^b [f(x) - g(x)]\,dx = \int_a^b f(x)\,dx - \int_a^b g(x)\,dx$

Proof: The proofs of (i) and (ii) depend on the linearity of Σ and the properties of limits. We show (ii)

$$\int_a^b [f(x) + g(x)]\,dx = \lim_{|P|\to 0}\sum_{i=1}^{n}[f(\bar{x}_i) + g(\bar{x}_i)]\Delta_i$$

$$= \lim_{|P|\to 0}\left[\sum_{i=1}^{n} f(\overline{x}_i)\Delta_i + \sum_{i=1}^{n} g(\overline{x}_i)\Delta_i\right]$$

$$= \lim_{|P|\to 0}\sum_{i=1}^{n} f(\overline{x}_i)\Delta_i + \lim_{|P|\to 0}\sum_{i=1}^{n} g(\overline{x}_i)\Delta_i$$

$$= \int_a^b f(x)\,dx + \int_a^b g(x)\,dx$$

Part (iii) follows from (i) and (ii) on writing $f(x) - g(x)$ as $f(x) + (-1)\, g(x)$.

REMARK

The definite integral is a Linear Operation. Earlier we learned that Dx, $\int dx$ and Σ are linear operations. You can add $\int_a^b ...dx$ to the list.

ILLUSTRATION 15: Find the algebraic summation of the area bounded by the function $f(x)$, x-axis and between the ordinates $x = -2$ to $x = 3$

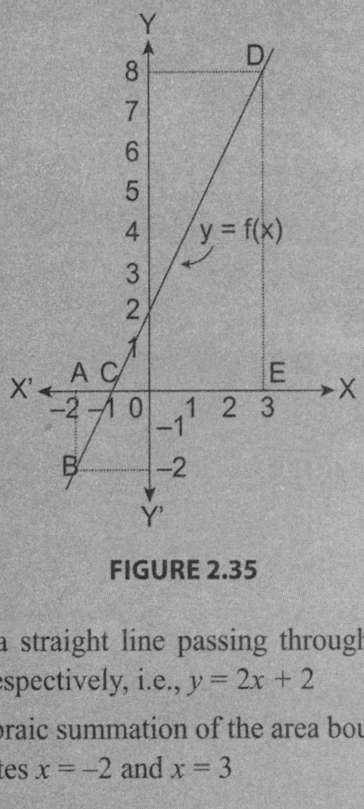

FIGURE 2.35

SOLUTION: Given function is a straight line passing through the points C and D having co-ordinates $(-1, 0)$ and $(3, 8)$ respectively, i.e., $y = 2x + 2$

We are to find algebraic summation of the area bounded by the figure $f(x) = 2x + 2$, x-axis and between the ordinates $x = -2$ and $x = 3$

i.e., $\int_{-2}^{3} (2x+2)dx$ ...(1)

Now let $F(x) = \int (2x+2)dx = x^2 + 2x + c$, then by second fundamental theorem of integral calculus, $\int_{-2}^{3} (2x+2)\,dx = F(3) - F(-2) = (9 + 6 + c) - (4 - 4 + c) = 15$ square units.

Verification: We can verify the above calculated answer by evaluating $-$(area of ΔABC) and area of ΔCED and adding.

i.e., $-(ar\ \Delta ABC) + (ar\ \Delta CED) = -\frac{1}{2}(1)(2) + \frac{1}{2}(4)(8) = 15$ square units.

ILLUSTRATION 16: Evaluate the algebraic summation of the area enclosed by the given parabolic curve, with x-axis and between the ordinates $x = -3$ and $x = 5$

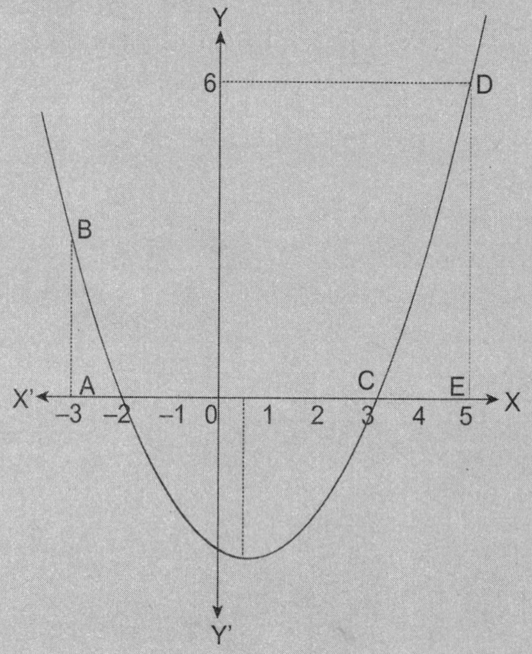

FIGURE 2.36

SOLUTION: It is given that the given function is parabolic.

Thus, we can suppose $f(x) = ax^2 + bx + c$.

Clearly $x = -2$ and $x = 3$ are its roots

$\Rightarrow$ $f(x) = a(x + 2)(x - 3)$

Also co-ordinates of D are (5, 6) and parabola pass through D.

$\Rightarrow$ $6 = a((7)(2)$

$\Rightarrow$ $a = 3/7$ $\quad\Rightarrow f(x) = \frac{3}{7}(x+2)(x-3)$

We are to find $\int_{-3}^{5} f(x)\,dx$ ...(1)

Let $F(x) = \int f(x)\,dx = \int \frac{3}{7}(x+2)(x-3)\,dx$

$$= \frac{3}{7}\left(\frac{x^3}{3} - \frac{x^2}{2} - 6x\right) + C = \frac{1}{7}x^3 - \frac{3}{14}x^2 - \frac{18}{7}x + C$$

$\therefore$ By second theorem of integral calculus $\int_{-3}^{5} f(x)\,dx = F(5) - F(-3)$

$$\Rightarrow \int_{-3}^{5} f(x)\,dx = F(5) - F(-3) = \left[\frac{1}{7}(5)^3 - \frac{3}{14}(5)^2 - \frac{18}{7}(5) + C\right]$$

$$-\left[\frac{1}{7}(-3)^3 - \frac{3}{14}(-3)^2 - \frac{18}{7}(-3) + C\right]$$

$$= \frac{1}{7}[125 + 27] - \frac{3}{14}(25 - 9) - \frac{18}{7}(5 + 3) = \frac{152}{7} - \frac{24}{7} - \frac{144}{7} = \frac{-16}{7} \text{ square units.}$$

NOTE

Here –ve sign shows that the area below x-axis is greater than the total area above x-axis.

ILLUSTRATION 17: Evaluate the algebraic summation of the area enclosed by the given cubic polynomial with x-axis and between the ordinates $x = 0$ to $x = 8$.

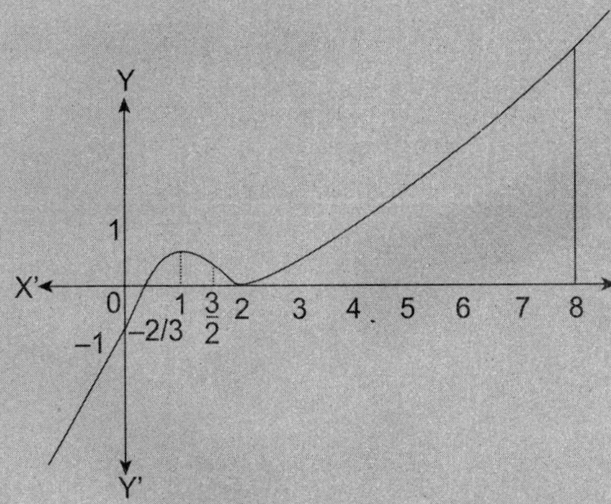

FIGURE 2.37

SOLUTION: We are to calculate the algebraic sum of shaded area

Given curve is a cubic polynomial

From diagram, it is clear that

(a) $x = 1$ and $x = 2$ are roots of $f'(x)$

$\Rightarrow f'(x) = k(x - 1)(x - 2)$

(b) $x = 2$ is a root of $f(x) \Rightarrow f(2) = 0$

(c) $f(0) = -2/3$

Now $f'(x) = k(x^2 - 3x + 2)$

$$\Rightarrow \quad f(x) = k\left(\frac{x^3}{3} - \frac{3x^2}{2} + 2x\right) + C \qquad \text{...(1)}$$

Now $f(0) = -\dfrac{2}{3}$ $\qquad \Rightarrow C = -\dfrac{2}{3}$

$$\Rightarrow \quad f(x) = k\left(\frac{x^3}{3} - \frac{3}{2}x^2 + 2x\right) - \frac{2}{3} \text{ and } f(2) = 0$$

$$\Rightarrow \quad 0 = k\left(\frac{8}{3} - 6 + 4\right) - \frac{2}{3}$$

$$\Rightarrow \quad 0 = k\left(\frac{2}{3}\right) - \frac{2}{3} \qquad \Rightarrow k = 1$$

$$\therefore \quad f(x) = \frac{x^3}{3} - \frac{3}{2}x^2 + 2x - \frac{2}{3}$$

$\therefore$ Required area $= \int_0^8 f(x)\,dx$ ...(2)

Let $F(x) = \int f(x)\,dx = \int\left(\frac{x^3}{3} - \frac{3}{2}x^2 + 2x - \frac{2}{3}\right)dx$

$= \frac{x^4}{12} - \frac{x^3}{2} + x^2 - \frac{2}{3}x + C$ ...(3)

By second theorem of integral calculus

$\int_0^8 f(x)\,dx = F(8) - F(0) = \left[\frac{1024}{3} - 256 + 64 - \frac{16}{3} + C\right] - [C]$

$= \frac{1008}{3} - 192 = 336 - 192 = 144$ square units.

ILLUSTRATION 18: Evaluate $\int_{-1}^{2} (4x - 6x^2)\,dx$

SOLUTION: Here we will do it by another way making use of the linearity of the definite integral.

Now, $\int_{-1}^{2} (4x - 6x^2)\,dx = 4\int_{-1}^{2} x dx - 6\int_{-1}^{2} x^2 dx = 4\left[\frac{x^2}{2}\right]_{-1}^{2} - 6\left[\frac{x^3}{3}\right]_{-1}^{2} = 4\left(\frac{4}{2} - \frac{1}{2}\right) - 6\left(\frac{8}{3} + \frac{1}{3}\right) = -12$

ILLUSTRATION 19: Evaluate $\int_0^4 \sqrt{x^2 + x}(2x+1)\,dx$

SOLUTION: Let $u = x^2 + x$; then $du = (2x + 1)dx$

Thus, $\int \sqrt{x^2 + x}(2x+1)\,dx = \int u^{1/2} du = \frac{2}{3}u^{3/2} + C = \frac{2}{3}(x^2 + x)^{3/2} + C = F(x)$

Therefore, by second fundamental theorem of integral calculus,

$\int_0^4 \sqrt{x^2 + x}(2x+1)\,dx = F(4) - F(0) = \left[\frac{2}{3}(16+4)^{3/2} + C\right]$

$= -[0 + C] = \left[\frac{2}{3}(20)^{3/2}\right] = \frac{2}{3}(20)^{3/2} = \frac{80}{3}\sqrt{5}$

ILLUSTRATION 20: Evaluate $\int_0^{\pi/4} \sin^3 2x \cos 2x\,dx$

SOLUTION: Let $u = \sin 2x$, then $du = 2\cos 2x\,dx$.

Thus, $\int \sin^3 2x \cos 2x\,dx = \frac{1}{2}\int (\sin^3 2x)2(\cos 2x)\,dx = \frac{1}{2}\int u^3 du = \frac{1}{2}\frac{u^4}{4} + C = \frac{\sin^4 2x}{8} + C$

$\therefore\ F(x) = \frac{\sin^4 2x}{8} + C$

$\therefore$ By second fundamental theorem of integral calculus $\int_0^{\pi/4} \sin^3 2x \cos 2x dx = F(\pi/4) - F(0)$

$= \left[\frac{1}{8}\sin^4\left(\frac{\pi}{2}\right) + C\right] - [0 + C] = \frac{1}{8}$

ILLUSTRATION 21: Evaluate the following definite integrals:

(i) $\int_0^2 x^3\,dx$ (ii) $\int_{-1}^2 (3x^3 - 2x + 3)\,dx$

(iii) $\int_1^4 (4x^3 + 7)\,dx$

SOLUTION: (i) $\int_0^2 x^3\,dx$ ...(1)

Let $F(x) = \int x^3 dx = \dfrac{x^4}{4} + C$

$\therefore$ By second fundamental theorem of integral calculus

$$\int_0^2 x^3\,dx = F(2) - F(0) = \left[\frac{(2)^4}{4} + C\right] - \left[\frac{(0)^4}{4} + C\right] = 4$$

(ii) To evaluate $\int_{-1}^2 (3x^3 - 2x + 3)\,dx$ ...(1)

Let $F(x) = \int (3x^3 - 2x + 3)\,dx = \dfrac{3x^4}{4} - \dfrac{2x^2}{2} + 3x + C = \dfrac{3}{4}x^4 - x^2 + 3x + C$

$\therefore$ By second fundamental theorem of integral calculus

$$\int_{-1}^2 (3x^3 - 2x + 3)\,dx = F(2) - F(-1)$$

$$= \left[\frac{3}{4}(2)^4 - (2)^2 + 3(2) + C\right] - \left[\frac{3}{4}(-1)^4 - (-1)^2 + 3(-1) + C\right]$$

$$= [12 - 4 + 6] - \left[\frac{3}{4} - 4\right] = 14 - \frac{3}{4} + 4 = \frac{69}{4}$$

(iii) To evaluate $\int_1^4 (4x^3 + 7)\,dx$ ...(1)

Let $F(x) = \int (4x^3 + 7)\,dx = \dfrac{4x^4}{4} + 7x + C = x^4 + 7x + C$

$\therefore$ By second fundamental theorem of integral calculus

$$\int_1^4 (4x^3 + 7)\,dx = F(4) - F(1) = (256 + 28) - (1 + 7) = 284 - 8 = 276.$$

ILLUSTRATION 22: Evaluate the following integrals:

(i) $\int_0^1 \cos x\,dx$ (ii) $\int_{\pi/6}^{\pi/2} 2\sin t\,dt$

(iii) $\int_{\pi/6}^{\pi/2} \sin^3 t\,dt$

SOLUTION: (i) $\int_0^1 \cos x\,dx = F(1) - F(0)$; where $F(x) = \int \cos x\,dx$

Here $F(x) = \sin x + C$

$$\therefore \int_0^1 \cos x\, dx = (\sin 1 + C) - (\sin 0 + C) = \sin 1$$

(ii) $\displaystyle\int_{\pi/6}^{\pi/2} 2\sin t\, dt = F\left(\frac{\pi}{2}\right) - F\left(\frac{\pi}{6}\right)$; where $F(t) = \int 2\sin t\, dt$

Here $F(t) = \int 2\sin t\, dt = -2\cos t + C$

$$\therefore \int_{\pi/6}^{\pi/2} 2\sin t\, dt = \left[-2\cos\left(\frac{\pi}{2}\right) + C\right] - \left[-2\cos\left(\frac{\pi}{6}\right) + C\right] = 2\left(\frac{\sqrt{3}}{2}\right) = \sqrt{3}$$

(iii) $\displaystyle\int_{\pi/6}^{\pi/2} \sin^3 t\, dt = F\left(\frac{\pi}{2}\right) - F\left(\frac{\pi}{6}\right)$; where $F(t) = \int \sin^3 t\, dt$ ...(1)

Here $F(t) = \int \sin^3 t\, dt = \int\left(\dfrac{3\sin t - \sin 3t}{4}\right) dt = \dfrac{3}{4}(-\cos t) + \dfrac{1}{12}\cos 3t + C$ ...(2)

$\therefore$ from (1) and (2)

$$\int_{\pi/6}^{\pi/2} \sin^3 t\, dt = \left[-\frac{3}{4}\cos\left(\frac{\pi}{2}\right) + \frac{1}{12}\cos\left(\frac{3\pi}{2}\right) + C\right] - \left[-\frac{3}{4}\cos\left(\frac{\pi}{6}\right) + \frac{1}{12}\cos\left(\frac{\pi}{2}\right) + C\right]$$

$$= \frac{3}{4}\left(\frac{\sqrt{3}}{2}\right) = \frac{3\sqrt{3}}{8}$$

ILLUSTRATION 23: Evaluate $\displaystyle\int_0^3 \frac{2x+4}{x^2+9}\, dx$

SOLUTION: $\displaystyle\int_0^3 \frac{2x+4}{x^2+9}\, dx = F(3) - F(0)$; where $F(x) = \displaystyle\int \frac{2x+4}{x^2+9}\, dx$ ...(1)

Here $\displaystyle\int \frac{2x+4}{x^2+9}\, dx = \int \frac{2x}{x^2+9}\, dx + 4\int \frac{dx}{x^2+9}$

$$= \ln(x^2+9) + 4.\frac{1}{3}\tan^{-1}\left(\frac{x}{3}\right) + C$$

$$= \ln(x^2+9) + \frac{4}{3}\tan^{-1}\left(\frac{x}{3}\right) + C \quad ...(2)$$

$$\therefore F(x) = \ln(x^2+9) + \frac{4}{3}\tan^{-1}\left(\frac{x}{3}\right) + C$$

$$\Rightarrow F(3) = \ln(18) + \frac{4}{3}\tan^{-1}(1) + C$$

$$= \ln 18 + \frac{4}{3}\left(\frac{\pi}{4}\right) + C = \ln 18 + \frac{\pi}{3} + C \quad ...(3)$$

and $F(0) = \ln 9 + \dfrac{4}{3}\tan^{-1} 0 + C = \ln 9 + C$ ...(4)

using (3) and (4) in (1) we have

$$\int_0^3 \frac{2x+4}{x^2+9}\, dx = \ln 18 + \frac{\pi}{3} - \ln 9 = \ln 2 + \frac{\pi}{3}$$

ILLUSTRATION 24: Evaluate $\int_{\pi/4}^{\pi/2}\left(x\ln x+\cos^2 x\right)dx$

SOLUTION: $\int_{\pi/4}^{\pi/2}\left(x\ln x+\cos^2 x\right)dx = \int_{\pi/4}^{\pi/2} x\ln x\,dx + \int_{\pi/4}^{\pi/2}\cos^2 x\,dx$

$$= \left[F\left(\frac{\pi}{2}\right)-F\left(\frac{\pi}{4}\right)\right]+\left[G\left(\frac{\pi}{2}\right)-G\left(\frac{\pi}{4}\right)\right] \quad \ldots(1)$$

where $F(x)=\int x\ln x\,dx$ and $G(x)=\int\cos^2 x\,dx$

Now $F(x)=\int \underset{II}{x}\,\underset{I}{\ln x}\,dx = (\ln x)\int x\,dx-\int\left(\frac{d}{dx}(\ln x)\int x\,dx\right)dx$

$$= (\ln x)\frac{x^2}{2}-\int\frac{1}{x}.\frac{x^2}{2}dx = \frac{1}{2}x^2\ln x-\frac{1}{2}\int x\,dx = \frac{1}{2}x^2\ln x-\frac{1}{4}x^2+C_1$$

$$\therefore\ F\left(\frac{\pi}{2}\right)-F\left(\frac{\pi}{4}\right)=\frac{1}{2}\left(\frac{\pi^2}{4}\right)\ln\left(\frac{\pi}{2}\right)-\frac{1}{4}\left(\frac{\pi^2}{4}\right)-\frac{1}{2}\left(\frac{\pi^2}{16}\right)\ln\left(\frac{\pi}{4}\right)+\frac{1}{4}\left(\frac{\pi^2}{16}\right)$$

$$= \frac{\pi^2}{8}\ln\left(\frac{\pi}{2}\right)-\frac{\pi^2}{32}\ln\left(\frac{\pi}{4}\right)-\left(\frac{\pi^2}{16}-\frac{\pi^2}{64}\right) = \frac{\pi^2}{8}\ln\frac{\pi}{2}-\frac{\pi^2}{32}\ln\left(\frac{\pi}{4}\right)-\frac{3}{64}\pi^2 \quad \ldots(2)$$

Also $G(x)=\int\cos^2 x\,dx = \int\frac{1+\cos 2x}{2}dx = \frac{1}{2}x+\frac{1}{4}\sin 2x+C_2$

$$\therefore\ G\left(\frac{\pi}{2}\right)-G\left(\frac{\pi}{4}\right)=\left(\frac{\pi}{4}+\frac{1}{4}\sin\pi+C_2\right)-\left(\frac{\pi}{8}+\frac{1}{4}\sin\frac{\pi}{2}+C_2\right)=\frac{\pi}{4}-\frac{\pi}{8}-\frac{1}{4}=\frac{\pi}{8}-\frac{1}{4} \quad \ldots(3)$$

Using (2) and (3) in (1) we get

$$\int_{\pi/4}^{\pi/2}\left(x\ln x+\cos^2 x\right)dx = \frac{\pi^2}{8}\ln\frac{\pi}{2}-\frac{\pi^2}{32}\ln\left(\frac{\pi}{4}\right)-\frac{3}{64}\pi^2+\frac{\pi}{8}-\frac{1}{4}$$

TEXTUAL EXERCISE–2: (SUBJECTIVE)

1. Evaluate the following integrals:

(a) $\int_0^{\pi/4}\cos^2 x\,dx$ (b) $\int_0^{\pi/2}\frac{dx}{1+\cos x}$

(c) $\int_0^{\pi/2}\sqrt{1+\cos x}\,dx$ (d) $\int_0^{\pi/2}\frac{\cos x\,dx}{1+\sin x}$

(e) $\int_0^{3}(x^2-2x)\,dx$

2. Evaluate $\int_0^1\left(xe^x+\sin\frac{\pi x}{4}\right)dx$

3. Evaluate $\int_0^4\left(4x^3-5x^2+6x+9\right)dx$

4. Evaluate $\int_0^4\left(x+x^{3/2}\right)dx$

5. Evaluate $\int_0^1\cos 2x\,dx$

6. Evaluate $\int_0^1\frac{1\,dx}{1+x^2}$

7. Evaluate $\int_2^3\frac{dx}{x^2-1}$

8. Evaluate $\int_0^1\frac{2x+3}{5x^2+1}dx$

9. Evaluate $\int_1^2 \frac{5x^2}{x^2+4x+3}dx$

10. Evaluate $\int_0^1 \left(xe^{2x}+\sin\frac{\pi x}{2}\right)dx$

11. Evaluate $\int_1^2 \frac{dx}{(x+1)(x+2)}$

12. Evaluate $\int_0^{\pi/4} \left(2\sec^2 x + x^3 + 2\right)dx$

13. Evaluate $\int_0^5 \sqrt{3t+1}\,dt$

14. Evaluate $\int_0^1 \sqrt{t}\left(t-\sqrt{t}\right)dt$

15. Evaluate $\int_1^4 \frac{x^2+x-1}{\sqrt{x}}dx$

16. Evaluate $\int_0^{0.5} \frac{6\,dx}{\sqrt{1-x^2}}$

17. Evaluate $\int_0^1 \frac{x^2-4}{x^2-2}dx$

18. Evaluate $\int_0^1 \frac{x^2-1}{x^2+1}dx$

19. Evaluate $\int_{-1}^{-1/\sqrt{3}} \cot^{-1} x\,dx$

20. Prove that $\int_0^{\pi/2} \sin^3 x\,dx = \int_0^{\pi/2} \cos^3 x\,dx = \frac{2}{3}$

21. Prove that $\int_0^{\pi/2} \sin^4 x\,dx = \int_0^{\pi/2} \cos^4 x\,dx = \frac{3\pi}{16}$

22. Find the area bounded by $f(x) = \frac{e^x}{1+e^x}$, x-axis from ordinate $x = 0$ to $x = \ln 2$.

23. Find the area bounded by $f(x) = xe^{-x}$, x-axis from ordinate bounded by $x = 0$ to $x = 1$.

24. Find the area bounded by $f(x) = xe^x$, x-axis from ordinate $x = 0$ to $x = \ln 2$.

25. Prove that $\int_{-\infty}^0 e^x\,dx = \int_0^\infty e^{-x}\,dx = \int_0^1 |\ln x|\,dx = 1$

Answer Keys

1. (a) $\left(\frac{\pi+2}{8}\right)$ (b) 1 (c) 2 (d) ln 2 (e) 0 **2.** $1+\frac{4}{\pi}-\frac{2\sqrt{2}}{\pi}$ **3.** $\frac{700}{3}$

4. $\frac{104}{5}$ **5.** $\frac{\sin 2}{2}$ **6.** $\frac{\pi}{4}$ **7.** $\frac{1}{2}\ln\frac{3}{2}$ **8.** $\frac{1}{5}\ln 6+\frac{3}{\sqrt{5}}\tan^{-1}\sqrt{5}$ **9.** $5-10\ln\left(\frac{15}{8}\right)+\frac{25}{2}\ln\left(\frac{6}{5}\right)$

10. $\frac{e^2}{4}+\frac{1}{4}+\frac{2}{\pi}$ **11.** $\ln\frac{9}{8}$ **12.** $\frac{\pi^4}{1024}+\frac{\pi}{2}+2$ **13.** 14 **14.** $-\frac{1}{10}$ **15.** $\frac{226}{15}$ **16.** π

17. $1+\frac{1}{\sqrt{2}}\ln\left(\frac{\sqrt{2}+1}{\sqrt{2}-1}\right)$ **18.** $\left(\frac{1}{2}-\frac{\pi}{2}\right)$ **19.** $\pi\left(\frac{3}{4}-\frac{2}{3\sqrt{3}}\right)+\frac{1}{2}\ln\left(\frac{2}{3}\right)$ **22.** $\ln\left(\frac{3}{2}\right)$ **23.** $\left(1-\frac{2}{e}\right)$ **24.** (ln4 – 1)

TEXTUAL EXERCISE–2: (OBJECTIVE)

1. $\int_0^{\pi/2} \frac{\cos x}{(1+\sin x)(2+\sin x)}dx =$

(a) $\log\frac{4}{3}$ (b) $\log\frac{2}{3}$

(c) $\log\frac{3}{4}$ (d) None of these

2. $\int_{\pi/3}^{\pi/2} \frac{\sqrt{1+\cos x}}{(1-\cos x)^{\frac{5}{2}}}dx =$

(a) $\frac{5}{2}$ (b) $\frac{3}{2}$

(c) $\frac{1}{2}$ (d) $\frac{2}{5}$

3. $\int_0^1 \sin^{-1}\left(\frac{2x}{1+x^2}\right)dx =$

(a) $\frac{\pi}{2}-2\log\sqrt{2}$ (b) $\frac{\pi}{2}+2\log\sqrt{2}$

(c) $\frac{\pi}{4}-\log\sqrt{2}$ (d) $\frac{\pi}{4}-\log\sqrt{2}$

4. $\int_1^e \frac{e^x}{x}(1+x\log x)\,dx =$

(a) e^e (b) $e^e - e$

(c) $e^e + e$ (d) None of these

5. The value $\int_{-2}^{2}(ax^3+bx+c)dx$ depends on

(a) the value of a (b) the value of b

(c) the value of c (d) both a and b

6. $\int_0^{\pi/2}\sqrt{\cos\theta}\sin^3\theta d\theta$ equals

(a) $\frac{20}{21}$ (b) $\frac{8}{21}$

(c) $\frac{-20}{21}$ (d) $\frac{-8}{21}$

7. $\int_0^1 \frac{dx}{[ax+b(1-x)]^2} =$

(a) a/b (b) b/a

(c) ab (d) 1/ab

8. If $\int_0^k \frac{dx}{2+8x^2}=\frac{\pi}{16}$, then k is

(a) 1 (b) 1/2

(c) 1/4 (d) None of these

9. $\int_0^{1/\sqrt{2}} \frac{\sin^{-1}x}{(1-x^2)^{3/2}}dx$ is equal to

(a) $\frac{\pi}{4}+\frac{1}{2}\log 2$ (b) $\frac{\pi}{4}-\frac{1}{2}\log 2$

(c) $\frac{\pi}{2}+\log 2$ (d) $\frac{\pi}{2}-\log 2$

10. The value of integral $\int_{1/\pi}^{2/\pi}\frac{\sin(1/x)}{x^2}dx$ is

(a) 2 (b) –1

(c) 0 (d) 1

11. $\int_0^{1/2}\frac{x\sin^{-1}x}{\sqrt{1-x^2}}dx$ is equal to

(a) $\frac{1}{2}+\frac{\sqrt{3}\pi}{12}$ (b) $\frac{1}{2}-\frac{\sqrt{3}\pi}{12}$

(c) $-\frac{1}{2}-\frac{\sqrt{3}\pi}{12}$ (d) None of these

12. $\int_0^2 \sqrt{\frac{2+x}{2-x}}dx$ is equal to

(a) $\pi + 2$ (b) $\pi + \frac{3}{2}$

(c) $\pi + 1$ (d) None of these

13. $\int_0^{\pi/8}\frac{\sec^2 2x}{2}\,dx$ is equal to

(a) $\frac{1}{4}$ (b) $\frac{1}{3}$

(c) $\frac{1}{2}$ (d) None of these

14. $\int_0^{2\pi}\sqrt{1+\sin\frac{x}{2}}dx$ is equal to

(a) 0 (b) 2

(c) 8 (d) 4

15. $\int_0^1 \cos^{-1}x\,dx$ is equal to

(a) 0 (b) 1

(c) 2 (d) None of these

16. $\int_0^2 \frac{x^3dx}{(x^2+1)^{\frac{3}{2}}}$ is equal to

(a) $(\sqrt{2}-1)^2$ (b) $\frac{(\sqrt{2}-1)^2}{\sqrt{2}}$

(c) $\frac{\sqrt{2}-1}{\sqrt{2}}$ (d) None of these

17. $\int_0^{\pi/4}\frac{4\sin 2\theta d\theta}{\sin^4\theta+\cos^4\theta} =$

(a) $\pi/4$ (b) $\pi/2$

(c) π (d) None of these

18. The value of $\int_a^b \frac{x}{|x|}dx,\ a<b<0$ is

(a) $-(|a|+|b|)$ (b) $|b|-|a|$

(c) $|a|-|b|$ (b) $|a|+|b|$

19. The points of intersection of $F_1(x)=\int_2^x(2t-5)dt =$ and $F_2(x)=\int_0^x 2t\,dt$, are

(a) $\left(\frac{6}{5},\frac{36}{25}\right)$ (b) $\left(\frac{2}{3},\frac{4}{9}\right)$

(c) $\left(\frac{1}{3},\frac{1}{9}\right)$ (d) $\left(\frac{1}{5},\frac{1}{25}\right)$

20. $\int_0^{b-c} f''(x+a)dx$ equals

(a) $f'(a) - f'(b)$ (b) $f'(b-c+a) - f'(a)$
(c) $f'(b+c-a) + f'(a)$ (d) None of these

21. $\int_0^1 \frac{d}{dx}\left[\sin^{-1}\left(\frac{2x}{1+x^2}\right)\right]dx$ is equal to

(a) 0 (b) π
(c) $\pi/2$ (d) $\pi/4$

22. $\int_0^{\infty} \frac{xdx}{(1+x)(1+x^2)}$ is equal to

(a) 0 (b) $\pi/2$
(c) $\pi/4$ (d) 1

23. Let (a, b) and (λ, μ) be two points on the curve $y = f(x)$. If the slope of the tangent to the curve at (x, y) be $\phi(x)$, then $\int_a^{\lambda} \phi(x)dx$ is

(a) $\lambda - a$ (b) $\mu - b$
(c) $\lambda + \mu - a - b$ (d) None of these

24. $\int_0^{\pi/4} \frac{dx}{\cos^4 x - \cos^2 x \sin^2 x + \sin^4 x}$ is equal to

(a) $\pi/2$ (b) $\pi/4$
(c) $\pi/3$ (d) None of these

25. The area of the region bounded by the curve $y = (x^2 + 1)$ and x-axis on $[-1, 1]$ is
(a) 5/3 (b) 8/3
(c) 7/3 (d) None of these

26. The area bounded by the curve $y = \sqrt{x}$ and x-axis on $[0, 1]$ equals
(a) 4/3 (b) 2/3
(c) 5/3 (d) None of these

27. The area bounded by the curve $y = \sec^2 x$ and x-axis on $\left[0, \frac{\pi}{4}\right]$ equals

(a) 2 (b) 1
(c) $\sqrt{2}$ (d) None of these

28. The area bounded by the function $y = \sin x + \cos x$ and x-axis on $\left[0, \frac{\pi}{2}\right]$ equals

(a) 2 (b) 1
(c) 3 (d) None of these

29. The area bounded by the function $y = e^x - x$ and x-axis on $[0, 1]$ equals
(a) $e - 1/2$ (b) $e + 1$
(c) $e - \frac{3}{2}$ (d) None of these

30. The area bounded by the function $y = (x^2 + x + 1)\sqrt{x}$, and x-axis on $[1, 4]$ equals

(a) $\frac{5602}{105}$ (b) $\frac{562}{35}$
(c) $\frac{801}{35}$ (d) None of these

31. The area bounded by the function $y = \frac{x^2 - 2x + 3}{x}$, and x-axis on $[1, 2]$ equals

(a) $3\ln 2 - 1$ (b) $3\ln 2 - \frac{1}{2}$
(c) $2\ln 3 - \frac{1}{2}$ (d) None of these

32. The area bounded by the function $y = \frac{2}{1+x^2}$ and x-axis on $[0, 1]$ equals

(a) $\frac{\pi}{4}$ (b) $\frac{2\pi}{3}$
(c) $\frac{\pi}{2}$ (d) None of these

33. The area bounded by the function $f(x) = |\sin x|$ and x-axis on $[\pi, 2\pi]$ equals
(a) 0 (b) 2
(c) 3 (d) None of these

Answer Keys

1. (a)	**2.** (b)	**3.** (a)	**4.** (a)	**5.** (c)	**6.** (b)	**7.** (d)	**8.** (b)	**9.** (b)	**10.** (d)
11. (b)	**12.** (a)	**13.** (a)	**14.** (c)	**15.** (b)	**16.** (d)	**17.** (c)	**18.** (b)	**19.** (a)	**20.** (b)
21. (c)	**22.** (c)	**23.** (b)	**24.** (a)	**25.** (b)	**26.** (b)	**27.** (b)	**28.** (a)	**29.** (c)	**30.** (a)
31. (b)	**32.** (c)	**33.** (b)							

PROPERTIES OF DEFINITE INTEGRAL

Property 1: Mere change of variable does not change the value of integral, i.e., $\int_a^b f(x)\,dx = \int_a^b f(t)\,dt$

Proof: Let $\int f(x)dx = \phi(x)$

$\Rightarrow \quad \int f(t)dt = \phi(t)$

$\Rightarrow \quad \int_a^b f(x)dx = [\phi(x)]_a^b = \phi(b) - \phi(a)$ ...(i)

And $\int_a^b f(t)dt = [\phi(t)]_a^b = \phi(b) - \phi(a)$ ...(ii)

Clearly from (i) and (ii)

$$\int_a^b f(x)dx = \int_a^b f(t)dt = \phi(b) - \phi(a)$$

ILLUSTRATION 25: Evaluate $\int_1^3 \frac{1-\cos 2t}{2}dt + \int_1^3 \frac{1+\cos 2u}{8}du + \int_1^3 \frac{1+\cos 2v}{4}dv + \int_1^3 \frac{2(1+\cos 2w)}{5}dw - \int_1^3 \frac{11(1+\cos 2x)}{40}dx$

SOLUTION: Since definite integral is independent of variable of integration, we can take variable of each integral same say (x)

$$I = \int_1^3 \frac{1-\cos 2x}{2}dx + \int_1^3 \frac{1+\cos 2x}{8}dx + \int_1^3 \frac{1+\cos 2x}{4}dx + \frac{2}{5}\int_1^3 (1+\cos 2x)\,dx - \frac{11}{40}\int_1^3 (1+\cos 2x)\,dx$$

$$= \int_1^3 \sin^2 x\,dx + \int_1^3 \left(\frac{1}{8}+\frac{1}{4}+\frac{2}{5}-\frac{11}{40}\right)(1+\cos 2x)\,dx$$

$$= \int_1^3 \sin^2 x\,dx + \int_1^3 \frac{1}{2}(1+\cos 2x)\,dx = \int_1^3 \sin^2 x\,dx + \int_1^3 \cos^2 x\,dx$$

$$= \int_1^3 \left(\sin^2 x + \cos^2 x\right)dx = \int_1^3 1\,dx = [x]_1^3 = (3-1) = 2$$

Property 2: By interchanging the limits of integration the value of integral becomes negative, i.e., $\int_a^b f(x)\,dx = -\int_b^a f(x)\,dx$

Proof: Let $\int f(x)\,dx = \phi(x)$,

Then $\int_a^b f(x)\,dx = [\phi(x)]_a^b = \phi(b) - \phi(a)$

And $-\int_b^a f(x)\,dx = -[\phi(x)]_a^b = -[\phi(b) - \phi(a)]$

Thus, $\int_a^b f(x)\,dx = -\int_b^a f(x)\,dx$

ILLUSTRATION 26: Evaluate $\int_2^5 \cos^2 x\,dx + \int_5^2 \sin^2 x\,dx$

SOLUTION: Given $I = \int_2^5 \cos^2 x\,dx + \int_5^2 \sin^2 x\,dx = \int_2^5 \cos^2 x\,dx - \int_2^5 \sin^2 x\,dx = \int_2^5 \left(\cos^2 x - \sin^2 x\right)dx$

$$= \int_2^5 \cos 2x\,dx = \left[\frac{\sin 2x}{2} + C\right]_2^5 = \frac{1}{2}\left(\sin 10 - \sin 4\right) = \frac{1}{2}\left(2\left(\cos 7 \sin 3\right)\right) = \cos 7 \sin 3$$

ILLUSTRATION 27: Evaluate $\int_0^1 \cos^{-1} x\,dx - \int_1^0 \sin^{-1} x\,dx$

SOLUTION: Given $I = \int_0^1 \cos^{-1} x\,dx - \int_1^0 \sin^{-1} x\,dx = \int_0^1 \cos^{-1} x\,dx + \int_0^1 \sin^{-1} x\,dx = \int_0^1 \left(\cos^{-1} x + \sin^{-1} x\right) dx$

$= \int_0^1 \left(\frac{\pi}{2}\right) dx = \frac{\pi}{2}(1-0) = \frac{\pi}{2}$ $\left(\because \sin^{-1} x + \cos^{-1} x = \frac{\pi}{2}\ \forall x \in [-1,1]\right)$

Property 3: $\int_a^b f(x)\,dx = \int_a^c f(x)\,dx + \int_c^b f(x)\,dx$ provided 'c' lies in the domain of continuity of $f(x)$.

Proof: **Geometrical Proof:**

Case (i): when $a < b < c$

Let $\int_a^b f(x)\,dx$ bounds the area as shown by shaded region as shown in Fig. 2.38.

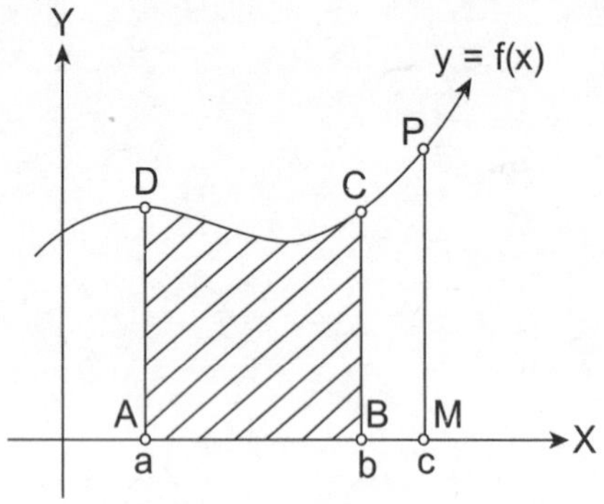

FIGURE 2.38

Now, $\int_a^b f(x)dx = \text{area } ABC\overset{\frown}{D}$ ...(i)

And $\int_a^c f(x)dx + \int_c^b f(x)dx = \int_a^c f(x)dx - \int_b^c f(x)dx$

$= \text{Area } AM\overset{\frown}{PD} - \text{Area } BM\overset{\frown}{PC} = \text{Area } AB\overset{\frown}{CD}$ ...(ii)

$\therefore$ from (i) and (ii) result follows

Case (ii): when $a < c < b$

Let $\int_a^b f(x)dx$ bounds the area as shown by shaded region as shown in Fig. 2.39.

Now, $\int_a^b f(x)dx = \text{Area } AB\overset{\frown}{CD}$ ...(iii)

And $\int_a^c f(x)dx + \int_c^b f(x)dx$

$= \text{Area } AM\overset{\frown}{PD} + \text{Area } MB\overset{\frown}{CP} = \text{Area } ABCD$ ...(iv)

Thus, from (iii) and (iv) result follows

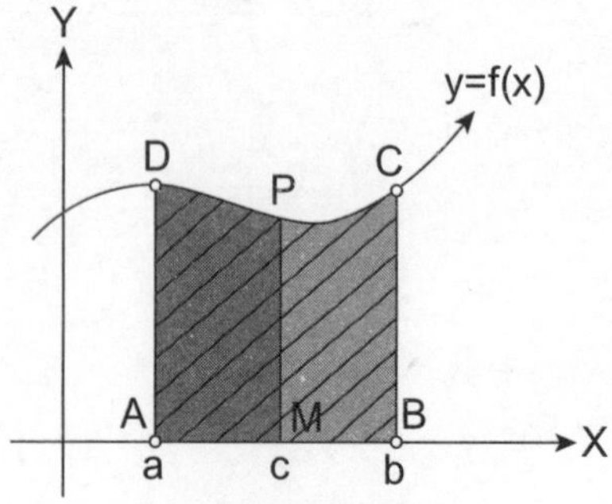

FIGURE 2.39

Aliter: Let $\int f(x)dx = F(x)$, then

$\int_a^b f(x)dx = F(b) - F(a)$ ...(i)

and $\int_a^c f(x)dx + \int_c^b f(x)dx$

$= [F(c) - F(a)] + [F(b) - F(c)] = F(b) - F(a)$ ...(ii)

From (i) and (ii), we get

$\int_a^b f(x)\,dx = \int_a^c f(x)\,dx + \int_c^b f(x)\,dx$

Generalization

The above property can be generalized into the following form:

$\int_a^b f(x)dx = \int_a^{c_1} f(x)dx + \int_{c_1}^{c_2} f(x)dx + ... + \int_{c_n}^b f(x)dx$;

where $c_1, c_2, c_3, \ldots, c_n$ lie in the domain of continuity of $f(x)$.

Conclusion

Although we can break limit of integration at any point but it is necessary to break limit at following points:

- ❑ where $f(x)$ is discontinuous.
- ❑ where $f(x)$ is not defined.
- ❑ where $f(x)$ changes its definition.

ILLUSTRATION 28: Evaluate $\int_{-\sqrt{2}}^{4} |2-x^2|\, dx$

SOLUTION: Given $f(x) = |2-x^2| = \begin{cases} 2-x^2; & 2 \ge x^2 \\ x^2-2; & 2 \le x^2 \end{cases}$

$$\Rightarrow f(x) = \begin{cases} 2-x^2; & x \in \left[-\sqrt{2}, \sqrt{2}\right] \\ x^2-2; & x \in \left(-\infty, -\sqrt{2}\right] \cup \left[\sqrt{2}, \infty\right) \end{cases}$$

∴ on interval [–√2, 4] we must have

$$f(x) = \begin{cases} (2-x^2); & x \in \left[-\sqrt{2}, \sqrt{2}\right] \\ (x^2-2); & x \in \left[\sqrt{2}, 4\right] \end{cases}$$

Thus, we must break the interval [–√2, 4] into two sub-intervals [–√2, √2] and [√2, 4] as the definition changes at $x = \sqrt{2}$.

$$\therefore \int_{-\sqrt{2}}^{4} |2-x^2|\, dx = \int_{-\sqrt{2}}^{\sqrt{2}} f(x)\, dx + \int_{\sqrt{2}}^{4} f(x)\, dx = \int_{-\sqrt{2}}^{\sqrt{2}} (2-x^2)\, dx + \int_{\sqrt{2}}^{4} (x^2-2)\, dx$$

$$= \left[2x - \frac{x^3}{3}\right]_{-\sqrt{2}}^{\sqrt{2}} + \left[\frac{x^3}{3} - 2x\right]_{\sqrt{2}}^{4}$$

$$= \left[2\left(\sqrt{2}+\sqrt{2}\right) - \frac{1}{3}\left(2\sqrt{2}+2\sqrt{2}\right)\right] + \left[\frac{1}{3}\left(64-2\sqrt{2}\right) - 2\left(4-\sqrt{2}\right)\right]$$

$$= 4\sqrt{2} - \frac{4\sqrt{2}}{3} + \frac{64}{3} - \frac{2\sqrt{2}}{3} - 8 + 2\sqrt{2} = 4\sqrt{2} + \frac{40}{3}$$

ILLUSTRATION 29: Evaluate $\int_{-\pi/2}^{\pi/2} |\sin x|\, dx$

SOLUTION: Here $f(x) = |\sin x| = \begin{cases} -\sin x; & -\dfrac{\pi}{2} \le x \le 0 \\ \sin x; & 0 \le x \le \dfrac{\pi}{2} \end{cases}$

Thus, the definition of function change at $x = 0$, although $f(x)$ is continuous on $\left[-\dfrac{\pi}{2}, \dfrac{\pi}{2}\right]$

Thus, $\int_{-\pi/2}^{\pi/2} |\sin x|\, dx = \int_{-\pi/2}^{0} (-\sin x)\, dx + \int_{0}^{\pi/2} (\sin x)\, dx$

$$= \left|\cos x\right|_{-\pi/2}^{0} - \left|\cos x\right|_{0}^{\pi/2} = (1-0) - (0-1) = 2$$

ILLUSTRATION 30: If $f(x) = \begin{cases} x+3; & \text{if } x < 3 \\ 3x^2+1; & \text{if } x \ge 3 \end{cases}$, then find $\int_{2}^{5} f(x)\, dx$

SOLUTION: $\int_{2}^{5} f(x)\, dx = \int_{2}^{3} f(x)\, dx + \int_{3}^{5} f(x)\, dx = \int_{2}^{3} (x+3)\, dx + \int_{3}^{5} (3x^2+1)\, dx = \left|\frac{x^2}{2} + 3x\right|_{2}^{3} + \left|x^3+x\right|_{3}^{5}$

$$= \frac{9-4}{2} + 3(3-2) + (5^3-3^3) + (5-3) = \frac{211}{2}$$

ILLUSTRATION 31: Evaluate $\int_0^3 x[x]\,dx$

SOLUTION: Here $f(x)$ is piece-wise continuous function on [0, 3], i.e., continuous on (0, 1); (1, 2) and (2, 3) having points of discontinuity of first kind at $x = 0, 1, 2, 3$.

Thus, we shall break the interval [0, 3] into sub-intervals (0, 1), (1, 2) and (2, 3).

i.e., $\int_0^3 f(x)\,dx = \int_0^1 f(x)\,dx + \int_1^2 f(x)\,dx + \int_2^3 f(x)\,dx$

Now we know that if $f(x)$ is continuous over (a, b), then $\int_a^b f(x)\,dx = F(b^-) - F(a^+)$; where $\int f(x)dx = F(x)$

$\therefore \quad \int_0^3 f(x)\,dx = |F(x)|_0^1 + |G(x)|_1^2 + |H(x)|_2^3$

Where $F(x) = \int f(x)dx$ for $x \in (0, 1)$

$G(x) = \int f(x)dx$ for $x \in (1, 2)$

And $H(x) = \int f(x)dx$ for $x \in (2, 3)$

$= [F(1^-) - F(0^+)] + [G(2^-) - G(1^+)] + [H(3^-) - H(2^+)]$ ...(1)

From (1) it is clear that we need not to find the value of function at the point of discontinuity

$$\therefore \quad f(x) = \begin{cases} x(0); & \text{for } 0 < x < 1 \\ x(1); & \text{for } 1 < x < 2 \\ x(2); & \text{for } 2 < x < 3 \end{cases} = \begin{cases} 0 & ; \; 0 < x < 1 \\ x & ; \; 1 < x < 2 \\ 2x & ; \; 2 < x < 3 \end{cases}$$

$$\therefore \quad \int_0^3 f(x)\,dx = \int_0^1 0\,dx + \int_1^2 x\,dx + \int_2^3 2x\,dx = \frac{1}{2}[x^2]_1^2 + [x^2]_2^3 = \frac{1}{2}[3] + [9-4] = \frac{13}{2}$$

ILLUSTRATION 32: Let $f(x)$ be the function defined by $f(x) = \begin{cases} -x^2; & \text{for } -\infty < x < 0 \\ 3 - x^3; & \text{for } 0 \le x < 2 \\ 2x - 3; & \text{for } 2 \le x < \infty \end{cases}$. Then evaluate $\int_{-2}^3 f(x)\,dx$

SOLUTION: Let us draw the graph of function $f(x)$ as shown below

Clearly $f(x)$ is piece-wise continuous function having discontinuity of first kind at $x = 0, 2$

Thus, we shall break the interval [–2, 3] into [–2, 0), (0, 2) and (2, 3] and hence

$$\int_{-2}^3 f(x)\,dx = \int_{-2}^0 f(x)\,dx + \int_0^2 f(x)\,dx + \int_2^3 f(x)\,dx$$

$$= \int_{-2}^0 (-x^2)\,dx + \int_0^2 (3 - x^3)\,dx + \int_2^3 (2x - 3)\,dx$$

$= [F(0^-) - F(-2^+)] + [G(2^-) - G(0^+)] + [H(3^+) - H(2^+)]$

Where $F(x) = \int -x^2\,dx$, $G(x) = \int (3 - x^3)\,dx$

and $H(x) = \int (2x - 3)\,dx$

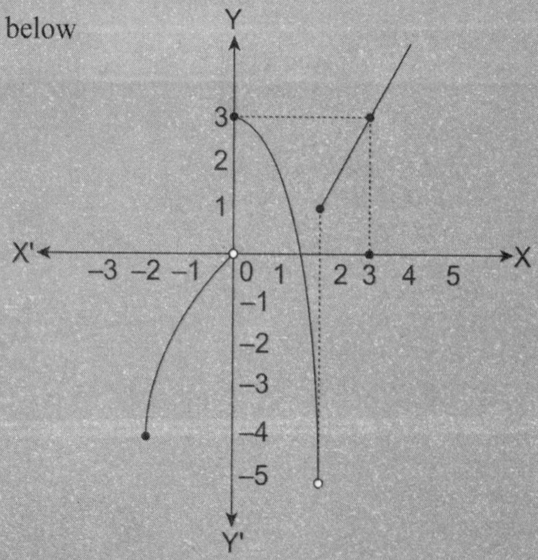

FIGURE 2.40

$$\therefore \int_{-2}^{3} f(x)\,dx = \frac{-1}{3}\left[(0)^3-(-2)^3\right] + 3[(2-0)] - \frac{1}{4}\left[(2)^4-(0)^4\right] + \frac{2}{2}\left[(3)^2-(2)^2\right] - 3(3-2)$$

$$= -\frac{8}{3}+6-4+(5)-3 = \frac{4}{3}$$

ILLUSTRATION 33: Evaluate $\int_1^2 \left[2x^2+1\right] dx$; where [.] is the greatest integer function.

SOLUTION: Let $f(x) = 2x^2 + 1;\ x \in [1, 2]$

$F'(x) = 4x > 0\ \forall\ x \in [1, 2]$

$\Rightarrow$ $f(x)$ is strictly increasing on [1, 2];

$\therefore$ Range of $f(x) = [3, 9]$ for $x \in [1, 2]$

Thus, $f(x)$ takes integer values 3, 4, 5, 6, 7, 8 and 9 and hence $f(x)$ is discontinuous function at each of the point of [1, 2] giving these integer values to $f(x)$.

Now let us find these points of discontinuity in [1, 2]

$2x^2 + 1 = 3 \quad \Rightarrow x = 1$

$2x^2 + 1 = 4 \quad \Rightarrow x = \sqrt{\frac{3}{2}}$

$2x^2 + 1 = 5 \quad \Rightarrow x = \sqrt{2}$

$2x^2 + 1 = 6 \quad \Rightarrow x = \sqrt{\frac{5}{2}}$

$2x^2 + 1 = 7 \quad \Rightarrow` x = \sqrt{3}$

$2x^2 + 1 = 8 \quad \Rightarrow x = \sqrt{\frac{7}{2}}$

$2x^2 + 1 = 9 \quad \Rightarrow x = 2$

$\therefore$ We are to divide the interval [1, 2] into sub-intervals $\left(1, \sqrt{\frac{3}{2}}\right)$; $\left(\sqrt{\frac{3}{2}}, \sqrt{2}\right)$; $\left(\sqrt{2}, \sqrt{\frac{5}{2}}\right)$; $\left(\sqrt{\frac{5}{2}}, \sqrt{3}\right)$; $\left(\sqrt{3}, \sqrt{\frac{7}{2}}\right)$; $\left(\sqrt{\frac{7}{2}}, 2\right)$

$$\therefore \int_1^2 \left[2x^2+1\right] dx = \int_1^{\sqrt{3/2}} \left[2x^2+1\right] dx + \int_{\sqrt{3/2}}^{\sqrt{2}} \left[2x^2+1\right] dx + \int_{\sqrt{2}}^{\sqrt{5/2}} \left[2x^2+1\right] dx + \int_{\sqrt{5/2}}^{\sqrt{3}} \left[2x^2+1\right] dx$$

$$+ \int_{\sqrt{3}}^{\sqrt{7/2}} \left[2x^2+1\right] dx + \int_{\sqrt{7/2}}^{2} \left[2x^2+1\right] dx$$

$$= \int_1^{\sqrt{3/2}} 3\,dx + \int_{\sqrt{3/2}}^{\sqrt{2}} 4\,dx + \int_{\sqrt{2}}^{\sqrt{5/2}} 5\,dx + \int_{\sqrt{5/2}}^{\sqrt{3}} 6\,dx + \int_{\sqrt{3}}^{\sqrt{7/2}} 7\,dx + \int_{\sqrt{7/2}}^{2} 8\,dx$$

$$= 3\left(\sqrt{\frac{3}{2}}-1\right)+4\left(\sqrt{2}-\sqrt{\frac{3}{2}}\right)+5\left(\sqrt{\frac{5}{2}}-\sqrt{2}\right)+6\left(\sqrt{3}-\sqrt{\frac{5}{2}}\right)+7\left(\sqrt{\frac{7}{2}}-\sqrt{3}\right)+8\left(2-\sqrt{\frac{7}{2}}\right)$$

$$= 13-\sqrt{\frac{3}{2}}-\sqrt{2}-\sqrt{\frac{5}{2}}-\sqrt{3}-\sqrt{\frac{7}{2}}$$

$$= 13-\left(\sqrt{\frac{3}{2}}+\sqrt{2}+\sqrt{\frac{5}{2}}+\sqrt{3}+\sqrt{\frac{7}{2}}\right)$$

ILLUSTRATION 34: Evaluate $\int_{-1}^{1}\left[x^2+x+1\right]dx$; where [.] is the greatest integer function.

SOLUTION: Given $f(x) = x^2 + x + 1$; $f'(x) = 2x + 1$

$\Rightarrow$ $f'(x) \leq 0$ for $x \leq -\dfrac{1}{2}$

And $f'(x) \geq 0$ for $x \geq -\dfrac{1}{2}$

$\Rightarrow$ $f(x)$ is a decreasing function in $\left[-1,-\dfrac{1}{2}\right]$ and increasing in $\left[-\dfrac{1}{2},1\right]$

$\therefore$ $f(x)$ has its range $=\left[f\left(-\dfrac{1}{2}\right),f(-1)\right]\cup\left[f\left(-\dfrac{1}{2}\right),f(1)\right]=\left[\dfrac{3}{4},1\right]\cup\left[\dfrac{3}{4},3\right]=\left[\dfrac{3}{4},3\right]$

$\therefore$ in $\left[\dfrac{3}{4},3\right]f(x)$ attains integer values 1, 2 and 3

So $f(x)$ will be discontinuous at the points giving these integer values. Let us obtain these integer values.

$f(x) = 1$

$\Rightarrow$ $x^2 + x + 1 = 1$ $\qquad\Rightarrow$ $x^2 + x = 0$

$\Rightarrow$ $x = 0$ or $x = -1$

$f(x) = 2$ $\qquad\Rightarrow$ $x^2 + x + 1 = 2$ $\qquad\Rightarrow$ $x^2 + x - 1 = 0$

$$\Rightarrow\quad x=\frac{-1\pm\sqrt{(1)^2-4(-1)}}{2(1)}=\frac{-1\pm\sqrt{5}}{2}$$

$f(x) = 3$ $\qquad\Rightarrow$ $x^2 + x + 1 = 3$ $\qquad\Rightarrow$ $x^2 + x - 2 = 0$

$$\Rightarrow\quad x=\frac{-1\pm\sqrt{(1)^2-4(-2)}}{2(1)}=\frac{-1\pm3}{2}=-2,1$$

i.e., on $[-1, 1]$; $f(x)$ has first kind of discontinuities at $x=-1,0,\dfrac{\sqrt{5}-1}{2},1$

So, we are to divide the interval $[-1, 1]$ into sub-intervals (1, 0); $\left(0,\dfrac{\sqrt{5}-1}{2}\right)$; $\left(\dfrac{\sqrt{5}-1}{2},1\right)$

Now $f(-1) = 1$, $f(0) = 1$, $f\left(\dfrac{\sqrt{5}-1}{2}\right)=2$, $f(1) = 3$

Clearly there is no integer in $(-1, 0)$ and in $(-1, 0)$, $f(x) \in (0, 1)$

$\Rightarrow$ $[f(x)] = 0$

In $\left(0,\dfrac{\sqrt{5}-1}{2}\right)$; $f(x) \in (1, 2)$ $\qquad\Rightarrow$ $[f(x)] = 1$

In $\left(\dfrac{\sqrt{5}-1}{2},1\right)$; $f(x) \in (2, 3)$ $\qquad\Rightarrow$ $[f(x)] = 2$

$$\therefore\quad \int_{-1}^{1}\left[x^2+x+1\right]dx=\int_{-1}^{0}0\,dx+\int_{0}^{\frac{\sqrt{5}-1}{2}}1\,dx+\int_{\frac{\sqrt{5}-1}{2}}^{1}2\,dx$$

$$=0+\left[x\right]_0^{\frac{\sqrt{5}-1}{2}}+2\left[x\right]_{\frac{\sqrt{5}-1}{2}}^{1}=\frac{\sqrt{5}-1}{2}+2\left(1-\frac{\sqrt{5}-1}{2}\right)=2-\left(\frac{\sqrt{5}-1}{2}\right)=\frac{5-\sqrt{5}}{2}$$

Let us analyze the above problem graphically.

Graph of $f(x) = x^2 + x + 1$ in $[-1, 1]$ is as shown below.

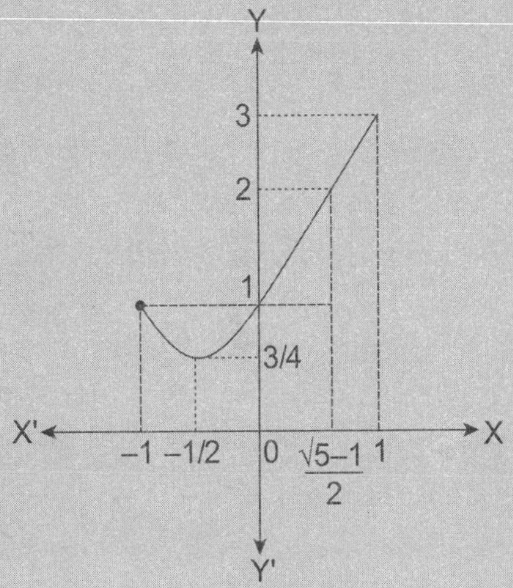

FIGURE 2.41

Therefore, graph of $[f(x)] = [x^2 + x + 1]$ in $[-1, 1]$ is as shown below

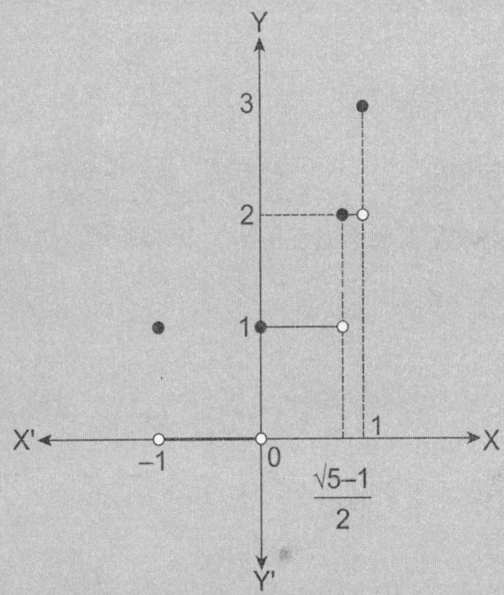

FIGURE 2.42

Clearly $\int_{-1}^{1}[f(x)]\,dx = \int_{-1}^{1}\left[x^2+x+1\right]dx$ represents the shaded region as shown in the figure given above

$$= (1)(0) + \left(\frac{\sqrt{5}-1}{2}\right)(1) + \left[1 - \left(\frac{\sqrt{5}-1}{2}\right)\right](2)$$

$$= \frac{\sqrt{5}-1}{2} + 2 - 2\left(\frac{\sqrt{5}-1}{2}\right) = 2 - \left(\frac{\sqrt{5}-1}{2}\right) = \frac{5-\sqrt{5}}{2}$$

ILLUSTRATION 35: Evaluate $\int_{-1}^{1}\left[2x^3-1\right]dx$

SOLUTION: For $x \in [-1, 1], x^3 \in [-1, 1]$

$\Rightarrow\ 2x^3 \in [-2, 2]$

$\Rightarrow\ 2x^3 - 1 \in [-3, 1]$

$\therefore$ for $x \in [-1, 1]$, $f(x)$ attains integer values $-3, -2, -1, 0, 1$. Also $f'(x) = 6x^2 \geq 0$

$\Rightarrow$ $f(x)$ is an increasing function.

Therefore, $f(x)$ has first kind of discontinuous at the points where the function attains these values in [–1, 1].

Let us find these values

$f(x) = -3 \quad \Rightarrow 2x^3 - 1 = -3 \quad \Rightarrow 2x^3 = -2 \quad \Rightarrow x = -1;$

$f(x) = -2 \quad \Rightarrow 2x^3 - 1 = -2 \quad \Rightarrow 2x^3 = -1 \quad \Rightarrow x = \sqrt[3]{-\frac{1}{2}};$

$f(x) = -1 \quad \Rightarrow 2x^3 - 1 = -1 \quad \Rightarrow x = 0;$

$f(x) = 0 \quad \Rightarrow 2x^3 - 1 = 0 \quad \Rightarrow x = \sqrt[3]{\frac{1}{2}};$

and $f(x) = 1 \quad \Rightarrow 2x^3 - 1 = 1 \quad \Rightarrow x = 1$

Thus, we are to divide the interval [–1, 1] into sub-intervals $\left(-1, \sqrt[3]{-\frac{1}{2}}\right); \left(\sqrt[3]{-\frac{1}{2}}, 0\right); \left(0, \sqrt[3]{\frac{1}{2}}\right)$

and $\left(\sqrt[3]{\frac{1}{2}}, 1\right)$ i.e., $\int_{-1}^{1}[f(x)]dx$

$$= \int_{-1}^{\sqrt[3]{-1/2}}[f(x)]dx + \int_{\sqrt[3]{-1/2}}^{0}[f(x)]dx + \int_{0}^{\sqrt[3]{1/2}}[f(x)]dx + \int_{\sqrt[3]{1/2}}^{1}[f(x)]dx$$

$$= \int_{-1}^{\sqrt[3]{-1/2}}(-3)\,dx + \int_{\sqrt[3]{-1/2}}^{0}(-2)\,dx + \int_{0}^{\sqrt[3]{1/2}}(-1)\,dx + \int_{\sqrt[3]{1/2}}^{1}0\,dx$$

$$= -3\left[\sqrt[3]{-\frac{1}{2}} - (-1)\right] - 2\left[0 - \sqrt[3]{-\frac{1}{2}}\right] - \left[\sqrt[3]{\frac{1}{2}} - 0\right] + 0$$

$$= -3\left(\sqrt[3]{-\frac{1}{2}}\right) - 3 + 2\left(\sqrt[3]{-\frac{1}{2}}\right) - \sqrt[3]{\frac{1}{2}}$$

$$= -\left(\sqrt[3]{-\frac{1}{2}}\right) - \left(\sqrt[3]{\frac{1}{2}}\right) - 3$$

$$= \sqrt[3]{\frac{1}{2}} - \sqrt[3]{\frac{1}{2}} - 3 = -3$$

Graphically

Graph of $y = [2x^3 - 1]$ in $[-1, 1]$ is as shown below

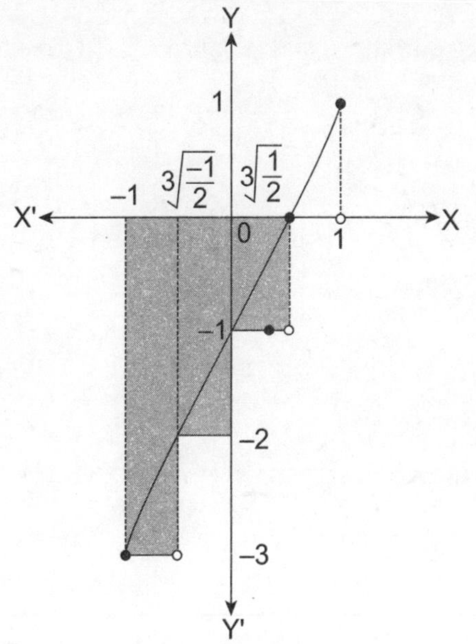

FIGURE 2.43

Clearly $\int_{-1}^{1}[f(x)]\,dx$ represents the area of region shown by shading in the above as shown in Fig. 2.43.

$$\therefore \int_{-1}^{1}[f(x)]\,dx = -\left[(3)\left(1-\sqrt[3]{\frac{1}{2}}\right)+(2)\left(\sqrt[3]{\frac{1}{2}}\right)+(1)\left(\sqrt[3]{\frac{1}{2}}\right)\right]$$

$$= -\left[3-3\left(\sqrt[3]{\frac{1}{2}}\right)+(2)\left(\sqrt[3]{\frac{1}{2}}\right)+\left(\sqrt[3]{\frac{1}{2}}\right)\right] = -3$$

Property 4: $\int_a^b f(x)\,dx = 0$ and $f(x)$ is continuous, then $f(x)$ has at least one root $\in (a, b)$

Proof: By the concept of area as an anti-derivative, we know that $\int_a^b f(x)\,dx$ represents the algebraic sum of areas bounded by the function $f(x)$, x-axis from the ordinate $x = a$ to $x = b$.

Further the area above x-axis has positive real value, whereas that below x-axis has negative.

Now if $f(x)$ is entirely above x-axis in $[a, b]$, i.e., $f(x) > 0\ \forall\ x \in [a, b]$, then $\int_a^b f(x)\,dx > 0$

And if $f(x)$ is entirely below y-axis in $[a, b]$, i.e., $f(x) < 0\ \forall\ x \in [a, b]$, then $\int_a^b f(x)\,dx < 0$. Thus, $f(x)$ must cross x-axis at least once in $[a, b]$, so that the algebraic sum of areas above x-axis and below x-axis vanishes. Graphically shown below

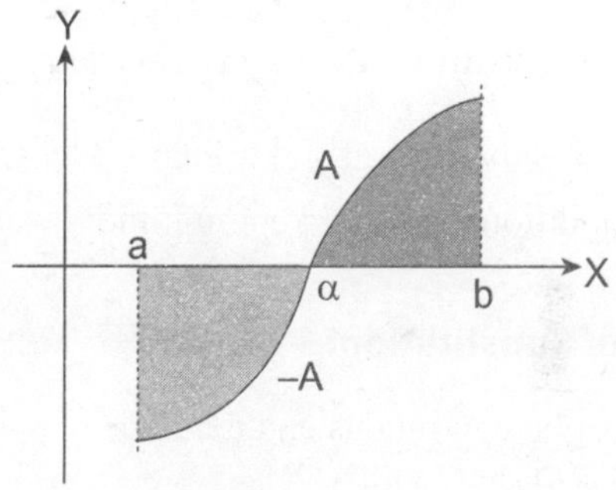

FIGURE 2.44

REMARKS

Converse of above property is not true, i.e., if f(x) has a root in (a, b) then $\int_a^b f(x)\,dx$ *need not be zero.*

e.g., if $f(x) = x^2 - 2x$ *has a root* $x = 2 \in (1, 3)$ *but* $\int_1^3 (x^2 - 2x)\,dx = \frac{1}{3}(27-1)-(9-1) = \frac{26}{3}-8 = \frac{2}{3} \neq 0$

ILLUSTRATION 36: Evaluate the integral $\int_0^3 (x^2 - 2x)\,dx$ and verify the fact 'If $f(x)$ is a continuous function $\forall\ x \in [a, b]$ such that $\int_a^b f(x)\,dx = 0$, then $f(x)$ has at least one root in (a, b)

SOLUTION: ***Proof:*** $\int_0^3 (x^2 - 2x)\,dx = \left[\frac{x^3}{3} - \frac{2x^2}{2}\right]_0^3 = \frac{1}{3}(27-0)-(9-0) = 9-9 = 0$

$\therefore$ $x^2 - 2x = 0$ has a root in (0, 3) which is true as $x^2 - 2x = 0$ has roots 0, 2 and $2 \in (0, 3)$.

Hence the statement is verified.

ILLUSTRATION 37: Show that $f(x) = x - \dfrac{(2+\sqrt{3})}{36}\pi^2 \sin x = 0$ has a root in $\left(0, \dfrac{\pi}{6}\right)$.

SOLUTION: It is sufficient to show that $\int_0^{\pi/6} f(x)\,dx = 0$

Now $\int_0^{\pi/6}\left[x - \dfrac{(2+\sqrt{3})}{36}\pi^2 \sin x\right]dx = \left|\dfrac{x^2}{2} + \dfrac{(2+\sqrt{3})\pi^2}{36}\cos x\right|_0^{\pi/6}$

$= \dfrac{1}{2}\left[\dfrac{\pi^2}{36}\right] + \dfrac{\pi^2}{36}(2+\sqrt{3})\left[\cos\dfrac{\pi}{6} - 1\right]$

$= \dfrac{\pi^2}{72} + \dfrac{\pi^2}{36}(2+\sqrt{3})\left(\dfrac{\sqrt{3}-2}{2}\right) = \dfrac{\pi^2}{72} + \dfrac{\pi^2}{36}\left(\dfrac{3-4}{2}\right) = \dfrac{\pi^2}{72} - \dfrac{\pi^2}{72} = 0$

Thus, $f(x) = 0$ has a root in $\left(0, \dfrac{\pi}{6}\right)$.

Property 5: **Substitution Property:** To evaluate $\int_a^b f(x)\,dx$ if we decide to substitute $g(x) = t$, then $x = g^{-1}(t)$. Then the following conditions must be kept in mind:

Condition of Substitution:

- ❑ $g(x)$ must be continuous and defined $\forall\, x \in [a, b]$.
- ❑ $g(x)$ must be monotonic $\forall\, x \in [a, b]$ (to ensure invertibility).

If the above two conditions are fulfilled, then we take the following steps:

Step 1: Change integrand $g(x) = t$, $g'(x)\,dx = dt$.

Step 2: Change the limits of integration

$$\int_{g(a)}^{g(b)} f(g^{-1}(t)).\frac{dt}{g'(g^{-1}(t))}$$

ILLUSTRATION 38: Evaluate $\int_0^3 \sqrt{2x+3}\,dx$ by using substitution method

SOLUTION: Given $\int_0^3 \sqrt{2x+3}\,dx$

Let us substitute $2x + 3 = t$ ...(1)

Clearly here $g(x) = 2x + 3$ which is continuous and monotonic on [0, 3]

Thus, there is no flaw in our substitution

Now at $x = 0$, $t = 3$ and at $x = 3$, $t = 9$

$\therefore$ limits of integration are from 3 to 9

Further differentiating (1) w.r.t. x we have $2dx = dt$

$\Rightarrow$ $dx = dt/2$

$\therefore$ $\int_0^3 \sqrt{2x+3}\,dx = \int_3^9 \sqrt{t}\left(\dfrac{dt}{2}\right) = \dfrac{1}{2}\left[\dfrac{(t)^{3/2}}{3/2}\right]_3^9 = \left(\dfrac{1}{2}\right)\left(\dfrac{2}{3}\right)\left[27 - 3\sqrt{3}\right] = \left(9 - \sqrt{3}\right)$

ILLUSTRATION 39: Compute the integral $\int_0^r \sqrt{r^2 - x^2}\,dx$

SOLUTION: Make a change of a variable $x = r \sin t$, $dx = r \cos t\, dt$

Determine the new limits:

$x = 0$ for $t = 0$

$x = r$ for $t = \pi/2$

consequently, $\int_0^r \sqrt{r^2 - x^2}\,dx = \int_0^{\pi/2} \sqrt{r^2 - r^2 \sin^2 t}\; r\cos t\, dt$

$$= r^2 \int_0^{\pi/2} \sqrt{1 - \sin^2 t}\, \cos t\, dt = r^2 \int_0^{\pi/2} \cos^2 t\, dt$$

$$= r^2 \int_0^{\pi/2} \left(\frac{1}{2} + \frac{1}{2}\cos 2t\right) dt = r^2 \left[\frac{t}{2} + \frac{\sin 2t}{4}\right]_0^{\pi/2} = \frac{\pi r^2}{4}$$

Geometrically

The computed integral is one-fourth area of the circle bounded by the circumference $x^2 + y^2 = r^2$.

ILLUSTRATION 40: Evaluate $\int_0^{\frac{\ell n 3}{2}} \frac{e^x + 1}{e^{2x} + 1}\, dx$

SOLUTION: Let $I = \int_0^{\frac{\ell n 3}{2}} \frac{e^x + 1}{e^{2x} + 1}\, dx$

$$= \int_0^{\frac{\ell n 3}{2}} \frac{e^x}{e^{2x} + 1}\, dx + \int_0^{\frac{\ell n 3}{2}} \frac{1}{e^{2x} + 1}\, dx = \int_0^{\frac{\ell n 3}{2}} \frac{e^x}{e^{2x} + 1}\, dx + \int_0^{\frac{\ell n 3}{2}} \frac{e^{-2x}}{e^{-2x} + 1}\, dx = I_1 + I_2 \text{ (say)}$$

$$\left.\begin{aligned} &\text{put } e^x = t \\ &\Rightarrow e^x dx = dt \end{aligned}\right\} \text{in } I_1$$

$\Rightarrow$ $t = 1$ at $x = 0$

and $t = \sqrt{3}$ at $x = \frac{\ln 3}{2}$

And put $1 + e^{-2x} = p$

$\Rightarrow$ $-2e^{-2x}\, dx = dp$ in I_2

$\Rightarrow$ $p = 2$ at $x = 0$

and $t = 4/3$ at $x = \frac{\ln 3}{2}$

$$\therefore \quad I = \int_1^{\sqrt{3}} \frac{dt}{1+t^2} + \frac{1}{2}\int_2^{4/3} \frac{-dp}{p} = |\tan^{-1} t| + \int_1^{\sqrt{3}} \frac{1}{2}\int_2^{4/3} \frac{-dp}{p}$$

$$= \frac{\pi}{3} - \frac{\pi}{4} - \frac{1}{2}|\ell np|_2^{4/3} = \frac{\pi}{12} - \frac{1}{2}\left(\ell n\frac{2}{3}\right) = \frac{1}{2}\left[\frac{\pi}{6} - \ell n\frac{2}{3}\right]$$

ILLUSTRATION 41: Evaluate $\int_0^{\pi/2} \sqrt{\frac{1 - \sin 2x}{1 + \sin 2x}}\, dx$

SOLUTION: Let $I = \int_0^{\pi/2} \sqrt{\frac{1 - \sin x}{1 + \sin x}} dx = \int_0^{\pi/2} \left|\frac{\cos x - \sin x}{\cos x + \sin x}\right| dx = \int_0^{\pi/4} \frac{\cos x - \sin x}{\cos x + \sin x}\, dx - \int_{\pi/4}^{\pi/2} \frac{\cos x - \sin x}{\cos x + \sin x}\, dx$

put $\cos x + \sin x = t \Rightarrow (\cos x - \sin x)\, dx = dt$

$$= \int_1^{\sqrt{2}} \frac{dt}{t} - \int_{\sqrt{2}}^1 \frac{dt}{t} = \left|\ell nt\right|_1^{\sqrt{2}} - \left|\ell nt\right|_{\sqrt{2}}^1 = \ell n\sqrt{2} + \ell n\sqrt{2} = \ell n2$$

ILLUSTRATION 42: Evaluate $\int_0^1 \frac{1-x}{1+x} \cdot \frac{dx}{\sqrt{x+x^2+x^3}} = I$

SOLUTION: $I = \int_0^1 \frac{1-x}{1+x} \frac{dx}{\sqrt{x+x^2+x^3}} = \int_0^1 \frac{(1-x^2)}{(1+x^2+2x)\sqrt{x+x^2+x^3}} dx$

$$= \int_0^1 \frac{-\left(1-\frac{1}{x^2}\right)}{\left(\frac{1}{x}+x+2\right)\sqrt{x+\frac{1}{x}+1}} dx$$ (dividing numerator and denominator by x^2)

put $x + \frac{1}{x} + 1 = t^2$ $\qquad \left(1-\frac{1}{x^2}\right)dx = 2t\,dt$

when $x \to 0 \Rightarrow t \to \infty$ and $x = 1 \Rightarrow t = \sqrt{3}$

$$\therefore \quad I = \int_\infty^{\sqrt{3}} \frac{-2t\,dt}{(t^2+1)t} = -2\int_\infty^{\sqrt{3}} \frac{dt}{1+t^2} = -2\left|\tan^{-1} t\right|_\infty^{\sqrt{3}} = -2(\tan^{-1}\sqrt{3} - \tan^{-1}\infty)$$

$$= -2\left(\frac{\pi}{3} - \frac{\pi}{2}\right) = -2\left(\frac{2\pi - 3\pi}{6}\right) = \frac{\pi}{3}$$

ILLUSTRATION 43: Evaluate $\int_1^{e^2} \frac{\ln x}{x} dx$

SOLUTION: Put $\ln x = t$

$\Rightarrow \quad \frac{1}{x} dx = dt$

For $x = 1$, $t = 0$; for $x = e^2$, $t = 2$

$$\therefore \quad \int_1^{e^2} \frac{\ln x}{x} dx = \int_0^2 t\,dt = \frac{1}{2}\left[t^2\right]_0^2 = \frac{1}{2}[4-0] = 2$$

ILLUSTRATION 44: Evaluate $\int_0^1 \frac{\cos^{-1} x}{\sqrt{1-x^2}} dx$

SOLUTION: Let $\cos^{-1}x = t$

$\Rightarrow \quad dt = \frac{-1}{\sqrt{1-x^2}} dx$

Clearly $\cos^{-1} x$ is decreasing and continuous on (0, 1)

For $x = 0$, $t = \pi/2$ and for $x = 1$, $t = 0$

$$\therefore \quad I = \int_{\pi/2}^0 t(-dt) = \int_0^{\pi/2} t\,dt = \left[\frac{t^2}{2}\right]_0^{\pi/2} = \frac{1}{2}\left[\frac{\pi^2}{4}\right] = \frac{\pi^2}{8}$$

ILLUSTRATION 45: Evaluate $\int_1^2 \frac{x^2 dx}{x^3 - 16}$

SOLUTION: Let $I = \int_1^2 \frac{x^2 dx}{x^3 - 16}$

Put $x^3 - 16 = t$

$\Rightarrow\ 3x^2\,dx = dt$

Clearly $y = x^3 - 16$ is continuous and increasing on (1, 2)

At $x = 1$, $t = -15$ and at $x = 2$, $t = -8$

$$\therefore\quad I = \int_{-15}^{-8} \frac{dt}{3t} = \frac{1}{3}\left[\ln|t|\right]_{-15}^{-8} = \frac{1}{3}\left[\ln 8 - \ln 15\right] = \frac{1}{3}\ln\left(\frac{8}{15}\right)$$

ILLUSTRATION 46: Compute $\int_0^{\pi/2} \frac{dx}{3+2\cos x}$ by using the substitution $t = \tan(x/2)$

SOLUTION: Let $I = \int_0^{\pi/2} \frac{dx}{3+2\cos x}$ clearly $\tan\frac{x}{2}$ is continuous and increasing on $\left[0, \frac{\pi}{2}\right]$

$\Rightarrow$ Let $\tan\frac{x}{2} = t$ $\qquad\therefore\ dt = \frac{1}{2}\sec^2\frac{x}{2}\,dx$

When $x = 0$, $t = 0$ and when $x = \frac{\pi}{2}, t = 1$

$$\therefore\quad I = \int_0^1 \frac{1}{3+2\left(\frac{1-\tan^2 x/2}{1+\tan^2 x/2}\right)}\left(\frac{2}{\sec^2 x/2}\right)dt = \int_0^1 \frac{\left(1+\tan^2 x/2\right)}{\left(3+3\tan^2\frac{x}{2}+2-2\tan^2\frac{x}{2}\right)}\left(\frac{2}{\sec^2 x/2}\right)dt$$

$$= \int_0^1 \frac{2}{5+\tan^2\frac{x}{2}}\,dt = 2\int_0^1 \frac{dt}{t^2+(\sqrt{5})^2} = 2\left(\frac{1}{\sqrt{5}}\right)\left|\tan^{-1}\left(\frac{t}{\sqrt{5}}\right)\right|_0^1$$

$$= \frac{2}{\sqrt{5}}\left|\tan^{-1}\frac{1}{\sqrt{5}} - \tan^{-1}(0)\right| = \frac{2}{\sqrt{5}}\tan^{-1}\left(\frac{1}{\sqrt{5}}\right)$$

ILLUSTRATION 47: Evaluate $\int_0^{\pi} \frac{dx}{(7+4\cos x)^2}$

SOLUTION: Let $I = \int_0^{\pi} \frac{dx}{\left[7+4\left(\frac{1-\tan^2 x/2}{1+\tan^2 x/2}\right)\right]^2}$

$$= \int_0^{\pi} \frac{\sec^4\frac{x}{2}}{\left[7+7\tan^2\frac{x}{2}+4-4\tan^2\frac{x}{2}\right]^2}\,dx = \int_0^{\pi} \frac{\sec^4\frac{x}{2}}{\left(11+3\tan^2\frac{x}{2}\right)^2}\,dx$$

Let us substitute, $\tan\frac{x}{2} = t$

$\Rightarrow\ \frac{1}{2}\sec^2\frac{x}{2}\,dx = dt$

Clearly $\tan\frac{x}{2}$ is increasing and continuous on $\left(0, \frac{\pi}{2}\right)$

$$\therefore\quad I = \int_0^{\infty} \frac{\left(1+t^2\right)2\,dt}{\left(11+3t^2\right)^2} = 2\int_0^{\infty} \frac{\left(1+t^2\right)dt}{\left(11+3t^2\right)^2} = \frac{2}{3}\int_0^{\infty} \frac{3+3t^2}{\left(11+3t^2\right)^2}\,dt = \frac{2}{3}\int_0^{\infty} \frac{11+3t^2-8}{\left(11+3t^2\right)^2}\,dt$$

$$= \frac{2}{3}\int_0^\infty \frac{dt}{(11+3t^2)} - \frac{16}{3}\int_0^\infty \frac{1}{(11+3t^2)^2}dt = \frac{2}{3}\times\frac{1}{3}\int_0^\infty \frac{dt}{\frac{11}{3}+t^2} - \frac{16}{3(9)}\int_0^\infty \frac{dt}{\left(\frac{11}{3}+t^2\right)^2}$$

$$= \frac{2}{9}\int_0^\infty \frac{dt}{\left(\sqrt{\frac{11}{3}}\right)^2+t^2} - \frac{16}{27}\int_0^\infty \frac{dt}{\left(\frac{11}{3}+t^2\right)^2} = \frac{2}{9}\times\frac{\sqrt{3}}{\sqrt{11}}\left|\tan^{-1}\left(\frac{\sqrt{3}t}{\sqrt{11}}\right)\right|_0^\infty - \frac{16}{27}\int_0^\infty \frac{dt}{\left(\frac{11}{3}+t^2\right)^2}$$

$$= \frac{2\sqrt{3}}{9\sqrt{11}}\left|\frac{\pi}{2}-0\right| - \frac{16}{27}\int_0^\infty \frac{dt}{\left(\frac{11}{3}+t^2\right)^2} = \frac{\sqrt{3}\pi}{9\sqrt{11}} - \frac{16}{27}\int_0^\infty \frac{dt}{\left(\frac{11}{3}+t^2\right)^2}$$

Now, let us substitute $t = \sqrt{\frac{11}{3}}\tan u \quad \Rightarrow dt = \sqrt{\frac{11}{3}}\sec^2 u du$

$$\therefore \quad I = \frac{\sqrt{3}}{9\sqrt{11}}\pi - \frac{16}{27}\int_0^{\pi/2} \frac{\sqrt{\frac{11}{3}}\sec^2 u\, du}{\left(\frac{11}{3}\right)^2(1+\tan^2 u)^2} = \frac{\sqrt{3}}{9\sqrt{11}}\pi - \frac{16}{27}\times\sqrt{\frac{11}{3}}\times\frac{9}{121}\int_0^{\pi/2}\frac{(1+\cos 2u)\, du}{2}$$

$$= \frac{\pi}{3\sqrt{33}} - \frac{16\sqrt{11}}{3\sqrt{3}(121)}\times\frac{1}{2}\left[u+\frac{\sin 2u}{2}\right]_0^{\pi/2} = \frac{\pi}{3\sqrt{33}} - \frac{8\sqrt{11}}{3\sqrt{3}(121)}\left[\frac{\pi}{2}\right] = \frac{\pi}{3\sqrt{33}} - \frac{4\sqrt{11}}{3\sqrt{3}(121)}\pi$$

Property 6: $\int_a^b f(x)dx$ is called improper integral. If

- $f(x)$ is discontinuous at atleast one point $c \in (a, b)$, whether the discontinuity is of first kind or infinite discontinuity. We already illustrated the process of finding definite integration of the type $\int_a^b f(x)dx$, such that $f(x)$ has a discontinuity of first kind at $c \in (a, b)$, i.e., $f(c^-) \neq f(c^+)$, inspite of each being finite.

To evaluate integrals having discontinuty at $c \in (a, b)$, we divide the limits interval at the point of discontinuity.

i.e., $\int_a^b f(x)dx = \int_a^{c^-} f(x)dx + \int_{c^+}^b f(x)dx$

or $\quad \int_a^b f(x)dx = \lim_{\varepsilon\to 0^+}\int_a^{c-\varepsilon} f(x)dx + \lim_{\delta\to 0^+}\int_{c+\delta}^b f(x)dx$

- Atleast one of a or b $\pm\infty$. In case b is infinite, then we take $\int_a^\infty f(x)dx = \lim_{b\to\infty}\int_a^b f(x)dx$;

  If a is $-\infty$, then we take

  $$\int_{-\infty}^b f(x)dx = \lim_{a\to-\infty}\int_a^b f(x)dx$$

If both a and b are $-\infty$ and ∞ respectively, then we take $\int_{-\infty}^\infty f(x)dx = \int_{-\infty}^0 f(x)dx + \int_0^\infty f(x)dx$

$$= \lim_{a\to-\infty}\int_a^0 f(x)dx + \lim_{b\to\infty}\int_0^b f(x)dx$$

- If $\int_a^b f(x)dx$ is such that $f(x)$ is unbounded as $x \to a^+$, then we take

  $$\int_a^b f(x)dx = \lim_{t\to 0^+}\int_{a+t}^b f(x)dx$$

  e.g., $\int_{-1}^2 \frac{1}{\sqrt{1+x}}dx = \lim_{t\to 0^+}\int_{-1+t}^2 \frac{1}{\sqrt{1+x}}dx$

  $$= \lim_{t\to 0^+}\left[2\sqrt{1+x}\right]_{-1+t}^2 = \lim_{t\to 0^+}\left[2\sqrt{3}-2\sqrt{t}\right] = 2\sqrt{3}$$

- If $\int_a^b f(x)\, dx$ is such that $f(x)$ is unbounded ∞ as $x \to b^-$, then we take

  $$\int_a^b f(x)\, dx = \lim_{t\to 0^+}\int_a^{b-t} f(x)\, dx$$

e.g., (i) Evaluate $\int_2^3 \frac{dx}{\sqrt{3-x}} dx = \lim_{t\to0^+}\int_2^{3-t}\frac{dx}{\sqrt{3-x}}$

$= \lim_{t\to0^+}\int_2^{3-t}(3-x)^{-1/2}\,dx$

$= \lim_{t\to0^+}\left[\frac{(3-x)^{1/2}}{(1/2)(-1)}\right]_2^{3-t}$

$= \lim_{t\to0^+}\left\{-2\left[(3-3+t)^{1/2}-(3-2)^{1/2}\right]\right\}$

$= \lim_{t\to0^+}\left\{-2\left[(t)^{1/2}-(1)^{1/2}\right]\right\} = 2$

(i) e.g., $\int_0^{\pi}\frac{\sin x}{1+\cos x}dx$, here $f(x)$ has a discontinuity at $x = \pi$

$\therefore$ we take $\int_0^{\pi}\frac{\sin x}{\sqrt{1+\cos x}}dx = \lim_{t\to0^+}\int_0^{\pi-t}\frac{\sin x}{\sqrt{1+\cos x}}dx$

$= \lim_{t\to0^+}\int_0^{\pi-t}(1+\cos x)^{-1/2}(\sin x)\,dx$

$= \lim_{t\to0^+}-\left\{\int_0^{\pi-t}(1+\cos x)^{-1/2}(-\sin x)\,dx\right\}$

$= -\lim_{t\to0^+}\left|\frac{(1+\cos x)^{1/2}}{1/2}\right|_0^{\pi-t}$

$= -2\lim_{t\to0^+}[\{1+\cos(\pi-t)\}^{1/2}-\{1+\cos 0\}^{1/2}]$

$= -2\,[0-(2)^{1/2}] = 2\sqrt{2}$

ILLUSTRATION 48: Evaluate the following definite integrals:

(i) $\int_{-\infty}^{0}\frac{1}{x^2+3}dx$

(ii) $\int_1^{\infty}x^2e^{-x^3}\,dx$

(iii) $\int_{-\infty}^{\infty}\frac{dx}{x^2+2x+2}dx$

SOLUTION: (i) $\int_{-\infty}^{0}\frac{1}{x^2+3}dx = \lim_{a\to-\infty}\int_a^0\frac{1}{x^2+3}dx = \lim_{a\to-\infty}\left[\frac{1}{\sqrt{3}}\tan^{-1}\left(\frac{x}{\sqrt{3}}\right)\right]_a^0$

$= \lim_{a\to-\infty}\left[\frac{1}{\sqrt{3}}\left(0-\tan^{-1}\left(\frac{a}{\sqrt{3}}\right)\right)\right] = -\frac{1}{\sqrt{3}}\left[\tan^{-1}(-\infty)\right] = \frac{-1}{\sqrt{3}}\left(\frac{-\pi}{2}\right) = \frac{\pi}{2\sqrt{3}}$

(ii) $\int_1^{\infty}x^2e^{-x^3}\,dx = \lim_{b\to\infty}\int_1^b x^2e^{-x^3}\,dx = \lim_{b\to\infty}\int_1^b\left(x^2e^{-x^3}\right)dx$

Put $e^{-x^3} = t$

$\Rightarrow -3x^2e^{-x^3}dx = dt$ $\Rightarrow t = e^{-1}$ for $x = 1$ and $t = e^{-b^3}$ for $x = b$

$\therefore I = \lim_{b\to\infty}\int_{e^{-1}}^{e^{-b^3}}-\frac{1}{3}dt = -\frac{1}{3}\lim_{b\to\infty}\left[e^{-b^3}-e^{-1}\right] = -\frac{1}{3}\left[e^{-\infty}-e^{-1}\right] = -\frac{1}{3}\left(0-\frac{1}{e}\right) = \frac{1}{3e}.$

(iii) $\int_{-\infty}^{\infty}\frac{dx}{x^2+2x+2}dx = \lim_{a\to-\infty}\int_a^0\frac{dx}{x^2+2x+2}+\lim_{b\to\infty}\int_0^b\frac{dx}{x^2+2x+2}$

$= \lim_{a\to-\infty}\int_a^0\frac{dx}{(x+1)^2+1}+\lim_{b\to\infty}\int_0^b\frac{dx}{(x+1)^2+1} = \lim_{a\to-\infty}\left|\tan^{-1}(x+1)\right|_a^0+\lim_{b\to\infty}\left|\tan^{-1}(x+1)\right|_0^b$

$= \lim_{a\to-\infty}\left[\tan^{-1}1-\tan^{-1}(a+1)\right] + \lim_{b\to\infty}\left[\tan^{-1}(b+1)-\tan^{-1}(1)\right]$

$= \frac{\pi}{4}+\left(\frac{\pi}{2}\right)+\frac{\pi}{2}-\frac{\pi}{4} = \pi$

CONVERGENT AND DIVERGENT IMPROPER INTEGRALS

A definite integral having either or both limits infinite (improper integral) is said to be convergent if its value is finite, i.e., if the area bounded by the continuous function $f(x)$, x-axis and between its limits is finite, otherwise it is said to be divergent. Thus,

(i) $\int_a^\infty f(x)\,dx$ is said to be divergent if $\lim_{b\to\infty}\int_a^b f(x)\,dx = L$ (finite)

e.g., $\int_{1/2}^\infty \frac{1}{x^2}dx$ expresses the area bounded by the function $f(x)=\frac{1}{x^2}$, x-axis and in $\left[\frac{1}{2},\infty\right)$ as shown below

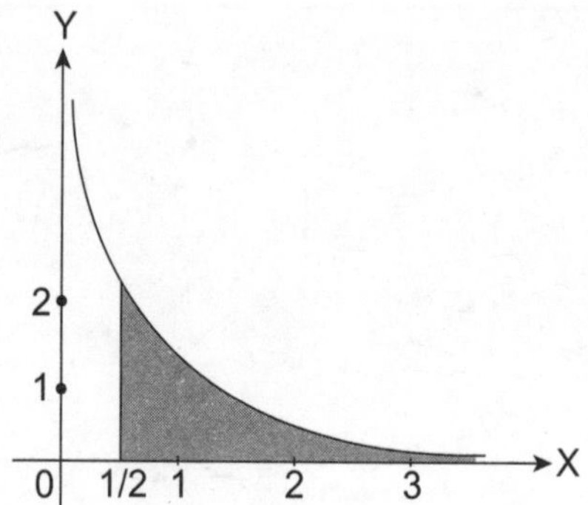

FIGURE 2.45

Now $\int_{1/2}^\infty \frac{1}{x^2}dx = \lim_{b\to\infty}\int_{1/2}^b \frac{1}{x^2}dx$

$= \lim_{b\to\infty}\left[\frac{-1}{x}\right]_{1/2}^b = \lim_{b\to\infty} -\left[\frac{1}{b}-2\right]$

Thus, $\int_{1/2}^\infty \frac{1}{x^2}dx = 2-\frac{1}{\infty} = 2 =$ finite and hence $\int_{1/2}^\infty \frac{1}{x^2}dx$ is convergent.

(ii) $\int_{-\infty}^b f(x)\,dx$ is said to be divergent if $\lim_{a\to-\infty}\int_a^b f(x)\,dx =$ L (finite)

e.g., $\int_{-\infty}^0 e^x\,dx$ expresses the area bounded by the function $y = e^x$, x-axis and in $(-\infty, 0]$ as shown figure.

Now $\int_{-\infty}^0 e^x\,dx = \lim_{a\to-\infty}\int_a^0 e^x\,dx = \lim_{a\to-\infty}\left[e^x\right]_a^0 =$ $\lim_{a\to-\infty}\left[1-e^a\right] = 1 - e^{-\infty} = 1 - 0 = 1$ which is finite, hence $\int_{-\infty}^0 e^x\,dx$ is convergent.

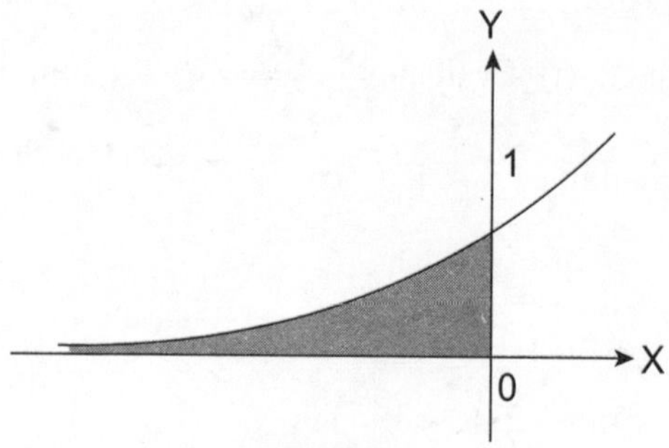

FIGURE 2.46

(iii) $\int_{-\infty}^\infty f(x)\,dx$ is said to be convergent if $\int_{-\infty}^\infty f(x)dx = \lim_{a\to-\infty}\int_a^0 f(x)\,dx + \lim_{b\to\infty}\int_0^b f(x)\,dx$, and each of the two integrals on right hand side is convergent. Note that if at least one of the two improper integrals on right side is divergent, then $\int_{-\infty}^\infty f(x)\,dx$ is said to be divergent.

e.g., $\int_{-\infty}^\infty \frac{1}{1+x^2}dx$ expresses the area bounded by the function $f(x)=\frac{1}{x^2+1}$, x-axis and in $(-\infty, \infty)$ as shown below

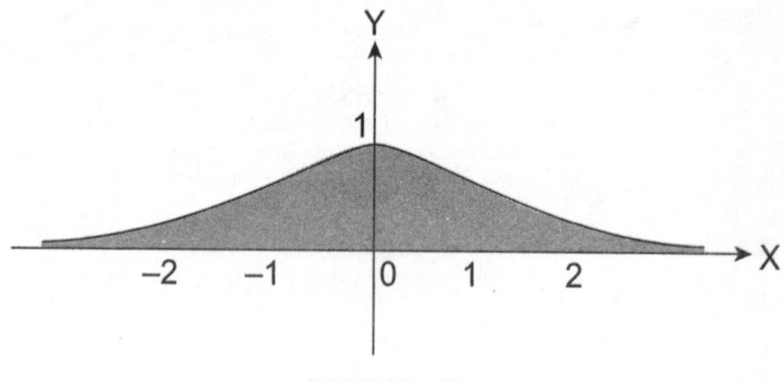

FIGURE 2.47

Now $\int_{-\infty}^\infty \frac{1}{1+x^2}dx = \lim_{a\to-\infty}\int_a^0 \frac{1}{1+x^2}dx + \lim_{b\to\infty}\int_0^b \frac{1}{1+x^2}dx$

$= \lim_{a\to-\infty}\left[\tan^{-1}x\right]_a^0 + \lim_{b\to\infty}\left[\tan^{-1}x\right]_0^b$

$= \lim_{a\to-\infty}\left[\tan^{-1}0-\tan^{-1}a\right] + \lim_{b\to\infty}\left[\tan^{-1}b-\tan^{-1}0\right]$

$= \lim_{a\to-\infty}\left[-\tan^{-1}a\right] + \lim_{b\to\infty}\left[\tan^{-1}b\right]$

$= -\tan^{-1}(-\infty) + \tan^{-1}(\infty) = -\left(-\frac{\pi}{2}\right)+\frac{\pi}{2} = \pi < \infty$

Thus, $\int_{-\infty}^\infty \frac{1}{1+x^2}dx$ is convergent.

ILLUSTRATION 49: Examine the improper integral $\int_1^{\infty}\frac{(x+1)}{(x+2)(x^2+4)}dx$ for convergent/divergent. If convergent, then evaluate it.

SOLUTION: Given integral is $\int_1^{\infty}\frac{(x+1)}{(x+2)(x^2+4)}dx = \int_1^{\infty}\left\{-\frac{1}{8}\left(\frac{1}{x+2}\right)+\frac{\left(\frac{1}{8}x+\frac{3}{4}\right)}{(x^2+4)}\right\}dx$

$$= \lim_{b\to\infty}\left\{-\frac{1}{8}[\ln|x+2|]_1^b+\frac{1}{16}\left[\ln\left(x^2+4\right)\right]_1^b+\frac{3}{8}\left[\tan^{-1}\left(\frac{x}{2}\right)\right]_1^b\right\}$$

$$= \lim_{b\to\infty}\left\{-\frac{1}{8}[\ln(b+2)-\ln(3)]+\frac{1}{16}\left[\ln\left(b^2+4\right)-\ln 5\right]+\frac{3}{8}\left[\tan^{-1}\frac{b}{2}-\tan^{-1}\frac{1}{2}\right]\right\}$$

$$= \lim_{b\to\infty}\left\{-\frac{1}{8}\ln(b+2)+\frac{1}{8}\ln 3+\frac{1}{16}\ln\left(b^2+4\right)-\frac{1}{16}\ln 5+\frac{3}{8}\tan^{-1}\frac{b}{2}-\frac{3}{8}\tan^{-1}\left(\frac{1}{2}\right)\right\}$$

$$= \lim_{b\to\infty}\left\{\frac{1}{16}\ln\left(\frac{b^2+4}{b^2+4+4b}\right)+\frac{1}{16}\ln\left(\frac{9}{5}\right)+\frac{3}{8}\tan^{-1}\frac{b}{2}-\frac{3}{8}\tan^{-1}\left(\frac{1}{2}\right)\right\}$$

$$= \lim_{b\to\infty}\frac{1}{16}\ln\left[\frac{1+4/b^2}{1+\frac{4}{b^2}+\frac{4}{b}}\right]+\frac{1}{16}\ln\left(\frac{9}{5}\right)+\frac{3}{8}\left(\frac{\pi}{2}\right)-\frac{3}{8}\tan^{-1}\left(\frac{1}{2}\right)$$

$$= \frac{1}{16}\ln(1)+\frac{1}{16}\ln\left(\frac{9}{5}\right)+\frac{3}{16}\pi-\frac{3}{8}\tan^{-1}\left(\frac{1}{2}\right) = \frac{1}{16}\ln\left(\frac{9}{5}\right)-\frac{3}{8}\tan^{-1}\left(\frac{1}{2}\right)+\frac{3}{16}\pi$$

ILLUSTRATION 50: Examine the improper integral $\int_{-\infty}^{0}x^2e^x\,dx$ for convergent/divergent. If convergent, then evaluate it.

SOLUTION: Given $I=\int_{-\infty}^{0}x^2e^x\,dx = \lim_{a\to-\infty}\int_a^0 x^2e^x\,dx = \lim_{a\to-\infty}\left[\left|x^2e^x\right|_a^0-\int_a^0 2xe^x\,dx\right]$

$$= \lim_{a\to-\infty}\left[0-a^2e^a-2\int_a^0 xe^x\,dx\right] = \lim_{a\to-\infty}\left\{-a^2e^a-2\left[\left|xe^x\right|_a^0-\int_a^0 1.e^x\,dx\right]\right\}$$

$$= \lim_{a\to-\infty}\left\{-a^2e^a-2\left[-ae^a-(1-e^a)\right]\right\} = \lim_{a\to-\infty}\left\{-a^2e^a+2ae^a+2-2e^a\right\}$$

$$= \lim_{a\to-\infty}\left\{-a^2e^a+2ae^a\right\}+2-2(0) = \lim_{a\to-\infty}\left[\frac{-a^2}{e^{-a}}\right]+\lim_{a\to-\infty}\left[\frac{2a}{e^{-a}}\right]+2$$

Both of the right hand limits are of $\frac{\infty}{\infty}$ form, therefore by L.H.L. rule of limits,

$$I=\lim_{a\to-\infty}\left[\frac{-2a}{-e^{-a}}\right]+\lim_{a\to-\infty}\left[\frac{2}{-e^{-a}}\right]+2,$$

Again by L.H. rule $I=\lim_{a\to-\infty}\left[\frac{2}{-e^{-a}}\right]+0+2=0+0+2=2<\infty$

Thus, the given improper integral is convergent and equal to 2.

ILLUSTRATION 51: Find whether the improper integral $\int_0^{\infty}\left[3e^{-x}\right]dx$ is convergent or divergent, if convergent, then evaluate it. ([.] is greatest integer function).

SOLUTION: For $x\in[0,\infty)$, $e^{-x}\in(0,1]$

$\Rightarrow$ $3e^{-x}\in(0,3]$ which contains integers 1, 2 and 3

Now $3e^{-x} = 1$

$\Rightarrow e^{-x} = 1/3$

$\Rightarrow -x = \ln(1/3)$

$\Rightarrow x = \ln 3$

$3e^{-x} = 2$ $\Rightarrow e^{-x} = 2/3$

$\Rightarrow -x = \ln(2/3)$ $\Rightarrow x = \ln(3/2)$

And $3e^{-x} = 3$ $\Rightarrow x = 0$

Further $3e^{-x}$ is a decreasing function on $\mathbb{R}$

$\Rightarrow 3e^{-x} \in (2, 3)$ for $x \in \left(0, \ln\frac{3}{2}\right)$; $3e^{-x} \in (1, 2)$ for $x \in \left(\ln\frac{3}{2}, \ln 3\right)$ and $3e^{-x} \in (0, 1)$ for $x \in (\ln 3, \infty)$

Thus, $[3e^{-x}] = \begin{cases} 2; & 0 < x < \ln(3/2) \\ 1; & \ln(3/2) < x < \ln 3 \\ 0; & \ln 3 < x < \infty \end{cases}$

$$\therefore \int_0^\infty \left[3e^{-x}\right] dx = \int_0^{\ln(3/2)} 2\, dx + \int_{\ln(3/2)}^{\ln 3} 1\, dx + \int_{\ln 3}^{\infty} 0\, dx$$

$$= 2\left[\ln\frac{3}{2} - 0\right] + \left[\ln 3 - \ln\frac{3}{2}\right] = \ln\frac{3}{2} + \ln 3 = \ln\frac{9}{2} < \infty$$

Thus, the given improper integral is convergent and equal to $\ln\frac{9}{2}$.

ILLUSTRATION 52: Evaluate the improper integral $\int_0^\infty \frac{x}{(1+x^2)^2}\, dx$ if it is convergent.

SOLUTION: $$I = \int_0^\infty \frac{x}{(1+x^2)^2}\, dx = \lim_{b\to\infty} \int_0^b \frac{x}{(1+x^2)^2}\, dx \quad \ldots(1)$$

Let us substitute $x = \tan\theta$

$\Rightarrow dx = \sec^2\theta\, d\theta$

$$\therefore \text{ (1) becomes, } I = \lim_{b\to\infty} \int_0^{\tan^{-1} b} \frac{\tan\theta}{\sec^4\theta}.\sec^2\theta\, d\theta = \lim_{b\to\infty} \int_0^{\tan^{-1} b} \tan\theta.\cos^2\theta\, d\theta$$

$$= \lim_{b\to\infty} \int_0^{\tan^{-1} b} \sin\theta.\cos\theta\, d\theta = \lim_{b\to\infty} \frac{1}{2} \int_0^{\tan^{-1} b} \sin 2\theta\, d\theta$$

$$= \lim_{b\to\infty} \frac{1}{2}\left[\frac{-\cos 2\theta}{2}\right]_0^{\tan^{-1} b} = \lim_{b\to\infty}\left\{-\frac{1}{4}[\cos 2\theta]_0^{\tan^{-1} b}\right\}$$

$$= -\frac{1}{4}\lim_{b\to\infty}\left[\cos 2(\tan^{-1} b) - \cos 0\right] = -\frac{1}{4}(-2) = \frac{1}{2}$$

Aliter: We take $\tan\theta = x$

$\Rightarrow dx = \sec^2\theta\, d\theta$

And $x \to 0$ $\Rightarrow \theta \to 0$ and $x \to \infty$ $\Rightarrow \theta \to \frac{\pi}{2}$

$$\therefore I = \int_0^{\pi/2} \frac{\tan\theta}{\sec^4\theta}.\sec^2\theta\, d\theta = \int_0^{\pi/2} \sin\theta.\cos\theta\, d\theta = -\frac{1}{2}\left[\frac{\cos 2\theta}{2}\right]_0^{\pi/2} = -\frac{1}{4}\left[\cos\pi - \cos 0\right] = \frac{1}{2}$$

Thus, an improper integral is transformed to ordinary definite integral, however conditions, of substitution i.e., continuity and monotonically must be kept in mind while transforming the improper integral using substitution.

ILLUSTRATION 53: Evaluate

(i) $\int_0^\infty e^{-x}x^n\,dx$, where n is a positive integer

(ii) Prove that $I_n = \int_0^\infty e^{-x}x^{n-1}\,dx = (n-1)\,I_{n-1}$, where n is a positive rational number.

SOLUTION: (i) Let $I_n = \int_0^\infty e^{-x}x^n\,dx,\ n \in \mathbb{N}$

$$= \lim_{b\to\infty}\int_0^b e^{-x}x^n\,dx = \lim_{b\to\infty}\left[\left|\frac{x^n.e^{-x}}{-1}\right|_0^b - \int_0^b \frac{nx^{n-1}.e^{-x}}{-1}\,dx\right] = \lim_{b\to\infty}\left[-\left(b^ne^{-b}\right)+n\int_0^b x^{n-1}e^{-x}\,dx\right]$$

As $\lim_{b\to\infty}\left(-b^ne^{-b}\right) = \lim_{b\to\infty}\left[\frac{-b^n}{e^b}\right] = -\lim_{b\to\infty}\left[\frac{n!}{e^b}\right] = 0$ (By L–H rule)

$$\therefore\ I_n = \lim_{b\to\infty} n\int_0^b x^{n-1}e^{-x}dx = nI_{n-1}$$

Repeating the above process again and again we get

$I_n = nI_{n-1} = n(n-1)\,I_{n-2} = n(n-1)\,(n-2)\,I_{n-3}\ \ldots.$

$\Rightarrow\ I_n = n(n-1)\,(n-2)\ \ldots.\ 2\cdot I_1 = n!\int_0^\infty e^{-x}xdx = n!(1) = n!$

Thus, $\int_0^\infty e^{-x}x^ndx = n!$

(ii) Let $I_n = \int_0^\infty e^{-x}x^{n-1}\,dx = \lim_{b\to\infty}\int_0^b e^{-x}x^{n-1}\,dx = \lim_{b\to\infty}\left[\left|\frac{x^{n-1}.e^{-x}}{-1}\right|_0^b - \int_0^b\frac{(n-1)x^{n-2}.e^{-x}}{-1}dx\right]$

$$= \lim_{b\to\infty}\left[-\left(b^{n-1}.e^{-b}\right)+(n-1)\int_0^b e^{-x}x^{n-2}dx\right] \qquad \ldots(1)$$

Now let us evaluate the limit $\lim_{b\to\infty}\left[-b^{n-1}e^{-b}\right] = L$ (say)

If $n \le 1$, then $n-1 \le 0$

$\Rightarrow\ 1-n \ge 0$

$\therefore\ L = \lim_{b\to\infty}\left[-\frac{1}{b^{1-n}.e^b}\right] = 0$

If $n > 1$, then $n-1 > 0$ therefore, $L = \lim_{b\to\infty}\left[-b^{n-1}.e^{-b}\right] = \lim_{b\to\infty}\left[\frac{-b^{(n-1)}}{e^b}\right]$

$\therefore$ By L–H rule $L = \lim_{b\to\infty}\left[\frac{-(n-1)b^{n-2}}{e^b}\right]$, if $(n-2) < 0$, then limit equals 0, otherwise we again apply L–H rule.

Since n is index of b, becomes –ve after some stage and hence the limit vanishes.

Thus, $L = \lim_{b\to\infty}\left[-(b)^{n-1}e^{-b}\right] = 0$

$$\therefore\ I_n = (n-1)\lim_{b\to\infty}\int_0^b e^{-x}x^{(n-2)}dx = (n-1)I_{n-1}$$

Continuing this way, we get $I_n = (n-1)\,I_{n-1} = (n-1)\,(n-2)\,I_{n-2}$ and so on. If n is a +ve integer, then $I_n = (n-1)!$

TEXTUAL EXERCISE–3: (SUBJECTIVE)

1. Evaluate the following integrals:

(a) $\int_0^{1/2} \frac{x\sin^{-1}x}{\sqrt{1-x^2}}dx$ (b) $\int_{-2}^{2}|1-x^2|\,dx$

(c) $\int_0^2 (x[x])\,dx$

2. Evaluate $\int_{-2}^{2} \frac{dx}{4+x^2}$ directly as well as by substitution $x = 1/t$ and examine why answer do not tally. Also mention correct answer.

3. Evaluate the integral $\int_0^{2\pi} \frac{dx}{2+\cos x}$ using substitution $\tan x/2 = t$ and explain the paradox as we know that the area represented by above integral must be positive.

4. Is it possible to substitute $x = \sec t$ to evaluate the integral $\int_0^1 \sqrt{2+x^2}\,dx$? If not, then explain the reason.

5. Show that $\int_0^{\pi/2} \frac{dx}{a^2\cos^2 x+b^2\sin^2 x} = \frac{\pi}{2ab}$; $(a, b > 0)$

6. Evaluate the following integrals:

(a) $\int_0^3 \frac{dx}{x^2+[x]^2+1-2x[x]}$

(b) $\int_0^{\pi} \sin^{-1}(\sin x)dx$

(c) $\int_0^{\pi/4} [\sin x+[\cos x+[\tan x]]]dx$

(d) $\int_{-2}^{2}[x]dx$

(e) $\int_{-2}^{3}\{x\}dx$

(f) $\int_0^3 [e^x]dx$

(g) $\int_1^5 [\log x]dx$

(h) $\int_1^{20} [\ln x]dx$

(i) $\int_0^x [x]dx$

(j) $\int_0^x e^{\{x\}}\,dx$

(k) $\int_0^x e^{[x]}\,dx$

(l) $\int_{\pi/2}^{3\pi/2} [2\sin x]dx$

(m) $\int_0^{n^2} [\sqrt{x}]dx$

(n) $\int_0^3 |(x-1)(x-2)(x-3)|\,dx$

(o) $\int_{-2}^{2} \min(x-\{x\}, -x-\{-x\})\,dx$

(p) $\int_3^8 \frac{\sin\sqrt{x+1}}{\sqrt{x+1}}dx$

(q) $\int_3^{29} \frac{\sqrt[3]{(x-2)^2}}{3+\sqrt[3]{(x-2)^2}}dx$

(r) $\int_2^4 \frac{\sqrt{x^2-4}}{x^4}\,dx$

(s) $\int_{-1}^{1} x^2 d(\ln|x|)$

Here $[x]$ denotes integer part and $\{x\}$ denotes fractional part of x.

7. Evaluate the following integrals:

(a) $\int_0^1 \frac{\sin^{-1}\sqrt{x}}{\sqrt{x\,(1-x)}}dx$ (b) $\int_0^{\ell n 2} x\,e^x dx$

8. Evaluate the following integrals:

(a) $\int_0^{\infty} \frac{1}{1+x^3}dx$ (b) $\int_0^{\infty} \frac{3x^2+4}{(x^3+4x+1)^3}dx$

9. Evaluate the Integrals: $\int_0^{\pi/2} \frac{dx}{1+4\cot^2 x}$

10. (i) Show that $\int_{-\infty}^{\infty} \frac{\cos x}{1+x^2}dx$ is convergent.

(ii) Which of the following integrals are improper and why? Also evaluate each if it is convergent.

(a) $\int_0^2 \frac{1}{2x-3}dx$ (b) $\int_0^1 \frac{1}{2x+1}dx$

(c) $\int_0^2 \frac{1}{x^2-2}dx$ (d) $\int_2^3 \ln(x-2)\,dx$

11. Explain the reason for each integral being improper. Also evaluate each if it is convergent.

(a) $\int_1^{\infty} xe^{-x^2}dx$ (b) $\int_0^{\pi/4} \operatorname{cosec} x\;dx$

(c) $\int_0^2 \frac{x^2dx}{x^2-3x+2}$ (d) $\int_0^{\infty} \tan^{-1}x\;dx$

(e) $\int_{-\infty}^{0} \frac{\tan^{-1}x}{1+x^2}\,dx$ (f) $\int_{-\infty}^{\infty} \frac{dx}{(x^2+4x+5)}$

12. Show that the improper integral $\int_0^3 \frac{1}{x^2-4x+3}dx$ is divergent.

13. Show that the following improper integrals are convergent and hence evaluate each:

(a) $\int_0^1 \frac{1}{\sqrt[3]{x}}dx$ (b) $\int_{-2}^{0} \frac{e^{\frac{1}{x}}}{x^3}dx$

(c) $\int_5^7 \frac{1}{\sqrt{x-5}}dx$ (d) $\int_0^1 \ln x\;dx$

Answer Keys

1. (a) $\frac{1}{2}-\frac{\pi}{4\sqrt{3}}$ (b) 4 (c) 3/2 **6.** (a) 3π/4 (b) π²/4 (c) 0 (d) –2 (e) 5/2

(f) $= \ln 2 + 2\ln\left(\frac{3}{2}\right) + 3\ln\left(\frac{4}{3}\right) + \ldots\ldots + \left(\left[e^3\right]-1\right)\ln\left(\frac{\left[e^3\right]}{\left[e^3\right]-1}\right) + \left[e^3\right]\ln\left(\frac{\left[e^3\right]}{\left[2^3\right]}\right)$ (g) $5 - e$ (h) $40 - e - e^2$

(i) $\frac{[x]}{2}[([x]-1)+2(x-[x])]$ (j) $[x](e-1)+(e^{\{x\}}-1)$ (k) $\left(\frac{e^{[x]}-1}{e-1}\right)+e^{[x]}\left(x-[x]\right)$ (l) –π/2

(m) $\frac{1}{6}n(n-1)(4n+1)$ (n) $\frac{11}{4}$ (o) –6 (p) 2 [cos2–cos3] (q) $8+\frac{3\sqrt{3}\,\pi}{2}$

(r) $\frac{\sqrt{3}}{32}$ (s) $\frac{1}{2}\left[e^2-e^{-2}\right]$ **7.** (a) $\frac{\pi^2}{4}$ (b) 2ln2 – 1 **8.** (a) $\frac{2\pi}{3\sqrt{3}}$ (b) $\frac{1}{2}$

9. (a) π/6 **10.** (ii) (a) $-\frac{1}{2}\ln 3$ (b) $\frac{1}{2}\ln 3$ (c) $\frac{1}{2\sqrt{2}}\ln\left(3-2\sqrt{2}\right)$ (d) –1

11. (a) $\frac{1}{2e}$ (b) Divergent (c) Divergent (d) Divergent (e) $-\frac{\pi^2}{8}$ (f) π

13. (a) $\frac{3}{2}$ (b) $-\frac{3}{2\sqrt{e}}$ (c) $2\sqrt{2}$ (d) –1

TEXTUAL EXERCISE–3: (OBJECTIVE)

1. If for a real number y, $[y]$ is the greatest integer less than or equal to y, then the value of the integral $\int_{\pi/2}^{3\pi/2}[2\sin x]dx$ is

(a) – π (b) 0
(c) $-\frac{\pi}{2}$ (d) $\frac{\pi}{2}$

2. If $\int_{-1}^{4} f(x)dx = 4$ and $\int_{2}^{4}(3-f(x))dx = 7$, then the value of $\int_{2}^{-1} f(x)dx$ is

(a) 2 (b) –3
(c) – 5 (d) None of these

3. The value of $\int_{-5}^{5}|x+2|\,dx$ is

(a) 25 (b) 29
(c) 33 (d) 0

4. The value of $\int_{-1}^{3/2}|x\sin \pi x|\,dx$ is

(a) $\frac{1}{\pi}+\frac{2}{\pi^2}$ (b) $\frac{2}{\pi}+\frac{1}{\pi^2}$
(c) $\frac{2}{\pi}+\frac{2}{\pi^2}$ (d) $\frac{3}{\pi}+\frac{1}{\pi^2}$

5. The value of $\int_{e^{-1}}^{e^2}\left|\frac{\log_e x}{x}\right|dx$ is

(a) 3/2 (b) 5/2
(c) 3 (d) 5

6. The value of $\int_0^1 \frac{\ln x}{\sqrt{1-x^2}}dx$ is

(a) π ln 2 (b) $-\frac{\pi}{2}$ ln 2
(c) $\frac{\pi}{2}$ ln 2 (d) None of these

7. The value of $\int_1^e \frac{\ln x}{x}\,dx$ equals

(a) 1 (b) 1/2
(c) 2 (d) None of these

8. The value of $\int_0^{\pi/2}\frac{dx}{1+\cos x}$ equals

(a) 2 (b) 3
(c) 1 (d) None of these

9. The value of $\int_0^{1/2}\frac{dx}{(1-2x^2)\sqrt{1-x^2}}$ equals

(a) $\ln(2+\sqrt{3})$ (b) $\ln\sqrt{(2+\sqrt{3})}$
(c) $\ln(2-\sqrt{3})$ (d) None of these

10. The value of $\int_0^2 \frac{x^2\,dx}{x^3-17}$ equals

(a) $\frac{1}{3}\ln\frac{9}{17}$ (b) $\ln\frac{9}{17}$

(c) $3\ln\frac{9}{17}$ (d) None of these

11. The value of $\int_\lambda^\mu \frac{dx}{x\sqrt{(x-\lambda)(\mu-x)}}$; where λ, μ are constants and (λ < μ), equals

(a) $\frac{\pi}{2\sqrt{\lambda\mu}}$ (b) $\frac{\pi}{\sqrt{\lambda\mu}}$

(c) $2\pi\sqrt{\lambda\mu}$ (d) None of these

12. The value of $\int_0^{\pi/2} \frac{dx}{\left(\sqrt{\sin x}+\sqrt{\cos x}\right)^4}$ equals

(a) 2/3 (b) 3

(c) 1/3 (d) None of these

13. The value of $\int_0^{3/4} \frac{dx}{(x+1)\sqrt{x^2+1}}$ equals

(a) $\frac{1}{\sqrt{2}}\ln\left(\frac{9+4\sqrt{2}}{7}\right)$ (b) $\frac{1}{\sqrt{2}}\ln\left(\frac{4\sqrt{2}-9}{7}\right)$

(c) $\ln\left(\frac{9+3\sqrt{2}}{7}\right)$ (d) None of these

14. The value of $\int_{-1}^{1} x^2 d(\ln x)$ equals

(a) $\frac{e^4-1}{2e^2}$ (b) $\frac{e^2-1}{2e^2}$

(c) $\frac{2e^4-1}{e^2}$ (d) None of these

15. The value of $\int_0^{\pi/2} \frac{\cos^2\theta\,d\theta}{\cos^2\theta+4\sin^2\theta}$ equals

(a) $\frac{\pi}{2}$ (b) $\frac{\pi}{3}$

(c) $\frac{\pi}{6}$ (d) None of these

16. The value of $\int_{-\infty}^{\infty} \frac{1}{e^x+e^{-x}}dx$ equals

(a) $\frac{\pi}{4}$ (b) $\frac{\pi}{2}$

(c) $\frac{3\pi}{4}$ (d) None of these

17. The value of $\int_1^{\infty} \frac{dx}{(x+1)x^2}$ equals

(a) ln 2 (b) ln2 – 1

(c) 1 – ln2 (d) None of these

Answer Keys

1. (c)	**2.** (c)	**3.** (b)	**4.** (d)	**5.** (b)	**6.** (b)	**7.** (b)	**8.** (c)	**9.** (b)	**10.** (a)
11. (b)	**12.** (c)	**13.** (a)	**14.** (a)	**15.** (c)	**16.** (b)	**17.** (c)			

Property 7: **Reflection Property:** $\int_a^b f(x)dx = \int_{-b}^{-a} f(-x)dx$

Proof: If $y = f(x)$ is a function, then $y = f(-x)$ represents the reflection of $f(x)$ on y–axis.

$$\text{R.H.S.} = \int_{-b}^{-a} f(-x)\,dx \text{ put } x = -t \Rightarrow dx = -dt$$

$$= -\int_b^a f(t)\,dt = \int_a^b f(t)\,dt = \int_a^b f(x)\,dx = \text{L.H.S.}$$

Geometrically: it can be observed that $\int_a^b f(x)dx$ represents the shaded area (right side of y-axis) under the curve $y = f(x)$ above x-axis and from ordinate $x = a$ to $x = b$ and $\int_{-b}^{-a} f(-x)dx$ represents the shaded area (left side of y-axis) under the curve $y = f(-x)$ above x-axis and from ordinate $x = -b$ to $-a$. Clearly the two areas are equal in magnitude.

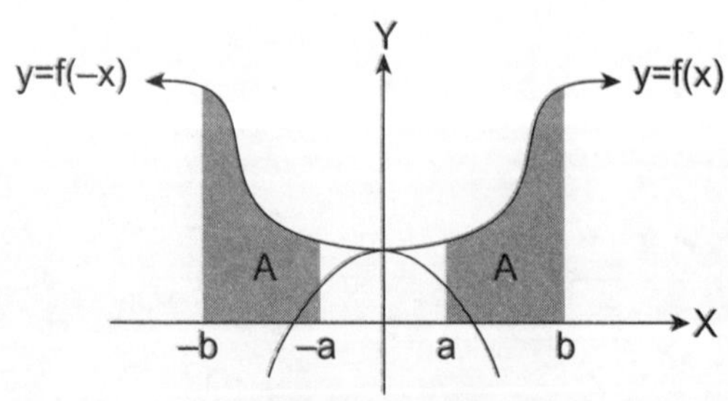

FIGURE 2.48

ILLUSTRATION 54: Evaluate $\int_{-2}^{-1} \ln|x|\,dx + \int_{1}^{2} \ln x\,dx$

SOLUTION: Given $I = \int_{-2}^{-1} \ln|x|\,dx + \int_{1}^{2} \ln x\,dx = \int_{-2}^{-1} \ln(-x)\,dx + \int_{1}^{2} \ln(x)\,dx$ ...(1)

But by reflection property

$\int_{-b}^{-a} f(-x)\,dx = \int_{a}^{b} f(x)\,dx$, therefore (1) becomes

$$I = \int_{1}^{2} \ln(x)\,dx + \int_{1}^{2} \ln x\,dx = 2\int_{1}^{2} \ln x\,dx = 2\int_{1}^{2} \underset{II}{1}.\underbrace{\ln x}_{I}\,dx$$

Integrating by parts we get,

$$I = 2\left[\left|\ln x \int 1\,dx\right|_1^2 - \int_1^2 \frac{1}{x}x\,dx\right] = 2\left[|x\ln x|_1^2 - |x|_1^2\right] = 2[(2\ln 2) - (2-1)]$$

$$= 2[\ln 4 - 1] = 2[\ln 4 - \ln e] = 2\ln\left(\frac{4}{e}\right) = \ln\left(\frac{16}{e^2}\right)$$

ILLUSTRATION 55: Evaluate $\int_{-\pi/2}^{\pi/2} |\tan^{-1} x|\,dx$

SOLUTION: Given $\int_{-\pi/2}^{\pi/2} |\tan^{-1} x|\,dx$ can be written as

$$I = \int_{-\pi/2}^{0} |\tan^{-1} x|\,dx + \int_{0}^{\pi/2} |\tan^{-1} x|\,dx = \int_{-\pi/2}^{0} -\tan^{-1} x\,dx + \int_{0}^{\pi/2} \tan^{-1} x\,dx$$

($\because \tan^{-1}x < 0$ for $x < 0$ and $\tan^{-1} x \geq 0$ for $x \geq 0$)

$$= \int_{-\pi/2}^{0} \tan^{-1}(-x)\,dx + \int_{0}^{\pi/2} \tan^{-1} x\,dx = 2\int_{0}^{\pi/2} \tan^{-1} x\,dx$$ ($\because \tan^{-1}(-x) = -\tan^{-1}x$)

($\because$ by reflection property $\int_{-\pi/2}^{0} \tan^{-1}(-x)\,dx = \int_{0}^{\pi/2} \tan^{-1}(x)\,dx$)

$$= 2\int_{0}^{\pi/2} \tan^{-1} x\,dx = 2\left[\left|(\tan^{-1} x)(x)\right|_0^{\pi/2} - \int_0^{\pi/2} \frac{1}{1+x^2}(x)\,dx\right]$$ (Integrating by parts)

$$= 2\left[\frac{\pi}{2}\tan^{-1}\left(\frac{\pi}{2}\right) - \frac{1}{2}\left|\ln(1+x^2)\right|_0^{\pi/2}\right] = 2\left[\frac{\pi}{2}\tan^{-1}\left(\frac{\pi}{2}\right) - \frac{1}{2}\left[\ln\left(1+\frac{\pi^2}{4}\right)\right]\right]$$

$$= \pi\tan^{-1}\left(\frac{\pi}{2}\right) - \ln\left(1+\frac{\pi^2}{4}\right)$$

ILLUSTRATION 56: If f is a continuous function satisfying the equation $f(x) + f(-x) = x^{12}$, then evaluate $\int_{-1}^{1} f(x)\,dx$

SOLUTION: Let $I = \int_{-1}^{1} f(x)\,dx = \int_{-1}^{0} f(x)\,dx + \int_{0}^{1} f(x)\,dx = \int_{0}^{1} f(-x)\,dx + \int_{0}^{1} f(x)\,dx$ (by reflection property)

$$= \int_0^1 \left(f(-x) + f(x)\right)dx = \int_0^1 x^{12}\,dx = \left[\frac{x^{13}}{13}\right]_0^1 = \frac{1}{13}$$

Hence $\int_{-1}^{1} f(x)\,dx = \frac{1}{13}$

ILLUSTRATION 57: Evaluate $\int\limits_{-\pi/2}^{\pi/2} \frac{dx}{e^{\tan x}+1}$

SOLUTION: Given $I = \int\limits_{-\pi/2}^{\pi/2} \frac{dx}{e^{\tan x}+1} = \int\limits_{-\pi/2}^{0} \frac{dx}{e^{\tan x}+1} + \int\limits_{0}^{\pi/2} \frac{dx}{e^{\tan x}+1} = \int\limits_{0}^{\pi/2} \frac{dx}{e^{-\tan x}+1} + \int\limits_{0}^{\pi/2} \frac{dx}{e^{\tan x}+1}$

(by reflection property)

$$= \int\limits_{0}^{\pi/2} \frac{e^{\tan x}}{1+e^{\tan x}} + \int\limits_{0}^{\pi/2} \frac{dx}{e^{\tan x}+1} = \int\limits_{0}^{\pi/2} 1\,dx = [x]_0^{\pi/2} = \frac{\pi}{2}$$

Thus, $I = \frac{\pi}{2}$

ILLUSTRATION 58: Prove that $\int_0^{\pi/2} f(\sin 2x)\sin x\,dx = \sqrt{2}\int_0^{\pi/4} f(\cos 2x)\cos x\,dx$

SOLUTION: Let $x = \pi/4 + t$ so that $dx = dt$ and $x = 0$ then

$t = -\pi/4$, $x = \pi/2$ then $t = \pi/4 = \int_0^{\pi/2} f(\sin 2x)\sin x\,dx = \int_{-\pi/4}^{\pi/4} f(\sin 2(\pi/4+t))\sin(\pi/4+t)dt$

$$= \int_{-\pi/4}^{\pi/4} f(\cos 2t)\sin(\pi/4+t)dt = \int\limits_{-\pi/4}^{0} f(\cos 2t)\sin(\pi/4+t)dt + \int\limits_{0}^{\pi/4} f(\cos 2t)\sin(\pi/4+t)dt$$

$$= \int_0^{\pi/4} [f(\cos 2t)\sin(\pi/4+t) + f(\cos(-2t))\sin(\pi/4-t)]dt$$ (using reflection property)

$$= \int_0^{\pi/4} f(\cos 2t)[\sin(\pi/4+t)+\sin(\pi/4-t)]dt = \int_0^{\pi/4} f(\cos 2t)[2\sin\pi/4\cos t]dt$$

$$= \sqrt{2}\int_0^{\pi/4} f(\cos 2t)\cos t\,dt = \sqrt{2}\int_0^{\pi/4} f(\cos 2x)\cos x\,dx$$

Property 8: **Shifting Property**

$\int\limits_{a}^{b} f(x)dx = \int\limits_{a+c}^{b+c} f(x-c)dx$, i.e., area under a part of function and above x-axis remains same when graph of function is shifted horizontally without having any change in the shape of curve.

Proof: Let $x = t - c$

$\Rightarrow$ $dx = dt$

When $x = a$,

$t = a + c$ and when $x = b$

$t = b + c$.

$\Rightarrow$ L.H.S. $= \int\limits_{a}^{b} f(x)dx = \int\limits_{a\ c}^{b\ c} f(t-c)dt$

$= \int\limits_{a+c}^{b+c} f(x-c)dx =$ R.H.S.

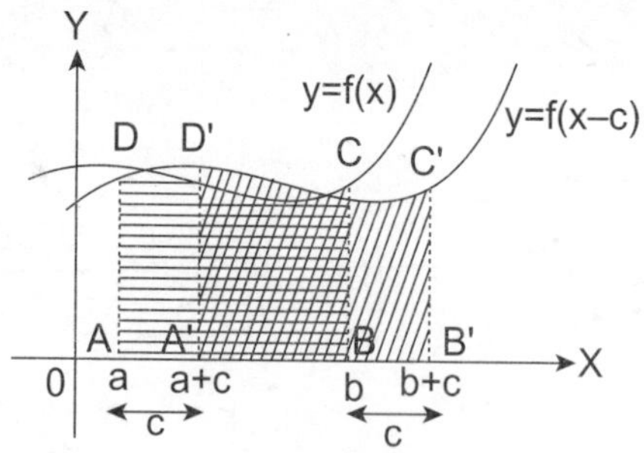

FIGURE 2.49

$f(x + c)$ is obtained by shifting $f(x)$ by $|c|$ unit opposite to sign of c.

Geometrically from above figure it can be observed that area $ABCD = \int\limits_{a}^{b} f(x)dx$ equals area

$A'B'C'D' = \int\limits_{a+c}^{b+c} f(x-c)dx$

ILLUSTRATION 59: Evaluate the integral $\int_2^3 x(x-1)^{2000}\,dx$

SOLUTION: By shifting property $\int_a^b f(x)\,dx = \int_{a+c}^{b+c} f(x-c)\,dx$

$$\therefore \int_2^3 x(x-1)^{2000}\,dx = \int_{2+(-1)}^{3+(-1)} (x-(-1))[(x-(-1)-1)]^{2000}\,dx$$

i.e., choosing $c = -1$

$$= \int_1^2 (x+1)(x)^{2000}\,dx = \int_1^2 \left(x^{2001}+x^{2000}\right)dx = \left|\frac{x^{2002}}{2002}\right|_1^2 + \left|\frac{x^{2001}}{2001}\right|_1^2$$

$$= \frac{1}{2002}\left[(2)^{2002}-1\right] + \frac{1}{2001}\left[(2)^{2001}-1\right] = \frac{(2^{2002}-1)}{2002} + \frac{(2^{2001}-1)}{2001}$$

ILLUSTRATION 60: Evaluate $\int_{1/3}^{2/3} \left(x-\frac{1}{2}\right)^2 e^{\left(x-\frac{1}{2}\right)^3}\,dx$

SOLUTION: By shifting property $\int_a^b f(x)\,dx = \int_{a+c}^{b+c} f(x-c)\,dx$

Let us take $c = -1/2$

$$\therefore \int_{1/3}^{2/3} \left(x-\frac{1}{2}\right)^2 e^{\left(x-\frac{1}{2}\right)^3}\,dx = \int_{1/3-1/2}^{2/3-1/2} \left(x+\frac{1}{2}-\frac{1}{2}\right)^2 e^{\left(x+\frac{1}{2}-\frac{1}{2}\right)^3}\,dx = \int_{-1/6}^{1/6} (x)^2 e^{x^3}\,dx$$

Let us substitute $x^3 = t$

$\Rightarrow 3x^2\,dx = dt$

When $x = -\frac{1}{6},\ t = \left(-\frac{1}{6}\right)^3 = -\frac{1}{216}$

and when $x = \frac{1}{6}, t = \left(\frac{1}{6}\right)^3 = \frac{1}{216}$

$$\therefore\ I = \int_{-1/216}^{1/216} \frac{1}{3}e^t\,dt = \frac{1}{3}\left[e^t\right]_{-1/216}^{1/216} = \frac{1}{3}\left[e^{1/216}-e^{-1/216}\right] = \frac{2}{3}\left[\frac{e^{\frac{1}{216}}-e^{-\frac{1}{216}}}{2}\right]$$

$$= \frac{2}{3}\sin h\left(\frac{1}{216}\right) \qquad \left(\because \sin hx = \frac{e^x-e^{-x}}{2}\right)$$

Property 9: $\int_0^a f(x)dx = \int_0^a f(a-x)dx$, i.e., area under a part of function above x-axis and that under its reversed part above x-axis are same.

Proof: Method I: Put $a - x = t$

$\Rightarrow -dx = dt$

$$\text{R.H.S.} = \int_a^0 f(t).(-dt) = -\int_a^0 f(t)dt = \int_0^a f(x)dx = \text{L.H.S.}$$

Method 2: Apply property 7, i.e., Reflection property

$$\text{L.H.S.} = \int_0^a f(x)dx = \int_{-a}^0 f(-x)dx$$ and shift by property 8, i.e., $x \to x - a$

$$= \int_{-a+a}^{0+a} f(-(x-a))dx = \int_0^a f(a-x)dx = \text{R.H.S.}$$

Method 3: (Graphically): The following figure shows the curves represented by $f(x)$, $f(-x)$, $f(a-x)$

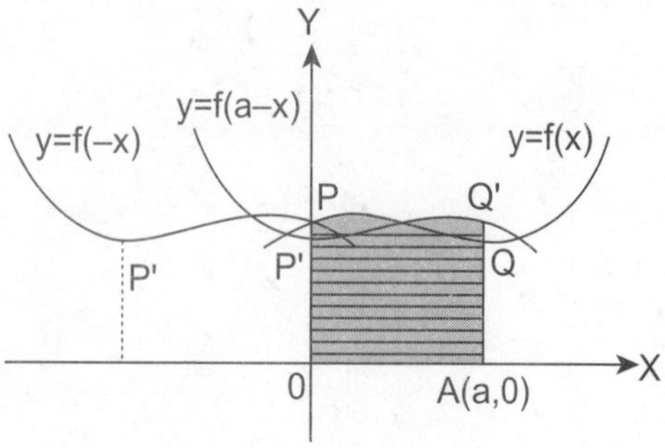

FIGURE 2.50

Applications: Clearly

$$\int_0^a f(x)dx = \text{Area } OA\widehat{QP} = \text{Area } OAQ'P' = \int_0^a f(a-x)dx$$

- If $f(a-x) = f(x)$, then to evaluate, $I = \int_0^a f(x).x\,dx$

  By using the above property, we have

$$I = \int_0^a (a-x)f(a-x)dx = \int_0^a (a-x)f(x)\,dx$$

$$(\because f(a-x) = f(x))$$

$$\Rightarrow \quad 2I = a\int_0^a f(x)dx$$

$$\Rightarrow \quad I = \frac{a}{2}\int_0^a f(x)\,dx$$

- If $f(x) + f(a-x) = \lambda$ (constant) then, to evaluate $I = \int_0^a f(x)dx$

  By using the above property, we have

$$\Rightarrow \quad I = \int_0^a f(a-x)dx$$

$$\Rightarrow \quad 2I = \int_0^a \left(f(x) + f(a-x)\right)dx$$

$$\Rightarrow \quad I = \frac{\lambda}{2}\int_0^a dx \qquad (\because f(x) + f(a-x) = f(x))$$

$$\Rightarrow \quad I = \frac{\lambda a}{2}$$

ILLUSTRATION 61: Evaluate the following definite integration :

(i) $\int_0^{\pi} x \sin x\, dx$ (ii) $\int_0^{\pi} x \cos^2 x\, dx$

SOLUTION: (i) Let $I = \int_0^{\pi} x \sin x\, dx = \int_0^{\pi} (\pi - x)\sin(\pi - x)\, dx = \int_0^{\pi} (\pi - x)\sin x\, dx$

$$= \pi\int_0^{\pi} \sin x\, dx - \int_0^{\pi} x\sin x\, dx = \pi\left[-\cos x\right]_0^{\pi} - I$$

$\therefore \quad I + I = -\pi[\cos\pi - \cos 0] = -\pi(-2)$

$\Rightarrow \quad 2I = 2\pi \qquad \Rightarrow I = \pi$

(ii) Let $I = \int_0^{\pi} x\cos^2 x\, dx$

$$= \int_0^{\pi} (\pi - x)\cos^2(\pi - x)\, dx = \int_0^{\pi} (\pi - x)(\cos^2 x)\, dx = \pi\int_0^{\pi} \cos^2 x\, dx - \int_0^{\pi} x\cos^2 x\, dx$$

$$\Rightarrow \quad I = \pi\int_0^{\pi} (\cos^2 x)\, dx - I \Rightarrow 2I = \pi\int_0^{\pi} \cos^2 x\, dx \Rightarrow 2I = \pi\int_0^{\pi} \frac{1+\cos 2x}{2}\, dx$$

$$\Rightarrow \quad I = \frac{\pi}{4}\int_0^{\pi} (1 + \cos 2x)\, dx = \frac{\pi}{4}\left[x + \frac{\sin 2x}{2}\right]_0^{\pi} = \frac{\pi}{4}[\pi] = \frac{\pi^2}{4}$$

ILLUSTRATION 62: Find the value of $\int_0^{\pi/2} \frac{\sqrt{\sin x}}{\sqrt{\sin x} + \sqrt{\cos x}}dx$

SOLUTION: Let $I = \int_0^{\pi/2} \frac{\sqrt{\sin x}}{\sqrt{\sin x} + \sqrt{\cos x}}dx$ ...(i)

$$= \int_0^{\pi/2} \frac{\sqrt{\sin(\pi/2-x)}}{\sqrt{\sin(\pi/2-x)}+\sqrt{\cos(\pi/2-x)}}\,dx$$

$$\Rightarrow\ I = \int_0^{\pi/2} \frac{\sqrt{\cos x}}{\sqrt{\cos x}+\sqrt{\sin x}}\,dx \qquad \ldots\text{(ii)}$$

Adding (i) and (ii) we get, $2I = \int_0^{\pi/2} \frac{\sqrt{\sin x}}{\sqrt{\sin x}+\sqrt{\cos x}}\,dx + \int_0^{\pi/2} \frac{\sqrt{\cos x}}{\sqrt{\cos x}+\sqrt{\sin x}}\,dx$

$$= \int_0^{\pi/2} \frac{\sqrt{\cos x}+\sqrt{\sin x}}{\sqrt{\cos x}+\sqrt{\sin x}}\,dx = \int_0^{\pi/2} dx = [x]_0^{\pi/2} = \pi/2 - 0 = \pi/2$$

$\therefore\ I = \pi/4$

ILLUSTRATION 63: Show that $\int_0^{\pi} x f(\sin x)dx = \frac{\pi}{2}\int_0^{\pi} f(\sin x)dx$

SOLUTION: $I = \int_0^{\pi} x f(\sin x)dx = \int_0^{\pi} (\pi - x) f \sin(\pi - x)dx \quad \left\{\because \int_0^a f(x)\,dx = \int_0^a f(a-x)dx\right\}$

$$= \int_0^{\pi} (\pi - x) f(\sin x)dx = \int_0^{\pi} \pi f(\sin x)dx - \int_0^{\pi} x f(\sin x)dx$$

$\Rightarrow\ I = \pi\int_0^{\pi} f(\sin x)dx - I \qquad \Rightarrow\ 2I = \pi\int_0^{\pi} f(\sin x)dx$

$$\Rightarrow\ I = \frac{\pi}{2}\int_0^{\pi} f(\sin x)dx$$

ILLUSTRATION 64: $\int_0^1 \frac{\sin^{-1}\sqrt{x}}{x^2 - x + 1}\,dx$

SOLUTION: Putting $\sin^{-1}\sqrt{x} = \theta$

$\Rightarrow \sqrt{x} = \sin\theta \Rightarrow x = \sin^2\theta \qquad \Rightarrow dx = \sin 2\theta\, d\theta$;

When $x = 0$, $\sin^{-1}0 = \theta \qquad \Rightarrow \theta = 0$

And $x = 1$, $\sin^{-1}1 = \theta \qquad \Rightarrow \theta = \pi/2$

$$\therefore\ I = \int_0^{\pi/2} \frac{(\theta \sin 2\theta)}{\sin^4\theta - \sin^2\theta + 1}\,d\theta \qquad \ldots(1)$$

By property $\int_0^a f(x)dx = \int_0^a f(a-x)dx$, we have

$$I = \int_0^{\pi/2} \frac{\left(\frac{\pi}{2}-\theta\right)\sin 2\theta}{\cos^4\theta - \cos^2\theta + 1}\,d\theta = \int_0^{\pi/2} \frac{\left(\frac{\pi}{2}-\theta\right)\sin 2\theta}{(1-\sin^2\theta)^2 - (1-\sin^2\theta)+1}\,d\theta$$

$$= \int_0^{\pi/2} \frac{\left(\frac{\pi}{2}-\theta\right)\sin 2\theta}{\sin^4\theta - \sin^2\theta + 1}\,d\theta \qquad \ldots(2)$$

Adding (1) and (2) we get $2I = \frac{\pi}{2}\int_0^{\pi/2} \frac{\sin 2\theta}{\sin^4\theta - \sin^2\theta + 1}\,d\theta$

put $\sin^2\theta = t \qquad \Rightarrow \sin 2\theta\, d\theta = dt$

$$\Rightarrow\ 2I = \frac{\pi}{2}\int_0^1 \frac{dt}{t^2 - t + 1} = \frac{\pi}{2}\int_0^1 \frac{dt}{\left(t-\frac{1}{2}\right)^2 + \left(\frac{\sqrt{3}}{2}\right)^2}$$

$$\Rightarrow\ 2I=\frac{\pi}{2}\cdot\frac{2}{\sqrt{3}}\tan^{-1}\left.\left(\frac{\left(t-\frac{1}{2}\right).2}{\sqrt{3}}\right)\right|_0^1=\frac{\pi}{\sqrt{3}}\left[\tan^{-1}\frac{1}{\sqrt{3}}-\tan^{-1}\left(\frac{-1}{\sqrt{3}}\right)\right]=\frac{\pi}{\sqrt{3}}\left[\frac{\pi}{6}+\frac{\pi}{6}\right]$$

$$\Rightarrow\ 2I=\frac{\pi}{\sqrt{3}}\left(\frac{2\pi}{6}\right)\qquad\Rightarrow\ I=\frac{\pi^2}{6\sqrt{3}}$$

ILLUSTRATION 65: Prove that $\int_0^{\pi/2}\frac{g(\sin x)}{g(\sin x)+g(\cos x)}dx=\int_0^{\pi/2}\frac{g(\cos x)}{g(\sin x)+g(\cos x)}dx=\frac{\pi}{4}$

SOLUTION: Let $I=\int_0^{\pi/2}\frac{g(\sin x)}{g(\sin x)+g(\cos x)}dx$ ...(i)

By using property $\int_0^a f(x)dx=\int_0^a f(a-x)dx$, we have

$$I=\int_0^{\pi/2}\frac{g\left(\sin\left(\frac{\pi}{2}-x\right)\right)}{g\left(\sin\left(\frac{\pi}{2}-x\right)\right)+g\left(\cos\left(\frac{\pi}{2}-x\right)\right)}dx=\int_0^{\pi/2}\frac{g(\cos x)}{g(\cos x)+g(\sin x)}dx \qquad \text{...(ii)}$$

On adding (i) and (ii); we obtain

$$2I=\int_0^{\pi/2}\left(\frac{g(\sin x)}{g(\sin x)+g(\cos x)}+\frac{g(\cos x)}{g(\cos x)+g(\sin x)}\right)dx=\int_0^{\pi/2}dx\qquad\Rightarrow\ I=\frac{\pi}{4}$$

ILLUSTRATION 66: Evaluate $\int_0^{\pi}\frac{dx}{1+2\sin^2 x}$

SOLUTION: Let $f(x)=\frac{1}{1+2\sin^2 x}$

$$\Rightarrow f(\pi-x)=f(x)\qquad\left(\because \int_0^{2a}f(x)dx=2\int_0^a f(x)dx \text{ if } f(2a-x)=f(x)\right)$$

$$\Rightarrow\ \int_0^{\pi}\frac{dx}{1+2\sin^2 x}=2\int_0^{\pi/2}\frac{dx}{1+2\sin^2 x}=2\int_0^{\pi/2}\frac{\sec^2 x\,dx}{1+\tan^2 x+2\tan^2 x}$$

$$=2\int_0^{\pi/2}\frac{\sec^2 x\,dx}{1+3\tan^2 x}=\frac{2}{\sqrt{3}}\left[\tan^{-1}\left(\sqrt{3}\tan x\right)\right]_0^{\pi/2}$$

$\because$ $\tan\frac{\pi}{2}$ is undefined, we take limit

$$=\frac{2}{\sqrt{3}}\left[\lim_{x\to\frac{\pi}{2}^-}\tan^{-1}\left(\sqrt{3}\tan x\right)-\tan^{-1}\left(\sqrt{3}\tan 0\right)\right]=\frac{2}{\sqrt{3}}\frac{\pi}{2}=\frac{\pi}{\sqrt{3}}$$

Alternatively: $\int_0^{\pi}\frac{dx}{1+2\sin^2 x}=\int_0^{\pi}\frac{\text{cosec}^2 x}{\text{cosec}^2 x+2}dx=\int_0^{\pi}\frac{\text{cosec}^2 x}{\cot^2 x+3}dx=-\int_0^{\pi}\frac{-\text{cosec}^2 x}{\left(\sqrt{3}\right)^2+(\cot x)^2}dx$

Observe that we are not converting in terms of $\tan x$ as it is not continuous in $(0, \pi)$

$$=-\frac{1}{\sqrt{3}}\left[\tan^{-1}\left(\frac{\cot x}{\sqrt{3}}\right)\right]_0^{\pi}=-\frac{1}{\sqrt{3}}\left[\lim_{x\to\pi^-}\tan^{-1}\left(\frac{\cot x}{\sqrt{3}}\right)-\lim_{x\to 0^+}\tan^{-1}\left(\frac{\cot x}{\sqrt{3}}\right)\right]$$

$$=-\frac{1}{\sqrt{3}}\left[-\frac{\pi}{2}-\frac{\pi}{2}\right]=\frac{\pi}{\sqrt{3}}.$$

ILLUSTRATION 67: If $n \geq 1$ is a positive integer, then evaluate $\int_0^1 \frac{\{nx\}}{1-x+x^2}dx$; where $\{nx\} = nx - [nx]$; where [.] denotes the greatest integer function

SOLUTION: Let $I = \int_0^1 \frac{\{nx\}}{1-x+x^2}dx$

$$= \int_0^1 \frac{\{n(1-x)\}}{1-(1-x)+(1-x)^2}dx \qquad \left[\because \int_0^a f(x)dx = \int_0^a f(a-x)dx\right]$$

$$= \int_0^1 \frac{\{n-nx\}}{1-x+x^2}dx = \int_0^1 \frac{1-\{nx\}}{1-x+x^2}dx \qquad [\because \{n-nx\} = \{-nx\} = 1 - \{nx\}]$$

$$\Rightarrow \quad 2I = \int_0^1 \frac{1}{1-x+x^2}dx = \int_0^1 \frac{1}{\left(x^2-x+\frac{1}{4}\right)+\left(\frac{\sqrt{3}}{2}\right)^2}dx$$

$$= \int_0^1 \frac{dx}{\left(x-\frac{1}{2}\right)^2+\left(\frac{\sqrt{3}}{2}\right)^2} = \frac{2}{\sqrt{3}}\left|\tan^{-1}\left(\frac{2x-1}{\sqrt{3}}\right)\right|_0^1 = \frac{2}{\sqrt{3}}\left(\frac{\pi}{6}+\frac{\pi}{6}\right) \qquad \Rightarrow \quad I = \frac{\pi}{3\sqrt{3}}$$

ILLUSTRATION 68: Evaluate $\int_0^{\pi/2} \frac{a\sin x + b\cos x}{\sin\left(\frac{\pi}{4}+x\right)}dx$

SOLUTION: Let $I = \int_0^{\pi/2} \frac{a\sin x + b\cos x}{\sin\left(\frac{\pi}{4}+x\right)}dx$

$$I = \int_0^{\pi/2} \frac{(a\sin x + b\cos x)\sqrt{2}}{\cos x + \sin x}dx \qquad \ldots(1)$$

Using property $\int_0^a f(x)\,dx = \int_0^a f(a-x)\,dx$ we have

$$I = \int_0^{\pi/2} \left(\frac{a\cos x + b\sin x}{\sin x + \cos x}\right)\sqrt{2}\,dx \qquad \ldots(2)$$

(1) + (2) gives $2I = \int_0^{\pi/2} \frac{(a+b)\,(\cos x + \sin x)}{(\cos x + \sin x)}\sqrt{2}\,dx$

$$\Rightarrow \quad I = \frac{a+b}{\sqrt{2}}\int_0^{\pi/2} dx \Rightarrow I = \frac{a+b}{2\sqrt{2}}\pi$$

ILLUSTRATION 69: Evaluate $\int_0^1 \frac{dx}{(3+x-x^2)(e^{3-6x}+1)}dx$

SOLUTION: Let $I = \int_0^1 \frac{dx}{(3+x-x^2)(e^{3-6x}+1)}$ $\qquad \ldots(1)$

Using the property $\int_0^a f(x)\,dx = \int_0^a f(a-x)\,dx$; we have

$$I=\int_0^1 \frac{dx}{\left[3+(1-x)-(1-x)^2\right](e^{3-6(1-x)}+1)}$$

$$=\int_0^1 \frac{dx}{\left(3+1-x-1-x^2+2x\right)(e^{-3+6x}+1)}=\int_0^1 \frac{dx}{\left(3+x-x^2\right)(e^{-3+6x}+1)}$$

or $I=\int_0^1 \frac{e^{3-6x}}{\left(3+x-x^2\right)(1+e^{3-6x})}dx$ ...(2)

Adding (1) and (2) we get $2I=\int_0^1 \frac{\left(1+e^{3-6x}\right)}{\left(3+x-x^2\right)(1+e^{3-6x})}dx$

or $2I=\int_0^1 \frac{dx}{3+x-x^2}$

$$\Rightarrow\quad 2I=\int_0^1 \frac{dx}{-\left[x^2-x-3\right]}=\int_0^1 \frac{dx}{-\left[x^2-x+\frac{1}{4}-3-\frac{1}{4}\right]}$$

$$=\int_0^1 \frac{dx}{-\left[\left(x-\frac{1}{2}\right)^2-\frac{13}{4}\right]}=\int_0^1 \frac{dx}{\left(\frac{\sqrt{13}}{2}\right)^2-\left(x-\frac{1}{2}\right)^2}$$

$$\Rightarrow\quad I=\frac{1}{2}\int_0^1 \frac{dx}{\left(\frac{\sqrt{13}}{2}\right)^2-\left(x-\frac{1}{2}\right)^2}=\left[\frac{1}{2}\left(\frac{1}{2\left(\sqrt{13}/2\right)}\right)\ln\left|\frac{\frac{\sqrt{13}}{2}+\left(x-\frac{1}{2}\right)}{\frac{\sqrt{13}}{2}-\left(x-\frac{1}{2}\right)}\right|\right]_0^1$$

$$=\frac{1}{2\sqrt{13}}\left[\ln\left(\frac{\frac{\sqrt{13}}{2}+\frac{1}{2}}{\frac{\sqrt{13}}{2}-\frac{1}{2}}\right)-\ln\left(\frac{\frac{\sqrt{13}}{2}-\frac{1}{2}}{\frac{\sqrt{13}}{2}+\frac{1}{2}}\right)\right]=\frac{1}{2\sqrt{13}}\left[\ln\left(\frac{\sqrt{13}+1}{\sqrt{13}-1}\right)+\ln\left(\frac{\sqrt{13}+1}{\sqrt{13}-1}\right)\right]$$

$$=\frac{1}{\sqrt{13}}\ln\left(\frac{\sqrt{13}+1}{\sqrt{13}-1}\right)$$

ILLUSTRATION 70: Evaluate $\int_{-1}^{0}\cot^{-1}\left(1+x+x^2\right)dx$

SOLUTION: Let $I=\int_{-1}^{0}\cot^{-1}\left(1+x+x^2\right)dx$

Using the property $\int_{-b}^{-a} f(-x)\,dx=\int_a^b f(x)\,dx$

i.e., reflection property, we have $I=\int_0^1\cot^{-1}\left(1+(-x)+(-x^2)\right)dx$ ...(1)

or $I=\int_0^1\cot^{-1}\left(1-x+x^2\right)dx=\int_0^1\cot^{-1}\left(1-x(1-x)\right)dx$

$\because\ x\in(0,1),\ 1-x+x^2\in\left[\frac{3}{4},1\right)$ and $\cot^{-1}x=\tan^{-1}\left(\frac{1}{x}\right)$ for $x>0$

$\Rightarrow \cot^{-1}(1-x(1-x)) = \tan^{-1}\left[\frac{1}{1-x(1-x)}\right] = \tan^{-1}\left[\frac{x+(1-x)}{1-x(1-x)}\right]$

$= \tan^{-1}x + \tan^{-1}(1-x)$, as $x(1-x) < 1$

$\therefore \quad I = \int_0^1 \left[\tan^{-1}x + \tan^{-1}(1-x)\right]dx = \int_0^1 \tan^{-1}x\, dx + \int_0^1 \tan^{-1}(1-(1-x))dx$

(using property $\int_0^a f(x)\,dx = \int_0^a f(a-x)\,dx$) $= 2\int_0^1 \tan^{-1}x\, dx = \frac{\pi}{2} - \ln 2$ on solving by parts.

ILLUSTRATION 71: Let $f(x)$ be a continuous function on [0, 6] and satisfying $f(x) \cdot f(6-x) = 4$, then evaluate $\int_0^6 \frac{2}{2+f(x)}dx$

SOLUTION: Let $I = \int_0^6 \frac{2}{2+f(x)}dx$ ...(1)

$= \int_0^6 \frac{2}{2+f(6-x)}dx \quad \left(\text{By using } \int_0^a f(x)dx = \int_0^a f(a-x)dx\right)$

$= \int_0^6 \frac{2}{2+\frac{4}{f(x)}}dx$ or $I = \int_0^6 \frac{2f(x)}{2f(x)+4}dx = \int_0^6 \frac{f(x)}{f(x)+2}dx$ ...(2)

Adding (1) and (2), we get

$2I = \int_0^6 \frac{2+f(x)}{2+f(x)}dx = \int_0^6 1\, dx \qquad \Rightarrow 2I = [x]_0^6 = 6$

$\Rightarrow I = 3$

ILLUSTRATION 72: Let f and g are two continuous functions on $[0, a]$ satisfying the equations

(i) $3f(x) = f(a-x)$

(ii) $11g(x) + 3g(a-x) = 12$, then show that $\int_0^a f(x)g(x)\,dx = \int_0^a f(x)\,dx$

SOLUTION: (i) Let $I = \int_0^a f(x)g(x)\,dx = \int_0^a f(a-x)g(a-x)\,dx$

$\left(\text{By using } \int_0^a f(x)dx = \int_0^a f(a-x)dx\right) = \int_0^a 3f(x)[g(a-x)]\,dx = \int_0^a 3f(x)\left[\frac{12-11g(x)}{3}\right]dx$

$= \int_0^a 12f(x)\,dx - 11\int_0^a f(x)g(x)dx$

$\Rightarrow I = 12\int_0^a f(x)\,dx - 11I \qquad \Rightarrow 12I = 12\int_0^a f(x)\,dx$

$\Rightarrow I = \int_0^a f(x)\,dx$

Hence $\int_0^a f(x)g(x)dx = \int_0^a f(x)\,dx$.

ILLUSTRATION 73: Evaluate $\int_0^{\infty}\frac{dx}{(1+x^a)(1+x^2)}$; $a>0$

SOLUTION: Given $I=\int_0^{\infty}\frac{dx}{(1+x^a)(1+x^2)}$

Put $x=\tan\theta$ $\Rightarrow dx=\sec^2\theta\, d\theta$

$\Rightarrow \frac{dx}{1+x^2}=d\theta$. When $x=0$, $\theta=0$ and when $x\to\infty, \theta\to\frac{\pi}{2}$

$$\therefore \quad I=\int_0^{\pi/2}\frac{d\theta}{1+(\tan\theta)^a}=\int_0^{\pi/2}\frac{(\cos\theta)^a}{(\cos\theta)^a+(\sin\theta)^a}d\theta \qquad \ldots(1)$$

By using the property $\int_0^a f(x)\,dx=\int_0^a f(a-x)\,dx$, we have

$$I=\int_0^{\pi/2}\frac{\left[\cos\left(\frac{\pi}{2}-\theta\right)\right]^a}{\left[\cos\left(\frac{\pi}{2}-\theta\right)\right]^a+\left[\sin\left(\frac{\pi}{2}-\theta\right)\right]^a}d\theta$$

$$\text{or} \quad I=\int_0^{\pi/2}\frac{(\sin\theta)^a}{(\sin\theta)^a+(\cos\theta)^a}d\theta \qquad \ldots(2)$$

Adding (1) and (2), we get $2I=\int_0^{\pi/2}1\,d\theta=\frac{\pi}{2}$ $\Rightarrow I=\frac{\pi}{4}$

ILLUSTRATION 74: Prove that $\int_0^{\pi/4}\ln(1+\tan\theta)\,d\theta=\frac{\pi}{8}\ln 2$

SOLUTION: Let $I=\int_0^{\pi/4}\ln(1+\tan\theta)\,d\theta$

$$\Rightarrow I=\int_0^{\pi/4}\ln\left(1+\tan\left(\frac{\pi}{4}-\theta\right)\right)d\theta=\int_0^{\pi/4}\ln\left[1+\frac{1-\tan\theta}{1+\tan\theta}\right]d\theta=\int_0^{\pi/4}\ln\left(\frac{2}{1+\tan\theta}\right)d\theta$$

$$=\int_0^{\pi/4}\{\ln 2-\ln(1+\tan\theta)\}\,d\theta=(\ln 2)\left[\frac{\pi}{4}\right]-\int_0^{\pi/4}\ln(1+\tan\theta)\,d\theta$$

$=\frac{\pi}{4}\ln 2-I$ $\Rightarrow 2I=\frac{\pi}{4}\ln 2$

$\Rightarrow I=\frac{\pi}{8}\ln 2$ Hence proved.

ILLUSTRATION 75: Evaluate $\int_0^{\pi/2}x\left|\cos^2 x-\frac{1}{2}\right|dx$

SOLUTION: Let $I=\int_0^{\pi/2}x\left|\frac{2\cos^2 x-1}{2}\right|dx=\int_0^{\pi/2}\frac{x}{2}|\cos 2x|\,dx=\frac{1}{2}\int_0^{\pi/2}x|\cos 2x|\,dx$

Put $2x=t$ $\Rightarrow dx=\frac{dt}{2}$

When $x=0$, $t=0$ and when $x=\frac{\pi}{2}$, $t=\pi$

$$\therefore \quad I=\frac{1}{2}\int_0^{\pi}\frac{t}{2}|\cos t|\frac{dt}{2} = \frac{1}{8}\int_0^{\pi} t|\cos t|\,dt = \frac{1}{8}\int_0^{\pi}(\pi-t)|\cos(\pi-t)|\,dt$$

(using the property $\int_0^a f(x)\,dx=\int_0^a f(a-x)\,dx$)

$$=\frac{\pi}{8}\int_0^{\pi}|\cos t|\,dt-\frac{1}{8}\int_0^{\pi}t|\cos t|\,dt = \frac{\pi}{8}\int_0^{\pi}|\cos t|\,dt - I$$

$$\Rightarrow \quad 2I=\frac{\pi}{8}\left\{\int_0^{\pi/2}\cos t\,dt+\int_{\pi/2}^{\pi}-\cos t\,dt\right\} = \frac{\pi}{8}\left\{|\sin t|_0^{\pi/2}-|\sin t|_{\pi/2}^{\pi}\right\}$$

$$=\frac{\pi}{8}\{(1-0)-(0-1)\}=\frac{\pi}{8}(2)$$

$$\Rightarrow \quad I=\frac{\pi}{8}$$

Property 10: $\int_a^b f(x)dx=\int_a^b f(a+b-x)dx$

Proof: ***Method 1:*** Let us substitute $x = a + b - t$, $dx = -dt$

$$\therefore \quad \text{L.H.S.} = -\int_b^a f(a+b-t)dt$$

$$=\int_a^b f(a+b-t)\,dt = \int_a^b f(a+b-x)\,dx \text{ R.H.S.}$$

Method 2: Applying property-7 and property-8, i.e., reflection and shifting property respectively we have,

$$\text{L.H.S.} = \int_a^b f(x)dx = \int_{-b}^{-a} f(-x)dx \text{ (by property–7)}$$

Shifting by $(a + b)$ towards right we have,

$$\int_{-b+a+b}^{-a+a+b} f(-(x-a-b)\,dx \text{ (property – 8)}$$

$$=\int_a^b f(a+b-x)dx = RHS$$

Method 3: **(Graphically)**

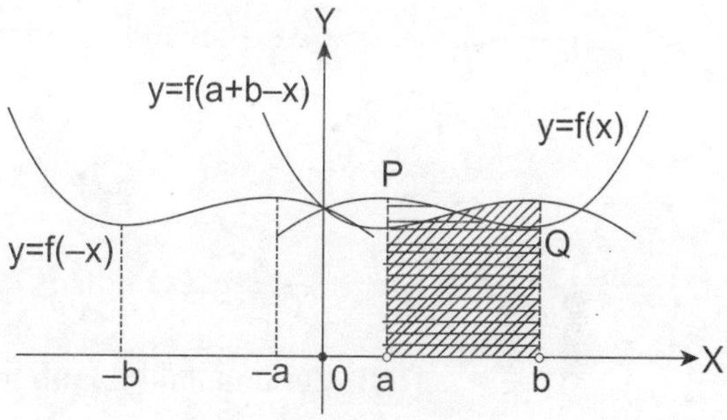

FIGURE 2.51

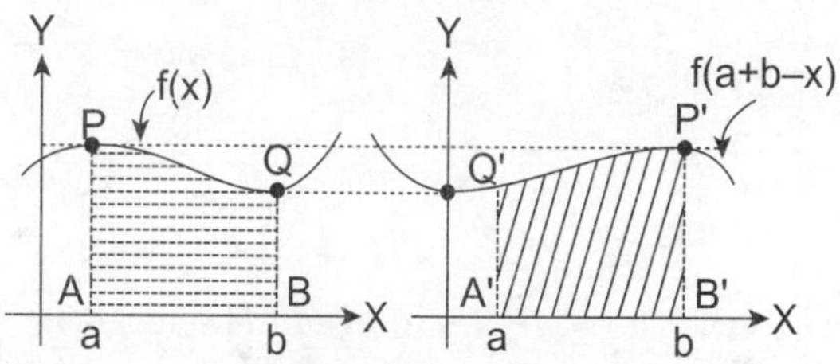

FIGURE 2.52

Clearly $\int_a^b f(x)\,dx = \square = \int_a^b f(a+b-x)\,dx = \square$

REMARKS

If a = 0 and we take b = a, then $\int_a^b f(x)\,dx=\int_a^b f(a+b-x)\,dx$

$\Rightarrow \quad \int_0^a f(x)\,dx=\int_0^a f(a-x)\,dx$ $\quad\Rightarrow$ *which is property 9.*

Applications

Application I: If $f(a+b-x)=f(x)$,

Then to evaluate $I=\int_a^b xf(x)\,dx$ ...(i)

By above property

$$\Rightarrow\quad I=\int_a^b (a+b-x)f(a+b-x)\,dx$$

$$=\int_a^b (a+b-x)f(x)\,dx \quad \text{...(ii)}$$

as $f(a+b-x)=f(x)$

Adding (i) and (ii) we get $2I=(a+b)\int_a^b f(x)\,dx$

$$\Rightarrow\quad I=\frac{(a+b)}{2}\int_a^b f(x)\,dx$$

Application II: If $f(x)+f(a+b-x)=\lambda$, then evaluate $I=\int_a^b f(x)\,dx$ ......(i)

By above property $I=\int_a^b f(a+b-x)\,dx$ ...(ii)

Adding (i) and (ii) we have,

$$2I=\int_a^b [f(a+b-x)+f(x)]dx=\int_a^b \lambda\,dx=\lambda[b-a]$$

$$\Rightarrow\quad I=\frac{\lambda(b-a)}{2}$$

ILLUSTRATION 76: Evaluate $\int_{\pi/6}^{\pi/3}\frac{\sqrt{\tan x}}{\sqrt{\tan x}+\sqrt{\cot x}}dx$

SOLUTION: Let $I=\int_{\pi/6}^{\pi/3}\frac{\sqrt{\tan x}}{\sqrt{\tan x}+\sqrt{\cot x}}dx$ ...(1)

By using the property $\int_a^b f(x)\,dx=\int_a^b f(a+b-x)\,dx$ we get

$$I=\int_{\pi/6}^{\pi/3}\frac{\sqrt{\tan\left(\frac{\pi}{2}-x\right)}}{\sqrt{\tan\left(\frac{\pi}{2}-x\right)}+\sqrt{\cot\left(\frac{\pi}{2}-x\right)}}dx=\int_{\pi/6}^{\pi/3}\frac{\sqrt{\cot x}}{\sqrt{\cot x}+\sqrt{\tan x}}dx \quad \text{...(2)}$$

Adding (1) and (2), we get $2I=\int_{\pi/6}^{\pi/3}1\,dx=\frac{\pi}{3}-\frac{\pi}{6}=\frac{\pi}{6}$

$\therefore\quad I=\frac{\pi}{12}$

ILLUSTRATION 77: Evaluate $\int_2^3\frac{x^2\,dx}{2x^2-10x+25}$

SOLUTION: Let $I=\int_2^3\frac{x^2\,dx}{2x^2-10x+25}=\int_2^3\frac{x^2\,dx}{x^2+(x-5)^2}$ ...(1)

Using the property $\int_a^b f(x)\,dx=\int_a^b f(a+b-x)\,dx$ we get

$$I=\int_2^3\frac{(5-x)^2\,dx}{(5-x)^2+x^2} \quad \text{...(2)}$$

Adding (1) and (2) we get $2I=\int_2^3 1\,dx=1$

$\Rightarrow\quad I=\frac{1}{2}$

ILLUSTRATION 78: Evaluate $\int_{\alpha}^{\beta} \frac{x}{\sqrt{(x-\alpha)(\beta-x)}}$; $\alpha < \beta$

SOLUTION: Let $I = \int_{\alpha}^{\beta} \frac{x}{\sqrt{(x-\alpha)(\beta-x)}}$ ...(1)

or $I = \int_{\alpha}^{\beta} \frac{(\alpha+\beta-x)}{\sqrt{(\alpha+\beta-x-\alpha)(\beta-\alpha-\beta+x)}} dx \left(\text{using} \int_a^b f(x)\,dx = \int_a^b f(a+b-x)\,dx\right)$

or $I = \int_{\alpha}^{\beta} \frac{(\alpha+\beta-x)}{\sqrt{(\beta-x)(x-\alpha)}} dx = (\alpha+\beta)\int_{\alpha}^{\beta} \frac{dx}{\sqrt{(\beta-x)(x-\alpha)}} - \int_{\alpha}^{\beta} \frac{x\,dx}{\sqrt{(\beta-x)(x-\alpha)}}$

$\Rightarrow I = (\alpha+\beta)\int_{\alpha}^{\beta} \frac{dx}{\sqrt{(\beta-x)(x-\alpha)}} - I$

$\Rightarrow I = \frac{(\alpha+\beta)}{2}\int_{\alpha}^{\beta} \frac{dx}{\sqrt{(\beta-x)(x-\alpha)}} = \frac{(\alpha+\beta)}{2}\int_{\alpha}^{\beta} \frac{dx}{\sqrt{-x^2+(\alpha+\beta)x-\alpha\beta}}$

(Here Disc. = $(\alpha-\beta)^2 > 0$)

$= \frac{(\alpha+\beta)}{2}\int_{\alpha}^{\beta} \frac{dx}{\sqrt{-\{x^2-(\alpha+\beta)x+\alpha\beta\}}}$

$= \frac{(\alpha+\beta)}{2}\int_{\alpha}^{\beta} \frac{dx}{\sqrt{-\left\{x^2-(\alpha+\beta)x+\frac{(\alpha+\beta)^2}{4}+\alpha\beta-\frac{(\alpha+\beta)^2}{4}\right\}}}$

$= \frac{(\alpha+\beta)}{2}\int_{\alpha}^{\beta} \frac{dx}{\sqrt{-\left\{\left(x-\frac{(\alpha+\beta)}{2}\right)^2+\alpha\beta-\frac{(\alpha+\beta)^2}{4}\right\}}}$

$= \frac{(\alpha+\beta)}{2}\int_{\alpha}^{\beta} \frac{dx}{\sqrt{\left(\frac{(\alpha+\beta)^2}{4}-\alpha\beta\right)-\left(x-\frac{(\alpha+\beta)}{2}\right)^2}}$

$= \frac{(\alpha+\beta)}{2}\int_{\alpha}^{\beta} \frac{dx}{\sqrt{\left[\frac{\beta-\alpha}{2}\right]^2-\left[x-\frac{(\alpha+\beta)}{2}\right]^2}}$ $(\because \beta > \alpha)$

$= \left(\frac{\alpha+\beta}{2}\right)\left[\sin^{-1}\left(\frac{x-\left(\frac{\alpha+\beta}{2}\right)}{\left(\frac{\beta-\alpha}{2}\right)}\right)\right]_{\alpha}^{\beta} = \left(\frac{\alpha+\beta}{2}\right)\left[\sin^{-1}\left(\frac{\beta-\alpha}{\beta-\alpha}\right)-\sin^{-1}\left(\frac{\alpha-\beta}{\beta-\alpha}\right)\right]$

$= \frac{\alpha+\beta}{2}\left[\frac{\pi}{2}-\left(-\frac{\pi}{2}\right)\right] = \frac{\alpha+\beta}{2}(\pi) = (\alpha+\beta).\frac{\pi}{2}$

ILLUSTRATION 79: Evaluate $\int_{1}^{4} \frac{\sqrt{x}}{\sqrt{x}+\sqrt{5-x}} dx$

SOLUTION: Let $I = \int_{1}^{4} \frac{\sqrt{x}}{\sqrt{x}+\sqrt{5-x}} dx$ ...(1)

$$= \int_1^4 \frac{\sqrt{1+4-x}}{\sqrt{1+4-x}+\sqrt{5-(1+4-x)}}\,dx \text{ or } I = \int_1^4 \frac{\sqrt{5-x}}{\sqrt{5-x}+\sqrt{x}}\,dx \quad \ldots(2)$$

(by using $\int_a^b f(x)\,dx = \int_a^b f(a+b-x)\,dx$)

Adding (1) and (2) we get, $2I = \int_1^4 1\,dx \quad \Rightarrow \quad I = \frac{3}{2}$

ILLUSTRATION 80: If $f(x)$ be a real valued continuous and bounded function, such that $f(a+b-x) = f(x)\ \forall\ x \in [a, b]$, then show that $\int_a^b x\,f(x)\,dx = \left(\frac{a+b}{2}\right)\int_a^b f(x)\,dx$

SOLUTION: Let $I = \int_a^b x\,f(x)\,dx \quad \ldots(1)$

Using the property $\int_a^b f(x)\,dx = \int_a^b f(a+b-x)\,dx$, we get

$$I = \int_a^b (a+b-x)f(a+b-x)\,dx = \int_a^b (a+b-x)f(x)\,dx$$

$(\because f(a+b-x) = f(x)\ \forall\ x \in [a, b])$

$$= (a+b)\int_a^b f(x)\,dx - \int_a^b x\,f(x)\,dx = (a+b)\int_a^b f(x)\,dx - I$$

$$\Rightarrow \quad 2I = (a+b)\int_a^b f(x)\,dx$$

$\Rightarrow \quad I = \frac{(a+b)}{2}\int_a^b f(x)\,dx$, hence the result.

ILLUSTRATION 81: Evaluate $\int_{\pi/6}^{\pi/3} |\cos 2x|\ln(\cot x)\,dx$

SOLUTION: Let $I = \int_{\pi/6}^{\pi/3} |\cos 2x|\ln(\cot x)\,dx$

Using the property $\int_a^b f(x)\,dx = \int_a^b f(a+b-x)\,dx$, we have

$$I = \int_{\pi/6}^{\pi/3}\left|\cos 2\left(\frac{\pi}{2}-x\right)\right|\ln\left(\cot\left(\frac{\pi}{2}-x\right)\right)dx \text{ or } I = \int_{\pi/6}^{\pi/3} |\cos(\pi-2x)|\ln(\tan x)\,dx$$

$$= \int_{\pi/6}^{\pi/3} |-\cos 2x|\ln(\cot x)^{-1}\,dx = \int_{\pi/6}^{\pi/3} |\cos 2x|(-\ln\cot x)\,dx = -\int_{\pi/6}^{\pi/3} |\cos 2x|\ln(\cot x)\,dx = -I$$

$\Rightarrow \quad 2I = 0 \qquad \Rightarrow \quad I = 0$

ILLUSTRATION 82: Evaluate $\int_{\pi/8}^{3\pi/8} \ln\left(\frac{8+5\sin x}{8+5\cos x}\right)dx$

SOLUTION: Let $I = \int_{\pi/8}^{3\pi/8} \ln\left(\frac{8+5\sin x}{8+5\cos x}\right)dx \quad \ldots(1)$

Using the property $\int_a^b f(x)\,dx = \int_a^b f(a+b-x)\,dx$, we have

$$I=\int_{\pi/8}^{3\pi/8}\ln\left(\frac{8+5\sin\left(\frac{\pi}{2}-x\right)}{8+5\cos\left(\frac{\pi}{2}-x\right)}\right)dx=\int_{\pi/8}^{3\pi/8}\ln\left(\frac{8+5\cos x}{8+5\sin x}\right)dx=-\int_{\pi/8}^{3\pi/8}\ln\left(\frac{8+5\sin x}{8+5\cos x}\right)dx=-I$$

$\Rightarrow\ 2I=0$

$\Rightarrow\ I=0$

ILLUSTRATION 83: Evaluate $\int_{\pi/4}^{3\pi/4}\frac{x\sin x}{1+\sin x}dx$

SOLUTION: Let $I=\int_{\pi/4}^{3\pi/4}\frac{x\sin x}{1+\sin x}dx$

$$\Rightarrow\ I=\int_{\pi/4}^{3\pi/4}\frac{(\pi-x)\sin(\pi-x)}{1+\sin(\pi-x)}dx$$

$$\Rightarrow\ I=\int_{\pi/4}^{3\pi/4}\frac{(\pi-x)\sin x}{1+\sin x}dx=\pi\int_{\pi/4}^{3\pi/4}\frac{\sin x}{1+\sin x}dx-\int_{\pi/4}^{3\pi/4}\frac{x\sin x}{1+\sin x}dx$$

$$\Rightarrow\ I=\pi\int_{\pi/4}^{3\pi/4}\frac{(1+\sin x-1)}{1+\sin x}dx-I \qquad \Rightarrow\ 2I=\pi\int_{\pi/4}^{3\pi/4}\left(1-\frac{1}{1+\sin x}\right)dx$$

$$\Rightarrow\ I=\frac{\pi}{2}[x]_{\pi/4}^{3\pi/4}-\frac{\pi}{2}\int_{\pi/4}^{3\pi/4}\frac{1-\sin x}{\cos^2 x}dx=\frac{\pi^2}{4}-\frac{\pi}{2}[\tan x-\sec x]_{\pi/4}^{3\pi/4}$$

$$=\frac{\pi^2}{4}-\frac{\pi}{2}\left[(-1-1)-\left(-\sqrt{2}-\sqrt{2}\right)\right]$$

$$\therefore\ I=\frac{\pi^2}{4}+\frac{\pi}{2}\left(2-2\sqrt{2}\right)=\frac{\pi^2}{4}-\left(\sqrt{2}-1\right)\pi$$

ILLUSTRATION 84: Evaluate $\int_{\pi/2}^{3\pi/2}[2\sin x]dx$; where [.] is greatest integer function.

SOLUTION: Let $I=\int_{\pi/2}^{3\pi/2}[2\sin x]dx$ ...(1)

$$\Rightarrow\ I=\int_{\pi/2}^{3\pi/2}\left[2\sin\left(\frac{\pi}{2}+\frac{3\pi}{2}-x\right)\right]dx$$

$$\Rightarrow\ I=\int_{\pi/2}^{3\pi/2}\left[2\sin(2\pi-x)\right]dx$$

$$\Rightarrow\ I=\int_{\pi/2}^{3\pi/2}[-2\sin x]dx \qquad ...(2)$$

Adding (1) and (2) we get, $2I=\int_{\pi/2}^{3\pi/2}\left([2\sin x]+[-2\sin x]\right)dx$

$$=\int_{\pi/2}^{5\pi/6}\left([2\sin x]+[-2\sin x]\right)dx+\int_{5\pi/6}^{\pi}\left([2\sin x]+[-2\sin x]\right)dx$$

$$+\int_{\pi}^{7\pi/6}([2\sin x]+[-2\sin x])\,dx+\int_{7\pi/6}^{3\pi/2}([2\sin x]+[-2\sin x])\,dx$$

Now $(2\sin x)\notin\mathbb{Z}$ for $x\in\left(\frac{\pi}{2},\frac{5\pi}{6}\right)\cup\left(\frac{5\pi}{6},\pi\right)\cup\left(\pi,\frac{7\pi}{6}\right)\cup\left(\frac{7\pi}{6},\frac{3\pi}{2}\right)$

$\Rightarrow$ $[2\sin x]+[-2\sin x]=-1$ for each of these open intervals

$$\therefore\quad 2I=\int_{\pi/2}^{5\pi/6}-1\,dx+\int_{5\pi/6}^{\pi}-1\,dx+\int_{\pi}^{7\pi/6}-1\,dx+\int_{7\pi/6}^{3\pi/2}-1+dx$$

$$\therefore\quad 2I=-\left\{\left(\frac{5\pi}{6}-\frac{\pi}{2}\right)+\left(\pi-\frac{5\pi}{6}\right)+\left(\frac{7\pi}{6}-\pi\right)+\left(\frac{3\pi}{2}-\frac{7\pi}{6}\right)\right\}$$

$$=-\left\{\frac{2\pi}{6}+\left(\frac{\pi}{6}\right)+\left(\frac{\pi}{6}\right)+\left(\frac{2\pi}{6}\right)\right\}=-\pi$$

$$\Rightarrow\quad I=-\frac{\pi}{2}$$

ILLUSTRATION 85: Let $f(x)=4x^3-6x^2+4x-\frac{1}{2}$; then evaluate $\int_{1/3}^{2/3}f(f(x))\,dx$

SOLUTION: Given $f(x)=4x^3-6x^2+4x-\frac{1}{2}$ ...(1)

To evaluate $\int_{1/3}^{2/3}f(f(x))\,dx=I$ (say) ...(2)

$$\therefore\quad I=\int_{1/3}^{2/3}f\left(f\left(\frac{2}{3}+\frac{1}{3}-x\right)\right)dx\qquad\left[\because\int_a^b f(x)\,dx=\int_a^b f(a+b-x)\,dx\right]$$

or $I=\int_{1/3}^{2/3}f(f(1-x))\,dx$ ...(3)

Now $f(1-x)=4(1-x)^3-6(1-x)^2+4(1-x)-\frac{1}{2}$

$$=4-4x^3-12x+12x^2-6-6x^2+12x+4-4x-\frac{1}{2}$$

$$=-4x^3+6x^2-4x+\frac{3}{2}$$ ...(4)

From (1) and (4), we have $f(x)+f(1-x)=1$ ...(5)

Replacing x by $f(x)$ we get $f(f(x))+f(1-f(x))=1$

or $f(f(x))+f(f(1-x))=1$ $(\because 1-f(x)=f(1-x))$

$$\Rightarrow\quad\int_{1/3}^{2/3}\left[f(f(x))+f(f(1-x))\right]dx=\int_{1/3}^{2/3}1\,dx$$

$$\Rightarrow\quad\int_{1/3}^{2/3}f(f(x))\,dx+\int_{1/3}^{2/3}f(f(1-x))\,dx=\left[\frac{2}{3}-\frac{1}{3}\right]$$

$\Rightarrow\quad I+I=\frac{1}{3}\quad\Rightarrow\quad 2I=\frac{1}{3}$ (from (2) and (3))

$$\Rightarrow\quad I=\frac{1}{6}$$

Property 11: $\int_a^b f(x)dx = \underbrace{\frac{1}{k}\int_{ak}^{bk} f\left(\frac{x}{k}\right)dx}_{\text{(Streching)}}$

$= \underbrace{k\int_{a/k}^{b/k} f(kx)dx}_{\text{(contraction)}}$, $k > 1$, i.e., when we stretch graph k times, area increases 'k' times. Therefore we divide by 'k' to keep the value of integral unchanged.

Proof: Substituting $\frac{x}{k} = t$ and $dx = k\,dt$ in $\frac{1}{k}\int_{ak}^{bk} f\left(\frac{x}{k}\right)dx$,

we get $\frac{1}{k}\int_a^b f(t).k\,dt = \int_a^b f(t)\,dt = \int_a^b f(x)\,dx$

Thus, $\int_a^b f(x)dx = \frac{1}{k}\int_{ak}^{bk} f\left(\frac{x}{k}\right)dx$

Similarly, if we substitute $kx = t$ and $dx = dt/k$ in $k\int_{a/k}^{b/k} f(kx)dx$ we get $k\int_{a/k}^{b/k} f(kx)dx = k\int_a^b f(t)\frac{dt}{k}$

$= \int_a^b f(t)dt = \int_a^b f(x)dx$

Thus, $\int_a^b f(x)dx = k\int_{a/k}^{b/k} f(kx)dx$

Geometrically:

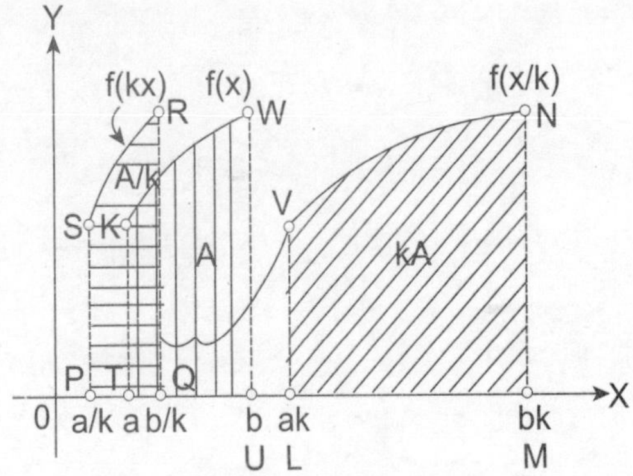

FIGURE 2.53

From figure

we observed, $\int_{a/k}^{b/k} f(kx)dx = \square = \frac{A}{k}$ = area $PQ\widehat{RS}$;

$\int_{ak}^{bk} f\left(\frac{x}{k}\right)dx = \square = KA$ = area $LM\widehat{NV}$ and

$\int_a^b f(x)dx$ = area $TU\widehat{WK} = \square = A$

Thus, $k\int_{a/k}^{b/k} f(kx)dx = \int_a^b f(x)dx = \frac{1}{k}\int_{ak}^{bk} f\left(\frac{x}{k}\right)dx$

ILLUSTRATION 86: Evaluate $\int_0^{\pi}\left(\cos^2 2x - \sin^2 2x\right)dx$

SOLUTION: Let $I = \int_0^{\pi}\left(\cos^2 2x - \sin^2 2x\right)dx = \int_0^{\pi} f(x)\,dx$

Replacing $2x$ by x, i.e., replacing $f(x)$ by $f\left(\frac{x}{2}\right)$; by contraction/stretching property, we have

$$I = \frac{1}{2}\int_0^{2\pi}\left(\cos^2 x - \sin^2 x\right)dx = \frac{1}{2}\int_0^{2\pi}\cos 2x\,dx = \frac{1}{2}\left[-\frac{\sin 2x}{2}\right]_0^{2\pi} = -\frac{1}{4}[0-0] = 0$$

ILLUSTRATION 87: Evaluate $\int_0^{\pi/4}\frac{\sqrt[3]{\sin 2x}}{\sqrt[3]{\sin 2x}+\sqrt[3]{\cos 2x}}dx$

SOLUTION: Given $I = \int_0^{\pi/4}\frac{\sqrt[3]{\sin 2x}}{\sqrt[3]{\sin 2x}+\sqrt[3]{\cos 2x}}dx$

$\therefore$ By contraction/stretching property, we have

$$I = \frac{1}{2}\int_0^{\pi/2}\frac{\sqrt[3]{\sin x}}{\sqrt[3]{\sin x}+\sqrt[3]{\cos x}}dx \quad \ldots(1)$$

Further by using the property $\int_0^a f(x)\,dx = \int_0^a f(a-x)\,dx$ we have

$$I = \frac{1}{2}\int_0^{\pi/2} \frac{\sqrt[3]{\sin\left(\frac{\pi}{2}-x\right)}}{\sqrt[3]{\sin\left(\frac{\pi}{2}-x\right)}+\sqrt[3]{\cos\left(\frac{\pi}{2}-x\right)}}dx \text{ or } I = \frac{1}{2}\int_0^{\pi/2}\frac{\sqrt[3]{\cos x}}{\sqrt[3]{\cos x}+\sqrt[3]{\sin x}}dx \quad ...(2)$$

Adding (1) and (2), we have $2I = \frac{1}{2}\int_0^{\pi/2} 1\,dx = \frac{1}{2}\left(\frac{\pi}{2}-0\right) = \frac{\pi}{4}$

$\therefore\ I = \frac{\pi}{8}$

ILLUSTRATION 88: Evaluate $\int_1^2 \left[16x(3-2x)(2+x)(3-x)(5-x)+\cos 2x\right]dx$

SOLUTION: Given $I = \int_1^2 \left[16x(3-2x)(2+x)(3-x)(5-x)+\cos 2x\right]dx$

Let us convert each x to $2x$ as given below

$$I = \int_1^2 \left[2x(3-2x)(4+2x)(6-2x)(10-2x)+\cos 2x\right]dx$$

Replacing $f(x)$ by $f\left(\frac{x}{2}\right)$ using contraction / stretching property we have

$$I = \frac{1}{2}\int_2^4 \left[x(3-x)(4+x)(6-x)(10-x)+\cos x\right]dx \quad ...(1)$$

Again using the property $\int_a^b f(x)\,dx = \int_a^b f(a+b-x)\,dx$, we have

$$I = \frac{1}{2}\int_2^4 \left[(6-x)[3-(6-x)][4+(6-x)][6-(6-x)][10-(6-x)]+\cos(6-x)\right]dx$$

$$\Rightarrow\ I = \frac{1}{2}\int_2^4 \left[(6-x)(x-3)(10-x)x(4+x)+\cos(6-x)\right]dx$$

or $$I = \frac{1}{2}\int_2^4 \left[-x(3-x)(4+x)(6-x)(10-x)+\cos(6-x)\right]dx \quad ...(2)$$

Adding (1) and (2) we get

$$2I = \frac{1}{2}\int_2^4 \left[\cos x+\cos(6-x)\right]dx \qquad \Rightarrow\ I = \frac{1}{4}\left[\sin x+\frac{\sin(6-x)}{-1}\right]_2^4$$

$$\Rightarrow\ I = \frac{1}{4}\left[\sin x-\sin(6-x)\right]_2^4 = \frac{1}{4}\left[(\sin 4-\sin 2)-(\sin 2-\sin 4)\right] = \frac{1}{4}\left[2(\sin 4-\sin 2)\right]$$

$$\Rightarrow\ I = \frac{1}{2}\left[2\cos 3\sin 1\right] = \cos 3 \sin 1.$$

Property 12: Transformation of a definite integral into other with new limits 0 to 1

Let $I = \int_a^b f(x)dx$ be the given definite integral.

Let $x = \lambda t + \mu$; (λ, μ constants), i.e., we can always choose a linear substitution such that $t = 0$ at $x = a$ and $t = 1$ at $x = b$.

$\therefore\ a = \lambda(0) + \mu$ and $b = \lambda(1) + \mu$

$\Rightarrow\ \mu = a$ and $\lambda = b - \mu = b - a$

$\therefore\ x = (b - a)t + a$

$\Rightarrow\ dx = (b - a)dt$

$\therefore\ I = (b-a)\int_0^1 f[(b-a)t+a]dt$

Thus, $\int_a^b f(x)dx = (b-a)\int_0^1 f\left[(b-a)x+a\right]dx$

ILLUSTRATION 89: Evaluate $\int_{-3}^{-2} e^{(u+4)^2} du + 2\int_{3/4}^{1/4} e^{4\left(v-\frac{5}{4}\right)^2} dv$

SOLUTION: Let $I = \int_{-3}^{-2} e^{(u+4)^2} du + 2\int_{3/4}^{1/4} e^{4\left(v-\frac{5}{4}\right)^2} dv = I_1 + I_2$ (say) ...(1)

Now $I_1 = \int_{-3}^{-2} e^{(u+4)^2} du$

$\therefore$ By property $\int_a^b f(x)dx = (b-a)\int_0^1 f[(b-a)t+a]dt$ we have

$$I_1 = (-2+3)\int_0^1 e^{[(-2+3)t+(-3)+4]^2} dt = \int_0^1 e^{(t+1)^2} dt \quad ...(2)$$

$$\text{And } I_2 = 2\int_{3/4}^{1/4} e^{4\left(v-\frac{5}{4}\right)^2} dv \;\; 2\left(\frac{1}{4}-\frac{3}{4}\right)\int_0^1 e^{4\left[\left(\frac{1}{4}-\frac{3}{4}\right)t+\frac{3}{4}-\frac{5}{4}\right]^2} dt$$

$$= 2\left(-\frac{1}{2}\right)\int_0^1 e^{4\left[-\frac{1}{2}t-\frac{1}{2}\right]^2} dt = -\int_0^1 e^{(t+1)^2} dt \quad ...(3)$$

By using (2) and (3) in (1), we get $I = \int_0^1 e^{(t+1)^2} dt - \int_0^1 e^{(t+1)^2} dt = 0$

ILLUSTRATION 90: If $\int_0^1 \frac{\sin x}{1+x} dx = \lambda$, then evaluate $\int_{4\pi-2}^{4\pi} \frac{\sin (x/2)}{4\pi+2-x} dx$

SOLUTION: Let us use the property $\int_a^b f(x)dx = (b-a)\int_0^1 f[(b-a)t+a]dt$ to integral $\int_{4\pi-2}^{4\pi} \frac{\sin (x/2)}{4\pi+2-x} dx$

$$= [4\pi-(4\pi-2)]\int_0^1 \frac{\sin\frac{1}{2}\left[\{4\pi-(4\pi-2)\}t+4\pi-2\right]}{4\pi+2-\left[\{4\pi-(4\pi-2)\}t+(4\pi-2)\right]} dt$$

$$= 2\int_0^1 \frac{\sin\frac{1}{2}\left[(2t-2)+4\pi\right]}{4\pi+2-\left[2t-2+4\pi\right]} dt = 2\int_0^1 \frac{\sin(2\pi+t-1)}{4-2t} dt$$

$$= \int_0^1 \frac{\sin(t-1)}{(2-t)} dt = \int_0^1 \frac{\sin(1-t-1)}{2-(1-t)} dt = \int_0^1 \frac{\sin(-t)}{1+t} dt = -\int_0^1 \frac{\sin t}{1+t} dt = -\lambda$$

TEXTUAL EXERCISE-4: (SUBJECTIVE)

1. Evaluate the following integrals:

(a) $\int_{\frac{\pi}{6}-a}^{\frac{\pi}{6}+a} \left[\sin\left(x-\frac{\pi}{6}\right)+\tan\left(\frac{\pi}{6}-x\right)\right] dx$

(b) $\int_0^1 x(1-x)^{50} dx$

(c) $\int_{\frac{\pi}{4}-a}^{\frac{\pi}{4}+a} \left(\sin\left(x-\frac{\pi}{4}\right)+\tan\left(x-\frac{\pi}{4}\right)\right)+\left|x-\frac{\pi}{4}\right|\left(x-\frac{\pi}{4}\right)^5 dx$

(d) $\int_{-3}^{1} (x+1)^5 \cos(x+1)+(x^3+3x^2+3x+2)dx$

2. Evaluate the following integrals, $[x]$ denotes Gint of x.

(a) $\int_0^{\pi/2} \frac{dx}{1+\sqrt{\tan x}}$

(b) $\int_{-a}^{3a} \frac{f(x)dx}{f(x)+f(2a-x)}$

(c) $\int_1^3 \frac{[x^2-8x+16]}{[(4-x)^2]+[x^2]}dx$

(d) $\int_0^{\pi/2} \frac{\sin 8x \log \cot x}{\cot 2x}dx$

(e) $\int_0^{\pi/2} \frac{\sin^3 x}{\sin x+\cos x}dx$

(f) $\int_0^{\pi/2} \frac{dx}{1+\tan^n x}$

3. Evaluate the following integrals:

(a) $\int_1^2 \frac{\ln x}{(1+\ln x)^2}dx$

(b) $\int_0^1 \cot^{-1}(1-x+x^2)dx$

4. Evaluate $\int_0^{\pi/4} \frac{\sin x+\cos x}{\cos^2 x+\sin^4 x}dx$

5. Solve the following integrals:

(a) $\int_0^{\pi} x\sin x\,dx$

(b) $\int_0^{\pi} \frac{x}{1+\sin x}dx$

(c) $\int_0^{\pi} \frac{x\tan x}{\sec x \operatorname{cosec} x}dx$

(d) $\int_0^{\pi} \frac{x\tan x}{\sec x+\tan x}dx$

(e) $\int_0^1 (1+x)(1-x)^{999}dx$

(f) $\int_0^{\pi} \frac{x\sin x}{1+\cos^2 x}dx$

(g) $\int_0^1 x(\ln x+\ln(1-x))dx$

6. If f and g are continuous function on $[0, a]$ satisfying $f(x) = f(a-x)$ and $g(x) + g(a-x) = 2$, then show that $\int_0^a f(x).g(x)dx = \int_0^a f(x)dx$.

7. Find out function $f(x)$,

(a) If $f(x) = \lambda\int_0^{\pi/2} \sin t\cos t\, f(t)\,dt + \sin x$

(b) If $f(x) = \lambda\int_0^{\pi/2} \sin t\cos x f(t)dt + \sin x$

8. Prove that $\int_0^1 x^m(1-x)^n dx = \int_0^1 x^n(1-x)^m dx$.

9. Evaluate the following integrals:

(a) $\int_{-\pi/2}^{\pi/2} \frac{dx}{e^{\tan x}+1}$

(b) $\int_0^{\pi} \frac{e^{\cos x}}{e^{\cos x}+e^{-\cos x}}dx$

10. Prove the following integrals:

(a) $\int_0^a f(x)dx = \int_0^{a/2} f(x)dx + \int_0^{a/2} f(a-x)dx$

(b) $\int_0^{2a} f(x)dx = \int_0^a f(a-x)dx + \int_0^a f(a+x)dx$

11. Evaluate the following:

(a) $\int_1^2 \frac{dx}{\sqrt{x^2+4x+3}}$ (b) $\int_{\pi/3}^{\pi/2} \frac{(1+\cos x)^{1/2}}{(1-\cos x)^{5/2}}dx$

(c) $\int_0^1 \cos^{-1}\left(\frac{1-x^2}{1+x^2}\right)dx$ (d) $\int_0^{1/\sqrt{2}} \frac{\sin^{-1} x}{(1-x^2)^{3/2}}dx$

(e) $\int_0^1 \frac{\log(1+x)}{1+x^2}dx$

12. Prove the following statements:

(a) $\int_a^b \frac{f(x)}{f(x)+f(a+b-x)}dx = \frac{b-a}{2}$

(b) $\int_0^1 x(1-x)^n dx = \frac{1}{(n+1)(n+2)}$

(c) $\int_a^{\pi/2} \sin 2x \log\tan x\,dx = 0$

13. Evaluate the following integrals:

(a) $\int_3^8 |x-4|\,dx$

(b) $\int_0^1 |\sin 2\pi x|\,dx$

(c) $\int_0^{\pi/2} |\sin x-\cos x|\,dx$

(d) $\int_1^{3/2} |x\sin \pi x|\,dx$

(e) $\int_2^5 f(x)dx$; where $f(x) = |x-2| + |x-3| + |x-4|$

14. Evaluate $\int_0^{\pi/2} \frac{(\tan x-\cot x)}{1+\tan x\cot x}dx$

15. Evaluate $\int_0^{\pi/2} \frac{\cos^2 x}{1-\sin x\cos x}dx$

16. Evaluate $\int_0^{\pi} x\sin^3 x\,dx$

17. Evaluate $\int_0^{\pi/4} \frac{x\,dx}{1+\sin 2x+\cos 2x}$

18. Evaluate $\int_0^{\pi/2} \frac{x\sin x\cos x}{\sin^4 x+\cos^4 x}dx$

19. Prove that $\int_0^{\pi/2n} \frac{dx}{1+\cot^n nx} = \frac{\pi}{4n}$

20. Prove that $\int_a^b \frac{|2-x|}{2-x}dx = |2-a|-|2-b|$

21. Show that $\int_{-1/3}^{1/3} \cos x \ln\left(\frac{1-x}{1+x}\right) dx = 0$

22. Evaluate $\int_{-\pi/4}^{\pi/4} \frac{x^9 - 3x^7 + 5x^3 - 2x + 1}{\cos^2 x} dx$

23. Prove that

(a) $\int_0^{b-c} f''(x+a)\,dx = f'(b-c+a) - f'(a)$

(b) $\int_0^{\pi/2} \left|\sin\left(x - \frac{\pi}{4}\right)\right| dx = 2 - \sqrt{2}$

24. Prove that $\int_a^b f(x)dx = (b-a)\int_0^1 f((b-a)x+a)dx$, hence or otherwise evaluate the integral $\int_{-4}^{-5} e^{(x+5)^2} dx + 3\int_{1/3}^{2/3} e^{9(x-2/3)^2} dx$.

25. If $\int_1^2 \frac{e^{\sin x}}{1+x^2} dx = \lambda$, then evaluate $\int_{2\pi}^{4\pi} \frac{e^{\sin\left(\frac{x}{2\pi}\right)}}{4\pi^2 + x^2} dx$ by converting the limits from 0 to 1.

Answer Keys

1. (a) 0 (b) 1/2652 (c) 0 (d) 4 **2.** (a) $\frac{\pi}{4}$ (b) 2a (c) 1 (d) 0 (e) $\frac{(\pi-1)}{4}$ (f) $\frac{\pi}{4}$ **3.** (a) $\frac{1-\ln 2}{1+\ln 2}$ (b) $\frac{\pi}{2} - \ln 2$ **4.** $\frac{\pi}{4} - \frac{1}{\sqrt{3}} \ln\left(\frac{\sqrt{3}-1}{\sqrt{2}}\right)$ **5.** (a) π (b) π (c) $\frac{\pi^2}{4}$ (d) $\frac{\pi}{2}(\pi - 2)$ (e) $\left(\frac{1002}{1001}\right) \times 10^{-3}$ (f) $\frac{\pi^2}{4}$ (g) –1 **7.** (a) $f(x) = \frac{2\lambda}{3(2-\lambda)} + \sin x$ (b) $\frac{(\pi-2)}{2(2-\lambda)} \cos x + \sin x$ **9.** (a) $\frac{\pi}{2}$ (b) $\frac{\pi}{2}$ **11.** (a) $\log\left|\frac{4+\sqrt{15}}{3+\sqrt{8}}\right|$ (b) 3/2 (c) π/2 – log2 (d) π/4 – (1/2) log 2 (e) $\frac{\pi}{8}\log 2$ **13.**(a) 17/2 (b) 2/π (c) 2(√2 – 1) (d) $\frac{\pi+1}{\pi^2}$ (e) 19/2 **14.** 0 **15.** $\frac{2\pi}{3\sqrt{3}}$ **16.** $\frac{2\pi}{3}$ **17.** $\frac{\pi}{16}\ln 2$ **18.** $\frac{\pi^2}{16}$ **22.** 2 **24.** 0 **25.** λ/2π

TEXTUAL EXERCISE–4: (OBJECTIVE)

1. $\int_0^{\pi} x f(\sin x) dx =$

(a) $\pi \int_0^{\pi} f(\sin x)dx$ (b) $\frac{\pi}{2}\int_0^{\pi} f(\sin x)dx$

(c) $\frac{\pi}{2}\int_0^{\pi/2} f(\sin x)dx$ (d) None of these

2. $\int_0^{\pi/2} \frac{d\theta}{1+\tan\theta}$ is equal to

(a) π (b) $\frac{\pi}{2}$

(c) $\frac{\pi}{3}$ (d) $\frac{\pi}{4}$

3. $\int_0^{\pi/2} \frac{\sin^{3/2} x\,dx}{\cos^{3/2} x + \sin^{3/2} x}$ is equal to

(a) 0 (b) π

(c) $\frac{\pi}{2}$ (d) $\frac{\pi}{4}$

4. For any integer *n*, the integral $\int_0^{\pi} e^{\sin^2 x} \cos^3(2n+1)x dx =$

(a) –1 (b) 0

(c) 1 (d) π

5. If $\int_0^{\pi} x\, f(\cos^2 x + \tan^4 x)dx = k\int_0^{\pi/2} f(\cos^2 x + \tan^4 x)dx$, then the value of *k* is

(a) $\frac{\pi}{2}$ (b) π

(c) $-\frac{\pi}{2}$ (d) None of these

6. The value of $\int_{\pi/4}^{3\pi/4} \frac{\phi}{1+\sin\phi} d\phi$, is

(a) $\pi \tan\frac{\pi}{8}$ (b) $\log \tan\frac{\pi}{8}$

(c) $\tan\frac{\pi}{8}$ (d) None of these

7. If $f(a + b - x) = f(x)$, then $\int_a^b x\ f(x)dx$ equals

(a) $\frac{a+b}{2}\int_a^b f(b-x)dx$ (b) $\frac{a+b}{2}\int_a^b f(x)dx$

(c) $\frac{b-a}{2}\int_a^b f(x)dx$ (d) None of these

8. The value of $\int_0^{\pi/2}\frac{2^{\sin x}}{2^{\sin x}+2^{\cos x}}dx$ is

(a) $\frac{\pi}{4}$ (b) $\frac{\pi}{2}$

(c) π (d) 2π

9. The value of $\int_0^{\pi/2}\frac{e^{x^2}}{e^{x^2}+e^{\left(\frac{\pi}{2}-x\right)^2}}dx$ is

(a) π/4 (b) π/2

(c) $e^{\pi^2/16}$ (d) $e^{\pi^2/4}$

10. Let $I_1 = \int_a^{\pi-a} xf(\sin x)dx$, $I_2 = \int_a^{\pi-a} f(\sin x)dx$, then I_2 is equal to

(a) $\frac{\pi}{2}I_1$ (b) πI_1

(c) $\frac{2}{\pi}I_1$ (d) $2I_1$

11. The value of the integral $\int_{\frac{1}{n}}^{\frac{an-1}{n}}\frac{\sqrt{x}}{\sqrt{a-x}+\sqrt{x}}dx$ is

(a) $\frac{a}{2}$ (b) $\frac{na+2}{2n}$

(c) $\frac{na-2}{2n}$ (d) None of these

12. $\int_0^1 \log\sin\left(\frac{\pi}{2}x\right)dx$ equals

(a) – log 2 (b) log 2

(c) $\frac{\pi}{2}\log 2$ (d) $-\frac{\pi}{2}\log 2$

13. If $f(x) = A\sin\left(\frac{\pi x}{2}\right)+B, f'\left(\frac{1}{2}\right)=\sqrt{2}$ and $\int_0^1 f(x)dx=\frac{2A}{\pi}$, then the constant A and B are respectively

(a) $\frac{\pi}{2}$ and $\frac{\pi}{2}$ (b) $\frac{2}{\pi}$ and $\frac{3}{\pi}$

(c) $\frac{4}{\pi}$ and 0 (d) 0 and $-\frac{4}{\pi}$

14. The value of $\int_0^{2\pi}\frac{dx}{e^{\sin x}+1}$ is

(a) π (b) 0

(c) 2π (d) π/2

15. If $f\left(\frac{1}{x}\right)+x^2 f(x)=0, \forall x>0$, then $\int_{\sin x}^{\operatorname{cosec} x} f(z)\,dz$ is (for $x\in(0, \pi/2)$)

(a) 1 (b) a function of x

(c) $\frac{\operatorname{cosec} x}{\tan x}$ (d) 0

16. The correct value of $\int_0^{\pi/2}\left|\sin\left(x-\frac{\pi}{4}\right)\right|dx$

(a) $2+\sqrt{2}$ (b) $2-\sqrt{2}$

(c) $-2+\sqrt{2}$ (d) 0

17. The value of $\int_0^{\pi/4}\ln\left(\cos\left(\frac{\pi}{4}+x\right)\right)^{\cot(\pi/4-x)}dx$ is

(a) 0 (b) 1

(c) 2 (d) Not defined

18. If f be continuous function of x, then $\frac{1}{c}\int_{ac}^{bc} f(x/c)dx$ is equal to

(a) $\int_a^b f(x)dx$ (b) $\frac{1}{c}\int_{a/c}^{b/c} f(cx)dx$

(c) $\int_{ac^2}^{bc^2} f(x)dx$ (d) $c\int_a^b f(x)dx$

19. The integral value $\int_{-2}^{0}(x^3+3x^2+3x+3+(x+1)\cos(x+1))dx$ is

(a) 2 (b) 4

(c) 0 (d) 8

20. The value of $\int_0^a\frac{x^5dx}{\left(2a^2-x^2\right)^3}$ is

(a) $\frac{\log 2}{2}-\frac{1}{2}$ (b) $\frac{\log 2}{2}-\frac{1}{4}$

(c) $-\frac{\log 2}{2}-\frac{1}{2}$ (d) None of these

21. Let $\int_0^a f(x)dx=\lambda$ and $\int_0^a f(2a-x)dx=\mu$. Then $\int_0^{2a} f(x)dx$ is equal to

(a) $\lambda+\mu$ (b) $\lambda-\mu$

(c) $2\lambda-\mu$ (d) $\lambda-2\mu$

22. $\int_{-\pi/2}^{\pi/2} \frac{\cos x}{1+e^x} dx =$

(a) 1 (b) 0
(c) –1 (d) None of these

23. The value of $\int_{-1}^{1} (\sqrt{1+x+x^2} - \sqrt{1-x+x^2}) dx$ is

(a) 0 (b) 1
(c) –1 (d) None of these

24. The value of $\int_{-\pi}^{\pi} \frac{\cos^2 x}{1+a^x} dx; a > 0$ is

(a) π (b) $a\pi$
(c) π/2 (d) 2π

25. If $f(x) = \frac{e^x}{1+e^x}$, $I_1 = \int_{f(-a)}^{f(a)} xg\{x(1-x)\}dx$, and $I_2 = \int_{f(-a)}^{f(a)} g\{x(1-x)\}dx$, then the value of $\frac{I_2}{I_1}$ is

(a) 1 (b) –3
(c) –1 (d) 2

Answer Keys

1. (b)	**2.** (d)	**3.** (d)	**4.** (b)	**5.** (b)	**6.** (a)	**7.** (b)	**8.** (a)	**9.** (a)	**10.** (c)
11. (c)	**12.** (a)	**13.** (c)	**14.** (a)	**15.** (d)	**16.** (b)	**17.** (d)	**18.** (a)	**19.** (b)	**20.** (b)
21. (a)	**22.** (a)	**23.** (a)	**24.** (c)	**25.** (d)					

Property 13:

$$\int_{-a}^{a} f(x)\,dx = \begin{cases} 0; \text{ if } f(-x) = -f(x); \text{ i.e., } f \text{ is odd function} \\ 2\int_0^a f(x)dx; \text{ if } f(-x) = f(x); \text{ i.e., } f \text{ is even function} \end{cases}$$

Proof: Let $I = \int_{-a}^{a} f(x)dx$

$= \int_{-a}^{0} f(x)\,dx + \int_{0}^{a} f(x)\,dx$; Using reflection property,

we have

$$I = \int_0^a f(-x)dx + \int_0^a f(x)dx = \int_0^a \big(f(x) + f(-x)\big)\,dx$$

$$= \begin{cases} 0; \text{ if } f(-x) = -f(x), \text{ i.e., } f \text{ is an odd function} \\ 2\int_0^a f(x)dx; \text{if } f(-x) = f(x), \text{i.e., } f(x) \text{ is an even function} \end{cases}$$

If $f(x)$ is odd, then I represents the algebraic sum of areas bounded by $f(x)$ and x–axis from ordinate $x = -a$ to $x = a$.

i.e., $I = -A + A = 0$

Where $-A = \int_{-a}^{0} f(x)dx$

and $A = \int_0^a f(x)dx$.

Geometrically shown below:

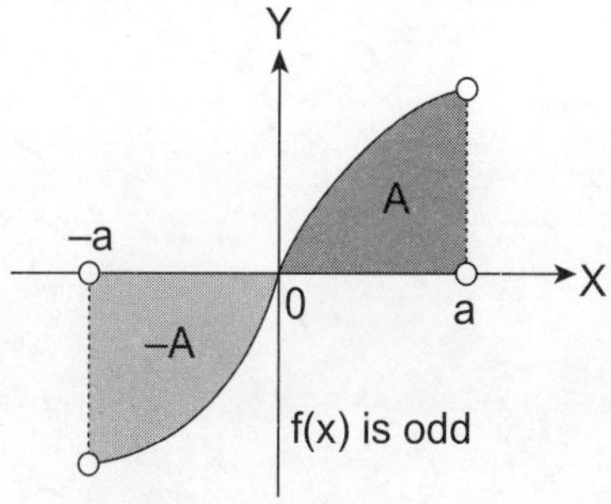

FIGURE 2.54

Further if $f(x)$ is an even function, then I represents the algebraic sum of areas bounded by $f(x)$ and x-axis from ordinate $x = -a$ to $x = a$

i.e., $I = \int_{-a}^{0} f(x)dx + \int_0^a f(x)dx = A + A$

$= 2A = 2\int_0^a f(x)dx$

Geometrically shown below:

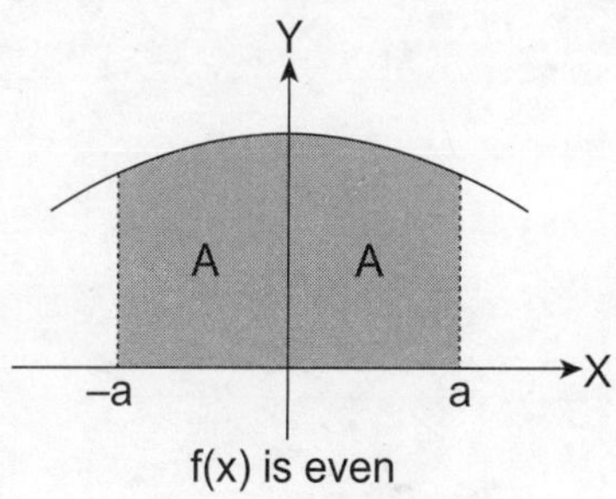

FIGURE 2.55

ILLUSTRATION 91: Evaluate the following integrals:

(a) $\int_{-\pi/2}^{\pi/2} x^2 \sin(x^3)dx$

(b) $\int_{-1}^{1}\left(\sin^{-1}x+\tan^{-1}x\right)dx$

(c) $\int_{-a}^{a}[f(x)-f(-x)]dx$; where $f(x)$ is a continuous and bounded function on [–a, a]

(d) $\int_{0}^{\pi/2}\left\{\sin^3\left(x-\frac{\pi}{4}\right)+\tan^3\left(x-\frac{\pi}{4}\right)\right\}dx$

SOLUTION: (a) $I=\int_{-\pi/2}^{\pi/2} x^2 \sin(x^3)dx$ hence $f(x) = x^2 \sin(x^3)$.

$\Rightarrow f(-x) = (-x)^2 \sin(-x)^2 = -x^2 (\sin(-x^3)) = -x^2 \sin x^3 = -f(x)$

$\Rightarrow f(x)$ is an odd function

$\therefore\ I = 0$ as $\int_{-a}^{a} f(x)dx = 0$ if $f(x)$ is an odd function.

(b) $I=\int_{-1}^{1}\left(\sin^{-1}x+\tan^{-1}x\right)dx$

$\because\ \sin^{-1}(-x) = -\sin^{-1}x$ and $\tan^{-1}(-x) = -\tan^{-1}x\ \forall\ x \in [-1, 1]$

$\Rightarrow \sin^{-1}(-x) + \tan^{-1}(-x) = -[\sin^{-1}x + \tan^{-1}x]$

$\therefore\ f(-x) = -f(x)$ $\Rightarrow f(x)$ is an odd function.

$\therefore\ \int_{-1}^{1}\left(\sin^{-1}x+\tan^{-1}x\right)dx=0$

(c) $\int_{-a}^{a}[f(x)-f(-x)]dx$

Let $g(x) = f(x) - f(-x)$

$\therefore\ g(-x) = f(-x) - f(x) = -g(x)$

$\Rightarrow g(x)$ is an odd function

$\therefore\ \int_{-a}^{a}[f(x)-f(-x)]dx=0$

(d) $I=\int_{0}^{\pi/2}\left\{\sin^3\left(x-\frac{\pi}{4}\right)+\tan^3\left(x-\frac{\pi}{4}\right)\right\}dx$

Using the property $\int_{a}^{b} f(x)dx=\int_{a+c}^{b+c} f(x-c)dx$ we have

$I=\int_{-\pi/4}^{\pi/4}\left\{\sin^3\left(x+\frac{\pi}{4}-\frac{\pi}{4}\right)+\tan^3\left(x+\frac{\pi}{4}-\frac{\pi}{4}\right)\right\}dx=\int_{-\pi/4}^{\pi/4}\left(\sin^3 x+\tan^3 x\right)dx$ (taking $c = -\pi/4$)

Clearly $(\sin^3 x + \tan^3 x)$ is an odd function

Therefore, $I=\int_{-\pi/4}^{\pi/4}\left(\sin^3 x+\tan^3 x\right)dx=0$

ILLUSTRATION 92: Evaluate $\int_{-\pi/4}^{\pi/4} \frac{x+\pi/4}{2-\cos 2x} dx$

SOLUTION: $I = \int_{-\pi/4}^{\pi/4} \frac{x}{2-\cos 2x} dx + \frac{\pi}{4}\int_{-\pi/4}^{\pi/4} \frac{dx}{2-\cos 2x} = I_1 + I_2$ (Say)

Let $f(x) = \frac{x}{2-\cos 2x}$

$\therefore \quad f(-x) = \frac{-x}{2-\cos 2x} = -\frac{x}{2-\cos 2x} = -f(x)$

$\therefore$ $f(x)$ is an odd function · Hence $I_1 = 0$

Let $f(x) = \frac{1}{2-\cos 2x}$

$\therefore \quad f(-x) = \frac{1}{2-\cos 2(-x)} = \frac{1}{2-\cos 2x} = f(x)$

$\therefore$ $f(x)$ is an even function.

$$\Rightarrow \quad I_2 = \frac{\pi}{4}\int_{-\pi/4}^{\pi/4} \frac{dx}{2-\cos 2x} = \frac{\pi}{4}\times 2\int_{0}^{\pi/4} \frac{dx}{2-\cos 2x}$$

$$= \frac{\pi}{2}\int_{0}^{\pi/4} \frac{dx}{2-\frac{1-\tan^2 x}{1+\tan^2 x}} = \frac{\pi}{2}\int_{0}^{\pi/4} \frac{\sec^2 x dx}{1+3\tan^2 x} = \frac{\pi}{2}\int_{0}^{1} \frac{dz}{1+3z^2} \quad \text{(putting } \tan x = z\text{)}$$

$$= \frac{\pi}{2}\int_{0}^{1} \frac{dz}{1+\left(\sqrt{3}z\right)^2} = \frac{\pi}{2}\left[\frac{\tan^{-1}\sqrt{3}z}{\sqrt{3}}\right]_0^1 = \frac{\pi}{2\sqrt{3}}.\frac{\pi}{3} = \frac{\pi^2}{6\sqrt{3}}$$

ILLUSTRATION 93: Evaluate $\int_{\frac{\pi}{3}-a}^{\frac{\pi}{3}+a} \left[\sin\left(x-\frac{\pi}{3}\right)+\tan\left(\frac{\pi}{3}-x\right)\right]^{15} dx;\ a \in \left(0, \frac{\pi}{2}\right)$

SOLUTION: By shifting property we have, $I = \int_{\frac{\pi}{3}-a}^{\frac{\pi}{3}+a} \left[\sin\left(x-\frac{\pi}{3}\right)+\tan\left(\frac{\pi}{3}-x\right)\right]^{15} dx$

$$= \int_{-a}^{a} \{\sin(x)+\tan(-x)\}^{15} dx = \int_{-a}^{a} (\sin x - \tan x)^{15} dx$$

$\because$ $(\sin x - \tan x)$ is an odd function

$\therefore$ $(\sin x - \tan x)^{15}$ is also an odd function

$\therefore \quad I = \int_{-a}^{a} (\sin x - \tan x)^{15} dx = 0$

ILLUSTRATION 94: Evaluate $\int_{0}^{\pi/2} \left|\tan\left(x-\frac{\pi}{4}\right)\right| dx$

SOLUTION: Using shifting property we get $I = \int_{0}^{\pi/2} \left|\tan\left(x-\frac{\pi}{4}\right)\right| dx$ or $I = \int_{-\pi/4}^{\pi/4} |\tan x| dx$

$\because$ $|\tan x|$ is an even function

Therefore $I = \int_{-\pi/4}^{\pi/4} |\tan x| dx = 2\int_{0}^{\pi/4} \tan x\, dx = 2[\ln \sec x]_0^{\pi/4} = 2\left[\ln\sec\frac{\pi}{4} - \ln\sec 0\right]$

$= 2\,[\ln(\sqrt{2}) - 0] = 2\ln\sqrt{2} = \ln 2$

ILLUSTRATION 95: Evaluate $\int\limits_{-\pi/6}^{\pi/6} \frac{x^5 - 3x^3 + 5x + 7\tan^2 x}{\cos^2 x} dx$

SOLUTION: Let $I = \int_{-\pi/6}^{\pi/6} \frac{x^5 - 3x^3 + 5x + 7\tan^2 x}{\cos^2 x} dx$

Now $(x^5 - 3x^3 + 5x)\sec^2 x$ is an odd function and $7\tan^2 x \sec^2 x$ is an even function

Therefore $I = \int\limits_{-\pi/6}^{\pi/6} (x^5 - 3x^3 + 5x)\sec^2 x\, dx + \int\limits_{-\pi/6}^{\pi/6} \tan^2 x \sec^2 x\, dx$

$= 0 + 2\int\limits_0^{\pi/6} \tan^2 x \sec^2 x\, dx = 2\int\limits_0^{1/\sqrt{3}} t^2\, dt = \frac{2}{3}[t^3]_0^{1/\sqrt{3}} = \frac{2}{3}\left[\frac{1}{3\sqrt{3}}\right] = \frac{2}{9\sqrt{3}}$

ILLUSTRATION 96: Evaluate $\int\limits_{-7}^{3} \left\{(x+2)^3 \cos(x+2) + \left(x^3 + 6x^2 + 12x + 9\right)\right\} dx$

SOLUTION: $I = \int\limits_{-7}^{3} \left\{(x+2)^3 \cos(x+2) + \left(x^3 + 6x^2 + 12x + 9\right)\right\} dx$

$= \int\limits_{-7}^{3} \left\{(x+2)^3 \cos(x+2) + \left((x+2)^3 + 1\right)\right\} dx$ using shifting property, we have

$= \int\limits_{-7+2}^{3+2} \left\{[x-2+2]^3 \cos(x-2+2) + \left[(x-2+2)^3 + 1\right]\right\} dx$

Now $(x^3 \cos x + x^3)$ is an odd function, and 1 is an even function.

$\therefore \quad I = 0 + 2\int\limits_0^5 1\, dx = 2[5-0] = 10$

ILLUSTRATION 97: Evaluate $\int\limits_{-a-\pi/4}^{a-\pi/4} \left\{\left(\sin\left(x+\frac{\pi}{4}\right) + \tan\left(x+\frac{\pi}{4}\right)\right)^5 + \left|x+\frac{\pi}{4}\right|\left(x+\frac{\pi}{4}\right)^3\right\} dx; a \in \left(0, \frac{\pi}{2}\right)$

SOLUTION: Let $I = \int\limits_{-a-\pi/4}^{a-\pi/4} \left\{\left(\sin\left(x+\frac{\pi}{4}\right) + \tan\left(x+\frac{\pi}{4}\right)\right)^5 + \left|x+\frac{\pi}{4}\right|\left(x+\frac{\pi}{4}\right)^3\right\} dx$

Using shifting property, we have

$\int\limits_{-a}^{a} \left\{\left(\sin\left(x-\frac{\pi}{4}+\frac{\pi}{4}\right) + \tan\left(x-\frac{\pi}{4}+\frac{\pi}{4}\right)\right)^5 + \left|x-\frac{\pi}{4}+\frac{\pi}{4}\right|\left(x-\frac{\pi}{4}+\frac{\pi}{4}\right)^3\right\} dx$

$\Rightarrow \quad I = \int\limits_{-a}^{a} \left\{(\sin x + \tan x)^5 + |x| x^3\right\} dx$

Clearly $(\sin x + \tan x)^5 + |x|\, x^3$ is an odd function

$\therefore \quad I = 0$

ILLUSTRATION 98: Evaluate $\int\limits_{-1}^{3} \left\{\tan^{-1}\left(\frac{x}{x^2+1}\right) + \tan^{-1}\left(\frac{x^2+1}{x}\right)\right\} dx$

SOLUTION: Let $I = \int\limits_{-1}^{3} \left\{\tan^{-1}\left(\frac{x}{x^2+1}\right) + \tan^{-1}\left(\frac{x^2+1}{x}\right)\right\} dx$

$$= \int_{-1}^{1}\left\{\tan^{-1}\left(\frac{x}{x^2+1}\right)+\tan^{-1}\left(\frac{x^2+1}{x}\right)\right\}dx + \int_{1}^{3}\left\{\tan^{-1}\left(\frac{x}{x^2+1}\right)+\tan^{-1}\left(\frac{x^2+1}{x}\right)\right\}dx$$

$$= \int_{-1}^{1} g(x)\,dx + \int_{1}^{3}\left\{\tan^{-1}\left(\frac{x}{x^2+1}\right)+\tan^{-1}\left(\frac{x^2+1}{x}\right)\right\}dx\,;$$

where $g(x)=\tan^{-1}\left(\frac{x}{x^2+1}\right)+\tan^{-1}\left(\frac{x^2+1}{x}\right)$

$$= 0+\int_{1}^{3}\left\{\tan^{-1}\left(\frac{x}{x^2+1}\right)+\cot^{-1}\left(\frac{x}{x^2+1}\right)\right\}dx$$

As $g(x)$ is an odd function and $\tan^{-1}x=\cot^{-1}\left(\frac{1}{x}\right)$ for $x>0$

$$\therefore\quad I=\int_{1}^{3}\frac{\pi}{2}dx \qquad \left(\because\ \tan^{-1}x+\cot^{-1}x=\frac{\pi}{2}\ \forall x\in\mathbb{R}\right)$$

$$= \frac{\pi}{2}(3-1)=\pi$$

Note that in above illustration students may do the following mistake

$$I=\int_{-1}^{3}\left\{\tan^{-1}\left(\frac{x}{x^2+1}\right)+\tan^{-1}\left(\frac{x^2+1}{x}\right)\right\}dx = \int_{-1}^{3}\left\{\tan^{-1}\left(\frac{x}{x^2+1}\right)+\cot^{-1}\left(\frac{x}{x^2+1}\right)\right\}dx$$

$$= \int_{-1}^{3}\frac{\pi}{2}dx=\frac{\pi}{2}[(3-(-1))]=2\pi,$$

Here we done a mistake at second step that $f(x)=\tan^{-1}\left(\frac{x}{x^2+1}\right)+\tan^{-1}\left(\frac{x^2+1}{x}\right)$ has a discontinuity at $x=0$ and hence $f(x)$ is not directly integral in $[-1, 3]$.

ILLUSTRATION 99: Evaluate $\int_{-\pi/4}^{\pi/4}\frac{x+\pi/4}{2-\cos 2x}dx$

SOLUTION: Let $I=\int_{-\pi/4}^{\pi/4}\frac{x}{2-\cos 2x}dx+\frac{\pi}{4}\int_{-\pi/4}^{\pi/4}\frac{1}{2-\cos 2x}dx$

$= 0+\frac{\pi}{4}\int_{-\pi/4}^{\pi/4}\frac{1}{2-\cos 2x}dx$ as $\frac{x}{2-\cos 2x}$ is an odd function

$= 2\left(\frac{\pi}{4}\right)\int_{0}^{\pi/4}\frac{1}{2-\cos 2x}dx$ as $\frac{1}{2-\cos 2x}$ is an even function

$$\therefore\quad I=\frac{\pi}{2}\int_{0}^{\pi/4}\frac{1}{2-\cos 2x}dx=\frac{\pi}{2}\int_{0}^{\pi/4}\frac{1}{2-(1-2\sin^2 x)}dx=\frac{\pi}{2}\int_{0}^{\pi/4}\frac{dx}{1+2\sin^2 x}$$

$= \frac{\pi}{2}\int_{0}^{\pi/4}\frac{\sec^2 x\,dx}{1+\tan^2 x+2\tan^2 x}=\frac{\pi}{2}\int_{0}^{1}\frac{dt}{1+3t^2}$; where $t=\tan x$

$$= \frac{\pi}{2}\times\frac{1}{3}\int_{0}^{1}\frac{dt}{t^2+1/3}=\frac{\pi}{6}\times\frac{\sqrt{3}}{1}\left[\tan^{-1}\left(\frac{t}{1/\sqrt{3}}\right)\right]_0^1$$

$$= \frac{\pi}{2\sqrt{3}}\left[\frac{\pi}{3}-0\right]=\frac{\pi^2}{6\sqrt{3}}$$

ILLUSTRATION 100: Evaluate $\int_{-1}^{1} \frac{x^3+|x|+1}{x^2+2|x|+1} dx$

SOLUTION: $I = \int_{-1}^{1} \frac{x^3+|x|+1}{(|x|+1)^2} dx = \int_{-1}^{1} \frac{x^3}{(|x|+1)^2} dx + \int_{-1}^{1} \frac{(|x|+1)}{(|x|+1)^2} dx$

$= 0 + \int_{-1}^{1} \frac{1}{(|x|+1)} dx$ as $\frac{x^3}{|x|+1}$ is an odd function

$= 2\int_{0}^{1} \frac{1}{|x|+1} dx$ as $\frac{1}{|x|+1}$ is an even function

$= 2\int_{0}^{1} \frac{1}{x+1} dx = 2[\ln(x+1)]_0^1 = 2\ln 2 = \ln 4$

ILLUSTRATION 101: Evaluate $\int_{-5}^{5} \frac{\sin^6 x}{\left[\frac{x}{\pi}+3\right]-\frac{7}{2}} dx$

SOLUTION: Let $f(x) = \frac{\sin^6 x}{\left[\frac{x}{\pi}+3\right]-\frac{7}{2}} = \frac{\sin^6 x}{\left[\frac{x}{\pi}\right]+3-\frac{7}{2}} = \frac{\sin^6 x}{\left[\frac{x}{\pi}\right]-\frac{1}{2}}$

$\therefore \quad f(-x) = \frac{\sin^6(-x)}{\left[-\frac{x}{\pi}\right]-\frac{1}{2}} = \frac{\sin^6 x}{\left[-\frac{x}{\pi}\right]-\frac{1}{2}}$

Now denominator is never zero as $\left[-\frac{x}{\pi}\right]$ is as integer,

whereas $\frac{1}{2}$ is non-integer

Also if $x = n\pi$; $n \in \mathbb{Z}$, then

$f(x) = f(-x) = 0$ so for $x \neq n\pi$, $\frac{-x}{\pi} \notin \mathbb{Z}$

Thus, $\left[\frac{-x}{\pi}\right] = 1 - \left[\frac{x}{\pi}\right]$ $\qquad (\because [x] + [-x] = -1 \text{ for } x \notin \mathbb{Z})$

$\therefore \quad f(-x) = \frac{\sin^6 x}{1-\left[\frac{x}{\pi}\right]-\frac{1}{2}} = \frac{\sin^6 x}{\frac{1}{2}-\left[\frac{x}{\pi}\right]} = -f(x)$

$\Rightarrow f(x)$ is an odd function

$\Rightarrow \int_{-5}^{5} \frac{\sin^6 x}{\left[\frac{x}{\pi}+3\right]-\frac{7}{2}} dx = 0$

Property 14: (a) $\int_0^{2a} f(x)dx = \int_0^a f(x)dx + \int_0^a f(2a-x)dx$

(b) $\int_0^{2a} f(x)dx = \int_0^a f(a-x)dx + \int_0^a f(a+x)dx$

Proof: (a) $\int_0^{2a} f(x)dx = \int_0^a f(x)dx + \int_a^{2a} f(x)dx$

By shifting property applied to second integral we have $\int_0^{2a} f(x)\,dx = \int_0^a f(x)\,dx + \int_{-a}^0 f(x+2a)\,dx$, now by reflection property, applied to second integral we have $\int_0^{2a} f(x)\,dx = \int_0^a f(x)\,dx + \int_0^a f(-x+2a)\,dx$

Therefore, $\int_0^{2a} f(x)\,dx = \int_0^a f(x)\,dx + \int_0^a f(2a-x)\,dx$

(b) $\int_0^{2a} f(x)dx = \int_0^a f(x)dx + \int_a^{2a} f(x)dx$

By shifting property applied to both integrals we have

$$\int_0^{2a} f(x)\,dx = \int_{-a}^0 f(x+a)\,dx + \int_0^a f(x+a)\,dx$$

By reflection property applied to first integral we have

$$\int_0^{2a} f(x)\,dx = \int_0^a f(-x+a)\,dx + \int_0^a f(x+a)\,dx$$

$$= \int_0^a f(a-x)\,dx + \int_0^a f(a+x)\,dx$$

ILLUSTRATION 102: Evaluate $\int_0^{\pi} x\sqrt{1+\sin x}\,dx$

SOLUTION: Using the property $\int_0^{2a} f(x)dx = \int_0^a f(x)dx + \int_0^a f(2a-x)dx$

we have $I = \int_0^{\pi} x\sqrt{1+\sin x}\,dx = \int_0^{\pi/2} x\sqrt{1+\sin x}\,dx + \int_0^{\pi/2} (\pi-x)\sqrt{1+\sin(\pi-x)}\,dx$

$$= \int_0^{\pi/2} x\sqrt{1+\sin x}\,dx + \int_0^{\pi/2} \pi\sqrt{1+\sin x}\,dx - \int_0^{\pi/2} x\sqrt{1+\sin x}\,dx$$

$$\Rightarrow \quad I = \pi\int_0^{\pi/2} \sqrt{1+\sin x}\,dx$$

$$\Rightarrow \quad I = \pi\int_0^{\pi/2} \sqrt{\left(\sin\frac{x}{2}+\cos\frac{x}{2}\right)^2}\,dx = \pi\int_0^{\pi/2} \left|\sin\frac{x}{2}+\cos\frac{x}{2}\right| dx = \pi\int_0^{\pi/2} \left(\sin\frac{x}{2}+\cos\frac{x}{2}\right) dx$$

$$= \pi\left[-2\cos\frac{x}{2}+2\sin\frac{x}{2}\right]_0^{\pi/2} = 2\pi\left[\sin\frac{x}{2}-\cos\frac{x}{2}\right]_0^{\pi/2} = 2\pi\left[\frac{1}{\sqrt{2}}-\left(\frac{1}{\sqrt{2}}-1\right)\right] = 2\pi$$

ILLUSTRATION 103: Evaluate $\int_0^{3\pi} \ln\left(\frac{4+\cos x}{4-\cos x}\right)dx$

SOLUTION: Let $I = \int_0^{3\pi} \ln\left(\frac{4+\cos x}{4-\cos x}\right)dx$

$$= \int_0^{3\pi/2} \ln\left(\frac{4+\cos\left(\frac{3\pi}{2}-x\right)}{4-\cos\left(\frac{3\pi}{2}-x\right)}\right)dx + \int_0^{3\pi/2} \ln\left(\frac{4+\cos\left(\frac{3\pi}{2}+x\right)}{4-\cos\left(\frac{3\pi}{2}+x\right)}\right)dx$$

(By using property $\int_0^{2a} f(x)dx = \int_0^a f(a-x)dx + \int_0^a f(a+x)dx$)

$$\therefore \quad I = \int_0^{3\pi/2} \ln\left(\frac{4-\sin x}{4+\sin x}\right)dx + \int_0^{3\pi/2} \ln\left(\frac{4+\sin x}{4-\sin x}\right)dx$$

$$= \int_0^{3\pi/2} \left\{\ln\left(\frac{4-\sin x}{4+\sin x}\right)+\ln\left(\frac{4+\sin x}{4-\sin x}\right)\right\}dx = \int_0^{3\pi/2} \ln 1\,dx = \int_0^{3\pi/2} 0\,dx = 0$$

Property 15:

$$\int_0^{2a} f(x)dx = \begin{cases} 0; & \text{if } f(2a-x) = -f(x) \\ 2\int_0^a f(x)dx; & \text{if } f(2a-x) = f(x) \end{cases}$$

$$\text{or } \int_0^{2a} f(x)dx = \begin{cases} 0; & \text{if } f(a+x) = -f(a-x) \\ 2\int_0^a f(x)dx; & \text{if } f(a+x) = f(a-x) \end{cases}$$

Equivalently $\int_0^{2a} f(x)dx$

$$= \begin{cases} 0; \text{ if graph of } f(x) \text{ is symmetric about point } (a, 0). \\ 2\int_0^a f(x)dx; \text{ if graph of } f(x) \text{ is symmetric about line } x = a. \end{cases}$$

Proof: L.H.S. $= \int_0^{2a} f(x)dx = \int_0^a f(x)dx + \int_a^{2a} f(x)dx$

Applying shifting property to second integral taking $c = -2a$ we have L.H.S.$= \int_0^a f(x)\,dx + \int_{-a}^0 f(x+2a)\,dx$

Now by reflection property applied to second integral we have,

$$\text{L.H.S.} = \int_0^a f(x)\,dx + \int_0^a f(-x+2a)\,dx \qquad \ldots\text{(i)}$$

Now if $f(2a-x) = -f(x)$ then from (i)

$$\text{L.H.S.} = \int_0^a f(x)\,dx + \int_0^a -f(x)dx = 0$$

and if $f(2a-x) = f(x)$, then from (i)

$$\text{L.H.S.} = \int_0^a f(x)\,dx + \int_0^a f(x)dx = 2\int_0^a f(x)dx$$

Geometrically:

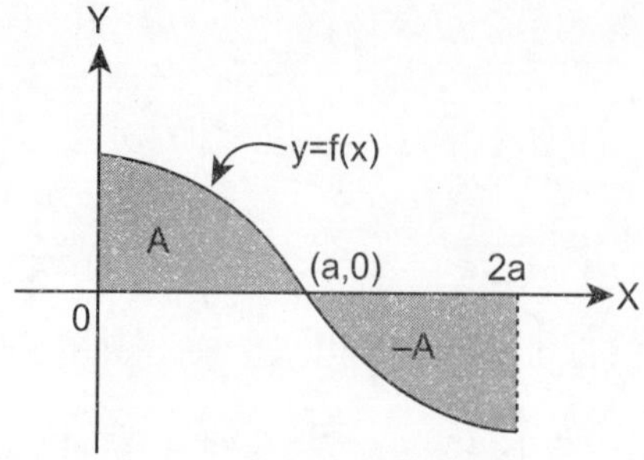

FIGURE 2.56

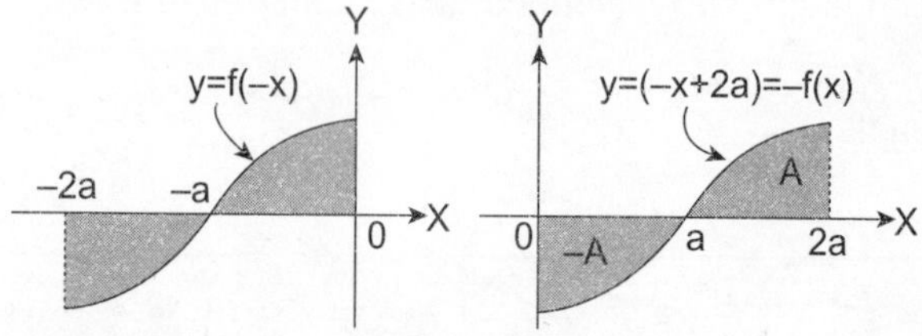

FIGURE 2.57

Clearly $\int_0^a f(x)\,dx = \int_0^a f(x)dx + \int_0^a f(2a-x)dx$
$= A + (-A) = 0$

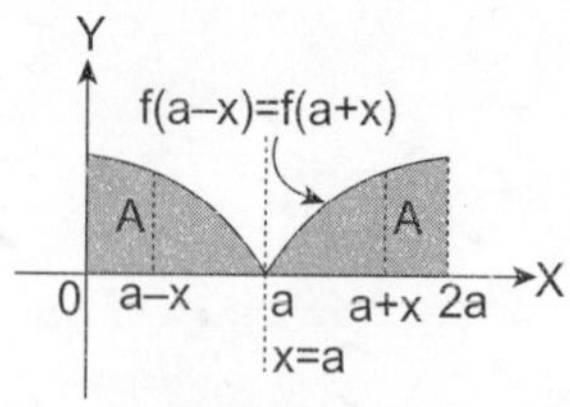

FIGURE 2.58

For above function clearly

$$\int_0^{2a} f(x)\,dx = \int_0^a f(x)dx + \int_a^{2a} f(x)dx = A + A = 2A$$

$$2\int_0^a f(x)\,dx$$

ILLUSTRATION 104: Evaluate $\int_0^{2\pi} \ln\left(\frac{2+\cos x}{2-\cos x}\right)dx$

SOLUTION: Here $f(x) = \ln\left(\frac{2+\cos x}{2-\cos x}\right)dx$

$$\therefore \quad f(2a-x) = f(2\pi - x) = \ln\left[\frac{2+\cos(2\pi-x)}{2-\cos(2\pi-x)}\right] = \ln\left[\frac{2+\cos x}{2-\cos x}\right] = f(x)$$

$$I = \int_0^{2\pi} \ln\left(\frac{2+\cos x}{2-\cos x}\right)dx = 2\int_0^{\pi} \ln\left(\frac{2+\cos x}{2-\cos x}\right)dx \qquad \text{(By property 13)}$$

$$\therefore \quad I = 2\int_0^{\pi} \ln\left(\frac{2+\cos x}{2-\cos x}\right)dx \qquad \ldots\ldots(1)$$

$\Rightarrow\ I = 2\int_0^{\pi} \ln\left(\frac{2+\cos(\pi - x)}{2-\cos(\pi - x)}\right)dx$ (by using $\int_0^a f(x)\,dx = \int_0^a f(a-x)\,dx$)

$\Rightarrow\ I = 2\int_0^{\pi} \ln\left(\frac{2-\cos x}{2+\cos x}\right)dx$ ...(2)

Adding (1) and (2) we get $2I = 2\int_0^{\pi}\left\{\ln\left(\frac{2+\cos x}{2-\cos x}\right) + \ln\left(\frac{2-\cos x}{2+\cos x}\right)\right\}dx$

$\therefore\ \ 2I = 2\int_0^{\pi} \ln 1\, dx$

$\Rightarrow\ I = 0$

ILLUSTRATION 105: Evaluate $\int_0^{\pi} \frac{x\,dx}{a^2\cos^2 x + b^2\sin^2 x} = \frac{\pi^2}{2ab}$

SOLUTION: $I = \int_0^{\pi} \frac{x\,dx}{a^2\cos^2 x + b^2\sin^2 x} = \int_0^{\pi} \frac{(\pi - x)\,dx}{a^2\cos^2 x + b^2\sin^2 x}$ $\left[\text{using } \int_0^a f(x)\,dx = \int_0^a f(a-x)dx\right]$

$\Rightarrow\ \ 2I = \pi\int_0^{\pi} \frac{dx}{a^2\cos^2 x + b^2\sin^2 x}$

Now if $f(x) = \frac{1}{a^2\cos^2 x + b^2\sin^2 x}$, $f(\pi - x) = f(x)$

$\therefore\ \ 2I = 2\pi\int_0^{\pi/2} \frac{dx}{a^2\cos^2 x + b^2\sin^2 x}$ (using $\int_0^{2a} f(x)dx = 2\int_0^a f(x)dx$ if $f(2a-x) = f(x)$)

$\Rightarrow\ \ I = \pi\int_0^{\pi/2} \frac{\sec^2 x}{a^2 + b^2\tan^2 x}dx = \pi\int_0^{\infty} \frac{dt}{a^2 + b^2t^2} = \frac{\pi}{b^2}\int_0^{\infty} \frac{dt}{\frac{a^2}{b^2} + t^2}$, where $t = \tan x$

$= \frac{\pi}{b^2}\times\frac{b}{a}\left[\tan^{-1}\left(\frac{bt}{a}\right)\right]_0^{\infty} = \frac{\pi}{ab}\left[\frac{\pi}{2}\right] = \frac{\pi^2}{2ab}$

ILLUSTRATION 106: Without integrating at any stage prove that $\int_{-\pi}^{\pi} \cos^4 2x.\sin^2 4x\,dx = \frac{5}{32}\int_0^{\pi/2} dx = \frac{5\pi}{64}$

SOLUTION: Since $\cos^4 2x\sin^2 4x$ is an even function, therefore $I = 2\int_0^{\pi} \cos^4 2x\sin^2 4x\,dx$

Now since $\cos^4 2(\pi - x)\sin^2 4(\pi - x) = \cos^4 2x\sin^2 4x$, by $\int_0^{2a} f(x)\,dx = 2\int_0^a f(x)dx$,

$I = 4\int_0^{\pi/2} \cos^4 2x\sin^2 4x\,dx$, by contraction/stretching property.

$I = \frac{4}{2}\int_0^{\pi} \cos^4 x\sin^2 2x\,dx$ or $I = 2\int_0^{\pi} \cos^4 x(4\sin^2 x\cos^2 x)\,dx$

$\therefore\ \ I = 8\int_0^{\pi} \sin^2 x\cos^6 x\,dx$

Again $\sin^2(\pi - x)\cos^6(\pi - x) = \sin^2 x\cos^6 x$, by $P : 15$

$\therefore\ \ I = 8(2)\int_0^{\pi/2} \sin^2 x\cos^6 x\,dx$. i.e., $I = 16\int_0^{\pi/2} \sin^2 x\cos^6 x\,dx$ ...(1)

Using the property $\int_0^a f(x)\,dx = \int_0^a f(a-x)\,dx$ we have,

$I = 16\int_0^{\pi/2} \sin^2\left(\frac{\pi}{2} - x\right)\cos^6\left(\frac{\pi}{2} - x\right)dx$

$\Rightarrow \quad I = 16\int_0^{\pi/2} \cos^2 x \sin^6 x \, dx$ ...(2)

Adding (1) and (2) we get $2I = 16\int_0^{\pi/2} \cos^2 x \sin^2 x\left(\cos^4 x + \sin^4 x\right) dx$

$\Rightarrow \quad I = 8\int_0^{\pi/2} \cos^2 x \sin^2 x\left[1 - 2\sin^2 x \cos^2 x\right] dx = 2\int_0^{\pi/2} \left\{\sin^2 2x - \frac{1}{2}(\sin^4 2x)\right\} dx$

Again by contraction / stretching property

$I = \frac{2}{2}\int_0^{\pi}\left(\sin^2 x - \frac{1}{2}\sin^4 x\right)dx = \int_0^{\pi}\left(\sin^2 x - \frac{1}{2}\sin^4 x\right)dx$

or $\quad I = 2\int_0^{\pi/2}\left(\sin^2 x - \frac{1}{2}\sin^4 x\right)dx$ ...(3)

Again by property $\int_0^a f(x)\,dx = \int_0^a f(a-x)\,dx$, we have

$I = 2\int_0^{\pi/2}\left(\cos^2 x - \frac{1}{2}\cos^4 x\right)dx$ ...(4)

Adding (3) and (4) we get $2I = 2\int_0^{\pi/2}\left\{1 - \frac{1}{2}\left(\sin^4 x + \cos^4 x\right)\right\}dx$

$= 2\int_0^{\pi/2} 1 - \frac{1}{2}\left[1 - 2\sin^2 x \cos^2 x\right]dx = 2\int_0^{\pi/2} \frac{1}{2} + \left(\sin^2 x \cos^2 x\right)dx$

$= 2\int_0^{\pi/2}\left(\frac{1}{2} + \frac{1}{4}\sin^2 2x\right)dx = \int_0^{\pi}\left(\frac{1}{2} + \frac{1}{4}\sin^2 x\right)dx$ (by stretching/contraction property)

$= \frac{1}{2}\int_0^{\pi/2}\left(\frac{1}{2} + \frac{1}{4}\sin^2 x\right)dx \qquad \left(\text{by } \int_0^{2a} f(x)\,dx = 2\int_0^a f(x)\,dx;\ f(2a-x) = f(x)\right)$

$\Rightarrow \quad I = \frac{1}{4}\int_0^{\pi/2}\left(\frac{1}{2} + \frac{1}{4}\sin^2 x\right)dx$ ...(5)

$\Rightarrow \quad I = \frac{1}{4}\int_0^{\pi/2}\left(\frac{1}{2} + \frac{1}{4}\cos^2 x\right)dx \qquad \left(\text{by } \int_0^a f(x)\,dx = \int_0^a f(a-x)dx\right)$ ...(6)

Adding (5) and (6) we get $2I = \frac{1}{4}\int_0^{\pi/2}\left(1 + \frac{1}{4}\right)dx$

or $\quad I = \frac{1}{8} \times \frac{5}{4}\int_0^{\pi/2} dx = \frac{5}{32}\int_0^{\pi/2} dx = \frac{5\pi}{64}$

ILLUSTRATION 107: Prove that $\int_0^{\pi/2} \log_e \sin x\,dx = \int_0^{\pi/2} \log_e \cos x\,dx = \int_0^{\pi/2} \log_e(\sin 2x)\,dx = -\frac{\pi}{2}\log_e 2$

SOLUTION: Let $I = \int_0^{\pi/2} \log_e \sin x\,dx$ ...(i)

$\Rightarrow \quad I = \int_0^{\pi/2} \log_e\left(\sin\left(\frac{\pi}{2} - x\right)\right)dx \qquad \left(\text{by } \int_0^a f(x)\,dx = \int_0^a f(a-x)dx\right)$

$\Rightarrow \quad I = \int_0^{\pi/2} \log_e(\cos x)dx$ ...(ii)

Adding (i) and (ii) we get $2I = \int_0^{\pi/2} \log_e(\sin x.\cos x)dx = \int_0^{\pi/2} \log_e\left(\frac{\sin 2x}{2}\right)dx$

$\Rightarrow\ 2I = \int_0^{\pi/2} \log_e(\sin 2x)\,dx - \int_0^{\pi/2} \log_e 2\ dx$

$\Rightarrow\ 2I = I_1 - \frac{\pi}{2}\log_e 2$ ...(iii)

Where $I_1 = \int_0^{\pi/2} \log_e(\sin 2x)\,dx$

By stretching/construction property, we have $I_1 = \frac{1}{2}\int_0^{\pi} \log_e(\sin x)dx$

Again since sin(π – x) = sinx, by P:12, we have $I_1 = \frac{1}{2}\times 2\int_0^{\pi/2} \log_e(\sin x)dx = I$ ...(iv)

$\therefore$ from (iii), $2I = I - \frac{\pi}{2}\log_e 2$

$\Rightarrow\ I = -\frac{\pi}{2}\log_e 2$ ...(v)

Thus, from (i), (ii), (iv) and (v), we have $\int_0^{\pi/2} \log_e \sin x dx$

$= \int_0^{\pi/2} \log_e \cos x dx = \int_0^{\pi/2} \log_e(\sin 2x)dx = -\frac{\pi}{2}\log e^2$

ILLUSTRATION 108: Evaluate $\int_0^1 \frac{x^2 \ell nx}{\sqrt{1-x^2}}dx$

SOLUTION: put $x = \sin\theta$ $\Rightarrow dx = \cos\theta\, d\theta$

when $x = 0 \Rightarrow \theta = 0$
and $x = 1$ $\Rightarrow\ \theta = \frac{\pi}{2}$

$\therefore\ I = \int_0^{\pi/2} \frac{\sin^2\theta\, \ell n(\sin\theta)}{\cos\theta}.\cos\theta\, d\theta = \int_0^{\pi/2}\left(\frac{1-\cos 2\theta}{2}\right).\ell n \sin\theta\, d\theta$

$= \frac{1}{2}\int_0^{\pi/2} \ell n \sin\theta\, d\theta - \frac{1}{2}\int_0^{\pi/2} \cos 2\theta\ \ell n(\sin\theta)d\theta$

$= \frac{1}{2}\left(-\frac{\pi}{2}\ell n2\right) - \frac{1}{2}\left\{\left[\ell n\sin\theta.\frac{\sin 2\theta}{2}\right]_0^{\pi/2} - \int_0^{\pi/2}\frac{\cos\theta}{\sin\theta}.\frac{\sin 2\theta}{2}d\theta\right\}$

$= -\frac{\pi}{4}\ell n2 + \frac{1}{2}\int_0^{\pi/2}\cos^2\theta\, d\theta = \frac{\pi}{8}(1-\ell n4)$

ILLUSTRATION 109: Evaluate $\int_0^{\pi} \frac{(ax+b)\sec x\tan x}{4+\tan^2 x}dx\ (a, b > 0)$

SOLUTION: Let $I = \int_0^{\pi} \frac{(ax+b)\sec x\tan x}{\sec^2 x+3}dx$ ...(1)

Using property $\int_0^a f(x)\,dx = \int_0^a f(a-x)\,dx$, we have

$I = \int_0^{\pi} \frac{(a\pi - ax + b)\sec x\tan x}{\sec^2 x+3}dx$ ...(2)

Adding (1) and (2), we get

$2I = \int_0^{\pi} \frac{(a\pi + 2b)\sec x\tan x}{\sec^2 x+3}dx$

Using property 12, we have $2I = 2(a\pi + 2b)\int_0^{\pi/2} \frac{\sec x\tan x}{\sec^2 x+3}dx$

put $\sec x = t \Rightarrow \sec x \tan x\, dx = dt$

when $x = 0 \Rightarrow t = 1$ and when

$x = \frac{\pi}{2} \Rightarrow t \to \infty$

$$\therefore \quad I = (a\pi + 2b)\int_1^{\infty} \frac{dt}{t^2 + (\sqrt{3})^2} = \left(\frac{a\pi + 2b}{\sqrt{3}}\right)\tan^{-1}\left(\frac{t}{\sqrt{3}}\right)_1^{\infty} = \left(\frac{a\pi + 2b}{\sqrt{3}}\right)\left(\frac{\pi}{2} - \frac{\pi}{6}\right)$$

$$= \left(\frac{a\pi + 2b}{3\sqrt{3}}\right)\pi$$

ILLUSTRATION 110: Evaluate $\int_0^{\pi}\left(\frac{(2x+3)\sin x}{1+\cos^2 x}\right)dx$

SOLUTION: Let $I = \int_0^{\pi} \frac{(2x+3)\sin x}{(1+\cos^2 x)}dx$ ...(1)

Using property $\int_0^a f(x)dx = \int_0^a f(a-x)dx$, we have $I = \int_0^{\pi} \frac{(2\pi - 2x + 3)\sin x}{1+\cos^2 x}$ ...(2)

(1) + (2) gives, $2I = \int_0^{\pi} \frac{(2\pi + 6)\sin x}{1+\cos^2 x}dx$

$\Rightarrow \quad I = (\pi + 3)\int_0^{\pi} \frac{\sin x}{1+\cos^2 x}dx$

Using property 12, we have $= (\pi+3).2\int_0^{\pi/2} \frac{\sin x}{1+\cos^2 x}dx$

Putting $\cos x = t \Rightarrow -\sin x\, dx = dt$, we have

$$I = (\pi+3).2\int_0^1 \frac{dt}{1+t^2} = 2(\pi+3)\left|\tan^{-1} t\right|_0^1 = (\pi+3)\frac{\pi}{2}$$

ILLUSTRATION 111: Evaluate $\int_{-\pi/4}^{\pi/4} \ln(\sin x + \cos x)dx$

SOLUTION: Let $I = \int_{-\pi/4}^{\pi/4} \ln\sqrt{2}\left(\sin\left(x + \frac{\pi}{4}\right)\right)dx$

By shifting property, $I = \int_0^{\pi/2} \ln\sqrt{2}(\sin x)dx$

$$= \int_0^{\pi/2} \frac{1}{2}\ln 2\, dx + \int_0^{\pi/2} \ln\sin x\, dx = (\ln 2)\left(\frac{\pi}{4}\right) + \left(-\frac{\pi}{2}\ln 2\right) = \frac{\pi}{4}\ln 2 - \frac{\pi}{2}\ln 2 = \frac{-\pi}{4}\ln 2$$

ILLUSTRATION 112: Evaluate $\int_0^1 \frac{\ln(1+x)}{1+x^2}dx$

SOLUTION: Let us substitute $x = \tan\theta$

$\Rightarrow \quad dx = \sec^2\theta\, d\theta$

For $x = 0$, $\theta = 0$ and for $x = 1$, $\theta = \frac{\pi}{4}$

$$\therefore \quad I = \int_0^{\pi/4} \frac{\ln(1+\tan\theta)}{(1+\tan^2\theta)}\sec^2\theta\, d\theta$$

$$\Rightarrow \quad I = \int_0^{\pi/4} \ln(1+\tan\theta)d\theta = \int_0^{\pi/4} \ln\left(1+\tan\left(\frac{\pi}{4}-\theta\right)\right)d\theta \qquad \left(\text{using} \int_0^a f(x)dx = \int_0^a f(a-x)dx\right)$$

$$= \int_0^{\pi/4} \ln\left[1+\frac{1-\tan\theta}{1+\tan\theta}\right]d\theta = \int_0^{\pi/4} \ln\left[\frac{2}{1+\tan\theta}\right]d\theta \qquad \ldots(1)$$

$$= \int_0^{\pi/4} \ln\left[\frac{2\cos\theta}{\cos\theta+\sin\theta}\right]d\theta = \int_0^{\pi/4} \ln 2\, d\theta - \int_0^{\pi/4} \ln\left(\frac{\cos\theta+\sin\theta}{\cos\theta}\right)d\theta$$

$$= (\ln 2)\frac{\pi}{4} - \int_0^{\pi/4} \ln\left[\frac{\sqrt{2}\sin\left(\frac{\pi}{4}+\theta\right)}{\cos\theta}\right]d\theta$$

$$= \frac{\pi}{4}(\ln 2) - \frac{1}{2}\ln 2\left(\frac{\pi}{4}\right) - \int_0^{\pi/4} \ln\sin\left(\frac{\pi}{4}+\theta\right)d\theta + \int_0^{\pi/4} \ln(\cos\theta)d\theta$$

$$= \frac{1}{2}\left[(\ln 2)\frac{\pi}{4}\right] - \int_{-\pi/4}^{0} \ln\sin\left(\frac{\pi}{4}+\frac{\pi}{4}+\theta\right)d\theta + \int_0^{\pi/4} \ln(\cos\theta)d\theta \text{ (by shifting property)}$$

$$= \frac{\pi}{8}\ln 2 - \int_{-\pi/4}^{0} \ln\cos\theta\, d\theta + \int_0^{\pi/4} \ln\cos\theta\, d\theta$$

$$= \frac{\pi}{8}\ln 2 - \int_0^{\pi/4} \ln\cos(-\theta)\, d\theta + \int_0^{\pi/4} \ln\cos\theta\,(d\theta) \text{ (by reflection property)}$$

$$= \frac{\pi}{8}\ln 2 \text{ } (\because 2^{\text{nd}} \text{ and } 3^{\text{rd}} \text{ integrals cancel out})$$

Alternatively: After proving $I = \int_0^{\pi/4} \ln\left(\frac{2}{1+\tan\theta}\right)d\theta$

$$= \int_0^{\pi/4} (\ln 2)\, d\theta - \int_0^{\pi/4} \ln(1+\tan\theta)\, d\theta = \int_0^{\pi/4} (\ln 2)\, d\theta - I$$

$$\Rightarrow \quad 2I = (\ln 2)\left[\frac{\pi}{4}-0\right] \qquad \Rightarrow \quad I = \frac{\pi}{8}\ln 2$$

ILLUSTRATION 113: Evaluate $\int_0^{\pi} \ln\sin\theta\, d\theta$ and hence evaluate $\int_0^{\pi} x^3 \ln\sin x\, dx$ in terms of $\int_0^{\pi} x^2 \ln\sin x\, dx$

SOLUTION: Let $I = \int_0^{\pi} \ln(\sin\theta)\, d\theta = 2\int_0^{\pi/2} \ln(\sin\theta)\, d\theta$ [$\because f(2a-\theta) = f(\pi-\theta) = f(\theta)$, Thus, by property 12]

$$= 2\left(-\frac{\pi}{2}\ln 2\right) \qquad \left[\because \int_0^{\pi/2} \ln\sin x\, dx = -\frac{\pi}{2}\ln 2\right]$$

$$= -\pi \ln 2$$

$$\therefore \quad \int_0^{\pi} \ln(\sin\theta)\, d\theta = -\pi\ln 2 \qquad \ldots(1)$$

Now let $I_1 = \int_0^{\pi} x^3 \ln\sin x\, dx = \int_0^{\pi} (\pi - x)^3 \ln\sin x\, dx \qquad \left(\text{using} \int_0^a f(x)dx = \int_0^a f(a-x)dx\right)$

$$= \int_0^{\pi} \left(\pi^3 - x^3 - 3\pi^2 x + 3\pi x^2\right)\ln\sin x\, dx$$

$$= \pi^3\int_0^{\pi} \ln\sin x\, dx - \int_0^{\pi} x^3 \ln\sin x\, dx - 3\pi^2\int_0^{\pi} x\ln\sin x\, dx + 3\pi\int_0^{\pi} x^2 \ln\sin x\, dx$$

$$= \pi^3(-\pi\ln 2) - I_1 - 3\pi^2 I_2 + 3\pi I_3 \text{ (using (1))}$$

$\therefore\ 2I_1 = -\pi^4 \ln 2 - 3\pi^2 I_2 + 3\pi I_3$

$\Rightarrow\ I_1 = -\dfrac{\pi^4}{2}\ln 2 - \dfrac{3\pi^2}{2} I_2 + \dfrac{3\pi}{2} I_3$ ...(2)

Where $I_2 = \int_0^{\pi} x \ln \sin x\, dx$ and $I_3 = \int_0^{\pi} x^2 \ln \sin x\, dx$

Let us evaluate $I_2 = \int_0^{\pi} x \ln \sin x\, dx$

$\Rightarrow\ I_2 = \int_0^{\pi} (\pi - x)\ln \sin(\pi - x)\, dx$ $\left(\text{using} \int_0^a f(x)dx = \int_0^a f(a-x)dx\right)$

$\Rightarrow\ I_2 = \pi \int_0^{\pi} \ln \sin x\, dx - \int_0^{\pi} x \ln \sin x\, dx$ $\Rightarrow\ 2I_2 = \pi \int_0^{\pi} \ln \sin x\, dx = \pi(-\pi \ln 2)$

$\Rightarrow\ I_2 = -\dfrac{\pi^2}{2}\ln 2$ ...(3)

Using (3) in (2) we get $I_1 = -\dfrac{\pi^4}{2}\ln 2 - \dfrac{3\pi^2}{2}\left(\dfrac{-\pi^2}{2}\ln 2\right) + \dfrac{3\pi}{2} I_3$

$= -\dfrac{\pi^4}{2}\ln 2 - \dfrac{3\pi^2}{2}\left(-\dfrac{\pi^2}{2}\ln 2\right) + \dfrac{3\pi}{2}\int_0^{\pi} x^2 \ln \sin x\, dx$

$= \left(\dfrac{\pi^4}{2}\ln 2\right)\left(\dfrac{3}{2} - 1\right) + \dfrac{3\pi}{2}\int_0^{\pi} x^2 \ln \sin x\, dx = \dfrac{\pi^4}{4}\ln 2 + \dfrac{3\pi}{2}\int_0^{\pi} x^2 \ln \sin x\, dx$

ILLUSTRATION 114: Evaluate $\displaystyle\int_0^{2\pi} \frac{x^2 \sin x}{3 + \sin^2 x} dx$

SOLUTION: Let $I = \displaystyle\int_0^{2\pi} \frac{x^2 \sin x}{3 + \sin^2 x} dx = \int_0^{2\pi} \frac{(2\pi - x)^2 \sin(2\pi - x)}{3 + \sin^2(2\pi - x)} dx$ $\left(\text{using} \int_0^a f(x)\, dx = \int_0^a f(a-x)\, dx\right)$

$= \displaystyle\int_0^{2\pi} \frac{-(4\pi^2 + x^2 - 4\pi x)\sin x}{3 + \sin^2 x} dx = -4\pi^2 \int_0^{2\pi} \frac{\sin x}{3 + \sin^2 x} dx - I + 4\pi \int_0^{2\pi} \frac{x \sin x}{3 + \sin^2 x} dx$ ...(i)

Now, $\dfrac{\sin(2\pi - x)}{3 + \sin^2(2\pi - x)} = \dfrac{-\sin x}{3 + \sin^2 x}$ thus, $\displaystyle\int_0^{2\pi} \frac{\sin x}{3 + \sin^2 x} dx = 0$, (by Property 13)

$\therefore$ from (i), $I = -I + 4\pi \displaystyle\int_0^{2\pi} \frac{x \sin x}{3 + \sin^2 x} dx$

$\Rightarrow\ I = 2\pi \displaystyle\int_0^{2\pi} \frac{x \sin x}{4 - \cos^2 x} dx$ ...(ii)

Let $I_1 = \displaystyle\int_0^{2\pi} \frac{x \sin x}{4 - \cos^2 x} dx = \int_0^{2\pi} \underset{I}{x} \underbrace{\left(\frac{\sin x}{4 - \cos^2 x}\right)}_{II} dx$ (using by parts)

$= \left| x \displaystyle\int \left(\frac{\sin x}{4 - \cos^2 x}\right) dx \right|_0^{2\pi} - \int_0^{2\pi} 1 . \int \left(\frac{\sin x}{4 - \cos^2 x}\right) dx$

$= \left| x . \dfrac{1}{2(2)} \ln \left|\dfrac{\cos x - 2}{\cos x + 2}\right| \right|_0^{2\pi} - \displaystyle\int_0^{2\pi} \frac{1}{2(2)} \ln \left|\frac{\cos x - 2}{\cos x + 2}\right| dx = \frac{1}{4}\left(2\pi \ln \left|-\frac{1}{3}\right|\right) - \frac{1}{4}\int_0^{2\pi} \ln \left|\frac{\cos x - 2}{\cos x + 2}\right| dx$

$$= \frac{\pi}{2}\ln\left(\frac{1}{3}\right) - \frac{1}{4}(2)\int_0^{\pi} \ln\left|\frac{\cos x - 2}{\cos x + 2}\right| dx \qquad (\because f(2a - x) = f(x), \text{ using property 15})$$

$$= \frac{\pi}{2}\ln\left(\frac{1}{3}\right) - \frac{1}{2}\int_0^{\pi} \ln\left|\frac{\cos x - 2}{\cos x + 2}\right| dx = -\frac{\pi}{2}\ln 3 - \frac{1}{2}(0)$$

$$\left[\begin{aligned} \because f(\pi - x) &= \ln\left|\frac{\cos(\pi - x) - 2}{\cos(\pi - x) + 2}\right| = \ln\left|\frac{-\cos x - 2}{-\cos x + 2}\right| \\ &= \ln\left|\frac{\cos x + 2}{\cos x - 2}\right| = -\ln\left|\frac{\cos x - 2}{\cos x + 2}\right| = -f(x) \end{aligned}\right]$$

$\therefore \quad I_1 = -\frac{\pi}{2}\ln 3$

$\therefore \quad$ from (ii) $I = 2\pi\left(-\frac{\pi}{2}\ln 3\right) = -\pi^2 \ln 3$

Property 16: **Integral of an Inverse Function:** If f is an invertible function and f' is continuous, then definite integral of f^{-1} can be expressed in terms of definite integral of function $f(x)$, i.e., $\int_{f(a)}^{f(b)} f^{-1}(y)\,dy = bf(b) - af(a) - \int_a^b f(x)\,dx$

Proof: Let us consider $I = \int_a^b f(x)\,dx = \int_a^b 1.f(x)\,dx$

$$= \left|f(x)\int 1\,dx\right|_a^b - \int_a^b f'(x).x\,dx \text{ (Integrating by parts)}$$

$$= |xf(x)|_a^b - \int_a^b f'(x).x\,dx$$

$$= bf(b) - af(a) - \int_a^b f'(x).x\,dx \qquad \ldots\text{(i)}$$

Let $f(x) = y$

$\Rightarrow f'(x)\,dx = dy$ and $x = f^{-1}(y)$

Where $x = a, y = f(a), x = b, y = f(b)$

$\therefore$ from (i), $I = \int_a^b f(x)\,dx$

$$= bf(b) - af(a) - \int_{f(a)}^{f(b)} f^{-1}(y)\,dy$$

$$\Rightarrow \int_{f(a)}^{f(b)} f^{-1}(y)\,dy = bf(b) - af(a) - \int_a^b f(x)\,dx \qquad \ldots\text{(ii)}$$

Now if we let $f(a) = c$ and $f(b) = d$ and $g(x) = f^{-1}(x)$, then (ii) can be written as

$$\int_c^d g(x)\,dx = bd - ac - \int_a^b f(x)\,dx$$

or $\int_a^b f(x)\,dx + \int_c^d g(x)\,dx = (bd - ac)$

Geometrically

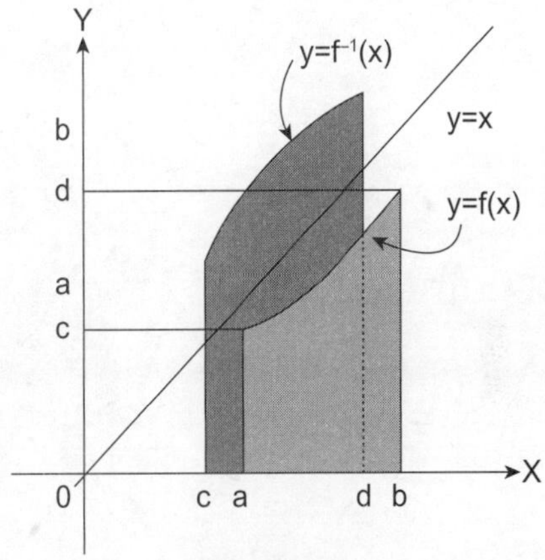

FIGURE 2.59

[dark shade] $= \int_c^d f^{-1}(x)dx$; [light shade] $= \int_a^b f(x)dx$

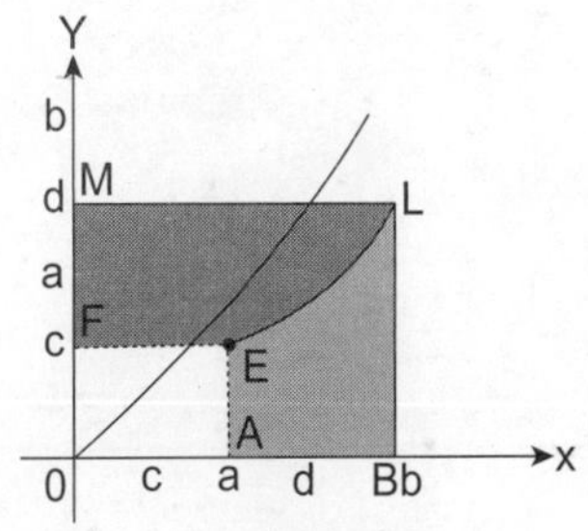

FIGURE 2.60

Also [shaded] $= \int_{y=c}^{d} x\,dy = \int_{y=c}^{d} f^{-1}(y)dy = \int_c^d f^{-1}(x)dx$

Thus, $\int_a^b f(x)dx + \int_c^d f^{-1}(x)dx =$

[shaded] $\int_a^d f^{-1}(y)dy = \int_c^d f^{-1}(x)dx$

– (Area of rectangle $OAEF$) = $(bd - ac)$

ILLUSTRATION 115: Evaluate $\int_1^3 (x^2-2x+5)\,dx + \int_4^8 \left(1+\sqrt{x-4}\right)dx$

SOLUTION: Let $f(x) = (x^2 - 2x + 5) = (x - 1)^2 + 4$

$\Rightarrow f'(x) = 2(x - 1) \geq 0 \ \forall \ x \geq 1$

$\Rightarrow f(x)$ is an injective function and hence is invertible on [1, 3]

Now $y = (x - 1)^2 + 4$ $\Rightarrow (x - 1)^2 = y - 4$

$\Rightarrow (x-1) = \pm\sqrt{y-4}$ $\Rightarrow x = 1 \pm \sqrt{y-4}$

But $x \geq 1$

$\therefore x = 1+\sqrt{y-4}$

$\Rightarrow f^{-1}(x) = 1+\sqrt{x-4}$ and $f(1) = 4, f(3) = 8$

$\therefore$ Given integral can be written as $\int_1^3 f(x)\,dx + \int_4^8 f^{-1}(x)\,dx$;

where $f(x) = (x^2-2x+5)$; $f^{-1}(x) = 1+\sqrt{x-4}$

Therefore by property, $\int_a^b f(x)\,dx + \int_c^d f^{-1}(x)\,dx = db - ac$

$\Rightarrow I = (3)(8) - (1)(4) = 20$

ILLUSTRATION 116: Evaluate $\int_0^{\pi/2} e^{\sin x}\,dx + \int_1^e \sin^{-1}(\ln x)\,dx$

SOLUTION: Let $I = \int_0^{\pi/2} e^{\sin x}\,dx + \int_1^e \sin^{-1}(\ln x)\,dx$ ...(1)

Let $f(x) = e^{\sin x}; x \in \left[0, \frac{\pi}{2}\right]$

$\Rightarrow f'(x) = \cos x . e^{\sin x}; x \in \left[0, \frac{\pi}{2}\right]$ $\Rightarrow f'(x) \geq 0 \ \forall \ x \in \left[0, \frac{\pi}{2}\right]$

Thus, $f(x)$ is injective function on $\left[0, \frac{\pi}{2}\right]$

Now $f(x) = e^{\sin x} \Rightarrow \ln f(x) = \sin x$

$\Rightarrow x = \sin^{-1}(\ln f(x))$ $\therefore f^{-1}(x) = \sin^{-1}(\ln x)$ when $x = 0$ $f(x) = e^0 = 1$

And when $x = \frac{\pi}{2}$; $f(x) = e^1 = e$

$\therefore$ (1) can be written as $I = \int_0^{\pi/2} f(x)\,dx + \int_1^e f^{-1}(x)\,dx = \frac{\pi}{2}(e) - (0)(1) = \frac{\pi}{2}e$

(using above property)

TEXTUAL EXERCISE–5: (SUBJECTIVE)

1. Evaluate the integral $\int_0^{\pi} \frac{|\sin x|}{|\sin x| + |\cos x|}dx$

2. Evaluate the following integrals:

(a) $\int_{\ln\lambda}^{\ln\frac{1}{\lambda}} \frac{f(x^2/2)[f(x)-f(-x)]}{g(x^2/4)[g(x)+g(-x)]}dx$

(b) $\int_0^{\pi} \sin^{-1}\sin x\,dx$

(c) $\int_0^{2\pi} \sin^{-1} \sin x \, dx$

(d) $\int_{-1}^{1} \sin^2 x \log\left(\frac{1-x}{1+x}\right) dx$

(e) $\int_{-2}^{2} \sin x \tan x \ln(x+\sqrt{x^2+1})\, dx$

(f) $\int_a^{-a} (f(x)+f(-x)) \tan^3 x \, dx$

(g) $\int_{-\pi/2}^{\pi/2} \sqrt{\cos x - \cos^3 x}\, dx$

(h) $\int_{-\pi/2}^{\pi/2} \frac{dx}{e^{\tan x}+1}$

(i) $\int_{-3}^{3} \frac{\sin^4 x}{[x/\pi]+0.5} dx$

(j) $\int_0^{\pi} \frac{e^{\cos x}}{e^{\cos x}+e^{-\cos x}} dx$

(k) $\int_0^{\pi} \frac{x \sin 2x \sin(\pi/2\cos x)}{(2x-\pi)} dx$

3. Evaluate $\int_0^{\pi} x\{\sin^2(\sin x)+\cos^2(\cos x)\}\, dx$

4. Evaluate $\int_0^{2\pi} \frac{x^2 \sin x}{8+\sin^2 x} dx$

5. Evaluate $\int_0^{\pi} x \sin(\cos^2 x)\cos(\sin^2 x) dx$

6. Evaluate $\int_0^{2\pi} \ln\left(\frac{\cos x - 4}{\cos x + 4}\right) dx$

7. Evaluate $\int_0^{\pi} \tan^{-1}(\cos x)\, dx$

8. Evaluate $\int_0^{\pi} \frac{x \sin x}{1+\cos^2 x} dx$

9. Evaluate $\int_{-\pi}^{\pi} (\cos px - \sin qx)^2 \, dx$; $p, q \in \mathbb{Z}$

10. Evaluate the following integrals:

(a) $\int_0^{2\pi} \cos^4 x \, dx$

(b) $\int_0^{\pi} \frac{dx}{1+2\sin^2 x} dx$

(c) $\int_0^{\pi} \frac{\sin x}{\sin 8x} dx$

(d) $\int_0^{\pi} \sin^5 x \cos^7 x \, dx$

(e) $\int_0^{\pi} \cos^{53} x \, dx$

11. Prove the following:

(a) $\int_0^{\pi} \ln(1-\cos x)\, dx = -\pi \ln 2$

(b) $\int_0^{\pi} \ln(1+\cos x)\, dx = -\pi \ln 2$

(c) $\int_0^{1} \frac{\sin^{-1} x}{x} dx = \frac{\pi}{2} \ln 2$

12. Evaluate $\int_0^{\pi} \frac{x^2 \sin x}{(2x-\pi)(1+\cos^2 x)} dx$

13. Evaluate $\int_0^{2\pi} \frac{x \sin^{2n} x}{\sin^{2n} x + \cos^{2n} x} dx$; $n \in \mathbb{Z}$

14. Let $f(x) = -\int_0^{x} \ln \cos y \, dy$, then prove that,

$$f(x) = 2f\left(\frac{\pi}{4}+\frac{x}{2}\right) - 2f\left(\frac{\pi}{4}-\frac{x}{2}\right) - x\ln 2$$

Answer Keys

1. $\pi/2$ **2.** (a) 0 (b) $\pi^2/4$ (c) $\pi^2/2$ (d) zero (e) zero (f) zero (g) 4/3 (h) $\pi/2$ (i) zero (j) $\pi/2$ (k) $8/\pi^2$ **3.** $\pi^2/2$ **4.** $\frac{-2\pi^2}{3}\ln 2$ **5.** $\frac{\pi^2}{4}(\sin 1)$ **6.** 0

7. 0 **8.** $\pi^2/4$ **9.** 2π **10.** (a) $3\pi/4$ (b) $\pi/\sqrt{3}$ (c) 0 (d) 0 (e) 0 **12.** $\frac{\pi^2}{4}$ **13.** π^2

TEXTUAL EXERCISE–5: (OBJECTIVE)

1. The value of $\int_0^{\pi} \frac{dx}{1+5^{\cos x}} + \int_{-2}^{2} \log\left(\frac{5-x}{5+x}\right) dx$ is

(a) π (b) π/2

(c) π + log 5 (d) None of these

2. Let f: |ℝ → |ℝ and g : |ℝ → |ℝ be continuous functions, then the value of the integral $\int_{-\pi/2}^{\pi/2} [f(x)+f(-x)][g(x)-g(-x)]dx$ is equal to

(a) π (b) 1

(c) – 1 (d) 0

3. The value of $\int_{-1}^{1} \log\left(\frac{2-x}{2+x}\right) dx$, is equal to

(a) 1/2 (b) 1

(c) – 1 (d) 0

4. $\int_{-1}^{1} \frac{\sin x - x^2}{3-|x|} dx$ equals

(a) 0 (b) $2\int_0^1 \frac{\sin x}{3-|x|} dx$

(c) $2\int_0^1 \frac{-x^2}{3-|x|} dx$ (d) $2\int_0^1 \frac{\sin x - x^2}{3-|x|} dx$

5. The equation $\int_{-\pi/4}^{\pi/4} \left(\lambda|\sin x| + \frac{\mu \sin x}{1+\cos x} + v\right) dx = 0,$ where λ, μ, ν are constants, gives an equation involving

(a) λ,μ, and ν (b) λ and ν

(c) λ and μ (d) μ and ν

6. If $f(x)$ is continuous and $n \in$ ℕ, then the value of $\int_{-2}^{2} \{f(x)-f(-x)\}x^{2n} dx$ is

(a) $nf(2)$ (b) $2n$

(c) 0 (d) None of these

7. If $\int_{-2}^{2} \{f(x)+f(-x)\}\{g(x)-g(-x)\}dx = 0$; then

(a) $f(x)$ must be an odd functions

(b) $g(x)$ must be on odd functions

(c) $g(x)$ as well as $f(x)$ must be an even function

(d) $f(x)$ or $g(x)$ can be either an odd or an even function

8. The value of $\int_{-10}^{10} x\left(|x| - e^{|x|}\right) dx$; is

(a) 1 (b) 2

(c) 3 (d) 0

9. If $\int_0^{\pi} \frac{x^3 \cos^4 x \sin^2 x}{\pi^2 - 3\pi x + 3x^2} dx = k \int_0^{\pi/2} \sin^2 x\, dx$,, then value of k is

(a) π/2 (b) π/4

c) π/8 (d) None of these

10. Let $I_1 = \int_0^{\pi/2} \frac{\sin x - \cos x}{1+\sin x.\cos x} dx; I_2 = \int_0^{2\pi} \cos^6 x dx;$

$I_3 = \int_{-\pi/2}^{\pi/2} \sin^3 x dx$ and $I_4 = \int_0^1 \ln\left(\frac{1}{x}-1\right) dx$, then:

(a) $I_1 = I_2 = I_3 = I_4 = 0$

(b) $I_1 = I_2 = I_3 = 0$ but $I_4 \neq 0$

(c) $I_1 = I_3 = I_4 = 0$ but $I_2 \neq 0$

(d) $I_1 = I_2 = I_4 = 0$ but $I_3 \neq 0$

11. Which of the following definite integral when simplified reduces to zero?

(a) $\int_{-1}^{1} \ln\left(\frac{1+x}{1-x}\right) dx$ (b) $\int_0^1 \tan^{-1}\left[\frac{2x-1}{1+x-x^2}\right] dx$

(c) $\int_0^{\pi} \sin^3 x.\cos^5 x\, dx$ (d) $\int_0^1 \ell n\left(\frac{1}{x}-1\right) dx$

12. Let f be integrable function. If we define

$I_1 = \int_0^{\pi/2} \cos\theta.f(\sin\theta + \cos^2\theta)d\theta$ and

$I_2 = \int_0^{\pi/2} \sin 2\theta.f(\sin\theta + \cos^2\theta)d\theta,$ then

(a) $I_1 = I_2$ (b) $I_1 = -I_2$

(c) $I_1 = 2I_2$ (d) $I_1 = -2I_2$

13. The value of $\int_{-1}^{1} [x[1+\sin\pi x]+1]dx$; ([.] denotes the greatest integer) is

(a) 2 (b) 0

(c) 1 (d) None of these

14. $\int_0^{\pi/2} \left(\frac{1+\sin 3x}{1+2\sin x}\right) dx$ is equal to

(a) $\int_0^{\pi/2} \frac{1-\cos 3x}{1+2\cos x} dx$ (b) $\int_0^{\pi/2} \frac{\cos 3x + 1}{2\cos x - 1} dx$

(c) $\frac{\pi}{2}$ (d) 1

15. The value of $\int_{-1/\sqrt{3}}^{1/\sqrt{3}}\left(\frac{x^4}{1-x^4}\right)\cos^{-1}\left(\frac{2x}{1+x^2}\right)dx$ equals

(a) $\frac{\pi}{3}\left\{\frac{\pi}{12}+\frac{1}{\sqrt{3}}-\frac{1}{4}\ln\left(2-\sqrt{3}\right)\right\}$

(b) $\pi\left\{\frac{\pi}{12}-\frac{1}{\sqrt{3}}+\frac{1}{4}\ln\left(2+\sqrt{3}\right)\right\}$

(c) $\pi\left\{\frac{\pi}{12}-\frac{1}{\sqrt{3}}-\frac{1}{2}\ln\left(2-\sqrt{3}\right)\right\}$

(d) None of these

16. The value of $\int_{-\pi}^{\pi}\frac{2x(1+\sin x)}{1+\cos^2 x}dx$ is

(a) π (b) π^2

(c) $\frac{\pi^2}{8}$ (d) None of these

17. The value of the definite integral

$I=\int_0^{\pi/2} e^x\left\{\cos(\sin x)\cos^2\frac{x}{2}+\sin(\sin x)\sin^2\frac{x}{2}\right\}dx$, is

(a) $\frac{1}{2}\left[e^{\pi/2}(\cos 1+\sin 1)-1\right]$

(b) $\frac{e^{\pi/2}}{2}(\cos 1+\sin 1)$

(c) $\frac{1}{2}\left(e^{\pi/2}\cos 1-1\right)$

(d) $\frac{e^{\pi/2}}{2}(\cos 1+\sin 1-1)$

18. Let $I_1=\int_0^3\frac{\sin x}{\left[\frac{x}{\pi}\right]+\frac{1}{2}}dx$ and $I_2=\int_{-3}^0\frac{\sin x}{\left[\frac{x}{\pi}\right]+\frac{1}{2}}dx$, then

(where [] represent greatest integer part)

(a) $I_1=3I_2$ (b) $I_2=3I_1$

(c) $I_1=I_2$ (d) $I_1+I_2=0$

19. Value of $\int_{-1}^{1}\frac{dx}{(1+x^2)(2^x+1)}$ is

(a) $\frac{\pi}{8}$ (b) $\frac{\pi}{4}\ell n\left(\frac{2}{3}\right)$

(c) $\frac{\pi}{4}$ (d) $\ell n\left(\frac{2}{3}\right)$

20. Which of the following integrals is/are not equal to zero?

(a) $\int_0^{\pi/2}\ell n(\cot x)dx$ (b) $\int_0^{2\pi}\sin^3 x dx$

(c) $\int_{1/e}^{e}\frac{dx}{x(\ell nx)^{1/3}}$ (d) $\int_0^{\pi}\sqrt{\frac{1+\cos 2x}{2}}dx$

21. The value of $\int_{-2\pi}^{5\pi}\cot^{-1}(\tan x)dx$ is equal to

(a) $\frac{5\pi^2}{2}$ (b) $\frac{7\pi^2}{2}$

(c) $\frac{9\pi^2}{2}$ (d) None of these

22. Value of the definite integral

$\int_{-1}^{1}\frac{\left(2x^{332}+x^{998}+4x^{1668}.\sin x^{691}\right)}{1+x^{666}}dx$, is

(a) $\frac{\pi+4}{666}$ (b) $\frac{\pi+2}{666}$

(c) $\frac{\pi+4}{333}$ (d) $\frac{\pi+2}{333}$

Answer Keys

1. (b)	2. (d)	3. (d)	4. (c)	5. (b)	6. (c)	7. (d)	8. (d)	9. (c)	10. (c)
11. (a,b,c,d)		12. (a)	13. (a)	14. (a,b,d)	15. (b)	16. (b)	17. (a)	18. (c)	19. (c)
20. (d)	21. (b)	22. (a)							

■ EVALUATION OF LIMIT UNDER INTEGRAL SIGN

The limit of a function expressed in the form of definite integral can also be evaluated by first finding the limit of the integrand function w.r.t. a quantity, of which the limit of integration are independent and subsequently integrating the result thus obtained.

e.g., $\lim_{x\to k}\int_\alpha^\beta f(x,t)dt=\int_\alpha^\beta\left(\lim_{x\to k}f(x,t)\right)dt$

ILLUSTRATION 117: Evaluate $\lim_{x\to\pi/4}\int_1^2 \frac{t}{t^2+\sin^2 x}dt$

SOLUTION: Given $\lim_{x\to\pi/4}\int_1^2 \frac{t}{t^2+\sin^2 x}dt = L\ (say)$

Since limits of integration are independent of x. we can first take limit of integrand and then integrate as follows

$$L=\int_1^2 \lim_{x\to\pi/4}\left(\frac{t}{t^2+\sin^2 x}\right)dt = \int_1^2\left(\frac{t}{t^2+1/2}\right)dt=\int_1^2\frac{2t}{2t^2+1}dt$$

$$=\frac{1}{2}\int_1^2\frac{4t}{2t^2+1}dt=\frac{1}{2}\mid \ln(2t^2+1)\mid_1^2=\frac{1}{2}[\ln(9)-\ln(3)]=\frac{1}{2}[\ln 3]=\ln\sqrt{3}$$

ILLUSTRATION 118: Evaluate $\lim_{x\to0^+}\int_{\pi/4}^{\pi/3}\left(x^2 t\operatorname{cosec} x\ln x+\cos x\sec^2 t\right)dt$

SOLUTION: Let $L=\lim_{x\to0^+}\int_{\pi/4}^{\pi/3}\left(x^2 t\operatorname{cosec} x\ln x+\cos x\sec^2 t\right)dt=\int_{\pi/4}^{\pi/3}\lim_{x\to0^+}\left(x^2 t\operatorname{cosec} x\ln x+\cos x\sec^2 t\right)dt$

$$=\int_{\pi/4}^{\pi/3}\lim_{x\to0^+}\left[t\frac{x}{\sin x}.(x\ln x)+\cos x\sec^2 t\right]dt=\int_{\pi/4}^{\pi/3}\left\{t\lim_{x\to0^+}\left[\frac{x}{\sin x}\right]\left(\frac{\ln x}{1/x}\right)+\sec^2 t\lim_{x\to0^+}\cos x\right\}dt$$

$$=\int_{\pi/4}^{\pi/3}\left\{t(1).\lim_{x\to0^+}\left[\frac{1/x}{-1/x^2}\right]+\sec^2 t(1)\right\}dt \text{ (By L–H rule)}$$

$$=\int_{\pi/4}^{\pi/3}\left\{t\lim_{x\to0^+}(-x)+\sec^2 t\right\}dt=\int_{\pi/4}^{\pi/3}\left(0+\sec^2 t\right)dt=\left[\tan t\right]_{\pi/4}^{\pi/3}=\left[\tan\frac{\pi}{3}-\tan\frac{\pi}{4}\right]=(\sqrt{3}-1)$$

ILLUSTRATION 119: Evaluate $\lim_{x\to0}\int_3^9\frac{(\ell nt)^x-1}{tx}dt; t>1$

SOLUTION: Let $L=\lim_{x\to0}\int_3^9\frac{(\ell nt)^x-1}{tx}dt=\int_3^9\lim_{x\to0}\left[\frac{(\ell nt)^x-1}{x}\right].\frac{1}{t}dt=\int_3^9\ell n(\ell nt).\frac{1}{t}dt$

Substituting $\ell n\, t=z$

$$\Rightarrow\ \frac{1}{t}dt=dz$$

and for $t=3$, $z=\ell n3$ and for $t=9$, $z=\ell n\,9$

$$\therefore\ L=\int_{\ln 3}^{\ln 9}\ln z\,dz=\int_{\ln 3}^{\ln 9}1.(\ln z)\,dz=\left|(\ln z)z\right|_{\ln 3}^{\ln 9}-\int_{\ln 3}^{\ln 9}\frac{1}{z}.z\,dz$$

$=[(\ell n\,9)\,\ell n(\ell n9)-\ell n3.\,\ell n\,(\ell n\,3)]-[\ell n\,9-\ell n3]$

$=2\ell n3\,[\ell n2+\ell n(\ell n\,3)]-\ell n3.\,\ell n\,(\ell n\,3)-\ell n3$

$=2\ell n\,3\,\ell n\,2+(\ell n\,3)\,\ell n(\ell n\,3)-\ell n3=(\ell n\,3)\,[2\ell n2+\ell n(\ell n\,3)-1]$

$=(\ell n\,3)\,[\ell n4+\ell n(\ell n\,3)-\ell n\,e]$

$$=(\ell n3)\left[\ell n\left[\frac{4\ell n3}{e}\right]\right]=(\ell n3)\left[\ell n\left(\frac{\ell n(81)}{e}\right)\right]$$

LEIBNITZ'S RULE FOR THE DIFFERENTIATION UNDER THE INTEGRAL SIGN

(a) If f is continuous on $[a, b]$ and $\phi(x)$ and $\psi(x)$ are differentiable functions of x whose values lie in $[a, b]$, then

$$\frac{d}{dx}\int_{\phi(x)}^{\psi(x)} f(t)dt = f\{\psi(x)\}.\frac{d\psi}{dx} - f\{\phi(x)\}.\frac{d\phi}{dx}$$

Proof: Let $F(x)$ be anti-derivative of $f(x)$, then $F'(t) = f(t)$.

$$\text{L.H.S.} = \frac{d}{dx}(F(\psi(x)) - F(\phi(x)))$$

$$= F'(\psi(x)).\psi'(x) - F'(\phi(x)).\phi'(x)$$

$$= f(\psi(x)).\psi'(x) - f(\phi(x)).\phi'(x)$$

(b) If the function $\phi(x)$ and $\psi(x)$ are defined on $[a, b]$ and differentiable at each point $x \in (a, b)$ and $f(x, t)$ is continuous, then

$$\frac{d}{dx}\left(\int_{\phi(x)}^{\psi(x)} f(x,t)\,dt\right) = \int_{\phi(x)}^{\psi(x)} \frac{\partial}{\partial x} f(x, t)\,dt + \frac{d\psi(x)}{dx}.f(x, \psi(x)) - \frac{d\phi(x)}{dx}.f(x, \phi(x))$$

(c) If $f(x, \alpha)$ be a continuous function of x for $x \in [a, b]$ and $\alpha \in [c, d]$, let $I(\alpha) = \int\limits_a^b f(x,\alpha)dx$ is a function of α, then

$$I'(\alpha) = \int\limits_a^b \frac{\partial}{\partial\alpha} f(x,\alpha)dx$$

ILLUSTRATION 120: Find the points of maxima/minima of $\int_0^{x^2} \frac{t^2 - 5t + 4}{2 + e^t}dt$

SOLUTION: Let $f(x) = \int_0^{x^2} \frac{t^2 - 5t + 4}{2 + e^t}dt$

$$\Rightarrow f'(x) = \frac{x^4 - 5x^2 + 4}{2 + e^{x^2}}2x - 0 = \frac{(x-1)(x+1)(x-2)(x+2)2x}{2 + e^{x^2}}$$

From the wavy curve, it is clear that $f(x)$ changes its sign at $x = \pm 1, \pm 2, 0$ and hence the points of maxima are -1, 1 and that of the minima are $-2, 0, 2$.

ILLUSTRATION 121: Find $\frac{d}{dx}\left(\int_{x^2}^{x^3} \frac{1}{\log t}dt\right)$

SOLUTION: $\frac{d}{dx}(x^3).\left(\frac{1}{\log x^3}\right) - \frac{d}{dx}(x^2).\left(\frac{1}{\log x^2}\right) = \frac{3x^2}{3\log x} - \frac{2x}{2\log x} = \frac{1}{\log x}(x^2 - x)$

ILLUSTRATION 122: If $\int_{\pi/3}^{x} \sqrt{3 - \sin^2 t}\, dt + \int_0^y \cos t\, dt = 0$ then evaluate $\frac{dy}{dx}$

SOLUTION: Differentiating with respect to x we have

$$\frac{d}{dx}\left(\int_{\pi/3}^{x} \sqrt{3 - \sin^2 t}\, dt\right) + \frac{d}{dx}\int_0^y (\cos t)dt = 0$$

$$\Rightarrow \sqrt{3 - \sin^2 x} + \cos y\frac{dy}{dx} = 0 \qquad \Rightarrow \frac{dy}{dx} = \frac{-\sqrt{3 - \sin^2 x}}{\cos y}$$

ILLUSTRATION 123: Evaluate $\int_0^1 \frac{x^b - 1}{\ln x}dx$; $(b \geq 0)$

SOLUTION: Clearly $\int\limits_0^1 \frac{x^b - 1}{\ell nx}dx$ is a function of b

So, let $I(b) = \int_0^1 \frac{x^b - 1}{\ln x} dx$

$$\Rightarrow I'(b) = \frac{d}{db}\int_0^1 \frac{x^b - 1}{\ell n x} dx = \int_0^1 \frac{\partial}{\partial b}\left(\frac{x^b - 1}{\ell nx}\right) dx = \int_0^1 \frac{x^b \ell nx}{\ell nx} dx = \int_0^1 x^b dx$$

$$\Rightarrow I'(b) = \left[\frac{x^{b+1}}{b+1}\right]_0^1 = \frac{1}{b+1} \qquad \Rightarrow I(b) = \int \frac{db}{b+1} = \ln(b+1) + c$$

If $b = 0$, then $I(0) = \int_0^1 \frac{x^0 - 1}{\log x} dx = 0$

$\Rightarrow c = 0 \qquad \Rightarrow I(b) = \ln(b + 1)$

ILLUSTRATION 124: Show that $\int_0^{\pi/2} \operatorname{cosec}\theta \cot^{-1}(a\sin\theta)\, d\theta$, is decreasing function of a.

SOLUTION: Given $\int_0^{\pi/2} \operatorname{cosec}\theta \cot^{-1}(a\sin\theta)\, d\theta$ ...(1)

Clearly (1) is a function of 'a' only

So, let $I(a) = \int_0^{\pi/2} \operatorname{cosec}\theta \cot^{-1}(a\sin\theta)\, d\theta$

$$\Rightarrow I'(a) = \int_0^{\pi/2} \frac{\partial}{\partial a}\left[\operatorname{cosec}\theta \cot^{-1}(a\sin\theta)\right] d\theta$$

$$= \int_0^{\pi/2} \operatorname{cosec}\theta.\left[\frac{-1}{1 + a^2\sin^2\theta}\right](\sin\theta) d\theta = -\int_0^{\pi/2} \frac{1}{1 + a^2\sin^2\theta} d\theta$$

$$= -\int_0^{\pi/2} \frac{\sec^2\theta}{\sec^2\theta + a^2\tan^2\theta} d\theta = -\int_0^{\infty} \frac{dz}{1 + z^2 + a^2z^2} = -\int_0^{\infty} \frac{dz}{1 + (a^2+1)z^2} = \frac{1}{(1+a^2)}\int_0^{\infty} \frac{-dz}{\left(\frac{1}{a^2+1}\right) + z^2}$$

$$= \frac{1}{\sqrt{1+a^2}} \cot^{-1}\left[\frac{z}{\frac{1}{\sqrt{a^2+1}}}\right]_0^{\infty} = \frac{1}{\sqrt{1+a^2}} \cot^{-1}\left[\sqrt{a^2+1}.z\right]_0^{\infty}$$

$$= \frac{1}{\sqrt{1+a^2}}\left[0 - \frac{\pi}{2}\right] = \frac{-\pi}{2\sqrt{1+a^2}} < 0$$

$\Rightarrow I(a)$ is a decreasing function $\forall$ a $\in \mathbb{R}$

ILLUSTRATION 125: Evaluate $\int_0^{\infty} \frac{\tan^{-1} ax - \tan^{-1} x}{x} dx;\ a > 0$

SOLUTION: Clearly, the given integral is a function of a

So, let $I(a) = \int_0^{\infty} \frac{\tan^{-1} ax - \tan^{-1} x}{x} dx$ ...(1)

$$\Rightarrow I'(a) = \frac{d}{da}\int_0^{\infty} \frac{\tan^{-1} ax - \tan^{-1} x}{x} dx = \int_0^{\infty} \frac{\partial}{\partial a}\left[\frac{\tan^{-1} ax - \tan^{-1} x}{x}\right] dx$$

$$= \int_0^{\infty} \frac{\partial}{\partial a}\left[\frac{\tan^{-1} ax}{x}\right] dx = \int_0^{\infty} \frac{1}{x}\left(\frac{1}{1 + a^2x^2}\right)(x)\, dx$$

$$= \int_0^\infty \frac{1}{1+a^2x^2}dx = \left|\frac{\tan^{-1}(ax)}{a}\right|_0^\infty = \frac{1}{a}|\tan^{-1}\infty - \tan^{-1}0| = \frac{1}{a}\left(\frac{\pi}{2}\right) = \frac{\pi}{2a}$$

$$\therefore \quad I(a) = \int \frac{\pi}{2a}da = \frac{\pi}{2}\ln(a) + C \qquad \ldots(2)$$

When $a = 1$, clearly $I(a) = I(1) = 0$. (from (1))

$$\therefore \quad 0 = \frac{\pi}{2}\ln(1) + C \qquad \Rightarrow C = 0 \qquad \text{(from (2))}$$

$\therefore$ from, (2) $I(a) = \frac{\pi}{2}\ln(a)$

ILLUSTRATION 126: Evaluate $\int_0^{\pi/2} \sec x \ln\left(\frac{1+a\cos x}{1-a\cos x}\right)dx; a \in (-1, 1)$

SOLUTION: Clearly the given integral is a function of a

So, let $I(a) = \int_0^{\pi/2} \sec x \ln\left(\frac{1+a\cos x}{1-a\cos x}\right)dx$

$$\therefore \quad I'(a) = \frac{d}{da}\int_0^{\pi/2} \sec x.\ln\left(\frac{1+a\cos x}{1-a\cos x}\right)dx = \int_0^{\pi/2} \sec x.\frac{\partial}{\partial a}\left\{\ln\left(\frac{1+a\cos x}{1-a\cos x}\right)\right\}dx$$

$$= \int_0^{\pi/2} \sec x\left[\left(\frac{1-a\cos x}{1+a\cos x}\right)\left\{\frac{(1-a\cos x)(\cos x)-(1+a\cos x)(-\cos x)}{(1-a\cos x)^2}\right\}\right]dx$$

$$= \int_0^{\pi/2} (\sec x)\left[\frac{1}{(1-a^2\cos^2 x)}\{2\cos x\}\right]dx = 2\int_0^{\pi/2}\frac{dx}{1-a^2\cos^2 x} = 2\int_0^{\pi/2}\frac{dx}{-a^2\cos^2 x+1}$$

$$= 2\int_0^{\pi/2}\frac{\sec^2 x\,dx}{-a^2+(1+\tan^2 x)} = 2\int_0^{\pi/2}\frac{\sec^2 x\,dx}{(-a^2+1+\tan^2 x)}$$

$$= 2\int_0^\infty \frac{dt}{\left[(1-a^2)+t^2\right]} \qquad (\because a^2 < 1)$$

$$= 2\int_0^\infty \frac{dt}{\left(\sqrt{1-a^2}\right)^2+t^2} = 2\times\frac{1}{\sqrt{1-a^2}}\left|\tan^{-1}\frac{t}{\sqrt{1-a^2}}\right|_0^\infty = \frac{2}{\sqrt{1-a^2}}\left|\frac{\pi}{2}-0\right| = \frac{\pi}{\sqrt{1-a^2}}$$

$$\therefore \quad I(a) = \int\frac{\pi}{\sqrt{1-a^2}}da = \pi\sin^{-1}a + C$$

Clearly at $a = 0$

$I(0) = 0 \qquad \Rightarrow C = 0$

$\therefore \quad I(a) = \pi\sin^{-1}(a)$

ILLUSTRATION 127: Evaluate $\int_0^\infty \frac{e^{-ax}\sin bx}{x}dx; a > 0$

SOLUTION: Clearly the given integral is a function of two variables a and b. Let us treat a as positive constant. Then

$\therefore$ Let $I(b) = \int_0^\infty \frac{e^{-ax}\sin bx}{x}dx$

$$\Rightarrow\ I'(b)=\int_0^\infty \frac{e^{-ax}}{x}\cos bx\,(x)\,dx$$

$$\Rightarrow\ I'(b)=\int_0^\infty e^{-ax}\cos bx\,dx=\left|\frac{e^{-ax}}{a^2+b^2}[-a\cos bx+b\sin bx]\right|_0^\infty$$

$$=\left(\frac{e^{-\infty}}{a^2+b^2}\right)(\text{finite quantity})-\frac{1}{a^2+b^2}[-a]=\frac{a}{a^2+b^2}$$

$$\therefore\ I'(b)=\frac{a}{a^2+b^2},\ a>0$$

$$\therefore\ I(b)=\int\frac{a}{a^2+b^2}db,\ a>0\ =\ a.\int\frac{1}{a^2+b^2}db=a.\frac{1}{a}\tan^{-1}\left(\frac{b}{a}\right)+C$$

$$\Rightarrow\ I(b)=\tan^{-1}\left(\frac{b}{a}\right)+C\text{. At } b=0,\ I(0)=\int_0^\infty\frac{e^{-ax}\sin 0x}{x}dx=0 \qquad \Rightarrow\ C=0$$

$$\therefore\ I(b)=\tan^{-1}\left(\frac{b}{a}\right)$$

ILLUSTRATION 128: Evaluate $\int_0^\infty \frac{\sin x}{x}dx$ by using Leibinitz's rule of differentiation under the integral sign.

SOLUTION: Let $I=\int_0^\infty\frac{e^{-ax}\sin bx}{x}dx;\ a>0$

Differentiating w.r.t. a and keeping b constant we get

$$I'(a)=\int_0^\infty\frac{e^{-ax}(-x)\sin bx}{x}dx=-\int_0^\infty e^{-ax}\sin bx\,dx=\left\{-\frac{e^{-ax}}{(a^2+b^2)}[-a\sin bx-b\cos bx]\right\}_0^\infty$$

$$=\left|\frac{e^{-ax}}{(a^2+b^2)}[a\sin bx+b\cos bx]\right|_0^\infty;\ a>0$$

$$=e^{-\infty}-\frac{1}{(a^2+b^2)}[b]=\frac{-b}{a^2+b^2}$$

$$\therefore\ I(a)=-b\int\frac{1}{a^2+b^2}da;\ a>0$$

$$\Rightarrow\ I(a)=-b.\frac{1}{b}\tan^{-1}\left(\frac{a}{b}\right)+C\ \text{ or }\ I(a)=-\tan^{-1}\left(\frac{a}{b}\right)+C \qquad \ldots(1)$$

At $b=0$, $I(a)=0$; $a>0$

$$\therefore\ 0=-\tan^{-1}\left(\frac{a}{b}\right)+C=-\frac{\pi}{2}+C$$

$$\Rightarrow\ C=\frac{\pi}{2}$$

$\therefore$ from (1) $I(a)=-\tan^{-1}\left(\frac{a}{b}\right)+\frac{\pi}{2}=\cot^{-1}\left(\frac{a}{b}\right)=\tan^{-1}\left(\frac{b}{a}\right)$ for $a,\ b>0$

Taking a $\to 0$, $b=1$, we have $I=\int_0^\infty\frac{\sin x}{x}dx=\lim_{a\to 0}\tan^{-1}\left(\frac{1}{a}\right)=\frac{\pi}{2}$

TEXTUAL EXERCISE-6: (SUBJECTIVE)

1. $f(x) = \int_{e^{2x}}^{e^{3x}} \frac{t}{\ell n\, t} dt;\ x > 0$. Find derivative of $f(x)$ w.r.t. $\ln x$; when $x = ln\, 2$.

2. $x = \int_0^y \frac{dt}{\sqrt{1+4t^2}}$. If $\frac{d^2y}{dx^2} = ky$, find k.

3. (a) If $x = \int_1^{t^2} \sqrt{z} \sin z\, dz$ and $y = \int_{\sqrt{t}}^{2} z^2 \cos z^2\, dz$, find $\frac{dy}{dx}$.

   (b) If $x = \int_1^{t^2} z \ln z\, dz$ and $y = \int_{t^2}^{1} z^2 \ln z\, dz$ find $\frac{dy}{dx}$

4. (a) Prove that $\int_{1/4}^{\sin^2 x} \sin^{-1}\sqrt{t}\,dt + \int_{1/4}^{\cos^2 x} \cos^{-1}\sqrt{t}\,dt = \frac{\pi}{8}$

   (b) If $y = \int_0^x f(t).\sin(k(x-t))dt$, then prove that $\frac{d^2y}{dx^2} + k^2 y = kf(x)$

5. Evaluate the $\frac{d}{dx}\int_x^{x^2} \frac{dt}{(x^2+t^2)} (x > 0)$

6. (i) Evaluate following limits:

   (a) $\lim_{x\to 0} \frac{\int_0^{x^2} \cos t^2 dt}{x \sin x}$

   (b) $\lim_{x\to 0} \frac{\int_0^x t\,dt}{x\tan(x+\pi)}$

   (c) $\lim_{x\to 0} \int_0^{x^2} \frac{\cos\sqrt{t}}{x^3} dt$

   (d) $\lim_{x\to\infty} \int_0^{2x} \frac{te^{t^2} dt}{e^{4x^2}}$

   (e) $\lim_{x\to 0} \int_0^{x^2} \frac{\sin\sqrt{t}}{x^3} dt$

   (ii) If $f: \mathbb{R} \to \mathbb{R}$ be differentiable function such that

   (a) $f(2) = 2$, then evaluate $\lim_{x\to 2} \int_2^{f(x)} \frac{4t^3}{x-2} dt$

   (b) $f(1) = 4$, then evaluate $\lim_{x\to 1} \int_4^{f(x)} \frac{2t}{(x-1)} dt$

   (iii) Let $f(x) = \int_0^x t(e^t - 1)(t-11)^9 (t+2)^3 (t+4)^4 \ln(t+1)\, dt$, then investigate maxima/minima and monotonicity of function.

7. If $F(x) = \int_a^{x^2} f(t)\,dt$; where $f(x^2) = x^2 - x$, then find the range of values of x in which $F(x)$ is concave upward/downward and also find the points of inflection.

8. Find the point of maxima/minima of function $f(x)$; where $f(x) = \int_0^x e^t (e^t - e)(t-3)^3 (t-4)^2\, dt$

9. If $y = \int_0^{z^2} \frac{dx}{1+x^3}$ find $\frac{d^2y}{dz^2}$ at $z = 1$

10. Evaluate the following limits:

    (a) $\lim_{x\to 0} \frac{1}{x^3}\int_0^x \frac{t^2}{t^4+1} dt$ (b) $\lim_{x\to\infty} x\int_0^x \left(e^{t^2-x^2}\right) dt$

11. Evaluate the limit $\left|\lim_{t\to\infty} t^2 \int_0^{\pi} \left(-1+\sqrt[t^2]{\sin x}\right) dx\right|$

12. If $x \in \left[0, \frac{\pi}{2}\right]$, then prove that

    $f(x) = \int_0^{\sin^2 x} \sin^{-1}\sqrt{t}\,dt + \int_0^{\cos^2 x} \cos^{-1}\sqrt{t}\,dt = \frac{\pi}{4}$

13. Prove that the function

    $f(x) = \int_{1/e}^{\tan x} \frac{tdt}{1+t^2} + \int_{1/e}^{\cot x} \frac{dt}{t(1+t^2)} = 1$

14. Evaluate the following limits as definite integrals

    $\lim_{x\to\infty} \frac{\left(\int_0^x e^{x^2} dx\right)^2}{\int_0^x e^{2x^2} dx}$

Answer Keys

1. 48/ln2 **2.** 4 **3.** (a) $\frac{-\cos t}{4\sqrt{t}(t)\sin t^2}$ (b) $-t^2$ **5.** $\frac{4[x-(x^2+1)\tan^{-1}x]+\pi(1+x^2)}{4x^2(1+x^2)}$

6. (i) (a) 1 (b) 1/2 (c) does not exist (d) 1/2 (e) 2/3 (ii) (a) $32f'(2)$ (b) $8f'(1)$

(iii) increasing for $x \in (-1, 0)$ and $(11, \infty)$; decreasing for $x \in (0, 11)$; $x = 0$ is the point of local maxima $x = 11$ is the point of local minima

7. $\left.\begin{array}{l}(-\infty,0)\cup(2/3,\infty) \text{ concave upward}\\ (0,2/3) \text{ concave downward}\end{array}\right\}$; point of inflection at $x = 0, 2/3$ **8.** increasing on $(-\infty, 1)$ and on $(3, \infty)$ decreasing on $(1, 3)$ **9.** -2 **10.** (a) 1/3 (b) 1/2 **11.** $\pi(\ln 2)$ **14.** 0

TEXTUAL EXERCISE-6: (OBJECTIVE)

1. The function $F(x)=\int_{x}^{x^2}\frac{dt}{\ln t}$ defined on $(1,\infty)$ is
(a) strictly increasing (b) strictly decreasing
(c) one–one (d) many–one

2. The function $F(x)=\int_{x}^{x^2}t\left(\ln\sqrt{t}\right)dt\ ;\ x\in(0,\infty)$ is
(a) increasing on $\left(0,\frac{1}{2}\right)$; decreasing on $\left(\frac{1}{2},1\right)$
(b) decreasing on $(1,\infty)$; increasing on $(0, 1)$
(c) point of minima at $x = 1$
(d) point of maxima at $x = 1/2$

3. If $F(x)=\frac{d}{dx}\left\{\pi\int_0^x\frac{1}{t}\sin\left(\frac{\pi}{4}t\right)dt-\int_0^x\tan^{-1}\left(\frac{t}{2}\right)dt\right\}$, then $F(2)$ equals
(a) π (b) $\pi/4$
(c) $\pi/2$ (d) None of these

4. Let $f:(0,\infty)\to\mathbb{R}$ be defined such that $F(x)=\frac{d}{dx}\int_0^x t\,f(t)\,dt$ and $F(x^2)=x^4+x^2$, then the value of $\sum_{k=1}^{5}f(k^2)$ is
(a) 60 (b) 70
(c) 80 (d) None of these

5. Let $f:(0,\infty)\to\mathbb{R}$ and $F(x)=\int_0^x t\,f(t)\,dt$. If $F(x^2)=x^4+x^5$, then the value of $\sum_{r=1}^{12}f(r^2)$ is
(a) 214 (b) 197
(c) 219 (d) None of these

6. The function $f(x)=\int_0^x\log_{\sin^2 t}\left(\sin^2 t+\frac{1}{2}\right)dt$; $x\in(0,2\pi)$ strictly increases in the interval
(a) $\left[\frac{3\pi}{4},\frac{5\pi}{4}\right]-\{\pi\}$
(b) $\left[\frac{7\pi}{4},2\pi\right)$
(c) $\left[\frac{5\pi}{4},\frac{7\pi}{4}\right]-\left\{\frac{3\pi}{2}\right\}$
(d) $\left[\frac{\pi}{4},\frac{3\pi}{4}\right]-\left\{\frac{\pi}{2}\right\}$

7. Let $f(x)$ be a continuous function for all real x, such that $(f(x))^2=\int_0^x f(t).\frac{2\sec^2 t}{(2+\tan t)}dt$ and $f(0) = 0$, then
(a) $f\left(\frac{\pi}{4}\right)=\ln\frac{5}{2}$
(b) $f\left(\frac{\pi}{4}\right)=\ln\frac{3}{2}$
(c) $f\left(\frac{\pi}{3}\right)=2\ln\left(\frac{\sqrt{3}+1}{2}\right)$
(d) None of these

8. $f(x)=\int_0^x(\sin t-\cos t)(e^t-2)(t-1)^3(t-2)^5\,dt$; $(0<x\le 3)$, then the number of points of local maxima of $f(x)$ is
(a) 3 (b) 2
(c) 1 (d) None of these

9. The value of $\lim_{x\to 1^+}\int_1^{x^2}\frac{t\sin\frac{\pi t}{2}}{(x^2-1)}dt$ equals
(a) 0 (b) 2
(c) 1 (d) None of these

10. If $f(x)=\int_0^x\frac{2\sin t}{\sqrt{1+\tan^2 x\sin^2 t}}dt$ for $0<x<\frac{\pi}{2}$, then
(a) $f\left(\frac{\pi}{4}\right)=\frac{\pi}{6}$
(b) $f(x)$ is continuous and differentiable on $\left(0,\frac{\pi}{2}\right)$
(c) $f(x)$ is continuous but not differentiable on $\left(0,\frac{\pi}{2}\right)$
(d) None of these

Answer Keys

1. (a, c) **2.** (a, c, d) **3.** (b) **4.** (a) **5.** (c) **6.** (a, b) **7.** (b, c) **8.** (b)
9. (c) **10.** (a,b)

Property 17: If $f(x)$ is an odd function of x, then $\int_a^x f(t)\,dt$ is an even function of x.

Proof: Given $f(x)$ is an odd function of x.

i.e., $f(-x) = -f(x)$

Let $g(x) = \int\limits_a^x f(t)\,dt$

$$\Rightarrow \quad g(-x) = \int\limits_a^{-x} f(t)\,dt$$

$$\Rightarrow \quad g(x) - g(-x) = \int_a^x f(t)\,dt - \int_a^{-x} f(t)\,dt$$

$$= \int\limits_a^x f(t)\,dt + \int\limits_{-x}^a f(t)\,dt = \int\limits_{-x}^a f(t)\,dt + \int\limits_a^x f(t)\,dt$$

$$= \int\limits_{-x}^x f(t)\,dt = 0$$

$\Rightarrow g(-x) = g(x) \qquad \therefore \quad g(x)$ is even.

e.g., Let $f(x) = x^2 \sin x$, then clearly $f(x)$ is an odd function $\forall\, x \in \mathbb{R}$

Let $a = \dfrac{\pi}{4}$, then $g(x) = \int\limits_{\pi/4}^x \underset{I}{\underbrace{x^2}}\, \underset{II}{\underbrace{\sin x}}\, dx$

$$= \left|x^2(-\cos x)\right|_{\pi/4}^x - \int\limits_{\pi/4}^x 2x(-\cos x)\,dx$$

$$= -\left|x^2 \cos x - \frac{\pi^2}{16}\frac{1}{\sqrt{2}}\right| + 2\int\limits_{\pi/4}^x \underset{I}{\underbrace{x}}\, \underset{II}{\underbrace{\cos x}}\, dx$$

$$= -x^2 \cos x + \frac{\pi^2}{16\sqrt{2}} + 2\left\{\left|x \sin x\right|_{\pi/4}^x - \int\limits_{\pi/4}^x 1.\sin x\,dx\right\}$$

$$= -x^2 \cos x + \frac{\pi^2}{16\sqrt{2}} + 2\left\{x \sin x - \frac{\pi}{4}\frac{1}{\sqrt{2}} + \cos x - \frac{1}{\sqrt{2}}\right\}$$

$$= -x^2 \cos x + \frac{\pi^2}{16\sqrt{2}} + 2x \sin x - \frac{\pi}{2\sqrt{2}} + 2\cos x - \sqrt{2}$$

Thus, $g(x) = (2 - x^2)\cos x + 2x \sin x + \dfrac{\pi^2}{16\sqrt{2}} - \dfrac{\pi}{2\sqrt{2}} - \sqrt{2}$

$\Rightarrow g(-x) = (2 - (-x)^2)\cos(-x) + 2(-x)$

$\sin(-x) + \dfrac{\pi^2}{16\sqrt{2}} - \dfrac{\pi}{2\sqrt{2}} - \sqrt{2}$

$= (2 - x^2)\cos x + 2x \sin x + \dfrac{\pi^2}{16\sqrt{2}} - \dfrac{\pi}{2\sqrt{2}} - \sqrt{2} = g(x)$

Thus, $g(-x) = g(x)$

$\Rightarrow g(x)$ is an even function.

Property 18: If $f(x)$ is an even function of x, then $\int_a^x f(t)\,dt$ is an odd function of x iff $\int_0^a f(t)\,dt = 0$

Proof: Given $f(x)$ is an even function of x.

i.e., $f(-x) = f(x)$

Let $g(x) = \int_a^x f(t)\,dt$

$$\Rightarrow \quad g(-x) = \int_a^{-x} f(t)\,dt$$

$$\Rightarrow \quad g(x) + g(-x) = \int_a^x f(t)\,dt + \underset{\text{apply reflection property}}{\underbrace{\int_a^{-x} f(t)\,dt}}$$

$$= \int_a^x f(t)\,dt + \int_x^{-a} f(t)\,dt$$

$$= \int_a^{-a} f(t)\,dt = -2\int_0^a f(t)\,dt = 0 \text{ iff } \int_0^a f(t)\,dt = 0$$

$\therefore \quad g(-x) = -g(x)$, i.e., $g(x)$ is an odd function.

e.g., Let $f(x) = \cos x$ and $a = \pi$, then clearly $f(x)$ is an even function, and $\int\limits_0^a f(t)\,dt = \int\limits_0^\pi \cos t\,dt = [\sin t]_0^\pi = \sin \pi - \sin 0 = 0$

Now consider $g(x) = \int\limits_\pi^x \cos t\,dt = |\sin t|_\pi^x = \sin x - \sin \pi = \sin x$, which is clearly an odd function of x

Property 19: If $f(x)$ is a periodic function with period T. i.e., $f(x) = f(x + T)$, then following properties hold good.

- $\int\limits_0^{nT} f(x)\,dx = n\int\limits_0^T f(x)\,dx$; where n is a positive integer.

Proof: L.H.S. $= \int\limits_0^T f(x)\,dx + \int\limits_T^{2T} f(x)\,dx + \ldots +$

$$\int\limits_{kT}^{(k+1)T} f(x)\,dx + \ldots + \int\limits_{(n-1)T}^{nT} f(x)\,dx$$

$$= \sum_{k=0}^{n-1} \int\limits_{kT}^{(k+1)T} f(x)\,dx = \sum_{k=0}^{n-1} \int\limits_0^T f(x + kT)\,dx$$

$$= \sum_{k=0}^{n-1} \int\limits_0^T f(x)\,dx = n\int\limits_0^T f(x)\,dx$$

(Graphically)

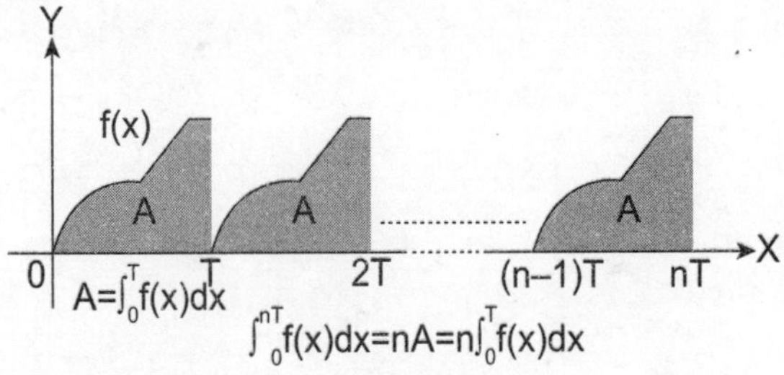

FIGURE 2.61

- $\int\limits_{mT}^{nT} f(x)\,dx = (n - m)\int\limits_0^T f(x)\,dx$; where $m, n \in \mathbb{Z}^+$.

Proof: L.H.S. $= \int_{mT}^0 f(x)\,dx + \int_0^{nT} f(x)\,dx$

$$= \int_0^{nT} f(x)\,dx - \int_0^{mT} f(x)\,dx = (n - m)\int_0^T f(x)\,dx$$

- $\int\limits_{a+nT}^{b+nT} f(x)\,dx = \int\limits_a^b f(x)\,dx$; where $m, n \in \mathbb{Z}^+$.

Proof: L.H.S. $= \int_a^b f(x + nT)\,dx = \int_a^b f(x)\,dx$

ILLUSTRATION 129: Evaluate the following integrals:

(i) $\int_0^{\frac{25}{6}\pi} |\cos x|\, dx$ (ii) $\int_{50\pi}^{100\pi} \frac{dx}{1+e^{-\cos x}}\, dx$

(iii) $\int_{50\pi}^{100\pi} \ln(2+x-[x])\, dx$ (iv) $\int_{2+3\pi}^{4+3\pi} |\sin^{-1}(\sin x)|\, dx$

SOLUTION: (i) Let $I = \int_0^{\frac{25}{6}\pi} |\cos x|\, dx$

Here $f(x) = |\cos x|$ which is periodic with period π

Now we can write $I = \int_0^{4\pi+(\pi/6)} |\cos x|\, dx = \int_0^{4\pi} |\cos x|\, dx + \int_{4\pi}^{4\pi+\pi/6} |\cos x|\, dx$

$= 4\int_0^{\pi} |\cos x|\, dx + \int_0^{\pi/6} |\cos x|\, dx$

$\left[\because \int_0^{n\pi} f(x)\,dx = n\int_0^{T} f(x)\,dx \text{ and } \int_{n\pi+a}^{n\pi+b} f(x)\,dx = \int_a^b f(x)\,dx\right]$

$= 4\int_0^{\pi/2} \cos x\, dx - 4\int_{\pi/2}^{\pi} \cos x\, dx + \int_0^{\pi/6} \cos x\, dx = 4|\sin x|_0^{\pi/2} - 4|\sin x|_{\pi/2}^{\pi} + |\sin x|_0^{\pi/6}$

$= 4 - 4(-1) + \left(\frac{1}{2}\right) = 8 + \frac{1}{2} = \frac{17}{2}$

(ii) Let $I = \int_{50\pi}^{100\pi} \frac{dx}{1+e^{-\cos x}}\, dx$

Here $f(x) = \frac{1}{1+e^{-\cos x}} = \frac{e^{\cos x}}{e^{\cos x}+1}$ and $f(2\pi+x) = \frac{e^{\cos(2\pi+x)}}{e^{\cos(2\pi+x)}+1} = \frac{e^{\cos x}}{e^{\cos x}+1} = f(x)$

$\Rightarrow f(x)$ is periodic with period $2\pi = T\,(say)$

$\therefore \quad I = \int_{25T}^{50T} f(x)\, dx = (50-25)\int_0^T f(x)\, dx$

$\because \quad \int_{mT}^{nT} f(x)\, dx = (n-m)\int_0^T f(x)\, dx; n,\ m \in \mathbb{Z}^+.$

$\therefore \quad I = 25\int_0^{2\pi} \frac{\cos x}{1+e^{\cos x}} dx = 50\int_0^{\pi} \frac{e^{\cos x}}{1+e^{\cos x}} dx$

Since $f(2a-x) = f(x)$, i.e., $f(2\pi - x) = f(x)$

$\therefore \quad I = 50\int_0^{\pi} \frac{e^{\cos x}}{1+e^{\cos x}} dx$ ...(1)

$\Rightarrow \quad I = 50\int_0^{\pi} \frac{e^{\cos(\pi-x)}}{1+e^{\cos(\pi-x)}} dx = 50\int_0^{\pi} \frac{e^{-\cos x}}{1+e^{-\cos x}} dx \Rightarrow I = 50\int_0^{\pi} \frac{1}{1+e^{\cos x}} dx$ ...(2)

Adding (1) and (2), we get $2I = 50\int_0^{\pi} \frac{1+e^{\cos x}}{1+e^{\cos x}} dx = 50\int_0^{\pi} 1.dx = 50\pi \Rightarrow I = 25\pi$

(iii) Let $I = \int_0^{1000} \ln(2+x-[x])\, dx = \int_0^{1000} \ln(2+\{x\})\, dx$

But $\{x\}$ is periodic with period 1

$$\therefore \quad I = 1000\int_0^1 \ln(2+\{x\})\,dx \qquad \left(\because \int_0^{nT} f(x)\,dx = n\int_0^T f(x)\,dx\right)$$

$$= 1000\int_0^1 \ln 2\, dx = (\ln 2)(1000) \qquad (\because \{x\} = 0 \text{ for } x \in (0, 1))$$

(iv) Let $I = \int_{2+3\pi}^{4+3\pi} |\sin^{-1}(\sin x)|\,dx$

Here $f(x) = |\sin^{-1}(\sin x)|$ is a periodic function with period π.

$$\therefore \quad I = \int_2^4 |\sin^{-1}(\sin x)|\,dx \text{ as } \int_{a+nT}^{b+nT} f(x)\,dx = \int_a^b f(x)\,dx \text{ for } n \in \mathbb{N}$$

From the graph of $\sin^{-1}(\sin x)$ given below

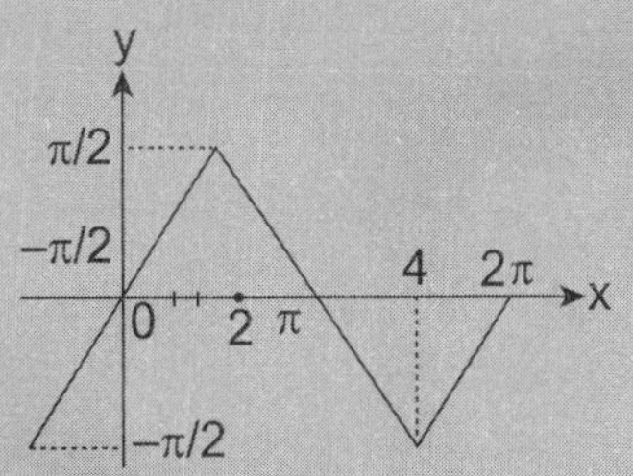

FIGURE 2.62

We have graph of $|\sin^{-1}(\sin x)|$ as

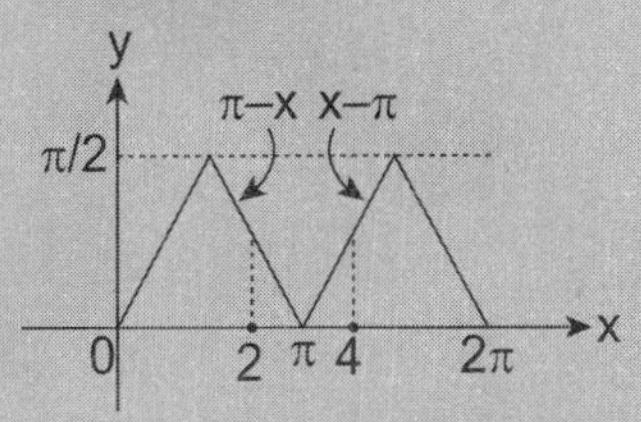

FIGURE 2.63

$$\therefore \quad I = \int_2^{\pi} |\sin^{-1}(\sin x)|\,dx + \int_{\pi}^4 |\sin^{-1}(\sin x)|\,dx = \int_2^{\pi}(\pi - x)\,dx + \int_{\pi}^4 (x-\pi)\,dx$$

$$= \pi(\pi-2) - \left(\frac{\pi^2}{2} - 2\right) + \left(8 - \frac{\pi^2}{2}\right) - \pi(4-\pi)$$

$$= \pi^2 - 2\pi - \frac{\pi^2}{2} + 2 + 8 - \frac{\pi^2}{2} - 4\pi + \pi^2 = (\pi^2 - 6\pi + 10)$$

Property 20: If $f(x)$ is a periodic function with period T, then $\int_a^{a+T} f(x)\,dx$ is independent of a. Hence prove that $\int_a^{a+T} f(x)\,dx = \int_0^T f(x)\,dx.$

Proof: Let $\phi(a) = \int_a^{a+T} f(x)\,dx$, then

$$\Rightarrow \quad \frac{d\phi(a)}{da} = \frac{d(a+T)}{da}.f(a+T) - \frac{d(a)}{da} f(a)$$

$= f(a+T) - f(a) = 0$

Since f is periodic with period T.

Thus, $\frac{d(\phi(a))}{da} = 0$

$\Rightarrow$ $\phi(a)$ is independent of a

Now, replacing a by 0, we have $\int_a^{a+T} f(x)\,dx = \int_0^T f(x)\,dx$

Aliter: $\int_a^{a+T} f(x)dx = \int_a^0 f(x)dx + \int_0^T f(x)dx + \int_T^{a+T} f(x)dx$

$$= \int_a^0 f(x)dx + \int_0^T f(x)dx + \int_0^a f(x)dx$$

as $\int_{a+nT}^{b+nT} f(x)dx = \int_a^b f(x)dx$

$$= -\int_0^a f(x)dx + \int_0^T f(x)dx + \int_0^a f(x)dx = \int_0^T f(x)dx$$

Corollary:

$\int_a^{a+nT} f(x)\,dx = n\int_0^T f(x)\,dx$; Where $n \in \mathbb{Z}^+$.

(Graphically)

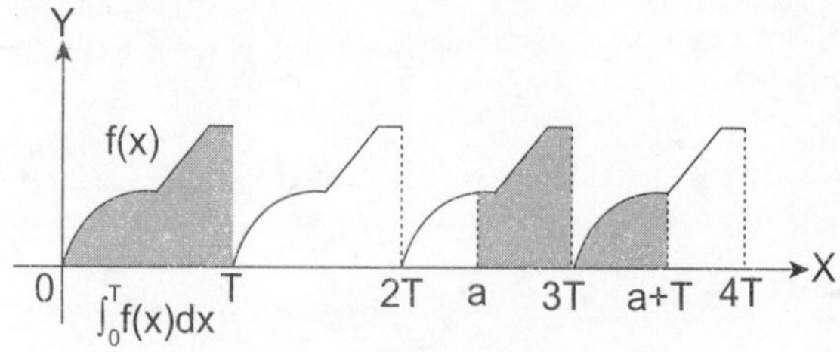

FIGURE 2.64

ILLUSTRATION 130: Evaluate $\int_{-1}^{2} e^{\{x\}} dx$

SOLUTION: $\int_{-1}^{2} e^{\{x\}}dx = \int_{-1}^{-1+3} e^{\{x\}}dx = 3\int_0^1 e^{\{x\}}dx = 3\int_0^1 e^x dx = 3(e-1)$ $\quad (\because \{x\} = x \text{ for } x \in (0, 1))$

ILLUSTRATION 131: Evaluate the following integrals:

(i) $\int_2^{2+\pi}\left(|\sin x| + \cos 2x + \left\{\frac{x}{\pi}\right\}\right)dx$; where | | and { } denotes modulus and fractional part functions, respectively

(ii) $\int_1^{1+\pi/2}\left\{|\sin x| + |\cos x| - \left[|\cos x| + \left[\frac{2x}{\pi}\right]\right] + \left(\frac{2x}{\pi}\right)\right\}dx$; where |.| and [.] denotes modulus and gint functions, respectively.

SOLUTION: (i) $\int_2^{2+\pi}\left(|\sin x| + \cos 2x + \left\{\frac{x}{\pi}\right\}\right)dx$

Clearly $|\sin x|$ is periodic with period π

$\cos 2x$ is periodic with period $\frac{2\pi}{2} = \pi$

Also $\left\{\frac{x}{\pi}\right\}$ is period with period $\frac{1}{1/\pi} = \pi$

so $|\sin x| + \cos 2x + \{x/\pi\}$ is periodic with period π (L.C.M.)

$\therefore$ $T = \pi$ for integrand. Thus, by property $\int_a^{a+T} f(x)\,dx = \int_0^T f(x)\,dx$,

$$I = \int_0^\pi\left(|\sin x| + \cos 2x + \left\{\frac{x}{\pi}\right\}\right)dx = \int_0^\pi\left(|\sin x| + \cos 2x + \frac{x}{\pi}\right)dx$$

$$= \int_0^\pi\left(\sin x + \cos 2x + \frac{x}{\pi}\right)dx \qquad \left(\because 0 < x < \pi \Rightarrow 0 < \frac{x}{\pi} < 1 \Rightarrow \left\{\frac{x}{\pi}\right\} = \frac{x}{\pi}\right)$$

$$= \left|-\cos x + \frac{\sin 2x}{2} + \frac{x^2}{2\pi}\right|_0^\pi = \left[-(-1-1) + \frac{1}{2}(0-0) + \frac{1}{2\pi}(\pi^2 - 0)\right] = \frac{\pi}{2} + 2$$

(ii) Let $I = \int_1^{1+\pi/2}\left\{|\sin x| + |\cos x| - \left[|\cos x| + \left[\frac{2x}{\pi}\right]\right] + \left(\frac{2x}{\pi}\right)\right\}dx$

By property $[x + m] = [x] + m$ for every $x \in \mathbb{R}$ and $m \in \mathbb{Z}$ we have

$$\left[|\cos x| + \left[\frac{2x}{\pi}\right]\right] = [|\cos x|] + \left[\frac{2x}{\pi}\right]$$

$\therefore\quad I = \int_1^{1+\pi/2}\left(|\sin x| + |\cos x| - [|\cos x|] - \left[\frac{2x}{\pi}\right] + \frac{2x}{\pi}\right)dx$

Now for $x \in \left(1, 1+\frac{\pi}{2}\right), |\cos x| \in [0, 1) \quad \Rightarrow [|\cos x|] = 0$

$\therefore\quad I = \int_1^{1+\pi/2}\left(|\sin x| + |\cos x| - \left[\frac{2x}{\pi}\right] + \frac{2x}{\pi}\right)dx = \int_1^{1+\pi/2}\left(|\sin x| + |\cos x| + \left(\frac{2x}{\pi} - \left[\frac{2x}{\pi}\right]\right)\right)dx$

$= \int_1^{1+\pi/2}\left(|\sin x| + |\cos x| + \left\{\frac{2x}{\pi}\right\}\right)dx$

Now $|\sin x| + |\cos x|$ is periodic a function with period $\pi/2$ and $\left\{\frac{2x}{\pi}\right\}$ is periodic with period $\frac{1}{(2/\pi)} = \frac{\pi}{2}$

Thus, integrand is periodic function with period $\frac{\pi}{2}$ (L.C.M.)

Therefore, by property $\int_a^{a+T} f(x)\,dx = \int_0^T f(x)\,dx$, we have

$I = \int_0^{\pi/2}\left(|\sin x| + |\cos x| + \left\{\frac{2x}{\pi}\right\}\right)dx$

Now $\sin x$, $\cos x \ge 0$ for $x \in \left[0, \frac{\pi}{2}\right]$

$\Rightarrow\quad |\sin x| = \sin x$ and $|\cos x| = \cos x$

Also $0 < x < \frac{\pi}{2}$

$\Rightarrow\quad 0 < 2x < \pi$

$\Rightarrow\quad 0 < \frac{2x}{\pi} < 1 \qquad\qquad \Rightarrow \left\{\frac{2x}{\pi}\right\} = \frac{2x}{\pi}$

Thus, $I = \int_0^{\pi/2}\left(\sin x + \cos x + \frac{2x}{\pi}\right)dx = -|\cos x|_0^{\pi/2} + |\sin x|_0^{\pi/2} + \frac{2}{\pi}\left|\frac{x^2}{2}\right|_0^{\pi/2}$

$= -(0-1) + (1-0) + \frac{1}{\pi}\left(\frac{\pi^2}{4} - 0\right) = 1 + 1 + \frac{\pi}{4} = 2 + \frac{\pi}{4}$

ILLUSTRATION 132: Find the value of the definite integral $I = \int_0^{\pi} |\sqrt{2}\sin x + 2\cos x|\,dx$

SOLUTION: Let $I = \int_0^{\pi} |\sqrt{2}\sin x + 2\cos x|\,dx = \sqrt{6}\int_0^{\pi}\left|\frac{1}{\sqrt{3}}\sin x + \frac{\sqrt{2}}{\sqrt{3}}\cos x\right|dx$

$= \sqrt{6}\int_0^{\pi} |\sin(x+\alpha)|\,dx$ where $\sin\alpha = \frac{\sqrt{2}}{\sqrt{3}}$ and $\cos\alpha = \frac{1}{\sqrt{3}}$

let $x + \alpha = t$ and $\tan\alpha = \sqrt{2}$

$\Rightarrow\quad \alpha = \tan^{-1}\sqrt{2}$

$\therefore\quad I = \sqrt{6}\int_{\alpha}^{\pi+\alpha} |\sin t|\,dt = \sqrt{6}\left[\int_{\alpha}^{0}|\sin t|\,dt + \int_0^{\pi}|\sin t|\,dt + \int_{\pi}^{\pi+\alpha}|\sin t|\,dt\right]$

$= \sqrt{6}\left[-\int_0^{\alpha}|\sin t|\,dt + \int_0^{\pi}\sin t\,dt + \int_0^{\alpha}|\sin t|\,dt\right]$

$= \sqrt{6}\left[\int_0^{\pi}\sin t\,dt\right] = \sqrt{6}[-\cos t]_0^{\pi} = -\sqrt{6}(-1-1) = 2\sqrt{6}$

ILLUSTRATION 133: Let $I_1 = \int_{k\pi}^{(k+2)\pi} \frac{|\sin 2x|}{|\sin x| + |\cos x|} dx$; $k \in \mathbb{N}$ and $I_2 = \int_0^{\pi/4} \frac{dx}{\sin x + \cos x} dx$, then prove that $I_1 = 4\int_0^{\pi/2} \frac{\sin 2x}{\sin x + \cos x} dx$ and $I_1 = 8 - 8I_2$

SOLUTION: Given $I_1 = \int_{k\pi}^{(k+2)\pi} \frac{|\sin 2x|}{|\sin x| + |\cos x|} dx$; $k \in \mathbb{N}$

Since $f(x)$ is periodic function, with period $\frac{\pi}{2} = T$ (say)

Thus, $I_1 = \int_{2kT}^{(k+2)(2T)} \frac{|\sin 2x|}{|\sin x| + |\cos x|} dx = \int_{2kT}^{(2k+4)T} \frac{|\sin 2x|}{|\sin x| + |\cos x|} dx$

$= (2k + 4 - 2k)\int_0^T \frac{|\sin 2x|}{|\sin x| + |\cos x|} dx$ as $\int_{mT}^{nT} f(x)\,dx = (n-m)\int_0^T f(x)\,dx$

$\therefore \quad I_1 = 4\int_0^{\pi/2} \frac{|\sin 2x|}{|\sin x| + |\cos x|} dx = 4\int_0^{\pi/2} \frac{\sin 2x}{\sin x + \cos x} dx$; this proves first part

$= 4\int_0^{\pi/2} \frac{(\sin x + \cos x)^2 - 1}{(\sin x + \cos x)} dx = 4\int_0^{\pi/2} (\sin x + \cos x)\,dx - 4\int_0^{\pi/2} \frac{1}{\sin x + \cos x} dx$

$= 4\left|-\cos x + \sin x\right|_0^{\pi/2} - 8\int_0^{\pi/4} \frac{1}{\sin x + \cos x} dx$

(By using property $\int_0^{2a} f(x)\,dx = 2\int_0^a f(x)\,dx$ if $f(2a - x) = f(x)$]

$= 4|-(0 - 1) + (1 - 0)| - 8I_2 = 8 - 8I_2$

Thus, $I_1 = 8 - 8I_2$.

ILLUSTRATION 134: Evaluate $\int_{-\pi/6}^{19\pi/4} \sqrt{|\tan^{-1}(\tan x)|}\, dx$

SOLUTION: Let us draw the graph of $y = \tan^{-1}(\tan x)$ and $y = |\tan^{-1}(\tan x)|$ as shown below $y = \tan^{-1}(\tan x)$

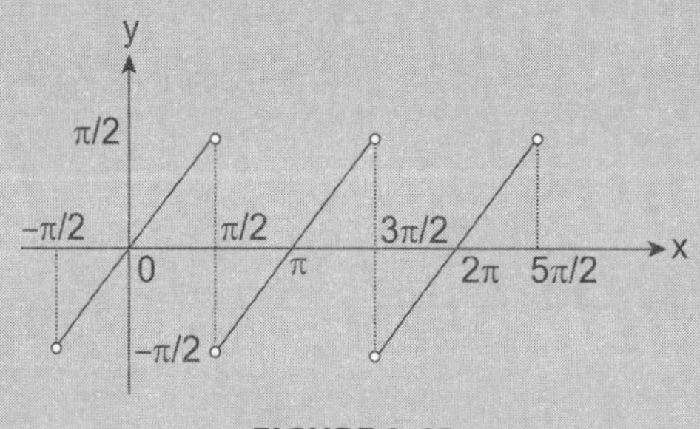

FIGURE 2.65

$y = |\tan^{-1}(\tan x)|$

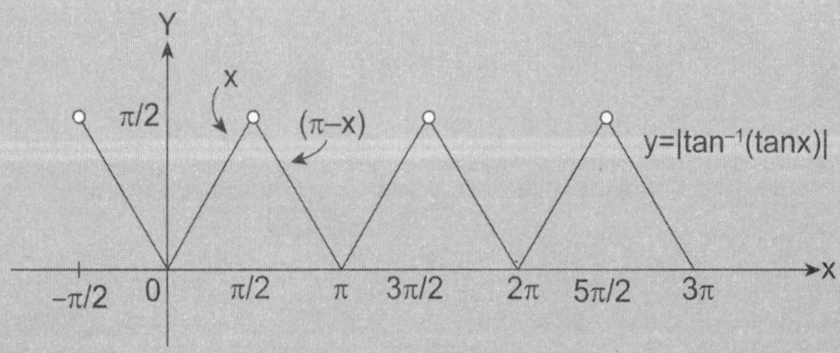

FIGURE 2.66

Clearly $y = |\tan^{-1}(\tan x)|$ is periodic with period π

$$\therefore \quad y = \int_{-\pi/6}^{19\pi/4} \sqrt{|\tan^{-1}(\tan x)|}\, dx$$

$$= \int_{-\pi/6}^{0} \sqrt{|\tan^{-1}(\tan x)|}\, dx + \int_{0}^{4\pi} \sqrt{|\tan^{-1}(\tan x)|}\, dx + \int_{4\pi}^{4\pi+\frac{3\pi}{4}} \sqrt{|\tan^{-1}(\tan x)|}\, dx$$

$$= \int_{-\pi/6}^{0} \sqrt{|x|}\, dx + 4\int_{0}^{\pi} \sqrt{|\tan^{-1}(\tan x)|}\, dx + \int_{0}^{\frac{3\pi}{4}} \sqrt{|\tan^{-1}(\tan x)|}\, dx$$

$$= \left[\frac{2}{3}\frac{(-x)^{3/2}}{-1}\right]_{-\pi/6}^{0} + 4\left[\int_{0}^{\pi/2} \sqrt{x}\, dx + \int_{\pi/2}^{\pi} \sqrt{(\pi - x)}\, dx\right] + \int_{0}^{\pi/2} \sqrt{x}\, dx + \int_{\pi/2}^{3\pi/4} \sqrt{\pi - x}\, dx$$

$$= -\frac{2}{3}\left[0 - \left(\frac{\pi}{6}\right)^{3/2}\right] + 4\left[\frac{2}{3}(x)^{3/2}\right]_{0}^{\pi/2} + \left[\frac{2}{3}\frac{(\pi - x)^{3/2}}{-1}\right]_{\pi/2}^{\pi} + \left[\frac{2}{3}(x)^{3/2}\right]_{0}^{\pi/4} + \left[\frac{2}{3}\frac{(\pi - x)^{3/2}}{-1}\right]_{\pi/2}^{3\pi/4}$$

$$= \frac{2}{3}\left(\frac{\pi}{6}\right)^{3/2} + \frac{8}{3}\left[\left(\frac{\pi}{2}\right)^{3/2}\right] - \frac{2}{3}\left[0 - \left(\frac{\pi}{2}\right)^{3/2}\right] + \frac{2}{3}\left[\left(\frac{\pi}{2}\right)^{3/2}\right] - \frac{2}{3}\left[\left(\frac{\pi}{4}\right)^{3/2} - \left(\frac{\pi}{2}\right)^{3/2}\right]$$

$$= \left(\pi^{3/2}\right)\left[\frac{2}{3}.\frac{1}{(6)^{3/2}} + \frac{8}{3\left(2\sqrt{2}\right)} + \frac{2}{3\left(2\sqrt{2}\right)} + \frac{2}{3}\frac{(3)^{3/2}}{2\sqrt{2}} - \frac{2}{3(8)} + \frac{2}{3}.\frac{1}{2\sqrt{2}}\right]$$

$$= \left(\pi^{3/2}\right)\left[\frac{2}{3\left(6\sqrt{6}\right)} + \frac{4}{3\sqrt{2}} + \frac{1}{3\sqrt{2}} + \frac{\sqrt{3}}{\sqrt{2}} - \frac{1}{12} + \frac{1}{3\sqrt{2}}\right] = \pi^{3/2}\left[\frac{1}{9\sqrt{6}} + \sqrt{2} + \frac{\sqrt{3}}{2} - \frac{1}{12}\right]$$

ILLUSTRATION 135: Evaluate $\int_{0}^{50\pi} [\sin x + \cos x]\, dx$; where [.] denotes greatest integer function.

SOLUTION: Here $[\sin x + \cos x] = \left[\sqrt{2}\sin\left(x + \frac{\pi}{4}\right)\right]$

Let us draw the graph of $y = \sqrt{2}\sin\left(x + \frac{\pi}{4}\right)$ in figure 2.67

Now $[\sin x + \cos x] = \left[\sqrt{2}\sin\left(x + \frac{\pi}{4}\right)\right]$

$$= \begin{cases} 1 & \text{for} \quad x \in \left[0, \frac{\pi}{2}\right] \\ 0 & \text{for} \quad x \in \left(\frac{\pi}{2}, \frac{3\pi}{4}\right] \\ -1 & \text{for} \quad x \in \left(\frac{3\pi}{4}, \pi\right] \\ -2 & \text{for} \quad x \in \left(\pi, \frac{3\pi}{2}\right) \\ -1 & \text{for} \quad x \in \left[\frac{3\pi}{2}, \frac{7\pi}{4}\right) \\ 0 & \text{for} \quad x \in \left[\frac{7\pi}{4}, 2\pi\right) \end{cases}$$

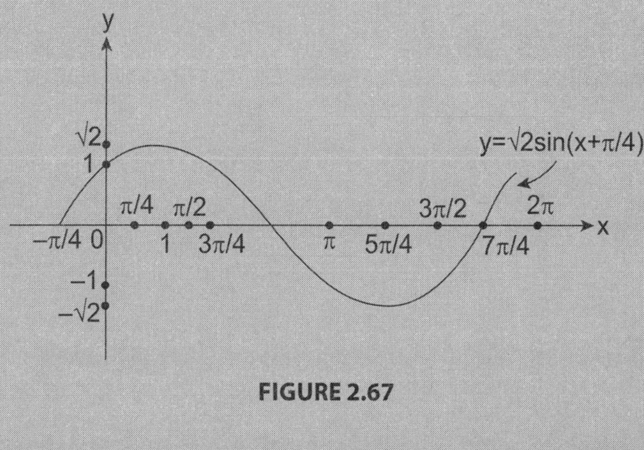

FIGURE 2.67

Also $\left[\sqrt{2}\sin\left(x+\frac{\pi}{4}\right)\right]$ is periodic function with period $2\pi = T\,(say)$

So $\int_0^{50\pi}[\sin x+\cos x]dx = \int_0^{25T}[\sin x+\cos x]dx = 25\int_0^{T}[\sin x+\cos x]dx$

$= 25\int_0^{2\pi}\left[\sqrt{2}\sin\left(x+\frac{\pi}{4}\right)\right]dx$

$= 25\left\{\int_0^{\pi/2}1\,dx+\int_{\pi/2}^{3\pi/4}0\,dx+\int_{3\pi/4}^{\pi}(-1)\,dx+\int_{\pi}^{3\pi/2}(-2)\,dx+\int_{3\pi/2}^{7\pi/4}(-1)\,dx+\int_{7\pi/4}^{2\pi}(0)\,dx\right\}$

$= 25\left\{\left(\frac{\pi}{2}-0\right)+0-\left(\pi-\frac{3\pi}{4}\right)-2\left(\frac{3\pi}{2}-\pi\right)-\left(\frac{7\pi}{4}-\frac{3\pi}{2}\right)+0\right\}$

$= 25\left\{\frac{\pi}{2}-\frac{\pi}{4}-\pi-\frac{\pi}{4}\right\} = 25\{-\pi\} = -25\pi$

ILLUSTRATION 136: Evaluate $\dfrac{\int_0^n [x+1]\,dx}{\int_0^n \{x+1\}\,dx}$; where [ ] and { } denotes gint and fractional part functions repectively.

SOLUTION: $\int_0^n [x+1]dx = \int_0^n ([x]+1)\,dx = |x|_0^n + \int_0^n [x]dx$

$= n+\int_0^1 0\,dx+\int_1^2 1\,dx+\int_2^3 2\,dx+\int_3^4 3\,dx+...+\int_{(n-1)}^{n}(n-1)\,dx$

$= n + 0 + (2-1) + 2(3-2) + 3(4-3) + ... + (n-1)\,(n-(n-1))$

$= n+1+2+3+...+(n-1) = 1+2+3+...+n = \frac{n(n+1)}{2}$

Also $\int_0^n \{x+1\}\,dx = \int_0^n \{x\}\,dx$ as $\{x + m\} = \{x\}\ \forall\ m \in \mathbb{Z}$

$= n\int_0^1\{x\}.dx$ as $\{x\}$ is a periodic function with period 1. $= n\int_0^1 x\,dx = \frac{n}{2}\left[x^2\right]_0^1 = \frac{n}{2}(1-0) = \frac{n}{2}$

$\therefore\ \dfrac{\int_0^n [x+1]dx}{\int_0^n \{x+1\}dx} = \dfrac{n(n+1)/2}{n/2} = (n+1)$

ILLUSTRATION 137: Evaluate $\left|\int_0^{10}\frac{\sin^{-1}([x]-x)}{\sqrt{1-([x]-x)^2}}dx\right|$

SOLUTION: Let $I = \int_0^{10}\frac{\sin^{-1}([x]-x)}{\sqrt{1-([x]-x)^2}}dx$

Since $\sin^{-1}(-x) = -\sin^{-1}x$, $\sin^{-1}([x]-x) = -\sin^{-1}(x-[x]) = -\sin^{-1}\{x\}$

$$\Rightarrow \quad I = -\int_0^{10} \frac{\sin^{-1}\{x\}}{\sqrt{1-(\{x\})^2}}\,dx$$

Now integrand is always defined as $\{x\} \in [0, 1)$ and also integrand is a periodic function with period 1.

$$\therefore \quad I = -(10)\int_0^1 \frac{\sin^{-1}\{x\}}{\sqrt{1-\{x\}^2}}\,dx = -(10)\int_0^1 \frac{\sin^{-1} x}{\sqrt{1-x^2}}\,dx = -10\int_0^{\pi/2} t\ dx = -10\left[\frac{\pi}{2}\right] = -5\pi$$

Thus, $|I| = 5\pi$.

ILLUSTRATION 138: Show that $\int_0^{2\pi} \sqrt[2m]{t+\sin^{2k-1} x}\ dx = \int_0^{2\pi} \sqrt[2m]{t+\cos^{2k-1} x}\ dx$, where $m, k \in \mathbb{N}$ and $t \ge 1$

SOLUTION: Let $I = \int_0^{2\pi} \sqrt[2m]{t+\sin^{2k-1} x}\ dx = \int_0^{2\pi} \sqrt[2m]{t+\cos^{2k-1}\left(\frac{\pi}{2}-x\right)}\ dx$

Let us put $\frac{\pi}{2} - x = z \qquad \Rightarrow dx = -dz$

When $x = 0$, $z = \pi/2$ and when $x = 2\pi$, $z = -3\pi/2$

$$\therefore \quad I = \int_{\pi/2}^{-3\pi/2} \sqrt[2m]{t+\cos^{2k-1}(z)}\ (-dz) = \int_{-3\pi/2}^{\pi/2} \sqrt[2m]{t+\cos^{2k-1}(z)}\ dz$$

Now $\sqrt[2m]{t+\cos^{2k-1}(z)}$ is a periodic function with period 2π.

we have, $I = \int_{-3\pi/2}^{-\frac{3\pi}{2}+2\pi} \sqrt[2m]{t+\cos^{2k-1}(z)}\,dz$

Since $\int_a^{a+T} f(x)\,dx = \int_0^T f(x)\,dx$

Thus, $I = \int_0^{2\pi} \sqrt[2m]{t+\cos^{2k-1} z}\ dz; t \ge 1$. Hence the result

Remark 1: If $m = 1, k = 1, t = 1$, we have $\int_0^{2\pi} \sqrt{1+\cos x}\ dx = \int_0^{2\pi} \sqrt{1+\sin x}\ dx$

If $m = 1, k = 2, t = 1$, we have $\int_0^{2\pi} \sqrt{1+\cos^3 x}\ dx = \int_0^{2\pi} \sqrt{1+\sin^3 x}\ dx$

If $m = 2, k = 3, t = 2$, we have $\int_0^{2\pi} \sqrt[6]{2+\cos^5 x}\ dx = \int_0^{2\pi} \sqrt[6]{2+\sin^5 x}\ dx$ and so on.

Remark 2: On the same steps, it can be proved that $\int_0^{\pi} \sqrt[n]{t+\sin^{2k} x}\ dx = \int_0^{\pi} \sqrt[n]{t+\cos^{2k} x}\ dx$;

where $n \in \mathbb{N}$; $k \in W$ (set of whole numbers) and t is any non-negative real number.

ILLUSTRATION 139: Prove that $\int_0^{2\pi} f(\sin nx)\,dx = \int_0^{2\pi} f(\cos nx)\,dx$; where $n \in \mathbb{N}$ and f is a continuous function defined on $[-1, 1]$.

SOLUTION: Let us consider $I = \int_0^{2\pi} f(\sin nx)\,dx \qquad \ldots(1)$

Clearly $f(\sin nx)$ and $f(\cos nx)$ are well defined as $\sin x, \cos x \in [-1, 1]$ and f is continuous on $[-1, 1]$.

Now $I = \int_0^{2\pi} f\left(\cos\left(\frac{\pi}{2} - nx\right)\right) dx$

Put $\frac{\pi}{2} - nx = nt$

$\Rightarrow -n\,dx = n\,dt \qquad \Rightarrow dx = -dt$

Thus, when, $x = 0$, $t = \pi/2n$ and when $x = 2\pi, t = \frac{\pi}{2n} - 2\pi$

$\therefore \quad I = \int_{\pi/2n}^{\frac{\pi}{2n}-2\pi} f(\cos nt)(-dt) = \int_{\frac{\pi}{2n}-2\pi}^{\pi/2n} f(\cos nt)(dt)$

Now cos nt is periodic with period $\frac{2\pi}{n} = T$ (*say*)

$\therefore \quad I = \int_{-2\pi+T}^{T} f(\cos nt)\,dt = \int_{-2\pi}^{0} f(\cos nt)\,dt$

Since $\int_{a+nT}^{b+nT} f(x)\,dx = \int_a^b f(x)\,dx$

$\therefore \quad I = \int_0^{2\pi} f(\cos n(-t))\,dt$ (by reflection property)

or $I = \int_0^{2\pi} f(\cos nt)\,dt = \int_0^{2\pi} f(\cos nx)\,dx$. Hence the proof.

ILLUSTRATION 140: Using the result $\int_0^{2\pi} f(\sin nx)\,dx = \int_0^{2\pi} f(\cos nx)\,dx$, $n \in \mathbb{N}$ and f continuous on [–1, 1] other-wise evaluate $\int_0^{2\pi} \cos^2(2013x)\,dx$

SOLUTION: Here $f(x) = x^2$; which is continuous and defined on [–1, 1]

Now $\int_0^{2\pi} \cos^2(2013x)\,dx = I$ (say), then by above result $\int_0^{2\pi} \sin^2(2013x)\,dx = I$

$\therefore \quad 2I = \int_0^{2\pi} \left[\cos^2(2013x) + \sin^2(2013x)\right] dx$

$\therefore \quad 2I = \int_0^{2\pi} 1\,dx = 2\pi \qquad \Rightarrow I = \pi$

Thus, $\int_0^{2\pi} \cos^2(2013x)\,dx = \pi$ otherwise $\int_0^{2\pi} \cos^2(2013x)\,dx = \frac{1}{2}\int_0^{2\pi} [1 + \cos(4026)x]\,dx$

$= \frac{1}{2}\left[x + \frac{\sin(4026)x}{4026}\right]_0^{2\pi} = \frac{1}{2}[2\pi - 0] + \frac{1}{8052}[\sin 2\pi(4026) - \sin 0] = \pi + 0 = \pi.$

ILLUSTRATION 141: Evaluate $I = \int_0^{2n\pi} f(x)\,dx$ such that $f(x) = \min\{\sin^{-1}(\sin x), \sin x\}$.

SOLUTION: Since the period of $\sin^{-1}(\sin x)$ and $\sin x$ both is 2π, so period of $f(x)$ is also 2π.

$\therefore$ Our problem reduces to find $I = n\int_0^{2\pi} f(x)\,dx$ ...(1)

Let us draw the graph of $y = \sin^{-1}(\sin x)$ and $y = \sin x$ on same $x - y$ plane for $x \in [0, 2\pi]$ as shown below

Thus, $f(x) = \min \{\sin^{-1}(\sin x), \sin x\}$

$$= \begin{cases} \sin x; & \text{for } x \in [0, \pi] \\ \sin^{-1}(\sin x); & \text{for } x \in (\pi, 2\pi] \end{cases}$$

$$= \begin{cases} \sin x; & \text{for } x \in [0, \pi] \\ \pi - x & \text{for } x \in \left(\pi, \frac{3\pi}{2}\right] \\ x - 2\pi; & \text{for } x \in \left(\frac{3\pi}{2}, \pi\right] \end{cases}$$

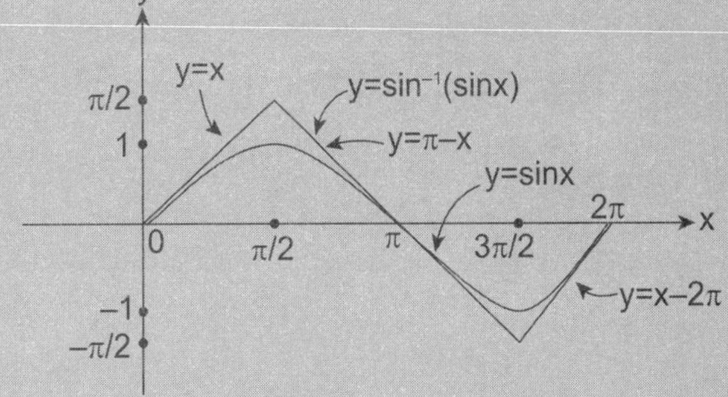

FIGURE 2.68

$$\therefore \quad I = n\int_0^{2\pi} f(x)dx = n\left[\int_0^{\pi} \sin x\, dx + \int_{\pi}^{3\pi/2} (\pi - x)\, dx + \int_{3\pi/2}^{2\pi} (x - 2\pi)\, dx\right]$$

$$= n\left[-[\cos x]_0^{\pi} + \pi[x]_{\pi}^{3\pi/2} - \frac{1}{2}\left[x^2\right]_{\pi}^{3\pi/2} + \frac{1}{2}\left[x^2\right]_{3\pi/2}^{2\pi} - 2\pi\left(2\pi - \frac{3\pi}{2}\right)\right]$$

$$= n\left[2 + \pi\left(\frac{\pi}{2}\right) - \frac{1}{2}\left[\frac{9}{4} - 1\right]\pi^2 + \frac{1}{2}\left[4 - \frac{9}{4}\right]\pi^2 - 2\pi\left(\frac{\pi}{2}\right)\right]$$

$$= n\left[2 + \frac{\pi^2}{2} - \frac{5}{8}\pi^2 + \frac{7}{8}\pi^2 - \pi^2\right] = n\left[2 + \left(-\frac{1}{4}\right)\pi^2\right] = 2n - \frac{\pi^2 n}{4} = \frac{n(8-\pi^2)}{4} = -\frac{(\pi^2 - 8)n}{4}$$

ILLUSTRATION 142: In the illustration, we evaluated $I = \int_0^{2n\pi} f(x)\, dx$; where $f(x) = \min\{\sin x, \sin^{-1}(\sin x)\}$. We found $I = \frac{-n(\pi^2 - 8)}{4}$

Now if $g(x)$ is a function defined by $g(x) = \max. \{\sin x, \sin^{-1}(\sin x)\}$. Then evaluate $\int_0^{2n\pi} g(x)\, dx$ without actually integrating.

SOLUTION: Since $\sin x$, $\sin^{-1}(\sin x)$ both are periodic functions with period $2\pi = T$ (say), $f(x)$ and $g(x)$ both are periodic with period 2π. Thus, our problem reduces to find $n\int_0^{2\pi} g(x)\, dx$.

The graph of $y = \sin x$ and $y = \sin^{-1}(\sin x)$ drawn on same Cartesian plane is shown below

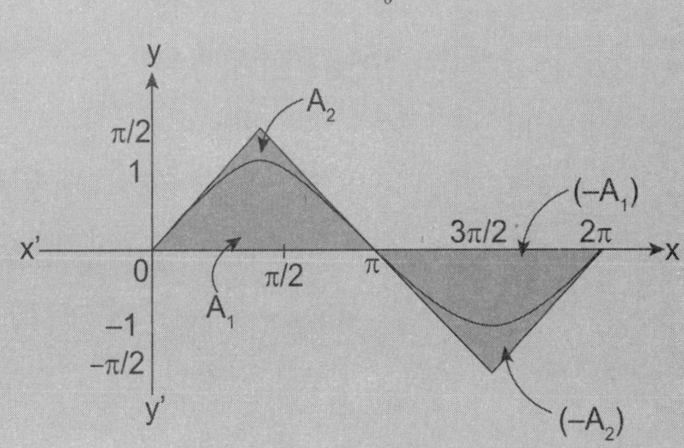

FIGURE 2.69

Now

$$\int_0^{2\pi} f(x)\, dx = \int_0^{\pi} f(x)\, dx + \int_{\pi}^{2\pi} f(x)\, dx$$

= (Area represented by horizontal lines in $[0, 2\pi]$) $= A_1 + (-A_2)$

and $\int_0^{2\pi} g(x)\, dx = \int_0^{\pi} g(x)\, dx + \int_{\pi}^{2\pi} g(x)\, dx$

= (Area represented by vertical lines in $[0\ 2\pi]$)

$= (A_2) + (-A_1) = -[A_1 + (-A_2)]$

$$\Rightarrow \int_0^{2\pi} g(x)\,dx = -\int_0^{2\pi} f(x)\,dx$$

$$\Rightarrow n\int_0^{2\pi} g(x)\,dx = -n\int_0^{2\pi} f(x)\,dx = -\int_0^{2n\pi} f(x)\,dx = \frac{n(\pi^2-8)}{4}$$

Thus, $\displaystyle\int_0^{2n\pi} g(x)\,dx = \frac{n(\pi^2-8)}{4}$

In the above problem A_1 is the area bounded by $y = \sin x$, x-axis and in the interval $[0, \pi]$ and A_2 is the area bounded by $y = \sin^{-1}(\sin x)$, x-axis and in the interval $[0, \pi]$.

$-A_1$ and $-A_2$ are the areas bounded by $y = \sin x$ and $y = \sin^{-1}(\sin x)$, respectively, with x-axis and in the interval $[\pi, 2\pi]$. Their magnitudes are negative, as they are bounded by the functions below x-axis.

ILLUSTRATION 143: Let $g(x) = \displaystyle\int_x^{x+\lambda} f(t)\,dt$ be independent of x; $\lambda, n \in \mathbb{N}$. Further consider $I_1 = \displaystyle\int_{20}^{20+n\lambda} f(z)\,dz$ and $I_2 = \displaystyle\int_{100}^{100+\lambda^n} f(z)\,dz$, then

(i) Show that $f(x)$ is periodic and hence find its period.

(ii) Evaluate I_1/I_2.

SOLUTION: (i) Given $g(x) = \displaystyle\int_x^{x+\lambda} f(t)\,dt$ is independent of x

$\Rightarrow g'(x) = 0$ $\qquad \Rightarrow f(x+\lambda) - f(x) = 0$

$\Rightarrow f(x+\lambda) = f(x)$ $\qquad \Rightarrow f(x)$ is a periodic function with period λ.

(ii) Now $I_1 = \displaystyle\int_{20}^{20+n\lambda} f(z)\,dz = \int_0^{n\lambda} f(z)\,dz$ as $\displaystyle\int_a^{a+nT} f(x)\,dx = \int_0^{nT} f(x)\,dx$

$\Rightarrow I_1 = n\displaystyle\int_0^{\lambda} f(z)\,dz$ as $\displaystyle\int_0^{nT} f(x)\,dx = n\int_0^{T} f(x)\,dx$

Then $I_1 = n\displaystyle\int_0^{\lambda} f(z)\,dz$ ...(1)

Further $I_2 = \displaystyle\int_{100}^{100+\lambda^n} f(z)\,dz = \int_0^{\lambda^n} f(z)\,dz = \int_0^{(\lambda^{n-1})\lambda} f(z)\,dz = \lambda^{n-1}\int_0^{\lambda} f(z)\,dz$

Since $\lambda, n \in \mathbb{N}$ and $\displaystyle\int_0^{nT} f(x)\,dx = n\int_0^{T} f(x)\,dx$ for $n \in \mathbb{N}$

Thus, $I_2 = \lambda^{n-1}\displaystyle\int_0^{\lambda} f(z)\,dz$ ...(2)

Dividing (1) by (2) we get $\dfrac{I_1}{I_2} = \dfrac{n}{\lambda^{n-1}}$ or $n\lambda^{(1-n)}$.

ILLUSTRATION 144: Let $f(x)$ be a continuous function defined on $\mathbb{R}$ is such that $f(x) + f\left(x + \dfrac{1}{4}\right) = 2, \forall x \in \mathbb{R}$, then show that $f(x)$ is a periodic function and hence evaluate $\displaystyle\int_0^{1000} f(x)\,dx$

SOLUTION: Given $f(x)+f\left(x+\frac{1}{4}\right)=2\ \forall\ x\in\mathbb{R},$ ...(1)

Replacing x by $x+\frac{1}{4}$, we get $f\left(x+\frac{1}{4}\right)+f\left(x+\frac{1}{4}+\frac{1}{4}\right)=2$

$\Rightarrow\ f\left(x+\frac{1}{4}\right)+f\left(x+\frac{1}{2}\right)=2\ \forall\ x\in\mathbb{R}$ ...(2)

from (1) and (2), we must have $f(x)=f\left(x+\frac{1}{2}\right)\ \forall\ x\in\mathbb{R}$

$\Rightarrow$ $f(x)$ is a periodic function with period ½ = T (say)

Now we are to evaluate $I=\int_0^{1000} f(x)\,dx=\int_0^{2000T} f(x)\,dx$

$=(2000)\int_0^T f(x)\,dx=2000\int_0^{1/2} f(x)\,dx\ =\ 2000\left\{\int_0^{1/4} f(x)\,dx+\int_{1/4}^{1/2} f(x)\,dx\right\}$

Let us substitute $x=t+\frac{1}{4}$ in second integral

$\Rightarrow$ $dx=dt$ and limits becomes $t=0$ to $t=1/4$

$\therefore\quad I=2000\left\{\int_0^{1/4} f(x)\,dx+\int_0^{1/4} f\left(t+\frac{1}{4}\right)dt\right\}\ =\ 2000\left\{\int_0^{1/4} f(x)\,dx+\int_0^{1/4} f\left(x+\frac{1}{4}\right)dx\right\}$

$=\ 2000\left\{\int_0^{1/4}\left\{f(x)+f\left(x+\frac{1}{4}\right)\right\}dx\right\}\ =\ 2000\left\{\int_0^{1/4} 2\,dx\right\}=4000\left[\frac{1}{4}-0\right]=1000$

TEXTUAL EXERCISE–7: (SUBJECTIVE)

1. Prove that $f(x)=\int_a^x \log(t+\sqrt{1+t^2})dt$ is an even function.

2. Prove that $\int_0^{nT} f(x).dx=n.\int_0^T f(x)dx$ if $f(x+T)=f(x)$, i.e., $f(x)$ is periodic with period T. Hence, and otherwise evaluate the following integrals:
   (a) $\int_0^{32\pi/3} |\sin x|\,dx$
   (b) $\int_0^{32\pi/3} \sqrt{1+\cos 2x}\,dx$
   (c) $\int_{-1}^{3/2} |x\sin \pi x|\,dx$
   (d) $\int_0^{41/4} e^{2x-[2x]}\,dx$; where [.] is gint function
   (e) $\int_0^{2n\pi} (\sin x+\cos x)dx$
   (f) $\int_0^{200\pi} \sqrt{1+\cos x}\,dx$
   (g) $\int_0^{2000\pi} \frac{dx}{1+e^{\sin x}}$

3. Evaluate the following integrals $\int_0^{2n\pi}\left(|\sin x|-\left[\left|\frac{\sin x}{2}\right|\right]\right)dx$; [] denotes greatest integer function; $n\in\mathbb{N}$.

4. Evaluate the integral $\int_0^{n\pi+v} |\cos x|\,dx$; where $\frac{\pi}{2}<v<\pi$ and $n\in\mathbb{N}$.

5. Evaluate
$$\int_{5n\pi}^{\frac{5\pi}{n}(n^2+1)} \frac{\left(\frac{8xn^2}{25}\right)dx}{\left[(a^2+b^2)+(a^2-b^2)\cos\frac{2nx}{5}\right]}\ a,b>0 \text{ and } n\in\mathbb{N}$$

6. Evaluate $\int_0^{\pi}\left|\sqrt{3}\sin x+\cos x\right|dx$

7. Evaluate $\int_{-5}^{55} e^{\{x\}}dx$; where $\{x\}$ denotes fractional part of x.

8. Evaluate $\int_{-\frac{52}{3}\pi}^{-12\pi}\left(\cos^{-1}(\cos 4x)+\|\sin x|-|\cos x\|\right)dx$

9. Evaluate $\int_{\pi/3}^{17\pi/3}\frac{\left|\sin^{-1}(\sin x)\right|+\left(\cos^{-1}(\cos 2x)\right)}{\sin^{-1}(\sin x)+\cos^{-1}(\sin x)}dx$

10. Evaluate $\int_{\frac{\pi}{2}}^{\frac{43\pi}{2}}\cos^{-1}(\sin x)\,dx$

11. Let $I_1=\int_{k\pi}^{(k+1)\pi}\frac{|\sin 2x|}{|\sin x|+|\cos x|}dx$; $k \in \mathbb{N}$ and $I_2=\int_0^{\pi/4}\frac{dx}{\sin x+\cos x}dx$, then prove that $I_1=2\int_0^{\pi/2}\frac{\sin 2x}{\sin x+\cos x}dx$ and $I_1+4I_2=4$.

Answer Keys

2. (a) 43/2 (b) $\left(\frac{44-\sqrt{3}}{\sqrt{2}}\right)$ (c) $\frac{3\pi+1}{\pi^2}$ (d) $10(e-1)+\frac{1}{2}(\sqrt{e}-1)$

(e) zero (f) $400\sqrt{2}$ (g) 1000π **3.** $4n$

4. $2n+2-\sin v$ **5.** $\frac{4\pi^2}{ab}$ **6.** 4 **7.** $60(e-1)$ **8.** $\frac{97}{36}\pi^2+12\sqrt{2}-\frac{\sqrt{3}}{2}-\frac{3}{2}$

9. $\frac{17\pi}{2}$ **10.** $\frac{21}{2}\pi^2$

TEXTUAL EXERCISE-7: (OBJECTIVE)

1. $\int_0^{1000} e^{x-[x]}dx$ is

(a) $e^{1000}-1$ (b) $\frac{e^{1000}-1}{e-1}$

(c) $1000(e-1)$ (d) $\frac{e-1}{1000}$

2. If $P=\int_0^{3\pi} f(cos^2x)dx$ and $Q=\int_0^{\pi} f(cos^2x)dx$, then

(a) $P-Q=0$ (b) $P-2Q=0$

(c) $P-3Q=0$ (d) $P-5Q=0$

3. The value of $\int_0^{2\pi}[|\sin x|+|\cos x|]dx$ equal to

(a) $\pi/2$ (b) π

(c) $3\pi/2$ (d) 2π

4. The value of $\int_{-2\pi}^{5\pi}\cot^{-1}(\tan x)\,dx$, is equal to

(a) $\frac{7\pi}{2}$ (b) $\frac{7\pi^2}{2}$

(c) $\frac{3\pi}{2}$ (d) π^2

5. The value of $\int_{-1}^{3}\{|x-2|+[x]\}dx$, where [.] denotes the greatest integer function, is equal to

(a) 5 (b) 6

(c) 7 (d) None of these

6. The value of $\int_{-1}^{3}(|x|+|x-1|)dx$, is equal to

(a) 9 (b) 6

(c) 3 (d) None of these

7. The value of $\int_{-1}^{1}\frac{d}{dx}\left(\tan^{-1}\frac{1}{x}\right)dx$, is equal to

(a) $\pi/2$ (b) $-\pi/2$

(c) $\pi/4$ (d) $3\pi/2$

8. If $I=\int_0^{100\pi}\sqrt{(1-\cos 2x)}dx$, then the value of I is

(a) $100\sqrt{2}$ (b) $200\sqrt{2}$

(c) $50\sqrt{2}$ (d) None of these

9. If $f(x)$ is periodic with period T, then $\left\{\int_{a+2T}^{b+2T} f(x)dx-\int_a^b f(x)dx\right\}$ is

(a) 1 (b) 2

(c) 3 (d) None of these

10. $\int_0^1|\sin 2\pi x|\,dx$, is equal to

(a) 0 (b) $-1/\pi$

(c) $1/\pi$ (d) $2/\pi$

11. If $f(x + 1) + f(x + 7) = 0, \forall x \in \mathbb{R}$, then possible value of 't' for which $\int_a^{a+t} f(x)\,dx$ is independent of 'a', is

(a) 6 (b) 8
(c) 12 (d) None of these

12. Let $f(x)$ be a given integrable function such that $f(x + k) = f(x)$ for all $x \in \mathbb{R}$. Then $\int_a^{a+k} f(x)dx$ depends for its value on

(a) a only (b) k only
(c) both a and k (d) neither a nor k

13. The value of $\int_{-\pi/3}^{13\pi/4} \sqrt{\cot^{-1}(\cot x)}\,dx$ equals

(a) $\left[\frac{33}{8}+\left(\frac{2}{3}\right)^{3/2}\right]\pi^{3/2}$ (b) $\frac{2}{3}\left(\frac{33}{8}-\left(\frac{2}{3}\right)^{3/2}\right)\pi^{3/2}$

(c) $\left(\frac{33}{8}-\left(\frac{2}{3}\right)^{3/2}\right)\pi^{3/2}$ (d) None of these

Answer Keys

1. (c)	**2.** (c)	**3.** (d)	**4.** (b)	**5.** (c)	**6.** (a)	**7.** (b)	**8.** (b)	**9.** (d)	**10.** (d)
11. (c)	**12.** (b)	**13.** (b)							

Property 21: If $f(x)$ is a function such that $f(x) \geq 0.\ \forall x \in [a, b]$, then $\int_a^b f(x)dx \geq 0$.

Proof: Since $f(x) \geq 0$ and a < b.

$\Rightarrow dx > 0 \qquad \Rightarrow f(x) \cdot dx \geq 0$

$\Rightarrow$ Sum of infinitely many positive infinitesimals is positive.

$$\Rightarrow \int_a^b f(x)dx \geq 0$$

e.g., $f(x) = \sin x \geq 0\ \forall x \in [0, \pi]$

$$\Rightarrow \int_0^\pi f(x)\,dx = \int_0^\pi \sin x\,dx = -[\cos x]_0^\pi$$

$$= -[\cos \pi - \cos 0] = -[-1 - 1] = 2 > 0$$

ILLUSTRATION 145: If $f(x)$ is a continuous function such that $f(x) \geq 0$ for all $x \in [2, 10]$ and $\int_4^8 f(x)dx = 0$, then find $f(6)$.

SOLUTION: $f(x)$ is above the x-axis or on the x-axis for all $x \in [2, 10]$. If $f(x)$ is greater than zero at any sub-interval of [4, 8], then $\int_4^8 f(x)dx$ must be greater than zero. But $\int_4^8 f(x)dx = 0$.

$\Rightarrow f(x) = 0$ for all $x \in [4, 8]$

$\Rightarrow f(6) = 0$

Property 22: If $f(x) > g(x)\ \forall x \in [a, b]$, then $\int_a^b f(x)dx > \int_a^b g(x)dx$

Analytical Proof:

$\because f(x) > g(x)\ \forall x \in (a, b]$

$\Rightarrow f(x) - g(x) > 0\ \forall x \in (a, b]$

$\Rightarrow \int_a^b (f(x) - g(x))dx > 0.$ (By property 21)

$$\Rightarrow \int_a^b f(x)dx - \int_a^b g(x)dx > 0$$

$$\Rightarrow \int_a^b f(x)dx > \int_a^b g(x)dx$$

Geometrical Proof:

As shown in figure 2.70 below, $f(x) > g(x)\ \forall x \in [a, b]$. The area under the graph of $y = f(x)$ above x-axis from x =

a to $x = b$ (represented by shading) is greater than the area under the graph of $y = g(x)$ above x-axis from $x = a$ to $x = b$ (represented by dots).

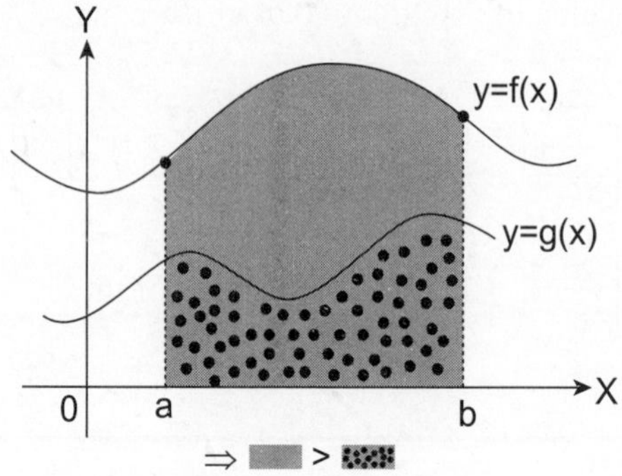

FIGURE 2.70

e.g., $\sin^{-1}(\sin x) > \sin x \ \forall \ x \in (0, \pi)$ as is clear from the figure given below

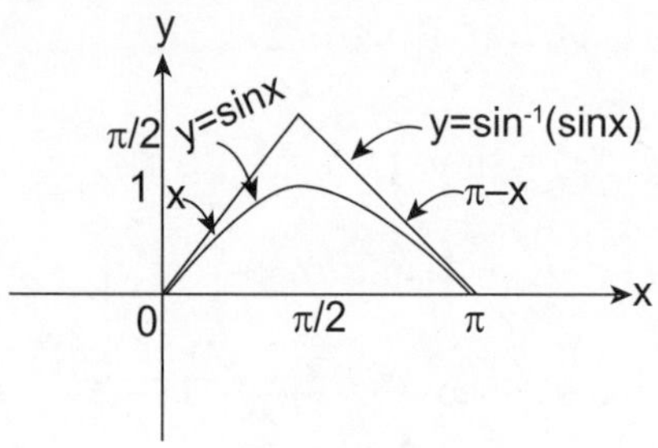

FIGURE 2.71

Now $\int_0^{\pi} \sin^{-1}(\sin x)\, dx$

$$= \int_0^{\pi/2} \sin^{-1}(\sin x)\, dx + \int_{\pi/2}^{\pi} \sin^{-1}(\sin x)\, dx$$

$$= \int_0^{\pi/2} x\, dx + \int_{\pi/2}^{\pi} (\pi - x)\, dx$$

$$= \frac{1}{2}\left[x^2\right]_0^{\pi/2} + \left[\pi x - \frac{x^2}{2}\right]_{\pi/2}^{\pi}$$

$$= \frac{1}{2}\left[\frac{\pi^2}{4}\right] + \pi\left(\frac{\pi}{2}\right) - \frac{1}{2}\left(\pi^2 - \frac{\pi^2}{4}\right)$$

$$= \frac{\pi^2}{8} + \frac{\pi^2}{2} - \frac{3\pi^2}{8} = \frac{1}{8}(1+4-3)\pi^2 = \frac{\pi^2}{4}$$

and $\int_0^{\pi} \sin x\, dx = -\left[\cos x\right]_0^{\pi} = 2$

Clearly $\frac{\pi^2}{4} > 2$ as $\pi \simeq 3.14$

i.e., $\int_0^{\pi} \sin^{-1}(\sin x)\, dx > \int_0^{\pi} \sin x\, dx$

Property 23: If $f(x)$, $g(x)$, $h(x)$ are continuous functions such that $g(x) \le f(x) \le h(x)$ in $[a, b]$, then $\int_a^b g(x)dx \le \int_a^b f(x)dx \le \int_a^b h(x)dx$

Analytical Proof:

By property 22

$g(x) \le f(x)$ for $x \in [a, b]$

$$\Rightarrow \int_a^b g(x)dx \le \int_a^b f(x)dx \quad \ldots\text{(i)}$$

Again $f(x) \le h(x)$ for $x \in [a, b]$

$$\Rightarrow \int_a^b f(x)dx \le \int_a^b h(x)dx \quad \ldots\text{(ii)}$$

$\therefore$ from (i) and (ii), we get $\int_a^b g(x)dx \le \int_a^b f(x)dx \le \int_a^b h(x)dx$

Geometrical Proof:

We can observe that $g(x) \le f(x) \le h(x)$

$\Rightarrow \int_a^b g(x)dx \le \int_a^b f(x)dx \le \int_a^b h(x)dx$ as shown below:

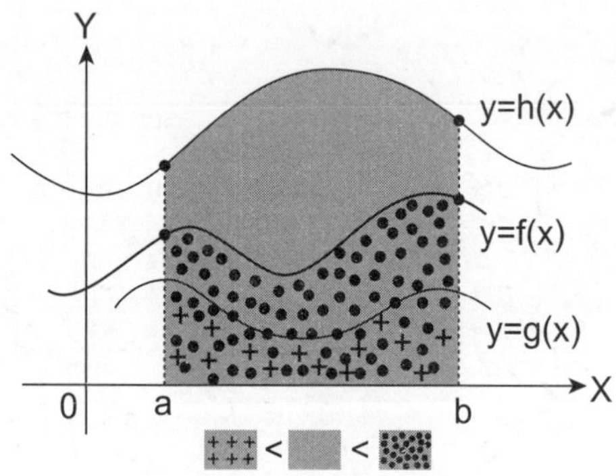

FIGURE 2.72

Application: To prove that $k_1 < \int_a^b f(x)\,dx < k_2$ where k_1, $k_2 \in \mathbb{R}$. It is suggested to find two functions $g(x)$ and $h(x)$. Such that $\int_a^b g(x)\,dx \ge k_1$ and $\int_a^b h(x)\,dx \le k_2$, then prove that $g(x) \le f(x) \le h(x)$

$$\Rightarrow \int_a^b g(x)dx < \int_a^b f(x)dx < \int_a^b h(x)dx$$

$$\Rightarrow k_1 \le \int_a^b g(x)dx < \int_a^b f(x)dx < \int_a^b h(x)dx \le k_2$$

$$\Rightarrow \quad k_1 < \int_a^b f(x)dx < k_2$$

e.g., Let $f(x) = \tan^{-1}x$, $g(x) = x$ and $h(x) = \tan x$, then on $\left(0, \frac{\pi}{4}\right)$, $f(x) < g(x) < h(x)$ as is clear from the figure given below

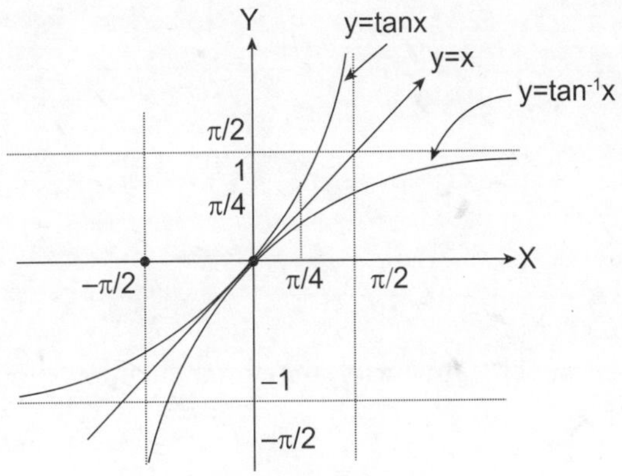

FIGURE 2.73

Now $\int_0^{\pi/4} h(x)\,dx = \int_0^{\pi/4} \tan x\,dx$

$= |\ln \sec x|_0^{\pi/4} = \ln\sqrt{2} = \frac{1}{2}\ln 2 = \ln\sqrt{2}$

$$\int_0^{\pi/4} g(x)\,dx = \int_0^{\pi/4} x\,dx = \frac{1}{2}\left[x^2\right]_0^{\pi/4} = \frac{\pi^2}{32} = \ln(e)^{\pi^2/32}$$

and $\int_0^{\pi/4} f(x)\,dx = \int_0^{\pi/4} \left(\tan^{-1} x\right) dx$

$$= \left|x \tan^{-1} x\right|_0^{\pi/4} - \int_0^{\pi/4} \frac{1.x}{1+x^2}\,dx$$

$$= \frac{\pi}{4} - \frac{1}{2}\int_0^{\pi/4} \frac{2x}{1+x^2}\,dx = \frac{\pi}{4} - \frac{1}{2}\left|\ln\left(1+x^2\right)\right|_0^{\pi/4}$$

$$= \frac{\pi}{4} - \frac{1}{2}\left[\ln\left(1+\frac{\pi^2}{4}\right)\right]$$

$$= \frac{\pi}{4} - \frac{1}{2}\ln\left(1+\frac{\pi^2}{4}\right) = \frac{\pi}{4} + \frac{1}{2}\ln\left(\frac{4}{4+\pi^2}\right)$$

$$= \ln e^{\pi/4} + \ln\frac{2}{\sqrt{4+\pi^2}} = \ln\left(\frac{2e^{\pi/4}}{\sqrt{4+\pi^2}}\right)$$

It can be shown that $\ln\sqrt{2} > \ln e^{\pi^2/32} > \ln\left(\frac{2e^{\pi/4}}{\sqrt{4+\pi^2}}\right)$

by proving $\sqrt{2} > \frac{\pi^2}{32} > \frac{2e^{\pi/4}}{\sqrt{4+\pi^2}}$ as $\log_e x$ is an increasing function.

ILLUSTRATION 146: If $\frac{2x}{\pi} < \sin x < x$ for $0 < x < \pi/2$, then express the integral $\int_0^{\pi/2} \frac{\sin x}{x}\,dx$ between two bounds.

SOLUTION: Given $\frac{2}{\pi} < \frac{\sin x}{x} < 1$ as $x > 0$

$$\Rightarrow \int_0^{\pi/2} \frac{2}{\pi}\,dx < \int_0^{\pi/2} \frac{\sin x}{x} < \int_0^{\pi/2} 1.dx$$

$$\Rightarrow 1 < \int_0^{\pi/2} \frac{\sin x}{x}\,dx < \frac{\pi}{2}$$

ILLUSTRATION 147: Show that $\int_0^1 e^{x^2}\,dx$ lies in between 1 and $(e-1)$ and hence evaluate $\left[\int_0^1 e^{x^2}\,dx\right]$; where [.] denotes greatest integer function.

SOLUTION: For $x \in [0, 1]$, $0 \le x^2 \le x$

$\Rightarrow e^0 \le e^{x^2} \le e^x$ as exponential function is an increasing function for base > 1.

$$\Rightarrow \int_0^1 e^0 dx \le \int_0^1 e^{x^2} dx \le \int_0^1 e^x\,dx \qquad \text{(By property 22)}$$

$$\Rightarrow 1 \le \int_0^1 e^{x^2} dx \le (e-1) \qquad \ldots(1)$$

Also from (1) clearly $\int_0^1 e^{x^2} dx \in [1, e-1]$; $e-1 \approx 1.7183$

$$\Rightarrow \left[\int_0^1 e^{x^2}dx\right] = 1\text{, i.e., greatest integer value of } \int_0^1 e^{x^2}dx \text{ is } 1.$$

ILLUSTRATION 148: Show that $\frac{1}{\sqrt{2}} < \int_0^1 \frac{1}{\sqrt{2-x^2+x^3}}dx < \frac{\pi}{4}$

SOLUTION: For $x \in [0, 1]$; $x^3 \le x^2$

$\Rightarrow -x^2 + x^3 \le 0$

$\Rightarrow 2 - x^2 + x^3 \le 2$ ...(1)

Also $1 \le 2 - x^2 \le 2 - x^2 + x^3$ as $x^3 \ge 0$ ...(2)

So from (1) and (2), we have, $1 \le 2 - x^2 \le 2 - x^2 + x^3 \le 2$

$\Rightarrow \sqrt{2-x^2} \le \sqrt{2-x^2+x^3} \le \sqrt{2}$

$\Rightarrow \frac{1}{\sqrt{2-x^2}} \ge \frac{1}{\sqrt{2-x^2+x^3}} \ge \frac{1}{\sqrt{2}}$ for $x \in [0, 1]$. Obviously the three functions follow equality only for $x = 0$.

$\Rightarrow \int_0^1 \frac{1}{\sqrt{2}}dx < \int_0^1 \frac{1}{\sqrt{2-x^2+x^3}}dx < \int_0^1 \frac{1}{\sqrt{2-x^2}}dx$ (By property 23)

$\Rightarrow \frac{1}{\sqrt{2}} < \int_0^1 \frac{1}{\sqrt{2-x^2+x^3}}dx < \left|\sin^{-1}\frac{x}{\sqrt{2}}\right|_0^1$

$\Rightarrow \frac{1}{\sqrt{2}} < \int_0^1 \frac{1}{\sqrt{2-x^2+x^3}}dx < \frac{\pi}{4}$; Hence the result.

ILLUSTRATION 149: Show that $\frac{1}{\sqrt{2}}\tan^{-1}\left(\frac{\sqrt{2}}{5}\right) < \int_{1/2}^1 \frac{1}{2+x^4}dx < \frac{1}{4}$

SOLUTION: For $x \in \left[\frac{1}{2}, 1\right]$, $x^2 \ge x^4$

$\Rightarrow 2 + x^2 \ge 2 + x^4 > 2$

$\Rightarrow \frac{1}{2+x^2} \le \frac{1}{2+x^4} < \frac{1}{2}$

$\Rightarrow \int_{1/2}^1 \frac{1}{2+x^2}dx < \int_{1/2}^1 \frac{1}{2+x^4}dx < \int_{1/2}^1 \frac{1}{2}dx$ (property 23)

$\Rightarrow \frac{1}{\sqrt{2}}\left|\tan^{-1}\left(\frac{x}{\sqrt{2}}\right)\right|_{1/2}^1 < \int_{1/2}^1 \frac{1}{2+x^4}dx < \frac{1}{2}\left(1-\frac{1}{2}\right)$

$\Rightarrow \frac{1}{\sqrt{2}}\left(\tan^{-1}\frac{1}{\sqrt{2}} - \tan^{-1}\frac{1}{2\sqrt{2}}\right) < \int_{1/2}^1 \frac{1}{2+x^4}dx < \frac{1}{4}$

$\Rightarrow \frac{1}{\sqrt{2}}\tan^{-1}\left(\frac{\frac{1}{\sqrt{2}} - \frac{1}{2\sqrt{2}}}{1+\frac{1}{\sqrt{2}}\times\frac{1}{2\sqrt{2}}}\right) < \int_{1/2}^1 \frac{1}{2+x^4}dx < \frac{1}{4}$

$$\Rightarrow \frac{1}{\sqrt{2}}\tan^{-1}\left(\frac{\frac{1}{2\sqrt{2}}}{\frac{5}{4}}\right) < \int_{1/2}^{1}\frac{1}{2+x^4}dx < \frac{1}{4}$$

$$\Rightarrow \frac{1}{\sqrt{2}}\tan^{-1}\left(\frac{\sqrt{2}}{5}\right) < \int_{1/2}^{1}\frac{1}{2+x^4}dx < \frac{1}{4}.$$

ILLUSTRATION 150: Find the greatest and least integral among I_1, I_2, I_3 , I_4 defined by $I_1 = \int_0^1 e^{-x}\sin^2 x\, dx$, $I_2 = \int_0^1 e^{-x^2}\sin^2 x\, dx$, $I_3 = \int_0^1 e^{-x^2}\, dx$ and $I_4 = \int_0^1 e^{-x^2/2}\, dx$

SOLUTION: For $x \in [0, 1]$, $\frac{x^2}{2} \le x^2 \le x$

$\Rightarrow -\frac{x^2}{2} \ge -x^2 \ge -x$

$\Rightarrow e^{-x^2/2} \ge e^{-x^2} \ge e^{-x}$ as exponential function is an increasing function.

$\Rightarrow e^{-x^2/2} \ge e^{-x^2}$ and $e^{-x^2} \ge e^{-x}$

$\Rightarrow e^{-x^2/2} \ge e^{-x^2}$ and

$e^{-x^2}\sin^2 x \ge e^{-x}\sin^2 x$ as $\sin^2 x \ge 0$ ...(1)

Also $e^{-x^2} \ge e^{-x^2}\sin^2 x$ as $\sin^2 x \le 1$ ...(2)

Combining (1) and (2) we have,

$e^{-x^2/2} \ge e^{-x^2} \ge e^{-x^2}(\sin^2 x) \ge e^{-x}\sin^2 x$ for $x \in [0, 1]$

∴ By property 23

$$\int_0^1 e^{-x^2/2}\, dx > \int_0^1 e^{-x^2}\, dx > \int_0^1 e^{-x^2}\sin^2 x\, dx > \int_0^1 e^{-x}\sin^2 x\, dx$$

$\Rightarrow I_4 > I_3 > I_2 > I_1$

Thus, I_1 is least and I_4 is greatest integral.

ILLUSTRATION 151: Express the integral $\int_0^1 \frac{dx}{1+x^2+3x^7}$ between two bounds by sandwiching the polynomial $1 + x^2 + 3x^7$ in between two quadratic polynomials.

SOLUTION: For $x \in (0, 1]$, $x^2 \ge x^7$ and equality holds only for $x = 0$ and $x = 1$

$\Rightarrow 1 + x^2 + 3x^7 \le 1 + x^2 + 3x^2$

$\Rightarrow 1 + x^2 + 3x^7 \le 1 + 4x^2$ ...(1)

Also $1 + x^2 \le 1 + x^2 + 3x^7$ as $x^7 \ge 0$ ...(2)

Combining (1) and (2) we have,

$1 + x^2 \le 1 + x^2 + 3x^7 \le 1 + 4x^2\ \forall\, x \in [0, 1]$

Here the first equality holds at $x = 0$ and second equality holds at $x = 1$

Thus, $(1 + x^2) < 1 + x^2 + 3x^7 < 1 + 4x\ \ \forall\, x \in (0, 1)$

$\Rightarrow \frac{1}{1+x^2} < \frac{1}{1+x^2+3x^7} < \frac{1}{1+4x^2}\ \forall\, x \in (0, 1)$ ∴ (By property 23)

$$\Rightarrow \int_0^1 \frac{1}{1+x^2}dx < \int_0^1 \frac{1}{1+x^2+3x^7}dx < \int_0^1 \frac{1}{1+4x^2}dx$$

$$\Rightarrow \left|\tan^{-1}x\right|_0^1 < \int_0^1 \frac{1}{1+x^2+3x^7}dx < \frac{1}{2}\left|\tan^{-1}(2x)\right|_0^1$$

$$\Rightarrow \frac{\pi}{4} < \int_0^1 \frac{1}{1+x^2+3x^7}dx < \frac{1}{2}\tan^{-1}(2)$$

ILLUSTRATION 152: Express $\int_0^{\pi/2} \sqrt{\sin x}\, dx$ between two bounds or prove that $1 < \int_0^{\pi/2} \sqrt{\sin x}\, dx < \frac{\pi}{2}$

SOLUTION: For $x \in \left(0, \frac{\pi}{2}\right)$, $\sin x \in (0, 1)$

$$\Rightarrow \sqrt{\sin x} > \sin x$$

$$\forall x \in \left(0, \frac{\pi}{2}\right) \quad \ldots(1)$$

Also $1 > \sqrt{\sin x}$

$$\forall x \in \left(0, \frac{\pi}{2}\right) \quad \ldots(2)$$

Combining (1) and (2) we have, $1 > \sqrt{\sin x} > \sin x$

$$\Rightarrow \int_0^{\pi/2} dx > \int_0^{\pi/2} \sqrt{\sin x}\, dx > \int_0^{\pi/2} \sin x\, dx$$

$$\Rightarrow \frac{\pi}{2} > \int_0^{\pi/2} \sqrt{\sin x}\, dx > -[\cos x]_0^{\pi/2}$$

$$\Rightarrow \frac{\pi}{2} > \int_0^{\pi/2} \sqrt{\sin x}\, dx > -[0-1]$$

$$\Rightarrow 1 < \int_0^{\pi/2} \sqrt{\sin x}\, dx < \frac{\pi}{2}$$

Property 24: $\left|\int_a^b f(x)dx\right| \le \int_a^b |f(x)|\,dx$; where $f(x)$ is continuous and bounded on (a, b)

Discussion: This is derived from generalized form of polygonal inequality and can be understood as below.

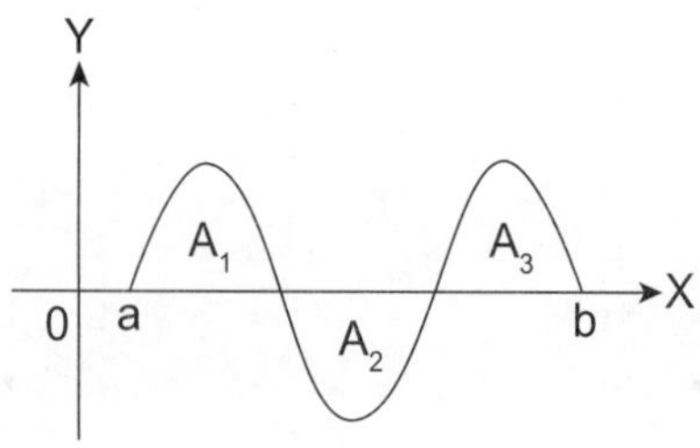

FIGURE 2.74

$\left|\int_a^b f(x)dx\right| = |A_1 - A_2 + A_3| \le \int_a^b |f(x)|\,dx = A_1 + A_2 + A_3$;

where A_1, A_2, A_3 are magnitudes of areas as shown above.

Here $\left|\int_a^b f(x)\,dx\right| \le \int_a^b |f(x)|\,dx$

$$\therefore \left|\sum_{k=1}^{n} f(x_k^*)\Delta x\right| \le \sum_{k=1}^{n} |f(x_k^*)\Delta x|$$

Proof: $\because f(x) \le |f(x)| \quad \Rightarrow -|f(x)| \le f(x) \le |f(x)|$

$$\Rightarrow -\int_a^b |f(x)|\,dx \le \int_a^b f(x)dx \le \int_a^b |f(x)|\,dx$$

$$\Rightarrow \left|\int_a^b f(x)dx\right| \le \int_a^b |f(x)|\,dx$$

ILLUSTRATION 153: Let $f(x) = -x^3 + 3x$, then prove that $\left|\int_{-2}^{3} f(x)\, dx\right| \le \int_{-2}^{3} |f(x)|\, dx$

SOLUTION: Here $f(x) = -x^3 + 3x$ which being a polynomial function is continuous and bounded in $[-2, 3]$ and hence is integrable.

Now $\int_{-2}^{3} f(x)\, dx = \int_{-2}^{3} (-x^3 + 3x)\, dx = \left|\frac{-x^4}{4} + \frac{3x^2}{2}\right|_{-2}^{3} = -\frac{1}{4}[81-16] + \frac{3}{2}(9-4)$

$$= \frac{-65}{4} + \frac{15}{2} = \frac{-65+30}{4} = \frac{-35}{4}$$

$$\therefore \left|\int_{-2}^{3} f(x)\, dx\right| = \left|\frac{-35}{4}\right| = \frac{35}{4}$$

Now $f(x) = -x^3 + 3x = -x(x^2 - 3) = -x(x + \sqrt{3})(x - \sqrt{3})$

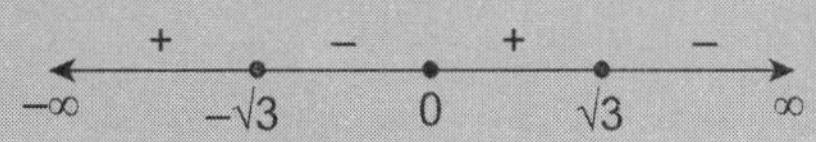

FIGURE 2.75

Thus, by sign scheme, we have $f(x) \ge 0$ for $x \in (-\infty, -\sqrt{3}] \cup [0, \sqrt{3}]$

and $f(x) < 0$ for $x \in (-\sqrt{3}, 0) \cup (\sqrt{3}, \infty)$

$$\therefore \; |f(x)| = \begin{cases} f(x); & \text{for } x \in \left(-\infty, -\sqrt{3}\right] \cup \left[0, \sqrt{3}\right] \\ -f(x); & \text{for } x \in \left(-\sqrt{3}, 0\right] \cup \left[\sqrt{3}, \infty\right] \end{cases}$$

$$= \begin{cases} -x^3 + 3x; & \text{for } x \in \left(-\infty, -\sqrt{3}\right] \cup \left[0, \sqrt{3}\right] \\ x^3 - 3x; & \text{for } x \in \left(-\sqrt{3}, 0\right) \cup \left(\sqrt{3}, \infty\right) \end{cases}$$

Thus, $\int_{-2}^{3} |f(x)|\, dx$

$$= \int_{-2}^{-\sqrt{3}} \left(-x^3 + 3x\right) dx + \int_{-\sqrt{3}}^{0} \left(x^3 - 3x\right) dx + \int_{0}^{\sqrt{3}} \left(-x^3 + 3x\right) dx + \int_{\sqrt{3}}^{3} \left(x^3 - 3x\right) dx$$

$$= -\frac{1}{4}\left[x^4\right]_{-2}^{-\sqrt{3}} + \frac{3}{2}\left[x^2\right]_{-2}^{-\sqrt{3}} + \frac{1}{4}\left[x^4\right]_{-\sqrt{3}}^{0} - \frac{3}{2}\left[x^2\right]_{-\sqrt{3}}^{0} - \frac{1}{4}\left[x^4\right]_{0}^{\sqrt{3}} + \frac{3}{2}\left[x^2\right]_{0}^{\sqrt{3}} + \frac{1}{4}\left[x^4\right]_{\sqrt{3}}^{3} - \frac{3}{2}\left[x^2\right]_{\sqrt{3}}^{3}$$

$$= -\frac{1}{4}[9-16] + \frac{3}{2}[3-4] + \frac{1}{4}[0-9] - \frac{3}{2}[0-3] - \frac{1}{4}[9-0] + \frac{3}{2}[3-0] + \frac{1}{4}[81-9] - \frac{3}{2}[9-3]$$

$$= \frac{7}{4} - \frac{3}{2} - \frac{9}{4} + \frac{9}{2} - \frac{9}{4} + \frac{9}{2} + 18 - 9$$

$$= \frac{7}{4} - \frac{3}{2} + \frac{9}{2} + 9 = \frac{7 - 6 + 18 + 36}{4} = \frac{55}{4}$$

Thus, $\left|\int_{-2}^{3} f(x)dx\right| < \int_{-2}^{3} |f(x)|dx$. Also geometrically as shown below

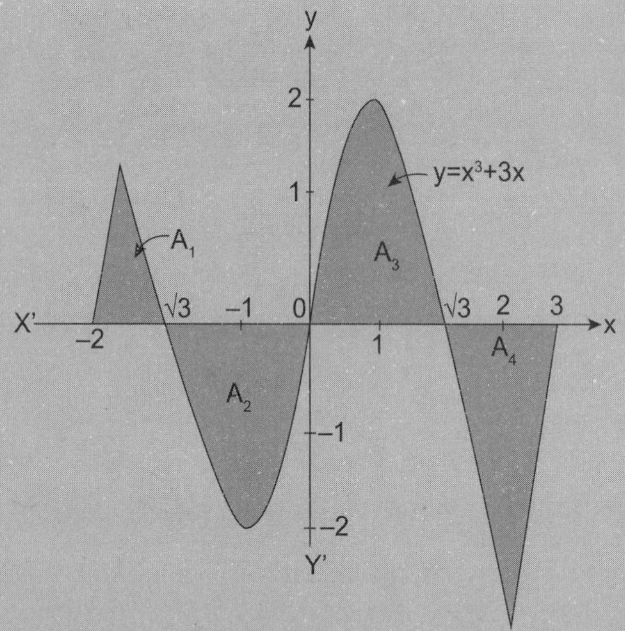

FIGURE 2.76

Clearly $\left|\int_{-2}^{3} f(x)\,dx\right| = |A_1 + A_2 + A_3 + A_4|$;

where $A_1, A_3 > 0$ and $A_2, A_4 < 0$

where as $\int_{-2}^{3} |f(x)|\,dx = |A_1| + |A_2| + |A_3| + |A_4|$

$$= A_1 + |A_2| + A_3 + |A_4|;\ A_1, A_3 > 0.$$

Property 25: (Max-Min inequality) If m and M are respectively the global min/max values of $f(x)$ in $[a, b]$, then

$$m(b-a) \le \int_a^b f(x)\,dx \le M(b-a)$$

Analytical Proof:

$\because$ $f(x)$ is continuous in $[a, b]$

$\Rightarrow$ $f(x)$ is bounded

$\Rightarrow$ Their exist $m, M \in \mathbb{R}$

Such that $m \le f(x) \le \mathrm{M}$

$$\Rightarrow \int_a^b m\ dx \le \int_a^b f(x)\,dx \le \int_a^b M\ dx$$

$$\Rightarrow m(b-a) < \int_a^b f(x)dx < M(b-a)$$

Also geometrically, it is clear that doted area = $m(b - a)$ is smaller than the area having vertical bars

$= \int_a^b f(x)dx$ which in turn is smaller than the area of shaded region = $M(b - a)$ as shown below:

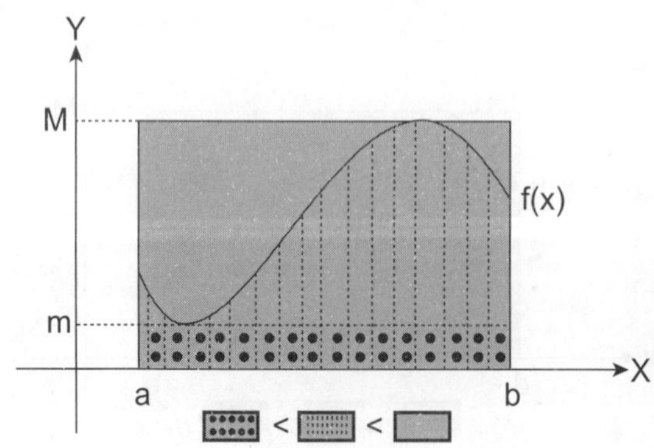

FIGURE 2.77

ILLUSTRATION 154: Show that $\left(e^{-1}\right)^{e^{-1}} < \int_0^1 (x)^x\,dx < 1$

SOLUTION: Let us first discuss about the monotonicity and concavity of the function $f(x) = x^x$ for $x > 0$

Taking natural log both sides we have $\ln f(x) = x \ln x$

Differentiating w.r.t. x we have $\frac{1}{f(x)} f'(x) = x.\frac{1}{x} + \ln x.1$

$\Rightarrow$ $f'(x) = f(x)\,[1 + \ln x]$

$\Rightarrow$ $f'(x) = (x)^x\,[1 + \ln x]$

Since for $x > 0$, $x^x > 0$, $f'(x) \geq 0$

$\Rightarrow$ $(1 + \ln x) \geq 0$

$\Rightarrow$ $\ln x \geq -1$

$\Rightarrow$ $x \geq e^{-1}$ and $f'(x) \leq 0$ $\qquad\qquad \Rightarrow x \leq e^{-1}$.

So $f(x)$ is strictly decreasing for $x \in (0, e^{-1})$ and strictly increasing for $x \in (e^{-1}, \infty)$

Clearly greatest lower bound of $f(x)$ occurs at $x = e^{-1}$

and is given by $m = \left(e^{-1}\right)^{e^{-1}}$ ...(1)

Since the functional values of $f(x)$ goes on increasing as we move away from either side of $x = \left(e^{-1}\right)^{e^{-1}}$, it means for $x \in (0, 1)$, least upper bound will be given by

$$M = \max.\left\{\lim_{x\to 0^+} f(x),\ f(1)\right\}$$

$$= \max.\left\{\lim_{x\to 0^+} (x)^x, 1\right\} \qquad ...(2)$$

Let $L = \lim_{x\to 0^+} (x)^x$

$\Rightarrow$ $\ln L = \lim_{x\to 0^+} x \ln x$

$$= \lim_{x\to 0^+}\left(\frac{\ln x}{1/x}\right) = \lim_{x\to 0^+}\left(\frac{1/x}{-1/x^2}\right) \qquad \text{(By L.H. rule)}$$

$$= \lim_{x\to 0^+}(-x) = 0$$

$\Rightarrow$ $L = e^0 = 1$

$\therefore$ from (2) $M = max.\ \{1, 1\} = 1$

$\because$ By Max.–Min. inequality

i.e., $m(b-a) < \int_a^b f(x)\,dx < M(b-a)$, we must have

$$(e^{-1})^{e^{-1}} < \int_a^b x^x\,dx < 1$$

ILLUSTRATION 155: Prove that $\frac{3}{257}\int_{-1}^{2}\frac{1}{x^8+1}dx<3$

SOLUTION: Let $I=\int_{-1}^{2}\frac{1}{x^8+1}dx$ Here $f(x)=\frac{1}{x^8+1}$

$f'(x)=\frac{-(8x^7)}{(x^8+1)^2}>0$ for $x<0$ and <0 for $x>0$

Thus, $f(x)$ increases on $(-\infty, 0)$ and decreases on $(0, \infty)$ and hence has least upper bound M at $x = 0$

$\therefore$ $M = f(0) = 1$

Now as we move away from $x = 0$ on either side, functional values decreases.

Thus, greatest lower bound of function would be the minimum among $f(-1)$ and $f(2)$.

Now $f(-1)=\frac{1}{2}$ and $f(2)=\frac{1}{257}$. Thus, $m=\frac{1}{257}$

$\therefore$ By min–max inequality, i.e., $(b-a)m<\int_a^b f(x)\,dx<(b-a)M$

$\Rightarrow$ $(2-(-1))\frac{1}{257}<\int_{-1}^{2}\frac{1}{x^8+1}dx<(2-(-1)).1$

$\Rightarrow$ $\frac{3}{257}<\int_{-1}^{2}\frac{1}{x^8+1}dx<3$

ILLUSTRATION 156: Show that $1<\int_0^2\frac{3-x}{5-x^2}dx<2$

SOLUTION: Let $f(x)=\frac{3-x}{5-x^2}$

$\Rightarrow$ $f'(x)=\frac{(5-x^2)(-1)-(3-x)(-2x)}{(5-x^2)^2}$

$\Rightarrow$ $f'(x)=\frac{-5+x^2+6x-2x^2}{(5-x^2)^2}=f'(x)=\frac{-x^2+6x-5}{(5-x^2)^2}$

$=-\frac{(x^2-6x+5)}{(5-x^2)^2}=-\frac{(x-1)(x-5)}{(5-x^2)^2}$

Now $f'(x)>0$ $\Rightarrow$ $(x-1)(x-5)<0$

$\Rightarrow$ $x\in(1, 5)$ and $f'(x)<0$ $\Rightarrow$ $(x-1)(x-5)>0$

$\Rightarrow$ $x\in(-\infty, 1)\cup(5, \infty)$

$\therefore$ $f(x)$ decreases on $(-\infty, 1)$ and $(5, \infty)$ and $f(x)$ increases on $(1, 5)$

Also $f(x)$ being a rational function is continuous on $[0, 2]$

Thus, $f(x)$ decreases on $(0, 1)$ and increases on $(1, 2)$.

Thus, in $[0, 2]$ greatest lower bound of $f(x)$ would occur at $x = 1$ and is given by $m=f(1)=\frac{3-1}{5-1}=\frac{2}{4}=\frac{1}{2}$

Also as we move with in the interval [0, 2] away from $x = 1$ on either side functional values goes on increasing and hence least upper bound of $f(x)$ would be given by

M = max. $\{f(0), f(2)\}$ = $\max.\left\{\frac{3}{5}, 1\right\} = 1$

$\therefore$ By max. – min inequality, i.e., $m(b-a) < \int_a^b f(x)\,dx < M(b-a)$

$\Rightarrow \frac{1}{2}(2-0) < \int_0^2 \frac{3-x}{5-x^2}dx < 2 \qquad \Rightarrow 1 < \int_0^2 \frac{3-x}{5-x^2}dx < 2$

ILLUSTRATION 157: Show that $\frac{\pi}{6} < \int_0^1 \frac{dx}{\sqrt{4-x^2-x^3}} < \frac{\pi}{4\sqrt{2}}$

SOLUTION: Clearly $4 - x^2 - x^3 > 0$, for $x \in [0, 1]$

Also, $4 - x^2 > 4 - x^2 - x^3$ because $0 < x \le 1$ and for $x = 0$ they are equal. Again, both sides are positive.

$\therefore \frac{1}{4-x^2} < \frac{1}{4-x^2-x^3} \qquad \Rightarrow \int_0^1 \frac{dx}{\sqrt{4-x^2}} < \int_0^1 \frac{dx}{\sqrt{4-x^2-x^3}} \qquad ...(1)$

Again, $4 - x^2 - x^3 > 4 - x^2 - x^2$ for $0 < x < 1$ and at $x = 0, 1$ they are equal. Also, both sides are positive.

$\therefore \frac{1}{4-x^2-x^3} < \frac{1}{4-2x^2}$

$\Rightarrow \int_0^1 \frac{dx}{\sqrt{4-x^2-x^3}} < \int_0^1 \frac{dx}{\sqrt{4-2x^2}} \qquad ...(2)$

Now, $\int_0^1 \frac{dx}{\sqrt{4-x^2}} = \left[\sin^{-1}\frac{x}{2}\right]_0^1 = \sin^{-1}\frac{1}{2} = \frac{\pi}{6} \qquad .....(3)$

And $\int_0^1 \frac{dx}{\sqrt{4-2x^2}} = \frac{1}{\sqrt{2}}\int_0^1 \frac{dx}{\sqrt{2-x^2}} = \frac{1}{\sqrt{2}}\left[\sin^{-1}\frac{x}{\sqrt{2}}\right]_0^1 = \frac{1}{\sqrt{2}}.\frac{\pi}{4} \qquad ....(4)$

$\therefore$ from (1), (2), (3) and (4) we get $\frac{\pi}{6} < \int_0^1 \frac{dx}{\sqrt{4-x^2-x^3}} < \frac{\pi}{4\sqrt{2}}$

ILLUSTRATION 158: Find the value of the integral $\int_0^1 e^{x^3}\,dx$

SOLUTION: Here, $f(x) = e^{x^3}$ on [0, 1];

$\Rightarrow f'(x) = 3x^2e^{x^3} \ge 0 \ \forall\ x \in [0, 1]$

$\Rightarrow f(x)$ is monotonically increasing

$\therefore$ least value = $e^0 = 1$; greatest value = $e^1 = e$

By property $m(b < a) < \int_a^b f(x)dx < M(b-a)$, we have

$\therefore 1(1-0) < \int_0^1 e^{x^3}\,dx < e(1-0)$

$\Rightarrow 1 < \int_0^1 e^{x^3}\,dx < e$

ILLUSTRATION 159: If $a < \int_0^{2\pi} \frac{1}{10+3\cos x} dx < b$, then find an ordered pair (*a*, *b*)

SOLUTION: We have $7 \le 10 + 3 \cos x \le 13$

$$\Rightarrow \frac{1}{13} \le \frac{1}{10+3\cos x} \le \frac{1}{7}$$

$$\Rightarrow \frac{2\pi}{13} \le \int_0^{2\pi} \frac{1}{10+3\cos x} \le \frac{2\pi}{7} \text{ (by max-min inequlity)}$$

Hence, ordered pair (*a*, *b*) is $\left(\frac{2\pi}{13}, \frac{2\pi}{7}\right)$

Remark: Clearly value of above integral may lie between infinitly many bounds (*a*, *b*). Thus, $\left(\frac{2\pi}{13}, \frac{2\pi}{7}\right)$ is not unique.

Property 26: If the function *f*(*x*) increases and has a concave graph in the interval [*a*, *b*], that is *f*′(*x*) and *f*″(*x*) both positive (+ve), then $(b-a)f(a) < \int_a^b f(x)dx < (b-a)\left(\frac{f(a)+f(b)}{2}\right)$

Geometrical Proof:

Clearly the area $(b - a) f(a)$ represented by + signs is smaller than the area represented by verticals bars

$= \int_a^b f(x)dx$ which in turn is smaller than the shaded region

$= (b-a)\left(\frac{f(a)+f(b)}{2}\right)$ = Area of trapezium *ABCD* as shown below

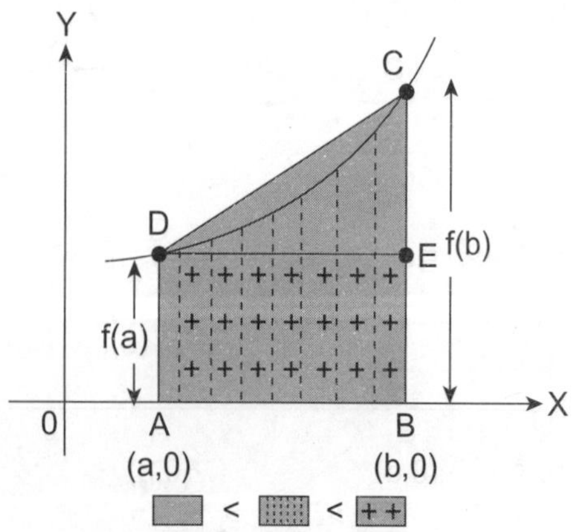

FIGURE 2.78

Thus, $(b-a)f(a) < \int_a^b f(x)dx < (b-a)\frac{f(a)+f(b)}{2}$

Analytical Proof: Equation of chord joining (a, *f*(*a*)) (*b*, *f*(*b*)) is $y - f(a) = \frac{f(b)-f(a)}{b-a}(x-a)$.

Let $\frac{f(b)-f(a)}{b-a} = m$, i.e., $y = m(x - a) + f(a)$

$\Rightarrow f(a) < f(x) < m(x - a) + f(a)$ applying property 22 (since curve is below the chord)

We have, $\int_a^b \{m(x-a)+f(a)\}dx$

$$= m\left[\frac{x^2-2ax}{2}\right]_a^b + f(a)(b-a)$$

$$= m\left\{\frac{b^2-2ab}{2} - \frac{(a^2-2a^2)}{2}\right\} + f(a)(b-a)$$

$$= m\left\{\frac{b^2+a^2-2ab}{2}\right\} + f(a)(b-a)$$

$$= \frac{f(b)-f(a)}{2(b-a)}(b-a)^2 + f(a)(b-a)$$

$$= \frac{f(b)+f(a)}{2}(b-a)$$

Thus, $\int_a^b f(a)dx < \int_a^b f(x)dx < \int_a^b \{m(x-a)+f(a)\}dx$

$$\Rightarrow (b-a)f(a) < \int_a^b f(x)dx < \left(\frac{f(a)+f(b)}{2}\right)(b-a)$$

ILLUSTRATION 160: Show that $1 < \int_0^1 e^{x^2} dx < \frac{e+1}{2}$

SOLUTION: Given $I = \int_0^1 e^{x^2} dx$ here $f(x) = e^{x^2}$

$\Rightarrow \; f'(x) = 2xe^{x^2} > 0$ for $x \in (0, 1)$

Now $f''(x) = 2\left[x.2xe^{x^2} + e^{x^2}\right] = 2e^{x^2}\left[2x^2+1\right] > 0 \; \forall \; x \in [0,1]$

Thus, $f(x)$ is strictly increasing and concave upwards on [0, 1]. Therefore by above property

i.e., $(b-a)f(a) < \int_a^b f(x)dx < (b-a).\frac{1}{2}[f(a)+f(b)]$

$$\Rightarrow \; (1-0)f(0) < \int_0^1 e^{x^2} dx < (1-0).\frac{1}{2}[f(0)+f(1)]$$

$$\Rightarrow \; 1.(1) < \int_0^1 e^{x^2} dx < \frac{1}{2}[1+e]$$

$$\Rightarrow \; 1 < \int_0^1 e^{x^2} dx < \frac{(e+1)}{2}$$

ILLUSTRATION 161: Show that $e^a < \frac{e^b - e^a}{(b-a)} < \frac{e^a + e^b}{2}$

SOLUTION: Let $a, b > 0$ be any two real numbers and $A(a, f(a))$, $B(b, f(b))$ be two points on the exponential curve $y = e^x$ as shown below

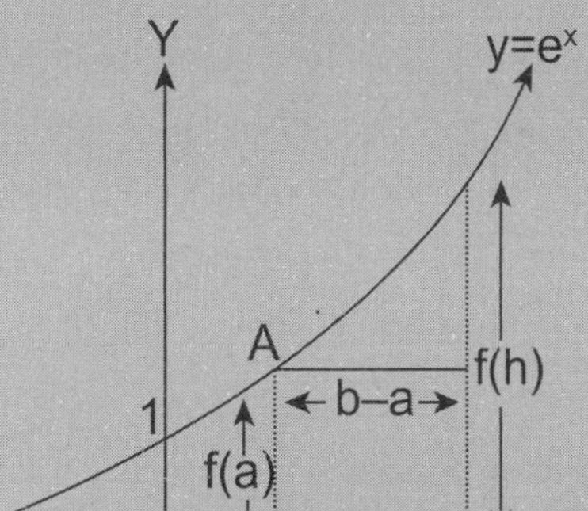

FIGURE 2.79

Clearly $y = e^x$ is strictly increasing and concave upwards

$\therefore$ By property 24 (A) $(b-a)f(a) < \int_a^b f(x)dx < (b-a)\frac{1}{2}(f(a)+f(b))$

$$\Rightarrow \; (b-a)e^a < \int_a^b e^x \, dx < \frac{(b-a)}{2}\left[e^a + e^b\right]$$

$$\Rightarrow \; (b-a)e^a < e^b - e^a < \frac{(b-a)}{2}(e^a+e^b) \qquad \Rightarrow \; e^a < \frac{e^b - e^a}{(b-a)} < \frac{e^a+e^b}{2}$$

ILLUSTRATION 162: Show that $1 < \int_0^1 \sqrt{1+x^3}\, dx < 1.25$

SOLUTION: Let $f(x) = \sqrt{1+x^3}$

$$\Rightarrow f'(x) = \frac{1}{2\sqrt{1+x^3}}(3x^2) = \frac{3x^2}{2\sqrt{1+x^3}} \geq 0 \ \forall x \in [0, 1]$$

$$\text{Also } f''(x) = \frac{3}{2}\left[\frac{\sqrt{1+x^3}(2x) - x^2.\frac{1}{2\sqrt{1+x^3}}(3x^2)}{(1+x^3)}\right] = \frac{3}{2}\left[\frac{(2x)2(1+x^3) - 3x^4}{2(1+x^3)^{3/2}}\right]$$

$$= \frac{3}{4(1+x^3)^{3/2}}\left[4x + 4x^4 - 3x^4\right] = \frac{3}{4(1+x^3)^{3/2}}\left[4x + x^4\right] > 0$$

$$\Rightarrow f''(x) = \frac{3}{4(1+x^3)^{3/2}}.x(4+x^3) \geq 0 \ \forall x \in [0, 1]$$

Thus, $f(x)$ is strictly increasing and concave upwards for $x \in [0, 1]$, therefore by property 24(A)

$$\text{i.e., } (b-a)f(a) < \int_a^b f(x)\, dx < (b-a).\frac{1}{2}[f(a) + f(b)]$$

$$\Rightarrow (1-0)f(0) < \int_0^1 \sqrt{1+x^3}\, dx < (1-0).\frac{1}{2}[f(0) + f(1)]$$

$$\Rightarrow 1 < \int_0^1 \sqrt{1+x^3}\, dx < \frac{1}{2}\left[1 + \sqrt{2}\right]$$

$$\Rightarrow 1 < \int_0^1 \sqrt{1+x^3}\, dx < \frac{1}{2} + \frac{\sqrt{2}}{2}$$

$$\Rightarrow 1 < \int_0^1 \sqrt{1+x^3}\, dx < 0.5 + 0.75 \qquad (\because \sqrt{2} \simeq 1.414 < 1.5 \Rightarrow \sqrt{2}/2 < 0.75)$$

$$\Rightarrow 1 < \int_0^1 \sqrt{1+x^3}\, dx < 1.25$$

Property 27: If the function $f(x)$ increases and has a convex upwards (or concave downwards) graph in the interval $[a, b]$, that is $f'(x)$ is positive (+ve) and $f''(x)$ is negative (–ve), then

$$(b-a)\left(\frac{f(a)+f(b)}{2}\right) < \int_a^b f(x)\,dx < (b-a)f(b)$$

Clearly we can see from the diagram that

Area of trapezium $ABCD$ < Area of curvilineal trapezium $AB\overset{\frown}{CD}$ < Area of rectangle $ABCE$

$$\Rightarrow (b-a)\left(\frac{f(a)+f(b)}{2}\right) < \int_a^b f(x)\,dx < (b-a)f(b)$$

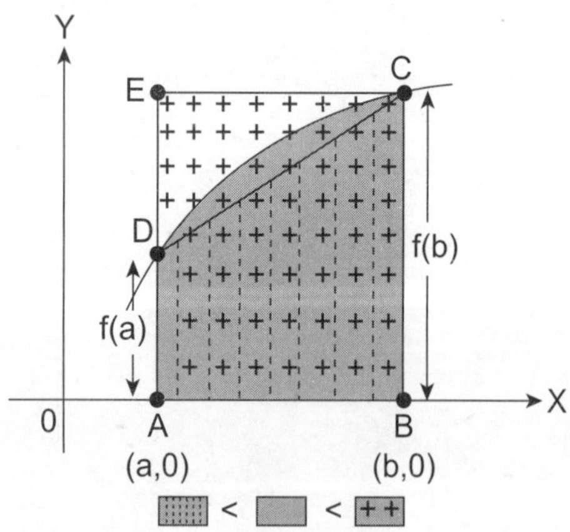

FIGURE 2.80

ILLUSTRATION 163: Show that $\ln 8 < \int_2^4 \ln x \, dx < \ln 16$

SOLUTION: Here $f(x) = \ln x$

$$\Rightarrow \quad f'(x) = \frac{1}{x} > 0 \ \forall \ x > 0 \ \text{ and}$$

$$f''(x) = -\frac{1}{x^2} < 0 \ \forall x > 0$$

Thus, $f(x)$ is strictly increasing function with its concavity downwards as shown below

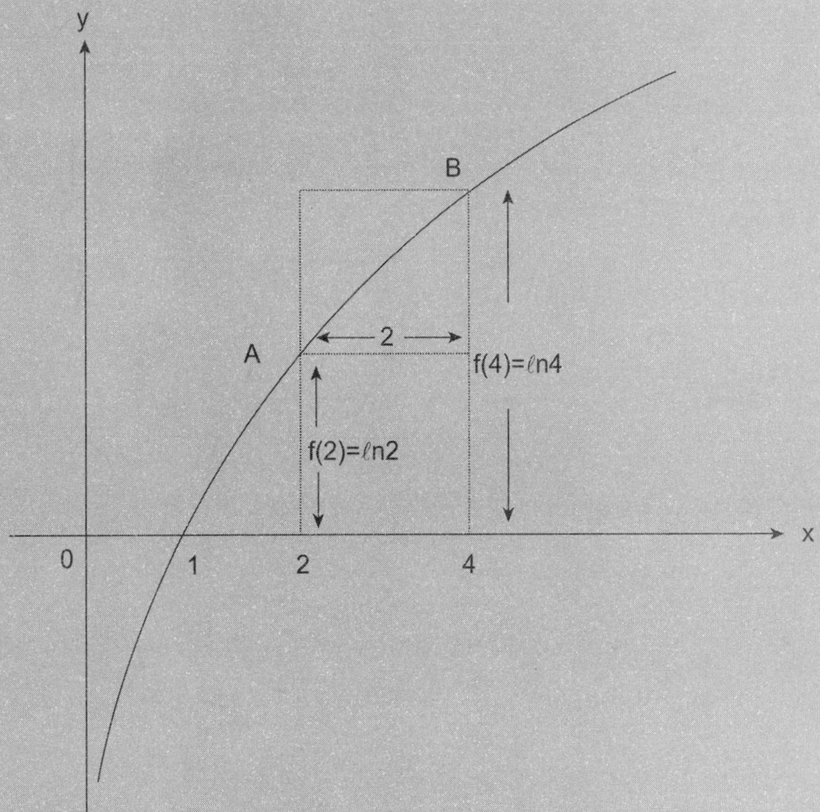

FIGURE 2.81

Therefore by property 27

i.e., $(b-a)\frac{1}{2}[f(a)+f(b)] < \int_a^b f(x)\,dx < (b-a)f(b)$

$$\Rightarrow \quad (4-2).\frac{1}{2}[\ln 2 + \ln 4] < \int_2^4 \ln x \, dx < (4-2)\ln 4$$

$$\Rightarrow \quad \ln 8 < \int_2^4 \ln x \, dx < \ln 16 \ \text{ hence the result.}$$

ILLUSTRATION 164: Show that $\frac{1}{2} < \frac{\sqrt{2}}{\sqrt{\pi - 2\cos 1}} \int_{-\sqrt{\frac{\pi}{2}-1}}^{0} \cos(x^2+1)\,dx < 1$

SOLUTION: Here $f(x) = \cos(x^2+1);\ x \in \left[-\sqrt{\frac{\pi}{2}-1}, 0\right]$

$\Rightarrow f'(x) = -2x\sin(x^2+1)$

Now $x \in \left[-\sqrt{\frac{\pi}{2}-1}, 0\right]$

$\Rightarrow x^2 \in \left[0, \frac{\pi}{2}-1\right]$

$\Rightarrow \sin(x^2+1) > 0$, but $x < 0$

$\Rightarrow f'(x) \geq 0\ \forall\ x \in \left[-\sqrt{\frac{\pi}{2}-1}, 0\right]$

$\Rightarrow f(x)$ is strictly increasing on $\left[-\sqrt{\frac{\pi}{2}-1}, 0\right]$

Further $f''(x) = -2\sin(x^2+1) - 2x(2x)\cos(x^2+1)$

$$= -2[\sin(x^2+1) + 2x^2\cos(x^2+1)] < 0 \text{ as } (x^2+1) \in \left[1, \frac{\pi}{2}\right]$$

so $f(x)$ is strictly increasing function with its concavity downwards.

Thus, by property 27

$$(b-a)\frac{1}{2}[f(a)+f(b)] < \int_a^b f(x)\,dx < (b-a)f(b)$$

$$\Rightarrow \left(\sqrt{\frac{\pi}{2}-1}\right).\frac{1}{2}[0+\cos 1] < \int_{-\sqrt{\frac{\pi}{2}-1}}^{0} f(x)\,dx < \left(\sqrt{\frac{\pi}{2}-1}(\cos 1)\right)$$

$$\Rightarrow \frac{\sqrt{\pi-2\cos 1}}{2\sqrt{2}} < \int_{-\sqrt{\frac{\pi}{2}-1}}^{0} f(x)\,dx < \frac{\sqrt{\pi-2\cos 1}}{\sqrt{2}}$$

$$\Rightarrow \frac{\sqrt{\pi-2\cos 1}}{2\sqrt{2}} < \int_{-\sqrt{\frac{\pi}{2}-1}}^{0} \cos(x^2+1)\,dx < \frac{\sqrt{\pi-2\cos 1}}{\sqrt{2}}$$

$$\Rightarrow \frac{1}{2} < \frac{\sqrt{2}}{\sqrt{\pi-2\cos 1}} \int_{-\sqrt{\frac{\pi}{2}-1}}^{0} \cos(x^2+1)\,dx < 1$$

Hence proved.

ILLUSTRATION 165: Show that $\dfrac{1}{15} < \displaystyle\int_1^2 \frac{1}{x^3+3x+1}dx < \frac{2}{15}$

SOLUTION: Here $f(x) = \dfrac{1}{x^3+3x+1}$; $x \in [1, 2]$

$$\Rightarrow \quad f'(x) = (x^3+3x+1)^{-2}(3x^2+3) = \frac{-3(x^2+1)}{(x^3+3x+1)^2}$$

$\Rightarrow$ $f'(x) < 0 \ \forall \ x \in [1, 2]$

$\Rightarrow$ $f(x)$ is a decreasing function

$$\text{Further } f''(x) = -3\left[\frac{(x^3+3x+1)^2(2x)-(x^2+1).2(x^3+3x+1)(3x^2+3)}{(x^3+3x+1)^4}\right]$$

$$= -3(x^3+3x+1)(2)\left[\frac{(x^3+3x+1)x-3(x^2+1)^2}{(x^3+3x+1)^4}\right]$$

$$= -6\left[\frac{x^4+3x^2+x-3x^4-3-6x^2}{(x^3+3x+1)^3}\right] = -6\left[\frac{-2x^4-3x^2-3+x}{(x^3+3x+1)^3}\right] = 6\left[\frac{(2x^4+3x^2)+(3-x)}{(x^3+3x+1)^3}\right]$$

Since for $x \in [1, 2]$, $3 > x$, i.e., $3 - x > 0$

$\Rightarrow$ $f'(x) > 0 \ \forall \ x \in [1, 2]$

$\Rightarrow$ $f(x)$ has upwards concavity, i.e., $f(x)$ would have its graph in the interval [1, 2] as of the type shown below (rough sketch)

Clearly we must have

$$(b-a)f(b) < \int_a^b f(x)\,dx < \frac{1}{2}(b-a)\left[f(a)+f(b)\right]$$

$$\Rightarrow \quad (1)f(2) < \int_1^2 \frac{1}{x^3+3x+1}dx < \frac{1}{2}\left[\frac{1}{5}+\frac{1}{15}\right]$$

$$\Rightarrow \quad \frac{1}{15} < \int_1^2 \frac{1}{x^3+3x+1}dx < \frac{2}{15}$$

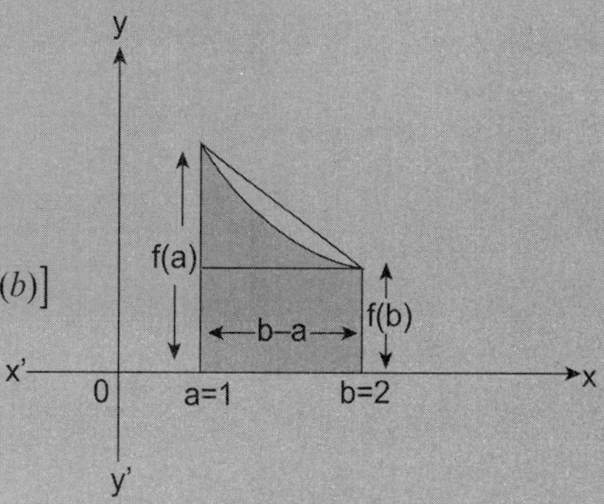

FIGURE 2.82

Property 28: **Schwarz-Bunyakovsky inequality:** If $f(x)$ and $g(x)$ are two functions such that $f^2(x)$ and $g^2(x)$ are integrable, then

$$\left|\int_a^b f(x)g(x)\,dx\right| \le \sqrt{\left(\int_a^b f^2(x)dx\right)\left(\int_a^b g^2(x)dx\right)}$$

Proof: Let $\phi(x) = (f(x) - \lambda g(x))^2$; where $\lambda \in \mathbb{R}$

$(f(x) - \lambda g(x))^2 \ge 0 \ \forall \ \lambda \in \mathbb{R}$

$\Rightarrow f^2(x) - 2f(x) \cdot g(x)\lambda + \lambda^2 g^2(x) \ge 0 \ \forall \ \lambda \in \mathbb{R}$

$$\Rightarrow \lambda^2\int_a^b g^2(x)\,dx - 2\lambda\int_a^b f(x).g(x)\,dx + \int_a^b f^2(x)\,dx \ge 0$$

i.e., $A\lambda^2 + B\lambda + C \ge 0 \ \forall \ \lambda \in \mathbb{R}$; where $A = \displaystyle\int_a^b g^2(x)\,dx$

$B = -2\displaystyle\int_a^b f(x).g(x)\,dx$, $C = \displaystyle\int_a^b f^2(x)\,dx$ and $\lambda \in \mathbb{R}$

$\Rightarrow$ Disc. ≤ 0, i.e., $B^2 - 4AC \le 0$ as $A > 0$

$$\Rightarrow \quad 4\left[\int_a^b f(x).g(x)\,dx\right]^2 - 4\int_a^b f^2(x)\,dx\int_a^b g^2(x)\,dx \le 0$$

$$\Rightarrow \quad \left(\int_a^b f(x).g(x)\,dx\right)^2 \le \int_a^b f^2(x)\,dx\int_a^b g^2(x)\,dx$$

$$\Rightarrow \quad \left|\int_a^b f(x).g(x)\,dx\right| \le \sqrt{\int_a^b f^2(x)\,dx\int_a^b g^2(x)\,dx}$$

Hence proved.

ILLUSTRATION 166: Show that $\int_0^1 x\sqrt{\sin 2x^2}\,dx$ cannot exceed the value $\left(\sin\frac{1}{2}\right)\sqrt{\sin 1}$

SOLUTION: Let $\int_0^1 x\sqrt{\sin 2x^2}\,dx = \int_0^1 x\sqrt{2\sin x^2 \cos x^2}\,dx = \sqrt{2}\int_0^1\left(\sqrt{x}\sqrt{\sin x^2}\right).\left(\sqrt{x}\sqrt{\cos x^2}\right)dx$

$\therefore$ By Schwartz-Bunyakovsky inequality, we have

$$\left|\sqrt{2}\int_0^1\left(\sqrt{x}\sqrt{\sin x^2}\right).\left(\sqrt{x}\sqrt{\cos x^2}\right)dx\right| \le \sqrt{2}\sqrt{\int_0^1 x\sin x^2\,dx.\int_0^1 x\cos x^2\,dx}$$

Since $\sqrt{x}\sqrt{\sin x^2}$ and $\sqrt{x}\sqrt{\cos x^2} > 0\ \forall\, x \in (0, 1)$, L.H.S. is non-negative.

$$\Rightarrow \int_0^1 x\sqrt{\sin 2x^2}\,dx \le \sqrt{2}\sqrt{\int_0^1 \frac{1}{2}\sin t\,dt.\int_0^1 \frac{1}{2}\cos t\,dt}$$

$$\Rightarrow \int_0^1 x\sqrt{\sin 2x^2}\,dx \le \frac{\sqrt{2}}{2}\sqrt{\left|-\cos t\right|_0^1.\left|\sin t\right|_0^1}$$

$$\Rightarrow \int_0^1 x\sqrt{\sin 2x^2}\,dx \le \frac{1}{\sqrt{2}}\sqrt{-(\cos 1-1)(\sin 1-0)}$$

$$\Rightarrow \int_0^1 x\sqrt{\sin 2x^2}\,dx \le \frac{1}{\sqrt{2}}\sqrt{(\sin 1)(1-\cos 1)} = \frac{1}{\sqrt{2}}\sqrt{2}\sin\frac{1}{2}\sqrt{\sin 1} = \left(\sin\frac{1}{2}\right)\sqrt{\sin 1}$$

Thus, $\int_0^1 x\sqrt{\sin 2x^2}\,dx \le \left(\sin\frac{1}{2}\right)\sqrt{\sin 1}$

ILLUSTRATION 167: Find the greatest value of the integral $\int_0^1 \sqrt{(2+x)(2+x^3)}\,dx$

SOLUTION: $\int_0^1 \sqrt{(2+x)(2+x^3)}\,dx \le \sqrt{\int_0^1 (2+x)\,dx.\int_0^1 (2+x^3)\,dx}$

$$= \sqrt{\left[2x+\frac{x^2}{2}\right]_0^1\left[2x+\frac{x^4}{4}\right]_0^1} = \sqrt{\frac{5}{2}\times\frac{9}{4}}.\ \text{Thus, } \int_0^1 \sqrt{(2x)(2+x^3)}\,dx \le \sqrt{\frac{45}{8}} = \sqrt{\frac{45}{8}}$$

ILLUSTRATION 168: Show that $\int_0^1 \sqrt{\left(1+3\sqrt{x}\right)\left(1+4x^3\right)}\,dx$; cannot exceed √6.

SOLUTION: By Schwartz-Bunyakovsky inequality

$$\left|\int_0^1 \sqrt{\left(1+3\sqrt{x}\right)\left(1+4x^3\right)}dx\right|$$

$$= \left|\int_0^1 \sqrt{\left(1+3\sqrt{x}\right)\left(1+4x^3\right)}dx\right| \le \sqrt{\int_0^1 \sqrt{\left(1+3\sqrt{x}\right)}\,dx.\int_0^1\left(1+4x^3\right)dx}$$

$$\Rightarrow \int_0^1 \sqrt{\left(1+3\sqrt{x}\right)\left(1+4x^3\right)}dx \le \sqrt{\left|x+2(x)^{3/2}\right|_0^1.\left|x+x^4\right|_0^1} = \sqrt{(3).(2)} = \sqrt{6}.$$

Thus, the given definite integral cannot exceed the value √6.

ILLUSTRATION 169: Show that $\frac{n+1}{n+2} \le \int_0^1 \frac{1}{1+x^n}dx < 1\ \forall\, n > 0$

SOLUTION: For $x \in [0, 1]$; $\frac{1}{1+x^n} \le 1$, $\therefore$ By dominance rule,

$$\int_0^1 \frac{1}{1+x^n}dx < \int_0^1 dx = 1$$

$$\Rightarrow \int_0^1 \frac{1}{1+x^n}dx < 1 \quad \ldots(1)$$

Now $\int_0^1 1\,dx = \int_0^1 \sqrt{1+x^n}.\frac{1}{\sqrt{1+x^n}}\,dx$

$$\Rightarrow 1 = \left|\int_0^1 \sqrt{1+x^n}.\frac{1}{\sqrt{1+x^n}}\,dx\right| \le \sqrt{\int_0^1 (1+x^n)\,dx.\int_0^1 \frac{1}{\sqrt{1+x^n}}dx}.$$

(By Schwartz's-Bunyakovsky Inequality)

$$\Rightarrow 1 \le \int_0^1 (1+x^n)\,dx.\int_0^1 \frac{1}{1+x^n}dx$$

$$\Rightarrow 1 \le \left|x+\frac{x^{n+1}}{n+1}\right|_0^1 .\int_0^1 \frac{1}{1+x^n}dx \quad (\because n>0)$$

$$\Rightarrow 1 \le \left[1+\frac{1}{n+1}\right].\int_0^1 \frac{1}{1+x^n}dx \qquad \Rightarrow \frac{n+1}{n+2} \le \int_0^1 \frac{1}{1+x^n}dx \quad \ldots(2)$$

$\therefore$ From (1) and (2), we have $\frac{n+1}{n+2} \le \int_0^1 \frac{1}{1+x^n}dx < 1$, hence proved.

ILLUSTRATION 170: Show that $\int_0^\pi \frac{\sin x}{\sqrt{x+1}}dx \le \sqrt{\pi \ln\sqrt{1+\pi}}$

SOLUTION: $\int_0^\pi \frac{\sin x}{\sqrt{x+1}}dx = \left|\int_0^\pi \frac{\sin x}{\sqrt{x+1}}dx\right| \le \sqrt{\int_0^\pi \sin^2 x\,dx\,.\int_0^\pi \frac{1}{1+x}dx}$

(By Schwartz's-Bunyakovsky Inequality)

$$= \sqrt{\int_0^\pi \frac{1-\cos 2x}{2}dx\,.\left|\ln(1+x)\right|_0^\pi} = \sqrt{\frac{1}{2}\left|x-\frac{\sin 2x}{2}\right|_0^\pi .\left(\ln(1+\pi)-\ln 1\right)}$$

$$= \sqrt{\frac{1}{2}(\pi).\ln(1+\pi)} = \sqrt{\pi \ln\sqrt{1+\pi}}$$

$$\therefore \int_0^\pi \frac{\sin x}{\sqrt{x+1}}dx \le \sqrt{\pi \ln\sqrt{1+\pi}}$$

ILLUSTRATION 171: Express

(a) $\int_0^1 \sqrt{1+x^5}\,dx$ between two bounds by using Schwartz-Bunyakovsky Inequality

(b) By using the inequality $1 \le \sqrt{1+x^5} \le \sqrt{1+x}\ \forall\ x \in [0,1]$

SOLUTION: (a) Clearly $\sqrt{1+x^5} > 0\ \forall\ x \in (0,1)$

$$\Rightarrow \int_0^1 \sqrt{1+x^5}\,dx > 0$$

$$\therefore \int_0^1 \sqrt{1+x^5}\,dx = \left|\int_0^1 \sqrt{1+x^5}\,dx\right| = \left|\int_0^1 1.\sqrt{1+x^5}\,dx\right| \le \sqrt{\int_0^1 1\,dx.\int_0^1 (1+x^5)\,dx}$$

(By schwartz's Bunyakovsky inequality)

$$= \sqrt{(1)\left[x+\frac{x^6}{6}\right]_0^1} = \sqrt{1+\frac{1}{6}} = \sqrt{\frac{7}{6}}$$

Thus, $0 < \int_0^1 \sqrt{1+x^5}\,dx < \sqrt{\frac{7}{6}}$

(b) Now $1 \le \sqrt{1+x^5} \le \sqrt{1+x}\ \forall\ x \in [0, 1]$

Since $x^5 \le x\ \forall\ x \in [0, 1]$

$$\Rightarrow \int_0^1 1\,dx < \int_0^1 \sqrt{1+x^5}\,dx < \int_0^1 \sqrt{1+x}\,dx \qquad \text{(By dominave rule)}$$

$$\Rightarrow 1 < \int_0^1 \sqrt{1+x^5}\,dx < \left[\frac{2}{3}(1+x)^{3/2}\right]_0^1$$

$$\Rightarrow 1 < \int_0^1 \sqrt{1+x^5}\,dx < \left[\frac{2}{3}(2)^{3/2} - \frac{2}{3}\right]$$

$$\Rightarrow 1 < \int_0^1 \sqrt{1+x^5}\,dx < \frac{2}{3}\left(2\sqrt{2}-1\right) < \frac{2}{3}[2(1.42)-1]$$

$$\Rightarrow 1 < \int_0^1 \sqrt{1+x^5}\,dx < 1.226$$

Thus, $\int_0^1 \sqrt{1+x^5}\,dx \in (1,\ 1.226)$

TEXTUAL EXERCISE–8: (SUBJECTIVE)

1. If $I_1 = \int_0^1 x^5 e^x dx$, $I_2 = \int_0^1 x^3 e^x dx$, $I_3 = \int_0^1 x^{10} e^x dx$, $I_4 = \int_0^1 x^{13} e^x dx$ then find the greatest and least integral out of I_1, I_2, I_3 and I_4.

2. Prove the inequality $\ln 2 < \int_0^1 \frac{dx}{\sqrt{1+x^6}} < \frac{\pi}{2}$

3. Prove the inequality $\ln(1+\sqrt{2}) < \int_0^1 \frac{dx}{\sqrt{1+x^6}} < \frac{\pi}{2}$

4. Prove the following inequalities:

   (a) $1 < \int_0^{\pi/2} \frac{\sin x}{x} dx < \frac{\pi}{2}$

   (b) $0 < \int_0^1 \frac{x}{x^3+16} dx < \frac{1}{17}$

   (c) $1 < \int_0^1 e^{x^2} dx < e$

5. Prove that $\left|\int_a^b f(x)\,dx\right| \le \int_a^b |f(x)|\,dx$

6. Prove that the value of $\int_1^3 \sqrt{3+x^3}\,dx$ lies in the interval $(4, 2\sqrt{30})$

7. Using $\int_0^\infty \frac{\sin x}{x} dx = \frac{\pi}{2}$, evaluate

   (a) $\int_0^\infty \frac{\sin ax}{x} dx$ (b) $\int_0^\infty \left(\frac{\sin x}{x}\right)^2 dx$

8. (a) Prove that $f(a).(b-a) \le \int_a^b f(x).dx \le (b-a)\left[\frac{f(a)+f(b)}{2}\right]$; where $f(x)$ is increasing function with concavity upward for all $x \in (a, b)$ and also discuss the change in nature of above relation when $f(x)$ is increasing function with concavity downwards.

(b) Using above result, find out the more precise interval in which $\int_0^{\pi/2}\frac{\sin x}{x}dx$ and $\int_0^1 e^{x^2}dx$ lie.

9. Prove that $\int_0^1\sqrt{(1+x)(1+x^3)}\,dx \le \sqrt{\frac{15}{8}}$

10. If $f(x) = x(x-1)$, $0 \le x \le 1$ and $f(x+1) = f(x)\ \forall\ x \in \mathbb{R}$, then prove that $\left|\int_2^4 f(x)dx\right| = 1/3$

11. Given that f satisfies $|f(u) - f(v)| \le |u - v|$ for u and v in $[a, b]$, then prove that f is continuous in $[a, b]$.

12. Prove that $\frac{1}{2} < \int_0^1 \frac{dx}{\sqrt{4-x^2+x^5}} < \frac{\pi}{6}$

13. Prove the following inequalities:

(a) $\frac{\pi}{128} < \int_{\pi/4}^{\pi/2}(\sin x)^{10}dx < \frac{\pi}{4}$

(b) $\frac{e-1}{3} < \int_1^e \frac{dx}{2+\ln x} < \frac{e-1}{2}$

Answer Keys

1. (a) Greatest : I_2 Least : I_4

7. (a) $\pi/2$ for $a > 0$, $-\pi/2$ for $a < 0$ (b) $\pi/2$

8. (a) $f(a)(b-a) \le (b-a)\frac{f(a)+f(b)}{2}\int_a^b f(x).dx \le f(b).(b-a)$

(b) $[(2+\pi)/4, 1][1, (e+1)/2]$

Hints. (i) Put $u = x + h$ and $v = x$

(ii) $LHS = \left|\int_a^b f(x)dx - \int_a^b f(a)dx\right| = \left|\int_a^b f(x) - f(a)dx\right| \le \int_a^b \{f(x) - f(a)\}dx \le \int_a^b |x-a|\,dx$

TEXTUAL EXERCISE–8: (OBJECTIVE)

1. The greater of $\int_0^{\pi/2}\frac{\sin x}{x}dx$ and $\frac{\pi}{2}$, is

(a) $\frac{\pi}{2}$

(b) $\int_0^{\pi/2}\frac{\sin x}{x}dx$

(c) Nothing can be said

(d) None of these

2. If $I_1 = \int_e^{e^2}\frac{dx}{\ln x}$ and $I_2 = \int_1^2 \frac{e^x}{x}dx$, then

(a) $I_1 = I_2$ (b) $I_1 > I_2$

(c) $I_1 < I_2$ (d) None of these

3. Let $I_1 = \int_1^2 \frac{dx}{\sqrt{1+x^2}}$ and $I_2 = \int_1^2 \frac{dx}{x}$, then

(a) $I_1 > I_2$ (b) $I_2 > I_1$

(c) $I_1 = I_2$ (d) $I_1 > 2I_2$

4. The minimum odd value of 'a' ($a > 1$) for which $\int_{10}^{19}\frac{\sin x}{1+x^a}dx < \frac{1}{9}$, is equal to

(a) 1 (b) 3

(c) 5 (d) 9

5. If $I = \int_0^{1/2}\frac{dx}{\sqrt{1-x^{2n}}}$ for $n \ge 1$, then the value of I is

(a) less than 1 (b) more than 1/2

(c) more than 1 (d) less than 1/4

6. The absolute value of $\int_{10}^{19}\frac{\sin x}{1+x^8}dx$ is

(a) less than 10^{-7} (b) more than 10^{-7}

(c) less than 10^{-6} (d) more than 10^{-6}

7. Let $\int_a^b f(x)dx = p$ and $\int_a^b |f(x)|\,dx = q$. Then

(a) $|p| \le q$ (b) $p > q$

(c) $p + q = 0$ (d) None of these

8. If $I_1 = \int_x^1 \frac{dt}{1+t^2}$ and $\int_1^{1/x}\frac{dt}{1+t^2}$, $x > 0$; then

(a) $I_1 = I_2$ (b) $I_1 > I_2$

(c) $I_2 > I_1$ (d) $I_2 = \pi/4 - \tan^{-1}x$

9. The value of the integral $\int_{-1}^{1}\sqrt{(8+x^3)}dx$ lies between $2\sqrt{7}$ and K. Then minimum positive integer value of K is
(a) 6 (b) 7
(c) 8 (d) 9

10. If $I=\int_{0}^{1}\sqrt{(1+x^3)}dx$; then
(a) $I<1$ (b) $I<1.1$
(c) $I<\sqrt{7}/2$ (d) None of these

11. Let $I_1=\int_0^1 e^{-x^2}dx,\ I_2=\int_0^1 e^{-x}\cos^2 x\,dx$ and $I_3=\int_0^1 e^{-x^2}\cos^2 x\,dx$. Then
(a) $I_1<I_2<I_3$ (b) $I_3<I_2<I_1$
(c) $I_2<I_1<I_3$ (d) $I_2<I_3<I_1$

12. State which of the following statements is/are true.
(a) If $f(x)$ is continuous in $[a, b]$ and $\int_a^b f(x)=0$; then the equation $f(x)=0$ has at least one root in (a, b)
(b) If $f(x)<g(x)\ \forall\, x\,(a, b)$, then $\int_a^b f(x)\,dx<\int_a^b g(x)dx$
(c) $\left|\int_a^b f(x)dx\right|\le\int_a^b|f(x)|\,dx$
(d) all of the above

Answer Keys

1. (a) 2. (a) 3. (b) 4. (b) 5. (a,b) 6. (a,c) 7. (a) 8. (a,d)
9. (a) 10. (b,c) 11. (d) 12. (d)

Property 29: If $f(x)$ is continuous in $[a, b]$, then there exists a point $c\in(a, b)$ such that $\int_a^b f(x)dx=f(c)(b-a)$

and the number $f(c)=\dfrac{1}{b-a}\int_a^b f(x)\,dx$ is called mean value of the function $f(x)$ on the interval $[a, b]$.

Proof: From Fermat's theorem $f(x)$ being continuous in $[a, b]$, there exist two real numbers m, and M such that

$m\le f(x)\le M$

$$\Rightarrow\ m(b-a)\le\int_a^b f(x)\,dx\le M(b-a)$$

(By max–min inequality)

$$\Rightarrow\ m\le\frac{1}{b-a}\int_a^b f(x)\,dx\le M$$

So from intermediate value theorem there exist at least one number $c\in(a, b)$: $f(c)=\dfrac{1}{b-a}\int_a^b f(x)\,dx$

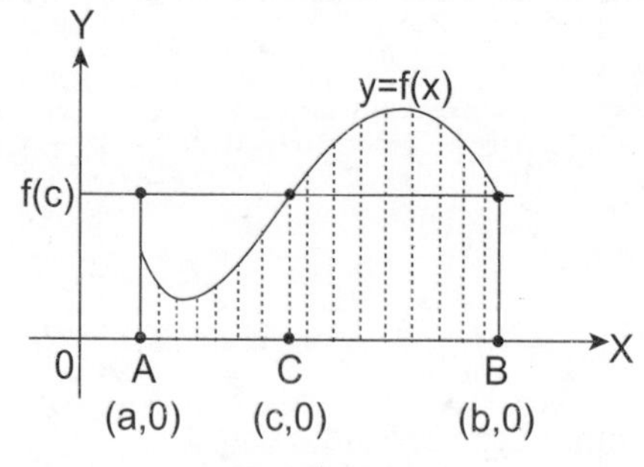

FIGURE 2.83

ILLUSTRATION 172: Estimate the value of integral $\int_0^1\sqrt{1+x^8}\,dx$ by using mean value theorem.

SOLUTION: By Mean value theorem, there exists $c\in(0, 1)$, such that

$$\int_0^1\sqrt{1+x^8}\,dx=(1-0)f(c)$$

$$\Rightarrow\int_0^1\sqrt{1+x^8}\,dx=\sqrt{1+c^8}<\sqrt{1+1}=\sqrt{2}$$

But $\sqrt{1+c^8}>1$

Thus, $1<\int_0^1\sqrt{1+x^8}\,dx<\sqrt{2}$

ILLUSTRATION 173: By using mean value theorem show that $0.7 < \int_0^1 \frac{dx}{\sqrt{1+x^4}} < 1$

SOLUTION: By mean value theorem there exists $c \in (0, 1)$, such that $\int_0^1 \frac{dx}{\sqrt{1+x^4}} = (1-0)f(c) = \frac{1}{\sqrt{1+c^4}}$

Now $c \in (0, 1)$

$\Rightarrow \; c^4 \in (0, 1)$

$\Rightarrow \; (1 + c^4) \in (1, 2)$

$\Rightarrow \; \sqrt{1+c^4} \in \left(1, \sqrt{2}\right) \qquad \Rightarrow \; \frac{1}{\sqrt{1+c^4}} \in \left(\frac{1}{\sqrt{2}}, 1\right)$

Thus, $\frac{1}{\sqrt{2}} < \int_0^1 \frac{dx}{\sqrt{1+x^4}} < 1$

$\Rightarrow \; 0.707 < \int_0^1 \frac{dx}{\sqrt{1+x^4}} < 1$

$\Rightarrow \; 0.7 < \int_0^1 \frac{1}{\sqrt{1+x^4}} dx < 1$

ILLUSTRATION 174: Show that $0 < \int_0^{\pi/2} \sqrt{\sin x}\; dx < \frac{\pi}{2}$

SOLUTION: By mean value theorem there exists $c \in (0, 1)$, such that $\int_0^{\pi/2} \sqrt{\sin x}\; dx = \left(\frac{\pi}{2} - 0\right) f(c)$

$\Rightarrow \; \int_0^{\pi/2} \sqrt{\sin x}\; dx = \frac{\pi}{2} \sqrt{\sin c}\; dc$ ...(1)

Now since $c \in \left(0, \frac{\pi}{2}\right)$ it implies $\sqrt{\sin c} \in (0,1)$

$\Rightarrow \; \int_0^{\pi/2} \sqrt{\sin x}\; dx \in \left(0, \frac{\pi}{2}\right)$ (using (1))

$\Rightarrow \; 0 < \int_0^{\pi/2} \sqrt{\sin x}\; dx < \frac{\pi}{2}$

ILLUSTRATION 175: If $f(a) > 0$, and $f(x)$ be a non decreasing continuous function in $[a, b]$, then find maximum/ minimum values of function $\left(\frac{1}{b-a}\right)\int_a^b f(x)dx$.

SOLUTION: $f(x)$ is monotonically increasing

Hence $f(a) < f(x) < f(b)$

$\Rightarrow \; \int_a^b f(a)\,dx \le \int_a^b f(x)\,dx \le \int_a^b f(b)\,dx$

$f(a)(b-a) \le \int_a^b f(x)\,dx \le f(b)(b-a)$

$\Rightarrow \; f(a) \le \frac{1}{b-a}\int_a^b f(x)dx \le f(b)$

$\Rightarrow$ Minimum value $f(a)$ and maximum value $f(b)$

■ EVALUATING INTEGRALS DEPENDENT ON A PARAMETER

Property 30: Suppose that $f(x, \alpha)$ and $f'(x, \alpha)$ are continuous functions:

when $c \le \alpha \le d$ and $a \le x \le b$, then $I'(\alpha) = \int_a^b f'(x,\alpha)dx$;

(where $I'(\alpha)$) is the derivative of $I(\alpha)$ w.r.t., α and $f'(x, \alpha)$ is the derivative of $f(x, \alpha)$ w.r.t., α, keeping x constant.

$$I(\alpha) = \int_a^b f(x,\alpha)dx \text{, then}$$

$$\frac{dI}{d\alpha} = I'(\alpha) = \int_a^b \frac{\partial}{\partial\alpha}\left(f(x,\alpha)\right)dx$$

REMARK

Since *x and* α *are independent parameters so the operations.*

(*a*) *Integration* w.r.t *x*

(*b*) *Differentiation* w.r.t. α *become independent of each other.*

$\therefore$ *final outcome becomes invariant of the order in which these operations are performed.*

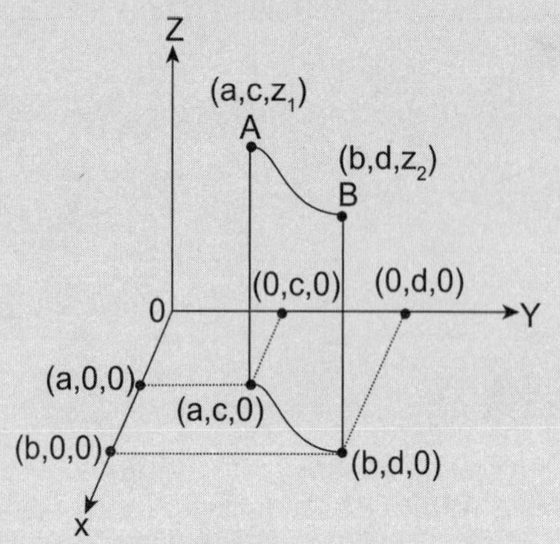

FIGURE 2.84

ILLUSTRATION 176: Verify the above property for the following integrals:

(a) $\int_0^1 \left(3\alpha^2x^2 + 2\alpha x + 1\right)dx$ (b) $\int_0^{\pi/2} \left(\sin(x+c)\right)dx$

SOLUTION: (a) $I(\alpha) = \int_0^1 \left(3\alpha^2x^2 + 2\alpha x + 1\right)dx$

$$= \left[3\alpha^2\frac{x^3}{3} + 2\alpha\frac{x^2}{2} + x\right]_0^1 = \alpha^2 + \alpha + 1$$

$$\Rightarrow \frac{d}{d\alpha}I(\alpha) = 2\alpha + 1 \qquad \text{...(1)}$$

Now $\int_0^1 \frac{\partial}{\partial\alpha}(3\alpha^2x^2 + 2\alpha x + 1)\,dx = \int_0^1 (6\alpha x^2 + 2x)\,dx = \left[\frac{6\alpha x^3}{3} + \frac{2x^2}{2}\right]_0^1 = 2\alpha + 1$ ...(2)

from (1) and (2) we observe that $\frac{d}{dx}(I(\alpha)) = \int_0^1 \frac{\partial}{\partial x}\left(3\alpha^2x^2 + 2\alpha x + 1\right)dx$

(b) Let $I_C = \int_0^{\pi/2} \left(\sin(x+c)\right)dx$

$\Rightarrow \quad I'(c) = \frac{d}{dc}\left[-\cos(x+c)\right]_0^{\pi/2} = \frac{-d}{dc}\left[-\cos\left(\frac{\pi}{2}+c\right) - \cos c\right]$

$= \frac{-d}{dc}\left[-\sin c - \cos c\right] = \frac{-d}{dc}\left[\sin c + \cos c\right]$ ...(1)

And $\int_0^{\pi/2} \frac{\partial}{\partial x}\left(\sin(x+c)\right)dx = \int_0^{\pi/2} \cos(x+c)\,dx = \left[\sin(x+c)\right]_0^{\pi/2}$

$= \sin\left(\frac{\pi}{2}+c\right) - \sin c = \cos c - \sin c$ ...(2)

$\therefore$ from (1) and (2) result is required.

ILLUSTRATION 177: Evaluate $\frac{d}{d\alpha}\int_0^1 \frac{x^\alpha - k}{\log x}\,dx$

SOLUTION: Let $I(\alpha) = \int_0^1 \frac{x^\alpha - k}{\log x}\,dx$.

Then $\frac{dI(\alpha)}{d\alpha} = \int_0^1 \frac{x^\alpha.\log x}{\log x}\,dx = \int_0^1 x^\alpha\,dx = \left[\frac{x^{\alpha+1}}{\alpha+1}\right]_0^1 = \frac{1}{\alpha+1}$

$\therefore \quad I(\alpha) = \log(\alpha + 1) + C$

If $\alpha = 0$, then $I(\alpha) = \int_0^1 \frac{x^0 - 1}{\log x}\,dx = 0$

$\therefore \quad 0 = \log(0 + 1) + C \qquad \Rightarrow C = 0$

Hence $I(\alpha) = \int_0^1 \frac{x^\alpha - 1}{\log x}\,dx = \frac{1}{\alpha+1}$

ILLUSTRATION 178: Evaluate $I = \int_0^1 \frac{\tan^{-1} a x}{x\sqrt{1-x^2}}\,dx$

SOLUTION: Let $I = \int_0^1 \frac{\tan^{-1} a x}{x\sqrt{1-x^2}}\,dx$ ...(1)

$\therefore \quad \frac{dI}{da} = \int_0^1 \frac{x\,dx}{x\sqrt{1-x^2}\,(1+a^2x^2)}$

Putting $x = \sin\theta$ we have

$\frac{dI}{da} = \int_0^{\pi/2} \frac{d\theta}{1+a^2\sin^2\theta} = \int_0^{\pi/2} \frac{\sec^2\theta\,d\theta}{a^2\tan^2\theta + 1 + \tan^2\theta}$

Further putting $\tan\theta = t$ we have

$\frac{dI}{da} = \int_0^\infty \frac{dt}{(1+a^2)t^2+1} = \frac{1}{1+a^2}\int_0^\infty \frac{dt}{t^2 + \left(\frac{1}{\sqrt{1+a^2}}\right)^2}$

$$= \frac{1}{1+a^2}\sqrt{1+a^2}\left[\tan^{-1} t\sqrt{1+a^2}\right]_0^{\infty} = \frac{1}{\sqrt{1+a^2}}\frac{\pi}{2}$$

$$\therefore \quad dI = \frac{\pi\, da}{2\sqrt{1+a^2}}$$

$$\Rightarrow \quad I = \frac{\pi}{2}\left[\ln\left(a+\sqrt{1+a^2}\right)\right] + C \text{; when } a = 0; I = 0 \text{ [from (1)]}$$

$$\Rightarrow \quad C = 0$$

$$\therefore \quad I = \frac{\pi}{2}\ln\left(a+\sqrt{1+a^2}\right)$$

ILLUSTRATION 179: Evaluate $\int\limits_0^1 \frac{\ell n\,(1-a^2x^2)}{x^2\sqrt{(1-x^2)}}dx\ (a^2 < 1)$

SOLUTION: $I = \int\limits_0^1 \frac{\ell n\,(1-a^2x^2)}{x^2\sqrt{(1-x^2)}}dx; |a| < 1$ ...(1)

$$\Rightarrow \quad \frac{dI}{da} = \int\limits_0^1 \frac{-2ax^2}{(1-a^2x^2)}\frac{dx}{x^2\sqrt{1-x^2}}$$

Putting $x = \sin\theta$, we have

$$\frac{dI}{da} = \int\limits_0^{\pi/2} \frac{2a\,d\theta}{a^2\sin^2\theta - 1} = \int\limits_0^{\pi/2} \frac{2a\sec^2\theta d\theta}{a^2\tan^2\theta - (1+\tan^2\theta)} = -\int\limits_0^{\pi/2} \frac{2a\sec^2\theta d\theta}{(1-a^2)\tan^2\theta + 1}$$

Further putting $\tan\theta = t$, we have

$$\frac{dI}{da} = \int\limits_0^{\infty} \frac{2a\,dt}{(1-a^2)t^2+1} = -\frac{2a}{(1-a^2)}\int\limits_0^{\infty} \frac{dt}{t^2 + \left(\frac{1}{\sqrt{1-a^2}}\right)^2}$$

$$\therefore \quad \frac{dI}{da} = -\frac{2a}{\sqrt{1-a^2}}\left[\tan^{-1} t\sqrt{1-a^2}\right]_0^{\infty} = -\frac{\pi.2a}{2\sqrt{1-a^2}} = -\frac{\pi a}{\sqrt{1-a^2}}$$

$$\Rightarrow \quad dI = \int \frac{-\pi a}{\sqrt{1-a^2}}da$$

$$\Rightarrow \quad I = \pi\sqrt{1-a^2} + C \text{; if } a = 0; I = 0 \text{ [from (1)]}$$

$$\Rightarrow \quad C = -\pi$$

$$\therefore \quad I = \pi\left[\sqrt{1-a^2} - 1\right]$$

ILLUSTRATION 180: $\int\limits_0^{\pi/2} \ln\left(\frac{1+a\sin x}{1-a\sin x}\right)\frac{dx}{\sin x}(|a| < 1)$

SOLUTION: Let $I = \int\limits_0^{\pi/2} \ln\left(\frac{1+a\sin x}{1-a\sin x}\right)\frac{dx}{\sin x}; (|a| < 1)$

$$\frac{dI}{da} = \int\limits_0^{\pi/2} \frac{2\sin x}{(1-a^2\sin^2 x)}.\frac{dx}{\sin x} = \int\limits_0^{\pi/2} \frac{2\sec^2 x}{(1+\tan^2 x - a^2\tan^2 x}dx = \int\limits_0^{\pi/2} \frac{2\sec^2 x}{(1-a^2)\tan^2 x + 1}dx$$

putting $\tan x = t$ we have

$$\frac{dI}{da} = \int_0^\infty \frac{2\,dt}{(1-a^2)t^2+1} = \frac{2}{(1-a^2)}\int_0^\infty \frac{dt}{t^2+\left(\frac{1}{\sqrt{1-a^2}}\right)^2}$$

$$= \frac{2}{\sqrt{1-a^2}}\left[\tan^{-1}\left(t\sqrt{1-a^2}\right)\right]_0^\infty = \frac{\pi}{\sqrt{1-a^2}} \qquad dI = \frac{\pi\, da}{\sqrt{1-a^2}}$$

$\Rightarrow$ $I = \pi \sin^{-1}a + C$; since for $a = 0$, $I = 0$.

$\Rightarrow$ $C = 0$

$\therefore$ $I = \pi \sin^{-1} a$

ILLUSTRATION 181: Evaluate $\int_0^{\pi/2} \ln(a^2\cos^2 x + b^2 \sin^2 x)\,dx$

SOLUTION: Let $I = \int_0^{\pi/2} \ln(a^2\cos^2 x + b^2\sin^2 x)dx$; $(a > 0, b > 0)$

$$= \int_0^{\pi/2} \ln\left\{a^2(\cos^2 x + K^2\sin^2 x)\right\}dx = \pi \ln a + \underbrace{\int_0^{\pi/2}\ln(\cos^2 x + k^2\sin^2 x)\,dx}_{I_1\text{ (say)}} \qquad \ldots(1)$$

Now $I_1 = \int_0^{\pi/2} \ln(\cos^2 x + k^2 \sin^2 x)\, dx$

$$\Rightarrow \frac{dI_1}{dk} = \int_0^{\pi/2} \frac{2k\sin^2 x}{\cos^2 x + k^2\sin^2 x}dx = 2k\int_0^{\pi/2}\frac{\tan^2 x\ \sec^2 x}{(1+k^2\tan^2 x)(1+\tan^2 x)}dx$$

Putting $\tan x = t$, we have

$$\frac{dI_1}{dk} = 2k\int_0^\infty \frac{t^2}{(1+k^2t^2)(1+t^2)}dt = \frac{2k}{k^2-1}\int_0^\infty \frac{(1+k^2t^2)-(1+t^2)}{(1+k^2t^2)(1+t^2)}dt$$

$$= \frac{2k}{k^2-1}\left[\int_0^\infty \frac{dt}{1+t^2} - \int_0^\infty \frac{dt}{1+k^2t^2}\right] = \frac{2k}{k^2-1}\left[\frac{\pi}{2} - \frac{1}{k}\tan^{-1} tk\right]_0^\infty$$

$$= \frac{2k}{k^2-1}\left[\frac{\pi}{2} - \frac{\pi}{2k}\right]$$

$$\frac{dI_1}{dk} = \frac{2k}{k^2-1}\frac{\pi}{2}\left(\frac{k-1}{k}\right) = \frac{\pi}{k+1}$$

$\therefore$ $I_1 = \pi \ln(1+k) + C$, if $k = 1$; $I_1 = 0$

$\Rightarrow$ $C = -\pi \ln 2$

$$\therefore\quad I_1 = \pi \ln\left(\frac{1+k}{2}\right) \qquad \text{or} \quad \pi\ln\left(\frac{1+\frac{b}{a}}{2}\right)$$

$$= \pi\ln\left(\frac{a+b}{2a}\right)$$

$$\therefore\quad I = \pi\ln a + \pi\ln\left(\frac{a+b}{2a}\right) = \pi\ln\left(\frac{a.(a+b)}{2a}\right) = \pi\ln\left(\frac{a+b}{2}\right)$$

TEXTUAL EXERCISE–9: (SUBJECTIVE)

1. Given the integral $\int_0^{\pi/2} \frac{dx}{a^2\sin^2 x + b^2\cos^2 x} = \frac{\pi}{2ab}$; then evaluate $\int_0^{\pi/2} \frac{dx}{\left(a^2\sin^2 x + b^2\cos^2 x\right)^2}$

2. Evaluate $I = \int_0^{\infty} \frac{e^{-\alpha x}\sin kx}{x} dx$ where α, k are parameters independent of each other (α > 0) and both are independent of x and hence evaluate the following integrals:

   (a) $I = \int_0^{\infty} \frac{\sin x}{x} dx.$

   (b) $I = \int_0^{\infty} \frac{\sin ax}{x} dx.$

   (c) $I = \int_0^{\infty} \left(\frac{\sin x}{x}\right)^2 dx.$

3. Find the integral $\int_0^{\pi} \frac{x\,dx}{\left(a^2\sin^2 x + b^2\cos^2 x\right)^2}$

4. Evaluate $\int_0^{\infty} \frac{\tan^{-1}(ax)}{x(1+x^2)} dx$

5. Prove that $\int_0^{\pi} \frac{\ell n\,(1 + a\cos x)}{\cos x} dx\ (|a|<1) = \pi \sin^{-1} a$

Answer Keys

1. $\frac{\pi}{4ab}\left(\frac{1}{a^2}+\frac{1}{b^2}\right)$

2. (a) $\tan^{-1}(k/a)$ (b) $\pi/2$ (c) $\pi/2$

3. $\frac{\pi^2(a^2+b^2)}{4a^3b^3}$

4. $\frac{\pi}{2}\ln|a+1|$

TEXTUAL EXERCISE–9: (OBJECTIVE)

1. The value of $\int_0^{\infty} \frac{\ln(1+a^2x^2)}{1+b^2x^2} dx$ equals

   (a) $\frac{\pi}{a}\ln\left(\frac{a+b}{b}\right)$ (b) $\frac{\pi}{b}\ln\left(\frac{a+b}{a}\right)$

   (c) $\frac{\pi}{b}\ln\left(\frac{a+b}{b}\right)$ (d) None of these

2. The value of $\int_0^{\pi/2} \sec\theta.\tan^{-1}\left(a\cos\theta\right)d\theta$ equals

   (a) $\frac{\pi}{4}\ln\left|a+\sqrt{1+a^2}\right|$ (b) $\frac{\pi}{2}\ln\left|a+\sqrt{1+a^2}\right|$

   (c) $\frac{\pi}{4}\ln\left|\sqrt{1+a^2}-a\right|$ (d) None of these

3. The value of $\int_0^{\infty} \frac{e^{-ax}\sin bx}{x} dx$ equals

   (a) $\tan^{-1}\left(\frac{b}{a}\right)$ (b) $\tan^{-1}\left(\frac{a}{b}\right)$

   (c) $\tan^{-1}\left(\frac{a+b}{a}\right)$ (d) None of these

4. The value of $\int_0^{\infty} \frac{\sin x}{x} dx$ equals

   (a) π/4 (b) π/2

   (c) –π/2 (d) None of these

5. The value of $\int_0^{\infty} \frac{\tan^{-1}\lambda x - \tan^{-1} x}{x} dx, \lambda > 0$ equals

   (a) $\frac{\pi}{2}\ln\lambda$ (b) π ln λ

   (c) ln λ (d) None of these

6. State which of the following statements is/are true

   (a) If m and M are the least and the greatest value of $f(x)$ in $[a, b]$, then $m(b-a) \le \int_a^b f(x)dx \le M(b-a)$

   (b) If $f^2(x)$ and $g^2(x)$ are integrable on $[a, b]$, then $\left|\int_a^b f(x)g(x)dx\right| \le \left(\int_a^b f^2(x)dx\right)^{1/2}\left(\int_a^b g^2(x)dx\right)^{1/2}$

   (c) If $f(x)$ is continuous on $[a, b]$, then there exists a point $c \in (a, b)$, such that $\int_a^b f(x)dx = f(c)(b-a)$

   (d) If $f(x)$ is periodic function with period T and $a \in R^+$, then $\int_a^{a+T} f(x)dx = \int_0^T f(x)dx$

Answer Keys

1. (c) **2.** (b) **3.** (a) **4.** (b) **5.** (a) **6.** (a,b,c,d)

DEFINITE INTEGRAL AS LIMIT OF INFINITE RIEMANN SUMMATION

To find the area of region enclosed by a continuous function $f(x)$ and x-axis between the ordinate $x = a$ and $x = b$.

Let us divide the interval $[a, b]$ into sub-intervals of equal width Δx.

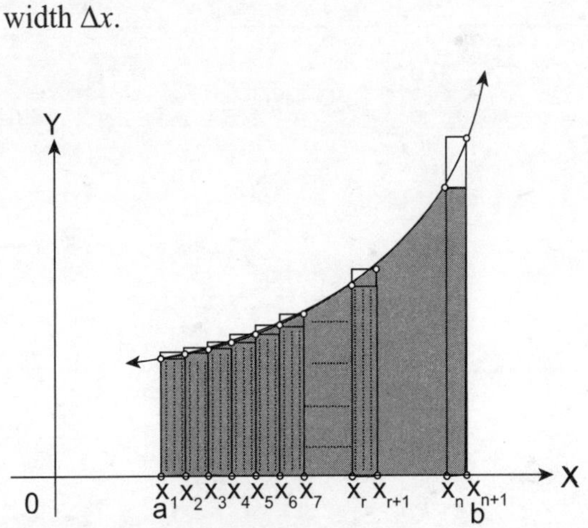

FIGURE 2.85

Clearly $\Delta x = \dfrac{b-a}{n}$.

Area of rth stripe

$$= f(x_{r+1})\,\Delta x = f\left(a + r\frac{b-a}{n}\right).\frac{b-a}{n}$$

⇒ Sum of areas of these 'n' rectangular strips

$$S = \sum_{r=1}^{n} f(x_{r+1}).\Delta x = \sum_{r=1}^{n} f\left(a + r\frac{b-a}{n}\right).\frac{b-a}{n}$$

❑ As number of strips 'n' increases to ∞, then the above sum (Riemann Sum) converges to the area enclosed which is given as integral sum.

$$\therefore \lim_{n\to\infty}\sum_{r=1}^{n} f\left(a + r\frac{(b-a)}{n}\right).\left(\frac{b-a}{n}\right) = \int_a^b f(x)\,dx$$

Detail Analysis: Area of kth strip

$$\Delta A_k = \Delta A_k = f(x_k^*).\,\Delta x = f(x_k^*)\left(\frac{b-a}{n}\right)$$

So two summations can be defined

$$\lim_{n\to\infty}\sum_{r=1}^{n} f(x_r)\Delta x \le \int_a^b f(x)\,dx \le \lim_{n\to\infty}\sum_{1}^{n} f(x_{r+1}).\Delta x$$

$$\Rightarrow \lim_{n\to\infty}\sum_{r=1}^{n} f(x_r)\Delta x = \int_a^b f(x)\,dx = \lim_{n\to\infty}\sum_{r=1}^{n} f(x_{r+1}).\Delta x$$

$$\Rightarrow \int_a^b f(x)\,dx = \lim_{n\to\infty}\sum_{r=1}^{n} f\left(a + \frac{r(b-a)}{n}\right)\left(\frac{b-a}{n}\right)$$

To evaluate a limit:

❑ Express it as $\lim\limits_{n\to\infty}\sum\limits_{r=1}^{n} f\left(a + \dfrac{r(b-a)}{n}\right)\left(\dfrac{b-a}{n}\right)$

$$\left(\frac{b-a}{n}\right) \to dx \text{ and } \left(a + \frac{r(b-a)}{n}\right) = x$$

$$\Rightarrow x_{\min} = \underbrace{\lim_{n\to\infty}\left(a + \frac{r_{\min}(b-a)}{n}\right)}_{\text{lower limit}} = a \text{ and}$$

$$x_{\max} = \underbrace{\lim_{x\to\infty}\left(a + \frac{r_{\max}(b-a)}{n}\right) = b}_{\text{upper limit}}$$

STEPS TO EVALUATE LIMIT OF INFINITE SUM USING INTEGRATION

To evaluate $\lim\limits_{n\to\infty} g(n)$ (when $g(n)$ can be expressed as infinite sum) using definite integral, follow the steps given:

Step I: Express the function $g(n)$ in terms of infinite summation, using sigma notation.

$$\text{i.e., } g(n) = \sum_{r=1}^{n} f\left(a + r\frac{(b-a)}{n}\right)\left(\frac{b-a}{n}\right)$$

Step II: Replace $a + r\left(\dfrac{b-a}{n}\right) \to x$ and $\left(\dfrac{b-a}{n}\right) \to dx$

Step III: $\lim\limits_{n\to\infty}\sum\limits_{r=1}^{n}$ converts to $\int\limits_{\alpha}^{\beta}$; where

$$\beta = \lim_{n\to\infty}\left(a + r_{\max}\frac{b-a}{n}\right) = b;\ \alpha = \lim_{n\to\infty}\left(a + r_{\min}\frac{b-a}{n}\right) = a$$

Step IV: $\lim\limits_{n\to\infty}\sum\limits_{r=1}^{n} f\left(a + r\left(\dfrac{b-a}{n}\right)\right).\left(\dfrac{b-a}{n}\right) = \int\limits_a^b f(x)dx$

❑ When domain of $f(x)$ is divided into unit length sub-intervals each of which further divided into n subintervals, Interval $[\alpha, \beta]$ contains $p(n)^{\text{th}}$ to $q(n)^{\text{th}}$ stripes. Then algorithm becomes

Step I: Express the function $g(n)$ in terms of infinite summation, using sigma notation.

i.e., $g(n)=\sum_{r=p(n)}^{q(n)} f\left(\frac{r}{n}\right).\left(\frac{1}{n}\right)$

Step II: Replace $\frac{r}{n}\rightarrow x$ and

$\left(\frac{1}{n}\right)\rightarrow dx$

Step III: $\lim_{n\to\infty}\sum_{r=p(n)}^{r=q(n)}$ converts to $\int_{\alpha}^{\beta}$; where

$\beta=\lim_{n\to\infty}\left(\frac{r_{\max}}{n}\right)=\lim_{n\to\infty}\left(\frac{q(n)}{n}\right)$;

$\alpha=\lim_{n\to\infty}\left(\frac{r_{\min}}{n}\right)=\lim_{n\to\infty}\left(\frac{p(n)}{n}\right)$

Step IV: $\lim_{n\to\infty}\sum_{r=p(n)}^{q(n)} f\left(\frac{r}{n}\right).\left(\frac{1}{n}\right)=\int_{\alpha}^{\beta} f(x)dx$

ILLUSTRATION 182: Evaluate $\lim_{n\to\infty}\left[\frac{1}{1+n}+\frac{1}{2+n}+\frac{1}{3+n}+...+\frac{1}{2n}\right]$

SOLUTION: $\lim_{n\to\infty}\left[\frac{1}{1+n}+\frac{1}{2+n}+\frac{1}{3+n}+...+\frac{1}{2n}\right]$

$$=\lim_{n\to\infty}\sum_{r=1}^{n}\frac{1}{r+n}=\lim_{n\to\infty}\sum_{r=1}^{n}\frac{1}{n}\frac{1}{\left(\frac{r}{n}\right)+1}=\int_0^1\frac{dx}{x+1}=\left[\log_e(x+1)\right]_0^1=\log_e 2$$

ILLUSTRATION 183: Evaluate $\lim_{n\to\infty}\left[\frac{n+r}{n^2+1^2}+\frac{n+2}{n^2+2^2}+\frac{n+3}{n^2+3^2}+...+\frac{3}{5n}\right]$

SOLUTION: Let $I=\lim_{n\to\infty}\sum_{r=1}^{2n}\frac{n+r}{n^2+r^2}=\lim_{n\to\infty}\sum_{r=1}^{2n}\frac{1}{n}\frac{1+\frac{r}{n}}{1+\left(\frac{r}{n}\right)^2}$

$\because$ $\lim_{n\to\infty}\left(\frac{r}{n}\right)=0$, when r = 1, lower limit = 0

and $\lim_{n\to\infty}\left(\frac{r}{n}\right)=\lim_{n\to\infty}\left(\frac{2n}{n}\right)=2$, when r = $2n$, upper limit = 2

$$\therefore\quad I=\int_0^2\frac{1+x}{1+x^2}dx=\int_0^2\frac{1}{1+x^2}dx+\frac{1}{2}\int_0^2\frac{2x}{1+x^2}dx$$

$$=\left[\tan^{-1}x\right]_0^2+\frac{1}{2}\left[\log_e\left(1+x^2\right)\right]_0^2=\tan^{-1}2+\frac{1}{2}\log_e 5$$

ILLUSTRATION 184: Evaluate $\lim_{n\to\infty}\left(\frac{n!}{n^n}\right)^{\frac{1}{n}}$

SOLUTION: Let $y=\lim_{n\to\infty}\left(\frac{n!}{n^n}\right)^{\frac{1}{n}}$

$$\log_e y=\lim_{n\to\infty}\frac{1}{n}\log_e\left(\frac{n!}{n^n}\right)=\lim_{n\to\infty}\frac{1}{n}\log_e\left(\frac{1.2.3....n}{n^n}\right)$$

$$=\lim_{n\to\infty}\frac{1}{n}\left(\log_e\left(\frac{1}{n}\right)+\log_e\left(\frac{2}{n}\right)+\log_e\left(\frac{3}{n}\right)+...+\log_e\left(\frac{n}{n}\right)\right)$$

$$=\lim_{n\to\infty}\frac{1}{n}\sum_{r=1}^{n}\log_e\left(\frac{r}{n}\right)=\int_0^1\log_e x\,dx=\left[x\log_e x-x\right]_0^1=(0-1)-\lim_{x\to 0}x\log_e x+0=-1-0=-1$$

$\Rightarrow\ y = \frac{1}{e}$ $\qquad \left(\because \lim_{x\to 0} x \lg_e x = \lim_{x\to 0} \frac{\log x}{y/x} = 0 \text{ by L.H.Rule}\right)$

ILLUSTRATION 185: $\lim_{n\to\infty}\left(\frac{1}{\sqrt{2n-1^2}}+\frac{1}{\sqrt{4n-2^2}}+\frac{1}{\sqrt{6n-3^2}}+....+\frac{1}{n}\right)$ has the value equal to

(a) π (b) π/2

(c) π/4 (d) 0

SOLUTION: $T_r = \frac{1}{\sqrt{2rn-r^2}} = \frac{1}{r\sqrt{\frac{2}{r/n}-1}} = \frac{1}{n}.\frac{1}{r/n}.\frac{1}{\sqrt{\frac{2}{r/n}-1}}$

$$\therefore\ S = \frac{1}{n}\sum_{r=1}^{n}\frac{1}{\frac{r}{n}\sqrt{\frac{2}{r/n}-1}} = \int_0^1 \frac{dx}{x\sqrt{\frac{2}{x}-1}} = \int_0^1 \frac{dx}{\sqrt{x}\sqrt{2-x}}$$

$$\Rightarrow\ S = \int_0^1 \frac{dx}{\sqrt{2x-x^2}} = \int_0^1 \frac{dx}{\sqrt{-(x^2-2x)}} = \int_0^1 \frac{dx}{\sqrt{-(x^2-2x+1)+1}} = \int_0^1 \frac{dx}{\sqrt{1-(x-1)^2}}$$

$$= \left|\sin^{-1}(x-1)\right|_0^1 = \sin^{-1} x - \sin^{-1}(-1) = \pi/2$$

ILLUSTRATION 186: Evaluate the following

(i) $S = \sum_{r=0}^{n-1}\frac{1}{\sqrt{4n^2-r^2}}$ as $n\to\infty$ (ii) $\lim_{n\to\infty}\left(\frac{1}{2n+1}+\frac{1}{2n+2}+.....+\frac{1}{6n}\right)$

SOLUTION: (i) $\sum_{r=0}^{n-1}\frac{1}{n\sqrt{4-(r/n)^2}} = \frac{1}{n}\sum_{r=0}^{n-1}\frac{1}{\sqrt{4-(r/n)^2}}$

Hence $S = \lim_{n\to 0} S_n = \lim_{n\to\infty}\frac{1}{n}\sum_{r=0}^{n-1}\frac{1}{\sqrt{4-(r/n)^2}} = \int_0^1 \frac{dx}{\sqrt{4-x^2}} = \left[\sin^{-1}\frac{x}{2}\right]_0^1 = \sin^{-1}\left(\frac{1}{2}\right) = -\frac{\pi}{6}$

(ii) Let $S = \lim_{n\to\infty}\left(\frac{1}{2n+1}+\frac{1}{2n+2}+.....+\frac{1}{6n}\right) = \lim_{n\to\infty}\sum_{r=1}^{4n}\frac{1}{2n+r} = \lim_{n\to\infty}\sum_{r=1}^{4n}\frac{1}{n}\frac{1}{2+(r/n)}$

$$\Rightarrow\ S = \int_0^4 \frac{dx}{2+x} = [\ln|2+x|]_0^4 = \ln 6 - \ln 2 = \ln 3$$

ILLUSTRATION 187: Evaluate $\lim_{n\to\infty}\left(\frac{n^{1/2}}{n^{3/2}}+\frac{n^{1/2}}{(n+3)^{3/2}}+\frac{n^{1/2}}{(n+6)^{3/2}}+...+\frac{n^{1/2}}{\{n+3(n-1)\}^{3/2}}\right)$

SOLUTION: Here r^{th} term $= \frac{\sqrt{n}}{\{n+3(r-1)\}^{3/2}} = \frac{1}{n}.\frac{1}{\left\{1+3\frac{r-1}{n}\right\}^{3/2}}$

Since the rth term contains $(r-1)$, so let us consider the $(r+1)$th term

The $(r+1)^{th}$ term $= \frac{\sqrt{n}}{\{n+3r\}^{3/2}} = \frac{1/n}{\{1+3(r/n)\}^{3/2}}$

Thus, the given sum $= \lim_{n\to\infty}\sum_{r=0}^{n-1}\frac{1/n}{\{1+3(r/n)\}^{3/2}} = \int_0^1 \frac{dx}{(1+3x)^{3/2}} = \frac{1}{3}$

TEXTUAL EXERCISE–10: (SUBJECTIVE)

1. (i) Evaluate the following limits:

(a) $\lim_{n\to\infty}\left(\frac{1}{n+1}+\frac{1}{n+2}+\frac{1}{n+3}+....+\frac{1}{6n}\right)$

(b) $\lim_{n\to\infty}\left[\frac{(n^3+1^3)(n^3+2^3)(n^3+3^3)....(n^3+n^3)}{n^{3n}}\right]^{1/n}$

(c) $\lim_{n\to\infty}\sum_{r=1}^{3n}\frac{n^2}{(3n+r)^3}$

(d) $\lim_{n\to\infty}\frac{n^2}{(n^2+1)^{3/2}}+\frac{n^2}{(n^2+2^2)^{3/2}}+.......+\frac{n^2}{\left[n^2+(n-1)^2\right]^{3/2}}$

(e) $\lim_{n\to\infty}\frac{\sqrt{1}+\sqrt{2}+\sqrt{3}+.........+2\sqrt{n}}{n\sqrt{n}}$

(f) $\lim_{n\to\infty}\left(\frac{1}{1+n^3}+\frac{4}{8+n^3}+..+\frac{r^2}{r^3+n^3}+..+\frac{1}{2n}\right)$

(g) $\lim_{n\to\infty}\left[\frac{1}{\sqrt{n^2-1}}+\frac{1}{\sqrt{n^2-4}}+..+\frac{1}{\sqrt{n^2-(n-1)^2}}\right]$

(h) $\lim_{n\to\infty}\frac{1}{n}\left[\sec^2\frac{\pi}{4n}+\sec^2\frac{2\pi}{4n}+.....+\sec^2\frac{n\pi}{4n}\right]$

(ii) Evaluate the following definite integrals (using first principle):

(a) $\int_1^4(ax^2+bx+c)dx$ (b) $\int_a^b e^x dx$

2. Evaluate the following integrals:

(a) $\lim_{n\to\infty}\frac{1}{n}\sum_{r=1}^{2n}\frac{r}{\sqrt{n^2+r^2}}$

(b) $\lim_{n\to\infty}\left(\frac{n}{n^2+1^2}+\frac{n}{n^2+2^2}+..+\frac{1}{2n}\right)$

(c) $\lim_{n\to\infty}\sum_{k=1}^{n}\log\left(1+\frac{k}{n}\right)^{1/n}$

(d) $\lim_{n\to\infty}\left(\frac{1}{na}+\frac{1}{na+1}+\frac{1}{na+2}+..+\frac{1}{nb}\right)$

3. Evaluate the given limits using definite integrals:

$\lim_{n\to\infty}\left[\frac{n+1}{n^2+1^2}+\frac{n+2}{n^2+2^2}+\frac{n+3}{n^2+3^2}+...+\frac{3}{5n}\right]$

4. Evaluate the following limits using definite integral:

(a) $\lim_{n\to\infty}\sum_{r=1}^{n}\frac{r}{n^2}\sec^2\frac{r^2}{n^2}$

(b) $\lim_{n\to\infty}\frac{[(n+1)(n+2)...(n+n)]^{1/n}}{n}$

5. Evaluate the given limits using definite integral:

$\lim_{n\to\infty}\frac{n}{(n+1)\sqrt{(2n+1)}}+\frac{n}{(n+2)\sqrt{2(2n+2)}}+\frac{n}{(n+3)\sqrt{3(2n+3)}}$.... upto n terms

6. Evaluate the given limits by using definite integral

$\lim_{n\to\infty}\sum_{r=1}^{n}\frac{\sqrt{n}}{\sqrt{r}\left(3\sqrt{r}+4\sqrt{n}\right)^2}$

7. Evaluate the given limits by using definite integral

$\lim_{n\to\infty}\left\{\frac{1}{1+n^4}+\frac{8}{16+n^4}+\frac{27}{81+n^4}+.....n\text{ terms}\right\}$

8. Compute $\lim_{n\to\infty}\left(\frac{1}{n}+\frac{1}{n+1}+\frac{1}{n+2}+...+\frac{1}{an}\right)$, where a is positive integer. Calculate approximately $\frac{1}{100}+\frac{1}{101}+\frac{1}{102}+...\frac{1}{300}$

Answer Keys

1. (i) (a) ln 6 (b) log4 –3 + $\pi/\sqrt{3}$ (c) 1/24 (d) $\frac{1}{\sqrt{2}}$ (e) $\frac{16}{3}$ (f) (1/3) log 9

(g) $\pi/2$ (h) $4/\pi$ (ii) (a) $21a+\frac{15}{2}b+3c$ (b) $e^b - e^a$

2. (a) $\sqrt{5}-1$ (b) $\pi/4$ (c) $\log_e\left(\frac{4}{e}\right)$ (d) $\log\left(\frac{b}{a}\right)$ 3. $\tan^{-1}2 + 1/2\ln 5$

4. (a) $\frac{1}{2}\tan 1$ (b) $4/e$ 5. $\frac{\pi}{3}$ 6. 1/14 7. $\frac{1}{4}\ln 2$ 8. ln 3

TEXTUAL EXERCISE–10: (OBJECTIVE)

1. Sum of the series

$$\lim_{n\to\infty}\left[\frac{1}{\sqrt{n^2-1^2}}+\frac{1}{\sqrt{n^2-2^2}}.....+\frac{1}{\sqrt{n^2-(n-1)^2}}\right]$$ is

(a) π/2 (b) π/4
(c) π/6 (d) None of these

2. $\lim_{n\to\infty}\left[\left(1+\frac{1}{n^2}\right)\left(1+\frac{2^2}{n^2}\right)......\left(1+\frac{n^2}{n^2}\right)\right]^{1/n}$ is

(a) $e^{\frac{1}{2}(\pi-4)}$ (b) $2.e^{\frac{1}{2}(\pi-4)}$
(c) $\frac{1}{2}.e^{2(\pi-4)}$ (d) None of these

3. $\lim_{n\to\infty}\frac{\sqrt[n]{n!}}{n}$ is equal to

(a) $1/e$ (b) e
(c) $\frac{2}{e}$ (d) None of these

4. $\lim_{n\to\infty}\left(\frac{n+1}{n^2+1^2}+\frac{n+2}{n^2+2^2}+.......+\frac{1}{n}\right)$ is

(a) $\frac{\pi}{4}+\frac{1}{2}$
(b) $\frac{1}{2}\log 2+\frac{\pi}{2}$
(c) $\frac{\pi}{4}+\frac{1}{2}\log 2$
(d) None of these

5. $\lim_{n\to\infty}\sum_{r=1}^{n}\frac{1}{n}e^{r/n}$ is

(a) e (b) $e-1$
(c) $1-e$ (d) $e+1$

6. $\lim_{n\to\infty}\sum_{r=1}^{n}\frac{1}{n}\sin\frac{r\pi}{2n}$ is

(a) π/2 (b) 2
(c) 2/π (d) None of these

7. $\lim_{n\to\infty}\left\{\frac{n!}{(kn)^n}\right\}^{1/n}$, where $k \neq 0$ is a constant and $n \in \mathbb{N}$, is equal to

(a) ke (b) $k^{-1}.e$
(c) ke^{-1} (d) $k^{-1}.e^{-1}$

8. $\lim_{n\to\infty}\sum_{r=1}^{n}\frac{1}{\sqrt{nr}}$ is equal to

(a) 2 (b) 1
(c) 0 (d) None of these

9. $\lim_{n\to\infty}\sum_{r=0}^{n-1}\frac{1}{\sqrt{n^2-r^2}}$ is

(a) π (b) π/2
(c) π/4 (d) None of these

10. $\lim_{n\to\infty}\sum_{r=1}^{4n}\frac{1}{n+r}$ is

(a) $\log_e 5$ (b) 0
(c) $\log_e 4$ (d) None of these

11. $\lim_{n\to\infty}\frac{2^k+4^k+6^k....+(2n)^k}{n^{k+1}}$, $k \neq -1$; is equal to

(a) 2^k
(b) $\frac{2^k}{k+1}$
(c) $\frac{1}{k+1}$
(d) None of these

12. $\lim_{n\to\infty}\frac{1}{n}\sum_{r=1}^{2n}\frac{r}{\sqrt{n^2+r^2}}$ equals

(a) $1+\sqrt{5}$ (b) $-1+\sqrt{5}$
(c) $-1+\sqrt{2}$ (d) $1+\sqrt{2}$

Answer Keys

1. (a) **2.** (b) **3.** (a) **4.** (c) **5.** (b) **6.** (c) **7.** (d) **8.** (a) **9.** (b) **10.** (a)
11. (b) **12.** (b)

MISCELLANEOUS CONCEPTS

WALLI'S Formulae

1. For $n \in \mathbb{N}, \int_0^{\pi/2} \sin^n x\, dx = \int_0^{\pi/2} \cos^n x\, dx$

$$= \begin{cases} \left\{\dfrac{(n-1)\times(n-3)\times(n-5)}{n\times(n-2)\times(n-4)}\cdots\right\}\dfrac{\pi}{2}; & \text{If } n \text{ is even} \\ \left\{\dfrac{(n-1)\times(n-3)\times(n-5)}{n\times(n-2)\times(n-4)}\cdots\right\}; & \text{If } n \text{ is odd} \end{cases}$$

2. For $m, n \in \mathbb{N}, \int_0^{\pi/2} \sin^m x \cos^n x\, dx$

$$= \frac{\{(m-1)\times(m-3)\ldots\}\{(n-1)\times(n-3)\ldots.\}}{(m+n)(m+n-2)\ldots\ldots..}.p;$$

Where $p = \pi/2$ if both m and n are even otherwise $p = 1$

Proof 1: Let $I_3 = \int_0^{\pi/2} \sin^n x\, dx = \int_0^{\pi/2} \underbrace{\sin^{n-1} x}_{I}.\underbrace{\sin x}_{II}\, dx$

$$= \left|(\sin^{n-1} x)(-\cos x)\right|_0^{\pi/2} - \int_0^{\pi/2} (n-1)\sin^{n-2} x \cos x(-\cos x)\, dx$$

$$= (n-1)\int_0^{\pi/2} \sin^{n-2} x(1-\sin^2 x)\, dx$$

$$= (n-1)\int_0^{\pi/2} \sin^{n-2} x\, dx - (n-1)\int_0^{\pi/2} \sin^n x\, dx$$

$$\Rightarrow \ln(1+(n-1)) = (n-1)\int_0^{\pi/2} \sin^{n-2} x\, dx$$

$$\Rightarrow I_n = \frac{(n-1)}{n}\int_0^{\pi/2} \sin^{n-2} x\, dx$$

$$\Rightarrow I_n = \frac{(n-1)}{n}.I_{n-2}$$

Using the above recurrence relation again and again we get

$$I_n = \frac{(n-1)}{n}.\frac{(n-3)}{(n-2)}.I_{n-4}$$

$= \dfrac{(n-1)}{n}.\dfrac{(n-3)}{(n-2)}.\dfrac{(n-5)}{(n-4)}.I_{n-6}$ and so on. Now there arise two cases as follows:

Case (i): **If n is odd**

As we go on diminishing $(n-1)$ by 4, we finally obtain 4 in numerator and in denominator, as we go on diminishing n by 2, we finally obtain 5. Hence I_n is given by

$$I_n = \frac{(n-1)(n-3)(n-5)\ldots.(2)}{n(n-2)(n-4)\ldots.3}.I_1$$

$$= \frac{(n-1)(n-3)(n-5)\ldots.(2)}{n(n-2)(n-4)\ldots.3}\int_0^{\pi/2} \sin x\, dx$$

$$= \frac{(n-1)(n-3)(n-5)\ldots.(2)}{n(n-2)(n-4)\ldots.3}[-\cos x]_0^{\pi/2}$$

Case (ii): **If n is even**

Then as we go on diminishing $(n-1)$ by 2, we finally obtain 3 in numerator and in denominator, as we go on diminishing n by 2, we finally obtain 4 in denominator. Hence I_n is given by

$$I_n = \frac{(n-1)(n-3)(n-5)\ldots.(1)}{n(n-2)(n-4)\ldots\ldots..(2)}.I_0$$

$$= \frac{(n-1)(n-3)(n-5)\ldots.(1)}{n(n-2)(n-4)\ldots\ldots..(2)}.\int_0^{\pi/2} \sin^{\circ} x\, dx$$

$$= \frac{(n-1)(n-3)(n-5)\ldots.(1)}{n(n-2)(n-4)\ldots\ldots.(2)}\times\frac{\pi}{2}$$

Combining above two cases, we have

$$\int_0^{\pi/2} \sin^n x\, dx = \frac{(n-1)(n-3)(n-5)\ldots.}{n(n-2)(n-4)\ldots\ldots..}.p,$$

where $p = 1$ if n is odd and $p = \dfrac{\pi}{2}$ if n is even

Similarly $I_n = \int_0^{\pi/2} \cos^n x\, dx = \int_0^{\pi/2} \cos^{n-1} x.\cos x\, dx$

$$= \left|\cos^{n-1} x \sin x\right|_0^{\pi/2} - \int_0^{\pi/2} (n-1)\cos^{n-2} x(-\sin x)\sin x\, dx$$

$$= 0 + (n-1)\int_0^{\pi/2} \cos^{n-2} x(1-\cos^2 x)\, dx$$

$= (n-1)\, I_{n-2} - (n-1)I_n$

$\Rightarrow I_n(1 + n - 1) = (n-1)\, I_{n-2}$

$$\Rightarrow I_n = \frac{(n-1)}{n}I_{n-2}$$

It is the same recurrence relation as we derived earlier for $\int_0^{\pi/2} \sin^2 ndx$. Thus, future can prove that

$$I_n = \int_0^{\pi/2} \cos^n x\, dx = \left\{\frac{(n-1)\times(n-3)\times\ldots\ldots}{n\times(n-2)\times\ldots\ldots\ldots..}\right\}.p,$$

where $p = 1$ for n an odd natural number and $p = \dfrac{\pi}{2}$ for n an even natural number.

Thus, $\int_0^{\pi/2} \sin^n x\, dx = \int_0^{\pi/2} \cos^n x\, dx$

$$= \left\{\frac{(n-1)\times(n-3)\times(n-5)\times\ldots\ldots}{n\times(n-2)\times(n-4)\times\ldots\ldots\ldots..}\right\}.p$$

where $p = 1$ for n an odd natural number and $p=\frac{\pi}{2}$ for n an even natural number.

2. Now consider

$$I_{(m,n)} = \int_0^{\pi/2} \sin^m x \cos^n x\, dx$$

$$= \int_0^{\pi/2} \underbrace{\sin^{m-1} x}_{I}.\underbrace{(\sin x.\cos^n x)}_{II}\, dx \text{ (integrating by parts)}$$

$$= \left|\sin^{m-1} x\int\left(\sin x \cos^n x\right)dx\right|_0^{\pi/2} -$$

$$\int_0^{\pi/2}\left\{(m-1)\sin^{m-2} x\cos x\int \sin x\cos^n x\, dx\right\}dx$$

$$= \left|\sin^{m-1} x\left[-\frac{\cos^{n+1} x}{n+1}\right]\right|_0^{\pi/2} -$$

$$(m-1)\int_0^{\pi/2} \sin^{m-2} x\cos x\left[-\frac{\cos^{n+1} x}{n+1}\right]dx$$

$$= -\frac{1}{n+1}[0-0]+\frac{(m-1)}{(n+1)}\int_0^{\pi/2} \sin^{m-2} x\cos^{n+2} x\, dx$$

$$= \frac{(m-1)}{(n+1)}\int_0^{\pi/2}\left(\sin^{m-2} x-\sin^m x\right)\cos^n x\, dx$$

$$= \frac{(m-1)}{(n+1)}\int_0^{\pi/2} \sin^{m-2} x\cos^n x\, dx-\frac{(m-1)}{(n+1)}I_{(m,n)}$$

$$\Rightarrow I_{(m,n)}\left(1+\frac{m-1}{n+1}\right)=\left(\frac{m-1}{n+1}\right)I_{(m-2,n)}$$

$$\Rightarrow I_{(m,n)} = \frac{(m-1)}{(m+n)}I_{(m-2,n)} \quad \ldots(1)$$

Using the above recurrence relations (1) again and again we get

$$I_{(m,n)} = \frac{(m-1)}{(m+n)}\cdot\frac{(m-3)}{(m+n-2)}I_{(m-4,n)}$$

$$= \frac{(m-1)}{(m+n)}\cdot\frac{(m-3)}{(m+n-2)}\cdot\frac{(m-5)}{(m+n-4)}I_{(m-6,n)} \text{ and so on.}$$

Now there arise two cases.

Case (i): If m is odd

As we go on diminishing $(m-1)$ by 2, we finally obtain factor 4 in numerator along with $I_{(3,n)}$ and on the other hand as we go on diminishing $(m+n)$ by 2, we finally obtain $(n+5)$ in numerator. i.e.,

$$I_n = \frac{(m-1)(m-3)(m-5)..........2}{(m+n)(m+n-2)(m+n-4)....(n+3)}.I_{(1,n)} \quad \ldots(2)$$

Now $I_{(m,n)} = \int_0^{\pi/2} \sin x\cos^n x\, dx$

$$= -\left[\frac{\cos^{n+1} x}{(n+1)}\right]_0^{\pi/2} = -\frac{1}{(n+1)}[0-1]=\frac{1}{(n+1)}$$

$$= -\left[\frac{\cos^{n+1} x}{n+1}\right]_0^{\pi/2} = \left[\frac{\cos^{n+3} 3}{n+3}\right]_0^{\pi/2}$$

$$= -\left[\frac{-1}{n+1}\right]+\frac{1}{n+3}[0-1]=\frac{1}{n+1}-\frac{1}{n+3}=\frac{2}{(x+1)(x+3)}$$

$\therefore$ from (2)

$$I_{(m,n)} = \frac{(m-1)(m-3)(m-5)....2.1}{(m+n)(m+n-2)(m+n-4)....(n+3)(n+1)}$$

$$(m-1)(m-3)(m-5).......2$$

or $$I_{(m,n)} = \frac{(1)(n-1)(n-3)(n-5).........2}{(m+n)(m+n-2)(m+n-4)....} \text{ if } n \text{ is odd.}$$

$$(n+3)(n+1)(n-1)(n-3)...2$$

and

$$I_{(m,n)} = \frac{\{(m-1)(m-3)(m-5).....\}\{(n-1)(n-3)......1\}}{(m+n)(m+n-2)(m+n-4)....(n+3)(n+1)....1}$$

if n is even

Case (ii): If m is even

As we go on diminishing $(m-1)$ by 2, we finally obtain factor 3 in numerator along with $I_{(2,n)}$. On the other hand as we go on diminishing $(m+n)$ by 2, we finally obtain $(n+4)$ in numerator, i.e.,

$$I_{(m,n)} = \frac{(m-1)(m-3)(m-5)....1}{(m+n)(m+n-2)(m+n-4).......(n+2)}.I_{(0,n)} \quad \ldots(3)$$

Now

$$I_{(0,n)} = \int_0^{\pi/2} \sin^0 x\cos^n x\, dx = \int_0^{\pi/2} \cos^n x\, dx$$

$$= \left\{\frac{(n-1)\times(n-3)\times....}{n\times(n-2)\times.......}\right\}.p\text{; where } p \text{ is 1 for } n \text{ an odd}$$

natural number and n an odd natural number and $p=\frac{\pi}{2}$ for n an even natural number

$\therefore$ From (3), we have,

$$I_{(m,n)} = \frac{\{(m-1)(m-3)(m-5)...1\}\{(n-1)(n-3)\times...\}}{\left\{\begin{matrix}(m+n)(m+n-2)(m+n-4)....\times\\(n+2)(n)(n-2)....\end{matrix}\right\}}.p;$$

Where p is 1 for n an odd natural number and $p=\frac{\pi}{2}$ for an even natural number.

From above two cases we conclude that

$$\int_0^{\pi/2} \sin^m x\cos^n x dx$$

$$= \frac{\{(m-1)\times(m-3)\times....\}.\{(n-1)\times(n-3)\times....\}}{\{(m+n)\times(m+n-2)\times(m+n-4).......\}}.p;$$

where $p=\frac{\pi}{2}$ if both m and n are even, otherwise $p=1$

ILLUSTRATION 188: Evaluate the following integrals:

(i) $\int_0^{\pi/2} \sin^7 x \, dx$ (ii) $\int_0^{\pi/2} \sin^8 x \, dx$

(iii) $\int_0^{\pi/4} \cos^8 (2x) \, dx$ (iv) $\int_0^{\infty} \frac{1}{(1+t^2)^4} dt$

SOLUTION: (i) $I = \int_0^{\pi/2} \sin^7 x \, dx$

Here $n = 7$ (odd natural number), therefore by Walli's formula

$$I = \left\{\frac{(n-1)\times(n-3)\times....}{n\times(n-2)\times.....}\right\} = \frac{6\times4\times2}{7\times5\times3} = \frac{16}{35}$$

(ii) $I = \int_0^{\pi/2} \sin^8 x \, dx$

Here $n = 8$ (even natural number), therefore by Walli's formula

$$I = \left\{\frac{(n-1)\times(n-3)\times(n-5)\times....}{n\times(n-2)\times(n-4)\times.....}\right\}.\frac{\pi}{2} = \frac{7\times5\times3\times1}{8\times6\times4\times2}\times\frac{\pi}{2} = \frac{35\pi}{256}$$

(iii) $I = \int_0^{\pi/4} \cos^8 (2x) \, dx$

Put $2x = t$

$\Rightarrow$ $dx = \frac{dt}{2}$; when $x = 0, t = 0$ and when $x = \frac{\pi}{4}, t = \frac{\pi}{2}$

$$\therefore \quad I = \int_0^{\pi/2} \cos^8 t \frac{dt}{2} = \frac{1}{2}\int_0^{\pi/2} \cos^8 t \, dt = \frac{1}{2}\left\{\frac{7\times5\times3\times1}{8\times6\times4\times2}\right\}\times\frac{\pi}{2} = \frac{35\pi}{512}$$

(iv) $I = \int_0^{\infty} \frac{1}{(1+t^2)^4} dt$

Let us substitute $t = \tan x$

$\Rightarrow$ $dt = \sec^2 x \, dx$

$\therefore$ when $t = 0, x = 0$ and when $t \to \infty, x \to \frac{\pi}{2}$

$$\therefore \quad I = \int_0^{\pi/2} \frac{\sec^2 x}{(1+\tan^2 x)^4} dx = \int_0^{\pi/2} \frac{1}{\sec^6 x} dx = \int_0^{\pi/2} \cos^6 x \, dx$$

$$= \frac{5\times3\times1}{6\times4\times2}\times\frac{\pi}{2}$$ (By Walli's Formula)

$$= \frac{5\pi}{32}$$

ILLUSTRATION 189: Evaluate the following integrals:

(i) $\int_0^{\pi/2} \sin^7 x \cos^4 x \, dx$ (ii) $\int_0^{\pi/2} \sin^6 x \cos^8 x \, dx$

(iii) $\int_0^{\pi/2} \sin^5 x \cos^7 x \, dx$

SOLUTION: (i) Let $I = \int_0^{\pi/2} \sin^7 x \cos^4 x\, dx$

Here $m = 7, n = 4$ (not both even)

∴ By Walli's formula

$$I = \frac{\{(m-1)\times(m-3)\times....\}\{(n-1)\times(n-3)\times....\}}{\{(m+n)(m+n-2)(m+n-4)\times....\}} = \frac{6\times4\times2\times3\times1}{11\times9\times7\times5\times3} = \frac{16}{3465}$$

(ii) $I = \int_0^{\pi/2} \sin^6 x \cos^8 x\, dx$

Here $m = 6, n = 8$ (both are even natural numbers)

∴ By Walli's formula

$$I = \frac{\{(m-1)\times(m-3)\times....\}\{(n-1)\times(n-3)\times....\}}{\{(m+n)(m+n-2)(m+n-4)\times....\}}.\frac{\pi}{2}$$

$$= \frac{5\times3\times1\times7\times5\times3\times1}{14\times12\times10\times8\times6\times4\times2}.\frac{\pi}{2} = \frac{5\pi}{4096}$$

(iii) Let $I = \int_0^{\pi/2} \sin^5 x \cos^7 x\, dx$

Here $m = 5, n = 7$ (not both even)

∴ By Walli's formula

$$I = \frac{\{(m-1)\times(m-3)\times....\}\{(n-1)\times(n-3)\times....\}}{\{(m+n)(m+n-2)(m+n-4)\times....\}} = \frac{4\times2\times6\times4\times2}{12\times10\times8\times6\times4\times2} = \frac{1}{120}$$

ILLUSTRATION 190: Evaluate the integral $\int_0^{\pi/4} \sin^5 4x \cos^2 2x\, dx$

SOLUTION: Let $I = \int_0^{\pi/4} \sin^5 4x \cos^2 2x\, dx = \int_0^{\pi/4} \left(32\sin^5 2x \cos^5 2x\right)\cos^2 2x\, dx = 32\int_0^{\pi/4} \sin^5 2x \cos^4 2x\, dx$

Put $2x = t$

$\Rightarrow \quad dx = \frac{dt}{2}$; when $x = 0, t = 0$ and when $x = \frac{\pi}{4}, t = \frac{\pi}{2}$

$\therefore \quad I = 32\times\frac{1}{2}\int_0^{\pi/2} \sin^5 t \cos^4 t\, dt;\ m = 5, n = 4$

$\Rightarrow \quad I = 16\times\frac{(4)\times(2)\times(3)\times(1)}{9\times7\times5\times3\times1} = \frac{128}{315}$

ILLUSTRATION 191: Evaluate the integral $\int_0^{\pi/4} \sin^4 4x\left(1-\cos 6x\right)dx$

SOLUTION: Let $I = \int_0^{\pi/4} \sin^4 4x\left(1-\cos 6x\right)dx = \int_0^{\pi/4} \sin^4 4x\, dx - \int_0^{\pi/4} \sin^4 4x \cos 6x\, dx$

$$= \int_0^{\pi/4} 16\sin^4 2x \cos^4 2x\, dx - \int_0^{\pi/4} \sin^4 4x\left[\cos 2x \cos 4x - \sin 2x \sin 4x\right]dx$$

$$= \frac{16}{2}\int_0^{\pi/2} \sin^4 t \cos^4 t\, dx - \int_0^{\pi/4} 16\sin^4 2x \cos^5 2x \cos 4x\, dx + \int_0^{\pi/4} 16\times2\sin^6 2x \cos^5 2x\, dx$$

$$= \frac{8(3)\times 1\times 3\times 1}{8\times 6\times 4\times 2}\times\frac{\pi}{2} - 16\int_0^{\pi/4}\sin^4 2x\cos^5 2x\left(2\cos^2 2x - 1\right)dx + 32\int_0^{\pi/4}\sin^6 2x\cos^5 2x\,dx$$

Substituting $2x = t$ in last two definite integrals, we get

$$I = \frac{3\pi}{32} - \frac{32}{2}\int_0^{\pi/2}\sin^4 t\cos^7 t\,dt + \frac{16}{2}\int_0^{\pi/2}\sin^4 t\cos^5 t\,dt + \frac{32}{2}\int_0^{\pi/2}\sin^6 t\cos^5 t\,dt$$

$$= \frac{3\pi}{32} - 16\frac{(3)(1)(6)(4)(2)}{11\times 9\times 7\times 5\times 3} + 8\frac{(3)(1)\times(4)\times(2)}{9\times 7\times 5\times 3\times 1} + 16\frac{5\times 3\times 1\times 4\times 2}{11\times 9\times 7\times 5\times 3}$$

$$= \frac{3\pi}{32} - \frac{256}{1155} + \frac{64}{315} + \frac{128}{693} = \frac{3\pi}{32} + \left\{\frac{64\times 11 - 256\times 3 + 640}{1155\times 3}\right\}$$

$$= \frac{3\pi}{32} + \left\{\frac{704 - 768 + 640}{3465}\right\} = \frac{3\pi}{32} + \frac{576}{3465}$$

ILLUSTRATION 192: Evaluate $\int_0^{\pi/4}(\cos 2\theta)^{5/2}\cos\theta\,d\theta$

SOLUTION: Here $I = \int_0^{\pi/4}(\cos 2\theta)^{5/2}\cos\theta\,d\theta = \int_0^{\pi/4}\left(1 - 2\sin^2\theta\right)^{5/2}\cos\theta\,d\theta$

Let us substitute $\sqrt{2}\sin\theta = \sin t$

$$\Rightarrow \cos\theta\,d\theta = \frac{\cos t\,dt}{\sqrt{2}}$$

when $\theta = 0$, $t = 0$ and $\theta = \frac{\pi}{4}$

$$\Rightarrow t = \frac{\pi}{2}$$

$$\therefore I = \int_0^{\pi/2}\left(1 - \sin^2 t\right)^{5/2}\frac{\cos t}{\sqrt{2}}\,dt = \frac{1}{\sqrt{2}}\int_0^{\pi/2}\cos^5 t\cos t\,dt = \frac{1}{\sqrt{2}}\int_0^{\pi/2}\cos^6 t\,dt$$

$$= \frac{1}{\sqrt{2}}\times\frac{(5)\times(3)\times(1)}{6\times 4\times 2}\times\frac{\pi}{2} = \frac{5\pi}{32\sqrt{2}}$$

ILLUSTRATION 193: Evaluate $\int_{-\pi/2}^{\pi/2}\tan x\left(\sin^2 x + 5\cos^3 x\sin^5 x\right)dx$

SOLUTION: Here $I = \int_{-\pi/2}^{\pi/2}\tan x\left(\sin^2 x + 5\cos^3 x\sin^5 x\right)dx$

$$= \int_{-\pi/2}^{\pi/2}\tan x\sin^2 x\,dx + 5\int_{-\pi/2}^{\pi/2}\cos^2 x\sin^6 x\,dx$$

$= 0 + 10\int_0^{\pi/2}\sin^6 x\cos^2 x\,dx$ as the integrand of first integral is an odd function, whereas that of second is an even function.

Thus, $I = \frac{10\times 5\times 3\times 1\times 1}{8\times 6\times 4\times 2}\times\frac{\pi}{2} = \frac{25\pi}{128}$

ILLUSTRATION 194: Evaluate $\int_0^{\pi} x\sin^7 x\cos^4 x\, dx$

SOLUTION: Let $I = \int_0^{\pi} x\sin^7 x\cos^4 x\, dx$

By property $\int_0^a f(x)\,dx = \int_0^a f(a-x)\,dx$, we have

$$I = \int_0^{\pi} (\pi - x)\sin^7(\pi - x)\cos^4(\pi - x)\,dx = \int_0^{\pi} (\pi - x)\sin^7 x\cos^4 x\,dx$$

$$= \pi\int_0^{\pi} \sin^7 x\cos^4 x\,dx - \int_0^{\pi} x\sin^7 x\cos^4 x\,dx$$

$$= \pi\int_0^{\pi} \sin^7 x\cos^4 x\,dx - I$$

$$\Rightarrow \quad 2I = \pi\int_0^{\pi} \sin^7 x\cos^4 x\,dx$$

$$\Rightarrow \quad I = \frac{\pi}{2}\int_0^{\pi} \sin^7 x\cos^4 x\,dx$$

$$\Rightarrow \quad I = \frac{\pi}{2} \times 2\int_0^{\pi/2} \sin^7 x\cos^4 x\,dx$$

$$(\because f(2a - x) = f(x) \Rightarrow \int_0^{2a} f(x)\,dx = 2\int_0^{a} f(x)\,dx)$$

$$\Rightarrow \quad I = \pi\int_0^{\pi/2} \sin^7 x\cos^4 x\,dx = \pi \times \frac{(6)\times 4\times 2\times 3\times 1}{11\times 9\times 7\times 5\times 3\times 1} = \frac{16\pi}{1155}$$

ILLUSTRATION 195: Evaluate $\int_0^{1} x^3(1-x)^4\,dx$

SOLUTION: Given $I = \int_0^{1} x^3(1-x)^4\,dx$

Let us substitute $x = \sin^2\theta$

$\Rightarrow \quad dx = 2\sin\theta\cos\theta\,d\theta$

$$\Rightarrow \quad I = \int_0^{\pi/2} \sin^6\theta\left(1-\sin^2\theta\right)^4(2\sin\theta\cos\theta)\,d\theta$$

$$= 2\int_0^{\pi/2} \sin^6\theta\cos^8\theta\sin\theta\cos\theta\,d\theta = 2\int_0^{\pi/2} \sin^7\theta\cos^9\theta\,d\theta$$

$$= \frac{2(6)\times 4\times 2\times 8\times 6\times 4\times 2}{16\times 14\times 12\times 10\times 8\times 6\times 4\times 2} = \frac{1}{280}$$

Walli's Product:

We can express π/2 in the form of infinite product given by

$$\frac{\pi}{2} = \lim_{n\to\infty}\left[\left(\frac{2.4.6....2n}{1.3.5.....(2n-1)}\right)^2 \cdot \frac{1}{(2n+1)}\right]$$

Proof: We have $I_n = \int_0^{\pi/2} \sin^n x\ dx$ ...(1)

$$\left\{\frac{(n-1)(n-3)(n-5)}{n(n-2)(n-4)}....\right\}.p\ ;\ p = \begin{cases} 1; & \text{if } n \text{ is odd} \\ \frac{\pi}{2}; & \text{if } n \text{ is even}\end{cases}$$

$$\Rightarrow\ I_{2n} = \frac{(2n-1)(2n-3)....5.3.1}{(2n)(2n-2)(2n-4)....4.2}\cdot\frac{\pi}{2} \quad .... (2)$$

$$\text{and } I_{2n+1} = \frac{(2n)(2n-2)....4.2}{(2n+1)(2n-1)(2n-3)....3.1} \quad ...(3)$$

(2) ÷ (3) gives,

$$\frac{I_{2n}}{I_{2n+1}} = \left[\frac{(2n-1)(2n-3)....5.3}{(2n)(2n-2).......4.2}\right]^2 .(2n+1)\frac{\pi}{2}$$

$$\Rightarrow\ \frac{\pi}{2} = \left(\frac{2.4.6........(2n-2)(2n)}{1.3.5..........(2n-3)(2n-1)}\right)^2 \frac{1}{(2n+1)}\frac{I_{2n}}{I_{2n+1}} \quad ...(4)$$

Now for $x \in \left(0, \frac{\pi}{2}\right)$, $\sin^{2n-1} x > \sin^{2n} x > \sin^{2n+1} x\ \forall$ $x \in \mathbb{N}$

∴ By dominance rule $\int_0^{\pi/2} \sin^{2n-1} x\ dx > \int_0^{\pi/2} \sin^{2n} x\ dx$ $> \int_0^{\pi/2} \sin^{2n+1} x\ dx$

$\Rightarrow\ I_{2n-1} > I_{2n} > I_{2n+1}$

Dividing the above inequality throughout by I_{2n+1}

$$\Rightarrow\ \frac{I_{2n-1}}{I_{2n+1}} > \frac{I_{2n}}{I_{2n+1}} > 1 \quad .... (5)$$

$$\text{Now } \frac{I_{2n-1}}{I_{2n+1}} = \frac{\int_0^{\pi/2} \sin^{2n-1} x\ dx}{\int_0^{\pi/2} \sin^{2n+1} x\ dx}$$

$$= \frac{\left\{\frac{(2n-2)(2n-4)....4.2}{(2n-1)(2n-3)....3.1}\right\}}{\left\{\frac{(2n)(2n-2)(2n-4)....4.2}{(2n+1)(2n-1)(2n-3)....3.1}\right\}} = \frac{2n+1}{2n}$$

$$\therefore\ \lim_{n\to\infty}\frac{I_{2n-1}}{I_{2n+1}} = 1 \quad .... (6)$$

∴ from (5), (6) and sandwitch theorem on limits, we have

$$\lim_{n\to\infty}\frac{I_{2n}}{I_{2n+1}} = 1 \quad ...(7)$$

Using (7) in (4) we have

$$\frac{\pi}{2} = \lim_{n\to\infty}\left[\left\{\frac{(2.4.6....2n}{1.3.5......(2n-1)}\right\}^2 \cdot \frac{1}{(2n+1)}\right]$$

■ INTEGRATION OF INFINITE SERIES

The integral of a series containing finitely many terms is equal to the sum of integrals of the terms of series.

i.e., if $f(x) = f_1(x) + f_2(x) + f_3(x) + ... + f_n(x)$,

then $\int f(x)\ dx = \int f_1(x)\ dx + \int f_2(x)\ dx + \int f_3(x)\ dx + ... + \int f_n(x)\ dx + C$

and $\int_a^b f(x)\ dx = \int_a^b f_1(x)\ dx + \int_a^b f_2(x)\ dx + \int_a^b f_3(x)\ dx + ...$ $\int_a^b f_n(x)\ dx$

Similarly a power series containing finitely many terms can be integrated term by term.

i.e., if $f(x) = a_0 + a_1x + a_2x^2 + ...+ a_nx^n$, then

$$\int_a^b f(x)\ dx = \int_a^b a_0\ dx + \int_a^b a_1x\ dx + \int_a^b a_2(x)^2\ dx + \int_a^b a_3(x)^3\ dx +....+ \int_a^b a_n(x)^n\ dx$$

$$\text{or } \int_a^b f(x)\ dx = \sum_{r=0}^{n}\int_a^b a_r\ x^r\ dx = \sum_{r=0}^{n} a_r \int_a^b x^r\ dx$$

However, is the same true if the series is infinite power series?

It is not true for every power series at all conditions. An infinite power series can be integrated term by term throughout any interval of convergence, not necessarily at end points of the interval. Its proof is beyond the scope of this book.

Example:

$$(1+x)^{-1} = 1 + (-1)x + \frac{(-1)(-2)x^2}{2!} + \frac{(-1)(-2)(-3)x^3}{3!} + ...\infty$$

for $|x| < 1$

$$\Rightarrow \int_0^x \frac{1}{(1+x)}dx = \int_0^x 1\,dx - \int_0^x x\,dx + \int_0^x x^2\,dx - \int_0^x x^3\,dx + ...\infty$$

$$\Rightarrow \left|\ln(1+x)\right|_0^x = \left(x - \frac{x^2}{2} + \frac{x^3}{3} - \frac{x^4}{4} + ...\infty\right)$$

$$\therefore \quad \ln(1+x) = x - \frac{x^2}{2} + \frac{x^3}{3} - \frac{x^4}{4} + ...\infty \qquad .... (1)$$

for $|x| < 1$

Thus, (1) represents the expression for $\ln(1 + x)$ for $|x| < 1$.

Further $\int_0^1 \frac{1}{(1+x)}dx$

$$= \left|\ln(1+x)\right|_0^1 = |x|_0^1 - \frac{1}{2}|x^2|_0^1 + \frac{1}{3}|x^3|_0^1 - .....$$

$$\Rightarrow \ln 2 = 1 - \frac{1}{2} + \frac{1}{3} - \frac{1}{4} + ...$$

Similarly, we can differentiate an infinite power series term by term throughout its interval of convergence.

ILLUSTRATION 196: Find the expansion of $\sin^{-1}x$ for $|x| < 1$ and hence find that of $\sin^{-1}1/4$.

SOLUTION: We know that $\int \frac{1}{\sqrt{1+x^2}}dx = \sin^{-1}x + C$,

$$\int \frac{1}{\sqrt{1-x^2}}dx = \int \left(1-x^2\right)^{-1/2} dx$$

$$= \int \left\{1 + \left(\frac{-1}{2}\right)(-x^2) + \frac{\left(\frac{-1}{2}\right)\left(\frac{-3}{2}\right)(-x^2)^2}{2!} + \frac{\left(\frac{-1}{2}\right)\left(\frac{-3}{2}\right)\left(\frac{-5}{2}\right)(-x^2)^3}{3!} + ...\right\} dx$$

for $|x| < 1$

$$\Rightarrow \int_0^x \frac{1}{\sqrt{1-x^2}}dx = \int \left\{1 + \frac{1}{2}x^2 + \frac{1.3}{2.4}x^4 + \frac{1.3.5}{2.4.6}x^6 + ...\right\} dx$$

By integrating term by term, we have $(\sin^{-1}x) = x + \frac{x^3}{2.3} + \frac{1.3.x^5}{2.4.5} + \frac{1.3.5}{2.4.6.7}x^7 + ...$

$$\therefore \quad \sin^{-1}x = x + \frac{x^3}{2.3} + \frac{1.3.x^5}{2.4.5} + \frac{1.3.5}{2.4.6.7}x^7 + ...$$

$$\Rightarrow \sin^{-1}\frac{1}{4} + \frac{1}{4} + \frac{1}{2.3}\left(\frac{1}{4}\right)^3 + \frac{1.3}{2.4.5}\left(\frac{1}{4}\right)^5 + \frac{1.3.5}{2.4.6.7}\left(\frac{1}{4}\right)^7 + ...$$

ILLUSTRATION 197: Find the expansion for $\tan^{-1}x$.

SOLUTION: Since $\int \frac{1}{1+x^2}dx = \tan^{-1}x$

$$\int \frac{1}{1+x^2}dx = \int \left(1+x^2\right)^{-1} dx$$

$$\therefore \quad \int_0^x \frac{1}{1+x^2}dx = \int_0^x \left(1 - x^2 + x^4 - x^6 + ...\right)dx; |x| < 1$$

By integrating term by tern in R.H.S, we have $\left|\tan^{-1}x\right|_0^x = x - \frac{x^3}{3} + \frac{x^5}{5} - \frac{x^7}{7} + ...$

$$\Rightarrow \tan^{-1}x = x - \frac{x^3}{3} + \frac{x^5}{5} - \frac{x^7}{7} + ...; |x| < 1$$

SOME IMPORTANT EXPANSIONS

Given below are few important expansions which can be used while evaluating the integrals of function having infinite expansions.

1. $\frac{1}{1^2}+\frac{1}{2^2}+\frac{1}{3^2}+\frac{1}{4^2}+.....\infty=\frac{\pi^2}{6}$ (derived from Fourier series)

2. $\frac{1}{1^2}+\frac{1}{3^2}+\frac{1}{5^2}+\frac{1}{7^2}+.....\infty=\frac{\pi^2}{8}$

Proof: Since $\frac{1}{1^2}+\frac{1}{2^2}+\frac{1}{3^2}+\frac{1}{4^2}+.....\infty=\frac{\pi^2}{6}$ [from (1)]

$$\Rightarrow \left(\frac{1}{1^2}+\frac{1}{3^2}+\frac{1}{5^2}+...\right)+\left(\frac{1}{2^2}+\frac{1}{4^2}+\frac{1}{6^2}+...\right)=\frac{\pi^2}{6}$$

$$\Rightarrow \left(\frac{1}{1^2}+\frac{1}{3^2}+\frac{1}{5^2}+...\right)+\frac{1}{2^2}\left(\frac{1}{1^2}+\frac{1}{2^2}+\frac{1}{3^2}+...\right)=\frac{\pi^2}{6}$$

$$\Rightarrow \left(\frac{1}{1^2}+\frac{1}{3^2}+\frac{1}{5^2}+...\right)=\frac{\pi^2}{6}-\frac{1}{4}\left(\frac{\pi^2}{6}\right)$$

$$=\frac{4\pi^2-\pi^2}{24}=\frac{\pi^2}{8}$$

3. $\frac{1}{1^2}-\frac{1}{2^2}+\frac{1}{3^2}-\frac{1}{4^2}+.....\infty=\frac{\pi^2}{12}$

Proof: $\frac{1}{1^2}-\frac{1}{2^2}+\frac{1}{3^2}-\frac{1}{4^2}+.....\infty$

$$=\left(\frac{1}{1^2}+\frac{1}{3^2}+\frac{1}{5^2}+...\right)-\left(\frac{1}{2^2}+\frac{1}{4^2}+...\right)$$

$$=\left(\frac{1}{1^2}+\frac{1}{3^2}+\frac{1}{5^2}+...\right)-\frac{1}{2^2}\left(\frac{1}{1^2}+\frac{1}{2^2}+\frac{1}{3^2}+...\right)$$

$$=\frac{\pi^2}{8}-\frac{1}{4}\left(\frac{\pi^2}{6}\right)$$

$$=\frac{\pi^2}{8}-\frac{\pi^2}{24}=\frac{3\pi^2-\pi^2}{24}=\frac{\pi^2}{12}$$

4. $\frac{1}{2^2}+\frac{1}{4^2}+\frac{1}{6^2}+\frac{1}{8^2}+....\infty=\frac{\pi^2}{24}$

Proof: $\frac{1}{2^2}\left(\frac{1}{1^2}+\frac{1}{2^2}+\frac{1}{3^2}+\frac{1}{4^2}+....\infty\right)$

$$=\frac{1}{4}\left(\frac{\pi^2}{6}\right)=\frac{\pi^2}{24}$$

5. $\ln 2=1-\frac{1}{2}+\frac{1}{3}-\frac{1}{4}+....\infty$

Proof: Since $\ln(1+x)=x-\frac{x^2}{2}+\frac{x^3}{3}-\frac{x^4}{4}+....\infty$; $|x|<1$

As $x\to 1^-$; $\ln(1+x)\to \ln 2$, thus, we take

$$\ln 2=1-\frac{1}{2}+\frac{1}{3}-\frac{1}{4}+....\infty$$

ILLUSTRATION 198: If $\frac{1}{1^2}+\frac{1}{2^2}+\frac{1}{3^2}+\frac{1}{4^2}+....=\frac{\pi^2}{6}$, then prove that $\int_0^1\frac{\ln(1+x^4)}{x}dx=\frac{\pi^2}{48}$

SOLUTION: $\int_0^1\frac{\ln(1+x^4)}{x}dx=\int_0^1\frac{1}{x}\left(x^4-\frac{x^8}{2}+\frac{x^{12}}{3}-\frac{x^{16}}{4}+....\right)dx$

$$=\int_0^1\left(x^3-\frac{x^7}{2}+\frac{x^{11}}{3}-\frac{x^{15}}{4}+....\right)dx=\left[\frac{x^4}{4}-\frac{x^8}{16}+\frac{x^{12}}{36}-\frac{x^{16}}{64}+....\right]_0^1=\left(\frac{1}{4}-\frac{1}{16}+\frac{1}{36}-\frac{1}{64}+....\right)$$

$$=\left(\frac{1}{2^2}-\frac{1}{4^2}+\frac{1}{6^2}-\frac{1}{8^2}+....\right)=\left(\frac{1}{2^2}+\frac{1}{4^2}+\frac{1}{6^2}+....\right)-2\left(\frac{1}{4^2}+\frac{1}{8^2}+....\right)$$

$$=\frac{1}{(2)^2}\left(\frac{1}{1^2}+\frac{1}{2^2}+\frac{1}{3^2}+....\right)-\frac{2}{4^2}\left(\frac{1}{1^2}+\frac{1}{2^2}+....\right)$$

$$=\frac{1}{4}\left(\frac{\pi^2}{6}\right)-\frac{1}{8}\left(\frac{\pi^2}{6}\right)=\left(\frac{1}{24}-\frac{1}{48}\right)\pi^2=\frac{\pi^2}{48}$$. Hence proved

ILLUSTRATION 199: If $\frac{1}{1^2}-\frac{1}{2^2}+\frac{1}{3^2}-\frac{1}{4^2}+\ldots\infty=\frac{\pi^2}{12}$, then show that $\int_0^1 \frac{\ln x}{(1+x)}dx=\frac{-\pi^2}{12}$

SOLUTION: Let $I=\int_0^1 \underbrace{\ln x}_{I}.\frac{1}{(x+1)}dx$

Integrating by parts we get $I=\left|\ln x\int\frac{1}{(1+x)}dx\right|_0^1-\int_0^1\left(\frac{1}{x}.\int\frac{1}{(1+x)}dx\right)dx$

$$=\left|\ln x.\ln(1+x)\right|_0^1-\int_0^1\frac{1}{x}.\ln(1+x)dx=-\lim_{x\to0^+}\ln x.\ln(1+x)-\int_0^1\frac{1}{x}.\ln(1+x)dx$$

$$=-\lim_{x\to0^+}x\ln x.\frac{\ln(1+x)}{x}-\int_0^1\frac{1}{x}.\ln(1+x)dx=-\lim_{x\to0^+}\left(\frac{\ln x}{1/x}\right).\lim_{x\to0^+}\frac{\ln(1+x)}{x}-\int_0^1\frac{1}{x}.\ln(1+x)dx$$

$$=-\lim_{x\to0^+}\left(\frac{1}{x}\times(-x-x^2)\right).(1)-\int_0^1\frac{1}{x}.\ln(1+x)dx \qquad \text{(By L.H. rule)}$$

$$=0-\int_0^1\frac{1}{x}\left[x-\frac{x^2}{2}+\frac{x^3}{3}-\frac{x^4}{4}+\ldots\right]dx \qquad \left\{\because \ln(1+x)=x-\frac{x^2}{2}+\frac{x^3}{3}-\frac{x^4}{4}+\ldots \text{ for } |x|<1\right\}$$

$$=-\int_0^1\left(1-\frac{x}{2}+\frac{x^2}{3}-\frac{x^3}{4}+\ldots\right)dx$$

$$=\left[-x+\frac{x^2}{4}-\frac{x^3}{9}+\frac{x^4}{16}-\ldots\right]_0^1=-\left[\frac{1}{1^2}-\frac{1}{2^2}+\frac{1}{3^2}-\frac{1}{4^2}+\ldots\right]=-\frac{\pi^2}{12} \text{ (given), hence proved.}$$

ILLUSTRATION 200: If $|x|<1$, then find the sum of the infinite series $\frac{1}{1+x}+\frac{2x}{1+x^2}+\frac{4x^3}{1+x^4}+\frac{8x^7}{1+x^8}+\ldots\infty$

SOLUTION: Let $S_\infty=\frac{1}{1+x}+\frac{2x}{1+x^2}+\frac{4x^3}{1+x^4}+\frac{8x^7}{1+x^8}+\ldots\infty$

$$\Rightarrow \int S_\infty dx=\ln(1+x)+\ln(1+x^2)+\ln(1+x^4)+\ln(1+x^8)+\ldots\infty$$

$$=\ln\{(1+x)(1+x^2)(1+x^4)\cdot(1+x^8)\ldots\ldots\};\ |x|<1$$

$$=\ln\left\{\frac{(1-x)(1+x)(1+x^2)(1+x^4)(1+x^8)}{(1-x)}\right\}$$

$$=\ln\left\{\frac{(1-x^2)(1+x^2)(1+x^4)(1+x^8)}{(1-x)}\right\}$$

$$=\lim_{n\to\infty}\ln\left\{\frac{\left(1-x^{2^n}\right)}{(1-x)}\right\};|x|<1=\ln\left(\frac{1}{(1-x)}\right)+C=\ln(1-x)+C$$

Thus, $\int S_\infty dx=-\ln(1+x)+C$

$$\Rightarrow S_\infty=-\frac{1}{(1-x)}(-1)$$

$$\Rightarrow \frac{1}{1+x}+\frac{2x}{1+x^2}+\frac{4x^3}{1+x^4}+\frac{8x^7}{1+x^8}+\ldots=\frac{1}{(1-x)}$$

ILLUSTRATION 201: Let $P_n(x)$ be a polynomial of degree n given by $P_n(x) = x + \frac{x^2}{2} + \frac{x^3}{3} + ... + \frac{x^n}{n} = \sum_{i=1}^{n}\left(\frac{x^i}{i}\right)$

Prove that $-\ln(1-x) = P_n(x) + \int_0^x \frac{t^n}{1-t}dt$ for $x < 1$ and $n \in \mathbb{N}$.

SOLUTION: Clearly $-\ln(1 - x)$ is valid for $x < 1$

Also $-\ln(1-x) = \int_0^x \frac{1}{(1-x)}dx = \int_0^x (1-x)^{-1}dx; x < 1$

$= \int_0^x \left(1 + x + x^2 + x^3 + ...\right)dx$ (By binomial theorem)

$= \left(x + \frac{x^2}{2} + \frac{x^3}{3} + \frac{x^4}{4} + ...\right)_0^x = x + \frac{x^2}{2} + \frac{x^3}{3} + \frac{x^4}{4} + ... + \frac{x^n}{n} + \frac{x^{n+1}}{n+1} + \frac{x^{n+2}}{(n+2)} + ...\infty$

$= P_n(x) + \frac{x^{n+1}}{n+1} + \frac{x^{n+2}}{(n+2)} + ...\infty = P_n(x) + \int_0^x \left(t^n + t^{n+1} + ...\right)dt$

$= P_n(x) + \int_0^x \frac{t^n}{1-t}dt$

($\because t^n + t^{n+1} + ... \infty$ is an infinite G.P. with first term $= t^n$ and common ratio $t \in (0, x); x < 1$)

■ ROOT MEAN SQUARE VALUE (R.M.S.V)

R.M.S.V. of a function $y = f(x)$ in the range (a, b) is given by $\sqrt{\frac{\int_a^b [f(x)]^2 dx}{(b-a)}}$

ILLUSTRATION 202: Find R.M.S.V. of the function $f(x) = \sqrt[4]{\left(\frac{1-\cos 2x}{2}\right)}$ in $(-\pi, 199\pi)$

SOLUTION: Here $f(x) = \sqrt[4]{\frac{1-\cos 2x}{2}} = \sqrt[4]{\frac{2\sin^2 x}{2}}$

$\Rightarrow (f(x))^2 = \sqrt{(\sin^2 x)} = |\sin x|$

$\Rightarrow \int_a^b f(x))^2 dx = \int_{-\pi}^{199\pi} |\sin x| dx = (199+1)\int_0^{\pi} |\sin x| dx$ (as $|\sin x|$ is periodic with period π)

$= 200\int_0^{\pi} \sin x\, dx = (200)[-\cos x]_0^{\pi} = -200\,[\cos \pi - \cos 0] = -200[-1 -1] = 400$

Now $\frac{\int_{-\pi}^{199\pi} [f(x)]^2 dx}{(199\pi + \pi)} = \frac{400}{200\pi} = \frac{2}{\pi}$

R.M.S.V of $f(x) = \sqrt{\frac{\int_{-\pi}^{199\pi} [f(x)]^2 dx}{[199\pi - (-\pi)]}} = \sqrt{\frac{2}{\pi}}$

BETA FUNCTION

It is denoted by $B\ (m,\ n)$ and is given by $B(m, n) = \int_0^1 x^{m-1}(1-x)^{n-1}dx$ where $m, n > 0$. It can be proved that for $m, n \in (0, 1)$ the above improper integral is convergent, however the proof is beyond the scope of this book. Clearly $B\ (m, n)$ is proper for $m, n \geq 1$

If $(2m–1)$ and $(2n–1)$ are positive integers, then $B(m, n) = \int_0^1 x^{m-1}(1-x)^{n-1}dx$

Let us substitute $x = \sin^2\theta$

$$\Rightarrow \quad B(m, n) = \int_0^{\pi/2} \sin^{2m-2}\theta(\cos\theta)^{2n-2}.\ 2\sin\theta\cos\theta d\theta$$

$$\Rightarrow \quad B(m, n) = 2\int_0^{\pi/2} \sin^{2m-1}\theta.\cos^{2n-1}\theta\, d\theta$$

$\therefore$ By Walli's formula

$$B(m,n) = \frac{2\{(2m-2)(2m-4)...\}\{(2n-2)(2n-4...\}}{(2m+2n-2)(2m+2n-4)......}\cdot p$$

Where $p = \pi/2$ if both $(2m–1)$ and $(2n–1)$ are even integers, otherwise $p = 1$

ILLUSTRATION 203: Evaluate

(i) $B\left(\frac{5}{2}, \frac{7}{2}\right)$ (ii) $\beta(3, 4)$

SOLUTION: (i) $B(m, n) = B(5/2,7/2)$

$$\Rightarrow \quad m = \frac{5}{2}, n = \frac{7}{2}$$

$$\therefore \quad B(m, n) = \int_0^1 (x)^{5/2}(1-x)^{\frac{7}{2}-1}dx = \int_0^1 x^{3/2}(1-x)^{5/2}dx$$

On substituting $x = \sin^2\theta$,

we have $B\left(\frac{5}{2}, \frac{7}{2}\right) = \int_0^{\pi/2} \sin^3\theta.\cos^5\theta.(2\sin\theta\cos\theta)d\theta$

$$= 2\int_0^{\pi/2} \sin^4\theta\cos^6\theta\, d\theta = \frac{2(3)(1)(5)(3)(1)}{10\times 8\times 6\times 4\times 2}.\frac{\pi}{2} = \frac{3\pi}{256}$$

(ii) $B(3\ 4) = \int_0^1 x^{3-1}(1-x)^{4-1}dx = \int_0^1 x^2(1-x)^3\, dx$

Put $x = \sin^2\theta$

$\Rightarrow \quad dx = 2\sin\theta\cos\theta d\theta$

$$\Rightarrow \quad B(3, 4) = \int_0^{\pi/2} \sin^4\theta\cos^6\theta(2\sin\theta\cos\theta)d\theta = 2\int_0^{\pi/2} \sin^5\theta\cos^7\theta\, d\theta = \frac{1}{60}$$

ILLUSTRATION 204: Evaluate $\int_0^1 \frac{x\,dx}{\sqrt{1-x^5}}$ in terms of Beta function

SOLUTION: Given $I = \int_0^1 \frac{x\ dx}{\sqrt{1-x^5}}$

Put $\sqrt{1-x^5} = t$

$$\Rightarrow \quad \frac{1}{2\sqrt{1-x^5}}(-5x^4)dx = dt$$

$$\Rightarrow \quad -\frac{5x^3}{2}\left(\frac{x}{\sqrt{1-x^5}}\right)dx = dt$$

$$\Rightarrow \quad \frac{x}{\sqrt{1-x^5}}dx = -\frac{2}{5}.x^{-3}dt = -\frac{2}{5}(1-t^2)^{-3/5}\,dt$$

$$\therefore \quad I=\int_1^0 -\frac{2}{5}\left(1-t^2\right)^{-3/5} dt=\frac{2}{5}\int_0^1 (1-t^2)^{-3/5} dt$$

Now Put $t^2 = z$

$\Rightarrow \quad 2tdt = dz$

$$\Rightarrow \quad dt=\frac{1}{2t}dz=\frac{1}{2}(z)^{-1/2}dz$$

$$\therefore \quad I=\frac{2}{5}\times\frac{1}{2}\int_0^1 (1-z)^{-3/5}.(z)^{-1/2}dz = \frac{1}{5}\int_0^1 (z)^{-1/2}(1-z)^{-3/5}dz=\frac{1}{5}\int_0^1 (z)^{\left(\frac{1}{2}-1\right)}(1-z)^{\left(\frac{2}{5}-1\right)}dz$$

$$=\frac{1}{5}B\left(\frac{1}{2},\frac{2}{5}\right)$$

ILLUSTRATION 205: Evaluate $\int_0^2 x^4(8-x^3)^{-1/3} dx$ in terms of beta function

SOLUTION: Given $I=\int_0^2 x^4(8-x^3)^{-1/3}dx=\int_0^2 x^4\frac{1}{2}\left(1-\frac{x^3}{8}\right)^{-1/3}dx=\frac{1}{2}\int_0^2 x^4\left(1-\left(\frac{x}{2}\right)^3\right)^{-1/3}dx$

Substituting $\left(\frac{x}{2}\right)^3=t$, we have $I=\frac{1}{2}\int_0^1 16t^{4/3}(1-t)^{-1/3}\frac{2}{3}(t)^{-2/3}dt=\frac{16}{3}\int_0^1 (t)^{2/3}(1-t)^{-1/3}dt$

$$=\frac{16}{3}\int_0^1 (t)^{\left(\frac{5}{3}-1\right)}(1-t)^{\left(\frac{2}{3}-1\right)}dt$$

$$=\frac{16}{3}B\left(\frac{5}{2},\frac{2}{3}\right)$$

ILLUSTRATION 206: Show that $\frac{\beta(p,q+1)}{q}=\frac{\beta(p+1,q)}{p}=\frac{\beta(p,q)}{p+q}$

SOLUTION: $\beta(p,q+1)=\int_0^1 \underbrace{x^{p-1}}_{I}\underbrace{(1-x)^q}_{II}\,dx$

Integrating by parts, we have

$$\beta(p,q+1)=\left|(1-x)^q.\frac{x^p}{p}\right|_0^1+\int_0^1 q(1-x)^{q-1}.\frac{x^p}{p}dx=0+\frac{q}{p}\int_0^1 x^p(1-x)^{q-1}dx=\frac{q}{p}\beta(p+1,q)$$

$$\Rightarrow \quad \frac{\beta(p,q+1)}{q}=\frac{(p+1,q)}{p} \qquad \ldots(i)$$

$\therefore$ By laws of proportionality, we have

$$\beta\frac{(p,q+1)}{q}=\frac{\beta(p+1,q)}{P}=\frac{\beta(p,q+1)+\beta(p+1,q)}{p+q} \qquad \ldots(2)$$

We shall show that $\beta(p, q+1)+\beta(p+1, q)=\beta(p, q)$

Now $\beta(p,q+1)+\beta(p+1,q)=\int_0^1 x^{p-1}(1-x)^q+x^p(1-x)^{q-1}dx$

$$=\int_0^1 x^{P-1}(1-x)^{q-1}[1-x+x]dx=\int_0^1 x^{p-1}(1-x)^{q-1}dx=\beta(p,q) \qquad \ldots(3)$$

$\therefore$ From (2) and (3) it follows that $\frac{\beta(p+1,q)}{p}=\frac{\beta(p,q+1)}{q}=\frac{\beta(p,q)}{p+q}$

ILLUSTRATION 207: Show that $\int_0^{\pi/2} \sin^p\theta\cos^q\theta\,d\theta = \frac{1}{2}\beta\left(\frac{p+1}{2},\frac{q+1}{2}\right)$; where $p, q > -1$

SOLUTIONS: Let $I = \int_0^{\pi/2} \sin^p\theta\cos^q\theta\,d\theta = \int_0^{\pi/2} (\sin^2\theta)^{p/2}(\cos 2\theta)^{q/2}\,d\theta$

$$= \int_0^{\pi/2} (\sin^2\theta)^{p/2}(1-\sin^2\theta)^{q/2}\,d\theta$$

Put $\sin^2\theta = t$

$\Rightarrow$ $2\sin\theta\cos\theta\,d\theta = dt$

$\Rightarrow$ $d\theta = \frac{1}{2\sin\theta\cos\theta}dt$

$\therefore$ $I = \int_0^1 (t)^{p/2}(1-t)^{q/2}\frac{1}{2\sqrt{t}(1-t)^{1/2}}dt = \frac{1}{2}\int_0^1 (t)^{\frac{p}{2}-\frac{1}{2}}(1-t)^{\frac{q}{2}-\frac{1}{2}}dt$

$$= \frac{1}{2}\int_0^1 (t)^{\frac{p-1}{2}}(1-t)^{\frac{q-1}{2}}dt = \frac{1}{2}\int_0^1 t^{\left(\frac{p+1}{2}-1\right)}(1-t)^{\left(\frac{q+1}{2}-1\right)}dt = \frac{1}{2}\beta\left(\frac{p+1}{2},\frac{q+1}{2}\right)$$

ILLUSTRATION 208: Evaluate $\int_0^{\pi/2} \sin^{3/2}\theta\cos^{5/3}\theta\,d\theta$ in terms of beta function

SOLUTION: We know that for $p, q > -1$

$$\int_0^{\pi/2} \sin^P\theta\cos^q\theta\,d\theta = \frac{1}{2}\beta\left(\frac{P+1}{2},\frac{q+1}{2}\right)$$

$$\therefore \int_0^{\pi/2} \sin^{3/2}\theta\cos^{5/3}\theta\,d\theta = \frac{1}{2}\beta\left(\frac{\frac{3}{2}+1}{2},\frac{\frac{5}{3}+1}{2}\right) = \frac{1}{2}\beta\left(\frac{5}{4},\frac{4}{3}\right)$$

■ GAMMA FUNCTION

The improper integral $\int_0^\infty e^{-x}x^{n-1}dx$; where n is a positive rational number is called gamma function and is denoted by Γn.

Thus, $\Gamma n = (n-1)\Gamma(n-1) = (n-1)(n-2)\Gamma(n-2)$ and so on (By previous illustration)

Properties of Gamma Function

(i) $\Gamma(n) = (n-1)!$ if n is a positive integer

(ii) $\Gamma 1 = (1-1)! = 0! = 1$

(iii) $\Gamma(n) = (n-1)\Gamma n-1$ e.g., $\Gamma 5 = 4\Gamma 4 = 4(3)\Gamma 3 = 4(3)(2)\Gamma 2$
$= 4(3)(2)(1)\Gamma 1 = 24$

(iv) $\Gamma 0 = \infty$

(v) $\Gamma\frac{1}{2} = \sqrt{\pi}$

ILLUSTRATION 209: Evaluate the following integrals:

(i) $\int_0^\infty e^{-x}(x)^{5/2}dx$

(ii) $\int_0^\infty e^{-t^2}(t)^7 dt$

(iii) $\Gamma\frac{9}{2}$

(iv) $\Gamma 7$

SOLUTION: (i) Given $\int_0^\infty e^{-x}(x)^{5/2}\,dx = \int_0^\infty e^{-x}(x)^{(7/2-1)}\,dx$

Comparing it with $\Gamma n = \int_0^\infty e^{-x}(x)^{n-1}dx$ we have; $\int_0^\infty e^{-x}(x)^{(7/2-1)}dx = \Gamma\frac{7}{2}$

$$= \left(\frac{5}{2}\right)\Gamma\frac{5}{2} = \left(\frac{5}{2}\right)\left(\frac{3}{2}\right)\Gamma\frac{3}{2} = \left(\frac{5}{2}\right)\left(\frac{3}{2}\right)\left(\frac{1}{2}\right)\Gamma\frac{1}{2} = \frac{5}{2}\times\frac{3}{2}\times\frac{1}{2}\times\sqrt{\pi} = \frac{15}{8}\sqrt{\pi}$$

(ii) Given $\int_0^\infty e^{-t^2}(t)^7\,dt$

Put $t^2 = z$

$\Rightarrow t = (z)^{1/2}; t = 0 \quad \Rightarrow z = 0, t = \infty$

$\Rightarrow z = \infty \quad \Rightarrow 2tdt = dz$

$$\therefore \int_0^\infty e^{-t^2}t^7dt = \int_0^\infty e^{-z}\left((z)^{1/2}\right)^7\frac{1}{2(z)^{1/2}}dz = \int_0^\infty e^{-z}.\frac{1}{2}(z)^3\,dz = \frac{1}{2}\int_0^\infty e^{-z}z^3dz$$

$$= \frac{1}{2}\int_0^\infty e^{-z}(z)^{4-1}dz = \frac{1}{2}\Gamma 4 = \frac{1}{2}(3)! \qquad (\because \Gamma n = (n-1)!\ for\ n\in\mathbb{N})$$

$$= \frac{1}{2}(6) = 3$$

(iii) $\Gamma\frac{9}{2} = \left(\frac{7}{2}\right)\Gamma\frac{7}{2} = \left(\frac{7}{2}\right)\left(\frac{5}{2}\right)\Gamma\frac{5}{2} = \frac{7}{2}.\frac{5}{2}.\frac{3}{2}\Gamma\frac{3}{2} = \frac{7}{2}.\frac{5}{2}.\frac{3}{2}.\frac{1}{2}\sqrt{\pi} = \frac{105}{16}\sqrt{\pi} \qquad \left(\because \Gamma\frac{1}{2} = \sqrt{\pi}\right)$

(iv) $\Gamma 7 = (7-1)! = 6! = 720 \qquad (\because \Gamma n = (n-1)!\,\forall n\in\mathbb{N})$

ILLUSTRATION 210: Evaluate $\int_0^\infty e^{-x}x^3dx$.

SOLUTION: By definition $\int_0^\infty e^{-x}x^3dx = \int_0^\infty e^{-x}x^{4-1}dx = \Gamma(4) = 3! = 6$

ILLUSTRATION 211: Solve $\int_0^\infty e^{-x}x^{2-1}dx$

SOLUTION: $\lim_{b\to\infty}\int_0^b e^{-x}x\,dx = \lim_{b\to\infty}[-xe^{-x}-e^{-x}]_0^b = \lim_{b\to\infty}[(-be^{-b}-e^{-b})-(0-1)]$

$$= \lim_{b\to\infty}\left(\frac{-b}{e^b}-\frac{1}{e^b}\right)+1 = \lim_{b\to\infty}\frac{(-b+1)}{e^b}+1 = \lim_{b\to\infty}-\frac{1}{e^b}+1 = 1 \qquad \text{(using L' Hospitals's Rule)}$$

ILLUSTRATION 212: When n is a positive integer, then evaluate $\int_0^1\left(\log\frac{1}{x}\right)^{n-1}dx$

SOLUTION: $I = \int_0^1\left(\log\frac{1}{x}\right)^{n-1}dx$; Put $\log\frac{1}{x} = t$

or $x = e^{-t} \quad \Rightarrow dx = -e^{-t}\,dt$

$$\therefore\ I = \int_\infty^0 t^{n-1}(-e^{-t})dt = \int_0^\infty e^{-t}t^{n-1}dt = \Gamma(n)$$

ILLUSTRATION 213: Show that $\beta(m, n) = \int_0^\infty \frac{x^{n-1}}{(1+x)^{m+n}} dx;\ m, n > 0$

SOLUTION: $B(m, n) = \int_0^1 x^{m-1}(1-x)^{n-1}\, dx$

Put $x = \frac{t}{1+t}; dx = \frac{(1+t)-t(1)}{(1+t)^2} dt = \frac{1}{(1+t)^2} dt$

$$\Rightarrow \beta(m, n) = \int_0^\infty \left(\frac{t}{1+t}\right)^{m-1} \left(\frac{1}{1+t}\right)^{n-1} \frac{1}{(1+t)^2} dt$$

$$= \int_0^\infty t^{m-1} \frac{1}{(1+t)^{m+n}} dt = \int_0^\infty \frac{x^{m-1}}{(1+x)^{m+n}} dx$$

Thus, $\beta(m, n) = \int_0^\infty \frac{x^{m-1}}{(1+x)^{m+n}} dx$ $\qquad \because \beta(m, n) = \beta(n, m)$

$$\therefore \quad \beta(m, n) = \beta(n, m) = \int_0^\infty \frac{x^{m-1}}{(1+x)^{m+n}} dx = \int_0^\infty \frac{x^{n-1} dx}{(1+x)^{m+n}}$$

RELATION BETWEEN BETA AND GAMMA FUNCTION

For $m, n > 0,\ B(m, n) = \frac{\overline{|m}\,\overline{|n}}{\overline{|m+n}}$

Proof: $\overline{|n} = \int_0^\infty x^{(n-1)} e^{-x} dx; n > 0$

Let us substitute $x = az;\ a > 0$

$\Rightarrow dx = adz$

$\Rightarrow \overline{|n} = \int_0^\infty (az)^{n-1} e^{-az} adz = a^n \int_0^\infty (z)^{n-1} e^{-az} dz$

$\Rightarrow \overline{|n} = a^n \int_0^\infty x^{n-1} e^{-ax}\, dx; a > 0$

Let us replace a by z,

We have $\overline{|n} = z^n \int_0^\infty x^{n-1}, e^{-zx}\, dx; z > 0$

Multiplying both sides by $e^{-z}.z^{m-1}$ and integrating with in the limits from $z = 0$ to $z = \infty$, we have

$$\overline{|n} \int_0^\infty e^{-z} z^{m-1} dz = \int_0^\infty z^n e^{-z} z^{m-1} \left(\int_0^\infty x^{n-1} e^{-zx}\, dx\right) dz$$

$$= \int_0^\infty z^{n+m-1} \left(\int_0^\infty x^{n-1} e^{-z(x+1)}\, dx\right) dz$$

$$\Rightarrow \overline{|n}.\overline{|m} = \int_0^\infty x^{n-1} \left(\int_0^\infty z^{(n+m-1)} e^{-z(x+1)} dz\right) dx$$

Put $z\,(x+1) = y$

$$\Rightarrow dz = \frac{dy}{(1+x)}$$

$$\therefore \quad \overline{|n}\ \overline{|m} = \int_0^\infty x^{n-1} \left(\int_0^\infty \left(\frac{y}{x+1}\right)^{x+m-1} e^{-y} \frac{dy}{1+x}\right) dx$$

$$= \int_0^\infty \frac{x^{n-1}}{(x+1)^{n+m}} \left(\int_0^\infty y^{n+m-1}.\ e^{-y} dy\right) dx$$

$$= \int_0^\infty \frac{x^{n-1}}{(1+x)^{n+m}} \overline{|(n+m)}\, dx$$

$$= \overline{|(n+m)} \int_0^\infty \frac{x^{n-1}}{(1+x)^{n+m}} dx$$

$= \overline{|(n+m)}\, \beta(m,n)$ (by result proved earlier)

$$\Rightarrow \beta(m,n) = \frac{\overline{|m}\ \overline{|n}}{\overline{|m+n}};\ m, n > 0$$

REMARK

If m, n are positive integers then $\beta(m, n) = \frac{\underline{|m-1}\,\underline{|n-1}}{\underline{|m+n-1}}$ *as* $\overline{|n} = \underline{|n-1}$ *for* $n \in \mathbb{N}$

ILLUSTRATION 214: Show that $\int_0^\infty \frac{x^3}{(1+x)^7}dx = \frac{1}{60}$

SOLUTION: Let $I = \int_0^\infty \frac{x^3}{(1+x)^7}dx = \int_0^\infty \frac{x^{4-1}}{(1+x)^{3+4}}dx = \beta(3,4)$; Since $\int_0^\infty \frac{x^{n-1}}{(1+x)^{m+n}}dx = \beta(m,n)$

$\therefore \quad I = \beta(3,4) = \frac{\lceil 3 \lceil 4}{\lceil 3+4} = \frac{\lfloor 2 \lfloor 3}{\lfloor 6} = \frac{2\times 6}{720} = \frac{1}{60}$ $\left(\because \beta(m,n) = \frac{\lceil m, \lceil n}{\lceil m+n} \text{ for } m,n>0\right)$

ILLUSTRATION 215: To show that $\left\lceil \frac{1}{2} \right. = \sqrt{\pi}$

SOLUTION: $B(m,n) = \frac{\lceil m \lceil n}{\lceil m+n}$; Taking $m = n = 1/2$, we have $B\left(\frac{1}{2},\frac{1}{2}\right) = \frac{\left(\lceil \frac{1}{2}\right)^2}{\lceil 1}$

$\Rightarrow \lceil \frac{1}{2} = \sqrt{B\left(\frac{1}{2},\frac{1}{2}\right)}$ as $\lceil 1 = \lfloor 0 = 1$ $= \sqrt{\int_0^1 (x)^{\frac{1}{2}-1}(1-x)^{\frac{1}{2}-1}dx} = \sqrt{\int_0^1 \frac{1}{\sqrt{x}\sqrt{1-x}}dx}$

Putting $x = \sin^2\theta$ we have $\lceil \frac{1}{2} = \sqrt{\int_0^{\pi/2} \frac{2\sin\theta\cos\theta d\theta}{\sin\theta\cos\theta}} = \sqrt{\int_0^{\pi/2} 2d\theta}$

Hence $\lceil \frac{1}{2} = \lceil \pi$

ILLUSTRATION 216: Show that

(i) $\int_0^\infty e^{-x^2}dx = \frac{\sqrt{\pi}}{2}$ (ii) $\int_{-\infty}^\infty e^{-x^2}dx = \sqrt{\pi}$

SOLUTION: (i) Let $I = \int_0^\infty e^{-x^2}dx$; Put $x^2 = t$

$\Rightarrow 2xdx = dt$ $\Rightarrow dx = \frac{1}{2x}dt = \frac{1}{2\sqrt{t}}dt$

When $x \to 0$, $t \to 0$ and when $x \to \infty$, $t \to \infty$

$\therefore \quad I = \int_0^\infty e^{-t}\frac{1}{2\sqrt{t}}dt = \frac{1}{2}\int_0^\infty (t)^{-1/2}e^{-t}dt = \frac{1}{2}\int_0^\infty (t)^{\frac{1}{2}-1}e^{-t}dt = \frac{1}{2}\lceil \frac{1}{2} = \frac{1}{2}\sqrt{\pi} = \frac{\sqrt{\pi}}{2}$

(ii) Let $I = \int_{-\infty}^\infty e^{-x^2}dx = 2\int_0^\infty e^{-x^2}dx$ as e^{-x^2} is an even function $= 2\frac{\sqrt{\pi}}{2} = \lceil \pi$

■ WEIGHED MEAN VALUE THEOREM

If $f(x)$ and $g(x)$ are two continuous functions on $[a, b]$ such that $g(x)$ does not change its sign in $[a, b]$, then there exists $c \in [a, b]$ such that $\int_a^b f(x)g(x)dx = f(c)\int_a^b g(x)dx$

Proof: Let m and M be greatest lower bound and least upper bounds of $f(x)$ respectively.

Then $m \le f(x) \le M$ ...(1)

Now $g(x)$ does not change sign in $[a, b]$. This means either $g(x)$ is non-negative or non-positive throughout in $[a, b]$

Let us suppose that $g(x) \ge 0\ \forall\ x \in [a, b]$

$\therefore$ from (1) $m\,g(x) \le f(x).g(x) \le M\,g(x)\ \forall\ x \in [a, b]$

Integrating both sides w.r.t x within the limits from $x = a$ to $x = b$, we have

$$m\int_a^b g(x)dx \le \int_a^b f(x).g(x)dx \le M\int_a^b g(x)dx \quad ......(2)$$

Now if $\int_a^b g(x)dx = 0$, then by inequality (2) we must have $0 \le \int_a^b f(x)g(x)dx \le 0$

$\Rightarrow \int_a^b f(x)g(x)dx = 0 = f(c)\int_a^b g(x)dx$ for every choice of c in $[a, b]$

Thus, the result is true in this case

So, let $\int_a^b g(x)d(x) > 0\ \forall x \in [a, b]$

Dividing (2) by $\int_a^b g(x)dx$, we get

$$m \le \frac{\int_a^b f(x)g(x)\,dx}{\int_a^b g(x)dx} \le M$$

Therefore, by intermediate value theorem there exists $c \in [a, b]$ such that

$$f(c) = \frac{\int_a^b f(x)g(x)dx}{\int_a^b g(x)dx}$$

$\Rightarrow f(x) = \int_a^b g(x)dx = \int_a^b f(x).g(x)dx$

Now if $g(x) < 0\ \forall\ x \in [a, b]$. Then replacing $g(x)$ by $-g(x)$ and by same arguments the result can be proved on same lines.

The above result is useful for estimating the integral of the product of two functions having required properties.

GENERALIZED MEAN VALUE THEOREM

If $g(x)$ is continuous $[a, b]$ and $f(x)$ has derivative function which is continuous and never changes its sign in $[a, b]$. Then there exists some $c \in [a, b]$ such that $\int_a^b f(x)g(x)dx = f(a)\int_a^c g(x)dx + f(b)\int_c^b g(x)\,dx$

Proof: Let $G(x) = \int_a^x g(x)\,dx$ ...(i)

Since $g(x)$ is continuous in $[a, b]$, $G'(x) = g(x)$

Now $\int_a^b f(x).g(x)dx = \int_a^b \underbrace{f(x)}_{I}\underbrace{G'(x)}_{II}dx$

On integrating by parts we have

$|f(x)\,G(x)|_a^b - \int_a^b f'(x)G(x)\,dx$

$= [f(b)G(b) - f(a)G(a)] - \int_a^b f'(x)G(x)\,dx$

$= f(b)G(b) - \int_a^b f'(x)G(x)dx$ as $G(a) = 0$

$= f(b).G)(b) - \left[G(c)\int_a^b f'(x)\,dx\right]$

($\because f'(x)$ does not change its sign in $[a, b]$ and hence by weighted mean value theorem]

$= f(b).G(b) - G(c)\,[f(b) - f(a)]$

$= f(a)\,G(c) + f(b)[G(b) - G(c)]$

$\therefore \int_a^b f(x)g(x)dx$

$= f(a)\int_a^c g(x)dx + f(b)\left[\int_a^b g(x)dx - \int_a^c g(x)\,dx\right]$

$= f(a)\int_a^c g(x)dx + f(b)\int_c^b g(x)\,dx$

ILLUSTRATION 217: Estimate the integral $\int_0^1 \frac{\tan x}{1+x^2}dx$ by using generalized mean value theorem

SOLUTION: Let $f(x) = \tan x$ and $g(x) = \frac{1}{1+x^2}$

Then $g(x)$ is continuous on $[0,1]$ and $f'(x) = \sec^2 x$ is also continuous on $[0,1]$ and is always non-negative

Thus, by generalized mean value theorem, there exists c in $[0,1]$ such that

$$\int_0^1 \frac{\tan x}{1+x^2}dx = f(0)\int_0^c \frac{1}{1+x^2}dx + f(1)\int_x^1 \frac{1}{1+x^2}dx$$

$= 0 + \tan 1 \int_0^1 \frac{1}{1+x^2}dx$

$= (\tan 1)\,[\tan^{-1}x]_c^1 = (\tan 1)\,[\tan^{-1}1 - \tan^{-1}c] = (\tan 1)\left[\frac{\pi}{4} - \tan^{-1}c\right]$ ...(1)

Since $\tan^{-1}x$ is an increasing function in [0,1]

$\Rightarrow \tan^{-1}0 < \tan^{-1} c < \tan^{-1} 1$ $\Rightarrow 0 < \tan^{-1}c < \pi/4$

$\Rightarrow -\pi/4 < -\tan^{-1} c < 0$

$\Rightarrow 0 < \frac{\pi}{4} - \tan^{-1} c < \frac{\pi}{4}$ $\Rightarrow 0 < (\tan 1)\left[\frac{\pi}{4} - \tan^{-1} c\right] < \frac{\pi}{4}\tan 1$ ...(2)

$\therefore$ from (1) and (2), $0 < \int_0^1 \frac{\tan x}{1+x^2}dx < \frac{\pi}{4}\tan 1 \Rightarrow 0 < \int_0^1 \frac{\tan x}{1+x^2}dx < \frac{\pi}{4}(0.0174) < 0.14$

Thus, $0 < \int_0^1 \frac{\tan, x}{1+x^2}dx < 0.14$

DETERMINATION OF FUNCTION BY USING INTEGRATION

Let $f(x)$ be a given continuous and differentiable function. Some times we are given a functional equation connecting the functional values at different points or function with some definite integral having integrand as $f(x)$ or $f'(x)$ or any other algebraic or trigonometric or exponential function. Then by differentiating and integrating we can find the function $f(x)$.

ILLUSTRATION 218: If $f(x)$ is a continuous function on the set of real numbers satisfying the functional equation $f(x + y) = f(x) + f(y)\ \forall\ x, y \in \mathbb{R}$, then show that $f(x) = kx$, k some real constant.

SOLUTION: Given equation is $f(x + y) = f(x) + f(y)$ ...(1)

Replacing y by z, we have $f(x + z) = f(x) + f(z)$

Integrating w.r.t. z within the limits $z = 0$ to $z = y$ and keeping x constant we get

$$\int_0^y f(x+z)dz = \int_0^y f(x)dz + \int_0^y f(z)dz \qquad ...(2)$$

Put $x + z = u$ $\Rightarrow dz = du$

when $z = 0$, $u = x$ and when $z = y$, $u = x + y$

$$\therefore \int_x^{x+y} f(u)du = f(x)[z]_0^y + \int_0^y f(z)dz$$

$$\Rightarrow \int_x^{x+y} f(u)du = yf(x) + \int_0^y f(z)dz \Rightarrow yf(x) = -\int_0^y f(z)dz + \int_x^{x+y} f(u)du$$

$$\Rightarrow yf(x) = -\int_0^y f(z)dz + \left(\int_x^0 f(u)du + \int_0^{x+y} f(u)du\right) = \int_0^{x+y} f(u)du - \int_0^x f(u)du - \int_0^y f(z)dz$$

$$\text{or} \quad yf(x) = \int_0^{x+y} f(u)du - \int_0^x f(u)du - \int_0^y f(u)du \qquad ...(3)$$

interchanging x and y we have $xf(y) = \int_0^{y+x} f(u)du - \int_0^y f(u)du - \int_0^x f(u)du$ ...(4)

Clearly R.H.S. of (3) and (4) are same

$\Rightarrow yf(x) = xf(y)$ $\Rightarrow \frac{f(x)}{x} = \frac{f(y)}{y}\ \forall x, y \in \mathbb{R}$

$\Rightarrow \frac{f(x)}{x} = k$ (constant) $\forall\ x, y \in \mathbb{R}$, $\Rightarrow f(x) = kx\ \forall\ x, y \in \mathbb{R}$,

ILLUSTRATION 219: Let $f(x)$ be a continuous function on $\mathbb{R}$ such that $f(x) > 0\ \forall\ x \in \mathbb{R}$, and satisfy the functional equation $f(x + y) = f(x) \cdot f(y)$, then show that $f(x) = a^{kx}$ for some real constant k and $a > 0$.

SOLUTION: Given equation is $f(x + y) = f(x).f(y)$ ...(1)

Taking logarithm with basc a on both sides we get

$\log_a f(x + y) = \log_a f(x) + \log_a f(y)$ ...(2)

Let $\log_a f(x) = g(x)$

Now $f(x) > 0\ \forall\ x \in \mathbb{R}$ and $f(x)$ is continuous on $\mathbb{R}$ and logarithm is a continuous function over every positive continuous interval. Therefore $g(x)$ is also continuous on $\mathbb{R}$ and from (2) $g(x + y) = g(x) + g(y)$

∵ From the last illustration, we have $g(x) = kx$ for some real constant k.

$\Rightarrow \log_a f(x) = kx \qquad \Rightarrow f(x) = a^{kx}$.

ILLUSTRATION 220: Find the value of real number 'a' such that $2a^{1/3} + \int_a^x \frac{f(y)}{y^3 dy} = (x)^{1/3} + 2$

SOLUTION: Given equation is $2a^{1/3} + \int_a^x \frac{f(y)}{y^3} dy = (x)^{1/3} + 2$

Differentiating both sides w.r.t. x we get

$\frac{f(x)}{x^3} = \frac{1}{3}(x)^{-2/3} \qquad \Rightarrow f(x) = \frac{1}{3}(x)^{3-\frac{2}{3}} = \frac{1}{3}(x)^{\frac{7}{3}}$

Substituting this value of function in given equation we get $2a^{1/3} + \int_a^x \frac{\frac{1}{3}(y)^{7/3}}{y^3} dy = (x)^{\frac{1}{3}} + 2$

$\Rightarrow 2a^{1/3} + \frac{1}{3}\int_a^x (y)^{-2/3} dy = (x)^{1/3} + 2 \Rightarrow 2a^{1/3} + \frac{1}{3}\left|\frac{(y)^{1/3}}{1/3}\right|_a^x = (x)^{1/3} + 2$

$\Rightarrow 2a^{1/3} + x^{1/3} - a^{1/3} = x^{1/3} + 2$

$\Rightarrow a^{1/3} = 2 \qquad \Rightarrow a = 8$

ILLUSTRATION 221: A function $f(x)$ is such that $8f(x) = -\cos x + \int_0^x f'(t)\left(\cos^3 t + 12\cos t - 6\cos^2 t\right)dt$, then find the analytical formula for $f(x)$ and hence evaluate $4f\left(\frac{\pi}{2}\right)$

SOLUTION: Given equation is $8f(x) = -\cos x + \int_0^x f'(t)\left(\cos^3 t + 12\cos t - 6\cos^2 t\right)dt$

Differentiating both sides w.r.t. x we get

$8f'(x) = \sin x + f'(x)(\cos^3 x + 12\cos x - 6\cos^2 x)$

$\Rightarrow f'(x)[8 - \cos^3 x - 12\cos x + 6\cos^2 x] = \sin x$

$\Rightarrow f'(x)[(2 - \cos x)^3] = \sin x$

$\Rightarrow f'(x) = \frac{\sin x}{(2-\cos x)^3} \qquad \Rightarrow f(x) = \int \frac{\sin x}{(2-\cos x)^3} dx$

$\Rightarrow f(x) = \frac{(2-\cos x)^{-2}}{-2} + C \qquad \Rightarrow f(x) = -\frac{1}{2(2-\cos x)^2} + C$ ...(1)

At $x = 0$, $8f(0) = -\cos 0 + 0 \qquad \Rightarrow f(0) = -\frac{1}{8}$ ...(2)

Using (2) in (1) we get $\frac{-1}{8} = -\frac{1}{2(1)^2} + C$

$\Rightarrow \; C = -\frac{1}{8} + \frac{1}{2} = \frac{-1+4}{8} = \frac{3}{8}$ $\qquad \therefore$ from (1) $f(x) = \frac{-1}{2(2-\cos x)^2} + \frac{3}{8}$

$\therefore \; f\left(\frac{\pi}{2}\right) = \frac{-1}{2(2-0)^2} + \frac{3}{8} = \frac{-1}{8} + \frac{3}{8} = \frac{1}{4}$ $\qquad \therefore \; 4f\left(\frac{\pi}{2}\right) = 1$

ILLUSTRATION 222: If $f(x)$ is a continuous function such that $f(x) > 0 \;\forall\; x \geq 0$ and $f(x)$ satisfies $f(x) = \sqrt[17]{2 + \int_0^x f(t)\,dt}$, then show that $f(x) = \sqrt[16]{\frac{16}{17}x + (2)^{16/17}}$

SOLUTION: Given $f(x) = \sqrt[17]{2 + \int_0^x f(t)\,dt}$ ...(1)

$\Rightarrow \; (f(x))^{17} = 2 + \int_0^x f(t)\,dt$

Differentiating both sides w.r.t. x we get $17(f(x))^{16}.f'(x) = f(x)$

$\Rightarrow$ $17(f(x))^{15}.f'(x) = 1$ as $f(x) > 0$ and hence $f(x) \neq 0$

$\Rightarrow \; (f(x))^{15}\, f'(x) = \frac{1}{17}$

Integrating both sides w.r.t. x we get $\int (f(x))^{15} f'(x)\,dx = \frac{1}{17}\int dx$

$\Rightarrow \; \frac{[f(x)]^{16}}{16} = \frac{1}{17}x + C$ ...(2)

At $x = 0$, from (1), $f(0) = \sqrt[17]{2}$ using $f(0) = \sqrt[17]{2}$ in (2) we get $\frac{(2)^{16/17}}{16} = C$

Using the value of C in (2) we get, $\frac{[f(x)]^{16}}{16} = \frac{x}{17} + \frac{(2)^{16/17}}{16}$

$\Rightarrow \; (f(x))^{16} = \frac{16}{17}x + (2)^{16/17}$ $\qquad \Rightarrow \; f(x) = \sqrt[16]{\frac{16}{17}x + (2)^{16/17}}$

ILLUSTRATION 223: If $\int_x^{x^2 y} f(t)\,dt$ is independent of x for $x > 0$. If $f(4) = 3$, then find the value of $\int_1^x f(t)\,dt$ at $x = e^2$.

SOLUTION: Given $\int_x^{x^2 y} f(t)\,dt$ is independent of x

$\Rightarrow$ keeping y constant $\int_x^{x^2 y} f(t)\,dt$ is independent of x

Differentiating above definite integral w.r.t. x and keeping y constant we get

$f(x^2 y)\,(2xy) - f(x) = 0$ ...(1)

Substituting $y = \frac{1}{x^2}$ in (1), we get

$f(1)\left(2x.\frac{1}{x^2}\right) - f(x) = 0$

$\Rightarrow \dfrac{2}{x} f(1) = f(x)$ ...(2)

$\because \int_1^x f(t)\, dt = \int_1^x \dfrac{2}{t} f(1)\, dt = 2f(1)\int_1^x \dfrac{1}{t}\, dt = 2f(1)[\ln|t|]_1^x = 2f(1)[\ln|x| - \ln 1]$

$= 2f(1) \ln|x| = 2f(1) \ln x$ as $x > 0$ ...(3)

Taking $x = 4$ in (2) we have, $\dfrac{2}{4} f(1) = f(4)$

$\Rightarrow f(1) = 2f(4) = 2(3) = 6$ ($\because f(4) = 3$ given)

$\therefore$ using $f(1) = 6$ in (3), we get

$\int_1^x f(t)\, dt = 12 \ln x$

$\therefore \int_1^{e^2} f(t)\, dt = 12 \ln e^2 = 24$

ILLUSTRATION 224: Consider a real valued continuous function $f(x)$ such that $f(x) = \cos x + \int_{-\pi/2}^{\pi/2} (\sin x + t\, f(t))\, dt$ Find the max*i*mum and minimum value of function $f(x)$.

SOLUTION: Given $f(x) = \sin x + \int_{-\pi/2}^{\pi/2} (\sin x + t\, f(t))\, dt$

$\Rightarrow f(x) = \sin x + (\sin x)\left(\dfrac{\pi}{2} + \dfrac{\pi}{2}\right) + \int_{-\pi/2}^{\pi/2} t\, f(t)\, dt$

$\Rightarrow f(x) = \sin x + \pi \sin x + M$

$\Rightarrow f(x) = (\pi + 1) \sin x + M;$ ...(1)

where $M = \int_{-\pi/2}^{\pi/2} t^2 f(t)\, dt$

Again $M = \int_{-\pi/2}^{\pi/2} t\{(\pi + 1)\sin t + M\}\, dt$

$= (\pi + 1)\int_{-\pi/2}^{\pi/2} t \sin t\, dt + M \int_{-\pi/2}^{\pi/2} t\, dt = 2(\pi + 1)\int_0^{\pi/2} t \sin t\, dt + M(0)$

$\Rightarrow M = 2(\pi + 1)\left[|t(-\cos t)|_0^{\pi/2} - \int_0^{\pi/2} 1(-\cos t)\, dt \right]$

$\Rightarrow M = 2(\pi + 1)\left[|\sin t|_0^{\pi/2} \right]$

$\Rightarrow M = 2(\pi + 1)$ ...(2)

Using (2) in (1) we get

$f(x) = (\pi + 1)\sin x + 2(\pi + 1)$

$\Rightarrow f_{max} = (\pi + 1) + 2(\pi + 1) = 3(\pi + 1)$

And $f_{min} = -(\pi + 1) + 2(\pi + 1) = (\pi + 1)$

ILLUSTRATION 225: In each part, calculate the corresponding value for continuous function $f(x)$ defined for non-negative real numbers.

(i) $\int_0^x f(t)\, dt = x(1 + x^2);\ f(3)$

(ii) $\int_0^{x^2} f(t)\, dt = x^2(1 - x);\ f(4)$

(iii) $\int_0^{f(x)} t^2\, dt = x^2(1+x);\ f(3)$

(iv) $\int_0^{x^2(1+x)} f(t)\, dt = \sqrt{x};\ f(80)$

SOLUTION: (i) Given equation is $\int_0^{x} f(t)\, dt = x(1+x^2)$ ...(1)

Differentiating both sides w.r.t. x we get $f(x) = 1 + 3x^2$

$\therefore\ f(3) = 1 + 3(3)^2 = 28$

(ii) Given equation is $\int_0^{x^2} f(t)\, dt = x^2 - x^3$

Differentiating w.r.t. x, we get $2xf(x^2) = 2x - 3x^2$

$\Rightarrow\ f(x^2) = 1 - \frac{3}{2}x$ $\qquad \Rightarrow\ f(t) = 1 - \frac{3}{2}\sqrt{t}$

$\therefore\ f(4) = 1 - \frac{3}{2}\sqrt{4} = 1 - 3 = -2$

(iii) Given equation is $\int_0^{f(x)} t^2\, dt = x^2(1+x)$ ...(1)

Differentiating w.r.t. x, we get

$\Rightarrow\ [f(x)]^2 f'(x) = 2x + 3x^2$

Now integrating both sides, we get $\frac{[f(x)]^3}{3} = x^2 + x^3 + C$ ...(2)

Let $f(0) = k$ $\qquad \therefore$ from (1) $\int_0^{k} t^2\, dt = 0$

$\Rightarrow\ \left[\frac{t^3}{3}\right]_0^k = 0$ $\qquad \Rightarrow\ k^3 = 0 \quad \Rightarrow k = 0$

$\Rightarrow f(0) = 0$ $\qquad \therefore$ from (2)

$C = 0$

$\Rightarrow\ \frac{[f(x)]^3}{3} = x^2 + x^3$ $\qquad \Rightarrow\ [f(x)]^3 = 3x^2(1 + x)$

$\Rightarrow\ f(x) = \sqrt[3]{3x^2(1+x)}$ $\qquad \therefore\ f(3) = \sqrt[3]{27(4)} = 3(4)^{1/3}$.

(iv) Given equation is $\int_0^{x^2(1+x)} f(t)\, dt = \sqrt{x}$

Differentiating w.r.t. x we get $[f(x^2 + x^3)](2x + 3x) = \frac{1}{2\sqrt{x}}$

$\Rightarrow\ f(x^2 + x^3) = \frac{1}{2\sqrt{x}(2x + 3x^2)}$

For $x = 4$, $x^2 + x^3 = 16 + 64 = 80$

$\therefore\ f(80) = \frac{1}{2\sqrt{4}\left(2(4) + 3(4)^2\right)} = \frac{1}{4(56)} = \frac{1}{224}$

TEXTUAL EXERCISE–11: (SUBJECTIVE)

1. Evaluate the following integrals:

(i) $\int_0^\infty e^{-x}x^{7/2}dx$ (ii) $\int_0^\infty e^{-x^2}x^8dx$

(iii) $\int_0^\infty e^{-x^2}x^5dx$ (iv) $\left|\left(\frac{5}{2}\right)\right.$

(v) $|\overline{8}$

2. Evaluate the sum of the series $\frac{x^2}{1.2}-\frac{x^3}{2.3}+\frac{x^4}{3.4}...(-1)^{n+1}\frac{x^{n+1}}{n(n+1)}+...;|x|<1$

3. If $f(x)=\frac{1}{2}\tan\frac{x}{2}+\frac{1}{2^2}\tan\frac{x}{2^2}+\frac{1}{2^3}\tan\frac{x}{2^3}+...\infty$. Then prove that $f(x) = 1/x - \cot x$

4. Evaluate the following:

(a) $\int_0^{\pi/2}\sin^5 x\,dx$ (b) $\int_0^{\pi/2}\sin^4 x\cos^6 x\,dx$

(c) $\int_0^{\pi} x\sin^5 x\cos^6 x\,dx$ (d) $\int_0^{\pi}\sin^5 x\cos^4 x\,dx$

(e) $\int_0^1 x^3(1-x)^5\,dx$

5. Evaluate ${}^{100}C_{30}\,I$, where $I=\int_0^1 x^{30}(1-x)^{70}\,dx$

6. Evaluate $\int_0^a x(a^2-x^2)^{7/2}dx$

7. Evaluate $\int_0^{2a} x^5\sqrt{2ax-x^2}\,dx$

8. Find the infinite series expansion of $\int_0^1\frac{x^{a-1}}{1+x^b}dx$ and hence show that $1-\frac{1}{4}+\frac{1}{7}-\frac{1}{10}+\frac{1}{13}-\frac{1}{16}+...=\frac{1}{3}\left(\frac{\pi}{\sqrt{3}}+\ell n2\right)$

9. Show that $-\ell n(1-x)=x+\frac{x^2}{2}+\int_0^x\frac{y^2}{1-y}dy\,;\,0<x<1$

10. Show that

(i) $\frac{x^3}{1.3}-\frac{x^5}{3.5}+\frac{x^7}{5.7}-...=\frac{1}{2}(1+x^2)\tan^{-1}x-\frac{1}{2}x$

(ii) $\int_0^x\frac{\sin x}{x}dx=x-\frac{x^3}{3.3!}+\frac{x^5}{5.5!}...$

(iii) $\int_a^b\frac{e^x}{x}dx=\ell n\frac{b}{a}+(b-a)+\frac{b^2-a^2}{2.2!}+\frac{b^3-a^3}{3.3!}+..$

11. Evaluate $\int_{\ell n2}^{\ell n3}f(x)dx$, if $f(x) = e^{-x} + 2e^{-2x} + 3e^{-3x} + ...\infty$

12. Evaluate the integrals in terms of beta function $\int_0^2\sqrt{x}(4-x^2)^{-1/4}dx$

13. Express $\int_0^1 x^m(1-x^n)^p dx$ in terms of Beta function $m, n, p > 0$ and hence evaluate $\int_0^1 x^5(1-x^3)^{10}dx$

14. Show that $\int_0^\infty\sqrt{x}\,e^{-x^3}dx=\frac{\sqrt{\pi}}{3}$

15. If $f(x)$ is a derivable function satisfying $f(x)=\int_0^x e^t\sin(x-t)dt$ and $g(x) = f'(x) - f(x)$, then find the range of function $g(x)$.

16. If $f(x)=x+\int_0^1(xy^2+x^2y)f(y)\,dy$, then find $f(x)$ and hence evaluate $119\,f(1)$.

17. If $f(x)$ is a continuous function and c is a constant satisfying $\int_0^x f(t)\,dt=e^x-ce^{2x}\int_0^1 f(t)e^{-t}\,dt$, then find $f(x)$ and the value of $(2e + c^{-1})$.

18. If $f(x)=e^x+\int_0^1(e^x+te^{-x})f(t)\,dt$, then find $f(x)$.

Answer Keys

1. (i) $\frac{105}{16}\sqrt{\pi}$ (ii) $\frac{105}{32}\sqrt{\pi}$ (iii) 1 (iv) $\frac{3}{4}\sqrt{\pi}$ (v) 5040

2. $(x + 1)\ln(1 + x) - x$ **4.** (a) $\frac{8}{15}$ (b) $\frac{3\pi}{512}$ (c) $\frac{8\pi}{693}$ (d) $\frac{16}{315}$ (e) $\frac{1}{504}$

5. $\frac{1}{101}$ **6.** $\frac{a^9}{9}$ **7.** $\frac{33}{16}\pi a^7$ **8.** $\frac{1}{a}-\frac{1}{b+a}+\frac{1}{2b+a}-\frac{1}{3b+a}+....$ **11.** $\frac{1}{2}$

12. $B\left(\frac{3}{4},\frac{3}{4}\right)$ **13.** $\frac{1}{3}\beta(2,11);\frac{1}{396}$ **15.** $[-\sqrt{2}, \sqrt{2}]$

16. $\frac{180x+80x^2}{119};260$ **17.** $f(x) = e^x - 2e^{2x}$; 3 **18.** $\frac{1}{(5-3e)}\left(2e^x+e^{1-x}\right)$

TEXTUAL EXERCISE–11: (OBJECTIVE)

1. The value of $\int_0^{\infty} e^{-x} x^{5/2} dx$ is

(a) An irrational No. (b) $\frac{105}{16}\sqrt{\pi}$

(c) $\frac{15}{8}\sqrt{\pi}$ (d) None of these

2. The value of $\int_0^{\infty} e^{-x^3} x^6 dx$ equals

(a) 720 (b) 120

(c) $\lceil 7$ (d) None of these

3. The value of $\int_0^{\pi/2} \frac{e^{-(\tan^{-1}x)}\left(\tan^{-1}x\right)^{7/2}}{(1+x^2)} dx$ is

(a) An irrational Number

(b) $\frac{7!}{2^7}\cdot\frac{\sqrt{\pi}}{3!}$

(c) $\frac{105}{16}\sqrt{\pi}$

(d) A rational number

4. The value of $\int_0^{\pi} \cos^4 2x.\sin^2 4x\, dx$ equals

(a) $\frac{5}{32}$ (b) $\frac{5\pi}{16}$

(c) $\frac{5\pi}{32}$ (d) None of these

5. The value of $\int_0^{\pi} x\cos^2 x \sin^4 x\, dx$ equals

(a) $\frac{\pi}{16}$ (b) $\frac{\pi^2}{32}$

(c) $\frac{\pi^2}{16}$ (d) None of these

6. The value of $\int_0^1 x^5(1-x^3)^3 dx$ equals

(a) $\frac{1}{90}$ (b) $\frac{1}{60}$

(c) $\frac{1}{45}$ (d) None of these

7. The value of $\int_0^{\infty} e^{-x^2} dx$ is

(a) $\sqrt{\pi}$ (b) $\frac{\sqrt{\pi}}{2}$

(c) $2\sqrt{\pi}$ (d) None of these

8. The value of $\int_0^{\infty} x^6 e^{-2x} dx$ is

(a) 45/4 (b) 45/2

(c) 45/8 (d) None of these

9. The value $\int_0^{\pi/2} \sin^3 x \cos^{5/2} x\, dx$ equals

(a) $\frac{8}{77}$ (b) $\frac{4}{77}$

(c) $\frac{77}{8}$ (d) None of these

10. $\int_0^1 \frac{\tan^{-1} x}{x} dx$ equals

(a) $\sum_{n=0}^{\infty}(-1)^n.\frac{1}{(2n+1)^2}$ (b) $\sum_{n=0}^{\infty}(-1)^n\frac{1}{(2n)^2}$

(c) $\sum_{n=0}^{\infty}(-1)^n\frac{1}{(n+1)^2}$ (d) None of these

11. If $f(x)$ is a continuous non-identically zero and differentiable function $\forall\ x \in \mathbb{R}$, such that $(f(x))^2 = 2\int_0^x f(t)\, dt$, then $f(x)$ equals

(a) 0 (b) x

(c) $2x$ (d) None of these

12. If $f(x)$ is a continuous function $\forall\ x \in \mathbb{R}$, such that $\int_c^x f(t)\, dt = \cos x - \frac{\sqrt{3}}{2}\ \forall x \in \mathbb{R}$, then a value of c is given by

(a) $\pi/2$ (b) $\pi/3$

(c) $\pi/6$ (d) None of these

13. If $\int_a^x tf(t)\, dt = \sin x - x\cos x - \frac{1}{2}x^2\ \forall\ x \in \mathbb{R}$, then

(a) $f(x) = \sin x - \cos x$ (b) $f(x) = \sin x - 1$

(c) $a = 0$ is possible (d) $a = \frac{\pi}{2}$ is possible

14. If $f(x)$ is a continuous function satisfying $\int_0^{x^2} f(t)\, dt = 1 - 3^{x^2}$ is given by

(a) $3^x \ln 3$ (b) $-3^x \ln 3$

(c) $3^{-x} \ln 3$ (d) None of these

Answer Keys

1. (a,c) **2.** (d) **3.** (a,b,c) **4.** (c) **5.** (b) **6.** (b) **7.** (b) **8.** (c) **9.** (d) **10.** (a)
11. (b) **12.** (c) **13.** (b,c) **14.** (b)

MULTIPLE CHOICE QUESTIONS

SECTION–I

OBJECTIVE-TYPE SOLVED EXAMPLES

1. If $f(x) = I = \int_0^{\sin x} \cos^{-1} t\,dt + \int_0^{\cos x} \sin^{-1} t\,dt,\quad 0 < x < \frac{\pi}{2}$, then $f\left(\frac{\pi}{4}\right)$ is

(a) $\pi/\sqrt{2}$ (b) $1 + \pi/(2\sqrt{2})$
(c) 1 (d) None of these

Solution: (b) $\because \cos\left(\frac{\pi}{4}\right) = \sin\left(\frac{\pi}{4}\right) = \frac{1}{\sqrt{2}}$

$\therefore\ I = \int_0^{1/\sqrt{2}} \left(\cos^{-1} x + \sin^{-1} x\right) dx$

$= \int_0^{1/\sqrt{2}} \frac{\pi}{2} dx = \frac{\pi}{2}\left(\frac{1}{\sqrt{2}} - 0\right) = \frac{\pi}{2\sqrt{2}}$

2. Let $f(x)$ be a continuous function such that $f(a - x) + f(x) = 0$ for all $x \in [0, a]$. Then $\int_0^a \frac{dx}{1+e^{f(x)}}$ is equal to

(a) a (b) $a/2$
(c) $f(a)$ (d) $1/2\, f(a)$

Solution: (b)

$I = \int_0^a \frac{dx}{1+e^{f(x)}} = \int_0^a \frac{dx}{1+e^{f(a-x)}} = \int_0^a \frac{dx}{1+e^{-f(x)}}$ A.T.Q.

$= \int_0^a \frac{e^{f(x)}dx}{e^{f(x)}+1}$

$\therefore\ I + I = \int_0^a \frac{dx}{1+e^{f(x)}} + \int_0^a \frac{e^{f(x)}}{1+e^{f(x)}} dx$

$\therefore\ I = \int dx = a \quad \Rightarrow I = \frac{a}{2}$

3. If $I = \int_0^1 \sqrt{1+x^3}\,dx$, then

(a) $I < 1$ (b) $I \neq \frac{\sqrt{5}}{2}$
(c) $I < \frac{\sqrt{7}}{2}$ (d) None of these

Solution: (c) We know that

$$\left|\int_a^b f(x)g(x)\,dx\right| \le \sqrt{\int_a^b f^2(x)dx}\sqrt{\int_a^b g^2(x)dx}$$

(Scwartz-Bunyakovsky inequality)

Putting $f(x) = 1$ and $g(x) = \sqrt{1+x^3}$, we get

$= \int_0^1 \sqrt{1+x^3} \le \sqrt{\int_0^1 (1+x^3)\,dx} = \sqrt{1+1/4} = \frac{\sqrt{5}}{2}$

$\Rightarrow\ I \le \frac{\sqrt{5}}{2} \qquad \Rightarrow\ I < \frac{\sqrt{7}}{2}$

4. The value of $\int_{1/2}^2 |\log_{10} x|\,dx$ is

(a) $\log_{10}(8/e)$ (b) $\frac{1}{2}\log_{10}(8/e)$
(c) $\log_{10}(2/e)$ (d) None of these

Solution: (b)

$\int_{1/2}^2 |\log_{10} x|\,dx = \int_{1/2}^2 |\log_e x.\log_{10} e|\,dx$

$= |\log_{10} e|\left[\int_{1/2}^1 -\log_e x\,dx + \int_1^2 \log_e x\,dx\right]$

$= \log_{10} e\left[-\{x\ln x - x\}_{1/2}^1 + \{x\ln x - x\}_1^2\right]$

$= \log_{10} e\left[1 + \left(-\frac{1}{2}\ln 2 - \frac{1}{2}\right) + 2\ln 2 - 2 + 1\right]$

$= \log_{10} e\left[-\frac{1}{2} + \frac{3}{2}\ln 2\right] = \frac{1}{2}.\log_{10} e(\ln 8 - 1)$

$= \frac{1}{2}\log_{10} e\log_e\left(\frac{8}{e}\right) = \frac{1}{2}.\log_{10}(8/e)$

5. The value of the integral $I = \int_1^\infty \frac{x^2-2}{x^3\sqrt{x^2-1}}dx$ is

(a) 0 (b) 2/3
(c) 4/3 (d) None of these

Solution: (a) Putting $x^2 - 1 = t^2$ and $x\,dx = t\,dt$ we get

$I = \int_0^\infty \frac{t^2-1}{(t^2+1)^2}dt$

$= \int_0^1 \frac{t^2-1}{(t^2+1)^2}dt + \int_1^\infty \frac{t^2-1}{(t^2+1)^2}dt = I_1 + I_2;$

where $I_1 = \int_0^1 \frac{t^2-1}{(t^2+1)^2}dt$ and $I_2 = \int_1^\infty \frac{t^2-1}{(t^2+1)^2}dt$

Putting $t = 1/u$ in I_2, we get

$I_2 = -\int_0^1 \frac{u^2-1}{(u^2+1)^2}du = -I_1$

$\therefore\ I = I_1 + I_2 = I_1 - I_1 = 0$

6. If $\int_0^1 \frac{e^t dt}{t+1} = a$, then $\int_{b-1}^{b} \frac{e^{-t} dt}{t-b-1}$ is equal to

(a) ae^{-b} (b) $-be^{-a}$

(c) $-ae^{-b}$ (d) None of these

Solution: (c) Let $I = \int_0^1 \frac{e^t}{(t+1)} dt$

and $I_1 = \int_{b-1}^{b} \frac{e^{-t}}{t-b-1} dt$

In I_1, putting $t = b - y$; $dt = -dy$, we have

$I_1 = \int_1^0 \frac{e^{-b+y}}{-(y+1)}(-dy) = -e^{-b}\int_0^1 \frac{e^y}{(y+1)} dy = -e^{-b} a$

7. If $x > 0$ and [.] denotes greatest integer function, then $\int_0^{100[p]} (2x-[2x])^2 dx$ is equal to, (p is any real number)

(a) $\frac{100[p]}{3}$ (b) $\frac{200}{3}[p]$

(c) $\frac{100}{3}p$ (d) None of these

Solution: (a) $I = \int_0^{100[p]} (2x-[2x])^2 dx$

Period of $2x - [2x] = 1/2$.

Also period of $(2x - [2x])^2$ is 1/2

$\therefore\ I = 200[p]\int_0^{1/2} (2x-[2x])^2 dx = 200[p]\int_0^{1/2} 4x^2 dx$

$= 200[p].\frac{4}{3}\left|x^3\right|_0^{1/2} = \frac{800}{3}[p]\left(\frac{1}{8}-0\right) = \frac{100[p]}{3}$

8. The integral $\int_0^{\pi/2} \frac{xdx}{\sin x}$ is equal to

(a) $2\int_0^1 \frac{\tan^{-1} z}{z} dz$ (b) $\int_0^1 \frac{\tan^{-1} z}{z} dz$

(c) $\frac{1}{2}\int_0^1 \frac{\tan^{-1} z}{z} dz$ (d) None of these

Solution: (a) Let $z = \tan \theta$; then $dz = \sec^2 \theta\, d\theta$

Also $z = 0$

$\Rightarrow \theta = 0; z = 1 \quad \Rightarrow \theta = \frac{\pi}{4}$

$\therefore \int_0^1 \frac{\tan^{-1} z}{z} dz = \int_0^{\pi/4} \frac{\theta}{\tan\theta}.\sec^2\theta\, d\theta$

$= \int_0^{\pi/4} \frac{\theta}{\sin\theta.\cos\theta} d\theta = \int_0^{\pi/4} \frac{2\theta}{\sin 2\theta} d\theta = \int_0^{\pi/2} \frac{1}{2}.\frac{xdx}{\sin x}$

(putting 2θ = x)

$\Rightarrow \int_0^{\pi/2} \frac{x}{\sin x} dx = 2\int_0^1 \frac{\tan^{-1} z}{z} dz$

9. If $f(x) = A\sin\left(\frac{\pi x}{2}\right) + B;\ f'\left(\frac{1}{2}\right) = \sqrt{2}$ and $\int_0^1 f(x)\, dx = \frac{2A}{\pi}$, then constants A and B are respectively:

(a) $\frac{\pi}{2}$ and $\frac{\pi}{2}$ (b) $\frac{2}{\pi}$ and $\frac{3}{\pi}$

(c) 0 and $\frac{4}{\pi}$ (d) $\frac{4}{\pi}$ and 0

Solution: (d) We have, $f(x) = A\sin\left(\frac{\pi x}{2}\right) + B$,

$\Rightarrow f'(x) = \frac{A\pi}{2}\cos\frac{\pi x}{2}$

$\Rightarrow f'\left(\frac{1}{2}\right) = \frac{A\pi}{2}\cos\frac{\pi}{4} = \frac{A\pi}{2\sqrt{2}} = \sqrt{2}$

$\left(\because f'\left(\frac{1}{2}\right) = \sqrt{2} \text{ given}\right)$

$\Rightarrow A = \frac{4}{\pi}$; Now, $\int_0^1 f(x)\, dx = \frac{2A}{\pi}$

$\Rightarrow \int_0^1 \left\{A\sin\left(\frac{\pi x}{2}\right) + B\right\} dx = \frac{2A}{\pi}$

$\Rightarrow \left[-\frac{2A}{\pi}\cos\frac{\pi x}{2} + Bx\right]_0^1 = \frac{2A}{\pi} \Rightarrow B + \frac{2A}{\pi} = \frac{2A}{\pi}$

$\Rightarrow B = 0$

10. Let f be a positive function such that $I_1 = \int_{1-k}^{k} xf[x(1-x)]dx$; $I_2 = \int_{1-k}^{k} f[x(1-x)]\, dx$; where $2k - 1 > 0$. Then $\frac{I_1}{I_2}$ is

(a) 2 (b) k

(c) 1/2 (d) 1

Solution: (c)

Applying $\int_a^b f(x)\, dx = \int_a^b f(a+b-x)\, dx$ for I_1, we get

$I = \int ((1-x)f(1-x)(x))\, dx$

$= \int_{1-k}^{k} f[(1-x)(x)]dx - \int_{1-k}^{k} x\, f[x(1-x)]dx = I_2 - I_1$

Thus, $I_1 = I_2 - I_1$

$\therefore\ 2I_1 = I_2 \quad \Rightarrow \frac{I_1}{I_2} = \frac{1}{2}$

11. If $g(x)=\int_0^x \cos^4 t\,dt$, then $g(x+\pi)$ equals

(a) $g(x)+g(\pi)$ (b) $g(x)-g(\pi)$

(c) $g(x)\,g(\pi)$ (d) $\dfrac{g(x)}{g(\pi)}$

Solution: (a) Given $g(x)=\int_0^x \cos^4 t\,dt$ (given)

$$\Rightarrow g(x+\pi)=\int_0^{\pi+x}\cos^4 t\,dt$$

$$=\int_0^{\pi}\cos^4 t\,dt+\int_{\pi}^{\pi+x}\cos^4 t\,dt$$

$$=\int_0^{\pi}\cos^4 t\,dt+\int_0^{x}\cos^4 t\,dt$$

(Since $\cos^4 t$ is periodic with period π and $\int_T^{T+x} f(x)\,dx=\int_0^x f(x)\,dx$ $= g(\pi)+g(x)$

Thus, $g(x+\pi)=g(x)+g(\pi)$

12. Let $g(x)=\int_0^x f(t)\,dt$; where f is such that $\frac{1}{2}\le f(t)\le 1$ for $t\in[0,1]$ and $0\le f(t)\le\frac{1}{2}$ for $t\in[1,2]$. Then $g(2)$ satisfies the inequality.

(a) $-\frac{3}{2}\le g(2)\le\frac{1}{2}$ (b) $0\le g(2)\le 2$

(c) $\frac{3}{2}< g(2)\le\frac{5}{2}$ (d) $2<g(2)<4$

Solution: (b) $g(x)=\int_0^x f(t)\,dt$

$$\Rightarrow g(2)=\int_0^2 f(t)\,dt=\int_0^1 f(t)\,dt+\int_1^2 f(t)\,dt$$

Now, $\frac{1}{2}\le f(t)\le 1$ for $t\in[0,1]$

$\therefore$ By dominance rule we have,

$$\Rightarrow \int_0^1\frac{1}{2}dt\le\int_0^1 f(t)\,dt\le\int_0^1 1\,dt$$

(apply line integral on inequality)

$$\Rightarrow \frac{1}{2}\le\int_0^1 f(t)\,dt\le 1 \quad \ldots(1)$$

Again, $0\le f(t)\le\frac{1}{2}$ for $t\in[1,2]$

$$\Rightarrow \int_1^2 0\,dt\le\int_1^2 f(t)\,dt\le\int_0^1\frac{1}{2}dt \quad\Rightarrow\quad 0\le\int_1^2 f(t)\,dt\le\frac{1}{2} \quad \ldots(2)$$

Adding (1) and (2), we get

$$\frac{1}{2}\le\int_0^1 f(t)\,dt+\int_1^2 f(t)\,dt\le\frac{3}{2}$$

or $\frac{1}{2}\le g(2)\le\frac{3}{2}$ $\Rightarrow 0\le g(2)\le 2$

13. The value of the integral $\int_{e^{-1}}^{e^2}\left|\frac{\log_e x}{x}\right|dx$ is

(a) 3/2 (b) 5/2

(c) 3 (d) 5

Solution: (b) $\frac{\log_e x}{x}>0$ for $x>1$

and $\frac{\log_e x}{x}<0$ for $0<x<1$

So let us break the interval $[e^{-1}, e^2]$ into two sub-intervals $[e^{-1}, 1]$ and $[1, e^2]$ and hence $\int_{e^{-1}}^{e^2}\left|\frac{\log_e x}{x}\right|dx$

$$=\int_{e^{-1}}^{1}\left|\frac{\log_e x}{x}\right|dx+\int_1^{e^2}\left|\frac{\log_e x}{x}\right|dx$$

$$=-\int_{e^{-1}}^{1}\frac{\log_e x}{x}dx+\int_1^{e^2}\frac{\log_e x}{x}dx$$

$$=-\frac{1}{2}\left[(\log_e x)^2\right]_{e^{-1}}^{1}+\frac{1}{2}\left[(\log_e x)^2\right]_1^{e^2}$$

$$=-\frac{1}{2}[-(1)]+\frac{1}{2}[4]=\frac{1}{2}+2=\frac{5}{2}$$

14. The value of $\int_{-\pi}^{\pi}\frac{\cos^2 x}{1+a^x}dx,\ a>0$ is

(a) π (b) $a\pi$

(c) $\pi/2$ (d) 2π

Solution: (c) Let $I=\int_{-\pi}^{\pi}\frac{\cos^2 x}{1+a^x}dx$ ...(1)

$$=\left(\text{using }\int_a^b f(x)\,dx=\int_a^b f(a+b-x)\,dx\right)$$

$$\Rightarrow I=\int_{-\pi}^{\pi}a^x\frac{\cos^2 x}{1+a^x}dx \quad \ldots(2)$$

On adding (1) and (2), we get

$$2I=\int_{-\pi}^{\pi}\left(\frac{1+a^x}{1+a^x}\right)\cos^2 x\,dx$$

$$=\int_{-\pi}^{\pi}\cos^2 x\,dx=2\int_0^{\pi}\frac{1+\cos 2x}{2}dx$$

$$=\int_0^{\pi}(1+\cos 2x)\,dx$$

$$=\int_0^{\pi}1\,dx+\int_0^{\pi}\cos 2x\,dx=[x]_0^{\pi}+2\int_0^{\pi/2}\cos 2x\,dx$$

$$\left(\because \int_0^{2a} f(x)dx = 2\int_0^a f(x)dx \text{ for } f(2a-x)=f(x)\right)$$

$= \pi + 0 \quad \Rightarrow 2I = \pi \quad \Rightarrow I = \pi/2$

15. Let $f(x) = \int_1^x \sqrt{2-t^2}\, dt$. Then the real roots of the equation $x^2 - f'(x) = 0$ are

(a) ± 1 (b) $\pm\frac{1}{\sqrt{2}}$

(c) $\pm\frac{1}{2}$ (d) 0 and 1

Solution: (a) Given $f(x) = \int_1^x \sqrt{2-t^2}\, dt$

$\Rightarrow f'(x) = \sqrt{2-x^2}$ $\quad\therefore x^2 - f'(x) = 0$ (given)

$\Rightarrow x^2 = \sqrt{2-x^2}$ $\quad\Rightarrow x^4 = 2 - x^2$

$\Rightarrow x^4 + x^2 - 2 = 0$ $\quad\Rightarrow (x^2+2)(x^2-1) = 0$

$\Rightarrow x^2 = 1$ $\quad\Rightarrow x = \pm 1$

16. Let $T > 0$ be a fixed real number. Suppose f is a continuous function such that for all $x \in \mathbb{R}$, $f(x + T) = f(x)$. If $I = \int_0^T f(x)\, dx$, then the value of $\int_3^{3+3T} f(2x)\, dx$ is

(a) $\frac{3}{2}I$ (b) I

(c) $3I$ (d) $6I$

Solution: (c) $\int_3^{3+3T} f(2x)\, dx$ put $2x = y$, the given integral reduces to $\frac{1}{2}\int_6^{6+6T} f(y)\, dy = \frac{1}{2}\int_0^{6T} f(y)\, dy$ as

$= \frac{1}{2}(6)\int_0^T f(y)\, dy$ as $\int_0^{nT} f(x)\, dx = n\int_0^T f(x)\, dx$

$= \frac{1}{2}6(I) = 3I$

17. If $I(m,n) = \int_0^1 t^m (1+t)^n\, dt$, then the expression for $I(m, n)$ in terms of $I(m + 1, n - 1)$ is

(a) $\frac{2^n}{m+1} - \frac{n}{m+1} I(m+1, n-1)$

(b) $\frac{n}{m+1} I(m+1, n-1)$

(c) $\frac{2^n}{m+1} + \frac{n}{m+1} I(m+1, n-1)$

(d) $\frac{m}{m+1} I(m+1, n-1)$

Solution: (a) Here $I(m,n) = \int_0^1 t^m (1+t)^n\, dt$ and to reduce it into $I(m + 1, n - 1)$, we apply integration by parts taking $(1 + t)^n$ as first and t^m as second function as we want to increase m and reduce n.

$$\therefore \quad I(m,n) = \left\{(1+t)^n . \frac{t^{m+1}}{m+1}\right\}_0^1 - \int_0^1 n(1+t)^{(n-1)} . \frac{t^{m+1}}{m+1} dt$$

$$= \frac{2^n}{m+1} - \frac{n}{m+1}\int_0^1 (1+t)^{(n-1)} . t^{m+1}\, dt$$

$$\therefore \quad I(m,n) = \frac{2^n}{m+1} - \frac{n}{m+1} I(m+1, n-1)$$

18. If $f(x) = \int_{x^2}^{x^2+1} e^{-t^2}\, dt$, then $f(x)$ increases in

(a) $(2, 2)$ (b) no value of x

(c) $(0, \infty)$ (d) $(-\infty, 0)$

Solution: (d) Here, $f(x) = \int_{x^2}^{x^2+1} e^{-t^2}\, dt$

Differentiating both sides using Newton's Leibnitz formula, we get

$$f'(x) = e^{-(x^2+1)^2} . \left\{\frac{d}{dx}(x^2+1)\right\} - e^{-(x^2)^2} . \left\{\frac{d}{dx}(x^2)\right\}$$

$$= e^{-x^4-1-2x^2}(2x) - e^{-x^4}(2x)$$

$$= e^{-x^4}(2x)\left[e^{-1-2x^2} - 1\right] = 2xe^{-x^4}\left[\frac{1-e^{2x^2+1}}{e^{2x^2+1}}\right]$$

$$= 2xe^{-(x^4+2x^2+1)}\left[1 - e^{2x^2+1}\right] = 2xe^{-(x^2+1)^2}\left[1 - e^{2x^2+1}\right]$$

Now $e^{2x^2+1} > 1, \forall\, x$ and $e^{-(x^2+1)^2} > 0\ \forall\, x$

$\therefore f'(x) > 0$ $\quad\Rightarrow 2x < 0$

$\Rightarrow x < 0$ $\quad\Rightarrow x \in (-\infty, 0)$

19. If $f(x)$ is differentiable and $\int_0^{t^2} x(f(x))\, dx = \frac{2}{5}t^5$, then $f\left(\frac{4}{25}\right)$ equals

(a) $\frac{2}{5}$ (b) $-\frac{5}{2}$

(c) 1 (d) $-\frac{2}{5}$

Solution: (a, d) Here $\int_0^{t^2} xf(x)\, dx = \frac{2}{5}t^5$

Differentiating both sides, w.r.t. x by Newton Leibnitz's formula, we have $t^2 f(t^2)\left\{\frac{d}{dt}(t^2)\right\} = 2t^4$

$\Rightarrow t^2 f(t^2) 2t = 2t^4$ $\Rightarrow f(t^2) = t$

$\Rightarrow f(t^2) = t$ $\Rightarrow f(t) = \sqrt{t}$ or $-\sqrt{t}$

$\therefore \quad f\left(\frac{4}{25}\right) = \pm\frac{2}{5}$

20. The value of the integral $\int\limits_0^{\infty} \frac{x\log x}{(1+x^2)^2} dx$ is

(a) 0 (b) 6

(c) 5 log 3 (d) 4 log 5

Solution: (a)

$$\int_0^{\infty} \frac{x\log x}{(1+x^2)^2} dx = \int_0^1 \frac{x\log x}{(1+x^2)^2} dx + \int_1^{\infty} \frac{x\log x}{(1+x^2)^2} dx \quad \ldots(i)$$

($\because$ function changes its nature on $x = 1$)

Consider $I = \int_1^{\infty} \frac{x\log x}{(1+x^2)^2} dx$, put $x = \frac{1}{y} \Rightarrow dx = -\frac{1}{y^2} dy$

$$\therefore \quad I = -\int_1^0 \frac{y\log\left(\frac{1}{y}\right) dy}{(1+y^2)^2}$$

$$= -\int_0^1 \frac{y\log y}{(1+y^2)^2} dy = -\int_0^1 \frac{x\log x}{(1+x^2)^2} dx, \text{ put it in (i)}$$

$$\Rightarrow \int_0^{\infty} \frac{x\log x}{(1+x^2)^2} dx = \int_0^1 \frac{x\log x}{(1+x^2)^2} dx - \int_0^1 \frac{x\log x}{(1+x^2)^2} dx = 0$$

21. The value of $\int_0^{\pi} \ln(1+\cos x) dx$ is

(a) $\frac{\pi}{2}\log 2$ (b) π log 2

(c) –π ln2 (d) 0

Solution: (c) $I = \int_0^{\pi} \ln(1-\cos x) dx$

$$\Rightarrow 2I = 2\int_0^{\pi} \ln(\sin^2 x) dx$$

$$\Rightarrow 2I = 4\int_0^{\pi/2} \ln(\sin x) dx$$

$$\Rightarrow 2I = -4\left(\frac{5}{2}\ln 2\right) \quad \Rightarrow I = -\pi \ln 2$$

22. The value of $\int_a^b (x-a)^3 (b-x)^4 dx$ is $\frac{(b-a)^m}{n}$. Then (m, n) is

(a) (6, 260) (b) (8, 280)

(c) (4, 240) (d) None of these

Solution: (b) Put $x = a\cos^2\theta + b\sin^2\theta$

$\Rightarrow dx = 2(b-a)\sin\theta\cos\theta\, d\theta$

$$\therefore \quad I = 2(b-a)\int\limits_0^{\pi/2} (a\cos^2\theta + b\sin^2\theta - a)^3 \times (b - a\cos^2\theta - b\sin^2\theta)^4 \sin\theta\cos\theta\, d\theta$$

$$= 2(b-a)^8 \int_0^{\pi/2} \sin^7\theta\cos^9\theta\, d\theta$$

$$= 2(b-a)^8 \int_0^{\pi/2} \sin^7\theta (1-\sin^2\theta)^4 \cos\theta\, d\theta$$

Let $\sin\theta = t \Rightarrow \cos\theta\, d\theta = dt$

$$\Rightarrow I = 2(b-a)^8 \int_0^1 t^7 (1-t^2)^4 dt$$

$$= 2(b-a)^8 \int_0^1 t^7 (1-4t^2+6t^4-4t^6+t^8) dt$$

$$= \frac{(b-a)^8}{280}$$

23. If $I_n = \int\limits_0^{\pi/2} \cos^n x . \cos(nx) dx$; I_1, I_2, I_3, are in

(a) A.P. (b) G.P.

(c) H.P. (d) None of these

Solution: (b) Let $I_{n+1} = \int_0^{\pi/2} \cos^{n+1} x . \cos(nx+x) dx$

$$= \int_0^{\pi/2} \left(\cos^n x \cos nx . \underbrace{\cos^2 x}_{1-\sin^2 x} - \cos^{n+1} x . \sin nx \sin x \right) dx$$

$$= \int_0^{\pi/2} \cos^n x \cos nx\, dx$$

$$\int_0^{\pi/2} [\cos^n x . \cos nx . \sin^2 x + \cos^{n+1} x \sin nx \sin x] dx$$

$$\Rightarrow I_{n+1} = I_n - \int_0^{\pi/2} \underbrace{\cos^n x . \sin x}_{II} . \underbrace{\sin(n+1)x}_{I} dx$$

Using integration by parts

$$\Rightarrow I_{n+1} = I_n - \sin(n+1)x\left(-\frac{\cos^{n+1} x}{n+1}\right)\Bigg|_0^{\pi/2} - \int_0^{\pi/2} (n+1).\cos(n+1)x \frac{(\cos^{n+1} x)}{n+1} dx$$

$$\Rightarrow 2I_{n+1} = I_n$$

$$\therefore \quad I_2 = \frac{1}{2} I_1 ; I_3 = \frac{1}{2} I_2$$

$\Rightarrow$ They are in G. P.

24. If $I_n = \int\limits_0^{\pi/2} x^n \cos x\, dx$, then the value of $2^8(I_8 + 56 I_6)$ is

(a) π^8 (b) 8^{π}

(c) 5^{π} (d) π^5

Solution: (a) $I_n = \int_0^{\pi/2} \underbrace{x^n}_{I} . \underbrace{\cos x}_{II} dx$ (intergrating by parts)

$$\Rightarrow I_n = x^n \sin x \Bigg|_0^{\pi/2} - \int_0^{\pi/2} \underbrace{n x^{n-1}}_{I} . \underbrace{\sin x}_{II} dx$$

$$= \left(\frac{\pi}{2}\right)^n - n(n-1)\int_0^{\pi/2} x^{n-2} \cos x\, dx$$

$\Rightarrow \ I_n = \left(\frac{\pi}{2}\right)^n - n(n-1)I_{n-2}$; Putting $n = 8$

$I_8 + 56I_6 = (\pi/2)^8 \Rightarrow (2)^8 (I_8 + 56I_6) = (\pi)^8$

25. $\int_{-1/2}^{1/2} \sqrt{\left\{\left(\frac{x+1}{x-1}\right)^2 + \left(\frac{x-1}{x+1}\right)^2 - 2\right\}}\, dx$ is

(a) $4\log\frac{3}{4}$ (b) $4\log\frac{4}{3}$

(c) $2\log\frac{16}{9}$ (d) None of these.

Solution: (b)

$$I = \int_{-1/2}^{1/2} \sqrt{\left(\frac{x+1}{x-1} - \frac{x-1}{x+1}\right)^2}\, dx = \int_{-1/2}^{1/2} \sqrt{\left(\frac{4x}{x^2-1}\right)^2}\, dx$$

$$= \int_{-1/2}^{1/2} \left|\frac{4x}{x^2-1}\right| dx$$

$$= 4\int_0^{1/2} \frac{2|x|}{|x^2-1|} dx \quad \left(\because \frac{|x|}{x^2-1} \text{ is an even function}\right)$$

$$= -4\int_0^{1/2} \frac{2x}{x^2-1} dx = -4\left[\log|x^2-1|\right]_0^{1/2}$$

$$= -4\log\left(\frac{3}{4}\right) = 4\log\left(\frac{4}{3}\right)$$

26. $\lim_{n\to\infty} \left[\left(1+\frac{1}{n^2}\right)\left(1+\frac{2^2}{n^2}\right)\cdots\cdots\left(1+\frac{n^2}{n^2}\right)\right]^{1/n}$ is

(a) $e^{\frac{1}{2}(\pi-4)}$ (b) $2.e^{\frac{1}{2}(\pi-4)}$

(c) $\frac{1}{2}.e^{2(\pi-4)}$ (d) None of these

Solution: (b) Let

$$S = \lim_{n\to\infty} \left[\left(1+\frac{1}{n^2}\right)\left(1+\frac{2^2}{n^2}\right)\cdots\left(1+\frac{n^2}{n^2}\right)\right]^{1/n}$$

Taking natural logarithms both sides, we get

$$\ln S = \lim_{n\to\infty} \frac{1}{n}\left[\ln\left(1+\frac{1}{n^2}\right) + \ln\left(1+\frac{2^2}{n^2}\right) + \ldots + \ln\left(1+\frac{n^2}{n^2}\right)\right]$$

$$= \lim_{n\to\infty} \sum_{r=1}^{n} \left\{\ln\left(1+\frac{r^2}{n^2}\right)\right\}\frac{1}{n} = \int_0^1 \ln(1+x^2)dx$$

$$= \left[x\ln(1+x^2)\right]_0^1 - \int_0^1 x.\frac{2x}{1+x^2}dx$$

$$= \ln 2 - 2\int_0^1 \left(1-\frac{1}{1+x^2}\right)dx$$

$$= \ln 2 - 2\left(x - \tan^{-1}x\right)\Big|_0^1 = \ln 2 - 2\,[1 - \pi/4]$$

$$\Rightarrow S = 2e^{\frac{1}{2}(\pi-4)}$$

27. If $I = \int_0^{\pi} \frac{\cos x}{(x+2)^2} dx$, then $\int_0^{\pi/2} \frac{\sin 2x}{x+1} dx$ is equal to

(a) $2I$ (b) $\frac{1}{\pi+2} - \frac{1}{2} - I$

(c) 0 (d) $\frac{1}{\pi+2} + \frac{1}{2} - I$

Solution: (d)

$$I = \int_0^{\pi} \cos x\, d\left(-\frac{1}{x+2}\right) = \left[\frac{-\cos x}{x+2}\right]_0^{\pi} - \int_0^{\pi} \frac{\sin x}{x+2} dx$$

$$= \frac{1}{\pi+2} + \frac{1}{2} - \int_0^{\pi/2} \frac{\sin 2t}{2t+2} 2dt, \text{ where } x = 2t$$

$$\therefore \ I = \frac{1}{\pi+2} + \frac{1}{2} - \int_0^{\pi/2} \frac{\sin 2x}{x+1} dx$$

$$\Rightarrow \int_0^{\pi/2} \frac{\sin 2x}{(x+1)} dx = \frac{1}{\pi+2} + \frac{1}{2} - I$$

28. If $\int_2^3 \frac{x^2 dx}{\sqrt{x^4 - x^2 + 1}} = I$, then the value of $\int_2^3 \frac{xdx}{\sqrt{1+\left(x-\frac{1}{x}\right)^2}} - \int_{1/2}^{1/3} \frac{dx}{x^3\sqrt{x^2+\frac{1}{x^2}-1}}$ is equal to

(a) $-I$ (b) 0

(c) I (d) $2I$

Solution: (d) $\int_2^3 \frac{xdx}{\sqrt{1+\left(x-\frac{1}{x}\right)^2}} - \int_{1/2}^{1/3} \frac{dx}{x^3\sqrt{1+\left(x-\frac{1}{x}\right)^2}}$

$$= \int_2^3 \frac{xdx}{\sqrt{1+\left(x-\frac{1}{x}\right)^2}} + \int_2^3 \frac{t\,dt}{\sqrt{1+\left(\frac{1}{t}-t\right)^2}}$$

(By substituting $x = 1/t$ in 2nd integral)

$$= \int_2^3 \frac{xdx}{\sqrt{1+\left(x-\frac{1}{x}\right)^2}} + \int_2^3 \frac{tdt}{\sqrt{1+\left(t-\frac{1}{t}\right)^2}} = I + I = 2I$$

29. The value of $\int_{-a}^{a} \left(\cos^{-1}x - \sin^{-1}\sqrt{1-x^2}\right)dx$ is $(a > 0)$

$\left(\text{where} \int_0^a \cos^{-1}x\,dx = A\right)$

(a) $\pi a - A$ (b) $\pi a + 2A$

(c) $\pi a - 2A$ (d) $\pi a + A$

Solution: (c) Let

$$I=\int_{-a}^{a}\left(\cos^{-1}x-\sin^{-1}\sqrt{1-x^2}\right)dx \quad (a>0)$$

$$\Rightarrow I=\int_{-a}^{0}\cos^{-1}x\,dx+A-2\int_{0}^{a}\sin^{-1}\sqrt{1-x^2}\,dx$$

$$\Rightarrow \int_{0}^{a}\cos^{-1}(-x)dx+A-2\int_{0}^{a}\sin^{-1}\sqrt{1-x^2}\,dx$$

$$=\int_{0}^{a}(\pi-\cos^{-1}x)\,dx+A-2\int_{0}^{a}\cos^{-1}x\,dx$$

$$=\pi a-A+A-2A=\pi a-2A$$

30. The value of $\int_{0}^{e-1}\frac{e^{\frac{x^2+2x-1}{2}}}{(x+1)}dx+\int_{1}^{e}x\ln x e^{\frac{x^2-2}{2}}\,dx$ is equal to

(a) $\sqrt{e}^{(e^2+1)}$ (b) $\left(\sqrt{e}\right)^{e^2-1}$

(c) 0 (d) $\left(\sqrt{e}\right)^{e^2-2}$

Solution: **(d)** In first integral, taking $t=x+1$,

we get $\int_{1}^{e}\frac{1}{t}e^{\left(\frac{t^2}{2}-1\right)}dt+\int_{1}^{e}t\ln t e^{\left(\frac{t^2}{2}-1\right)}dt$

(Replacing x by t in II_{nd} integral)

$$=\int_{1}^{e}\frac{1}{t}e^{\left(\frac{t^2}{2}-1\right)}dt+\left|(\ln t)\int te^{\left(\frac{t^2}{2}-1\right)}dt\right|_{1}^{e}-\int_{1}^{e}\frac{1}{t}\int te^{\left(\frac{t^2}{2}-1\right)}dt$$

$$=\int_{1}^{e}\frac{1}{t}e^{\left(\frac{t^2}{2}-1\right)}dt+\left|(\ln t)e^{\frac{t^2}{2}-1}\right|_{1}^{e}-\int_{1}^{e}\frac{1}{t}e^{\left(\frac{t^2}{2}-1\right)}dt$$

$$=e^{\left(\frac{e^2}{2}-1\right)}=(\sqrt{e})^{(e^2-2)}$$

31. If $f:\mathbb{R}\to\mathbb{R}$; $f(x)=\sin x+x$, then the value of $\int_{0}^{\pi}(f^{-1}(x))dx$ is equal to

(a) π^2 (b) $\frac{\pi^2}{2}-2$

(c) $\frac{\pi^2}{2}+2$ (d) cannot be evaluated

Solution: (b) $\int_{0}^{x}f^{-1}(x)dx=\int_{f^{-1}(0)}^{f^{-1}(x)}tf'(t)dt$

$$=tf(t)\Big|_{f^{-1}(0)}^{f^{-1}(x)}-\int_{f^{-1}(0)}^{f^{-1}(x)}f(t)dt$$

(by substituting $x=f(t)$)

$$\Rightarrow \int_{0}^{\pi}f^{-1}(x)dx=\pi^2-\int_{0}^{\pi}(x+\sin x)dx=\frac{\pi^2}{2}-2$$

32. The value of $\int_{0}^{1/2}e^x\left(\sin^{-1}x-\frac{x}{(1-x^2)^{3/2}}\right)dx$ is

(a) 0 (b) $\frac{\sqrt{e}\pi}{6}-\frac{2}{3\sqrt{3}}$

(c) $\frac{\sqrt{e}\pi}{6}-\frac{4}{3\sqrt{3}}$ (d) $\sqrt{e}\left(\frac{\pi}{6}-\frac{2}{\sqrt{3}}\right)+1$

Solution: (d)

$$\int_{0}^{1/2}e^x\left\{\left(\sin^{-1}x+\frac{1}{\sqrt{1-x^2}}\right)-\left(\frac{1}{\sqrt{1-x^2}}+\frac{x}{(1-x^2)^{3/2}}\right)\right\}dx$$

(adding and subtracting $\frac{1}{\sqrt{1-x^2}}$)

$$=\int_{0}^{1/2}e^x\left(\sin^{-1}x+\frac{d}{dx}(\sin^{-1}x)\right)dx-$$

$$\int_{0}^{1/2}e^x\left\{\frac{1}{\sqrt{1-x^2}}+\frac{d}{dx}\left(\frac{1}{\sqrt{1-x^2}}\right)\right\}dx$$

$$=\left|e^x\left(\sin^{-1}x-\frac{1}{\sqrt{1-x^2}}\right)\right|_{0}^{1/2}=e^{1/2}\left(\frac{\pi}{6}-\frac{2}{\sqrt{3}}\right)+1$$

Since $\int e^x(f(x)+f'(x))dx=e^x f(x)+C$

33. The value of $\lim_{n\to\infty}\left(\frac{n!}{n^n}\right)^{\left(\frac{2n^4+1}{5n^5+1}\right)}$ is equal to

(a) 1 (b) 0

(c) $\left(\frac{1}{e}\right)^{2/5}$ (d) $e^{2/5}$

Solution: **(c)** We know that $\lim_{x\to\infty}f(x)=e^{\lim_{x\to\infty}\ln f(x)}$ ...(i)

Here, $\lim_{n\to\infty}\log\left(\frac{n!}{n^n}\right)^{1/n}=\lim_{n\to\infty}\frac{1}{n}\log\left(\frac{1\cdot2\cdot3\cdot\ldots\ldots n}{n\cdot n\cdot n\cdot\ldots\ldots n}\right)$

$$=\lim_{n\to\infty}\frac{1}{n}\sum_{r=1}^{n}\log\frac{r}{n}=\int_{0}^{1}\log x\,dx$$

$$=\left[(\log x)\cdot x-\int x.\frac{1}{x}dx\right]_{0}^{1}=[x\log x-x]_{0}^{1}$$

$$=-1-\lim_{x\to0}x\log x=-1-\lim_{x\to0}\frac{\log x}{1/x}=-1-\lim_{x\to0}\frac{1/x}{-1/x^2},$$

using L L.H rule $=-1-\lim_{x\to0}(-x)=-1$

$\therefore$ using (1), $\lim_{n\to\infty}\left(\frac{n!}{n^n}\right)^{1/n}=e^{-1}=\frac{1}{e}$

$$\therefore \lim_{n\to\infty}\left(\frac{n!}{n^n}\right)^{\left(\frac{2n^4+1}{5n^5+1}\right)}=\left(\frac{1}{e}\right)^{\lim_{n\to\infty}\left(\frac{2n^5+n}{5n^5+1}\right)}=\left(\frac{1}{e}\right)^{2/5}$$

SECTION–II

SUBJECTIVE-TYPE SOLVED EXAMPLES

1. Evaluate the following (where [.] denotes the greatest integer function).

(i) $\int_0^{2\pi} [|\sin x| + |\cos x|]dx$

(ii) $\int_{\cos(\cos^{-1}\alpha)}^{\sin(\sin^{-1}\beta)} \left|\frac{\cos(\cos^{-1}x)}{\sin(\sin^{-1}x)}\right| dx$

Solution: (i) $I = \int_0^{2\pi} [|\sin x| + |\cos x|]dx$

We know that $[|\sin x| + |\cos x|] = 1$ for $x \in \mathbb{R}$

$\Rightarrow I = \int_0^{2\pi} 1.dx$

$\therefore I = 2\pi$

(ii) we know that cos ($\cos^{-1}x$) and sin ($\sin^{-1}x$) could be plotted as

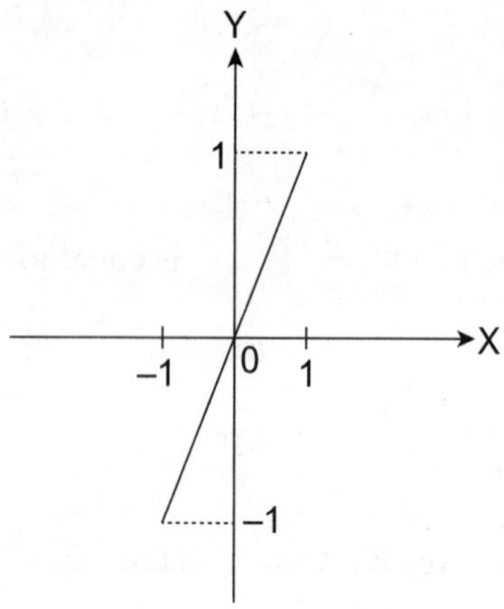

$\therefore$ $\sin(\sin^{-1}x)$ and $\cos(\cos^{-1}x)$ are identical functions

$\therefore \int_\alpha^\beta \left|\frac{\cos(\cos^{-1}x)}{\sin(\sin^{-1}x)}\right| dx = \int_\alpha^\beta 1.dx = (\beta - \alpha)$

2. Show that

$$\int_0^{\pi/2} f(\sin 2x)\sin x dx = \int_0^{\pi/2} f(\sin 2x)\cos x dx$$

$$= \sqrt{2}\int_0^{\pi/4} f(\cos 2x)\cos x dx$$

Solution: Let $I = \int_0^{\pi/2} f(\sin 2x)\sin x dx$ ...(1)

$\Rightarrow I = \int_0^{\pi/2} f\left[\sin 2\left(\frac{\pi}{2} - x\right)\right]\sin\left(\frac{\pi}{2} - x\right)dx$

$\Rightarrow I = \int_0^{\pi/2} f[\sin(\pi - 2x)]\cos x dx$ ...(2)

$\Rightarrow I = \int_0^{\pi/2} f(\sin 2x)\cos x\, dx$

Hence the first part is proved

Now, $I = \int_0^{\pi/2} f(\sin 2x)\sin x dx$

$= \int_0^{\pi/4} f(\sin 2x)\sin x dx + \int_0^{\pi/4} f[\sin 2(\pi/2 - x)]$
$\sin(\pi/2 - x)dx$

$= \int_0^{\pi/4} f(\sin 2x)\sin x dx + \int_0^{\pi/4} f(\sin 2x)\cos x dx$

$= \int_0^{\pi/4} f(\sin 2x)(\sin x + \cos x)dx$

$= \int_0^{\pi/4} f\left[\sin 2\left(\frac{\pi}{4} - x\right)\right]\left[\sin\left(\frac{\pi}{4} - x\right) + \cos\left(\frac{\pi}{4} - x\right)\right]dx$

$= \int_0^{\pi/4} f(\cos 2x)$

$\left[\frac{1}{\sqrt{2}}\cos x - \frac{1}{\sqrt{2}}\sin x + \frac{1}{\sqrt{2}}\cos x + \frac{1}{\sqrt{2}}\sin x\right]dx$

$= \sqrt{2}\int_0^{\pi/4} f(\cos 2x)\cos x dx$

Hence the second part is also proved.

3. Evaluate the $\int_1^{10\pi} ([\sec^{-1}x] + [\cot^{-1}x])dx$; (where $[x]$ denotes the greatest integer function)

Solution: $I = \int_1^{10\pi} ([\sec^{-1}x] + [\cot^{-1}x])dx$

$= \int_0^{\sec 1} ([\sec^{-1}x] + [\cot^{-1}x])dx +$

$\int_{\sec 1}^{10\pi} ([\sec^{-1}x] + [\cot^{-1}x])dx$

$= \int_0^{\sec 1} (0+0).dx + \int_{\sec 1}^{10\pi} (1+0).dx$

$= 0 + (x)_{\sec 1}^{10\pi} = 10\pi - \sec 1$

4. Evaluate $\int_0^x [\cos t]dt$; where $x \in \left(2n\pi, (4n+1)\frac{\pi}{2}\right)$; $n \in \mathbb{N}$ and [.] denotes the greatest integer function.

Solution: Let $I = \int_0^x [\cos t]dt$

$= \int_0^{2n\pi} [\cos t]dt + \int_{2n\pi}^{x} [\cos t]dt$

$= n\int_0^{2\pi}[\cos t]dt + \int_{2n\pi}^{x}[\cos t]dt$

$= n\left(\int_0^{\pi/2}[\cos t]dt + \int_{\pi/2}^{3\pi/2}[\cos t]dt + \int_{3\pi/2}^{2\pi}[\cos t]dt\right) + \int_{2n\pi}^{x}[\cos t]dt$

$= n\left(\int_0^{\pi/2}0.dt + \int_{\pi/2}^{3\pi/2}(-1)\,dt + \int_{3\pi/2}^{2\pi}0.dt\right) + \int_{2n\pi}^{x}0.dt$

$= n\left(0 - \left(\frac{3\pi}{2} - \frac{\pi}{2}\right) + 0\right) + 0 = -n\pi$

5. If $\int_0^\infty \frac{\sin x}{x}dx = \frac{\pi}{2}$, then compute the following:

(i) $\int_0^\infty \frac{\sin^2 x}{x^2}dx$ (ii) $\int_0^\infty \frac{\sin^3 x}{x}dx$

Solution: (i)

$$\int_0^\infty \frac{\sin^2 x}{x^2}dx = \left[\sin^2 x\left(\frac{-1}{x}\right)\right]_0^\infty - \int_0^\infty 2\sin x\cos x\left(-\frac{1}{x}\right)dx$$

$$= \int_0^\infty \frac{\sin 2x}{x}dx$$

$$\left(\because \lim_{x\to\infty}\frac{\sin^2 x}{x} = 0, \lim_{x\to 0}\frac{\sin^2 x}{x} = \lim_{x\to 0}\frac{\sin x}{x}\sin x = 1\times 0 = 0\right)$$

$$= \int_0^\infty \frac{\sin t}{t/2}\cdot\frac{dt}{2} = \int_0^\infty \frac{\sin t}{t}dt = \int_0^\infty \frac{\sin x}{x}dx = \frac{\pi}{2}$$

where $2x = t,\ dx = \frac{1}{2}dt$

(ii) $\int_0^\infty \frac{\sin^3 x}{x}dx = \frac{1}{4}\int_0^\infty \frac{3\sin x - \sin 3x}{x}dx$

$$= \frac{3}{4}\int_0^\infty \frac{\sin x}{x}dx - \frac{1}{4}\int_0^\infty \frac{\sin 3x}{x}dx$$

$$= \frac{3}{4}\int_0^\infty \frac{\sin x}{x}dx - \frac{1}{4}\int_0^\infty \frac{\sin t dt}{t}$$

$= \frac{3}{4}\cdot\frac{\pi}{2} - \frac{1}{4}\cdot\frac{\pi}{2}$ (Put $3x = t$ in the second integral)

$$= \frac{\pi}{4}$$

6. Prove that $\int_0^\infty \frac{dx}{1+x^4} = \int_0^\infty \frac{x^2dx}{1+x^4} = \frac{\pi}{2\sqrt{2}}$

Solution: Put $x = \frac{1}{z}$ in the first integral

$\int_0^\infty \frac{dx}{1+x^4} = I(\text{Say})$. Then $dx = \frac{-1}{z^2}dz$; also

$x = 0 \Rightarrow z \to \infty;\ x \to \infty \Rightarrow z \to 0$

$$I = \int_0^\infty \frac{dx}{1+x^4} = \int_\infty^0 -\frac{1}{z^2}\cdot\frac{1}{1+1/z^4}dz = \int_0^\infty \frac{z^2dz}{1+z^4} = \int_0^\infty \frac{x^2dx}{1+x^4},$$

(using property of changing of variable)

$$\Rightarrow 2I = \int_0^\infty \frac{dx}{1+x^4} + \int_0^\infty \frac{x^2dx}{1+x^4} = \int_0^\infty \frac{1+x^2}{1+x^4}dx$$

$$= \int_0^\infty \frac{1+x^2}{x^2}\cdot\frac{1}{x^2+\frac{1}{x^2}}dx = \int_0^\infty \frac{1+\frac{1}{x^2}}{(x-1/x)^2+2}dx$$

Put $x - \frac{1}{x} = z$; then $\left(1+\frac{1}{x^2}\right)dx = dz$

Also, $x \to 0 \Rightarrow z \to -\infty$ and $x \to \infty \Rightarrow z \to \infty$

$$\therefore\ 2I = \int_{-\infty}^\infty \frac{dz}{z^2+2} = \left[\frac{1}{\sqrt{2}}\tan^{-1}\left(\frac{z}{\sqrt{2}}\right)\right]_{-\infty}^\infty$$

$$= \frac{1}{\sqrt{2}}\left[\tan^{-1}\infty - \tan(-\infty)\right]$$

$$= \frac{1}{\sqrt{2}}\left[\frac{\pi}{2} - \left(-\frac{\pi}{2}\right)\right] = \frac{\pi}{\sqrt{2}} \quad \therefore\ I = \frac{1}{2}\cdot\frac{\pi}{\sqrt{2}} = \frac{\pi}{2\sqrt{2}}$$

7. If $f(x) = -\int_0^x \log\cos y\,dy$; prove that $f(x) = 2f\left(\frac{\pi}{4}+\frac{x}{2}\right) - 2f\left(\frac{\pi}{4}-\frac{x}{2}\right) - x\log 2$. Hence or otherwise, show that $f\left(\frac{\pi}{2}\right) = \frac{\pi}{2}\log 2$

Solution: On putting $y = \frac{\pi}{2} - z,\ dy = -dz$

we get $f(x) = -\int_{\pi/2}^{\pi/2-x} \log\cos\left(\frac{\pi}{2} - z\right)(-dz)$

($\because$ when $y = 0$, $z = \frac{\pi}{2}$ and when $y = x, z = \frac{\pi}{2} - x$)

$$= \int_{\pi/2}^{\pi/2-x} \log\sin z dz = \int_{\pi/2}^{\pi/2-x} \log\left(2\sin\frac{z}{2}\cos\frac{z}{2}\right)dz$$

$$= \int_{\pi/2}^{\pi/2-x} \log 2dz + \int_{\pi/2}^{\pi/2-x} \log\sin\frac{z}{2}dz + \int_{\pi/2}^{\pi/2-x} \log\cos\frac{z}{2}dz$$

$$= -x\log 2 + I_1 + I_2 \qquad \text{...(i)}$$

now $I_1 = \int_{\pi/2}^{\pi/2-x} \log\sin\frac{z}{2}dz = \int_{\pi/2}^{\pi/2-x} \log\cos\left(\frac{\pi}{2} - \frac{z}{2}\right)dz$

$= \int_{\pi/4}^{\pi/4+x/2} \log\cos u(-2du)$; where

$\frac{\pi}{2} - \frac{z}{2} = u,\ dz = -2du$

$$\therefore\ I_1 = -2\int_{\pi/4}^{0} \log\cos u du - 2\int_0^{(\pi/4+x/2)} \log\cos u du$$

$$= -2\int_{\pi/4}^{0} \log\cos u \, du + 2f\left(\frac{\pi}{4}+\frac{x}{2}\right) \quad \ldots\text{(ii)}$$

Similarly, by putting $\frac{z}{2} = v$ in I_2,

we get $I_2 = 2\int_{\pi/4}^{0} \log\cos v \, dv - 2f\left(\frac{\pi}{4}-\frac{x}{2}\right)$ ...(iii)

Putting the values of I_1 and I_2 in (i) we get equation to be proved. Finally putting $x = \frac{\pi}{2}$ in this relation, we obtain $f\left(\frac{\pi}{2}\right) = 2f\left(\frac{\pi}{2}\right) - \frac{\pi}{2}\log 2$

or $f\left(\frac{\pi}{2}\right) = \frac{\pi}{2}\log 2$

8. Evaluate $\int_0^{2\pi} \frac{\sin^2\theta}{a - b\cos\theta} d\theta \ (a > b > 0)$

Solution: Using property we get

$$I = \int_0^{\pi} \frac{\sin^2\theta}{a-b\cos\theta} d\theta + \int_0^{\pi} \frac{(\sin(2\pi-\theta))^2}{a-b\cos(2\pi-\theta)} d\theta$$

$$= 2\int_0^{\pi} \frac{\sin^2\theta}{a-b\cos\theta} d\theta$$

$$= 2\left\{\int_0^{\pi/2} \frac{\sin^2\theta}{a-b\cos\theta} d\theta + \int_0^{\pi/2} \frac{(\sin(\pi-\theta))^2}{a-b\cos(\pi-\theta)} d\theta\right\}$$

$$= 4a\int_0^{\pi/2} \frac{\sin^2\theta}{a^2-b^2\cos^2\theta} d\theta \quad \ldots\text{(i)}$$

(Now numerator $= \sin^2\theta = 1 - \cos^2\theta$)

$$= \frac{1}{b^2}(b^2 - b^2\cos^2\theta) = \frac{1}{b^2}(b^2 + a^2 - b^2\cos^2\theta - a^2)$$

$$= \frac{1}{b^2}(b^2 - a^2) + \frac{1}{b^2}(a^2 - b^2\cos^2\theta) \quad \ldots\text{(ii)}$$

∴ From (i) and (ii)

$$I = 4a\int_0^{\pi/2} \left\{\frac{\frac{1}{b^2}(b^2-a^2) + \frac{1}{b^2}(a^2-b^2\cos^2\theta)}{(a^2-b^2\cos^2\theta)}\right\} d\theta$$

$$= 4a\int_0^{\pi/2} \left\{\frac{b^2-a^2}{b^2}\cdot\frac{1}{(a^2-b^2\cos^2\theta)} + \frac{1}{b^2}\right\} d\theta$$

$$\Rightarrow I = 4a\left[\frac{1}{b^2}\int_0^{\pi/2} d\theta + \frac{b^2-a^2}{b^2}\int_0^{\pi/2} \frac{1}{a^2-b^2\cos^2\theta} d\theta\right]$$

$$= 4a\left[\frac{1}{b^2}\left(\frac{\pi}{2}\right) + \frac{b^2-a^2}{b^2} \times \frac{\pi}{2a\sqrt{a^2-b^2}}\right]$$

$$= \frac{2\pi}{b^2}\left[a - \sqrt{a^2-b^2}\right]$$

9. Prove that $\int_0^{\pi} \frac{\sin n\theta}{\sin\theta} d\theta$ is equal to 0 or π according as n is an even or odd positive integer.

Solution: ***Case I:*** n is even.

Let $n = 2m$, $m \in \mathbb{N}$; $I_m = \int_0^{\pi} \frac{\sin 2m\theta}{\sin\theta} d\theta$

Consider $I_m - I_{m-1} = \int_0^{\pi} \frac{\sin(2m)\theta - \sin(2m-2)\theta}{\sin\theta} d\theta$

$$= \int_0^{\pi} \frac{2\sin\theta\cos(2m-1)\theta}{\sin\theta} d\theta = 0$$

$\Rightarrow I_m = I_{m-1}$

$\Rightarrow I_m = I_{m-1} = I_{m-2} = \ldots\ldots\ldots = I_2 = I_1$

$\Rightarrow I_m = I_{m-1} = \int_0^{\pi} \frac{\sin 2\theta}{\sin\theta} d\theta = 0$

Case II: If n is odd. Let $n = 2m + 1$, $m \in$ W;

$$I_m = \int_0^{\pi} \frac{\sin(2m+1)\theta}{\sin\theta} d\theta$$

Consider $I_m - I_{m-1} = \int_0^{\pi} \frac{(\sin(2m+1)\theta - \sin(2m-1)\theta)}{\sin\theta} d\theta$

$$= \int_0^{\pi} \frac{2\sin\theta\cos 2m\theta}{\sin\theta} d\theta = 0$$

$\Rightarrow I_m = I_{m-1} = I_{m-2} = \ldots\ldots = I = \int_0^{\pi} \frac{\sin\theta}{\sin\theta} d\theta = \pi$

10. Evaluate $\int_0^{\pi} \frac{(ax+b)\sec x\tan x}{4+\tan^2 x} dx$

Solution: $I = \int_0^{\pi} \frac{(ax+b)\sec x\tan x}{4+\tan^2 x} dx$ ....(i)

$$= \int_0^{\pi} \frac{(a(\pi-x)+b)\sec(\pi-x)\tan(\pi-x)}{4+(\tan(\pi-x))^2} dx$$

$\Rightarrow I = \int_0^{\pi} \frac{(a(\pi-x)+b)\sec x\tan x}{4+\tan^2 x} dx$ ...(ii)

Adding (i) and (ii) we get,

$2I = (a\pi + 2b)\int_0^{\pi} \frac{\sec x\tan x}{3+\sec^2 x} dx = (a\pi+2b)I'$ ...(iii)

consider, $I' = \int_0^{\pi} \frac{\sec x\tan x}{3+\sec^2 x} dx$

$$= 2\int_0^{\pi/2} \frac{\sec(\pi-x)\tan(\pi-x)}{3+\sec^2(\pi-x)} dx = 2\int_0^{\pi/2} \frac{\sec x\tan x}{3+\sec^2 x} dx$$

Let $\sec x = t \Rightarrow \sec x\tan x dx = dt$

$$\Rightarrow \; I' = 2\int_1^{\infty} \frac{dt}{3+t^2} = 2.\frac{1}{\sqrt{3}}\left[\tan^{-1}\frac{t}{\sqrt{3}}\right]_1^{\infty}$$

$$= \frac{2}{\sqrt{3}}\,[\pi/2 - \pi/6] = \frac{2}{\sqrt{3}}\cdot\frac{\pi}{3} = \frac{2\pi}{3\sqrt{3}} \quad \text{...(iv)}$$

From (iii) and (iv), we get, $I = \dfrac{(a\pi + 2b)\pi}{3\sqrt{3}}$

11. Prove that $4 < \int_1^3 \sqrt{3+x^3}\,dx < 2\sqrt{30}$

Solution: Since the function $f(x) = \sqrt{3+x^3}$ increases monotonically on the interval, $[1, 3]$, $m = 2$, $M = \sqrt{30}$, $b - a = 2$

By max-min inequality

Hence $2.(2) \le \int_1^3 \sqrt{3+x^3}\,dx < 2\sqrt{30}$

$$\Rightarrow \; 4 < \int_1^3 \sqrt{3+x^3}\,dx < 2\sqrt{30}$$

12. Evaluate $\int_0^{\infty}[ne^{-x}]dx$; where n is a natural number greater than 1 and [.] denotes the greatest integer function.

Solution: $[ne^{-x}] = k, k \ge 0, k \in \mathbb{Z}$

$\Rightarrow k \le ne^{-x} < k + 1$

$$\Rightarrow \; \frac{k}{n} \le e^{-x} < \frac{k+1}{n} \quad \Rightarrow \; \ln\left(\frac{n}{k+1}\right) < x \le \ln\left(\frac{n}{k}\right)$$

Therefore

$$\int_0^{\infty}[ne^{-x}]dx = \int_{\ln\left(\frac{n}{n}\right)}^{\ln\left(\frac{n}{n-1}\right)} (n-1)\,dx + \int_{\ln\left(\frac{n}{n-1}\right)}^{\ln\left(\frac{n}{n-2}\right)} (n-2)dx + ...+$$

$$\int_{\ln\left(\frac{n}{2}\right)}^{\ln n} 1.dx + \int_{\ln n}^{\infty} 0.dx$$

$$= (n-1).\ln\left(\frac{n}{n-1}\right) + (n-2)$$

$$\left[\ln\frac{n}{n-2} - \ln\frac{n}{n-1}\right] + ... + [\ln n - \ln(n/2)]$$

$$= (n-1).\ln\left(\frac{n}{n-1}\right) + (n-2)\ln\left(\frac{n-1}{n-2}\right) + ... + \ln 2$$

$$= \ln\left\{\left(\frac{n}{n-1}\right)^{n-1}\cdot\left(\frac{n-1}{n-2}\right)^{n-2}\cdot\left(\frac{n-2}{n-3}\right)^{n-3} + ...(2/1)^1\right\}$$

$$= \ln\frac{n^{n-1}}{(n-1)(n-2)(n-3)...2.1} = \ln\frac{n^n}{n!}$$

13. If f, g, h be continuous function on $[0, a]$ such that $f(a - x) = f(x)$, $g(a - x) = g(x)$ and $3h(x) - 4h(a - x) = 5$, then prove that $\int_0^a f(x)g(x)dx = -\frac{1}{5}\int_0^a f(x)g(x)h(x)dx$

Solution: Let $I = \int_0^a f(x)g(x)h(x)dx$

$$= \int_0^a f(a-x)g(a-x)h(a-x)dx$$

$$= \int_0^a f(x)g(x)h(a-x)dx = \int_0^a f(x)g(x)\left(\frac{3h(x)-5}{4}\right)dx$$

$$\Rightarrow \; I = \int_0^a f(x)g(x)\left[\frac{3h(x)-5}{4}\right]dx$$

$$\Rightarrow \; I = \frac{3}{4}\int_0^a f(x)g(x)h(x) - \frac{5}{4}\int_0^a f(x)g(x)dx$$

$$\Rightarrow \; I = \left(1 - \frac{3}{4}\right) = -\frac{5}{4}\int_0^a f(x)g(x)dx$$

$$\Rightarrow \; I = -5\int_0^a f(x)g(x)dx$$

$$\Rightarrow \; \int_0^a f(x)g(x)dx = -\frac{1}{5}I$$

14. Let $I_n = \int_0^{\pi/4} \tan^n x\,dx$ ($n > 1$ and is an integer). Show that

(i) $I_n + I_{n-2} = \dfrac{1}{n-1}$ (ii) $\dfrac{1}{2(n+1)} < I_n < \dfrac{1}{2(n-1)}$

Solution: (i) $I_n = \int_0^{\pi/4} \tan^n x\,dx$

$$= \int_0^{\pi/4} \tan^2 x.\tan^{n-2} x\,dx = \int_0^{\pi/4} (\sec^2 x - 1).\tan^{n-2} x\,dx$$

$$= \int_0^{\pi/4} \sec^2 x.\tan^{n-2} x\,dx - \int_0^{\pi/4} \tan^{n-2} x\,dx$$

$$\Rightarrow \; I_n + I_{n-2} = \int_0^{\pi/4} \tan^{n-2} x\,d(\tan x)$$

$$= \left.\frac{\tan^{n-1} x}{n-1}\right|_0^{\pi/4} = \frac{1}{n-1}$$

(ii) For $0 < x < \pi/4$, we have $\tan^{n+2} x < \tan^n x < \tan^{n-2} x$

so that $I_{n+2} < I_n < I_{n-2}$

Therefore $I_n + I_{n+2} < 2I_n < I_n + I_{n-2}$

$$\Rightarrow \; \frac{1}{n+1} < 2I_n < \frac{1}{n-1} \quad \Rightarrow \; \frac{1}{2(n+1)} < I_n < \frac{1}{2(n-1)}$$

15. If for every non-zero x, $af(x) + bf(1/x) = \frac{1}{x} - 5$; where $a \neq b$, then find $\int_1^2 f(x)\,dx$.

Solution: $af(x) + bf(1/x) = \frac{1}{x} - 5$ ...(i)

Integrating, we get

$$a\int_1^2 f(x)\,dx + b\int_1^2 f(1/x)\,dx = (\ln x - 5x)|_1^2$$

$= \ln 2 - 5$ ...(ii)

Replacing x by $1/x$ in (i) we get, $af(1/x) + bf(x) = x - 5$

Integrating, we get

$$a\int_1^2 f(1/x)\,dx + b\int_1^2 f(x)\,dx = \left[\left(\frac{x^2}{2} - 5x\right)\right]_1^2 = -\frac{7}{2}$$ ...(iii)

Eliminating $\int_1^2 f(1/x)\,dx$ from (ii) and (iii) by multiplying (ii) by a and (iii) by b and subtracting, $(a^2 - b^2)\int_1^2 f(x)\,dx$

$= a(\ln 2 - 5) + \frac{7}{2}b$

$$\Rightarrow \int_1^2 f(x)\,dx = \frac{1}{a^2 - b^2}\left[a(\ln 2 - 5) + \frac{7b}{2}\right]$$

16. If $\int_0^x [x]dx = \int_0^{[x]} x\,dx$, then prove that either x is purely fractional or x is such that $\{x\} = 1/2$, (where [.] and {.} denotes the greatest and fractional part, respectively.

Solution: Let $x = I + f \Rightarrow [x] = I$.

Now $\int_0^{[x]} x\,dx = \int_0^I x\,dx = \frac{I^2}{2}$

and $\int_0^x [x]dx = \int_0^{I+f} [x]dx = \int_0^1 0.dx + \int_1^2 1.dx + ... +$

$\int_{I-1}^I (I-1)dx + \int_I^{I+f} I.dx$

$= \{1 + 2 + 3 + ...+ (I - 1)\} + I(I + f - I)$

$= \frac{I(I-1)}{2} + I(f) = \frac{I(I-1)}{2} + I(x - I)$

given $\int_0^x [x]dx = \int_0^{[x]} x\,dx \Rightarrow \frac{I^2}{2} = \frac{I^2}{2} - \frac{I}{2} + I(x - I)$

$\Rightarrow I = 0$ or $x = I + \frac{1}{2}$

i.e., $[x] = 0$ or $x = I + \frac{1}{2}$

$\Rightarrow 0 \le x < 1$ or $x = [x] + 1/2$

$\Rightarrow 0 \le x < 1$ or $\{x\} = 1/2$

17. Compute the following integrals:

(a) $\int_0^\infty f(x^n + x^{-n}) \ln x \frac{dx}{x} = 0$

(b) $\int_0^\infty f(x^n + x^{-n}) \ln x \frac{dx}{1+x^2} = 0$

Solution: (a) Let $t = \ln x$

$\Rightarrow x = e^t$ $\Rightarrow dx = e^t\,dt$

or $\frac{dx}{x} = dt$ also $x \to 0$

$\Rightarrow t \to -\infty$ and $x \to \infty \Rightarrow t \to \infty$

Thus, $\int_0^\infty f(x^n + x^{-n}) \ln x \frac{dx}{x} = \int_{-\infty}^\infty f(e^{nt} + e^{-nt}).t\,dt$

$= 0$ {integrand is an odd function of t}

(b) $\int_0^\infty f(x^n + x^{-n}) \ln x.\frac{dx}{1+x^2}$

$= \int_{-\infty}^\infty f(e^{nt} + e^{-nt}).t.\frac{e^t}{1+e^{2t}}dt$

Now if $h(t) = f(e^{nt} + e^{-nt}) \frac{te^t}{1+e^{2t}}$.

then $h(-t) = f(e^{-nt} + e^{nt}) \cdot (-t) \frac{1}{e^t + e^{-t}}$.

$= -f(e^{nt} + e^{-nt})\frac{te^t}{(e^{2t} + 1)}$

$\Rightarrow h(-t) = -h(t)$

Thus, integrand is again an odd function and hence $\int_0^\infty f(x^n + x^{-n}) \ln x.\frac{dx}{1+x^2} = 0$.

18. Evaluate $\int_0^1 (tx + 1 - x)^n\,dx$; where n is a positive integer and t is a parameter independent of x. Hence show that $\int_0^1 x^k (1-x)^{n-k}\,dx = [{}^nC_k\,(n + 1)]^{-1}$.

Solution: We have, $I = \int_0^1 (tx + 1 - x)^n\,dx$

$$= \int_0^1 \{(t-1)x + 1\}^n\,dx = \left\{\frac{((t-1)x + 1)^{n+1}}{(n+1)(t-1)}\right\}_0^1$$

$$= \frac{1}{n+1}\left\{\frac{t^{n+1} - 1}{t-1}\right\} = \frac{1}{n+1}\{1 + t + t^2 + ... + t^n\} \quad ...(1)$$

again $I = \int_0^1 (tx + 1 - x)^n\,dx = \int_0^1 ((1-x) + tx)^n\,dx$

$$= \int_0^1 \{{}^nC_0(1-x)^n + {}^nC_1(1-x)^{n-1}(tx) + {}^nC_2(1-x)^{n-2}(tx)^2 + ... + {}^nC_n(tx)^n\}\,dx$$

$$= \int_0^1 \left\{ \sum_{r=0}^{n} {}^nC_r (1-x)^{n-r} (tx)^r \right\} dx$$

$$= \sum_{r=0}^{n} {}^nC_r \left\{ \int_0^1 (1-x)^{n-r} . x^r \, dx \right\} t^r \quad \ldots(2)$$

From (1) and (2) we have

$$\sum_{r=0}^{n} {}^nC_r \left\{ \int_0^1 (1-x)^{n-r} . x^r \, dx \right\} t^r = \frac{1}{n+1} \{1 + t + \ldots + t^n\}$$

Equating coefficient of t^k on both sides, we have,

$${}^nC_k \int_0^1 (1-x)^{n-k} . x^k \, dx = \frac{1}{n+1}$$

$$\Rightarrow \int_0^1 (1-x)^{n-k} . x^k \, dx = \frac{1}{(n+1)\, {}^nC_k} = [(n+1).{}^nC_k]^{-1}$$

19. Prove that for any positive integer k,

$$\frac{\sin 2kx}{\sin x} = 2[\cos x + \cos 3x + \ldots + \cos(2k-1)x].$$

Hence prove that $\int_0^{\pi} \sin 2kx \cot x \, dx = \frac{\pi}{2}$

Solution: Consider the sum, $2\sin x \{\cos x + \cos 3x + \cos 5x + \ldots + \cos (2k-1)x\}$

$= 2 \sin x \cos x + 2\sin x \cos 3x + 2 \sin x \cos 5x + \ldots + 2\sin x \cos (2k-1)x$

$= \sin 2x + (\sin 4x - \sin 2x) + (\sin 6x - \sin 4x) + \ldots + \{\sin 2kx - \sin(2k-2)x\} = \sin 2kx$

$\therefore\ 2\{\cos x + \cos 3x + \cos 5x + \ldots + \cos(2k-1)x\} = \dfrac{\sin 2kx}{\sin x} \quad \ldots(1)$

Now, $\sin 2kx \cdot \cot x = \dfrac{\sin 2kx}{\sin x}.\cos x$

$= 2\cos x\{\cos x + \cos 3x + \cos 5x + \ldots + \cos (2k-1)x\}$ {using (1)}

$= \{2\cos^2 x + 2\cos x \cos 3x + 2\cos x \cos 5x + \ldots + 2\cos x \cos(2k-1)x\}$

$= (1 + \cos 2x) + (\cos 4x + \cos 2x) + (\cos 6x + \cos 4x) + \ldots + (\cos 2kx + \cos (2k-2)x)$

$= 1 + 2\{\cos 2x + \cos 4x + \cos 6x + \ldots + \cos (2k-2)x\} + \cos 2kx$

$$\therefore \int_0^{\pi/2} (\sin 2kx).\cot x \, dx = \int_0^{\pi/2} 1 \, dx + 2\int_0^{\pi/2} (\cos 2x + \cos 4x + \ldots \cos(2k-2)x)\, dx + \int_0^{\pi/2} \cos(2k)x . \, dx$$

$$= \frac{\pi}{2} + 2\left[\frac{\sin 2x}{2} + \frac{\sin 4x}{4} + \ldots + \frac{\sin(2k-2)x}{(2k-2)}\right]_0^{\pi/2} + \left[\frac{\sin(2k)x}{2k}\right]_0^{\pi/2} = \frac{\pi}{2}$$

20. Show that

$$\int_0^{\pi/2} f(\sin 2x) \sin x \, dx = \sqrt{2} \int_0^{\pi/4} f(\cos 2x) \cos x \, dx$$

Solution: Let, $I = \int_0^{\pi/2} f(\sin 2x).\sin x \, dx \quad \ldots(1)$

Then, $I = \int_0^{\pi/2} f\left\{\sin 2\left(\frac{\pi}{2} - x\right)\right\}.\sin\left(\frac{\pi}{2} - x\right) dx$

$$= \int_0^{\pi/2} f\{\sin 2x\}.\cos x \, dx \quad \ldots(2)$$

Adding (1) and (2), we get

$$2I = \int_0^{\pi/2} f(\sin 2x).(\sin x + \cos x) \, dx$$

$$= 2\int_0^{\pi/4} f(\sin 2x).(\sin x + \cos x) \, dx$$

$$\left(\because \int_0^{2a} f(x)\, dx = 2\int_0^{a} f(x) \text{ if } f(2a - x) = f(x)\right)$$

$$= 2\sqrt{2} \int_0^{\pi/4} f(\sin 2x).\sin\left(x + \frac{\pi}{4}\right) dx$$

$$= 2\sqrt{2} \int_0^{\pi/4} f\left(\sin 2\left(\frac{\pi}{4} - x\right)\right).\sin\left(-x + \frac{\pi}{2}\right) dx$$

$$= 2\sqrt{2} \int_0^{\pi/4} f(\cos 2x).\cos x \, dx$$

$$\therefore\ I = \sqrt{2} \int_0^{\pi/4} f(\cos 2x).\cos x \, dx$$

Hence $\int_0^{\pi/2} f(\sin(2x)).\sin x \, dx$

$$= \sqrt{2} \int_0^{\pi/4} f(\cos 2x).\cos x \, dx$$

21. If 'f' is a continuous function with $\int_0^x f(t)dt \to \infty$ as $|x| \to \infty$, then show that every line $y = mx$ intersects the curve $y^2 + \int_0^x f(t)dt = 2$!

Solution: We are given that f is continuous function and $\int_0^x f(t)dt \to \infty$, as $|x| \to \infty$.

To show that every line $y = mx$ intersects the curve $y^2 + \int_0^x f(t)dt = 2$

If possible, let $y = mx$ intersect the given curve, then substituting $y = mx$ in the curve, we get

$$m^2x^2 + \int_0^x f(t)dt = 2 \quad \ldots(1)$$

Consider, $F(x) = m^2x^2 + \int_0^x f(t)dt - 2$

Then $F(x)$ is a continuous function as $f(x)$ is given to be continuous.

Also $F(x) \to \infty$ as $|x| \to \infty$; But $F(0) = -2$

Thus, $F(0) = -$ve and $F(b) = +$ve, where b is some value of x and $F(x)$ is continuous

$\therefore$ $F(x) = 0$ for some value of $x \in (0, b)$ or equation (1) is solvable for x.

Hence, $y = mx$ intersects the given curve.

22. Show that $\int_0^{n\pi+v} |\sin x|\, dx = 2n + 1 - \cos v$; where n is a positive integer and $0 \le v < \pi$.

Solution: $\int_0^{n\pi+v} |\sin x|\, dx = \int_0^{\pi} |\sin x|\, dx + \int_{\pi}^{2\pi} |\sin x|\, dx$

$+ \ldots + \int_{(n-1)\pi}^{n\pi} |\sin x|\, dx + \int_{n\pi}^{n\pi+v} |\sin x|\, dx$

$= \sum_{r=1}^{n} \int_{(r-1)\pi}^{r\pi} |\sin x|\, dx + \int_{n\pi}^{n\pi+v} |\sin x|\, dx$

Now to solve, $\int_{(r-1)\pi}^{r\pi} |\sin x|\, dx$, we have $x = (r-1)\pi + t$

$\Rightarrow \sin x = \sin[(r-1)\pi + t] = (-1)^{r-1} \sin t$ and when $x = (r-1)\pi$, $t = 0$ and when $x = r\pi$, $t = \pi$

$\Rightarrow \int_{(r-1)\pi}^{r\pi} |\sin x|\, dx = \int_0^{\pi} |(-1)^{r-1} \sin t|\, dt = \int_0^{\pi} |\sin t|\, dt$

$= \int_0^{\pi} \sin t\, dt = [-\cos t]_0^{\pi} = -\cos\pi + \cos 0 = 2$

again $\int_{n\pi}^{n\pi+v} |\sin x|\, dx$, putting $x = n\pi + t$

Then $\int_{n\pi}^{n\pi+v} |\sin x|\, dx = \int_0^{v} |(-1)^n \sin t|\, dt = \int_0^{v} \sin t\, dt$

$= [-\cos t]_0^{v} = -\cos v + \cos 0 = 1 - \cos v$

Therefore $\int_0^{n\pi+v} |\sin x|\, dx$

$= \sum_{r=1}^{n} \int_{(r-1)\pi}^{r\pi} |\sin x|\, dx + \int_{n\pi}^{n\pi+v} |\sin x|\, dx$

$= \sum_{r=1}^{n} 2 + \int_{n\pi}^{n\pi+v} |\sin x|\, dx = 2n + 1 - \cos v$

23. Determine the value of $\int_{-\pi}^{\pi} \frac{2x(1+\sin x)}{1+\cos^2 x} dx$

Solution: Let $I = \int_{-\pi}^{\pi} \frac{2x(1+\sin x)}{1+\cos^2 x} dx$

$\Rightarrow I = \int_{-\pi}^{\pi} \frac{2x}{1+\cos^2 x} dx + \int_{-\pi}^{\pi} \frac{2x\sin x}{1+\cos^2 x} dx = I_1 + I_2;$

where $I_1 = \int_{-\pi}^{\pi} \frac{2x}{1+\cos^2 x} dx$ and $I_2 = \int_{-\pi}^{\pi} \frac{2x\sin x}{1+\cos^2 x} dx$

Now $I_1 = \int_{-\pi}^{\pi} \frac{2x}{1+\cos^2 x} dx$; Let $f(x) = \frac{2x}{1+\cos^2 x}$

$\Rightarrow f(-x) = \frac{-2x}{1+\cos^2(-x)} = \frac{-2x}{1+\cos^2 x} = -f(x)$

$\Rightarrow f(-x) = -f(x)$ which shows that $f(x)$ is an odd function

$\therefore I_1 = 0$ Again let $g(x) = \frac{2x\sin x}{1+\cos^2 x}$

$\Rightarrow g(-x) = \frac{2(-x)\sin(-x)}{1+\cos^2(-x)} = \frac{2x\sin x}{1+\cos^2 x} = g(x)$

$\Rightarrow g(-x) = g(x)$ which shows that $g(x)$ is an even function

Therefore $I_2 = \int_{-\pi}^{\pi} \frac{2x\sin x}{1+\cos^2 x} dx = 2.2\int_0^{\pi} \frac{x\sin x}{1+\cos^2 x} dx$

$= 4\int_0^{\pi} \frac{(\pi - x)\sin(\pi - x)}{1+[\cos(\pi - x)]^2} dx = 4\int_0^{\pi} \frac{(\pi - x)\sin x}{1+\cos^2 x} dx$

$= 4\int_0^{\pi} \frac{\pi \sin x}{1+\cos^2 x} dx - 4\int_0^{\pi} \frac{x\sin x}{1+\cos^2 x} dx$

$\Rightarrow I_2 = 4\pi \int_0^{\pi} \frac{\sin x}{1+\cos^2 x} dx - I_2$

$\Rightarrow 2I_2 = 4\pi \int_0^{\pi} \frac{\sin x}{1+\cos^2 x} dx$

Now put $\cos x = t$, $-\sin x\, dx = dt$; where $x = 0$, $t = 1$ and $x = \pi$, $t = -1$

$\therefore I_2 = -2\pi \int_1^{-1} \frac{dt}{1+t^2} dx = 2\pi \int_{-1}^{1} \frac{dt}{1+t^2} dx$

$= 4\pi \int_0^{1} \frac{dt}{1+t^2} dx$, as $\frac{1}{1+t^2}$ is an even function

$= 4\pi \left[\tan^{-1} t\right]_0^1 = 4\pi \left\{\tan^{-1} 1 - \tan^{-1} 0\right\}$

$4\pi\left(\frac{\pi}{4} - 0\right) = \pi^2$

Thus, $I = I_1 + I_2 = 0 + \pi^2 = \pi^2$.

24. Let $a + b = 4$, where $a < 2$ and let $g(x)$ be a differentiable and increasing function $\forall\, x \in \mathbb{R}$, then show that $\int_0^a g(x)\,dx + \int_0^b g(x)\,dx$ increases as $(b - a)$ increases.

Solution: Let $t = b - a$ and $a + b = 4$ given

$\Rightarrow t = 4 - 2a \qquad \Rightarrow \frac{t}{2} = 2 - a$

$\Rightarrow a = 2 - t/2$ and $t = b - (4 - b)$

$\Rightarrow t = 2b - 4 \qquad \Rightarrow \frac{t}{2} = b - 2$

$\Rightarrow b = 2 + \frac{t}{2}$; Now $a < 2$ (given)

$\Rightarrow 2 - t/2 < 2 \qquad \Rightarrow \frac{t}{2} > 0$

$\Rightarrow t > 0$; Again $\int_0^a g(x)\,dx + \int_0^b g(x)\,dx$

$$= \int_0^{2-t/2} g(x)\,dx + \int_0^{2+t/2} g(x)\,dx$$

Let $F(t) = \int_0^{2-t/2} g(x)\,dx + \int_0^{2+t/2} g(x)\,dx$

for $t > 0$; $F'(t) = -\frac{1}{2} g\left(2 - \frac{t}{2}\right) + \frac{1}{2} g\left(2 + \frac{t}{2}\right)$

(by Leibnitz rule)

$$= \frac{1}{2} g\left(2 + \frac{t}{2}\right) - \frac{1}{2} g\left(2 - \frac{t}{2}\right).$$

Again $\frac{dg}{dx} > 0\ \forall x$ (given); Now $2 - \frac{t}{2} < 2 + \frac{t}{2}$

$\because\ t > 0$; We get $g\left(2 + \frac{t}{2}\right) - g\left(2 - \frac{t}{2}\right) > 0\ \forall\, t > 0$

So $F'(t) > 0\ \forall\, t > 0$

Hence $F(t)$ increases with t, therefore,

$F(t)$ increases as $(b - a)$ increases.

25. Prove that $\int_0^1 \tan^{-1}\left(\frac{1}{1 - x + x^2}\right) dx = 2\int_0^1 \tan^{-1} x\, dx$

Hence or otherwise, evaluate the integral $\int_0^1 \tan^{-1}\left(1 - x + x^2\right) dx$

Solution: $\int_0^1 \tan^{-1}\left(\frac{1}{1 - x + x^2}\right) dx$

$$= \int_0^1 \tan^{-1}\left[\frac{1 - x + x}{1 - x(1 - x)}\right] dx$$

$$= \int_0^1 \left[\tan^{-1}(1 - x) + \tan^{-1} x\right] dx$$

$$= \int_0^1 \tan^{-1}(1 - x)\,dx + \int_0^1 \tan^{-1} x\,dx$$

$$= \int_0^1 \tan^{-1}\{1 - (1 - x)\}\,dx + \int_0^1 \tan^{-1} x\,dx = 2\int_0^1 \tan^{-1} x\,dx$$

$$\left[\because \int_0^a f(x)\,dx = \int_0^a f(a - x)\,dx\right]$$

Now $\int_0^1 \tan^{-1}(1 - x + x^2)\,dx$

$$= \int_0^1 \left[\frac{\pi}{2} - \cot^{-1}(1 - x + x^2)\right] dx$$

$$= \frac{\pi}{2} - \int_0^1 \cot^{-1}(1 - x + x^2)\,dx$$

$$= \frac{\pi}{2} - \int_0^1 \tan^{-1}\left(\frac{1}{1 - x + x^2}\right) dx = \frac{\pi}{2} - 2I_1; \quad \text{(proved)}$$

where $I_1 = \int_0^1 \tan^{-1} x\,dx = \left[x.\tan^{-1} x\right]_0^1 - \int_0^1 \frac{x\,dx}{1 + x^2}$

(by parts, taking 1 as first function)

$$= \frac{\pi}{4} - \frac{1}{2}\left[\ln\left(1 + x^2\right)\right]_0^1 \quad \left(\because \int \frac{f'(x)}{f(x)} dx = \ln f(x)\right)$$

$$= \frac{\pi}{4} - \frac{1}{2}\ln 2$$

$$\therefore\ \int_0^1 \tan^{-1}\left(1 - x + x^2\right) dx = \frac{\pi}{2} - 2\left(\frac{\pi}{4} - \frac{1}{2}\ln 2\right)$$

$$= \frac{\pi}{2} - \frac{\pi}{2} + \ln 2 = \ln 2$$

26. For $x > 0$, let $f(x) = \int_1^x \frac{\ln t}{1 + t}\,dt$. Find the function $f(x) + f(1/x)$ and show that $f(e) + f(1/e) = 1/2$.

Solution: Given $f(x) = \int_1^x \frac{\ln t}{1 + t}\,dt$; for $x > 0$

Now $f\left(\frac{1}{x}\right) = \int_1^{1/x} \frac{\ln t}{1 + t}\,dt$

Put $t = 1/u$, so that $dt = \left(-\frac{1}{u^2}\right) du$

$$\therefore\ f\left(\frac{1}{x}\right) = \int_1^x \frac{\ln(1/u)}{1 + 1/u} \cdot \frac{(-1)}{u^2}\,du = \int_1^x \frac{\ln u}{u(u + 1)}\,du$$

$$= \int_1^x \frac{\ln t}{t(1 + t)}\,dt$$

Now $f(x) + f\left(\frac{1}{x}\right) = \int_1^x \frac{\ln t}{(1 + t)}\,dt + \int_1^x \frac{\ln t}{t(1 + t)}\,dt$

$$= \int_1^x \frac{(1 + t)\ln t}{t(1 + t)}\,dt = \int_1^x \frac{\ln t}{t}\,dt = \frac{1}{2}\left[(\ln t)^2\right]_1^x = \frac{1}{2}(\ln x)^2$$

Put $x = e$

$\Rightarrow f(e) + f\left(\frac{1}{e}\right) = \frac{1}{2}(\ln e)^2 = \frac{1}{2}$, hence proved.

27. If $f(x)=x+\int_0^1 t(x+t)f(t)\,dt$, then find the value of $\int_0^1 f(x)\,dx$

Solution: Given $f(x)=x+\int_0^1 t(x+t)f(t)\,dt$

$\Rightarrow f(x)=x+x\int_0^1 t\,f(t)\,dt+\int_0^1 t^2 f(t)\,dt$

$\Rightarrow f(x) = (\lambda + 1)x + \mu$; ...(1)

Where $\lambda=\int_0^1 t\,f(t)\,dt$ and $\mu=\int_0^1 t^2 f(t)\,dt$

Clearly both λ and μ are constants to be evaluated.

Now using $f(t) = (\lambda + 1)t + \mu$ in $\lambda=\int_0^1 t\,f(t)\,dt$ and $\mu=\int_0^1 t^2 f(t)\,dt$, we get

$$\lambda=\int_0^1\{t^2(\lambda+1)+\mu t\}\,dt \text{ and } \mu=\int_0^1\{(\lambda+1)t^3+\mu t^2\}\,dt$$

$$\Rightarrow \lambda=\left|\frac{\lambda t^3}{3}+\frac{t^3}{3}+\frac{\mu t^2}{2}\right|_0^1 \text{ and } \mu=\left|\frac{(\lambda+1)t^4}{4}+\frac{\mu t^3}{3}\right|_0^1$$

$$\Rightarrow \lambda=\frac{\lambda}{3}+\frac{1}{3}+\frac{\mu}{2} \text{ and } \mu=\frac{\lambda+1}{4}+\frac{\mu}{3}$$

$$\Rightarrow \frac{2\lambda}{3}-\frac{\mu}{2}=\frac{1}{3} \text{ and } \frac{\lambda}{4}-\frac{2}{3}\mu=\frac{-1}{4}$$

$\Rightarrow 4\lambda - 3\mu = 2$ ...(2)

and $3\lambda - 8\mu = -3$ ...(3)

Solving above equations for λ and μ we get

$$\lambda=\frac{25}{23} \text{ and } \mu=\frac{18}{23}$$

$\therefore$ from (1), $f(x)=\frac{48}{23}x+\frac{18}{23}$

$$\therefore \int_0^1 f(x)\,dx = \int_0^1\left(\frac{48}{23}x+\frac{18}{23}\right)dx = \frac{48}{46}+\frac{18}{23}=\frac{42}{23}$$

28. Let f be a function continuous on $\mathbb{R}$ satisfying the equation

$$\int_0^x f(t)\,dt = \int_0^1 t^2 f(t)\,dt + \frac{x^{16}}{8}+\frac{x^{18}}{9}+C \quad ...(1)$$

Find the function $f(x)$ and the constant C.

Solution: Given equation is

$$\int_0^x f(t)\,dt = \int_0^1 t^2 f(t)\,dt + \frac{x^{16}}{8}+\frac{x^{18}}{9}+C$$

Differentiating w.r.t. x, we get

$$f(x)=0+\frac{16x^{15}}{8}+\frac{18x^{17}}{9}$$

$\Rightarrow f(x) = 2x^{15} + 2x^{17}$

Substituting $f(t) = 2t^{15} + 2t^{17}$ in (1) we get

$$\int_0^x\left(2t^{15}+2t^{17}\right)dt$$

$$= \int_0^1\left(2t^{17}+2t^{19}\right)dt + \frac{x^{16}}{8}+\frac{x^{18}}{9}+C$$

$$\Rightarrow \frac{x^{16}}{8}+\frac{x^{18}}{9}=\left(\frac{1}{9}+\frac{1}{10}\right)+\frac{x^{16}}{8}+\frac{x^{18}}{9}+C$$

$$\Rightarrow C=-\left(\frac{1}{9}+\frac{1}{10}\right)=-\left(\frac{10+9}{90}\right)=-\frac{19}{90}$$

Thus, $f(x) = 2x^{15} + 2x^{17}$ and $C=-\frac{19}{90}$

29. Find the value of the definite integral $\int_0^\pi\left|\sqrt{2}\sin x+2\cos x\right|dx$.

Solution: Let $I=\int_0^\pi\left|\sqrt{2}\sin x+2\cos x\right|dx$.

Multiplying and dividing by $\sqrt{6}$ we get,

$$I=\sqrt{6}\int_0^\pi\left|\frac{1}{\sqrt{3}}\sin x+\frac{\sqrt{2}}{\sqrt{3}}\cos x\right|dx$$

$$=\sqrt{6}\int_0^\pi|\sin(x+\alpha)|\,dx;$$

where $\sin\alpha=\frac{\sqrt{2}}{\sqrt{3}}$ and $\cos\alpha=\frac{1}{\sqrt{3}}$;

$\therefore$ $\tan\alpha = \sqrt{2}$ $\Rightarrow$ $\alpha = \tan^{-1}(\sqrt{2}) \in (0, \pi/2)$

Let $x + \alpha = t$ $\Rightarrow$ $dx = dt$

$$\therefore\ I=\sqrt{6}\int_\alpha^{\pi+\alpha}|\sin t|\,dt$$

$$=\sqrt{6}\left[\int_\alpha^0|\sin t|\,dt+\int_0^\pi|\sin t|\,dt+\int_\pi^{\pi+\alpha}|\sin t|\,dt\right]$$

$$=\sqrt{6}\left[-\int_0^\alpha|\sin t|\,dt+\int_0^\pi\sin t\,dt+\int_0^\alpha|\sin t|\,dt\right]$$

$$=\sqrt{6}\left[-\int_0^\alpha\sin t\,dt+\int_0^\pi\sin t\,dt+\int_0^\alpha\sin t\,dt\right]$$

$$=\sqrt{6}\,[-\cos t]_0^\pi=2\sqrt{6}$$

30. $\int_0^{\pi/2} e^x\left\{\cos(\sin x)\cos^2\frac{x}{2}+\sin(\sin x)\sin^2\frac{x}{2}\right\}dx$

Solution: $\int_0^{\pi/2} e^x(\cos(\sin x).\cos^2\frac{x}{2}\,dx+$

$\int_0^{\pi/2} e^x\sin(\sin x)\sin^2\frac{x}{2}\,dx$

$$= \int_0^{\pi/2} e^x \cos(\sin x)\left(\frac{1+\cos x}{2}\right)dx +$$

$$\int_0^{\pi/2} e^x \sin(\sin x)\left(\frac{1-\cos x}{2}\right)dx$$

$$= \int_0^{\pi/2} e^x \left(\frac{\cos(\sin x)}{2} - \frac{\sin(\sin x)\cos x}{2}\right)dx +$$

$$\int_0^{\pi/2} e^x \left(\frac{\sin(\sin x)}{2} + \frac{\cos(\sin x).\cos x}{2}dx\right)$$

$$= \frac{1}{2}\left[e^x \cos(\sin x)\big|_0^{\pi/2} + e^x \sin(\sin x)\big|_0^{\pi/2}\right]$$

$$= \frac{1}{2}\left[(e^{\pi/2}\cos 1 - e^0) + (e^{\pi/2}\sin 1)\right]$$

$$= \frac{1}{2}\left[e^{\pi/2}(\cos 1 - \sin 1) - 1\right]$$

31. If

$$\int_0^{\pi} \sqrt{(\cos x + \cos 2x + \cos 3x)^2 + (\sin x + \sin 2x + \sin 3x)^2}$$

dx has the value equal to $\left(\frac{\pi}{k} + \sqrt{w}\right)$, where k and w are positive integers, then find the value of $(k^2 + w^2)$

Solution:

$$I = \int_0^{\pi} \sqrt{\begin{matrix} 3 + 2(\cos x \cos 2x + \cos 2x \cos 3x + \cos x \cos 3x) + \\ 2(\sin x \sin 2x + \sin 2x \sin 3x + \sin x \sin 3x) \end{matrix}}$$

$$= \int_0^{\pi} \sqrt{3 + 4\cos x + 2\cos 2x}\ dx$$

$$= \int_0^{\pi} \sqrt{1 + 2(1 + \cos 2x) + 4\cos x}\ dx$$

$$= \int_0^{\pi} \sqrt{1 + 2.2\cos^2 x + 4\cos x}\ dx$$

$$= \int_0^{\pi} \sqrt{4\cos^2 x + 4\cos x + 1}\ dx$$

$$= \int_0^{\pi} |2\cos x + 1|\ dx$$

$$\int_0^{2\pi/3} (2\cos x + 1)dx - \int_{2\pi/3}^{\pi} (2\cos x + 1)dx = 2\sqrt{3} + \frac{\pi}{3}$$

$= \frac{\pi}{3} + \sqrt{12}$. Comparing with $\left(\frac{\pi}{k} + \sqrt{w}\right)$, we have

$k = 3$; $w = 12$

So $k^2 + w^2 = 9 + 144 = 153$

32. Evaluate the integral $\int_1^{16} \tan^{-1}\left(\sqrt{\sqrt{x} - 1}\right) dx$

Solution: Let $I = \int_1^{16} \tan^{-1}\left(\sqrt{\sqrt{x} - 1}\right) dx$

Put $\sqrt{x} = \sec^2\theta$; when $x = 1$; $\sec^2\theta = 1$; $\sec\theta = 1$; $x = \sec^4\theta$; $\theta = 0$; $dx = 4\sec^3\theta.\ \sec\theta \tan\theta\ d\theta$; $x = 16$; $\sec^2\theta = \sqrt{16}$; $\sec^2\theta = 4$; $\sec\theta = 2$

$\Rightarrow \theta = \pi/3$

$$\therefore\ I = \int_0^{\frac{\pi}{3}} \tan^{-1}\sqrt{\sec^2\theta - 1}\ ;\ 4\sec^4\theta \tan\theta\ d\theta$$

$$= 4\int_0^{\frac{\pi}{3}} \theta \sec^4\theta \tan\theta\ d\theta$$

$$= 4\int_0^{\frac{\pi}{3}} \theta \sec^3\theta(\sec\theta \tan\theta)d\theta$$

$$= 4\left(\left[\theta\frac{\sec^4\theta}{4}\right]_0^{\pi/3} - \int_0^{\frac{\pi}{3}} \frac{\sec^4\theta}{4}d\theta\right)$$

(using by parts)

$$= \left(\frac{\pi}{3}(2)^4\right) - \int_0^{\frac{\pi}{3}} \sec^4\theta\ d\theta$$

$$= \frac{16\pi}{3} - \int_0^{\frac{\pi}{3}} \sec^4\theta\, d\theta = \frac{16\pi}{3} - \int_0^{\frac{\pi}{3}} \sec^4\theta\ d\theta$$

$$= \frac{16\pi}{3} - \int_0^{\frac{\pi}{3}} \sec^2\theta.(1 + \tan^2\theta)d\theta$$

$$= \frac{16\pi}{3} - \left(\int_0^{\frac{\pi}{3}} \sec^2\theta + \int_0^{\frac{\pi}{3}} \sec^2\theta \tan^2\theta d\theta\right)$$

$$= \frac{16\pi}{3} - \left[\tan\theta + \frac{\tan^3\theta}{3}\right]_0^{\frac{\pi}{3}}$$

$$= \frac{16\pi}{3} - \left(\sqrt{3} + \frac{3\sqrt{3}}{3}\right) = \frac{16\pi}{3} - 2\sqrt{3}$$

33. Show that $\int_0^{p+q\pi} |\cos x|\, dx = 2q + \sin p$; where $q \in \mathbb{N}$ and $-\frac{\pi}{2} < p < \frac{\pi}{2}$

Solution: $I = \int_0^{p} \cos x dx + \int_p^{p+q\pi} |\cos x|\, dx$

$$= [|\sin x|]\int_0^{p} + q\int_0^{\pi} |\cos x|\, dx$$

$$= \sin p + q\left[\int_0^{\pi/2} \cos x\ dx - \int_{\pi/2}^{\pi} \cos x\, dx\right]$$

$= \sin p + q\,(1 + 1) = 2q + \sin p.$

34. Comment upon the nature of roots of the quadratic equation $x^2 + 2x = k + \int_0^1 |t + k|\, dt$ depending on the value of $k \in \mathbb{R}$.

Solution: $D = 4 + 4\left(k + \int_0^1 |k + t|\, dt\right)$

$$= 4 + 4k + 4\int_0^1 |k + t|\, dt$$

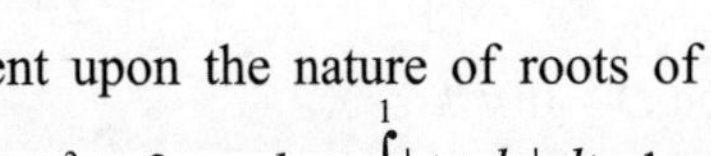

Case (i): $k \geq 0$

$$I = \int_0^1 |k+t|\,dt = \int_0^1 (k+t)dt = kt + \left.\frac{t^2}{2}\right|_0^1 = k + \frac{1}{2}$$

$$\therefore \quad D = 4 + 4k + 4\left(k + \frac{1}{2}\right)$$

$$= 4 + 8k + 2 = 8k + 6 > 0 = 4\left(2k + \frac{3}{2}\right)$$

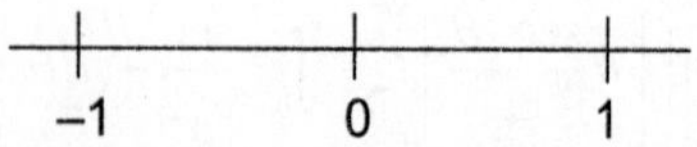

Case (ii): $k \leq -1$;

$$I = -\int_0^1 (k+t)\,dt = -\left[kt + \frac{t^2}{2}\right]_0^1 = -\left[k + \frac{1}{2}\right]$$

$$\therefore \quad D = 4 + 4k - 4\left(k + \frac{1}{2}\right) \quad \Rightarrow \quad D = 2 > 0$$

Case (iii): $-1 < k < 0 \quad \therefore \quad I = \int_0^1 |k+t|\,dt$

Let $k = -y \quad \Rightarrow \quad 0 < y < 1$

$$I = \int_0^1 |t-y|\,dt = \int_0^y (y-t)\,dt + \int_y^1 (t-y)\,dt$$

$$= \left[ty - \frac{t^2}{2}\right]_0^y + \left[\frac{t^2}{2} - yt\right]_y^1$$

$$= \left(y^2 - \frac{y^2}{2}\right) + \left(\frac{1}{2} - y\right) - \left(\frac{y^2}{2} - y^2\right) = y^2 - y + \frac{1}{2}$$

$$= k^2 + k + \frac{1}{2}$$

$$\therefore \quad D = 4 + 4k + 4\left(k^2 + k + \frac{1}{2}\right)$$

$$= 4\left[1 + k + k^2 + k + \frac{1}{2}\right]$$

$$= 4\left[k^2 + 2k + \frac{3}{2}\right] = 4\left[(k+1)^2 + \frac{1}{2}\right] > 0$$

Hence $D > 0 \ \forall \ k \in \mathbb{R}$

⇒ roots of given equation are real and distinct.

Assertion and Reason Type Questions

35. A: $\int_0^{\pi/4} \sec x \sqrt{\frac{1-\sin x}{1+\sin x}} = 2 - \sqrt{2}$

R: $\int_0^{\pi/4} \frac{\sec x}{1 + 2\sin^2 x} dx = \frac{1}{2}\log(\sqrt{2} - 1) + \frac{\pi}{6\sqrt{2}}$

Solution: (c) **A:** Let

$$I = \int_0^{\pi/4} \frac{1}{\cos x}\sqrt{\frac{1-\sin x}{1+\sin x}}dx = \int_0^{\pi/4} \frac{1-\sin x}{\cos x.\cos x}dx$$

$$= \int_0^{\pi/4} \left(\sec^2 x - \sec x \tan x\right)dx$$

$$= (\tan x - \sec x)_0^{\pi/4} = 2 - \sqrt{2} \quad \Rightarrow \text{Assertion is true}$$

R: $I = \int_0^{\pi/4} \frac{\sec x\, dx}{1 + 2\sin^2 x}$

$$= \int_0^{\pi/4} \frac{\cos x}{\left(1 - \sin^2 x\right)\left(1 + 2\sin^2 x\right)}dx$$

$$= \int_0^{1/\sqrt{2}} \frac{dt}{\left(1-t^2\right)\left(1+2t^2\right)} \quad \text{(on substituting } \sin x = t\text{)}$$

$$= \frac{1}{3}\int_0^{\frac{1}{\sqrt{2}}} \left(\frac{1}{1-t^2} + \frac{2}{1+2t^2}\right)dt$$

$$= \left(\frac{1}{3}\frac{1}{2}\ell n\frac{1+t}{1-t} + \frac{2}{3\sqrt{2}}\tan^{-1}\sqrt{2}t\right)_0^{1/\sqrt{2}}$$

$$= \frac{1}{6}\ell n\frac{\sqrt{2}+1}{\sqrt{2}-1} + \frac{\sqrt{2}}{3}\left(\frac{\pi}{4}\right) = \frac{1}{6}\ell n\left(3 + 2\sqrt{2}\right) + \frac{\pi}{6\sqrt{2}}$$

⇒ Reason is false

36. A: $\int_0^1 e^{\sin^{-1}x}\left(1 - \frac{x}{\sqrt{1-x^2}}\right)dx = -1$

R: $\int_0^1 e^{g(x)}.\{f(x)g'(x) + f'(x)\}\,dx = e^{g(x)}f(x) + C$

Solution: (a) **R:** $\int e^{g(x)}\{f(x)g'(x) + f'(x)\}\,dx$

$$= \int f(x).e^{g(x)}.g'(x)\,dx + \int e^{g(x)}.f'(x)\,dx$$

$$= f(x).e^{g(x)} - \int f'(x)e^{g(x)}dx + \int e^{g(x)}.f'(x)\,dx$$

$$= e^{g(x)} f(x) + C$$

A: Since $g(x) = \sin^{-1} x$

$$\therefore \quad \int e^{\sin^{-1}x}\left(1 - \frac{x}{\sqrt{1-x^2}}dx\right)$$

$$= \int e^{\sin^{-1}x}\left(\frac{1}{\sqrt{1-x^2}}.\sqrt{1-x^2} - \frac{x}{\sqrt{1-x^2}}\right)$$

$$= \int e^{\sin^{-1}x}\left(\sqrt{1-x^2}.\frac{1}{\sqrt{1-x^2}} + \frac{d}{dx}\sqrt{1-x^2}\right)dx$$

$$\Rightarrow \quad f(x) = \sqrt{1-x^2}\ ;\ g(x) = \sin^{-1}x$$

$$\therefore \quad \int e^{\sin^{-1}x}\left(1 - \frac{x}{\sqrt{1-x^2}}\right)dx$$

$$= e^{\sin^{-1}x}.\sqrt{1-x^2} + C \text{ by reason.}$$

$$\Rightarrow \int_0^1 e^{\sin^{-1}x}\left(1-\frac{x}{\sqrt{1-x^2}}\right)dx = 0 - e^0(1) = -1$$

37. A: If $\frac{d}{dx}f(x)=\frac{e^{\sin x}}{x}, x>0$ and $\int_1^4 \frac{3e^{\sin x^3}}{x}dx$ = $f(k)-f(1)$, then one possible value of k is 64.

R: If $f(x)$ is a function satisfying $f(1/x)+x^2f(x)=0\ \forall$ $x\in\mathbb{R}\sim\{0\}$, then $\int_{\sin\theta}^{\operatorname{cosec}\theta} f(x)dx = \sin\theta - \operatorname{cosec}\theta$

Solution: (c) **A:** $\frac{d}{dx}f(x)=\frac{e^{\sin x}}{x}, x>0$

$$\Rightarrow f(x)=\int\frac{e^{\sin x}dx}{x}$$

Now, $I=\int_1^4\frac{3e^{\sin x^3}}{x}dx=\int_1^4\frac{3x^2e^{\sin x^3}}{x^3}dx = \int_1^{64}\frac{e^{\sin t}}{t}dt$

$$=\left[f(t)\right]_1^{64} = f(64)-f(1)$$

$\therefore\ f(64)-f(1)=f(k)-f(1)$

$\Rightarrow k=64$ $\quad\Rightarrow$ Assertion is true

R: $I=\int_{\sin\theta}^{\operatorname{cosec}\theta} f(x)dx=\int_{\operatorname{cosec}\theta}^{\sin\theta} f\left(\frac{1}{t}\right)\left(-\frac{1}{t^2}\right)dt$

$$=\int_{\operatorname{cosec}\theta}^{\sin\theta} f(t)dt=-I\ \left(\because x^2f(x)+f(1/x)=0\right)$$

$\therefore\ I=0$ $\quad\Rightarrow$ Reason is false.

38. A: $\int_{-\pi}^{\pi}\frac{2x(1+\sin^2x)}{1+\cos^2x}dx=0$

R: $\int_0^{\pi/2}\sin^2x\cos^2x(\sin x+\cos x)dx=\frac{4}{15}$

Solution: (b) **A:** $I=\int_{-\pi}^{\pi}\frac{2x\left(1+\sin^2x\right)}{1+\cos^2x}dx$

$I=0$ $\quad(\because f(x)=-f(-x))$

$\Rightarrow$ Assertion is true.

R: Let $I_1=\int_0^{\pi/2}\sin^2x\cos^2x(\sin x+\cos x)dx$

and $\sin x-\cos x=t$

$\Rightarrow 1-2\sin x\cos x=t^2$ and $(\cos x+\sin x)dx=dt$

$\Rightarrow \frac{1-t^2}{2}=\sin x\cos x$

$$\therefore\ I_1=\int_{-1}^{1}\left(\frac{1-t^2}{2}\right)^2dt$$

$$=\frac{1}{2}\int_0^1\left(1-2t^2+t^4\right)dt=\frac{1}{2}\left(t-\frac{2t^3}{3}+\frac{t^5}{5}\right)_0^1$$

$$=\frac{1}{2}\left[\frac{15t-10t^3+3t^5}{15}\right]_0^1=\frac{1}{2}\left(\frac{15-10+3}{15}\right)=\frac{4}{15}$$

$\Rightarrow$ Reason is also true, but there is no connectivity between the assertion and reason.

39. A: $\int_0^n[x]dx=\frac{n(n-1)}{2}$; where $[x]$ represents greatest integer of x and $n\in\mathbb{N}$.

R: $\int_0^n\{x\}dx=\frac{n}{2}$; where $\{x\}$ represents fractional part of x and $n\in\mathbb{N}$

Solution: **R:** Here $I=\int_0^n\{x\}dx = n\int_0^1x\,dx$ = $n\left[\frac{x^2}{2}\right]_0^1=\frac{n}{2}$ as $\{x\}$ is a periodic function with period 1.

A: $\int_0^n[x]dx=\int_0^n(x-\{x\})dx=\int_0^nxdx-\int_0^n\{x\}dx$

$$=\left[\frac{x^2}{2}\right]_0^n-\frac{n}{2}=\frac{n^2}{2}-\frac{n}{2}=\frac{n}{2}(n-1)$$

(By using reason)

40. A: $\int_0^{\pi}x\sin x\cos^2x\,dx=\frac{\pi}{2}\int_0^{\pi}\sin x\cos^2x\,dx$

R: $\int_a^b x\,f(x)\,dx=\frac{a+b}{2}\int_a^b f(x)dx$

Solution: (c)

A: $\int_a^b x\,f(x)dx = \int_a^b(a+b-x)f(a+b-x)dx$

$$=(a+b)\int_a^b f(a+b-x)dx - \int_a^b x\,f(a+b-x)dx$$

$\therefore$ Reason is true only when $f(a+b-x)=f(x)$ which holds in assertion.

$\Rightarrow$ Reason is not always true which holds in assertion as $f(x)=\sin x\cos x$

$\Rightarrow f(0+\pi-x)$

$\Rightarrow \sin(\pi-x)\cos^2x(\pi-x)=\sin x\cos^2x=f(x)$

$\therefore\ \int_0^{\pi}x\sin x(\cos^2x)\,dx=\frac{0+\pi}{2}\int_0^{\pi}\sin x\cos^2x\,dx$

$\therefore$ Assertion is true

41. A: $\int_0^{2\pi}\tan^2x\,dx=4\int_0^{\pi/2}\tan^2x\,dx$

R: $\int_0^{nT}f(x)dx=n\int_0^T f(x)\,dx$, where n is an integer and T is a period of $f(x)$ and

$$\int_0^{2a} f(x)dx = \int_0^a f(x)dx + \int_0^a f(2a-x)dx$$

Solution: (b) **A:** $\int_0^{2\pi} \tan^2 x\, dx = 2\int_0^{\pi} \tan^2 x\, dx$

as $f(2a-x) = f(x)$

$= 2\left[\int_0^{\pi/2} \tan^2 x\, dx + \int_0^{\pi/2} \tan^2(\pi - x)\, dx\right]$

$= 4\int_0^{\pi/2} \tan^2 x\, dx$ (By same reason)

∴ Assertion is true; Reason is a standard result.

∴ Both assertion and reason are correct but there is no connectivity between the two.

42. A: If

$\lim_{n\to\infty}\left(\frac{1}{2n+1}+\frac{1}{2n+3}+\frac{1}{2n+5}+\ldots+\frac{1}{4n-1}\right) = \frac{a}{b}\ell nc$, then

least value of $a+b+c$ equals 5; $a, b, c \in \mathbb{N}$.

R: Given limit equals $\int_0^1 \frac{1}{2+x}dx - \int_0^1 \frac{1}{2+2x}dx$

Solution: (c) Let

$$L = \lim_{n\to\infty}\left(\frac{1}{2n+1}+\frac{1}{2n+3}+\frac{1}{2n+5}+\ldots+\frac{1}{4n-1}\right)$$

$$= \lim_{n\to\infty}\left(\frac{1}{2n+1}+\frac{1}{2n+3}+\frac{1}{2n+5}+\ldots+\frac{1}{2n+(2n-1)}\right)$$

$$= \lim_{n\to\infty}\left(\frac{1}{2n+1}+\frac{1}{2n+2}+\frac{1}{2n+3}+..+\frac{1}{2n+2n}\right)$$

$$= -\lim_{n\to\infty}\left(\frac{1}{2n+2}+\frac{1}{2n+4}+\frac{1}{2n+6}+\ldots+\frac{1}{2n+2n}\right)$$

$$= \lim_{n\to\infty}\sum_{r=1}^{2n}\frac{1}{2n+r} - \lim_{n\to\infty}\sum_{r=1}^{n}\frac{1}{2n+2r}$$

$$= \lim_{n\to\infty}\frac{1}{n}\sum_{r=1}^{2n}\frac{1}{2+(r/n)} - \lim_{n\to\infty}\frac{1}{n}\sum_{r=1}^{n}\frac{1}{2+2(r/n)}$$

$= \int_0^2 \frac{1}{2+x}dx - \int_0^1 \frac{1}{2+2x}$ ⇒ Reason is incorrect

$$= \left|\ell n(2+x)\right|_0^2 - \frac{1}{2}\left|\ell n(1+x)\right|_0^1$$

$$= (\ell n\,(4) - \ell n 2) - \frac{1}{2}(\ln 2)$$

$$= 2\ell n2 - \ell n2 - \frac{1}{2}(\ln 2) = \frac{1}{2}(\ln 2)$$

$$= \frac{n}{2n^2}\ln(2)^n \;\forall n \in \mathbb{N} = \frac{a}{b}\ell n c\,(given)$$

⇒ $a = n$, $b = 2n^2$, $c = (2)^n$

∴ $a + b + c = n + 2n^2 + (2)^n = f(n)$; $n \in \mathbb{N}$ (say)

∴ $f'(n) = 1 + 4n + (2)^n \ln 2 > 0 \;\forall n \in \mathbb{N}$

⇒ $f(n)$ is increasing function of n

∴ $f(n)$ will be least at $n = 1$ and least value will be $= 1 + 2(1)^2 + (2)^1 = 1 + 2 + 2 = 5$

⇒ Assertion is correct

43. A: If H_n denotes the sum of first n terms of the harmonic progression $\left\langle \frac{1}{n+1}, \frac{1}{n+2} \ldots\ldots \right\rangle$, then $\lim_{n\to\infty} H_n = \ell n2$

R: $\lim_{n\to\infty} H_n = \int_0^1 \frac{dx}{1+x}$

Solution: (a) Here, H_n = sum of first n-terms of Harmonic progression $\left\langle \frac{1}{n+1}, \frac{1}{n+2}, \ldots \right\rangle$

$$= \left(\frac{1}{n+1}+\frac{1}{n+2}+\ldots+\frac{1}{n+n}\right) = \sum_{r=1}^{n}\frac{1}{n+r}$$

$$\therefore \lim_{n\to\infty} H_n = \lim_{n\to\infty}\sum_{r=1}^{n}\frac{1}{(n+r)} = \lim_{n\to\infty}\sum_{r=1}^{n}\frac{1}{n}\frac{1}{(1+r/n)}$$

$$= \int_0^1 \frac{1}{(1+x)}dx = \left|\ell n(1+x)\right|_0^1 = \ell n2$$

Clearly assertion is true and reason correctly explains the assertion.

44. A: If $f(x) = \int_1^x \frac{\ell nt}{(t+1)}dt$ for $x > 0$, then $f(2) + f(1/2) = \frac{1}{2}(\ln 2)^2$

R: $f(x) + f(1/x) = \frac{1}{x}\ell n^2 x \; for\; x > 0$

Solution: (c)

$$f(x) + f\left(\frac{1}{x}\right) = \int_1^x \frac{\ell nt}{(t+1)}dt + \int_1^{1/x}\frac{\ell nt}{(t+1)}dt$$

In second integral , put $t = 1/u$

$$dt = \frac{-1}{u^2}dt$$

$$\therefore\; f(x) + f\left(\frac{1}{x}\right) = \int_1^x \frac{\ell nt}{(t+1)}dt + \int_1^x \frac{\ell n\left(\frac{1}{u}\right)}{\left(\frac{1}{u}+1\right)}\left(\frac{-1}{u^2}\right)du$$

$$= \int_1^x \frac{\ell nt}{(t+1)}dt + \int_1^x \frac{\ell nu}{(u^2+u)}du$$

$$= \int_1^x \frac{\ln t}{t+1}dt + \int_1^x \frac{\ln u}{u(1+u)}dt = \int_1^x \frac{\ell nt}{t+1}dt + \int_1^x \frac{\ell nt}{t(t+1)}dt$$

$$= \int_1^x \left(1+\frac{1}{t}\right)\left(\frac{\ell nt}{t+1}\right)dt$$

$$= \int_1^x \frac{\ell nt}{t}dt = \left|\frac{1}{2}(\ell nt)^2\right|_1^x = \frac{1}{2}(\ell nx)^2$$

$\Rightarrow$ Reason is incorrect but $f(2)+f\left(\frac{1}{2}\right)=\frac{1}{2}(\ln 2)^2$

$\Rightarrow$ Assertion is correct.

Comprehension-Type Questions

A: Definite integral of any discontinuous or non-differentiable function is normally solved by the property $\int_a^b f(x)dx = \int_a^c f(x)dx + \int_c^b f(x)dx$, where $c \in (a, b)$ is the point of discontinuity or non-differentiability.

45. The value of $A = \int_1^\infty [\text{cosec}^{-1}x]dx$, ; (where [.] denotes greatest integer function), is equal to

(a) cosec 1 –1 (b) 1

(c) 1 – sin1 (d) None of these

46. The value of $B = \int_1^{100} [\sec^{-1} x]dx$, {where [.] denotes greatest integer function}, is equal to

(a) sec 1 (b) 100 – sec 1

(c) 99 – sec 1 (d) None of these

47. The value of integral $\int_A^B [\tan^{-1} x]dx$, {where [.] denotes greatest integer function}, is equal to

(a) tan 1 (b) 100 – tan 1 – sec1

(c) 99 – sec 1 (d) None of these

Solutions:

45. (a) $A = \int_1^\infty [\text{cosec}^{-1}x]dx$

$$= \int_1^{\text{cosec}1} 1\,dx + \int_{\text{cosec}1}^\infty 0\,dx = \text{cosec } 1 - 1$$

46. (b) $\int_1^{100} [\sec^{-1} x]dx = \int_1^{\sec 1} 0\,dx + \int_{\sec 1}^{100} 1dx = 100 - \sec 1$

47. (b) From above two parts of passage, $A = \text{cosec } 1 - 1$ and $B = 100 - \sec 1$

$$\therefore\ I = \int_{\text{cosec}1-1}^{100-\sec 1} [\tan^{-1} x]\,dx$$

$$= \int_{\text{cosec}1-1}^{\tan 1} 0\,dx + \int_{\tan 1}^{100-\sec 1} 1\,dx = 100 - \sec 1 - \tan 1$$

D: (i) If $f(2a - x) = k - f(x)$, then $\int_0^{2a} f(x)\,dx$

$$= \int_0^a f(x)\,dx + \int_0^a f(2a-x)\,dx = \int_0^a k\,dx = ka$$

(ii) If $f(a + x) = k - f(x)$, then $\int_0^{2a} f(x)\,dx$

$$= \int_0^a f(x)\,dx + \int_0^a f(2a-x)\,dx$$

$$= \int_0^a f(x)\,dx + \int_0^a f(2a-(a-x))\,dx$$

$$= \int_0^a f(x)\,dx + \int_0^a f(a+x)\,dx = \int_0^a k\,dx = ka$$

On the basis of above information answer the following questions:

48. Value of integral $I = \int_0^4 \ell n\left(\sqrt{(x-2)^2+4}+(x-2)\right)dx$ is

(a) $\ell n2$ (b) $2\ell n2$

(c) $4\ell n2$ (d) 0

49. Value of integral $I = \int_0^\pi \cos^{-1}(\cos 2x)dx$ is

(a) π/4 (b) $\pi^2/2$

(c) π/2 (d) 0

50. Value of integral $I = \int_0^\pi \sin^{-1}(\cos 2x)dx$ is

(a) π/4 (b) $\pi^2/4$

(c) π/2 (d) 0

Solutions:

48. (c) Here $2a = 4$

$\Rightarrow a = 2$

Let $f(x) = \ell n\left(\sqrt{(x-2)^2+4}+(x-2)\right)$

Then $f(2a - x) = \ell n\left(\sqrt{(4-x-2)^2+4}+(4-x-2)\right)$

$$= \ell n\left(\sqrt{(x-2)^2+4}-(x-2)\right)$$

$$= \ell n\left(\frac{4}{\sqrt{(x-2)^2+4}+(x-2)}\right) = \ell n\ 4 - f(x)$$

$= k - f(x)$

$\Rightarrow k = \ln 4$

$\therefore\ I = ka = (\ln 4)\,(2)$ (using part (i))

$= 2\ln 4 = 4\ln 2$

49. (b) Let $f(x) = \cos^{-1}(\cos 2x)$; $2a = \pi$

$\Rightarrow\ a = \dfrac{\pi}{2}$

Then $f(a+x) = f\left(\dfrac{\pi}{2}+x\right) = \cos^{-1}\left(\cos 2\left(\dfrac{\pi}{2}+x\right)\right)$

$= \cos^{-1}(\cos(\pi + 2x))$

$= \cos^{-1}(-\cos 2x) = \pi - \cos^{-1}(\cos 2x)$

$= \pi - f(x) = k - f(x) \quad \Rightarrow \quad k = \pi$

$\therefore\ I = ka = \pi\left(\dfrac{\pi}{2}\right) = \dfrac{\pi^2}{2}$ (using part (ii)

50. (d) Let $f(x) = \sin^{-1}(\cos 2x)$ and $2a = \pi$

$\Rightarrow\ a = \dfrac{\pi}{2}$; Then $f(a+x) = f\left(\dfrac{\pi}{2}+x\right)$

$= \sin^{-1}\left(\cos 2\left(\dfrac{\pi}{2}+x\right)\right) = \sin^{-1}(\cos(\pi + 2x))$

$= \sin^{-1}(-\cos 2x) = -\sin^{-1}(\cos 2x) = -f(x) = k - f(x)$

$\Rightarrow\ k = 0 \qquad \therefore\ I = ka = 0\left(\dfrac{\pi}{2}\right) = 0$

E: Let $f(x)$ be a polynomial of the form x^n for some $n \in \mathbb{N}$ and is one–one and onto. Let $f^{-1}(x)$ be the inverse of $f(x)$. Further define a function $g(x) = \min.\ \{f(x), f^{-1}(x)\}$ such that $\lim\limits_{x\to 1}\left[\dfrac{g(x)-x}{h(x)} + \dfrac{|x-1|}{x^2+2x-3}\right]$ is non-zero finite for least possible value of n, and $h(x)$ is a second degree polynomial even function. On the basis of above information answer the following questions:

51. The value of $\int_1^2 h(x)\,dx$ equals

(a) $\dfrac{24}{9}$ (b) $\dfrac{32}{9}$

(c) $\dfrac{32}{3}$ (d) None of these

52. The value of $\int_0^3 g(x)\,dx$ equals

(a) $\dfrac{3}{4}\left((3)^{4/3}-1\right)$ (b) $\dfrac{1}{4}\left((3)^{4/3}-1\right)$

(c) $\dfrac{1}{4}\left((3)^{7/3}-2\right)$ (d) None of these

53. The value of $\int_0^L \dfrac{g(x)-x}{h(x)}\,dx$; (where L is the given limit) is

(a) $\dfrac{3}{1024}$ (b) $\dfrac{3}{512}$

(c) $\dfrac{5}{256}$ (d) None of these

Solutions:

Let $f(x) = x^n$; $n \in \mathbb{N}$

Since $f(x)$ is given to be one–one and onto

$\Rightarrow$ $f(x)$ cannot be an even function

$\Rightarrow$ n must be odd

$\Rightarrow$ $n \in \{1, 3, 5, \ldots.,\}$

For $n = 1$, $f(x) = x$

$\Rightarrow$ $f^{-1}(x) = x$

$\Rightarrow$ $g(x) = \min\{f(x), f^{-1}(x)\} = \min\{x, x\} = x \quad \ldots(1)$

Further $h(x)$ is a second degree polynomial even function

$\Rightarrow$ $h(x) = ax^2 + b$ for some $a, b \in \mathbb{R}$ to be determined such that $\lim\limits_{x\to 1}\left[\dfrac{g(x)-x}{ax^2+b} + \dfrac{|x-1|}{x^2+2x-3}\right]$ exists non-zero finitely, i.e., here,

$\lim\limits_{x\to 1}\left[\dfrac{x-x}{ax^2+b} + \dfrac{|x-1|}{x^2+2x-3}\right] = l(\neq 0, < \infty)$

$= \lim\limits_{x\to 1}\left[\dfrac{|x-1|}{x^2+2x-3}\right]$

$\Rightarrow$ L.H.L. $= -\dfrac{1}{4}$ and R.H.L. $= \dfrac{1}{4}$

$\Rightarrow$ Limit does not exist non-zero finitely.

Thus, $n = 1$ is rejected

So let $n = 3$, then $f(x) = (x)^3$

$\Rightarrow$ $g(x) = \min\{f(x), f^{-1}(x)\} = \min\{x^3, x^{1/3}\}$

$= \begin{cases} x^3; & 0 < x \le 1 \\ x^{1/3}; & 1 \le x < \infty \end{cases}$

$\therefore\ \lim\limits_{x\to 1}\left[\dfrac{g(x)-x}{h(x)} + \dfrac{|x-1|}{x^2+2x-3}\right]$

$\therefore$ L.H.L. $= \lim\limits_{x\to 1^-}\left[\dfrac{x^3-x}{ax^2+b} + \dfrac{|x-1|}{x^2+2x-3}\right]$

Since $x^3 - x \to 0$ as $x \to 1^-$.

$\Rightarrow$ $ax^2 + b = 0$ at $x = 1$ (As otherwise again L.H.L $= -1/4$, R.H.L. $= 1/4$ as before)

$\Rightarrow\ a + b = 0 \qquad \Rightarrow\ b = -a$

$$\Rightarrow \text{L.H.L.} = \lim_{x\to1^-}\left[\frac{x^3-x}{ax^2-a}+\frac{|x-1|}{x^2+2x-3}\right]$$

$$= \lim_{x\to1^-}\left[\frac{x(x^2-1)}{a(x^2-1)}+\frac{-(x-1)}{x^2+2x-3}\right]$$

$$= \lim_{x\to1^-}\left[\frac{x}{a}-\frac{(x-1)}{(x-1)(x+3)}\right]$$

$$= \lim_{x\to1^-}\left[\frac{x}{a}-\frac{1}{x+3}\right]=\frac{1}{a}-\frac{1}{4} \quad ...(2)$$

$$\text{And R.H.L.} = \lim_{x\to1^+}\left[\frac{x^{1/3}-x}{ax^2-a}+\frac{(x-1)}{(x-1)(x+3)}\right]$$

($\because$ $a + b = 0$ by same reason)

$$= \lim_{x\to1^+}\left(\frac{x^{1/3}(1-x^{2/3})}{a(x^2-1)}+\frac{1}{x+3}\right)$$

$$= \lim_{x\to1^+}\left(\frac{x^{1/3}(1+x^{1/3})(1-x^{1/3})}{a(x-1)(x+1)}+\frac{1}{x+3}\right)$$

$$= \lim_{x\to1^+}\left[\frac{x^{1/3}(1+x^{1/3})(1-x)}{a(x-1)(x+1)\left(1+x^{1/3}+x^{2/3}\right)}+\frac{1}{x+3}\right]$$

$$= \lim_{x\to1^+}\left(\frac{-x^{1/3}(1+x^{1/3})}{a(x+1)\left(1+x^{1/3}+x^{2/3}\right)}+\frac{1}{x+3}\right)=\frac{-1}{3a}+\frac{1}{4}$$

$\therefore$ for existence of limit, L.H.L. = R.H.L.

$$\Rightarrow \frac{1}{a}-\frac{1}{4}=-\frac{1}{3a}+\frac{1}{4} \quad \Rightarrow \left(\frac{1}{3}+1\right)\frac{1}{a}=\frac{1}{2}$$

$$\Rightarrow \frac{4}{3}.\frac{1}{a}=\frac{1}{2} \quad \Rightarrow a=\frac{8}{3}$$

Since $a + b = 0 \quad \Rightarrow b=-\dfrac{8}{3}$

$$\therefore \; h(x)=\frac{8}{3}x^2-\frac{8}{3}=\frac{8}{3}(x^2-1)$$

51. (b) Given $\int_1^2 h(x)\,dx = \int_1^2 \frac{8}{3}(x^2-1)\,dx = \frac{8}{3}\left[\frac{x^3}{3}-x\right]_1^2$

$$= \frac{8}{3}\left(\frac{8}{3}-\frac{1}{3}\right)-\frac{8}{3}(2-1)=\frac{56}{9}-\frac{8}{3}=\frac{56-24}{9}=\frac{32}{9}$$

52. (c) We proved $g(x)=\begin{cases} x^3; & 0<x\le1 \\ x^{1/3}; & 1\le x<\infty\end{cases}$

$$\therefore \int_0^3 g(x)\,dx = \int_0^1 g(x)\,dx+\int_1^3 g(x)\,dx$$

$$= \int_0^1 x^3\,dx+\int_1^3 x^{1/3}\,dx = \frac{1}{4}+\frac{3}{4}\left|x^{4/3}\right|_1^3$$

$$= \frac{1}{4}+\frac{3}{4}\left((3)^{4/3}-1\right) = \frac{1}{4}(3)^{7/3}-\frac{2}{4} = \frac{1}{4}\left((3)^{7/3}-2\right)$$

53. (a) $L = \text{L.H.L.} = \dfrac{1}{a}-\dfrac{1}{4}=\dfrac{1}{8/3}-\dfrac{1}{4}$

$$=\frac{3}{8}-\frac{1}{4}=\frac{1}{8} \text{ and hence } x\in\left(0,\frac{1}{8}\right)$$

$$\Rightarrow g(x)=x^3 \text{ and } h(x)=\frac{8}{3}(x^2-1)$$

$$\therefore \int_0^L \frac{g(x)-x}{h(x)}dx = \frac{3}{8}\int_0^{1/8}\frac{x^3-x}{(x^2-1)}dx$$

$$=\frac{3}{8}\int_0^{1/8} x\,dx = \frac{3}{8}\left(\frac{x^2}{2}\right)_0^{1/8} = \frac{3}{16}\left[\frac{1}{64}-0\right]=\frac{3}{1024}$$

F: There exists a G.P. with first term and its common ratio (say α and β, respectively) satisfying the equation $ax^2 + bx + a = 0$ for some $a, b \in \mathbb{R}$. On adding 1 to twice the sum of n terms of G.P., we get the quantity equal to the number of ways of selecting objects out of n different objects. Further, on interchanging the first term and common ratio of G.P. the sum of new obtained infinite G.P. becomes λ, and we have $3\int_{\beta-2}^{\lambda-2}(x+1)^n dx = 364$. On the basis of above information answer the following questions:

54. The value of $\int_0^{\pi/4}\sin^n(2x)\,dx$ equals

(a) $\dfrac{15}{16}$ (b) $\dfrac{2\pi}{15}$

(c) $\dfrac{4}{15}$ (d) None of these

55. The value of $\int_0^{\pi/2}\sin^{2\beta}x\cos^{2\lambda}x\,dx$ equals

(a) $\dfrac{7\pi}{(2)^{11}}$ (b) $\dfrac{7}{(2)^{10}}$

(c) $\dfrac{(2)^{10}}{7}$ (d) None of these

56. The value of $\int_0^{\beta\pi} x|\sin^6 x\cos^n x|\,dx$ equals

(a) $\dfrac{2}{5}$ (b) $\dfrac{5}{2}$

(c) $\dfrac{5\pi}{4}$ (d) None of these

Solutions:

Given α = first term of G.P., β = common ratio of G.P. Now α, β satisfy the equation $ax^2 + bx + a = 0$, $a, b \in \mathbb{R}$

$\Rightarrow$ α, β are roots of $ax^2 + bx + a = 0$

But roots of $ax^2 + bx + a = 0$ are reciprocal of each other

$$\Rightarrow \alpha = \frac{1}{\beta} \quad ...(1)$$

Now A.T.Q. $2(S_n) + 1$ = Number of ways of selecting objects out of n-different objects

$= ({}^nC_0 + {}^nC_1 + {}^nC_2 + ... + {}^nC_n) = (2)^n$.

$$\Rightarrow 2\left[\frac{\alpha(\beta^n - 1)}{(\beta - 1)}\right] + 1 = (2)^n$$

$$\Rightarrow 2\left[\frac{\frac{1}{\beta}(\beta^n - 1)}{(\beta - 1)}\right] + 1 = (2)^n$$

$$\Rightarrow \left[\frac{\beta^n - 1}{\beta(\beta - 1)}\right] = \frac{2^n - 1}{2} = \frac{2^n - 1}{2(2-1)} \Rightarrow \beta = 2$$

$\therefore$ First term $\alpha = \frac{1}{2}$, common ratio β = 2

On interchanging common ratio and first term, we get first term of new infinite G.P. = 2 and common ratio = $\frac{1}{2}$

$\therefore$ Sum $= S_\infty = \frac{2}{1-(1/2)} = 4 \quad \therefore \quad ATQ, \lambda = 4$

Now given $3\int_{\beta-2}^{\lambda-2} (x+1)^n dx = 364$

$$\Rightarrow 3\int_0^2 (x+1)^n dx = 364 \Rightarrow 3\left[\frac{(x+1)^{n+1}}{n+1}\right]_0^2 = 364$$

$$\Rightarrow 3\left[\frac{(3)^{n+1} - 1}{(n+1)}\right] = 364$$

$$\Rightarrow \frac{(3)^{n+1} - 1}{(n+1)} = \frac{364}{3} = \frac{728}{6} = \frac{729 - 1}{6}$$

$$\Rightarrow \frac{(3)^{n+1} - 1}{(n+1)} = \frac{(3)^6 - 1}{6} \Rightarrow n = 5$$

54. (c) Let $\int_0^{\pi/4} \sin^n(2x)dx = \int_0^{\pi/4} \sin^5(2x)dx$

On substituting $2x = t$,

$\Rightarrow dx = \frac{dt}{2}$ when $x = 0, t = 0$

and when $x = \frac{\pi}{4}, t = \frac{\pi}{2} \quad \therefore \quad I = \frac{1}{2}\int_0^{\pi/2} \sin^5 t\, dt$

$= \frac{1}{2} \times \frac{(4)\times(2)}{5\times 3} = \frac{4}{15}$ (By Walli's formula)

55. (a) Let $I = \int_0^{\pi/2} \sin^{2\beta} x \cos^{2\lambda} x\, dx$

$= \int_0^{\pi/2} \sin^4 x \cos^8 x\, dx$ (By Walli's formula)

$$= \frac{(3\times1)\times(7\times5\times3)}{12\times10\times8\times6\times4\times2} \times \frac{\pi}{2} = \frac{7\pi}{(2)^{11}}$$

56. (d) Let $I = \int_0^{\beta\pi} x|\sin^6 x \cos^n x|\, dx$

$= \int_0^{2\pi} x|\sin^6 x \cos^5 x|\, dx \quad (\because \beta = 2, n = 5)$

$= \int_0^{2\pi} (2\pi - x)|\sin^6 x \cos^5 x|\, dx$

$\left(\because \int_0^a f(x)\, dx = \int_0^a f(a-x)\, dx\right)$

$= 2\pi\int_0^{2\pi} |\sin^6 x \cos^5 x|\, dx - I$

$\Rightarrow 2I = 2\pi\int_0^{2\pi} |\sin^6 x \cos^5 x|\, dx$

$\Rightarrow I = \pi\int_0^{2\pi} |\sin^6 x \cos^5 x|\, dx$

$= 2\pi\int_0^{\pi} |\sin^6 x \cos^5 x|\, dx$ as

$f(2\pi - x) = |\sin^6(2\pi - x)\cos^5(2\pi - x)|$

$= |\sin^6 x \cos^5 x| = f(x)$

$= 4\pi\int_0^{\pi/2} \sin^6 x \cos^5 x\, dx$

$$= \frac{4\pi(5\times3\times1)(4\times2)}{11\times9\times7\times5\times3} = \frac{32\pi}{693}$$

Column Matching

57. Column I

(a) If $\int_0^1 \frac{\cos x}{1+x} dx = k$ and $\int_{6\pi-3}^{6\pi} \frac{\cos(x/3)}{6\pi+3-x} dx = mk$, then m is

(b) If $\int_{-1}^{1}\left(\sin^{-1}\left[x + \frac{3}{4}\right]\right)dx = \frac{\pi}{k}$, then k is

{where [.] denotes greatest integer function}

(c) If $f(x)$ = max $\{x - |x|, x + [x]\}$ and $\int_{-3}^{3} f(x)dx = -\frac{3}{k}$, then k is

{where [.] denotes greatest integer function}

(d) If, $\int_0^{20} \sqrt{1 - \cos \pi x}\, dx = \frac{8k\sqrt{2}}{\pi}$, then k is

Column II

(p) 4

(q) 1

(r) 5

(s) 2

Ans. (a) → (q); (b) → (p);
(c) → (s); (d) → (r)

Solution: (a) Let $I = \int_{6\pi-3}^{6\pi} \frac{\cos(x/3)}{6\pi+3-x}dx$

Substituting $6\pi - 3t = x$

$\Rightarrow \frac{x}{3} = 2\pi - t$; $6\pi - x + 3 = 3t + 3$ and $dx = -3dt$

When $x = 6\pi - 3$, then $t = 1$

And when $x = 6\pi$, then $t = 0$

$\therefore \int_0^1 \frac{3\cos(2\pi-t)}{3(1+t)}dt = \int_0^1 \frac{\cos t}{1+t}dt = \int_0^1 \frac{\cos x}{1+x}dx = k$

$= mk$ (given)

$\Rightarrow m = 1$

$\therefore$ (a) → (q)

(b) $\int_{-1}^{1}\left(\sin^{-1}\left[x+\frac{3}{4}\right]\right)dx = \int_{-1}^{-3/4} -\frac{\pi}{2}dx + \int_{-3/4}^{1/4} 0\,dx + \int_{1/4}^{1}\frac{\pi}{2}dx$

$= -\frac{\pi}{8} + \frac{\pi}{2} \times \frac{3}{4} = \frac{2\pi}{8} = \frac{\pi}{4} = \frac{\pi}{k} \Rightarrow k = 4$

(c) $\because -|x| \le [x]\ \forall\ x \ge 0,\ -|x| \ge [x]\ \forall\ x \le 0$

$\Rightarrow \int_{-3}^{3} f(x)dx = \int_{-3}^{0}(x-|x|)dx + \int_{0}^{3}(x+[x])dx$

$= \int_{-3}^{0} 2x\,dx + \int_{0}^{3} x\,dx + \int_{0}^{3}[x]\,dx$

$= |x^2|_{-3}^{0} + \frac{1}{2}|x^2|_{0}^{3} + \int_0^1 0\,dx + \int_1^2 1dx + \int_2^3 2\,dx$

$= [0-9] + \frac{1}{2}[9-0] + 0 + (2-1) + 2(3-2)$

$= -9 + \frac{9}{2} + 1 + 2 = -\frac{3}{2} = \frac{-3}{k} \Rightarrow k = 2$

$\therefore$ (c) → (s)

(d) $\int_0^{20}\sqrt{1-\cos\pi x}\,dx = \int_0^{20}\sqrt{2}\left|\sin\frac{\pi x}{2}\right|dx$

$= 10\sqrt{2}\int_0^2\left|\sin\frac{\pi x}{2}\right|dx$

$\{\because \left|\sin\frac{\pi x}{2}\right|$ is periodic with period 2}

$= 10\sqrt{2}\int_0^2 \sin\left(\frac{\pi x}{2}\right)dx$

$= 10\sqrt{2}\left[-\frac{\cos\left(\frac{\pi x}{2}\right)}{\frac{\pi}{2}}\right]_0^2 = \frac{40\sqrt{2}}{\pi} = \frac{8k\sqrt{2}}{\pi}$ (given)

$\Rightarrow k = 5$

$\therefore$ (d) → (r)

58. **Column I**

(a) $\int_5^{10}\left[\frac{x-5}{5}\right]dx =$

(b) $\int_{-\tan 1}^{0}\left[-\tan^{-1}x\right]dx =$

(c) $\frac{12}{\pi}\int_{\pi/6}^{\pi/3}[2\sin x]dx =$

(d) $\int_{-1}^{1}\frac{\cot^{-1}x}{\pi}dx =$

where [.] represents greatest integer function.

Column II

(p) 1

(q) 2

(r) 0

(s) 3

Ans. (a) → (r); (b) → (r);
(c) → (q); (d) → (p)

Solution: (a) $5 < x < 10$

$\Rightarrow 0 < x - 5 < 5 \quad \Rightarrow 0 < \frac{x-5}{5} < 1$

$\therefore \left[\frac{x-5}{5}\right] = 0 \quad \Rightarrow \int_5^{10}\left[\frac{x-5}{5}\right]dx = \int_5^{10} 0\,dx = 0$

$\therefore$ (a) → (r)

(b) $-\tan 1 < x < 0$

$\Rightarrow \tan(-1) < x < 0 \quad \Rightarrow -1 < \tan^{-1}x < 0$

$\Rightarrow 0 < -\tan^{-1}x < 1 \quad \therefore [-\tan^{-1}x] = 0$

$\Rightarrow \int_{-\tan 1}^{0}\left[-\tan^{-1}x\right]dx = \int_{-\tan 1}^{0} 0dx = 0$

$\therefore$ (b) → (r)

(c) $\frac{\pi}{6} < x < \frac{\pi}{3}$

$\Rightarrow \frac{1}{2} < \sin x < \frac{\sqrt{3}}{2} \quad \Rightarrow 1 < 2\sin x < \sqrt{3}$

$\therefore\ [2\sin x] = 1 \qquad \Rightarrow \dfrac{12}{\pi}\int_{\pi/6}^{\pi/3}[2\sin x]dx$

$= \dfrac{12}{\pi}\int_{\pi/6}^{\pi/3} 1\,dx = \dfrac{12}{\pi}\left(\dfrac{\pi}{3}-\dfrac{\pi}{6}\right) = \dfrac{12}{\pi}\left(\dfrac{\pi}{6}\right) = 2$

$\therefore$ (c) $\to$ (q)

(d) $I = \displaystyle\int_{-1}^{1}\frac{\cot^{-1}x}{\pi}dx = \int_{-1}^{1}\frac{\cot^{-1}(-x)}{\pi}dx$

$= \displaystyle\int_{-1}^{1}\frac{\pi-\cot^{-1}x}{\pi}dx = \int_{-1}^{1}1dx - \int_{-1}^{1}\frac{\cot^{-1}x}{\pi}dx$

$\Rightarrow I = |x|_{-1}^{1} - I \qquad \Rightarrow 2I = 1-(-1) = 2$

$\Rightarrow I = 1 \qquad \therefore$ (d) $\to$ (p)

Integer Type

59. If $\displaystyle\int_{\sin x}^{1} t^2 f(t)\,dt = 1 - \sin x\ \forall\ x \in (0, \pi/2)$, then evaluate $f\left(\dfrac{1}{\sqrt{3}}\right)$.

Solution: Since $\displaystyle\int_{\sin x}^{1} t^2 f(t)\,dt = 1 - \sin x$,

Differentiating both sides w.r.t. x, we get

$$\frac{d}{dx}\int_{\sin x}^{1} t^2 f(t)\,dt = \frac{d}{dx}(1-\sin x)$$

$\Rightarrow (1^2 f(1))\cdot(0) - (\sin^2 x)\cdot f(\sin x)\cdot\cos x = -\cos x$ (by Newton Leibnitz's formula)

$\Rightarrow f(\sin x) = \dfrac{1}{\sin^2 x}\left(\because\ x \in \left(0,\dfrac{\pi}{2}\right); \sin x \neq 0; \cos x \neq 0;\right)$

Putting $\sin x = \dfrac{1}{\sqrt{3}}$

we get $f\left(\dfrac{1}{\sqrt{3}}\right) = \left(\sqrt{3}\right)^2 = 3$.

60. Find the value of

$$\int_{-2}^{0}\left[x^3+3x^2+3x+3+(x+1)\cos(x+1)\right]dx$$

Solution: Here

$$I = \int_{-2}^{0}\left[x^3+3x^2+3x+3+(x+1)\cos(x+1)\right]dx$$

$$= \int_{-2}^{0}\left\{x^3+3x^2+3x+1+2+(x+1)\cos(x+1)\right\}dx$$

$$= \int_{-2}^{0}\left\{(x+1)^3+2+(x+1)\cos(x+1)\right\}dx$$

Substituting, $x + 1 = t$

$\Rightarrow dx = dt$, we have,

$$I = \int_{-1}^{1}\left\{t^3+2+t\cos t\right\}dt$$

$$= \int_{-1}^{1}t^3\,dt + 2\int_{-1}^{1}1\,dt + \int_{-1}^{1}t\cos t\,dt$$

Since t^3 and $t\cos t$ are odd functions

$$\int_{-1}^{1}t^3\,dt = \int_{-1}^{1}t\cos t\,dt = 0$$

$\Rightarrow I = 2(1-(-1)) = 4$

61. Let $f : (0, \infty) \to \mathbb{R}$ and $F(x) = \displaystyle\int_0^x f(t)\,dt$. If $F(x^2) = x^2(1 + x)$, then find $f(4)$.

Solution: $F(x) = \displaystyle\int_0^x f(t)\,dt$ (given)

By Leibnitz rule, $F'(x) = f(x)$

But $F(x^2) = x^2(1 + x) = x^2 + x^3$

$\Rightarrow F(x) = x + x^{3/2}$

$\Rightarrow F'(x) = 1+\dfrac{3}{2}x^{1/2} \qquad \Rightarrow f(x) = F'(x) = 1+\dfrac{3}{2}x^{1/2}$

$\Rightarrow f(4) = 1+\dfrac{3}{2}(4)^{1/2} \qquad \Rightarrow f(4) = 1+\dfrac{3}{2}\times 2 = 4$

62. A function f is defined for all real x satisfying the equation $f(x) = 5+\displaystyle\int_0^x\frac{1+\sin t}{2+t^2}dt$. Find a quadratic polynomial $p(x) = a + bx + cx^2$ such that $p(0) = f(0)$, $p'(0) = f'(0)$ and $p''(0) = f''(0)$. Hence find $p(2)$.

Solution: Given equation is $f(x) = 5+\displaystyle\int_0^x\frac{1+\sin t}{2+t^2}dt$

$\Rightarrow f'(x) = \dfrac{1+\sin x}{2+x^2}$

$\Rightarrow f''(x) = \dfrac{(2+x^2)(\cos x)-(1+\sin x)(2x)}{(2+x^2)^2}$

$\Rightarrow f'(0) = \dfrac{1}{2}$ and $f''(0) = \dfrac{2}{4} = \dfrac{1}{2}$; Also $f(0) = 5$

$\therefore\ p(x) = a + bx + cx^2 \Rightarrow p'(x) = b + 2cx$

$\Rightarrow p''(x) = 2c \qquad \Rightarrow p(0) = a = f(0) = 5$

$\Rightarrow a = 5$ and $p'(0) = b = f'(0) = \dfrac{1}{2}$;

$\Rightarrow b = \dfrac{1}{2}$ and $P''(0) = 2c = f''(0) = \dfrac{1}{2}$;

$\Rightarrow c = \dfrac{1}{4}$; Thus, $p(x) = 5+\dfrac{1}{2}x+\dfrac{1}{4}x^2$

$\therefore\ p(2) = 5+\dfrac{1}{2}(2)+\dfrac{1}{4}(4) = 7$

63. If p is the number of points of extrema of the function $\int_4^{x^2} \frac{t(t-1)(t-9)^2}{e^t-1}dt$ and $q = \int_{-10}^{20}\left\{\frac{x}{15}\right\}dx$; where $\{.\}$ denotes fractional part function and $r = \int_0^{2\pi} \ell n\left(\sin x+\sqrt{1+\sin^2 x}\right)dx$, then evaluate $p+q+r$.

Solution: $f(x) = \int_4^{x^2} \frac{t(t-1)(t-9)^2}{(e^t-1)}dt$

$$f'(x) = \frac{x^2\left(x^2-1\right)\left(x^2-9\right)^2}{e^{x^2}-1}.2x = 0$$

$\Rightarrow x = 0, \pm 1, \pm 3$

But f' changes sign only around $x = 0, \pm 1$

$\Rightarrow p = 3$, period of $\left\{\frac{x}{15}\right\}$ is 15 and $20-(-10) = 30$

$$\Rightarrow q = 2\int_0^{15}\left\{\frac{x}{15}\right\}dx = 2\int_0^{15}\frac{x}{15}dx.2.\left.\frac{x^2}{30}\right|_0^{15} = 15$$

$$r = \int_0^{2\pi} \ell n\left(\sin x+\sqrt{1+\sin^2 x}\right)dx$$

$$= \int_0^{2\pi} \ell n\left(-\sin x+\sqrt{1+\sin^2 x}\right)dx$$

$$\left(\because \int_0^a f(x)dx = \int_0^a f(a-x)dx\right)$$

$$r = -\int_0^{2\pi} \ell n\left(\sin x+\sqrt{1+\sin^2 x}\right)dx = -r$$

$\therefore r = 0$ $\qquad\therefore p+q+r = 18$

64. Let $f(x) = \sqrt{x}$ and $g(x) = e^x - 1$, then $\int_0^x fog(x)\,dx = A\,fog(x) + B\tan^{-1}(fog(x))$, then evaluate $(A - B)$

Solution: $fog(x) = \sqrt{g(x)} = \sqrt{e^x-1}$

$\therefore \int_0^x fog(x)\,dx = \int_0^x \sqrt{e^x-1}\,dx$; Put $\sqrt{e^x-1} = t$

$\Rightarrow e^x - 1 = t^2 \qquad \Rightarrow e^x\,dx = 2t\,dt$

$\Rightarrow dx = \frac{2t\,dt}{t^2+1} \qquad \therefore \int_0^x fog(x)\,dx$

$$= \int_0^{\sqrt{e^x-1}} \frac{2t^2}{t^2+1}dt = \int_0^{\sqrt{e^x-1}}\left(2-\frac{2}{t^2+1}\right)dt$$

$$= \left|2t-2\tan^{-1}t\right|_0^{\sqrt{e^x-1}} = 2\sqrt{e^x-1}-2\tan^{-1}\left(\sqrt{e^x-1}\right)$$

$= 2\,fog(x) + (-2)\tan^{-1}(fog(x))$

$\Rightarrow A = 2, B = -2 \qquad \therefore A - B = 4.$

65. Let α, β be the distinct positive roots of the equation $\tan x = 2x$, then evaluate $\int_0^1(\sin\alpha x\cdot\sin\beta x)\,dx$, independent of α and β.

Solution: Let $I = \frac{1}{2}\int_0^1(2\sin\alpha x\cdot\sin\beta x)\,dx$

$$\Rightarrow I = \frac{1}{2}\int_0^1 2\sin\alpha x\cdot\sin\beta x\,dx$$

$$= \frac{1}{2}\int_0^1(\cos(\alpha-\beta)x-\cos(\alpha+\beta)x)\,dx$$

$$= \frac{1}{2}\left[\frac{\sin(\alpha-\beta)x}{\alpha-\beta}-\frac{\sin(\alpha+\beta)x}{\alpha+\beta}\right]_0^1$$

$$= \frac{1}{2}\left[\frac{\sin(\alpha-\beta)}{\alpha-\beta}-\frac{\sin(\alpha+\beta)}{\alpha+\beta}\right] \quad ...(1)$$

Now α, β are distinct positive roots of equation $\tan x = 2x$

$\Rightarrow 2\alpha = \tan\alpha$ and $2\beta = \tan\beta$

$\Rightarrow 2(\alpha - \beta) = \tan\alpha - \tan\beta$ and $2(\alpha + \beta) = \tan\alpha + \tan\beta$

$$\therefore 2(\alpha-\beta) = \frac{\sin(\alpha-\beta)}{\cos\alpha\cos\beta} \text{ and } 2(\alpha+\beta) = \frac{\sin(\alpha+\beta)}{\cos\alpha\cos\beta} \quad ...(2)$$

Substituting the value of $\frac{\sin(\alpha-\beta)}{2(\alpha-\beta)}$ and $\frac{\sin(\alpha+\beta)}{2(\alpha+\beta)}$ from (2),we get

$I = (\cos\alpha\cdot\cos\beta) - (\cos\alpha\cdot\cos\beta) = 0.$

66. If a_1, a_2 and a_3 are the three values of a which satisfy the equation $\int_0^{\pi/2}(\sin x+a\cos x)^3\,dx - \frac{4a}{\pi-2}\int_0^{\pi/2} x\cos x\,dx = 2$, then find the value of $1000(a_1^2+a_2^2+a_3^2)$.

Solution: Given

$$\int_0^{\pi/2}(\sin x+a\cos x)^3\,dx - \frac{4a}{\pi-2}\int_0^{\pi/2} x\cos x\,dx = 2,$$

Let $I_1 = \int_0^{\pi/2}(\sin x+a\cos x)^3\,dx$

$$= \int_0^{\pi/2}(\sin^3 x+a^3\cos^3 x+3a\sin^2 x\cos x+3a^2\sin x\cos^2 x)dx$$

$$= \int_0^{\pi/2}\sin^3 x\,dx + a^3\int_0^{\pi/2}\cos^3 x\,dx + 3a\int_0^{\pi/2}\sin^2 x\cos x\,dx + 3a^2\int_0^{\pi/2}\sin x\cos^2 x\,dx$$

$$= \frac{2}{3} + a^3\left(\frac{2}{3}\right) + 3a\int_0^{\pi/2}(1-\cos^2 x)\cos x\,dx +$$

$$3a^2\int_0^{\pi/2}\sin x(1-\sin^2 x)\,dx = \frac{2}{3} + \frac{2a^3}{3} + a + a^2$$

$$\therefore\ I_1 = \frac{2a^3}{3} + a^2 + a + \frac{2}{3};\ \text{Now let } I_2 = \int_0^{\pi/2}\underbrace{x}_{I}\cdot\underbrace{\cos x}_{II}\,dx$$

$$= x\sin x\Big|_0^{\pi/2} - \int_0^{\pi/2}\sin x\,dx$$

$$\Rightarrow\ I_2 = x\sin x + \cos x\Big|_0^{\pi/2}\ \Rightarrow\ I_2 = \frac{\pi}{2} - 1 = \frac{\pi-2}{2}$$

$$\therefore\ I = \frac{2a^3}{3} + a^2 + a + \frac{2}{3} - \frac{4a}{\pi-2}\cdot\frac{\pi-2}{2}$$

$$= \frac{2a^3}{3} + a^2 - a + \frac{2}{3} = 2\ \text{(Given)}$$

$$\Rightarrow\ 2a^3 + 3a^2 - 3a + 2 = 6$$

$$\Rightarrow\ 2a^3 + 3a^2 - 3a - 4 = 0$$

$$\Rightarrow\ a_1 + a_2 + a_3 = -\frac{3}{2}\ \text{and}\ \sum a_1a_2 = -\frac{3}{2}$$

$$\therefore\ \sum a_1^2 = \frac{9}{4} + \frac{6}{2} = \frac{21}{4}$$

$$\therefore\ 1000\sum a_1^2 = 1000\times\frac{21}{4} = 250\times 21 = 5250$$

67. Evaluate $\lim\limits_{n\to\infty} n^2\int_{-1/n}^{1/n}(2006\sin x + 2007\cos x)|x|\,dx$

Solution: Consider

$$I = \underbrace{\int_{-1/n}^{1/n}(2006\sin x)|x|\,dx}_{\text{vanishes as odd}} + \int_{-1/n}^{1/n}(2007\cos x)|x|\,dx$$

$$\therefore\ I = \int_{-1/n}^{1/n}(2007\cos x)|x|\,dx = 2\int_0^{1/n}(2007\cos x)\cdot x\,dx$$

[as function is even]

$$= 2\cdot 2007\int_0^{1/n}\underbrace{x}_{I}\ \underbrace{\cos x}_{II}\,dx$$

$$= 2\cdot 2007\left[\left|x\sin x\right|_0^{1/n} - \int_0^{1/n}\sin x\,dx\right]$$

$$= 2\cdot 2007\left[\frac{1}{n}\sin\frac{1}{n} + \cos\frac{1}{n} - 1\right]$$

Substituting $n = 1/y$, we have,

Given limit $\lim\limits_{y\to 0}\frac{1}{y^2}2.(2007)\left[y\sin y + \cos y - 1\right]$

$$= 2\cdot 2007\lim_{y\to 0}\frac{y\sin y + \cos y - 1}{y^2}$$

$$= 2\cdot 2007\left[1 - \lim_{y\to 0}\frac{1-\cos y}{y^2}\right] = 2\cdot 2007\ \frac{1}{2} = 2007$$

68. If $\int_1^2 \frac{(x^2-1)dx}{x^3\sqrt{2x^4-2x^2+1}} = \frac{u}{v}$; where u and v are in their lowest form, then find the value of $(1000)\ \frac{u}{v}$

Solution: Let $I = \int_1^2 \frac{(x^2-1)dx}{x^3\sqrt{2x^4-2x^2+1}}$

$$= \int_1^2 \frac{(x^2-1)\,dx}{x^5\sqrt{2-\frac{2}{x^2}+\frac{1}{x^4}}} = \int_1^2 \frac{(x^{-3}-x^{-5})}{\sqrt{2-2x^{-2}+x^{-4}}}\,dx$$

put $2 - 2x^{-2} + x^{-4} = t^2 \Rightarrow (x^{-3} - x^{-5})\,dx = \frac{1}{2}\ tdt$

when $x = 1$, then $t = 1$ and $x = 2$, then $t = \frac{5}{4}$

$$\therefore\ I = \frac{1}{2}\int_1^{5/4}\frac{t}{t}dt = \frac{1}{2}\left(\frac{5}{4} - 1\right) = \frac{1}{8}$$

$$I = \frac{u}{v} = \frac{1}{8},\ \text{then}\ (1000)\left(\frac{u}{v}\right) = \left(1000\left(\frac{1}{8}\right)\right) = 125$$

69. Let $u = \int_0^{\pi/4}\left(\frac{\cos x}{\sin x + \cos x}\right)^2 dx$ and $v = \int_0^{\pi/4}\left(\frac{\sin x + \cos x}{\cos x}\right) dx$, find the value of $\frac{v}{u}$.

Solution: $u = \int_0^{\pi/4}\left(\frac{\cos x}{\sin x + \cos x}\right)^2 dx$

$$= \int_0^{\pi/4}\left(\frac{\cos(\pi/4 - x)}{\sin(\pi/4 - x) + \cos(\pi/4 - x)}\right)^2 dx$$

$$= \int_0^{\pi/4}\left(\frac{\frac{1}{\sqrt{2}}(\cos x + \sin x)}{\frac{1}{\sqrt{2}}\cos x - \frac{1}{\sqrt{2}}\sin x + \frac{1}{\sqrt{2}}\cos x + \frac{1}{\sqrt{2}}\sin x}\right)^2 dx$$

$$= \int_0^{\pi/4}\left(\frac{\cos x + \sin x}{2\cos x}\right)^2 dx;\ u = \frac{1}{4}\ v;\ \frac{v}{u} = 4\ \text{Ans}$$

70. If

$$\int_{\frac{\pi}{4}}^{\pi/3}\frac{(\sin^3\theta - \cos^3\theta - \cos^2\theta)(\sin\theta + \cos\theta + \cos^2\theta)^{2007}}{(\sin\theta)^{2009}(\cos\theta)^{2009}}d\theta$$

$= \frac{(a+\sqrt{b})^d - (1+\sqrt{c})^d}{d}$, where a, b, c and d are all positive integers. Find the value of $(a + b + c + d)$

Solution: $I = \int_{\pi/4}^{\pi/3}\frac{(\sin^3\theta - \cos^3\theta - \cos^2\theta)}{\sin^2\theta\cos^2\theta}$

$$\left(\frac{\sin\theta + \cos\theta + \cos^2\theta}{\sin\theta\cos\theta}\right)^{2007} d\theta$$

$$= \int_{\pi/4}^{\pi/3} (\tan\theta\sec\theta - \cot\theta\,\text{cosec}\,\theta - \text{cosec}^2\theta)$$

$$(\sec\theta + \text{cose}\,\theta + \cot\theta)^{2007}\,d\theta$$

put $\sec\theta + \text{cosec}\,\theta + \cot\theta = t$

$\Rightarrow$ $(\sec\theta\tan\theta - \text{cosec}\,\theta\cot\theta - \text{cosec}^2\theta)\,d\theta = dt$

when $\theta = \pi/4$; $t = \sqrt{2}+\sqrt{2}+1 = 1+2\sqrt{2}$

when $\theta = \pi/3$,

$$t = \frac{2}{\sqrt{3}} + 2 + \frac{1}{\sqrt{3}} = 2+\sqrt{3}$$

$$\therefore\ I = \int_{1+\sqrt{8}}^{2+\sqrt{3}} t^{2007}\,dt = \left.\frac{t^{2008}}{2008}\right|_{1+\sqrt{8}}^{2+\sqrt{3}}$$

$$= \frac{(2+\sqrt{3})^{2008} - (1+\sqrt{8})^{2008}}{2008}$$

$a = 2$; $b = 3$; $c = 8$;

$d = 2008$, then

$(a + b + c + d) = 2021$

71. Given $\lim_{n\to\infty}\left(\frac{{}^{3n}C_n}{{}^{2n}C_n}\right)^{1/n} = \frac{a}{b}$; where a and b are relatively prime, find the value of $(a + b)$.

Solution: Consider $\frac{{}^{3n}C_n}{{}^{2n}C_n} = \frac{(3n)!}{n!(2n)!}\cdot\frac{n!n!}{(2n)!}$

$$= \frac{3n(3n-1)......(2n+1)(2n)!n!}{(2n)!(2n)(2n-1)....(n+1)n!}$$

$$= \frac{(2n+1)(2n+2)(2n+3).....(2n+n)}{(n+1)(n+2)(n+3)..........(n+n)}$$

$$\therefore\ P = \lim_{n\to\infty}\left(\frac{{}^{3n}C_n}{{}^{2n}C_n}\right)^{1/n}$$

$$= \lim_{n\to\infty}\left[\frac{(2n+1)(2n+2)....(2n+n)}{(n+1)(n+2)(n+3)....(n+n)}\right]^{1/n}$$

$$\Rightarrow\ P = \lim_{n\to\infty}\left[\left(1+\frac{n}{n+1}\right)\left(1+\frac{n}{n+2}\right)......\left(1+\frac{n}{n+n}\right)\right]^{1/n}$$

Taking natural logarithm both sides, we get

$$\ell n P = \lim_{n\to\infty}\frac{1}{n}\left[\begin{array}{l}\ln\left(1+\frac{n}{n+1}\right)+\ln\left(1+\frac{n}{n+2}\right)+...+\\ \ln\left(1+\frac{n}{n+n}\right)\end{array}\right]$$

$$= \lim_{n\to\infty}\sum_{r=1}^{n} T_r$$

Where $T_r = \frac{1}{n}\ln\left(1+\frac{n}{n+r}\right) = \frac{1}{n}\ln\left(1+\frac{1}{1+(r/n)}\right)$

$$\therefore\ \ell n P = \lim_{n\to\infty}\frac{1}{n}\sum_{r=1}^{n}\ln\left(1+\frac{1}{1+(r/n)}\right)$$

$$= \int_0^1 \ln\left(1+\frac{1}{1+x}\right)dx = \int_0^1 \ln\left(\frac{x+2}{x+1}\right)dx$$

$$= \int_0^1 \ln(x+2)dx - \int_0^1 \ln(x+1)dx$$

$$= \left|(x+2)\ln(x+2)-(x+2)\right|_0^1 - \left|(x+1)\ln(x+1)-(x+1)\right|_0^1$$

$= [(3 \ln 3 - 3) - (2 \ln 2 - 2)] - [(2 \ln 2 - 2) - (0 - 1)]$

$= [\ln 27 - 3] - [\ln 4 - 2] - [\ln 4 - 1] = [\ln 27 - 2\ln 4]$

$= \ln 27 - \ln 16$

$\therefore\ \ell n P = \ell n\frac{27}{16}$ $\Rightarrow$ $P = \frac{27}{16} = \frac{a}{b}$ (given)

$\Rightarrow$ $a = 27$; $b = 16$ $\Rightarrow$ $a + b = 43$

72. Let $F(x) = \int_{-1}^{x}\sqrt{4+t^2}\,dt$ and $G(x) = \int_{x}^{1}\sqrt{4+t^2}\,dt$; then compute the value of $(FG)'(0)$, where dash denotes the derivative.

Solution: $F(x) = \int_{-1}^{x} f(t)\,dt$ and $G(x) = \int_{x}^{1} f(t)\,dt$;

where $f(t) = \sqrt{4+t^2}$

Let $H(x) = F(x)\cdot G(x) = (FG)(x)$

$\Rightarrow$ $H'(x) = F(x)\cdot G'(x) + G(x)\cdot F'(x)$

$$\Rightarrow\ H'(x) = \left(\int_{-1}^{x} f(t)\,dt\right)\left(-\sqrt{4+x^2}\right) + \left(\int_{x}^{1} f(t)\,dt\right)\left(\sqrt{4+x^2}\right)$$

$$\Rightarrow\ H'(x) = \sqrt{4+x^2}\left[\int_{x}^{1}\sqrt{4+t^2}\,dt - \int_{-1}^{x}\sqrt{4+t^2}\,dt\right]$$

$$\Rightarrow\ (FG)'(0) = H'(0) = 2\left[\int_{0}^{1}\sqrt{4+t^2}\,dt - \int_{-1}^{0}\sqrt{4+t^2}\,dt\right]$$

$$= 2\left[\int_{0}^{1}\sqrt{4+t^2}\,dt + \int_{1}^{0}\sqrt{4+y^2}\,dy\right]$$

(by reflection property)

$$= 2\left[\int_{1}^{1}\sqrt{4+t^2}\,dt\right] = 0$$

73. If the value of definite integral $\int_e^{e^{2010}} \frac{1}{x}\left(1+\frac{1-\ell n x}{\ell n x\,\ell n\left(\frac{x}{\ell n x}\right)}\right)dx = \lambda - \ln(\mu - \ln\mu)$ then evaluate $(\mu - \lambda)$.

Solution: Let $I = \int_e^{e^{2010}} \frac{1}{x}\left(1 + \frac{1-\ln x}{\ell nx\,\ell n\left(\frac{x}{\ell nx}\right)}\right)dx$

Put $\ell nx = t \Rightarrow \frac{1}{x}dx = dt$ for $x = e$, $t = 1$ and for $x = e^{2010}$, $t = 2010$

$$\therefore \quad I = \int_1^{2010}\left(1 + \frac{1-t}{t(t-\ell nt)}\right)dt$$

$$= \int_1^{2010} dt + + \int_1^{2010}\left(\frac{1-t}{t(t-\ell nt)}\right)dt$$

Again put $(t - \ell nt) = z$ in second integral

$$\Rightarrow \left(1 - \frac{1}{t}\right)dt = dz$$

$$\therefore \quad I = (2010-1) + \int_1^{2010-\ln(2010)}\left(-\frac{dz}{z}\right)$$

$$= 2009 - [\ell nz]_1^{2010-\ell n2010}$$

$= 2009 - [\ell n\,(2010 - \ell n2010) - \ell n1]$

$= 2009 - \ell n\,(2010 - \ell n\,2010) = \lambda - \ell n\,(\mu - \ell n\mu)$

$\Rightarrow \lambda = 2009,\ \mu = 2010$

$\Rightarrow \mu - \lambda = 1$

74. Let A_k denotes the area of triangle with vertices at O (origin); P and Q_K such that $OP = \pi^3$ and $OQ_k = 3k$; when $k \in \{1,2,3,\ldots.n\}$, and $\angle POQ_k = \frac{k\pi}{2n}$. Then evaluate $\lim\limits_{n\to\infty}\frac{1}{n^2}\sum\limits_{k=1}^{n} A_k$

Solution: The triangle is as shown below

Now area of triangle $OPQ_k = A_k$

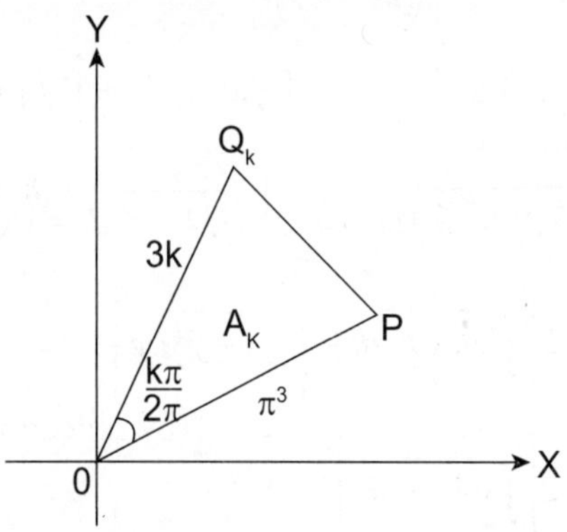

$$= \frac{1}{2}(OP)(OQ_k)\sin\angle POQ_k$$

$$= \frac{1}{2}(\pi)^3(3k)\sin\frac{k\pi}{2n}\left(\because \Delta = \frac{1}{2}ab\sin\theta\right)$$

$$= \frac{3}{2}k\pi^3\sin\left(\frac{k\pi}{2n}\right)$$

$$\therefore \quad L = \lim_{n\to\infty}\frac{1}{n^2}\sum_{k=1}^{n}A_k = \lim_{n\to\infty}\frac{1}{n^2}\sum_{k=1}^{n}\left(\frac{3}{2}\right)k\pi^3\sin\left(\frac{k\pi}{2n}\right)$$

$$= \lim_{n\to\infty}\sum_{k=1}^{n}\frac{\pi^3}{n}\left(\frac{3}{2}\right)\frac{k}{n}\sin\left(\frac{\pi}{2}\cdot\frac{k}{n}\right)$$

Substituting $\frac{k}{n} = x, \frac{1}{n} = dx$, we have

$$L = \int_0^1 \pi^3\left(\frac{3}{2}\right)x\sin\left(\frac{\pi}{2}x\right)dx$$

$$= \frac{3\pi^3}{2}\int_0^1 x\sin\left(\frac{\pi}{2}x\right)dx$$

$$= \frac{3\pi^3}{2}\left[\left|\frac{-x\cos\left(\frac{\pi}{2}x\right)}{\frac{\pi}{2}}\right|_0^1 + \int_0^1\frac{\cos\left(\frac{\pi}{2}x\right)}{\frac{\pi}{2}}\right]$$

$$= \frac{3\pi^3}{2}\left(\frac{2}{\pi}\right)\left[\left|-x\cos\left(\frac{\pi}{2}x\right)\right|_0^1 + \frac{4}{\pi^2}\left|\sin\left(\frac{\pi}{2}x\right)\right|_0^1\right]$$

$$= 3\pi^2\left[0 + \frac{4}{\pi^2}(1-0)\right] = 3\pi^2\left(\frac{4}{\pi^2}\right) = 12$$

75. If $\int_a^b|\sin x|dx = 8$ and $\int_{-a}^{b}|\cos x|dx = 9$, then evaluate $\int_0^{a+b}\sin x\,dx$

Solution: Since $\int_0^{\pi}|\sin x|dx = \int\limits_0^{\pi}\sin x\ dx$

$= |-\cos x|_0^{\pi} = -(\cos\pi - \cos 0) = 2$

$\therefore \quad \int_a^b|\sin x|dx = 8$

$\Rightarrow b - a = 4\pi$ ...(1)

Also $\int_0^{\pi}|\cos x|dx = \int_0^{\pi/2}\cos xdx + \int_{\pi/2}^{\pi} -\cos x\,dx$

$= |\sin x|_0^{\pi/2} - |\sin x|_{\pi/2}^{\pi} = (1 - 0) - (0 - 1) = 2$

$\therefore \quad \int_{-a}^{b}|\cos x|dx = 9 \quad \Rightarrow b - (-a) = 4\pi + \frac{\pi}{2}$

$\Rightarrow b + a = \frac{9\pi}{2}$ ...(2)

Solving (1) and (2) we get

$b = 4\pi + \frac{\pi}{4}$ and $a = \pi/4$

$$\therefore \quad \int_0^{a+b}\sin x\,dx = \int_0^{\left(4\pi+\frac{\pi}{2}\right)}(\sin x)dx$$

$$= \int_0^{4\pi}\sin x\,dx + \int_{4\pi}^{4\pi+\frac{\pi}{2}}\sin x\,dx$$

$$= 0 + (-\cos x)_{4\pi}^{4\pi+\frac{\pi}{2}} = (0-1) = 1 = 1$$

TUTORIAL EXERCISE

SECTION–III

ONLY ONE CORRECT ANSWER

1. $\int_{\pi/3}^{\pi/2} \frac{\sqrt{1+\cos x}}{(1-\cos x)^{\frac{5}{2}}} dx$ is equal to
(a) 5/2 (b) 3/2
(c) 1/2 (d) 2/5

2. $\int_1^e \frac{e^x}{x}(1+x\log x)\, dx$ is equal to
(a) e^e (b) $e^e - e$
(c) $e^e + e$ (d) None of these

3. $\int_0^{b-c} f''(x+a)dx$ is equal to
(a) $f'(a) - f'(b)$
(b) $f'(b - c + a) - f'(a)$
(c) $f'(b + c - a) + f'(a)$
(d) None of these

4. $\int_0^1 \frac{d}{dx}\left[\sin^{-1}\left(\frac{2x}{1+x^2}\right)\right] dx$ is equal to
(a) 0 (b) π
(c) π/2 (d) π/4

5. Let (a, b) and (λ, μ) be two points on the curve $y = f(x)$. If the slope of the tangent to the curve at (x, y) be $\phi(x)$, then $\int_a^{\lambda} \phi(x)dx$ is
(a) $\lambda - a$ (b) $\mu - b$
(c) $\lambda + \mu - a - b$ (d) None of these

6. $\int_0^{\pi/4} \frac{dx}{\cos^4 x - \cos^2 x \sin^2 x + \sin^4 x}$ is equal to
(a) π/2 (b) π/4
(c) π/3 (d) None of these

7. For any integer n, the integral $\int_0^{\pi} e^{\sin^2 x} \cos^3(2n+1)x dx$ is equal to
(a) –1 (b) 0
(c) 1 (d) π

8. If $\int_0^{\pi} x\, f(\cos^2 x + \tan^4 x)dx = k\int_0^{\pi/2} f(\cos^2 x + \tan^4 x)dx$, then the value of k is
(a) $\frac{\pi}{2}$ (b) π
(c) $-\frac{\pi}{2}$ (d) None of these

9. The value of the integral $\int_{\frac{1}{n}}^{\frac{an-1}{n}} \frac{\sqrt{x}}{\sqrt{a-x}+\sqrt{x}} dx$ is
(a) $\frac{a}{2}$ (b) $\frac{na+2}{2n}$
(c) $\frac{na-2}{2n}$ (d) None of these

10. If $f(x) = \frac{e^x}{1+e^x}$, $I_1 = \int_{f(-a)}^{f(a)} xg\{x(1-x)\}dx$, and $I_2 = \int_{f(-a)}^{f(a)} g\{x(1-x)\}dx$, then the value of $\frac{I_2}{I_1}$ is
(a) 1 (b) –3
(c) –1 (d) 2

11. The equation $\int_{-\pi/4}^{\pi/4}\left(\lambda|\sin x| + \frac{\mu \sin x}{1+\cos x} + v\right)dx = 0$, where λ, μ, v are constants, gives an equation involving
(a) λ, μ and v (b) λ and v
(c) λ and μ (d) μ and v

12. If $f(x)$ and $g(x)$ are continuous functions, then $\int_{\ln \lambda}^{\ln 1/\lambda} \frac{f\left(\frac{x^2}{4}\right)[f(x)-f(-x)]}{g\left(\frac{x^2}{4}\right)[g(x)+g(-x)]} dx$ is
(a) dependent on λ (b) a non-zero constant
(c) zero (d) None of these

13. If $I_1 = \int_e^{e^2} \frac{dx}{\log x}$ and $I_2 = \int_1^2 \frac{e^x}{x} dx$ then
(a) $I_1 = I_2$ (b) $I_1 > I_2$
(c) $I_1 < I_2$ (d) None of these

14. Let $I_1 = \int_1^2 \frac{dx}{\sqrt{1+x^2}}$ and $I_2 = \int_1^2 \frac{dx}{x}$ then
(a) $I_1 > I_2$ (b) $I_2 > I_1$
(c) $I_1 = I_2$ (d) $I_1 > 2I_2$

15. Let $\int_a^b f(x)dx = p$ and $\int_a^b |f(x)|dx = q$. Then

(a) $|p| \le q$ (b) $p > q$
(c) $p + q = 0$ (d) None of these

16. If $\int_n^{n+1} f(x)dx = n^2 + n, \forall n \in \mathbb{Z}$, then value of $\int_{-3}^{3} f(x)dx$ is equal to

(a) 6 (b) 10
(c) 16 (d) 12

17. The value of $\int_0^{\sin^2 x} \sin^{-1}\sqrt{t}\,dt + \int_0^{\cos^2 x} \cos^{-1}\sqrt{t}dt$ is

(a) π/2 (b) 1
(c) π/4 (d) None of these

18. Let $\int_0^1 f(x)dx = 1$, $\int_0^1 x f(x)dx = a$ and $\int_0^1 x^2 f(x)dx = a^2$, then the value of $\int_0^1 (x-a)^2 f(x)dx =$

(a) 0 (b) a^2
(c) $a^2 - 1$ (d) $a^2 - 2a + 2$

19. Let $f(x)$ be a continuous function such that $f(a - x) + f(x) = 0$ for all $x \in [0, a]$. Then $\int_0^a \frac{dx}{1+e^{f(x)}}$ is equal to

(a) a (b) $a/2$
(c) $f(a)$ (d) $1/2\, f(a)$

20. If $\int_0^1 \frac{e^t dt}{t+1} = a$, then $\int_{b-1}^{b} \frac{e^{-t}dt}{t-b-1}$ is equal to

(a) ae^{-b} (b) $-be^{-a}$
(c) $-ae^{-b}$ (d) None of these

21. If f is continuous functions, then

(a) $\int_{-2}^{2} f(x)dx = \int_0^2 [f(x) - f(-x)]dx$

(b) $\int_{-3}^{5} 2f(x)dx = \int_{-6}^{10} f(x-1)dx$

(c) $\int_{-3}^{5} f(x)dx = \int_{-4}^{4} f(x-1)dx$

(d) $\int_{-3}^{5} f(x)dx = \int_{-2}^{6} f(x-1)dx$

22. If $\int_a^b f(t)g(h(t))dt = \int_a^b f(h(t))g(t)dt$; where f, g, h are non-negative continuous function on $[a, b]$, then $h(t)$ is equal to

(a) t (b) $a - b - t$
(c) $a + b - t$ (d) $b - t$

23. If f: ℝ → ℝ: $f(x) = \sin x + x$, then the value of $\int_0^\pi (f^{-1}(x))dx$, is equal to

(a) $\frac{\pi^2}{2} - 2$ (b) π^2
(c) $\frac{\pi^2}{2} + 2$ (d) None of these

24. The value of $\int_0^{100} [\tan^{-1} x]\, dx$ is equal to (where [.] denotes the greatest integer function)

(a) tan 1 – 100 (b) π/2 – tan 1
(c) 100 – tan 1 (d) None of these

25. The value of $\int_0^2 f(x)dx$; where $f(x) = \begin{cases} 0; & \text{when } x = \frac{n}{n+1}, n = 1, 2, 3, \ldots \\ 1; & \text{else where} \end{cases}$ is equal to

(a) 1 (b) 2
(c) 3 (d) None of these

26. If $f(x) = \cos x - \int_0^x (x-t)f(t)dt$, then $f''(x) + f(x)$ is equal to

(a) $-\cos x$ (b) $-\sin x$
(c) $\int_0^x (x-t)f(t)dt$, (d) 0

27. $\int_{-1/2}^{1/2} \sqrt{\left\{\left(\frac{x+1}{x-1}\right)^2 + \left(\frac{x-1}{x+1}\right)^2 - 2\right\}}dx$ is

(a) $4 \log \frac{3}{4}$ (b) $4 \log \frac{4}{3}$
(c) $2 \log \frac{16}{9}$ (d) None of these

28. If $I = \int_0^1 \cos\left(2\cot^{-1}\sqrt{\left(\frac{1-x}{1+x}\right)}\right)dx$, then

(a) $I > 1/2$ (b) $I = -1/2$
(c) $0 < I < 1/2$ (d) None of these

29. The value of

$$\int_{-\sqrt{2}}^{\sqrt{2}} \frac{2x^7 + 3x^6 - 10x^5 - 7x^3 - 12x^2 + x + 1}{x^2 + 2}dx \text{ is}$$

(a) $2\int_0^{\sqrt{2}} \frac{3x^6 - 12x^2 + 1}{x^2 + 2}dx$

(b) 0

(c) $\frac{-14}{5}\sqrt{2} + \frac{\pi}{2\sqrt{2}}$

(d) $\frac{-16}{5}\sqrt{2} - \frac{\pi}{2\sqrt{2}}$

30. The value of the integral $I=\int_1^{\infty}\frac{(x^2-2)}{x^3\sqrt{(x^2-1)}}dx$ is

(a) 0 (b) 2/3
(c) 4/3 (d) None of these

31. The value of the integral $\int_0^{\infty}\frac{x\log x}{(1+x^2)^2}dx$ is

(a) 0 (b) 7
(c) 5 log 13 (d) 2 log 5

32. If $\int_0^{\pi/3}\frac{\cos x}{3+\sin x}dx=k\ln\left(\frac{3+\sqrt{3}/2}{3}\right)$, then k is

(a) 1/2 (b) 1/3
(c) 1/4 (d) None of these

33. If $I_1=\int_0^1\frac{dx}{\sqrt{1+x^2}}$ and $I_2=\int_0^1\frac{dx}{|x|}$, then

(a) $I_1>I_2$ (b) $I_1=I_2$
(c) $I_1<I_2$ (d) None of these

34. $\int_{\pi/2}^{\pi}\sqrt{\sin x-\sin^3 x}dx$ is equal to

(a) 2/3 (b) –2/3
(c) 4/3 (d) 0

35. $\int_0^a f(x)\,dx$ is equal to

(a) $\int_0^a f(a+x)\,dx$

(b) $\int_0^a f(x-a)dx$

(c) $\int_0^{a/2} f(x)dx+\int_0^{a/2} f\left(\frac{a}{2}-x\right)dx$

(d) $\int_0^{a/2} f(x)dx+\int_0^{a/2} f\left(\frac{a}{2}+x\right)dx$

36. $\int_1^{\sqrt{3}}\sin^{-1}\frac{2x}{1+x^2}dx$ is equal to

(a) $\frac{2-\sqrt{3}}{2\sqrt{3}}\pi+\log 2$ (b) $\frac{4-\sqrt{3}}{2\sqrt{3}}\pi-\log 2$

(c) $\log 2-\frac{4-\sqrt{3}}{2\sqrt{3}}\pi$ (d) None of these

37. The set of all the values of α for which the inequality $\frac{1}{\sqrt{\alpha}}\int_1^{\alpha}\left(\frac{3}{2}\sqrt{x}+1-\frac{1}{\sqrt{x}}\right)dx<4$ holds is given by

(a) [0, 4] (b) (0, 4)
(c) (0, 1) (d) None of these

38. If $\int_0^1\left(\frac{\tan^{-1}x}{x}\right)dx=l\int_0^{\pi/2}\frac{x}{\sin x}dx$, then the value of ℓ is

(a) 1 (b) 1/2
(c) 2/π (d) π/2

39. The value of $\int_{-\pi/4}^{\pi/4}\frac{dx}{\sec^2 x(1+\sin x)}$ is

(a) π/4 (b) π
(c) π/2 (d) 2π

40. If $f(x)=\frac{1}{x^2}\int_4^x(4t^2-2f'(t))dt$, then $f'(4)$ is

(a) $\frac{32}{9}$ (b) 32

(c) $\frac{32}{3}$ (d) None of these

41. The value of $\int_{-\pi}^{\pi}(\cos px-\sin qx)^2dx$; where p and q are integers is

(a) π (b) 0
(c) 4π (d) 2π

42. The value of the integral $\int_0^{\pi}\frac{x^2\sin x}{(2x-\pi)(1+\cos^2 x)}dx$ is

(a) $\frac{\pi^2}{4}$ (b) $\frac{\pi^2}{2}$

(c) $\frac{\pi^2}{6}$ (d) None of these

43. If f: ℝ → ℝ is continuous and differentiable function such that $\int_3^x f(t)dt+f''(3)\int_{-1}^0 dt=\int_x^x t^3dt$ – $f'(1)\int_0^x t^2dt+f''(2)\int_x^1 t\,dt$, then the value of $f'(4)$ is

(a) 48 – 8f'(1) – f''(2) (b) 48 + 8f'(1) – f''(2)
(c) 48 – 8f'(1) + f''(2) (d) 48 + 8f'(1) + f''(2)

44. If $f(a-x)=f(x)$ and $\int_0^{a/2}f(x)dx=p$, then $\int_0^a f(x)dx$ is equal to

(a) 2p (b) 0
(c) p (d) None of these

45. Let $I_1=\int_{\sec^2 z}^{2-\tan^2 z}xf(x(3-x))dx$ and $I_2=\int_{\sec^2 z}^{2-\tan^2 z}f(x(3-x))dx$; where f is a continuous function and z is any real number, then $\frac{I_1}{I_2}=$

(a) $\frac{3}{2}$ (b) $\frac{1}{2}$
(c) 1 (d) None of these

46. The value of the integral $\int_1^2 \sqrt{(2x+3)(3x^2+4)}dx$ cannot exceed

(a) $\sqrt{48}$ (b) $\sqrt{66}$
(c) $\sqrt{73}$ (d) None of these

47. If $I = \int_1^2 \frac{dx}{\sqrt{2x^3 - 9x^2 + 12x + 4}} dx$, then

(a) $\frac{1}{2} < I < \frac{1}{3}$ (b) $\frac{1}{4} < I < \frac{1}{3}$
(c) $\frac{1}{4} < I < 1$ (d) None of these

48. $f(x)$ is a continuous function for all real values of x and satisfies $\int_0^x f(t)dt = \int_x^1 t^2 f(t)dt + \frac{x^{16}}{8} + \frac{x^6}{3} + k$. The value of k is

(a) $\frac{167}{840}$ (b) $-\frac{167}{840}$
(c) $\frac{17}{38}$ (d) None of these

49. If $\int_0^1 \frac{\sin t}{1+t} dt = \alpha$, then the value of the integral $\int_{4\pi-2}^{4\pi} \frac{\sin t/2}{4\pi + 2 - t} dt$ in terms of α is given by

(a) 2α (b) –2α
(c) α (d) –α

50. If $I_1 = \int_0^{\pi/2} \cos(\sin x)dx$, $I_2 = \int_0^{\pi/2} \sin(\cos x)\, dx$ and $I_3 = \int_0^{\pi/2} \cos x\, dx$, then

(a) $I_1 > I_3 > I_2$ (b) $I_3 > I_1 > I_2$
(c) $I_1 > I_2 > I_3$ (d) $I_3 > I_2 > I_1$

51. $\int_0^1 \frac{dx}{1+x^2+2x^5}$ lies between

(a) $\frac{\pi}{6\sqrt{3}}$ and $\frac{\pi}{4}$ (b) $\frac{\pi}{3\sqrt{3}}$ and $\frac{\pi}{2}$
(c) $\frac{\pi}{3\sqrt{3}}$ and $-\frac{\pi}{4}$ (d) None of these

52. If $f(x)$ satisfies the relation $\int_{-2}^x f(t)dt + xf'''(3) = \int_1^x x^3 dx + f'(1)\int_2^x x^2 dx + f''(2)\int_3^x x\, dx$, then

(a) $f(x) = x^3 + 5x^2 + 2x - 6$
(b) $f(x) = x^3 - 5x^2 + 2x + 6$
(c) $f(x) = x^3 + 5x^2 + 2x - 6$
(d) $f(x) = x^3 - 5x^2 + 2x - 6$

53. $\lim_{x\to 0} \frac{1}{x}\left[\int_0^{x+y} e^{\sin^2 t}dt - \int_0^y e^{\sin^2 t}dt\right]$; where y is a constant independent of x, is equal to

(a) $e^{\sin^2 y}$ (b) $2e^{\sin^2 y}$
(c) $-e^{\sin^2 y}$ (d) None of these

54. $\int_{-2\pi}^{5\pi} \cot^{-1}(\tan x)dx$ is equal to

(a) $7\pi^2$ (b) $\frac{7\pi^2}{2}$
(c) 0 (d) $\frac{3\pi^2}{2}$

55. $\int_0^{\sqrt{3}} \frac{1}{1+x^2} . \sin^{-1}\left(\frac{2x}{1+x^2}\right) dx =$

(a) $\frac{7}{72}\pi^2$ (b) $\frac{3}{42}\pi^2$
(c) $\frac{17}{72}\pi^2$ (d) None of these

56. If f and g are two continuous functions being even and odd, respectively, then $\int_{-a}^a \frac{f(x)}{b^{g(x)}+1} dx$ is equal to (a being any non-zero number and b is positive real number, $b \neq 1$)

(a) independent of f
(b) independent of g
(c) independent of both f and g
(d) None of these

57. The sum $\int_{-3}^{-7} \tan\left(x^2 - 6\right)dx + \int_{-6}^{-2} \tan\left(x^2 + 18x + 75\right)dx$ is equal to

(a) 0 (b) 1
(c) 2 (d) None of these

58. If $A = \int_1^{\sin\theta} \frac{tdt}{1+t^2}$ and $B = \int_1^{\operatorname{cosec}\theta} \frac{dt}{t(1+t^2)}$, then the value of $\begin{vmatrix} A & A^2 & B \\ e^A e^B & B^2 & -1 \\ 1 & A^2 + B^2 & -1 \end{vmatrix}$ is

(a) sin θ (b) cosec θ
(c) 0 (d) 1

59. If $\int_0^{\pi/2} \frac{dx}{a^2\cos^2 x + b^2\sin^2 x} = \frac{\pi}{2ab}$, then the value of $\int_0^{\pi/2} \frac{dx}{(4\cos^2 x + 9\sin^2 x)^2}$

(a) $\frac{11\pi}{864}$ (b) $\frac{13\pi}{864}$

(c) $\frac{17\pi}{864}$ (d) None of these

60. If α, β; (β > α) are the roots of $g(x) = ax^2 + bx + c = 0$ and $f(x)$ is an even function, then $\int_\alpha^\beta \frac{e^{f\left(\frac{g(x)}{x-\alpha}\right)}}{e^{f\left(\frac{g(x)}{x-\alpha}\right)} + e^{f\left(\frac{g(x)}{x-\beta}\right)}} dx$ is equal to

(a) $\left|\frac{b}{2a}\right|$ (b) $\frac{\sqrt{b^2-4ac}}{|2a|}$

(c) $\left|\frac{b}{a}\right|$ (d) None of these

SECTION–IV

MORE THAN ONE CORRECT ANSWER

1. If $I_1 = \int_x^1 \frac{dt}{1+t^2}$ and $\int_1^{1/x} \frac{dt}{1+t^2}$, $x > 0$; then

(a) $I_1 = I_2$ (b) $I_1 > I_2$

(c) $I_2 > I_1$ (d) $I_2 = \pi/4 - \tan^{-1}x$

2. State which of the following statements are true?

(a) If m and M are the least and the greatest value of $f(x)$ in $[a, b]$, then $m(b-a) \le \int_a^b f(x)dx \le M(b-a)$

(b) If $f^2(x)$ and $g^2(x)$ are integrable on $[a, b]$, then $\left|\int_a^b f(x)g(x)dx\right| \le \left(\int_a^b f^2(x)dx\right)^{1/2}\left(\int_a^b g^2(x)dx\right)^{1/2}$

(c) If $f(x)$ is continuous on $[a, b]$, then there exists a point $c \in (a, b)$, such that $\int_a^b f(x)dx = f(c)(b-a)$

(d) If $f(x)$ is periodic function with period T and $a \in R^+$, then $\int_a^{a+T} f(x)dx = \int_0^T f(x)dx$

3. Let $f(a) > 0$, and let $f(x)$ be a non-decreasing continuous function in $[a, b]$. Then $\left(\frac{1}{b-a}\right)\int_a^b f(x)dx$ has the

(a) minimum value $f(a)$

(b) maximum value $f(b)$

(c) maximum value $b\,f(b)$

(d) minimum value $f(a)/(b-a)$

4. State which of the following statements are true?

(a) If $f(x)$ is an odd function of x, then $\int_a^x f(t)dt$ is an even function of x

(b) If $f(x)$ is an even function of x then $\int_0^x f(t)\,dt$ is an odd function of x

(c) If $I(x) = \int_{g(x)}^{h(x)} \phi(x)dx$, then $I'(x) = \phi(h(x))\,h'(x) - \phi(g(x))g'(x)$

(d) All of the above

5. State which of the following statements are true?

(a) If $f(x)$ is continuous in $[a, b]$ and $\int_a^b f(x) = 0$; then the equation $f(x) = 0$ has at least one root in (a, b)

(b) If $f(x) < g(x)\ \forall\, x \in (a, b)$, then $\int_a^b f(x)\,dx < \int_a^b g(x)dx$

(c) $\left|\int_a^b f(x)dx\right| \le \int_a^b |f(x)|\,dx$

(d) all of the above

6. If $I_n = \int_0^{\pi/4} \tan^n x\,dx$, $n \in W$

(a) $I_n + I_{n-2} = \frac{1}{n-1}$ for $n \ge 2$

(b) $I_{n+1} + I_{n-1} = 1/n$ for $n \ge 1$

(c) $\frac{1}{n+1} < 2I_n < \frac{1}{n-1}$; where $n > 1$

(d) $(I_{n+2} + I_n)(n+1) = 1$ for $n \ge 1$

7. Let $I_n = \int_0^{\pi/2} \cos^n x\,dx$, $n \in W$. Then

(a) $I_{n-2} > I_n\ \forall\, n \ge 2$

(b) $n(I_{n-2} - I_n) = I_{n-2}\ \forall\, n \ge 2$

(c) $I_n : I_{n-1} = n : (n-1)\ \forall\, n \ge 1$

(d) None of these

8. In order to find the numerical value of $I = \int_{-2}^{2} (ax^2 + bx + c)\,dx$, it is necessary to know the value of the constant

(a) a (b) b

(c) c (d) None of these

9. If $I_n = \int_0^1 \frac{dx}{(1+x^2)^n}$, $n \in \mathbb{N}$, then which of the following statements hold good?

(a) $2nI_{n+1} = 2^{-n} + (2n-1)I_{n-1}$

(b) $I_2 = \frac{\pi}{8} + \frac{1}{4}$

(c) $I_2 = \frac{\pi}{8} - \frac{1}{4}$

(d) $I_3 = \frac{\pi}{16} - \frac{5}{48}$

10. If $f(2-x) = f(2+x)$ and $f(4-x) = f(4+x)$ and $f(x)$ is a function for which $\int_0^2 f(x)dx = 5$, then $\int_0^{50} f(x)dx$ is equal to

(a) 125 (b) $\int_{-4}^{46} f(x)dx$

(c) $\int_1^{51} f(x)dx$ (d) $\int_2^{52} f(x)dx$

11. If $F(x) = \frac{1}{x^2}\int_4^x (4t^2 - 2F'(t))dt$, then $F'(4)$ equals

(a) $\frac{32}{9}$ (b) $\frac{64}{9}$

(c) $\frac{(2+F(4))^5}{9}$ (d) $\frac{11F(8)}{28}$

12. Which of the following is are true?

(a) $\int_0^1 \sin\left(x^2+2x+1\right) dx - \int_1^2 \sin x^2 dx = 0$

(b) $\int_{-1}^1 e^{\sin x} dx - \int_0^1 e^{\sin(2x+1)} dx = 0$

(c) $\int_{-5}^{-4} \sin\left(x^2-3\right) dx + \int_{-2}^{-1} \sin\left(x^2+12x+33\right) dx = 0$

(d) $\int_{-4}^4 \cos x^2 \, dx - 8\int_0^1 \cos\ 16(2x-1)^2 \, dx = 0$

13. If $\int_0^x f(t)dt = x^2 + 2x + \int_0^x tf(t)\, dt$, $x \in (0, \infty)$. Then $f(x)$ is

(a) Not periodic

(b) Periodic but fundamental period does not exists

(c) Periodic but fundamental period exists

(d) Nothing can be said

14. If $f(x+1) + f(x+7) = 0$, $\forall\, x \in \mathbb{R}$, then possible value of t for which $\int_a^{a+t} f(x)dx$ is independent of a, is

(a) 6 (b) 24

(c) 12 (d) None of these

15. If $f(x) = \int_0^x 2|t|\, dt$, the tangent lines which are parallel to the bisector of the first quadrant angle is

(a) $y = x - \frac{1}{4}$ (b) $y = x - \frac{3}{2}$

(c) $y = x + \frac{3}{2}$ (d) $y = x + \frac{1}{4}$

16. Let $f(x)$ be a non constant twice differentiable function defined on $(-\infty, \infty)$ such that $f(x) = f(1-x)$ and $f'\left(\frac{1}{4}\right) = 0$. Then

(a) $f'(x)$ vanishes at least twice on [0, 1]

(b) $f'\left(\frac{1}{2}\right) = 0$

(c) $\int_{-1/2}^{1/2} f\left(x + \frac{1}{2}\right) \sin x \, dx = 0$

(d) $\int_0^{1/2} f(t) e^{\sin \pi t} \, dt = \int_{1/2}^1 f(1-t) e^{\sin \pi t} \, dt$

17. If $I_n = \int_{-\pi}^{x} \frac{\sin nx}{(1+\pi^x)\sin x} dx$; $n = 0, 1, 2, \ldots$, then

(a) $I_n = I_{n+2}$ (b) $\sum_{m=1}^{10} I_{2m+1} = 10\pi$

(c) $\sum_{m=1}^{10} I_{2m} = 0$ (d) $I_n = I_{n+1}$

18. If $I_n = \int_0^{\pi/4} \tan^n x \, dx$; $n = 0, 1, 2, 3, \ldots$, then

(a) $I_7 + I_5 = \frac{1}{6}$ (b) $I_{10} + I_8 = \frac{1}{9}$

(c) $I_8 - I_{12} = \frac{2}{99}$ (d) $I_{12} + 2I_{10} + I_8 = \frac{20}{99}$

19. The value of $\int_{-\pi}^{\pi} \sin mx \cos nx \, dx$ $(m, n \in \mathbb{N})$ is equal to

(a) 0 (b) $\int_{-\pi/8}^{\pi/8} x^8 \sin^9 x \, dx$

(c) $\int_{-\pi/2}^{\pi/2} \sin x f(\cos x) dx$ (d) None of these

20. The value of $\int_{\pi}^{5\pi/4} \frac{\sin 2x}{\cos^4 x + \sin^4 x} dx$ is

(a) $\pi/4$ (b) π

(c) $\int_0^1 \frac{2t}{1+t^4} dt$ (d) None of these

21. The value of $\int_3^4 \frac{dx}{\sqrt[3]{\log x}}$ is

(a) less than one (b) greater than 1/2

(c) less than two (d) greater than 1/4

SECTION–V

ASSERTION AND REASON TYPE QUESTIONS

1. A: $\int_{-100}^{100\pi} (\sin^4 x + \cos^4 x)dx = 200\pi$

R: $\sin^4 x + \cos^4 x$ is a periodic function of period $\frac{\pi}{2}$

2. A: $\int_{1/3}^{11/2} \{x\}dx = \frac{185}{72}$ (where $\{x\}$ denotes the fractional part of x)

R: If $f(x)$ is a periodic function having period T, then $\int_a^{b+nT} f(x)dx = n\int_0^T f(x)dx + \int_a^b f(x)dx$

3. A: If $f(x) = \int_0^x g(t)dt$, where g is an even function and $f(x + 5) = g(x)$, then $g(0) - g(x) = \int_0^x f(t)dt.$

R: f is an odd function.

4. A: If f, g and h be continuous functions on $[0, a]$ such that $f(x) = f(a - x)$, $g(x) = -g(a - x)$ and $3h(x) - 4h(a - x) = 5$, then $\int_0^a f(x)g(x)h(x)dx = 0$

R: $\int_0^a f(x)g(x)dx = 0$

5. A: If $f(x) = \int_1^x \frac{\log t dt}{1+t+t^2}$; $(x > 0)$; $f(x) = -f\left(\frac{1}{x}\right)$

R: If $f(x) = \int_1^x \frac{\log t}{t+1}dt$, then $f(x) + f\left(\frac{1}{x}\right) = \frac{1}{2}(\log x)^2$

6. A: $\int_0^{10} \frac{2^x}{2^{[x]}}dx = \frac{10}{\ln 2}$ (where [.] denotes the greatest integer function)

R: $\int_0^{nT} f(x)dx = n\int_0^T f(x)dx$ if T is the fundamental period of $f(x)$; n is rational number.

7. Let $I_n = \int_0^{\pi/2} \log\cos x \cos 2nx\, dx$

A: $I_n = -\frac{n-1}{n}I_{n-1}$

R: $I_n = \frac{1}{2n}\int_0^{\pi/2} \tan x \sin 2nx\, dx$

8. Let $f(x) = \begin{cases} 1; & \text{if } 2 \le x < 3 \\ 3; & \text{if } 3 \le x \le 5 \end{cases}$

A: The mean value of f is attained

R: f is a bounded function but not continuous on [2, 5]

9. A: $\int_0^{\pi/2} x\cot x\, dx = \frac{\pi}{2}\log 2$

R: $\int_0^{\pi/2} \log\sin x\, dx = -\frac{\pi}{2}\log 2$

10. A: $I = \int_a^b \frac{|x|}{x}dx = |b| - |a|$

R: (i) For $a < b \le 0$; $\frac{|x|}{x} = -1$

(ii) For $a < 0 < b$; $I = \int_a^0 \frac{|x|}{x}dx + \int_0^b \frac{|x|}{x}dx$

(iii) For $0 \le a < b$; $\frac{|x|}{x} = 1$

11. A: $\int_0^{\sqrt{3}} \frac{dx}{1+x^2} + \left|\frac{1}{2}\tan^{-1}\left(\frac{2x}{1-x^2}\right)\right|_0^{\sqrt{3}} = \frac{-\pi}{6}$

R: $\frac{d}{dx}\left\{\frac{1}{2}\tan^{-1}\left(\frac{2x}{1-x^2}\right)\right\} = \frac{1}{1+x^2}$

12. A: $\int_0^{\pi} \frac{dx}{1+2\sin^2 x} = \frac{1}{\sqrt{3}}\left|\tan^{-1}\left(\sqrt{3}\tan x\right)\right|_0^{\pi} = 0$

R: $\frac{d}{dx}\left(\frac{1}{\sqrt{3}}\tan^{-1}\left(\sqrt{3}\tan x\right)\right) = \frac{\left(\sqrt{3}\sec^2 x\right)}{\sqrt{3}\left[1+\left(\sqrt{3}\tan x\right)^2\right]}$

$= \frac{\sec^2 x}{1+3\tan^2 x} = \frac{1}{\cos^2 x + 3\sin^2 x} = \frac{1}{1+2\sin^2 x}$

13. A: $\int_0^{\pi} \sqrt{\frac{1+\cos 2x}{2}}dx = \int_0^{\pi} \sqrt{\cos^2 x}dx = \int_0^{\pi} \cos x\, dx = 0$

R: Definite integral of a non-negative (not identically zero function) is always positive.

14. A: $1 < \int_0^1 e^{x^2} dx < e$

R: If $f(x) \le g(x) \le h(x)$ for $x \in [a, b]$, then $\int_a^b f(x)\,dx \le \int_a^b g(x)\,dx \le \int_a^b h(x)\,dx$

15. A: $\int_0^1 x^2 (\ln x)^4\,dx = \frac{8}{81}$

R: $I(m,n) = \int_0^1 x^m (\ln x)^n\,dx = \frac{n}{(m+1)} I_{(m,n-1)}$

SECTION–VI

COMPREHENSION-TYPE QUESTIONS

A: Consider a continuous and differentiable function $f(x)$ satisfying the equation $f\left(\frac{x+y}{2}\right) = \frac{f(x)+f(y)}{2}$ $\forall x, y \in \mathbb{R}$ and $f(1) = f'(1) = 4$. Let $y = h \pm \sqrt{g(x)}$ be a parabola having its focus at $(I, 4)$; where $I = \int_0^\pi f(\sin x)\,dx + \int_0^\pi f\left(\frac{4}{\pi} - \sin x\right) dx$ and having its directrix perpendicular to x-axis and passing through the point of intersection of curve $y = f(x)$ and $y = 4$.

On the basis of above information answer the following questions:

1. The value of $\left|\int_h^{h+2} g(x)dx\right|$ equals

(a) 960
(b) 210
(c) 1120
(d) None of these

2. If $I_1 = \int_0^h f(x)dx$ and $I_2 = \int_0^h g(x)dx$, then

(a) $I_1 = I_2$ (b) $I_1 > I_2$
(c) $I_2 > I_1$ (d) $I_1 \cdot I_2 < 0$

3. The value of $\frac{d}{dx}\int_0^{f(x)} (g(x)+255)dx$ equals

(a) $240x - 60$ (b) $60x^2 - 2x$
(c) $480\,x$ (d) None of these

B: Two vectors $\vec{a}$ and $\vec{b}$ have unit modulus and angle between them is θ. Further let $g(\theta) = \int_{-(\vec{a}.\vec{b})^2}^{(\vec{a}\times\vec{b})^2} f^2(x)dx$; where $f(x)$ is continuous and differentiable for all $x \in \mathbb{R} \sim \{0\}$ and satisfy the functional equation $f(x) + f(y) = \frac{x+y}{xy}$ $\forall x, y \in \mathbb{R} \sim \{0\}$.

On the basis of above information answer the following questions:

4. The value of $\int_{\pi/6}^{\pi/3} g(\theta)d\theta$ equals

(a) $\frac{-4}{\sqrt{3}}$ (b) $\frac{2}{\sqrt{3}}$
(c) $-4\sqrt{3}$ (d) None of these

5. The value of $\int_0^{10\pi} \left|\frac{1}{g(\theta)}\right| d\theta$ equals

(a) $\frac{3\pi}{2}$ (b) $\frac{5\pi}{4}$
(c) $\frac{5}{2}$ (d) None of these

6. The value of $\int_{-\pi/4}^{\pi/4} [g(\theta)]^{-4} d\theta$ equals

(a) $\frac{35\pi}{(2)^8}$ (b) $\frac{35\pi}{(2)^{16}}$
(c) $\frac{35}{(2)^{16}}$ (d) None of these

C: If $f(x, \alpha)$ be a continuous function of x and $\alpha\ \forall x \in [a, b]$ and $\alpha \in [c,d]$ where x and α be two independent parameters and $I(\alpha) = \int_a^b f(x,\alpha)dx$ then $I'(\alpha) = \frac{dI(\alpha)}{d\alpha} = \int_a^b \left(\frac{\partial}{\partial\alpha} f(x,\alpha)\right) dx$. That is, integrating $f(x, \alpha)$ with respect to x and then differentiating the result with respect to α results into same output as when we differentiate $f(x, \alpha)$ with respect to α first and then integrate the result with respect to parameter x. e.g. $f(x,\alpha)=3\alpha^2x^2+2\alpha x+\alpha$

$$I(\alpha)=\int_0^1 f(x,\alpha)dx=\left[\alpha^2x^3+\alpha x^2+\alpha x+c\right]_0^1$$

$$=\alpha^2+\alpha+\alpha \Rightarrow I'(\alpha)=2\alpha+2$$

$$f'(x,\alpha)=\frac{d}{d\alpha}f(x,\alpha)=6\alpha x^2+2x+1$$

$$\Rightarrow \int_0^1 f'(x,\alpha)dx=\left[\frac{6\alpha x^3}{3}+\frac{2x^2}{2}+x\right]_0^1=2\alpha+2$$

Based on the above theorem answer the following problems:

7. Let $I(\alpha, k) = \int_0^\infty \frac{e^{-\alpha x}\sin kx}{3x}dx$, then $\int_0^\infty \frac{\sin 2x}{3x}dx$ is equal to; $\alpha > 0$

(a) $\frac{\pi}{2}$ (b) Not integrable

(c) $\frac{\pi}{6}$ (d) None of these

8. If the value of integral $\int_0^\pi \frac{dx}{a-\cos x}=\frac{\pi}{2\sqrt{a^2-1}}$, the value of integral $\int_0^\pi \frac{dx}{(a-\cos x)^2}$ is equal to

(a) $\frac{\pi a}{2(a^2-1)^{1/2}}$ (b) $\frac{\pi a}{2(a^2-1)^{3/2}}$

(c) $\frac{\pi a}{(a^2-1)^{3/2}}$ (d) None of these

9. The value of the integral $= \int_0^l \frac{\ell n(1-a^2x^2)}{x^2\sqrt{(1-x^2)}}dx$ $(a^2 < 1)$ is equal to

(a) $\frac{\pi}{\sqrt{1-a^2}-1}$ (b) $\frac{\pi}{\sqrt{1-a^2}+1}$

(c) $\pi\left(\sqrt{1-a^2}-1\right)$ (d) $\pi\left(\sqrt{1-a^2}+1\right)$

D: Suppose we define the definite integral using the following formula $\int_a^b f(x)dx=F\left(\frac{a+b}{2}\right)$, for more accurate result for $c \in (a, b)$; $F(c)=\frac{c-a}{2}$ ($f(a)$ + $f(c)$) + $\frac{b-c}{2}$ ($f(b)$ + $f(c)$). When $c=\frac{a+b}{2}$; $F(c)=\int_a^b f(x)dx=\frac{b-a}{4}\left(f(a)+f(b)+2f(c)\right)$. On the basis of above information answer the following questions:

10. $\int_0^{\pi/2} \sin x\, dx$ is equal to

(a) $\frac{\pi}{8}\left(1+\sqrt{2}\right)$ (b) $\frac{\pi}{4}\left(1+\sqrt{2}\right)$

(c) $\frac{\pi}{8\sqrt{2}}$ (d) $\frac{\pi}{4\sqrt{2}}$

11. If $f''(x) < 0\ \forall\ x \in (a, b)$ and c is a point such that $a < c < b$, and $(c, f(c))$ is the point lying on the curve for which $F(c)$ is maximum, then $f'(c)$ is equal to

(a) $\frac{f(b)-f(a)}{b-a}$ (b) $\frac{2(f(b)-f(a))}{b-a}$

(c) $\frac{2f(b)-f(a)}{2b-a}$ (d) 0

E: Consider the function defined implicitly by the equation $y^3 - 3y + x = 0$ on various intervals in the real line.

If $x \in (-\infty, -2) \cup (2, \infty)$, the equation implicitly define a unique real valued differentiable function $y = f(x)$.

If $x \in (-2, 2)$, the equation implicitly define a unique real valued differentiable function $y = g(x)$ satisfying $g(0) = 0$. On the basis of above information answer the following questions:

12. If $f(-10\sqrt{2}) = 2\sqrt{2}$, then $f''(-10\sqrt{2})$ equals

(a) $\frac{4\sqrt{2}}{7^3 3^2}$ (b) $-\frac{4\sqrt{2}}{7^3 3^2}$

(c) $\frac{4\sqrt{2}}{7^3 3}$ (d) $-\frac{4\sqrt{2}}{7^3 3}$

13. The area of the region bounded by the curves $y = f(x)$, the x-axis, and the line $x = a$ and $x = b$, where $-\infty < a < b < -2$ is

(a) $\int_a^b \frac{x}{3(f(x)^2-1)}dx+bf(b)-af(a)$

(b) $-\int_b^a \frac{x}{3((f(x)^2)-1)}dx+bf(b)-bf(b)+af(a)$

(c) $\int_a^b \frac{x}{3((f(x)^2)-1)}dx-bf(b)+af(a)$

(d) $-\int_a^b \frac{x}{3((f(x)^2)-1)}dx-bf(b)+af(a)$

14. $\int_{-1}^{1} g'(x)\,dx$ equals

(a) $2g(-1)$
(b) $2g(1)$
(c) $-2g(1)$
(d) None of these

F: Consider the function $f: (-\infty, \infty) \to (-\infty, \infty)$ defined by $f(x) = \dfrac{x^2 - ax + 1}{x^2 + ax + 1}, 0 < a < 2$. On the basis of above information answer the following questions:

15. Which of the following is true?
(a) $(2 + a)^2 f''(1) + (2 - a)^2 f''(-1) = 0$
(b) $(2 - a)^2 f''(1) - (2 + a)^2 f''(-1) = 0$
(c) $f'(1) f'(-1) = (2 - a)^2$
(d) $f'(1) f'(-1) = -(2 + a)^2$

16. Which of the following is true?
(a) $f(x)$ is decreasing on $(-1,1)$ and has a local minimum at $x = 1$
(b) $f(x)$ is increasing on $(-1,1)$ and has a local maximum at $x = 1$
(c) $f(x)$ is increasing on $(-1,1)$ but has neither a local maximum nor a local minimum at $x = 1$
(d) $f(x)$ is decreasing on $(-1,1)$ but has neither a local maximum nor a local maximum at $x = 1$

17. Let $g(x) = \int_0^{e^x} \dfrac{f'(t)}{1+t^2}\,dt$, which of the following is true?
(a) $g'(x)$ is positive on $(-\infty, 0)$ and negative on $(0, \infty)$
(b) $g'(x)$ is negative on $(-\infty, 0)$ and positive on $(0, \infty)$
(c) $g'(x)$ changes sign on both $(-\infty, 0)$ and $(0, \infty)$
(d) $g'(x)$ does not change sign on $(-\infty, \infty)$

G: Let $[a, b]$ be an interval that does not contain 0 in its interior and let f be a non-negative continuous function on $[a, b]$ (say $a > 0$). If the region bounded by the graph of f and the x-axis is revolved around y-axis, then a solid is generated. The volume of this solid is given $V = 2\pi \int_a^b x f(x)\,dx$. On the basis of above information answer the following questions:

18. The region bounded by $f(x) = 4x - x^2$ and the x-axis between $x = 1$ and $x = 4$ is rotated about the y-axis. The volume of the solid generated is
(a) $\dfrac{81}{2}\pi$ (b) $\dfrac{41}{2}\pi$
(c) $\dfrac{83}{2}\pi$ (d) None of these

19. Let $f(x) = \begin{cases} \sqrt{3}x; & 0 \le x < 1 \\ \sqrt{4 - x^2}; & 1 \le x \le 2 \end{cases}$ and A be the region between the graph of f and x-axis. On revolving A around y-axis, the volume of the solid, thus obtained is
(a) $\dfrac{4\sqrt{3}}{3}\pi$ (b) $\dfrac{8\sqrt{3}}{3}\pi$
(c) $\dfrac{2\sqrt{3}}{3}\pi$ (d) None of these

20. An ellipse whose major axis is $2a$ and the minor axis is $2b$ revolves about the minor axis. The volume of the solid is equal to
(a) $\dfrac{4}{3}\pi ab^2$ (b) $\dfrac{2}{3}\pi ab^2$
(c) $\dfrac{4}{3}\pi a^2 b$ (d) None of these

SECTION–VII

MATRIX MATCHING-TYPE QUESTIONS

1. **Column I**

(i) $\int_{-1}^{3} (|x-2| + [x])\,dx =$ ($[x]$ stands for greatest integer less than or equal to x)

(ii) $\int_{-1}^{1} \dfrac{\sin^2 x}{\left[\dfrac{x}{\sqrt{2}}\right] + \dfrac{1}{2}}\,dx =$ ($[x]$ stands for greatest integer less than or equal to x)

(iii) If $\int_1^b (b - 4x)\,dx \ge 6 - 5b, b > 1$, then $b =$

(iv) If $I_1 = \int_0^{3\pi} f(\cos^2 x)dx$ and $I_2 = \int_0^{\pi} f(\cos^2 x)dx$, then $I_1 = kI_2$, where $k =$

Column II

(a) 2
(b) 3
(c) 7
(d) 0

2. **Column I**

(i) $\int_0^{\pi/2} (\sin x)^{\cos x}\left(\cos x \cot x - \log(\sin x)^{\sin x}\right)dx =$

(ii) $\left|\int_0^1 (1-y^2)dy\right| + \left|\int_1^0 (y^2-1)dy\right| =$

(iii) $f(x) = \frac{1}{x^2}\int_4^x (4t^2 - 2f'(t))dt$, then $f'(4)$ is equal to

(iv) $\int_0^{\pi} (|\sin 4x| + |\cos 4x|)dx$ is equal to

Column II

(a) $\frac{4}{3}$
(b) $\frac{32}{9}$
(c) 1
(d) 4

3. If $F(x) = \int_0^x f(t)dt$, then

Column I

(i) $f(x) = \begin{cases} \cos\frac{\pi}{2}x; & 0 \le x < 1 \\ \sin \pi x; & x \ge 1 \end{cases}$

(ii) $f(x) = \begin{cases} \sqrt{3-x}; & 0 \le x \le 2 \\ (5x-9)^{1/3}; & x > 2 \end{cases}$

(iii) $f(x) = \begin{cases} x^4; & 0 \le x \le 1 \\ \cos 2\pi x; & x > 1 \end{cases}$

(iv) $f(x) = \begin{cases} \sin\frac{3\pi}{2}x; & 0 \le x < 1 \\ -\sqrt{3-2x}; & \frac{3}{2} \ge x > 1 \end{cases}$

Column II

(a) $F'(2) = 1$
(b) $F'(7.2) = 3$
(c) $F'\left(\frac{3}{2}\right) = -1$
(d) $F'\left(\frac{3}{2}\right) = 0$

4. **Column I**

(i) $\lim_{x\to 0} \frac{1}{x}\left(\int_y^a e^{\sin^3 t}dt - \int_{x+y}^a e^{\sin^3 t}dt\right)$ equals

(ii) $\lim_{x\to\infty} \frac{\left(\int_0^{x+y} e^{t^2}dt\right)^2}{\int_0^{x+y} e^{2t^2}dt}$ equals

(iii) $\lim_{x\to 0} \frac{\int_0^{x^2} \sin\sqrt{x}\, dx}{x^3}$ equals

(iv) $\lim_{x\to 0} \frac{\int_0^x \cos t^2\, dt}{x}$ equals

Column II

(a) 1
(b) $e^{\sin^3 y}$
(c) 0
(d) $\frac{2}{3}$

SECTION–VIII

INTEGER-TYPE QUESTIONS

1. If $\int_0^{\pi/2} \frac{dx}{\left(\sqrt{\cos x} + \sqrt{\sin x}\right)^4} = \lambda$, then evaluate λ^{-1}.

2. If $\int_0^{\pi/4} \frac{\ln(\cot x).(\sin 2x)^{2008}dx}{\left[(\sin x)^{2009} + (\cos x)^{2009}\right]^2} = \frac{(\lambda)^{\mu}\ln\lambda}{\nu^2}$, then evaluate $(\lambda + \mu + \nu)$

3. If $\int_{-1}^{1} x^2 d(\ell nx) = \frac{e^k - 1}{2e^\ell}$, then evaluate $(k + \ell)$

4. Evaluate $\lim_{n\to\infty} \frac{(m+1)}{n^{(m+1)}}(1^m + 2^m + 3^m + ... + n^m)$; $m > -1$

5. Evaluate $\lim_{n\to\infty} \sum_{r=1}^{n} \frac{12}{\sqrt{n^2 + 3rn}}$

6. Evaluate $\lim_{n\to\infty} \left[C_0^2 + C_1^2 + C_2^2 + ... + C_n^2\right]^{1/n}$; where $C_r = {}^nC_r$

7. For $x > 0$, $f(x) = \int_0^x \frac{1}{1+t^2} dt + \int_0^{1/x} \frac{1}{1+t^2} dt$ and $f(2) = 4$, then evaluate $f(2) + f(1/2)$

8. If $f(x)$ is an even differentiable function, then find the value of the integral $\int_{-2}^{2} (x^3 f(x) + xf''(x) + 2)\, dx$

9. If $f(x) = 4x^3 - x^2 - 2x + 1$ and $g(x) = \begin{cases} \min\{f(t) : 0 \le t \le x\} & ; 0 \le x \le 1 \\ 3 - x & : 1 < x \le 2 \end{cases}$, then find the value of $\int_0^2 \left\{ g\left(\frac{1}{4}\right) + g\left(\frac{3}{4}\right) + g\left(\frac{5}{4}\right) + \frac{1}{2} \right\} dx$.

10. Find the number of solutions of the equation $\frac{d}{dx} \int_{\cos x}^{\sin x} \frac{dt}{1-t^2} = 2\sqrt{2}$ in $[0, \pi]$.

11. If $f(\pi) = 2$ and $\int_0^{\pi} [f(x) + f''(x)] \sin x \, dx$ has the value equal to 5, then find $f(0)$.

12. The tangent to the graph of the function $y = f(x)$ at the point with abscissa $x = a$ forms with the x-axis an angle of $\pi/3$ and at the point with abscissa $x = b$ at an angle of $\pi/4$, then find the value of $\int_a^b f'(x).f''(x)\, dx$ [assume $f''(x)$ to be continuous].

13. Let $f(x)$ be continuous function in $\mathbb{R}$ such that $f(x) + f(y) = f(x + y)$. If $\int_0^3 f(x) dx = k$, then find $\int_{-3}^{3} f(x) dx$.

14. The true set of values of x for which $f(x) = \int_1^x (3y^2 - 12y - 36)\, dy$ is increasing is $(-\infty, a] \cup [b, \infty)$, then evaluate $a + b$.

15. Let $f(x) = \left\{ b^2 + (a-1)b - \frac{1}{4} \right\} x + \int_0^x (\sin^4 x + \cos^4 x)\, dx$.

If $f(x)$ be a non-decreasing function of x $\forall x \in \mathbb{R}$ and $\forall b \in \mathbb{R}$, then find the greatest permissible values of parameter a.

16. Find the value of $\frac{(\sqrt{2}+1)198}{\pi} \int_{\pi/4}^{3\pi/4} \frac{\phi}{1+\sin\phi} d\phi$

17. For any $t \in \mathbb{R}$ and f a continuous function, let $I_1 = \int_{\sin^2 t}^{1+\cos^2 t} xf(x(2-x))dx$ and $I_2 = \int_{\sin^2 t}^{1+\cos^2 t} f(x(2-x))dx$, then find $\frac{I_1}{I_2}$.

18. Find $\lim_{x\to 0} \frac{\int_{-x}^{x} f(t)\, dt}{\int_0^{2x} f(t+4)\, dt}$; where f is a continuous function and $f(x) > 0$ for all x satisfying $f(0) = 48 f(4)$.

19. If $I = 636 \int_0^{\pi/4} \left(\sqrt{\sin x} + \sqrt{\cos x}\right)^{-4} dx$, then find I.

20. If $I = \int_0^{\pi} \frac{x^2 \sin x}{(2x-\pi)(1+\cos^2 x)} dx$, then find the value of $\frac{4}{\pi^2} I + 198$

21. For $x > 0$, let $f(x) = \int_1^x \frac{\log t}{t+1} dt$. Find the value of $98(f(e) + f(1/e))$.

Answer Keys

SECTION–III

1. (b)	**2.** (a)	**3.** (b)	**4.** (c)	**5.** (b)	**6.** (a)	**7.** (b)	**8.** (b)	**9.** (c)	**10.** (d)
11. (b)	**12.** (c)	**13.** (a)	**14.** (b)	**15.** (a)	**16.** (c)	**17.** (c)	**18.** (a)	**19.** (b)	**20.** (c)
21. (d)	**22.** (c)	**23.** (a)	**24.** (c)	**25.** (b)	**26.** (a)	**27.** (b)	**28.** (b)	**29.** (a)	**30.** (a)
31. (a)	**32.** (d)	**33.** (c)	**34.** (a)	**35.** (d)	**36.** (a)	**37.** (b)	**38.** (b)	**39.** (c)	**40.** (a)
41. (d)	**42.** (a)	**43.** (a)	**44.** (a)	**45.** (a)	**46.** (b)	**47.** (c)	**48.** (b)	**49.** (d)	**50.** (a)
51. (a)	**52.** (d)	**53.** (a)	**54.** (b)	**55.** (a)	**56.** (b)	**57.** (a)	**58.** (c)	**59.** (b)	**60.** (b)

SECTION–IV

1. (a,d)	**2.** (a,b,c,d)	**3.** (a,b)	**4.** (a,b,c,d)	**5.** (a,b,c,d)	**6.** (a,b,c,d)
7. (a,b)	**8.** (a,c)	**9.** (a,b)	**10.** (a,b,c,d)	**11.** (a,c,d)	**12.** (a,d)
13. (a)	**14.** (b,c)	**15.** (a,d)	**16.** (a,b,c,d)	**17.** (a,b,c)	**18.** (a,b,c,d)
19. (a,b,c)	**20.** (a,c)	**21.** (a,b,c,d)			

SECTION–V

1. (d)	**2.** (a)	**3.** (a)	**4.** (a)	**5.** (d)	**6.** (c)	**7.** (a)	**8.** (d)	**9.** (a)	**10.** (a)
11. (d)	**12.** (d)	**13.** (d)	**14.** (a)	**15.** (c)					

SECTION–VI

1. (b)	**2.** (b), (d)	**3.** (c)	**4.** (a)	**5.** (b)	**6.** (b)	**7.** (c)	**8.** (b)	**9.** (c)	**10.** (a)
11. (a)	**12.** (b)	**13.** (a)	**14.** (b)	**15.** (a)	**16.** (a)	**17.** (b)	**18.** (a)	**19.** (b)	**20.** (c)

SECTION–VII

1. (i) → (c) (ii) → (d) (iii) → (a) (iv) → (b)
2. (i) → (c) (ii) → (a) (iii) → (b) (iv) → (d)
3. (i) → (c) (ii) → (a, b) (iii) → (a, c) (iv) → (d)
4. (i) → (b) (ii) → (c) (iii) → (d) (iv) → (a)

SECTION–VIII

1. 3	**2.** 4019	**3.** 6	**4.** 1	**5.** 8	**6.** 4	**7.** 8	**8.** 8	**9.** 6	**10.** 2
11. 3	**12.** –1	**13.** 0	**14.** 4	**15.** 2	**16.** 198	**17.** 1	**18.** 48	**19.** 106	
20. 199	**21.** 98								

HINTS AND SOLUTIONS

TEXTUAL EXERCISE–I: (SUBJECTIVE)

1. $\int_0^8 f(x)dx$ = area boundary by curve of two and x-axis

= area of Trapezium $OABF$ + area of $FBKCG$ + area of trapezium $GCDE$

$$=\left[\frac{1}{2}(2+3)\times 2\right]+\left[(2\times 2)+\frac{1}{2}\pi(1)^2\right]+\left[\frac{1}{2}(1+3)\times 2\right]$$

$$=5+4+\frac{\pi}{2}+4=\left(13+\frac{\pi}{2}\right)\text{sq. unit}$$

2. $\int_0^{12} f(x)dx$ = area boundary by the curve of $f(x)$ and x-axis

= area of ΔOAM + 2 ar.($MABCGN$) + 2 ar.($KFHN$)

$$=\left[\frac{1}{2}(2)\times 2\right]+2\left[\left(\frac{\pi(1)^2}{2}\right)+1\times 2+1\times 3+1\times 4+\frac{1}{2}(1)(2)\right]$$

$$+2\left[2\times 2+\frac{1}{2}(2)(4)\right]+2+2\left[\frac{\pi}{2}+2+3+4+1\right]+2[4+4]$$

$= 2 + \pi + 36 = (38 + \pi)$ sq. units

3. $\int_0^{13}|f(x)|dx$ = area of trapezium $OLMA$ + area of $\frac{1}{4}$th of circle of radius $\sqrt{2}$ – area of right angled ΔACB + area of trapezium $BNPQ$ + area of trapezium $QRST$

$$=\left[\frac{1}{2}(1+2)\times 1\right]+\left[\frac{1}{4}\pi\left(\sqrt{2}\right)^2\right]-\left[\frac{1}{2}\times\sqrt{2}\times\sqrt{2}\right]$$

$$+\left[\frac{1}{2}(3+1)\times 1\right]+\left[\frac{1}{2}(6+3)\times 2\right]$$

$$=\frac{3}{2}+\frac{\pi}{2}-1+2+9=\frac{(23+\pi)}{2}\text{sq. units}$$

4. $\int_0^6|f(x)|dx+\int_6^{13}|g(x)|dx$ = area of ΔOAH + area of rectangle $AHML$ $-\left(\frac{1}{4}\text{ area of circle of radius 2}\right)$ + area of ΔMBI + area of ΔIJK + area of trapezium $KDEP$ + area of rectangle $TPQF$ $-\left(\frac{1}{4}\text{area of circle of radius 2}\right)$ + area of rectangle $QFRG$ $-\left(\frac{1}{4}\text{area of circle of radius 3}\right)$

$$=\frac{1}{2}(2)(3)+2(3)-\frac{1}{4}\pi(2)^2+2\times\frac{1}{2}(1)(1)+\frac{1}{2}(3+1)$$

$$\times(2)+(2)(3)-\frac{1}{4}\pi(2)^2+(3)(3)-\frac{1}{4}\pi(3)^2$$

$$=3+6-\pi+1+4+6-\pi+9-\frac{9\pi}{4}=\left(29-\frac{17\pi}{4}\right)\text{sq. units}$$

5. (a) $\int_{-1}^{1}\{x\}dx$ = area represented by shaded region

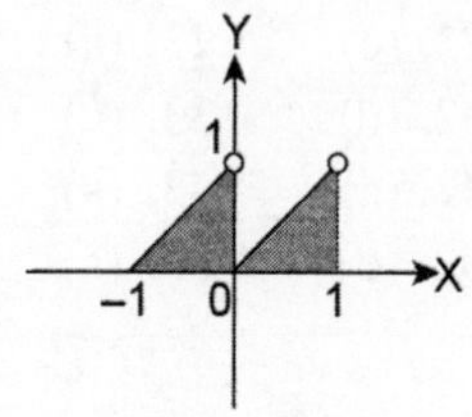

$$=2\left[\frac{1}{2}(1)(1)\right]=1\text{sq. units.}$$

(b) $\int_0^2[x-1]dx$ = area represented by shaded region

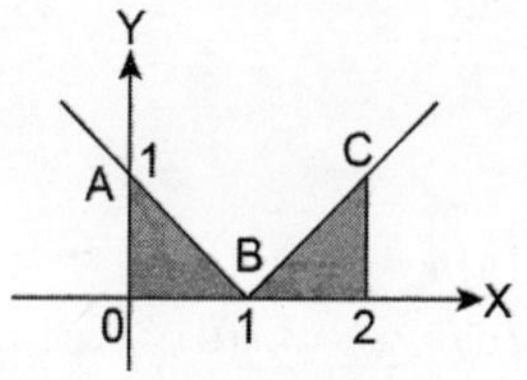

$$=2\left[\frac{1}{2}(1)(1)\right]=1\text{ sq. units.}$$

(c) $\int_0^a\sqrt{a^2-x^2}dx$ = Area represented by shaded region.

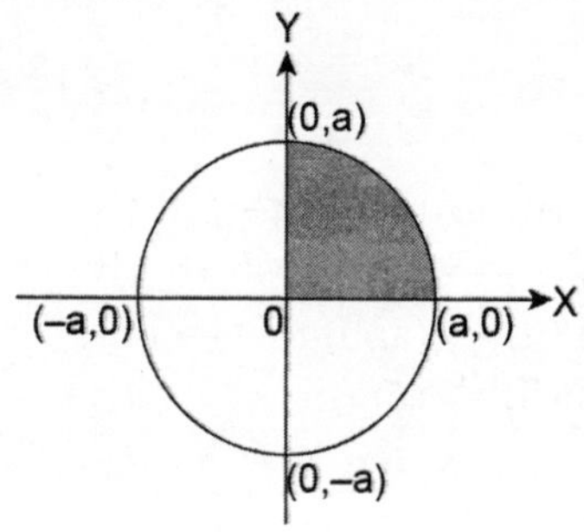

$$=\frac{1}{4}\pi(a)^2\text{ sq. units}$$

6. $\int_{-2}^{-2}\left(1+\sqrt{4-x^n}\right)dx$ = area of region represented by shaded portion.

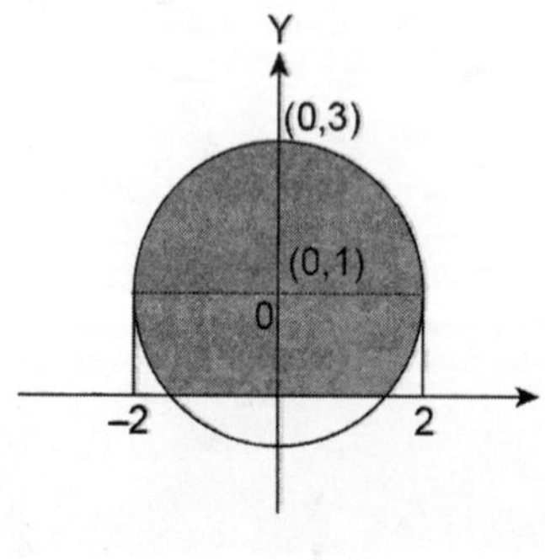

$$=4+\frac{1}{2}\pi(2)^2=(4+2\pi)\text{ sq. units.}$$

7. $\int_0^4 \sqrt{4-(x-2)^2}\,dx + \int_4^6 ||x-5|-1|\,dx$

The value of above expression is equal to the sum of areas represented by shaded region.

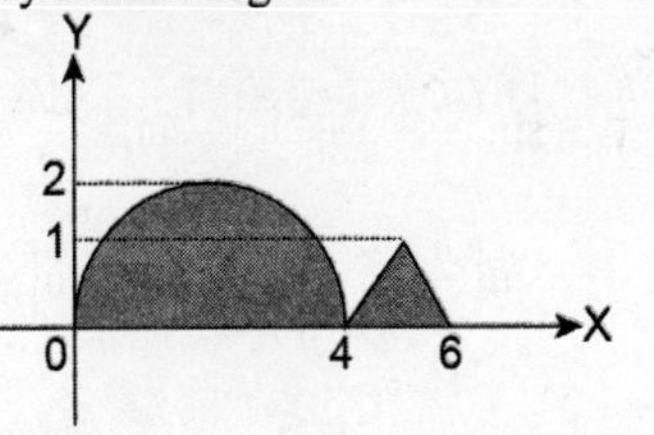

$$=\frac{1}{2}\pi(2)^2+\frac{1}{2}(2)(1) = (2\pi+1)\text{sq.units.}$$

8. **(a)** $\int_0^3 (x^2+1)dx$

$$=\lim_{\substack{h\to 0\\ n\to\infty}} h\left[f(0)+f(h)+f(2h)+...+f((n-1)h)\right]$$

where $f(x) = x^2+1$ and $h=\frac{3-0}{n}=\frac{3}{n}$ or $3=nh$

$$= \lim_{\substack{h\to 0\\ n\to\infty}} h\left[(0^2+1)+(h^2+1)+(2^2h^2+1)+(3^2h^2+1)+....+\left((n-1)^2h^2+1\right)\right]$$

$$= \lim_{\substack{h\to 0\\ n\to\infty}} h\left[h^2\left(1^2+2^2+3^2+....+(n-1)^2\right)+\underbrace{(1+1+1+....+1)}_{n-times}\right]$$

$$= \lim_{\substack{h\to 0\\ n\to\infty}} h\left[h^2.\frac{(n-1)(n)(2n-1)}{6}+n\right]$$

$$= \lim_{\substack{h\to 0\\ n\to\infty}} \left[\frac{(nh-h)(nh)(2nh-h)}{6}+nh\right]$$

$$= \lim_{\substack{h\to o\\ n\to\infty}} \left[\frac{(3-h)(3)(6-h)}{6}+3\right] = 12\text{sq.units}$$

(b) $\int_0^4 (2x^3+5)dx$

$$= \lim_{\substack{h\to o\\ n\to\infty}} h\left[f(0)+f(x)+f(2h)+....+f\left((n-1)h\right)\right]$$

where $h=\frac{4-0}{n} \Rightarrow nh=4$ and $f(x)=2x^3+5$

$$= \lim_{\substack{h\to 0\\ n\to\infty}} h\Big[\left[2(0)^3+5\right]+\left[2(1)^3h^3+5\right]+\left[2(2)^3h^3+5\right]+$$

$$\left[2(3)^3h^3+5\right]+....+\left[2(n-1)^3h^3+5\right]\Big]$$

$$= \lim_{\substack{h\to 0\\ n\to\infty}} h\Big[2h^3\left(1^3+2^3+3^3+....+(n-1)^3\right)+$$

$$(5+5+5+...+5)(n-times)\Big]$$

$$=\lim_{\substack{h\to 0\\ n\to\infty}} h\left[2\left[\frac{(n-2)(n)}{2}\right]^2h^3+5n\right]$$

$$= \lim_{\substack{h\to 0\\ n\to\infty}} \left[\frac{1}{2}[(nh-h)(nh)]^2+5nh\right]$$

$$= \lim_{\substack{h\to 0\\ n\to\infty}} \left[\frac{1}{2}\{(4-h)(4)\}^2+5(4)\right] = \frac{1}{2}(16)^2+20 = 148$$

(c) $\int_0^2 (2x+1)dx \;= \lim_{\substack{h\to 0\\ n\to\infty}} h\big[2\left(h+2h+3h+.....+(n-1)h\right)+$

$$(1+1+.....+1)(n-times)\big];$$

where $nh = 2-0 = 2$

$$= \lim_{\substack{h\to 0\\ n\to\infty}} h\left[2h\frac{(n-1)(n)}{2}+n\right] = \lim_{\substack{h\to 0\\ n\to\infty}}\left[(nh)(nh-h)+nh\right]$$

$$= \lim_{\substack{h\to 0\\ n\to\infty}}\left[2(2-h)+2\right] = 6$$

(d) $\int_a^b x^2dx$

$$= \lim_{\substack{h\to o\\ x\to\infty}} h\left[a^2+(a+h)^2+(a+2h)^2+......+\left(a+(n-1)h\right)^2\right];\ nh=b-a$$

$$= \lim_{\substack{h\to o\\ n\to\infty}} h\left[a^2(n)+h^2\left(1^2+2^2+3^2+.....+(n-1)^2\right)+2a(h)\left(1+2+3+......+(n-1)\right)\right]$$

$$= \lim_{\substack{h\to 0\\ n\to\infty}}\left[a^2(nh)+h^3\frac{(n-1)(n)(2n-1)}{6}+2ah^2\frac{(n-1)(n)}{2}\right]$$

$$= \lim_{\substack{h\to 0\\ n\to\infty}}\left[a^2(b-a)+\frac{(nh-h)(nh)[2nh-h]}{6}+a(nh-h)(nh)\right]$$

$$= \lim_{\substack{h\to 0\\ n\to\infty}}\left[a^2(b-a)+\frac{[(b-a)-h](b-a)[2(b-a)-h]}{6}+a((b-a)-h(b-a))\right]$$

$$= a^2(b-a)+\frac{2(b-a)^3}{6}+a(b-a)^2$$

$$= \frac{(b-a)}{3}\left[3a^2+(b-a)^2+3a(b-a)\right]$$

$$= \frac{(b-a)}{3}\left[a^2+b^2+ab\right] = \frac{1}{3}\left(a^3-b^3\right)$$

9. **(a)** $\int_1^2 e^{-x}dx \;= \lim_{\substack{h\to 0\\ x\to\infty}} h\left[e^{-1}+e^{-(1+h)}+^{-(1+h)}+......+e^{-(1+(n-1)h)}\right];$

where $h=\frac{2-1}{n}=\frac{1}{n}$

$$= \lim_{\substack{h\to 0\\ n\to\infty}} h\left[e^{-1}\left(1+e^{-h}+e^{-2h}+.....+e^{-(n-1)h}\right)\right]$$

$$= \lim_{\substack{h\to 0\\ n\to\infty}} h\left[e^{-1}\left\{\frac{1\left(1-(e^{-h})^n\right)}{1-e^{-h}}\right\}\right] \quad = \lim_{\substack{h\to 0\\ n\to\infty}} h\left[e^{-1}\left\{\frac{1-e^{-nh}}{1-e^{-h}}\right\}\right]$$

$$= \lim_{\substack{h\to 0\\ n\to\infty}}\left\{e^{-1}\left\{\frac{1-e^{-1}}{1-e^{-h}}\right\}h\right\} \quad = \lim_{h\to 0}\left(e^{-1}-e^{-2}\right).\left\{\frac{-h}{e^{-h}-1}\right\}$$

$$\left[\because\ \lim_{x\to 0}\frac{e^x-1}{x}=1\right]$$

$$= \left(e^{-1}-e^{-2}\right)$$

(b) $\int_3^5 e^{3x+4}\,dx$

$$=\lim_{\substack{h\to 0\\ n\to\infty}} h\Big[e^{3(3)+4}+e^{3(3+h)+4}+e^{3(3+2h)+4}+$$

$$e^{3(3+3h)+4}+.....+e^{3(3+(n-1)h)+4}\Big];nh=5-3=2$$

$$= \lim_{\substack{h\to 0\\ n\to\infty}} h\left[e^9.e^4.\left(1+e^{3h}+e^{6h}+e^{9h}+......+e^{3(n-1)h}\right)\right]$$

$$= \lim_{\substack{h\to 0\\ n\to\infty}} h\left[e^{13}.\left(\frac{1-(e^{3h})^n}{1-e^{3h}}\right)\right]$$

$$= \lim_{\substack{h\to 0\\ n\to\infty}} h\left[\frac{3h}{e^{3h}-1}\right]\left[\frac{-1}{3}\left(1-e^{3(2)}\right)\right].e^{13}$$

$$=(1)\left(\frac{e^6-1}{3}\right)e^{13}=\left(\frac{e^{19}-e^{13}}{3}\right)$$

(c) $\int_1^2 e^{-2x+4}\,dx$

$$= \lim_{\substack{h\to 0\\ n\to\infty}} h\left[e^{-2(1)+4}+e^{-2(1+h)+4}+e^{-2(1+2h)+4}+.....+e^{-2(1+(n-1)h)+4}\right];$$

$nh = 2-1 = 1$

$$= \lim_{\substack{h\to 0\\ n\to\infty}} h\left[e^{-2}.e^4\left(1+e^{-2h}+e^{-4h}+e^{-6h}+.....+e^{-2(n-1)h}\right)\right]$$

$$= \lim_{\substack{h\to 0\\ n\to\infty}} h\left[e^2\left\{\frac{1-(e^{-2h})^n}{1-e^{-2h}}\right\}\right]=\lim_{\substack{h\to 0\\ n\to\infty}}\left[\frac{he^2\left(1-e^{-2nh}\right)}{1-e^{-2h}}\right]$$

$$= \lim_{\substack{h\to 0\\ n\to\infty}}\left[\frac{he^2\left(1-e^{-2}\right)}{1-e^{-2h}}\right]=\lim_{h\to 0}\left[\frac{-2h}{e^{-2h}-1}\right]\left[\frac{1}{2}\left(e^2-1\right)\right]$$

$$=\frac{1}{2}(e^2-1)$$

(d) $\int_0^1\left(x+e^{2x}\right)dx$

$$= \lim_{\substack{h\to 0\\ n\to 0}} h\left[\left(0+e^{2(0)}\right)+\left(h+e^{2h}\right)+\left(2h+e^{2(2h)}\right)+\right.$$

$$\left.\left(3h+e^{2(3h)}\right)+......+\left((n-1)h+e^{2[(n-1)h]}\right)\right];$$

$nh = 1-0 = 1$

$$=\lim_{\substack{h\to 0\\ n\to\infty}} h\left[1+e^{2h}+e^{4h}+e^{6h}+....e^{2(n-1)h}+h\left(1+2+3+....+(n-1)\right)\right]$$

$$= \lim_{\substack{h\to 0\\ n\to\infty}} h\left[\frac{1-(e^{2h})^n}{1-e^{2h}}+\frac{h(n-1)(n)}{2}\right]$$

$$=\lim_{\substack{h\to 0\\ n\to\infty}}\left\{\left[\frac{2h}{e^{2h}-1}\right]\left(\frac{-1}{2}\right)\left(1-e^{2nh}\right)+\frac{(nh)(nh-h)}{2}\right\}$$

$$=\frac{-1}{2}\left(1-e^2\right)+\frac{1}{2}=\frac{1}{2}e^2$$

10. (a) $\int_a^b \cos x\,dx$

$$= \lim_{\substack{h\to 0\\ n\to\infty}} h\left[\cos a+\cos(a+h)+\cos(a+2h)+\right.$$

$$\left.\cos(a+3h)+......+\cos\left(a+(n-1)h\right)\right]$$

$$= \lim_{\substack{h\to 0\\ n\to\infty}}\frac{h}{2\sin\frac{h}{2}}\left[2\sin\frac{h}{2}\cos a+2\sin\frac{h}{2}\cos(a+h)+\right.$$

$$\left.2\sin\frac{h}{2}\cos(a+2h)+....+2\sin\frac{h}{2}\cos\left[a+(n-1)h\right]\right]$$

$$= \lim_{\substack{h\to o\\ n\to\infty}}\frac{\frac{h}{2}}{\sin\frac{h}{2}}\left\{\begin{array}{l}\sin\left(\frac{h}{2}+a\right)+\sin\left(\frac{h}{2}-a\right)\\ +\sin\left(\frac{h}{2}+a+\mathrm{h}\right)+\sin\left(-\frac{h}{2}-a\right)\\ +\sin\left(\frac{h}{2}+a+2\mathrm{h}\right)+\sin\left(-\frac{3h}{2}-a\right)+....\\ +\sin\left(\frac{h}{2}+a+(n-1)\mathrm{h}\right)+\sin\left(-\frac{h}{2}-a-(n-1)h\right)\end{array}\right\}$$

$$= \lim_{\substack{h\to o\\ n\to\infty}}\frac{\frac{h}{2}}{\sin\frac{h}{2}}\left\{\sin\left(\frac{h}{2}-a\right)++\sin\left(\frac{h}{2}+a+(n-1)\mathrm{h}\right)\right\}$$

$$=\left(\sin b-\sin a\right)$$

(b) $\int_a^b \sin^2 x\,dx = \int_a^b\frac{(1-\cos 2x)}{2}dx$

$$= \lim_{\substack{h\to 0\\ n\to\infty}} h\left\{\left(\frac{1-\cos 2a}{2}\right)+\left(\frac{1-\cos 2(a+h)}{2}\right)+\right.$$

$$\left.\left(\frac{1-\cos 2(a+2h)}{2}\right)+....+\left(\frac{1-\cos 2(a+(n-1)h)}{2}\right)\right\}$$

$$=\lim_{\substack{h\to 0\\ n\to\infty}} h\left\{\frac{n}{2}-\frac{1}{2}\left[\cos 2a+\cos(2a+2h)+\right.\right.$$

$$\left.\left.\cos(2a+4h)+....+\cos\left(2a+2(n-1)h\right)\right]\right\}$$

$$= \lim_{\substack{h\to 0\\ n\to\infty}} h\left\{\frac{n}{2}-\frac{1}{4\sin h}\left[\begin{array}{l}2\sin h\cos 2a+2\sin h\cos(2a+2h)+\\ 2\sin h\cos(2a+4h)+...+\\ 2\sin h\cos(2a+2(n-1)h\end{array}\right]\right\}$$

$$= \lim_{\substack{h\to 0\\ n\to\infty}}\left\{\frac{nh}{2}-\frac{h}{4\sin h}\left[\sin(h-2a)+\sin\left(h+2a+2(n-1)h\right)\right]\right\}$$

$$= \lim_{\substack{h\to 0\\ n\to\infty}}\left\{\frac{nh}{2}-\frac{h}{4\sin h}\left[\sin(h-2a)+\sin\left(2a+2nh-h\right)\right]\right\}$$

$$=\frac{(b-a)}{2}-\frac{1}{4}\left[\sin(-2a)+\sin\left(2a+2b-2a\right)\right]$$

$$=\frac{(b-a)}{2}-\frac{1}{4}[\sin(2b)-\sin(2a)]$$

$$=\frac{(b-a)}{2}-\frac{1}{2}\cos(b+a)\sin(b-a)$$

(c) $\int_a^b \sin^3 x\,dx=\int_a^b\left(\frac{3\sin x-\sin 3x}{4}\right)dx$

$$= \lim_{\substack{h\to 0\\ n\to\infty}} h\left\{\frac{3}{4}\left[\sin a+\sin(a+h)+\sin(a+2h)+....+\sin(a+n-1h)\right]\right\}$$

$$-\frac{1}{4}\left\{\sin 3a+\sin 3(a+h)+\sin 3(a+2h)+....+\sin 3(a+(n-1)h)\right\}$$

$$= \lim_{\substack{h\to 0\\ n\to\infty}} h\left[\frac{3}{8}\sin\frac{h}{2}\left\{\begin{array}{l}2\sin\frac{h}{2}\sin a+2\sin\frac{h}{2}\sin(a+h)+\\ 2\sin\frac{h}{2}\sin(a+2h)+...+2\sin\frac{h}{2}\sin(a+n-1)h\end{array}\right]\right]$$

$$-\frac{1}{8\sin\frac{3h}{2}}\left\{\begin{array}{l}2\sin\frac{3h}{2}\sin 3a+2\sin\frac{3h}{2}\sin(3a+3h)+\\ 2\sin\frac{3h}{2}(3a+6h)+.....+2\sin\frac{3h}{2}\sin(3a+3(n-1)h)\end{array}\right\}$$

$$=\lim_{\substack{h\to 0\\ n\to\infty}}\left[\frac{3h}{8\sin^{h/2}}\left\{\cos\left(\frac{h}{2}-a\right)-\cos\left(\frac{h}{2}+a\right)\right.\right.$$

$$+\cos\left(-a-\frac{h}{2}\right)-\cos\left(\frac{3h}{2}+a\right)$$

$$\left.\left.+\cos\left(-a-nh+\frac{3h}{2}\right)-\cos\left(a+nh-\frac{h}{2}\right)\right\}\right]$$

$$-\frac{h}{8\sin\frac{3h}{2}}\left\{\begin{array}{l}\cos\left(\frac{3h}{2}-3a\right)-\cos\left(\frac{3h}{2}+3a\right)+\\ \cos\left(-3a-\frac{3h}{2}\right)-\cos\left(3a+\frac{ah}{2}\right)\end{array}\right.$$

$$\left.\left.+....+\cos\left(\frac{3h}{2}-3a-3nh+3h\right)-\cos\left(\frac{3h}{2}+3a+3nh-3h\right)\right\}\right]$$

$$=\frac{3}{4}\{\cos(-a)-\cos(a+(b-a))\}-\frac{1}{12}$$

$$\{\cos(-3a)-\cos(3a+3b-3a)\}$$

$$=\frac{3}{4}\{\cos a-\cos b\}-\frac{1}{12}\{\cos 3a-\cos 3b\}$$

$$=\frac{-3}{4}\{\cos b-\cos a\}+\frac{1}{12}\{\cos 3b-\cos 3a\}$$

11. $\int_a^b \sqrt{x}\,dx$

Let us make the partition of $[a, b]$ as $\{a, ar^2, ar^4, ar^6,...,ar^{2n-2}, ar^{2n}\}$ with length of subinterval $\Delta_i = ar^{2i} - ar^{2(i-1)}$, $1 \le i \le n$, $i \in \mathbb{N}$

then, $b = ar^{2n} \Rightarrow r = \left(\frac{b}{a}\right)^{1/2n} \to 1$ as $n \to \infty$ and $\Delta_i = ar^{2(i-1)}$

$(r^2 - 1) \to 0$ as $r \to 1$

$\therefore$ Length of each subinterval approach to zero when $n \to \infty$

$$\therefore\ \int_a^b \sqrt{x}\,dx=\lim_{\substack{n\to\infty\\ r\to 1}}\left[\sum_{i=1}^{n} f\left(ar^{2(i-1)}\right).\Delta_i\right]$$

$$=\lim_{\substack{n\to\infty\\ r\to 1}}\left[\sum_{i=1}^{n}\sqrt{ar^{2(i-1)}}.\ ar^{2(i-1)}.(r^2-1)\right]$$

$$=\lim_{\substack{n\to\infty\\ r\to 1}}\left[a^{3/2}\sum_{i=1}^{n} r^{3(i-1)}(r^2-1)\right]$$

$$=\lim_{\substack{n\to\infty\\ r\to 1}} a^{3/2}\sum_{i=1}^{n}\left\{r^{3i-1}-r^{3(i-1)}\right\}$$

$$=\lim_{\substack{n\to\infty\\ r\to 1}} a^{3/2}\left[\begin{array}{l}\left(r^2+r^5+r^8+.....+r^{3n-1}\right)-\\ \left(1+r^3+r^6+....+r^{3(n-1)}\right)\end{array}\right]$$

$$=\lim_{\substack{n\to\infty\\ r\to 1}} a^{3/2}\left[\frac{r^2(r^{3n}-1)}{r^3-1}-\frac{1(r^{3n}-1)}{r^3-1}\right]$$

$$=\lim_{\substack{n\to\infty\\ r\to 1}} a^{3/2}\left[\frac{(r^2-1)(r^{3n})}{r^3-1}-\frac{(r^2-1)}{r^3-1}\right]$$

$$=\lim_{\substack{n\to\infty\\ r\to 1}} a^{3/2}\left[\frac{(r+1)r^{3n}}{(r^2+r+1)}-\frac{(r+1)}{r^2+r+1}\right]$$

$$=\lim_{\substack{n\to\infty\\ r\to 1}} a^{3/2}\left(\frac{r+1}{r^2+r+1}\right)\left[r^{3n}-1\right]$$

$$=\lim_{\substack{r\to 1\\ n\to\infty}} a^{3/2}\frac{(r+1)}{r^2+r+1}\left[\left(\frac{b}{a}\right)^{\frac{3n}{2n}}-1\right] = \frac{2a^{3/2}}{3}\left(\frac{b^{3/2}-a^{3/2}}{a^{3/2}}\right)$$

$$=\frac{2}{3}\left(b^{3/2}-a^{3/2}\right)$$

12. Equation of AB is $\frac{x}{a}+\frac{y}{h}=1 \Rightarrow y=h\left(1-\frac{x}{b}\right)$

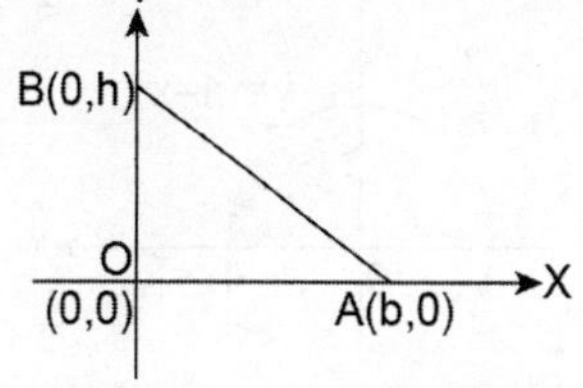

area of $\Delta OAB=\int_0^b f(x)\,dx$; where $f(x)=h\left(1-\frac{x}{b}\right)$

$$=\lim_{\substack{t\to 0\\ n\to\infty}} t\left[\begin{array}{l}h\left(1-\frac{0}{b}\right)+h\left(1-\frac{t}{b}\right)+h\left(1-\frac{2t}{b}\right)+\\ h\left(1-\frac{3t}{b}\right)+......+h\left(1-\frac{(n-1)t}{b}\right)\end{array}\right]$$

$$=\lim_{\substack{t\to 0\\ n\to\infty}}\left[n^{th}-\frac{ht^2}{b}(1+2+3)+....+(n-1)\right];nt=b$$

$$=\lim_{\substack{t\to o\\ n\to\infty}}\left[h(b)-\frac{ht^2}{b}\frac{(n-1)(n)}{2}\right]$$

$$=\lim_{\substack{t\to o\\ n\to\infty}}\left[h(b)-\frac{h}{2b}(nt)(nt-t)\right]=\left[h(b)-\frac{h}{2b}(b-0)(b)\right]$$

$$=h\left[b-\frac{b}{2}\right]=\frac{1}{2}bh \text{ sq.units.}$$

13. Required area $=\int_1^2 2x^2\,dx, h=\frac{2-1}{n}=\frac{1}{n}$

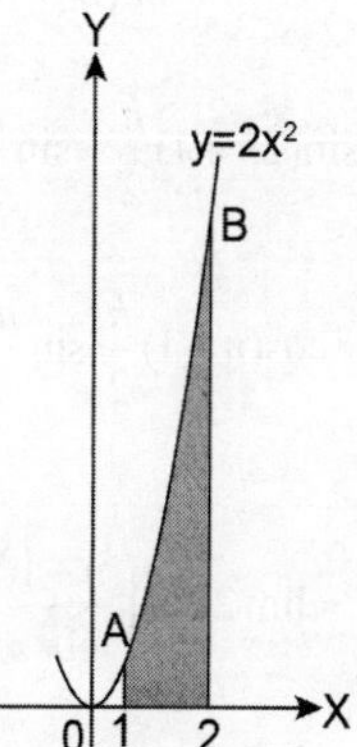

$$= \lim_{\substack{h\to o\\ n\to\infty}} h\left[2(1)^2 + 2(1+h)^2 + 2(1+2h)^2 + ... + 2(1+(n-1)h)^2\right]$$

$$= \lim_{\substack{h\to o\\ n\to\infty}} h\left[\begin{matrix}2(1^2+1^2+...+1^2)+2h^2\left(1^2+2^2+....(n-1)^2\right)+\\ 4h(1+2+3+....+(n-1))\end{matrix}\right]$$

$$= \lim_{\substack{h\to o\\ n\to\infty}} h\left[2n + 2h^2\frac{(n-1)(n+1)(2n-1)}{6} + 4h\frac{(n-1)(n)}{2}\right]$$

$$= \lim_{\substack{h\to 0\\ n\to\infty}} \left[2nh + \frac{1}{3}(nh-h)(nh+h)(2nh-h) + 2(nh-h)(nh)\right]$$

$$= 2(1) + \frac{1}{3}(1)(1)(2) + 2 = 4 + \frac{2}{3} = \frac{14}{3}$$

14. Required area $= \int_{-1}^{1}\sqrt{1-x^2}\,dx$

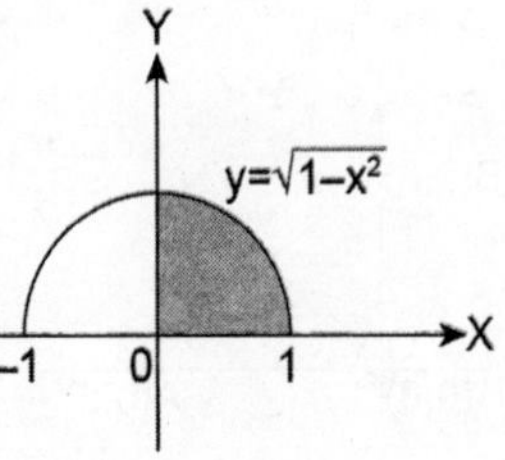

$= 2\int_0^1 \sqrt{1-x^2}\,dx$ as function is even; $h = 1/n$ breaking the interval [0, 1] at $\sin h$, $\sin 2h$, $\sin 3h$, ……, $\sin(n)h$ where $h = \frac{\pi}{2n}$

Required area $= 2\int_0^1 \sqrt{1-x^2}\,dx$

$$= 2\lim_{\substack{h\to 0\\ n\to\infty}} h\left(\begin{matrix}\sqrt{1-\sin^2 h}+\sqrt{1-\sin^2 2h}+\\ \sqrt{1-\sin^2 3h}+....+\sqrt{1-\sin^2 nh}\end{matrix}\right)$$

$$= 2\lim_{\substack{h\to 0\\ n\to\infty}} h\left(\cos h + \cos 2h + \cos 3h + ... + \cos nh\right)$$

$$= \lim_{\substack{h\to 0\\ n\to\infty}} \frac{h}{\sin\frac{h}{2}}\left(\begin{matrix}2\sin\frac{h}{2}\cos h + 2\sin\frac{h}{2}\cos 2h+\\ 2\sin\frac{h}{2}\cos 3h+....+2\sin\frac{h}{2}\cos nh\end{matrix}\right)$$

$$= \lim_{\substack{h\to 0\\ n\to\infty}} \frac{h}{\frac{h}{2}}\left(\begin{matrix}\sin\frac{3h}{2}-\sin\frac{h}{2}+\sin\frac{5h}{2}-\sin\frac{3h}{2}+\sin\frac{7h}{2}-\\ \sin\frac{5h}{2}+...+\sin(2n+1)\frac{h}{2}-\sin(2n-1)\frac{h}{2}\end{matrix}\right)$$

$$= \lim_{\substack{h\to 0\\ n\to\infty}} \frac{h}{\sin\frac{h}{2}}\left(\sin(2n+1)\frac{h}{2} - \sin\frac{h}{2}\right)$$

$$= \lim_{\substack{h\to 0\\ n\to\infty}} \frac{h}{\sin\frac{h}{2}}\left(2\cos(n+1)\frac{h}{2}.\sin\frac{nh}{2}\right)$$

$$= 4\lim_{h\to 0}\frac{\frac{h}{2}}{\sin\frac{h}{2}} = \lim_{h\to\infty} 2\cos\left(\frac{n+1}{4n}\right)\pi.\sin\frac{\pi}{4}$$

$$= 4\times 2\cos\frac{\pi}{4}.\sin\frac{\pi}{4} = 4$$

15. Displacement $= \int_1^2 v(t)dt$, $nh = 2-1 = 1$; $n\to\infty$, $h\to 0$

$$= \int_1^2 t^3\,dt = \lim_{\substack{h\to o\\ n\to\infty}} h\left[(1)^3 + (1+h)^3 + (1+2h)^3 + ... + (1+(n-1)h)^3\right]$$

$$= \lim_{\substack{h\to 0\\ n\to\infty}} h\left[\begin{matrix}\underbrace{(1^3+1^3+...1^3)}_{n-times}+h^3\left(1^3+2^3+3^3+...+(n-1)^3\right)+\\ 3(1)^2h(1+2+3+...+(n-1)+\\ 3(1)h^2(1^2+2^2+3^2+...+(n-1)^2)\end{matrix}\right]$$

$$= \lim_{\substack{h\to o\\ n\to\infty}} h\left[\begin{matrix}n + h^3\left[\frac{(n-1)(n)}{2}\right]^2 + 3h\frac{(n-1)(n)}{2}+\\ 3h^2\frac{(n-1)(n)(2n-1)}{6}\end{matrix}\right]$$

$$= 1 + \left[\frac{(1-0)(1)}{2}\right]^2 + \frac{3}{2}(1-0)(1) + \frac{1}{2}(1-0)(1)(2(1)-0)$$

$$= 1 + \frac{1}{4} + \frac{3}{2} + 1 = \frac{15}{4} \text{ units.}$$

16. $f(x) = \begin{cases} 2; & -1 \le x \le 1 \\ 3-x; & 1<x<4 \\ 2x-9; & 4\le x\le 5\end{cases}$

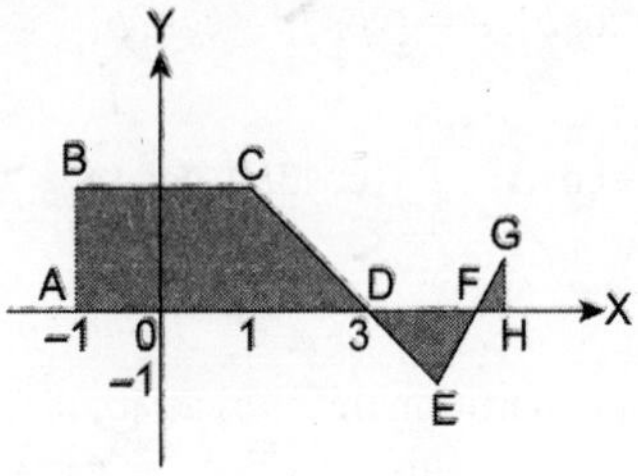

$$\int_{-1}^{5} f(x)dx = \text{area } ABCD - \text{area } DEF + \text{area } FGH$$

$$= \frac{1}{2}(2+4)\times 2 - \frac{1}{2}(1.5)\times(1) + \frac{1}{2}\left(\frac{1}{2}\right)\times 1$$

$$= 6 - \frac{3}{4} + \frac{1}{4} = 6 - \frac{1}{2} = \frac{11}{2}$$

TEXTUAL EXERCISE-1: (OBJECTIVE)

1. **(c), (d)** ∵ $\int_a^b f(x)dx$ represents the Algebraic sum of area boundary by function $f(x)$, x-axis and ordinates $x = a$, $x = b$. Also if $f(x) \ge 0$, then it represents the area bounded by curve $y = f(x)$, x-axis and the ordinates $x = a$ and $x = b$.

2. **(b)** $\int_0^5 f(x)dx$ = Area under the curve $y = f(x)$, bounded by x-axis and ordinates $x = 0$ and $x = 5$.

$$= (1)(2) + (2)(2) - \frac{1}{2}\pi(1)^2 + \frac{1}{2}(2)(2) = \left(8 - \frac{\pi}{2}\right)$$

3. **(c)** $\int_{-4}^{7} f(x)dx = \frac{1}{2}(4+2)(2) + \frac{1}{2}(2+3)(2)$

$$+\frac{1}{2}(3+2)(2) + (1)(2) + (2)^2 - \frac{1}{4}\pi(2)^2$$

$$= 6 + 5 + 5 + 2 + 4 - \pi = 22 - \pi$$

4. (a) $\int_0^4 f(x)dx + \int_4^8 f(x)dx = \left[\frac{1}{4}\left(\pi(2)^2\right) + \frac{1}{2}(2+4)\times 2\right]$

$+\left[(2)^2 - \frac{1}{4}\pi(2)^2\right] + \left[(2)^2\right] = 14$

5. (b) $\int_0^2 f(x)dx + \int_2^4 f(x)dx$

$+\int_4^6 f(x)dx + \int_6^8 f(x)dx + \int_8^{10} f(x)dx$

$= 2\left[\int_0^2 f(x)dx + \int_2^4 f(x)dx\right] + \int_8^{10} f(x)dx$

$= 2\left[\frac{1}{4}\pi(2)^2 + (2)^2 - \frac{1}{4}\pi(2)^2\right] + \left[\frac{1}{4}\pi(2)^2\right] = 8 + \pi$

6. (a), (b) $\int_a^b f(x)dx$ can usages to

$\lim_{\substack{h\to 0\\ n\to\infty}} h\left[f(a) + f(a+h) + f(a+2h) + ... + f\left(a + \overline{n-1}\,h\right)\right];$

$h = \frac{b-a}{n} = \lim_{\substack{h\to 0\\ n\to\infty}} \sum_{r=1}^{n} h.f\left(a + \overline{(r-1)}\,h\right)$ or

$= \lim_{\substack{h\to 0\\ n\to\infty}} h\left[f(a+h) + f(a+2h) + ... + f(a+nh)\right]$

$= \lim_{\substack{h\to 0\\ n\to\infty}} \sum_{r=1}^{n} hf(a+rh); h = \frac{b-a}{n}$

7. (b), (c) Here $f(x)$ is non-decreasing and non-constant function.

$\Rightarrow \lim_{\substack{h\to 0\\ n\to 0}} \sum_{r=1}^{n} hf\left(a + \overline{r-1}\,h\right) < \int_a^b f(x)dx < \lim_{\substack{h\to 0\\ n\to 0}} \sum_{r=1}^{n} h\,f(a+rh)$

8. (c) Displacement = velocity × time = Area under the curve.
= (Area under circular arcs OA) + (Area under line segment AB) + (Area under circular arc BC)

$= (2)^2 - \frac{1}{4}\pi(2)^2 + (2)^2 + (2)^2 + \frac{1}{4}\pi(2)^2 = 12 + \pi$

9. (b) Required Area $= \frac{1}{2}(1)(2) + \frac{1}{2}(2)(2)$

$+\frac{1}{2}(1)(2) + (2)^2 + \left[(2)^2 - \frac{1}{4}\pi(2)^2\right]$

$+\left[(2)^2 - \frac{1}{4}\pi(2)^2\right] + \frac{1}{2}(2)(2)$

$= 1 + 2 + 1 + 4 + 2\,(4 - \pi) + 2 = 18 - 2\pi$

10. (c) Given $\sum_{r=1}^{n}\left(\frac{2}{n}\right).f\left((r).\frac{2}{n}\right) = \frac{8}{n^3}\sum_{r=1}^{n} r^2$

Put $\frac{2r}{n} = x$ and $\frac{2}{n} = dx$

when n → ∞, we get

$\int_0^2 f(x)dx = \lim_{n\to\infty} \frac{8}{n^3} \times \left(\frac{n(n+1)(2n+1)}{6}\right)$

$\Rightarrow \int_0^2 f(x)dx = 8\lim_{n\to\infty}\left(1.\frac{\left(1+\frac{1}{n}\right)\left(2+\frac{1}{n}\right)}{6}\right) = \frac{8(1)(2)}{6} = \frac{8}{3}$

TEXTUAL EXERCISE–2: (SUBJECTIVE)

1. (a) $\int_0^{\frac{\pi}{4}} \cos^2 x\, dx = \int_0^{\frac{\pi}{4}} \left(\frac{1+\cos 2x}{2}\right) dx$

$= \left[\frac{1}{2}x + \frac{1}{4}\sin 2x\right]_0^{\frac{\pi}{4}} = \frac{\pi}{8} + \frac{1}{4} = \left(\frac{\pi+2}{8}\right)$

(b) $\int_0^{\frac{\pi}{2}} \frac{dx}{1+\cos x} = \int_0^{\frac{\pi}{2}} \frac{dx}{2\cos^2\frac{x}{2}}$

$= \frac{1}{2}\int_0^{\frac{\pi}{2}} \sec^2\frac{x}{2}dx = \frac{1}{2}\left[\frac{\tan\frac{x}{2}}{\frac{1}{2}}\right]_0^{\frac{\pi}{2}} = 1$

(c) $\int_0^{\frac{\pi}{2}} \sqrt{1+\cos x}\, dx = \int_0^{\frac{\pi}{2}} \sqrt{2}\left|\cos\frac{x}{2}\right| dx$

$= \sqrt{2}\int_0^{\frac{\pi}{2}} \cos\frac{x}{2}dx = \sqrt{2}\left[\frac{\sin\frac{x}{2}}{\frac{1}{2}}\right]_0^{\frac{\pi}{2}} = 2\sqrt{2}\left[\frac{1}{\sqrt{2}} - 0\right] = 2$

(d) $\int_0^{\frac{\pi}{2}} \frac{\cos x\, dx}{1+\sin x} = \left[\ln|1+\sin x|\right]_0^{\frac{\pi}{2}} = \ln 2 - \ln 1$

$\left(\because \int \frac{f'(x)}{f(x)}dx = \ln|f(x)| + C\right)$

= ln 2

(e) $\int_0^3 \left(x^2 - 2x\right)dx = \left|\frac{x^3}{3} - x^2\right|_0^3 = (9-9) = 0$

2. $\int_0^1 \left(xe^x + \sin\frac{\pi x}{4}\right)dx = \left|xe^x\right|_0^1 - \int_0^1 1.e^x dx - \left|\frac{\cos\frac{\pi x}{4}}{\frac{\pi}{4}}\right|_0^1$

$= e - [e-1] - \frac{4}{\pi}\left(\frac{1}{\sqrt{2}} - 1\right) = 1 + \frac{4}{\pi} - \frac{2\sqrt{2}}{\pi}$

3. $\int_0^4 \left(4x^3 - 5x^2 + 6x + 9\right)dx = \left|4\frac{x^4}{4} - 5\frac{x^3}{3} + 6\frac{x^2}{2} + 9x\right|_0^4$

$= 256 - \frac{5}{3}(64) + 3(16) + 9(4) = 256 - \frac{320}{3} + 48 + 36$

$= \frac{1020 - 320}{3} = \frac{700}{3}$

4. $\int_0^4 \left(x + x^{\frac{3}{2}}\right)dx = \left[\frac{x^2}{2} + \frac{x^{\frac{5}{2}}}{\frac{5}{2}}\right]_0^4 = \left[\frac{x^2}{2} + \frac{2}{5}x^{\frac{5}{2}}\right]_0^4 = 8 + \frac{2}{5}(32)$

$= \frac{104}{5}$

5. $\int_0^1 \cos 2x\, dx = \left[\frac{\sin 2x}{2}\right]_0^1 = \frac{1}{2}[\sin 2 - 0] = \frac{\sin 2}{2}$

6. $\int_0^1 \frac{1}{1+x^2}dx = \left|\tan^{-1} x\right|_0^1 = \tan^{-1}1 - \tan^{-1}0 = \frac{\pi}{4} - 0 = \frac{\pi}{4}$

7. $\int_2^3 \frac{dx}{x^2-1} = \int_2^3 \frac{dx}{x^2-(1)^2} = \left(\frac{1}{2(1)}\ln\left|\frac{x-1}{x+1}\right|\right)_2^3$

$= \frac{1}{2}\left[\ln\left|\frac{2}{4}\right| - \ln\left|\frac{1}{3}\right|\right] = \frac{1}{2}\left(\ln\left(\frac{1}{2}\right) - \ln\left(\frac{1}{3}\right)\right) = \frac{1}{2}\ln\left(\frac{3}{2}\right)$

8. $\int_0^1 \frac{2x+3}{5x^2+1}dx = \frac{1}{5}\int_0^1 \frac{10x+15}{5x^2+1}dx$

$= \frac{1}{5}\int_0^1 \frac{10x}{5x^2+1}dx + 3\int_0^1 \frac{1}{5x^2+1}dx$

$= \frac{1}{5}\left[\ln\left|5x^2+1\right|\right]_0^1 + \frac{3}{\sqrt{5}}\left[\tan^{-1}\left(\frac{\sqrt{5}x}{1}\right)\right]_0^1$

$= \frac{1}{5}[\ln 6] + \frac{3}{\sqrt{5}}\left[\tan^{-1}\left(\sqrt{5}\right) - 0\right] = \frac{1}{5}\ln 6 + \frac{3}{\sqrt{5}}\tan^{-1}\left(\sqrt{5}\right)$

9. $\int_1^2 \frac{5x^2}{x^2+4x+3} = 5\int_1^2\left[\frac{(x^2+4x+3)-(4x+3)}{(x^2+4x+3)}\right]dx$

$= 5\int_1^2\left[1 - \frac{4x+3}{x^2+4x+3}\right]dx = 5[x]_1^2 - 5\times 2\int_1^2 \frac{\left(2x+\frac{3}{2}\right)dx}{x^2+4x+3}$

$= 5 - 10\int_1^2 \frac{2x+4-4+\frac{3}{2}}{x^2+4x+3}dx$

$= 5 - 10\left|\ln\left|x^2+4x+3\right|\right|_1^2 + \frac{50}{2}\int_1^2 \frac{dx}{x^2+4x+3}$

$= 5 - 10\left|\ln\left(\frac{15}{8}\right)\right| + 25\int_1^2 \frac{dx}{(x+2)^2-1}$

$= 5 - 10\ln\left(\frac{15}{8}\right) + 25\times\frac{1}{2(1)}\left|\ln\left|\frac{x+1}{x+3}\right|\right|_1^2$

$= 5 - 10\ln\left(\frac{15}{8}\right) + \frac{25}{2}\left[\ln\left(\frac{3}{5}\right) - \ln\left(\frac{2}{4}\right)\right]$

$= 5 - 10\ln\left(\frac{15}{8}\right) + \frac{25}{2}\left[\ln\left(\frac{3}{5}\times\frac{2}{1}\right)\right]$

$= 5 - 10\ln\left(\frac{15}{8}\right) + \frac{25}{2}\ln\left(\frac{6}{5}\right)$

10. $\int_0^1\left(xe^{2x} + \sin\frac{\pi x}{2}\right)dx = \left|\frac{xe^{2x}}{2}\right|_0^1 - \int_0^1 \frac{1.e^{2x}}{2}dx - \left[\frac{\cos x\frac{\pi}{2}}{\frac{\pi}{2}}\right]_0^1$

$= \frac{e^2}{2} - \frac{1}{4}(e^2-1) - \frac{2}{\pi}(0-1) = \frac{e^2}{4} + \frac{1}{4} + \frac{2}{\pi}$

11. $\int_1^2 \frac{dx}{(x+1)(x+2)} = \int_1^2 \frac{(x+2)-(x+1)}{(x+1)(x+2)}dx$

$= \int_1^2\left(\frac{1}{(x+1)} - \frac{1}{(x+2)}\right)dx$

$= \left|\ln|x+1|\right|_1^2 - \left|\ln|x+2|\right|_1^2 = \ln\left(\frac{3}{2}\right) - \ln\left(\frac{4}{3}\right) = \ln\left(\frac{9}{8}\right)$

12. $\int_0^{\frac{\pi}{4}}(2\sec^2 x + x^3 + 2)dx = 2\left|\tan x\right|_0^{\frac{\pi}{4}} + \left[\frac{x^4}{4}\right]_0^{\frac{\pi}{4}} + 2[x]_0^{\frac{\pi}{4}}$

$= 2[1-0] + \frac{1}{4}\left[\frac{\pi^4}{256}\right] + 2\left(\frac{\pi}{4}\right) = 2 + \frac{\pi^4}{1024} + \frac{\pi}{2}$

13. $\int_0^5 \sqrt{3t+1}\,dt = \left|\frac{(3t+1)^{3/2}}{3\left(\frac{3}{2}\right)}\right|_0^5 = \frac{2}{9}\left[\left(16^{3/2} - (1)^{3/2}\right)\right] = \frac{2}{9}[64-1]$

$= 14$

14. $\int_0^1 \sqrt{t}\left(t - \sqrt{t}\right)dt = \int_0^1\left[(t)^{3/2} - t\right]dt$

$= \left[\frac{2}{5}t^{5/2} - \frac{t^2}{2}\right]_0^1 = \left(\frac{2}{5} - \frac{1}{2}\right) = \frac{4-5}{10} = \frac{-1}{10}$

15. $\int_1^4 \frac{x^2+x-1}{\sqrt{x}}dx = \int_1^4\left(x^{3/2} + x^{1/2} - x^{-1/2}\right)dx$

$= \left|\frac{2}{5}x^{5/2} + \frac{2}{3}x^{3/2} - \frac{2}{1}(x)^{1/2}\right|_1^4 = \left(\frac{64}{5} + \frac{16}{3} - 4\right) - \left(\frac{2}{5} + \frac{2}{3} - 2\right)$

$= \frac{62}{5} + \frac{14}{3} - 2 = \frac{226}{15}$

16. $\int_0^{0.5} \frac{6dx}{\sqrt{1-x^2}} = 6\left[\sin^{-1} x\right]_0^{1/2} = 6\left[\frac{\pi}{6}\right] = \pi$

17. $\int_0^1 \frac{x^2-4}{x^2-2}dx = \int_0^1 \frac{x^2-2-2}{x^2-2}dx = \int_0^1 1\,dx - 2\int_0^1 \frac{1}{x^2-2}dx$

$= [x]_0^1 - 2\times\frac{1}{2\sqrt{2}}\left|\ln\left|\frac{x-\sqrt{2}}{1+\sqrt{2}}\right|\right|_0^1 = 1 - \frac{1}{\sqrt{2}}\left|\ln\left|\frac{1-\sqrt{2}}{1+\sqrt{2}}\right|\right|$

$= 1 + \frac{1}{\sqrt{2}}\ln\left(\frac{\sqrt{2}+1}{\sqrt{2}-1}\right)$

18. $\int_0^1 \frac{x^2-1}{x^2+1}dx = \int_0^1 \frac{x^2+1-2}{x^2+1}dx = \int_0^1\left(1 - \frac{2}{x^2+1}\right)dx$

$= \int_0^1 x\,dx - 2\int_0^1 \frac{1}{x^2+1}dx$

$= \left[\frac{x^2}{2}\right]_0^1 - 2\left[\tan^{-1} x\right]_0^1 = \frac{1}{2} - 2\tan^{-1}(1) = \left(\frac{1}{2} - \frac{\pi}{2}\right)$

19. $\int_{-1}^{-1/\sqrt{3}} \cot^{-1} x\,dx = \int_{-1}^{-1/\sqrt{3}} 1.\cot^{-1} x\,dx =$

$\left|x\cot^{-1} x\right|_{-1}^{-1/\sqrt{3}} - \int_{-1}^{-1/\sqrt{3}} \frac{-1}{1+x^2}(x)dx$

$= \frac{1}{\sqrt{3}}\left(\frac{2\pi}{3} - \frac{3\pi}{4}\right) + \frac{1}{2}\left|\ln\left(1+x^2\right)\right|_{-1}^{-1/\sqrt{3}}$

$= \left(\frac{\sqrt{3}}{4} - \frac{2}{3\sqrt{3}}\right)\pi + \frac{1}{2}\left|\ln\left(\frac{4}{3}\right) - \ln 2\right|$

$= \left(\frac{\sqrt{3}}{4} - \frac{2}{3\sqrt{3}}\right)\pi + \frac{1}{2}\ln\left(\frac{2}{3}\right)$

20. Let $I_1 = \int_0^{\pi/2} \sin^3 x\, dx; I_2 = \int_0^{\pi/2} \cos^3 x\, dx$

$\Rightarrow\ I_1 = \int_0^{\pi/2} (1-\cos^2 x)\sin x\, dx;$

Put $\cos x = t$

$\Rightarrow\ I_1 = -\int_1^0 (1-t^2)dt = \int_0^1 (1-t^2)dt = \left[t - \frac{t^3}{3}\right]_0^1 = 1 - \frac{1}{3} = \frac{2}{3}$

and $I_2 = \int_0^{\pi/2} (1-\sin^2 x).\cos x\ dx$

$= \int_0^1 (1-t^2)dt = \left[t - \frac{t^3}{3}\right]_0^1 = \frac{2}{3}$

Thus, $I_1 = I_2 = \frac{2}{3}$

21. Let $I_1 = \int_0^{\pi/2} \sin^4 x\ dx$ and $I_2 = \int_0^{\pi/2} \cos^4 x\ dx$

$\therefore\ I_1 = \int_0^{\pi/2} \left(\frac{1-\cos 2x}{2}\right)^2 dx$

$= \frac{1}{4}\int_0^{\pi/2} (1+\cos^2 2x - 2\cos 2x)dx$

$= \frac{1}{4}[x]_0^{\pi/2} + \frac{1}{4}\int_0^{\pi/2} \frac{1+\cos 4x}{2}dx - \frac{1}{4}[\sin 2x]_0^{\pi/2}$

$= \frac{\pi}{8} + \frac{1}{8}\left[x + \frac{\sin 4x}{4}\right]_0^{\pi/2} - \frac{1}{4}(0) = \left(\frac{\pi}{8} + \frac{\pi}{16}\right) = \frac{3\pi}{16}$

similarly, $I_2 = \int_0^{\pi/2} \left(\frac{1+\cos^2 x}{2}\right)^2 dx$

$= \frac{1}{4}\int_0^{\pi/2} (1+\cos^2 2x + 2\cos 2x)dx$

$= \frac{1}{4}[x]_0^{\pi/2} + \frac{1}{8}\int_0^{\pi/2} (1+\cos 4x)dx + \frac{1}{4}[\sin 2x]_0^{\pi/2}$

$= \frac{\pi}{8} + \frac{\pi}{16} = \frac{3\pi}{16}$

Hence, $I_1 = I_2 = \frac{3\pi}{16}$

22. Required Area $= \int_0^{\ln 2} f(x)dx = A$ (say)

$= \int_0^{\ln 2} \frac{e^x}{1+e^x}dx;$ Put $1+e^x = t$

$\Rightarrow\ e^x dx = dt$ for $x = 0,\ t = 2$ and for $x = \ln 2,\ t = 3$

$\therefore\ A = \int_2^3 \frac{dt}{t} = [\ln t]_2^3 = \ln\left(\frac{3}{2}\right)$

23. $A = \int_0^1 xe^{-x}dx = \left|\frac{xe^{-x}}{-x}\right|_0^1 = \frac{-1}{e} - (e^{-1} - 1) = \left(1 - \frac{2}{e}\right)$

24. $A = \int_0^{\ln 2} xe^x dx = \left|xe^x\right|_0^{\ln 2} - \int_0^{\ln 2} 1.e^x dx = 2\ln 2 - \left[e^x\right]_0^{\ln 2}$

$= 2\ln 2 - [2-1] = 2\ln 2 - 1 = \ln 4 - 1$ or $\ln\left(\frac{4}{e}\right)$

25. $I = \int_{-\infty}^0 e^x dx$

Put $x = -t \qquad \Rightarrow\ dx = -dt$

For $x = -\infty,\ t = \infty$ and for $x = 0,\ t = 0$

$\therefore\ I = \int_\infty^0 e^{-t}(-dt) = \int_0^\infty e^{-t}dt = -\left[e^{-t}\right]_0^\infty = -[0-1] = 1$

Also $\int_0^1 |\ln x|dx = \int_0^1 -\ln x\ dx \qquad (\because \ln x < 0 \text{ for } x \in (0,1))$

$= -\left[\left|(\ln x).x\right|_0^1 - \int_0^1 \frac{1}{x}.x\ dx\right]$

$= -\left[0 - \int_0^1 dx\right] = -[-(1-0)] = 1$

Hence $\int_{-\infty}^0 e^x dx = \int_0^\infty e^{-x}dx = \int_0^1 dx = \int_0^1 |\ln x|dx = 1$

TEXTUAL EXERCISE–2: (OBJECTIVE)

1. (a) $I = \int_0^{\pi/2} \frac{\cos x}{(1+\sin x)(2+\sin x)}dx$

Put $\sin x = t \qquad \Rightarrow\ \cos x\ dx = dt$

$\therefore\ I = \int_0^1 \frac{dt}{(1+t)(t+2)} = \int_0^1 \frac{[(t+2)-(t+1)]}{(t+1)(t+2)}dt$

$= \int_0^1 \left(\frac{1}{t+1} - \frac{1}{t+2}\right)dt$

$= \left|\ln|t+1| - \ln|t+2|\right|_0^1 = \left|\ln\left|\frac{t+1}{t+2}\right|\right|_0^1 = \ln\left|\frac{2}{3}\right| - \ln\left|\frac{1}{2}\right|$

$= \ln\frac{4}{3}$

2. (b) $\int_{\pi/3}^{\pi/2} \frac{\sqrt{1+\cos x}}{(1-\cos x)^{5/2}}dx = \int_{\pi/3}^{\pi/2} \frac{\sqrt{2}\cos\frac{x}{2}}{\left(2\sin^2\frac{x}{2}\right)^{5/2}}dx$

$= \int_{\pi/3}^{\pi/2} \frac{\sqrt{2}\cos\frac{x}{2}}{4\sqrt{2}\sin^5\frac{x}{2}}dx = \frac{1}{4}\int_{\pi/3}^{\pi/2} \frac{\cos\frac{x}{2}}{\sin^5\frac{x}{2}}dx$

Put $\sin\frac{x}{2} = t \qquad \Rightarrow\ \frac{1}{2}\cos\frac{x}{2}dx = dt$

$\Rightarrow\ I = \frac{1}{2}\int_{1/2}^{1/\sqrt{2}} \frac{dt}{t^5} = \frac{1}{2}\left[\frac{t^{-4}}{-4}\right]_{1/2}^{1/\sqrt{2}} = -\frac{1}{8}[4-16] = \frac{3}{2}$

3. (a) $\int_0^1 \sin^{-1}\left(\frac{2x}{1+x^2}\right)dx$

Put $\theta = \tan^{-1} x;\ x \in (0,1)$

$\Rightarrow\ x = \tan\theta$ and $\theta \in \left(0, \frac{\pi}{4}\right)$

$\Rightarrow\ dx = \sec^2\theta d\theta$

$\therefore\ I = \int_0^{\pi/4} \sin^{-1}\left(\frac{2\tan\theta}{1+\tan^2\theta}\right)\sec^2\theta d\theta$

$= \int_0^{\pi/4} \sin^{-1}(\sin 2\theta).\sec^2\theta d\theta = \int_0^{\pi/4} 2\theta.\sec^2\theta d\theta$

$= 2\left[\left|\theta.\tan\theta\right|_0^{\pi/4} - \int_0^{\pi/4} 1.\tan\theta d\theta\right] = 2\left[\frac{\pi}{4} - \left|\ln\ \sec\theta\right|_0^{\pi/4}\right]$

$= 2\left[\frac{\pi}{4} - \left\{\frac{1}{2}\ln 2\right\}\right] = \frac{\pi}{2} - 2\ln\sqrt{2}$

4. (a) $\int_1^e \frac{e^x}{x}(1+x\log x)dx = \int_1^e e^x\left(\log x+\frac{1}{x}\right)dx$

$=\left|e^x \log x\right|_1^e = e^e - 0 = e^e$

5. (c) $\int_{-2}^{2}(ax^3+bx+c)dx = \left|\frac{ax^4}{4}+\frac{bx^2}{2}+cx\right|_{-2}^{2}$

$=\frac{a}{4}[16-16]+\frac{b}{2}[4-4]+c[2-(-2)]=4c$

6. (b) $\int_0^{\pi/2}\sqrt{\cos\theta}.\sin^3\theta\, d\theta$

$=\int_0^{\pi/2}-\sqrt{\cos\theta}.(1-\cos^2\theta).d(\cos\theta) = -\int_1^0 \sqrt{t}(1-t^2)dt$

$=-\left[\frac{2}{3}(t)^{3/2}-\frac{2}{7}(t)^{7/2}\right]_1^0 = +\left[\frac{2}{3}-\frac{2}{7}\right]=\frac{8}{21}$

7. (d) $\int_0^1 \frac{dx}{[ax+b(1-x)]^2} = \int_0^1 \frac{dx}{[b+(a-b)x]^2}$

$=\left|\frac{[b+(a-b)x]^{-2+1}}{(-2+1)(a-b)}\right|_0^1 = \left|\frac{-1}{(a-b)[b+(a-b)x]}\right|_0^1$

$=\frac{-1}{(a-b)}\left[\frac{1}{a}-\frac{1}{b}\right]=\frac{1}{ab}$

8. (b) $\int_0^k \frac{dx}{2+8x^2}=\frac{\pi}{16} \quad\Rightarrow\quad \frac{1}{8}\int_0^k \frac{dx}{x^2+\left(\frac{1}{2}\right)^2}=\frac{\pi}{16}$

$\Rightarrow \frac{1}{8}\times\frac{1}{1/2}\left|\tan^{-1}\left|\frac{x}{1/2}\right|\right|_0^k=\frac{\pi}{16}$

$\Rightarrow \frac{1}{4}\left[\tan^{-1}2k\right]=\frac{\pi}{16} \quad\Rightarrow\quad \tan^{-1}(2k)=\frac{\pi}{4}$

$\Rightarrow 2k=1=k-1$

9. (b) $\int_0^{1/\sqrt{2}} \frac{\sin^{-1}x}{(1-x^2)^{3/2}}dx$

Let $\theta=\sin^{-1}x$ as $x\in\left(0,1/\sqrt{2}\right)$

$\Rightarrow \sin^{-1}x\in(0,\pi/4)$ and $d\theta=\frac{1}{\sqrt{1-x^2}}dx,\ x=\sin\theta$

$\therefore\quad I=\int_0^{\pi/4}\frac{\theta\, d\theta}{(1-\sin^2\theta)}=\int_0^{\pi/4}\theta\sec^2\theta d\theta$

$=\left|\theta\tan\theta\right|_0^{\pi/4}-\int_0^{\pi/4}1.\tan\theta d\theta$

$=\frac{\pi}{4}-\left|\ln\ \sec\theta\right|_0^{\pi/4}=\frac{\pi}{4}-\ln\sqrt{2}=\frac{\pi}{4}-\frac{1}{2}\ln 2$

10. (d) $\int_{1/\pi}^{2/\pi}\frac{\sin\left(\frac{1}{x}\right)}{x^2}dx$ Put $\frac{1}{x}=t$

$\Rightarrow \frac{1}{x^2}dx=-dt \ = -\int_\pi^{\pi/2}\sin t\ dt \ = \int_{\pi/2}^{\pi}\sin t\ dt = -[\cos t]_{\pi/2}^{\pi}$

$=-[-1-0]=1$

11. (b) $\int_0^{1/2}\frac{x\sin^{-1}x}{\sqrt{1-x^2}}dx$

Put $\sin^{-1}x=t \quad\Rightarrow\quad \frac{1}{\sqrt{1-x^2}}dx=dt$

$\therefore\quad I=\int_0^{\pi/6}t\sin t\ dt = \left[\left|t(-\cos t)\right|_0^{\pi/6}-\int_0^{\pi/6}1.(-\cos t)dt\right.$

$=\left[-\frac{\pi}{6}\times\frac{\sqrt{3}}{2}+\left|\sin t\right|_0^{\pi/6}\right]=-\frac{\sqrt{3}\pi}{12}+\frac{1}{2}=\frac{1}{2}-\frac{\sqrt{3}\pi}{12}$

12. (a) $\int_0^2\sqrt{\frac{2+x}{2-x}}dx$

Put $x=2\cos\theta$ and $\theta\in(0,\pi/2)$

$=\int_{\pi/2}^{0}\sqrt{\frac{2(1+\cos\theta)}{2(1-\cos\theta)}}.(-2\sin\theta)d\theta$

$=2\int_0^{\pi/2}\sqrt{\frac{1+\cos\theta}{1-\cos\theta}}.\sin\theta\ d\theta \ =2\int_0^{\pi/2}\sqrt{\frac{2\cos^2\frac{\theta}{2}}{2\sin^2\frac{\theta}{2}}}.\sin\theta\ d\theta$

$=2\int_0^{\pi/2}\left(\cos\frac{\theta}{2}\right)\left(2\sin\frac{\theta}{2}\cos\frac{\theta}{2}\right)d\theta$

$=4\int_0^{\pi/2}\left(\cos^2\frac{\theta}{2}\right)d\theta=$

$2\int_0^{\pi/2}(1+\cos\theta)d\theta=2[\theta+\sin]_0^{\pi/2} \ =2\left[\frac{\pi}{2}+1\right]\pi+2$

13. (a) $\int_0^{\pi/8}\frac{\sec^2 2x}{2}dx \ =\frac{1}{2}\left[\frac{\tan 2x}{2}\right]_0^{\pi/8} \ =\frac{1}{4}\left[\tan\frac{\pi}{4}-0\right]=\frac{1}{4}$

14. (c) $\int_0^{2\pi}\sqrt{1+\sin\frac{x}{2}}\ dx \ =\int_0^{2\pi}\sqrt{1+\cos\left(\frac{\pi}{2}-\frac{x}{2}\right)}\ dx$

$=\int_0^{2\pi}\sqrt{2\cos^2\left(\frac{\pi}{4}-\frac{x}{4}\right)}\ dx \ =\sqrt{2}\int_0^{2\pi}\left|\cos\left(\frac{\pi}{4}-\frac{x}{4}\right)\right|\ dx$

$\because\quad x\in(0,2\pi)$

$\Rightarrow \frac{x}{4}\in\left(0,\frac{\pi}{2}\right) \quad\Rightarrow\quad \frac{-x}{4}\in\left(\frac{-\pi}{2},0\right)$

$\Rightarrow \left(\frac{\pi}{4}-\frac{x}{4}\right)\in\left(\frac{-\pi}{4},\frac{\pi}{4}\right)$

$\Rightarrow \cos\left(\frac{\pi}{4}-\frac{x}{4}\right)>0 \quad\Rightarrow\quad \left|\cos\left(\frac{\pi}{4}-\frac{x}{4}\right)\right|=\cos\left(\frac{\pi}{4}-\frac{x}{4}\right)$

$\therefore\quad I=\sqrt{2}\int_0^{2\pi}\cos\left(\frac{\pi}{4}-\frac{x}{4}\right)dx=\frac{\sqrt{2}\left|\sin\left(\frac{\pi}{4}-\frac{x}{4}\right)\right|_0^{2\pi}}{\frac{-1}{4}}$

$=-4\sqrt{2}\left[\sin\left(\frac{-\pi}{4}\right)-\sin\left(\frac{\pi}{4}\right)\right]$

$=-4\sqrt{2}\left[-2\sin\frac{\pi}{4}\right]=8\sqrt{2}\sin\frac{\pi}{4}=8\sqrt{2}\left(\frac{1}{\sqrt{2}}\right)=8$

15. (b) $\int_0^1 \cos^{-1} x\, dx = \left|x\cos^{-1} x\right|_0^1 - \int_0^1 \frac{-1}{\sqrt{1-x^2}} x\, dx$ (Integrating by parts).

$$= 0 - 0 + \frac{1}{-2}\int_0^1 \frac{-2x}{\sqrt{1-x^2}} dx = -\frac{1}{2}\left|\frac{\sqrt{1-x^2}}{\frac{1}{2}}\right|_0^1 = -[0-1] = 1$$

16. (d) $\int_0^2 \frac{x^3 dx}{\left(x^2+1\right)^{3/2}} = \int_0^2 \frac{\left(x^2+1-1\right)}{\left(x^2+1\right)^{3/2}}$

Put $x^2+1=t \qquad \Rightarrow \quad x\,dx = dt/2$

$$\Rightarrow \quad I = \int_1^5 \frac{(t-1)dt}{2t^{3/2}} = \frac{1}{2}\int_1^5\left(\frac{1}{t^{1/2}} - \frac{1}{t^{3/2}}\right)dt = \frac{1}{2}\left[2t^{1/2} + 2t^{-1/2}\right]_1^5$$

$$= \left[\left(\sqrt{5} + \frac{1}{\sqrt{5}}\right) - (1+1)\right] = \frac{5+1-2\sqrt{5}}{\sqrt{5}} = \frac{6-2\sqrt{5}}{\sqrt{5}}$$

17. (c) $\int_0^{\pi/4} \frac{4\sin 2\theta\, d\theta}{\left(\sin^4\theta + \cos^4\theta\right)}$

Put $\sin^2\theta = t$

$\Rightarrow \quad 2\sin\theta\cos\theta\, d\theta = dt$

$\Rightarrow \quad \sin 2\theta\, d\theta = dt$

$$\therefore \quad I = 4\int_0^{1/2} \frac{dt}{\left[t^2 + (1-t)^2\right]} =$$

$$4\int_0^{1/2} \frac{dt}{\left(2t^2 - 2t + 1\right)} = \frac{4}{2}\int_0^{1/2} \frac{dt}{t^2 - t + \frac{1}{4} + \frac{1}{4}}$$

$$= 2\int_0^{1/2} \frac{dt}{\left(t-\frac{1}{2}\right)^2 + \left(\frac{1}{2}\right)^2}$$

$$= \frac{2}{(1/2)}\left|\tan^{-1}\frac{t-\frac{1}{2}}{\frac{1}{2}}\right|_0^{1/2} = 4\left|\tan^{-1}(2t-1)\right|_0^{1/2}$$

$$= 4\left|\tan^{-1} 0 - \tan^{-1}(-1)\right| = 4\tan^{-1}(1) = \pi$$

18. (b) $\int_a^b \frac{x}{|x|} dx\ ;\ a < b < 0$

$\because \quad x \in (a,b)$ and $b<0 \Rightarrow \quad x<0$

$\Rightarrow \quad |x| = -x$

$$\therefore \quad I = \int_a^b \frac{x}{-x} dx = \int_a^b -1 dx = -[x]_a^b = (a-b) =$$

$$-(-a) + (-b) = -|a| + |b| = |b| - |a|$$

19. (a) $F_1(x) = \int_2^x (2t-5)dt,\ F_2(x) = \int_0^x 2t\, dt$

$\Rightarrow \quad F_1(x) = \left|t^2 - 5t\right|_2^x, F_2(x) = \left|t^2\right|_0^x$

$\Rightarrow \quad F_1(x) = (x^2 - 5x) - (4-10), F_2(x) = x^2$

$\Rightarrow \quad F_1(x) = x^2 - 5x + 6, F_2(x) = x^2$

$\therefore$ At the point of intersection, $x^2 - 5x + 6 = x^2$

$\Rightarrow \quad 5x = 6 \qquad \Rightarrow \quad x = \frac{6}{5}$

$\Rightarrow \quad y = \frac{36}{25}$

$\therefore$ Point of intersection is $\left(\frac{6}{5}, \frac{36}{25}\right)$

20. (b) $\int_0^{b-c} f''(x+a)dx$

Put $x+a=t \qquad \Rightarrow \quad dx = dt$

$$\therefore \quad I = \int_a^{a+b-c} f''(t)dt = \left|f'(t)\right|_a^{a+b-c} = f'(a+b-c) - f'(a)$$

21. (c) $\int_0^1 \frac{d}{dx}\left[\sin^{-1}\left(\frac{2x}{1+x^2}\right)\right]dx = \left|\sin^{-1}\left(\frac{2x}{1+x^2}\right)\right|_0^1$

$$= \sin^{-1}(1) - \sin^{-1}(0) = \left(\frac{\pi}{2} - 0\right) = \frac{\pi}{2}$$

22. (c) $\int_0^\infty \frac{x\, dx}{(1+x)(1+x^2)}$

Let $\frac{x}{(1+x)(1+x^2)} = \frac{A}{1+x} + \frac{Bx+C}{1+x^2}$

$\Rightarrow \quad x = A(1+x^2) + (1+x)(Bx+C)$

$\Rightarrow \quad A + C = 0$ (putting $x = 0$)

$\Rightarrow \quad A = \frac{-1}{2}, C = \frac{1}{2}, B = \frac{1}{2}$

$$\Rightarrow \quad \int_0^\infty \frac{x}{(1+x)(1+x^2)} dx = \int_0^\infty \left(\frac{\frac{-1}{2}}{(1+x)} + \frac{\frac{1}{2}(x+1)}{(1+x^2)}\right)dx$$

$$= \frac{-1}{2}\left|\ln|1+x|\right|_0^\infty + \frac{1}{2\times 2}\int_0^\infty \frac{2x}{1+x^2}dx + \frac{1}{2}\int_0^\infty \frac{1}{1+x^2}dx$$

$$= \frac{-1}{2\times 2}\left[\ln|1+x|^2\right]_0^\infty + \frac{1}{4}\left|\ln\left(1+x^2\right)\right|_0^\infty + \frac{1}{2}\left|\tan^{-1} x\right|_0^\infty$$

$$= \frac{1}{4}\left[\ln\left[\frac{1+x^2}{(1+x)^2}\right]\right]_0^\infty + \frac{1}{2}\tan^{-1}\infty - 0$$

$$= \frac{1}{4}\left[\lim_{x\to\infty} \ln\left(\frac{1+x^2}{(1+x)^2}\right)\right] + \frac{\pi}{4}$$

$$= \frac{1}{4}\lim_{x\to\infty} \ln\left(\frac{1+\frac{1}{x^2}}{\frac{1}{x^2}+1+\frac{2}{x}}\right) + \frac{\pi}{4} = 0 + \frac{\pi}{4} = \frac{\pi}{4}$$

23. (b) $\int_a^\lambda \phi(x)dx = \int_a^\lambda f'(x)dx = [f(x)]_a^\lambda$

$$= f(\lambda) - f(a) = (\mu - b)$$

24. (a) $\int_0^{\pi/4} \frac{dx}{\cos^{4x} - \cos^2 x\sin^2 x + \sin^4 x}$

$$= \int_0^{\pi/4} \frac{dx}{(\cos^2 x + \sin^2 x)^2 - 3\sin^2 x + \cos^2 x}$$

$$= \int_0^{\pi/4} \frac{dx}{1-\frac{3}{4}(2\sin x\ \cos x)^2} = \int_0^{\pi/4} \frac{dx}{1-\frac{3}{4}\sin^2 2x} =$$

$$4\int_0^{\pi/4} \frac{dx}{4-3\sin^2 2x}$$

$$= 4\int_0^{\pi/4} \frac{\sec^2 2x\ dx}{4\sec^2 2x - 3\tan^2 2x} = 4\int_0^{\pi/4} \frac{\sec^2 2x\ dx}{(4+\tan^2 2x)}$$

Put $\tan 2x = t$

$\Rightarrow\ 2\sec^2 2x\ dx = dt$

$$\Rightarrow\ \text{I} = 2\int_0^{\infty} \frac{dt}{4+t^2} = \frac{2}{2}\left[\tan^{-1}\left(\frac{t}{2}\right)\right]_0^{\infty} = \tan^{-1}\infty = \frac{\pi}{2}$$

25. (b) $A = \int_{-1}^{1}(x^2+1)dx = \left[\frac{x^3}{3}+x\right]_{-1}^{1}$

$$= \frac{1}{3}(1-(-1)) + (1-(-1)) = \frac{2}{3}+2 = \frac{8}{3}$$

26. (b) $A = \int_0^1 \sqrt{x}\ dx = \left[\frac{2}{3}x^{\frac{3}{2}}\right]_0^1 = \frac{2}{3}(1-0) = \frac{2}{3}$

27. (b) $A = \int_0^{\pi/4} \sec^2 x\ dx = [\tan x]_0^{\pi/4} = \left[\tan\frac{\pi}{4} - 0\right] = 1$

28. (a) $A = \int_0^{\pi/2} (\sin x + \cos x)dx = [-\cos x + \sin x]_0^{\frac{\pi}{2}}$

$$= -[0-1] + [1-0] = 2$$

29. (c) $\int_0^1 (e^x - x)dx = \left[e^x - \frac{x^2}{2}\right]_0^1 = \left(e-\frac{1}{2}\right) - (1-0) = e - \frac{3}{2}$

30. (a) $A = \int_1^4 \left(x^2+x+1\right)\sqrt{x}\ dx = \int_1^4 \left(x^{5/2}+x^{3/2}+x^{1/2}\right)dx$

$$= \left[\frac{2}{7}x^{7/2} + \frac{2}{5}x^{5/2} + \frac{2}{3}x^{3/2}\right]_1^4$$

$$= \frac{2}{7}(127) + \frac{2}{5}(31) + \frac{2}{3}(7) = \frac{254}{7} + \frac{62}{5} + \frac{14}{3}$$

$$= \frac{254\times 15 + 62\times 21 + 14\times 35}{105} = \frac{5602}{105}$$

31. (b) $\int_1^2 \left(\frac{x^2-2x+3}{x}\right)dx = \int_1^2 \left(x-2+\frac{3}{x}\right)dx$

$$= \left[\frac{x^2}{2} - 2x + 3\ln x\right]_1^2$$

$$= \left[(2-4+3\ln 2) - \left(\frac{1}{2}-2+3\ln 1\right)\right]$$

$$= \left[-2+3\ln 2+\frac{3}{2}\right] = 3\ln 2 - \frac{1}{2}$$

32. (c) $A = \int_0^1 \frac{2}{1+x^2}dx = 2\left|\tan^{-1}x\right|_0^1 = 2\left[\tan^{-1}1 - \tan^{-1}0\right] = \frac{\pi}{2}$

33. (b) $\int_{\pi}^{2\pi} |\sin x|\,dx = \int_{\pi}^{2\pi}(-\sin x)dx = |\cos x|_{\pi}^{2\pi}$

$$= (\cos 2\pi - \cos\pi) = 1-(-1) = 2$$

TEXTUAL EXERCISE–3: (SUBJECTIVE)

1. (a) $\int_0^{1/2} \frac{x\sin^{-1}x}{\sqrt{1-x^2}}dx$

Put $\sin^{-1}x = t \qquad \Rightarrow\ x = \sin t,\ dx = \cos t\ dt$

$\Rightarrow$ At $x=0,\ t=0$ and at $x = \frac{1}{2}, t = \frac{\pi}{6}$

$$\therefore\ \text{I} = \int_0^{\pi/6} \frac{t\sin t\ \cos t\ dt}{\cos t} = \int_0^{\pi/6} t\sin t\ dt$$

$$= -|t\cos t|_0^{\pi/6} + \int_0^{\pi/6} 1.\cos t\ dt$$

$$= -\left[\frac{\pi}{6}\times\frac{\sqrt{3}}{2}\right] + [\sin t]_0^{\pi/6} = \frac{-\pi}{4\sqrt{3}} + \left[\frac{1}{2}\right] = \frac{1}{2} - \frac{\pi}{4\sqrt{3}}$$

(b) $\int_{-2}^{2} |1-x^2|\,dx$

$\because\ 1-x^2 < 0$ for $x\in(-\infty,-1)\cup(1,\infty)$ and $1-x^2 \ge 0$ for $x\in[-1,1]$

$$\therefore\ \text{I} = \int_{-2}^{-1}|1-x^2|\,dx + \int_{-1}^{1}|1-x^2|\,dx + \int_1^2 |1-x^2|\,dx$$

$$= \int_{-2}^{-1}(x^2-1)dx + \int_{-1}^{1}(1-x^2)dx + \int_1^2 (x^2-1)dx$$

$$= \left|\frac{x^3}{3}-x\right|_{-2}^{-1} + \left|x-\frac{x^3}{3}\right|_{-1}^{1} + \left|\frac{x^3}{3}-x\right|_1^2$$

$$= \left[\left(\frac{-1}{3}+1\right) - \left(\frac{-8}{3}+2\right)\right] + \left[(1+1) - \frac{1}{3}(1+1)\right] + \left[\left(\frac{8}{3}-2\right) - \left(\frac{1}{3}-1\right)\right]$$

$$= \frac{4}{3}+\frac{4}{3}+\frac{4}{3} = 4$$

(c) $\int_0^2 (x[x])dx = \int_0^1 x[x]\ dx + \int_1^2 x[x]dx$

$$= \int_0^1 0\ dx + \int_1^2 x\ dx = \left[\frac{x^2}{2}\right]_1^2 = \frac{1}{2}[4-1] = \frac{3}{2}$$

2. Directly: $\text{I} = \int_{-2}^{2}\frac{dx}{4+x^2} = \int_{-2}^{2}\frac{dx}{(2)^2+x^2} = \frac{1}{(2)}\left|\tan^{-1}\frac{x}{2}\right|_{-2}^{2}$

$$= \frac{1}{2}\left[\tan^{-1}(1) - \tan^{-1}(-1)\right] = \frac{1}{2}\left[\frac{\pi}{4}+\frac{\pi}{4}\right] = \frac{\pi}{4}$$

By Substitution:-

Put $x = \frac{1}{t}$

$$\Rightarrow\ \text{I} = \int_{-1/2}^{1/2} \frac{dx}{4+\frac{1}{t^2}}\left(\frac{-1}{t^2}\right)dt = \int_{-1/2}^{1/2}\frac{-dt}{4t^2+1} = \left[\frac{\frac{-1}{(1)}\tan^{-1}\left(\frac{2t}{1}\right)}{2}\right]_{-1/2}^{1/2}$$

$= -\frac{1}{2}\left[\tan^{-1}1 - \tan^{-1}(-1)\right] = \left(-\frac{1}{2}\right)\left(2\tan^{-1}1\right) = -\frac{\pi}{4}$

$\because$ By substituting $x = \frac{1}{t}$

$\Rightarrow t = \frac{1}{x}$ which is discontinuous in [–2, 2] having discontinuity at $x = 0$, i.e., the substitution is not valid.

Thus, correct answer will be π/4 as obtained by direct method

3. $\int_0^{2\pi} \frac{dx}{2+\cos x} = \int_0^{2\pi} \frac{dx}{2 + \left(\frac{1-\tan^2\frac{x}{2}}{1+\tan^2\frac{x}{2}}\right)} = \int_0^{2\pi} \frac{\sec^2\frac{x}{2}dx}{\tan^2\frac{x}{2}+3}$

Put $\tan\frac{x}{2} = t \quad \Rightarrow \quad \frac{1}{2}\sec^2\frac{x}{2}dx = dt$

$\therefore \quad I = \int_0^{\pi} \frac{2dt}{t^2 + \left(\sqrt{3}\right)^2} = 0$

Clearly $\frac{1}{2+\cos x} > 0 \ \forall x \in [0, 2\pi]$

$\Rightarrow I > 0.$

Here the problem is in substitution $\tan\frac{x}{2} = t$; $x \in [0, 2\pi]$.

As $y = \tan\frac{x}{2}$ is discontinuous in [0, 2π] at x = π.

Hence the above integral should be evaluated as given by

$I = \int_0^{\pi} \frac{\sec^2\frac{x}{2}dx}{\tan^2\frac{x}{2}+3} + \int_{\pi}^{2\pi} \frac{\sec^2\frac{x}{2}dx}{\tan^2\frac{x}{2}+3}$

Put $\tan\frac{x}{2} = t \quad \Rightarrow \quad \sec^2\frac{x}{2}dx = 2dt$

$\therefore \quad I = \int_0^{\infty} \frac{2dt}{t^2+3} + \int_{-\infty}^{0} \frac{2dt}{t^2+3}$

$= \frac{2}{\sqrt{3}}\left|\tan^{-1}\frac{t}{\sqrt{3}}\right|_0^{\infty} + \frac{2}{\sqrt{3}}\left|\tan^{-1}\frac{t}{\sqrt{3}}\right|_{-\infty}^{0}$

$= \frac{2}{\sqrt{3}}\left(\frac{\pi}{2}\right) + \frac{2}{\sqrt{3}}\left(0 + \frac{\pi}{2}\right) = \frac{\pi}{\sqrt{3}} + \frac{\pi}{\sqrt{3}} = \frac{2}{\sqrt{3}}\pi$

4. It is not possible to substitute x = sec t as here x ∈ (0, 1); where as sec t ∈ (–∞, –1]∪ [1, ∞).

5. $I = \int_0^{\pi/2} \frac{dx}{a^2\cos^2 x + b^2\sin^2 x} = \int_0^{\pi/2} \frac{\sec^2 x\, dx}{a^2 + b^2\tan^2 x}$

Put tan x = t as y = tan x is continuous in (0, π/2)

$\Rightarrow \sec^2 x\, dx = dt$

$\therefore \quad I = \int_0^{\infty} \frac{dt}{a^2 + b^2t^2} = \frac{\frac{1}{a}\left|\tan^{-1}\left(\frac{bt}{a}\right)\right|_0^{\infty}}{b}$

$= \frac{1}{ab}\left[\tan^{-1}\infty - \tan^{-1}(0)\right] = \frac{\pi}{2b}$

6. (a) $\int_0^3 \frac{dx}{x^2 + [x]^2 + 1 - 2x[x]}$

$= \int_0^1 \frac{dx}{x^2+1} + \int_1^2 \frac{dx}{x^2-2x+2} + \int_2^3 \frac{dx}{x^2-4x+5}$

$= \left|\tan^{-1}x\right|_0^1 + \int_1^2 \frac{dx}{(x-1)^2+1} + \int_2^3 \frac{dx}{(x-2)^2+1}$

$= \frac{\pi}{4} + \left|\tan^{-1}(x-1)\right|_1^2 + \left|\tan^{-1}(x-2)\right|_2^3 = \frac{\pi}{4} + \frac{\pi}{4} + \frac{\pi}{4} = \frac{3\pi}{4}$

(b) $\int_0^{\pi} \sin^{-1}(\sin x)dx$

$= \int_0^{\pi/2} \sin^{-1}(\sin x)dx + \int_{\pi/2}^{\pi} \sin^{-1}(\sin x)dx$

$= \int_0^{\pi/2} x\, dx + \int_{\pi/2}^{\pi} \sin^{-1}\left(\sin(\pi - x)\right)dx$

$\left[\because \sin^{-1}(\sin x) = x \forall x \in \left[\frac{-\pi}{2}, \frac{\pi}{2}\right]\right]$

$= \int_0^{\pi/2} x\, dx + \int_{\pi/2}^{\pi} (\pi - x)dx = \left[\frac{x^2}{2}\right]_0^{\pi/2} + \left[\pi x - \frac{x^2}{2}\right]_{\pi/2}^{\pi}$

$= \frac{1}{2}\left[\frac{\pi^2}{4}\right] + \left[\left(\pi^2 - \frac{\pi^2}{2}\right) - \left(\frac{\pi^2}{2} - \frac{\pi^2}{8}\right)\right]$

$= \frac{\pi^2}{8} + \left[\frac{\pi^2}{8}\right] = \frac{\pi^2}{4}$

(c) $\int_0^{\pi/4} \left[\sin x + \left[\cos x + [\tan x]\right]\right]dx$

$= \int_0^{\pi/4} \left([\sin x] + [\cos x] + [\tan x]\right)dx$

$\left(\because [m + x] = m + [x] \forall m \in \mathbb{Z}\right)$

$= \int_0^{\frac{\pi}{4}} 0\, dx + \int_0^{\pi/4} 0\, dx + \int_0^{\pi/4} 0\, dx = 0$

(d) $\int_{-2}^{2} [x]dx = \int_{-2}^{-1} -2dx + \int_{-1}^{0} (-1)dx + \int_0^1 0\, dx + \int_1^2 1dx$

$= -2[x]_{-2}^{-1}[x]_{-1}^{0} + 0 + [x]_1^2$

$= -2[-1+2] - [0+1] + [2-1] = -2 - 1 + 1 = 2$

(e) $\int_{-2}^{3} \{x\}dx = \int_{-2}^{3} \left(x - [x]\right)dx$

$= \int_{-2}^{-1} (x+2)dx + \int_{-1}^{0} (x+1)dx + \int_0^1 (x-0)dx$

$+ \int_1^2 (x-1)dx + \int_2^3 (x-2)dx$

$= \left[\frac{x^2}{2} + 2x\right]_{-2}^{-1} + \left[\frac{x^2}{2} + x\right]_{-1}^{0} + \left[\frac{x^2}{2}\right]_0^1$

$+ \left[\frac{x^2}{2} - x\right]_1^2 + \left[\frac{x^2}{2} - 2x\right]_3^2 = \frac{5}{2}$

(f) $\int_0^3 [e^x]dx$

$0 < e^x < 1$ for $-\infty < x < 0$,

$1 < e^x < 2$ for $0 < x < \ln 2$,

$2 < e^x < 3$ for $\ln 2 < x < \ln 3$,

$3 < e^x < 2$ for $\ln 3 < x < \ln 4$, and so on.

$$\therefore \quad I = \int_0^{\ln 2} 1\,dx + \int_{\ln 2}^{\ln 3} 2\,dx + \int_{\ln 3}^{\ln 4} 3\,dx + \ldots\ldots$$

$$+\int_{\ln 2([e^3]-1)}^{\ln[e^3]} \left([e^3]-1\right)dx + \int_{\ln[e^3]}^{\ln e^3} [e^3]dx$$

$$= [\ln 2 - 0] + 2[\ln 3 - \ln 2] + 3[\ln 4 - \ln 3] +$$

$$\ldots\ldots + \left(\left[e^3\right]-1\right)\left[\ln\left[e^3\right] - \ln\left(\left[e^3\right]-1\right)\right]$$

$$+\left[e^3\right]\left[\ln e^3 - \ln\left[e^3\right]\right]$$

$$= \ln 2 + 2\ln\left(\frac{3}{2}\right) + 3\ln\left(\frac{4}{3}\right) + \ldots\ldots$$

$$+\left(\left[e^3\right]-1\right)\ln\left(\frac{\left[e^3\right]}{\left[e^3\right]-1}\right) + \left[e^3\right]\ln\left(\frac{\left[e^3\right]}{\left[2^3\right]}\right)$$

(g) $\int_1^5 [\log x]dx$; at $x = 1, \log x = 0$; $0 < \log x < 1$

for $1 < x < e$, $1 < \log x < 2$

for $e < x < e^2$, $2 < \log < 3$

for $e^2 < x < e^3$ and so on but $5 < e^2$

$$\therefore \quad I = \int_1^e 0\,dx + \int_e^5 1\,dx = (5-e)$$

(h) $\int_1^{20} [\ln x]dx$; at $x = 1$, $\ln x = 0$;

$0 < \ln x < 1$ for $1 < x < e$,

$1 < \ln x < 2$ for $e < x < e^2$,

$2 < \ln x < 3$ for $e^2 < x < e^3$ but $20 < e^3$

$$\therefore \quad I = \int_1^e 0\,dx + \int_e^{e^2} 1.dx + \int_{e^2}^{20} 2\,dx$$

$$= \left(e^2 - e\right) + 2\left(20 - e^2\right) = 40 - e - e^2$$

(i) $\int_0^x [x]\,dx = \int_0^1 0\,dx + \int_1^2 1\,dx + \int_2^3 2\,dx + \int_3^4 3\,dx + \ldots..$

$$+\int_{[x]-1}^{[x]} \left([x]-1\right)dx + \int_{[x]}^x [x]dx$$

$$= (2-1) + 2(3-2) + 3(4-3) + 4(5-4) + \ldots..$$

$$+\left([x]-1\right)\left[[x] - \left([x]-1\right)\right] + [x]\left(x - [x]\right)$$

$$= 1 + 2 + 3 + 4 + \ldots.. + \left([x]-1\right) + [x]\{n\}$$

$$= \frac{\left([x]-1\right)\left([x]\right)}{2} + [x].\{x]$$

$$= \frac{[x]}{2}\left[\left([x]-1\right) + 2\left(x - [x]\right)\right]$$

(j) $\int_0^x e^{\{x\}}dx = \int_0^x e^{x-[x]}dx = \int_0^1 e^x dx + \int_1^2 e^{x-1}dx + \int_2^3 e^{x-2}dx +$

$$\ldots.. + \int_{[x]-1}^{[x]} e^{x-([x]-1)}dx + \int_{[x]}^x e^{x-[x]}dx$$

$$= (e-1) + (e - e^0) + (e - e^0) + \ldots..$$

$$+(e - e^0) + \left(e^{x-[x]} - e^0\right) = [x](e-1) + \left(e^{\{x\}} - 1\right)$$

(k) $\int_0^x e^{[x]}dx = \int_0^1 e^0 dx + \int_1^2 e^1 dx + \int_2^3 e^2 dx + \int_3^4 e^3 dx +$

$$\ldots.. + \int_{[x]-1}^{[x]} e^{[x]-1}dx + \int_{[x]}^x e^{[x]}dx$$

$$= (1-0) + e(2-1) + e^2(3-2) + e^3(4-3) + \ldots..$$

$$+e^{[x]-1}\left([x] - \left([x]-1\right)\right) + e^{[x]}\left(x - [x]\right)$$

$$= 1 + e + e^2 + e^3 + \ldots.. + e^{[x]-1} + e^{[x]}.\{x\}$$

$$= 1.\frac{\left(e^{[x]}-1\right)}{(e-1)} + e^{[x]}.\{x\} = \frac{e^{[x]}-1}{(e-1)} + e^{[x]}\left(x - [x]\right)$$

(l) $\int_{\pi/2}^{3\pi/2} [2\sin x]dx$

At $x = \frac{\pi}{2}$, $2\sin x = 2$

At $x = \frac{5\pi}{6}$, $2\sin x = 1$

At $x = \pi$, $2\sin x = 0$

At $x = \frac{7\pi}{6}$, $2\sin x = -1$

At $x = \frac{3\pi}{2}$, $2\sin x = -2$

$$\therefore \quad I = \int_{\pi/2}^{5\pi/6} 1\,dx + \int_{5\pi/6}^{\pi} 0\,dx + \int_{\pi}^{7\pi/6} -1\,dx + \int_{7\pi/6}^{3\pi/2} -2\,dx$$

$$= \left[\frac{5\pi}{6} - \frac{\pi}{2}\right] + 0 - \left[\frac{7\pi}{6} - \pi\right] - 2\left[\frac{3\pi}{2} - \frac{7\pi}{6}\right]$$

$$= \left[\frac{5\pi - 3\pi}{6}\right] - \left[\frac{\pi}{6}\right] - 2\left[\frac{9\pi - 7\pi}{6}\right]$$

$$= \frac{\pi}{3} - \frac{\pi}{6} - \frac{2\pi}{3} = -\frac{\pi}{2}$$

(m) $I = \int_0^{n^2} \left[\sqrt{x}\right]dx = \int_0^1 0\,dx +$

$$\int_1^4 1\,dx + \int_4^9 2\,dx + \int_9^{16} 3\,dx + \ldots.. + \int_{(n-1)^2}^{n^2} (n-1)dx$$

$$= 0 + (4-1) + 2(9-4) + 3(16-9) + \ldots..$$

$$+(n-1)\left[(n)^2 - (n-1)^2\right]$$

$$= 1.3 + 2.5 + 3.7 + \ldots.. + (n-1)(2n-1)$$

$$T_m = m\,(2m+1)$$

$$\therefore \quad I = \sum_{m=1}^{n-1} T_m = \sum_{m=1}^{n-1}(2m^2 + m) = 2\sum_{m=1}^{n-1} m^2 + \sum_{m=1}^{n-1} m$$

$$= 2\left[\frac{(n-1)(n)(2n-1)}{6} + \frac{(n-1)(n)}{4}\right]$$

$$= \frac{2(n-1)(n)}{2}\left[\frac{2n-1}{3} + \frac{1}{2}\right] = \frac{1}{6}n(n-1)(4n+1)$$

(n) $\int_0^3 |(x-1)(x-2)(x-3)|\,dx$

Clearly $(x-1)(x-2)(x-3) > 0$ for $x \in (1,2) \cup (3,\infty)$

and < 0 for $x \in (-\infty,1) \cup (2,3)$

$$\therefore \quad I = \int_0^1 -(x-1)(x-2)(x-3)dx$$

$$+\int_1^2 (x-1)(x-2)(x-3)dx + \int_2^3 -(x-1)(x-2)(x-3)dx$$

Put $x - 2 = t \qquad \Rightarrow \quad dx = dt$

$$\therefore \quad I = \int_{-2}^{-1} -(t+1)t(t-1)dt + \int_{-1}^{0} (t+1)t(t-1)dt$$

$$+\int_0^1 -(t+1)t(t-1)dt$$

$$=\int_{-2}^{-1}(t-t^3)dt+\int_{-1}^{0}(t^3-t)dt+\int_{0}^{1}(t-t^3)dt$$

$$=\left|\frac{t^2}{2}-\frac{t^4}{4}\right|_{-2}^{-1}+\left|\frac{t^4}{4}-\frac{t^2}{2}\right|_{-1}^{0}+\left|\frac{t^2}{2}-\frac{t^4}{4}\right|_{0}^{1}=\frac{11}{4}$$

(o) $\int_{-2}^{2}\min.(x-\{x\},-x-\{x\})dx \quad =\int_{-2}^{2}\min.([x],[-x])dx$

$$=\int_{-2}^{0}[x]dx+\int_{0}^{2}[-x]dx$$

$$=\int_{-2}^{-1}-2\,dx+\int_{-1}^{0}-1\,dx+\int_{0}^{1}-1\,dx+\int_{1}^{2}-2\,dx$$

$$=-2[-1+2]-1(0-(-1))-1(1-0)-2(2-1)$$

$$=-2-1-1-2=-6$$

(p) $\int_{3}^{8}\frac{\sin\sqrt{x+1}}{\sqrt{x+1}}dx$

Put $\sqrt{x+1}=t \qquad \Rightarrow \qquad \frac{1}{2\sqrt{x+1}}=dx=dt$

$\Rightarrow \quad \frac{dx}{\sqrt{x+1}}=2\,dt$

$\therefore \quad I=\int_{2}^{3}2\sin t\,dt=-2[\cos t]_{2}^{3}$

$$=-2[\cos 3-\cos 2]=2[\cos 2-\cos 3]$$

(q) $\int_{3}^{29}\frac{\sqrt[3]{(x-2)^2}}{3+\sqrt[3]{(x-2)^2}}dx=\int_{3}^{29}\frac{(x-2)^{2/3}}{3+(x-2)^{2/3}}dx$

$$=\int_{3}^{29}\frac{(x-2)(x-2)^{-1/3}}{3+(x-2)^{2/3}}dt$$

Put $(x-2)^{2/3}=t$

$\Rightarrow \quad (x-2)^{-1/3}dx=\frac{3}{2}dt=\int_{1}^{9}\frac{t^{3/2}\left(\frac{3}{2}\right)dt}{3+t} \quad =\frac{3}{2}\int_{1}^{9}\left(t^{1/2}-\frac{3t^{1/2}}{3+t}\right)dt$

$$=\frac{3}{2}\left[\frac{t^{3/2}}{3/2}\right]_{1}^{9}-\frac{9}{2}\int_{1}^{9}\frac{t^{1/2}dt}{3+t}dt$$

In second integral, Put $t^{1/2}=u$

$\Rightarrow \quad \frac{1}{2t^{1/2}}dt=du$

$\Rightarrow \quad (27-1)-\frac{9}{2}\int_{1}^{3}\frac{u.2udu}{3+u^2}=26-\frac{9}{2}\int_{1}^{3}\frac{2u^2}{3+u^2}du$

$$=26-9\int_{1}^{3}\frac{u^2+3-3}{3+u^2}du$$

$$=26-9\int_{1}^{3}du+27\int_{1}^{3}\frac{du}{3+u^2} \quad =26-9\int_{1}^{3}du+27\int_{1}^{3}\frac{du}{3+u^2}$$

$$=26-9(3-1)+27\times\frac{1}{\sqrt{3}}\left|\tan^{-1}\left(\frac{u}{\sqrt{3}}\right)\right|_{1}^{3}$$

$$=26-18+\frac{27}{\sqrt{3}}\left[\tan^{-1}\sqrt{3}-\tan^{-1}\left(\frac{1}{\sqrt{3}}\right)\right]$$

$$=8+\frac{27}{\sqrt{3}}\left[\frac{\pi}{3}-\frac{\pi}{6}\right]=8+\frac{27}{\sqrt{3}}\times\frac{\pi}{6}=8+\frac{3\sqrt{3}\pi}{2}$$

(r) $\int_{2}^{4}\frac{\sqrt{x^2-4}}{x^4}dx \;=\int_{2}^{4}\frac{x\sqrt{1-\frac{4}{x^2}}}{x^4}dx=\int_{2}^{4}\sqrt{1-\frac{4}{x^2}}.\frac{1}{x^3}dx$

Put $1-\frac{4}{x^2}=t$

$\Rightarrow \quad \frac{8}{x^3}dx=dt \qquad \Rightarrow \quad \frac{1}{x^3}dx=\frac{dt}{8}$

$\therefore \quad \int_{0}^{3/4}t^{1/2}.\frac{dt}{8}=\frac{1}{8}.\frac{2}{3}\left|t^{3/2}\right|_{0}^{3/4}=\frac{1}{2}\left[\frac{3\sqrt{3}}{8}\right]=\frac{\sqrt{3}}{32}$

(s) $I=\int_{-1}^{1}x^2d(\ln|x|)$

$\ln|x|=-1 \qquad \Rightarrow \quad |x|=e^{-1}$ and $\ln|x|=1$

$\Rightarrow \quad |x|=e$

$\therefore \quad I=\int_{-1}^{1}e^{2\ln|x|}.d(\ln|x|)=\int_{-1}^{1}e^{2t}\,dt=\left|\frac{e^{2t}}{2}\right|_{-1}^{1}$

$$=\frac{1}{2}\left[e^2-e^{-2}\right]$$

7. (a) $\int_{0}^{1}\frac{\sin^{-1}\sqrt{x}}{\sqrt{x(1-x)}}dx$

Put $\sin^{-1}\sqrt{x}=t$

$\Rightarrow \quad \frac{1}{\sqrt{1-x}}\times\frac{1}{2\sqrt{x}}dx=dt$

$\therefore \quad I=\int_{0}^{\pi/2}2t\,dt=\left|t^2\right|_{0}^{\pi/2}=\frac{\pi^2}{4}$

(b) $\int_{0}^{\ln 2}xe^xdx=\left|xe^x\right|_{0}^{\ln 2}-\int_{0}^{\ln 2}1.e^xdx$

$$=2\ln 2-[2-1]=2\ln 2-1$$

8. (a) $\int_{0}^{\infty}\frac{1}{1+x^3}dx \;=\int_{0}^{\infty}\frac{1}{(1+x)(x^2-x+1)}dx$

$$=\int_{0}^{\infty}\left(\frac{A}{1+x}+\frac{Bx+C}{x^2-x+1}\right)dx=\int_{0}^{\infty}\left(\frac{\frac{1}{3}}{1+x}+\frac{\frac{-1}{3}x+\frac{2}{3}}{x^2-x+1}\right)dx$$

$$=\frac{1}{3}\int_{0}^{\infty}\frac{1}{1+x}dx-\frac{1}{3}\int_{0}^{\infty}\frac{x-2}{x^2-x+1}dx$$

$$=\frac{1}{3}\int_{0}^{\infty}\frac{1}{1+x}dx-\frac{1}{2\times 3}\int_{0}^{\infty}\frac{2x-1-3}{x^2-x+1}dx$$

$$=\frac{1}{3}\left|\ln(1+x)\right|_{0}^{\infty}-\frac{1}{6}\left|\ln\left|x^2-x+1\right|\right|_{0}^{\infty}+\frac{1}{2}\int_{0}^{\infty}\frac{1.dx}{(x^2-x+1)}$$

$$=\frac{1}{6}\lim_{x\to\infty}\ln\left|\frac{(1+x)^2}{x^2-x+1}\right|+\frac{1}{2}\int_{0}^{\infty}\frac{1dx}{\left(x-\frac{1}{2}\right)^2+\frac{3}{4}}$$

$$=\frac{1}{6}\lim_{x\to\infty}\ln\left|\frac{x^2+2x+1}{x^2-x+1}\right|+\frac{1}{2}\times\frac{2}{\sqrt{3}}\left|\tan^{-1}\left|\frac{\left(x-\frac{1}{2}\right)}{\frac{\sqrt{3}}{2}}\right|\right|_{0}^{\infty}$$

$$=\frac{1}{6}\lim_{x\to\infty}\ln\left|\frac{1+\frac{2}{x}+\frac{1}{x^2}}{1-\frac{1}{x}+\frac{1}{x^2}}\right|+\frac{1}{\sqrt{3}}\left[\tan^{-1}(\infty)-\tan^{-1}\left(\frac{-1}{\sqrt{3}}\right)\right]$$

$$=\frac{1}{6}\ln 1+\frac{1}{\sqrt{3}}\left[\frac{\pi}{2}+\frac{\pi}{6}\right]=\frac{1}{\sqrt{3}}\left[\frac{3\pi+\pi}{6}\right]$$

$$=\frac{1}{\sqrt{3}}\left(\frac{2\pi}{3}\right)=\frac{2\pi}{3\sqrt{3}}$$

(b) $$\int_0^{\infty}\frac{3x^2+4}{(x^3+4x+1)^3}dx=\left[\frac{(x^3+4x+1)^{-2}}{-2}\right]_0^{\infty}$$

$$=\frac{-1}{2}[0-1]=\frac{1}{2}$$

9. $$\int_0^{\pi/2}\frac{dx}{1+4\left(\frac{\cos^2 x}{\sin^2 x}\right)}=\int_0^{\pi/2}\frac{\sin^2 x}{\sin^2 x+4\cos^2 x}dx$$

$$=\int_0^{\pi/2}\frac{\tan^2 x\sec^2 x}{\tan^2 x\sec^2 x+4\sec^2 x}dx$$

$$=\int_0^{\infty}\frac{t^2dt}{t^2(1+t^2)+4(1+t^2)};t=\tan x$$

$$=\int_0^{\infty}\frac{t^2dt}{t^4+5t^2+4}dt=\int_0^{\infty}\frac{t^2}{(t^2+1)(t^2+4)}dt$$

$$=\frac{-1}{3}\int_0^{\infty}\frac{1}{t^2+1}dt+\frac{4}{3}\int_0^{\infty}\frac{1}{t^2+4}dt$$

$$=\frac{-1}{3}\left|\tan^{-1}t\right|_0^{\infty}+\frac{4}{3}\times\frac{1}{2}\left|\tan^{-1}\frac{t}{2}\right|_0^{\infty}=\frac{-1}{3}\left|\frac{\pi}{2}-0\right|+\frac{2}{3}\left[\frac{\pi}{2}-0\right]$$

$$=\frac{\pi}{3}-\frac{\pi}{6}=\frac{\pi}{6}$$

10. (i) $$I=\int_{-\infty}^{\infty}\frac{\cos x}{1+x^2}dx$$

$$\therefore\ \int_{-\infty}^{\infty}\frac{-1}{1+x^2}\le I\le\int_{-\infty}^{\infty}\frac{1}{1+x^2}dx$$

$$\Rightarrow\ -2\int_0^{\infty}\frac{1}{1+x^2}dx\le I\le 2\int_0^{\infty}\frac{1}{1+x^2}dx$$

$$\Rightarrow\ -2\left|\tan^{-1}x\right|_0^{\infty}\le I\le 2\left|\tan^{-1}x\right|_0^{\infty}$$

$$\Rightarrow\ -2\left[\frac{\pi}{2}-0\right]\le I\le 2\left[\frac{\pi}{2}-0\right]$$

$\Rightarrow\ -\pi\le I\le\pi$ $\qquad\Rightarrow\ |I|\le\pi$

$\Rightarrow$ I is convergent

(ii) (a), (c) and (d) are improper as their denominator approaches to zero at $x=\frac{3}{2}$, $\sqrt{2}$ and 2 respectively.

(a) $$I=\int_0^2\frac{1}{2x-3}dx=\int_0^{3/2}\frac{1}{2x-3}+$$

$$\int_{3/2}^2\frac{1}{2x-3}dx=\lim_{h\to0^+}\int_0^{\frac{3}{2}-h}\frac{1}{(2x-3)}x+\lim_{h'\to0^+}\int_{\frac{3}{2}+h}^2\frac{1}{2x-3}dx$$

$$=\lim_{h\to0^+}\left[\frac{\ln|2x-3|}{2}\right]_0^{\frac{3}{2}-h}+\lim_{h'\to0^+}\left[\frac{\ln|2x-3|}{2}\right]_{\frac{3}{2}+h}^2$$

$$=\lim_{h\to0^+}\left[\frac{1}{2}\ln|-2h|\right]+\lim_{h'\to0^+}\left[\frac{1}{2}\ln|1|-\frac{1}{2}\ln|2h|\right]-\frac{1}{2}\ln|3|$$

$$=\lim_{h\to0^+}\frac{1}{2}\ln|2h|-\lim_{h'\to0^+}\frac{1}{2}\ln|2h'|-\frac{1}{2}\ln 3=-\frac{1}{2}\ln 3$$

(b) $$I=\int_0^1\frac{1}{2x+1}dx=\frac{1}{2}\left[\ln|2x+1|\right]_0^1=\frac{1}{2}[\ln 3]$$

(c) $$I=\int_0^2\frac{1}{x^2-2}dx=\frac{1}{2\sqrt{2}}\lim_{h\to0^+}\left[\ln\left|\frac{x-\sqrt{2}}{x+\sqrt{2}}\right|\right]_0^{\sqrt{2}-h}$$

$$+\frac{1}{2\sqrt{2}}\lim_{h'\to0^+}\left[\ln\left|\frac{x-\sqrt{2}}{x+\sqrt{2}}\right|\right]_{\sqrt{2}+h}^2$$

$$=\frac{1}{2\sqrt{2}}\lim_{h\to0^+}\left|\frac{-h}{2\sqrt{2}-h}\right|+\frac{1}{2\sqrt{2}}\lim_{h'\to0^+}\left\{\ln\left|\frac{2-\sqrt{2}}{2+\sqrt{2}}\right|-\ln\left|\frac{h'}{2\sqrt{2}+h'}\right|\right\}$$

$$=\frac{1}{2\sqrt{2}}\ln\left|\frac{2-\sqrt{2}}{2+\sqrt{2}}\right|=\frac{1}{2\sqrt{2}}\ln\left(3-2\sqrt{2}\right)$$

(d) $$I=\int_2^3\ln(x-2)dx=\lim_{h\to0^+}\int_{2-h}^3\ln(x-2)dx=$$

$$\lim_{h\to0^+}\left[\left|x\ln(x-2)\right|_{2-h}^3-\int_{2-h}^3\frac{1}{(x-2)}.x\,dx\right]$$

$$=\lim_{h\to0^+}\left[-(2-h)\ln|h|-\int_{2-h}^3\frac{x-2+2}{x-2}dx\right]$$

$$=\lim_{h\to0^+}\left[(h-2)\ln|h|-\int_{2-h}^3 1dx-2\int_{2-h}^3\frac{1}{x-2}dx\right]$$

$$=\lim_{h\to0^+}\left[(h-2)\ln|h|-[3-(2-h)]-2[\ln 1-\ln|h|]\right]$$

$$=\lim_{h\to0^+}\left[(h-2)\ln|h|-3+(2-h)+2\ln|h|\right]$$

$$=\lim_{h\to0^+}\left[h\ln|h|-1-h\right]=\lim_{h\to0^+}\frac{\ln h}{\frac{1}{h}}-1$$

$$=\lim_{h\to0^+}\left[\frac{\frac{1}{h}}{\frac{1}{h^2}}\right]-1=0-1=-1$$

11. (a) $$\int_1^{\infty}xe^{-x^2}dx=\lim_{t\to\infty}\int_1^t xe^{-x^2}dx=\lim_{t\to\infty}\int_1^{t^2}e^{-u}\frac{du}{2};u=x^2$$

$$=\frac{1}{2}\lim_{t\to\infty}\int_1^{t^2}e^{-u}du$$

$$=\frac{1}{2}\lim_{t\to\infty}\left[\frac{e^{-u}}{-1}\right]_1^{t^2}=\frac{-1}{2}\left[e^{-t^2}-e^{-1}\right]_{t\to\infty}$$

$$=\frac{-1}{2}\left[e^{-\infty}-e^{-1}\right]=\frac{1}{2e}$$

(b) $$I=\int_0^{\pi/4}\text{cosec}\,x\,dx=\lim_{t\to0^+}\int_t^{\pi/4}\text{cosec}\,x\,dx$$

$$=\lim_{t\to0^+}\left[\ln\left|\text{cosec}x-\cot x\right|\right]_t^{\pi/4}$$

$$=\lim_{t\to0^+}\left[\ln\left(\sqrt{2}-1\right)-\ln\left|\text{cosec}t-\cot t\right|\right]$$

$$=\ln\left(\sqrt{2}-1\right)-\lim_{t\to0^+}\ln\left|\frac{1-\cos t}{\sin t}\right|$$

$$= \ln\left(\sqrt{2}-1\right) - \lim_{t\to 0^+} \ln\left|\frac{2\sin^2 \in/2}{2\sin\frac{\in}{2}\cos\frac{\in}{2}}\right|$$

$$= \ln\left(\sqrt{2}-1\right) - \lim_{\in\to 0^+} \ln\left|\tan \in/2\right| = \ln\left(\sqrt{2}-1\right) - (-\infty) = \infty$$

⇒ I is divergent is not convergent

(c) $$I = \int_0^2 \frac{x^2 dx}{x^2-3x+2} = \int_0^2 \frac{\left(x^2-3x+2\right)+(3x-2)}{\left(x^2-3x+2\right)}dx$$

$$= \int_0^1 \frac{\left(x^2-3x+2\right)+(3x-2)}{\left(x^2-3x+2\right)}dx + \int_1^2 \frac{\left(x^2-3x+2\right)+(3x-2)}{\left(x^2-3x+2\right)}dx$$

$$= \lim_{\in\to 0^+}\int_0^{1-\in}\left[1+\frac{3x-2}{x^2-3x+2}\right]dx + \lim_{\substack{\in_1\to 0^+\\ \in_2\to 0^+}}\int_{1-\in_1}^{2-\in_2}\left[1+\frac{3x-2}{x^2-3x+2}\right]dx$$

$$= 1 + \lim_{\in\to 0^+}\int_0^{1-\in}\frac{3x-2}{x^2-3x+2}dx + 1 + \lim_{\in_1,\in_2\to 0^+}\int_{1+\in_1}^{2-\in_2}\frac{3x-2}{x^2-3x+2}dx$$

$$= 2 + \lim_{\in\to 0^+}\int_0^{1-\in}\frac{3x-2}{x^2-3x+2}dx + 1 + \lim_{\in_1,\in_2\to 0^+}\int_{1+\in_1}^{2-\in_2}\frac{3x-2}{x^2-3x+2}dx$$

$$= 2 + \lim_{\in\to 0^+}\left[\frac{3}{2}\ln\left|x^2-3x+2\right| + \frac{5}{2}\ln\left|\frac{x-2}{x-1}\right|\right]_0^{1-\in} + \lim_{\in_1,\in_2\to 0^+}\left[\frac{3}{2}\ln\left|x^2-3x+2\right| + \frac{5}{2}\ln\left|\frac{x-2}{x-1}\right|\right]_{1+\in_1}^{2-\in_2}$$

$$= 2 + \lim_{\in\to 0^+}\left[\frac{3}{2}\ln\in(\in+1) + \frac{5}{2}\ln\left|\frac{\in+1}{\in}\right| - \frac{3}{2}\ln 2 + \frac{5}{2}\ln 2\right]$$

$$+ \lim_{\in_1,\in_2\to 0^+}\left[\begin{matrix}\frac{3}{2}\ln\in_2(1-\in_2) + \frac{5}{2}\ln\left[\frac{\in_2}{1-\in_2}\right] - \\ \frac{3}{2}\ln\in_1(1-\in_1) - \frac{5}{2}\ln\left(\frac{1-\in_1}{\in_1}\right)\end{matrix}\right]$$

$$= 2 + \lim_{\in\to 0^+}\left[\frac{3}{2}\ln\in(\in+1) + \frac{5}{2}\ln\left(\frac{\in+1}{\in}\right)\right] + \lim_{\in_1,\in_2\to 0^+}\left[\frac{5}{2}\ln\left(\frac{\in_2}{1-\in_2}\right) + \frac{5}{2}\ln\left(\frac{\in_1}{1-\in_1}\right)\right]$$

$$= 2 + \lim_{\in\to 0^+}\left[\frac{3}{2}\ln\in(\in+1) + \frac{5}{2}\ln\left(\frac{\in+1}{\in}\right) + 5\ln\left(\frac{\in}{1-\in}\right)\right]$$

$$= 2 + \lim_{\in\to 0^+}\left[4\ln\in + 4\ln(\in+1) - 5\ln(1-\in)\right]$$

$$= 2 + \lim_{\in\to 0^+}\left[4\ln\in\right] = 2 + \infty = \infty$$

⇒ I is divergent. Ans

(d) $$\int_0^\infty \tan^{-1}x\,dx = \lim_{t\to\infty}\int_0^t 1.\tan^{-1}x\,dx$$

$$= \lim_{t\to\infty}\left[\left|x.\tan^{-1}x\right|_0^t - \int_0^t \frac{1}{1+x^2}(x)dx\right]$$

$$= \lim_{t\to\infty}\left[t\tan^{-1}t - \frac{1}{2}\left[\ln\left(1+x^2\right)\right]_0^t\right]$$

$$= \lim_{t\to\infty}\left[t\tan^{-1}t - \frac{1}{2}\ln\left(1+t^2\right)\right]$$

$$= \lim_{t\to\infty}\left[t.\tan^{-1}t\left(1 - \frac{\frac{1}{2}\ln\left(1+t^2\right)}{t.\tan^{-1}t}\right)\right]$$

$$= \lim_{t\to\infty}\left[(\infty).\left(\frac{\pi}{2}\right)(1-0)\right] = \infty = \text{Divergent}$$

(e) $$I = \int_{-\infty}^0 \frac{\tan^{-1}x}{1+x^2}dx = \lim_{t\to\infty}\int_{-t}^0 \frac{\tan^{-1}x}{1+x^2}dx =$$

$$\lim_{t\to\infty}\int_{-\tan^{-1}(t)}^0 u\,du = \lim_{t\to\infty}\left[\frac{u^2}{2}\right]_{-\tan^{-1}t}^0$$

$$= \frac{1}{2}\lim_{t\to\infty}\left[0 - \left(\tan^{-1}t\right)^2\right] = \frac{1}{2}\left[-\left(\frac{\pi}{2}\right)^2\right] = -\frac{\pi^2}{8}$$

(f) $$I = \int_{-\infty}^\infty \frac{dx}{x^2+4x+5}dx = \lim_{t\to\infty}\int_{-t}^t \frac{dx}{(x+2)^2+1}$$

$$= \lim_{t\to\infty}\left[\tan^{-1}(x+2)\right]_{-t}^t$$

$$= \lim_{\to\infty}\left[\tan^{-1}(t+2) - \tan^{-1}(-t+2)\right]$$

$$= \lim_{t\to\infty}\left[\tan^{-1}(t+2) + \tan^{-1}(t-2)\right]$$

$$= \tan^{-1}(\infty) + \tan^{-1}(\infty) = \frac{\pi}{2} + \frac{\pi}{2} = \pi$$

12. $$I = \int_0^3 \frac{1}{x^2-4x+3}dx = \int_0^3 \frac{1}{\left(x^2 4x+4\right)-(1)}dx$$

$$= \int_0^3 \frac{1}{\left(x^2-2\right)^2-(1)^2}dx$$

$$= \int_0^1 \frac{1}{(x-2)^2-(1)^2}dx + \int_1^3 \frac{1}{(x-2)^2-(1)^2}dx$$

$$= \lim_{\in_1\to 0^+}\int_0^{1-\in_1}\frac{1}{(x-2)^2-(1)^2}dx + \lim_{\substack{\in_2\to 0^+\\ \in_3\to 0^+}}\int_{1+\in_2}^{3-\in_3}\frac{1}{(x-2)^2-(1)^2}dx$$

$$= \lim_{\in_1\to 0^+}\frac{1}{2}\left[\ln\left|\frac{x-2-1}{x-2+1}\right|\right]_0^{1-\in_1} + \lim_{\substack{\in_2\to 0^+\\ \in_3\to 0^+}}\frac{1}{2}\left[\ln\left|\frac{x-2-1}{x-2+1}\right|\right]_{1+\in_2}^{3-\in_3}$$

$$= \lim_{\in_1\to 0^+}\frac{1}{2}\left[\ln\left(\frac{\in_1+2}{\in_1}\right) - \ln 3\right] + \lim_{\substack{\in_2\to 0^+\\ \in_3\to 0^+}}\frac{1}{2}\left[\ln\left(\frac{\in_3}{2-\in_3}\right) - \ln\left(\frac{2-\in_2}{\in_2}\right)\right]$$

$$=-\frac{1}{2}\ln 3+\frac{1}{2}\lim_{\epsilon_1\to 0^+}\ln\left(\frac{\epsilon_1+2}{\epsilon_1}\right)+\lim_{\epsilon_2\to 0^+}\frac{1}{2}\left[2\ln\left(\frac{\epsilon_2}{2-\epsilon_2}\right)\right]$$

$$=-\frac{1}{2}\ln 3+\frac{1}{2}\lim_{\epsilon_1\to 0^+}\ln\left(\frac{\epsilon_1+2}{\epsilon_1}\right)+\lim_{\epsilon_2\to 0^+}\ln\left(\frac{\epsilon_2}{2-\epsilon_2}\right)$$

$$=-\frac{1}{2}\ln 3+\frac{1}{2}\ln 2-\ln 2+\lim_{\epsilon\to 0^+}\frac{1}{2}\ln\epsilon$$

$$=-\frac{1}{2}\ln 3-\frac{1}{2}\ln 2+\infty=\infty$$

⇒ I is divergent

13. (a) $\int_0^1\frac{1}{\sqrt[3]{x}}dx=\lim_{\epsilon\to 0^+}\int_\epsilon^1(x)^{-1/3}dx$

$$=\lim_{\epsilon\to 0^+}\left[\frac{3}{2}(x)^{2/3}\right]_\epsilon^1=\lim_{\epsilon\to 0^+}\frac{3}{2}\left[1-(\epsilon)^{2/3}\right]=\frac{3}{2}(1-0)=\frac{3}{2}$$

(b) $I=\int_{-2}^{0}\frac{e^{\frac{1}{x}}}{x^3}dx=\lim_{\epsilon\to 0^+}\int_{-2}^{-\epsilon}\frac{e^{1/x}}{x^3}dx$

Put $\frac{1}{x}=t \Rightarrow \frac{-1}{x^2}dx=dt$

$$\therefore\ I=\lim_{\epsilon\to 0^+}\int_{-1/2}^{-1/\epsilon}te^t(-dt)=\lim_{\epsilon\to 0^+}\int_{-1/\epsilon}^{-1/2}te^t dt$$

$$=\lim_{\epsilon\to 0^+}\left[\left[te^t\right]_{-1/\epsilon}^{-1/2}-\int_{-1/\epsilon}^{-1/2}1.e^t dt\right]$$

$$=\lim_{\epsilon\to 0^+}\left[-\frac{1}{2}e^{-1/2}+\frac{1}{\epsilon}e^{-1/\epsilon}-\left[e^{-1/2}-e^{-1/\epsilon}\right]\right]$$

$$=-\frac{1}{2}e^{-1/2}+\lim_{\epsilon\to 0^+}\frac{e^{-1/\epsilon}}{\epsilon}-e^{-1/2}+0$$

$$=-\frac{3}{2}e^{-1/2}+\lim_{\epsilon\to 0^+}e^{-1/\epsilon}.\left(\frac{1}{\epsilon}\right)=-\frac{3}{2}e^{-1/2}+\lim_{\epsilon\to 0^+}\left[\frac{1}{\epsilon\left(e^{1/\epsilon}\right)}\right]$$

$$=-\frac{3}{2}e^{-1/2}+\lim_{\epsilon\to 0^+}\left[\frac{1}{\epsilon\left[1+\frac{1}{\epsilon}+\frac{1}{2!\epsilon^2}+\frac{1}{3!\epsilon^3}+....\infty\right]}\right]$$

$$=-\frac{3}{2}e^{-1/2}+\lim_{\epsilon\to 0^+}\left[\frac{1}{\epsilon+1+\frac{1}{2!\epsilon}+\frac{1}{3!\epsilon^2}+....\infty}\right]$$

$$=-\frac{3}{2}e^{-1/2}+0=-\frac{3}{2}e^{-1/2}$$

(c) $I=\int_5^7\frac{1}{\sqrt{x-5}}dx=\lim_{\epsilon\to 0^+}\int_{5+\epsilon}^{7}\frac{1}{\sqrt{x-5}}dx$

$$=\lim_{\epsilon\to 0^+}\int_{5+\epsilon}^{7}(x-5)^{-1/2}dx$$

$$=\lim_{\epsilon\to 0^+}\left[2(x-5)^{1/2}\right]_{5+\epsilon}^{7}$$

$$=\lim_{\epsilon\to 0^+}2\left[(2)^{1/2}-(\epsilon)^{1/2}\right]=2\sqrt{2}$$

(d) $I=\int_0^1\ln x\,dx=\lim_{\epsilon\to 0^+}\int_\epsilon^1\ln x\,dx$

$$=\lim_{\epsilon\to 0^+}\left[\left[(\ln x)x\right]_\epsilon^1-\int_\epsilon^1\frac{1}{x}x\,dx\right]$$

$$=\lim_{\epsilon\to 0^+}\left[0-\epsilon\ln\epsilon-[x]_\epsilon^1\right]=\lim_{\epsilon\to 0^+}\left[-\epsilon\ln\epsilon-(1-\epsilon)\right]$$

$$=\lim_{\epsilon\to 0^+}\left[-\left(\frac{\ln\epsilon}{1/\epsilon}\right)\right]-1=\lim_{\epsilon\to 0^+}\left[-\frac{1/\epsilon}{-1/\epsilon^2}\right]-1$$

$$=\lim_{\epsilon\to 0^+}\left[\frac{1}{\epsilon}\times\frac{\epsilon^2}{1}\right]-1=-1$$

TEXTUAL EXERCISE-3: (OBJECTIVE)

1. (c) $I=\int_{\pi/2}^{3\pi/2}[2\sin x]dx$

For $x\in\left[\frac{\pi}{2},\frac{3\pi}{2}\right],(\sin x)\in[-1,1]$

⇒ |2 sinx ∈ [–2, 2], i.e., take integer values –1, 0, 1 in (–2, 2) at $x=\frac{7\pi}{6},\pi,\frac{5\pi}{6}$

$$\therefore\ I=\int_{\pi/2}^{\frac{5\pi}{6}}[2\sin x]dx+\int_{\frac{5\pi}{6}}^{\pi}[2\sin x]dx$$

$$+\int_{\pi}^{7\pi/6}[2\sin x]dx+\int_{7\pi/6}^{3\pi/2}[2\sin x]dx$$

$$=\int_{\pi/2}^{5\pi/6}1dx+\int_{5\pi/6}^{\pi}0dx+\int_{\pi}^{7\pi/6}(-1)dx+\int_{7\pi/6}^{3\pi/2}(-2)dx$$

$$=\left(\frac{5\pi}{6}-\frac{\pi}{2}\right)-\left(\frac{7\pi}{6}-\pi\right)-2\left(\frac{3\pi}{2}-\frac{7\pi}{6}\right)$$

$$=\left(\frac{5\pi-3\pi}{6}\right)-\left(\frac{7\pi-6\pi}{6}\right)-2\left(\frac{9\pi-7\pi}{6}\right)$$

$$=\frac{\pi}{3}-\frac{\pi}{6}-\frac{2\pi}{3}=\frac{-\pi}{2}$$

2. (c) Given $\int_{-1}^{4}f(x)dx=4;\int_2^4(3-f(x))dx=7$,

To find: $I=\int_2^{-1}f(x)dx$ ...(1)

Now $\int_2^4(3-f(x))dx=7$

$$\Rightarrow\ 3\,(2)-\int_2^4 f(x)dx=7$$

$$\Rightarrow\ \int_2^4 f(x)dx=-1\text{ and }\int_{-1}^4 f(x)dx=\int_{-1}^2 f(x)dx+\int_2^4 f(x)dx$$

$$\Rightarrow\ 4=\int_{-1}^2 f(x)dx+(-1)$$

$$\Rightarrow\ \int_{-1}^2 f(x)dx=5$$

$$\Rightarrow\ \int_2^{-1}f(x)dx=-5$$

3. (b) $\int_{-5}^{5}|x+2|dx=\int_{-5}^{-2}|x+2|dx+\int_{-2}^{5}|x+2|dx$

$$=\int_{-5}^{-2}(-x-2)dx+\int_{-2}^{5}(x+2)dx$$

$$=-\left[\frac{x^2}{2}+2x\right]_{-5}^{-2}+\left[\frac{x^2}{2}+2x\right]_{-2}^{5}$$

$$=-\left[\frac{1}{2}(4-25)+2(3)\right]+\left[\frac{1}{2}(21)+2(7)\right]$$

$$=21+14-6=29$$

4. (d) $I=\int_{-1}^{3/2}|x\sin\pi x|\,dx$

For $x\in[-1,0]$, $\pi x\in[-\pi,0]$ and for $x\in[0,1]$, $\pi x\in[\pi,0]$, and for $x\in\left[1,\frac{3}{2}\right]$, $\pi x\in\left[\pi,\frac{3\pi}{2}\right]$

$\Rightarrow$ for $x\in(-1,0)$, $x\sin\pi x>0$,
for $x\in(0,1)$, $x\sin\pi x>0$,
for $x\in(1,3/2)$, $x\sin\pi x<0$,

$$\therefore\quad I=\int_{-1}^{1}x\sin\pi x\,dx+\int_{1}^{3/2}-x\sin\pi x\,dx$$

$$=2\int_0^1 x\sin\pi x\,dx-\int_1^{3/2}x\sin\pi x\,dx$$

$$=2\left[\left[\frac{-x\cos\pi}{\pi}\right]_0^1+\int_0^1\frac{1.\cos\pi x}{\pi}dx\right]-\left[\left[\frac{-x\cos\pi}{\pi}\right]_1^{3/2}+\int_1^{3/2}\frac{1.\cos\pi x}{\pi}dx\right]$$

$$=-\frac{2}{\pi}[(-1)]+\frac{2}{\pi^2}[0]+\frac{1}{\pi}[0-(-1)]-\frac{1}{\pi^2[-1-(0)]}$$

$$=\frac{2}{\pi}+\frac{1}{\pi}+\frac{1}{\pi^2}=\frac{3}{\pi}+\frac{1}{\pi^2}$$

5. (b) $I=\int_{e^{-1}}^{e^2}\left|\frac{\log e^x}{x}\right|dx=\int_{e^{-1}}^{e^2}|\ln x|\frac{dx}{2}$

Put $\ln x=t$

$$\Rightarrow\quad \frac{1}{x}dx=dt=\int_{-1}^{2}|t|\,dt=\int_{-1}^{0}-t\,dt+\int_0^2 t\,dt$$

$$=-\left[\frac{t^2}{2}\right]_{-1}^{0}+\left[\frac{t^2}{2}\right]_0^2$$

$$=\frac{-1}{2}[0-1]+\frac{1}{2}[4-0]=\frac{1}{2}+2=\frac{5}{2}$$

6. (b) $I=\int_0^1\frac{\ln x}{\sqrt{1-x^2}}dx$

Put $x=\sin\theta$ $\quad\Rightarrow\quad dx=\cos\theta\,d\theta$

$$\Rightarrow\quad I=\int_0^{\pi/2}\frac{\ln(\sin\theta)}{\cos\theta}\cos\theta\,d\theta$$

$$\Rightarrow\quad I=\int_0^{\pi/2}\ln(\sin\theta)d\theta\qquad\ldots(1)$$

Also, $I=\int_0^{\pi/2}\ln\left(\sin\left(\frac{\pi}{2}-\theta\right)\right)d\theta$

$$\Rightarrow\quad I=\int_0^{\pi/2}\ln(\cos\theta)\qquad\ldots(2)$$

Adding (1) and (2), we get $2I=\int_0^{\pi/2}\ln(\sin\theta.\cos\theta)d\theta$

$$2I=\int_0^{\pi/2}\ln(\sin 2\theta)d\theta-(\ln.2)\frac{\pi}{2}$$

Put $2\theta=t$ $\quad\Rightarrow\quad d\theta=\frac{dt}{2}$

$$\Rightarrow\quad 2I=\int_0^{\pi}(\sin t)\frac{dt}{2}-\frac{\pi}{2}\ln 2=\frac{1}{2}\int_0^{\pi}\ln(\sin t)dt-\frac{\pi}{2}\ln 2$$

$$=2\left(\frac{1}{2}\right)\int_0^{\pi/2}\ln(\sin t)dt-\frac{\pi}{2}\ln 2$$

$$\Rightarrow\quad 2I=I=\frac{\pi}{2}\ln 2\qquad\Rightarrow\quad I=-\frac{\pi}{2}\ln 2$$

7. (b) $I=\int_1^e\frac{\ln x}{x}dx$

Put $\ln x=t$ $\quad\Rightarrow\quad \frac{1}{x}dx=dt$

$$\Rightarrow\quad I=\int_0^1 t\,dt=\frac{1}{2}\left[t^2\right]_0^1=\frac{1}{2}$$

8. (c) $I=\int_0^{\pi/2}\frac{dx}{1+\cos x}=\int_0^{\pi/2}\frac{dx}{2\cos^2\frac{x}{2}}=\frac{1}{2}\int_0^{\pi/2}\sec^2\frac{x}{2}dx$

$$=\frac{1}{2}\left[\frac{\tan\frac{x}{2}}{\frac{1}{2}}\right]_0^{\pi/2}=[1-0]=1$$

9. (b) $I=\int_0^{1/2}\frac{dx}{(1-2x^2)\sqrt{1-x^2}}$

Put $x=\cos\theta$
$\Rightarrow\ dx=-\sin\theta\,d\theta$

$$\Rightarrow\quad I=\int_{\pi/2}^{\pi/3}\frac{-\sin\theta.d\theta}{(1-2\cos^2\theta)\sqrt{1-\cos^2\theta}}=\int_{\pi/2}^{\pi/3}\frac{d\theta}{(2\cos^2\theta-1)}$$

$$=-\int_{\pi/3}^{\pi/2}\frac{d\theta}{\cos 2\theta}=-\int_{\pi/3}^{\pi/2}\sec 2\theta\,d\theta$$

$$\Rightarrow\quad -\frac{1}{2}\left[\ln|\sec 2\theta+\tan 2\theta|\right]_{\pi/3}^{\pi/2}=-\frac{1}{2}\left[\ln|-1|-\ln\left|-2-\sqrt{3}\right|\right]$$

$$=\frac{1}{2}\ln\left|2+\sqrt{3}\right|=\ln\sqrt{2+\sqrt{3}}$$

10. (a) $I=\int_0^2\frac{x^2dx}{x^3-17}=\frac{1}{3}\int_0^2\frac{3x^2dx}{x^3-17}=\frac{1}{3}\left[\ln\left|x^3-17\right|\right]_0^2$

$$=\frac{1}{3}[\ln 9-\ln 17]=\frac{1}{3}\ln\left(\frac{9}{17}\right)$$

11. (b) $I=\int_{\lambda}^{\mu}\frac{dx}{x\sqrt{(x-\lambda)(\mu-x)}}$

Put $x=\frac{1}{t}$ $\quad\Rightarrow\quad dx=\frac{-1}{t^2}dt$

$$\therefore\quad I=\int_{\frac{1}{\lambda}}^{\frac{1}{\mu}}\frac{-\frac{1}{t^2}dt}{\left(\frac{1}{t}\right)\sqrt{\left(\frac{1}{t}-\lambda\right)\left(\mu-\frac{1}{t}\right)}}=\int_{\frac{1}{\lambda}}^{\frac{1}{\mu}}\frac{-dt}{\sqrt{(1-\lambda t)(\mu t-1)}}$$

$$= \int_{1/\mu}^{1/\lambda} \frac{dt}{\sqrt{-\lambda\mu t^2 + \lambda t + \mu t - 1}}$$

$$= \int_{1/\mu}^{1/\lambda} \frac{dt}{\sqrt{-\lambda\mu\left(t^2 - \frac{1}{\mu}t - \frac{t}{\lambda} + \frac{1}{\lambda\mu}\right)}}$$

$$= \int_{1/\mu}^{1/\lambda} \frac{dt}{-\lambda\mu\left[t^2 - \left(\frac{1}{\mu} - \frac{1}{\lambda}\right)t + \frac{1}{\lambda\mu}\right]}$$

$$= \int_{1/\mu}^{1/\lambda} \frac{dt}{\sqrt{-\lambda\mu\left[t^2 - \left(\frac{1}{\mu} + \frac{1}{\lambda}\right)t + \frac{1}{4}\left(\frac{1}{\lambda} + \frac{1}{\mu}\right)^2 - 1 + \frac{\lambda\mu}{4}\left(\frac{1}{\lambda} + \frac{1}{\mu}\right)^2\right]}}$$

$$= \int_{1/\mu}^{1/\lambda} \frac{dt}{\sqrt{-\lambda\mu\left[t - \frac{1}{2}\left(\frac{1}{\lambda} + \frac{1}{\mu}\right)^2 - 1 + \frac{\lambda\mu}{4}\left(\frac{1}{\lambda} + \frac{1}{\mu}\right)^2\right]}}$$

$$= \int_{1/\mu}^{1/\lambda} \frac{dt}{\sqrt{\left\{\frac{\lambda\mu}{4}\left(\frac{1}{\lambda} + \frac{1}{\mu}\right)^2 - 1\right\} - \lambda\mu\left[t - \frac{1}{2}\left(\frac{1}{\lambda} + \frac{1}{\mu}\right)\right]^2}}$$

$$= \left[\frac{1}{\sqrt{\lambda}\sqrt{\mu}}\sin^{-1}\left[\frac{\sqrt{\lambda}\sqrt{\mu}\left(t - \frac{1}{2}\right)\left(\frac{1}{\lambda} + \frac{1}{\mu}\right)}{\frac{\lambda\mu}{4}\left(\frac{1}{\lambda} + \frac{1}{\mu}\right)^2 - 1}\right]\right]_{\frac{1}{\mu}}^{\frac{1}{\lambda}}$$

$$= \frac{1}{\sqrt{\lambda}\sqrt{\mu}}\sin^{-1}\left[\frac{\sqrt{\lambda}\sqrt{\mu}\left(\frac{1}{2\lambda} + \frac{1}{2\mu}\right)}{\frac{\sqrt{\lambda}\sqrt{\mu}}{2}\left[\sqrt{\left(\frac{1}{\lambda} + \frac{1}{\mu}\right)^2 - \frac{4}{\lambda\mu}}\right]}\right]$$

$$- \frac{1}{\sqrt{\lambda}\sqrt{\mu}}\sin^{-1}\left\{\frac{\sqrt{\lambda}\sqrt{\mu}\left(\frac{1}{2\mu} - \frac{1}{2\lambda}\right)}{\frac{\sqrt{\lambda}\sqrt{\mu}}{2}\left[\sqrt{\left(\frac{1}{\lambda} + \frac{1}{\mu}\right)^2 - \frac{4}{\lambda\mu}}\right]}\right\}$$

$$= \frac{1}{\sqrt{\lambda}\sqrt{\mu}}\sin^{-1}(1) - \frac{1}{\sqrt{\lambda}\sqrt{\mu}}\sin^{-1}(-1)$$

$$\left[\because \lambda < \mu \Rightarrow \frac{1}{\lambda} > \frac{1}{\mu} \Rightarrow \frac{1}{\lambda} - \frac{1}{\mu} > 0\right]$$

$$= \frac{2}{\sqrt{\lambda}\sqrt{\mu}}\sin^{-1}(1) = \frac{\pi}{\sqrt{\lambda\mu}}$$

12. (c) $I = \int_0^{\pi/2} \frac{dx}{\left(\sqrt{\sin x} + \sqrt{\cos x}\right)^4} = \int_0^{\pi/2} \frac{dx}{\cos^2 x\left(\sqrt{\tan x} + 1\right)^4}$

$$= \int_0^{\pi/2} \frac{\sec^2 x\, dx}{\left(\sqrt{\tan x} + 1\right)^4}$$

Put $\tan x = t \quad \Rightarrow \quad \sec 2x\, dx = dt$

$$\Rightarrow \quad I = \int_0^{\infty} \frac{dt}{\left(\sqrt{t} + 1\right)^4}$$

Put $\sqrt{t} = u \quad \Rightarrow \quad \frac{1}{2\sqrt{t}}dt = du$

$$\Rightarrow \quad dt = 2\sqrt{t}du = 2u\, du$$

$$\therefore \quad I = \int_0^{\infty} \frac{2u\, du}{(u+1)^4} = 2\int_0^{\infty} \frac{(u+1) - 1}{(u+1)^4}du$$

$$= 2\left[\int_0^{\infty} \frac{1}{(u+1)^3}du - \int_0^{\infty} \frac{1}{(u+1)^4}du\right]$$

$$= 2\left[\frac{(u+1)^{-2}}{-2} - \frac{(u+1)^{-3}}{-3}\right]_0^{\infty}$$

$$= 2\left[\frac{-1}{2(u+1)^2} + \frac{1}{3(u+1)^3}\right]_0^{\infty}$$

$$= 2\left[0 - \left(-\frac{1}{2} + \frac{1}{3}\right)\right] = 2\left[\frac{1}{2} - \frac{1}{3}\right] = 2\left[\frac{3-2}{6}\right] = \frac{1}{3}$$

13. (a) $I = \int_0^{3/4} \frac{dx}{(x+1)\sqrt{x^2+1}}$

Put $(x+1) = \frac{1}{t} \quad \Rightarrow \quad dx = \frac{-1}{t^2}dt$

$$\therefore \quad I = \int_1^{4/7} \frac{\left(-1/t^2\right)dt}{\left(\frac{1}{t}\right)\sqrt{\left(\frac{1}{t} - 1\right)^2 + 1}} = \int_1^{4/7} \frac{\left(-1/t^2\right)dt}{\left(\frac{1}{t^2}\right)\sqrt{(1-t)^2 + t^2}}$$

$$= \int_{4/7}^{1} \frac{dt}{\sqrt{2t^2 - 2t + 1}}$$

$$= \int_{4/7}^{1} \frac{dt}{\sqrt{2}\sqrt{t^2 - t + \frac{1}{2}}} = \int_{4/7}^{1} \frac{1}{\sqrt{2}} \cdot \frac{dt}{\sqrt{\left(t - \frac{1}{2}\right)^2 + \left(\frac{1}{2}\right)^2}}$$

$$= \left[\frac{1}{\sqrt{2}}\ln\left|\left(t - \frac{1}{2}\right) + \sqrt{t^2 - t + \frac{1}{2}}\right|\right]_{4/7}^{1}$$

$$= \frac{1}{\sqrt{2}}\ln\left|\frac{1}{2} + \sqrt{\frac{1}{2}}\right| - \frac{1}{\sqrt{2}}\ln\left|\frac{1}{14} + \sqrt{\frac{25}{98}}\right|$$

$$= \frac{1}{\sqrt{2}}\ln\left|\frac{1}{2} + \frac{1}{\sqrt{2}}\right| - \frac{1}{\sqrt{2}}\ln\left|\frac{1}{14} + \frac{5}{7\sqrt{2}}\right|$$

$$= \frac{1}{\sqrt{2}}\ln\left|\frac{\left(\frac{1+\sqrt{2}}{2}\right)}{\left(\frac{1+5\sqrt{2}}{14}\right)}\right| = \frac{1}{\sqrt{2}}\ln\left(\frac{\left(1+\sqrt{2}\right)(7)}{1+5\sqrt{2}}\right)$$

$$= \frac{1}{\sqrt{2}}\ln\left(\frac{7\left(1+\sqrt{2}\right)\left(5\sqrt{2}-1\right)}{49}\right)$$

$$=\frac{1}{\sqrt{2}}\ln\left(\frac{5\sqrt{2}+10-\sqrt{2}-1}{7}\right)=\frac{1}{\sqrt{2}}\ln\left(\frac{5\sqrt{2}+9}{7}\right)$$

14. (a) $I=\int_{-1}^{1}x^2d\left(\ln(x)\right)$

Put $\ln x = t \quad \Rightarrow x = e^t$

$$\therefore\quad I=\int_{-1}^{1}e^{2t}dt=\left[\frac{e^{2t}}{2}\right]_{-1}^{1}=\frac{1}{2}\left[e^2-e^{-2}\right]=\frac{e^4-1}{2e^2}$$

15. (c) $I=\int_0^{\pi/2}\frac{\cos^2\theta\,d\theta}{\cos^2\theta+4\sin^2\theta}=\int_0^{\pi/2}\frac{\sec^2\theta\,d\theta}{\sec^2\theta=4\sec^2\theta.\tan^2\theta}$

$$=\int_0^{\pi/2}\frac{\sec^2\theta\,d\theta}{1+\tan^2\theta+4\left(1+\tan^2\theta\right).\tan^2\theta}$$

$$=\int_0^{\pi/2}\frac{\sec^2\theta\,d\theta}{4\tan^4\theta+5\tan^2\theta+1}=\int_0^{\infty}\frac{dt}{4t^4+5t^2+1}$$

$$=\int_0^{\infty}\frac{dt}{\left(4t^2+1\right)\left(t^2+1\right)}=\int_0^{\infty}\frac{4/3}{\left(4t^2+1\right)}dt+\int_0^{\infty}\frac{-1/3}{t^2+1}$$

$$=\frac{4}{3}\times\left|\frac{\tan^{-1}(2t)}{2}\right|_0^{\infty}-\frac{1}{3}\left|\tan^{-1}t\right|_0^{\infty}$$

$$=\frac{2}{3}\left[\tan^{-1}\infty-\tan^{-1}0\right]-\frac{1}{3}\left[\tan^{-1}\infty-\tan^{-1}0\right]$$

$$=\frac{2}{3}\left[\frac{\pi}{2}\right]-\frac{1}{3}\left[\frac{\pi}{2}\right]=\frac{\pi}{3}-\frac{\pi}{6}=\frac{\pi}{6}$$

16. (b) $I=\int_{-\infty}^{\infty}\frac{1}{e^x+e^{-x}}dx=\int_{-\infty}^{\infty}\frac{e^x}{\left(e^{2x}+1\right)}dx$

$$=\int_0^{\infty}\frac{dt}{1+t^2}=\left|\tan^{-1}t\right|_0^{\infty}=\frac{\pi}{2}$$

17. (c) $I=\int_1^{\infty}\frac{dx}{(x+1)x^2}=\int_1^{\infty}\frac{dx}{x^3\left(1+\frac{1}{x}\right)}$

Put $\frac{1}{x}=t \quad\Rightarrow\quad -\frac{1}{x^2}dx=dt$

$$\Rightarrow\quad I=\int_1^{0}\frac{(-t)dt}{(1+t)}=\int_0^{1}\frac{t\,dt}{t+1}=\int_0^{1}\left(1-\frac{1}{1+t}\right)dt$$

$$=\left[t-\ln|1+t|\right]_0^1=1-\ln 2$$

TEXTUAL EXERCISE–4: (SUBJECTIVE)

1. (a) $I=\int_{\frac{\pi}{6}-a}^{\frac{\pi}{6}+a}\left[\sin\left(x-\frac{\pi}{6}\right)+\tan\left(\frac{\pi}{6}-x\right)\right]dx$

$$\Rightarrow\quad I=\int_{\frac{\pi}{6}-a}^{\frac{\pi}{6}+a}\sin\left[\left(\frac{\pi}{6}+a+\frac{\pi}{6}-a-x\right)-\frac{\pi}{6}\right]$$

$$+\tan\left(\frac{\pi}{6}-\left(\frac{\pi}{6}-a+\frac{\pi}{6}+a-x\right)\right)dx$$

$$\Rightarrow\quad I=\int_{\frac{\pi}{6}-a}^{\frac{\pi}{6}+a}\left[\sin\left(\frac{\pi}{6}-x\right)+\tan\left(x-\frac{\pi}{6}\right)\right]dx=-I$$

$\Rightarrow\quad 2I=0$

$\Rightarrow\quad I=0$

(b) $I=\int_0^1 x(1-x)^{50}dx$

$$\Rightarrow\quad I=\int_0^1(1-x)\left[1-(1-x)\right]^{50}dx$$

$$=\int_0^1(1-x)(x)^{50}dx=\int_0^1\left(x^{50}-x^{51}\right)dx$$

$$=\left[\frac{x^{51}}{51}-\frac{x^{52}}{52}\right]_0^1=\left(\frac{1}{51}-\frac{1}{52}\right)=\frac{1}{51\times 52}=\frac{1}{2652}$$

(c) $I=\int_{\frac{\pi}{4}-a}^{\frac{\pi}{4}+a}\left(\sin\left(x-\frac{\pi}{4}\right)+\tan\left(x-\frac{\pi}{4}\right)\right)+$

$$\left|x-\frac{\pi}{4}\right|\left(x-\frac{\pi}{4}\right)^5dx$$

Using the property, we get $\int_a^b f(x)dx=\int_a^b f(a+b-x)dx$

we see, that I = – I

$\Rightarrow\ 2I=0 \qquad \Rightarrow\ I=0$

(d) $I=\int_{-3}^{1}\left[(x+1)^5\cos(x+1)+\left(x^3+3x^2+3x+2\right)\right]dx$

Using the property, we get

$$I=\int_a^b f(x)dx=\int_a^b f(a+b-x)dx,$$

$$I=\int_{-3}^{1}(-2-x+1)^5\cos(-2-x+1)$$

$$+(-x-1)^3+3(-x-1)^2+3(-x-1)+2]dx$$

$$\Rightarrow\quad I=\int_{-3}^{1}\left[-(x+1)^5\cos(x+1)+\left[(-2-x+1)^3+1\right]\right]dx$$

$$=\int_{-3}^{1}\left(-(x+1)^5\cos(x+1)+\left[-(x+1)^3+1\right]\right)dx$$

$$=-\int_{-3}^{1}\left[(x+1)^5\cos(x+1)+(x+1)^3+1-2\right]dx$$

$$=-I+2\int_{-3}^{1}dx$$

$\Rightarrow\ 2I=2[1+3] \qquad \Rightarrow\ I=4$

2. (a) $I=\int_0^{\pi/2}\frac{dx}{1+\sqrt{\tan x}}$

$$\Rightarrow\quad I=\int_0^{\pi/2}\frac{\sqrt{\cos x}}{\sqrt{\cos x}+\sqrt{\sin x}}dx \qquad \text{...(i)}$$

$$\Rightarrow\quad I=\int_0^{\pi/2}\frac{\sqrt{\cos\left(\frac{\pi}{6}-x\right)}}{\cos\left(\frac{\pi}{2}-x\right)+\sqrt{\sin\left(\frac{\pi}{2}-x\right)}}dx$$

$$\Rightarrow\quad I=\int_0^{\pi/2}\frac{\sqrt{\sin x}}{\sqrt{\sin x}+\sqrt{\cos x}}dx \qquad \text{...(ii)}$$

$\therefore$ (i) + (ii) gives, $2I=\int_0^{\pi/2}1\,dx=\frac{\pi}{2}$

$$\Rightarrow\quad I=\frac{\pi}{4}$$

(b) $I=\int_{-a}^{3a}\frac{f(x)dx}{f(x)+f(2a-x)}$ ...(i)

$\Rightarrow\ I=\int_{-a}^{3a}\frac{f(-a+3a-x)}{f(-a+3a-x)+f(2a-(-a+3a-x))}dx$

$\Rightarrow\ I=\int_{-a}^{3a}\frac{f(2a-x)}{f(2a-x)+f(x)}$ ...(ii)

$\therefore$ (i) + (ii) gives, $2I=\int_{-a}^{3a}\left\{\frac{f(x)+f(2a-x)}{f(2a-x)+f(x)}\right\}dx$

$\Rightarrow\ 2I=\int_{-a}^{3a}1\,dx=3a+a=4a$

$\Rightarrow$ I = 2a

(c) $I=\int_1^3\frac{[x^2-8x+16]}{[(4-x)^2]+[x^2]}dx$

$\Rightarrow\ I=\int_1^3\frac{[(x-4)^2]}{[(4-x)^2]+[x^2]}$ ...(i)

$\Rightarrow\ I=\int_1^3\frac{[(4-x-4)^2]}{[(4-(4-x))^2]+[(4-x)^2]}dx$

$\Rightarrow\ I=\int_1^3\frac{[x^2]}{[x^2]+[(4-x)^2]}$ ...(ii)

$\therefore$ (i) + (ii), gives, $2I=\int_1^3 1\,dx=2$

$\Rightarrow$ I = 1

(d) $I=\int_0^{\pi/2}\frac{\sin 8x\log\cot x}{\cot 2x}dx$

$\Rightarrow\ I=\int_2^{\pi/2}\frac{\sin 8\left(0+\frac{\pi}{2}-x\right)\log\cot\left(0+\frac{\pi}{2}-x\right)}{\cot 2\left(0+\frac{\pi}{2}x\right)}dx$

$=\int_0^{\pi/2}\frac{\sin(4\pi-8x)\log\cot\left(\frac{\pi}{2}-x\right)}{\cot(\pi-2x)}dx$

$=\int_0^{\pi/2}\frac{-\sin 8x\log\tan x}{-\cot 2x}dx$

$=-\int_0^{\pi/2}\frac{\sin 8x\log\tan x}{-\cot 2x}dx=-I$

$\Rightarrow\ 2I=0$ $\Rightarrow\ I=0$

(e) $I=\int_0^{\pi/2}\frac{\sin^3 x}{\sin x+\cos x}dx$ ...(1)

$\Rightarrow\ I=\int_0^{\pi/2}\frac{\sin^3\left(\frac{\pi}{2}-x\right)}{\sin\left(\frac{\pi}{2}-x\right)+\cos\left(\frac{\pi}{2}-x\right)}dx$

$\Rightarrow\ I=\int_0^{\pi/2}\frac{\cos^3 x}{\cos x+\sin x}dx$ ...(2)

$\therefore$ (1) + (2) gives, $2I=\int_0^{\pi/2}\frac{\sin^3 x+\cos^3 x}{(\sin x+\cos x)}dx$

$\Rightarrow\ 2I=\int_0^{\pi/2}\left(\sin^2 x-\sin x\cos x+\cos^2 x\right)dx$

$\Rightarrow\ 2I=\int_0^{\pi/2}(1-\sin x\cos x)dx$

$\Rightarrow\ 2I=[x]_0^{\pi/2}-\frac{1}{2}\left[\frac{-\cos 2x}{2}\right]_0^{\pi/2}$

$\Rightarrow\ 2I=\frac{\pi}{2}+\frac{1}{4}[-1-1]$

$\Rightarrow\ 2I=\frac{\pi}{2}-\frac{1}{2}$ $\Rightarrow\ I=\frac{\pi}{4}-\frac{1}{4}$

Thus, $I=\frac{(\pi-1)}{4}$

(f) $I=\int_0^{\pi/2}\frac{dx}{1+\tan^n x}$

$\Rightarrow\ I=\int_0^{\pi/2}\frac{\cos^n x}{\cos^n x+\sin^n x}dx$ ...(1)

Also $I=\int_0^{\pi/2}\frac{\left(\cos\left(\frac{\pi}{2}-x\right)\right)^n}{\left(\cos\left(\frac{\pi}{2}-x\right)\right)^n+\left(\sin\left(\frac{\pi}{2}-x\right)\right)^n}dx$

$\Rightarrow\ I=\int_0^{\pi/2}\frac{\sin^n x\,dx}{\sin^n x+\cos^n x}$ ...(2)

$\therefore$ (1) + (2) gives, $2I=\int_0^{\pi/2}1\,dx=\frac{\pi}{2}-0$

$\Rightarrow\ I=\frac{\pi}{4}$

3. (a) $I=\int_1^2\frac{\ln x}{(1+\ln x)^2}dx=\int_1^2\left[\frac{1}{(1+\ln x)}-\frac{1}{(1+\ln x)^2}\right]dx$

Put $\ln x=t$

$\Rightarrow\ \frac{1}{x}dx=dt$

$\Rightarrow\ dx=e^t dt$

$\therefore\ I=\int_0^{\ln 2}e^t\left(\frac{1}{(1+t)}-\frac{1}{(1+t)^2}\right)dt=\left|e^t\left(\frac{1}{1+t}\right)\right|_0^{\ln 2}$

$=\left[\frac{2}{1+\ln 2}-1\right]=\frac{1-\ln 2}{1+\ln 2}$

(b) $\int_0^1\cot^{-1}(1-x+x^2)dx=\int_0^1\tan^{-1}\left[\frac{1}{1+x^2-x}\right]dx$

$\left[\because \text{ for } x\in(0,1); 1+x^2-x>0 \text{ and } \cot^{-1}x=\tan^{-1}\left(\frac{1}{x}\right) \text{ for } x>0\right]$

$=\int_0^1\tan^{-1}\left[\frac{x-(x-1)}{1+x(x-1)}\right]dx=\int_0^1\left[\tan^{-1}x-\tan^{-1}(x-1)\right]dx$

$\Rightarrow\ I=\int_0^1\left(\tan^{-1}x-\tan^{-1}(x-1)\right)dx$ ...(1)

Also $\int_0^1 \tan^{-1}(x-1)dx = \int_0^1 \tan^{-1}(1-x-1)dx$

$= \int_0^1 \tan^{-1}(-x)dx = -\int_0^1 \tan^{-1} x\, dx$ ...(2)

$\therefore$ From (1) and (2), we get $I = 2\int_0^1 \tan^{-1} x\, dx$

$= 2\left[\left|x\tan^{-1}x\right|_0^1 - \frac{1}{2}\int_0^1 \frac{2x}{1+x^2}dx\right]$

$= 2\left[\frac{\pi}{4} - \frac{1}{2}\left|\ln\left(1+x^2\right)\right|_0^1\right] = 2\left[\frac{\pi}{4} - \frac{1}{2}(\ln 2)\right] = \frac{\pi}{2} - \ln 2$

4. $I = \int_0^{\pi/4} \frac{\sin x + \cos x}{\cos^2 x + \sin^4 x}dx = \int_0^{\pi/4} \frac{\sin x + \cos x}{\cos^2 x + (1-\cos^2 x)^2}dx$

$= \int_0^{\pi/4} \frac{(\sin x + \cos x)}{\cos^2 x + 1 - 2\cos^2 x + \cos^4 x}dx$

$= \int_0^{\pi/4} \frac{\sin x + \cos x}{1 + \cos^4 x - \cos^2 x}dx = \int_0^{\pi/4} \frac{(\sin x + \cos x)}{1 - \cos^2 x(1-\cos^2 x)}dx$

$= \int_0^{\pi/4} \frac{(\sin x + \cos x)}{1 - \cos^2 x \sin^2 x}dx = \int_0^{\pi/4} \frac{(\sin x + \cos x)}{1 - (\sin x \cos x)^2}dx$

Put $\sin x - \cos x = t$

$\Rightarrow I = \int_{-1}^{0} \frac{dt}{1 - \left(\frac{1-t^2}{2}\right)^2} = \int_{-1}^{0} \frac{-4}{t^4 - 2t^2 - 3}dt$

$= -4\int_{-1}^{0} \frac{1}{t^2-3}dt + \int_{-1}^{0} \frac{1}{t^2+1}dt$

$= \frac{1}{2\sqrt{3}}\ln\left|\frac{\sqrt{3}+t}{\sqrt{3}-t}\right|_{-1}^{0} + \left|\tan^{-1} t\right|_{-1}^{0} = \frac{\pi}{4} - \frac{1}{2\sqrt{3}}\ln\left|\frac{\sqrt{3}-1}{\sqrt{3}+1}\right|$

$= \frac{\pi}{4} - \frac{1}{\sqrt{3}}\ln\left|\frac{\sqrt{3}-1}{\sqrt{2}}\right|$

5. (a) $I = \int_0^{\pi} x \sin dx$ ...(1)

$\Rightarrow I = \int_0^{\pi} (\pi - x)\sin(\pi - x)dx$

$\Rightarrow I = \int_0^{\pi} (\pi - x)\sin x\, dx$

$\Rightarrow I = \pi\int_0^{\pi} \sin x\, dx - \int_0^{\pi} \sin x\, dx$

$\Rightarrow I = \pi\int_0^{\pi} \sin x\, dx - I$ ...(2)

$\Rightarrow 2I = \pi\int_0^{\pi} \sin x\, dx$

$\Rightarrow I = \frac{\pi}{2}\int_0^{\pi} \sin x\, dx = \frac{\pi}{2}[-\cos x]_0^{\pi}$

$\Rightarrow I = \frac{-\pi}{2}[-1-1] = \pi$

(b) $I = \int_0^{\pi} \frac{x}{1+\sin x}dx$ ...(1)

$\Rightarrow I = \int_0^{\pi} \frac{\pi - x}{1 + \sin(\pi - x)}dx$

$\Rightarrow I = \pi\int_0^{\pi} \frac{1}{1+\sin x}dx - I$

$\Rightarrow 2I = \pi\int_0^{\pi}\left(\frac{1-\sin x}{\cos^2 x}\right)dx$

$\Rightarrow I = \int_0^{\pi}\left(\sec^2 x - \sec x \tan x\right)dx$

$\Rightarrow I = \frac{\pi}{2}[\tan x - \sec x]_0^{\pi} \Rightarrow I = \frac{\pi}{2}[0 - (-1-1)] = \pi$

(c) $I = \int_0^{\pi} \frac{x \tan x}{\sec x\ \mathrm{cosec} x}dx$

By property, we get $I = f(x)dx = \int_0^a f(a-x)dx$,

$I = \int_0^{\pi} \frac{(\pi - x)\tan(\pi - x)}{\sec(\pi - x)\mathrm{cosec}(\pi - x)}dx$

$\Rightarrow I = \int_0^{\pi} \frac{-(\pi - x)\tan x}{-\sec x\ \mathrm{cosec} x}dx$

$\Rightarrow I = \pi\int_0^{\pi} \frac{\tan x}{\sec x\ \mathrm{cosec} x}dx - \int_0^{\pi} \frac{x \tan x}{\sec x\ \mathrm{cosec} x}dx$

$\Rightarrow 2I = \pi\int_0^{\pi} \frac{\tan x}{\sec x.\mathrm{cosec} x}dx$

$\Rightarrow I = \frac{\pi}{2}\int_0^{\pi} \frac{\sin^2 x}{\cos x.\sec x}dx$

$\Rightarrow I = \frac{\pi}{2}\int_0^{\pi} \frac{(1-\cos 2x)}{2}dx$

$\Rightarrow I = \frac{\pi}{4}\left[x - \frac{\sin 2x}{2}\right]_0^{\pi}$

$\Rightarrow I = \frac{\pi}{4}[\pi] = \frac{\pi^2}{4}$

(d) $I = \int_0^{\pi} \frac{x \tan x}{\sec x + \tan x}dx$ ...(1)

By property, $\int_0^a f(x)dx = \int_0^a f(a-x)dx$

$I = \int_0^{\pi} \frac{(\pi - x)\tan(\pi - x)}{\sec(\pi - x) + \tan(\pi - x)}dx$

$\Rightarrow I = \int_0^{\pi} \frac{-(\pi - x)\tan x}{-\sec x - \tan x}dx$

$\Rightarrow I = \pi\int_0^{\pi} \frac{\tan x}{\sec x + \tan x}dx - \int_0^{\pi} \frac{x \tan x}{(\sec x + \tan x)}$

$\Rightarrow 2I = \pi\int_0^{\pi} \frac{\tan x}{\sec x + \tan x}dx$

$\Rightarrow 2I = \pi\int_0^{\pi}\left(\sec x \tan x - \tan^2 x\right)dx$

$\Rightarrow 2I = \pi\int_0^{\pi}\left(\sec x \tan x + 1 - \sec^2 x\right)dx$

$\Rightarrow I = \frac{\pi}{2}[\sec x + x - \tan x]_0^{\pi}$

$\Rightarrow I = \frac{\pi}{2}[-2 + \pi] = \frac{\pi}{2}(\pi - 2)$

(e) $I = \int_0^1 (1+x)(1-x)^{999}dx$ ...(1)

$\Rightarrow I = \int_0^1 (1+1-x)(1-(1-x))^{999}dx$

$\Rightarrow \ \mathrm{I}=\int_0^1(2-x)(x)^{999}dx \ \Rightarrow \ \mathrm{I}=\int_0^1\left(2x^{999}-x^{1000}\right)dx$

$\Rightarrow \ \mathrm{I}=2\left[\frac{x^{1000}}{1000}\right]_0^1-\left[\frac{x^{1001}}{1001}\right]_0^1=\left(\frac{2}{1000}-\frac{1}{1001}\right)$

$=\left(\frac{2002-1000}{1001}\right)\times10^{-3}=\left(\frac{1002}{1001}\right)\times10^{-3}$

(f) $\mathrm{I}=\int_0^\pi\frac{x\sin x}{1+\cos^2x}dx \ \Rightarrow \ \mathrm{I}=\int_0^\pi\frac{(\pi-x)\sin(\pi-x)}{1+\cos^2(\pi-x)}dx$

$\Rightarrow \ \mathrm{I}=\int_0^\pi\frac{(\pi-x)\sin x}{1+\cos^2x}dx$

$\Rightarrow \ \mathrm{I}=\pi\int_0^\pi\frac{\sin x}{1+\cos^2x}dx-\int_0^\pi\frac{x\sin x}{1+\cos^2x}dx$

$\Rightarrow \ 2\mathrm{I}=\pi\int_0^\pi\frac{\sin x}{1+\cos^2x}dx$

Put $-\cos x=t \quad \Rightarrow \quad \sin x dx=dt$

$\Rightarrow \ 2\mathrm{I}=\pi\int_{-1}^1\frac{dt}{1+t^2} \quad \Rightarrow \quad 2\mathrm{I}=\pi\left[\tan^{-1}t\right]_{-1}^1$

$\Rightarrow \ 2\mathrm{I}=\pi\left[\frac{\pi}{4}+\frac{\pi}{4}\right]=\frac{\pi^2}{2}$

$\Rightarrow \ \mathrm{I}=\frac{\pi^2}{4}$

(g) $\mathrm{I}=\int_0^1x\left(\ln x+\ln(1-x)\right)dx$

$\Rightarrow \ \mathrm{I}=\int_0^1(1-x)\left(\ln(1-x)+\ln\left(1-(1-x)\right)\right)dx$

$\Rightarrow \ \mathrm{I}=\int_0^1\left(\ln(1-x)+\ln x\right)dx-\mathrm{I}$

$\Rightarrow \ \mathrm{I}=\frac{1}{2}\int_0^1\left(\ln(1-x)+\ln x\right)dx$

$=\frac{1}{2}\int_0^1\ln(1-x)dx+\frac{1}{2}\int_0^1\ln x dx$

$=\frac{1}{2}\lim_{h\to0^+}\int_0^{1-h}\ln(1-x)dx+\frac{1}{2}\lim_{\epsilon\to0^+}\int_\epsilon^1\ln x dx$

$=\frac{1}{2}\mathrm{I}_1+\frac{1}{2}\mathrm{I}_2$ (Say).

Now, $\mathrm{I}_1=\lim_{h\to0^+}\int_0^{1-h}\ln(1-x)dx$

$=\lim_{h\to0^+}\left[\left|x\ln(1-x)\right|_0^{1-h}-\int_0^{1-h}\frac{-1}{(1-x)}xdx\right]$

$=\lim_{h\to0^+}\left[(1-h)\ln(h)-\int_0^{1-h}\frac{1-x-1}{1-x}dx\right]$

$=\lim_{h\to0^+}\left[(1-h)\ln(h)-\int_0^{1-h}1dx+\int_0^{1-h}\frac{1}{1-x}dx\right]$

$=\lim_{h\to0^+}\left[(1-h)\ln h-[1-h]-\left|\ln|1-x|\right|_0^{1-h}\right]$

$=\lim_{h\to0^+}\left[(1-h)\ln h-(1-h)-\ln h\right]$

$=\lim_{h\to0^+}\left[-h\ln h-1+h\right]$

$=-1-\lim_{h\to0^+}(h\ln h)=-1-\lim_{h\to0^+}\left(\frac{\ln h}{\frac{1}{h}}\right)$

$=-1-\lim_{h\to0^+}\frac{\left(\frac{1}{h}\right)}{\left(\frac{-1}{h^2}\right)}=-1$

Now, $\mathrm{I}_2=\lim_{\epsilon\to0^+}\int_\epsilon^1\ln x\,dx=\lim_{\epsilon\to0^+}\left[\left|x\ln x\right|_\epsilon^1-\int_\epsilon^1\frac{1}{x}.xdx\right]$

$=\lim_{\epsilon\to0^+}\left[0-\epsilon\ln\epsilon-(1-\epsilon)\right]$

$=\lim_{\epsilon\to0^+}\left[-0-1+\epsilon\right]=-1\left(\because\lim_{\epsilon\to0^+}\epsilon\ln\epsilon=0\right)$

$\therefore \ \mathrm{I}=\frac{1}{2}(-1)+\frac{1}{2}(-1)=-1$

6. $f(x)=f(a-x)$ and $g(x)+g(a-x)=2$.

Let $\mathrm{I}=\int_0^af(x).g(x)dx$

$\Rightarrow \ \mathrm{I}=\int_0^af(a-x).g(a-x)dx$

$\Rightarrow \ \mathrm{I}=\int_0^af(x).\left[2-g(x)\right]dx$

$\Rightarrow \ \mathrm{I}=\int_0^af(x)dx-\int_0^af(x).g(x)dx$

$\Rightarrow \ 2\mathrm{I}=2\int_0^af(x)dx \quad \Rightarrow \quad \mathrm{I}=\int_0^af(x)dx$

7. (a) $f(x)=\lambda\int_0^{\pi/2}\sin t\cos t\,f(t)dt+\sin x$

$\Rightarrow \ f(x)=\lambda\int_0^{\pi/2}\sin t\cos t$

$\left(\lambda\int_0^{\pi/2}\sin t\cos t\,f(t)dt+\sin t\right)dt+\sin x$

$=\lambda^2\int_0^{\pi/2}\sin t\cos t\ \mu\ dt\ \lambda\int_0^{\pi/2}\sin^2t\cos t\ dt;+\sin x$,

where $\mu=\int_0^{\pi/2}\sin t\cos t\,f(t)dt$

$\Rightarrow \ f(x)=\lambda^2\mu\int_0^{\pi/2}\sin t\cos t\ dt+\lambda\left[\frac{\sin^3t}{3}\right]_0^{\pi/2}+\sin x$

$\Rightarrow \ f(x)=\lambda^2\mu\left[\frac{\sin^2t}{2}\right]_0^{\pi/2}+\frac{\lambda}{3}+\sin x$

$\Rightarrow \ f(x)=\frac{\lambda^2\mu}{2}+\frac{\lambda}{3}+\sin x$

Also $f(0)=\lambda\mu$

$\Rightarrow \ \lambda\mu=\frac{\lambda^2\mu}{2}+\frac{\lambda}{3} \quad \Rightarrow \quad \mu\left(\lambda-\frac{\lambda^2}{2}\right)=\frac{\lambda}{3}$

$\Rightarrow \ \mu=\frac{\lambda}{3}\left(\frac{2}{2\lambda-\lambda^2}\right)=\frac{2}{3(2-\lambda)}$

$\therefore \ f(x)=\frac{\lambda^2}{2}\left(\frac{2}{3(2-\lambda)}\right)+\frac{\lambda}{3}+\sin x$

$\Rightarrow \ f(x)=\frac{\lambda^2}{3(2-\lambda)}+\frac{\lambda}{3}+\sin x=\frac{\lambda}{3}\left[\frac{\lambda}{2-\lambda}+1\right]+\sin x$

$=\frac{\lambda}{3}\left[\frac{\lambda+2-\lambda}{2-\lambda}\right]+\sin x$

$\therefore \ f(x)=\frac{2}{3}\left(\frac{\lambda}{2-\lambda}\right)+\sin x$

(b) $f(x)=\lambda\int_0^{\pi/2}\sin t\cos x\, f(t)dt+\sin x$

$=\lambda\cos x\int_0^{\pi/2}\sin t\, f(t)dt+\sin x;$

Let $\mu=\int_0^{\pi/2}\sin t\, f(t)dt$

Now, $f(x)=(\lambda\cos x)(\mu)+\sin x$

$\therefore\quad f(x)=\lambda\cos x\int_0^{\pi/2}\sin t\, f(t)dt+\sin x$

$\Rightarrow\quad f(x)=\lambda\cos x\int_0^{\pi/2}\sin t\left[\lambda.\mu\cos t+\sin t\right]dt+\sin x$

$\Rightarrow\quad f(x)=\lambda\cos x\left[\int_0^{\pi/2}\lambda\mu\sin t\cos t\, dt+\int_0^{\pi/2}\sin^2 t\, dt+\sin x\right]$

$\Rightarrow\quad f(x)=\lambda\cos x\left[\lambda\mu\left[\frac{\sin^2 t}{2}\right]_0^{\pi/2}+\frac{1}{2}\left(t-\frac{\sin^2 t}{2}\right)_0^{\pi/2}\right]+\sin x$

$\Rightarrow\quad f(x)=(\lambda\cos x)\left[\frac{\lambda\mu}{2}+\frac{1}{2}\left(\frac{\pi}{2}\right)\right]+\sin x$

$\Rightarrow\quad f(x)=\frac{\lambda^2\mu}{2}\cos x+\frac{\lambda\pi}{4}\cos x+\sin x$

Also $f(0)=\lambda\mu$

$\Rightarrow\quad \lambda\mu=\frac{\lambda^2\mu}{2}+\frac{\lambda\pi}{4}\quad\Rightarrow\quad \mu\left(\lambda-\frac{\lambda^2}{2}\right)=\frac{\lambda\pi}{4}$

$\Rightarrow\quad \mu=\frac{\lambda\pi}{4}\left(\frac{2}{2\lambda-\lambda^2}\right)\quad\Rightarrow\quad \mu=\frac{\pi}{2(2-\lambda)}$

$\therefore\quad f(x)=\frac{\pi\lambda\cos x}{2(2-\lambda)}+\sin x$

8. $\mathrm{I}=\int_0^1 x^m(1-x)^n dx\ =\int_0^1(1-x)^m\left(1-(1-x)\right)^n dx$

$=\int_0^1(1-x)^m(x)^n dx$

9. (a) $\mathrm{I}=\int_{-\pi/2}^{\pi/2}\frac{dx}{e^{\tan x}+1}$ ...(1)

$\Rightarrow\quad \mathrm{I}=\int_{-\pi/2}^{\pi/2}\frac{dx}{e^{\tan\left(-\frac{\pi}{2}+\frac{\pi}{2}-x\right)}+1}$

$\Rightarrow\quad \mathrm{I}=\int_{-\pi/2}^{\pi/2}\frac{dx}{e^{\tan(-x)}+1}$

$\Rightarrow\quad \mathrm{I}=\int_{-\pi/2}^{\pi/2}\frac{e^{\tan x}}{1+2^{\tan x}}dx$ ...(2)

Equation (1)+(2) gives, $2\mathrm{I}=\int_{-\pi/2}^{\pi/2}\frac{1+e^{\tan x}}{e^{\tan x}+1}dx=\int_{-\pi/2}^{\pi/2}1\, dx$

$\Rightarrow\quad 2\mathrm{I}=[x]_{-\pi/2}^{\pi/2}=\pi\quad\Rightarrow\quad \mathrm{I}=\pi/2$

(b) $\mathrm{I}=\int_0^{\pi}\frac{e^{\cos x}}{e^{\cos x}+e^{-\cos x}}dx$ ...(1)

$\Rightarrow\quad \mathrm{I}=\int_0^{\pi}\frac{e^{\cos(\pi-x)}}{e^{\cos(\pi-x)}+e^{-\cos(\pi-x)}}dx$

$\Rightarrow\quad \mathrm{I}=\int_0^{\pi}\frac{e^{-\cos x}}{e^{-\cos x}+e^{\cos x}}dx$ ...(2)

Equation (1) + (2) gives, $2\mathrm{I}=\int_0^{\pi}1\, dx=\pi$

$\Rightarrow\quad \mathrm{I}=\frac{\pi}{2}$

10. (a) $\int_0^a f(x)dx=\int_0^{a/2}f(x)dx+\int_{a/2}^a f(x)dx=\mathrm{I}_1+\mathrm{I}_2$ (say) ...(1)

In I_2, put $x=a-y$

$\Rightarrow\quad dx=-dy$

$\Rightarrow\quad \mathrm{I}_2=\int_{a/2}^0 f(a-y)(-dy)=\int_0^a f(a-y)dy$ or

$\mathrm{I}_2=\int_0^{a/2}f(a-x)dx$ ...(2)

Using (2) in (1), we get $\mathrm{I}=\int_0^{a/2}f(x)dx+\int_0^{a/2}f(a-x)dx$

(b) $\mathrm{I}=\int_0^{2a}f(x)dx=\int_0^a f(x)dx+\int_0^{2a}f(x)dx=\mathrm{I}_1+\mathrm{I}_2$ (say) ...(1)

In I_1, put $x=a-y$ and In I_2, put $x=a-y$

$\Rightarrow\quad \mathrm{I}_1=\int_a^0 f(a-y)(-dy)=\int_0^a f(a-y)dy$ or

$\mathrm{I}_1=\int_0^a f(a-x)dx$ ...(2)

and $\mathrm{I}_2=\int_0^a f(a+y)dy$ or $\mathrm{I}_2=\int_0^a f(a+x)dx$ ...(3)

Using (2) and (3) in (1), we get

$\mathrm{I}_2=\int_0^a f(a-x)dx+\int_0^a f(a+x)dx$

11. (a) $\int_1^2\frac{dx}{\sqrt{x^2+4x+3}}=\int_1^2\frac{dx}{\sqrt{(x^2+4x+4)-1}}=\int_1^2\frac{dx}{\sqrt{(x+2)^2-(1)^2}}$

$=\left[\ln\left|(x+2)+\sqrt{x^2+4x+3}\right|\right]_1^2$

$=\ln\left|4+\sqrt{15}\right|-\ln\left|3+\sqrt{8}\right|=\ln\left|\frac{4+\sqrt{15}}{3=\sqrt{8}}\right|$

(b) $\int_{\pi/3}^{\pi/2}\frac{(1+\cos x)^{1/2}}{(1-\cos x)^{5/2}}dx=\int_{\pi/3}^{\pi/2}\frac{(2\cos^2 x/2)^{1/2}}{(2\sin^2 x/2)^{5/2}}dx=\int_{\pi/3}^{\pi/2}\frac{\cos x/2}{4\sin^5 x/2}dx$

$=\frac{1}{2}\int_{\pi/3}^{\pi/2}\frac{1}{2}\left(\sin\frac{x}{2}\right)^{-5}.\left(\cos\frac{x}{2}\right)dx=\frac{1}{2}\left[\frac{\left(\sin\frac{x}{2}\right)^{-4}}{-4}\right]_{\pi/3}^{\pi/2}$

$=\frac{-1}{8}\left[\left(\sin\frac{\pi}{4}\right)^{-4}\left(\sin\frac{\pi}{6}\right)^{-4}\right]$

$=\frac{-1}{8}\left[\left(\sqrt{2}\right)^4-(2)^4\right]=\frac{-1}{8}[4-16]=\frac{3}{2}$

(c) $\int_0^1\cos^1\left(\frac{1-x^2}{1+x^2}\right)dx$

Put $\theta=\tan^{-1}x; x\in(0,1)$

$\Rightarrow\quad \theta\in(0,\pi/4)$

$\Rightarrow\ I=\int_0^{\pi/4}\cos^{-1}\left(\frac{1-\tan^2\theta}{1+\tan^2\theta}\right)\sec^2\theta d\theta=$

$\int_0^{\pi/4}\cos^{-1}(\cos 2\theta).\sec^2\theta d\theta=\int_0^{\pi/4}2\theta\sec^2\theta d\theta$

$=2\left[|\theta.\tan\theta|_0^{\pi/4}-\int_0^{\pi/4}1.\tan\theta d\theta\right]=2\left[\frac{\pi}{4}-|\ln|\sec\theta||_0^{\pi/4}\right]$

$=\frac{\pi}{2}-2\left[\ln(\sqrt{2})-\ln 1\right]=\frac{\pi}{2}-\frac{2}{2}\ln 2=\frac{\pi}{2}-\ln 2$

(d) $I=\int_0^{1/\sqrt{2}}\frac{\sin^{-1}x}{(1-x^2)^{3/2}}dx$

Put $\sin^{-1}=t,\frac{1}{\sqrt{1-x^2}}dx=dt$ and $x\in(0,1/\sqrt{2})$

$\Rightarrow\ t\in(0,\pi/4)$ and $x=\sin t$

$\therefore\ I=\int_0^{\pi/4}\frac{t\ dt}{(1-x^2)}=\int_0^{\pi/4}\frac{t}{\cos^2 t}dt=\int_0^{\pi/4}t\sec^2 t\ dt$

$=|t\tan t|_0^{\pi/4}-\int_0^{\pi/4}1.\tan t\ dt$

$=\frac{\pi}{4}-|\ln\sec t|_0^{\pi/4}=\frac{\pi}{4}-\{\ln\sqrt{2}-\ln 1\}=\frac{\pi}{4}-\frac{1}{2}\ln 2$

(e) $I=\int_0^1\frac{\log(1+x)}{1+x^2}dx$

$\Rightarrow\ I=\int_0^{\pi/4}\ln(1+\tan\theta)d\theta; x=\tan\theta$

$\Rightarrow\ I=\int_0^{\pi/4}\ln\left[1+\tan\left(\frac{\pi}{4}-\theta\right)\right]d\theta=\int_0^{\pi/4}\ln\left(\frac{2}{1+\tan\theta}\right)d\theta$

$=\int_0^{\pi/4}\ln 2d\theta-\int_0^{\pi/4}(1+\tan\theta)d\theta$

$\Rightarrow\ 2I=\ln 2\int_0^{\pi/4}d\theta\quad\Rightarrow\ I=\frac{\pi}{8}\ln 2$

12. (a) $I=\int_a^b\frac{f(x)}{f(x)+f(a+b-x)}dx\quad\quad ...(1)$

$\Rightarrow\ I=\int_a^b\frac{f(a+b-x)}{f(a+b-x)+f(x)}dx\quad\quad ...(2)$

Adding (1) and (2), $2I=\int_a^b\frac{f(x)+f(a+b-x)}{f(a+b-x)+f(x)}dx$

$\Rightarrow\ 2I=\int_a^b 1\ dx-(b-a)\ \Rightarrow\ I=\left(\frac{b-a}{2}\right)$

(b) $I=\int_0^1 x(1-x)^n dx$

$\Rightarrow\ I=\int_0^1(1-x)(1-(1-x))^n dx$

$\Rightarrow\ I=\int_0^1(1-x)x^n dx=\int_0^1(x^n-x^{n+1})dx=\left[\frac{x^{n+1}}{x+1}-\frac{x^{n+2}}{n+2}\right]_0^1$

$=\frac{1}{n+1}-\frac{1}{n+2}=\frac{1}{(n+1)(n+2)}$

(c) $I=\int_0^{\pi/2}\sin 2x\ \log\ \tan x\ dx$

$\Rightarrow\ I=\int_0^{\pi/2}\sin 2\left(\frac{\pi}{2}-x\right)\log\tan\left(\frac{\pi}{2}-x\right)dx$

$\Rightarrow\ I=\int_0^{\pi/2}\sin(\pi-2x)\log\cot x\ dx$

$=\int_0^{\pi/2}-\sin 2x\log\tan x\ dx=-I$

$\Rightarrow\ 2I=0\quad\quad\Rightarrow\ I=0$

13. (a) $\int_3^8|x-4|dx=\int_3^4|x-4|dx+\int_4^8|x-4|dx$

$=\int_3^4(-x+4)dx+\int_4^8(x-4)dx$

$=\left|\frac{-x^2}{2}+4x\right|_3^4+\left|\frac{x^2}{2}-4x\right|_4^8$

$=\frac{-1}{2}(7)+4(1)+\frac{1}{2}(48)-4(4)=\frac{1}{2}+24-16=\frac{17}{2}$

(b) $I=\int_0^1|\sin 2\pi x|dx=\int_0^{1/2}|\sin 2\pi x|dx+$

$\int_{1/2}^1|\sin 2\pi x|dx=\int_0^{1/2}\sin 2\pi x\ dx+\int_{1/2}^1-\sin 2\pi x\ dx$

$=\left[\frac{-\cos 2\pi x}{2\pi}\right]_0^{1/2}+\left[\frac{\cos 2\pi x}{2\pi}\right]_{1/2}^1$

$=\frac{-1}{2\pi}(-1-1)+\frac{1}{2\pi}(1+1)=\frac{1}{\pi}+\frac{1}{\pi}=\frac{2}{\pi}$

(c) $\int_0^{\pi/2}|\sin x-\cos x|dx$

$=\int_0^{\pi/4}|\sin x-\cos x|dx+\int_{\pi/4}^{\pi/2}|\sin x-\cos x|dx$

$=\int_0^{\pi/4}(-\sin x+\cos x)dx+\int_{\pi/4}^{\pi/2}(\sin x-\cos x)dx$

$=[\cos x+\sin x]_0^{\pi/4}+[-\cos x-\sin x]_{\pi/4}^{\pi/2}$

$=[\sqrt{2}-1]-[1-(\sqrt{2})]=2(\sqrt{2}-1)$

(d) $\int_1^{3/2}|x\sin\pi x|dx=\int_1^{3/2}-x\sin\pi x\ dx$

$=-\left[\left|\frac{-x\cos\pi x}{\pi}\right|_1^{3/2}-\int_1^{3/2}-1.\frac{\cos\pi x}{\pi}dx\right]$

$=-\left[\frac{-1}{\pi}(0-(-1))+\frac{1}{\pi}\left[\frac{\sin\pi x}{\pi}\right]_1^{3/2}\right]=-\left[\frac{-1}{\pi}+\frac{1}{\pi^2}(-1)\right]$

$=\frac{1}{\pi}+\frac{1}{\pi^2}=\frac{\pi+1}{\pi^2}$

(e) $\int_2^5 f(x)dx; f(x)=|x-2|+|x-3|+|x-4|$

$=\int_2^3(x-2-x+3-x+4)dx$

$+\int_3^4[(x-2)+(x-3)-x+4]dx$

$+\int_4^5((x-2)+(x-3)+(x-4))dx$

$I=\int_2^3(-x+5)dx+\int_3^4(x-1)dx+\int_4^5(3x-9)dx$

$=\left|\frac{-x^2}{2}+5x\right|_3^2+\left|\frac{x^2}{2}-x\right|_3^4+\left|\frac{3x^2}{2}-9x\right|_4^5$

$$= \frac{-1}{2}(5) + 5(1) + \frac{1}{2}(7) - 1 + \frac{3}{2}(9) - 9(1) = \frac{19}{2}$$

14. $I = \int_0^{\pi/2} \frac{\tan x - \cot x}{1 + \tan x . \cot x} dx$

$$\Rightarrow \quad I = \int_0^{\pi/2} \frac{\tan\left(\frac{\pi}{2} - x\right) - \cot\left(\frac{\pi}{2} - x\right)}{1 + \tan\left(\frac{\pi}{2} - x\right).\cot\left(\frac{\pi}{2} - x\right)}$$

$$= \int_0^{\pi/2} \frac{\cot x - \tan x}{1 + \cot x . \tan x} dx = -I$$

$\therefore \quad 2I = 0 \qquad \Rightarrow \quad I = 0$

15. $I = \int_0^{\pi/2} \frac{\cos^2 x}{1 - \sin x . \cos x} dx$ ...(1)

$$\Rightarrow \quad I = \int_0^{\pi/2} \frac{\cos^2\left(\frac{\pi}{2} - x\right)}{1 - \sin\left(\frac{\pi}{2} - x\right)\cos\left(\frac{\pi}{2} - x\right)} dx$$

$$\Rightarrow \quad I = \int_0^{\pi/2} \frac{\sin^2 x}{1 - \cos x . \sin x} dx \qquad ...(2)$$

$\therefore$ (1) + (2) gives,

$$2I = \int_0^{\pi/2} \frac{1\, dx}{1 - \sin x \cos x} = \int_0^{\pi/2} \frac{2\, dx}{2 - \sin 2x}$$

$$= \int_0^{\pi/2} \frac{2\, dx}{2 - \left(\frac{2\tan x}{1 + \tan^2 x}\right)}$$

$$= \int_0^{\pi/2} \frac{\sec^2 x\, dx}{\tan^2 x - \tan x + 1} = \int_0^{\infty} \frac{dt}{t^2 - t + 1}$$

$$= \int_0^{\infty} \frac{dt}{\left(t - \frac{1}{2}\right)^2 + \left(\frac{\sqrt{3}}{2}\right)^2}$$

$$= \frac{2}{\sqrt{3}}\left[\tan^{-1}\left|\frac{2t-1}{\sqrt{3}}\right|\right]_0^{\infty} = \frac{2}{\sqrt{3}}\left[\tan^{-1}(\infty) - \tan^{-1}\left(\frac{-1}{\sqrt{3}}\right)\right]$$

$$\therefore \quad 2I = \frac{2}{\sqrt{3}}\left[\frac{\pi}{2} + \frac{\pi}{6}\right] = \frac{4\pi}{3\sqrt{3}}$$

$$\Rightarrow \quad I = \frac{2\pi}{2\sqrt{3}}$$

16. $I = \int_0^{\pi} x \sin^3 x\, dx$ ...(1)

$$\Rightarrow \quad I = \int_0^{\pi} (\pi - x)\sin^3(\pi - x) dx$$

$$\Rightarrow \quad I = \int_0^{\pi} (\pi - x)\sin^3 x\, dx$$

$$\Rightarrow \quad I = \pi\int_0^{\pi} \sin^3 x\, dx - \int_0^{\pi} x \sin^3 x\, dx$$

$$\Rightarrow \quad 2I = \pi\int_0^{\pi}\left(\frac{3}{4}\sin x - \frac{\sin 3x}{4}\right)dx$$

$$\Rightarrow \quad I = \frac{\pi}{2 \times 4}\int_0^{\pi}(3\sin x - \sin 3x)dx$$

$$\Rightarrow \quad I = \frac{\pi}{8}\left[-3\cos x + \frac{\cos 3x}{3}\right]_0^{\pi}$$

$$\Rightarrow \quad I = \frac{\pi}{8}\left[-3(-1-1) + \frac{1}{3}(-1-1)\right] = \frac{2\pi}{3}$$

17. $I = \int_0^{\pi/4} \frac{x\, dx}{1 + \sin 2x + \cos 2x}$

$$\Rightarrow \quad I = \int_0^{\pi/4} \frac{\left(\frac{\pi}{4} - x\right)dx}{1 + \sin 2\left(\frac{\pi}{4} - x\right) + \cos 2\left(\frac{\pi}{4} - x\right)}$$

$$\Rightarrow \quad I = \int_0^{\pi/4} \frac{\left(\frac{\pi}{4} - x\right)dx}{1 + \cos 2x + \sin 2x}$$

$$\Rightarrow \quad I = \frac{\pi}{4}\int_0^{\pi/4} \frac{dx}{1 + \cos 2x + \sin 2x} - I$$

$$\Rightarrow \quad I = \frac{\pi}{8}\int_0^{\pi/4} \frac{dx}{1 + \sin 2x + \cos 2x}$$

$$= \frac{\pi}{8}\int_0^{\pi/4} \frac{dx}{1 + \left(\frac{2\tan x}{1 + \tan^2 x}\right) + \left(\frac{1 - \tan^2 x}{1 + \tan^2 x}\right)}$$

$$I = \frac{\pi}{8}\int_0^{\pi/4} \frac{dx}{1 + \sin 2x + \cos 2x}$$

$$= \frac{\pi}{8}\int_0^{\pi/4} \frac{dx}{1 + \left(\frac{2\tan x}{1 + \tan^2 x}\right) + \left(\frac{1 - \tan^2 x}{1 + \tan^2 x}\right)}$$

$$= \frac{\pi}{8}\int_0^{\pi/4} \frac{\sec^2 x\, dx}{2(1 + \tan x)}$$

$$= \frac{\pi}{8}\int_0^{1} \frac{dt}{2(1+t)} = \frac{\pi}{16}\left[\ln|1+t|\right]_0^1 = \frac{\pi}{16}[\ln 2 - 0] = \frac{\pi}{16}\ln 2$$

18. $I = \int_0^{\pi/2} \frac{x \sin x \cos x}{\sin^4 x + \cos^4 x} dx$

$$= \int_0^{\pi/2} \frac{\left(\frac{\pi}{2} - x\right)\sin\left(\frac{\pi}{2} - x\right)\cos\left(\frac{\pi}{2} - x\right)}{\sin^4\left(\frac{\pi}{2} - x\right) + \cos^4\left(\frac{\pi}{2} - x\right)} dx$$

$$= \int_0^{\pi/2} \frac{\left(\frac{\pi}{2} - x\right)\cos x \sin x\, dx}{(\cos^4 x + \sin^4 x)}$$

$$\Rightarrow \quad I = \frac{\pi}{2}\int_0^{\pi/2} \frac{\sin x . \cos x\, dx}{\sin^4 x + \cos^4 x} - I$$

$$\Rightarrow \quad I = \frac{\pi}{4}\int_0^{\pi/2} \frac{\sin x . \cos x\, dx}{\sin^4 x + \cos^4 x}$$

$$\Rightarrow \quad I = \frac{\pi}{4 \times 2}\int_0^{1} \frac{dt}{t^2 + (1-t)^2}$$

$$\Rightarrow \quad I = \frac{\pi}{8}\int_0^1 \frac{dt}{2t^2 - 2t + 1}$$

$$\Rightarrow \quad I = \frac{\pi}{16}\int_0^1 \frac{dt}{\left(t^2 - t + \frac{1}{2}\right)} \quad \Rightarrow \quad I = \frac{\pi}{16}\int_0^1 \frac{dt}{\left(t - \frac{-1}{2}\right)^2 + \frac{1}{4}}$$

$$\Rightarrow \quad I = \frac{\pi}{16} \times 2\left[\tan^{-1}\left(\frac{t - \frac{1}{2}}{\frac{1}{2}}\right)\right]_0^1$$

$$\Rightarrow \quad I = \frac{\pi}{8}\left[\tan^{-1}(2t - 1)\right]_0^1$$

$$= \frac{\pi}{8}\left[\tan^{-1}(1) - \tan^{-1}(-1)\right] = \frac{\pi^2}{16}$$

19. $I = \int_0^{\pi/2n} \frac{dx}{1 + \cot^n nx} \Rightarrow I = \int_0^{\pi/2n} \frac{\sin^n nx\ dx}{(\sin^n xn + \cos^n nx)}$ ...(1)

$$\Rightarrow \quad I = \int_0^{\pi/2n} \frac{\sin^n n\left(\frac{\pi}{2n} - x\right) dx}{\sin^n n\left(\frac{\pi}{2n} - x\right) + \cos^n n\left(\frac{\pi}{2n} - x\right)}$$

$$\Rightarrow \quad I = \int_0^{\pi/2n} \frac{\sin^n\left(\frac{\pi}{2} - nx\right) dx}{\sin^n\left(\frac{\pi}{2} - nx\right) + \cos^n\left(\frac{\pi}{2} - nx\right)}$$

$$\Rightarrow \quad I = \int_0^{\pi/2n} \frac{\cos^n nx\ dx}{\cos^n nx + \sin^n nx} \quad ...(2)$$

Equation (1) + (2) gives, $2I = \int_0^{\pi/2n} 1\, dx = \frac{\pi}{2n}$

$$\Rightarrow \quad I = \frac{\pi}{4n}$$

20. $I = \int_a^b \frac{|2 - x|}{(2 - x)} dx$

Put $2 - x = t$ $\quad \Rightarrow \quad dx = -dt$

$$\Rightarrow \quad I = \int_{2-a}^{2-b} \frac{-|t|}{t} dt$$

Case-(i): $2 - b < 0$;

$$I = \int_{2-a}^{2-b} 1\, dt = (2 - b) - (2 - a) = |2 - a| - |2 - b|$$

$(\because 2 - a < 0, 2 - b < 0)$

Case-(ii): $2 - a > 0$;

$$I = \int_{2-a}^{2-b} -dt = (2 - a) - (2 - b) = |2 - a| - |2 - b|$$

Case-(iii): $2 - a < 0 < 2 - b$;

$$I = \int_{2-a}^{0} 1\, dt + \int_0^{2-b} -1 dt = -(2 - a) - (2 - b) = |2 - a| - |2 - b|$$

Hence $I = |2 - a| - |2 - b|$

21. $I = \int_{-1/3}^{1/3} \cos x \ln\left(\frac{1 - x}{1 + x}\right) dx$

$$\Rightarrow \quad I = \int_{-1/3}^{1/3} \cos\left(\frac{-1}{3} + \frac{1}{3} - x\right) \ln\left(\frac{1 - \left(\frac{1}{3} + \frac{1}{3} - x\right)}{1 + \left(\frac{-1}{3} + \frac{1}{3} - x\right)}\right) dx$$

$$= \int_{-1/3}^{1/3} \cos(-x) \ln\left(\frac{1 + x}{1 - x}\right) dx$$

$$= -\int_{-1/3}^{1/3} \cos x \ln\left(\frac{1 - x}{1 + x}\right) dx = -I$$

$\Rightarrow \quad 2I = 0$

$\Rightarrow \quad I = 0$; hence proved

22. $I = \int_{-\pi/4}^{\pi/4} \left(\frac{x^9 - 3x^7 + 5x^3 - 2x + 1}{\cos^2 x}\right) dx$

$$= \underbrace{\int_{-\pi/4}^{\pi/4} (x^9 - 3x^7 + 5x^3 - 2x) \sec^2 dx}_{\text{(odd function)}\times\text{(even function)}} + \int_{-\pi/4}^{\pi/4} \sec^2 x dx$$

$$= 0 + 2\int_0^{\pi/4} \sec^2 x dx$$

$$\left(\because \int_{-a}^{a} (\text{odd function}) dx = 0 \text{ and } \int_{-a}^{a} (\text{even function}) dx = 2\int_0^a (\text{even function}) dx\right)$$

$$= 2|\tan x|_0^{\pi/4} = 2(1 - 0) = 2$$

23. (a) $\int_0^{b-c} f''(x + a) dx$

Put $x + a = t = \int_a^{a+b-c} f''(t) dt$

$$= [f'(t)]_a^{a+b-c} = f'(a + b - c) - f'(a)$$

(b) $\int_0^{\pi/2} \left|\sin\left(x - \frac{\pi}{4}\right)\right| dx$

$$= \int_0^{\pi/4} \left|\sin\left(x - \frac{\pi}{4}\right)\right| dx + \int_{\pi/4}^{\pi/2} \left|\sin\left(x - \frac{\pi}{4}\right)\right| dx$$

$$= \int_0^{\pi/4} -\sin\left(x - \frac{\pi}{4}\right) dx + \int_{\pi/4}^{\pi/2} \sin\left(x - \frac{\pi}{4}\right) dx$$

$$= \left[\cos\left(x - \frac{\pi}{4}\right)\right]_0^{\pi/4} - \left[\cos\left(x - \frac{\pi}{4}\right)\right]_{\pi/4}^{\pi/2}$$

$$= \left(1 - \frac{1}{\sqrt{2}}\right) - \left(\frac{1}{\sqrt{2}} - 1\right) = 2\left(1 - \frac{1}{\sqrt{2}}\right) = 2 - \sqrt{2}$$

24. $I = \int_a^b f(x) dx$

Put $x = (b - a)t + a$

$$\Rightarrow \quad I = \int_0^1 f[(b - a)t + a](b - a) dt$$

$$= (b - a)\int_0^1 f[(b - a)t + a] dt$$

$$= (b - a)\int_0^1 f[(b - a)x + a] dx \quad ...(1)$$

Hence proved, Let $I_1 = \int_{-4}^{-5} e^{(x+5)^2} dx$ and

$$I_2 = \int_{1/3}^{2/3} e^{9(x - 2/3)^2} dx$$

$$\therefore \quad I_1 = (-5 + 4)\int_0^1 e^{[(-5+4)x - 4 + 5]^2} dx = -\int_0^1 e^{(-x+1)^2} dx$$

$$= -\int_0^1 e^{(x-1)^2} dx \quad ...(2)$$

$$I_2 = 3\left(\frac{2}{3} - \frac{1}{3}\right)\int_0^1 e^{9\left[\left(\frac{2}{3} - \frac{1}{3}\right)x + \frac{1}{3} - \frac{2}{3}\right]^2} dx$$

$$= \int_0^1 e^{9\left[\frac{x}{3}-\frac{1}{3}\right]^2} dx = \int_0^1 e^{(x-1)^2} dx$$

$$\therefore \quad I_1 + I_2 = -\int_0^1 e^{(x-1)^2} dx + \int_0^1 e^{(x-1)^2} dx = 0$$

25. $\int_1^2 \frac{e^{\sin x}}{1+x} dx = \lambda$ ...(1)

$$\Rightarrow (2-1)\int_0^1 \frac{e^{\sin[(2-1)x+1]}}{1+[(2-1)x+1]^2} dx = \lambda$$

$$\Rightarrow \int_0^1 \frac{e^{\sin(x+1)}}{1+[x+1]^2} dx = \lambda \quad ...(2)$$

Now, $\int_{2\pi}^{4\pi} \frac{e^{\sin\left(\frac{x}{2\pi}\right)}}{4\pi^2+x^2} dx$

$$= (4\pi - 2\pi)\int_0^1 \frac{e^{\sin\left(\frac{(4\pi-2\pi)x+2\pi}{2\pi}\right)}}{4\pi^2\left[(4\pi-2\pi)x+2\pi\right]^2} dx$$

$$= 2\pi\int_0^1 \frac{e^{\sin(x+1)}}{4\pi^2+(2\pi x+2\pi)^2} dx = \frac{2\pi}{4\pi^2}\int_0^1 \frac{e^{\sin(x+1)}}{1+(x+1)^2} dx$$

$$= \frac{1}{2\pi}\lambda = \frac{\lambda}{2\pi} \text{ (using (2))}$$

TEXTUAL EXERCISE–4: (OBJECTIVE)

1. (b) $I = \int_0^\pi x f(\sin x) dx$

$$\Rightarrow I = \int_0^\pi (\pi - x) f(\sin(\pi - x)) dx = \int_0^\pi (\pi - x) f(\sin x) dx$$

$$= \pi\int_0^\pi f(\sin x) dx - \int_0^\pi x f(\sin x) dx$$

$$\Rightarrow 2I = \pi\int_0^\pi f(\sin x) dx \Rightarrow I = \frac{\pi}{2}\int_0^\pi f(\sin x) dx$$

2. (d) $I = \int_0^{\pi/2} \frac{d\theta}{1+\tan\theta}$

$$\Rightarrow I = \int_0^{\pi/2} \frac{\cos\theta}{\cos\theta + \sin\theta} d\theta \quad ...(1)$$

$$\Rightarrow I = \int_0^{\pi/2} \frac{\cos\left(\frac{\pi}{2}-\theta\right)}{\cos\left(\frac{\pi}{2}-\theta\right)+\sin\left(\frac{\pi}{2}-\theta\right)} d\theta$$

$$\Rightarrow I = \int_0^{\pi/2} \frac{\sin\theta}{\sin\theta + \cos\theta} d\theta \quad ...(2)$$

Equation (1) + (2) gives, $2I = \int_0^{\pi/2}\left(\frac{\sin\theta + \cos\theta}{\cos\theta + \sin\theta}\right) d\theta$
$= \int_0^{\pi/2} 1 d\theta$

$$\Rightarrow I = \frac{\pi}{4}$$

3. (d) $I = \int_0^{\pi/2} \frac{\sin^{3/2} x \, dx}{\cos^{3/2} x + \sin^{3/2} x} dx$ ...(1)

$$\Rightarrow I = \int_0^{\pi/2} \frac{\sin^{3/2}\left(\frac{\pi}{2}-x\right)}{\cos^{3/2}\left(\frac{\pi}{2}-x\right)+\sin^{3/2}\left(\frac{\pi}{2}-x\right)} dx$$

$$\Rightarrow I = \int_0^{\pi/2} \frac{\cos^{3/2} x}{\sin^{3/2} x + \cos^{3/2} x} dx \quad ...(2)$$

$\therefore$ Equation (1) + (2) gives, $2I = \int_0^{\pi/2} 1 \, dx = \frac{\pi}{2}$

$$\Rightarrow I = \frac{\pi}{4}$$

4. (b) $I = \int_0^\pi e^{\sin^2 x}.\cos^3(2n+1)x \, dx$

$$\Rightarrow I = \int_0^\pi e^{\sin^2(\pi - x)}.\cos^3(2n+1)(\pi - x) dx$$

$$\Rightarrow I = \int_0^\pi -e^{\sin^2 x}.\cos^3(2n+1)x \, dx = -I$$

$$\Rightarrow 2I = 0 \qquad \Rightarrow I = 0$$

5. (b) Let $I = \int_0^\pi x f\left(\cos^2 x + \tan^4 x\right) dx$

Applying $\int_0^a f(x)dx = \int_0^a f(a-x)dx$

$$\Rightarrow I = \frac{\pi}{2}\int_0^\pi f(\cos^2 x + \tan^4 x) dx$$

$$= \frac{\pi}{2}\left[2\int_0^{\pi/2} f(\cos^2 x + \tan^4 x) dx\right]$$

$$\left(\because \int_0^{2a} f(x)dx = 2\int_0^a f(x)dx \text{ if } f(2a-x) = f(x)\right)$$

$$\Rightarrow \pi\int_0^{\pi/2} f(\cos^2 x + \tan^4 x) dx$$

$$\Rightarrow k = \pi$$

6. (a) $I = \int_{\pi/4}^{3\pi/4} \frac{\phi}{1+\sin\phi} d\phi = \int_{\pi/4}^{3\pi/4} \frac{\left(\frac{\pi}{4}+\frac{3\pi}{4}-\phi\right)}{1+\sin\left(\frac{\pi}{4}+\frac{3\pi}{4}-\phi\right)} d\phi$

$$= \int_{\pi/4}^{3\pi/4} \frac{(\pi - \phi)}{1+\sin\phi} d\phi = \pi\int_{\pi/4}^{3\pi/4} \frac{1}{1+\sin\phi} d\phi - I$$

$$\Rightarrow I = \frac{\pi}{2}\int_{\pi/4}^{3\pi/4} \frac{1}{1+\sin\phi} d\phi$$

$$\Rightarrow I = \frac{\pi}{2}\int_{\pi/4}^{3\pi/4} \frac{(1-\sin\phi)}{\cos^2\phi} d\phi$$

$$\Rightarrow I = \frac{\pi}{2}\int_{\pi/4}^{3\pi/4} \left(\sec^2\phi - \sec\phi\tan\phi\right) d\phi$$

$$\Rightarrow I = \frac{\pi}{2}\left[\tan\phi - \sec\phi\right]_{\pi/4}^{3\pi/4}$$

$$\Rightarrow I = \frac{\pi}{2}\left[(-1-1) - \left(\sqrt{2} - \sqrt{2}\right)\right]$$

$$\Rightarrow I = \frac{\pi}{2}\left[-2 + 2\sqrt{2}\right]$$

$$\Rightarrow I = \pi\left(\sqrt{2} - 1\right) \quad ...(1)$$

$$\Rightarrow \tan\left[2\left(\frac{\pi}{8}\right)\right] = \frac{2\tan\frac{\pi}{8}}{1-\tan^2\frac{\pi}{8}}$$

$$\Rightarrow \tan^2\frac{\pi}{8} + 2\tan\frac{\pi}{8} - 1 = 0$$

$\Rightarrow \tan\frac{\pi}{8} = \frac{-2+\sqrt{8}}{2} = \sqrt{2}-1$ ...(2)

$\therefore$ From equation (1) and (2), we get $I = \pi\tan\left(\frac{\pi}{8}\right)$

7. (b) $I = \int_a^b xf(x)dx = \int_a^b (a+b-x)f(a+b-x)dx$

$= (a+b)\int_a^b f(a+b-x)dx - \int_a^b xf(a+b-x)dx$

$= (a+b)\int_a^b f(x) - \int_a^b f(x)dx$

$\Rightarrow 2I = (a+b)\int_a^b f(x)dx$

$\Rightarrow I = \frac{(a+b)}{2}\int_a^b f(x)dx$

8. (a) $I = \int_0^{\pi/2} \frac{2^{\sin x}}{2^{\sin x}+2^{\cos x}}dx$ ...(1)

$\Rightarrow I = \int_0^{\pi/2} \frac{2^{\sin\left(\frac{\pi}{2}-x\right)}}{2^{\sin\left(\frac{\pi}{2}-x\right)}+2^{\cos\left(\frac{\pi}{2}-x\right)}}dx$

$\Rightarrow I = \int_0^{\pi/2} \frac{2^{\cos x}}{2^{\cos x}+2^{\sin x}}dx$ ...(2)

Equation (1) + (2) gives, $2I = \int_0^{\pi/2} 1\, dx$

$\Rightarrow I = \frac{\pi}{4}$

9. (a) $I = \int_0^{\pi/2} \frac{e^{x^2}}{e^{x^2}+e^{\left(\frac{\pi}{2}-x\right)^2}}dx$ ...(1)

$\Rightarrow I = \int_0^{\pi/2} \frac{e^{\left(\frac{\pi}{2}-x\right)^2}}{e^{\left(\frac{\pi}{2}-x\right)^2}+e^{x^2}}dx$ ...(2)

Adding (1) and (2), $2I = \int_0^{\pi/2} 1\, dx$

$\Rightarrow I = \frac{\pi}{4}$

10. (c) $I_1 = \int_a^{\pi-a} xf(\sin x)dx$ ...(1)

$I_2 = \int_a^{\pi-a} f(\sin x)dx$ ...(2)

$I_1 = \int_a^{\pi-a} xf(\sin x)dx$

$= \int_a^{\pi-a} (a+\pi-a-x)f\left(\sin(a+\pi-a-x)\right)dx$

$= \int_a^{\pi-a} (\pi-x)f\left(\sin(\pi-x)\right)dx$

$= \pi\int_a^{\pi-a} f(\sin x)dx - \int_a^{\pi-a} xf(\sin x)dx = \pi I_2 - I_1$

$\Rightarrow 2I_1 = \pi I_2 \quad \Rightarrow I_2 = \frac{2}{\pi}I_1$

11. (c) $I = \int_{1/n}^{\frac{an-1}{n}} \frac{\sqrt{x}}{\sqrt{a-x}+\sqrt{x}}dx$ ...(1)

$\Rightarrow I = \int_{\frac{1}{n}}^{a-\frac{1}{n}} \frac{\sqrt{\frac{1}{n}+a-\frac{1}{n}-x}}{\sqrt{a-\frac{1}{n}-a+\frac{1}{n}+x}+\sqrt{\frac{1}{n}+a-\frac{1}{n}-x}}$

$\Rightarrow I = \int_{\frac{1}{n}}^{a-\frac{1}{n}} \frac{\sqrt{a-x}}{\sqrt{x}+\sqrt{a-x}}dx$ ...(2)

$\therefore$ Equation (1) + (2) gives, $2I = \int_{\frac{1}{n}}^{a-\frac{1}{n}} 1dx = \left(a-\frac{1}{n}-\frac{1}{n}\right)$

$\Rightarrow I = \frac{na-2}{2n}$

12. (a) $I = \int_0^1 \log\sin\left(\frac{\pi}{2}x\right)dx$

Put $\frac{\pi}{2}x = t \quad \Rightarrow dx = \frac{2}{\pi}dt$

$\Rightarrow I = \frac{2}{\pi}\int_0^{\pi/2} \log\sin t\, dt$ ...(1)

$= \frac{2}{\pi}\int_0^{\pi/2} \log\sin\left(\frac{\pi}{2}-t\right)dt$

$I = \frac{2}{\pi}\int_0^{\frac{\pi}{2}} \log\cos t\, dt$ ...(2)

Equation (1) + (2) gives, $2I = \frac{2}{\pi}\int_0^{\pi/2} \log(\sin t\cos t)dt$

$= \frac{2}{\pi}\int_0^{\pi/2} \log\left(\frac{\sin 2t}{2}\right)dt$

$= \frac{2}{\pi}\int_0^{\pi/2} \log(\sin 2t)dt - \frac{2}{\pi}\times\frac{\pi}{2}\log 2$

$2I = \frac{2}{\pi}\int_0^{\pi/2} \log(\sin 2t)dt - \log 2$

Put $2t = u \quad \Rightarrow dt = \frac{du}{2}$

$\Rightarrow 2I = \frac{2}{\pi}\int_0^{\pi} \log\sin u\frac{du}{2} - \log 2 = \frac{1}{\pi}\int_0^{\pi} \log\sin u\, du - \log 2$

$= \frac{2}{\pi}\int_0^{\pi/2} \log\sin u\, du - \log 2$

$\therefore 2I = I - \log 2$

$\Rightarrow I = -\log 2$

13. (c) $f(x) = A\sin\left(\frac{\pi x}{2}\right) + B$

$\Rightarrow f'(x) = A\left(\frac{\pi}{2}\right)\cos\left(\frac{\pi x}{2}\right)$

$\Rightarrow f'\left(\frac{1}{2}\right) = \frac{A\pi}{2}\cos\left(\frac{\pi}{2}\right) = \frac{A\pi}{2\sqrt{2}} = \sqrt{2}$

$\Rightarrow A = \frac{4}{\pi}$ ...(1)

$\int_0^1 f(x)dx = \int_0^1 \left\{\frac{4}{\pi}\sin\left(\frac{\pi x}{2}\right) + B\right\}dx$

$= \left|-\frac{4}{\pi}\times\frac{1}{\pi/2}\cos\left(\frac{\pi x}{2}\right)\right|_0^1 + B = \frac{-8}{\pi^2}[0-1] + B$

$\Rightarrow \frac{2A}{\pi} = \frac{8}{\pi^2} + B \quad \left(\because \int_0^1 f(x)dx = \frac{2A}{\pi} \text{ given}\right)$

$\Rightarrow \frac{2}{\pi}\left(\frac{4}{\pi}\right) = \frac{8}{\pi^2} + B \quad \Rightarrow B = 0$

14. (a) $I=\int_0^{2\pi}\frac{dx}{e^{\sin x}+1}$ ...(1)

$\Rightarrow\ I=\int_0^{2\pi}\frac{dx}{e^{\sin(2\pi-x)}+1}$

$\Rightarrow\ I=\int_0^{2\pi}\frac{e^{\sin x}}{1+e^{\sin x}}dx$ ...(2)

Equation (1) + (2) gives, $2I=\int_0^{2\pi}1\,dx=2\pi$

$\Rightarrow\ I=\pi$

15. (d) $I=\int_{\sin x}^{\operatorname{cosec} x}f(z)dz=\int_{\sin x}^{\operatorname{cosec} x}-\frac{1}{z^2}f\left(\frac{1}{z}\right)dz$

Put $\frac{1}{z}=u$ $\Rightarrow\ -\frac{1}{z^2}dz=du$

$=\int_{\operatorname{cosec} x}^{\sin x}f(u)du=-\int_{\sin x}^{\operatorname{cosec} x}f(u)du$

$\Rightarrow\ I=-I$ $\Rightarrow\ 2I=0$

$\Rightarrow\ I=0$

16. (b) $I=\int_0^{\pi/2}\left|\sin\left(x-\frac{\pi}{4}\right)\right|dx$

Put $x-\frac{\pi}{4}=t$ $\Rightarrow\ dx=dt$

$\therefore\ I=\int_{-\pi/4}^{\pi/4}|\sin t|\,dt=\int_{-\pi/4}^{0}-\sin t\,dt+\int_0^{\pi/4}\sin t\,dt$

$=|\cos t|_{-\pi/4}^{0}-|\cos t|_0^{\pi/4}=\left(1-\frac{1}{\sqrt2}\right)-\left(\frac{1}{\sqrt2}-1\right)=2-\sqrt2$

17. (d) $I=\int_0^{\pi/4}\ln\left(\cos\left(\frac{\pi}{4}+x\right)\right)^{\cos\left(\frac{\pi}{4}-x\right)}dx$

Put $\frac{\pi}{4}+x=t, dx=dt$

$\Rightarrow\ I=\int_{\pi/4}^{\pi/2}\ln(\cos t)^{\cot\left(\frac{\pi}{2}-t\right)}dt$

$\Rightarrow\ I=\int_{\pi/4}^{\pi/2}\ln(\cos t)^{\tan t}dt=\int_{\pi/4}^{\pi/2}(\tan t)(\ln\cos t)dt$

Put $\ln(\cos t)=u$

$\Rightarrow\ -\tan t\,dt=du$

$\Rightarrow\ I=\int_{\ln(1/\sqrt2)}^{-\infty}-u\,du=-\left[\frac{u^2}{2}\right]_{\ln\left(\frac{1}{\sqrt2}\right)}^{-\infty}=\frac{-1}{2}\left[\infty-\left(\ln\frac{1}{\sqrt2}\right)^2\right]=$

Not defined.

18. (a) $I=\frac{1}{c}\int_{ac}^{bc}f\left(\frac{x}{c}\right)dx$

Put $\frac{x}{c}=t$ $\Rightarrow\ dx=c\,dt$

$\therefore\ I=\frac{1}{c}\int_a^b f(t)c\,dt=\int_a^b f(t)dt=\int_a^b f(x)dx$

19. $I=\int_{-2}^{0}\left(\left(x^3+3x^2+3x+3\right)+(x+1)\cos(x+1)\right)dx$

Put $(x+1)=t$

$\Rightarrow\ I=\int_{-1}^{1}\left((t-1)^3+3(t-1)^2+3(t-1)+3+t\cos t\right)dt$

$=\int_{-1}^{1}\left[\left(t^3-3t^2+3t-1\right)+3t^2-6t+3+3t+t\cos t\right]dt$

$=\int_{-1}^{1}\left(t^3+2+t\cos t\right)dt=2\int_0^1 2\,dt=4(1-0)=4$

20. (b) $I=\int_0^a\frac{x^5dx}{\left(2a^2-x^2\right)^3}$

Put $x=\sqrt2 a\sin\theta$

$\Rightarrow\ dx=\sqrt2 a\cos\theta d\theta$

$\therefore\ I=\int_0^{\pi/4}\frac{\left(\sqrt2 a\sin\theta\right)^5\left(\sqrt2 a\cos\theta d\theta\right)}{\left(2a^2-2a^2\sin^2\theta\right)^3}$

$=\int_0^{\pi/4}\frac{8a^6\sin^5\theta\cos d\theta}{\left(2a^2\right)^3\left(\cos^2\theta\right)^3}=\int_0^{\pi/4}\frac{\sin^5\theta}{\cos^5\theta}d\theta=\int_0^{\pi/4}\tan^5\theta d\theta$

$=\int_0^{\pi/4}\left(\tan^3\theta\right)\left(\sec^2\theta-1\right)d\theta$

$=\left[\frac{\tan^4\theta}{4}\right]_0^{\pi/4}-\int_0^{\pi/4}(\tan\theta)\left(\sec^2\theta-1\right)d\theta$

$=\frac{1}{4}[1]-\left[\frac{\tan^2\theta}{2}\right]_0^{\pi/4}+|\ln\sec\theta|_0^{\frac{\pi}{4}}$

$=\frac{1}{4}-\frac{1}{2}+\ln\sqrt2=\frac{1}{2}\ln2-\frac{1}{4}$

21. (a) $\int_0^a f(x)dx=\lambda;\ \int_0^a f(2a-x)dx=\mu$

$\Rightarrow\ I=\int_0^{2a}f(x)dx=\int_0^a f(x)dx+\int_a^{2a}f(x)dx$

In second integral, put $x=2a-t$

$\Rightarrow\ I=\int_0^a f(x)dx+\int_a^0 f(2a-t)(-dt)$

$=\int_0^a f(x)dx+\int_0^a f(2a-x)dx=\lambda+u$

22. (a) $I=\int_{-\pi/2}^{\pi/2}\frac{\cos x}{1+e^x}dx$ ...(1)

Also $I=\int_{-\pi/2}^{\pi/2}\frac{\cos\left(-\frac{\pi}{2}+\frac{\pi}{2}-x\right)dx}{1+e^{\left(-\frac{\pi}{2}+\frac{\pi}{2}-x\right)}}$

$=\int_{-\pi/2}^{\pi/2}\frac{\cos x}{1+e^{-x}}dx=\int_{-\pi/2}^{\pi/2}\frac{e^x\cos x}{1+e^x}dx$ ...(2)

$\therefore$ Equation (1) + (2) gives,

$2I=\int_{-\pi/2}^{\pi/2}\cos x\,dx=[\sin x]_{-\pi/2}^{\pi/2}=2$

$\Rightarrow\ I=1$

23. (a) $I=\int_{-1}^{1}\left(\sqrt{1+x+x^2}-\sqrt{1-x+x^2}\right)dx$

Let $f(x)=\sqrt{1+x+x^2}-\sqrt{1-x+x^2}$

$\Rightarrow\ f(-x)=\sqrt{1+x+x^2}-\sqrt{1-x+x^2}=-f(x)$

$\Rightarrow\ f(x)$ is an odd function.

$\therefore\ I=0$

24. (c) $I=\int_{-\pi}^{\pi}\frac{\cos^2 x}{1+a^x}dx\ ;\ a>0$ ...(1)

$\Rightarrow\ I=\int_{-\pi}^{\pi}\frac{\cos^2(-\pi+\pi-x)}{1+a^{(-\pi+\pi-x)}}dx$

$\Rightarrow\ I=\int_{-\pi}^{\pi}\frac{\cos^2 x}{1+a^{-x}}dx$

$\Rightarrow\ I=\int_{-\pi}^{\pi}\frac{a^x\cos^2 x}{a^x+1}dx$ ...(2)

Equation (1) + (2) gives, $2I=\int_{-\pi}^{\pi}\cos^2 x\,dx$

$\Rightarrow\ 2I=2\int_0^{\pi}\cos^2 x\,dx \quad \Rightarrow\ 2I=2\int_0^{\pi}(1+\cos 2)\,dx$

$\Rightarrow\ 2I=\left|x+\frac{\sin 2x}{2}\right|_0^{\pi}=\pi \Rightarrow\ I=\frac{\pi}{2}$

25. (d) $f(x)=\frac{e^x}{1+e^x}$

$I_1=\int_{f(-a)}^{f(a)}g\{x(1-x)\}dx;\ I_2=\int_{f(-a)}^{f(a)}g\{x(1-x)\}dx$

Now, $f(a)+f(-a)=\frac{e^a}{1+e^a}+\frac{e^{-a}}{1+e^{-a}}$

$=\frac{e^a}{1+e^a}+\frac{1}{e^a+1}=1$

$\therefore\ I_1=\int_{f(-a)}^{f(a)}(f(a)+f(-a)-x)g\{(1-x)(x)\}dx$

$=\int_{f(-a)}^{f(a)}(1-x)g\{x(1-x)\}dx$

$=\int_{f(-a)}^{f(a)}g\{x(1-x)\}dx-\int_{f(-a)}^{f(a)}xg\{x(1-x)\}dx$

$\Rightarrow\ I_1=I_2-I_1 \quad \Rightarrow\ 2I_1=I_2$

$\Rightarrow\ \frac{I_2}{I_1}=2$

TEXTUAL EXERCISE–5: (SUBJECTIVE)

1. $I=\int_0^{\pi}\frac{|\sin x|}{|\sin x|+|\cos x|}dx$

$\Rightarrow\ I=2\int_0^{\pi/2}\frac{|\sin x|}{|\sin x|+|\cos x|}dx$ ...(1)

$\left(\because \int_0^{2a}f(x)dx=2\int_0^{a}(x)dx \text{ if } f(2a-x)=f(x)\right)$

$\therefore\ I=2\int_0^{\pi/2}\frac{\left|\sin\left(\frac{\pi}{2}-x\right)\right|dx}{\left|\sin\left(\frac{\pi}{2}-x\right)\right|+\left|\cos\left(\frac{\pi}{2}-x\right)\right|}$

$\Rightarrow\ I=2\int_0^{\pi/2}\frac{|\cos x|}{|\cos x|+|\sin x|}dx$ ...(2)

Equation (1) + 2 gives, $2I=2\int_0^{\pi/2}1\,dx=2\left(\frac{\pi}{2}\right)$

$\Rightarrow\ I=\frac{\pi}{2}$

2. (a) $I=\int_{\ln\lambda}^{\ln\frac{1}{\lambda}}\frac{f\left(\frac{x^2}{2}\right)[f(x)-f(-x)]}{g\left(\frac{x^2}{4}\right)[g(x)+g(-x)]}dx$

$\Rightarrow\ I=\int_{\ln\lambda}^{\ln\frac{1}{\lambda}}\frac{f\left(\frac{(-x)^2}{2}\right)[f(-x)-f(x)]}{g\left(\frac{(-x)^2}{4}\right)[g(-x)+g(x)]}dx$

$\left(\because a+b=\ln\lambda+\ln\frac{1}{\lambda}=0 \text{ using} \int_a^b f(x)dx = \int_a^b f(a+b-x)dx=\int_a^b f(-x)dx\right)$

$\Rightarrow\ I=\int_{\ln\lambda}^{\ln\frac{1}{\lambda}}\frac{-f\left(\frac{x^2}{2}\right)[f(x)-f(-x)]}{g\left(\frac{x^2}{4}\right)[g(x)+g(-x)]}dx$

$\Rightarrow\ I=-I \qquad \Rightarrow\ 2I=0$

$\Rightarrow\ I=0$

(b) $I=\int_0^{\pi}\sin^{-1}(\sin x)dx$

$\therefore\ I=\int_0^{\pi/2}x\,dx+\int_{\pi/2}^{\pi}(-x+\pi)\,dx$

$=\left[\frac{x^2}{2}\right]_0^{\pi/2}+\left[\frac{-x^2}{2}\right]_{\pi/2}^{\pi}+\pi[x]_{\pi/2}^{\pi}$

$=\frac{1}{2}\left[\frac{\pi^2}{4}\right]-\frac{1}{2}\left[\pi^2-\frac{\pi^2}{4}\right]+\pi\left[\pi-\frac{\pi}{2}\right]$

$\Rightarrow\ \frac{\pi^2}{8}-\frac{3\pi^2}{8}+\frac{\pi^2}{2}=\left(\frac{1}{8}-\frac{3}{8}+\frac{4}{8}\right)\pi^2=\frac{\pi^2}{4}$

(c) $\int_0^{2\pi}\sin^{-1}(\sin x)dx=\int_0^{\pi/2}xdx+\int_{\pi/2}^{\pi}(-x+\pi)dx$

$+\int_{\pi}^{3\pi/2}(x-\pi)dx+\int_{3\pi/2}^{2\pi}(-x+2\pi)dx$

$=\frac{1}{2}\left[\frac{\pi^2}{4}\right]+\left[\frac{-1}{2}\left(\pi^2-\frac{\pi^2}{4}\right)+\pi\left(\frac{\pi}{2}\right)\right]$

$+\left[\frac{1}{2}\left(\frac{9\pi^2}{4}-\pi^2\right)-\pi\left(\frac{\pi}{2}\right)\right]$

$+\frac{-1}{2}\left[4\pi^2-\frac{9\pi^2}{4}\right]+2\pi\left(2\pi-\frac{3\pi}{2}\right)$

$=\frac{\pi^2}{8}-\frac{3\pi^2}{8}+\frac{\pi^2}{2}+\frac{5\pi^2}{8}-\frac{\pi^2}{2}-\frac{7\pi^2}{8}+\pi^2$

$=\left(\frac{1}{8}-\frac{3}{8}+\frac{5}{8}-\frac{7}{8}+\frac{8}{8}\right)\pi^2=\frac{4\pi^2}{8}=\frac{\pi^2}{2}$

(d) $I=\int_{-1}^{1}\underbrace{\sin^2 x}_{\text{even}}\underbrace{\log\left(\frac{1-x}{1+x}\right)}_{\text{odd function}}dx$

$\Rightarrow$ Integer and is an odd function

$\Rightarrow\ I=0$

(e) $I=\int_{-2}^{2}\underbrace{\underbrace{\underbrace{\sin x}_{\text{odd}}.\underbrace{\tan x}_{\text{odd}}.\underbrace{\ln\left(x+\sqrt{x^2+1}\right)}_{\text{odd function.}}}_{\text{odd function.}}}dx$

$\Rightarrow\ I=0$

(f) $\int_a^{-a}\underbrace{\underbrace{(f(x)+f(-x))}_{\text{even function}}\ \underbrace{\tan^3 x}_{\text{odd function}}}_{\text{odd function}}\ dx$

$=\int_a^{-a}(\text{odd function})\,dx=0$

(g) $I=\int_{-\pi/2}^{\pi/2}\sqrt{\cos x-\cos^3 x}\ dx=\int_{-\pi/2}^{\pi/2}\underbrace{\sqrt{\cos x}\,|\sin x|}_{\text{even function.}}dx$

$\therefore\ I=2\int_0^{\pi/2}\sqrt{\cos x}\,|\sin x|\,dx=2\int_0^{\pi/2}\sqrt{\cos x}\,(\sin x)\,dx$

$=2\int_1^0-\sqrt{t}\ dt=2\int_0^1\sqrt{t}\ dt=2\left|\frac{(t)^{3/2}}{\frac{3}{2}}\right|_0^1=\frac{4}{3}$

(h) $I=\int_{-\pi/2}^{\pi/2}\frac{dx}{e^{\tan x}+1}$ ...(1)

$\Rightarrow\ I=\int_{-\pi/2}^{\pi/2}\frac{dx}{e^{\tan\left(\frac{-\pi}{2}+\frac{\pi}{2}-x\right)}+1}$

$\Rightarrow\ I=\int_{-\pi/2}^{\pi/2}\frac{dx}{e^{\tan(-x)}+1}$

$\Rightarrow\ I=\int_{-\pi/2}^{\pi/2}\frac{e^{\tan x}}{1+e^{\tan x}}dx$ ...(2)

Equation (1) + (2) gives, $2I=\int_{-\pi/2}^{\pi/2}1\ dx=\pi$

$\Rightarrow\ I=\frac{\pi}{2}$

(i) $I=\int_{-3}^{3}\frac{\sin^4 x}{\left[\frac{x}{\pi}\right]+0.5}dx$

Let $f(x)=\frac{\sin^4 x}{\left[\frac{x}{\pi}\right]+0.5}\quad\Rightarrow\quad f(-x)=\frac{\sin^4 x}{\left[-\frac{x}{\pi}\right]+0.5}$

$\left(\because [x]+[-x]=-1 \text{ for } x\notin\mathbb{Z} \text{ and } \frac{x}{\pi}\notin\mathbb{Z} \text{ for } x\in(-3,3)\right)$

$\Rightarrow\ f(-x)=\frac{\sin^4 x}{-1-\left[\frac{x}{\pi}\right]+0.5}$

$\Rightarrow\ f(-x)=\frac{\sin^4 x}{-\left[\frac{x}{\pi}\right]-0.5}\ \Rightarrow\ f(-x)=\frac{-\sin^4 x}{\left[\frac{x}{\pi}\right]+0.5}=-f(x)$

$\Rightarrow$ $f(x)$ is an odd function

$\Rightarrow\ I=\int_{-3}^{3}f(x)\ dx=0$

(j) $I=\int_0^{\pi}\frac{e^{\cos x}}{e^{\cos x}+e^{-\cos x}}dx$ ...(1)

$\Rightarrow\ I=\int_0^{\pi}\frac{e^{\cos(\pi-x)}}{e^{\cos(\pi-x)}+e^{-\cos(\pi-x)}}dx$

$\Rightarrow\ I=\int_0^{\pi}\frac{e^{-\cos x}}{e^{-\cos x}+e^{\cos x}}dx$ ...(2)

$\therefore$ (1) + (2) gives, $2I=\int_0^{\pi}1\ dx=\pi$

$\Rightarrow\ I=\frac{\pi}{2}$

(k) $I=\int_0^{\pi}\frac{x\sin 2x\sin\left(\frac{\pi}{2}\cos x\right)}{(2x-\pi)}dx$

Put $2x-\pi=t\quad\Rightarrow\quad 2dx=dt$

$\Rightarrow\ I=\frac{1}{2}\int_{-\pi}^{\pi}\frac{(\pi+t)\sin(\pi+t)\sin\left(\frac{\pi}{2}\cos\left(\frac{\pi}{2}+\frac{t}{2}\right)\right)}{t}\frac{dt}{2}$

$=\frac{1}{2}\int_{-\pi}^{\pi}\frac{-(\pi+t)\sin t\sin\left(\frac{-\pi}{2}\sin\frac{t}{2}\right)}{t}\frac{dt}{2}$

$=\frac{1}{4}\int_{-\pi}^{\pi}\frac{(\pi+t)\sin t\sin\left(\frac{\pi}{2}\sin\frac{t}{2}\right)}{t}dt$

$=\frac{\pi}{4}\underbrace{\int_{-\pi}^{\pi}\frac{\sin t\sin\left(\frac{\pi}{2}\sin\frac{t}{2}\right)}{t}dt}_{\text{odd function}}+\frac{1}{4}\underbrace{\int_{-\pi}^{\pi}\frac{\sin t\sin\left(\frac{\pi}{2}\sin\frac{t}{2}\right)}{t}dt}_{\text{even function}}$

$=0+\frac{1}{4}\times 2\int_0^{\pi}\sin t.\sin\left(\frac{\pi}{2}\sin\frac{t}{2}\right)dt$

$=\frac{2}{4}\int_0^{\pi}2\sin\frac{t}{2}\cos\frac{t}{2}\sin\left(\frac{\pi}{2}\sin\frac{t}{2}\right)dt$

Put $\sin\frac{t}{2}=u\quad\Rightarrow\quad\frac{1}{2}\cos\frac{t}{2}dt=du$

$\therefore\ I=\int_0^1 u\sin\left(\frac{\pi}{2}u\right)(2du)$

$\Rightarrow\ I=0\int_0^1 u\sin\left(\frac{\pi}{2}u\right)du$

Put $\frac{\pi u}{2}=y\quad\Rightarrow\quad du=\frac{2}{\pi}dy$

$\therefore\ I=2\int_0^{\pi/2}\frac{2}{\pi}y\sin y\left(\frac{2}{\pi}dy\right)=\frac{8}{\pi^2}\int_0^{\pi/2}y\sin y\ dy$

$=\frac{8}{\pi^2}\left[|-y\cos y|_0^{\pi/2}-\int_0^{\pi/2}1.(-\cos y)dy\right]$

$=\frac{8}{\pi^2}\left[(\sin y)\right]_0^{\pi/2}=\frac{8}{\pi^2}[1-0]=\frac{8}{\pi^2}$

3. $I=\int_0^{\pi}x\{\sin^2(\sin x)+\cos^2(\cos x)\}dx$

$I=\int_0^{\pi}(\pi-x)\{\sin^2(\sin(\pi-x))+\cos^2(\cos(\pi-x))\}dx$

$=\pi\int_0^{\pi}\left[\sin^2(\sin x)+\cos^2(\cos x)\right]dx-I$

$\Rightarrow \quad I=\frac{\pi}{2}\int_0^{\pi}\left[\sin^2(\sin x)+\cos^2(\cos x)\right]dx$

$=\frac{\pi}{2}[\pi-0]=\frac{\pi^2}{2}$

4. $I=\int_0^{2\pi}\frac{x^2\sin x}{8\sin^2 x}dx=\int_0^{2\pi}\frac{x^2\sin x}{9-\cos^2 x}$

$\therefore \quad I=\int_0^{2\pi}\frac{(2\pi-x)^2\sin(2\pi-x)}{9-\cos^2(2\pi-x)}dx$

$\Rightarrow \quad I=\int_0^{2\pi}\frac{-(4\pi^2-4\pi x+x^2)\sin x}{9-\cos^2 x}dx$

$\Rightarrow \quad I=-4\pi^2\int_0^{2\pi}\frac{\sin x}{9-\cos^2 x}dx$

$+4\pi\int_0^{2\pi}\frac{x\sin x}{9-\cos^2 x}dx-\int_0^{2\pi}\frac{x^2\sin x}{9-\cos^2 x}dx$

$\left[\begin{array}{l}\because \int_0^{2a} f(x)dx=0 \text{ if } f(2a-x)=-f(x)\\ \therefore \int_0^{2\pi}\frac{x\sin x}{9-\cos^2 x}dx=0\end{array}\right]$

$\therefore \quad I=4\pi\int_0^{2\pi}\frac{x\sin x}{9-\cos^2 x}dx-I$

$\Rightarrow \quad I=2\pi\int_0^{2\pi}\frac{x\sin x}{9-\cos^2 x}dx$

$\Rightarrow \quad I=2\pi\left\{\left|x\int\frac{\sin x}{9-\cos^2 x}dx\right|_0^{2\pi}-\int_0^{2\pi}\left(1.\int\frac{\sin x}{9-\cos^2}\right)dx\right\}$

$\Rightarrow \quad I=2\pi\left\{\left|x\int\frac{dt}{t^2-(3)^2}\right|_0^{2\pi}-\int_0^{2\pi}\int\frac{dt}{t^2-(3)^2}dx\right\};$

Where $t=\cos x$

$=2\pi\left\{\left|x\frac{1}{6}\ln\left|\frac{t-3}{t+3}\right|\right|_0^{2\pi}-\int_0^{2\pi}\frac{1}{6}\ln\left|\frac{t-3}{t+3}\right|dx\right\}$

$=2\pi\left\{\left[\frac{x}{6}\ln\left|\frac{\cos x-3}{\cos x+3}\right|\right]_0^{2\pi}-\frac{1}{6}\int_0^{2\pi}\ln\left|\frac{\cos x-3}{\cos x+3}\right|dx\right\}$

$=2\pi\left\{\frac{2\pi}{6}\ln\left|\frac{-2}{4}\right|\frac{-1}{6}\int_0^{2\pi}\ln\left|\frac{\cos x-3}{\cos x+3}\right|dx\right\}$

$=2\pi\left\{\frac{\pi}{3}\ln\left(\frac{1}{2}\right)-\frac{1}{6}\int_0^{2\pi}\ln\left|\frac{\cos x-3}{\cos x+3}\right|dx\right\}$ ...(1)

If $g(x)=\ln\left|\frac{\cos x-3}{\cos x+3}\right|$; then $g(2\pi-x)=\ln\left|\frac{\cos x-3}{\cos x+3}\right|$

$\Rightarrow \quad \int_0^{2\pi}\ln\left|\frac{\cos x-3}{\cos x+3}\right|dx=2\int_0^{\pi}\ln\left|\frac{\cos x-3}{\cos x+3}\right|dx$

Also if $g(x)=\ln\left|\frac{\cos x-3}{\cos x+3}\right|$

$\Rightarrow \quad g(\pi-x)=\ln\left|\frac{-\cos x-3}{-\cos x+3}\right|=-\ln\left|\frac{\cos x-3}{\cos x+3}\right|=-g(x)$

$\Rightarrow \quad \int_0^{\pi}\ln\left|\frac{\cos x-3}{\cos x+3}\right|dx=0$

$\Rightarrow \quad \int_0^{2\pi}\ln\left|\frac{\cos x-3}{\cos x+3}\right|dx=0$

$\therefore \quad$ From (1), $I=\frac{2\pi^2}{3}\ln\left(\frac{1}{2}\right)=\frac{-2\pi^2}{3}\ln 2$

5. $I=\int_0^{\pi}x\sin(\cos^2 x)\cos(\sin^2 x)dx$

$\Rightarrow \quad I=\int_0^{\pi}(\pi-x)\sin(\cos^2 x)\cos(\sin^2 x)dx$

$\Rightarrow \quad I=\pi\int_0^{\pi}\sin(\cos^2 x)\cos(\sin^2 x)dx-I$

$\Rightarrow \quad I=\frac{\pi}{2}\int_0^{\pi}\sin(\cos^2 x)\cos(\sin^2 x)dx$

$=\frac{\pi}{2\times 2}\int_0^{\pi}\left[\sin(\cos^2 x+\sin^2 x)+\sin(\cos^2 x-\sin^2 x)\right]dx$

$=\frac{\pi}{4}\int_0^{\pi}\left[(\sin 1)+\sin(\cos 2x)\right]dx$

$=\frac{\pi}{4}(\sin 1)[\pi]+\frac{\pi}{4}\int_0^{\pi}\sin(\cos 2x)dx$

$=\frac{\pi^2}{4}\sin 1+\frac{\pi}{4}\int_4^{\pi}\sin(\cos 2x)dx$

$=\frac{\pi^2}{4}\sin 1+\frac{\pi}{4}.2\int_0^{\pi/2}\sin(\cos 2x)dx$

$=\frac{\pi^2}{4}\sin 1+\frac{\pi}{2}\int_0^{\pi/2}\sin(\cos 2x)dx$

$\because \quad f(x)=\sin(\cos 2x)$

$\Rightarrow \quad f\left(\frac{\pi}{2}-x\right)=\sin\left(\cos 2\left(\frac{\pi}{2}-x\right)\right)=\sin(\cos(\pi-2x))$

$=\sin(-\cos 2x)=-\sin(\cos 2x)=-f(x)$

$\Rightarrow \quad \int_0^{\pi/2}\sin(\cos 2x)dx=0$

$\Rightarrow \quad I=\frac{\pi^2}{4}\sin 1+(0)=\frac{\pi^2}{4}\sin 1$

6. $I=\int_0^{2\pi}\ln\left(\frac{\cos x-4}{\cos x+4}\right)dx=2\int_0^{\pi}\ln\left(\frac{\cos x-4}{\cos x+4}\right)dx=2(0)=0$

$\left[\begin{array}{l}\because \int_0^{2a} f(x)dx=2\int_0^{a} f(x)dx\\ \text{if } f(2a-x)=f(x)\end{array}\right]$ and $\left[\begin{array}{l}\int_0^{2a} f(x)dx=0\\ \text{if } f(2a-x)=-f(x)\end{array}\right]$

$=0$

7. $I=\int_0^{\pi}\tan^{-1}(\cos x)dx$ If $f(x)=\tan^{-1}(\cos x)$

$\Rightarrow \quad f(\pi-x)=\tan^{-1}(\cos(\pi-x))$

$=\tan^{-1}(-\cos x)=-\tan^{-1}(\cos x)=-f(x)$

$\Rightarrow \quad I=\int_0^{\pi}f(x)dx=0$

8. $I=\int_0^{\pi}\frac{x\sin x}{1+\cos^2 x}dx \Rightarrow I=\int_0^{\pi}\frac{(\pi-x)\sin(\pi-x)}{1+\cos^2(\pi-x)}dx$

$\Rightarrow \quad I=\int_0^{\pi}\frac{(\pi-x)\sin x}{1+\cos^2 x}dx \Rightarrow I=\pi\int_0^{\pi}\frac{\sin x}{1+\cos^2 x}dx-I$

$\Rightarrow \quad I = \frac{\pi}{2}\int_0^{\pi} \frac{\sin x}{1+\cos^2 x}dx$

$\Rightarrow \quad I = \frac{-\pi}{2}\int_0^{\pi} \frac{-dt}{1+t^2} = \frac{\pi}{2}\int_1^{-1}\frac{-dt}{1+t^2}$

$\Rightarrow \quad I = \frac{\pi}{2}\int_{-1}^{1}\frac{dt}{1+t^2} = \frac{\pi}{2}\times 2\int_0^1 \frac{dt}{1+t^2}$

$\Rightarrow \quad I = \pi\left[\tan^{-1} t\right]_0^1 = \pi\left(\frac{\pi}{4}\right) = \frac{\pi^2}{4}$

9. $I = \int_{-\pi}^{\pi}(\cos px - \sin qx)^2\,dx;\ p, q \in \mathbb{Z}$

$= \int_{-\pi}^{\pi}\left(\cos^2 px + \sin^2 qx - 2\sin qx\cos px\right)dx$

$= 2\int_0^{\pi}\left(\cos^2 px + \sin^2 qx\right)dx$

$-\int_{-\pi}^{\pi}\left[\sin(q+p)x + \sin(q-p)x\right]dx$

$= \int_0^{\pi}(1+\cos 2px)dx + \int_0^{\pi}(1-\cos 2qx)dx - (0+0)dx$

$\left[\because\ \sin(q+p)x \text{ and } \sin(q-p)x \text{ are odd functions}\right]$

$= \pi + [(1-1)] + \pi[1-1] = 2\pi$

10. (a) $\int_0^{2\pi}\cos^4 x\,dx = \frac{1}{4}\int_0^{2\pi}\left(1+\cos^2 x\right)^2$

$= \frac{1}{4}\int_0^{2\pi}\left(1+\cos^2 x + 2\cos 2x\right)dx$

$= \frac{1}{4}[2\pi] + \frac{1}{8}[1+\cos 4x]_0^{2\pi} + \frac{1}{4}[0] = \frac{\pi}{2} + \frac{1}{8}[2\pi] = \frac{3\pi}{4}$

(b) $I = \int_0^{\pi}\frac{dx}{1+2\sin^2 x} = \int_0^{\pi}\frac{\sec^2 x\,dx}{\sec^2 + 2\tan^2 x} = \int_0^{\pi}\frac{\sec^2 x\,dx}{1+3\tan^2 x}$

$= \int_0^{\pi/2}\frac{\sec^2 x\,dx}{1+3\tan^2 x} + \int_{\pi/2}^{\pi}\frac{\sec^2 x\,dx}{1+3\tan^2 x}$

$= \int_0^{\infty}\frac{dt}{1+3t^2} + \int_{-\infty}^{0}\frac{dt}{1+3t^2}$

$= \left[\frac{\tan^{-1}\left(\sqrt{3}\,t\right)}{\sqrt{3}}\right] + \left[\frac{\tan^{-1}\left(\sqrt{3}\,t\right)}{\sqrt{3}}\right]_{-\infty}^{0}$

$= \frac{1}{\sqrt{3}}\left[\frac{\pi}{2} - 0\right] + \frac{1}{\sqrt{3}}\left[0 + \frac{\pi}{2}\right] = \frac{\pi}{\sqrt{3}}$

(c) $I = \int_0^{\pi}\frac{\sin x}{\sin 8x}dx = \int_0^{\pi/2}\frac{\sin x}{\sin 8x}dx + \int_{\pi/2}^{\pi}\frac{\sin x}{\sin 8x}dx$

$= 0 \quad \left[\begin{array}{l}\because\ \dfrac{\sin(\pi - x)}{\sin 8(\pi - x)} = \dfrac{\sin x}{-\sin 8x} \\ \therefore f(\pi - x) = -f(x)\end{array}\right]$

(d) $I = \int_0^{\pi}\sin^5 x\cos^7 x\,dx$

Let $f(x) = \sin^5 x\cos^7 x$ and

$f(\pi - x) = \sin^5(\pi - x)\cos^7(\pi - x)$

$\Rightarrow \quad f(\pi - x) = -\sin^5 x.\cos^7 x$

$\Rightarrow \quad f(\pi - x) = -f(x)$

$\Rightarrow I = 0$

(e) $I = \int_0^{\pi}\cos^{53} x\,dx$

Let $f(x) = \cos^{53} x$

$\Rightarrow \quad f(\pi - x) = -\cos^{53} = -f(x)$

$\Rightarrow I = 0$

11. (a) $I = \int_0^{\pi}\ln(1-\cos x)dx$ ...(1)

$I = \int_0^{\pi}\ln(1-\cos(\pi - x))dx$

$\Rightarrow \quad I = \int_0^{\pi}\ln(1+\cos)dx$ ...(2)

$\therefore$ Equation (1) + (2) gives, $\int_0^{\pi}\ln\left(1-\cos^2 x\right)dx$

$\Rightarrow \quad 2I = \int_0^{\pi}\ln\sin^2 x\,dx$

$\Rightarrow \quad 2I = 2\int_0^{\pi}\ln\sin x\,dx$

$\Rightarrow \quad I = \int_0^{\pi}\ln(\sin x)dx$

$\Rightarrow \quad I = 2\int_0^{\pi/2}\ln(\sin x)dx$ ...(3)

$\left[\begin{array}{l}\because f(2a - x) = f(x) \\ \text{i.e., } f(\pi - x) = f(x)\end{array}\right]$

$\Rightarrow \quad I = 2\int_0^{\pi/2}\ln\left(\sin\left(\frac{\pi}{2} - x\right)\right)dx$

$\Rightarrow \quad I = 2\int_0^{\pi/2}\ln(\cos x)dx$ ...(4)

$\therefore$ Equation (3) + (4) gives, $2I = 2\int_0^{\pi/2}\ln(\sin x\cos x)dx$

$\Rightarrow \quad I = \int_0^{\pi/2}\ln(\sin x\cos x)dx$

$\Rightarrow \quad I = 2\int_0^{\pi/2}\ln(\sin 2x)dx - \int_0^{\pi/2}\ln 2\,dx$

Put $2x = t \quad \Rightarrow \quad dx = \frac{dt}{2}$

$I = \frac{1}{2}\int_0^{\pi}\ln\sin t\,dt - (\ln 2)\left(\frac{\pi}{2}\right)$

$\Rightarrow \quad I = \frac{1}{2}I - \frac{\pi}{2}\ln 2 \quad \Rightarrow \quad \frac{1}{2}I = \frac{-\pi}{2}\ln 2$

$\Rightarrow \quad I = -\pi\ln 2$

(b) $I = \int_0^{\pi}\ln(1+\cos x)dx$

$\Rightarrow \quad I = \int_0^{\pi}\ln(1+\cos(\pi - x))dx$

$\Rightarrow \quad I = \int_0^{\pi}\ln(1-\cos x)dx = -\pi\ln 2$ (as done in part (a))

(c) $I = \int_0^{1}\frac{\sin^{-1} x}{x}dx$

Put $\sin^{-1} x = t \quad \Rightarrow \quad x = \sin t$

$\Rightarrow \quad dx = \cos t\,dt$

$\therefore \quad I = \int_0^{\pi/2}\frac{t}{\sin t}\cos t\,dt$

$\Rightarrow \quad I = \int_0^{\pi/2} t\cot t\,dt$

$\Rightarrow \ I = \left|t\ln\sin t\right|_0^{\pi/2} - \int_0^{\pi/2} - \int_0^{\pi/2} 1.(\ln\sin t)\,dt$

$\Rightarrow \ I = 0 - \lim_{t\to 0}\left(\frac{\ln\sin t}{1/t}\right) - \left[\frac{-\pi}{2}\ln 2\right]$

$\Rightarrow \ I = -\lim_{t\to 0}\left[\frac{\frac{1}{\sin t}.\cos t}{\frac{-1}{-t^2}}\right] + \frac{\pi}{2}\ln 2$

$\Rightarrow \ I = \lim_{t\to 0}\left[t\left(\frac{t}{\tan t}\right)\right] + \frac{\pi}{2}\ln 2$

$\Rightarrow \ I = 0 + \frac{\pi}{2}\ln 2 = \frac{\pi}{2}\ln 2$

12. $I = \int_0^{\pi} \frac{x^2\sin x\,dx}{(2x-\pi)(1+\cos^2 x)}$

$\Rightarrow \ I = \int_0^{\pi} \frac{(\pi-x)^2\sin(\pi-x)}{(2(\pi-x)-\pi)(1+\cos^2(\pi-x))}dx$

$\Rightarrow \ I = \int_0^{\pi} \frac{(\pi^2+x^2-2x\pi)\sin x}{(\pi-2x)(1+\cos^2)x}dx$

$\Rightarrow \ I = \int_0^{\pi} \frac{x^2\sin x \ \ dx}{(\pi-2x)(1+\cos^2 x)} + \pi\int_0^{\pi}\frac{(\pi-2x)}{(\pi-2x)}.\frac{\sin x\ dx}{(1+\cos^2 x)}$

$\Rightarrow \ I = -I + \pi\int_0^{\pi}\frac{\sin x}{1+\cos^2 x}dx$

$\Rightarrow \ 2I = \pi\int_0^{\pi}\frac{\sin x}{1+\cos^2 x}dx$

$\Rightarrow \ I = \frac{1}{2}\pi\int_0^{\pi}\frac{\sin x}{1+\cos^2}dx \Rightarrow \ I = \frac{\pi}{2}(2)\int_0^{\pi/2}\frac{\sin x}{1+\cos^2}dx$

$\Rightarrow \ I = \pi\int_0^{\pi/2}\frac{\sin x}{1+\cos^2 x}dx$

$\Rightarrow \ I = \pi\int_1^0\frac{-dt}{1+t^2} = \pi\int_0^1\frac{1}{1+t^2}dt$

$\Rightarrow \ I = \pi\left[\tan^{-1}t\right]_0^1 = \frac{\pi^2}{4}$

13. $I = \int_0^{2\pi}\frac{x\sin^{2n}x}{\sin^{2n}x+\cos^{2n}x}dx \ ; n\in\mathbb{Z}$

$\Rightarrow \ I = \int_0^{2\pi}\frac{(2\pi-x)\sin^{2n}(2\pi-x)}{\sin^{2n}(2\pi-x)+\cos^{2n}(2\pi-x)}dx$

$\Rightarrow \ I = \int_0^{2\pi}\frac{(2\pi-x)\sin^{2n}x}{\sin^{2n}x+\cos^{2n}x}dx$

$\Rightarrow \ I = 2\pi\int_0^{2\pi}\frac{\sin^{2n}x}{\sin^{2n}x+\cos^{2n}x}dx - I$

$\Rightarrow \ I = \pi\int_0^{2\pi}\frac{\sin^{2n}x}{\sin^{2n}x+\cos^{2n}x}dx$

$\Rightarrow \ I = 2\pi\int_0^{\pi}\frac{\sin^{2n}x}{\sin^{2n}x+\cos^{2n}x}dx$

$\Rightarrow \ I = 4\pi\int_0^{\pi/2}\frac{\sin^{2n}x}{\sin^{2n}x+\cos^{2n}x}dx \quad \ldots(1)$

Clearly, $I_1 = \int_0^{\pi/2}\frac{\sin^{2n}x}{\sin^{2n}x+\cos^{2n}x}dx = \frac{\pi}{4}$

$\therefore \ I = 4\pi\left(\frac{\pi}{4}\right) = \pi^2$

14. $f(x) = -\int_0^x \ln\cos y\ dy$

$\Rightarrow \ f\left(\frac{\pi}{4}+\frac{x}{2}\right) = -\int_0^{\frac{\pi}{4}+\frac{x}{2}}\ln(\cos y)dy$ and

$f\left(\frac{\pi}{4}-\frac{x}{2}\right) = -\int_0^{\frac{\pi}{4}-\frac{x}{2}}\ln(\cos y)dy$

$\Rightarrow \ f\left(\frac{\pi}{4}-\frac{x}{2}\right) = \int_{\frac{\pi}{4}-\frac{x}{2}}^0\ln(\cos y)dy$

$\therefore \ f\left(\frac{\pi}{4}+\frac{x}{2}\right) = \left(\frac{\pi}{4}-\frac{x}{2}\right)$

$= -\int_0^{\frac{\pi}{4}+\frac{x}{2}}\ln(\cos y)dy - \int_{\pi/4-x/2}^0\ln(\cos y)dy$

$\Rightarrow \ I = -\left[\int_{\frac{\pi}{4}-\frac{x}{2}}^{\frac{\pi}{4}+\frac{x}{2}}\ln(\cos y)dy\right]$ (say) $\quad \ldots..(1)$

$\Rightarrow \ I = -\int_{\frac{\pi}{4}-\frac{x}{2}}^{\frac{\pi}{4}+\frac{x}{2}}\ln\cos\left(\frac{\pi}{2}-y\right)dy$

$\Rightarrow \ I = -\int_{\frac{\pi}{4}-\frac{x}{2}}^{\frac{\pi}{4}+\frac{x}{2}}\ln\sin(y)dy \quad \ldots(2)$

$\Rightarrow \ 2I = -\int_{\left(\frac{\pi}{4}-\frac{x}{2}\right)}^{\left(\frac{\pi}{4}+\frac{x}{2}\right)}\ln\sin(y)(\cos y)dy$

$\Rightarrow \ 2I = -\int_{\frac{\pi}{4}-\frac{x}{2}}^{\frac{\pi}{4}+\frac{x}{2}}(\ln\sin 2y - \ln 2)dy$

$\Rightarrow \ 2I = -\int_{\frac{\pi}{4}-\frac{x}{2}}^{\frac{\pi}{4}+\frac{x}{2}}(\sin 2y)dy + \ln 2(x)$

$\therefore \ 2f\left(\frac{\pi}{4}+\frac{x}{2}\right) - 2f\left(\frac{\pi}{4}-\frac{x}{2}\right) = -\int_{\pi/4-x/2}^{\pi/4+x/2}\ln(\sin 2y)dy$

Put $2y = t \quad \Rightarrow \ dy = \frac{dt}{2}$

$\Rightarrow \ 2f\left(\frac{\pi}{4}+\frac{x}{2}\right) - 2f\left(\frac{\pi}{4}-\frac{x}{2}\right) - x\ln 2 = \frac{-1}{2}\int_{\frac{\pi}{2}-x}^{\frac{\pi}{2}+x}\ln(\sin t)dt$

Put $t = \frac{\pi}{2}+u \quad \Rightarrow \ dt = du$

$\Rightarrow \ \frac{-1}{2}\int_{-x}^{x}\ln\left(\sin\left(\frac{\pi}{2}+u\right)\right)du = \frac{-1}{2}\int_{-x}^{x}\ln(\cos u)du$

$= -2\left(\frac{1}{2}\right)\int_0^x\ln(\cos u)du = -\int_0^x\ln(\cos u)du = f(x)$

Thus, $f(x) = 2f\left(\frac{\pi}{4}+\frac{x}{2}\right) - 2f\left(\frac{\pi}{4}-\frac{x}{2}\right) - x\ln 2$

TEXTUAL EXERCISE-5: (OBJECTIVE)

1. (b) $I=\int_0^{\pi}\frac{dx}{1+5^{\cos x}}+\int_{-2}^{2}\log\left(\frac{5-x}{5+x}\right)dx=I_1+I_2$ (say)

Now $I_2=0$ as $\log\left(\frac{5-x}{5+x}\right)$ is an odd function and

$$I_1=\int_0^{\pi}\frac{dx}{1+5^{\cos(\pi-x)}} \quad ...(1)$$

$$\Rightarrow I_1=\int_0^{\pi}\frac{dx}{1+5^{-\cos x}}$$

$$\Rightarrow I_1=\int_0^{\pi}\frac{5^{\cos x}}{5^{\cos x}+1}dx \quad ...(2)$$

Equation (1) + (2) gives, $2I_1=\int_0^{\pi}1\,dx=\pi$

$$\Rightarrow I_1=\frac{\pi}{2}$$

$$\therefore I=\frac{\pi}{2}+0=\frac{\pi}{2}$$

2. (d) $I=\int_{-\pi/2}^{\pi/2}[f(x)+f(-x)][g(x)-g(-x)]dx$

Clearly integrand is an odd function

$\Rightarrow I=0$

3. (d) $I=\int_{-1}^{1}\log\left(\frac{2-x}{2+x}\right)dx$

$\because$ Integrand is an odd function, I = 0

4. (c) $I=\int_{-1}^{1}\frac{\sin x-x^2}{3-|x|}dx$

$$\Rightarrow I=\int_{-1}^{1}\frac{\sin x}{3-|x|}dx-\int_{-1}^{1}\frac{x^2}{3-|x|}dx$$

$\because \frac{\sin x}{3-|x|}$ = odd function and $\frac{x^2}{3-|x|}$ = even function.

$$\Rightarrow I=0-2\int_0^1\frac{x^2}{3-|x|}dx=2\int_0^1\frac{-x^2}{3-|x|}dx$$

5. (b) Let $I=\int_{-\pi/4}^{\pi/4}\left(\lambda|\sin x|+\frac{\mu\sin x}{1+\cos x}+v\right)dx$

$$\Rightarrow I=2\lambda\int_0^{\pi/4}|\sin x|dx+0+2v\int_0^{\pi/4}1\,dx$$

$$\Rightarrow I=2\lambda\int_0^{\pi/4}\sin x\,dx+2v\left[\frac{\pi}{4}\right]$$

$$\Rightarrow I=2\lambda[-\cos x]_0^{\pi/4}+\frac{v\pi}{2}$$

$\therefore I=0$

$$\Rightarrow 2\lambda-\sqrt{2}\lambda+\frac{v\pi}{2}=0$$

$$\Rightarrow 4\lambda-2\sqrt{2}\lambda+v\pi=0$$

$$\Rightarrow 2\sqrt{2}\left(\sqrt{2}\lambda-1\right)+v\pi=0$$

6. (c) $I=\int_{-2}^{2}\{f(x)-f(-x)\}x^{2n}dx=0$ as integrand is an odd function

7. (d) $I=\int_{-2}^{2}\{f(x)+f(-x)\}\{g(x)-g(-x)\}dx=0$

Let $F(x)=\{f(x)+f(x)\}\{g(x)-g(-x)\}$, then

$$I=\int_{-2}^{2}F(x)dx=0$$

$\Rightarrow$ $F(x)$ must be an odd function.

Now, $F(-x)=\{f(-x)+f(x)\}\{g(-x)-g(x)\}=-F(x)$

$\Rightarrow$ $F(x)$ is an odd function for every function $f(x)$ and $g(x)$

8. (d) $I=\int_{-10}^{10}x\left(|x|-e^{|x|}\right)dx=\int_{-10}^{10}x|x|dx-\int_{-10}^{10}xe^{|x|}dx=0$ as $x|x|$ as well as $xe^{|x|}$ both are odd functions

9. (c) $I_1=\int_0^{\pi}\frac{x^3\cos^4 x\sin^2 x}{\pi^2-3\pi x+3x^2}dx=k\int_0^{\pi/2}\sin^2 x\,dx$

$$I_1=\int_0^{\pi}\frac{(\pi-x)^3\cos^4(\pi-x).\sin^2(\pi-x)}{\pi^2-3\pi(\pi-x)+3(\pi-x)^2}dx$$

$$=\int_0^{\pi}\frac{\left(\pi-3\pi^2x+3\pi x^2-x^3\right)\cos^4 x.\sin^2 x}{\pi^2-3\pi^2+3\pi x+3\pi^2+3x^2-6\pi x}dx$$

$$=\int_0^{\pi}\frac{\left(\pi^3-3\pi^2x+3\pi x^2-x^3\right)\cos^4 x.\sin^2 x\,dx}{\left(\pi^2-3\pi x+3x^2\right)}$$

$$=\pi\int_0^{\pi}\cos^4 x\sin^2 x\,dx-I_1$$

$$\Rightarrow I_1=\frac{\pi}{2}\int_0^{\pi}\cos^4 x\sin^2 x\,dx$$

$$\Rightarrow I_1=\frac{\pi}{2}\times 2\int_0^{\pi/2}\cos^4 x\sin^2 x\,dx$$

$$\Rightarrow I_1=\pi\int_0^{\pi/2}\cos^4 x\sin^2 x\,dx \quad ...(1)$$

$$\Rightarrow I_1=\pi\int_0^{\pi/2}\sin^4 x\cos^2 x\,dx \quad ...(2)$$

$\left(\text{using } \int_0^a f(x)dx=\int_0^a f(a-x)dx\right)$

Adding (1) and (2), we get

$$2I_1=\pi\int_0^{\pi/2}\sin^2 x\cos^2 x\left(\cos^2 x+\sin^2 x\right)dx$$

$$\Rightarrow 2I_1=\pi\int_0^{\pi/2}\sin^2 x\cos^2 x\,dx$$

$$\Rightarrow 2I_1=\frac{\pi}{4}\int_0^{\pi/2}4\sin^2 x\cos^2 x\,dx$$

$$\Rightarrow 2I_1=\frac{\pi}{4}\int_0^{\pi/2}\sin^2 2x\,dx$$

Put $2x=t \quad \Rightarrow dx=\frac{dt}{2}$

$$\Rightarrow 2I_1=\frac{\pi}{8}\int_0^{\pi}\sin^2 t\,dt$$

$$\Rightarrow 2I_1=\frac{\pi}{8}\times 2\int_0^{\pi/2}\sin^2 t\,dt$$

$$\left[\begin{array}{l}\text{using } \int_0^{2a} f(x)dx = 2\int_0^a f(x)dx \\ \text{if } f(2-ax) = f(x)\end{array}\right]$$

$$\Rightarrow \ I_1 = \frac{\pi}{8}\int_0^{\pi/2} \sin t\, dt \quad \Rightarrow \quad k = \frac{\pi}{8}$$

10. (c) $I_1 = \int_0^{\pi/2} \frac{(\sin x - \cos x)dx}{1+\sin x.\cos x}$

$$\Rightarrow \ I_1 = \int_0^{\pi/2} \frac{\sin x - \cos x}{1+\cos x.\sin x} dx = -I_1$$

$$\Rightarrow \ 2I_1 = 0$$

$$\Rightarrow \ I_1 = 0$$

Now, $I_2 = 2\int_0^{2\pi} \cos^6 x\, dx$ $\left[\begin{array}{l}\because \int_0^{2a} f(x)dx = 2\int_0^a f(x)dx \\ \text{if } f(2a-x) = f(x)\end{array}\right]$

Similarly $I_2 = 4\int_0^{\pi/2} \cos^6 x\, dx$

$$\Rightarrow \ I_2 = 4\int_0^{\pi/2} \sin^6 x\, dx$$

$$\Rightarrow \ 2I_2 = 4\int_0^{\pi/2} \left(\cos^6 x + \sin^6 x\right)dx$$

$$\Rightarrow \ I_2 = 2\int_0^{\pi/2} \left(1 - 3\sin^2 x \cos^2 x\right)dx$$

$$\Rightarrow \ I_2 = 2\left(\frac{\pi}{2}\right) - \frac{3}{2}\int_0^{\pi/2} \sin^2 2x\, dx$$

$$\Rightarrow \ I_2 = \pi - \frac{3}{2}\int_0^{\pi/2} \frac{(1-\cos 4x)}{2} dx$$

$$\Rightarrow \ I_2 = \pi - \frac{3}{4}\left[\left(\frac{\pi}{2}\right) - (0)\right]$$

$\Rightarrow \ I_2 = \left(1 - \frac{3}{8}\right)\pi = \frac{5}{8}\pi, \ I_3 = \int_{-\pi/2}^{\pi/2} \sin^3 x\, dx = 0$ as $\sin 3x$ is an odd function and $I_4 = \int_0^1 \ln\left(\frac{1}{x} - 1\right)dx$

$$= \int_0^1 \{\ln(1-x) - \ln x\}dx = \int_0^1 \ln(1-x)dx - \int_0^1 \ln x\, dx$$

$$= \int_0^1 \ln(1-x)dx - \int_0^1 \ln(1-x)dx$$

using $\int_0^a f(x)dx = \int_0^a f(a-x)dx = 0$

Thus, $I_1 = I_3 = I_4 = 0$ and $I_2 \neq 0$

11. (a), (b), (c), (d)

(a) $I_1 = \int_{-1}^1 \ln\left(\frac{1+x}{1-x}\right)dx = 0$ as $\ln\left(\frac{1+x}{1-x}\right)$ is an odd function.

(b) $I_2 = \int_0^1 \tan^{-1}\left[\frac{2x-1}{1+x-x^2}\right]dx = \int_0^1 \tan^{-1}\left(\frac{x+x-1}{1-x(x-1)}\right)dx$

$$\left[\because \tan^{-1}(x) + \tan^{-1}(y) = \tan^{-1}\left(\frac{x+y}{1-xy}\right) \text{ if } xy < 1\right]$$

Here $x \in (0,1)$

$$\Rightarrow \ x(x-1) < 0$$

$$\Rightarrow \ x(x-1) < 1$$

$$\Rightarrow \ \tan^{-1}\left[\frac{x+(x-1)}{1-x(x-1)}\right] = \tan^{-1} x + \tan^{-1}(x-1)$$

$$\therefore \ I_2 = \int_0^1 \left[\tan^{-1} x + \tan^{-1}(x-1)\right]dx$$

$$= \int_0^1 \tan^{-1} x\, dx + \int_0^1 \tan^{-1}(x-1)dx$$

$$= \int_0^1 \tan^{-1} x\, dx + \int_0^1 \tan^{-1}(1-x-1)dx$$

$$= \int_0^1 \tan^{-1} x\, dx + \int_0^1 \tan^{-1}(-x)dx = 0$$

(c) $I_3 = \int_0^\pi \sin^3 x \cos^5 x\, dx = \int_0^\pi \sin^3(\pi - x).\cos^5(\pi - x)dx$

$$= \int_0^\pi -\sin^3 x \cos^5 x\, dx = -I_3$$

$$\Rightarrow \ 2I_3 = 0$$

$$\Rightarrow \ I_3 = 0$$

(d) $\int_0^1 \ln\left(\frac{1}{x} - 1\right)dx = \int_0^1 \ln\left(\frac{1-x}{x}\right)dx$

$$= \int_0^1 \ln(1-x)dx - \int_0^1 \ln x\, dx$$

$$= \int_0^1 \ln(1-(1-x))dx - \int_0^1 \ln x\, dx$$

$$= \int_0^1 \ln(x)dx - \int_0^1 \ln x\, dx = 0$$

12. (a) $I_1 = \int_0^{\pi/2} \cos\theta.f(\sin\theta + \cos^2\theta)d\theta$

$I_2 = \int_0^{\pi/2} \sin 2\theta.f(\sin\theta + \cos^2\theta)d\theta$

Put $\sin\theta = t$ in I_1,

$$\Rightarrow \ I_1 = \int_0^1 f(t + 1 - t^2)dt$$

Also, put $\sin\theta = t$ in I_2,

$$\Rightarrow \ I_2 = \int_0^{\pi/2} 2\sin\theta\cos\theta.f(\sin\theta + 1 - \sin^2\theta)d\theta$$

$$\Rightarrow \ I_2 = \int_0^1 2t\, f(t + 1 - t^2)dt$$

$$= \int_0^1 2(1-t)f(1-t+1-1-t)^2 dt$$

$$= \int_0^1 2f(2-t-1-t^2+2t)dt - \int_0^1 2t\, f(1+t-t^2)dt$$

$$= 2\int_0^1 f(1+t-t^2)dt - 2\int_0^1 t\, f(1+t-t^2)dt$$

$$\Rightarrow \ I_2 = 2I_1 - I_2 \qquad \Rightarrow \ 2I_2 = 2I_1$$

$$\Rightarrow \ I_1 = I_2$$

13. (a) $I = \int_{-1}^1 \left[x[1 + \sin\pi x] + 1\right]dx$

$f(x) = \left[x[1+\sin\pi x] + 1\right] = \left[x + x[\sin\pi x] + 1\right]$

$= 1 + \left[x + x[\sin\pi x]\right]$

$$\Rightarrow \ f(-x) = 1 + \left[-x - x[-\sin\pi x]\right]$$

$f(0) = 1 + [0+0] = 1$ for $x \neq 0, x \neq \frac{-1}{2}, \frac{1}{2}, \frac{-1}{2}, 1, \sin\pi x \notin \mathbb{Z}$

$\Rightarrow\ [-\sin\pi x] = -1-[\sin\pi x]$

$\therefore\ f(-x) = 1+\left[-x-x\{-1-[\sin\pi x]\}\right]$

$= 1+\left[-x+x+x[\sin\pi x]\right] = 1+\left[x[\sin\pi x]\right] = f(x)$

For $x = \frac{1}{2}, f\left(-\frac{1}{2}\right) = 1+\left[\frac{1}{2}+\frac{1}{2}\left[+\sin\frac{\pi}{2}\right]\right]$

$= 1+\left[\frac{1}{2}+\frac{1}{2}\right] = 2$

$\& f\left(\frac{1}{2}\right) = 1+\left[+\frac{1}{2}+\frac{1}{2}\left[+\sin\frac{\pi}{2}\right]\right] = 1+\left[+\frac{1}{2}+\frac{1}{2}\right] = 2$

Thus, $f(-x) = f(x)\ \forall x(-1,1)$

$\Rightarrow$ $f(x)$ is an even function in $(-1,1)$

$\Rightarrow\ I = 2\int_0^1 \left[x[1+\sin\pi x]+1\right]dx$

$\Rightarrow\ I = 2\int_0^1 1+\left[x+x[\sin\pi x]\right]dx$

$\Rightarrow\ I = 2+2\int_0^1 \left[x+x[\sin\pi x]\right]dx$

$= 2+2\int_0^{1/2}\left[x+x[\sin\pi x]\right]dx + 2\int_{1/2}^1\left[x+x[\sin\pi x]\right]dx$

$= 2+2\int_0^{1/2}[x+x(0)]dx + 2\int_{1/2}^1[x+x(0)]dx$

$= 2+2\int_0^{1/2} 0dx + 2\int_{1/2}^1 0dx = 2$

14. (a), (b), (d)

$I = \int_0^{\pi/2}\left(\frac{1+\sin 3x}{1+2\sin x}\right)dx$

$\Rightarrow\ I = \int_0^{\pi/2}\frac{1+\sin 3\left(\frac{\pi}{2}-x\right)}{1+2\sin\left(\frac{\pi}{2}-x\right)}dx = \int_0^{\pi/2}\frac{1+\sin\left(\frac{3\pi}{2}-3x\right)}{1+2\cos x}dx$

$= \int_0^{\pi/2}\frac{1-\cos 3x}{1+2\cos x}dx$

$= \int_0^{\pi/2}\frac{\sin\left(2\sin^2\frac{3x}{2}\right)}{(\sin x+\sin 2x)}dx = \int_0^{\pi/2}\frac{(\sin x)\left(2\sin^2\frac{3x}{2}\right)}{2\sin\frac{3x}{2}\cos\frac{x}{2}}dx$

$= \int_0^{\pi/2}\frac{\left(2\sin\frac{x}{2}\cos\frac{x}{2}\right)\left(2\sin^2\frac{3x}{2}\right)}{2\sin\frac{3x}{2}\cos\frac{x}{2}}dx$

$= \int_0^{\pi/2}\left(2\sin\frac{3x}{2}\sin\frac{x}{2}\right)dx = \int_0^{\pi/2}(\cos x-\cos 2x)dx$

$= \left[\sin x-\frac{\sin 2x}{2}\right]_0^{\pi/2} = [(1-0)]-\frac{1}{2}[0] = 1$

Now, $\int_0^{\pi/2}\frac{\cos 3x+1}{2\cos x-1}dx = \int_0^{\pi/2}\frac{2\cos^2\frac{3x}{2}.\sin x}{\sin 2x-\sin x}dx$

$= \int_0^{\pi/2}\frac{2\cos^2\frac{3x}{2}.\sin x}{2\cos\frac{3x}{2}\sin\frac{x}{2}} = \int_0^{\pi/2}\frac{2\cos^2\frac{3x}{2}.2\sin\frac{x}{2}\cos\frac{x}{2}}{2\cos\frac{3x}{2}.\sin\frac{x}{2}}dx$

$= \int_0^{\pi/2}2\cos\frac{3x}{2}.\cos\frac{x}{2}dx = \int_0^{\pi/2}(\cos 2x+\cos x)dx$

$= \left[\frac{\sin x}{2}\right]_0^{\pi/2} + [\sin x]_0^{\pi/2} = 0+(1-0) = 1$

15. (b) $I = \int_{-1/\sqrt{3}}^{1/\sqrt{3}}\left(\frac{x^4}{1-x^4}\right)\cos^{-1}\left(\frac{2x}{1+x^2}\right)dx$

$= \int_{-1/\sqrt{3}}^{1/\sqrt{3}}\left(\frac{x^4}{1-x^4}\right)\cos^{-1}\left(\frac{2(-x)}{1+x^2}\right)dx$

$\left[\because \int_a^b f(x)dx = \int_a^b f(a+b-x)dx\right]$

$\Rightarrow\ I = \int_{-1/\sqrt{3}}^{1/\sqrt{3}}\left(\frac{x^4}{1-x^4}\right)\left[\pi\cos^{-1}\left(\frac{2x}{1+x^2}\right)\right]dx$

$= \pi\int_{-1/\sqrt{3}}^{1/\sqrt{3}}\frac{x^4}{1-x^4}dx - \int_{-1/\sqrt{3}}^{1/\sqrt{3}}\left(\frac{x^4}{1-x^4}\right)\cos^{-1}\left(\frac{2x}{1+x^2}\right)dx$

$\Rightarrow\ 2I = \pi\int_{-1/\sqrt{3}}^{1/\sqrt{3}}\frac{x^4}{1-x^4}dx \Rightarrow\ 2I = 2\pi\int_0^{1/\sqrt{3}}\frac{x^4}{1-x^4}dx$

$\Rightarrow\ I = -\pi\int_0^{1/\sqrt{3}}\frac{x^4-1+1}{x^4-1}dx$

$\Rightarrow\ I = -\pi\int_0^{1/\sqrt{3}}\left(1+\frac{1}{x^4-1}\right)dx = -\frac{\pi}{\sqrt{3}}-\pi\int_0^{1/\sqrt{3}}\frac{1}{x^4-1}dx$

$= -\frac{\pi}{\sqrt{3}}-\frac{\pi}{2}\int_0^{1/\sqrt{3}}\frac{(x^2+1)-(x^2-1)dx}{(x^4-1)}dx$

$= \frac{-\pi}{\sqrt{3}}-\frac{\pi}{2}\int_0^{1/\sqrt{3}}\left(\frac{1}{x^2-1}-\frac{1}{x^2+1}\right)dx$

$= \frac{-\pi}{\sqrt{3}}-\frac{\pi}{2}\left[\frac{1}{2}\left\{\ln\left|\frac{x-1}{x+2}\right|\right\}_0^{1/\sqrt{3}} - \left[\tan^{-1}x\right]_0^{1/\sqrt{3}}\right]$

$= \frac{-\pi}{\sqrt{3}}-\frac{\pi}{2}\left\{\frac{1}{2}\ln\left|\frac{1-\sqrt{3}}{1+\sqrt{3}}\right| - \tan^{-1}\frac{1}{\sqrt{3}}\right\}$

$= \frac{-\pi}{\sqrt{3}}-\frac{\pi}{4}\ln\left|\frac{\sqrt{3}-1}{\sqrt{3}+1}\right| + \frac{\pi}{2}\left(\frac{\pi}{6}\right)$

$\Rightarrow\ I = \frac{-\pi}{\sqrt{3}}-\frac{\pi}{4}\ln\left|\frac{\sqrt{3}-1}{\sqrt{3}+1}\right| + \frac{\pi^2}{12}$

$\Rightarrow\ I = \pi\left[\frac{\pi}{12}-\frac{1}{\sqrt{3}}-\frac{1}{4}\ln\left(\frac{\sqrt{3}-1}{\sqrt{3}+1}\right)\right]$

$\Rightarrow\ I = \pi\left[\frac{\pi}{12}-\frac{1}{\sqrt{3}}-\frac{1}{4}\ln\left(\frac{4-2\sqrt{3}}{2}\right)\right]$

$\Rightarrow\ I = \pi\left[\frac{\pi}{12}-\frac{1}{\sqrt{3}}-\frac{1}{4}\ln\left(2-\sqrt{3}\right)\right]$

$\Rightarrow\ I = \pi\left[\frac{\pi}{12}-\frac{1}{\sqrt{3}}-\frac{1}{4}\ln\left(2+\sqrt{3}\right)\right]$

16. (b) $I=\int_{-\pi}^{\pi}\frac{2x(1+\sin x)}{1+\cos^2 x}dx$

$\Rightarrow\ I=2\int_{-\pi}^{\pi}\frac{x\,dx}{1+\cos^2 x}+2\int_{-\pi}^{\pi}\frac{x\sin x}{1+\cos^2 x}dx$

$\Rightarrow\ I=2(0)+4\int_0^{\pi}\frac{x\sin x}{1+\cos^2}dx$

$\left(\because \frac{x\sin x}{1+\cos^2 x}\text{ is an even function}\right)$

$\Rightarrow\ I=4\int_0^{\pi}\frac{(\pi-x)\sin x}{1+\cos^2 x}dx$

$\Rightarrow\ I=4\pi\int_0^{\pi}\frac{\sin x}{1+\cos^2 x}dx-\int_0^{\pi}\frac{4x\sin x}{1+\cos^2 x}dx$

$\Rightarrow\ I=2\pi\int_0^{\pi}\frac{\sin x}{1+\cos^2 x}dx$

$\Rightarrow\ I=4\pi\int_0^{\pi/2}\frac{\sin x}{1+\cos^2 x}dx\qquad[\because f(\pi-x)=f(x)]$

$\Rightarrow\ I=-4\pi\int_1^0\frac{dt}{1+t^2}=4\pi\left[\tan^{-1}t\right]_0^1$

$\Rightarrow\ I=4\pi\left[\frac{\pi}{4}\right]=\pi^2$

17. (a) $I=\int_0^{\pi/2}e^x\left\{\cos(\sin x)\cos^2\frac{x}{2}+\sin(\sin x)\sin^2\frac{x}{2}\right\}dx$

$\Rightarrow\ I=\int_0^{\pi/2}e^x\left\{\cos(\sin x)\left(\frac{1+\cos x}{2}\right)+\sin(\sin x)\left(\frac{1-\cos x}{2}\right)\right\}dx$

$\Rightarrow\ I=\frac{1}{2}\int_0^{\pi/2}e^x\{\cos(\sin x)+\cos(\sin x).\cos x+\sin(\sin x)-\sin(\sin x).\cos x\}dx$

$\Rightarrow\ I=\frac{1}{2}\int_0^{\pi/2}e^x\{[\cos(\sin x)+\sin(\sin x)]+[-\sin(\sin x).\cos x+\cos(\sin x)\cos x]\}dx$

$\Rightarrow\ I=\frac{1}{2}\left[e^x\left[\cos(\sin x)+\sin(\sin x)\right]\right]_0^{\frac{\pi}{2}}$

$\left(\because\int e^x(f(x)+f'(x))dx=e^xf(x)+c\right)$

$\Rightarrow\ I=\frac{1}{2}\left[e^{\pi/2}(\cos(1)+\sin(1))-e^{\circ}(1+0)\right]$

$\Rightarrow\ I=\frac{1}{2}\left[e^{\pi/2}(\cos1+\sin1)-1\right]$

18. (c) $I_1=\int_0^3\frac{\sin x}{\left[\frac{x}{\pi}\right]+\frac{1}{2}}dx$

Put $x=-y\quad\Rightarrow\quad dx=-dy$

$\Rightarrow\ I_1=\int_0^{-3}\frac{\sin(-y)}{\left[\frac{-y}{\pi}\right]+\frac{1}{2}}(-dy)$

$\Rightarrow\ I_1=\int_0^{-3}\frac{\sin y\,dy}{\left[\frac{-y}{\pi}\right]+\frac{1}{2}}$

$\because\ y\in(-3,0)\quad\Rightarrow\quad\frac{-y}{\pi}\in\left(0,\frac{3}{\pi}\right)$

$\Rightarrow\ -\frac{y}{\pi}\notin\mathbb{Z}$

$\Rightarrow\ \left[\frac{-y}{\pi}\right]=-1-\left[\frac{y}{\pi}\right]$

$\therefore\ I_1=\int_0^{-3}\frac{\sin y\,dy}{-1-\left[\frac{y}{\pi}\right]+\frac{1}{2}}=\int_0^{-3}\frac{\sin y\,dy}{-\left[\frac{y}{\pi}\right]-\frac{1}{2}}$

$=\int_{-3}^{0}\frac{\sin y\,dy}{\left[\frac{y}{\pi}\right]+\frac{1}{2}}=I_2\text{ (given)}$

$\therefore\ I_1=I_2$

19. (c) $I=\int_{-1}^{1}\frac{dx}{(1+x^2)(2^x+1)}\qquad\ldots(1)$

$\Rightarrow\ I=\int_{-1}^{1}\frac{dx}{(1+(-x)^2)(2^{-x}+1)}$

$\left(\text{using }\int_a^b f(x)dx-\int_a^b f(a+b-x)dx\right)$

$\Rightarrow\ I=\int_{-1}^{1}\frac{2^x\,dx}{(1+x^2)(1+2^x)}\qquad\ldots(2)$

$\therefore$ Equation (1) + (2) gives, $2I=\int_{-1}^{1}\frac{1}{1+x^2}dx=2\int_0^1\frac{1}{1+x^2}dx$

$\Rightarrow\ I=\left[\tan^{-1}\right]_0^1=\frac{\pi}{4}$

20. (d) (a) $I_1=\int_0^{\pi/2}\ln(\cot x)dx\qquad\ldots(1)$

$\Rightarrow\ I_1=\int_0^{\pi/2}\ln\left(\cot\left(\frac{\pi}{2}-x\right)\right)dx$

$\Rightarrow\ I_1=\int_0^{\pi/2}\ln(\tan x)dx\qquad\ldots(2)$

Equation (1) + (2) gives, $2I_1=\int_0^{\pi/2}\ln1\,dx=0$

$\Rightarrow\ I_1=0$

(b) $I_2=\int_0^{2\pi}\sin^3x\,dx=0$ as $\sin^3(2\pi-x)=-\sin^3x$

(c) $I_3=\int_{1/e}^{e}\frac{dx}{x(\ln x)^{1/3}}=\int_{1/e}^{e}\frac{1}{x}(\ln x)^{-1/3}dx=\left[\frac{(\ln x)^{2/3}}{2/3}\right]_{1/e}^{e}$

$=\frac{3}{2}\left[1-(-1)^{2/3}\right]=0$

$I_4=\int_0^{\pi}\sqrt{\frac{1+\cos2x}{2}}dx=\int_0^{\pi}\sqrt{(\cos^2x)}dx=\int_0^{\pi}|\cos x|dx$

$=\int_0^{\pi/2}\cos x\,dx+\int_{\pi/2}^{\pi}-\cos x\,dx=1-[0-(1)]=2$

21. (b) $\int_{-2\pi}^{5\pi}\cot^{-1}(\tan x)dx=\int_{-2\pi}^{5\pi}\cot^{-1}\left(\cot\left(\frac{\pi}{2}-x\right)\right)dx$

$\because\ \cot^{-1}(\cot x)$ is a periodic function with period π

$\Rightarrow \cot^{-1}\left(\cot\left(\frac{\pi}{2}-x\right)\right)$ is also Periodic function with period π

$$\therefore \int_{-2\pi}^{5\pi}\cot^{-1}\left(\cot\left(\frac{\pi}{2}-x\right)\right)dx = 7\int_0^{\pi}\cot^{-1}\left(\cot\left(\frac{\pi}{2}-x\right)\right)dx$$

$$= 7\int_0^{\pi}\cot^{-1}(\cot x)dx = 7\int_0^{\pi}x\,dx = 7\left[\frac{x^2}{2}\right]_0^{\pi} = \frac{7\pi^2}{2}$$

22. (a) $\int_{-1}^{1}\frac{\left(2x^{332}+x^{998}+4x^{1668}.\sin x^{691}\right)}{1+x^{666}}dx = \int_{-1}^{1}\frac{2x^{332}+x^{998}}{1+x^{666}}dx$

$$= 2\int_0^1\frac{2x^{332}+x^{998}}{1+x^{666}}dx = 2\int_0^1\frac{x^{332}+x^{332}+x^{998}}{1+x^{666}}dx$$

$$= 2\int_0^1\left[\frac{x^{332}}{1+x^{666}}+\frac{x^{332}\left(1+x^{666}\right)}{1+x^{666}}\right]dx$$

$$= 2\int_0^1\frac{x^{332}}{1+x^{666}}dx + 2\int_0^1 x^{332}dx$$

Put $x^{333}=t$

$\Rightarrow 333x^{332}dx = dt$

$$\Rightarrow \text{I} = \frac{2}{333}\int_0^1\frac{dt}{1+t^2}+2\left[\frac{x^{333}}{333}\right]_0^1$$

$$\Rightarrow \text{I} = \frac{2}{333}\left|\tan^{-1}t\right|_0^1+\frac{2}{333}(1-0)$$

$$\Rightarrow \text{I} = \frac{2}{333}\left[\frac{\pi}{4}\right]+\frac{2}{333} \Rightarrow \text{I} = \frac{2}{333}\left[\frac{\pi}{4}+1\right] = \left(\frac{\pi+4}{666}\right)$$

TEXTUAL EXERCISE-6: (SUBJECTIVE)

1. $f(x) = \int_{e^{2x}}^{e^{3x}}\frac{t}{\ln t};x>0$

$$f'(x) = \frac{e^{3x}}{\ln e^{3x}}\times e^{3x}\times 3 - \frac{e^{2x}}{\ln e^{2x}}\times e^{2x}\times 2$$

$\Rightarrow f'(x)$ at $x = \ln 2$

i.e., $f'(\ln 2) = \frac{8}{3\ln 2}\times 8\times 3 - \frac{4}{2\ln 2}\times 4\times 2$

$$= \frac{64}{\ln 2}-\frac{16}{\ln 2} = \frac{48}{\ln 2}$$

2. $x = \int_0^y\frac{dt}{\sqrt{1+4t^2}} = f(y)$

$$\Rightarrow \frac{dx}{dy} = \frac{1}{\sqrt{1+4y^2}} \quad \Rightarrow \frac{dy}{dx} = \sqrt{1+4y^2}$$

$$\Rightarrow \frac{d^2y}{dx^2} = \frac{d}{dx}\left(\frac{dy}{dx}\right) = \frac{d}{dy}\left(\frac{dy}{dx}\right)\times\frac{dy}{dx}$$

$$= \frac{d}{dy}\left(\sqrt{1+4y^2}\right)\times\sqrt{1+4y^2}$$

$$= \frac{1}{2}\frac{(8y)}{\sqrt{1+4y^2}}\times\sqrt{1+4y^2} = 4y = ky \text{ (given)}$$

$\Rightarrow$ k = 4

3. (a) $x = \int_1^{t^2}\sqrt{z}.\sin z dz = f(t)$ (say) and

$y = \int_{\sqrt{t}}^{2} z^2\cos z^2\,dz = g(t)$ (say)

$$\therefore \frac{dy}{dx} = \frac{\frac{dy}{dt}}{\frac{dx}{dt}} = \frac{g'(t)}{f'(t)} = \frac{0-(t\cos t)\frac{1}{2\sqrt{t}}}{(t\sin t^2)(2t)-0}$$

$$= -\frac{\sqrt{t}\cos t}{4t^2\sin t^2} = \frac{-\cos t}{4t\sqrt{t}\sin t^2}$$

(b) $x = \int_1^{t^2}z\ln z dz = f(t)$ (say) and $y = \int_{t^2}^{1}z^2\ln z dz = g(t)$ (say)

$$\therefore \frac{dy}{dx} = \frac{\frac{dy}{dt}}{\frac{dx}{dt}} = \frac{g'(t)}{f'(t)} = \frac{0-t^4\left(\ln t^2\right)(2t)}{\left(t^2\ln t^2\right)(2t)-0} = -t^2$$

4. (a) $\text{I} = \int_{1/4}^{\sin^2 x}\sin^{-1}\sqrt{t}\,dt + \int_{1/4}^{\cos^2 x}\cos^{-1}\sqrt{t}\,dt$

$$= \int_{1/4}^{\sin^2 x}\sin^{-1}\sqrt{t}\,dt + \int_{1/4}^{\sin^2 x}\cos^{-1}\sqrt{t}\,dt + \int_{\sin^2 x}^{\cos^2}\cos^{-1}\sqrt{t}\,dt$$

$$= \int_{1/4}^{\sin^2 x}\frac{\pi}{2}dt + \int_{\sin^2 x}^{\cos^2 x}\cos^{-1}\sqrt{t}\,dt$$

$$= \frac{\pi}{2}\left(\sin^2 x-\frac{1}{4}\right)+\int_{\sin^2 x}^{\cos^2 x}\cos^{-1}\sqrt{t}\,dt$$

Put $\sqrt{t}=u$

$$\Rightarrow \frac{1}{2\sqrt{t}}dt = du$$

$$\Rightarrow \text{I} = \frac{\pi}{2}\sin^2 x - \frac{\pi}{8}+\int_{\sin x}^{\cos x}\left(\cos^{-1}u\right)2udu$$

$$= \frac{\pi}{2}\sin^2 x-\frac{\pi}{8}+2\left[\left|\left(\cos^{-1}u\right)\frac{u^2}{2}\right|_{\sin x}^{\cos x} - \int_{\sin x}^{\cos x}\frac{-1}{\sqrt{1-u^2}}\times\frac{u^2}{2}du\right]$$

$$= \frac{\pi}{2}\sin^2 x-\frac{\pi}{8}+\left[\left(\cos^2 x\right)x-\left(\sin^2 x\right)\left(\cos^{-1}\left(\cos\left(\frac{\pi}{2}-x\right)\right)\right)\right.$$

$$\left.-\int_{\sin x}^{\cos x}\frac{1-u^2-1}{\sqrt{1-u^2}}du\right]$$

$$= \frac{\pi}{2}\sin^2 x-\frac{\pi}{8}+\left[x\cos^2 x-\left(\frac{\pi}{2}-x\right)\sin^2 x\right]$$

$$-\int_{\sin x}^{\cos x}\left(\sqrt{1-u^2}-\frac{1}{\sqrt{1-u^2}}\right)du$$

$$= \frac{\pi}{2.}\sin^2 x-\frac{\pi}{8}+x\cos^2 x-\frac{\pi}{2}\sin^2 x+x\sin^2 x$$

$$-\left[\frac{4\sqrt{1-u^2}}{2}+\frac{1}{2}\sin^{-1}u\right]_{\sin x}^{\cos x}+\left[\sin^{-1}u\right]_{\sin x}^{\cos x}$$

$$= x - \frac{\pi}{8} - \left[\frac{\cos x \sin x}{2} + \frac{1}{2}\sin^{-1}\left(\sin\left(\frac{\pi}{2} - x\right)\right)\right.$$

$$\left. - \frac{\sin x \cos x}{2} - \frac{1}{2}x\right] + \left[\left(\frac{\pi}{2} - x\right) - x\right]$$

$$= x - \frac{\pi}{8} - \left[\frac{\pi}{4} - x\right] + \frac{\pi}{2} - x - x = \frac{\pi}{8}$$

(b) $y = \int_0^x f(t)\sin(k(x-t))dt$

$$\Rightarrow \frac{dy}{dx}\int_0^x \frac{\partial}{\partial x}\{f(t).\sin(k(x-t))\}dt + (f(0).\sin 0).1. - 0$$

$$\Rightarrow \frac{dy}{dx} = \int_0^x f(t).\cos(k(x-t)).k\,dt$$

$$\Rightarrow \frac{dy}{dx} = k\int_0^x f(t).\cos(k(x-t))dt$$

$$\Rightarrow \frac{d^2y}{dx^2} = k\left[\int_0^x \frac{\partial}{\partial x}\{f(t).\cos k(x-t)\}dt + f(x) - 0\right]$$

$$\Rightarrow \frac{d^2y}{dx^2} = k\left[\int_0^x -f(t)k.\sin k(x-t)dt + f(x)\right]$$

$$\Rightarrow \frac{d^2y}{dx^2} = k\left[-k\int_0^x f(t)\sin k(x-t)dt + f(x)\right]$$

$$\Rightarrow \frac{d^2y}{dx^2} = k[-ky + f(x)] \Rightarrow \frac{d^2y}{dx^2} + k^2y = kf(x)$$

5. $\frac{d}{dx}\int_x^{x^2}\frac{dt}{x^2+t^2}; x > 0$

$$= \int_x^{x^2}\frac{\partial}{\partial x}\left(\frac{1}{x^2+t^2}\right)dt + \frac{1}{(x^2+x^4)}(2x) - \frac{1}{(x^2+x^2)} \quad \ldots\text{(i)}$$

$$= \int_x^{x^2}\frac{-1}{(x^2+t^2)^2}(2x)dt + \frac{2}{x+x^3} - \frac{1}{2x^2}$$

$$= -2x\int_x^{x^2}\frac{1}{(x^2+t^2)^2}dt + \frac{2}{x(1+x^2)} - \frac{1}{2x^2}$$

Put $t = x\tan\theta \quad \Rightarrow \quad dt = x\sec^2\theta d\theta$

$$\Rightarrow \text{I} = -2x\int_{\pi/4}^{\tan^{-1}(x)}\frac{1}{x^4(1+\tan^2\theta)^2}x\sec^2\theta d\theta + \frac{2}{x(1+x^2)} - \frac{1}{2x^2}$$

$$\Rightarrow \text{I} = \frac{-2x^2}{x^4}\int_{\pi/4}^{\tan^{-1}x}\cos^2\theta d\theta + \frac{2}{x(1+x^2)} - \frac{1}{2x^2}$$

$$\Rightarrow \text{I} = \frac{-2}{x^2}\int_{\pi/4}^{\tan^{-1}x}\frac{(1+\cos 2\theta)}{2}d\theta + \frac{2}{x(1+x^2)} - \frac{1}{2x^2}$$

$$\Rightarrow \text{I} = \frac{-1}{x^2}\left[\theta + \frac{\sin 2\theta}{2}\right]_{\pi/4}^{\tan^{-1}x} + \frac{2}{x(1+x^2)} - \frac{1}{2x^2}$$

$$\Rightarrow \text{I} = \frac{-1}{x^2}\left[\tan^{-1}x - \frac{\pi}{4} + \frac{1}{2}\sin 2(\tan^{-1}x) - \frac{1}{2}\right] + \frac{2}{x(1+x^2)} - \frac{1}{2x^2}$$

$$\Rightarrow \text{I} = \frac{-1}{x^2}\left[\tan^{-1}x - \frac{\pi}{4} + \frac{x}{1+x^2} - \frac{1}{2}\right] + \frac{2}{x(1+x^2)} - \frac{1}{2x^2}$$

$$\Rightarrow \text{I} = \frac{-1}{x^2}\tan^{-1}x + \frac{\pi}{4x^2} - \frac{1}{x(1+x^2)} + \frac{1}{2x^2} + \frac{2}{x(1+x^2)} - \frac{1}{2x^2}$$

$$\Rightarrow \text{I} = \frac{-1}{x^2}\tan^{-1}x + \frac{1}{x(1+x^2)} + \frac{\pi}{4x^2}$$

$$\Rightarrow \text{I} = \frac{-4(1+x^2)\tan^{-1}x + 4x + \pi(1+x^2)}{4x^2(1+x^2)}$$

$$\Rightarrow \text{I} = \frac{4\left[x - (1+x^2)\tan^{-1}x\right] + \pi(1+x^2)}{4x^2(1+x^2)}$$

6. (i) (a) $\lim_{x\to 0}\frac{\int_0^{x^2}\cos t^2 dt}{x\sin x}$

By L.H. Rule, $\lim_{x\to 0}\frac{\frac{d}{dx}\int_0^{x^2}\cos t^2 dt}{[x\cos x + \sin x]} = \lim_{x\to 0}\frac{[\cos(x^4)](2x)}{[x\cos x + \sin x]}$

$$= \lim_{x\to 0}\left[\frac{2\cos x^4}{\cos x + \frac{\sin x}{x}}\right] = \frac{2}{1+1} = 1$$

(b) $\lim_{x\to 0}\frac{\int_0^x t\,dt}{x\tan(x+\pi)}$

By L.H. Rule, $\lim_{x\to 0}\frac{\frac{d}{dx}\int_0^x t\,dt}{\frac{d}{dx}(x\tan(x+\pi))}$

$$= \lim_{x\to 0}\frac{x}{[x\sec^2(x+\pi) + \tan(x+\pi)]}$$

$$= \lim_{x\to 0}\left[\frac{1}{\sec^2(x+\pi) + \frac{\tan(x+\pi)}{x}}\right]$$

$$= \lim_{x\to 0}\left[\frac{1}{\sec^2 x + \frac{\tan x}{x}}\right] = \frac{1}{1+1} = \frac{1}{2}$$

(c) $\lim_{x\to 0}\int_0^{x^2}\frac{\cos\sqrt{t}\,dt}{x^3} = \lim_{x\to 0}\frac{\int_0^{x^2}\cos\sqrt{t}\,dt}{x^3}$

By L.H. Rule $= \lim_{x\to 0}\frac{(\cos x)(2x)}{3x^2} = \lim_{x\to 0}\frac{(2\cos x)}{3x} = \pm\infty$

$\Rightarrow$ Limit does not exist

(d) $\lim_{x\to\infty}\int_0^{2x}\frac{te^{t^2}dt}{e^{4x^2}} = \lim_{x\to\infty}\left(\frac{\int_0^{2x}te^{t^2}dt}{e^{4x^2}}\right) = \lim_{x\to\infty}\frac{\int_0^{4x^2}\frac{1}{2}e^z dz}{e^{4x^2}}$

$$\left(\because t^2 = z \Rightarrow tdt = \frac{dz}{2}\right)$$

$$= \lim_{x\to\infty} \frac{\frac{1}{2}\left(e^{4x^2}-1\right)}{e^{4x^2}} = \lim_{x\to\infty}\left(\frac{1}{2}-\frac{1}{2}e^{-4x^2}\right) = \frac{1}{2}-\frac{1}{2}(0) = \frac{1}{2}$$

(e) $\lim_{x\to 0}\int_0^{x^2}\frac{\sin\sqrt{t}}{x^3}dt = \lim_{x\to 0}\frac{\int_0^{x^2}\sin\sqrt{t}\,dt}{x^3}$

By L.H. Rule $= \lim_{x\to 0}\left(\frac{(\sin x)(2)}{3x^2}\right) = \frac{2}{3}\lim_{x\to 0}\left(\frac{\sin x}{x}\right)$

$= \frac{2}{3}(1) = \frac{2}{3}$

(ii) (a) $\lim_{x\to 2}\int_2^{f(x)}\frac{4t^3}{(x-2)}dt = \lim_{x\to 2}\frac{\int_2^{f(x)}4t^3dt}{(x-2)}; f(2)=2$

$\therefore$ By L.H. Rule, $\lim_{x\to 2}\frac{4\left(f(x)\right)^3.f'(x)}{1}$

$= 4\left(f(2)\right)^3 f'(2) = 32.f'(2)$

(b) $\lim_{x\to 1}\int_4^{f(x)}\frac{2t}{(x-1)}dt; f(1)=4$

By L.H. Rule, $\lim_{x\to 1}\frac{2f(x).f'(x)}{(1)} = 2f(1).f'(1)$

$= 2(4).f'(1) = 8f'(1)$

(iii) $f(x) = \int_0^x t(e^t-1)(t-11)^9(t+2)^3(t+4)^4\ln(t+1)dt$

$\Rightarrow\ f'(x) = x(e^x-1)(x-11)^9(x+2)^3(x+4)^4\ln(x+1)$

Clearly $n>-1$

$\therefore\ f'(x)=0 \qquad \Rightarrow\ x = 0, 11, -2, -4$

$f'(x)>0$

$\Rightarrow\ x(e^x-1)(x-11)^9(x+2)^3\ln(x+1)>0$

For $x>11, f'(x)>0$ and for $x\in(0,11), f'(x)<0$

Also $f'(x)>0$ for $x\in(-1,0)$

$\therefore$ $f(x)$ increase on (–1, 0) and (11, ∞) and decrease on (0, 11)

$\therefore$ Local maxima at x = 0 and local minima at x = 11

7. $F(x) = \int_a^{x^2} f(t)dt \qquad \ldots(1)$

$F'(x) = f(x^2).(2x)$

$F''(x) = (2x)^2 f'(x^2) + f(x^2)(2)$

Here $f(x^2) = x^2 - x$

$\Rightarrow\ f(x) = x-\sqrt{x} \qquad \Rightarrow\ f'(x) = 1-\frac{1}{2\sqrt{x}}$

$\Rightarrow\ f'(x^2) = 1-\frac{1}{2\sqrt{x^2}} \qquad \Rightarrow\ f'(x^2) = 1-\frac{1}{2x}$

$\therefore\ F''(x) = 4x^2\left(1-\frac{1}{2x}\right)+\left(x^2-x\right)(2)$

$\Rightarrow\ F''(x) = 4x^2\left(\frac{2x-1}{2x}\right)+2x^2-2x$

$\Rightarrow\ F''(x) = 4x^2-2x+2x^2-2x$

$\Rightarrow\ F''(x) = 6x^2-4x = 2x(3x-2)$

$\therefore$ For concave upwards, $F''(x)>0$

$\Rightarrow\ x(3x-2)>0 \qquad \Rightarrow\ x\in(-\infty,0)\cup\left(\frac{2}{3},\infty\right)$ and

For concave downwards, $F''(x)>0$

$\Rightarrow\ x(3x-2)<0 \qquad \Rightarrow\ x\in\left(0,\frac{2}{3}\right)$ and $F''(x)=0$

$\Rightarrow\ x = 0$ or $\frac{2}{3}$, i.e., Point of inflexion

8. $f(x) = \int_0^x e^t(e^t-e)(t-3)^3(t-4)^2dt$

$\Rightarrow\ f'(x) = e^x(e^x-e)(x-3)^3(x-4)^2$

$\therefore\ f'(x)=0$ at $x=1,3,4$

$\therefore\ f'(x)>0$ for $x\in(-\infty,1)$,

$f'(x)<0$ for $x\in(1,3)$, and

$f'(x)>0$ for $x\in(3,4)\cup(4,\infty)$

Hence $f(x)$ is increasing in (–∞, 1) and on (3, ∞) and decreasing on (1, 3)

9. $y = \int_0^{z^2}\frac{dx}{1+x^3} \ \Rightarrow\ \frac{dy}{dz} = \frac{1}{1+z^6}(2z)$

$\Rightarrow\ \frac{d^2y}{dz^2} = 2\left[\frac{\left(1+z^6\right)-z\left(6z^5\right)}{\left(1+z^6\right)^2}\right] = 2\left[\frac{1-5z^6}{\left(1+z^6\right)^2}\right]$

$\Rightarrow\ \left(\frac{d^2y}{dz^2}\right)_{z=1} = 2\left(\frac{1-5}{4}\right) = -2$

10. (a) $\lim_{x\to 0}\frac{1}{x^3}\int_0^x\frac{t^2}{t^4+1}dt = \lim_{x\to 0}\frac{\int_0^x\frac{t^2}{t^4+1}}{x^3}$

$\therefore$ By L.H. Rule $= \lim_{x\to 0}\left[\frac{\left(\frac{x^2}{x^4+1}\right)}{3x^2}\right] = \lim_{x\to 0}\left[\frac{1}{3(x^4+1)}\right] = \frac{1}{3}$

(b) $\lim_{x\to\infty} x\int_0^x\left(e^{t^2-x^2}\right)dt = \lim_{x\to\infty} xe^{-x^2}\int_0^x e^{t^2}dt = \lim_{x\to\infty}\frac{\int_0^x e^{t^2}dt}{\left(\frac{e^{x^2}}{x}\right)}$

$\ldots\left(\frac{\infty}{\infty}\text{ form}\right)$

$\therefore$ By L.H. Rule, $\lim_{x\to\infty}\frac{e^{x^2}}{\left[\frac{2x^2e^{x^2}-e^{x^2}.1}{x^2}\right]} = \lim_{x\to\infty}\frac{x^2}{\left(2x^2-1\right)} = \frac{1}{2}$

11. $\left|\lim_{t\to\infty}t^2\int_0^\pi\left(-1+\sqrt[t^2]{\sin x}\right)dx\right| = \left|\lim_{t\to\infty}t^2\left\{-\pi+\int_0^\pi\sqrt[t^2]{\sin x}\,dx\right\}\right|$ a s

$\lim_{t\to\infty}\int_0^\pi\left(\sin x\right)^{1/t^2}dt = \int_0^\pi\lim_{t\to\infty}\left(\sin x\right)^{1/t^2} = \pi$

$$\therefore \left|\lim_{t\to\infty}\left\{\frac{-\pi+\int_0^{\pi}(\sin x)^{1/t^2}dx}{1/t^2}\right\}\right|$$

Now, the limit inside modulus is of $\frac{0}{0}$ form, by L.H. Rule,

$$=\left|\lim_{t\to\infty}\left\{\frac{\frac{d}{dt}\int_0^{\pi}(\sin x)^{1/t^2}dx}{\left(\frac{-2}{t^3}\right)}\right\}\right|=\left|\lim_{t\to\infty}\frac{\left\{\int_0^{\pi}\frac{\partial}{\partial t}(\sin x)^{1/t^2}dx\right\}}{\frac{-2}{t^3}}\right|$$

$$=\left|\lim_{t\to\infty}\frac{\left\{\int_0^{\pi}(\sin x)^{1/t^2}.\ln(\sin x)\left(\frac{-2}{t^3}\right)dx\right\}}{\left(\frac{-2}{t^3}\right)}\right|$$

$$=\left|\lim_{t\to\infty}\int_0^{\pi}(\sin x)^{1/t^2}\ln(\sin x)dx\right|$$

$$=\left|\int_0^{\pi}\ln(\sin x).\lim_{t\to\infty}(\sin x)^{1/t^2}dx\right|=\left|\int_0^{\pi}(\sin x)(1)dx\right|$$

$$=\left|2\int_0^{\pi/2}\ln(\sin x)dx\right|=\left|2\left(\frac{-\pi}{2}\ln 2\right)\right|=\pi\ln 2$$

12. Here, $x\in\left[0,\frac{\pi}{2}\right]$

$$f(x)=\int_0^{\sin^2 x}\sin^{-1}\sqrt{t}\,dt+\int_0^{\cos^2 x}\cos^{-1}\sqrt{t}\,dt$$

$$\Rightarrow f'(x)=\sin^{-1}(\sin x).2\sin x\cos x+\cos^{-1}(\cos x)(2\cos x)(-\sin x)$$

$$=(2\sin x\cos x)\left[\sin^{-1}(\sin x)-\cos^{-1}(\cos x)\right]$$

$$=(2\sin x\cos x)(x-x)=0$$

$$\Rightarrow f(x)=\text{Constant}=C\text{ (say)}$$

$$\Rightarrow f\left(\frac{\pi}{4}\right)=\text{C}$$

$$\Rightarrow \int_0^{1/2}\sin^{-1}\sqrt{t}\,dt+\int_0^{1/2}\cos^{-1}\sqrt{t}\,dt$$

$$=\int_0^{1/2}\left(\sin^{-1}\sqrt{t}+\cos^{-1}\sqrt{t}\right)dt=\int_0^{1/2}\frac{\pi}{2}dt=\frac{\pi}{4}$$

$$\therefore f(x)=\frac{\pi}{4}$$

13. $f(x)=\int_{1/e}^{\tan x}\frac{t\,dt}{1+t^2}+\int_{1/e}^{\cot x}\frac{dt}{t(1+t^2)}=1$

Here $f'(x)=\frac{(\tan x)}{1+\tan^2 x}.\sec^2 x-\frac{(\text{cosec}^2 x)}{(\cot x)(1+\cot^2 x)}$

$$\Rightarrow f'(x)=\frac{\tan x}{1+\tan^2 x}.\sec^2 x-\frac{\tan^3 x.\text{cosec}^2 x}{(\tan^2 x+1)}$$

$$\Rightarrow f'(x)=\left(\tan x-\frac{1}{\cot x}\right)=0$$

$$\Rightarrow f(x)=\text{Constant}=C\text{ (say)}$$

$$\therefore f\left(\frac{\pi}{4}\right)=\text{C}=f(x)$$

$$\Rightarrow f(x)=\int_{1/e}^{1}\left[\frac{t}{1+t^2}+\frac{1}{t(1+t^2)}\right]dt=\int_{1/e}^{1}\left[\frac{t^2+1}{t(1+t^2)}\right]dt$$

$$=\int_{1/e}^{1}\frac{1}{t}dt=[\ln t]_{1/e}^{1}=\ln 1-\ln(1/e)=1$$

Hence, $f(x)=1$

14. $\lim_{x\to\infty}\frac{\left(\int_0^x e^{x^2}dx\right)^2}{\int_0^x e^{2x^2}dx}=\frac{\infty}{\infty}$ form

$\therefore$ By L.H. Rule, $\lim_{x\to\infty}\frac{\left(2\int_0^x e^{x^2}\right)e^{x^2}}{e^{2x^2}(1)}=\lim_{x\to\infty}\left(\frac{2\int_0^x e^{x^2}dx}{e^{x^2}}\right)=\frac{\infty}{\infty}$ from

Again, by L.H. Rule, $=\lim_{x\to\infty}\frac{2e^{x^2}}{e^{x^2}(2x)}=\lim_{x\to\infty}\frac{1}{x}=0$

TEXTUAL EXERCISE–6: (OBJECTIVE)

1. **(a), (c)** $F(x)=\int_x^{x^2}\frac{dt}{\ln t};x\in(0,\infty)$

$$\Rightarrow F'(x)=\frac{1}{\ln x^2}(2x)-\frac{1}{\ln x}=\frac{x}{\ln x}-\frac{1}{\ln x}$$

$$=\frac{(x-1)}{\ln x};x\in(0,\infty)$$

$\therefore$ $F'(x)>0$ for $\frac{(x-1)}{\ln x}>0;\ x\in(0,1)\cup(1,\infty)$

$\Rightarrow$ $F(x)$ is increasing on $(1,\infty)$ and hence one–one

2. **(a), (c), (d)**

$$F(x)=\int_x^{x^2}t\left(\ln\sqrt{t}\right)dt;x\in(0,\infty)$$

$$\Rightarrow F'(x)=(x^2\ln x)(2x)-x\ln\sqrt{x}=2x^3\ln x-\frac{x}{2}\ln x$$

$$=(x\ln x)\left[2x^2-\frac{1}{2}\right]=\frac{1}{2}(4x^2-1)x.\ln x$$

Thus, $F'(x)=\frac{1}{2}(2x+1)(x)(2x-1)\ln x;x\in(0,\infty)$

For $x\in(0,1),\ln x<0$ and for $x\in(0,\infty),\ln x>0$ and

$(2x+1)(x)(2x-1)>0$ for $x\in\left(-\frac{1}{2},0\right)\cup\left(\frac{1}{2},\infty\right)$ and

$(2x+1)(x)(2x-1)<0$ for $x\in\left(-\infty,-\frac{1}{2}\right)\cup\left(0,\frac{1}{2}\right)$

$\therefore$ $F'(x)>0$ for $x\in\left(0,\frac{1}{2}\right)\cup(1,\infty)$ and $F'(x)<0$ for $x\in\left(\frac{1}{2},1\right)$

3. **(b)** $F(x)=\frac{d}{dx}\left\{\pi\int_0^x\frac{1}{t}\sin\left(\frac{\pi}{4}t\right)dt-\int_0^x\tan^{-1}\left(\frac{t}{2}\right)dt\right\}$

$$\Rightarrow F(x)=\pi\left(\frac{1}{x}\sin\frac{\pi x}{4}\right)-\tan^{-1}\frac{x}{2}$$

$\Rightarrow \quad F(2)=\frac{\pi}{2}\sin\frac{\pi}{2}-\tan^{-1}1$

$\Rightarrow \quad F(2)=\frac{\pi}{2}-\frac{\pi}{4}=\frac{\pi}{4}$

4. (a) $f:(0,\infty)\to\mathbb{R};$

$F(x)=\frac{d}{dx}\int_0^x t.f(t)dt;$

$\Rightarrow \quad F(x)=xf(x)$

$\Rightarrow \quad F(x^2)=x^2f(x^2)=x^4+x^2$ (given)

$\Rightarrow \quad f(x^2)=x^2+1 \quad \Rightarrow \quad f(r^2)=r^2+1$

$\Rightarrow \quad \sum_{k=1}^{5}f(k^2)=\sum_{k=1}^{5}(k^2+1)=\sum_{k=1}^{5}k^2+\sum_{k=1}^{5}1$

$=\frac{(5)(6)(11)}{6}+5=60$

5. (c) $F(x)=\int_0^x t.f(t)dt$

$\Rightarrow \quad F'(x)=x.f(x) \qquad ...(1)$

Also $F(x^2)=x^4+x^5$

$\Rightarrow \quad \left[F'(x^2)\right].(2x)=4x^3+5x^4$

$\Rightarrow \quad F'(x^2)=2x^2+\frac{5}{2}x^3 \qquad ...(2)$

$\Rightarrow$ From (1), $F'(x^2)=x^2.f(x^2) \qquad ...(3)$

$\therefore$ From (2) and (3), $x^2.f(x^2)=2x^2+\frac{5}{2}x^3$

$\Rightarrow \quad f(x^2)=2+\frac{5}{2}x$

$\Rightarrow \quad f(r^2)=2+\frac{5}{2}r$

$\therefore \quad \sum_{r=1}^{12}f(r^2)=\sum_{r=1}^{12}2+\frac{5}{2}\sum_{r=1}^{12}r=(24)+\frac{5}{2}.\frac{(12)(13)}{(2)}$

$=24+195=219$

6. (a), (b) $f(x)=\int_0^x \log_{\sin^2 x}\left(\sin^2 t+\frac{1}{2}\right)dt; x\in(0,2\pi)$

$\Rightarrow \quad f'(x)=\log_{\sin^2 x}\left(\sin^2 x+\frac{1}{2}\right); x\in(0,2\pi)$

For $x\in\left(0,\frac{\pi}{2}\right)$ or $\left(\frac{\pi}{2},\pi\right)$ or $\left(\pi,\frac{3\pi}{2}\right)$ or $\left(\frac{3\pi}{2},2\pi\right)$, $\sin^2 x\in(0,1)$

$\therefore$ For $f'(x)\le 0, \sin^2 x+\frac{1}{2}\ge 1$

$\Rightarrow \quad \sin^2 x\ge\frac{1}{2}$

$\Rightarrow \quad \sin^2 x\in\left[\frac{1}{2},1\right)$ and for $f'(x)\ge 0, \sin^2 x+\frac{1}{2}\in(0,1]$

$\Rightarrow \quad \sin^2 x\in\left(0,\frac{1}{2}\right]$

$\therefore \quad f'(x)\ge 0$ for $\sin^2 x\in\left(0,\frac{1}{2}\right]$

$\Rightarrow \quad x\in\left(0,\frac{\pi}{4}\right]$ or $\left[\frac{3\pi}{4},\frac{5\pi}{4}\right]-\{\pi\},\left[\frac{7\pi}{4},2\pi\right)$

7. (b), (c) $\left(f(x)\right)^2=\int_0^x f(t).\frac{2\sec^2 t}{(2+\tan t)}dt; f(0)=0$

$\Rightarrow \quad 2f(x).f'(x)=f(x).\frac{2\sec^2 x}{(2+\tan x)}$

$\Rightarrow \quad f'(x)=\frac{\sec^2 x}{2+\tan x}$

$\Rightarrow \quad f(x)=\int\frac{\sec^2 x}{2+\tan x}dx \Rightarrow f(x)=\ln|2+\tan x|+C$

$\because \quad f(0)=0$ (given)

$\Rightarrow \quad 0=\ln|2|+C \quad \Rightarrow \quad C=-\ln 2$

$\therefore \quad f(x)=\ln|2+\tan x|-\ln 2$

$\Rightarrow \quad f(x)=\ln\left|\frac{2+\tan x}{2}\right|$

$\therefore \quad f\left(\frac{\pi}{4}\right)=\ln\left|\frac{3}{2}\right|=\ln\left(\frac{3}{2}\right)$ and $f\left(\frac{\pi}{3}\right)=\ln\left|\frac{2+\sqrt{3}}{2}\right|$

$\Rightarrow \quad f\left(\frac{\pi}{3}\right)=\ln\left(\frac{2+\sqrt{3}}{2}\right)=\ln\left(\frac{4+2\sqrt{3}}{4}\right)=\ln\left(\frac{\left(\sqrt{3}+1\right)^2}{4}\right)$

$=2\ln\left(\frac{\sqrt{3}+1}{2}\right)$

8. (b) $f(x)=\int_0^x(\sin t-\cos t)(e^t-2)(t-1)^3(t-2)^5dt; 0\le x\le 3,$

$\Rightarrow \quad f'(x)=(\sin x-\cos x)(e^x-2)(x-1)^3(x-2)^5; x\in(0,3);$

$\therefore \quad f'(x)=0$

$\Rightarrow \quad x=\frac{\pi}{4}, x=\ln 2, x=1, x=2$

For $x\in\left[0,\frac{\pi}{4}\right]; \sin x-\cos x\le 0;$

Also $\ln 1<\ln 2<\ln e$

$\Rightarrow \quad \ln 2\in(0,1)$ Now, $\ln 2<\frac{\pi}{4}$

$\Rightarrow \quad 2<e^{\pi/4}$

$\Rightarrow \quad 2^4<e^{\pi} \qquad \Rightarrow \quad 16 \quad (2.73)^{3.14}$ which is true

$\Rightarrow$ Thus, $0<\ln 2<\frac{\pi}{4}<1<2<3$

$\therefore$ For $x\in(0,\ln 2), \sin x-\cos x<0, (e^x-2)<0$ and $(x-1)^3(x-2)^5>0$

$\therefore$ For $x\in(0,\ln 2), f'(x)>0$

For $x\in\left(\ln 2,\frac{\pi}{4}\right), (\sin x-\cos x)<0,$

$\left(e^x-2\right)>0, \left(x-1\right)^3\left(x-2\right)^5>0$

$\Rightarrow \quad f'(x)<0$

For $x\in\left(\frac{\pi}{4},1\right); \sin x-\cos x>0,$

$e^x-2>0, (x-1)^3(x-2)^5>0$

$\Rightarrow \quad f'(x) > 0$

For $x \in (1,2); \sin x - \cos x > 0, e^x - 2 > 0, (x-1)^3(x-2)^5 < 0$

$\Rightarrow \quad f'(x) < 0$

For $x \in (2,3); f'(x) > 0$

$\Rightarrow$ It has two points of maxima, $x = \ln 2$ and $x = 1$

9. (c) $\lim_{x \to 1^+} \int_1^{x^2} \frac{t \sin\left(\frac{\pi t}{2}\right)}{(x^2-1)} dt \quad \ldots\left(\frac{0}{0}\text{ from}\right)$

By L.H., Rule, $= \lim_{x\to 1^+} \frac{x^2 \sin\left(\frac{\pi x^2}{2}\right)(2x)}{2x} = 1$

10. (a), (b) $f(x) = \int_0^x \frac{2\sin t\, dt}{\sqrt{1+\tan^2 x \sin^2 t}}$

$= \int_0^x \frac{2\sin t\, dt}{\sqrt{1+\tan^2 x(1-\cos^2 t)}} = \int_0^x \frac{2\sin t\, dt}{\sqrt{\sec^2 x - \tan^2 x \cos^2 t}}$

Put $\cos t = u \quad \Rightarrow \quad \sin dt = -du$

$\Rightarrow \quad f(x) = 2\int_1^{\cos x} \frac{-du}{\sqrt{\sec^2 x - u^2 \tan^2 x}}$

$\Rightarrow \quad f(x) = \frac{-2}{\tan x}\int_1^{\cos x} \frac{du}{\sqrt{\text{cosec}^2 x - u^2}}$

$\Rightarrow \quad f(x) = 2\cot x \int_{\cos x}^1 \frac{du}{\sqrt{\text{cosec}^2 x - u^2}}$

$= 2(\cot x)\left[\sin^{-1}\left(\frac{u}{\text{cosec}\, x}\right)\right]_{\cos x}^1$

$= 2(\cot x)\left[\sin^{-1}(\sin x) - \sin^{-1}(\sin x \cos x)\right]$

$f(x) = 2(\cot x)\left[x - \sin\ (\sin x \cos x)\right]$

$\therefore \quad f\left(\frac{\pi}{4}\right) = 2\left[\frac{\pi}{4} - \sin^{-1}\left(\frac{1}{2}\right)\right] = \frac{\pi}{2} - 2\sin^{-1}\frac{1}{2} = \frac{\pi}{2} - \frac{\pi}{3}$

$= \frac{3\pi - 2\pi}{6} = \frac{\pi}{6}$

Clearly, in $\left(0, \frac{\pi}{2}\right)$

$f(x) = \frac{2x - 2\sin^{-1}(\sin x \cos x)}{\tan x}$ is continuous and differentiable.

TEXTUAL EXERCISE–7: (SUBJECTIVE)

1. $f(x) = \int_a^x \log\left(t + \sqrt{1+t^2}\right) dt$

$\Rightarrow \quad f(-x) = \int_a^{-x} \log\left(t + \sqrt{1+t^2}\right) dt$

$\therefore \quad f(x) - f(-x) = \int_a^x \log\left(t + \sqrt{1+t^2}\right) dt$

$-\int_a^{-x} \log\left(t + \sqrt{1+t^2}\right) dt$

$= \int_{-x}^a \log\left(t + \sqrt{1+t^2}\right) dt + \int_a^x \log\left(t + \sqrt{1+t^2}\right) dt$

$= \int_{-x}^x \log\left(t + \sqrt{1+t^2}\right) dt = 0$ as $\log\left(t + \sqrt{1+t^2}\right)$ is odd function.

$\Rightarrow \quad f(-x) = f(x)$

$\Rightarrow \quad f(x)$ is an even function.

2. $\int_0^{nT} f(x)dx = n\int_0^T f(x)dx$ has been already proved in property (19)

(a) $\text{I} = \int_0^{32\pi/3} |\sin x|\, dx = \int_0^{10\pi} |\sin x|\, dx + \int_{10\pi}^{\left(10\pi + \frac{2\pi}{3}\right)} |\sin x|\, dx$

$\because \quad |\sin x|$ is periodic with period π,

Hence, $\text{I} = 10\int_0^\pi |\sin x|\, dx + \int_0^{2\pi/3} |\sin x|\, dx$

$= 10\int_0^\pi \sin x\, dx + \int_0^{2\pi/3} \sin x\, dx$

$= 10[-\cos x]_0^\pi + [-\cos x]_0^{2\pi/3}$

$= -10[-1-1] - \left[\frac{-1}{2} - 1\right] = 20 + \frac{3}{2} = \frac{43}{2}$

(b) $\int_0^{32\pi/3} \sqrt{1+\cos 2x}\, dx = \int_0^{32\pi/3} \sqrt{2\cos^2 x}\, dx$

$= \sqrt{2}\int_0^{32\pi/3} |\cos x|\, dx$

$= \sqrt{2}\int_0^{10} |\cos x|\, dx + \sqrt{2}\int_{10\pi}^{10\pi + \frac{2\pi}{3}} |\cos x|\, dx$

$= \sqrt{2}(10)\int_0^\pi |\cos x|\, dx + \sqrt{2}\int_0^{2\pi/3} |\cos x|\, dx$

$= 10\sqrt{2}\left[\int_0^{\pi/2} \cos x\, dx - \int_{\pi/2}^\pi \cos x\, dx\right]$

$+\sqrt{2}\left[\int_0^{\pi/2} \cos x\, dx + \int_{\pi/2}^{2\pi/3} -\cos x\, dx\right]$

$= 10\sqrt{2}[(1) - (0-1)] + \sqrt{2}\left[(1-0) - \left(\frac{\sqrt{3}}{2} - 1\right)\right]$

$= \left(10\sqrt{2}\right)(2) + \sqrt{2}\left[2 - \frac{\sqrt{3}}{2}\right]$

$= 20\sqrt{2} + 2\sqrt{2} - \frac{\sqrt{3}}{\sqrt{2}} = 22\sqrt{2} - \frac{\sqrt{3}}{\sqrt{2}} = \frac{44-\sqrt{3}}{\sqrt{2}}$

(c) $\int_{-1}^{3/2} |x \sin \pi x| dx = \int_{-1}^0 (x\sin \pi x)dx + \int_0^1 (x\sin \pi x)dx$

$+\int_1^{3/2} -(x\sin \pi x)dx$

$= \int_{-1}^1 (x\sin \pi x)dx - \int_1^{3/2} (x\sin \pi x)dx$

$[\because \ x\sin \pi x$ is an even function$]$

$= 2\int_0^1 (x\sin \pi x)dx - \int_1^{3/2} (x\sin \pi x)dx$

$= 2\left[\left|\frac{-x\cos \pi x}{\pi}\right|_0^1 + \int_0^1 \frac{\cos \pi x}{\pi} dx\right]$

$-\left[\left|\frac{-x\cos \pi x}{\pi}\right|_1^{3/2} + \int_1^{3/2} \frac{\cos \pi x}{\pi} dx\right]$

$$= 2\left[\frac{1}{\pi} + \frac{1}{\pi}\left[\frac{\sin \pi x}{\pi}\right]_0^1\right] - \left[0 - \left(\frac{1}{\pi}\right) + \frac{1}{\pi^2}[\sin \pi x]_1^{3/2}\right]$$

$$= \frac{2}{\pi} + \frac{1}{\pi} - \frac{1}{\pi^2}[-1] = \frac{3}{\pi} + \frac{1}{\pi^2} = \frac{3\pi + 1}{\pi^2}$$

(d) $\int_0^{41/4} e^{2x-[2x]} dx = \int_0^{41/4} e^{\{2x\}} dx$

Put $2x = t \Rightarrow dx = \frac{dt}{2}$

$\therefore \quad I = \int_0^{41/2} e^{\{t\}} \frac{dt}{2} = \frac{1}{2}\int_0^{41/2} e^{\{t\}} dt$

$\because \quad e^{\{t\}}$ is periodic with period 1

$$\Rightarrow I = \frac{1}{2}\int_0^{20} e^{\{t\}} dt + \frac{1}{2}\int_{20}^{20+\frac{1}{2}} e^{\{t\}} dt = \frac{1}{2}(20)\int_0^1 e^t dt + \frac{1}{2}\int_0^{1/2} e^t dt$$

$$= 10[e-1] + \frac{1}{2}\left(e^{1/2} - 1\right)$$

(e) $I = \int_0^{2n\pi} [\sin x + \cos x] dx$

$(\sin x + \cos x)$ is periodic with period 2π

$$\therefore \quad I = \int_0^{n(2\pi)} (\sin x + \cos x) dx = n\int_0^{2\pi} (\sin x + \cos x) dx$$

$$= n[-\cos x + \sin x]_0^{2\pi} = n[-(1-1) + (0-0)] = 0$$

(f) $\int_0^{200\pi} \sqrt{1 + \cos x}\, dx = \int_0^{200\pi} \sqrt{2\cos^2 \frac{x}{2}} dx$

$$= \sqrt{2}\int_0^{200\pi} \left|\cos\frac{x}{2}\right| dx$$

$\because \quad |\cos x|$ is periodic with period π,

$$= \sqrt{2}\int_0^{100(2\pi)} \left|\cos\frac{x}{2}\right| dx = \left(\sqrt{2}\right)(100)\int_0^{2\pi} \left|\cos\frac{x}{2}\right| dx$$

$$= \left(100\sqrt{2}\right)\int_0^{\pi} \left|\cos\frac{x}{2}\right| dx + \left(100\sqrt{2}\right)\int_{\pi}^{2\pi} \left|\cos\frac{x}{2}\right| dx$$

$$= 100\sqrt{2}\int_0^{\pi} \cos\frac{x}{2} + 100\sqrt{2}\int_{\pi}^{2\pi} -\cos\frac{x}{2} dx$$

$$= 100\sqrt{2}\left[\frac{\sin\frac{x}{2}}{\frac{1}{2}}\right] - 100\sqrt{2}\left[\frac{\sin\frac{x}{2}}{\frac{x}{2}}\right]_{\pi}^{2\pi}$$

$$= 200\sqrt{2}[1-0] - 200\sqrt{2}[0-1]$$

$$= 200\sqrt{2} + 200\sqrt{2} = 400\sqrt{2}$$

(g) $\int_0^{2000\pi} \frac{dx}{1 + e^{\sin x}}$

$$\Rightarrow I = 1000\int_0^{2\pi} \frac{dx}{1 + e^{\sin x}} \quad \ldots(1)$$

$$\Rightarrow I = 1000\int_0^{2\pi} \frac{dx}{1 + e^{\sin(2\pi - x)}}$$

$$\Rightarrow I = 1000\int_0^{2\pi} \frac{dx}{1 + e^{-\sin x}}$$

$$\Rightarrow I = 1000\int_0^{2\pi} \frac{e^{\sin x}}{e^{\sin x} + 1} dx \quad \ldots(2)$$

$\therefore$ Equation (1) + (2) gives, $2I = 1000\int_0^{2\pi} 1 dx$

$\Rightarrow 2I = 1000(2\pi)$

$\Rightarrow 2I = 1000\pi$

3. $I = \int_0^{2n\pi} \left(|\sin x| - \left[\left|\frac{\sin x}{2}\right|\right]\right) dx$

$$= (2n)\int_0^{\pi} \left(|\sin x| - \left[\left|\frac{\sin x}{2}\right|\right]\right) dx$$

$$= (2n)\int_0^{\pi} \left((\sin x) - \left[\frac{\sin x}{2}\right]\right) dx$$

$$= (2n)\int_0^{\pi} (\sin x - (0)) dx \quad = 2n[-\cos x]_0^{\pi} = (-2n)(-1-1)$$

$$= 4n$$

4. $I = \int_0^{n\pi + v} |\cos x| dx; \frac{\pi}{2} < v < \pi; n \in \mathbb{N}$

$$= n\int_0^{\pi} |\cos x| dx + \int_{n\pi}^{n\pi + v} |\cos x| dx$$

$$= n\int_0^{\pi/2} \cos x\, dx - n\int_{\pi/2}^{\pi} \cos x\, dx + \int_0^{v} |\cos x| dx$$

$$= n[\sin x]_0^{\pi/2} - n[\sin x]_{\pi/2}^{\pi} + \int_0^{\pi/2} \cos x\, dx + \int_{\pi/2}^{v} (-\cos x) dx$$

$$= n[1-0] - (0-1) + (1-0) - (\sin v - 1) = 2n + 2 - \sin v$$

5. $I = \int_{5n\pi}^{\frac{5\pi}{n}(n^2+1)} \frac{\left(\frac{8xn^2}{25}\right) dx}{\left[\left(a^2 + b^2\right) + \left(a^2 - b^2\right)\cos\frac{2nx}{5}\right]}; a, b > 0$ and $n \in \mathbb{N}$.

$$\Rightarrow I = \frac{8n^2}{25}\int_{5n\pi}^{\left(5n\pi + \frac{5\pi}{n}\right)} \frac{x^n dx}{\left[\left(a^2 + b^2\right) + \left(a^2 - b^2\right)\cos\left(\frac{2nx}{5}\right)\right]} \quad \ldots(1)$$

$$\Rightarrow I = \frac{8n^2}{25}\int_{5n\pi}^{5n\pi + \frac{5\pi}{n}} \frac{\left(\frac{5\pi}{n} - x\right) dx}{\left[\left(a^2 + b^2\right) + \left(a^2 - b^2\right)\cos\left[\frac{2n}{5}\left(\frac{5n}{n} - x\right)\right]\right]}$$

$$\Rightarrow I = \frac{8n^2}{25}\int_{5n\pi}^{5n\pi + \frac{5\pi}{n}} \frac{\left(\frac{5\pi}{n} - x\right) dx}{\left[\left(a^2 + b^2\right) + \left(a^2 - b^2\right)\cos\left[2\pi - \frac{2nx}{5}\right]\right]}$$

$$\Rightarrow I = \frac{8n^2}{25}\int_{5n\pi}^{5n\pi + \frac{5\pi}{n}} \frac{\left(\frac{5\pi}{n} - x\right) dx}{\left(a^2 + b^2\right) + \left(a^2 - b^2\right)\cos\frac{2nx}{5}} \quad \ldots(2)$$

$\therefore$ (1) + (2) gives,

$$I = \frac{4n^2}{25} \times \frac{5\pi}{n}\int_{5n\pi}^{5n\pi + \frac{5\pi}{n}} \frac{dx}{\left(a^2 + b^2\right) + \left(a^2 - b^2\right)\cos\frac{2nx}{5}}$$

$$\Rightarrow \quad I=\frac{4n\pi}{5}\int_{5n\pi}^{5n\pi+\frac{5\pi}{n}}\frac{dx}{\left(a^2+b^2\right)+\left(a^2-b^2\right)\cos\frac{2nx}{5}}$$

Now integrand is periodic with period $\frac{2\pi}{2n/5}=\frac{5\pi}{n}$

$$\Rightarrow \quad I=\frac{4n\pi}{5}\int_0^{5\pi/n}\frac{dx}{\left(a+b^2\right)+\left(a^2-b^2\right)\cos\left(\frac{2nx}{5}\right)}$$

Put $\frac{2nx}{5}=t \quad \Rightarrow \quad dx=\frac{5}{2n}dt$

$$\Rightarrow \quad I=\frac{4n\pi}{5}\times\frac{5}{2n}\int_0^{2\pi}\frac{dt}{\left(a^2+b^2\right)+\left(a^2-b^2\right)\cos t}$$

$$\Rightarrow \quad I=2\pi\int_0^{2\pi}\frac{dt}{\left(a^2+b^2\right)+\left(a^2-b^2\right)\cos t}$$

$$\Rightarrow \quad I=4\pi\int_0^{\pi}\frac{dt}{\left(a^2+b^2\right)+\left(a^2-b^2\right)\cos t}$$

$$=4\pi\int_0^{\pi}\frac{dt}{a^2(1+\cos t)+b^2(1-\cos t)}$$

$$=4\pi\int_0^{\pi}\frac{dt}{2a^2\cos^2\frac{t}{2}+2b^2\sin^2\frac{t}{2}}$$

$$=2\pi\int_0^{\pi/2}\frac{\sec^2\frac{t}{2}dt}{a^2+b^2\tan^2\frac{t}{2}}+2\pi\int_{\pi/2}^{\pi}\frac{\sec^2\frac{t}{2}}{a^2+b^2\tan^2\frac{t}{2}}dt$$

$$=2\pi\int_0^{\infty}\frac{2du}{a^2+b^2u^2}+2\pi\int_{-\infty}^{0}\frac{2du}{a^2+b^2u^2}$$

$$=4\pi\int_0^{\infty}\frac{du}{a^2+b^2u^2}+4\pi\int_{-\infty}^{0}\frac{du}{a^2+b^2u^2}$$

$$=4\pi\frac{1}{ab}\left[\tan^{-1}\left(\frac{bu}{a}\right)\right]_0^{\infty}+\frac{4\pi}{ab}\left[\tan^{-1}\left(\frac{bu}{a}\right)\right]_{-\infty}^{0}$$

$$=\frac{4\pi}{ab}\left[\frac{\pi}{2}\right]+\frac{4\pi}{ab}\left[0-\left(\frac{-\pi}{2}\right)\right]=\frac{4\pi^2}{ab}$$

6. $I=\int_0^{\pi}\left|\sqrt{3}\sin x+\cos x\right|dx$

$$\Rightarrow \quad I=\int_0^{\pi}2\left|\frac{\sqrt{3}}{2}\sin x+\frac{1}{2}\cos x\right|dx$$

$$\Rightarrow \quad I=2\int_0^{\pi}\left|\sin x\cos\frac{\pi}{6}+\cos x\sin\frac{\pi}{6}\right|dx$$

$$\Rightarrow \quad I=2\int_0^{\pi}\left|\sin\left(x+\frac{\pi}{6}\right)\right|dx$$

Put $x+\frac{\pi}{6}=t \quad \Rightarrow \quad dx=dt$

$$\Rightarrow \quad I=2\int_{\pi/6}^{7\pi/6}|\sin t|\,dt$$

$$\Rightarrow \quad I=2\int_{\pi/6}^{\pi}\sin t\,dt+2\int_{\pi}^{7\pi/6}-\sin t\,dt$$

$$\Rightarrow \quad I=-2[\cos t]_{\pi/6}^{\pi}+2[\cos t]_{\pi}^{7\pi/6}$$

$$\Rightarrow \quad I=-2\left[-1-\frac{\sqrt{3}}{2}\right]+2\left[-\frac{\sqrt{3}}{2}+1\right]$$

$$\Rightarrow \quad I=4$$

7. $I=\int_{-5}^{55}e^{\{x\}}dx \quad (\because e^{\{x\}}\text{is Periodic with Period }1)$

$$=60\int_0^1 e^{\{x\}}dx=60\int_0^1 e^x dx=60(e-1)$$

8. $\int_{-\frac{52}{3}\pi}^{-12\pi}\left\{\cos^{-1}(\cos 4x)+|\sin x|-|\cos x|\right\}dx$

Replacing x by −x, we get

$$I=-\int_{-\frac{52}{3}\pi}^{12\pi}\left\{\cos^{-1}(\cos 4x)+|\sin x|-|\cos x|\right\}dx$$

$$=\int_{12\pi}^{\frac{52}{3}\pi}\left\{\cos^{-1}(\cos 4x)+|\sin x|-|\cos x|\right\}dx$$

Integrand is Periodic with period π

$$\therefore \quad I=\int_{12\pi}^{17\pi}\left\{\cos^{-1}(\cos 4x)+|\sin x|-|\cos x|\right\}dx+I$$

$$=\int_{12\pi}^{17\pi+\frac{\pi}{3}}\left\{\cos^{-1}(\cos 4x)+|\sin x|-|\cos x|\right\}dx$$

$$\Rightarrow \quad I=5\int_0^{\pi}\left\{\left(\cos^{-1}(\cos 4x)\right)+|\sin x+\cos x|\right\}dx+\int_0^{\pi/3}\left\{\cos^{-1}(\cos 4x)+|\sin x-\cos x|\right\}dx$$

$$\Rightarrow \quad I=5\int_0^{\pi}\left\{\cos^{-1}(\cos 4x)+\sqrt{2}\left|\sin\left(x+\frac{\pi}{4}\right)\right|\right\}dx+\int_0^{\pi/3}\left\{\cos^{-1}(\cos 4x)+\sqrt{2}\left|\cos\left(x+\frac{\pi}{4}\right)\right|\right\}dx$$

$=\cos^{-1}(\cos 4x)$ is periodic with period $\frac{\pi}{2}$

$$\therefore \quad I=10\int_0^{\pi/2}\cos^{-1}(\cos 4x)dx+\int_0^{\pi/3}\cos^{-1}(\cos 4x)dx+5\sqrt{2}\int_0^{3\pi/4}\sin\left(x+\frac{\pi}{4}\right)dx$$

$$-5\sqrt{2}\int_{3\pi/4}^{\pi}\sin\left(x+\frac{\pi}{4}\right)dx+\sqrt{2}\int_0^{\pi/4}\cos\left(x+\frac{\pi}{4}\right)dx-\sqrt{2}\int_{\pi/4}^{\pi/3}\cos\left(x+\frac{\pi}{4}\right)dx$$

$$=20\int_0^{\pi/4}4x\,dx+\int_0^{\pi/4}4x\,dx+\int_{\pi/4}^{\pi/3}(-4x+2\pi)dx-5\sqrt{2}\left[\cos\left(x+\frac{\pi}{4}\right)\right]_0^{3\pi/4}$$

$$+5\sqrt{2}\left[\cos\left(x+\frac{\pi}{4}\right)\right]_{3\pi/4}^{\pi}+\sqrt{2}\left[\sin\left(x+\frac{\pi}{4}\right)\right]_0^{\pi/4}-\sqrt{2}\left[\sin\left(x+\frac{\pi}{4}\right)\right]_{\pi/4}^{\pi/3}$$

$$=\frac{97}{36}\pi^2+12\sqrt{2}-\frac{\sqrt{3}}{2}-\frac{3}{2}$$

9. $I=\int_{\pi/3}^{17\pi/3}\frac{|\sin^{-1}(\sin x)|+(\cos^{-1}(\cos 2x))}{\sin^{-1}(\sin x)+\cos^{-1}(\sin x)}dx$

$\because\ \sin^{-1}(\sin x)+\cos^{-1}(\sin x)=\frac{\pi}{2}$

$\therefore\ I=\frac{2}{\pi}\int_{\pi/3}^{17\pi/3}\{|\sin^{-1}(\sin x)|+(\cos^{-1}(\cos 2x))\}dx$

$\Rightarrow\ I=\frac{2}{\pi}\times 5\int_0^{\pi}|\sin^{-1}(\sin x)|dx\ +\frac{2}{\pi}\int_{\pi/3}^{17\pi/3}\cos^{-1}(\cos 2x)dx$

$+\frac{2}{\pi}\int_{\pi/3}^{2\pi/3}x\,dx$

$=\frac{20}{\pi}\int_0^{\pi/2}x\,dx+\frac{2}{\pi}\times 5\int_0^{\pi}\cos^{-1}(\cos 2x)dx\ +\frac{2}{\pi}\int_{\pi/3}^{2\pi/3}x\,dx$

$+\frac{2}{\pi}\int_{\pi/3}^{2\pi/3}\cos^{-1}(\cos 2x)dx$

$=\frac{10}{\pi}\left[\frac{\pi^2}{4}\right]+\frac{10}{\pi}\times 2\int_0^{\pi/2}\cos^{-1}(\cos 2x)dx$

$+\frac{1}{\pi}\left[\frac{\pi^2}{3}\right]+\frac{2}{\pi}\left[\frac{\pi^2}{3}\right]$

$=\frac{5}{2}\pi+\frac{20}{\pi}\left[\frac{\pi^2}{4}\right]+\frac{\pi}{3}+\frac{2\pi}{3}$

$=\frac{5}{2}\pi+5\pi+\pi=6\pi+\frac{5}{2}\pi=\frac{17}{2}\pi$

10. $I=\int_{\pi/2}^{\frac{43\pi}{2}}\cos^{-1}(\sin x)dx=\int_{\pi/2}^{43\pi/2}\cos^{-1}\left(\cos\left(\frac{\pi}{2}-x\right)\right)dx$

Put $\frac{\pi}{2}-x=t \quad\Rightarrow\quad dx=-dt$

$\therefore\ I=\int_0^{-21\pi}\cos^{-1}(\cos t)(-dt)$ (Replacing t by $-t$)

$=\int_0^{21\pi}\cos^{-1}(\cos t)dt$

$=10\int_0^{2\pi}\cos^{-1}(\cos t)dt+\int_0^{\pi}t\,dt$

$=10\times 2\int_0^{\pi}\cos^{-1}(\cos t)dt+\int_0^{\pi}t\,dt$

$=20\frac{\pi^2}{2}+\frac{\pi^2}{2}=\frac{21}{2}\pi^2$

11. $I_1=\int_{k\pi}^{(k+1)\pi}\frac{|\sin 2x|}{|\sin x|+|\cos x|}dx; k\in\mathbb{N}$ and

$I_2=\int_0^{\pi/4}\frac{dx}{\sin x+\cos x}dx$

Here $I_1=(k+1-k)\int_0^{\pi}\frac{|\sin 2x|}{|\sin x|+|\cos x|}dx$ (as integrand is periodic with period π)

$\Rightarrow\ I_1=2\int_0^{\pi/2}\frac{|\sin 2x|}{|\sin x|+|\cos x|}dx \qquad (\because f(2a-x)=f(x))$

$\Rightarrow\ I_1=2\int_0^{\pi/2}\frac{\sin 2x}{\sin x+\cos x}dx$

This proves the first part, now I_1+4I_2

$=2\int_0^{\pi/2}\frac{\sin 2x}{\sin x+\cos x}dx+4\int_0^{\pi/4}\frac{1dx}{\sin x+\cos x}$

$\left(\because 2\int_0^{\pi/2}\frac{1}{\sin x+\cos x}dx=4\int_0^{\pi/4}\frac{1}{\sin x+\cos x}\right)$

$\Rightarrow\ I_1+4I_2=2\int_0^{\pi/2}\frac{\sin 2x}{\sin x+\cos x}dx\ +2\int_0^{\pi/2}\frac{1}{\sin x+\cos x}dx$

$=2\int_0^{\pi/2}\frac{\sin 2x+2}{\sin x+\cos x}dx$

$=2\int_0^{\pi/2}\frac{(\sin x+\cos x)^2}{(\sin x+\cos x)}dx\ =2\int_0^{\pi}(\sin x+\cos x)dx$

$=2[\sin x-\cos x]_0^{\pi/2}\ =2[(1-0)-(0-1)]=4$

TEXTUAL EXERCISE–7: (OBJECTIVE)

1. (c) $I=\int_0^{1000}e^{x-[x]}dx=\int_0^{1000}e^{\{x\}}dx$

$=1000\int_0^1 e^{\{x\}}dx=1000\int_0^1 e^x dx\ =1000(e-1)$

2. (c) $P=\int_0^{3\pi}f(\cos^2 x)dx$ and $Q=\int_0^{\pi}f(\cos^2 x)dx$

Clearly $P=3\int_0^{\pi}f(\cos^2 x)dx=3Q$

$\Rightarrow\ P-3Q=0$

3. (d) $I=\int_0^{2\pi}[|\sin x|+|\cos x|]dx\ =4\int_0^{\pi/2}[|\sin x|+|\cos x|]dx$

$=4\int_0^{\pi/2}[\sin x+\cos x]dx$

$=4\int_0^{\pi/2}\left[\sqrt{2}\sin\left(x+\frac{\pi}{4}\right)\right]dx=4\int_0^{\pi/2}1dx$

$\left[\because \text{for } x\in\left[0,\frac{\pi}{2}\right] \text{ integrand } \in\left[1,\sqrt{2}\right]\right]$

$=4\frac{\pi}{2}=2\pi$

4. (b) $I=\int_{-2\pi}^{5\pi}\cot^{-1}(\tan x)dx\ =\int_{-2\pi}^{5\pi}\cot^{-1}\left(\cot\left(\frac{\pi}{2}-x\right)\right)dx$

Put $\frac{\pi}{2}-x=t \qquad\Rightarrow\quad dx=-dt$

$\therefore\ I=\int_{\frac{5\pi}{2}}^{\frac{9\pi}{2}}\cot^{-1}(\cot(t))(-dt)\ =\int_{-9\pi/2}^{5\pi/2}\cot^{-1}(\cot t)dt$

$=7\int_0^{\pi}\cot^{-1}(\cot t)dt\ =7\int_0^{\pi}t\,dt=\frac{7}{2}\pi^2$

5. (c) $I=\int_{-1}^{3}\{|x-2|+[x]\}dx\ \ =\int_{-1}^{2}(-x+2)dx+\int_2^3(x-2)dx$

$+\int_1^0(-1)dx+\int_0^1 0dx+\int_1^2 1dx+\int_2^3 2dx$

$=-\frac{1}{2}(3)+2(3)+\frac{1}{2}(5)-2(1)-(1)+(2-1)+2(3-2)$

$=\frac{-3}{2}+6+\frac{5}{2}-3+3=7$

6. (a) $\mathrm{I}=\int_{-1}^{3}\left(|x|+|x-1|\right)dx$

$$=\int_{-1}^{0}-x dx+\int_{0}^{3}x dx+\int_{-1}^{1}(-x+1)dx+\int_{1}^{3}(x-1)dx$$

$$=\frac{-1}{2}[0-1]+\frac{1}{2}[9-0]+2+\frac{1}{2}(8)-(2)$$

$$=\frac{1}{2}+\frac{9}{2}+2+4-2=9$$

7. (b) $\mathrm{I}=\int_{-1}^{1}\frac{d}{dx}\left(\tan^{-1}\frac{1}{x}\right)dx=\int_{-1}^{0}\frac{d}{dx}\left(\tan^{-1}\frac{1}{x}\right)dx$

$$+\int_{0}^{1}\frac{d}{dx}\left(\tan^{-1}\frac{1}{x}\right)dx$$

$$=\int_{-1}^{0}\frac{1}{\left(1+\frac{1}{x^2}\right)}\left(\frac{-1}{x^2}\right)dx+\int_{0}^{1}\left(\frac{1}{1+\frac{1}{x^2}}\right)\left(\frac{-1}{x^2}\right)dx$$

$$=\int_{0}^{-1}\frac{1}{x^2+1}dx-\int_{0}^{1}\frac{1}{1+x^2}dx$$

$$=\int_{0}^{1}\frac{-dx}{x^2+1}-\int_{0}^{1}\frac{dx}{1+x^2}=-2\left[\tan^{-1}x\right]=-2\left[\tan^{-1}1\right]=-\frac{\pi}{2}$$

8. (b) $\mathrm{I}=\int_{0}^{100\pi}\sqrt{1-\cos 2x}\,dx=\int_{0}^{100\pi}\sqrt{2\sin^2 x}\,dx$

$$=\int_{0}^{100}\sqrt{2}|\sin x|dx=\sqrt{2}(100)\int_{0}^{\pi}|\sin x|dx$$

$$=\left(\sqrt{2}\right)(100)\int_{0}^{\pi}(\sin x)dx \qquad =100\sqrt{2}\left[-\cos x\right]_{0}^{\pi}$$

$$=-100\sqrt{2}[-1-1]=200\sqrt{2}$$

9. (d) $\left\{\int_{a+2T}^{b+2T}f(x)dx-\int_{a}^{b}f(x)dx\right\}=\int_{a}^{b}f(x)dx-\int_{a}^{b}f(x)dx=0$

10. (d) $\mathrm{I}=\int_{0}^{1}|\sin 2\pi x|dx=2\int_{0}^{1/2}|\sin 2\pi x|dx=2\int_{0}^{1/2}(\sin 2\pi x)dx$

$$=\frac{-2}{2\pi}\left[\cos 2\pi x\right]_{0}^{1/2}=\frac{-2}{2\pi}[-1-1]=\frac{4}{2\pi}=\frac{2}{\pi}$$

11. (c) $f(x+1)+f(x+7)=0\ \forall x\in\mathbb{R}$

$\int_{a}^{a+t}f(x)dx$ will be independent of a if t is the period of $f(x)$

Now $f(x+1)=-f(x+7)$

Replacing x by $x-1$, we get $f(x)=-f(x+6)$

$\Rightarrow\ f(x)=-\left[-f(x+6+6)\right]$

$\Rightarrow\ f(x)=f(x+12)$

$\Rightarrow\ f(x)$ is periodic with period 12. Hence possible value t is 12

12. (b) $f(x+k)=f(x)\ \forall x\in\mathbb{R}$

$\Rightarrow\ f(x)$ is periodic with period 'k'

$\therefore\ \int_{a}^{a+k}f(x)dx=\int_{0}^{k}f(x)dx$ which is independent of 'a' and depends only on 'k'.

13. (b) $\mathrm{I}=\int_{-\pi/3}^{13\pi/4}\sqrt{\cot^{-1}(\cot x)}dx=\int_{-\pi/3}^{0}\sqrt{\cot^{-1}(\cot x)}dx$

$$+\int_{0}^{3\pi}\sqrt{\cot^{-1}(\cot x)}dx+\int_{3\pi}^{3\pi+\frac{\pi}{4}}\sqrt{\cot^{-1}(\cot x)}dx$$

$$=\int_{-\pi}^{0}\sqrt{\cot^{-1}(\cot x)}dx-\int_{0}^{2\pi/3}\sqrt{\cot^{-1}(\cot x)}dx$$

$$+3\int_{0}^{\pi}\sqrt{\cot^{-1}(\cot x)}dx+\int_{0}^{\pi/4}\sqrt{\cot^{-1}(\cot x)}dx$$

$$=4\int_{0}^{\pi}\sqrt{x}+\int_{0}^{\pi/4}\sqrt{x}\,dx-\int_{0}^{2\pi/3}\sqrt{x}\,dx$$

$$=4\left|\frac{\frac{x^3}{2}}{\frac{3}{2}}\right|_{0}^{\pi}+\left|\frac{\frac{x^3}{2}}{\frac{3}{2}}\right|_{0}^{\pi/4}-\left|\frac{\frac{x^3}{2}}{\frac{3}{2}}\right|_{0}^{2\pi/3}$$

$$=4\left(\frac{2}{3}\right)\left[\pi^{3/2}\right]+\frac{2}{3}\left|\left(\frac{\pi}{4}\right)^{3/2}\right|-\frac{2}{3}\left|\left(\frac{2\pi}{3}\right)^{3/2}\right|$$

$$=\left[\frac{8}{3}+\frac{2}{3(8)}-\frac{2}{3}\left(\frac{2}{3}\right)^{3/2}\right](\pi)^{3/2}$$

$$=\left[\frac{64+2}{24}-\left(\frac{2}{3}\right)^{5/2}\right](\pi)^{3/2}=\left[\frac{33}{12}-\left(\frac{2}{3}\right)\left(\frac{2}{3}\right)^{3/2}\right](\pi)^{3/2}$$

$$=\frac{2}{3}\left[\frac{33}{8}-\left(\frac{2}{3}\right)^{3/2}\right](\pi)^{3/2}$$

TEXTUAL EXERCISE–8: (SUBJECTIVE)

1. $\mathrm{I}_1=\int_{0}^{1}x^5e^x dx,\ \mathrm{I}_2=\int_{0}^{1}x^3e^x dx,\ \mathrm{I}_3=\int_{0}^{1}x^{10}e^x dx,$

$\mathrm{I}_4=\int_{0}^{1}x^{13}.e^x dx$

For $x\in(0,1), x^{13}<x^{10}<x^5<x^3$ and $e^x>0$

$\Rightarrow\ x^{13}e^x<x^{10}e^x<x^5e^x<x^3e^x$

$\Rightarrow\ \mathrm{I}_4<\mathrm{I}_3<\mathrm{I}_1<\mathrm{I}_2$

$\therefore$ Greatest $=I_2$, Least $=I_4$

2. Consider $g(x)=\frac{1}{1+x},\ f(x)=\frac{1}{\sqrt{1+x^6}},\ h(x)=\frac{1}{\sqrt{1-x^2}}$

Now For $x\in(0,1);\ 1>x>x^6>0$

$\Rightarrow\ 2>1+x>1+x^6>\sqrt{1+x^6}$

$\Rightarrow\ 2>(1+x)>\sqrt{1+x^6}>0$

$\Rightarrow\ 0<\frac{1}{(1+x)}<\frac{1}{\sqrt{1+x^6}}$

$\Rightarrow\ 0<g(x)<f(x)$ ...(1)

Also for $x\in(0,1),\ -1<-x^2<0<x^6$

$\Rightarrow\ 0<\sqrt{1-x^2}<1<\sqrt{1+x^6}$

$\Rightarrow\ 0<\frac{1}{\sqrt{1-x^2}}>\frac{1}{\sqrt{1+x^6}}$ ...(2)

$\therefore$ Combining (1) & (2), we get $\frac{1}{1+x}<\frac{1}{\sqrt{1+x^6}}<\frac{1}{\sqrt{1-x^2}}$

i.e., $g(x)<f(x)<h(x)$ for $x\in(0,1)$

$\Rightarrow \int_0^1 \frac{1}{1+x}dx < \int_0^1 \frac{1}{\sqrt{1+x^6}}dx < \int_0^1 \frac{1}{\sqrt{1-x^2}}dx$

$\Rightarrow |\ln(1+x)|_0^1 < \int_0^1 \frac{1}{\sqrt{1+x^6}}dx < |\sin^{-1}x|_0^1$

$\Rightarrow \ln 2 < \int_0^1 \frac{1}{\sqrt{1+x^6}}dx < \frac{\pi}{2}$

3. Let $g(x) = \frac{1}{\sqrt{1+x^2}}, f(x) = \frac{1}{\sqrt{1+x^6}}$ and $h(x) = \frac{1}{\sqrt{1-x^2}}; x \in (0,1)$ then, clearly

$1+x^2 > 1+x^6 > 1-x^2 > 0$

$\Rightarrow \sqrt{1+x^2} > \sqrt{1+x^6} > \sqrt{1-x^2}$

$\Rightarrow \frac{1}{\sqrt{1+x^2}} < \frac{1}{\sqrt{1+x^6}} > \frac{1}{\sqrt{1-x^2}}$

$\Rightarrow \int_0^1 \frac{1}{\sqrt{1+x^2}}dx < \int_0^1 \frac{1}{\sqrt{1+x^6}}dx < \int_0^1 \frac{1}{\sqrt{1-x^2}}dx$

$\Rightarrow \left[\ln\left|x+\sqrt{x^2+1}\right|\right]_0^1 < \int_0^1 \frac{1}{\sqrt{1+x^6}}dx < \left[\sin^{-1}x\right]_0^1$

$\Rightarrow \ln\left(1+\sqrt{2}\right) < \int_0^1 \frac{1}{\sqrt{1+x^6}}dx < \frac{\pi}{2}$

4. (a) $f(x) = \frac{\sin x}{x} \downarrow$ as x increases from 0 to $\frac{\pi}{2}$

$\therefore \frac{\sin x}{x} \uparrow$ as $x \to 0^+ \quad \Rightarrow \quad f\left(\frac{\pi}{2}\right) < f(x) < f\left(0^+\right)$

$\Rightarrow \frac{2}{\pi} < \frac{\sin x}{x} < 1$

$\Rightarrow \frac{2}{\pi}\int_0^{\pi/2} 1dx < \int_0^{\pi/2} \frac{\sin x}{x}dx < \int_0^{\pi/2} 1dx$

$\Rightarrow \frac{2}{\pi}\left(\frac{\pi}{2}\right) < \int_0^{\pi/2} \frac{\sin x}{x}dx < \frac{\pi}{2}$

$\Rightarrow 1 < \int_0^{\pi/2} \frac{\sin x}{x}dx < \frac{\pi}{2}$

(b) Let $f(x) = \frac{x}{x^3+16}$

$\Rightarrow f'(x) = \frac{\left(x^3+16\right).(1) - x\left(3x^2+0\right)}{\left(x^3+16\right)^2}$

$\Rightarrow f'(x) = \frac{x^3+16-3x^3}{\left(x^3+16\right)^2} = \frac{16-2x^3}{\left(x^3+16\right)^2}$

$\Rightarrow f'(x) = \frac{2\left(8-x^3\right)}{\left(x^3+16\right)^2} > 0$ for $x \in (0,1)$

$\Rightarrow f(x)$ is an increasing function,

$\Rightarrow (1-0)f(0) < \int_x^1 \frac{x}{x^3+16}dx < (1-0)f(1)$

$\Rightarrow 0 < \int_0^1 \frac{x}{x^3+16}dx < \frac{1}{17}$

(c) For $x \in (0,1), e^{x^2}$ is increasing

$\Rightarrow e^0 < e^{x^2} < e$

$\Rightarrow \int_0^1 1dx < \int_0^1 e^{x^2}dx < \int_0^1 e\,dx$

$\Rightarrow 1 < \int_0^1 e^{x^2}dx < e$

5. Clearly $-|f(x)| \le f(x) \le |f(x)| \forall x \in (a,b)$

$\therefore$ By sand witch theorem

$\int_a^b -|f(x)|dx \le \int_a^b f(x)dx \le \int_a^b |f(x)|dx$ and

$\int_a^b |f(x)|dx \ge 0$

$\Rightarrow \left|\int_a^b f(x)dx\right| \le \int_a^b |f(x)|dx$

6. Let $f(x) = (3+x^3)^{1/2}$

$\Rightarrow f'(x) = \frac{1}{2}(3x^2).\frac{1}{\sqrt{3+x^3}}$

$\Rightarrow f'(x) = \frac{3x^2}{2\sqrt{3+x^3}} > 0 \ \forall x \in (1,3)$

$\Rightarrow (b-a)\left(f(a)\right) < \int_a^b f(x)dx < (b-a)f(b)$

where $a = 1, b = 3$

$\Rightarrow (2)\ f(1) < \int_1^3 f(x)dx < 2f(3)$

$\Rightarrow 2(2) < \int_1^3 f(x)dx < 2\left(\sqrt{30}\right)$, i.e., $\int_1^3 f(x)dx \in \left(4, 2\sqrt{30}\right)$

7. (a) $I = \int_0^\infty \frac{\sin ax}{x}dx;$

Put $ax = t \quad \Rightarrow \quad dx = dt/a$

$\therefore I = \int_0^\infty \frac{\sin t}{t/a} \times \frac{dt}{a}$ for $a > 0$, i.e., $I = \int_0^\infty \frac{\sin t}{t}dt$; for $a > 0$

$\Rightarrow I = \frac{\pi}{2}$ and $I = \int_0^{-\infty} \frac{\sin t}{t}dt$, for $a < 0$

Replacing t by $-u \quad \Rightarrow \quad dt = -du$

$\therefore I = \int_0^\infty \frac{\sin(-u)}{-u}(-du) = -\int_0^\infty \frac{\sin u}{u}du = -\frac{\pi}{2}$

$\therefore I = \frac{\pi}{2}$ for $a > 0$, $\frac{-\pi}{2}$ for $a < 2$

(b) Let $I = \int_0^\infty \left(\frac{\sin x}{x}\right)^2 dx$

$= \left|(\sin x)^2\right| \left|\int x^{-2}dx - \int_0^\infty \left((2\sin x\cos x)\int x^{-2}dx\right)\right.$

$= \left|\sin^2 x\left(\frac{-1}{x}\right)\right|_0^\infty - \int_0^\infty (\sin 2x)\left(\frac{-1}{x}\right)dx$

$= -\left[\lim_{x\to\infty}\frac{\sin^2}{x^2} - \lim_{x\to 0}\frac{\sin^2 x}{x}\right] + \int_0^\infty \frac{\sin x}{x}dx$

$= -[0-(0)(1)] + \frac{\pi}{2}$ (By part (a)) $= \frac{\pi}{2}$

8. (a) Clearly, the area of rectangle ABCD $\le$ area under the curve DFC $\le$ area of trapezium ABCD.

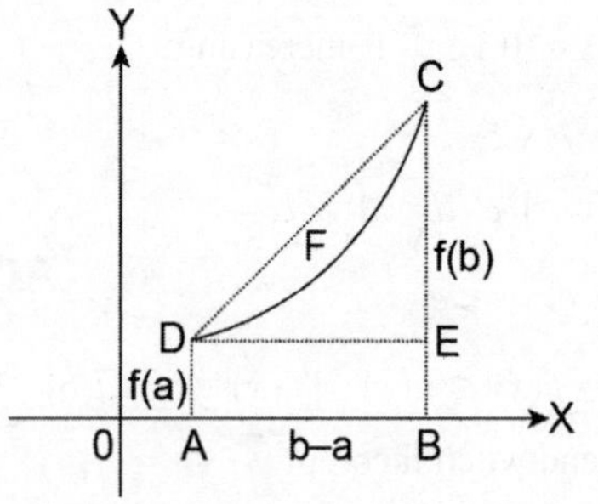

$\Rightarrow\ (b-a)f(a)\le\int_a^b f(x)dx\le\frac{1}{2}(b-a)[f(a)+f(b)]$

For $f(x)$ increasing and concave downwards

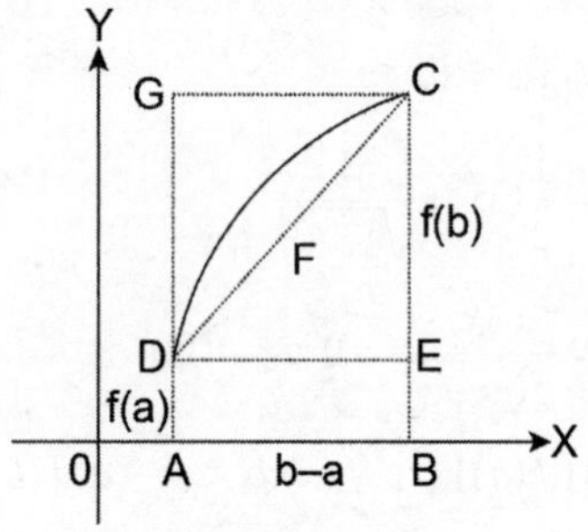

Clearly, the area of trapezium $ABCD\le$ area under the curve $DFC\le$ area of rectangle $ABCG$

$\Rightarrow\ \frac{1}{2}(b-a)[f(a)+f(b)]\le\int_a^b f(x)dx$

(b) Let $f(x)=\frac{\sin x}{x}$ we know that $\frac{\sin x}{x}$ is a decreasing function with its concavity downwards in $\left(0,\frac{\pi}{2}\right)$.

$\Rightarrow\ \frac{1}{2}\left[\frac{\pi}{2}-0\right]\left(f(0^+)+f\left(\frac{\pi}{2}\right)\right)$

$\le\int_0^{\pi/2}\frac{\sin x}{x}dx\le\left(\frac{\pi}{2}-0\right).f\left(\frac{\pi}{2}\right)$

$\Rightarrow\ \frac{1}{2}\left(\frac{\pi}{2}\right)\left(1+\frac{2}{\pi}\right)\le\int_0^{\pi/2}\frac{\sin x}{x}dx\le1$

$\Rightarrow\ \int_0^{\pi/2}\frac{\sin x}{x}dx\in\left[\left(\frac{\pi}{4}+\frac{1}{2}\right),1\right]$ i.e., $\left[\frac{(\pi+2)}{4},1\right]$

Let $g(x)=e^{x^2}$

$\Rightarrow\ g'(x)=2xe^{x^2}>0\ \forall x\in(0,1)$

$\Rightarrow\ g'(x)=4x^2e^{x^2}+2e^{x^2}>0\ \forall x\in(0,1)$

$\Rightarrow\ g(x)$ is increasing function, with its concavity upwards.

$\therefore\ (1-0)g(0)\le\int_0^1 e^{x^2}dx\le\frac{1}{2}(1-0)[g(0)+g(1)]$

$\Rightarrow\ 1\le\int_0^1 e^{x^2}dx\le\frac{1}{2}[1+e]$

Thus, $\int_0^1 e^{x^2}dx\in\left[1,\frac{(e+1)}{2}\right]$

9. By Schwartz-Bunyakovsky inequality, $\left|\int_0^1\sqrt{1+x}.\sqrt{1+x^3}dx\right|$ $\le\sqrt{\int_0^1(1+x)dx\int_0^1(1+x^3)dx}$

$\Rightarrow\ \left|\int_0^1\sqrt{(1+x)(1+x^3)}dx\right|\le\sqrt{\left[x+\frac{x^2}{2}\right]_0^1\left[x+\frac{x^4}{4}\right]_0^1}$

$\Rightarrow\ \int_0^1\sqrt{(1+x)(1+x^3)}dx\le\sqrt{\left(\frac{3}{2}\right)\left(\frac{5}{4}\right)}=\sqrt{\frac{15}{8}}$

10. $f(x)=x(x-1);\ 0\le x\le1$ …. (i) and $f(x+1)=f(x)\ \forall x\in\mathbb{R}$,

$\because\ |f(x)|$ is periodic with period, 1

$\therefore\ \int_2^4|f(x)|dx=2\int_0^1|f(x)|dx$

$=2\int_0^1|x(x-1)|dx=-2\int_0^1 x(x-1)dx$

$=-2\left[\frac{x^3}{3}-\frac{x^2}{2}\right]_0^1=2\left[\frac{1}{2}-\frac{1}{3}\right]=2\left[\frac{3-2}{6}\right]=\frac{1}{3}$

11. Let $x_0\in[a,b]$ and $\lim_{x\to x0}f(x)-f(x_0)=L$ (say), then

$|L|=\lim_{x\to x0}|f(x)-f(x_0)|\le\lim_{x\to x0}|x-x_0|=0$

$\Rightarrow\ |L|\le0$, But $|L|\ge0$

$\Rightarrow\ |L|=0\qquad\Rightarrow\ L=0$

$\Rightarrow\ \lim_{x\to x_0}f(x)=f(x_0)$

$\Rightarrow\ f(x)$ is continuous at $x=x_0\ \forall\ x_0\in[a,b]$

$\Rightarrow\ f(x)$ is a continuous function on $[a,b]$

12. For $x\in(0,1)$; $1>x^2>x^5>0$

$\Rightarrow\ 1<x^2-x^5>0\qquad\Rightarrow\ -1<(x^2-x^5)<0$

$\Rightarrow\ 3<4-(x^2-x^5)<4\ \Rightarrow\ 3<4-x^2+x^5<4$

$\Rightarrow\ \sqrt{4-x^2+x^5}<2\qquad\Rightarrow\ \frac{1}{\sqrt{4-x^2+x^5}}>\frac{1}{2}$ …(1)

Also, $0<4-x^2<4-x^2+x^5$

$\Rightarrow\ \sqrt{4-x^2}<\sqrt{4-x^2+x^5}$

$\Rightarrow\ \frac{1}{\sqrt{4-x^2}}>\frac{1}{\sqrt{4-x^2+x^5}}$ …(2)

$\therefore$ From (1) and (2), we get $\frac{1}{2}<\frac{1}{\sqrt{4-x^2+x^5}}<\frac{1}{\sqrt{4-x^2}}$ for $x\in(0,1)$

$\Rightarrow\ \int_0^1\frac{1}{2}dx<\int_0^1\frac{1}{\sqrt{4-x^2+x^5}}dx<\int_0^1\frac{1}{\sqrt{4-x^2}}$

$\Rightarrow\ \frac{1}{2}<\int_0^1\frac{1}{\sqrt{4-x^2+x^5}}dx<\left[\sin^{-1}\left(\frac{x}{2}\right)\right]_0^1$

$\Rightarrow\ \frac{1}{2}<\int_0^1\frac{1}{\sqrt{4-x^2+x^5}}dx<\frac{\pi}{6}$

13. **(a)** For $x\in\left(\frac{\pi}{4},\frac{\pi}{2}\right)$

$(\sin x)^{10}$ is an increasing function

$\Rightarrow\ \left(\sin\frac{\pi}{4}\right)^{10}<(\sin x)^{10}<\left(\sin\frac{\pi}{2}\right)\forall x\in\left(\frac{\pi}{4},\frac{\pi}{2}\right)$

$\Rightarrow\ \frac{1}{32}<(\sin x)^{10}<1\ \forall x\in\left(\frac{\pi}{4},\frac{\pi}{2}\right)$

$$\Rightarrow \frac{1}{32}\int_{\pi/4}^{\pi/2} 1dx < \int_{\pi/4}^{\pi/2}(\sin x)^{10}dx < \int_{\pi/4}^{\pi/2} 1dx$$

$$\Rightarrow \frac{1}{32}\left(\frac{\pi}{2}-\frac{\pi}{4}\right) < \int_{\pi/4}^{\pi/2}(\sin x)^{10}dx < \left(\frac{\pi}{2}-\frac{\pi}{4}\right)$$

$$\Rightarrow \frac{\pi}{128} < \int_{\pi/4}^{\pi/2}(\sin x)^{10}dx < \frac{\pi}{4}$$

(b) $f(x) = \frac{1}{2+\ln x}; x \in (1, e)$

$$\Rightarrow f'(x) = \frac{-1}{(2+\ln x)^2}\left(\frac{1}{x}\right) = \frac{-1}{x(2+\ln x)^2} < 0 \ \forall x \in (1, e)$$

$$\Rightarrow f(e) < f(x) < f(1) \quad \Rightarrow \frac{1}{3} < \frac{1}{2+\ln x} < \frac{1}{2}$$

$$\Rightarrow \frac{1}{3}\int_1^e 1dx < \int_1^e \frac{1}{2+\ln x}dx < \int_1^e \frac{1}{2}dx$$

$$\Rightarrow \frac{1}{3}(e-1) < \int_1^e \frac{1}{2+\ln x}dx, \frac{1}{2}(e-1)$$

TEXTUAL EXERCISE–8: (OBJECTIVE)

1. (a) $I = \int_0^{\pi/2} \frac{\sin x}{x}dx$

For $x \in \left(0, \frac{\pi}{2}\right); \frac{\sin x}{x}$ is a decreasing function and $\frac{\sin x}{x} \to 1$ as $x \to 0^+$

$$\Rightarrow f\left(\frac{\pi}{2}\right) < \frac{\sin x}{x} < f(0^+)$$

$$\Rightarrow \frac{2}{\pi} < \frac{\sin x}{x} < 1$$

$$\Rightarrow \int_0^{\pi/2}\frac{\sin x}{x}dx < \int_0^{\pi/2} 1dx$$

$$\Rightarrow \int_0^{\pi/2}\frac{\sin x}{x}dx < \frac{\pi}{2}$$

2. (a) $I_1 = \int_e^{e^2}\frac{dx}{\ln x}$

Put $\ln x = t \quad \Rightarrow \frac{1}{x}dx = dt$

$\Rightarrow dx = x\,dt = e^t dt \quad \therefore I_1 = \int_1^2 \frac{e^t dt}{t} = I_2$

3. (b) $I_1 = \int_1^2 \frac{dx}{\sqrt{1+x^2}}, I_2 = \int_1^2 \frac{dx}{x}$

For $x \in (1, 2)$

$1 + x^2 \quad \Rightarrow \sqrt{1+x^2} > \sqrt{x^2}$

$\Rightarrow \sqrt{1+x^2} > x \quad \Rightarrow \frac{1}{\sqrt{1+x^2}} < \frac{1}{x}$

$$\Rightarrow \int_1^2 \frac{1}{\sqrt{1+x^2}}dx < \int_1^2 \frac{1}{x}dx$$

$\Rightarrow I_1 < I_2$

4. (b) $x \in [10, 19]$;

$\Rightarrow x^a \in [10^a, 19^a]$

$\Rightarrow 1 + x^a \in [1 + 10^a, 1 + 19^a]$

$$\Rightarrow \frac{1}{1+x^a} \in \left[\frac{1}{1+19^a}, \frac{1}{1+10^a}\right]$$

Also $|\sin x| \le 1$

$$\Rightarrow \frac{\sin x}{1+x^a} \le \frac{1}{1+10^a}$$

$$\Rightarrow \int_{10}^{19}\frac{\sin x}{1+x^a}dx \le \int_{10}^{19}\frac{1}{1+10^a}dx = \frac{9}{1+10^a}$$

Given, $\int_{10}^{19}\frac{\sin x}{1+x^a}dx < \frac{1}{9}$

$\Rightarrow \frac{9}{1+10^a} < \frac{1}{9} \quad \Rightarrow 1 + 10^a > 81$

$\Rightarrow 10^a > 80; a > 1 \quad \Rightarrow a \ge 2$

$\Rightarrow$ Minimum odd value of $a = 3$

5. (a), (b) $I = \int_0^{1/2}\frac{dx}{\sqrt{1-x^{2n}}}$, for $n \ge 1$,

For $n \ge 1$, $2n \ge 2$

Also $x \in \left(0, \frac{1}{2}\right)$

$\Rightarrow x^{2n} \le x^2$

$\Rightarrow 1 - x^{2n} \ge 1 - x^2 > 0$

$\Rightarrow \sqrt{1-x^{2n}} \ge \sqrt{1-x^2} > 0$

$$\Rightarrow \frac{1}{\sqrt{1-x^{2n}}} \le \frac{1}{\sqrt{1-x^2}}$$

$$\Rightarrow \int_0^{1/2}\frac{dx}{\sqrt{1-x^{2n}}} \le \int_0^{1/2}\frac{1}{\sqrt{1-x^2}}dx = \left[\sin^{-1}x\right]_0^{1/2} = \frac{\pi}{6} < 1$$

Also $\sqrt{1-x^{2n}} < 1$ for $x \in \left(0, \frac{1}{2}\right)$ and $n \ge 1$

$$\Rightarrow \frac{1}{\sqrt{1-x^{2n}}} > 1$$

$$\Rightarrow \int_0^{1/2}\frac{1}{\sqrt{1-x^{2n}}}dx > \int_0^{1/2} 1dx = \frac{1}{2}$$

$\therefore \frac{1}{2} < I < 1$

6. (a), (c) $\left|\frac{\sin x}{1+x^8}\right| \le \frac{1}{1+x^8}$ ...(1)

Also $x \in [10, 19]$

$\Rightarrow x^8 \in [10^8, (19)^8]$

$\Rightarrow 1 + x^8 > x^8 \ge 10^8$

$\Rightarrow \frac{1}{1+x^8} < \frac{1}{x^8} \le \frac{1}{10^8}$ ...(2)

$\therefore$ From (1) and (2), we get $\left|\frac{\sin x}{1+x^8}\right| \le \frac{1}{10^8}$

$$\Rightarrow \frac{-1}{10^8} \le \frac{\sin x}{1+x^8} \le \frac{1}{10^8}$$

$\Rightarrow \left|\int_{10}^{19} \frac{\sin x}{1+x^8}dx\right| \le \int_{10}^{19}\frac{1}{10^8}dx = \frac{9}{10^8} = \frac{10-1}{10^8} = \frac{1}{10^7} - \frac{1}{10^8}$

$= 10^{-7} - \frac{1}{10^8} < 10^{-7} < 10^{-6}$

7. (a) $\int_a^b f(x)dx = p$ and $\int_a^b |f(x)|dx = q$

$\because \quad -|f(x)| \le f(x) \le |f(x)|$

$\Rightarrow \quad -\int_a^b |f(x)|dx \le \int_a^b f(x)dx \le \int_a^b |f(x)|dx$

$\Rightarrow \quad \left|\int_a^b f(x)dx\right| \le \int_a^b |f(x)|dx$

$\Rightarrow \quad |p| \le q$

8. (a), (d) $I_1 = \int_x^1 \frac{dt}{1+t^2} = \tan^{-1}1 - \tan^{-1}x = \frac{\pi}{4} - \tan^{-1}x$ and

$I_2 = \tan^{-1}\left(\frac{1}{x}\right) - \tan^{-1}(1); x > 0$

$= \cot^{-1}x - \frac{\pi}{4} = \left(\frac{\pi}{2} - \tan^{-x}\right) - \frac{\pi}{4} = \frac{\pi}{4} - \tan^{-1}x$

9. (a) $I = \int_{-1}^1 \left(\sqrt{8+x^3}\right)dx; -1 < x^3 < 1$

$\Rightarrow 7 < x^3 + 8 < 9$

$\Rightarrow \sqrt{7} < \sqrt{8+x^3} < 3$

$\Rightarrow \int_{-1}^1 \sqrt{7}dx < \int_{-1}^1 \sqrt{8+x^3} < \int_{-1}^1 3dx$

$\Rightarrow 2\sqrt{7} < \int_{-1}^1 \sqrt{8+x^3} < 6$

$\Rightarrow$ The minimum value of k = 6

10. (b), (c) $I = \int_0^1 \sqrt{1+x^3}dx$

Clearly for $x \in (0, 1)$, $1 < \sqrt{1+x^3} < \sqrt{2}$

$\Rightarrow 1 < \int_0^1 \sqrt{1+x^3}dx < \sqrt{2} = 1.414$

Also by Schwartz Bunyakovsky inequality,

$\left|\int_0^1 \sqrt{1+x^3}dx\right| \le \sqrt{\int_0^1 (1)^2 dx . \int_0^1 \left(\sqrt{1+x^3}\right)^2 dx}$

$\Rightarrow \int_0^1 \sqrt{1+x^3}dx \le \sqrt{\left(x + \frac{x^4}{4}\right)_0^1} = \sqrt{1+\frac{1}{4}} = \frac{\sqrt{5}}{2} < \frac{\sqrt{7}}{2}$

Hence $I < \frac{\sqrt{7}}{2}$

11. (d) For $x \in (0, 1)$; $0 < x^2 < x$

$\Rightarrow 0 > -x^2 > -x$

$\Rightarrow e^0 > e^{-x^2} > e^{-x} \qquad \Rightarrow 1 > e^{-x^2} > e^{-x}$

Also $1 > \cos^2$ for $x \in (0, 1)$

$\Rightarrow 1 > e^{-x^2}\cos^2 x > e^{-x}\cos^2 x$ and $e^{-x^2} > e^{-x^2}\cos^2 x$

$\Rightarrow \int_0^1 e^{-x^2}\cos^2 x\,dx > \int_0^1 e^{-x}\cos^2 x\,dx$ and

$\int_0^1 e^{-x^2}dx > \int_0^1 e^{-x^2}\cos^2 x$

$\Rightarrow I_3 > I_2$ and $I_1 > I_3$

Hence $I_1 > I_3 > I_2$

12. (d) If $f(x) > 0 \ \forall\ x \in [a, b]$, then $\int_a^b f(x)dx > 0$ and if $f(x) < 0 \ \forall\ x \in [a, b]$, then $\int_a^b f(x)dx < 0$

So, $\int_a^b f(x)dx = 0$

$\Rightarrow$ $f(x)$ must intersect x-axis at some $k \in (a, b)$, i.e., $f(k) = 0$

$\Rightarrow$ Option (a) is correct

Also (b) is correct

Also $-|f(x)| \le f(x) \le |f(x)| \ \forall x \in (a,b)$

$\Rightarrow \quad -\int_a^b |f(x)|dx \le \int_a^b f(x)dx \le \int_a^b |f(x)|dx$

$\Rightarrow \quad \left|\int_a^b f(x)dx\right| \le \int_a^b |f(x)|dx$

$\Rightarrow$ (c) is correct

Thus, all the option are correct

TEXTUAL EXERCISE-9: (SUBJECTIVE)

1. Let $I(a, b) = \int_0^{\pi/2} \frac{dx}{a^2\sin^2 x + b^2\cos^2 x}$

Differentiating w. r. t. a, keeping b constant

$\Rightarrow I_1'(a, b) = \frac{\partial}{\partial a}\left(\frac{\pi}{2ab}\right) = \int_0^{\pi/2} \frac{\partial}{\partial a}\left[\frac{1}{a^2\sin^2 x + b^2\cos^2 x}\right]dx$

$\Rightarrow \frac{\pi}{2b}\left(\frac{-1}{a^2}\right) = \int_0^{\pi/2} \frac{-(2a\sin^2 x)dx}{(a^2\sin^2 x + b^2\cos^2 x)^2}$

$\Rightarrow \frac{-\pi}{2a^2b} = -2a\int_0^{\pi/2} \frac{\sin^2 x\,dx}{(a^2\sin^2 x + b^2\cos^2 x)^2} \qquad \ldots(1)$

Now differentially I(a, b) w. r. t. b, keeping a constant

$\Rightarrow I_2'(a, b) = \frac{\partial}{\partial b}\left(\frac{\pi}{2ab}\right)$

$= \int_0^{\pi/2} \frac{\partial}{\partial b}\left[\frac{1}{a^2\sin^2 x + b^2\cos^2 x}\right]dx$

$\Rightarrow \frac{\pi}{2a}\left(\frac{-1}{b^2}\right) = \int_0^{\pi/2} \frac{-(2b\cos^2 x)}{(a^2\sin^2 x + b^2\cos^2 x)^2}dx \qquad \ldots(2)$

$\therefore$ From (1), $\frac{\pi}{4a^3b} = \int_0^{\pi/2} \frac{\sin^2 x\,dx}{(a^2\sin^2 x + b^2\cos^2 x)^2} \qquad \ldots(3)$

From (2), $\frac{\pi}{4ab^3} = \int_0^{\pi/2} \frac{\cos^2 x\,dx}{(a^2\sin^2 x + b^2\cos^2 x)^2}$

Adding (3) and (4), we get $\frac{\pi}{4ab}\left[\frac{1}{a^2} + \frac{1}{b^2}\right]$

$= \int_0^{\pi/2} \frac{1\,dx}{(a^2\sin^2 x + b^2\cos^2 x)^2}$

$\Rightarrow \frac{\pi}{4a^3b^3}\left(a^2 + b^2\right) = \int_0^{\pi/2} \frac{1}{(a^2\sin^2 x + b^2\cos^2 x)^2}dx$

$\therefore \quad \frac{\pi}{4ab}\left(\frac{1}{a^2} + \frac{1}{b^2}\right)$

2. $I=\int_0^{\infty}\frac{a^{-ax}\sin kx}{x}dx$

Let $I(k)=\int_0^{\infty}\frac{e^{-ax}\sin kx}{x}dx$

$\Rightarrow \frac{\partial I}{ak}=\int_0^{\infty}\frac{e^{-ax}}{x}.(\cos kx)(x)dx$

$\Rightarrow \frac{\partial I}{\partial k}=\int_0^{\infty}e^{-ax}.\cos kx\,dx$

$\Rightarrow \frac{\partial I}{\partial k}=\left|\frac{e^{-ax}}{(a^2+k^2)}[-a\cos kx+k\sin kx]\right|_0^{\infty}$

$\Rightarrow \frac{\partial I}{\partial k}=0-\frac{1}{(a^2+k^2)}[-a]=\frac{a}{a^2+k^2}$

$\Rightarrow I=\int\frac{a}{a^2+k^2}dk$

$\Rightarrow I=a\times\frac{1}{a}\tan^{-1}\left(\frac{k}{a}\right)+C$

$\Rightarrow I(k)=\tan^{-1}\left(\frac{k}{a}\right)+C$

$\Rightarrow I(0)=0=\tan^{-1}(0)+C$

$\Rightarrow C=0$

$\therefore\ I(k)=\tan^{-1}\left(\frac{k}{a}\right)$

(a) $I=\int_0^{\infty}\left(\frac{\sin x}{x}\right)dx=I(a=0,k=1)$

$=I(k=1,a=0)=\tan^{-1}(\infty)=\frac{\pi}{2}$

(b) $I=\int_0^{\infty}\left(\frac{\sin x}{x}\right)dx=I(a=0,k=a)$

$=\tan^{-1}\left(\frac{a}{0}\right)=\tan^{-1}(\infty)=\frac{\pi}{2}$

(c) $\int_0^{\infty}\left(\frac{\sin x}{x}\right)^2dx=\int_0^{\infty}\underset{\text{I}}{(\sin^2x)}.\underset{\text{II}}{(x^{-2})}dx$

$=\left|(\sin^2x)\left(\frac{x^{-1}}{-1}\right)\right|_0^{\infty}-\int_0^{\infty}(2\sin x\cos x)\left(\frac{x^{-1}}{-1}\right)dx$

$=\left|\frac{\sin^2x}{x}\right|_0^{\infty}+2\int_0^{\infty}\frac{\sin 2x}{2x}dx$

$=0-\lim_{x\to0}\left(\frac{\sin^2x}{x^2}.x\right)+2\int_0^{\infty}\frac{\sin t}{t}.\frac{dt}{2}$

$=-0(1)^2+\int_0^{\infty}\frac{\sin t}{t}dt=\frac{\pi}{2}$

3. $\int_0^{\pi}\frac{x\,dx}{(a^2\sin^2x+b^2\cos^2x)^2}$

Let $I(a,b)=\int_0^{\pi}\frac{1}{(a^2\sin^2x+b^2\cos^2x}dx$

$\therefore\ \frac{\partial I}{\partial a}(I(a,b))=\int_0^{\pi}\frac{-2a\sin^2x\,dx}{(a^2\sin^2x+b^2\cos^2x)^2}$ …(1) and

$\frac{\partial I}{\partial b}(I(a,b))=\int_0^{\pi}\frac{-2b\cos^2x}{(a^2\sin^2x+b^2\cos^2x)^2}$ …(2)

Now, $I(a,b)=\int_0^{\pi}\frac{1}{(a^2\sin^2x+b^2\cos^2x)^2}dx$

$=2\int_0^{\pi/2}\frac{1\,dx}{a^2\sin^2x+b^2\cos^2x}dx=2\int_0^{\pi/2}\frac{\sec^2x\,dx}{a^2\tan^2x+b^2}$

Put $\tan x=t\ \Rightarrow\ \sec2x\,dx=dt$

$\therefore\ I(a,b)=2\int_0^{\infty}\frac{dt}{a^2t^2+b^2}=2\times\frac{1}{ab}\left|\tan^{-1}\left(\frac{at}{b}\right)\right|_0^{\infty}$

$=\frac{2}{ab}\left[\frac{\pi}{2}-0\right]=\frac{\pi}{ab}$

$\Rightarrow \frac{\partial I}{\partial a}=\frac{-\pi}{a^2b}$ and $\frac{\partial I}{\partial b}=\frac{-\pi}{ab^2}$ …(3)

Adding(1)and(2)andusing(3),weget, $\frac{-\pi}{(-2a)a^2b}-\frac{\pi}{ab^2(-2b)}$

$=\int_0^{\pi}\frac{1\,dx}{(a^2\sin^2x+b^2\cos^2x)^2}$

$\Rightarrow \frac{\pi}{2ab}\left(\frac{1}{a^2}+\frac{1}{b^2}\right)=\int_0^{\pi}\frac{1\,dx}{(a^2\sin^2x+b^2\cos^2x)^2}$ …(4)

Now, $I=\int_0^{\pi}\frac{x\,dx}{(a^2\sin^2x+b^2\cos^2x)^2}$

$\Rightarrow I=\int_0^{\pi}\frac{(\pi-x)dx}{(a^2\sin^2x+b^2\cos^2x)^2}$

$\Rightarrow 2I=\pi\int_0^{\pi}\frac{dx}{(a^2\sin^2x+b^2\cos^2x)^2}$

$\Rightarrow I=\frac{\pi}{2}\int_0^{\pi}\frac{dx}{(a^2\sin^2x+b^2\cos^2x)^2}$

$\Rightarrow I=\frac{\pi}{2}\times\frac{\pi}{2ab}\left(\frac{1}{a^2}+\frac{1}{b^2}\right)$ (using (4))

$\Rightarrow I=\frac{\pi^2}{4a^3b^3}(a^2+b^2)$

4. $I(a)=\int_0^{\infty}\frac{\tan^{-1}(ax)}{x(1+x^2)}dx$

$\Rightarrow \frac{dI}{da}=\int_0^{\infty}\frac{1}{(1+a^2x^2)}\times\frac{x}{x(1+x^2)}dx$

$\Rightarrow \frac{dI}{da}=\int_0^{\infty}\frac{1}{(1+a^2x^2)}\times\frac{x}{(1+x^2)}dx$

$\Rightarrow \frac{dI}{da}=\int_0^{\infty}\frac{1}{(a^2-1)}\left[\frac{a^2}{1+a^2x^2}-\frac{1}{1+x^2}\right]dx$

$\Rightarrow \frac{\partial I}{\partial a}=\int_0^{\infty}\frac{1}{(a^2-1)}\left[\frac{a^2}{1+a^2x^2}-\frac{1}{1+x^2}\right]dx$

$=\frac{1}{(a^2-1)}\times a^2\times\frac{1}{a}\left|\tan^{-1}(ax)\right|_0^{\infty}-\frac{1}{(a^2-1)}\left|\tan^{-1}(x)\right|_0^{\infty}$

$=\frac{a}{(a^2-1)}\left[\frac{\pi}{2}\right]-\frac{1}{(a^2-1)}\left[\frac{\pi}{2}\right]$

$\Rightarrow \dfrac{dI}{da} = \dfrac{1}{(a^2-1)}.\dfrac{\pi}{2}[a-1] = \dfrac{\pi}{2(a+1)}$

$\Rightarrow \text{I} = \dfrac{\pi}{2}\int \dfrac{1}{a+1}da$

$\Rightarrow \text{I(a)} = \dfrac{\pi}{2}\ln|a+1| + \text{C}$

Also $\text{I}(0) = 0 = \dfrac{\pi}{2}\ln 1 + \text{C} \Rightarrow \text{C} = 0$

$\Rightarrow \text{I} = \dfrac{\pi}{2}\ln|a+1|$

5. Let $\text{I (a)} = \int_0^\pi \dfrac{\ln(1+a\cos x)}{\cos x}dx; |a| < 1$

$\Rightarrow \dfrac{\partial \text{I}}{\partial a} = \int_0^\pi \dfrac{1}{(1+a\cos x)} \times \dfrac{\cos x}{\cos x}dx$

$\Rightarrow \dfrac{\partial \text{I}}{\partial a} = \int_0^\pi \dfrac{1}{(1+a\cos x)}dx = \int_0^\pi \dfrac{1}{1+a\left(\dfrac{1-\tan^2\frac{x}{2}}{1+\tan^2\frac{x}{2}}\right)}dx$

$= \int_0^\pi \dfrac{\sec^2\frac{x}{2}dx}{(1+a)+(1-a)\tan^2\frac{x}{2}}$

Put $\tan^2\dfrac{x}{2}$ $\quad\Rightarrow \sec^2\dfrac{x}{2}dx = 2dt$

$\Rightarrow \dfrac{\partial \text{I}}{\partial a} = \int_0^\infty \dfrac{2dt}{(1+a)+(1-a)t^2} = \dfrac{2}{(1-a)}\int_0^\infty \dfrac{dt}{\left(\dfrac{1+a}{1-a}\right)+t^2}$

$= \dfrac{2}{(1-a)} \times \sqrt{\dfrac{1-a}{1+a}}.\left|\tan^{-1}\left(t\sqrt{\dfrac{1-a}{1+a}}\right)\right|_0^\infty = \dfrac{2}{\sqrt{1-a^2}}\left[\dfrac{\pi}{2}-0\right]$

$= \dfrac{\pi}{\sqrt{1-a^2}}$

$\Rightarrow \text{I}(a) = \pi\int \dfrac{1}{\sqrt{1-a^2}}da$

$\Rightarrow$ I(a) = $\pi\sin^{-1}$ (a) + c

$\Rightarrow$ I(0) = $\pi\sin^{-1}$ (0) + c but $I(0) = 0$, from given integral.

$\Rightarrow$ 0 = 0 + c $\quad\Rightarrow c = 0$

$\therefore$ I(a) = $\pi \sin^{-1} (a)$

TEXTUAL EXERCISE–9: (OBJECTIVE)

1. (c) Let $\text{I}(a,b) = \int_0^\infty \dfrac{\ln(1+a^2x^2)}{1+b^2x^2}dx$

$\therefore \quad \dfrac{\partial \text{I}}{\partial a} = \int_0^\infty \dfrac{2ax^2}{(1+a^2x^2)(1+b^2x^2)}dx$

Let $\dfrac{2ax^2}{(1+a^2x^2)(1+b^2x^2)} = \dfrac{\text{A}}{1+a^2x^2} + \dfrac{\text{B}}{1+b^2x^2}$

$\Rightarrow 2ax^2 = A(1+b^2x^2) + B(1+a^2x^2)$

$\Rightarrow 2a\left(\dfrac{-1}{a^2}\right) = \text{A}\left(1+b^2\left(\dfrac{-1}{a^2}\right)\right)$

$\Rightarrow -\dfrac{2}{a} = \text{A}\left(\dfrac{a^2-b^2}{a^2}\right)$

$\Rightarrow \text{A} = \dfrac{2a}{b^2-a^2}$ and $2a\left(\dfrac{-1}{b^2}\right) = \text{B}\left(1+a\left(\dfrac{-1}{b^2}\right)\right)$

$\Rightarrow \text{B} = \dfrac{2a}{a^2-b^2}$

$\therefore \dfrac{\partial \text{I}}{\partial a} = \int_0^\infty \left\{\dfrac{2a}{(b^2-a^2)(1+a^2x^2)} + \dfrac{2a}{(a^2-b^2)(1+b^2x^2)}\right\}dx$

$= \dfrac{2a}{(b^2-a^2)} \times \left[\dfrac{\tan^{-1}}{a}(ax)\right]_0^\infty + \dfrac{2a}{(a^2-b^2)}\left[\dfrac{\tan^{-1}}{b}dx\right]_0^\infty$

$= \dfrac{2}{(b^2-a^2)}\left[\dfrac{\pi}{2}-0\right] + \dfrac{2a}{b(a^2-b^2)} + \dfrac{2a}{b(a^2-b^2)}\left[\dfrac{\pi}{2}-0\right]$

$= \dfrac{\pi}{(b^2-a^2)} + \dfrac{a\pi}{(a^2-b^2)}$

$\therefore \dfrac{\partial \text{I}}{\partial a} = \dfrac{(a-b)\pi}{b(a^2-b^2)} = \dfrac{\pi}{b(a+b)}$

$\Rightarrow \text{I} = \dfrac{\pi}{b}\int \dfrac{1}{a+b}da \quad \Rightarrow \dfrac{\pi}{b}\ln|a+b| + \text{C}$

For $a = 0$, I = 0

$\Rightarrow 0 = \dfrac{\pi}{b}\ln b + c \quad \Rightarrow c = \dfrac{-\pi}{b}\ln b$

$\Rightarrow \text{I} = \dfrac{\pi}{b}\ln|a+b| - \dfrac{\pi}{b}\ln b = \dfrac{\pi}{b}\ln\left|\dfrac{a+b}{b}\right|$

2. (b) $\text{I}(a) = \int_0^{\pi/2} \sec\theta.\tan^{-1}(a\cos\theta)d\theta$

$\Rightarrow \text{I}'(a) = \int_0^{\pi/2} \sec\theta.\dfrac{1}{1+a^2\cos^2\theta}.\cos\theta\, d\theta$

$\Rightarrow \dfrac{\partial \text{I}}{\partial a} = \int_0^{\pi/2} \dfrac{d\theta}{1+a^2\cos^2\theta} = \int_0^{\pi/2} \dfrac{\sec^2\theta\, d\theta}{\sec^2\theta + a^2}$

$= \int_0^{\pi/2} \dfrac{\sec^2\theta\, d\theta}{(a^2+1+\tan^2\theta)}$

Put $\tan\theta = t$

$\Rightarrow \dfrac{\partial \text{I}}{\partial a} = \int_0^\infty \dfrac{dt}{a^2+1+t^2} = \int_0^\infty \dfrac{dt}{\left(\sqrt{a^2+1}\right)^2 + t^2}$

$\Rightarrow \dfrac{\partial \text{I}}{\partial a} = \dfrac{1}{\sqrt{a^2+1}}\left|\tan^{-1}\left(\dfrac{t}{\sqrt{a^2+1}}\right)\right|_0^\infty$

$\Rightarrow \dfrac{\partial \text{I}}{\partial a} = \dfrac{1}{\sqrt{a^2+1}}\left[\dfrac{\pi}{2}-0\right]$

$\Rightarrow \text{I} = \dfrac{\pi}{2}\int \dfrac{da}{\sqrt{a^2+1}}$

$\Rightarrow \text{I}(a) = \dfrac{\pi}{2}\ln\left|a+\sqrt{a^2+1}\right| + \text{C}$

$I(0) = 0 \qquad \Rightarrow \quad 0 = \frac{\pi}{2}\ln 1 + C$

$\Rightarrow \quad C = 0$

$\therefore \quad I(a) = \frac{\pi}{2}\ln\left|a + \sqrt{a^2+1}\right|$

3. (a) $I(a,b) = \int_0^{\infty} \frac{e^{-ax}.\sin bx}{x}dx \qquad ...(1)$

Keeping 'a' constant and different partially w.r.t 'b' get

$$\frac{\partial I}{\partial b} = \int_0^{\infty}\frac{e^{-ax}}{x}(\cos bx)(x)dx = \int_0^{\infty} e^{-ax}\cos bx\, dx$$

$$= 0 - \frac{1}{a^2+b^2}[-a] = \frac{a}{a^2+b^2}$$

$\Rightarrow \quad I = \int \frac{a}{a^2+b^2}db \qquad \Rightarrow \quad I = a\int\frac{1}{a^2+b^2}db$

$\Rightarrow \quad I = a \times \frac{1}{a}\tan^{-1}\left(\frac{b}{a}\right) + C$

$\Rightarrow \quad I = \tan^{-1}\left(\frac{b}{a}\right) + C$

$I(a,b) = \tan^{-1}\left(\frac{b}{a}\right) + C$ from (1), I (a, 0) = 0

$\Rightarrow \quad 0 = \tan^{-1}(0) + C \qquad \Rightarrow \quad C = 0$

$\therefore \quad I(a, b) = \tan^{-1}\left(\frac{b}{a}\right)$

4. (b) $I = \int_0^{\infty}\frac{\sin x}{x}dx$

$\because \quad \int_0^{\infty}\frac{e^{-ax}\sin bx}{x}dx = \tan^{-1}\left(\frac{b}{a}\right)$

$\therefore \quad \int_0^{\infty}\frac{\sin x}{x}dx = \tan^{-1}\left(\frac{1}{0}\right) = \tan^{-1}(\infty) = \frac{\pi}{2}$

5. (a) $I(\lambda) = \int_0^{\infty}\left(\frac{\tan^{-1}\lambda x - \tan^{-1}x}{x}dx\right); \lambda > 0$

$$\Rightarrow \quad \frac{dI}{d\lambda} = \int_0^{\infty}\frac{\frac{1}{1+\lambda^2x^2}\times x}{x}dx; \lambda > 0$$

$$\Rightarrow \quad \frac{dI}{d\lambda} = \int_0^{\infty}\frac{1}{1+\lambda^2x^2}dx = \left[\frac{\tan^{-1}(\lambda x)}{\lambda}\right]_0^{\infty}$$

$$= \frac{1}{\lambda}\left[\tan^{-1}(\infty) - \tan^{-1}(0)\right] = \frac{\pi}{2}\left(\frac{1}{\lambda}\right)$$

$\Rightarrow \quad I = \frac{\pi}{2}\int\frac{1}{\lambda}d\lambda$

$\Rightarrow \quad I(\lambda) = \frac{\pi}{2}\ln\lambda + C \qquad \Rightarrow \quad I(1) = 0 = \frac{\pi}{2}\ln(1) + C$

$\Rightarrow \quad C = 0 \qquad \therefore \quad I(\lambda) = \frac{2}{\pi}\ln\lambda$

6. (a), (b), (c), (d)

(a) $\because \quad m \le f(x) \le M \;\forall\; x \in [a, b]$

$\Rightarrow \quad m\int_a^b 1dx \le \int_a^b f(x)dx \le \int_a^b M\,dx$

$\Rightarrow \quad m(b-a) \le \int_a^b f(x)dx \le M(b-a)$

$\Rightarrow$ Which is true.

(b) It is Schwartz-Bunyakovsky inequality. Hence true.

(c) If m and M are g.l.b. and l.u.b. of $f(x)$, then $m \le f(x) \le M \;\forall\; x \in [a, b]$

$\Rightarrow \quad m(b-a) \le \int_a^b f(x)dx \le M(b-a)$

$\Rightarrow \quad m \le \frac{1}{(b-a)}\int_a^b f(x)dx \le M$

$\therefore$ By intermediate value theorem $f(x)$ will take value $\frac{1}{(b-a)}\int_a^b f(x)dx$ at some $c \in (a, b)$, i.e., $f(c) = \frac{1}{(b-a)}\int_a^b f(x)dx$ or $\int_a^b f(x)dx = (b-a).f(c)$

for some $c \in (a, b)$

$\Rightarrow$ It is true

(d) Let $I(a) = \int_a^{a+T} f(x)dx$

$\Rightarrow \quad \frac{d}{da}I(a) = f(a+T) - f(a) = 0$

$(\because f(a+T) = f(a))$

$\Rightarrow$ I(a) = Constant, independent of 'a'

$\therefore$ Replacing 'a' by '0', we get I(a) = I(0) $= \int_0^T f(x)dx$

$\therefore$ It is true

TEXTUAL EXERCISE–10: (SUBJECTIVE)

1. (i) (a) $\lim_{n\to\infty}\left(\frac{1}{n+1} + \frac{1}{n+2} + \frac{1}{n+3} + ... + \frac{1}{n+5n}\right)$

$$= \lim_{n\to\infty}\left(\sum_{r=1}^{5n}\frac{1}{n+r}\right)$$

$$= \lim_{n\to\infty}\sum_{r=1}^{5n}\frac{1}{n}\left(\frac{1}{1+\frac{r}{n}}\right) = \int_0^5\frac{1}{1+x}dx\left[\ln|1+x|\right]_0^5 = \ln 6$$

(b) $\lim_{n\to\infty}\left[\frac{(n^3+1^3)(n^3+2^3)(n^3+3^3)....(n^3+n^3)}{n^{3n}}\right]^{1/n}$

$$= \lim_{n\to\infty}\left[\frac{(n^3)^n}{n^{3n}}\left(1+\frac{1^3}{n^3}\right)\left(1+\frac{2^3}{n^3}\right)\left(1+\frac{3^3}{n^3}\right)....\left(1+\frac{n^3}{n^3}\right)\right]^{1/n}$$

$$= \lim_{n\to\infty}\left[\prod_{r=1}^{n}\left(1+\frac{r^3}{n^3}\right)\right]^{1/n} = L \text{ (say)}$$

$$\Rightarrow \quad \ln L = \lim_{n\to\infty}\sum_{r=1}^{n}\frac{1}{n}\ln\left(1+\frac{r^3}{n^3}\right) = \int_0^1 \ln(1+x^3)dx$$

$$= \left[\ln(1+x^3)\right].(x)\Big|_0^1 - \int_0^1\frac{3x^3}{1+x^3}.x\,dx = \ln 2 - \int_0^1\frac{3x^3}{x^3+1}dx$$

$$= \ln 2 - 3\int_0^1 \frac{x^3+1-1}{x^3+1}dx = \ln 2 - 3\int_0^1\left(1-\frac{1}{x^3+1}\right)dx$$

$$= \ln 2 - 3 + 3\int_0^1 \frac{1}{x^3+1}dx$$

$$= \ln 2 - 3 + 3\int_0^1 \frac{1}{(x+1)(x^2-x+1)}dx$$

$$= \ln 2 - 3 + \ln 2 + \int_0^1 \frac{-x+2}{x^2-x+1}dx$$

$$= 2\ln 2 - 3 - \frac{1}{2}\int_0^1 \frac{2x-1-3}{x^2-x+1}dx$$

$$= \ln 4 - 3 - \frac{1}{2}\left[\ln\left|x^2-x+1\right|\right]_0^1 + \frac{3}{2}\int_0^1 \frac{1}{\left(x-\frac{1}{2}\right)+\left(\frac{\sqrt{3}}{2}\right)^2}$$

$$= \ln 4 - 3 - \frac{1}{2}[0] + \frac{3}{2}\times\frac{2}{\sqrt{3}}\left|\tan^{-1}\left(\frac{2x-1}{\sqrt{3}}\right)\right|_0^1$$

$$= \ln 4 - 3 + \sqrt{3}\left(\frac{\pi}{3}\right) = \ln 4 - 3 + \frac{\pi}{\sqrt{3}}$$

(c) $\lim_{n\to\infty}\sum_{r=1}^{3n}\frac{n^2}{(3n+r)^3} = \lim_{n\to\infty}\sum_{r=1}^{3n}\frac{1}{n\left(3+\frac{r}{n}\right)^3} = \int_0^3 \frac{1}{(3+x)^3}dx$

$$= \left|\frac{(3+x)^{-2}}{-2}\right|_0^3 = \frac{-1}{2}\left[\frac{1}{36}-\frac{1}{9}\right] = \frac{-1}{2}\left[\frac{1-4}{36}\right] = \frac{1}{24}$$

(d) $\lim_{n\to\infty}\sum_{r=1}^{(n-1)}\frac{n^2}{\left(n^2+r^2\right)^{3/2}} = \lim_{n\to\infty}\sum_{r=1}^{(n-1)}\frac{1}{\left(1+\frac{r^2}{n^2}\right)^{3/2}}\cdot\frac{1}{n}$

$$= \int_0^1 \frac{1}{\left(1+x^2\right)^{3/2}}dx$$

Put x = tanθ

⇒ Limit $= \int_0^{\pi/4}\cos^3\theta.\sec^2\theta d\theta = \int_0^{\pi/4}\cos\theta d\theta = [\sin\theta]_0^{\pi/4}$

$$= \frac{1}{\sqrt{2}}$$

(e) $\lim_{n\to\infty}\sum_{r=1}^{4n}\frac{\sqrt{r}}{n\sqrt{n}} = \lim_{n\to\infty}\sum_{r=1}^{4n}\frac{1}{n}\sqrt{\frac{r}{n}} = \int_0^4\sqrt{x}\,dx$

$$= \left[\frac{2}{3}(x)^{3/2}\right]_0^4 = \frac{2}{3}[(8)-0] = \frac{16}{3}$$

(f) $\lim_{n\to\infty}\sum_{r=1}^{2n}\frac{r^2}{r^3+n^3} = \lim_{n\to\infty}\sum_{r=1}^{2n}\frac{1}{n}\left(\frac{r^2}{\frac{r^3}{n}+n^2}\right)$

$$= \lim_{n\to\infty}\sum_{r=1}^{2n}\frac{1}{n}\left(\frac{\frac{r^2}{n^2}}{\frac{r^3}{n^3}+1}\right) = \int_0^2\left(\frac{x^2}{x^3+1}\right)dx = \frac{1}{3}\left[\ln\left(1+x^3\right)\right]_0^2$$

$$= \frac{1}{3}[\ln 9]$$

(g) $\lim_{n\to\infty}\left[\frac{1}{\sqrt{n^2-1}}+\frac{1}{\sqrt{n^2-4}}+....+\frac{1}{\sqrt{n^2-(n-1)^2}}\right]$

$$= \lim_{n\to\infty}\sum_{r=1}^{(n-1)}\frac{1}{\sqrt{n^2-(r^2)}} = \lim_{n\to\infty}\sum_{r=1}^{(n-1)}\frac{1}{n}\cdot\frac{1}{\sqrt{1-\left(\frac{r}{n}\right)^2}}$$

$$= \int_0^1\frac{1}{\sqrt{1-x^2}}dx = \left[\sin^{-1}x\right]_0^1 = \frac{\pi}{2}$$

(h) $\lim_{n\to\infty}\frac{1}{n}\left[\sec^2\frac{\pi}{4n}+\sec^2\frac{2\pi}{4n}+....+\sec^2\frac{n\pi}{4n}\right]$

$$= \lim_{n\to\infty}\sum_{r=1}^{n}\sec^2\left(\frac{r\pi}{4n}\right).dx$$

$$= \int_0^1\sec^2\left(\frac{\pi}{4}x\right)dx = \left[\frac{\tan\left(\frac{\pi}{4}x\right)}{\left(\frac{\pi}{4}\right)}\right]_0^1 = \frac{\pi}{4}[1-0] = \frac{4}{\pi}$$

(ii) (a) $I = \int_1^4\left(ax^2+bx+c\right)dx$

Let $f(x) = ax^2+bx+c;\ a_1 = 1, b_1 = 4$

∴ $I = \lim_{h\to 0}[f(a_1)+f(a_1+h)+f(a_1+2h)+....$

$+f(a_1+(n-1)h)]$; where

$h = \frac{b_1-a_1}{n} = \frac{4-1}{n} = \frac{3}{n}; n\to\infty; nh = 3$

$= \lim_{\substack{h\to 0\\ n\to\infty}} h\,[(a+b+c)+a(1+h)^2+b(1+h)+c+a(1+2h)^2$

$+b(1+2h)+c+....+a(1+\overline{n-1}\,h)^2+b(1+\overline{n-1}\,h)+c]$

$= \lim_{\substack{h\to 0\\ n\to\infty}} h\,[a(n)+a(1^2+2^2+3^3+....+(n-1)^2)h^2+2ah(1+2$

$+3+....+\overline{n-1})+nb+bh(1+2+3+....+\overline{n-1})+nc]$

$= \lim_{\substack{h\to 0\\ n\to\infty}} h\left[na+\frac{ah^2(n-1)(n)(2n-1)}{6}+2ah\frac{n(n-1)}{2}+\right.$

$\left.nb+bh\frac{(n-1)(n)}{2}+nc\right]$

$= \lim_{\substack{h\to 0\\ n\to\infty}}\left[nha+\frac{(nh-h)(nh)(2nh-h)a}{6}+a(nh)(nh-h)+\right.$

$\left.b(nh)+\frac{b}{2}(nh)(nh-h)+c(nh)\right]$

$= a(3)+\frac{(3-0)(3)(6-0)a}{6}+a(3)(3-0)+b(3)+$

$\frac{b}{2}(3)(3-0)+3c$

$= 3a+9a+9a+3b+\frac{9}{2}b+3c = 21a+\frac{15}{2}b+3c$

(b) $I = \int_a^b e^x dx$

Let $f(x) = e^x; h = \frac{b-a}{n}; h\to 0, n\to\infty$ and $h = (b-a)$

$= \lim_{\substack{n\to\infty\\ h\to 0}} h[f(a)+f(a+h)+f(a+2h)+....+f(a+(n-1)h)]$

$$= \lim_{\substack{n\to\infty \\ h\to 0}} h\left[e^a + e^{a+h} + e^{a+2h} + ... + e^{a+(n+1)h}\right]$$

$$= \lim_{\substack{n\to\infty \\ h\to 0}} h\left[e^a(1+e^h+e^{2h}+....+e^{(n-1)h})\right] = \lim_{\substack{n\to\infty \\ h\to 0}} h\left[e^a\frac{(e^{nh}-1)}{(e^h-1)}\right]$$

$$= \lim_{\substack{n\to\infty \\ h\to 0}} e^a\left(e^{(b-a)}-1\right).\left(\frac{h}{e^h-1}\right) = \left(e^b - e^a\right)$$

2. (a) $\lim_{n\to\infty}\frac{1}{n}\sum_{r=1}^{2n}\frac{r}{\sqrt{n^2+r^2}} = \lim_{n\to\infty}\frac{1}{n}\sum_{r=1}^{2n}\frac{\frac{r}{n}}{\sqrt{1+\frac{r^2}{n^2}}} = \int_0^2\frac{x}{\sqrt{1+x^2}}dx$

$$= \frac{1}{2}\int_0^2\frac{2x\ dx}{(1+x^2)^{1/2}} = \frac{1}{2}\left[\frac{(1+x)^{1/2}}{1/2}\right]_0^2 = \left(\sqrt{5}-1\right)$$

(b) $\lim_{n\to\infty}\sum_{r=1}^{n}\frac{n}{n^2+r^2} = \lim_{n\to\infty}\sum_{r=1}^{n}\frac{1}{n\left(1+\frac{r^2}{n^2}\right)} = \int_0^1\frac{1}{1+x^2}dx$

$$= \left[\tan^{-1}x\right]_0^1 = \frac{\pi}{4}$$

(c) $\lim_{n\to\infty}\sum_{k=1}^{n}\log_e\left(1+\frac{k}{n}\right)^{1/n} = \lim_{n\to\infty}\sum_{k=1}^{n}\frac{1}{n}\log_e\left(1+\frac{k}{n}\right)$

$$= \int_0^1\log_e(1+x)dx$$

$$= \left[x\log_e(1+x)\right]_0^1 - \int_0^1\frac{1}{(1+x)}x\ dx$$

$$= \log_e 2 - \int_0^1\left(1-\frac{1}{1+x}\right)dx$$

$$= \log_e 2 - \left[x-\ln(1+x)\right]_0^1 = \log_e 2[1-\ln 2]$$

$$= 2\ln 2 - 1 = \ln\left(\frac{4}{e}\right)$$

(d) $\lim_{n\to\infty}\left(\frac{1}{na}+\frac{1}{na+1}+\frac{1}{na+2}+....+\frac{1}{nb}\right)$

$$= \lim_{n\to\infty}\sum_{r=0}^{(nb-na)}\frac{1}{na+r} = \lim_{n\to\infty}\sum_{r=0}^{n(b-a)}\frac{1}{n\left(a+\frac{r}{n}\right)}$$

$$= \int_0^{b-a}\frac{1}{a+x}dx = \left[\ln(a+x)\right]_0^{b-a}$$

$$= \ln(b) - \ln(a) = \ln\left(\frac{b}{a}\right)$$

3. $\lim_{n\to\infty}\sum_{r=1}^{2n}\frac{n+r}{n^2+r^2} = \lim_{n\to\infty}\sum_{r=1}^{2n}\frac{1}{n}\left[\frac{1+\frac{r}{n}}{1+\frac{r^2}{n^2}}\right] = \int_0^2\left(\frac{1+x}{1+x^2}\right)dx$

$$= \int_0^2\frac{1}{1+x^2}dx + \int_0^2\frac{1}{2}\left(\frac{2x}{1+x^2}\right)dx$$

$$= \left[\tan^{-1}x\right]_0^2 + \frac{1}{2}\left[\ln\left(1+x^2\right)\right]_0^2 = \tan^{-1}2 + \frac{1}{2}[\ln(5)]$$

4. (a) $\lim_{n\to\infty}\sum_{r=1}^{n}\frac{r}{n^2}\sec^2\left(\frac{r^2}{n^2}\right) = \lim_{n\to\infty}\sum_{n^2}^{n}\frac{1}{n}.\left(\frac{r}{n}\right)\sec^2\left(\frac{r}{n}\right)^2$

$$= \int_0^1 x\sec^2 x^2 dx$$

$$= \int_0^1\frac{1}{2}\sec^2 t\ dt = \frac{1}{2}[\tan t]_o^1 = \frac{1}{2}\tan 1$$

(b) $\lim_{n\to\infty}\frac{\left[(n+1)(n+2)....(n+n)\right]^{1/n}}{n}$

$$= \lim_{n\to\infty}\frac{\left[\left(n^n\right)\left(1+\frac{1}{n}\right)\left(1+\frac{2}{n}\right)....\left(1+\frac{n}{n}\right)\right]^{1/n}}{n}$$

$$= \lim_{n\to\infty}\left[\left(1+\frac{1}{n}\right)\left(1+\frac{2}{n}\right)....\left(1+\frac{n}{n}\right)\right]^{1/n} = \text{L (say)}$$

$$\Rightarrow \ln \text{L} = \lim_{n\to\infty}\ln\left[\pi\left(1+\frac{r}{n}\right)\right]^{1/n} = \lim_{n\to\infty}\frac{1}{n}\sum_{r=1}^{n}\ln\left(1+\frac{r}{n}\right)$$

$$= \int_0^1\ln(1+x)dx$$

$$= \left|x\ln(1+x)\right|_0^1 - \int_0^1\frac{1}{(1+x)}(x)dx$$

$$= \ln 2 - \int_0^1\left(1-\frac{1}{1+x}\right)dx = \ln 2 - \left[x-\ln(1+x)\right]_0^1$$

$$= 2\ln 2 - 1$$

5. $\lim_{n\to\infty}\frac{n}{(n+1)\sqrt{2n+1}} + \frac{n}{(n+2)\sqrt{2(2n+2)}} + \frac{n}{(n+3)\sqrt{3(2n+3)}} + ...$ upto n-terms

$$= \lim_{n\to\infty}\sum_{r=1}^{n}\frac{n}{(n+r)\sqrt{r(2n+r)}} = \lim_{n\to\infty}\sum_{r=1}^{n}\frac{\frac{1}{n}}{\left(1+\frac{r}{n}\right)\sqrt{2\frac{r}{n}+\frac{r^2}{n^2}}}$$

$$= \int_0^1\frac{1}{(1+x)\sqrt{x^2+2x}}dx$$

$$= \int_0^1\frac{1}{(x+1)\sqrt{(x+1)^2-1}}dx = \int_1^2\frac{1}{t\sqrt{t^2-1}}dt = \left[\sec^{-1}t\right]_0^2$$

$$= \sec^{-1}2 - \sec^{-1}1 = \frac{\pi}{3} - 0 = \frac{\pi}{3}$$

6. $\lim_{n\to\infty}\sum_{r=1}^{n}\frac{\sqrt{n}}{\sqrt{r}\left(3\sqrt{r}+4\sqrt{n}\right)^2} = \lim_{n\to\infty}\sum_{r=1}^{n}\frac{1}{n}.\frac{1}{\sqrt{\frac{r}{n}}\left(3\sqrt{\frac{r}{n}}+4\right)^2}$

$$= \int_0^1\frac{1}{\sqrt{x}\left(3\sqrt{x}+4\right)^2}$$

Put $3\sqrt{x}+4 = t \quad\Rightarrow\quad \frac{3}{2\sqrt{x}}dx = dt$

$$\Rightarrow \text{Limit} = \int_4^7\frac{2}{3(t)^2} = \frac{2}{3}\left[\frac{t^{-1}}{-1}\right]_4^7 = \left(\frac{-2}{3}\right)\left[\frac{1}{7}-\frac{1}{4}\right]$$

$$= \frac{-2}{3}\left(\frac{-3}{28}\right) = \frac{1}{14}$$

7. $\lim_{n\to\infty}\left\{\frac{1}{1+n^4}+\frac{8}{16+n^4}+\frac{27}{81+n^4}+....+\text{upto n terms}\right\}$

$= \lim_{n\to\infty}\sum_{r=1}^{n}\frac{r^3}{r^4+n^4} = \lim_{n\to\infty}\sum_{r=1}^{n}\frac{1}{n}.\frac{\frac{r^3}{n^3}}{\left(\frac{r^4}{n^4}+1\right)}$

$= \int_0^1\left(\frac{x^3}{x^4+1}\right)dx = \frac{1}{4}\int_4^1\frac{4x^3}{x^4+1}dx = \frac{1}{4}\left[\ln\left(1+x^4\right)\right]_0^1 = \frac{1}{4}[\ln 2]$

8. $\lim_{n\to\infty}\left(\frac{1}{n}+\frac{1}{n+1}+\frac{1}{n+2}+....+\frac{1}{an}\right); a>0$

$= \lim_{n\to\infty}\sum_{r=0}^{an-n}\frac{1}{n+r} = \lim_{n\to\infty}\sum_{r=0}^{n(a-1)}\frac{1}{n+r}$

$= \lim_{n\to\infty}\sum_{r=0}^{n(a-1)}\frac{1}{n\left(1+\frac{r}{n}\right)} = \int_0^{a-1}\frac{1}{1+x}dx = \left[\ln(1+x)\right]_0^{a-1} = \ln a$

$S = \frac{1}{100}+\frac{1}{101}+\frac{1}{102}+....+\frac{1}{300}$

$= \frac{1}{n}+\frac{1}{n+1}+\frac{1}{n+2}+....+\frac{1}{n+200}$, where $n = 100$ and $n + 200 = n + 2n = 3n = an$

$\Rightarrow a = 3$

$\therefore$ By first part, given sum $S = \ln 3$

TEXTUAL EXERCISE–10: (OBJECTIVE)

1. (a) $\lim_{n\to\infty}\left[\frac{1}{\sqrt{n^2-12}}+\frac{1}{\sqrt{n^2-2^2}}+....+\frac{1}{\sqrt{n^2-(n-1)^2}}\right]$

$= \lim_{n\to\infty}\sum_{r=1}^{(n-1)}\frac{1}{\sqrt{n^2-r^2}}$

$= \lim_{n\to\infty}\sum_{r=1}^{n-1}\frac{1}{n}.\frac{1}{\sqrt{1-\left(\frac{r}{n}\right)^2}} = \int_0^1\frac{1}{\sqrt{1-x^2}}dx = \left[\sin^{-1}\right]_0^1 = \frac{\pi}{2}$

2. (b) $\lim_{n\to\infty}\left[\left(1+\frac{1}{n^2}\right)\left(1+\frac{2^2}{n^2}\right)....\left(1+\frac{n^2}{n^2}\right)\right]^{1/n}$

$= \lim_{n\to\infty}\left[\prod_{r=1}^{n}\left(1+\frac{r^2}{n^2}\right)\right]_n^{1/n} = L \text{ (say)}$

$\Rightarrow \ln L = \lim_{n\to\infty}\frac{1}{n}\sum_{r=1}^{n}\ln\left(1+\frac{r^2}{n^2}\right)$

$\Rightarrow \ln L = \int_0^1\ln\left(1+x^2\right)dx = \left|x\ln\left(1+x^2\right)\right|_0^1 - \int_0^1\frac{2x}{\left(1+x^2\right)}.x\,dx$

$= \ln 2 - 2\int_0^1\left(\frac{x^2+1-1}{x^2+1}\right)dx$

$= \ln 2 - 2\int_0^1\left(1-\frac{1}{1+x^2}\right)dx \quad = \ln 2 - 2\left[x-\tan^{-1}x\right]_0^1$

$= \ln 2 - 2\left[\left(1-\tan^{-1}1\right)-0\right] = \ln 2 - 2 + \frac{\pi}{2}$

$\Rightarrow \quad L = e^{\left(\ln 2-2+\frac{\pi}{2}\right)}$

$\Rightarrow \quad L = 2.e^{\left(\frac{\pi}{2}-2\right)} = 2e^{\frac{1}{2}(\pi-4)}$

3. (a) $\lim_{n\to\infty}\frac{\sqrt[n]{n!}}{n} = \lim_{n\to\infty}\frac{(n!)^{1/n}}{n} = \lim_{n\to\infty}\left[\frac{(1.2.3....n)^{1/n}}{n}\right]$

$= \lim_{n\to\infty}\left[\frac{(1.2.3....n)}{(n)^n}\right]$

$= \lim_{n\to\infty}\left[\frac{1}{n}.\frac{2}{n}.\frac{3}{n}.....\frac{n}{n}\right]^{1/n} = \lim_{n\to\infty}\left[\prod_{r=1}^{n}\left(\frac{r}{n}\right)\right]^{1/n} = L \text{ (say)}$

$\Rightarrow \quad \ln L = \lim_{n\to\infty}\left[\frac{1}{n}\sum_{r=1}^{n}\ln\left(\frac{r}{n}\right)\right] = \int_0^1\ln x\,dx$

$= \left|x\ln x\right|_0^1 - \int_0^1\frac{1}{x}.x\,dx$

$= 0 - \lim_{x\to 0}\left(\frac{\ln x}{\frac{1}{x}}\right) - [x]_0^1 = -\lim_{x\to 0}\left[\frac{\frac{1}{x}}{-\frac{1}{x^2}}\right] - 1$

$= \lim_{x\to 0}[x] - 1 = -1$

$\Rightarrow \quad L = e^{-1} = \frac{1}{e}$

4. (c) $\lim_{n\to\infty}\left(\frac{n+1}{n^2+1^2}+\frac{n+2}{n^2+2^2}+....+\frac{1}{n}\right) = \lim_{n\to\infty}\sum_{r=1}^{n}\frac{n+r}{n^2+r^2}$

$= \lim_{n\to\infty}\sum_{r=1}^{n}\frac{\frac{1}{n}\left(1+\frac{r}{n}\right)}{1+\frac{r^2}{n^2}}$

$= \int_0^1\frac{(1+x)}{1+x^2}dx = \int_0^1\frac{1}{1+x^2}dx + \frac{1}{2}\int_0^1\frac{2x}{1+x^2}$

$= \left[\tan^{-1}x\right]_0^1 + \frac{1}{2}\left[\ln\left(1+x^2\right)\right]_0^1$

$= \left[\tan^{-1}1\right] + \frac{1}{2}[\ln 2] = \frac{\pi}{4} + \frac{1}{2}\ln 2$

5. (b) $\lim_{n\to\infty}\sum_{r=1}^{n}\frac{1}{n}e^{r/n} = \int_0^1 e^x dx = \left[e^x\right]_0^1 = (e-1)$

6. (c) $\lim_{n\to\infty}\sum_{r=1}^{n}\frac{1}{n}\sin\left(\frac{r\pi}{2n}\right) = \int_0^1\sin\left(\frac{\pi}{2}x\right)dx = -\frac{2}{\pi}\left[\cos\frac{\pi}{2}x\right]_0^1$

$= \left(\frac{-2}{\pi}\right)[0-1] = \frac{2}{\pi}$

7. (d) $\lim_{n\to\infty}\left\{\frac{n!}{(kn)^n}\right\}^{1/n}$ k = constant, $n \in \mathbb{N}$

$= \lim_{n\to\infty}\left\{\frac{1.2.3.......n}{k^n(n.n.n.......n)}\right\}^{1/n} = \lim_{n\to\infty}\frac{1}{k}\left\{\frac{1}{n}.\frac{2}{n}.\frac{3}{n}....\frac{n}{n}\right\}^{1/n}$

$= \lim_{n\to\infty}\frac{1}{k}\left\{\prod_{r=1}^{n}\frac{r}{n}\right\}^{1/n} = L \text{ (say)}$

$$\Rightarrow \ln L = \lim_{n\to\infty}\left\{\left(\ln\frac{1}{k}\right)+\frac{1}{n}\sum_{r=1}^{n}\ln\left(\frac{r}{n}\right)\right\}$$

$$\Rightarrow \ln L = \ln\left(\frac{1}{k}\right)+\int_0^1 \ln x\,dx$$

$$\Rightarrow \ln L = \ln\left(\frac{1}{k}\right)+\left[\left[x\ln x\right]_0^1-\int_0^1 1\,dx\right]$$

$$\Rightarrow \ln L = \ln\left(\frac{1}{k}\right)+\left[-\lim_{x\to 0}\left(\frac{\ln x}{\frac{1}{x}}\right)-1\right]$$

$$\Rightarrow \ln L = \ln\left(\frac{1}{k}\right)+\lim_{x\to 0}\left[\frac{1}{x}\times\frac{x^2}{1}\right]-1$$

$$\Rightarrow \ln L = \ln\left(\frac{1}{k}\right)-1$$

$$\Rightarrow \ln L = \ln\left(\frac{\frac{1}{k}}{e}\right)=\ln\left(\frac{1}{ke}\right)$$

$$\Rightarrow L=\frac{1}{ke}=k^{-1}e^{-1}$$

8. (a) $\lim\limits_{n\to\infty}\sum\limits_{r=1}^{n}\frac{1}{\sqrt{n^r}}=\lim\limits_{n\to\infty}\sum\limits_{r=1}^{n}\frac{1}{n}\times\sqrt{\frac{n}{r}}=\lim\limits_{n\to\infty}\sum\limits_{r=1}^{n}\frac{1}{n}\times\frac{1}{\sqrt{\frac{r}{n}}}$

$$=\int_0^1\frac{1}{\sqrt{x}}dx=\int_0^1(x)^{-1/2}dx=\left[2x^{1/2}\right]_0^1=2$$

9. (b) $\lim\limits_{n\to\infty}\sum\limits_{r=0}^{n-1}\frac{1}{\sqrt{n^2-r^2}}=\lim\limits_{n\to\infty}\sum\limits_{r=0}^{n-1}\frac{1}{n}\times\frac{1}{\sqrt{1-\left(\frac{r}{n}\right)^2}}$

$$=\int_0^1\frac{1}{\sqrt{1-x^2}}dx=\left[\sin^{-1}x\right]_0^1=\sin^{-1}1=\frac{\pi}{2}$$

10. (a) $\lim\limits_{n\to\infty}\sum\limits_{r=1}^{4n}\frac{1}{n+r}=\lim\limits_{n\to\infty}\sum\limits_{r=1}^{4n}\frac{1}{n}\times\frac{1}{\left(1+\frac{r}{n}\right)}$

$$=\int_0^4\frac{1}{1+x}dx=\left[\ln(1+x)\right]_0^4=\ln 5$$

11. (b) $\lim\limits_{n\to\infty}\frac{2^k+4^k+6^k+....+(2n)^k}{n^{k+1}},k\neq -1=\lim\limits_{n\to\infty}\sum\limits_{r=1}^{n}\frac{(2r)^k}{n^{k+1}}$

$$=\lim_{n\to\infty}\sum_{r=1}^{n}2^k.\frac{1}{n}\left(\frac{r}{n}\right)^k=2^k\int_0^1(x)^k dx=2^k\left[\frac{x^{k+1}}{k+1}\right]_0^1=\frac{2^k}{k+1}$$

12. (b) $\lim\limits_{n\to\infty}\frac{1}{n}\sum\limits_{r=1}^{2n}\frac{r}{\sqrt{n^2+r^2}}=\lim\limits_{n\to\infty}\frac{1}{n}\sum\limits_{r=1}^{2n}\frac{\frac{r}{n}}{\sqrt{1+\frac{r^2}{n^2}}}$

$$=\int_0^2\frac{x}{\sqrt{1+x^2}}=\frac{1}{2}\int_0^2\frac{2x}{\sqrt{1+x^2}}=\frac{1}{2}\left[\frac{\left(1+x^2\right)^{1/2}}{\frac{1}{2}}\right]_0^2=\sqrt{5}-1$$

TEXTUAL EXERCISE–11: (SUBJECTIVE)

1. (i) $\int_0^\infty e^{-x}.x^{7/2}dx=\int_0^\infty e^{-x}.x^{\left(\frac{9}{2}-1\right)}dx$

$$\left(\because \Gamma n=\int_0^\infty e^{-x}(x)^{n-1}dx; n>0\right)$$

$$=\Gamma\tfrac{9}{2}=\frac{7}{2}\Gamma\tfrac{7}{2}=\frac{7}{2}.\frac{5}{2}\Gamma\tfrac{5}{2}=\frac{7}{2}.\frac{5}{2}.\frac{3}{2}\Gamma\tfrac{3}{2}=\frac{7}{2}.\frac{5}{2}.\frac{3}{2}.\frac{1}{2}\Gamma\tfrac{1}{2}$$

$$=\frac{7}{2}\times\frac{5}{2}\times\frac{3}{2}\times\frac{1}{2}\times\sqrt{\pi}=\frac{105}{16}\sqrt{\pi}$$

$$\left(\because \Gamma n=(n-1)\Gamma(n-1);\ \Gamma\tfrac{1}{2}=\sqrt{\pi}\right)$$

(ii) $I=\int_0^\infty e^{-x^2}.x^8dx$

Put $x^2=t$ $\Rightarrow x\,dx=dt/2$

$$\therefore\ I=\int_0^\infty e^{-t}\left(\sqrt{t}\right)^7.\frac{dt}{2}=\frac{1}{2}\int_0^\infty e^{-t}.(t)^{7/2}dt=\frac{1}{2}\int_0^\infty e^{-t}(t)^{\left(\frac{9}{2}-1\right)}$$

$$=\frac{1}{2}\Gamma\tfrac{9}{2}=\frac{1}{2}\left(\frac{105}{16}\sqrt{\pi}\right)=\frac{105}{32}\sqrt{\pi}$$

(iii) $I=\int_0^\infty e^{-x^2}.x^5dx$

Put $x^2=t$ $\Rightarrow x\,dx=dt/2$

$$\therefore\ I=\int_0^\infty e^{-t}\left(\sqrt{t}\right)^4.\frac{dt}{2}\Rightarrow I=\frac{1}{2}\int_0^\infty e^{-t}.t^2dt$$

$$\Rightarrow I=\frac{1}{2}\int_0^\infty e^{-t}(t)^{3-1}dt=\frac{1}{2}\Gamma 3=\frac{1}{2}(2).\Gamma 2=\frac{1}{2}(2).1.\Gamma 1$$

$$=\frac{1}{2}(2)(1).\underline{|0}=1\qquad\left(\because \Gamma n=\underline{|n-1}\text{ for } n\in\mathbb{N}\right)$$

(iv) $\Gamma\left(\frac{5}{2}\right)=\frac{3}{2}\Gamma\tfrac{3}{2}=\frac{3}{2}.\frac{1}{2}\Gamma\tfrac{1}{2}=\left(\frac{3}{2}\right)\left(\frac{1}{2}\right)\left(\sqrt{\pi}\right)=\frac{3}{4}\sqrt{\pi}$

(v) $\Gamma 8=7!=5040\qquad\left(\because \Gamma n=\underline{|(n-1)}\text{ for } n\in\mathbb{N}\right)$

2. $\frac{x^2}{1.2}-\frac{x^3}{2.3}+\frac{x^4}{3.4}.....(-1)^{n+1}.\frac{x^{n+1}}{n(x+1)}+....;|x|<1$

$$=\sum_{n=1}^{\infty}\frac{(-1)^{n+1}.x^{n+1}}{n(n+1)};|x|<1$$

$$=\sum_{n=1}^{\infty}\left[\frac{(n+1)-n}{n(n+1)}\right]x^{n+1}(-1)^{n+1}=\sum_{n=1}^{\infty}\left[\frac{1}{n}-\frac{1}{n+1}\right]x^{n+1}(-1)^{n+1}$$

$$=-x\sum_{n=1}^{\infty}\frac{(-1)^n x^n}{n}-\sum_{n=1}^{\infty}\frac{(-1)^{n+1}.x^{n+1}}{(n+1)}$$

$$=-x\sum_{n=1}^{\infty}\frac{(-x)^n}{n}-\sum_{n=1}^{\infty}\frac{(-x)^{n+1}}{(n+1)}$$

$$=x\ln(1+x)+\left[\ln(1+x)-x\right]=(x+1)\ln(1+x)-x$$

3. $f(x)=\frac{1}{2}\tan\frac{x}{2}+\frac{1}{2^2}\tan\frac{x}{2^2}+\frac{1}{2^3}\tan\frac{x}{2^3}+...\infty$

$$=\lim_{n\to\infty}\sum_{r=1}^{n}\frac{1}{2^r}\tan\left(\frac{x}{2^r}\right)$$

$$= \lim_{n\to\infty}\sum_{r=1}^{n}\frac{d}{dx}\left(\ln\sec\frac{x}{2^r}\right) = \lim_{n\to\infty}\frac{d}{dx}\sum_{r=1}^{n}\ln\left(\sec\frac{x}{2^r}\right)$$

$$= \lim_{n\to\infty}\frac{d}{dx}\left(\ln\left(\sec\frac{x}{2}.\sec\frac{x}{2^2}\sec\frac{x}{2^3}....\sec\frac{x}{2^n}\right)\right)$$

$$= \lim_{n\to\infty}\frac{d}{dx}\left[\ln\left(\frac{1}{\cos\frac{x}{2}}.\frac{1}{\cos\frac{x}{2^2}}.\frac{1}{\cos\frac{x}{2^3}}....\frac{1}{\cos\frac{x}{2^n}}\right)\right]$$

$$= \lim_{n\to\infty}\frac{d}{dx}\left[\ln\left(\frac{2\sin\frac{x}{2^n}}{\cos\frac{x}{2}.\cos\frac{x}{2^2}....\cos\frac{x}{2^{x-1}}.\cos\frac{x}{2^n}\sin\frac{x}{2^n}}\right)\right]$$

$$= \lim_{n\to\infty}\frac{d}{dx}\left[\ln\left(\frac{2\sin\frac{x}{2^n}}{\sin x}\right)\right]$$

$$= \lim_{n\to\infty}\left[\frac{1}{2\sin\left(\frac{x}{2^n}\right)}\times 2\cos\frac{x}{2^n}\times\frac{1}{2^n}-\cot x\right]$$

$$= \lim_{n\to\infty}\left[\frac{1}{x}.\frac{\left(\frac{x}{2^n}\right)}{\tan\left(\frac{x}{2^n}\right)}\right]-\cot x = \frac{1}{x}-\cot x$$

4. **(a)** $\int_0^{\pi/2}\sin^5 x\,dx = \frac{4\times 2}{5\times 3\times 1} = \frac{8}{15}$

(b) $\int_0^{\pi/2}\sin^4 x\cos^6 x\,dx = \frac{3\times 1\times 5\times 3\times 1}{10\times 8\times 6\times 4\times 2}\times\frac{\pi}{2} = \frac{3\pi}{512}$

(c) $I = \int_0^{\pi} x\sin^5 x\cos^6 x\,dx$

$\Rightarrow I = \int_0^{\pi}(\pi - x)\sin^5 x\cos^6 x\,dx = \pi\int_0^{\pi}\sin^5 x\cos^6 x\,dx - I$

$\Rightarrow I = \frac{\pi}{2}\int_0^{\pi}\sin^5 x\cos^6 x\,dx = \frac{\pi}{2}\times 2\int_0^{\pi/2}\sin^5 x\cos^6 x\,dx$

$= \pi\int_0^{\pi/2}\sin^5\cos^6 x\,dx$

$= \pi\left[\frac{4\times 2\times 5\times 3\times 1}{11\times 9\times 7\times 5\times 3}\right] = \frac{8\pi}{693}$

(d) $I = \int_0^{\pi}\sin^5 x\cos^4 x\,dx = 2\int_0^{\pi/2}\sin^5 x\cos^4 x\,dx$

$= 2\left[\frac{4\times 2\times 3\times 1}{9\times 7\times 5\times 3}\right] = \frac{16}{315}$

(e) $I = \int_0^1 x^3(1-x)^5\,dx$

Put $x = \sin^2\theta$

$\Rightarrow dx = 2\sin\theta\cos\theta\,d\theta$

$\Rightarrow I = \int_0^{\pi/2}\sin^6\theta.\cos^{10}\theta\times(2\sin\theta\cos\theta)d\theta$

$= 2\int_0^{\pi/2}\sin^7\theta.\cos^{11}\theta d\theta$

$= 2\frac{(6\times 4\times 2\times 10\times 8\times 6\times 4\times 2)}{18\times 16\times 14\times 12\times 10\times 8\times 6\times 4\times 2} = \frac{1}{504}$

5. $I = \int_0^1 x^{30}(1-x)^{70}dx$

Put $x = \sin^2\theta$ $\Rightarrow dx = 2\sin\theta\cos\theta\,d\theta$

$\Rightarrow I = \int_0^{\pi/2}\sin^{60}\theta(\cos^{140}\theta)(2\sin\theta\cos\theta)d\theta$

$= 2\int_0^{\pi/2}\sin^{61}\theta\cos^{141}\theta d\theta$

$= \frac{2\times 60\times 58\times 56\times....2\times 140\times 138\times....\times 2}{202\times 200\times 198\times....\times 2}$

$= \frac{2\times(2)^{30}(30!)\times(2)^{70}(70!)}{(2)^{101}(101)!} = \frac{(2)^{101}(30!)\times(70)!}{(2)^{101}(101)!}$

$\Rightarrow {}^{100}C_{30}I = \frac{100!}{30!70!}\times\frac{30!\times 70!}{(101)!} = \frac{1}{101}$

6. $I = \int_0^a x(a^2-x^2)^{7/2}dx$

Put x = a sinθ $\Rightarrow$ dx = a coxθ dθ

$\Rightarrow I = \int_0^{\pi/2}(a\sin\theta)a^7(\cos^7\theta)a\cos\theta\,d\theta$

$= a^9\int_0^{\pi/2}\sin\theta.\cos^8\theta\,d\theta$

$= a^9\times\left[-\frac{\cos^9\theta}{9}\right]_0^{\pi/2} = \frac{-a^9}{9}[0-1] = \frac{a^9}{9}$

7. $I = \int_0^{2a}x^5\sqrt{2ax-x^2}\,dx = \int_0^{2a}x^5.\sqrt{x}\sqrt{2a-x}\,dx$

Put $x = 2a\sin^2\theta$

$= \int_0^{\pi/2}(2a)^5\sin^{10}\theta.(2a\sin^2\theta)^{1/2}$

$\times\sqrt{2a-2a\sin^2\theta}\times 2a(\sin\theta\cos\theta)d\theta$

$= \int_0^{\pi/2}(2a)^7\sin^{12}\theta\cos^2\theta\,d\theta$

$= 128a^7\int_0^{\pi/2}\sin^{12}\theta\cos^2\theta\,d\theta$

$= 128a^7\frac{(11\times 9\times 7\times 5\times 3\times 1)}{14\times 12\times 10\times 8\times 6\times 4\times 2}\times\frac{\pi}{2} = \frac{33}{32}\pi a^7$

8. $\int_0^1\frac{x^{a-1}}{1+x^b}dx$

Put $x^a = t$ $\Rightarrow ax^{a-1}\,dx = dt$

$\Rightarrow I = \int_0^1\frac{dt}{a\left(1+(t)^{b/a}\right)} = \frac{1}{a}\int_0^1\left(1+t^{b/a}\right)^{-1}dt;\left|t^{b/a}\right|$

$= \left|x^b\right|\in(0,1)$ as $x\in(0,1)$

$= \frac{1}{a}\int_0^1\left(1-t^{b/a}+t^{2b/a}-t^{3b/a}+....\right)dx$

(using binomial theorem)

$$= \frac{1}{a}\left[t-\frac{t^{\frac{b}{a}+1}}{\left(\frac{b}{a}+1\right)}+\frac{t^{\frac{2b}{a}+1}}{\frac{2b}{a}+1}-\frac{t^{\frac{3b}{a}+1}}{\frac{3b}{a}+1}+...\right]_0^1$$

$$= \frac{1}{a}\left[1-\frac{1}{\left(\frac{b}{a}+1\right)}+\frac{1}{\left(\frac{2b}{a}+1\right)}-\frac{1}{\frac{3b}{a}+1}+...\right]$$

$$=\frac{1}{a}-\frac{1}{b+a}+\frac{1}{2b+a}-\frac{1}{3b+a}+....$$

Put $a = 1, b = 3$

$$\Rightarrow \quad I=\int_0^1 \frac{1}{1+x^3}dx = 1-\frac{1}{4}+\frac{1}{7}-\frac{1}{10}+...$$

$$\Rightarrow \quad 1-\frac{1}{4}+\frac{1}{7}-\frac{1}{10}+... = \int_0^1 \frac{1}{(1+x)(x^2-x+1)}dx$$

$$=\int_0^1 \left\{\frac{\frac{1}{3}}{(1+x)}+\frac{\left(-\frac{1}{3}x+\frac{2}{3}\right)}{x^2-x+1}\right\}dx$$

$$=\frac{1}{3}\left[\ln(x+1)\right]_0^1-\frac{1}{3}\int_0^1\frac{(x-2)}{x^2-x+1}dx$$

$$=\frac{1}{3}\ln 2-\frac{1}{2\times 3}\int_0^1\frac{2x-4}{x^2-x+1}dx$$

$$=\frac{1}{3}\ln 2-\frac{1}{6}\int_0^1\left\{\frac{2x-1}{x^2-x+1}-\frac{3}{\left(x-\frac{1}{2}\right)^2+\left(\frac{\sqrt{3}}{2}\right)^2}\right\}dx$$

$$=\frac{1}{3}\ln 2-\frac{1}{6}\left[\ln\left(x^2-x+1\right)\right]_0^1+\frac{1}{2}\times\frac{2}{\sqrt{3}}\tan^{-1}\left[\frac{2x-1}{\sqrt{3}}\right]_0^1$$

$$=\frac{1}{3}\ln 2-\frac{1}{6}[0]+\frac{2}{\sqrt{3}}\tan^{-1}\frac{1}{\sqrt{3}}$$

$$=\frac{1}{3}\ln 2+\frac{2}{\sqrt{3}}\left(\frac{\pi}{6}\right)=\frac{1}{3}\ln 2+\frac{\pi}{3\sqrt{3}}=\frac{1}{3}\left(\frac{\pi}{\sqrt{3}}+\ln 2\right)$$

9. R.H.S. $=x+\frac{x^2}{2}+\int_0^x\frac{y^2}{1-y}dy=x+\frac{x^2}{2}-\int_0^x\frac{y^2-1+1}{y-1}dy$

$$=x+\frac{x^2}{2}-\int_0^x\left\{(y+1)+\frac{1}{y-1}\right\}dy$$

$$=x+\frac{x^2}{2}-\left[\frac{y^2}{2}+y\right]_0^x-\left[\ln|y-1|\right]_0^x$$

$$=x+\frac{x^2}{2}-\left[\frac{x^2}{2}+x\right]-\ln|x-1|$$

$$=x+\frac{x^2}{2}-\frac{x^2}{2}-x-\ln(1-x) \qquad [\because 0<x<1]$$

$$=-\ln(1-x)=\text{R.H.S.}$$

10. **(i)** $\frac{x^3}{1.3}-\frac{x^5}{3.5}+\frac{x^7}{5.7}-....=\sum_{r=1}^{\infty}\frac{(-1)^{r-1}.(x)^{2r+1}}{(2r-1)(2r+1)}$

$$=\sum_{r=1}^{\infty}\frac{1}{2}(-1)^{r-1}\left[\frac{(2r+1)-(2r-1)}{(2r-1)(2r+1)}\right].x^{2r+1}$$

$$=\frac{1}{2}\sum_{r=1}^{\infty}\frac{(-1)^{r-1}.x^{2r+1}}{(2r-1)}-\frac{1}{2}\sum_{r=1}^{\infty}\frac{(-1)^{r+1}.x^{2r+1}}{(2r+1)}$$

$$=\frac{1}{2}x^2\sum_{r=1}^{\infty}\frac{(-1)^{r-1}.x^{2r-1}}{(2r-1)}-\frac{1}{2}\sum_{r=1}^{\infty}\frac{(-1)^{r+1}.x^{2r+1}}{(2r+1)}$$

$$=\frac{1}{2}x^2\left[x-\frac{x^3}{3}+\frac{x^5}{5}-\frac{x^7}{7}+....\right]-\frac{1}{2}\left[\frac{x^3}{3}-\frac{x^5}{5}+\frac{x^7}{7}-....\right]$$

$$=\frac{1}{2}\left(x^2+1\right)\left[x-\frac{x^3}{3}+\frac{x^5}{5}-\frac{x^7}{7}+....\right]-\frac{1}{2}x$$

$$=\frac{1}{2}\left(x^2+1\right)\int_0^x\left(1-x^2+x^4-x^6+....\right)dx-\frac{1}{2}dx$$

$$=\frac{1}{2}\left(x^2+1\right)\int_0^x\left(1+x^2\right)^{-1}dx-\frac{1}{2}x$$

$$=\frac{1}{2}\left(x^2+1\right)\tan^{-1}x-\frac{1}{2}x$$

(ii) $\int_0^x\frac{\sin x}{x}dx=\int_0^x\frac{1}{x}\left(x-\frac{x^3}{3!}+\frac{x^5}{5!}-\frac{x^7}{7!}+....\right)dx$

$$=\int_0^x\left(1-\frac{x^2}{3!}+\frac{x^4}{5!}-\frac{x^6}{7!}+....\right)dx$$

$$=x-\frac{x^3}{3.3!}+\frac{x^5}{5.5!}-\frac{x^7}{7.7!}+....$$

(iii) $\int_a^b\frac{e^x}{x}dx=\int_a^b\frac{1}{x}\left(1+x+\frac{x^2}{2!}+\frac{x^3}{3!}+....\right)dx$

$$=\int_a^b\left(\frac{1}{x}+1+\frac{x}{2!}+\frac{x^2}{3!}+....\right)dx$$

$$=\left[\ln x+x+\frac{x^2}{2.(2!)}+\frac{x^3}{3.(3!)}+....\right]_a^b$$

$$=\ln\left(\frac{b}{a}\right)+(b-a)+\frac{\left(b^2-a^2\right)}{2.2!}+\frac{\left(b^3-a^3\right)}{3.(3!)}+....$$

11. $\int_{\ln 2}^{\ln 3}f(x)dx=\int_{\ln 2}^{\ln 3}\left(e^{-x}+2e^{-2x}+3e^{-3x}+....\infty\right)dx$

$$=\left[\frac{e^{-x}}{-1}+\frac{2.e^{-2x}}{-2}+\frac{3.e^{-3x}}{-3}+....\infty\right]_{\ln 2}^{\ln 3}$$

$$=-\left[e^{-x}+e^{-2x}+e^{-3x}+....\infty\right]_{\ln 2}^{\ln 3}$$

$$=-\left[e^{-x}+\left(e^{-x}\right)^2+\left(e^{-x}\right)^3+....\infty\right]_{\ln 2}^{\ln 3}=-\left[\frac{e^{-x}}{1-\left(e^{-x}\right)}\right]_{\ln 2}^{\ln 3}$$

$$\left[\begin{array}{l}\because \ln 2<x<\ln 3\\ \Rightarrow 2<e^x<3\\ \Rightarrow \frac{1}{3}<\frac{1}{e^x}<\frac{1}{2}\\ \Rightarrow \left|e^{-x}\right|<1\end{array}\right]$$

$$=-\left[\frac{e^{\ln 1/3}}{1-e^{\ln 1/3}}\right]+\left[\frac{e^{\ln 1/2}}{1-e^{\ln 1/2}}\right]=-\left[\frac{\frac{1}{3}}{1-\frac{1}{3}}\right]+\left[\frac{\frac{1}{2}}{1-\frac{1}{2}}\right]$$

$$=-\left[\frac{\frac{1}{3}}{\frac{2}{3}}\right]+1=\frac{1}{2}$$

12. $I=\int_0^2 \sqrt{x}\left(4-x^2\right)^{-1/4}dx$

Put x = 2 sinθ $\Rightarrow dx = 2\cos\theta\, d\theta$

$\Rightarrow I=\int_0^{\pi/2}\sqrt{2\sin\theta}\left(4-4\sin^2\theta\right)^{-1/4}(2\cos\theta d\theta)$

$=\frac{\sqrt{2}(2)}{(4)^{1/4}}\int_0^{\pi/2}\frac{\sqrt{\sin\theta}}{(\cos\theta)^{1/2}}\cos\theta d\theta$

$=\frac{2\sqrt{2}}{\sqrt{2}}\int_0^{\pi/2}(\cos\theta)^{1/2}(\sin\theta)^{1/2}d\theta$

$=2\int_0^{\pi/2}(\sin\theta)^{2\left(\frac{3}{4}\right)-1}.(\cos\theta)^{2\left(\frac{3}{4}\right)-1}d\theta=2\beta\left(\frac{3}{4},\frac{3}{4}\right)$

13. $I=\int_0^1 x^m\left(1-x^n\right)^p dx$

Put $x^n = t$ $\Rightarrow dx = dt$

$\Rightarrow dx=\frac{dt}{nx^{n-1}}$

$\therefore I=\int_0^1 x^m(1-t)^p.\frac{dt}{nx^{n-1}}=\frac{1}{n}\int_0^1 x^{m-n+1}(1-t)^p dt$

$=\frac{1}{n}\int_0^1\left(t^{1/n}\right)^{m-n+1}(1-t)^p dt$

$=\frac{1}{n}\int_0^1(t)^{\frac{m+1}{n}-1}(1-t)^{(p+1)-1}=\frac{1}{n}\beta\left(\frac{m+1}{n},p+1\right)$

$\therefore \int_0^1 x^5\left(1-x^3\right)^{10}dx=\frac{1\beta}{3}\left(\frac{5+1}{3},10+1\right)=\frac{1}{3}\beta(2,11)$

$=\frac{1}{3}\frac{\lceil 2\lceil 11}{\lceil 13}=\frac{1}{3}\frac{(1!)\lceil 11}{12.11\lceil 11}=\frac{1}{396}$

14. $I=\int_0^\infty\sqrt{x}\,e^{-x^3}dx$

Put $x^3 = t$ $\Rightarrow 3x^2\,dx = dt$

$\Rightarrow dx=\frac{dt}{3x^2}$

$\therefore I=\int_0^\infty\sqrt{x}\,e^{-t}\frac{dt}{3x^2}=\frac{-1}{3}\int_0^\infty(x)^{-3/2}.e^{-t}dt$

$=\frac{1}{3}\int_0^\infty\left[(t)^{1/3}\right]^{-3/2}.e^{-t}dt=\frac{1}{3}\int_0^\infty e^{-t}.(t)^{-1/2}dt$

$=\frac{1}{3}\int_0^\infty e^{-t}.(t)^{\frac{1}{2}-1}.dt=\frac{1}{3}\left\lceil\frac{1}{2}\right.=\frac{\sqrt{\pi}}{3}\left(\because\left\lceil\frac{1}{2}\right.=\sqrt{\pi}\right)$

15. $f(x)=\int_0^x e^t.\sin(x-t)dt$

$g(x)=f''(x)-f(x)$ ...(1)

Now, $f'(x)=\int_0^x e^t\cos(x-t)dt+e^x$

$\Rightarrow f''(x)=\int_0^x e^t(-\sin(x-t))dt+e^x$

$=-\int_0^x e^t\sin(x-t)dt+e^x=-f(x)+e^x$

$\Rightarrow f''(x)-f(x)=e^x-2f(x)$

$\Rightarrow g(x)=e^x-2f(x)$ ...(2)

Now, $f(x)=\int_0^x e^t[\sin x\cos t-\cos x\sin t]dt$

$=\sin x\int_0^x e^t\cos t\,dt-\cos x\int_0^x e^t\sin t\,dt$

$=(\sin x)\left[\frac{e^t}{2}(\cos t+\sin t)\right]_0^x$

$-(\cos x)\left[\frac{e^t}{2}(\sin t-\cos t)\right]_0^x$

$=\frac{(\sin x)e^x}{2}(\cos x+\sin x)-\frac{\sin x}{2}$

$-\frac{(\cos x)e^x}{2}(\sin x-\cos x)+\frac{\cos x}{2}(-1)$

$=\frac{e^x}{2}\left[\sin x\cos x+\sin^2 x-\sin x\cos x+\cos^2 x\right]$

$-\frac{1}{2}(\sin x+\cos x)$

$=\frac{e^x}{2}-\frac{1}{2}(\sin x+\cos x)$ ...(3)

$\therefore$ From (2) and (3), $g(x)=e^x-e^x+(\sin x+\cos x)$

$\Rightarrow g(x)=(\sin x+\cos x)$ and hence range of $g(x)=\left[-\sqrt{2},\sqrt{2}\right]$

16. $f(x)=x+\int_0^1\left(xy^2+x^2y\right).f(y)dy$

$\Rightarrow f(x)=x+\int_0^1\left(xy+x^2\right).y\,f(y)dy$

$\Rightarrow f'(x)=1+\int_0^1(y+2x).y\,f(y)dy$

$=1+\int_0^1\left(y^2+2xy\right)f(y).dy$

$=1+\int_0^1 y^2f(y)dy+2x\int_0^1 y\,f(y)dy$

$=1+\int_0^1 y^2f(y)dy+2x\int_0^1 y\,f(y)dy=1+2x\,c_2+c_1$ (say)

$\therefore f'(x)=2x\,c_2+1+c_1$

$\Rightarrow f(x)=c_2x^2+(c_1+1)x$ ...(1)

$\therefore c_1=\int_0^1 y^2\left(c_2y^2+(c_1+1)y\right)dy$

$\Rightarrow c_1=\int_0^1\left[c_2y^4+(c_1+1)y^3\right]dy=\left[\frac{c_2y^5}{5}+\frac{(c_1+1)y^4}{4}\right]_0^1$

$\Rightarrow c_1=\frac{c_2}{5}+\frac{c_1+1}{4}$ ...(2)

Also, $c_2=\int_0^1 y\,f(y)dy=\int_0^1 y\left(c_2y^2+(c_1+1)y\right)dy$

$\Rightarrow c_2=\int_0^1\left[c_2y^3+(c_1+1)y^2\right]dy=\left[\frac{c_2y^4}{4}+\frac{(c_1+1)y^3}{3}\right]_0^1$

$\Rightarrow c_2=\frac{c_2}{4}+\frac{c_1+1}{3}$ ...(3)

Solving, (2) and (3), we get, $c_1=\frac{61}{119},c_2=\frac{80}{119}$

Using above values in (1), we get, $f(x)=\frac{80}{119}x^2+\left(\frac{180}{119}\right)x$

$\Rightarrow f(x)=\frac{80x^2+180x}{119}$ $\Rightarrow 119.f(1)=260$

17. $\int_0^x f(t)dt = e^x - ce^{2x}\underbrace{\int_0^1 f(t).e^{-t}dt}_{C_1\text{ (say)}}$

$\Rightarrow f(x) = e^x - ce^{2x}(0) - cC_1\left(2e^{2x}\right)$ ...(1); where

$C_1 = \int_0^1 f(t).e^{-t}dt$

$\Rightarrow C_1 = \int_0^1\left(e^x - 2cC_1e^{2x}\right)e^{-x}dx = \int_0^1\left(1 - 2cC_1e^x\right)dx$

$= \left[x - 2cC_1e^x\right]_0^1 \; C_1 = 1 - 2cC_1e + 2cC_1$

$\Rightarrow C_1(1 + 2ce - 2c) = 1 \Rightarrow C_1 = \dfrac{1}{(1 - 2ce - 2c)}$

$\therefore f(x) = e^x - 2ce^{2x}\left(\dfrac{1}{1 + 2ce - 2c}\right)$

$\Rightarrow f(x) = \dfrac{(1 + 2ce - 2c)e^x - 2ce^{2x}}{(1 + 2ce - 2c)}$

$\Rightarrow f(x) = e^x - \dfrac{2c.e^{2x}}{(1 + 2ce - 2c)}$ ...(2)

$\therefore \int_0^x f(t)dt = e^x - ce^{2x}c_1 = e^x - ce^{2x}\left[\dfrac{1}{1 + 2ce - 2c}\right]$ at

$x = 0$, L.H.S. = 0

$\Rightarrow 0 = 1 - c\left[\dfrac{1}{1 + 2ce - 2c}\right]$

$\Rightarrow 1 + 2ce - 2c - c = 0$

$\Rightarrow 2e + c^{-1} = 3$

$\Rightarrow f(x) = e^x - \dfrac{2e^x}{(c^{-1} + 2e - 2)}$

$\Rightarrow f(x) = e^x - \dfrac{2e^x}{(3 - 2)}$

$\Rightarrow f(x) = e^x - 2e^x$

Thus, $f(x) = e^x - 2e^x$, $2e + c^{-1} = 3$

18. $f(x) = e^x + \int_0^1\left(e^x + te^{-x}\right)f(t)dt$

$\Rightarrow f(x) = e^x + e^x\int_0^1 f(t)dt + e^{-x}\int_0^1 t.f(t)dt$

$\Rightarrow f(x) = e^x + e^x.\, k_1 + e^{-x}.\, k_2$ ...(1)

where $k_1 = \int_0^1 f(x)dx$ and $k_2 = \int_0^1 x\, f(x)dx$

$\therefore k_1 = \int_0^1\left[(1 + k_1)e^x + k_2e^{-x}\right]dx$

$\Rightarrow k_1 = (1 + k_1)(e - 1) + k_2\left(-e^{-1} + 1\right)$ ...(2)

and $k_2 = \int_0^1 x\left(e^x + k_1e^x + k_2e^{-x}\right)dx$

$\Rightarrow k_2 = \int_0^1 (k_1 + 1)x.e^x dx + k_2\int_0^1 x.e^{-x}dx$

$\Rightarrow k_2 = (k_1 + 1)\left[\left|xe^x\right|_0^1 - \int_0^1 e^x\right] + k_2\left[\left|\dfrac{xe^{-x}}{-1}\right|_0^1 - \int_0^1 \dfrac{e^{-x}}{-1}dx\right]$

$\Rightarrow k_2 = (k_1 + 1)\left[e - [e - 1]\right] + k_2\left[-e^{-1} - \left[e^{-1} - 1\right]\right]$

$\Rightarrow k_2 = (k_1 + 1) + k_2\left(1 - 2e^{-1}\right)$ ...(3)

Solving (2) and (3), we get $k_1 = \dfrac{3(e - 1)}{5 - 3e}$ and $k_2 = \dfrac{e}{5 - 3e}$

$\therefore f(x) = (k_1 + 1)e^x + k_2e^{-x}$

$\Rightarrow f(x) = \dfrac{2}{5 - 3e}.e^x + \dfrac{e}{5 - 3e}.e^{-x}$

$\Rightarrow f(x) = \dfrac{1}{(5 - 3e)}\left(2e^x + e^{1-x}\right)$

TEXTUAL EXERCISE–11: (OBJECTIVE)

1. (a), (c) $I = \int_0^\infty e^{-x}.5^{5/2}dx = \int_0^\infty e^{-x}(x)^{\frac{7}{2}-1}dx$

$= \left|\dfrac{7}{2} = \dfrac{5}{2} \times \dfrac{3}{2} \times \dfrac{1}{2} \times \right|\dfrac{1}{2} = \dfrac{15}{8}\sqrt{\pi}$

2. (d) $I = \int_0^\infty e^{-x^3}.x^6 dx$

Put $x^3 = t$ $\Rightarrow 3x^2\, dx = dt$

$\Rightarrow dx = \dfrac{1}{3x^2}dt$

$\therefore I = \int_0^\infty e^{-t}\left(t^2\right)\dfrac{1}{3x^2}dt = \dfrac{1}{3}\int_0^\infty e^{-t}(t)^{-2/3}dt$

$= \dfrac{1}{3}\int_0^\infty e^{-t}(t)^{4/3}dt = \dfrac{1}{3}\int_0^\infty e^{-t}.(t)^{\frac{7}{3}-1}dt = \dfrac{1}{3}\left|\dfrac{7}{3}\right.$

3. (a), (b), (c) $I = \int_0^{\pi/2} \dfrac{e^{-\left(\tan^{-1}x\right)}\left(\tan^{-1}x\right)^{7/2}}{\left(1 + x^2\right)}dx$

Put $\tan^{-1}x = t$ $\Rightarrow \dfrac{1}{1 + x^2}dx = dt$

$\Rightarrow I = \int_0^\infty e^{-t}(t)^{7/2}.dt = \int_0^\infty e^{-t}(t)^{\frac{9}{2}-1}dt$

$= \left|\dfrac{9}{2} = \dfrac{7}{2} \times \dfrac{5}{2} \times \dfrac{3}{2} \times \dfrac{1}{2} \times \right|\dfrac{1}{2} = \dfrac{105}{16}\sqrt{\pi}$

$= \dfrac{7 \times 6 \times 5 \times 4 \times 3 \times 2}{6 \times 4 \times 2 \times (2)^4} \times \sqrt{\pi} = \dfrac{7!}{3 \times 2 \times 1} \times \dfrac{\sqrt{\pi}}{(2)^7} = \dfrac{7!\sqrt{\pi}}{3!(2)^7}$

4. (c) $I = \int_0^\pi\left(\cos^4 2x \sin^2 4x\right)dx$

Put $2x = t$ $\Rightarrow dx = \dfrac{dt}{2}$

$\therefore I = \int_0^{2\pi} \cos^4 t \sin^2 2t\dfrac{dt}{2} = \dfrac{1}{2}\int_0^{2\pi} 4\sin^2 t\cos^6 t\, dt$

$= \int_0^\pi 4\sin^2 t\cos^6 t\, dt$

$= 8\int_0^{\pi/2} \sin^2 t\cos^6 t\, dt = 4 \times \dfrac{\left|\frac{3}{2}\right.\left|\frac{7}{2}\right.}{\left|5\right.}$

$= 4 \times \dfrac{\frac{1}{2} \times \left|\frac{1}{2}\right. \times \frac{5}{2} \times \frac{3}{2} \times \frac{1}{2}\left|\frac{1}{2}\right.}{4!}$

$= 4 \times \dfrac{15}{4!} \times \dfrac{1}{16} \times \pi = \dfrac{5}{4 \times 3 \times 2} \times \dfrac{1}{16}\pi = 4 \times \dfrac{5\pi}{128} = \dfrac{5\pi}{32}$

5. (b) $I = \int_0^\pi x\cos^2 x\sin^4 x\, dx$

$\Rightarrow I = \int_0^\pi (\pi - x)\cos^2(\pi - x)\sin^4(\pi - x)dx$

$= \int_0^\pi (\pi - x)\cos^2 x\sin^4 x\, dx = \int_0^\pi \cos^2 x\sin^4 x\, dx = I$

$\Rightarrow\ I=\frac{\pi}{2}\int_0^{\pi}\cos^2 x\sin^4 x\,dx=\frac{\pi}{2}\times 2\int_0^{\pi/2}\cos^2 x\sin^4 x\,dx$

$=\pi\int_0^{\pi/2}\cos^2 x\sin^4 x\,dx=\pi\times\frac{1}{2}\beta\left(\frac{3}{2},\frac{5}{2}\right)$

$=\frac{\pi}{2}\frac{\overline{|\frac{3}{2}}\,\overline{|\frac{5}{2}}}{\overline{|4}}=\frac{\frac{\pi}{2}\times\frac{1}{2}\overline{|\frac{1}{2}}\times\frac{3}{2}\times\frac{1}{2}\overline{|\frac{1}{2}}}{3!}=\frac{\pi^2}{32}$

6. (b) $I=\int_0^1 x^5(1-x^3)^3\,dx$

Put $x^3=t \Rightarrow 3x^2\,dx=dt$

$\Rightarrow\ I=\frac{1}{3}\int_0^1 t(1-t)^3\,dt=\frac{1}{3}\int_0^1 t^{2-1}(1-t)^{4-1}\,dt=\frac{1}{3}\beta(2,4)$

$=\frac{1}{3}\times\frac{\overline{|2}\,\overline{|4}}{\overline{|6}}=\frac{1}{3}\times\frac{1!\times 3!}{5!}=\frac{2}{120}=\frac{1}{60}$

7. (b) $\int_0^{\infty}e^{-x^2}dx$

Put $x^2=t \Rightarrow 2x\,dx=dt$

$\Rightarrow\ \int_0^{\infty}e^{-t}\left(\frac{dt}{2\sqrt{t}}\right)=\frac{1}{2}\int_0^{\infty}e^{-t}(t)^{\frac{1}{2}-1}dt=\frac{1}{2}\overline{|\frac{1}{2}}=\frac{\sqrt{\pi}}{2}$

8. (c) $I=\int_0^{\infty}x^6.e^{-2x}dx$

Put $2x=t \Rightarrow dx=\frac{dt}{2}$

$\Rightarrow\ I=\int_0^{\infty}\left(\frac{t}{2}\right)^6 e^{-t}.\frac{dt}{2}=\frac{1}{128}\int_0^{\infty}e^{-t}(7)^{7-1}dt$

$=\frac{1}{128}\overline{|7}=\frac{1}{128}\times 6!=\frac{720}{128}=\frac{180}{32}=\frac{45}{8}$

9. (d) $I=\int_0^{\pi/2}\sin^3 x.\cos^{5/2}x\,dx=\int_0^{\pi/2}\sin^{2(2)-1}x.\cos^{2\left(\frac{7}{4}\right)-1}x\,dx$

$=\frac{1}{2}\beta\left(2,\frac{7}{4}\right)$

10. (a) Consider, $\int\frac{1}{1+x^2}dx=\tan^{-1}x$

$\Rightarrow\ \tan^{-1}x=\int(1+x^2)^{-1}dx=\int(1-x^2+x^4-x^6+....)dx$

$=\left(x-\frac{x^3}{3}+\frac{x^5}{5}-\frac{x^7}{7}+....\right)+c$

$\Rightarrow\ \frac{\tan^{-1}x}{x}=\left(1-\frac{x^2}{3}+\frac{x^4}{5}-\frac{x^6}{7}+....\right)dx$

$\Rightarrow\ \int_0^1\frac{\tan^{-1}x}{x}dx=\int_0^1\left(1-\frac{x^2}{3}+\frac{x^4}{5}-\frac{x^6}{7}+....\right)dx$

$=\left[x-\frac{x^3}{9}+\frac{x^5}{(5)^2}-\frac{x^7}{(7)^2}+....\right]_0^1=1-\frac{1}{9}+\frac{1}{25}-\frac{1}{49}+....$

$=\sum_{n=0}^{\infty}\frac{(-1)^n}{(2n+1)^2}$

11. (b) $(f(x))^2=2\int_0^x f(t)dt$ ...(1)

$\Rightarrow\ 2.f(x).f'(x)=2f(x)$

$\Rightarrow\ 2f(x).[f'(x)-1]=0$

$\Rightarrow\ f'(x)=1$ as $f(x)\neq 0$ identically

$\Rightarrow\ f(x)=\int 1\,dx \Rightarrow f(x)=x+c$ ...(2)

From (1); $f(0)=0 \Rightarrow C=0$ (using (2))

$\Rightarrow\ f(x)=x$

12. (c) $\int_c^x f(t)dt=\cos x-\frac{\sqrt{3}}{2}\ \forall x\in\mathbb{R}$

Differentiating both sides, we get $f(x)=-\sin x\ \forall x\in\mathbb{R}$

$\therefore\ \int_c^x(-\sin t)dt=\cos x-\frac{\sqrt{3}}{2}\forall x\in\mathbb{R}$

$\Rightarrow\ [\cos t]_c^x=\cos x-\frac{\sqrt{3}}{2}\forall x\in\mathbb{R}$

$\Rightarrow\ \cos x-\cos c=\cos x-\frac{\sqrt{3}}{2}\forall x\in\mathbb{R}$

$\Rightarrow\ \cos c=\frac{\sqrt{3}}{2} \Rightarrow c=\frac{\pi}{6}$

13. (b), (c) $\int_a^x t\,f(t)dt=\sin x-x\cos x\frac{-1}{x}x^2\ \forall x\in\mathbb{R}$,

$\Rightarrow\ x\,f(x)=\cos x+x\sin x-\cos x-x\ \forall x\in\mathbb{R}$

$\Rightarrow\ x\,f(x)=x(\sin x-1)\forall x\in\mathbb{R}$

$\Rightarrow\ f(x)=(\sin x-1)\forall x\in\mathbb{R}$

$\Rightarrow\ \int_a^x t(\sin t-1)dt=\sin x-x\cos x-\frac{1}{2}x^2$

$\Rightarrow\ \int_a^x(t\sin t-t)dt=\sin x-x\cos x-\frac{1}{2}x^2$

$\Rightarrow\ |-t\cos t|_a^x-\int_a^x 1(-\cos t)dt-\left[\frac{t^2}{2}\right]_a^x$

$=\sin x-x\cos x-\frac{1}{2}x^2$

$\Rightarrow\ -x\cos x+a\cos a+(\sin x-\sin a)-\frac{x^2}{2}+\frac{a^2}{2}$

$=\sin x-x\cos x-\frac{1}{2}x^2$

$\Rightarrow\ a\cos a-\sin a+\frac{a^2}{2}=0$

$\Rightarrow$ a = 0 is a possible value, where as $a=\frac{\pi}{2}$ is impossible.

14. (b) $\int_0^{x^2}f(t)dt=1-3^{x^2}$

$\Rightarrow\ f(x^2)(2x)=0-3^{x^2}(\ln 3)(2x)$

$\Rightarrow\ f(x^2)=-3^{x^2}(\ln 3)$

$\Rightarrow\ f(x)=-3^{x}.(\ln 3)$

TUTORIAL SHEET SECTION–III

1. (b) $I=\int_{\pi/3}^{\pi/2}\frac{\sqrt{1+\cos x}}{(1-\cos x)^{5/2}}dx=\int_{\pi/3}^{\pi/2}\frac{\sqrt{2\cos^2\frac{x}{2}}}{\left(2\sin^2\frac{x}{2}\right)^{5/2}}dx$

$=\int_{\pi/3}^{\pi/2}\frac{\sqrt{2}}{(2)^{5/2}}.\frac{\cos\frac{x}{2}}{\sin^5\frac{x}{2}}dx=\frac{1}{4}\int_{\pi/3}^{\pi/2}\frac{\cos\frac{x}{2}}{\sin^5\frac{x}{2}}dx$

Put $\sin\frac{x}{2}=t$ $\Rightarrow$ $\frac{1}{2}\cos\frac{x}{2}dx=dt$

$\Rightarrow$ $I=\frac{1}{2}\int_{1/2}^{1/\sqrt{2}}\frac{dt}{t^5}=\frac{1}{2}\left(\frac{t^{-4}}{-4}\right)_{1/2}^{1/\sqrt{2}}$ $=-\frac{1}{8}\left[\left(\sqrt{2}\right)^4-(2)^4\right]$

$=\frac{-1}{8}[4-16]=\frac{3}{2}$

2. (a) $\int_1^e\frac{e^x}{x}(1+x\log x)dx$

$=\int_1^e e^x\left(\frac{1}{x}+\log x\right)dx=\left[e^x\log x\right]_1^e=e^x f(x)$

$\left(\because\int e^x\left(f(x)+f'(x)\right)\right)dx$

$=e^e-0=e^e$

3. (b) $\int_0^{b-c}f''(x+a)dx$

Put $x+a=t$ $\Rightarrow$ $dx=dt$

$\therefore$ $I=\int_a^{b-c+a}f''(t)dt=\left[f'(t)\right]_a^{a+b-c}=f'(a+b-c)-f'(a)$

4. (c) $\int_0^1\frac{d}{dx}\left[\sin^{-1}\left(\frac{2x}{1+x^2}\right)\right]dx=\int_0^1\frac{d}{dx}\left(2\tan^{-1}x\right)dx$

$\left(\because 2\tan^{-1}x=\sin^{-1}\left(\frac{2x}{1+x^2}\right)\right.$ for $\left.-1\le x\le 1\right)$

$=2\int_0^1\frac{1}{1+x^2}dx=2\left[\tan^{-1}x\right]_0^1=\frac{\pi}{2}$

5. (b) $\phi(x)=f'(x)$ and $f(a)=b, f(\lambda)=\mu$

$\therefore$ $\int_a^\lambda\phi(x)dx=\int_a^\lambda f'(x)dx=\left[f(x)\right]_a^\lambda=f(\lambda)-f(a)$

$=(\mu-b)$

6. (a) $\int_0^{\pi/4}\frac{dx}{\cos^4x-\cos^2x\sin^2x+\sin^4x}$

$=\int_0^{\pi/4}\frac{dx}{\left(\cos^2x+\sin^2x\right)^2-3\sin^2x\cos^2x}=\int_0^{\pi/4}\frac{dx}{1-\frac{3}{4}\sin^2 2x}$

$=\int_0^{\pi/4}\frac{\sec^2 2x\,dx}{\sec^2 2x-\frac{3}{4}\tan^2 2x}=\int_0^{\pi/4}\frac{\sec^2 2x\,dx}{1+\frac{1}{4}\tan^2 2x}$

Put $\tan x=t$ $\Rightarrow$ $2\sec^2 2x\,dx=dt$

$\therefore$ $I=\int_0^\infty\frac{4dt}{2\left(4+\tan^2 2x\right)}=\int_0^\infty\frac{2dt}{4+t^2}=2\left(\frac{1}{2}\right)\left[.\tan^{-1}\left(\frac{t}{2}\right)\right]_0^\infty$

$=\frac{\pi}{2}$

7. (b) $I=\int_0^\pi e^{\sin^2x}\cos^3(2n+1)x\,dx$

$=\int_0^\pi e^{\sin^2(\pi-x)}.\cos^3\left[(2n+1)(\pi-x)\right]dx$

$=\int_0^\pi -e^{\sin^2x}\cos^3(2n+1)x\,dx=-I$

$\Rightarrow$ $2I=0$ $\Rightarrow$ $I=0$

8. (b) $\int_0^\pi x f\left(\cos^2x+\tan^4x\right)dx=k\int_0^{\pi/2}f\left(\cos^2x+\tan^4x\right)dx$

$\Rightarrow$ $I=\int_0^\pi(\pi-x).f\left(\cos^2(\pi-x)+\tan^4(\pi-x)\right)dx$

$\Rightarrow$ $I=\int_0^\pi(\pi-x).f\left(\cos^2x+\tan^4x\right)dx$

$=\pi\int_0^\pi f\left(\cos^2x+\tan^4x\right)dx-I$

$\Rightarrow$ $I=\frac{\pi}{2}\int_0^\pi f\left(\cos^2x+\tan^4x\right)dx$

$=\frac{\pi}{2}\times 2\int_0^{\pi/2}f\left(\cos^2x+\tan^4x\right)dx$

$=\pi\int_0^{\pi/2}f\left(\cos^2x+\tan^4x\right)dx$

$\left[\because\int_0^{2a}f(x)dx=2\int_0^a f(x)dx \text{ if } f(2a-x)=f(x)\right]$

$\Rightarrow$ $k=\pi$

9. (c) $I=\int_{1/n}^{a-\frac{1}{n}}\frac{\sqrt{x}}{\sqrt{a-x}+\sqrt{x}}dx$ ...(1)

$\Rightarrow$ $I=\int_{1/n}^{a-\frac{1}{n}}\frac{\sqrt{a-x}}{\sqrt{x}+\sqrt{a-x}}dx$ ...(2)

$\left[\because\int_a^b f(x)dx=\int_a^b f(a+b-x)dx\right]$

Adding (1) and (2), we get $2I=\int_{1/n}^{a-\frac{1}{n}}1\,dx=a-\frac{2}{n}$

$\Rightarrow$ $I=\frac{a}{2}-\frac{1}{n}=\frac{na-2}{2n}$

10. (d) $f(x)=\frac{e^x}{1+e^x}, I_1=\int_{f(-a)}^{f(a)}x.g\{x(1-x)\}dx$ and

$I_2=\int_{f(-a)}^{f(a)}g\{x(1-x)\}dx,$

Hence $f(a)+f(-a)=\frac{e^a}{1+e^a}+\frac{e^{-a}}{1+e^{-a}}=1$

$\therefore$ $I_1=\int_{f(-a)}^{f(a)}(1-x).g\{x(1-x)\}dx$

$=\int_{f(-a)}^{f(a)}(1-x)g\{x(1-x)\}dx=\int_{f(-a)}^{f(a)}g\{x(1-x)\}dx$

$-\int_{f(-a)}^{f(a)}x.g\{x(1-x)\}dx$

$\Rightarrow$ $I_1=I_2-I_1$ $\Rightarrow$ $2I_1=I_2$

$\Rightarrow$ $\frac{I_2}{I_1}=2$

11. (b) $\int_{-\pi/4}^{\pi/4}\left(\lambda|\sin x|+\frac{\mu\sin x}{1+\cos x}+v\right)dx=0$

$\because$ $\frac{\mu\sin x}{1+\cos x}$ = odd function and $\lambda|\sin x|+v$ = even function

$\therefore$ $=2\int_0^{\pi/4}\left(\lambda|\sin x|+v\right)dx=2\int_0^{\pi/4}\left(\lambda\sin x+v\right)dx$

$=-2\lambda\left[\frac{1}{\sqrt{2}}-1\right]+2v\left(\frac{\pi}{4}\right)=2\lambda-\sqrt{2}\lambda+\frac{v\pi}{2}$

12. (c) $I=\int_{\ln\lambda}^{\ln(1/\lambda)}\frac{f\left(\frac{x^2}{4}\right)[f(x)-f(-x)]}{g\left(\frac{x^2}{4}\right)[g(x)+g(-x)]}$

Hence $\ln\lambda+\ln\frac{1}{\lambda}=\ln 1=0$

$\therefore\quad I=\int_{\ln\lambda}^{\ln\left(\frac{1}{\lambda}\right)}.\frac{f\left(\frac{x^2}{4}\right)[f(-x)-f(x)]}{g\left(\frac{x^2}{4}\right)[g(-x)+g(x)]}dx=-I$

$\Rightarrow\ 2I=0 \qquad \Rightarrow\ I=0$

13. (a) $I_1=\int_e^{e^2}\frac{dx}{\log x}$ and $I_2=\int_1^2\frac{e^x}{x}dx$

$I_1=\int_e^{e^2}\frac{dx}{\log x}$

Put $\log x=t \qquad \Rightarrow\ \frac{1}{x}dx=dt$

$\Rightarrow\ dx=x\,dt \qquad \Rightarrow\ dx=e^t\,dt$

$\therefore\quad I_1=\int_1^2\frac{1}{t}e^t dt=I_2$

14. (b) $I_1=\int_1^2\frac{dx}{\sqrt{1+x^2}}$ and $I_2=\int_1^2\frac{dx}{x}$

$\because\quad \sqrt{x^2}=x$ for $x\in(1,2)$ and $\sqrt{1+x^2}>\sqrt{x^2}=x$

$\Rightarrow\ \sqrt{1+x^2}>x\ \forall x\in(1,2)$

$\Rightarrow\ \frac{1}{\sqrt{1+x^2}}<\frac{1}{x}\ \forall x\in(1,2)$

$\Rightarrow\ I_1<I_2$

15. (a) $\int_a^b f(x)dx=p$ and $\int_a^b|f(x)|dx=q$

$\because\quad |f(x)|\ge f(x)\ \forall x\in(a,b)$

$\Rightarrow\ \int_a^b|f(x)|dx\ge\int_a^b f(x)dx$

$\Rightarrow\ q\ge p$ ...(1)

Also $|f(x)|\ge -f(x)$

$\Rightarrow\ \int_a^b|f(x)|dx\ge-\int_a^b f(x)dx$

$\Rightarrow\ q\ge -p$ ...(2)

$\therefore$ From (1) and (2), $q\ge|p|$

18. (c) $\int_n^{n+1}f(x)dx=n^2+n\ \forall n\in\mathbb{Z}$,

$\Rightarrow\ \int_{-3}^3 f(x)dx=\int_{-3}^{-2}f(x)dx+\int_{-2}^{-1}f(x)dx$

$+\int_{-1}^0 f(x)dx+\int_0^1 f(x)dx+\int_1^2 f(x)dx+\int_2^3 f(x)dx$

$=\sum_{-3}^{2}n^2+\sum_{-3}^{2}n=[9+4+1+0+1+4]$

$+[-3-2-1+0+1+2]=19-3=16$

17. (c) $f(x)=\int_0^{\sin^2 x}\sin^{-1}\sqrt{t}dt+\int_0^{\cos^2}\cos^{-1}\sqrt{t}dt$ (say)

$\Rightarrow\ f'(x)=\sin^{-1}(\sin x).2\sin x\cos x$

$+\cos^{-1}(\cos x).2\cos x(-\sin x)$

$\Rightarrow\ f'(x)=x\sin 2x-x\sin 2x=0$

$\Rightarrow\ f(x)=\text{constant}\ \forall x\in\mathbb{R}$

$\Rightarrow\ f(x)=f\left(\frac{\pi}{4}\right)=\int_0^{1/2}\sin^{-1}\sqrt{t}dt+\int_0^{1/2}\cos^{-1}\sqrt{t}dt$

$=\int_0^{1/2}\left(\sin^{-1}\sqrt{t}+\cos^{-1}\sqrt{t}\right)dt=\frac{\pi}{2}\left[\frac{1}{2}-0\right]=\frac{\pi}{4}$

18. (a) $\int_0^1 f(x)dx=1,\ \int_0^1 xf(x)dx=a,\ \int_0^1 x^2f(x)dx=a^2$,

$I=\int_0^1(x-a)^2.f(x)dx$

$=\int_0^1\left(x^2-2ax+a^2\right)f(x)dx=a^2-2a(a)+a^2=0$

19. (b) $f(a-x)+f(x)=0\ \forall x\in[0,a]$ ...(1)

$I=\int_0^a\frac{dx}{1+e^{f(x)}}$ ...(2)

$=\int_0^a\frac{dx}{1+e^{f(a-x)}}=\int_0^a\frac{dx}{1+e^{f(x)}}$ (By (1))

$\Rightarrow\ I=\int_0^a\frac{e^{f(x)}}{e^{f(x)}+1}dx$ ...(3)

Adding (2) and (3) gives, $2I=\int_0^a 1dx=a$

$\Rightarrow\ I=\frac{a}{2}$

20. (c) $I=\int_{b-1}^b\frac{e^{-t}}{t-b-1}$

Put $t-b-1=z+1\ \Rightarrow\ dt=dz$

$\therefore\quad I=\int_{-3}^{-2}\frac{e^{(-b-1-z-1)}}{z+1}dz=\int_{-3}^{-2}\frac{e^{(-b-z-2)}}{z+1}dz=e^{-b-2}\int_{-3}^{-2}\frac{e^{-z}}{z+1}dz$

Put $z=-u-2 \qquad \Rightarrow\ dz=-du$

$\therefore\quad I=e^{-b-2}\int_1^0\frac{e^{u+2}}{-u-1}(-du) \qquad =e^{-b-2}\int_1^0\frac{e^{u+2}}{u+1}du$

$=-e^{-b}\int_0^1\frac{e^4}{u+1}du=-e^{-b}.a=-ae^{-b}$

21. (d) (a) $\int_{-2}^2 f(x)dx=\int_{-2}^0 f(x)dx+\int_0^2 f(x)dx$

$=\int_2^0-f(-x)dx+\int_0^2 f(x)dx$

$=\int_0^2 f(-x)dx+\int_0^2 f(x)dx=\int_0^2[f(-x)+f(x)]dx$

$\Rightarrow$ (a) is not correct

(b) $I=\int_{-6}^{10}f(x-1)dx$

Put $t=\frac{x}{2} \qquad \Rightarrow\ dt=\frac{1}{2}dx$

$\therefore\quad I=\int_{-3}^5 2f(2t-1)dt\ne\int_{-3}^5 2f(t)dt$

$\Rightarrow$ (b) is not correct

(c) $I=\int_{-4}^{4} f(x-1)dx$

Put t = x + 1

$\Rightarrow\ I=\int_{-3}^{5} f(t-2)dt \neq \int_{-3}^{5} f(t)dt$

$\Rightarrow$ (c) is not correct

(d) $I=\int_{-2}^{6} f(x-1)$;

Put t = x − 1

$\Rightarrow\ I=\int_{-3}^{5} f(t)dt=\int_{-3}^{5} f(x)dx$

$\Rightarrow$ option (d) is correct

22. (c) $\int_a^b f(t).g(h(t))dt=\int_a^b f(h(t)).g(t)dt;$

L.H.S. $=\int_a^b f(a+b-t).g(h(a+b-t))dt$

(using property) and R.H.S. $=\int_a^b f(h(t)).g(t)dt$

Clearly if $h(t)=a+b-t$

$\Rightarrow\ h(a+b-t)=a+b-(a+b-t)=t$

Thus, $h(t)=a+b-t$

23. (a) $f:\mathbb{R}\to\mathbb{R};\ f(x)=\sin x+x$,

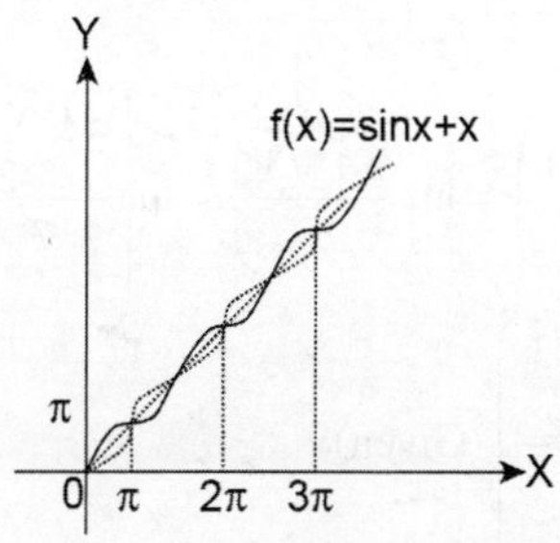

Here $\pi^2=\int_0^{\pi} f^{-1}(x)dx+\int_0^{\pi} f(x)dx$

$\Rightarrow\ \int_0^{\pi} f^{-1}(x)dx=\pi^2-\int_0^{\pi} f(x)dx=\pi^2-\int_0^{\pi}(\sin x+x)dx$

$=\pi^2-\left[-\cos x+\frac{x^2}{2}\right]_0^{\pi}=\pi^2-\left[-(-1-1)+\frac{1}{2}\pi^2\right]$

$=\frac{\pi^2}{2}-2$

24. (c) $\therefore\ I=\int_0^{100}\left[\tan^{-1}x\right]dx$

$=\int_0^{\tan 1}\left[\tan^{-1}x\right]dx+\int_{\tan 1}^{100}\left[\tan^{-1}x\right]dx$

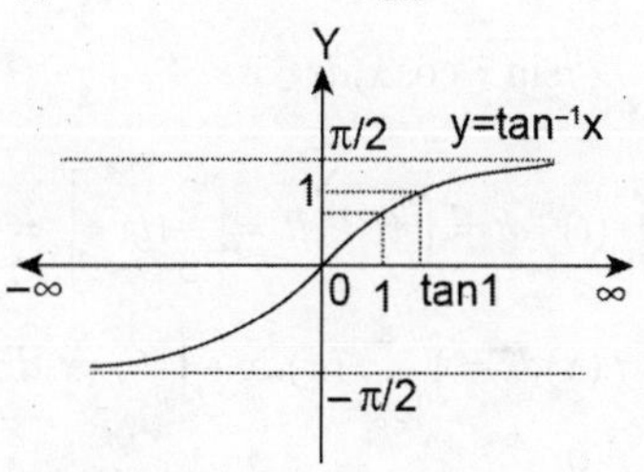

$=\int_0^{\tan 1} 0dx+\int_{\tan 1}^{100} 1dx=(100-\tan 1)$

25. (b) $f(x)=\begin{cases}0; x=\dfrac{n}{n+1}, n=1,2,3....\\ 1;\quad \text{elsewhere.}\end{cases}$

$\int_0^2 f(x)dx=\int_0^{1/2}1dx+\int_{1/2}^{2/3}1dx+\int_{2/3}^{3/4}1dx+\int_{3/4}^{4/5}+....$

$+\lim_{x\to\infty}\int_{\frac{n-1}{n}}^{\frac{n}{n+1}}1dx+\int_1^2 1dx$

$=\lim_{n\to\infty}\left[\frac{n}{n+1}\right]+1=2$

26. (a) $f(x)=\cos x-\int_0^x (x-t)f(t)dt$

$f'(x)=-\sin x-\left[\int_0^x 1f(t)dt\right]$

$\Rightarrow\ f'(x)=-\sin x-\int_0^x f(t)dt$

$\Rightarrow\ f''(x)=-\cos x-f(x)$

$\Rightarrow\ f''(x)+f(x)=-\cos x$

27. (b) $\int_{-1/2}^{1/2}\sqrt{\left\{\left(\frac{x+1}{x-1}\right)^2+\left(\frac{x-1}{x+1}\right)^2-2\right\}}dx$

$=\int_{-1/2}^{1/2}\sqrt{\left\{\left(\frac{x+1}{x-1}\right)-\left(\frac{x-1}{x+2}\right)\right\}^2}dx$

$=\int_{-1/2}^{1/2}\sqrt{\left\{\frac{4x}{x^2-1}\right\}^2}dx=\int_{-1/2}^{1/2}\left|\frac{4x}{x^2-1}\right|dx=2\int_0^{1/2}\left|\frac{4x}{x^2-1}\right|dx$

$\left(\because\left|\frac{4x}{x^2-1}\right| \text{ is an even function}\right)$

Now $\frac{4x}{x^2-1}\le 0$

$\Rightarrow\ x^2-1<0$ as $x\in\left[0,\frac{1}{2}\right]$

$\Rightarrow$ x ∈ (−1, 1)

$\Rightarrow\ \frac{4x}{x^2-1}\le 0\ \forall x\in\left[0,\frac{1}{2}\right]$

$\Rightarrow\ I=2\int_0^{1/2}\frac{-4x}{x^2-1}dx=-8\int_0^{1/2}\frac{x-1+1}{x^2-1}dx$

$=-8\int_0^{1/2}\frac{1}{x+1}dx-8\int_0^{1/2}\frac{1}{x^2-1}dx$

$=-8\left[\ln|x+1|\right]_0^{1/2}-8\times\frac{1}{2(1)}\left[\ln\left|\frac{x-1}{x+1}\right|\right]_0^{1/2}$

$=-8\left[\ln\frac{3}{2}\right]-4\left[\ln\frac{1}{3}\right]$

$=-4\left[\ln\frac{9}{4}+\ln\frac{1}{3}\right]=-4\ln\left(\frac{3}{4}\right)=4\ln\left(\frac{4}{3}\right)$

28. (b) $I=\int_0^1\cos\left(2\cot^{-1}\sqrt{\left(\frac{1-x}{1+x}\right)}\right)dx$

Put x = cosθ, $dx=-\sin\theta\, d\theta$

$\Rightarrow\ I=\int_{\pi/2}^{0}\cos\left(2\cot^{-1}\sqrt{\frac{2\sin^2\frac{\theta}{2}}{2\cos^2\frac{\theta}{2}}}\right)(-\sin\theta)d\theta$

$=\int_0^{\pi/2}\cos\left(2\cot^{-1}\left(\tan\frac{\theta}{2}\right)\right)(\sin\theta)d\theta$

$$=\int_0^{\pi/2}\cos\left(2\cot^{-1}\left(\cot\left(\frac{\pi}{2}-\frac{\theta}{2}\right)\right)\right)(\sin\theta)d\theta$$

$$=\int_0^{\pi/2}\cos\left(2\left(\frac{\pi}{2}-\frac{\theta}{2}\right)\right)(\sin\theta)d\theta$$

$$=\int_0^{\pi/2}\cos(\pi-\theta)\sin\theta\,d\theta \qquad =-\int_0^{\pi/2}\sin\theta.\cos\theta\,d\theta$$

$$=-\frac{1}{2}\int_0^{\pi/2}\sin 2\theta d\theta=\frac{1}{2}\left[\frac{\cos 2\theta}{2}\right]_0^{\pi/2}$$

$$=\frac{1}{4}[\cos\pi-\cos 0]=\frac{-1}{2}$$

29. (a) $I=\int_{-\sqrt{2}}^{\sqrt{2}}\frac{2x^7+3x^6-10x^5-7x^3-12x^2+x+1}{x^2+2}dx$

$$=\frac{2x^7-10x^5-7x^3+x}{x^2+2}=\text{odd function and}$$

$$\frac{3x^6-12x^2+1}{x^2+2}=\text{even function}$$

$$\therefore\quad I=2\int_0^{\sqrt{2}}\frac{3x^6-12x^2+1}{x^2+2}dx$$

$$=2\int_0^{\sqrt{2}}\left(3x^4-6x^2+\frac{1}{x^2+2}\right)dx$$

$$=2\left[\frac{3\times 5}{5}-2x^3+\frac{1}{\sqrt{2}}\tan^{-1}\left(\frac{x}{\sqrt{2}}\right)\right]_0^{\sqrt{2}}$$

$$=2\left[\frac{3}{5}(4\sqrt{2})-2(2\sqrt{2})+\frac{1}{\sqrt{2}}\left(\frac{\pi}{4}\right)\right]$$

$$=\frac{24}{5}\sqrt{2}-8\sqrt{2}+\frac{\pi}{2\sqrt{2}}=\frac{-16}{5}\sqrt{2}+\frac{\pi}{2\sqrt{2}}$$

30. (a) $I=\int_1^{\infty}\frac{(x^2-2)}{x^3\sqrt{x^2-1}}dx=\int_1^{\infty}\frac{1}{x\sqrt{x^2-1}}dx-2\int_1^{\infty}\frac{1dx}{x^3\sqrt{x^2-1}}$

$$=\left[\sec^{-1}x\right]_1^{\infty}-2\int_1^{\infty}\frac{1}{x^3\sqrt{x^2-1}}dx$$

$$=\left(\frac{\pi}{2}-0\right)-2\int_1^{\infty}\frac{1}{x^3\sqrt{x^2-1}}dx$$

Put x = sec θ, dx = sec θ tan θ dθ

$$\Rightarrow\quad I=\frac{\pi}{2}-2\int_0^{\pi/2}\frac{1}{\sec^3\theta.\tan\theta}\times\sec\theta\tan\theta\,d\theta$$

$$=\frac{\pi}{2}-2\int_0^{\pi/2}\cos^2\theta\,d\theta$$

$$=\frac{\pi}{2}-\int_0^{\pi/2}(1+\cos 2\theta)d\theta=\frac{\pi}{2}-\left[\theta+\frac{\sin 2\theta}{2}\right]_0^{\pi/2}$$

$$=\frac{\pi}{2}-\left[\frac{\pi}{2}+\frac{1}{2}(0)\right]=0$$

31. (a) $I=\int_0^{\infty}\frac{x\ln x}{(1+x^2)^2}dx$

Put x = tan θ ⇒ dx = sec² θ dθ

$$\Rightarrow\quad I=\int_0^{\pi/2}\frac{\tan\theta\ln(\tan\theta)\sec^2\theta d\theta}{\sec^4\theta}$$

$$=\int_0^{\pi/2}\tan\theta.\ln(\tan\theta).\cos^2\theta d\theta$$

$$=\int_0^{\pi/2}\sin\theta\cos\theta.\ln(\tan\theta)d\theta$$

$$\Rightarrow\quad I=\int_0^{\pi/2}\sin\left(\frac{\pi}{2}-\theta\right).\cos\left(\frac{\pi}{2}-\theta\right)\ln\left(\tan\left(\frac{\pi}{2}-\theta\right)\right)d\theta$$

$$=\int_0^{\pi/2}\cos\theta\sin\theta\ln(\cot\theta)d\theta$$

$$=-\int_0^{\pi/2}\cos\theta.\sin\theta\ln(\tan\theta)d\theta=-I$$

$$\Rightarrow\quad 2I=0$$

$$\Rightarrow\quad I=0$$

32. (d) $I=\int_0^{\pi/3}\frac{\cos x}{3+\sin x}dx$

Put 3 + sin x = t ⇒ cos x dx = dt

$$\Rightarrow\quad I=\int_3^{3+\frac{\sqrt{3}}{2}}\frac{dt}{t}=\left[\ln|t|\right]_3^{3+\frac{\sqrt{3}}{2}}=\ln\left(3+\frac{\sqrt{3}}{2}\right)-\ln 3$$

$$=\ln\left(1+\frac{1}{2\sqrt{3}}\right)$$

$$=\ln\left(\frac{2\sqrt{3}+1}{2\sqrt{3}}\right)=\ln\left(\frac{6+\sqrt{3}}{6}\right)=\ln\left(\frac{3+\frac{\sqrt{3}}{2}}{3}\right)$$

$$=k\ln\left(\frac{3+\frac{\sqrt{3}}{2}}{3}\right)\text{ (Given)}$$

⇒ $k = 1$, i.e., none of these.

33. (c) $I_1=\int_0^1\frac{dx}{\sqrt{1+x^2}}$ and $I_2=\int_0^1\frac{dx}{|x|}$

$$\because\quad\sqrt{1+x^2}>\sqrt{x^2}=|x|$$

$$\Rightarrow\quad\frac{1}{\sqrt{1+x^2}}<\frac{1}{|x|}\qquad\Rightarrow\quad I_1<I_2$$

34. (a) $I=\int_{\pi/2}^{\pi}\sqrt{\sin x-\sin^3 x}\,dx=\int_{\pi/2}^{\pi}\sqrt{\sin x}|\cos x|dx$

$$=\int_{\pi/2}^{\pi}-\sqrt{\sin x}.\cos x\,dx$$

$$=-\int_1^0(t)^{1/2}dt=\int_0^1(t)^{1/2}dt=\left[\frac{2}{3}(t)^{3/2}\right]_0^1=\frac{2}{3}$$

35. (d) $I=\int_0^a f(x)dx=\int_0^{a/2}f(x)dx+\int_{a/2}^a f(x)dx$

Put $x=\frac{a}{2}+t$ ⇒ $dx = dt$

$$\Rightarrow\quad I=\int_0^{a/2}f(x)dx+\int_0^{a/2}f\left(\frac{a}{2}+t\right)dt$$

$$=\int_0^{a/2}f(x)dx+\int_0^{a/2}f\left(\frac{a}{2}+x\right)dx$$

36. (a) $I=\int_1^{\sqrt{3}}\sin^{-1}\left(\frac{2x}{1+x^2}\right)dx$

$$\because\quad 2\tan^{-1}x=\begin{cases}\sin^{-1}\left(\frac{2x}{1+x^2}\right); -1\le x\le 1\\ -\pi-\sin^{-1}\left(\frac{2x}{1+x^2}\right);\ x<-1\\ \pi-\sin^{-1}\left(\frac{2x}{1+x^2}\right); x>1\end{cases}$$

$$\therefore\quad I=\int_1^{\sqrt{3}}\left(\pi-2\tan^{-1}x\right)dx=\pi\left(\sqrt{3}-1\right)-2\int_1^{\sqrt{3}}\tan^{-1}x\,dx$$

$$=\pi\left(\sqrt{3}-1\right)-2\left[\left|x\tan^{-1}x\right|_1^{\sqrt{3}}-\int_1^{\sqrt{3}}\frac{1}{1+x^2}.x\,dx\right]$$

$$=\pi\left(\sqrt{3}-1\right)-2\left[\left(\sqrt{3}.\frac{\pi}{3}-\frac{\pi}{4}\right)-\frac{1}{2}\int_1^{\sqrt{3}}\frac{2x}{1+x^2}dx\right]$$

$$=\pi\left(\sqrt{3}-1\right)-2\left[\frac{\pi}{\sqrt{3}}-\frac{\pi}{4}\right]+\left[\ln\left(1+x^2\right)\right]_1^{\sqrt{3}}$$

$$=\pi\left(\sqrt{3}-1\right)-2\pi\left(\frac{1}{\sqrt{3}}-\frac{1}{4}\right)+\left[\ln(4)-\ln 2\right]$$

$$=\pi\left(\sqrt{3}-1\right)-2\pi\left(\frac{4-\sqrt{3}}{4\sqrt{3}}\right)+\ln 2$$

$$=\pi\left[\sqrt{3}-1-\frac{\left(4-\sqrt{3}\right)}{2\sqrt{3}}\right]+\ln 2$$

$$=\pi\left[\frac{6-2\sqrt{3}-4+\sqrt{3}}{2\sqrt{3}}\right]+\ln 2=\pi\left[\frac{2-\sqrt{3}}{2\sqrt{3}}\right]+\ln 2$$

37. (b) $\frac{1}{\sqrt{\alpha}}\int_1^{\alpha}\left(\frac{3}{2}\sqrt{x}+1-\frac{1}{\sqrt{x}}\right)dx<4$

$$\Rightarrow\ \frac{1}{\sqrt{\alpha}}\left[\frac{3}{2}\frac{(x)^{3/2}}{\frac{3}{2}}+x-\frac{(x)^{1/2}}{\frac{1}{2}}\right]_1^{\alpha}<4$$

$$\Rightarrow\ \frac{1}{\sqrt{\alpha}}\left[(x)^{3/2}+x-2(x)^{1/2}\right]_1^{\alpha}<4$$

$$\Rightarrow\ \frac{1}{\sqrt{\alpha}}\left[\alpha^{3/2}-1+\alpha-1-2\sqrt{\alpha}+2\right]<4$$

$$\Rightarrow\ \frac{1}{\sqrt{\alpha}}\left[\alpha^{3/2}-2\sqrt{\alpha}+\alpha\right]<4$$

$$\Rightarrow\ \alpha^{3/2}-2\sqrt{\alpha}+\alpha<4\sqrt{\alpha}$$

$$\Rightarrow\ \alpha^{3/2}-6\sqrt{\alpha}+\alpha<0$$

$$\Rightarrow\ \sqrt{\alpha}\left(\alpha-6+\sqrt{\alpha}\right)<0\ \Rightarrow\ \sqrt{\alpha}\left(\sqrt{\alpha}+3\right)\left(\sqrt{\alpha}-2\right)<0$$

$$\Rightarrow\ -3<\sqrt{\alpha}<2\qquad\Rightarrow\ \sqrt{\alpha}\in[0,2)$$

$$\Rightarrow\ \alpha\in[0,4)\text{; But }\alpha>0\Rightarrow\ \alpha\in(0,4)$$

38. (b) $\int_0^1\left(\frac{\tan^{-1}}{x}\right)dx=l\int_0^{\pi/2}\frac{x}{\sin x}dx$ (given)

L.H.S. $=\int_0^1\frac{\tan^{-1}}{x}dx$

Put $\tan^{-1}x=t\quad\Rightarrow\quad\frac{1}{1+x^2}dx=dt$

$\Rightarrow\ dx=(1+x^2)\,dt\quad\Rightarrow\ dx=(1+\tan^2 t)\,dt$

$\Rightarrow\ dx=\sec^2 t\,dt$

$\Rightarrow$ L.H.S. $=\int_0^{\pi/4}\frac{t}{\tan t}\sec^2 t\,dt=\int_0^{\pi/4}\frac{t}{\sin t\cos t}dt$

$=2\int_0^{\pi/4}\frac{t}{\sin 2t}dt$

Put $2t=u\quad\Rightarrow\ 2\,dt=du$

$\Rightarrow$ L.H.S. $=\frac{1}{2}\int_0^{\pi/2}\frac{u}{\sin u}du=l\int_0^{\pi/2}\frac{x}{\sin x}dx$ (given)

$\Rightarrow\ l=\frac{1}{2}$

39. (c) $\int_{-\pi/4}^{\pi/4}\frac{dx}{\sec^2 x(1+\sin x)}dx=\int_{-\pi/4}^{\pi/4}\frac{\cos^2 x}{1+\sin x}dx$

$=\int_{-\pi/4}^{\pi/4}(1-\sin x)dx$

$=\left[x+\cos x\right]_{-\pi/4}^{\pi/4}=\frac{\pi}{2}+\left[\frac{1}{\sqrt{2}}-\frac{1}{\sqrt{2}}\right]=\frac{\pi}{2}$

40. (a) $f(x)=\frac{1}{x^2}\int_4^x\left(4t^2-2f'(t)\right)dt, f'(4)=?$

$\Rightarrow\ x^2 f(x)=\int_4^x\left(4t^2-2f'(t)\right)dt$

$\Rightarrow\ x^2.f'(x)+f(x)(2x)=4x^2-2f'(x)$

$\Rightarrow\ \left(x^2+2\right)f'(x)=4x^2-2x\,f(x)$

Put x = 4

$\Rightarrow\ 18.f'(4)=64-8f(4)$ …. (1) and $f(4)=0$ …. (2)

$\Rightarrow\ 18f'(4)=64-8(0)$

$\Rightarrow\ f'(4)=\frac{64}{18}=\frac{32}{9}$

41. (d) $I=\int_{-\pi}^{\pi}\left(\cos px-\sin qx\right)^2dx;\ p,q\in\mathbb{Z}$

$$=\int_{-\pi}^{\pi}\left(\cos^2 px+\sin^2 qx\underbrace{-2\sin qx.\cos px}_{\text{odd function.}}\right)dx$$

$=2\int_0^{\pi}\left(\cos^2 px+\sin^2 qx\right)dx$

$=\int_0^{\pi}\left(1+\cos 2px\right)dx+\int_0^{\pi}\left(1-\cos 2qx\right)dx$

$=2\pi+\int_0^{\pi}\cos 2px\,dx-\int_0^{\pi}\cos 2qx\,dx$

$=2\pi+\left[\frac{\sin 2px}{2p}\right]_0^{\pi}-\left[\frac{\sin 2qx}{2q}\right]_0^{\pi}$

$=2\pi+\frac{1}{2p}\left[\sin 2p\pi\right]-\frac{1}{2q}\left[\sin 2q\pi\right]$

$=2\pi+\frac{1}{2p}(0)-\frac{1}{2q}(0)=2\pi\qquad[\because p,q\in\mathbb{Z}]$

42. (a) $I=\int_0^{\pi}\frac{x^2\sin x}{(2x-\pi)(1+\cos^2 x)}dx$

$=\int_0^{\pi}\frac{(\pi-x)^2\sin(\pi-x)}{[2(\pi-x)-\pi][1+\cos^2(\pi-x)]}dx$

$=\int_0^{\pi}\frac{(\pi^2+x^2-2\pi x)\sin x}{(\pi-2x)(1+\cos^2 x)}dx$

$=\int_0^{\pi}\frac{\pi(\pi-2x)}{(\pi-2x)}.\frac{\sin x}{(1+\cos^2 x)}dx-I$

$\Rightarrow\ 2I=\pi\int_0^{\pi}\frac{\sin x}{(1+\cos^2 x)}dx$

Put $\cos x = t$

$\Rightarrow\ 2I=\pi\int_1^{-1}\frac{-dt}{1+t^2}$ \

$\Rightarrow\ I=\frac{\pi}{2}\int_{-1}^{1}\frac{1}{1+t^2}dt=\frac{\pi}{2}\left[\tan^{-1}t\right]_{-1}^{1}=\frac{\pi}{2}\left[\frac{\pi}{4}+\frac{\pi}{4}\right]=\frac{\pi^2}{4}$

43. (a) $\int_{-1}^{x}f(t)dt+f'''(3)\int_x^0 dt$

$=\int_1^x t^3dt-f'(1)\int_0^x t^2dt+f''(2)\int_x^3 t\,dt$

$\Rightarrow\ \int_{-1}^{x}f(t)dt+(-x)f'''(3)$

$=\frac{1}{4}(x^4-1)-f'(1)\frac{1}{3}(x^3)+f''(2)\frac{1}{2}(9-x^2)$

$\Rightarrow\ \int_{-1}^{x}f(t)dt-xf'''(3)-\frac{x^4}{4}$

$-\frac{1}{4}-\frac{x^3}{3}f'(1)+\left(\frac{9}{2}-\frac{x^2}{2}\right)f''(2)$

$\Rightarrow\ f(x)-f'''(3)=x^3-x^2f''(1)-xf''(2)$

$\Rightarrow\ f(x)=x^3-x^2f'(1)-xf''(2)+f'''(3)$ ...(1)

$\Rightarrow\ f'(x)=3x^2-2xf'(1)-f''(2)$ ...(2)

$\Rightarrow\ f''(x)=6x-2f'(1)$ ...(3)

$\Rightarrow\ f'''(x)=6x \quad\Rightarrow\ f'''(3)=6$ ...(4)

$\Rightarrow\ f''(2)=12-2f'(1)$ (using (3)) ...(5)

$f'(1)=3-2f'(1)-f''(2)$ (using (2))

$\Rightarrow\ f'(1)=3-2f'(1)-12+2f'(1)$ (using (5))

$\Rightarrow\ f'(1)=-9, f''(2)=12-2(-9)=30, f'''(3)=6$

$\therefore$ From (1), $f(x)=x^3+9x^2-30x+6$

$\Rightarrow\ f'(x)=3x^2+18x-30$

$\Rightarrow\ f'(4)=48+72-30=90$

Also $f'(4)=48-8f'(1)-f''(2)$

44. (a) $f(a-x)=f(x)$ ...(1)

$\Rightarrow\ \int_0^a f(x)dx=\int_0^{a/2}f(x)dx+\int_{a/2}^{a}f(x)dx$

In second integral, Put $x = a - t$, $dx = -dt$

$\Rightarrow\ \int_0^a f(x)dx=\int_0^{a/2}f(x)dx+\int_{a/2}^{0}f(a-t)(-dt)$

$=\int_0^{a/2}f(x)dx+\int_0^{a/2}f(a-t)dt$

$=\int_0^{a/2}f(x)dx+\int_0^{a/2}f(a-x)dx$

$=\int_0^{a/2}f(x)dx+\int_0^{a/2}f(x)dx=2p$

45. (a) $I_1=\int_{\sec^2 z}^{2-\tan^2 z}x.f(x(3-x))dx;$

$I_2=\int_{\sec^2 z}^{2-\tan^2 z}f(x(3-x))dx;$

Here $\sec^2 z + 2 - \tan^2 z = 3$

$\therefore\ I_1=\int_{\sec^2 z}^{2-\tan^2 z}(3-x)f((3-x)x)dx$

$=3\int_{\sec^2 z}^{2-\tan^2 z}f((3-x)x)dx-I_1$

$\Rightarrow\ 2I_1=3I_2 \quad\Rightarrow\ \frac{I_1}{I_2}=\frac{3}{2}$

46. (b) $I=\int_1^2\sqrt{(2x+3)(3x^2+4)}dx$ by Schwartz - Bunyakovsky inequality,

$\int_1^2\left(\sqrt{2x+3}\right)\left(\sqrt{3x^2+4}\right)dx$

$\le\sqrt{\int_1^2(2x+3)dx.\int_1^2(3x^2+4)dx}$

$\Rightarrow\ I\le\sqrt{\left[x^2+3x\right]_1^2.\left[x^3+4x\right]_1^2}=\sqrt{(3+3)(7+4)}=\sqrt{66}$

47. (c) $I=\int_1^2\frac{dx}{\sqrt{2x^3-9x^2+12x+4}}$

Let $f(x)=\left(2x^3-9x^2+12x+14\right)^{-1/2}$

$\Rightarrow\ f'(x)=\frac{-1}{2\left(2x^3-9x^2+12x+4\right)^{3/2}}\left(6x^2-18x+12\right)$

$=\frac{-\left(3x^2-9x+6\right)}{\left(2x^3-9x^2+12x+4\right)^{3/2}}$

$=\frac{-3\left(x^2-3x+2\right)}{\left(2x^3-9x^2+12x+4\right)^{3/2}}=\frac{-3(x-1)(x-2)}{\left(2x^3-9x^2+12x+4\right)^{3/2}}$

$\Rightarrow$ For $x \in (1, 2)$, $f'(x) > 0$

$\Rightarrow$ $f(x)$ is a +ve increasing function

$\Rightarrow$ $(2-1).f(1) < I < (2-1).f(2)$

$\Rightarrow\ \frac{1}{\sqrt{9}}<I<\frac{1}{\sqrt{8}}$

$\Rightarrow\ \frac{1}{3}<I<\frac{1}{\sqrt{8}}$ But $\frac{1}{4}<\frac{1}{3}<I<\frac{1}{\sqrt{8}}<1$

$\Rightarrow\ \frac{1}{4}<I<1$

48. (b) $\int_0^x f(t)dt=\int_x^1 t^2.f(t)dt+\frac{x^{16}}{8}+\frac{x^6}{3}+k$

$\Rightarrow\ f(x)=-\left[x^2.f(x)\right]+2x^{15}+2x^5$

$\Rightarrow\ \left(1+x^2\right)f(x)=2x^{15}+2x^5$

$\Rightarrow\ f(x)=\frac{2x^{15}+2x^5}{x^2+1} \quad\Rightarrow\ f(x)=2x^5\frac{\left(x^{10}+1\right)}{\left(x^2+1\right)}$

$\Rightarrow \quad f(x) = 2x^5\left(x^8 - x^6 + x^4 - x^2 + 1\right)$

$\Rightarrow \quad f(x) = 2x^{13} - 2x^{11} + 2x^9 - 2x^7 + 2x^5$

$\Rightarrow \quad \int_0^x f(t)dt = \int_0^x \left(2t^{13} - 2t^{11} + 2t^9 - 2t^7 + 2t^5\right)dt$

$= \frac{2x^{14}}{14} - \frac{2x^{12}}{12} + \frac{2x^{10}}{10} - \frac{2x^8}{8} + \frac{2x^6}{6}$

$= \frac{x^{14}}{7} - \frac{x^{12}}{6} + \frac{x^{10}}{5} - \frac{x^8}{4} + \frac{x^6}{3}$ .... (1)

and $\int_x^1 t^2.f(t)dt + \frac{x^{16}}{8} + \frac{x^6}{3} + k$

$= \int_x^1 \left(2t^{15} - 2t^{13} + 2t^{11} - 2t^9 + 2t^7\right)dt + \frac{x^{16}}{8} + \frac{x^6}{3} + k$

$= \left[2\frac{t^{16}}{16} - \frac{2t^{14}}{14} + \frac{2t^{12}}{12} - \frac{2t^{10}}{10} + \frac{2t^8}{8}\right]_x^1 + \frac{x^{16}}{8} + \frac{x^6}{3} + k$

$= \frac{1}{8}\left(1 - x^{16}\right) - \frac{1}{7}\left(1 - x^{14}\right) + \frac{1}{6}\left(1 - x^{12}\right)$

$-\frac{1}{5}\left(1 - x^{10}\right) + \frac{1}{4}\left(1 - x^8\right) + \frac{x^{16}}{8} + \frac{x^6}{3} + k$

$= \left(\frac{1}{8} - \frac{1}{7} + \frac{1}{6} - \frac{1}{5} + \frac{1}{4} + k\right) + \frac{x^{14}}{7} - \frac{x^{12}}{6} + \frac{x^{10}}{5} - \frac{x^8}{4} + \frac{x^6}{3}$ ...(2)

Equating (1) and (2), we get $k = -\frac{1}{8} + \frac{1}{7} - \frac{1}{6} + \frac{1}{5} - \frac{1}{4}$

$= \frac{-105 + 120 - 140 + 168 - 210}{840} = \frac{-167}{840}$

49. (d) $I_1 = \int_0^1 \frac{\sin t}{1+t} dt = \alpha$ ...(1)

$I_2 = \int_{4\pi-2}^{4\pi} \frac{\sin\left(\frac{t}{2}\right)}{4\pi + 2 - t} dt$ ...(2)

From (1), $I_1 = \int_0^1 \frac{\sin(1+t-1)}{(1+t)} dt$

Put $(1 + t) = z$ $\Rightarrow dt = dz$

$\Rightarrow \quad I_1 = \int_1^2 \frac{\sin(z-1)}{z} dz = \alpha$ ...(3)

From (2), $I_2 = \int_{4\pi-2}^{4\pi} \frac{\sin\left(\frac{t}{2}\right)}{4\pi + 2 - t} dt$

Put $\frac{t}{2} = \theta$ $\Rightarrow dt = 2d\theta$

$\therefore \quad I_2 = \int_{2\pi-1}^{2\pi} \frac{\sin(\theta)}{4\pi + 2 - 2\theta}(2d\theta) = \int_{2\pi-1}^{2\pi} \frac{\sin\theta d\theta}{2\pi + 1 - \theta}$

Put $\theta - (2\pi - 2) = t$, $d\theta = dt$

$\therefore \quad I_2 = \int_1^2 \frac{\sin\left[2\pi + (t-2)\right]dt}{2\pi + 1 - [2\pi - 2 + t]} = \int_1^2 \frac{\sin(t-2)dt}{(3-t)}$

$= \int_1^2 \frac{-\sin(2-t)}{(3-t)} dt = \int_1^2 \frac{-\sin(3-t-1)}{(3-t)} dt$

Put $3 - t = u$, $dt = -du$

$\Rightarrow \quad I_2 = \int_2^1 -\frac{\sin(u-1)}{u}(-du) = -\int_1^2 \frac{\sin(u-1)}{u} du = -\alpha$

(using (3))

50. (a) $I_1 = \int_0^{\pi/2} \cos(\sin x)dx$, $I_2 = \int_0^{\pi/2} \sin(\cos x)dx$,

$I_3 = \int_0^{\pi/2} \cos x \, dx$

For $x \in \left(0, \frac{\pi}{2}\right)$, $\sin x < x$ and in $\left(0, \frac{\pi}{2}\right)$, $\cos x$ is decreasing function

$\Rightarrow$ cos (sin x) > cos x

$\Rightarrow \quad \int_0^{\pi/2} \cos(\sin x)dx > \int_0^{\pi/2} \cos x \, dx$

$\Rightarrow \quad I_1 > I_3$ ...(1)

Also for $x \in \left(0, \frac{\pi}{2}\right)$, cos x decreases from 1 to 0

$\Rightarrow$ sin (cos x) decreases from sin 1 to 0, whereas cos x decreases from 1 to 0, i.e., for $x \in \left(0, \frac{\pi}{2}\right)$, cos x > sin (cos x)

$\Rightarrow \quad I_3 > I_2$ ...(2)

From (1) and (2), $I_1 > I_3 > I_2$

51. (a) $I = \int_0^1 \frac{dx}{1 + x^2 + 2x^5}$ for $x \in (0, 1)$, $1 + x^2 + 2x^5 > 1 + x^2$

$\Rightarrow \quad \frac{1}{1 + x^2 + 2x^5} < \frac{1}{1 + x^2}$

$\Rightarrow \quad \int_0^1 \frac{1}{1 + x^2 + 2x^5} dx < \int_0^1 \frac{1}{1 + x^2} dx = \frac{\pi}{4}$

$\Rightarrow \quad I < \frac{\pi}{4}$ ...(1)

Also for $x \in (0, 1)$, $1 + x^2 + 2x > 1 + x^2 + 2x^5$

$\Rightarrow \quad (1 + x)^2 > 1 + x^2 + 2x^5$

$\Rightarrow \quad \frac{1}{(1+x)^2} < \frac{1}{1 + x^2 + 2x^5}$

$\Rightarrow \quad \int_0^1 \frac{1}{(1+x)^2} dx < \int_0^1 \frac{1}{1 + x^2 + 2x^5} dx$

$\Rightarrow \quad \left[\frac{-1}{(1+x)}\right]_0^1 < I$

$\Rightarrow \quad -\left[\frac{1}{2} - 1\right] < I \qquad \Rightarrow \quad I > \frac{1}{2}$ ...(2)

From (1) and (2), $\frac{1}{2} < I < \frac{\pi}{4}$

Also $\frac{\pi}{6\sqrt{3}} < \frac{1}{2}$

$\Rightarrow \quad I \in \left(\frac{\pi}{6\sqrt{3}}, \frac{\pi}{4}\right)$

Also, $1 + x^2 + 2x^5 < 1 + x^2 + 2x^2$

$\Rightarrow \quad 1 + x^2 + 2x^5 < 1 + 3x^2 \Rightarrow \quad \frac{1}{1 + x^2 + 2x^5} > \frac{1}{1 + 3x^2}$

$\Rightarrow \quad \frac{1}{1 + 3x^2} < \frac{1}{1 + x^2 + 2x^5}$

$\Rightarrow \int_0^1 \frac{1}{1+3x^2}dx < \int_0^1 \frac{1}{1+x^2+2x^5}dx$

$\Rightarrow \left[\frac{1}{\sqrt{3}}\tan^{-1}\left(\sqrt{3}x\right)\right]_0^1 < \text{I}$

$\Rightarrow \frac{1}{\sqrt{3}}.\frac{\pi}{3} < \text{I}$ ...(3)

$\therefore$ From (1) and (3) $\text{I} \in \left(\frac{\pi}{3\sqrt{3}}, \frac{\pi}{4}\right)$

52. (d) $\int_{-2}^{x} f(t)dt + x f'''(3)$

$= \int_1^x x^3 dx + f'(1)\int_2^x x^2 dx + f''(2)\int_3^x x\, dx$

Differentiating both sides,

$\Rightarrow f(x) + f'''(3) = x^3 + f'(1)x^2 + f''(2)x$ ...(1)

$\Rightarrow f'(x) = 3x^2 + 2x f'(1) + f''(2)$ ...(2)

$\Rightarrow f''(x) = 6x + 2f'(1)$ ...(3)

$\Rightarrow f'''(x) = 6$ ...(4)

From (4), $f'''(3) = 6$;

$f''(2) = 12 + 2f'(1)$ ...(5) (using (3)) and

$f'(1) = 3 + 2f'(1) + f''(2)$ (using (2))

$\Rightarrow f'(1) = 3 + 2f'(1) + 12 + 2f'(1)$

$\Rightarrow 3f'(1) = -15 \quad \Rightarrow f'(1) = -5$

$\therefore$ From (5), $f''(2) = 12 - 10 = 2$ i.e., $f''(2) = 2$

$\therefore$ From (1), $f(x) = x^3 + f'(1)x^2 + f''(2)x - f'''(3)$

$\Rightarrow f(x) = x^3 - 5x^2 + 2x - 6$

53. (a) $\lim_{x\to 0}\frac{1}{x}\left[\int_0^{x+y} e^{\sin^2 t}dt - \int_0^{y} e^{\sin^2 t}dt\right]$

By L.H. Rule, $= \lim_{x\to 0}\frac{\left[e^{\sin^2(x+y)} - 0\right]}{1} = e^{\sin^2 y}$

54. (b) $\text{I} = \int_{-2\pi}^{5\pi} \cot^{-1}(\tan x)dx$

$\because \cot^{-1}\left(\tan\left(\pi + x\right)\right) = \cot^{-1}\left(\tan x\right)$; Integrand is periodic with period π

$\therefore \text{I} = 7\int_0^{\pi} \cot^{-1}(\tan x)dx = 7\int_0^{\pi}\cot^{-1}\left(\cot\left(\frac{\pi}{2} - x\right)\right)$

$= 7\int_0^{\pi/2}\cot^{-1}\left(\cot\left(\frac{\pi}{2} - x\right)\right)dx$

$+7\int_{\pi/2}^{\pi}\cot^{-1}\left(\cot\left(\frac{\pi}{2} - x\right)\right)dx$

$= 7\int_0^{\pi/2}\left(\frac{\pi}{2} - x\right)dx + 7\int_{\pi/2}^{\pi}\left[\left(\frac{\pi}{2} - x\right) + \pi\right]dx$

$= \frac{7\pi^2}{4} - \frac{7}{2}\left[\frac{\pi^2}{4}\right] + \frac{7\pi^2}{4} - \frac{7}{2}\left[\pi^2 - \frac{\pi^2}{4}\right] + 7\pi\left(\frac{\pi}{2}\right)$

$= \frac{7\pi^2}{8} + \frac{7\pi^2}{4} - \frac{7}{2}\left(\frac{3\pi^2}{4}\right) + \frac{7\pi^2}{2}$

$= \frac{\pi^2}{8}(7 + 14 - 21 + 28) = \frac{7\pi^2}{2}$

55. (a) $\text{I} = \int_0^{\sqrt{3}} \frac{1}{1+x^2}\sin^{-1}\left(\frac{2x}{1+x^2}\right)dx$

$$\because \quad 2\tan^{-1}x = \begin{cases} \sin^{-1}\left(\frac{2x}{1+x^2}\right); -1 \le x \le 1 \\ -\pi - \sin^{-1}\left(\frac{2x}{1+x^2}\right); x < -1 \\ \pi - \sin^{-1}\left(\frac{2x}{1+x^2}\right); x > 1 \end{cases}$$

$\therefore \quad \text{I} = \int_0^{\sqrt{3}} \frac{1}{\left(1+x^2\right)}\left\{\sin^{-1}\left(\frac{2x}{1+x^2}\right)\right\}dx$

$= \int_0^1 \frac{1}{\left(1+x^2\right)}\left\{2\tan^{-1}x\right\}dx$

$+\int_1^{\sqrt{3}} \frac{1}{\left(1+x^2\right)}\left\{\pi - 2\tan^{-1}x\right\}dx$

$= 2\int_0^1 \frac{\tan^{-1}x}{1+x^2}dx + \pi\int_1^{\sqrt{3}}\frac{1}{1+x^2}dx - 2\int_1^{\sqrt{3}}\frac{\tan^{-1}x}{1+x^2}dx$

$= 2\int_0^{\pi/4} t\, dt + \pi\left[\tan^{-1}x\right]_1^{\sqrt{3}} - 2\int_{\pi/4}^{\pi/3} t\, dt$

$= \left[t^2\right]_0^{\pi/4} + \pi\left[\frac{\pi}{3} - \frac{\pi}{4}\right] - \left[t^2\right]_{\pi/4}^{\pi/3}$

$= \frac{\pi^2}{16} + \pi\left(\frac{\pi}{12}\right) - \left[\frac{\pi^2}{9} - \frac{\pi^2}{16}\right]$

$= \frac{\pi^2}{16} + \frac{\pi^2}{12} - \left[\frac{16-9}{144}\right]\pi^2 = \frac{\pi^2}{16} + \frac{\pi^2}{12} - \frac{7\pi^2}{144}$

$= \left(\frac{9\pi^2 + 12\pi^2 - 7\pi^2}{144}\right) = \frac{7}{72}\pi^2$

56. (b) $\int_{-a}^{a}\frac{f(x)}{b^{g(x)}+1}dx$

Let $F(x) = \frac{f(x)}{b^{g(x)}+1}$

$F(-x) = \frac{f(-x)}{b^{g(-x)}+1} = \frac{f(x)}{b^{-g(x)}+1}$

$\Rightarrow F(-x) = \frac{f(x)}{1+b^{g(x)}}.b^{g(x)}$ ...(1)

Now $\int_{-a}^{a}F(x)dx = \int_{-a}^{a}F(-a+a-x)dx = \int_{-a}^{a}F(-x)dx$

$= \int_{-a}^{a}\frac{f(x).b^{g(x)}}{1+b^{g(x)}}dx$

$\Rightarrow 2\text{I} = \int_{-a}^{a}\frac{f(x)}{b^{g(x)}+1} + \int_{-a}^{a}\frac{f(x).b^{g(x)}}{1+b^{g(x)}}dx$

$= \int_{-a}^{a}f(x)dx = 2\int_0^a f(x)dx$

($\because f(x)$ is an even function)

$\Rightarrow \text{I} = \int_0^a f(x)dx$, which is independent of $g(x)$

57. (a) $\int_{-3}^{-7}\tan\left(x^2-6\right)dx+\int_{-6}^{-2}\tan\left(x^2+18x+75\right)dx$

$=\int_{-3}^{-7}\tan\left(x^2-6\right)dx+\int_{-6}^{-2}\tan\left\{(x+9)^2-6\right\}dx$

In second integral, put $x + 9 = t$, $dx = dt$

$\Rightarrow$ For $x = -6$, $t = 3$ and For $x = -2$, $t = 7$

$\therefore\quad I=\int_{-3}^{-7}\tan\left(x^2-6\right)dx+\int_{3}^{7}\tan\left(t^2-6\right)dx$

Put $t = -z$ $\qquad \Rightarrow\quad dt = -dz$

$\Rightarrow\quad I=\int_{-3}^{-7}\tan\left(x^2-6\right)dx-\int_{-3}^{-7}\tan\left(z^2-6\right)dz=0$

58. (c) $A=\int_1^{\sin\theta}\frac{t}{1+t^2}dt;\ B=\int_1^{\operatorname{cosec}\theta}\frac{dt}{t\left(1+t^2\right)}$

$=\frac{1}{2}\ln\left(\frac{1+\sin^2\theta}{2}\right)$ and $B=\int_1^{\operatorname{cosec}\theta}\frac{1}{t\left(1+t^2\right)}dt$

Put $t=\frac{1}{z}$ $\qquad\Rightarrow\quad dt=\frac{-1}{z^2}dz$

$\Rightarrow\quad B=\int_1^{\sin\theta}\frac{1}{\frac{1}{z}\left(1+\frac{1}{z^2}\right)}\left(-\frac{1}{z^2}\right)dz$

$=-\int_1^{\sin\theta}\frac{1}{\left(z^2+1\right)}dz=-A=\frac{-1}{2}\ln\left(\frac{1+\sin^2\theta}{2}\right)$

Thus, $B=-A=\frac{-1}{2}\ln\left(\frac{1+\sin^2\theta}{2}\right)$ and $A + B = 0$

Now $\Delta=\begin{vmatrix}A & A^2 & B\\ e^{A+B} & B^2 & -1\\ 1 & A^2+B^2 & -1\end{vmatrix}$

$=\begin{vmatrix}A & A^2 & B\\ 1 & B^2 & -1\\ 1 & -2AB & -1\end{vmatrix}$

$= A(-B^2 - 2AB) - A^2 (0) + B(-2AB - B^2) = -AB^2 - 2A^2B - 2AB^2 - B^3$

$= -2A^2B - 3AB^2 - B^3 = -[2A^2B + 3AB^2 + B^3] = -B\,[2A^2 + 3AB + B^2]$

$= -B\,[(2A + B)(A + B)] = 0$

59. (b) $\int_0^{\pi/2}\frac{dx}{a^2\cos^2x+b^2\sin^2x}=\frac{\pi}{2ab}$ $\qquad$ ...(1)

Differentially both sides of (1) partially w.r.t. 'a', we get

$\int_0^{\pi/2}\frac{-1\left(2a\cos^2x\right)}{\left(a^2\cos^2x+b^2\sin^2x\right)^2}dx=\frac{\pi}{2b}\left(\frac{-1}{a^2}\right)$ $\qquad$ ...(2)

Parallely differentiating both sides of (1) partially w.r.t. 'b' we get $\int_0^{\pi/2}\frac{-\left(2b\sin^2x\right)}{\left(a^2\cos^2x+b^2\sin^2x\right)^2}dx=\frac{\pi}{2a}\left(\frac{-1}{b^2}\right)$ $\qquad$ ...(3)

$\therefore$ From (2), $\int_0^{\pi/2}\frac{\cos^2x\,dx}{\left(a^2\cos^2x+b^2\sin^2x\right)^2}=\frac{\pi}{4a^3b}$ .... (4)

and and from (3), $\int_0^{\pi/2}\frac{\sin^2x\,dx}{\left(a^2\cos^2x+b^2\sin^2x\right)^2}=\frac{\pi}{4ab^3}$ .... (5)

Adding (4) and (5), we get $\int_0^{\pi/2}\frac{dx}{\left(a^2\cos^2x+b^2\sin^2x\right)^2}$

$=\frac{\pi}{4ab}\left(\frac{1}{a^2}+\frac{1}{b^2}\right)$

$\therefore\quad\int_0^{\pi/2}\frac{dx}{\left(4\cos^2x+9\sin^2x\right)^2}=\frac{\pi}{24}\left(\frac{1}{4}+\frac{1}{9}\right)$

$=\frac{\pi}{24}\left(\frac{13}{36}\right)=\frac{13\pi}{864}$

60. (b) $I=\int_\alpha^\beta\frac{e^{f\left(\frac{g(x)}{x-\alpha}\right)}}{e^{f\left(\frac{g(x)}{x-\alpha}\right)}+e^{f\left(\frac{g(x)}{x-\beta}\right)}}dx$; where α, β; (β > α) are roots of $g(x)=ax^2+bx+c=0$ and $f(x)$ is even.

$\Rightarrow\quad g(x)=a(x-\alpha)(x-\beta);\ f(-x)=f(x)$

$\therefore\quad I=\int_\alpha^\beta\frac{e^{f(a(x-\beta))}}{e^{f(a(x-\beta))}+e^{f(a(x-\alpha))}}dx$ $\qquad$ ...(1)

$\Rightarrow\quad I=\int_\alpha^\beta\frac{e^{f(a[(\alpha+\beta-x)-\beta])}}{e^{f(a[(\alpha+\beta-x)-\beta])}+e^{f(a[(\alpha+\beta-x)-\alpha])}}dx$

$\Rightarrow\quad I=\int_\alpha^\beta\frac{e^{f(a(\alpha-x))}}{e^{f(a(\alpha-x))}+e^{f(a(\beta-x))}}dx$

$\Rightarrow\quad I=\int_\alpha^\beta\frac{e^{f(a(x-\alpha))}\,dx}{e^{f(a(x-\alpha))}+e^{f(a(x-\beta))}}$ $(\because f(x)$ is even$)$ $\qquad$ ...(2)

Adding (1) and (2), we get $2I=\int_\alpha^\beta 1dx=(\beta-\alpha)$

$\Rightarrow\quad I=\frac{\beta-\alpha}{2}=\frac{\sqrt{D}}{2|a|}=\frac{\sqrt{b^2-4ac}}{2|a|}=\frac{\sqrt{b^2-4ac}}{|2a|}$

TUTORIAL SHEET SECTION–IV

1. (a), (d) $I_1=\int_x^1\frac{dt}{1+t^2}$ and $\int_1^{1/x}\frac{dt}{1+t^2},x>0$

$\Rightarrow\quad I_1=\left[\tan^{-1}t\right]_x^1;I_2=\left[\tan^{-1}t\right]_x^{1/x}$

$\Rightarrow\quad I_1=\frac{\pi}{4}-\tan^{-1}x;I_2=\tan^{-1}\frac{1}{x}-\frac{\pi}{4}$

$\because\quad x>0,\ \tan^{-1}\frac{1}{x}=\cot^{-1}x=\frac{\pi}{2}-\tan^{-1}x$

$\therefore\quad I_2=\frac{\pi}{2}-\tan^{-1}x-\frac{\pi}{4}$

$\Rightarrow\quad I_2=\frac{\pi}{4}-\tan^{-1}x$

$\therefore\quad I_1=I_2$

2. (a), (b), (c), (d)

(a) $\because\quad m\le f(x)\le M$

$\Rightarrow\quad\int_a^b m\,dx\le\int_a^b f(x)dx\le\int_a^b M\,dx$

$\Rightarrow\quad m(b-a)\le\int_a^b f(x)dx\le M(b-a)$

$\Rightarrow$ (a) is correct

(b) Schwartz – Bunyakovsky inequality

$\Rightarrow$ (b) is correct

(c) $\because$ $m(b-a) \le \int_a^b f(x)dx \le M(b-a) \exists\, c \in (a, b)$ such that, $m < f(c) < M$ and $\int_a^b f(x)dx = (b-a).f(c)$

$\Rightarrow$ (c) is correct

(d) $I = \int_a^{a+T} f(x)dx$

Put $x = a + t$; $dx = dt$

$\Rightarrow$ $I = \int_0^T f(a+t)dt = \int_0^T f(x)dx$ as $f(x)$ is periodic with period T

$\Rightarrow$ (d) is correct

3. (a), (b) $\because f(x)$ is non-decreasing function on $[a, b]$,

$f(b) \ge f(x) \ge f(a)\ \forall\ x \in [a, b]$

$\Rightarrow \int_a^b f(x)dx \ge \int_a^b f(a)dx = f(a)(b-a)$

$\Rightarrow \frac{1}{(b-a)}\int_a^b f(x)dx \ge f(a)$

$\Rightarrow \frac{1}{(b-a)}\int_a^b f(x)dx$ has its minimum value $f(a)$. Also

$\int_a^b f(x)dx \le \int_a^b f(b)dx$

$\Rightarrow \frac{1}{(b-a)}\int_a^b f(x)dx$ has its maximum value $f(b)$

4. (a), (b), (c), (d)

(a) Let $F(x) = \int_a^x f(t)dt$

$\Rightarrow F(-x) = \int_a^{-x} f(t)dt$

$\Rightarrow F(x) - F(-x) = \int_a^x f(t)dt - \int_a^{-x} f(t)dt$

$= \int_a^x f(t)dt - \int_{-a}^x f(-z)(-dz)$

$= \int_a^x f(t)dt - \int_x^{-a} f(-z)dz = \int_a^x f(t)dt + \int_x^{-a} f(z)dz$

($\because$ f is odd)

$= \int_a^{-a} f(t)dt = 0$ ($\because$ f is odd)

$\Rightarrow F(x) - F(-x) = 0$

$\Rightarrow F(x) = F(-x)$

$\Rightarrow F(x) = \int_a^x f(t)dt$ is an even function

$\Rightarrow$ option (a) is correct

(b) Let $F(x) = \int_a^x f(t)dt$

$\Rightarrow F(-x) = \int_a^{-x} f(t)dt$

$\therefore F(x) + F(-x) = \int_a^x f(t)dt + \int_a^{-x} f(t)dt$

$= \int_a^x f(t)dt + \int_{-a}^x f(-z)(-dz)$

$= \int_a^x f(t)dt + \int_{-a}^x f(z)dz$ ($\because f(x)$ is even function)

$= \int_a^x f(t)dt + \int_x^{-a} f(t)dt = \int_a^{-a} f(t)dt = 0$

$\Rightarrow F(-x) = -F(x)$

$\Rightarrow F(x) = \int_a^x f(t)dt$ is an odd function and hence $\int_a^x f(t)dt$ is odd function (taking a = 0)

(c) It is Leibinitiz Rule of differentiation under integral sign.

Thus, (a), (b), (c), (d) are correct

5. (a), (b), (c), (d)

If $f(x) = 0$ has no root in [a, b], then either $\int_a^b f(x)dx < 0$ or $\int_a^b f(x) > 0$

$\therefore \int_a^b f(x)dx = 0$ and $f(x)$ being continuous, implies $f(x) = 0$ has at least one root in (a, b).

(b) and (c) are standard results

6. (a),(b), (c), (d)

$I_n = \int_0^{\pi/4} \tan^n x\, dx;\ n \in \mathbb{N}$

$\Rightarrow I_n = \int_0^{\pi/4} \tan^{n-2} x.\tan^2 x\, dx$ for $n \ge 2$

$= \int_0^{\pi/4} \tan^{n-2} x\left(\sec^2 x - 1\right)dx,$

$= \int_0^{\pi/4} \tan^{n-2} x.\sec^2 x\, dx - \int_0^{\pi/4} \tan^{n-2} x\, dx$

$= \int_0^1 (t)^{n-2}.dt - I_{n-2} = \left[\frac{t^{n-1}}{n-1}\right]_0^1 - I_{n-2}; n \ge 2$

$\Rightarrow I_n = \frac{1}{n-1} - I_{n-2}; n \ge 2$

$\Rightarrow I_n + I_{n-2} = \frac{1}{n-1}$ for $n \ge 2$

$\Rightarrow$ Option (a) is correct

Replacing 'n' by 'n + 1', we get $I_{n+1} + I_{n-1} = \frac{1}{n}$ for $n \ge 2$

$\Rightarrow$ option (b) is correct

Replacing n by 'n + 1' in above, we get $I_{n+2} + I_n = \frac{1}{n+1}$ $\forall\ n \ge 1$

$\Rightarrow (I_{n+2} + I_n)(n + 1) = 1\ \forall n \in \mathbb{N}$

$\Rightarrow$ option (d) is correct.

Now, as $\tan^n x > 0$ for each n and $x \in \left(0, \frac{\pi}{4}\right)$

$\Rightarrow I_n > 0\ \forall x \in \mathbb{N}$

Also for $x \in (0, \pi/4)$, $\tan \in (0,1)$

$\Rightarrow \tan^n x$ decreases an increasing power n.

$\Rightarrow I_1 > I_2 > I_3 \ldots$ $\therefore I_{n+2} < I_n$

$\therefore I_{n+2} + I_n = \frac{1}{n+1}$

$\Rightarrow I_n + I_n > I_{n+2} + I_n = \frac{1}{n+1}$

$\Rightarrow 2I_n > \frac{1}{n+1}\ \forall\ n \ge 1$ ...(1)

Also, $I_n < I_{n-2}$

$\Rightarrow 2I_n < I_{n-2} + I_n = \frac{1}{n-1}\ \forall n \ge 2$

$\Rightarrow \quad 2I_n < \dfrac{1}{n-1} \; \forall n \geq 2$ ...(2)

$\therefore$ From (1) and (2), $\dfrac{1}{n+1} < 2I_n < \dfrac{1}{n-1} \; \forall n \geq 2$

7. (a), (b) $I_n = \int_0^{\pi/2} \cos^n x \, dx = \int_0^{\pi/2} \cos^{n-1} x.\cos x \, dx$

$= \left|(\cos x)^{n-1}(\sin x)\right|_0^{\pi/2}$

$-\int_0^{\pi/2}(n-1)(\cos x)^{n-2}(-\sin x)(\sin x)dx$

$= 0 + (n-1)\int_0^{\pi/2}(\cos x)^{n-2}.(1-\cos^2 x)dx$

$I_n = (n-1)\int_0^{\pi/2}(\cos x)^{n-2}dx - (n-1)\int_0^{\pi/2}(\cos x)^n dx$

$\Rightarrow I_n(1+n-1) = (n-1)I_{n-2}$

$\Rightarrow I_n = \dfrac{(n-1)}{n}.I_{n-2} \quad \Rightarrow \quad \dfrac{n}{n-1} = I_{n-2} : I_n$

$\Rightarrow$ option (c) is correct

$\Rightarrow nI_n = nI_{n-2} - I_{n-2}$

$\Rightarrow n(I_{n-2} - I_n) = I_{n-2} \quad \Rightarrow$ option (b) is correct

For $x \in (0, \pi/2)$, $\cos x \in (0, 1)$

$\Rightarrow (\cos x)^n$ decreasing with n increasing

$\Rightarrow I_1 > I_2 > I_3 > ....$

$\Rightarrow I_{n-2} > I_n \; \forall n \geq 2 \quad \Rightarrow$ option (a) is correct

8. (a), (c) $I = \int_{-2}^{2}\left(\underbrace{ax^2}_{\text{even}} + \underbrace{bx}_{\text{odd}} + \underbrace{c}_{\text{even}}\right)dx = 2\int_0^2(ax^2+c)dx$

$= 2\left[\dfrac{ax^3}{3} + cx\right]_0^2 = 2\left[\dfrac{8a}{3} + 2c\right] = \dfrac{16a}{3} + 4c$

which can be evaluated by knowing the values of 'a' and 'c'

9. (a), (b) $I_n = \int_0^1 \dfrac{dx}{(1+x^2)^n}$

Put $x = \tan\theta$, $dx = \sec^2\theta \, d\theta$

$\therefore \quad I_n = \int_0^{\pi/4}\dfrac{\sec^2\theta \, d\theta}{(\sec^2\theta)^n} = \int_0^{\pi/4}\dfrac{1}{\sec^{2n-2}\theta}d\theta$

$= \int_0^{\pi/4}\cos^{2n-2}\theta \, d\theta = \int_0^{\pi/4}(\cos\theta)^{2n-3}.(\cos\theta)d\theta$

$= \left|(\cos\theta)^{2n-3}\sin\theta\right|_0^{\pi/4} + \int_0^{\pi/4}(2n-3)(\cos\theta)^{2n-4}\sin^2\theta \, d\theta$

$= \left(\dfrac{1}{\sqrt{2}}\right)^{2n-3}.\left(\dfrac{1}{\sqrt{2}}\right) + (2n-3)$

$\int_0^{\pi/4}(\cos\theta)^{2n-4}(1-\cos^2\theta)d\theta$

$= \left(\dfrac{1}{\sqrt{2}}\right)^{2n-2} + (2n-3)$

$\int_0^{\pi/4}\left[(\cos\theta)^{2n-4} - (\cos\theta)^{2n-2}\right]d\theta$

$I_n = \left(\dfrac{1}{2}\right)^{n-1} + (2n-3).I_{n-2} - (2n-3)I_n$

$\Rightarrow \quad (2n-2)I_n = \dfrac{1}{(2)^{n-1}} + (2n-3).I_{n-2}$

$\Rightarrow \quad (n-1)I_n = \dfrac{1}{2^n} + \dfrac{(2n-3)}{2}I_{n-2}$

Replacing n by (n + 1), we get $nI_{n+1} = \dfrac{1}{2^{n+1}} + \dfrac{(2n-1)}{2}I_{n-1}$

$\Rightarrow 2n\,I_{n+1} = 2^{-n} + (2n-1)\,I_{n-1}$

Put $n = 1 \quad \Rightarrow \quad 2I_2 = \dfrac{1}{2} + I_0$

$\Rightarrow \quad I_2 = \dfrac{1}{4} + \dfrac{1}{2}\int_0^1 \dfrac{1}{(1+x^2)}dx$

$\Rightarrow \quad I_2 = \dfrac{1}{4} + \dfrac{1}{2}\left(\dfrac{\pi}{4}\right) = \dfrac{\pi}{8} + \dfrac{1}{4}$

10. (a), (b), (c), (d)

Given: $\left.\begin{aligned} f(2-x) &= f(2+x) \\ f(4-x) &= f(4+x) \end{aligned}\right\}$ .... (1) and

$\int_0^2 f(x)dx = 5$ ...(2)

$I = \int_0^{50} f(x)dx = ?$

From (1), $f(2-x) = f(2+x)$

Replacing x by $(2-x), f(2-(2-x)) = f(2+2-x)$

$\Rightarrow \quad f(x) = f(4-x)$

$\Rightarrow \quad f(x) = f(4+x) \qquad [\because f(4-x) = f(4+x)]$

$\Rightarrow \quad f(x)$ is a periodic function with period 4. Also $f(2-x) = f(2+x)$

$\Rightarrow \quad f(x)$ is symmetric about x = 2

$\therefore \quad \int_0^2 f(x)dx = \int_2^4 f(x)dx$

$\Rightarrow \quad \int_0^4 f(x)dx = 2\int_0^2 f(x)dx = 10$

$\therefore \quad I = \int_0^2 f(x)dx + \int_2^{50} f(x)dx$

$= 5 + 12\int_0^4 f(x)dx = 5 + 12(10) = 125$

$\Rightarrow$ option (a) is correct

Also $I = \int_0^{50} f(x)dx = \int_{-4}^{46} f(x)dx$ and

$I = \int_0^{50} f(x)dx = \int_1^{51} f(x)dx = \int_2^{52} f(x)dx$

$\Rightarrow$ Options (a), (b), (c) and (d) are correct

11. (a), (c), (d) $F(x) = \dfrac{1}{x^2}\int_4^x \left(4t^2 - 2F'(t)\right)dt$

$\Rightarrow \quad x^2.F(x) = \int_4^x \left(4t^2 - 2F'(t)\right)dt$

$\Rightarrow x^2 F'(x) + 2x.\, F(x) = 2x^2 - 2F'(x)$

Put $x = 4$

$\Rightarrow \quad 16\,F'(4) + 8\,F(4) = 64 - 2F'(4)$

$\Rightarrow \quad 16\,F'(4) = 64 - 2\,F'(4)$

$(\because F(4) = 0)$

$\Rightarrow \quad 18F'(4) = 64 \qquad \Rightarrow \quad F'(4) = \dfrac{32}{9}$

Also $\dfrac{(2+F(4))^5}{9}=\dfrac{(2+(0))^5}{9}=\dfrac{32}{9}$ $\quad (\because F(4)=0)$

Put x = 8

⇒ 64F′(8) + 16F(8) = 256 – 2F′(8)

⇒ 66F′(8) = 256 – 16F(8) ...(1) and

$$F(8)=\frac{1}{64}\int_4^8\left(4t^2-2F'(t)\right)=\frac{1}{16}\left[\frac{t^3}{3}\right]_4^8-\frac{1}{32}\int_4^8 F'(t)dt$$

$$\Rightarrow F(8)=\frac{1}{48}[512-64]-\frac{1}{32}[F(8)-F(4)]$$

$$\Rightarrow F(8)=\frac{448}{48}-\frac{F(8)}{32}+\frac{F(4)}{32}$$

$$\Rightarrow \frac{33}{32}F(8)=\frac{28}{3}$$

$$\Rightarrow F(8)=\frac{28}{3}\times\frac{32}{33}$$

$$\therefore \frac{11}{28}F(8)=\frac{11}{28}\times\frac{28}{3}\times\frac{32}{33}=\frac{32}{9}$$

$$\therefore F'(4)=\frac{11}{28}F(8)$$

12. (a), (d) $\int_0^1\sin\left(x^2+2x+1\right)dx-\int_1^2\sin x^2dx$

$=\int_0^1\sin(x+1)^2dx-\int_1^2\sin x^2dx$

In first integral, put $(x+1)=t$ $=\int_1^2\sin t^2dt-\int_1^2\sin x^2dx=0$

⇒ option (a) is correct

(b) $I=\int_{-1}^1 e^{\sin x}dx-\int_0^1 e^{\sin(2x+1)}dx$

In second integral, put 2x + 1 = t

$\Rightarrow I=\int_{-1}^1 e^{\sin x}dx-\int_1^3 e^{\sin t}\frac{dt}{2}\neq 0$

(c) $\int_{-5}^{-4}\sin\left(x^2-3\right)dx+\int_{-2}^{-1}\sin\left(x^2+12x+33\right)dx$

$$=\int_{-5}^{-4}\sin\left(x^2-3\right)dx+\int_{-2}^{-1}\sin\left[(x+6)^2-3\right]dx$$
$$=\int_{-5}^{-4}\sin\left(x^2-3\right)dx+\int_4^5\sin\left(t^2-3\right)dx$$
$$=\int_{-5}^{-4}\sin\left(x^2-3\right)dx+\int_{-5}^{-4}\sin\left(t^2-3\right)dt$$
$$=2\int_{-5}^{-4}\sin\left(x^2-3\right)dx\neq 0$$

(d) $I=\int_{-4}^4\cos x^2dx-8\int_0^1\cos 16(2x-1)^2dx$

In second integral, put 4(2x – 1) = t

$\Rightarrow I=\int_{-4}^4\cos x^2\,dx-8\int_{-4}^4\cos t^2\frac{dt}{8}=0$

⇒ Option (d) is correct

13. (a) $\int_0^x f(t)dt=x^2+2x+\int_0^x t.f(t)dt$

Differentiating both sides, w.r.t. x, we get

$f(x)=2x+2+x\,f(x)$

$\Rightarrow f(x)[1-x]=2(x+1)$

$\Rightarrow f(x)=\dfrac{2(1+x)}{(1-x)}$ which is not periodic.

14. (b), (c) $f(x+1)+f(x+7)=0,\ \forall x\in\mathbb{R}$

$\Rightarrow f(x+1)=-f(x+7)$

Replacing x by x – 1, $f(x)=-f(x+6)$

$=-[-f(x+6+6)]=f(x+12)$

⇒ $f(x)$ is periodic with period 12

$\therefore \int_a^{a+t}f(x)dx=\int_0^t f(x)dx$ if t = T = 12

⇒ Option (c) is correct

Also T = 12 ⇒ T = 24 is a period

⇒ Option (b) is also correct

15. (a), (d) $f(x)=\int_0^x 2|t|dt=\begin{cases}-\int_x^0 2|t|dt & \text{if } x<0\\ \int_0^x 2|t|dt & \text{if } x>0\end{cases}$

$$=\begin{cases}\int_x^0 2t\,dt & \text{if } x<0\\ \int_0^x 2t\,dt & \text{if } x>0\end{cases}=\begin{cases}\left[x^2\right]_x^0 & \text{if } x<0\\ \left[x^2\right]_0^x & \text{if } x\geq 0\end{cases}=\begin{cases}-x^2 & \text{if } x<0\\ x^2 & \text{if } x\geq 0\end{cases}$$

$$\Rightarrow f'(x)=\begin{cases}-2x & \text{if } x<0\\ 2x & \text{if } x>0\end{cases}$$

$\therefore f'(x)=1 \quad\Rightarrow\quad x=\frac{-1}{2},\frac{1}{2}$

⇒ Point $\left(\frac{-1}{2},\frac{-1}{4}\right)$ and $\left(\frac{1}{2},\frac{1}{4}\right)$ are the points on $f(x)$ where tangents are parallel to bisector of first quadrant, hence tangents are given by $\frac{1}{2}\left(y-\frac{1}{4}\right)=-x\left(\frac{-1}{2}\right)$ and $\frac{1}{2}\left(y+\frac{1}{4}\right)=x\left(\frac{1}{2}\right)$ or $y=x+\frac{1}{4}$ and $y=x\frac{-1}{4}$

16. (a), (b), (c), (d) $f(x)=f(1-x);f'\left(\frac{1}{4}\right)=0$

$\Rightarrow f'(x)=-f'(1-x)$ ...(1)

$\Rightarrow f'\left(\frac{1}{4}\right)=-f'\left(\frac{3}{4}\right)$

$\Rightarrow f'\left(\frac{1}{4}\right)=0$ and $f'\left(\frac{3}{4}\right)=0$

⇒ $f'(x)$ vanishes at least twice on [0, 1]

⇒ (a) is correct

Also from (1) $f'\left(\frac{1}{2}\right)=-f'\left(\frac{1}{2}\right)$

$\Rightarrow 2f'\left(\frac{1}{2}\right)=0 \quad\Rightarrow\quad f'\left(\frac{1}{2}\right)=0$

⇒ (b) is correct

Now, $I=\int_{-1/2}^{1/2}f\left(x+\frac{1}{2}\right)\sin x\,dx$

Let $g(x)=f\left(x+\frac{1}{2}\right)$

$\Rightarrow\ g(-x)=f\left(-x+\frac{1}{2}\right)\quad =f\left(1-\left(-x+\frac{1}{2}\right)\right)$

$=f\left(\frac{1}{2}+x\right)=g(x)$

$\Rightarrow$ $g(x)$ is an even function

$\Rightarrow$ $g(x)$ sinx $=f\left(x+\frac{1}{2}\right)\sin x$ is an odd function.

$\Rightarrow\ \mathrm{I}=\int_{-1/2}^{1/2}f\left(x+\frac{1}{2}\right)\sin x\,dx=0$

$\Rightarrow$ (c) is correct

Now, $\mathrm{I}_1=\int_0^{1/2}f(t).e^{\sin\pi t}dt$ and $\mathrm{I}_2=\int_{1/2}^{1}f(1-t)e^{\sin\pi t}\,dt$

In I_2, put $(1-t)=z\ \Rightarrow\ dt=-dz$

$\Rightarrow\ \mathrm{I}_2=\int_{1/2}^{0}f(z)e^{\sin\pi(1-z)}(-dz)=\int_0^{1/2}f(z)e^{\sin\pi z}dz=\mathrm{I}_1$

17. (a), (b), (c)

$\mathrm{I}_n=\int_{-\pi}^{\pi}\frac{\sin nx}{(1+\pi^x)\sin x}dx;\ n\in I,\ n\geq 0\quad\ldots(1)$

Put $x=-t,\ dx=-dt$

$\therefore\ \mathrm{I}_n=\int_{\pi}^{-\pi}\frac{\sin n(-t)(-dt)}{\left[1+(\pi)^{-t}\right](\sin(-t))}=\int_{-\pi}^{\pi}\frac{\pi^t.\sin nt\ dt}{(\pi^t+1)\sin t}$ or

$\mathrm{I}_n=\int_{-\pi}^{\pi}\frac{\pi^x\sin nx}{(\pi^x+1)\sin x}dx\quad\ldots(2)$

Adding (1) and (2), we get $2\mathrm{I}_n=\int_{-\pi}^{\pi}\frac{(1+\pi^x)}{(\pi^x+1)}.\frac{\sin nx}{\sin x}dx$

$\Rightarrow\ \mathrm{I}_n=\frac{1}{2}\int_{-\pi}^{\pi}\frac{\sin nx}{\sin x}dx$

$\Rightarrow\ \mathrm{I}_{n+2}=\frac{1}{2}\int_{-\pi}^{\pi}\frac{\sin(n+2)x}{\sin x}dx$

$\therefore\ \mathrm{I}_{n+2}-\mathrm{I}_n=\frac{1}{2}\int_{-\pi}^{\pi}\frac{\sin(n+2)x-\sin nx}{\sin x}dx$

$=\frac{1}{2}\int_{-\pi}^{\pi}\frac{2\cos(n+1)x\sin(x)}{\sin x}dx=\int_{-\pi}^{\pi}\cos(n+1)x\,dx$

$=\left[\frac{\sin(n+1)x}{(n+1)}\right]_{-\pi}^{\pi}=0$

$\Rightarrow\ I_n=I_{n+2}\ \forall\ n\geq 0$

$\Rightarrow\ I_0=I_2=I_4=I_6\ \ldots.=I_{20}=\ldots.$

$\Rightarrow\ \sum_{m=1}^{10}\mathrm{I}_{2m}=10.(\mathrm{I}_0)=0$

Thus, $\sum_{m=1}^{10}\mathrm{I}_{2m}=0$ and $I_1=I_3=I_5=\ldots.\ I_{21}=\ldots.$

$\Rightarrow\ \sum_{m=1}^{10}\mathrm{I}_{2m+1}=10\mathrm{I}_1=10\int_{-\pi}^{\pi}\frac{\sin x}{(1+\pi^x)\sin x}dx$

$=10\int_{-\pi}^{\pi}\frac{1}{1+\pi^x}dx$

$\therefore\ 10\,\mathrm{I}_1=10\int_{-\pi}^{\pi}\frac{1}{1+\pi^{-x}}dx=10\int_{-\pi}^{\pi}\frac{\pi x}{\pi^x+1}dx$

$\Rightarrow\ 20\,\mathrm{I}_1=10\int_{-\pi}^{\pi}1dx=20\pi$

$\Rightarrow\ 10\,I_1=10\pi$

Thus, $\sum_{m=1}^{10}\mathrm{I}_{2m+1}=10\pi$

18. (a), (b), (c), (d) $\mathrm{I}_n=\int_0^{\pi/4}\tan^n x\,dx$,

$\Rightarrow\ \mathrm{I}_n=\int_0^{\pi/4}\tan^{n-2}x.\tan^2x\,dx$ for $n\geq 2$

$=\int_0^{\pi/4}\tan^{n-2}x\left(\sec^2x-1\right)dx$

$\Rightarrow\ \mathrm{I}_n=\left[\frac{(\tan x)^{n-1}}{n-1}\right]_0^{\pi/4}-\mathrm{I}_{n-2}$ for $n\geq 2$

$\Rightarrow\ \mathrm{I}_n+\mathrm{I}_{n-2}=\frac{1}{n-1}$ for $n\geq 2$

$\therefore$ For $n=7$, $I_7+I_5=\frac{1}{6}\quad\ldots(1)$

For $n=10$, $I_8+I_{10}=\frac{1}{9}\quad\ldots(2)$

For $n=12$, $I_{12}+I_{10}=\frac{1}{11}\quad\ldots(3)$

Adding (2) and (3), we get $I_8+2I_{10}+I_{12}=\frac{1}{9}+\frac{1}{11}=\frac{20}{99}$

Also (2) – (3) gives, $I_8-I_{12}=\frac{1}{9}-\frac{1}{11}=\frac{2}{99}$

19. (a), (b), (c)

$\mathrm{I}=\int_{-\pi}^{\pi}\sin mx.\cos nx\ dx;m,n\in\mathbb{N}$

$=\frac{1}{2}\int_{-\pi}^{\pi}\left[\sin(m+n)x+\sin(m-n)x\right]dx$

$=\frac{1}{2}\int_{-\pi}^{\pi}\sin(m+n)x\,dx+\frac{1}{2}\int_{-\pi}^{\pi}\sin(m-n)x\ dx=0$

($\because$ Both are odd functions or simply the integrand of I is a odd function)

Also $\int_{-\pi/8}^{\pi/8}x^8\sin^9x\ dx=\int_{-\pi/2}^{\pi/2}\sin x.f(\cos x)dx=0$ as both have odd integrand functions.

20. (a), (c) $\mathrm{I}=\int_{\pi}^{5\pi/4}\frac{2\sin x\cos x}{\cos^4x+\sin^4x}dx$

Dividing Nr. and Dr. by cos2x, we get

$\mathrm{I}=\int_{\pi}^{5\pi/4}\frac{2\frac{\sin x}{\cos x}.\frac{1}{\cos^2x}dx}{1+\tan^4x}=\int_{\pi}^{5\pi/4}\frac{2\tan x.\sec^2x\ dx}{1+\tan^4x}$

Put $\tan x=t$, $\sec^2x\ dx=dt$

$\Rightarrow\ \mathrm{I}=\int_0^1\frac{2t}{1+t^4}dt$

Put $t^2=2$, $2t\ dt=dz$

$\Rightarrow\ \mathrm{I}=\int_0^1\frac{dz}{1+z^2}=\left[\tan^{-1}z\right]_0^1=\tan^{-1}1-\tan^{-1}0=\frac{\pi}{4}$

21. (a), (b), (c), (d) $\mathrm{I}=\int_3^4\frac{dx}{\sqrt[3]{\log x}}$

$\log_e x=\ln x$ is an increasing function on $(0,\infty)$

Now, e < 3 < 4 and x ∈ (3, 4)

⇒ ln e < ln 3 < ln 4; ln 3 < ln x < ln 4

⇒ 1 < ln 3 < ln x < ln 4

⇒ 1 < ln x and 1 < $(\ln x)^{1/3}$

⇒ $\frac{1}{\sqrt[3]{\ln x}} < 1$ ⇒ $I < \int_3^4 1 dx$

⇒ I < 1 ⇒ I < 2

⇒ options (a) and (c) are correct.

Also 1 < ln 3 < ln x < ln 4 ln (e^2) = 2

⇒ $1 < \ln x < 2;\ 3 < x < 4$

⇒ $\sqrt[3]{\ln x} < 2$ ⇒ $\frac{1}{\sqrt[3]{\ln x}} > \frac{1}{2}$

⇒ $I > \int_3^4 \frac{1}{2} dx = \frac{1}{2}$ ⇒ $I > \frac{1}{2}$ and $I > \frac{1}{4}$

ASSERTION / REASON TYPE

1. (d) $f(x) = \sin^4 x \cos^4 x = \left(\sin^2 x + \cos^2 x\right)^2 - 2\sin^2 x\cos^2 x$

$= 1 - \frac{1}{2}\sin^2 2x$

$= 1 - \frac{1}{2}\left[\frac{1-\cos 4x}{2}\right] = 1 - \frac{1}{4} + \frac{1}{4}\cos 4x = \frac{3}{4} + \frac{1}{4}\cos 4x,$

which is periodic with period $\frac{2\pi}{4} = \frac{\pi}{2}$

⇒ Reason is correct

∴ $I = \int_{-100\pi}^{100\pi}\left(\sin^4 x + \cos^4 x\right)dx = 2\int_0^{100\pi}\left(\sin^4 x + \cos^4 x\right)dx$

$= \int_0^{200\left(\frac{\pi}{2}\right)}\left(\sin^4 x + \cos^4 x\right)dx$

$= 2(200)\int_0^{\pi/2}\left(\sin^4 x + \cos^4 x\right)dx$

$= 400\int_0^{\pi/2}\left(\frac{3}{4} + \frac{1}{4}\cos 4x\right)dx$

$= 400\left[\frac{3}{4}\left(\frac{\pi}{2}\right) + \frac{1}{16}[0]\right] = 150\pi$

⇒ Assertion is correct

2. (a) $\int_a^{b+nT} f(x)dx = \int_a^b f(x)dx + \int_b^{b+nT} f(x)dx$

$= \int_a^b f(x)dx + n\int_0^T f(x)dx$

⇒ Reason is correct

Now {x} is periodic function with period 1,

∴ $\int_{1/3}^{11/2}\{x\}dx = \int_{1/3}^{(½)+5}\{x\}dx = \int_{1/3}^{\frac{1}{2}+5(1)}\{x\}dx$

$= \int_{1/3}^{1/2}\{x\}dx + 5\int_0^1\{x\}dx = \int_{1/3}^{1/2} x\,dx + 5\int_0^1 x\,dx$

$= \frac{1}{2}\left[x^2\right]_{1/3}^{1/2} + \frac{5}{2}\left[x^2\right]_0^1 = \frac{1}{2}\left[\frac{1}{4} - \frac{1}{9}\right] + \frac{5}{2}$

$= \frac{1}{2}\left(\frac{9-4}{36}\right) + \frac{5}{2} = \frac{5}{72} + \frac{5}{2} = \frac{5+180}{72} = \frac{185}{72}$

⇒ Assertion is correct and is explained by reason

3. (a) $f(x) = \int_0^x g(t)dt$

⇒ $f(-x) = \int_0^{-x} g(t)dt$

⇒ $f(x) + f(-x) = \int_0^x g(t)dt + \int_0^{-x} g(t)dt$

Put t = –z in second integrals, $dt = -dz$

⇒ $f(x) + f(-x) = \int_0^x g(t)dt + \int_0^x g(-z)(-dz)$

$= \int_0^x g(t)dt - \int_0^x g(z)dz = 0$

(∵ $g(x)$ is an even function)

⇒ $f(x)$ is an odd function

⇒ Reason is correct

Now, $\int_0^x f(t)dt = \int_0^x f(t-5+5)dt = \int_0^x g(t-5)dt$

Put $t - 5 = z$, $dt = dz$ $= \int_{-5}^{x-5} g(z)dz$ ...(1)

Now, $f(x) = \int_0^x g(t)dt$

⇒ $f'(x) = g(x)$

∴ $\int_0^x f(t)dt = \int_{-5}^{x-5} f'(z)dz$ (From (1))

$= f(x-5) - f(-5) = -f(-5) + f(x-5)$

$= f(5) - f(5-x)$ [∵ f is odd]

$= g(0) - f(-x+5) = g(0) - g(-x) = g(0) - g(x)$

[∵ g is an even function]

⇒ Assertion is correct

⇒ Both assertion and reason are correct and reason correctly explains the assertion

4. (a) $I = \int_0^a f(x).g(x)dx = \int_0^a f(a-x).g(a-x)dx$

$= \int_0^a -f(x).g(x)dx = -I$

⇒ $2I = 0$ ⇒ $I = 0$

Now, $I_1 = \int_0^a f(x).g(x).h(x)dx$

$= \int_0^a f(x)g(x)\left[h(a-x)\right]dx$

$= \int_0^a f(x).g(x)\frac{[3h(x)-5]}{4}dx$

$I_1 = \frac{3}{4}\int_0^a f(x).g(x).h(x)dx - \frac{5}{4}\int_0^a f(x)g(x)dx$

∴ $I_1 = \frac{3}{4}I_1 - \frac{5}{4}I = \frac{3}{4}I_1$

⇒ $\left(1 - \frac{3}{4}\right)I_1 = 0$

⇒ $I_1 = 0$

Thus, both assertion and reason both are correct and reason is the correct explanation of assertion.

5. (d) $f(x) = \int_1^x \frac{\log t}{t+1}dt$ ...(1)

and $f\left(\frac{1}{x}\right) = \int_1^{1/x} \frac{\log t}{t+1}dt$ ...(2)

Putting $t = \frac{1}{z}$ in (1); $dt = \frac{-1}{z^2}dz$

$\Rightarrow f(x) = \int_1^{1/x} \frac{-\log z}{\left(\frac{1}{z}+1\right)}\left(-\frac{1}{z^2}dz\right) = \int_1^{1/x} \frac{\log z}{z(z+1)}dz$

$= \int_1^{1/z} \frac{[(z+1)-z]\log z}{z(z+1)}dz$

$= \int_1^{1/x}\left(\frac{1}{z}-\frac{1}{z+1}\right)\log z\,dz = \int_1^{1/x}\frac{\log z}{z}dz - \int_1^{1/x}\frac{\log z}{z+1}dz$

$= \int_1^{1/x}\frac{\log z}{z}dz - f\left(\frac{1}{x}\right)$ (using 2)

$\Rightarrow f(x)+f\left(\frac{1}{x}\right) = \int_1^{1/x}\left(\frac{\log z}{z}\right)dz$

$\Rightarrow f(x)+f\left(\frac{1}{x}\right) = \frac{1}{2}\left|(\log z)^2\right|_1^{1/x} = \frac{1}{2}(\log x)^2$

$\Rightarrow$ Reason is correct

Now, $f(x) = \int_1^x \frac{\log t}{1+t+t^2}dt = \int_1^x \frac{\log t}{1+t(1+t)}$

Put $t = \frac{1}{z}; dt = \frac{-1}{z^2}dz$

$= \int_1^{1/x} \frac{\log\left(\frac{1}{z}\right)\left(\frac{-1}{z^2}dz\right)}{1+\frac{1}{z}\left(1+\frac{1}{z}\right)} = \int_1^{1/x}\frac{-\frac{1}{z^2}(-\log z)}{1+\frac{1}{z^2}+\frac{1}{z}}dz$

$= \int_1^{1/x}\frac{\log z\,dz}{z^2+1+z} = f\left(\frac{1}{x}\right)$

$\Rightarrow$ Assertion is incorrect

6. (c) Reason is not correct as it holds for natural number 'n'

Now $\int_0^{10}\frac{2^x}{2^{[x]}}dx = \int_0^1 2^{2x}dx + \int_1^2 2^{x-1}dx$

$+\int_2^3 x^{x-2}dx + \int_3^4 2^{x-3}dx + ... + \int_9^{10} 2^{x-9}dx$

$= \left[\frac{2^x}{\ln 2}\right]_0^1 + \left[\frac{2^{x-1}}{\ln 2}\right]_1^2 + \left[\frac{2^{x-2}}{\ln 2}\right]_2^3 + ... + \left[\frac{2^{x-9}}{\ln 2}\right]_9^{10}$

$= \frac{1}{\ln 2}(2-1) + \frac{1}{\ln 2}(2-1) + \frac{1}{\ln 2}(2-1)$

$+ .... + \frac{1}{\ln 2}(2-1) = \frac{10}{\ln 2}$

$\Rightarrow$ Assertion is correct

7. (a) Let $I = \frac{1}{2n}\int_0^{\pi/2}\tan x.\sin 2nx\,dx$

Here, $I_n = \int_0^{\pi/2}\log\cos x.\cos 2nx\,dx$

$= \left[\log(\cos x)\frac{\sin 2nx}{2n}\right]_0^{\pi/2} - \int_0^{\pi/2} -\frac{\tan x.\sin 2nx}{2n}dx$

$= \frac{1}{2n}\lim_{x\to\pi/2}\left[\ln(\cos x).\sin 2nx\right] + \frac{1}{2n}\int_0^{\pi/2}\tan x.\sin 2nx\,dx$

$= \frac{1}{2n}\lim_{x\to\pi/2}(\cos x)^{\sin 2nx} + I$

$= \frac{1}{2n}\lim_{x\to\pi/2}\ln\left[(1+\cos)-1\right]^{\sin 2nx} + I$

$= \frac{1}{2n}\lim_{x\to\pi/2}\ln\left[1+(\cos x-1)\right]^{\sin 2nx} + I$

$= \frac{1}{2n}\lim_{x\to\frac{\pi}{2}}(1)(\sin 2nx)(\cos x-1) + I$

$= \frac{1}{2n}(0)(0-1) + I = I = \frac{1}{2n}\int_0^{\pi/2}\tan x\sin 2nx\,dx$

$\Rightarrow$ Reason is correct

Also $I_{n-1} = \frac{1}{2(n-1)}\int_0^{\pi/2}\tan x\sin 2(n-1)x\,dx$

$= \frac{1}{2(n-1)}\int_0^{\pi/2}\tan x[\sin 2nx\cos 2x - \cos 2nx.\sin 2x]dx$

$\Rightarrow I_{n-1} = \frac{1}{2(n-1)}\int_0^{\pi/2}\tan x\sin 2x\left(2\cos^2 x-1\right)dx$

$- \frac{1}{2(n-1)}\int_0^{\pi/2}\tan x\cos 2nx\sin 2x\,dx$

$\Rightarrow I_{n-1} = \frac{1}{2(n-1)}\int_0^{\pi/2}\sin 2nx\sin 2x\,dx$

$- \frac{1}{2(n-1)}\int_0^{\pi/2}\tan x.\sin 2nx\,dx$

$- \frac{1}{2(n-1)}\int_0^{\pi/2}2\sin^2 x\cos 2nx\,dx$

$\Rightarrow I_{n-1} = \frac{1}{2(n-1)}\int_0^{\pi/2}\sin 2nx\sin 2x\,dx$

$- \frac{n}{(n-1)}.I_n - \frac{1}{2(n-1)}\int_0^{\pi/2}2\sin^2 x\cos 2nx\,dx$

$\Rightarrow I_{n-1} = \frac{1}{2(n-1)}\int_0^{\pi/2}\sin 2nx\sin 2x\,dx$

$- \frac{n}{(n-1)}I_n - \frac{1}{2(n-1)}\int_0^{\pi/2}(1+\cos 2x)\cos 2nx\,dx$

$\Rightarrow I_{n-1} + \frac{n}{n-1}I_n = \frac{-1}{2(n-1)}\int_0^{\pi/2}\cos(2n+2)x\,dx$

$- \frac{1}{2(n-1)}\int_0^{\pi/2}\cos 2nx\,dx$

$= \frac{-1}{2(n-1)}.\left[\frac{\sin(2n+2)x}{2n+2}\right]_0^{\pi/2} - \frac{1}{2(n-1)}\left[\frac{\sin 2nx}{2n}\right]_0^{\pi/2} = 0$

$\Rightarrow I_n = -\frac{(n-1)}{n}I_{n-1}$

$\Rightarrow$ Assertion is correct and correctly explained by reason

8. (d) $\int_2^5 f(x) = \int_2^3 f(x)dx + \int_3^5 f(x)dx$

$= \int_2^3 1dx + \int_3^5 3dx = (1)+(3)(2) = 7$

∴ $\frac{1}{(b-a)}\int_a^b f(x)dx = \frac{1}{(5-2)}(7) = \frac{7}{3}$, which is not attained in [2, 5]

⇒ Assertion is incorrect

Clearly, $f(3^-) = 1, f(3^+) = 3$ and range of $f(x) = \{1,3\}$

⇒ $f(x)$ is bounded but not continuous on [2, 5]

⇒ Reason is correct

9. (a) Reason is a standard result, that $\int_0^{\pi/2} \log\sin x\, dx = \int_0^{\pi/2} \log\cos x\, dx = \frac{-\pi}{2}\ln 2$

Now, $\int_0^{\pi/2} x\cot x\, dx = \left[x\ln(\sin x)\right]_0^{\pi/2} - \int_0^{\pi/2} 1.\ln\sin x\, dx$

$= -\lim_{x\to 0}\frac{\ln(\sin x)}{\frac{1}{x}} + \frac{\pi}{2}\ln 2 = -\lim_{x\to 0}\frac{\cot x}{\frac{-1}{x^2}} + \frac{\pi}{2}\ln 2$

$= 0\frac{\pi}{2}\ln 2$

⇒ $\int_0^{\pi/2} x\cot x\, dx = \frac{\pi}{2}\ln 2$

⇒ Assertion is correct and correctly explained by reason.

10. (a) $I = \int_a^b \frac{|x|}{x}dx = ?$

Case (i): $a < b \le 0$ and $a < x < b \le 0$

⇒ $I = \int_a^b \frac{-x}{x}dx = \int_a^b -1dx = -(b-a)$

$= (-b) - (-a) = |b| - |a|$

Case (ii): $a < 0 < b;\ a < x < b$

⇒ $I = \int_a^b \frac{|x|}{x}dx = \int_a^0 \frac{|x|}{x}dx + \int_0^b \frac{|x|}{x}dx = \int_a^0 -1dx + \int_0^b 1dx$

$= -[0-a] + [b-0] = b - (-a) = |b| - |a|$

Case (iii): $0 \le a < b;\ a < x < b;$

⇒ $I = \int_a^b \frac{|x|}{x}dx = \int_a^b 1dx = b - a = |b| - |a|$

Thus, assertion and reason both are correct and reason correctly explains the assertion.

11. (d) $\frac{d}{dx}\left\{\frac{1}{2}\tan^{-1}\left(\frac{2x}{1-x^2}\right)\right\}$

Put x = tan θ, i.e., θ = tan⁻¹x

⇒ $\frac{d}{dx}\left\{\frac{1}{2}\tan^{-1}\left(\frac{2\tan\theta}{1-\tan^2\theta}\right)\right\} = \frac{d}{dx}\left\{\frac{1}{2}\tan^{-1}(\tan 2\theta)\right\}$

$= \frac{d}{dx}\left\{\frac{1}{2}(2\theta - n\pi)\right\}$; where $n \in \mathbb{Z}$

⇒ $\frac{d}{dx}\left\{\frac{1}{2}\frac{d}{dx}\left\{\theta - \frac{n\pi}{2}\right\}(2\theta)\right\} = \frac{d\theta}{dx} = \frac{d}{dx}\{\tan^{-1}x\} = \frac{1}{1+x^2}$

⇒ Reason is correct

Now $\int_0^{\sqrt{3}} \frac{1}{1+x^2}dx = \left|\frac{1}{2}\tan^{-1}\left(\frac{2x}{1-x^2}\right)\right|_0^{\sqrt{3}}$

$= \frac{1}{2}\tan^{-1}\left(\tan 2\left(\frac{\pi}{3}\right)\right)$

$= \frac{1}{2}\tan^{-1}\left(\tan\left(\pi - \frac{\pi}{3}\right)\right) = \frac{1}{2}\tan^{-1}\left(-\tan\frac{\pi}{3}\right)$.

$= \frac{1}{2}\left(\frac{-\pi}{3}\right) = \frac{-\pi}{6}$

⇒ $\int_0^{\sqrt{3}} \frac{1}{1+x^2}dx + \left|\frac{1}{2}\tan^{-1}\left(\frac{2x}{1-x^2}\right)\right|_0^{\sqrt{3}} = \frac{-\pi}{3}$

⇒ Assertion is incorrect

12. (d) $\frac{d}{dx}\left(\frac{1}{3}\tan^{-1}\left(\sqrt{3}\tan x\right)\right) = \frac{1}{\sqrt{3}}\left[\frac{1}{1+3\tan^2 x}\right] \times \sqrt{3}\sec^2 x$

$= \frac{\sec^2 x}{1+3\tan^2 x} = \frac{1}{\cos^2 x + 3\sin^2 x} = \frac{1}{1+2\sin^2 x}$

⇒ Reason is correct.

∴ $\int_0^{\pi}\frac{dx}{1+2\sin^2 x} = \left|\frac{1}{\sqrt{3}}\tan^{-1}\left(\sqrt{3}\tan x\right)\right|_0^{\pi}$ but assertion is incorrect

as $\int_0^{\pi}\frac{dx}{1+2\sin^2 x} = \int_0^{\pi/2}\frac{dx}{1+2\sin^2 x} + \int_{\pi/2}^{\pi}\frac{dx}{1+2\sin^2 x}$

(∵ For dividing by cos² which should be ≠ 0)

$= \int_0^{\pi/2}\frac{\sec^2 x\, dx}{\sec^2 x + 2\tan^2 x} + \int_{\pi/2}^{\pi}\frac{\sec^2 x\, dx}{\sec^2 x + 2\tan^2 x}$

$= \int_0^{\pi/2}\frac{\sec^2 x\, dx}{1+3\tan^2 x} + \int_{\pi/2}^{\pi}\frac{\sec^2 x\, dx}{1+3\tan^2 x}$

$= \int_0^{\infty}\frac{dt}{1+\left(\sqrt{3}\,t\right)^2} + \int_{-\infty}^{0}\frac{dt}{1+\left(\sqrt{3}\,t\right)^2}$

$= \left|\frac{1}{\sqrt{3}}\tan^{-1}\left(\sqrt{3}\,t\right)\right|_0^{\infty} + \left|\frac{1}{\sqrt{3}}\tan^{-1}\left(\sqrt{3}\,t\right)\right|_{-\infty}^{0}$

$= \frac{1}{\sqrt{3}}\left[\frac{\pi}{2} - 0\right] + \frac{1}{\sqrt{3}}\left[0 - \left(\frac{-\pi}{2}\right)\right] = \frac{\pi}{2\sqrt{3}} + \frac{\pi}{2\sqrt{3}}$

$= 2\left(\frac{\pi}{2\sqrt{3}}\right) = \frac{\pi}{\sqrt{3}}$

13. (d) Reason is obviously correct, i.e., definite integral of a non-negative (not identically zero) function is always positive.

Now $\int_0^{\pi}\sqrt{\frac{1+\cos 2x}{2}}dx = \int_0^{\pi}\sqrt{\cos^2 x}\, dx = \int_0^{\pi}|\cos x|dx$

$= \int_0^{\pi/2}\cos x\, dx + \int_{\pi/2}^{\pi} -\cos x\, dx$

$= [\sin x]_0^{\pi/2}[\sin x]_{\pi/2}^{\pi} = (1-0) - (0-1) = 2$

⇒ Assertion is incorrect

14. (a) Reason is correct, as it is a standard result.

Now for x ∈(0, 1), x^2∈(0, 1) and e^x is an increasing function

$\Rightarrow \quad e^0 < e^{x^2} < e$ for x ∈ (0, 1)

$\Rightarrow \quad 1 < e^{x^2} < e$

$\Rightarrow \quad \int_0^1 1dx < \int_0^1 e^{x^2} dx < \int_0^1 e\, dx$

$\Rightarrow \quad 1 < \int_0^1 e^{x^2} dx < e$

⇒ Assertion is correct and is supported by reason

15. (c) $I(m, n) = \int_0^1 \underbrace{x^m}_{\text{II}} \underbrace{(\ln x)^n}_{\text{I}} dx$

$$= \left[\frac{(\ln x)^n . x^{m+1}}{m+1}\right]_0^1 - \int_0^1 n\frac{(\ln x)^{n-1} . x^{m+1}}{x(m+1)} dx$$

$$= \frac{-1}{m+1} . \lim_{x\to 0^+} x^{m+1} . (\ln x)^n - \frac{n}{(m+1)}\int_0^1 x^m . (\ln x)^{n-1} dx$$

$$= \frac{-1}{m+1} \lim_{x\to 0^+} \frac{(\ln x)^n}{\left(\frac{1}{x^{m+1}}\right)} - \frac{n}{(m+1)} \mathrm{I}(m, n-1)$$

$$= \frac{-1}{m+1} \lim_{x\to 0^+} \left[\frac{n(\ln x)^{n-1}}{-(m+1) . \frac{1}{x^{(m+2)}}} . \frac{1}{x}\right] \frac{-n}{m+1} \mathrm{I}(m, m-1)$$

$$= -\frac{1}{(m+1)} \lim_{x\to 0^+} \left[\frac{-n}{(m+1)} . \frac{(\ln x)^{n-1}}{\left(\frac{1}{x^{m+1}}\right)}\right] - \frac{n}{(m+1)} I(m, n-1)$$

In the first limit power of (ln x) goes on decreasing on applying L.H. Rule again and again, but power of, x i.e., x^{m+1} will remain same. After applying L.H. Rule n-times, the power of (ln x) will become zero and hence, the limit becomes zero as it converts to $\lim_{x\to 0^+} \left[\frac{(-1)^n n!}{(m+1)^n} . x^{m+1}\right] = 0$.

Thus, $\mathrm{I}(m,n) = 0 - \frac{n}{(m+1)} \mathrm{I}(m, n-1)$ ...(1)

⇒ Reason is incorrect,

Now, by result (1),

$$\mathrm{I}(2,4)\int_0^1 x^2 (\ln x)^4 dx = -\frac{4}{3} \mathrm{I}(2,3)$$

$$= \left(-\frac{4}{3}\right)\left(-\frac{3}{3}\right)\mathrm{I}(2,2)$$

$$= \left(\frac{-4}{3}\right)\left(\frac{-3}{3}\right)\left(\frac{-2}{3}\right)\mathrm{I}(2,1)$$

$$= \left(-\frac{4}{3}\right)\left(-\frac{3}{3}\right)\left(-\frac{2}{3}\right)\left(-\frac{1}{3}\right)\mathrm{I}(2,0)$$

$$= \frac{24}{81}\int_0^1 x^2 dx = \frac{24}{81}\left[\frac{x^3}{3}\right]_0^1 = \frac{8}{81}$$

⇒ Assertion is correct

TUTORIAL SHEET SECTION–VI

PASSAGE – A

$$f\left(\frac{x+y}{2}\right) = \frac{f(x) + f(y)}{2} \quad \forall x, y \in \mathbb{R}$$

Differentiating both sides partially w.r.t. x and keeping y-constants,

$$\Rightarrow \quad \frac{1}{2} f'\left(\frac{x+y}{2}\right) = \frac{1}{2} f'(x)$$

$$\Rightarrow \quad f'\left(\frac{x+y}{2}\right) = f'(x) \; \forall x, y \in \mathbb{R}$$

$\Rightarrow \quad f'(x) = \text{constant} = k$ (say)

$\Rightarrow \quad f'(x) = kx + k_1$

$\Rightarrow \quad f'(x) = k$

Now $f(1) = f'(1) = 4$

$\Rightarrow \quad 4 = k + k_1, k = 4 \quad \Rightarrow \quad k = 4, k_1 = 0$

$\Rightarrow \quad f(x) = 4x$ ...(1)

$$\therefore \quad \mathrm{I} = \int_0^\pi f(\sin x) dx + \int_0^\pi f\left(\frac{4}{\pi} - \sin x\right) dx$$

$$= \int_0^\pi 4\sin x\, dx + \int_0^\pi \left(\frac{16}{\pi} - 4\sin x\right) dx = \frac{16}{\pi}\int_0^\pi 1\, dx = 16$$

$\Rightarrow \quad I = 16$ ...(2)

∴ Focus of parabola $(y - h)^2 = g(x)$ is $(I, 4) \equiv (16, 4)$

Let $(y - h)^2 = 4a (x - k_2) = g(x)$

⇒ Focus of parabola $\equiv (k_2 + a, h)$

$\Rightarrow \quad k_2 + a = 16, h = 4$ ...(3)

It is given that directing of parabola, i.e., $x = k_2 - a$ passes through the point of intersection of curve $y = hx$ and line $y = 4$, i.e., through (1, 4)

$\Rightarrow \quad 1 = k_2 - a$ ...(4)

Solving (3) and (4), we get $k_2 = \frac{17}{2}, a = \frac{15}{2}$

$\Rightarrow \quad g(x) = 4a(x - k_2)$

$$\Rightarrow \quad g(x) = 4\left(\frac{15}{2}\right)\left(x - \frac{17}{2}\right) = 15(2x - 17)$$

$\therefore \quad g(x) = 30x - 255$ ...(5)

1. (b) $\mathrm{I} = \left|\int_h^{h+2} g(x)dx\right| = \left|\int_4^6 (30x - 255)dx\right|$

$$= \left|\left[\frac{30x^2}{2} - 255x\right]_4^6\right|$$

$$= \left|\left[15x^2 - 255x\right]_4^6\right| = \left|15(20) - 255(2)\right| = \left|300 - 510\right|$$

$$= |-210| = 210$$

2. (b), (d) $\mathrm{I}_1 = \int_0^h f(x)dx = \int_0^4 4x\, dx$

$$= \frac{4}{2}\left[x^2\right]_0^4 = 2(16 - 0) = 32 \text{ and}$$

$$\mathrm{I}_2 = \int_0^h g(x) = \int_0^4 (30x - 255)dx$$

$$= \left[\frac{30x^2}{2} - 255x\right]_0^4 = 15(16) - 1020$$

$$= 240 - 1020 = -780$$

$$\Rightarrow I_1 > I_2 \text{ and } I_1 \cdot I_2 < 0$$

3. (c) $\frac{d}{dx}\int_0^{f(x)} (g(x)+255)dx = \frac{d}{dx}\int_0^{4x} (30x - 255 + 255)dx$

$$= \frac{d}{dx}\int_0^{4x} 30x\, dx = \frac{d}{dx}\left[\frac{30x^2}{2}\right]_0^{4x}$$

$$= \frac{d}{dx}\left[15(16x^2)\right] = 15(16)(2x) = 480x$$

PASSAGE-(B)

$|\vec{a}| = |\vec{b}| = 1$, Angle between $\vec{a}$ and $\vec{b}$ is θ ...(1)

$\Rightarrow \vec{a}.\vec{b} = \cos\theta$ and $\left(\vec{a}\times\vec{b}\right)^2 = \left(|\vec{a}||\vec{b}|\sin\theta.\hat{n}\right)^2$

$$= (\sin\theta.\hat{n})^2 = |\sin\theta.\hat{n}|^2 = \sin^2\theta$$

$\therefore \quad g(\theta) = \int_{-\cos^2\theta}^{\sin^2\theta} f^2(x)dx$ ...(2)

Also, $f(x) + f(y) = \frac{x+y}{xy} \quad \forall\ x, y \in \mathbb{R} - \{0\}$

$\Rightarrow f(x) + f(y) = \frac{1}{y} + \frac{1}{x} \ \forall x, y \in \mathbb{R}$

Keeping y constant and differentially partially w.r.t. x, we get $f'(x) = -\frac{1}{x^2}$

$\Rightarrow f(x) = -\int x^{-2}dx \quad \Rightarrow f(x) = \frac{-x^{-1}}{-1} + c$

$\Rightarrow f(x) = \frac{1}{x} + c$ But $f(x) + f(y) = \frac{1}{x} + \frac{1}{y}$

$\Rightarrow \frac{1}{x} + c + \frac{1}{y} + c = \frac{1}{x} + \frac{1}{y}$

$\Rightarrow$ c = 0

$\therefore \quad f(x) = \frac{1}{x} \ \forall x \in \mathbb{R} - \{0\}$

$\therefore \quad g(\theta) = \int_{-\cos^2\theta}^{\sin^2\theta} \frac{1}{x^2} dx = \left[\frac{-1}{x}\right]_{-\cos^2\theta}^{\sin^2\theta}$

$$= -\left[\frac{1}{\sin^2\theta} - \frac{1}{-\cos^2\theta}\right] = -\left[\frac{\cos^2\theta + \sin^2\theta}{\sin^2\theta.\cos^2\theta}\right]$$

$$= \frac{-1}{\sin^2\theta.\cos^2\theta} = \frac{-4}{4\sin^2\theta.\cos^2\theta}$$

$$= \frac{-4}{\sin^2 2\theta} = -4\text{cosec}^2 2\theta$$

4. (a) $\int_{\pi/6}^{\pi/3} -4\text{cosec}^2 2\theta\, d\theta = -4\left[-\frac{\cot 2\theta}{2}\right]_{\pi/6}^{\pi/3}$

$$= 2\left[\cot\frac{2\pi}{3} - \cot\frac{\pi}{3}\right] = 2\left[-2\cot\frac{\pi}{3}\right] = -\frac{4}{\sqrt{3}}$$

5. (b) $\text{I} = \int_0^{10\pi}\left|\frac{1}{g(\theta)}\right| d\theta = \int_0^{10\pi}\left|\frac{1}{-4\text{cosec}^2 2\theta}\right| d\theta$

$$= \frac{1}{4}\int_0^{10\pi} \sin^2 2\theta\, d\theta = \frac{1}{4}\int_0^{10\pi}\left(\frac{1-\cos 4\theta}{2}\right)d\theta$$

$$= \frac{1}{8}\left[\theta - \frac{\sin 4\theta}{4}\right]_0^{10\pi} = \left[\frac{\theta}{8} - \frac{1}{32}\sin 4\theta\right]_0^{10\pi}$$

$$= \frac{1}{8}(10\pi) = \frac{5}{4}\pi$$

6. (b) $\text{I} = \int_{-\pi/4}^{\pi/4} [g(\theta)]^{-4} d\theta = \int_{-\pi/4}^{\pi/4}\left[\frac{1}{-4\text{cosec}^2 2\theta}\right]^4 d\theta$

$$= \frac{1}{256}\int_{-\pi/4}^{\pi/4} (\sin^2 2\theta)^4 d\theta = \frac{1}{128}\int_0^{\pi/4} \sin^8 2\theta\, d\theta$$

Put 2θ = t $\Rightarrow$ $d\theta = dt/2$

$$\Rightarrow \text{I} = \frac{1}{128}\int_0^{\pi/2} \sin^8 t \frac{dt}{2} = \frac{1}{256}\times\frac{7\times5\times3}{8\times6\times4\times2}\times\frac{\pi}{2} = \frac{35\pi}{(2)^{16}}$$

PASSAGE-C

7. (c) $\text{I}(\alpha, k) = \int_0^\infty \frac{e^{-\alpha x}.\sin kx}{3x} dx$

$$\Rightarrow \text{I}'(k) = \int_0^\infty \frac{e^{-\alpha x}.(\cos kx)x}{3x} dx$$

$$\Rightarrow \text{I}'(k) = \frac{1}{3}\int_0^\infty e^{-\alpha x}\cos kx\, dx$$

$$= \frac{1}{3}.\left\{\frac{e^{-\alpha x}}{(\alpha^2+k^2)}[-\alpha\cos kx + k\sin kx]\right\}_0^\infty$$

$$= \frac{1}{3(\alpha^2+k^2)}\{0 - 1[-\alpha]\}$$

$$\Rightarrow \text{I}'(k) = \frac{\alpha}{3(\alpha^2+k^2)}$$

$$\Rightarrow \int \text{I}'(k)dk = \frac{\alpha}{3}\int\frac{1}{\alpha^2+k^2}dk = \frac{\alpha}{3}.\frac{1}{\alpha}.\tan^{-1}\left(\frac{k}{\alpha}\right) + c$$

$$\Rightarrow \text{I}(\alpha, k) = \frac{1}{3}\tan^{-1}\left(\frac{k}{\alpha}\right) + c$$

Clearly I (α, 0) = 0

$\Rightarrow$ c = 0

$$\Rightarrow \text{I}(\alpha, k) = \frac{1}{3}\tan^{-1}\left(\frac{k}{\alpha}\right).$$

$$\therefore \int_0^\infty \frac{\sin 2x}{3x}dx = \int_0^\infty \frac{e^{-(0)x}.\sin 2x}{3x}dx = \text{I}(0, 2)$$

$$= \frac{1}{3}\tan^{-1}\left(\frac{2}{0}\right) = \frac{1}{3}\left(\frac{\pi}{2}\right) = \frac{\pi}{6}$$

8. (b) Let $\text{I}(a) = \int_0^\pi \frac{dx}{a - \cos x} = \frac{\pi}{2\sqrt{a^2-1}}$

$$\Rightarrow \text{I}'(a) = \int_0^\pi \frac{-1}{(a-\cos x)^2}dx = \frac{\pi}{2}.\left(\frac{-1}{2}\right).(a^2-1)^{-3/2}(2a)$$

$$\Rightarrow \quad I'(a)=\int_0^{\pi}\frac{-1\ dx}{(a-\cos x)^2}=\frac{-a\pi}{2(a^2-1)^{3/2}}$$

$$\Rightarrow \quad \int_0^{\pi}\frac{dx}{(a-\cos x)^2}=\frac{a\pi}{2(a^2-1)^{3/2}}$$

9. (c) Let $I(a)=\int_0^1\frac{\ln(1-a^2x^2)}{x^2\sqrt{(1-x^2)}}dx$

$$\Rightarrow \quad I'(a)=\int_0^1\frac{1}{(1-a^2x^2)}\times\frac{(-2ax^2)}{x^2\sqrt{1-x^2}}dx$$

$$\Rightarrow \quad I'(a)=\int_0^1\frac{-2a}{(1-a^2x^2)\sqrt{1-x^2}}dx$$

$$\Rightarrow \quad I'(a)=(-2a)\int_0^1\frac{dx}{(1-a^2x^2)\sqrt{1-x^2}}$$

Put $x=\frac{1}{t}$

$$\Rightarrow \quad I'(a)=-2a\int_{\infty}^{1}\frac{-\frac{1}{t^2}dt}{\left(1-\frac{a^2}{t^2}\right)\sqrt{1-\frac{1}{t^2}}}$$

$$=-2a\int_{\infty}^{1}\frac{-t\ dt}{(t^2-a^2)\sqrt{t^2-1}}=-2a\int_1^{\infty}\frac{t\ dt}{(t^2-a^2)\sqrt{t^2-1}}$$

Put $t^2=u \quad \Rightarrow \quad 2t\ dt=du$

$$\Rightarrow \quad I'(a)=(-a)\int_1^{\infty}\frac{du}{(u-a^2)\sqrt{u-1}}$$

Put $\sqrt{u-1}=v \quad \Rightarrow \quad \frac{1}{2\sqrt{u-1}}du=dv$

$$\Rightarrow \quad I'(a)=(-a)\int_0^{\infty}\frac{2dv}{(v^2+1-a^2)}=-2a\int_0^{\infty}\frac{dv}{v^2+\left(\sqrt{1-a^2}\right)^2}$$

$(\because a^2<1)$

$$=-2a\times\left[\frac{1}{\sqrt{1-a^2}}\tan^{-1}\left(\frac{v}{\sqrt{1-a^2}}\right)\right]_0^{\infty}$$

$$=\frac{-2a}{\sqrt{1-a^2}}\left[\frac{\pi}{2}\right]=\frac{-a\pi}{\sqrt{1-a^2}}$$

$$\Rightarrow \quad I(a)=\frac{\pi}{2}\int\frac{-2a}{\sqrt{1-a^2}}da=\frac{\pi}{2}\left[\frac{\sqrt{1-a^2}}{\frac{1}{2}}\right]+c$$

$= \pi\sqrt{1-a^2}+c$ at a = 0, I(0) = 0

$\Rightarrow$ I(0) = 0 = π + c $\quad \Rightarrow$ c = –π

$\Rightarrow \quad I(a)=\pi\sqrt{1-a^2}+(-\pi)=\pi\left(\sqrt{1-a^2}-1\right)$

PASSAGE-D

Here $\int_a^b f(x)dx=F\left(\frac{a+b}{2}\right)$; where for $c\in(a,b)$,

$$F(c)=\left(\frac{c-a}{2}\right)(f(a)+f(c))+\frac{(b-c)}{2}(f(b)+f(c)) \text{ and}$$

$$c=\frac{a+b}{2}$$

$$\Rightarrow \quad \int_a^b f(x)dx=F\left(\frac{a+b}{2}\right)$$

$$=F(c)=\frac{b-a}{4}(f(a)+f(b)+2f(c))$$

10. (a) $\int_0^{\pi/2}\sin x\,dx=F\left(\frac{0+\frac{\pi}{2}}{2}\right)=F\left(\frac{\pi}{4}\right)$

$$=\left(\frac{\frac{\pi}{2}-0}{4}\right)\left(\sin 0+\sin\frac{\pi}{2}+2\sin\frac{\pi}{4}\right)$$

$$=\frac{\pi}{8}\left(1+2\left(\frac{1}{\sqrt{2}}\right)\right)=\frac{\pi}{8}\left(1+\sqrt{2}\right)$$

11. (a) For x ∈(a, b)

$$F(x)=\left(\frac{x-a}{2}\right)(f(a)+f(x))+\frac{b-x}{2}(f(b)+f(x))$$

$$\Rightarrow \quad F'(x)=\left(\frac{x-a}{2}\right)(f'(x))+\frac{1}{2}(f(a)+f(x))+\left(\frac{b-x}{2}\right)$$

$$(f'(x))-\frac{1}{2}(f(b)+f(x))$$

$$\Rightarrow \quad F'(c)=\left(\frac{c-a}{2}+\frac{b-c}{2}\right)f'(c)+\frac{1}{2}(f(a)-f(b))$$

$\because \quad f(x)$ is maximum at 'c'

$\Rightarrow \quad F'(c)=0$

$$\Rightarrow \quad 0=\left(\frac{b-a}{2}\right).f'(c)+\left(\frac{f(a)-f(b)}{2}\right)$$

$$\Rightarrow \quad f'(c)=\frac{f(b)-f(a)}{(b-a)}$$

PASSAGE-E

$y^3-3y+x=0 \qquad$ ...(1)

$$\Rightarrow \quad 3y^2\frac{dy}{dx}-3\frac{dy}{dx}+1=0 \Rightarrow (3y^2-3)\frac{dy}{dx}=-1$$

$\Rightarrow \quad \frac{dy}{dx}=\frac{-1}{3y^2-3} \qquad$ ...(2)

$$\Rightarrow \quad f'\left(-10\sqrt{2}\right)=\frac{-1}{3y^2-3}=\frac{-1}{3\left(2\sqrt{2}\right)^2-3}=\frac{-1}{3(7)}=\frac{-1}{21}$$

...(3)

$$\Rightarrow \quad \frac{d^2y}{dx^2}=-\frac{1}{3}.\frac{-(1)(2yy')}{(y^2-1)^2}=\frac{2yy'}{3(y^2-1)^2}$$

$\therefore \quad f''\left(-10\sqrt{2}\right)=\frac{2\left(2\sqrt{2}\right)}{3(8-1)^2}\left(\frac{-1}{21}\right)$ (using (3))

$$\Rightarrow \quad =\frac{-4\sqrt{2}}{(3)^2(7)^3}$$

12. (b)

13. (a) Now Area $= \int_a^b 1.f(x)dx = [x f(x)]_a^b - \int_a^b x f'(x)dx$

$= b f(b) - af(a) - \int_a^b \frac{-x}{3(y^2-1)}dx$

$= \int_a^b \frac{x}{3((f(x)^2)-1)}dx + b f(b) - a f(a)$

14. (b) For x ∈(–2, 2), $(g(x))^3 - 3g(x) + x = 0$ and

$(g(-x))^3 - 3g(-x) + (-x) = 0$

Adding, we get

$(g(x))^3 + (g(-x))^3 - 3[g(x) + g(-x)] = 0$

$\Rightarrow (g(x)+g(x))[(g(x))^2 + (g(-x))^2 - g(x).g(-x)]$

$-3(g(x)+g(-x)) = 0$

$\Rightarrow [g(x)+g(-x)][(g(x))^2 + (g(-x))^2 - g(x).g(-x) - 3] = 0$

$\Rightarrow g(x) + g(-x) = 0$ or ...(4)

$\Rightarrow (g(x))^2 + (g(-x))^2 - g(x).g(-x) - 3 = 0$ ...(5)

Given g(0) = 0

From (5), – 3 = 0, (false)

$\Rightarrow g(x) + g(-x) = 0$

$\Rightarrow g(x) = -g(-x)$

$\therefore \int_{-1}^{1} g'(x)dx = [g(x)]_{-1}^{1} = g(1) - g(-1) = 2g(1)$

PASSAGE-F

$f: (-\infty, \infty) \to (-\infty, \infty),\ f(x) = \frac{x^2 - ax + 1}{x^2 + ax + 1}; 0 < a < 2$

$\Rightarrow f(x) = \frac{x^2 + ax + 1 - 2ax}{x^2 + ax + 1}$

$\Rightarrow f(x) = 1 - \frac{2ax}{x^2 + ax + 1}$

$\Rightarrow f'(x) = 0 - 2a\left[\frac{(x^2+ax+1) - x(2x+a)}{(x^2+ax+1)^2}\right]$

$\Rightarrow f'(x) = -2a\left[\frac{1-x^2}{(x^2+ax+1)^2}\right]$

$\Rightarrow f'(x) = \frac{2a(x^2-1)}{(x^2+ax+1)^2}$ ...(1)

$\Rightarrow f''(x) = 2a\left[\frac{(x^2+ax+1)^2(2x) - (x^2-1)2(2x+a)(x^2+ax+1)}{(x^2+ax+1)^4}\right]$

$\Rightarrow f''(x) = \frac{(2a)(2)(x^2+ax+1)[x^3+ax^2+x-(x^2-1)(2x+a)]}{(x^2+ax+1)^4}$

$\Rightarrow f''(x) = \frac{4a[x^3+ax^2+x-2x^3-ax^2+2x+a]}{(x^3+ax+1)^3}$

$\Rightarrow f''(x) = \frac{4a(-x^3+3x+a)}{(x^2+ax+1)^3}$

$\Rightarrow f''(x) = \frac{4a[-(x-1)^2(x+2)+(a+2)]}{(x^2+ax+1)^3}$

$\Rightarrow f''(x) = \frac{4a[(a+2)-(x+2)(x-1)^2]}{(x^2+ax+1)^3}$

$\Rightarrow f''(1) = \frac{4a[(a+2)]}{(a+2)^3} = \frac{4a}{(2-a)^2}$

$\Rightarrow f''(-1) = \frac{4a[(a+2)-4]}{(2-a)^3} = \frac{-4a}{(2-a)^2}$

15. (a) Clearly $(a+2)^2 f''(1) = 4a$ and $(2-a)^2 f''(-1) = -4a$

Adding above two equations, we get

$(a+2)^2 f''(1) + (2-a)^2 f''(-1) = 0$

16. (a) From (1), $f'(x) < 0$ for $x^2 - 1 < 0$, i.e., $x \in (-1, 1)$

$\Rightarrow$ $f(x)$ is a decreasing function on (–1, 1) and increasing on (–∞, –1) and (1, ∞).

$\Rightarrow$ $f(x)$ has a local maxima at $x = -1$ and a local minima at $x = 1$

17. (b) $g(x) = \int_0^{e^x} \frac{f'(t)}{1+t^2}dt \quad \Rightarrow g'(x) = \frac{f'(e^x)}{1+e^{2x}}.e^x$

$\Rightarrow g'(x) = \frac{2a(e^{2x}-1)e^x}{(e^{2x}+1)(e^{2x}+ae^x+1)^2}; a \in (0,2)$

$\Rightarrow$ g′(x) < 0 for e2x – 1 < 0

$\Rightarrow -1 < e^x < 1 \qquad \Rightarrow 0 < e^x < 1$

$\Rightarrow x \in (-\infty, 0)$ and $g'(x) > 0$ for $x \in (0, \infty)$

PASSAGE-G

$f: [a, b] \to [0, \infty)$; $a > 0$ and f is continuous.

Volume of solid of revolution is given by, $V = 2\pi\int_x^b x f(x)dx$

18. (a) Volume of solid of revolution $= 2\pi\int_1^4 x(4x - x^2)dx$

$= 2\pi\int_1^4 (4x^2 - x^3)dx = 2\pi\left[\frac{4x^3}{3} - \frac{x^4}{4}\right]_1^4$

$= 2\pi\left[\left(\frac{256}{3} - 64\right) - \left(\frac{4}{3} - \frac{1}{4}\right)\right] = 2\pi\left[\frac{64}{3} - \left(\frac{16-3}{12}\right)\right]$

$= 2\pi\left[\frac{64}{3} - \frac{13}{2}\right] = \frac{81\pi}{2}$ cubic units

19. (b) $f(x) = \begin{cases} \sqrt{3}x\ ; & 0 \le x \le 1 \\ \sqrt{4-x^2}\ ; & 1 \le x \le 2 \end{cases}$

Volume of revolution $= 2\pi\int_0^2 x f(x)dx$

$= 2\pi\int_0^1 x.\sqrt{3}x\, dx + 2\pi\int_1^2 x\sqrt{4-x^2}dx$

$= 2\sqrt{3}\pi\int_0^1 x^2dx + 2\pi\int_1^2 x\sqrt{4-x^2}dx$

$= 2\sqrt{3}\pi\left[\frac{1}{3}\right] + \frac{2\pi}{-2}\left[\int_1^2 -2x\sqrt{4-x^2}dx\right]$

$= \frac{2\sqrt{3}\pi}{3} - \pi\left(\frac{2}{3}(4-x^2)^{3/2}\right)_1^2$

$= \frac{2\sqrt{3}\pi}{3} - \frac{2\pi}{3}(0-3\sqrt{3}) = \frac{8\sqrt{3}\pi}{3}$

20. **(c)** Let the equation of ellipse be $\frac{x^2}{a^2}+\frac{y^2}{b^2}=1$

$\therefore$ Volume of solid of revolution of ellipse

$= 2\left(2\pi\int_0^a x f(x)dx\right) = 4\pi\int_x^a x.\frac{b}{a}\sqrt{a^2-x^2}dx$

$= \frac{4\pi b}{(-2)a}\int_0^a (-2x)(a^2-x^2)^{1/2}dx$

$= \frac{-2\pi b}{a}\left[(a^2-x^2)^{3/2}\left(\frac{2}{3}\right)\right]_0^a = -\frac{2\pi b}{a}\left[\frac{2}{3}(0-a^3)\right]$

$= \frac{4\pi a^2 b}{3}$

SECTION–VII: (TUTORIAL SHEET)

1. **(i) → (c); (ii) → (d); (iii) → (a); (iv) → (b)**

(i) $\int_{-1}^3 (|x-2|+[x])dx \quad = \int_{-1}^2(-x+2)dx + \int_2^3(x-2)dx$

$+\int_{-1}^0(-1)dx + \int_0^1 0dx + \int_1^2 1dx + \int_2^3 2dx$

$= \left[\frac{-x^2}{2}+2x\right]_{-1}^2 + \left[\frac{x^2}{2}-2x\right]_2^3$

$-[0-(-1)]+[2-1]+2(3-2)$

$= -\frac{1}{2}(3)+2(3)+\frac{1}{2}(5) - 2(1) - 1 + 1 + 2 = 7$

(ii) $I = \int_{-1}^1 \frac{\sin^2 x\, dx}{\left[\frac{x}{\sqrt{2}}\right]+\frac{1}{2}} = \int_{-1}^1 \frac{\sin^2(-x)}{\left[\frac{-x}{\sqrt{2}}\right]+\frac{1}{2}}dx$

$\left(\because \frac{-x}{\sqrt{2}} \in \left(\frac{-1}{\sqrt{2}},\frac{1}{\sqrt{2}}\right) \neq \mathbb{Z} \text{ for } x\in[-1,1]-\{0\}\right)$

$\therefore \quad I = \int_{-1}^0 \frac{\sin^2 x}{\left[\frac{-x}{\sqrt{2}}\right]+\frac{1}{2}}dx + \int_0^1 \frac{\sin^2 x}{\left[\frac{-x}{\sqrt{2}}\right]+\frac{1}{2}}dx$

$= \int_{-1}^0 \frac{\sin^2 x}{-1-\left[\frac{x}{\sqrt{2}}\right]+\frac{1}{2}}dx + \int_0^1 \frac{\sin^2 x}{-1-\left[\frac{x}{\sqrt{2}}\right]+\frac{1}{2}}dx$

$(\because [-x] = -1-[x] \text{ for } x\notin\mathbb{Z}, = [-x] = -[x] \text{ for } x\in\mathbb{Z})$

$= \int_{-1}^0 \frac{\sin^2 x}{-\left(\left[\frac{x}{2}\right]+\frac{1}{2}\right)}dx + \int_0^1 \frac{\sin^2 x}{-\left(\left[\frac{x}{\sqrt{2}}\right]+\frac{1}{2}\right)}dx$

$= -\int_{-1}^1 \frac{\sin^2 x}{\left(\left[\frac{x}{2}\right]+\frac{1}{2}\right)}dx = -I$

$\Rightarrow 2I = 0 \qquad \Rightarrow I = 0$

(iii) $I = \int_1^b (b-4x)dx \geq 6-5b, b>1$

$\Rightarrow (bx-2x^2)_1^b \geq 6-5b, b>1$

$\Rightarrow (b^2-2b^2)-(b-2) \geq 6-5b, b>1$

$\Rightarrow -b^2+4b+2-6 \geq 0, b>1$

$\Rightarrow b^2-4b+4 \leq 0, b>1$

$\Rightarrow (b-2)^2 \leq 0, b>1 \quad \Rightarrow b=2$

(iv) $I_1 = \int_0^{3\pi} f(\cos^2 x)dx;$

$\because$ $f(\cos^2 x)$ is periodic with period π

$\therefore$ $I_1 = 3\int_0^{\pi} f(\cos^2 x)dx = 3I_2$

$\Rightarrow k = 3$

2. **(i) → (c); (ii) → (a); (iii) → (b); (iv) → (d)**

(i) $\int_0^{\pi/2}(\sin x)^{\cos x}.\left(\cos x\cot x - \log(\sin x)^{\sin x}\right)dx$

Let $t = (\sin x)^{\cos x}$

$\Rightarrow$ $\ln t = \cos x \ln \sin x$

$\Rightarrow \frac{1}{t}dt = \frac{\cos x}{\sin x}.\cos x - \sin x \ln \sin x$

$\Rightarrow dt = (\sin x)^{\cos x}\left[\cos x dt\, x - \ln(\sin x)^{\sin x}\right]$

$\therefore$ $I = \int_0^1 dt = 1$

(ii) $\left|\int_0^1(1-y^2)dy\right| + \left|\int_1^0(y^2-1)dy\right|$

$= \int_0^1(1-y^2)dy + \left|\int_0^1(1-y^2)dy\right|$

$= 2\int_0^1(1-y^2)dy = 2\left[y-\frac{y^3}{3}\right]_0^1 = 2\left(1-\frac{1}{3}\right) = \frac{4}{3}$

(iii) $f(x) = \frac{1}{x^2}\int_4^x(4t^2-2f'(t))dt,$

$\Rightarrow f'(x) = \frac{1}{x^2}\left[4x^2-2f'(x)\right]$

$\Rightarrow f'(4) = \frac{1}{16}[64-2f'(4)]$

$\Rightarrow f'(4)\left(1+\frac{1}{8}\right) = 4 \qquad \Rightarrow f'(4) = \frac{32}{9}$

(iv) $\int_0^{\pi}(|\sin 4x|+|\cos 4x|)dx = 2\int_0^{\pi/2}(|\sin 4x|+|\cos 4x|)dx$

$= 4\int_0^{\pi/4}(|\sin 4x|+|\cos 4x|)dx$

$= 8\int_0^{\pi/8}(\sin 4x+\cos 4x)dx = 8\left[\frac{-\cos 4x}{4}+\frac{\sin 4x}{4}\right]_0^{\pi/8}$

$= 2[-(0-1)+(1-0)] = 4$

3. **(i) → (c); (ii) → (a, b); (iii) → (a, c); (iv) → (d)**

(i) $F(x) = \int_a^x f(x)dx$

$$\Rightarrow \quad F'(x) = f(x) = \begin{cases} \cos\frac{\pi}{2}x \; ; \; 0 \le x < 1 \\ \sin \pi x \; ; \; x \ge 1 \end{cases}$$

$\Rightarrow \quad F'(2) = f(2) = \sin 2\pi = 0,$

$\Rightarrow \quad F'\left(\frac{3}{2}\right) = f\left(\frac{3}{2}\right) = \sin\frac{3\pi}{2} = -1$ and

F′(7.2) = sin (7.2π) ≠ 3

(ii) $f(x) = F'(x) = \begin{cases} \sqrt{3-x} \; ; \; 0 \le x \le 2 \\ (5x-9)^{1/3} \; ; x > 2 \end{cases}$

$\Rightarrow \quad F'(2) = \sqrt{3-2} = 1,$

$F'(7.2) = (36-9)^{1/3} = 3,$

$F'\left(\frac{3}{2}\right) = \sqrt{\frac{3}{2}} \ne 0, -1$

(iii) $F'(x) = f(x) = \begin{cases} x^4 \; ; \; 0 \le x \le 1 \\ \cos 2\pi x \; ; x > 1 \end{cases}$

∴ F′(2) = cos 4π = 1,

F′(3/2) = cos 3π = –1

F′(7.2) = cos (14.4π) ≠ 3

(iv) $F'(x) = f(x) = \begin{cases} \sin\frac{3\pi}{2}x; \; 0 \le x < 1 \\ -\sqrt{3-2x}; \; 1 < x \le \frac{3}{2} \end{cases}$

⇒ F′(2) = not defined and F′(7.2) = not defined as is defined only for $x \in [0, 3/2]$ and $F'\left(\frac{3}{2}\right) = -\sqrt{3-2\left(\frac{3}{2}\right)} = 0$

4. (i) → (b); (ii) → (c); (iii) → (d); (iv) → (a)

(i) $\lim_{x\to 0}\frac{1}{x}\left(\int_y^a e^{\sin^3 t}dt - \int_{x+y}^a e^{\sin^3 t}.dt\right)$

By L.H. Rule $= \lim_{x\to 0}\frac{0 - \left[0 - e^{\sin^3(x+y)}\right]}{1}$

$= \lim_{x\to 0}\left[e^{\sin^3(x+y)}\right] = e^{\sin^3 y}$

(ii) $\lim_{x\to\infty}\frac{\left(\int_0^{x+y} e^t dt\right)^2}{\left(\int_0^{x+y} e^{2t^2} dt\right)}$

By L.H. Rule $\lim_{x\to\infty}\frac{\left(2\int_0^{x+y} e^{t^2}dt\right).\left(e^{(x+y)^2}\right)}{e^{2(x+y)^2}} = \lim_{x\to\infty}\frac{2\int_0^{x+y} e^{t^2}dt}{\left(e^{(x+y)^2}\right)}$

Again using L.H. Rule, $\lim_{x\to\infty}\frac{2e^{(x+y)^2}}{e^{(x+y)^2}.2(x+y)}$

$= \lim_{x\to\infty}\left[\frac{1}{(x+y)}\right] = 0$

(iii) $\lim_{x\to 0}\frac{\int_0^{x^2}\sin\sqrt{x}\,dx}{x^3}$

By L.H. Rule, $\lim_{x\to 0}\frac{(\sin x)(2x)}{3x^3} = \lim_{x\to 0}\frac{2}{3}\frac{(\sin x)}{x} = \frac{2}{3}$

(iv) $\lim_{x\to 0^+}\frac{\int_0^x \cos t^2 dt}{x}$

By L.H. Rule $= \lim_{x\to 0^+}\left(\frac{\cos x^2}{1}\right) = 1$

∴ **(iv) → (a)**

INTEGER TYPE

1. $\int_0^{\pi/2}\frac{dx}{\left(\sqrt{\cos x}+\sqrt{\sin x}\right)^4} = \int_0^{\pi/2}\frac{dx}{\cos^2 x\left(1+\sqrt{\tan x}\right)^4}$

$= \int_0^{\pi/2}\frac{\sec^2 x\,dx}{\left(1+\sqrt{\tan x}\right)^4}$

Put tan $x = t$ ⇒ sec2x $dx = dt$

$\Rightarrow \quad I = \int_0^\infty \frac{dt}{\left(1+\sqrt{t}\right)^4} = \int_0^\infty \frac{dt}{t^2\left(1+\frac{1}{\sqrt{t}}\right)^4}$

$= \int_0^\infty \frac{dt}{(t)^{3/2}\left(1+\frac{1}{\sqrt{t}}\right)^4.\sqrt{t}}$

Put $\frac{1}{\sqrt{t}} = z$ ⇒ $\frac{-1}{2(t)^{3/2}}dt = dz$

$\Rightarrow \quad \frac{1}{\sqrt{t}(t)^{3/2}}dt = \frac{-2}{\sqrt{t}}dz = -2zdz$

$\therefore \quad I = \int_\infty^0 \frac{-2z\,dz}{(1+z)^4} = \int_0^\infty \frac{2z}{(z+1)^4}dx = 2\int_0^\infty \frac{(z+1-1)}{(z+1)^4}dz$

$= 2\int_0^\infty \frac{1}{(z+1)^3}dz - 2\int_0^\infty \frac{1}{(z+1)^4}dz$

$= 2\left[\frac{(z+1)^{-2}}{-2}\right]_0^\infty - 2\left[\frac{(z+1)^{-3}}{-3}\right]_0^\infty$

$= -\left[\frac{1}{(z+1)^2}\right]_0^\infty + \frac{2}{3}\left[\frac{1}{(z+1)^3}\right]_0^\infty = -[0-1] + \frac{2}{3}[0-1]$

$= 1 - \frac{2}{3} = \frac{1}{3} = \frac{1}{\lambda}$

⇒ λ = 3

2. $I = \int_0^{\pi/4}\frac{\ln(\cot x).(\sin 2x)^{2008}.dx}{\left[(\sin x)^{2009}+(\cos x)^{2009}\right]^2}$

$= \int_0^{\pi/4}\frac{-\ln(\tan x)(2)^{2008}.(\sin x)^{2008}.(\cos x)^{2008}dx}{(\cos x)^{4018}.\left[1+(\tan x)^{2009}\right]^2}$

$= \int_0^{\pi/4}\frac{-(2)^{2008}.\ln(\tan x).(\tan x)^{2008}.\sec^2 x\,dx}{\left[1+(\tan x)^{2009}\right]^2}$

Put $(\tan x)^{2009} = t$; ln (tan x) $= \frac{\ln t}{2009}$

⇒ (2009) $(\tan x)^{2008}$. $\sec^2 x\,dx = dt$

$$\Rightarrow \quad I=\int_0^1 \frac{-(2)^{2008}\cdot\left(\frac{\ln t}{2009}\right)\cdot\frac{dt}{(2009)}}{(1+t)^2}$$

$$\Rightarrow \quad I=\frac{-(2)^{2008}}{(2009)^2}\int_0^1\frac{\ln t}{(1+t)^2}$$

$$=\frac{-(2)^{2008}}{(2009)^2}\left[\left|\frac{-\ln t}{(1+t)}\right|_0^1-\int_0^1\frac{1}{t}\left(\frac{-1}{1+t}\right)dt\right]$$

$$=\frac{-(2)^{2008}}{(2009)^2}\left[+\lim_{t\to0^+}\left(\frac{\ln t}{1+t}\right)+\int_0^1\frac{(1+t)-t}{t(1+t)}dt\right]$$

$$=-\frac{(2)^{2008}}{(2009)^2}\left[\lim_{t\to0^+}\frac{\ln t}{1+t}+\int_0^1\left(\frac{1}{t}-\frac{1}{1+t}\right)dt\right]$$

$$=\frac{-(2)^{2008}}{(2009)^2}\left[\lim_{t\to0^+}\ln t+\left(0-\lim_{t\to0^+}(\ln t)\right)-(\ln 2-\ln 1)\right]$$

$$=\frac{(2)^{2008}.\ln 2}{(2009)^2}=\frac{(\lambda)^u\ln\lambda}{v^2}$$

$\Rightarrow$ λ = 2, u = 2008, v = 2009

$\Rightarrow$ (λ + u + v) = 4019

3. $I=\int_{-1}^1 x^2 d(\ln x)$

Put ln x = t $\qquad \Rightarrow \quad x = e^t$

$$\Rightarrow \quad I=\int_{-1}^1\left(e^{2t}\right)dt=\left[\frac{e^{2t}}{2}\right]_{-1}^1=\frac{1}{2}\left(e^2-e^{-2}\right)=\frac{e^4-1}{2e^2}=\frac{e^k-1}{2e^l}$$

$\Rightarrow$ k = 4, l = 2 $\qquad \Rightarrow$ (k + l) = 6

4. $\lim_{n\to\infty}\frac{(m+1)}{(n)^{m+1}}\left(1^m+2^m+3^m+....+n^m\right);m>-1$

$$=\lim_{n\to\infty}\frac{(m+1)}{n}\left(\left(\frac{1}{n}\right)^m+\left(\frac{2}{n}\right)^m+....+\left(\frac{n}{n}\right)^m\right)$$

$$=\lim_{n\to\infty}\frac{(m+1)}{n}\sum_{r=1}^n\left(\frac{r}{n}\right)^m=\lim_{n\to\infty}(m+1).\sum_{r=1}^n\frac{1}{n}\left(\frac{r}{n}\right)^m$$

$$=(m+1).\int_0^1(x)^m\,dx=\left[(x)^{m+1}\right]_0^1=1$$

5. $\lim_{n\to\infty}\sum_{r=1}^n\frac{12}{\sqrt{n^2+3rn}}=\lim_{n\to\infty}\sum_{r=1}^n\frac{12}{n\sqrt{1+3\left(\frac{r}{n}\right)}}=\int_0^1\frac{12}{\sqrt{1+3x}}dx$

$$=\left[\frac{12(1+3x)^{1/2}}{3\left(\frac{1}{2}\right)}\right]_0^1=24\left[\frac{(2-1)}{3}\right]=8$$

6. $\lim_{n\to\infty}\left[C_0^2+C_1^2+C_2^2+....+C_n^2\right]^{1/n}=\lim_{n\to\infty}\left[{}^{2n}C_n\right]^{1/n}$

$$=\lim_{n\to\infty}\left[\frac{(2n)!}{n!.\,n!}\right]^{1/n}$$

$$=\lim_{n\to\infty}\left[\frac{1.2.3....n.(n+1)(n+2)....(2n)}{n!.\,n!}\right]^{1/n}$$

$$=\lim_{n\to\infty}\left[\frac{(n+1)(n+2)(n+3)....(n+n)}{1\,.\,2\,.\,3\,.\,4\,.......\,n}\right]^{1/n}$$

$$=\lim_{n\to\infty}\left[\left(\frac{n}{1}+1\right)\left(\frac{n}{2}+1\right)\left(\frac{n}{3}+1\right)....\left(\frac{n}{n}+1\right)\right]^{1/n}=\text{L (say)}$$

$$=\lim_{n\to\infty}\left[\prod_{r=1}^n\left(1+\frac{n}{r}\right)\right]^{1/n}$$

$$\Rightarrow \quad \ln L=\lim_{n\to\infty}\frac{1}{n}\sum_{r=1}^n\ln\left(1+\frac{n}{r}\right)=\int_0^1\ln\left(1+\frac{1}{x}\right)dx$$

$$=\left|x\ln\left(1+\frac{1}{x}\right)\right|_0^1-\int_0^1\left(\frac{x}{x+1}\right)\times\left(0-\frac{1}{x^2}\right)x$$

$$=\left|x\ln(x+1)-x\ln x\right|_0^1+\int_0^1\frac{1}{x+1}dx$$

$$=(\ln 2)-\left(0-\lim_{x\to0}\frac{\ln x}{\frac{1}{x}}\right)+\left[\ln(x+1)\right]_0^1$$

$$=\ln 2+\lim_{x\to0}\left(\frac{1}{x}\left(-\frac{x^2}{1}\right)\right)+\ln 2=2\ln 2=\ln 4$$

$\therefore \quad$ ln L = ln 4 $\qquad \Rightarrow$ L = 4

7. For x > 0, $f(x)=\int_0^x\frac{1}{1+t^2}dt+\int_0^{1/x}\frac{1}{1+t^2}dt$

$f(2)=\int_0^2\frac{1}{1+t^2}dt+\int_0^{1/2}\frac{1}{1+t^2}dt$ and

$$f\left(\frac{1}{2}\right)=\int_0^{1/2}\frac{1}{1+t^2}dt+\int_0^2\frac{1}{1+t^2}dt$$

$$\Rightarrow \quad f\left(\frac{1}{2}\right)=f(2)$$

Thus, $f(2)+f\left(\frac{1}{2}\right)=2f(2)=2(4)=8$

8. $\int_{-2}^2\left(x^3f(x)+xf''(x)+2\right)dx$

$$=\int_{-2}^2x^3.f(x)dx+\int_{-2}^2\left(xf''(x)+2\right)dx$$

$$=0+\int_{-2}^2\left(xf''(x)+2\right)dx$$

[$\because$ $x^3f(x)$ = odd function)

$$=\left[\left|xf'(x)\right|_{-2}^2-\int_{-2}^2 1.f'(x)dx\right]+4\int_0^2 1.dx$$

$$=\left[2f'(2)+2f'(-2)\right]-\int_{-2}^2f'(x)dx+4(2-0)$$

$\because$ $f(x)$ is even
$\Rightarrow f(-x)=f(x)$
$\Rightarrow -f'(-x)=f'(x)$
$\Rightarrow f'(x)$ = odd function

$$=2f'(2)-2f'(2)-0+8=8$$

9. $f(x)=4x^3-x^2-2x+1$;

$$g(x)=\begin{cases}\min\{f(t):0\le t\le x\};0\le x\le 1\\3-x;\ 1<x\le 2\end{cases}$$

$f'(x)=12x^2-2x-2=2(6x^2-x-1)=2[6x^2-3x+2x-1]$
$=2(3x+1)(2x-1)$

$\Rightarrow\ f'(x) > 0$ for $x < -\frac{1}{3}$ and $x > \frac{1}{2}$; whereas $f'(x) < 0$ for $x \in \left(-\frac{1}{3}, \frac{1}{2}\right)$

$\Rightarrow\ f'(x) \uparrow$ on $\left(-\infty, -\frac{1}{3}\right), \downarrow$ on $\left(-\frac{1}{3}, \frac{1}{2}\right)$ and again $\uparrow$ on $\left(\frac{1}{2}, \infty\right)$

$\therefore\ g\left(\frac{1}{4}\right) = \min\left\{f(t); 0 \le t \le \frac{1}{4}\right\}$

$= f\left(\frac{1}{4}\right) = 4\left(\frac{1}{4^3}\right) - \left(\frac{1}{4^2}\right) - \frac{2}{4} + 1 = \frac{1}{16} - \frac{1}{16} - \frac{1}{2} + 1 = \frac{1}{2}$

$g\left(\frac{3}{4}\right) = \min\left\{f(t): 0 \le t \le \frac{3}{4}\right\}$

$= f\left(\frac{1}{2}\right) = 4\left(\frac{1}{8}\right) - \left(\frac{1}{4}\right) - \frac{2}{2} + 1 = \frac{1}{2} - \frac{1}{4} = \frac{1}{4};$

$g\left(\frac{5}{4}\right) = 3 - \frac{5}{4} = \frac{7}{4}$

$\therefore\ g\left(\frac{1}{4}\right) + g\left(\frac{3}{4}\right) + g\left(\frac{5}{4}\right) + \frac{1}{2} = \frac{1}{2} + \frac{1}{4} + \frac{7}{4} + \frac{1}{2} = 3$

$\Rightarrow\ \int_0^2 \left\{g\left(\frac{1}{4}\right) + g\left(\frac{3}{4}\right) + g\left(\frac{5}{4}\right) + \frac{1}{2}\right\} dx$

$= \int_0^2 3dx = 3(2-0) = 6$

10. $\frac{d}{dx}\int_{\cos x}^{\sin x} \frac{dt}{1-t^2} = 2\sqrt{2}\ ; x \in [0, \pi]$

$\Rightarrow\ \left(\frac{1}{1-\sin^2 x}\right)(\cos x) - \left(\frac{1}{1-\cos^2 x}\right)(-\sin x) = 2\sqrt{2}$

$\Rightarrow$ sec x + cosec x $= 2\sqrt{2}$

$\Rightarrow\ \frac{1}{\cos x} + \frac{1}{\sin x} = 2\sqrt{2}$

$\Rightarrow\ \sin x + \cos x = \sqrt{2}(\sin 2x)$ ...(1)

From (1); $\sin x.\frac{1}{\sqrt{2}} + \cos x.\frac{1}{\sqrt{2}} = \sin 2x$

$\Rightarrow\ \sin\left(x + \frac{\pi}{4}\right) = \sin 2x = x + \frac{\pi}{4} = n\pi + (-1)^n(2x);\ n \in \mathbb{Z}$

$\Rightarrow\ x\left(1 - (-1)^n(2)\right) = n\pi - \frac{\pi}{4}$ ...(2)

For n = 0, x = π/4 ∈ [0, π]
For n = 1, x = π/4
For n = –1, x = –5π/12 ∉ [0, π]
For n = 2, x = –7π/4 ∉ [0, π]
For n = –2, x = 9π/4 ∉ [0, π]
For n = 3, $x = 11\frac{\pi}{12}$ ∈ [0, π]
For n = –3, x = –13π/12 ∉ [0, π]
For n = 4, x = –15π/4,
For n = –4, $x = \frac{17\pi}{4}$

$\therefore$ From $n \le -3$ and $n \ge 4$
No value of x given by equation (2) will lie in [0, π].
Thus, only 2 solutions in [0, π] are possible.

11. Given $f(\pi) = 2$ and $\int_0^\pi [f(x) + f''(x)]\sin x\, dx = 5, f(0) = ?$

$I = \int_0^\pi [f(x) + f''(x)]\sin x\, dx$

$= \int_0^\pi f(x)\sin x\, dx + \int_0^\pi f''(x).\sin x\, dx$

$= \int_0^\pi f(x)\sin x\, dx + |\sin x\, f'(x)|_0^\pi - \int_0^\pi \cos x. f'(x) dx$

$= \int_0^\pi f(x)\sin x\, dx - \left[|\cos x. f(x)|_0^\pi - \int_0^\pi -\sin x\, f(x) dx\right]$

$= -[\cos\pi f(\pi) - (\cos 0) f(0)] = -[2(-1) - 1 f(0)] = 5$ (given)

$\Rightarrow\ 2 + f(0) = 5$

$\Rightarrow\ f(0) = 3$

12. $f'(a) = \sqrt{3}, f'(b) = 1,\ I = \int_b^a \underbrace{f'(x)}_{I}.\underbrace{f''(x)}_{II} dx$

$= |f'(x).f'(x)|_a^b - \int_a^b f''(x).f'(x) dx$

$\Rightarrow\ 2I = [f'(b)]^2 - [f'(a)]^2$

$\Rightarrow\ I = \frac{(1)^2 - (\sqrt{3})^2}{2} = -1$

13. $f(x) + f(y) = f(x+y)$ ...(1)

$\forall x, y \in \mathbb{R}$ and $\int_0^3 f(x) dx = k$ ...(2)

Differentiating (1) partially w.r.t. x, we get

$f'(x) = f'(x+y)\ \forall x, y \in \mathbb{R}$

$\Rightarrow\ f'(x) = \text{constant} = C$ (say)

$\Rightarrow\ f(x) = Cx + D$ ...(3)

From (1), $2f(0) = f(0)$, [Putting $x = y = 0$]

$\Rightarrow\ f(0) = 0$

$\therefore$ From (3), $D = 0$ ...(4)

Also $\int_0^3 f(x) dx = k \Rightarrow \frac{9C}{2} = k$

$\Rightarrow\ C = \frac{2k}{9}$

$\therefore\ f(x) = \frac{2k}{9}x$

Clearly $f(x) =$ odd function

$\therefore\ \int_{-3}^3 f(x) dx = 0$

14. $f(x) = \int_1^x (3y^2 - 12y - 36) dy$

$\Rightarrow\ f'(x) = 3x^2 - 12x - 36 = 3(x^2 - 4x - 12) = 3(x-6)(x+2)$

$\therefore\ f(x) \uparrow$

$\Rightarrow\ f'(x) \ge \ge 0$

$\Rightarrow\ x \in (-\infty, -2] \cup [6, \infty)$

$\Rightarrow\ a = -2, b = 6$

$\Rightarrow\ a + b = 4$

15. $f(x)=\left\{b^2+(a-1)b-\frac{1}{4}\right\}x+\int_0^x\left(\sin^4 x+\cos^4 x\right)dx$

$\Rightarrow\ f'(x)=\left\{b^2+(a-1)b-\frac{1}{4}\right\}+\left(\sin^4 x+\cos^4 x\right)$

$\therefore\ f(x)$ is non-decreasing

$\Rightarrow\ f'(x)\geq 0\ \ \forall x,b\in\mathbb{R}$

$\Rightarrow\ b^2+(a-1)b-\frac{1}{4}+\sin^4 x+\cos^4 x\geq 0\ \forall x,b\in\mathbb{R}$

$\Rightarrow\ b^2+(a-1)b-\frac{1}{4}+1-2\sin^2 x\cos^2 x\geq 0$

$\Rightarrow\ b^2+(a-1)b+\frac{3}{4}-\frac{1}{2}\sin^2 2x\geq 0\ \forall x,b\in\mathbb{R}$

$\Rightarrow\ b^2+(a-1)b+\frac{3}{4}\geq\frac{1}{2}\sin^2 2x\ \forall x,b\in\mathbb{R}$

$\Rightarrow\ b^2+(a-1)b+\frac{3}{4}\geq\frac{1}{2}$

$\Rightarrow\ b^2+(a-1)b+\frac{1}{4}\geq 0$

$\Rightarrow\ 4b^2+4(a-1)b+1\geq 0\ \forall b\in\mathbb{R}$

$\Rightarrow$ Disc. ≤ 0

$\Rightarrow\ [4(a-1)]^2-4(4)(1)\leq 0$

$\Rightarrow\ (a-1)^2-1\leq 0$

$\Rightarrow\ -1\leq(a-1)\leq 1\qquad\Rightarrow\ 0\leq a\leq 2$

$\Rightarrow$ Greatest permissible value of 'a' = 2

16. $\frac{\left(\sqrt{2}+1\right)}{\pi}(198).\int_{\pi/4}^{3\pi/4}\frac{\phi}{1+\sin\phi}d\phi$

Let $\mathrm{I}=\int_{\pi/4}^{3\pi/4}\frac{(\phi)}{1+\sin\phi}d\phi$

$\Rightarrow\ \mathrm{I}=\int_{\pi/4}^{3\pi/4}\frac{(\pi-\phi)\,d\phi}{1+\sin(\pi-\phi)}$

$\Rightarrow\ \mathrm{I}=\pi\int_{\pi/4}^{3\pi/4}\frac{d\phi}{1+\sin\phi}-\mathrm{I}$

$\Rightarrow\ \mathrm{I}=\frac{\pi}{2}\int_{\pi/4}^{3\pi/4}\frac{1}{1+\sin\phi}d\phi=\frac{\pi}{2}\int_{\pi/4}^{3\pi/4}\frac{(1-\sin\phi)}{\cos^2\phi}d\phi$

$=\frac{\pi}{2}\int_{\pi/4}^{3\pi/4}\left(\sec^2\phi-\sec\phi\tan\phi\right)d\phi$

$=\frac{\pi}{2}[\tan\phi-\sec\phi]_{\pi/4}^{3\pi/4}=\frac{\pi}{2}\left[(-1-1)-\left(-\sqrt{2}-\sqrt{2}\right)\right]$

$=\frac{\pi}{2}\left[-2+2\sqrt{2}\right]=\pi\left(\sqrt{2}-1\right)$

$\therefore\ \frac{\left(\sqrt{2}+1\right)}{\pi}(198).\,\mathrm{I}=\frac{\left(\sqrt{2}+1\right)}{\pi}(198).\pi\left(\sqrt{2}-1\right)=198$

17. $\mathrm{I}_1=\int_{\sin^2 t}^{1+\cos^2 t}x f\left(x(2-x)\right)dx;\ \mathrm{I}_2=\int_{\sin^2 t}^{1+\cos^2 t}f\left(x(2-x)\right)dx$

$\mathrm{I}_1=\int_{\sin^2 t}^{1+\cos^2 t}(2-x)f\left((2-x)(x)\right)dx=2\mathrm{I}_2-\mathrm{I}_1$

$\Rightarrow\ I_1=I_2$

$\Rightarrow\ \frac{\mathrm{I}_1}{\mathrm{I}_2}=1$

18. $\lim\limits_{x\to 0}\frac{\int_{-x}^{x}f(t)dt}{\int_0^{2x}f(t+4)dt}$;

By L.H. Rule $=\lim\limits_{x\to 0}\frac{f(x)-f(-x)(-1)}{f(2x+4)(2)}$

$=\lim\limits_{x\to 0}\frac{f(x)+f(-x)}{2f(2x+4)}=\frac{2f(0)}{2f(4)}=\frac{f(0)}{f(4)}=48$

$(\because f(0)=48f(4)$ given$)$

19. $\mathrm{I}=636\int_0^{\pi/4}\left(\sqrt{\sin x}+\sqrt{\cos x}\right)^{-4}dx$

Let $\mathrm{I}_1=\int_0^{\pi/4}\frac{1}{\left(\sqrt{\sin x}+\sqrt{\cos x}\right)^4}dx=\int_0^{\pi/4}\frac{\sec^2 x\,dx}{\left(1+\sqrt{\tan x}\right)^4}$

Put $\sqrt{\tan x}=t\qquad\Rightarrow\ \frac{1}{2\sqrt{\tan x}}\sec^2 x\,dx=dt$

$\Rightarrow\ \sec 2x\,dx=2t\,dt$

$\therefore\ \mathrm{I}_1=\int_0^1\frac{2t\,dt}{(1+t)^4}=2\int_0^1\frac{(t+1-1)}{(t+1)^4}dt$

$=2\int_0^1\left[\frac{1}{(t+1)^3}-\frac{1}{(t+1)^4}\right]dt=2\left[\frac{-1}{2(t+1)^2}-\frac{1}{-3(t+1)^3}\right]_0^1$

$=2\left[-\frac{1}{2}\left(\frac{1}{4}-1\right)+\frac{1}{3}\left(\frac{1}{8}-1\right)\right]$

$=2\left[\left(\frac{-1}{2}\right)\left(\frac{-3}{4}\right)+\frac{1}{3}\left(\frac{-7}{8}\right)\right]=2\left[\frac{3}{8}-\frac{7}{24}\right]=2\left(\frac{9-7}{24}\right)=\frac{1}{6}$

$\therefore\ \mathrm{I}=636\ \mathrm{I}_1=(636)\frac{1}{6}=106$

20. $\mathrm{I}=\int_0^{\pi}\frac{x^2\sin x}{(2x-\pi)\left(1+\cos^2 x\right)}dx\qquad\ldots(1)$

$\Rightarrow\ \mathrm{I}=\int_0^{\pi}\frac{(\pi-x)^2\sin(\pi-x)dx}{\left(2(\pi-x)-\pi\right)\left(1+\cos^2(\pi-x)\right)}$

$\Rightarrow\ \mathrm{I}=\int_0^{\pi}\frac{(\pi-x)^2\sin\ dx}{(\pi-2x)\left(1+\cos^2 x\right)}$

$\Rightarrow\ \mathrm{I}=-\int_0^{\pi}\frac{(\pi-x)^2\sin\ dx}{(2x-\pi)\left(1+\cos^2 x\right)}\qquad\ldots(2)$

Equation (1)+(2) gives, $2\mathrm{I}=\int_0^{\pi}\frac{\left[x^2-(\pi-x)^2\right]\sin x}{(2x-\pi)\left(1+\cos^2 x\right)}dx$

$\Rightarrow\ 2\mathrm{I}=\int_0^{\pi}\frac{\left(-\pi^2+2\pi x\right)\sin x}{(2x-\pi)\left(1+\cos^2 x\right)}dx$

$\Rightarrow\ 2\mathrm{I}=\int_0^{\pi}\frac{\pi(2x-\pi)}{(2x-\pi)}.\frac{\sin x}{\left(1+\cos^2 x\right)}dx$

$\Rightarrow\ \mathrm{I}=\frac{\pi}{2}\int_0^{\pi}\frac{\sin x}{1+\cos^2 x}dx=\frac{\pi}{2}(2)\int_0^{\pi/2}\frac{\sin x}{1+\cos^2}dx$

$=\pi\int_0^{\pi/2}\frac{\sin x}{1+\cos^2 x}dx$

Put $\cos x = t$ $\Rightarrow$ $\sin x\, dx = -\,dt$

$$\Rightarrow \quad I = \pi\int_1^0 \frac{-dt}{1+t^2} = \pi\int_0^1 \frac{dt}{t^2+1} = \pi\left[\tan^{-1} t\right]_0^1 = \frac{\pi^2}{4}$$

$$\therefore \quad \frac{4}{\pi^2} I + 198 = 199$$

21. For $x > 0, f(x) = \int_1^x \frac{\log t}{t+1} dt$ ....(1)

$$f\left(\frac{1}{x}\right) = \int_1^{1/x} \frac{\log t}{t+1} dt \quad ...(2)$$

In (1), putting t by $\frac{1}{z}$, we get $f(x) = \int_1^{1/x} \frac{-\log z}{\frac{1}{z}+1}\left(\frac{-1}{z^2}\right) dz$

$$= \int_1^{1/x} \frac{\log z\, dz}{z+z^2} = \int_1^{1/x} \frac{\log z\, dz}{z(z+1)} = \int_1^{1/x}\left(\frac{z+1-z}{z(z+1)}\right)\log z\, dz$$

$$= \int_1^{1/x} \frac{\log z}{z} dz - \int_1^{1/x} \frac{\log z}{z+1} dz = \int_1^{1/x} \frac{\log z}{z} dz - f\left(\frac{1}{x}\right)$$

$$\Rightarrow \quad f(x) + f\left(\frac{1}{x}\right) = \int_1^{1/x} \frac{\log z}{z} dz = \left[\frac{(\log z)^2}{2}\right]_1^{1/x}$$

$$= \frac{1}{2}\left[\left(\log\frac{1}{x}\right)^2\right] = \frac{1}{2}(\log x)^2$$

$$\Rightarrow \quad f(e) + f\left(\frac{1}{e}\right) = \frac{1}{2} + \frac{1}{2} = 1$$

$$\Rightarrow \quad 98\left(f(e) + f\left(\frac{1}{e}\right)\right) = 98(1) = 98$$

Area Under the Curves

CHAPTER 3

■ INTRODUCTION

Origin of integral calculus is related to the method of exhaustion developed by the mathematician of ancient Greeks to calculate the area of plane figures, surface area and volume of solid bodies, which can also be regarded as early method of integration. It was greatly applied in the works of Eudoxus (440 BC) and Archimedes (300 BC).

A systematic approach for the above purposes called as the theory of integral calculus began in the 17th century AD by Newton, Leibnitz, Euler, Fermat, Cauchy and other prominent mathematicians of that era.

In the previous chapter, we have learnt that the definite integral between two values of independent variable (two ordinate) represents the area bounded by the curve, the axis of the independent variable and the two ordinates.

Further, as we can find the area under one curve and area under another curve and so we can find the area enclosed between the two curves.

Depending upon the nature of the curves, this area can have different shapes, and thus, the tool of definite integral can be employed to find the areas of different shapes. As a matter of fact, you will realize that the standard formulae to find the areas of different shapes can be derived by definite integral by choosing the appropriate area elements for various situations.

This chapter is devoted to find these areas and various types of problems related to it. The application of areas is done in the various fields like health, management, photography, geology etc.

■ AREAS OF CURVES GIVEN BY CARTESIAN EQUATIONS

Let $y = f(x)$ be a finite and continuous function in the interval $[a, b]$ and A denote the variable area $DARP$, bounded by the curve $y = f(x)$, the x-axis, the fixed ordinate DA and the variable ordinate PR. Thus, it is clear that area A is a function of x and has a unique value corresponding to each value of x (see Fig. 3.1).

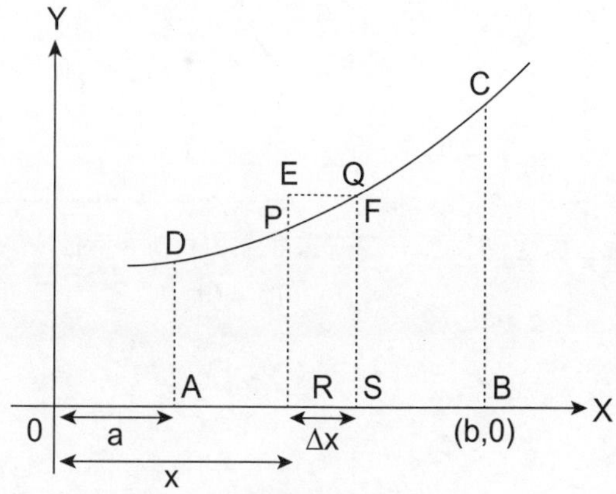

FIGURE 3.1

When x is increased by an amount Δx (= RS), area A assumes an increment ΔA = the trapezoidal area $PQSR$. Clearly this trapezoidal area $PQSR$ lies inbetween the areas of the inscribed and circumscribed rectangles $PFSR$ and $EQSR$ respectively.

Let $OA = a$, $OB = b$ and $OR = x$

Also, we have ar.($PFSR$) < ar. ($PQ\ SR$) < ar. ($EQ\ SR$)

$\Rightarrow f(x).\Delta x < \Delta A < f(x + \Delta x).(\Delta x)$

$$\Rightarrow \quad f(x) < \frac{\Delta A}{\Delta x} < f(x+\Delta x)$$

Taking the limit $\Delta x \to 0$, we have

$$\lim_{\Delta x \to 0} f(x) \le \lim_{\Delta x \to 0} \frac{\Delta A}{\Delta x} \le \lim_{\Delta x \to 0} f(x+\Delta x)$$

i.e., $f(x) \le \lim\limits_{\Delta x \to 0} \dfrac{\Delta A}{\Delta x} \le f(x)$ (because of the continuity of $f(x)$ at x, we have $\lim\limits_{\Delta x \to 0} f(x+\Delta x) = f(x)$)

$\Rightarrow \quad \dfrac{dA}{dx} = f(x)$

$\therefore$ By definition $dA = f(x)\, dx$

i.e., $A = \int f(x)dx = F(x) + C$, where C is an arbitrary constant of integration and $f(x)$ is an indefinite integral of $F(x)$.

Now when $x = OA = a$, PR coincides with DA and the area becomes zero.

Also, when $x = OB = b$, the area becomes the required area A, we get, $0 = F(a) + C$ and $A = F(b) + C$

$\therefore \quad A = F(b) - F(a) = \int_a^b f(x)dx$

AREA BOUNDED BY SINGLE CURVES

The area bounded by single curve with x-axis can be evaluated by first finding the area of vertical curvilinear trapezoid of thickness dx ($\rightarrow 0$) given by $|y|dx$ and summing up all such areas from $x = a$ to $x = b$, i.e., taking the definite integral $\int_a^b |y|\, dx$.

Similarly the area bounded by a single curve with y-axis can be evaluated by first finding the area of horizontal curvilinear trapezoid of thickness dy ($\rightarrow 0$) given by $|x|dy$ and summing up all such areas from $y = c$ to $y = d$ ($c < d$), i.e., taking the definite integral $\int_c^d |x|\, dy$.

(a) Area Enclosed by y = f(x) and x-axis

To calculate the area enclosed by $y = f(x)$ and x-axis between the ordinates $x = a$ and $x = b$ (where $a < b$) is defined by $A = \int_0^A dA = \int_a^b |y|\, dx = \int_a^b |f(x)|\, dx$; where dA is the area element of width dx as shown in Fig. 3.2.

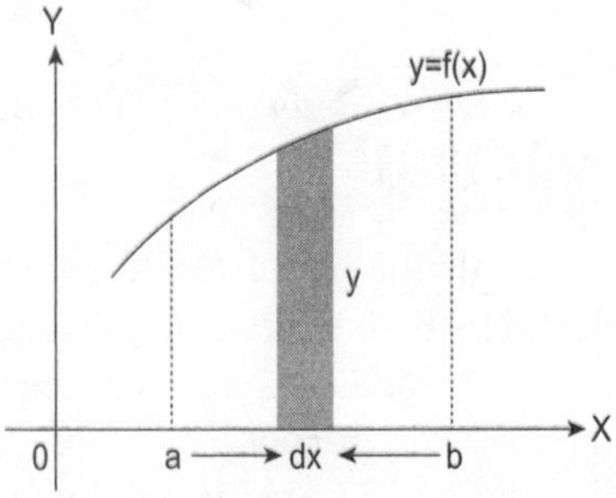

FIGURE 3.2

ILLUSTRATION 1: Find the area bounded by $y = x^3$ and x-axis between ordinates $x = -1$ and $x = 1$.

SOLUTION: $f(x) = x^3$

$$\Rightarrow \quad |f(x)| = |x^3| = \begin{cases} -x^3; & -1 < x \le 0 \\ x^3; & 0 < x < 1 \end{cases}$$

The graph of $y = x^3$ is as shown in Fig. 3.3.

Therefore, required area $= \int_{-1}^{1} |x^3|\, dx$

$$= \int_{-1}^{0} -x^3\, dx + \int_0^1 x^3\, dx = -\left[\frac{x^4}{4}\right]_{-1}^{0} + \left[\frac{x^4}{4}\right]_0^1$$

$$= 0 - \left(\frac{-1}{4}\right) + \frac{1}{4} - 0 = \frac{1}{2}$$

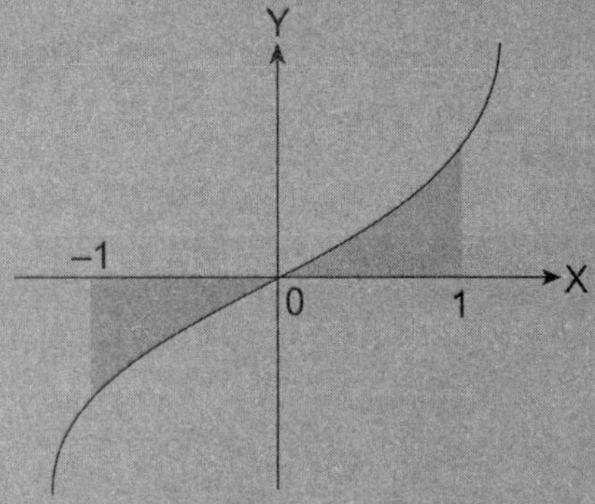

FIGURE 3.3

ILLUSTRATION 2: Calculate the area of the plane figure bounded by the interval $\left[-\frac{5\pi}{6}, \frac{3\pi}{2}\right]$ of the x-axis, the graph of the function $f(x) = \cos x$, and segments of the straight lines $x = -\frac{5\pi}{6}$ and $x = \frac{3\pi}{2}$

SOLUTION: The graph of $f(x) = \cos x$ is shown in Fig. 3.4.

Solving the equation $\cos x = 0$, we find that the graph of the function $y = \cos x$ on the interval $\left[-\frac{5\pi}{6}, \frac{3\pi}{2}\right]$ intersects the x-axis at the points $x_1 = -\frac{\pi}{2}$, $x_2 = \frac{\pi}{2}$, $x_3 = \frac{3\pi}{2}$

Consequently, the require area $= \int_{-5\pi/6}^{3\pi/2} |\cos x|\, dx$

$$= \int_{-5\pi/6}^{-\pi/2} -\cos x\, dx + \int_{-\pi/2}^{\pi/2} \cos x\, dx + \int_{\pi/2}^{3\pi/2} -\cos x\, dx$$

$$= -[\sin x]_{-5\pi/6}^{-\pi/2} + [\sin x]_{-\pi/2}^{\pi/2} - [\sin x]_{\pi/2}^{3\pi/2}$$

$$= -\left[(-1)-\left(-\frac{1}{2}\right)\right] + [1-(-1)] - [-1-1]$$

$$= -\left[\frac{-1}{2}\right] + 2 + 2$$

$$= 4 + \frac{1}{2} = \frac{9}{2} \text{ square units}$$

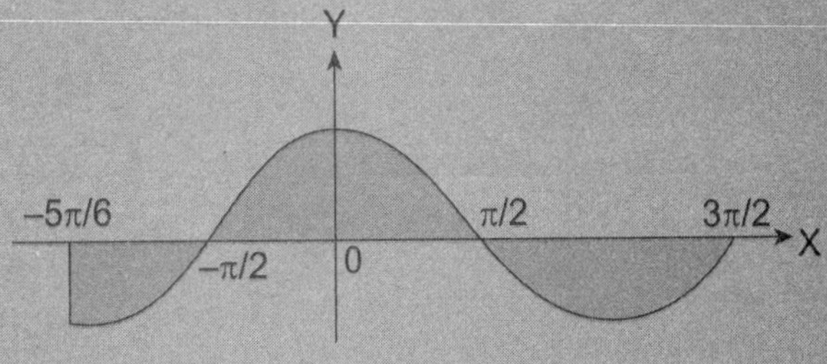

FIGURE 3.4

REMARK

If f(x) ≥ 0 ∀ x ∈ (a, b) and is continuous on (a, b), then the area bounded by function f(x) with x-axis and from the ordinates x = a to x = b is given by $A = \int_a^b y\,dx = \int_a^b f(x)\,dx$, *since |f(x)| = f(x) for x ∈ (a, b), geometrically shown in Fig. 3.5.*

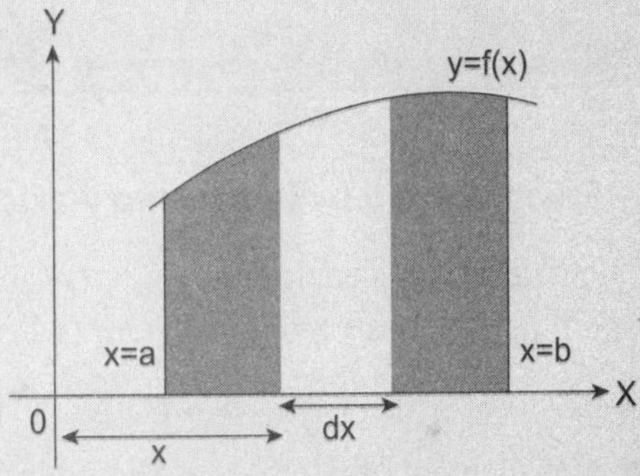

FIGURE 3.5

ILLUSTRATION 3: Find the area enclosed by $y = x{\cdot}e^x$ and x-axis between the ordinates $x = 0$ and $x = 2$.

SOLUTION: Here $f(x) = xe^x > 0$ for $x \in (0, 2)$

$\therefore\ |f(x)| = |xe^x| = xe^x$.

$\therefore$ Required area $= \int_0^2 |f(x)|\,dx = \int_0^2 xe^x\,dx = \left|xe^x\right|_0^2 - \int_0^2 1.e^x\,dx$

$= 2e^2 - (e^2 - 1) = e^2 + 1$

REMARK

If f(x) ≤ 0 ∀ x ∈ (a, b) and is continuous on (a, b), then the area bounded by function f(x) with x-axis and from the ordinates x = a to x = b is given by $A = \int_a^b -y\,dx = -\int_a^b f(x)\,dx$, since |f(x)| = –f(x) *for x ∈ (a, b), geometrically shown in Fig.3.6.*

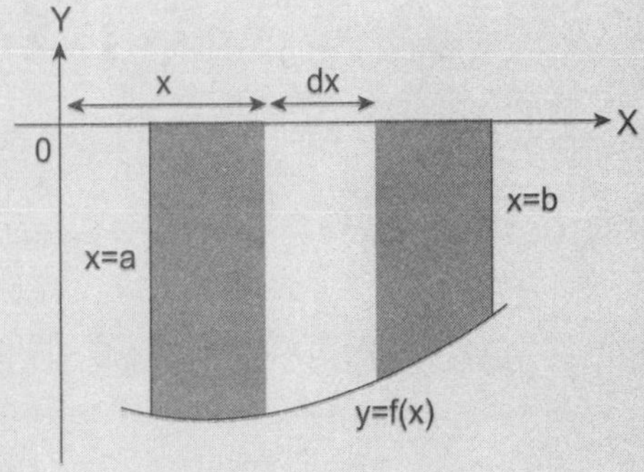

FIGURE 3.6

ILLUSTRATION 4: Find the area bounded by $y = log_{1/2}\, x$ and x-axis between $x = 1$ and $x = 2$.

SOLUTION: We know that $\log_a x < 0$ for $a \in (0, 1)$ and $x > 1$ and $\log_a x > 0$ for $a \in (0, 1)$ and $0 < x < 1$.

$\therefore$ A rough sketch of $y = log_{1/2}\, x$ is as shown in Fig. 3.7.

Now $|f(x)| = \begin{cases} \log_{1/2} x; & 0 < x \le 1 \\ -\log_{1/2} x; & 1 < x < \infty \end{cases}$

$$\therefore \text{ Area } = \int_1^2 |\log_{1/2} x|\, dx$$

$$= -\int_1^2 \log_{1/2} x\, dx = -\int_1^2 \log_e x\, dx . \log_{1/2} e\, dx$$

$$= -\log_{1/2} e \cdot \left[x \log_e x - x\right]_1^2$$

$$= -\log_{1/2} e \cdot (2 \log_e 2 - 2 - 0 + 1)$$

$$= -\log_{1/2} e \cdot (2 \log_e 2 - 1)$$

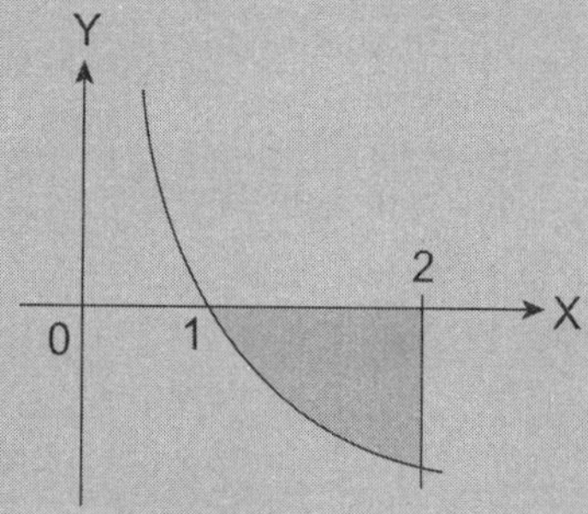

FIGURE 3.7

(b) Area Enclosed by $y = f(x)$ and y-axis

To calculate the area enclosed by $y = f(x)$ and y-axis between the abscissa $y = c$ and $y = d$; (where $c < d$) is defined by $A = \int_0^A dA = \int_c^d |x|\, dy = \int_c^d |f^{-1}(y)|\, dy$; where dA is the area element of width dy as shown in Fig. 3.8.

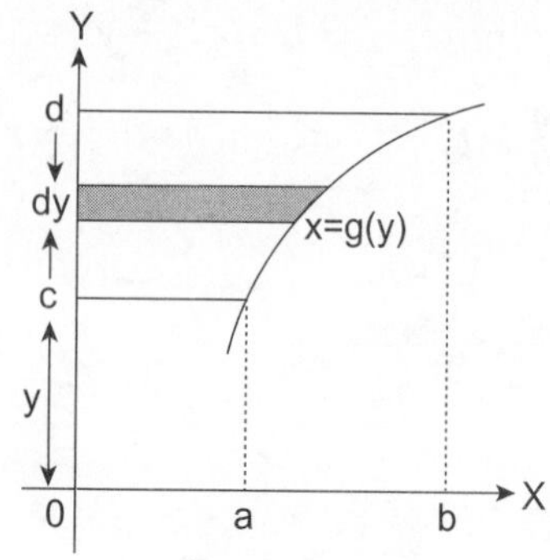

FIGURE 3.8

ILLUSTRATION 5: Find the area bounded between $y = \sin^{-1}x$ and y-axis between $y = 0$ and $y = \dfrac{\pi}{2}$

SOLUTION: $y = \sin^{-1} x$

$\Rightarrow x = \sin y$

The graph of $y = \sin^{-1}x$ is shown in Fig. 3.9 and the shaded region represents the area bounded by function $y = \sin^{-1}x$ and y-axis.

$$\therefore \text{ Required area } = \int_0^{\pi/2} x\, dy = \int_0^{\pi/2} \sin y\, dy$$

$$= \left|-\cos y\right|_0^{\pi/2} = -(0 - 1) = 1$$

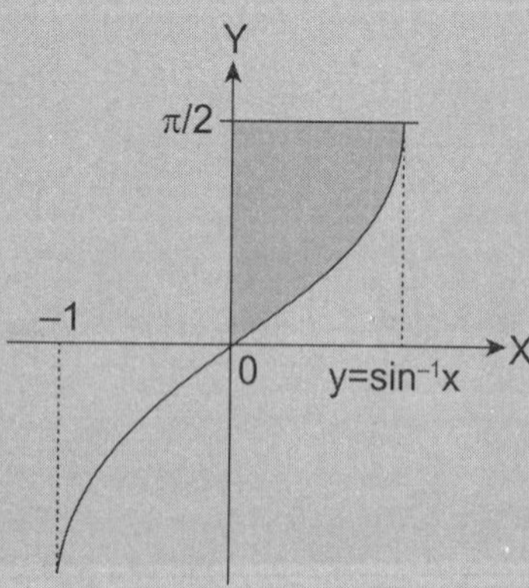

FIGURE 3.9

ILLUSTRATION 6: Find the area bounded by $y = \sin x$ with y-axis for $x \in [-\pi/2, \pi/2]$

SOLUTION: The graph of $y = \sin x$ for $x \in [-\pi/2, \pi/2]$ is as shown in Fig. 3.10.

Now here $|x| = |\sin^{-1} y| = \begin{cases} -\sin^{-1} y; & -1 \le y < 0 \\ \sin^{-1} y; & 0 \le y \le 1 \end{cases}$

Therefore, required area $= \int_{-1}^{1} |x|\, dy = \int_{-1}^{0} -\sin^{-1} y\, dy + \int_{0}^{1} \sin^{-1} y\, dy$

$= -\left| y\sin^{-1} y + \sqrt{1-y^2} \right|_{-1}^{0} + \left| y\sin^{-1} y + \sqrt{1-y^2} \right|_{0}^{1}$

$= -\left[1-(-1)\left(-\frac{\pi}{2}\right)\right] + \left[1\cdot\frac{\pi}{2} - 1\right]$

$= -1 + \frac{\pi}{2} + \frac{\pi}{2} - 1 = (\pi - 2)$ square units.

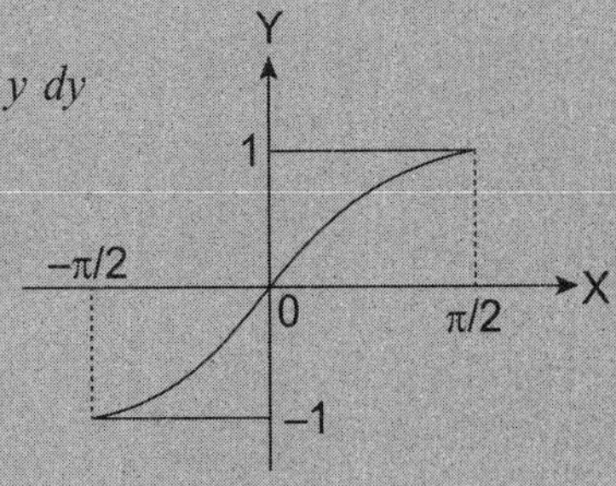

FIGURE 3.10

ILLUSTRATION 7: Find the area bounded by $y = x^2 + 2$ and y-axis from $y = 2$ to $y = 3$ in the first quadrant.

SOLUTION: Given equation is $y = x^2 + 2$

$\Rightarrow \quad x = \pm\sqrt{y-2}$

In the first quadrant x is positive, so take $x = \sqrt{y-2}$

Therefore, the required area $= A = \int_2^3 \sqrt{y-2}\, dy$

let $y - 2 = t$

$\Rightarrow \quad dy = dt$ and when $y = 2$, $t = 0$ and when $y = 3$, $t = 1$

$\therefore \quad A = \int_0^1 \sqrt{t}\, dt = \frac{2}{3} | t^{3/2} |_0^1 = \frac{2}{3} - 0 = \frac{2}{3}$ square units

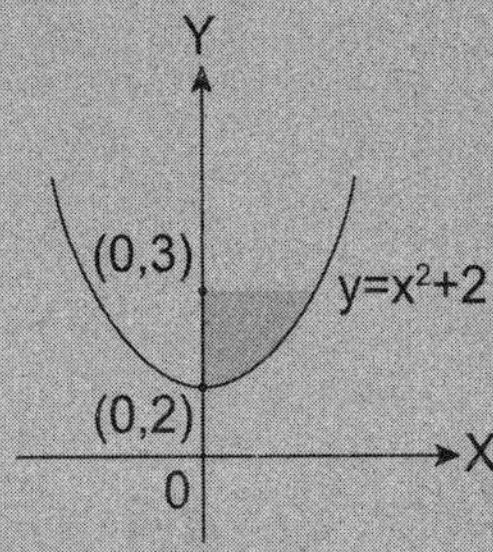

FIGURE 3.11

REMARK

Sometimes calculation of area becomes more convenient by using horizontal strips method as compared to vertical strips method.

ILLUSTRATION 8: Evaluate the area represented by shaded portion as shown in the Fig. 3.12.

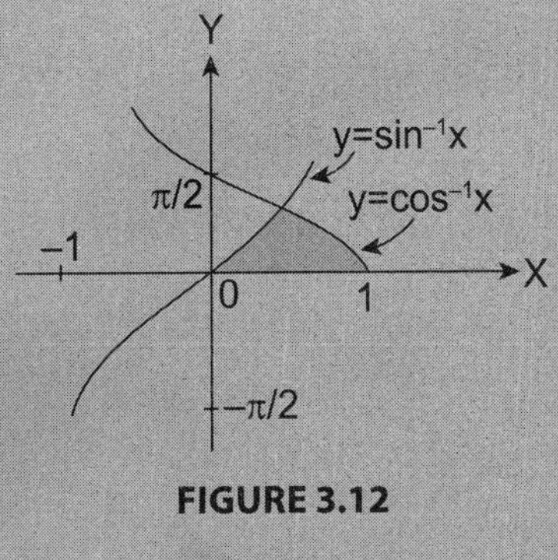

FIGURE 3.12

SOLUTION: Let us evaluate the shaded area by two methods, i.e., considering vertical strips and horizontal strips

Method 1:

Note that P is the point of intersection of $y = \sin^{-1}x$ and $y = \cos^{-1}x$, i.e., $P\left(\frac{1}{\sqrt{2}}, \frac{\pi}{4}\right)$

$\therefore$ To evaluate the required area we are to find area below the curve $\overparen{OP}$ above x-axis from $x = 0$ to $x = 1/\sqrt{2}$ and area below the curve $\overparen{PQ}$ above x-axis from $x = 1/\sqrt{2}$ to $x = 1$ and then add up.

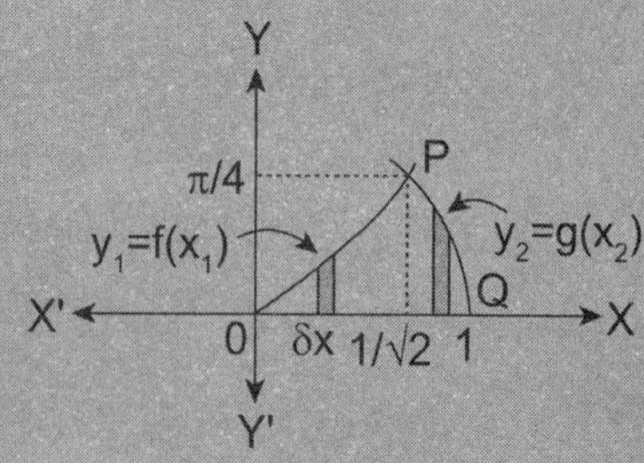

FIGURE 3.13

$$\therefore \text{ Required area} = \int_0^{1/\sqrt{2}} y_1\,dx + \int_{1/\sqrt{2}}^{1} y_2\,dx$$

$$= \int_0^{1/\sqrt{2}} \sin^{-1}x\,dx + \int_{1/\sqrt{2}}^{1} \cos^{-1}x\,dx$$

$$= \left|x\sin^{-1}x\right|_0^{1/\sqrt{2}} - \int_0^{1/\sqrt{2}} \frac{1}{\sqrt{1-x^2}}.x\,dx$$

$$+ \left|x\cos^{-1}x\right|_{1/\sqrt{2}}^{0} - \int_{1/\sqrt{2}}^{1} \frac{-1}{\sqrt{1-x^2}}x\,dx$$

$$= \frac{1}{\sqrt{2}}\left(\frac{\pi}{4}\right) + \frac{1}{2}\int_0^{1/\sqrt{2}} (-2x)(1-x^2)^{-1/2}\,dx + (1)(0) - \frac{1}{\sqrt{2}}\left(\frac{\pi}{4}\right)$$

$$-\frac{1}{2}\int_{1/\sqrt{2}}^{1} -2x(1-x^2)^{-1/2}\,dx = \frac{1}{2}\left|\frac{(1-x^2)^{1/2}}{1/2}\right|_0^{1/\sqrt{2}} - \frac{1}{2}\left|\frac{(1-x^2)^{1/2}}{1/2}\right|_{1/\sqrt{2}}^{1}$$

$$= \left[\frac{1}{\sqrt{2}} - 1\right] - \left[0 - \left(\frac{1}{\sqrt{2}}\right)\right] = \sqrt{2} - 1 \text{ square units.}$$

Method:2 Now let us evaluate the shaded area by considering the horizontal strips of width dy and from limits $y = 0$ to $y = \pi/4$.

The required area can be evaluated by taking the difference of area bounded by curves $y = \sin^{-1}x$ and $y = \cos^{-1}x$ with y-axis from $y = 0$ to $y = \pi/4$.

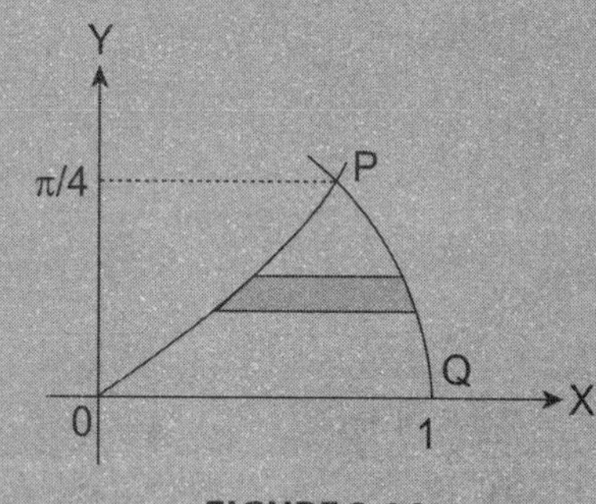

FIGURE 3.14

$$\therefore \text{ required area} = \int_0^{\pi/4} x_2\,dy - \int_0^{\pi/4} x_1\,dy$$

$$= \int_0^{\pi/4} (x_2 - x_1)\,dy = \int_0^{\pi/4} (\cos y - \sin y)\,dy$$

$$= \left|\sin y + \cos y\right|_0^{\pi/4} = \left(\sin\frac{\pi}{4} + \cos\frac{\pi}{4}\right) - (\sin 0 + \cos 0)$$

$$= \left(\frac{1}{\sqrt{2}} + \frac{1}{\sqrt{2}}\right) - 1 = \sqrt{2} - 1 \text{ square units}$$

Thus, we observe that the area of shaded region obtained by two methods is same, whereas method 2 is easier than method 1. Therefore, sometimes using horizontal strips to evaluate area proves to be more convenient than using vertical strips.

ILLUSTRATION 9: Find the area of the region bounded by the parabola $y^2 = 4ax$ and x-axis between the ordinate $x = 0$ and $x = a$.

SOLUTION: Area of shaded region, as shown in the Fig. 3.15 is given by,

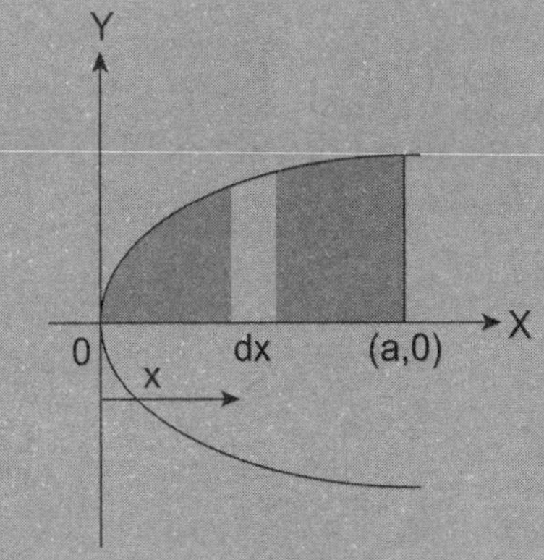

FIGURE 3.15

$$A=\int_0^a y\,dx=\int_0^a 2\sqrt{ax}\,dx = 2\sqrt{a}\left[\frac{x^{3/2}}{3/2}\right]_0^a = 2\sqrt{a}.\frac{2}{3}a^{3/2} = \frac{4}{3}a^2 \text{ square units.}$$

REMARK:

In some problems we are to find area enclosed by a function from ordinate x = a to x = b and the function is symmetric about x-axis. In such cases we evaluate the area under the given function above x-axis from ordinate x = a to x = b and double it.

ILLUSTRATION 10: Find the area bounded by ellipse $\frac{x^2}{a^2}+\frac{y^2}{b^2}=1$ and the ordinate $x = ae$ and $x = 0$, where $b^2 = a^2(1 - e^2)$ and $e < 1$.

SOLUTION: Clearly the given function is symmetric about x-axis.

Thus, the required area $= 2\int_0^{ae} y\,dx$

$$=\frac{2b}{a}\int_0^{ae}\sqrt{a^2-x^2}\,dx = \frac{2b}{a}\left[\frac{x}{2}\sqrt{a^2-x^2}+\frac{a^2}{2}\sin^{-1}\frac{x}{a}\right]_0^{ae}$$

$$=\frac{2b}{2a}\left[ae\sqrt{a^2-a^2e^2}+a^2\sin^{-1}e\right] = ab\left[e\sqrt{1-e^2}+\sin^{-1}e\right]$$

THE SIGN CONVENTION FOR FINDING THE AREAS USING INTEGRATION

Case I: In the expansion $\int_a^b f(x)\,dx$ if $b > a$ and $f(x) > 0$ for all $a \le x \le b$, then this integration will give the area enclosed between the curve $f(x)$, x-axis and the line $x = a$ and $x = b$ which is positive. No need of any modification.

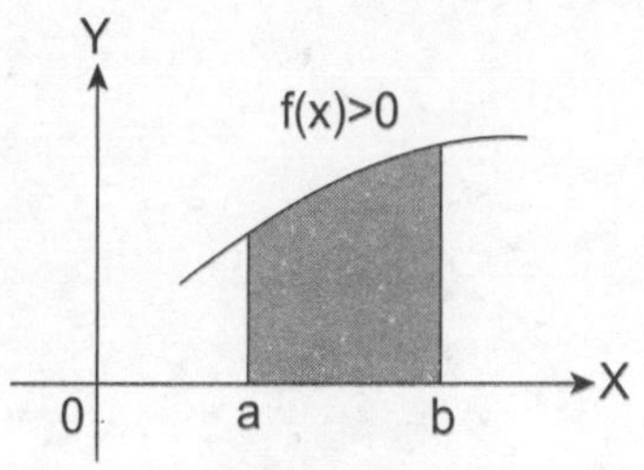

FIGURE 3.16

Case II: In the expansion $\int_a^b f(x)\,dx$ if $b > a$ and $f(x) < 0$ for all $a \le x \le b$, this integration will give negative value. But the numerical or the absolute value is to be taken to mean the area enclosed between the curve $y = f(x)$, x-axis and the lines $x = a$ and $x = b$

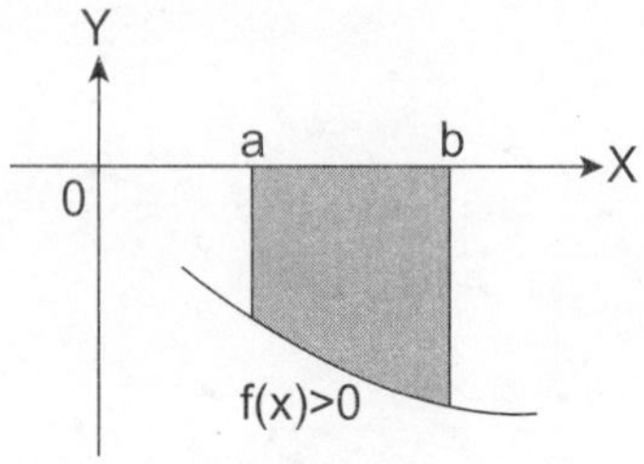

FIGURE 3.17

Case III: If $f(x) > 0$ but $a > b$, then $\int_a^b f(x)\,dx$ represents negative of area.

Case IV: If in the integral $\int_a^b f(x)\,dx$; where $b > a$ but $f(x)$ changes its sign a number of times in the interval $[a, b]$, then we must divide the region $[a, b]$ in such a way that we clearly get the points lying between $[a, b]$; where $f(x)$ changes its sign. For the region where $f(x) > 0$ we just integrate to get the area in that region. Then add the absolute value of the integration calculated in the region where $f(x) < 0$ to get the desired area between the curve $y = f(x)$, x-axis and the line $x = a$ and $x = b$.

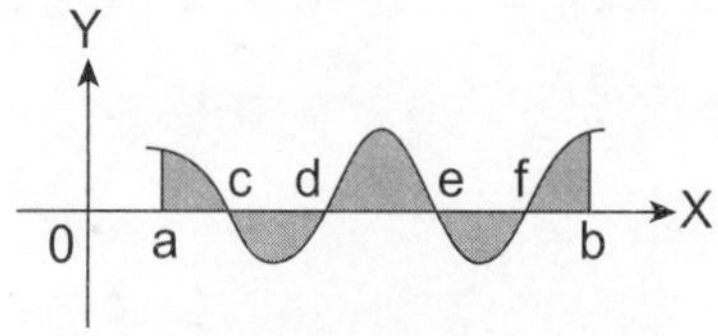

FIGURE 3.18

Hence if $f(x)$ is as shown in the Fig. 3.18, then the area enclosed by $y = f(x)$, x-axis and the lines $x = a$ and $x = b$ is given by, $A = \int_a^c f(x)\,dx + \left|\int_c^d f(x)\,dx\right| + \int_d^e f(x)\,dx$ + $\left|\int_e^f f(x)\,dx\right| + \int_f^b f(x)\,dx$

Conclusion:

Area (A) enclosed by function $y = f(x)$ and x-axis between the ordinate $x = a$ and $x = b$ $(a < b)$ is $A = \int_a^b |f(x)|\,dx$

ILLUSTRATION 11: Find the positive values of the parameter 'a' for which the area of the figure bounded by the curve $y = \cos ax$, $y = 0$, $x = \dfrac{\pi}{6a}$, $x = \dfrac{5\pi}{6a}$ is greater than 3, $(a > 0)$.

SOLUTION: When $x = \pi/6a$, $ax = \pi/6$ and when $x = 5\pi/6a$, $ax = 5\pi/6$. Thus, we are to work for $ax \in [\pi/6, 5\pi/6]$

Now $\cos ax = 0$ in above interval for $ax = \dfrac{\pi}{2}$ is shown in the Fig. 3.19.

Let A_1 and A_2 be the areas bounded by function above and below x-axis, respectively

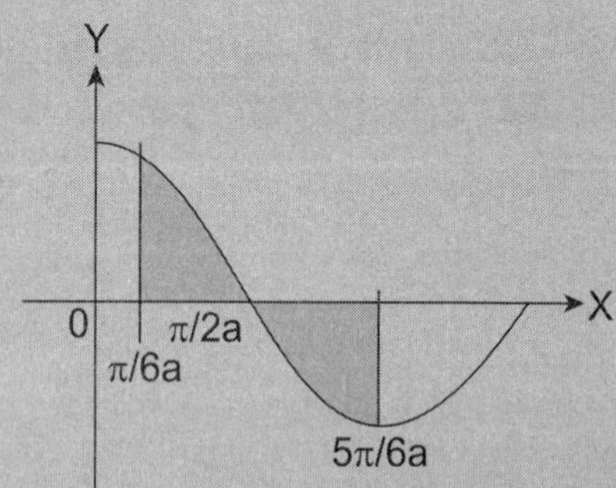

FIGURE 3.19

$$\therefore \quad A_1 = \int_{\frac{\pi}{6a}}^{\frac{\pi}{2a}} \cos ax\,dx = \frac{1}{a}\int_{\pi/6}^{\pi/2} \cos t\,dt = \frac{1}{a}[\sin t]_{\pi/6}^{\pi/2} = \frac{1}{2a}$$

Similarly

$$A_2 = \int_{\frac{\pi}{2a}}^{\frac{5\pi}{6a}} |\cos ax|\,dx = \int_{\frac{\pi}{2a}}^{\frac{5\pi}{6a}} -\cos ax\,dx = \frac{1}{a}\int_{\frac{\pi}{2}}^{\frac{5\pi}{6}} -\cos t\,dt = -\frac{1}{a}(\sin t)_{\pi/2}^{5\pi/6} = \frac{1}{2a}$$

$$\therefore \quad \text{Total area} = \frac{1}{a} > 3;$$

$$\therefore \quad 0 < a < \frac{1}{3}.$$

ILLUSTRATION 12: Find the area bounded by the curves $y = x\,(1 - \ln x)$; $x = e^{-1}$ and positive x-axis between $x = e^{-1}$ and $x = e$.

SOLUTION: Given function is $y = x\,(1 - \ln x)$

Therefore, $y = 0$

$\Rightarrow\ x = e$ (as $x > 0$)

Now $\dfrac{dy}{dx} = -\ln x > 0$ for $x \in (0, 1)$ and < 0 for $x \in (1, \infty)$

$\Rightarrow\ f(x)$ is increasing (↑) in (0, 1) and decreasing (↓) in $(1, \infty)$

Since $f(x)$ is not defined at $x = 0$, we shall take limiting value of function at $x = 0$

i.e., $\lim\limits_{x\to 0} x(1-\ln x) = \lim\limits_{x\to 0}\dfrac{(1-\ln x)}{1/x}\ \left(\dfrac{\infty}{\infty}\text{ form}\right)$

$= \lim\limits_{x\to 0}\dfrac{(-1/x)}{-1/x^2} = \lim\limits_{x\to 0}(x) = 0$ (by L.H. rule)

$\therefore$ The graph of function will be as shown in the Fig. 3.20.

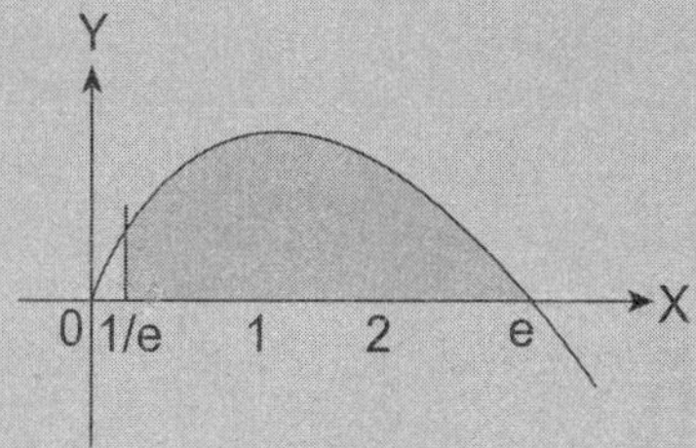

FIGURE 3.20

Therefore, the required area $= A = \displaystyle\int_{1/e}^{e} x(1-\ln x)\,dx$

$$= \left[\frac{x^2}{2}\right]_{1/e}^{e} - \int_{1/e}^{e}(x\ln x)\,dx$$

$$= \frac{1}{2}\left[e^2 - \frac{1}{e^2}\right] - \left[\left|\frac{x^2}{2}\ln x\right|_{1/e}^{e} - \int_{1/e}^{e}\frac{1}{x}\cdot\frac{x^2}{2}dx\right] = \frac{1}{2}\left(e^2 - \frac{1}{e^2}\right) - \left[\frac{e^2}{2} + \frac{1}{2e^2} - \frac{1}{2}\left|\frac{x^2}{2}\right|_{1/e}^{e}\right]$$

$$= \frac{1}{2}\left(e^2 - \frac{1}{e^2}\right) - \left[\frac{e^2}{2} + \frac{1}{2e^2} - \frac{e^2}{4} + \frac{1}{4e^2}\right] = \frac{e^2}{4} - \frac{5}{4e^2} = \left(\frac{e^2 - 5e^{-2}}{4}\right)$$

ILLUSTRATION 13: Find the area bounded by the curve $y = x^2 + 4x + 5$, the axes of co-ordinates and the minimum ordinate.

SOLUTION: Given function is $y = x^2 + 4x + 5 = (x + 2)^2 + 1$

Clearly the vertex of above curve is $(-2, 1)$, therefore, the minimum ordinate is at $x = -2$.

Thus, we are to find the area bounded by $x = -2$, $x = 0$, $y = 0$ and the curve $y = x^2 + 4x + 5$

i.e., $A = \displaystyle\int_{-2}^{0}\left(x^2 + 4x + 5\right)dx = \left[\frac{x^3}{3} + 2x^2 + 5x\right]_{-2}^{0}$

$$= -\left[-\frac{8}{3} + 8 - 10\right] = 2 + \frac{8}{3} = \frac{14}{3} = 4\frac{2}{3}\ \text{square units.}$$

ILLUSTRATION 14: If $y = 2\sin x + \sin 2x$ for $0 \le x \le 2\pi$, then find the area enclosed by the curve and the x-axis.

SOLUTION: Given function is $y = 2\sin x + \sin 2x = 2\sin x\,(1 + \cos x) = 0$

$\Rightarrow\ \sin x = 0$ or $\cos x = -1$, $x \in [0, 2\pi]$

$\Rightarrow\ x = 0, \pi$ or 2π

Also $f'(x) = 2\cos x + 2\cos 2x = 2\cos x + 4\cos^2 x - 2$.

Therefore, $f'(x) > 0$

$\Rightarrow\ 2(2\cos x - 1)(\cos x + 1) > 0\ \Rightarrow \cos x \dfrac{1}{2}$

$\Rightarrow x \in [0, \pi/3)$ and $(5\pi/3, 2\pi]$

Similarly $f'(x) < 0$

$\Rightarrow x \in (\pi/3, 5\pi/3)$

Thus, graph of given function would be as shown in the Fig. 3.21.

Also the function $|f(x)|$ is periodic with period 2π

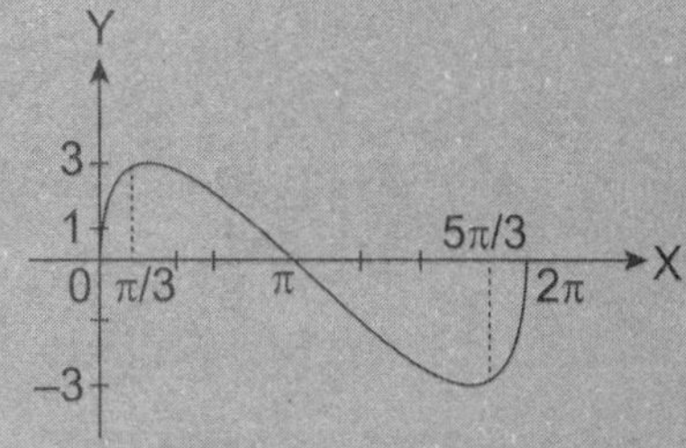

FIGURE 3.21

Therefore, $A = \int_0^{2\pi} |2\sin x + \sin 2x|\, dx$

$= \int_0^{\pi} |2\sin x + \sin 2x|\, dx + \int_{\pi}^{2\pi} |2\sin x + \sin 2x|\, dx$

$= \int_0^{\pi} (2\sin x + \sin 2x)\, dx - \int_{\pi}^{2\pi} (2\sin x + \sin 2x)\, dx$

$= -2|\cos x|_0^{\pi} - \left|\frac{\cos 2x}{2}\right|_0^{\pi} + 2|\cos x|_{\pi}^{2\pi} + \frac{1}{2}|\cos 2x|_{\pi}^{2\pi}$

$= -2(-2) - \frac{1}{2}(0) + 2(2) + \frac{1}{2}(0) = 8$ square units.

ILLUSTRATION 15: Find the area bounded by the curve given by $x = 2y - y^2$ and the y-axis

SOLUTION: Given curve is $x = 2y - y^2$, which represents a left handed parabola as shown in Fig. 3.22. Clearly the curve cuts y-axis at $y = 0$ and $y = 2$

Now $\frac{dx}{dy} = 2 - 2y = 0$

$\Rightarrow y = 1$;

Thus, the required area is the region bounded by y-axis, and the curve having its vertex at $x = 1$

given by, $A = \int_0^2 |x|\, dy = \int_0^2 (2y - y^2)\, dy = \left[y^2 - \frac{y^3}{3}\right]_0^2 = 4 - \frac{8}{3} = \frac{4}{3}$ square units

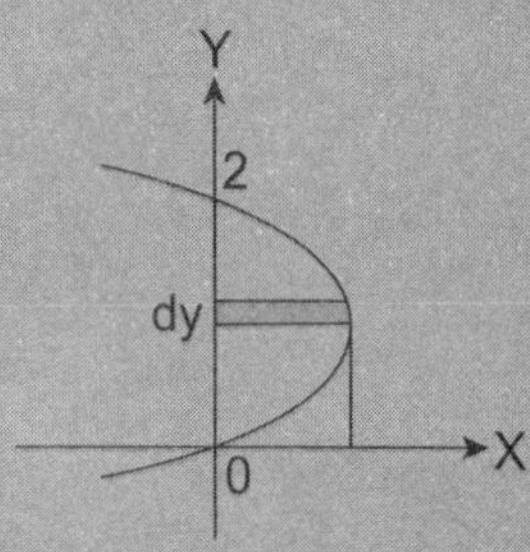

FIGURE 3.22

Aliter: The above area can also be calculated by taking vertical strips (shown in Fig. 3.23) as follows.

Here $y^2 - 2y + x = 0$

$\Rightarrow y = \frac{2 \pm \sqrt{4 - 4x}}{2}$

$\Rightarrow y = 1 + \sqrt{1 - x}\,;\ (y_2)$

(portion of parabola above the line $y = 1$)

and $y = 1 - \sqrt{1 - x}\,;\ (y_1)$

(Portion of parabola below the line $y = 1$)

$\therefore \quad A = \int_0^1 (y_2 - y_1)\, dx \ = \ 2\left[\frac{(1-x)^{3/2}}{-3/2}\right]_0^1 = -\frac{4}{3}(-1)$

$(-1) = \frac{4}{3}$ square units.

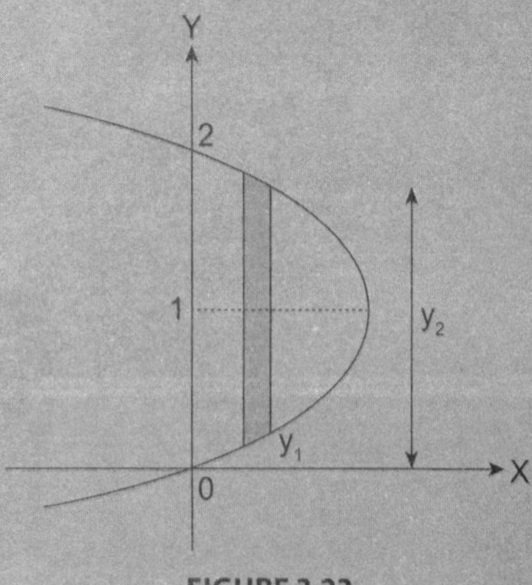

FIGURE 3.23

ILLUSTRATION 16: Find the area bounded by $y^2 = -4x$, and its latus-rectum.

SOLUTION: The given curve is a left handed parabola with its vertex at origin and latus – rectum $x = -1$. Thus, the required area is the region bounded by the straight line $x = -1$ and curve $y^2 = -4x$

Therefore, $A = 2\int_{-1}^{0}\sqrt{-4x}\,dx = \left|2\times\frac{2}{3}\frac{(-4x)^{3/2}}{-4}\right|_{-1}^{0} = -\frac{1}{3}[0-(4)^{3/2}] = \frac{8}{3}$ square units

Aliter: The above area can be calculated by taking horizontal strips.

Here $x = -y^2/4$. Now w.r.t. y, the area enclosed can be calculated as $A = \int_{-2}^{2}|g_2(y) - g_1(y)|\,dy$

$\Rightarrow\ A = \left|\int_{-2}^{2}\left(-\frac{y^2}{4}+1\right)dy\right|$ which is an even function in y

$\therefore\ A = \left|2\int_{0}^{2}\left(-\frac{y^2}{4}+1\right)dy\right|$

$= \left|2\left(-\frac{y^3}{12}+y\right)\right|_0^2 = \left|2\left(-\frac{8}{12}+2\right)\right| = \frac{8}{3}$ square units.

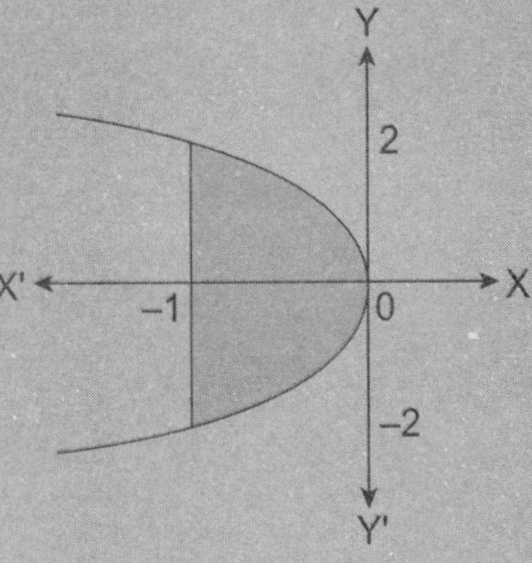

FIGURE 3.24

ILLUSTRATION 17: Find the area of the region bounded by the curve $y = \frac{1}{1+(\tan x)^{1/2}}$ and the x-axis between the ordinates $x = \pi/6$ and $x = \pi/3$.

SOLUTION: The given curve is $y = \frac{1}{1+(\tan x)^{1/2}}$, $x \in \left[\frac{\pi}{6}, \frac{\pi}{3}\right]$

Clearly $f(x) > 0$ in the given interval.

Therefore, required area $A = \int_{\pi/6}^{\pi/3}\frac{1}{1+(\tan x)^{1/2}}dx = \int_{\pi/6}^{\pi/3}\frac{(\cos x)^{1/2}}{(\sin x)^{1/2}+(\cos x)^{1/2}}dx$

Also $A = \int_{\pi/6}^{\pi/3}\frac{(\sin x)^{1/2}}{(\sin x)^{1/2}+(\cos x)^{1/2}}$

Adding $2A = \int_{\pi/6}^{\pi/3} dx$

$\Rightarrow\ A = \frac{1}{2}\left[\frac{\pi}{3}-\frac{\pi}{6}\right] = \frac{\pi}{12}$ square units

ILLUSTRATION 18: Let $f(x)$ = minimum ($\tan x$, $\cot x$, $1/\sqrt{3}$) $\forall\ x \in (0, \pi/2)$, then find area bounded by $y = f(x)$ and the x-axis.

SOLUTION: We have $f(x) = \min(\tan x, \cot x, 1/\sqrt{3})$, $\forall\ x \in \left(0, \frac{\pi}{2}\right)$

The given function is given by

$$f(x) = \begin{cases} \tan x; & 0 < x \le \pi/6 \\ 1/\sqrt{3}; & \pi/6 < x \le \pi/3 \\ \cot x; & \pi/3 < x < \pi/2 \end{cases}$$

$\therefore$ The required area

$= \int_{0}^{\pi/6}\tan x\,dx + \int_{\pi/6}^{\pi/3}\frac{1}{\sqrt{3}}dx + \int_{\pi/3}^{\pi/2}\cot x\,dx$

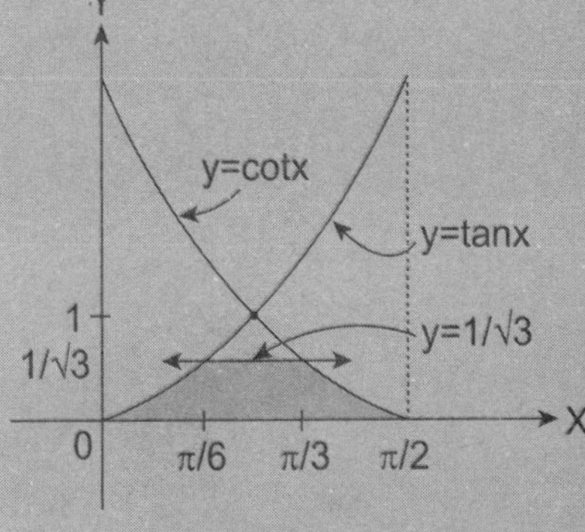

FIGURE 3.25

$$= \left(\ln \sec x\right)_0^{\pi/6} + \frac{1}{\sqrt{3}} \cdot \frac{\pi}{6} + \left(\ln \sin x\right)_{\pi/3}^{\pi/2}$$

$$= \log\frac{2}{\sqrt{3}} + \frac{\pi}{6\sqrt{3}} + \log\frac{2}{\sqrt{3}}$$

$$\Rightarrow \log\frac{4}{3} + \frac{\pi}{6\sqrt{3}} \text{ square units.}$$

ILLUSTRATION 19: Find the area enclosed by the parabola $ay = 3(a^2 - x^2)$ and the x-axis.

SOLUTION: The parabola cuts the x-axis at points $(-a, 0)$ and $(a, 0)$. Therefore, the required area is given by

$$A = \int_{-a}^{a} y\, dx = 2\frac{3}{a}\int_0^a \left(a^2 - x^2\right) dx = 4a^2 \text{ square units.}$$

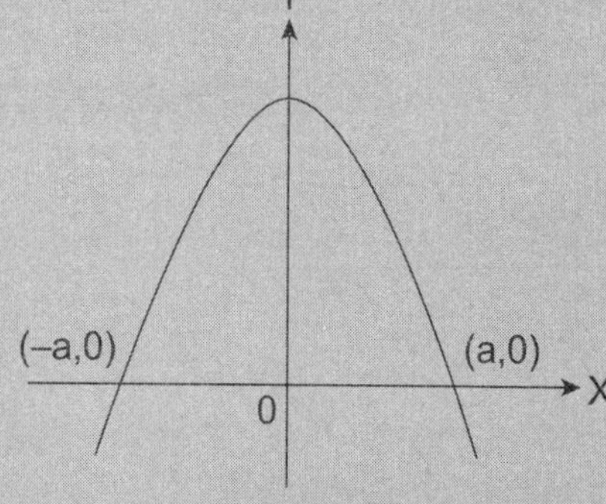

FIGURE 3.26

ILLUSTRATION 20: If $y = f(x) = x^4 - 2x^3 + x^2 + 3$ and α, β are two minima of $f(x)$ and A represents the area bounded by $y = f(x)$, the x-axis and the ordinates corresponding to the minimum of function $f(x)$, then find A.

SOLUTION: We have $f(x) = x^4 - 2x^3 + x^2 + 3$

To find minimum, $f'(x) = 4x^3 - 6x^2 + 2x = 0$

$\Rightarrow 2x(x - 1)(2x - 1) = 0$

$\Rightarrow x = 0, 1, 1/2$

$f''(x) = 12x^2 - 12x + 2 = 2(6x^2 - 6x + 1)$

$f''(x)_{x=0} > 0 \quad \Rightarrow$ Minimum exists at $x = 0$

$f''(x)_{x=1/2} < 0 \quad \Rightarrow$ Maximum exists at $x = 1/2$

$f''(x)_{x=1} > 0 \quad \Rightarrow$ Minimum exists at $x = 1$

$\Rightarrow$ The required area is bounded by the curve and the ordinates $x = 0$ and $x = 1$ and x-axis.

$$\therefore \text{ Required area } = A = \int_0^1 \left(x^4 - 2x^3 + x^2 + 3\right) dx$$

$$= \left|\left(\frac{x^5}{5} - \frac{x^4}{2} + \frac{x^3}{3} + 3x\right)\right|_0^1 = \frac{91}{30} \text{ square units.}$$

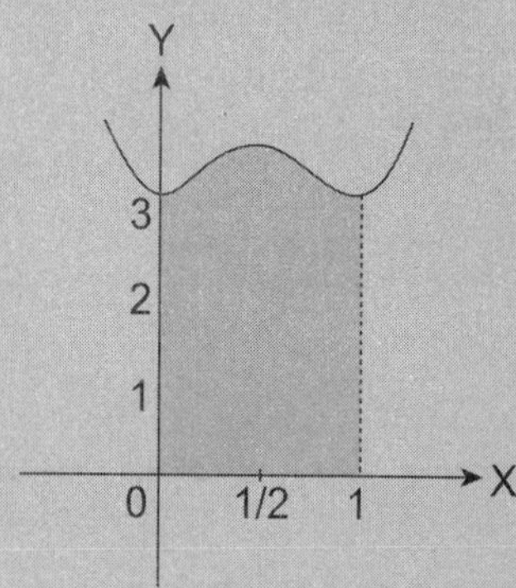

FIGURE 3.27

ILLUSTRATION 21: Find the area bounded by the graph of $y = \max\{\sin x, \cos x\}$ with x-axis.

SOLUTION: The graph of $\sin x$ and $\cos x$ represented on same xy plane is shown in Fig. 3.28. Here the bold line represents the graph of $y = \max\{\sin x, \cos x\}$.

$\therefore$ Required area

$$= \int_0^{\pi/4} \cos x\, dx + \int_{\pi/4}^{\pi} \sin x\, dx - \int_{\pi}^{5\pi/4} \sin x\, dx$$

$$- \int_{5\pi/4}^{3\pi/2} \cos x\, dx + \int_{3\pi/2}^{2\pi} \cos x\, dx$$

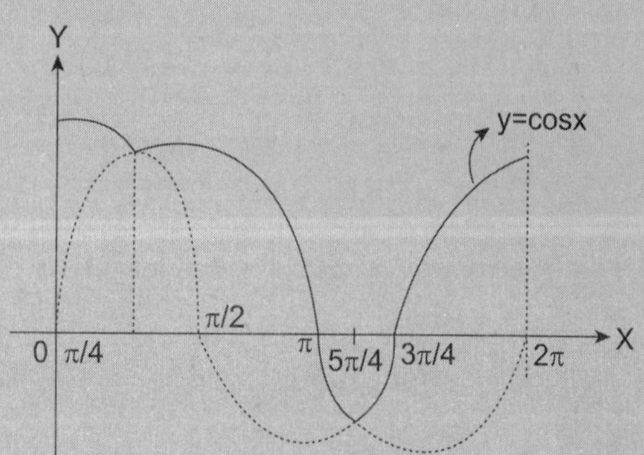

FIGURE 3.28

$= \left|\sin x\right|_0^{\pi/4} - \left|\cos x\right|_{\pi/4}^{\pi} + \left|\cos x\right|_{\pi}^{5\pi/4} - \left|\sin x\right|_{5\pi/4}^{3\pi/2} + \left|\sin x\right|_{3\pi/2}^{2\pi}$

= 4 square units.

ILLUSTRATION 22: Find the area enclosed between $y = \tan x$; $y = \cot x$ and x-axis in first quadrant.

SOLUTION: We are to find shaded area bounded by $\tan x$, $\cot x$ above x-axis

= Area under the curve $\overparen{OP}$ + Area under the curve $\overparen{PQ}$

$$= \int_0^{\pi/4} \tan x\,dx + \int_{\pi/4}^{\pi/2} \cot x\,dx = \left|\ln\sec x\right|_0^{\pi/4} + \left|\ln\sin x\right|_{\pi/4}^{\pi/2}$$

$$= \left[\ln\sec\frac{\pi}{4} - \ln\sec 0\right] + \left[\ln\sin\frac{\pi}{2} - \ln\sin\frac{\pi}{4}\right]$$

$$= \left[\ln\sqrt{2} - 0\right] + \left[0 - \ln\left(\frac{1}{\sqrt{2}}\right)\right] = \ln\sqrt{2} + \ln\sqrt{2} = 2\ln\sqrt{2} = \ln 2$$

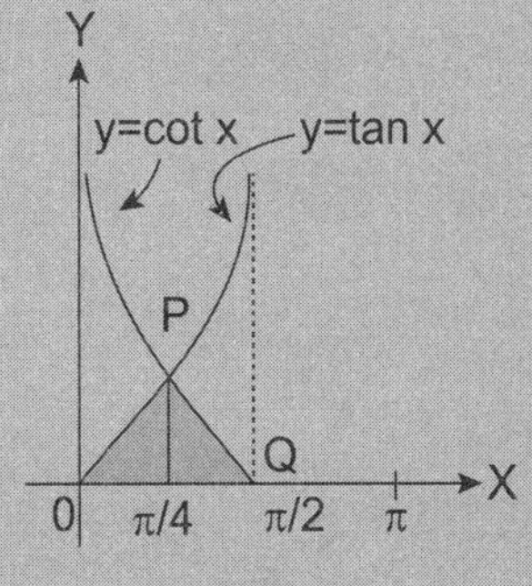

FIGURE 3.29

ILLUSTRATION 23: Find the area enclosed between $y = \tan^{-1}x$; $y = \cot^{-1}x$ and y-axis in first quadrant.

SOLUTION: We are to find the shaded area bounded by functions $\tan^{-1}x$, $\cot^{-1}x$ and y-axis

= Area OPL + Area PLQ

$$= \int_0^{\pi/4} (\tan y)\,dy + \int_{\pi/4}^{\pi/2} (\cot y)\,dy$$

$$= \left|\ln\sec y\right|_0^{\pi/4} + \left|\ln\sin y\right|_{\pi/4}^{\pi/2}$$

$$= \left(\ln\sqrt{2} - 0\right) + \left(0 - \ln\frac{1}{\sqrt{2}}\right) = 2\ln\sqrt{2} = \ln 2$$

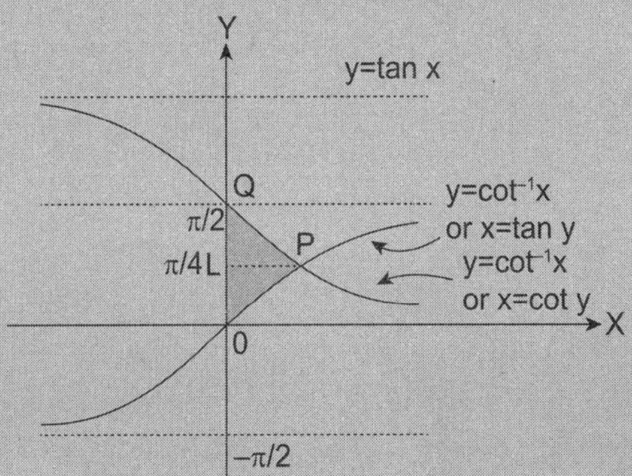

FIGURE 3.30

REMARK

From above two illustrations we conclude that the area enclosed by function f(x), g(x) and x-axis is the same as that enclosed by $f^{-1}(x)$, $g^{-1}(x)$ and y-axis.

ILLUSTRATION 24: Find the area enclosed by $y = \sin^{-1}(\cos x)$ with x-axis from $x = -\frac{\pi}{2}$ to $x = \frac{3\pi}{2}$

SOLUTION: The given function is $y = \sin^{-1}(\cos x)$

The graph of $y = \sin^{-1}(\cos x)$ is as shown in Fig. 3.31.

Here $y = \sin^{-1}\left(\sin\left(\frac{\pi}{2} + x\right)\right)$

Now graph of $\sin^{-1}\left(\sin\left(x + \frac{\pi}{2}\right)\right)$ can be obtained by shifting the graph of $\sin^{-1}(\sin x)$ by $\pi/2$ units towards left of y-axis shown in Fig. 3.31.

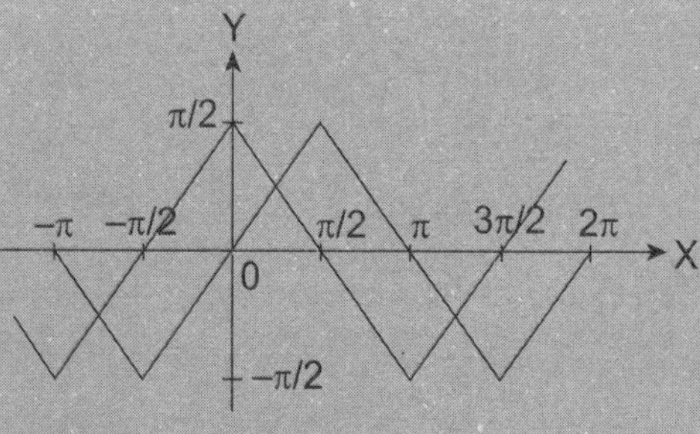

FIGURE 3.31

Clearly $f(x) \geq 0$ for $x \in \left[-\frac{\pi}{2}, \frac{\pi}{2}\right]$ and $f(x) \leq 0$ for $x \in \left[\frac{\pi}{2}, \frac{3\pi}{2}\right]$

$$\therefore \text{ Required area } = \int_{-\pi/2}^{3\pi/2} |f(x)|\,dx = \int_{-\pi/2}^{\pi/2} f(x)\,dx + \int_{\pi/2}^{3\pi/2} -f(x)\,dx$$

$$= \int_{-\pi/2}^{0}\left(x+\frac{\pi}{2}\right)dx + \int_{0}^{\pi/2} -\left(x-\frac{\pi}{2}\right)dx + \int_{\pi/2}^{\pi}\left(x-\frac{\pi}{2}\right)dx - \int_{\pi}^{3\pi/2}\left(x-\frac{3\pi}{2}\right)dx$$

$$= \left|\frac{x^2}{2}+\frac{\pi}{2}x\right|_{-\pi/2}^{0} - \left|\frac{x^2}{2}-\frac{\pi}{2}x\right|_{0}^{\pi/2} + \left|\frac{x^2}{2}-\frac{\pi}{2}x\right|_{\pi/2}^{\pi} - \left|\frac{x^2}{2}-\frac{3\pi x}{2}\right|_{\pi}^{3\pi/2}$$

$$= -\left(\frac{\pi^2}{8}-\frac{\pi^2}{4}\right) - \left(\frac{\pi^2}{8}-\frac{\pi^2}{4}\right) - \left(\frac{\pi^2}{8}-\frac{\pi^2}{4}\right) - \left[\left(\frac{9\pi^2}{8}-\frac{9\pi^2}{4}\right)-\left(\frac{\pi^2}{2}-\frac{3\pi^2}{2}\right)\right]$$

$$= 4\left(\frac{\pi^2}{8}\right) = \frac{\pi^2}{2} \text{ square units.}$$

The above area can be easily calculated geometrically since area of each of the two triangles

$$= \frac{1}{2}\pi \times \frac{\pi}{2} = \frac{\pi^2}{4}$$

$$\therefore \text{ Required area } = 2\left(\frac{\pi^2}{4}\right) = \frac{\pi^2}{2} \text{ square units}$$

ILLUSTRATION 25: Find the value of c for which the area of the figure bounded by the curves $y = \sin 2x$, the straight lines $x = \pi/6$, $x = c$ and the abscissa axis is equal to 1/2; given that $c \in \left(-\frac{\pi}{2}, \frac{\pi}{2}\right)$

SOLUTION: The graph of $y = \sin 2x$ is as shown in the Fig. 3.32.

Case I: If $c < 0$ then A.T.Q. $\int_{c}^{\pi/6} |\sin 2x|\,dx = \frac{1}{2}$

$$\Rightarrow \int_{c}^{0} -\sin 2x\,dx + \int_{0}^{\pi/6} \sin 2x\,dx = \frac{1}{2}$$

$$\Rightarrow \frac{1}{2}[\cos 2x]_{c}^{0} - \frac{1}{2}[\cos 2x]_{0}^{\pi/6} = \frac{1}{2}$$

$$\Rightarrow \frac{1}{2}[1-\cos 2c] - \frac{1}{2}\left[\frac{1}{2}-1\right] = \frac{1}{2}$$

$$\Rightarrow \frac{1}{2} - \frac{1}{2}\cos 2c + \frac{1}{4} = \frac{1}{2}$$

$$\Rightarrow \cos 2c = \frac{1}{2} \quad \Rightarrow \quad 2c = \frac{-\pi}{3} \quad \Rightarrow c = \frac{-\pi}{6}$$

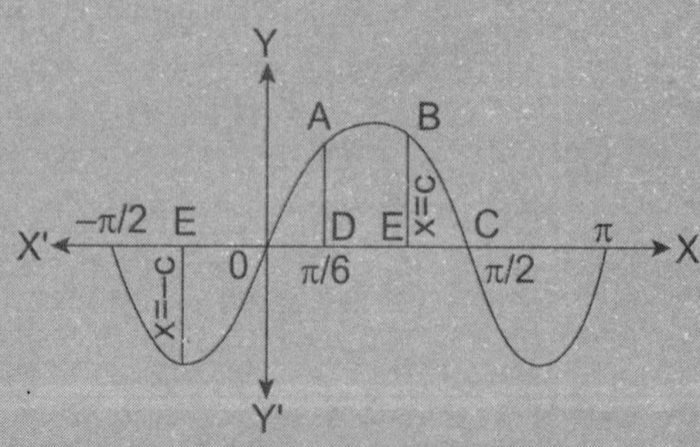

FIGURE 3.32

Case II: If $c > 0$,

$\Rightarrow \int_{\pi/6}^{c} \sin 2x dx = \frac{1}{2}$ $\Rightarrow -\frac{1}{2}[\cos 2x]_{\pi/6}^{c} = \frac{1}{2}$

$\Rightarrow -\left[\cos 2c - \frac{1}{2}\right] = 1$ $\Rightarrow \cos 2c = -\frac{1}{2}$

$\Rightarrow 2c = \frac{2\pi}{3}$

or $2c = \pi + \frac{\pi}{3}$ $\Rightarrow c = \frac{\pi}{3}$ or $c = \frac{2\pi}{3}$

But $0 < c < \frac{\pi}{2}$ $\Rightarrow c \neq \frac{2\pi}{3}$

$\therefore c = \frac{\pi}{3}$ $\therefore c = -\frac{\pi}{6}$ or $\frac{\pi}{3}$

TEXTUAL EXERCISE–1: (SUBJECTIVE)

1. Find the area of the region bounded by $y^2 = x - 2$, $x = 4$, $x = 6$ and the x-axis in the first quadrant.
2. Find the area of the region bounded by $x^2 = 4y$, $y = 2$, $y = 4$ and the y-axis in the first quadrant.
3. Find the area of the region bounded by the ellipse $\frac{x^2}{16} + \frac{y^2}{9} = 1$.
4. Find the area of the region bounded by the function $f(x) = (x)^{1/3}$, the x-axis and lines $x = -1$ and $x = 1$.
5. Find the area of the region bounded by the x-axis, the function $y = -x^2 + 4x - 8$ and the lines $x = -1$ and $x = 4$.
6. Find the area bounded by the hyperbola $x^2 - y^2 = a^2$ between the straight lines $x = a$ and $x = 2a$.
7. Evaluate area enclosed by $f(x)$ and x-axis between the mentioned ordinates:
   (a) $f(x) = \sin^2 \pi x$, $x = 0$ to 1
   (b) $f(x) = \log x$, $x = 0$ to 1
   (c) $f(x) = \cos x$, $x = 0$ to $\pi/2$
   (d) $f(x) = \cos(2x + \pi/4)$, $x = -\pi/8$ to $\pi/8$
8. Find the area under $y = \ln x$, x-axis and the two ordinates at $x = \frac{1}{e}$ and $x = e$.
9. Find the area enclosed by $y = e^{-|x|}$ and the x-axis
10. Determine the area of region bounded by the curve $f(x) = \max\left\{\sin x, \cos x, \frac{1}{2}\right\}$ and x-axis between $x = 0$ and $x = 2\pi$
11. If the area bounded by curves $y = f(x)$ and x-axis between the ordinates $x = 0$ and $x = a$; where $a \geq 0$ is $(e^{a^2} - 1)$ square units $\forall\ a \geq 0$, then find all such possible curves.
12. If a curve $y = a\sqrt{x} + bx$ passes through the point $(1, 2)$ and the area bounded by the curve, line $x = 4$ and x-axis is 8 square units, then find the value of a and b.
13. If the area above the x-axis, bounded by the curves $y = 2^{kx}$ and $x = 0$ and $x = 2$ is $\frac{3}{In\ 2}$, then find the value of k.
14. Find the area bounded by the curve $xy - 3x - 2y - 10 = 0$, x-axis and the lines $x = 3$, $x = 4$.

Answer Keys

1. $\frac{16 - 4\sqrt{2}}{3}$ **2.** $\frac{32 - 8\sqrt{2}}{3}$ **3.** 12π **4.** $3/2$ **5.** $31\frac{1}{2}$ **6.** $2a^2\sqrt{3} - a^2 \log(2 + \sqrt{3})$

7. (a) 1/2 (b) 1 (c) 1 (d) 1/2 **8.** $2 - \frac{2}{e}$ **9.** 2 sq. units **10.** $\left(\frac{15\pi}{12} + \sqrt{2} + \sqrt{3}\right)$ Square units

11. $\pm 2xe^{x^2}$ **12.** $a = 3$, $b = -1$ **13.** **14.** $16 \log 2 + 3$

TEXTUAL EXERCISE–1: (OBJECTIVE)

1. Area bounded by the curve $y = \ln x$, x-axis and the ordinates $x = 1, x = 2$ is
   (a) ln 4 square units
   (b) (ln 4 + 1) square units
   (c) (ln 4 – 1) square units
   (d) None of these

2. Area bounded by the curve $y = xe^{x^2}$, x-axis and the ordinates $x = 0, x = a$ is
   (a) $\dfrac{e^{a^2} - 1}{2}$ square units
   (b) $\dfrac{e^{a^2} + 1}{2}$ square units
   (c) $\left(e^{a^2} + 1\right)$ square units
   (d) $\left(e^{a^2} - 1\right)$ square units

3. Area bounded by curve $xy = c$, x-axis between $x = 1$ and $x = 4$, is
   (a) $c \log 3$ square units
   (b) $2 \log c$ square units
   (c) $2c \log 2$ square units
   (d) $2c \log 5$ square units

4. Area bounded by $y = x \sin x$ and x-axis between $x = 0$ and $x = 2\pi$, is
   (a) 0 (b) 2π square units
   (c) π square units (d) 4π square units

5. The area of smaller part between the circle $x^2 + y^2 = 4$ and the line $x = 1$ is
   (a) $\dfrac{4\pi}{3} - \sqrt{3}$ (b) $\dfrac{8\pi}{3} - \sqrt{3}$
   (c) $\dfrac{4\pi}{3} + \sqrt{3}$ (d) $\dfrac{5\pi}{3} + \sqrt{3}$

6. Area inside the parabola $y^2 = 4ax$, between the lines $x = a$ and $x = 4a$ is equal to
   (a) $4a^2$ (b) $8a^2$
   (c) $28\dfrac{a^2}{3}$ (d) $35\dfrac{a^2}{3}$

7. The area enclosed by the curve $|y| = \sin 2x$, when $x \in [0, 2\pi]$ is
   (a) 1 (b) 2
   (c) 3 (d) 4

8. The area of the loop between the curve $y = a \sin x$ and x-axis is:
   (a) a (b) $2a$
   (c) $3a$ (d) None of these

9. Area lying between the parabola $y^2 = 4ax$ and its latus-rectum is
   (a) $\dfrac{8}{3}a^2$ (b) $\dfrac{8}{3}a$
   (c) $\dfrac{4}{3}a$ (d) $\dfrac{4}{3}a^2$

10. The area of the upper half of the circle whose equation is, $(x - 1)^2 + y^2 = 1$ is given by
    (a) $\int_0^2 \sqrt{2x - x^2}\,dx$ (b) $\int_0^1 \sqrt{2x - x^2}\,dx$
    (c) $\int_0^2 \sqrt{2x - x^2}\,dx$ (d) $\dfrac{\pi}{4}$

11. Area bounded by the curves $y^2(2a - x) = x^3$ and the line $x = 2a$ is
    (a) $3\pi a^2$ (b) $\dfrac{3\pi a^2}{2}$
    (c) $\dfrac{3\pi a^2}{4}$ (d) None of these

12. The area bounded by $y = x\, e^{|x|}$ and lines $|x| = 1, y = 0$ is
    (a) 4 (b) 6
    (c) 1 (d) 2

13. The area of the figure bounded by the curve $|y| = 1 - x^2$ is
    (a) 2/3 (b) 4/3
    (c) 8/3 (d) None of these

14. The area bounded by the curve $y^2 = x$ and the ordinate $x = 36$ is divided in the ratio 1 : 7 by the ordinate $x = a$. Then a is
    (a) 8 (b) 9
    (c) 7 (d) 0

15. The value of c for which the area of the figure bounded by the curve $y = 8x^2 - x^5$, the straight lines $x = 1$ and $x = c$ and the x-axis is equal to 16/3, is
    (a) 2 (b) $3\sqrt{8 - \sqrt{17}}$
    (c) 3 (d) –1

Answer Keys

1. (c)	**2.** (a)	**3.** (a)	**4.** (d)	**5.** (b)	**6.** (c)	**7.** (d)	**8.** (b)	**9.** (a)	**10.** (a)
11. (a)	**12.** (d)	**13.** (c)	**14.** (b)	**15.** (d)					

■ AREA BOUNDED BETWEEN TWO CURVES

The area bounded by the straight lines $x = a$, $x = b$ $(a < b)$ and the curves $y = f_1(x)$ and $y = f_2(x)$, or the area bounded by $y = f_1(x)$ and $f_2(x)$ when the two curves intersect each other at $x = a$ and $x = b$ is given by,

(i) $A = \int_a^b [f_2(x) - f_1(x)]dx$; provided $f_1(x) \le f_2(x)$; where $(a \le x \le b)$,

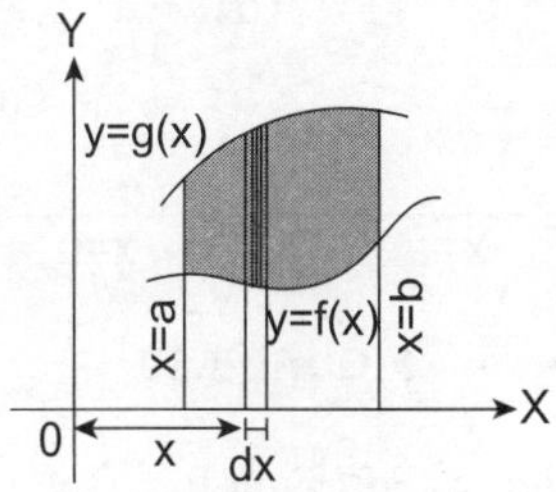

FIGURE 3.33

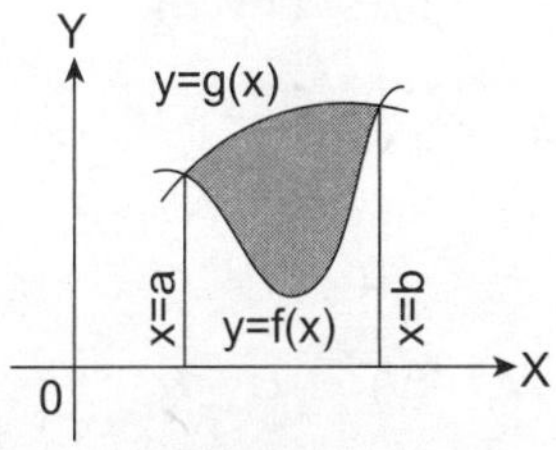

FIGURE 3.34

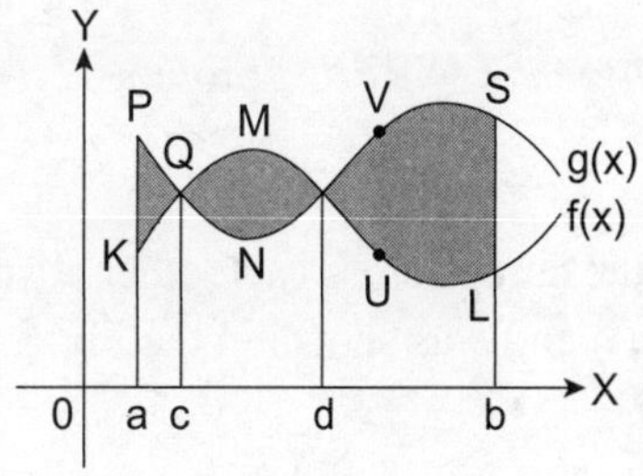

FIGURE 3.35

Proof: Consider the diagram given below. Here signs of y_1 and y_2 are given. Now $(y_1 - y_2)$ gives the height of strip (irrespective of signs of y_1 and y_2).

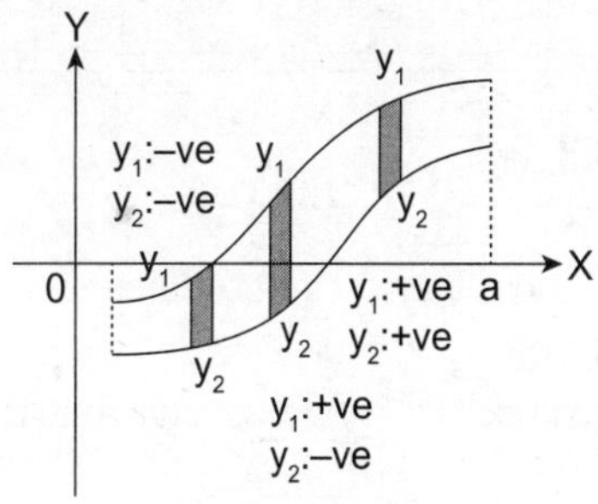

FIGURE 3.36

So, area element dA = height of strip × width

$$\Rightarrow \quad A = \int_0^A dA = \int_a^b (y_1 - y_2)dx$$

NOTE

Consider the adjacent figure. If you are uncomfortable with negative values simply shift the graph upward by a certain number c.

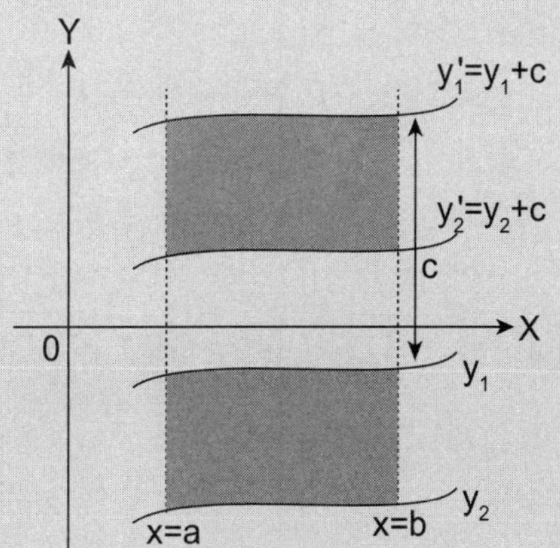

FIGURE 3.37

Writing $y_1' = y_1 + c$ *and* $y_2' = y_2 + c$. *The required area* $A = \int_a^b (y_1' - y_2')dx$

$$= \int_a^b (y_1 + c) - (y_2 + c)dx = \int_a^b (y_1 - y_2)dx$$

(ii) $A = \int_a^b [f_1(x) - f_2(x)]\,dx$; provided $f_2(x) \le f_1(x)$; where $(a \le x \le b)$.

(iii) If both the curves cross each other at some point c, d between a and b as shown in the Fig. 3.38.

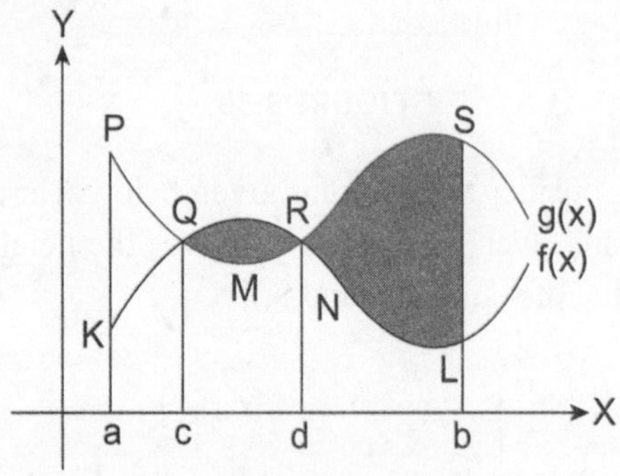

FIGURE 3.38

Then to find the area enclosed between the curves we proceed as follows:

Required area = A = Area of curvilinear triangle PQK
+ Area of loop $QMRQ$
+ Area of loop $RNLSR$

$$= \int_a^c [g(x) - f(x)]\,dx + \int_c^d [f(x) - g(x)]\,dx + \int_d^b [g(x) - f(x)]\,dx$$

$$= \left|\int_a^c [f(x) - g(x)]\,dx\right| + \int_c^d [f(x) - g(x)]\,dx + \left|\int_d^b [f(x) - g(x)]\,dx\right|$$

$$= \int_a^c |f(x) - g(x)|\,dx + \int_c^d |f(x) - g(x)|\,dx + \int_d^b |f(x) - g(x)|\,dx$$

$$= \int_a^b |f(x) - g(x)|\,dx$$

Conclusion:

From the above discussion one can easily conclude that area enclosed between two curves $f(x)$ and $g(x)$ and ordinate $x = a$ and $x = b$ is given by $\left|\int_a^b |f(x) - g(x)|\,dx\right|$ irrespective of their mutual position and their position w.r.t. x-axis.

How We Take Strip and Limit of Integration

1. For the regions as in the Fig. 3.39, use the formula:

Area = $\int_a^b (y_1 - y_2)\,dx$

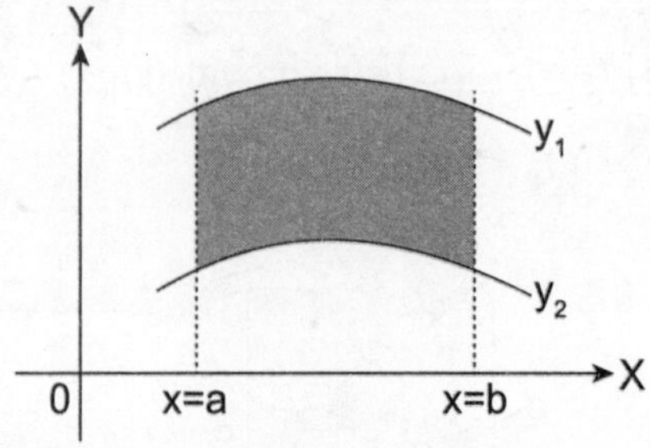

FIGURE 3.39

2. For the regions as in given Fig. 3.40.

Area $A = \int_c^d |f(y) - \phi(y)|\,dy$

$\Rightarrow dA = |(x_2 - x_1)|\,dy$

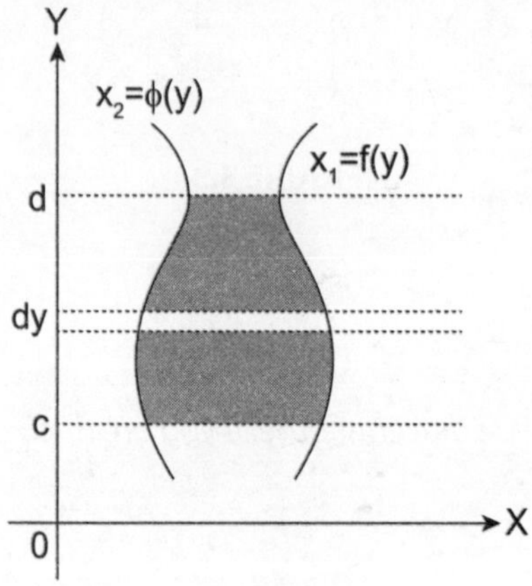

FIGURE 3.40

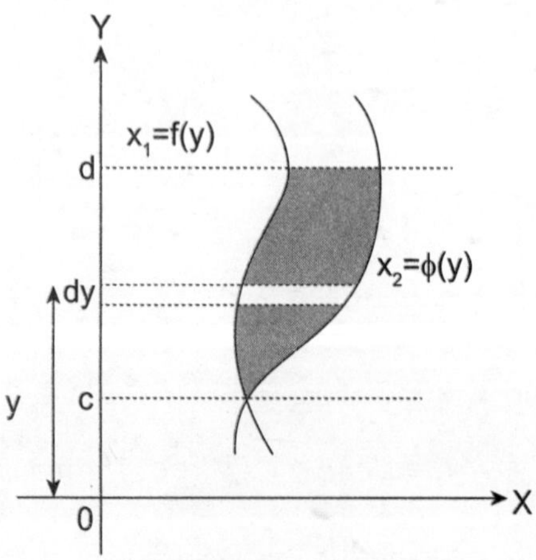

FIGURE 3.41

3. For the regions as in given Fig. 3.42, use the formula:

$$A = \int_{x_B}^{x_A} [g(x) - h(x)]dx + \int_{x_A}^{x_C} [f(x) - h(x)]dx$$

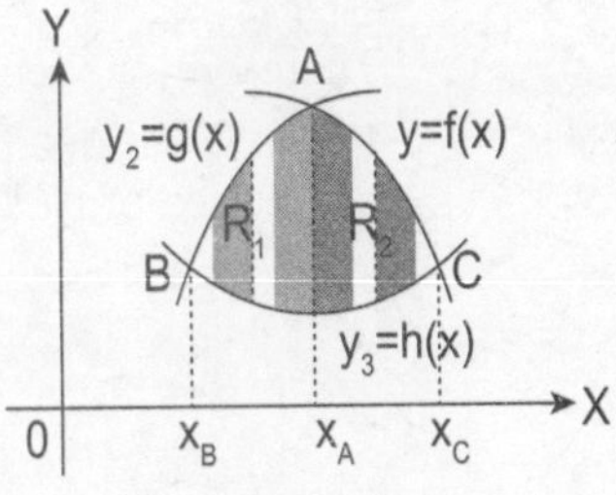

FIGURE 3.42

ILLUSTRATION 26: Find the area of region R bounded by graphs of $y = 2x - 1$ and $y = x^2 - 4$ and vertical lines $x = 1$ and $x = 2$.

SOLUTION: The figure representing the graph of $y = 2x - 1$ and $y = x^2 - 4$ is as shown Fig. 3.43.

Clearly for $x = 1$ to $x = 2$ the graph of function $y_2 = x^2 - 4$ is below the graph of function $y_1 = 2x - 1$

Therefore, the required area is given by $A = \int_1^2 (y_1 - y_2)\, dx$

$$= \int_1^2 [(2x-1) - (x^2 - 4)]\, dx = \int_1^2 (-x^2 + 2x + 3)\, dx$$

$$= \left[-\frac{1}{3}x^3 + x^2 + 3x\right]_1^2 = \frac{11}{3} \text{ square units.}$$

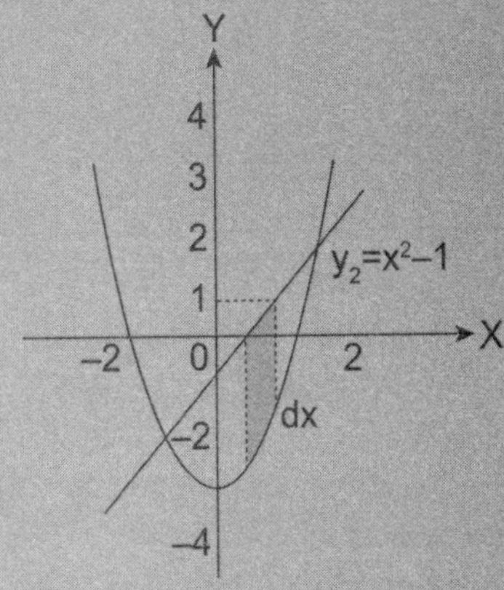

FIGURE 3.43

ILLUSTRATION 27: Find the area of the region bounded by $x = y^2$ and $x = y + 2$ in first quadrant for the points of intersection of curves.

SOLUTION: Solving $y^2 = y + 2$

$\Rightarrow y^2 - y - 2 = 0$

$\Rightarrow (y + 1)(y - 2) = 0$

$\Rightarrow y = -1, 2$

Therefore, the point of intersection of $x = y + 2$ and $x = y^2$ is $A \equiv (4, 2)$

Thus, the required area $= \int_0^2 (y + 2 - y^2)dy$

$$= \frac{y^2}{2} + 2y - \frac{y^3}{3}\Big|_0^2 = \frac{10}{3} \text{ square units.}$$

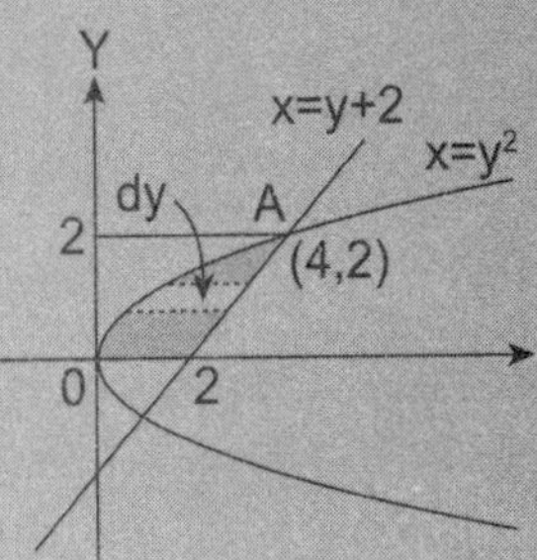

FIGURE 3.44

ILLUSTRATION 28: Find the area of the region bounded by curve $y = \cos^{-1}(\cos x)$ and the curve $f(x)$ given by $f(x) = \begin{cases} 2x + 3; & x < 0 \\ -x + 3; & x > 0 \end{cases}$

SOLUTION: As we know that $\cos^{-1}(\cos x) = \begin{cases} x; & 0 \le x \le \pi \\ -x; & -\pi \le x \le 0 \end{cases}$ and $f(x) = \begin{cases} 2x + 3; & x < 0 \\ -x + 3; & x \ge 0 \end{cases}$

The graph of $y = \cos^{-1}(\cos x)$ and $f(x)$ for $x \in [-\pi, \pi]$ is as shown Fig. 3.45.

From the diagram, the point of intersection of $f(x)$ and $\cos^{-1}(\cos x)$ are given by $R\left(\frac{3}{2}, \frac{3}{2}\right)$ and $P(-1, 1)$

Therefore, the required enclosed area is given by

A = area of quadrilateral $OPQR$ = area of ΔOPQ + area of ΔOQR

$$= \int_{-1}^{0}\{2x+3-(-x)\}\,dx + \int_{0}^{3/2}(3-x-x)\,dx$$

$$= 3\left[\frac{x^2}{2}+x\right]_{-1}^{0} + \left[3x-x^2\right]_{0}^{3/2} = 3\left(-\left(-\frac{1}{2}\right)\right)+\left(\frac{9}{2}-\frac{9}{4}\right)$$

$$= \frac{3}{2}+\frac{9}{4} = \frac{15}{4} \text{ square units}$$

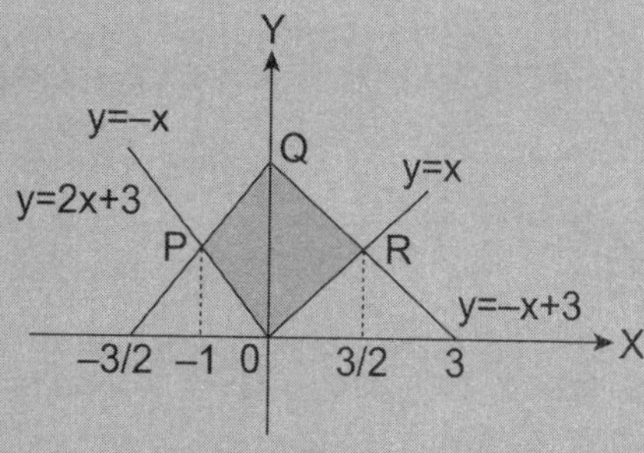

FIGURE 3.45

Alternatively, area of the above shaded region can also be obtained geometrically without application of calculus as below.

The area enclosed $OPQR$ = area of ΔOPQ + area of ΔOQR

$$= \frac{1}{2}OQ(1)+\frac{1}{2}OQ\left(\frac{3}{2}\right) = \frac{3}{2}+\frac{9}{4} = \frac{15}{4} \text{ square units.}$$

■ AREA BOUNDED BETWEEN TWO STANDARD CURVES

(i.e., straight line, circle, parabola, ellipse, hyperbola, trigonometric functions, exponential and logarithmic functions)

Straight Line with Straight Line

Area of region R bounded by straight line $L_1 = 0$, $L_2 = 0$ and $L_3 = 0$ as represented in Fig. 3.46.

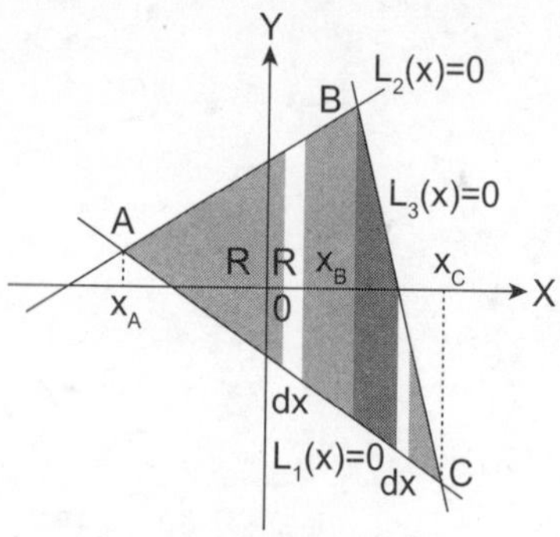

FIGURE 3.46

is given by $A = \int_{x_A}^{x_B}\{L_2(x)-L_1(x)\}\,dx + \int_{x_B}^{x_C}\{L_3(x)-L_1(x)\}\,dx$

ILLUSTRATION 29: Find the area of the triangular region bounded by the lines $y = 2x+1$, $y = 3x+1$, and $x = 4$.

SOLUTION: The given lines are $y = 2x+1$ ....(i)

$y = 3x+1$, ...(ii)

$x = 4$ ....(iii)

Solving (i) and (ii), we get (0, 1) as point of intersection of (i) and (ii) Let it be A.

Solving (i) and (iii), we get point of intersection of (i) and (iii) as $x = 4$, $y = 9$ i.e., (4, 9). Let it be B.

Solving (ii) and (iii), we get the point of intersection C as (4, 13).

Therefore, line (i) is AB, line (ii) is AC and line (iii) is BC. (parallel to y-axis) and the graph is given as in Fig. 3.47, so clearly,

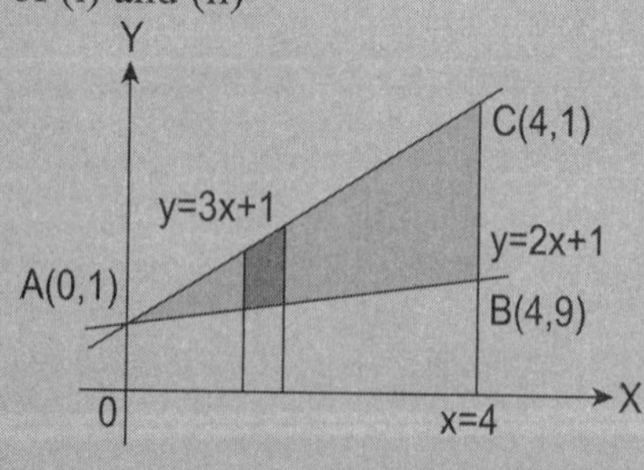

FIGURE 3.47

Required area $= \int_0^4 (y_{AC}-y_{AB})\,dx = \int_0^4 [(3x+1)-(2x+1)]\,dx$

$$= \int_0^4 x\,dx = \left[\frac{1}{2}x^2\right]_0^4 = 8-0 = 8 \text{ square units}$$

Straight Line with Circle

(i) Area of region R (minor segment of circle) bounded by the straight line and circle as shown in Fig. 3.48.

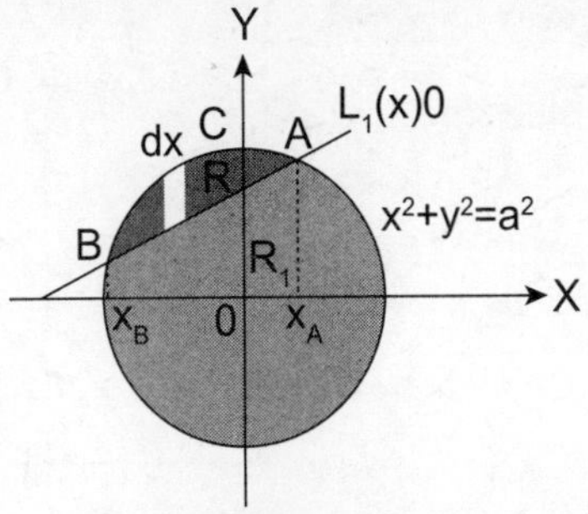

FIGURE 3.48

is given by $A = \text{area}\ (x_B x_A \widehat{ACB})$ –

$$\text{area}\ (x_B x_A AB) = \int_{x_B}^{x_A} (\sqrt{a^2 - x^2} - L_1(x))dx$$

(ii) Area of region R_1 (major segment of circle)
= area of circle – area of region

$$R = \pi a^2 - \int_{x_B}^{x_A}\left[\sqrt{a^2 - x^2} - L_1(x)\right]dx$$

ILLUSTRATION 30: Find the area of smaller region bounded by the circle $x^2 + y^2 = 4$ and the straight line $x - y = 2$.

SOLUTION: Evidently straight line $x - y = 2$ intersect the circle $x^2 + y^2 = 4$ in two points $A(2, 0)$ and $B(0, -2)$. Therefore, the required area is as shown the in Fig. 3.49.

$\therefore$ required area $= \int_0^2 (y_{AB} - y_{\widehat{BA}})dx$; where $\widehat{BA}$ is the arc of circle traversed anti-clockwise from B to A.

Now $y_{AB} = y_{\text{st.line}} = x - 2;\ y_{\widehat{BA}} = y_{\text{circle(lower half)}} = -\sqrt{4 - x^2}$

$$\therefore\ \text{Area} = BQAPB = \int_0^2 \left\{ (x-2) - \left(-\sqrt{4-x^2}\right)\right\} dx$$

$$= \int_0^2 \left\{ (x-2) + \sqrt{4-x^2} \right\} dx$$

$$= \left[\frac{x^2}{2} - 2x + \frac{1}{2}\left\{x\sqrt{4-x^2} + 4\sin^{-1}\left(\frac{x}{2}\right)\right\}\right]_0^2$$

$$= \left[2 - 4 + \frac{1}{2}\left(0 + 4.\frac{\pi}{2}\right)\right] - [0] = (\pi - 2) \text{ square units}$$

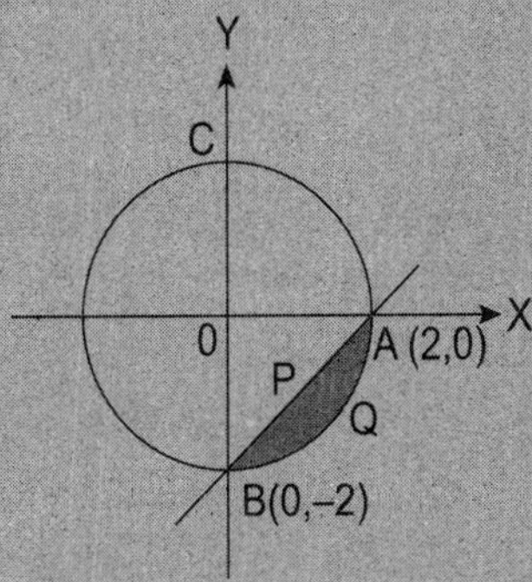

FIGURE 3.49

Straight line with Parabola

Area of region R bounded by parabola $y^2 = 4ax$ and the straight line $L_1(x) = 0$ as shown in Fig. 3.50, is given by R = Area of region.

$$(R_1 + R_2) = 2\int_0^{x_A} (\sqrt{4ax})\,dx + \int_{x_A}^{x_B} [\sqrt{4ax} - L_1(x)]\,dx$$

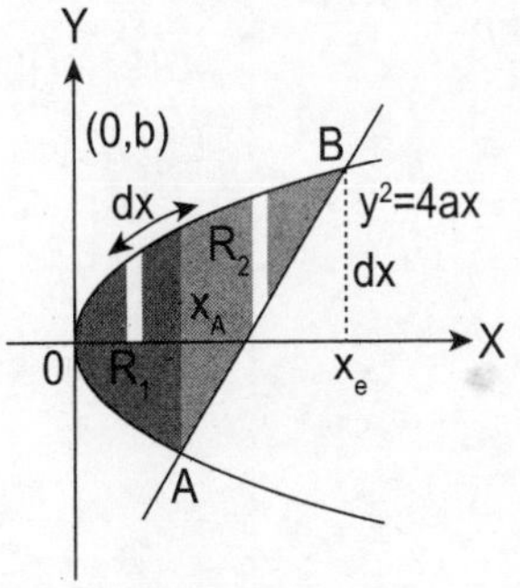

FIGURE 3.50

ILLUSTRATION 31: Find the area of the region bounded by the parabola $y = x^2 + 2$ and the lines $y = x$, $x = 0$ and $x = 3$.

SOLUTION: The equation of the parabola $y = x^2 + 2$ and $y = x$ is the equation of a straight lines lying below the parabola.

The line $x = 3$ meets the parabola at $P(3, 11)$ and the line $y = x$ meets the line $x = 3$ at $Q(3, 3)$.

The region, whose area is required, is shaded in the Fig. 3.51.

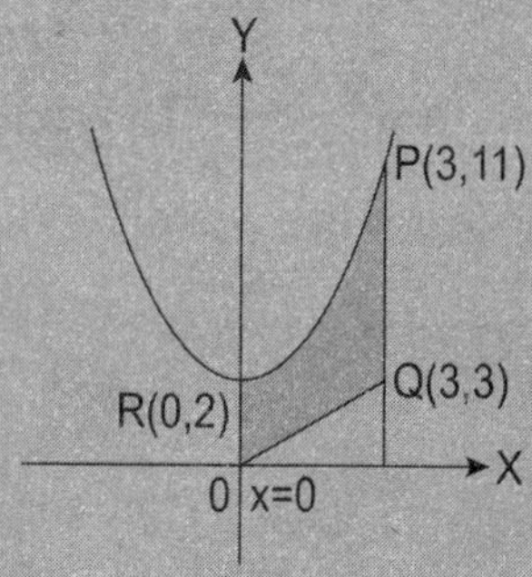

FIGURE 3.51

Here $R_1 = \int_0^3 (x^2+2)\,dx$, represents the area enclosed by $y = x^2 + 2$, $x = 0$, $y = 0$ and $x = 3$

And $R_2 = \int_0^3 x\,dx$; represents the area enclosed by $y = x$, $x = 0$ and $x = 3$.

Thus, it is clear from the Fig. 3.51 that the required area $OQPR = R_1 - R_2$

$$= \int_0^3 (x^2+2)dx - \int_0^3 x\,dx = \left[\frac{x^3}{3}+2x\right]_0^3 - \left[\frac{x^2}{2}\right]_0^3 = 9+6-\frac{9}{2} = \frac{21}{2} \text{ square units.}$$

ILLUSTRATION 32: Find the area bounded on the right by the line $x + y = 2$, on the left by the parabola $y = x^2$ and below by the x-axis.

SOLUTION: The required area is as shown by shaded of in Fig. 3.52.

Now, point of intersection of $x + y = 2$ and $y = x^2$ are given by $x + x^2 = 2$

$\Rightarrow (x + 2)(x - 1) = 0$

$\Rightarrow x = -2, 1$

$\Rightarrow B(1, 1)$ is the point of intersection of straight line and parabola with in the required area.

So required Area

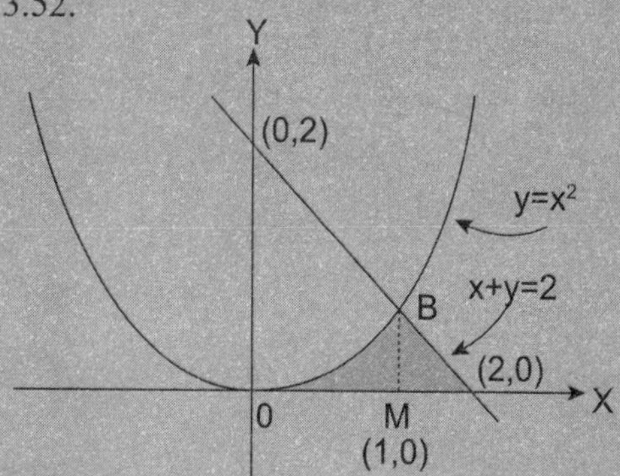

FIGURE 3.52

$$OBAM = \int_0^1 x^2dx + \int_1^2 (2-x)\,dx$$

$$= \left(\frac{x^3}{3}\right)_0^1 + \left|2x-\frac{x^2}{2}\right|_1^2 = \frac{5}{6} \text{ square units}$$

Straight Line with Ellipse

Area of a region R bounded by the ellipse $\frac{x^2}{a^2}+\frac{y^2}{b^2}=1$ and the line $L_1(x) = 0$ is as represented below:

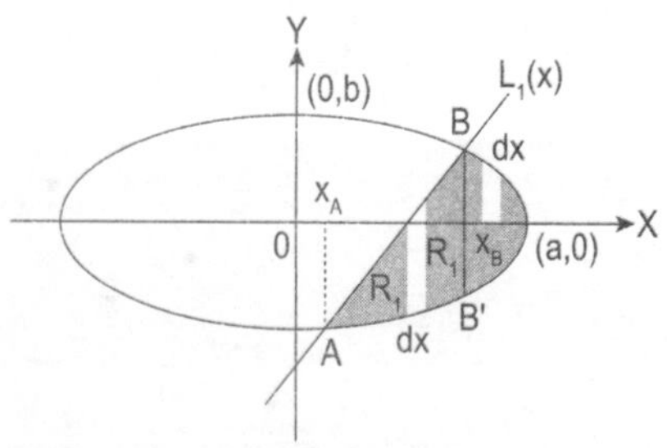

FIGURE 3.53

is given by, $A = \int_{x_A}^{x_B} (y_{AB} - y_{\widehat{AB'}})\,dx + 2\int_{x_B}^{a} (y_{\widehat{CB}})\,dx$; where

$\widehat{AB'}$ is the arc of ellipse traversed anti-clockwise from A to B'.

$$= \int_{x_A}^{x_B}\left[L_1(x) - \left(-b\sqrt{\left(1-\frac{x^2}{a^2}\right)}\right)\right]dx + 2\int_{x_B}^{a} b\sqrt{\left(1-\frac{x^2}{a^2}\right)}\,dx$$

REMARKS

Note that above shaded area is the minor area between the straight line and ellipse, to find major area subtract the above area from total area of ellipse (i.e., πab).

ILLUSTRATION 33: Find the area of larger region enclosed between ellipse $\frac{x^2}{9}+\frac{y^2}{4}=1$ and straight line $2x+3y=6$ and ratio of areas of smaller to larger region:

SOLUTION: The equation of ellipse is $y=\pm\frac{2}{3}\sqrt{9-x^2}$

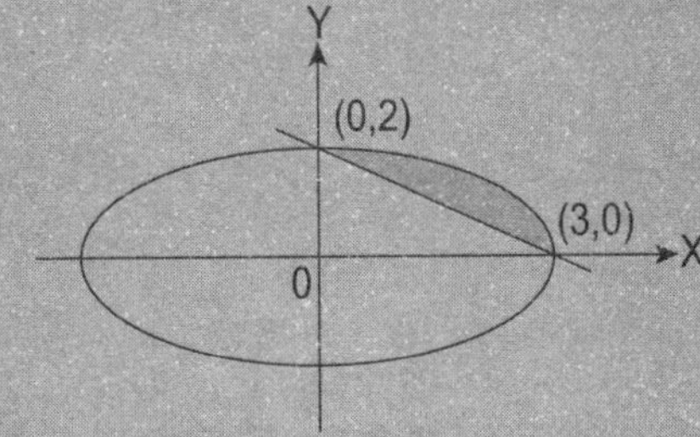

FIGURE 3.54

The equation of given straight line is $2x+3y=6$ which intersects the ellipse at points $P(0, 2)$ and $Q(3, 0)$ as shown in Fig. 3.54.

Therefore, the area of shaded region $A_1=\int_0^3\left(y_{\widehat{QP}}-y_{QP}\right)dx$;

where $y_{\widehat{QP}}$ is the y coordinate of any point on the arc QP of the ellipse traversed anti-clockwise from Q to P and is given by $y_{\widehat{QP}}=\sqrt{b^2\left(1-\frac{x^2}{a^2}\right)}$

$=\sqrt{4\left(1-\frac{x^2}{9}\right)}=\frac{2}{3}\sqrt{9-x^2}$ and y_{QP} is ordinate of straight line given by $y_{QP}=\left(\frac{6-2x}{3}\right)$

Thus, $A_1=\int_0^3\left(\frac{2}{3}\sqrt{9-x^2}-\frac{6-2x}{3}\right)dx=\frac{2}{3}\left[\frac{x}{2}\sqrt{9-x^2}+\frac{9}{2}\sin^{-1}\frac{x}{3}\right]_0^3-\left[2x-\frac{x^2}{3}\right]_0^3$

$=\left(\frac{3\pi}{2}-3\right)$ square units

Now area of the ellipse $=\pi ab=\pi(3)(2)=6\pi$ square units

Thus, area of non-shaded region (larger region) $=A_2=6\pi-A_1=\frac{9\pi}{2}+3$ square units.

So ratio of areas of smaller to larger region $=\frac{A_1}{A_2}=\frac{A_1}{6\pi-A_1}=\frac{\frac{3\pi}{2}-3}{\frac{9\pi}{2}+3}=\frac{3\pi-6}{9\pi+6}$

ILLUSTRATIOR 34: The line $3x+2y=13$ divides the area enclosed by the curve, $9x^2+4y^2-18x-16y-11=0$ into two parts. Find the ratio of the larger area to the smaller area.

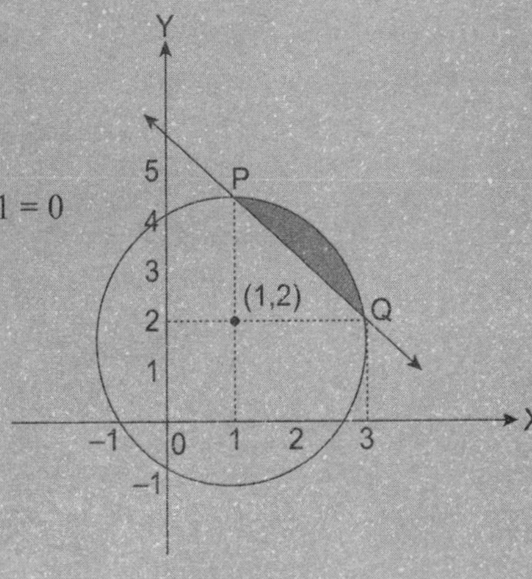

FIGURE 3.55

SOLUTION: Given equation of curve is $9x^2+4y^2-18x-16y-11=0$

or $\frac{(x-1)^2}{(2)^2}+\frac{(y-2)^2}{(3)^2}=1$ which is the equation of ellipse having its centre at (1, 2) and axes parallel to coordinate axes and with semi-major axis length 3, semi-minor axis length 2 as shown in Fig. 3.55.

Area of ellipse is $\pi ab=\pi(2)(3)=6\pi$

The points of inter section of $9x^2 + 4y^2 - 18x - 16y - 11 = 0$ and line $3x + 2y = 13$ are given by $P(1, 5)$ and $Q(3, 2)$

$\therefore$ Minor area between ellipse and line $= \int_1^3 (y_1 - y_2)\,dx$

$$= \int_1^3 \left[\frac{3}{2}\sqrt{4-(x-1)^2} + 2 - \left(\frac{13-3x}{2}\right)\right] dx$$

$$= \frac{3}{2}\left\{\frac{x-1}{2}\sqrt{4-(x-1)^2} + \frac{4}{2}\sin^{-1}\left(\frac{x-1}{2}\right)\right\} + \left[2x - \frac{1}{2}\left(13x - \frac{3x^2}{2}\right)\right]_1^3 = \frac{3\pi}{2} - 3$$

$$\therefore \quad \frac{\text{Area of larger region}}{\text{Area of smaller region}} = \frac{6\pi - \left(\frac{3\pi}{2} - 3\right)}{\frac{3\pi}{2} - 3} = \frac{3\pi + 2}{\pi - 2}$$

Circle with Circle

Area of region R bounded by two circles $C_1: x^2 + y^2 = a^2$ and $C_2: (x - a)^2 + (y - a)^2 = a^2$ is as shown in Fig. 3.56.

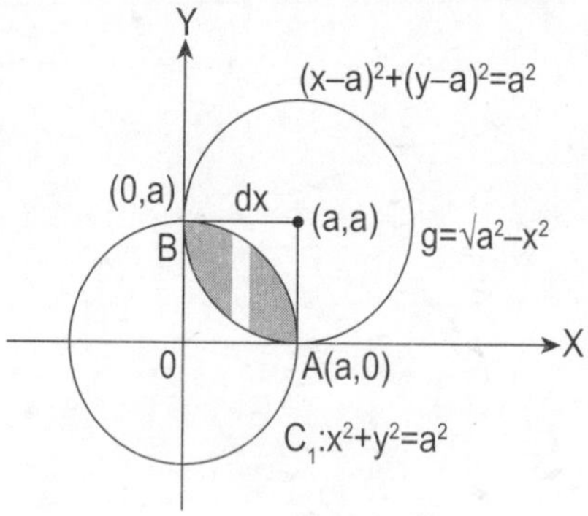

FIGURE 3.56

is given by $A = \int_0^a (y_1 - y_2)\,dx$; where y_1 and y_2 are respectively the ordinates of points lying on upper half and lower half of circle C_1 and C_2.

Here $y_1 = \sqrt{a^2 - x^2}$

and $y_2 = a - \sqrt{a^2 - (x-a)^2}$

Thus, required shaded area

$$A = \int_0^a \left[\sqrt{a^2 - x^2} - \left(a - \sqrt{a^2 - (x-a)^2}\right)\right] dx$$

ILLUSTRATION 35: Find the ratio of the area outside the circle $x^2 + y^2 = 4$ but inside the circle $x(x - 2) + y(y - 2) = 0$ to the area of IInd circle.

SOLUTION: Given $C_1 : x^2 + y^2 = 4$ ....(i)

and $C_2 : x(x - 2) + y(y - 2) = 0$ ....(ii)

First circle has its radius 2 and centred at origin, whereas second circle has diameters with end points $O(0, 0)$, $Q(2, 2)$; $A(2, 0)$ and $B(0, 2)$, i.e., having centre at (1, 1) and radius $\sqrt{2}$ is geometrically shown in Fig. 3.57.

Required area is shaded in the given in Fig. 3.57, A_1 (say)

$\Rightarrow A_1$ = area of semicircle C_2 – (area of quarter circle C_1 – area of triangle OAB)

$$= \frac{\pi(\sqrt{2})^2}{2} - \left[\frac{\pi(2)^2}{4} - \frac{1}{2}(2)(2)\right] = \pi - \pi + 2 = 2 \text{ square units}$$

Area of IInd circle (say) region A_2 is 2π square units

Therefore, the ratio $\dfrac{A_1}{A_2} = \dfrac{2}{2\pi} = \dfrac{1}{\pi}$

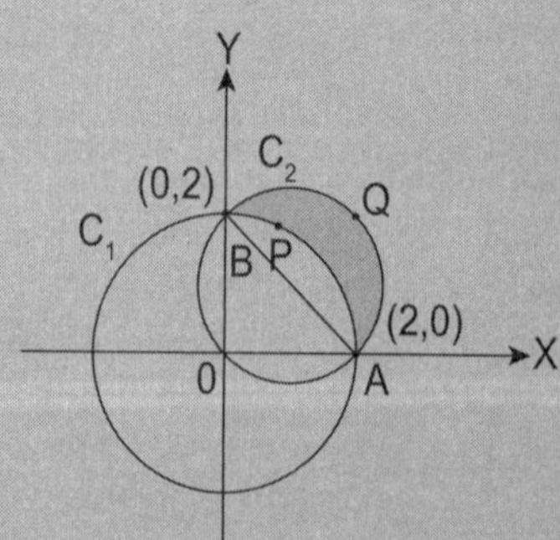

FIGURE 3.57

Circle with Parabola

Area of region R: (shaded region) is given by,

$$A = 2\int_0^{x_A}\left[\sqrt{4ax}\right]dx + 2\int_{x_A}^{a}\sqrt{a^2-x^2}\,dx$$

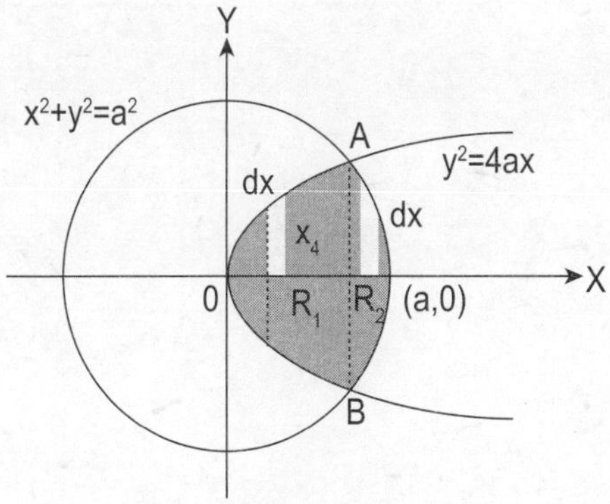

FIGURE 3.58

ILLUSTRATION 36: Find the area of the region inside the circle $x^2 + y^2 - 2ax = 0$ but outside the parabola $y^2 = ax$ $(a > 0)$.

SOLUTION: Equation of given circle is $x^2 - 2ax + y^2 = 0$ or $(x - a)^2 + y^2 = a^2$ which has its centre at $(a, 0)$ and radius 'a'.

Equation of parabola is $y^2 = 4ax$, the right handed parabola. The area inside the circle and outside the parabola is shown shown by shaded region in the Fig. 3.59.

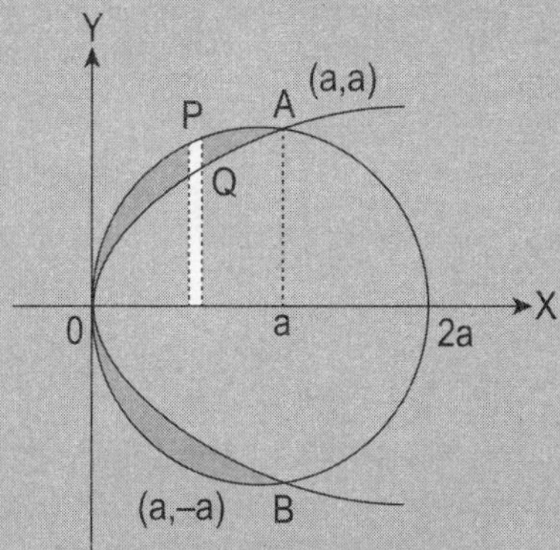

FIGURE 3.59

For points of intersections, solving $x^2 + y^2 - 2ax = 0$ and $y^2 = ax$ simultaneously we get, $x^2 - ax = 0$

$\Rightarrow x = 0, x = a$

Now, $x = 0$

$\Rightarrow y = 0$ and $x = a$

$\Rightarrow y = \pm a$

Therefore, $O(0, 0)$; $A(a, a)$ and $B(a, -a)$ are points of intersections.

By symmetry about x-axis

Required area = 2 area $OQAPO = 2\int_0^a (y_P - y_Q)dx$

$$= 2\int_0^a \left(\sqrt{a^2-(x-a)^2} - \sqrt{a}\sqrt{x}\right)dx$$

$$= 2\left\{\frac{1}{2}\left[(x-a)\sqrt{a^2-(x-a)^2} + a^2\sin^{-1}\frac{x-a}{a}\right] - \sqrt{a}.\frac{2}{3}x^{3/2}\right\}_0^a$$

$$= \{a^2(0-\sin^{-1}(-1)\} - \frac{4}{3}\sqrt{a}\{a^{3/2}-0\} = \frac{\pi a^2}{2} - \frac{4}{3}a^2$$

$$= \left(\frac{\pi}{2} - \frac{4}{3}\right)a^2 \text{ square units}$$

ILLUSTRATION 37: Find the area common to the curve $y = \sqrt{9-x^2}$ and $x^2 + y^2 = 6x$.

SOLUTION: Given equations are $y = \sqrt{9-x^2}$ which represents upper half of circle $x^2 + y^2 = 9$ ...(i)

and $x^2 - 6x + y^2 = 0$ ....(ii)

Which represent circle with centre at (3, 0) and radius 3. We are to find common region between two as shown by shaded region in the Fig. 3.60.

For point of intersection, we get on solving, $x = 3/2$;
$y^2 = 9 - 9/4 = 27/4$

$\Rightarrow \quad y = \dfrac{3\sqrt{3}}{2}$, i.e., $P\left(\dfrac{3}{2}, \dfrac{3\sqrt{3}}{2}\right)$

$\therefore \quad A = 2\int_{3/2}^{3} \sqrt{9-x^2}\, dx$

($\because$ Both circles have same radius 3, $x = \dfrac{3}{2}$ is the line of symmetry for two circles).

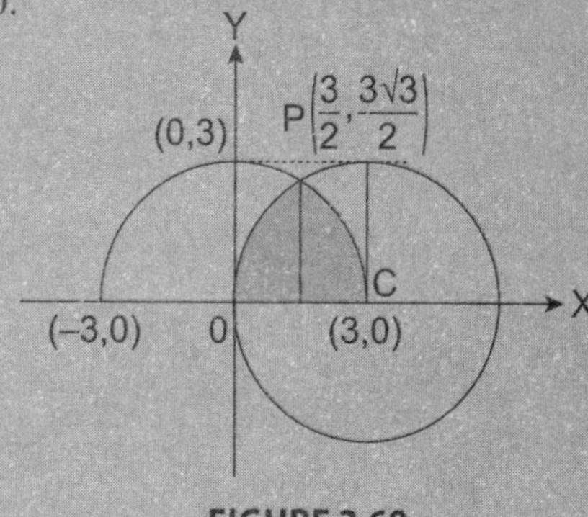

FIGURE 3.60

$$= \left[\frac{x\sqrt{9-x^2}}{2} + \frac{9}{2}\sin^{-1}\left(\frac{x}{3}\right)\right]_{3/2}^{3} = \left[\frac{9\pi}{2} - \frac{3}{2}\sqrt{9-\frac{9}{4}} - 9.\frac{\pi}{6}\right] = \left(3\pi - \frac{9\sqrt{3}}{4}\right) \text{ square units.}$$

ILLUSTRATION 38: Find the area enclosed by the curve $y = \sqrt{x}$ and $x = -\sqrt{y}$, the circle $x^2 + y^2 = 2$ above the x-axis.

SOLUTION: $x = -\sqrt{y}$ represents the branch of parabola $x^2 = y$ on the left of y-axis which intersects the given circle $x^2 + y^2 = 2$, where $x < 0$, $y > 0$ and $y^2 + y = 2$

$\Rightarrow$ $x = -1$, $y = 1$, i.e., at $A(-1, 1)$. Further $y = \sqrt{x}$ represents parabola $y^2 = x$, above x-axis which intersects the circle $x^2 + y^2 = 2$, where $x, y > 0$ and $x^2 + x = 2$

$\Rightarrow$ $x = 1, y = 1$, i.e., at $B(1, 1)$ geometrically shown in Fig. 3.61.

Thus, the required area shown by shaded region is $\int_{-1}^{0}\left(\sqrt{2-x^2} - x^2\right)dx + \int_{0}^{1}\left(\sqrt{2-x^2} - \sqrt{x}\right)dx$

$\Rightarrow \quad 2\int_{0}^{1}\sqrt{2-x^2}\,dx - \dfrac{1}{3}(0+1) - \dfrac{2}{3}(1)$

$\Rightarrow \quad \left|x\sqrt{2-x^2} + 2\sin^{-1}\left(\dfrac{x}{\sqrt{2}}\right)\right|_{0}^{1} - 1$

$\Rightarrow \quad 1 + \dfrac{\pi}{2} - 1 = \dfrac{\pi}{2}$ square units

Note that the area is equal to the sector AOB with central angle 90^0

= 1/4 (the area of the circle)

$= \dfrac{1}{4}\pi(2) = \dfrac{\pi}{2}$ square units.

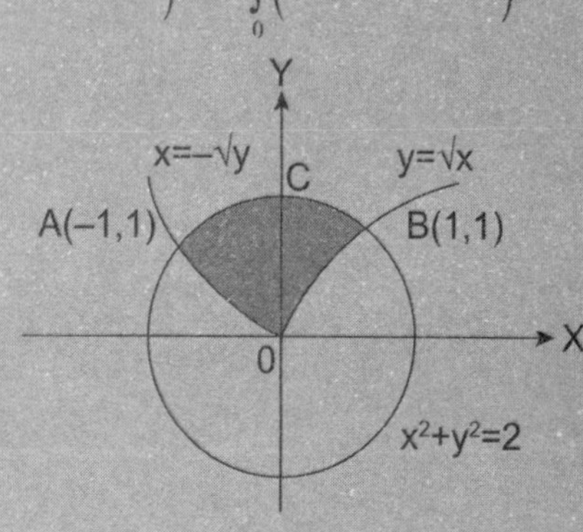

FIGURE 3.61

Parabola with Parabola

The following illustration explains the method to find the area enclosed between two parabolas.

ILLUSTRATION 39: If the area enclosed by the parabolas $y = a^2 - x^2$ and $y = x^2$ is $18\sqrt{2}$ sq. units, find the value of 'a'.

SOLUTION: The point of intersection of $y = x^2$ and $y = a^2 - x^2$ is given by $a^2 - x^2 = x^2$

$\Rightarrow \quad x = \pm\dfrac{a}{\sqrt{2}}$

Now, given area $OABC = 18\sqrt{2}$

$$\Rightarrow \quad 2\int_0^{\frac{a}{\sqrt{2}}} (y_1 - y_2)dx = 18\sqrt{2}$$

$$\Rightarrow \quad 2\int_0^{\frac{a}{\sqrt{2}}} (a^2 - x^2 - x^2)dx = 18\sqrt{2}$$

$$\Rightarrow \quad 2\int_0^{\frac{a}{\sqrt{2}}} (a^2 - 2x^2)dx = 18\sqrt{2} \Rightarrow 2\left[a^2x - \frac{2x^3}{3}\right]_0^{\frac{a}{\sqrt{2}}} = 18\sqrt{2}$$

$$\Rightarrow \quad \left[\frac{a^3}{\sqrt{2}} - \frac{2}{3}\cdot\frac{a^3}{2\sqrt{2}}\right] = 9\sqrt{2} \quad \Rightarrow \frac{a^3}{\sqrt{2}}\left(1 - \frac{1}{3}\right) = 9\sqrt{2} \quad \Rightarrow a = 3$$

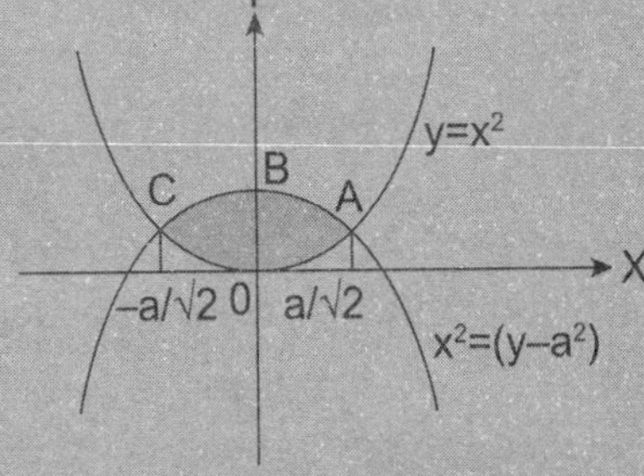

FIGURE 3.62

ILLUSTRATION 40: The line $y = mx$ bisects the area enclosed by the lines $x = 0$, $y = 0$, $x = 3/2$ and the curve $y = 1 + 4x - x^2$. Find the value of m, given that the line $y = mx$ intersects the line $x = \frac{3}{2}$ inside the parabola.

SOLUTION: Given $y = 1 + 4x - x^2$.

$\Rightarrow$ $y - 5 = -(x - 2)^2$ which is a downwards parabola with its vertex at (2, 5).

The region bounded by curve $y = 1 + 4x - x^2$, straight line $x = \frac{3}{2}$ and x-axis, y-axis is shown in Fig. 3.63.

$\therefore$ Area bounded by $x = 0, y = 0, x = 3/2$ and $y = 1 + 4x - x^2$ is given by

$$A = \int_0^{3/2} (-x^2 + 4x + 1)\,dx = \left[\frac{-x^3}{3} + 2x^2 + x\right]_0^{3/2}$$

$$= \left[\frac{-9}{8} + \frac{9}{2} + \frac{3}{2}\right] = \frac{39}{8}$$

Since, it is given that straight line $y = mx$ intersects the line $x = \frac{3}{2}$ inside the parabola and bisects the area $A = \frac{39}{8}$

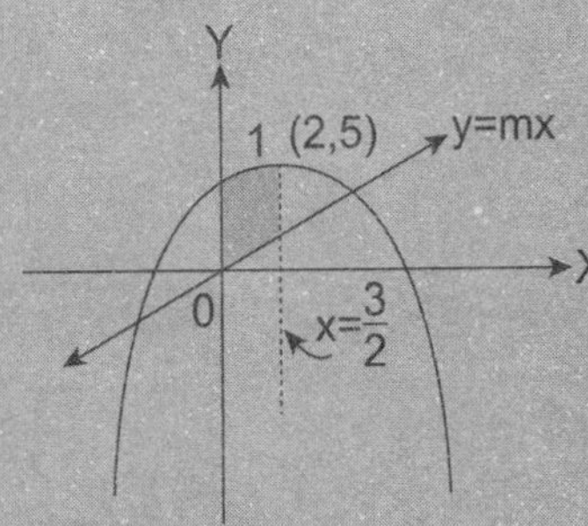

FIGURE 3.63

$\Rightarrow$ The area of the region bounded by $y = mx$, $y = 0$ and $x = 3/2$ must be $\frac{39}{16}\left(= \frac{A}{2}\right)$

$$\Rightarrow \quad \frac{1}{2} \times \frac{3}{2} \times \frac{3m}{2} = \frac{39}{16} \qquad \Rightarrow \quad m = \frac{13}{6}$$

ILLUSTRATION 41: Show that the area cut off from a parabola by any of its double ordinate is two-third of the corresponding rectangle contained by the double ordinate and its distance from the vertex.

SOLUTION: Let us consider the parabola be $y^2 = 4ax$ and BC be any double ordinates with end points $B\left(x_0, -\sqrt{4ax_0}\right)$ and $C\left(x_0, \sqrt{4ax_0}\right)$ as shown in Fig. 3.64.

We need to prove that the area shown by the region $OBECO$ is two-third of the area of rectangle $ABCD$. Let $OE = x_0$

Hence area of shaded region $= A_1 = 2\int_0^{x_0} \sqrt{4ax}\,dx = 4\sqrt{a}\left[\frac{x^{3/2}}{3/2}\right]_0^{x_0}$

$$= \frac{8\sqrt{a}\, x_0^{3/2}}{3}$$

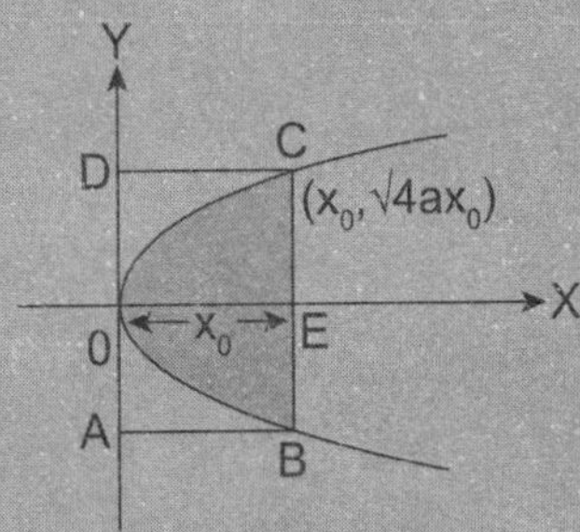

FIGURE 3.64

Now area of rectangle $ABCD = A_2 = AB \times BC$

$$= x_0 \times 2\sqrt{4ax_0} = 4\sqrt{a}\, x_0^{3/2}$$

Clearly $\dfrac{A_1}{A_2} = \dfrac{2}{3}$

ILLUSTRATION 42: Find the area of the smaller region bounded by the circle $x^2 + y^2 = 1$ and the line $|y| = x + 1$.

SOLUTION: Graph of $|y| = x + 1$ can be obtained by replacing the graph of $y = (x + 1)$ below x-axis by the reflection of line $y = (x + 1)$ above x-axis on x-axis.

At the point of intersection of $y = x + 1$ and $x^2 + y^2 = 1$

$\Rightarrow x^2 + (x + 1)^2 = 1$

$\Rightarrow x^2 + x^2 + 2x + 1 = 1$

$\Rightarrow 2x^2 + 2x = 0$

$\Rightarrow 2x\,(x + 1) = 0$

$\Rightarrow x = 0$ or $x = -1$

Similarly the line $y = -(x + 1)$ intersect the circle $x^2 + y^2 = 1$ at $x = 0$ and $x = -1$ as shown in Fig. 3.65.

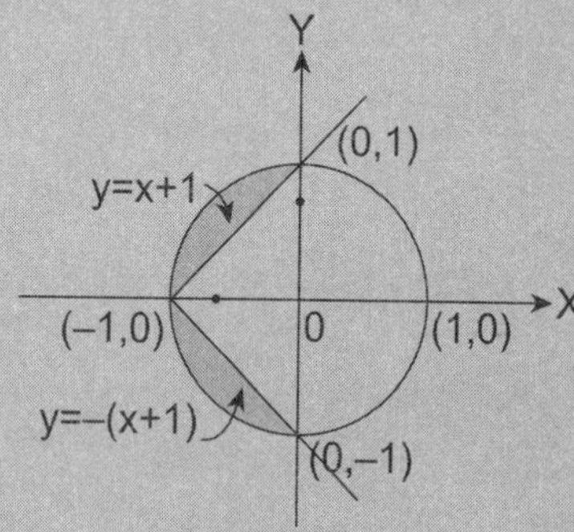

FIGURE 3.65

$$\therefore \text{ Required area} = 2\int_{-1}^{0}\left[y_{\text{circle (upper half)}} - y_{\text{st. line } (y\ge 0)}\right]dx$$

$$= 2\int_{-1}^{0}\left[\sqrt{1-x^2} - (x+1)\right]dx$$

$$= 2\left[\frac{x\sqrt{1-x^2}}{2} + \frac{1}{2}\sin^{-1}\left(\frac{x}{1}\right) - \frac{x^2}{2} - x\right]_{-1}^{0} = 2\left[0 - \left(\frac{1}{2}\left(-\frac{\pi}{2}\right) - \frac{1}{2} + 1\right)\right]$$

$$= 2\left[-\left(\frac{-\pi}{4} + \frac{1}{2}\right)\right] = 2\left[\frac{\pi}{4} - \frac{1}{2}\right] = \left(\frac{\pi}{2} - 1\right) \text{ square units.}$$

ILLUSTRATION 43: Find the area bounded by the curve $x = \cos^{-1}y$ and the line $|x| = 1$

SOLUTION: ***Case (i):*** If $x = \cos^{-1}y$ is treated as a function, $x = \cos^{-1}y$ is defined for $y \in [-1, 1]$ and range of $x = [0, \pi]$

Thus, $x = \cos^{-1}y$ can be drawn with its domain $[-1, 1]$ along y-axis and range $[0, \pi]$ along x-axis.

or $y = \cos x$ with principle domain $[0, \pi]$ and range $[-1, 1]$ as shown in the Fig. 3.66.

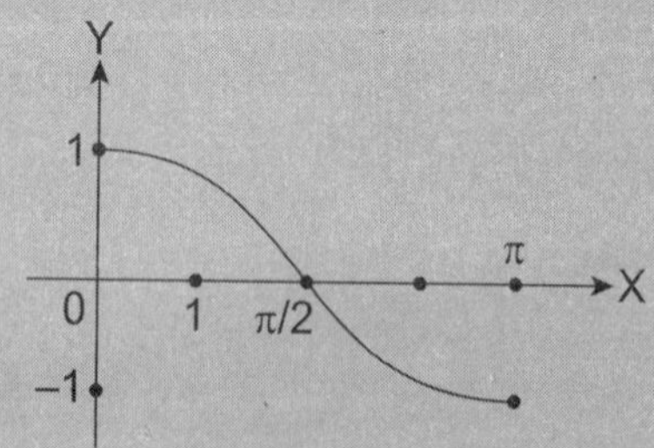

FIGURE 3.66

We are to find the area of shaded region $R = \int_0^1 \left(y_{\widehat{AB}}\right)dx = \widehat{AB}$

= concave from A to B cosine function.

$$= \int_0^1 (\cos x)\,dx = (\sin x)_0^1 = \sin 1$$

Case (ii): If $x = \cos^{-1}y$ is treated as a relation, i.e., it can be one-many.

So $x = \cos^{-1}y$ is defined for $y \in [-1, 1]$ along y-axis but range $= \mathbb{R}$. Equivalently we can consider the graph of $y = \cos x$ with domain $\mathbb{R}$ along x-axis and range $= [-1, 1]$ along y-axis as shown in Fig. 3.67.

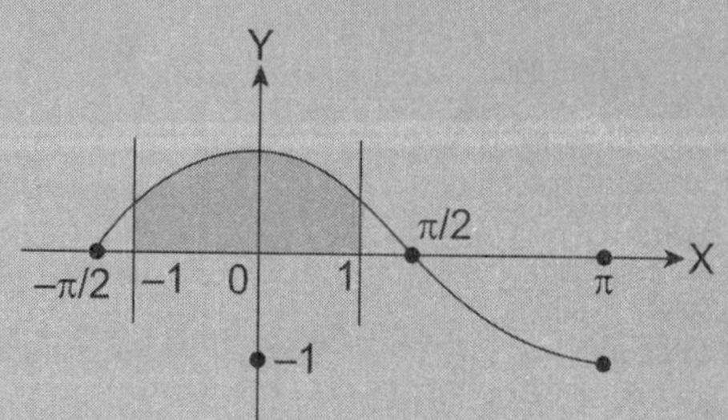

FIGURE 3.67

$\therefore$ The required area is the shaded region

$= 2\int_0^1 \cos x\, dx = 2\sin 1$ square units.

ILLUSTRATION 44: Find between two parabolas the area of the figure bounded by $y^2 + 8x = 16$ and $y^2 = 24x + 48$.

SOLUTION: Given equations are $y^2 = -8x + 16$

or $y^2 = -8(x - 2)$ ...(1)

and $y^2 = 24x + 48$

or $y^2 = 24(x + 2)$ ...(2)

Therefore, (1) and (2) represent left-handed and right-handed parabola respectively with their vertices at (2, 0) and (–2, 0) as shown in Fig. 3.68.

At the point of intersection of two curves $-8x + 16 = 24x + 48$

$\Rightarrow 32x = -32 \qquad \Rightarrow x = -1$

$\therefore$ The required area $= 2\left[\int_{-2}^{-1} y_{\widehat{AP}}\, dx + \int_{-1}^{2} y_{\widehat{BP}}\, dx\right]$

$= 2\left[\int_{-2}^{-1}\sqrt{24x+48}\, dx + \int_{-1}^{2}\sqrt{16-8x}\, dx\right]$

$= 2\left[\sqrt{24}\int_{-2}^{-1}\sqrt{x+2}\, dx + \sqrt{8}\int_{-1}^{2}\sqrt{2-x}\, dx\right]$

$= 2\left[\sqrt{24}\left\{\frac{2}{3}(x+2)^{3/2}\right\}_{-2}^{-1} + \sqrt{8}\left\{\frac{2}{3}\frac{(2-x)^{3/2}}{(-1)}\right\}_{-1}^{2}\right]$

$= 2\left[\frac{2\sqrt{24}}{3}[1] - \frac{2\sqrt{8}}{3}\left[0-3\sqrt{3}\right]\right] = 2\left[\frac{2\sqrt{24}}{3} + 2\sqrt{24}\right] = 2\left[\left(2\sqrt{24}\right).\left(\frac{4}{3}\right)\right]$

$= \frac{16\sqrt{24}}{3} = \frac{16\times 2\sqrt{6}}{3} = \frac{32\sqrt{6}}{3}$ square units.

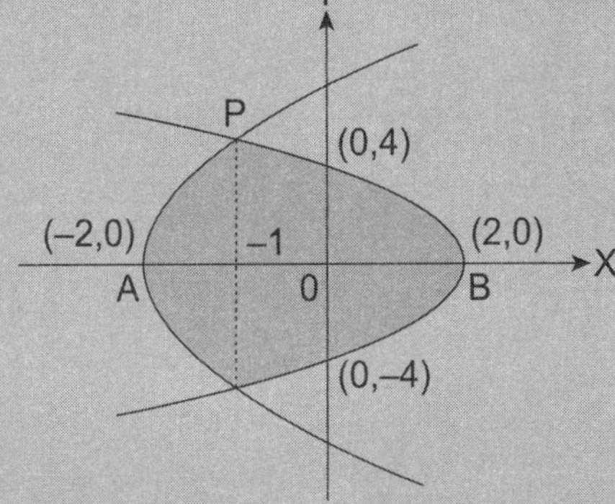

FIGURE 3.68

ILLUSTRATION 45: Find the area of the region bounded by the curve $y = xe^x$, $y = e^x$ and the line $x = \pm 1$ and y-axis.

SOLUTION: $f(x) = xe^x = 0$

$\Rightarrow x = 0$ $(\because e^x > 0)$

i.e., the function $y = xe^x$ intersects the x-axis at origin (0, 0)

Now, $f'(x) = xe^x + e^x = (1 + x)\, e^x$

$\therefore f'(x) > 0$ for $x > -1$ and $f'(x) < 0$ for $x < -1$

$\Rightarrow f(x)$ is decreasing function for $x < -1$ and is increasing for $x > -1$

and $f(x)$ has a stationary point at $x = -1$

$f''(x) = xe^x + 2e^x = (x + 2)\, e^x >$a 0 for $x > -2$ and < 0 for $x < -2$

Thus, the graph of $y = xe^x$ and $y = e^x$ drawn on same x - y plane is as shown in Fig. 3.69.

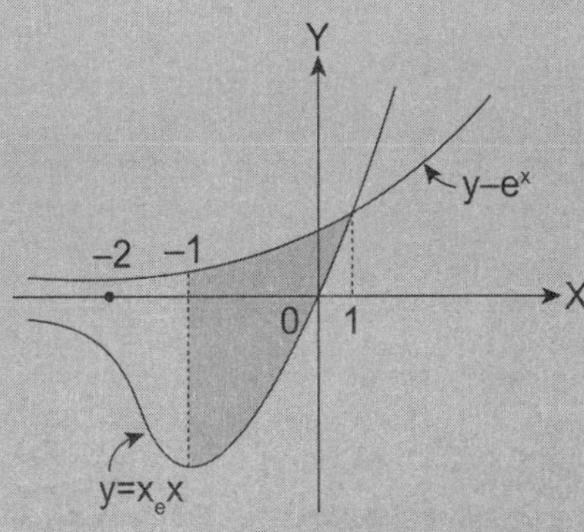

FIGURE 3.69

We are to find the shaded area $= \int_{-1}^{1}\left(y_{\text{upper}} - y_{\text{lower}}\right) dx$

$$= \int_{-1}^{1}(e^x - xe^x)dx = |e^x|_{-1}^{1} - \left[|xe^x|_{-1}^{1} - \int_{-1}^{1} 1.e^x\,dx\right] = (e-e^{-1}) - \left[(e+e^{-1})-(e-e^{-1})\right]$$

$$= e - 3e^{-1} = e - \frac{3}{e}.$$

ILLUSTRATION 46: Find the area enclosed between the curves $y = \ln(x + e)$; $x = \ln(1/y)$ and x-axis

SOLUTION: Given functions are $y = \ln(x + e)$ and $x = \ln\left(\frac{1}{y}\right) = -\ln y$

$\Rightarrow \ln y = -x$

$\Rightarrow y = e^{-x}; x > -e, y > 0$

$\therefore$ The required area is shaded region

$$= \int_{1-e}^{0} \ln(x+e)\,dx + \int_{0}^{\infty} e^{-x}\,dx$$

$$= |x\ln(x+e)|_{1-e}^{0} - \int_{1-e}^{0}\frac{x}{x+e}dx + \left[\frac{e^{-x}}{-1}\right]_0^{\infty}$$

$$= -\int_{1-e}^{0}\left(1 - \frac{e}{x+e}\right)dx + 1$$

$$= -[x]_{1-e}^{0} + e|\ln(x+e)|_{1-e}^{0} + 1 = 0 - (1-e) + e[\ln(0+e) - \ln(1)] + 1$$

$$= 1 - e + e(1 - 0) + 1 = 1 - e + e + 1 = 2 \text{ square units.}$$

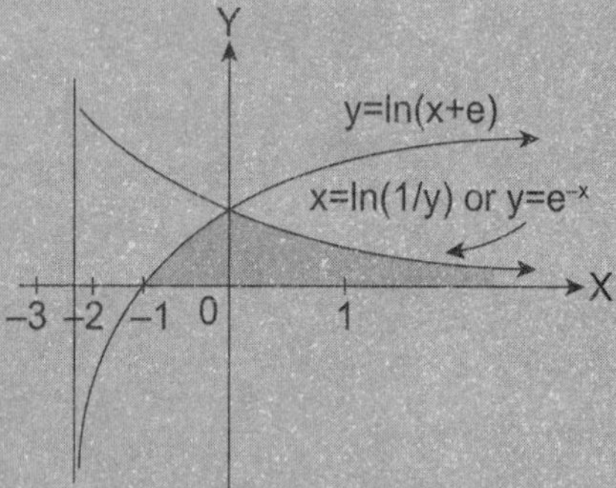

FIGURE 3.70

ILLUSTRATION 47: Compute the area of the curvilinear triangle bounded by the y-axis and the curve, $y = \tan x$ and $y = (2/3)\cos x$.

SOLUTION: Given curve is

$y = \tan x$ ...(i)

$y = \frac{2}{3}\cos x$ ...(ii)

The points of intersection of (i) and (ii) are given for $\tan x = \frac{2}{3}\cos x$

$\Rightarrow \sin x = \frac{2}{3}\cos^2 x$

$\Rightarrow (\sin x + 2)(2\sin x - 1) = 0$

$\Rightarrow \sin x = \frac{1}{2}$ as $\sin x \neq -2$

$\Rightarrow x = \frac{\pi}{6}$ (as for bounded region $x \in \left(-\frac{\pi}{2}, \frac{\pi}{2}\right)$)

so required area $= \int_{0}^{\pi/6}(y_1 - y_2)dx$

$$= \int_0^{\pi/6}\left(\frac{2}{3}\cos x - \tan x\right)dx = \left(\frac{2}{3}\sin x - \ln\sec x\right)_0^{\pi/6}$$

$$= \left[\frac{2}{3}\left(\frac{1}{2} - 0\right) - \ln\frac{2}{\sqrt{3}}\right] = \frac{1}{3} + \ln\frac{\sqrt{3}}{2}$$

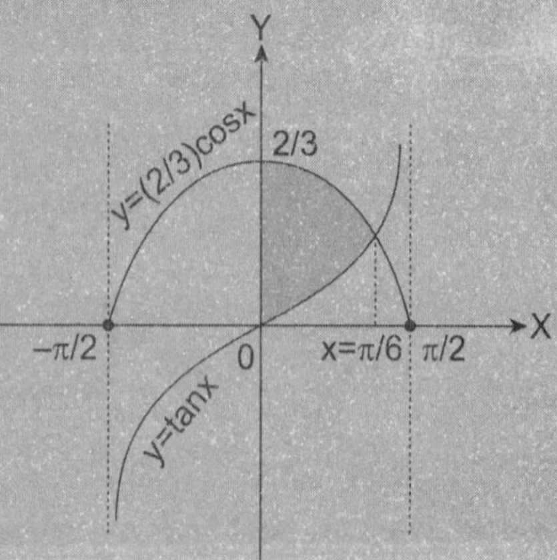

FIGURE 3.71

ILLUSTRATION 48: Find the area bounded by the curve $y = \min\{\sin^2 x, \cos^2 x\}$ and x-axis between the ordinates $x = 0$ and $x = \frac{5\pi}{4}$.

SOLUTION: The graph of $\sin^2 x$ and $\cos^2 x$ for $x \in \left[0, \frac{5\pi}{4}\right]$ is as shown in Fig. 3.69.

We are to find the area bounded by minimum of minimum of $\sin^2 x$ and $\cos^2 x$ and y-axis. The required area is as shown by shaded region in the Fig. 3.72.

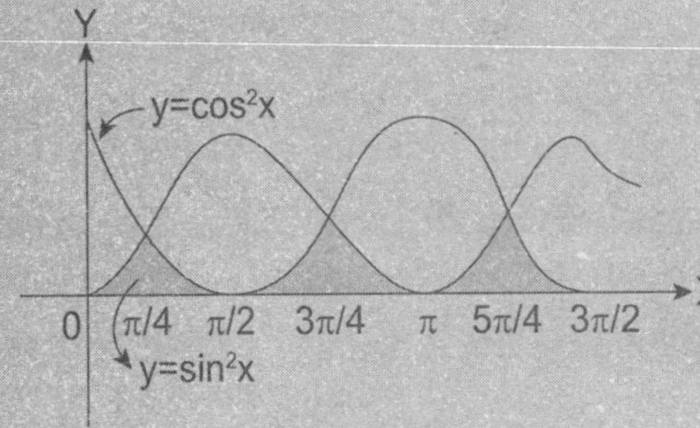

FIGURE 3.72

$\therefore$ Required area = A

$$= \int_0^{\pi/4} \sin^2 x\,dx + \int_{\pi/4}^{3\pi/4} \cos^2 x\,dx + \int_{3\pi/4}^{5\pi/4} \sin^2 x\,dx$$

$$= \frac{1}{2}\left[x - \frac{\sin 2x}{2}\right]_0^{\frac{\pi}{4}} + \frac{1}{2}\left[x + \frac{\sin 2x}{2}\right]_{\frac{\pi}{4}}^{\frac{3\pi}{4}} + \frac{1}{2}\left[x - \frac{\sin 2x}{2}\right]_{\frac{3\pi}{4}}^{\frac{5\pi}{4}}$$

$$= \frac{1}{2}\left[\frac{\pi}{4} - \frac{1}{2}\right] + \frac{1}{2}\left[\left(\frac{3\pi}{4} - \frac{1}{2}\right) - \left(\frac{\pi}{4} + \frac{1}{2}\right)\right] + \frac{1}{2}\left[\left(\frac{5\pi}{4} - \frac{1}{2}\right) - \left(\frac{3\pi}{4} + \frac{1}{2}\right)\right]$$

$$= \frac{\pi}{8} - \frac{1}{4} + \frac{3\pi}{8} - \frac{1}{4} - \frac{\pi}{8} - \frac{1}{4} + \frac{5\pi}{8} - \frac{1}{4} - \frac{3\pi}{8} - \frac{1}{4} = \frac{5\pi}{8} - \frac{5}{4} = \frac{5}{8}(\pi - 2)$$

ILLUSTRATION 49: Find the area enclosed by the curves $y = \cos x$, $y = 1 + \sin 2x$ and $x = \frac{3\pi}{2}$

SOLUTION: Required area is given by

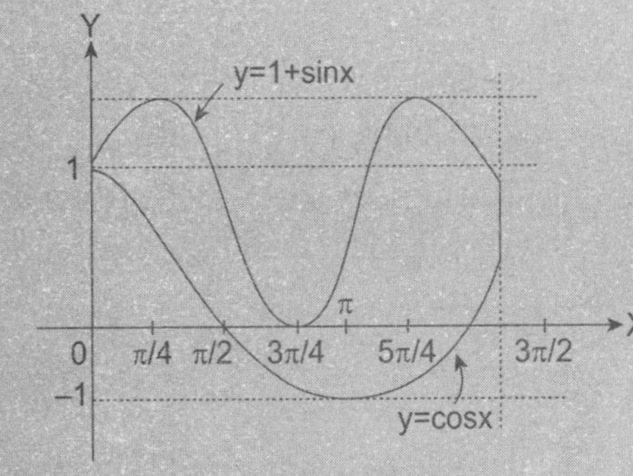

FIGURE 3.73

$$A = \int_0^{3\pi/2} (1 + \sin 2x - \cos x)\,dx;$$

$$= \left(x - \frac{1}{2}\cos 2x - \sin x\right)_0^{\frac{3\pi}{2}}$$

$$= \left(\frac{3\pi}{2} + \frac{1}{2} + 1\right) - \left(0 - \frac{1}{2}\right)$$

$$= 2 + \frac{3\pi}{2} \text{ square units.}$$

TEXTUAL EXERCISE–2: (SUBJECTIVE)

1. Find the area of region bounded by x-axis and curve defined by $y = \tan x, -\frac{\pi}{3} \le x \le \frac{\pi}{3}$; $y = \cot x, \frac{\pi}{6} \le x \le \frac{\pi}{2}$

2. Find the area enclosed by the
(a) curve $|x| + |y| = 1$.
(b) curves $x + y = 1$, $x + 3y = 6$, $y = x - 1$ and $y = x + 1$.

3. Sketch the region $|x + 1| + |y + 1| = 2$ and also evaluate the area bounded.

4. Find the area enclosed by x-axis and $|x| + y = 1$

5. Find the area enclosed by $y = \ln x$, $y = \ln |x|$, $y = |\ln x|$, $y = |\ln |x||$.

6. (a) Find the area enclosed by the parabolas $5x^2 - y = 0$ and $2x^2 - y + 9 = 0$.
(b) Find the area enclosed between $y = x(1 - x)$ and $y = 2^x$ between $x = 0$, $x = 1$.

7. Find the area of region bounded by the curves defined by $x^2 + y^2 = 4$, $x^2 = -\sqrt{2}\,y$ and $y = x$ lying below the line $y = x$ and x-axis.

8. Find the area bounded by the curves $x = y^2$ and $x = 3 - 2y^2$.

9. The parabola $y^2 = 2x$ divides the circle $x^2 + y^2 = 8$ in two parts. Find the ratio of the areas of the both parts.

10. Find the area bounded by the curves $x^2 + y^2 = 25$ and $4y = |4 - x^2|$ and $x = 0$ above the x-axis.

11. Find the area of region bounded by $y = 2^x$, $y = 2x - x^2$ between the ordinates $x = 0$ and $x = 2$.

12. Sketch the curve $x = 1/2$, $x = 2$, $y = ln x$ and $y = 2^x$ and find the area of region bounded by them.

13. Find area included between the parabola $y^2 = 4a(x + a)$, $y^2 = 4b(b - x)$ is

14. Find the area of region represented by $|x - y| \le 2$ and $x^2 + y^2 - 4 \le 0$.

15. Consider a square with vertices (1, 1), (–1, 1), (–1, –1) and (1, –1). Let S be region consisting of all points inside square which are nearer to origin than to any edge. Sketch the region S and find its area.

16. Sketch the region bounded by the curves $y = x^2$ and $y = \dfrac{2}{1+x^2}$. Find this area. 3

17. Calculate the area enclosed between $y = 2 - |2 - x|$ and $y = 3/|x|$

18. Find the area of region bonded by curves $y = \log_e x$ and $y = \sin^4 \pi x$ and y-axis ($x = 0$).

19. Calculate the area enclosed between the curves $y = ln\, x$ and $y = (\ln x)^2$.

20. Find the area bounded by the curves $y = ex \log x$ and $y = \dfrac{\log x}{ex}$

21. Find the area of figure bounded by the parabola $(y - 2)^2 = x - 1$ and its tangent at the point with ordinate 3 and x-axis.

22. Find the area of the region bounded by the curve c: $y = \tan x$, tangent drawn to c at $x = \pi/4$ and the positive x-axis, (above the x-axis).

23. Find area of common region represented by $x^2 + y^2 - 4 \le 0$, $y \ge \sin\left(\dfrac{\pi x}{4}\right)$.

24. If $ABCD$ is square of side '$2a$' circles of radius $2a$ are drawn with centres A, B, C, D. Find the common area.

25. Sketch the region between the curves $x^2 + y^2 = a^2$ and $\sqrt{|x|} + \sqrt{|y|} = \sqrt{a}\ (a > 0)$; find its area.

26. Find the area included between the parabola $y = \dfrac{x^2}{4a}$ and the curve $y = \dfrac{8x^3}{(x^2 + 4a^2)}$.

27. Find the total area bounded by the curves $y = \cos x - \cos^2 x$ and $y = x^2\left(x^2 - \dfrac{\pi^2}{4}\right)$.

28. A normal to the curve $x^2 + kx - y + 2 = 0$ at the point with abscissa 1, is parallel to the line $y = x$. Find the area bounded by the curve, this normal and x-axis lying in the first quadrant.

29. Find the area enclosed by the circle $x^2 + y^2 = 4$, parabola $y = x^2 + x + 1$, the curve $y = \left[\sin^2 \dfrac{x}{4} + \cos \dfrac{x}{4}\right]$ and the x-axis (where [.] denotes the greater integer function).

30. If the area bounded by x-axis the curve $y = f(x)$ and the line $x = a$, $x = b$ is equal to $\sqrt{b^2 - a^2}\ \forall\ a < b$; where a is given positive real number. Find the function $f(x)$.

31. Show that the area enclosed between; $y = e^{-\alpha x} \sin \beta x$ and x-axis can be expressed as the sum of areas S_0, S_1, S_2,....∞ which forms an infinite GP and find its common ratio.

32. Let $O(0, 0)$, $A(2, 0)$ and $B\left(1, \dfrac{1}{\sqrt{3}}\right)$ be the vertices of a triangle. Let R be the region consisting of all those points P inside ΔOAB which satisfy $d(P, OA) \le$ min. $\{d(P,OB), d(P,AB)\}$, (where 'd' denotes the distance from the point to the corresponding line). Sketch the region R and find its area.

33. Let A_n the be area bounded by $y = \tan^n x$, $x = \pi/4$, $y = 0$. Prove that $\forall\ n \ge 2$.

(i) $A_n + A_{n-2} = \dfrac{1}{n-1}$ (ii) $\dfrac{1}{2(n+1)} < A_n < \dfrac{1}{2(n-1)}$

34. Let C_1 and C_2 be the graphs of the function $y = x^2$ and $y = 2x$, $0 \le x \le 1$ respectively. Let C_3 be the graph of a function $y = f(x)$; $0 \le x \le 1$, $f(0) = 0$. For a point P on C_1, let the lines through P parallel to the axes, meets C_2 and C_3 at Q and R respectively (see figure). If for every position of P on (C_1), the areas of the shaded region OPQ and ORP are equal, determine the function $f(x)$.

35. If area bounded by the line $y = x$, curve $y = f(x)$, ($f(x) > x$ for all $x > 1$) and the lines $x = 1$, $x = t$ is $(t + \sqrt{1+t^2}) - (1 + \sqrt{2})$ for all $t > 1$, then find the function $f(x)$?

36. Calculate the whole area contained between the curve $y^2(a - x) = x^2(a + x)$ and the line $x = a\ (a > 0)$.

37. Let $f(x)=\begin{cases}-2, -3\le x\le 0\\ x-2, 0<x\le 3\end{cases}$; where g(x) = min {$f(|x|$ + $|f(x)|, f(|x| - |f(x)|\}$. Find the area bounded by the curve g(x) and the x-axis between the ordinates at x = 3 and x = –3.

38. For any real t, $x=2+\frac{e^t+e^{-t}}{2}$, $y=2+\frac{e^t-e^{-t}}{2}$ is a point on the hyperbola $x^2 - y^2 - 4x + 4y - 1 = 0$. Find the area bounded by the hyperbola and the lines joining the centre to the points corresponding to t_1 and $-t_1$.

39. If $(x - y) f(x + y) - (x + y) f(x - y) = 4xy(x^2 - y^2)$, then find the area common to both the curves $\{f(y)\}^{2/3} + \{f(x)\}^{1/3} = 0$ and $\{f(y)\}^{2/3} + \{f(x)\}^{2/3} = 12$.

40. Find the area of region enclosed by; $2x^2 + 6xy + 5y^2 = 1$.

Answer Keys

1. 2ln 2 **2.** (a) 2 sq. units (b) 2 sq. units **3.** 8 sq. units **4.** 1 sq. unit
5. 4 sq. units **6.** (a) $12\sqrt{3}$ sq. units (b) $\log_2 e - 1/6$ **7.** (π+ 1/3) **8.** 4 sq. units
9. $\frac{2+3\pi}{9\pi-2}$ **10.** $25\sin^{-1}(4/5) + 4$ **11.** $\frac{3}{\ln 2}-\frac{4}{3}$ **12.** $\frac{4-\sqrt{2}}{\log 2}-\frac{5}{2}\ln 2+\frac{3}{2}$
13. $\frac{8}{3}\sqrt{ab}(a+b)$ sq. units **14.** $2\pi + 4$ sq. units **15.** $\frac{4}{3}(4\sqrt{2}-5)$
16. $2\left(\frac{\pi}{2}-\frac{1}{3}\right)$ **17.** $(2-3\ln\sqrt{3})$ **18.** 11/8 sq. units **19.** (3 – e) sq. units
20. $\frac{e^2-5}{4e}$ **21.** 9 sq. units **22.** $\frac{1}{2}\left(\log 2-\frac{1}{2}\right)$ **23.** 2π sq. units
24. $4a^2\left[1+\frac{\pi}{3}-\sqrt{3}\right]$ sq. units **25.** $\left(\pi-\frac{2}{3}\right)a^2$ **26.** $\frac{2}{3}a^2(3\pi-2)$ **27.** $\left(2-\frac{\pi}{2}+\frac{\pi^5}{120}\right)$ sq. units
28. 7/6 sq. units **29.** $\left(\frac{2\pi}{3}+\sqrt{3}-\frac{1}{6}\right)$ sq. units **30.** $\pm\frac{x}{\sqrt{x^2-a^2}}$ **31.** $e^{-\frac{\pi\alpha}{\beta}}$
32. (2 – $\sqrt{3}$) sq. units **34.** $x^3 - x^2$ **35.** $1+x+\frac{x}{\sqrt{1+x^2}}$ **36.** $2a^2\left(1+\frac{\pi}{4}\right)$
37. $\frac{23}{2}$ sq. units **38.** t_1 **39.** $2\pi - 3\sqrt{3}$ **40.** π sq. units

TEXTUAL EXERCISE–2: (OBJECTIVE)

1. If the area bounded by the curves $y^2 = 4ax$ and $y = mx$ is $\frac{a^2}{3}$, then the value of m is
(a) 2 (b) –2
(c) 1/2 (d) None of these

2. For $0 \le x \le \pi$ the area bounded by $y = x$ and $y = x + \sin x$, is
(a) 2 (b) 4
(c) 2π (d) 4π

3. The area of the triangle formed by the tangent to the hyperbola $xy = a^2$ and co-ordinate axes is
(a) a^2 (b) $2a^2$
(c) $3a^2$ (d) $4a^2$

4. The area bounded by the curve $y^2 = 4x$ and the circle $x^2 + y^2 - 2x - 3 = 0$ is equal to
(a) $2\pi+\frac{8}{3}$ (b) $4\pi+\frac{8}{3}$
(c) $\pi+\frac{8}{3}$ (d) $\pi-\frac{8}{3}$

5. The ratio of the areas between the curves $y = \cos x$ and $y = \cos 2x$ and x-axis from $x = 0$ to $x=\frac{\pi}{3}$ is:
(a) 1 : 3 (b) 2 : 1
(c) $\sqrt{3}:1$ (d) None of these

6. The area enclosed between the parabolas $y^2 = 4ax$ and $x^2 = 4by$ is:

(a) $\frac{8}{3}ab$ (b) $\frac{16}{3}ab$

(c) $\frac{4}{3}ab$ (d) None of these

7. The area of the region in first quadrant bounded by the curve $y = x^3$ and $y = \sqrt{x}$, is

(a) 12/5 (b) 5/12

(c) 5/3 (d) 3/5

8. The area of the region bounded by the curve $y = x^2 - 2x$ and $y = x$, is

(a) 9/2 (b) 7/2

(c) 5/2 (d) None of these

9. The area of the region bounded by the curve $y = x$ and $y = 2 - (x - 2)^2$, is

(a) 1/3 (b) 1/6

(c) 1/9 (d) None of these

10. The ratio in which the area bounded by the curves $y^2= 12x$ and $x^2 = 12y$ is divided by the line $x = 3$, is

(a) 15 : 16 (b) 15 : 49

(c) 1 : 2 (d) None of these

11. The area of figure bounded by $y^2 + 8x = 16$ and $|y| = 24x + 48$, is

(a) $32\sqrt{6}$ (b) $16\sqrt{6}/3$

(c) $8\sqrt{6}$ (d) $32\sqrt{6}/3$

12. The area of the smaller region bounded by the circle $x^2 + y^2 = 1$ and the lines $|y| = x + 1$ is

(a) $\frac{\pi}{4}-\frac{1}{2}$ (b) $\frac{\pi}{2}-1$

(c) $\frac{\pi}{2}$ (d) $\frac{\pi}{2}+1$

13. The area of figure bounded by $y^2 + 8x = 16$ and $|y| = 24x + 48$, is

(a) $32\sqrt{6}$ (b) $16\sqrt{6}/3$

(c) $8\sqrt{6}$ (d) $32\sqrt{6}/3$

14. The area of the region bounded by $x^2 + y^2 - 2y - 3 = 0$ and $y = |x| + 1$ is

(a) π (b) 2π

(c) 4π (d) $\pi/2$

15. The area of the region bounded by $1 - y^2 = |x|$ and $|x| + |y| = 1$

(a) 1/3 (b) 2/3

(c) 4/3 (d) 1

16. The area of the figure bounded by the curves $y = |x - 1|$ and $y = 3 - |x|$ is

(a) 2 (b) 3

(c) 4 (d) 1

17. The area bounded by the curve $y = x^2 + 2x + 1$ and tangent at (1, 4) and y-axis is

(a) 2/3 square units (b) 1/3 square units

(c) 2 square units (d) None of these

18. Area of the region bounded by the curve $y = e^x$, $y = e^{-x}$ and the straight line $x = 1$ is given by

(a) $e - e^{-1} + 2$ (b) $e - e^{-1} - 2$

(c) $e + e^{-1} - 2$ (d) None of these

19. The area bounded by $y = 2 - |2 - x|$, $y = \frac{3}{|x|}$ is

(a) $\frac{5-4\ln 2}{3}$ (b) $\frac{2-\ln 3}{2}$

(c) $\frac{4-3\ln 3}{2}$ (d) None of these

20. The area inside the parabola $5x^2 - y = 0$ but outside the parabola $2x^2 - y + 9 = 0$ is

(a) $12\sqrt{3}$ (b) $6\sqrt{3}$

(c) $8\sqrt{3}$ (d) $4\sqrt{3}$

21. A polynomial P is positive for $x > 0$ and the area of the region bounded by $P(x)$ the x-axis, and the vertical lines $x = 0$ and $x = k$ is $k^2(k + 3)/3$

(a) $x^2 + x + 1$ (b) $x^2 + 2x + 1$

(c) $x^2 + 2x$ (d) $x^3 + 1$

22. The area bounded by $y = \frac{|x|}{x}, x \neq 0$, and the curve $y = x(x - 1)(x - 3)$, is

(a) 1 (b) 2

(c) 3 (d) 4

23. The area bounded by the curve $x = \cos^{-1}y$ and the lines $|x| = 1$, is

(a) 2 cos 1 (b) 2 tan 1

(c) 2 sin 1 (d) None of these

24. The area of figure bounded by $y^2 + 8x = 16$ and $y^2 = 24x + 48$, is

(a) $32\sqrt{6}$ (b) $\frac{16\sqrt{6}}{3}$

(c) $8\sqrt{6}$ (d) $\frac{32\sqrt{6}}{3}$

25. The area of the region bounded by the curves $y = xe^x$, $y = e^x$ and the lines $x = \pm 1$ and y-axis is

(a) e (b) $e+\frac{2}{e}$

(c) $e-\frac{3}{e}$ (d) $e+\frac{3}{e}$

26. The area of the smaller region bounded by the circle $x^2 + y^2 = 1$ and the lines $|y| = x + 1$ is

(a) $\frac{\pi}{4}-\frac{1}{2}$ (b) $\frac{\pi}{2}-1$

(c) $\frac{\pi}{2}$ (d) $\frac{\pi}{2}+1$

27. For which of the following values of m, is the area of the region bounded by the curve $y = x - x^2$ and the line $y = mx$ equals 9/2 ?

(a) –4 (b) –2

(c) 2 (d) 4

28. The slope of the tangent to a curve $y = f(x)$ at $(x, f(x))$ is $2x + 1$. If the curve passes through the point (1, 2), then the area of the region bounded byt he curve, the x-axis and the line $x = 1$ is

(a) 5/6 (b) 6/5

(c) 1/6 (d) 6

29. The area of the closed figure bounded by $x = -1$, $x = 2$ and $y\begin{cases}-x^2+2, & x \le 1\\ 2x-1, & x>1\end{cases}$ and the abscissa axis is

(a) 16/3 sq. units (b) 10/3 sq. units

(c) 13/3 sq.units (d) 7/3 sq.units

30. The area of the closed figure bounded by the curves $y = \sqrt{x}$, $y = \sqrt{(4-3x)}$ and $y = 0$

(a) 4/9 (b) 8/9

(c) 16/9 (b) None of these

Answer Keys

1. (a)	**2.** (a)	**3.** (b)	**4.** (a)	**5.** (b)	**6.** (b)	**7.** (b)	**8.** (a)	**9.** (b)	**10.** (b)
11. (b)	**12.** (b)	**13.** (b)	**14.** (a)	**15.** (b)	**16.** (c)	**17.** (d)	**18.** (c)	**19.** (c)	**20.** (a)
21. (c)	**22.** (b)	**23.** (c)	**24.** (a)	**25.** (c)	**26.** (b)	**27.** (b, d)	**28.** (b)	**29.** (a)	**30.** (b)

AREA ENCLOSED BY INVERSE FUNCTION

Area enclosed by $y = f^{-1}(x)$ and x-axis between ordinate $x = a$ and $x = b$ is same as area enclosed $y = f(x)$ and y-axis from $y = a$ to $y = b$.

Clearly, from Fig. 3.74, the area bounded by $y = f(x)$ with y-axis from $y = a$ to $y = b$ and $f^{-1}(x)$ with x-axis from $x = a$ to $x = b$ are same as $y = f(x)$ and $y^{-1}(x)$ are reflection of each other on line $y = x$.

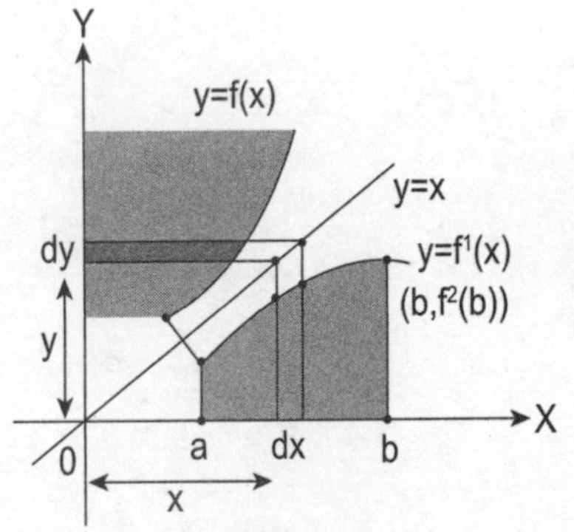

FIGURE 3.74

ILLUSTRATION 50: Let $f(x) = x^3 - x^2 + 2x - 8$ and $g(x)$ is the inverse of $f(x)$. Find the area bounded by $g(x)$, x-axis and from $x = -12$ to $x = 16$.

SOLUTION: We know that the area bounded by function $y = f(x)$ from $x = a$ to $x = b$ with x-axis is the same as the area bounded by $y = f^{-1}(x)$ with y-axis from $y = a$ to $y = b$. Similarly the area bounded by function $y = f^{-1}(x)$ with x-axis from $x = a$ to $x = b$ is same as the area bounded by function $y = f(x)$ with y-axis from $y = a$ to $y = b$.

Here $g(x) = f^{-1}(x)$ and we are to find area bounded by $f^{-1}(x)$, x-axis, $x = -12$ and $x = 16$.

Since here it is difficult to find $f^{-1}(x)$ for $f(x) = x^3 - x^2 + 2x - 8$, so we shall avoid it and find the equivalent area bounded by $y = f(x) = x^3 - x^2 + 2x - 8$ y-axis from $y = -12$ to $y = 16$.

Here $f'(x) = 3x^2 - 2x + 2 > 0$ as disc. $= (-2)^2 - 4(3)(2) < 0$

$\Rightarrow f(x)$ is an increasing function.

$\Rightarrow$ $f(x) = 0$ has exactly one root.

Now $f(x) = 0$

$\Rightarrow x^3 - x^2 + 2x - 8 = 0$

$\Rightarrow x^3 - 8 - (x^2 - 2x) = 0$

$\Rightarrow [x^3 - (2)^3] - x(x - 2) = 0$

$\Rightarrow (x - 2)(x^2 + 2x + 4) - x(x - 2) = 0$

$\Rightarrow (x - 2)(x^2 + x + 4) = 0 \qquad \Rightarrow x = 2$

$\therefore$ $f(x)$ intersects x-axis at point (2, 0), also on y-axis, $x = 0$

$\Rightarrow y = -8$

Thus, $f(x)$ intersects y-axis at (0, –8)

Now $y = -12$

$\Rightarrow x^3 - x^2 + 2x - 8 = -12$

$\Rightarrow x^3 - x^2 + 2x + 4 = 0$

$\Rightarrow x^3 + 1 - x^2 + 2x + 3 = 0$

$\Rightarrow (x + 1)(x^2 - x + 1) - (x^2 - 2x - 3) = 0$

$\Rightarrow (x + 1)(x^2 - x + 1) - (x + 1)(x - 3) = 0$

$\Rightarrow (x + 1)(x^2 - x + 1 - x + 3) = 0$

$\Rightarrow (x + 1)(x^2 - 2x + 4) = 0$

$\Rightarrow x = -1$

Further $y = 16$

$\Rightarrow x^3 - x^2 + 2x - 8 = 16$

$\Rightarrow x^3 - x^2 + 2x - 24 = 0$

$\Rightarrow x^3 - 27 - x^2 + 2x + 3 = 0$

$\Rightarrow (x - 3)(x^2 + 3x + 9) - (x + 1)(x - 3) = 0$

$\Rightarrow (x - 3)(x^2 + 3x + 9 - x - 1) = 0$

$\Rightarrow (x - 3)(x^2 + 2x + 8) = 0$

$\Rightarrow x = 3$

Thus, the graph of $f(x)$ and $f^{-1}(x)$ would be as shown in Fig. 3.75.

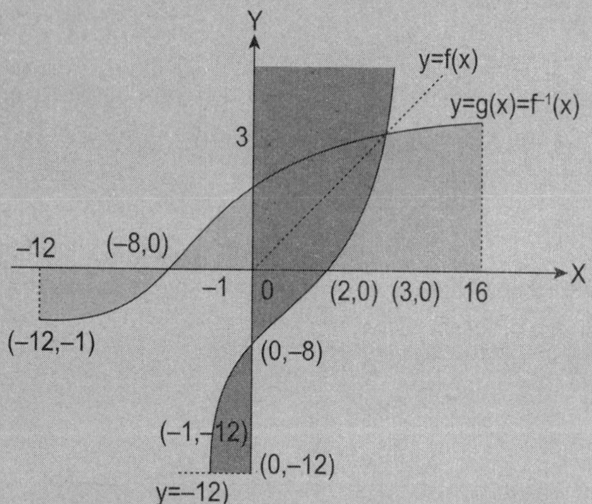

FIGURE 3.75

Thus, we are to find the shaded area shown in Fig. 3.75.

$$= \int_0^3 \left[16 - (x^3 - x^2 + 2x - 8)\right] dx + \int_{-1}^0 \left[(x^3 - x^2 + 2x - 8) - (-12)\right] dx$$

$$= \int_0^3 \left(24 - x^3 + x^2 - 2x\right) dx + \int_{-1}^0 \left(x^3 - x^2 + 2x + 4\right) dx$$

$$= \left|24x - \frac{x^4}{4} + \frac{x^3}{3} - x^2\right|_0^3 + \left|\frac{x^4}{4} - \frac{x^3}{3} + x^2 + 4x\right|_{-1}^0$$

$$= \left[72 - \frac{81}{4} + \frac{27}{3} - 9\right] + \left[0 - \left(\frac{1}{4} + \frac{1}{3} + 1 - 4\right)\right]$$

$$= \left[\frac{288-81}{4}\right] + \left[-\left(\frac{1}{4}+\frac{1}{3}-3\right)\right]$$

$$= \left[\frac{207}{4}\right] + \left[\frac{29}{12}\right] = \frac{621+29}{12} = \frac{325}{6} = 54\frac{1}{6} \text{ square units.}$$

ILLUSTRATION 51: Let $f(x) = \sin x + x$ and $g(x)$ be the inverse of $f(x)$, then find the area bounded by $g(x)$ with y-axis from $y = 0$ to $y = 2\pi$.

SOLUTION: Given function is $f(x) = \sin x + x$ and $g(x) = f^{-1}(x)$, but it is difficult to find $f^{-1}(x)$. So to evaluate the area bounded by $f^{-1}(x)$ and y-axis from $y = 0$ to $y = 2\pi$, we shall find the equivalent area bounded by $f(x)$ with x-axis from $x = 0$ to $x = 2\pi$. The graph of $f(x)$ and $f^{-1}(x)$ would be as shown in Fig. 3.76.

Thus, required area = R_1 (light shaded)

$$= \int_0^{2\pi} f^{-1}(y)\,dy$$

$$= R_2 \text{(dark shaded)} = \int_0^{2\pi} f(x)dx = \int_0^{2\pi} (\sin x + x)\,dx$$

$$= \left[-\cos x + \frac{x^2}{2}\right]_0^{2\pi}$$

$$= \left[-(\cos 2\pi - \cos 0) + \frac{1}{2}(4\pi^2 - 0)\right]$$

$= 2\pi^2$ square units.

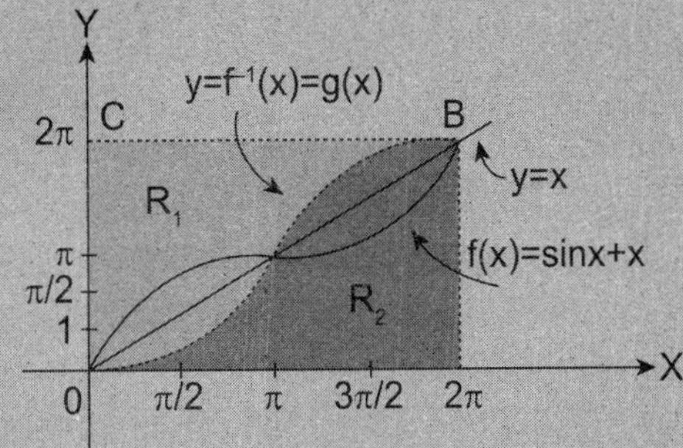

FIGURE 3.76

Aliter: Geometrically, area of square $OABC$ $= (2\pi)(2\pi)\ 4\pi^2$ square units

We can see that shaded and dotted areas are equal having their sum $4\pi^2$

Thus, each portion area $= \dfrac{4\pi^2}{2} = 2\pi^2$ square units.

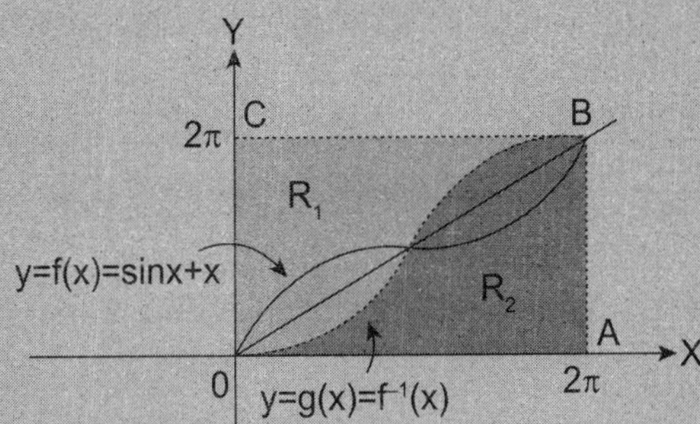

FIGURE 3.77

■ VARIABLE AREA ITS OPTIMIZATION AND DETERMINATION OF PARAMETERS

If the region bounded by curve is continuously changing due to some variable ordinate or abscissae or any other parameter present in the boundary curve, then we obtain a variable area function that can be optimized with respect to involved parameters e.g.

A triangle OAB is inscribed in the region enclosed by a parabola $f(x) = \frac{1}{4}x^2$ and the straight line $4y = t^2$ as shown in the Fig.3.78. Find the limit of the ratio of the area of the Δ to the area of the parabolic region as t approaches zero.

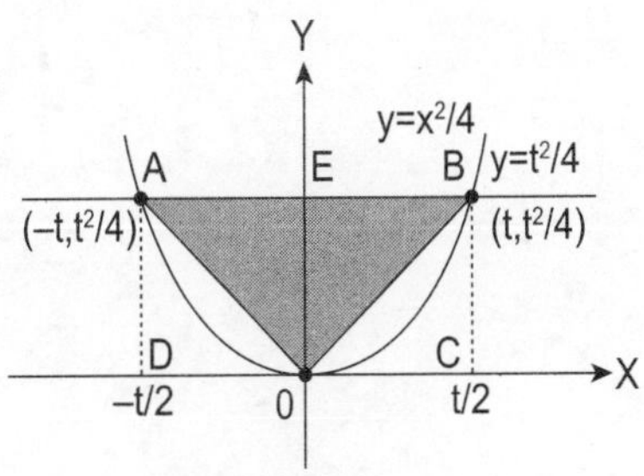

FIGURE 3.78

Here, $\left(t, \frac{t^2}{4}\right)$ are the parametric coordinates of any point on the parabola $y = \frac{1}{4}x^2$. Let $A\left(-t, \frac{t^2}{4}\right)$ and $B\left(t, \frac{t^2}{4}\right)$

be any two points on the parabola. Clearly AD and BC are the straight lines represented by $4y = t^2$, i.e., $y = -\frac{t}{2}$ and $y = \frac{t}{2}$ respectively.

Now area of $\Delta OAB = A_1$

$$= \frac{1}{2}(AB)\times(EO) = \frac{1}{2}(2t)\times\left(\frac{t^2}{4}\right) = \frac{t^3}{4}$$

Next, area of parabolic region $A_2 = 2\int_0^{\frac{t^2}{4}} x\,dy$

$$= 2\int_0^{\frac{t^2}{4}} 2\sqrt{y}\,dy = 4\left(\frac{2y^{3/2}}{3}\right)_0^{\frac{t^2}{4}} = \frac{8}{3}\left[\frac{t^3}{8}\right] = \frac{t^3}{3}$$

$$\therefore \quad \frac{A_1}{A_2} = \frac{\frac{t^3}{4}}{\frac{t^3}{3}} = \frac{3}{4}$$

$$\Rightarrow \quad \lim_{t\to 0}\frac{A_1}{A_2} = \frac{3}{4}$$

ILLUSTRATION 52: Let $a \in [0, 4]$. Show that the maximum area bounded by the curves $y = 1 - |x - 1|$ and $y = |2x - a|$ is 1/3.

SOLUTION: Given curves have equations $y = 1 - |x - 1|$ .... (1)

and $y = |2x - a|$ ...(2)

Graph of $y = 1 - |x - 1|$ is as shown Fig. 3.79.

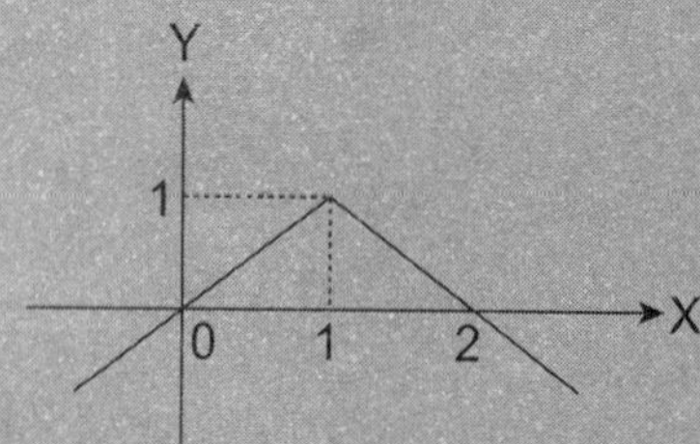

FIGURE 3.79

Graph of $y = |2x - a|$ for $a \in [0, 4]$ or $\frac{a}{2} \in [0, 2]$ is as shown in Fig. 3.80.

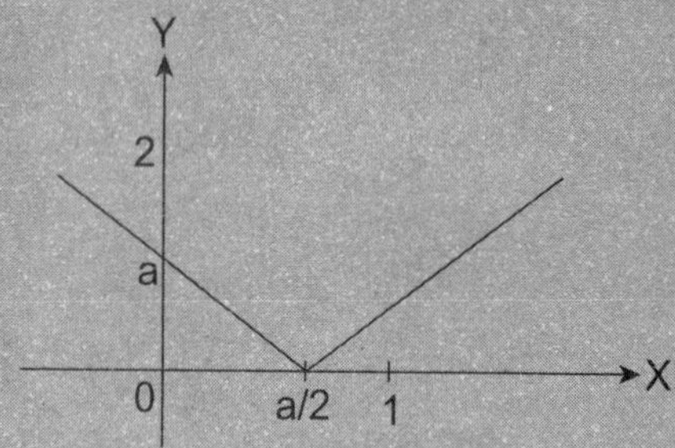

FIGURE 3.80

So let us analyse for five cases.

Case (i): For $0 < \frac{a}{2} < 1$ or $a \in (0, 1)$

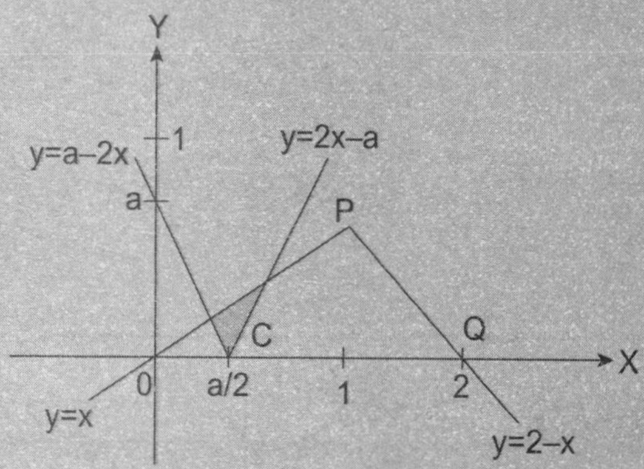

FIGURE 3.81

At point A, $y = x$ and $y = a - 2x$ intersect

$\Rightarrow \; x = a - 2x \;\; \Rightarrow 3x = a$

$\Rightarrow \; x = a/3$

$\therefore \quad A = \left(\frac{a}{3}, 0\right)$

At point B, $y = a - 2x$ and $y = 0$

$\Rightarrow \; x = a/2$

$\therefore \quad B = \left(\frac{a}{2}, 0\right)$

At point C, $y = 2x - a$ and $y = x$

$\Rightarrow x = 2x - a \qquad \Rightarrow x = a$

$\therefore \quad C = (a, a)$

$\therefore$ Required area = area of $\Delta ACB = \int_{a/3}^{a/2} [x - (a - 2x)]dx + \int_{a/2}^{a} x - (2x - a)dx$

$$= \int_{a/3}^{a/2} (3x - a)\,dx + \int_{a/2}^{a} (-x + a)dx = \left[\frac{3x^2}{2} - ax\right]_{a/3}^{a/2} + \left[\frac{-x^2}{2} + ax\right]_{a/2}^{a}$$

$$= \frac{3}{2}\left[\frac{a^2}{4} - \frac{a^2}{9}\right] - a\left[\frac{a}{2} - \frac{a}{3}\right] - \frac{1}{2}\left[a^2 - \frac{a^2}{4}\right] + a\left(a - \frac{a}{2}\right)$$

$$= \frac{3}{2}\left[\frac{9a^2}{36} - 4a^2\right] - a\left[\frac{a}{6}\right] - \frac{3a^2}{8} + \frac{a^2}{2} = \frac{5a^2}{24} - \frac{a^2}{6} - \frac{3a^2}{8} + \frac{a^2}{2} = \frac{5a^2 - 4a^2 - 9a^2 + 12a^2}{24} = \frac{a^2}{6}$$

$< \frac{1}{6}$ as $a \in (0, 1)$

Case (ii): For $a = 1$

$\Rightarrow \quad \frac{a}{2} = \frac{1}{2}$

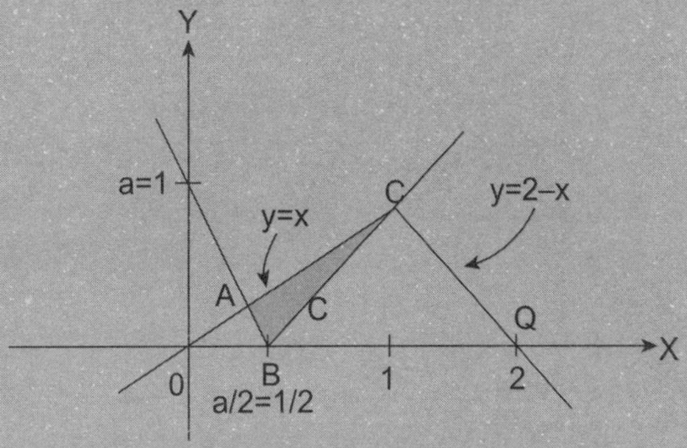

FIGURE 3.82

As above area $ABC = \frac{a^2}{6} = \frac{1}{6} < \frac{1}{3}$

Case (iii): For $1 < a < 2$, i.e., $\frac{1}{2} < \frac{a}{2} < 1$

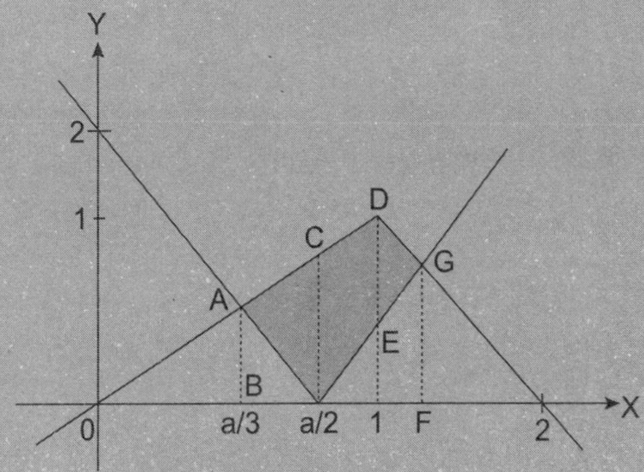

FIGURE 3.83

At the point of intersection $A \equiv \left(\frac{a}{3}, \frac{a}{3}\right); B \equiv \left(\frac{a}{2}, 0\right); G \equiv \left(\frac{a}{3}+\frac{2}{3}, \frac{4}{3}-\frac{a}{3}\right)$

$$\therefore \text{ Required area } = \int_{a/3}^{a/2} [x-(a-2x)]dx + \int_{a/2}^{1} [x-(2x-a)]dx + \int_{1}^{\frac{a}{3}+\frac{2}{3}} [2-x-(2x-a)]dx$$

$$= \frac{a^2}{24} - \frac{1}{2}\left[1-\frac{a^2}{4}\right] + a\left(1-\frac{a}{2}\right) + (2+a)\left[\frac{a}{3}-\frac{1}{3}\right] - \frac{3}{2}\left[\left(\frac{a}{3}+\frac{2}{3}\right)^2 - 1\right]$$

$$= \frac{a^2}{24} - \frac{1}{2} + \frac{a^2}{8} + a - \frac{a^2}{2} + \frac{2a}{3} - \frac{2}{3} + \frac{a^2}{3} - \frac{a}{3} - \frac{3}{2}\left[\frac{a^2}{9} + \frac{4}{9} + \frac{4a}{9} - 1\right]$$

$$= -\frac{1}{6}\left(a^2 - 4a + 2\right) \le -\frac{1}{6}\left(\frac{-D}{4}\right) = \frac{1}{24}(8) = \frac{1}{3}$$

Case (iv): For $\frac{a}{2} = 1$, i.e., $a = 2$

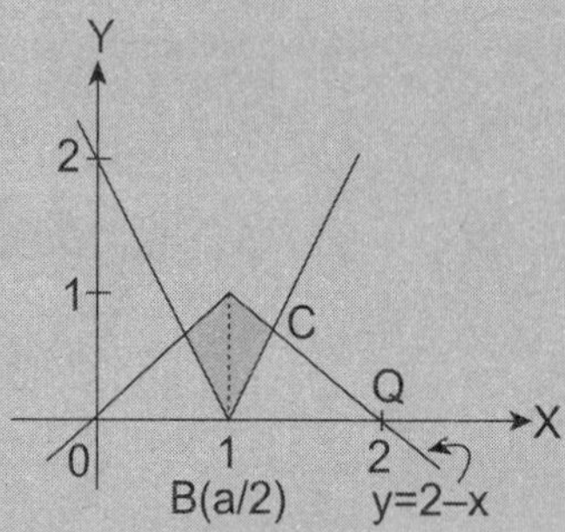

FIGURE 3.84

At point $A \equiv \left(\frac{a}{3}, \frac{a}{3}\right) \equiv \left(\frac{2}{3}, \frac{2}{3}\right)$

At point C, $y = 2x - a$, $y = 2 - x$

$\Rightarrow 2x - a = 2 - x$

$\Rightarrow 3x = a + 2$

$\Rightarrow x = \frac{a+2}{3}$

$\Rightarrow C \equiv \left(\frac{a+2}{3}, \frac{4-a}{3}\right) \equiv \left(\frac{4}{3}, \frac{2}{3}\right)$ as $a = 2$

Required area $= \int_{2/3}^{1} \left[x-(2-2x)\right]dx + \int_{1}^{4/3} \left[(2-x)-(2x-2)\right]dx$

or $2\int_{2/3}^{1} (3x-2)\,dx$ (By symmetry)

$$= 2\times\frac{3}{2}\left[x^2\right]_{2/3}^{1} - \left[x\right]_{2/3}^{1} = 3\left(1-\frac{4}{9}\right) - 4\left(1-\frac{2}{3}\right) = \frac{5}{3} - \frac{4}{3} = \frac{1}{3} \text{ square units}$$

Case (v): For $1 < \frac{a}{2} < 2$ or $a \in (2, 4)$

By symmetry of bounded region about line $x = 1$ is as shown in Fig. 3.85.

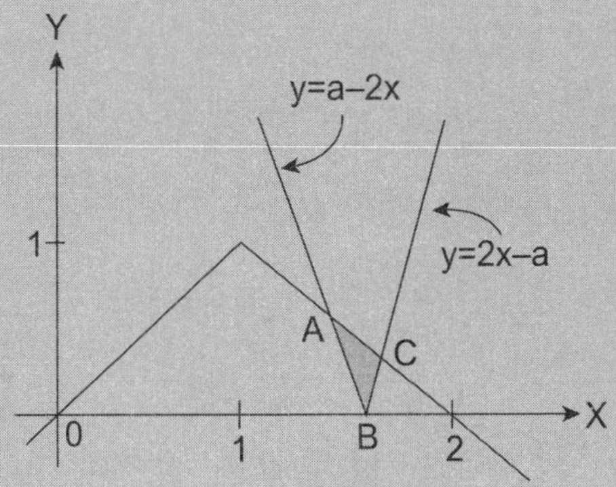

FIGURE 3.85

Similar to case (i) to (iv), maximum value of bounded region will be 1/3.

Thus, the maximum value of bounded region is 1/3, $a \in (1, 3)$

ILLUSTRATION 53: If the least area bounded by the straight line having constant slope 'm', passing through the point $(1, c)$; where $c > 1$ and the parabola $y = x^2$ is $\frac{32}{3}$ square units, then evaluate '$c + m$'

SOLUTION: Equation of straight line with slope m is $(y - c) = m(x - 1)$

or $y = mx + (c - m)$ ...(1)

Now the bounded area is given by $A = \int_a^b [mx + (c-m) - x^2]\,dx$;

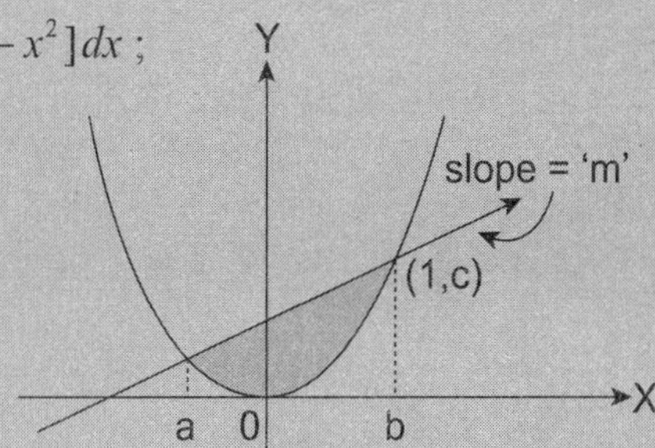

FIGURE 3.86

Where a and b are the points of intersection of parabola and straight line, i.e., roots of equation $x^2 = mx + (c - m)$ and $a < b$.

$\Rightarrow x^2 - mx - (c - m) = 0$

$\Rightarrow a + b = m;\ a.b = m - c$ ...(2)

Now, $A = \int_a^b (mx + (c-m) - x^2)\,dx$

$$= m\left[\frac{x^2}{2}\right]_a^b + (c-m)[x]_a^b - \frac{1}{3}\left[x^3\right]_a^b = \frac{m}{2}(b^2 - a^2) + (c-m)(b-a) - \frac{1}{3}(b^3 - a^3)$$

$$= (b-a)\left[\frac{m}{2}(b+a) + (c-m) - \frac{1}{3}(b^2 + a^2 + ab)\right]$$

$$= \sqrt{(b+a)^2 - 4ab}\left[\frac{m}{2}(m) + (c-m) - \frac{1}{3}[(a+b)^2 - ab]\right]$$

$$= \sqrt{m^2 - 4(m-c)}\left[\frac{m^2}{2} + (c-m) - \frac{1}{3}\{m^2 - (m-c)\}\right]$$

$$= \sqrt{m^2 - 4m + 4c}\left[\left(\frac{1}{2} - \frac{1}{3}\right)m^2 + \left(1 - \frac{1}{3}\right)(c-m)\right]$$

$$= \sqrt{m^2 - 4m + 4c}\left[\frac{1}{6}m^2 - \frac{2}{3}m + \frac{2}{3}c\right] = \frac{1}{6}\sqrt{m^2 - 4m + 4c}\left[m^2 - 4m + 4c\right]$$

$$= \frac{1}{6}(m^2 - 4m + 4c)^{3/2} = \frac{1}{6}\left[(m-2)^2 + 4(c-1)\right]^{3/2}$$

$\therefore$ A is least for $m = 2$ and least value of A will be

$$= \frac{1}{6}[4(c-1)]^{3/2} = \frac{1}{6}(8)(c-1)^{3/2} = \frac{4}{3}(c-1)^{3/2}$$

Now it is given, that least value of $A = 32/3$

$$\therefore \quad \frac{4}{3}(c-1)^{3/2} = \frac{32}{3} \qquad \Rightarrow \quad (c-1)^{3/2} = 8$$

$$\Rightarrow \quad (c-1) = (8)^{2/3} = 4 \qquad \Rightarrow \quad c = 5$$

Thus, $m = 2$ and $c = 5$

$\therefore \quad c + m = 7$

ILLUSTRATION 54: Three points $O(0, 0)$; $A(a, a^2)$; $B(-b, b^2)$; where $a > 0, b > 0$ lie on the parabola $y = x^2$ and let S_1 be the area bounded by line segment AB and parabola, and S_2 be the area of ΔOAB. Find the minimum value of S_1/S_2.

SOLUTION: S_1 is the shaded area bounded by parabola and straight line and S_2 is the dotted area of ΔOAB.

$$\therefore \quad S_1 = \int_{-b}^{a} \left(y_{\text{straght line}} - y_{\text{parabola}}\right) dx \qquad \ldots(1)$$

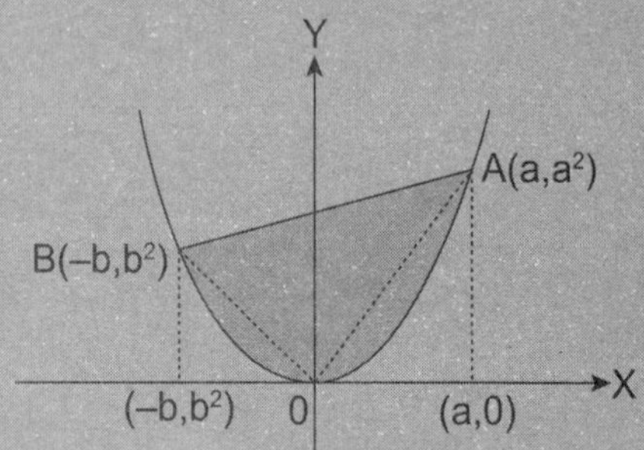

FIGURE 3.87

Equation of straight line AB will be

$$(y-a^2) = \frac{b^2-a^2}{-b-a}(x-a)$$

$$\Rightarrow \quad y-a^2 = \frac{(b^2-a^2)}{-(b+a)}(x-a)$$

$$\Rightarrow \quad y - a^2 = -(b-a)(x-a)$$

$$\Rightarrow \quad y - a^2 = (a-b)(x-a) = ax - a^2 - bx + ab$$

$$\Rightarrow \quad y = (a-b)x + ab \qquad \ldots(2)$$

$\therefore$ from (1) and (2),

$$S_1 = \int_{-b}^{a} \left[(a-b)x + ab - x^2\right] dx = \frac{(a-b)}{2}[a^2-b^2] + ab(a+b) - \frac{1}{3}(a^3+b^3)$$

$$= (a+b)\left[\frac{(a-b)^2}{2} + ab - \frac{1}{3}(a^2-ab+b^2)\right]$$

$$= (a+b)\left[\frac{3a^2+3b^2-6ab+6ab-2a^2+2ab-2b^2}{6}\right]$$

$$= (a+b)\left[\frac{a^2+b^2+2ab}{6}\right] = \frac{(a+b)^3}{6} \qquad \ldots(3)$$

Further area of $\Delta OAB = S_2 = \frac{1}{2}\begin{vmatrix} 0 & 0 & 1 \\ a & a^2 & 1 \\ -b & b^2 & 1 \end{vmatrix}$

$$= \frac{1}{2}(ab^2+ba^2) = \frac{1}{2}ab(a+b) \qquad \ldots(4)$$

$$\therefore \quad \frac{S_1}{S_2} = \frac{(a+b)^2}{3ab}$$

Since $a, b > 0$, A.M. $\geq$ G.M. implies $a+b \geq 2\sqrt{ab}$

$\Rightarrow\ (a+b)^2 \geq 4ab$

$\Rightarrow\ \dfrac{(a+b)^2}{3ab} \geq \dfrac{4ab}{3ab} = \dfrac{4}{3}$

$\therefore$ Minimum value of $\dfrac{S_1}{S_2}$ is $\dfrac{4}{3}$

ILLUSTRATION 55: Find the value of 'a' ($a > 0$) for which the area bounded by a function $f(x) = \dfrac{x}{6} + \dfrac{1}{x^2}$ with x-axis from $x = a$ to $x = 2a$ is least. Also find the least value of area.

SOLUTION: Given curve is $y = \dfrac{x}{6} + \dfrac{1}{x^2} > 0\ \forall\ x > 0$

$\therefore$ Area bounded by $f(x) = \dfrac{x}{6} + \dfrac{1}{x^2};\ x = a, x = 2a$ for $a > 0$ is given by,

$$A = \int_a^{2a}\left(\frac{x}{6} + \frac{1}{x^2}\right)dx = \frac{1}{6}\left[\frac{x^2}{2}\right]_a^{2a} + \left[\frac{x^{-1}}{-1}\right]_a^{2a} = \frac{1}{12}\left[4a^2 - a^2\right] - \left[\frac{1}{2a} - \frac{1}{a}\right] = \frac{a^2}{4} + \frac{1}{2a}$$

$\therefore\quad A = \dfrac{a^2}{4} + \dfrac{1}{4a} + \dfrac{1}{4a},\ a > 0$

$\therefore$ By A.M. $\geq$ G.M. we have, $A \geq 3\left(\dfrac{a^2}{4} \times \dfrac{1}{4a} \times \dfrac{1}{4a}\right)^{1/3} = \dfrac{3}{4}$

$\therefore$ Least value of area = 3/4 and it would occur, for $\dfrac{a^2}{4} = \dfrac{1}{4a}$, i.e., $a = 1$

Aliter: $A = \displaystyle\int_a^{2a}\left(\frac{x}{6} + \frac{1}{x^2}\right)dx = \frac{dA}{da} = \left(\frac{2a}{6} + \frac{1}{4a^2}\right)(2) - \left(\frac{a}{6} + \frac{1}{a^2}\right)(1) = \frac{a}{2} - \frac{1}{2a^2}$

For maxima/minima, $\dfrac{dA}{da} = 0$

$\Rightarrow\ \dfrac{a}{2} - \dfrac{1}{2a^2} = 0$

$\Rightarrow\ a^3 = 1 \qquad\qquad \Rightarrow\ a = 1$

And $\dfrac{d^2A}{da^2} = \dfrac{1}{2} - \dfrac{1}{2}(-2a^{-3}) > 0$ for $a = 1$

$\therefore$ a will be minimum at $a = 1$ and is given by,

$$A = \int_1^2\left(\frac{x}{6} + \frac{1}{x^2}\right)dx = \frac{1}{12}\left[x^2\right]_1^2 + \frac{1}{(-1)}\left(x^{-1}\right)_1^2 = \frac{1}{12}[4-1] - \left(\frac{1}{2} - 1\right)$$

$= \dfrac{1}{4} + \dfrac{1}{2} = \dfrac{3}{4}$ square units.

ILLUSTRATION 56: Find the values of m ($m > 0$) for which the area bounded by the line $y = mx + 2$ and $x = 2y - y^2$ is,

(i) 9/2 square units (ii) minimum

Also find the minimum area.

SOLUTION: Given equations are

$y = mx + 2 \qquad \ldots(i)$

$x = 2y - y^2$ ...(ii)

point of inter-section of curve (i) and (ii) are given by $\frac{y-2}{m} = 2y - y^2$

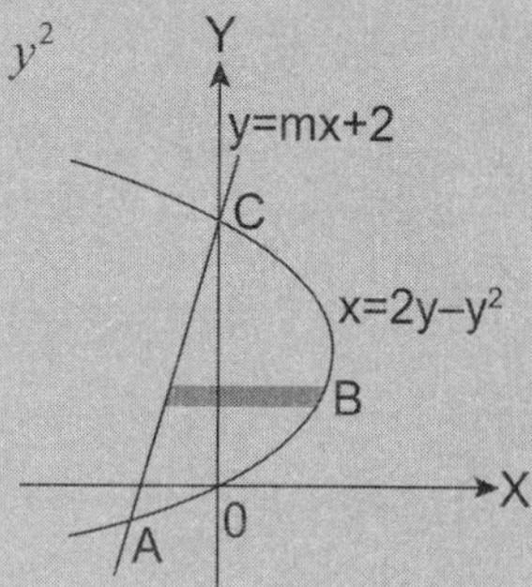

FIGURE 3.88

$\Rightarrow$ $(my + 1)(y - 2) = 0$ $\Rightarrow$ $y = 2, -\frac{1}{m}$

$\therefore$ Points of intersection are $A\left(-\frac{1}{m^2} - \frac{2}{m}, -\frac{1}{m}\right)$ and $C(0, 2)$

(i) Given that Area of $APBC = \frac{9}{2}$

$$\Rightarrow \int_{-\frac{1}{m}}^{2}\left[(2y - y^2) - \left(\frac{y-2}{m}\right)\right]dy = \frac{9}{2}$$

$$\Rightarrow \left[y^2 - \frac{y^3}{3} - \frac{y^2}{2m} + \frac{2y}{m}\right]_{-1/m}^{2} = \frac{9}{2} \quad \Rightarrow 19m^3 - 12m^2 - 6m - 1 = 0$$

$\Rightarrow m = 1$

(ii) $\int_{-\frac{1}{m}}^{2}\left[(2y - y^2) - \left(\frac{y-2}{m}\right)\right]dy = f(m)$ (say)

$$\Rightarrow f(m) = \frac{1}{6m^3} + \frac{1}{m^2} + \frac{2}{m} + \frac{4}{3}; (m > 0) \quad \Rightarrow f(m) \text{ is minimum when } m \to \infty$$

So, $A_{\min} = f_{\min} = \frac{4}{3}$; when $m \to \infty$

ILLUSTRATION 57: For what value of 'a' is the area bounded by the curve $y = a^2x^2 + ax + 1$ and the straight line $y = 0$, $x = 0$ and $x = 1$ is least? Also find the least value of area.

SOLUTION: Given equation is $y = a^2x^2 + ax + 1$

$\Rightarrow \left(x + \frac{1}{2a}\right)^2 = \frac{1}{a^2}\left(y - \frac{3}{4}\right)$ which is an upward parabola

with vertex at $\left(\frac{-1}{2a}, \frac{3}{4}\right)$

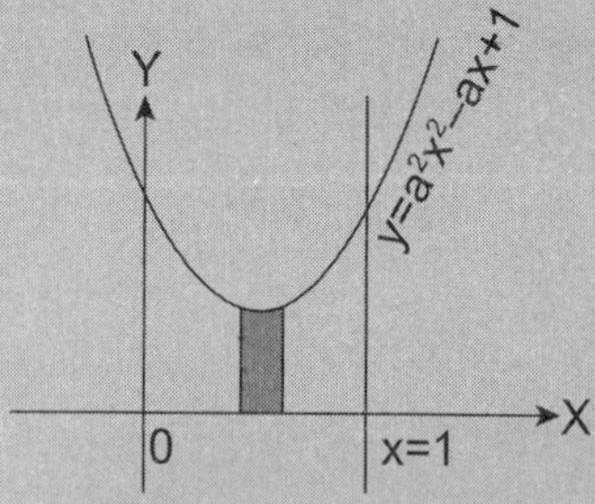

FIGURE 3.89

$\therefore$ Bounded area $f(a) = \int_0^1 (a^2x^2 + ax + 1)\,dx$

$\Rightarrow f(a) = \frac{a^2}{3} + \frac{a}{2} + 1$

Now, $f(a)$ is least when $f'(a) = 0$

$\Rightarrow \frac{2a}{3} + \frac{1}{2} = 0$ $\Rightarrow a = -\frac{3}{4}$, also $f''(a) = \frac{2}{3}$

$\Rightarrow f''(a) > 0$ at $a = -\frac{3}{4}$

So $f(a)$ is least at $a = -\frac{3}{4}$

Also least area $= f\left(-\frac{3}{4}\right) = \frac{9}{48} - \frac{3}{8} + 1 = \frac{13}{16}$ square units.

LEAST VALUE OF VARIABLE AREA

Let $f(x)$ be a monotonic function with $f'(x) \neq 0$ in (a, b), then the area bounded by function $y = f(x)$, $y = f(c)$; $(a < c < b)$. And ordinates $x = a$, $x = b$ is minimum for $c = \frac{a+b}{2}$.

Proof: Let us suppose that $f(x)$ is monotonically decreasing function as shown in Fig. 3.90.

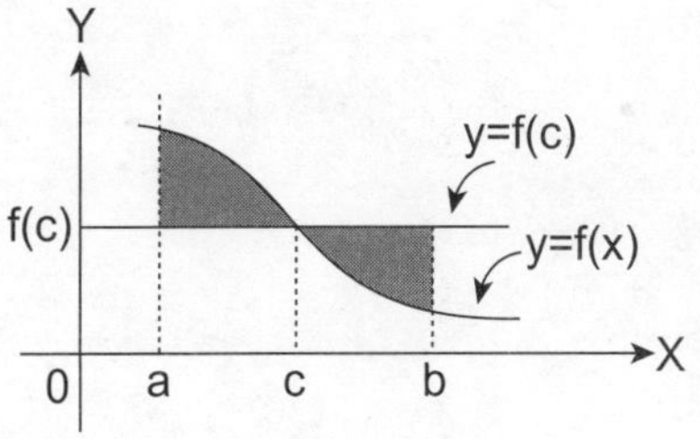

FIGURE 3.90

Here, required area

$$= A = \int_a^c [f(x) - f(c)]dx + \int_c^b [f(c) - f(x)]dx$$

$$= \int_a^c f(x)dx - f(c)(c-a) + f(c)(b-c) - \int_c^b f(x)dx$$

$$= f(c)(b-c-c+a) + \int_a^c f(x)dx - \int_c^b f(x)dx$$

$$= f(c)(a+b-2c) + \int_a^c f(x)dx - \int_c^b f(x)dx$$

Differentiating w.r.t. c (variable) we get

$$\frac{dA}{dc} = f'(c)(a+b-2c) + f(c)(-2) + f(c) - [0 - f(c)]$$

$= f'(c)\ (a + b - 2c)$

For minima or maxima, $\frac{dA}{dc} = 0$

$\Rightarrow f'(c)\ (a + b - 2c) = 0$

$\Rightarrow c = \frac{a+b}{2}$ as $f'(x) < 0\ \forall\ x \in (a, b)$

Now $\frac{d^2A}{dc^2} = f''(c)(a+b-2c) + f'(c)(-2)$

$\therefore \left[\frac{d^2A}{dc^2}\right]_{c=\frac{a+b}{2}} = 0 - 2f'(c) = -2f'\left(\frac{a+b}{2}\right) > 0,$

as $f'(x) < 0\ \forall\ x \in (a, b)$

$\Rightarrow$ A will be least for $c = \frac{a+b}{2}$.

ILLUSTRATION 58: Let $f(x) = x^3 + 5x + \lambda$ encloses minimum area with x-axis from ordinate $x = 1$ to $x = 3$, then find the value of λ.

SOLUTION: Given function is $f(x) = x^3 + 5x + \lambda$

$\Rightarrow f'(x) = 3x^2 + 5 > 0\ \forall\ x \in (1, 3)$

i.e., $f(x)$ is strictly monotonicity increasing with $f'(x) \neq 0$ on the interval $(1, 3)$

Since the area bounded by $y = f(x)$, x-axis, i.e., $y = 0 = f(c)$ from ordinate $x = 1$ to $x = 3$ is minimum,

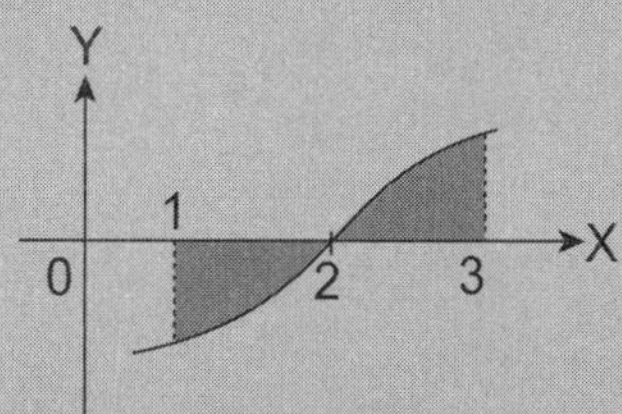

FIGURE 3.91

$\Rightarrow c = \frac{a+b}{2} = \frac{1+3}{2} = 2$

$\therefore f(c) = 0$

$\Rightarrow f(2) = 0 \qquad \Rightarrow (2)^3 + 5(2) + \lambda = 0$

$\Rightarrow \lambda = -18$

ILLUSTRATION 59: If A is the area bounded by $y = \tan x$, $y = c$; $c > 0$ from ordinate $x = 0$ to $x = \frac{\pi}{3}$, then find the least value of A.

SOLUTION: The area bounded by $y = \tan x$ and $y = c = f(k)$; $(c > 0)$

and $0 < k < \pi/3$ will be minimum for $k = \frac{a+b}{2} = \frac{0+\pi/3}{2} = \frac{\pi}{6}$

$\Rightarrow f\left(\frac{\pi}{6}\right) = c$ $\qquad\qquad \Rightarrow \tan\frac{\pi}{6} = c$

$\Rightarrow c = \frac{1}{\sqrt{3}}$

$\therefore$ Least value of

$$A = \int_0^{\pi/6}\left(\frac{1}{\sqrt{3}} - \tan x\right)dx + \int_{\pi/6}^{\pi/3}\left(\tan x - \frac{1}{\sqrt{3}}\right)dx$$

$$= \frac{1}{\sqrt{3}}[x]_0^{\pi/6} - [\log\sec x]_0^{\pi/6} + [\log\sec x]_{\pi/6}^{\pi/3} - \frac{1}{\sqrt{3}}[x]_{\pi/6}^{\pi/3}$$

$$= \frac{1}{\sqrt{3}}\left[\frac{\pi}{6}\right] - \left[\ln\left(\frac{2}{\sqrt{3}}\right)\right] + \left[\ln 2 - \ln\frac{2}{\sqrt{3}}\right] - \frac{1}{\sqrt{3}}\left(\frac{\pi}{6}\right)$$

$$= \ln 2 - 2\ln\frac{2}{\sqrt{3}} = \ln 2 - 2\ln\frac{4}{3} = \ln\left(2\times\frac{3}{4}\right) = \ln\left(\frac{3}{2}\right)$$

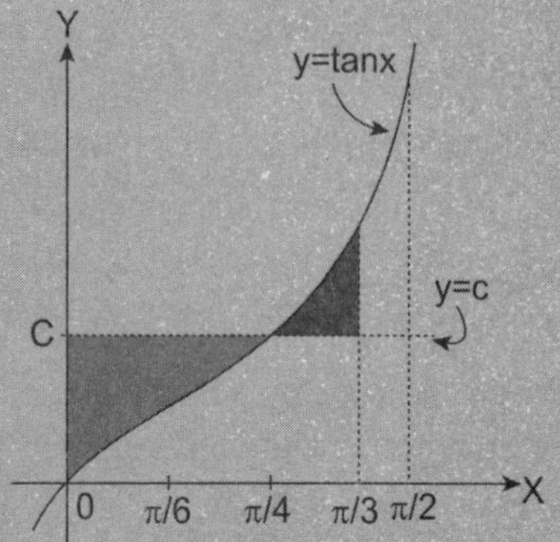

FIGURE 3.92

METHOD OF TRACING THE REGION REPRESENTED BY INEQUALITY

Each curve $f(x, y) = 0$ divides the enire x - y plane into three set of points as given in Fig. 3.93.

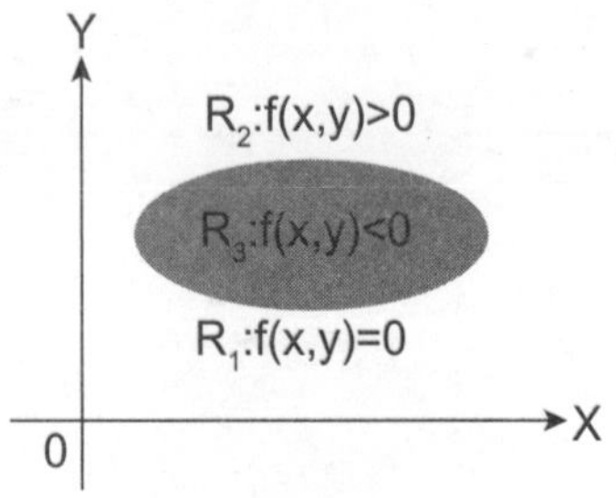

FIGURE 3.93

$R_1 = \{(x, y): f(x, y) = 0, x, y \in \mathbb{R}\}$, i.e., the points lying on the curve $f(x, y) = 0$

$R_2 = \{(x, y): f(x, y) > 0, x, y \in \mathbb{R}\}$, i.e., the points lying on one side of the curve $f(x, y) = 0$ (outside the curve if closed).

$R_3 = \{(x, y): f(x, y) < 0, x, y \in \mathbb{R}\}$, i.e., the points lying on other side of $f(x, y) = 0$ (inside the curve if closed).

Steps to identify the region represented by a given inequality (say) $f(x, y) > 0$.

Step I: Consider the equality and draw the curve using the symmetry and other concepts of curve sketching and transformation of graphs.

Step II: Consider any points (α, β) not lying on the curve preferably $(0, 0)$ {or point on coordinate axis} and determine the sign of $f(\alpha, \beta)$.

Step III: If $f(\alpha, \beta) > 0$, then $f(x, y) > 0$ represents the region containing (α, β). If $f(\alpha, \beta) < 0$, then the region which does not contains point (α, β) will be represented by inequality $f(x, y) > 0$

Note that the region represented by inequality $f(x, y) > 0$ or $f(x, y) < 0$ does not contain the points on the curve whereas the region represented by inequality $f(x, y) \geq 0$ and $f(x, y) \leq 0$ contains the points on the curve.

ILLUSTRATION 60: Sketch the region represented by the following inequalities.

(a) $y > x$

(b) $y < -x$

(c) $y \geq |x - 1|$

(d) $x - 3y + 15 \leq 0$, $y + 5 \leq 5x$ and $4y + 28 \geq 7x$

(e) $(x^2 - x) < (y - xy)$

SOLUTION: (a) To find the region represented by inequality $y > x$ or $y - x > 0$, first of all draw the group of straight line $y = x$

Since the line is passing through the origin, we shall not take the point (α, β) as origin. Let us take the point $(\alpha, \beta) \equiv (1, 0)$.

Substituting (1, 0) in the expression $f(x, y)$, where $f(x, y) = y - x$

$f(1, 0) = 0 - 1 = -1 < 0$

so, the region represented by inequality $y - x > 0$ is the region of plane on the side of straight line $y - x = 0$ not containing the point (1, 0) as shown in Fig. 3.94.

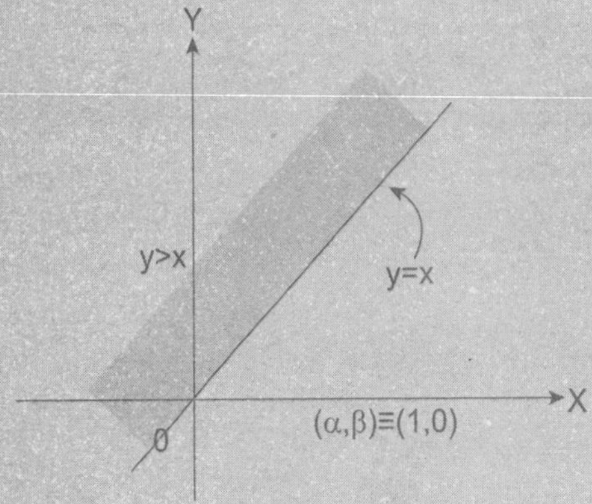

FIGURE 3.94

(b) $y < -x$

$\Rightarrow x + y < 0 \qquad \Rightarrow f(x, y) = x + y < 0$

Taking $(\alpha, \beta) \equiv (1, 0)$

We have $f(\alpha, \beta) = f(1, 0) = L + 0 = 1 \geq 0$

$\therefore$ The required region will be on the side of line $x + y = 0$ not containing the point (α, β) shown in Fig. 3.95. by shaded region.

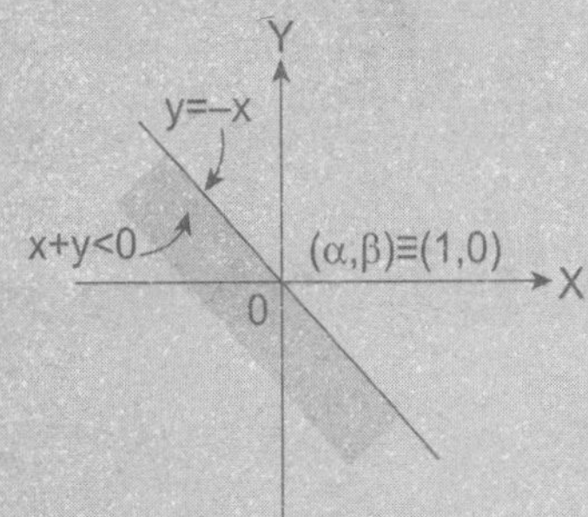

FIGURE 3.95

(c) $y \geq |x - 1|$

or $y - |x - 1| \geq 0$

$\Rightarrow f(x, y) \equiv y - |x - 1| \geq 0$

Let us first draw the graph of $f(x, y) = 0$

i.e., $y = |x - 1|$ as shown in Fig. 3.96.

If we consider $(\alpha, \beta) \equiv (1, 1)$, then $f(\alpha, \beta) = f(1, 1)$ $= 1 - |1 - 1| = 1 > 0$

$\therefore$ The required region will be on the side of graph of $y = |x - 1|$ containing the point (α, β) as shown by shaded region.

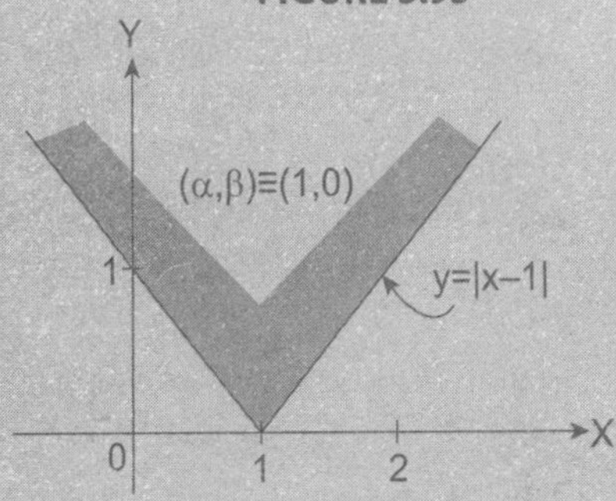

FIGURE 3.96

(d) $x - 3y + 15 \leq 0$

$\Rightarrow f(x, y) \equiv x - 3y + 15 \leq 0 \qquad$ ...(i)

$y + 5 \leq 5x$

$\Rightarrow g(x, y) \equiv 5x - y + 5 \geq 0 \qquad$ ...(ii)

$4y + 28 \geq 7x$

$\Rightarrow h(x, y) \equiv 7x - 4y - 28 \leq 0 \qquad$ ...(iii)

To draw the region represented by above system of inequalities, first of all we draw the three straight lines $f(x, y) = 0$, $g(x, y) = 0$ and $h(x, y) = 0$ and then draw the regions represented by each linear inequality.

The common region of three inequalities will represent the required region as shown in Fig. 3.97.

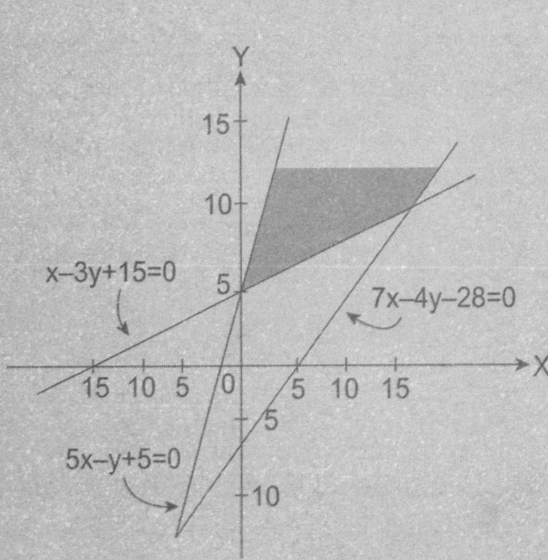

FIGURE 3.97

If we take $(\alpha, \beta) = (0, 0)$, then $f(0, 0) = 15 > 0$
$g(0, 0) = 5 > 0$ and $h(0, 0) = -28 < 0$
Thus, the inequality (i) , (ii) and (iii) contains the points on the side of corresponding lines not containing the origin, containing the origin, respectively. The common region of three inequalities is shown in the Fig. 3.98 by shaded portion.

(e) $(x^2 - x) < (y - xy)$
$\Rightarrow x^2 + xy - x - y < 0$
$\Rightarrow x(x + y) - (x + y) < 0$
$\Rightarrow (x - 1)(x + y) < 0$
$\therefore f(x, y) \equiv (x - 1)(x + y) = 0$
represents a pair of straight line $x - 1 = 0$ and $x + y = 0$
Let us take $(\alpha, \beta) \equiv (0, 1)$
$\therefore f(\alpha, \beta) \equiv f(0, 1) = (0 - 1)(0 + 1) = -1 < 0$
$\therefore$ The required region will be on the side of pair of straight line containing the point (α, β), i.e., (0, 1) as shown by the shaded portion in in Fig. 3.98. Note that the shaded region does not contain the pair of straight line as the strict inequality is given.

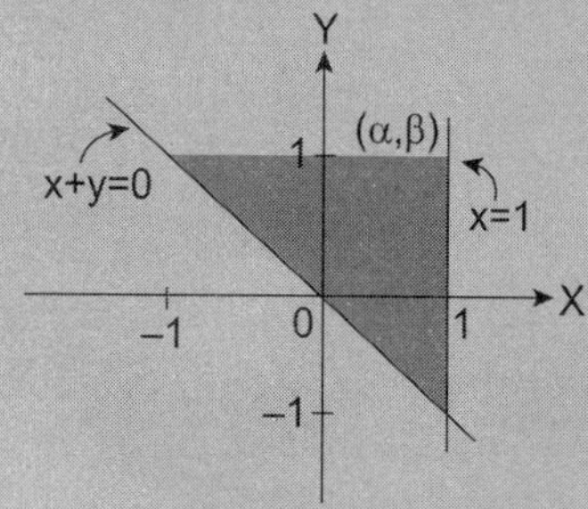

FIGURE 3.98

ILLUSTRATION 61: Sketch the curve of the following:

(a) $y \leq -x$ (b) $x > |y|$
(c) $|x + y| \geq 1$ (d) $|x - y| \leq 2$
(e) $|x| + |y| \leq 2$ (f) $|x| + |y| \geq 2$

Also find the area bounded by the curve $x^2 + y^2 \leq 4$ from the region of inequality in each of the above cases.

SOLUTION: (a) $y \leq -x$

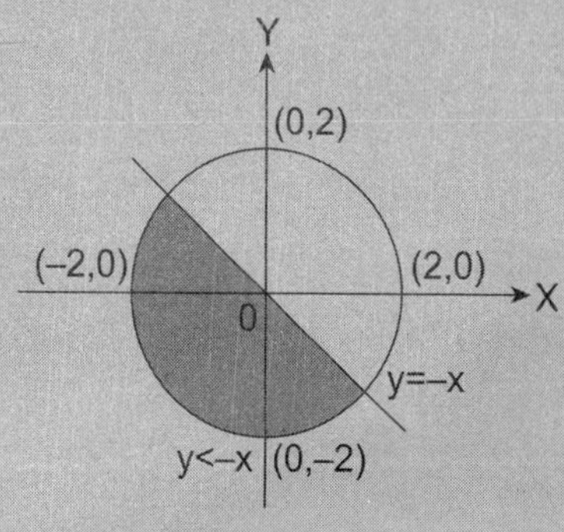

FIGURE 3.99

Required area = dark shaded area $\frac{1}{2}\pi(2^2) = 2\pi$ square units.

(b) $x > |y|$

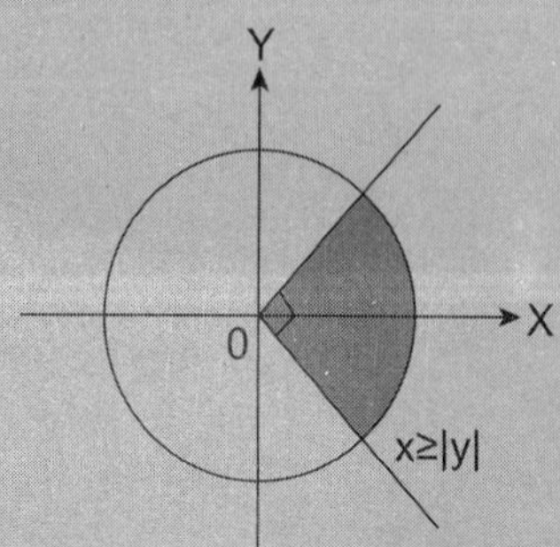

FIGURE 3.100

Required area = dark shaded area $\frac{1}{4}\pi\,(2^2) = \pi$ square units.

(c) $|x + y| \geq 1$ ……….(i)

$$\Rightarrow \begin{cases} x+y \geq 1; & x+y \geq 0 \\ -(x+y) \geq 1; & x+y \leq 0 \end{cases}$$

$$\Rightarrow \begin{cases} x+y \geq 1; & y \geq -x \\ x+y \leq -1; & y \leq -x \end{cases}$$

$$\Rightarrow \begin{cases} y \geq -x+1; & y \geq -x \\ y \leq -x-1; & y \leq -x \end{cases}$$

Thus, the region (i) is the union of two regions

$R_1 = \{(x, y) : y \geq -x \text{ and } y \geq -x + 1\}$ and

$R_2 = \{(x, y) : y \leq -x \text{ and } y \leq -x + 1\}$ or

$R_1 = \{(x, y) : y \geq -x + 1\}$ and

$R_2 = \{(x, y) : y \leq -x + 1\}$

Further we want to find the region bounded by curve $x^2 + y^2 \leq 4$ from the region $R_1 \cup R_2$ as shown by dark shaded portion in Fig. 3.101.

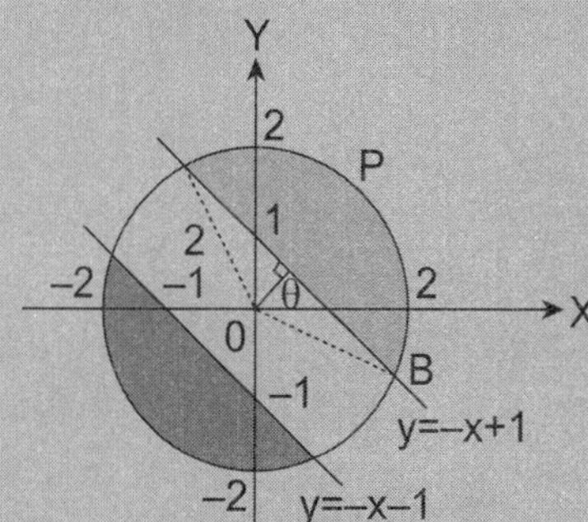

FIGURE 3.101

In $\Delta OAL = OL = \frac{|0+0-1|}{\sqrt{2}} = \frac{1}{\sqrt{2}}$

$$\therefore \quad \cos\theta = \frac{OL}{OA} = \frac{1/\sqrt{2}}{2} = \frac{1}{\sqrt{2}}$$

$$\Rightarrow \quad \sin\theta = \sqrt{1 - \frac{1}{8}}$$

$$\Rightarrow \quad \sin\theta = \frac{\sqrt{7}}{2\sqrt{2}}$$

$\therefore$ Required area = 2[area of sector $OBPAO$ – area of ΔOBA]

$$= 2\left[\frac{2\theta}{2\pi}(\pi(4)) - \frac{1}{2}(2)^2 \sin 2\theta\right]$$

$$= 2\left[4\sin^{-1}\left(\sqrt{\frac{7}{8}}\right) - 4\left(\sqrt{\frac{7}{8}} \times \frac{1}{\sqrt{8}}\right)\right]$$

$$= 8\sin^{-1}\sqrt{\frac{7}{8}} - \sqrt{7}$$

(d) $|x - y| \leq 2$ …(i)

$$\Rightarrow \begin{cases} x-y \leq 2 \text{ for } x-y \geq 0 \\ -(x-y) \leq 2 \text{ for } x-y < 0 \end{cases}$$

$$\Rightarrow \begin{cases} x-y-2 \leq 0 \text{ for } y \leq x \\ x-y+2 \geq 0 \text{ for } y \geq x \end{cases} = \begin{cases} R_1\{(x,y) : x-y-2 \leq 0, y \leq x\} \\ R_2 = \{(x,y) : x-y+2 \geq 0, y \geq x\} \end{cases}$$

The region (R) represented by inequality (i) is the union of region R_1 and R_2. Further we require to find the region of R common with region $R' = \{(x, y) : x^2 + y^2 \leq 4\}$, i.e., $R \cap R'$.

The shaded region shown above is the required region = 2[area of curvilinear ΔOED + area of ΔDOB + area of curvilinear ΔOBA]

= 2[1/8 (area of circle) + 1/2 (2) (2) + 1/8 (area of circle)]

= 2[1/4 (area of circle) + 2] = [1/4 (π) $(2)^2$+2] = 2π + 4 square units.

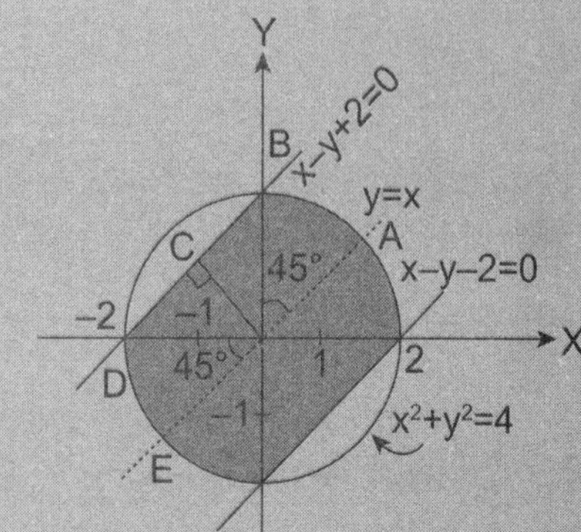

FIGURE 3.102

(e) $|x| + |y| \le 2$ ...(i)

$$\Rightarrow \begin{cases} x+y\le 2 \;\; ; x\ge 0, y\ge 0 \\ x-y\le 2 \;\; ; x\ge 0, y\le 0 \\ -x-y\le 2 ; x\le 0, y\le 0 \\ -x+y\le 2 ; x\le 0, y\ge 0 \end{cases}$$

$$= \begin{cases} R_1 = \{(x,y); x+y-2\le 0, x, y\ge 0\} \\ R_2 = \{(x,y); x-y-2\le 0, x\ge 0, y\le 0\} \\ R_3 = \{(x,y); x+y+2\ge 0, x, y\le 0\} \\ R_4 = \{(x,y); x-y+2\ge 0, x\le 0, y\ge 0\} \end{cases}$$

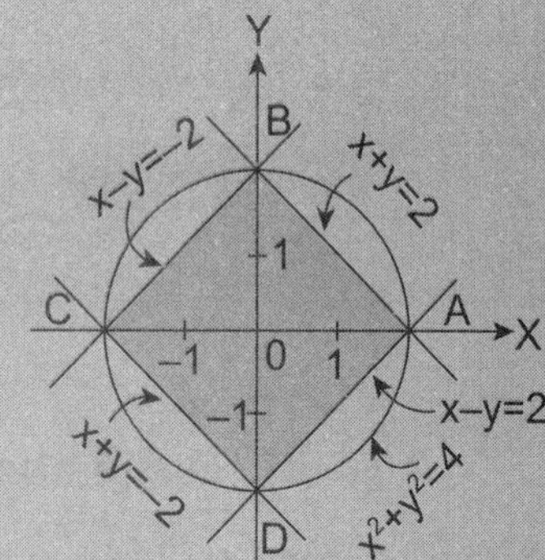

FIGURE 3.103

Thus, the region (R) (1) is the union of above four regions R_1, R_2, R_3 and R_4. Further we require to find the region common to R and that of $x^2 + y^2 \le 4$.

The required region (shaded) = 4 (area ΔOAB) = 4 [1/2(2) (2)] = 8 square units

(f) $|x| + |y| \ge 2$ is the region outside the quadrilateral $ABCD$ shown in the above diagram.

The region of $|x| + |y| \ge 2$ common with the region $x^2 + y^2 \le 4$ is unshaded region of circle shown in Fig. 3.103 and equals

= [(area of circle) –8] square units = π $(2)^2$= 8 – (4π –8) square units

ILLUSTRATION 62: Sketch the following curves:

(i) $|x + y| + |x - y| \le 4$ (ii) $|x + y| + |x - y| \ge 4$

SOLUTION: (i) Given inequalities are $|x + y| + |x - y| \le 4$ ...(i)

Now if we replace x by $-x$ and y by $-y$, there will be no change in the inequality (i) . It implies the region represented by inequality (i) is symmetric about the coordinate axes.

So to draw the region represented by inequality (i), we draw the region contained I[st] quadrant and copy the same in rest of the quadrants. So let us take $x \ge 0$, $y \ge 0$, then inequality (i) becomes $x + y + |x - y| \le 4$

$$\Rightarrow \begin{cases} x+y+x-y\le 4; x\ge y \\ x+y-x+y\le 4; x\le y \end{cases}$$

$$= \begin{cases} R_1 = \{(x,y): 0\le y\le x\le 2\} \\ R_2 = \{(x,y): 0\le x\le y\le 2\} \end{cases}$$

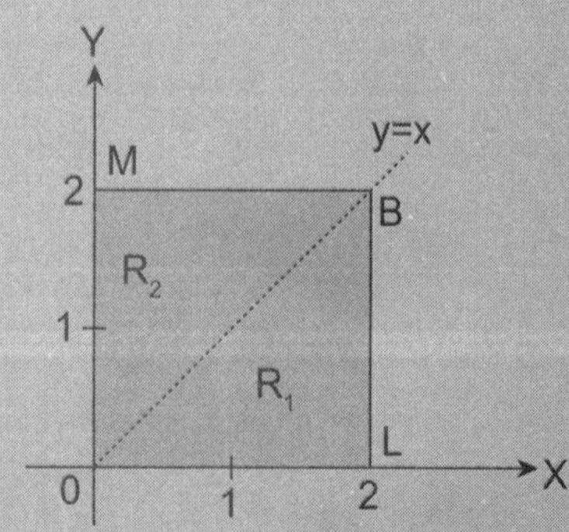

FIGURE 3.104

Thus, the region of inequality (i) contained in I[st] quadrant is the union two regions R_1 and R_2 as represented by following diagram by shaded region

Thus, the total region represented by inequality (i) will be as shown Fig. 3.105.

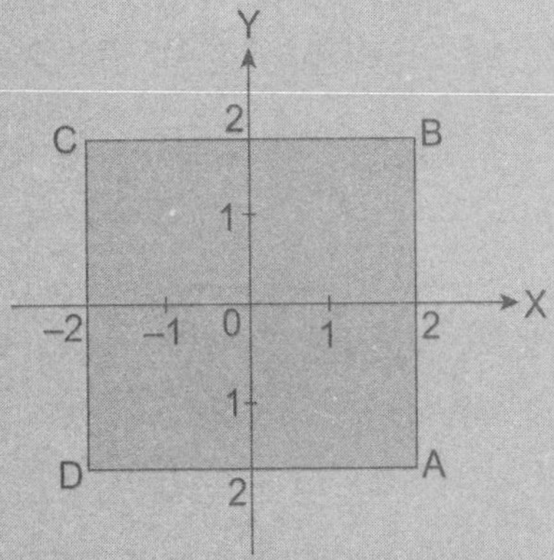

FIGURE 3.105

Thus, the area of above shaded region = area of square $ABCD = (4)^2 = 16$ square units.

Aliter: $|x + y| + |x - y| \le 4$

$$\Rightarrow \begin{cases} x+y+x-y \le 4; & x+y \ge 0, x-y \ge 0 \\ x+y-x+y \le 4; & x+y \ge 0, x-y \le 0 \\ -x-y-x+y \le 4; & x+y \le 0, x-y \le 0 \\ -x-y+x-y \le 4; & x+y \le 0, x-y \ge 0 \end{cases}$$

$$= \begin{cases} R_1 = \{(x,4) : x \le 2; y \ge -x; y \le x\} \\ R_2 = \{(x,y) : y \le 2; y \ge x, y \ge -x\} \\ R_3 = \{(x,y) : x \ge -2, x \le y \le -x\} \\ R_4 = \{(x,y) : y \ge -2, y \le x, y \le -x\} \end{cases}$$

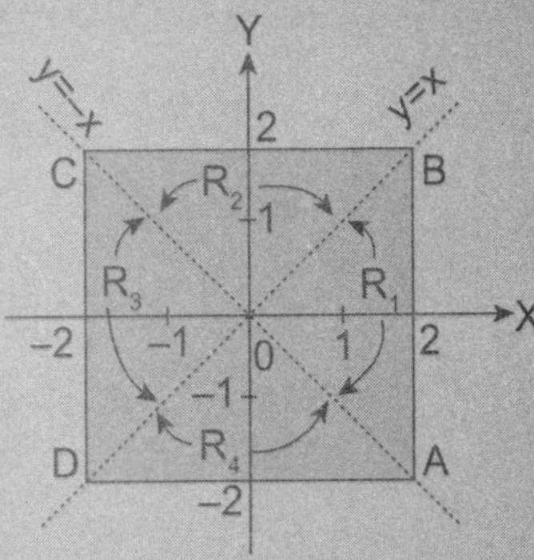

FIGURE 3.106

Thus, the required region R is the union of region R_1, R_2, R_3 and R_4. i.e., $R = R_1 \cup R_2 \cup R_3 \cup R_4$ as shown in Fig. 3.106 by shaded region.

In above Fig. 3.106 R_1 = *area* of ΔOAD

R_2 = area of ΔOBC

R_3 = area of ΔOCD

R_4 = area of ΔODA

$\therefore$ R = area of square $ABCD = (4)^2 = 16$ square unit

(ii) $|x + y| + |x - y| \ge 4$

Clearly as $|x + y| + |x - y| \le 4$ is the region inside the square $ABCD$, $|x + y| + |x - y| \ge 4$ will represent region on the boundary and outside the square $ABCD$ as shown in Fig. 3.107:

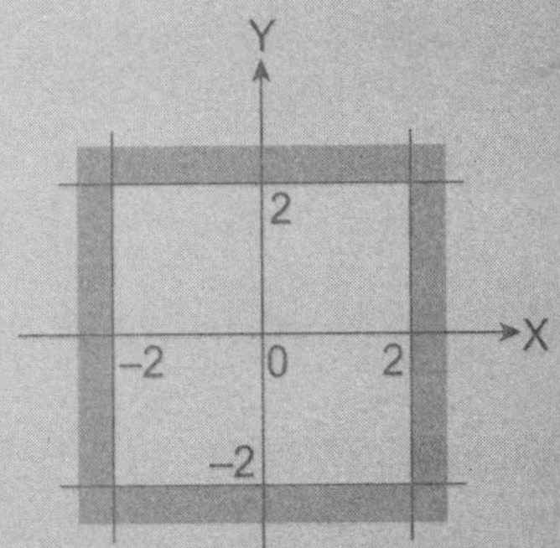

FIGURE 3.107

Clearly the region is unbounded and hence is infinite.

ILLUSTRATION 63: Draw the graphs of the solution set of the following system of inequations:

(a) $x^2 + y \le 0$; $2x^2 + y - 1 \le 0$

(b) $y + x^2 \le 0$; $y - 2x + 3 \ge 0$ and $y + 1 \le 0$

(c) $x + y \le 6$; $x^2 + y^2 \le 6y$ and $y^2 \le 8x$

(d) $|x - 2y| + |x + 2y| \le 8$ and $xy \ge 2$

And also find the corresponding area.

SOLUTION: (a) First given inequality is $x^2 + y \le 0$

$\Rightarrow$ $x^2 \le -y$ which represents the interior region of the downwards parabola $x^2 = -y$ .....(i)

Second given inequality is $2x^2 + y - 1 \le 0$

or $x^2 \le -\frac{1}{2}(y-1)$ which represents the interior region of the downwards parabola $x^2 = -\frac{1}{2}(y-1)$ ....(ii)

Curves (i) and (ii) intersect at $(\pm 1, -1)$ as shown below:

The region common to interior of (i) and (ii) is shown by shaded portion in the Fig. 3.108 and is given by, $\int_{-1}^{1}(1-2x^2)-(-x^2) = \frac{4}{3}$ square units.

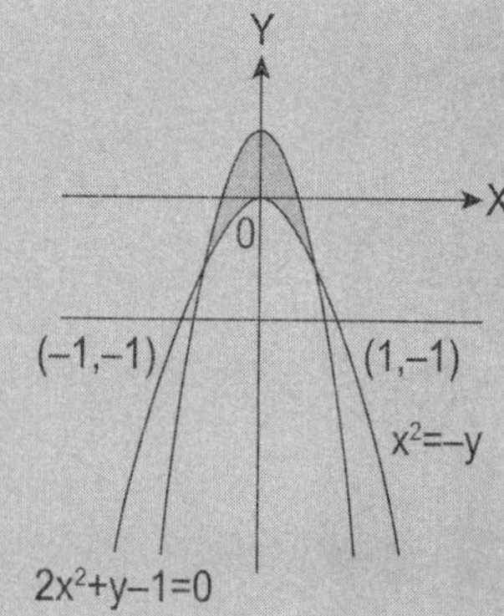

FIGURE 3.108

(b) First givnen inequality is $y + x^2 \le 0$ or $x^2 \le -y$

which represents the interior of parabola $x^2 = -y$ ...(i)

second given inequality is $y - 2x + 3 \ge 0$ or $y - 2x \ge -3$ ...(ii)

third inequality is $y + 1 \le 0$ or $y \le -1$ ...(iii)

now $y = -1$ and $x^2 = -y$ intersects at $(\pm1, -1)$ and the straight line $y - 2x = -3$ intersects parabola $x^2 = -y$ at points $(1, -1)$ and $(-3, -9)$ as shown in Fig. 3.109.

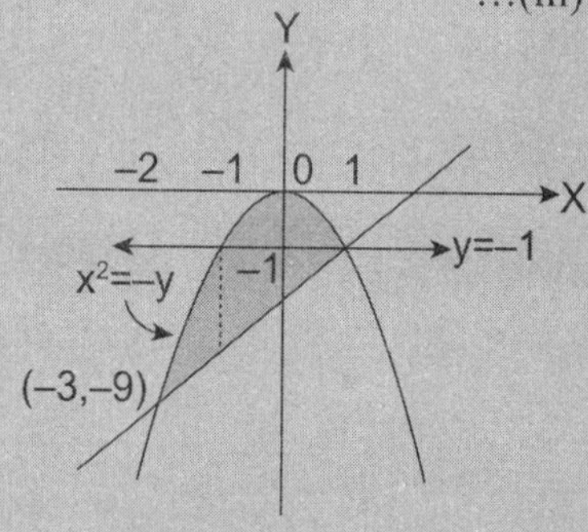

FIGURE 3.109

The shaded region represents the required area

$$= \int_{-3}^{-1}\left[-x^2-(2x-3)\right]dx + \int_{-1}^{1}\left[-1-(2x-3)\right]dx$$

$$= -\frac{1}{3}\left[x^3\right]_{-3}^{-1} - \left[x^2\right]_{-3}^{-1} + 3\left[x^3\right]_{-3}^{-1} - \left[x\right]_{-1}^{1}$$

$$-\left[x^2-3x\right]_{-1}^{1} = \frac{28}{3} \text{ square units}$$

(c) Given inequities are

$x + y \le 6$ ...(i)

$x^2 + y^2 - 6y \le 0$ ...(2)

$y^2 - 8x \le 0$ ...(3)

$x^2 + y^2 - 6y \le 0$ represents the interior region of circle $x^2 + (y-3)^2 = 9$; where $y^2 - 8x \le 0$ represents interior region of parabola $y^2 = 8x$.

$x + y \le 6$ represents the region of plane on the side of line $x + y = 6$ containing the origin. Thus, the required region is as shown by shaded portion in the given in Fig. 3.110.

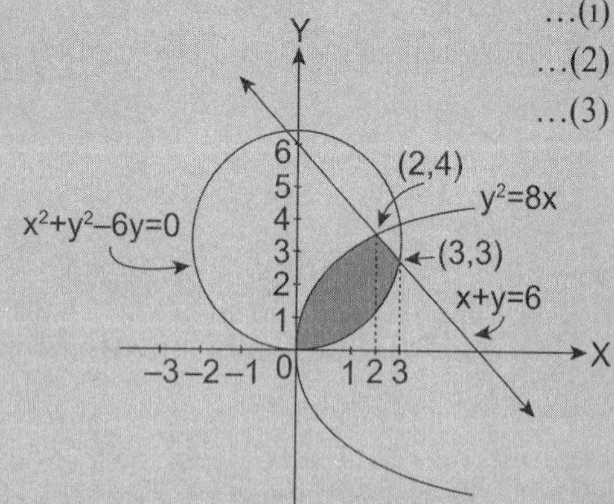

FIGURE 3.110

∴ The required region =

$$\int_{0}^{2}\left[\sqrt{8}\sqrt{x}-(3-\sqrt{9-x^2})\right]dx + \int_{2}^{3}\left[(6-x)-(3-\sqrt{9-x^2})\right]dx$$

$$= \sqrt{8}\left[\frac{2}{3}x^{3/2}\right]_0^2 - 3(2) + \left|\frac{x\sqrt{9-x^2}}{2} + \frac{9}{2}\sin^{-1}\left(\frac{x}{3}\right)\right|_0^2 +$$

$$6(1) - \frac{1}{2}(9-4) - 3(1) + \left|\frac{x\sqrt{9-x^2}}{2} + \frac{9}{2}\sin^{-1}\left(\frac{x}{3}\right)\right|_2^3$$

$$= \frac{2\sqrt{8}}{3}(2\sqrt{2}) - 6 + \left[\sqrt{5} + \frac{9}{2}\sin^{-1}\frac{2}{3}\right] + 6 - \frac{5}{2} - 3 + \frac{9}{2} \times \frac{\pi}{3} - \sqrt{5} - \frac{9}{2}\sin^{-1}\left(\frac{2}{3}\right)$$

$$= \frac{16}{3} - \frac{11}{2} + \frac{9}{4}\pi = \frac{32-33}{6} + \frac{9}{4}\pi = \left(\frac{9}{4}\pi - \frac{1}{6}\right) \text{ sq. units}$$

(d) Given inequalities

$|x - 2y| + |x + 2y| \leq 8$ ...(i)

and $xy \geq 2$ ...(ii)

Replacing x by $-x$ and y by $-y$ does not effect the inequality (i), Thus, the relation represented by inequality (i) is symmetric about x-axis and y-axis. Let us draw the sketch when $x - 2y \geq 0$ and $x + 2y \geq 0$

i.e., $y \leq \frac{x}{2}$ and $y \geq -\frac{x}{2}$

Then (1) becomes $(x - 2y) + (x + 2y) \geq 8$

$\Rightarrow$ $2x \leq 8$

$\Rightarrow$ $x \leq 4$

$\therefore$ The region

$R_1 = \left\{(x, y) : -\frac{x}{2} \leq y \leq \frac{x}{2} \text{ and } x \leq 4\right\}$ is as in Fig. 3.111.

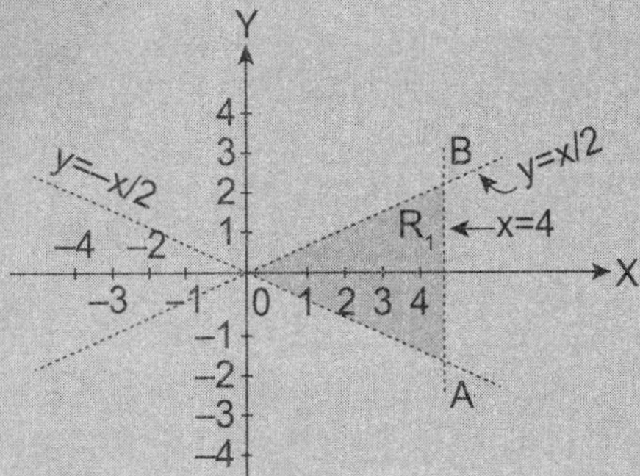

FIGURE 3.111

Next for $x - 2y \leq 0$ and $x + 2y \geq 0$

i.e., $y \geq \frac{x}{2}$ and $y \geq -\frac{x}{2}$

Also (i) becomes $-x + 2y + x + 2y \leq 8$

$\Rightarrow$ $y \leq 2$

$\therefore$ The region

$R_2 = \left\{(x, y) : y \geq \frac{x}{2}, y \geq -\frac{x}{2} \text{ and } y \leq 2\right\}$ is as shown in Fig. 3.112.

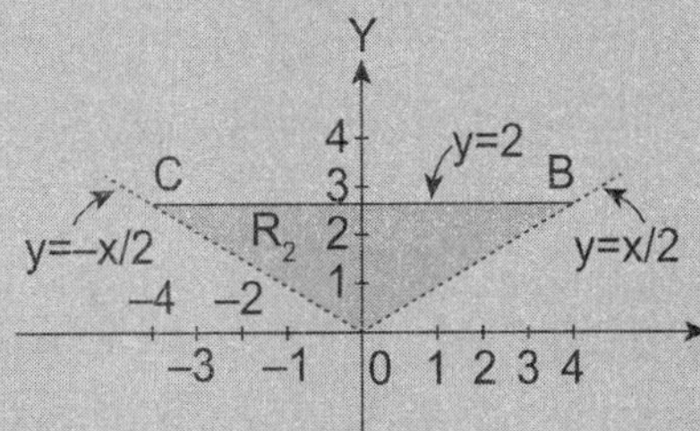

FIGURE 3.112

Since the region $|x - 2y| + |x + 2y| \leq 8$ is symmetric about x-axis and y-axis, from above two cases we conclude that the interior of rectangle bounded by straight line $x = \pm 4$ and $y = \pm 2$ will be the region represented by the inequality $|x - 2y| + |x + 2y| \leq 8$ as shown in Fig. 3.113.

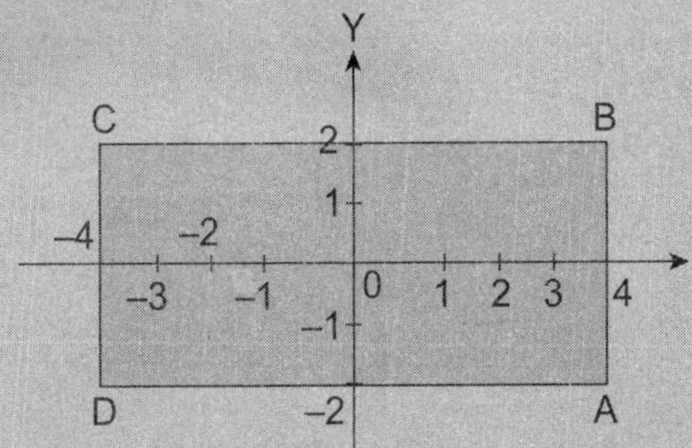

FIGURE 3.113

Further we are required to find the region common to interior of above rectangle and the region represented by inequality $xy \geq 2$ or $xy - 2 \geq 0$

Here $xy = 2$ represents the rectangular hyperbola since $f(0, 0) = 0.0 - 2 = -2 < 0$

$\therefore$ $xy - 2 \geq 0$ will be the region on the side of the hyperbola $xy = 2$ not containing the origin as shown below.

Thus, the required region is the area common to interior of rectangle $ABCD$ and the region of hyperbola shown in Fig. 3.115, as represented below

$\therefore$ The required area $= 2\int_1^4 \left[2 - +\left(\frac{2}{x}\right)\right] dx$

$= 2[2x - 2\ell nx]_1^4$

$= 2[(8 - 2ln4) - (2)]$

$= 2[6 - 2ln4] = (12 - 4ln4)$ square units.

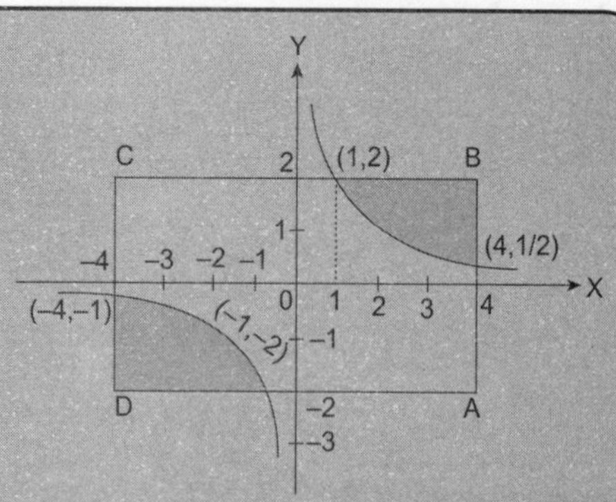

FIGURE 3.115

ILLUSTRATION 64: Find the area of the region $\{(x, y): 0 \le y \le x^2 + 1, 0 \le y \le x + 1, 0 \le x \le 2\}$.

SOLUTION: The required area is bounded by parabola $y = x^2 + 1$, straight lines $y = x + 1$, $x = 2$ and in Ist quadrant.

The point of intersection of $y = x^2 + 1$ and $y = x + 1$ is given by $x^2 + 1 = x + 1$

$\Rightarrow x = 0$ or $x = 1$

i.e., $A(0, 1)$ and $B(1, 2)$

Thus, the required area is shown by shaded region

$\therefore$ Required Area $OABCDO = \int_0^1 (x^2+1)dx + \int_1^2 (x+1)dx$

$= \left(\frac{x^3}{3}+x\right)_0^1 + \left(\frac{x^2}{2}+x\right)_1^2 = \frac{23}{6}$ square units.

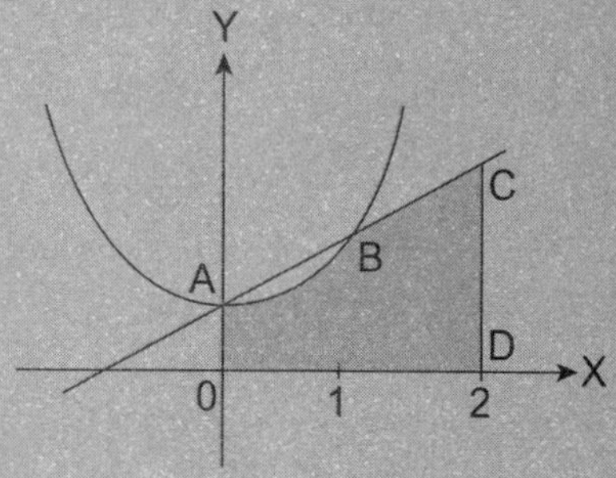

FIGURE 3.116

DETERMINATION OF CURVE WHEN AREA FUNCTION IS GIVEN

If the area bounded by some function and x-axis between $x = a$ and $x = b$ is given $g(a, b)\ \forall\ a > b$, where a is a given real number and b is a real parameter, then the function can be obtained as described below. Let the unknown function be $y = f(x)$.

$\because \int_a^b |f(x)|dx$ represents area enclosed between $f(x)$ and x-axis between the semi-variable boundaries $x = a$ and $x = b$ as b is a real parameter and it is given as $g(a, b)$. Of course area changes by variation in 'b' but always the value of area shall be represented by a function $g(a, b)$.

Thus, $\int_a^b |f(x)|dx = g(a, b)$

Now differentiating both sides w.r.t. b we get $|f(b)| = \frac{d}{db}(g(a,b)) = g'(a,b)$ (say)

$\Rightarrow f(b) = \pm g'(a, b)$

Consequently determining two curves $f(x) = g'(a, x)$ or $f(x) = -g'(a, x)$

ILLUSTRATION 65: If the area bounded by x-axis, the curve $y = f(x)$ and the line $x = a$, $x = b$ is given $a \sin^2 b + b\sin^2 a\ \forall\ a < b$, where a is a fixed given positive real number, then find the function $f(x)$.

SOLUTION: We are given $\int_a^b |f(x)|dx = (a\sin^2 b + b\sin^2 a)$, where $0 < a \in \mathbb{R}$ and $a < b$ and b is a variable parameter.

Differentiating both sides w.r.t b we get $|f(b)| = 2a \sin b \cos b + \sin^2 a$

$\Rightarrow f(b) = \pm (2a \sin b \cos b + \sin^2 a)$

$\Rightarrow f(x) = \pm (a \sin^2 x + \sin^2 a)$

ILLUSTRATION 66: If the area bounded by x-axis, the curve $y = f(x)$ and the line $x = 1/\sqrt{2}$ and $x = a$; $a \in \left(\frac{1}{\sqrt{2}}, \frac{\pi}{2}\right)$ is given by $\sec^2 a - 1/2$, then find the function $f(x)$

SOLUTION: we are given $\int_{1/\sqrt{2}}^{a} |f(x)| dx = (\sec^2 a - 1/2)$

Differentiating both sides w.r.t. a we get $|f(a)| = 2\sec^2 a \tan a$

$\Rightarrow f(x) = \pm (2\sec^2 x \tan x)$

TEXTUAL EXERCISE–3: (SUBJECTIVE)

1. Let $g(x)$ be the inverse of $f(x) = x^3 + 3x + 2$. Find the area bounded by $g(x)$, the x-axis and the ordinate at $x = -2$ and $x = 6$.

2. The possible values of $b > 0$, so that the area of the bounded region enclosed between the parabola $y = x - bx^2$ and $y = \frac{x^2}{b}$ is maximum.

3. The Fig. 3.117 shows two regions in the first quadrant. $f(t)$ is the area under the curve $y = \sin x^2$ from 0 to t and $g(t)$ is the area of the triangle with vertices O, P and $M(t, 0)$. Determine the ratio $\lim_{t\to 0} \frac{f(t)}{g(t)}$

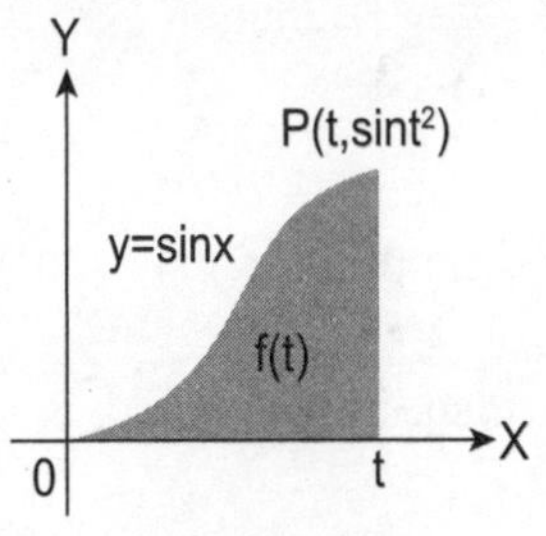

FIGURE 3.117

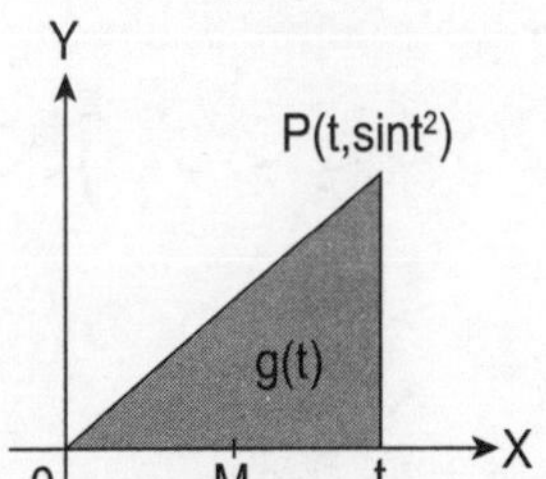

FIGURE 3.118

4. If the area bounded by $y = x^2 + 2x - 3$ and the line $y = kx + 1$ is the least, find k and also the least area.

5. Consider two curves $C_1: y = e^x$, $C_2: y = e^{t-x}$ where 't' be a positive parameter. Let A be the area of the part surrounded by C_1, C_2 and the y-axis, then find $\lim_{t\to 0}\left(\frac{A}{t^2}\right)$.

6. Find the area of the region represented by the following linear in-equations:

(a) $|x| + |y| \geq 2$; $x^2 + y^2 \leq 4$

(b) $x^2 + xy - 4 \leq 0$, $y - 3 \leq 0$ and $x > 0$, $y > 0$

7. Find the area of the region represented by the following linear in-equations:

(a) $x > |y - 1|$; $x \leq 1$

(b) $|x - y| \leq 2$; $|x + y| \leq 2$

(c) $|x| - |y| \geq 1$; $1 \leq |x| \leq 2$

(d) $|x| + |y| \leq 2$; $|x| \leq 1$; $|y| \geq 1$

8. Find the area of the region represented by the following linear in equations:

(a) $|x + y| + |x - y| \leq 3$ (b) $|x + 2| + |y + 1| \leq 3$

9. Find the area of the region represented by the following in equation:

(a) $|x + y| + |x - y| \leq 4$, $|x| \leq 1$ and $y \geq \sqrt{x^2 - 2x + 1}$

(b) $x^2 + y^2 \leq 2(|x| + |y|)$

(c) $4 \leq x^2 + y^2 \leq 2(|x| + |y|)$

10. Find the area of the following regions:

(a) $4 \leq x^2 + y^2 \leq 2(|x| + |y|)$ $|x| \leq \sqrt{2} + 1$; $0 \leq y \leq \sqrt{2} + 1$

(b) $2^{|x|}|y| + 2^{|x|-1} \leq 1$, $|x| \leq \frac{1}{2}$ and $|y| \leq \frac{1}{2}$

11. If the area bounded by x-axis the curve $y = f(x)$ and the line $x = a$, $x = b$ is equal to $\sqrt{b^2 - a^2}$ $\forall\, a < b$

where a is given positive real number, find the function $f(x)$.

12. If the area bounded by curves $y = f(x)$ and x-axis between the ordinates $x = 0$ and $x = a$ where $a \geq 0$ is $(e^{a^2} - 1)$ square unit $\forall\ a \geq 0$ then find all such possible curves.

13. Find the area bounded by
(i) $|xy| = 1$ and $x^2 + y^2 \leq 4$
(ii) $|xy| \leq 1$ and $x^2 + y^2 \leq 4$

14. Find the area bounded by the region common to the inequality $\dfrac{|x|+|y|}{2} + \left|\dfrac{|x|+|y|}{2}\right| \leq 2$ and $x^2 + y^2 \leq 36$

15. Find the area of the figure whose set of points satisfies the system of inequalities $x^2 + y^2 \leq r^2$, $r > 0$, $x - y \geq 0$ and $y \geq 0$.

16. Find the area bounded by $|y| + \dfrac{1}{2} \geq 2^{-|x|}$ and $\max(|x|, |y|) \leq \dfrac{1}{2}$

17. Find the area common to the regions $y \geq \sin \pi x$ and $x(x - 2) + y^2 \leq 0$

18. Find the area common to the regions $y \geq \sin x$ and $y \leq \sin^{-1} \sin x$ for all $x \in [0, \pi]$.

19. Find the area common to the regions $y \geq x^2 + 1$ and $y \leq x + 1$

20. Find the area common to the regions $y \leq |x^2 - 1|$ and $y \geq x^2 - 4$

21. Find the area common to the regions $\dfrac{x^2}{a^2} + \dfrac{y^2}{b^2} \leq 1$ and $ay + bx \leq ab$.

22. Find the area enclosed by the curves $\min(|x + y|, |x - y|) = 1$ and $x^2 + y^2 > 1$ between the ordinates $x = -1$ to $x = 1$.

23. Find the area of the regions represented by the following relations:
(a) $[y] = 4 - [x]; x \geq 0, y \geq 0$
(b) $[|y|] = 4 - [|x|]$
(c) $[y] = [\cos x]; 0 \leq x \leq 2\pi$

24. Find all the points, in the plane, whose coordinates x and y satisfy inequality
(a) $\cos x - \cos y > 0$ and hence find the area for $(x + y); (x - y) \in [0, y\pi]$
(b) $\log_{|\sin x|} y > 0$ and hence find the area of aring for $x \in (0, 2\pi)$

25. Sketch on x - y plane and find the area
(a) $\max([|x - 3|], [|y - 1|]) \leq 2$
(b) $\min([x - 1], [y + 2], 3) \geq 2$ and $y \leq 3; x \leq 5$

Answer Keys

1. 9/2 sq. units **2.** $b = 1$ **3.** 2/3 **4.** $k = 2$ and $A_{min} = 32/3$ **5.** 1/4

6. (a) $(4\pi - 8)$ sq. units (b) $\dfrac{3}{2} + 4\ln 2$ sq. units

7. (a) 1 sq. units (b) 8 sq. units (c) 2 sq. units (d) 2 sq. units

8. (a) 9 sq. units (b) 18 sq. units

9. (a) 2 sq. units (b) $(4\pi + 8)$ sq. units (c) 8 sq. units

10. (a) 4 sq. units (b) $(4 - 2\sqrt{2}) \log_2 e - 1$ **11.** $f(x) = \pm\dfrac{x}{\sqrt{x^2 - a^2}}$ **12.** $f(x) = \pm 2xe^{x^2}$

13. (i) $4\sqrt{3} - 4\ln(2 + \sqrt{3})$ (ii) $4\pi - 4\sqrt{3} + 4\ln(2 + \sqrt{3})$ **14.** 8 **15.** $\dfrac{1}{8}\pi r^2$

16. $2 - (4 - 2\sqrt{2})\log_2 e$ **17.** $\pi/2$ sq. units **18.** $\dfrac{\pi^2}{8}$ **19.** $\dfrac{1}{6}$ sq. units

20. $\dfrac{44}{3}$ sq. units **21.** $\dfrac{(3\pi + 2)ab}{4}$ **22.** $6 - \pi$

23. (a) 5 sq. units (b) 20 sq. units (c) 2π sq. units

24. (a) $4\pi^2$ sq. units (b) 2π sq. units

25. (a) 36 sq. units (b) 6 sq. units

TEXTUAL EXERCISE–3: (OBJECTIVE)

1. The area of the region defined by $||x| - |y|| \le 1$ and $x^2 + y^2 \le 1$ in the $x - y$ coordinate plane is
(a) π (b) 2π
(c) 3π (d) 1

2. The area defined by $1 \le |x - 2| + |y + 1| \le 2$ is
(a) 2 (b) 4
(c) 6 (d) None of these

3. The area bounded by the curves, $|y| = e^{-|x|} - \frac{1}{2}$ and $\frac{|x|+|y|}{2} + \left|\frac{|x|-|y|}{2}\right| \le 2$ is
(a) (7 + log 4) sq units
(b) (7 – log 2) sq units
(c) (14 + 2 log 2) sq units
(d) (14 – 2 log 2) sq. units

4. The area bounded by the curves $|x| + |y| \ge 1$ and $x^2 + y^2 \le 1$ is
(a) 2 sq. units (b) π sq. units
(c) (π – 2) sq. units (d) (π + 2) sq. units

5. The area common to the region determined by $y \ge \sqrt{x}$ and $x^2 + y^2 < 2$ has the value
(a) π (b) (2π – 1)
(c) $\frac{\pi}{4} - \frac{1}{6}$ (d) None of these

6. The area enclosed in the region $\frac{x^2}{a^2} + \frac{y^2}{b^2} \le 1$ and $\frac{x}{a} + \frac{y}{b} \ge 1$ is
(a) $\frac{\pi ab}{4} - \frac{1}{2}ab$ (b) $\frac{\pi ab}{4}$
(c) πab (d) None of these

7. The area defined by $|y| + \frac{1}{2} \le e^{-|x|}$ is
(a) 2(1 – ln 2) (b) 2(1 + ln 2)
(c) 2 ln 2 (d) None of these

8. The area defined by $2 \le |x + y| + |x - y| \le 4$ is
(a) 4 (b) 8
(c) 12 (d) None of these

9. The area defined by $|x + 1| + |2y - 3| \le 1$ in the $x - y$ coordinate plane is
(a) 1 (b) 2
(c) 4 (d) None of these.

10. The area defined by $||x + y| - |x - y|| \le 1$, $x^2 + y^2 \le \frac{1}{2}$ in the $x - y$ coordinate plane is
(a) π (b) $\frac{\pi}{2}$
(c) $\frac{\pi}{4}$ (d) None of these

11. The area of the region for which $0 < y < 3 - 2x - x^2$ and $x > 0$ is
(a) $\int_1^3 (3 - 2x - x^2)dx$ (b) $\int_0^3 (3 - 2x - x^2)dx$
(c) $\int_0^1 (3 - 2x - x^2)dx$ (d) None of these

12. Area of common region bounded by $x \ge y - 4$; $4 \le x^2 + y^2$ and $3y + 16x - 48 \le 0$ which lies above x-axis is (in square units)
(a) 8 – 2p (b) 16
(c) 8 + 2p (d) None of these

Answer Keys

1. (a) 2. (c) 3. (c) 4. (c) 5. (c) 6. (a) 7. (a) 8. (c) 9. (a) 10. (b)
11. (c) 12. (d)

■ AREA ENCLOSED IN CURVED LOOP

Any curve forming loop is multi-valued function so first of all solve the equation of curve for y to find its functional branches and obtain the domain of function say [α, β]

e.g., $ax^2 + by^2 + 2hxy + 2gx + 2fy + c = 0$ (say) solving for y, we get

$$y_1 = \frac{f(x) + \sqrt{g(x)}}{2}; \; y_2 = \frac{f(x) - \sqrt{g(x)}}{2}$$

Clearly there two functions are forming the loop.

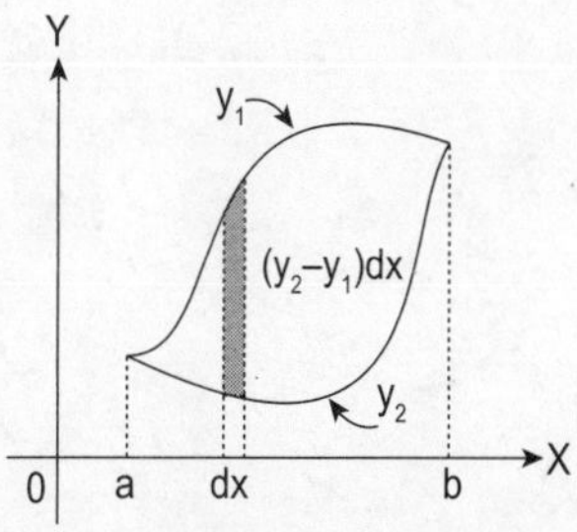

FIGURE 3.119

$$\text{Area of loop} = \int_\alpha^\beta |y_2 - y_1| dx = \int_\alpha^\beta \sqrt{g(x)}\, dx$$

ILLUSTRATION 67: Find the area enclosed by the curve $5x^2 + 6xy + 2y^2 + 7x + 6y + 6 = 0$.

SOLUTION: $2y^2 + (6x + 6)y + 5x^2 + 7x + 6 = 0$

$$y = \frac{-6(x+1) \pm \sqrt{36(x+1)^2 - 8(5x^2+7x+6)}}{4} = \frac{-6(x+1) \pm \sqrt{-4x^2+16x-12}}{4}$$

$$= \frac{-3(x+1) \pm \sqrt{-(x^2-4x+3}}{2}$$

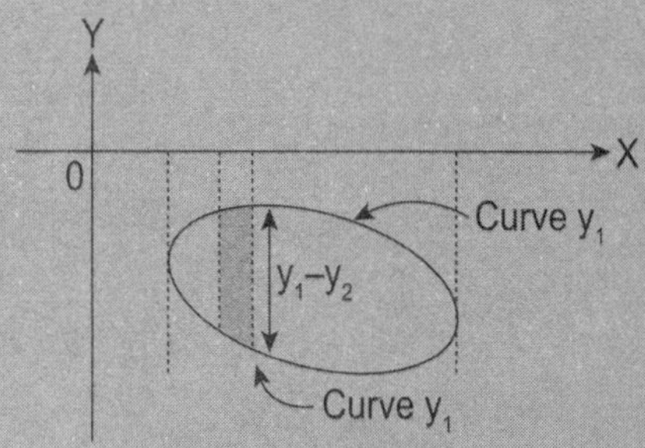

FIGURE 3.120

Two functional branches of above relation are

$$\left.\begin{aligned} y_1 &= \frac{-3(x+1) + \sqrt{(x-1)(3-x)}}{2} \\ y_2 &= \frac{-3(x+1) - \sqrt{(x-1)(3-x)}}{2} \end{aligned}\right\} \text{with common domain } x \in [1, 3]$$

$$A = \int_1^3 (y_1 - y_2)dx = \int_1^3 \sqrt{(x-1)(3-x)}dx$$

Put $x = \cos^2\theta + 3\sin^2\theta$

$Dx = (3\sin 2\theta - \sin 2\theta)d\theta = 2\sin 2\theta d\theta$

$x - 1 = 2\sin^2\theta$

$3 - x = 2\cos^2\theta$

If $x = 3 = 3\sin^2\theta + \cos^2\theta$

$\cos^2\theta = 0$

$\theta = \pi/2$

$$A = \int_0^{\pi/2} 2\sin\theta\cos\theta.2\sin 2\theta\, d\theta = 2\int_0^{\pi/2} \sin^2 2\theta\, d\theta = \int_0^{\pi} \sin^2\theta\, d\theta = 2\int_0^{\pi/2} \sin^2\theta\, d\theta$$

$$= 2\left(\frac{1}{2}\right)\frac{\pi}{2} = \frac{\pi}{2} \text{ square units}$$

ILLUSTRATION 68: Find the area bounded by the curve $a^2x^2 = y^3(2a - y)$; $a > 0$.

SOLUTION: Let us first draw the graph of given relation by analyzing its following features.

1. **Symmetry about axes:** Replacing x by $-x$ causes no change in the given relation implying the curve is symmetric about y-axis. But the relation changes on replacing y by $-y$ implying the curve is not symmetric about x-axis.
2. **Points of Intersection of curve and axes:** On x-axis $y = 0$

   $\Rightarrow a^2x^2 = 0$ $\qquad\qquad \Rightarrow a = 0$

   i.e., the curve passes through origin $O(0, 0)$

   On y-axis $x = 0$ $\qquad\qquad \Rightarrow 0 = y^3(2a - y)$

   $\Rightarrow y = 0$ or $y = 2a$

   $\Rightarrow$ the curve passes through the point $(0, 2a)$
3. **Domain of relation:** $a^2x^2 = y^3(2a - y)$

   $\Rightarrow x^2 = \dfrac{y^3(2a-y)}{a^2}$ $\qquad\qquad \Rightarrow x = \pm\sqrt{\dfrac{y^3(2a-y)}{a^2}}$

   For x to be real, $y^3(2a - y) \geq 0$ as $a > 0$

   $\Rightarrow y \geq 0$ and $2a - y \geq 0$ or $y \leq 0$, $2a - y \leq 0$

$\Rightarrow\; y \geq 0, y \leq 2a$ or $y \leq 0, y \geq 2a$ (impossible as $a > 0$)

$\Rightarrow\; y \in [0, 2a]$

$\therefore$ No portion of curve lies for $y < 0$ and $y > 2a$

4. To find stationary points: On differentiating given explicit relation w.r.t. x are get

$$2a^2x = 6ay^2\frac{dy}{dx} - 4y^3\frac{dy}{dx}$$

$$\Rightarrow\; 2a^2x = (6ay^2 - 4y^3)\frac{dy}{dx} \qquad \Rightarrow\; \frac{dy}{dx} = \frac{2a^2x}{2y^2(3a-2y)}$$

$$\therefore\; \frac{dy}{dx} = 0 \qquad \Rightarrow\; x = 0;\; y \neq 0,\; y \neq \frac{3a}{2}$$

Now $x = 0$ $\qquad \Rightarrow\; y^3(2a - y) = 0$

$\Rightarrow\; y = 0$ or $y = 2a$

But $y \neq 0$

$\Rightarrow\; P(0, 2a)$ is the stationary point.

5. Vertical Tangent: For vertical tangent $\frac{dy}{dx} \to \infty$

$$\Rightarrow\; \frac{dy}{dx} \to 0$$

$$\Rightarrow\; \frac{2y^2(3a-2y)}{2a^2x} = 0;\; y = \frac{3a}{2} \text{ or } y = 0$$

(Since $y \to 0$ and $x \to 0$)

$\Rightarrow$ Fraction value zero as numerator is of higher order infinitesimal as compared to denominator.

$\therefore$ curve has vertical tangent at point $Q\left(\frac{3\sqrt{3a}}{4}, \frac{3a}{2}\right)$; $R\left(\frac{-3\sqrt{3a}}{4}, \frac{3a}{2}\right)$ and $O(0, 0)$.

From above points, we find that the graph of curve would be as shown in Fig. 3.121.

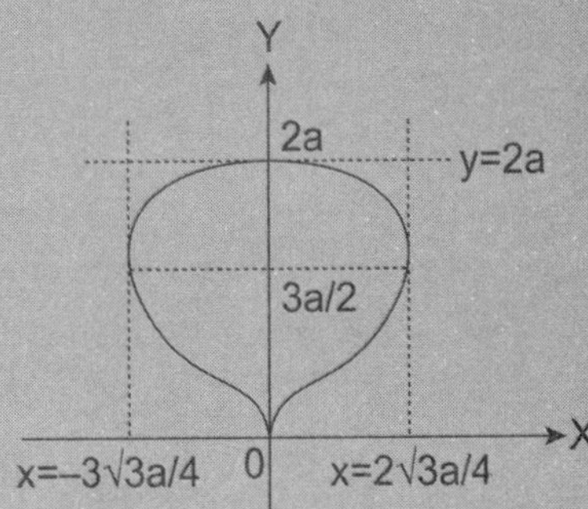

FIGURE 3.121

Thus, we are to find the area bounded by the above loop having equation $a^3x^2 = y^3(2a - y)$

$$\Rightarrow\; x = \pm\sqrt{\frac{y^3(2a-y)}{a^2}}$$

$$\therefore\; \text{Required area} = A = 2\int_0^{2a} |x|\, dy = \frac{2}{a}\int_0^{2a} y^{3/2}(2a-y)^{1/2}\, dy$$

Substitute $y = 2a\sin^2\theta$ $\qquad \Rightarrow\; dy = 4a\sin\theta\cos\theta\, d\theta$

For $y = 0$, $\theta = 0$ and for $y = 2a$, $\theta = \frac{\pi}{2}$

$$\therefore\; A = \frac{2}{a}\int_0^{\pi/2} \left(2a\sin^2\theta\right)^{3/2}(2a)^{1/2}(\cos\theta).4a\sin\theta\cos\theta\, d\theta = 2(16)a^2\int_0^{\pi/2}\sin^4\theta\cos^2\theta\, d\theta$$

$$= 32a^2\int_0^{\pi/2}\sin^4\theta\cos^2\theta\, d\theta = 32a^2\left[\frac{3\times1\times1}{6\times4\times2}\times\frac{\pi}{2}\right] = \pi a^2 \text{ square units.}$$

ILLUSTRATION 69: Find the area of a loop of the curve $xy^2 + (x + a)2\ (x + 2a) = 0;\ a > 0$.

SOLUTION: Given curve is $xy^2 + (x + a)^2\ (x + 2a) = 0$ .....(1)

Replacing y by $-y$ does not effect the given equation. So the curve is symmetric about x-axis.

The given curve cuts x-axis, where $y = 0$

$\Rightarrow\ (x + a)^2(x + 2a) = 0 \qquad \Rightarrow\ x = -a$ or $x = -2a$

i.e., points of intersection of curve and x-axis are $(-a, 0)$ and $(-2a, 0)$

Also $y = \pm\sqrt{\dfrac{-(x+a)^2(x+2a)}{x}}$

$\therefore$ For y to be real $\dfrac{-(x+a)^2)(x+2a)}{x} \geq 0$

$\Rightarrow\ \dfrac{(x+a)^2(x+2a)}{x} \leq 0$

$\Rightarrow\ x = -a$ or $(x + 2a)\,x \leq 0;\ x \neq 0$

$\Rightarrow\ x = -a$ or $x \in [-2a, 0)$

$\therefore$ The curve lie entirely on the left of y-axis but no portion of curve lies on the left of line $x = -2a$.

Thus, the curve has a loop intersecting x-axis at point $(-2a, 0)$ and $(-a, 0)$ and composed of function.

$$y = \sqrt{\frac{-(x+a)^2(x+2a)}{x}} = f_1(x) \qquad \text{(say)}$$

above x-axis and function $y = -\sqrt{\dfrac{-(x+a)^2(x+2a)}{x}} = f_2(x)$ (say)

below x-axis as shown in Fig. 3.122.

$\therefore$ Area of loop $= A = \displaystyle\int_{-2a}^{-a} (f_1(x) - f_2(x))\,dx$

$$= 2\int_{-2a}^{-a} \sqrt{\frac{-(x+a)^2(x+2a)}{x}}\,dx$$

For simplicity of integrand let us shift the origin to point $B(-a, 0)$ or translating the curve horizontally by 'a' units towards right, i.e., replacing x by $x - a$,

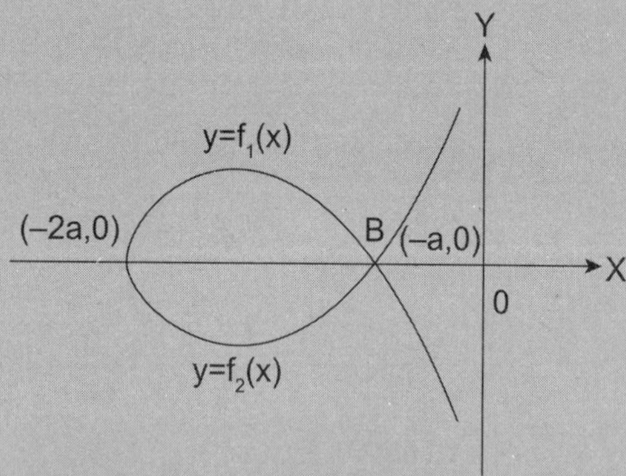

FIGURE 3.122

$$\therefore\ A = 2\int_{-a}^{0} \sqrt{\frac{-x^2(x+a)}{(x-a)}}\,dx$$

$$= 2\int_{-a}^{0} |x|\sqrt{-\frac{(x+a)}{x-a}}\,dx = 2\int_{-a}^{0} -x\sqrt{-\frac{(x+a)}{x-a}}\,dx$$

$$= 2\int_{0}^{a} x\sqrt{-\frac{(-x+a)}{-x-a}}\,dx \text{ (replacing } x \text{ by } -x) = 2\int_{0}^{a} x\sqrt{\frac{a-x}{a+x}}\,dx$$

Put $x = a\cos\theta \qquad \Rightarrow\ dx = -a\sin\theta\,d\theta$

For $x = 0 \qquad \Rightarrow\ \theta = \dfrac{\pi}{2}$

and for $x = a$ $\Rightarrow \theta = 0$

$$= 2\int_{\pi/2}^{0} a\cos\theta\sqrt{\frac{1-\cos\theta}{1+\cos\theta}}(-a\sin\theta)d\theta = 2a^2\int_0^{\pi/2}\sin\theta\cos\theta\sqrt{\frac{2\sin^2\theta/2}{2\cos^2\theta/2}}d\theta$$

$$= 2a^2\int_0^{\pi/2}\sin\theta\cos\theta\cdot\frac{\sin\frac{\theta}{2}}{\cos\frac{\theta}{2}}d\theta = 2a^2\int_0^{\pi/2}2\sin\frac{\theta}{2}\cos\frac{\theta}{2}\left(2\cos^2\frac{\theta}{2}-1\right)\frac{\sin\theta/2}{\cos\theta/2}d\theta$$

$$= 2a^2\int_0^{\pi/2}2\sin^2\frac{\theta}{2}\left(2\cos^2\frac{\theta}{2}-1\right)d\theta = 8a^2\int_0^{\pi/2}\sin^2\frac{\theta}{2}\cos^2\frac{\theta}{2}d\theta - 4a^2\int_0^{\pi/2}\sin^2\frac{\theta}{2}d\theta$$

$$= 2a^2\int_0^{\pi/2}\sin^2\theta\,d\theta - 2a^2\int_0^{\pi/2}(1-\cos\theta)\,d\theta = a^2\int_0^{\pi/2}(1-\cos 2\theta)d\theta - 2a^2\int_0^{\pi/2}(1-\cos\theta)\,d\theta$$

$$= a^2\left[\theta - \frac{\sin 2\theta}{2}\right]_0^{\pi/2} - 2a^2[\theta - \sin\theta]_0^{\pi/2} = a^2\left[\frac{\pi}{2}\right] - 2a^2\left[\frac{\pi}{2}-1\right]$$

$$= \frac{a^2\pi}{2} - a^2\pi + 2a^2 = 2a^2 - \frac{a^2\pi}{2} = 2a^2\left[1-\frac{\pi}{4}\right] \text{ square units.}$$

ILLUSTRATION 70: Find the area of the loop of the curve $x^2 - (y - 1)y^2 = 0$.

SOLUTION: We have, $x^2 = (1 - y)y^2$

$\Rightarrow 1 - y \geq 0$ $\Rightarrow y \leq 1$

Thus, for the loop, $y \in [0, 1]$

$$\text{Area of required loop} = 2\int_0^1 y\sqrt{1-y}\,dy$$

$$= 2\int_0^1 (1-y)\sqrt{y}\,dy$$

$$= 2\int_0^1\left(\sqrt{y} - y^{3/2}\right)dy = 2\left(\frac{2}{3}y^{3/2} - \frac{2}{5}y^{5/2}\right)_0^1$$

$$= \frac{8}{15} \text{ square units.}$$

AREA ENCLOSED BY CURVE BETWEEN TWO RADIUS VECTORS WHEN ITS EQUATION IS GIVEN IN POLAR FORM

If $r = f(\theta)$ is the equation of curve in polar form, where $f(\theta)$ is a continuous function of θ, then the area enclosed by curve $r = f(\theta)$, and the radius vectors $r = f(\theta_1)$ and $r = f(\theta_2)$; $(\theta_1 < \theta_2)$ is given by $A = \frac{1}{2}\int_{\theta_1}^{\theta_1} r^2\,d\theta = \frac{1}{2}\int_{\theta_1}^{\theta_1}[f(\theta)]^2\,d\theta$

Proof: The region is shown in Fig. 3.123. To find the area bounded by the graphs of the polar functions, partition the region between $\theta = \alpha$ and $\theta = \beta$ a collection of rays, say θ_0, θ_1, …, θ_n. Let $\alpha = \theta_0$ and $\beta = \theta_n$.

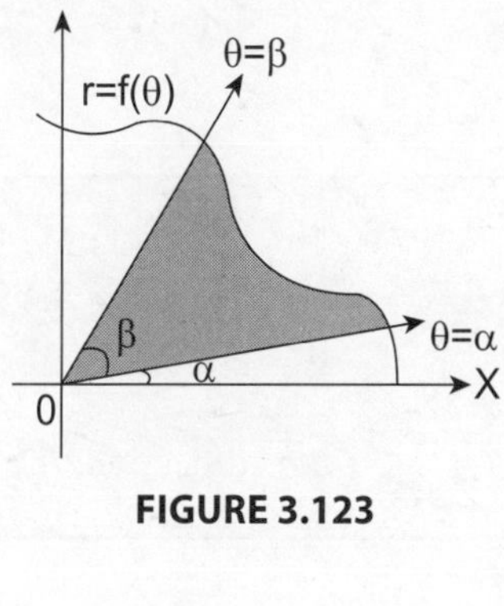

FIGURE 3.123

The region bounded by the polar curver r = f(θ) and the rays θ = a and θ = b

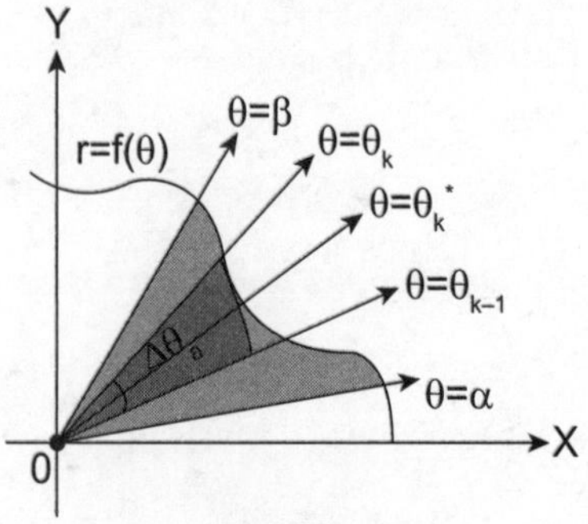

FIGURE 3.124

The area A can be estimated by adding the area of "small" (gray) circular sectors.

Pick any ray $\theta = \theta_k^*$, with $\theta_{k-1} \le \theta_k^* \le \theta_k$. Then the area ΔA_k of the circular sector is approximately the same as the area of the region bounded by the graph of f and the lines $\theta = \theta_{k-1}$ and $\theta = \theta_k$. Because this circular sector has radius $f(\theta_k^*)$ and central angle $\Delta\theta_k$, its area is $\Delta A_k \approx \frac{1}{2}$ (radius)^2 (central angle) $= \frac{1}{2}\left[f(\theta_k^*)\right]^2 \Delta\theta_k$

The sum $\sum_{k=1}^{n} \Delta A_k$ is an approximation to total area A bounded by the polar curve, and by taking the limit as $n \to \infty$, we obtain

$$A = \lim_{n\to\infty}\sum_{k=1}^{n}\Delta A_k = \lim_{n\to\infty}\frac{1}{2}\sum_{k=1}^{n}\left[f(\theta_k^*)\right]^2\Delta\theta_k$$

(Riemann sum)

$$= \frac{1}{2}\int_{\alpha}^{\beta}[f(\theta)]^2\, d\theta$$

You will probably find that the most difficult part of the problem is deciding on the limits of integration. A decent sketch of the region will help with this.

Aliter Proof: Consider infinitesimal area element at an angle θ with central angle $d\theta$ in the form of circular sector as shown Fig. 3.125.

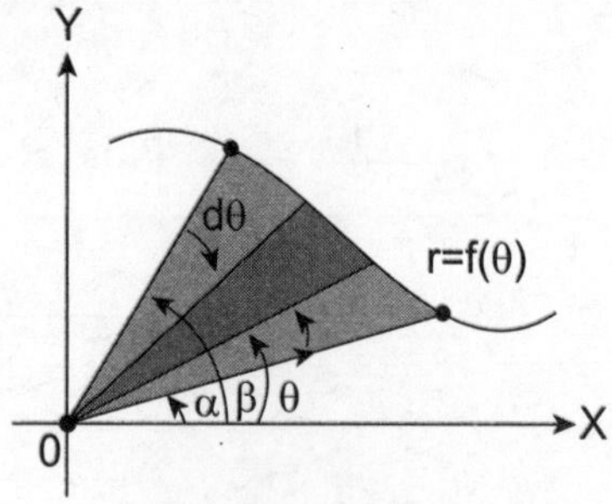

FIGURE 3.125

∴ Area of circular sector = $\frac{1}{2}$ (radius)^2 (central angle) $= \frac{1}{2}r^2 d\theta$

i.e., $dA = \frac{1}{2}r^2 d\theta = 1$

$$\Rightarrow \quad A = \int_0^A dA = \frac{1}{2}\int_\alpha^\beta r^2 d\theta$$

$$\therefore \quad A = \frac{1}{2}\int_\alpha^\beta f^2(\theta)d\theta$$

NOTE

In order to transform the cartesian equation of a curve to polar form we replace x by r cosθ and y by rsinθ

$$\therefore \quad \underbrace{f(x,y)}_{\text{catesian equation}} \xrightarrow[y = r\sin\theta]{x = r\cos\theta} \frac{f(r\cos\theta, r\sin\theta) = 0}{\text{polar equation}}$$

ILLUSTRATION 71: Find the area of elliptical sector of an ellipse having centre at pole and major axis as initial line between θ = 0 to $\theta = \frac{\pi}{4}$ (Length of semi major and semi minor axes are a, b respectively)

SOLUTION: The equation of such ellipse in cartesian form is $\frac{x^2}{a^2}+\frac{y^2}{b^2}=1$

$\Rightarrow$ Polar equation of ellipse is $\frac{r^2\cos^2\theta}{a^2}+\frac{r^2\sin^2\theta}{b^2}=1$

$$\Rightarrow \frac{1}{r^2}=\frac{\cos^2\theta}{a^2}+\frac{\sin^2\theta}{b^2}$$

$\therefore$ Required Area (A)

$$=\frac{1}{2}\int_{\theta=0}^{\pi/4} r^2 d\theta=\frac{1}{2}\int_0^{\pi/4}\frac{a^2b^2}{b^2\cos^2\theta+a^2\sin^2\theta}d\theta$$

$$=\frac{1}{2}a^2b^2\int_0^{\pi/4}\frac{\sec^2\theta d\theta}{b^2+a^2\tan^2\theta}$$

Put $\tan\theta = t$; $\sec^2\theta\, d\theta = dt$

$$\therefore \quad A=\frac{a^2b^2}{2}\int_0^1\frac{dt}{b^2+a^2t^2}=\frac{a^2b^2}{2ab}\left[\tan^{-1}\left(\frac{at}{b}\right)\right]_0^1=\frac{ab}{2}\tan^{-1}\left(\frac{a}{b}\right)$$

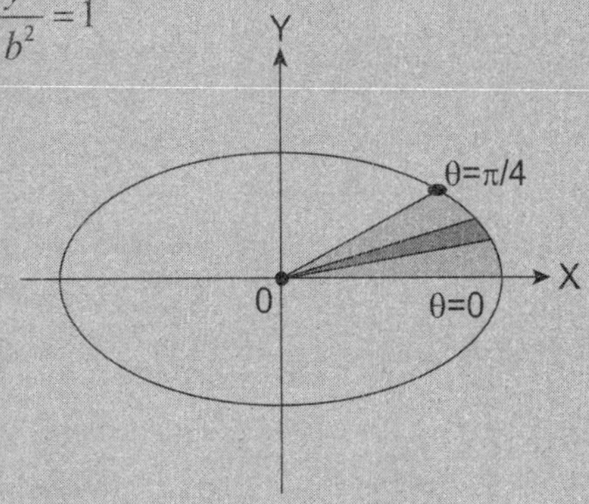

FIGURE 3.126

ILLUSTRATION 72: Find the area of cardioid whose polar equation is given by $r = a(1 + \cos\theta)$.

SOLUTION: The figure of cardiod $r = a(1 + \cos\theta)$ is as shown in Fig. 3.127.

$$\therefore \text{ Required area } = 2.\frac{1}{2}\int_0^{\pi} r^2\, d\theta = \int_0^{\pi} a^2(1+\cos\theta)^2\, d\theta$$

$$=a^2\int_0^{\pi}\left\{1+2\cos\theta+\left(\frac{1+\cos 2\theta}{2}\right)\right\}d\theta$$

$$=a^2\left[\frac{3\theta}{2}+2\sin\theta+\frac{1}{2}\frac{\sin 2\theta}{2}\right]_0^{\pi}$$

$$=a^2\left[\left(\frac{3\pi}{2}+0+0\right)-(0)\right]=\frac{3\pi a^2}{2} \text{ square units.}$$

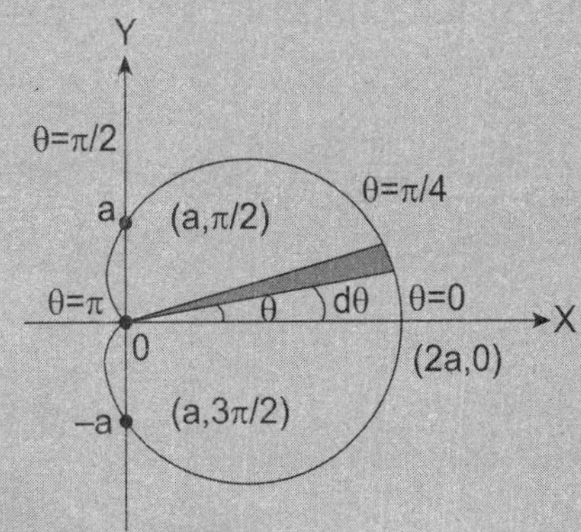

FIGURE 3.127

ILLUSTRATION 73: Find the area enclosed by lemniscate $r = a\sqrt{\cos 2\theta}$

SOLUTION: The radius vector describes one fourth loop as θ varies from 0 to π/4

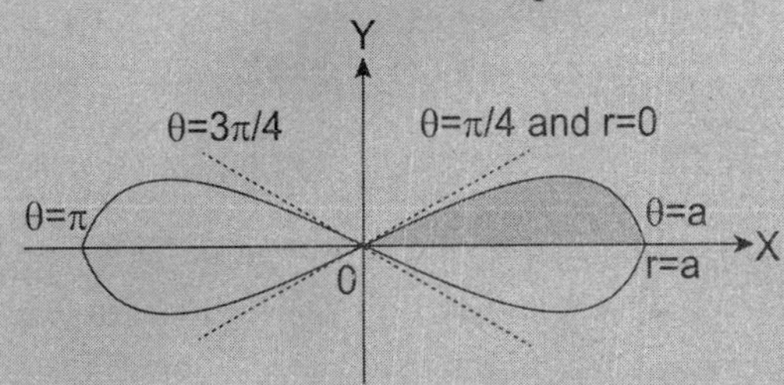

FIGURE 3.128

$$\therefore \quad \text{Required area } = 4\left(\frac{1}{2}\int_0^{\pi/4} r^2 d\theta\right)$$

$$= 2a^2\int_0^{\pi/4}\cos 2\theta\, d\theta = a^2\int_0^{\pi/2}\cos\theta\, d\theta = a^2\left|\sin\theta\right|_0^{\pi/2} = a^2$$

■ INTERSECTION OF POLAR FORM CURVES

In previous discussion we calculated areas bounded by curves having their equations in polar form and two radius vectors. Now in coming concept we desire to calculate areas bounded between two curves having their equations in polar form for which we need to find their points of intersection.

To find the points of intersection of graphs in rectangular form, you need to find only the simultaneous solution of the equations that define those graphs. It is not even necessary to draw the graphs, because there is a one-to-one correspondence between ordered pairs satisfying an equation and points on its graph. However, in polar form, this one-to-one property is lost, so that without drawing the graphs you may fail to find all points of intersection. For this reason, our method for finding the intersection of polar-form curves will include sketching the graphs.

ILLUSTRATION 74: Find the points of intersection of the circles $r = 2\cos\theta$ and $r = 2\sin\theta$ for $0 \le \theta < \pi$.

SOLUTION: ***Step 1:*** First, consider the simultaneous solution of the system of equations.

$2\cos\theta = 2\sin\theta$

$\Rightarrow\ 1 = \dfrac{2\sin\theta}{2\cos\theta} \qquad \Rightarrow\ 1 = \tan\theta$

$\Rightarrow\ \theta = \dfrac{\pi}{4}, \dfrac{5\pi}{4}$

Step 2: Then find r using either of two given equations: For $\theta = \dfrac{\pi}{4}$

$r = 2\cos\dfrac{\pi}{4} = \sqrt{2}$ And, For $\theta = \dfrac{5\pi}{4}$; $r = 2\cos\dfrac{5\pi}{4} = -\sqrt{2}$

But $r > 0$, so we get only one point of intersection $P\left(\sqrt{2}, \dfrac{\pi}{4}\right)$.

Thus, simultaneous solution yields one point of intersection. Next, consider the graphs of these circles shown in Fig. 3.129. It looks that (0, 0) is also a point of intersection. Check this point in each of the given equations:

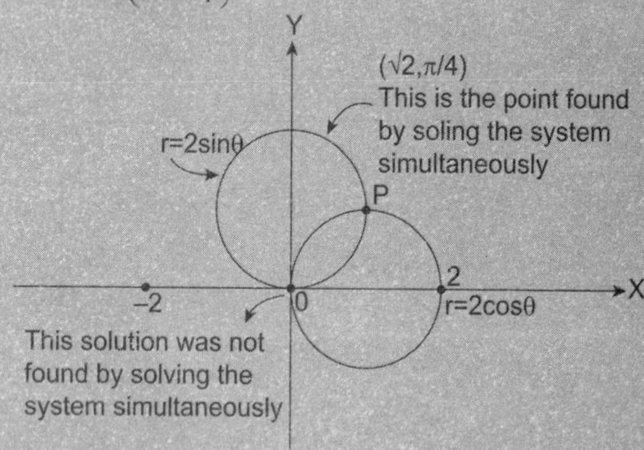

FIGURE 3.129

If $r = 0$ in $r = 2\cos\theta$, then $\theta = \dfrac{\pi}{2}$;

If $r = 0$ in $r = 2\sin\theta$, then $\theta = 0$ or π.

At first it does not seem that the pole satisfies the equation, because $r = 0$ gives $\left(0, \dfrac{\pi}{2}\right)$ and $(0, \pi)$, respectively. Notice that these coordinates are different and do not satisfy the equations simultaneously. But if you plot the point with the coordinates, you will see that $\left(0, \dfrac{\pi}{2}\right)$; $(0, \pi)$ and $(0, 0)$ are all the same point. It's as if two ants were crawling along the curves and came to the origin at different times and they would pass each other without colliding. In most of the polar curves pole is a solution for a system of polar equations, even though it may not satisfy the equations simultaneously. This is because when $r = 0$, all values of θ will yield the point – namely, the pole. For this reason, it is necessary to check separately to see whether the pole lies on the given graph or not.

GRAPHICAL SOLUTION OF THE INTERSECTION OF POLAR CURVES

Following steps are taken to find the points of intersection of polar curves.

Step 1: Find all simultaneous solutions of the given system of equations.

Step 2: Determine whether the pole lies on the two graphs.

Step 3: Graph the curves to look for other points of intersection.

ILLUSTRATION 75: Find the points of intersection of the curves $r=\frac{3}{2}-\cos\theta$ and $\theta=\frac{2\pi}{3}$.

SOLUTION: ***Step 1:*** Solve the system by substitution: $r=\frac{3}{2}-\cos\frac{2\pi}{3}=\frac{3}{2}-\left(-\frac{1}{2}\right)=2$

$\Rightarrow \left(2,\frac{2\pi}{3}\right)$ is a point of intersection.

Step 2: If $r = 0$, the first equation has no solution because $0=\frac{3}{2}-\cos\theta$ or $\cos\theta=\frac{3}{2}$ and a cosine cannot be larger than 1.

Step 3: Now look at the graph.

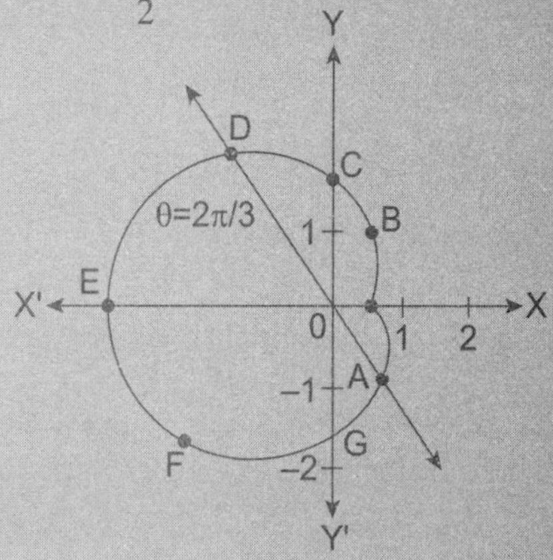

FIGURE 3.130

From the graph we see that $\left(1,\frac{2\pi}{3}\right)$ may also be a point of intersection. It satisfies the equation $\theta=\frac{2\pi}{3}$, but what about $r=\frac{3}{2}-\cos\theta$?

Let us check $1=\frac{3}{2}-\cos\left(\frac{2\pi}{3}\right)$

$\Rightarrow 1=\frac{3}{2}-\left(-\frac{1}{2}\right)=2$

Not satisfied

However, if you check for the alternative representation of $\left(1,\frac{2\pi}{3}\right)$, namely $\left(1,\frac{5\pi}{3}\right)$, then $1=\frac{3}{2}-\cos\left(\frac{5\pi}{3}\right)=\frac{3}{2}-\frac{1}{2}=1$ Satisfied

Be sure to check for points of intersection that you may have missed.

AREA BOUNDED BETWEEN TWO CURVES HAVING THEIR EQUATIONS IN POLAR FORM

The following examples illustrattes the procedure to find the area bounded between two curves having their equations in polar form.

ILLUSTRATION 76: Find the area common to circles $r = a\sqrt{2}$ and $r = 2a\cos\theta$; $a > 0$. Hence find the area inside the circle $r = a\sqrt{2}$ and outside the circle $r = 2a\cos\theta$.

SOLUTION: Let us first of all find the points of intersection of two curves by equating their radius vectors

$\Rightarrow a\sqrt{2} = 2a\cos\theta$ $\quad\Rightarrow \cos\theta = 1/\sqrt{2}$

$\Rightarrow \theta=\frac{\pi}{4}$ or $-\frac{\pi}{4}$

At $\theta=\pm\frac{\pi}{4}, r=a\sqrt{2}$

∴ $P(a\sqrt{2}, \pi/4)$ and $Q(a\sqrt{2}, -\pi/4)$ are points of intersection of two curves.

Now, pole (0, 0) does not lie on $r = a\sqrt{2}$, whereas it lies on $r = 2a\cos\theta$ at $\theta = \dfrac{\pi}{2}$.

Thus, pole is not a point of intersection of two curves. For more information let us draw their graphs.

Clearly $r = a\sqrt{2}$ is a circle with its centre at origin and radius $= a\sqrt{2}$, whereas $r = 2a\cos\theta$ is a circle with radius $2a$ and having its centre at $C(a, 0)$ as shown in Fig. 3.131.

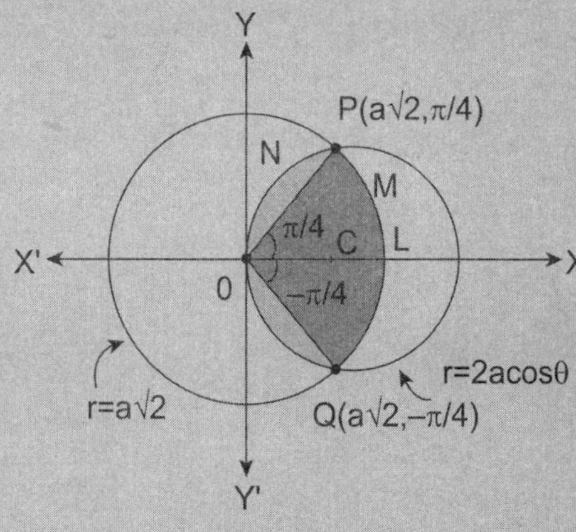

FIGURE 3.131

Then we are to find the shaded area shown above and is given by A = 2 (Area of region $OLMPNO$)

= 2[Area of curvilinear $\Delta OLMPO$ + area of region $OPNO$]

$$= 2\Bigg[\underbrace{\frac{1}{2}\int_0^{\pi/4} r^2\, d\theta}_{\text{cirlce with centre at origin}} + \underbrace{\frac{1}{2}\int_{\pi/4}^{\pi/2} r^2\, d\theta}_{\text{cirlce with centre at origin } C(a,0)}\Bigg] = \int_0^{\pi/4} 2a^2 d\theta + \int_{\pi/4}^{\pi/2} 4a^2\cos^2\theta\, d\theta$$

$$= 2a^2\left(\frac{\pi}{4}\right) + 4a^2\int_{\pi/4}^{\pi/2}\left(\frac{1+\cos 2\theta}{2}\right)d\theta = \frac{a^2\pi}{2} + 2a^2\left[\theta + \frac{\sin 2\theta}{2}\right]_{\pi/4}^{\pi/2}$$

$$= \frac{a^2\pi}{2} + 2a^2\left[\left(\frac{\pi}{2} - \frac{\pi}{4}\right) + \frac{1}{2}(0-1)\right] = \frac{a^2\pi}{2} + 2a^2\left[\frac{\pi}{4} - \frac{1}{2}\right] = \frac{a^2\pi}{2} + \frac{a^2\pi}{2} - a^2 = a^2\pi - a^2$$

$= a^2(\pi - 1)$ square units

Finally area of circle inside the circle $r = a\sqrt{2}$ and outside the circle $r = 2a\cos\theta = \pi(a\sqrt{2})^2 - [a^2\pi - a^2] = a^2\pi + a^2 = a^2(\pi + 1)$ square units.

ILLUSTRATION 77: Find the area common to circle $r = a$ and the cardioid $r = a(1 + \cos\theta)\, d\theta$.

SOLUTION: For the point of intersection $a = a(1 + \cos\theta)$

$\Rightarrow \cos\theta = 0 \qquad \Rightarrow \theta = \dfrac{\pi}{2}$ or $\dfrac{3\pi}{2}$

Clearly the pole does not lie on the circle $r = a$, however the pole lies on the curve $r = a(1 + \cos\theta)$ at $\theta = \pi$.

For further information, let us draw the graphs of two curves as shown in Fig. 3.132.

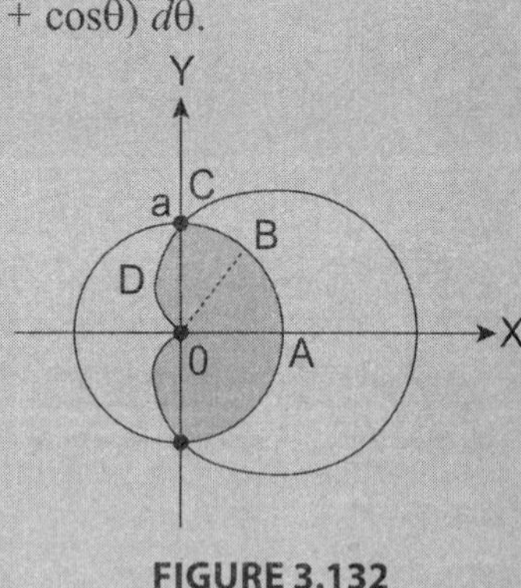

FIGURE 3.132

Thus, the required shaded area = 2[Area of region ($OABC$) + Area of region ($OCDO$)]

$$= 2\Bigg[\underbrace{\frac{1}{2}\int_0^{\pi/2} r^2\, d\theta}_{\text{(circle)}} + \underbrace{\frac{1}{2}\int_{\pi/2}^{\pi} r^2\, d\theta}_{\text{(cardioid)}}\Bigg] = \int_0^{\pi/2} a^2\, d\theta + \int_{\pi/2}^{\pi} a^2(1+\cos\theta)^2\, d\theta$$

$$= a^2\left[\frac{\pi}{2} + \int_{\pi/2}^{\pi}\left(1 + \cos^2\theta + 2\cos\theta\right)d\theta\right] = a^2\left[\frac{\pi}{2} + \frac{\pi}{2} + 2\left|\sin\theta\right|_{\pi/2}^{\pi} + \frac{1}{2}\left|\theta + \frac{\sin 2\theta}{2}\right|_{\pi/2}^{\pi}\right]$$

$$= a^2\left[\pi + \frac{1}{2}\left(\frac{\pi}{2}\right) - 2\right] = a^2\left(\frac{5\pi}{4} - 2\right) \text{ square units}$$

ILLUSTRATION 78: Find the area common to the interior of closed curve $r = 2 - \cos 2\theta$ and interior of closed curve obtained by reflection of given curve on the line $y = x$.

SOLUTION: Given curve is $r = 2 - \cos 2\theta$ ....(1)

Let us find some points on the curve (1)

At $\theta = 0, r = 1 \Rightarrow A(1, 0)$

At $\theta = \frac{\pi}{4}, r = 2 \Rightarrow B\left(2, \frac{\pi}{4}\right)$

At $\theta = \frac{\pi}{2}, r = 3 \Rightarrow C\left(3, \frac{\pi}{2}\right)$

At $\theta = \frac{3\pi}{4}\theta, r = 2 \Rightarrow D\left(2, \frac{3\pi}{4}\right)$

At $\theta = \pi, r = 1 \Rightarrow E(1, \pi)$

At $\theta = \frac{5\pi}{4}, r = 2 \Rightarrow F\left(2, \frac{5\pi}{4}\right)$

At $\theta = \frac{3\pi}{2}, r = 3 \Rightarrow G\left(3, \frac{3\pi}{2}\right)$

At $\theta = \frac{7\pi}{4}, r = 2 \Rightarrow H\left(2, \frac{7\pi}{4}\right)$

At $\theta = 2\pi, r = 1 \Rightarrow I(1, 2\pi)$

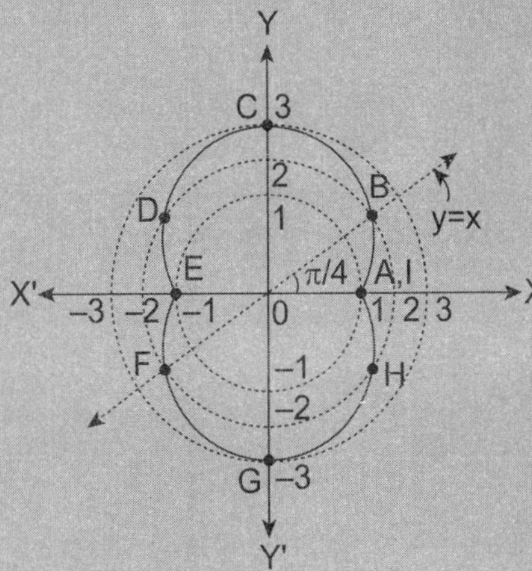

FIGURE 3.133

Thus, the above points on the curve lies on the concentric circles having its centre at origin and with radii 1, 2 and 3. Thus, the graph of curve would be as shown in Fig. 3.133.

Clearly if we take reflection of above curve about the line $y = x$, the loop generated by reflected curve along x-axis would be as shown in Fig. 3.134.

Thus, the area common to the interior of curve $y = 2 - \cos 2\theta$ and its reflection on line $y = x$ would be the area of bounded region $ABLDEFMHA$ and equals four times the shaded area.

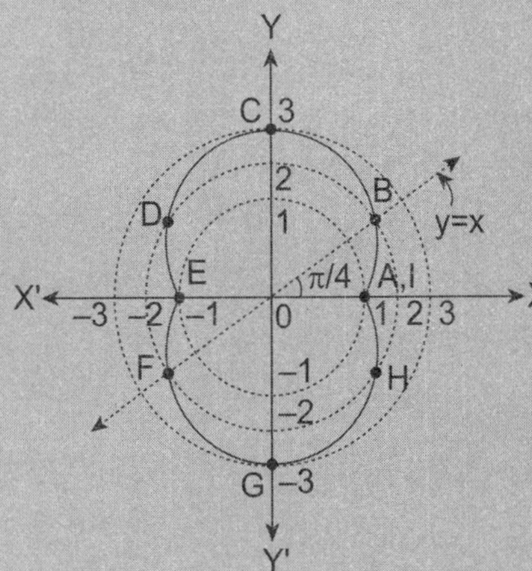

FIGURE 3.133

$$\therefore \text{ Required area } A = \frac{1}{2}\int_{-\pi/4}^{\pi/4} r^2\, d\theta = \frac{1}{2}\int_{-\pi/4}^{\pi/4} (2 - \cos 2\theta)^2\, d\theta$$

$$= \frac{1}{2}\int_{-\pi/4}^{\pi/4} \left(4 + \cos^2 2\theta - 4\cos 2\theta\right) d\theta = \frac{1}{2} \times 2\int_{0}^{\pi/4} \left(4 + \cos^2 2\theta - 4\cos 2\theta\right) d\theta$$

$$= \int_0^{\pi/4} 4\, d\theta + \frac{1}{2}\int_0^{\pi/4} (1 + \cos 4\theta)\, d\theta - 4\int_0^{\pi/4} \cos 2\theta\, d\theta$$

$$= 4\left(\frac{\pi}{4}\right) + \frac{1}{2}\left(\frac{\pi}{4}\right) + \frac{1}{2}\left[\frac{\sin 4\theta}{4}\right]_0^{\pi/2} - 4\left[\frac{\sin 2\theta}{2}\right]_0^{\pi/4}$$

$$= \pi + \frac{\pi}{8} + \frac{1}{8}(0 - 0) - 2(1 - 0) = \left(\frac{9\pi}{8} - 2\right) \text{ square units.}$$

AREA ENCLOSED BY CURVE HAVING THEIR EQUATIONS IN PARAMETRIC FORM

Let $y = f(x)$ be a continuous function on closed interval $[a, b]$ and let $x = g(t)$ and $y = h(t)$ be its parametric equations with domain $t \in [t_1, t_2]$ such that $g(t_1) = a$ and $g(t_2) = b$. Let the traced curve be simple. Its derivative function $g'(t)$ is continuous on $[t_1, t_2]$, then the area under the curve is given by

$$A = A = \int_a^b y\,dx = \int_a^b h(t)d(g(t))$$

$$= \int_{t_1}^{t^2} h(t)g'(t)dt \;;y \geq 0 \text{ for } t \in [t_1, t_2]$$

ILLUSTRATION 79: Find the area bounded by the following curves defined parametrically over the prescribed intervals and with x-axis

(i) $x = t + 1; y = t - 1 ; 0 \leq t \leq 2$ (ii) $x = 30t, y = 60\,t - 9t^2 ; -1 \leq t \leq 2$

(iii) $x = t^3 ; y = 3\ln t ; 0 < t \leq 2$ (iv) $x = e^t, y = 2e^t + 1 ; 0 \leq t \leq 1$

SOLUTION: (i) Graph of $x = t + 1 ; y = t + 1 ; 0 \leq t \leq 2$ is as shown in Fig. 3.135.

The Cartesian form of curve can be obtained by eliminating 't', i.e., $x - 1 = y + 1$

$\Rightarrow y = x - 2$

$\Rightarrow$ Required Area bounded by the curve and x-axis is

$$= \int_1^2(-x+2)dx + \int_2^3(x-2)dx$$

$$= \left|\frac{-x^2}{2}+2x\right|_1^2 + \left|\frac{x^2}{2}-2x\right|_2^3$$

$$= (-2+4) - \left(-\frac{1}{2}+2\right) + \left(\frac{9}{2}-6\right) - (2-4)$$

$$= \left(2-\frac{3}{2}\right) + \left(\frac{9}{2}-6\right) + 2 = 1 \text{ square units}$$

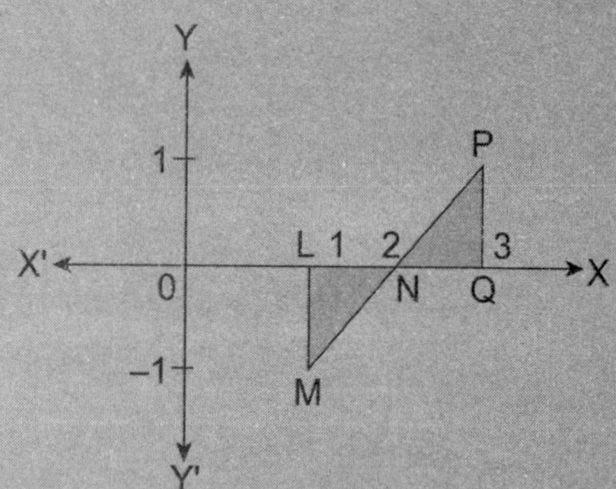

FIGURE 3.135

Also by geometry required area = ar. $\Delta\,LMN$ + ar. $\Delta NPQ = \frac{1}{2}\times1\times1+\frac{1}{2}\times1\times1 = 1$ square units

Also $A = \int_0^2 h(t)g'(t)dt$. Here $h(t) = t - 1 < 0$ for $t < 1$ and > 0 for $t > 1$

$$\therefore \quad A = \int_0^1(-t+1)(1)dt + \int_1^2(t-1)(1)dt$$

$$= \left|\frac{-t^2}{2}+t\right|_0^1 + \left|\frac{t^2}{2}-t\right|_1^2 = \left(\frac{-1}{2}+1\right) - 0 + (2-2) - \left(\frac{1}{2}-1\right)$$

$$= \frac{1}{2}+\frac{1}{2} = 1 \text{ square units}$$

(ii) $x = 30t, y = 60t - 9t^2 ; -1 \leq t \leq 2$

Here $y < 0$ $\Rightarrow -9t^2 + 60t < 0$

$\Rightarrow 9t^2 - 60t > 0$

$\Rightarrow 3t\,(3t - 20) > 0$ $\Rightarrow t \in (-\infty, 0) \cup \left(\frac{20}{3}, \infty\right)$

$\therefore$ $h(t) \leq 0$ for $t \in [-1,0)$ and $h(t) > 0$ for $t \in (0,2)$

$$\therefore \text{ Required Area} = \int_{t_1}^{t_2} h(t)g'(t)dt = \int_{-1}^{0}(9t^2 - 60\,t)\,dt + \int_0^2(-9t^2 + 60\,t)dt$$

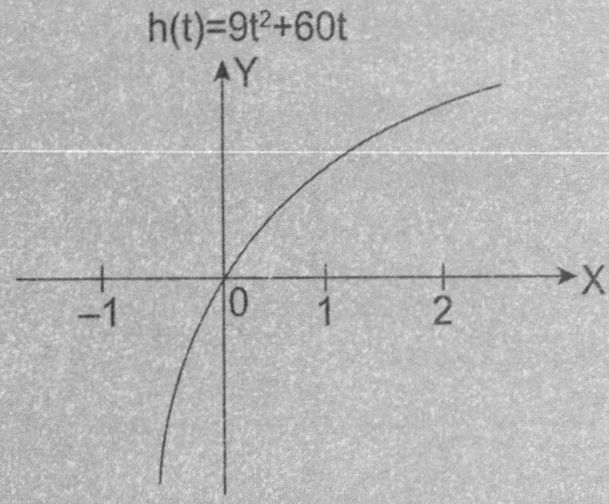

FIGURE 3.136

$$= \left[\frac{9t^3}{3} - \frac{60t^2}{2}\right]_{-1}^{0} + \left[\frac{-9t^3}{3} + \frac{60t^2}{2}\right]_{0}^{2} = (0) - (-3-30) + (-24+120) - (0)$$

$= 33 + 96 = 129$ square units.

(iii) $x = t^3,\ y = 3\ \text{ln}t\ ;\ 0 < t \le 2$

Here $y = 3\ln t < 0$ for $t \in (0,1)$ and $y = 3\ln t \ge 0$ for $t > 1$

$\therefore$ Required Area $= \int_0^1 (-3\ln t)(3t^2)dt + \int_1^2 (3\ln t)(3t^2)dt$

$$= -9\int_0^1 t^2 \ln t\ dt + 9\int_1^2 t^2 \ln t\ dt \quad \ldots(1)$$

Let $I = \int t^2 \ln t\ dt = (\ln t)\left(\frac{t^3}{3}\right) - \int \frac{1}{t}\left(\frac{t^3}{3}\right)dt = \frac{1}{3}t^3 \ln t - \frac{1}{3}\int t^2 dt$

$$= \frac{1}{3}t^3 \ln t - \frac{1}{3}\left(\frac{t^3}{3}\right) + C = \frac{1}{3}t^3 \ln t - \frac{1}{9}t^3 + C$$

$\therefore$ From (1); required Area $= -9\left[\frac{1}{3}t^3 \ln t - \frac{1}{9}t^3\right]_0^1 + 9\left[\frac{1}{3}t^3 \ln t - \frac{1}{9}t^3\right]_1^2$

$$= -9\left[\left(\frac{-1}{9}\right) - 0\right] + 9\left[\left(\frac{8}{3}\ln 2 - \frac{8}{9}\right) - \left(0 - \frac{1}{9}\right)\right] = 1 + 24\ln 2 - 8 + 1 = 24\ln 2 - 6$$

(iv) $x = e^t\ ;\ y = 2e^t + 1\ ;\ 0 \le t \le 1$

Clearly $h(t) = 2e^t + 1 \ge 0$ for $0 \le t \le 1\ ;\ g(t) = e^t$

$\therefore$ The required area $= \int_0^1 h(t)g'(t)dt = \int_0^1 (2e^t + 1)e^t dt = \int_0^1 (2e^{2t} + e^t)dt = \left|2\frac{e^{2t}}{2}\right|_0^1 + \left|e^t\right|_0^1$

$= (e^2 - 1) + (e - 1) = e^2 + e - 2$

ILLUSTRATION 80: Find the area bounded by the cycloid $x = a(t - \sin t)\ ;\ y = a(1 - \cos t);\ 0 \le t \le 2\pi$ and x-axis

SOLUTION The graph of cycloid with parametric equation $x = a(t - \sin t);\ y = a(1 - \cos t);\ 0 \le t \le 2\pi$ is as shown in Fig. 3.137.

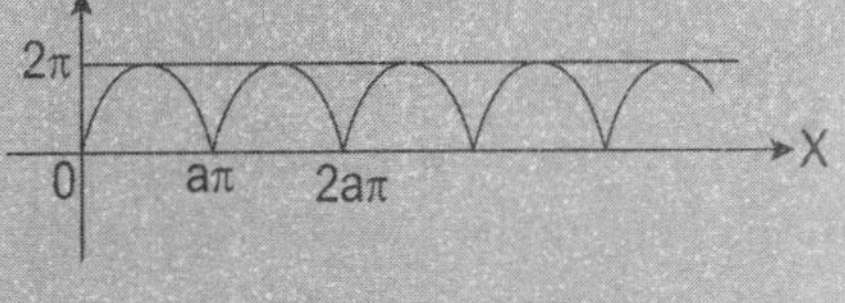

FIGURE 3.137

∴ The area of bounded region is given by,

$$A=\int_{t_1}^{t_2} h(t)g'(t);h(t)=a(1-\cos t)\geq 0\,\forall t\in[0,2\pi]=\int_0^{2\pi} a(1-\cos t)a(1-\cos t)dt$$

$$=a^2\int_0^{2\pi}(1-\cos t)^2dt=a^2\int_0^{2\pi}(1+\cos^2 t-2\cos t)dt=a^2\int_0^{2\pi}\left(1+\frac{1+\cos 2t}{2}-2\cos t\right)dt$$

$$=a^2\left[\frac{3}{2}t+\frac{1}{4}\sin 2t-2\sin t\right]_0^{2\pi}=a^2\left[\frac{3}{2}(2\pi)\right]=3\pi a^2.$$

Aliter: Equation of cycloid in parametric form is $x = a(t - \sin t)$; $y = a(1 - \cos t)$; $t \in \mathbb{R}$. Clearly $x \in (-\infty, \infty)$ for $t \in (-\infty, \infty)$ and $y \in [0, 2a]$.

Also $\cos t$ being periodic function with period 2π, $y = (1 - \cos t)$ is also periodic function of t with period 2π.

Let us obtain few points on cycloid.

At $t = 0$, $x = 0$, $y = 0$

At $t=\frac{\pi}{4}$, $x=a\left(\frac{\pi}{4}-\frac{1}{\sqrt{2}}\right)$, $y=a\left(1-\frac{1}{\sqrt{2}}\right)$ $\Rightarrow A(0.08a, 0.3a)$

At $t=\frac{\pi}{2}$, $x=a\left(\frac{\pi}{2}-1\right)$, $y=a$ $\Rightarrow B(0.57a, a)$

At $t = \pi$, $x = a\pi$, $y = 2a$ $\Rightarrow C(a\pi, 2a)$

At $t=\frac{3\pi}{2}$, $x=a\left(\frac{3\pi}{2}+1\right)$, $y=a$ $\Rightarrow D(5.71a, a)$

At $t = 2\pi$, $x = 2a\pi$, $y = 0$ $\Rightarrow E(2a\pi, 0)$

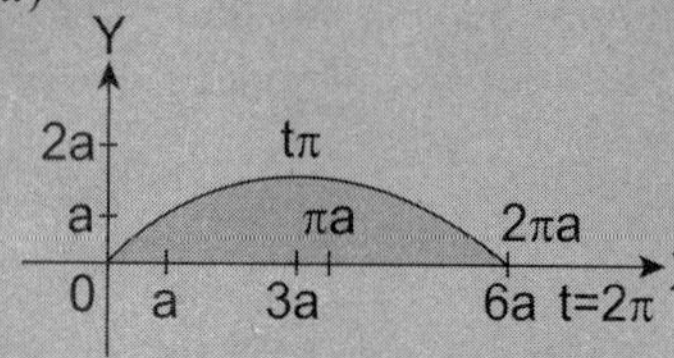

FIGURE 3.138

Thus, area of each arc of cycloid for $t \in [0, 2\pi]$ will be as shown in Fig. 3.138.

∴ Required area of one each of cycloid bounded by x-axis will be $\int_{x=0}^{x=2a\pi} y\,dx$

$$=\int_{t=0}^{2\pi} a(1-\cos t)d(a(t-\sin t))=a^2\int_{x=0}^{2\pi} a(1-\cos t)(1-\cos t)\,dt$$

$$=a^2\int_0^{2\pi}(1-\cos t)^2\,dt=a^2\int_0^{2\pi}\left(1+\cos^2 t-2\cos t\right)dt=a^2(2\pi)+\frac{a^2}{2}\int_0^{2\pi}(1+\cos 2t)\,dt$$

$$=-2a^2\left|\sin t\right|_0^{2\pi}=2a^2\pi+a^2\pi=3a^2\pi \text{ square units}$$

■ AREA BOUNDED BY A CLOSED CURVE DEFINED IN PARAMETRIC FORM

"We now consider a formula which gives the area enclosed by any closed curve which does not intersect itself; there being no restriction as to the manner in which the curve is situated relative to the co-ordinate axes. Consider a closed curve represented by the parametric equations $x = f(t)$, $y = \phi(t)$. 't' being the parameter. We suppose that the curve does not intersect itself. Also suppose that as the parameter 't' increases from value t_1 to the value t_2, the point $P(x, y)$ describes the curve completely in the counter clockwise sense. The curve being closed, the point on it corresponding to the value t_2 of the parameter is the same as the point corresponding to the value t_1 of the parameter. Let this point be C.

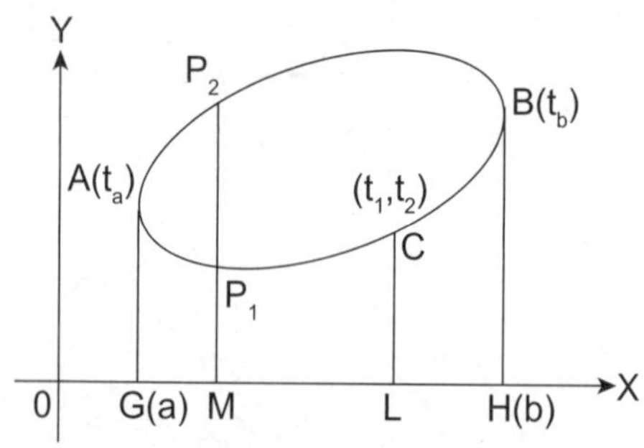

FIGURE 3.139

It will now be shown that the area of the region bounded by such a curve is $\frac{1}{2}\int_{t_1}^{t_2}\left(x\frac{dy}{dt}-y\frac{dx}{dt}\right)dt$

Let the points on the curve with greatest and least abscissae be A, B.

We suppose that the curve is such that every line parallel to y-axis and lying between the ordinates $x = a$, $x = b$ of the points A, B meets it in two and only two points P_1 and P_2; P_1 lying on the arc ACB and P_2 on the arc BP_2A

The area of the region = Area $AGH\ BP_2AG$ – Area $AGHBCAG$

$$= \int_a^b MP_2 dx - \int_a^b MP_1 dx \quad \text{...(i)}$$

We now express these integrals in terms of the variable t. Let t_a, t_b denote the values of the parameter t for the points A, B.

As $P(x, y)$ moves along the arc BP_2A from B to A, the parameter t increases from t_b to t_a; as $P(x, y)$ moves along the arc AC from A to C, the parameter t increases from t_a to t_2; as $P(x, y)$ moves along the arc CB from C to B, the parameter t increases from t_1 to t_b.

$$\therefore \int_a^b MP_2 dx = -\int_{t_b}^{t_a} y\frac{dx}{dt}dt,$$

$$\text{and } \int_a^b MP_1 dx = \int_a^{OL} MP_1\, dx + \int_{OL}^b MP_1\, dx$$

$$= \int_{t_a}^{t_2} y\frac{dx}{dt}dt + \int_{t_1}^{t_b} y\frac{dx}{dt}dt$$

∴ area of the region by equation (i) is given by,

$$A = -\int_{t_b}^{t_a} y\frac{dx}{dt}dt - \int_{t_a}^{t_2} y\frac{dx}{dt}dt - \int_{t_1}^{t_b} y\frac{dx}{dt}dt.$$

$$= -\int_{t_1}^{t_b} y\frac{dx}{dt}dt - \int_{t_b}^{t_a} y\frac{dx}{dt}dt - \int_{t_a}^{t_2} y\frac{dx}{dt}dt.$$

$$= -\int_{t_1}^{t_2} y\frac{dx}{dt}dt \quad \text{...(ii)}$$

It can similarly be shown that the area of the same region is also equal to

$$A = \int_{t_1}^{t_2} x\frac{dy}{dt}dt \quad \text{...(iii)}$$

Adding the two expressions in equations (ii) and (iii), we see that the area of the region is given by,

$$2A = \int_{t_1}^{t_2}\left(x\frac{dy}{dt} - y\frac{dx}{dt}\right)dt \text{ or } A = \frac{1}{2}\int_{t_1}^{t_2}\left(x\frac{dy}{dt} - y\frac{dx}{dt}\right)dt$$

REMARKS

1. *Suppose that the curve intersects itself once as shown in Fig. 3.140.*

   Let t vary from t_1 to t_1' as P (x, y) moves along the curve OAB from O to O.
   Also, let t vary from t'_1 to t_2 as P(x, y) moves along the curve OCD from O to O.

   The area OABO is described in the counter clock-wise but the area OCD in the clock wise sence

   The area of the loop $OABO = \frac{1}{2}\int_{t_1}^{t_1'}\left(x\frac{dy}{dt} - y\frac{dx}{dt}\right)dt$ *(from above result)*

   The area of the loop $OCDO = -\frac{1}{2}\int_{t_1'}^{t_2}\left(x\frac{dy}{dt} - y\frac{dx}{dt}\right)dt$

   Area OABO – area $OCDO = \frac{1}{2}\int_{t_1}^{t_2}\left(x\frac{dy}{dt} - y\frac{dx}{dt}\right)dt$

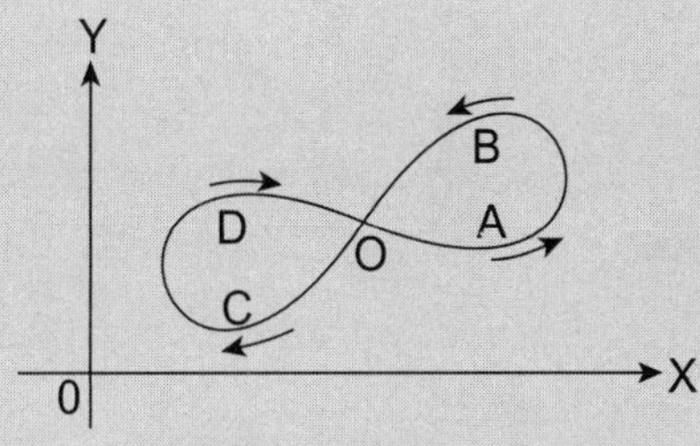

FIGURE 3.140

   So, that the formula gives the difference of the areas of the two loops and not their sum. In order to find the whole area, we have to find each area separately and then obtain their sum

2. *The definite integral* $\frac{1}{2}\int\left(x\frac{dy}{dt} - y\frac{dx}{dt}\right)dt$ *is sometimes briefly written as* $\frac{1}{2}\int(xdy - ydx)$

ILLUSTRATION 81: Find the area enclosed by the following closed curves defined parametrically

(i) $x = 3\cos\theta$, $y = 3\sin\theta$; $0 \le \theta \le 2\pi$

(ii) $x = 1 + \sin t$, $y = -2 + \cos t$; $0 \le t \le 2\pi$

SOLUTION: (i) $x = 3\cos\theta$, $y = 3\sin\theta$; $0 \le \theta \le 2\pi$

Given equations are parametric equations of circle $x^2 + y^2 = 9$, which is a closed curve as shown in Fig. 3.141.

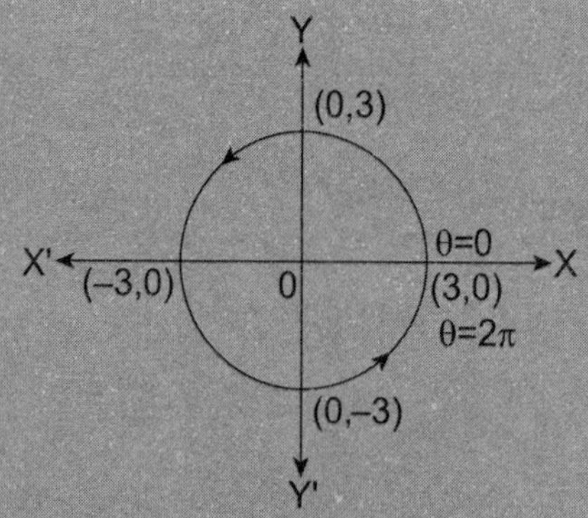

FIGURE 3.141

∴ Enclosed area is given by, $A=\frac{1}{2}\int_{t_1}^{t_2}\left(x\frac{dy}{dt}-y\frac{dx}{dt}\right)dt$

Here $t=\theta$, $t_1=0$, $t_2=2\pi$

$$\Rightarrow\ A=\frac{1}{2}\int_0^{2\pi}\left\{(3\cos\theta)\frac{d}{d\theta}(3\sin\theta)-(3\sin\theta)\frac{d}{d\theta}(3\cos\theta)\right\}d\theta$$

$$=\frac{1}{2}\int_0^{2\pi}[(3\cos\theta)(3\cos\theta)-(3\sin\theta)(-3\sin\theta)]d\theta=\frac{9}{2}\int_0^{2\pi}d\theta=\frac{9}{2}(2\pi)=9\pi \text{ square units.}$$

(ii) $x=1+\sin t$, $y=-2+\cos t$, $0\le t\le 2\pi$

Given equations are parametric equations of circle $(x-1)^2+(y+2)^2=1$ as shown in Fig. 3.142.

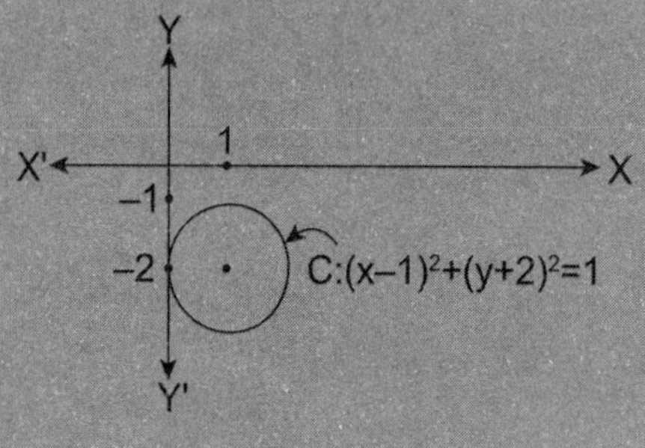

FIGURE 3.142

Enclosed area is given by, $A=\frac{1}{2}\int_{t_1}^{t_2}\left(x\frac{dy}{dt}-y\frac{dx}{dt}\right)dt$

$$=\frac{1}{2}\int_0^{2\pi}\left\{(1+\sin t)\frac{d}{dt}(-2+\cos t)-(-2+\cos t)\frac{d}{dt}(1+\sin t)\right\}dt$$

$$=\frac{1}{2}\int_0^{2\pi}\left(-\sin t-\sin^2 t+2\cos t-\cos^2 t\right)dt=\frac{1}{2}[2\sin t+\cos t-t]_0^{2\pi}=\frac{1}{2}\left[-(2\pi-0)\right]=-\pi$$

Numerically, $A=\pi$ square units.

REMARK

In above illustration, $y<0$ for $\theta\in[0, 2\pi]$, thus, area comes out to be –ve. In such cases absolute (numerical) value of area should be considered.

ILLUSTRATION 82: Find the area enclosed by the ellipse $x = a\cos\theta, y = b\sin\theta$; $0 \le \theta \le 2\pi$

SOLUTION: $\text{Area} = \frac{1}{2}\int_0^{2\pi}\left(x\frac{dy}{d\theta} - y\frac{dx}{d\theta}\right)d\theta = \frac{1}{2}\int_0^{2\pi}\{(a\cos\theta)(b\cos\theta)-(b\sin\theta)(-a\sin\theta)\}d\theta$

$= \frac{1}{2}ab\int_0^{2\pi}(\cos^2\theta + \sin^2\theta)d\theta = \frac{1}{2}ab(2\pi - 0) = \pi ab$ square units

ILLUSTRATION 83: Find the area enclosed by the curve $x = a\cos^3 t$; $y = a\sin^3 t$

SOLUTION: We know that $x^{2/3} + y^{2/3} = a^{2/3}$ is the equation of astroid, having its parametric equation $x = a\cos^3 t$ and $y = a\sin^3 t$; $0 \le t < 2\pi$ as shown in Fig. 3.143.

$\therefore$ Enclosed Area $= \frac{1}{2}\int_0^{2\pi}\left(x\frac{dy}{dt} - y\frac{dx}{dt}\right)dt$

$= \frac{1}{2}\int_0^{2\pi}\{(a\cos^3 t)(3a\sin^2 t\cos t) -$

$(a\sin^3 t)(-3a\cos^2 t\sin t)\}dt$

$= \frac{1}{2}\int_0^{2\pi}3a^2(\sin^2 t\cos^4 t + \sin^4 t\cos^2 t)dt$

$= \frac{3a^2}{2}\int_0^{2\pi}\sin^2 t\cos^2 t(\cos^2 t + \sin^2 t)dt$

$= \frac{3a^2}{8}\int_0^{2\pi}\sin^2 2t\,dt = \frac{3a^2}{8}\int_0^{2\pi}\left(\frac{1-\cos 4t}{2}\right)dt$

$\frac{3a^2}{16}\left[t - \frac{\sin 4t}{4}\right]_0^{2\pi} = \frac{3a^2}{16}[2\pi] = \frac{3a^2\pi}{8}$ square units

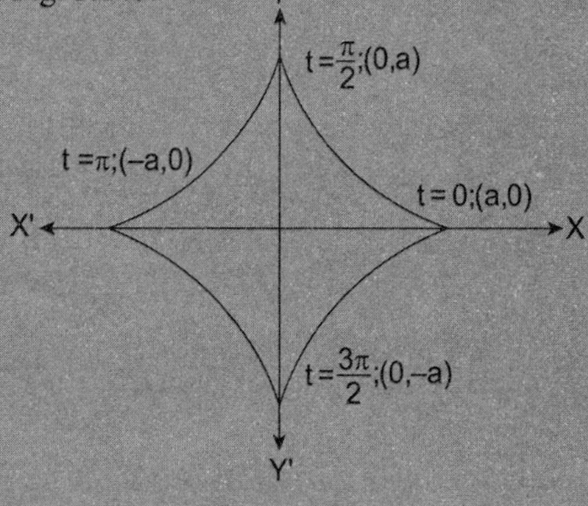

FIGURE 3.143

TEXTUAL EXERCISE–4: (SUBJECTIVE)

1. Find the area enclosed by the loop of the curve $y^2 = (x - 1)(x - 2)^2$.

2. Find the area enclosed by the curve $y^2 = (1 - x^2)^3$.

3. Calculate the area enclosed by the loop of the curve $4(y^2 - x^2) + x^3 = 0$

4. Calculate the areas enclosed by the loops of the curves
   (a) $x = t^2 - 1, y = t^3 - t$
   (b) $x = 2t - t^2, y = 2t^2 - t^3$
   (c) $x = t^2, y = \frac{t}{3}(3 - t^2)$

5. Find the area of the region enclosed by the curve $x = a\cos t, y - b\sin^3 t$.

6. Calculate the area of the region enclosed by the curve $x = a\cos t$; $y = b\sin t\cos^2 t$

7. Calculate the area enclosed by the cardioid $x = a\cos t(1 + \cos t)$; $y = a\sin t(1 + \cos t)$

8. Find the area of the parabola $r = \frac{2a}{(1-\cos\phi)}$ bounded by the line $y = x - a$ and $y = a$.

9. Find the area of the region enclosed by
   (a) Cardioid $r = 1 + \cos\theta$
   (b) $r = a\cos\theta$

10. Find the area of the figure bounded by the circle $3\sqrt{2}\,a\cos\theta$ and $r = 3a\sin\theta$.

11. Calculate the area area enclosed by the curve $(y - \sin^{-1}x)^2 = x - x^2$.

12. Calculate the area of the region enclosed by the curve $r = a\sin\theta\cos^2\theta, a > 0$

13. Calculate the area of the region enclosed by the curve $r = a\cos^3\theta, a > 0$.

14. Calculate the area of the portion lying inside the circle $r = a/\sqrt{2})$ of the figure bounded by the Bernouli's lemniscate $r = a\sqrt{\cos 2\theta}$

15. Convert the equation of curve $(x^2 + y^2)^3 = 4a^2x^2y^2$ into polar form and hence find the area of enclosed region.

16. Convart the equation of curve $(x^4 + y^4) = a^2(x^2 + y^2)$ into polar form and hence find the area of enclosed region.

Answer Keys

1. 8/15 2. 0.75 π 3. 128/15 4. (a) 8/15 (b) 8/15 (c) $\frac{8\sqrt{3}}{5}$

5. 0.75 π*ab* 6. 0.25 π*ab* 7. $\frac{3}{2}\pi a^2$ 8. $2a^2\left(1+\frac{4}{3}\sqrt{2}\right)$

9. (a) $\frac{3\pi}{2}$ (b) $\frac{\pi a^2}{4}$ 10. $\frac{9}{4}a^2\left(\pi-\tan^{-1}\sqrt{2}-\sqrt{2}\right)$ 11. π /4

12. $\frac{\pi a^2}{32}$ 13. $\frac{5}{32}\pi a^2$ 14. $a^2\left(1+\frac{\pi}{6}-\frac{\sqrt{3}}{2}\right)$ 15. $\frac{\pi a^2}{2}$ 16. $\sqrt{2}\pi a^2$.

TEXTUAL EXERCISE-4: (OBJECTIVE)

1. The area of the figure enclosed by the curve $y^2 = x^2(1 - x^2)$ is
   (a) 2/3 (b) 4/3
   (c) 5/3 (d) None of these

2. The area bounded by the *y*-axis and the curve $x = y^2(1 - y)$ is
   (a) 1/2 (b) 1/6
   (c) 3/4 (d) None of these

3. The area of the region enclosed by the curve $x = a \sin t$ and $y = b\sin 2t$ is
   (a) $\frac{2}{3}ab$ (b) $\frac{7}{3}ab$
   (c) $\frac{8}{3}ab$ (d) None of these

4. The area of the region enclosed by the loop of the curve $x=\frac{t}{3}(6-t)$; $x=\frac{t^2}{5}(6-t)$
   (a) 5 (b) 27/5
   (c) 32/5 (d) None of these

5. The area enclosed by the loop of the curve $x = t^2$ and $y=t-\frac{t^3}{3}$
   (a) 2/5 (b) 3/5
   (c) 8/5 (d) None of these

6. The area of the region enclosed by one loop of the curves $r = a \cos 2\theta$ is
   (a) $\frac{\pi a}{8}$ (b) $\frac{\pi a^2}{4}$
   (c) $\frac{\pi a^2}{8}$ (d) None of these

7. The area of the region enclosed by one loop of the curve $r = a \sin 2\theta$ is
   (a) $\frac{\pi a^2}{8}$ (b) $\frac{\pi a^2}{4}$
   (c) $\frac{\pi a^2}{2}$ (d) None of these

8. The area of the figure bounded by the cardioid $r = a(1 - \cos\theta)$ and $r = a$ is
   (a) $2a^2\left(\frac{5\pi}{8}-1\right)$ (b) $a^2\left(\frac{5\pi}{8}-2\right)$
   (c) $2a^2\left(\frac{5\pi}{8}-2\right)$ (d) None of these

9. The area enclosed by the portion of the cardioid $r = a(1 - \cos\theta)$ lying inside the circle $r = a \cos\theta$ is
   (a) $a^2\left(\frac{5\pi}{12}-\sqrt{3}\right)$ (b) $a^2\left(\frac{7\pi}{12}-\sqrt{3}\right)$
   (c) $a^2\left(\frac{7\pi}{12}+\sqrt{3}\right)$ (d) None of these

10. The area of the figure cut out by the circle $r = \sqrt{3} \sin\theta$ from the cardioid $r = 1 + \cos\theta$ is
    (a) $\frac{3}{4}\left(\pi-\sqrt{3}\right)$ (b) $\frac{3}{4}\left(\pi+\sqrt{2}\right)$
    (c) $\frac{1}{4}\left(\pi-\sqrt{3}\right)$ (d) None of these

Answer Keys

1. (b) 2. (a) 3. (c) 4. (b) 5. (c) 6. (c) 7. (a) 8. (a) 9. (b) 10. (a)

MULTIPLE CHOICE QUESTIONS

SECTION-I

OBJECTIVE-TYPE SOLVED EXAMPLES

1. Compute the area bounded by the curve $y = x^4 - 2x^3 + x^2 + 3$, the axis of abscissa and two ordinates corresponding to the points of minima of the function $y(x)$

(a) $\frac{91}{30}$ Square units (b) $\frac{93}{30}$ Square units

(c) $\frac{1}{30}$ Square units (d) None of these

Solution: (a) The given curve is $y = x^4 - 2x^3 + x^2 + 3$, since f is differentiable function

$\Rightarrow \frac{dy}{dx} = 4x^3 - 6x^2 + 2x = 2x(2x^2 - 3x + 1)$

$\Rightarrow$ Thus, $x = 0, 1/2, 1$ are critical points

$\Rightarrow \frac{d^2y}{dx^2} = 12x^2 - 12x + 2$

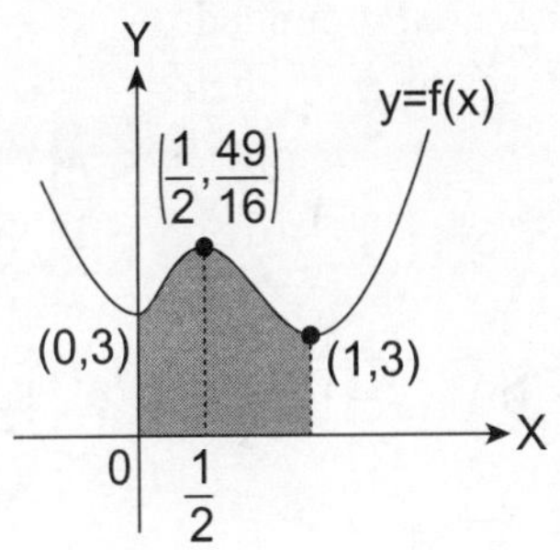

$\Rightarrow$ Now taking the sign of $\frac{d^2y}{dx^2}$ at the critical point,

we get $\left(\frac{d^2y}{dx^2}\right)_{x=0} = 2$, $\left(\frac{d^2y}{dx^2}\right)_{x=1/2} = -1$, $\left(\frac{d^2y}{dx^2}\right)_{x=1} = 2$

Curve has minima at $x = 0$

and $x = 1$; $f(-\infty) = \infty$, $f(0) = 3$, $f(1) = 3$, $f(\infty) = \infty$

$\therefore f(x) > 0 \ \forall x \in \mathbb{R}$

$\therefore$ Required area $= \int_0^1 y\,dx = \int_0^1 (x^4 - 2x^3 + x^2 + 3)dx$

$= \left[\frac{x^5}{5} - \frac{x^4}{2} + \frac{x^3}{3} + 3x\right]_0^1 = \frac{91}{30}$ square units

2. If A_1 is the area of the parabola $y^2 = 4ax$ lying between vertex and the latus rectum and A_2 is the area between the latus rectum and the double ordinate $x = 2a$, then $\frac{A_1}{A_2} =$

(a) $2\sqrt{2} - 1$ (b) $\frac{1}{7}(2\sqrt{2}+1)$

(c) $\frac{1}{7}(2\sqrt{2}-1)$ (d) None of these

Solution: (b) The areas A_1 and A_2 are shown below:

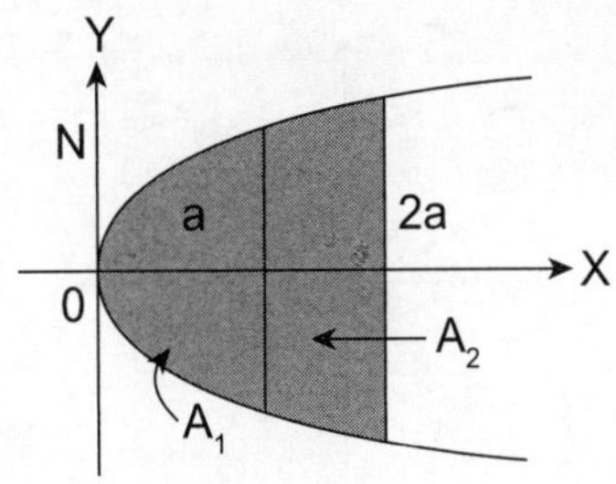

Now, $A_1 = 2\int_0^a \sqrt{4ax}\,dx = \frac{8a^2}{3}$ and

$A_2 = 2\left[\int_0^{2a} \sqrt{4ax} - \int_0^a \sqrt{4ax}\right] = \frac{16\sqrt{2}}{3}a^2 - \frac{8a^2}{3}$

$= \frac{8a^2}{3}\left(2\sqrt{2}-1\right) \Rightarrow \frac{A_1}{A_2} = \frac{1}{2\sqrt{2}-1} = \frac{2\sqrt{2}+1}{7}$

3. Area enclosed between the curves $y^2 = x$ and $x^2 = y$ is equal to

(a) $2\int_0^1 (x - x^2)\,dx$

(b) 1/3

(c) area of region $\{(x, y) : x^2 \le y \le |x|\}$

(d) 2/3

Solution: (a,b,c) The $y^2 = x$ and $x^2 = y$ intersect each other at point (0, 0) and (1, 1) as shown below.

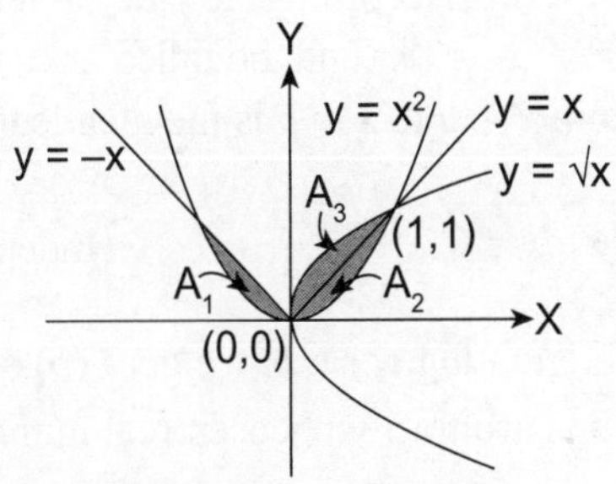

$\therefore$ The required area is given by,

$A = \int_0^1 (\sqrt{x} - x^2)dx = 2A_2$

Where A_2 = area between $y = x$ and $y = x^2$ between $x = 0$ and $x = 1$ = $\{(x, y) : x^2 \le y \le |x|\}$

$$= 2\int_0^1 (x-x^2)dx = 2\left[\frac{x^2}{2}-\frac{x^3}{3}\right]_0^1$$

$$= 2\left[\frac{1}{2}-\frac{1}{3}\right] = \frac{1}{3} \text{ square units.}$$

4. The area bounded by curves $y = x^3$; $y = (x)^{1/3}$
(a) lies in Ist quadrant (b) lies is IIIrd quadrant
(c) is equal to 1 unit² (d) is equal to 4 unit²

Solution: (a, b, c) $y = x^3$ and $y = x^{1/3}$ are mirror images of each other about the line $y = x$ as shown below:

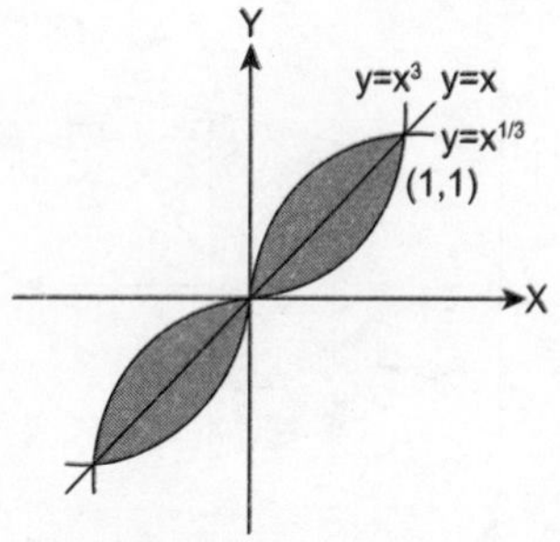

Clearly the bounded area lies in Ist and IIIrd quadrant and is equal to $4\left[\int_0^1 (x-x^3)dx\right]$

$$= 4\left[\frac{x^2}{2}-\frac{x^4}{4}\right]_0^1 = 4\left[\frac{1}{2}-\frac{1}{4}\right] = 1 \text{ square units}$$

5. If the area bounded by the x-axis, the curve $y = f(x) \geq 0\ \forall\ x \in \mathbb{R}$ and the lines $x = a$ and $x = b$ is independent of b, $b > a$ (a is a constant), then f is
(a) The zero function for $x > 0$
(b) The identity function
(c) A non-zero constant function
(d) None of these

Solution: (a) According to the given condition; $f(x) \geq 0\ \forall\ x \in \mathbb{R}$ and bounded area by $f(x)$ and x-axis from $x = a$ to $x = b$ is independent of b.

$$\Rightarrow \int_a^b f(x)dx = C \qquad \text{(Independent of b)}$$

Differentiating w.r.t. b, we get $f(b) = 0$
But b is arbitrarily choosen real number $> a$
$\Rightarrow f(x) = 0\ \forall\ x \in \mathbb{R}$ and $x > 0$

6. If f is a differentiable function satisfying $f(x + y) = f(x).f(y)$, $f'(0) = \ln 2$ and $f(x) \neq 0$ for any x, then area bounded by $y = f(x)$, the x-axis, the y-axis and $x = 2$ is equal to
(a) $\frac{3}{\ln 2}$ (b) $\frac{2}{\ln 2}$
(c) $\frac{\ln 2}{2}$ (d) $2 \ln 2$

Solution: (a) Using the given functional equation, we obtain the function $y = f(x) = 2^x$

$$\text{Required Area} = \int_0^2 2^x\, dx = \left|\frac{2^x}{\ln 2}\right|_0^2 = \frac{1}{\ln 2}(4-1) = \frac{3}{\ln 2}$$

7. If the area bounded by $y = f_i(x)$, the x-axis, the y-axis and $x = t$ are same for $i = 1, 2$ for any $t > 0$, then for $x > 0$
(a) $f_1(x)$ and $f_2(x)$ are equal
(b) $f_1(x)$ and $f_2(x)$ may be unequal as well as equal
(c) Always unequal
(d) $f_1(x) = 2f_2(x)$

Solution: (a) We have $\int_0^t f_1(x)dx = \int_0^t f_2(x)dx; t > 0$

On differentiating, we get $f_1(t) = f_2(t)\ \forall\ t > 0$
$\Rightarrow f_1(x) = f_2(x)\ \forall\ x > 0$

8. If A_n is the area bounded by $y = (1 - x^2)^n$ and coordinate axes, n ∈ ℕ, then
(a) $A_n = A_{n-1}$ (b) $A_n < A_{n-1}$
(c) $A_n > A_{n-1}$ (d) $A_n = 2A_{n-1}$

Solution: (b) $A_n = \int_0^1 (1-x^2)^n dx < \int_0^1 (1-x^2)^{n-1} dx$

as $0 < x < 1$
$\Rightarrow -1 < -x^2 < 0$
$\Rightarrow 0 < 1 - x^2 < 1$
$\Rightarrow (1 - x^2)^n < (1 - x^2)^{n-1}$
$\Rightarrow A_n < A_{n-1}$

9. The interval $[a, b]$ such that the value of $\int_a^b (2+x-x^2)dx$ is maximum, is
(a) [–1, 2] (b) [–2, 1]
(c) –2, –1 (d) [1, 2]

Solution: (a) The integral $\int_a^b (2+x-x^2)dx$ will give us the algebraic sum of areas bounded by the parabola $y = 2 + x - x^2$, x-axis and the lines $x = a$ and $x = b$. The expression $2 + x - x^2$ is non-negative in [–1, 2] as shown below:

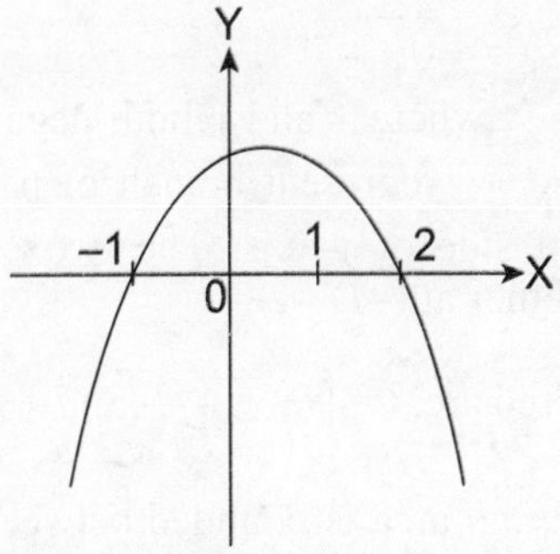

Thus, $[a, b]$ should be $[-1, 2]$.

10. Area enclosed by the curve $y = f(x)$ that is being defined parametrically as $x = \frac{1-t^2}{1+t^2}$, $y = \frac{2t}{1+t^2}$ is equal to

(a) π square units (b) $\pi/2$ square units

(c) $\frac{3\pi}{4}$ square units (d) $\frac{3\pi}{2}$ square units

Solution: (a) Clearly 't' can be any real number.

Let $t = \tan\theta$ $\Rightarrow x = \frac{1-\tan^2\theta}{1+\tan^2\theta}$

$\Rightarrow x = \cos 2\theta$ and $y = \frac{2\tan\theta}{1+\tan^2\theta} = \sin 2\theta$

$\Rightarrow x^2 + y^2 = 1$, which is the equation of circle with radius 1.

Thus, required area $= \pi .1^2 = \pi$ square units.

11. The ratio in which the x-axis divides the area of the region bounded by the curves $y = x^2 - 4x$ and $y = 2x - x^2$ is:

(a) $\frac{4}{23}$ (b) $\frac{4}{27}$

(c) $\frac{4}{19}$ (d) None of these

Solution: (a) For the points of intersection of given curves $x^2 - 4x = 2x - x^2$

$\Rightarrow x = 0$ or $x = 3$, i.e., the two curves intersect each other at $(0, 0)$ and $(3, -3)$.

Let x-axis divides the bounded area into two parts, i.e., above the x-axis $= A_1$ and below x-axis $= A_2$ as shown in figure

Total area

$$= \int_0^3 [(2x - x^2) - (x^2 - 4x)]dx = \int_0^3 (6x - 2x^2)dx$$

$$= \left|3x^2 - \frac{2}{3}x^3\right|_0^3 = 27 - 18 = 9 \text{ square units}$$

Now, $A_1 = \int_0^2 (2x - x^2)dx = \left|x^2 - \frac{x^3}{3}\right|_0^2 = \frac{4}{3}$ square units

$$A_2 = 9 - \frac{4}{3} = \frac{23}{3} \Rightarrow \frac{A_1}{A_2} = \frac{4}{23}$$

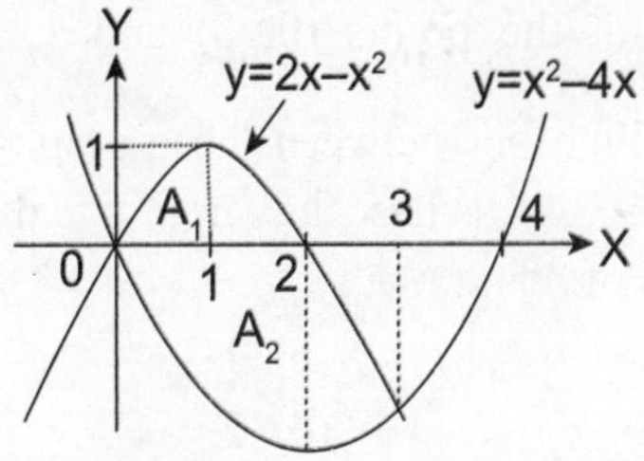

12. The area bounded by the curve $y = f(x)$, the x-axis and the ordinates $x = 1$ and $x = b$ is $(b - 1)\sin(3b + 4)$. Then $f(x)$ is ($f(x) > 0$ for $x \in (1, b)$).

(a) $(x - 1)\cos(3x + 4)$

(b) $\sin(3x + 4)$

(c) $\sin(3x + 4) + 3(x - 1).\cos(3x + 4)$

(d) None of these

Solution: (c) since $f(x) > 0$ for $x \in (1, b)$, we have

$$\int_1^b f(x)\,dx = (b-1)\sin(3b+4)$$

i.e., Area function $= \int_1^x f(x)\,dx = (x - 1)\sin(3x + 4)$,

on differentiating we have

$\therefore f(x) = \sin(3x + 4) + 3(x - 1) . \cos(3x + 4)$

13. A curve is such that the area of the region bounded by the co-ordinate axes, the curve and the ordinate of any point on it is equal to the cube of that ordinate. The curve represents

(a) a pair of straight lines

(b) a circle

(c) a parabola

(d) an ellipse

Solution: (c) According to question $\int_0^x f(x)\,dx = y^3$

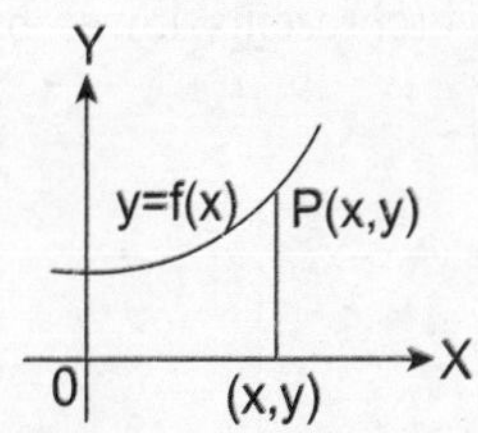

On differentiating, we get $f(x) = 3y^2 . \frac{dy}{dx}$

$\Rightarrow y = 3y^2 \frac{dy}{dx}$ $\Rightarrow y = 0$ (rejected) or $3y\,dy = dx \quad \Rightarrow \quad \dfrac{3y^2}{2} = x + C$

⇒ Which represents parabola.

14. The graphs of $f(x) = x^2$ and $g(x) = cx^3$ $(c > 0)$ intersect at the points (0, 0) and $\left(\dfrac{1}{c}, \dfrac{1}{c^2}\right)$. If the region which lies between these graphs and over the interval [0, 1/c] has the area equal to 2/3, then the value of c is

(a) 1 (b) 1/3

(c) 1/2 (d) 2

Solution: (c) Required area $= \displaystyle\int_0^{1/c} |cx^3 - x^2|\,dx$

$\Rightarrow \left|\dfrac{cx^3}{4} - \dfrac{x^3}{3}\right|_0^{1/c} = \left|\dfrac{c}{4}\left(\dfrac{1}{c^4}\right) - \dfrac{1}{3}\left(\dfrac{1}{c^3}\right)\right|$

$\Rightarrow \left|-\dfrac{1}{12c^3}\right| = \dfrac{1}{12c^3} \quad \Rightarrow \quad \dfrac{1}{12c^3} = \dfrac{2}{3} \quad \Rightarrow \quad c = \dfrac{1}{2}$

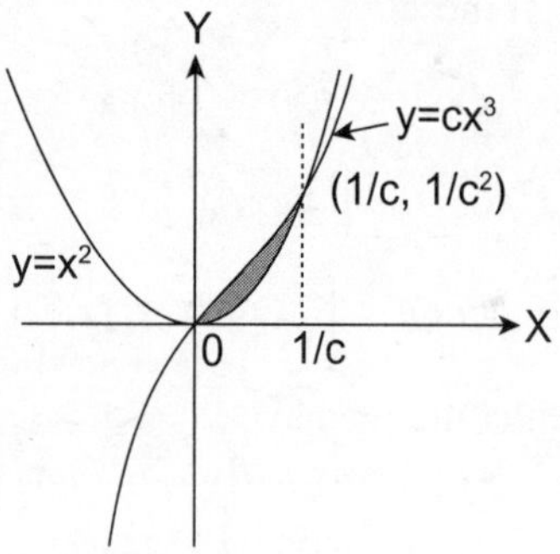

15. The area bounded by the curves $y = -\sqrt{-x}$ and $x = -\sqrt{-y}$; where x, $y \le 0$

(a) cannot be determined

(b) is 1/3

(c) is 2/3

(d) is same as that of the figure bounded by the curves $y = \sqrt{-x}$; $x \le 0$ and $x = \sqrt{-y}$; $y \le 0$

Solution: (b) $y = -\sqrt{-x}$

⇒ $y^2 = -x$; where x and y both (–) negative, i.e., $y = -\sqrt{-x}$ represents lower branch of parabola $y^2 = -x$

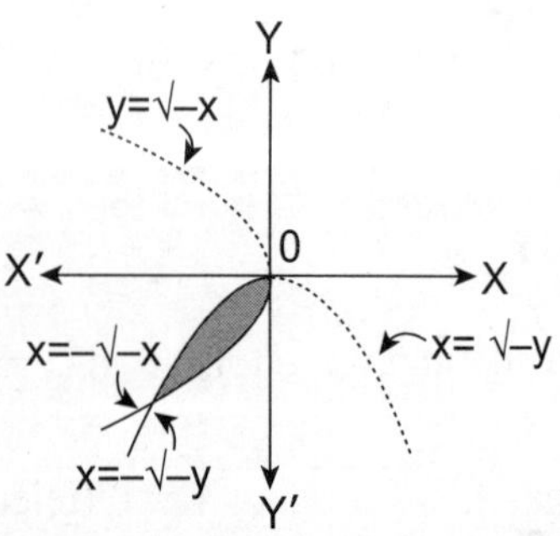

Now, $x = -\sqrt{-y}$

⇒ $x^2 = -y$; where x and y both negative (–ve), i.e., $x = -\sqrt{-y}$ represent branch of parabola $x^2 = -y$ on left side of y-axis. The two curves intersect each other at (–1, –1).

∴ Required area $= \displaystyle\int_1^0 (-x^2 + \sqrt{-x})dx = \dfrac{1}{3}$ square units

Clearly no area is bounded between the branches $y = \sqrt{-x}$; $x \le 0$ and $x = \sqrt{-y}$; $y \le 0$.

Hence $A = \dfrac{16ab}{3}$; where $a = b = \dfrac{1}{4}$

∴ $A = \dfrac{1}{3}$

16. The curvilinear trapezoid is bounded by the curve $y = x^2 + 1$ and the straight lines $x = 1$ and $x = 2$. The co-ordinates of the point (on the given curve) with abscissa $x \in [1, 2]$ where tangent drawn cut off from the curvilinear trapezoid an ordinary trapezium of the greatest area, is

(a) (1, 2) (b) (2, 5)

(c) $\left(\dfrac{3}{2}, \dfrac{13}{4}\right)$ (d) None of these

Solution: (c) Let $R(x_1, y_1)$ be point on parabola $y = x^2 + 1$, for which $x_1 \in [1, 2]$.

∴ $\left[\dfrac{dy}{dx}\right]_{x_1 y_1} = 2x_1$ = slope of tangent to given parabola at point $R(x_1, y_1)$

∴ Equation of tangent to given parabola at point $R(x_1, y_1)$ is given by $y - y_1 = 2x_1 (x - x_1)$ ...(1)

For co-ordinates of the point P put $x = 1$ in (1)

⇒ $y = y_1 + 2x_1 (1 - x_1)$
$= 1 + x_1^2 + 2x_1 - 2x_1^2 = 1 + 2x_1 - x_1^2$

∵ (x_1, y_1) lies $y = x^2 + 1 \Rightarrow y_1 = x_1^2 + 1)$

Hence $P \equiv (1, 1 + 2x_1 - x_1^2)$

For Q, put $x = 2$ in (1)

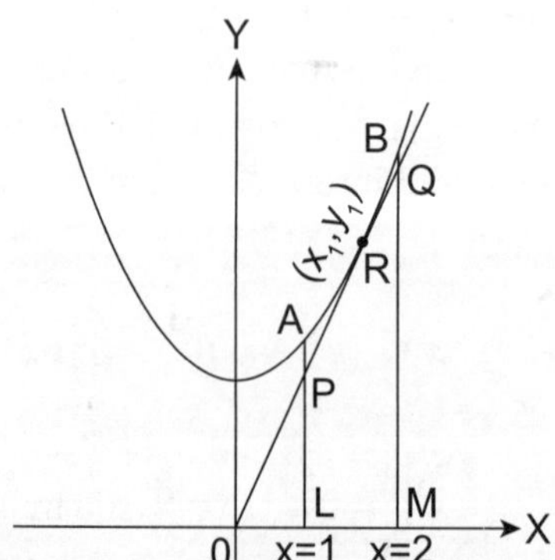

$\Rightarrow y = y_1 + 2x_1(2 - x_1) = 1 + x_1^2 + 4x_1 - 2x_1^2$

$= 1 + 4x_1 - x_1^2$; Hence, $Q \equiv (2, 1 + 4x_1 - x_1^2)$

$\therefore$ Area of trapezium

$LMPQ = A = \frac{1}{2}[(1 + 2x_1 - x_1^2) + (1 + 4x_1 - x_1^2)]$

$= 1 + 3x_1 - x_1^2 \quad \Rightarrow \quad \frac{dA}{dx_1} = 3 - 2x_1$

$\therefore$ For maximum area $\frac{dA}{dx_1} = 0$

$\Rightarrow x_1 = \frac{3}{2} \qquad \therefore \quad \frac{d^2A}{dx_1^2} = -2 < 0$

$\Rightarrow R\left(\frac{3}{2}, \frac{13}{4}\right)$ is the required point.

17. Area of the region enclosed between the curves $x = y^2 - 1$ and $x = |y|\sqrt{1-y^2}$ is

(a) 1 (b) 4/3

(c) 2/3 (d) 2

Solution: (d) $x = |y|\sqrt{1-y^2}$

$\Rightarrow x \geq 0$ and $1 - y^2 \geq 0$; Also corresponding to each x there are two values of y, i.e., (x, y) and $(x, -y)$ lie on the curve.

$\Rightarrow x \geq 0$ and $y - 1 \leq 0 \quad \Rightarrow \quad x \geq 0$ and $-1 \leq y - 1$

$\Rightarrow$ on x-axis $y = 0 \quad \Rightarrow \quad x = 0$ and on y-axis $x = 0$

$\Rightarrow y = 0$ or $y = \pm 1$

$\therefore$ curve passes through origin, $A(0, 1)$ and $B(0, -1)$, clearly replacing y by $-y$ does not affect the equation $x = |y|\sqrt{1-y^2}$

$\Rightarrow$ curve is symmetric about x-axis

Also $\frac{dx}{dy} = 0 \quad \Rightarrow \quad y = \pm\frac{1}{\sqrt{2}}$

i.e., tangent is parallel to y-axis at $y = \pm\frac{1}{\sqrt{2}}$

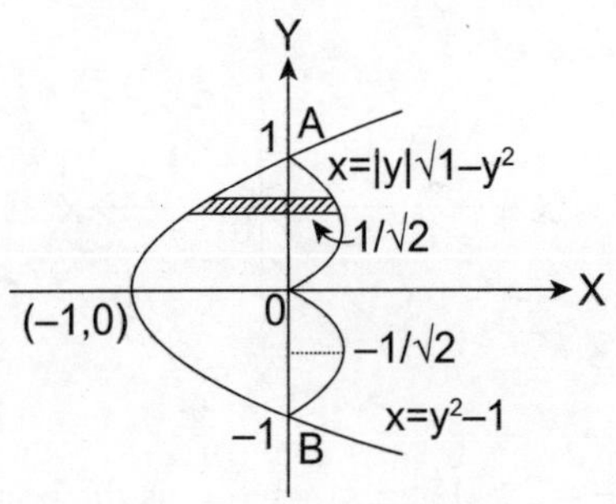

$$A = 2\int_0^1 \left[y\sqrt{1-y^2} - (y^2 - 1)\right] dy$$

$$= -\left[\frac{2}{3}(1-y^2)^{3/2}\right]_0^1 - 2\left[\frac{y^3}{3} - y\right]_0^1 = 2 \text{ square units}$$

18. Let $y = g(x)$ be the inverse of a bijective mapping f: $\mathbb{R} \to \mathbb{R}$, $f(x) = 3x^3 + 2x$. The area bounded by the graph of $g(x)$, the x-axis and the ordinate at $x = 5$ is:

(a) $\frac{5}{4}$ (b) $\frac{7}{4}$

(c) $\frac{9}{4}$ (d) $\frac{13}{4}$

Solution: (d) We know that

$$\int_a^b f(x)dx + \int_c^d f^{-1}(x)dx = (bd - ac);$$

where $f(a) = c$, $f(b) = d$

i.e., required area = Area of rectangle $-\int_0^1 f(x)\,dx$;

since $f(x)$ passes through (0, 0); $a = 0$, $c = 0$ and $d = 5$

$\Rightarrow 3b^3 + 2b = 5 \qquad \Rightarrow b = 1$

$$\therefore \quad \int_0^1 f(x)dx + \int_0^5 g(x)dx = (1)(5) - 0.0$$

$$\Rightarrow \quad \int_0^5 g(x)dx = 5 - \int_0^1 f(x)dx$$

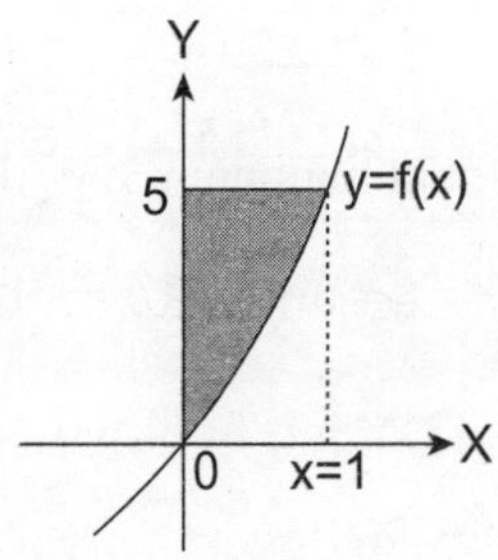

$$= 5 - \int_0^1 (3x^3 + 2x)\,dx = 5 - \left(\frac{3}{4} + 1\right)\frac{1}{4} = \frac{13}{4}$$

19. If the tangent to the curve $y = 1 - x^2$ at $x = \alpha$, where $0 < \alpha < 1$, meets the axes at P and Q. Also α varies, the minimum value of the area of the triangle OPQ is k times the area bounded by the axes and the part of the curve for which $0 < x < 1$, then k is equal to

(a) $\frac{2}{\sqrt{3}}$ (b) $\frac{75}{16}$

(c) $\frac{25}{18}$ (d) $\frac{2}{3}$

Solution: (a) Let A_1 = area under the curve and axes

$$= \int_0^1 (1 - x^2)\,dx = \left[x - \frac{x^3}{3}\right]_0^1 = \frac{2}{3} \qquad \text{...(1)}$$

Now $y = 1 - x^2 \qquad \therefore \quad y' = -2x$

$\therefore \quad y'(\alpha, 1 - \alpha^2) = -2\alpha$ = slope of tangent to curve at $R(\alpha, 1 - \alpha^2)$

Equation of tangent to the curve $y = 1 - x^2$ at $R(\alpha, 1 - \alpha^2)$ is $[y - (1 - \alpha] = -2\alpha(x - \alpha)$

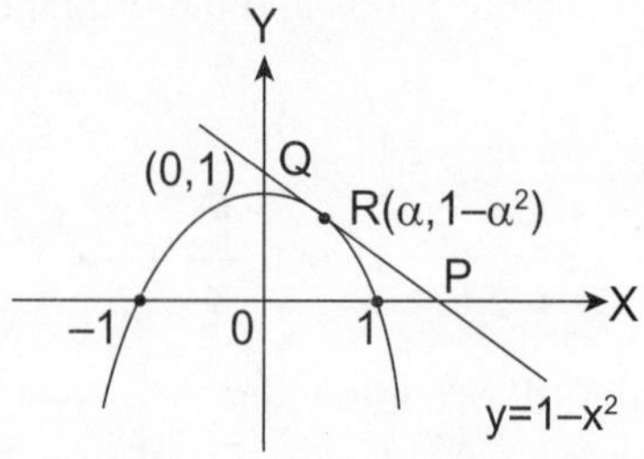

$\Rightarrow 2\alpha x + y = \alpha^2 + 1$, on x-axis $y = 0$

$\Rightarrow x = \dfrac{\alpha^2+1}{2\alpha} \quad \therefore P \equiv \left(\dfrac{\alpha^2+1}{2\alpha}, 0\right)$, on y-axis, $x = 0$

$\Rightarrow y = \alpha^2 + 1 \qquad \Rightarrow Q \equiv (0, \alpha^2 + 1)$

$\therefore A =$ Area of triangle $POQ = \dfrac{1}{2}(OP)(OQ)$

$= \dfrac{1}{4}\dfrac{(\alpha^2+1)^2}{\alpha}$

$\therefore A' = \dfrac{1}{4}\dfrac{\alpha 2(\alpha^2+1)2\alpha - (\alpha^2+1)^2}{\alpha^2}$

$= \dfrac{1}{4}\dfrac{3\alpha^4 + 2\alpha^2 - 1}{\alpha^2}$

For maximum/minimum, $A' = 0$

$\Rightarrow 3\alpha^4 + 2\alpha^2 - 1 = 0 \Rightarrow \alpha^2 = -1, \dfrac{1}{3}$

$\Rightarrow \alpha = \pm\dfrac{1}{\sqrt{3}} \qquad \because 0 < \alpha < 1$

$\Rightarrow \alpha = \dfrac{1}{\sqrt{3}}$, $A'' > 0$, hence, A is minimum and is given by

$$A = \frac{1}{4}\frac{\left(\frac{1}{3}+1\right)^2}{\frac{1}{\sqrt{3}}} = \frac{4}{3\sqrt{3}} \qquad \ldots(2)$$

Since $A = kA_1$ (given)

From (1) and (2); $\dfrac{4}{3\sqrt{3}} = k.\dfrac{2}{3} \Rightarrow k = \dfrac{2}{\sqrt{3}}$

20. If (a, 0); $a > 0$ is the point where the curve $y = \sin 2x - \sqrt{3}\sin x$ cuts the x-axis first, A is the area bounded by this part of the curve, the origin and the positive x-axis, then

(a) $4A + 8\cos a = 7$ (b) $4A + 8\sin a = 7$

(c) $4A - 8\sin a = 7$ (d) $4A - 8\cos a = 7$

Solution: (a) (a, 0) lies on the given curve

$\therefore 0 = \sin 2a - \sqrt{3}\sin a$

$\Rightarrow \sin a = 0$ or $\cos a = \sqrt{3}/2$

$\Rightarrow a = \dfrac{\pi}{6}$ (as $a > 0$ and the first point of intersection with positive X-axis)

And $A = \displaystyle\int_0^{\pi/6} (\sin 2x - \sqrt{3}\sin x)\,dx$

$= \left(-\dfrac{\cos 2x}{2} + \sqrt{3}\cos x\right)_0^{\pi/6}$

$= \left(-\dfrac{1}{4} + \dfrac{3}{2}\right) - \left(-\dfrac{1}{2} + \sqrt{3}\right) = \dfrac{7}{4} - \sqrt{3}$

$\Rightarrow 4A + 8\cos a = 7$

21. The curve $y = ax^2 + bx + c$ passes through the point (1, 2) and its tangent at origin is the line $y = x$. The area bounded by the curve, the ordinate of the curve at minima and the tangent line is

(a) $\dfrac{1}{24}$ (b) $\dfrac{1}{12}$

(c) $\dfrac{1}{8}$ (d) $\dfrac{1}{6}$

Solution: (a) Since point (1, 2) lies on curve $y = ax^2 + bx + c$,

Substituting $x = 1; y = 2$, we get $2 = a + b + c$

Also tangent at origin means curve passes through origin

$\Rightarrow x = 0, y = 0 \qquad \Rightarrow c = 0$

$\Rightarrow a + b = 2$; Now $\left[\dfrac{dy}{dx}\right]_{(0,0)} = 2a(0) + b = 1$

(since the tangent at origin is $y = x$)

$\therefore b = 1; a = 1$; Hence, the curve is $y = x^2 + x$

$\Rightarrow \dfrac{dy}{dx} = 2x + 1 = 0 \qquad \Rightarrow x = -\dfrac{1}{2}$

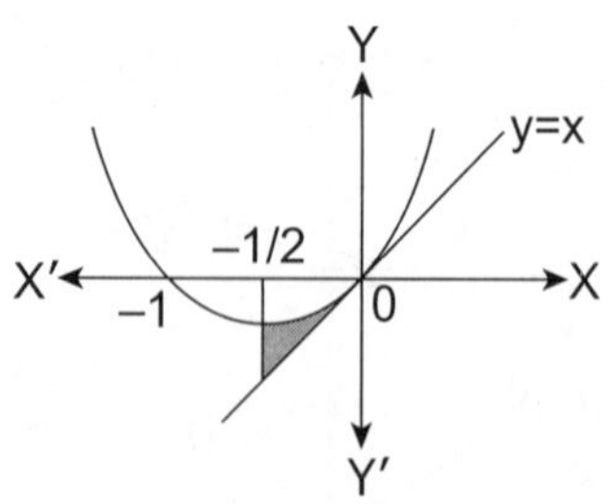

$\Rightarrow \dfrac{d^2y}{dx^2} = 2 > 0 \quad \Rightarrow x = -\dfrac{1}{2}$ is the point of minima

$\therefore$ Required area $= A = \displaystyle\int_{-\frac{1}{2}}^{0} (x^2 + x - x)\,dx$

$= \displaystyle\int_{-\frac{1}{2}}^{0} (x^2)\,dx = \dfrac{1}{24}$ square units.

22. The polynomial $f(x)$ satisfies the condition $f(x+1) = x^2 + 4x$. The area enclosed by $y = f(x-1)$ and the curve $x^2 + y = 0$, is

(a) $\dfrac{16\sqrt{2}}{3}$ (b) $\dfrac{16}{3}$

(c) $\dfrac{8\sqrt{2}}{3}$ (d) None of these

Solution: (a) $f(x+1) = x^2 + 4x$ ...(i)
Putting $x = x - 2$ in (i), we get $f(x-1) = (x-2)^2 + 4(x-2)$, i.e., $f(x-1) = x^2 - 4$; Thus, we are to find area enclosed curves $y = x^2 - 4$ and $y = -x^2$ as shown below to shaded portion.

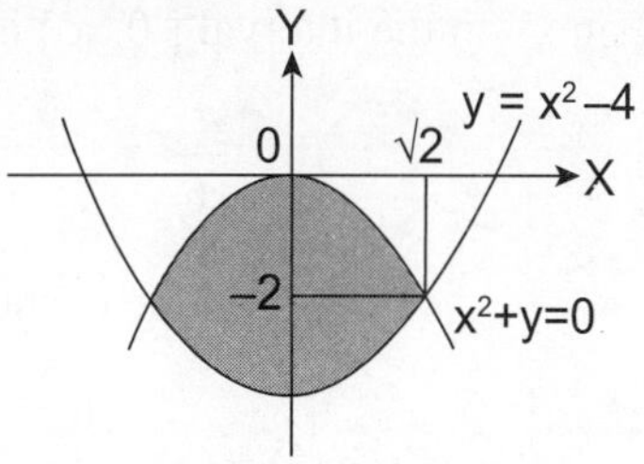

$\therefore$ Required Area $= A = 2\int_0^{\sqrt{2}} [(-x^2) - (x^2 - 4)]\,dx$

$= 2\int_0^{\sqrt{2}} (4 - 2x^2)\,dx = \dfrac{16\sqrt{2}}{3}$

23. Area bounded by curves $y = [\cos A + \cos B + \cos C]$, $y = \left[7\sin\frac{A}{2}\sin\frac{B}{2}\sin\frac{C}{2}\right]$; (where [.] denotes the greatest integer function and A, B, C are angles of a triangle) and curve $|x-4| + |y| = 2$ is

(a) 2 (b) 3

(c) 4 (d) 6

Solution: (b) We know $1 < \cos A + \cos B + \cos C \le \dfrac{3}{2}$ and $0 < \sin\dfrac{A}{2}\sin\dfrac{B}{2}\sin\dfrac{C}{2} \le \dfrac{1}{8}$

$\Rightarrow [\cos A + \cos B + \cos C] = 1$

and $\left[7\sin\dfrac{A}{2}\sin\dfrac{B}{2}\sin\dfrac{C}{2}\right] = 0$

$\therefore$ Curves are $y = 1$, $y = 0$ and $|x-4| + |y| = 2$

For $x \ge 4$, $x - 4 + |y| = 2$

$\Rightarrow x + |y| = 6$

$\Rightarrow x + y = 6$ as $y \in [0, 1]$ and

For $x \le 4$, $-x + 4 + |y| = 2$

$\Rightarrow x - y = 2$

$\therefore$ The required area is shaded portion as shown below

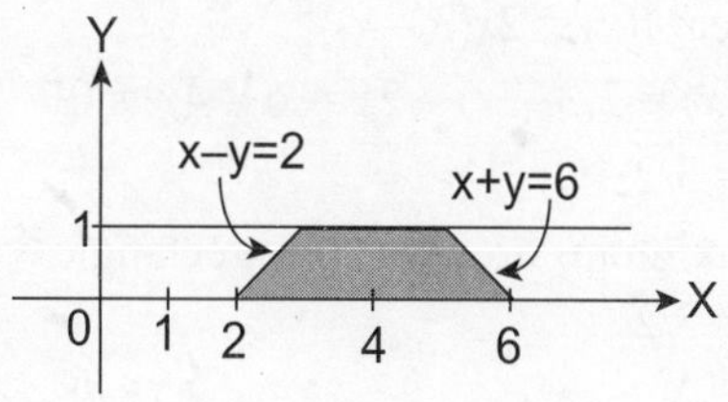

$\therefore$ Required area $= \dfrac{1}{2}(2+4).1 = 3$ square units

24. The area defined by $[x] + [y] = 1$, $-1 \le x, y \le 3$ in the $x - y$ coordinate plane is

(a) 8 (b) 6

(c) 4 (d) 2

Solution: (c) For $-1 \le x < 0$, $[x] = -1$, $[x] + [y] = 1$

$\Rightarrow [y] = 2$ $\Rightarrow y \in [2, 3)$

Similarly, For $x \in [0, 1)$; $[x] = 0$ and $[x] + [y] = 1$

$\Rightarrow 0 + [y] = 1$ $\Rightarrow [y] = 1$

$\Rightarrow y \in [1, 2)$ and for $x \in [1, 2)$; $y \in [0, 1)$

for $x \in [2, 3)$; $y \in [-1, 0)$

$\therefore$ The required area consists of four squares each having unit are as shown below:

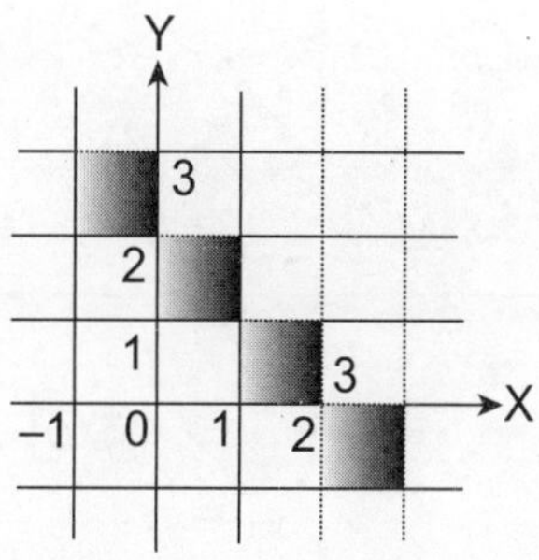

$\therefore$ The required area $= 4 \times 1 = 4$ square units

25. The maximum area of a rectangle whose two vertices lie on the x-axis and two on the curve $y = 3 - |x|$, $-3 \le x \le 3$ is

(a) 9 (b) 9/2

(c) 3 (d) None of these

Solution: (b) The area bounded by the lines $y = 3 - |x|$; $-3 \le x \le 3$ is shown in the figure.

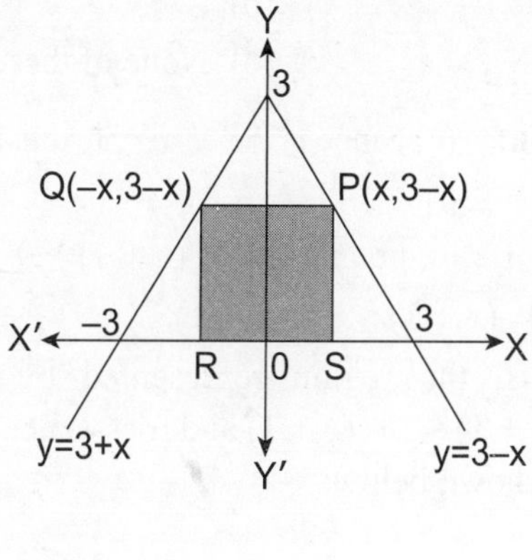

$\therefore$ Area $A(x) = 2x(3 - x)$

$\Rightarrow$ $A'(x) = 2(3 - x) - 2x = 6 - 4x = 0$

$\Rightarrow$ $x = 3/2$

$\therefore$ Maximum area of the rectangle occurs when $x = 3/2$

$\therefore$ Maximum area $= 2.\frac{3}{2}\left(3-\frac{3}{2}\right) = \frac{9}{2}$ square units.

26. The area of the region defined by $||x| - |y|| \le 1$ and $x^2 + y^2 \le 1$ in the x-y coordinate plane is

(a) 1 (b) 2

(c) π (d) None of these

Solution: (c) $||x| - |y|| \le 1$ ...(i)

$\Rightarrow -1 \le |x| - |y| \le 1$

$$\Rightarrow \begin{cases} -1 \le x - y \le 1 & \text{in I}^{\text{st}} \text{ qudrant} \\ -1 \le -x - y \le 1 & \text{in II}^{\text{nd}} \text{ qudrant} \\ -1 \le -x + y \le 1 & \text{in III}^{\text{rd}} \text{ qudrant} \\ -1 \le x + y \le 1 & \text{in IV}^{\text{th}} \text{ qudrant} \end{cases}$$

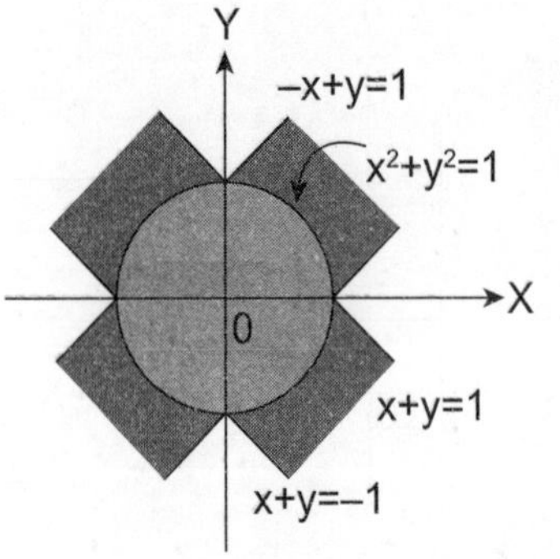

Thus, the region given by inequality (i) is represented by shaded in the figure given above: Also $x^2 + y^2 \le 1$ represents the interior area of circle $x^2 + y^2 = 1$ shown by shaded portion, which is also the common region.

$\therefore$ Required area = area of the circle $= \pi(1)^2 = \pi$ square units

27. The area bounded by $e^{\ln(x+1)} \ge |y|$, $|x| \le 1$ is

(a) 1 (b) 2

(c) 4 (d) None of these

Solution: (c) Since $e^{\ln(x+1)} = x + 1$, thus, $e^{\ln(x+1)} \ge |y|$

$\Rightarrow x + 1 \ge |y|$

$\Rightarrow x + 1 \not< 0$, i.e., $x \ge -1$ or $(x + 1) \ge 0$

and $-(x + 1) \le y < (x + 1)$.

Thus, the region represented by inequalities $-(x + 1) \le y \le (x + 1)$ and $|x| \le 1$, i.e., $-1 \le x \le 1$ is as shown below:

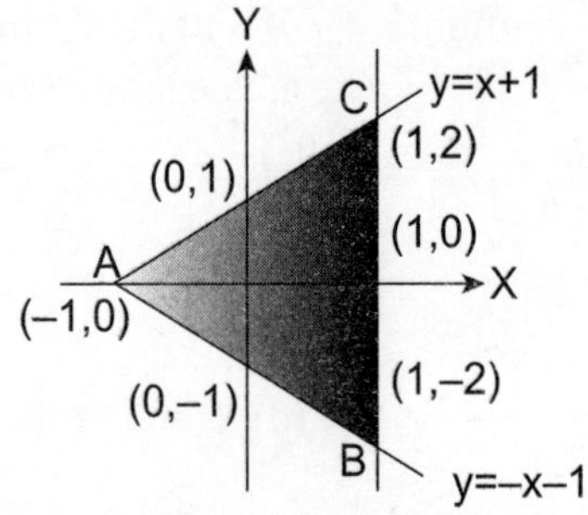

Thus, required area is the area of $\Delta ABC = \frac{1}{2}(4)(2) = 4$ square units.

28. The area bounded by $y = \cos^{-1}(\sin x)$ and $y = \sin^{-1}(\sin x)$ on the interval $[0, \pi]$ is

(a) $\frac{\pi^2}{8}$ (b) $\frac{\pi^2}{6}$

(c) $\frac{\pi^2}{4}$ (d) None of these

Solution: (a) $\cos^{-1}(\sin x) = \frac{\pi}{2} - \sin^{-1}(\sin x)$ ...(i)

$$\left(\because \sin^{-1} x + \cos^{-1} x = \frac{\pi}{2} \text{ for } x \in [-1,1] \text{ and } \sin x \in [-1,1]\right)$$

$$\text{But } \sin^{-1}(\sin x) = \begin{cases} x, & 0 \le x \le \frac{\pi}{2} \\ \pi - x, & \frac{\pi}{2} \le x \le \pi \end{cases} \quad \text{......(ii)}$$

Given that $x \in [0, \pi]$

$$\therefore \cos^{-1}(\sin x) = \begin{cases} \frac{\pi}{2} - x; & 0 \le x \le \frac{\pi}{2} \\ \frac{\pi}{2} - (\pi - x); & \frac{\pi}{2} \le x \le \pi \end{cases}$$

$$= \begin{cases} \frac{\pi}{2} - x; & 0 \le x \le \frac{\pi}{2} \\ x - \frac{\pi}{2}; & \frac{\pi}{2} \le x \le \pi \end{cases} \quad \text{.........(iii)}$$

$\therefore$ From (ii) and (iii) the graph of $\sin^{-1}(\sin x)$ and $\cos^{-1}(\sin x)$ is as shown below:

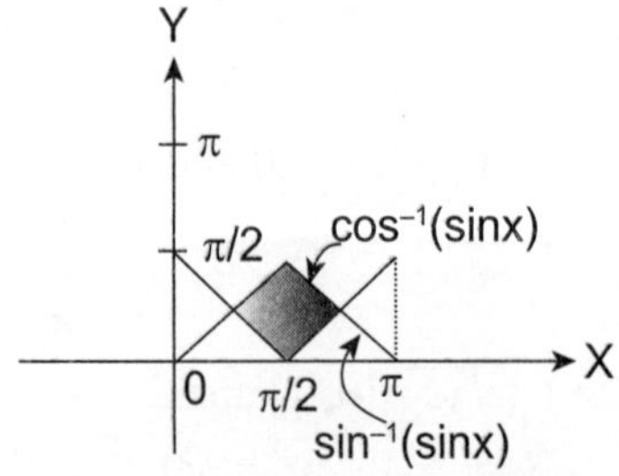

$\therefore$ The required shaded area $= \frac{\pi^2}{8}$ square units

29. The area bounded by the curves $y = \begin{cases} x^{1/\ln x}, & x \neq 1 \\ e, & x = 1 \end{cases}$ and $y = |x - e|$ is

(a) $e^2/2$ (b) e^2
(c) $2e^2$ (d) 1

Solution: (b) Given that $y = x^{1/\ln x}$

$\Rightarrow \ln y = \frac{1}{\ln x}\ln x = 1$; when $\ell n\, x \neq 0$

i.e., $x \neq 1, x > 0 \quad \Rightarrow y = e$

Thus, $y = \begin{cases} e; & x > 0; x \neq 1 \\ e; & x = 1 \end{cases}$ ...(i)

$\Rightarrow y = e \;\forall\; x > 0$

Also $y = |x - e| = \begin{cases} -x + e & \text{for } x \leq 3 \\ x - e & \text{for } x \geq 3 \end{cases}$ ...(ii)

Thus, the area bounded by (i) and (ii) is shown by shaded portion in the figure given below:

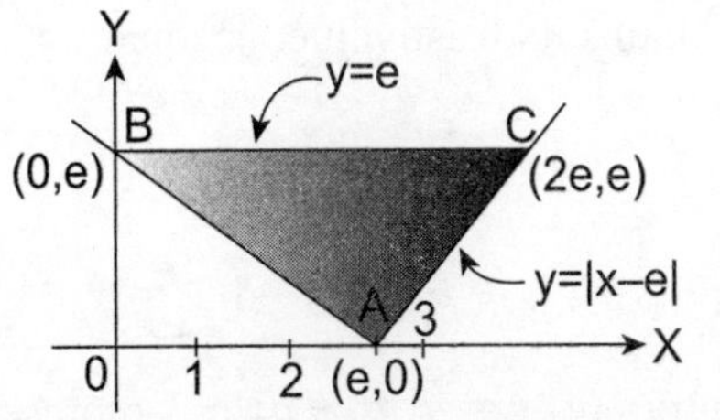

Hence the required area of $\Delta ABC = e^2$.

30. The area enclosed by the curves $y = \sqrt{4 - x^2}, y \geq \sqrt{2}\sin\left(\frac{x\pi}{2\sqrt{2}}\right)$ and x-axis is divided by y-axis in the ratio

(a) $\frac{\pi^2 - 8}{\pi^2 + 8}$ (b) $\frac{\pi^2 - 4}{\pi^2 + 4}$

(c) $\frac{\pi - 4}{\pi - 4}$ (d) None of these

Solution: (d) Given curves are

$y = \sqrt{4 - x^2}, y \geq \sqrt{2}\sin\left(\frac{x\pi}{2\sqrt{2}}\right)$

Which intersect at $x = \sqrt{2}$ (By inspection)

Area of the left of y-axis is $A_1 = \pi = \frac{1}{4}$th area of circle

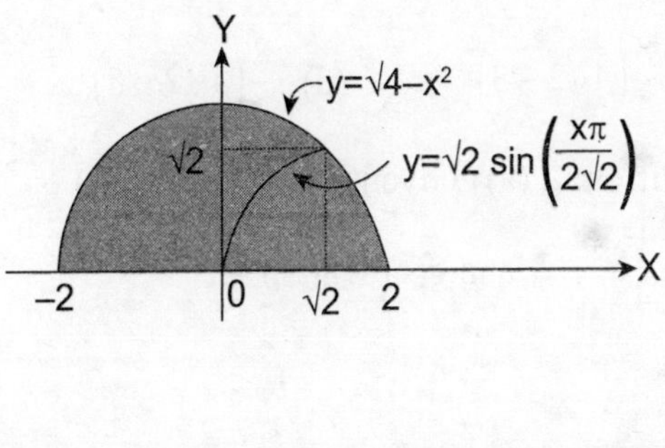

Area to the right of y-axis is

$$A_2 = \int_0^{\sqrt{2}}\left(\sqrt{4 - x^2} - \sqrt{2}\sin\frac{x\pi}{2\sqrt{2}}\right)dx$$

$$= \left(\frac{x\sqrt{4 - x^2}}{2} + \frac{4}{2}\sin^{-1}\frac{x}{2}\right)_0^{\sqrt{2}} + \frac{4}{\pi}\cos\frac{x\pi}{2\sqrt{2}}\Bigg|_0^{\sqrt{2}}$$

$$= \left(1 + 2.\frac{\pi}{4}\right) + \frac{4}{\pi}(0 - 1) = 1 + \frac{\pi}{2} - \frac{4}{\pi} = \frac{2\pi + \pi^2 - 8}{2\pi}$$

$$\Rightarrow \frac{A_1}{A_2} = \frac{\pi}{\left(\frac{2\pi + \pi^2 - 8}{2\pi}\right)} \quad \therefore \quad \frac{2\pi^2}{2\pi + \pi^2 - 8}$$

31. If $f(x) = \sin x \;\forall\; x \in \left[0, \frac{\pi}{2}\right]$; $f(x) + f(\pi - x) = 2$ $\forall\; x \in \left(\frac{\pi}{2}, \pi\right]$ and $f(x) = f(2\pi - x) \;\forall\; x \in (\pi, 2\pi]$, then the area enclosed by $y = f(x)$ and x-axis is

(a) π (b) 2π
(c) 2 (d) 4

Solution: (b) Given $f(x) = \sin x \;\forall x \in \left[0, \frac{\pi}{2}\right]$

and $f(x) + f(\pi - x) = 2 \;\forall x \in \left(\frac{\pi}{2}, \pi\right]$

$\Rightarrow f(x) = 2 - f(\pi - x) = 2 - \sin(\pi - x)$

$= 2 - \sin x;\; x \in \left(\frac{\pi}{2}, \pi\right]$

$\left(\because \text{ for } x \in \left(\frac{\pi}{2}, \pi\right]; \pi - x \in \left[0, \frac{\pi}{2}\right)\right)$

Also given $f(x) = f(2\pi - x) \;\forall\; x \in (\pi, 2\pi]$

$\Rightarrow (2\pi - x) \in [0, \pi)$

$\therefore f(x) = f(2\pi - x) = 2 - \sin(2\pi - x)$ for

$(2\pi - x) \in \left(\frac{\pi}{2}, \pi\right]$, i.e., for $x \in \left[\pi, \frac{3\pi}{2}\right)$

or $f(x) = 2 + \sin x$ for $x \in \left[\pi, \frac{3\pi}{2}\right)$

Now, for $x \in \left(\frac{3\pi}{2}, 2\pi\right]$

$f(x) = f(2\pi - x) = \sin(2\pi - x) = -\sin x$

$$\left(\begin{array}{l} \because \frac{3\pi}{2} \leq x \leq 2\pi \\ \Rightarrow -2\pi \leq -x \leq -\frac{3\pi}{2} \\ \Rightarrow 0 \leq 2\pi - x \leq \frac{\pi}{2} \end{array}\right)$$

Thus, $f(x)=\begin{cases}\sin x; & x\in\left[0,\frac{\pi}{2}\right]\\ 2-\sin x; & x\in\left(\frac{\pi}{2},\pi\right]\\ 2+\sin x; & \left(\pi,\frac{3\pi}{2}\right)\\ -\sin x; & \left[\frac{3\pi}{2},2\pi\right]\end{cases}$

⇒ The graph of function $f(x)$ would be as shown below:

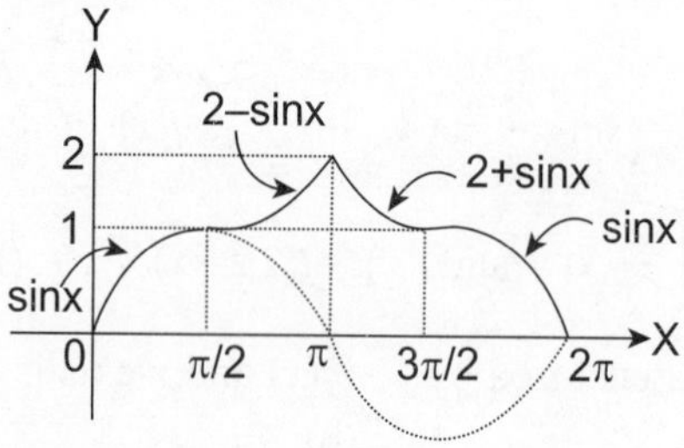

∴ The required area

$$=\int_0^{\pi/2}\sin x\,dx+\int_{\pi/2}^{\pi}(2-\sin x)dx+\int_{\pi}^{3\pi/2}(2+\sin x)dx+\int_{3\pi/2}^{2\pi}(-\sin x)dx$$

$= 1 + 2 \times \frac{\pi}{2} - 1 + 2 \times \frac{\pi}{2} - 1 + 1$

$= 2\pi$ square units.

32. $y=\frac{1-x^2}{1+x^2}$ divides the area enclosed by $y=\frac{1}{1+x^2}$, x-axis y-axis in the first quadrant in the ratio

(a) $\frac{\pi-2}{2}$ (b) $\frac{4-\pi}{4}$

(c) $\frac{2\pi-4}{\pi}$ (d) $\frac{\pi-1}{\pi+1}$

Solution: (a) Since $y=\frac{1}{1+x^2}>0\forall x\geq 0$ and $f(x)$ is a decreasing function for $x \geq 0$ and $f(x) \to 0$ as $x \to \infty$, the area bounded by $f(x)=\frac{1}{1+x^2}, x>0, y>0$ is given by $\int_0^{\infty}\frac{1}{1+x^2}dx=\left|\tan^{-1}x\right|_0^{\infty}=\frac{\pi}{2}$

∴ $A=\frac{\pi}{2}$

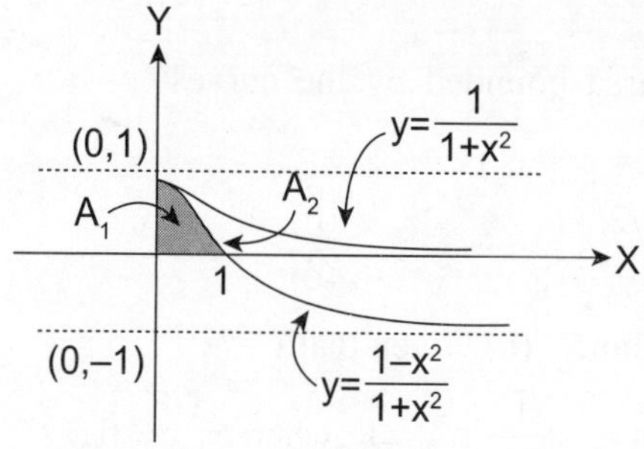

Now, $A_1=\int_0^1\left(\frac{2}{1+x^2}-1\right)dx=\left(\frac{\pi}{2}-1\right)$

∴ $A_2=A-A_1=\frac{\pi}{2}-\left(\frac{\pi}{2}-1\right)=1$

∴ $A_1:A_2=\left(\frac{\pi}{2}-1\right):1 = \pi - 2 : 2$

33. Value of the parameter 'a' such that the area bounded by $y = a^2x^2 + ax + 1$, co-ordinate axes and the line $x = 1$, attains its least value, is equal to:

(a) $-\frac{1}{4}$ (b) $-\frac{1}{2}$

(c) $-\frac{3}{4}$ (d) -1

Solution: (c) $y = a^2 x^2 + ax + 1$ represents upwards parabola with discriminant $-3a^2 < 0$

⇒ $y > 0\ \forall\ x \in \mathbb{R}$

∴ Required area $A=\int_0^1\left(a^2x^2+ax+1\right)dx$

$$=\left(a^2\frac{x^3}{3}+\frac{ax^2}{2}+x\right)\Bigg|_0^1=\frac{a^2}{3}+\frac{a}{2}+1$$

$$==\frac{1}{3}\left(a^2+\frac{3}{2}a+\frac{9}{16}\right)+1-\frac{9}{48}=\frac{1}{3}\left(a+\frac{3}{4}\right)^2+\frac{39}{48}$$

attains its least value, when $a=-\frac{3}{4}$

34. If $f(x) = x - 1$ and g $(x) =\left|f(|x|)-2\right|$, then the area bounded by $y = g(x)$ and the curve $x^2 - 4y + 8 = 0$ is equal to

(a) $\frac{4}{3}\left(4\sqrt{2}-5\right)$ (b) $\frac{4}{3}\left(4\sqrt{2}-3\right)$

(c) $\frac{8}{3}\left(4\sqrt{2}-3\right)$ (d) $\frac{8}{3}\left(4\sqrt{2}-5\right)$

Solution: (a) Given curves are $f(x) = x - 1$; $y=\frac{1}{4}x^2+2$ and $g(x) = |f(|x|) - 2|$

$$= \begin{cases} f(|x|)-2 & \text{for } f(|x|)-2 \geq 0 \\ 2-f(|x|) & \text{for } f(|x|)-2 \leq 2 \end{cases}$$

$$= \begin{cases} f(x)-2 & \text{for } f(x)-2 \geq 0; x \geq 0 \\ f(-x)-2 & \text{for } f(-x)-2 \geq 0; x < 0 \\ 2-f(x) & \text{for } f(x)-2 \leq 0; x \geq 0 \\ 2-f(-x) & \text{for } f(-x)-2 \leq 0; x < 0 \end{cases}$$

$$= \begin{cases} x-3 & \text{for } x \geq 3 \\ -x-3 & \text{for } x \leq -3 \\ 3-x & \text{for } 0 \leq x \leq 3 \\ x+3 & \text{for } -3 \leq x < 0 \end{cases}$$

$\therefore$ Graph of $g(x)$ will be as shown below:

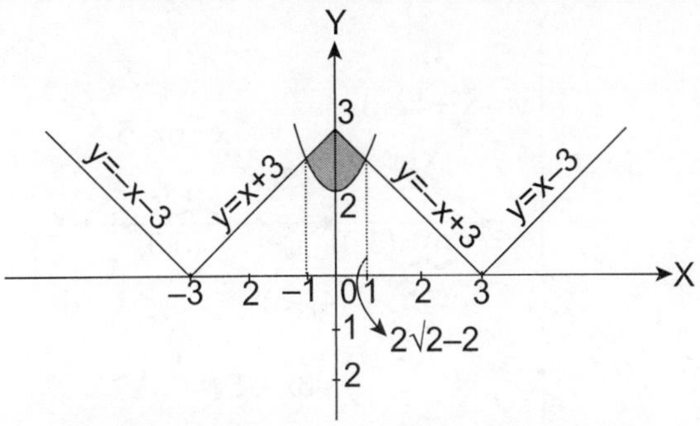

The above graph can also be obtained with the help of transformation of graphs. Now, the second given curve is $y = \frac{1}{4}x^2 + 2$ which cuts y-axis at (0, 2) and cuts the function $g(x)$ symmetrically about y-axis at $x = \pm 2\sqrt{2} - 2$

$\therefore$ Required area $= 2 \int_0^{2\sqrt{2}-2} \left[(-x+3) - \left(\frac{x^2}{4} + 2\right)\right] dx$

$$= \frac{16\sqrt{2}}{3} - \frac{20}{3} = \frac{4}{3}(4\sqrt{2} - 5)$$

35. Area bounded by the curve

$$f(x) = \begin{cases} \log_e |x|, |x| \geq \frac{1}{e} \\ |x| - 1 - \frac{1}{e}, \quad |x| < \frac{1}{e} \end{cases}$$ and x-axis is

(a) $\frac{1}{e^2} + 2 - \frac{2}{e}$ (b) $\frac{1}{e^2} + 2 + \frac{2}{e}$

(c) $\frac{1}{e^2} + \frac{2}{e}$ (d) None of these

Solution: (a) Given curve is

$$f(x) = \begin{cases} \log_e |x|, |x| \geq \frac{1}{e} \\ |x| - 1 - \frac{1}{e}, \quad |x| < \frac{1}{e} \end{cases}$$

Graph of $f(x)$ is as figure shown below:

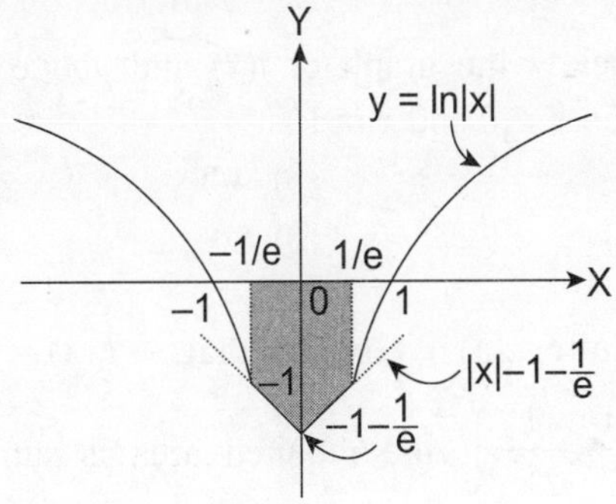

$\therefore$ Required shaded area

$$= 2\left[\int_0^{1/e} -\left(x - 1 - \frac{1}{e}\right) dx + \int_{1/e}^{1} -\ln x \, dx\right]$$

$$= 2\left[-\left\{\frac{x^2}{2} - \left(1 + \frac{1}{e}\right)x\right\}_0^{1/e} - \left(x(\ln x - 1)\right)_{1/e}^{1}\right]$$

$$= -2\left[\frac{1}{2e^2} - \frac{1}{e} - \frac{1}{e^2}\right] - 2\left[(-1) + \left(\frac{2}{e}\right)\right]$$

$$= -\frac{1}{e^2} + \frac{2}{e} + \frac{2}{e^2} + 2 - \frac{4}{e} = \frac{1}{e^2} + 2 - \frac{2}{e} \text{ square units}$$

36. If A_n is the area bounded by $y = x$ and $y = x^n$, $n \in \mathbb{N}$, then, $A_2 \,.\, A_3 \, ... \, A_n =$

(a) $\frac{1}{n(n+1)}$ (b) $\frac{1}{2^n n(n+1)}$

(c) $\frac{1}{2^{n-1} n(n+1)}$ (d) $\frac{1}{2^{n-2} n(n+1)}$

Solution: (d) $y = x$ and $y = x^n$; $n \in \mathbb{N}$ intersect at $x = 0$ and $x = 1$ and for $x \in (0, 1)$, $x > x^n$ as figure shown below:

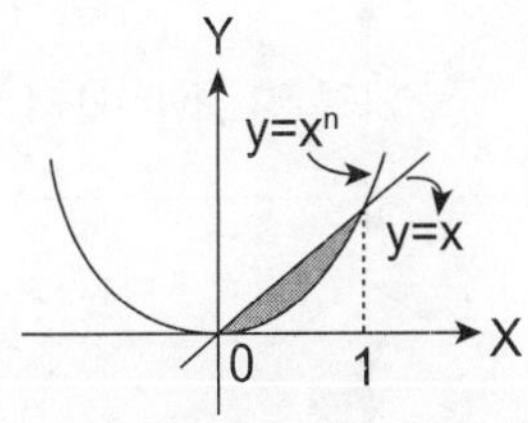

Thus, the area bounded by $y = x$ and $y = x^n$ is given by $A_n = \int_0^1 (x - x^n) dx = \left[\frac{x^2}{2} - \frac{x^{n+1}}{n+1}\right]_0^1$

$$= \frac{1}{2} - \frac{1}{n+1} = \frac{n-1}{2(n+1)}; \text{ Thus, } A_2 \,.\, A_3 \,.\, A_4 \, ... \, A_n$$

$$= \frac{1}{2^{n-1}}\left(\frac{1}{3} \cdot \frac{2}{4} \cdot \frac{3}{5} \cdots \frac{n-1}{n+1}\right) = \frac{1}{2^{n-2} . n(n+1)}$$

37. If $f(x)=\frac{1}{2^{n-1}}, \frac{1}{2^n}<x<\frac{1}{2^{n-1}}; n\geq 0$ and $n\in\mathbb{Z}$, then the area below the graph of $f(x)$ and above the x-axis between $x = 0$ and $x = 1$ is

(a) 8/3 (b) 4/3

(c) 2/3 (d) 2

Solution: (a) Given that $f(x)=\frac{1}{2^{n-1}}$ for $x\in\left(\frac{1}{2^n},\frac{1}{2^{n-1}}\right)$, the required area is sum of areas $\left(\frac{1}{2^{n-1}}\right)\left(\frac{1}{2^{n-1}}-\frac{1}{2^n}\right)$.

Thus, the required area is given by, $\sum_{n=0}^{\infty}\frac{1}{2^{n-1}}\left(\frac{1}{2^{n-1}}-\frac{1}{2^n}\right)$

$=\sum_{n=0}^{\infty}\frac{1}{2^{2n-1}}=\frac{8}{3}$

38. The area enclosed by $|y|-|x|\leq 1; x^2+y^2\geq 1$ and $|x| = 1$ is

(a) $6 + \pi$ units (b) $6 - \pi$ units

(c) infinite units (d) None of these

Solution: (b) Graph of $x^2 + y^2 \geq 1$ is the region outer of circle as shown below:

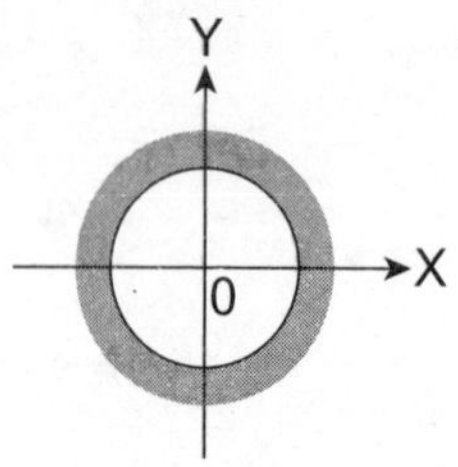

and the region of $|y|-|x|\leq 1$ and $|x| = 1$ is as shown below:

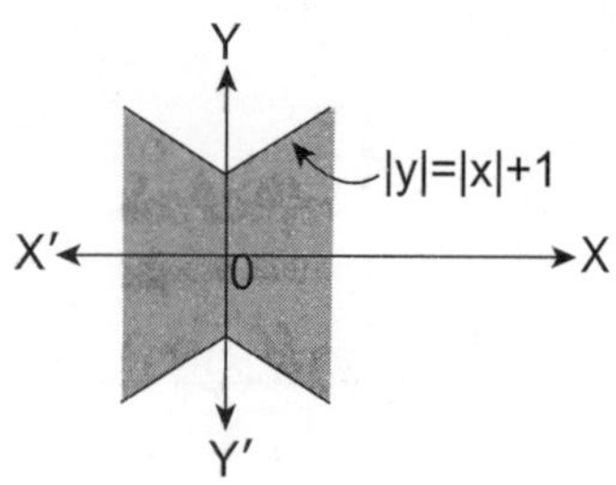

So, area enclosed by two graphs is as shown below:

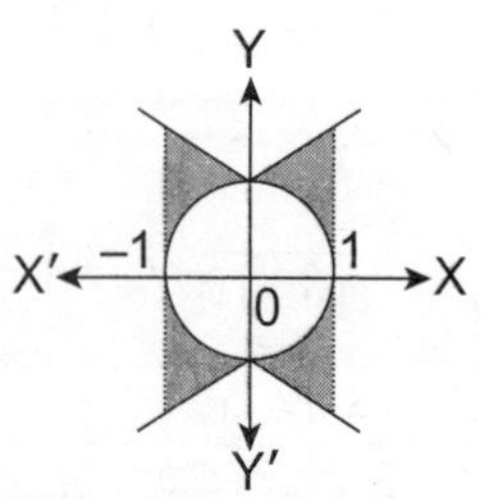

Thus, the required area $=4\int_0^1\left\{(x+1)-\left(\sqrt{1-x^2}\right)\right\}dx$

$= (6 - \pi)$ square units. or

$= \{2(\text{area of Trapezium}) - (\text{area of circle})\}$

$= \{(2 + 4) - \pi(1)^2\} = (6 - \pi)$ square units

39. Area bounded by $y = -x^2 + 6x - 5$, $y = -x^2 + 4x - 3$ and $y = 3x - 15$, for $x > 1$, is (in sq. units)

(a) 73 (b) 13/6

(c) 73/6 (d) None of these

Solution: (c) The two parabolas intersect each other at (1, 0) and are intersect by line $y = 3x - 15$ at (4, –3) and (5, 0) as shown below:

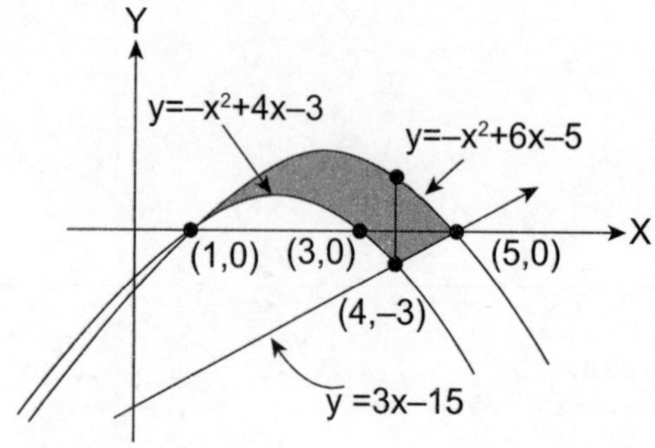

∴ Required area

$$= A = \int_1^4\{(-x^2+6x-5)-(-x^2+4x-3)\}dx + \int_4^5\{(-x^2+6x-5)-(3x-15)\}dx$$

$\Rightarrow A = \frac{73}{6}$ square units

40. The area of the region bounded by the curve $y=\frac{16-x^2}{4}$ and $y = \sec^{-1}[-\sin^2 x]$; (where [.] denotes the greatest integer function) is

(a) $\frac{1}{3}(4-\pi)^{3/2}$ (b) $8(4-\pi)^{3/2}$

(c) $\frac{8}{3}(4-\pi)^{3/2}$ (d) $\frac{8}{3}(4-\pi)^{1/2}$

Solution: (c) $0 \leq \sin^2 x \leq 1$

$\Rightarrow -1 \leq -\sin^2 x \leq 0$

∴ $[-\sin^2 x] = 0$ or -1 but $\sec^{-1}(0)$ is not defined

Hence, $y = \sec^{-1}[-\sin^2 x] = \sec^{-1}(-1) = \pi$; at the point of intersection of $y=\frac{16-x^2}{4}$ & $y=\pi$

$\Rightarrow \pi = \frac{16-x^2}{4}$ $\Rightarrow x^2 = 16 - 4\pi = 4(4 - \pi)$

$\Rightarrow x = \pm 2\sqrt{4-\pi}$; Thus, the area bounded by curves

$y = \pi$ & $y = \dfrac{16-x^2}{4}$ is as shown below figure

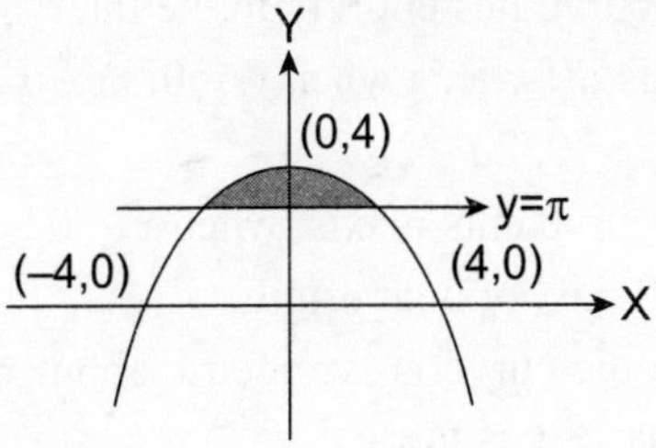

$\therefore$ The required area $= \displaystyle\int_{-2\sqrt{4-\pi}}^{2\sqrt{4-\pi}} \left(\frac{16-x^2}{4} - \pi\right) dx$

$= \dfrac{8}{3}(4-\pi)^{3/2}$ square units.

41. Find the area enclosed between $x^2 + y^2 \le 9\pi^2$ and $\sin(x-y) \ge 0$

(a) $\dfrac{9\pi^3}{4}$ (b) $\dfrac{9\pi^3}{2}$

(c) $3\pi^3$ (d) π^3

Solution: (b) $\sin(x-y) \ge 0$

$\Rightarrow (x-y) \in [2n\pi, (2n+1)\pi]$; $n \in \mathbb{Z}$

$\Rightarrow x - (2n+1)\pi \le y \le x - 2n\pi$; $n \in \mathbb{Z}$

$$\Rightarrow \begin{cases} x-\pi \le y \le x & \text{for } n=0 \\ x-3\pi \le y \le x-2\pi & \text{for } n=1 \\ x-5\pi \le y \le x-4\pi & \text{for } n=2 \\ x-7\pi \le y \le x-6\pi & \text{for } n=3 \\ x+\pi \le y \le x+2\pi & \text{for } n=-1 \\ x+3\pi \le y \le x+4\pi & \text{for } n=-2 \end{cases}$$

and so on........

$\therefore$ The shaded area represents the required bounded area as shown below:

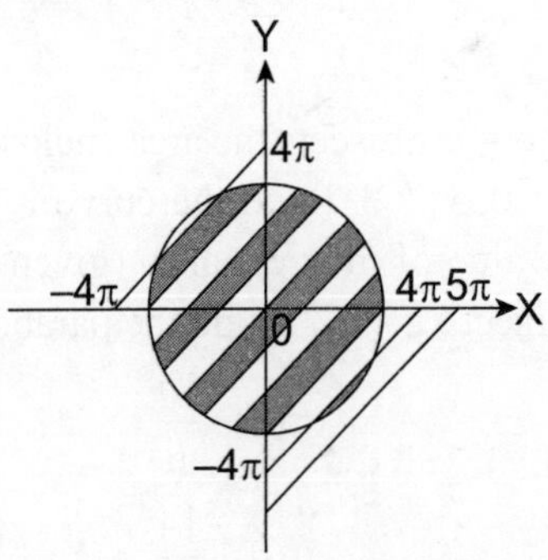

Clearly the shaded and unshaded areas are equally inside the circle, i.e., they are half of circular area.

Thus, the shaded area equals $= \dfrac{\pi(9\pi^2)}{2} = \dfrac{9\pi^3}{2}$

square units

42. The area bounded by $y = x^2 + 2$ and $y = 2|x| - \cos \pi x$ is equal to

(a) 2/3 (b) 8/3

(c) 4/3 (d) 1/3

Solution: (b) The two curves intersect where $x^2 + 2 = 2|x| - \cos \pi x$

$\Rightarrow x^2 - 2|x| + 2 = -\cos \pi x$

$\Rightarrow (|x| - 1)^2 + 1 = -\cos \pi x$

($\because$ Left expression ≥ 1, where as right expression ≤ 1)

$\Rightarrow (|x|-1)^2 = 0$; $\cos \pi x = -1 \Rightarrow x = \pm 1$

Also $(|x|-1)^2 + 1 \ge 1$ and $-\cos \pi x \le 1$

$\Rightarrow (|x|-1)^2 + 1 + \cos \pi x \ge 0$

$\Rightarrow x^2 + 2 \ge 2|x| - \cos \pi x$ and equally holds at $x = \pm 1$

$\therefore$ The bounded area is given by $\displaystyle\int_{-1}^{1} (y_1 - y_2) dx$;

where $y_1 = x^2 + 2$ and $y_2 = 2|x| - \cos \pi x$

$\therefore$ The required area $= \displaystyle\int_{-1}^{1} (x^2 + 2 - 2|x| + \cos \pi x)\, dx$

$= \dfrac{8}{3}$ square units.

43. Area bounded by the curve $y^2(2a - x) = x^3$ and the line $x = 2a$ is

(a) $3\pi a^2$ (b) $\dfrac{3\pi a^2}{2}$

(c) $\dfrac{3\pi a^2}{4}$ (d) None of these

Solution: (a) $y^2(2a-x) = x^3$ is symmetrical about x-axis because even power of y is present.

It also passes through (0, 0). The line $x = 2a$ is asymptote as $y \to \infty$ when $x = 2a$.

Also $y_1 = \sqrt{\dfrac{x^3}{2a-x}}$ for curve above x-axis and

$y_2 = -\sqrt{\dfrac{x^3}{2a-x}}$ for curve below x-axis.

$$\Rightarrow y_1' = \frac{\sqrt{2a-x}.\frac{3}{2}\sqrt{x} - x^{3/2}.\frac{1}{2\sqrt{2a-x}}(-1)}{(2a-x)}$$

$$\Rightarrow \frac{3(2a-x)\sqrt{x} + x\sqrt{x}}{2(2a-x)^{3/2}} \quad \Rightarrow \quad \frac{\sqrt{x}(6a-2x)}{2(2a-x)^{3/2}}$$

$\Rightarrow y_1' > 0$ for $x > 0$, $6a - 2x > 0$ and $2a - x > 0$

$\Rightarrow 0 < x < 2a$

$\therefore$ curve is increasing for $0 < x < 2a$

Similarly $y_2' < 0$ for $0 < x < 2a$

Thus, the curve would be as shown below.

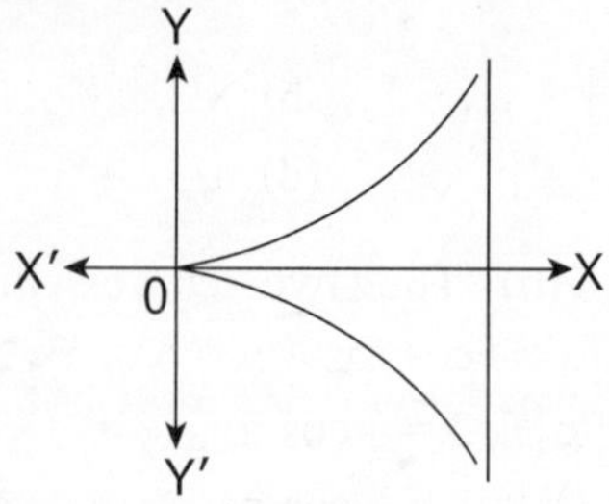

$\therefore$ Required area $= 2\int_0^{2a} y dx = 2\int_0^{2a} \sqrt{\frac{x^3}{2a-x}} dx$

Put $x = 2a \sin^2 \theta \Rightarrow dx = 4a \sin \theta \cos \theta \, d\theta$

$\therefore$ Required area $= 2\int_0^{\pi/2} 2a \frac{\sin^3 \theta}{\cos \theta} .4a \sin \theta \cos \theta \, d\theta$

$= 16a^2 \int_0^{\pi/2} \sin^4 \theta \, d\theta = 16a^2 \frac{3.1}{4.2} . \frac{\pi}{2} = 3\pi a^2.$

44. The area of the figure bounded by two branches of the curve $(y - x)^2 = x^3$ and the straight line $x = 1$ is

(a) 1/3 square units (b) 4/5 square units
(c) 5/4 square units (d) 3 square units

Solution: (b) Given curve is $(y - x)^2 = x^3$

$\Rightarrow y - x = \pm x\sqrt{x}$ or $y = x \pm x\sqrt{x}$

Clearly the curves $y = x + x\sqrt{x}$; $y = x - x\sqrt{x}$ intersect each other at origin (0, 0). Further $y = x + x\sqrt{x}$ intersect $x = 1$ at (1, 2) and $y = x - x\sqrt{x}$ intersect $x = 1$ at (1, 0). Since we are to find area bounded by two branches of $(y - x)^2 = x^3$ and $x = 1$; $x \in [0, 1]$ for which $y = x + x\sqrt{x} > 0$ and also $y = x - x\sqrt{x} > 0$.

Also $x + x\sqrt{x} > x - x\sqrt{x}$ for $x \in [0, 1]$

$\therefore$ The bounded region will be as shown below:

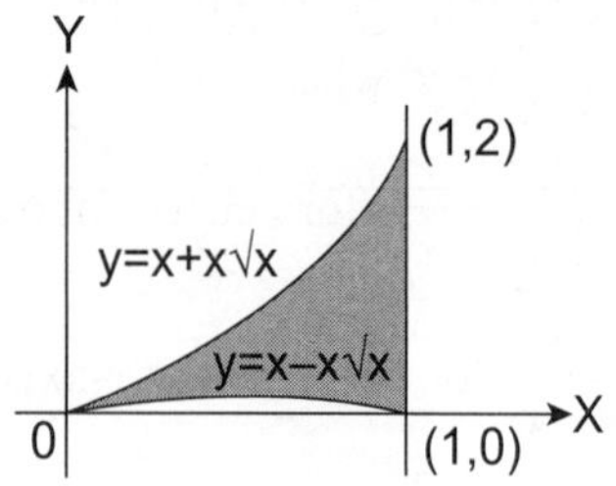

$\therefore$ The required area $= \int_0^1 [(x + x\sqrt{x} - (x - x\sqrt{x})] dx$

$= 2\int_0^1 x^{3/2} dx = 2.\frac{2}{5} = \frac{4}{5}$ square units.

45. The area of the region bounded by the curve $a^4y^2 = (2a - x) x^5$ is to that of the circle whose radius is a, is given by the ratio

(a) 4 : 5 (b) 5 : 8
(c) 2 : 3 (d) 3 : 2

Solution: (b) Given curve is $a^4y^2 = (2a - x) x^5$

$\Rightarrow y = \pm \frac{\sqrt{(2a-x)x^5}}{a^2} = \pm \frac{x^2}{a^2} = \sqrt{x(2a-x)}$

$\Rightarrow$ The curve lies entirely in the interval $x \in [0, 2a]$

It cuts off x-axis when $y = 0$, i.e., $0 = (2a - x) x^5$

i.e., $x = 0, 2a$

The curve cuts y-axis, when $x = 0$

$\Rightarrow y = 0$, i.e., only at origin.

Also the curve is symmetric about x-axis as even power of y is present.

Thus, the shape of curve will be as shown in figure:

Hence, the area bounded by the curve

$a^4y^2 = (2a - x) x^5$ is $A_1 = \int_0^{2a} \frac{\sqrt{(2a-x)}}{a^2} x^{5/2} dx$

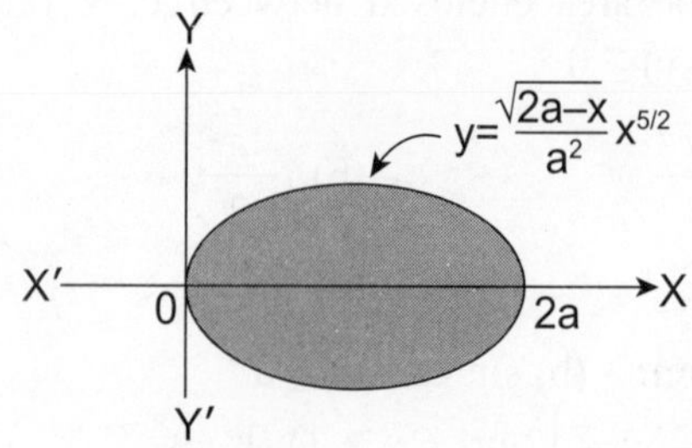

Put $x = 2a \sin^2 \theta$ $\therefore dx = 4a \sin \theta \cos \theta \, d\theta$

$\therefore A_1 = \int_0^{\pi/2} \frac{\sqrt{2a}.\cos\theta(2a)^{5/2}.\sin^5\theta \; 4a \sin\theta\cos\theta}{a^2} d\theta$

$= \int_0^{\pi/2} 32a^2 \sin^6\theta . \cos^2\theta \, d\theta$

$= 32a^2 \frac{(5.3.1)(1)}{8.6.4.2} . \frac{\pi}{2} = \frac{5\pi a^2}{8}$

(By walli's formula)

Also area of circle $A_2 = \pi a^2$

$\therefore \frac{A_1}{A_2} = \frac{5}{8}$ $\Rightarrow A_1 : A_2 = 5 : 8.$

46. If the line $y = mx$ bisects the area enclosed by the lines $x = 0, y = 0, x = 3/2$ and the curve $y = 1 + 4x - x^2$. Then the value of m is equal to (given that the line $y = mx$ intersect $x = 3/2$ inside the parabola)

(a) $\frac{13}{6}$ (b) $\frac{15}{6}$

(c) $\frac{13}{2}$ (d) $\frac{14}{4}$

Solution: (a) We have, $y = 1 + 4x - x^2$

$\Rightarrow x^2 - 4x = -y + 1 \Rightarrow (x - 2)^2 = -(y - 5)$

This equation represents a parabola having vertex at (2, 5) and opens downward. The area enclosed by this parabola and the line $x = 0, y = 0, x = 3/2$ is shown by shaded region in the figure given below:

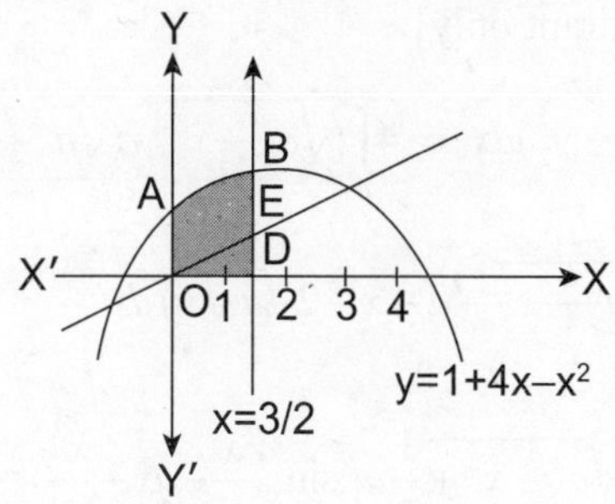

Since $y = mx$ bisects the area of the shaded region. Therefore, Area of the region $ODBAO$ = 2 (Area of triangle ODE)

$$\Rightarrow \int_0^{3/2}\left(1+4x-x^2\right)dx = 2\int_0^{3/2} mx\,dx$$

$$\Rightarrow \left[x+2x^2-\frac{x^3}{3}\right]_0^{3/2} = 2m\left[\frac{x^2}{2}\right]_0^{3/2}$$

$$\Rightarrow \frac{3}{2}+\frac{9}{2}-\frac{9}{8} = m\times\frac{9}{4} \Rightarrow \frac{39}{8}=\frac{9m}{4} \Rightarrow m=\frac{13}{6}.$$

47. The area bounded by the curve $y = f(x)$, $y = x$ and the lines $x = 1$, $x = t$ is $\left(t+\sqrt{1+t^2}\right)-\sqrt{2}-1$ square units, for all $t > 1$. If $f(x)$ satisfying $f(x) > x$ for all $x > 1$, then $f(x)$ is equal to

(a) $x+1+\dfrac{x}{\sqrt{1+x^2}}; x>1$

(b) $x+\dfrac{x}{\sqrt{1+x^2}}; x>1$

(c) $1+\dfrac{x}{\sqrt{1+x^2}}; x>1$

(d) $\dfrac{x}{\sqrt{1+x^2}}; x>1$

Solution: (a) It is given that $f(x) > x$, for all $x > 1$ and we are to find the area bounded by $y = f(x)$; $y = x$; $x = 1$ and $x = t(>1)$. The required region will be as shown below:

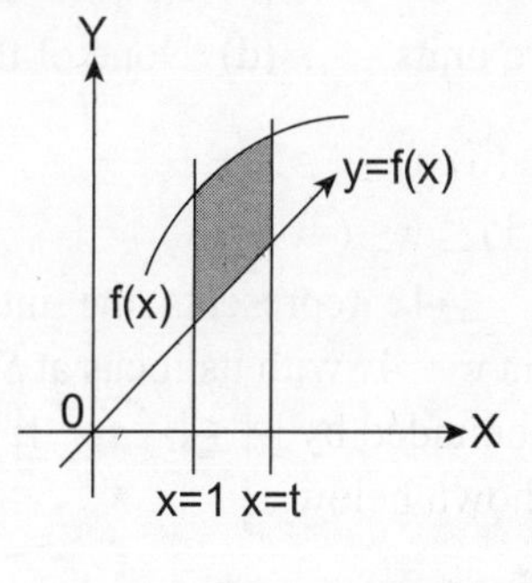

The required area will be given by $\int_1^t \{f(x)-x\}dx$

But this area is given equal to $\left(t+\sqrt{1+t^2}\right)-\sqrt{2}-1$ sq. units.

Therefore, $\int_1^t |f(x)-x|dx = \left(t+\sqrt{1+t^2}\right)-\sqrt{2}-1$, for all $t > 1$

On differentiating both sides w.r.t. 't', we get

$$\left(f(t)-t\right)=1+\frac{t}{\sqrt{1+t^2}} \text{ for all } t>1 \quad (\because f(t)>t)$$

$$\Rightarrow f(t)=t+1+\frac{t}{\sqrt{1+t^2}} \text{ for all } t>1$$

$$\text{Hence } f(x)=x+1+\frac{x}{\sqrt{1+x^2}} \text{ for all } x>1.$$

48. The area of the region bounded by the ellipse $\dfrac{x^2}{a^2}+\dfrac{y^2}{b^2}=1$ and its pair of latus recta; e is eccentricity of ellipse and $e < 1$, is given by

(a) $2ab\left(e\sqrt{1-e^2}+\sin^{-1}e\right)$ square units

(b) $2ab\left(e\sqrt{1-e^2}-\sin^{-1}e\right)$ square units

(c) $ab\left(e\sqrt{1-e^2}-\sin^{-1}e\right)$ square units

(d) None of these

Solution: (a) We are to find area bounded ellipse $\dfrac{x^2}{a^2}+\dfrac{y^2}{b^2}=1$ and the straight lines $x = \pm ae$ passing through the foci of ellipse as shown below figure:

$$\therefore \text{ The required area } = 4\int_0^{ae} y\,dx = \frac{4b}{a}\int_0^{ae}\sqrt{a^2-x^2}\,dx$$

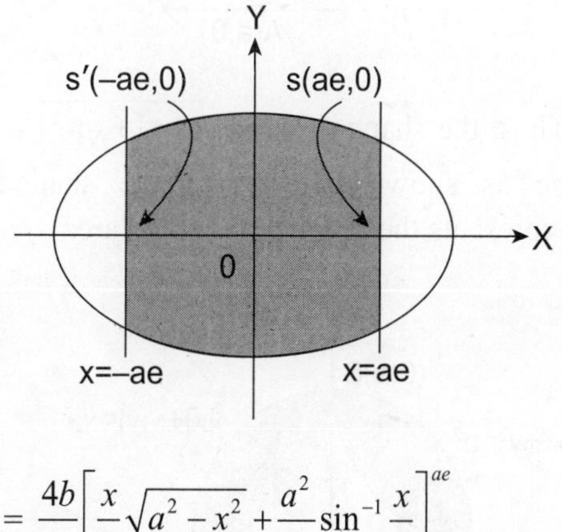

$$= \frac{4b}{a}\left[\frac{x}{2}\sqrt{a^2-x^2}+\frac{a^2}{2}\sin^{-1}\frac{x}{a}\right]_0^{ae}$$

$$= \frac{4b}{2a}\left[ae\sqrt{a^2-a^2e^2}+a^2\sin^{-1}e\right]$$

$$= 2ab\left(e\sqrt{1-e^2}+\sin^{-1}e\right) \text{ square units.}$$

49. The area bounded by the curve $\sqrt{|x|}+\sqrt{|y|}=\sqrt{a}$ and $x^2 + y^2 = a^2$, $a > 0$ is

(a) $\left\{\pi a^2 - \frac{2}{3}a^2\right\}$ square units

(b) $\left\{\pi a^2 - \frac{a^2}{3}\right\}$ square units

(c) $\left\{\pi a^2 - \frac{3a^2}{2}\right\}$ square units

(d) None of these

Solution: (a) Replacing x by $-x$ and y by $-y$ does not change the equation $\sqrt{|x|}+\sqrt{|y|}=\sqrt{a}$. It implies the curve is symmetric about x-axis and y-axis. In first quadrant $\sqrt{|x|}+\sqrt{|y|}=\sqrt{a} = \sqrt{y}=\sqrt{a}-\sqrt{x}$

$\Rightarrow \sqrt{a}\geq\sqrt{x}; x\geq 0 \Rightarrow 0\leq x\leq a$; similarly $0\leq y\leq a$

Thus, the curve $\sqrt{|x|}+\sqrt{|y|}=\sqrt{a}$ is entirely contained in the region $0 \leq x \leq a$ and $0 \leq y \leq a$

$\Rightarrow \sqrt{y}=\sqrt{a}-\sqrt{x} \quad \Rightarrow \quad y=\left(\sqrt{a}-\sqrt{x}\right)^2$,

which intersects x-axis at $(a, 0)$ and y-axis at $(0, a)$

Further $y' = \frac{\left(\sqrt{a}-\sqrt{x}\right)}{\sqrt{x}} < 0$ and $y'' = \frac{\sqrt{a}}{2x\sqrt{x}} > 0$.

Thus, the curve is decreasing having upwards concavity as shown below:

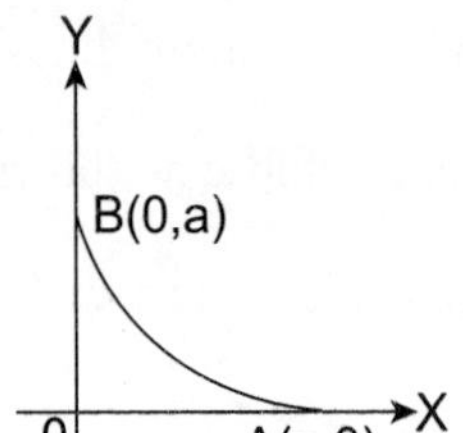

Thus, the shape of curve $\sqrt{|x|}+\sqrt{|y|}=\sqrt{a}$ will be as shown below and the shaded region represents the required bounded area.

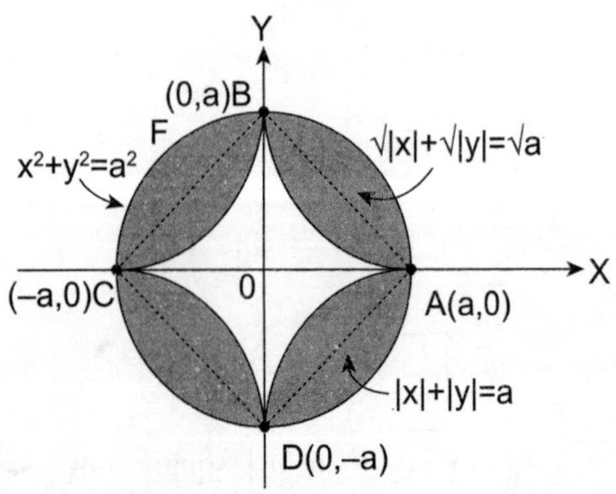

From the symmetry, it is evident that required area = 4 [Area of the region bounded by the two curves in first quadrant only]

$$= 4\int_0^a (y_1 - y_2)dx = 4\int_0^a \{\sqrt{a^2-x^2} - (\sqrt{a}-\sqrt{x})^2\}dx$$

$$= 4\int_0^a (\sqrt{a^2-x^2} - a - x + 2\sqrt{a}\sqrt{x})\,dx$$

$$= 4\left[\frac{1}{2}x\sqrt{a^2-x^2}+\frac{1}{2}a^2\sin^{-1}\frac{x}{a} - ax - \frac{x^2}{2}+\frac{4\sqrt{a}}{3}x^{3/2}\right]_0^a$$

$$= 4\left[\left\{\frac{1}{2}a^2\times\frac{\pi}{2} - a^2 - \frac{a^2}{2}+\frac{4}{3}a^2\right\} - 0\right]$$

$$= \left\{\pi a^2 - \frac{2}{3}a^2\right\} \text{ square units.}$$

50. The area bounded by the curve $f(x) = Ce^x$ $(C > 0)$, the x-axis and the two ordinates $x = p$ and $x = q$, is equal to

(a) $f(p)\,f(q)$ (b) $|f(p) - f(q)|$

(c) $f(p) + f(q)$ (d) $\sqrt{f(p)f(q)}$

Solution: (b) The area bounded by $y = Ce^x$, $y = 0$, $x = p$ and $x = q$ is shown below:

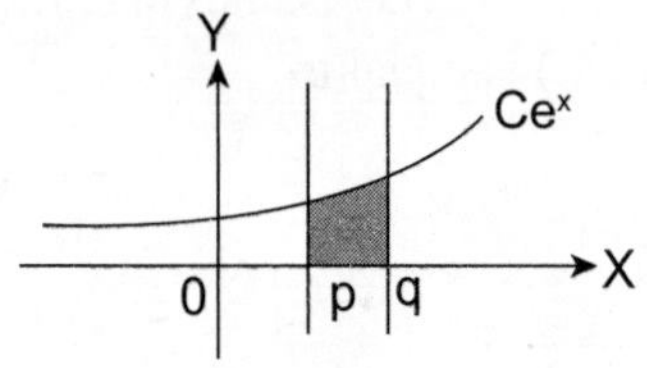

$\therefore$ Required area $= \int_p^q C\,e^x dx = C\left|e^x\right|_p^q$

$\Rightarrow C\,(e^q - e^p)$

$\Rightarrow (f(q) - f(p))$

Next in above figure we assumed $p < q$, if had we started with $p > q$, we get area $= (f(p) - f(q))$.

Thus, the required area $= |f(p) - f(q)|$.

51. The area bounded by $|y| \leq |-x + 1|$ and $y^2 \leq 4x$ is

(a) 1 square unit (b) 2 square units

(c) 3 square units (d) None of these

Solution: (d) $|y| \leq |-x + 1|$

$\Rightarrow -(-x + 1) \leq y \leq (-x + 1)$ ...(i)

Also $y^2 \leq 4x$ represents the interior region of parabola $y^2 = 4x$ with its focus at $S(1, 0)$. Thus, the region bounded by $|y| \leq |-x + 1|$ and $y^2 \leq 4x$ will be as shown below.

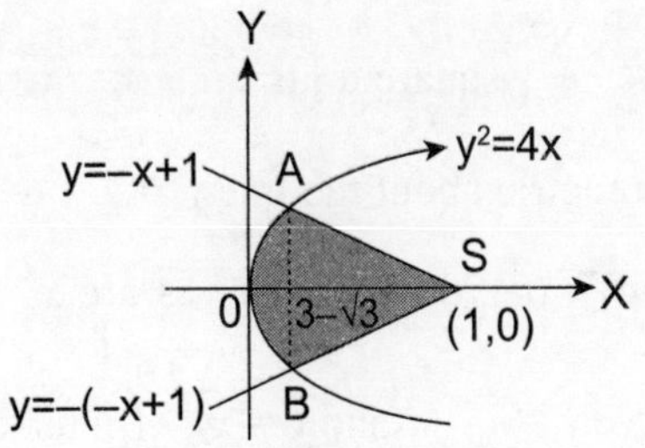

$\therefore$ Required area $= 2\int_0^{3-\sqrt{8}} \sqrt{4x}\,dx$ + area of ΔABS

$$= 2\left[\frac{4}{3}\left(x^{3/2}\right)_0^{3-\sqrt{8}} + \frac{1}{2}\left(2\sqrt{2}-2\right)^2\right]$$

$$= 2\left[\frac{4}{3}(5\sqrt{2}-7)+6-4\sqrt{2}\right] \text{ Square units}$$

52. A curve is given by $y = \begin{cases}\sqrt{(4-x^2)} & ; 0 \le x < 1 \\ \sqrt{(3x)} & ; 1 \le x \le 3\end{cases}$. The area lying between the curve and the x-axis is equal to

(a) $(2\pi - \sqrt{3} + 36)/6$

(b) $(2\pi - \sqrt{3} + 36)/12$

(c) $(2\pi - \sqrt{3} + 36)/3$

(d) None of these

Solution: (a) Given curves are $y = \sqrt{4-x^2}$ or $x^2 + y^2 = 4$; $y \ge 0$; $0 \le x < 1$, i.e., a semi-circle of radius 2 and having its centre at origin. and $y^2 = 3x$; $1 \le x \le 3$, $y \ge 0$.

Thus, the bounded area will be as shown below:

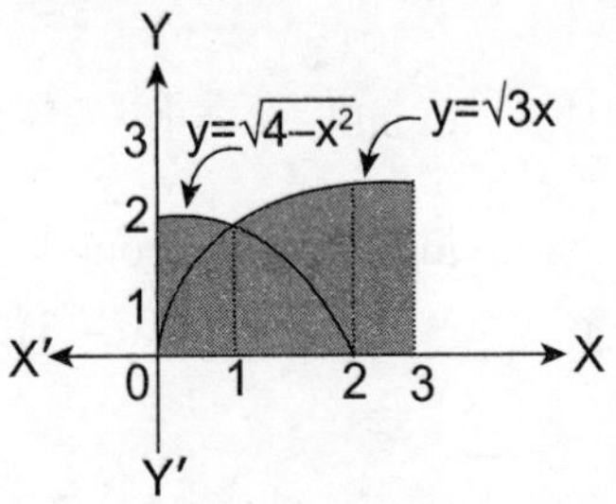

$\therefore$ Required area $= \int_0^1 \sqrt{4-x^2}\,dx + \int_1^3 \sqrt{3x}dx$

$$= \frac{2\pi - \sqrt{3} + 36}{6} \text{ square units.}$$

53. The area in the first quadrant between $x^2 + y^2 = \pi^2$ and $y = \sin x$ is

(a) $\dfrac{(\pi^3 - 8)}{4}$ (b) $\dfrac{\pi^3}{4}$

(c) $\dfrac{(\pi^3 - 16)}{4}$ (d) $\dfrac{(\pi^3 - 8)}{2}$

Solution: (a) $x^2 + y^2 = \pi^2$ represents a circle with its centre at origin and radius π. Area bounded by $y = \sin x$ and given circle in first quadrant is as shown below:

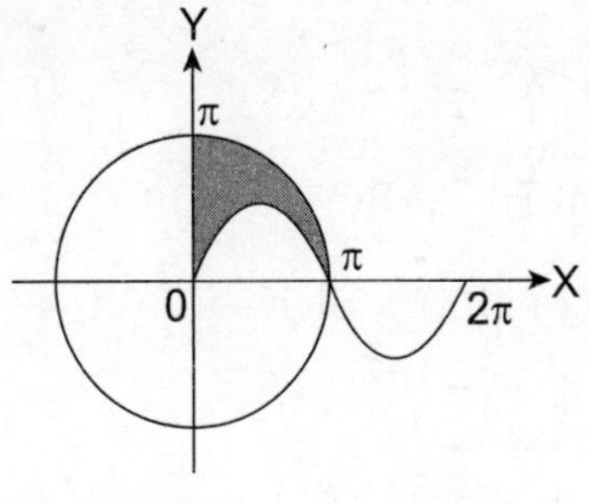

And is given by $\int_0^{\pi} (y_2 - y_1)dx$

$$= \int_0^{\pi}\{\sqrt{\pi^2 - x^2} - \sin x\}dx = \int_0^{\pi}\sqrt{\pi^2 - x^2}\,dx - 2$$

$$= \left|\frac{x\sqrt{\pi^2 - x^2}}{2} + \frac{\pi^2}{2}\sin^{-1}\left(\frac{x}{\pi}\right)\right|_0^{\pi} - 2$$

$$= \frac{\pi^3}{4} - 2 = \left(\frac{\pi^3 - 8}{4}\right)$$

54. The shaded area of the equilateral triangle, in which three coins of radius 1 cm are placed as shown in the figure given below, is

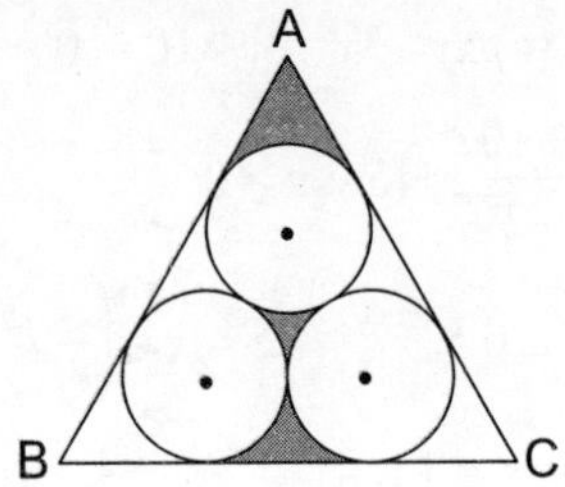

(a) $2(\sqrt{3} + 1 - 2\pi/3)$ (b) $4\sqrt{3} - 6$

(c) $7 + 4\sqrt{3}$ (d) $4\sqrt{3}$

Solution: (a) In ΔBLM, $BM = LM \cot 30^o = \sqrt{3}$

Similarly, $CP = \sqrt{3}$

Also MP = 2(radius) = 2

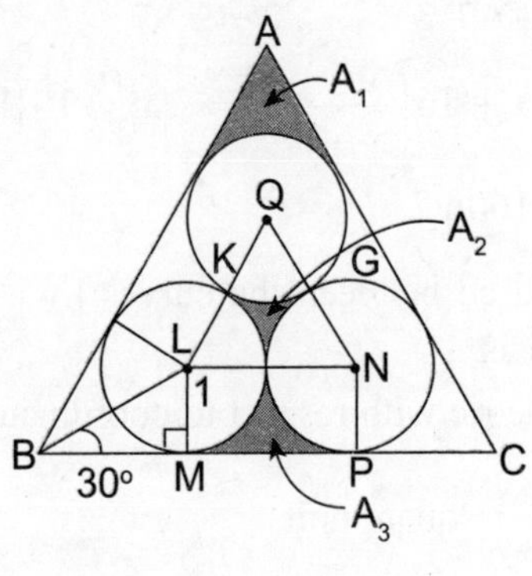

$\therefore$ Each side of equilateral $\Delta ABC = BC = BM + MP + CP = 2 + 2\sqrt{3}$

We are to find sum of areas A_1, A_2 and A_3

Now, A_2 = area of ΔLNQ – 3(area of sector QKG)

$$= \frac{\sqrt{3}}{4}(LN)^2 - 3\left(\frac{1}{6}\pi(1)^2\right) = \frac{\sqrt{3}}{4}(2)^2 - \frac{\pi}{2} = \sqrt{3} - \frac{\pi}{2}$$

Now, area of $\Delta ABC = \Delta = 3A_1 + A_2 + 3A_3 + 3\pi(1)^2$

$$\Rightarrow \frac{\sqrt{3}}{4}(2+2\sqrt{3})^2 = 3[A_1 + A_3] + A_2 + 3\pi$$

$$\Rightarrow 3(A_1 + A_3) = \sqrt{3}(1+\sqrt{3})^2 - A_2 - 3\pi$$

$$\Rightarrow A_1 + A_3 = \frac{1}{\sqrt{3}}(1+\sqrt{3})^2 - \frac{A_2}{3} - \pi$$

$$\Rightarrow A_1 + A_2 + A_3 = \frac{1}{\sqrt{3}}(1+\sqrt{3})^2 + \frac{2}{3}A_2 - \pi$$

$$\Rightarrow \frac{1}{\sqrt{3}}(4+2\sqrt{3}) + \frac{2}{3}\left(\sqrt{3} - \frac{\pi}{2}\right) - \pi$$

$$\Rightarrow \frac{4}{\sqrt{3}} + 2 + \frac{2}{\sqrt{3}} - \frac{4\pi}{3} \Rightarrow 2\sqrt{3} + 2 - \frac{4\pi}{3}$$

$$\Rightarrow 2\left(\sqrt{3} + 1 - \frac{2\pi}{3}\right) \text{ square units.}$$

55. The area bounded by the curve $xy - 3x - 2y - 10 = 0$, x-axis and straight lines $x = 3$, $x = 4$ is

(a) 16 log 2 –13 (b) 16 log 2 – 3
(c) 16 log 2 + 3 (d) None of these

Solution: (c) $xy - 3x - 2y - 10 = 0$

$$\Rightarrow y = \frac{3x+10}{x-2}; \text{ Now } y \ge 0$$

$$\Rightarrow \frac{3x+10}{x-2} \ge 0 \quad \Rightarrow x \in \left(-\infty, -\frac{10}{3}\right] \cup (2, \infty)$$

$\Rightarrow y > 0$ for $x \in [3, 4]$

$\therefore$ The area bounded by $xy - 3x - 2y - 10 = 0$, x-axis and straight lines $x = 3$ and $x = 4$ is given by $\int_3^4 \left(\frac{3x+10}{x-2}\right)dx = \int_3^4 \frac{3x+10}{x-2}dx$

$$= \int_3^4 \frac{3(x-2)+16}{x-2}dx = \int_3^4 \frac{3(x-2)}{x-2}dx + \int_3^4 \frac{16}{x-2}dx$$

$$= 3\int_3^4 dx + 16\int_3^4 \frac{1}{x-2}dx = 3|x|_3^4 + 16\{\ln(x-2)\}_3^4$$

$= 3 + 16 \ln 2$

56. Area enclosed between the curves $|y| = 1 - x^2$ and $x^2 + y^2 = 1$ is

(a) Symmetric with respect to coordinate axis

(b) $\left(\pi - \frac{8}{3}\right)$ square unit

(c) $\left(2\pi - \frac{8}{3}\right)$ square units

(d) Symmetric about the line $y = 2$

Solution: (*a*, *b*) Given curves are $x^2 + y^2 = 1$ and $|y| = 1 - x^2 \quad \Rightarrow y = \pm(1 - x^2)$

The curve $y = 1 - x^2$ and $y = x^2 - 1$ intersect each other on x-axis at points $A(-1, 0)$ and $B(1, 0)$.

$y = 1 - x^2$ intersect y-axis at $C(0, 1)$ and $y = x^2 - 1$ intersect y-axis at $D(0, -1)$. Therefore, the area bounded by given curves as represented by given below is given by figure

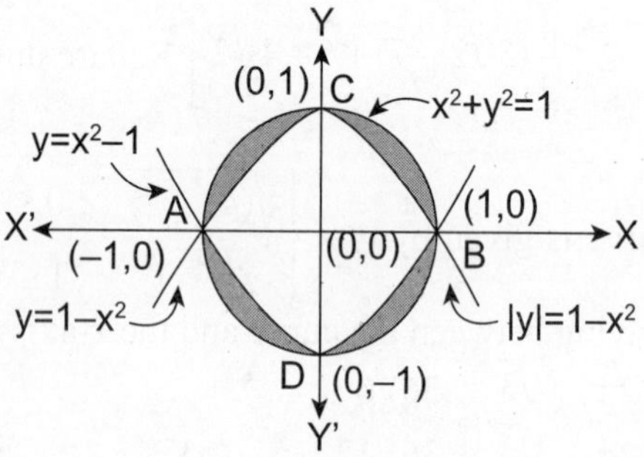

Area of circle – 4(area bounded by parabola $y = 1 - x^2$ from $x = 0$ to $x = 1$)

$$= \text{Area of circle} - 4\left[\int_0^1 (1-x^2)\,dx\right]$$

$$= \pi - 4\left[\int_0^1 (1-x^2)\,dx\right] = \pi - \frac{8}{3} \text{ square units.}$$

Also clearly the bounded area is symmetric about coordinate axis.

57. Let $A_1 = \int_1^2 |y|\,dx$ and $A_2 = \int_2^3 y\,dx$. If the ratio in which x-axis divides the area bounded by x-axis and the curve $y = (x-1)(x-2)(x-3)$ in two parts is $\frac{a}{b}$, then

(a) $a = |A_1|$ (b) $b = |A_2|$
(c) $a = A_1$ (d) $A_1 = A_2 = 1/4$

Solution: (a,b,c,d) Given function is $y = (x-1)(x-2)(x-3) = x^3 - 6x^2 + 11x - 6$

$\Rightarrow y > 0$ for $x \in (1, 2)$ and $y < 0$ for $x \in (2, 3)$ as shown below:

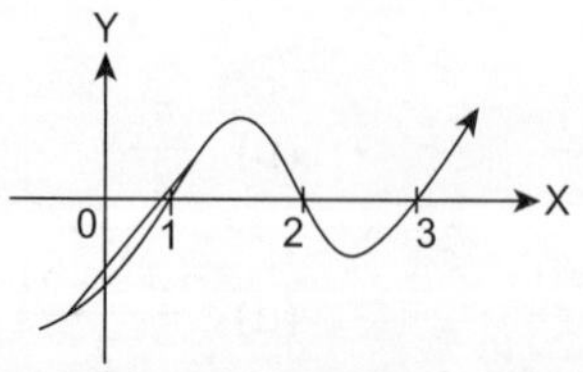

Thus, $A_1 = \int_1^2 |y|\,dx = \int_1^2 (x-1)(x-2)(x-3)dx$

$= \int_1^2 (x^3 - 6x^2 + 11x - 6)dx$

$= \frac{1}{4}(15) - \frac{6}{3}(7) + \frac{11}{2}(3) - 6(1) = \frac{1}{4}$

and $A_2 = \int_2^3 ydx = \int_2^3 (x^3 - 6x^2 + 11x - 6)dx$

$= \frac{1}{4}(65) - 2(19) + \frac{11}{2}(5) - 6(1) = \frac{65}{4} - 44 + \frac{55}{2}$

$= \frac{65+110-176}{4} = -\frac{1}{4} \quad \Rightarrow \quad A_1 = |A_2| = \frac{1}{4}$

Clearly x-axis divides the area bounded by $y = (x-1)(x-2)(x-3)$ into two parts are $\int_1^2 ydx$ and $\int_2^3 |y|\,dx$ or $\int_1^2 |y|\,dx \,\&\, \left|\int_2^3 ydx\right|$

i.e., $A_1 : |A_2| = a : b$ (given)

$\Rightarrow a = A_1$ and $b = |A_2|$ or $a = A_1 = |A_1|;\ b = |A_2|$

$\therefore$ a, b, c, d are correct answer

58. If A_i is the area bounded by $|x - a_i| + |y| = b_i$, $i \in \mathbb{N}$, where $a_{i+1} = a_i + \frac{3}{2}b_i$ and $b_{i+1} = \frac{b_i}{2}$, $a_1 = 0$, $b_1 = 32$, then:

(a) $A_3 = 128$

(b) $A_3 = 256$

(c) $\lim_{n\to\infty} \sum_{i=1}^{n} A_i = \frac{8}{3}(32)^2$

(d) $\lim_{n\to\infty} \sum_{i=1}^{n} A_i = \frac{4}{3}(16)^2$

Solution: (a,c) Given $a_1 = 0$, $b_1 = 32$, $a_2 = a_1 + \frac{3}{2}b_1 = 48$, $b_2 = \frac{b_1}{2} = 16$; $a_3 = 48 + \frac{3}{2} \times 16 = 72$, $b_3 = \frac{16}{2} = 8$

Now, A_1 is the area bounded by $|x - 0| + |y| = 32$ i.e., $|x| + |y| = 32$ represented by square area $ABCD$.

Next, A_2 is the area bounded by $|x - 48| + |y| = 16$ i.e., $|y| = 16 - |x - 48|$

$\Rightarrow y = \pm(16 - |x - 48|) \Rightarrow \begin{cases} \pm(x-32) \text{ for } x \le 48 \\ \pm(64-x) \text{ for } x \ge 48 \end{cases}$

Similarly A_3 is the area bounded by $|x - 72| + |y| = 8$ i.e., $y = \pm\{8 - |x - 72|\}$

$\Rightarrow \begin{cases} \pm(x-64) \text{ for } x \le 72 \\ \pm(80-x) \text{ for } x \ge 72 \end{cases}$ and so on.

Thus, the areas A_1, A_2, A_3.........looks like as given below.

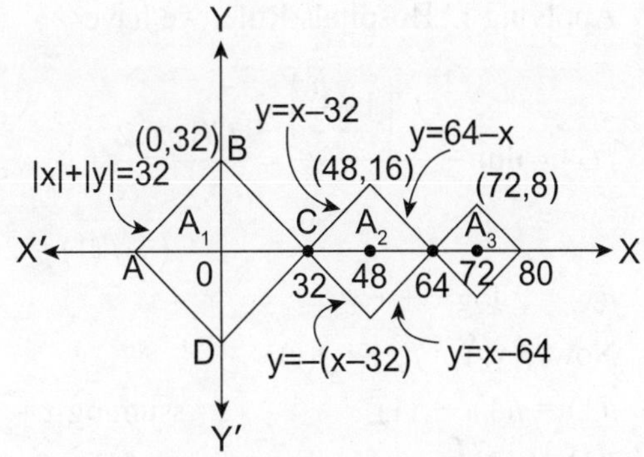

So the three loops from $i = 1$ to $i = 3$ are alike

Now area of ith loop (square) $= \frac{1}{2}(\text{diagonal})^2$

$\Rightarrow A_i = \frac{1}{2}(2b_i)^2 = 2(b_i)^2 \Rightarrow A_3 = 2(b_3)^2 = 2(8)^2 = 128$

Now, $\frac{A_{i+1}}{A_i} = \frac{2(b_{i+1})^2}{2(b_i)^2} = \frac{1}{4}$

So the areas form a $G.P.$ series with common ratio 1/4.

So, the sum of the $G.P.$ upto infinite terms

$= \sum_{i=1}^{\infty} A_i = \frac{A_1}{1-r} = 2(32)^2 \times \frac{1}{1-\frac{1}{4}} = \frac{8}{3}(32)^2$ units^2

59. If $f(x.\ y) = f(x) + f(y)$ $x > 0$, $y > 0$ and $f(1) = 2$ and A represents the area bounded by the curves $y = f(x)$, $x = 2$ and the axis of abscissa, then

(a) $f(x) = 2\log_e x$ (b) $f(x) = 2\log_2 x$

(c) $A = 2(2\log_e 2 - 1)$ (d) $A = 4\log_e\left(\frac{2}{\sqrt{e}}\right)$

Solution: (a,c,d) $f'(x) = \lim_{h\to 0} \frac{f(x+h) - f(x)}{h}$

$\Rightarrow f'(x) = \lim_{h\to 0} \frac{f\left(x\left(1+\frac{h}{x}\right)\right) - f(x)}{h}$

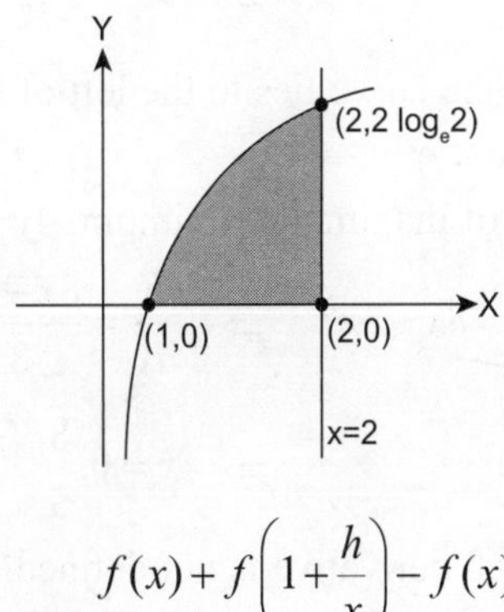

$\Rightarrow f'(x) = \lim_{h\to 0} \frac{f(x) + f\left(1+\frac{h}{x}\right) - f(x) - f(1)}{h}$

$\Rightarrow f'(x) = \lim_{h\to 0} \frac{f\left(1+\frac{h}{x}\right) - f(1)}{h}$; $\left\{\frac{0}{0} \text{ from}\right\}$

Applying L' Hospitals Rule, we have

$$\Rightarrow f'(x) = \lim_{h\to 0} \frac{\frac{1}{x} f'\left(1+\frac{h}{x}\right)}{1} = \frac{f'(1)}{x} = \frac{2}{x}$$

$(\because f'(1) = 2 \text{ given})$

$\therefore\ f(x) = 2\log_e x + C$ ...(1)

Now, $f(xy) = f(x) + f(y)$

$\Rightarrow f(1) = f(1) + f(1)$ {Assuming $x = y = 1$}

$\Rightarrow f(1) = 0$; Now, from (1), we have $f(1) = 0 + C$

$\Rightarrow C = 0$

$\Rightarrow f(x) = 2\ln x$

Required Area $(A) = \int_1^2 2\ln x dx$

$$\Rightarrow A = 2\left\{x\log_e x\Big|_1^2 - \int_1^2 x.\frac{1}{x}dx\right\}$$

{using integration by parts}

$$\Rightarrow A = 2\{2\log_e 2 - 1\} = 4\log_e\left(\frac{2}{\sqrt{e}}\right).$$

Hence a, c and d are correct answers.

SECTION–II

SUBJECTIVE-TYPE SOLVED EXAMPLES

1. Sketch the curve and find the area enclosed by the loop in the curve $4y^2 = 4x^2 - x^3$

Solution: The given curve is $4y^2 = 4x^2 - x^3$

To draw the rough sketch of the given curve, consider the following steps:

1. On replacing y by-y, there is no change in function. It means the graph is symmetric about x-axis.
2. For $y = 0$, $x = 0$ or $x = 4$ and for $x = 0$, $y = 0$, i.e., the curve intersect x-axis at (4, 0) and at origin.
3. In the given curve, LHS is positive for all values of y.

$$\Rightarrow RHS \geq 0 \quad \Rightarrow 4x^2\left(1 - \frac{x}{4}\right) \geq 0$$

$$\Rightarrow 1 - \frac{x}{4} \geq 0 \quad \Rightarrow 1 \geq \frac{x}{4} \quad \Rightarrow x \leq 4$$

Hence the curve lies to the left of $x = 4$

4. As $x \to -\infty$, $y \to \pm\infty$
5. Points of maximum/minimum: $4y^2 = 4x^2 - x^3$

$$\Rightarrow 8y\frac{dy}{dx} = 8x - 3x^2 \quad \Rightarrow \frac{dy}{dx} = \frac{8x - 3x^2}{8y}$$

$$\therefore \frac{dy}{dx} = 0 \quad \Rightarrow x = 0, \frac{8}{3}$$

At, $x = 0$ derivative is not defined.

By checking for $\frac{d^2y}{dx^2}$, $x = \frac{8}{3}$ is a point of local maximum (above x-axis)

Thus, the graph of curve would be as shown below:

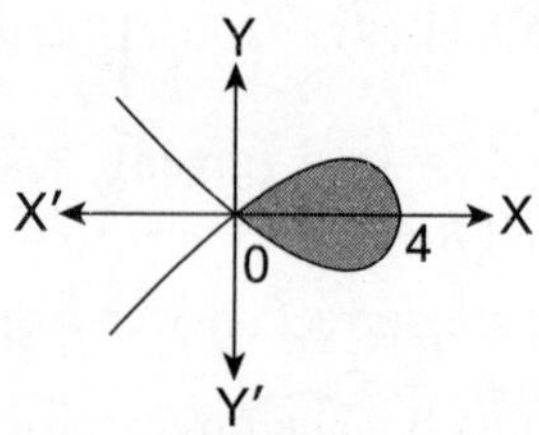

From graph. Shaded area $(A) = 2 \times$ (area of portion above x-axis)

$$\Rightarrow A = 2\int_0^4 \frac{x}{2}\sqrt{4-x}\, dx = \int_0^4 x\sqrt{4-x}\, dx$$

$$\Rightarrow A = \int_0^4 (4-x)\sqrt{4-(4-x)}\, dx$$

$$\Rightarrow A = \int_0^4 (4-x)\sqrt{x}\, dx$$

$$\Rightarrow A = 4\left|\frac{2}{3}x\sqrt{x}\right|_0^4 - \left|\frac{2}{5}x^2\sqrt{x}\right|_0^4$$

$$\Rightarrow A = \frac{128}{15} \text{ square units}$$

2. Find the area bounded by the curves $y = -\sqrt{4-x^2}$, $x^2 = -\sqrt{2}y$ and $x = y$.

Solution: Given curves are $x^2 + y^2 = 4$ ...(1)

$x^2 = -\sqrt{2}y$ ...(2)

And $x = y$ ...(3)

Here (1) represents a semi-circle with radius 2 and centre at (0, 0); (2) is a downwards parabola with vertex at (0, 0) and axis as y-axis, while (3) is a straight line making an angle of 45° with x-axis and passing through (0,0).

By solving (1) and (2), we get point of intersection $A\left(\sqrt{2}, -\sqrt{2}\right)$, $B\left(-\sqrt{2}, -\sqrt{2}\right)$

Clearly line (3) passes through B. Now draw the figure. Shaded area in the figure is the required area as shown below:

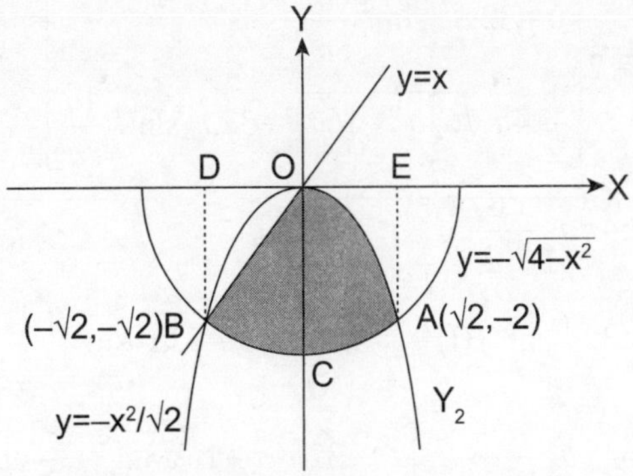

$\therefore$ The required area $= A =$ Area $OEACBDO$ – Area $OBDO$ – Area $OAEO$

$= 2$ Area $OCAE$ – Area $OBDO$ – Area $OAEO$

$$= 2\left[\int_0^{\sqrt{2}} \sqrt{4-x^2}\right] - \left[\int_0^{\sqrt{2}} \frac{x^2}{\sqrt{2}}dx\right] - \left[\int_{\sqrt{2}}^{0} -xdx\right]$$

$$= 2\left[\frac{x}{2}\sqrt{4-x^2} + \frac{1}{2}4\sin^{-1}\left(\frac{x}{2}\right)\right]_0^{\sqrt{2}} -$$

$$\left(\frac{x^3}{3\sqrt{2}}\right)\Bigg|_0^{\sqrt{2}} + \left|\left(\frac{x^2}{2}\right)\right|_{-\sqrt{2}}^{0}$$

$$= (2+\pi) - \frac{2}{3} - 1 = \frac{1}{3}(3\pi + 1) \text{ square units}$$

3. Find out the area enclosed by the polynomial function of least degree satisfying $\lim\limits_{x\to 0}\left[1+\frac{f(x)}{x^3}\right]^{1/x} = e$ and circle $x^2+y^2=2$ above the x-axis.

Solution: Since $\lim\limits_{x\to 0}\left[1+\frac{f(x)}{x^3}\right]^{1/x}$ exist and $f(x)$ is of least degree. So $f(x)$ must be of the form $f(x) = ax^4$

Solving the limit, we get $a = 1$, so $f(x) = x^4$.

Hence we have two curves $y = x^4$ ...(i)

and $y = \sqrt{2-x^2}$ ...(ii)

Now, at the point of intersection, $\sqrt{2-x^2} = x^4$

$\Rightarrow x^8 + x^2 - 2 = 0 \Rightarrow (x^2-1)(x^6+x^4+x^2+2) = 0$

$\Rightarrow x^2 - 1 = 0$ or $x^6 + x^4 + x^2 + 2 \neq 0 \Rightarrow x = \pm 1$

$\therefore$ $A(-1, 1)$ and $B(1, 1)$ are points of intersection of (i) and (ii) and the required bounded area is as shown below.

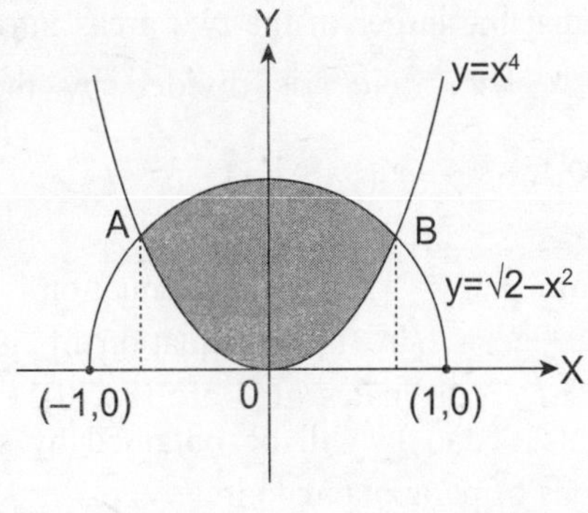

$$\therefore \text{ Required Area } = 2\int_0^1\left(\sqrt{2-x^2} - x^4\right)dx$$

$$= 2\left[\frac{x}{2}\sqrt{2-x^2} + \frac{2}{2}\sin^{-1}\frac{x}{\sqrt{2}} - \frac{x^5}{5}\right]_0^1$$

$$= \left(\frac{\pi}{2} + \frac{3}{5}\right) \text{ square units.}$$

4. Find the area of the figure enclosed by the curve $5x^2+6xy+2y^2+7x+6y+6=0$.

Solution: Equation of curve can be re-written as

$2y^2 + 6(1+x)y + 5x^2 + 7x + 6 = 0$

or $y^2 + 3(1+x)y + \frac{1}{2}(5x^2+7x+6) = 0$

$$y_1 = \frac{-3(1+x)+\sqrt{(3-x)(x-1)}}{2};$$

$$y_2 = \frac{-3(1+x)-\sqrt{(3-x)(x-1)}}{2}$$

Therefore, the curves (y_1 and y_2) are defined for values of x for which $(3-x)(x-1) \geq 0$, i.e., $1 \leq x \leq 3$

Actually the given equation denotes an ellipse, because $\Delta \neq 0$ and $h^2 < ab$ as shown below:

$\therefore$ Required area will be given by $A = \int_1^3 (y_1 - y_2)dx$

$\Rightarrow \int_1^3 \sqrt{(3-x)(x-1)}dx$ put $x = 3\cos^2\theta + \sin^2\theta$

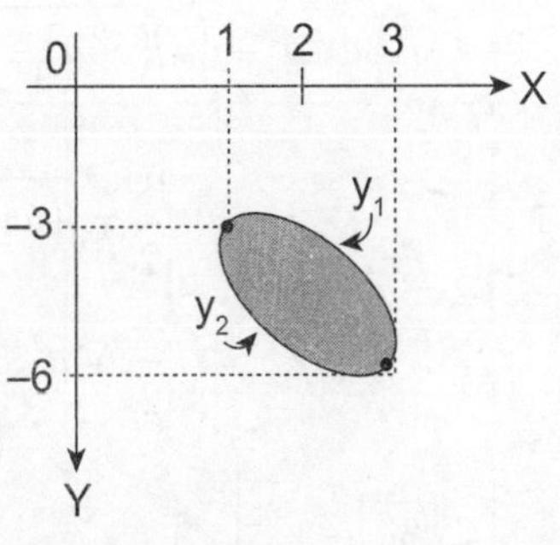

i.e., $dx = -2\sin 2\theta \, d\theta$

$$\Rightarrow A = 2\int_0^{\pi/2} \sin^2 2\theta \, d\theta = \frac{\pi}{2} \text{Sq.unit}$$

5. Show that the larger of the two areas into which the circle $x^2+y^2=64a^2$ is divided by the parabola $y^2=12ax$ is $\frac{16}{3}a^3\left(8\pi-\sqrt{3}\right)$

Solution: $y^2 = 12ax$ is the equation of parabola and $x^2 + y^2 = 64a^2$ is the equation of the circle of radius $8a$. Coordinates of A are $(8a, 0)$. Coordinates of points P and P' will be obtained by solving the equations of parabola and circle.

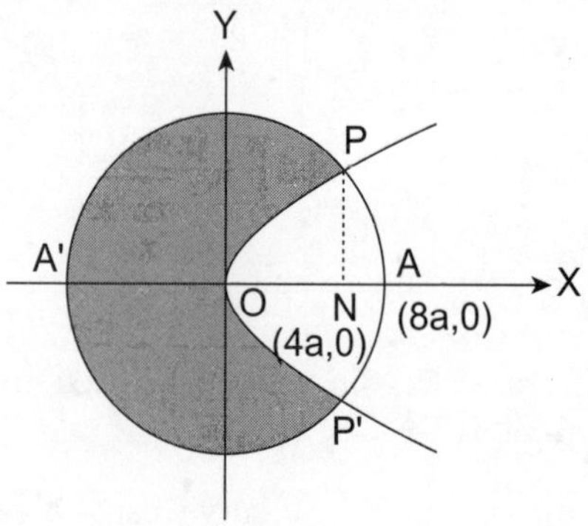

Putting $y^2=12ax$ in the equation of circle, we have

$x^2+12ax=64a^2$

$\Rightarrow\ x^2+12ax-64a^2=0\ \Rightarrow\ (x+16a)(x-4a)=0$

$\Rightarrow\ x=4a\ \ (\because x\neq -16a)$

$\therefore$ Coordinates of point N are $(4a\ ,0)$

Required area = Shaded area in the above figure

= Area of circle – Area $OPAP'O$

$=\pi\ (8a)^2-2(\text{Area of OPA})$

$=\pi\ (8a)^2-2\ (\text{Area of ONP}+\text{Area of PNA})$

$$=64\pi a^2-2\left[\int_0^{4a} y_1dx+\int_{4a}^{8a} y_2dx\right]$$

(y_1 for parabola and y_2 for circle)

$$=64\pi a^2-2\left[\int_0^{4a}\sqrt{12ax}.dx+\int_{4a}^{8a}\sqrt{(64a^2-x^2)}\ dx\right]$$

$$=64\pi a^2-2\left[2\sqrt{3a}\int_0^{4a}\sqrt{x}.dx+\left|\begin{matrix}\frac{1}{2}.x\sqrt{(64a^2-x^2)}+\\ \frac{1}{2}.64a^2\sin^{-1}\left(\frac{x}{8a}\right)\end{matrix}\right|_{4a}^{8a}\right]$$

$$=64\pi a^2-2\left[\begin{matrix}2\sqrt{3a}\left|\frac{2}{3}.x^{3/2}\right|_0^{4a}+\\ \left|\frac{1}{2}.x\sqrt{(64a^2-x^2)}+32a^2\sin^{-1}\frac{x}{8a}\right|_{4a}^{8a}\end{matrix}\right]$$

$$=64\pi a^2-4\sqrt{3a}\left[\frac{2}{3}.(4a)^{3/2}\right]$$

$$-2\left[\begin{matrix}0+32.a^2.\sin^{-1}\frac{8a}{8a}-\\ \frac{1}{2}.4a.\sqrt{64a^2-16a^2}-32a^2\sin^{-1}\frac{4a}{8a}\end{matrix}\right]$$

$$=64\pi a^2-\frac{64}{3}.\sqrt{3}.a^2-2$$

$$\left[32a^2\sin^{-1}(1)-\frac{1}{2}.4a.4a.\sqrt{3}-32a^2\sin^{-1}\left(\frac{1}{2}\right)\right]$$

$$=64\pi a^2-\frac{64}{3}.\sqrt{3}.a^2-32a^2\pi+16\sqrt{3}.a^2+\frac{32}{3}a^2\pi$$

$$\left[\because \sin^{-1}(1)=\frac{\pi}{2}\text{ and }\sin^{-1}\left(\frac{1}{2}\right)=\frac{\pi}{6}\right]$$

$$=\frac{16}{3}.a^2\left(8\pi-\sqrt{3}\right)\ \text{Square units}$$

6. Find the value(s) of the parameter 'a' ($a > 0$) for each of which the area of the figure bounded by the straight line, $y = \dfrac{a^2+ax}{1+a^4}$ and the parabola $y=\dfrac{x^2+2ax+3a^2}{1+a^4}$ is the greatest .

Solution:

$$A=\left|\int_{x_1}^{x_2}\frac{(a^2-ax)-(x^2+2ax+3a^2)}{1+a^4}dx\right|;\ \text{where}$$

x_1 and x_2 are the roots of $x^2 + 2ax + 3a^2 = a^2 - ax$

$\Rightarrow x = -a$ or $x = -2a \Rightarrow\ A=\dfrac{a^3}{6\left(1+a^4\right)}$;

for greatest value of area A, $\dfrac{dA}{da}=0$

Now, $\dfrac{dA}{da}=0$

$$\Rightarrow\ \frac{1}{6}\left[\frac{(1+a^4)(3a^2)-a^3(4a^3)}{(1+a^4)^2}\right]=0$$

$\Rightarrow\ a = 0$ or $a = (3)^{1/4}$; But $a > 0$ (given)

$\Rightarrow\ a = 3^{1/4}$

7. Sketch the curves $y = 2x^2e^x$ and $y = -x^3e^x$ and compute the area of the finite portion of the figure bounded by these curves.

Solution: Solving the two curves for points of intersection, we get $x = 0$ or -2.

Now $y = 2x^2 e^x \Rightarrow \frac{dy}{dx} = 2xe^x(x + 2) = 0$

$\Rightarrow x = 0$ or $x = -2 \Rightarrow$ Horizontal tangent at $x = 0, -2$.

Also increasing for $x < -2$ and $x > 0$ and decreasing in $(-2, 0)$.

Thus, the graph of curve $y = 2x^2e^x$ will be as shown below:

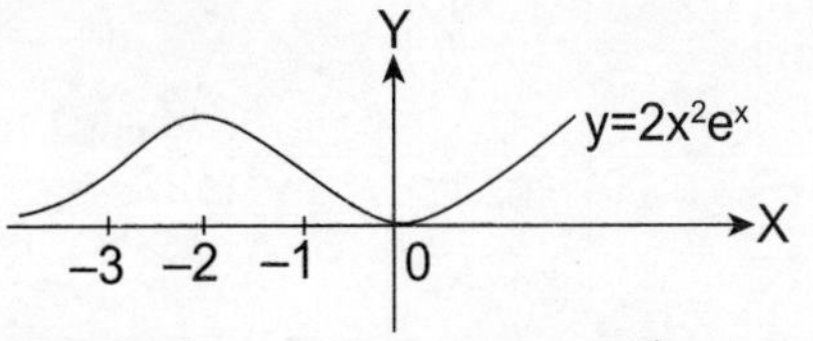

Similarly for $y = -x^3 e^x$; we have $\frac{dy}{dx} = -x^2e^x(x + 3)$

$\Rightarrow \frac{dy}{dx} = 0$ for $x = 0$ and $x = -3$

$\Rightarrow$ increasing in $(-\infty, -3)$ and decreasing in $(-3, \infty)$

Thus, the graph of $y = -x^3e^x$ will as shown below:

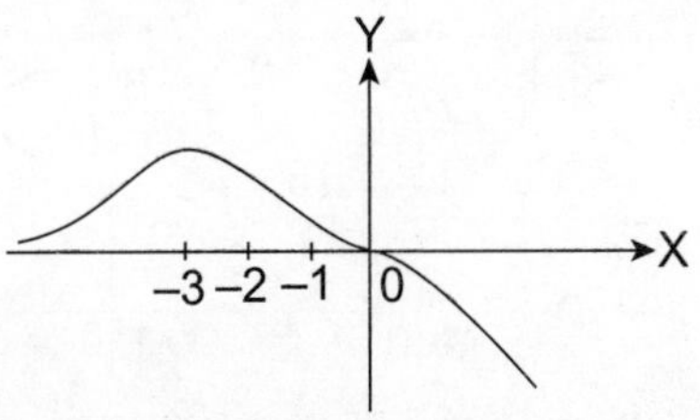

Thus, the bounded area will be as shown below:

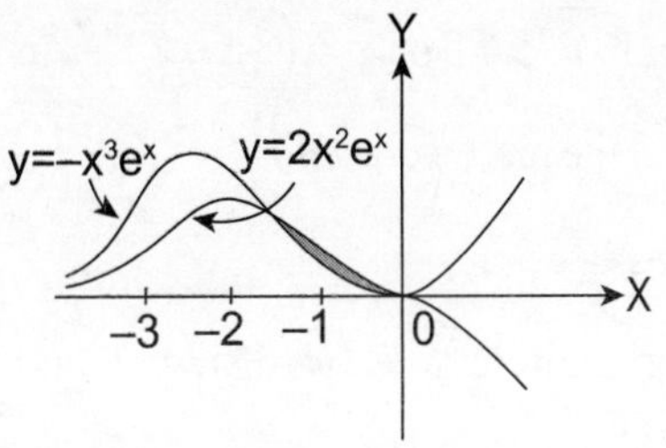

$\therefore$ The required area $A = \int_{-2}^{0} (2x^2e^x + x^3e^x)dx$.

Integrating by parts we get the result as $18e^{-2} - 2$

8. A figure is bounded by the curves $y = \left|\sqrt{2}\sin\frac{\pi x}{4}\right|, y = 0, x = 2 \,\&\, x = 4$. At what angles to the positive x-axis straight lines must be drawn through $(4, 0)$ so that these lines partition the figure into three parts of the same size and each part is bounded by $x = 2$.

Solution: Area of region $GCDK = \int_{2}^{4} \sqrt{2}\sin\frac{\pi x}{4}dx$

$$= -\frac{4\sqrt{2}}{\pi}\left|\cos\frac{x\pi}{4}\right|_2^4 = -\frac{4\sqrt{2}}{\pi}|-1-0| = \frac{4\sqrt{2}}{\pi} \text{ square units}$$

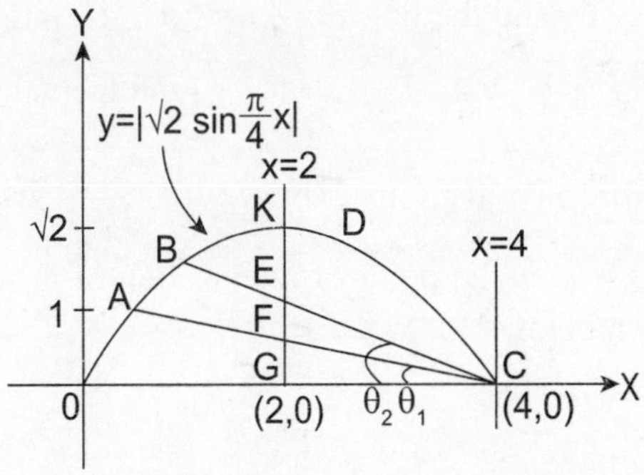

Let the lines segments CA and CB be drawn at angles θ_1 and θ_2 as shown in above figure

Now equation of CA will be given by

$(y - 0) = \tan(180^o - \theta_1)(x - 4)$

or $y = -\tan\theta_1(x - 4)$ ...(i)

similarly equation of CB will be given by

$y = -\tan\theta_2(x - 4)$ ...(ii)

Now, according to question

Area of ΔCFG = Area $\Delta CEF = \frac{1}{3}\left(\frac{4\sqrt{2}}{\pi}\right)$

$\Rightarrow \int_{2}^{4} -\tan\theta_1(x-4)dx$

$$= \int_{2}^{4} \{-\tan\theta_2(x-4) + \tan\theta_1(x-4)\}dx = \frac{4\sqrt{2}}{3\pi}$$ ...(iii)

Let $D_1 = (-\tan\theta_1)\left[\frac{x^2}{2} - 4x\right]_2^4$

$= (-\tan\theta_1)[(8-16)-(2-8)]$

$= (-\tan\theta_1)[(-8+6)] = 2\tan\theta_1$

$\Rightarrow D_1 = 2\tan\theta_1 = \frac{4\sqrt{2}}{3\pi}$

$\therefore$ Angle subtended by line AC with positive x-axis will be $\left(\pi - \frac{2\sqrt{2}}{3\pi}\right)$; Similarly Δ_2 = area of

$\Delta GCE = \frac{1}{2}(2) \times 2\tan\theta_2 = 2\tan\theta_2$

$\therefore$ area of $\Delta EFC = \Delta_2 - \Delta_1 = 2\tan\theta_2 - \frac{4\sqrt{2}}{3\pi} = \frac{4\sqrt{2}}{3\pi}$

$\Rightarrow \pi - \left(\frac{4\sqrt{2}}{3\pi}\right)$ will be the angle subtended by the AB with positive direction of x-axis.

9. Consider two curves $C_1: y = \frac{1}{x}$ and $C_2: y = \ell nx$ on the xy plane. Let D_1 denotes the region enclosed by C_1, C_2 and the line $x = 1$ and D_2 denotes the region enclosed by C_1, C_2 and the line $x = a$ ($> c$; C_1, C_2 intersect at $x = c$). If $D_1 = D_2 + 1 - \frac{1}{a^2} - \ln a$. Find the value of '$a$'.

Solution: Given that $D_1 = D_2 + 1 - \frac{1}{a^2} - \ln a$ ...(i)

and $x = c$ is the point of intersection of C_1 and C_2 as shown below:

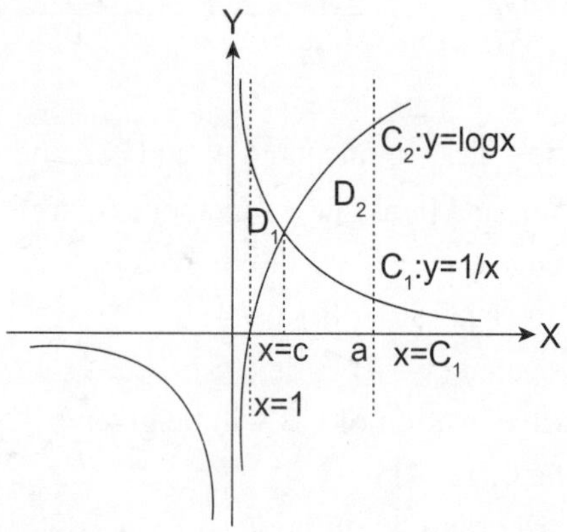

Now,

$$\text{A.T.Q} \int_1^c \left(\frac{1}{x} - \log x\right) dx = \int_c^a \left(\log x - \frac{1}{x}\right) dx + 1 - \frac{1}{a^2} - \ln a$$

$$\Rightarrow \left(\frac{-1}{x^2} - x(\log x - 1)\right)_1^c = \left(x(\log x - 1) + \frac{1}{x^2}\right)_c^a + 1 - \frac{1}{a^2} \ln a$$

$$\Rightarrow -\frac{1}{c^2} - c\ln c + c + 1 + 0 - 1$$

$$= a\ln a - a + \frac{1}{a^2} - c\ln c + c - \frac{1}{c^2} + 1 - \frac{1}{a^2} - \ln a$$

$$\Rightarrow 0 = a\ln a - a + 1 - \ln a$$

$$\Rightarrow a(\ln a - 1) - 1(\ln a - 1) = 0$$

$$\Rightarrow (a - 1)(\ln a - 1) = 0$$

$$\Rightarrow a = 1 \text{ or } a = e, \text{ but } a > c > 1 \Rightarrow a = e$$

10. Find the value of 'c' for which the area of the figure bounded by the curve, $y = 8x^2 - x^5$, the straight lines $x = 1$ and $x = c$ and the abscissa axis is equal to 16/3.

Solution: Given curve is $y = 8x^2 - x^5$

It intersect x-axis, where $y = 0$

$$\Rightarrow x^2(8 - x^3) = 0 \qquad \Rightarrow x = 0 \text{ or } x = 2$$

$$\text{Now, } \frac{dy}{dx} = 16x - 5x^4 = 0$$

$$\Rightarrow x = 0 \text{ or } x = \left(\frac{16}{5}\right)^{1/3}; \text{ also } \frac{d^2y}{dx^2} = 16 - 20x^3$$

$$\text{At } x = 0, \frac{d^2y}{dx^2} = 16 > 0 \text{ and at } x = \left(\frac{16}{5}\right)^{1/3};$$

$$\Rightarrow \frac{d^2y}{dx^2} = 16 - 20\left(\frac{16}{5}\right) = -48 < 0$$

$\therefore$ $f(x)$ has a local minima at $x = 0$ and local maxima at $x = \left(\frac{16}{5}\right)^{1/3}$

Thus, the slope of curve will be shown below:

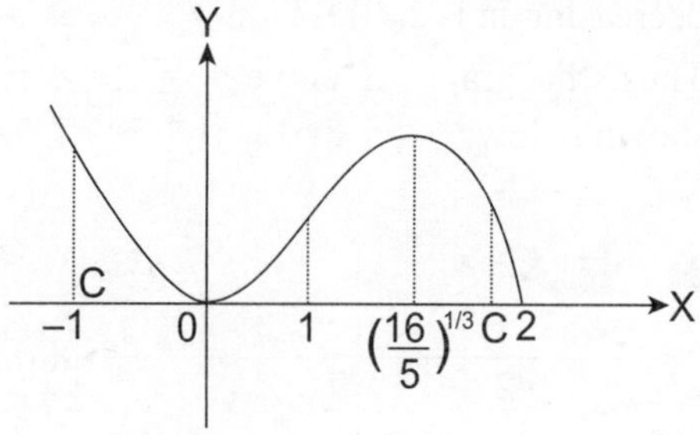

$$\text{Now, given that } \left|\int_1^c y\,dx\right| = \frac{16}{3}$$

$$\Rightarrow \left|\int_1^c (8x^2 - x^5)dx\right| = \frac{16}{3} \quad \Rightarrow \quad \int_1^c (8x^2 - x^5)dx = \pm\frac{16}{3}$$

$$\Rightarrow \left[\frac{8}{3}x^3 - \frac{x^6}{6}\right]_1^c = \pm\frac{16}{3}$$

$$\Rightarrow \frac{8}{3}c^3 - \frac{c^6}{6} - \frac{8}{3} + \frac{1}{6} = \pm\frac{16}{3}$$

$$\Rightarrow 16c^3 - c^6 = 47 \text{ or } -17$$

$$\Rightarrow c^6 - 16c^3 - 17 = 0 \text{ or } c^6 - 16c^3 + 47 = 0$$

$$\Rightarrow c^3 = 17, -1 \text{ or } c^3 = 8 \pm \sqrt{22}$$

$$\Rightarrow c = (17)^{1/3}, -1 \text{ or } c = \left(8 \pm \sqrt{22}\right)^{1/3}$$

$\therefore$ $c = (17)^{1/3}, -1, \left(8 \pm \sqrt{22}\right)^{1/3}$ are possible values of (c).

11. Consider a circle $x^2 + (y - 1)^2 = 1$ and the parabola $y = -\frac{x^2}{4}$. The common tangents to the two curves constitute a triangle ABC, the point A and B being on the x-axis and C on the y-axis. CA produced touches the parabola at P and CB produced touches the parabola at Q.

(a) Find the equation of the common tangent BC.

(b) Find the area of the portion between the upper arc of the circle and the common tangents QC and PC.

(c) Find the area enclosed by the parabola $y = -\frac{x^2}{4}$, the x-axis and the lines AP and BQ.

Solution: (a) $x^2 + (y - 1)^2 = 1^2$ ...(i)

$x^2 = -4y$ ...(ii)

Equation of tangent to (ii) $y = mx + m^2$ ...(iii)

$\because$ equation (iii) touches circle (i)

$\Rightarrow$ Perpendicular distance of (iii) from point (0, 1) will be equal to the radius of circle

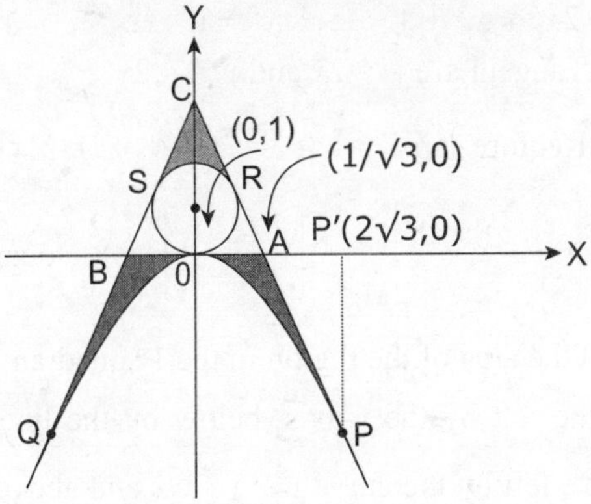

$\Rightarrow \left|\dfrac{m^2-1}{\sqrt{m^2+1}}\right| = 1 \quad \Rightarrow \quad (m^2-1) = \pm\sqrt{m^2+1}$

$\Rightarrow m^2(m^2 - 3) = 0$

$\Rightarrow m = \sqrt{3}, -\sqrt{3}$ $\qquad (\because m = 0$ gives x-axis)

(a) Equation of tangents are given by

$BC: y = \sqrt{3}x + 3$ and $AC: y = -\sqrt{3}x + 3$

$\Rightarrow$ Coordinates of $A \equiv (\sqrt{3}, 0)$; $B \equiv (-\sqrt{3}, 0)$;

$Q \equiv (-2\sqrt{3}, -3)$; $P \equiv (2\sqrt{3}, -3)$;

$S \equiv \left(-\dfrac{\sqrt{3}}{2}, \dfrac{3}{2}\right)$; $R \equiv \left(\dfrac{\sqrt{3}}{2}, \dfrac{3}{2}\right)$

(b) Area of region SCR $= 2\displaystyle\int_{-\frac{\sqrt{3}}{2}}^{0} (y_1 - y_2)dx$

$= 2\displaystyle\int_{-\frac{\sqrt{3}}{2}}^{0} ((\sqrt{3}x + 3) - \sqrt{1-x^2} - 1)\,dx = \left(\sqrt{3} - \dfrac{\pi}{3}\right)$ square units

(c) Area of region OAP + OBQ = $2\left[\left|\displaystyle\int_0^{2\sqrt{3}} \dfrac{x^2}{-4}dx\right| - \left|\displaystyle\int_{\sqrt{3}}^{2\sqrt{3}} (-\sqrt{3}x + 3)\,dx\right|\right] = \sqrt{3}$ square units

12. Find the area bounded by $y = g(x)$, x-axis and the lines $x = -2$, $x = 3$, where $g(x) = \begin{cases} \max.\{f(t); -2 \le t \le x\}; & -2 \le x < 0 \\ \min.\{f(t); 0 \le t \le x\}; & 0 \le x \le 3 \end{cases}$ and $f(x) = x^2 - |x|$.

Solution: ***Case I:*** For $-2 \le x < 0$ and $-2 \le t \le x$

In this interval $f(t)$ is a decreasing function and hence the maximum value would occur at -2

$\therefore$ $g(x) = g(-2) = 2$ for $-2 \le x < 0$

Case II: For $0 \le x \le \dfrac{1}{2}$; $f(t)$ is again a decreasing function, thus, giving minimum value at x for $0 \le t \le x$.

Thus, $g(x) = f(x)$

Case III: For $x \ge \dfrac{1}{2}$; $f(t)$ is an increasing function, so $f(t)$ is minimum at $x = \dfrac{1}{2}$; $g(x) = g\left(\dfrac{1}{2}\right)$

Thus, $g(x) = \begin{cases} 2; & -2 \le x < 0 \\ x^2 - x; & 0 \le x \le \dfrac{1}{2} \\ -\dfrac{1}{4}; & \dfrac{1}{2} < x \le 3 \end{cases}$

The graph of $g(x)$ is as shown in figure:

The required area is $\displaystyle\int_{-2}^{0} 2dx + \int_0^{1/2} (x - x^2)dx + \int_{1/2}^{3} \frac{1}{4}dx$

$= (2x)_{-2}^{0} + \left(\dfrac{x^2}{2} - \dfrac{x^3}{3}\right)_0^{1/2} + \dfrac{5}{8} = \dfrac{113}{24}$ square units

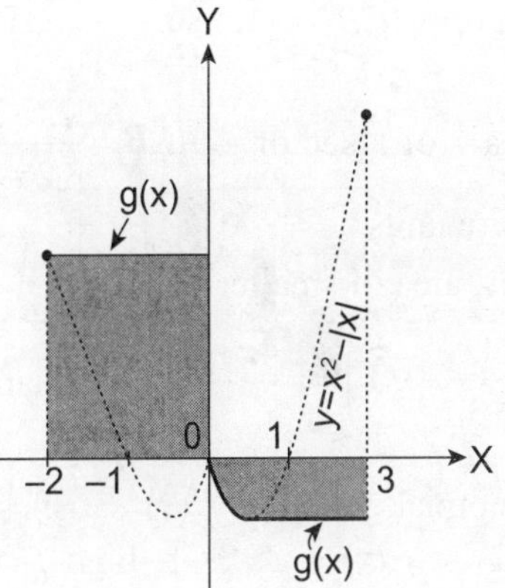

13. Find the area of the smaller region in which the curve $y = \left[\dfrac{x^3}{100} + \dfrac{x}{50}\right]$, where [.] denotes the greatest integer function, divides the circle $(x - 2)^2 + (y + 1)^2 = 4$.

Solution: Circle has (2, –1) as it's center and radius of this circle is 2. Thus, if $P(x, y)$ be any point on it then $x \in [0, 4]$ and $y \in [-3, 1]$

Let $g(x) = \dfrac{x^3}{100} + \dfrac{x}{50}$

$\Rightarrow g'(x) = \dfrac{3x^3}{100} + \dfrac{1}{50} > 0 \ \forall x \in [0, 4]$

Thus, $g(x)$ is increasing in [0, 4]. $g(0) = 0$, $g(4) = \dfrac{18}{25}$. Hence, $g(x) \in \left[0, \dfrac{18}{25}\right] \ \forall x \in [0, 4]$

$\Rightarrow [g(x)] = 0 \ \forall \ x \in [0, 4]$

Thus, $y = \left[\dfrac{x^3}{100} + \dfrac{x}{50}\right]$, simply represents the x-axis.

Thus, we are to find the shaded area as shown below:

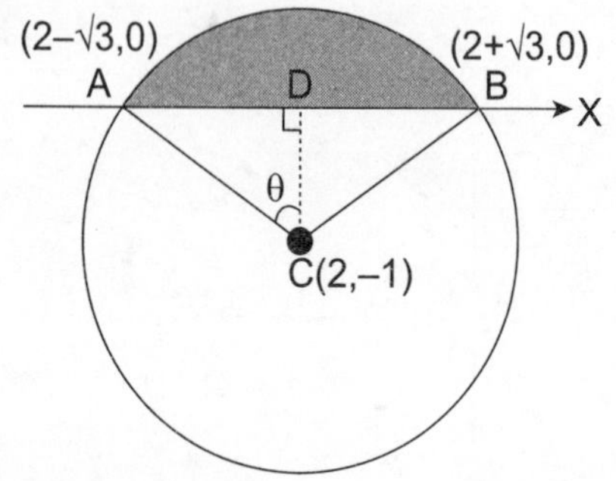

$\Rightarrow CA = CB = 2, CD = 1$

$\Rightarrow \cos\theta = \dfrac{CD}{CA} = \dfrac{1}{2}$

$\Rightarrow \theta = \dfrac{\pi}{3} \qquad \Rightarrow \angle ACB = \dfrac{2\pi}{3}$

$\therefore$ area of $\Delta ACB = \dfrac{1}{2}.2^2.\sin\dfrac{2\pi}{3} = \sqrt{3}$ square units.

$\therefore$ Area of sector $ACB = \dfrac{2\pi/3}{2\pi} \times \pi(2)^2 = \dfrac{4\pi}{3}$ square units

Thus, area of smaller segment

$= \left(\dfrac{4\pi}{3} - \sqrt{3}\right) = \left(\dfrac{4\pi - 3\sqrt{3}}{3}\right)$ square units.

14. A polynomial function $f(x)$ satisfies the condition $f(x + 1) = f(x) + 2x + 1$. Find $f(x)$ if $f(0) = 1$. Find also the equations of the pair of tangents from the origin on the curve $y = f(x)$ and compute the area enclosed by the curve and the pair of tangents.

Solution: $f(x + 1) - f(x) = 2x + 1$ (linear function) Obviously $f(x)$ must be a quadratic polynomial as if we take $f(x) = ax + b$, than $f(x + 1)\ f(x)$ would be independent of x. So, let $f(x) = ax^2 + bx + c$

$\therefore [a(x + 1)^2 + b(x + 1) + c] - [ax^2 + bx + c] = 2x + 1$

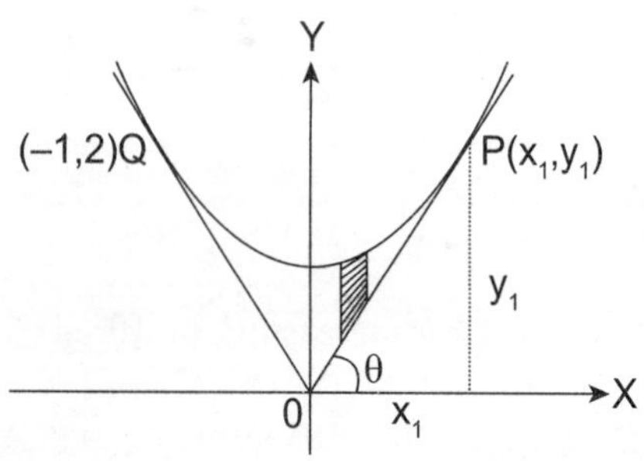

$\Rightarrow a + 2ax + b \equiv 2x + 1 \Rightarrow 2a = 2, a + b = 1$

$\Rightarrow a = 1$ and $b = 0 \quad \therefore f(x) = x^2 + C$

$\Rightarrow f(x) = 2x \Rightarrow f(x_1) = 2x_1 = \dfrac{y_1}{x_1} = \dfrac{x_1^2 + 1}{x_1}$

$\therefore 2x_1^2 = x_1^2 + 1 \Rightarrow x_1^2 = 1 \Rightarrow x_1 = 1$ or -1

$\therefore$ Tangent are $y = 2x$ and $y = -2x$

$\therefore$ Require area $= A = 2\displaystyle\int_0^1 [(x^2 + 1) - 2x]dx = 2$

$\left[\dfrac{x^3}{3} - x^2 + x\right]_0^1 = 2\left[\dfrac{1}{3} - 1 + 1\right] = \dfrac{2}{3}$ square units.

15. Find the area of the region in the 1st quadrant bounded on the left by the y-axis, below by the line $y = \dfrac{x}{4}$, above left by the curve $y = 1 + \sqrt{x}$ and above right by the curve $y = \dfrac{2}{\sqrt{x}}$.

Solution: Given curves are y-axis, i.e., $x = 0$ ...(i)

Straight line $y = \dfrac{x}{4}$ ......(ii)

Upper branch of parabola $(y - 1)^2\ x$

i.e., $y = 1 + \sqrt{x}$ ......(iii)

and the curve $y = \dfrac{2}{\sqrt{x}}$ ......(iv)

Straight line (i) and (ii) intersect at origin O; straight line (i) and parabola (iii) intersect at $A(0, 1)$; parabola (iii) and curve (iv) intersect at $B(1, 2)$. Parabola (iv) and straight line (ii) intersect at $C(4, 1)$.

Thus, $OABCO$ is the required area as shown below:

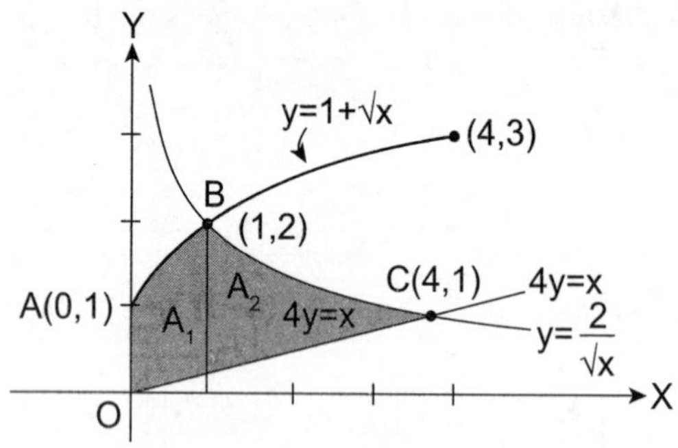

$\therefore$ The required area is given by $A = A_1 + A_2$

$= \displaystyle\int_0^1 \left(1 + \sqrt{x} - \dfrac{x}{4}\right)dx + \int_1^4 \left(\dfrac{2}{\sqrt{x}} - \dfrac{x}{4}\right)dx$

$= \left[x + \dfrac{2}{3}x^{3/2} - \dfrac{x^2}{8}\right]_0^1 + \left[\dfrac{2x^{1/2}}{1/2} - \dfrac{x^2}{8}\right]_1^4$

$= \left(1 + \dfrac{2}{3} - \dfrac{1}{8}\right) + \left[4(2) - 2 - \left(4(1) - \dfrac{1}{8}\right)\right]$

$= \dfrac{11}{3}$ square units

16. Find the value of 'a' ($a > 2$) for which the reciprocal of the area enclosed between $y = \frac{1}{x^2}$; $y = \frac{1}{4(x-1)}$; $x = 2$ and $x = a$ is 'a' itself and for what values of $b \in (1, 2)$, the area of the figure bounded by the lines $x = b$ and $x = 2$ is $1 - \frac{1}{b}$.

Solution: Given curve are $y = \frac{1}{x^2}$; $y = \frac{1}{4(x-1)}$, at the point of intersection $x^2 = 4(x - 1)$

$\Rightarrow x^2 - 4x + 1 = 0 \quad \Rightarrow (x - 2)^2 = 0$

$\Rightarrow$ curves touch each other at $\left(2, \frac{1}{4}\right)$

Also $x^2 > 4(x - 1)$ as $x^2 - 4x + 4 > 0$, i.e., $(x - 2)^2 > 0$

$\Rightarrow \frac{1}{x^2} < \frac{1}{4(x-1)}$ foe $x > 1$

Thus, the curve $y = \frac{1}{x^2}$ is always above the curve $y = \frac{1}{4(x-1)}$ for $x > 1$ except for the point $P\left(2, \frac{1}{4}\right)$ where they touch each other. As $x \to 1^+, y = \frac{1}{4(x-1)} \to +\infty$.

Similarly $x \to 0, \frac{1}{x^2} \to \infty$. Thus, the graph representing the curves would be as shown below.

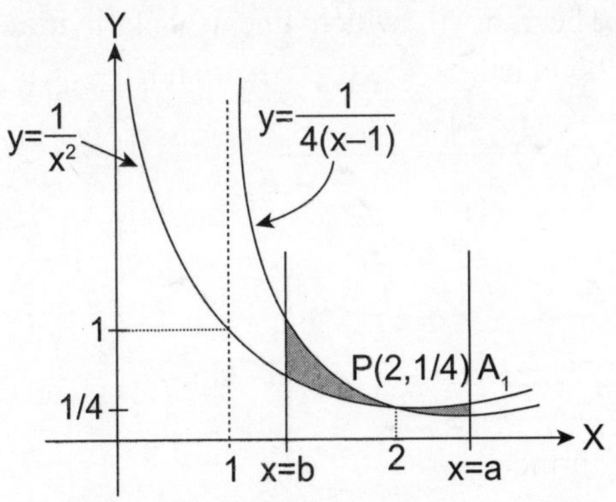

The shaded area A_1 represent the area bounded by $x = a \in (2, \infty)$ and the curves $y = \frac{1}{x^2}$, $y = \frac{1}{4(x-1)}$ and is given by,

$$A_1 = \int_2^a \left(\frac{1}{4(x-1)} - \frac{1}{x^2}\right) dx = \frac{1}{a} \text{ (Given)}$$

$$\Rightarrow \frac{1}{4}\left|\ln|x-1|\right|_2^a - \left[-\frac{1}{x}\right]_2^a = \frac{1}{a}$$

$$\Rightarrow \frac{1}{4}\ln|a-1| + \left(\frac{1}{a} - \frac{1}{2}\right) = \frac{1}{a} \quad \Rightarrow \ln|a - 1| = 2$$

$\Rightarrow a - 1 = e^2 \quad \Rightarrow a = e^2 + 1$

Further the region bounded by $x = b$, $x = 2$ and the curves is given by $A_2 = \int_b^2 \left(\frac{1}{4(x-1)} - \frac{1}{x^2}\right) dx = 1 - \frac{1}{b}$ (given)

$$\Rightarrow \frac{1}{4}\left|\ln|x-1|\right|_b^2 + \left[\frac{1}{x}\right]_b^2 = 1 - \frac{1}{b}$$

$$\Rightarrow \frac{1}{4}\left(-\ln|b-1|\right) + \left(\frac{1}{a} - \frac{1}{2}\right) = 1 - \frac{1}{b}$$

$\Rightarrow b = 1 + e^{-2}$

17. For what value of 'a' is the area of the figure bounded by the lines, $y = \frac{1}{x}$, $y = \frac{1}{2x-1}$, $x = 2$ and $x = a$ equal to $\ln\frac{4}{\sqrt{5}}$?

Solution: Given curves are $y = 2x - 1$ ...(i)

$y = \frac{1}{x}$ ......(ii)

Solving these two equation we get, $x = 1$, $y = 1$. i.e., $P(1, 1)$ as the point of their intersection.

As $x \to \frac{1}{2}^+, y = \frac{1}{2x-1} \to +\infty$ and as $x \to 0^+, y \to \pm\infty$.

The graphs representing the given curves would be as shown below.

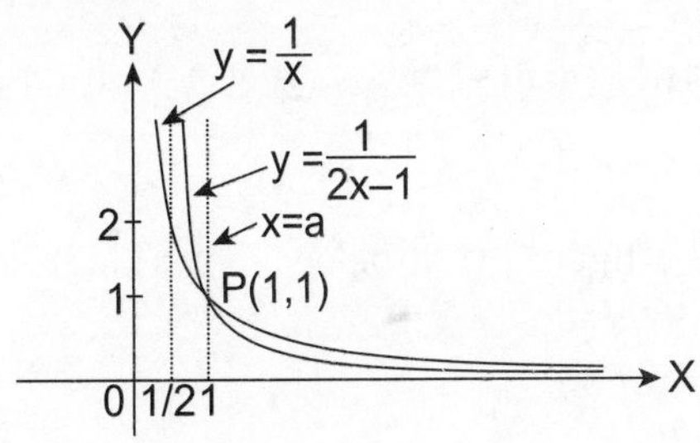

Clearly for bounded region, $a \in \left(\frac{1}{2}, 1\right)$ or a $\in (1, \infty)$

A.T.Q. $\left|\int_2^a \left(\frac{1}{x} - \frac{1}{2x-1}\right) dx\right| = \ln\frac{4}{\sqrt{5}}$

$$= \int_2^a \left(\frac{1}{x} - \frac{1}{2x-1}\right) dx = \pm\ln\frac{4}{\sqrt{5}}$$

$$= \left[\ln x - \frac{1}{2}\ln(2x-1)\right]_2^a = \pm\ln\frac{4}{\sqrt{5}}$$

$$\Rightarrow (\ln a - \ln 2) - \frac{1}{2}\ln(2a-1) + \frac{1}{2}\ln 3 = \pm\ln\frac{4}{\sqrt{5}}$$

$\Rightarrow \ln\left(\frac{(a/2)}{\sqrt{|2a-1|}}.\sqrt{3}\right) = \pm\ln\frac{4}{\sqrt{5}}$

$\Rightarrow \frac{\sqrt{3}a}{2\sqrt{12a-11}} = \frac{4}{\sqrt{5}} \text{ or } \frac{\sqrt{5}}{4}$

$\Rightarrow \frac{3a^2}{4(2a-1)} = \frac{16}{5} \text{ or } \frac{5}{16}$

$\Rightarrow 15a^2 = 128a - 64$ or $12a^2 = 10a - 5$

$\Rightarrow a = 8$ or $\frac{8}{15}$ or $12a^2 - 10a + 5 = 0$ has imaginary roots

Thus, $a = \frac{8}{15}$ or $a = 8$

18. Consider the two curves $C_1 : y = 1 + \cos x$ and $C_2 : y = 1 + \cos(x - \alpha)$ for $\alpha \in (0, \pi/2)$; $x \in [0, \pi]$. Find the value of α, for which the area of the figure bounded by the curves C_1, C_2 and $x = 0$ is same as that of the figure bounded by C_2, $y = 1$ and $x = \pi$. For this value of α, find the ratio in which the line $y = 1$ divides the area of the figure by the curves C_1, C_2 and $x = \pi$.

Solution: The two curves intersect when $1 + \cos x = 1 + \cos(x - \alpha)$

$\Rightarrow \alpha = 0$ or $x = \alpha - x$; But $\alpha > 0$

$\Rightarrow x = \frac{\alpha}{2}$ $\quad \left[\because \alpha \in \left(0, \frac{\pi}{2}\right) \Rightarrow \frac{\alpha}{2} \in \left(0, \frac{\pi}{4}\right)\right]$

Thus, two given curves intersect in $x \in \left(0, \frac{\pi}{4}\right)$

Clearly $f(x) = 1 + \cos x > g(x) = 1 + \cos(x - \alpha)$ for $0 \le x < \frac{\alpha}{2} < \frac{\pi}{4}$

The figure given below shows the rough sketch of C_1 and C_2

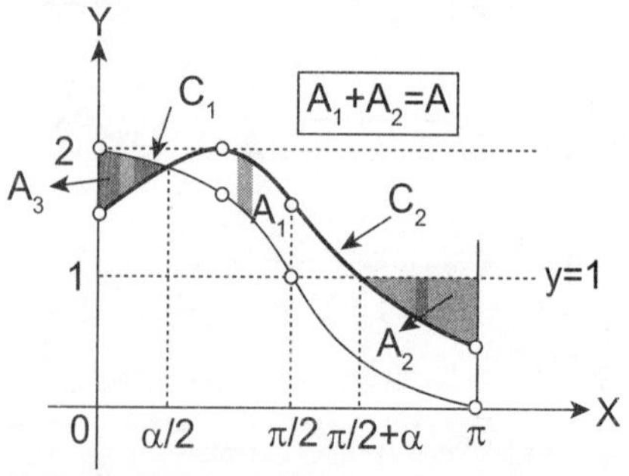

$\therefore$ The area bounded by C_1, C_2 and $x = \frac{\alpha}{2}$ will be

$A_3 = \int_0^{\alpha/2} (y_{C_1} - y_{C_2})dx = \int_0^{\alpha/2} [\cos x - \cos(x - \alpha)]dx$

$= |\sin x - \sin(x - \alpha)|_0^{\alpha/2} = \sin\frac{\alpha}{2} + \sin\frac{\alpha}{2} - \sin\alpha$

$= 2\sin\frac{\alpha}{2} - \sin\alpha$ ......(i)

When $y = 1$, $1 + \cos(x - \alpha) = 1$

$\Rightarrow (x - \alpha) = \frac{\pi}{2} \qquad \Rightarrow x = \alpha + \frac{\pi}{2}$

Now, area bounded by C_2, $y = 1$ and $x = \pi$ will be

$A_2 = \int_{\alpha+\frac{\pi}{2}}^{\pi} \{1 - 1 - \cos(x - \alpha)\}dx$

$= -\int_{\alpha+\frac{\pi}{2}}^{\pi} \cos(x - \alpha)dx = -[\sin(x - \alpha)]_{\alpha+\frac{\pi}{2}}^{\pi}$

$= -\left[\sin(\pi - \alpha) - \sin\left(\frac{\pi}{2}\right)\right]$

$= 1 - \sin\alpha$ ......(ii)

$\therefore$ A.T.Q areas represented by (i) and (ii) are equal, i.e., $A_3 = A_2$

$\Rightarrow 2\sin\frac{\alpha}{2} = 1 \qquad \Rightarrow \sin\frac{\alpha}{2} = \frac{1}{2}$

$\Rightarrow \frac{\alpha}{2} = \frac{\pi}{6} \qquad \Rightarrow \alpha = \frac{\pi}{3}$

Now let A_1 = area bounded by $C_1, C_2; x = \frac{\alpha}{2}$ & $y \ge 1$

Now for $\alpha = \frac{\pi}{3}$; $A_3 = A_2$

$\therefore$ The ratio in which line $y = 1$ divides the area bounded by C_1, C_2, $x = 0$ and $x = \pi$ is given by

$r = \frac{A_3 + A_1}{A_2} = \frac{A_3}{A_2} + \frac{A_1}{A_2}$

Thus, $r = 1 + \frac{A_1}{A_2}$ $\qquad (\because A_2 = A_3)$

Now at $\alpha = \frac{\pi}{3}$; $A_2 = 1 - \sin\frac{\pi}{3} = 1 - \frac{\sqrt{3}}{2} = \frac{2-\sqrt{3}}{2}$

Further

$A_1 = \int_{\pi/6}^{\pi/2} [\cos(x - \alpha) - \cos x]dx + \int_{\pi/2}^{5\pi/6} [\cos(x - \alpha)]dx$

$= [\sin(x - \alpha)]_{\pi/6}^{\pi/2} - [\sin x]_{\pi/6}^{\pi/2} + |\sin(x - \alpha)|_{\pi/2}^{5\pi/6}$

$= \sin\left(\frac{\pi}{2} - \frac{\pi}{3}\right) - \sin\left(\frac{\pi}{6} - \frac{\pi}{3}\right) -$

$\left(\sin\frac{\pi}{2} - \sin\frac{\pi}{6}\right) + \left(\sin\frac{\pi}{2} - \sin\frac{\pi}{6}\right) = 1$

$\therefore$ From (ii), $r = 1 + \frac{2}{2-\sqrt{3}} = \frac{4-\sqrt{3}}{2-\sqrt{3}} = 5 + 2\sqrt{3}$

19. If the area bounded by $f(x)=\frac{x^3}{3}-x^2+a$ and the straight lines $x = 0$; $x = 2$ and the x-axis is minimum then find the value of 'a'.

Solution: Given curve is $f(x)=\frac{x^3}{3}-x^2+a$.

$\Rightarrow f'(x) = x^2 - 2x = x(x - 2) = 0$

$\Rightarrow f'(x) = 0$ at $x = 0$ and $x = 2$ $\Rightarrow$ $f'(x) < 0$ for $x \in (0, 2)$ and $f'(x) > 0$ for $x < 0$ or $x > 2$.

Thus, $f(x)$ is of the form as shown below:

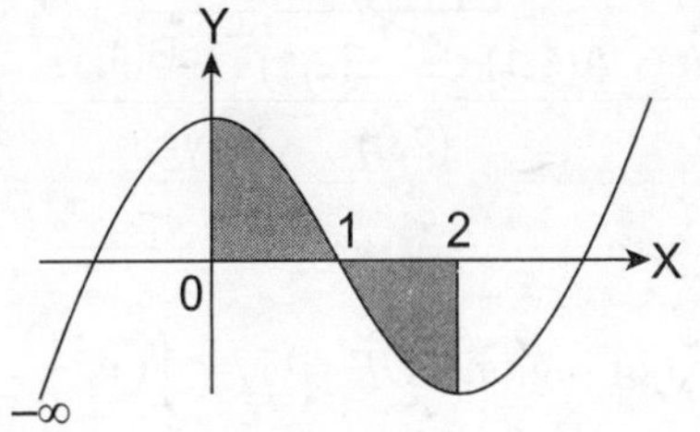

Now, $y = 0$ cuts the shaded area bounded by $f(x)$, $x = 0$ and $x = 2$.

Thus, minimum value of area exists for

$C=\frac{a+b}{2}=\frac{0+2}{2}=1$. Thus, $f(1) = 0$

$\Rightarrow f(1)=\frac{1}{3}-1+a=0 \Rightarrow a=\frac{2}{3}$

20. Let $f(x)$ be a continuous function given by $f(x)=\begin{cases}2x & ;|x|\le 1\\ x^2+ax+b; & |x|>1\end{cases}$. Find the area of the region in the third quadrant bounded by the curve $x = -2y^2$ and $y = f(x)$ lying on the left of the line $8x + 1 = 0$.

Solution: $f(x)=\begin{cases}2x, & -1\le x\le 1\\ x^2+ax+b, & x<-1,\quad x>1\end{cases}$

Since $f(x)$ is continuous, so it must be continuous at $x = 1, -1$

$\Rightarrow \lim\limits_{x\to 1^-} f(x)=\lim\limits_{x\to 1^+} f(x)=f(1)$

$\Rightarrow \lim\limits_{x\to 1^-} 2x=\lim\limits_{x\to 1^+} x^2+ax+b=2$

$\Rightarrow 2-1+a+b \Rightarrow a+b=1$

Also $\lim\limits_{x\to -1^-} f(x)=\lim\limits_{x\to -1^+} f(x)=f(-1)$

$\Rightarrow \lim\limits_{x\to 1^-}+ax+b=\lim\limits_{x\to 1^+} 2x=-2$

$\Rightarrow -a+b=-3$ ...(2)

Solving (1) and (2), we have $b = -1$, $a = 2$

Thus, $f(x)=\begin{cases}2x; & -1\le x\le 1\\ x^2+2x-1; & x\in(-\infty,-1)\cup(1,\infty)\end{cases}$

thus, the graph of $f(x)$, $x = -2y^2$ and line $8x + 1 = 0$ will be as shown below:

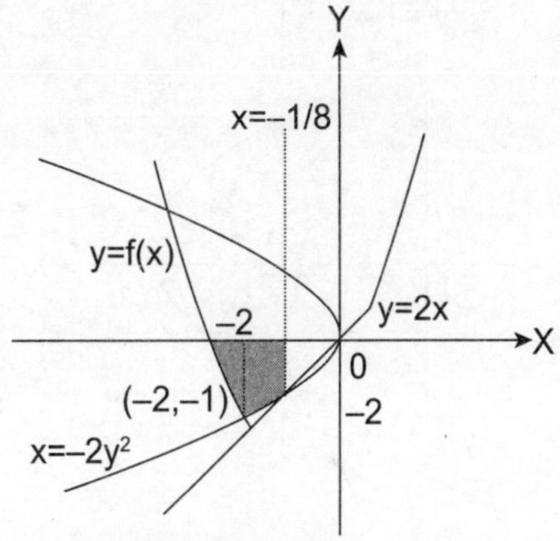

$\therefore$ The required area is

$$\int_{-1-\sqrt{2}}^{-2}(-x^2-2x+1)dx+\int_{-2}^{-1/8}\sqrt{-\frac{x}{2}}dx$$

$$=\left[-\frac{1}{3}x^3-x^2+x\right]_{-1-\sqrt{2}}^{-2}-2\left[\left(-\frac{x}{2}\right)^{3/2}\cdot\frac{2}{3}\right]_{-2}^{-1/8}$$

$$=-\frac{1}{3}\left[-8+(5\sqrt{2}+7)\right]-(4-3-2\sqrt{2})+(-2+1+\sqrt{2})-\frac{4}{3}\left[\frac{1}{64}-1\right]$$

$$=\frac{4\sqrt{2}-5}{3}+\frac{21}{16}=\frac{64\sqrt{2}-80+63}{48}$$

$$=\frac{64\sqrt{2}-17}{48}\text{ Sq units.}$$

21. Calculate the area bounded by parabola $y^2 = 1 - x$; $y\ge -1$ and $y=\frac{|x|}{x}$, $x\ne 0$ in side the parabola and for $x\in\left[-1,\frac{1}{2}\right]$

Solution: Given curves are

$y^2 = 1 - x = -(x - 1)$ ....(i)

which represents left handed parabola with its vertex at $(1, 0)$ and $y=\frac{|x|}{x}=\begin{cases}1 \text{ for } x>0\\ -1 \text{ for } x<0\end{cases}$ ......(ii)

We are to find the region inside the parabola where $y\ge -1$ and $x\in\left[-1,\frac{1}{2}\right]$.

Hence required bounded area is

$$A=\int_{-1}^{0}\left\{\sqrt{1-x}-(-1)\right\}dx+2\int_{0}^{1/2}\sqrt{1-x}\,dx$$

Thus, the required region will be as shown below:

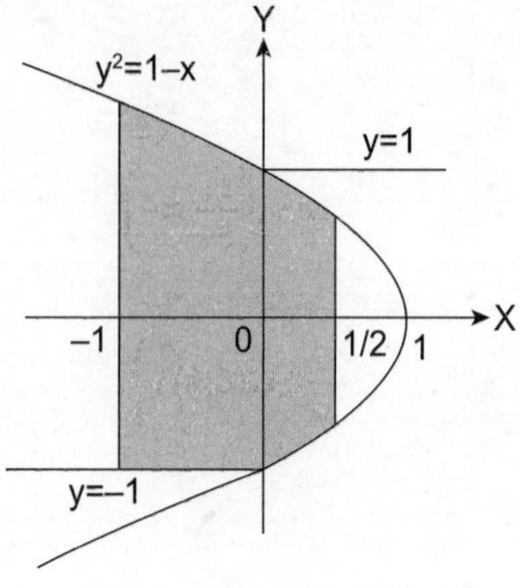

$$A=\int_{-1}^{0}\sqrt{1-x}\,dx+\int_{-1}^{0}dx+2\int_{0}^{\frac{1}{2}}\sqrt{1-x}\,dx=\sqrt{2}+\frac{5}{3}\text{ sq. units}$$

$$=\left[\frac{2}{3}\frac{(1-x)^{3/2}}{(-1)}\right]_{-1}^{0}+[x]_{-1}^{0}+2\times\frac{2}{3}\left[\frac{(1-x)^{3/2}}{(-1)}\right]_{0}^{1/2}$$

$$=-\frac{2}{3}\left[1-2\sqrt{2}\right]+[1]-\frac{4}{3}\left[\frac{1}{2\sqrt{2}}-1\right]$$

$$=\sqrt{2}+\frac{5}{3}\text{ Square units}$$

22. Let $[x]$ denotes the greatest integer function. Draw a rough sketch of the portions of the curves $x^2 = 4[\sqrt{x}]\,y$ and $y^2 = 4[\sqrt{y}]\,x$ that lie within the square $\{(x, y)|\ 1 \le x \le 4,\ 1 \le y \le 4\}$. Find the area of the part of the square that is enclosed by the two curves and the line $x + y = 3$.

Solution: Since we are the find the area with in the square we have $1 < x < 4$ and $1 < y < 4$

$\Rightarrow 1 < \sqrt{x} < 2$ and $1 < \sqrt{y} < 2$

$\Rightarrow [\sqrt{x}\,] = 1$ and $[\sqrt{y}\,] = 1$ for all (x, y) lying within the square.

Thus, the curves $x^2 = 4[\sqrt{x}\,]y$ and $y^2 = 4[\sqrt{y}\,]\,x$ are the parts of the two parabolas $x^2 = 4y$ and $y^2 = 4x$ respectively lying within the given squares as shown in figure. We have to find the area of the shaded region. Let us slice this region into vertical strips. We observe that the vertical strips change their character at point E. So, we draw a line EG parallel to y-axis which divides the area into two regions EGF and ECG.

In the region EGF, the approximating rectangle has length $= (y_2 - y_1)$ and width $= \Delta x$ and it can, move from $x = 1 \to x = 2$.

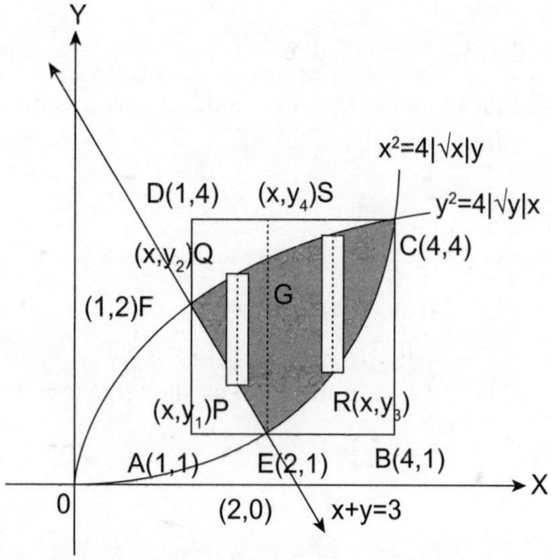

$\Rightarrow$ Area of region $EGF = A_1 = \int_1^2 (y_2 - y_1)\,dx$

$$=\int_1^2[\sqrt{4x}-(3-x)]\,dx$$

$$\left[\begin{array}{c}\because P(x,y_1)\text{ and }Q(x,y_2)\\ y^2=4x\text{ and }x+y=3\text{ respectively}\end{array}\right]$$

Further A_2 = Area of region ECG

$$=\int_2^4 (y_4-y_3)\,dx=\int_2^4\left(\sqrt{4x}-\frac{x^2}{4}\right)dx$$

$$\left[\begin{array}{l}\because R(x,y_3)\text{ and }S(x,y_4)\text{ lie on }x^2=4y\text{ and}\\ y^2=4x\ \text{ respectively}\therefore y_3=\dfrac{x^2}{4}\text{ and }y_4=\sqrt{4x}\end{array}\right]$$

Hence, required area $= A_1 + A_2$

$$=\int_1^2(2\sqrt{x}-3+x)\,dx+\int_2^4\left(2\sqrt{x}-\frac{x^2}{4}\right)dx$$

$$=\left[\frac{4}{3}x^{3/2}-3x+\frac{x^2}{2}\right]_1^2+\left[\frac{4}{3}x^{3/2}-\frac{x^3}{12}\right]_2^4$$

$$=\left(\frac{8\sqrt{2}}{3}-6+2\right)-\left(\frac{4}{3}-3+\frac{1}{2}\right)+\left(\frac{32}{3}-\frac{64}{12}\right)-\left(\frac{8\sqrt{2}}{3}-\frac{8}{12}\right)$$

$$=\frac{8\sqrt{2}}{3}-4+\frac{7}{6}+\frac{16}{3}-\frac{8\sqrt{2}}{3}+\frac{2}{3}=\frac{19}{6}\text{ sq. units.}$$

23. The parabola $y^2 = ax$ cuts $x^2 - y^2 = 2a^2$ at P and Q. Tangent at P to the hyperbola cuts the parabola again in R. Find the area of the curvilinear triangle PQR.

Solution: Solving $y^2 = ax$ and $x^2 - y^2 = 2a^2$ together, we obtain the coordinates of P and Q as $(2a, a\sqrt{2})$ and $(2a, -a\sqrt{2})$ respectively. The equation of the tangent to $x^2 - y^2 = 2a^2$ at $P(2a, a\sqrt{2})$ is $2ax - a\sqrt{2}\,y = 2a^2$

or, $2x - \sqrt{2}\,y = 2a$ ...(i)

Solving this equation with $y^2 = ax$, we obtain the coordinates fo R as $(a/2, -a/\sqrt{2})$

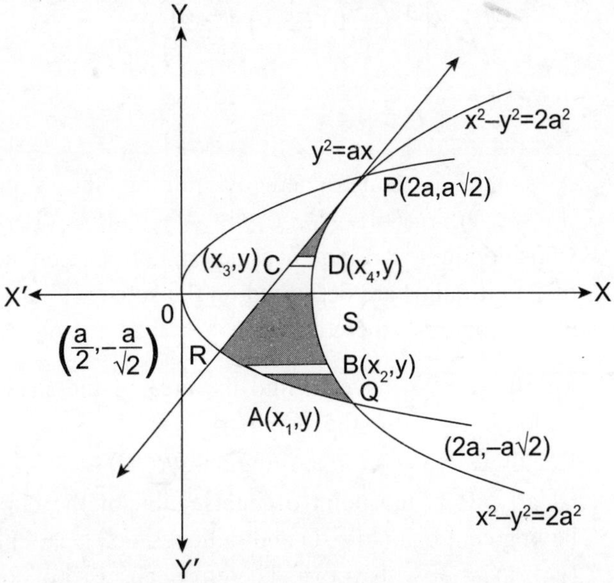

Now, Area of curve linear $\Delta\ PQR$ = Area of curvilinear ΔQRS + Area of curvilinear triangle PRS.

$$= \int_{-a\sqrt{2}}^{-a/\sqrt{2}} (x_2 - x_1)\,dy + \int_{-a/\sqrt{2}}^{a\sqrt{2}} (x_4 - x_3)\,dy$$

$$= \int_{-a\sqrt{2}}^{-a/\sqrt{2}} \left(\sqrt{2a^2 + y^2} - \frac{y^2}{a}\right) dy + \int_{-a/\sqrt{2}}^{a\sqrt{2}} \left\{\sqrt{2a^2 + y^2} - \left(a + \frac{1}{\sqrt{2}}y\right)\right\} dy$$

$$= \int_{-a\sqrt{2}}^{-a/\sqrt{2}} \sqrt{2a^2 + y^2}\,dy + \int_{-a/\sqrt{2}}^{a\sqrt{2}} \sqrt{2a^2 + y^2}\,dy - \int_{-a\sqrt{2}}^{-a/\sqrt{2}} \frac{y^2}{a}\,dy - \int_{-a/\sqrt{2}}^{a\sqrt{2}} \left(a + \frac{y}{\sqrt{2}}\right) dy$$

$$= \int_{-a\sqrt{2}}^{a\sqrt{2}} \sqrt{2a^2 + y^2}\,dy - \frac{1}{a}\int_{-a\sqrt{2}}^{a/\sqrt{2}} y^2\,dy - \int_{-a/\sqrt{2}}^{a\sqrt{2}} \left(a + \frac{y}{\sqrt{2}}\right) dy$$

$$= 2\int_{0}^{a\sqrt{2}} \sqrt{2a^2 + y^2}\,dy - \frac{1}{a}\int_{-a\sqrt{2}}^{-a/\sqrt{2}} y^2\,dy - \int_{-a/\sqrt{2}}^{a\sqrt{2}} \left(a + \frac{y}{\sqrt{2}}\right) dy$$

$$= \left[y\sqrt{2a^2 + y^2} + 2a^2 \ln\{y + \sqrt{2a^2 + y^2}\}\right]_0^{a\sqrt{2}} - \frac{1}{3a}\left[y^3\right]_{-a\sqrt{2}}^{-a/\sqrt{2}} - \left[ay + \frac{y^2}{2\sqrt{2}}\right]_{-a/\sqrt{2}}^{a\sqrt{2}}$$

$$= [2\sqrt{2}\,a^2 + 2a^2 \ln(a\sqrt{2} + 2a) - 2a^2 \log(\sqrt{2}\,a)] - \frac{1}{3a}\left[\frac{-a^3}{2\sqrt{2}} + 2\sqrt{2}a^3\right] - \left[\left(\sqrt{2}a^2 + \frac{a^2}{\sqrt{2}}\right) - \left(\frac{-a^2}{\sqrt{2}} + \frac{a^2}{4\sqrt{2}}\right)\right]$$

$$= \left[2\sqrt{2}a^2 + 2a^2 \ln(1+\sqrt{2}) - \frac{7a^2}{6\sqrt{2}} - \frac{3a^2}{\sqrt{2}} - \frac{3a^2}{4\sqrt{2}}\right]$$

$$= \left[2a^2 \log(1+\sqrt{2}) - \frac{11\sqrt{2}}{24}a^2\right] \text{ sq. units.}$$

24. Find all values of the parameter $a (a \geq 1)$ for which the area of the figure bounded by the pair of straight lines $y^2 - 3y + 2 = 0$ and the curves $y = [a]\,x^2$, $y = \frac{1}{2}[a]\,x^2$ is the greatest. Here [.] denotes the greatest integer function. Also find the greatest area.

Solution: The curves $y = [a]\,x^2$ and $y = \frac{1}{2}[a]\,x^2$ represent parabolas which are symmetric about y-axis. The equation $y^2 - 3y + 2 = 0$ gives a pair of straight lines $y = 1$, $y = 2$ which are parallel to x-axis. The shaded region in figure given below:

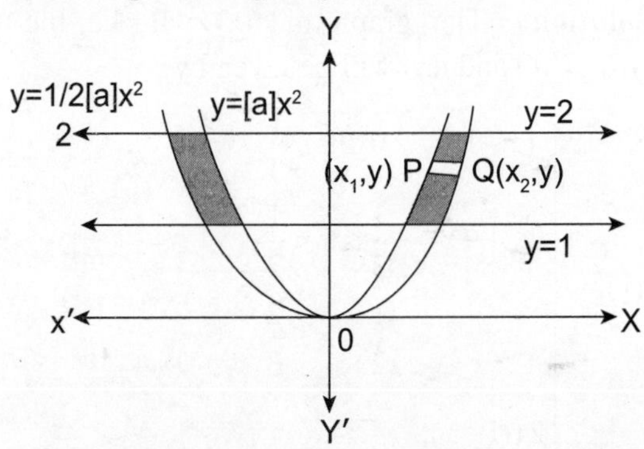

determines the area bounded by the two parabolas and two lines. Let us slice this region into horizontal strips. For the approximating rectangle shown in figure, we have

Length = $x_2 - x_1$, Width = Δy, Area= $(x_2 - x_1)\,dy$

As it can move vertically between $y = 1$ and $y = 2$.

So, required area $= 2\int_1^2 (x_2 - x_1)\,dy$

$$= 2\int_1^2 \left(\sqrt{\frac{2y}{[a]}} - \sqrt{\frac{y}{[a]}}\right) dy$$

$$\left[\begin{array}{c} \because P(x_1, y) \text{ and } Q(x_2, y) \text{ lie on} \\ y = [a]x^2 \text{ and } y = \frac{1}{2}[a]x^2 \text{ respectively} \\ \therefore [a]x_1^2 = y \text{ and } \frac{1}{2}[a]x_2^2 = y \end{array}\right]$$

$$= 2\int_1^2 \left(\frac{\sqrt{2}-1}{\sqrt{[a]}}\right)\sqrt{y}\, dy = \frac{2(\sqrt{2}-1)}{\sqrt{[a]}}\int_1^2 \sqrt{y}\, dy$$

$$= \frac{2(\sqrt{2}-1)}{\sqrt{[a]}} \times \frac{2}{3}\left[y^{3/2}\right]_1^2 = \frac{4(\sqrt{2}-1)}{3\sqrt{[a]}}(2^{3/2}-1)$$

$$= \frac{4}{3}\frac{(5-\sqrt{2}-2\sqrt{2})}{\sqrt{[a]}} = \frac{4(5-3\sqrt{2})}{3\sqrt{[a]}}$$

Clearly, area will be greatest, if $[a]$ is least. It is given that $a \geq 1$. Therefore, the least value of $[a]$ is 1.
Thus, area is greatest when $[a] = 1$
$\Rightarrow a \in [1, 2)$

Also the greatest area will be $\frac{4(5-3\sqrt{2})}{3}$ sq. units.

25. Let $f(x) = \begin{cases} \max\{(x-1)^2, 2x(1-x)\}, & \text{if } 0 \leq x < 1/2 \\ \min.\{2x(1-x), x^2\}, & \text{if } \frac{1}{2} \leq x \leq 1 \end{cases}$.

Draw a rough sketch of the curve $y = f(x)$ and find the area bounded by the curve and x-axis.

Solution: The graph of $f(x)$ will be the curve $OBFGNO$ and $f(x)$ will be given by

$$f(x) = \begin{cases} (x-1)^2, & 0 \leq x \leq \frac{1}{3} \\ 2x(1-x), & \frac{1}{3} \leq x < \frac{1}{2} \\ x^2, & \frac{1}{2} \leq x \leq \frac{2}{3} \\ 2x(1-x), & \frac{2}{3} \leq x \leq 1 \end{cases}$$

Required area = Area of the region $OLBA$ + Area of the region $BLGQ$ + Area of the region $FCMG$ + Area of the region $CMNC$

$$= \int_0^{1/3} (1-x)^2\, dx + \int_{1/3}^{1/2} 2x(1-x)dx + \int_{1/2}^{2/3} x^2\, dx + \int_{2/3}^{1} 2x(1-x)\, dx = \frac{11}{24} \text{ sq. units.}$$

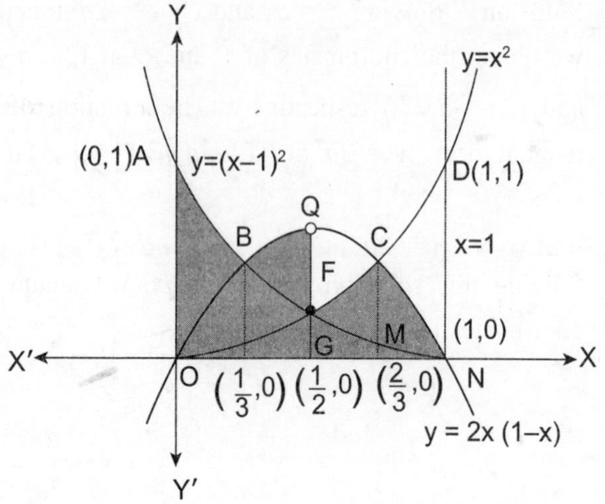

26. A square is constructed by joining the points A (–1, 1), B (–1, –1), C (1, –1) and D (1, 1). Considering A, B, C and D as centre, four circles each of 2 unit radius are described on the square. Find the area common to these circles.

Solution: We have to find the area of the shaded region in fig. From the symmetry,
Required area = 4 (area of region $ORQO$) ...(i)
Clearly, R is the point of intersection of the circle having centre at (–1, –1) and radius 2, i.e., $(x + 1)^2 + (y + 1)^2 = 2^2$ with x-axis. Therefore, abscissa of R is given by $(x + 1)^2 + (0 + 1)^2 = 2^2 \Rightarrow x = \sqrt{3} - 1$

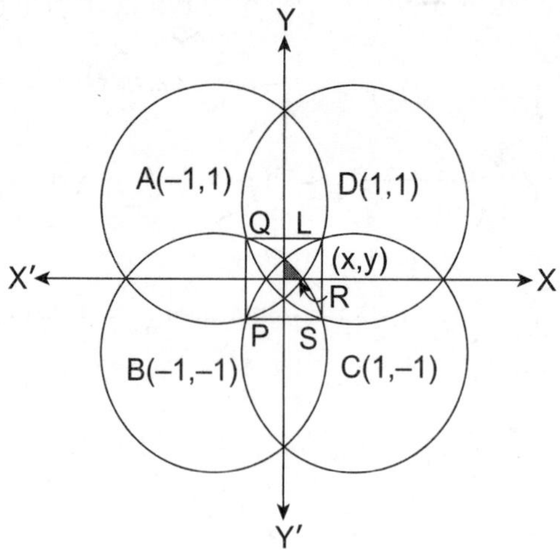

$\therefore$ Area of the region $ORQO = \int_0^{\sqrt{3}-1} y\, dx$

$$= \int_0^{\sqrt{3}-1} \{-1 + \sqrt{2^2 - (x+1)^2}\}dx$$

$$\left[\begin{array}{c} \because L(x, y) \text{ lies on } (x+1)^2 + (y+1)^2 = 2^2 \\ \therefore y = -1 + \sqrt{2^2 - (x+1)^2} \end{array}\right]$$

$$= \left[-x + \frac{1}{2}(x+1)\sqrt{2^2-(x+1)^2} + \frac{4}{2}\sin^{-1}\left(\frac{x+1}{2}\right)\right]_0^{\sqrt{3}-1}$$

$$= \left\{-(\sqrt{3}-1) + \frac{\sqrt{3}}{2} + \frac{4}{2}\sin^{-1}\frac{\sqrt{3}}{2}\right\} - \left\{\frac{1}{2}\sqrt{3} + \frac{4}{2}\sin^{-1}\left(\frac{1}{2}\right)\right\}$$

$$= -\sqrt{3} + 1 + \frac{\sqrt{3}}{2} + 2 \times \frac{\pi}{3} - \frac{\sqrt{3}}{2} - 2 \times \frac{\pi}{6}$$

$$= \left(1 + \frac{\pi}{3} - \sqrt{3}\right)$$

Hence, required area $= 4\left(1 + \frac{\pi}{3} - \sqrt{3}\right)$ sq. units.

27. Find a continuous function $f(x)$ satisfying $x^4 - 4x^2 \le f(x) \le 2x^2 - x^3$ for all $x \in [0, 2]$, such that the area bounded by $y = f(x)$, $y = x^4 - 4x^2$, the y-axis and the line $x = t$ $(0 \le t \le 2)$ is k times the area bounded by $y = f(x)$, $y = 2x^2 - x^3$, y-axis and the line $x = t(0 \le t \le 2)$

Solution: Let A_1 be the area bounded by $y = f(x)$, $y = x^4 - 4x^2$, y-axis and $x = t$.

Graph of $y = x^4 - 2x^2$ and $y = 2x^2 - x^3$ are as shown below:

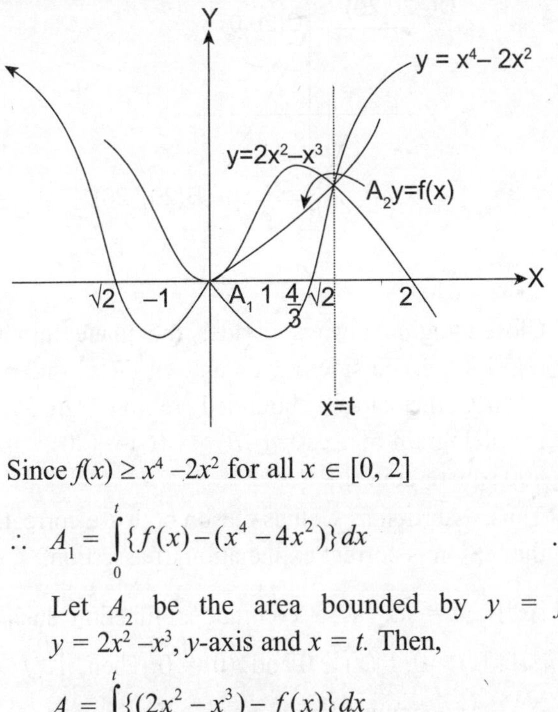

Since $f(x) \ge x^4 - 2x^2$ for all $x \in [0, 2]$

$$\therefore\ A_1 = \int_0^t \{f(x) - (x^4 - 4x^2)\}\,dx \qquad \ldots\text{(i)}$$

Let A_2 be the area bounded by $y = f(x)$, $y = 2x^2 - x^3$, y-axis and $x = t$. Then,

$$A_2 = \int_0^t \{(2x^2 - x^3) - f(x)\}\,dx$$

$$[\because f(x) \le (2x^2 - x^3)\ for\ all\ x \in [0,2]]$$

It is given that $A_1 = kA_2$

$$\Rightarrow \int_0^t \{f(x) - (x^4 - 4x^2)\}\,dx = k\left[\int_0^t \{(2x^2 - x^3) - f(x)\}\,dx\right]$$

Differentiating both sides w.r.t. t, we get

$f(t) - (t^4 - 4t^2) = k\,[(2t^2 - t^3) - f(t)]$

$\Rightarrow (1 + k)\,f(t) = k\,(2t^2 - t^3) + (t^4 - 4t^2)$

$\Rightarrow f(t) = \frac{k}{k+1}(2t^2 - t^3) + \frac{t^4 - 4t^2}{k+1}$ for all $t \in [0, 2]$

Hence $f(x) = \frac{k}{k+1}(2x^2 - x^3) + \frac{(x^4 - 4x^2)}{k+1}$

$= \frac{1}{k+1}\{x^4 - kx^3 + 2(k-2)\,x^2\}$

Assertion and Reasoning

(a) If both assertion and reason are correct and reason is the correct explanation of the assertion.
(b) If both assertion and reason are correct but reason is not correct explanation of the assertion.
(c) If assertion is correct, but reason is incorrect
(d) If assertion is incorrect, but reason is correct

28. A: The area of the region $\{(x, y) : x^2 + y^2 \le 5,\ ||x| - |y|| \ge 1\}$ is $5\left(\pi - \tan^{-1}\frac{24}{7}\right) - 3$.

R: $4\tan^{-1}\frac{1}{2} = \pi - \tan^{-1}\frac{24}{7}$

Solution: (d) $x^2 + y^2 \le 5$ represents a circle with its centre at origin and radius $\sqrt{5}$. $||x| - |y|| \ge 1$ represents symmetric region about x-axis and y-axis in first quadrant $|x - y| \ge 1$.

$$\Rightarrow \begin{cases} x - y \ge 1 \text{ for } x \ge y \\ -(x - y) \ge \text{for } x \le y \end{cases} \Rightarrow \begin{cases} y \le x - 1 \text{ for } y \le x \\ y \ge x + 1 \text{ for } y \ge x \end{cases}$$

$\therefore$ In the first quadrant, region bounded by inequality $||x| - |y|| \ge 1$ will be as shown below

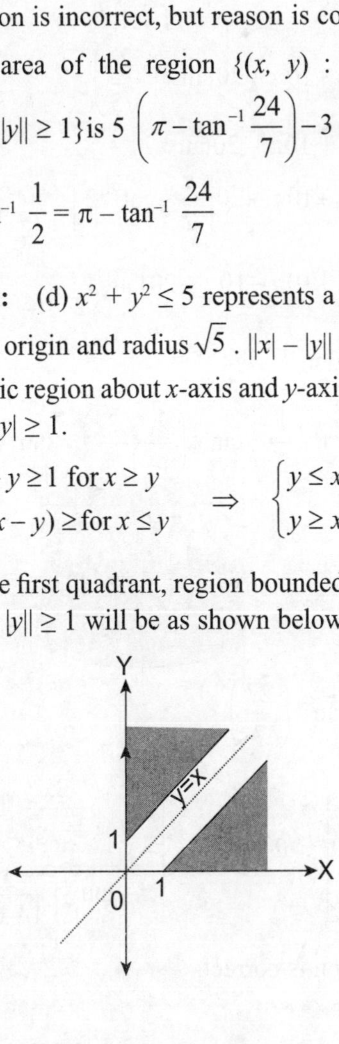

Hence the region bounded by circle $x^2 + y^2 \leq 5$ and $||x| - |y|| \geq 1$ will be as shown below:

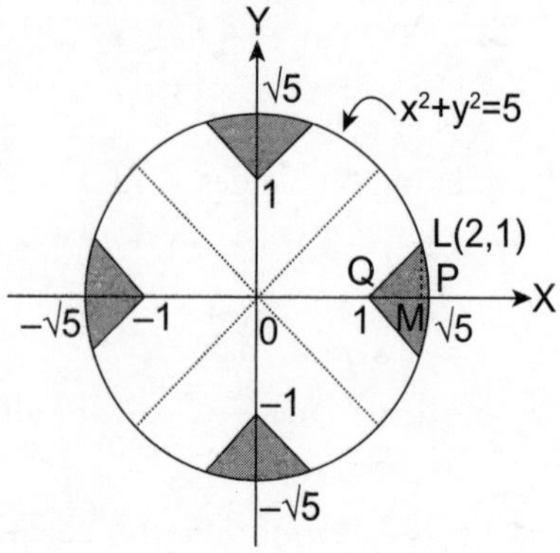

$\therefore$ The required area = 8[area of ΔMQL + area of curvilinear ΔMPL)

$$= 8\left[\frac{1}{2}(1)(1) + \int_2^{\sqrt{5}} \sqrt{5-x^2}\,dx\right]$$

$$= 8\left[\frac{1}{2} + \frac{x\sqrt{5-x^2}}{2} + \frac{5}{2}\sin^{-1}\left(\frac{x}{\sqrt{5}}\right)\right]_2^{\sqrt{5}}$$

$$= 4 + 4[0 - 2(1)] + 4\left[5\left(\frac{\pi}{2}\right) - 5\sin^{-1}\left(\frac{2}{\sqrt{5}}\right)\right]$$

$$= -4 + 10\pi - 20\sin^{-1}\left(\frac{2}{\sqrt{5}}\right)$$

$$= -4 + 10\pi - 20\tan^{-1} 2$$

$$= -4 + 10\pi - 20\left[\frac{\pi}{2} - \cot^{-1} 2\right]$$

$$= -4 + 10\pi - 10\pi + 20\tan^{-1}\frac{1}{2}$$

$$= 20\tan^{-1}\frac{1}{2} - 4 \quad \text{...(i)}$$

Now, $2\tan^{-1}\frac{1}{2} = \tan^{-1}\left(\frac{2(1/2)}{1-1/4}\right) = \tan^{-1}\frac{4}{3}$

$$\Rightarrow 4\tan^{-1}\frac{1}{2} = 2\tan^{-1}\frac{4}{3} = \pi + 2\tan^{-1}\frac{1}{2} = \tan^{-1}\left(\frac{2\left(\frac{4}{3}\right)}{1-\frac{16}{9}}\right)$$

$$\Rightarrow \pi - \tan^{-1}\left(\frac{27}{7}\right) \quad \text{......(ii)}$$

$$\left(\because 2\tan^{-1} x = \begin{cases} \tan^{-1}\left(\dfrac{2x}{1-x^2}\right) \text{for} -1 < x < 1 \\ \pi + \tan^{-1}\left(\dfrac{2x}{1-x^2}\right) \text{for } x > 1 \end{cases}\right)$$

$\therefore$ Reason is correct.

Now, from (i) and (ii), $A = 5\left(\pi - \tan^{-1}\frac{24}{7}\right) - 4$

$\Rightarrow$ Assertion is incorrect

29. A: The graph of $y^2 + 2xy + 40|x| = 400$ divides the plane into two regions. The area of bounded region is 800 (units)^2

R: The bounded region is a parallelogram.

Solution: (a) Given equation is $y^2 + 2xy + 40|x| = 400$

$$\Rightarrow \begin{cases} y^2 + 2xy + 40x = 400 \text{ for } x \geq 0 \\ y^2 + 2xy - 40x = 400 \text{ for } x < 0 \end{cases}$$

$$\Rightarrow \begin{cases} (y^2 + 2xy + x^2) - (x^2 - 40x + 400) = 0 \text{ for } x \geq 0 \\ (y^2 + 2xy + x^2) - (x^2 + 40x + 400) = 0 \text{ for } x < 0 \end{cases}$$

$$\Rightarrow \begin{cases} (y + x)^2 - (x - 20)^2 = 0 \text{ for } x \geq 0 \\ (y + x)^2 - (x + 20)^2 = 0 \text{ for } x < 0 \end{cases}$$

$$\Rightarrow \begin{cases} (2x + y - 20)(y + 20) = 0 \text{ for } x \geq 0 \\ (2x + y + 20)(y - 20) = 0 \text{ for } x < 0 \end{cases}$$

Which represents four straight lines $2x + y - 20 = 0$; $y = -20$ for $x \geq 0$ and $2x + y + 20 = 0$; $y = 20$ for $x < 0$

Hence representing the closed region as shown below

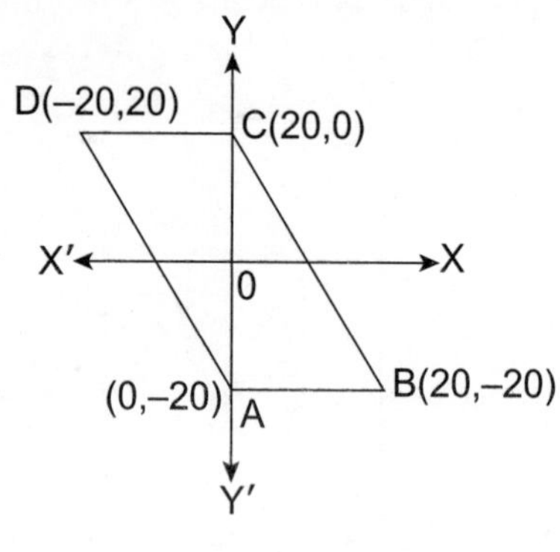

Closed region always divides the plane into three regions, i.e., outside, inside and on the closed curve. Clearly the closed bounded region $ABCD$ is a parallelogram of area = $(AB) \times (AC) = (20) \times (40) = 800$ square unit.

Thus, assertion as well as reason both are correct, and the reason is correct explanation of assertion.

30. A: If $y = f(x)$ is a continuous function such that $f'(x) > 0$, $f''(x) > 0$ and $f(0) = 0$. Then, $\int_{-1}^{1} f(x)\,dx$ $\neq$ Area bounded by $x = \pm 1$ and $y = f(x)$ and x-axis.

R: curve lies above the x-axis in between $1 \leq x \leq 1$

Solution: (c) Given that $y = f(x)$ is a continuous function and $f'(x) > 0$, $f''(x) > 0$ and $f(0) = 0$

⇒ $y = f(x)$ passes through origin, and is an increasing function with its concavity upwards as shown below.

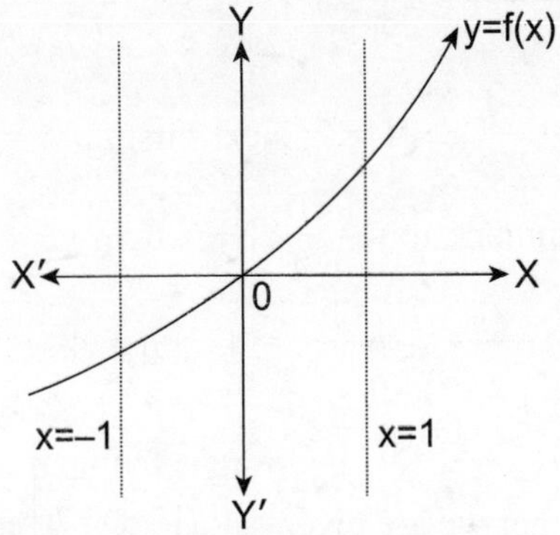

Thus, the area bounded by $y = f(x)$, x-axis and $x = \pm 1$ will be given by $A = \int_{-1}^{0} -f(x)\,dx + \int_{0}^{1} f(x)\,dx$

(since $f(x) < 0$ for $x < 0$ and $f(x) > 0$ for $x > 0$)

Thus, $A \neq \int_{-1}^{1} f(x)\,dx$ ∴ Assertion is correct

Clearly the curve is not always above x-axis for $x \in [-1,1]$, showing that reason is incorrect.

Thus, (C) must be right option

Passage type

A: Consider a triangle OAB formed by the points $O = (0, 0)$, $A = (2, 0)$, $B = \left(1, \sqrt{3}\right)$). $P(x, y)$ is an arbitrary interior point of the triangle, moving in such a way that $d(P, OA) + d(P, AB) + d(P, OB) = \sqrt{3}$, where $d(P, OA)$, $d(P, AB)$, $d(P, OB)$ represent the distance of 'P' from the sides OA, AB and OB respectively. On the basis of information answer the following questions.

31. Area of the region representing all possible positions of the point 'P' is equal to

(a) $2\sqrt{3}$ sq. units (b) $\sqrt{6}$ sq. units

(c) $\sqrt{3}$ sq. units (d) None of these

32. In above problem, if the point 'P' moves in such a way that $d(P, OA) \le \min \{d(P, OB)\}, d(P, AB)\}$, then area of the region representing all possible positions of the point 'P' is equal to

(a) $\sqrt{3}$ sq. units (b) $\sqrt{6}$ sq. units

(c) $\frac{1}{\sqrt{3}}$ sq. units (d) $\frac{1}{\sqrt{6}}$ sq. units

33. In the above problem if the point 'P' moves in such a way that $d(P, OA) \le \max \{d(P, OB), d(P, AB)\}$, then the area of the region representing all possible positions of the point P is equal to

(a) $\frac{\sqrt{3}}{2}$ (b) $\frac{1}{\sqrt{3}}$

(c) $\frac{2}{\sqrt{3}}$ (d) None of these

Solutions:

31. vertices of ΔOAB is $O(0,0)$; $A(2,0)$; $B(1,\sqrt{3})$

⇒ $OA = OB = AB = 2$ units.

⇒ ΔOAB is equilateral Δ

Let $P(x, y)$ be the point in the interior of ΔOAB as shown below:

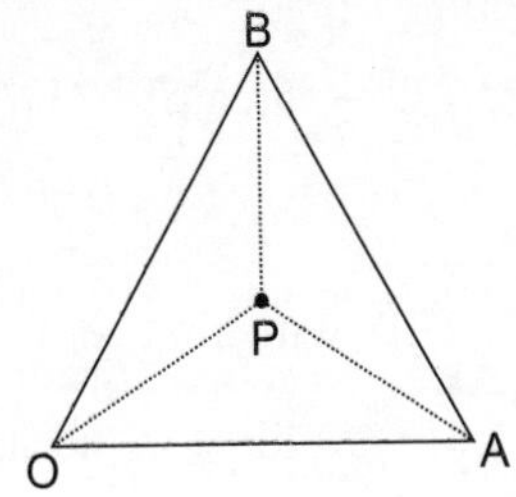

Now as $\Delta_{OAB} = \Delta_{OPA} + \Delta_{APB} + \Delta_{OPB}$

⇒ $\frac{\sqrt{3}}{4}.4 = \frac{1}{2}.2.$ $[d(P, OA) + d(P, AB) + d(P, OB)]$

⇒ $d(P, OA) + d(P, AB) + d(P, OB) = \sqrt{3}$

Thus, point 'P' can be any interior point of the triangle. Hence area of required region $= \Delta_{OAB} = \sqrt{3}$ square units.

∴ c is the correct option

32. Now $d(P,OA) \le \min \{d(P,OB), d(P,AB)\}$

⇒ we must have $d(P, OA) \le d(P, OB)$ as well as $d(P, OA) \le d(P, AB)$.

Thus, 'P' lies either on or below the angle bisectors of $\angle BOA$ and $\angle BAO$

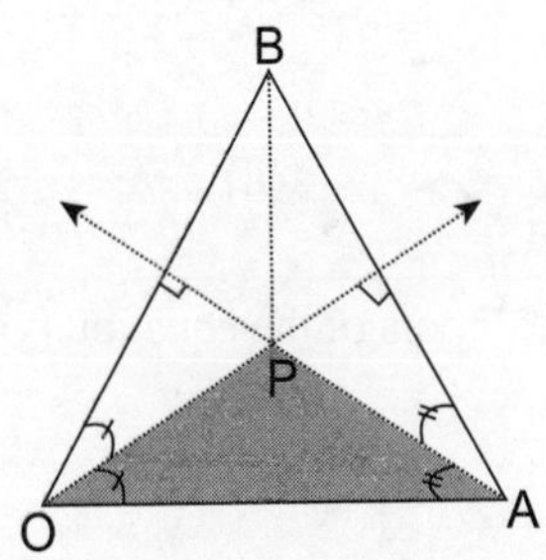

Required area $= \frac{1}{3} \cdot \Delta_{OAB} = \frac{1}{\sqrt{3}}$ square units.

∴ c must be the right option.

33. We must have $d(P, OA) \geq d(P, OB)$ as well as $d(P, OA) \geq d(P, AB)$. Thus, 'P' must lie above the bisectors of $\angle BOA$ and $\angle BAO$ as shown below

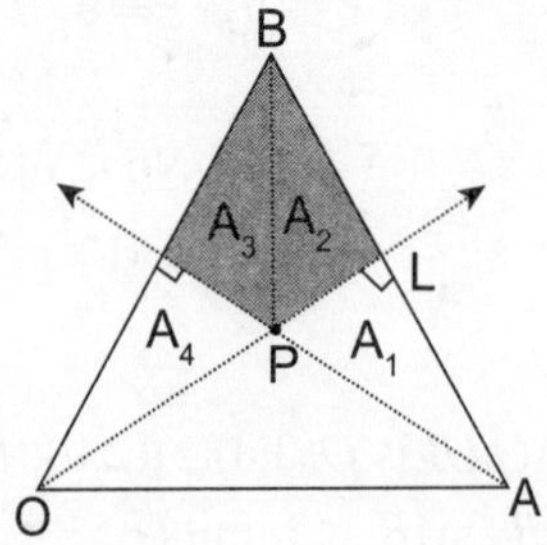

Required area $= A_2 + A_3 = \frac{1}{2}$ (area of Δ PAB) + $\frac{1}{2}$ (area of ΔPOB) = $\frac{1}{2}$(2area of ΔPAB)

= area of ΔPAB = $\frac{1}{3}$ area of ΔOAB = $\frac{1}{3}(\sqrt{3}) = \frac{1}{\sqrt{3}}$ square units

B: There exists a G.P. with first term $\frac{1}{A}$ and common ratio A ($A > 1$). If we add $\frac{1}{2}$ in the sum of first n terms of the sequence, it equals to the sum of the coefficients of even power of x in the expansion of $(1 + x)^n$; $n \in \mathbb{N}$. If we interchange the first term and common ratio of given G.P., the sum of new infinitely decreasing G.P. is equal to B, where A, B and n are related by the relation $\left|\int_{A-2}^{B-2} (1+x)^n\, dx\right| = \frac{364}{3}$. On the basis of above information answer the following questions.

34. The value of $\lim\limits_{x\to A}\frac{(1+x)^A - n - B}{x - A}$ is

(a) 3 (b) 6
(c) e (d) 8

35. Area bounded by $f(x) = x^A$ and $g(x) = x^B$ is

(a) $\frac{A+B}{n}$ (b) $\frac{B-A}{n}$

(c) $\frac{2A}{A+2B+n}$ (d) $\frac{B}{n+A+B}$

36. Number of real roots of the equation $(x^B - nx^A)^{1/A} = 6$ are

(a) 2 (b) 4
(c) 1 (d) 0

Solutions:

First terms of G.P = $\frac{1}{A}$

Common ratio (r) = A(>1)

A.T.Q $S_n + \frac{1}{2} = ({}^nC_0 + {}^nC_2 + ...)$

$\Rightarrow \frac{1}{A}\frac{(A^n-1)}{(A-1)} + \frac{1}{2} = 2^{n-1} \Rightarrow \frac{(A^n-1)}{A(A-1)} = 2^{n-1} - \frac{1}{2}$

$= \frac{2^n - 1}{2} \Rightarrow A = 2$; Next, first term = A

Common ratio = $\frac{1}{A}$; $S_\infty = B$

$\Rightarrow B = \frac{A}{1-\frac{1}{A}} = \frac{2}{1-\frac{1}{2}} = 4 \Rightarrow B = 4$

Further we are given $\left|\int_{A-2}^{B-2}(1+x)^n\, dx\right| = \frac{364}{3}$

$\Rightarrow \int_0^2 (1+x)^n\, dx = \frac{364}{3} \Rightarrow \left[\frac{(1+x)^{n+1}}{n+1}\right]_0^2 = \frac{364}{3}$

$\Rightarrow \frac{3^{n+1}-1}{n+1} = \frac{364}{3} \Rightarrow n = 5$

34. $\lim\limits_{x\to A}\frac{(1+x^A) - n - B}{x - A} = \lim\limits_{x\to 2}\frac{(1+x)^2 - 9}{x-2}$

$= \lim\limits_{x\to 2}\frac{x^2+2x-8}{x-2} = \lim\limits_{x\to 2}(x+4) = 6$

$\therefore$ b is the correct option

35. $f(x) = x^A = x^2$ and $g(x) = x^B = x^4$

The graph of $f(x) = x^2$ and $g(x) = x^4$ are as given below

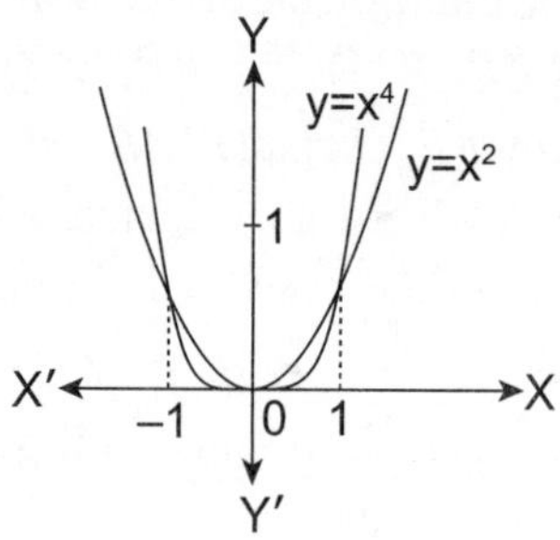

Thus, the required shaded area bounded by x^2 and x^4 equals

$= 2\int_0^1 (x^2 - x^4)\, dx = \frac{4}{15} = \frac{2A}{A+2B+n}$

$\therefore$ c will be the right option

36. We are to find the real roots of the equation $(x^B - nx^A)^{1/A} = 6$

$\Rightarrow (x^4 - 5x^2)^{1/2} = 6 \Rightarrow x^4 - 5x^2 = 36$

$\Rightarrow x^4 - 5x^2 - 36 = 0 \Rightarrow (x^2 - 9)(x^2 + 4) = 0$

$\Rightarrow x = \pm 3$,so there will be two real roots.

$\Rightarrow$ option (a) will be correct option

C: Consider the region R which is enclosed by the curve $y \geq \sqrt{1-x^2}$ and $\max\{|x|, |y|\} \leq 4$. The slope of a family of lines defined as $m(t) = -\sin^2 t + \sin t + 1$, where $(t, 2t + 0.4)$ lies inside the region R. On the basis of above information, answer the following questions.

37. The area of region R is

(a) $8 + \frac{\pi}{2}$ (b) $8 - \frac{\pi}{2}$

(c) $4 + \frac{\pi}{2}$ (d) $4 - \frac{\pi}{2}$

38. All possible values of t are represented by the interval

(a) [0.14, 1.0] (b) [0.14, 0.5]

(c) [0.28, 0.8] (d) [0.28, 1.0]

39. The maximum slope of any member of family is for t is equal to

(a) $\frac{\pi}{6}$ (b) 1

(c) 0.28 (d) None of these

Solutions:

Given bounding curve is $y = \sqrt{1-x^2}$, i.e., upper half part of circle $x^2 + y^2 = 1$. Further $y \geq \sqrt{1-x^2}$ is the region of plane outside the circle $x^2 + y^2 = 1$ above x-axis as shown below

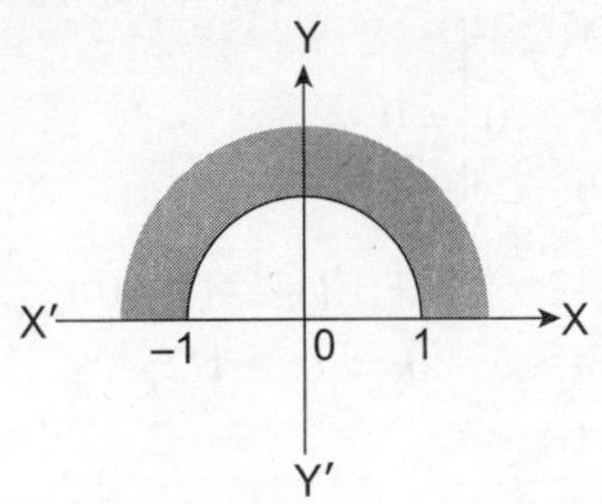

Further max. $\{|x|, |y|\} \leq 4$

$$\Rightarrow \begin{cases} |x| \leq 4; |x| \geq |y| \\ |y| \leq 4; |y| \geq |x| \end{cases} \begin{cases} -2 \leq x \leq 2; |x| \geq |y| \\ -2 \leq y \leq 2; |y| \geq |x| \end{cases}$$

Thus, the above region is as given below

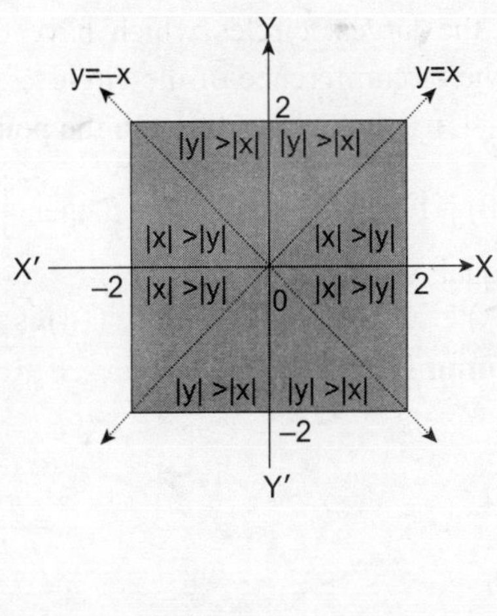

Thus, the region R bounded by two inequalities is as shown below

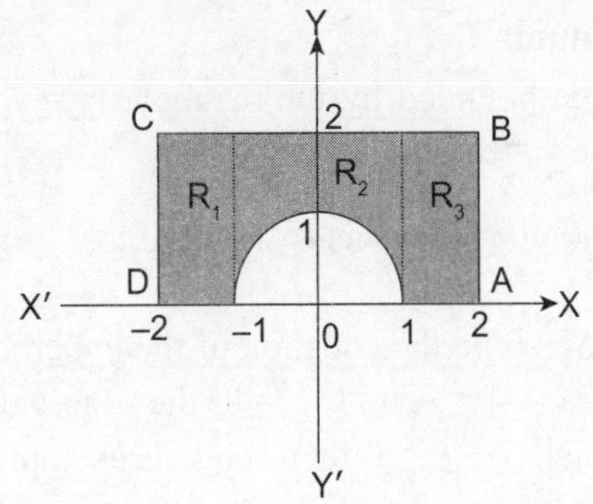

37. Area of region R = (Area of rectangle $ABCD$) – (Area of semi-circle) $= 8 - \frac{1}{2}(\pi(1)^2) = 8 - \frac{\pi}{2}$.

$\therefore$ (b) will be the correct option

38. Since the point $(t, 2t + 0.4)$ lies inside the region R. If it lies in R_2

$\Rightarrow -1 \leq t \leq 1$ and $\sqrt{1-t^2} \leq y \leq 2$

$\Rightarrow -1 \leq t \leq 1$; $\sqrt{1+t^2} \leq 2t + 0.4 \leq 2$

$\Rightarrow t \in [-1, 1]$; $t - t^2 \leq (2t + 0.4)^2 \leq 4$

$\Rightarrow t \in [-1, 1]$; $t - t^2 \leq 4t^2 + 0.16 + 1.6t \leq 4$

$\Rightarrow t \in [-1, 1]$; $t \in (-\infty, 0.6] \cup [0.28, \infty)$ and $t \in [-1.2, 0.8]$

$\Rightarrow t \in [0.28, 0.8]$

But if $(t, 2t + 0.4)$ lies in region R_1, $t \in [-2, 1]$; and $0 \leq 2t + 0.4 \leq 2$

$\Rightarrow t \in [-2, -1] \cap [-0.2, 0.8] = \phi$

If $(t, 2t + 0.4)$ lies in Region R_3 $t \in [1, 2]$ and $0 \leq 2t + 0.4 \leq 2$

$\Rightarrow t \in [1, 2] \cap [-0.2, 0.8] = \phi$

$\therefore$ $t \in [0.28, 0.8]$

$\therefore$ (c) must be the option.

39. slope of family of straight lines is given by,

$m(t) = -\sin^2 t + \sin t + 1 = -\left(\sin t - \frac{1}{2}\right)^2 + \frac{5}{4}$

$\Rightarrow m(t) \leq \frac{5}{4}$ and occurs for $\sin t = \frac{1}{2}$

$\Rightarrow t \in \left\{\frac{\pi}{6}, \frac{7\pi}{6}, \ldots\right\}$; but $t \in [0.28, 0.8]$

$\Rightarrow t = \frac{\pi}{6}$

$\therefore$ (a) option is correct

Column Matching Problems

40. Match the following

Column I

(a) Area bounded by the parabola $y^2 = -4x$ and the line $y = x$ is

(b) $\int_0^{\pi/2} (\sin^5 x + \cos^5 x)dx$ is equal to

(c) If $S = 0$ be the equation of the hyperbola $x^2 + 4xy + 3y^2 - 4x + 2y + 1 = 0$, then the value of k for which $S + k = 0$ represents its asymptotes is

(d) The value of α for which $\alpha\hat{i} + 2\hat{j} + \hat{k}$, lies in the plane containing three points $\hat{i} + \hat{j} + \hat{k}$, $2\hat{i} + 2\hat{j} + \hat{k}$ and $3\hat{i} - \hat{k}$, is

Column II

(i) 1/2
(ii) 22
(iii) 8/3
(iv) 16/15
(v) –22

Ans: (a) → (iii); (b) → (iv); (c) → (v); (d) → (i)

Solution: (a) Given curves are $y^2 = -4a$ and $y = x$

The curve intersect each other where $x^2 = -4x$

$\Rightarrow x^2 + 4x = 0$

$\Rightarrow x = 0$ or $x = -4$

The bounded region is as shown below by shaded portion

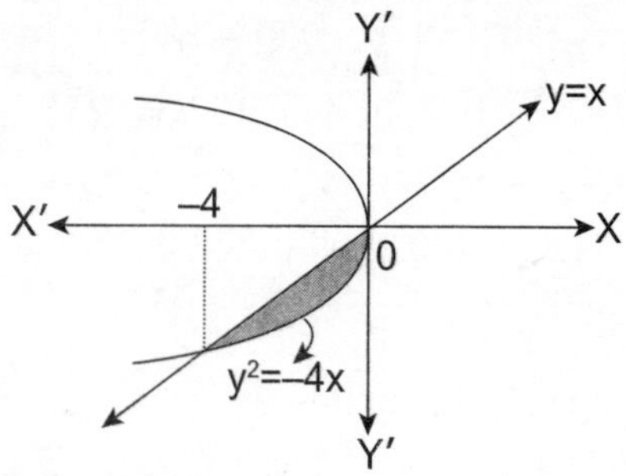

∴ required area

$$= \int_{-4}^{0} \{x - (-\sqrt{-4x})\}dx = \left[\frac{x^2}{2}\right]_{-4}^{0} + \left[\frac{(2)}{(-1)}(-x)^{3/2}.\frac{2}{3}\right]_{-4}^{0}$$

$$= \frac{1}{2}(0-16) - \frac{4}{3}[0-8] = -8 + \frac{32}{3} = \frac{8}{3} \text{square units}$$

∴ (a) → (ii)

(b) $\int_0^{\pi/2} (\sin^5 x + \cos^5 x)dx$

$$= \int_0^{\pi/2} \sin^5 x\, dx + \int_0^{\pi/2} \cos^5 x\, dx$$

$$= \frac{(5-1)\times(2)}{5\times3\times1} + \frac{(5-1)\times2}{5\times3\times1}$$

(By using walli's formula)

$$= 2\left[\frac{8}{15}\right] = \frac{16}{15}.$$

∴ (b) → (iv)

(c) The given equation of hyperbola is S ≡ 0

i.e., $x^2 + 4xy + 3y^2 - 4x + 2y + 1 = 0$

Now $S + k = 0$ will represent asymptotes to parabola if it represent a pair of straight lines

$\Rightarrow \Delta = 0$

i.e., $x^2 + 3y^2 + 4xy - 4x + 2y + (k + 1) = 0$ has

$$\begin{vmatrix} a & h & g \\ h & b & f \\ g & f & c \end{vmatrix} = 0 \Rightarrow \begin{vmatrix} 1 & 2 & 2 \\ 2 & 3 & 1 \\ -2 & 1 & k+1 \end{vmatrix} = 0$$

$\Rightarrow 1(3k + 3 - 1) - 2(2k + 2 + 2) - 2(2 + 6) = 0$

$\Rightarrow 3k + 2 - 4k - 8 - 16 = 0 \Rightarrow k = -22$

∴ (c) → (v)

(d) Let $A \equiv (1,1,1); B \equiv (2,2,1); C \equiv (3,0,-1)$

$\Rightarrow \overrightarrow{AB} = \hat{i} + \hat{j}; \overrightarrow{BC} = \hat{i} - 2\hat{j} - 2\hat{k}$

∴ The vector $\vec{a} = \alpha\hat{i} + 2\hat{j} + \hat{k}$ lies in the plane containing $\overrightarrow{AB}$ *and* $\overrightarrow{BC}$ if they are coplanar

$$\Rightarrow \begin{vmatrix} \alpha & 2 & 1 \\ 1 & 1 & 0 \\ 1 & -2 & -2 \end{vmatrix} = 0$$

$\Rightarrow \alpha(-2) - 2(-2) + 1(-2 - 1) = 0$

$-2\alpha + 4 - 3 = 0 \Rightarrow \alpha = 1/2$

∴ (d) → (i)

41. Column I

(a) Area between $y = |\cos^{-1}(\sin x)| - |\sin^{-1}(\cos x)|$ and x-axis, where $x \in \left[\frac{3\pi}{2}, 2\pi\right]$ is $\frac{k\pi^2}{4}$, then k is equal to

(b) The difference between the radii of the smallest and the largest circles which have their centres on the circumference of the circle $x^2 + y^2 + 2x + 4y - 4 = 0$ and passes through the point (2, 2) is

(c) If $f(0) = 1, f(2) = 3$ and $f'(2) = 5$, then $\int_0^1 xf''(2x)\,dx$ is equal to

(d) If $f(x) = x^3 + 4x^2 + 6x$, then $f^{-1}(-4)$ is

Column II

(p) 1
(q) 6

(r) 2

(s) –2

Solution: (a) $y = |\cos^{-1}(\sin x)| - |\sin^{-1}(\cos x)|$ ...(i)

Now $\cos^{-1}x \in [0,\pi] \Rightarrow \cos^{-1}x \geq 0$

$\Rightarrow \cos^{-1}(\sin x) \geq 0$

$\Rightarrow |\cos^{-1}(\sin x)| = \cos^{-1}(\sin x)$ ...(ii)

Now $-1 \leq \cos x \leq 1$; $\sin^{-1}x \leq 0$ for $x \leq 0$

And $\sin^{-1}x \geq 0$ for $x \geq 0$

$$\therefore\ |\sin^{-1}(\cos x)| = \begin{cases} -\sin^{-1}(\cos x); \cos x \leq 0 \\ \sin^{-1}(\cos x); \cos x \geq 0 \end{cases} \quad ...(iii)$$

$\therefore$ Using (ii) and (iii) in (i), we get

$$y = \begin{cases} \cos^{-1}(\sin x) + \sin^{-1}(\cos x); \cos \leq 0 \\ \cos^{-1}(\sin x) - \sin^{-1}(\cos x); \cos \geq 0 \end{cases} \quad ...(iv)$$

Further given that $x \in \left[\frac{3\pi}{2}, 2\pi\right]$

$\Rightarrow \sin x \in [-1,0]$ and $\cos x \in [0,1]$

$\Rightarrow \cos x \geq 0$

$\therefore$ From (iv) $y = \cos^{-1}(\sin x) - \sin^{-1}(\cos x)$;

$x \in \left[\frac{3\pi}{2}, 2\pi\right]$

$$= \cos^{-1}\left[\cos\left(\frac{\pi}{2} - x\right)\right] - sin^{-1}\left[\sin\left(\frac{\pi}{2} - x\right)\right]$$

$$= \left\{\left(\frac{\pi}{2} - x\right) + 2\pi\right\} - \left\{-\left(\frac{\pi}{2} - x\right) - \pi\right\}$$

$$\left(\begin{array}{l} \because \cos^{-1}(\cos x) = x + 2\pi \text{ for } x \in [-2\pi, -\pi] \\ \text{and} \sin^{-1}(\sin x) = -x - \pi \text{ for } x \in \left[\frac{-3\pi}{2}, \frac{-\pi}{2}\right] \end{array}\right)$$

$$= \frac{5\pi}{2} - x + \frac{\pi}{2} - x + \pi = 4\pi - 2x$$

Bounded area is as shown below by shaded area

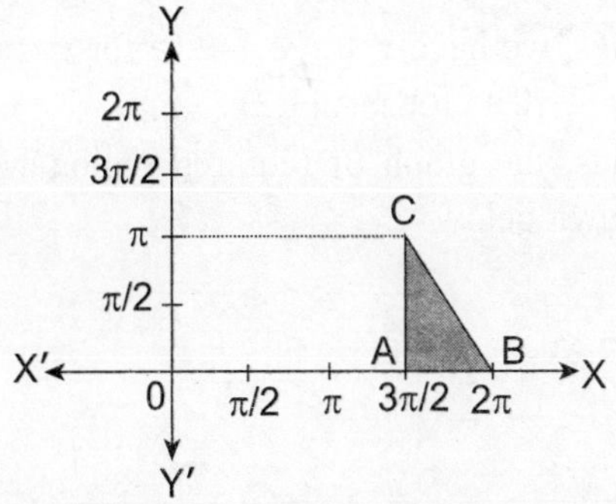

$= \text{area of } \Delta ABC = \frac{1}{2}(\pi/2) \times \pi = \pi^2/4$ square units

$= k\pi^2/4$ (given) $\Rightarrow k = 1$

$\therefore$ (a) → (i)

(b) Given circle is $x^2 + y^2 + 2x + 4y - 4 = 0 = 0$; having its centre at (–1,–2) and radius = 3 as shown below:

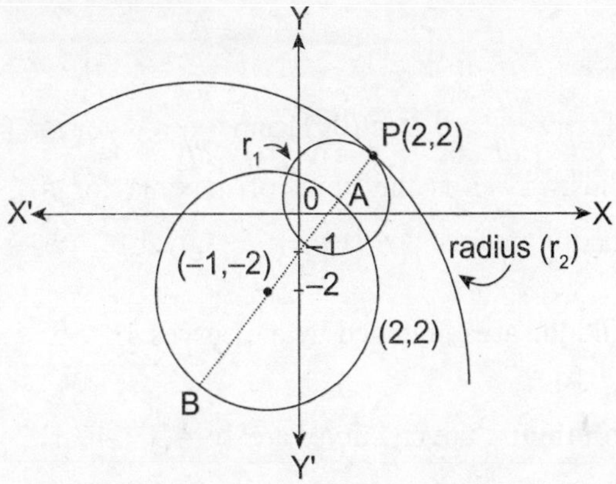

$\therefore$ Smallest circle having its centre on circumcentre and has radius $r_1 = AP$

and tanget circle having its centre on circumference and has radius $r_2 = BP$

$\therefore\ |r_2 - r_1| = (BP - AP) = AB = 6$

$\therefore$ (b) → (ii)

(c) $f(0) = 1$; $f(2) = 3$; $f'(2) = 5$

$$\text{Now, } I = \int_0^1 x f''(2x)\,dx = \left|\frac{x f'(2x)}{2}\right|_0^1 - \int_0^1 \frac{1.f'(2x)\,dx}{2}$$

$$= \frac{f'(2)}{2} - \frac{1}{2}\int_0^1 f'(2x)dx = \frac{f'(2)}{2} - \frac{1}{4}|f(2x)|_0^1$$

$$= \frac{f'(2)}{2} - \frac{1}{4}f(2) + \frac{1}{4}f(0) = \frac{5}{2} - \frac{3}{4} + \frac{1}{4} = 2$$

$\therefore$ (c) → (iii)

(d) $\because f^{-1}(y) = x \Rightarrow y = f(x)$

$\therefore\ f^{-1}(-4) = x \Rightarrow f(x) = -4$; $x = ?$

$\Rightarrow x^3 + 4x^2 + 6x + 4 = 0$

$\Rightarrow (x + 2)(x^2 + 2x + 2) = 0$

$\Rightarrow x = -2$ or $x = \frac{-2 \pm \sqrt{-4}}{2} \Rightarrow x = -2$ is the real root

$\therefore\ f^{-1}(-4) = -2 \qquad \therefore$ (d) → (iv)

Solved Integer Type

42. The maximum area of a rectangle whose two consecutive vertices lie on the x-axis and another two lie on the curve $y = e^{-|x|}$, is equal to ke^{-1}, then evaluate k

Solution: Let the rectangle be $ABCD$, with $A \equiv (t, 0)$, $B \equiv (t, e^{-t})$. $C \equiv (-t, e^{-t})$, $D \equiv (-t, 0)$; where $t \in R^+$. Area of rectangle $ABCD = 2t.e^{-t} = f(t)$ (say)

Now $\frac{df}{dt} = 2(t(-e^{-t}) + e^{t}) = 2e^{-t}(1 - t)$.

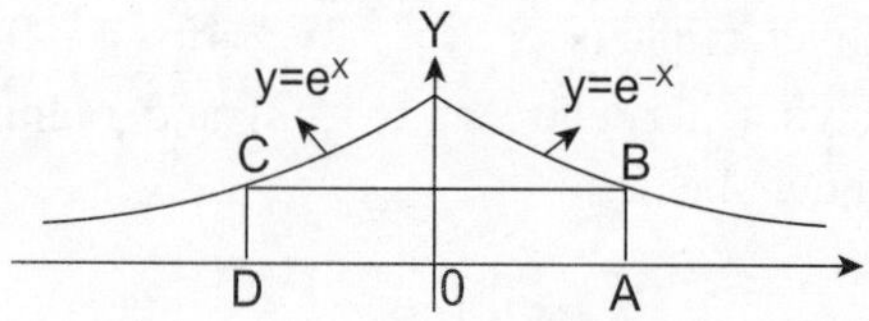

Clearly $\frac{df}{dt} > 0$, t ∈ (0, 1) and $\frac{df}{dt} < 0$ for $t \in (1, \infty)$. Thus, $t = 1$ is the point of maxima for $f(t)$. Thus, maximum area $= f(1) = \frac{2}{e} = \frac{k}{e}$ (given) $\Rightarrow k = 2$

43. Find the area bounded by the curves $4y = |x^2 - 4|$ and $y + |x| = 7$.

Solution: Given curves are $4y = |x^2 - 4|$ or

$$\Rightarrow y = \frac{1}{4}|x^2 - 4| = \begin{cases} \frac{1}{4}(x^2 - 4); x \le -2 \text{ or } x \ge 2 \\ -\frac{1}{4}(x^2 - 4); -2 < x \le 2 \end{cases} \quad \ldots\text{(i)}$$

and $y + |x| = 7$

$$\Rightarrow y = 7 - |x| \begin{cases} 7 - x \text{ for } x \le 0 \\ 7 + x \text{ for } x < 0 \end{cases} \quad \ldots\text{(ii)}$$

Curve (i) and (ii) intersect each other for $x \le 0$ where $\frac{1}{4}(x^2 - 4) = 7 - x$

$\Rightarrow x^2 - 4 + 4x - 28 = 0$; $x^2 + 4x - 32 = 0$

$\Rightarrow (x + 8)(x - 4) = 0$

$\Rightarrow x = 4$

Similarly curve (i) and (ii) intersect each other for $x < 0$, where $x = -4$

The graph of curves (i) and (ii) will be as shown below:

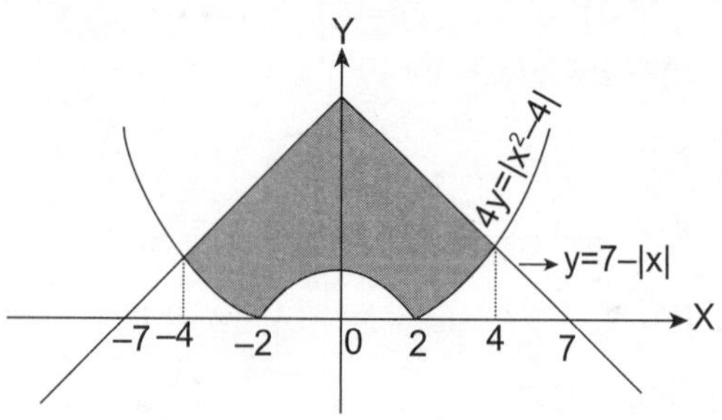

∴ required area

$$= 2\left(\int_0^2 \left(7 - x - \left(\frac{4 - x^2}{4}\right)\right) dx + \int_2^4 \left(7 - x - \left(\frac{x^2 - 4}{4}\right)\right) dx\right)$$

$$= 2\left(\int_0^2 \left(6 - x - \frac{x^2}{4}\right) dx + \int_2^4 \left(8 - x - \frac{x^2}{4}\right) dx\right)$$

$$= 2\left(6x - \frac{x^2}{2} + \frac{x^3}{12}\right)_0^2 + 2\left(8x - \frac{x^2}{2} - \frac{x^3}{12}\right)_2^4 = 32 \text{ sq. units.}$$

44. A point 'P' moves in xy plane in such a way that $[|x|] + [|y|] = 1$, where [.] denotes the greatest integer function, then find the area of the region representing all possible positions of the point 'P'.

Solution: Clearly $[|x|] = 1$, $[|y|] = 0$

$\Rightarrow 1 \le |x| < 2$, $0 \le |y| < 1$

$\Rightarrow x \in (-2, -1] \cup [1, 2)$, $y \in (-1, 1)$

or $[|x|] = 0$, $[|y|] = 1$

$\Rightarrow 0 \le |x| < 1$ and $1 \le |y| < 2$

$\Rightarrow y \in (-2, -1] \cup [1, 2)$

i.e., $x \in (-1, 1)$ and $y \in (-2, -1) \cup [1, 2]$

∴ These points would represent the area as shown below by shaded region

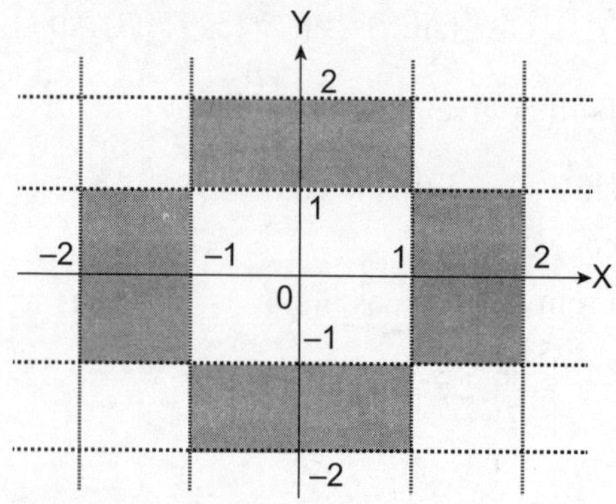

∴ Area of required region = 4(2 – 1) (1 – (–1)) = 8sq. units

45. A point 'P' moves in xy plane in such a way that $[x + y + 1] = [x]$, where [.] represents the greatest integer function, and $x \in (0, 2)$. Find the area of the region representing all possible positions of the point 'P'.

Solution: $[x + y + 1] = [x] \Rightarrow [x + y] + 1 = [x]$.

If $x \in (0, 1) \Rightarrow [x] = 0 \Rightarrow [x + y] = -1$

$\Rightarrow -1 \le x + y < 0$; If $x \in (1, 2)$

$\Rightarrow [x] = 1 \Rightarrow [x + y] = 0 \Rightarrow 0 \le x + y < 1$

Thus, we have $x + y \in [-2, 0)$ for $x \in (0,1)$ and $x + y \in [0,1)$ for $x \in [1,2)$

Thus, the graph of required region would be as shown below

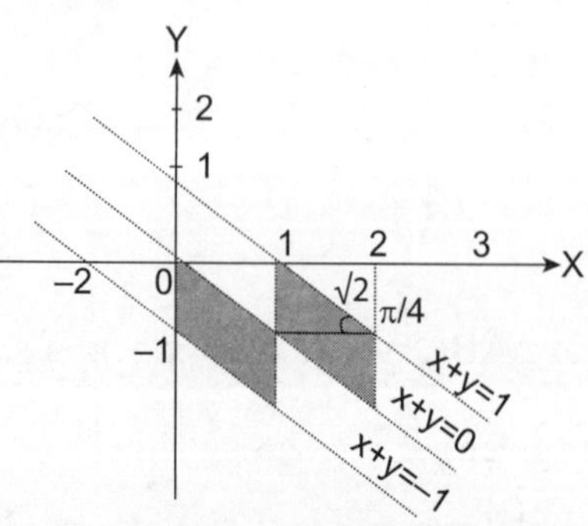

Shaded region represents all possible positions of point 'P'.

It's area $= 4\left(\frac{1}{2}.1.\sqrt{2}\sin\frac{\pi}{4}\right) = 2$ sq. units.

46. A point $P(x, y)$ moves in xy plane in such a way that $\sqrt{2} \le |x+y| + |x-y| \le 2\sqrt{2}$. Find the area of the region representing all possible positions of the point 'P'

Solution: If we replace x by $-x$, then there will be no change in inequality. Thus, the region is symmetric about y-axis. Similiarly the region is symmetric about x-axis. Let $x + y \ge 0$ and $x - y \ge 0$

$\Rightarrow \sqrt{2} \le x + y + x - y \le 2\sqrt{2} \Rightarrow \frac{1}{\sqrt{2}} \le x \le \sqrt{2}$

Thus, in this case the region will be as represented below

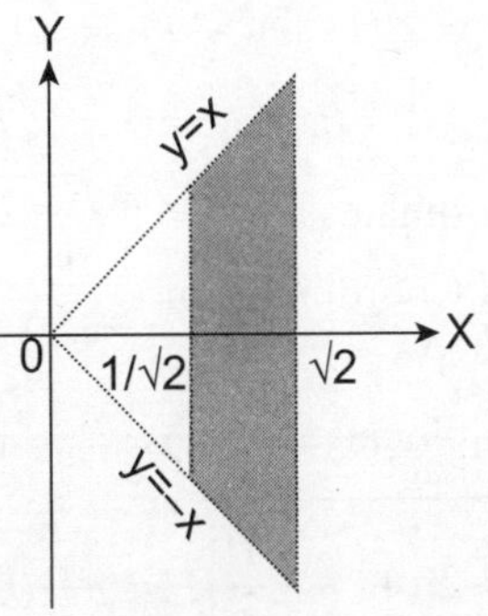

∴ By symmetry, the total required region will be as shown below.

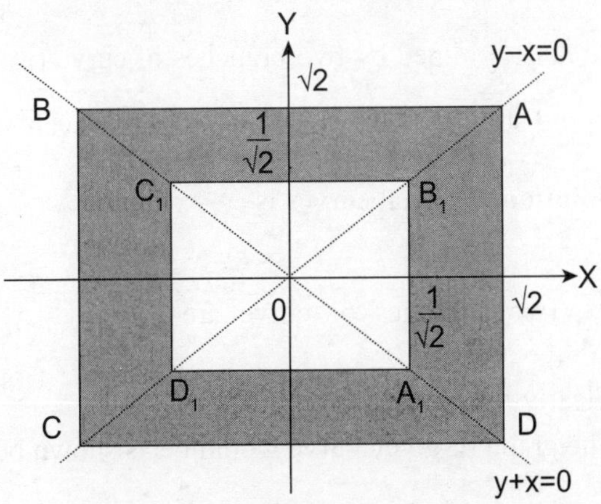

The shaded region represents all positions of point P. It's area is equal to area of $\angle ABCD$ – area of $\angle A_1B_1C_1D_1 = (2\sqrt{2})^2 - (\sqrt{2})^2$, i.e., 6 square units

47. Consider a rectangle $ABCD$ formed by the points $A \equiv (0, 0)$, $B \equiv (6, 0)$, $C \equiv (6, 4)$ and $D \equiv (0, 4)$. $P(x, y)$ is a moving interior point of the rectangle, moving in such a way that $d(P, AB) <$ mini. $\{d(P, BC), d(P, CD), d(P, AD)\}$. Here $d(P, AB)$, $d(P, BC)$, $d(P, CD)$ and $d(P, AD)$ represents the distances of the point P from the sides AB, BC, CD and AD respectively. Find the area of the region representing all possible positions of the point P

Solution: Given the coordinates of $P \equiv (x, y)$ the interior point of rectangle $ABCD$

$d(P, AB) = y$, $d(P, BC) = 6 - x$,

$d(P, CD) = 4 - y$, $d(P, AD) = x$,

We must have $y \le 6 - x$, $y \le 4 - y$, $y \le x$

$\Rightarrow x + y \le 6$, $y \le 2$, $y \le x$

∴ Shaded region represents the required area as shown below

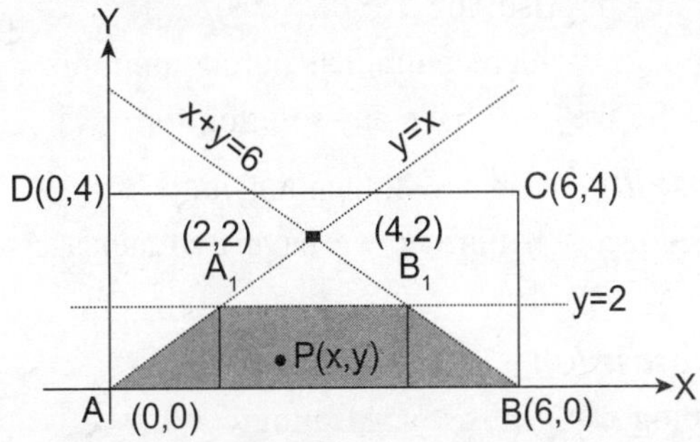

This area is equal to area of trapezium ABB_1A_1A

$= \frac{1}{2}(6 + 2).2 = 8$ sq. units

48. In last questions, if the point P moves in such a way that $d(P, AB) \ge$ maxi. $\{d(P, BC), d(P, CD), d(P, DA)\}$, then find the area of the region, representing all possible positions of the point P.

Solution: In this case, we must have, $y \ge x$, $x + y \ge 6$, $y \ge 2$. Shaded region represents the required area.

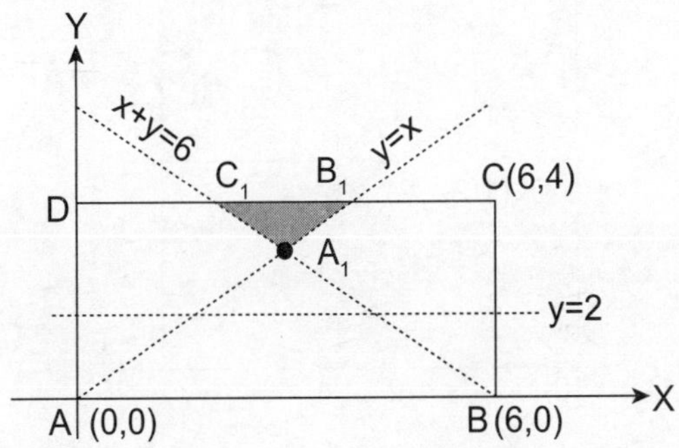

For $A_1 : y = x = 6 - x \Rightarrow x = 3, y = 3$

$\Rightarrow A_1 \equiv (3, 3)$, $B_1 \equiv (4, 4)$, $C_1 \equiv (2, 4)$.

∴ required area = area of $\Delta_{A_1B_1C_1} = \frac{1}{2}.2.1$

= 1 square units.

49. Find eight times the area of the region bounded by the point $P(x, y)$ satisfying $\log_x \log_y x > 0$ and $\frac{1}{2} < x < 2$

Solution: Let us analyse for two cases

Case I: If $\frac{1}{2} < x < 1$

$\log_x \log_y x > 0 \Rightarrow 0 < \log_y x < 1$

Now there arises two sub cases for the values of y

Subcase(a) if $0 < y < 1$,

then $\log_y x < 1 \Rightarrow x > y$

also $\log_y x > 0 \Rightarrow x < 1$

Thus, we have $0 < y < 1$, $\frac{1}{2} < x < 1$ and $x > y$ ...(i)

Subcase(b) : If $y > 1$, then $\log_y x < 1$

$\Rightarrow x < y$; Also, $\log_y x > 0$

$\Rightarrow x > 1$ which contradicts our assumption.

So we don't have any solution for $y > 1$

Case II: If $1 < x < 2$, then $\log_x \log_y x > 0$

$\Rightarrow \log_y x > 1$. Further we have two subcases for the values of y.

Subcase (a): If $0 < y < 1$

So $\log_y x > 1 \Rightarrow x < y$; Also $\log_y x > 0$

$\Rightarrow x < 1$ which contradicts our assumption.

Subcase(b): If $y > 1$

So $\log_y x > 1 \Rightarrow x > y$

Also $\log_y x > 0 \Rightarrow x > 1$.

So we have $1 < x < 2$; $y > 1$ and $x > y$ ...(ii)

Thus, we conclude $P(x, y)$ will lie in the region satisfying (i) and (ii)

So the region of $P(x, y)$ is shown in the figure given below

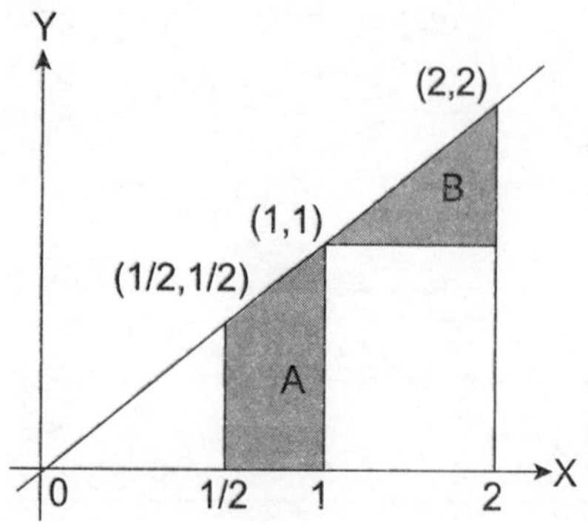

Thus, the area of the shaded region

$$= A + B = \frac{1}{2}\left(\frac{1}{2}+1\right)\left(\frac{1}{2}\right) + \frac{1}{2}(1)(1) = \frac{3}{8} + \frac{1}{2} = \frac{7}{8} \text{ sq. units.}$$

$\therefore$ eight times the area of bounded region = 7 square units.

50. Two circles of radii 'a' and 'b' touching externally are inscribed in the area bounded by $y = \sqrt{1-x^2}$ and x-axis. If $b = \frac{1}{2}$ and $a = \frac{1}{k}$, then find k.

Solution: $y = \sqrt{1-x^2}$ represents upper half of circle $x^2 + y^2 = 1$. Let C_1 and C_2 be the centers of circles with radius 'a'

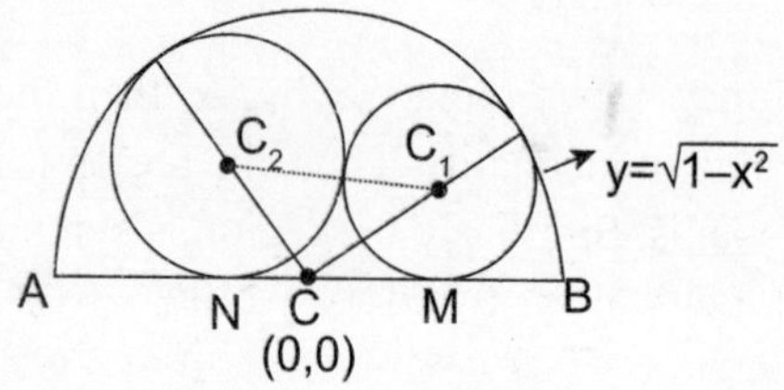

Now , $AC = BC = 1$

Let $r_1 = a$, $r_2 = b$

Now $CC_1 = 1 - a$, $C_1M = a$

$\Rightarrow CM = \sqrt{(1-a)^2 - a^2} = \sqrt{1-2a}$

$CC_2 = 1 - b$, $C_2N = b \Rightarrow CN = \sqrt{1-2b}$

$\therefore$ Coordinates of $C_1 \equiv (\sqrt{1-2a}, a)$

And Coordinates of $C_2 \equiv (-\sqrt{1-2b}, b)$

$= (0, 1/2)$ ($\because b = 1/2$ given)

Using $C_1C_2 = r_1 + r_2$

$$\Rightarrow \sqrt{1-2a+\left(a-\frac{1}{2}\right)^2} = a + b$$

$$\Rightarrow \sqrt{1-2a+\left(a-\frac{1}{2}\right)^2} = a + \frac{1}{2} \Rightarrow a = \frac{1}{4} \Rightarrow k = 4$$

51. Area determined by two branches of curve $(y - x)^2 = x^3$ and straight line $x = 1$ is $\frac{\lambda}{\lambda+1}$. Then evaluate λ

Solution: Given curves is $(y - x)^2 = x^3$

$\Rightarrow y - x = \pm x^{3/2}$ $\Rightarrow t = x \pm x^{3/2}$

$\therefore$ Two branches of curve are $y = x - x^{3/2}$ and $y = x + x^{3/2}$

Clearly for $x > 0$, $x + x^{3/2} > x - x^{3/2}$

The graph of given curve would be as shown below:

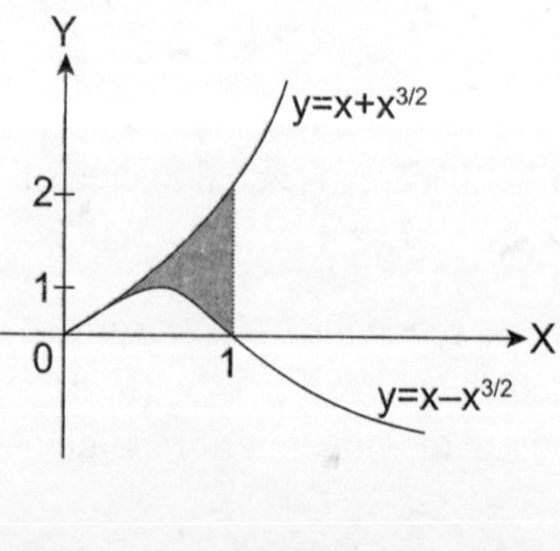

$\therefore$ Required area $A = \int_0^1 [(x + x^{3/2}) - (x - x^{3/2})]\, dx$

$= 2\int_0^1 x^{3/2} dx = 2\left(\frac{2}{5}\right) = \frac{4}{5} = \frac{\lambda}{\lambda+1}$ (given)

$\Rightarrow \lambda = 5$

52. Let $f : \mathbb{R} \to \mathbb{R}$ defined as $f(x)=\begin{cases} |x-[x]| & ; when [x] is\ odd \\ |x-[x]-1| & ; when [x] is\ even \end{cases}$. where [.] denotes greatest integer function. What will be the area bounded by the curve $y = f(x)$, x-axis with in $x \in [0, 4]$?

Solution: $f(x)=\begin{cases} |\{x\}| & ; [x] is\ odd \\ |\{x\}-1| & ; [x] is\ even \end{cases}$

$= \begin{cases} \{x\};[x]\text{is odd} \\ \{x\}-1;\{x\}\geq 1;[x]\text{is even} \\ 1-\{x\};\{x\}<1;[x]\text{ is even} \end{cases}$

But $\{x\} \not\geq 1$

$\Rightarrow f(x) = \begin{cases} \{x\};[x]\text{is odd} \\ 1-\{x\};[x]\text{is even} \end{cases} = \begin{cases} 1-x;0\leq x<1 \\ x-1;1\leq x<2 \\ 3-x;2\leq x<3 \\ x-3;3\leq x<4 \end{cases}$

Thus, the graph of $f(x)$ for $x \in [0,4]$ would be as shown below.

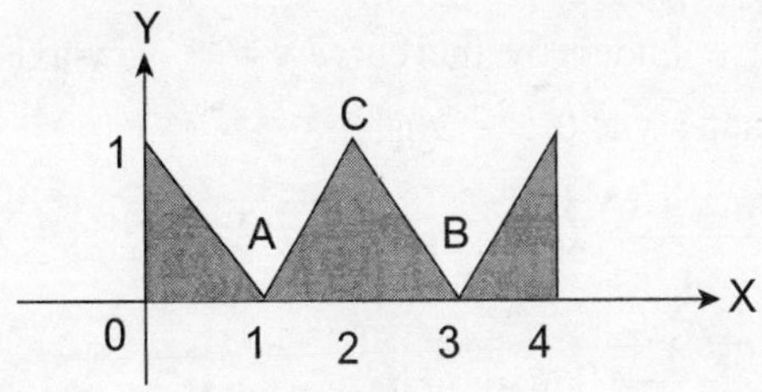

$\therefore$ Required area $= 2(ar\Delta ABC) = 2.\frac{1}{2}(2)(1) = 2$ square units.

TUTORIAL EXERCISE

SECTION–III

ONLY ONE COREECT ANSWER

1. Area bounded by the curve $y = xe^{x^2}$, x-axis and the ordinates $x = 0$, $x = a$ is
(a) $\frac{e^{a^2}-1}{2}$ Square unit
(b) $\frac{e^{a^2}+1}{2}$ Square unit
(c) $(e^{a^2}+1)$ Square unit
(d) $(e^{a^2}-1)$ Square unit

2. The area bounded by the x-axis, the curve $y = f(x)$ and the lines $x = 1$, $x = b$ is equal to $\sqrt{b^2+1}-\sqrt{2}$ for all $b > 1$, then $f(x)$ is
(a) $\sqrt{x-1}$ (b) $\sqrt{x+1}$
(c) $\sqrt{x^2+1}$ (d) $\frac{x}{\sqrt{1+x^2}}$

3. The area bounded by the curve $y = f(x)$, x-axis and ordinates $x = 1$ and $x = b$ is $(b - 1)\sin(3b + 4)$, then $f(x)$ is
(a) $3(x-1)\cos(3x + 4) + \sin(3x + 4)$
(b) $(b - 1)\sin(3x + 4) + 3\cos(3x + 4)$
(c) $(b - 1)\cos(3x + 4) + 3\sin(3x + 4)$
(d) None of these

4. Area bounded by the curve $xy - 3x - 2y - 10 = 0$, x–axis and the lines $x = 3$, $x = 4$ is
(a) $16 \log 2 - 13$ (b) $16 \log 2 - 3$
(c) $16 \log 2 + 3$ (d) None of these

5. Area bounded by the curves $y^2(2a - x) = x^3$ and the line $x = 2a$ is:
(a) $3\pi a^2$ (b) $\frac{3\pi a^2}{2}$
(c) $\frac{3\pi a^2}{4}$ (d) None of these

6. If the ordinate $x = a$ divides the area bounded by the curve $y = 1+\frac{8}{x^2}$ and the ordinates $x = 2$, $x = 4$ into two equal parts, then a is equal to
(a) $2\sqrt{3}$ (b) $2\sqrt{2}$
(c) 3 (d) None of these

7. The latus rectum of the parabola $y^2 = 4ax$ for which the area bounded by the curve and the double ordinate $x = 6$ is three times the area bounded by the curve and the double ordinate through the focus is
(a) 2 (b) $2\sqrt[3]{3}$
(c) $8\sqrt[3]{3}$ (d) None of these

8. If the area bounded by the curves $y^2 = 4ax$ and $y = mx$ is $\frac{a^2}{3}$, then the value of m is
(a) 2 (b) –2
(c) 1/2 (d) None of these

9. The area of the triangle formed by the tangent to the hyperbola $xy = a^2$ and co-ordinate axes is
(a) a^2 (b) $2a^2$
(c) $3a^2$ (d) $4a^2$

10. If $f(x) = \begin{cases} \sqrt{\{x\}}; & x \notin \mathbb{Z} \\ 1; & x \in \mathbb{Z} \end{cases}$ and $g(x) = \{x\}^2$, (where {.} denotes fractional part of x), then area bounded by $f(x)$ and $g(x)$ for $x \in [0, 10]$ is
(a) 5/3 (b) 5
(c) 10/3 (d) None of these

11. Let $f(x) = x^2$, $g(x) = \cos x$ and α, β $(\alpha < \beta)$ be the roots of the equation $18x^2 - 9\pi x + \pi^2 = 0$. Then the area bounded by the curves $y = fog(x)$, the ordinates $x = \alpha$, $x = \beta$ and the x-axis is
(a) $\frac{1}{2}(\pi-3)$ (b) $\frac{\pi}{3}$
(c) $\frac{\pi}{4}$ (d) $\frac{\pi}{12}$

12. Area included between the parabolas $y = \frac{x^2}{4a}$; $a > 0$ and the curve $y = \frac{8a^3}{x^2+4a^2}$; $a > 0$ is
(a) $\frac{a^2}{3}(6\pi-4)$ (b) $\frac{a^2}{3}(4\pi+3)$
(c) $\frac{a^2}{3}(8\pi+3)$ (d) None of these

13. The value of b; ($b > 0$) so that the area of the bounded region enclosed between the parabolas $y = x - bx^2$ and $y = \frac{x^2}{b}$ is maximum, is

(a) 1 (b) 2
(c) 3 (d) 4

14. Area bounded by the curve $xy^2 = a^2(a - x)$ and y-axis is

(a) $\pi a^2/2$ (b) πa^2
(c) $3\pi a^2$ (d) None of these

15. The area bounded by $y = x^2$ and $y = x^3/3$ is.

(a) 9/5 (b) 9/4
(c) 9 (d) None of these

16. The area bounded by the curve $y = x^4 - 2x^3 + x^2 + 3$, the axis of abscissas and two ordinates corresponding to the points of minima of the function $y(x)$ is

(a) $\frac{91}{30}$ square units (b) $\frac{93}{30}$ square units
(c) $\frac{1}{30}$ square units (d) None of these

17. If A_n is the area bounded by $y = (1 - x^2)^n$ and coordinate axes, $n \in \mathbb{N}$, then

(a) $A_n = A_{n-1}$ (b) $A_n < A_{n-1}$
(c) $A_n > A_{n-1}$ (d) $A_n = 2A_{n-1}$

18. The area bounded by the curve $y^2 + x^4 = x^2$ is

(a) $\frac{2}{3}$ (b) $\frac{4}{3}$
(c) $\frac{8}{3}$ (d) None of these

19. The area bounded by $x^2 + y^2 - 2x = 0$ and $y = \sin\frac{\pi x}{2}$ in the upper half of the circle is

(a) $\frac{\pi}{2} - \frac{4}{\pi}$ (b) $\frac{\pi}{4} - \frac{2}{\pi}$
(c) $\pi - \frac{8}{\pi}$ (d) None of these

20. The area from 1 to x under a certain graph is given by $A = (1 + 3x)^{1/2} - 1$, $x \geq 0$. The average value of y w.r. t. x as x increases from 0 to 8 is:

(a) $\frac{3}{7}$ (b) $\frac{1}{2}$
(c) $\frac{3}{8}$ (d) $\frac{4}{7}$

21. The area included between the curve $xy^2 = a^2(a - x)$ and its asymptote is:

(a) $\frac{\pi a^2}{2}$ (b) $2\pi a^2$
(c) πa^2 (d) None of these

22. Area bounded by the curves $y = \left[\frac{x^2}{64} + 2\right]$, $y = x - 1$ and $x = 0$ above x-axis is ([.] denotes the greatest integer function) is

(a) 2 (b) 3
(c) 4 (d) None of these

23. The area of the region bounded by the curve $a^4 y^2 = (2a - x) x^5$ is to that of the circle whose radius is a, is given by the ratio

(a) 5 : 4 (b) 5 : 8
(c) 2 : 3 (d) 3 : 2

24. The area bounded by the curves $y = x(1 - \ln x)$ $x = e^{-1}$ and a positive x-axis between $x = e^{-1}$ and $x = e$ is:

(a) $\left(\frac{e^2 - 4e^{-2}}{5}\right)$ (b) $\left(\frac{e^2 - 5e^{-2}}{4}\right)$
(c) $\left(\frac{4e^2 - e^{-2}}{5}\right)$ (d) $\left(\frac{5e^2 - e^{-2}}{4}\right)$

25. The positive values of the parameter 'a' for which the area of the figure bounded by the curve $y = \cos ax$, $y = 0$, $x = \frac{\pi}{6a}$, $x = \frac{5\pi}{6a}$ is greater than 3 constitute the set:

(a) ϕ (b) (0, 1/3)
(c) $(3, \infty)$ (d) None of these

26. Let $f(x)$ be a continuous function such that the area bounded by the curve $y = f(x)$, the x-axis and the two ordinates $x = 0$ and $x = a$ is $\frac{a^2}{2} + \frac{a}{2}\sin a + \frac{\pi}{2}\cos a$, then $f(\pi/2)$ is

(a) 1/2 (b) $\frac{\pi^2}{8} + \frac{\pi}{4}$
(c) $\frac{\pi + 1}{2}$ (d) None of these

27. Let $f(x) = x - x^2$ and $g(x) = ax$. If the region above the graph of g and below the graph of f has an area equal to 9/2, then 'a' is equal to

(a) 2 (b) 4
(c) −2 (d) 3

28. The area of the figure bounded by the curve $(y - x - 2)^2 = 9x$, y-axis and x-axis is

(a) $\frac{1}{2}$ (b) $\frac{3}{4}$
(c) 1 (d) None of these

29. The slope of the tangent to curve $y = f(x)$ at any of its point is given by $2x - 4$. If the curve passes through the point $(-2, 12)$, then the area of the region bounded by the curve, the x-axis and the line $x + 1 = 0$ is

(a) 3/7 (b) 7/3
(c) 1/7 (d) None of these

30. The ratio in which the curve $y = x^2$ divides the region bounded by the curve ; $y = \sin\left(\frac{\pi x}{2}\right)$ and the x-axis as x varies from 0 to 1, is:

(a) $2 : \pi$ (b) $1 : 3$
(c) $3 : \pi$ (d) $(6 - \pi) : \pi$

31. A figure is bounded by the curves $y = x^2 + 6x + 9$ and the co-ordinate axes. The angles which the straight lines passing through the point (0, 9) must make with positive semi axes so that they partition the figure into three parts of equal areas are

(a) $\cos^{-1}\frac{27}{2}$ and $\cos^{-1}\frac{27}{4}$
(b) $\sin^{-1}\frac{27}{2}$ and $\sin^{-1}\frac{27}{4}$
(c) $\tan^{-1}\frac{27}{2}$ and $\tan^{-1}\frac{27}{4}$
(d) None of these

32. The area of the region bounded by the curve $y^2 = -x - 16$, the x-axis and the tangent drawn to the curve from the origin is

(a) $\frac{3}{64}$ (b) $\frac{64}{3}$
(c) $\frac{1}{3}$ (d) $\frac{1}{64}$

33. Consider the graph of continuous function $y = f(x)$ for $x \in [a - b, a + b]$ $a, b \in R^+$ and $b > a$. If the origin is shifted to $(a + b, 0)$ such that new axes are parallel to the old axes, then the area bounded by the given curve, the X-axis and the new ordinates $X = -a$, $X = -b$ can be written as

(a) $\int_{\frac{b-a}{2}}^{\frac{a+b}{2}} f(x)\, dx$ (b) $\int_{-a}^{-b} f(x) dx$
(c) $\int_{a}^{b} f(a+b-x) dx$ (d) $\frac{1}{2}\int_{a-b}^{a+b} f(x)\, dx$

34. P is any point inside or on the boundary of ΔABC having perimeter p and area Δ. R is any point in the plane of $\Delta\, ABC$ such that $PR \leq 5$. The area of the region in which the point R lies is

(a) $25\pi + 5p + \Delta$ (b) $5\pi + 25p + \Delta$
(c) $5\pi + 5p + \Delta$ (d) $5(\pi + p) + 25\Delta$

35. The area bounded by $y = f(x)$, x-axis and the line $y = 1$, where $f(x) = 1 + \frac{1}{x}\int_1^x f(t)\, dt$ is

(a) $2(e + 1)$ (b) $2\left(1 - \frac{1}{e}\right)$
(c) $2(e - 1)$ (d) None of these

36. The area bounded by the curves $y = \frac{\sin x}{e^x}$ $\forall\ x \in [0, 2\pi]$ and the axes of abscissae

(a) $\frac{e^{-2\pi}}{2} - e^{-\pi} + \frac{1}{2}$ (b) $\frac{e^{-2\pi}}{2} + e^{-\pi} - \frac{1}{2}$
(c) $\frac{e^{-2\pi}}{2} + e^{-\pi} + \frac{1}{2}$ (d) None of these

37. The area bounded by the curves $y = \sin^{-1}|\sin x|$ and $y = (\sin^{-1}|\sin x|)^2$, $0 \leq x \leq 2\pi$ is

(a) $\left(\frac{\pi^3}{3} + \frac{4}{3}\right)$ square unit
(b) $\left(\frac{\pi^3}{6} - \frac{\pi^2}{2} + \frac{4}{3}\right)$ square unit
(c) $\left(\frac{\pi^2}{2} - \frac{4}{3}\right)$ square unit
(d) $\left(\frac{\pi^3}{6} - \frac{\pi}{4} + \frac{4}{3}\right)$ square unit

38. Let Z be a complex number such that $Re(Z) = \sqrt{x^2 + 4}$, and $\ell m\ (Z) = \sqrt{y - 4}$ satisfying $|Z| = \sqrt{10}$. Area enclosed by the set of points (x, y) on the complex plane, is

(a) $8\sqrt{6}$ (b) $4\sqrt{6}$
(c) $\frac{20\sqrt{10}}{3}$ (d) $\frac{40\sqrt{10}}{3}$

39. The area bounded by $y = x^2$ and $y = [x + 1]$, where [ ] stands for greatest integer function, $x \leq 1$ and the y-axis is

(a) 1 (b) 2/3
(c) 1/3 (d) None of these

40. If A_1 is the area enclosed by the curve $xy = 1$, x-axis and the ordinates $x = 1$, $x = 2$; and A_2 is the area enclosed by the curve $xy = 1$, x-axis and the coordinates $x = 2$, $x = 4$; then

(a) $A_2 = 2A_1$ (b) $A_1 = 2A_2$
(c) $A_2 = 3A_1$ (d) $A_1 = A_2$

41. The triangle formed by the tangent to the curve $f(x) = x^2 + bx - b$ at the point (1, 1) and the coordinates axes, lies in the first quadrant. If its area is 2, then the value of b is

(a) – 1 (b) 3

(c) – 3 (d) 1

42. The area of the region between the curves $y=\sqrt{\dfrac{1+\sin x}{\cos x}}$ and $y=\sqrt{\dfrac{1-\sin x}{\cos x}}$ bounded by the lines $x = 0$ and $x=\dfrac{\pi}{4}$ is

(a) $\int_0^{\sqrt{2}-1}\dfrac{t}{(1+t^2)\sqrt{1-t^2}}dt$

(b) $\int_0^{\sqrt{2}-1}\dfrac{4t}{(1+t^2)\sqrt{1-t^2}}dt$

(c) $\int_0^{\sqrt{2}+1}\dfrac{4t}{(1+t^2)\sqrt{1-t^2}}dt$

(d) $\int_0^{\sqrt{2}+1}\dfrac{t}{(1+t^2)\sqrt{1-t^2}}dt$

43. The area contained between the x-axis and one arc of the curve $y = \cos 9x$ is:

(a) $\dfrac{1}{3}$ (b) $\dfrac{2}{3}$

(c) $\dfrac{2}{7}$ (d) $\dfrac{2}{9}$

44. The area bounded by $y = 4 - x^2$ and $y=\left[3+\dfrac{x^2}{4}\right]$ is, (where [.] is *G. I. F.*):

(a) 1 square unit (b) $\dfrac{1}{3}$ square units

(c) $\dfrac{2}{3}$ square units (d) $\dfrac{4}{3}$ square units

45. Let $f(x)$ be a non-negative continuous function such that the area bounded by the curve $y = f(x)$, x-axis and the ordinates $x=\dfrac{\pi}{4}$ and $x=\beta>\dfrac{\pi}{4}$ is $\left(\beta\sin\beta+\dfrac{\pi}{4}\cos\beta+\sqrt{2}\beta\right)$. Then $f\left(\dfrac{\pi}{2}\right)$ is

(a) $\left(1-\dfrac{\pi}{4}-\sqrt{2}\right)$ (b) $\left(1-\dfrac{\pi}{4}+\sqrt{2}\right)$

(c) $\left(\dfrac{\pi}{4}+\sqrt{2}-1\right)$ (d) $\left(\dfrac{\pi}{4}-\sqrt{2}+1\right)$

46. If the ordinate $x = a$ divides the area bounded by the curve $y=1+\dfrac{8}{x^2}$ and the ordinates $x = 2$, $x = 4$ into two equal parts, then a is equal to

(a) $2\sqrt{3}$ (b) $2\sqrt{2}$

(c) 3 (d) None of these

47. Area enclosed by the curve $x = a\cos^3 t$, $y = a\sin^3 t$, $0 \le t \le 2\pi$

(a) $\dfrac{3}{2}a^2\pi$ (b) $\dfrac{3}{4}a^2\pi$

(c) $\dfrac{3}{8}a^2\pi$ (d) None of these

48. Area of the loop of the curve $x = a(1 - t^2)$, $y = at(1 - t^2)$, $-1 \le t \le 1$ must be

(a) $\dfrac{2}{15}a^2$ (b) $\dfrac{4}{15}a^2$

(c) $\dfrac{8}{15}a^2$ (d) $\dfrac{a^2}{5}$

49. The area of the curve $x = 2\cos t$, $y = 2\sin t$ must be

(a) 4π (b) 2π

(c) 8π (d) None of these

SECTION–IV

MORE THAN ONE COREECT ANSWER

1. The equation $(y - x - 2)^2 = 9x$ represents a curve:

(a) Which is an ellipse?

(b) Which cuts the x-axis at two distinct points?

(c) Which touches the y-axis

(d) Which encloses an area equal to unity with the co-ordinate axes.

2. The area bounded between the curves $x^2 = y$ and $y^2 = x$ is equal to

(a) Area of the region $\{(x, y) : x^2 \le y \le |x|\}$

(b) 1/3

(c) $2\int_0^1 (x-x^2)\,dx$

(d) None of these

3. The area of quadrilateral, combined equation of whose sides are $(x^2 - y^2)(x^2 - y^2 - 8x + 16) = 0$, is

(a) 8 (b) >5

(c) $2\sqrt{2}$ (d) 9

4. If $A\left(\frac{3}{\sqrt{2}},\sqrt{2}\right)$, $B\left(\frac{-3}{\sqrt{2}},\sqrt{2}\right)$, $C\left(\frac{-3}{\sqrt{2}},-\sqrt{2}\right)$ and $D(3\cos\theta, 2\sin\theta)$ are four points, then the value of θ for which the area of quadrilateral ABCD is maximum, $\left(\frac{3\pi}{2} \le \theta \le 2\pi\right)$ is

(a) $2\pi - \sin^{-1}\frac{1}{3}$ (b) $\frac{7\pi}{4}$

(c) $2\pi - \cos^{-1}\frac{3}{\sqrt{85}}$ (d) $\tan\left(\tan^{-1}\frac{17\pi}{4}\right)$

5. The value (s) of 'a' for which the area of the triangle included between the axes and any tangent to the curve $x^a y = \lambda^a$ is constant, is / are

(a) $-\frac{1}{2}$ (b) -1

(c) $\frac{1}{2}$ (d) 1

6. Let f and g be continuous function on $a \le x \le b$ and set $p(x) = \max\{f(x), g(x)\}$ and $q(x) = \min\{f(x), g(x)\}$, the area bounded by the curves $y = p(x)$, $y = q(x)$ and the ordinates $x = a$ and $x = b$ is given by

(a) $\int_a^b (f(x)-g(x))dx$ (b) $\int_a^b (p(x)-q(x))dx$

(c) $\int_a^b |p(x)-q(x)|dx$ (d) $\int_a^b |f(x)-g(x)|dx$

7. Family of curves whose tangent at a point with its intersection with the curve $xy = c^2$ form an angle of $\frac{\pi}{4}$ is

(a) $y^2 - 2xy - x^2 = k$

(b) $y^2 + 2xy - x^2 = k$

(c) $y = x - 2c\tan^{-1}\left(\frac{x}{c}\right) + k$

(d) $y = c\ln\left|\frac{c+x}{c-x}\right| - x + k$

Where k is an arbitrary constant.

8. The area bounded by a curve, the axis of co-ordinates and the ordinate of some point of the curve is equal to the length of the corresponding arc of the curve. If the curve passes through the point $P(0, 1)$ then the equation of this curve can be

(a) $y = \frac{1}{2}(e^x - e^{-x} + 2)$ (b) $y = \frac{1}{2}(e^x + e^{-x})$

(c) $y = 1$ (d) $y = \frac{2}{e^x + e^{-x}}$

9. Let $f(x) = |x| - 2$ and $g(x) = |f(x)|$. Now area bounded by x-axis and $f(x)$ is A_1 and area bounded by x-axis and $g(x)$ is A_2 then

(a) $A_1 = 3$

(b) $A_1 = A_2$

(c) $A_2 = 4$

(d) $A_1 + A_2 = 8$

10. Let L: $x - y - 1 = 0$ be a line and $C : y^2 = 2x + 1$ be a parabola, then

(a) Area bounded by L and C lying in the upper half plane is $\frac{32}{3}$

(b) Area bounded by L and C lying in the plane is $\frac{16}{3}$

(c) Area bounded by L and C in the upper half plane is $\frac{9}{2}$

(d) Area bounded by L and C in the lower half plane is $\frac{5}{6}$

11. If $C_1 \equiv y = \frac{1}{1+x^2}$ and $C_2 \equiv y = \frac{x^2}{2}$ be two curve lying in XY plane. Then

(a) Area bounded by curve $y = \frac{1}{1+x^2}$ and $y = 0$ is π

(b) Area bounded by C_1 and C_2 is $\frac{\pi}{2} - \frac{1}{3}$

(c) Area bounded by C_1 and C_2 is $1 - \frac{\pi}{2}$

(d) Area bounded by curve $y = \frac{1}{1+x^2}$ and x-axis is $\frac{\pi}{2}$

12. Area of the region bounded by the curve $y = e^x$ and lines $x = 0$ and $y = e$ is

(a) $e - 1$ (b) $\int_1^e \ell n(e+1-y)\,dy$

(c) $e - \int_0^1 e^x dx$ (d) $\int_1^e \ell n\, y\, dy$

14. Which statement/statements is/are correct

(a) Area enclosed by the curve $\max(|x + y|, |x - y|) = 1$ is 2

(b) Area enclosed by the curve $\max(|x|, |y|) = 1$ is 4

(c) Area enclosed by the curve $\max(|2x|, |2y|) = 1$ is 1

(d) Area enclosed by the curve $\min(|x + y|, |x - y|) = 1$ is 2

SECTION–V

ASSERTION AND REASON TYPE QUESTIONS

The questions given below consist of an assertion (A) and the reason (R). Use the following key to choose the appropriate answer.

(a) If both assertion and reason are correct and reason is the correct explanation of the assertion.

(b) If both assertion and reason are correct but reason is not correct explanation of the assertion.

(c) If assertion is correct, but reason is incorrect

(d) If assertion is incorrect, but reason is correct

Now consider the following statements:

1. **A:** Area of the region satisfying the inequalities $x^2 + y^2 \le 25$ and $\sin(x + y) \ge 0$ is $\frac{25\pi}{2}$.

   R: Using symmetry of opposite quadrants area of the region is half the area of the circle.

2. **A:** Let $ABCD$ and $BEFG$ are two parallelograms such that E lies on AD and C lies on FG, then $\frac{ar(ABCD)}{ar(BEFG)} = 1$.

   R: $ar(ABCD) = 2.\ ar\ (\Delta BEC) = ar(BEFG)$.

3. Let $P(x, y)$ be a point inside the equilateral ΔABC such that $d(P, AB) + d(P, AC) + d(P, BC) = k$ where k is the altitude of the Δ, then

   A: area of the region of $P(x, y) = ar$ of (ΔABC)

   R: For equilateral triangle if $d(P, AB) + d(P, AC) + d(P, BC) = k$, then P will lie inside the pedal triangle of $\Delta\ ABC$.

4. **A:** The area of the curve $y = \sin^2 x$ from 0 to π will be more than that of curve $y = \sin x$ from 0 to π.

   R: $t^2 > t$ if $t > 1$.

5. **A:** If $b > 0$, the area bounded by the parabolas $y = x - bx^2$ and $y = \frac{x^2}{b}$ is maximum if $b = 1$.

   R: The area bounded by the parabolas $y = x - bx^2$ and $y = \frac{x^2}{b}$ is $2 - (b - 1)^2$.

6. **A:** The area bounded by curves $3y = -x^2 + 8x - 7$ and $y+1 = \frac{4}{x-3}$ is equal to area bounded by curves $3y = -x^2 + 2x + 11$ and $y = \frac{4}{x}$.

   R: Area is invariant, i.e., it does not depend upon origin and axes.

7. **A:** The area bounded by the curves $y = x^2 + 2x - 3$ and the line $y = \lambda x + 1$ is least, if $\lambda = 2$.

   R: The area bounded by the curve $y = x^2 + 2x - 3$ and $y = \lambda x + 1$ is $\{(\lambda - 2)^2 + 16^{3/2}\}$ square units.

8. **A:** The area of the ellipse $2x^2 + 3y^2 = 6$ will be more than the area bounded by $2|x| + 3|y| \le 6$.

   R: The length of major axis of the ellipse $2x^2 + 3y^2 = 6$ is less than the distance between the points of $2|x| + 3|y| \le 6$ on x-axis.

9. **A:** The area of the ellipse $2x^2 + 3y^2 = 6$ will be more than the area of the circle $x^2 + y^2 - 2x + 4y + 4 = 0$.

   R: The length of the semi-major axis of ellipse $2x^2 + 3y^2 = 6$ is more than the radius of the circle $x^2 + y^2 - 2x + 4y + 4 = 0$.

10. **A:** The area bounded by the curves $y = x^2 - 3$ and $y = kx + 2$ is least if $k = 0$.

    R: The area bounded by the curves $y = x^2 - 3$ and $y = kx + 2$ is $\sqrt{k^2 + 20}$

11. **A:** Area bounded by curves $y = 3x - x^2$ and $y = x^2 - x$ is $\frac{4}{3}$

    R: Area bounded by two curve $y = f(x)$ and $y = g(x)$ between $x = a, x = b\ (b > a)$ is $\int_a^b |f(x) - g(x)|\,dx$

12. **A:** Area bounded by curve $y = \cos x$ with $y = 0$, $x = 0$ and $x = \frac{3\pi}{4}$ is $2 - \frac{1}{\sqrt{2}}$

    R: Area of curve $y = f(x)$ with x-axis between ordinates $x = a$ and $x = b$ is $\int_a^b f(x)\,dx$

SECTION–VI

COMPREHENSION-TYPE QUESTIONS

A: Let $O(0, 0)$ and $A(2, 0)$ be the vertices of an isosceles triangle inscribed in an ellipse $(x - 1)^2 + 3y^2 = 1$. Let S represents the region consisting of all those points P inside the given triangle such that the distance of point P from OA is not more than the minimum distance of point P from the other two sides of the triangle. On the basis of above information answer the following questions.

1. The coordinates of third vertex of the triangle is/are given by

(a) $(1, 2)$ (b) $(1, \sqrt{3})$

(c) $\left(1, \frac{1}{\sqrt{3}}\right)$ (d) None of these

2. If the third vertex of the triangle lies in the 1st quadrant, then the region S is represented by

(a) 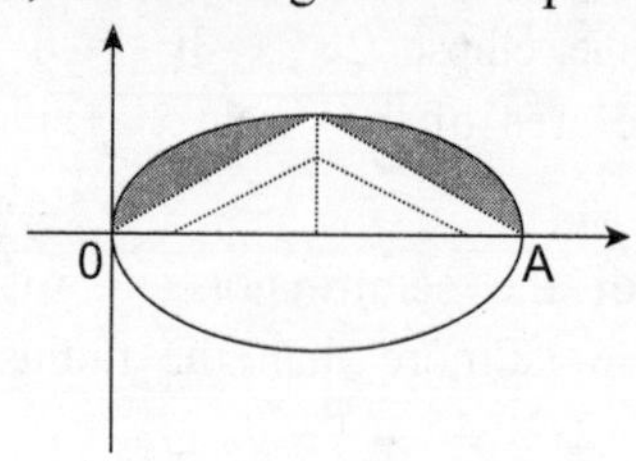

(b) 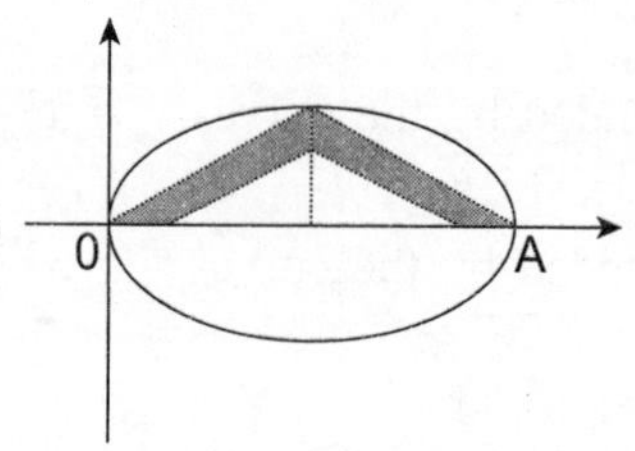

(c) 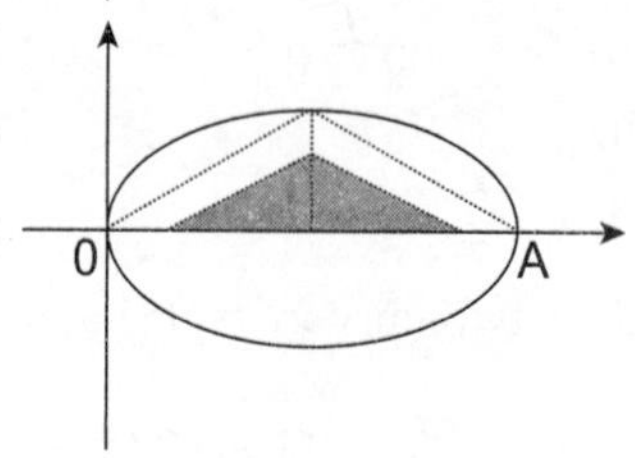

(d) 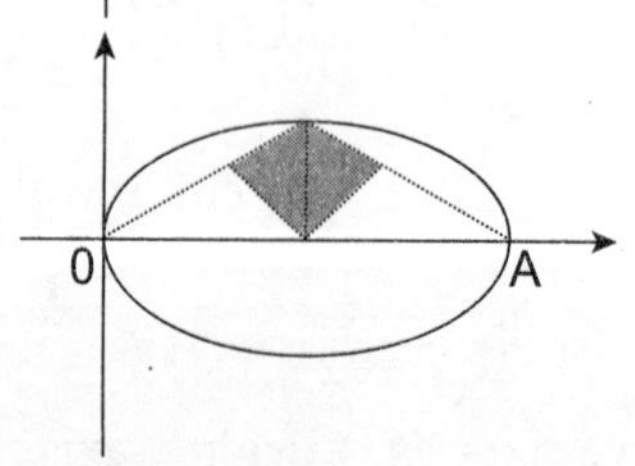

3. The area represented by the region S is

(a) $2 - \sqrt{3}$ (b) $2 + \sqrt{3}$

(c) $\sqrt{2} - 3$ (d) $\sqrt{2} + 3$

B: If the boundary of a curve is represented by parametric equations, i.e., $x = x(t)$, $y = y(t)$, then area of the figure is evaluated by one of the three formulas, $S = \int_{\alpha}^{\beta} y(t).x'(t)dt$, $S = \int_{\alpha}^{\beta} x(t).y'(t)dt$, $S = \frac{1}{2}\int_{\alpha}^{\beta}(xy' - yx')dt$; where α and β are the values of the parameter 't' corresponding respectively to the beginning and the end of the traversal of the curves corresponding to increasing 't'.

4. The area enclosed by the asteroid $\left(\frac{x}{a}\right)^{2/3} + \left(\frac{y}{a}\right)^{2/3} = 1$ is

(a) $\frac{3}{4}a^2\pi$ (b) $\frac{3}{18}\pi a^2$

(c) $\frac{3}{8}\pi a^2$ (d) $\frac{3}{4}\pi a$

5. The area of the region bounded by an arc of the cycloids $x = a(t - \sin t)$, $y = a(1 - \cos t)$ and the x-axis is

(a) $6\pi a^2$ (b) $3\pi a^2$

(c) $4\pi a^2$ (d) None of these

6. Area of the loop described as $x = \frac{t}{3}(6 - t)$, $y = \frac{t^2}{8}(6 - t)$ is

(a) $\frac{27}{5}$ (b) $\frac{24}{5}$

(c) $\frac{27}{6}$ (d) $\frac{21}{5}$

7. The area of the region enclosed by the curve $x = a \sin t$, $y = b \sin 2t$ is

(a) $\frac{3}{4}ab$ (b) $-\frac{4}{3}ab$

(c) $\frac{3}{8}ab$ (d) $\frac{8}{3}ab$

8. The area enclosed by the curve $x = \frac{c^2}{a}\cos^3 t$, $y = \left(-\frac{c^2}{b}\right)\sin^3 t$ is $\frac{3c^2(a^2 - b^2)\pi}{8ab}$, then

(a) $c^2 = ab$ (b) $c^2 = a^2 + b^2$

(c) $c^2 = a^2 - b^2$ (d) $c^2 = \frac{a^2b^2}{(a^2 + b^2)}$

C: Let there are three functions described here: $f(x) = \{\sin x\}$, $g(x) = \{\cos x\}$, $h(x) = [x/\pi]$, where $[x]$ is greatest integral part of x and $\{x\}$ is the fractional part of x. On the basis of above information, answer the following questions.

9. If the area bounded by x-axis, $x = 0$, $x = \pi$ and $f(x)$ is t_1 and the area bounded by x-axis, $x = \pi$, $x = 2\pi$ and $f(x)$ is t_2, than

(a) $\frac{t_2}{t_1} > \frac{1}{2}$ (b) $0 < \frac{t_2}{t_1} < \frac{1}{2}$

(c) $\frac{t_2}{t_1} > 1$ (d) None of these

10. The area bounded by $f(x)$, $h(x)$, $x = \pi$ and $x = 2\pi$

(a) 2 (b) $\pi - 2$

(c) $\frac{\pi-2}{2}$ (d) None of these

11. The area bounded by $f(x)$, $g(x)$, $x = \pi$ and $x = \frac{3\pi}{2}$ is

(a) $\frac{\pi}{2} - \frac{1}{\sqrt{2}}$ (b) $(\pi - 1)$

(c) $\frac{\pi}{2} - \frac{1}{2}$ (d) None of these

D: Five curves defined as follows:

$C_1 : |x + y| \le 1$ $C_2 : |x - y| \le 1$

$C_3 : |x| \le \frac{1}{2}$ $C_4 : |y| \le \frac{1}{2}$

$C_5 : 3x^2 + 3y^2 = 1$. On the basis of above information, answer the following questions

12. The ratio of region bounded by C_1, C_2 and C_3, C_4 is

(a) 1.5 (b) 2

(c) $\frac{1}{2}$ (d) None of these

13. The area bounded by C_1 and C_2 which does not contain the area of C_5 is

(a) $2 - \frac{\pi}{4}$ (b) $2 - \frac{\pi}{6}$

(c) $2 - \frac{\pi}{3}$ (d) None of these

14. The area of part which is bounded by C_1 and C_2 but not bounded by C_3 and C_4 is

(a) 1 (b) $\frac{1}{2}$

(c) $\frac{1}{3}$ (d) None of these

E: Let there are two function defined here: $f(x) = \min(|x - 2|, |x + 2|)$ and $g(x) = \min(e^x, e^{-x})$. Now the root of the equation $e^{-x} + x - 2 = 0$ is α. Where $\alpha \in \mathbb{R}$. On the basis of above information, answer the following questions.

15. The area bounded by $f(x)$ and x-axis is

(a) 1 square units (b) 4 square units

(c) 6 square units (d) None of these

16. Which statement is correct?

(a) $\alpha \in (2, 3)$ (b) $\alpha \in (-1, 0)$

(c) $\alpha \in (0, 2)$ (d) None of these

17. The area bounded by $f(x)$, $g(x)$ and $x = 0$ in first quadrant is

(a) $e^{-\alpha-1}$ (b) $2 - e^{-\alpha}$

(c) $1 + e^{-\alpha}$ (d) None of these

F: In the adjacent figure, the graphs of two functions $y = f(x)$ and $y = \sin x$ are given. They intersect at origin, $A(a , f(a))$, $B(\pi, 0)$ and $C(2\pi, 0)$. A_i $(i = 1, 2, 3)$ is the area bounded by the curves as shown in the figure respectively for $x \in (0, a)$, $x \in (a, \pi)$, $x \in (\pi, 2\pi)$. If $A_1 = 1 + (a - 1)\cos a - \sin a$. On the basis of above information, answer the following questions.

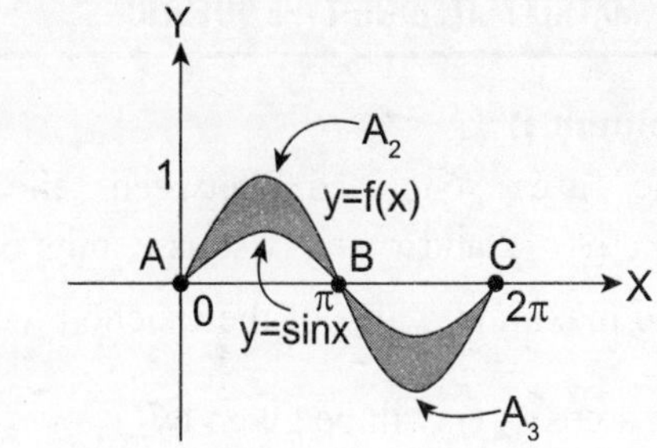

18. The function $f(x)$ is

(a) $x^2 \sin x$ (b) $x \sin x$

(c) $2x \sin x$ (d) $x^3 \sin x$

19. Value of A_2 for $a = 1$, is

(a) $(\pi - 1)$ units^2 (b) $(\pi/2 - 1)$ units^2

(c) $(\pi - \sin 1 - 1)$ units^2 (d) $\pi/2$ units^2

20. Value of A_3 is

(a) $(2\pi - 1)$ units^2 (b) $(3\pi - \sin 2)$ units^2

(c) $(3\pi - 2)$ units^2 (d) $(\pi - 2)$ units^2

G: Area enclosed by curve $y = f(x)$ and $y = x^2 + 2$ between the abscissa $x = 2$ and $x = \alpha$ is given as $(\alpha^3 - 4\alpha^2 + 8)$ square unit. It is known that curve $y = f(x)$ lies below the parabola $y = x^2 + 2$.

21. Area enclosed by curve $y = f(x)$ with x-axis, $x = 0$, $x = 1$ is

(a) $\frac{8}{3}$ (b) $\frac{16}{3}$

(c) $\frac{16}{7}$ (d) $\frac{4}{3}$

22. If $f(x)$ lies above x-axis in $x \in (p, q)$, then $(q + p)$ is equal to

(a) 2 (b) 3

(c) 4 (d) 8

23. Value of area bounded by line $y = x + 2$ and $y = f(x)$, $x = 2$ and $x = 4$ is

(a) $\frac{36}{5}$ (b) $\frac{7}{5}$

(c) $\frac{123}{13}$ (d) None of these

H: Let A, O, B & C are fixed points on a straight line such that $AO = OB = BC = 1$ unit. The points A and B are also joined by a semicircle of radius 1 unit, and P is a variable point on this semicircle such that $\angle POC = \theta$. Consider the region R bounded by the arc AP of the semi circle and the straight lines PC and AC.

24. Area of region R is maximum when θ is

(a) $\pi/6$ (b) $\pi/2$

(c) $\pi/3$ (d) π

25. Minimum value of perimeter of region R is

(a) 3 units (b) π units

(c) 4 units (d) 6 units

26. The graphs of area and perimeter of the region R are being drawn, w.r.t., θ. Tangents to the two graphs are parallel

(a) No where (b) at least once

(c) At least twice (d) at least thrice

SECTION–VII

MATRIX MATCHING-TYPE QUESTIONS

1. **Column I**

(i) The area enclosed between the curves $|x| + |y| = 2$ and $x^2 = y$ in square units is

(ii) The maximum value of the function $f(x) = 3 \sin x - 4 \cos x - \frac{7}{3}$ will be given by

(iii) The length of common chord of two circles of radii 3 and 4 units which intersect orthogonally

(iv) The length of chord intercepted by the parabola $y^2 = 4(x + 1)$ passing through its focus and inclined at 60° with positive x-axis is

Column II

(a) 24/5

(b) 7/3

(c) 16/3

(d) 8/3

2. **Column I**

(i) The area bounded by the curve $y = x + \sin x$ and its inverse function between the ordinates $x = 0$ to $x = 2\pi$ is $4s$ Then the value of s is

(ii) The area bounded by $y = x\,e^{|x|}$ and lines $|x| = 1$, $y = 0$ is

(iii) The area bounded by the curves $y^2 = x^3$ and $|y| = 2x$

(iv) The smaller area included between the curves $\sqrt{x} + \sqrt{|y|} = 1$ *and* $|x| + |y| = 1$

Column II

(a) 2

(b) 1

(c) 32/5

(d) 2/3

3. Let $f(x) = |x|$,. $g(x) = |x - 1|$ and $h(x) = |x + 1|$.

Column I

(i) Area bounded by min $(f(x), g(x))$ and x-axis is

(ii) Area bounded by min $(f(x), h(x))$ and x-axis is

(iii) Area bounded by min $(f(x), g(x), h(x))$ and x-axis is

(iv) Area bounded by min $(f(x), g(x), h(x))$, x-axis and $y = \frac{1}{2}$ is

Column II

(a) $\frac{1}{8}$ square units

(b) $\frac{1}{4}$ square units

(c) $\frac{1}{2}$ square units

(d) 1 square unit

4. **Column I**

(i) Let area of the figure bounded by $y = -3x^2 - |x| + 2$ and $y = 0$ is $\frac{22}{a^3}$ square units then a is

(ii) Let $I_{n,m} = \int \frac{\sin^n x}{\cos^m x} dx$ $m \neq 1$, If $I_{n,m} = \frac{\sin^{n-1} x}{(m-1)\cos^{m-1} x} + \frac{a(n-1)}{2(m-1)} I_{n-2,m-2}$ then a is

(iii) Let $f(x) = x - x^2$; $g(x) = ax$; If the area of the region above the graph of $g(x)$ and below the graph of $f(x)$ is $\frac{9}{2}$ square units, then a is

(iv) Let $f_n(x) = \int \cot^n x\, dx$, then $3\left(f_2\left(\frac{3\pi}{4}\right) + f_4\left(\frac{3\pi}{4}\right)\right)$ is

Column II

(a) 4

(b) 3

(c) –2

(d) 1

5. **Column I**

(i) Area bounded by $y = x^2$ and $y = \frac{2}{1+x^2}$

(ii) Area of the region bounded by $y^2 = 16ax$ and $x^2 = 16ay$

(iii) Area bounded by curves $xy^2 = a^2(a - x)$ and y-axis, is; $(a > 0)$

(iv) Area bounded by $y = x^2 + 2$, $y = -x$, $x = 0$ and $x = 1$, is

Column II

(a) $\frac{256}{3}a^2$

(b) πa^2

(c) $\frac{17}{6}$

(d) $\left(\pi - \frac{2}{3}\right)$

6. **Column I**

(i) Area bounded by $f(x) = \max(\sin x, \cos x)$ $\forall\ 0 \le x \le \frac{\pi}{2}$ and the coordinate axis is

(ii) Area bounded by $y = x + \sin x$ and its inverse function between the ordinate $x = 0$ and $x = 2\pi$ is

(iii) Area bounded by curve $y^2 = x^2(1 - x^2)$ is

(iv) Area bounded by the curves $\frac{y}{x} = \log x$ and $\frac{y}{2} = -x^2 + x$ is

Column II

(a) 7/12

(b) 4/3

(c) 8

(d) $\sqrt{2}$

SECTION–VIII

INTEGER-TYPE QUESTIONS

1. If A denotes the area of a loop of the curve $y^2 = x^2(4 - x^2)$, then evaluate $3A$.

2. The area bounded by the curve $y = \sqrt{x - [x]}$, between the ordinates $x = 1$, $x = 3/2$ and x-axis is (here [ ] is the greatest integer function) is $1/3\sqrt{k}$, then evaluate k.

3. The ratio in which the curve $y = 3x - 1$ divides the area of rectangle with vertices (1/2, 0), (1, 0), (1, 1) and (1/2, 1) is 1: b, then evaluate b.

4. Area bounded by the curve $y = \sqrt{\sin[x] + [\sin x]}$; (where [ ] is greatest integer function), lines $x = 1$ and $x = \pi/2$ and the x-axis is given by $\sqrt{\sin k}\ (\pi/2 - k)$, then evaluate k.

5. Find the area of the figure lying between the curve $y = xe^{-\frac{x^2}{2}}$ and its asymptote.

6. From the square with sides $x = 0$; $y = 0$; $x = 2$ and $y = 2$, the portion bounded by the curves, $y = e^x$ and $y = \ln x$ is removed. If the area of the remaining figure is given by $a - b\ln 2$, then evaluate $a + b$.

7. If the area of the finite portion of the figure bounded by the curves $y = 2x^2 e^x$ and $y = -x^3 e^x$ is given by $ae^{-2} - b$, then evaluate $a - b$.

8. If area bounded by the function $f(x) = 2x + b$ and its inverse and positive co-ordinate axes is 2 square units, then find the value of b^2.

9. Find the value of twice the area of the region in first quadrant bounded on the left by y-axis, below by the curve $x = 2\sqrt{y}$, above left by $x = (y - 1)^2$ and above right by the line $x + y = 3$.

10. Compute the area of the figure bounded by the straight lines, $y = 1$ and $y = 2$ and the curve $y = ax^2$; $y = \frac{1}{2}(ax^2)$. Find also the values of the parameter a (a ≥ 1) for which the area is greatest.

11. The area bounded by the curve $y = \left[\frac{x^2}{64} + 2\right]$, $y = x - 1$ and $x = 0$ above the x-axis will be; (Where [ ] represents greatest integer function)

12. The area between the curves $y = \log x$ and $y = \log 1/x$ when $1 \le x \le e$ is

13. Let $f(x)$ be a twice differentiable function defined as $R \to R$ such that the equation $\lambda^2 f(x) - 2\lambda f'(x) + f''(x) = 0$ provides two equal values of λ for all x. If $f(0) = 1$ and $f'(0) = 2$, then find the area bounded by the curve $y = f(x)$ and x-axis in the region $x + y < 1$.

14. The maximum area of a rectangle whose two consecutive vertices lie on the x-axis and another two lie on the curve $y = e^{-|x|}$, is equal to k/e, then evaluate k.

15. Let 'c' be the constant number such that $c > 1$. If the least area of the figure given by the line passing through the point (1, c) with gradient 'm' and the parabola $y = x^2$ is 36 sq. units, find the value of $(c^2 + m^2)$.

16. Find the maximum area bounded by the curves $y^2 = 4ax$, $y = ax$ and $y = x/a$ $(1 \le a \le 2)$.

17. Find the area of region bounded by $[x]^2 = [y]^2$ if $x \in [1, 5]$; where [.] represents the greatest integer function.

18. Find the area bounded by the graph $y = |[x - 3]|$ the x-axis and the lines $x = -2$ and $x = 3$ is ([.] denotes the greatest integer function).

19. If the area above the x-axis, bounded by the curves $y = 2^{kx}$ and $x = 0$ and $x = 2$ is $\frac{3}{\log 2}$, then find the value of k.

20. Find the area enclosed between the curve $y = \log_e(x + e)$ and the coordinate axes.

21. Let there are four curves defined here C_1: $|x + y| \le 1$, C_2: $|x - y| \le 1$, C_3: $|x| \le \frac{1}{2}$ and C_4: $|y| \le \frac{1}{2}$, then find the ratio of the area bounded by C_1 and C_2, and area bounded by C_3 and C_4.

22. Area bounded between maxima and minima of function $y = x^3 - 3x + 4$ with curve and X-axis is A. Find number of positive even divisors of $3A$.

23. Area bounded by curves $y = \ell n\, x$ and $y = (\ell n\, x)^2$ is of form $(a - e)$ sq. units. Find $\lim\limits_{x \to a} \frac{x^2 - 4}{x - 2}$.

24. Area bounded by $y = x^2 - 3$ and $y = kx + 2$ is least for some value of 'k'. Find the value of $k + 7$

25. Area bounded by curves $\sqrt{|x|} + \sqrt{|y|} = \sqrt{a}$ and $x^2 + y^2 = a^2$, $a > 0$ is divided by line $|x| + |y| = a$ into two parts and ratio of area of these two parts in first quadrant is $\frac{A}{3(B\pi - 2)}$. Then find $A + B$.

26. If the area bounded by the curves $y = \cos^{-1}x$; $y = \sin^{-1}x$ and $y = -\pi x^3$; where $-1 \le x \le 1$, is A sq. units, then find $[A]$. Where $[A]$ represents integral value of A.

27. Find the area enclosed between the curves $y = \log_e (x + e)$, $x = \log_e \left(\frac{1}{y}\right)$ and the x-axis.

Answer Keys

SECTION–III

1. (a)	**2.** (d)	**3.** (a)	**4.** (c)	**5.** (a)	**6.** (b)	**7.** (c)	**8.** (a)	**9.** (b)	**10.** (c)
11. (d)	**12.** (a)	**13.** (a)	**14.** (b)	**15.** (b)	**16.** (a)	**17.** (b)	**18.** (b)	**19.** (a)	**20.** (b)
21. (c)	**22.** (c)	**23.** (a)	**24.** (b)	**25.** (b)	**26.** (a)	**27.** (c)	**28.** (a)	**29.** (b)	**30.** (d)
31. (c)	**32.** (b)	**33.** (c)	**34.** (a)	**35.** (c)	**36.** (c)	**37.** (b)	**38.** (a)	**39.** (b)	**40.** (d)
41. (c)	**42.** (b)	**43.** (d)	**44.** (d)	**45.** (b)	**46.** (b)	**47.** (c)	**48.** (c)	**49.** (a)	

SECTION–IV

1. (b,c,d)	**2.** (a,b,c)	**3.** (a,b)	**4.** (b,d)	**5.** (b,d)	**6.** (a,c,d)	**7.** (a,b,c,d)
8. (b,c)	**9.** (b,c,d)	**10.** (b,c,d)	**11.** (a,b)	**12.** (b,c,d)	**13.** (a,b,c)	

SECTION–V

1. (a)	**2.** (a)	**3.** (c)	**4.** (d)	**5.** (c)	**6.** (a)	**7.** (c)	**8.** (a)	**9.** (b)	**10.** (c)
11. (d)	**12.** (c)								

SECTION–VI

1. (c)	**2.** (c)	**3.** (a)	**4.** (c)	**5.** (b)	**6.** (a)	**7.** (b)	**8.** (c)	**9.** (a)	**10.** (a)
11. (b)	**12.** (b)	**13.** (c)	**14.** (a)	**15.** (b)	**16.** (c)	**17.** (d)	**18.** (b)	**19.** (c)	**20.** (c)
21. (b)	**22.** (c)	**23.** (d)	**24.** (c)	**25.** (d)	**26.** (b)				

SECTION–VII

1. (i) → (b) (ii) → (d) (iii) → (a) (iv) → (c)
2. (i) → (a) (ii) → (a) (iii) → (c) (iv) → (d)
3. (i) → (b) (ii) → (b) (iii) → (c) (iv) → (c)
4. (i) → (b) (ii) → (c) (iii) → (a,c) (iv) → (d)
5. (i) → (d) (ii) → (a) (iii) → (b) (iv) → (c)
6. (i) → (d) (ii) → (c) (iii) → (b) (iv) → (a)

SECTION–VIII

1. 16	**2.** 2	**3.** 11	**4.** 1	**5.** 2	**6.** 10	**7.** 16	**8.** 2	**9.** 5	**10.** 1
11. 4	**12.** 2	**13.** 1	**14.** 2	**15.** 104	**16.** 84	**17.** 8	**18.** 15	**19.** 1	**20.** 1
21. 2	**22.** 6	**23.** 5	**24.** 7	**25.** 5	**26.** 3	**27.** 2			

HINTS AND SOLUTIONS

TEXTUAL EXERCISE–1: (SUBJECTIVE)

1. Points of intersection of $y^2 = x - 2$, $x = 4$, $x = 6$ are $(4, \pm\sqrt{2})$, $(6, \pm 2)$.
   In the first quadrant, points of intersection are $P(4, \sqrt{2})$ and $Q(6, 2)$
   Also, $y^2 = x - 2$ intersect x-axis at $R(2, 0)$

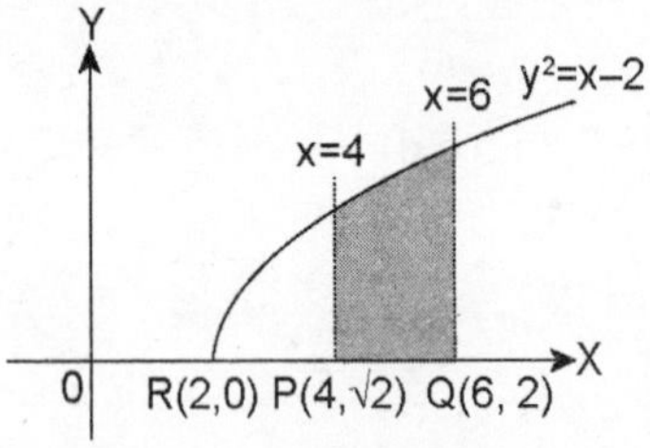

$\therefore$ The Required area $= \int_4^6 \left(\sqrt{x-2}\right)dx = \left[\frac{2}{3}(x-2)^{3/2}\right]_4^6$

$= \frac{2}{3}\left[8 - 2\sqrt{2}\right] = \frac{16 - 4\sqrt{2}}{3}$ sq. units

2. Required Area $= \int_2^4 2\sqrt{y}dy = 2\left[\frac{2}{3}y^{3/2}\right]_2^4$

$= \frac{4}{3}\left[8 - 2\sqrt{2}\right] = \frac{32 - 8\sqrt{2}}{3}$ sq. units

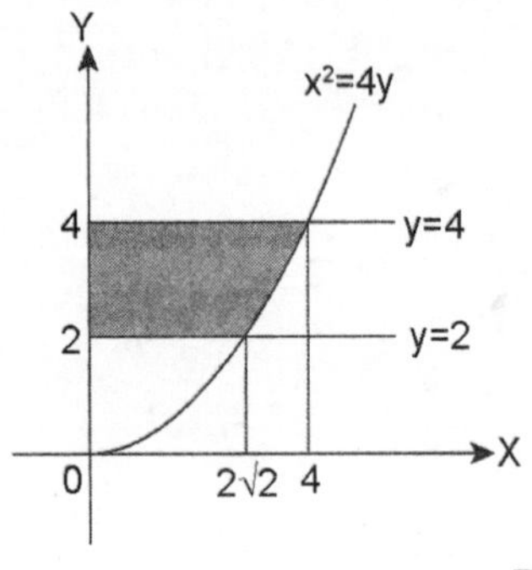

3. Required Area = 4(Area OAB) $= 4(3)\int_0^4 \sqrt{\left(1 - \frac{x^2}{16}\right)}dx$
   $= \frac{12}{4}\int_0^4 \sqrt{16 - x^2}dx$

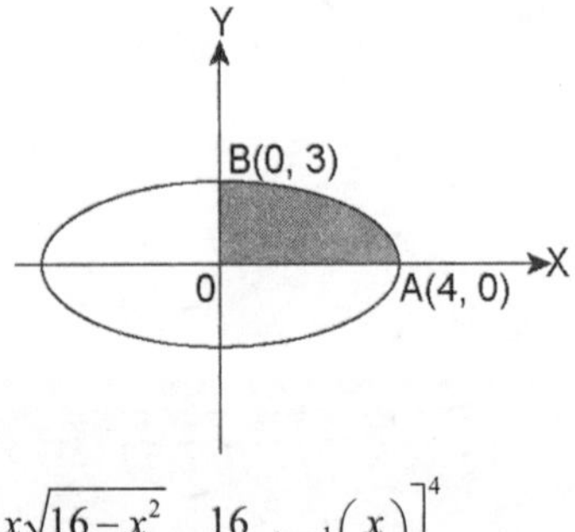

$= 3\left[\frac{x\sqrt{16-x^2}}{2} + \frac{16}{2}\sin^{-1}\left(\frac{x}{4}\right)\right]_0^4$

$= 3\left[8\sin^{-1}(1)\right] = 24\left(\frac{\pi}{2}\right) = 12\pi$ sq. units

4. Required Area = 2 (Area OAB) $= 2\int_0^1 x^{1/3}dx = 2\left[\frac{3}{4}x^{4/3}\right]_0^1 = \frac{3}{2}$ sq. units

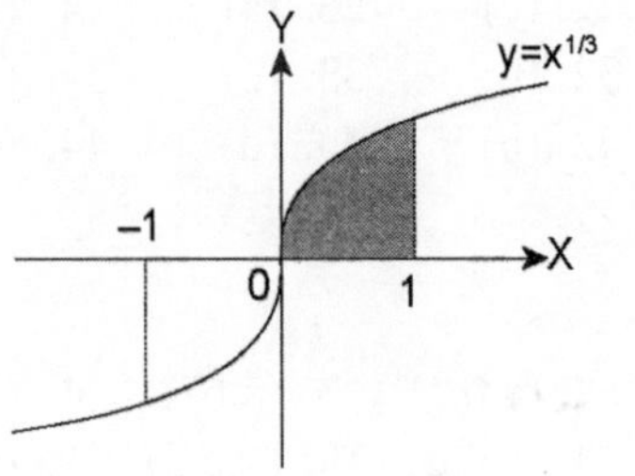

5. $y = -(x^2 - 4x + 4) - 4$
   $\Rightarrow y = -(x-2)^2 - 4$
   $\Rightarrow y + 4 = -(x-2)^2$
   $\Rightarrow (x-2)^2 = -(y+4)$ which is a downwards parabola having its vertex at $(2, -4)$

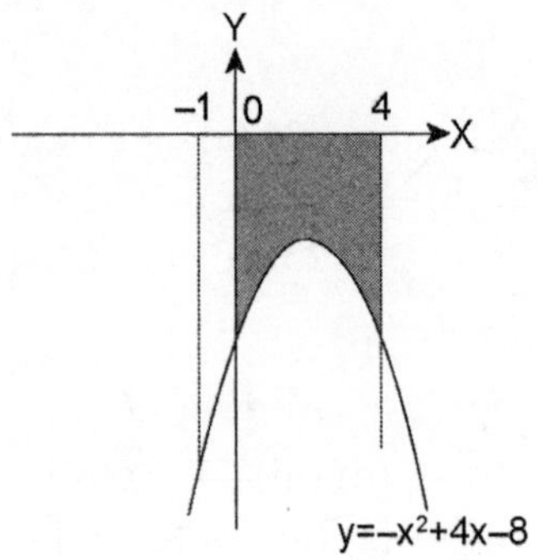

$\therefore$ Required Area $= \int_{-1}^4 \left[0 - (-x^2 + 4x - 8)\right]dx$

$= \int_{-1}^4 (x^2 - 4x + 8)dx = \left[\frac{x^3}{3} - \frac{4x^2}{2} + 8x\right]_{-1}^4$

$= \frac{1}{3}[64+1] - 2[16-1] + 8[4+1]$

$= \frac{65}{3} - 30 + 40 = \frac{95}{3} = 31\frac{2}{3}$ sq. units

6. Required Area $= 2\int_a^{2a} \sqrt{x^2 - a^2}dx$

$= 2\left[\frac{x\sqrt{x^2-a^2}}{2} - \frac{a^2}{2}\ln\left|x + \sqrt{x^2 - a^2}\right|\right]_a^{2a}$

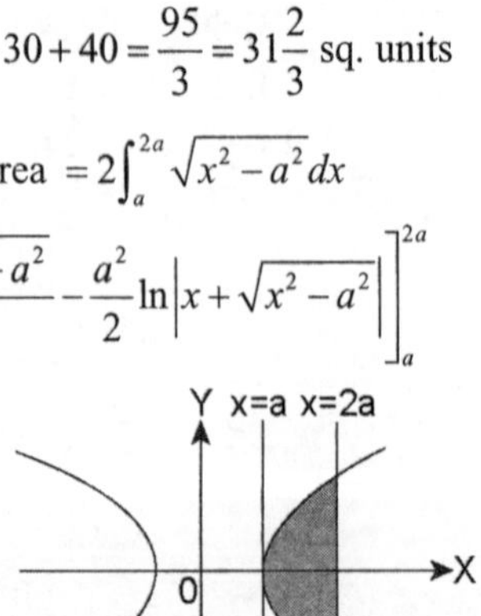

$= \left[2a\sqrt{3a^2} - a^2\ln\left|2a + \sqrt{3a^2}\right| + a^2\ln|a|\right]$

$=\left[2\sqrt{3}a^2-a^2\ln\left[\left(2+\sqrt{3}\right)a\right]+a^2\ln a\right]$

$=2a^2\sqrt{3}-a^2\ln(2+\sqrt{3})$ sq. units

7. **(a)** $f(x)=\sin 2p\,x$, $x=0$ to 1

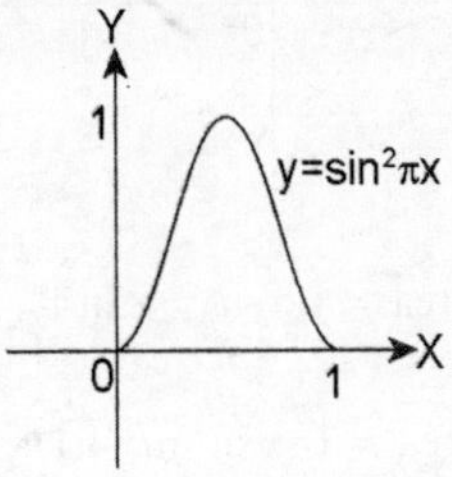

$\therefore$ Required Area $=\int_0^1\sin^2\pi x dx=\int_0^1\frac{(1-\cos 2\pi x)}{2}dx$

$=\frac{1}{2}\left[x-\frac{\sin 2\pi x}{2\pi}\right]_0^1=\frac{1}{2}[1-0]=\frac{1}{2}$ sq. units

(b) $f(x)=\ln x$, $x=0$ to 1

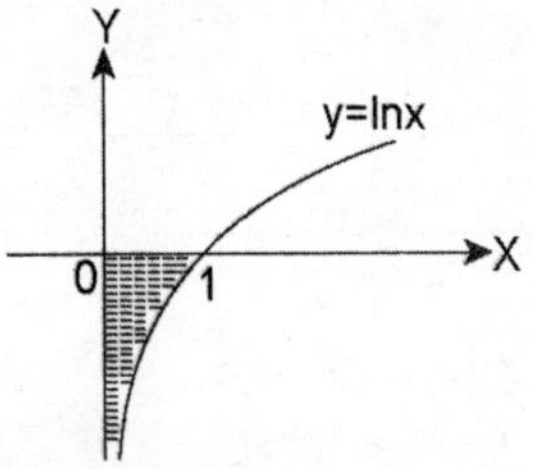

$\therefore$ Required Area $=\int_0^1(0-\ln x)dx=-\int_0^1(\ln x)dx$

$=-\left[|x\ln x|_0^1-\int_0^1\left(\frac{1}{x}.x\right)dx\right]$

$=-\left[-\lim_{x\to 0}(x\ln x)\right]+[x]_0^1=\lim_{x\to 0}\left[\frac{\ln x}{1/x}\right]+1$

$=\lim_{x\to 0}\left[\frac{1}{x}\times\left(\frac{-x^2}{1}\right)\right]+1=1$ sq. units

(c) $f(x)=\cos x$, $x=0$ to $\pi/2$

Required Area $=\int_0^{\pi/2}\cos x dx=[\sin x]_0^{\pi/2}=(1-0)=1$ sq. units

(d) $f(x)=\cos(2x+\pi/4)$; $x=-\pi/8$ to $\pi/8$

For $x\in\left[\frac{-\pi}{8},\frac{\pi}{8}\right]$; $\left(2x+\frac{\pi}{4}\right)\in[0,\pi/2]$

$\Rightarrow\ f(x)\geq 0\ \forall x\in\left[\frac{-\pi}{8},\frac{\pi}{8}\right]$

$\therefore$ Required Area $=\int_{-\pi/8}^{\pi/8}\cos(2x+\pi/4)dx$

$=\left[\frac{\sin(2x+\pi/4)}{2}\right]_{-\pi/8}^{\pi/8}=\frac{1}{2}[1-(0)]=\frac{1}{2}$ sq. units

8. $y=\ln x$, x-axis and two ordinates $x=\frac{1}{e}$ and $x=e$

For $x\in\left[\frac{1}{e},1\right]$, $f(x)\leq 0$ and for $x\in[1,e]$, $f(x)\geq 0$

$\therefore$ Required Area $=\int_{1/e}^{1}-\ln x dx+\int_1^e\ln x dx$

$=-\left[|x\ln x|_{1/e}^{1}-[x]_{1/e}^{1}\right]+\left[|x\ln x|_1^e-[x]_1^e\right]$

$=-\left[-\frac{1}{e}(-1)-\left(1-\frac{1}{e}\right)\right]+[e-(e-1)]$

$=-\frac{1}{e}+1-\frac{1}{e}+1=\left(2-\frac{2}{e}\right)$ sq. units

9. $y=e^{-|x|}$ and x-axis

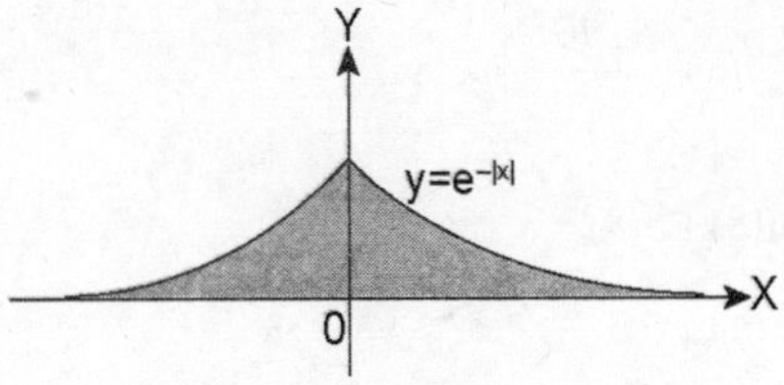

Required Area $=2\int_0^{\infty}e^{-x}dx=2\left[\frac{e^{-x}}{-1}\right]_0^{\infty}=-2[0-1]=2$ sq. units

10. $f(x).\max.\left\{\sin x,\cos x,\frac{1}{2}\right\};x\in[0,2\pi]$

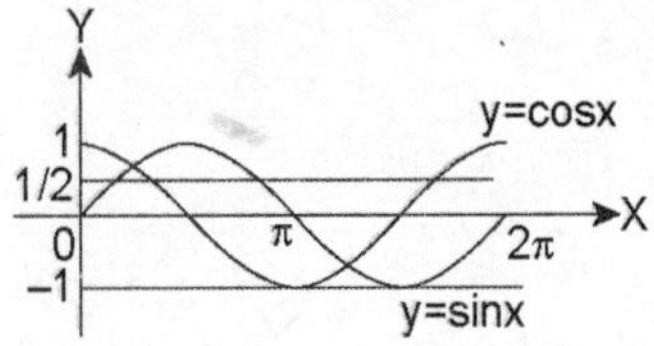

Clearly, $f(x)=\begin{cases}\cos x \text{ for } 0\leq x\leq\frac{\pi}{4}\\ \sin x \text{ for } \frac{\pi}{4}<x\leq\frac{5\pi}{6}\\ \frac{1}{2} \text{ for } \frac{5\pi}{6}<x\leq\frac{5\pi}{3}\\ \cos x \text{ for } \frac{5\pi}{3}<x\leq 2\pi\end{cases}$

$\therefore$ Required area $=\int_0^{\pi/4}\cos x dx+\int_{\pi/4}^{5\pi/6}\sin x dx$

$+\int_{5\pi/6}^{5\pi/3}\frac{1}{2}dx+\int_{5\pi/3}^{2\pi}\cos x dx$

$=[\sin x]_0^{\pi/4}-[\cos x]_{\pi/4}^{5\pi/6}+\frac{1}{2}\left[\frac{5\pi}{3}-\frac{5\pi}{6}\right]+[\sin x]_{5\pi/3}^{2\pi}$

$=\left[\frac{1}{\sqrt{2}}-0\right]-\left[\frac{-\sqrt{3}}{2}-\frac{1}{\sqrt{2}}\right]+\frac{5\pi}{12}+\frac{\sqrt{3}}{2}$

$=\sqrt{2}+\frac{\sqrt{3}}{2}+\frac{\sqrt{3}}{2}+\frac{\sqrt{3}}{2}+\frac{5\pi}{12}=\left(\sqrt{2}+\sqrt{3}+\frac{5\pi}{12}\right)$ sq. units.

11. Given $\int_0^a|f(x)|dx=(e^{a^2}-1)$

Differentiating both sides w.r.t. a, we get

$|f(a)|-|f(0)|=e^{a^2}(2a)$

Let $|f(0)|=k$

$\Rightarrow\ |f(a)|=2ae^{a^2}+k\quad\Rightarrow\ f(a)=\pm 2ae^{a^2}+C$

$\Rightarrow\ f(x)=\pm\ 2xe^{x^2}+C$

But the area a bounded is $(e^{a^2}-1)$ from $x=0$ to $x=a$

$\Rightarrow C = 0$

$\Rightarrow f(x) = \pm 2xe^{x^2}$

12. $y = a\sqrt{x} + bx$ passes through (1, 2)

$\Rightarrow 2 = a + b$ ...(1)

Also, $\int_0^4 \left(a\sqrt{x} + bx\right)dx = 8$

$$\Rightarrow \left[\frac{2}{3}a(x)^{3/2} + \frac{bx^2}{2}\right]_0^4 = 8$$

$$\Rightarrow \frac{2}{3}a(8) + b(8) = 8$$

$\Rightarrow 2a + 3b = 3$ ...(2)

Solving (1) and (2), we get $a = 3$, $b = -1$

13. $y = 2^{kx} > 0 \ \forall \ x \in [0, 2]$

$$\therefore \int_0^2 2^{kx}\,dx = \frac{3}{\ln 2}$$

$$\Rightarrow \left[\frac{2^{kx}}{k\ln 2}\right]_0^2 = \frac{3}{\ln 2}; k \neq 0$$

$$\Rightarrow \frac{1}{k}[2^{2k} - 1] = 3; k \neq 0$$

$\Rightarrow 2^{2k} - 1 = 3k;\ k \neq 0 \quad \Rightarrow 2^{2k} = 3k + 1;\ k \neq 0$

$\Rightarrow k = 0, 1;\ k \neq 0$

$\Rightarrow k = 1$ is the only possible value

14. $xy - 3x - 2y - 10 = 0$

$\Rightarrow y(x - 2) = 3x + 10$

$$\Rightarrow y = \frac{3x+10}{x-2}; x \in [3,4]$$

$$\Rightarrow y' = \frac{(x-2)(3) - (3x+10)(1)}{(x-2)^2}$$

$$\Rightarrow y' = \frac{-16}{(x-2)^2} < 0$$

$\Rightarrow y = f(x)$ is *a* decreasing function and continuous on [3, 4]

$\Rightarrow$ Range of $f(x)$ for $x \in [3, 4]$ is [11, 19]

$\Rightarrow f(x) > 0 \ \forall \ x \in [3, 4]$

$\therefore$ Area bounded by curve with x-axis, $x = 3$ and $x = 4$

$$= \int_3^4 \left(\frac{3x+10}{x-2}\right)dx = \int_3^4 \frac{3x - 6 + 16}{x-2}dx = \int_3^4 \left(3 + \frac{16}{x-2}\right)dx$$

$= \left[3x + 16\ln|x-2|\right]_3^4 = 3 + 16\,[\ln 2] = 3 + 16\ln 2$

TEXTUAL EXERCISE–1: (OBJECTIVE)

1. (c) Required Area $= \int_1^2 \ln x\,dx$ as $\ln x \geq 0 \ \forall \ x \in [1, 2]$

$= |x\ln x|_1^2 - \int_1^2 1dx = 2\ln 2 - 1 = \ln 4 - 1$

2. (a) Required Area $= \int_0^a xe^{x^2}dx = \frac{1}{2}\int_0^a 2xe^{x^2}dx$

$$= \frac{1}{2}\int_0^{a^2} e^t\,dt = \frac{e^{a^2} - 1}{2}$$

3. (c) $xy = c;\ c > 0$

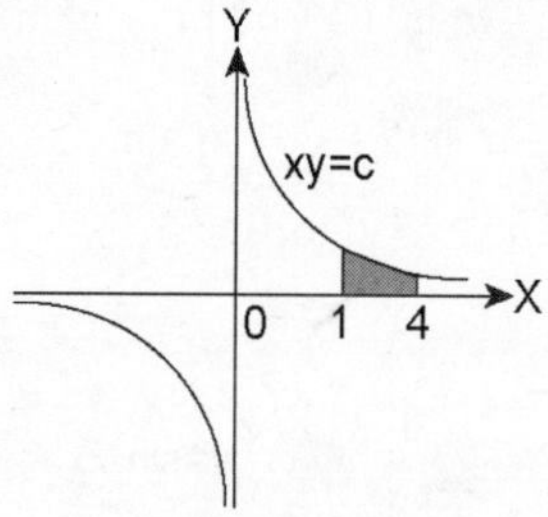

$\therefore$ Required Area $= \int_1^4 \frac{c}{x}dx = c\ln 4 = 2c\ln 2$

4. (d) Required Area $= \int_0^{\pi} x\sin x\,dx + \int_{\pi}^{2\pi} -x\sin x\,dx$

$= |-x\cos x|_0^{\pi} - \int_0^{\pi} 1.(-\cos x)dx$

$- \left[|-x\cos x|_{\pi}^{2\pi} - \int_{\pi}^{2\pi} 1.(-\cos x)dx\right]$

$= \pi + [\sin x]_0^{\pi} + [2\pi + \pi] - [0] = 4\pi$

5. (a) Required Area $= 2\int_1^2 \sqrt{4 - x^2}\,dx$

$$= 2\left[\frac{x\sqrt{4-x^2}}{2} + \frac{4}{2}\sin^{-1}\left(\frac{x}{2}\right)\right]_1^2$$

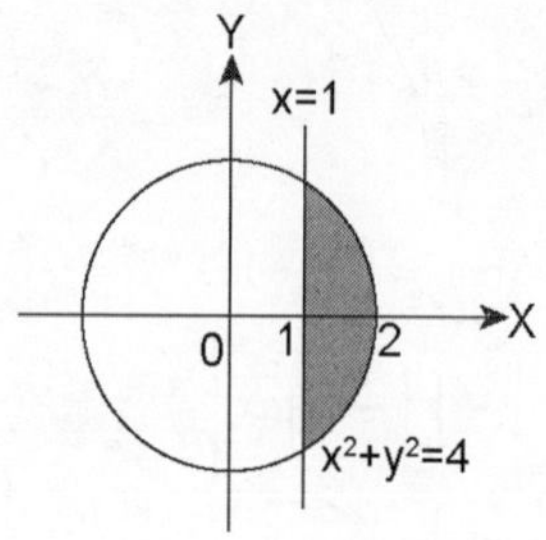

$$= 2\left[2\left(\frac{\pi}{2}\right) - \frac{\sqrt{3}}{2} - 2\left(\frac{\pi}{6}\right)\right] = 2\left[\pi - \frac{\sqrt{3}}{2} - \frac{\pi}{3}\right] = \frac{4\pi}{3} - \sqrt{3}$$

6. (c) Required Area $= \int_a^{4a} 2\sqrt{a}\sqrt{x}dx = 2\sqrt{a}\left[\frac{2}{3}(x)^{3/2}\right]_a^{4a}$

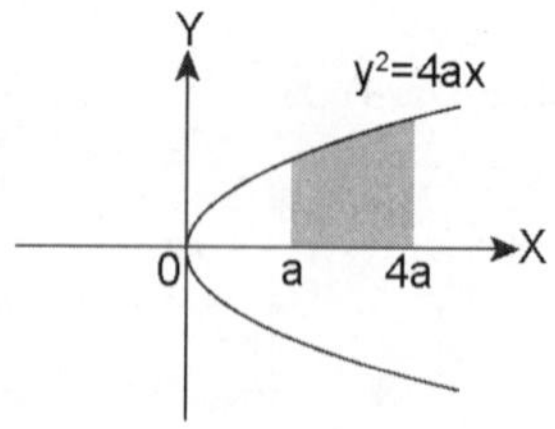

$$= \frac{4\sqrt{a}}{3}\left[(4a)^{3/2} - (a)^{3/2}\right] = \frac{4\sqrt{a}}{3}(7a^{3/2}) = \frac{28}{3}a^2$$

7. (d) $|y| = \sin 2x; x \in [0, 2\pi]$

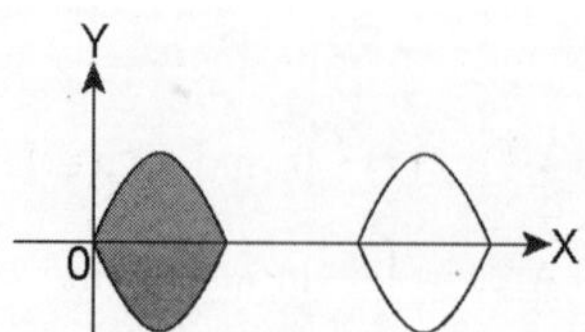

Required Area $=4\int_0^{\pi/2}\sin 2x dx=4\left[\frac{-\cos 2x}{2}\right]_0^{\pi/2}$

$=-2[-1-1]=4$

8. (b) Area of loop between the curve $y=a$ sinx and x-axis is

$\int_a^{\pi} a\sin x dx=-a[\cos x]_0^{\pi}=-a[-1-1]=2a$

9. (a) Required Area $=2\int_0^a 2\sqrt{a}\sqrt{x}dx$

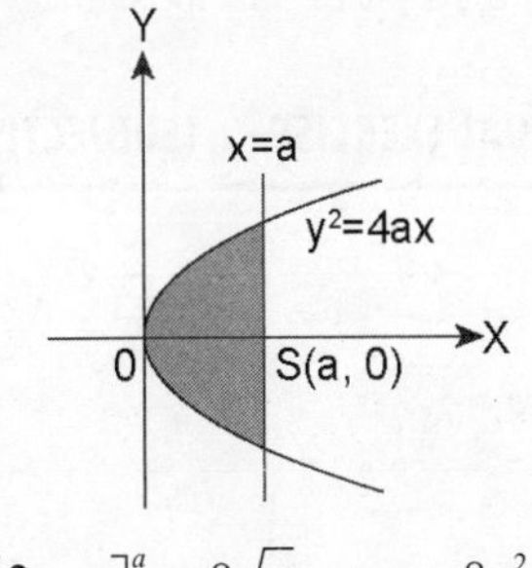

$=4\sqrt{a}\left[\frac{2}{3}x^{3/2}\right]_0^a=\frac{8\sqrt{a}}{3}[a^{3/2}]=\frac{8a^2}{3}$

10. (a) Required Area $=\int_0^2\sqrt{1-(x-1)^2}dx$

$=\left[\frac{(x-1)\sqrt{1-(x-1)^2}}{2}+\frac{1}{2}\sin^{-1}\left(\frac{x-1}{1}\right)\right]_0^2$

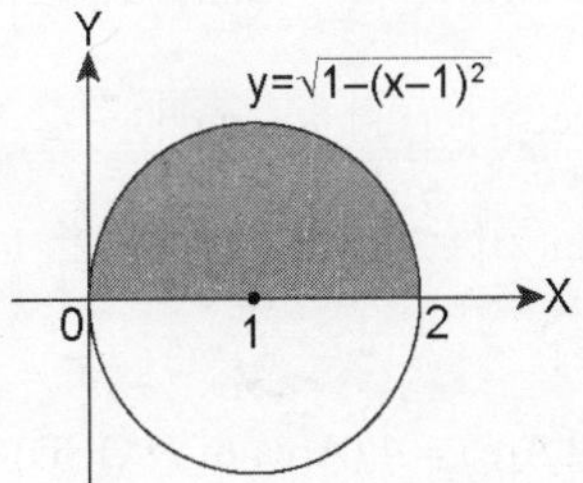

$=\frac{1}{2}\left[\frac{\pi}{2}-\left(\frac{-\pi}{2}\right)\right]=\frac{\pi}{2}=\int_0^2\sqrt{2x-x^2}$

11. (a) $y^2(2a-x)=x^3;\ x=2a$

$y^2=\frac{x^3}{2a-x}$

$\Rightarrow\ y=\pm\sqrt{\frac{x^3}{2a-x}}=\pm\frac{x^{3/2}}{\sqrt{2a-x}}$

As $x\to 2a^-, y=\pm\sqrt{\frac{8a^3}{0^+}}=\pm\infty$

Also curve passes through and

$y'=\pm\left(\frac{\sqrt{2a-x}.\frac{3}{2}\sqrt{x}+x^{3/2}.\frac{1}{2\sqrt{2a-x}}}{(2a-x)}\right)$

$\Rightarrow\ y'=\pm\frac{(2a-x)(3\sqrt{x})+x^{3/2}}{2(2a-x)^{3/2}}$

$\Rightarrow\ y'=\pm\frac{6a\sqrt{x}-2x\sqrt{x}}{2(2a-x)^{3/2}}$

$\Rightarrow\ y'=\pm\frac{(3a-x)\sqrt{x}}{(2a-x)^{3/2}}$

$\Rightarrow\ y'\geq 0$ for $y=\sqrt{\frac{x^3}{2a-x}};x\in[0,2a)$ and $y'\leq 0$ for

$y=-\sqrt{\frac{x^3}{2a-x}};x\in[0,2a)$

Group of $y=f(x)$ will be as shown below:

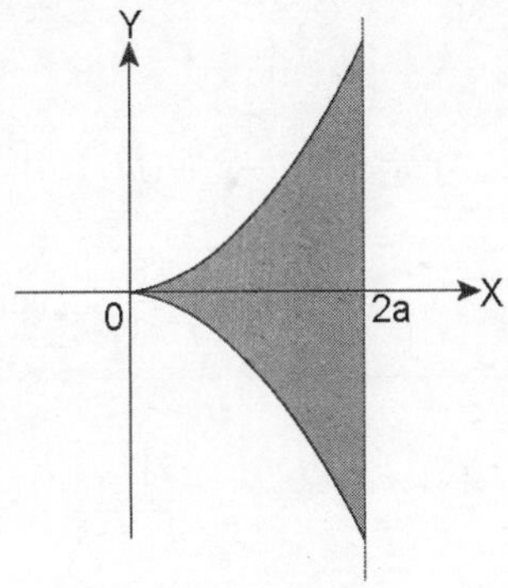

$\therefore$ Required Area $=2\int_0^{2a}\frac{x^{3/2}}{\sqrt{2a-x}}dx$

Put $x=2a\sin^2\theta\qquad\Rightarrow\ dx=(2a)(2\sin\theta\cos\theta)d\theta$

$\therefore\quad A=2\int_0^{\pi/2}\frac{(2a)^{3/2}\sin^3\theta}{(2a)^{1/2}\cos\theta}(4a\sin\theta\cos\theta)d\theta$

$=2(2a^2)(4)\int_0^{\pi/2}\sin^4\theta d\theta=16a^2\int_0^{\pi/2}\left(\frac{1-\cos 2\theta)}{2}\right)^2 d\theta$

$=4a^2\int_0^{\pi/2}(1+\cos^2 2\theta-2\cos 2\theta)d\theta$

$=4a^2\int_0^{\pi/2}\left[1+\frac{1+\cos 4\theta}{2}-2\cos 2\theta\right]d\theta$

$=4a^2\left[\frac{3}{2}\theta+\frac{1}{8}\sin 4\theta-\sin 2\theta\right]_0^{\pi/2}=4a^2\left[\frac{3}{2}\left(\frac{\pi}{2}\right)\right]=3a^2\pi$

12. (d) $y=x.e^{|x|};|x|=1;y=0$

$y=xe^{|x|}=\begin{cases}xe^x & \text{for } x\geq 0\\ xe^{-x} & \text{for } x<0\end{cases}$ is shown by curve AOB for $x\in[-1,1]$.

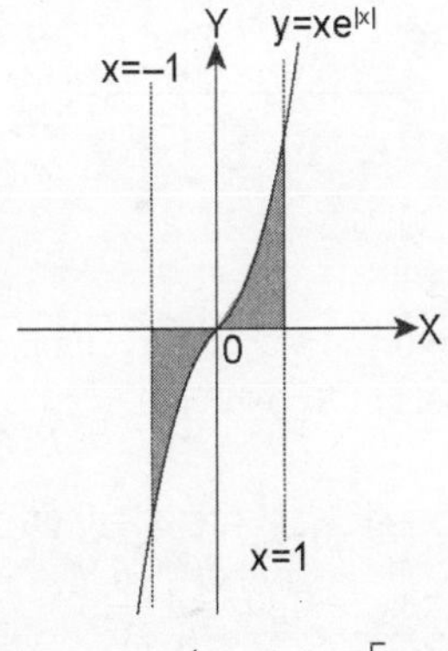

$\therefore$ Required Area $=2\int_0^1 xe^x dx=2\left[\left|xe^x\right|_0^1-\int_0^1 1.e^x dx\right]$

$=2[e-[e-1]]=2$ sq. units

13. (c) $|y| = 1 - x^2$

$\Rightarrow y = \pm(1 - x^2) \quad \Rightarrow y = -x^2 + 1$ or $y = x^2 - 1$

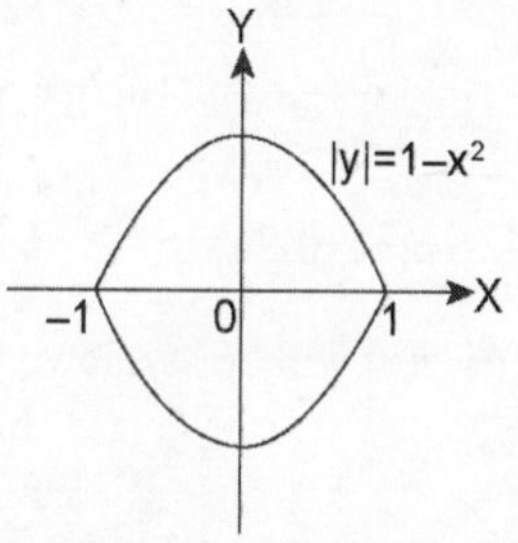

$\therefore$ Required Area $= 2\int_{-1}^{1}(-x^2+1)dx = 4\int_0^1(-x^2+1)dx$

$= 4\left[\dfrac{-x^3}{3}+x\right]_0^1 = 4\left[\dfrac{-1}{3}+1\right] = \dfrac{8}{3}$ sq. units

14. (b) $y^2 = x$; $x = 36$ $y^2 = x$

A.T.Q., $\dfrac{A_1}{A_7} = \dfrac{1}{7} \quad \Rightarrow \dfrac{2\int_0^a \sqrt{x}dx}{2\int_a^{36}\sqrt{x}dx} = \dfrac{1}{7}$

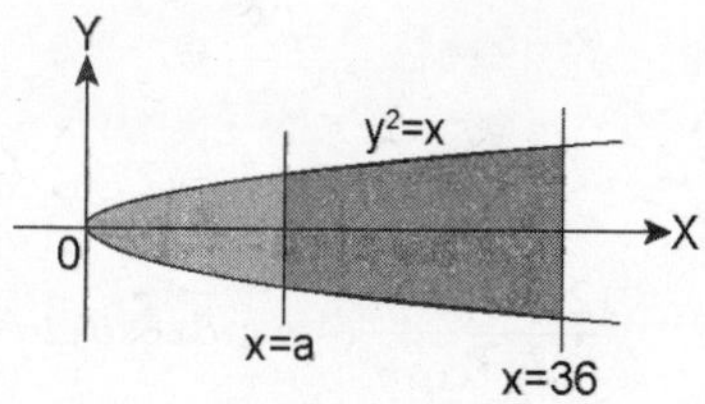

$\Rightarrow \dfrac{\frac{2}{3}\left[(x)^{3/2}\right]_0^a}{\frac{2}{3}\left[x^{3/2}\right]_a^{36}} = \dfrac{1}{7} \quad \Rightarrow \dfrac{a^{3/2}}{216 - a^{3/2}} = \dfrac{1}{7}$

$\Rightarrow 8a^{3/2} = 216 \quad \Rightarrow a^{3/2} = 27$

$\Rightarrow \sqrt{a} = 3 \quad \Rightarrow a = 9$

15. (d) $y = 8x^2 - x^5$, $x = 1$, $x = c$, $y = 0$

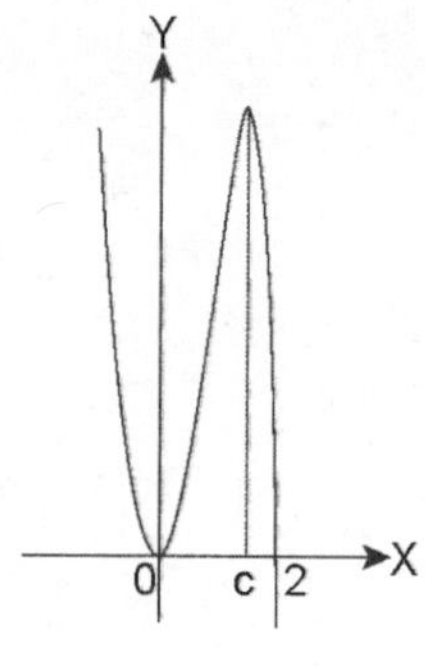

$\Rightarrow y' = 16x - 5x^4$

$\therefore y = 0$

$\Rightarrow x^2(8 - x^3) = 0 \quad \Rightarrow x = 0$ or $x = 2$

$\therefore$ 0, 2 are roots of $8x^2 - x^5 = 0$

$y' = 0$

$\Rightarrow x(16 - 5x^3) = 0 \quad \Rightarrow x = 0$ or $x = \left(\dfrac{16}{5}\right)^{1/3}$

Given:- $\int_1^c (8x^2 - x^5)dx = \pm\dfrac{16}{3}$

$\Rightarrow \left[\dfrac{8x^3}{3} - \dfrac{x^6}{6}\right]_1^c = \pm\dfrac{16}{3} \quad \Rightarrow \dfrac{8}{3}(c^3-1) - \dfrac{1}{6}(c^6-1) = \pm\dfrac{16}{3}$

$\Rightarrow 16(c^3 - 1) - (c^6 - 1) = \pm 32$

$\Rightarrow -c^6 + 16c^3 - 15 = \pm 32$

$\Rightarrow c^6 - 16c^3 + 15 \pm 32 = 0$

$\Rightarrow c^6 - 16c^3 - 17 = 0$ or $c^6 - 16c^3 + 47 = 0$

$\Rightarrow (c^3 - 17)(c^3 + 1) = 0$ or $c^3 = \dfrac{16 \pm \sqrt{68}}{2}$

$\Rightarrow c = (17)^{1/3}$ or $c = -1$ or $c = (8 \pm \sqrt{17})^{1/3}$

$\therefore c = \sqrt[3]{17}, -1, \sqrt[3]{8 \pm \sqrt{17}}$ are possible values of c

TEXTUAL EXERCISE–2: (SUBJECTIVE)

1. $y = \tan x; \dfrac{-\pi}{3} \le x \le \dfrac{\pi}{3}$; $y = \cot x$; $\dfrac{\pi}{6} \le x \le \dfrac{\pi}{2}$

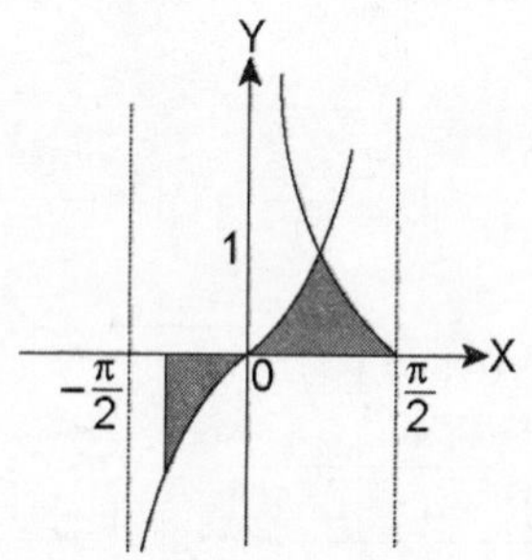

Required Area $= \int_{-\pi/3}^{0}(-\tan x)dx + 2\int_0^{\pi/4}\tan x dx$

$= -\left[\ln|\sec x|\right]_{-\pi/3}^{0} + \left[\ln|\sec x|\right]_0^{\pi/4}$

$= -[0 - \ln(2)] + 2[\ln\sqrt{2} - 0] = \ln 2 + \ln 2 = 2\ln 2$

2. (a) $|x| + |y| = 1$

Required Area = 4 (Area of D OCD)

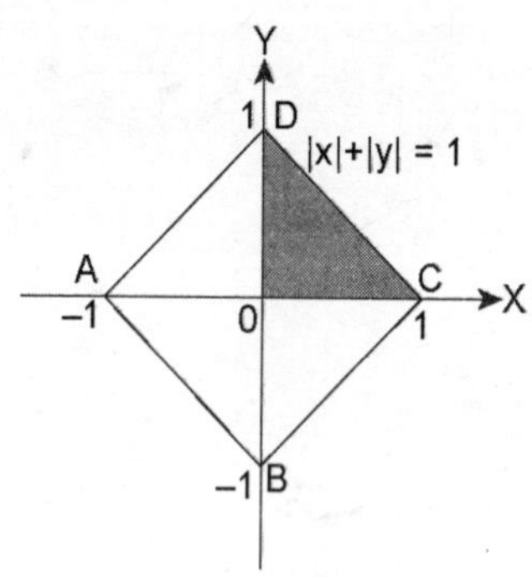

$= 4\int_0^1(1-x)dx = 4\left[x - \dfrac{x^2}{2}\right]_0^1 = 4\left[(1-0) \dfrac{-1}{2}(1-0)\right] = 2$

sq. units

(b) Given curves are $x + y = 1$; $x + 3y = 6$; $y = x - 1$; $y = x + 1$

Required Area = area of trapezium $ABCD = \dfrac{1}{2}$ $(AD + CB) \times (\sqrt{2})$; where $\sqrt{2}$ = DC or by using definite integral;

Point $B\left(\dfrac{9}{4}, \dfrac{5}{4}\right)$ and $A\left(\dfrac{3}{7}, \dfrac{7}{4}\right)$

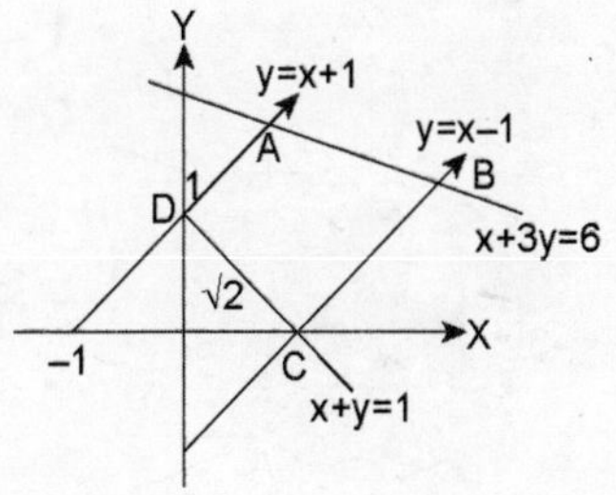

Required Area

$$= \int_0^{3/4}(x+1)dx + \int_{3/4}^{9/4}\frac{1}{3}(6-x)dx - \int_0^1(1-x)dx - \int_1^{9/4}(x-1)dx$$

$$= \left[\frac{x^2}{2}+x\right]_0^{3/4} + \frac{1}{3}\left[6x-\frac{x^2}{2}\right]_{3/4}^{9/4} - \left[x-\frac{x^2}{2}\right]_0^1 - \left[\frac{x^2}{2}-x\right]_1^{9/4}$$

$$= \frac{33}{32}+\frac{1}{3}\left[\frac{351-135}{32}\right]-1-\frac{9}{32}$$

$$= \frac{1}{32}-\frac{9}{32}+\frac{1}{3}\left(\frac{216}{32}\right) = \frac{-8}{32}+\frac{72}{32} = 2 \text{ sq. units}$$

3. The graph of $|x+1|+|y+1|=2$ is *a* square with centre at (–1, –1) and diagonals parallel to coordinates axis and of length 4 as shown in

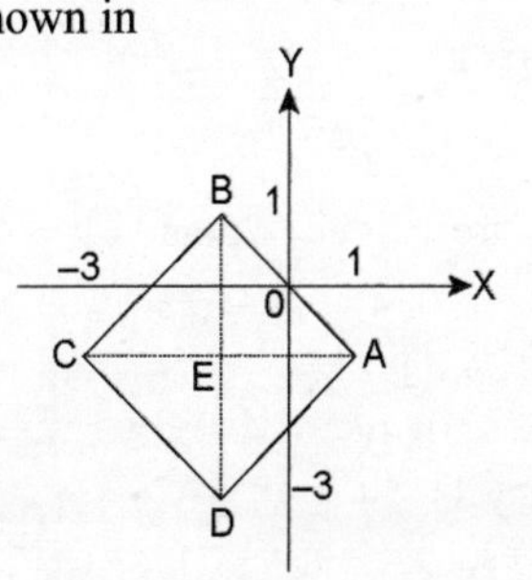

$\therefore$ Required Area = 4 (area of D BEA) $= 4\left(\frac{1}{2}(2)(2)\right) = 8$ sq. units

4. Given curve is $|x|+y=1$ or $y=1-|x|$

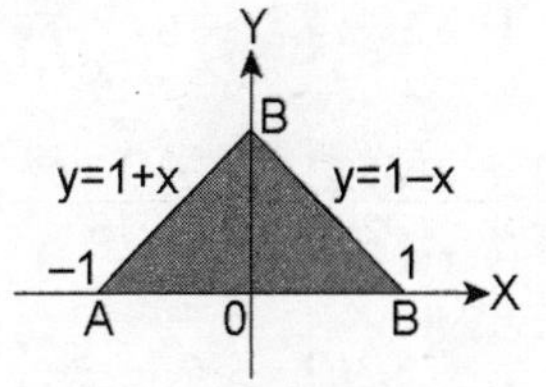

$\therefore$ Required Area = 2 (area of D OBC) $= 2\left(\frac{1}{2}(1)(1)\right) = 1$ sq. units

5. $y=\ln x,\ y=\ln|x|,\ y=|\ln x|,\ y=|\ln|x||$

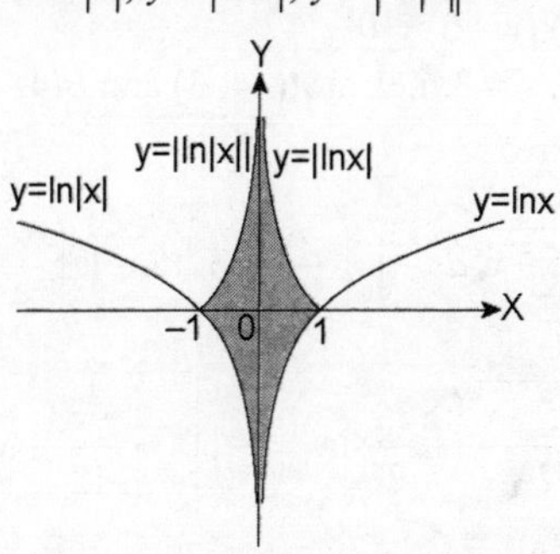

$\therefore$ Required Area $= 4\int_0^1|\ln x|dx = 4\int_0^1(-\ln x)dx$

$$= -4\left[x[\ln x]_0^1 - \int_0^1\left(\frac{1}{x}.x\right)dx\right]$$

$$= -4\left[0-\lim_{x\to 0}\left(\frac{\ln x}{1/x}\right)-[x]_0^1\right] = -4[0-(1-0)] = 4 \text{ sq. units}$$

6. (a) Given parabola are. $5x^2 - y = 0$; $2x^2 - y + 9 = 0$, i.e., $x^2 = \frac{1}{5}y$ and $x^2 = \frac{1}{2}(y-9)$

The two parabolas intersect each other, where $5x^2 = 2x^2 + 9$

$\Rightarrow$ $3x^2 = 9$ $\qquad\Rightarrow$ $x^2 = 3$

$\Rightarrow$ $x = \pm\sqrt{3}$

$\therefore$ Points intersection are $A(-\sqrt{3},15)$ and $B(\sqrt{3},15)$

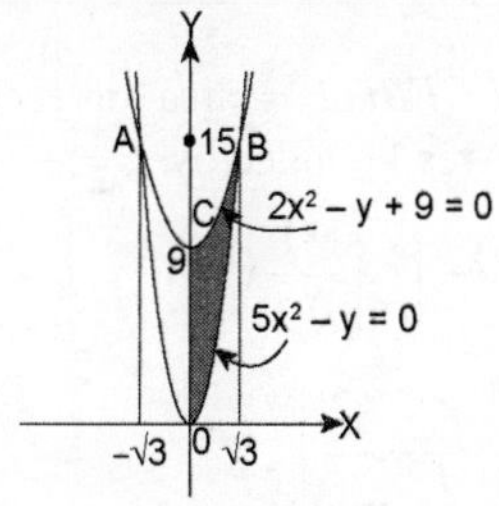

Required bounded area = (area OCB)

$$= 2\int_0^{\sqrt{3}}\left[(2x^2+9)-(5x^2)\right]dx = 2\int_0^{\sqrt{3}}(9-3x^2)dx$$

$$= 2\left[9x-\frac{3x^2}{3}\right]_0^{\sqrt{3}} = 2\left[9\sqrt{3}-(3\sqrt{3})\right] = 12\sqrt{3} \text{ sq. units}$$

(b) Given curves are $y = x(1-x)$ and $y = 2^x$; $x \in [0, 1]$

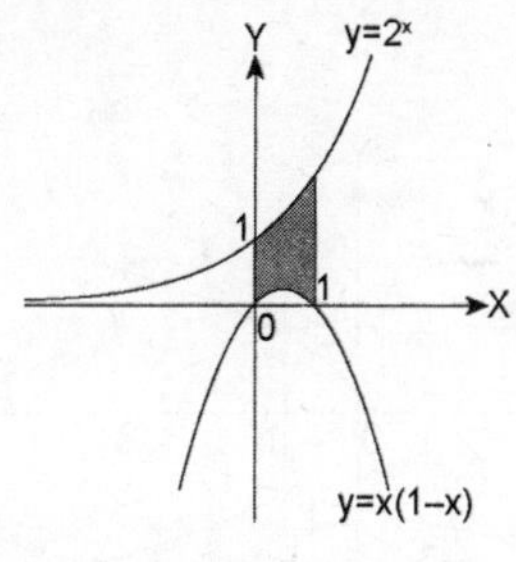

$\therefore$ Required Area $= \int_0^1[2^x - x(1-x)]dx = \left[\frac{2^x}{\ln 2}-\frac{x^2}{2}+\frac{x^3}{3}\right]_0^1$

$$= \left[\left(\frac{2}{\ln 2}-\frac{1}{2}+\frac{1}{3}\right)-\left(\frac{1}{\ln 2}\right)\right] = \frac{1}{\ln 2}-\frac{1}{6} = \left(\log_2 e-\frac{1}{6}\right) \text{ sq. units}$$

7. Given curves are $x^2 + y^2 = 4$; $x^2 = -\sqrt{2}y$; $y \le x, y \le 0$

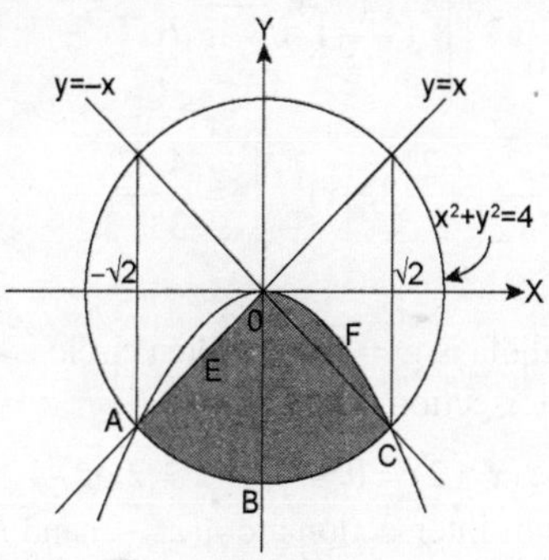

The parabola $x^2 = -\sqrt{2}y$ and circle $x^2 + y^2 = 4$ intersect, each other, where, $y^2 - \sqrt{2}y = 4$

$$\Rightarrow \quad y = \frac{\sqrt{2} \pm \sqrt{2+16}}{2} \qquad \Rightarrow \quad y = \frac{\sqrt{2} \pm 3\sqrt{2}}{2}$$

$$\Rightarrow \quad y = \frac{1}{\sqrt{2}} \pm \frac{3}{\sqrt{2}}$$

$$\Rightarrow \quad y = \frac{4}{\sqrt{2}} \text{ or } \frac{-2}{\sqrt{2}} \qquad \Rightarrow \quad y = 2\sqrt{2} \text{ or } -\sqrt{2}$$

But for $y = 2\sqrt{2}$, $x^2 = -4$ which is impossible

$\therefore \quad y = -\sqrt{2}$

$\therefore$ Point of their intersection are $A(\sqrt{2}, -\sqrt{2})$ and $B(\sqrt{2}, -\sqrt{2})$

The region bounded by $x^2 + y^2 = 4$; $x^2 = -\sqrt{2}$ y, $y \le x$ and $y \le 0$,

= Area $AEOFBDA$ = area of sector $AOBD$ (quarter circle) + (Area bounded by $x^2 = -\sqrt{2}$ and $y \ge -x$)

$$= \frac{1}{4}(\pi(2)^2) + \int_0^{\sqrt{2}} \left[\frac{-1}{\sqrt{2}}x^2 - (-x)\right] dx$$

$$= \pi + \left[\frac{-1}{\sqrt{2}} \cdot \frac{x^3}{3} + \frac{x^2}{2}\right]_0^{\sqrt{2}}$$

$$= \pi - \frac{1}{3\sqrt{2}}(2\sqrt{2} - 0) + \frac{1}{2}(2) = \left(\pi + \frac{1}{3}\right) \text{ sq. units}$$

8. $x = y^2$ and $x = 3 - 2y^2$, i.e., $y^2 = x$ and $y^2 = \frac{-1}{2}(x-3)$

The two parabola intersect, where, $x = \frac{-1}{2}(x-3)$

$\Rightarrow \quad 3x = 3 \qquad \Rightarrow \quad x = 1$

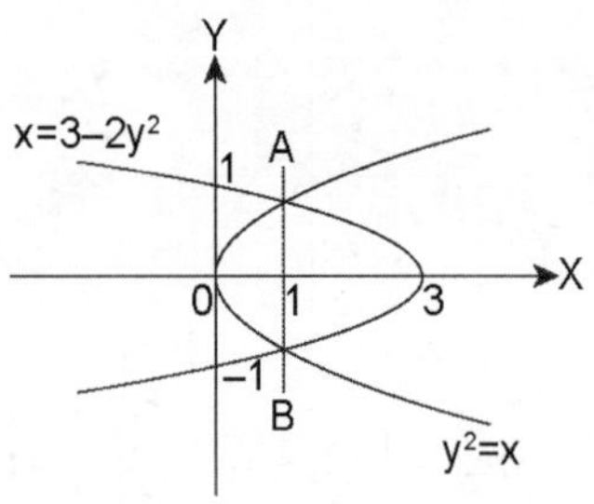

$\therefore \quad A(1, -1)$ and $B(1, 1)$

$$\therefore \quad \text{Required Area} = 2\left[\int_0^1 \sqrt{x}dx + \int_1^3 \sqrt{\frac{-1}{2}(x-3)}dx\right]$$

$$= 2\left[\left|\frac{2}{3}x^{3/2}\right|_0^1\right] + \frac{1}{\sqrt{2}}\int_1^3 \sqrt{3-x}dx$$

$$= \frac{4}{3} + \frac{2}{\sqrt{2}}\left[\frac{-2}{3}(3-x)^{3/2}\right]_1^3 = \frac{4}{3} \frac{-2\sqrt{2}}{3}(-2\sqrt{2}) = 4 \text{ sq.}$$

units

9. Given parabola is $y^2 = 2x$ and given circle is $x^2 + y^2 = 8$ at the point of intersection, $x^2 + 2x - 8 = 0$

$\Rightarrow \quad (x + 4)(x - 2) = 0 \qquad \Rightarrow \quad x = 2$ or -4

$\therefore$ Points of intersection are $A(2, -2)$ and $B(2, 2)$

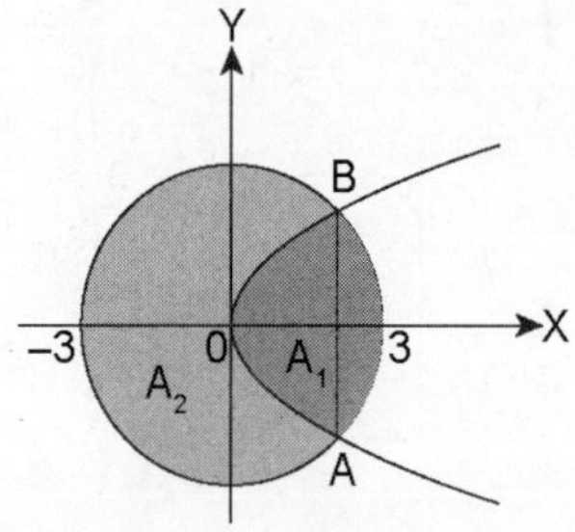

$$\therefore \quad \text{Area } (A_1) = 2\left[\int_0^2 \sqrt{2}\sqrt{x}dx + \int_2^{2\sqrt{2}} \sqrt{8-x^2}dx\right]$$

$$= 2\left[\left|\frac{2\sqrt{2}}{3}(x)^{3/2}\right|_0^2 + \left[\frac{x\sqrt{8-x^2}}{2} + \frac{8}{2}\sin^{-1}\left(\frac{x}{2\sqrt{2}}\right)\right]_2^{2\sqrt{2}}\right]$$

$$= 2\left[\frac{2\sqrt{2}}{3}(2\sqrt{2}) + \left[4\left(\frac{\pi}{2}\right) - \left(2 + 4\left(\frac{\pi}{4}\right)\right)\right]\right]$$

$$= 2\left[\frac{8}{3} + [2\pi - 2 - \pi]\right] = 2\pi + \frac{4}{3} = A_1$$

$$\therefore \quad A_2 = \pi(2\sqrt{2})^2 - A_1 = 8\pi - \left(2\pi + \frac{4}{3}\right) = 6\pi - \frac{4}{3}$$

$$\therefore \quad \frac{A_1}{A_2} = \frac{6\pi + 4}{18\pi - 4} = \frac{3\pi + 2}{9\pi - 2}$$

10. Given curves are $x^2 + y^2 = 25$ and $4y = |4 - x^2|$; $x = 0$; $y \ge 0$

For, $4 - x^2 \ge 0$, $4y = 4 - x^2$

$\Rightarrow \quad x^2 = -4(y - 1)$

For $4 - x^2 < 0$, $4y = -4 + x^2$

$\Rightarrow \quad x^2 = 4(y + 1)$

The curves, $x^2 = -4(y - 1)$; $x \in (-2, 2)$ and $x^2 + y^2 = 25$ intersect where, $y^2 - 4y - 21 = 0$

$\Rightarrow \quad (y - 7)(y + 3) = 0$, i.e., at $(-4, -3)$ and $(4, -3)$

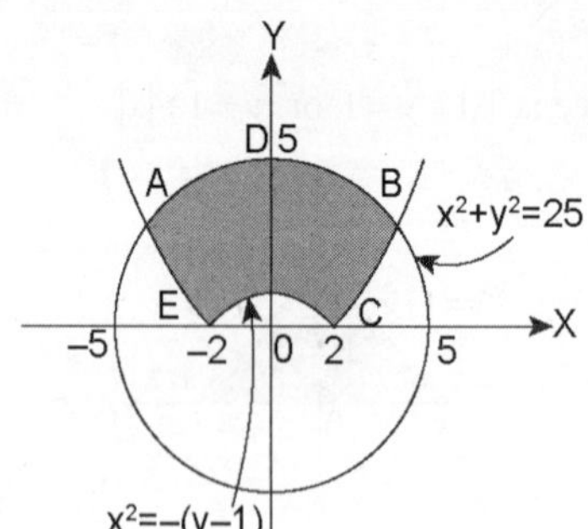

The curves, $x^2 = 4(y + 1)$; $x \in (-\infty, -2) \cup (2, \infty)$ and $x^2 + y^2 = 25$ intersect, where, $y^2 + 4y - 21 = 0$

$\Rightarrow \quad (y + 7)(y - 3) = 0$

$\Rightarrow \quad y = -7, y = 3$, i.e., at $A(-4, 3)$ and $B(4, 3)$

Required Area

$$= 2\left\{\int_0^4 \sqrt{25 - x^2}dx - \int_0^2 \left(\frac{-x^2}{4} + 1\right)dx - \int_2^4 \left(\frac{x^2}{4} - 1\right)dx\right\}$$

$$= 2\left\{\left[\frac{x\sqrt{25-x^2}}{2} + \frac{25}{2}\sin^{-1}\left(\frac{x}{5}\right)\right]_0^4 - \left[\frac{-x^3}{12} + x\right]_0^2 - \left[\frac{x^3}{12} - x\right]_2^4\right\}$$

$$=2\left\{\left[6+\frac{25}{2}\sin^{-1}\left(\frac{4}{5}\right)-\left[\frac{-2}{3}+2\right]-\left[\left(\frac{16}{3}-\frac{2}{3}\right)-2\right]\right]\right\}$$

$$=2\left\{6+\frac{25}{2}\sin^{-1}\left(\frac{4}{5}\right)-\frac{4}{3}-\frac{16}{3}+\frac{2}{3}+2\right\}$$

$$=2\left\{8+\frac{25}{2}\sin^{-1}\left(\frac{4}{5}\right)-6\right\}$$

$$=2\left\{2+\frac{25}{2}\sin^{-1}\left(\frac{4}{5}\right)\right\}=4+25\sin^{-1}\left(\frac{4}{5}\right) \text{ sq. units}$$

11. Given curves are $y = 2^x$, $y = 2x - x^2$, $0 \le x \le 2$

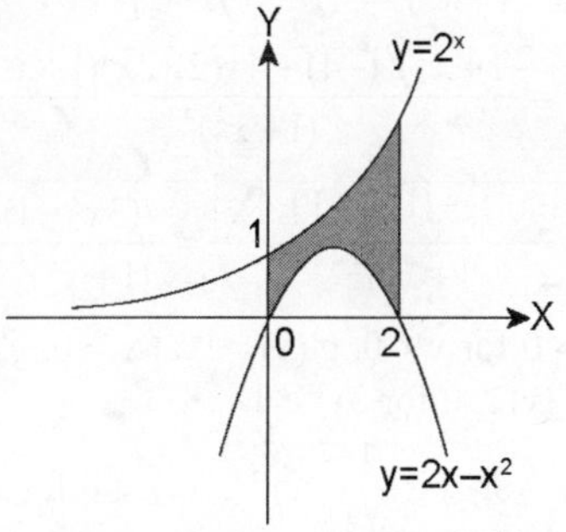

$\therefore$ Required Area $= \int_0^2 [2^x - (2x - x^2)]dx$

$$=\left[\frac{2^x}{\ln 2}-x^2+\frac{x^3}{3}\right]_0^2$$

$$=\left(\frac{4}{\ln 2}-4+\frac{8}{3}-\frac{1}{\ln 2}\right)=\left(\frac{3}{\ln 2}-\frac{4}{3}\right) \text{ sq. units}$$

12. Required Area $= \int_{1/2}^2 (2^x - \ln x)dx$

$$=\left[\frac{2^x}{\ln 2}\right]_{1/2}^2-\left[|x\ln 2|_{1/2}^2-\int_{1/2}^2 x.\frac{1}{x}dx\right]$$

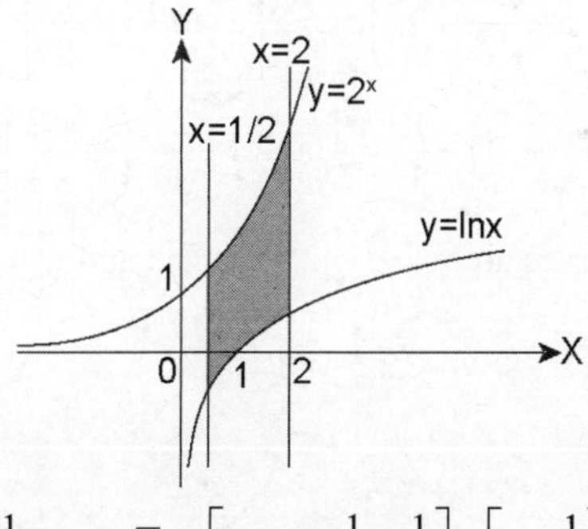

$$=\frac{1}{\ln 2}[4-\sqrt{2}]-\left[2\ln 2-\frac{1}{2}\ln\frac{1}{2}\right]+\left[2-\frac{1}{2}\right]$$

$$=\frac{1}{\ln 2}[4-\sqrt{2}]-\frac{5}{2}\ln 2+\frac{3}{2} \text{ sq. units}$$

13. Given parabola are $y^2 = 4a(x + a)$ and $y^2 = 4b(b - x)$

The two parabolas intersect each other, where $4a(x + a) = 4b(b - x)$

$\Rightarrow$ $ax + a^2 = b^2 - bx$

$\Rightarrow$ $(a + b)x = (b^2 - a^2)$

$\Rightarrow$ $x = (b - a)$

$\therefore$ Points of intersection are $A(b - a, -2\sqrt{ab})$; $B(b - a, 2\sqrt{ab})$

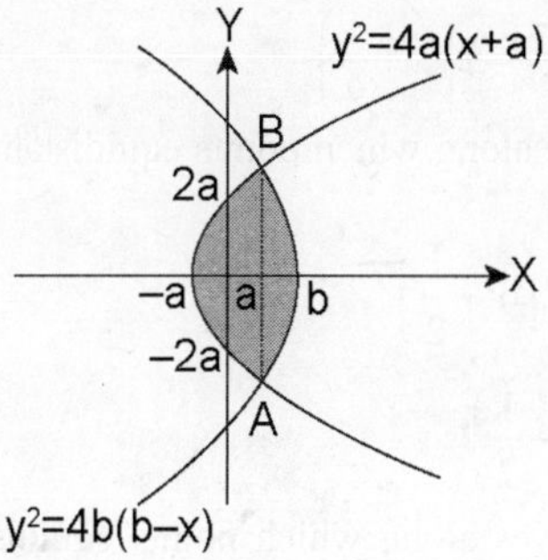

$\therefore$ Required Area

$$=2\left[\int_{-a}^{b-a} 2\sqrt{a}\sqrt{x+a}dx+\int_{b-a}^{b} 2\sqrt{b}\sqrt{b-x}dx\right]$$

$$=4\sqrt{a}\left[\frac{2}{3}(x+a)^{3/2}\right]_{-a}^{b-a}+4\sqrt{b}\left[\left(\frac{-2}{3}\right)(b-x)^{3/2}\right]_{b-a}^{b}$$

$$=\frac{8\sqrt{a}}{3}\left[(b)^{3/2}-0\right]-\frac{8\sqrt{b}}{3}\left[0-(a)^{3/2}\right]$$

$$=\frac{8\sqrt{a}\sqrt{b}}{3}+\frac{8\sqrt{b}\sqrt{aa}}{3}=\frac{8\sqrt{a}\sqrt{b}}{3}(b+a) \text{ sq. units}$$

14. $|x-y| \le 2$ ...(1)

and $x^2 + y^2 \le 4$ ...(2)

For $x \ge y$, (1) $\Rightarrow$ $x - y \le 2$

$\Rightarrow$ $y \ge x - 2$

For $x \le y$, (1) $\Rightarrow$ $-x + y \le 2$

$\Rightarrow$ $y \le x + 2$

$\therefore$ Required Area $= 2\int_0^2\left[\sqrt{4-x^2}-(x-2)\right]dx$

$$=2\left[\frac{x\sqrt{4-x^2}}{2}+\frac{4}{2}\sin^{-1}\left(\frac{x}{2}\right)\right]_0^2-2\left[\frac{x^2}{2}-2x\right]_0^2$$

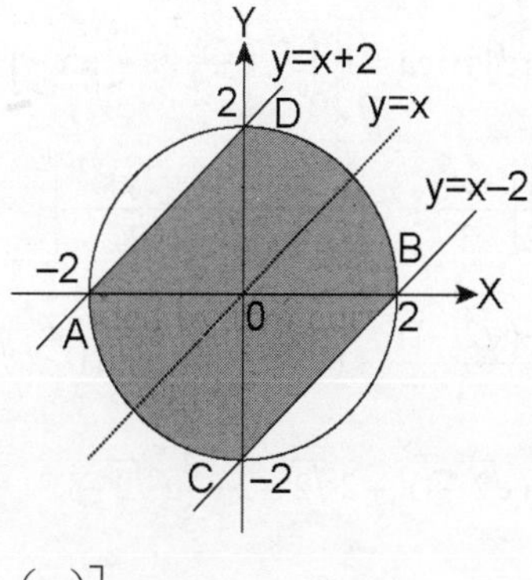

$$=2\left[2\left(\frac{\pi}{2}\right)\right]-2[2-(4)]=(2\pi+4) \text{ sq. units}$$

15. If $P(x, y)$ is any point which is equidistant from origin and line $x = 1$

$\Rightarrow$ $OP = PM$

$\Rightarrow$ $\sqrt{x^2+y^2}=(1-x)$

$\Rightarrow$ $x^2 + y^2 = x^2 + 1 - 2x$

$\Rightarrow$ $y^2 = -2x + 1$

$\Rightarrow$ $y^2 = -2\left(x - \frac{1}{2}\right)$ ...(1)

Similarly $y^2 = 2\left(x + \frac{1}{2}\right)$ ...(2)

is the curve along which points equidistant from origin and $x = -1$ lie

Also $x^2 = 2\left(y + \frac{1}{2}\right)$ ...(3)

$x^2 = -2\left(y - \frac{1}{2}\right)$ ...(4)

are the curves along which points equidistant from origin and sides $y = -1$ and $y = 1$ respectively lie.

Thus, *ABCD* is the reqd. area = 4 (Area *OECF*)

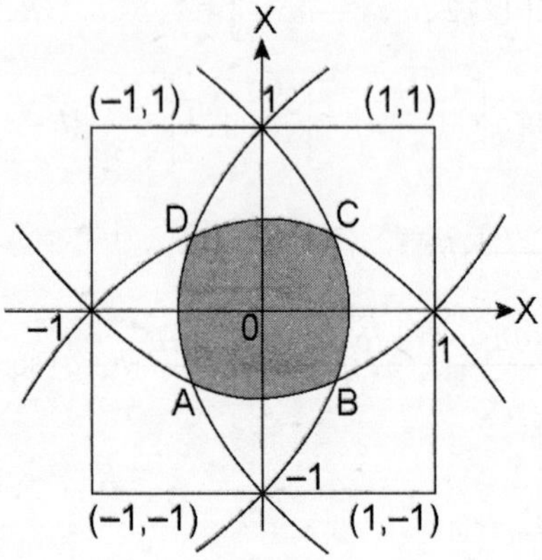

Curves $y^2 = -2\left(x - \frac{1}{2}\right)$ and $x^2 = -2\left(y - \frac{1}{2}\right)$ intersect, which $y = x$ due to symmetry

$\Rightarrow$ $x^2 = -2\left(x - \frac{1}{2}\right)$ $\Rightarrow$ $x^2 = -2x + 1$

$\Rightarrow$ $x^2 + 2x - 1 = 0$

$\Rightarrow$ $x^2 + 2x + 1 = 2$ $\Rightarrow$ $(x + 1)^2 = 2$

$\Rightarrow$ $x = -1 \pm \sqrt{2}$, i.e., at $C\ (\sqrt{2}-1, \sqrt{2}-1)$

$\therefore$ Required Area $= 4\left[\int_0^{\sqrt{2}-1}\left(\frac{-x^2}{2} + \frac{1}{2}\right)dx + \int_{\sqrt{2}-1}^{1/2}\sqrt{1-2x}\,dx\right]$

$= 4\left[\frac{1}{2}\left(\frac{-x^3}{3} + x\right)_0^{\sqrt{2}-1} + \left[\frac{2}{3}\frac{(1-2x)^{3/2}}{(-2)}\right]_{\sqrt{2}-1}^{1/2}\right]$

$= 2\left[\frac{-(\sqrt{2}-1)^3}{3} + (\sqrt{2}-1)\right] - \frac{4}{3}\left[-(1-2\sqrt{2}+2)^{3/2}\right]$

$= -\frac{2}{3}(\sqrt{2}-1)^3 + 2\sqrt{2} - 2 + \frac{4}{3}(\sqrt{2}-1)^3$

$= \frac{2}{3}(\sqrt{2}-1)^3 + 2(\sqrt{2}-1) = (\sqrt{2}-1)\left[\frac{2}{3}(\sqrt{2}-1)^2 + 2\right]$

$= (\sqrt{2}-1)\left[\frac{2}{3}(3-2\sqrt{2}) + 2\right]$

$= (\sqrt{2}-1)\left[2 - \frac{4\sqrt{2}}{3} + 2\right] = (\sqrt{2}-1)\left[4 - \frac{4\sqrt{2}}{3}\right]$

$= 4\sqrt{2} - \frac{8}{3} - 4 + \frac{4\sqrt{2}}{3}$

$= \frac{4}{3}(4\sqrt{2}) - \frac{20}{3} = \frac{4}{3}(4\sqrt{2} - 5)$ sq. units

16. Given curve are $y = x^2$ ...(1)

and $y = \frac{2}{1+x^2}$ ...(2)

Let $g(x) = \frac{2}{1+x^2}; f(x) = x^2$

$\Rightarrow$ $g'(x) = \frac{-2(2x)}{(1+x^2)^2} = \frac{-4x}{(1+x^2)^2}$ and

$g''(x) = \frac{(1+x^2)^2(-4) + 4x(2)(2x)(1+x^2)}{(1+x^2)^4}$

$= \frac{4(1+x^2)\left[-(1+x^2) + 4x\right]}{(1+x^2)^4} = \frac{4(3x^2-1)}{(1+x^2)^3}$

$\Rightarrow$ $g'(x) > 0$ for $x < 0$, $g'(x) = 0$ at $x = 0$, $g'(x) < 0$ for $x > 0$ and $g''(x) \geq 0$ for $3x^2 \geq 1$

$\Rightarrow$ $x \leq \frac{-1}{\sqrt{3}}$ or $x \geq \frac{1}{\sqrt{3}}$ and $g''(x) < 0$ for $x \in \left(-\frac{1}{\sqrt{3}}, \frac{1}{\sqrt{3}}\right)$;

$g(\pm\infty) \to 0$; $g(0) = 2$

Graphically,

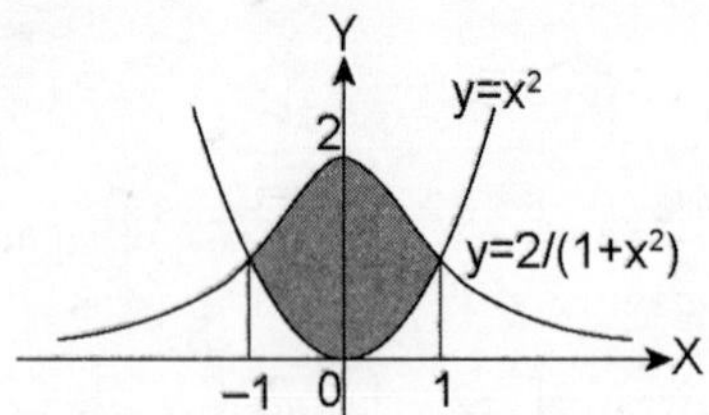

The curves (1) and (2) will intersect each other at *A* (–1, 1) and *B* (1, 1)

$\therefore$ The Required Area

$= 2\int_0^1\left(\frac{2}{1+x^2} - x^2\right)dx = 2\left[2\tan^{-1}x - \frac{x^3}{3}\right]_0^1$

$= 2\left[2\tan^{-1}1 - \frac{1}{3}\right] = 4\tan^{-1}1 - \frac{2}{3} = \left(\pi - \frac{2}{3}\right)$ sq. units

17. Given curves are $y = 2 - |2 - x|$ ...(1) and $y = 3/|x|$ ...(2)

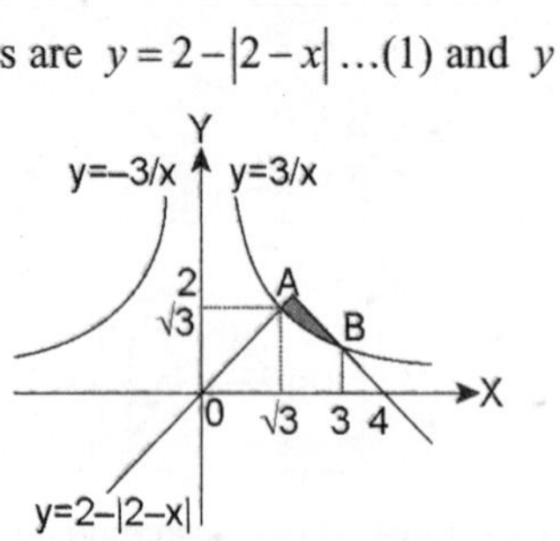

The curves (1) and (2) will intersect each other at A $(\sqrt{3}, \sqrt{3})$ and $B(3, 1)$

$\therefore$ The Required Area $= \int_{\sqrt{3}}^{3}\left[(2 - |2-x|) - \frac{3}{x}\right]dx$

$= \int_{\sqrt{3}}^{2} x\,dx + \int_2^3 (4-x)dx - 3\int_{\sqrt{3}}^{3}\frac{1}{x}dx$

$$=\frac{1}{2}[4-3]+\left[4(1)-\frac{1}{2}(5)\right]-3\left[\ln\left(\frac{3}{\sqrt{3}}\right)\right]$$

$$=\frac{1}{2}+\frac{3}{2}-3\ln\sqrt{3}=(2-3\ln\sqrt{3})\text{ sq. units}$$

18. Given curves are $y = \ln x$ and $y = \sin^4 px$; $x = 0$

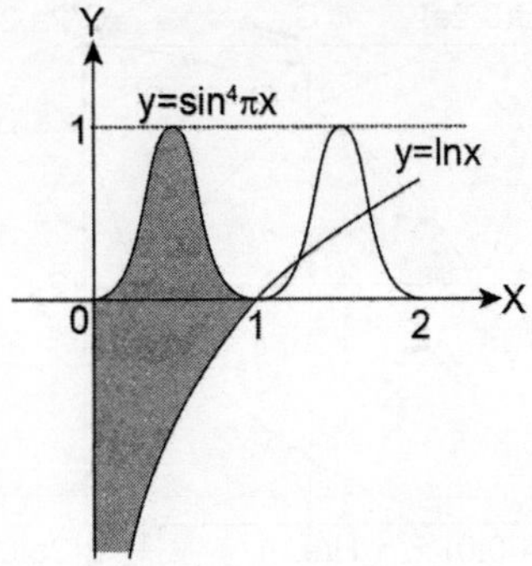

Required Area $=\int_0^1(\sin^4\pi-\ln x)dx$

$$=\int_0^1\left(\frac{1-\cos 2\pi x}{2}\right)^2dx-\int_0^1(\ln x).1dx$$

$$=\frac{1}{4}\int_0^1(1+\cos^2 2\pi x-2\cos 2\pi x)dx-\left[|x\ln x|_0^1-\int_0^1\frac{1}{x}.xdx\right]$$

$$=\frac{1}{4}-\frac{1}{2}\left[\frac{\sin 2\pi x}{2\pi}\right]_0^1+\frac{1}{4}\int_0^1\left(\frac{1+\cos 4\pi x}{2}\right)dx-[0-1]$$

$$=\frac{1}{4}-\frac{1}{4\pi}[0-0]+\frac{1}{8}+\frac{1}{32\pi}[1-1]+1=\frac{3}{8}+1=\frac{11}{8}\text{ sq.}$$
units

19. Given curves are $y = \ln x$ and $y = (\ln x)^2$

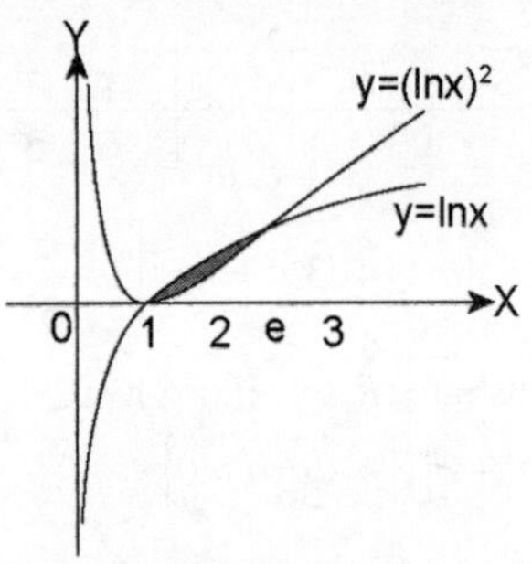

$\therefore$ Required Area $=\int_1^e[\ln x-(\ln x)^2]dx$

$$=\int_1^e(\ln x)dx-\int_1^e(\ln x)^2dx$$

$$=|x\ln x|_1^e-\int_1^e\frac{1}{x}.xdx-\left\{|x(\ln x)^2|_1^e-\int_1^e 2\frac{\ln x}{x}.xdx\right\}$$

$$=e-[e-1]-\left\{e-2\left[|x\ln x|_1^e-(e-1)\right]\right\}=1-e+2[e-e$$
$+ 1] = (3 - e)$ sq. units

20. Given curves are $y = ex\ln x$; $y=\frac{\ln x}{ex}$

Two curves will intersect where, $ex\ln x-\frac{\ln x}{ex}=0$

$$\Rightarrow (\ln x)\left(ex-\frac{1}{ex}\right)=0\quad\Rightarrow (\ln x)\left[\frac{e^2x^2-1}{ex}\right]=0$$

$$\Rightarrow \ln x=0 \text{ or } x=\frac{1}{e}\quad\Rightarrow \ln x=1\text{ or } x=\frac{1}{e}$$

For $f(x) = y = ex\ln x$

$y' = e[1 + \ln x] < 0$ for $x\in\left(0,\frac{1}{e}\right)$ and $y' > 0$ for

$x\in\left(\frac{1}{e},\infty\right)$ and $f(0^+)=\lim_{x\to 0^+}\frac{(e\ln x)}{1/x}=0^-$

$f\left(\frac{1}{e}\right)=-1$; $f(1) = 0$, $f(\infty) = \infty$

$f''(x)=\frac{e}{x}>0\ \forall\, x>0$

For $g(x)=y=\frac{\ln x}{ex}$

$$y'=\frac{1}{e}\left[\frac{x.\frac{1}{x}-\ln x}{x^2}\right]=\frac{1}{ex^2}[1-\ln x]>0\text{ for } x<e\text{ and }<0$$

for $x > e$

$g(0^+)=-\infty$, $g\left(\frac{1}{e}\right)=-1$, $g(\infty)=0^+$, $g(e)=\frac{1}{e^2}$, $g(1)=0$

Graphs of $f(x)$ and $g(x)$ are as given below:

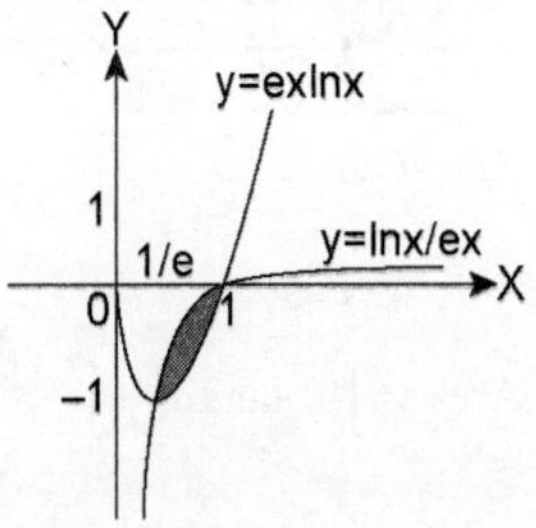

$\therefore$ Required area $=\int_{1/e}^1\left(\frac{\ln x}{ex}-ex\ln x\right)dx$

$$=\frac{1}{e}\int_{1/e}^1\frac{\ln x}{x}dx-e\int_{1/e}^1 x\ln x dx$$

$$=\frac{1}{e}\left[\frac{(\ln x)^2}{2}\right]_{1/e}^1-e\left[\left|\frac{x^2}{2}\ln x\right|_{1/e}^1-\int_{1/e}^1\frac{1}{x}.\frac{x^2}{2}dx\right]$$

$$=\frac{1}{2e}[0-1]-e\left[0-\frac{1}{2}(-e^{-2})\right]+\frac{1}{2}e\left[\frac{x^2}{2}\right]_{1/e}^1$$

$$=-\frac{1}{2e}-\frac{1}{2e}+\frac{e}{4}\left[1-\frac{1}{e^2}\right]$$

$$=-\frac{1}{e}=\frac{2}{4}-\frac{1}{4e}=\frac{e}{4}-\frac{5}{4e}=\left(\frac{e^2-5}{4e}\right)\text{ sq. units}$$

21. Given parabola is $(y - 2)^2 = (x - 1)$

$\therefore$ Equation of tangent at (2, 3) is $(y - 2)(3 - 2)$

$$=\frac{(x-1)+(2-1)}{2}$$

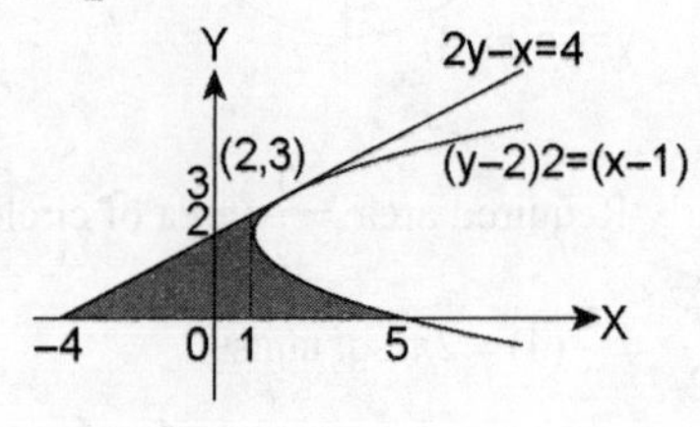

∴ The Required area

$$= \int_{-4}^{1}\left(\frac{x+4}{2}\right)dx + \int_{1}^{2}\left[\frac{x+4}{2} - \left(\sqrt{x-1}+2\right)\right]dx +$$

$$\int_{1}^{5}\left(-\sqrt{x-1}+2\right)dx$$

$$= \frac{1}{4}[x^2]_{-4}^{1} + 2[1+4] + \frac{1}{4}[x^2]_{1}^{2} + 2[1] - 2(1)$$

$$-\left[\frac{2}{3}(x-1)^{3/2}\right]_{1}^{2} - \left[\frac{2}{3}(x-1)^{3/2}\right]_{1}^{5} + 2(4)$$

$$= \frac{1}{4}(-15) + 10 + \frac{1}{4}(3) + 2 - 2 - \frac{2}{3}[1] - \frac{2}{3}[8-0] + 8$$

$$= -\frac{15}{4} + 10 + \frac{3}{4} - \frac{2}{3} - \frac{16}{3} + 8 = 9 \text{ sq. units}$$

22. Given curve is $y = \tan x$.
Equation of tangent to curve at $x = \pi/4$ is $(y - 1) = 2(x - \pi/4)$

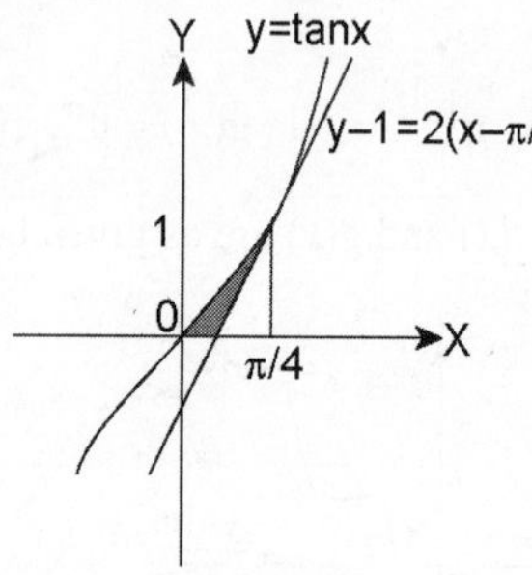

$$\therefore \text{ Required Area } = \int_0^{\pi/4}\tan x dx - \int_{\frac{\pi}{4}-\frac{1}{2}}^{\pi/4}\left(2x - \frac{\pi}{2} + 1\right)dx$$

$$= \left[\ln|\sec x|\right]_0^{\pi/4} = \left[x^2\right]_{\frac{\pi}{4}-\frac{1}{2}}^{\pi/4} + \frac{\pi}{2}\left[\frac{1}{2}\right] - \frac{1}{2}$$

$$= \frac{1}{2}.\ln 2 - \left[\frac{\pi^2}{16} - \frac{\pi^2}{16} - \frac{1}{4} + \frac{\pi}{4}\right] + \frac{\pi}{4} - \frac{1}{2}$$

$$= \frac{1}{2}\ln 2 + \frac{1}{4} - \frac{1}{2} = \frac{1}{2}\ln 2 - \frac{1}{4} = \frac{1}{2}\left(\ln 2 - \frac{1}{2}\right) \text{ sq. units}$$

23. Given regions are $R_1 = \{(x, y): x^2 + y^2 \le 4\}$ and $R_2 = \left\{(x, y): y \ge \sin\left(\frac{\pi x}{4}\right)\right\}$

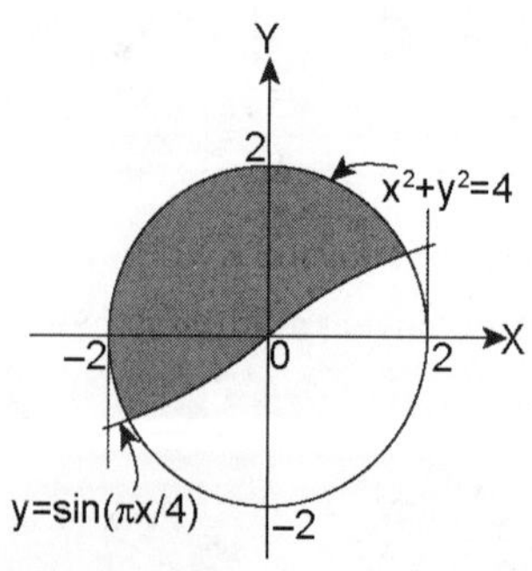

Clearly Required area $= \frac{1}{2}$ (area of circle)

$$= \frac{\pi r^2}{2} = \frac{\pi}{2}(4) = 2\pi \text{ sq. units}$$

24. Equation of circle having arc AC through G:
$(x - 2a)^2 + y^2 = 4a^2$ ...(1)
Equation of circle having arc BD through G:
$x^2 + y^2 = 4a^2$ ...(2)
Equation of circle having arc BD through E:
$(x - 2a)^2 + (y - 2a)^2 = 4a^2$ ...(3)

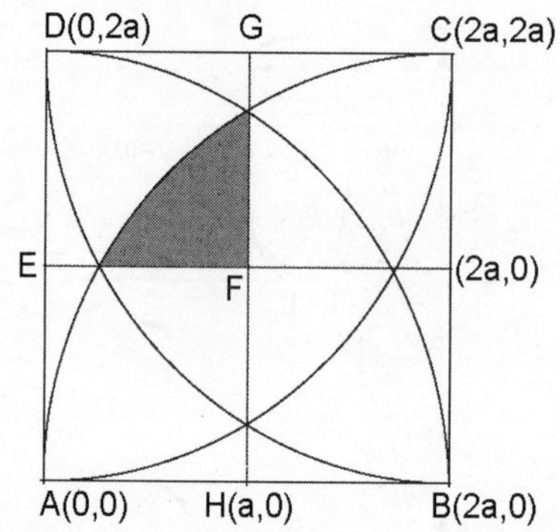

Now, G is the point of intersection of (1) and (2) given by $(x - 2a)^2 = x^2$

$\Rightarrow\ -4ax + 4a^2 = 0$

$\Rightarrow\ x = a,\ y = \sqrt{3}\,a$, i.e., $G \equiv (a, \sqrt{3}\,a)$. Similarly $E \equiv (2a - \sqrt{3}\,a, a)$

$$\therefore \text{ Required Area } = 4\left[\int_{(2-\sqrt{3})a}^{a}\left\{\sqrt{4a^2 - (x-2a)^2} - a\right\}\right]dx$$

Put $x - 2a = t$, $\Rightarrow$ $dx = dt$

∴ Required Area

$$= 4\int_{-\sqrt{3}a}^{-a}\sqrt{(2a)^2 - t^2}\,dt - 4a\left[a - \left(2 - \sqrt{3}\right)a\right]$$

$$= 4\left[\frac{t\sqrt{4a^2 - t^2}}{2} + \frac{4a^2}{2}\sin^{-1}\left(\frac{t}{2a}\right)\right]_{-\sqrt{3}a}^{-a} - 4a^2\left[1 - 2 + \sqrt{3}\right]$$

$$= 4\left[\frac{-a^2\sqrt{3}}{2} + \frac{\sqrt{3}a^2}{2}\right] + 8a^2\left[-\frac{\pi}{6} + \frac{\pi}{3}\right] + 4a^2 - 4\sqrt{3}a^2$$

$$= \frac{4}{3}\pi a^2 + 4a^2 - 4\sqrt{3}a^2 = 4a^2\left[1 + \frac{\pi}{3} - \sqrt{3}\right] \text{ sq. units.}$$

25. Given regions are $R_1 = \{(x, y): x^2 + y^2 \le a^2\}$ and $R_2 = \left\{(x, y): \sqrt{|x|} + \sqrt{|y|} < \sqrt{a}, a > 0\right\}$

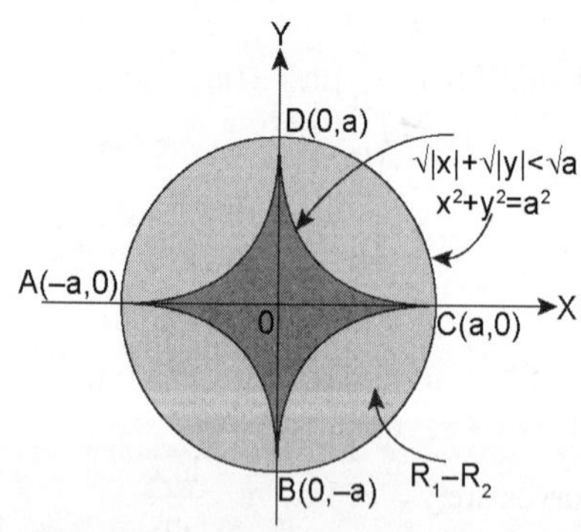

$$\therefore \text{ Required Area } = 4\int_0^a\left(\sqrt{a^2 - x^2} - \left(\sqrt{a} - \sqrt{x}\right)^2\right)dx$$

$$= 4\int_0^a\sqrt{a^2 - x^2}\,dx - 4\int_0^a\left(a + x - 2\sqrt{a}\sqrt{x}\right)dx$$

$$= 4\left[\frac{x\sqrt{a^2-x^2}}{2}+\frac{a^2}{2}\sin^{-1}\left(\frac{x}{a}\right)\right]_0^a$$

$$-4\left[a^2+\frac{1}{2}a^2-2\sqrt{a}\left(\frac{2}{3}\right)a^{3/2}\right]$$

$$= 4\left[\frac{a^2}{2}.\frac{\pi}{2}\right]-4\left[\frac{3}{2}a^2-\frac{4}{3}a^2\right]=\left(\pi-\frac{2}{3}\right)a^2$$

$$= a^2\pi-4\left[\frac{1}{6}\right]a^2 = a^2\pi-\frac{2}{3}a^2 \text{ sq. units}$$

26. Given curves are $y=\frac{x^2}{4a}, y=\frac{x^3}{x^2+4a^2}$, $a > 0$

Two curve intersect where $\frac{x^2}{4a}=\frac{x^3}{x^2+4a^2}$

$\Rightarrow$ $x^4 - 4ax^3 + 4a2x^2 = 0 \Rightarrow x^2 (x^2 - 4ax + 4a^2) = 0$

$\Rightarrow$ $x^2 (x - 2a)^2 = 0$

$\Rightarrow$ $x = 0, 2a$

$\therefore$ $O(0, 0)$ and $A(2a, a)$

For the curve, $y=\frac{x^3}{x^2+4a^2}$

$$y'=\frac{(x^2+4a^2)3x^2-x^3(2x)}{(x^2+4a^2)^2}$$

$$\Rightarrow \quad y'=\frac{x^4+12a^2x^2}{(x^2+4a^2)^2}$$

$\Rightarrow$ $y' = 0$ at $x = 0$ and $y' > 0\ \forall\ x \in R - \{0\}$

$\therefore$ Required Area $=\int_0^{2a}\left(\frac{x^3}{x^2+4a^2}-\frac{x^2}{4a}\right)dx$

$$=\int_0^{2a}\left(\frac{x^3+4a^2x-4a^2x}{x^2+4a^2}-\frac{x^2}{4a}\right)dx$$

$$=\int_0^{2a}xdx-2a^2\int_0^{2a}\frac{2x}{x^2+4a^2}dx-\frac{1}{4a}\int_0^{2a}x^2dx$$

$$=\frac{1}{2}[4a^2]-2a^2\left|\ln\left|x^2+4a^2\right|\right|_0^{2a}-\frac{1}{4a}\left[\frac{8a^3}{3}\right]$$

$$= 2a^2 - 2a^2 [\ln 8a^2 - \ln 4a^2] -\frac{2}{3}a^2$$

$$= 2a^2 - 2a^2 [\ln 2] -\frac{2}{3}a^2 = 2 (1 - \ln 2) a^2 -\frac{2}{3}a^2$$

$$=\left[2a^2\ln\left(\frac{e}{2}\right)-\frac{2}{3}a^2\right] \text{ sq. units}$$

$$= 2a^2\left[\ln\left(\frac{e}{2}\right)-\frac{1}{3}\right] \text{ sq. units}$$

27. Given curves are $y = \cos x - \cos 2x$ and

$$y=x^2\left(x^2-\frac{\pi^2}{4}\right)=x^4-\frac{\pi^2}{4}x^2$$

Clearly two curves will intersect each other at (0, 0) and $\left(\frac{\pi}{2},0\right)$.

For curve, $y=x^4-\frac{\pi^2}{4}x^2$, $y'=4x^3-\frac{\pi^2x}{2}=\left(4x^2-\frac{\pi^2}{2}\right)$

$\Rightarrow$ $x=0$ or $x=\pm\frac{\pi}{2\sqrt{2}}$

$y' < 0$ for $x\in\left(-\infty,\frac{-\pi}{2\sqrt{2}}\right)\cup\left(0,\frac{\pi}{2\sqrt{2}}\right)$ and $y' > 0$ for $x\in\left(\frac{-\pi}{2\sqrt{2}},0\right)\cup\left(\frac{\pi}{2\sqrt{2}},\infty\right)$

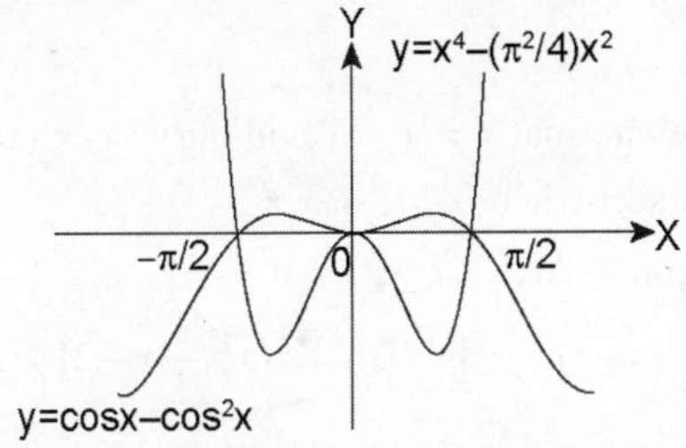

For curve $y = \cos x - \cos 2x$

$y' = - \sin x + 2\cos x \sin x$

$\Rightarrow$ $y' = (\sin x) (2\cos x - 1)$

$\therefore$ $y' = 0$

$\Rightarrow$ $\sin x = 0$ or $\cos x = 1/2$

$\Rightarrow$ $x = 0$ or $x=\frac{\pi}{3},\frac{-\pi}{3}$ and $y' > 0$ for

$x\in\left(\frac{-\pi}{2},\frac{-\pi}{3}\right)\cup\left(0,\frac{\pi}{3}\right)$ and $y' < 0$ for

$x\in\left(\frac{-\pi}{3},0\right)\cup\left(\frac{\pi}{3},\frac{\pi}{2}\right)$

$$f\left(\frac{-\pi}{2}\right)=f\left(\frac{\pi}{2}\right)=0,\ f\left(\pm\frac{\pi}{3}\right)=\frac{1}{4}$$

$\therefore$ Required Area $=2\int_0^{\pi/2}\left(\cos x-\cos^2 x-x^4+\frac{\pi^2}{4}x^2\right)dx$

$$=2\left[\sin x-\frac{1}{2}x+\frac{1}{4}\sin 2x-\frac{x^5}{5}+\frac{\pi^2x^3}{12}\right]_0^{\pi/2}$$

$$=2\left[1-\frac{\pi}{4}-\frac{\pi^5}{160}+\frac{\pi^5}{96}\right]$$

$$=2\left[1-\frac{\pi}{4}+\frac{\pi^5}{480}\right]=2\left(1-\frac{\pi}{4}+\frac{\pi^5}{240}\right)=\left(2-\frac{\pi}{2}+\frac{\pi^5}{120}\right) \text{ sq. units}$$

28. Given curve is $y = x^2 + kx + 2$

$$\Rightarrow \quad \frac{dy}{dx}=2x+k$$

$\Rightarrow$ Slope of normal $=\frac{-1}{2x+k}=m'$ (say)

At $x = 1$, $m'=\frac{-1}{k+2}=1$ (given)

$\Rightarrow$ $k + 2 = - 1$

$\Rightarrow$ $k = - 3$

$\therefore$ Curve is $y = x^2 - 3x + 2 = (x - 1) (x - 2)$ and equation of normal will be $(y - 0) = 1 (x - 1)$ or $y = x - 1$

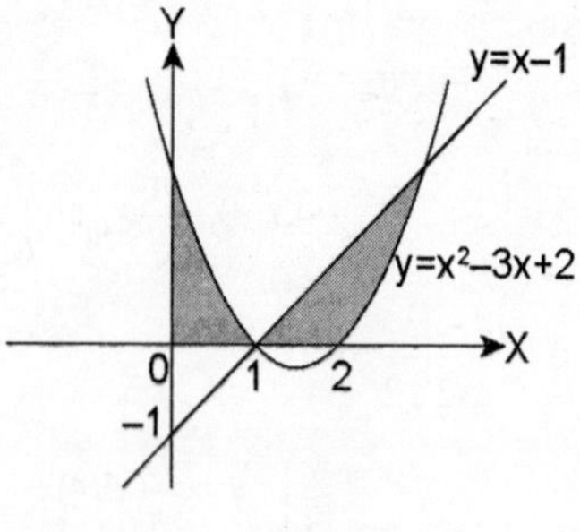

Now, normal $y = x - 1$ and curve $y = (x - 1)(x - 2)$ intersect where $x = 1$ or $x = 3$

∴ Required Area

$$= \int_1^2 (x-1)dx + \int_1^3 \left[(x-1)-(x^2-3x+2)\right]dx$$

$$= \left[\frac{x^2}{2} - x\right]_1^2 + \left[-\frac{x^3}{3} + \frac{4x^2}{2} - 3x\right]_2^3$$

$$= \frac{1}{2}(3) - 1 - \frac{1}{3}(19) + 2(5) - 3$$

$$= \frac{1}{2} - \frac{19}{3} + 7 = \frac{15}{2} - \frac{19}{3} = \frac{45-38}{6} = \frac{7}{6} \text{ sq. units}$$

29. Given curves are $x^2 + y^2 = 4$ ...(1); $x \in [-2, 2]$

$y = x^2 + x + 1$ ...(2)

$y = \left[\sin^2\frac{x}{4} + \cos\frac{x}{4}\right]$ ...(3)

Where [.] is gint function and $y = 0$ ...(4)

Here $y = \left[1 - \cos^2\frac{x}{4} + \cos\frac{x}{4}\right]$

$$\Rightarrow y = \left[-\left(\cos^2\frac{x}{4} - \cos\frac{x}{4} + \frac{1}{4}\right) + \frac{5}{4}\right]$$

$$\Rightarrow y = \left[\frac{5}{4} - \left(\frac{1}{2} - \cos\frac{x}{4}\right)^2\right]$$

For $x \in [-2, 2]$; $\frac{x}{4} \in \left[-\frac{1}{2}, \frac{1}{2}\right] \cos\frac{x}{4} \in \left[\cos\frac{1}{2}, 1\right]$

$$\Rightarrow -\cos\frac{x}{4} \in \left[-1, -\cos\frac{1}{2}\right]$$

$$\Rightarrow \frac{1}{2} - \cos\frac{x}{4} \in \left[\frac{-1}{2}, \frac{1}{2} - \cos\frac{1}{2}\right]$$

$$\Rightarrow \left(\frac{1}{2} - \cos\frac{x}{4}\right)^2 \in \left[\left(\frac{1}{2} - \cos\frac{1}{2}\right)^2, \frac{1}{4}\right]$$

$$\Rightarrow \frac{5}{4} - \left(\frac{1}{2} - \cos\frac{x}{4}\right)^2 \in \left[1, \frac{5}{4} - \left(\frac{1}{2} - \cos\frac{1}{2}\right)^2\right]$$

$$= \left[1, 1 + \cos\frac{1}{2} - \cos^2\frac{1}{2}\right]$$

$$\Rightarrow y = \left[1 - \cos^2\frac{x}{4} + \cos\frac{x}{4}\right] = 1$$

∴ (3) is equivalent to $y = 1$

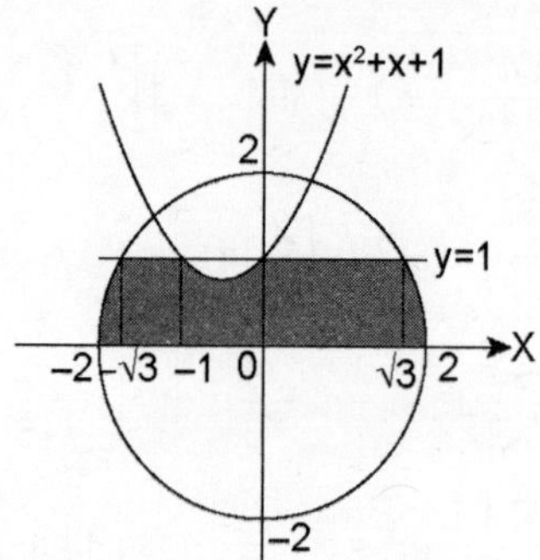

∴ Required Area

$$= 2\int_{-2}^{-\sqrt{3}} \sqrt{4-x^2}\,dx + \int_{-3}^{-1} 1dx + \int_1^0 (x^2+x+1)dx + \int_0^{\sqrt{3}} 1dx$$

$$= 2\left[\frac{x\sqrt{4-x^2}}{2} + \frac{4}{2}\sin^{-1}\left(\frac{x}{2}\right)\right]_{-2}^{-\sqrt{3}}$$

$$+\left[-1+\sqrt{3}\right] - \left[\frac{(-1)}{3} + \frac{1}{2} + (-1)\right] + \sqrt{3}$$

$$= 2\left[-\frac{\sqrt{3}}{2} + 2\left\{-\frac{\pi}{3} + \frac{\pi}{2}\right\}\right] - 1 + \sqrt{3} + \frac{1}{3} + \frac{1}{2} + \sqrt{3}$$

$$= -\sqrt{3} + 4\left[\frac{\pi}{6}\right] - \frac{1}{2} + \frac{1}{3} + 2\sqrt{3} = \left(\sqrt{3} - \frac{1}{6} + \frac{2\pi}{3}\right) \text{ sq. units}$$

30. **Case (i):** If $f(x) \geq 0 \;\forall\; x \in [a, b]$, then

$$\int_a^b f(x)dx = \sqrt{b^2 - a^2}$$

$$\Rightarrow \int_a^x f(x)dx = \sqrt{x^2 - a^2}$$

$$\Rightarrow f(x) = \frac{x}{\sqrt{x^2 - a^2}}$$

Case (ii): If $f(x) \leq 0 \;\forall\; x \in [a, b]$, then $\int_a^b |f(x)|dx = \sqrt{b^2 - a^2}$

$$\Rightarrow \int_a^x f(x)dx = -\sqrt{x^2 - a^2}$$

$$\Rightarrow f(x) = \frac{-x}{\sqrt{x^2 - a^2}}$$

31. $y = e^{-\alpha x}\sin \beta x$ ...(1)

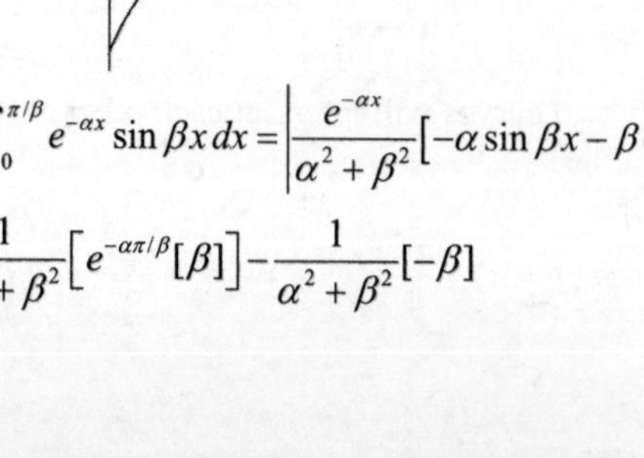

$$S_0 = \int_0^{\pi/\beta} e^{-\alpha x}\sin \beta x\,dx = \left|\frac{e^{-\alpha x}}{\alpha^2+\beta^2}\left[-\alpha\sin\beta x - \beta\cos\beta x\right]_0^{\pi/\beta}\right|$$

$$= \frac{1}{\alpha^2+\beta^2}\left[e^{-\alpha\pi/\beta}[\beta]\right] - \frac{1}{\alpha^2+\beta^2}[-\beta]$$

$$=\frac{\beta}{(\alpha^2+\beta^2)}[1+e^{-\alpha\pi/\beta}]$$

$$S_1=\int_{\pi/\beta}^{\frac{2\pi}{\beta}}-e^{-\alpha x}.\sin\beta x dx=\frac{1}{\alpha^2+\beta^2}\left[e^{\frac{-2\pi}{\beta}}(+\beta)\right]+\frac{1}{\alpha^2+\beta^2}\left[e^{\frac{-\alpha\pi}{\beta}}(\beta)\right]$$

$$=\frac{+e^{-\frac{\alpha\pi}{\beta}}\beta}{\alpha^2+\beta^2}\left[1+e^{\frac{\alpha\pi}{\beta}}\right]$$

$$S_2=\int_{2\pi/\beta}^{3\pi/\beta}e^{-\alpha x}\sin\beta x dx=\frac{e^{-\alpha\left(\frac{3\pi}{\beta}\right)}}{\alpha^2+\beta^2}(\beta)-\frac{e^{-\alpha\left(\frac{2\pi}{\beta}\right)}}{\alpha^2+\beta^2}(-\beta)$$

$$=\frac{e^{-\frac{2\pi}{\beta}\alpha}\beta}{\alpha^2+\beta^2}[1+e^{-\alpha\pi/\beta}]$$

Clearly S_0, S_1, S_2 and so on, are in infinite G.P. with common ration $e^{-\frac{\alpha\pi}{\beta}}$ having sum

$$\frac{a}{1-r}=\frac{S_0}{1-e^{-\alpha\pi/\beta}}=\frac{\left(\frac{\beta}{\alpha^2+\beta^2}\right)[1+e^{-\alpha\pi/\beta}]}{[1-e^{-\alpha\pi/\beta}]}$$

$$=\frac{\beta}{(\alpha^2+\beta^2)}\left[\frac{1+e^{-\alpha\pi/\beta}}{1-e^{-\alpha\pi/\beta}}\right]\text{ sq. units}$$

32. Let the coordinates of P be (x, y), then $d(P, OA) = y$

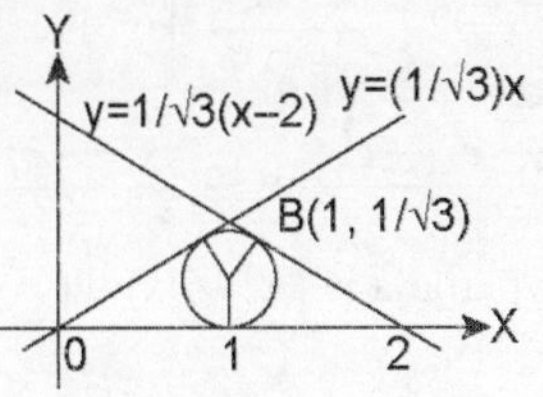

$$d(P,OB)=\frac{\left|\frac{1}{\sqrt{3}}x-y\right|}{\sqrt{\left(\frac{4}{3}\right)}}\text{ and } d(P,AB)=\frac{\left|-\frac{1}{\sqrt{3}}x-y+\frac{2}{\sqrt{3}}\right|}{\frac{2}{\sqrt{3}}}$$

A.T.Q., $d(P, OA) \le \min\{d(P, OB), d(P, AB)\}$

$$\Rightarrow\ y\le\min\left\{\frac{\left|\frac{1}{\sqrt{3}}x-y\right|}{\frac{2}{\sqrt{3}}},\frac{\left|\frac{-1}{\sqrt{3}}x-y+\frac{2}{\sqrt{3}}\right|}{2/\sqrt{3}}\right\}$$

$$\Rightarrow\ y\le\min\left\{\frac{\frac{1}{\sqrt{3}}x-y}{2/\sqrt{3}},\frac{\frac{-1}{\sqrt{3}}x-y+\frac{2}{\sqrt{3}}}{2/\sqrt{3}}\right\}$$

Clearly the distances of points on Angle of $\angle OBA$ from OB and AB are same

$\therefore$ for $x < 1$, $d(P,OB) < d(P,BA)$ and for $x > 1$, $d(P,OB) > d(P,BA)$ and for $x = 1$, $d(P,OB) = d(P,BA)$

$$\therefore\quad y\le\frac{\frac{1}{\sqrt{3}}x-y}{2/\sqrt{3}}\text{ for } x\le1\text{ and } y\le\frac{\frac{1}{\sqrt{3}}x-y+\frac{2}{\sqrt{3}}}{2/\sqrt{3}}\text{ for } x>1$$

$$\Rightarrow\ \frac{2}{\sqrt{3}}y\le\frac{1}{\sqrt{3}}x-y\ \text{ for } x\le 1 \text{ and } \frac{2}{\sqrt{3}}y\le\frac{-1}{\sqrt{3}}x-y+\frac{2}{\sqrt{3}}$$

for $x > 1$

$$\Rightarrow\ \begin{cases}\frac{1}{\sqrt{3}}x-\left(1+\frac{2}{\sqrt{3}}\right)y\ge0 & ;x\le1\\ \frac{-1}{\sqrt{3}}x-\left(1+\frac{2}{\sqrt{3}}\right)y+\frac{2}{\sqrt{3}}\ge0 & ;x>1\end{cases}$$

$$\Rightarrow\ \begin{cases}x-(2+\sqrt{3})y\ge0 & ;x\le1\\ -x-(2+\sqrt{3})y+2\ge0 & ;x<1\end{cases}$$

$$\Rightarrow\ \begin{cases}y\le\frac{1}{2+\sqrt{3}}x & ;x\le1\\ y\le\frac{-1}{2+\sqrt{3}}x+\frac{2}{2+\sqrt{3}} & ;x>1\end{cases}$$

$\therefore$ Required Area

$$=\int_0^1\frac{1}{2+\sqrt{3}}xdx+\int_1^2\left(\frac{-1}{2+\sqrt{3}}x+\frac{2}{2+\sqrt{3}}\right)dx$$

$$=\frac{1}{2+\sqrt{3}}.\frac{1}{2}-\frac{1}{2+\sqrt{3}}.\frac{(3)}{2}+\frac{2}{2+\sqrt{3}}$$

$$=\left(\frac{1}{2+\sqrt{3}}\right)\left(\frac{1}{2}-\frac{3}{2}-2\right)=\left(\frac{1}{2+\sqrt{3}}\right)(1)=(2-\sqrt{3})\text{ sq. units}$$

33. Given curves are $y = \tan^n x$; $x = \pi/4$, $y = 0$

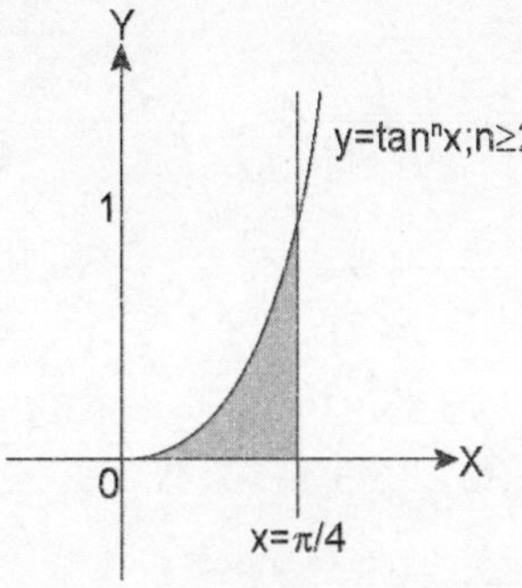

(i) $A_n=\int_0^{\pi/4}\tan^n xdx\ ;n\ge3;\ A_2=\int_0^{\pi/4}(\sec^2 x-1)=\left(1-\frac{\pi}{4}\right)$

$$A_n=\int_0^{\pi/4}\tan^{n-2}x.\tan^2 xdx=\int_0^{\pi/4}\tan^{n-2}x(\sec^2 x-1)dx$$

$$=\int_0^{\pi/4}\tan^{n-2}x\sec^2 dx-A_{n-2}$$

$$\Rightarrow\ A_n=\int_0^1 t^{n-2}dt-A_{n-2}$$

$$\Rightarrow\ A_n=\frac{1}{n-1}-A_{n-2}\ ;n\ge3$$

$$\Rightarrow\ A_n+A_{n-2}=\frac{1}{n-1}\ ;n\ge3$$

For $n = 2$, $A_2 + A_0 = 1 - \frac{\pi}{4} + \frac{\pi}{4} = \frac{1}{2-1}$

$\therefore \quad A_n + A_{n-2} = \frac{1}{n-1} \quad \forall\, n \geq 2$

(ii) $A_n + A_{n-2} = \frac{1}{n-1}$ ...(1)

$\Rightarrow \quad A_{n+2} + A_n = \frac{1}{n+1}$ ...(2)

$\because \quad \tan x \in [0, 1]$ for $x \in [0, \pi/4]$

$\Rightarrow \quad (\tan x)^n \downarrow$ as $n \uparrow$

$\Rightarrow \quad A_{n-2} > A_n > A_{n+2}$

$\therefore$ From (1), $A_n + A_n < \frac{1}{n-1}$ and from (2), $A_n + A_n > \frac{1}{n+1}$

$\Rightarrow \quad \frac{1}{2(n+1)} > A_n < \frac{1}{2(n-1)}$

34. A.T.Q. $\int_1^t (f(x) - x)dx = (t + \sqrt{1+t^2}) - (1+\sqrt{2})$

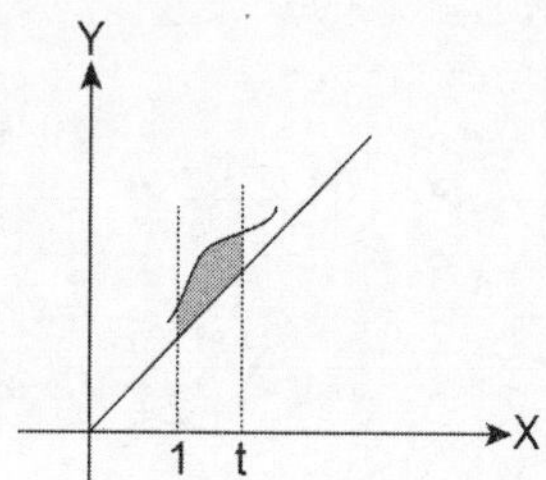

$\Rightarrow \quad \int_1^t f(x)dx - \frac{(t^2-1)}{2} = t + \sqrt{1+t^2} - (1+\sqrt{2})$

$\Rightarrow \quad f(t) - \frac{1}{2}(2t) = 1 + \frac{t}{\sqrt{1+t^2}}$

$\Rightarrow \quad f(t) = 1 + t + \frac{t}{\sqrt{1+t^2}}$

$\Rightarrow \quad f(x) = 1 + x + \frac{x}{\sqrt{1+x^2}}$

35. $f(x) = \begin{cases} -2, & -3 \leq x \leq 0 \\ x-2, & 0 < x \leq 3 \end{cases}$

$f(|x|) = \begin{cases} -x-2; & -3 \leq x \leq 0 \\ x-2; & 0 < x \leq 3 \end{cases};$

$|f(x)| = \begin{cases} 2 \ ; & -3 \leq x \leq 0 \\ -x+2 \ ; & 0 < x < 2 \\ 2x-4 \ ; & 2 \leq x \leq 3 \end{cases}$

$\Rightarrow \quad f|x| + |f(x)| = \begin{cases} -x; & -3 \leq x \leq 0 \\ 0; & 0 < x < 2 \\ 2x-4; & 2 \leq x \leq 3 \end{cases}$ and

$f|x| - |f(x)| = \begin{cases} -x-4 \ ; & -3 \leq x \leq 0 \\ 2x-4 \ ; & 0 < x < 2 \\ 0 \ ; & 2 \leq x \leq 3 \end{cases}$

$\Rightarrow \quad g(x) = \min.\{f|x| + |f(x)|, f|x| - |f(x)|\}$

$= \min \begin{cases} -x-4 \ ; & -3 \leq x \leq 0 \\ 2x-4 \ ; & 0 < x < 2 \\ 0 \ ; & 2 \leq x \leq 3 \end{cases}$

$\therefore$ Required Area = area of trapezium $ABCD$ + area of ΔOCD

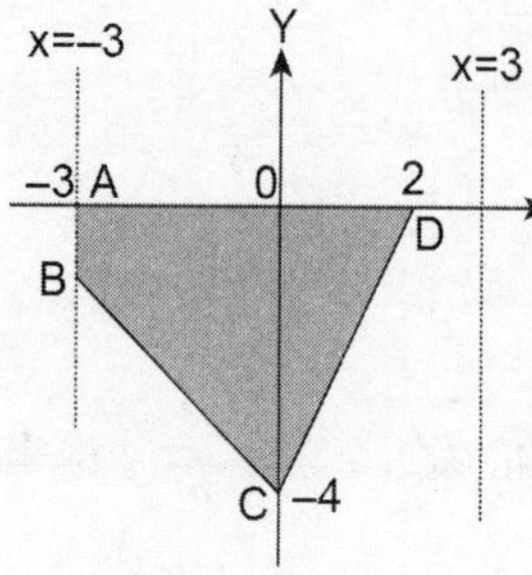

$= \frac{1}{2}(1+4)(3) + \frac{1}{2}(2)(4) = 7.5 + 4 = 11.5$ sq. units

36. $x = 2 + \frac{e^t + e^{-t}}{2}; y = 2 + \frac{e^t - e^{-t}}{2}$

$f(x, y) = x^2 - y^2 - 4x + 4y - 1 = 0$

$\Rightarrow \quad \frac{\partial f}{\partial x} = 2x - 4; \frac{\partial f}{\partial y} = -2y + 4$

$\therefore \quad \frac{\partial f}{\partial x} = 0 \qquad \Rightarrow \quad x = 2$ and $\frac{\partial f}{\partial y} = 0$

$\Rightarrow \quad y = 2$

$\therefore$ Centre $\equiv (2, 2) \equiv C$

Also $P : x = 2 + \left(\frac{e^{t_1} + e^{-t_1}}{2}\right); y = 2 + \left(\frac{e^{t_1} - e^{-t_1}}{2}\right)$ and

$Q : x = 2 + \frac{e^{-t_1} + e^{t_1}}{2}; y = 2 + \frac{e^{-t_1} - e^{t_1}}{2}$

Given hyperbola is, $(x^2 - 4x) - (y^2 - 4y) = 1$

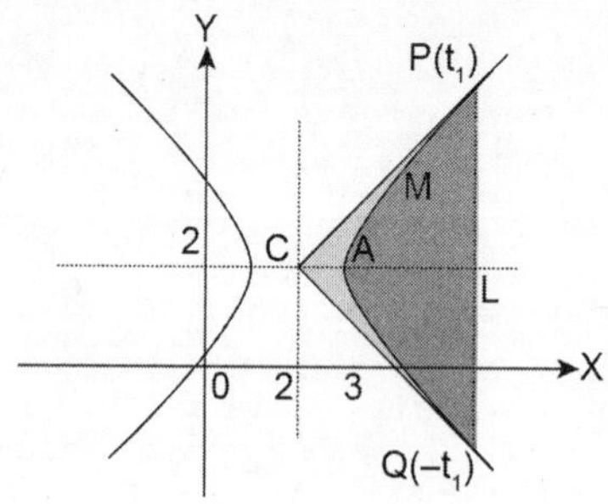

$\Rightarrow \quad (x^2 - 4x + 4) - (y^2 - 4y + 4) = 1$

$\Rightarrow \quad (x - 2)^2 - (y - 2)^2 = 1$

$\therefore$ Required Area = 2 [area of $D\ CPL$ – area under the curve AMP]

$= 2\left[\frac{1}{2}\left(\frac{e^{t_1} + e^{-t_1}}{2}\right)\left(\frac{e^{t_1} - e^{-t_1}}{2}\right) - \int_{x(t=0)}^{x(t_1)} \left\{\sqrt{(x-2)^2 - 1}\right\} dx\right]$

$= \frac{e^{2t_1} - e^{-2t_1}}{4}$

$-2\left[\frac{(x-2)\sqrt{(x-2)^2-1}}{2} - \frac{1}{2}\ln\left|(x-2) + \sqrt{(x-2)^2 - 1}\right|\right]_{x(t=0)}^{x(t_1)}$

$$= \frac{e^{2t_1} - e^{-2t_1}}{4}$$

$$-\left[(x-2)\sqrt{(x-2)^2-1} - \ln\left|(x-2)+\sqrt{(x-2)^2-1}\right|\right]_3^{x(t_1)}$$

$$= \frac{e^{2t_1} - e^{-2t_1}}{4}$$

$$-\left[\left(\frac{e^{t_1}+e^{-t_1}}{2}\right)\sqrt{\left(\frac{e^{t_1}+e^{-t_1}}{2}\right)^2 - 1} - \ln\left|\frac{e^{t_1}+e^{-t_1}}{2} + \sqrt{\left(\frac{e^{t_1}+e^{-t_1}}{2}\right)^2 - 1}\right|\right]$$

$$= \frac{e^{2t_1} - e^{-2t_1}}{4} - \left[\frac{e^{2t_1} - e^{-2t_1}}{4}\right] + \ln(e^{t_1}) = t_1$$

37. $(x-y)f(x+y) - (x+y)f(x-y) = 4xy(x^2-y^2)$ ...(1)

For $x = 0$,

$-yf(y) - yf(-y) = 0$

$\Rightarrow f(y) = -f(-y)$

$\Rightarrow f(x)$ is an odd function

For $x = y$, $-2x f(0) = 0 \ \forall x \in \mathbb{R}$

$\Rightarrow f(0) = 0$ ...(2)

From (1), $\dfrac{f(x+y)}{x+y} - \dfrac{f(x-y)}{(x-y)} = 4xy$ for $y \neq \pm x$

Put $x + y = u$, $x - y = v$

$\Rightarrow \dfrac{f(u)}{u} - \dfrac{f(v)}{v} = (u+v)(u-v)$

$\Rightarrow \dfrac{f(u)}{u} - \dfrac{f(v)}{v} = u^2 - v^2$

Different partially w.r.t. u, we get

$\dfrac{f'(u)}{u} + f(u)\left(-\dfrac{1}{u^2}\right) = 2u$

$\Rightarrow uf'(u) - f(u) = 24^3 \quad \Rightarrow f'(u) - \dfrac{1}{u}\,\text{f(u)} = 24^2$

$\text{I.F} = e^{\int -\frac{1}{u}du} = e^{-\ln u} = \dfrac{1}{u}$

$\Rightarrow \dfrac{1}{u}f(u) = \int 2u^2.\dfrac{1}{u}du + C$

$\Rightarrow \dfrac{f(u)}{u} = u^2 + C$

$\Rightarrow f(u) = u^3 + \text{u.C}$

For $u = 0$, $f(0) = 0 \quad \Rightarrow C = 0$

$\Rightarrow f(u) = u^3$

$\therefore$ $y^2 + x = 0$ and $y^2 + x^2 = 12$;

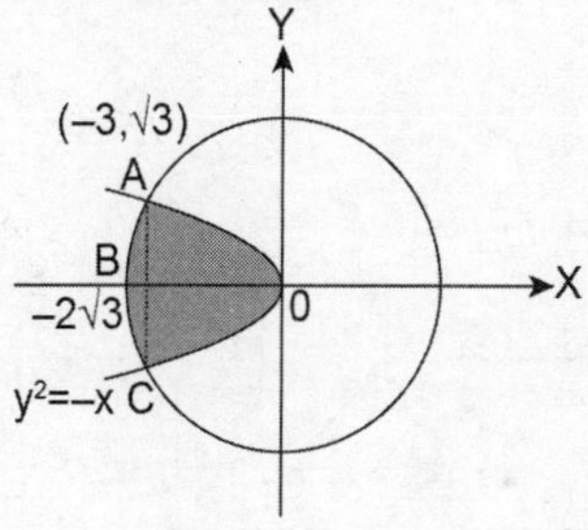

At the points of intersect: $x^2 - x - 12 = 0$

$\Rightarrow (x-4)(x+3) = 0$

$\Rightarrow x = 4$ or $x = -3 \qquad \therefore \quad A \equiv (-3, \sqrt{3})$

$\therefore$ Required Area $= 2\int_{-2\sqrt{3}}^{-3}\sqrt{12-x^2}\,dx + 2\int_{-3}^{0}\sqrt{-x}\,dx$

$$= 2\left[\frac{x\sqrt{12-x^2}}{2} + \frac{12}{2}\sin^{-1}\left(\frac{x}{2\sqrt{3}}\right)\right]_{-2\sqrt{3}}^{-3} + 2\left[\frac{-2}{3}(-x)^{3/2}\right]_{-3}^{0}$$

$$= 2\left[\frac{-3}{2}.\sqrt{3} + 6\left(\frac{-\pi}{3}\right) + 6\left(\frac{\pi}{2}\right)\right] - \frac{4}{3}[0 - 3\sqrt{3}]$$

$= -3\sqrt{3} - 4p + 6p + 4\sqrt{3} = (\sqrt{3} + 2p)$ sq. units

38. Given curve is $2x^2 + 6xy + 5y^2 - 1 = 0$ ...(1)

$\Rightarrow 5y^2 + (6x)y + (2x^2 - 1) = 0$

$\Rightarrow y = \dfrac{-6x \pm \sqrt{36x^2 - 20(2x^2-1)}}{10}$

$\Rightarrow y = \dfrac{-6x \pm \sqrt{20 - 4x^2}}{10}$

$\Rightarrow y = \dfrac{-3x \pm \sqrt{5 - x^2}}{5}$

$\Rightarrow y_1 = \dfrac{-3x}{5} - \dfrac{\sqrt{5-x^2}}{5}$ or $y_2 = \dfrac{-3x}{5} + \dfrac{\sqrt{5-x^2}}{5}$ ...(2)

From (1) $4x + 6xy' + 6y + 10yy' = 0$

$\Rightarrow y'(6x + 10y) = -4x - 6y$

$\Rightarrow y' = \dfrac{-4x - 6y}{6x + 10y}$

$\Rightarrow y' = \pm\infty$ for $6x + 10y = 0$, i.e., $y = \dfrac{-3}{5}x$

Clearly the center of conic is C(0, 0)

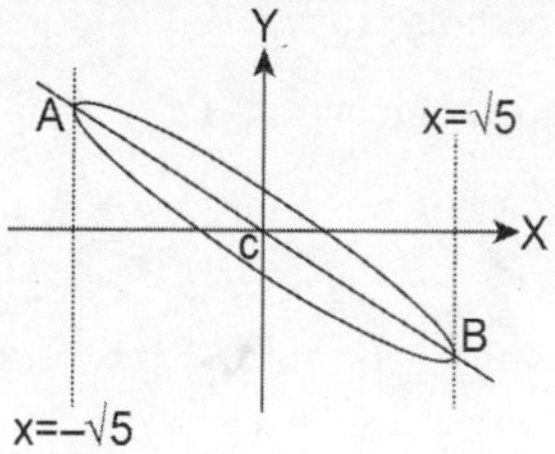

At A and B, $\dfrac{-3}{5}x = y_1$ or y_2

$\Rightarrow x = -\sqrt{5}$ and $x = \sqrt{5}$

$\therefore$ Required Area $= \int_{-\sqrt{5}}^{\sqrt{5}}(y_2 - y_1)dx = \dfrac{2}{5}\int_{-\sqrt{5}}^{\sqrt{5}}\sqrt{5-x^2}\,dx$

$$= \frac{2}{5}\left[\frac{x\sqrt{5-x^2}}{2} + \frac{5}{2}\sin^{-1}\left(\frac{x}{\sqrt{5}}\right)\right]_{-\sqrt{5}}^{\sqrt{5}} = \frac{1}{5}\left[5\frac{\pi}{2} + \frac{5\pi}{2}\right] = \pi \text{ sq.}$$

units

TEXTUAL EXERCISE–2: (OBJECTIVE)

1. (a) Given equations are $y^2 = 4ax$ ...(1) and $y = mx$ ...(2)

At the points of intersection, $m^2x^2 - 4ax = 0$

$\Rightarrow x(m^2x - 4a) = 0 \qquad \Rightarrow x = 0$ or $x = 4a/m^2$

$\therefore$ Required area $= \int_0^{4a/m^2}(2\sqrt{a}\sqrt{x} - mx)dx$

$$= 2\sqrt{a}\left|(x)^{3/2}\left(\frac{2}{3}\right)\right|_0^{4a/m^2} - \frac{m}{2}\left[\frac{16a^2}{m^4}\right]$$

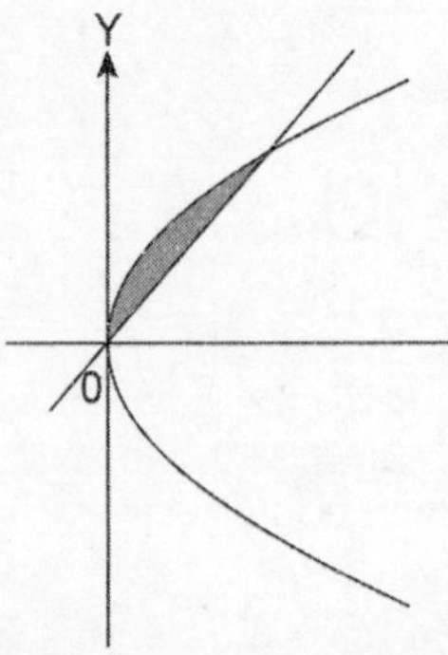

$$= \frac{4\sqrt{a}}{3}\left(\frac{4a}{m^2}\right)^{3/2} - \frac{8a^2}{m^3} = \frac{32a^3}{3m^3} - \frac{8a^2}{m^3}$$

$$= \frac{32a^2 - 24a^2}{3m^3} = \frac{8a^2}{3m^3} = \frac{a^2}{3}$$

$\Rightarrow \ m = 2$

2. (a) Required Area $= \int_0^{\pi} (x + \sin x - x)dx = \int_0^{\pi} \sin x dx$

$$= |-\cos x|_0^{\pi} = 1 + 1 = 2$$

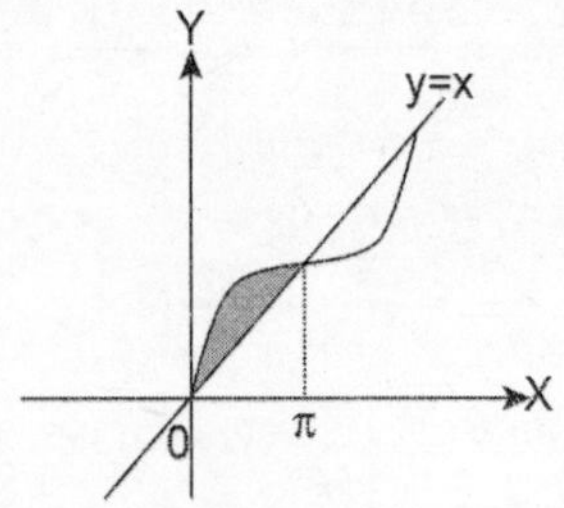

3. (b) Given hyperbola is $xy = a^2$

Equation of tangent at P: $\left(y - \frac{a}{h}\right) = \frac{-1}{h^2}(x - ah)$ or

$$y - \frac{a}{h} = -\frac{x}{h^2} + \frac{a}{h}$$

$$\Rightarrow \ y = \frac{-x}{h^2} + \frac{2a}{h} \qquad \ldots(1)$$

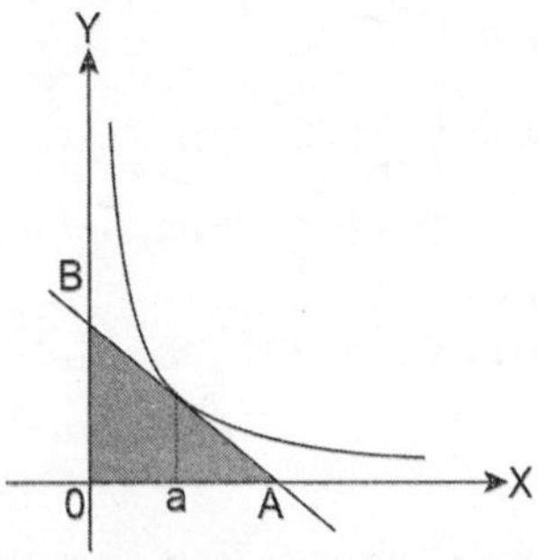

It will intersect x-axis, $A(2ah, 0)$ and y-axis, where B $\left(0, \frac{2a}{h}\right) 2ah$

$\therefore$ Required Area $-\int_0^{2ah} \left(\frac{-x}{h^2} + \frac{2a}{h}\right)dx$

$$= \frac{-1}{2h^2}(4a^2h^2) + \frac{2a}{h}(2ah) = -2a^2 + 4a^2 = (2a^2) \text{ sq. units}$$

4. (a) Given curves are $y^2 = 4x$ ...(1) and $x^2 + y^2 - 2a - 3 = 0$ or $(x^2 - 2x + 1) + y^2 = 4$ or $(x - 1)^2 + (y - 0)^2 = (2)^2$ ...(2)

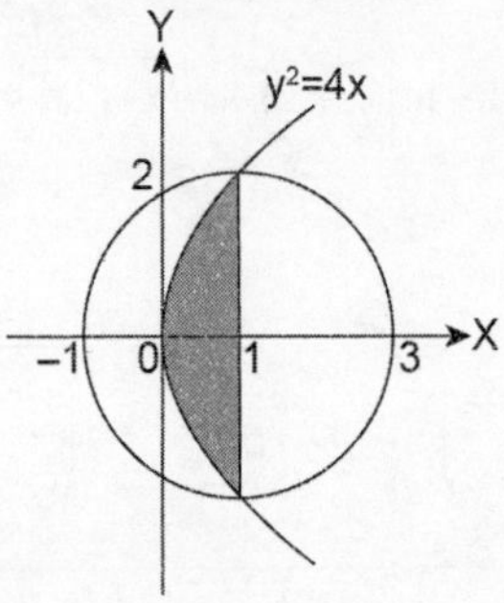

$\therefore$ Required Area $= 2\int_2^1 (2\sqrt{x})dx + \frac{1}{2}\pi(4)$

$$= 4\left[\frac{2}{3}(x)^{3/2}\right]_0^1 + 2\pi$$

$$= \frac{8}{3}[(1) - (0)] + 2\pi = \left(\frac{8}{3} + 2\pi\right) \text{ sq. units}$$

5. (c) Let A_1 = Area bounded by $y = \cos x$; $x = 0$, $x = \pi/3$ and above x-axis

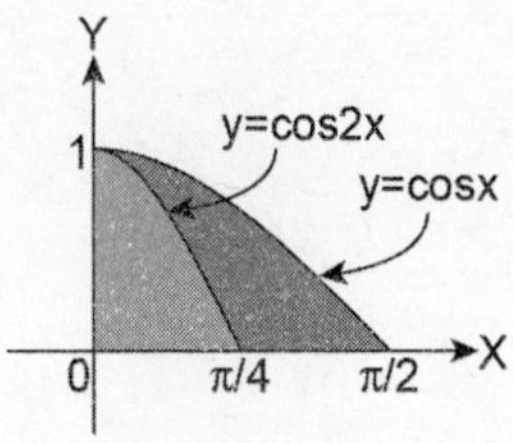

$$= \int_0^{\pi/3} \cos x d = [\sin x]_0^{\pi/3} = \frac{\sqrt{3}}{2}$$

A_2 = Area bounded by $y = \cos 2x$, $x = 0$, $x = \pi/3$, but above x-axis

$$= \int_0^{\pi/4} \cos 2x dx = \frac{1}{2}[\sin 2x]_0^{\pi/4} = \frac{1}{2}[1 - 0] = \frac{1}{2}$$

$\therefore \ A_1 : A_2 = \sqrt{3} : 1$

6. (b) $x^2 = 4by$ and $y^2 = 4ax$ will intersect each other, where $x^4 = 16\,b^2\,(4ax)$

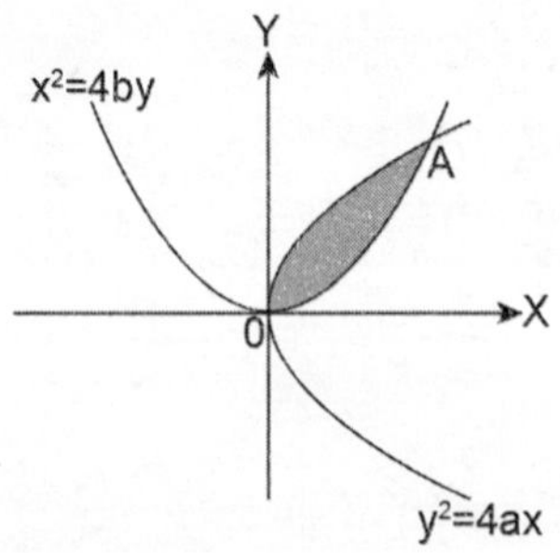

$\Rightarrow \ x(x^3 - 64\,ab^2) = 0 \quad \Rightarrow \ x = 0$ or $x = 4a^{1/3}.\,b^{2/3}$

$\therefore$ Required Area $= \int_0^{4a^{1/3}b^{2/3}} \left(2\sqrt{a}\sqrt{x} - \frac{x^2}{4b}\right)dx$

$$= \left[\frac{2\sqrt{a}(x)^{3/2}}{3/2}\right]_0^{4a^{1/3}b^{2/3}} - \frac{1}{4b}\left[\frac{x^3}{3}\right]_0^{4a^{1/3}b^{2/3}}$$

$= \frac{4\sqrt{a}}{3}\left[8\sqrt{ab}\right] - \frac{1}{12b}[64ab^2] = \frac{32ab}{3} - \frac{16ab}{3} = \frac{16ab}{3}$ sq. units

7. (b) At the point of intersection, $x^3 = \sqrt{3}$

$\Rightarrow \sqrt{3}\,(x^{5/2} - 1) = 0$

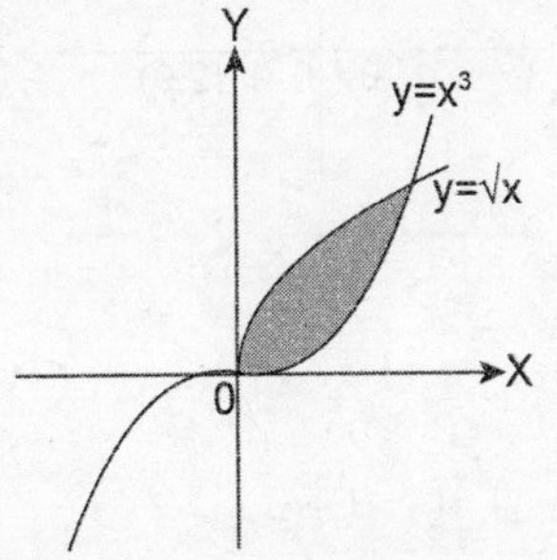

$\Rightarrow x = 0$ or $x = 1$ $\Rightarrow O(0, 0)$ and $A(1, 1)$

$\therefore$ Required Area $= \int_0^1 \left(\sqrt{x} - x^3\right)dx = \left[\frac{2}{3}(x)^{3/2} - \frac{x^4}{4}\right]_0^1$

$= \left(\frac{2}{3} - \frac{1}{4}\right) = \frac{5}{12}$ sq. units

8. (a) Given curves are $y = x^2 - 2x$ and $y = x$

At the points of intersection $x^2 - 2x = x$

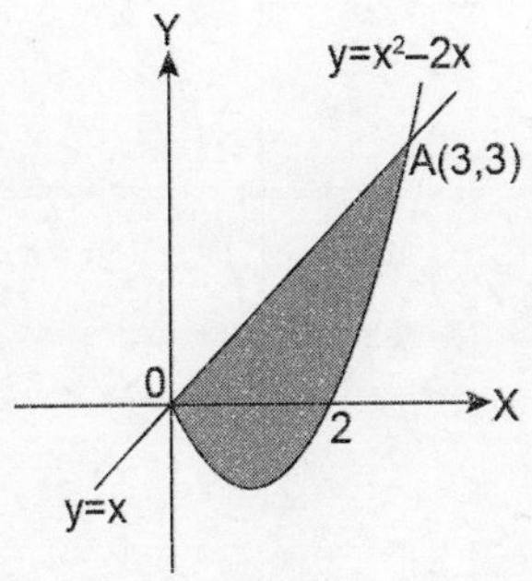

$\Rightarrow x^2 - 3x = 0$ $\Rightarrow x(x - 3) = 0$

$\Rightarrow x = 0$ or $x = 3$, i.e., 0(0,0) and A (3, 3)

$\therefore$ Required Area

$= \int_0^3 x - (x^2 - 2x)dx = \int_0^3 (-x^2 + 3x)dx = \frac{-1}{3}[27] + \frac{3}{2}[9] = \frac{9}{2}$

sq. units

9. (b) Given curves are $y = x$ and $(y - 2) = -(x - 2)^2$

The points of intersection $(x - 2) = -(x - 2)^2$

$\Rightarrow (x - 2)[x - 1] = 0$

$\Rightarrow x = 1$ or $x = 2$

$\therefore$ Points of intersection are A(1, 1) and B(2, 2)

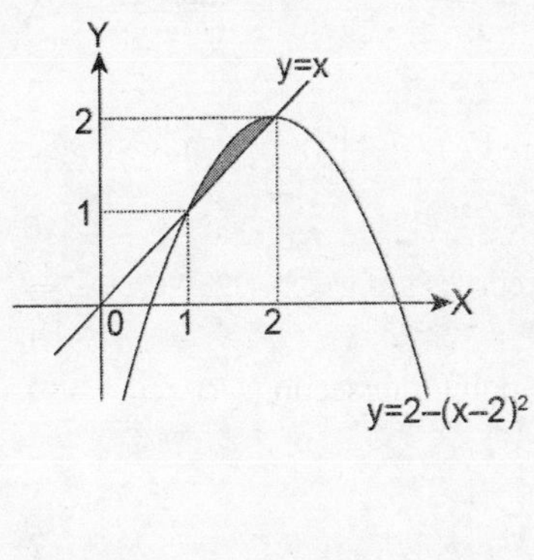

$\therefore$ Required Area $= \int_1^2 [2 - (x - 2)^2 - x]dx$

$= \int_1^2 (-x^2 + 3x - 2)dx$

$= -\frac{1}{3}[x^3]_1^2 + \frac{3}{2}[x^2]_1^2 - 2[x]_1^2 = -\frac{1}{3}[7] + \frac{3}{2}[3] - 2[1]$

$= \frac{9}{2} - \frac{13}{3} = \frac{27 - 26}{6} = \frac{1}{6}$ sq. units

10. (b) Given curves are $y^2 = 12x$ and $x^2 = 12y$

At the point of intersection $x^4 = 144\,(12x)$

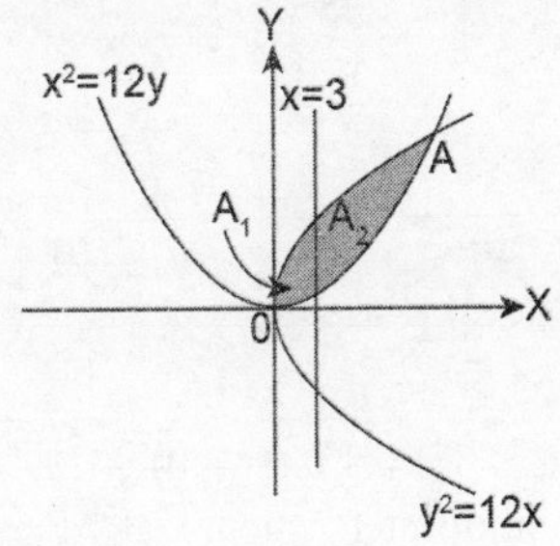

$\Rightarrow x(x^3 - (12)^3) = 0$

$\Rightarrow x = 0$ or $x = 12$

$\Rightarrow O \equiv (0, 0)$ and A (12, 12)

Total area $= \int_0^{12}\left(\sqrt{12}\sqrt{x} - \frac{x^2}{12}\right)dx$

$= \sqrt{12}\left[\frac{2}{3}(x)^{3/2}\right]_0^{12} - \frac{1}{12}\left[\frac{x^3}{3}\right]_0^{12}$

$= \frac{2}{3}\left(2\sqrt{3}\right)\left[(12)^{3/2}\right] - \frac{1}{36}[(12)^3] = \frac{4}{\sqrt{3}}\left(24\sqrt{3}\right) - \frac{144}{3}$

$= 96 - 48 = 49$ sq. units $= (A_1 + A_2)$

Now, $A_1 = \int_0^3\left(\sqrt{12}\sqrt{x} - \frac{x^2}{12}\right)dx = \frac{4}{\sqrt{3}}(3)^{3/2} - \frac{1}{36}(3)^3$

$= 12 - \frac{3}{4} = \frac{45}{4}$

$\therefore$ $A_2 = 48 - \frac{45}{4} = \frac{147}{4}$

$\therefore$ $A_1 : A_2 = 45 : 147 = 15 : 49$

11. (b) Required area $= 2\int_{-1}^{0}\left\{\sqrt{1 - x^2} - (x + 1)\right\}dx$

$= 2\left[\frac{x\sqrt{1 - x^2}}{2} + \frac{1}{2}\sin^{-1}\left(\frac{x}{1}\right)\right]_{-1}^{0} - 2\left[\frac{x^2}{2} + x\right]_{-1}^{0}$

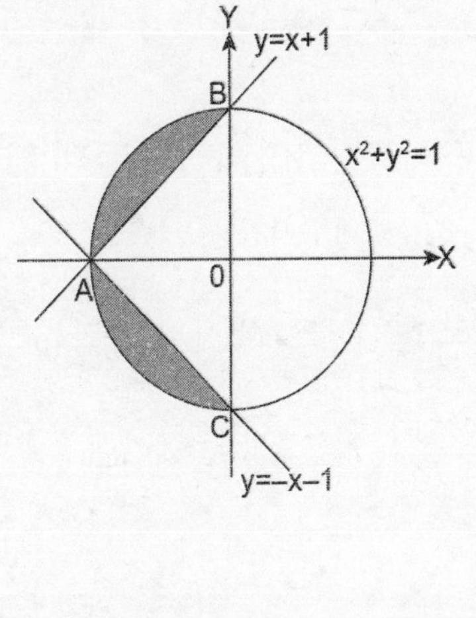

$$=\left[x\sqrt{1-x^2}+\sin^{-1}x\right]_{-1}^{0}-[x^2+2x]_1^0$$

$$=\left[0-\left\{\frac{-\pi}{2}\right\}\right]-[0-\{-1\}]=\left(\frac{\pi}{2}-1\right) \text{ sq. units}$$

12. (a) Given curves are $x^2 + y^2 - 2y - 3 = 0$ ...(1) and $y = 1 + |x|$ ...(2)

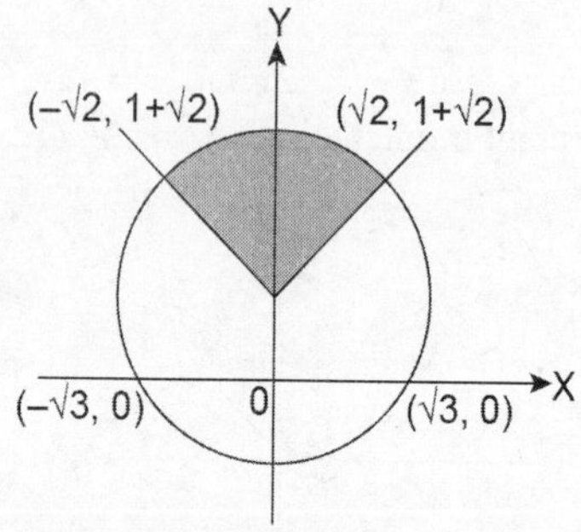

i.e., $x^2 + (y-1)^2 = 4$ or $(x-0)^2 + (y-1)^2 = (2)^2$

At the point of intersection, $x^2 + |x|^2 = 4$

$\Rightarrow$ $2x^2 = 4$ $\qquad\Rightarrow$ $x^2 = 2$

$\Rightarrow$ $x = \pm\sqrt{2}$

$\therefore$ Required Area $=2\int_0^{\sqrt{2}}\left\{1+\sqrt{4-x^2}-1-1x\right\}dx$

$$=2\int_0^{\sqrt{2}}\left(\sqrt{4-x^2}-x\right)dx$$

$$=2\left[\frac{x\sqrt{4-x^2}}{2}+\frac{4}{2}\sin^{-1}\left(\frac{x}{2}\right)\right]_0^{\sqrt{2}}-[x^2]_0^{\sqrt{2}}$$

$$=\left[x\sqrt{4-x^2}+4\sin^{-1}\left(\frac{x}{2}\right)_0^{\sqrt{2}}-[2]\right]$$

$$=\left[\sqrt{2}\sqrt{2}+4\left(\frac{\pi}{4}\right)\right]-2=\pi \text{ sq. units}$$

13. (b) Given curves are $1 - y^2 = |x|$ and $|x| + |y| = 1$

For $x \geq 0$, $y^2 = -(x-1)$

For $x < 0$, $y^2 = x + 1$

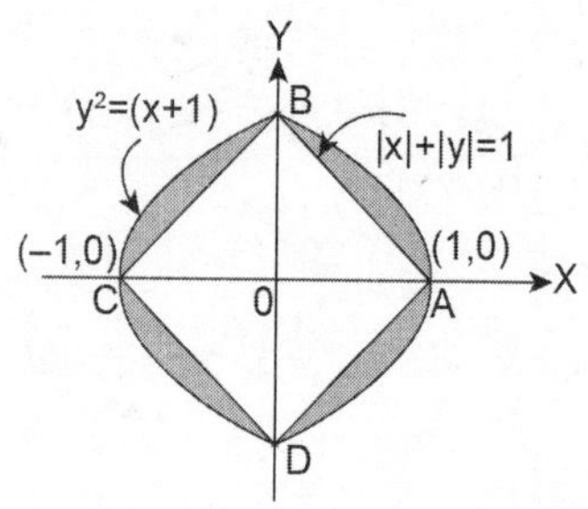

$\therefore$ Required Area $=4\int_0^1\left\{\sqrt{1-x}-(1-x)\right\}dx$

$$=4\int_0^1\left(\sqrt{1-x}-1+x\right)dx$$

$$=4\left[\frac{-2}{3}(1-x)^{3/2}-x+\frac{x^2}{2}\right]_0^1=4\left[\frac{-2}{3}(0-1)-1+\frac{1}{2}\right]$$

$$=4\left[\frac{2}{3}-\frac{1}{2}\right]=4\left(\frac{4-3}{6}\right)=\frac{2}{3} \text{ sq. units}$$

14. (c) Give curves are $y = |x-1|$ and $y = 3 - |x|$

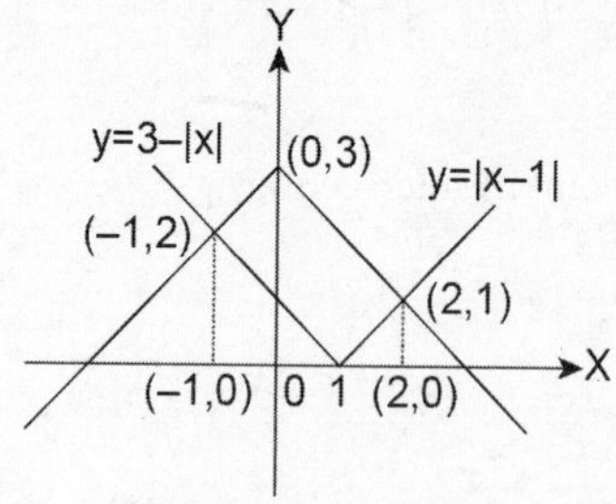

$\therefore$ The given area $=\int_{-1}^{2}\{3-|x|-|x-1|\}\,dx$

$$=\int_{-1}^{0}(3+x+x-1)dx+\int_0^1\{(3-x)+(x-1)\}\,dx$$

$$+\int_1^2\{(3-x)-(x-1)\}\,dx$$

$$=\int_{-1}^{0}(2+2x)dx+\int_0^1(2)dx+\int_1^2(4-2x)dx=[0-(-2)-1]$$

$+ 2[1-0] + [4(2-1)]\ [4-1]$

$= 1 + 2 + 4 - 3 = 4$ sq. units

15. (b) Given curves are $y = x^2 + 2x + 1$ and tangent at (1, 4),

i.e., $\frac{y+4}{2} = x(1) + (x+1) + 1$

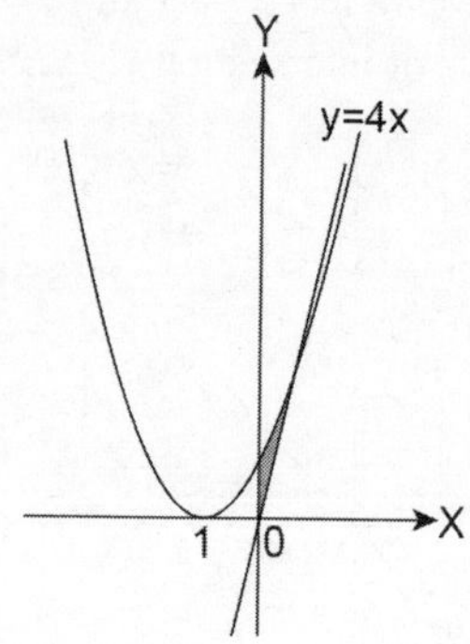

$\Rightarrow$ $y + 4 = 4x + 4$ $\qquad\Rightarrow$ $y = 4x$

$\therefore$ Required area $=\int_0^1(x^2+2x+1-4x)dx=\int_0^1(x-1)^2dx$

$$=\left[\frac{1}{3}(x-1)^3\right]_0^1=\frac{1}{3} \text{ sq. units}$$

16. (c) Given curve are $y = e^x$, $y = e^{-x}$ and the straight line $x = 1$

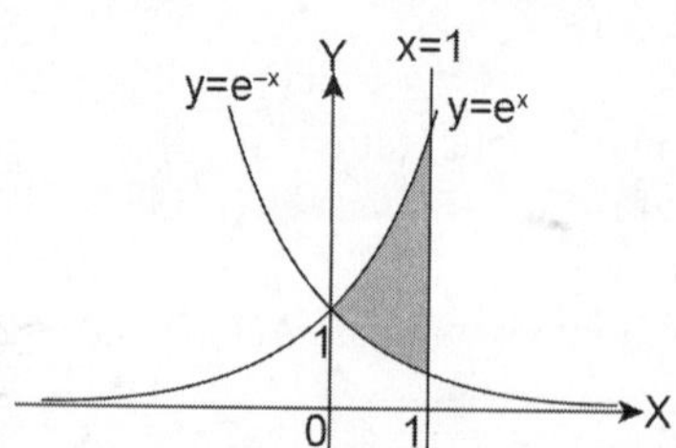

$\therefore$ Required Area $=\int_0^1(e^x-e^{-x})dx=[e^x+e^{-x}]_0^1$

$=[e+e^{-1}-2]$

17. (c) Given curves are $y = 2 - |2-x|$, $y=\frac{3}{|x|}$

At the point intersection (B), $y = 4 - x = \frac{3}{x}$

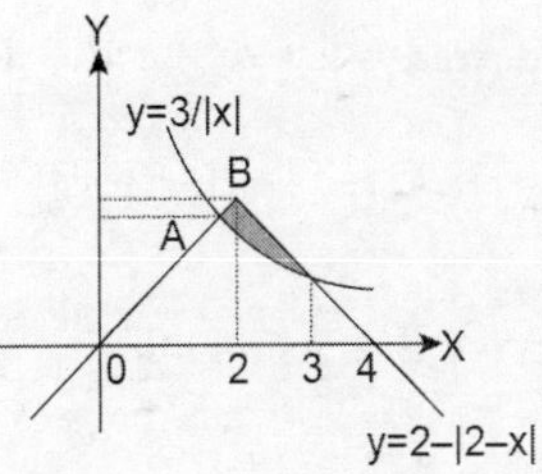

$\Rightarrow\ -x^2 + 4x - 3 = 0 \qquad \Rightarrow\ x^2 - 4x + 3 = 0$

$\Rightarrow\ (x - 1)(x - 3)$

$\Rightarrow\ x = 1$ or $x = 3 \qquad \Rightarrow\ B \equiv (3, 1)$

Also, to point intersect (A), $x = \dfrac{3}{x}$

$\Rightarrow\ x^2 = 3 \qquad \Rightarrow\ x = \sqrt{3}$

$\Rightarrow\ A \equiv (\sqrt{3}, \sqrt{3})$

$\therefore$ Required Area $= \int_{\sqrt{3}}^{2}\left(x - \dfrac{3}{x}\right)dx + \int_{2}^{3}\left(4 - x - \dfrac{3}{x}\right)dx$

$= \dfrac{1}{2}[4 - 3] - 3[\ln 2 - \ln\sqrt{3}\,] + 4(1) - \dfrac{1}{2}(5) - 3[\ln 3 - \ln 2]$

$= \dfrac{1}{2} - 3\ln 2 + 3\ln\sqrt{3} + \dfrac{3}{2} - 3\ln 3 + 3\ln 2$

$= 2 - \dfrac{3}{2}\ln 3 = \dfrac{4 - 3\ln 3}{2}$ sq. units

18. (a) Given parabola are $y = 5x^2$ ...(1) and $2x^2 = (y - 9)$ ...(2)

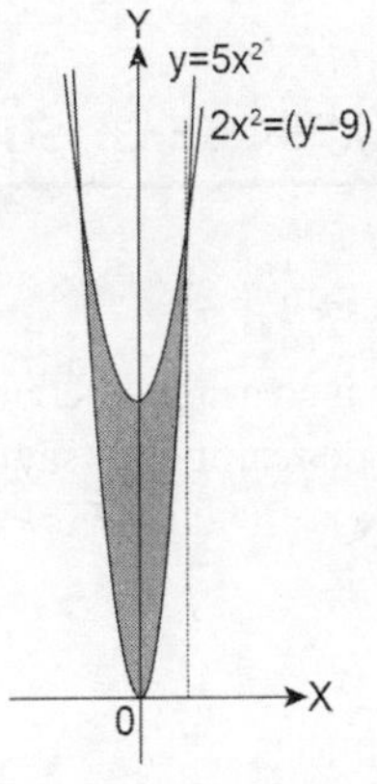

At the point of intersection $5x^2 = 2x^2 + 9$

$\Rightarrow\ 3x^2 = 9 \qquad \Rightarrow\ x^2 = 3$

$\Rightarrow\ x = \pm\sqrt{3}$

$\therefore$ Required Area $= 2\int_0^{\sqrt{3}}\{(2x^2 + 9) - 5x^2\}dx$

$= 2\int_0^{\sqrt{3}}(9 - 3x^2)dx$

$= 2[9x - x^3]_0^{\sqrt{3}} = 2[9\sqrt{3} - 3\sqrt{3}] = 12\sqrt{3}$ sq. units

19. (c) $P(x) > 0\ \forall\ x > 0$

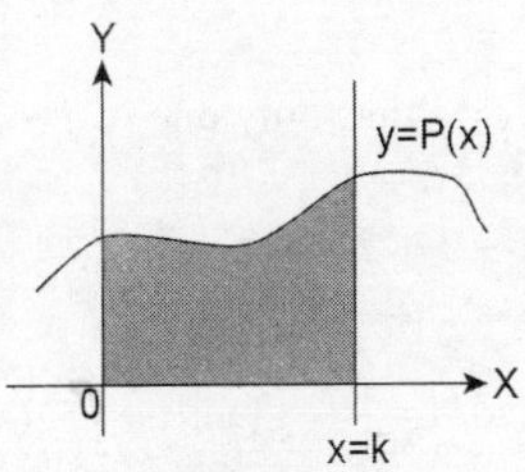

Given : $\int_0^k P(x)dx = \dfrac{k^2(k + 3)}{3}$

$\Rightarrow\ P(k) = \dfrac{1}{3}[3k^2 + 6k] \qquad \Rightarrow\ P(k) = k^2 + 2k$

$\therefore\ P(x) = x^2 + 2x$

20. (c) Given curve are $|x| = \cos^{-1}y$ and the lines $|x| = 1$

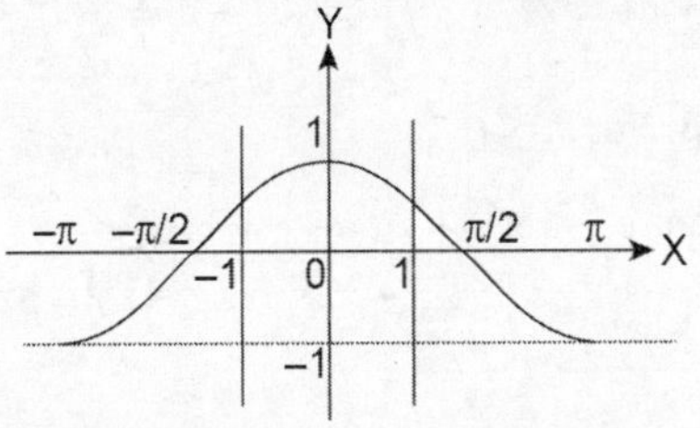

$\Rightarrow\ |x| = \cos^{-1}(y)$

$\Rightarrow\ \cos|x| = \cos(\cos^{-1}y)$

$\Rightarrow\ \cos|x| = y$ for $|x| \in [0, \pi]$ and $y \in [-1, 1]$

$\Rightarrow\ x \in [\pi, \pi]$ and $y \in [-1, 1]$

$\therefore$ Required Area $= 2\int_0^1 \cos x\,dx = 2|\sin x|_0^1 = 2\sin 1$

21. (c) The given curve are $y = xe^x$ and $y = e^x$; $x = \pm 1$ and y-axis

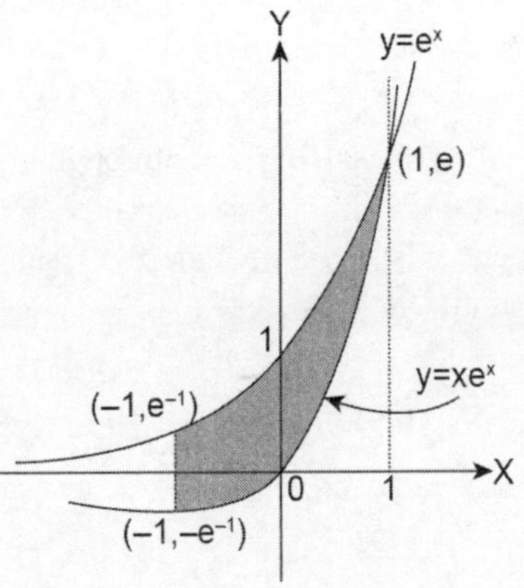

$\therefore$ Required Area $= \int_{-1}^{1}(e^x - xe^x)dx = [e^x]_{-1}^{1} - \int_{-1}^{1}xe^x dx$

$= (e - e^{-1}) - \left[|xe^x|_{-1}^{1} - \int_{-1}^{1}1.e^x dx\right] = (e - e^{-1}) - [e + e^{-1} - (e - e^{-1})] = e - e^{-1} - 2e^{-1} = e - 3e^{-1}$

22. (b), (d) Given curve are $y = x - x^2$ and $y = mx$

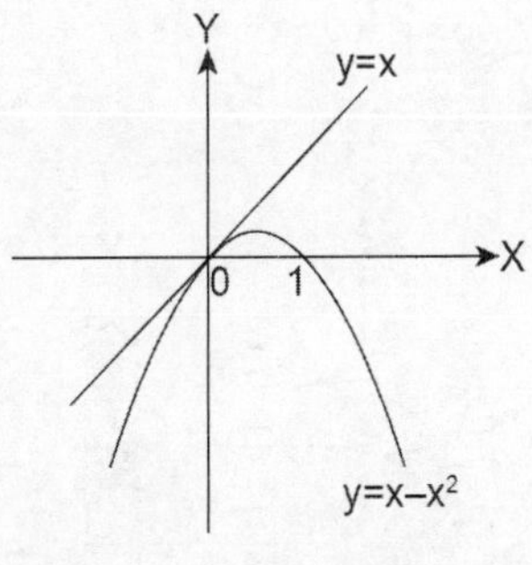

$y' = 1 - 2x$

$\Rightarrow\ y''(0) = 1$

$\Rightarrow$ For bounded area $m \neq 1$

Case (i): For $m < 1$,

$\therefore$ Required bounded Area $= \int_0^{1-m} (x - x^2 - mx)dx$

$$= \left[\frac{x^2}{2} - \frac{x^3}{3} - \frac{mx^2}{2}\right]_0^{(1-m)}$$

$$= \frac{1}{2}(1-m)(1-m)^2 - \frac{1}{3}(1-m)^3 = \frac{1}{6}(1-m)^3 = \frac{9}{2}$$

$\Rightarrow (1-m)^3 = 27 \qquad \Rightarrow 1 - m = 3$

$\Rightarrow m = -2$

Case (ii): For $m > 1$

$\therefore$ Required Area $= \int_{1-m}^{0} (x - x^2 - mx)dx$

$$= \left[\frac{x^2}{2} - \frac{x^3}{3} - \frac{mx^2}{2}\right]_{(1-m)}^{0}$$

$$= 0 - \frac{1}{2}(1-m)(1-m)^2 + \frac{1}{3}(1-m)^3$$

$$= \left(\frac{1}{3} - \frac{1}{2}\right)(1-m)^3 = \frac{9}{2}$$

$\Rightarrow -\frac{1}{6}(1-m)^3 = \frac{9}{2} \qquad \Rightarrow (1-m)^3 = -27$

$\Rightarrow 1 - m = -3 \qquad \Rightarrow m = 4$

23. (a) $\left(\frac{dy}{dx}\right)_{(x, f(x))} = (2x+1)$

$\Rightarrow y = x^2 + x + c$ curve passes through (1, 2)

$\Rightarrow 2 = 2 + c \qquad \Rightarrow c = 0$

$\therefore$ The curve is $y = x^2 + x$, line $x = 1$ cuts the curve $y = x^2 + x$ at (1, 2)

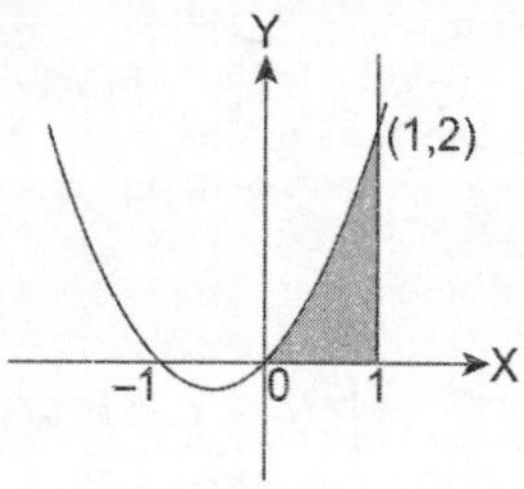

The Required area is $= \int_0^1 (x^2 + x)dx = \left[\frac{x^3}{3} + \frac{x^2}{2}\right]_0^1$

$$= \frac{1}{3} + \frac{1}{2} = \frac{5}{6} \text{ sq. units}$$

24. (a) $y = \begin{cases} -x^2 + 2 \; ; & -1 \le x \le 1 \\ 2x - 1 \; ; & 1 < x < 2 \end{cases}$

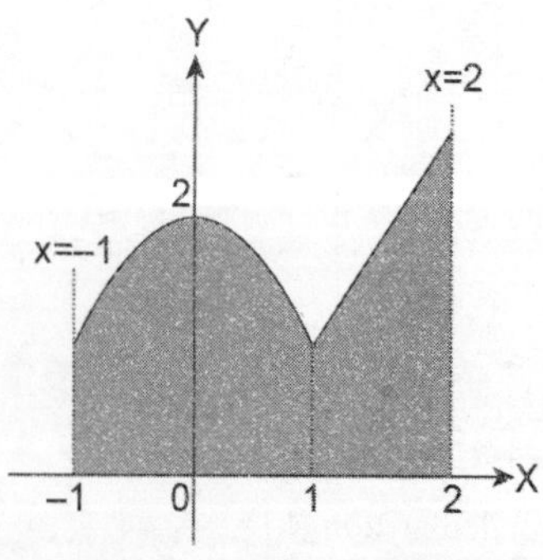

$\therefore$ Required Area $= \int_{-1}^{1} (-x^2 + 2)dx + \int_1^2 (2x - 1)dx$

$$= \frac{-1}{3}\left|x^3\right|_{-1}^{1} + 2(2) + [4-1] - [2-1]$$

$$= \frac{-2}{3} + 4 + 3 - 1 = \frac{16}{3} \text{ sq. units}$$

25. (b) Given curve are $y = \sqrt{x}$ and $y = \sqrt{4-3x}$ clearly, $x \in \left[0, \frac{4}{3}\right]$

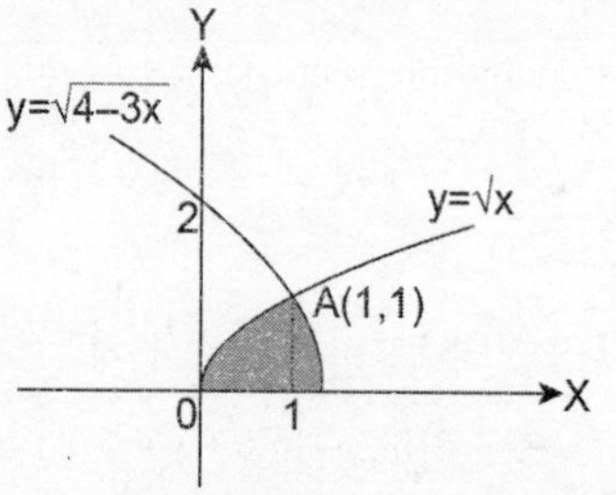

$\therefore$ Required Area $= \int_0^1 \sqrt{x}dx + \int_1^{4/3} \sqrt{4-3x}dx$

$$= \left|\frac{2}{3}(x)^{3/2}\right|_0^1 + \frac{2}{3}\left|\frac{(4-3x)^{3/2}}{(-2)}\right|_1^{4/3}$$

$$= \frac{3}{2} - \frac{2}{9}[0 - (1)] = \frac{2}{3} + \frac{2}{9} = \frac{8}{9} \text{ sq. units}$$

TEXTUAL EXERCISE-3: (SUBJECTIVE)

1. $f(x) = x^3 + 3x + 2$

$f'(x) = 3x^2 + 3 > 0 \; \forall \, x \in \mathbb{R}$,

$\Rightarrow f(x)$ is strictly increasing function

$\Rightarrow f(x)$ has a single real root a (say) As $f(0) = 2$

$\Rightarrow a < 0$ and $f''(x) = 6x < 0$ for $x < 0$ and > 0 for $x > 0$ on $y = x$

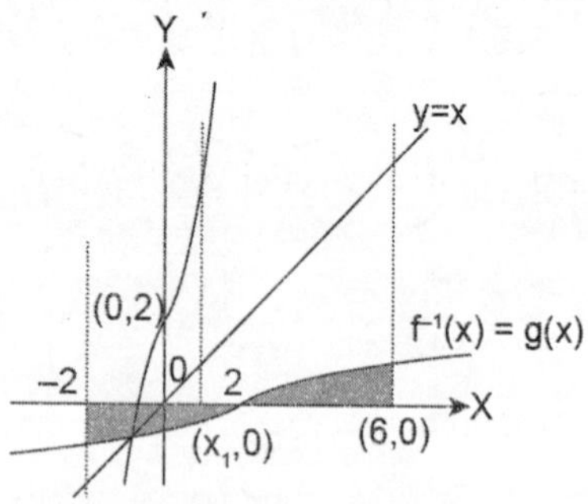

$x = x^3 + 3x + 2$

$\Rightarrow x^3 + 2x + 2 = 0 \qquad \Rightarrow g(x) = 0$

$\Rightarrow g'(x) = 3x^2 + 2 > 0$

$\Rightarrow x^3 + 2x + 2 = 0$ has only one real root.

$f(-2) = -8 - 6 + 2 = -12$

$f(-1) = -1 - 3 + 2 = -2$

$f(6) = 216 + 18 + 2 = 236$

We are to find $A = \int_{-2}^{2} -g(x)dx + \int_2^6 g(x)dx \qquad \ldots(1)$

Equivalently, $\int_0^{x_1}(6-f(x))dx+\int_{x_2}^{0}(f(x)-(-2))dx$ ...(2)

Where $f(x_1) = 6$ and $f(x_2) = -2$

$\Rightarrow x_1^3 + 3x_1 + 2 = 6$ and $x_2^3 + 3x_2 + 2 = -2$

$\Rightarrow x_1^3 + 3x_1 - 4 = 0$ and $x_2^3 + 3x_2 + 4 = 0$

$\Rightarrow x_1 = 1$ and $x_2 = -1$

$\therefore$ Required Area $=\int_0^1(-x^3-3x+4)dx+\int_{-1}^{0}(x^3+3x+4)dx$

$$=-\frac{1}{4}-\frac{3}{2}+4+\left[0-\left(\frac{1}{4}+\frac{3}{2}-4\right)\right]$$

$$=-\frac{1}{4}-\frac{3}{2}+4-\frac{1}{4}-\frac{3}{2}+4=\frac{9}{2}\text{ sq. units}$$

2. Given parabolas are $y = x - bx^2$ ...(1) and $y=\frac{x^2}{b}$ ...(2)

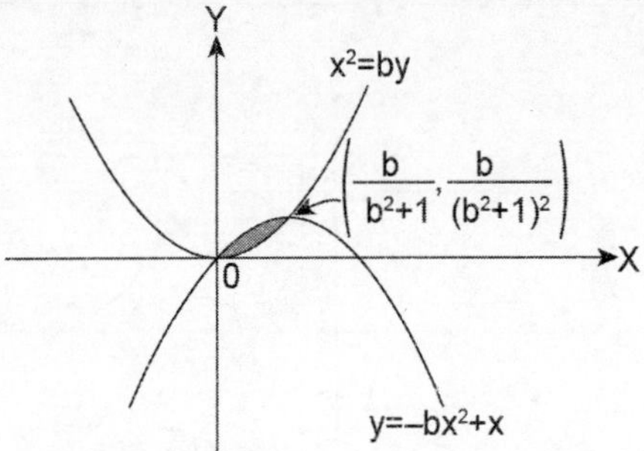

At the point of intersection, $x-bx^2=\frac{x^2}{b}$

$\Rightarrow bx - b2x^2 = x^2$

$\Rightarrow bx - (b^2 + 1)x^2 = 0$

$\Rightarrow x[b - (b^2 + 1)x] = 0$

$\Rightarrow x = 0$ or $x=\frac{b}{b^2+1}$; $b > 0$

$\therefore$ Required Area $=\int_0^{\frac{b}{b^2+1}}\left(-bx^2+x-\frac{x^2}{b}\right)dx$

$$=\left|-\frac{b}{3}x^3+\frac{1}{2}x^2-\frac{1}{3b}x^3\right|_0^{\frac{b}{b^2+1}}$$

$$=-\frac{b}{3}\left[\frac{b^3}{(b^2+1)^3}\right]+\frac{1}{2}\left[\frac{b^2}{(b^2+1)^2}\right]-\frac{1}{3b}\left[\frac{b^3}{(b^2+1)^3}\right]$$

$$=\frac{-b^4}{3(b^2+1)^3}+\frac{b^2}{2(b^2+1)^2}-\frac{b^2}{3(b^2+1)^3}$$

$$=\frac{-b^2}{(b^2+1)^2}\left[\frac{b^2}{3(b^2+1)}-\frac{1}{2}+\frac{1}{3(b^2+1)}\right]$$

$$=\frac{-b^2}{(b^2+1)^2}\left[\frac{2b^2-3(b^2+1)+2}{6(b^2+1)}\right]$$

$$=\frac{-b^2}{6(b^2-11)^3}[-b^2-1]=\frac{b^2}{6(b^2+1)^2}$$

$\therefore A(b)=\frac{b^2}{6(b^2+1)^2}$

$\Rightarrow A'(b)=\frac{1}{6}\left[\frac{(b^2+1)^2(2b)-b^2(2)(b^2+1)(2b)}{(b^2+1)^4}\right]$

$$=\frac{1}{6(b^2+1)^4}[(2b)(b^2+1)[b^2+1-2b^2]]$$

$$=\frac{2b(b^2+1)(1-b^2)}{6(b^2+1)^4}=\frac{b(b^2+1)(1-b^2)}{3(b^2+1)^4}$$

$$=\frac{b(1-b^2)}{3(b^2+1)^3}=0\text{ for }b=0,\pm 1$$

$A(b = 0) = 0$; $A(b=\pm 1)=\frac{1}{24}$

$\therefore$ For $b = 1$, area will be maximum, i.e., $\frac{1}{24}$

3. $f(t)=\int_0^t(\sin x^2)dx$ and $g(t)=\frac{1}{2}(t).\sin t^2$

$\therefore \lim_{t\to 0}\frac{f(t)}{g(t)}=\lim_{t\to 0}\frac{\int_0^t(\sin x^2)dx}{\frac{1}{2}(t\sin t^2)}$

By *L*- Hospitals rule

$$=\lim_{t\to 0}\frac{\sin t^2}{\frac{1}{2}[t(2t)\cos t^2+\sin t^2]}=\lim_{t\to 0}\frac{2\sin t^2}{[2t^2\cos t^2+\sin t^2]}$$

$$=\lim_{t\to 0}\frac{(2\cos t^2)(2t)}{-2t^2(2t)\sin t^2+2t\cos t^2+(\cos t^2)(4t)}$$

$$=\lim_{t\to 0}\frac{2\cos t^2}{[-2t^2\sin t^2+\cos t^2+2\cos t^2]}=\frac{2}{3}$$

4. Given parabola is $y = x^2 + 2x - 3$ or $y = (x + 3)(x - 1)$

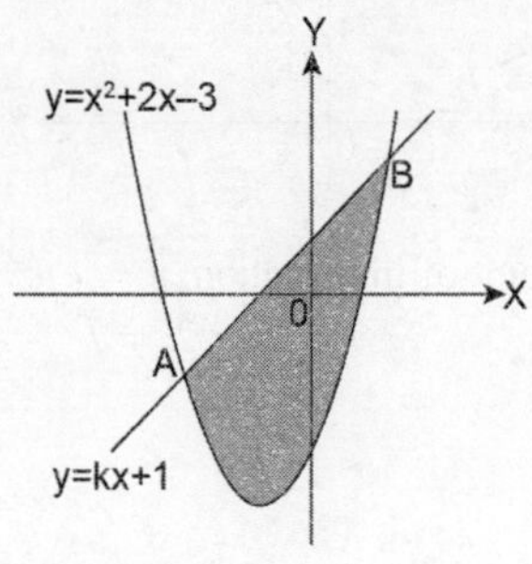

$\Rightarrow x = 1$ and $x = -3$ are roots of $y = x^2 + 2x - 3 = 0$

At the point of intersection, $x^2 + 2x - 3 = kx + 1$

$\Rightarrow x^2 + (2 - k)x - 4 = 0$

$\Rightarrow x=\frac{(k-2)\pm\sqrt{(2-k)^2+16}}{2}=\alpha,\beta$ (say for – and +ve)

$\therefore$ Required area $=\int_\alpha^\beta[(kx+1)-(x^2+2x-3)]dx$

$$=\left[\frac{k}{2}x^2+x-\frac{x^3}{3}-x^2+3x\right]_\alpha^\beta$$

$$=\left[-\frac{x^3}{3}+\left(\frac{k}{2}-1\right)x^2+4x\right]_\alpha^\beta$$

$$=-\frac{1}{3}(\beta^3-\alpha^3)+\left(\frac{k}{2}-1\right)(\beta^2-\alpha^2)+4(\beta-\alpha)$$

$$=(\beta-\alpha)\left[-\frac{1}{3}(\beta^2+\alpha^2+\alpha\beta)+\left(\frac{k}{2}-1\right)(\beta+\alpha)+4\right]$$

$$=\sqrt{(2-k)^2+16}\left[-\frac{1}{3}\left[(2-k)^2+4\right]+\left(\frac{k}{2}-1\right)(k-2)+4\right]$$

$$=\sqrt{(2-k)^2+16}\left[-\frac{1}{3}\left[(2-k)^2+4\right]+\frac{(k-2)^2}{2}+4\right]$$

$$=\sqrt{(k-2)^2+16}\left[\frac{-2(2-k)^2-8+3(k-2)^2+24}{6}\right]$$

$$=\frac{1}{6}\left[(k-2)^2+16\right]^{3/2}=A(k)\text{ (say)}$$

$$\therefore\quad A'(k)=\frac{1}{6}\left(\frac{3}{2}\right)(2)(k-2)\sqrt{(k-2)^2+16}$$

$$=\frac{1}{2}(k-2)\sqrt{(k-2)^2+16}=0\text{ for }k=2\text{ and }A''(\text{k})$$

$$=\frac{1}{2}\sqrt{(k-2)^2+16}+\frac{1}{4}\times\frac{2(k-2)^2}{\sqrt{(k-2)^2+16}}$$

$$=\frac{1}{2}\left[\frac{2(k-2)^2+16}{\sqrt{(k-2)^2+16}}\right]=\frac{(k-2)^2+8}{\sqrt{(k-2)^2+16}}=2>0\text{ for }k=2$$

$\Rightarrow$ Area will be least equal to $\frac{32}{3}$ sq. units at $k = 2$

5. $C_1 : y = e^x$ and $C_2 : y = e^{t-x}; t > 0$

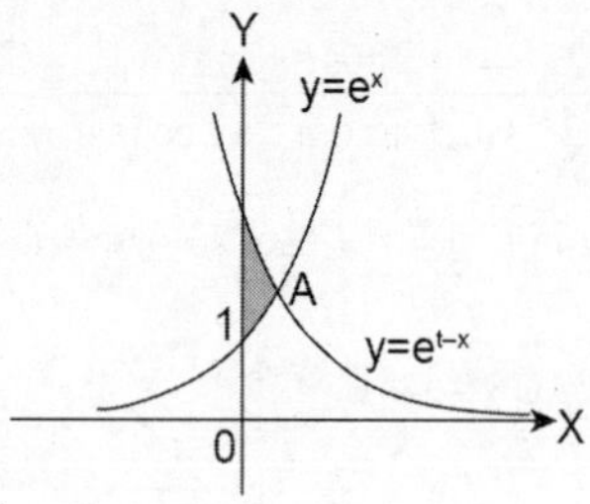

At the point of intersection, $e^x = e^t/e^x$

$\Rightarrow\ e^{2x} = e^t \qquad \Rightarrow\ 2x = t$

$\Rightarrow\ x = t/2$

$$\therefore\quad A\equiv\left(\frac{t}{2},e^{t/2}\right)$$

$$\therefore\quad \text{Required Area }=A=\int_0^{t/2}(e^{t-x}-e^x)dx=\left[\frac{e^{t-x}}{-1}-x^2\right]_0^{t/2}$$

$$=-[e^{t/2}-e^t]-[e^{t/2}-1]=e^t-2e^{t/2}+1=(e^{t/2}-1)^2$$

$$\Rightarrow\quad \lim_{t\to 0}\left(\frac{A}{t^2}\right)=\frac{1}{4}\lim_{t\to 0}\left[\left(\frac{e^{t/2}-1}{t/2}\right)^2\right]=\frac{1}{4}(1)^2=\frac{1}{4}\text{ sq. units}$$

6. (a) $|x| + |y| \geq 2;\ x^2 + y^2 \leq 4$

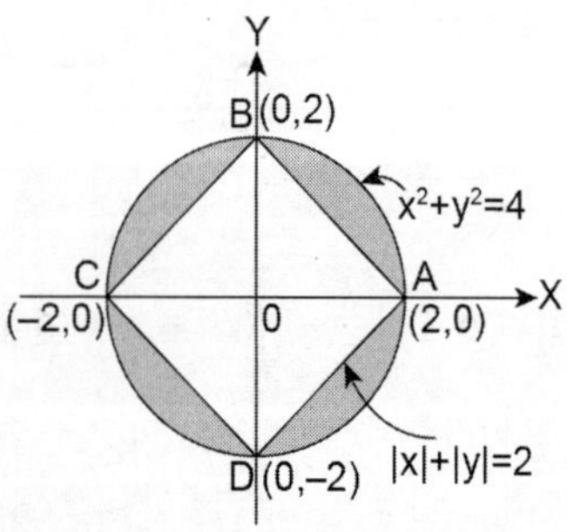

$$\therefore\quad \text{Required Area }=4\int_0^2\left\{\sqrt{4-x^2}-(2-x)\right\}dx$$

$$=4\left\{\frac{x\sqrt{4-x^2}}{2}+\frac{4}{2}\sin^{-1}\frac{x}{2}-2x+\frac{x^2}{2}\right\}_0^2$$

$$=4\left\{2\left[\frac{\pi}{2}\right]-2(2)+\frac{1}{2}(4)\right\}=(4P-8)\text{ sq. units}$$

(B) $X^2 + XY - 4 \leq 0,\ Y - 3 \leq 0,\ X > 0,\ Y > 0$

$\Rightarrow\ X^2 + XY - 4 = 0$

$$\Rightarrow\quad y=\frac{4-x^2}{x}=\frac{4}{x}-x=0\text{ AT }X=\pm 2$$

$$\Rightarrow\quad y'=-\frac{4}{x^2}-1<0\ \forall\ x\neq 0$$

$\therefore$ Required Area = Area of rectangle $\Delta ABCD$ + Area under the curve BD

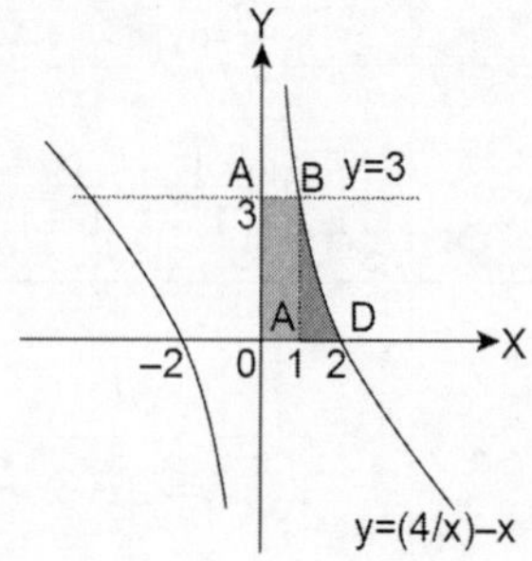

$$=(1)\ (3)+\int_1^2\left(\frac{4}{x}-x\right)dx=3+4[\ln x]_1^2-\frac{1}{2}[x^2]_1^2$$

$$=3+4\ [\ln 2]-\frac{1}{2}(4-1)=\left(\frac{3}{2}+4\ln 2\right)\text{ sq. units}$$

7. (a) $x > |y - 1|;\ x \leq 1$

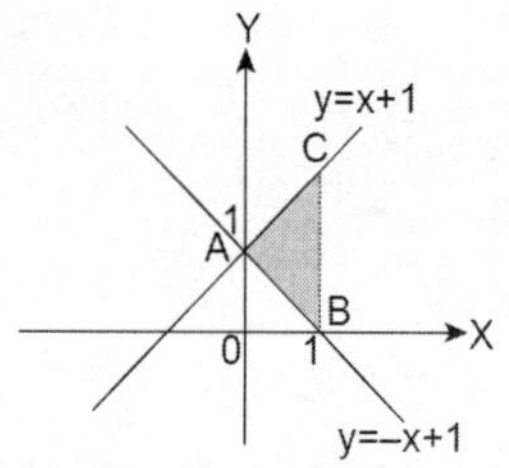

For $y < 1;\ x > -y + 1$ or $y > -x + 1$

For $y \geq 1;\ x > y - 1$ or $y < x + 1$

$$\therefore\quad \text{Required Area }=\int_0^1\{(x+1)-(-x+1)\}dx$$

$$=\int_0^1(2x)dx=[x^2]_0^1=1\text{ sq. units}$$

(b) $|x-y|\leq 2;|x+y|\leq 2$

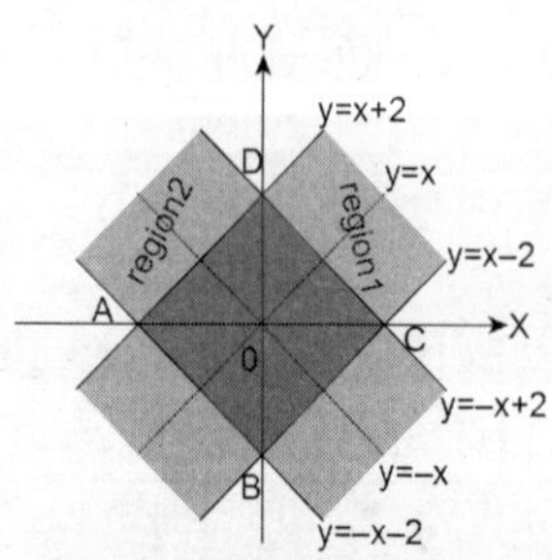

For $x \ge y$; $x - y \le 2$ and $x < y$; $-x + y \le 2$ ...
(1) (Region I)
For $x + y \ge 0$; $x + y \le 2$ and $x + y < 0$; $-x - y \le 2$ ...
(2) (Region II)
Square $ABCD$ represents the area common to region (1) and (2), we get

$$= \frac{1}{2}(d_1 d_2) = \frac{1}{2}(AC)(BD) = \frac{1}{2}(4)(4) = 8 \text{ sq. units}$$

(c) $|x| - |y| \ge 1; 1 \le |x| \le$

In Ist quadrant, $x, y > 0$

$\Rightarrow x - y \ge 1$ (Region R_1)

In IInd quadrant, $x < 0, y > 0$

$\Rightarrow -x - y \ge 1$ (Region R_2)

In IIIrd quadrant, $x < 0, y < 0$

$\Rightarrow -x + y \ge 1$ (Region R_3)

In IVth quadrant, $x > 0, y < 0$

$\Rightarrow x + y \ge 1$ (Region R_4)

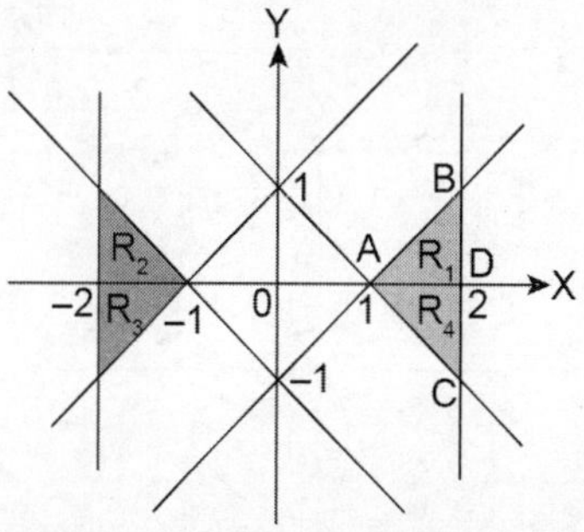

$\therefore$ Required Area $= 2\left[\frac{1}{2}(BC)(AD)\right] = (2)(1) = 2$ sq. units

(d) $|x| + |y| \le 2; |x| \le 1; |y| \ge 1$

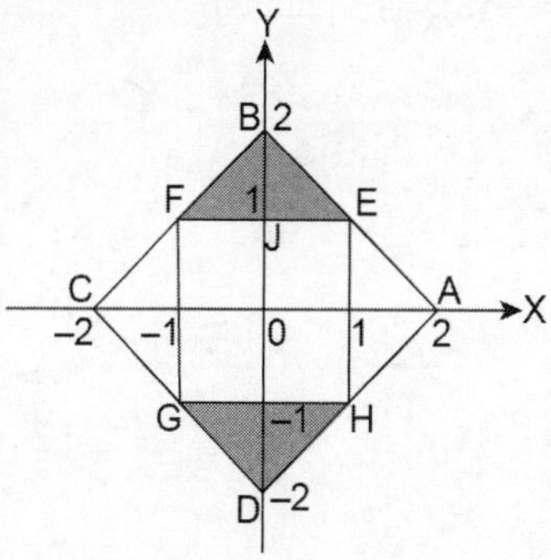

$\therefore$ Required are $= 2\left(\frac{1}{2}(EF) \times (BJ)\right) = (EF) \times (BJ) = (2)$ (1) = sq. units

8. (a) $|x + y| + |x - y| \le 3$

Case (i): For $x + y \ge 0, x - y \ge 0$

$\Rightarrow y \ge -x$ and $y \le x$ $\Rightarrow (x + y) + (x - y) \le 3$

$\Rightarrow x \le 3/2$ (Region R_1)

Case (ii): For $x + y \ge 0, x - y \le 0$

$\Rightarrow y \ge -x$ and $y \ge x$ $\Rightarrow (x + y) + (-x + y) \le 3$

$\Rightarrow y \le 3/2$ (Region R_2)

Case (iii): For $x + y \le 0, x - y \le 0$

$\Rightarrow y \le -x$ and $y \ge x$ $\Rightarrow -x - y + x - y \le 3$

$\Rightarrow x \ge -3/2$ (Region R_3)

Case (iv): For $x + y \le 0, x - y \ge 0$

$\Rightarrow y \le -x$ and $y \le x$ $\Rightarrow -x - y + x - y \le 3$

$\Rightarrow y \ge -3/2$ (Region R_4)

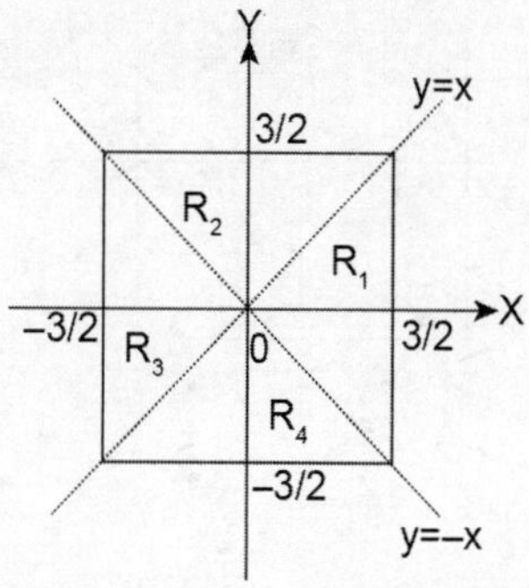

$\therefore$ Required Area = Area of square $ABCD = (3)^2 = 9$ sq. units

(b) $|x + 2| + |y + 1| \le 3$

Case (i): For $x + 2 \ge 0, y + 1 \ge 0$

$\Rightarrow x + y \le 0$ (Region R_1)

Case (ii): For $x + 2 \ge 0, y + 1 \le 0$

$\Rightarrow x - y \le 2$ (Region R_2)

Case (iii): For $x + 2 \le 0, y + 1 \le 0$

$\Rightarrow -x - y \le 6$ (Region R_3)

Case (iv): For $x + 2 \le 0, y + 1 \ge 0$

$\Rightarrow -x + y \le 4$ (Region R_4)

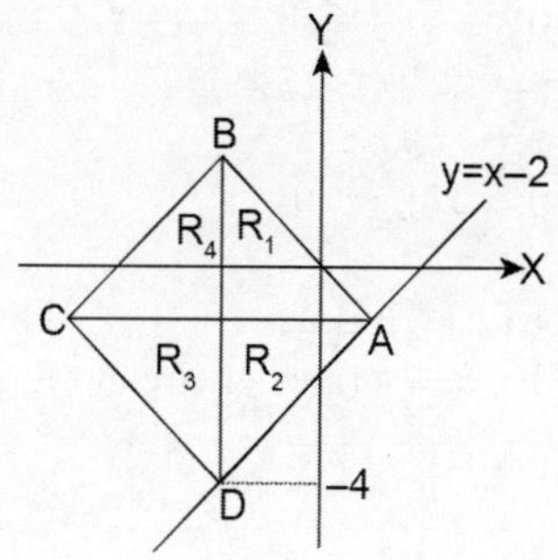

$\therefore$ Required Area = Area of square $ABCD = \frac{1}{2}(AC)(BD)$
$= \frac{1}{2}(6)(6) = 18$ sq. units

Aliter:
Shifting the origin at $(-2, -1)$ we have, $|x| + |y| \le 3$

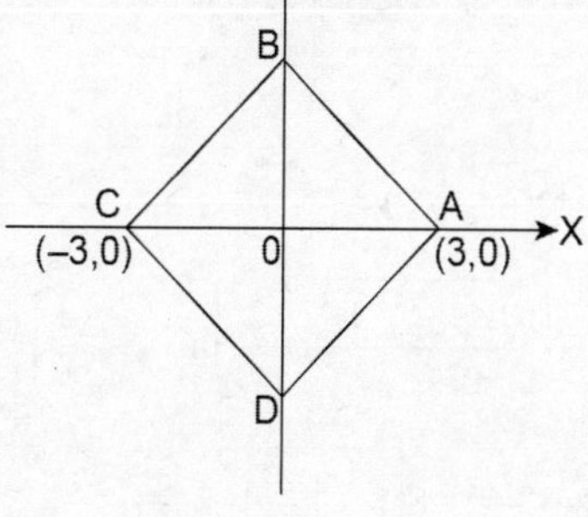

Area of square $ABCD = \frac{1}{2}(AC)(BD) = \frac{1}{2}(6)(6) =$ sq. units

9. (a) $|x+y|+|x-y|\le 4$; $|x|\le 1$ and $y\ge\sqrt{x^2-2x+1}$

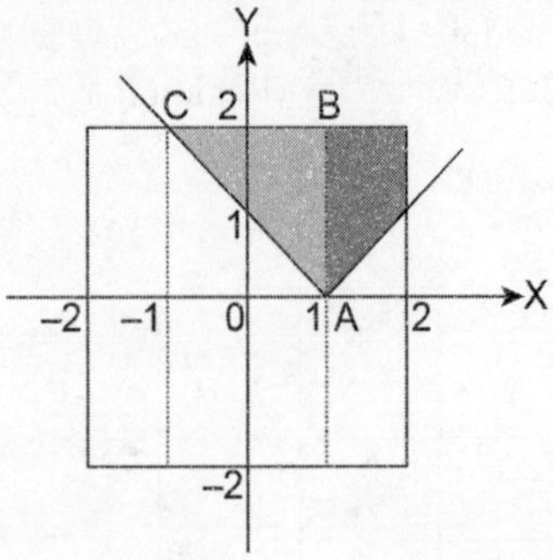

$\Rightarrow\ |x+y|+|x-y|\le 4$ ...(1)

$\Rightarrow\ |x|\le 1$ ...(2) and $y\ge|x-1|$ ...(3)

$\therefore$ Required area = area of $\Delta ABC = \frac{1}{2}(2)(2) = 2$ sq. units

(b) $(x^2+y^2)\le 2(|x|+|y|)$

Case (i): $x\ge 0, y\ge 0$

$\Rightarrow\ x^2+y^2-2x-2y\le 0$

$\Rightarrow\ (x^2-2x+1)+(y^2-2y+1)\le 2$

$\Rightarrow\ (x-1)^2+(y-1)^2\le 2$

Case (ii): $x\le 0, y\ge 0$

$\Rightarrow\ x^2+y^2+2x-2y\le 0$

$\Rightarrow\ x^2+y^2+2x-2y+1+1\le 2$

$\Rightarrow\ (x+1)^2+(y-1)^2\le 2$

Case (iii): $x\le 0, y\le 0$

$\Rightarrow\ x^2+y^2+2x+2y+2\le 2$

$\Rightarrow\ (x+1)^2+(y+1)^2\le 2$

Case (iv): $x\ge 0, y\le 0$

$\Rightarrow\ x^2+y^2-2x+2y+2\le 2$

$\Rightarrow\ (x-1)^2+(y+1)^2\le 2$

$\therefore$ Required area = 4 (area of circle of radius $\sqrt{2}$)

$$-8\int_0^2\left(-1+\sqrt{2-(x-1)^2}\right)dx$$

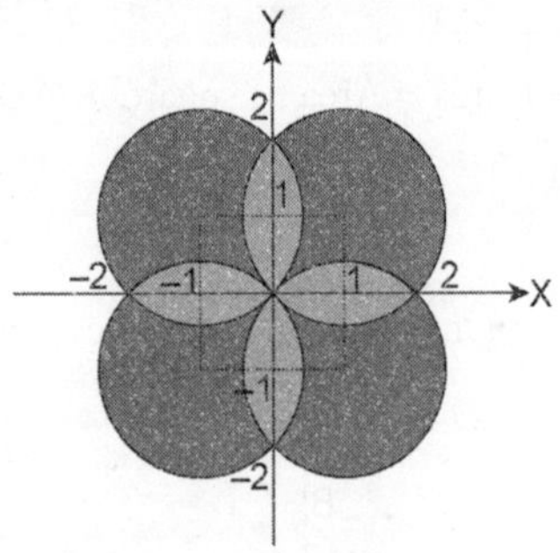

$$=4\left(\pi\left(\sqrt{2}\right)^2\right)-8\left[|-x|_0^2\right]-$$

$$8\left[\frac{(x-1)\sqrt{2-(x-1)^2}}{2}+\frac{2}{2}\sin^{-1}\left(\frac{x-1}{\sqrt{2}}\right)\right]_0^2$$

$$=8\pi-8[-2]-8\left[\left(\frac{1}{2}+\frac{\pi}{4}\right)-\left(\frac{-1}{2}-\frac{\pi}{4}\right)\right]$$

$= 8p + 16 - 4 - 2p - 4 - 2p = (4p + 8)$ sq. units

(c) $4\le x^2+y^2\le 2(|x|+|y|)$

$\Rightarrow\ x^2+y^2\ge 4$ ...(1) and $x^2\le y^2\le 2(|x|+|y|)$ ...(2)

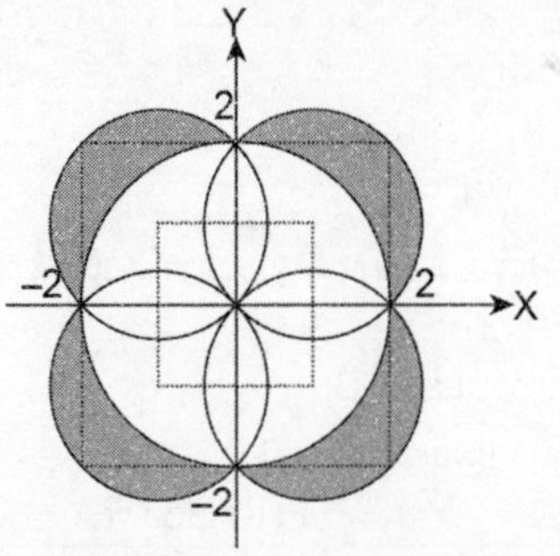

$\therefore$ Required Area = (Area found in part (*b*)) – (Area of circle $x^2+y^2=4$)

$= (4p + 8) - [\pi(2)^2] = 8$ sq. units

10. (a) $4\le x^2+y^2\le 2(|x|+|y|)$ ...(1)

$|x|\le\sqrt{2}+1$ ...(2)

and $0\le y\le\sqrt{2}+1$ ...(3)

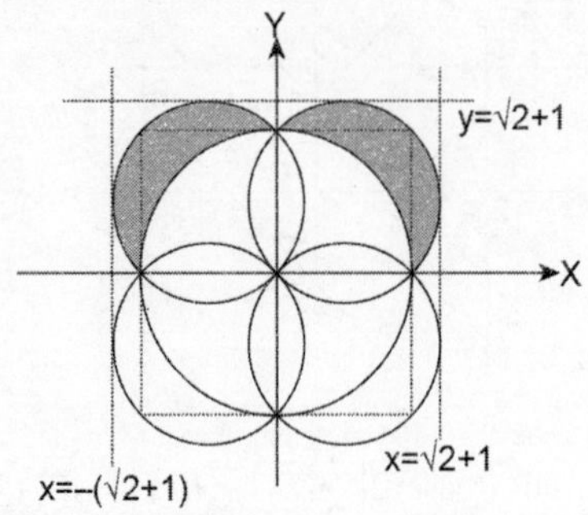

Clearly the required area $=\frac{1}{2}$ [area found un part (c) of $Q(9) = \frac{1}{2}(8) = 4$ sq. units]

(b) $2^{|x|}(|y|)+2^{|x|-1}\le 1, |x|\le\frac{1}{2}; |y|\le\frac{1}{2}$

$\Rightarrow\ 2^{|x|}\left(|y|+\frac{1}{2}\right)\le 1 \quad\Rightarrow\ \left(|y|+\frac{1}{2}\right)\le\frac{1}{2^{|x|}}$

$$\Rightarrow\begin{cases} y+\frac{1}{2}\le\frac{1}{2^x} & \text{for } x, y\ge 0\\ y+\frac{1}{2}\le 2^x & \text{for } x\le 0, y\ge 0\\ -y+\frac{1}{2}\le 2^x & \text{for } x\le 0, y\le 0\\ -y+\frac{1}{2}\le\frac{1}{2^x} & \text{for } x\ge 0, y\le 0\end{cases}$$

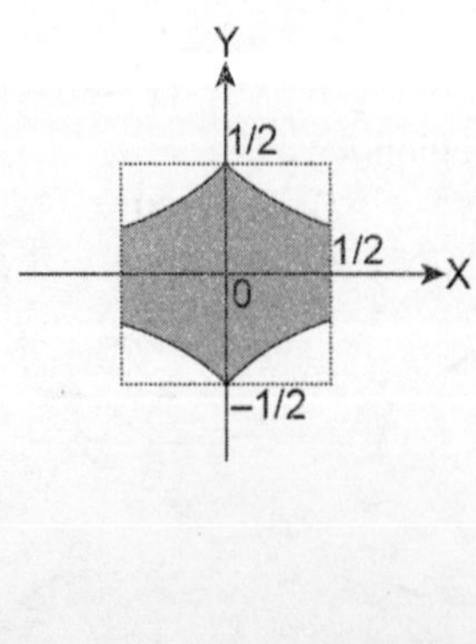

$\therefore$ Required Area $= 4\int_0^{1/2}\left(\frac{1}{2^x}-\frac{1}{2}\right)dx = 4\left[\frac{2^{-x}}{\ln\left(\frac{1}{2}\right)}-\frac{1}{2}x\right]_0^{1/2}$

$= 4\left[-2^{-x}\log 2^e - \frac{x}{2}\right]_0^{1/2}$

$= 4\left[-2^{-1/2}\log_2^e - \frac{1}{4} + \log_2^e\right] = \left(-\frac{4}{\sqrt{2}}+4\right)\log_2^e - 1$

$= \left[\left(4-2\sqrt{2}\right)\log_2^e - 1\right]$ sq. units

11. $\int_0^a |f(x)|dx = (e^{a^2}-1) \quad \Rightarrow \quad |f(a)| = 2ae^{a^2}$

$\Rightarrow \quad f(a) = \pm 2ae^{a^2} \quad \Rightarrow \quad f(x) = \pm 2xe^{x^2}$

12. (i) $|xy| = 1$ and $x^2 + y^2 \le 4$

At the point of intersection (in Ist quadrant) $xy = 1$ and $x^2 + y^2 = 4$

$\Rightarrow \quad x^2 + \frac{1}{x^2} = 4 \quad \Rightarrow \quad x4 - 4x^2 + 1 = 0$

$\Rightarrow \quad x^2 = \frac{4 \pm \sqrt{16-4}}{2}$

$\Rightarrow \quad x = \sqrt{2 \pm \sqrt{3}} \qquad (\because x > 0)$

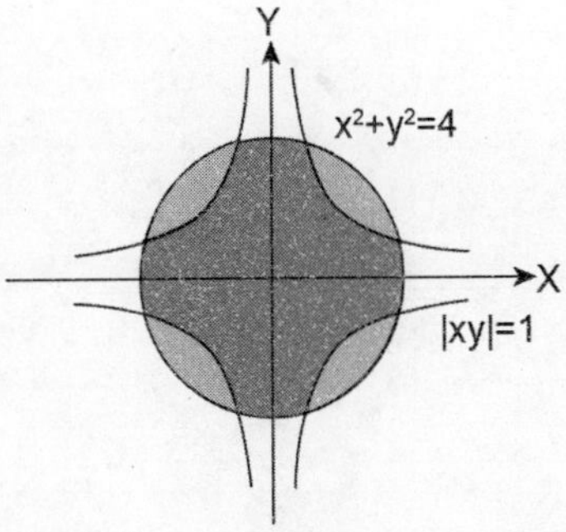

$\therefore$ Required Area $= 4\int_{\sqrt{2-\sqrt{3}}}^{\sqrt{2+\sqrt{3}}}\left(\sqrt{4-x^2}-\frac{1}{x}\right)dx$

$= 4\left[\frac{x\sqrt{4-x^2}}{2}+\frac{4}{2}\sin^{-1}\left(\frac{x}{2}\right)\right]_{\sqrt{2-\sqrt{3}}}^{\sqrt{2+\sqrt{3}}} - 4\left[\ln x\right]_{\sqrt{2-\sqrt{3}}}^{\sqrt{2+\sqrt{3}}}$

$= 4\left[\frac{\sqrt{(2+\sqrt{3})}\sqrt{2-\sqrt{3}}}{2}+2\sin^{-1}\left(\frac{\sqrt{2+\sqrt{3}}}{2}\right)\right]$

$-\left[\frac{\sqrt{(2-\sqrt{3})}\sqrt{2+\sqrt{3}}}{2}+2\sin^{-1}\left(\frac{\sqrt{2-\sqrt{3}}}{2}\right)\right]$

$-4\left[\ln\sqrt{2+\sqrt{3}} - \ln\sqrt{2-\sqrt{3}}\right]$

$= 8\left[\sin^{-1}\left(\frac{\sqrt{2+\sqrt{3}}}{2}\right) - \sin^{-1}\left(\frac{\sqrt{2-\sqrt{3}}}{2}\right)\right] - 4\ln\left[\sqrt{\frac{2+\sqrt{3}}{2+\sqrt{3}}}\right]$

$= 8\left[\pi - \left(\sin^{-1}\left\{\frac{\sqrt{2+\sqrt{3}}}{2}.\sqrt{1-\left(\frac{2-\sqrt{3}}{4}\right)} - \frac{\sqrt{2-\sqrt{3}}}{2}.\sqrt{1-\left(\frac{2+\sqrt{3}}{4}\right)}\right\}\right)\right]$

$-4\ln\left[2+\sqrt{3}\right]$

$= 8\left[\sin^{-1}\left\{\left(\frac{2+\sqrt{3}}{4}\right)-\left(\frac{2-\sqrt{3}}{4}\right)\right\}\right] - 4\ln(2+\sqrt{3})$

$= 8\left[\sin^{-1}\left(\frac{\sqrt{3}}{2}\right)\right] - 4\ln\left(2+\sqrt{3}\right) = 8\left(\frac{\pi}{3}\right) - 4\ln\left(2+\sqrt{3}\right)$ sq. units

(ii) $|xy| \le$ and $x^2 + y^2 \le 4$

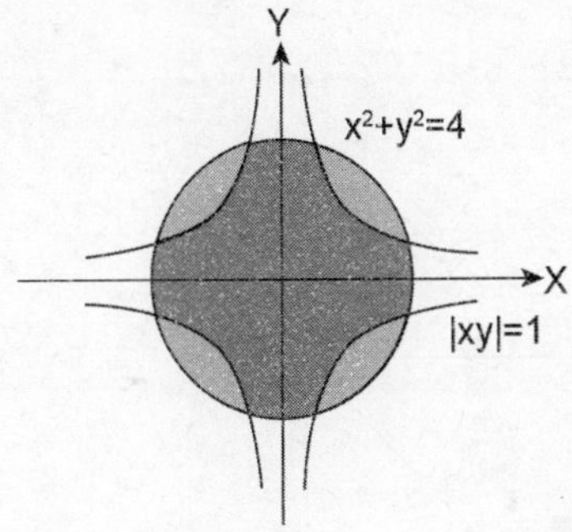

$\therefore$ Required Area $= 4p -$ (Area found in part a)

$= \frac{4\pi}{3} + 4\ln\left(2+\sqrt{3}\right)$

13. Given inequalities are $\frac{|x|+|y|}{2} + \left|\frac{|x|-|y|}{2}\right| \le 2$

$\Rightarrow \quad \begin{cases} |x| \le 2 \text{ for } |x| \ge |y|; (R_1) \\ |y| \le 2 \text{ for } |x| \le |y|; (R_2) \end{cases}$ ...(i)

Area of Square $ABCD = (4)^2 = 16$ and Area of circle $x^2 + y^2 = 6$ ...(ii)

$\therefore$ Area bounded by (i) and (ii) = Area of square ABCD – 4[Area of curvilinear ΔEFB]

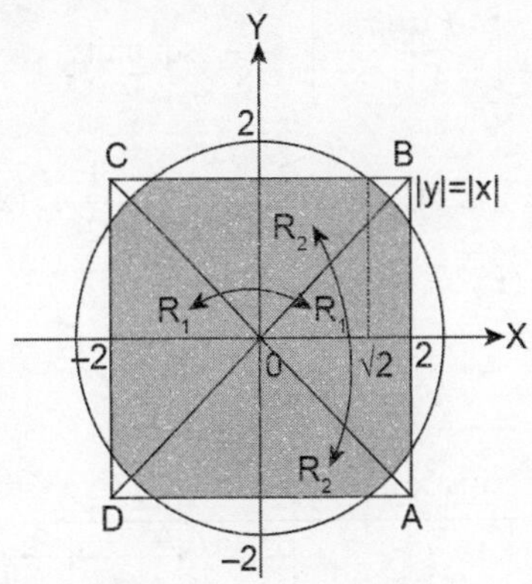

$= 16 - 4\left[(2-\sqrt{2})(2) - \int_{\sqrt{2}}^{2}\sqrt{6-x^2}\,dx\right]$

$= 16 - \left[(16-8\sqrt{2})\right] + 4\left[\frac{x\sqrt{6-x^2}}{2}+\frac{6}{2}\sin^{-1}\left(\frac{x}{\sqrt{6}}\right)\right]_{\sqrt{2}}^{2}$

$= 8\sqrt{2} + 4\left[3\left[\sin^{-1}\left(\frac{\sqrt{2}}{\sqrt{3}}\right) - \sin^{-1}\left(\frac{1}{\sqrt{3}}\right)\right]\right]$

$= 8\sqrt{2} + 12\left[\sin^{-1}\sqrt{\frac{2}{3}} - \sin^{-1}\left(\frac{1}{\sqrt{3}}\right)\right]$

$$= 8\sqrt{2} + 12\left[\sin^{-1}\left(\sqrt{\frac{2}{3}}.\sqrt{\frac{2}{3}} - \frac{1}{\sqrt{3}}.\frac{1}{\sqrt{3}}\right)\right]$$

$$= 8\sqrt{2} + 12\left[\sin^{-1}\left[\left(\frac{2}{3}\right) - \frac{1}{3}\right]\right] = 8\sqrt{2} + 12\sin^{-1}\left(\frac{1}{3}\right) \text{ sq. units}$$

14. $x^2 + y^2 \le r^2, r > 0$ ...(1)
$x - y \ge 0$ ...(2)
$y \ge 0$ ...(3)

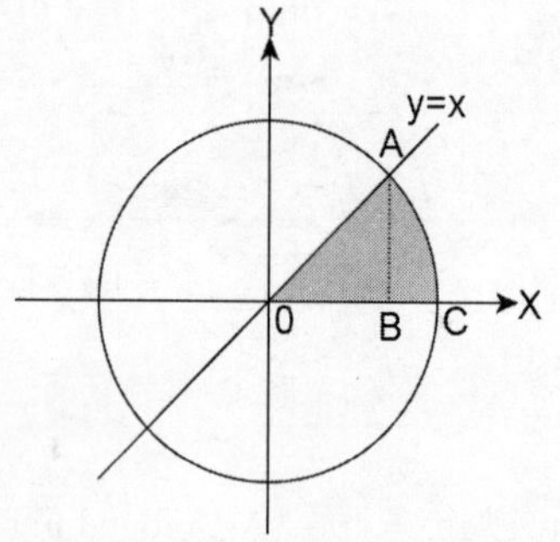

$\therefore$ The required area = (area of ΔOAB) + (area under the arc AC)

$$= \frac{1}{2}\left(\frac{r}{\sqrt{2}}\right)\left(\frac{r}{\sqrt{2}}\right) + \int_{r/\sqrt{2}}^{r} \sqrt{r^2 - x^2}\,dx$$

$$= \frac{1}{4}r^2 + \left[\frac{x\sqrt{r^2 - x^2}}{2} + \frac{r^2}{2}\sin^{-1}\left(\frac{x}{r}\right)\right]_{r/\sqrt{2}}^{r}$$

$$= \frac{1}{4}r^2 + \left[0 - \frac{r}{2\sqrt{2}}.\frac{r}{\sqrt{2}} + \frac{r^2}{2}\left(\frac{\pi}{2} - \frac{\pi}{4}\right)\right]$$

$$= \frac{r^2}{4} + \left[-\frac{r^2}{4} + \frac{\pi r^2}{8}\right] = \frac{\pi r^2}{8} \text{ sq. units}$$

15. $|y| + \frac{1}{2} \ge 2^{-|x|}$ ...(1) and max $(|x|, |y|) \le \frac{1}{2}$ ...(2)

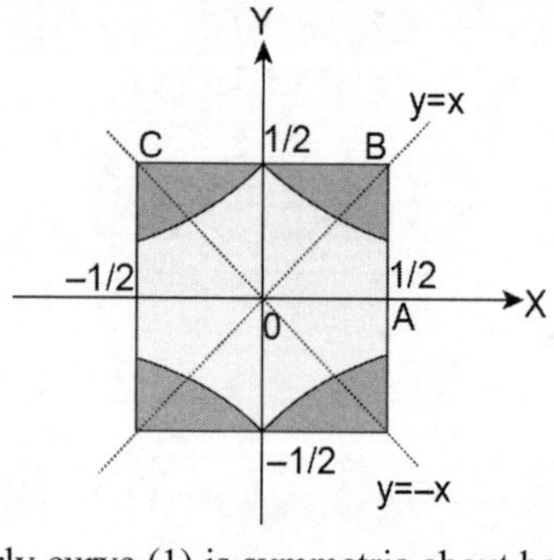

Clearly curve (1) is symmetric about both axes.
In first quadrant, $|x| = x$ and $|y| = y$

$$\Rightarrow \quad y + \frac{1}{2} \ge 2^{-x} \text{ or } y + \frac{1}{2} \ge \frac{1}{2^x} \text{ or } y \ge \frac{1}{2^x} - \frac{1}{2}$$

$\therefore$ Required area $= 4\left[ar.OABC - \int_0^{1/2}\left(\frac{1}{2^x} - \frac{1}{2}\right)dx\right]$

$$= 4\left[\frac{1}{4} - \left[\frac{1/(2)^x}{\ln 1/2} - \frac{1}{2}x\right]_0^{1/2}\right]$$

$$= 1 - 4\left[\frac{1}{\ln(1/2)}.\frac{1}{\sqrt{2}} - \frac{1}{4} + \frac{1}{\ln 2}\right] = \frac{+4}{\sqrt{2}\ln 2} + 2\frac{-4}{\ln 2}$$

$$= \frac{-4}{\ln 2}\left[1 - \frac{1}{\sqrt{2}}\right] + 2 = 2\log_2^e\left[4 - 2\sqrt{2}\right] \text{ sq. units}$$

16. Required Area $= \int_0^1 (x - x^2)dx = \left[\frac{x^2}{2} - \frac{x^3}{3}\right]_0^1$

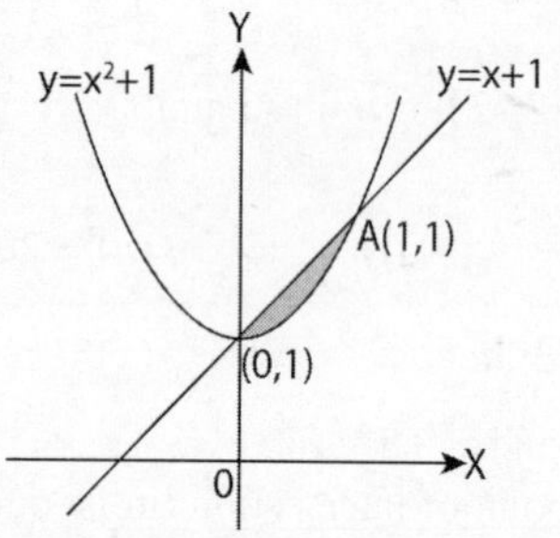

$$= \frac{1}{2} - \frac{1}{3} = \frac{3-2}{6} = \frac{1}{6} \text{ sq. units}$$

17. $y \le |x^2 - 1|$ ...(1)
$y \ge x^2 - 4$ ...(2)
$|x| = 2$ ...(3)

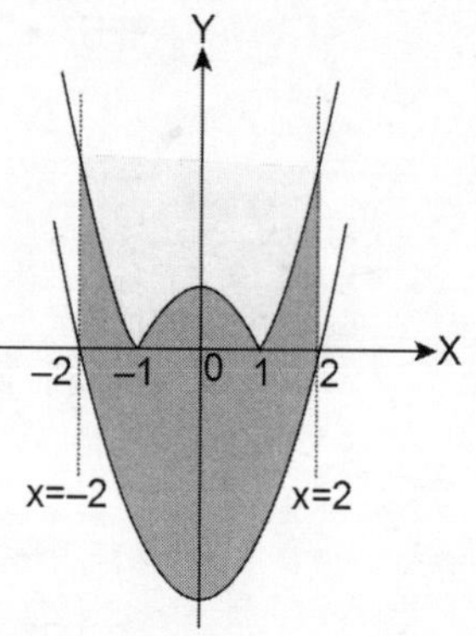

In $(-\infty, -1) \cup (1, \infty)$, $x^2 - 1 > x^2 - 4$, i.e., two curves will never intersect

$\therefore$ Required Area

$$= 2\int_0^1 (-x^2 + 1 - x^2 + 4)dx + 2\int_1^2 (x^2 - 1 - x^2 + 4)dx$$

$$= 2\int_2^1 (-2x^2 + 5)dx + 2\int_1^2 3dx$$

$$= 2\left[-\frac{2x^3}{3} + 5x\right]_0^1 + 6 = 2\left[5 - \frac{2}{3}\right] + 6 = \frac{26}{3} + 6 = \frac{44}{3}$$

sq. units

18. $\frac{x^2}{a^2} + \frac{y^2}{b^2} \le 1$ ...(1) and $\frac{y}{b} + \frac{x}{a} \le 1$ ...(2)

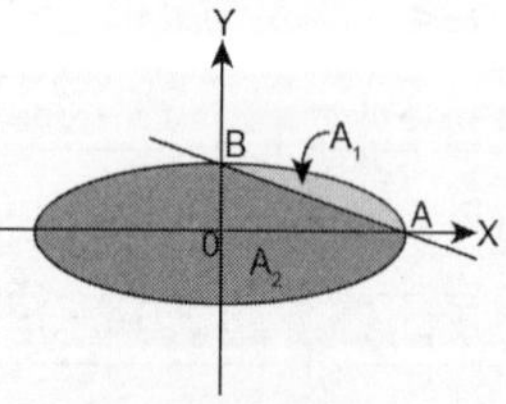

Area $(A_1) = \int_0^a \frac{b}{a}\sqrt{a^2 - x^2}\,dx - \int_0^a \frac{b}{a}(a - x)dx$

$$=\frac{b}{a}\left[\frac{x\sqrt{a^2-x^2}}{2}+\frac{a^2}{2}\sin^{-1}\left(\frac{x}{a}\right)\right]_0^a-\frac{b}{a}\left[ax-\frac{x^2}{2}\right]_0^a$$

$$=\frac{b}{a}\left[\frac{a^2}{2}\left(\frac{\pi}{2}\right)\right]-\frac{b}{a}\left[a^2-\frac{a^2}{2}\right]$$

$$=\frac{\pi ab}{4}-ab+\frac{ab}{2}=\frac{\pi ab}{4}-\frac{ab}{2}=\left(\frac{\pi}{2}-\frac{1}{2}\right)ab \text{ sq. units}$$

$\therefore$ Area A_2 = Area of ellipse – A_1 $=\pi ab-\left(\frac{\pi}{4}ab-\frac{ab}{2}\right)$

$$=\frac{3}{4}\pi ab+\frac{ab}{2}=\frac{(3\pi+2)ab}{4} \text{ sq. units}$$

19. $\min.(|x+y|,|x-y|)=1$ ...(1) and $x^2+y^2>1$...(2)

$\Rightarrow$ $x=-1$ to $x=1$

Case (i): $x+y\geq 0, x-y\geq 0$

$\Rightarrow$ $y\geq -x$ and $y\leq x$

min. $(x+y, x-y)=1$

Now $x+y\leq x-y$ iff $y\leq 0$

$\therefore$ $x+y=1$

Also $x+y\geq x-y$

iff $y\geq 0$

$\therefore$ $x-y=1$

Case (ii): $x+y\geq 0, x-y\leq 0$

$\Rightarrow$ $y\geq -x, y\geq x$

min. $(x+y, -x+y)=1$

$x+y\leq -x+y \Leftrightarrow x\leq 0$ and $x+y=1$

Also, $x+y\geq -x+y \Leftrightarrow x\geq 0$ and $-x+y=1$

Case (iii): $x+y\leq 0, x-y\leq 0$

$\Rightarrow$ $y\leq -x, y\geq x$

$\Rightarrow$ min $(-x-y, -x+y)=1$

$\Rightarrow$ $-x-y\leq -x+y \Leftrightarrow y\geq 0$ and $-x-y=1$

Also $-x-y\geq -x+y \Leftrightarrow y\leq 0$ and $-x+y=1$

Case (iv): $x+y\leq 0, x-y\geq 0$

$\Rightarrow$ $y\leq -x, y\leq x$

$\Rightarrow$ min $\{-x-y, x-y\}=1$

Here $-x-y\leq x-y \Leftrightarrow x\geq 0$ and $-x-y=1$

Also $-x-y\geq x-y \Leftrightarrow x\leq 0$ and $x-y=1$

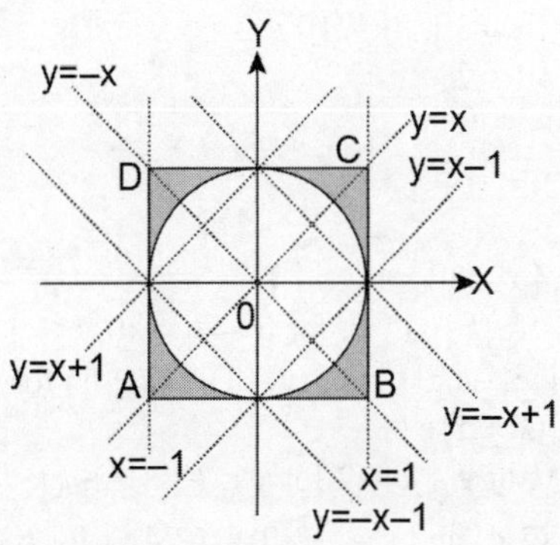

$\therefore$ The required area = Area of square $ABCD$ – Area of circle = $4-p$ square units

20. (a) $[y]=4-[x]$; $x\geq 0, y\geq 0$

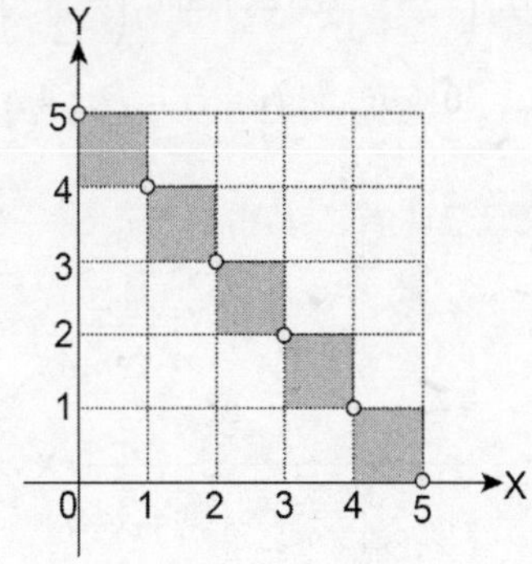

Clearly the required area = 5 sq. units

(b) $[|y|]=4-[|x|]$ ...(1)

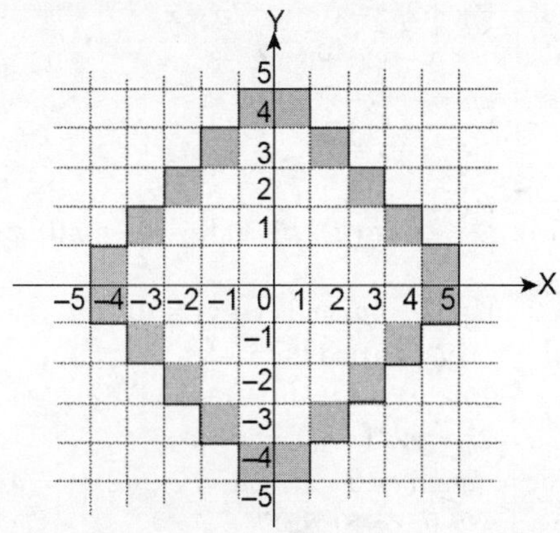

For $x, y\geq 0$; $[y]=4-[x]$ ...(2)

Clearly (1), will be represent relation symmetric about x-axis and y-axis as shown above.

$\therefore$ The required area = 20 square units

(c) $[y]=[\cos x]$; $0\leq x\leq 2p$

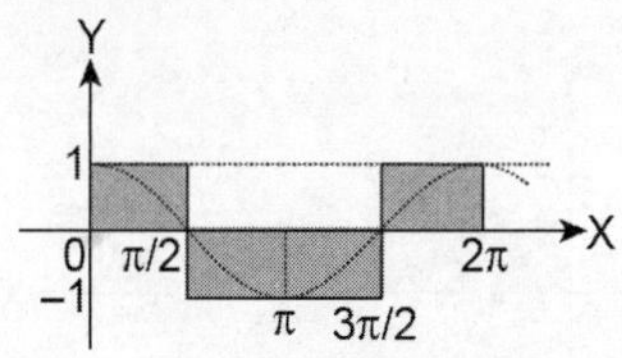

Clearly the required area $=4\left[\frac{\pi}{2}(1)\right]=2\pi$ sq. units

21. (a) $\cos x-\cos y>0$

$$\Rightarrow \quad -2\sin\left(\frac{x+y}{2}\right).\sin\left(\frac{x-y}{2}\right)>0$$

$$\Rightarrow \quad \sin\left(\frac{x+y}{2}\right).\sin\left(\frac{x-y}{2}\right)<0 \qquad ...(1)$$

Now, $(x+y), (x-y)\in[0, 4p]$

$$\Rightarrow \quad \frac{x+y}{2},\frac{x-y}{2}\in[0,2\pi] \qquad ...(2)$$

From (1) and (2), $\left(\frac{x+y}{2}\right)\in(0,\pi)$ and $\left(\frac{x-y}{2}\right)\in(\pi, 2p)$

or $\left(\frac{x+y}{2}\right)\in(\pi, 2p)$ and $\left(\frac{x-y}{2}\right)\in(0,\pi)$

Case (i): $\left(\frac{x+y}{2}\right) \in (0,\pi)$ and $\left(\frac{x-y}{2}\right) \in (\pi,2\pi)$

$\Rightarrow$ $(x + y) \in (0, 2p)$ and $(x - y) \in (2p, 4p)$

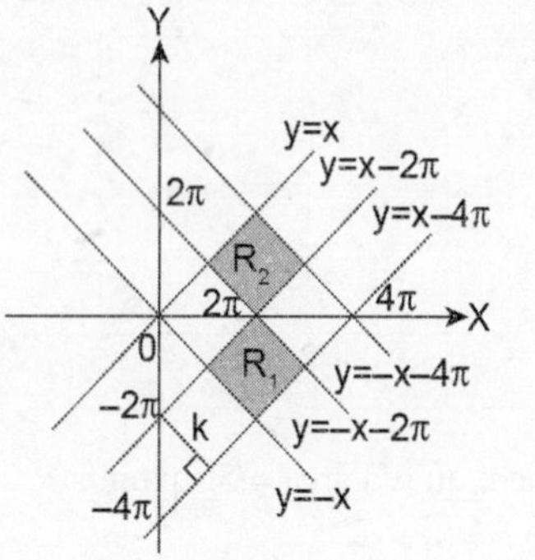

$\Rightarrow$ $0 < x + y < 2p; - x < y < 2p - x$

Also $2p < x - y < 4p$

$\Rightarrow$ $- x + 2p < - y < - x + 4p$

$\Rightarrow$ $x - 4p < y < x - 2p$

Case (ii): $\left(\frac{x+y}{2}\right) \in (\pi,2\pi)$ and $\left(\frac{x-y}{2}\right) \in (0,\pi)$

$\Rightarrow$ $(x + y) \in (2p, 4p)$ and $(x - y) \in (0, 2p)$

$\Rightarrow$ $2p < x + y < 4p$ and $0 < x - y < 2p$

$\Rightarrow$ $- x + 2p < y < -x + 4p$ ...(3) and $- x < - y < - x + 2p$ or $x - 2p < y < x$ ...(4)

$\therefore$ The required area $= R_1 + R_2 = 2(\sqrt{2}\,\pi)^2 = 4p^2$ sq. units

(b) $\log_{|\sin x|} y > 0, x \in (0, 2p)$

As $|\sin x| \neq 0, 1$ and $x \in (0, 2p)$

$\Rightarrow$ $x \neq \frac{\pi}{2}, \pi, \frac{3\pi}{2}$ and for $x \in (0, 2p) - \left\{\frac{\pi}{2}, \pi \frac{3\pi}{2}\right\}$, $|\sin x| < 1$

Thus, $\log_{|\sin x|} y > 0$

$\Rightarrow$ $0 < y < 1$

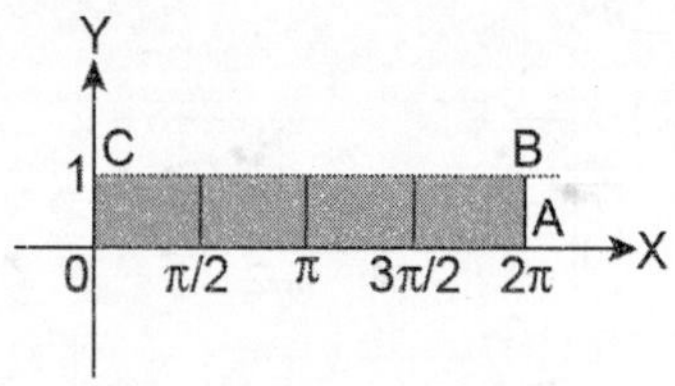

$\therefore$ Required Area $= (2p) \times 1 = 2p$ sq. units

22. (a) max.$([|x - 3|], [|y - 1|]) \leq 2$

Case (i): $[|x - 3|] \geq [|y - 1|]$

$\Rightarrow$ $|x - 3|, |y - 1| \in [k, k + 1)$ for some $k \in \mathbb{Z}$, so that $[|x - 3|] = [|y - 1|] = k$

or $|x - 3| \in [k + 1, \infty)$ for $|y - 1| \in [0, k + 1)$

Sub Case (i): $k \leq |x - 3| < k + 1; k \leq |y - 1| < k + 1; k \geq 0$

$\Rightarrow$ $-(k + 1) < x - 3 \leq -k$ or $k \leq x - 3 < k + 1$ and $-(k + 1) < y - 1 \leq -k$ or $k \leq y - 1 < k + 1$

$\Rightarrow$ $2 - k < x \leq 3 - k$ or $k + 3 \leq x < k + 4$ and $-k < y \leq 1 - k$ or $k + 1 \leq y < k + 2$

$\Rightarrow$ $\{x \in (2, 3] \cup [3, 4) = (2, 4)$ and $y \in (0, 2)$ for $k = 0$; $x \in (1, 2] \cup [4, 5)$ and $y \in (-1, 0] \cup [2, 3)$ for $k = 0$; $x \in (0, 1] \cup [5, 6)$ and $y \in (-2, -1] \cup [3, 4)$ for $k = 2$

$\therefore$ max. $([|x - 3|], [|y - 1|]) \leq 2$

$\Rightarrow$ $[|x - 3|] = [|y - 1|] \leq 2$

$\Rightarrow$ $0 \leq |x - 3| < 3$ and $0 \leq |y - 1| < 3$

$\Rightarrow$ $-3 < x - 3 < 3$ and $-3 < y - 1 < 3$

$\Rightarrow$ $0 < x < 6$ and $- 2 < y < 4$

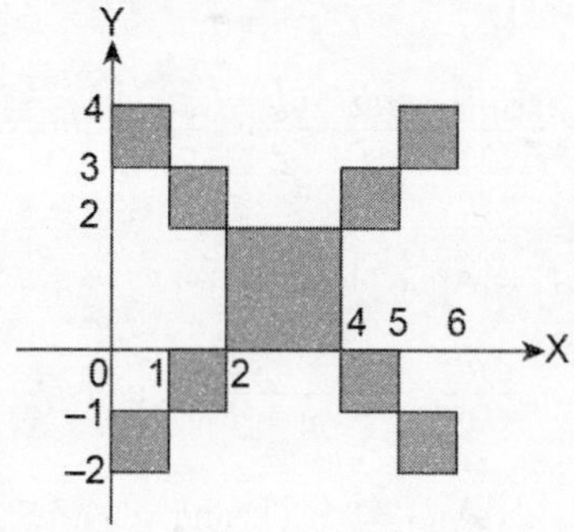

Sub Case (ii): $|x - 3| \in [k + 1, \infty)$ and $|y - 1| \in [0, k + 1)$

$\Rightarrow$ $[|x - 3|] > [|y - 1|]$

$\Rightarrow$ $(x - 3) < - (k + 1)$ or $(x - 3) > k + 1$ and $-(k + 1) < y - 1 < (k + 1)$

$\Rightarrow$ $x < - k + 2$ or $x > k + 4$ and $-k < y < k + 2$

$$\Rightarrow \begin{cases} x < 2 \text{ or } x > 4 \text{ and } \ 0 < y < 2 & \text{for } k = 2 \\ x < 1 \text{ or } \ x > 5 \ \text{ and } \ -1 < y < 3 & \text{for } k = 1 \\ x < 0 \text{ or } x > 6 \text{ and } \ -2 < y < 4 & \text{for } k = 2 \end{cases}$$

Also max. $[|x - 3|], [|y - 1|] \leq 2$

$\Rightarrow$ $[|x - 3|] \leq 2$

$\Rightarrow$ $0 \leq |x - 3| < 3$

$\Rightarrow$ $-3 < x - 3 < 3$

$\Rightarrow$ $0 < x < 6$

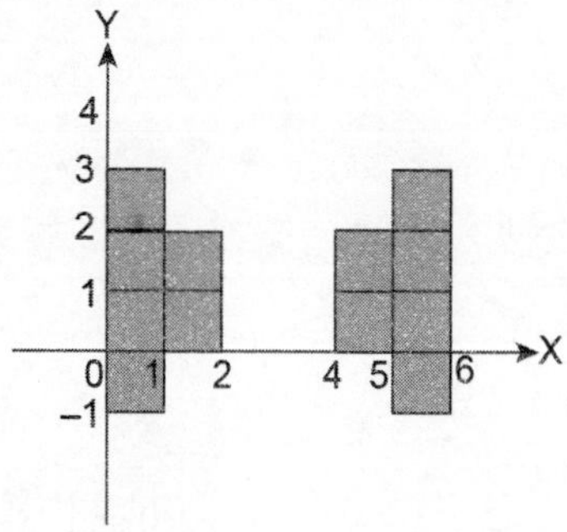

Case (iii): $[|x - 3|] < [|y - 1|]$

$\therefore$ max. $[|x - 3|], [|y - 1|] \leq 2$

$\Rightarrow$ $[|y - 1|] \leq 2$

$\Rightarrow$ $0 \leq |y - 1| < 3$

$\Rightarrow$ $-3 < y - 1 < 3$

$\Rightarrow$ $-2 < y < 4$

Now, $[|x - 3|] < [|y - 1|]$

$\Rightarrow$ $|y - 1| \in [k + 1, \infty)$ for $|x - 3| \in [0, k + 1)$

$\Rightarrow$ $(y - 1) \leq - (k + 1)$ or $(y - 1) \geq (k + 1)$ for $(x - 3) \in (-(k + 1), (k + 1))$

$\Rightarrow$ $y \leq - k$ or $y \geq k + 2$ for $x \in (-k + 2, k + 4)$

$$\Rightarrow \begin{cases} x \in (2,4) \text{ and } y \in (-2,0) \cup (2,4) & \text{for } k = 0 \\ x \in (1,5) \ \text{ and } y \in (-2,-1) \cup (3,4) & \text{for } k = 1 \\ x \in (0,6) \text{ and } y \in (0,6) & \text{for } k = 2 \end{cases}$$

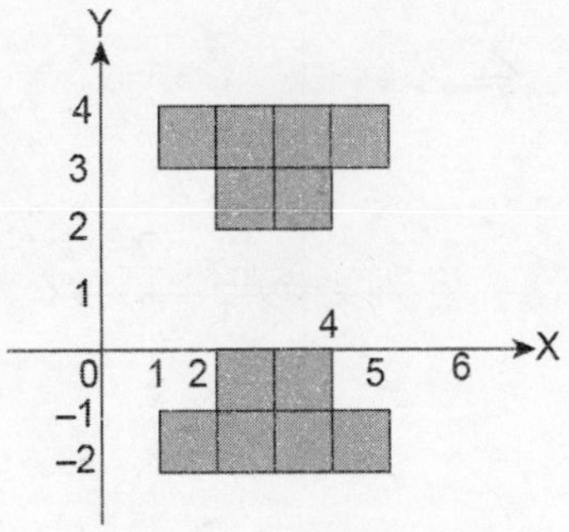

$\therefore$ Final areas will be as shown below

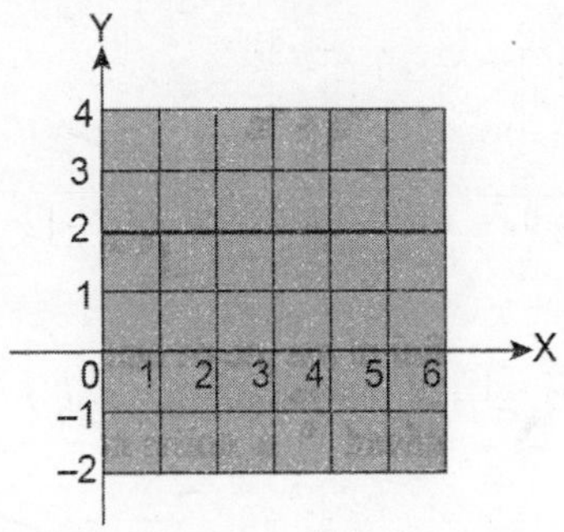

Clearly the required area = 36 sq. units

(b) Case (i): $[x-1] < [y+2], 3$

$\Rightarrow [x-1] \geq 2$

$\Rightarrow (x-1) \geq 2 \quad \Rightarrow x \geq 3 \qquad \ldots(1)$

Also $[x-1] < 3 \quad \Rightarrow (x-1) < 3$

$\Rightarrow x < 4 \qquad \ldots(2)$

$\therefore$ From (1) and (2) $x \in [3, 4) \qquad \ldots(3)$

Now for $x \in [3, 4) \quad \Rightarrow (x-1) \in [2, 3)$

$\Rightarrow [x-1] = 2 \quad \therefore 2 < [y+2], 3$

$\Rightarrow [y+2] > 2 \quad \Rightarrow (y+2) \geq 3$

$\Rightarrow y \geq 1$, but $y \leq 3$ (given)

$\Rightarrow y \in [1, 3] \qquad \ldots(4)$

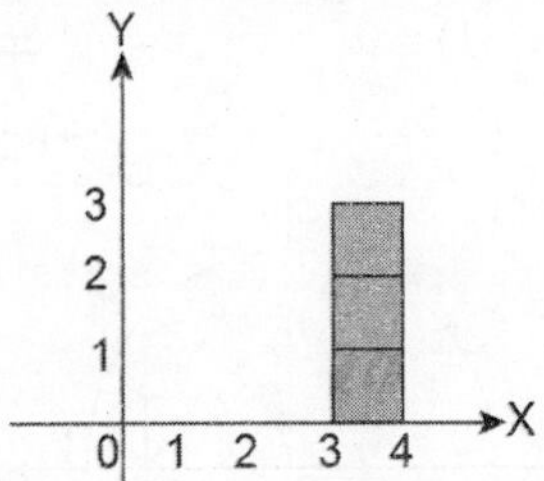

Case (ii): $[y+2] < [x-1], 3$

$\Rightarrow [y+2] \geq 2$

$\Rightarrow (y+2) \geq 2 \quad \Rightarrow y \geq 0 \qquad \ldots(5)$

Also $[y+2] < 3$

$\Rightarrow (y+2) < 3 \quad \Rightarrow y < 1 \qquad \ldots(6)$

$\therefore$ Form (5) and (6), $y \in [0, 1) \qquad \ldots(7)$

$\therefore$ For $y \in [0, 1) \quad \Rightarrow (y+2) \in [2, 3)$

$\Rightarrow [y+2] = 2 \quad \Rightarrow 2 < [x-1], 3$

$\Rightarrow [x-1] > 2 \quad \Rightarrow (x-1) \geq 3$

$\Rightarrow x \geq 4$ but $x \leq 5$

$\Rightarrow x \in [4, 5] \qquad \ldots(8)$

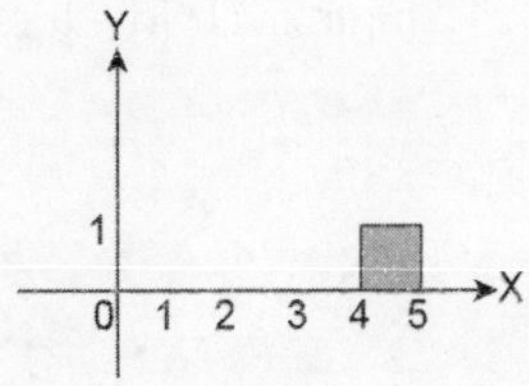

Case (iii): $3 < [x-1], [y+2] \qquad \ldots(9)$, then $3 \geq 2$ which is true $\forall$ x and y satisfying (9)

$\Rightarrow [x-1] > 3$ and $[y+2] > 3$

$\Rightarrow (x-1) \geq 4$ and $(y+2) \geq 4$

$\Rightarrow x \geq 5$ and $y \geq 2$

$\Rightarrow x = 5, y \in [2, 3]$ as $x \leq 5$ (given)

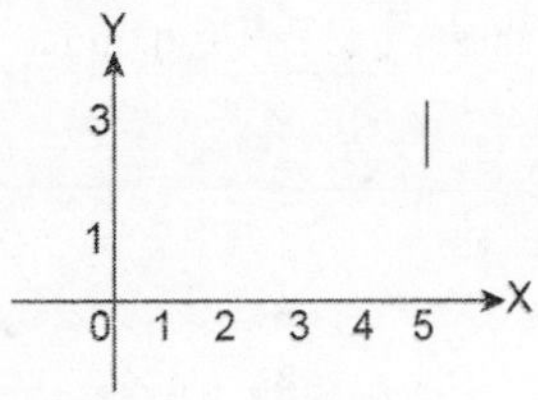

Case (iv): $[x-1] = [y+2] = 3$

$\Rightarrow 3 \geq 2$ (true)

$\Rightarrow (x-1) \in [3, 4)$ and $(y+2) \in [3, 4)$

$\Rightarrow x \in [4, 5)$ and $y \in [1, 2)$

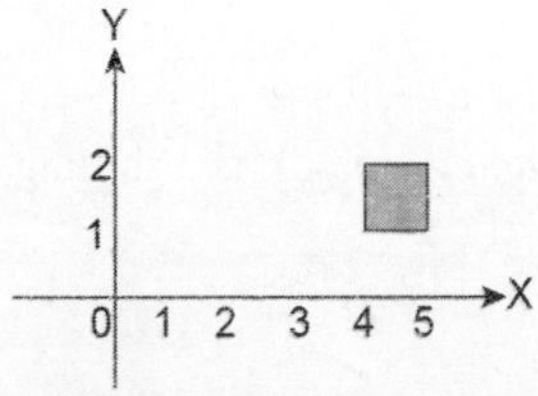

Thus, the total region for min $[x-1], [y+2] \geq 2$ and $y \leq 3$; $x \leq 5$ is as shown below

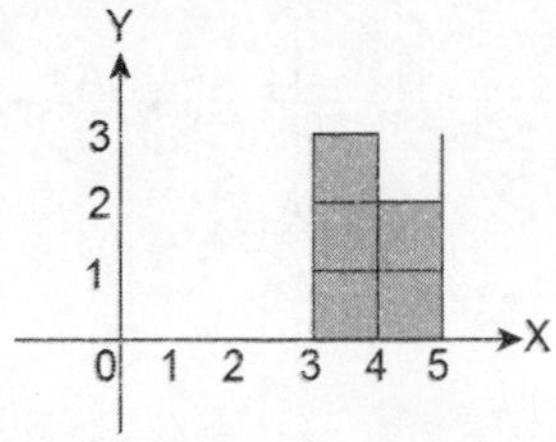

Clearly the required area = 6 sq. units

TEXTUAL EXERCISE-3: (OBJECTIVE)

1. (a) $\big||x| - |y|\big| \leq 1 \qquad \ldots(1)$

$x^2 + y^2 \leq 1 \qquad \ldots(2)$

Case (i): For $|x| \geq |y|$, from (1) $|x| - |y| \leq 1$ (Region R_1)

Which is symmetric about x-and y-axis

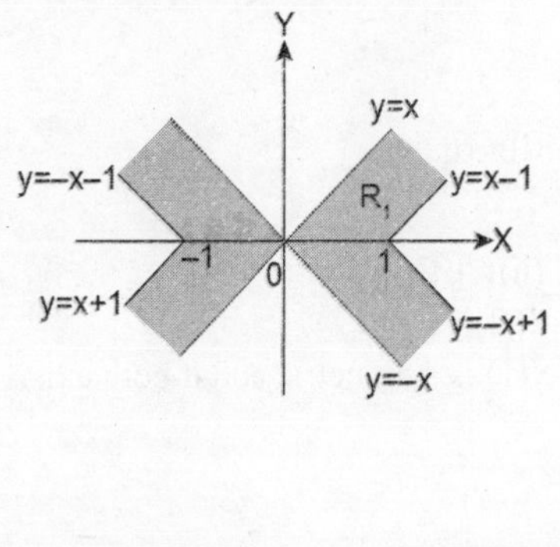

Case (ii): For $|x| \le |y|$, from (1) $|y| - |x| \le 1$ (Region R_2)

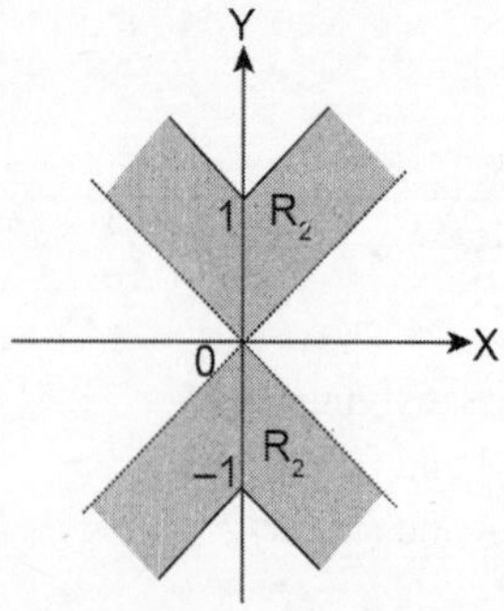

Thus, the required region is as shown below intersection of dotted and dashes = $p\ (1)^2 = p$ sq. units

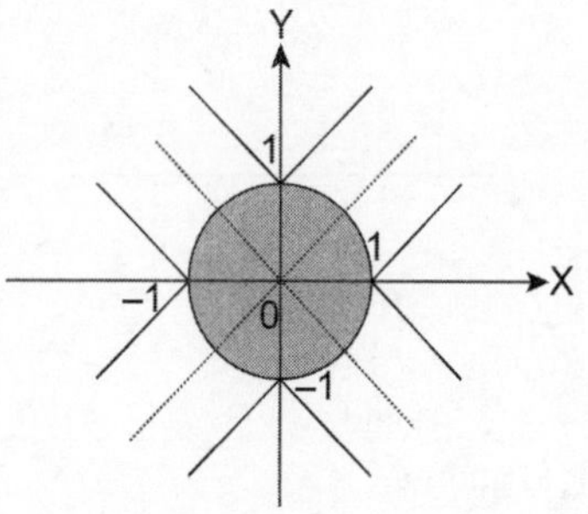

2. (c) $1 \le |x - 2| + |y + 1| \le 2$ ...(1)
Put $x - 2 = X$ *abd* $y + 1 = Y$, i.e., shifting the origin at (2, −1)
$\Rightarrow\ 1 \le |X| + |Y| \le 2$ ...(2)

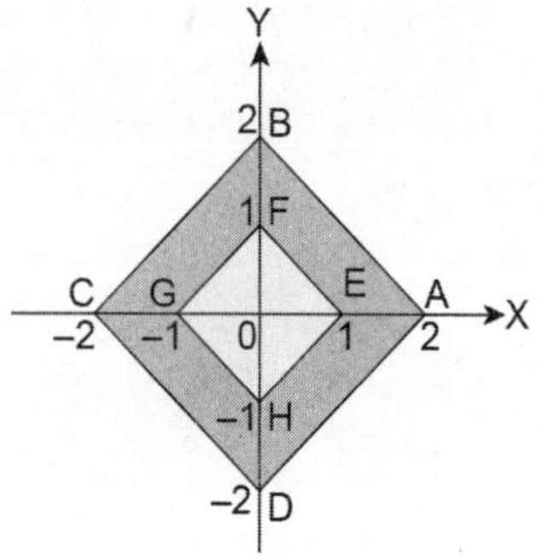

$\therefore$ Required Area = (Area of square *ABCD*) – (Area of square EFGH)

$$= \frac{1}{2}(4)(4)\frac{-1}{2}(2)(2) = (8 - 2) = 6 \text{ sq. units}$$

3. (c) C_1: $|y| \ge e^{-|x|} - \dfrac{1}{2}$ ...(1)

$$C_2: \frac{|x| + |y|}{2} + \left|\frac{|x| - |y|}{2}\right| \le 2 \qquad ...(2)$$

For C_2:
Case (i): $|x| \ge |y| \quad \Rightarrow \quad |x| \le 2$
$\Rightarrow$ x$\in [-2, 2]$
Case (ii): $|x| \le |y| \quad \Rightarrow \quad |y| \le 2$
$\Rightarrow$ $y \in [-2, 2]$
Curve (1) is symmetric about both axis

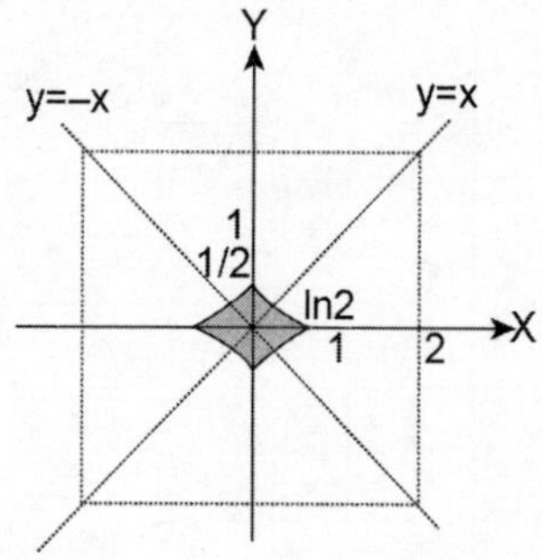

$$\therefore \text{ Required Area } = 16 - \left[4\int_0^{\ln 2}\left(e^{-x} - \frac{1}{2}\right)dx\right]$$

$$= 16\left\{4\left[-e^{-x} - \frac{1}{2}x\right]_0^{\ln 2}\right\}$$

$$= 16 - 4\left[-\left(\frac{1}{2}\right) - \frac{1}{2}(\ln 2) + 1\right] = 16 - [2 - 2\ln 2] = 14 + 2\ln 2$$

4. (c) $|x| + |y| \ge 1$...(1) and $x^2 + y^2 \le 1$ ...(2)

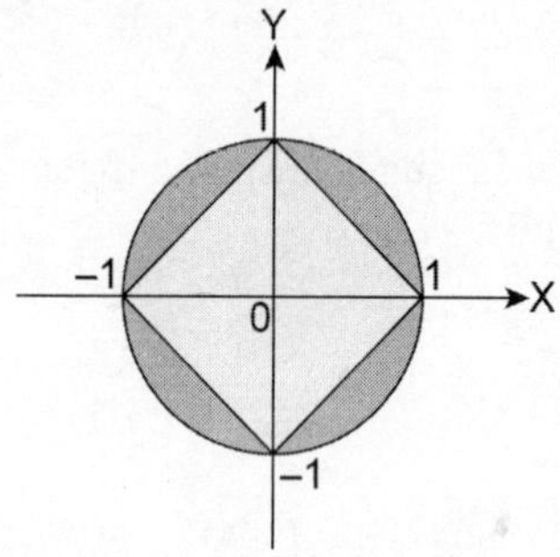

$\therefore$ Required Area = $\pi(1)^2 - \dfrac{1}{2}(2)(2) = (\pi - 2)$ sq. units

5. (c) $y \ge \sqrt{x}$ ...(1) and $x^2 + y^2 < 2$....(2)
At the point of intersection $x^2 + x - 2 = 0$
$\Rightarrow\ (x + 2)(x - 1) = 0 \quad \Rightarrow\ x = -2$ or $x = 1$, i.e., at (1, 1)

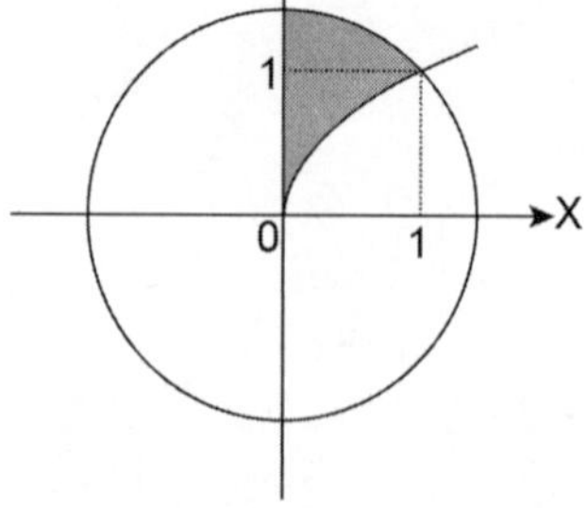

$$\therefore \text{ Required area } = \int_0^1\left(\sqrt{2 - x^2} - \sqrt{x}\right)dx$$

$$= \left[\frac{x\sqrt{2 - x^2}}{2} + \frac{2}{2}\sin^{-1}\left(\frac{x}{\sqrt{2}}\right)\right]_0^1 - \left[\frac{2}{3}(x)^{3/2}\right]_0^1$$

$$= \left[\frac{1}{2} + \frac{\pi}{4}\right] - \frac{2}{3} = \left(\frac{\pi}{4} - \frac{1}{6}\right) \text{ sq. units}$$

6. (a) $\frac{x^2}{a^2}+\frac{y^2}{b^2}\le 1$ …(1) and $\frac{x}{a}+\frac{y}{b}\ge 1$ …(2)

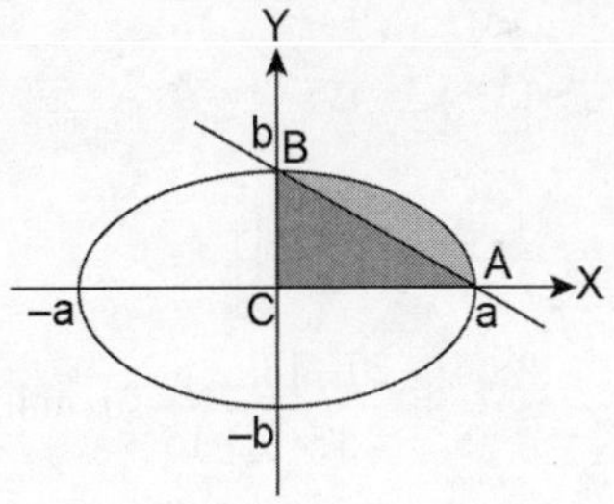

$\therefore$ Required Area = Area of 4th part of ellipse – Area of D *ABC*

$=\left(\frac{1}{4}\pi ab-\frac{1}{2}ab\right)$ sq. units

7. (a) $|y|+\frac{1}{2}\le e^{-|x|} \Rightarrow |y|\le e^{-|x|}-\frac{1}{2}$

It is symmetric about both axes

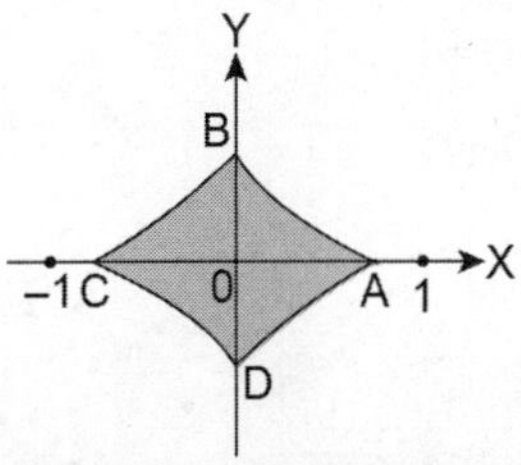

$\therefore$ Required Area $=4\int_0^{\ln 2}\left(e^{-x}-\frac{1}{2}\right)dx=4\left[-e^{-x}-\frac{1}{2}x\right]_0^{\ln 2}$

$=4\left[-\left(\frac{1}{2}\right)-\frac{1}{2}(\ln 2)+1\right]$

$=4\left(\frac{1}{2}-\frac{1}{2}\ln 2\right)=2-\ln 2=2(1-\ln 2)$ sq. units

8. (c) $2\le|x+y|+|x-y|\le 4$ …(1)

Clearly $|x+y|+|x-y|=2$ or 4 are symmetric about *x*-axis and *y*-axis

For, $x+y\ge 0$ and $x-y\ge 0$

$\Rightarrow 1\le x\le 2$

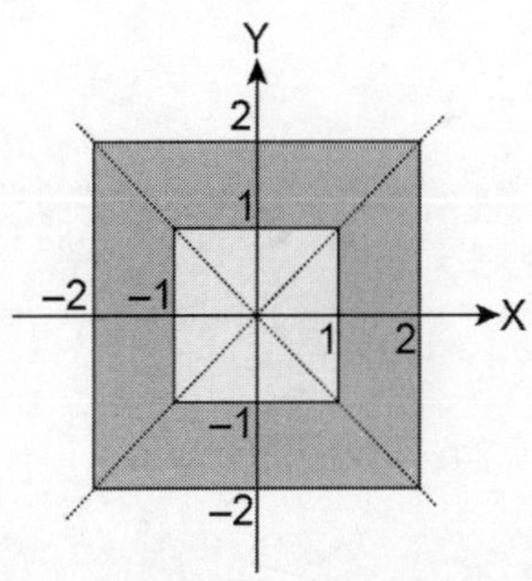

$\therefore$ Required area = $(4)^2-(2)^2=12$ sq. units

9. (b) $|x+1|+|2y-3|\le 1$ …(1)

Shift the origin at (–1, 3/2), i.e., $|X|+|Y|\le 1$; where $X=x+1$ and $Y=2y-3$

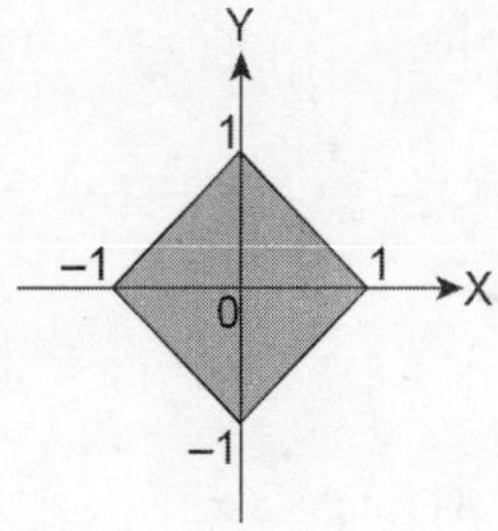

$\therefore$ Required area $=\frac{1}{2}(2)(2)=2$ sq. units

10. (b) $\left||x+y|-|x-y|\right|\le 1,\ x^2+y^2\le\frac{1}{2}$

$\Rightarrow -1\le|x+y|-|x-y|\le 1$ …(1)

and $x^2+y^2\le\frac{1}{2}$ …(2)

Case (i): For $x+y\ge 0,\ x-y\ge 0$, i.e., $y\ge -x,\ y\le x$

We have $\frac{-1}{2}\le y\le\frac{1}{2}$

Case (ii): For $x+y\ge 0,\ x-y\le 0$, i.e., $y\ge -x,\ y\ge x$,

We have, $\frac{-1}{2}\le x\le\frac{1}{2}$

Case (iii): For $x+y\le 0,\ x-y\le 0$, i.e., $y\le -x,\ y\ge x$,

We have, $\frac{1}{2}\ge y\ge\frac{-1}{2}$

Case (iv): For $x+y\le 0,\ x-y\ge 0$, i.e., $y\le -x,\ y\le x$,

We have, $\frac{1}{2}\ge x\ge\frac{-1}{2}$

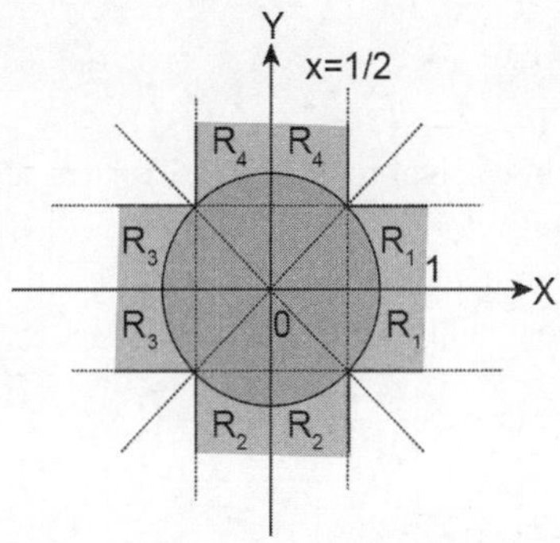

Clearly the required area = (area of circle radius $\frac{1}{\sqrt{2}}$)

$=\pi\left(\frac{1}{\sqrt{2}}\right)=\left(\frac{\pi}{2}\right)$ sq. units

11. (c) $0<y<3\pm 2x-x^2$ …(i)

From (i); $y<-(x^2\pm 2x-3)$

$\Rightarrow y<-(x^2\pm 2x+1)+4$

$\Rightarrow y<-(x\pm 1)^2+4$ …(ii) and $y>0,\ x>0$ …(iii)

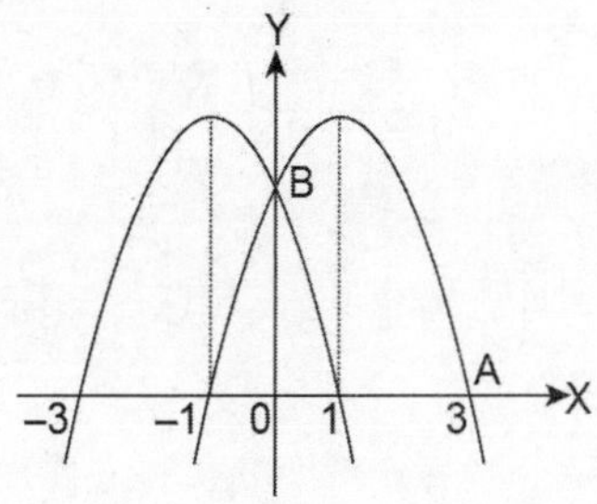

$\therefore$ Required Area $= 2\int_0^3 [-(x-1)^2 + 4]dx$

$= 2\left[-\frac{(x-1)^3}{3} + 4x\right]_0^3$

$= \frac{-2}{3}[8 + 1] + 8(3 - 0) = 18$ sq. units

12. (d) $x \geq y - 4$ ...(1) and $4 \leq x^2 + y^2$ ...(2)

And $3y + 16x - 48 \leq 0$ ...(3)

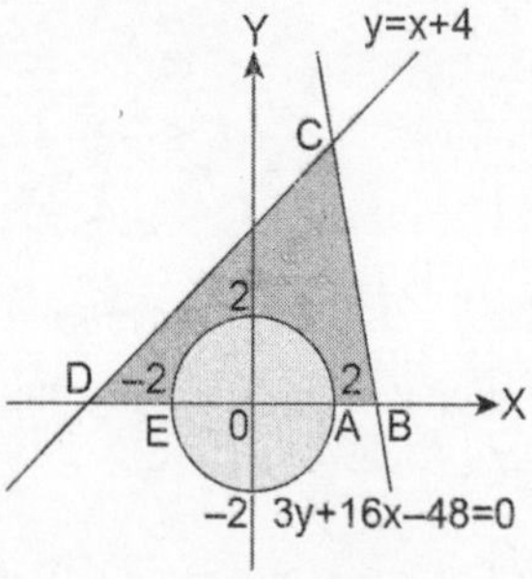

$\therefore$ Required area = (area of $D\ BCD$) – (area of semi-circle)

$= \frac{1}{2}$ (BD) × (Ordinate of point C) – $\pi(2)^2$

$= \frac{1}{2}(7)\left(\frac{112}{19}\right) - 4\pi = \left(\frac{392}{19} = 4\pi\right)$ sq. units

TEXTUAL EXERCISE–4: (SUBJECTIVE)

1. $y^2 = (x - 1)(x - 2)^2$ ...(i)

$\Rightarrow y = \pm(x-2)\sqrt{(x-1)}$

Clearly y is real for $x \geq 1$, i.e., for $x \in [1, \infty)$

$y = 0$ at $x = 1, 2$

i.e., curve intersects x-axis at $x = 1$ and $x = 2$ ...(ii)

Differentiating w.r.t.x, we get

$\frac{dy}{dx} = \pm(x-2).\frac{1}{2\sqrt{x-1}} + \sqrt{x-1}(\pm 1)$

$\Rightarrow \frac{dy}{dx} = \frac{\pm(x-2) \pm 2(x-1)}{\left(2\sqrt{x-1}\right)}$

$\Rightarrow \frac{dy}{dx} = \frac{\pm(x-2+2x-2)}{2\sqrt{x-1}} = \frac{\pm(3x-4)}{2\sqrt{x-1}}$

$\Rightarrow \frac{dy}{dx} = 0$ at $x = 4/3$ and $\pm\infty$ at $x = 1$

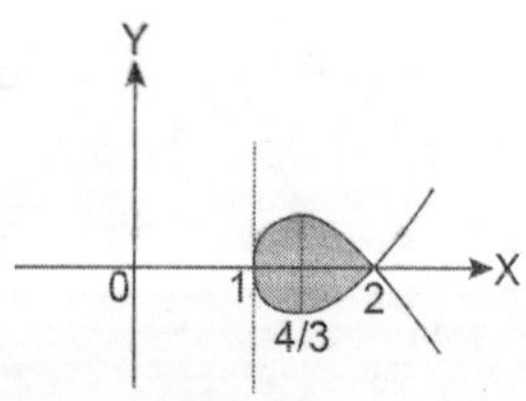

$\Rightarrow f\left(\frac{4}{3}\right) = \pm\left(\frac{4}{3} - 2\right)\sqrt{\frac{4}{3} - 1} = \pm\left(\frac{-2}{3}\right)\sqrt{\frac{1}{3}} = \mp\frac{2}{3}\sqrt{\frac{1}{3}}$

$= \mp\frac{2\sqrt{3}}{3}$

$\therefore$ Required area $= 2\int_1^2 -(x-2)\sqrt{x-1}dx$

$= -2\int_1^2 (x-1)\sqrt{x-1}dx$

$= -2\int_1^2 (x-1)^{3/2}dx + 2\int_1^2 \sqrt{x-1}dx$

$= -2\left[\frac{2}{5}(x-1)^{5/2}\right]_1^2 + 2\left[(x-1)^{3/2}\left(\frac{2}{3}\right)\right]_1^2$

$= -\frac{4}{5}[1] + \frac{4}{3}[1-0] = \frac{4}{3} - \frac{4}{5} = \frac{20-13}{15} = \frac{8}{15}$ sq. units

2. Given curve is $y^2 = (1 - x^2)^3$

$\Rightarrow y = \pm(1 - x^2)^{3/2}$

For y to be real, $1 - x^2 \geq 0$

$\Rightarrow x^2 \leq 1$

$\Rightarrow x \in [-1, 1]$ ...(1)

Differentiating w.r.t.x, we get $\frac{dy}{dx} = \pm\frac{3}{2}(-2x)\sqrt{1-x^2}$

$\Rightarrow \frac{dy}{dx} = \mp 3x\sqrt{1-x^2}$

$\Rightarrow \frac{dy}{dx} = 0$ at $x = 0, \pm 1$

Also $y = 0$ at $x = \pm 1$

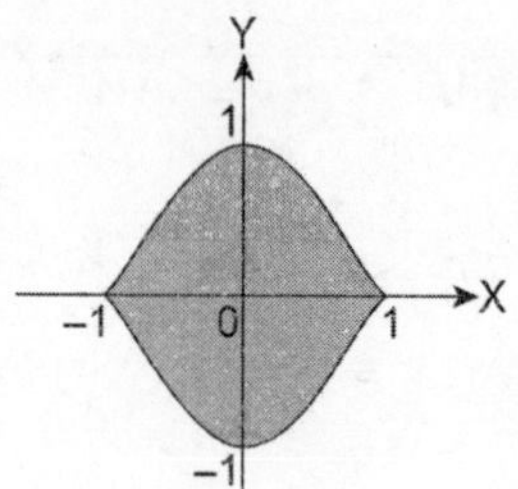

$\therefore$ Required Area $= 2\int_{-1}^{1}(1-x)^{3/2}dx = 4\int_0^1 (1-x)^{3/2}dx$

Put $x = \sin\theta$ $\Rightarrow dx = \cos\theta\, d\theta$

$\therefore$ $A = 4\int_0^{\pi/2}(\cos^2\theta)^{3/2}\cos\theta d\theta = 4\int_0^{\pi/2}(\cos^4\theta d\theta)$

$= 4\left[\frac{3.1}{4.2}\left(\frac{\pi}{2}\right)\right] = \frac{3\pi}{4} = (0.75)\,p$ sq. units

3. Given curve is $4(y^2 - x^2) + x^3 = 0$

$\Rightarrow y^2 - x^2 = -\frac{x^3}{4}$

$\Rightarrow y^2 = x^2 - \frac{x^3}{4}$ $\Rightarrow y = \pm\sqrt{\frac{4x^2 - x^3}{4}}$

$\Rightarrow y = \pm\frac{1}{2}\sqrt{4x^2 - x^3}$ ...(i)

For $y \in \mathbb{R}$, $4x^2 - x^3 \geq 0$

$\Rightarrow x^2(4 - x) \geq 0$

$\Rightarrow 0 \leq x \leq 4$ ...(ii)

From (i), $\frac{dy}{dx} = \pm\frac{1}{2} \times \frac{1}{2\sqrt{4x^2 - x^3}}(8x - 3x^2)$

$= \pm\frac{1}{4}\frac{(8x - 3x^2)}{\sqrt{4x^2 - x^3}} = \pm\frac{1}{4}\frac{(8 - 3x)}{\sqrt{4 - x}}$

$\Rightarrow \dfrac{dy}{dx} = 0$ for $(8-3x)=0$

$\Rightarrow x = 8/3$ and $\dfrac{dy}{dx} = \pm\infty$ at $x = 4$

$$\Rightarrow f\left(\frac{8}{3}\right) = \pm\frac{1}{2}\sqrt{4\left(\frac{8}{3}\right)^2 - \left(\frac{8}{3}\right)^3} = \pm\frac{1}{2}\sqrt{\frac{256}{9} - \frac{512}{27}}$$

$$= \pm\frac{1}{2}\sqrt{\frac{768-512}{27}}$$

$$= \pm\frac{1}{2}\sqrt{\frac{256}{27}} = \pm\frac{1}{2}\left(\frac{16}{3\sqrt{3}}\right) = \pm\frac{8}{3\sqrt{3}} = \pm\frac{8\sqrt{3}}{9}$$

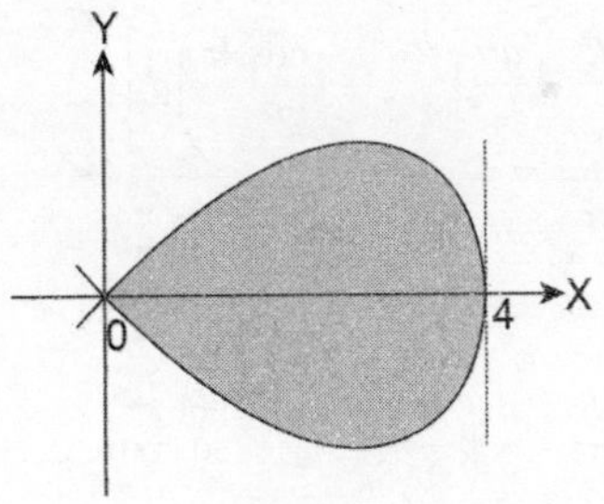

$$\therefore \text{ Required Area } = 2\int_0^4 \frac{1}{2}\sqrt{4x^2 - x^3}\,dx = \int_0^4 \sqrt{4x^2-x^3}\,dx$$

$$= \int_0^4 x\sqrt{4-x}\,dx$$

$$= -\int_0^4 (4-x-4)\sqrt{4-x}\,dx$$

$$= -\int_0^4 (4-x)^{3/2}dx + 4\int_0^4 \sqrt{4-x}\,dx$$

$$= -\left[\frac{-2}{5}(4-x)^{5/2}\right]_0^4 + \left[\frac{-2}{3}(4-x)^{3/2}\right]_0^4$$

$$= \frac{2}{5}[0-(32)] - \frac{8}{3}[0-(8)]$$

$$= +\frac{64}{3} - \frac{64}{5} = \frac{64(5-3)}{15} = \frac{128}{15} \text{ sq. units}$$

4. (a) $x = t^2 - 1, y = t^3 - t$

$\Rightarrow t^2 = x + 1 \qquad \Rightarrow \quad t = \pm\sqrt{x+1}$

$\Rightarrow y = \pm (x+1)^{3/2} \mp \sqrt{x+1}$

$\Rightarrow y = \pm\sqrt{(x+1)}\,((x+1)-1)$

$\Rightarrow y = \pm\sqrt{(x+1)}\,.\,(x)$ ...(1)

$\therefore$ Clearly (1) passes through origin (0, 0)

Now, $\dfrac{dy}{dx} = \pm\sqrt{x+1} \pm x.\dfrac{1}{2\sqrt{x+1}} = \pm\left(\dfrac{2x+2+x}{2\sqrt{x+1}}\right)$

$$= \pm\left(\frac{3x+2}{2\sqrt{x+1}}\right)$$

$\therefore \dfrac{dy}{dx} = 0$

$\Rightarrow x = -2/3$ and $\dfrac{dy}{dx} = \pm\infty$ at $x = -1$ and $x \geq -1$

Also f(0) = 0, $f\left(\dfrac{-2}{3}\right) = \mp\dfrac{2}{3}\sqrt{\dfrac{1}{3}} = \mp\dfrac{2\sqrt{3}}{9}$; $f(-1) = 0$

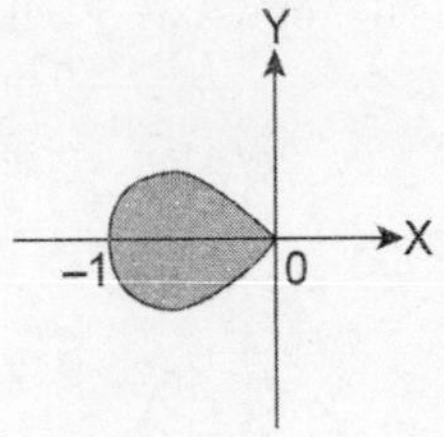

$\therefore$ The required area enclosed by the loop $= 2\int_{-1}^{0} -x\sqrt{x+1}\,dx$

$$= -2\int_{-1}^{0}(x+1-1)\sqrt{x+1}\,dx$$

$$= -2\left[\frac{(x+1)^{5/2}}{5/2}\right]_{-1}^{0} + 2\left[\frac{(x+1)^{3/2}}{3/2}\right]_{-1}^{0}$$

$$= -2\left(\frac{2}{5}\right)[1] + (2)\left(\frac{2}{3}\right)[1] = -\frac{4}{5} + \frac{4}{3} = \frac{-12+20}{15} = \frac{8}{15} \text{ sq. units}$$

(b) $x = 2t - t^2, y = 2t^2 - t^3$ on x-axis, $y = 0$

$\Rightarrow 2t^2 - t^3 = 0$

$\Rightarrow t^2(2-t) = 0 \qquad \Rightarrow \quad t = 0$ or $t = 2$

$\therefore$ Area of loop $= \dfrac{1}{2}\displaystyle\int_0^2 x\left(\frac{dy}{dx} - y\frac{dx}{dt}\right)dt$

$$= \frac{1}{2}\int_0^2 \left[(2t-t^2)(4t-3t^2) - (2t^2-t^3)(2-2t)\right]dt$$

$$= \frac{1}{2}\int_0^2 (8t^2 - 6t^3 - 4t^3 + 3t^4 - 4t^2 + 4t^3 + 2t^3 - 2t^4)dt$$

$$= \frac{1}{2}\int_0^2 (t^4 - 4t^3 + 4t^2)dt$$

$$= \frac{1}{2}\left[\frac{t^5}{5} - \frac{4t^4}{4} + \frac{4t^3}{3}\right]_0^2 = \frac{1}{2}\left[\frac{32}{5} - 16 + \frac{32}{3}\right]$$

$$= \frac{1}{2}\left[\frac{96-240+160}{15}\right] = \frac{1}{2}\left[\frac{16}{15}\right] = \frac{8}{15} \text{ sq. units}$$

(c) $x = t^2,\ y = \dfrac{t}{3}(3-t^2)$

The loop will intersect x-axis, where $y = 0$

$\Rightarrow t = 0$ or $t = \pm\sqrt{3}$

$\therefore$ Required area = area enclosed two loops

$$= \frac{1}{2}(2)\int_0^{\sqrt{3}}\left(x\frac{dy}{dt} - y\frac{dx}{dt}\right)dt$$

$$= \int_0^{\sqrt{3}}\left[t^2.\frac{1}{3}(3-3t^2) - \frac{t}{3}(3-t^2)(2t)\right]dt$$

$$= \int_0^{\sqrt{3}}\left[(t^2-t^4) - \left(t - \frac{t^3}{3}\right)(2t)\right]dt$$

$$= \int_0^{\sqrt{3}}\left(t^2 - t^4 - 2t^2 + \frac{2}{3}t^4\right)dt = \left[\frac{t^3}{3} - \frac{t^5}{5} - \frac{2t^3}{3} + \frac{2t^5}{15}\right]_0^{\sqrt{3}}$$

$$= \sqrt{3} - \frac{9\sqrt{3}}{5} - 2\sqrt{3} + \frac{2}{15}(9\sqrt{3}) = -\sqrt{3} - \frac{3\sqrt{3}}{5} = -\frac{8\sqrt{3}}{5}$$

$\Rightarrow$ Area $= \dfrac{8\sqrt{3}}{5}$ (in magnitude)

5. $x = a\cos t$, $y = b\sin^3 t$ on x-axis, $y = 0$

$\Rightarrow$ $b\sin 3t = 0$ $\qquad \Rightarrow$ $t = 0$ or π

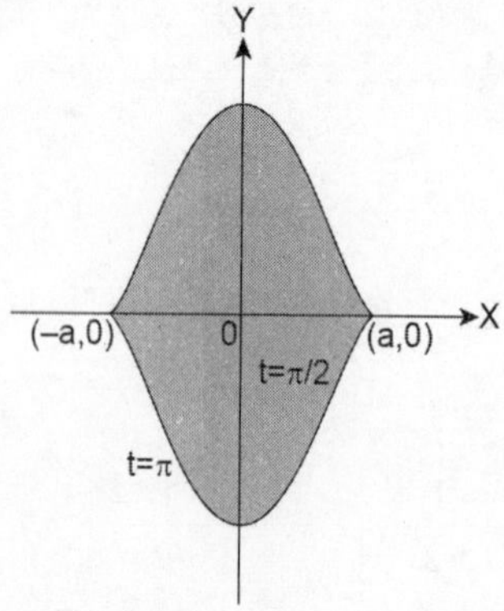

$$\Rightarrow \frac{dy}{dx} = \frac{3b\sin^2 t\cos t}{-a\sin t} = -3\frac{b}{a}\sin t\cos t = 0 \text{ at } t = 0 \text{ or}$$

$t = \pi/2, p$

$$\therefore \text{ The required Area } = \left|\frac{1}{2}\int_0^{\pi}\left(x\frac{dy}{dt} - y\frac{dx}{dt}\right)dt\right|$$

$$= \left|\frac{1}{2}\int_0^{\pi}\left[(a\cos t)(3b\sin^2 t\cos t) - (b\sin^3 t)(-a\sin t)\right]dt\right|$$

$$= \left|\frac{1}{2}\int_0^{\pi}(3ab\sin^2 t\cos^2 t + ab\sin^4 t)dt\right|$$

$$= \left|\frac{1}{2}\int_0^{\pi}\left(\frac{3ab}{4}\sin^2 2t + ab\sin^4 t\right)dt\right|$$

$$= \left|\frac{3ab}{8}\int_0^{\pi}\sin^2 2t dt + \frac{ab}{2}\int_0^{\pi}\sin^4 t dt\right|$$

$$= \left|\frac{3ab}{8}\int_0^{\pi}\left(\frac{1-\cos 4t}{2}\right)dt + \frac{ab}{2}(2)\int_0^{\pi/2}\sin^4 t dt\right|$$

$$= \left|\frac{3ab}{16}\left[t - \frac{\sin 4t}{4}\right]_0^{\pi} + ab\left[\frac{3\times 1}{4\times 2}\times\frac{\pi}{2}\right]\right|$$

$$= \left|\frac{3ab}{16}[\pi] + \frac{3ab\pi}{16}\right| = \frac{6ab\pi}{16} = \frac{3ab\pi}{8}$$

6. $x = a\cos t$; $y = b\sin t\cos 2t$ on x=axis, $y = 0$

$\Rightarrow$ $b\sin t\cos^2 t = 0$ $\qquad \Rightarrow$ $t = 0$ or $\pi/2, \pi, 3p/2, 2p$

$$\Rightarrow \frac{dx}{dt} = -a\sin t\,; \quad \frac{dy}{dt} = b\cos 3t - b\sin 2t\,(2\cos t)$$

$$\therefore \frac{dy}{dx} = \frac{b\cos t(\cos^2 t - 2\sin^2 t)}{-a\sin t}$$

$$\therefore \frac{dy}{dx} = 0$$

$$\Rightarrow t = \pi/2 + \pi/4 \text{ and } \frac{dy}{dx} = \pm\infty \text{ at } t = 0, \pi, 2p$$

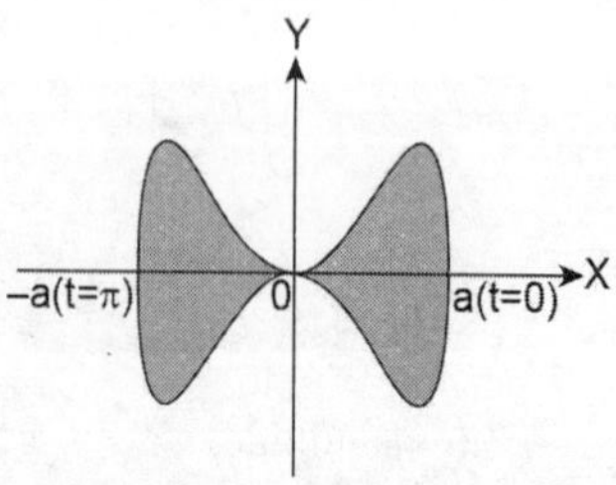

$$\therefore \text{ Required Area} = \left|2\left(\frac{1}{2}\right)\int_0^{\pi/2}\left(x\frac{dy}{dt} - y\frac{dx}{dt}\right)dt\right|$$

$$= \left|\int_0^{\pi/2}\{(a\cos t)(b\cos^3 t) - 2b\sin^2 t\cos t - (b\sin t\cos^2 t)(-a\sin t)\}dt\right|$$

$$= \left|\int_0^{\pi/2}\{ab\cos^4 t - 2ab\sin^2 t\cos^2 t + ab\sin^2 t\cos^2 t\}dt\right|$$

$$= \left|\int_0^{\pi/2}(ab\cos^4 t - ab\sin^2 t\cos^2 t)dt\right|$$

$$= \left|ab\left[\frac{3.1}{4.2}\left(\frac{\pi}{2}\right) - \frac{ab}{4}\int_0^{\pi/2}\sin^2 2t dt\right]\right|$$

$$= \left|\frac{3\pi ab}{16} - \frac{ab}{4}\int_0^{\pi/2}\left(\frac{1-\cos 4t}{2}\right)dt\right|$$

$$= \left|\frac{3\pi ab}{16} - \frac{ab}{8}\left[t - \frac{\sin 4t}{4}\right]_0^{\pi/2}\right|$$

$$= \left|\frac{3\pi ab}{16} - \frac{ab}{8}\left(\frac{\pi}{2}\right)\right| = \frac{\pi ab}{8} \text{ sq. units}$$

7. $x = a\cos t\,(1 + \cos t)$; $y = a\sin t\,(1 + \cos t)$ on x-axis, $y = 0$

$\Rightarrow$ $\sin t = 0$ or $\cos t = -1$

$\Rightarrow$ $t = 0, \pi, 2p....$ or $t = 0, \pi, 3p$

On y-axis, $x = 0$ $\qquad \Rightarrow$ $\cos t = 0$ or $\cos t = -1$

$$\Rightarrow t = \frac{\pi}{2}, \frac{3\pi}{2} \text{ .... or } t = \pi, 3p, \text{ ....}$$

$$\Rightarrow \frac{dy}{dx} = \frac{a\sin t(-\sin t) + a(1+\cos t)\cos t}{a\cos t(-\sin t) + a(1+\cos t)(-\sin t)}$$

$$= \frac{a(\cos^2 t - \sin^2 t) + a\cos t}{-a\sin t - 2a\sin t\cos t} = \frac{a\cos 2t + a\cos t}{-(a\sin t + a\sin 2t)}$$

$$= \frac{\cos 2t + \cos t}{-(\sin t + \sin 2t)}$$

$$\therefore \frac{dy}{dt} = 0 \qquad \Rightarrow \cos 2t + \cos t = 0$$

$$\Rightarrow 2\cos\left(\frac{3t}{2}\right)\cos\left(\frac{t}{2}\right) = 0$$

$$\Rightarrow \cos\left(\frac{3t}{2}\right) = 0 \text{ or } \cos\left(\frac{t}{2}\right) = 0$$

$$\Rightarrow \frac{3t}{2} = \frac{\pi}{2} \text{ or } \frac{t}{2} = \frac{\pi}{2}$$

$\Rightarrow$ $t = \pi/3$ or $t = \pi$

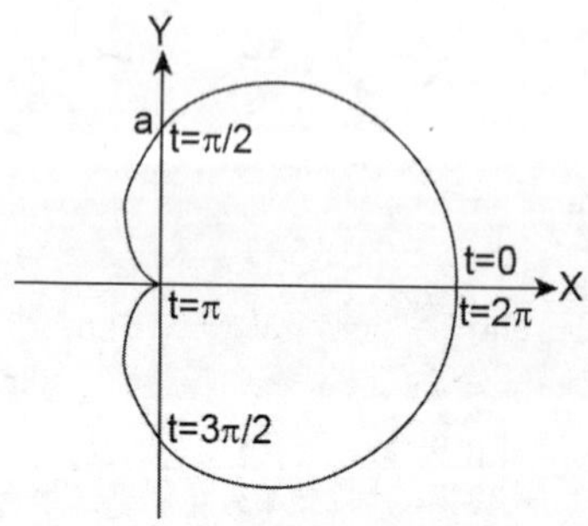

$\Rightarrow \quad \frac{dy}{dt} = \infty$ at $\sin 2t + \sin t = 0$

$\Rightarrow \quad 2\sin\left(\frac{3t}{2}\right)\cos\left(\frac{t}{2}\right) = 0$

$\Rightarrow \quad \frac{3t}{2} = 0$, π, 2p or $\frac{t}{2} = \frac{\pi}{2}, \frac{3\pi}{2}, \frac{2\pi}{2}$

$\Rightarrow \quad t = 0, \frac{2\pi}{3}, \frac{4\pi}{3}$ or t = π, 3p, 5p

Here $x^2 + y^2 = a^2 (1 + \cos t)^2$

$\Rightarrow \quad r^2 = a^2 (1 + \cos t)^2$

$\Rightarrow \quad r = \pm a (1 + \cos t)$

$\therefore$ Required area $= 2\left(\frac{1}{2}\right)\int_0^{\pi} r^2 dt = \int_0^{\pi} a^2(1+\cos t)^2 dt$

$= a^2\int_0^{\pi} 4\cos^4\frac{t}{2}dt = 4a^2\int_0^{\pi}\cos^4\frac{t}{2}dt$

Put $\frac{t}{2} = \phi \qquad \Rightarrow \quad dt = 3d\phi$

$\therefore \quad A = 4a^2\int_0^{\pi/2}\cos^4\phi(2d\phi) = 8a^2\int_0^{\pi/2}\cos^4\phi d\phi$

$= 8a^2\left[\frac{3\times 1}{4\times 2}\times\frac{\pi}{2}\right] = \frac{3\pi a^2}{2}$

8. (a) $r = 1 + \cos\theta$

$\therefore$ Required Area $= 2\left(\frac{1}{2}\right)\int_0^{\pi} r^2 d\theta = \int_0^{\pi}(1+\cos\theta)^2 d\theta$

$= \int_0^{\pi}\left(2\cos^2\frac{\theta}{2}\right)d\theta$

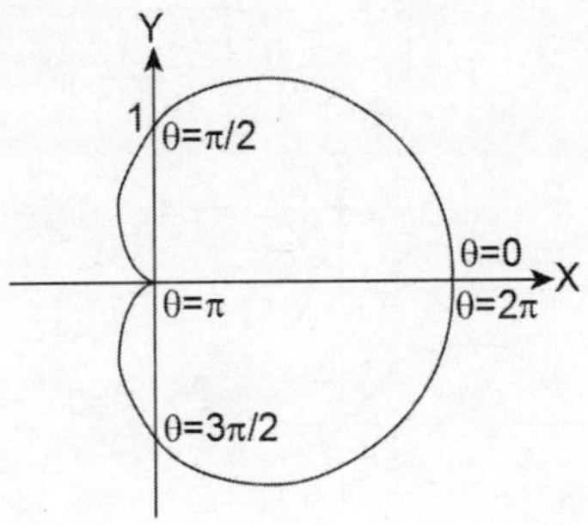

$= 4\int_0^{\pi}\cos^4\frac{\theta}{2}d\theta = 4\int_0^{\pi/2}\cos^4 t(2dt) = 8\left[\frac{3\times 1}{4\times 2}\times\frac{\pi}{2}\right]$

$= \frac{3\pi}{2}$ sq. units

(b) $r = a\cos\theta$

$\therefore$ Required Area $= 2\left(\frac{1}{2}\right)\int_0^{\pi/2} r^2 d\theta = \int_0^{\pi/2} a^2\cos^2\theta d\theta$

$= \frac{a^2}{2}\int_0^{\pi/2}(1+\cos 2\theta)d\theta$

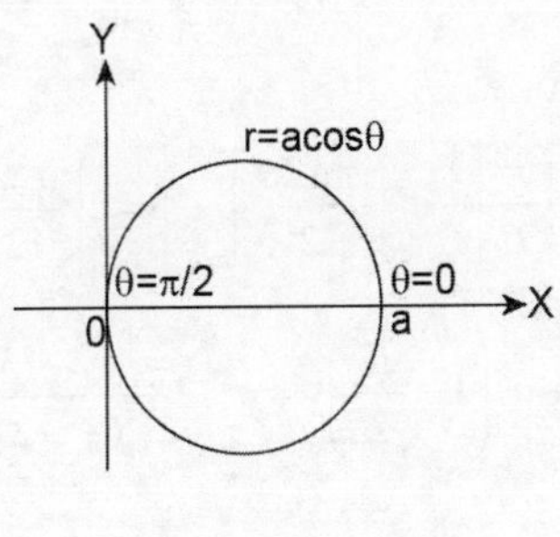

$= \frac{a^2}{2}\left[\theta + \frac{\sin 2\theta}{2}\right]_0^{\pi/2} = \frac{a^2\pi}{4}$ sq. units

9. $r = 3\sqrt{2}$ a cos q ...(1)

$r = 3a\sin q$ ...(2)

At the point of intersection $3a\sin q = 3\sqrt{2}\ a\cos\theta$

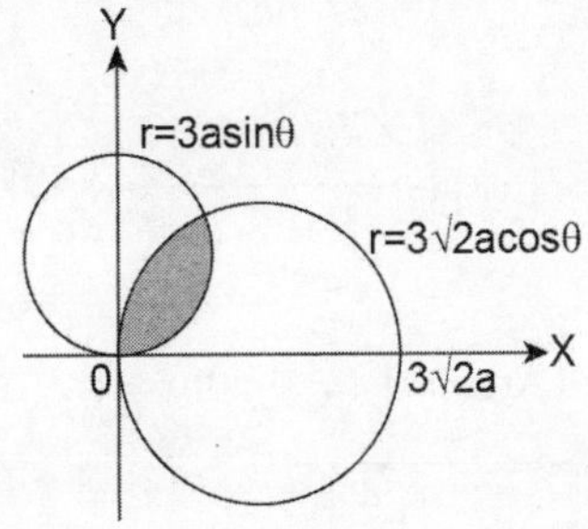

$\Rightarrow \tan\theta = \sqrt{2} \qquad \Rightarrow \quad q = \tan^{-1}\sqrt{2}$

$\therefore$ Required Area $= \left(\frac{1}{2}\right)\int_0^{\tan^{-1}(\sqrt{2})} r^2 d\theta + \frac{1}{2}\int_{\tan^{-1}\sqrt{2}}^{\pi/2} r^2 d\theta$

$= \frac{1}{2}\int_0^{\tan^{-1}\sqrt{2}} 9a^2\sin^2\theta d\theta + \frac{1}{2}\int_{\tan^{-1}\sqrt{2}}^{\pi/2} 18a^2\cos^2\theta d\theta$

$= \frac{9a^2}{4}\int_0^{\tan^{-1}\sqrt{2}}(1-\cos 2\theta)d\theta +$

$\frac{9a^2}{2}\int_{\tan^{-1}\sqrt{2}}^{\pi/2}(1+\cos 2\theta)d\theta$

$= \frac{9a^2}{4}\left[\theta - \frac{\sin 2\theta}{2}\right]_0^{\tan^{-1}(\sqrt{2})} + \frac{9a^2}{2}\left[\theta + \frac{\sin 2\theta}{2}\right]_{\tan^{-1}\sqrt{2}}^{\pi/2}$

$= \frac{9a^2}{4}\left[\tan^{-1}\sqrt{2} - \frac{1}{2}\left[\frac{2(\sqrt{2})}{1+2}\right]\right]$

$+ \frac{9a^2}{2}\left[\frac{\pi}{2} - \tan^{-1}\sqrt{2} + \frac{1}{2}(0 - \sin(2\tan^{-1}\sqrt{2}))\right]$

$= \frac{9a^2}{4}\left[\tan^{-1}\sqrt{2} - \frac{\sqrt{2}}{3}\right]$

$+ \frac{9a^2}{2}\left[\frac{\pi}{2} - \tan^{-1}\sqrt{2} - \frac{1}{2}\sin(2\tan^{-1}\sqrt{2})\right]$

$= \frac{9a^2}{4}\left[\tan^{-1}\sqrt{2} - \frac{\sqrt{2}}{3} + \pi - 2\tan^{-1}\sqrt{2} - \sin(2\tan^{-1}\sqrt{2})\right]$

$= \frac{9a^2}{4}\left[\pi - \tan^{-1}\sqrt{2} - \frac{\sqrt{2}}{3} - \left(\frac{2\sqrt{2}}{1+2}\right)\right]$

$= \frac{9a^2}{4}\left[\pi - \tan^{-1}\sqrt{2} - \sqrt{2}\right]$ sq. units

10. $(y - \sin^{-1}x)^2 = x - x^2$

$\Rightarrow \quad y - \sin^{-1}x = \pm\sqrt{x(1-x)}$ ...(1)

From (1), $x \in [-1, 1]$ and $x(1 - x) \geq 0$

$\Rightarrow \quad x \in [0, 1]$ ...(2)

From (1), $y = \sin^{-1} \pm \sqrt{x(1-x)}$ on x-axis, $y = 0$

$\Rightarrow\ \sin^{-1}x = \mp\sqrt{x(1-x)}\ \Rightarrow\ x = 0$ on y-axis, $x = 0$

$\Rightarrow\ y = 0$

$\Rightarrow$ Curve intersects x-axis and y-axis only at origin.

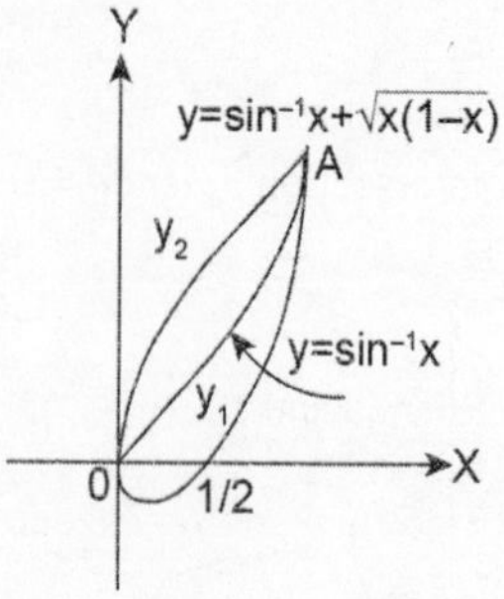

$\therefore$ Required Area $= \int_0^1 (y_2 - y_1)dx = \int_0^1 2\sqrt{x(1-x)}dx$

$$= 2\int_0^1 \sqrt{-\left(x^2 - x + \frac{1}{4}\right) + \frac{1}{4}}dx$$

$$= 2\int_0^1 \sqrt{\left(\frac{1}{2}\right)^2 - \left(x - \frac{1}{2}\right)^2}\ dx$$

$$= 2\left[\frac{\sqrt{x-x^2}}{2}\left(x - \frac{1}{2}\right) + \frac{\left(\frac{1}{2}\right)^2}{2}\sin^{-1}\left(\frac{x - \frac{1}{2}}{\frac{1}{2}}\right)\right]_0^1$$

$$= \left[\left(x - \frac{1}{2}\right)\sqrt{x - x^2} + \frac{1}{4}\sin^{-1}\left(\frac{x - \frac{1}{2}}{\frac{1}{2}}\right)\right]_0^1$$

$$= \left[\frac{\pi}{8} + \frac{\pi}{8}\right] = \left(\frac{\pi}{4}\right) \text{ sq. units}$$

11. $r = a\sin\theta\cos 2q,\ a > 0$

Clearly $r > 0$ for $\theta \in (0, \pi)$ and $r < 0$ for $\theta \in (\pi, 2p)$

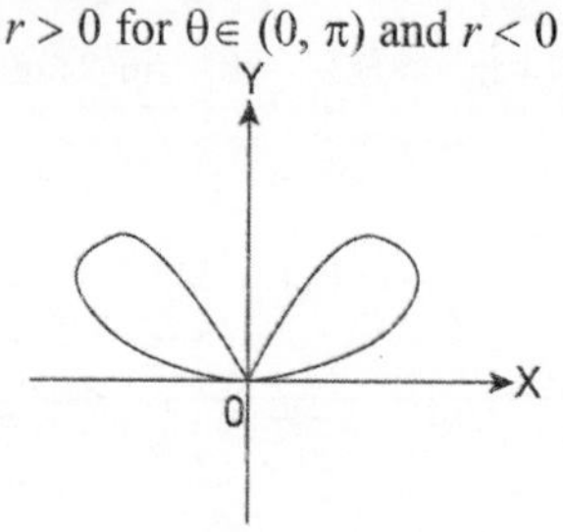

$\therefore$ Required area $= 2\left(\frac{1}{2}\right)\int_0^{\pi/2} r^2 d\theta$

$$= \int_0^{\pi/2} a^2\sin^2\theta\cos^4\theta d\theta = a^2\int_0^{\pi/2}(\cos^4\theta - \cos^6)d\theta$$

$$= a^2\left[\frac{3\times1}{4\times2} - \frac{5\times3\times1}{6\times4\times2}\right]\frac{\pi}{2} = \frac{a^2\pi}{2}\left(\frac{3}{8}\right)\left(1 - \frac{5}{6}\right)$$

$$= \frac{a^2\pi}{2}\left(\frac{3}{48}\right) = \frac{a^2\pi}{32} \text{ sq. units}$$

12. $r = a\cos 3q,\ a > 0$

Clearly, $r > 0$ for $q \in (0, \pi/2) \cup \left(\frac{3\pi}{2}, 2\pi\right)$

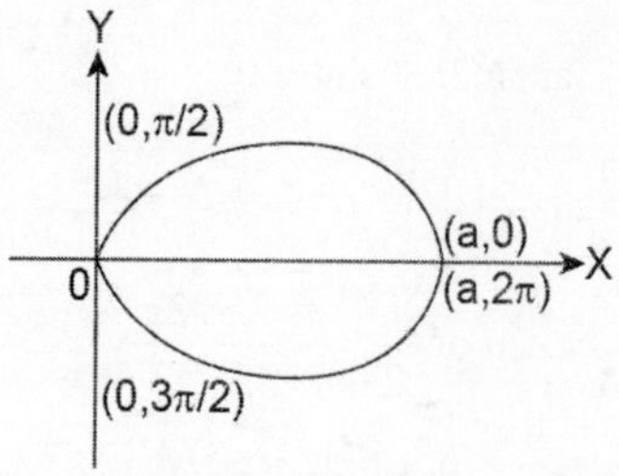

$\therefore$ Required Area $= 2\left(\frac{1}{2}\right)\int_0^{\pi/2} r^2 d\theta = \int_0^{\pi/2} a^2\cos^6\theta d\theta$

$$= \int_0^{\pi/2} a^2\cos^6\theta d\theta$$

$$= a^2\int_0^{\pi/2}\cos^6\theta d\theta = a^2\left[\frac{5\times3\times1}{6\times4\times2}\times\frac{\pi}{2}\right] = \frac{5\pi a^2}{32} \text{ sq. units}$$

13. Given curves is $r = a/\sqrt{2}$ ...(1)

and $r = a\sqrt{\cos 2\theta}$ ...(2)

For lemniscate, $r = a\sqrt{\cos 2\theta}$, $r > 0$ for $\cos 2q \geq 0$,

$$\Rightarrow\ 2\theta \in \left[0, \frac{\pi}{2}\right] \cup \left[\frac{3\pi}{2}, 2\pi\right]$$

$$\Rightarrow\ \theta \in \left[0, \frac{\pi}{4}\right] \cup \left[\frac{3\pi}{4}, \pi\right]$$

Also $r > 0$ for $2\theta \in \left[2\pi, \frac{5\pi}{2}\right] \cup \left[\frac{7\pi}{2}, 4\pi\right]$,

i.e., $\theta \in \left[\pi, \frac{5\pi}{4}\right] \cup \left[\frac{7\pi}{4}, 2\pi\right]$

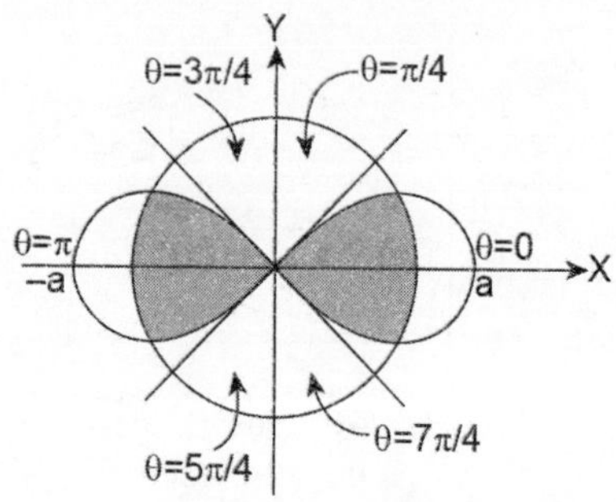

At point A, $\frac{a}{\sqrt{2}} = a\sqrt{\cos 2\theta}$

$\Rightarrow\ 1 = \sqrt{2\cos 2\theta}$ $\qquad\Rightarrow\ 1/2 = \cos 2q$

$\Rightarrow\ 2q = \pi/3$ $\qquad\Rightarrow\ q = \pi/6$

$$\therefore \text{ Required Area} = 4\left[\underbrace{\frac{1}{2}\int_0^{\pi/6}\left(\frac{a^2}{2}\right)d\theta}_{\text{circle}} + \underbrace{\frac{1}{2}\int_{\pi/6}^{\pi/4} a^2\cos 2\theta d\theta}_{\text{lemniscate}}\right]$$

$$= 2\left[\frac{a^2}{2}\left[\frac{\pi}{6}\right] + a^2\left[\frac{\sin 2\theta}{2}\right]_{\pi/6}^{\pi/4}\right] = 2\left[\frac{a^2\pi}{12} + \frac{a^2}{2}\left[1 - \frac{\sqrt{3}}{2}\right]\right]$$

$$= \frac{a^2\pi}{6} + a^2\left(1 - \frac{\sqrt{3}}{2}\right) = a^2\left(1 + \frac{\pi}{6} - \frac{\sqrt{3}}{2}\right) \text{ sq. units}$$

14. Given curve is $(x^2 + y^2)^3 = 4a^2 x^2 y^2$ ...(1)

Put $x = r\cos\theta$, $y = r\sin\theta$

$\Rightarrow r^6 = 4a^2 r^4 \cos 2q \sin 2q$

$\Rightarrow r^2 = a^2 \sin^2 2q$

$\Rightarrow r = |a \sin 2q|$

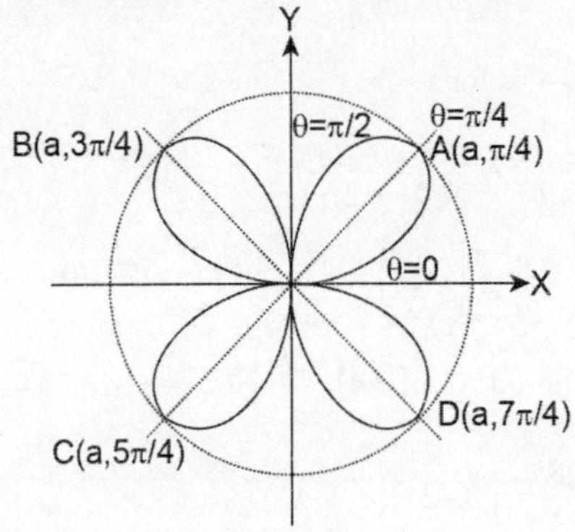

$\therefore$ Required Area $= 4\left(\dfrac{1}{2}\right)\displaystyle\int_0^{\pi/2} r^2 d\theta = = 2\int_0^{\pi/2} a^2 \sin^2 2\theta d\theta$

$$= = a^2 \int_0^{\pi/2} (1+\cos 4\theta) d\theta$$

$$= a^2\left[\theta + \frac{\sin 4\theta}{4}\right]_0^{\pi/2} = a^2\left[\frac{\pi}{2} + \frac{1}{4}(0-0)\right] = \frac{a^2\pi}{2} \text{ sq. units}$$

15. Given curve is $(x^4 + y^4) = a^2(x^2 + y^2)$ ...(1)

Put $x = r\cos\theta$, $y = r\sin\theta$ in (i)

$\Rightarrow r^4(\cos^4 q + \sin 4q) = a^2 r^2$

$\Rightarrow r^2(1 - 2\sin 2q \cos 2q) = a^2$

$$\Rightarrow r^2\left(1 - \frac{1}{2}\sin^2 2\theta\right) = a^2$$

$\Rightarrow r^2(2 - \sin^2 2q) = 2a^2$

$\Rightarrow r^2(1 + \cos^2 2q) = 2a^2 \Rightarrow r^2 = \dfrac{2a^2}{(1+\cos^2 2\theta)}$

$$\Rightarrow r = \frac{\sqrt{2}a}{\sqrt{1+\cos^2 2\theta}} \quad ...(1)$$

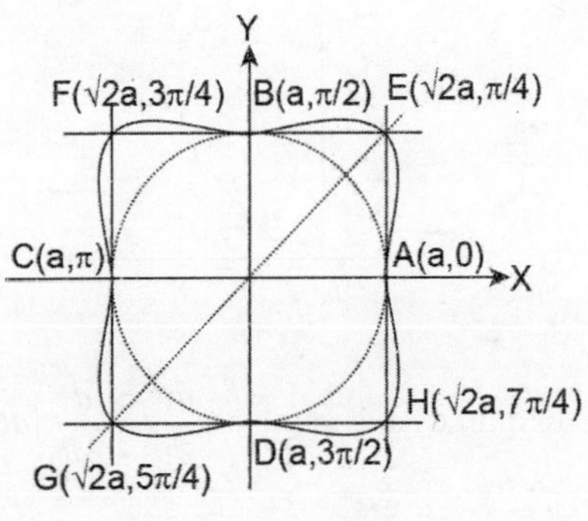

which is the required. Polar form of (1)

$\therefore$ Required Area $= 8\left(\dfrac{1}{2}\right)\displaystyle\int_0^{\pi/4} r^2 d\theta = 4\int_0^{\pi/4} \frac{2a^2}{1+\cos^2 2\theta} d\theta$

$$= 8a^2 \int_0^{\pi/2} \frac{1}{1+\left(\dfrac{1+\cos 4\theta}{2}\right)} d\theta = 16a^2 \int_0^{\pi/4} \frac{1}{3+\cos 4\theta} d\theta$$

Put $4q = t \quad \Rightarrow 4\,d\theta = dt$

$$= 16a^2 \int_0^{\pi} \frac{1}{3+\cos t}\left(\frac{dt}{4}\right) = 4a^2 \int_0^{\pi} \frac{1}{3+\cos t} dt$$

$$= 4a^2 \int_0^{\pi} \frac{1}{3 + \left(\dfrac{1-\tan^2 t/2}{1+\tan^2 t/2}\right)} dt$$

$$= 4a^2 \int_0^{\pi} \frac{1+\tan^2 t/2}{(4+2\tan^2 t/2)} = 2a^2 \int_0^{\pi} \frac{\sec^2 t/2}{(2+\tan^2 t/2)}$$

Put $\tan\dfrac{t}{2} = u \quad \Rightarrow \dfrac{1}{2}\sec^2\dfrac{t}{2} dt = du$

$\Rightarrow \sec^2\dfrac{t}{2}\, dt = 2du$

$$= 2a^2 \int_0^{\infty} \frac{2du}{2+u^2} = 4a^2\left[\frac{1}{\sqrt{2}}\tan^{-1}\left(\frac{u}{\sqrt{2}}\right)\right]_0^{\infty}$$

$$= \frac{4a^2}{\sqrt{2}}\left[\frac{\pi}{2} - 0\right] = \sqrt{2}\pi a^2 \text{ sq units}$$

TEXTUAL EXERCISE-4: (OBJECTIVE)

1. (b) $y^2 = x^2(1 - x^2)$

The graph is symmetric about both axes.

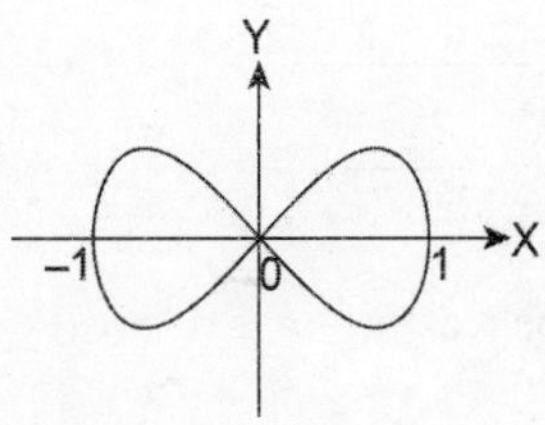

On x-axis, $y = 0 \quad \Rightarrow x = 0, \pm 1$

On y-axis, $x = 0 \quad \Rightarrow y = 0$

i.e., curve passes through the origin.

Now, $y = \pm\sqrt{x^2(1-x^2)}$

$\therefore$ For y – to be real, $x^2(1 - x^2) \ge 0$

$\Rightarrow x = 0$ or $1 - x^2 \ge 0$

$\Rightarrow x = 0$ or $x^2 \le 1$

$\Rightarrow x \in [-1, 1]$

$\Rightarrow$ Required Area $= 4\displaystyle\int_0^1 x\sqrt{1-x^2}\, dx$

$$= 4\left(-\frac{1}{2}\right)\int_0^1 (-2x)(1-x^2)^{1/2} dx$$

$$= (-2)\left[\frac{2}{3}(1-x^2)^{3/2}\right]_0^1 = -\frac{4}{3}[0-1] = \frac{4}{3} \text{ sq. units}$$

2. (a) Given curve is $x = y^2(1 - y)$

On x-axis, $y = 0 \quad \Rightarrow x = 0$

On y-axis, $x = 0 \quad \Rightarrow y^2(1 - y) = 0$

$\Rightarrow y = 0$ or 1

$x = -y^3 + y^2 > 0$ for $y^2(1 - y) > 0$

$\Rightarrow y < 1$

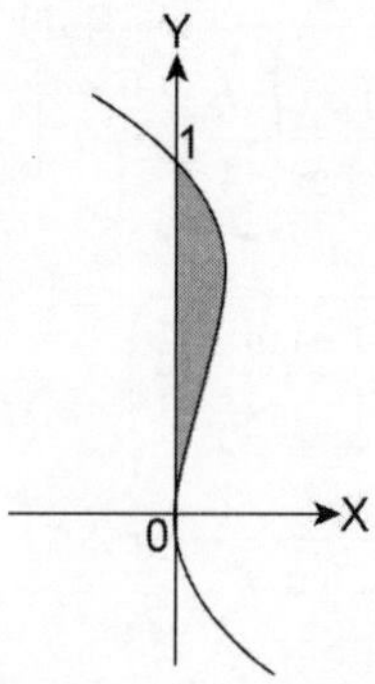

$$\frac{dx}{dy} = -3y^2 + 2y = 0 \Rightarrow y(2-3y) = 0$$

$\Rightarrow y = 0$ or $y = 2/3$ and $\frac{d^2x}{dy^2} = -6y + 2 > 0$ for $y < 1/3$

$\therefore$ Required Area $= \int_0^1 x\,dy = \int_0^1 (y^2 - y^3)dy$

$$= \left[\frac{y^3}{3} - \frac{y^4}{4}\right]_0^1 = \frac{1}{3} - \frac{1}{4} = \frac{4-3}{12} = \frac{1}{12} \text{ sq. units}$$

3. (c) $x = a$ sin$t$ and $y = b$ sin$2t$

$$y = b(2 \sin t \cos t) = \pm 2b\left(\frac{x}{a}\right)\sqrt{1 - \frac{x^2}{a^2}}$$

$$\Rightarrow y = \pm\frac{2b}{a}.\frac{x\sqrt{a^2 - x^2}}{a}$$

$$\Rightarrow y = \pm\frac{2b}{a^2}.x.\sqrt{a^2 - x^2}$$

For y to be real, $a^2 - x^2 \geq 0$

$\Rightarrow x \in [-a, a]$

$$\Rightarrow y' = \pm\frac{2b}{a^2}\left[x.\frac{1}{2\sqrt{a^2 - x^2}}(-2x) + \sqrt{a^2 - x^2}\right]$$

$$\Rightarrow y' = \pm\frac{2b}{a^2}\left[\frac{-x^2 + a^2 - x^2}{\sqrt{a^2 - x^2}}\right]$$

$$\Rightarrow y' = \pm\frac{2b}{a^2}\left[\frac{a^2 - 2x^2}{\sqrt{a^2 - x^2}}\right]$$

$\therefore$ $y' = 0$ for $x = \pm\frac{a}{\sqrt{2}}$ and $y' > 0$ for $a^2 - 2x^2 > 0$

For the branch $y = \frac{2b}{a^2}x\sqrt{a^2 - x^2}$ and

$y' < 0$ for $a^2 - 2x^2 < 0$

For the branch $y = \frac{2b}{a^2}x\sqrt{a^2 - x^2}$, i.e., for the branch

$$y = \frac{2b}{a^2}x\sqrt{a^2 - x^2}$$

$y \uparrow$ for $x \in \left[\frac{-a}{\sqrt{2}}, \frac{a}{\sqrt{2}}\right]$ and $y \downarrow$ for

$$x \in \left(-\infty, \frac{-a}{\sqrt{2}}\right) \cup \left(\frac{a}{\sqrt{2}}, \infty\right)$$

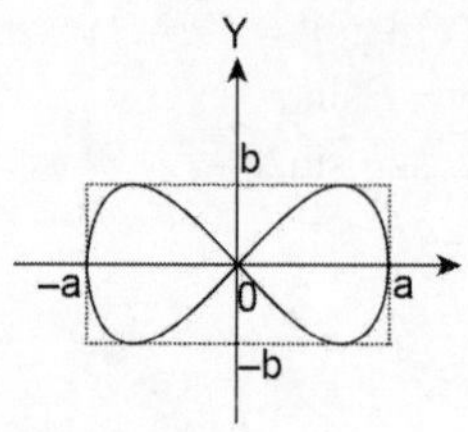

Also $y' \to \infty$ for $x = \pm$ a

$$f\left(\pm\frac{a}{\sqrt{2}}\right) = \pm\frac{2b}{a^2}\left(\pm\frac{a}{\sqrt{2}}\right)\sqrt{a^2 - \frac{a^2}{2}}$$

$= \pm\frac{2b}{a^2}\left(\pm\frac{a}{\sqrt{2}}\right)\left(\frac{a}{\sqrt{2}}\right) = \pm$ b and $f(\pm a) = f(0) = 0$

$\therefore$ Required Area $= 4\int_0^a \frac{2b}{a^2}x\sqrt{a^2 - x^2}\,dx$

$$= \frac{8b}{-2a^2}\int_0^a (-2x)(a^2 - x^2)^{1/2}dx$$

$$= -\frac{4b}{a^2}\left[\frac{(a^2 - x^2)^{3/2}}{3/2}\right]_0^a = -\frac{4b}{a^2}\left(\frac{2}{3}\right)[0 - a^3] = \frac{8}{3}ab \text{ sq. units}$$

4. (b) $\frac{dx}{dt} = \frac{1}{3}[6 - 2t]$ and $\frac{dy}{dt} = \frac{1}{5}[12t - 3t^2]$

$$\therefore \frac{dy}{dx} = \frac{\frac{1}{5}[3t(4-t)]}{\frac{1}{3}(2)(3-t)} = \frac{3}{5}\times\frac{3}{2}\times\frac{t(4-t)}{(3-t)} = \frac{9}{10}\frac{t(4-t)}{(3-t)} = 0 \text{ at}$$

$t = 0, 4$

$\Rightarrow$ At A (0, 0); $\beta\left(\frac{8}{3}, \frac{32}{5}\right)$

Also $\frac{dy}{dx} \to \infty$ at $t = 3$, i.e., at $C\left(3, \frac{27}{5}\right)$

On x-axis $y = 0$

$\Rightarrow t = 0, t = 6$, i.e., at A(0, 0) only

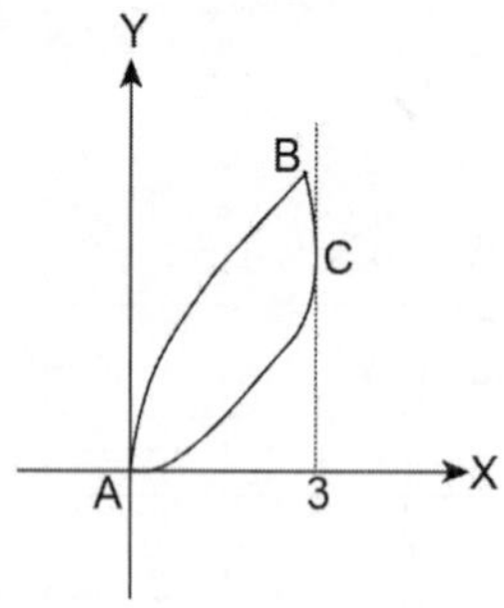

$\therefore$ Required Area $= \frac{1}{2}\int_0^6 \left(x\frac{dy}{dt} - y\frac{dx}{dt}\right)dt$ As at A, $t = 0$ and $t = 6$

$$= \frac{1}{2}\int_0^6 \left[\frac{t}{3}(6-t)\left[\frac{6}{5}2t, -\frac{1}{5}(3t^2)\right] - \frac{t^2}{5}(6-t)\left(2 - \frac{1}{3}(2t)\right)\right]dt$$

$$= \frac{1}{2}\int_0^6 \left\{\left(2t - \frac{1}{3}t^2\right)\left(\frac{12}{5}t - \frac{3}{5}t^2\right) - \left(\frac{6}{5}t^2 - \frac{t^3}{5}\right)\left(2 - \frac{2}{3}t\right)\right\}dt$$

$$= \frac{1}{2}\int_0^6 \left(\frac{24}{5}t^2 - \frac{6}{5}t^3 - \frac{4}{5}t^3 + \frac{1}{5}t^4 - \frac{12}{5}t^2 + \frac{4}{5}t^3 + \frac{2t^3}{5} - \frac{2}{15}t^4\right)dt$$

$$=\frac{1}{2}\int_0^6\left(\frac{1}{5}t^4-\frac{4}{5}t^3+\frac{12}{5}t^2\right)dt=\frac{1}{2}\left[\frac{1}{15}\left(\frac{t^5}{5}\right)-\frac{1}{5}(t^4)+\frac{4}{5}t^3\right]_0^6$$

$$=\frac{1}{2}\left[\frac{t^5-15t^4+60t^3}{75}\right]_0^6=\frac{1}{150}\left[t^3(t^2-15t+60)\right]_0^6$$

$$=\frac{1}{150}(216)(36-90+60)=\frac{216}{150}\times 6=\frac{216}{25}$$

5. **(c)** $x = t^2$ and $y = t - \frac{t^3}{3}$ on x-axis, $y = 0$

$\Rightarrow\ t\left(1-\frac{t^2}{3}\right)=0 \qquad \Rightarrow\ t = 0$ or $t = \pm\sqrt{3}$

$\Rightarrow\ \frac{dx}{dt}=2t,\ \frac{dy}{dt}=1-t^2 \quad \therefore \quad \frac{dy}{dx}=\frac{1-t^2}{2t}$

$\Rightarrow\ \frac{dy}{dx}=0$ at $t = \pm 1$ and $\frac{dy}{dx}\to\infty$ at $t = 0$

At, $t = 1, x = 1, y = 2/3$ and At, $t = -1, x = 1, y = -2/3$

At, $t = -\sqrt{3}$; $x = 3, y = 0$

At, $t = \sqrt{3}$; $x = 3, y = 0$

At, $t = 0$; $x = 0, y = 0$

At, $t = \pm\sqrt{2}$; $x = 2, y = \pm\sqrt{2}/3$

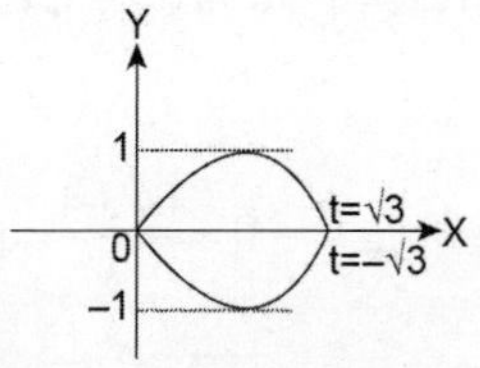

$\therefore$ Required Area $=\frac{1}{2}\left|\int_{-\sqrt{3}}^{\sqrt{3}}\left(x\frac{dy}{dt}-y\frac{dx}{dt}\right)\right|$

$$=\frac{1}{2}\int_{-\sqrt{3}}^{\sqrt{3}}\left\{t^2(1-t^2)-\left(t-\frac{t^3}{3}\right)(2t)\right\}dt$$

$$=\frac{1}{2}\int_{-\sqrt{3}}^{\sqrt{3}}\left(t^2-t^4-2t^2+\frac{2}{3}t^4\right)dt=\frac{1}{2}\int_{-\sqrt{3}}^{\sqrt{3}}\left(-\frac{1}{3}t^4-t^2\right)dt$$

$$=\int_0^{\sqrt{3}}\left(-\frac{1}{3}t^4-t^2\right)dt=-\frac{1}{3}\left[\frac{t^5}{5}\right]_0^{\sqrt{3}}-\frac{1}{3}[t^3]_0^{\sqrt{3}}$$

$$=\left|-\frac{1}{15}\left[9\sqrt{3}\right]-\frac{1}{3}\left[3\sqrt{3}\right]\right|=\left|-\frac{3}{5}\sqrt{3}-\sqrt{3}\right|$$

$$=\left|-\frac{8}{5}\sqrt{3}\right|=\frac{8\sqrt{3}}{5}\text{ sq. units}$$

6. **(c)** $r = a$ cos2q

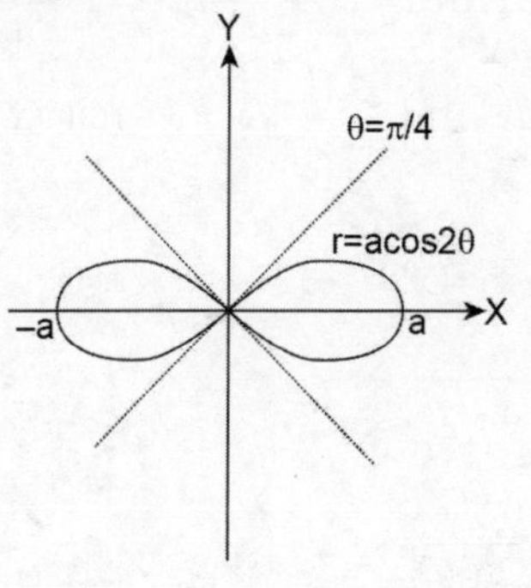

$\therefore$ Required Area of one loop $=2\left(\frac{1}{2}\right)\int_0^{\pi 4}r^2d\theta$

$$=\int_0^{\pi/4}a^2\cos^2 2\theta d\theta=\frac{a^2}{2}\int_0^{\pi/4}(1+\cos 4\theta)d\theta$$

$$=\frac{a^2}{2}\left[\theta+\frac{\sin 4\theta}{4}\right]_0^{\pi/4}=\frac{a^2\pi}{8}\text{ sq. units}$$

7. **(a)** $r = a$ sin2q

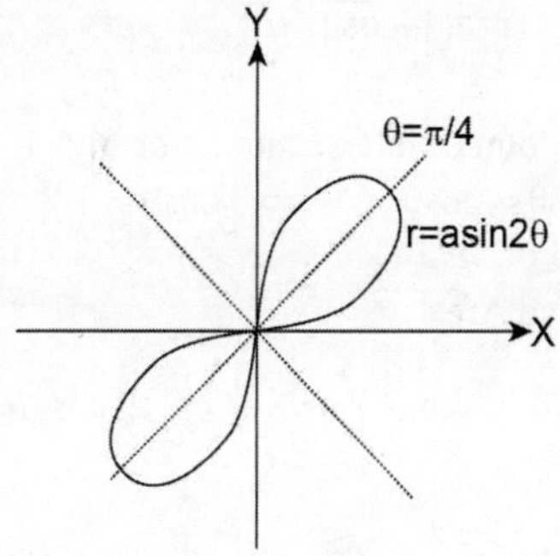

$\therefore$ The Required area of one loop $=\left(\frac{1}{2}\right)\int_0^{\pi/2}r^2d\theta$

$$=\frac{1}{2}\int_0^{\pi/2}a^2\sin^2 2\theta d\theta=\frac{a^2}{4}\int_0^{\pi/2}2\sin^2 2\theta d\theta$$

$$=\frac{a^2}{4}\int_0^{\pi/2}(1-\cos 4\theta)d\theta=\frac{a^2}{4}\left[\theta-\frac{\sin 4\theta}{4}\right]_0^{\pi/2}$$

$$=\frac{a^2}{4}\left(\frac{\pi}{2}\right)=\frac{a^2\pi}{8}\text{ sq. units}$$

8. **(a)** $r = a\,(1 - \cos\theta)$; $r = a$ or $r = a - a\cos\theta$; $r = a$

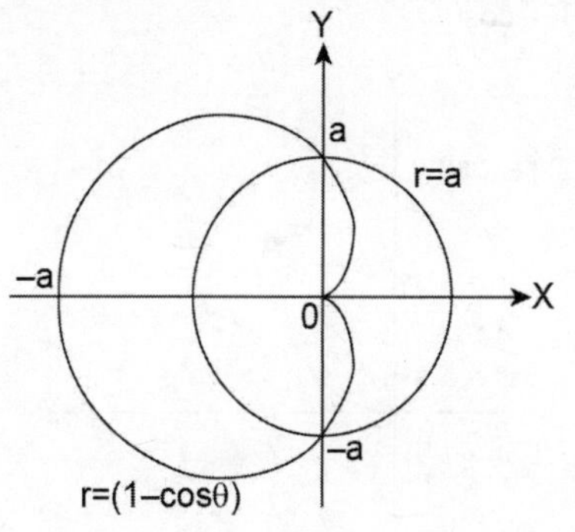

The required area $=2\left[\frac{1}{2}\int_0^{\pi/2}a^2(1-\cos\theta)^2d\theta+\frac{1}{2}\int_{\pi/2}^{\pi}a^2d\theta\right]$

$$=a^2\left[\int_0^{\pi/2}4\sin^4\frac{\theta}{2}d\theta+\frac{\pi}{2}\right]$$

$$=a^2\frac{\pi}{2}+a^2\int_0^{\pi/2}(1+\cos^2\theta-2\cos\theta)d\theta$$

$$=a^2\frac{\pi}{2}+a^2\frac{\pi}{2}-2a^2[1-0]+a^2\left[\frac{\pi}{4}\right]$$

$$=5a^2\frac{\pi}{4}-2a^2=2a^2\left(\frac{5\pi}{8}-1\right)\text{ sq. units}$$

9. (b) $r = a(1 - \cos\theta)$; $r = a\cos\theta$

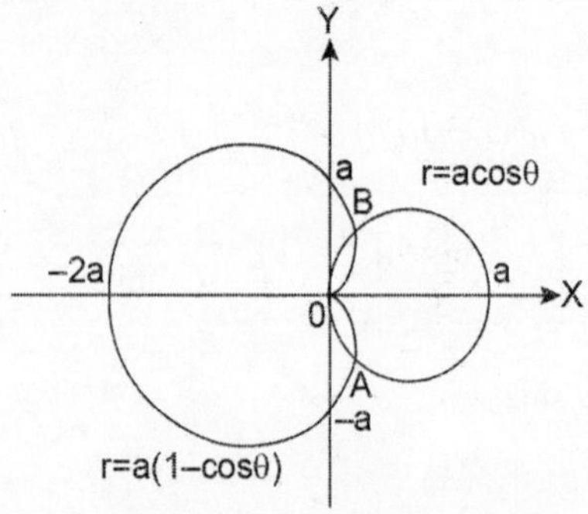

At the point of intersection, A or B; $a(1 - \cos\theta) = a\cos\theta$

$\Rightarrow$ $1 - \cos\theta = \cos\theta$ $\quad\Rightarrow$ $\cos\theta = 1/2$

$\Rightarrow$ $q = \pi/3$ or $5p/3$

$\therefore$ Required Area

$$= 2\left[\frac{1}{2}\int_0^{\pi/3} a^2(1-\cos\theta)^2 d\theta + \frac{1}{2}\int_{\pi/3}^{\pi/2} a^2\cos^2\theta d\theta\right]$$

$$= a^2\left[\int_0^{\pi/3} 1+\cos^2\theta - 2\cos\theta d\theta + \int_{\pi/3}^{\pi/2}\cos^2\theta d\theta\right]$$

$$= a^2\left[\theta - 2\sin\theta + \frac{1}{2}\left(\theta + \frac{\sin 2\theta}{2}\right)\right]_0^{\pi/3} + \frac{a^2}{2}\left[\theta + \frac{\sin 2\theta}{2}\right]_{\pi/3}^{\pi/2}$$

$$= a^2\left[\frac{\pi}{3} - 2\left(\frac{\sqrt{3}}{2}\right) + \frac{1}{2}\left(\frac{\pi}{3}\right) + \frac{1}{4}\left(\frac{\sqrt{3}}{2}\right)\right] + \frac{a^2}{2}\left[\frac{\pi}{6} + \frac{1}{2}\left(0 - \frac{\sqrt{3}}{2}\right)\right]$$

$$= a^2\left[\frac{\pi}{2} - \frac{7}{8}\sqrt{3}\right] + a^2\left[\frac{\pi}{12} - \frac{\sqrt{3}}{8}\right] = a^2\left[\frac{7\pi}{12} - \sqrt{3}\right] \text{ sq. units}$$

10. (a) $r = \sqrt{3}\,\sin\theta$ ...(1)

$r = 1 + \cos\theta$ ...(2)

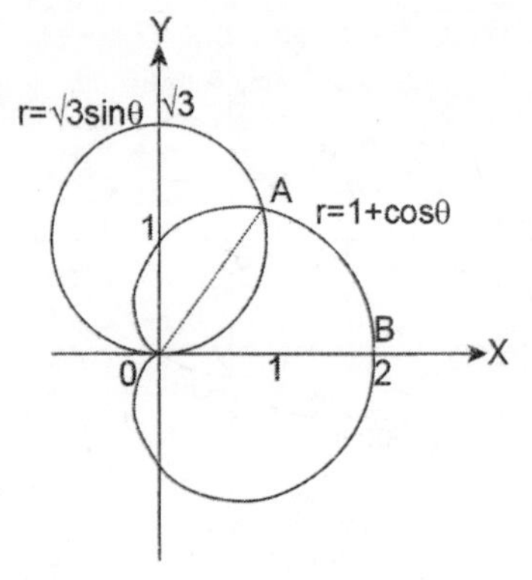

At the point of intersection, $r = \sqrt{3}\sin\theta = 1 + \cos\theta$

$\Rightarrow$ $\sqrt{3}\sin\theta - \cos\theta = 1$ $\Rightarrow$ $\frac{\sqrt{3}}{2}\sin\theta - \frac{1}{2}\cos\theta = \frac{1}{2}$

$\Rightarrow$ $\sin\theta\cos\frac{\pi}{6} - \cos\theta.\sin\frac{\pi}{6} = \frac{1}{2}$

$\Rightarrow$ $\sin\left(\theta - \frac{\pi}{6}\right) = \sin\left(\frac{\pi}{6}\right)$

$\Rightarrow$ $\theta - \frac{\pi}{6} = \frac{\pi}{6}$ $\quad\Rightarrow$ $q = \pi/3$

$\Rightarrow$ $A \equiv \left(\frac{3}{2}, \frac{\pi}{3}\right)$

$\therefore$ Required Area $= \frac{1}{2}\int_0^{\pi/3} 3\sin^2\theta d\theta + \frac{1}{2}\int_{\pi/3}^{\pi}(1+\cos\theta)^2 d\theta$

$$= \frac{3}{4}\int_0^{\pi/3}(1-\cos 2\theta)d\theta + \frac{1}{2}\int_{\pi/3}^{\pi}(1+\cos^2\theta + 2\cos\theta)d\theta$$

$$= \frac{3}{4}\left[\frac{\pi}{3} - \frac{1}{2}\left(\frac{\sqrt{3}}{2} - 0\right)\right] + \frac{1}{2}\left[\frac{2\pi}{3} + 2\left(0 - \frac{\sqrt{3}}{2}\right) + \frac{1}{2}\left(\frac{2\pi}{3} + \frac{1}{2}\left(0 - \frac{\sqrt{3}}{2}\right)\right)\right]$$

$$= \frac{\pi}{4} - \frac{3\sqrt{3}}{16} + \frac{\pi}{3} - \frac{\sqrt{3}}{2} + \frac{\pi}{6} - \frac{\sqrt{3}}{16}$$

$$= \left(\frac{3\pi}{4} - \frac{3\sqrt{3}}{4}\right) = \frac{3}{4}\left(\pi - \sqrt{3}\right) \text{ sq. units}$$

SECTION–III (ONLY ONE CORRECT ANSWER)

1. (a) Given curve is $y = xe^{x^2}$ ...(1)

For $x \in [0, a]$; $y \geq 0$

$\therefore$ Required Area $= \int_0^a xe^{x^2}dx = \frac{1}{2}\int_0^a (2x)e^{x^2}dx$

Put $x^2 = t$ $\quad\Rightarrow$ $2xdx = dt$

$$= \frac{1}{2}\int_0^{a^2} e^t dt = \frac{1}{2}[e^{a^2} - 1] = \frac{e^{a^2} - 1}{2} \text{ sq. units}$$

2. (d) A.T.Q., $\int_1^b f(x)dx = \sqrt{b^2+1} - \sqrt{2}\ \forall\ b > 1$

$\Rightarrow$ $\int_1^x f(x)dx = \sqrt{x^2+1} - \sqrt{2}\ \forall\ x > 1$

$\Rightarrow$ $f(x) = \frac{x}{\sqrt{x^2+1}}$

3. (a) A.T.Q., $\int_1^b f(x)dx = (b-1)\sin(3b+4)\ \forall\ b > 1$

$\Rightarrow$ $\int_1^x f(x)dx = (x-1)\sin(3x+4)\ \forall\ x > 1$

$\Rightarrow$ $f(x) = 3(x-1)\cos(3x+4) + \sin(3x+4)$

4. (c) $xy - 3x - 2y - 10 = 0$ ...(1)

$\Rightarrow$ $y(x-2) = 3x + 10$ ...(2)

$\Rightarrow$ $y = \frac{3x+10}{(x-2)}$ ...(3)

For $x \in (3, 4)$, $y > 0$

$\Rightarrow$ Required Area $= \int_3^4 \frac{3x+10}{x-2}dx = \int_3^4 \frac{3x-6+16}{(x-2)}dx$

$= 3\int_3^4 1.dx + 16\int_3^4 \frac{1}{x-2}dx = 3 + 16|\ln(x-2)|_3^4 = 3 + 16$ [ln 2]

5. (a) $y^2(2a - x) = x^3$

$\Rightarrow$ $y^2 = \frac{x^3}{(2a-x)}$ ...(1)

$\Rightarrow$ $y = \pm\frac{(x)^{3/2}}{\sqrt{2a-x}}$ ...(2)

From (1), $\dfrac{x^3}{(2a-x)} \geq 0$

$\Rightarrow x^3(2a-2x) \geq 0$

$\Rightarrow x^3(x-2a) \leq 0 \qquad \Rightarrow x \in [0, 2a)$

As $x \to 2a^-, y \to \pm\infty$

$\Rightarrow y(0) = 0$

Also, curve is symmetric about x-axis because of having even power of y

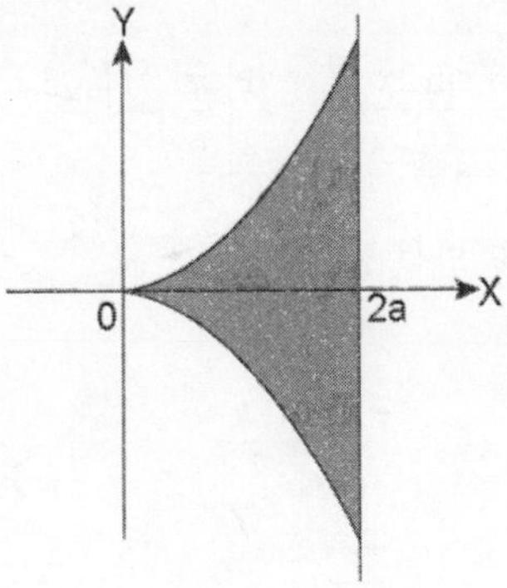

$\therefore$ Required Area $= 2\int_0^{2a} \dfrac{x^{3/2}}{\sqrt{2a-x}}dx$

Put $x = 2a \sin 2q \qquad \Rightarrow dx = 4a \sin\theta \cos\theta \, d\theta$

$$\Rightarrow A = 2\int_0^{\pi/2} \frac{(2a)^{3/2}.\sin^3\theta}{\sqrt{2a-2a\sin^2\theta}} (4a \sin\theta \cos\theta)d\theta$$

$$= 2\int_0^{\pi/2} \frac{(2a)\sin^3\theta}{\cos\theta}(4a \sin\theta \cos\theta)d\theta$$

$$= 16a^2\int_0^{\pi/2} \sin^4\theta d\theta = 16a^2\left[\frac{3\times1}{4\times2}\times\frac{\pi}{2}\right] = 3\pi a^2 \text{ sq. units}$$

6. (b) $y = 1+\dfrac{8}{x^2} \qquad \Rightarrow y' = 8\left(\dfrac{-2}{x^3}\right) = \dfrac{-16}{x^3} < 0$ for $x > 0$

$\Rightarrow f(2) = 3; f(4) = 3/2; y'' = \dfrac{48}{x^4} > 0 \forall x$

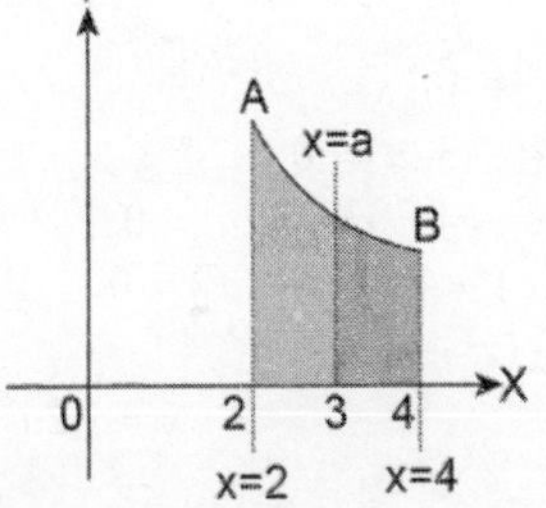

A.T.Q. $\int_2^a \left(1+\dfrac{8}{x^2}\right)dx = \int_a^4\left(1+\dfrac{8}{x^2}\right)dx$

$$\Rightarrow [x]_2^a + 8\left[\frac{x^{-1}}{-1}\right]_2^a = [x]_a^4 + 8\left[\frac{x^{-1}}{-1}\right]_a^4$$

$$\Rightarrow (a-2) - 8\left[\frac{1}{a}-\frac{1}{2}\right] = [4-a] - 8\left[\frac{1}{4}-\frac{1}{a}\right]$$

$$\Rightarrow a - 2 - \frac{8}{a} + 4 = 4 - a - 2 + \frac{8}{a}$$

$\Rightarrow 2a - \dfrac{16}{a} = 0 \qquad \Rightarrow 2a^2 = 16$

$\Rightarrow a^2 = 8 \qquad \Rightarrow a = 2\sqrt{2} \qquad [\because a > 0]$

7. (c) $y^2 = 4ax$ ...(1)

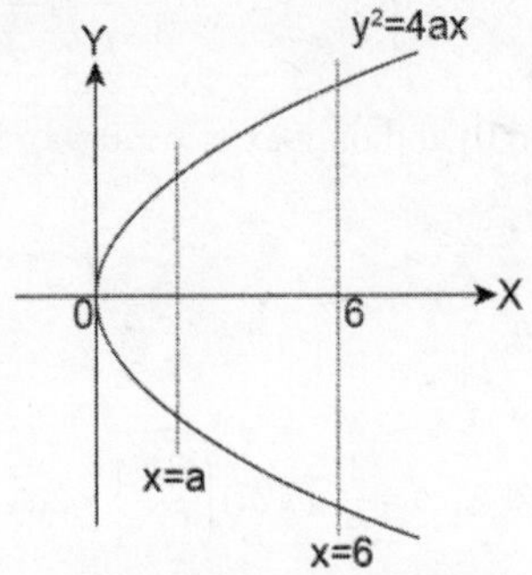

A.T.Q., $2\int_0^6 2\sqrt{a}\sqrt{x}dx = 3(2)\int_0^a 2\sqrt{a}\sqrt{x}dx$

$\Rightarrow \int_0^6 \sqrt{x}dx = 3\int_0^a \sqrt{x}dx \quad \Rightarrow \left[\dfrac{2}{3}(x)^{3/2}\right]_0^6 = 3\left[\dfrac{2}{3}(x)^{3/2}\right]_0^a$

$\Rightarrow \dfrac{2}{3}(6)\sqrt{6} = 2\left[a\sqrt{a}\right] \quad \Rightarrow 2\sqrt{6} = a\sqrt{a}$

$\Rightarrow (a)^{3/2} = 2\sqrt{6} \qquad \Rightarrow a\left(2\sqrt{6}\right)^{2/3}$

$\Rightarrow 4a = 4\,((2)^{3/2}\,(3)^{1/2})^{2/3} \Rightarrow 4a = 4\,(2)(3)^{1/3}$

$\Rightarrow$ Length of Latus-Rectum $= 8\sqrt[3]{3}$ sq. units

8. (a) $y^2 = 4ax, y = mx$

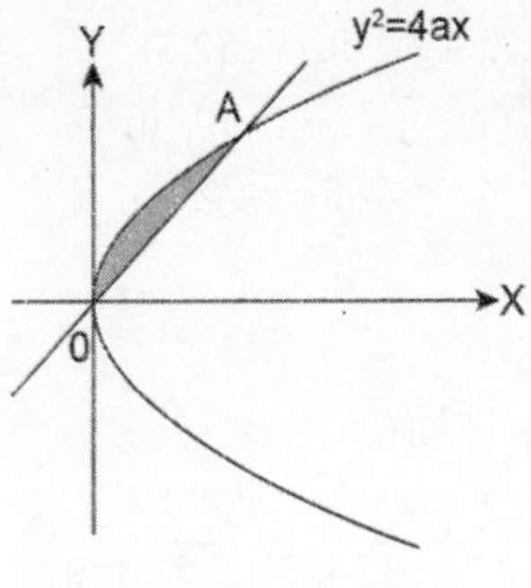

At the point of intersection, $m2x^2 = 4ax$

$\Rightarrow x(m^2x - 4a)$

$\Rightarrow x = 0$ or $x = 4a/m^2$

$\Rightarrow 0 \equiv (0, 0)$ and $A\left(\dfrac{4a}{m^2}, \dfrac{4a}{m}\right)$

$\therefore$ Required Area $= \int_0^{4a/m^2}\left(2\sqrt{a}\sqrt{x} - mx\right)dx$

$$= 2\sqrt{a}\left[\frac{2}{3}x^{3/2}\right]_0^{\frac{4a}{m^2}} - m\left[\frac{x^2}{2}\right]_0^{4a/m^2}$$

$$= \frac{4\sqrt{a}}{3}\left[\left(\frac{4a}{m^2}\right)^{3/2}\right] - \frac{m}{2}\left(\frac{16a^2}{m^4}\right)$$

$$= \frac{32a^2}{3m^3} - \frac{8a^2}{m^3} = \left(\frac{32}{3}-8\right)\frac{a^3}{m^3} = \frac{8}{3}\frac{a^2}{m^3} = \frac{a^2}{3}$$

$\Rightarrow m = 2$

9. (b) Equation of tangent to hyperbola $xy = a^2$ at $P\left(at, \frac{a}{t}\right)$ is

$$\left(y-\frac{a}{t}\right)=\frac{-1/t^2}{1}(x-at)$$

$\Rightarrow$ on x-axis, $y = 0$ $\quad\Rightarrow\quad 0-\frac{a}{t}=-\frac{1}{t^2}(x-at)$

$\Rightarrow at = x - at \quad\Rightarrow\quad x = 2at$

$\Rightarrow A \equiv (2at, 0)$ and on y-axis, $x = 0$

$\Rightarrow y-\frac{a}{t}=\frac{a}{t} \quad\Rightarrow\quad y=\frac{2a}{t}$

$\Rightarrow B\equiv\left(0,\frac{2a}{t}\right)$

$\therefore$ Required Area $=\frac{1}{2}(2at)\left(\frac{2a}{t}\right)=2a^2$ sq. units

10. (c) $f(x)=\begin{cases}\sqrt{\{x\}} & ; x\notin\mathbb{Z}\\ 1 & ; x\in\mathbb{Z}\end{cases}$ and $g(x) = \{x\}^2$; $x\in[0, 10]$

$$\Rightarrow f(x)=\begin{cases}\sqrt{x} & \text{for } x\in(0,1)\\ \sqrt{x-1} & \text{for } x\in(1,2)\\ \sqrt{x-2} & \text{for } x\in(2,3)\\ \sqrt{x-9} & \text{for } x\in(9,10)\\ 1 & \text{for } x\in\mathbb{Z}\end{cases} \text{ and}$$

$$g(x)=\begin{cases}x^2 & \text{for } x\in(0,1)\\ (x-1)^2 & \text{for } x\in(1,2)\\ (x-2)^2 & \text{for } x\in(2,3)\\ (x-9)^2 & \text{for } x\in(9,10)\\ 0 & \text{for } x\in\mathbb{Z}\end{cases}$$

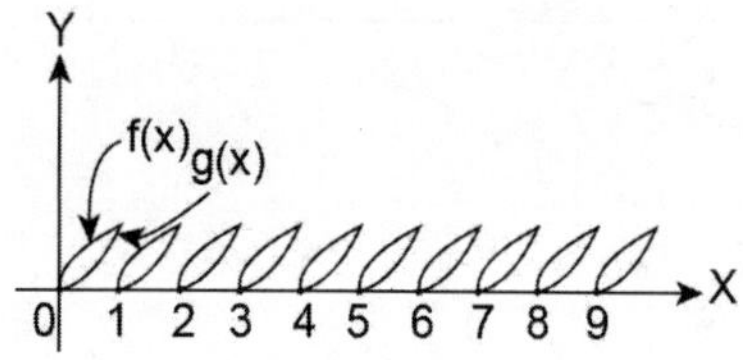

$\therefore$ Required Area $=10\int_0^1[f(x)-g(x)]dx$

$$=10\int_0^1\left(\sqrt{x}-x^2\right)dx$$

$$=10\left[\frac{2}{3}(x)^{3/2}-\frac{x^3}{3}\right]_0^1=10\left[\frac{2}{3}-\frac{1}{3}\right]=\frac{10}{3}\text{ sq. units}$$

11. (d) $f(x) = x^2$, $g(x) = \cos x$; α, b ($\alpha < \beta$) are roots of equation $18x^2 - 9px + \pi^2 = 0$

$\Rightarrow 18x^2 - 6px - 3px + \pi^2 = 0$

$\Rightarrow 6x(3x - \pi) - p(3x - \pi) = 0$

$\Rightarrow (6x - \pi)(3x - \pi) = 0$

$\Rightarrow x = \pi/6, x = \pi/3$

$\Rightarrow \alpha=\frac{\pi}{6}, \beta=\frac{\pi}{3}$ as $a < \beta$

$y = fog(x) = f(g(x)) = f(\cos x) = \cos 2x$

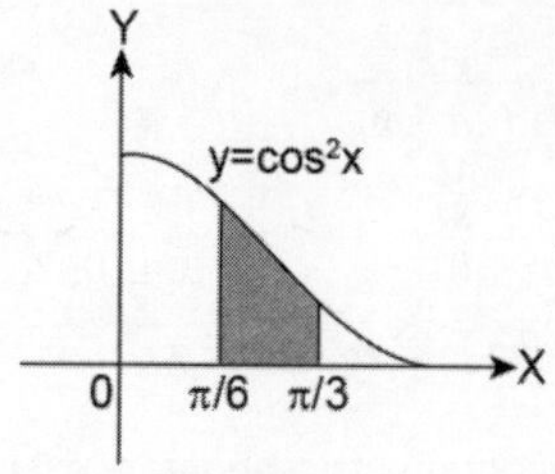

$\therefore$ Required Area $=\int_{\pi/6}^{\pi/3}\cos^2 x\,dx=\frac{1}{2}\int_{\pi/6}^{\pi/3}(1+\cos 2x)dx$

$$=\frac{1}{2}\left[x+\frac{\sin 2x}{2}\right]_{\pi/6}^{\pi/3}=\frac{1}{2}\left[\frac{\pi}{6}+\frac{1}{2}\left(\frac{\sqrt{3}}{2}-\frac{\sqrt{3}}{2}\right)\right]$$

$$=\frac{\pi}{12}\text{ sq. units}$$

12. (a) $y=\frac{x^2}{4a}$ ...(1)

$f(x)=y=\frac{8a^3}{x^2+4a^2}$ ...(2)

Curve (2) is symmetric about y-axis

At, $x = 0$, $f(0) = 2a$

$$f'(x)=(8a^3)\left[\frac{-1}{(x^2+4a^2)^2}(2x)\right]=\frac{-16}{(x^2+4a^2)^2}$$

$\Rightarrow f'(x) > 0$ for $x < 0$ and $f'(x) < 0$ for $x > 0$; $f'(x) = 0$ at $x = 0$

$$\Rightarrow f''(x)=-16a^3\left[\frac{(x^2+4a^2)^2-x(2)(2x)(x^2+4a^2)}{(x^2+4a^2)^4}\right]$$

$$=\frac{-16a^3}{(x^2+4a^2)^3}\left[(x^2+4a^2)-4x^2\right]$$

$$=\frac{-16a^3}{(x^2+4a^2)^3}(4a^2-3x^2)$$

$\Rightarrow f''(x)>0$ for $x^2>\frac{4a^2}{3}$ and $f''(x)<0$ for $x^2<\frac{4a^2}{3}$

At the point of intersection $\frac{8a^3}{x^2+4a^2}=\frac{x^2}{4a}$

$\Rightarrow 32a^4 = x^4 + 4a^2x^2$

$\Rightarrow x^4 + 4a^2x^2 - 32a^4 = 0$

$\Rightarrow x^4 + 8a^2x^2 - 4a^2x^2 - 32a^4 = 0$

$\Rightarrow x^2(x^2 + 8a^2) - 4a^2(x^2 + 8a^2) = 0$

$\Rightarrow (x^2 + 8a^2)(x^2 - 4a^2) = 0$

$\Rightarrow x^2 = 4a^2 \quad\Rightarrow\quad x = \pm 2a$

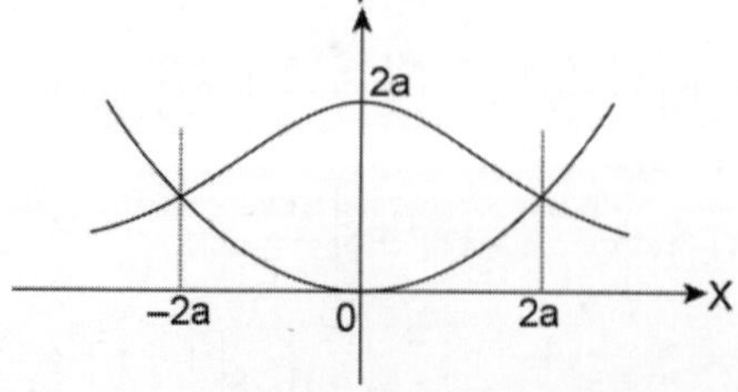

$\therefore$ Required Area $=2\int_0^{2a}\left(\frac{8a^3}{x^2+4a^2}-\frac{x^2}{4a}\right)dx$

$$= 16a^3\left[\frac{1}{2a}\tan^{-1}\left(\frac{x}{2a}\right)\right]_0^{2a} - \frac{1}{2a}\left[\frac{x^3}{3}\right]_0^{2a}$$

$$= 8a^2\left[\frac{\pi}{4}\right] - \frac{1}{6a}[8a^3]$$

$$= 2a^2\pi - \frac{4}{3}a^2 = \frac{a^2}{3}(6\pi - 4) \text{ sq. units}$$

13. (a) $y = x - bx^2$ and $y = \frac{x^2}{b}$

$\Rightarrow \quad y = -b\left(x^2 - \frac{1}{b}x + \frac{1}{4b^2}\right) + \frac{1}{4b}$

$\Rightarrow \quad \left(y - \frac{1}{4b}\right) = -b\left(x - \frac{1}{2b}\right)^2$

$\Rightarrow \quad \left(x - \frac{1}{2b}\right)^2 = -\frac{1}{b}\left(y - \frac{1}{4b}\right)$

At the point of intersection, $x - bx^2 = \frac{x^2}{b}$

$\Rightarrow \quad bx - b2x^2 = x^2 \qquad \Rightarrow \quad (b^2 + 1)x^2 - bx = 0$

$\Rightarrow \quad x[(b^2 + 1)x - b] = 0 \quad \Rightarrow \quad x = 0$ or $x = \frac{b}{(b^2+1)}$

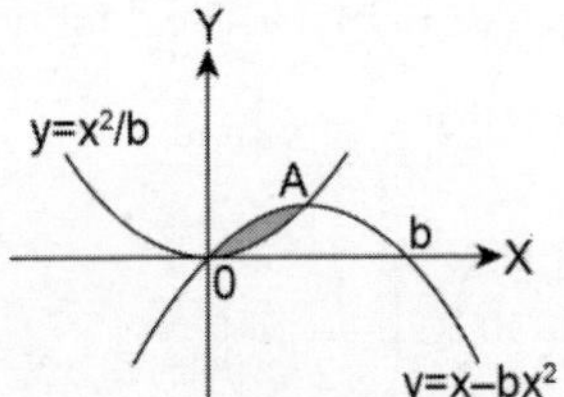

$\therefore \quad$ Required Area $= \int_0^{b/(b^2+1)}\left[\left(x - bx^2\right) - \left(\frac{x^2}{b}\right)\right]dx$

$$= \left[\frac{x^2}{2} - \frac{bx^3}{3} - \frac{x^3}{3b}\right]_0^{b/b^2+1}$$

$$= \frac{1}{2}\left[\frac{b^2}{(b^2+1)^2}\right] - \frac{1}{3}\left(b + \frac{1}{b}\right)\left(\frac{b^3}{(b^2+1)^3}\right)$$

$$= \frac{1}{2}\frac{b^2}{(b^2+1)^2} - \frac{1}{3}\frac{b^2}{(b^2+1)^2} = \frac{1}{6}\frac{b^2}{(b^2+1)^2} = \frac{1}{6}\left[\frac{1}{\left(\frac{b^2+1}{b}\right)^2}\right]$$

$$= \frac{1}{6}\left[\frac{1}{\left(b + \frac{1}{b}\right)^2}\right]$$

$\because \quad b + \frac{1}{b} \geq 2 \ \forall\ b > 0$, equality holds at $b = 1$

$\Rightarrow \quad \frac{1}{\left(b + \frac{1}{b}\right)^2} \leq \frac{1}{4}$

$\Rightarrow$ Area will be maximum $= \frac{1}{6}\left(\frac{1}{4}\right) = \frac{1}{24}$ at $b = 1$

14. (b) Given curve $xy^2 = a^2(a - x)$ ...(1)

Clearly curve is symmetric about x-axis and

$y^2 = \frac{a^2(a-x)}{x}$

$\Rightarrow \quad y = \pm a\sqrt{\frac{a-x}{x}}$

For y to be real, $\frac{a-x}{x} \geq 0$

$\Rightarrow \quad \frac{x-a}{x} \leq 0 \qquad \Rightarrow \quad x \in (0, a]$

From (1); $x(2yy') + y^2 = a^2(-1)$

$\Rightarrow \quad 2xyy' = -a^2 - y^2$

$\Rightarrow \quad y' = \frac{-a^2 - y^2}{2xy} = \frac{-(a^2 + y^2)}{2xy}$

$\therefore \quad$ For $y < 0$, $y' > 0$ and $y > 0$, $y' < 0$

Also $y \to \pm\infty$ as $x \to 0^+$ and $f(a) = 0$

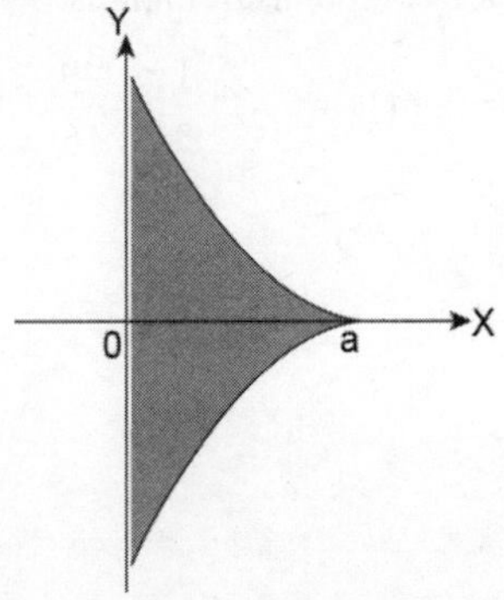

$\therefore \quad$ Required Area $= 2\int_0^a a\sqrt{\frac{a-x}{x}}dx = 2a\int_0^a \sqrt{\frac{a-x}{x}}dx$

Put $x = a\sin 2q \qquad \Rightarrow \quad dx = 2a\sin\theta\cos\theta\, d\theta$

$\therefore \quad A = 2a\int_0^{\pi/2}\sqrt{\frac{\cos^2\theta}{\sin^2\theta}}\,(2a\sin\theta\cos\theta)\,d\theta$

$$= 4a^2\int_0^{\pi/2}\cos^2\theta\, d\theta = 2a^2\int_0^{\pi/2}[1 + \cos 2\theta]d\theta$$

$$= 2a^2\left[\theta + \frac{\sin 2\theta}{2}\right]_0^{\pi/2} = 2a^2\left(\frac{\pi}{2}\right) = (a^2\pi) \text{ sq. units}$$

15. (b) Given curves are $y = x^2$ and $y = x^3/3$

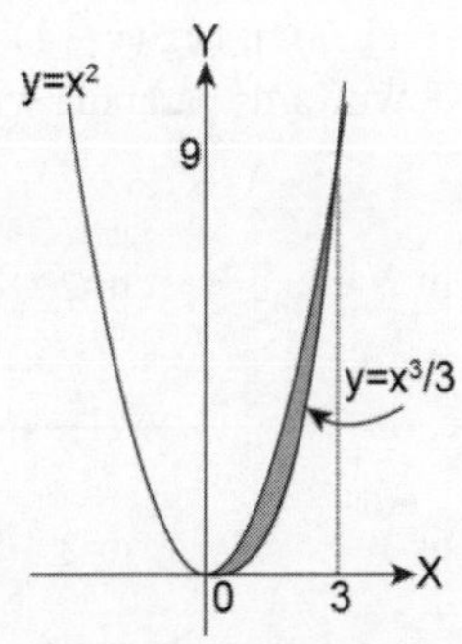

At the point of intersection, $x^2 = \frac{x^3}{3}$

$\Rightarrow \; x^3 - 3x^2 = 0 \qquad \Rightarrow \; x^2(x-3) = 0$

$\Rightarrow \; x = 0$ or $x = 0$

$\therefore$ The required area $= \int_0^3 \left(x^2 - \frac{x^3}{3}\right) dx = \left[\frac{x^3}{3} - \frac{x^4}{12}\right]_0^3$

$= \frac{1}{3}(27) - \frac{1}{27}(81) = 9 - \frac{27}{4} = \frac{9}{4}$ sq. units

16. (a) $y = x^4 - 2x^3 + x^2 + 3,$

$y' = 4x^3 - 6x^2 + 2x = 2x(2x^2 - 3x + 1)$

$= 2x\,[2x^2 - 2x - x + 1] = 2x[2x\,(x-1) - 1(x-1)]$

$= (2x)\,(x-1)\,(2x-1)$

$\Rightarrow \; x = 0, \frac{1}{2}, 1$

$y'' = 12x^2 - 12x + 2 = 2(6x^2 - 6x + 1)$

$y''(0) = 2,\; y''(1) = 2,\; y''\left(\frac{1}{2}\right) = 2\left(\frac{3}{2} - 3 + 1\right) = -1 < 0$

$\Rightarrow \; x = 0, 1$ are two points of minima

$\Rightarrow f(0) = 3, f(1) = 3,\; f\left(\frac{1}{2}\right) = \frac{49}{16}$

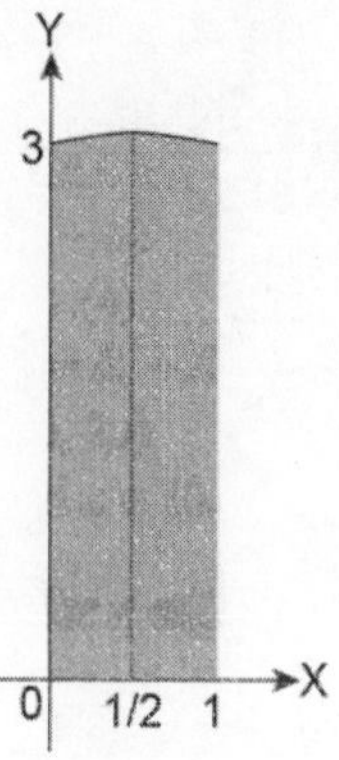

$\therefore$ Required Area $= \int_0^1 \left(x^4 - 2x^3 + x^2 + 3\right) dx$

$= \left|\frac{x^5}{5} - \frac{2x^4}{4} + \frac{x^3}{3} + 3x\right|_0^1$

$= \left(\frac{1}{5} - \frac{1}{2} + \frac{1}{3} + 3\right) = \frac{6 - 15 + 10 + 90}{30} = \frac{91}{30}$ sq. units

17. (b) $y = (1 - x^2)^n$; $n \in \infty$

For $n = 1$, $y = (1 - x^2)$, i.e., $(y - 1) = (x - 0)^2$

Which is *a* downwards parabola with vertex at (0, 1)

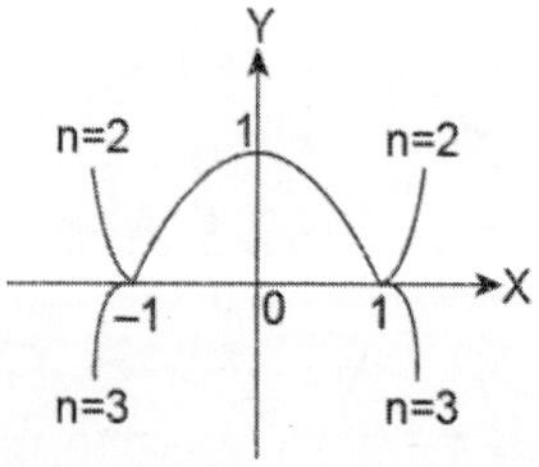

Clearly $f(x) = (1 - x^2)^n > 0$ for $x \in (-1, 1)$

Now $A_n = 2\int_0^1 (1 - x^2)^n dx$

Put $x = \sin\theta \qquad \Rightarrow \; dx = \cos\theta \, d\theta$

$\Rightarrow \; A_n = 2\int_0^{\pi/2} (\cos^2\theta)^n (\cos\theta) d\theta = 2\int_0^{\pi/2} \cos^{(2n+1)}\theta d\theta$

$= 2\left[\frac{(2n)(2n-2)(2n-4)}{(2n+1)(2n-1)(2n-3)}\right]$

$\Rightarrow \; A_{n-1} = 2\left[\frac{(2n-2)(2n-4)}{(2n-1)(2n-3)}\right]$

$\Rightarrow \; A_n = \frac{2n}{(2n+1)} . A_{n-1} \qquad \Rightarrow \; A_n < A_{n-1}$

18. (b) Given curve is $y^2 + x^4 = x^2$

$\Rightarrow \; y^2 = x^2 - x^4 = x^2\,(1 - x^2)$

$\Rightarrow \; y = \pm x\sqrt{1 - x^2}$

Clearly curve is symmetric about x and y-axis

Curve intersects x-axis at $x = 0, \pm 1$ and for $y \in \mathbb{R}$; $x \in [-1, 1]$

Also $2yy' = 2x - 4x^3$

$\Rightarrow \; y' = \frac{x - 2x^3}{y} = \frac{x(1 - 2x^2)}{y}$

For $y < 0$, $y' > 0$ for $x(1 - 2x^2) < 0$

$\Rightarrow \; x(2x^2 - 1) > 0$

$\Rightarrow \; (\sqrt{2}x + 1)x(\sqrt{2}x - 1) > 0$, i.e., for $y < 0$, $y' > 0$ for $x \in \left(\frac{-1}{\sqrt{2}}, 0\right) \cup \left(\frac{1}{\sqrt{2}}, \infty\right)$ and for $y > 0$, $y' < 0$, $x(1 - 2x^2) < 0$

$\Rightarrow \; x \in \left(-\frac{1}{\sqrt{2}}, 0\right) \cup \left(\frac{1}{\sqrt{2}}, \infty\right)$

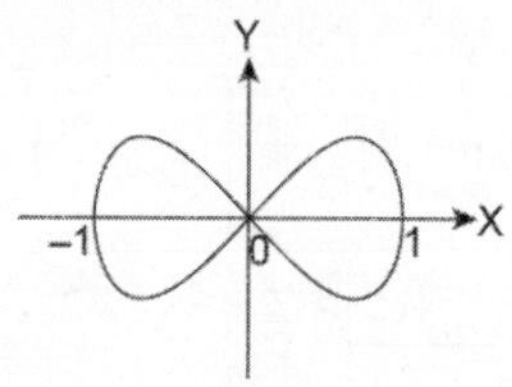

$\therefore$ The required Area $= 4\int_0^1 x\sqrt{1 - x^2}\, dx$

$= \frac{4}{-2}\int_0^1 (-2x)(1 - x^2)^{1/2} dx$

$= -2\left[\frac{2}{3}(1 - x^2)^{3/2}\right]_0^1 = -\frac{4}{3}[0 - 1] = \frac{4}{3}$ sq. units

19. (a) $x^2 + y^2 - 2x = 0 \qquad$ ...(1)

$y = \sin\frac{\pi x}{2} \qquad$ ...(2)

From (1); $x^2 - 2x + y^2 + 1 = 1$

$\Rightarrow \; (x - 1)^2 + (y - 0)^2 = 1 \qquad$ ...(3)

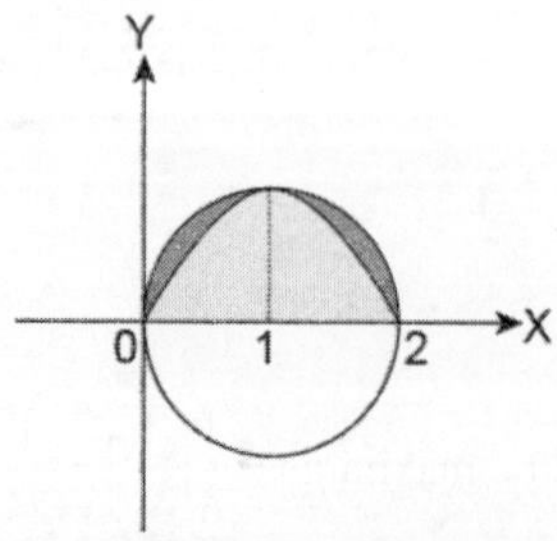

$\therefore$ Required Area $= 2\int_1^2\left(\sqrt{1-(x-1)^2}-\sin\dfrac{\pi x}{2}\right)dx$

$$= 2\left[\frac{(x-1)\sqrt{1-(x-1)^2}}{2}+\frac{1^2}{2}\sin^{-1}\left(\frac{x-1}{1}\right)\right]_1^2$$

$$-2\left[\frac{-\cos\pi x/2}{\pi/2}\right]_1^2$$

$$= 2\left[\frac{1}{2}\left[\frac{\pi}{2}-0\right]\right]+\frac{4}{\pi}[-1-0] = \left(\frac{\pi}{2}-\frac{4}{\pi}\right) \text{ sq. units}$$

20. (b) $\int_1^x ydx = (1+3x)^{1/2}-1$

$\Rightarrow f(x) = \dfrac{1}{2}(1+3x)^{-1/2}(3)$

$\Rightarrow f(x) = \dfrac{3}{2\sqrt{1+3x}}$

$$\therefore \frac{\int_0^8 f(x)dx}{(8-0)} = \frac{\int_0^8 \frac{3}{2\sqrt{1+3x}}dx}{8} = \frac{3}{16}\int_0^8 (1+3x)^{-1/2}dx$$

$$= \frac{3}{16}\left[\frac{2}{3}(1+3x)^{1/2}\right]_0^8 = \frac{1}{8}[5-1] = \frac{1}{2} \text{ sq. units}$$

21. (c) $xy^2 = a^2(a-x)$

$y = \pm a\sqrt{\dfrac{a-x}{x}}$; as $x \to 0^+, y \to \pm\infty$

$\Rightarrow$ y-axis is the asymptote and $y(a) = 0$

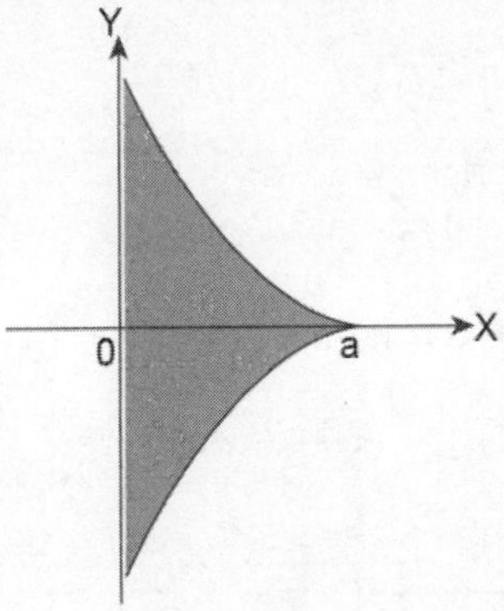

$\therefore$ Required Area $= 2\int_0^a a\sqrt{\dfrac{a-x}{x}}dx = 2a\int_0^a\sqrt{\dfrac{a-x}{x}}dx$

Put $x = a$ sin2q $\Rightarrow$ $dx = 2a \sin\theta\cos\theta\, d\theta$

$\Rightarrow$ Area $= 2\int_0^{\pi/2}\sqrt{\dfrac{\cos^2\theta}{\sin^2\theta}}\,(2a\sin\theta\cos\theta)d\theta$

$$= 4a^2\int_0^{\pi/2}\cos^2\theta d\theta = 2a^2\int_0^{\pi/2}(2\cos^2\theta)d\theta$$

$$= 2a^2\int_0^{\pi/2}(1+\cos 2\theta)d\theta = 2a^2\left[\frac{\pi}{2}\right]+\frac{2a^2}{2}[\sin 2\theta]_0^{\pi/2}$$

$= (a^2\pi)$ sq. units

22. (c) $y = \left[\dfrac{x^2}{64}+2\right]$; $y = x-1$; $x = 0$

For $x \in [0, 8)$; $y = \left[\dfrac{x^2}{64}+2\right] = 2$

For $x \in [8, \sqrt{128})$; $y = \left[\dfrac{x^2}{64}+2\right] = 3$

For $x \in \left[\sqrt{128}\sqrt{192}\right) = 4$

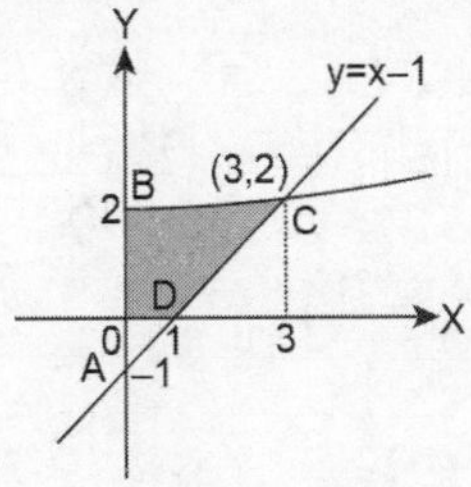

$\therefore$ Required Area = are of trapezium $OBCD = \dfrac{1}{2}(OD + BC) \times (OB)$

$= \dfrac{1}{2}(1+3)\times(2) = 4$ sq. units

23. (a) $a^4y^2 = (2a-x)x^5$ ...(1)

Curve is symmetric about x-axis as it contains even power of y and $y = \pm\dfrac{x^2}{a^2}\sqrt{x(2a-x)}$

For y, to be real, $x(2a-x) \geq 0$ or $x(x-2a) \leq 0$

$\Rightarrow x \in [0, 2a]$

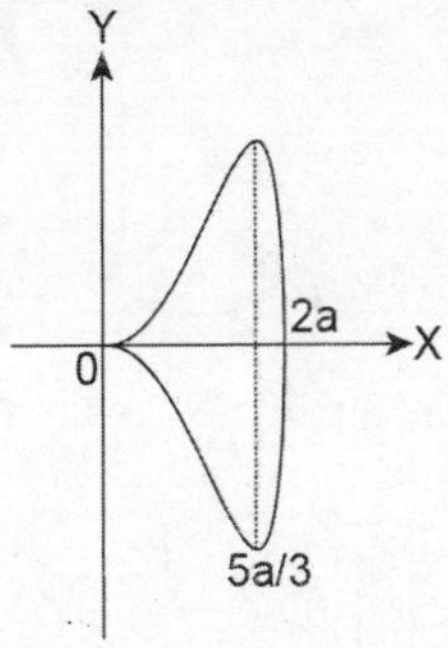

Also $a^4(2yy') = (2a-x)(5x^4) + x^5(-1) = x^4[10a-5x-x]$

$\Rightarrow y' = \dfrac{x^4(10a-6x)}{2a^4y}$

As, $y \to 0^+, x = 0$ $\Rightarrow y' = 0$

Also $y' = 0$ at $x = \dfrac{5}{3}a$

$\therefore$ Required Area

$$= 2\int_0^{2a}\frac{x^2}{a^2}\sqrt{x(2a-x)}dx = \frac{2}{a^2}\int_0^{2a}x^2\sqrt{x(2a-x)}dx$$

Put $x = 2a\sin^2\theta$

$\Rightarrow dx = 4a\sin\theta\cos\theta\, d\theta$

$$= \frac{2}{a^2}\int_0^{\pi/2}4a^2\sin^4\theta\sqrt{2a\sin^2\theta.2a\cos^2\theta}\,.(4a\sin\theta\cos\theta)\,d\theta$$

$$= \frac{32a^3}{a^2}\int_0^{\pi/2} 2a\sin^6\theta\cos^2\theta d\theta = 64a^2\int_0^{\pi/2}\sin^6\theta\cos^2\theta d\theta$$

$= 64a^2\left[\frac{5\times3\times1\times1}{8\times6\times4\times2}\times\frac{\pi}{2}\right] = \frac{5}{4}a^2\pi$ and Area of circle having radius 'a' = πa^2

$$\therefore \text{ Required ratio} = \frac{\frac{5}{4}\pi a^2}{\pi^2} = \frac{5}{4}$$

24. (b) Given curve are $y = x(1 - \ln x)$; $x > 0$

On x-axis, $y = 0 \quad \Rightarrow \quad x = e$

$$\text{Now } \lim_{x\to0^+} x(1-\ln x) = \lim_{x\to0^+}\frac{(1-\ln x)}{1/x}$$

$$= \lim_{x\to0^+}(-1/x)\left(\frac{-x^2}{1}\right) = 0$$

$$y' = x\left(\frac{-1}{x}\right) + (1-\ln x)$$

$\Rightarrow$ $y' = -\ln x = 0$ at $x = 1$

Also, $y' > 0$ for $\ln x < 0$

$\Rightarrow$ $0 < x < 1$ and $y' < 0$ for $\ln x > 0$

$\Rightarrow$ $x > 1$

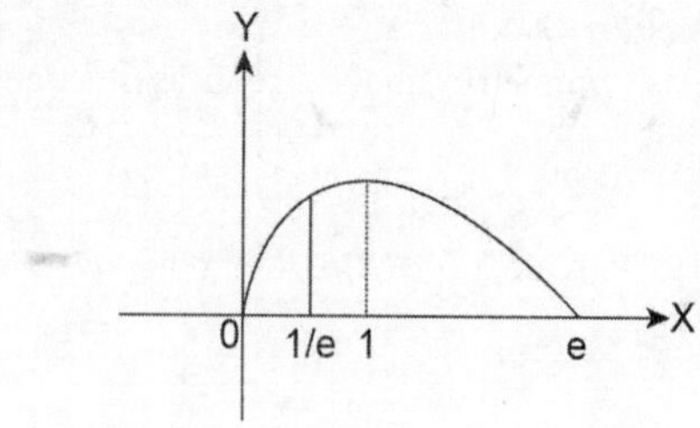

$y'' = \frac{-1}{x} < 0$ for $x \in (0, e)$

$\therefore$ Required Area

$$= \int_{1/e}^{e}(x - x\ln x)dx = \left[\frac{x^2}{2}\right]_{1/e}^{e} - \int_{1/e}^{e}(x\ln x)dx$$

$$= \frac{1}{2}\left[e^2 - \frac{1}{e^2}\right] - \left[\left[(\ln x)\frac{x^2}{2}\right]_{1/e}^{e} - \int_{1/e}^{e}\frac{1}{x}.\frac{x^2}{2}dx\right]$$

$$= \frac{1}{2}e^2 - \frac{1}{2}\left(\frac{1}{e^2}\right) - \left[\frac{e^2}{2} + \frac{1}{2e^2}\right] + \frac{1}{4}\left[e^2 - \frac{1}{e^2}\right]$$

$$= -\frac{1}{e^2} + \frac{1}{4}e^2 - \frac{1}{4e^2} = \frac{1}{4}e^2 - \frac{5}{4e^2} = \left(\frac{e^2 - 5e^{-2}}{4}\right) \text{ sq. units}$$

25. (b) Required Area $= \int_{\frac{\pi}{6a}}^{\frac{\pi}{2a}}\cos ax dx + \int_{\frac{\pi}{2a}}^{\frac{5\pi}{6a}} -\cos ax dx$

$$= \left[\frac{\sin ax}{a}\right]_{\frac{\pi}{6a}}^{\frac{\pi}{2a}} - \left[\frac{\sin ax}{a}\right]_{\frac{\pi}{2a}}^{\frac{5\pi}{6a}}$$

$$= \frac{1}{a}\left[1 - \frac{1}{2}\right] - \frac{1}{a}\left[\frac{1}{2} - 1\right] = \frac{1}{2a} + \frac{1}{2a} = \frac{1}{a} > 3$$

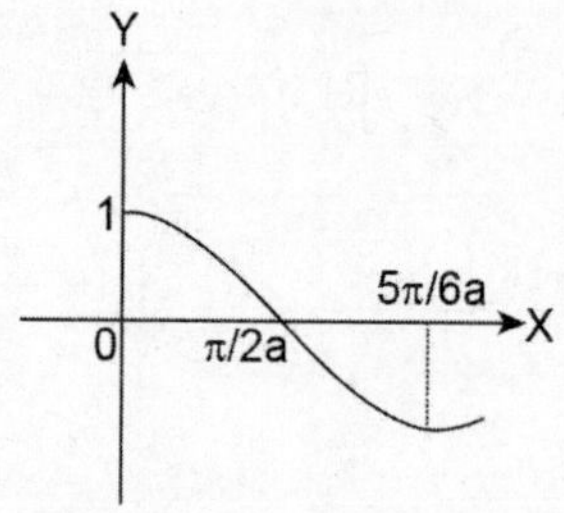

$$\Rightarrow a \in \left(0, \frac{1}{3}\right)$$

26. (a) Given $\int_0^a f(x)dx = \frac{a^2}{2} + \frac{a}{2}\sin a + \frac{\pi}{2}\cos a$

$$\Rightarrow \int_0^x f(x)dx = \frac{x^2}{2} + \frac{x}{2}\sin x + \frac{\pi}{2}\cos x$$

$$\Rightarrow f(x) = x + \frac{x}{2}\cos x + \frac{1}{2}\sin x - \frac{\pi}{2}\sin x$$

$$\Rightarrow f(\pi/2) = \frac{\pi}{2} + \frac{1}{2}(1) - \frac{\pi}{2} = \frac{1}{2}$$

27. (c) $f(x) = x - x^2$; $g(x) = ax$

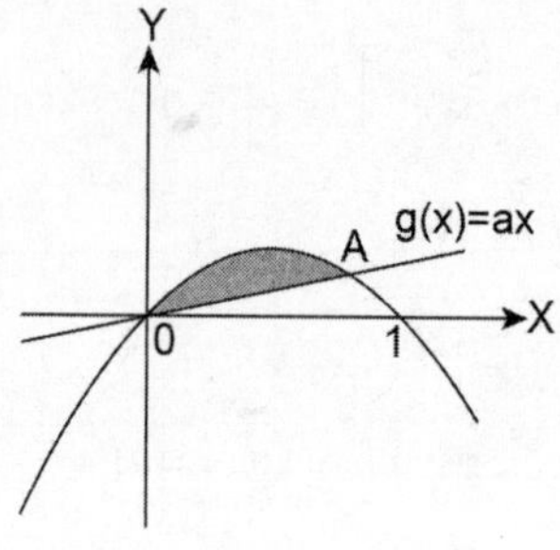

A.T.Q., $\int_0^{x_0}[f(x) - g(x)]dx = \frac{9}{2}$ ...(1)

Now, at A, $ax_0 = x_0 - x_0^2$

$\Rightarrow$ $x_0^2 + (a - 1)x_0 = 0$

$\Rightarrow$ $x_0[x_0 + (a - 1)] = 0$

$\Rightarrow$ $x_0 = 0$ or $x_0 = 1 - a$

$\therefore$ From (1), $\int_0^{1-a}(x - x^2 - ax)dx = \frac{9}{2}$

$$\Rightarrow \left[\frac{x^2}{2} - \frac{x^3}{3} - \frac{ax^2}{2}\right]_0^{1-a} = \frac{9}{2}$$

$$\Rightarrow \frac{1}{2}(1-a)^2 - \frac{1}{3}(1-a)^3 - \frac{a}{2}(1-a)^2 = \frac{9}{2}$$

$$\Rightarrow (1-a)^2\left[\frac{1}{2} - \frac{1}{3}(1-a) - \frac{a}{2}\right] = \frac{9}{2}$$

$$\Rightarrow (1-a)^2\left[\frac{3 - 2 + 2a - 3a}{6}\right] = \frac{9}{2}$$

$\Rightarrow$ $(1 - a)^2(1 - a) = 27$

$\Rightarrow$ $(1 - a) = 3 \quad \Rightarrow \quad a = -2$

28. (a) Given curve is $(y - x - 2)^2 = 9x$; $x \geq 0$

$\Rightarrow$ $(y - x - 2) = \pm 3\sqrt{x} \quad \Rightarrow \quad y = (x + 2) \pm 3\sqrt{x}$

On x-axis, $y = 0$

$\Rightarrow (x + 2) = m\ 3\sqrt{x} \quad \Rightarrow (x + 2)^2 = 9x$

$\Rightarrow x^2 + 4x - 9x + 4 = 0 \Rightarrow x^2 - 5x + 4 = 0$

$\Rightarrow (x - 1)(x - 4) = 0 \quad \Rightarrow x = 1, x = 4$

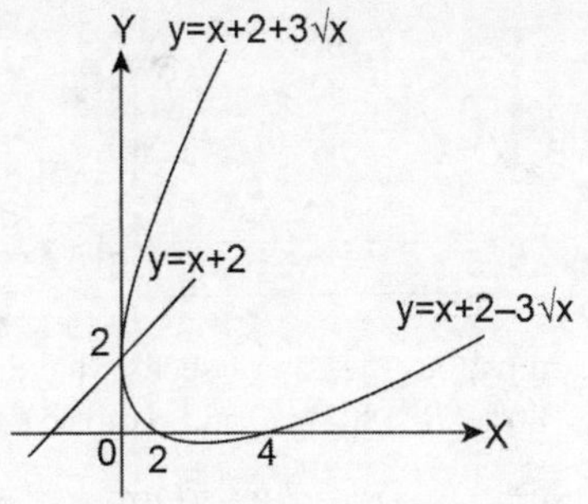

$\therefore\ y = (x + 2) - 3\sqrt{x}$ intersect x-axis, at $x = 1, 4$

$y = (x + 2) - 3\sqrt{x}$

$\Rightarrow y' = 1 - \dfrac{3}{2\sqrt{x}} = 0$

$\Rightarrow \dfrac{3}{2\sqrt{x}} = 1 \quad \Rightarrow \sqrt{x} = 3/2$

$\Rightarrow x = 9/4 = 2.25$

$y\left(\dfrac{9}{4}\right) = \dfrac{9}{4} + 2 - 3\left(\dfrac{3}{2}\right) = \dfrac{-1}{4}$

$\Rightarrow y'' = \dfrac{3}{2}\left(\dfrac{1}{2}\right)(x)^{-3/2} > 0 \forall x > 0$

$\therefore$ The required Area $= \int_0^1 \left[(x+2) - 3\sqrt{x}\right] dx$

$= \left[\dfrac{x^2}{2} + 2x - 3(x)^{3/2}\left(\dfrac{2}{3}\right)\right]_0^1 = \dfrac{12}{2} + 2 - 2 = \dfrac{1}{2}$ sq. units

29. **(b)** $y = f(x)$; $f'(x) = 2x - 4$

$\Rightarrow f(x) = \int (2x - 4) dx \quad \Rightarrow f(x) = x^2 - 4x + c$

$\Rightarrow y = x^2 - 4x + c$ ...(1)

As (1) passes through (–2, 12)

$\Rightarrow 12 = 4 + 8 + c \quad \Rightarrow c = 0$

$\Rightarrow y = x^2 - 4x = (x - 2)^2 - 4$

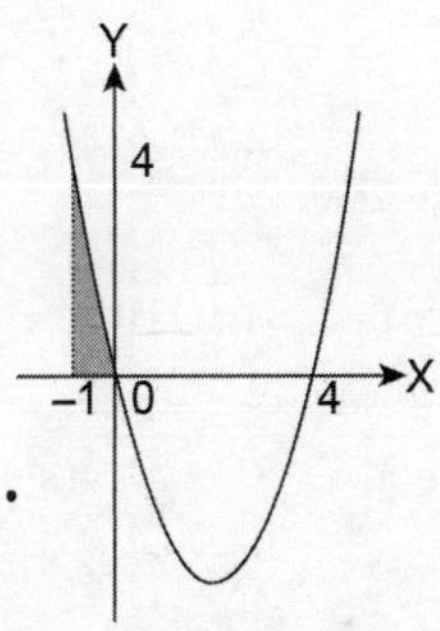

$\therefore$ The required area $= \int_{-1}^0 (x^2 - 4x) dx = \left[\dfrac{x^3}{3} - 2x^2\right]_1^0$

$= -\left(\dfrac{-1}{3}\right) - 2(0 - 1)\dfrac{1}{3} + 2 = \dfrac{7}{3}$

30. **(d)** $y = x^2$...(i) and $y = \sin\left(\dfrac{\pi x}{2}\right)$...(ii)

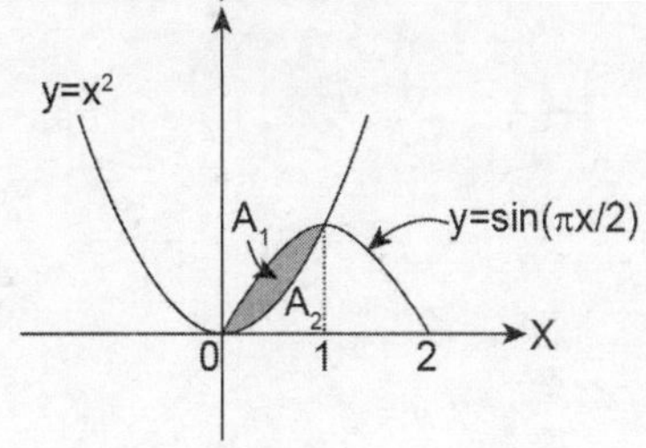

(A_1) Area $= \int_0^1 \left[\sin\left(\dfrac{\pi x}{2}\right) - x^2\right] dx = \left[\dfrac{-\cos\left(\dfrac{\pi x}{2}\right)}{\pi/2}\right]_0^1 - \left[\dfrac{x^3}{2}\right]_0^1$

$= -\dfrac{2}{\pi}[0 - 1] - \dfrac{1}{3} = \left(\dfrac{2}{\pi} - \dfrac{1}{3}\right)$

Area $(A_2) = \int_x^1 x^2 dx = \dfrac{1}{3}$

$\therefore\ \dfrac{A_1}{A_2} = \dfrac{\left(\dfrac{6-\pi}{3\pi}\right)}{\dfrac{1}{3}} = \dfrac{6-\pi}{\pi}$

31. **(c)** $y = x^2 + 6x + 9$

$\Rightarrow y = (x + 3)^2$ ...(1)

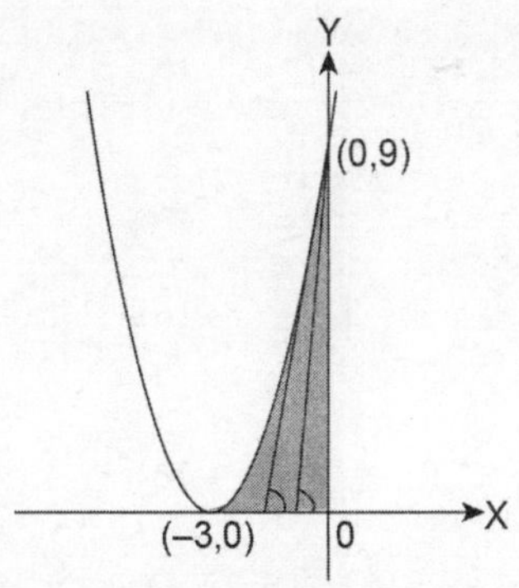

$\therefore$ Equation lies be $y = (\tan\alpha)\,x + c_1$ and $y = (\tan\beta)\,x + c_2$

They pass through (0, 9)

$\Rightarrow 9 = c_1$ and $9 = c_2$

$\Rightarrow y = (\tan\alpha)\,x + 9$...(2) and $y = (\tan\beta)\,x + 9$...(3)

A.T.Q. $\dfrac{1}{3}\int_{-3}^0 (x+3)^2 dx = \dfrac{1}{2}\int_{-9\cot\alpha}^0 ((\tan\alpha)x + 9) dx$

$= \int_{-9\cot\beta}^0 [(\tan\beta)x + 9] dx$

$\Rightarrow \dfrac{1}{3}\left[\dfrac{(x+3)^3}{3}\right]_{-3}^0 = \dfrac{1}{2}\left[\dfrac{(\tan\alpha)x^2}{2} + 9x\right]_{-9\cot\alpha}^0$

$= \left[\dfrac{(\tan\beta)x^2}{2} + 9x\right]_{-9\cot\beta}^0$

$\Rightarrow \quad \frac{1}{9}[27] = \frac{1}{4}(\tan\alpha)(0 - 81\cot^2\beta) + \frac{9}{2}(9\cot\alpha)$

$= \frac{\tan\beta}{2}[-81\cot^2\beta] + 9[9\cot\beta]$

$\Rightarrow \quad 3 = -\frac{81}{4}\cot\alpha + \frac{81}{2}\cot\alpha = -\frac{81}{2}\cot\beta + 81\cot\beta$

$\Rightarrow \quad 3 = \frac{81}{4}\cot\alpha = \frac{81}{2}\cot\beta$

$\Rightarrow \quad \cot\alpha = \frac{4}{27}; \cot\beta = \frac{2}{27}$

$\Rightarrow \quad \tan\alpha = \frac{27}{4}, \ \tan\beta = \frac{27}{2}$

$\Rightarrow \quad \alpha = \tan^{-1}\left(\frac{27}{4}\right), \ \beta = \tan^{-1}\left(\frac{27}{2}\right)$

32. **(b)** $y^2 = -x - 16 \quad \Rightarrow (y - 0)^2 = -(x + 16)$ ...(1)

$\therefore$ (1) is *a* parabola (left handed) with its vertex at (–16, 0)

Let the equation of tangent be

$(y - 0) = m(x + 16) - \frac{1}{4m}$ ...(2)

As it passes through the origin

$\Rightarrow \quad 0 = m(16) - \frac{1}{4m} \qquad \Rightarrow \quad 64m^2 - 1 = 0$

$\Rightarrow \quad m^2 = \frac{1}{64} \qquad \Rightarrow \quad m = \pm\frac{1}{8}$

$A \equiv \left(X = \frac{-1/4}{1/64}, Y = \frac{-2(1/4)}{-1/8}\right) \equiv (X = -16, Y = +4)$

$\Rightarrow \quad A = (x = -32, y = 4)$

$\therefore$ Required area $= \int_{32}^{0}\left[\frac{-1}{8}(x+16)+2\right]dx - \int_{-32}^{-16}\sqrt{-x-16}\,dx$

$= -\frac{1}{16}\left[0-(32)^2\right] - \left[\frac{-2}{3}(-x-16)^{3/2}\right]_{-32}^{16}$

$= 64 + \frac{2}{3}[0 - 64] = 64\left(1 - \frac{2}{3}\right) = \frac{65}{3}$ square unit.

33. **(c)** $y = f(x)$ be the equation of function w.r.t. old co-ordinate system *m*.

i.e., $x - (a + b) = X, y - 0 = Y$

$\Rightarrow \quad x = X + (a + b), y = Y$

$\therefore$ Equation of curve w.r.t. new coordinate system will be $Y = f(x + (a + b))$

$\int_{x=-b}^{x=-a} Y dx = \int_{x=-b}^{x=-a} f(X + a + b) dX$

Put, $X + a + b = x$

$\Rightarrow \quad A = \int_a^b f(x)dx = \int_a^b f(a+b-x)dx$

34. **(a)** Area of $\Delta ABC = D$ and perimeter of $\Delta ABC = p$

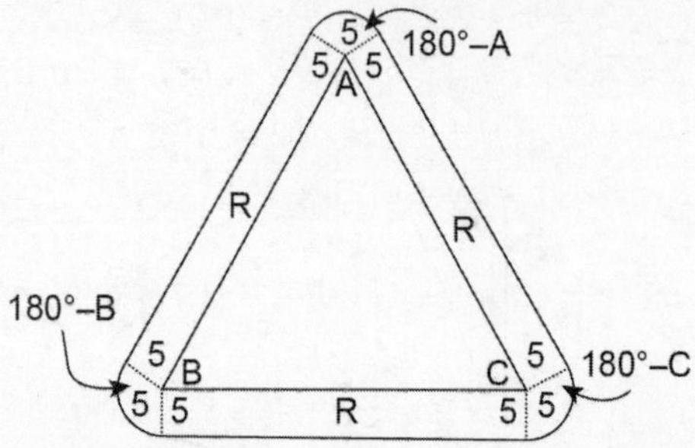

Total Area must be = [Area of sectors having central angle 180° – *A*, 180° – *B*, 180° – *C* and radius 5] + 5(*p*) + Δ

$= \frac{1}{2}(5)^2[(180° - A) + (180° - B) + (180° - C)] \times \frac{\pi}{180} + 5p + \Delta$

$= \frac{25}{2}\left(\frac{\pi}{180}\right)[360] + 5p + \Delta = (25p + 5p + \Delta)$ square unit.

35. **(c)** $f(x) = 1 + \frac{1}{x}\int_1^x f(t)dt = x f(x) = x + \int_1^x f(t)dt$

$\Rightarrow \quad x f'(x) + f(x) = 1 + f(x)$

$\Rightarrow \quad xf'(x) = 1 \qquad \Rightarrow \quad f'(x) = 1/x$

$\Rightarrow \quad f(x) = \int \frac{1}{x}dx \qquad \Rightarrow \quad f(x) = \ln x$

$\therefore$ Required area $= \int_0^e (1 - f(x))dx$

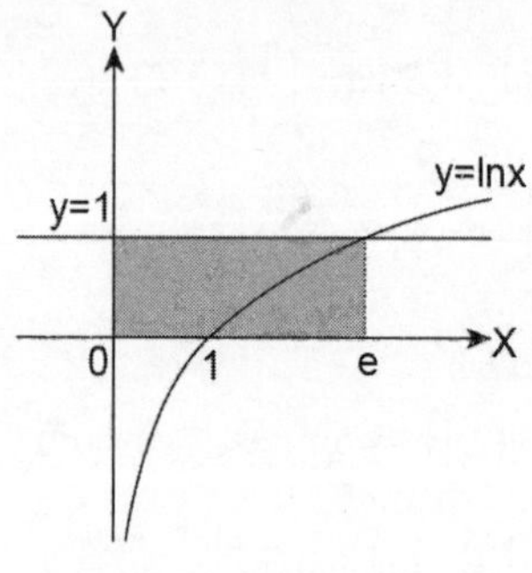

$= e - \int_1^e (\ln x)dx = e - \left[|x\ln x|_1^e - |x|_1^e\right] = e - [(1 - 0)$

$(e - 1)] = 2e - 2$

36. **(c)** $y = \frac{\sin x}{e^x} \ \forall\, x \in [0, 2p]$

$y(0) = 0, y(2p) = 0, y(\pi) = 0$

$y' = \frac{e^x\cos x - \sin x.e^x}{(e^x)^2} = \frac{e^x(\cos x - \sin x)}{(e^x)^2}$

$\therefore \quad y' = 0 \qquad \Rightarrow \quad \cos x = \sin x; x \in [0, 2p]$

$\Rightarrow \quad x = \frac{\pi}{4}, \frac{5\pi}{4}$

$\Rightarrow \quad y' > 0$ for $\cos x > \sin x$; i.e., $\left[0, \frac{\pi}{4}\right) \cup \left(\frac{5\pi}{4}, 2\pi\right]$ and y' < 0 for $x \in \left(\frac{\pi}{4}, \frac{5\pi}{4}\right)$

$\therefore$ Required area $= \int_0^{\pi} \frac{\sin x}{e^x} dx + \int_{\pi}^{-2\pi} \frac{-\sin x}{e^x} dx$

$= \int_0^{\pi} e^{-x} \sin x \, dx - \int_{\pi}^{2\pi} e^{-x} \sin x \, dx$

$= \left[\frac{e^{-x}}{2}(-\sin x - \cos x)\right]_0^{\pi} - \left[\frac{e^{-x}}{2}(-\sin x - \cos x)\right]_{\pi}^{2\pi}$

$= \frac{-1}{2}\left[e^{-x}(\sin x + \cos x)\right]_0^{\pi} + \frac{1}{2}\left[e^{-x}(\sin x + \cos x)\right]_{\pi}^{2\pi}$

$= \frac{-1}{2}\left[e^{-\pi}(-1) - (1)\right] + \frac{1}{2}\left[e^{-2\pi} - e^{-\pi}(-1)\right]$

$= \frac{1}{2}e^{-\pi} + \frac{1}{2} + \frac{1}{2}e^{-2\pi} + \frac{1}{2}e^{-\pi} = e^{-\pi} + \frac{1}{2}e^{-2\pi} + \frac{1}{2}$

37. (b) $y = \sin^{-1}|\sin x|$; and $y = (\sin^{-1}|\sin x|)^2$; $0 \le x \le 2p$.

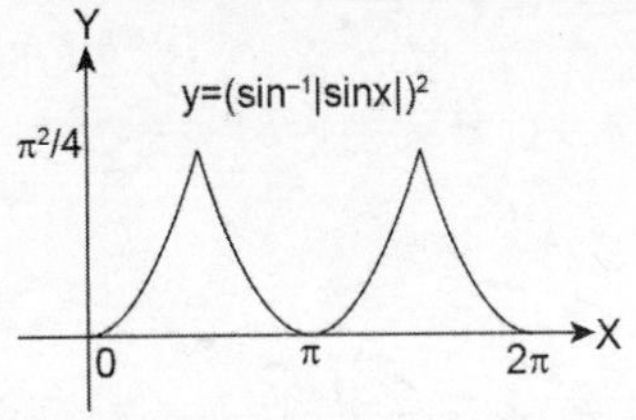

$\therefore$ Required Area $= 4\int_0^1 \left[x - \left(\sin^{-1}(\sin x)\right)^2\right] dx +$

$4\int_1^{\pi/2} \left[\left(\sin^{-1}(\sin x)\right)^2 - x\right] dx$

$= 4\left(\frac{1}{2}\right) - 4\int_0^1 \left(\sin^{-1}(\sin x)\right)^2 dx +$

$4\int_1^{\pi/2} \left(\sin^{-1}(\sin x)\right)^2 dx - \frac{4}{2}\left(\frac{\pi^2}{4} - 1\right)$

$= 4 - \frac{\pi^2}{2} - 4\int_0^1 \left(\sin^{-1}(\sin x)\right)^2 dx + 4\int_0^{\pi/2} \left(\sin^{-1}(\sin x)\right)^2 dx$

$= 4 - \frac{\pi^2}{2} - 4\int_0^1 x^2 dx + 4\int_1^{\pi/2} x^2 dx$

$= 4 - \frac{\pi^2}{2} - \frac{4}{3} + \frac{4}{3}\left[\frac{\pi^3}{8} - 1\right]$

$= 4 - \frac{\pi^2}{2} - \frac{8}{3} + \frac{\pi^3}{6} = \left(\frac{4}{3} - \frac{\pi^2}{2} + \frac{\pi^3}{6}\right)$ square units.

38. (a) $z = \sqrt{x^2 + 4} + i\sqrt{y - 4}$; $|z| = \sqrt{x^2 + 4 + y - 4} = \sqrt{10}$

$\Rightarrow$ $x^2 + y - 10$; $y \ge 4$ $\Rightarrow$ $x^2 = -(y - 10)$; $y \ge 4$

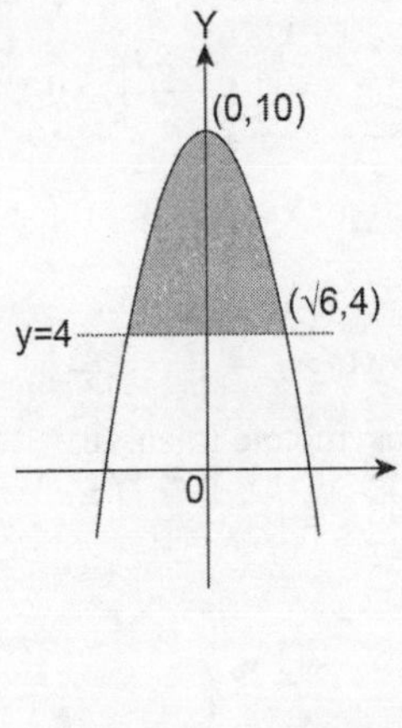

$\therefore$ Required Area $= 2\int_0^{\sqrt{6}} \left[(10 - x^2) - 4\right] dx$

$= 2\left[6\sqrt{6} - \frac{1}{3}(6\sqrt{6})\right] = (8\sqrt{6})$ square units.

39. (b) $y = x^2$ and $y = [x + 1]$; $x \le 1$

$$y = [x+1] = \begin{cases} -1 \text{ for } & 2 \le x < -1 \\ 0 \text{ for } & -1 \le x < 0 \\ 1 \text{ for } & 0 \le x < 1 \\ 2 \text{ for } & 1 \le x < 2 \end{cases}$$

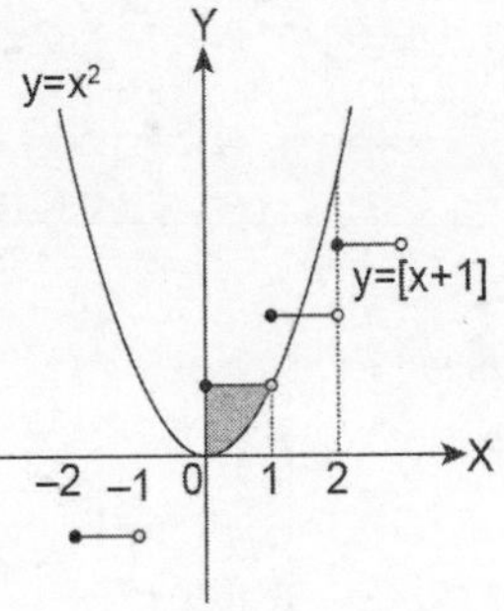

$\therefore$ Required Area $= \int_0^1 (1 - x^2) dx = \left[x - \frac{x^3}{3}\right]_0^1 = 1 - \frac{1}{3} = \frac{2}{3}$ square units

40. (d) $xy = 1$ or $y = 1/x$

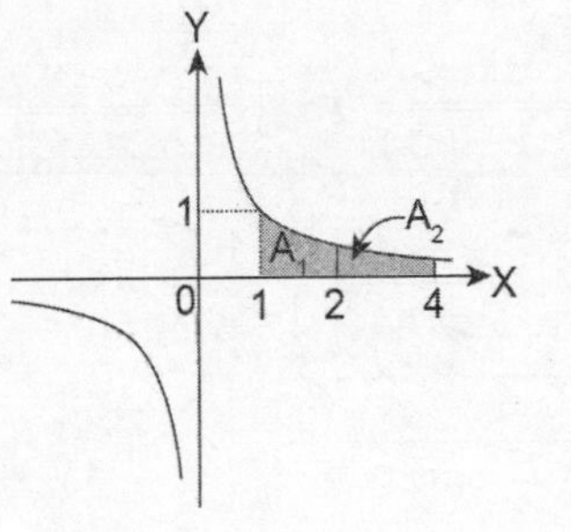

Now, $A_1 = \int_1^2 \frac{1}{x} dx = [\ln x]_1^2 = \ln 2$ and $A_2 = \int_2^4 \frac{1}{x} dx = [\ln x]_2^4$

$= \ln 4 - \ln 2 = \ln 2$

$\therefore$ $A_1 = A_2$.

41. (c) Given curve is $f(x) = x^2 + bx - b$ ...(1)

$f'(x) = 2x + b$; $f'(1) = 2 + b$

Equation of tangent to curve at $P(1, 1)$ is

$(y - 1) = (2 + b)(x - 1)$ or $y = (2 + b)(x - 1) + 1$ ...(2)

Eqn. (2) intersects x-axis, whose $y = 0$

$\Rightarrow$ $0 = (2 + b)(x - 1) + 1$

$\Rightarrow$ $(x - 1) = \frac{-1}{2 + b}$ $\Rightarrow$ $x = \frac{2 + b - 1}{2 + b} = \frac{1 + b}{2 + b}$

i.e., at $A\left(\frac{b+1}{b+2}, 0\right)$ and on y-axis, $x = 0$

$\Rightarrow$ $y = -2 - b + 1 = -1 - b$, i.e., at $\beta(0, -1-b)$

$\therefore$ Area of $\Delta = \frac{1}{2}|b + 1|\left(\frac{b+1}{b+2}\right) = 2$

$\Rightarrow\ (b+1)^2 = \pm 4(b+2)$

$\Rightarrow\ b^2 - 2b - 7 = 0$ or $b^2 + 6b + 9 = 0$

$\Rightarrow\ b = \dfrac{2 \pm \sqrt{32}}{2}$ or $b = -3 \quad \Rightarrow b = 1 \pm 2\sqrt{2}$ or $b = 3$

42. (b) Given curve are $y = \sqrt{\dfrac{1+\sin x}{\cos x}}$, $y = \sqrt{\dfrac{1-\sin x}{\cos x}}$

OR $y = \sqrt{\dfrac{\left(\cos\frac{x}{2} \pm \sin\frac{x}{2}\right)^2}{\left(\cos^2\frac{x}{2} - \sin^2\frac{x}{2}\right)}} = \sqrt{\dfrac{\cos\frac{x}{2} \pm \sin\frac{x}{2}}{\cos^2\frac{x}{2} \mp \sin^2\frac{x}{2}}}$,

i.e., $y = \sqrt{\tan\left(\dfrac{\pi}{4} \pm \dfrac{x}{2}\right)}$

$x \in \left(0, \dfrac{\pi}{4}\right) \quad \Rightarrow \quad \dfrac{x}{2} \in \left(0, \dfrac{\pi}{8}\right)$

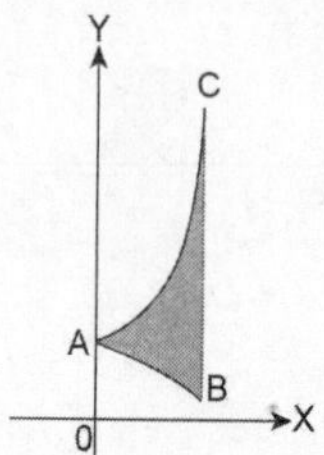

$\therefore$ Required area $= \displaystyle\int_0^{\pi/4} \left\{\sqrt{\tan\left(\frac{\pi}{4} + \frac{x}{2}\right)} - \sqrt{\tan\left(\frac{\pi}{4} - \frac{x}{2}\right)}\right\} dx$

$= \displaystyle\int_0^{\pi/4} \frac{\cos x}{\sqrt{\cos x(1-\sin x)}} dx - \int_0^{\pi/4} \frac{\cos x}{\sqrt{\cos x(1+\sin x)}} dx$

$= \displaystyle\int_0^{\pi/4} \sqrt{\cos x}\left[\frac{1}{\sqrt{1-\sin x}} - \frac{1}{1+\sin x}\right] dx$

$= \displaystyle\int_0^{\pi/4} \left[\frac{\sqrt{1+\sin x} - \sqrt{1-\sin x}}{\cos x}\right] \sqrt{\cos x}\, dx$

$= \displaystyle\int_0^{\pi/4} \frac{\left(\cos\frac{x}{2} + \sin\frac{x}{2}\right) - \left(\cos\frac{x}{2} - \sin\frac{x}{2}\right)}{\sqrt{\cos x}} dx$

$= \displaystyle\int_0^{\pi/4} \frac{2\sin\frac{x}{2}}{\sqrt{\cos x}} dx = \int_0^{\pi/4} \frac{2\tan\frac{x}{2}.\cos\frac{x}{2}}{\sqrt{\cos x}} dx$

$= \displaystyle\int_0^{\pi/4} \frac{2\tan\frac{x}{2}.\sec^2\frac{x}{2}}{\sec^3\frac{x}{2}\sqrt{2\cos^2\frac{x}{2} - 1}} dx = \int_0^{\pi/4} \frac{2\tan\frac{x}{2}.\sec^2\frac{x}{2}}{\sec^3\frac{x}{2}.\cos\frac{x}{2}\sqrt{2 - \sec^2\frac{x}{2}}} dx$

$= \displaystyle\int_0^{\pi/4} \frac{2\tan\frac{x}{2}.\sec^2\frac{x}{2}}{\sec^2\frac{x}{2}\sqrt{2 - \left(1 + \tan^2\frac{x}{2}\right)}} dx$

$= \displaystyle\int_0^{\pi/4} \frac{2\tan\frac{x}{2}.\sec^2\frac{x}{2}}{\sec^2\frac{x}{2}\sqrt{1 - \tan^2\frac{x}{2}}} dx$

Put $\tan\dfrac{x}{2} = t$

$\Rightarrow\ \dfrac{1}{2}\sec^2\dfrac{x}{2} dx = dt = \displaystyle\int_0^{\sqrt{2}-1} \frac{2t(2dt)}{(1+t^2)\sqrt{1-t^2}}$

$= \displaystyle\int_0^{\sqrt{2}-1} \frac{4t\, dt}{(1+t^2)\sqrt{1-t^2}}$

43. (d) Required Area $= \displaystyle\int_{-\pi/18}^{\pi/18} \cos 9x\, dx = \left[\frac{\sin 9x}{9}\right]_{-\pi/18}^{\pi/18}$

$= \dfrac{1}{9}[1+1] = \dfrac{2}{9}$

44. (d) $y = 4 - x^2$; $y = \left[3 + \dfrac{x^2}{4}\right]$

$\Rightarrow\ y = \left[3 + \dfrac{x^2}{4}\right] = \begin{cases} 3 \text{ for} & -2 < x < 2 \\ 4 \text{ for} & x \in (-\sqrt{8}, -2] \cup [2, \sqrt{8}) \text{ and so on} \end{cases}$

$\Rightarrow\ y = -x^2 + 4$ or $x^2 = -(y - 4)$

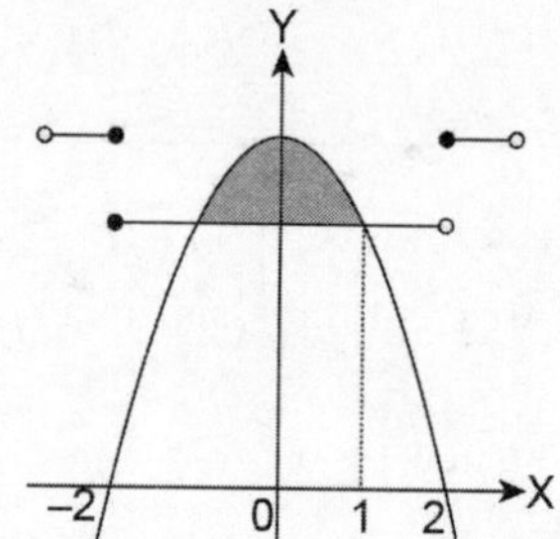

$\therefore$ Required area $= 2\displaystyle\int_0^1 \left(-x^2 + 4 - 3\right) dx = \int_0^1 \left(-x^2 + 1\right) dx$

$= 2\left[\dfrac{-x^3}{3} + x\right]_0^1 = 2\left[\dfrac{-1}{3} + 1\right]_0^1 = \dfrac{4}{3}$ square units.

45. (b) $f(x) \geq 0$ and is continuous.

A.T.Q. $\displaystyle\int_{\pi/4}^{x} f(x)dx = x\sin x + \frac{\pi}{4}\cos x + \sqrt{2}x$; where $x > \pi/4$

$f(x) = x\cos x + \sin x - \dfrac{\pi}{4}\sin x + \sqrt{2}$

$= x\cos + \left(1 - \dfrac{\pi}{4}\right)\sin x + \sqrt{2}$

$\Rightarrow\ f\left(\dfrac{\pi}{2}\right) = 1 - \dfrac{\pi}{4} + \sqrt{2}$

46. (b) Given curve is $y = \left(1 + \dfrac{8}{x^2}\right) > 0\ \forall\ x \in \mathbb{R}$

$\Rightarrow\ y' = \dfrac{-16}{x^3} < 0$ for $x > 0$ and > 0 for $x < 0$

$y' \to +\infty$ for $x \to 0^-$ and $y' \to -\infty$ for $x \to 0^+$

$y(x \to 0) \to y(+\infty) \to 1$

$\Rightarrow\ y = 1$ is an asymptote to curve.

Also $y'' = \dfrac{48}{x^4} > 0\ \forall\ x \in \mathbb{R}$

$\Rightarrow$ Curve is concave upwards $\forall\, x \in R$

Also curve is symmetric about y-axis as it has even power of x.

A.T.Q. $\int_2^a \left(1+\frac{8}{x^2}\right)dx = \int_2^4 \left(1+\frac{8}{x^2}\right)dx$

$\Rightarrow \left[x+8\left(\frac{-1}{x}\right)\right]_2^a = \left[x+8\left(\frac{-1}{x}\right)\right]_a^4$

$\Rightarrow (a-2)-8\left(\frac{1}{a}-\frac{1}{2}\right) = (4-a)-8\left(\frac{1}{4}-\frac{1}{a}\right)$

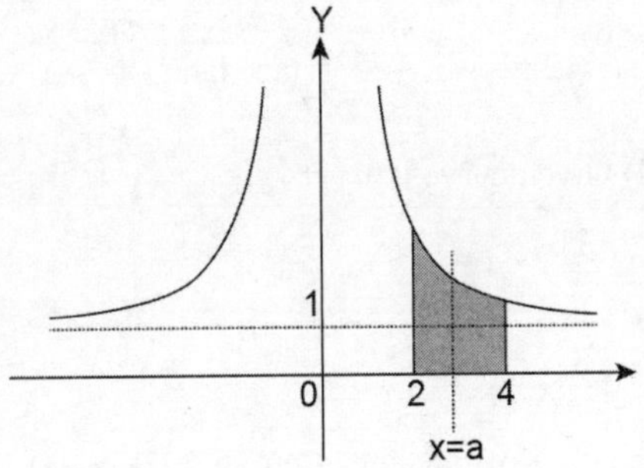

$\Rightarrow 2a-6-\frac{16}{a}+4+2=0$

$\Rightarrow 2a-\frac{16}{a}=0$

$\Rightarrow 2a^2-16=0 \qquad \Rightarrow a^2-8=0$

$\Rightarrow a = \pm\sqrt{8}$

But $a > 0 \qquad \Rightarrow a = \sqrt{8}$ or $2\sqrt{2}$

47. **(c)** $x = a\cos^3 t,\ y = a\sin^3 t,\ 0 \le x \le 2p.$

$\therefore$ The required area $= \frac{1}{2}\int_0^{2\pi}\left(x\frac{dy}{dx} - y\frac{dx}{dt}\right)dt$

$= \frac{1}{2}\int_0^{2\pi}\left[a\cos^3 t(3a\sin^3 t\cos t) - a\sin^3 t(3a\cos^2 t - \sin t)\right]dt$

$= \frac{3}{2}a^2\int_0^{2\pi}\sin^2 t\cos^2 t\,dt = \frac{3}{8}a^2\int_0^{2\pi}\sin^2 2t\,dt$

$= \frac{3}{8}a^2\int_0^{2\pi}\left(\frac{1-\cos 4t}{2}\right)dt = \frac{3}{16}a^2\left[t-\frac{\sin 4t}{4}\right]_0^{2\pi}$

$= \frac{3}{16}a^2(2\pi) = \frac{3}{8}a^2\pi$ square units.

48. **(c)** $x = a(1-t^2),\ y = at(1-t^2);\ -1 \le t \le 1$

Required area $= \frac{1}{2}\int_{-1}^{1}\left(x\frac{dy}{dx} - y\frac{dx}{dt}\right)dt$

$= \frac{1}{2}\int_{-1}^{1}\left[a(1-t^2)\left[a-3at^2\right] - at(1-t^2)a(-2t)\right]dt$

$= \frac{1}{2}\int_{-1}^{1}a^2\left[(1-t^2)(1-3t^2)+2t^2(1-t^2)\right]dt$

$= \frac{1}{2}a^2\int_{-1}^{1}\left(1-4t^2+3t^4+2t^2-2t^4\right)dt = \frac{1}{2}a^2\int_{-1}^{1}\left(t^4-2t^2+1\right)dt$

$= a^2\int_{-1}^{1}\left(t^4+1-2t^2\right)dt$

$= a^2\left[\frac{t^5}{5}+t-\frac{2t^3}{3}\right]_0^1 = a^2\left[\frac{1}{5}+1-\frac{2}{3}\right] = a^2\left[\frac{1}{5}+\frac{1}{3}\right] = \frac{8}{15}a^2$

square unit.

49. **(a)** $x = 2\cos t;\ y = 2\sin t$

Clearly $x^2+y^2=4$; which represents a circle of radius 2.

$\therefore$ Area $= \pi(2)^2 = 4p$.

SECTION-IV (MORE THAN ONE ARE CORRECT)

1. **(b), (c), (d)**

$(y-x-2)^2 = 9x;\ x \ge 0$

$\Rightarrow y = x+2 \pm 3\sqrt{x}$

On x-axis, $y = 0$

$\Rightarrow x+2 \pm 3\sqrt{x} = 0$

$\Rightarrow x+2 = \mp 3\sqrt{x}$

$\Rightarrow (x+2)^2 = 9x$

$\Rightarrow x^2+4x+4-9x=0$

$\Rightarrow x^2-5x+4=0$

$\Rightarrow (x-1)(x-4)=0 \qquad \Rightarrow x = 1$ or $x = 4$

For $y = x+2+\sqrt{3x}$, Clearly $y \ne 0$ at $x = 1, 4$

$y = x+2-3\sqrt{x}$, Clearly $y = 0$ at $x = 1$ and $x = 4$

$\therefore\ y = x+2-3\sqrt{x}$ intersects x-axis at $x = 1$ and $x = 4$.

On $y = x+2 \pm 3\sqrt{x}$ intersects y-axis at $(0, 2)$; $y' = 1 \pm \frac{3}{2\sqrt{x}}$

The curve will be of following shape

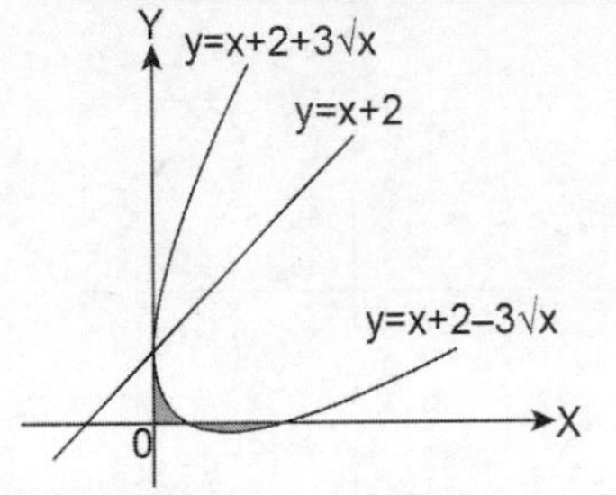

Clearly branches $y = x+2+3\sqrt{x}$ and $y = x+2-3\sqrt{x}$ will intersect each other only when

$x+2+3\sqrt{x} = x+2-3\sqrt{x}$

$\Rightarrow x = 0$, i.e., at $(0, 2)$

Area enclosed by the curve with (0 ordinate axis)

$= \int_0^1\left(x+2-3\sqrt{x}\right)dx + \int_1^4 0-\left(x+2-3\sqrt{x}\right)dx$

$= \left[\frac{x^2}{2}+2x-3(x)^{3/2}\left(\frac{2}{3}\right)\right]_0^1 - \left[\frac{x^2}{2}+2x-2x^{3/2}\right]_1^4$

$= \left(\frac{1}{2}+2-2\right) - \left[\frac{16}{2}+8-16-\frac{1}{2}-2+2\right] = \left(\frac{1}{2}+\frac{1}{2}\right) = 1$

square units.

2. **(a), (b), (c)**

Given curves are $x^2 = y$ and $y^2 = x$.

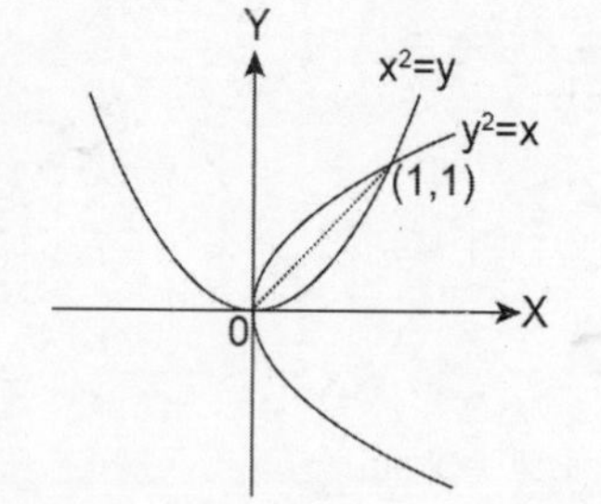

Required area = $\{(x, y)\} : x^2 \le y \le \sqrt{x}\} = A_1$

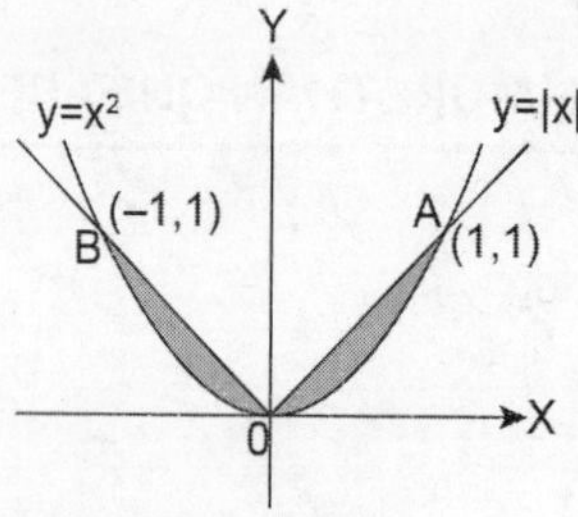

$A_2 = \{(x, y) : x^2 \le y \le |x|\}$

$\therefore$ Required Area = $2\int_0^1 (x - x^2)dx = 2\left[\frac{x^2}{2} - \frac{x^3}{3}\right]_0^1$

$= 2\left(\frac{1}{2} - \frac{1}{3}\right) = 2\left(\frac{3-2}{6}\right) = \frac{1}{3}$ square units.

3. (a), (b) $(x^2 - y^2)(x^2 - y^2 - 8x + 16) = 0$

$\Rightarrow (x - y)(x + y)(x - 4 - y)(x - 4 + y) = 0$

$\Rightarrow y = x, y = -x, y = x - 4, y = -x + 4$

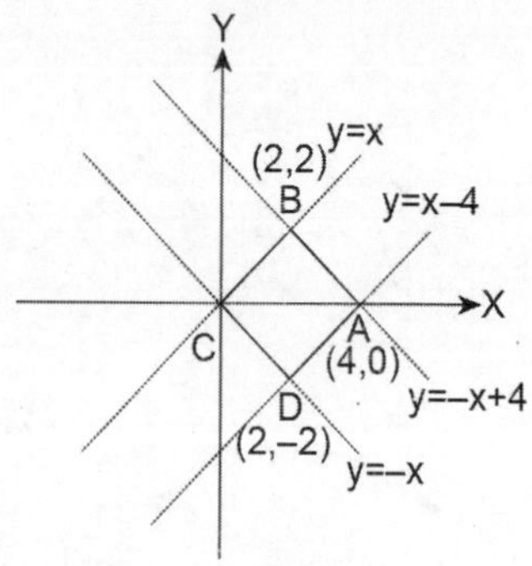

Area of quadrilateral $ABCD$ =

$\frac{1}{2}(AC)(BD) = \frac{1}{2}(4)(4) = 8$ square units

4. (b), (d) Area of quadrilateral $ABCD$ will be maximum if ar ΔACD, i.e., $\frac{1}{2}(AC)(FD)$

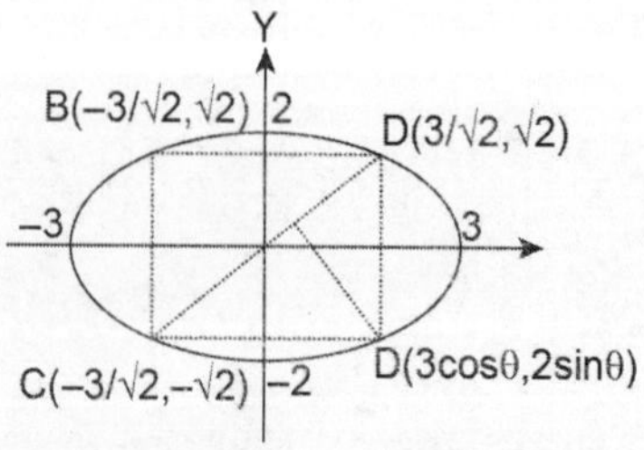

$\Rightarrow$ FD is maximum

Equation of AC is $y = \left(\frac{\sqrt{2}}{3/\sqrt{2}}\right)x$, i.e., $y = \frac{2}{3}x$ or $2x - 3y = 0$

$\Rightarrow DF = \left|\frac{2(3\cos\theta) - 3(2\sin\theta)}{\sqrt{4+9}}\right| = \frac{6}{\sqrt{13}}|\cos\theta - \sin\theta|;$

$\frac{3\pi}{2} \le \theta \le 2\pi$

Which has its maximum value $= \frac{6}{\sqrt{13}}\left(\sqrt{2}\right)$

At $\theta = 2\pi - \frac{\pi}{4} = \frac{7\pi}{4} = \tan\left(\tan^{-1}\left(\frac{7\pi}{4}\right)\right)$

5. (b), (d) Given curve is $x^a y = \lambda^a$

$\Rightarrow y = \frac{\lambda^a}{x^a}$ ....(i)

$\Rightarrow y' = \lambda^a\left(-ax^{-a-1}\right)$

$\therefore$ Equation of tangent to curve at $P(x_0, y_0)$ is $(y - y_0) = \frac{-a\lambda^a}{(x_0)^{a+1}}(x - x_0)$ ...(2)

Eqn. (2) intersects x-axis, where $y = 0$

i.e., at $-y_0 = \frac{-a\lambda^a}{(x_0)^{a+1}}(x - x_0)$

$\Rightarrow x - x_0 = \frac{(x_0)^{a+1}.y_0}{a\lambda^a}$

$\Rightarrow x = x_0 + \frac{(x_0)^{a+1}y_0}{a\lambda^a}$ ...(3)

Also Eqn. (2) intersects y-axis, where $x = 0$

$\Rightarrow y - y_0 = \frac{-a\lambda^a}{(x_0)^{a+1}}(-x_0)$

$\Rightarrow y = \frac{a\lambda^a}{(x_0)^a} + y_0$ ...(4)

$\Rightarrow$ Area of triangle bounded by co-ordinate axes and tangent at $P(x_0, y_0)$

$= \frac{1}{2}x_0\left[1 + \frac{x_0^a y_0}{a\lambda^a}\right]\left[\frac{a\lambda^a}{(x_0)^a} + y_0\right]$

$= \frac{1}{2}x_0\left[\frac{a\lambda^a + x_0^a y_0}{a\lambda^a}\right]\left[\frac{a\lambda^a + y_0 x_0^a}{(x_0)^a}\right]$

$= \frac{1}{2}\frac{\left(a\lambda^a + x_0^a y_0\right)^2}{a\lambda^a(x_0)^{a-1}} = \frac{1}{2}\frac{\left(a\lambda^a + \lambda_0\right)^2}{[a\lambda^a(x_0)^{a-1}]}$ $[\because x_0^a y_0 = \lambda^a]$

Or Area $= \frac{1}{2}\frac{(a+1)^2\lambda^{2a}}{a.\lambda^a.(x_0)^{a-1}} = \frac{1}{2}\frac{(a+1)^2}{(x_0)^{a-1}} = 0$; if $a = -1$

$\therefore a = \pm 1$

6. (a), (c), (d)

$P(x) = \max. \{f(x), g(x)\}$ and $g(x) = \min, \{f(x), g(x)\}$

Clearly for $x \in [a, b]$, $p(x) \ge q(x)$

∴ Area bounded by $P(x)$, $q(x)$ ordinates $x = a$, $x = b$ will be

$$= \int_a^b [p(x) - q(x)]dx = \int_a^b | p(x) - q(x) | dx = \int_a^b | f(x) - g(x) | dx$$

7. (a), (b), (c), (d)

Let $y = f(x)$ be the required curve, let $P(x_0, y_0)$ be any point on the above curve tangent at which makes angle $\pi/4$ with the intersection of tangent and the given curve $xy = c^2$.

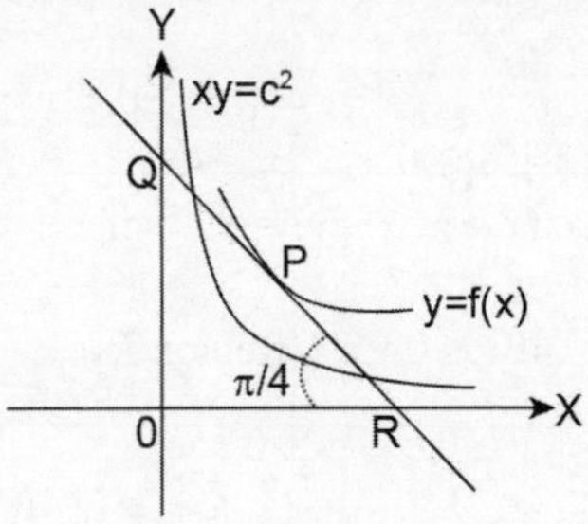

Equation to

$y = f(x)$ at $P(x_0, y_0)$ is $(y - y_0) = f'(x_0)(x - x_0)$ .....(1)

At the point of intersection of (1) and the curve $xy = c^2$ ....(2)

Is given by $\left(\dfrac{c^2}{x} - y_0\right) = f'(x_0)(x - x_0)$

$\Rightarrow$ $(c_2 - xy_0) = f'(x)(x^2 - x\,x_0)$

$\Rightarrow$ $f'(x_0)x^2 + (y_0 - x_0 f'(x_0))\,x - c^2 = 0$

$\Rightarrow$ $x_1 + x_2 = \dfrac{x_0 f'(x_0) - y_0}{f'(x_0)}$ ...(3)

And $x_1 x_2 = \dfrac{-c^2}{f'(x_0)}$ ...(4)

Now slopes of tangents at $Q\left(x_1, \dfrac{c^2}{x_1}\right)$ and $R\left(x_2, \dfrac{c^2}{x_2}\right)$

will be $m_1 = \dfrac{-c^2}{x_1^2}$ and $m_2 = \dfrac{-c^2}{x_2^2}$ ...(5)

$\therefore$ $m_1 . m_2 = -1$ $\Rightarrow$ $\left(\dfrac{-c^2}{x_1^2}\right)\left(\dfrac{-c^2}{x_2^2}\right) = -1$

$\Rightarrow$ $x_1^2 x_2^2 = -c^4$ ...(6)

$\therefore$ From (4) and (5), we get $\dfrac{c^4}{(f'(x_0))^2} = -c^4$

$\Rightarrow$ $(f'(x_0)) = -1$

8. (b), (c) A.T.Q. $\int_0^a f(x)dx = \int_0^a \sqrt{1 + (f'(x))^2}\,dx$

$\Rightarrow$ $f(a) = \sqrt{1 + (f'(a))^2}\,dx$

$\Rightarrow$ $(f(a))^2 = 1 + (f'(a))^2 = (f'(x))^2 = (f(x))^2 - 1$

$\Rightarrow$ $f'(x) = \pm\sqrt{(f(x))^2 - 1}$; $\left(\dfrac{dy}{dx}\right)^2 - y^2 + 1 = 0$;

$\dfrac{dy}{dx} = \pm\sqrt{y^2 - 1}$

$\Rightarrow$ $\dfrac{dy}{\sqrt{y^2 - 1}} = \pm dx$ $\Rightarrow$ $\int \dfrac{dy}{\sqrt{y^2 - 1}} = \pm dx$

$\Rightarrow$ $\ln\left|y + \sqrt{y^2 - 1}\right| = \pm x + C$

It passes through (0, 1)

$\Rightarrow$ $\ln 1 = \pm 0 + C$ $\Rightarrow$ $C = 0$

$\Rightarrow$ $\ln\left|y + \sqrt{y^2 - 1}\right| = \pm x$ $\Rightarrow$ $y + \sqrt{y^2 - 1} = e^{\pm x}$

$\Rightarrow$ $\sqrt{y^2 - 1} = e^{\pm x} - y$

$\Rightarrow$ $y^2 - 1 = e^{\pm 2}x + y^2 - 2ye^{\pm x}$

$\Rightarrow$ $-1 = e^{\pm 2x} - 2ye^{\pm x}$ $\Rightarrow$ $2ye^{\pm x} = 1 + e^{\pm 2x}$

$\Rightarrow$ $y = \dfrac{e^{\pm 2x} + 1}{2e^{\pm x}}$ or $y = \dfrac{1}{2}\left(e^x + \dfrac{1}{e^x}\right)$ or $y = \dfrac{1}{2}\left(e^{-x} + \dfrac{1}{e^{-x}}\right)$

or $y = \dfrac{1}{2}\left(e^x + e^{-x}\right)$

Also if $y = 1$, then (1) is satisfied.

9. (b), (c), (d)

$f(x) = |x| - 2$ and $g(x) = |f(x)|$

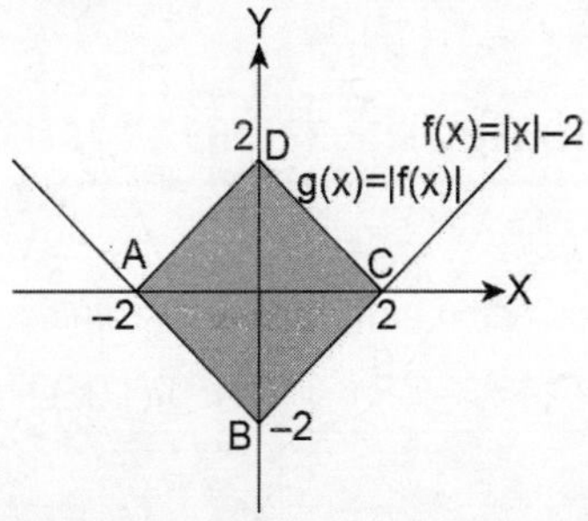

$\therefore$ Required bounded area by $f(x)$ or $g(x) = 1/2$ [area of square $ABCD$]

$= \dfrac{1}{2}\left[\dfrac{1}{2}(4)(4)\right] = 4$ square units

$\Rightarrow$ $A_1 = A_2 = 4$ square units.

10. (b), (c), (d)

L: $x - y - 1 = 0$ ...(1)

C: $y^2 = 2x + 1$ ...(2)

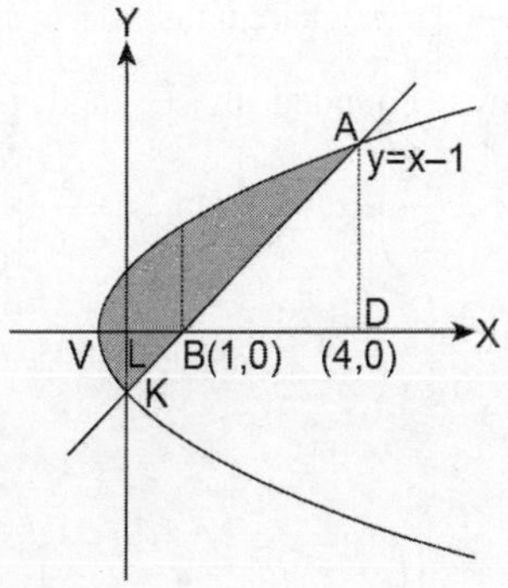

$\therefore$ Area bounded by L and C by the upper half plane =

$\int_{-1/2}^{1} \sqrt{2x + 1}\,dx + \int_1^4 \left[\sqrt{2x + 1} - (x - 1)\right]dx$

$\Rightarrow$ $\left[\dfrac{2(2x + 1)^{3/2}}{3(2)}\right]_{-1/2}^{1} + \left[\dfrac{2(2x + 1)^{3/2}}{3(2)}\right]_1^4 - \dfrac{15}{2} + 3$

$\Rightarrow\ \frac{1}{3}\left[3\sqrt{3}-0\right]+\frac{1}{3}\left[27-3\sqrt{3}\right]-\frac{9}{2}=9-\frac{9}{2}=\frac{9}{2}$ square units

Area bounded by L and C in the plane

Plane = Above found area $=(9/2)+\int_{-1/2}^{0}\sqrt{2x+1}\,dx$ + area of ΔBLK

$=\frac{9}{2}+\left[\frac{2}{3}\frac{(2x+1)^{3/2}}{(2)}\right]_{-1/2}^{0}+\frac{1}{2}(1)(1)$

$=\frac{9}{2}+\frac{1}{3}(1-0)+\frac{1}{2}=5+\frac{1}{3}=\frac{16}{3}$ square units.

Area bounded by L and C in the lower half plane

$=\frac{1}{3}+\frac{1}{2}=\frac{5}{6}$ square units.

11. (a), (b) $C_1:\ y=\frac{1}{1+x^2}$ ...(1)

And $C_2=\ y=\frac{1}{1+x^2}$ ...(2)

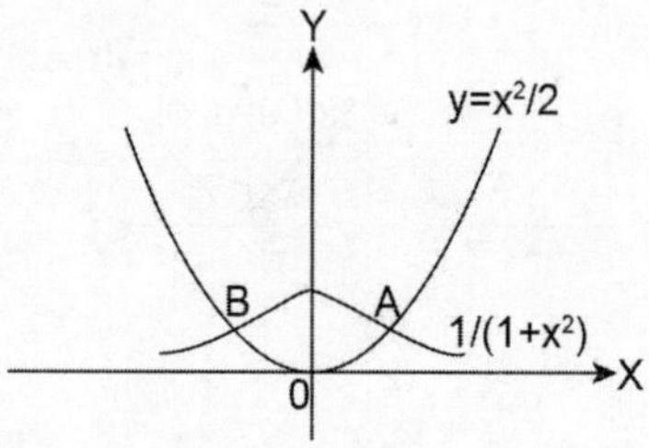

Clearly C_1 is symmetric about x-axis as $x\to 0,\ y\to\infty^+$ and as $x\to\pm\infty,\ y\to 0^+$

$\Rightarrow$ x–axis and y-axis are asymptotes to the curve C_1.

At the point of intersection of C_1 and C_2, $\frac{1}{1+x^2}=\frac{x^2}{2}$

$\Rightarrow\ x^4+x^2-2=0\qquad\Rightarrow\ (x^2+2)(x^2-1)=0$

$\Rightarrow\ x^2=1\qquad\Rightarrow\ x=1$

$\therefore$ Area bounded by C_1 and $y=0=2\int_0^{\infty}\frac{1}{1+x^2}dx=2\left[\tan^{-1}x\right]_0^{\infty}$

$=2\left[\frac{\pi}{2}-0\right]=\pi$ square units

Now, area bounded by C_1 and C_2 and x-axis is $\int_0^1\left(\frac{1}{1+x^2}-\frac{x^2}{2}\right)dx=2\left[\tan^{-1}x-\frac{x^3}{6}\right]_0^1$

$=2\left[\frac{\pi}{4}-\frac{1}{6}\right]=\left(\frac{\pi}{2}-\frac{1}{3}\right)$ square units.

12. (b), (c), (d)

Required area $=\int_0^1\left(e-e^x\right)dx=e-(e-1)=1=e-\int_0^1 e^x dx$

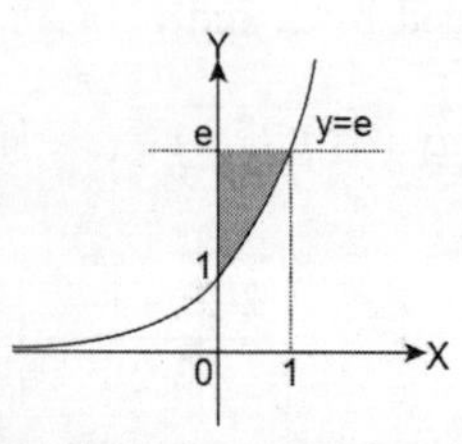

$=\int_1^e x\,dy=\int_1^e \ln y\,dy=\int_1^e \ln(1+e-y)\,dy$

By property of definite integral $\int_a^b f(x)dx=\int_a^b f(a+b-x)dx$

13. (a), (b), (c)

Case (i): $x+y\ge 0,\ x-y\ge 0$

$\Rightarrow$ max. $(|x+y|,|x-y|)=$ max. $(x+y,x-y)=x+y$ if $x+y\ge x-y$

$\Rightarrow\ 2y\ge 0\qquad\Rightarrow\ y\ge 0$

$\therefore\ x+y=1$ if $y\ge 0$

Also max$(x+y,x-y)=x-y$ if $x+y\le x-y$

$\Rightarrow\ y\le 0$

$\therefore\ x-y=1$ if $y\le 0$ (Region R_1)

Case (ii): $x+y\ge 0,\ x-y\le 0$

$\Rightarrow$ max$(x+y,-x+y)=\begin{cases}x+y & \text{if } x+y\ge -x+y\\ -x+y & \text{if } -x+y\ge x+y\end{cases}$

$=\begin{cases}x+y & \text{if } x\ge 0\\ -x+y & \text{if } x\le 0\end{cases}$

$\therefore\ x+y=1$ if $x\ge 0$ and $-x+y=1$ if $x\le 0$

Case (iii): $x+y\le 0,\ x-y\le 0,$

$\Rightarrow$ max. $(-x-y,-x+y)=\begin{cases}-x-y & \text{if } -x-y\ge -x+y\\ -x+y & \text{if } -x+y\ge -x-y\end{cases}$

$\Rightarrow\ \begin{cases}-x-y & \text{if } y\le 0\\ -x+y & \text{if } y\ge 0\end{cases}$ (Region R_3)

Case (iv): $x+y\le 0,\ x-y\ge 0$

$\therefore$ max. $\{-x-y,x-y\}=\begin{cases}-x-y & \text{if } -x-y\ge -x-y\\ x-y & \text{if } x-y\ge -x-y\end{cases}$

$=\begin{cases}-x-y=1 & \text{if } x\le 0\\ x-y=1 & \text{if } x\ge 0\end{cases}$

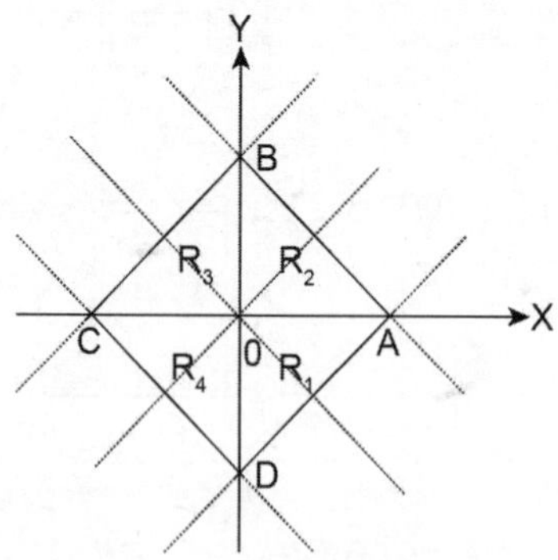

$\therefore$ Required area = Area of square $ABCD$ = 1/2 (2)(2) = 2 square units

(b) max. $\{|x|,|y|\}=1$

Case (i): $x\ge 0,\ y\ge 0$; max $\{x,y\}=\begin{cases}x & \text{if } x\ge y\\ y & \text{if } y\ge x\end{cases}$

$=\begin{cases}x=1 & \text{if } x\ge y\\ y=1 & \text{if } y\ge x\end{cases}$ (region R_1)

Case (ii): $x \geq 0, y \leq 0$

$$\Rightarrow \text{max. }\{x, -y\} = \begin{cases} x & \text{if } x \geq -y \text{ or } y \geq -x \\ -y & \text{if } -y \geq x \text{ or } y \leq -x \end{cases}$$

$$\Rightarrow \begin{cases} x = 1 & \text{if } y \geq -x \\ -y = 1 & \text{if } y \leq -x \end{cases} \text{(Region } R_2\text{)}$$

Case (iii): $x \leq 0, y \leq 0$

$$\Rightarrow \text{max. }\{-x, -y\} = \begin{cases} -x & \text{if } -x \geq -y \text{ or } x \leq y \\ -y & \text{if } -y \geq -x \text{ or } y \leq x \end{cases}$$

$$\Rightarrow \begin{cases} -x = 1 & \text{if } y \geq x \\ -y = 1 & \text{if } y \leq x \end{cases} \text{(Region } R_3\text{)}$$

Case (iv): $x \leq 0, y \leq 0$

$$\Rightarrow \text{max. }\{-x, y\} = \begin{cases} -x & \text{if } -x \geq y \\ y & \text{if } y \geq -x \end{cases}$$

$$= \begin{cases} -x = 1 & \text{if } y \geq -x \\ y = 1 & \text{if } y \geq -x \end{cases}$$

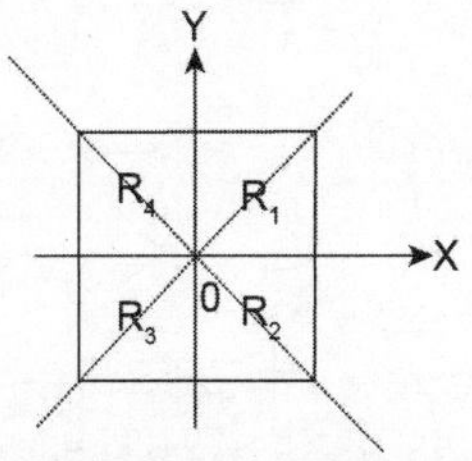

∴ Required area = $(2)^2 = 4$ square units

(c) As in above case, we will get,

$x = \frac{1}{2}$ if $x \geq y$

$y = \frac{1}{2}$ if $y \geq x$

For $x \geq 0, y \geq 0$

For region R_1

∴ Total region = $4\left(\frac{1}{2} \times \frac{1}{2}\right)$ square units.

(d) Required area (unbounded region) = infinite

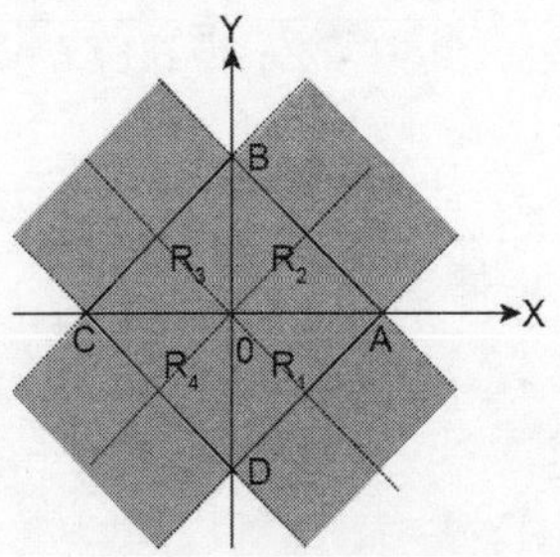

SECTION–V (ASSERTION AND REASON TYPE)

1. (a) Given inequalities are $x^2 + y^2 \leq 25$ ...(1)

And $\sin(x + y) \leq 0$ ...(2)

$$(x + y) \in \bigcup_{n \in \mathbb{Z}} [(2n\pi, (2n+1)\pi]$$

For $n = 0$, $x + y \in [0, \pi]$

$\Rightarrow 0 \leq x + y \leq \pi$

$\Rightarrow -x \leq y \leq -x + \pi$

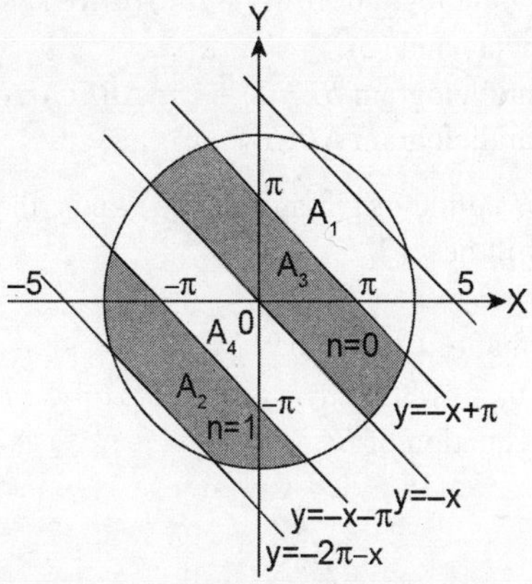

For $n = 1$, $(x + y) \in [2p, 3p]$ ⇒

$2p \leq x + y \leq 3p$ ⇒ $2p - x \leq y \leq 3p - x$

For $n = -1$, $(x + y) \in [-2p, -\pi]$

$\Rightarrow -2p \leq x + y \leq -\pi$ ⇒ $-2p - x \leq y \leq -\pi - x$

Clearly PQ and RS being equidistance from origin are equal. Hence area A, (without shading of circle and shaded portion of circle A_2 are equal. Also symmetry A_3 and A_4 are equal. Hence common region to (1) and (2) equals.

$(A_3 + A_1)$ = half the area of circle = $(25p)$ square units.

∴ Both assertion and reason are correct and reason correctly expansion assertion.

2. (a) Produce AD and CF to H

Now $EH \parallel BC$ and $BE \parallel CH$

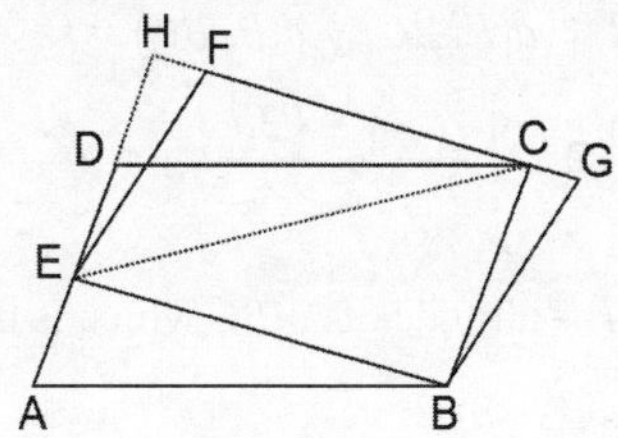

⇒ $BEHC$ is *a* parallelogram.

⇒ $SH = BC$ and $EF = GB$ (∵ BEFG is *a* parallelogram)

And $\angle HEF = \angle CBG = \alpha$

⇒ $\Delta FHE \approx \Delta GCB$

⇒ (ar $BEFC$) + *ar* ΔFHE = (ar $BEFC$) + (ar ΔGCB)

⇒ ar (parallelogram $BEHC$) = ar(parallelogram $BEFG$)

⇒ 1/2 ar(parallelogram $BEHC$) = 1/2 ar(parallelogram $BEFG$) = arΔBEC

= 1/2 ar (parallelogram $BEFG$)

Or ar. (parallelogram $BEFG$) = 2 ar. ΔBEC ...(1)

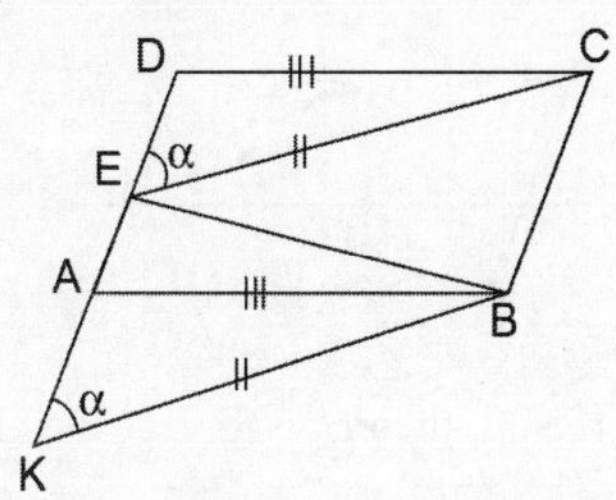

Produce DA to K and draw BK parallel to CE.

Clearly, $\Delta ABK \simeq \Delta DCE$

$\Rightarrow$ ar parallelogram ABCD = *ar* parallelogram EKBC

$\Rightarrow$ ar. Parallelogram AB (i) = 2*ar* (ΔBEC) ...(2)

$\therefore$ From (1) and (2)

ar(parallelogram $BEFG$) = 2*ar*(ΔBEC) =

ar(parallelogram ABCD)

3. (c) Let B be the origin and BC be x-axis, then equation of BA will be

$y = \sqrt{3}x$ ...(i)

and that of CA will be

$(y - 0) = -\sqrt{3}(x - a)$, i.e., $y = -\sqrt{3}x + \sqrt{3}a$ ...(ii)

and equation of BC is $y = 0$ ...(iii)

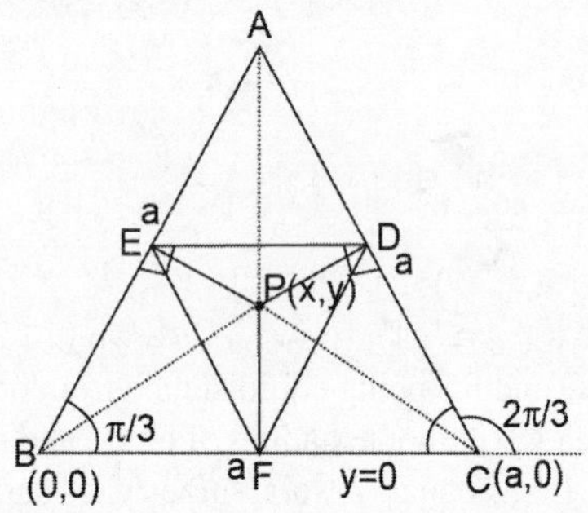

$\therefore \quad d(P, AB) = \dfrac{|\sqrt{3}x - y|}{2} = \dfrac{\sqrt{3}x - y}{2}$

$d(P, AC) = \dfrac{|-\sqrt{3}x - y + \sqrt{3}a|}{2} = \dfrac{-\sqrt{3}x - y + \sqrt{3}a}{2}$

$d(P, BC) = |y| = y$

$\therefore \quad d(P, AB) + d(P, AC) + d(P, BC) = k$

$\Rightarrow \quad \dfrac{\sqrt{3}x - y}{2} + \dfrac{-\sqrt{3}x - y + \sqrt{3}a}{2} + y = k$

$\Rightarrow \quad \dfrac{\sqrt{3}a}{2} = k =$ altitude of ΔABC which is true for all $P(x, y)$ inside the ΔABC.

$\therefore$ Required area of point $P(x, y)$ = ar(ΔABC)

$\therefore$ Assertion is true.

Clearly as, $d(P, AB) + d(P, AC) + d(P, BC) = k$ holds $\forall$ $P(x, y)$ inside the ΔABC, hence, these types of points need not necessarily lies in pedal triangle of ΔABC, hence reason is incorrect.

4. (d) $y = \sin^2 x$; $x \in [0, \pi]$ ...(i)

$y = \sin x$; $x \in [0, \pi]$ ...(ii)

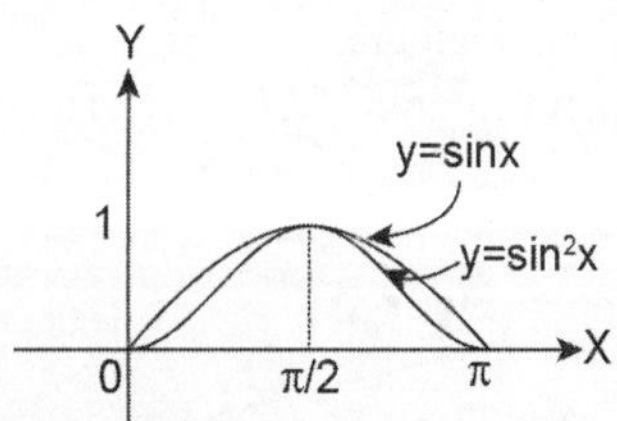

Clearly if $t >$ i, then $t^2 > t$

$\Rightarrow$ if $0 < t < 1$, then $t^2 < t$

$\Rightarrow$ Area bounded by $\sin 2x$ will be less than that of bounded by $\sin x$.

$\Rightarrow$ Assertion is incorrect, but reason is correct.

5. (c) Equation of given parabolas is $y = x - bx^2$ ...(i)

And $\quad y = \dfrac{x^2}{b}$ ...(ii)

At the point of intersection, $x - bx^2 = \dfrac{x^2}{b}$

$\Rightarrow bx - b2x^2 = x^2$

$\Rightarrow (1 + b^2)x^2 - bx = 0$

$\Rightarrow x = 0$ or $x = \dfrac{b}{1+b^2}$

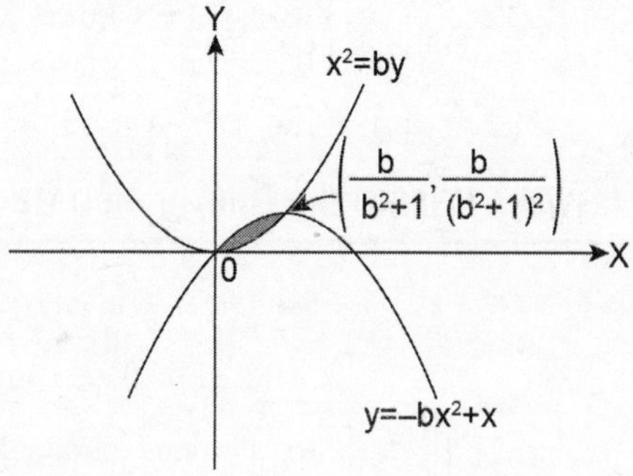

$\therefore$ Bounded area = $\displaystyle\int_0^{\frac{b}{1+b^2}} \left(-bx^2 + x - \frac{x^2}{b}\right) dx$

$= \left[-\dfrac{bx^3}{3} + \dfrac{x^2}{2} - \dfrac{x^3}{3b}\right]_0^{\frac{b}{1+b^2}}$

$= \dfrac{-b}{3}\left(\dfrac{b^3}{(1+b^2)^3}\right) + \dfrac{b^2}{2(1+b^2)^2} - \dfrac{1}{3b}\left(\dfrac{b^3}{(1+b^2)^3}\right)$

$= \dfrac{-b^4}{3(1+b^2)^3} + \dfrac{b^2}{2(1+b^2)^2} - \dfrac{b^2}{3(1+b^2)^3}$

$= \dfrac{-2b^4 + 3b^2(1+b^2) - 2b^2}{6(1+b^2)^3} = \dfrac{-b^2\left(+2b^2 - 3(1+b^2) + 2\right)}{6(1+b^2)^3}$

$= \dfrac{-b^2\left(-b^2 - 1\right)}{6(1+b^2)^3} = \dfrac{b^2\left(b^2 + 1\right)}{6(1+b^2)^3} = \dfrac{b^2}{6(1+b^2)^2}$

$= \dfrac{1}{6\left(\dfrac{1+b^2}{b}\right)^2} = \dfrac{1}{6\left(\dfrac{1}{b} + b\right)^2}$

$\therefore \quad b + \dfrac{1}{b} \geq 2 \quad \Rightarrow \quad \dfrac{1}{\left(b + \dfrac{1}{b}\right)} \leq \dfrac{1}{2}$

$\Rightarrow$ Area will be maximum $= \dfrac{1}{6}\left(\dfrac{1}{4}\right) = \dfrac{1}{24}$ at $b = 1$

$\Rightarrow$ Assertion is correct, but reason is incorrect.

6. (a) Equation of curve is $3y = -x^2 + 8x - 7$ ...(i)

And $(y + 1) = \dfrac{4}{x-3}$ ...(ii)

Shifting the origin at (3, –1), equation becomes replacing $x-3$ by x and $y+1$ by y.

$3(y-1) = -(x+3)^2 + 8(x+3) - 7$ and $y = \frac{4}{x}$

i.e., $3y = -x^2 + 2x + 11$ ...(iii)

and

$y = \frac{4}{x}$ ...(iv)

∴ Area bounded by (i) and (ii) will be same as that by (iii) and (iv) as the reason is correct.

∴ Both assertion and reason are correct and reason correctly explains the assertion.

7. (c) Given curves are $y = x^2 + 2x - 3$ ...(i)

And $y = \lambda x + 1$ ...(ii)

At the point of intersection $x^2 + 2x - 3 = \lambda x + 1$

⇒ $x^2 + (2-\lambda)x - 4 = 0$ ...(iii)

Equation (i) can be written as $y = x^2 + 2x + 1 - 4$ or $y = (x+1)^2 - 4$ or $(x+1)^2 = (y+4)$

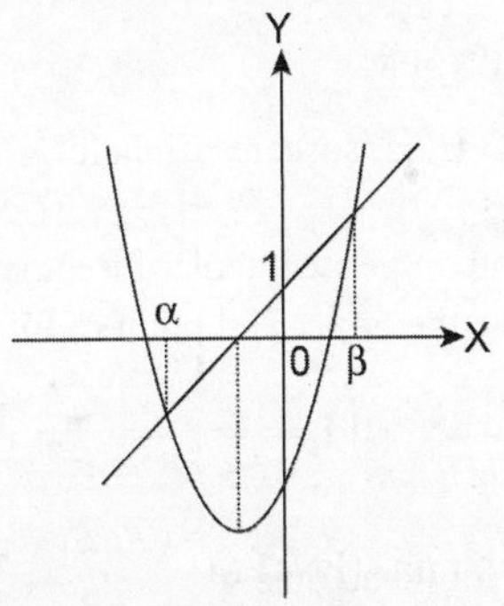

Hence α, b are roots of (iii)

∴ Area bounded by (i) and (ii) will be

$$A = \int_\alpha^\beta \left(\lambda x + 1 - x^2 - 2x + 3\right) dx$$

$$= \left[\lambda \frac{x^2}{2} + x - \frac{x^3}{3} - x^2 + 3x\right]_\alpha^\beta$$

$$= \left[\left(\frac{\lambda}{2} - 1\right)x^2 + 4x - \frac{x^3}{3}\right]_\alpha^\beta$$

$$= \left(\frac{\lambda}{2} - 1\right)\left(\beta^2 - \alpha^2\right) + 4(\beta - \alpha) - \frac{1}{3}\left(\beta^3 - \alpha^3\right)$$

$$= (\beta - \alpha)\left[\left(\frac{\lambda}{2} - 1\right)(\beta + \alpha) + 4 - \frac{1}{3}(\beta^2 + \alpha^2 + \alpha\beta)\right]$$

$$= \sqrt{(2-\lambda)^2 + 16}\left[\left(\frac{\lambda}{2} - 1\right)(\lambda - 2) + 4 - \frac{1}{3}\left[(2-\lambda)^2 + 4\right]\right]$$

$$= \sqrt{(2-\lambda)^2 + 16}\left[\frac{(\lambda - 2)^2}{2} + 4 - \frac{1}{3}(2-\lambda)^2 - \frac{4}{3}\right]$$

$$= \sqrt{(2-\lambda)^2 + 16}\left[\frac{(\lambda - 2)^2}{6} + \frac{8}{3} - \frac{1}{12}(2 - \lambda^2)\right]$$

$$= \sqrt{(2-\lambda)^2 + 16}\left[\frac{1}{12}(2-\lambda)^2 + \frac{8}{3}\right]$$

$$= \frac{1}{12}\left[(2-\lambda)^2 + 32\right]\sqrt{(2-\lambda)^2 + 16} \text{ square units}$$

It will be least at $l = 2$

∴ Assertion is correct, but reason is incorrect.

8. (a) Given curves are $2x^2 + 3y^2 = 6$ ...(i)

And $2|x| + 3|y| \le 6$ or $\frac{|x|}{3} + \frac{|y|}{2} = 1$ ...(ii)

Clearly ellipse $2x^2 + 3y^2 = 6$ is well inside the curve $2|x| + 3|y| \le 6$.

∴ Area of ellipse is less than that of $2|x| + 3|y| \le 6$

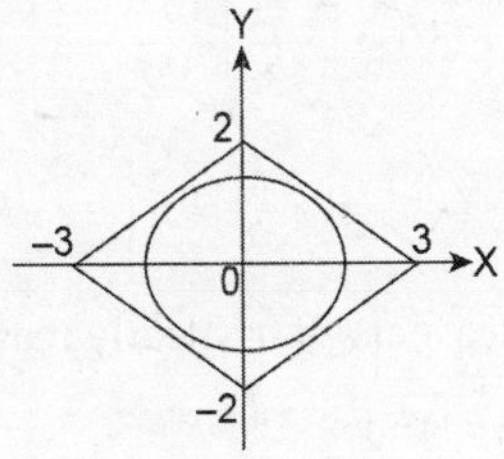

⇒ Assertion is incorrect.

Clearly length of major of ellipse = 2√3 is less than the distance between the points of

$2|x| + 3|y| \le 6$ on x-axis which is 6 units

⇒ Reason is correct.

9. (b) Given curve are $2x^2 + 3y^2 = 6$ or $\frac{x^2}{3} + \frac{y^2}{2} = 1$ ...(i)

And $x^2 + y^2 - 2x + 4y + 4 = 0$ or $(x^2 - 2x + 1) + (y^2 + 4y + 4) = 1$ or $(x-1)^2 + (y+2)^2 = 1$ ...(ii)

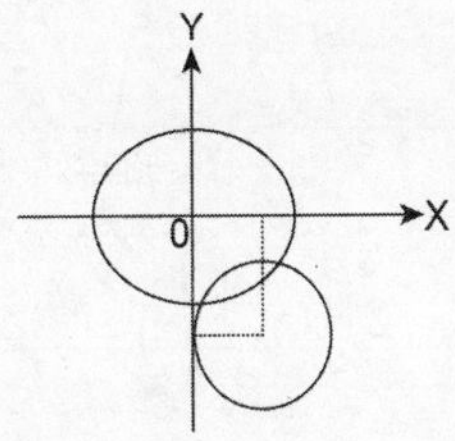

Area of ellipse (i) is πab = p (√3) (√2) = √6 p square units.

And area of circle (2) is $\pi r^2 = \pi$. Clearly √6p > π

⇒ Assertion is correct but reason is not complete.

As for πab to be greater than πr^2, (a, b) must be greater than r^2. 'a' lone is not sufficient to be greater than 'r'.

∴ Reason is correct, but not complete.

10. (c) Given curve are $y = x^2 - 3$ ...(1)

And $y = kx + 2$ ...(2)

At the point of intersection

$x^2 - 3 = kx + 2$ or $x^2 - kx - 5 = 0$ ...(3)

Let α, b points two roots.

⇒ $a + b = k$, αβ = –5 ...(4)

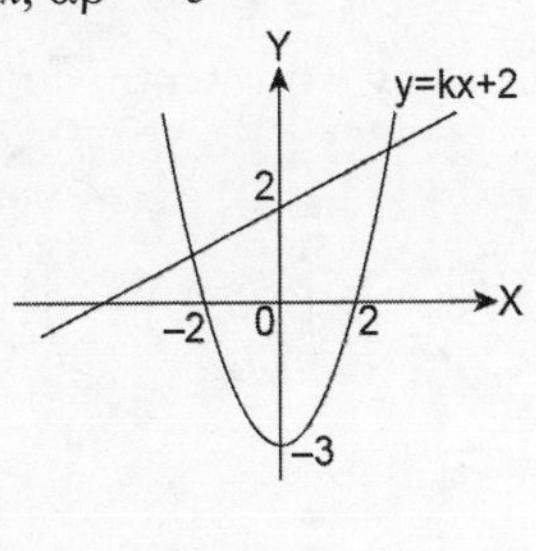

$\therefore$ Required bounded area $= \int_{\alpha}^{\beta}\left[(kx+2)-(x^2-3)\right]dx$

$= \int_{\alpha}^{\beta}(-x^2+kx+5)dx = \left[\frac{-x^3}{3}+\frac{kx^2}{2}+5x\right]_{\alpha}^{\beta}$

$= \frac{-1}{3}(\beta^3-\alpha^3)+\frac{k}{2}(\beta^2-\alpha^2)+5(\beta-\alpha)$

$= (\beta-\alpha)\left[(\beta^2+\alpha^2\alpha\beta)\left(\frac{-1}{3}\right)+\frac{k}{2}(\beta+\alpha)+5\right]$

$= \left(\sqrt{k^2+20}\right)\left[\left[k^2+5\right]\left(\frac{-1}{3}\right)+\frac{k^2}{2}+5\right]$

$= \sqrt{k^2+20}\left[\frac{-1}{3}(k^2+5)+\frac{k^2}{2}+5\right] = \sqrt{k^2+20}\left[\frac{1}{6}k^2+\frac{10}{3}\right]$

Which is least at $k = 0$. Clearly reason is incorrect.

11. (d) Given curve are $y = 3x - x^2$ ...(i)

And $y = x^2 - x$ ...(ii)

At the point of intersection $3x - x^2 = x^2 - x$

$\Rightarrow 2x^2 - 4x = 0$

$\Rightarrow 2x(x-2) = 0 \quad \Rightarrow x = 0, 2$

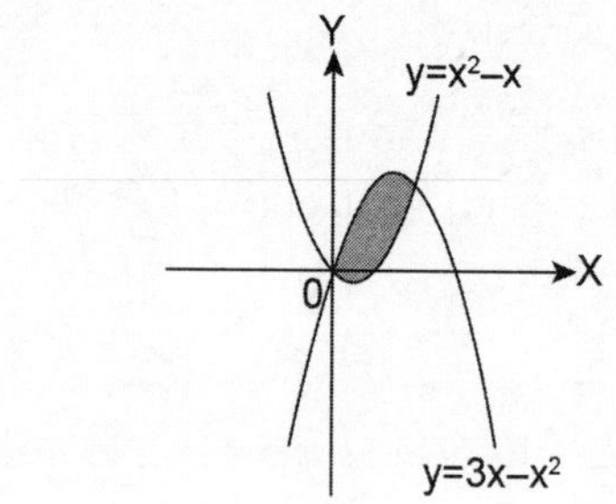

$\therefore$ Required area $= \int_0^2 (3x-x^2)-(x^2-x)dx$

$= \int_0^2 \left[-2x^2+4x\right]dx$

$= -2\left[\frac{x^3}{3}\right]_0^2+\frac{4}{2}\left[x^2\right]_0^2 = \frac{-2}{3}[8-0]+2(4-0)$

$= 8-\frac{16}{3}=\frac{8}{3}$ square units.

$\Rightarrow$ Assertion is incorrect. Obviously reason is correct.

12. (c) Given curve is $y = \cos x$ ...(1)

Clearly, reason is incorrect as area bounded by $y = f(x)$, x-axis, between ordinates.

$x = a$ and $x = b$ is given by $\int_a^b |f(x)|\,dx$

$\therefore$ Area bounded by $y = \cos x$, $y = 0$, $x = 0$ and $x = \frac{3\pi}{4}$ must be

$= \int_0^{3\pi/4} |\cos x|\,dx = \int_0^{\pi/2} \cos x\,dx + \int_{\pi/2}^{3\pi/4} (-\cos x)\,dx$

$= \left[\sin x\right]_0^{\pi/2} - \left[\sin x\right]_{\pi/2}^{3\pi/4}$

$= (1-0)-\left(\frac{1}{\sqrt{2}}-1\right)=\left(2-\frac{1}{\sqrt{2}}\right)$ square units.

$\Rightarrow$ Assertion is correct.

SECTION–VI (COMPREHENSION TYPE)

PASSAGE-A:

Given ellipse is $(x-1)^2 + 3y^2 = 1$ or $\frac{(x-1)^2}{1}+\frac{y^2}{1/3}=1$ ...(1)

Having its centre at (1, 0)

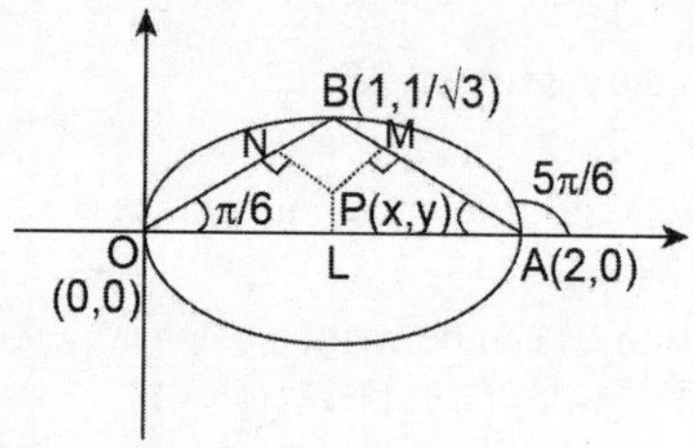

LP $\le$ min. {PN, PM}

1. (c) Clearly OAB is isosceles triangle

$\Rightarrow$ OB = AB

$\Rightarrow$ B must lie on perpendicular bisector of OA

$\Rightarrow$ B must be the upper end point of minor axis

$\Rightarrow \; B \equiv \left(1,\frac{1}{\sqrt{3}}\right)$ or $\left(1,-\frac{1}{\sqrt{3}}\right)$

2. (c) Now LP $\le$ min. {PN, PM}

$\Rightarrow \; y \le \min.\left\{\frac{\left|\frac{1}{\sqrt{3}}x-y\right|}{\frac{2}{\sqrt{3}}},\frac{\left|-\frac{1}{\sqrt{3}}x-y+\frac{2}{\sqrt{3}}\right|}{\frac{2}{\sqrt{3}}}\right\}$

$\Rightarrow \; y \le \min.\left\{\frac{\frac{1}{\sqrt{3}}x-y}{\left(\frac{2}{\sqrt{3}}\right)},\frac{-\frac{1}{\sqrt{3}}x-y+\frac{2}{\sqrt{3}}}{\left(\frac{2}{\sqrt{3}}\right)}\right\}$

$\Rightarrow \; y \le \min.\left\{\frac{1}{2}\left(x-\sqrt{3}y\right),\frac{1}{2}\left(-x-\sqrt{3}y+2\right)\right\}$

$\Rightarrow \; y \le \min.\left\{\frac{1}{2}x-\frac{\sqrt{3}}{2}y,\frac{-1x}{2}-\frac{\sqrt{3}}{2}y+1\right\}$

Now,

Case (i): $\frac{1}{2}x-\frac{\sqrt{3}}{2}y \le \frac{-x}{2}-\frac{\sqrt{3}}{2}y+1$

$\Rightarrow x \le 1$

$\therefore \quad y \le \frac{1}{2}x-\frac{\sqrt{3}}{2}y \quad \Rightarrow \quad \left(1+\frac{\sqrt{3}}{2}\right)y \le \frac{1}{2}x$

$\Rightarrow \; y \le \frac{1}{\left(\sqrt{3}+2\right)^x}$

$\Rightarrow y \le (2-\sqrt{3})x \qquad \Rightarrow y \le (\tan 15°)x$

Case (ii): $\frac{1}{2}x-\frac{\sqrt{3}}{2}y \geq -\frac{x}{2}-\frac{\sqrt{3}}{2}y+1$

$\Rightarrow \ x \geq 1$

$\therefore \quad y \leq \frac{-x}{2}-\frac{\sqrt{3}}{2}y+1 \text{ for } x \geq 1$

$\Rightarrow \quad \left(1+\frac{\sqrt{3}}{2}\right)y \leq \frac{-x}{2}+1$

$\Rightarrow \quad y \leq \frac{-1}{\left(\sqrt{3}+2\right)}x+\frac{2}{\left(\sqrt{3}+2\right)}$

$\Rightarrow \quad y \leq -\frac{\left(2-\sqrt{3}\right)x}{1}+\frac{2}{\sqrt{3}+2}$

$\Rightarrow \quad y \leq -(2 - \sqrt{3})x + 2(2 - \sqrt{3})$

$\Rightarrow \quad y \leq \tan(165°)x + (4 - 2\sqrt{3})$

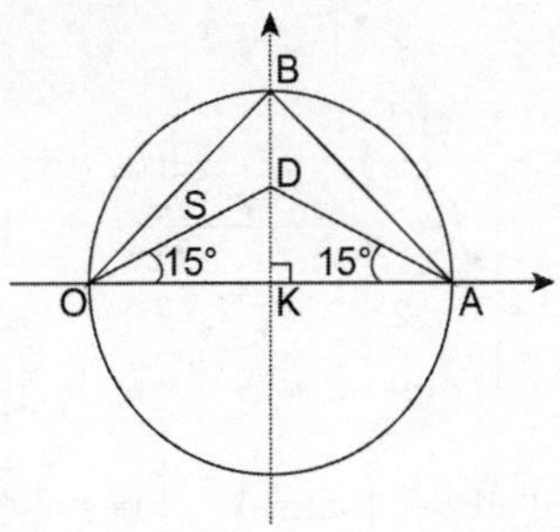

Which is same as given in option (c)

3. (a) Area of triangle represent by $S=\frac{1}{2}(OA).(DK)$

$= \quad \frac{1}{2}(2)(OK)\tan 15^\circ = (1)\ (2 - \sqrt{3}) = (2 - \sqrt{3})$ square unit

Passage-B:

4. (c) $\left(\frac{x}{a}\right)^{2/3}+\left(\frac{y}{a}\right)^{2/3}=1 \qquad \ldots(1)$

$\Rightarrow$ $x = a\cos 3t$, $y = a\sin 3t$ is the parametric equation of (1) and $a = 0$, $b = 2p$

$\therefore$ Required area

$=\frac{1}{2}\int_0^{2\pi}\left[a\cos^3 t+\left(3a\sin^2 t\cos t\right)-a\sin^3 t\left(-3a\cos^2 t\sin t\right)\right]$

$=\frac{3a^2}{2}\int_0^{2\pi}\left(\cos^4 t\sin^2 t+\sin^4 t\cos^2 t\right)dt \ = \ \frac{3a^2}{2}\int_0^{2\pi}\cos^2 t\sin^2 t\,dt$

$=\frac{3a^2}{8}\int_0^{2\pi}\sin^2 2t\,dt$

$=\frac{3a^2}{8}\int_0^{2\pi}\left[\frac{1-\cos 4t}{2}\right]dt \ = \ \frac{3a^2}{16}\left[t-\frac{\sin 4t}{4}\right]$

$=\frac{3a^2}{16}[2\pi]=\frac{3a^2\pi}{8}$ square units.

5. (b) $x = a(t - \sin t)$, $y = a(1 - \cos t)$

$\therefore$ Required area $= \int_0^{2\pi a} y\,dx$

$=\int_0^{2\pi} a(1-\cos t)a(1-\cos t)dt$

$=a^2\int_0^{2\pi}\left(1-2\cos t+\cos^2 t\right)dt$

$=a^2\int_0^{2\pi}\left[1-2\cos t+\frac{(1+\cos 2t)}{2}\right]dt$

$= \ \frac{3a^2}{2}[2\pi]-2a^2(0)+\frac{1}{4}a^2[\sin 2t]_0^{2\pi}$

$= 3a2p$ square units.

6. (a) $x=\frac{t}{3}(6-t)\ ;\ y=\frac{t^2}{8}(6-t)$

Required area

$=\frac{1}{2}\int_0^6\left\{\frac{t}{3}(6-t)\frac{1}{8}\left[12t-3t^2\right]-\frac{t^2}{8}(6-t)\frac{1}{3}[6-2t]\right\}dt$

$=\frac{1}{2}\int_0^6\left\{\frac{t}{8}(6-t)(4t-t^2)-\frac{t^2}{24}(6-t)(6-2t)\right\}dt$

$=\frac{1}{2}\int_0^6\left[\frac{1}{8}\left(t^3-10t^2+24t\right)t-\frac{t^2}{24}\left(2t^2-18t+36\right)\right]dt$

$=\frac{1}{16}\int_0^6\left(t^4-10t^3+24t^2\right)dt \ - \ \frac{1}{24}\int_0^6\left(t^4-9t^3+18t^2\right)dt$

$=\frac{1}{16}\left[\frac{t^5}{5}-\frac{10t^4}{4}-\frac{24t^3}{3}\right]_0^6-\frac{1}{24}\left[\frac{t^5}{5}-\frac{9t^4}{4}+\frac{18t^3}{3}\right]_0^6$

$=\left[(6)^5\left[\frac{1}{80}-\frac{1}{120}\right]+\left[\frac{9}{96}-\frac{10}{64}\right]\right](6)^4+\left(\frac{1}{2}-\frac{1}{4}\right)(6)^3$

$=(6)^5\left[\frac{1}{240}\right]+\left[\frac{9-15}{96}\right](6)^4+\left(\frac{1}{4}\right)(6)^3$

$=(6)^3\left[\frac{36}{240}-\frac{6}{16}+\frac{1}{4}\right]=(6)^3\left[\frac{6}{40}-\frac{3}{8}+\frac{1}{4}\right]$

$= \ (6)^3\left[\frac{6-15+10}{40}\right] \ = \ 216\times\frac{1}{40}=\frac{27}{5}$ square units.

7. (b) Given curve is $x = a\sin t$, $y = b\sin 2t$.

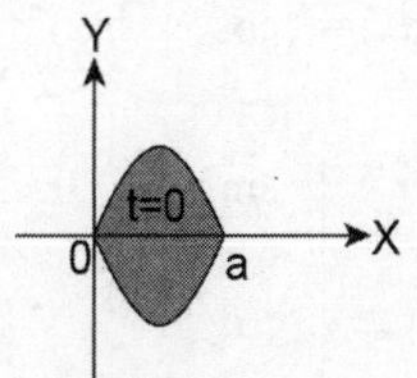

Required area $=\frac{1}{2}\int_0^{\pi}\left(x\frac{dy}{dx}-y\frac{dx}{dt}\right)dt$

$=\frac{1}{2}\int_0^{\pi}\left[(a\sin t)(2b\cos 2t)-b\sin 2ta\cos t\right]dt$

$=\frac{1}{2}\int_0^{\pi}\left[2ab\sin t\cos 2t-ab\sin 2t\cos t\right]dt$

$$= \frac{ab}{2}\int_0^{\pi}[\sin 3t + \sin(-t)]dt - \frac{ab}{4}\int_0^{\pi}[\sin 3t + \sin t]dt$$

$$= \left(\frac{ab}{2} - \frac{ab}{4}\right)\int_0^{\pi}\sin 3t\,dt + \left(-\frac{ab}{2} - \frac{ab}{4}\right)\int_0^{\pi}\sin t\,dt$$

$$= \frac{-ab}{12}[\cos 3t]_0^{\pi} + \frac{3ab}{4}[\cos t]_0^{\pi} = \frac{-ab}{12}[-1-1] + \frac{3ab}{4}[-1-1]$$

$$= \frac{ab}{6} - \frac{3ab}{2} = \left(\frac{1}{6} - \frac{3}{2}\right)ab$$

$$= \left[\frac{1-9}{6}\right]ab = \frac{-4}{3} \text{ square units}$$

8. (c) $x = \frac{C^2}{a}\cos^3 t,\ y = \frac{-C^2}{b}\sin^3 t$

Required area $= \frac{1}{2}\int_0^{2\pi}\left(x\frac{dy}{dx} - y\frac{dx}{dt}\right)dt$

$$= \frac{1}{2}\int_0^{2\pi}\left(\frac{C^2}{a}\cos^3 t\left(-\frac{C^2}{b}.3\sin^2 t\cos t\right) + \frac{C^2}{b}\sin^3 t\left(-3\frac{C^2}{a}\cos^2 t\sin t\right)\right)dt$$

$$= \frac{1}{2}\int_0^{2\pi}\left(-\frac{3C^4}{ab}\sin^2 t\cos^4 t - \frac{3C^4}{ab}\sin^4 t\cos^2 t\right)dt$$

$$= \frac{-3C^4}{2ab}\int_0^{2\pi}\sin^2 t\cos^2 t\,dt = \frac{-3C^4}{8ab}\int_0^{2\pi}\sin^2 2t\,dt$$

$$= \frac{-3C^4}{8ab}\int_0^{2\pi}\left(\frac{1-\cos 4t}{4}\right)dt = \frac{-3C^4}{16ab}\left[t - \frac{\sin 4t}{4}\right]_0^{2\pi}$$

$$= \frac{-3C^4}{16ab}[2\pi] = \frac{-3C^4\pi}{8ab}$$

Required area $= \frac{3C^4\pi}{8ab}$ (in magnitude)

$= \frac{3C^2(a^2-b^2)\pi}{8ab}$ (given)

$\Rightarrow C^2 = a^2 - b^2.$

Paragraph-C

$F(x) = \{\sin x\}$; $g(x) = \{\cos x\}$; $h(x) = \{x/\pi\}$

9. (a) $f(x) = \{\sin x\} = \begin{cases} \sin x, & 0 < x < \pi;\ x \neq \frac{\pi}{2} \\ 0; & x = \frac{\pi}{2}, \frac{3\pi}{2} \\ \sin x + 1; & \pi < x < 2\pi; x = \frac{3\pi}{2} \end{cases}$

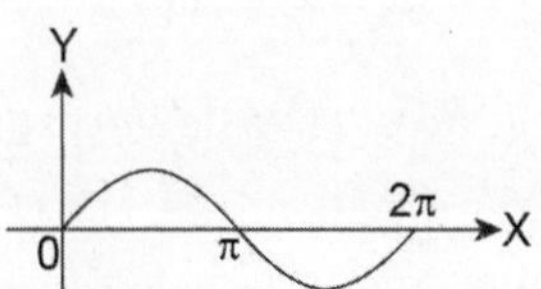

$$\therefore\quad t_1 = \int_0^{\pi/2}\sin x\,dt + \int_{\pi/2}^{\pi}\sin x\,dt = -[\cos x]_0^{\pi/2} = [\cos x]_{\pi/2}^{\pi}$$

$= -[0 - 1] - [-1 - 0] = 2$ square unit

And $t_2 = \int_{\pi}^{3\pi/2}(\sin x + 1)dx + \int_{3\pi/2}^{2\pi}(\sin x + 1)dx =$

$$-[\cos x]_{\pi}^{3\pi/2} + \frac{\pi}{2} - [\cos x]_{3\pi/2}^{2\pi} + \frac{\pi}{2}$$

$= -[0 - (-1)] + p - [1 - 0] = (\pi - 2)$ square unit

$$\therefore\quad \frac{t_2}{t_1} = \frac{\pi - 2}{2} = \frac{\pi}{2} - 1 \in \left(\frac{1}{2}, 1\right)$$

10. (a) $h(x) = [x/\pi] = \begin{cases} 0; & \text{for } 0 \le x < \pi \\ 1; & \text{for } \pi \le x < 2\pi \\ 2; & \text{for } x = 2\pi \end{cases}$

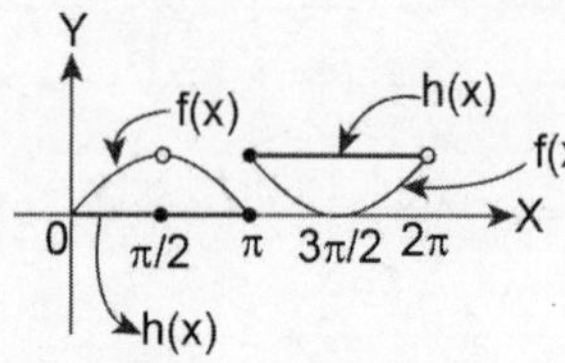

$$\therefore\quad \text{Required area} = \int_0^{\pi}\sin x\,dx = \int_{\pi}^{2\pi}(-\sin x)dx$$

$$= [-\cos x]_0^{\pi} = [1 + 1] = 2 \text{ square units}$$

11. (b) $g(x) = \{\cos x\} = \left\{-1 \text{ for } \pi < x < \frac{3\pi}{2}\right\}$

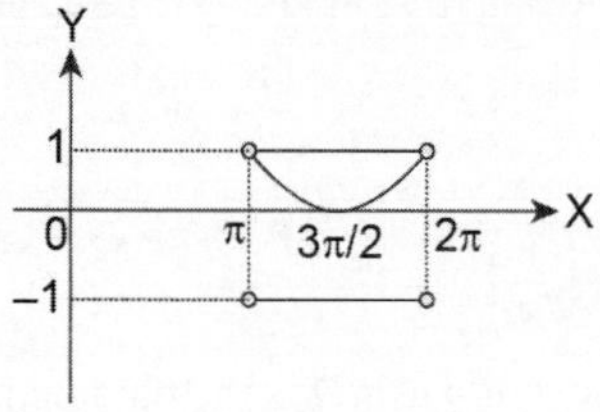

$$= \int_{\pi}^{3\pi/2}[1 + \sin x - (-1)]dx = \int_{\pi}^{3\pi/2}(2 + \sin x)dx$$

$= 2\left[\frac{\pi}{2}\right] + [-\cos]_{\pi}^{3\pi/2} = p - [0 - (-1)] = (\pi - 1)$

$= (\pi - 1)$ square units

Passage -D

C_1: $|x + y| \le 1$ …(i)

C_2: $|x - y| \le 1$ …(ii)

C_3: $|x| \le \frac{1}{2}$ …(iii)

C_4: $|y| \le \frac{1}{2}$ …(iv)

$C_5 : 3x^2 + 3y^2 = 1$

12. (b)

C_1: $-1 \le x + y \le 1 \Rightarrow -x - 1 \le y \le -x + 1$ …(v)

C_2: $-1 \le x - y \le 1 \Rightarrow -x - 1 \le -y \le -x + 1$ …(vi)

$\Rightarrow x-1 \le y \le x+1$

C_3: $-1/2 \le x \le 1/2$ ...(vii)

C_4: $-1/2 \le y \le 1/2$ ...(viii)

C_5: $x^2 + y^2 = 1/3$ ...(ix)

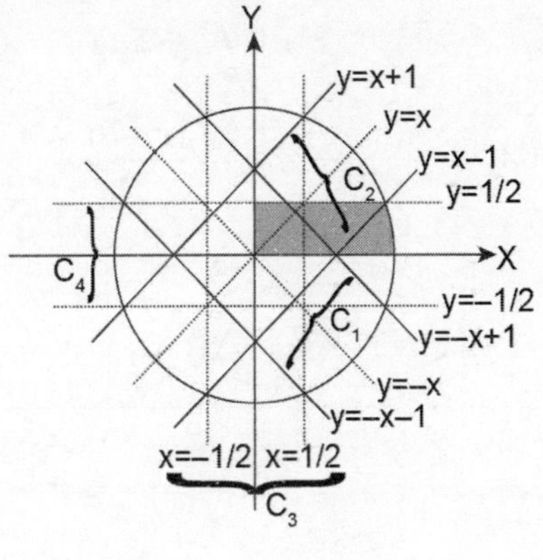

Required area = Area bounded by C_1 and C_2

$A_1 = 1/2\ (2)\ (2) = 2$ square units and area bounded C_3 and C_4

$A_2 = (1)\ (1) = 1$ square units

$\therefore \dfrac{A_1}{A_2} = \dfrac{2}{1} = 2$

13. (c) Area bounded by C_1 and C_2 which does not contains C_5.
$= 1/2\ (2)(2) - p\ (1/\sqrt{3})^2 = (2 - \pi/3)$ square units.

14. (a) Area bounded by C_1 and C_2 but not bounded by C_3 and C_4
$= 1/2\ (2)\ (2) - (1)\ (1) = (2 - 1) = 1$ square units.

Passage – E

$f(x) = \min. (|x-2|, |x+2|)$ and $g(x) = \min. (e^x, e^{-x})$ ...(1)

α is *a* roots of $e^{-x} + x - 2 = 0$ ...(2)

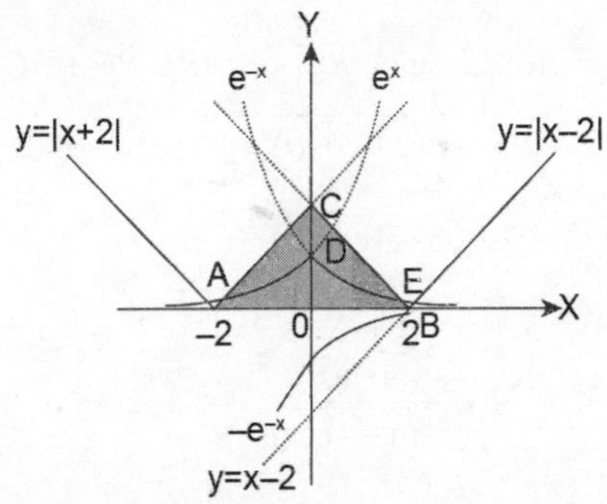

15. (b) Area bounded by $f(x)$ and x-axis = area of $\Delta ABC = 1/2\ (2)\ (4) = 4$ square units.

16. (c) $e^{-x} + x - 2 = 0 \Rightarrow e^{-x} = x - 2$

$\because -e^{-x} < 0 \qquad \Rightarrow x - 2 < 0$

$\Rightarrow x < 2$

At $x = 2$, $e^{-2} + 2 - 2 = e^{-2} > 0$.

At $x = 1$, $e^{-1} + 1 - 2 = e^{-1} - 1 < 0$

$\Rightarrow a \in (1, 2) \qquad \Rightarrow a \in (0, 2)$

17. (d) If $y = e^x$

$\Rightarrow y' = e^x > 0$ and for $y = x - 2$ or $x + 2$; $y' = 1$

$\therefore \dfrac{d}{dx}(e^x) > \dfrac{d}{dx}(x \pm 2)$ for $x > 0$

Area bounded by $f(x)$, $g(x)$, $x = 0$ in the first quadrant equals area ECD

At the point of intersection of $y = e^{-x}$ and $y = -x + 2$, $e^{-x} = -x + 2$

$\Rightarrow e^{-x} + x - 2 = 0$ whose one roots is $a \in (1, 2)$

$\therefore$ Required area $ECD = \displaystyle\int_0^{\alpha} \left(-x + 2 - e^{-x}\right) dx$

$= \left[-\dfrac{x^2}{2} + 2x + e^{-x}\right]_0^{\alpha} = -\dfrac{1}{2}\alpha^2 + 2\alpha + (e^{-\alpha} - 1)$

$= -\dfrac{1}{2}\alpha^2 + \left(e^{-\alpha} + \alpha - 2\right) + \alpha + 1 = -\dfrac{1}{2}\alpha^2 + \alpha + 1$

$= -\dfrac{1}{2}(2 - e^{-\alpha})^2 + (2 - e^{-\alpha}) + 1$

$= -\dfrac{1}{2}\left[4 + e^{-2\alpha} - 4e^{-\alpha}\right] + (2 - e^{-\alpha}) + 1$

$= -2 - \dfrac{1}{2}e^{-2\alpha} - 2e^{-\alpha} + 3 - e^{-\alpha} = -\dfrac{1}{2}e^{-2\alpha} + e^{-\alpha} + 1$

None of the given option correct.

Passage F:

18. (b) $A_1 = \displaystyle\int_0^{a} \left(\sin x - f(x)\right) dx = 1 + (a - 1)\cos a - \sin a$

$\Rightarrow \sin a - f(a) = (a - 1)(-\sin a) + \cos a - \cos a$

$\Rightarrow \sin a - f(a) = \sin a - a \sin a$

$\Rightarrow f(a) = a \sin a \qquad \Rightarrow f(x) = x \sin x$

19. (c) $A_2 = \displaystyle\int_a^{\pi} [f(x) - \sin x]\, dx = \int_a^{\pi} [x\sin x - \sin x]\, dx$

$= [-x\cos x]_a^{\pi} - \displaystyle\int_a^{\pi} [-1.\cos x]\, dx + [\cos x]_a^{\pi}$

$= -[\pi \cos p - a \cos a] + [0 - \sin a] - 1 - \cos a$

$= p + a \cos a - \sin a - 1 - \cos a$

For $a = 1$

$A_2 = (\pi - \sin^1 - 1)$ square units.

20. (c) $A_3 = \displaystyle\int_{\pi}^{2\pi} (\sin x - f(x))\, dx = [-\cos x]_{\pi}^{2\pi} - \int_{\pi}^{2\pi} x \sin x\, dx$

$-[1+1] - [|-\cos x|]_{\pi}^{2\pi} - \displaystyle\int_{\pi}^{2\pi} (-1.\cos x)\, dx$

$= -2 - [(-2p) - \pi] + [0 - 0] = (3p - 2)$ square units.

Passage –G:

A.T.Q.; $\displaystyle\int_2^{\alpha} \left(x^2 + 2 - f(x)\right) dx = (\alpha^3 - 4a^2 + 8)$

$\Rightarrow \alpha^2 + 2 - f(\alpha) = 3a^2 - 8a$

$\Rightarrow -f(\alpha) = 2a^2 - 8a - 2 \Rightarrow f(\alpha) = -2a^2 + 8a + 2$

$\Rightarrow f(x) = -2x^2 + 8x + 2$

21. **(b)** Required area = $\int_0^1 \left(-2x^2+8x+2\right)dx$

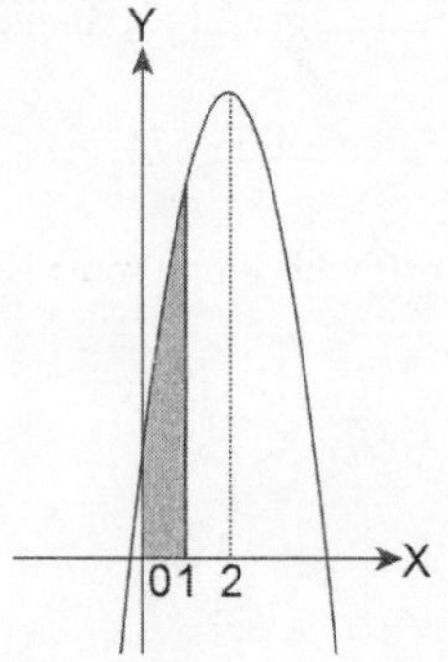

$=-2\left[\frac{x^3}{3}\right]_0^1+4\left[x^2\right]_0^1+2\left[x\right]_0^1=\frac{-2}{3}+4+2=\left(\frac{16}{3}\right)$ square units.

22. **(c)** $f(x) = -2x^2 + 8x + 2$; $f(x)$ is above axis for $x \in (p, q)$

$\Rightarrow$ p and q must be the roots of $f(x) = 0$

$\Rightarrow$ $p + q$ = sum of roots = $-8/-2 = 4$

23. **(d)** $y = x + 2$ and $y = -2x^2 + 8x + 2$ intersect each other, where $-2x^2 + 8x = x$.

$\Rightarrow$ $-x^2 + 7x = 0$

$\Rightarrow$ $2x^2 - 7x = 0$

$\Rightarrow$ $x(2x - 7) = 0$, i.e., at $x = 0$ and $x = 7/2$.

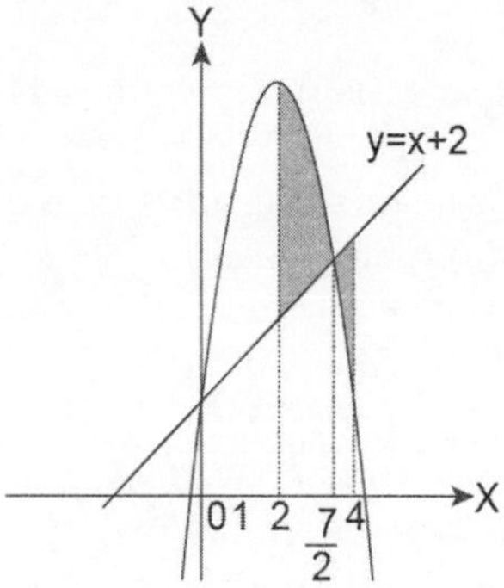

Required area = $\int_2^{7/2}\left[\left(-2x^2+8x+2\right)-\left(x+2\right)\right]dx$

$+\int_{7/2}^{4}\left[\left(x+2\right)\left(-2x^2+8x+2\right)\right]dx$

$=\left[-\frac{2}{3}x^3+4x^2+2x-\frac{x^2}{2}-2x\right]_2^{7/2}$

$+\left[\frac{x^2}{2}+2x+\frac{2}{3}x^3-4x^2-2x\right]_2^{7/2}$

$=\left[-\frac{2}{3}x^3+\frac{7}{2}x^2\right]_2^{7/2}+\left[\frac{2}{3}x^3-\frac{7}{2}x^2\right]_{7/2}^{4}$

$=-\frac{2}{3}\left(\frac{343}{8}-8\right)+\frac{7}{2}\left(\frac{49}{4}-4\right)+\frac{2}{3}\left(64-\frac{343}{8}\right)-\frac{7}{2}\left(16-\frac{49}{4}\right)$

$=-\frac{4}{3}\left(\frac{343}{8}\right)+7\left(\frac{49}{4}\right)+\frac{16}{3}-14+\frac{128}{3}-56$

$=-\frac{343}{6}+\frac{343}{4}+48-70$

$=343\left(\frac{1}{4}-\frac{1}{6}\right)-22=\frac{343}{12}-22=\frac{79}{12}$ square units.

Passage – H:

Area of sector $AOP = \frac{(\pi-\theta)}{2\pi}\times\pi r^2=\frac{(\pi-\theta)}{2}.r^2$ ...(1)

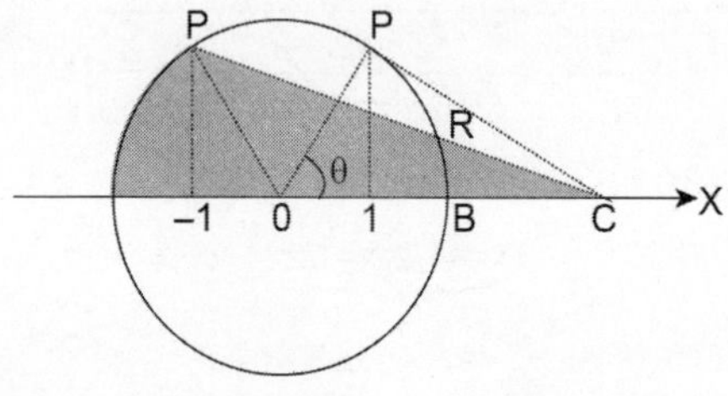

Area of ΔOPC = 1/2 $(OC) \times (OP \sin(\pi - \theta))$

= 1/2 (2) × (1 sin θ) = sinθ ...(2)

$\therefore$ R = (area of sector AOP) + (Area of ΔOPC)

$R(\theta)=\left(\frac{\pi-\theta}{2}\right).r^2+\sin\theta$

$\Rightarrow$ $R'(\theta)=\frac{1}{2}r^2(-1)+\cos\theta$

24. **(c)** For maximum value of θ, $R'(\theta) = 0$

$\Rightarrow$ $\cos\theta - 1/2r^2 = 0$

$\Rightarrow$ $\cos=\frac{1}{2}r^2=\frac{1}{2}$ ...(3)

And $R''(\theta) = -\sin\theta < 0$ for $q \in (0, \pi)$

$\therefore$ For $q \in (0, \pi)$, for which $\cos q = 1/2$ will be maximum and in given by R = for $q = \pi/3$.

25. **(d)** Perimeter of region $R = arc\,\widehat{AP} + PC + AC$

$=(\pi-\theta).r+\sqrt{(2-\cos\theta)^2+(\sin\theta)^2}+3$

$=(\pi-\theta)+\sqrt{5-4\cos\theta}+3$

$\Rightarrow$ $P(\theta) = 3 + p - q + \sqrt{5-4\cos\theta}$

$\Rightarrow$ $P'(\theta)=-1+\frac{4\sin\theta}{2\sqrt{5-4\cos\theta}}$

$\therefore$ $P'(\theta) = 0$ $\Rightarrow$ $\frac{2\sin\theta}{\sqrt{5-4\cos\theta}}=1$

$\Rightarrow$ $2\sin\theta=\sqrt{5-4\cos\theta}$

$\Rightarrow$ $4\sin 2q = 5 - 4\cos\theta$

$\Rightarrow$ $4(1 - \cos 2q) = 5 - 4\cos\theta$

$\Rightarrow$ $4\cos 2q - 4\cos q + 1 = 0$

$\Rightarrow$ $(2\cos\theta - 1)^2 = 0$ $\Rightarrow$ $\cos\theta = 1/2$

$\Rightarrow$ $q = \pi/3$.

$\therefore$ For $\pi/3$, $P(\theta)=3+\pi-\frac{\pi}{3}+\sqrt{5-2}=3+\frac{2\pi}{3}+\sqrt{3}$

But for $q = \pi$, P will be at A

$\Rightarrow$ $(\pi-\pi)+\sqrt{5-4\cos\pi}+3=6\,\text{units}$

26. (b) $R(\theta) = \frac{1}{2}r^2(\pi - \theta_1) + \sin\theta_1$ ...(1)

And $P(\theta) = 3 + (\pi - \theta) + \sqrt{5 - 4\cos\theta}$ ...(2)

$R'(\theta) = \frac{1}{2}r^2(-1) + \cos\theta_1 = \cos\theta_1 - \frac{1}{2}r^2$ ...(3)

And $P'(\theta) = (-1) + \frac{4\sin\theta}{2\sqrt{5-4\cos\theta}}$

$P'(\theta) = \frac{2\sin\theta}{\sqrt{5-4\cos\theta}} - 1$ ...(4)

Tangent will be parallel, if $\cos\theta_1 - \frac{1}{2}r^2 = \frac{2\sin\theta}{\sqrt{5-4\cos\theta}} - 1$

Here $r = 1$ $\Rightarrow$ $\cos\theta_1 - \frac{2\sin\theta}{\sqrt{5-4\cos\theta}} = \frac{-1}{2}$

At $\theta_1 = q = \pi/3$

$\Rightarrow$ $\cos\theta_1 - \frac{2\sin\theta}{\sqrt{5-4\cos\theta}} = \frac{1}{2} - \frac{2\frac{\sqrt{3}}{2}}{\sqrt{3}} = \frac{-1}{2}$

$\therefore$ At $\theta_1 = q = \pi/3$, $R(\theta)$ and $P(\theta)$ have parallel tangents. Thus, tangent to two graphs are parallel at, at least one point.

SECTION–VI (MATRIX MATCH)

1. (i) – (b); (ii) → (d); (iii) → (a); (iv) → (c)

(i) At the point of intersection in first quadrant, $2 - x = x^2$

$\Rightarrow$ $x^2 + x - 2 = 0$

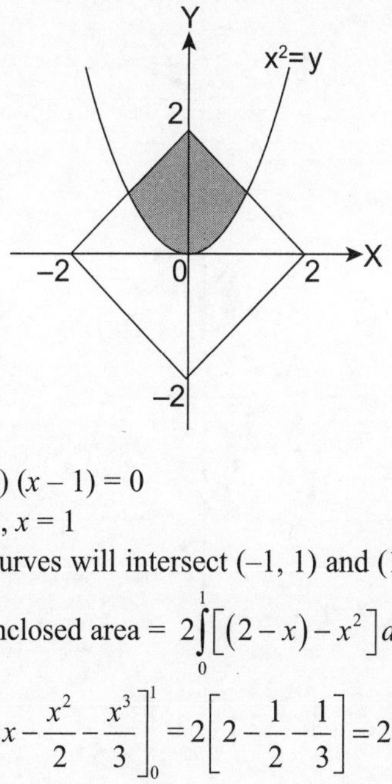

$\Rightarrow$ $(x + 2)(x - 1) = 0$

$\Rightarrow$ $x = -2, x = 1$

$\therefore$ Two curves will intersect (–1, 1) and (1, 1)

$\therefore$ The enclosed area $= 2\int_0^1 \left[(2-x) - x^2\right]dx$

$= 2\left[2x - \frac{x^2}{2} - \frac{x^3}{3}\right]_0^1 = 2\left[2 - \frac{1}{2} - \frac{1}{3}\right] = 2\left(\frac{7}{6}\right) = \frac{7}{3}$ square units.

(ii) $f(x) = 3\sin x - 4\cos x - 7/3$

Max. value of $f(x) = \sqrt{(3)^2 + (-4)^2} - \frac{7}{3} = 5 - \frac{7}{3} = \frac{8}{3}$

(iii) $\Delta AC_1D \sim \Delta C_2C_1A$

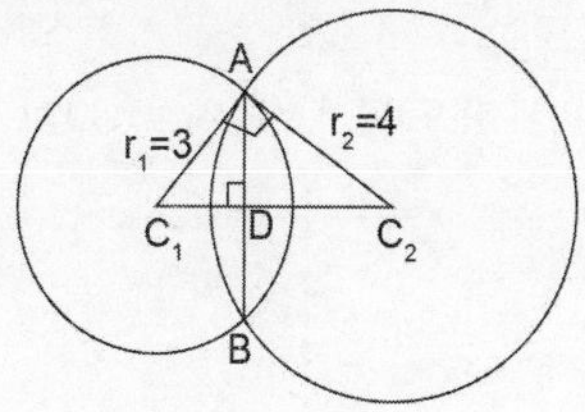

$\Rightarrow$ $\frac{AC_1}{C_2C_1} = \frac{C_1D}{C_1A} = \frac{AD}{C_2A}$ $\Rightarrow$ $\frac{3}{5} = \frac{C_1D}{3} = \frac{AD}{4}$

$\Rightarrow$ $C_1D = 9/5$; $AD = 12/5$

$\Rightarrow$ $AB = 2AD = 24/5$

(iv) Equation of AB is $\frac{x-0}{\cos 60°} = \frac{y-0}{\sin 60°} = r$

$\Rightarrow$ $x = r\cos 60°, y = r\sin 60°$

$\Rightarrow$ $x = \frac{r}{2}, y = \frac{\sqrt{3}r}{2}$

If it lies on parabola, i.e., A or B, then it will satisfy $y^2 = 4(x + 1)$

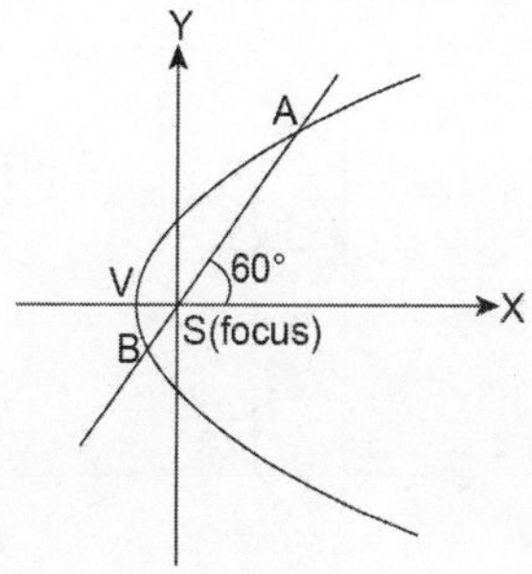

$\Rightarrow$ $\frac{3r^2}{2} = 4\left(\frac{r}{2} + 1\right)$

$\Rightarrow$ $3r^2 = 8(r + 2)$

$\Rightarrow$ $3r^2 - 8r - 16 = 0$

$\Rightarrow$ $3r^2 - 12r + 4r - 16 = 0$

$\Rightarrow$ $3r(r - 4) + 4(r - 4) = 0$

$\Rightarrow$ $(3r + 4)(r - 4) = 0$

$\Rightarrow$ $r = -4/3$ or $r = 4$

$\therefore$ Length of chord AB $= \left|\frac{-4}{3}\right| + 4 = \frac{4}{3} + 4 = \frac{16}{3}$ units

2. (i) →(a); (ii) → (a); (iii) → (c); (iv) → (d)

(i) Area bounded by $f(x)$ and $f^{-1}(x)$ for $x \in [0, 2p]$ =

$4\int_0^{\pi}(x + \sin x - x)dx$

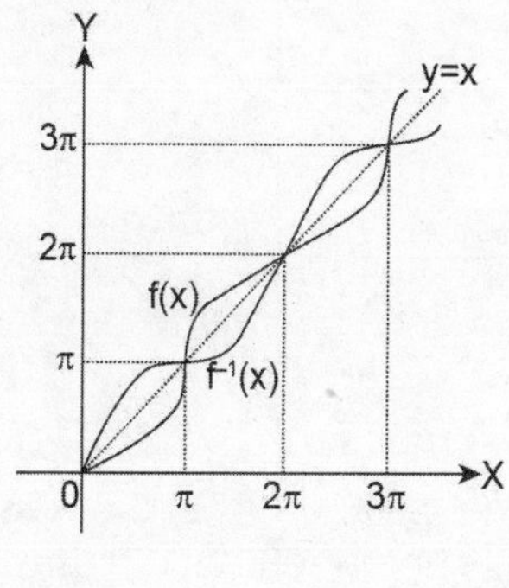

$= 4[-\cos x]_0^{\pi} = 4[-1-1] = 8 = 4s$ (given)

$\Rightarrow s = 2$

(ii) Given curve are $y = x.e^{|x|}$; $|x| = 1$, $y = 0$

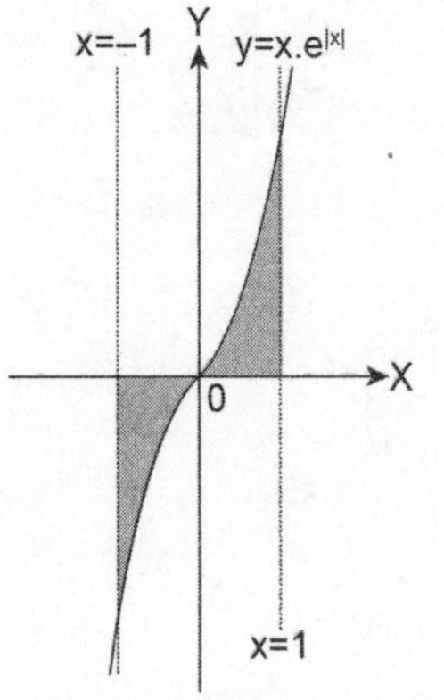

$\therefore$ Required $= 2\int_0^1 xe^x dx = 2\left[|xe^x|_0^1 - \int_0^1 1.e^x dx\right]$

$= 2[e - (e - 1)] = 2$ square units

(iii) Given curves are $y^2 = x^3$ and $|y| = 2x$

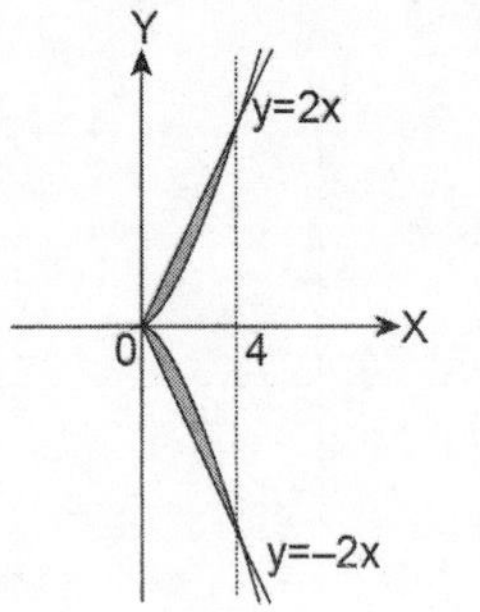

At the point of intersection of $y = 2x$ and $y = e^{3/2}$ is $2x = x^{3/2}$

$\Rightarrow 4x^2 = x^3$

$\Rightarrow x^2(4 - x) \qquad \Rightarrow x = 0, x = 4$

$\therefore \quad 2\int_0^4 \left(2x - x^{3/2}\right)dx = 2\left[x^2 - \frac{2x^{5/2}}{5}\right]_0^4 = 2\left[16 - \frac{2}{5}(32)\right]$

$= 2\left[\frac{80-64}{5}\right] = \frac{32}{5}$ square units.

(iv) Required area $= 2\int_0^1 \left[(1-x) - \left(1-\sqrt{x}\right)^2\right]dx$

$= 2\int_0^1 \left[(1-x) - (1+x-2\sqrt{x})\right]dx = 2\int_0^1 \left(-2x + 2\sqrt{x}\right)dx$

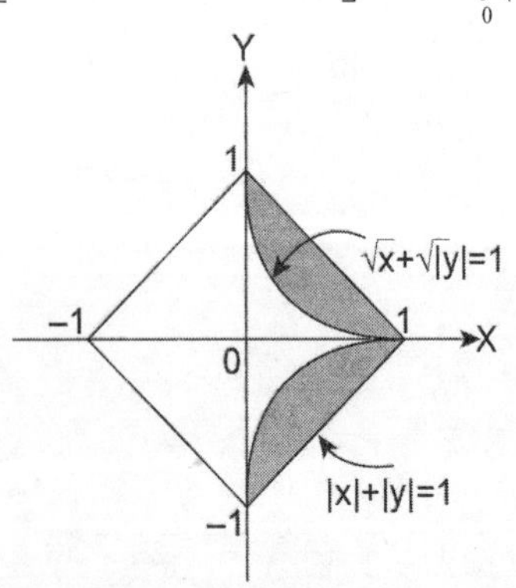

$= 2\left[-x^2 + 2(x)^{3/2}\left(\frac{2}{3}\right)\right]_0^1 = 2\left[-1 + \frac{4}{3}\right] = \frac{2}{3}$

3. (i) → (b); (ii) → (b); (iii) → (c); (iv) → (c)

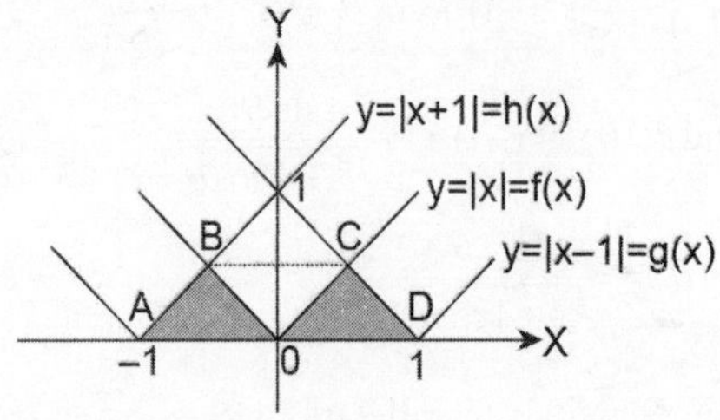

(i) Area bounded by min. $f(x)$, $g(x)$ and x-axis = area of $\Delta OCD\left(\frac{1}{2}(1)\times\frac{1}{2}\right) = \frac{1}{4}$ square units.

(ii) Area bounded by min. $(f(x), h(x))$ = area of ΔAOB = $\frac{1}{2}\times 1\times\frac{1}{2} = \frac{1}{4}$ square units

(iii) Area bounded by min. $(f(x), g(x), h(x))$ = area of ΔAOB + area of $\Delta OCD = \left(\frac{1}{4}+\frac{1}{4}\right) = \frac{1}{2}$ square units

(iv) Area bounded by min. $(f(x), g(x), h(x))$, x-axis and $y = 1/2$ = area of ΔAOB + area of ΔOCD

$= \frac{1}{4} + \frac{1}{4} = \frac{1}{2}$ square units

4. (i) → (b); (ii) → (c); (iii) →(a), (c); (iv) → (d)

(i) $y = -3x^2 - |x| + 2 = \begin{cases} -3x^2 - x + 2 \text{ for } x \geq 0 \\ -3x^2 + x + 2 \text{ for } x < 0 \end{cases}$ and $y = 0$

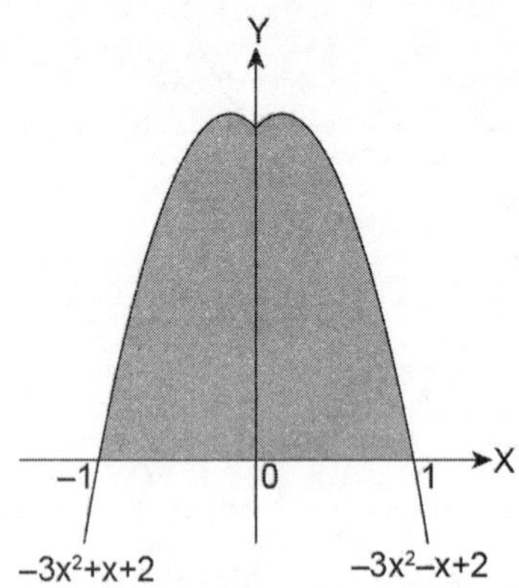

Bounded area $= 2\int_0^{2/3} \left(-3x^2 - x + 2\right)dx$

$= 2\left\{(-3)\left[\frac{x^3}{3}\right]_0^{2/3} - \left[\frac{x^2}{2}\right]_0^{2/3} + 2[x]_0^{2/3}\right\}$

$= 2\left\{-\left[\frac{8}{27}\right] - \frac{1}{2}\left[\frac{4}{9}\right] + 2\left(\frac{2}{3}\right)\right\}$

$$= -\frac{16}{27} - \frac{4}{9} + \frac{8}{3} = \frac{-16-12+72}{27} = \frac{44}{27} = \frac{44}{a^3}$$

$\Rightarrow a = 3$

(ii) In, $m = \int \frac{\sin^n x}{\cos^m x} dx$; $m \neq 1$,

$$= \int \underbrace{\cos^{-m} x . \sin x}_{II} . \underbrace{\sin^{n-1} x}_{I} dx$$

$$= -\sin^{-1} x . \int -\cos^{-m} \sin x \, dx$$

$$+ \int (n-1)\sin^{n-2} x \cos x . \frac{(\cos x)^{-m+1}}{(-m+1)} dx$$

$$= \left(\sin^{n-1} x\right)\left[\frac{(\cos x)^{-m+1}}{-m+1}\right] - \frac{(n-1)}{(m-1)}\left[\frac{(\sin x)^{n-2}}{(\cos x)^{m-2}} dx\right]$$

$$= \frac{\sin^{n-1} x}{(m-1)\cos^{m-1} x} - \frac{n-1}{m-1} . I_{n-2,m-2}$$

$\Rightarrow$ a/2 = –1 $\qquad \Rightarrow a = -2$

(iii) $f(x) = x - x^2$; $g(x) = ax$;

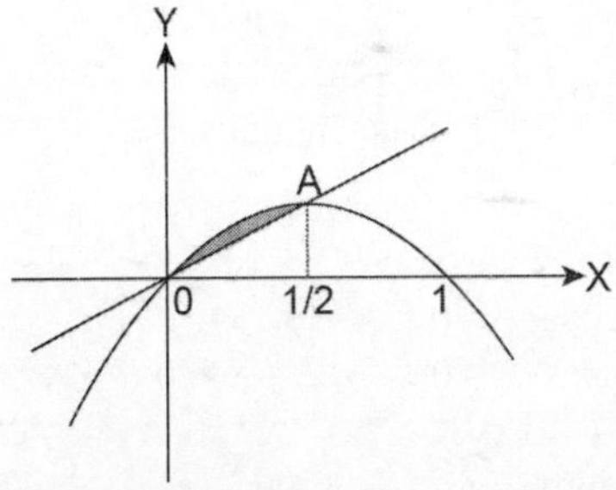

Area bounded = $\int_0^{1-a} \left[ax - (x - x^2)\right] dx = \pm\frac{9}{2}$

$\because$ At the point of intersection, $ax = x - x^2$

$\Rightarrow x^2 + (a-1)x = 0$

$\Rightarrow x = 0$ or $x = 1 - a$

$$\Rightarrow \left[(a-1)\frac{x^2}{2} + \frac{x^3}{3}\right]_0^{1-a} = \pm\frac{9}{2}$$

$$\Rightarrow \frac{(a-1)}{2}\left[(1-a)^2\right] + \frac{1}{3}(1-a)^3 = \pm\frac{9}{2}$$

$$\Rightarrow \frac{-1}{6}(1-a)^3 = \pm\frac{9}{2}$$

$\Rightarrow (1-a)^3 = \pm 27$

$\Rightarrow (1-a) = \pm 3 \qquad \Rightarrow a = 4$ or $a = -2$

(iv) $f_n(x) = \int \cot^n(x)\, dx \quad \Rightarrow \quad f_n(x) = \int \cot^{n-2} x . \left(\cot^2 x\right) dx$

$$\Rightarrow \int \left(\cot^{n-2} x\right)\left(\text{cosec}^2 x - 1\right) dx$$

$$= \int (\cot x)^{n-2} \text{cosec}^2 x \, dx - \int \cot x^{n-2} x dx$$

$$= -\frac{(\cot x)^{n-1}}{n-1} - \int \cot^{n-2} x \, dx = -\frac{1}{(n-1)}(\cot x)^{n-1} - f_{n-2}(x)$$

$$\Rightarrow f_n(x) + f_{n-2}(x) = \frac{-1}{(n-1)}(\cot x)^{n-2}$$

$$\Rightarrow f_4(x) + f_2(x) = \frac{-1}{3}(\cot x)^3$$

$$\Rightarrow 3\left(f_4\left(\frac{3\pi}{4}\right) + f_2\left(\frac{3\pi}{4}\right)\right) = -\left(\cot\frac{3\pi}{4}\right)^3 = 1$$

5. (i) → (d); (ii) → (a); (iii) → (b); (iv) → (c)

(i) Required area = $2\int_0^1 \left(\frac{2}{1+x^2} - x^2\right) dx$

$$= 4\left[\tan^{-1} x\right]_0^1 - \frac{2}{3}\left[x^3\right]_0^1 = 4\left(\frac{\pi}{4} - 0\right) - \frac{2}{3} = \left(\pi - \frac{2}{3}\right)$$

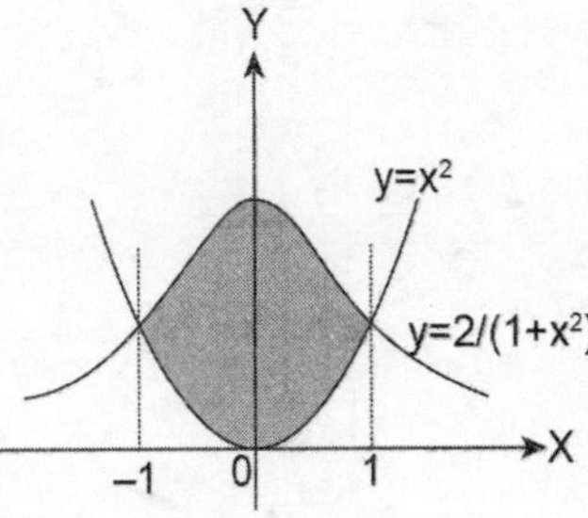

(ii) At the point of intersection, $x = 16a$, $y = 16a$, i.e., $A \equiv (16a, 16a)$

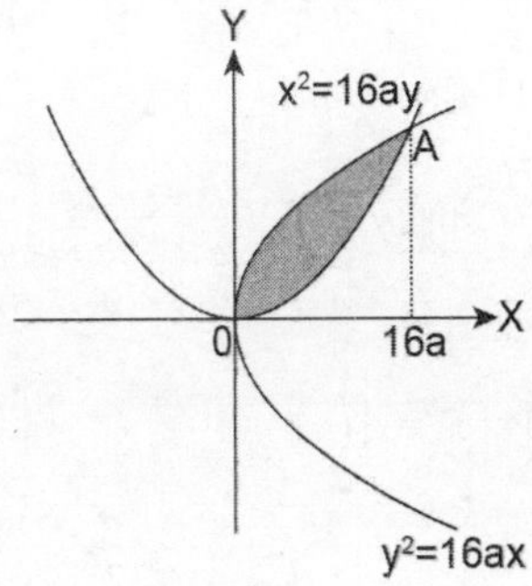

$\therefore$ Required area = $2\int_0^{16a} \left(4\sqrt{a}\sqrt{x} - x\right) dx$

$$= \left[8\sqrt{a}\frac{(x)^{3/2}}{3/2}\right]_0^{16a} - \frac{2}{2}\left[x^2\right]_0^{16a}$$

$$= 8\sqrt{a} . \frac{2}{3}(64)a\sqrt{a} - \left(256a^2\right)$$

$$= \left(\frac{1024}{3} - 256\right)a^2 = \left(\frac{1024 - 768}{3}\right)a^2 = \frac{256}{3}a^2$$

(iii) $xy^2 = a^2(a - x)$, curve is symmetric about x-axis. On x-axis, $x = a$ and $y = \pm a\sqrt{\frac{a-x}{x}}$

For y to be real, $\frac{a-x}{x} \geq 0$

$\Rightarrow x \in (0, a]$ for $y > 0$, $y = a\sqrt{\frac{a-x}{x}}$

$$\Rightarrow y' = a\left(\frac{1}{2}\right)\sqrt{\frac{x}{a-x}}\left(-\frac{a}{x^2} - 1\right)$$

$\Rightarrow\ y' = \frac{-a}{2}\sqrt{\frac{x}{a-x}}\left(\frac{a+x^2}{x^2}\right)$

$\Rightarrow\ y' < 0$ for $x \to (0, a]$ and $y' \to \mu$ at $x \to a^-$.

Also $y = \pm a\sqrt{\frac{a-x}{x}}$. As $x \to 0^+, y \to \pm\infty$

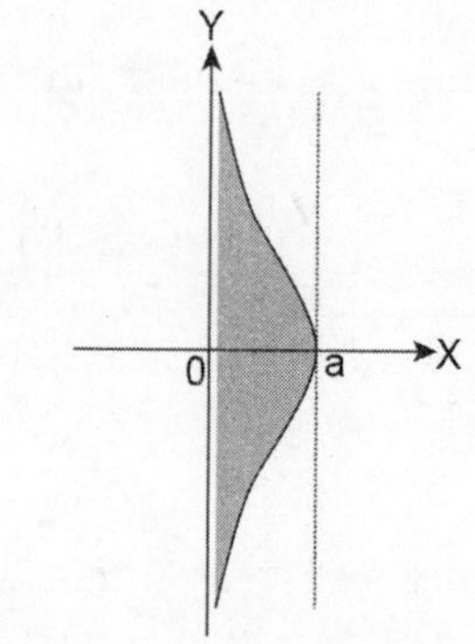

$\therefore$ Required area $= 2\int_0^a a\sqrt{\frac{a-x}{x}}\,dx$

Put $x = a$ sin2q, $dx = 2a$ sinθ cosθ dθ

$\Rightarrow\ 2\int_0^{\pi/2} a.\sqrt{\frac{a(\cos^2\theta)}{a\sin^2\theta}}.(2a\sin\theta\cos\theta)d\theta = 4a^2\int_0^{\pi/2}\cos^2\theta\,d\theta$

$= 2a^2\int_0^{\pi/2}(1+\cos^2\theta)d\theta$

$= 2a^2\left[\theta + \frac{\sin 2\theta}{2}\right]_0^{\pi/2} = 2a^2\left[\frac{\pi}{2}\right] = a^2\pi$

(iv) Required area $= \int_0^1 (x^2+2+x)dx = \left[\frac{x^3}{3} + 2x + \frac{x^2}{2}\right]_0^1$

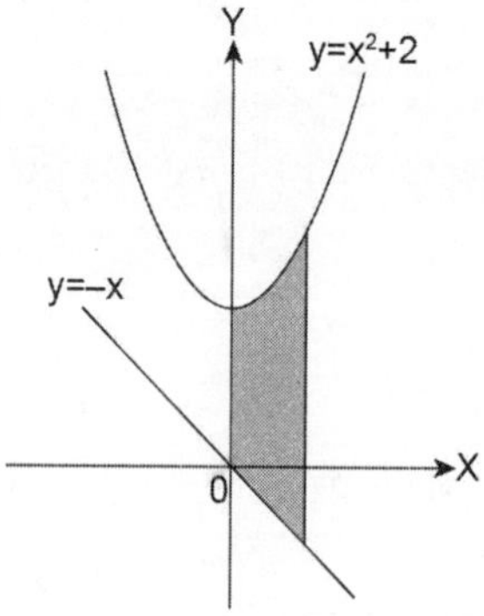

$= \frac{1}{3} + 2 + \frac{1}{2} = \frac{17}{6}$ square units.

6. (i) → (d); (ii) → (c); (iii) → (b); (iv) → (a)

(i) $f(x) = \max.(\sin x, \cos x);\ 0 \le x \le \pi/2$

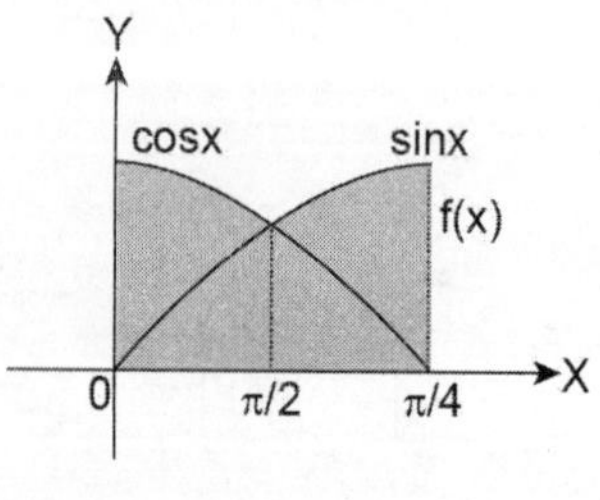

Required bounded area $= \int_0^{\pi/4}\cos x\,dx + \int_{\pi/4}^{\pi/2}\sin x\,dx =$ $[\sin x]_0^{\pi/4} - [\cos x]_{\pi/4}^{\pi/2}$

$= \left[\frac{1}{\sqrt{2}} - 0\right] - \left[0 - \frac{1}{\sqrt{2}}\right] = \sqrt{2}$

(ii) Required bounded area $= 4\int_0^{\pi}(x + \sin x - x)dx$

$= 4\int_0^{\pi}\sin x\,dx = -4[\cos x]_0^{\pi}$

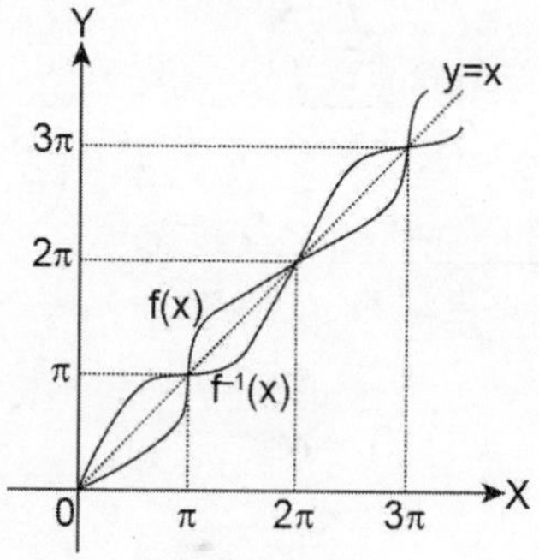

$= -4[-1 - 1] = 8$ square units.

(iii) Given curve is $y^2 = x^2(1 - x^2)$ it is symmetric about x-axis and y-axis.

On x-axis, $y = 0$ $\Rightarrow\ x = 0, \pm 1$

On y-axis, $x = 0$ $\Rightarrow\ y = 0$

Also $y = \pm x\sqrt{1-x^2}$

For y to be real, $1 - x^2 \ge 0$

$\Rightarrow\ x \in [-1, 1]$

For, $y \ge 0$, i.e., $x \in [0, 1]$ and $y = x\sqrt{1-x^2}$

$\Rightarrow\ y' = x.\frac{1}{2\sqrt{1-x^2}}(-2x) + \sqrt{1-x^2}$

$\Rightarrow\ y' = \frac{-x^2+1-x^2}{\sqrt{1-x^2}} = \frac{1-2x^2}{\sqrt{1-x^2}}$

$\Rightarrow\ y' = 0$ at $x = 1/\sqrt{2}$, $y' \to -\infty$ as $x \to 1^-$ and $y' > 0$ for $x \in \left(0, \frac{1}{\sqrt{2}}\right)$ and $y' < 0$ for $x \in \left(\frac{1}{\sqrt{2}}, 1\right)$

$\Rightarrow\ y(0) = 0,\ y(\pm 1) = 0,\ y\left(\pm\frac{1}{\sqrt{2}}\right) = \pm\frac{1}{2}$

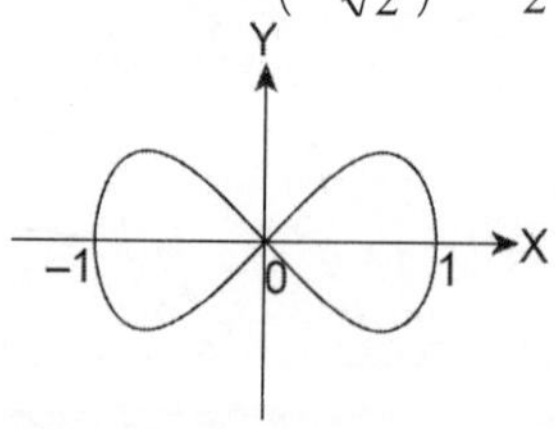

$\therefore$ Required area $= 4\int_0^1 x\sqrt{1-x^2}\,dx = \frac{-4}{2}\int_0^1 -2x(1-x^2)^{1/2}\,dx$

$= \frac{-4}{2}\left[\frac{2}{3}(1-x^2)^{3/2}\right]_0^1 = \frac{-4}{3}[0-1] = \frac{4}{3}$ square units

(iv) $\frac{y}{x} = \ln x$ and $\frac{y}{2} = -x^2 + x$ or $y = x\ln x$ and $y = -2x^2 + 2x$

For bounded area $x > 0$

Now $\lim_{x\to 0^+} x\ln x = \lim_{x\to 0^+}\left(\frac{\ln x}{1/x}\right) = 0$ and $y' = 1 + \ln x > 0$

for $x \in \left(\frac{1}{e}, \infty\right)$ and $y' < 0$ for $x \in \left(0, \frac{1}{e}\right)$; $y' = 0$ at $x =$ 1/e

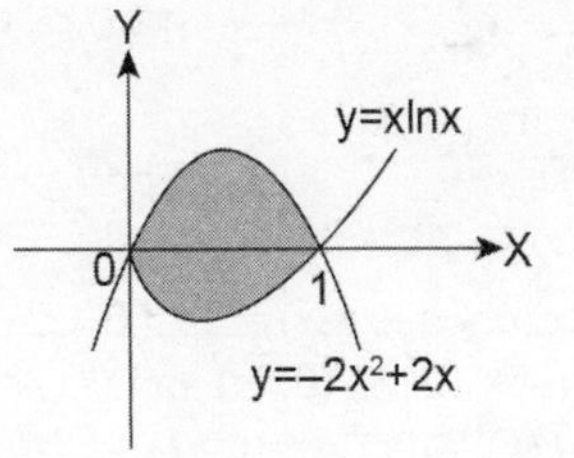

$\therefore$ Required area $= \int_0^1 \left(-2x^2 + 2x - x\ln x\right)dx$

$$= \frac{-2}{3}\left[x^3\right]_0^1 + \left[x^2\right]_0^1 - \left[\left|\ln x.\frac{x^2}{2}\right|_0^1 - \int_0^1 \frac{1}{x}.\frac{x^2}{2}dx\right]$$

$$= \frac{-2}{3} + 1 - \left[0 - \frac{1}{2}\left[\frac{x^2}{x}\right]_0^1\right] = \frac{1}{3} + \frac{1}{4} = \frac{7}{12} \text{ square units}$$

SECTION–VIII (INTEGER TYPE QUESTIONS)

1. Given curve is $y^2 = x^2(4 - x^2)$ the curve is symmetric about x and y-axis and $y = \pm x\sqrt{4 - x^2}$

$\Rightarrow$ y is real for $x \in [-2, 2]$ and for $x \in [0, 2]$; $y > 0$ and $y = x\sqrt{4 - x^2}$

$$\Rightarrow y' = x.\frac{1}{2\sqrt{4 - x^2}}(-2x) + \sqrt{4 - x^2}$$

$$\Rightarrow y' = \frac{-x^2 + \left(\sqrt{4 - x^2}\right)^2}{\sqrt{4 - x^2}}$$

$$\Rightarrow y' = \frac{4 - 2x^2}{\sqrt{4 - x^2}} = \frac{2(2 - x^2)}{\sqrt{4 - x^2}}$$

$\Rightarrow$ $y' = 0$ at $x = \sqrt{2}$ and $y' < 0$ for $x \in (\sqrt{2}, 1]$ and $y' > 0$ for $x \in [0, \sqrt{2})$ and $y' = 0$ at $x = \sqrt{2}$

On x-axis, $x = 0$ or ± 2; On y-axis, $y = 0$

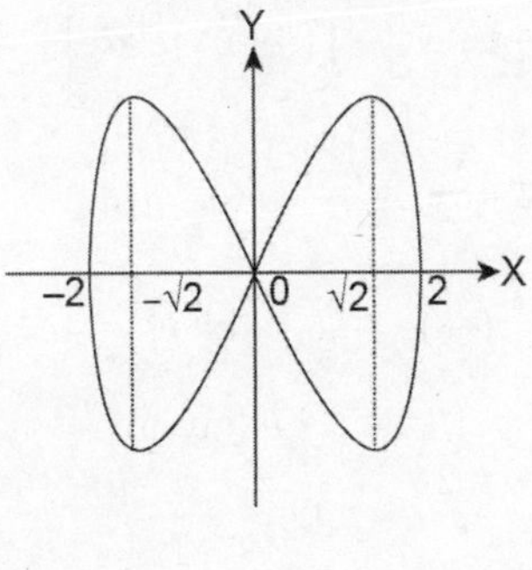

Area of one loop $A = 2\int_0^2 x\sqrt{4 - x^2}\,dx = -\int_0^2 -2x\left(4 - x^2\right)^{1/2}dx$

$$= \frac{-2}{3}\left[\left(4 - x^2\right)^{3/2}\right]_0^2 = -\frac{2}{3}[0 - 8] = \frac{16}{3}$$

$\Rightarrow$ $3A = 16$

2. $y = \sqrt{x - [x]}$

For $x \in (1, 3/2)$; $[x] = 1$

$\Rightarrow$ $y = \sqrt{x - 1}$ $\Rightarrow$ $x \in [1, \infty)$

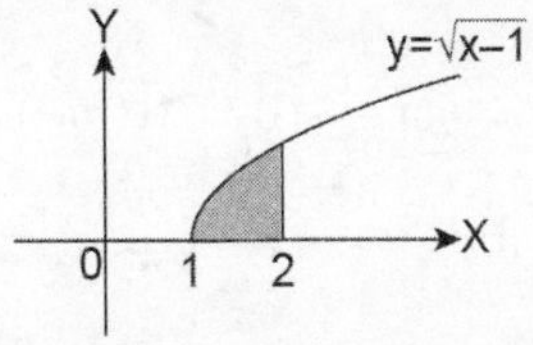

$\therefore$ Required bounded area $= \int_1^{3/2} \sqrt{x - 1}\,dx$

$$= \left[\frac{2}{3}(x - 1)^{3/2}\right]_1^{3/2} = \frac{2}{3}\left[\frac{1}{2\sqrt{2}}\right] = \frac{1}{3\sqrt{2}} = \frac{1}{\sqrt{k}} \text{ (given)}$$

$\Rightarrow$ $k = 2$

3. A.T.Q., $\dfrac{\int_{1/2}^{2/3}[1 - (3x - 1)]dx}{\left(\frac{1}{2}\right)(1) - \int_{1/2}^{2/3}[1 - (3x - 1)]dx} = \dfrac{1}{b}$

$$\Rightarrow \frac{2\left(\frac{2}{3} - \frac{1}{2}\right) - \frac{3}{2}\left(\frac{4}{9} - \frac{1}{4}\right)}{\frac{1}{2} - \left[2\left(\frac{2}{3} - \frac{1}{2}\right) - \frac{3}{2}\left(\frac{4}{9} - \frac{1}{4}\right)\right]} = \frac{1}{b}$$

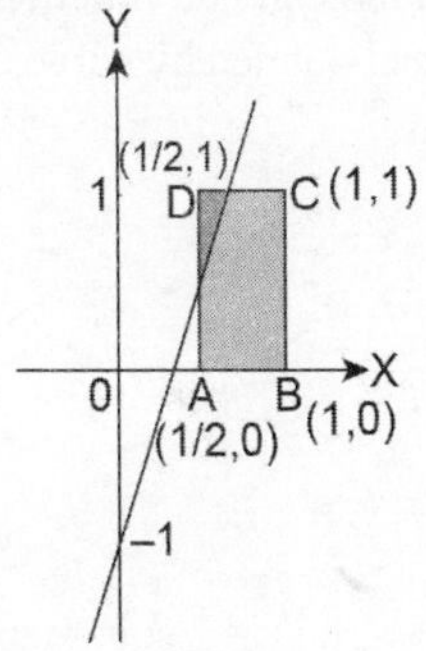

$$\Rightarrow \frac{2\left(\frac{4 - 3}{6}\right) - 3\left(\frac{16 - 9}{36}\right)}{\frac{1}{2} - \left[2\left(\frac{4 - 3}{6}\right) - \frac{3}{2}\left(\frac{16 - 9}{36}\right)\right]} = \frac{1}{b}$$

$$\Rightarrow \frac{\frac{1}{3} - \frac{7}{24}}{\frac{1}{2} - \left[\frac{1}{3} - \frac{7}{24}\right]} = \frac{1}{b} \quad \Rightarrow \frac{1/24}{\left(\frac{1}{2} - \frac{1}{24}\right)} = \frac{1}{b}$$

$$\Rightarrow \frac{1}{24} \times \frac{24}{11} = \frac{1}{b} \quad \Rightarrow b = 11$$

4. $y=\sqrt{\sin[x]+[\sin x]}$

For $x \in [1, \pi/2)$; $[x] = 1$ and $[\sin x] = 0$

$\Rightarrow \quad y=\sqrt{\sin 1+0} \qquad \Rightarrow \quad y=\sqrt{\sin 1}$

$\therefore$ Bounded area $= \int_1^{\pi/2} \sqrt{\sin 1}dx = \sqrt{\sin 1}\left(\frac{\pi}{2}-1\right)$

$\Rightarrow k = 1$

5. Given curve is $y = xe^{\frac{-x^2}{2}}$

As $x \to +\infty$, $y = \lim_{x\to\infty} xe^{-\frac{x^2}{2}} = \lim_{x\to\infty} \frac{x}{e^{\frac{x^2}{2}}} = \lim_{x\to\infty} \frac{1}{xe^{\frac{x^2}{2}}} = 0^+$ and

$y = \lim_{x\to-\infty} xe^{-\frac{x^2}{2}} = \lim_{x\to-\infty} \frac{x}{e^{\frac{x^2}{2}}}$ (By L.H. rule)

$= \lim_{x\to-\infty} \frac{1}{xe^{\frac{x^2}{2}}} = 0^-$

$F(0) = 0$; clearly $y < 0$ for $x < 0$ and $y > 0$ for $x > 0$

Now $y' = xe^{-x^2/2}(-x) + e^{-x^2/2}.(1) = (1-x^2).e^{-x^2/2} < 0$ for $x^2 - 1 > 0$, i.e., $x \in (-\infty, -1) \cup (1, \infty)$ and $y' > 0$ for $x \in (-1, 1)$; $y' = 0$ at $x = \pm 1$

Now, $y'' = (1-x^2)\left[-xe^{-\frac{x^2}{2}}\right] + e^{-x^2/2}(-2x)$

$= e^{-x^2/2}(-2x-x+x^3) = x(x^2-3)x^{-x^2/2}$

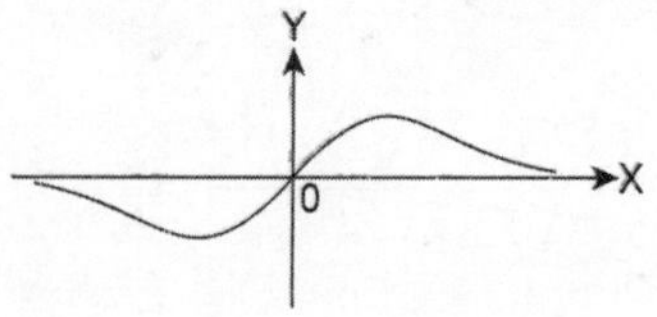

Given function is an odd function

$\therefore$ Required area bounded by curve and its asymptote (i.e., x-axis)

$A = 2\int_0^{\infty} xe^{-x^2/2}dx$

Put $e^{-x^2/2} = t \qquad \Rightarrow \quad (e^{-x^2/2})(-x)dx = dt$

$\Rightarrow \quad xe^{-x^2/2}dx = -dt$

$\therefore \quad A = 2\int_1^0 -dt = -2[t]_1^0 = 2$ square units

6. A.T.Q. Since $y = e^x$ and $y = \ln x$ are inverse of each other, $R_1 = R_2$

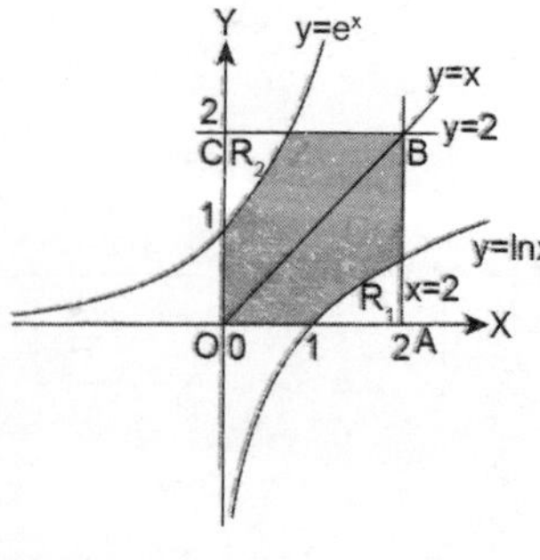

$\Rightarrow$ Area of square $OABC - 2R_1 = a - b\ln 2$

$\Rightarrow \quad 4 - 2\int_1^2 \ln x\,dx = a - b\ln 2$

$\Rightarrow \quad 4 - 2\left[\int_1^2 |(\ln x)x|_1^2 - \int_1^2 \frac{1}{x}.x\,dx\right] = a - b\ln 2$

$\Rightarrow \quad 4 - 2[2\ln 2 - 1] = a - b\ln 2$

$\Rightarrow \quad 6 - 4\ln 2 = a - b\ln 2$

$\Rightarrow \quad a = 6, b = 4 \qquad \Rightarrow \quad a + b = 10$

7. Given curve are $y = 2x2e^x$ ...(1)

And $y = -x^3.e^x$ ...(2)

$f(x) = 2e2x^x$

$\Rightarrow \quad f'(x) = 2x2ex + 2e^x(2x) = 2e^x(x^2 + 2x) = 2xe^x(x + 2) > 0$ for $x \in (-\infty, -2) \cup (0, \infty)$ and $f'(x) < 0$ for $x \in (-2, 0)$

Further $f'(x) = 0$ at $x = 0, -2$

$f(0) = 0, f(-2) = 8e^{-2}$.

Now, $g(x) = -x^3.e^x$

$\Rightarrow \quad g'(x) = -x3e^x - 3x2e^x = -x2e^x(x + 3)$

$\therefore \quad g'(x) < 0$ for $x > -3$ and $g'(x) < 0$ for $x < -3$; $g'(x) = 0$ at $x = 0, -3$

$g(0) = 0, g(-3) = 27e^{-3}, g(-2) = 8e^{-2}$

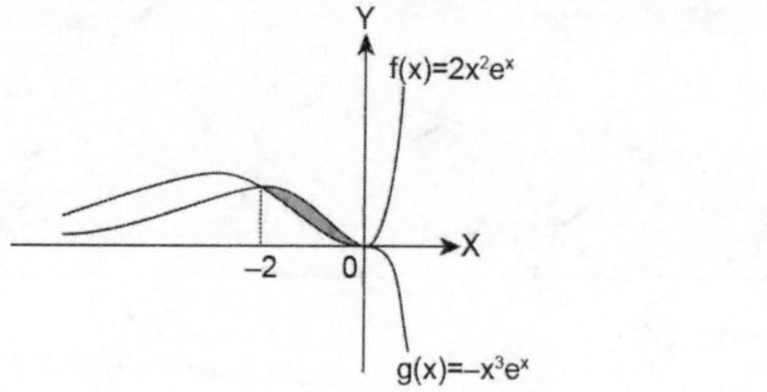

A.T.Q., $\int_{-2}^{0} |g(x) - f(x)|dx = ae^{-2} - b$

$\Rightarrow \quad \int_{-2}^{0}[2x^2e^x + x^3e^x]dx$

$= \int_{-2}^{0}(2x^2+x^3)e^x dx = [(2x^2+x^3)e^x]_{-2}^{0} - \int_{-2}^{0}(4x+3x^2).e^x dx$

$= -(8-8)e^{-2} - \int_{-2}^{0}(4x+3x^2).e^x dx$

$= -\left[|(4x+3x^2)e^x|_{-2}^{0} - \int_{-2}^{0}(4+6x)e^x dx\right]$

$= -\left[|0-(8+12)e^{-2}| - \int_{-2}^{0}(4+6x)e^x dx\right]$

$= 4e^{-2} + \left[|(4+6x)e^x|_{-2}^{0} - \int_{-2}^{0}(6)e^x dx\right]$

$= 4e^{-2} + [4-(-8)e^{-2} - 6(1-e^{-2})] = 4e^{-2} + 4 + 8e^{-2} - 6 + 6e^{-2} = (18e^{-2} - 2) = ae^{-2} - b$ (given)

$\Rightarrow \quad a = 18, b = 2 \qquad \Rightarrow \quad a - b = 16$

8. $f(x) = 2x + b$ and inverse of $f(x)$ is $g(x) = \frac{1}{2}(x - b)$

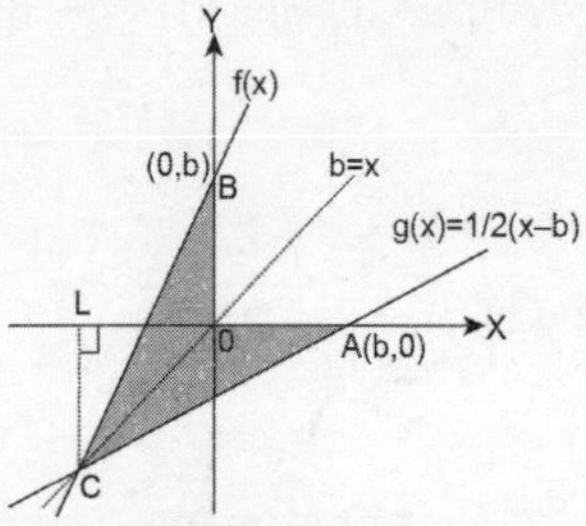

A.T.Q, area $OABC$ = 2 units

At point C, $x = 1/2(x - b)$

$\Rightarrow 2x = x - b \qquad \Rightarrow x = -b$

$\Rightarrow C \equiv (-b, -b)$

$\therefore$ Area $\Delta OAC = \frac{1}{2}(OA) \times CL = \frac{1}{2}(b) \times (b) = \frac{1}{2}b^2$

$\Rightarrow$ Area bounded by $f(x)$, $g(x)$ and positive co-ordinate axes = 2(area of ΔOAC) = b^2 (given)

$\therefore b^2 = 2$ square units

9. Given curve area $x = 2\sqrt{y}$ ...(1)

$x = (y - 1)^2$ ...(2)

$x + y = 3$ ...(3)

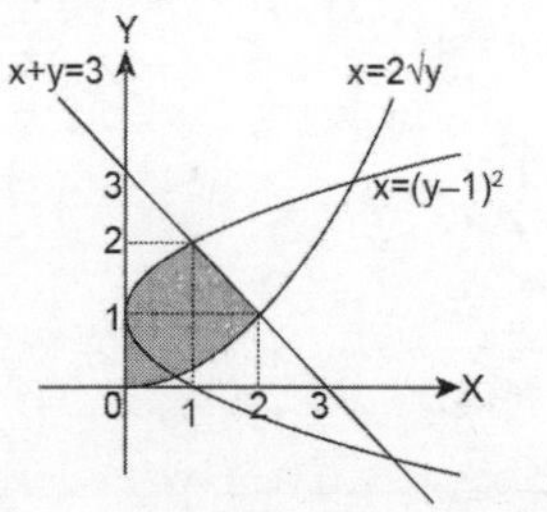

$$\Rightarrow 2A = 2\left[\int_0^1\left(1+\sqrt{x}-\frac{x^2}{4}\right)dx + \int_1^2\left[(3-x)-\frac{x^2}{4}\right]dx\right]$$

$$= 2\left[1+\frac{2}{3}-\frac{1}{12}+3-\frac{1}{2}(3)-\frac{1}{12}(7)\right]$$

$$= 2\left[4+\frac{2}{3}-\frac{1}{12}-\frac{3}{2}-\frac{7}{12}\right]$$

$$= 2\left[\frac{48+8-1-18-7}{12}\right] = 2\left[\frac{30}{12}\right] = 5 \text{ square units}$$

10. Required area bounded = $\int_1^2\left(\frac{\sqrt{2y}}{\sqrt{a}}-\sqrt{\frac{y}{a}}\right)dy$

$= \frac{1}{\sqrt{a}}\int_1^2\left(\sqrt{2}-1\right)\sqrt{y}\,dy$

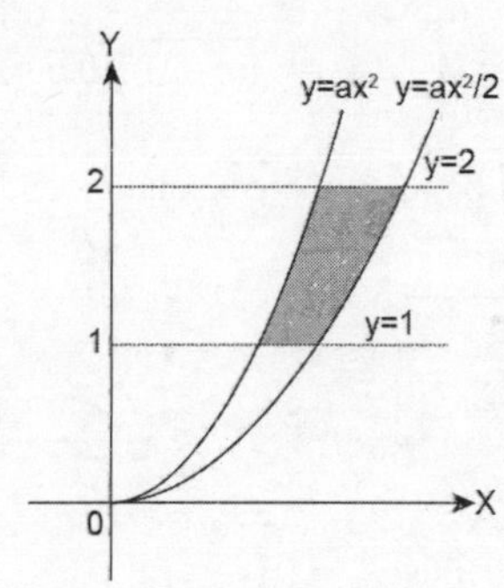

$$= \frac{\sqrt{2}-1}{\sqrt{a}}\left[\frac{2}{3}(y)^{3/2}\right]_1^2 = \frac{2\left(\sqrt{2}-1\right)}{3\sqrt{a}}\left[2\sqrt{2}-1\right]$$

Now $a \geq 1$

$\therefore$ For maximum area, $a = 1$.

11. Given curve are $y = \left[\frac{x^2}{64}+2\right]$ ...(1)

$y = x - 1$ ...(2)

$x = 0$ ...(3)

and $y = 0$ ...(4)

$$\text{Now } y = \left[\frac{x^2}{64}+2\right] = \begin{cases} 2 & \text{for } 0 \leq x < 8 \\ 3 & \text{for } 8 \leq x < 8\sqrt{2} \\ 4 & \text{for } 8\sqrt{2} \leq x < 8\sqrt{3} \\ \text{and so on} \end{cases}$$

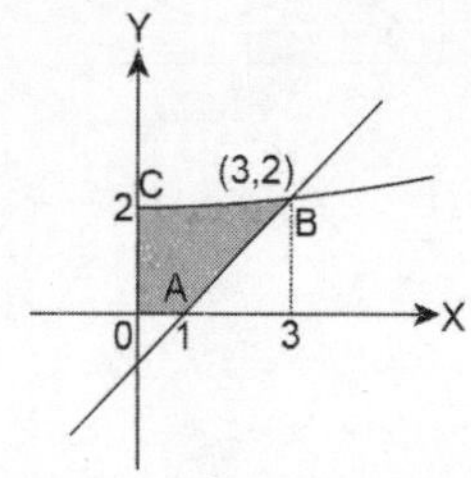

$\therefore$ Required area = 1/2 (OA + CB) × (OC) = 1/2 (1 + 3) × (2) = 4 square.

12. Given curve are

$y = \ln x$ ...(i)

And

$y = \ln(x)^{-1}$ ...(ii)

$1 \leq x \leq e$

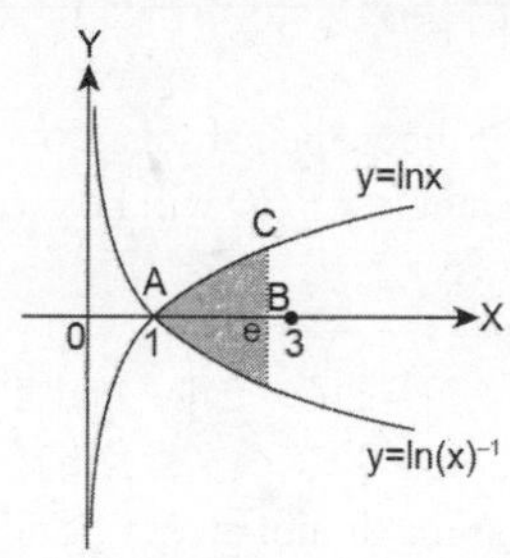

$\therefore$ Required area $= 2\int_1^e \ln x\,dx = 2\left[\left|x\ln x\right|_1^e - \int_1^e \frac{1}{x}\times x\,dx\right]$

$= 2[e - (e - 1)] = 2$ square units.

13. $\lambda^2 f(x) - 2lf'(x) + f''(x) = 0$ provides two equal values of a for all x.

$\Rightarrow$ Disc. = 0

$\Rightarrow 4(f'(x))^2 - 4f(x).f''(x) = 0$

$\Rightarrow 4.\frac{f'(x)}{f(x)} - 4\frac{f''(x)}{f'(x)} = 0 \Rightarrow \int\frac{f'(x)}{f(x)}dx = \int\frac{f''(x)}{f(x)}dx$

$\Rightarrow \ln f(x) = \ln f'(x) + \ln c \Rightarrow f(x) = c.f'(x)$ ...(i)

$\Rightarrow \frac{f'(x)}{f(x)} = \frac{1}{c} \qquad \Rightarrow \ln f(x) = x/c + k$

$\Rightarrow f(x) = e^{x/}c^{+k}$ ....(ii)

Now, $f(0) = 1 \qquad \Rightarrow 1 = e^k$

$\Rightarrow f(x) = e^{x/c}$

$\Rightarrow f'(x) = 1/c\ e^{x/c}$

Also $f'(0) = 2 \qquad \Rightarrow 2 = 1/c$

$\Rightarrow f(x) = e^{2x}$ .....(iii)

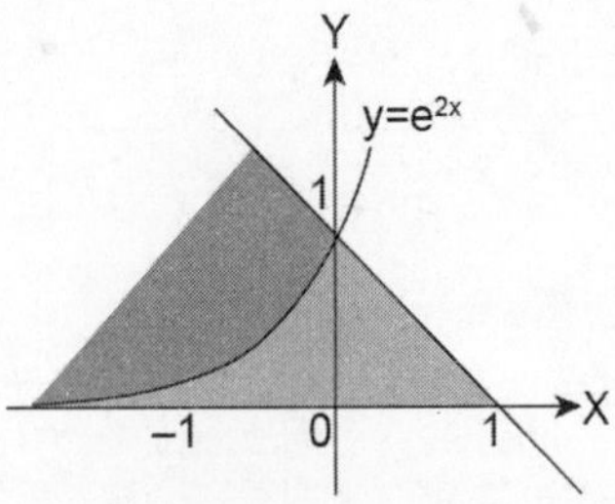

$\therefore$ Area of required region $= \int_{-\infty}^{0} e^{2x}dx + \int_{0}^{1}(-x+1)dx$

$= \left[\frac{e^{2x}}{2}\right]_{-\infty}^{2} + \left[\frac{-x^2}{2}+x\right]_0^1$

$= \frac{1}{2}(1-0) + \left[\frac{-1}{2}(1-0)+(1-0)\right] = \frac{1}{2} - \frac{1}{2} + 1 = 1$ square units.

14. Given curve is $y = e^{-|x|}$

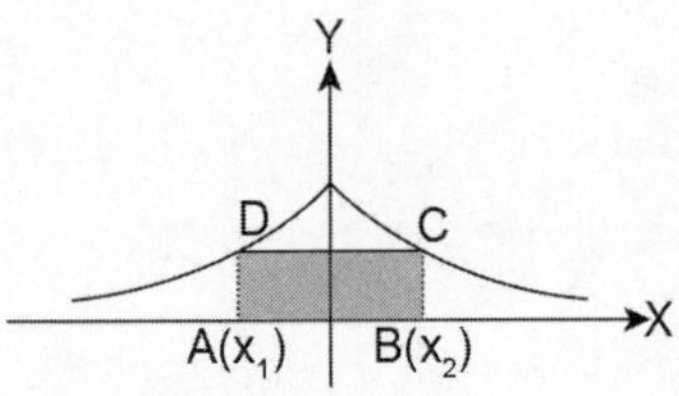

Since $ABCD$ is a rectangle

$\Rightarrow AD = BC \qquad \Rightarrow e^{|-x_1|} = e^{-|x_2|}$

$\Rightarrow |x_1| = |x_2| \qquad \Rightarrow x_2 = -x_1$ as $x_1 < 0, x_2 > 0$

Let abscissa of B be x, then abscissa of A will be $-x$.

$\therefore$ Area of rectangle $ABCD$ will be $= (AB) \times (BC) = (2x) \times e^{-x} = A(x)$ (say)

$\Rightarrow A'(x) = 2[x(-e^{-x}) + e^{-x}(1)] = 2(1-x)e^{-x}$ and $A''(x) = 2[(1-x)(-e^{-x}) + e^{-x}(1)] = 2[(x-2)]e^{-x}$ and $A'(x) = 0$ at $x = 1$

$\Rightarrow A''(1) = -2e^{-1} < 0$

$\Rightarrow A(x)$ will be maximum at $x = 1$ and is given by $A(1) = 2e^{-1} = 2/e = k/e$ (given)

$\Rightarrow k = 2$

15. Equation of line passing through $P(1, c)$ with gradient 'm' is given by $(y - c) = m(x - 1)$

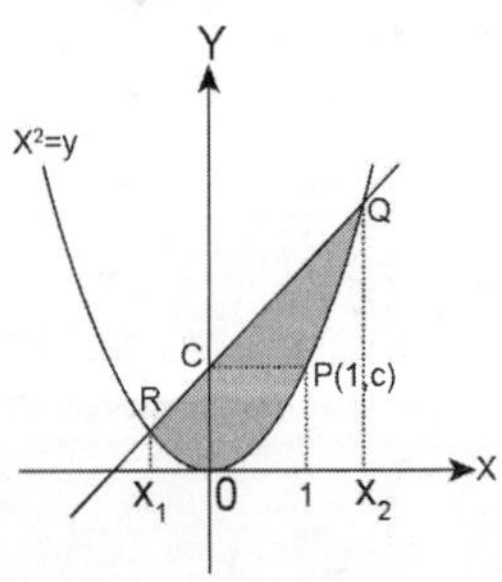

All the point of intersection Q and R; $(x^2 - c) = m(x - 1)$

$\Rightarrow x^2 - mx + (m - c)$ ...(1)

$\Rightarrow x_1$ and x_2 are roots of (i)

$\Rightarrow x_1 + x_2 = m$ and $x_1.x_2 = (m - c)$

Bounded area $A(m) = \int_{x_1}^{x_2}\left[m(x-1)+c-x^2\right]dx$

$= \left[m\left(\frac{x^2}{2}-x\right)+cx-\frac{x^3}{3}\right]_{x_1}^{x_2}$

$= \frac{m}{2}\left[x_2^2 - x_1^2\right] + (c-m)(x_2-x_1) - \frac{1}{3}(x_2^3 - x_1^3)$

$= (x_2 - x_1)\left[\frac{m}{2}(x_2+x_1)+(c-m)-\frac{1}{3}(x_2^2+x_1^2+x_1.x_2)\right] = 36$

$= \sqrt{m^2-4(m-c)}\left[\frac{m}{2}(m)+(c-m)-\frac{1}{3}(m^2-(m-c))\right]$

$= \sqrt{m^2-4m+4c}\left[m^2\left(\frac{1}{2}-\frac{1}{3}\right)+\frac{2}{3}(c-m)\right]$

$= \sqrt{m^2-4m+4c}\left[\frac{m^2}{6}+\frac{2}{3}(c-m)\right]$

$= \sqrt{\frac{m^2-4m+4c}{6}}\left[m^2+4c-4m\right]$

$= \frac{1}{6}\left(m^2-4m+4c\right)^{3/2}$

$\therefore \quad A(m) = \frac{1}{6}\left(m^2-4m+4c\right)^{3/2}$

$\Rightarrow A'(m) = \frac{1}{6}\times\frac{3}{2}(2m-4)(m^2-4m+4c)^{1/2}$

$= \frac{1}{2}(m-2)(m^2-4m+4c)^{1/2}$

For maximum / minimum, $A(m)$, $A'(m) = 0$

$\Rightarrow m = 2$ or $m = \frac{4 \pm \sqrt{16-16c}}{2}$

i.e., $m = 2$ or $m = 2 \pm 2\sqrt{1-c}$

But $c > 1$

$\Rightarrow m = 2$ is the only real value.

$= A''(m) = \frac{1}{2}\times\frac{1}{2}(2m-4)(m-2)(m^2-4m+4c)^{-1/2} + \frac{1}{2}(m^2-4m+4c)^{1/2}$

$= \frac{\frac{1}{2}(m-2)^2+\frac{1}{2}(m^2-4m+4c)}{\sqrt{(m^2-4m+4c)}}$

$\Rightarrow A''(2) = \frac{\frac{1}{2}(4c-4)}{\sqrt{4c-4}} = \sqrt{(c-1)} > 0$ as $c > 1$

$\therefore$ Area will be least at $m = 2$ and given by $A(2) = \frac{(4c-4)^{3/2}}{6}$

$= \frac{8(c-1)^{3/2}}{6} = 36$ (given)

$\Rightarrow (c-1)^{3/2} = \frac{36\times 6}{8} = 27$

$\Rightarrow (c-1)(27)^{2/3} = 9 \qquad \Rightarrow c = 10$

$\therefore c^2 + m^2 = 100 + 4 = 104$

16. Given curves are $y^2 = 4ax$ ...(1)

$y = ax$ ...(2)

And $y = x/a$ ...(3)

$(1 \le a \le 2)$

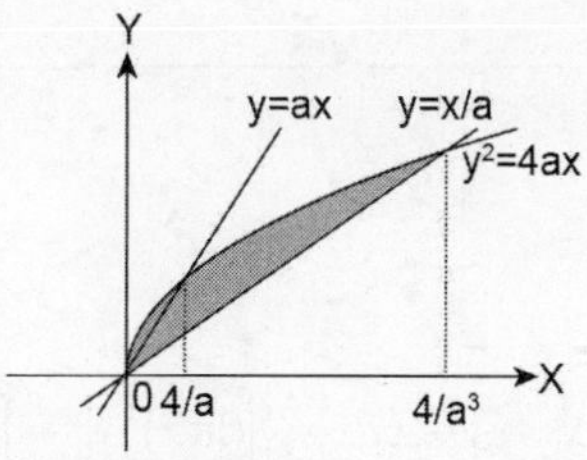

At the point if intersection A, B;

$a2x^2 = 4ax$ and $\dfrac{x^2}{a^2} = 4ax$

$\Rightarrow ax(ax - 4) = 0$ and $x(x - 4a^3) = 0$

$\Rightarrow x = 0$ or $x = 4/a$ and $x = 0, 4a^3$

$\Rightarrow A \equiv \left(\dfrac{4}{a}, 4\right)$ and $B \equiv (4a^3, 4a^2)$

$\therefore$ Bounded area

$$A(a) = \int_0^{4/a}\left(ax - \frac{x}{a}\right)dx + \int_{4/a}^{4a^3}\left(2\sqrt{a}\sqrt{x} - \frac{x}{a}\right)dx$$

$$= \frac{a}{2}\left(\frac{16}{a^2}\right) - \frac{1}{2a}\left(\frac{16}{a^2}\right) + 2\sqrt{a}\left(\frac{2}{3}\right)$$

$$\left[(4a^3)^{3/2} - \left(\frac{4}{a}\right)^{3/2}\right] - \frac{1}{2a}\left[16a^6 - \frac{16}{a^2}\right]$$

$$= \frac{8}{a^2}\left(a - \frac{1}{a}\right) + \frac{32\sqrt{a}}{3}\left[a^{9/2} - \frac{1}{a^{3/2}}\right] - \frac{8}{a}\left(a^6 - \frac{1}{a^2}\right)$$

$$= \frac{8}{a^2}\left(a - \frac{1}{a}\right) + \frac{32}{3}\left(a^5 - \frac{1}{a}\right) - \frac{8}{a}\left(a^6 - \frac{1}{a^2}\right)$$

$$= \frac{8}{a} - \frac{8}{a^3} + \frac{32}{3}a^5 - \frac{32}{3a} - 8a^5 + \frac{8}{a^3}$$

$$= \left(\frac{32}{3} - 8\right)a^5 + \frac{1}{a}\left(8 - \frac{32}{3}\right) = \frac{8}{3}\left(a^5 - \frac{1}{a}\right)$$

$\therefore \quad A'(a) = \dfrac{8}{3}\left(5a^4 + \dfrac{1}{a^2}\right) > 0 \ \forall\ a \in [1, 2]$

$\Rightarrow A$ is an increasing function of a

$\Rightarrow A$ will be maximum at $a = 2$

$\therefore$ Maximum bounded area $= \dfrac{8}{3}\left((2)^5 - \dfrac{1}{2}\right)$

$= \dfrac{8}{3}\left(32 - \dfrac{1}{2}\right) = \dfrac{8}{3}\left(\dfrac{63}{2}\right) = 4(21) = 84$ square units.

17. $[x]^2 = [y]^2 \quad \Rightarrow \quad ([x] - [y])([x] + [y]) = 0$

$\Rightarrow [y] = [x]$ or $[y] = -[x]$

$$\text{Now } [x] = \begin{cases} 1 & \text{for } x \in [1,2) \\ 2 & \text{for } x \in [2,3) \\ \text{and so on} \end{cases}$$

$$\therefore \quad y \in \begin{cases} [-1,0) \cup [1,2) & \text{for } x \in [1,2) \\ [-2,-1) \cup [2,3) & \text{for } x \in [2,3) \\ [-3,-2) \cup [3,4) & \text{for } x \in [3,4) \\ [-4,-3) \cup [4,5) & \text{for } x \in [4,5) \end{cases}$$

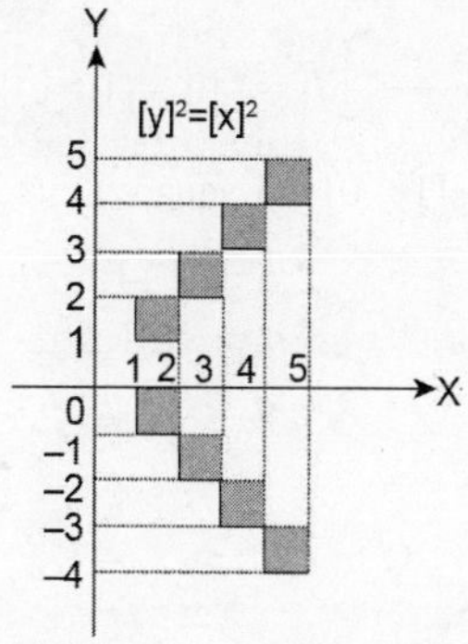

Clearly the bounded region consists of 8 squares each having 1 square unit = 8

$$\text{18. } y = |[x-3]| = \begin{cases} 5 & \text{for } x \in [-2,-1) \\ 4 & \text{for } x \in [-1,0) \\ 3 & \text{for } x \in [0,1) \\ 2 & \text{for } x \in [1,2) \\ 1 & \text{for } x \in [2,3) \end{cases}$$

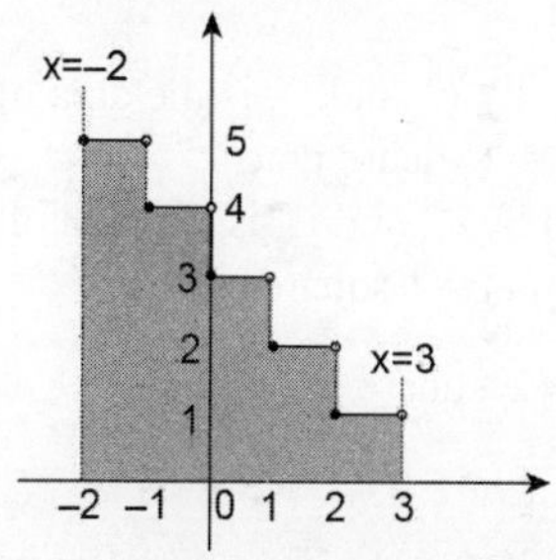

$\therefore$ Required bounded area = 5 + 4 + 3 + 2 + 1 = 15 square units.

19. Given curves are $y = 2^{kx}$, $x = 0$ and $x = 2$

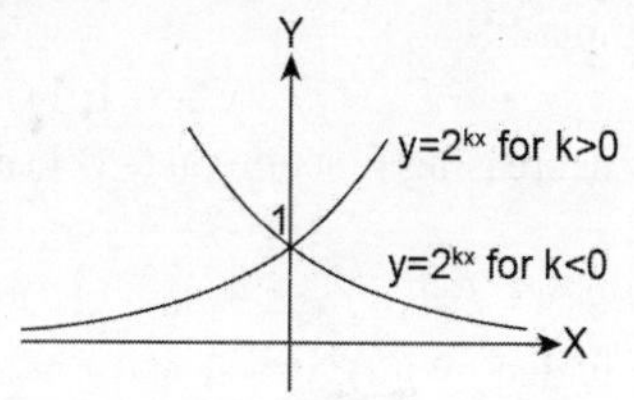

A.T.Q., $\displaystyle\int_0^2 2^{kx}\,dx = \frac{3}{\log^2} = \left[\frac{2^{kx}}{k\ln 2}\right]_0^2 = \frac{3}{\ln 2} = \frac{1}{k}\left[2^{kx} - 1\right]_0^2 = 3$

$\Rightarrow 2^{2k} - 1 = 3k \qquad \Rightarrow 2^{2k} = (3k + 1)$

$\Rightarrow k = 1$

20. Given curve is $y = \ln(x + e)$

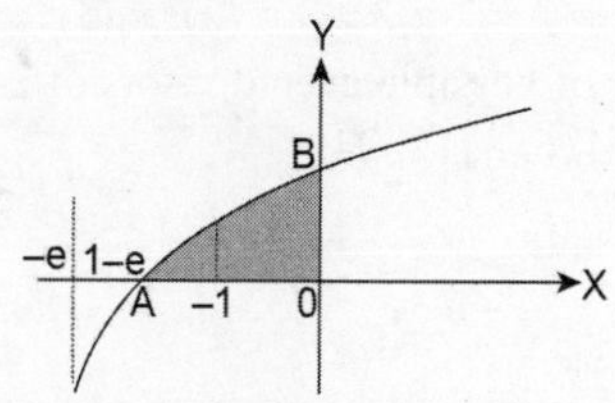

Required area $= \displaystyle\int_{1-e}^{0} \ln(x+e)dx$

$= |\,x\ln(x+e)\,|_{1-e}^{0} - \displaystyle\int_{1-e}^{0} \frac{1}{(x+e)}(x)dx$

$$= -\int_{1-e}^{0}\left(1-\frac{e}{x+e}\right)dx = -[0-(1-e)] + e[\ln(x+e)]_{1-e}^{0} =$$

$1 - e + e[1 - 0] = 1$ square units.

21. $C_1 : |x + y| \le 1 \quad \Rightarrow \quad -1 \le x + y \le 1$

$C_2 : |x - y| \le 1 \quad \Rightarrow \quad -1 \le x - y \le 1$

$C_3 : |x| \le 1/2 \quad \Rightarrow \quad -\frac{1}{2} \le x \le \frac{1}{2}$

$C_4 : |y| \le 1/2 \quad \Rightarrow \quad -\frac{1}{2} \le y \le \frac{1}{2}$

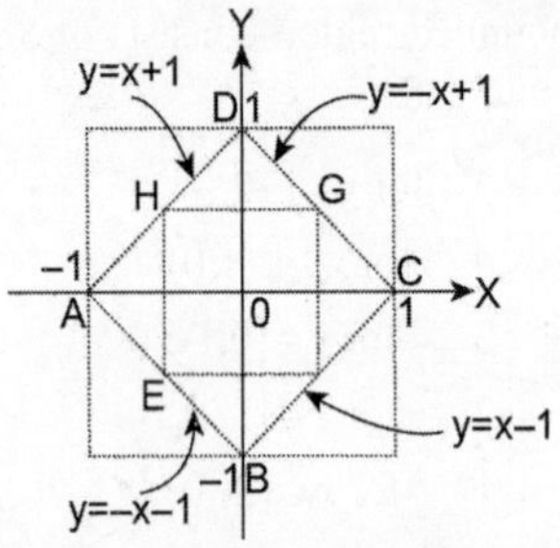

Area bounded by C_1 and C_2 is the area of square (A_1 (say)) $= 1/2 \times 2 \times 2 = 2$ square units.

Area bounded by C_3 and C_4 is the area of square *EFGH* (A_2 (say)) $= (1) \times (1) = 1$ square units.

$\therefore \quad \frac{A_1}{A_2} = \frac{2}{1} = 2$ square units.

22. $y = x^3 - 3x + 4$

$y' = 3x^2 - 3 = 3(x^2 - 1) \quad \therefore \quad y' = 0, x = \pm 1$

$y'' = 6x$

$\Rightarrow \; y''(-1) = -6 < 0$ and $y''(1) = 6 > 0$

$\Rightarrow \; x = -1$ and $x = 1$ are respectively the points of maxima and minima.

$y' < 0 \quad \Rightarrow \quad x \in (-1, 1)$

$\Rightarrow \; f(x)$ is *a* decreasing function on $(-1, 1)$ and $f(-1) = 6$ and $f(1) = 2$

$\Rightarrow \; f(x) > 0 \;\forall\; x \in (-1, 1)$

$\Rightarrow$ Area bounded by $f(x)$, $x = -1$ and $x = 1$, above x-axis

$$A = \int_{-1}^{1}\left(x^3 - 3x + 4\right)dx$$

$$= \left[\frac{x^4}{4} - \frac{3x^2}{2} + 4x\right]_{-1}^{1} = \frac{1}{4}(1-1) - \frac{3}{2}(1-1) + 4(2)$$

$\Rightarrow \; A = 8$ square units

$\Rightarrow \; 3A = 24 = 2 \times 2 \times 2 \times 3 = (2)^3 \times (3)^1$

Number of possible even divisors of $24 = (3) \times (2) = 6$ (Viz, 2, 4, 6, 8, 12, 24)

23. Given curves are

$x = \ln x$ ....(1)

And

$y = (\ln x)^2$ ....(2)

$\therefore$ Required bounded area $= \int_{1}^{e}\left[\ln x - (\ln x)^2\right]dx$

$$= \int_{1}^{e}(\ln x)dx - \int_{1}^{e}(\ln x)^2 dx$$

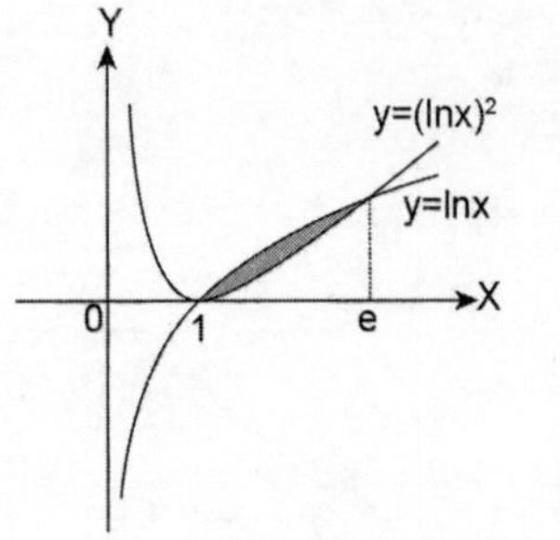

$$= |(\ln x)x|_1^e - \int_1^e \frac{1}{x}.x\,dx - \left\{|(\ln x)^2 x|_1^e - \int_1^e 2\frac{\ln x}{x}.x\,dx\right\} = e -$$

$$[e-1] - \left\{e - 2\int_1^e \ln x\,dx\right\}$$

$$= 1 - e + 2\left[|x\ln x|_1^e - \int_1^e \frac{1}{x}.x\,dx\right] = 1 - e + 2[e - (e-1)] =$$

$1 - e + 2 = 3 - e = (a - e)$ square units.

$\Rightarrow \; a = 3$

$$\therefore \quad \lim_{x \to a}\frac{x^2-4}{x-2} = \lim_{x \to 3}\frac{x^2-4}{x-2} = 5$$

24. Given curves are $y = x^2 - 3$ and $y = kx + 2$

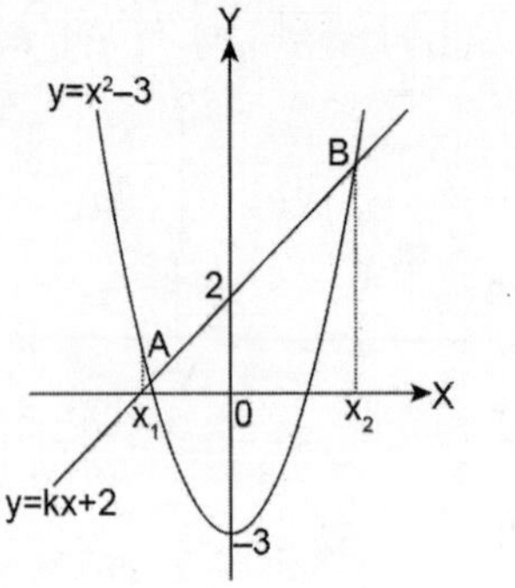

Area bounded by $y = x^2 - 3$ and $y = kx + 2$ is given by

$$A(k) = \int_{x_1}^{x_2}\left[kx + 2 - (x^2 - 3)\right]dx \qquad ...(1)$$

Where x_1, x_2 are roots of quadratic $x^2 - 3 = kx + 2$, i.e., $x^2 - kx - 5 = 0$

$$\therefore \quad A(k) = \int_{x_1}^{x_2}\left(-x^2 + kx + 5\right)dx$$

$$= -\frac{1}{3}\left(x_2^3 - x_1^3\right) + \frac{k}{2}\left(x_2^2 - x_1^2\right) + 5(x_2 - x_1)$$

$$= (x_2 - x_1)\left[-\frac{1}{3}\left(x_2^2 - x_1^2 + x_1x_2\right) + \frac{k}{2}(x_2 + x_1) + 5\right]$$

$$= \sqrt{k^2+20}\left[-\frac{1}{3}\left[\left(k^2\right)+5\right] + \frac{k^2}{2} + 5\right]$$

$$= \sqrt{k^2+20}\left[k^2\left(\frac{1}{2}-\frac{1}{3}\right) + 5 - \frac{5}{3}\right]$$

$$= \sqrt{k^2+20}\left[\frac{1}{6}k^2 + \frac{10}{3}\right] = \frac{1}{6}(k^2+20)^{3/2}$$ which is least for $k = 0$

$\Rightarrow \; k + 7 = 7$

25. Given curves are $\sqrt{|x|}+\sqrt{|y|}=\sqrt{a}$ ...(1)

$x^2+y^2=a^2,\ a>0$ ...(2)

$|x|+|y|=a$ ...(3)

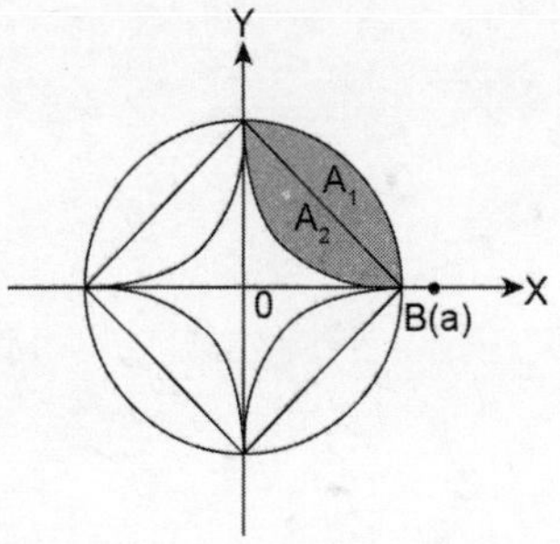

$$A_1=\int_0^a\left[\sqrt{a^2-x^2}-(a-x)\right]dx$$

$$=\left[\frac{x\sqrt{a^2-x^2}}{2}+\frac{a^2}{2}\sin^{-1}\left(\frac{x}{a}\right)\right]_0^a-a^2+\frac{1}{2}(a^2)$$

$$=\frac{a^2}{2}\left(\frac{\pi}{2}\right)-\frac{a^2}{2}=\frac{a^2}{2}\left(\frac{\pi}{2}-1\right)$$

$$A_2=\int_0^a\left[(a-x)-\left(\sqrt{a}-\sqrt{x}\right)^2\right]dx$$

$$=\int_0^a\left(a-x-a-x+2\sqrt{a}\sqrt{x}\right)dx=\int_0^a\left(2\sqrt{a}\sqrt{x}-2x\right)dx$$

$$=2\sqrt{a}\frac{2}{3}\left[(x)^{3/2}\right]_0^a-\left[a^2-0\right]$$

$$=\frac{4}{3}\sqrt{a}.a^{3/2}-a^2=\left(\frac{4}{3}-1\right)a^2=\frac{1}{3}a^2$$

$$=\frac{A_1}{A_2}=\frac{\frac{a^2}{2}\left(\frac{\pi-2}{2}\right)}{\frac{1}{3}a^2}\text{ and }\frac{A_2}{A_1}=\frac{\frac{1}{3}a^2}{\frac{1}{2}a^2(\pi-2)}=\frac{4}{3(\pi-2)}$$

$$=\frac{A}{3(B\pi-2)}$$

$\Rightarrow A=4,\ B=1$

So, $A+B=5$

26. Given curves area $y=\cos^{-1}x$ ...(1)

$y=\sin^{-1}x$ ...(2)

and $y=-\pi x^3$ ...(3)

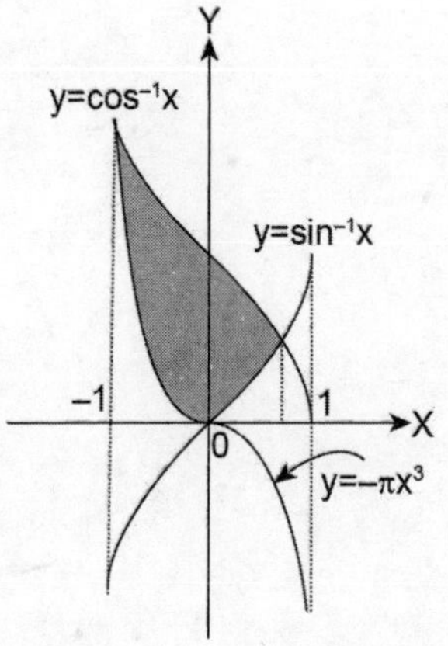

$$\therefore\ \text{Bounded area}=\int_{-1}^{0}\left(\cos^{-1}x+\pi x^3\right)dx$$

$$+\int_0^{1/\sqrt{2}}\left(\cos^{-1}x-\sin^{-1}x\right)dx$$

$$=\left|x\cos^{-1}x\right|_{-1}^{0}-\int_{-1}^{0}\frac{-1}{\sqrt{1-x^2}}.x\,dx+\frac{\pi}{4}\left[x^4\right]_{-1}^{0}$$

$$+\int_0^{1/\sqrt{2}}\left(2\cos^{-1}x-\frac{\pi}{2}\right)dx$$

$$=0-(-\pi)-\frac{1}{2}\int_{-1}^{0}\frac{-2x}{\sqrt{1-x^2}}dx+\frac{\pi}{4}(-1)$$

$$+2\left\{\left|x\cos^{-1}x\right|_0^{1/\sqrt{2}}-\int_0^{1/\sqrt{2}}\frac{-1}{\sqrt{1-x^2}}.x\,dx-\frac{\pi}{2}\left(\frac{1}{\sqrt{2}}\right)\right\}$$

$$=\pi-\frac{1}{2}\left[\frac{2}{1}\left(1-x^2\right)^{1/2}\right]_{-1}^{0}-\frac{\pi}{4}$$

$$+2\left\{\frac{1}{\sqrt{2}}\times\frac{\pi}{4}-\frac{1}{2}\left[\frac{2}{1}\left(1-x^2\right)^{1/2}\right]_0^{1/\sqrt{2}}\right\}-\frac{\pi}{2\sqrt{2}}$$

$$=\frac{3\pi}{4}-[1-0]+\frac{\pi}{2\sqrt{2}}-2.\left[\frac{1}{\sqrt{2}}-1\right]-\frac{\pi}{2\sqrt{2}}$$

$$=\frac{3\pi}{4}-1+\frac{\pi}{2\sqrt{2}}-\sqrt{2}+2-\frac{\pi}{2\sqrt{2}}$$

$$A=\frac{3\pi}{4}+1-\sqrt{2}$$

$$[A]=1+\left[\frac{3\pi}{4}-\sqrt{2}\right]=1+\left[\frac{3\times3.14-1.414}{4}\right]$$

$$=1+\left[\frac{9.42-1.41}{4}\right]=1+\left[\frac{8.01}{4}\right]=3$$

27. $y=f(x)=\ln(x+e)$ ...(1)

$x=\ln(1/y)$ or $1/y=e^x$ or $y=e^{-x}$ ...(2)

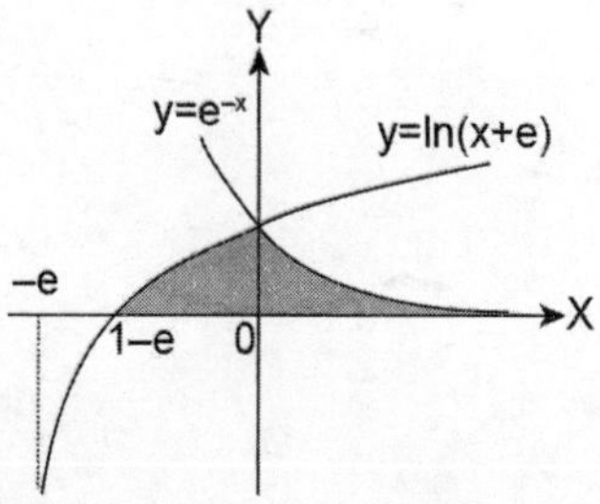

$$\text{Required bounded area}=\int_{1-e}^{0}\left(\ln(x+e)\right)dx+\int_{1-e}^{0}e^{-x}\,dx$$

$$=\left|x\ln(x+e)\right|_{1-e}^{0}-\int_{1-e}^{0}\frac{1}{x+e}.x\,dx+1$$

$$=1+(0-0)-\int_{1-e}^{0}\frac{x+e-e}{x+e}dx=1-\int_{1-e}^{0}\left(1-\frac{e}{x+e}\right)dx$$

$$=1-[0-(1-e)]+e\left|\ln(x+e)\right|_{1-e}^{0}$$

$=(2-e)+e[1-0]=2$ square units.

Differential Equation

CHAPTER 4

INTRODUCTION

We are familiar with word "Equation" and have dealt with linear and quadratic equations in Algebra. An equation equates the two quantities, so, it has great importance in Mathematics. Problems in any field can be solved, if from the given problem we can form the equation involving the unknowns. These equations of unknown can be then solved to find the values of the unknowns.

Mathematics is a tool to demystify the mysteries of nature and life. Problems in nature do not exist in numerical form or in the form of equation but they exist in the form of events. The observation are made and based on the collected data, the unknowns are related and equation/inequalities are formed. Therefore, for solving real life problems, only the ability to solve a given set of equations/inequalities is not enough. The ability to form a set of equations from the given problem is where the genius of a mathematician actually lies.

This chapter deals with differential equations. As the term signifies, these equations involve derivatives equated with the variables by means of equations. We'll learn in this chapter how to solve a real life problem by forming and then solving differential equations. You will appreciate that since these problems involve derivatives, we'll be making extensive use of our ability not only to differentiate the given equation having some parameters and to use the various techniques of eliminating the parameter (formation of differential equation) but also to integrate the given function (solving the differential equation).

Mastering the skills of this chapter will enhance your ability to apply your genius in Applied Mathematics and Technical Studies. Although the differential equation may be ordinary (only one independent variable) or partial (more than one independent variable) in present topic our concern will remain only ordinary differential equation.

BASICS OF DIFFERENTIAL EQUATIONS

Definition

An equation involving independent variable x, dependent variable y and differential coefficients of one or more dependent variables with respect to one or more than one independent variables is called a differential equation.

e.g., $\left(\frac{dy}{dx}\right)^2+\left(\frac{d^2y}{dx^2}\right)^3=x,\ \sqrt{1+\left(\frac{d^2y}{dx^2}\right)^2+\left(\frac{dy}{dx}\right)^3}=x^2,$

$\sqrt{\frac{dy}{dx}}+y=x,\ z^2\frac{dz}{dx}+y\frac{dy}{dx}=x^2$

or $\left(\frac{\partial z}{\partial x}\right)^2-\frac{\partial^2 z}{\partial x^2}=4x^2\frac{\partial^2 z}{\partial y^2}$ etc.,

Depending upon the nature of derivatives involved these are broadly classified into two types.

TYPES OF DIFFERENTIAL EQUATION

Ordinary Differential Equations

An equation involving only one independent variable and ordinary derivatives with respect to that is known as ordinary differential equation (O.D.E.). For instance, $F\left(x, y, \frac{dy}{dx}, \frac{d^2y}{dx^2}, ...\right)=0$ is a standard form of an ordinary differential equation.

e.g., $\sin 2x\, dx + e^{2y}\, dy = 0,\ \frac{d^2y}{dx^2}+ky=0$

or $\left[1+\left(\frac{dy}{dx}\right)^2\right]^{3/2}=\left(\frac{d^3y}{dx^3}\right)^2$ etc.

Partial Differential Equations

Differential equation involving two or more independent variables and partial derivatives with respect to these is known as partial differential equation (P.D.E.).

e.g., $y^2\frac{\partial z}{\partial x}+xy\frac{\partial x}{\partial y}=x^2z$, $\frac{\partial y}{yz}+\frac{\partial x}{yx}+\frac{\partial z}{xz}=0$ etc.

ORDER AND DEGREE OF DIFFERENTIAL EQUATION

Order

It is the order of the highest order derivative appearing in the differential equation. The order of differential equation states about the number of times the family of curve has been differentiated in order to eliminate all its parameters to form the given differential equation.

Therefore, the order of differential equation is same as the number of effective arbitrary constants present in the family of curves from which the differential equation is derived.

e.g., $x\frac{dy}{dx}+x^2y\sin x=\log x$ is of 1st order whereas $\frac{d^2y}{dx^2}-3x\frac{dy}{dx}=x^2e^x$ is second order differential equation.

Degree

Degree of differential equation is the degree, i.e., power of the highest order derivative present in the differential equation after the equation is made free from all radicals and fractions as far as derivatives are concerned and is written in terms of a polynomial in all differential coefficients (i.e., derivative involved in differential equation.

To get the degree of the differential equation, we first try to convert it into the following form:

$$f(x,y)\left[\frac{d^my}{dx^m}\right]^p+g(x,y)\left[\frac{d^{m-1}(y)}{dx^{m-1}}\right]^{n_1}+h(x,y)\left[\frac{d^{m-2}(y)}{dx^{m-2}}\right]^{n_2}+\ldots=0$$

is of order m and degree p. ...(1)

Where $m, n_1, n_2, \ldots, n_k$ are positive integers.

For example, the differential equation

$\left(y-x\frac{dy}{dx}\right)^2=k^2\left[1+\left(\frac{dy}{dx}\right)^2\right]$ is of degree 2.

Note that in the differential equation $e^{\left(\frac{d^3y}{dx^3}\right)^2}+x\frac{d^2y}{dx^2}+y=0$

Order is three but degree of equation is not defined because it cannot be reduced to the form (1).

ILLUSTRATION 1: Find the order and degree of the following differential equation.

(i) $\left(\frac{d^3y}{dx^3}\right)^2-x\left(\frac{dy}{dx}\right)^3=0$ (ii) $y=x\frac{dy}{dx}+\sqrt{1+\left(\frac{dy}{dx}\right)^2}$

SOLUTION: (i) $\left(\frac{d^3y}{dx^3}\right)^2-x\left(\frac{dy}{dx}\right)^3=0$

The highest derivative of this equation is order 3. Therefore, the order of the differential equation is 3

The power to which the highest derivative is raised is 2.

Hence, the degree of the equation is 2.

(ii) $y=x\frac{dy}{dx}+\sqrt{1+\left(\frac{dy}{dx}\right)^2}$ squaring both sides in order to make the derivatives free from radical sign (√)

$\Rightarrow\left(y-x\frac{dy}{dx}\right)^2=\left\{1+\left(\frac{dy}{dx}\right)^2\right\}$ $\Rightarrow y^2+x^2\left(\frac{dy}{dx}\right)^2-2xy\left(\frac{dy}{dx}\right)=1+\left(\frac{dy}{dx}\right)^2$

Clearly, the order of the differential equation is 1 and the degree of the differential equation is 2.

ILLUSTRATION 2: Obtain the degree and order of following differential equations:

(a) $\frac{dy}{dx} = x\ln\left(\frac{d^2y}{dx^2}\right)$ (b) $\frac{d^2y}{dx^2} = 3\left(\frac{dy}{dx}\right)^2 + x^2\sin\left(\frac{d^2y}{dx^2}\right)$

(c) $\frac{d^3y}{dx^3} = \sin\left(\frac{d^2y}{dx^2}\right)$

SOLUTION: (a) Clearly, it shows that order of the differential equation is 2, whereas degree of the differential equation is not defined because the right hand side cannot be expressed as a polynomial in $\frac{dy}{dx}$.

(b) Clearly, order of the differential equation is 2 whereas degree of the differential equation is not defined, because the right hand side cannot be expressed as a polynomial in $\frac{d^2y}{dx^2}$.

(c) Highest order derivative present in the differential equation is $\frac{d^3y}{dx^3}$, so the order of the differential equation is 3.
But the degree of differential equation is not defined because the right hand side cannot be expressed as a polynomial in derivative $\frac{d^2y}{dx^2}$.

ILLUSTRATION 3: Find the order and degree of following differential equations:

(i) $\frac{d^2y}{dx^2} = \left[y + \left(\frac{dy}{dx}\right)^6\right]^{1/4}$ (ii) $y = e^{\left(\frac{dy}{dx} + \frac{d^2y}{dx^2}\right)}$

(iii) $\sin\left(\frac{dy}{dx} + \frac{d^2y}{dx^2}\right) = y$ (iv) $e^{y'''} - xy'' + y = 0$

SOLUTION: (i) Given differential equation is $\frac{d^2y}{dx^2} = \left[y + \left(\frac{dy}{dx}\right)^6\right]^{1/4}$

$\Rightarrow \left(\frac{d^2y}{dx^2}\right)^4 = y + \left(\frac{dy}{dx}\right)^6$

Since highest order of differential equation is 2 and its power is 4.

$\Rightarrow$ order = 2, degree = 4

(ii) Given differential equation is $y = e^{\left(\frac{dy}{dx} + \frac{d^2y}{dx^2}\right)}$

$\Rightarrow \frac{d^2y}{dx^2} + \frac{dy}{dx} = \ell ny$

$\Rightarrow$ order = 2, degree = 1

(iii) Given differential equation is $\sin\left(\frac{dy}{dx} + \frac{d^2y}{dx^2}\right) = y$

$\Rightarrow \frac{d^2y}{dx^2} + \frac{dy}{dx} = \sin^{-1} y$

$\Rightarrow$ order = 2, degree = 1

(iv) Given differential equation is $e^{y'''} - xy'' + y = 0$

$\Rightarrow e^{\frac{d^3y}{dx^3}} - x\frac{d^2y}{dx^2} + y = 0$

$\because$ Equation can not be expressed as a polynomial in differential coefficients, so degree is not applicable but order is 3.

REMARK:

Linear and Non-linear Differential Equation:

If the dependent variables and all its derivatives present occur in the first degree only that is neither the product of dependent variables nor product of derivative, nor product of derivative and dependent variables are present in the differential equation, then it is known as a linear differential equation. A differential equation which is not linear is termed as a non-linear differential equation.

For instance, the differential equation $2x^3\frac{d^2y}{dx^2}-x\frac{dy}{dx}+x^2y=0$ *is linear, while* $\frac{d^3y}{dx^3}+x\frac{d^2y}{dx^2}-3y\frac{dy}{dx}=0$ *is non-linear.*

TEXTUAL EXERCISE–1: (SUBJECTIVE)

1. Find the order and degree of the following differential equations:
   (a) $(x^2+y^2)dx-2x\,dy=0$
   (b) $\sqrt{1+\left(\frac{dy}{dx}\right)^2}=x^3$
   (c) $\frac{dy}{dx}=\cos x$
   (d) $\sqrt{\frac{d^3y}{dx^3}}=\sqrt[4]{\left(\frac{dy}{dx}+5\right)}$
   (e) $y=x\left(\frac{dy}{dx}\right)+r\sqrt{1+\left(\frac{dy}{dx}\right)^2}$
   (f) $\frac{d^2y}{dx^2}=0$
   (g) $\frac{\left\{1+\left(\frac{dy}{dx}\right)^2\right\}^{3/2}}{d^2y/dx^2}=r$
   (h) $y=x\frac{dy}{dx}+\frac{a}{(dy/dx)}$
   (i) $(y+c)^2\frac{dx}{dz}+z\frac{dy}{dz}-(y+a)=0$

2. Find the order and degree of the following differential equation:
   (a) $y=\frac{dy}{dx}.x+\sqrt{a^2\left(\frac{dy}{dx}\right)^2+b^2}$
   (b) $x^2\left(\frac{d^2y}{dx^2}\right)^3+y\left(\frac{dy}{dx}\right)^4+y^4=0$
   (c) $x\frac{\partial z}{\partial x}+y\frac{\partial z}{\partial y}=nz$
   (d) $\frac{\partial^2 z}{\partial x^2}-a^2\frac{\partial^2 z}{\partial y^2}=0$

3. Find the order and degree of the differential equation $y=1+\left(\frac{dy}{dx}\right)+\frac{1}{2!}\left(\frac{dy}{dx}\right)^2+\frac{1}{3!}\left(\frac{dy}{dx}\right)^3+....$

4. Find the order and degree of the differential equation $\frac{d^2y}{dx^2}+3\left(\frac{dy}{dx}\right)^2=x\log\left(\frac{d^2y}{dx^2}\right)$.

5. Find the order and degree of the given equations
   (a) $y'+\sin y'=0$
   (b) $y''+2y'+\sin y=0$

Answer Keys

1. (a) Order = 1; Degree = 1 (b) Order = 1; Degree = 2 (c) Order = 1; Degree = 1
   (d) Order = 3; Degree = 2 (e) Order = 1; Degree = 2 (f) Order = 2; Degree = 1
   (g) Order = 2; Degree = 2 (h) Order = 1; Degree = 2 (i) Order = 1; Degree = 2
2. (a) Order = 1; Degree = 2 (b) Order = 2; Degree = 3 (c) Order = 1; Degree = 1
   (d) Order = 2; Degree = 1
3. Order = 1; Degree = 1
4. Order = 2; Degree = Not defined
5. (a) Order = 1; Degree = Not defined (b) Order = 2; Degree = 1

TEXTUAL EXERCISE–1: (OBJECTIVE)

1. The order of the differential equation of all tangent lines to the parabola $y = x^2$ is
(a) 1 (b) 2
(c) 3 (d) 4

2. The degree and order of the differential equation of all parabolas whose axis is x-axis is
(a) 2, 1 (b) 1, 2
(c) 3, 2 (d) None of these

3. The degree of the differential equation $y_3^{2/3} + 2 + 3y_2 + y_1 = 0$ is
(a) 1 (b) 2
(c) 3 (d) None of these

4. The degree of the differential equation $y(x) = 1 + \frac{dy}{dx} + \frac{1}{1.2}\left(\frac{dy}{dx}\right)^2 + \frac{1}{1.2.3}\left(\frac{dy}{dx}\right)^3 + ...$ is
(a) 2 (b) 3
(c) 1 (d) None of these

5. If m and n are order and degree of the equation $\left(\frac{d^2y}{dx^2}\right)^5 + 4.\frac{\left(\frac{d^2y}{dx^2}\right)^3}{\frac{d^3y}{dx^3}} + \frac{d^3y}{dx^3} = x^2 - 1$, then
(a) $m = 3, n = 3$ (b) $m = 3, n = 2$
(c) $m = 3, n = 5$ (d) $m = 3, n = 1$

6. The order of the differential equation of a family of curves represented by an equation containing four arbitrary constants will be
(a) 2 (b) 4
(c) 6 (d) None of these

7. A differential equation of first order and first degree is
(a) $x\left(\frac{dy}{dx}\right)^2 - x + a = 0$ (b) $\frac{d^2y}{dx^2} + xy = 0$
(c) $dy + dx = 0$ (d) None of these

8. The order of the differential equation of all circles of radius r, having centre on y-axis and passing through the origin is
(a) 1 (b) 2
(c) 3 (d) 4

9. The differential equation of all circles in the first quadrant which touch the coordinate axes is of order
(a) 1 (b) 2
(c) 3 (d) None of these

10. Order and degree of differential equation $\frac{d^2y}{dx^2} = \left\{y + \left(\frac{dy}{dx}\right)^2\right\}^{1/4}$ are
(a) 4 and 2 (b) 1 and 2
(c) 1 and 4 (d) 2 and 4

11. The order and degree of the differential equation $\frac{d^2y}{dx^2} + \left(\frac{dy}{dx}\right)^{\frac{1}{3}} + x^{\frac{1}{4}} = 0$ are respectively
(a) 2,3 (b) 3,3
(c) 2,6 (d) 2,4

12. The degree of the differential equation $\left(1 + \left(\frac{dy}{dx}\right)^2\right)^{3/4} = \left(\frac{d^2y}{dx^2}\right)^{1/3}$ is
(a) 1/3 (b) 4
(c) 9 (d) 3/4

Answer Keys

1. (a) **2.** (b) **3.** (b) **4.** (c) **5.** (b) **6.** (b) **7.** (c) **8.** (a) **9.** (a) **10.** (d)
11. (a) **12.** (b)

■ FORMATION OF DIFFERENTIAL EQUATION

We know that differential equations are used to represent a family of curves. Family of curves is defined as a set of infinite curves having some common charactristics and at-least one variable characteristic, which is represented by unknown parameter involved in the equation family of curves (i.e., atleast one parameter). By assigning different values to these parameters (arbitrary constants) different members of the family of curves can be obtained.

Single Parameter Family

The family of curves having only one arbitrary constant. e.g., $y = mx + 2$: family of lines passing through $y = 2$;

$x^2 + y^2 = k^2$: family of concentric circles; $y^2 = kx$: family of parabolas; $y = x + k$: set of parallel lines

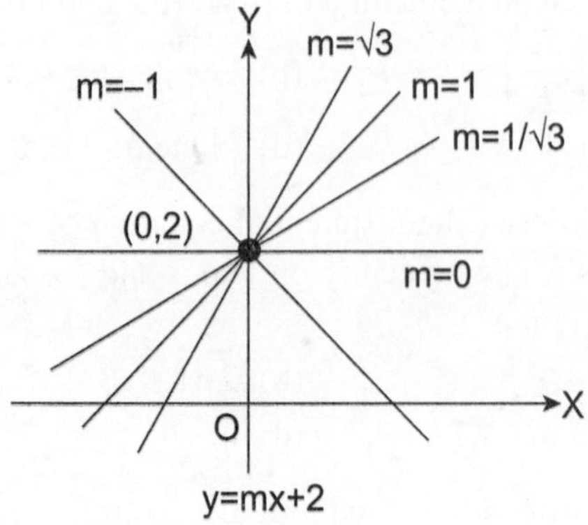

FIGURE 4.1

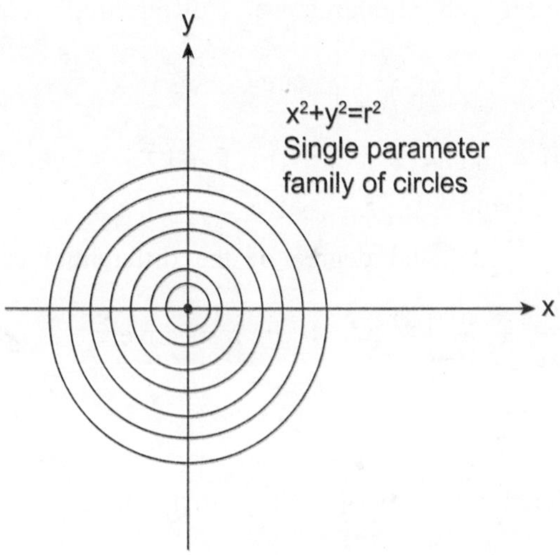

FIGURE 4.2

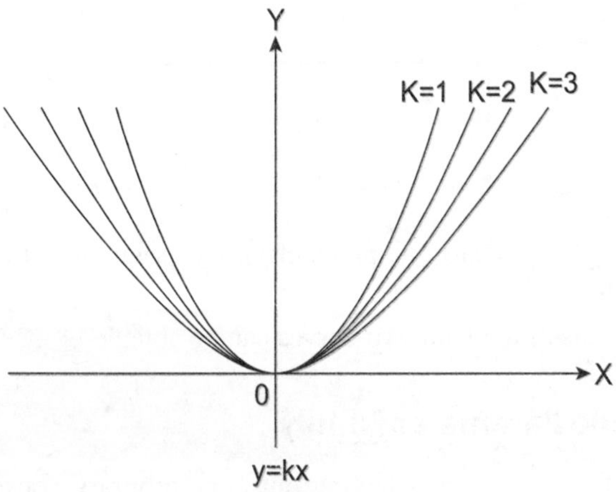

FIGURE 4.3

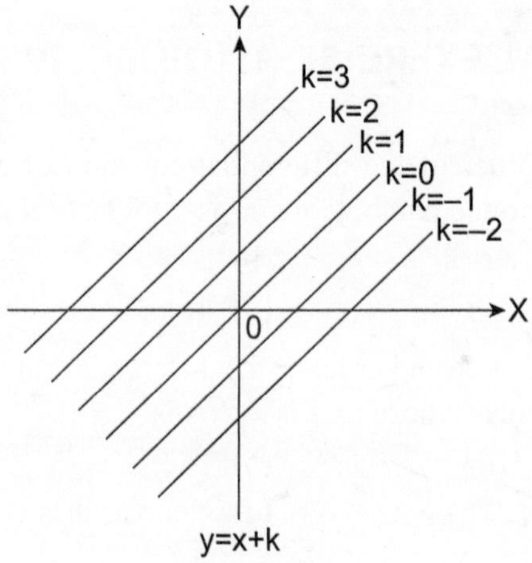

FIGURE 4.4

Double Parameter Family

These are the equations having two parameters, so called family of family of curves.

e.g., $y = mx + c$: denoting family of family of lines in xy-plane

e.g., two families of the above family of family of lines as shown in Fig. 4.5.

$y = x + k$; when $m = 1$

$y = mx + 2$; when $c = 2$

Similarly other two parameter family of curves are $(x - h)^2 + y^2 = r^2$ (circles), $y = A \sin x + B \cos x$, $y = Ax^2 + Bx$ etc.

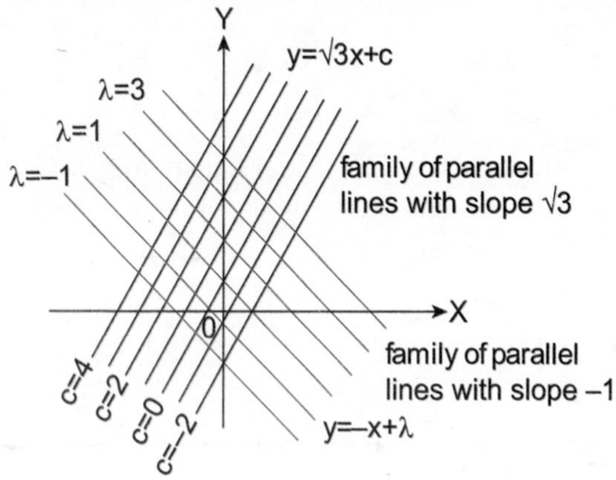

FIGURE 4.5

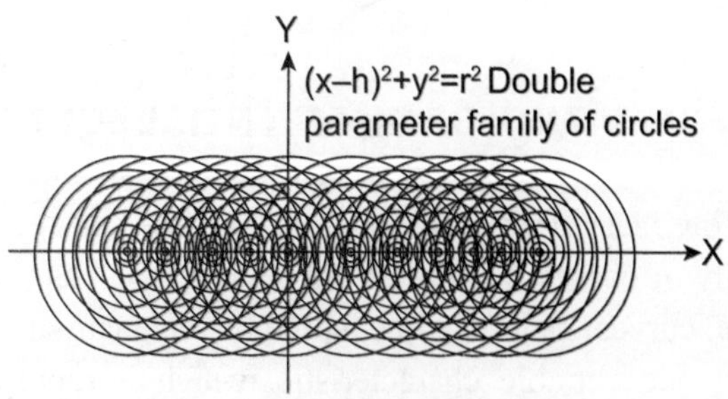

FIGURE 4.6

FORMATION OF DIFFERENTIAL EQUATION

Consider a family of curves involving a set of n arbitrary constants $f(x, y, C_1, C_2, C_3, ...C_n) = 0$ ...(i); where $C_1, C_2, ...C_n$ are n independent effective parameters is known as n parameter family of curves. The differential equation corresponding to above family of curves is a relation between x, y and derivatives of y up to order n, not containing any of the n arbitrary constants. It is obtained by eliminating arbitrary constants occurring in its equation, for instance if we differentiate the above equation (i) n times, w.r.t. x, one can get n more equations in $x, y, C_1, ... C_n$ other than equation (i). We have Therefore, $n + 1$ equations all together involving n parameters.

Now, by eliminating n parameters with the help of these $(n + 1)$ equations obtained one can get the differential equation of the above family of curves. As we have differentiated the equation of family of curve n times Therefore, resulting differential equation is of nth order and due to this reason the equation of family of curve is also known as primitive of the differential equation.

e.g., consider the family of parabolas $y^2 = 4ax$ ...(ii) with vertex at the origin and axis as the x-axis, here a is a parameter.

Differentiating w.r.t x, we get $2y\frac{dy}{dx} = 4a$ and from equation (ii), we have $4a = \frac{y^2}{x}$. Therefore, eliminating the parameter a from the above two equations, we get $2x\frac{dy}{dx} - y = 0$, which is the differential equation of (i) and clearly it is of order 1.

NOTES

1. *The order of the differential equation of family of curves is number of effective arbitrary constants present in the equation of family of curves. (Effective arbitrary constants means the parameter when they are reduced to be in minimum in number)*
2. *The equations obtained by varying the arbitrary constants in the primitive represent a certain system or family of curves; the differential equation (in which these constants do not appear) expresses some property common to all these curves.*
3. *If arbitrary constants appear in addition, subtraction, multiplication, or division, then we can club them to reduce into one new arbitrary constant. Hence, the differential equation corresponding to a family of curves will have order exactly same as number of essential arbitrary constants in the equation of curve.*
4. *On the other hand, it is evident that a differential equation of the nth order cannot have more than n arbitrary constants in its solution; for, if it had, say (n + 1), on eliminating them there would appear, not an equation of the nth order, but one of the (n + 1)th order. Finally, the differential equation corresponding to a family of curves is obtained by using the following steps:*
   (a) Identify the number of essential arbitrary constants (say n) in the equation of the curve.
   (b) Differentiate the equation n times.
   (c) Eliminate the arbitrary constants from the equation of curve and n additional equations obtained in step (b).

ILLUSTRATION 4: Find the differential equation of the family of curves $y = e^x (A \cos x + B \sin x)$; where A, B are arbitrary constants. Also write its order and degree.

SOLUTION: Here, the equation has two arbitrary constants. So, its differential equation will be of the second order.

We have $y = e^x (A \cos x + B \sin x)$ ...(i)

Differentiating (i) w.r.t. x, $\frac{dy}{dx} = e^x(A\cos x + B\sin x) + e^x(-A\sin x + B\cos x)$

or $\frac{dy}{dx} = y + e^x(-A\sin x + B\cos x)$ ...(ii)

Differentiating (ii) w.r.t. x, $\frac{d^2y}{dx^2}=\frac{dy}{dx}+e^x(-A\sin x+B\cos x)+e^x(-A\cos x-B\sin x)$

or $\frac{d^2y}{dx^2}=\frac{dy}{dx}+\left(\frac{dy}{dx}-y\right)-y$, by using (ii) and (i)

$\therefore$ $\frac{d^2y}{dx^2}-2\left(\frac{dy}{dx}-y\right)=0$ is the required differential equation

ILLUSTRATION 5: Find the differential equation representing the family of curves $xy = ae^x + be^{-x}$.

SOLUTION: Let $xy = ae^x + be^{-x}$ ...(i)

Differentiating (i) with respect to x, we get $x\frac{dy}{dx}+y=ae^x-be^{-x}$ ...(ii)

Now differentiating (ii) with respect to x, we get

$x\frac{d^2y}{dx^2}+\frac{dy}{dx}+\frac{dy}{dx}=ae^x+be^{-x}=xy$ [from (i)]

Therefore, $x\frac{d^2y}{dx^2}+2\frac{dy}{dx}=xy$ is the required differential equation.

ILLUSTRATION 6: Find the differential equation representing the family of curves $c(y + c)^2 = x^3$.

SOLUTION: Given family of curve is $c(y + c)^2 = x^3$ ...(i)

Differentiating with respect to x, we get

$c[2(y+c)]\frac{dy}{dx}=3x^2$ ...(ii)

Dividing (i) by (ii), we have $\frac{y+c}{2\frac{dy}{dx}}=\frac{x}{3}$

$\Rightarrow$ $c=\frac{2xdy}{3dx}-y$

Hence, $c=\frac{2x}{3}\left[\frac{dy}{dx}\right]-y$.

Substituting c, back into equation (i), we get

$\left[\frac{2x}{3}\left(\frac{dy}{dx}\right)-y\right]\left[\frac{2x}{3}\frac{dy}{dx}\right]^2=x^3$, which is the required differential equation.

ILLUSTRATION 7: Find the differential equation of the family of straight lines at a constant distance p from the origin such that the perpendicular from origin to these lines makes angle θ with positive direction of x-axis. (Given θ is a parameter)

SOLUTION: Given equation is $x\cos\theta + y\sin\theta = p$ ...(1)

Differentiating w.r.t. x, we get

$\cos\theta+\frac{dy}{dx}\sin\theta=0$ ...(2)

$\therefore$ from (1) and (2) by eliminating $\cos\theta$, we get

These gives $\left(y-x\frac{dy}{dx}\right)\sin\theta=p$ ...(3)

Parallelly by eliminating $\sin\theta$, we get

$\left(y-x\frac{dy}{dx}\right)\cos\theta=-p\frac{dy}{dx}$ ...(4)

Squaring and adding (3) and (4), we get

$$\left(y-x\frac{dy}{dx}\right)^2 = p^2\left\{1+\left(\frac{dy}{dx}\right)^2\right\}$$

ILLUSTRATION 8: Form a differential equation of a family of circles touching y-axis at origin.

SOLUTION: The required equation of circle will be

$x^2 + y^2 + 2gx = 0$

$(f = c = 0)$ ...(1)

(where g is the parameter)

i.e., circle with centre $(-g, 0)$ and radius $= |g|$

That is for different values of g, we get different circles belonging to the above family as shown below

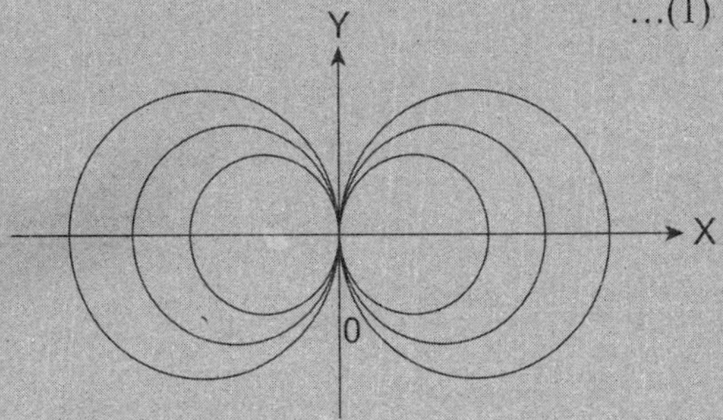

FIGURE 4.7

Differentiating (1) w.r.t., x, we get

$$2x+2y\frac{dy}{dx}+2g=0$$

or $\quad x+y\dfrac{dy}{dx}+g=0$ ...(2)

Now eliminating 'g' using (1) and (2), we get $x^2+y^2+2x\left(-x-y\dfrac{dy}{dx}\right)=0$

i.e., $y^2-x^2-2xy\dfrac{dy}{dx}=0$ is the required differential equation.

ILLUSTRATION 9: Show that $y = A\cos x + \sin x$ is a solution of $\cos x\dfrac{dy}{dx}+y\sin x=1$.

SOLUTION: Given family of curve is $y = A\cos x + \sin x$ ...(1)

and given differential equation is $\cos x\dfrac{dy}{dx}+y\sin x=1$ ...(2)

Differentiating (i), we get $\dfrac{dy}{dx}=-A\sin x+\cos x$ ...(3)

Substituting the values of y and $\dfrac{dy}{dx}$ in the equation (2),

We see that equation (2) reduces to $\cos x\,(-A\sin x + \cos x) + (A\cos x + \sin x)\sin x = 1$,

so, the given differential equation is satisfied

ILLUSTRATION 10: Determine the differential equation to represent a family of circles such that their centers move along x-axis with constant radius unity.

SOLUTION: The equation of a circle having centre on the x-axis, say, at $(a, 0)$ and radius unity is $(x-a)^2 + y^2 = 1$

So, the family C of all circles with centre on the x-axis and radius unity as shown in Fig. 4.8.

Hence, $C : (x-a)^2 + y^2 = 1$ ...(i)

For different values of a, we get different members of the family C.

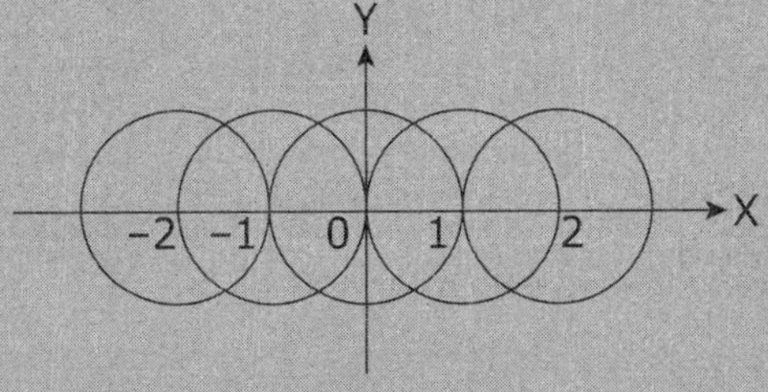

FIGURE 4.8

$\therefore\ x^2 + y^2 = 1$ (for $a = 0$);

$(x-1)^2 + y^2 = 1$ (for $a = 1$);

$(x+1)^2 + y^2 = 1$ (for $a = -1$); are member of family C

In order to form the relation that will represent family C, and is free from the parameter a, we obtain on differentiating (i), $(x-a)+y\frac{dy}{dx}=0$ ...(ii)

Note that it is not still free from the parameter a. To obtain the required relation (free from a) we are to eliminate a from (i) and (ii), giving $y^2\left(\frac{dy}{dx}\right)^2+y^2=1$ ...(iii)

The relation (iii) represents the differential equation of the family C of circles (having centers on the x-axis and radius unity), being free from the parameter a, and Therefore, this relation represents the differential equation of the above family of circle.

ILLUSTRATION 11: Find the differential equation of the system of hyperbolas $\frac{x^2}{a^2}-\frac{y^2}{b^2}=1$, where b is a fixed constant and a is a parameter.

SOLUTION: Consider the equation $\frac{x^2}{a^2}-\frac{y^2}{b^2}=1.$ ...(1)

Differentiating this equation with respect to x, we get

$\frac{2x}{a^2}-\frac{2yy'}{b^2}=0$ i.e., $b^2x = a^2yy'$ ...(2)

Multiplying both sides by x, gives $\frac{x^2}{a^2}=\frac{xyy'}{b^2}.$ ...(3)

From equations (1) and (3) eliminating a^2 we obtain

$1+\frac{y^2}{b^2}=\frac{xyy'}{b^2}$

$\Rightarrow b^2 + y^2 = xyy'$

Therefore, the differential equation of the family of hyperbolas is $xyy' - y^2 = b^2$.

ILLUSTRATION 12: Form a differential equation representing the family of curves $y = a\cos(x + b)$, where a, b are arbitrary constants.

SOLUTION: Given $y = a\cos(x + b)$ ...(i)

Differentiating (i) with respect to x, we get

$y' = -a\sin(x + b)$ ...(ii)

Differentiating (ii) with respect to x, we get

$y'' = -a\cos(x + b)$ ...(ii)

Eliminating a, b from the equations (i), (ii) and (iii), we get $\frac{d^2y}{dx^2}+y=0$, which is the required differential equation.

ILLUSTRATION 13: Form the differential equation corresponding to $y^2 = m(a^2 - x^2)$ by eliminating m and a.

SOLUTION: Given $y^2 = m(a^2 - x^2)$ ...(i)

Differentiating (i) with respect to x, we get $2yy' = -2mx$

or $yy' = -mx$ ...(ii)

Differentiating (ii) with respect to x, we get

$(y')^2 + yy'' = -m$ ...(iii)

Eliminating 'm' from the equation (ii) and (iii), we get

$yy'' - x[(y')^2 + yy'']$

$\Rightarrow xyy'' + x(y')^2 - yy' = 0$

$\Rightarrow xy\dfrac{d^2y}{dx^2} + x\left(\dfrac{dy}{dx}\right)^2 - y\left(\dfrac{dy}{dx}\right) = 0$ is the required differential equation.

TEXTUAL EXERCISE–2: (SUBJECTIVE)

1. Show that $Ax^2 + By^2 = 1$ is the solution of $x\left[y\dfrac{d^2y}{dx^2} + \left(\dfrac{dy}{dx}\right)^2\right] - y\dfrac{dy}{dx} = 0$.

2. By the elimination of the constants h and k, find the differential equation of which $(x - h)^2 + (y - k)^2 = a^2$ is a solution.

3. By the elimination of the constants a and b, find the differential equation of which $xy = ce^x + be^{-x} + x^2$ is a solution.

4. By the elimination of the constants a find the differential equation of which $y^2 = 4a(x + a)$ is a solution.

5 Show that the differential equation of the family of circles of fixed radius r with centers on y-axis is $(x^2 - r^2)\left(\dfrac{dy}{dx}\right)^2 + x^2 = 0$

6. Find the order of the following curves:
(a) $y = C_1 \tan^2 x + C_2 \sec^2 x + C_3$
(b) Family of ellipses having fixed directrix
(c) $xy = C_1e^x - C_2e^{-x} + x^2$
(d) $y = C_1x + C_2x^2$
(e) $y = C_1x + \dfrac{C_2}{x} + C_3$
(f) $y = C_1e^{3x} + C_2e^{2x} + C_3e^x$
(g) $y = (\sin^{-1} x)^2 + A\sin^{-1} x + B$

7. Find the order of the differential equation whose general solution is $y = (c_1 + c_2)\sin(x + c_3) - c_4e^{x+c_2}$

8. Find the differential equation of the family of curves $y = e^x(A\cos x + B\sin x)$, where A and B are arbitrary constants.

9. A series circuit contains an inductor, resistor and capacitor. Determine the differential equation for the charge $q(t)$.

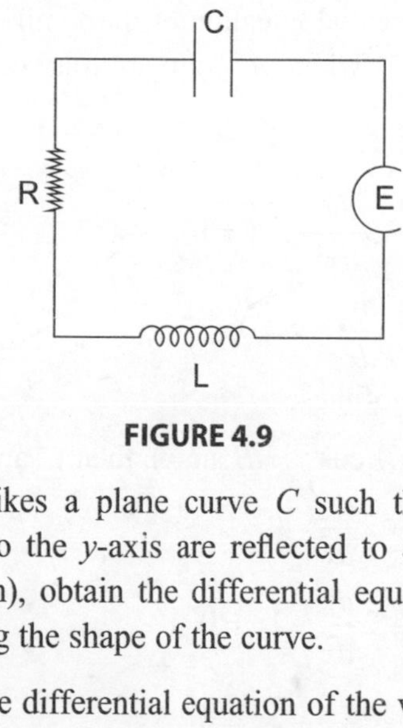

FIGURE 4.9

10. Light strikes a plane curve C such that all beams parallel to the y-axis are reflected to a single point O (Origin), obtain the differential equation $y = f(x)$ describing the shape of the curve.

11. Obtain the differential equation of the velocity v of a body of mass m falling vertically downwards through a medium offering a resistance proportional to the square of the instantaneous velocity.

Answer Keys

2. $\left[1+\left(\frac{dy}{dx}\right)^2\right]^3 = a^2\left(\frac{d^2y}{dx^2}\right)^2$

3. $x\frac{d^2y}{dx^2}+2\frac{dy}{dx}-xy+x^2-2=0$

4. $y\left[1-\left(\frac{dy}{dx}\right)^2\right]=2x\frac{dy}{dx}$

6. (a) 2nd order (b) order 3 (c) $xy'' + 2y' = xy - x^2 + 2$ (d) $y = xy_1 - \frac{1}{2}x^2y_2$

(e) $y'''+\frac{3}{x}y''=0$ (f) $\frac{d^3y}{dx^3}-6\frac{d^2y}{dx^2}+11\frac{dy}{dx}-6y=0$ (g) $(1-x^2)\frac{d^2y}{dx^2}-x\frac{dy}{dx}=2$

7. order = 3.

8. $\frac{d^2y}{dx^2}-2\frac{dy}{dx}+2y=0$

9. $L\frac{d^2q}{dt^2}+R\frac{dq}{dt}+\frac{q}{C}=E(t)$

10. $x\left(\frac{dx}{dy}\right)^2+2y\frac{dx}{dy}=x$

11. $\frac{dv}{dt}=g-\frac{k}{m}v^2$

TEXTUAL EXERCISE–2: (OBJECTIVE)

1. The equation of the curve whose subnormal is equal to a constant a is
   (a) $y = ax + b$ (b) $y^2 = 2\,ax + 2b$
   (c) $a\,y^2 - x^3 = a$ (d) None of these

2. The differential equation of all parabolas with axis parallel to the axis of y is
   (a) $yy_2 + (y_1)^2 = 0$ (b) $y_3 = 2y_1$
   (c) $y_3^2 = y_1$ (d) None of these

3. The differential equation of all ellipses centred at the origin would be of order
   (a) 4 (b) 3
   (c) 2 (d) None of these

4. The differential equation of the family of curves $y = Ae^{3x} + Be^{5x}$, where A, B are arbitrary constants is:
   (a) $\frac{d^2y}{dx^2}+8\frac{dy}{dx}+15y=0$
   (b) $\frac{d^2y}{dx^2}-8\frac{dy}{dx}+15y=0$
   (c) $\frac{d^2y}{dx^2}-\frac{dy}{dx}+y=0$
   (d) None of these

5. If $y = e^{-x}(A\cos x + B\sin x)$, then y satisfies:
   (a) $\frac{d^2y}{dx^2}+2\frac{dy}{dx}=0$
   (b) $\frac{d^2y}{dx^2}-2\frac{dy}{dx}+2y=0$
   (c) $\frac{d^2y}{dx^2}+2\frac{dy}{dx}+2y=0$
   (d) $\frac{d^2y}{dx^2}+2y=0$

6. The differential equation of all non-vertical lines in a plane is given by
   (a) $\frac{d^2y}{dx^2}=0$
   (b) $\frac{d^2x}{dy^2}=0$
   (c) $\frac{d^2x}{dy^2}=0$ and $\frac{d^2y}{dx^2}=0$
   (d) All of these

7. Family $y = Ax + A^3$ of curve represented by the differential equation has degree
   (a) Three (b) Two
   (c) One (d) None of these

8. The differential equation for all the straight lines which are at a distance p from the origin is
   (a) $\left(y-x\frac{dy}{dx}\right)^2=p^2\left(1-\left(\frac{dy}{dx}\right)^2\right)$
   (b) $\left(y+x\frac{dy}{dx}\right)^2=p^2\left(1+\left(\frac{dy}{dx}\right)^2\right)$
   (c) $\left(y-x\frac{dy}{dx}\right)^2=p^2\left(1+\left(\frac{dy}{dx}\right)^2\right)$
   (d) None of these

9. The differential equation whose solution is $y = c_1\cos ax + c_2\sin ax$ is (Where c_1,c_2 are arbitrary constants)
   (a) $\frac{d^2y}{dx^2}+y^2=0$ (b) $\frac{d^2y}{dx^2}+a^2y=0$
   (c) $\frac{d^2y}{dx^2}+ay^2=0$ (d) $\frac{d^2y}{dx^2}-a^2y=0$

10. Differential equation whose solution is $y = cx + c - c^3$, is

(a) $\frac{dy}{dx} = c$ (b) $y = x\frac{dy}{dx} + \frac{dy}{dx} - \left(\frac{dy}{dx}\right)^3$

(c) $\frac{dy}{dx} = c - 3c^3$ (d) None of these

11. The elimination of the arbitrary constants A, B and C from $y = A + Bx + Ce^{-x}$ leads to the differential equation

(a) $y''' - y' = 0$ (b) $y''' - y'' + y' = 0$

(c) $y''' + y'' = 0$ (d) $y''' + y'' - y' = 0$

12. $y = ae^{mx} + be^{-mx}$ satisfies which of the following differential equations

(a) $\frac{dy}{dx} - my = 0$ (b) $\frac{dy}{dx} + my = 0$

(c) $\frac{d^2y}{dx^2} + m^2y = 0$ (d) $\frac{d^2y}{dx^2} - m^2y = 0$

13. If $x^2 + y^2 = 1$, then $\left(\text{given } y' = \frac{dy}{dx}, y'' = \frac{d^2y}{dx^2}\right)$

(a) $yy'' - 2(y')^2 + 1 = 0$ (b) $yy'' + (y')^2 + 1 = 0$

(c) $yy'' - (y')^2 - 1 = 0$ (d) $yy'' + 2(y')^2 + 1 = 0$

14. Differential equation of $y = \sec(\tan^{-1}x)$ is

(a) $(1+x^2)\frac{dy}{dx} = y + x$ (b) $(1+x^2)\frac{dy}{dx} = y - x$

(c) $(1+x^2)\frac{dy}{dx} = xy$ (d) $(1+x^2)\frac{dy}{dx} = \frac{x}{y}$

15. The differential equation of all circles of radius r, is given by

(a) $\{1 + (y_1)^2\}^2 = r^2y^3_2$ (b) $\{1 + (y_1)^2\}^3 = r^2 y^3_2$

(c) $\{1 + (y_1)^2\}^3 = r^2 y^2_2$ (d) None of these

16. The differential equations of all circles touching the x-axis at origin is

(a) $(y^2 - x^2) = 2xy\left(\frac{dy}{dx}\right)$

(b) $(x^2 - y^2)\frac{dy}{dx} = 2xy$

(c) $(x^2 - y^2) = 2xy\left(\frac{dy}{dx}\right)$

(d) None of these

17. The differential equation of all circles in the first quadrant which touch the coordinate axes is

(a) $(x - y)^2 (1 + (y')^2) = (x + yy')^2$

(b) $(x + y)^2 (1 + (y')^2) = (x + y')^2$

(c) $(x - y)^2 (1 + y') = (x + yy')^2$

(d) None of these

18. The differential equation of all circles touching the y-axis at origin is,

(a) $y^2 - x^2 = 2xy\frac{dy}{dx}$ (b) $y^2 - x^2 = 2xy\frac{dx}{dy}$

(c) $x^2 - y^2 = 2xy\frac{dy}{dx}$ (d) $x^2 - y^2 = 2xy\frac{dx}{dy}$

19. The differential equation of all parabolas having their axes of symmetry coincident with the axes of x is,

(a) $yy_2 + y_1^2 = y + y_1$ (b) $yy_2 + y_1^2 = 0$

(c) $yy_2 + y_1^2 = y_1$ (d) None of these

Answer Keys

1. (b)	**2.** (d).	**3.** (b)	**4.** (b)	**5.** (c)	**6.** (a)	**7.** (a)	**8.** (c)	**9.** (b)	**10.** (b)
11. (c)	**12.** (d)	**13.** (b)	**14.** (c)	**15.** (c)	**16.** (b)	**17.** (a)	**18.** (a)	**19.** (b)	

SOLUTION OF DIFFERENTIAL EQUATIONS

Solving a differential equation is an inverse process of forming differential equation of a family of curves by integrating the given differential equation to obtain a general relation between the independent and dependent variables. Therefore, the solution/integral/primitive of a differential equation of a family of curves is a relation between the variables free from derivatives which or derivatives obtained there from satisfy the differential equation. That means the curve which satisfies the differential equation in the domain of differential equation is called solution of differential equation.

e.g., $y = \sin x + c$ is solution of differential equation $dy = \cos x\, dx$.

"A family of curve $f(x, y, c_1, c_2, ...) = 0$; from which the differential equation $F(x, y, dy/dx, ...)$ obtained at any point, always satisfies the differential equation is called **solution/integral/primitive.**"

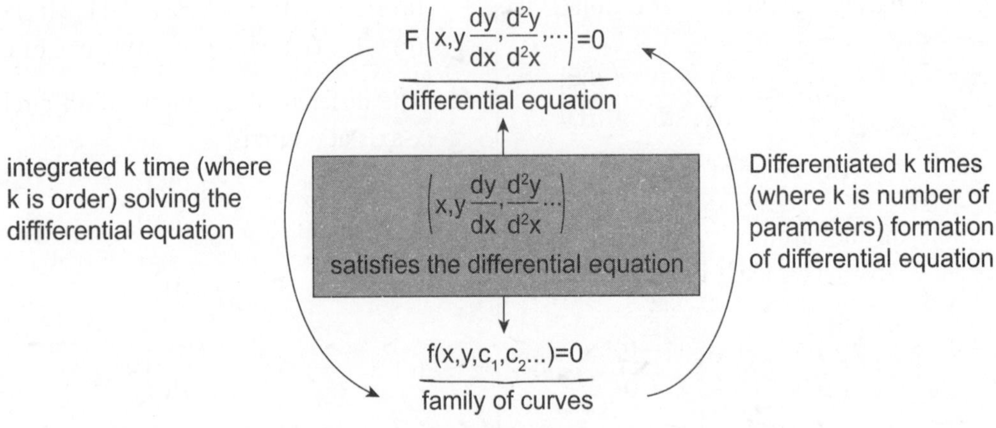

FIGURE 4.10

ILLUSTRATION 14: Explain with proper reason, why the functions with the given graphs cannot be solutions of the differential equation $\frac{dy}{dx} = e^{2x}(y-2)^2$.

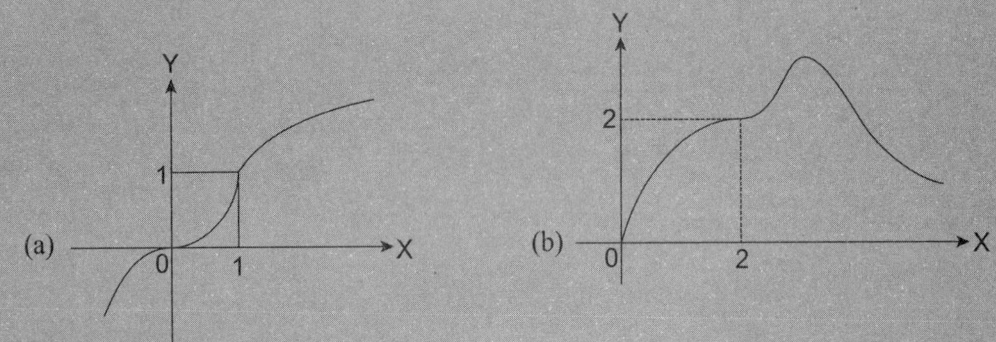

SOLUTION: (a) The curve given cannot be a solution of given differential equation because of two primary reasons.

(i) Derivative at (0, 0) is zero on the curve on the other hand differential equation don't exhibit that value.

(ii) Curve is not differentials at (1, 1) which is again not true from the differential equation.

The curve in figure (2) cannot be solution of differential equation because it is non-monotonic; whereas the differential equation generates positive (+ve) slope at each point (x, y) in the domain.

ILLUSTRATION 15: The function illustrated by the given graph is a solution of exactly one of the following equations. Find out which one is the correct equation and justify your answers with proper argument.

(i) $\frac{dy}{dx} = 3 + xy$

(ii) $\frac{dy}{dx} = 1 - xy$

(iii) $\frac{dy}{dx} = -4xy^2$

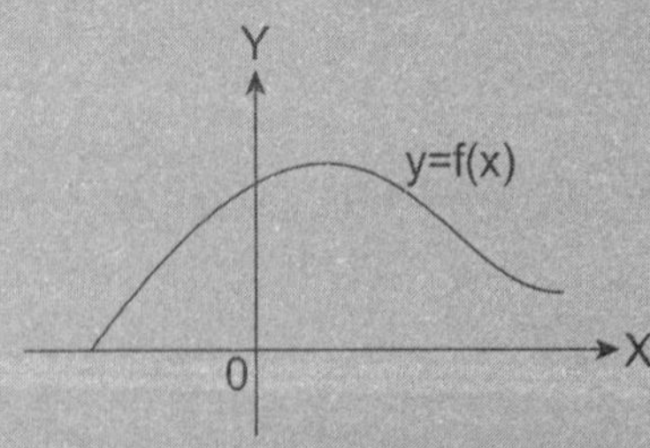

FIGURE 4.11

SOLUTION: Since exactly one equation has solution as the graph shown, Therefore, to single out that equation let us rule out the possibilities of other.

Given curve cannot be solution of equation

(i) indeed the solutions of equation;

(ii) must be non-monotonic in 2nd quadrant as the sign of $\frac{dy}{dx}$ change at $xy = -3$

Similarly equation (iii) can never have the function shown in graph as solution because its derivative at $x = 0$ is not zero.

■ CLASSIFICATION OF SOLUTIONS

Solutions are classified in to the following three types:

(i) General Solution
(ii) Particular Solution
(iii) Singular Solution

General Solution

A family of curves (i.e., relation in variables x and y) satisfying the given differential equation which contains exactly as many effective arbitrary constants as the order of differential equation is known as General solution or Complete integral or Complete primitives. Let the equation involving the variables x, y and n independent arbitrary constants be

$$f(x, y, C_1, C_2, \ldots C_n) = 0 \quad \ldots(i)$$

and the differential equation obtained from (i) be

$$F\left(x, y, \frac{dy}{dx}, \frac{d^2y}{dx^2}, \ldots, \frac{d^ny}{dx^n}\right) = 0 \quad \ldots(ii)$$

Then (i) is called the general solution of (ii).

ILLUSTRATION 16: Show that $V = Ar + B/r$ is a solution of the differential equation $r^2\frac{d^2V}{dr^2} + r\frac{dV}{dr} - V = 0$

SOLUTION: If $V = Ar + \frac{B}{r}$ ...(i)

$\Rightarrow \frac{dV}{dr} = A - \frac{B}{r^2}$ ...(ii)

multiplying by r, we get

$\Rightarrow r\frac{dV}{dr} = Ar - \frac{B}{r}$ ...(iii)

Differentiating (ii) w.r.t. r again, we get $\frac{d^2V}{dr^2} = \frac{2B}{r^3}$

Therefore, $\frac{1}{2}r^2\frac{d^2V}{dr^2} = \frac{B}{r}$ ...(iv)

From (i) and (iii), we get (substituting the value of $\frac{B}{r}$ from (iii) in (i))

$Ar = \frac{1}{2}\left(V + r\frac{dV}{dr}\right)$ ...(v)

Substituting the value of Ar and $\frac{B}{r}$ in equation (i),

we get $\frac{1}{2}\left(V + r\frac{dV}{dr}\right) + \frac{1}{2}r^2\frac{d^2V}{dr^2} = V$

$\Rightarrow r^2\frac{d^2V}{dr^2} + r\frac{dV}{dr} - V = 0$

Thus, $V = Ar + \frac{B}{r}$ is solution of equation $r^2\frac{d^2V}{dr^2} + \frac{rdV}{dr} - V = 0$.

GENERAL SOLUTION FOR MODELING THE POPULATION GROWTH

For modeling the unrestricted growth of population $x(t)$ of a colony of any living organism (bacteria, humans or other animals), it is reasonable to assume the relative rate of change of population to be constant.

In other words $\dfrac{\frac{dy}{dt}}{y} = k$ (constant) i.e.,

$$\frac{dy}{dt} = ky \qquad \ldots(1)$$

(Here y and $\dfrac{dy}{dt}$ are instantaneous population and its rate of reproduction at time 't')

Clearly both y and $\dfrac{dy}{dt}$ are positive, consequently k is also positive.

As long as the colony has plenty of food and living space, its population will obey the above unrestricted growth rate formula and known as exponential growth rate formula, because y will continue to grow as exponential function of 't'.

Now we like to obtain the unknown y as a function of t (say $y = f(t)$) that is involved in the differential equation (1) along with its derivative $\dfrac{dy}{dt}$.

$$\because \frac{dy}{dt} = ky \quad \Rightarrow \quad \frac{dy}{y} = kdt$$

$$\Rightarrow \int \frac{dy}{y} = k\int dt \quad \Rightarrow \quad \ln y = kt + c_0$$

$$\Rightarrow y = e^{kt+c_0} = e^{c_0}.e^{kt}$$

$\Rightarrow y = \lambda e^{kt}$ (where λ is an arbitrary constant)

Indeed it can be easily verified that any function $f(t)$ of the type $y = \lambda e^{kt}$ satisfies the differential equation (1) because $\dfrac{dy}{dt} = \dfrac{d}{dt}(\lambda e^{kt}) = k\lambda e^{kt} = ky$ and consequently all the solutions of differential equation are given by above formula and are known as general solution.

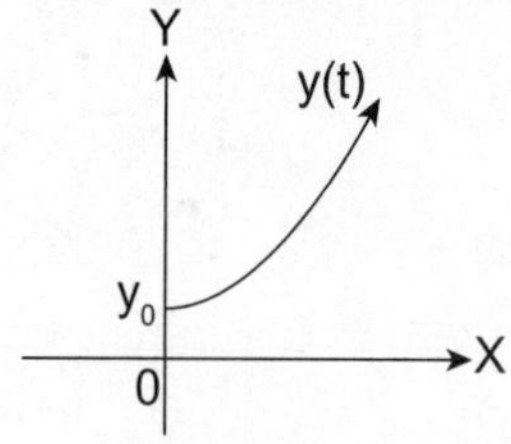

FIGURE 4.12

However, in practice, there often comes a time when environmental factors begin to restrict the further expansion of the colony and at this point, the growth ceases to be purely exponential in nature. To construct a population model that takes into account the effect of diminishing resources and cramping we assume that the initial population is y_0, then, the relative rate of change of population is proportional to the size of the remaining population. That is,

$$\frac{\frac{dy}{dt}}{y} = k(y_0 - y) \text{ or } \frac{dy}{dt} = ky(y_0 - y)$$

This is termed as a **Logistic equation,** and it arises not only in connection with population models, but also in a variety of other situations of problem solving.

A differential equation of the first order can be expressed in general form as:

$$\frac{dy}{dx} = F(x, y) \qquad \ldots(1)$$

The function $f(x)$, $\forall\, x \in (\alpha, \beta)$), is called a solution of the equation (1) if it has a derivative $f'(x)$ over (α, β) and if the equation $f'(x) = F(x, f(x))$ $\forall\, x \in (\alpha, \beta)$ holds good. On the other hand we can say that when the function $f(x)$ $\forall\, x \in (\alpha, \beta)$ substituted instead of y in the differential equation (1) the equation turns into an identity with respect to x on the interval (α, β).

A curve specified by the equation $y = f(x)$, $\forall\, x \in (\alpha, \beta)$; of equation (1), is also known as the **integral curve** of differential equation (1).

NOTES:

(i) *The general solution of an ordinary differential equation of nth order contains n independent parameters (essential arbitrary constant) which means the general solution of an ordinary differential equation of order one contains one arbitrary parameter and of second order contains two independent parameters and so on.*

(ii) *The general solution of a differential equation contains exactly as many essential parameters as the degree of equation. While counting the parameters in the general solution, it must be seen that they are essential and are not equivalent to a lesser number of parameters. The parameters in the solution of a differential equation are said to be essential, if it is impossible to deduce from the solution an equivalent relation containing lesser number of parameters.*

e.g., $y = (A + B)e^x + Ce^{D-x}$ = has apparently four parameters but number of essential parameter is two this can be observed as below $y = (A + B)e^x + Ce^D e^{-x}$

$\Rightarrow y = C_1e^x + C_2e^{-x}$; where $C_1 = A + B$ and $C_2 = Ce^D$

Hence, the four parameters A, B, C, D are not independent parameters, they are equivalent to two essential parameter C_1 and C_2.

The general solution of a differential equation can be written in more than one way, but parameters in one form must always be related to parameters of another form.

e.g., $y = e^{x^2+C}$ and $y = ke^{x^2}$ are both the general solutions of equation $dy - 2xy\,dx = 0$

Comparing both, we can see $e^{x^2}.e^C = ke^{x^2}$

$\Rightarrow k = e^C$ or $C = \ln k$

Hence, establishing the relationship between essential parameters of general solution of both type.

ILLUSTRATION 17: Mentioned below are differential equations and their general solutions in different forms. Compare them and establish the relation between their essential parameters.

(a) $\dfrac{d^2y}{dx^2} + \dfrac{dy}{dx} = 0$; $y = C_2 - e^{C_1 - x}$, and $y = C_3 + C_4e^{-x}$

(b) $\dfrac{d^2y}{dx^2} = -y$; $y = C_1 \sin x + C_2 \cos x$ and $y = C_3 \sin(x - C_4)$

SOLUTION: (a) Given two general solutions $y = C_2 - e^{C_1 - x}$ and $y = C_3 + C_4e^{-x}$ each containing two essential parameters.

Rearranging the first equation as $y = C_2 - e^{C_1}e^{-x}$ and comparing it with the second $y = C_3 + C_4e^{-x}$, we get $C_2 = C_3$ and $C_4 = -e^{C_1}$.

Consider the General solutions $y = C_1 \sin x + C_2 \cos x$ and $y = C_3 \sin(x - C_4)$

Being a general solution of an equation of order two,containing two essential parameters. symplifying the equation $y = C_3 \sin(x - C_4)$ and comparing it with the first, we get

$C_1 = C_3 \cos C_4$, and $C_2 = C_3 \sin C_4$

$\Rightarrow C_3 = \sqrt{C_1^2 + C_2^2}$ and $C_4 = -\tan^{-1}\left(\dfrac{C_2}{C_1}\right)$,

Hence, we get the relationship between the parameters involved in the given two general solutions.

ILLUSTRATION 18: Find the order of the differential equation whose general solution is represented by $y = C_1e^{2x+C_2} + (C_3 + C_4)\ln(C_5x)$, where C_1, C_2, C_3, C_4, C_5 are parameters.

SOLUTION: Given complete primitive is $y = C_1e^{2x+C_2} + (C_3 + C_4)\ln(C_5x)$

The expression on R.H.S. can be arranged and regrouped as $y = C_1e^{C_2}.e^{2x} + (C_3 + C_4)\ln C_5 + (C_3 + C_4)\ln x$

which can be rewritten as $y = Ae^{2x} + B \ln x + C$; where $A = C_1e^{C_2}$, $B = C_3 + C_4$ and $C = (C_3 + C_4) \ln C_5$.

Indeed it contains minimum number of parameters 3.

Consequently the order of its differential equation shall be 3.

ILLUSTRATION 19: The rate at which an epidemic spreads through a community is proportional to the product of the number of residents who have been infected and the number of susceptible residents. Express the number of residents who have been infected as a function of time.

SOLUTION: Let $y(t)$ denotes the number of residents who have been infected by time t and y_m the total number of residents. Then the number of susceptible residents who have not been infected is $y_m - y$, and the differential equation describing the spread of the epidemic is $\frac{dy}{dt} = ky(y_m - y)$; ($k$ is the constant of proportionality)

$\Rightarrow \frac{dy}{y(y_m - y)} = k\,dt$; Integrating both sides, we get

$$\Rightarrow \int \frac{dy}{y(y_m - y)} = \int k\,dt$$

The integral on the left requires partial fractions

$$\Rightarrow \frac{1}{y_m}\int \frac{dy}{y} + \frac{1}{y_m}\int \frac{dy}{y_m - y} = \int k\,dt$$

$$\Rightarrow \frac{1}{y_m}\ln|y| - \frac{1}{y_m}\ln|y_m - y| = kt + C$$

$$\Rightarrow \frac{1}{y_m}\ln\left|\frac{y}{y_m - y}\right| = kt + C \quad \text{(Applying division property of logs)}$$

$$\Rightarrow \ln\left(\frac{y}{y_m - y}\right) = y_m(kt + C) \qquad \text{(Note that } y > 0, y_m > y)$$

$$\Rightarrow \frac{y}{y_m - y} = e^{y_m(kt+C)} \quad \text{(Applying the definition of log)}$$

$$\Rightarrow y = (y_m - y)e^{y_m(kt+C)}$$

$$\Rightarrow y = (y_m - y)e^{y_m kt}e^{y_m C} \qquad \text{(Because } e^{y_m C} \text{ is a constant, take it as } A_1)$$

$$\Rightarrow y = A_1 y_m e^{y_m kt} - A_1 y e^{y_m kt}$$

$$\Rightarrow y(1 + A_1 e^{y_m kt}) = A_1 y_m e^{y_m kt}$$

$\Rightarrow y = \frac{A_1 y_m e^{y_m kt}}{(1 + A_1 e^{y_m kt})}$ to simplify the equation, let $A = \frac{1}{A_1}$, so that we have

$$y = \frac{y_m}{\left(1 + Ae^{-y_m kt}\right)}$$

The graph of $y(t)$ is as shown in Fig. 4.13.

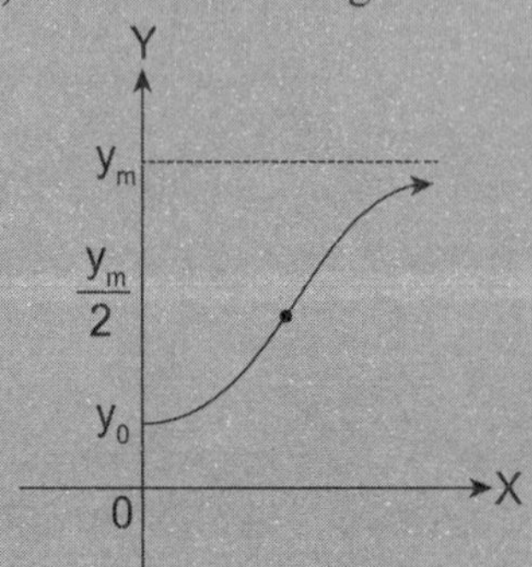

FIGURE 4.13

Particular Solution

A solution obtained from the general solution by giving particular values to the arbitrary constants (parameters) is called a particular solution of that differential equation.

e.g., $y = \sin x + 1$ is one particular solution of equation $dy - \cos x\, dx = 0$.

Therefore, the set of all particular solutions is known as general solution.

ILLUSTRATION 20: Show that $y = 2e^x - 3e^{-x}$ is a particular solution of differential equation $\frac{d^2y}{dx^2} - y = 0$

SOLUTION: We are given $y = 2e^x - 3e^{-x}$ differentiating with respect to x, we get

$$\frac{dy}{dx} = 2e^x + 3e^{-x}$$

differentiating once again w.r.t. x, we get

$$\frac{d^2y}{dx^2} = 2e^x - 3e^{-x}$$

$\Rightarrow \quad \frac{d^2y}{dx^2} = y$, is thus the differential equation of $y = 2e^x - 3e^{-x}$.

Cauchy's Initial Value Problem

The problem of determining the particular solution of

equation $\frac{dy}{dx} = F(x, y)$ ...(1)

satisfying the condition $y(x_0) = y_0$ ...(2)

where x_0, y_0 are given numbers, is referred to as **Cauchy's initial value problem.** Condition (2) is called the initial condition (boundary condition). The particular integral of equation (1), satisfying the initial condition (2), is called the solution of Cauchy problem. Geometrical meaning of solving Cauchy's problem means to find the integral curve of equation (1) which passes through the given point (x_0, y_0).

ILLUSTRATION 21: Verify that the function f defined by $f(x) = \ln x$ for all $x \in (0, \infty)$ satisfies the initial value problem $xy' = 1$ $(x \neq 0)$, $y(1) = 0$.

SOLUTION: If $f(x) = \ln x$ for all $x \in (0, \infty)$ we have $f'(x) = \frac{1}{x}$ for all $x \in (0, \infty)$ $x \in (0, \infty)$.

Hence, if we put $f'(x)$ for y' in the given differential equation, the equation becomes an identity on $(0, \infty)$.

Thus, the given function f satisfies the given differential equation. Further $f(1) = 0$. Hence, the given function f satisfies the given initial value problem.

ILLUSTRATION 22: Show that the function f defined by $f(x) = \cos x$; $(x \in \mathbb{R})$, satisfies the initial value problem $y'' + y = 0$, $y(0) = 0$, $y'(0) = 1$

SOLUTION: $f(x) = \cos x$; $(x \in \mathbb{R})$ implies that $f'(x) = -\sin x$ and $f''(x) = -\cos x$

Hence, if we put y for f, the given function f satisfies the given differential equation for all $x \in \mathbb{R}$.

Further $f(0) = 1$ and $f'(0) = 0$, i.e., satisfies the initial conditions. So, the given function f satisfies the given initial value problem.

ILLUSTRATION 23: Find the particular solution of $\log\left(\frac{dy}{dx}\right) = 3x + 4y$, $y(0) = 0$

SOLUTION: The given equation is $\log\left(\frac{dy}{dx}\right) = 3x + 4y$

$\Rightarrow \quad \frac{dy}{dx} = e^{3x+4y} = e^{3x}e^{4y} \qquad \Rightarrow \quad e^{-4y}\,dy = e^{3x}\,dx$

Integrating the above, we have $\frac{e^{-4y}}{-4} = \frac{e^{3x}}{3} + C$

Putting $x = 0$, $y = 0$, we have $-\frac{1}{4} - \frac{1}{3} = C$

$\Rightarrow \quad C = -\frac{7}{12}$

Hence, $\frac{e^{-4y}}{-4} = \frac{e^{3x}}{3} - \frac{7}{12}$

$\Rightarrow \quad 4e^{3x} + 3e^{-4y} - 7 = 0$ is a particular solution.

Singular Solutions

General solution of differential equations may not include all possible solutions, consequently the differential equation may also possess other solutions than the general solution. "The solution which cannot be obtained by giving any value to arbitrary constants present in the general solution are termed as singular solution". Geometrically they act as an envelope to the family of curves represented by general solutions.

In order to realize the existence of singular solution consider an example of family of circles $(x - h)^2 + y^2 = a^2$, where h is parameter and a is fixed constant.

It is the general solution of differential equation $\left(\frac{dy}{dx}\right)^2 = \frac{a^2}{y^2} - 1$. Clearly $y = \pm a$ also satisfies the above differential equation but it can never be obtained by providing any real value for the parameter h from the general solution. Therefore, $y = \pm a$ is indeed the singular solution of the above differential equation.

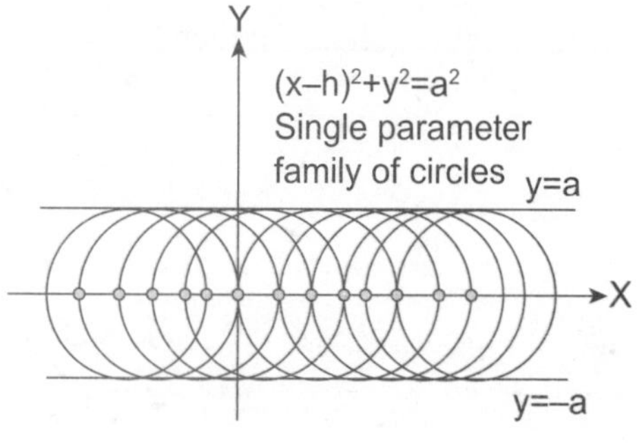

FIGURE 4.14

e.g., equation $y = x\frac{dy}{dx} \pm r\sqrt{1+\left(\frac{dy}{dx}\right)^2}$ has solutions $y = mx \pm r\sqrt{1+m^2}$ (family of tangents) called as general solution but the circle $x^2 + y^2 = r^2$ also satisfies the above differential equation, but it is not contained in general solution, so, it is termed as singular solution.

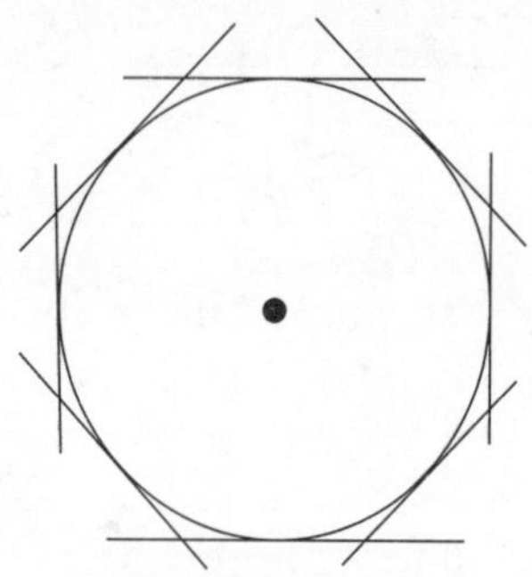

FIGURE 4.15

■ GEOMETRIC SIGNIFICANCE

Geometrically, singular solution represents envelope of the family of the curves and it is defined as a curve touching some member of the family of curves given by general solution at each of its points.

Let the family of curves be $f(x, y, c) = 0$ ...(i)

is the complete integral (*general solution*) of the differential equation $F\left(x, y, \frac{dy}{dx}\right) = 0$ ...(ii)

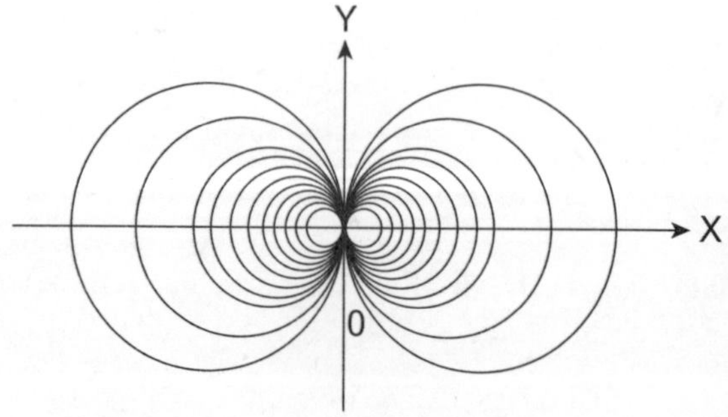

FIGURE 4.16

and if the family of curve possess an envelope $\phi(x, y) = 0$, then at any point P (x, y) on the envelope $\phi(x, y) = 0$, there always exist a member of the family of curves say $f(x, y, c_1) = 0$ touching the envelope $\phi(x, y) = 0$ at P. And therefore, $x, y, dy/dx$ for the curve as well as envelope at point P must be same and these satisfy the differential equation. So, we can say that the values of $x, y, dy/dx$ at every point of the envelope always satisfies the differential equation. That is why singular solution are the envelope of family of curves given by general solution.

For example, for the differential equation $x^2 + y^2 - 2x\left(x + y\dfrac{dy}{dx}\right) = 0$, the general solution is given as $x^2 + y^2 - 2kx = 0$ (family of coaxial circles touching y-axis) and the singular solution of the differential equation is given as $x = 0$, i.e., y-axis

ILLUSTRATION 24: The family of non-parallel straight lines $y = cx + 1/c$ are evidently the general solution of the differential equation $y = x\dfrac{dy}{dx} + \dfrac{1}{dy/dx}$. Find the singular solution of this differential equation if any and discuss its geometrical significance.

SOLUTION: Given $y = x\dfrac{dy}{dx} + \dfrac{1}{dy/dx}$. ...(i)

Let $m = \dfrac{dy}{dx}$ $\Rightarrow$ $y = m.x + \dfrac{1}{m}$

Differentiating w.r.t. x, we get $m = x\dfrac{dm}{dx} + m - \dfrac{1}{m^2}\dfrac{dm}{dx}$

$\Rightarrow$ $\dfrac{dm}{dx}\left(x - \dfrac{1}{m^2}\right) = 0$ $\Rightarrow$ $\dfrac{dm}{dx} = 0$ or $x = \dfrac{1}{m^2}$

$\Rightarrow$ $m = c$ or $y = \pm\dfrac{x}{\sqrt{x}} \pm \sqrt{x}$

$\Rightarrow$ $m = c$ or $y = \pm 2\sqrt{x}$ i.e., $y^2 = 4x$.

Substituting $m = c$ in the differential equation (i), we get general solution as $y = cx + \dfrac{1}{c}$, $c \in \mathbb{R}$

This family of straight lines possesses an envelope, that is, a curve having the property that at each of its points it is tangent to one of the members of the family. The envelope here is $y^2 = 4x$ and its graph is indicated by the curve drawn in gray scale as shown in Fig. 4.17.

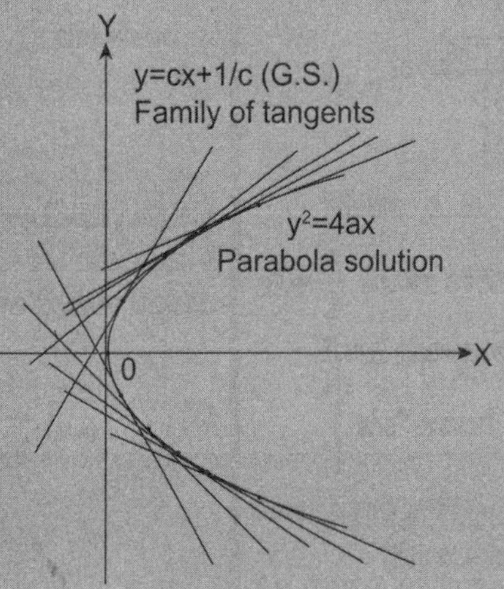

FIGURE 4.17

The envelope of a family of complete integral is itself an integral curve because the slope (derivative) and coordinates at a point of the envelope are the same as those of one of the integral curves of the family of curve represented by the general solution. In this illustration, it is easy to verify directly that $y^2 = 4x$ is a solution of (i). Thus, $y^2 = 4x$ is its singular solution, since $y^2 = 4x$ does satisfy the differential equation but parabola is not a member of family of tangents, thus can never be obtained from general solution by assigning any value for parameter c.

It is interesting to know that we can construct other singular solutions defined non-uniformly by clubbing together a portion of envelope cut between any of its two points say A and B and some part of the members of general solutions touching the envelope at such two points.

For intake look at the example illustrated below

Consider the envelope $y = 2\sqrt{x}$ between points $A(1, 2)$ and $B(4, 4)$ and tangent to $y = 2\sqrt{x}$ at these two points $y = x + 1$ at A and $y = \frac{1}{2}x + 2$ at B Therefore, an integral curve can be constructed as shown in the Fig. 4.18 given below:

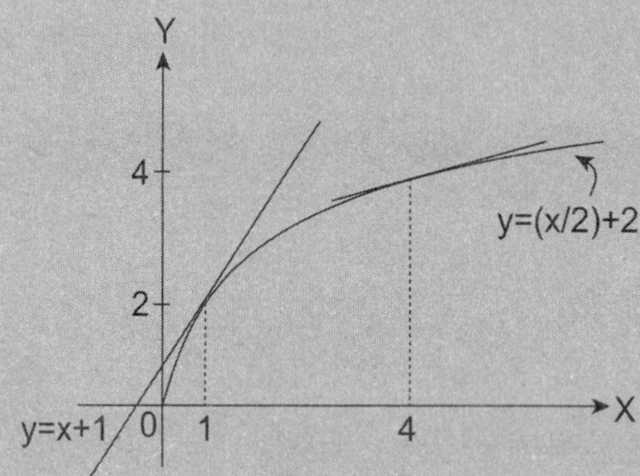

FIGURE 4.18

$$f(x) = \begin{cases} x+1 \ ; \ x<1 \\ 2\sqrt{x} \ ; \ 1 \le x \le 4 \\ \frac{1}{2}x+2 \, ; 4 < x < \infty \end{cases}$$

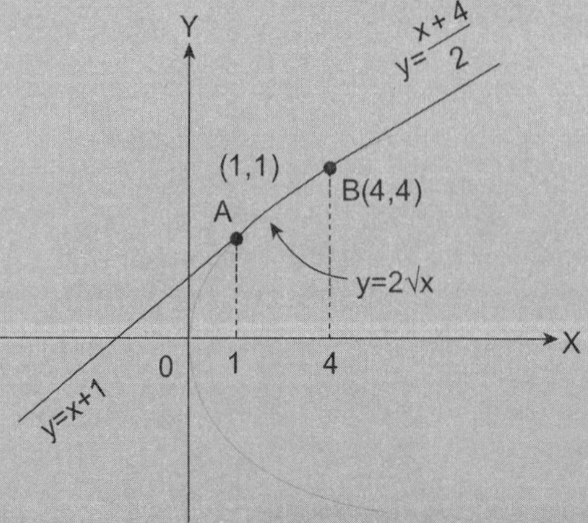

FIGURE 4.19

The function $f(x)$ is differentiable everywhere and the $\left(x, y, \frac{dy}{dx}\right)$ obtained from it always satisfies the differential equation but indeed $f(x)$ is not a member of complete integral. Thus, $f(x)$ is also one singular solution.

It is, therefore, clear that an infinitely many singular solutions can be constructed as described above. Of course it also illustrates impossibility of finding all solutions represented by a differential equation.

GEOMETERICAL INTERPRETATION OF DIFFERENTIAL EQUATION

Let us consider an ordinary differential equation of Ist order and Ist degree $\frac{dy}{dx} = f(x, y)$ ...(i).

At times it can be expressed in the form $M\ dx + N\ dy = 0$ where M and N are functions of x and y. Corresponding to any point in $x - y$ plane, we get a definite direction assigned by the differential equation (known as direction field). Imagine any point, beginning from any position in xy plane (where differential equation is defined) that moves always along the direction as, indicated, it will trace out an integral curve known as primitive or particular solution of the considered differential equation. Elaborating the idea let $Q(x, y)$ be any point, then slope $m = \frac{dy}{dx}$ can be obtained from the equation (i) provided x and y are known. If m_0 be value of slope at (x_0, y_0) the tangent line of slope m_0 through Q_0 shows direction of motion at (x_0, y_0) and Therefore, determines the position of neighboring point $(x_0 + h, y_0 + k)$ at which the slope of tangent changes according to equation (i) changing the direction of motion and fixing the another neighboring point and this process continues till one complete member of the family of curves is traced.

So, we can clearly see that for different initial points like (x_1, y_1), (x_2, y_2),..... the various members of the family of the curve traced out using the single differential equation. Hence, we can say that every differential equation of Ist order represent a family of curves (∞ curves) and every differential equation of 2nd order represents a family of family of curves (∞^2 curves).

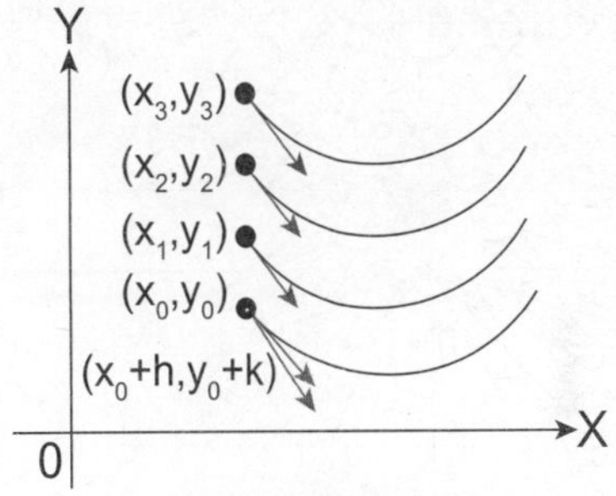

FIGURE 4.20

Geometric Significance of Order

Order of differential equation represents number of essential parameters present in the family of curve given by it. In order to find the solution of differential equation, the differential equation is to be integrated exactly that many times as its order. Hence, introducing same number of arbitrary constants. To have better idea of this observe the following cases. For differential equation $y = x\frac{dy}{dx} + 2$.

Since its order is 1 it represents Single infinity (∞) of straight lines as shown in the Fig. 4.21.

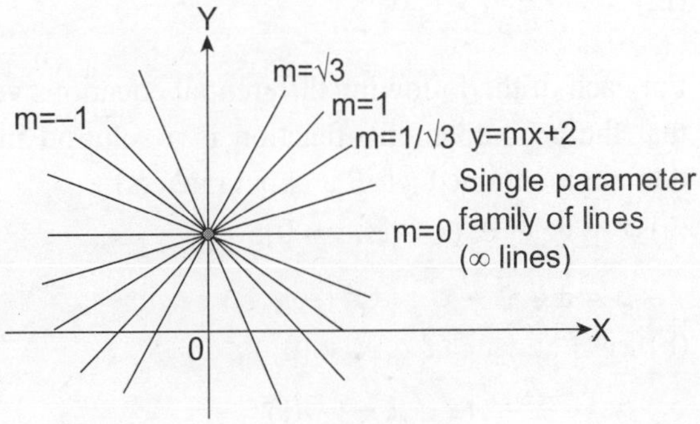

FIGURE 4.21

For differential equation $\frac{d^2y}{dx^2} = 0$. Since its order is 2 it represents ∞^2 ($\infty \times \infty$) number of straight lines as shown in the Fig. 4.22.

FIGURE 4.22

Geometric Significance of Degree

In case of first order differential equations, the degree of differential equation represents the maximum number of possible directions on the graph of the family of curve at any point. e.g., $y = x\frac{dy}{dx} + \left(\frac{dy}{dx}\right)^2$ (degree = 2)

Let (α, β) is a point on a family of curve and $\left(\frac{dy}{dx}\right)$ at (α, β) = m

$\Rightarrow m^2 + m\alpha - \beta = 0$

Therefore, at the most two real values of m at (α, β)

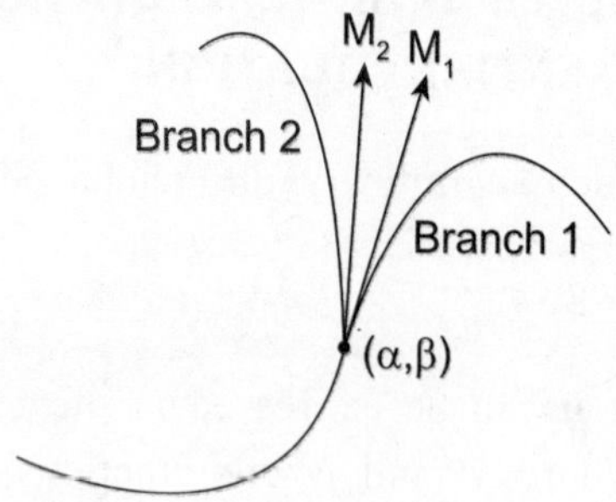

FIGURE 4.23

TEXTUAL EXERCISE–3: (SUBJECTIVE)

1. Given a function $f(x)$. State if $f(x)$ is a solution to the function of differential equation given adjacent to $f(x)$.

   (i) $y = x - \frac{1}{x}; xy' + y = 2x$

   (ii) $y = 2x^2 + C; y'^2 - 2xy' - 8x^2 = 0$ {C is an arbitrary constant}

   (iii) $y = -\frac{x^2}{4}; y = xy' + y'^2$

2. For each of the following differential equations verify that the accompanying function is a solution in the domain mentioned (A, B are: parameters)

   (a) $x + yy' = 0; (x \in \mathbb{R}, y \neq 0);$

   $y = \pm\sqrt{A^2 - x^2}; (x \in (-A, A))$

   (b) $xy' + y = y^2; (x \in \mathbb{R} \sim \{0\});$

   $y = \frac{A}{x + A}; (x \in \mathbb{R} \sim \{-A\})$

   (c) $x^3y'' = 1; (x \in \mathbb{R} \sim \{0\});$

   $y = \frac{1}{2x} + Ax + B; (x \in \mathbb{R} \sim \{0\})$

3. Which out of the given are solutions to the differential equation $2yy' = x(y'^2 + 4)$?

   (i) $y^2 - 4x^2 = 0$ (ii) $y = (x^2 - x)\,e^x$

   (iii) $y = 3x^2 + 1/3$

4. Verify that each of the following function $\phi : \mathbb{R} \to \mathbb{R}$, as defined below, is the solution of the accompanying initial value theorem

   (a) $\phi(x) = e^{-x} + 2; y' + y = 2, y(0) = 3$

   (b) $\phi(x) = x^2 + 2x + 1; y''' = 0, y(0) = 1, y'(0) = 2, y''(0) = 2$

5. Does there exist differential equations having no solution?

6. Does there exist a differential equation having no general solution but has particular solution?

7. Can you figure out if $A = p\tan^{-1}\left(\frac{A + l}{p}\right) + C$ is a solution of $(A + l)^2 \frac{dA}{dl} = p^2$?

8. Consider the differential equation $y - y'' = 0$. Verify that $e^x, e^{-x}, k_1e^x, k_2e^{-x}$ are all solutions to the equation.

9. For what value of 'a' is $y = ax^2$ a solution to the differential equation $y'^2 - 4xy' + 2y + 2x^2 = 0$?

10. We define solution as a function of x such that if $y = f(x)$ is given as an input to the differential equation

the required output is achieved. Moreover if arbitrary constants are involved in the solution they simply signify certain constraints to the differential equation. Consider the differential equation $y'' = -1/y^3$. Check if $(C_1x + C_2)^2 - C_1y^2 = 1$ is a solution of this differential equation. Can you eliminate C_1, C_2 if given that $y(1) = 0$ and $y''(0) = 0$. If not then give a set of conditions that can eliminate C_1, C_2 from the solution curve.

11. Given three functions of derivatives (differential equations) as

(i) $y' = x^2$

(ii) $y' = e^x$

(iii) $y' = \sqrt{x}$ can the following graph be solution to any of these;

If not, predict the nature of the solution curves on cartesian planes.

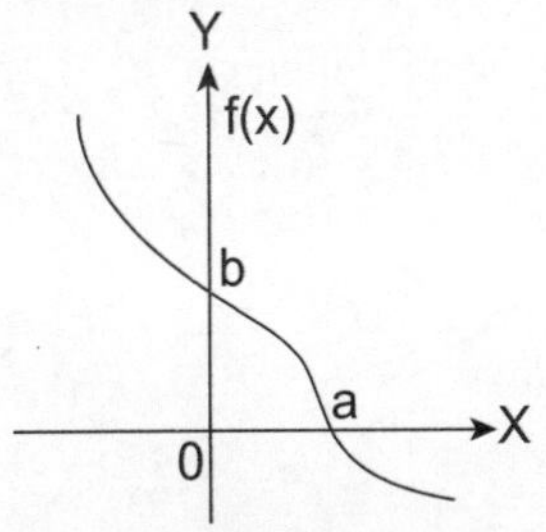

FIGURE 4.24

12. Consider a function having its graph as shown below:

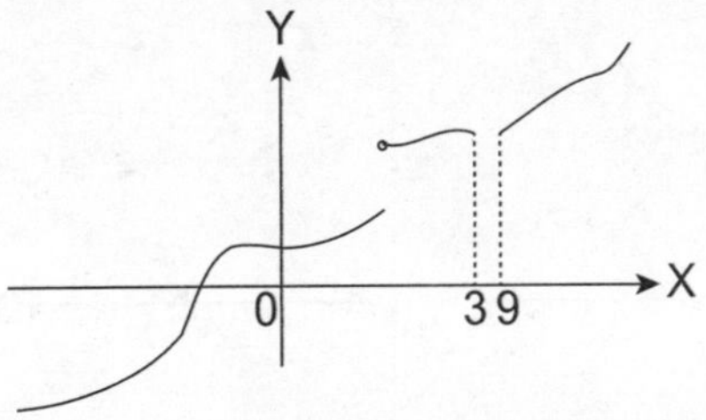

FIGURE 4.25

Can this function be a solution to the differential equation of the form $y' = ax^2 + bx + c$ $(a \geq 0)$

13. Given a differential equation $y' = 1 - \sin x$. Which of the following can be a possible solution curve?

(i)

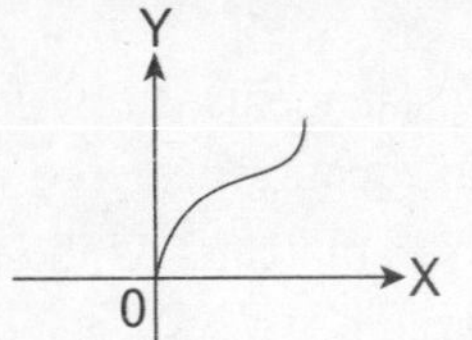

(ii)

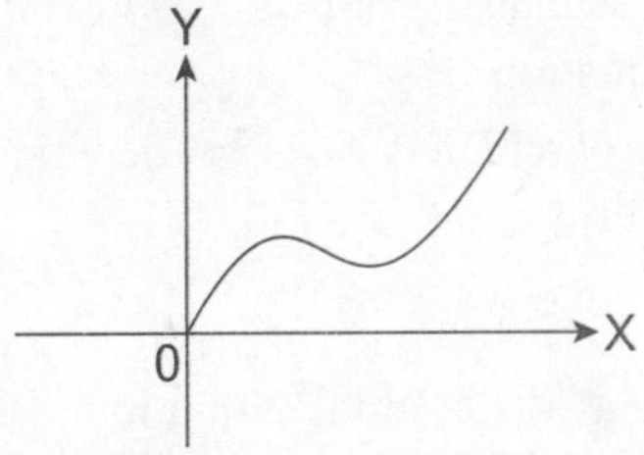

(iii)

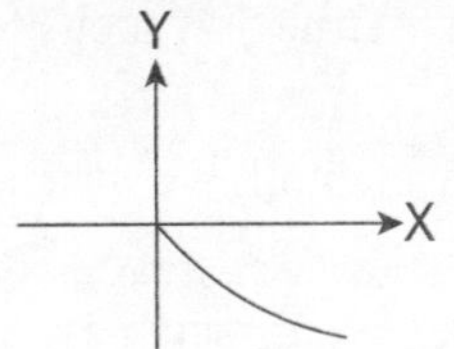

(iv)

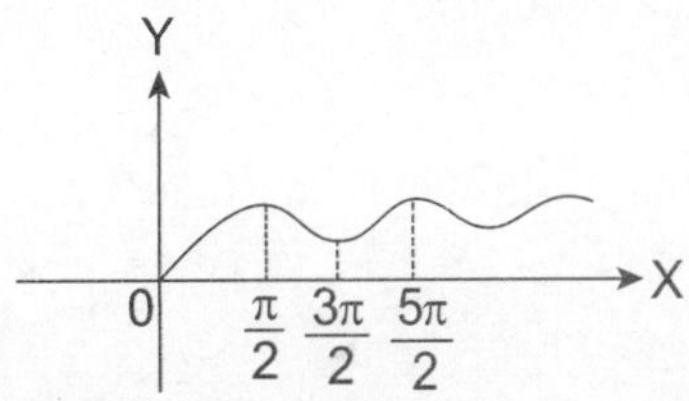

14. Consider the function having its graph as shown below:

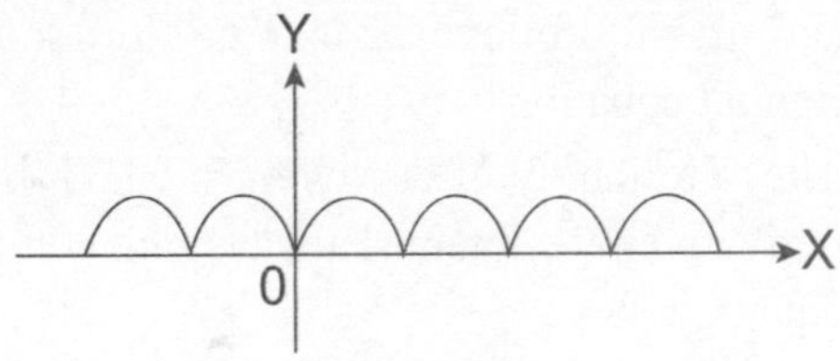

FIGURE 4.26

Can this be a solution for the equation

$$y' = \left|e^x + \sin e^{-x} + \sqrt{1-x^2}\right|$$

Answer Keys

1. (i) Yes (ii) Yes (iii) No **3.** (i) Yes (ii) No (iii) Yes

5. Yes e.g. $\left(\frac{dy}{dx}\right)^2 + a^2 = 0; \forall\, a \in \mathbb{R} \sim \{0\}$ **6.** Yes $\left(\frac{dy}{dx}\right)^2 + y^2 = 0$ $y = 0$, i.e., x-axis is only particular integral

7. Yes **9.** $a = 1$ or $1/2$ **10.** No; $y(1) = 1$, $y'(1) = 2$

11. (i) No (ii) No (iii) No; $f(x) = \frac{(c_1a + b)}{a^4}(x^4 - 2ax^3) + c_1x + b$; where $c_1 > -\frac{b}{a}$

12. No **13.** (i) Yes (ii) No (iii) No (iv) No **14.** No

TEXTUAL EXERCISE–3: (OBJECTIVE)

1. Which of the following statements is true for general solution of a differential equation?

(a) It contains as many parameters as the degree of differential equation

(b) It contains as many parameters as the order of differential equation

(c) Number of parameters may not depend on order/degree of differential equation

(d) all of the above

2. If degree of a differential equation is 2, then which of the following is true for such differential equation?

(a) It has two direction of motion at each point on solution

(b) It can have more than two directions

(c) It has atmost two directions

(d) None of these

3. Which of the following is false for singular solution?

(a) It has no parameter

(b) It cannot be derived from general solution

(c) It is the envelope of the general solution

(d) All the above are false

4. Which of the following is true for solution of differential equation?

(a) They are family of curves from which if x, y and derivatives are obtained always satisfy differential equation

(b) Solution are of three type particular, general and singular

(c) These are parameter family of curves if $k \in \mathbb{N}$ is order of differential equation

(d) None of these

5. Which of the following is true about the differential equation $y = x\frac{dy}{dx} + \left(\frac{dy}{dx}\right)^2$?

(a) It represents infinitely many linear curve

(b) A non-linear curve is solution of the differential equation

(c) At any point of its general solution there can be atmost two direction of motion.

(d) None of the above is true.

6. State which of the following is not true for the differential equation having complete integral $2y + 3Ax - A^2 = 0$; where A is essential parameter.

(a) has degree 3

(b) has degree 2

(c) is of 1st order

(d) is of 2nd order

7. Given a differential equation $\frac{dy}{dx} = \frac{2x}{1+x^2}$. Which of the following will be a solution curve for it?

(a) 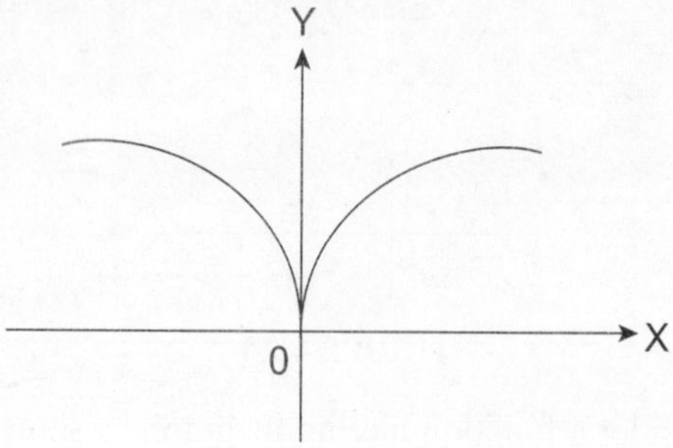

(b) 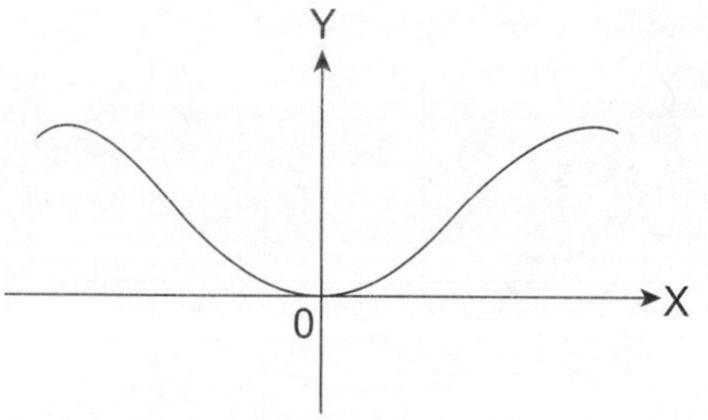

(c) 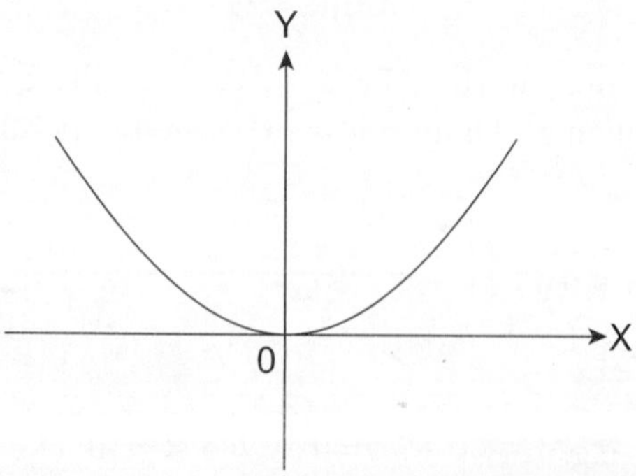

(d) None of these

Answer Keys

1. (b) **2.** (c) **3.** (d) **4.** (a,b) **5.** (a,b,c) **6.** (b,c) **7.** (b)

■ METHODS OF SOLVING A DIFFERENTIAL EQUATION OF ORDER AND DEGREE ONE

Given an ordinary differential equation of Ist order and Ist degree $\frac{dy}{dx} = f(x, y)$ ...(i).

A differential equation of such type is not always solvable. However they can be solved when they belong to any of the standard type discussed in present articles.

When f(x.y) is function of only x or only y

If the equation is of the form $\frac{dy}{dx} = f(x)$ ...(i)

and $\frac{dy}{dx} = f(y)$ ...(ii)

The equation of type (i) will reduce to $y = \int f(x)dx + C$.

Whereas the equation of type (ii) will reduce to $\frac{dy}{f(y)} = dx$ that can be solved as $\int \frac{dy}{f(y)} = x + C$; where C is parameter.

ILLUSTRATION 25: Find the equation of curve satisfying the differential equation $xdy - dx = 2x^2dx$, $x \neq 0$ and passing through the point (–1, 1).

SOLUTION: The given differential equation can be rewritten as $xdy = (2x^2 + 1)dx$ ...(i)

$\Rightarrow \quad dy = \left(\frac{2x^2+1}{x}\right)dx \because x \neq 0.$

Integrating both sides, we get

$\Rightarrow \quad \int dy = \int \left(2x + \frac{1}{x}\right)dx$

$\Rightarrow \quad y = x^2 + \ell n|x| + C$ ...(ii)

∴ which is the General solution of the above differential equation.

But we are interested in that integral curve of the above family of curves which passes through the

Point (–1, 1). Therefore, substituting $x = -1$ and $y = 1$, we obtain $C = 0$ consequently the desired curve obtain has equation $y = x^2 + \ell n|x|$.

ILLUSTRATION 26: Find the equation of family of curve whose sub-normal has constant value $k/2$.

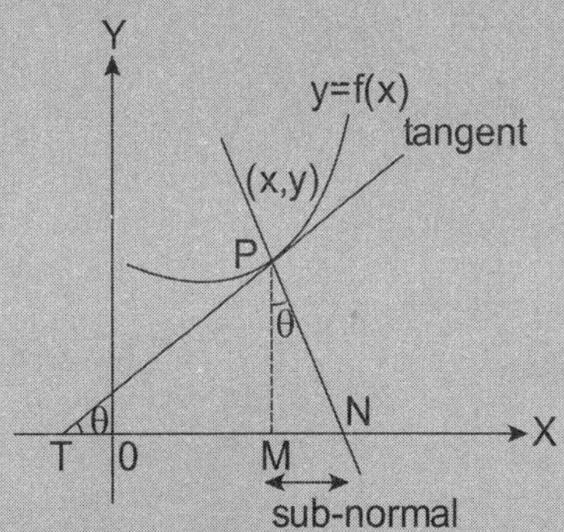

FIGURE 4.27

SOLUTION: As the sub-normal is given as $y\frac{dy}{dx} = \frac{k}{2}$

$\Rightarrow \quad \frac{k}{2}dx = ydy$ Integrating both sides, we get $\frac{k}{2}\int dx = \int y\, dy$

$\Rightarrow \quad \frac{k}{2}x = \frac{y^2}{2} + C_0 \qquad \Rightarrow y^2 = kx - 2C_0$

Let $-2C_0 = C$; where C is real parameter.

$\Rightarrow \quad y^2 = kx + C$ as desired family of parabolas.

VARIABLE SEPARABLE FORM

The differential equation of the form $\frac{dy}{dx} = f(x).g(y)$ or $\frac{dy}{dx} = \frac{f(x)}{g(y)}$ is called variable separable form because when expressed in form $M\,dx + N\,dy = 0$, the coefficient of dx is a function of x and dy is a function of y that means variables are separated by little rearrangement in the differential equation, thus called as variable separable form.

So, the general form of such equation is $N(y)dy = M(x)$ dx which can be solved by integrating both sides i.e., $\int M(x)\,dx = \int N(y)dy$ as described as below for $\frac{dy}{dx} = f(x)g(y)$.

Step I: Rearrange the expression to express it in the form $f(x)dx = g(y)dy$.

Step II: Integrating both sides, we get $\int f(x)\,dx = \int g(y)dy$. Say $F(x)$, $G(y)$ be some anti-derivatives of $f(x)$ and $g(y)$ respectively, we get $G(y) = F(x) + C$.

Step III: Solving the equation, $G(y) = F(x) + C$ for y, we express the general solution as $y = H(x, C)$.

ILLUSTRATION 27: Solve the following differential equations $xy\frac{dy}{dx} = 2 + x + 2y + xy$

SOLUTION: Given $xy\frac{dy}{dx} = 2 + x + 2y + xy$ ...(1)

$\Rightarrow xy\frac{dy}{dx} = (2+x) + y(2+x)$

$\Rightarrow xy\frac{dy}{dx} = (2+x) + (1+y)$; Separating the variable, we have $\frac{ydy}{1+y} = \frac{2+x}{x}dx$

Integrating both sides, we get $\int \frac{ydy}{1+y} = \int \frac{2+x}{x}dx$

$\Rightarrow \int \frac{1+y-1}{1+y}dy = 2\int \frac{1}{x}dx + \int 1dx$

$\Rightarrow \int \left\{1 - \frac{1}{(1+y)}\right\}dy = 2\ln|x| + C$

$\Rightarrow y - \ln|1 + y| = 2\ln|x| + x + C$

$\Rightarrow y = \ln x^2\, |y + 1| + x + C$

ILLUSTRATION 28: Solve the differential equation $\frac{dy}{dx} = e^{x-y} + x^2 e^{-y}$. And find the integral curve satisfying $y(0) = 0$.

SOLUTION: Let $\frac{dy}{dx} = \frac{e^x}{e^y} + \frac{x^2}{e^y}$

$\Rightarrow \int e^y dy = \int (e^x + x^2)\,dx$

$\Rightarrow e^y = e^x + \frac{x^3}{3} + C$

Expressing y as a function of x, we get $y = \ell n\left(e^x + \frac{x^3}{3} + C\right)$ which is the general solution of the above differential equation.

But we are also required to find the integral curve of the above family of curves which passes through the point (0,0). Therefore, substituting $x = 0$ and $y = 0$, we obtain $C = 0$.

Consequently the desired curve obtained has equation $e^y = e^x + \frac{x^3}{3}$. i.e., $y = \ell n\left(e^x + \frac{x^3}{3}\right)$.

ILLUSTRATION 29: Solve the differential equation $y - x\frac{dy}{dx} = a\left(y^2 + \frac{dy}{dx}\right)$. Also find the integral curve satisfying $y(0) = 1$.

SOLUTION: Rewriting the given equation as $y - ay^2 = (x+a)\frac{dy}{dx}$

$$\Rightarrow \frac{dy}{y(1-ay)} = \frac{dx}{(x+a)}$$

This is variable separable form; integrating both sides

$$\Rightarrow \int \frac{dy}{y(1-ay)} = \int \frac{dx}{(x+a)} \qquad \Rightarrow \int \left(\frac{1}{y} + \frac{a}{1-ay}\right)dy = \int \frac{dx}{(x+a)}$$

$$\Rightarrow \ln y - \frac{a}{a}\ln(1-ay) + \ln c = \ln(a+x) \qquad \Rightarrow \ln\left(\frac{(a+x)(1-ay)}{y}\right) = \ln(c)$$

or $cy = (a + x)(1 - ay)$ which is the general solution. Now to find the particular solution of the above family of curves which passes through the point (0, 1) substituting $x = 0$ and $y = 1$, we obtain $C = a(1 - a)$. Consequently the desired curve obtained has equation $y = \frac{(a+x)(1-ay)}{a(1-a)}$.

ILLUSTRATION 30: Solve the differential equation: $(1 + x)y\,dx + (1 - y)x\,dy = 0$.

SOLUTION: Given differential equation is $(1+x)y.\,dx = -(1-y)\,x.dy$

Isolating the term of x and y, we get $\frac{1+x}{x}dx = \frac{y-1}{y}dy$

Integrating both sides, we get $\int\left(\frac{1+x}{x}\right)dx = \int\frac{y-1}{y}dy$

$\Rightarrow \ell nx + x = y - \ell ny + C$

$\Rightarrow \ell n(xy) + x - y = C$ is the desired general solution.

To obtain y in terms of x is definitely not possible but we can say that the general solution of the given differential equation is given by above implicit relation in x and y.

ILLUSTRATION 31: Solve the differential equation: $xy^2\frac{dy}{dx} = 1 - x^2 + y^2 - x^2y^2$

SOLUTION: The given differential equation is $xy^2\frac{dy}{dx} = 1 - x^2 + y^2 - x^2y^2$

$$\Rightarrow xy^2\frac{dy}{dx} = \left(1-x^2\right)\left(1+y^2\right) \qquad \Rightarrow \frac{y^2dy}{1+y^2} = \frac{\left(1-x^2\right)dx}{x}$$

$$\Rightarrow \int\frac{y^2}{1+y^2}dy = \int\left(\frac{1}{x} - x\right)dx \qquad \Rightarrow y - \tan^{-1}y = \ln x - \frac{x^2}{2} + C$$

To obtain y in terms of x is definitely not possible but we can say that the general solution of the given differential equation is given by the above implicit relation in x and y.

ILLUSTRATION 32: Solve the initial value problem $\sqrt{1+x^2+y^2+x^2y^2} = -xy\frac{dy}{dx}$; such that $y(0) = 0$.

SOLUTION: $\sqrt{\left(1+y^2\right)\left(1+x^2\right)} = -xy\frac{dy}{dx}$

$\Rightarrow \; -\dfrac{\sqrt{1+x^2}}{x}dx = +\dfrac{ydy}{\sqrt{1+y^2}}$ $\qquad \Rightarrow \; -\int \dfrac{\sqrt{1+x^2}}{x}dx = \int \dfrac{ydy}{\sqrt{1+y^2}}$

$\Rightarrow \; -\left[\sqrt{1+x^2} + \dfrac{1}{2}\log\left(\dfrac{\sqrt{1+x^2}-1}{\sqrt{1+x^2}+1}\right)\right] = \sqrt{1+y^2} + C$

This is the solution to the above equation.

ILLUSTRATION 33: Solve the initial value problem $y' = 2xy$, $y(0) = 1$

SOLUTION: We rewrite the given differential equation in the alternative form as $\dfrac{dy}{y} = 2x\,dx$ if $y \neq 0$

Hence, on integration, we get the associated one-parameter family of curves to be

Log $|y| = x^2 + c$; $(y \neq 0)$ (c: parameter)

This gives $|y| = Ae^{x^2}$ $(A = e^c)$

Since $y(0) = 1$, we have $A = 1$. So, $y = e^{x^2}$

Hence, the required solution of the given initial value problem is the function $\phi : \mathbb{R} \to \mathbb{R}$, defined by $\phi(x) = e^{x^2}$ $x \in \mathbb{R}$.

ILLUSTRATION 34: Solve the differential equation $\dfrac{\ell n(\sec x + \tan x)}{\cos x}dx = \dfrac{\ell n(\sec y + \tan y)}{\cos y}dy$

SOLUTION: Given differential equation is $\dfrac{\ell n(\sec x + \tan x)}{\cos x}dx = \dfrac{\ell n(\sec y + \tan y)}{\cos y}dy$ ...(i)

Let $\ell n(\sec x + \tan x) = t$ and $\ell n(\sec y + \tan y) = p$

$\Rightarrow \; (\sec x \tan x + \sec^2 x)\left(\dfrac{1}{\sec x + \tan x}\right) = \dfrac{dt}{dx}$

$\Rightarrow \; \dfrac{dx}{\cos x} = dt$, similarly $\dfrac{dy}{\cos y} = dp$

$\Rightarrow \; t\,dt = p\,dp$ (from (i))

$\Rightarrow \; \dfrac{t^2}{2} = \dfrac{p^2}{2} + C_1$

$\Rightarrow \; (\ell n(\sec x + \tan x))^2 = (\ell n(\sec y + \tan y))^2 + 2C$

or $[\ln(\sec x + \tan x)]^2 = [\ln(\sec y + \tan y)]^2 + C$

is the required solution of the given differential equation.

ILLUSTRATION 35: Show that the equation $\dfrac{dy}{dx} = \dfrac{y}{x}$ subject to the initial condition $y(0) = 0$ has an infinite number of solutions of the form $y = cx$. Also find the number of solutions for $y(0) = k \neq 0$.

SOLUTION: Given differential equations $\dfrac{dy}{dx} = \dfrac{y}{x}$

$\Rightarrow \; \dfrac{dy}{y} = \dfrac{dx}{x}$ $\qquad \Rightarrow \; \ln|y| = \ln|x| + \ln|C_1|$

$\Rightarrow \; |y| = |C_1 x|$ $\qquad \Rightarrow \; y = Cx$; where $C = \pm C_1$

Given $y(0) = 0$

$\Rightarrow \; 0 = C(0)$ which is true for all real values of C.

Thus, $y = Cx$ is a family of solution curve having infinitely many numbers.

Further, if we are given $y(0) = k \neq 0$, then $k = C(0)$

$\Rightarrow$ $k = 0$, which is impossible as $k \neq 0$ (given)

$\therefore$ There exist no solution, when $y(0) = k \neq 0$

ILLUSTRATION 36: The population P of a town decreases at a rate proportional to the number by which the population exceeds 1000, proportionality constant being $k > 0$. Find

(a) Population at any time t, given initial population of the town being 2500 and it is 1900 after 10 years.

(b) Find the time when the population will be 1500.

(c) Predict about the population of the town in the long run.

SOLUTION: Let p be the population at time 't'

Now, the excess of population over 1000, equals $(p - 1000)$

According to question $\dfrac{dp}{dt} = -k(p - 1000)$; $k > 0$

$$\frac{dp}{p-1000} = -kdt$$

Integrating, we get $\log(p - 1000) = -kt + C_1$

$\Rightarrow p - 1000 = e^{-kt + C1}$

$\Rightarrow p = Ae^{-kt} + 1000$ (where $A = e^{C1}$)

(a) Now, at $t = 0$; $p = 2500$ (given) (initial population)

$\Rightarrow 2500 = A + 1000$ $\qquad\qquad \Rightarrow A = 1500$

So, $p = 1500\, e^{-kt} + 1000$

Given at $t = 10$ year; $p = 1900$

$\Rightarrow 1900 = 1500e^{-kt} + 1000$

$\Rightarrow e^{-10k} = 3/5$

Taking log both sides, we have $k = \dfrac{1}{10}\ln\left(\dfrac{5}{3}\right)$

(b) Let after t years, the population will be 1500

$\Rightarrow 1500 = 1500\, e^{-kt} + 1000$ $\qquad\qquad \Rightarrow 500 = 1500\, e^{-kt}$

$\Rightarrow \dfrac{1}{3} = e^{-kt} \Rightarrow -kt = \ln(1/3) = -\ln 3$ $\qquad\qquad \Rightarrow t = \dfrac{1}{k}\ln 3$

$$\Rightarrow T = t = \frac{1}{\frac{1}{10}\ln 5/3}\ln 3 = 10\frac{\ln 3}{(\ln 5/3)}$$

$= 10 \ln_{5/3}(3)$

(c) $p = 1500\, e^{-kt} + 1000$; In the long run $t \to \infty$

$\Rightarrow e^{-kt} \to e^{-\infty} \to 0 \text{ as } k > 0$ $\qquad\qquad \therefore p \to 1000$

ILLUSTRATION 37: It is known that the decay rate of radium and is directly proportional to its quantity at each given instant. Find the law of variation of a mass of radium as a function of time, if at $t = 0$ the mass of the radium was m_0 and during time t_0, $\alpha\%$ of the original mass of radium decays.

SOLUTION: Let m be the mass of radium at any instant t. Since in decay process mass decreases rate of change of mass w.r.t time is negative, i.e., $\dfrac{dm}{dt}$ is negative. Further this rate is proportional to mass of radium at that instant $\dfrac{dm}{dt} = -km$; $k > 0$

$$\Rightarrow \frac{dm}{m} = -kdt$$

$$\Rightarrow \ln m = -kt + C_1$$

$$\Rightarrow m = e^{-kt} \cdot e^{C1} \text{ (on Integrating)}$$

$$\Rightarrow m = Ae^{-kt}; \text{ where } A = e^{C1}$$

Now, at $t = 0$ given $m = m_0$ (initial mass)

$$\Rightarrow A = m_0$$

$$\Rightarrow m = m_0 e^{-kt}$$

Now, given time t_o during to α% mass of radius decays, so, at $t = t_0$,

$$m = m_0 - (\alpha\% \text{of } m_0) = m_0 - \frac{\alpha m_0}{100}$$

$$\Rightarrow m_0 - \frac{\alpha m_0}{100} = m_0 e^{-kt_0}$$

$$\Rightarrow 1 - \frac{\alpha}{100} = e^{-kt_0} \qquad \Rightarrow -kt_0 = \ln\left(1 - \frac{\alpha}{100}\right)$$

$$\Rightarrow k = -\frac{1}{t_0}\ln\left(1 - \frac{\alpha}{100}\right).$$

ILLUSTRATION 38: A nomral is drawn at a point $P(x, y)$ of a curve. It meets the x-axis at Q. If PQ is of constant length k, then show that the differential equation describing such curves is $y\frac{dy}{dx} = \pm\sqrt{k^2 - y^2}$. Find the equation of such a curve passing through $(0, k)$.

SOLUTION: Let $y = f(x)$ be the curve such that the normal at $P(x, y)$ to this curve meets x-axis at Q, as shown below:

Now, PQ = length of the normal at P = $y\sqrt{1 + \left(\frac{dy}{dx}\right)^2}$

put $PQ = k$ (constant given)

$$\Rightarrow y\sqrt{1 + \left(\frac{dy}{dx}\right)^2} = k$$

$$\Rightarrow y^2\left(1 + \left(\frac{dy}{dx}\right)^2\right) = k^2$$

$$\Rightarrow y^2\left(\frac{dy}{dx}\right)^2 = k^2 - y^2$$

$$\Rightarrow y\frac{dy}{dx} = \pm\sqrt{k^2 - y^2}$$

$$\Rightarrow \frac{ydy}{\sqrt{k^2 - y^2}} = \pm\, dx$$

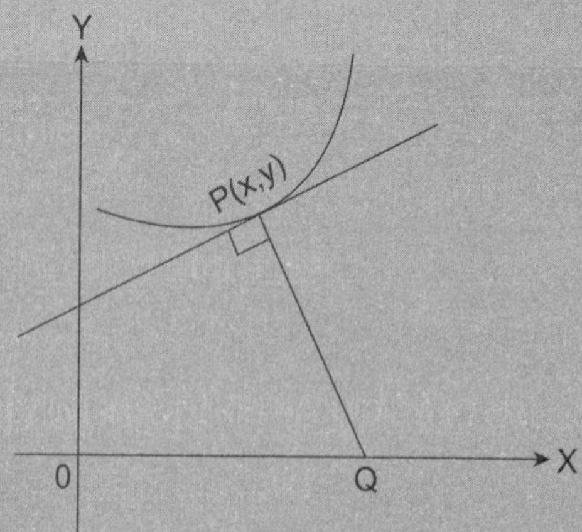

FIGURE 4.28

$$\Rightarrow \int \frac{ydy}{\sqrt{k^2 - y^2}} = \int \pm dx$$

$\Rightarrow -\sqrt{k^2 - y^2} = \pm x + C$

Now, it passes through the point (0, k) $\Rightarrow C = 0$

$\Rightarrow -\sqrt{k^2 - y^2} = \pm x$

$\Rightarrow k^2 - y^2 = x^2$

$\Rightarrow x^2 + y^2 = k^2$, i.e., circle with centre at origin and radius k.

ILLUSTRATION 39: Let C be a curve such that the normal at any point P on it meets x-axis and y-axis at A and B respectively. If $BP : PA = 1 : 3$ (internally) and the curve passes through the point (0, 2), then show that the curve is a parabola.

SOLUTION: The equation of normal at $P(x, y)$ is $(Y - y) = \frac{-1}{\frac{dy}{dx}}(X - x)$

$\therefore \quad A\left(x + y\frac{dy}{dx}, 0\right)$ and $B\left(0, y + \frac{x}{\frac{dy}{dx}}\right)$

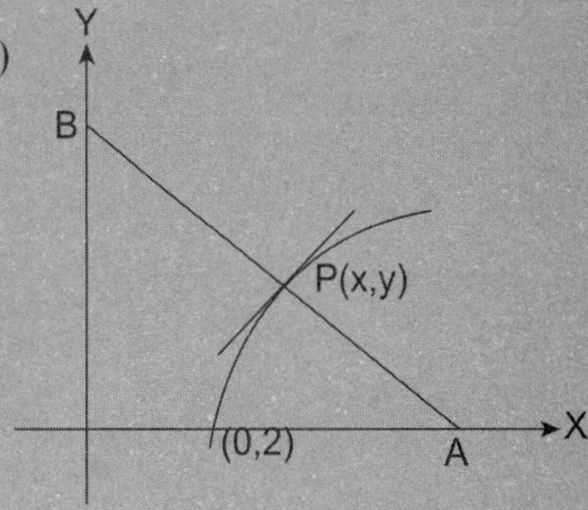

FIGURE 4.29

Now $BP = PA = 1 : 3$

$\Rightarrow \frac{1\left(x + y\frac{dy}{dx}\right) + 3(0)}{1+3} = x$

$\Rightarrow x + y\frac{dy}{dx} = 4x \qquad \therefore \quad y\frac{dy}{dx} = 3x$

$\Rightarrow \int y\, dy = \int 3x\, dx \qquad \Rightarrow \frac{y^2}{2} = \frac{3}{2}x^2 + C$

Also (0, 2) satisfy it, so, $C = 2$.

$\Rightarrow y^2 = 3x^2 + 4$ is the equation of the curve which represents a hyperbola.

ILLUSTRATION 40: A conic C passes through the point (3, 2) and is such that the segment of any of its tangents at any point contained between the co-ordinate axes is bisected at the point of tangency. Find the equation of a circle described on the latus rectum of the conic C as diameter.

SOLUTION: Let m be the slope of tangent at point $P(x, y)$ on the curve.

Thus, equation of tangent at P will be $Y - y = m(X - x)$ if

$Y = 0$, then $X = x - \frac{y}{m}$ and if $X = 0$, then $Y = y - mx$

Since $P(x, y)$ is mid point of $A\left(x - \frac{y}{m}, 0\right)$ and $B(0, y - mx)$

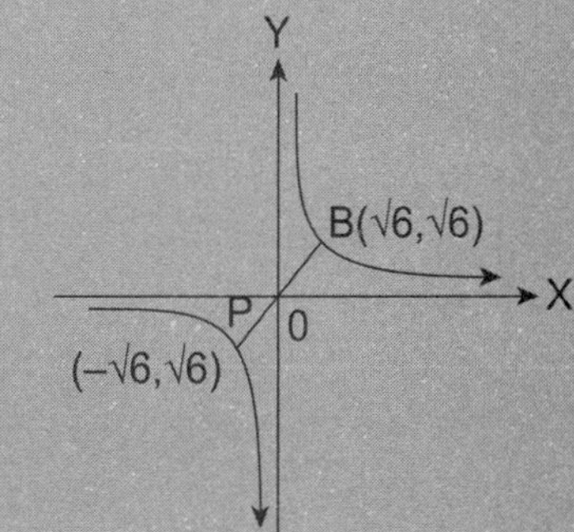

FIGURE 4.30

Hence, $x - \frac{y}{m} = 2x$ and $y = -mx$; $\frac{dy}{dx} = -\frac{y}{x}$

$\Rightarrow \int\frac{dy}{y} + \int\frac{dx}{x} = C_1 \qquad \Rightarrow xy = C$

Since it passes through (3, 2) the equation of conic is $xy = 6$.

It is a rectangular hyperbola with $e = \sqrt{2}$

Hence, the two foci are $(2\sqrt{3}, 2\sqrt{3})$ and $(-2\sqrt{3}, -2\sqrt{3})$.

Equation to the latus rectum is $x + y = 4\sqrt{3}$.

Solving with $xy = 6$, we get $x^2 - 4\sqrt{3}x + 6 = 0$

Similarly, $y^2 - 4\sqrt{3}y + 6 = 0$

Hence, the equation of circle is, $x^2 + y^2 - 4\sqrt{3}(x + y) + 12 = 0$.

ILLUSTRATION 41: A curve $y = f(x)$ passes through the origin. Lines drawn parallel to the coordinates axes through an arbitrary point of the curve form a rectangle with two side on the axes. The curve divides every such rectangle into two region R_1 and R_2 one of which has an area equal to 3 times the other. Find the function f.

SOLUTION: Let $y = f(x)$ be the function representing the given curve and passing through origin.

Let PL and PM be the lines drawn parallel to y and x-axis respectively as shown below $y = f(x)$.

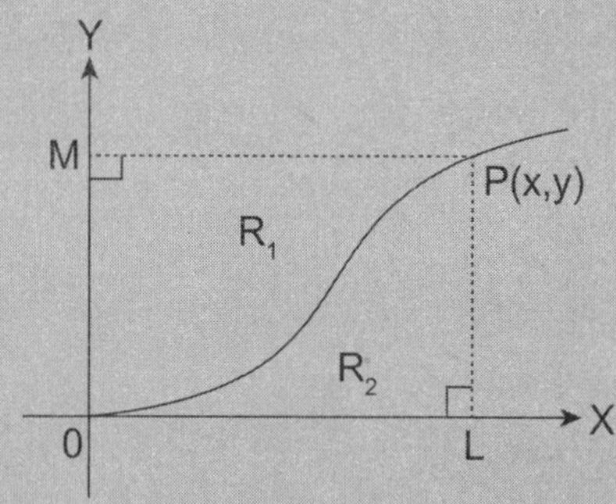

FIGURE 4.31

Further let $R_1 = 3R_2$ or $xy - R_2 = 3R_2$

$\Rightarrow xy = 4R_2$ $\qquad (\because R_1 + R_2 = xy)$

$\Rightarrow 4\int_0^x f(x)\,dx$

$\Rightarrow$ Differentiating both sides w.r.t. x, we get

$$x\frac{dy}{dx} + y = 4f(x) = 4y$$

$\Rightarrow x\dfrac{dy}{dx} = 3y \qquad \Rightarrow \dfrac{dy}{y} = \dfrac{3}{x}dx$

$\Rightarrow \ln|y| = 3\ln|x| + \ln C_1 \qquad \Rightarrow |y| = C_1|x|^3$

or $y = Cx^3$; where $C \pm C_1$ had we taken $R_2 = 3R_1$, then $R_2 = 3[xy - R_2]$

$\Rightarrow 3xy = 4R_2$

$\Rightarrow 3xy = 4\int_0^x f(x)\,dx \qquad \Rightarrow 3x\dfrac{dy}{dx} + 3y = 4f(x) = 4y$

$\Rightarrow 3x\dfrac{dy}{dx} = y \qquad \Rightarrow \dfrac{dy}{y} = \dfrac{1}{3}\dfrac{dx}{x}$

$\Rightarrow \ln|y| = 1/3\ln|x| + \ln C_1 \qquad \Rightarrow \ln|y| = \ln C_1|x|^{1/3}$

$\Rightarrow |y| = C_1|x|^{1/3}$

$\Rightarrow y = Cx^{1/3}$; where $C = \pm C_1$

Thus, $f(x) = Cx^3$ or $y = Cx^{1/3}$ are the required functions representing the given curves.

ILLUSTRATION 42: A normal $P(x, y)$ on curve meets the x-axis at Q and N is the foot of the ordinate at P. If $NQ = \dfrac{2x(1+y^2)}{(1+x^2)}$ find the equation of the curve, given that it passes through the point $(1, \sqrt{3})$.

SOLUTION: Given that $NQ = \dfrac{2x(1+y^2)}{(1+x^2)}$ ...(1)

Now $NQ = OQ - ON = OQ - x$ ...(2)

Equation of normal to curve at point $P(x, y)$ will be $(Y - y) = -\dfrac{1}{dy/dx}(X - x)$, which intersects x-axis, where $Y = 0$

$\Rightarrow \; -y = -\dfrac{1}{dy/dx}(X - x)$

$\Rightarrow \; y\dfrac{dy}{dx} + x = X$

$\therefore$ coordinates of Q are $\left(y\dfrac{dy}{dx} + x, 0\right)$

$\Rightarrow \; OQ = y\dfrac{dy}{dx} + x$ ...(3)

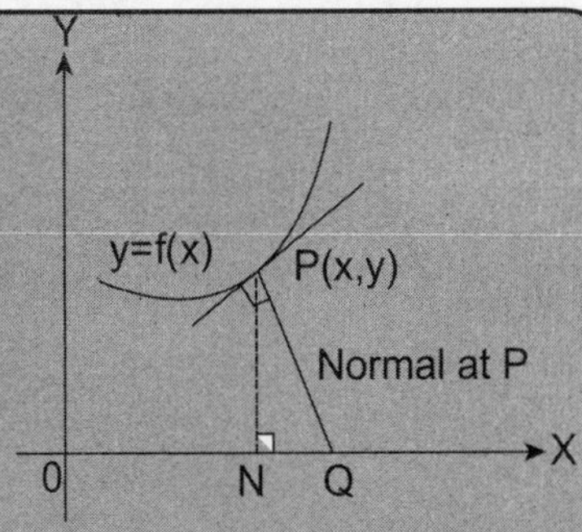

FIGURE 4.32

$\therefore$ from (2) and (3), $NQ = y\dfrac{dy}{dx} + x - x = y\dfrac{dy}{dx}$ = length of sub-normal

A.T.Q., $NQ = \dfrac{2x(1+y^2)}{(1+x^2)}$ $\quad\Rightarrow \; y\dfrac{dy}{dx} = \dfrac{2x(1+y^2)}{(1+x^2)}$

$\Rightarrow \; \dfrac{y}{1+y^2}dy = \dfrac{2x}{1+x^2}dx$

$\Rightarrow \; \dfrac{1}{2}\int\dfrac{2y}{1+y^2}dy = \int\dfrac{2x}{1+x^2}dx$ $\quad\Rightarrow \; \dfrac{1}{2}\ln(1+y^2) = \ln(1+x^2) + \ln C_1$

$\Rightarrow \; \ln\sqrt{1+y^2} = \ln C_1(1+x^2)$ $\quad\Rightarrow \; \sqrt{1+y^2} = C_1(1+x^2)$

Since the given curve passes through $(1, \sqrt{3})$, we have $2 = C_1(2)$

$\Rightarrow \; C_1 = 1$

$\therefore$ The curves are given by $\sqrt{1+y^2} = (1+x^2)$

■ EQUATIONS REDUCIBLE TO VARIABLE SEPARABLE FORM

Type A: $\dfrac{dy}{dx} = f(ax+by+c)$; where $b \neq 0$

Algorithm: The differential equations are of the form $\dfrac{dy}{dx} = f(ax+by+c)$ are reducible to variable separable form by substituting $ax + by + c = t$. The substitution reduces the differential equation to, $a + b\dfrac{dy}{dx} = \dfrac{dt}{dx}$

$\Rightarrow \; \dfrac{1}{b}\left(\dfrac{dt}{dx} - a\right) = f(t)$ $\quad\Rightarrow \; \dfrac{dt}{dx} = bf(t) + a$

$\Rightarrow \; \int\dfrac{dt}{bf(t)+a} = \int dx$

which can be solved as it is clearly in variable separable form.

ILLUSTRATION 43: Solve the following differential equations $\cos(x + y)dy = dx$

SOLUTION: Given differential equation is $\cos(x + y)dy = dx$ ...(1)

$\Rightarrow \; \dfrac{dy}{dx} = \sec(x+y)$ ...(2)

Put $x + y = t$

$\Rightarrow \; 1 + \dfrac{dy}{dx} = \dfrac{dt}{dx}$

$\Rightarrow \; \dfrac{dy}{dx} = \dfrac{dt}{dx} - 1$ ...(3)

$\therefore$ From (2) and (3); $\frac{dt}{dx} - 1 = \sec t$

$\Rightarrow \frac{dt}{dx} = 1 + \sec t \qquad \Rightarrow \frac{dt}{1+\sec t} = dx$

Integrating both sides, we get $\int \frac{dt}{1+\sec t} = \int dx$

$\Rightarrow \int \frac{\cos t}{1+\cos t} dt = \int dx \qquad \Rightarrow \int \frac{\cos^2\frac{t}{2} - \sin^2\frac{t}{2}}{2\cos^2\frac{t}{2}} dt = \int dx$

$\Rightarrow \frac{1}{2}\int\left(1 - \tan^2\frac{t}{2}\right)dt = \int dx \qquad \Rightarrow \frac{1}{2}\int\left\{1 - \left(\sec^2\frac{t}{2} - 1\right)\right\}dt = \int dx$

$\Rightarrow \frac{1}{2}\int\left(2 - \sec^2\frac{t}{2}\right)dt = \int dx \qquad \Rightarrow \frac{1}{2}\left[2t - 2\tan\frac{t}{2}\right] = x$

$\Rightarrow t - \tan\frac{t}{2} = x + C \qquad \Rightarrow (x+y) - \tan\left(\frac{x+y}{2}\right) = x + C$

$\Rightarrow y - \tan\left(\frac{x+y}{2}\right) = C \qquad \Rightarrow y = \tan\left(\frac{x+y}{2}\right) + C \qquad \ldots(4)$

Equation (4) can be further simplified as follows:

$$y = \frac{\sin\left(\frac{x+y}{2}\right)}{\cos\left(\frac{x+y}{2}\right)} + C = \frac{2\sin\left(\frac{x+y}{2}\right)\sin\left(\frac{x+y}{2}\right)}{2\cos\left(\frac{x+y}{2}\right)\sin\left(\frac{x+y}{2}\right)} + C = \frac{2\sin^2\left(\frac{x+y}{2}\right)}{\sin(x+y)} + C$$

$$= \frac{1-\cos(x+y)}{\sin(x+y)} + C = \operatorname{cosec}(x+y) - \cot(x+y) + C$$

Ans: $y = \operatorname{cosec}(x+y) - \cot(x+y) + C$ is also a general solution of given differential equation.

ILLUSTRATION 44: Solve the differential equation $\sin^{-1}\left(\frac{dy}{dx}\right) = ax + by$; $|b| < |a|$.

SOLUTION: $\therefore \frac{dy}{dx} = \sin(ax+by)$, Substitute $ax + by = t$.

$\Rightarrow a + b\frac{dy}{dx} = \frac{dt}{dx} \qquad \Rightarrow \frac{dy}{dx} = \frac{1}{b}\left(\frac{dt}{dx} - a\right)$

$\Rightarrow \frac{1}{b}\left(\frac{dt}{dx} - a\right) = \sin t \qquad \Rightarrow \int \frac{dt}{a + b\sin t} = \int dx$

Put $\tan\frac{t}{2} = z$

$\Rightarrow dt = \frac{2dz}{1+z^2}$ and $\sin t = \frac{2z}{1+z^2} \qquad \Rightarrow \int \frac{2dz}{(1+z^2)} \cdot \frac{1}{a + b\frac{(2z)}{1+z^2}} = \int dx$

$\Rightarrow \frac{2}{\sqrt{a^2-b^2}} \tan^{-1}\left(\frac{az+b}{\sqrt{a^2-b^2}}\right) = x + C$; where $z = \tan\left(\frac{ax+by}{2}\right)$

ILLUSTRATION 45: Solve $(x+2y)(dx-dy)=dx+dy$

SOLUTION: The given equation is $(x + 2y - 1)\, dx = (x + 2y + 1)\, dy$;

$$\Rightarrow \frac{dy}{dx}=\frac{x+2y-1}{x+2y+1}$$

Put $x + 2y = z$; then $1+2\frac{dy}{dx}=\frac{dz}{dx}$, the equation becomes $\frac{1}{2}\left(\frac{dz}{dx}-1\right)=\frac{z-1}{z+1}$

$$\Rightarrow \frac{dz}{dx}=\frac{2z-2}{z+1}+1=\frac{3z-1}{z+1}$$

$$\therefore \frac{z+1}{3z-1}dz=dx\text{, we get } x+c=\int\frac{z+1}{3z-1}dz=\frac{1}{3}\int\frac{(3z-1)+4}{3z-1}dz=\frac{1}{3}\int\left(1+\frac{4}{3z-1}\right)dz$$

$$\Rightarrow x+c=\frac{z}{3}+\frac{4}{9}\ln|3z-1|$$

$$\Rightarrow x=\frac{x+2y}{3}+\frac{4}{9}\ln|3x+6y-1|-C$$

or $6y - 6x + 4 \ln |3x + 6y - 1| - C = 0$

Type B: **Equation of type:** $\frac{dy}{dx}=\frac{a_1x+b_1y+c_1}{a_2x+b_2y+c_2}$;

where $b_1 + a_2 = 0$.

Consider $\frac{dy}{dx}=\frac{a_1x+b_1y+c_1}{a_2x+b_2y+c_2}$; where $b_1 + a_2 = 0$.

Cross multiply and observe the perfect differential of xy, and then Integrate term by term.

$\Rightarrow a_2xdy + b_2ydy + c_2dy = a_1xdx + c_1dx + b_1ydx$

$\Rightarrow a_2(xdy + ydx) + (b_2y + c_2)dy = (a_1x + c_1)\, dx$.

Now integrate

$\Rightarrow a_2d(xy) + (b_2y + x_2)dy = (a_1x + c_1)dx$

on integration, we get

$$a_2(xy)+\frac{b_2y^2}{2}+c_2y=\frac{a_1x^2}{2}+c_1x+C$$

ILLUSTRATION 46: Solve the differential equation $\frac{dy}{dx}=\frac{4x-3y}{3x-2y}$

SOLUTION: Given equation is $\frac{dy}{dx}=\frac{4x-3y}{3x-2y}$

$\Rightarrow 3xdy - 2ydy = 4xdx - 3ydx$

$\Rightarrow 3(xdy + ydx) - 2y\, dy - 4xdx = 0$

$\Rightarrow 3\, d(xy) - 2ydy - 4xdx = 0$

Integrating, we get $3xy - y^2 - 2x^2 = C$

Type C. **Equation of type:** Any equation of the form: $R(x^2 + y^2, x\, dx + ydy, x\, dy - ydx) = 0$

Some times transformation to the polar co-ordinates facilitates separation of variables.

Substitute: $x = r \cos \theta$ and $y = r \sin \theta$

$\Rightarrow x^2 + y^2 = r^2$ ...(1)

and $\frac{y}{x} = \tan\theta$ ...(2)

Differentiating (1) w.r.t. any variable, we get

$xdx + ydy = rdr$ ...(3)

Differenting (ii) w.r.t. x.

$$\Rightarrow \frac{\frac{xdy}{dx} - y}{x^2} = \sec^2\theta \frac{d\theta}{dx}$$

$\Rightarrow\ xdy - ydx = x^2\sec^2\theta d\theta = r^2 d\theta$ ...(4)

Now the equation reduces to

$R\,(r^2, rdr, r^2 d\theta) = 0$

ILLUSTRATION 47: Solve the differential equation $\frac{xdx + ydy}{xdy - ydx} = \sqrt{\frac{a^2 - (x^2 + y^2)}{x^2 + y^2}}$

SOLUTION: $\frac{rdr}{r^2 d\theta} = \sqrt{\frac{a^2 - r^2}{r^2}}$

$$\Rightarrow \frac{1}{r} \cdot \frac{dr}{d\theta} = \frac{\sqrt{a^2 - r^2}}{r}$$

$$\Rightarrow \int \frac{dr}{\sqrt{a^2 - r^2}} = \int d\theta$$

$$\Rightarrow \sin^{-1}\frac{r}{a} = \theta + C$$

$$\Rightarrow \sqrt{x^2 + y^2} = a \sin\left\{C + \tan^{-1}\left(\frac{y}{x}\right)\right\}.$$

Which is the required solution of given differential equation.

Type D. **Equation of type:** Any equation of the form: $R(x^2 - y^2, x\,dx - ydy, xdy - ydx) = 0$

Substitute: $x = r \sec\theta$ and $y = r \tan\theta$

$\Rightarrow\ x^2 - y^2 = r^2$ ...(1)

and $\frac{y}{x} = \sin\theta$ ...(2)

differentiate (1) w.r.t. any variable, we get

$xdx - ydy = rdr$ ...(3)

Differentiate (2) w.r.t. x, we get $\frac{xdy - ydx}{x^2} = \cos\theta d\theta$

$\Rightarrow\ xdy - ydx = r^2 \sec\theta d\theta$ ...(4)

Now the equation gets reduced to

$R(r^2, rdr, r^2 \sec\theta d\theta) = 0.$

ILLUSTRATION 48: Solve the differential equation $\frac{xdx - ydy}{xdy - ydx} = \sqrt{\frac{1 + x^2 - y^2}{x^2 - y^2}}$

SOLUTION: $\frac{rdr}{r^2 \sec\theta d\theta} = \sqrt{\frac{1 + r^2}{r^2}}$

$$\Rightarrow \frac{dr}{\sec\theta\, d\theta} = \sqrt{1 + r^2}$$

$$\Rightarrow \int \frac{dr}{\sqrt{1 + r^2}} = \int \sec\theta\, d\theta$$

$$\Rightarrow \ln\left|r + \sqrt{1 + r^2}\right| = \ln|\sec\theta + \tan\theta| + \ln|c|$$

$$\Rightarrow \sqrt{x^2 - y^2} + \sqrt{1 + x^2 - y^2} = \left|\frac{cx}{\sqrt{x^2 - y^2}} + \frac{cy}{\sqrt{x^2 - y^2}}\right|$$

$$\Rightarrow \sqrt{x^2 - y^2} + \sqrt{1 + x^2 - y^2} = \left|\frac{c(x + y)}{\sqrt{x^2 - y^2}}\right|$$

REMARKS:

Memorising the following differentials of course helps:

If $x = r\cos\theta$; $y = r\sin\theta$, then

(a) $x\,dx + y\,dy = r\,dr$

(b) $(dx)^2 + (dy)^2 = (dr)^2 + r^2(d\theta)^2$

(c) $x\,dy - y\,dx = r^2\,d\theta$

If $x = r\sec\theta$ and $y = r\tan\theta$, then

(a) $x\,dx - y\,dy = r\,dr$

(b) $x\,dy - y\,dx = r^2\sec\theta\,d\theta$

Type E. **Equation of type:** In an equation of the form: $yf_1(xy)\,dx + xf_2(xy)\,dy = 0$, the variable can be separated by the substitution $xy = v$.

Proof: $xy = v$

$$\Rightarrow\ y = \frac{v}{x} \qquad \Rightarrow\ dy = \frac{xdv - vdx}{x^2},$$

$$\Rightarrow\ xdy = dv - \frac{v}{x}dx \qquad \ldots\text{(i)}$$

Using (i), $xy = v$ and $y = \frac{v}{x}$ in given differential equation $yf_1(xy)dx + xf_2(xy)dy = 0$, we get

$$\frac{v}{x}f_1(v)dx + f_2(v)\left\{dv - \frac{v}{x}dx\right\} = 0$$

$$\Rightarrow\ \frac{f_2(v)dv}{v\{f_1(v) - f_2(v)\}} + \frac{dx}{x} = 0$$

Thus, the variables are separated.

ILLUSTRATION 49: Solve $(x^3y^3 + x^2y^2 + xy + 1)dx + (x^3y^3 - x^2y^2 - xy + 1)xdy = 0$

SOLUTION: Here we put $xy = v$

$$\Rightarrow\ y = \frac{v}{x} \qquad \Rightarrow\ dy = \frac{xdv - vdx}{x^2},$$

$$\Rightarrow\ xdy = dv - \frac{v}{x}dx$$

Now, given equation is $(x^3y^3 + x^2y^2 + xy + 1)dx + (x^3y^3 - x^2y^2 - xy + 1)xdy = 0$

$$\Rightarrow\ (xy + 1)\{(x^2y^2 + 1)ydx + (x^2y^2 + 1 - 2xy).xdy\} = 0$$

$$\Rightarrow\ (v^2 + 1)\frac{vdx}{x} + (v^2 - 2v + 1)\left[dv - \frac{v}{x}dx\right] = 0$$

$$\Rightarrow\ \frac{dx}{x}\left[v(v^2 + 1) - v^3 + 2v^2 - v\right] = -(v^2 - 2v + 1)dv$$

$$\Rightarrow\ \frac{dx}{x}\left[2v^2\right] = -(v^2 - 2v + 1)dv$$

The equation reduces to $\int \frac{v^2 - 2v + 1}{v^2}dv = -2\int \frac{dx}{x}$

$$\Rightarrow\ xy - 2\ln|xy| - \frac{1}{xy} + 2\ln|x| = C$$

$$\Rightarrow\ xy - 2\ln|y| - \frac{1}{xy} = C$$, which is the required solution.

ILLUSTRATION 50: Solve the following differential equations:

(a) $\frac{dy}{dx}=\frac{x+y+4}{x+y-4}$ (b) $\left(\frac{x+y-2}{x+y-4}\right)\frac{dy}{dx}=\frac{x+y+2}{x+y+4}$

(c) $(2x+3y+1)dy+(4x+6y-1)dx=0$ (d) $(x-y)(dx+dy)=dx-dy$

SOLUTION: **(a)** Given differential equation is $\frac{dy}{dx}=\frac{x+y+4}{x+y-4}$ ...(1)

Put $(x+y)=t$

$\Rightarrow 1+\frac{dy}{dx}=\frac{dt}{dx}$ $\Rightarrow \frac{dy}{dx}=\frac{dt}{dx}-1$ ...(2)

$\therefore$ from (1) and (2) $\frac{dt}{dx}-1=\frac{t+4}{t-4}$

$\Rightarrow \frac{dt}{dx}=\frac{t+4}{t-4}+1=\frac{2t}{t-4}$

Separating the variables, we have $\frac{t-4}{2t}dt=dx$; integrating both sides, we get

$\frac{1}{2}\int\frac{t-4}{t}dt=\int dx$

$\Rightarrow \frac{1}{2}\int\left(1-\frac{4}{t}\right)dt=\int dx$ $\Rightarrow \frac{t}{2}-2\ln|t|=x+C'$

$\Rightarrow \frac{x+y}{2}-2\ln|x+y|=x+C'$

$\Rightarrow (x+y)-\ln(x+y)^4=2x+2C'$

$\Rightarrow y=x+\ln(x+y)^4=2x+2C'$.

(b) Given differential equation $\left(\frac{x+y-2}{x+y-4}\right)\frac{dy}{dx}=\frac{x+y+2}{x+y+4}$

$\Rightarrow \left(\frac{x+y-2}{x+y-4}\right)\frac{dy}{dx}=\left(\frac{x+y+2}{x+y+4}\right)$ ...(1)

$\Rightarrow \frac{dy}{dx}=\left(\frac{x+y+2}{x+y-2}\right).\left(\frac{x+y-4}{x+y+4}\right)$ ...(2)

Substituting $x+y=t$ and $1+\frac{dy}{dx}=\frac{dt}{dx}$, in (2), we have

$\frac{dt}{dx}-1=\frac{(t+2)}{(t-2)}.\frac{(t-4)}{(t+4)}$ or $\frac{dt}{dx}=\frac{t^2-2t-8}{t^2+2t-8}+1$

$\Rightarrow \frac{dt}{dx}=\frac{2t^2-16}{t^2+2t-8}=\frac{2(t^2-8)}{(t^2+2t-8)}$

Separating the variable, we have $\left(\frac{t^2+2t-8}{t^2-8}\right)dt=2dx$

$\Rightarrow \left(1+\frac{2t}{t^2-8}\right)dt=2dx$ Integrating both sides, we have

$$\int\left(1+\frac{2t}{t^2-8}\right)dt = 2\int dx \qquad \Rightarrow t + \ln|t^2 - 8| = 2x + C$$

$\Rightarrow\ y = x - \ln|(x + y)^2 - 8| + C$

(c) Given differential equation

$(2x + 3y + 1)dy + (4x + 6y - 1)dx = 0$ ...(1)

$$\Rightarrow \frac{dy}{dx} = \frac{-(4x+6y-1)}{(2x+3y+1)} \quad ...(2)$$

$$\text{or} \quad \frac{dy}{dx} = \frac{[2(2x+3y)-1]}{[(2x+3y)+1]} \quad ...(3)$$

Putting $(2x + 3y) = t$ and $2+3\frac{dy}{dx}=\frac{dt}{dx}$ in (3), we have

$$\Rightarrow \frac{1}{3}\left[\frac{dt}{dx}-2\right]=\left[\frac{2t-1}{t+1}\right] = \frac{1}{3}\left(\frac{dt}{dx}\right)=\frac{2t-1}{t+1}+\frac{2}{3}$$

$$\Rightarrow \frac{dt}{dx}=3\left[\frac{6t-3+2t+2}{3(t+1)}\right]$$

$$\Rightarrow \frac{dt}{dx}=\left[\frac{8t-1}{t+1}\right] \qquad \Rightarrow \frac{(t+1)}{8t-1}dt = dx$$

Integrating both sides, we have $\int\left(\frac{t+1}{8t-1}\right)dt = \int dx$

$$\Rightarrow \frac{1}{8}\int\left(\frac{8t+8}{8t-1}\right)dt = \int dx \qquad \Rightarrow \frac{1}{8}\int\left(\frac{8t-1+9}{8t-1}\right)dt = \int dx$$

$$\Rightarrow \frac{1}{8}\int\left(1+\frac{9}{8t-1}\right)dt = \int dx \qquad \Rightarrow \frac{t}{8}+\frac{9}{8}\frac{\ln|8t-1|}{8}=x+C$$

$$\Rightarrow \frac{2x+3y}{8}+\frac{9}{64}\ln|16x+24y-1|=x+C'$$

$\Rightarrow\ 16x + 24y + 9\ln|16x + 24y - 1| = 64x + 64 + C'$

$\Rightarrow\ 48x - 24y - 9\ln|16x + 24y - 1| + C = 0$

Where $C = 64C'$

(d) Given differential equation

$(x - y)(dx + dy) = dx - dy$ ...(1)

$(x - y - 1)\,dx = -(x - y + 1)dy$

$$\Rightarrow \frac{dy}{dx}=\frac{-(x-y-1)}{(x-y+1)} \quad ...(2)$$

Putting $x - y = t$ and $1-\frac{dy}{dx}=\frac{dt}{dx}$ in (2), we have

$$1-\frac{dt}{dx}=-\frac{(t-1)}{(t+1)} \qquad \Rightarrow \frac{dt}{dx}=1+\frac{(t-1)}{(t+1)}=\frac{2t}{t+1}$$

$$\Rightarrow \frac{t+1}{2t}dt = dx \qquad \Rightarrow \frac{1}{2}\int\left(1+\frac{1}{t}\right)dt = \int dx$$

$$\Rightarrow \frac{1}{2}(t+\ln|t|)=x+C_1$$

$$\Rightarrow \frac{1}{2}[(x-y)+\ln|x-y|]=x+C_1$$

Or $x - y + \ln|x - y| = 2x + 2C_1$

$\Rightarrow y = -x + \ln|x - y| + C$; where $C = -2C_1$.

TEXTUAL EXERCISE–4: (SUBJECTIVE)

1. Solve the following differential equation

(a) $\frac{dy}{dx}=(x+y)^2$ (b) $\frac{dy}{dx}=e^{x-y}+x^2e^{-y}$

(c) $\sin^{-1}\frac{dy}{dx}=x+y$

2. Solve the following differential equations

(a) $(xy^2 + x)dx + (yx^2 + y)dy = 0$

(b) $y\sqrt{(1+x^2)}dx+x\sqrt{(1+y^2)}dy=0$

(c) $\frac{dy}{dx}=\frac{\sin x+x\cos x}{y(2\log y+1)}$

(d) $\frac{dy}{dx}=e^{x+y}+x^2e^y$

3. Solve the differential equation $\cos y \log(\sec x + \tan x)dx = \cos x \log(\sec y + \tan y)dy$

4. Solve the following differential equations:

(a) $\frac{dy}{dx}=\frac{6x^2}{2y+\cos y}; y(1)=\pi$

(b) $\sec^2 x \tan y\, dx + \sec^2 y \tan x\, dy = 0$

(c) $\frac{dy}{dx}=\cos(x+y)+\sin(x+y)$

5. Find the equation of the curve for which the cartesian sub tangent varies as the reciprocal of the square of the abscissa.

6. Solve the following initial value problems and find the corresponding solution curves

(a) $\sin x \cos y dx + \cos x \sin y dy = 0, y(0) = \pi/4$

(b) $xdy + ydx = xydx, y(-1) = -e^{-2}$

(c) $x(dy - ydx) = ydx, y(-1) = -e^{-2}$

Answer Keys

1. (a) $\tan^{-1}(x + y) = x + c$ (b) $e^4 - e^x = \frac{x^3}{3}+c$

(c) $\tan(x + y) - \sec(x + y) = x + c$

2. (a) $(x^2 + 1)(y^2 + 1) = c$ (b) $\sqrt{1+x^2}+\sqrt{1+y^2}+\log\frac{[\sqrt{1-x^2}-1][\sqrt{1+y^2}-1]}{|xy|}=C$

(c) $y^2\log y = x \sin x + c$ (d) $e^x+e^{-y}=-\frac{x^3}{3}+C$

3. $[\log(\sec x + \tan x)]^2 - [\log(\sec y + \tan y)]^2 = c$

4. (a) $y^2 \sin y = 2x^3 + \pi^2 - 2$ (b) $\tan x \,.\, \tan y = c$

(c) $\log\left|1+\tan\frac{(x+y)}{2}\right|=x+c$

5. $y=ce^{\frac{x^3}{3k}}$

6. (a) $y=\cos^{-1}\left(\frac{\sec x}{\sqrt{2}}\right)\left(-\frac{\pi}{4}\le x\le\frac{\pi}{4}\right)$

(b) $y=\frac{1}{x}e^{x-1}\ (x\in\mathbb{R}\setminus\{0\})$ (c) $y=xe^{x-1}\ (x>0)$

TEXTUAL EXERCISE–4: (OBJECTIVE)

1. The solution of the equation $\frac{dy}{dx}=\frac{3x-4y-2}{3x-4y-3}$ is

(a) $(x-y)^2+C=\log(3x-4y+1)$

(b) $x-y+C=\log(3x-4y+4)$

(c) $x-y+C=\log(3x-4y-3)$

(d) $x-y+C=\log(3x-4y+1)$

2. The solution of the equation $dy/dx=\cos(x-y)$ is

(a) $y+\cot\left(\frac{x-y}{2}\right)=C$

(b) $x+\cot\left(\frac{x-y}{2}\right)=C$

(c) $x+\tan\left(\frac{x-y}{2}\right)=C$

(d) None of these

3. $y=ae^{-1/x}+b$ is a solution of $\frac{dy}{dx}=\frac{y}{x^2}$ when

(a) $a=1, b=0$ (b) $a=3, b=0$

(c) $a=1, b=1$ (d) $a=2, b=2$

4. Solution of $\frac{dy}{dx}=e^{y+x}+e^{y-x}$ is

(a) $e^x(x+1)=y$ (b) $e^x(x+1)+1=y$

(c) $e^x(x-1)+1=y$ (d) None of these

5. The solution of the differential equation $2x\frac{dy}{dx}-y=3$ represents:

(a) straight line (b) circle

(c) parabola (c) ellipse

6. The number of solutions of $y'=\frac{y+1}{x-1}, y(1)=2$ is

(a) none (b) 1

(c) 2 (d) infinite

7. A continuously differentiable function $y=f(x)$, $x\in(0,\pi)$ satisfying $y'=1+y^2, y(0)=0=y(\pi)$ is:

(a) $\tan x$ (b) $x(x-\pi)$

(c) $(x-\pi)(1-e^x)$ (d) not possible

8. The solution of the equation $\frac{dy}{dx}=e^{x-y}+x^2e^{-y}$ is

(a) $e^y=e^x+\frac{x^3}{3}+C$ (b) $e^y=e^x+2x+C$

(c) $e^y=e^x+x^3+C$ (d) $y=e^x+C$

9. The solution of the differential equation $(\sin x+\cos x)\,dy+(\cos x-\sin x)dx=0$ is

(a) $e^x(\sin x+\cos x)+c=0$

(b) $e^y(\sin x+\cos x)=c$

(c) $e^y(\cos x-\sin x)=c$

(d) $e^x(\sin x-\cos x)=c$

10. The solution of the differential equation $\frac{dy}{dx}=(1+x)(1+y^2)$ is

(a) $y=\tan(x^2+x+c)$ (b) $y=\tan(2x^2+x+c)$

(c) $y=\tan(x^2-x+c)$ (d) $y=\tan\left(\frac{x^2}{2}+x+c\right)$

11. The solution of the differential equation $\frac{dy}{dx}=1+x+y+xy$ is

(a) $\log(1+y)=x+\frac{x^2}{2}+c$

(b) $(1+y)^2=x+\frac{x^2}{2}+c$

(c) $\log(1+y)=\log(1+x)+c$

(d) None of these

12. The solution of differential equation $x\frac{dy}{dx}+y=y^2$ is

(a) $y^2=y+cx$ (b) $y=\log\{cxy\}$

(c) $y-1=cxy$ (d) $y=c+xy$

13. If $\frac{dy}{dx}=\frac{xy+y}{xy+x}$, then the solution of the differential equation is

(a) $y=xe^x+c$ (b) $y=e^x+c$

(c) $y=Axe^{x-y}$ (d) $y=x+A$

14. The solution of the differential equation $\frac{dy}{dx}=\frac{(1+x)y}{(y-1)x}$ is

(a) $\log xy+x+y=c$

(b) $\log\left(\frac{x}{y}\right)+x-y=c$

(c) $\log xy+x-y=c$

(d) None of these

15. The solution of the differential equation $\frac{dy}{dx}=\frac{x-y+3}{2(x-y)+5}$ is

(a) $2(x-y)+\log|x-y|=x+c$

(b) $2(x-y)-\log|x-y+2|=x+c$

(c) $2(x-y)+\log|x-y+2|=x+c$

(d) None of these

16. The solution of the differential equation $(1+x^2)(1+y)dy+(1+x)(1+y^2)dx=0$ is

(a) $\tan^{-1}x+\log(1+x^2)+\tan^{-1}y+\log(1+y^2)=c$

(b) $\tan^{-1}x+\frac{1}{2}\log(1+x^2)+\tan^{-1}\frac{y-1}{2}+\log(1+y^2)=c$

(c) $\tan^{-1}x+\frac{1}{2}\log(1+x^2)+\tan^{-1}y+\frac{1}{2}\log(1+y^2)=c$

(d) None of these

17. Solution of the differential equation $\sin\left(\frac{dy}{dx}\right)=a$ with $y(0)=1$ is

(a) $\sin^{-1}\frac{(y-1)}{x}=a$ (b) $\sin\frac{(y-1)}{x}=a$

(c) $\sin\frac{(1-y)}{(1+x)}=a$ (d) $\sin\frac{y}{(x+1)}=a$

18. If $\left(\frac{2+\sin x}{1+y}\right)\frac{dy}{dx}=\cos x,\ y(0)=1$, then $y\left(\frac{\pi}{2}\right)=$

(a) 1 (b) 1/2

(c) 2 (d) 1/4

19. The solution of $e^{dy/dx}=(x+1),\ y(0)=3$ is

(a) $y=x\log x-x+2$

(b) $y=(x+1)\log|x+1|-x+3$

(c) $y=(x+1)\log|x+1|+x+3$

(d) $y=x\log x+x+3$

(e) $y=-(x+1)\log|x+1|+x+3$

20. The equation of a curve passing through $\left(2,\frac{7}{2}\right)$ and having gradient $1-\frac{1}{x^2}$ at (x, y) is

(a) $y=x^2+x+1$ (b) $xy=x^2+x+1$

(c) $xy=x+1$ (d) None of these

21. The equation of the curve through the point (1, 0) and whose slope is $\frac{y-1}{x^2+x}$ is

(a) $(y-1)(x+1)+2x=0$

(b) $2x(y-1)+x+1=0$

(c) $x(y-1)(x+1)+2=0$

(d) None of these

22. The slope of a curve at any point is the reciprocal of twice the ordinate at the point and it passes through the point (4, 3). The equation of the curve is

(a) $x^2=y+5$ (b) $y^2=x-5$

(c) $y^2=x+5$ (d) $x^2=y-5$

23. Solution of differential equation $x\,dy-y\,dx=0$ represents

(a) Rectangular hyperbola

(b) Straight line passing through origin

(c) Parabola whose vertex is at origin

(d) Circle whose centre is at origin

24. The solution of $\frac{dy}{dx}=(x+y-1)+\frac{x+y}{\log(x+y)}$ is given by

(a) $\{1+\log(x+y)\}-\log\{1+\log(x+y)\}=x+c$

(b) $\{1+\log(x+y)\}-\log\{1-\log(x+y)\}=x+c$

(c) $\{1+\log(x+y)\}^2-\log\{1+\log(x+y)\}=x+c$

(d) None of the above

25. Solution of the differential equation $(x-y)^2\frac{dy}{dx}=a^2$ is

(a) $y=\frac{a}{2}\log\left|\frac{x-y-a}{x-y+a}\right|+C$

(b) $y=\frac{a}{2}\log\left|\frac{x-y+a}{x-y-a}\right|+C$

(c) $y^2=a\log\left|\frac{x-y+a}{x-y-a}\right|+C$

(d) None of these

26. Solution of the differential equation $xdy-ydx=0$ represents.

(a) hyperbola (b) straight line

(c) parabola (d) circle

27. Equation of curve through point (1,0) which satisfies the differential equation$(1+y^2)dx-xydy=0$ is

(a) $x^2+y^2=1$ (b) $x^2-y^2=1$

(c) $2x^2+y^2=2$ (d) None of these

28. The differential equation $y\frac{dy}{dx}+x=a$ (a is any constant) represents

(a) A set of circles having centre on the y-axis

(b) A set of circles centre on the x-axis

(c) A set of ellipses

(d) None of these

Answer Keys

1. (d)	**2.** (b)	**3.** (a,b)	**4.** (d)	**5.** (c)	**6.** (a)	**7.** (a)	**8.** (a)	**9.** (b)	**10.** (d)
11. (a)	**12.** (c)	**13.** (c)	**14.** (c)	**15.** (c)	**16.** (c)	**17.** (b)	**18.** (c)	**19.** (b)	**20.** (b)
21. (a)	**22.** (c)	**23.** (b)	**24.** (a)	**25.** (a)	**26.** (b)	**27.** (b)	**28.** (b)		

HOMOGENEOUS DIFFERENTIAL EQUATION

Homogeneous Function

$f(x, y)$ is said to be homogenous expression of its variable of degree n, iff it can expressed as $f(x,y)=x^n\phi\left(\frac{y}{x}\right)$ or $y^n\psi\left(\frac{x}{y}\right)$ it satisfies the identity $f(tx, ty) = t^n f(x, y)$.

For instance $f(x, y) = x^3 - 3xy + y^3$ is homogenous expression of degree 3 as

$$f(tx, ty) = t^3x^3 - 3(tx)(ty) + 2(ty)^3$$
$$= t^3(x^3 - 3ty + 2y^3) = t^3 f(x, y)$$

Example:

(i) $f(x, y) = x^3 + x^2y + y^3 + xy^2 = x^3\left(1+\frac{y}{x}+\frac{y^2}{x^2}+\frac{y^3}{x^3}\right)$ is homogenous expression of degree 3.

(ii) $f(x,y)=\tan^{-1}\left(\frac{xy}{x^2+y^2}\right) = x^\circ\tan^{-1}\left(\frac{y/x}{1+y^2/x^2}\right)$ is homogenous expression of degree 0.

Homogeneous Differential Equation

A differential equation of the form $\frac{dy}{dx}=\frac{f(x,y)}{\phi(x,y)}$; where $f(x, y)$ and $\phi(x, y)$ are homogenous functions of x, y and of the same degree, is said to be homogenous differential equation, or $\frac{dy}{dx}=F(x,y)$, is called homogenous differential equation iff F is homogenous function of zero degree in variable x and y. Since the above equation can be reduced to the form $\frac{dy}{dx}=G\left(\frac{y}{x}\right)$ Therefore, it can be solved by reducing them to variable separable form using the substitution $\frac{y}{x}=v$, i.e., $y = vx$.

SOLUTION OF HOMOGENEOUS DIFFERENTIAL EQUATION

By using proper substitution each homogeneous differential equation can be converted to variables separable type differential equation:

Type A: Differential equation of type $\frac{dy}{dx}=f\left(\frac{y}{x}\right)$

To solve this kind of equation substitute $\frac{y}{x}=v$

$\Rightarrow \frac{dy}{dx}=v+x\frac{dv}{dx}$ replacing in the differential equation the equation reduces to

$$\Rightarrow v+x\frac{dv}{dx}=f(v)$$

$\Rightarrow \frac{dv}{f(v)-v}=\frac{dx}{x}$ which is variable separable form, and thus directly integrable.

Now integrating both sides, we get the required general solution.

$$\Rightarrow \int\frac{dv}{f(v)-v}=\int\frac{dx}{x}=\ln x+c$$

ILLUSTRATION 51: Solve the differential equation $(x^2 + y^2)dx - 2xy\,dy = 0$.

SOLUTION: Given differential equation is $(x^2 + y^2)dx - 2xy\,dy = 0$.

$$\Rightarrow \frac{dy}{dx}=\frac{x^2+y^2}{2xy}=\frac{1+(y/x)^2}{2(y/x)} \qquad \ldots(i)$$

Putting $y = vx$, and $\frac{dy}{dx}=v+x\frac{dv}{dx}$ in (i), we get

$$\Rightarrow v+x\frac{dv}{dx}=\frac{1+v^2}{2v} \qquad \Rightarrow x\frac{dv}{dx}=\frac{1+v^2}{2v}-v=\frac{1-v^2}{2v}$$

$\Rightarrow \int \frac{2v}{1-v^2} dv = \int \frac{dx}{x}$

$\Rightarrow -\ln(1 - v^2) = \ln x - \ln C$

$\Rightarrow \ln C = \ln x(1 - v^2)$

$\Rightarrow C = x(1 - v^2)$

$\Rightarrow x\left(1-\frac{y^2}{x^2}\right) = C$

$\Rightarrow (x^2 - y^2) = Cx$

Hence, $x^2 - y^2 - Cx = 0$ is the required solution.

ILLUSTRATION 52: Solve the differential equation $(1 + e^{x/y})dx + e^{x/y}(1 - x/y)dy = 0$

SOLUTION: The given differential equation is $(1 + e^{x/y})dx + e^{x/y}(1 - x/y)dy = 0$ ...(i)

which is a homogenous differential equation of the form $\frac{dx}{dy} = f\left(\frac{x}{y}\right)$

So, put $x = my$ and $\frac{dx}{dy} = m + y\frac{dm}{dy}$ in (i), we get

The given equation reduces to $(1+e^m)\left(m+y\frac{dm}{dy}\right)+e^m(1-m)=0$

$\Rightarrow (m+me^m+e^m-me^m)=-(1+e^m)y\frac{dm}{dy} \quad \Rightarrow \frac{dy}{y} = -\frac{1+e^m}{m+e^m}dm$

Integrating both sides, we get $\ln y + \ln (m + e^m) = C_1$

$\Rightarrow \ln y\left(\frac{x}{y}+e^{x/y}\right) = C_1$

$\Rightarrow x + ye^{\frac{x}{y}} = C$ is the required general solution.

ILLUSTRATION 53: Solve $\left(xe^{y/x} - y\sin\frac{y}{x}\right)dx + \left(x\sin\frac{y}{x}\right)dy = 0$

SOLUTION: Given equation is a homogeneous equation.

So, put $y = vx$ and $\frac{dy}{dx} = v + x\frac{dv}{dx}$.

So, the given equation $xe^{\frac{y}{x}} - y\sin\frac{y}{x} + \left(x\sin\frac{y}{x}\right).\frac{dy}{dx} = 0$ becomes,

$\Rightarrow xe^v - vx\sin v + x\sin v.\left(v+x\frac{dv}{dx}\right) = 0 \quad \Rightarrow xe^v + x^2\sin v\frac{dv}{dx} = 0$

$\Rightarrow \frac{dx}{x} + e^{-v}\sin v dv = 0 \quad \Rightarrow \int\frac{dx}{x} + \int e^{-v}\sin v dv = c$ ...(i)

Now, $I = \int e^{-v}\sin v dv = \sin v.\frac{e^{-v}}{-1} - \int\frac{e^{-v}}{-1}.\cos v dv = -e^{-v}\sin v + \int e^{-v}\cos v dv$

$= -e^{-v}\sin v + \cos v.\frac{e^{-v}}{-1} - \int\frac{e^{-v}}{-1}.(-\sin v)dv = -e^{-v}(\sin v + \cos v) - I$

$\therefore \; 2I = -e^{-v}(\sin v + \cos v)$

$\Rightarrow I = \frac{-1}{2}e^{-v}(\sin v + \cos v)$

From equation (i),

$\ln x + \frac{-1}{2}.e^{-v}(\sin v + \cos v) = C$ or $\ln x = C + \frac{1}{2}e^{-y/x}\left\{\sin\frac{y}{x} + \cos\frac{y}{x}\right\}$

REMARKS:

(i) While solving homogeneous equations it is not necessary to transform them to the form $\frac{dy}{dx} = G\left(\frac{y}{x}\right)$. The equation can be transformed to variable separable form by making a direct substitution y = vx.

(ii) After the integration, replace v by y/x, and express the solution of the equation in variable x and y.

(iii) While solving the equation it is assumed that f(v) – v ≠ 0. Because if f(v) –v = 0, then equation reduces to $\frac{dy}{dx} = \frac{y}{x}$ which is in variables separable form, and thus, no substitution is needed. It is also important to notice that if the denominator f(v) – v turn out to be zero only for an isolated value v = k, then the function v = k is a solution of the transformed equation and Therefore, the straight line y = kx, satisfies the original differential equation.

ILLUSTRATION 54: Find the equation of a curve passing through points (1, 2) and (3, –4) for which the area contained between the x-axis the curve and two ordinates, one of which is a constant and the other a variable is equal to the ratio of the cube of the variable ordinate to the corresponding abscissa.

SOLUTION: $\int_a^x |f(x)|\,dx = \frac{f^3(x)}{x}$ differentiating both sides w.r.t x

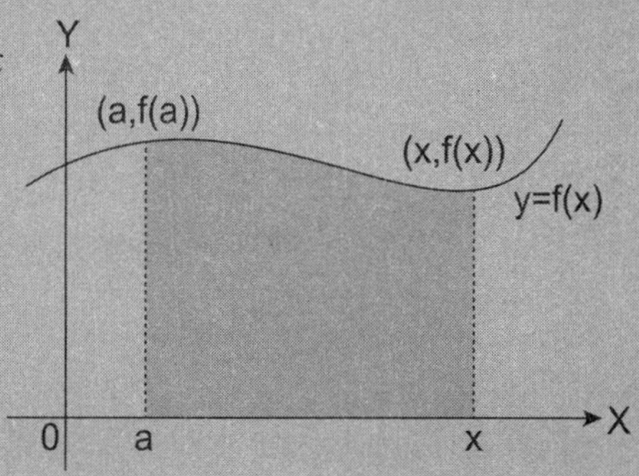

FIGURE 4.33

$|f(x)| = \frac{3xy^2y' - y^3}{x^2}$

$\pm x^2 y = (3xyy' - y^2)y$

Hence, $y = 0$ is an obviously solution. For $y \neq 0$, we have $\begin{cases} x^2 + y^2 = 3xyy'; & \text{for } y > 0 \\ y^2 - x^2 = 3xyy'; & \text{for } y < 0 \end{cases}$

$$\Rightarrow \frac{dy}{dx} = \frac{y^2 \pm x^2}{3xy} \Rightarrow \begin{cases} \frac{dy}{dx} = \frac{y^2 + x^2}{3xy}; & \text{for } y > 0 \\ \frac{dy}{dx} = \frac{y^2 - x^2}{3xy}; & \text{for } y < 0 \end{cases}$$

Substituting $y = vx$ and $\frac{dy}{dx} = v + x\frac{dv}{dx}$; we have

$$\Rightarrow v + x\frac{dv}{dx} = \frac{v^2+1}{3v} \text{ or } v + x\frac{dv}{dx} = \frac{v^2-1}{3v}$$

$$\Rightarrow x\frac{dv}{dx} = \frac{v^2+1-3v^2}{3v} = \frac{1-2v^2}{3v} \text{ or } \frac{-1-2v^2}{3v}$$

$$\Rightarrow \int \frac{3v}{1-2v^2}dv = \int \frac{dx}{x} \text{ or } \int \frac{3v}{-1-2v^2}dv = \int \frac{dx}{x}$$

$$\Rightarrow -\frac{3}{4}\int \frac{4v}{2v^2-1}dv = \int \frac{dx}{x} \text{ or } -\frac{3}{4}\int \frac{4v}{2v^2+1}dv = \int \frac{dx}{x}$$

$$\Rightarrow -\frac{3}{4}\ln|2v^2-1| = \ln|x| + \ln C_1 \text{ or } -\frac{3}{4}\ln|2v^2+1| = \ln|x| + \ln C_2$$

$$\Rightarrow (2v^2-1)^{3/4}x = C \text{ or } x(2v^2+1)^{3/4} = C'$$

$$\Rightarrow \left[\frac{2y^2}{x^2} - 1\right]^{3/4} x = C \text{ or } x\left[\frac{2y^2}{x^2} + 1\right]^{3/4} = C'$$

$\Rightarrow (2y^2 - x^2)^{3/4} = C\,(x)^{1/2}$ or $(2y^2 + x^2)^{3/4} = C'\,(x)^{1/2}$

$\Rightarrow (2y^2 - x^2) = C\,x^{2/3}$ or $2y^2 + x^2 = C'x^{2/3}$ $\Rightarrow (2y^2 - x^2)^3 = C\,x^2$ or $(2y^2 + x^2)^3 = C'x^2$

for $y > 0$ and $y < 0$ respectively

Now the curve passes through (1, 2) and (3, –4)

$\Rightarrow (8 - 1)^3 = C$ $\Rightarrow C = (7)^3 = 343$ and $(32 + 9)^3 = C'(9)$

$$\Rightarrow C' = \frac{(41)^3}{9}$$

$\therefore$ The required curve is given by $\begin{cases} (2y^2 - x^2)^3 = (7)^3 x^2; & \text{for } y > 0 \\ (2y^2 + x^2)^3 = \dfrac{(41)^3}{9} x^2; & \text{for } y < 0 \end{cases}$

ILLUSTRATION 55: A line is drawn from a point P(x, y) on curve $y = f(x)$, making an angle with the x-axis which is supplementary to the one made by the tangent to the curve at $P(x, y)$. The line meets the x-axis at A. Another line perpendicular to the first is drawn from $P(x, y)$ meeting the y-axis at B. If $OA = 2OB$, where O is the origin, find the curve which passes through (2, –2).

SOLUTION: The equation of the line through $P(x, y)$ making an angle with the x-axis which is supplementary to the angle made by the tangent at $P(x, y)$ is $Y - y = -\dfrac{dy}{dx}(X - x)$ ...(i)

At the point where it meets the x-axis

$$Y = 0,\ X = x + \frac{y}{\frac{dy}{dx}} \quad \Rightarrow \quad OA = x + \frac{y}{\frac{dy}{dx}}$$

The line through $P(x, y)$ and perpendicular to (1) is

$$Y - y = \frac{dx}{dy}(X - x)$$

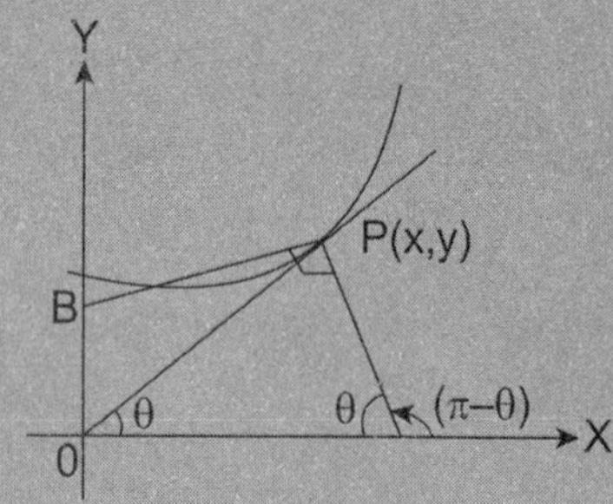

FIGURE 4.34

At the point where it meets the y-axis.

$$X = 0,\ Y = y - \frac{x}{\frac{dy}{dx}} \quad \Rightarrow \quad OB = y - \frac{x}{\frac{dy}{dx}}$$

Since $OA = 2OB$,

$$\Rightarrow x + \frac{y}{\frac{dy}{dx}} = 2\left(y - \frac{x}{\frac{dy}{dx}}\right) \quad \Rightarrow \quad (x - 2y) = -\frac{y}{\frac{dy}{dx}} - \frac{2x}{\frac{dy}{dx}}$$

$$\Rightarrow 2y - x = \frac{1}{\left(\frac{dy}{dx}\right)}(2x + y) \quad \Rightarrow \quad \frac{dy}{dx} = \frac{2x + y}{2x - y} \quad \text{...(ii)}$$

Put $y = vx$ and $\dfrac{dy}{dx} = v + x\dfrac{dv}{dx}$ in equation (ii)

$$\Rightarrow v + x\frac{dv}{dx} = \frac{2x + vx}{2vx - x} = \frac{2 + v}{2v - 1} \quad \Rightarrow \quad x\frac{dv}{dx} = \frac{2 + v - 2v^2 + v}{2v - 1} = \frac{-2(v^2 - v - 1)}{(2v - 1)}$$

$$\Rightarrow \frac{2v - 1}{v^2 - v - 1}dv = -2\frac{dx}{x}$$

$\Rightarrow \int\left(\frac{2v-1}{v^2-v-1}\right)dv = -2\int\frac{dx}{x}$

$\Rightarrow \ln(v^2 - v - 1) = -2\ln|x| + \ln C_1$

$\Rightarrow |v^2 - v - 1| = \frac{C_1}{x^2}$ $\Rightarrow \left|\frac{y^2}{x^2} - \frac{y}{x} - 1\right| = \frac{C_1}{x^2}$

$\Rightarrow |y^2 - xy - x^2| = C_1$ $\Rightarrow y^2 - xy - x^2 = C$

Now, the curve passes through (2, –2).

$\Rightarrow c = 4$

$\therefore$ The required curve is $y^2 - xy - x^2 = 4$.

ILLUSTRATION 56: The tangent and a normal to a curve at any point P meet the x and y-axis at A, B, C and D respectively. Find the equation of the curve passing through $(1, \sqrt{3})$, if the centre of circle through O, C, P and B lies on the line $y = 2x$ (where O is origin)

SOLUTION: Let $P(x, y)$ be a point on the curve

$C \equiv \left(x + y\frac{dx}{dy}, 0\right)$; $B \equiv \left(0, y - x\frac{dy}{dx}\right)$

Circle passing through O, C, P and B has its centre at mid-point of BC.

Let the centre of the circle be (α, β)

$\Rightarrow 2\alpha = x + y\frac{dx}{dy}$ and $2\beta = y - x\frac{dy}{dx}$. Now centre lies on $y = 2x$

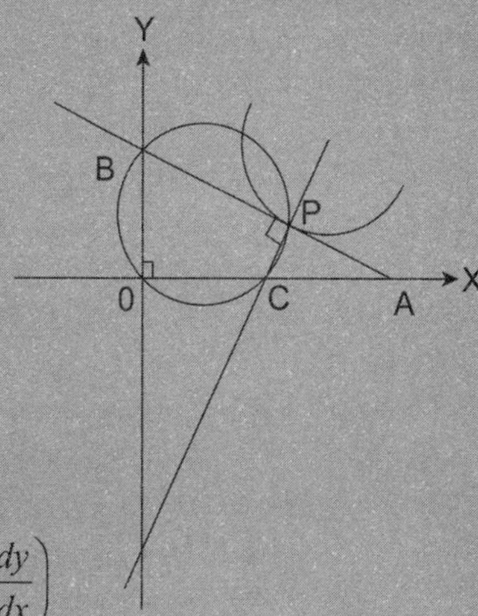

FIGURE 4.35

$\Rightarrow \beta = 2\alpha$ $\Rightarrow \frac{\left(y - x\frac{dy}{dx}\right)}{2} = \left(x + y\frac{dy}{dx}\right)$

$\Rightarrow y - x\frac{dy}{dx} = 2x + 2y\frac{dy}{dx}$ $\Rightarrow y - 2x = (x + 2y)\frac{dy}{dx}$

$\Rightarrow \frac{dy}{dx} = \frac{y - 2x}{x + 2y}$ ...(i)

It is a homogeneous equation, so, put $y = vx$ and $\frac{dy}{dx} = v + x\frac{dv}{dx}$ in (i)

$\Rightarrow v + x\frac{dv}{dx} = \frac{vx - 2x}{x + 2vx} = \frac{v - 2}{2v + 1}$ $\Rightarrow x\frac{dv}{dx} = \frac{v - 2 - 2v^2 - v}{2v + 1}$

$\Rightarrow x\frac{dv}{dx} = \frac{-2(1 + v^2)}{2v + 1}$ $\Rightarrow \frac{2v + 1}{v^2 + 1}dv = -2\frac{dx}{x}$

$\Rightarrow \int\frac{2v}{v^2 + 1}dv + \int\frac{1}{v^2 + 1}dv = -2\int\frac{dx}{x}$ $\Rightarrow \ln|v^2 + 1| + \tan^{-1}(v) + 2\ln|x| = C$

$\Rightarrow \ln x^2(v^2 + 1) + \tan^{-1}v = c$ $\Rightarrow \ln x^2\left(\frac{y^2 + x^2}{x^2}\right) + \tan^{-1}\left(\frac{y}{x}\right) = C$

$\Rightarrow \ln(x^2 + y^2) + \tan^{-1}\left(\frac{y}{x}\right) = C$ ...(ii)

Since it passes through $(1, \sqrt{3})$

$$\Rightarrow \ln(4)+\tan^{-1}\left(\frac{\sqrt{3}}{1}\right)=C \qquad \Rightarrow 2\ln 2+\frac{\pi}{3}=C$$

$\therefore$ (ii) becomes $\ln(x^2+y^2)+\tan^{-1}\left(\frac{y}{x}\right)=2\ln 2+\frac{\pi}{3}$

$$\Rightarrow \ln\left(\frac{x^2+y^2}{4}\right)+\tan^{-1}\left(\frac{y}{x}\right)=\frac{\pi}{3}$$

ILLUSTRATION 57: The light rays emanating from a point source of a search light are reflected as beam parallel to the x-axis. Show that the surface is parabolic, by first forming the differential equation and then solving it.

SOLUTION: Let $P(x, y)$ be the incident point on the reflecting surface and let O (origin) be the source of light. Then OP will be the incident ray to reflecting surface at point P. Now, the equation of normal NP will be $Y-y=-\frac{1}{m}(X-x)$, on x-axis $Y = 0$.

$\Rightarrow X = x + my$

$\therefore$ Coordinates of N will be $(x + my, 0)$

Now, $(OP)^2 = (ON)^2$

$\Rightarrow x^2 + y^2 = (x + my)^2$

$$\Rightarrow m=\frac{-x\pm\sqrt{x^2+y^2}}{y}=\frac{dy}{dx}$$

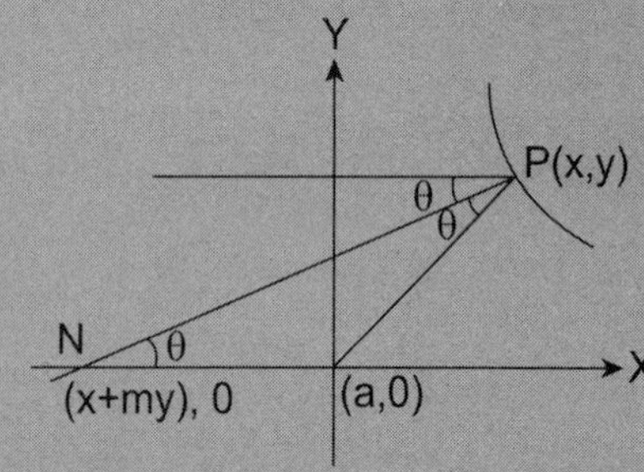

FIGURE 4.36

Put $y = vx$ to get $\int\frac{v}{\sqrt{1+v^2}\left[\pm1-\sqrt{1+v^2}\right]}dv=\int\frac{dx}{x}$

Put $\pm1-\sqrt{1+v^2}=t \qquad \Rightarrow -\frac{1}{2\sqrt{1+v^2}}(+2v)dv=dt$

$\Rightarrow -\frac{v}{\sqrt{1+v^2}}dv=dt \qquad \Rightarrow -\int\frac{dt}{t}=\ln x+C$

Now we proceed to get $y^2 = c^2 \pm 2cx$.

$\Rightarrow -\ln|t| = \ln|x| + C_1 \qquad \Rightarrow \ln|xt| = C_1$

$\Rightarrow xt = C_2 \qquad \Rightarrow x\left[\pm1-\sqrt{1+v^2}\right]=C_2$

Type B: Differential equation of type

$$y\,f(x\,y)\,dx + xg(xy)dy = 0 \qquad \ldots\text{(i)}$$

Substitute: $xy = u$

Differentiating w.r.t. x, we get $x\frac{dy}{dx}+y=\frac{du}{dx}$

$$\Rightarrow \frac{u}{x}f(xy)+x\,g(xy)\frac{dy}{dx}=0$$

$$\Rightarrow \frac{u}{x}f(u)+x\,g(u).\frac{\left(\frac{du}{dx}-\frac{u}{x}\right)}{x}$$

$$\Rightarrow \frac{u}{x}f(u)+x\,g(u).\frac{du}{dx}-\frac{u}{x}=0$$

$$\Rightarrow \frac{u}{x}(f(u)-1)=-g(u).\frac{du}{dx}$$

$\Rightarrow \frac{dx}{x}=\frac{g(u)du}{u(1-f(u))}$; which is a variable separable form and can be further integrated

ILLUSTRATION 58: Solve the differential equation $y(xy + e^{xy})dx + x(xy - e^{xy})dy = 0$.

SOLUTION: Let $xy = u$

$\Rightarrow xdy + ydx = du$

Now given equation can be written as $xy^2\,dx + x^2\,y\,dy + y\,.e^{xy}\,dx - x\,e^{xy}\,dy = 0$

$\Rightarrow xy\,(y\,dx + x\,dy) + e^{xy}\,(y\,dx - x\,dy) = 0$

$\Rightarrow xy\,(y\,dx + x\,dy) + e^{xy}\,(y\,dx + xdy - 2x\,dy) = 0$

$\Rightarrow udu + e^{u}\left(du - 2.\frac{u}{y}dy\right) = 0 \qquad \Rightarrow udu + e^{u}du - \frac{2u.e^{u}}{y}dy = 0$

$\Rightarrow \frac{1}{2}\int\left(\frac{u+e^{u}}{u.e^{u}}\right)du - \int\frac{dy}{y} = 0 \qquad \Rightarrow \frac{1}{2}\left(\log|u| - e^{-u}\right) = \ln|y| + c$

$\Rightarrow \frac{1}{2}(\ln|xy| - e^{-xy}) = \ln|y| + c$ is the required general solution

ILLUSTRATION 59: A curve is such that the length of the polar radius of any point on the curve is equal to the length of the tangent drawn at this point. Form the differential equation and solve it to find the equation of the curve.

SOLUTION: Let $y = f(x)$ is a curve and $p(x, y)$ be a point on curve at which tangent is drawn given length of tanget = polar radius

$\Rightarrow y\sqrt{1+\left(\frac{dx}{dy}\right)^2} = \sqrt{x^2+y^2}$

Squaring both sides, we get $y^2 + y^2\left(\frac{dx}{dy}\right)^2 = x^2 + y^2$

$\Rightarrow y^2 = x^2\left(\frac{dy}{dx}\right)^2 \qquad \Rightarrow \frac{dy}{dx} = \pm\frac{y}{x}$

Taking + sign, we have $\frac{dy}{y} = \frac{dx}{x}$

$\ln = \ln x + \log c$

$\Rightarrow \frac{y}{x} = C \qquad \Rightarrow y = cx$

Taking – ve sign, we have $\frac{dy}{dx} = -\frac{y}{x}$

$\Rightarrow \frac{dy}{y} = -\frac{dx}{x}$, on integrating, we have $\ln y = -\ln x + \ln C$

$\Rightarrow xy = C$. Thus, $y = Cx$ and $y = C/x$ are two possible curves.

ILLUSTRATION 60: Solve $x\,dy - ydx = \sqrt{x^2+y^2}\,dx$

SOLUTION: Let $x\,dy - ydx = \sqrt{x^2+y^2}\,dx$ ...(i)

The given differential equation can be written as $\frac{dy}{dx} = \frac{y+\sqrt{x^2+y^2}}{x}$ if $x \neq 0$ ...(ii)

As the right-hand side of (ii), can be written as $\frac{y}{x} + \sqrt{1+\frac{y^2}{x^2}}$

It is a homogenous function of degree zero; so, we put $y = vx$ to obtain

$$x\frac{dv}{dx} + v = \frac{vx + \sqrt{x^2+v^2x^2}}{x} = v + \sqrt{1+v^2},\ x \neq 0$$

$$\Rightarrow \frac{dv}{\sqrt{1+v^2}} = \frac{dx}{x}$$

Hence, on integrating, we get $\ln|v+\sqrt{1+v^2}| = \log|cx|, x \neq 0$ (c : parameter)

$$\Rightarrow |v+\sqrt{1+v^2}| = |cx| \qquad \Rightarrow \left|\frac{y}{x}+\sqrt{1+\frac{y^2}{x^2}}\right| = |cx|$$

$\Rightarrow (y+\sqrt{x^2+y^2})^2 = c^2x^4, x \neq 0$. Which is the required solution of given differential equation.

EQUATIONS REDUCIBLE TO THE HOMOGENEOUS FORM

To solve the equation of form $\dfrac{dy}{dx} = \dfrac{ax+by+c}{a_1x+b_1y+c_1}$

Case I: If $\dfrac{a}{a_1} = \dfrac{b}{b_1} \neq \dfrac{c}{c_1}$, then $ax + by + c = 0$ and $a_1x + b_1y + c_1 = 0$ represent parallel lines.

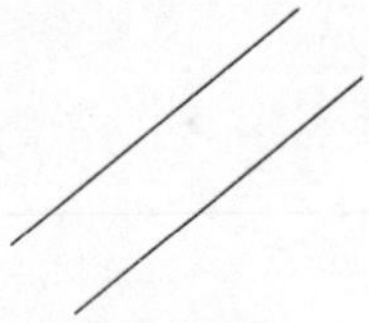

FIGURE 4.37

Let $\dfrac{a}{a_1} = \dfrac{b}{b_1} = k$

$\Rightarrow a = ka_1, b = kb_1$

$\Rightarrow ax + by = k(a_1x + b_1y)$ ...(i)

On substituting $a_1x + b_1y = v$

$\Rightarrow ax + by = kv$

$\Rightarrow ax + by + c = kv + c$ ...(ii)

And $a_1x + b_1y + c_1 = v + c_1$ ...(iii)

Also $a_1x + b_1y = v$

$$\Rightarrow a_1 + b_1\frac{dy}{dx} = \frac{dv}{dx}$$

$$\Rightarrow \frac{dy}{dx} = \frac{1}{b_1}\left(\frac{dv}{dx} - a_1\right) \qquad \text{......(iv)}$$

Using (ii), (iii) and (iv) in given differential equation,

we get $\dfrac{1}{b_1}\left(\dfrac{dv}{dx} - a_1\right) = \dfrac{kv+c}{v+c_1}$

$$\Rightarrow \frac{dv}{dx} = \frac{b_1(kv+c)}{v+c_1} + a_1$$

$$\Rightarrow \frac{(v+c_1)dv}{[(kb_1+a_1)v+(b_1c+a_1c_1)]} = \int dx$$

$$\Rightarrow \int\frac{(v+c_1)dv}{[(kb_1+a_1)v+(b_1c+a_1c_1)]} = \int dx$$

Which can be solved further, to get the general solution of given differential equation.

Case II: If $\dfrac{a}{a_1} = \dfrac{b}{b_1} = \dfrac{c}{c_1} = k$, then $ax + by + c = 0$ and $a_1x + b_1y + c_1 = 0$ are coincident lines.

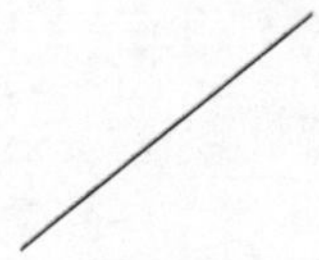

FIGURE 4.38

$\Rightarrow ax + by + c = k(a_1x + b_1y + c_1)$

On substituting $a_1x + b_1y + c_1 = v$ ...(i)

$\Rightarrow a_1 + \dfrac{dy}{dx} = \dfrac{dv}{dx}$ ...(ii)

And $ax + by + c = kv$ ......(iii)

Using (i), (ii) and (iii) in given differential equation,

we get $\dfrac{dv}{dx} - a_1 = \dfrac{kv}{v} = k$

$\Rightarrow \dfrac{dv}{dx} = k + a$

$\Rightarrow dv = (k + a_1)\,dx$

$\Rightarrow v = (k + a_1)x + c_1$

$\Rightarrow (a_1x + b_1y + c_1) = (k + a_1)x + c_1$

Which gives us the required solutions of given differential equation.

Case III: If $a_1 + b = 0$, then on cross multiplication we have $a_1(xdy + ydx) = (ax + c)dx - (b_1y + c_1)dy$

Or $a_1d(xy) = (ax + c)dx - (b_1y + c_1)dy$

$$\Rightarrow a_1xy = \left(\frac{ax^2}{2} + cx\right) - \left(\frac{b_1y^2}{2} + c_1y\right) + C'$$

Which gives us the general solution of given differential equation

Case IV: Equation of the form $\frac{dy}{dx}=\frac{ax+by+c}{a_1x+b_1y+c_1}$; where $\frac{a}{a_1}\neq\frac{b}{b_1}$ can be reduced to a homogeneous form by substituting $x = X + h$ and $y = Y + k$; where h and k are constants which are to be determined.

Such that the given differential equation has no constant terms in numerator and denominator

Now, $\frac{a}{a_1}\neq\frac{b}{b_1}$

$\Rightarrow$ $ax + by + c = 0$ and $a_1x + b_1y + c_1 = 0$ have unique solution say (h, k). That is, unique point of intersection.

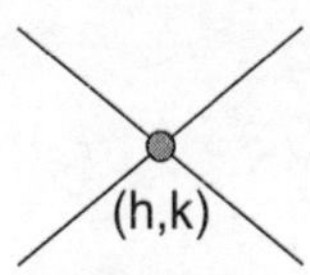

FIGURE 4.39

Now, $x = X + h$; $y = Y + k$

$\Rightarrow$ $dx = dX$; $dy = dY$

$\therefore$ gives $\frac{dy}{dx}=\frac{dY}{dX}$

Now, given differential equation becomes

$$\frac{dY}{dX}=\frac{a(X+h)+b(Y+k)+c}{a_1(X+h)+b(Y+k)+c_1}$$

$\Rightarrow$ $\frac{dY}{dX}=\frac{aX+bY}{a_1X+b_1Y}$; choosing h, k so that $ah + bk + c = 0$ and $a_1h + bk + c_1 = 0$(say); $(h = h_1, k = k_1)$

Now, put $Y = VX$

$$\Rightarrow \frac{dY}{dX}=V+X\frac{dV}{dX}$$

$$\Rightarrow V+X\frac{dV}{dX}=\frac{a+bV}{a_1+b_1V}$$

Which is in variable separable form and can be solved further for giving a relation in X, Y and V. Resubstituting $X = x - h_1$ and $Y = y - k_1$ and $V = Y/X$, we get required general solution of given differential equation.

ILLUSTRATION 61: Solve the differential equation $\frac{dy}{dx}=\frac{x+2y+3}{2x+3y+4}$

SOLUTION: The given equation is $\frac{dy}{dx}=\frac{x+2y+3}{2x+3y+4}$

By putting $x = X + h$; $y = Y + k$

We have $\frac{dY}{dX}=\frac{X+2Y+(h+2k+3)}{2X+3Y+(2h+3k+4)}$

To determine h and k, we have $h + 2k + 3 = 0$, $2h + 3k + 4 = 0$

$\Rightarrow$ $h = 1$, $k = -2$

$$\therefore \frac{dY}{dX}=\frac{X+2Y}{2X+3Y}$$

Putting $Y = VX$, we get $V+X\frac{dV}{dX}=\frac{1+2V}{2+3V}$

$$\Rightarrow \frac{2+3V}{3V^2-1}dV=-\frac{dX}{X}$$

$$\Rightarrow \left[\frac{2+\sqrt{3}}{2\left(\sqrt{3}V-1\right)}-\frac{2-\sqrt{3}}{2\left(\sqrt{3}V+1\right)}\right]dV=-\frac{dX}{X}$$

$$\Rightarrow \frac{2+\sqrt{3}}{2}\log\left(\sqrt{3}V-1\right)-\frac{2-\sqrt{3}}{2}\log\left(\sqrt{3}V+1\right)=\left(-\log X+c\right)\sqrt{3}$$

$$\Rightarrow \left(\frac{2+\sqrt{3}}{2}\right)\ln\left(\frac{\sqrt{3}Y}{X}-1\right)-\left(\frac{2-\sqrt{3}}{2}\right)\ln\left(\frac{\sqrt{3}Y}{X}+1\right)=(\ln X+C)\sqrt{3}$$

where A is another constant and $X = x - 1$, $Y = y + 2$

ILLUSTRATION 62: Solve the differential equation $(x - y)dy = (x + y + 1)\, dx$

SOLUTION: Given differential equation is $\frac{dy}{dx}=\frac{x+y+1}{x-y}$ ...(i)

Let $x = X + h$, $y = Y + K$ $\Rightarrow \frac{dY}{dX}=\frac{dy}{dx}$ ...(ii)

$\therefore$ from (i) $\frac{dy}{dx}=\frac{X+Y+h+k+1}{X-Y+h-k}\Rightarrow\frac{dY}{dX}=\frac{X+Y+h+k+1}{X-Y+h-k}$ (using (2)) ...(iii)

Setting h and k such that

$$\left.\begin{matrix}h+k+1=0\\ h-k=0\end{matrix}\right\}\Rightarrow h=k=-\frac{1}{2}$$

From (iii) $\frac{dY}{dX}=\frac{X+Y}{X-Y}$

put $Y = vX$ and $\frac{dY}{dX}=v+X\frac{dv}{dX}$ in (iv), we get $v+X\frac{dv}{dX}=\frac{X+vX}{X-vX}$

$$\Rightarrow X\frac{dv}{dX}=\frac{1+v}{1-v}-v \qquad \Rightarrow X\frac{dv}{dX}=\frac{1+v-v+v^2}{1-v}$$

$$\Rightarrow X\frac{dv}{dX}=\frac{1+v^2}{1-v} \qquad \Rightarrow \frac{1-v}{1+v^2}dv=\frac{dX}{X}$$

$$\Rightarrow \int\frac{1}{1+v^2}dv-\frac{1}{2}\int\frac{2v}{1+v^2}dv=\int\frac{dX}{X}$$

$$\Rightarrow \tan^{-1}v-\frac{1}{2}\ln(1+v^2)=\ln X+\ln C$$

$$\Rightarrow \tan^{-1}v-\frac{1}{2}\ \ell n(1+v^2)=\ell n(CX) \qquad \Rightarrow \tan^{-1}v=\ell n(CX)+\ell n\sqrt{1+v^2}$$

$$\Rightarrow \tan^{-1}v=\ell n\ (cX\sqrt{1+v^2})$$

$$\Rightarrow \tan^{-1}\left(\frac{Y}{X}\right)=\ell n\left(CX\sqrt{1+\left(\frac{Y}{X}\right)^2}\right)$$

$$\Rightarrow \tan^{-1}\left(\frac{y-k}{x-h}\right)=\ell n\left(C\sqrt{X^2+Y^2}\right)$$

$$\Rightarrow \tan^{-1}\left(\frac{2y+1}{2x+1}\right)=\ell nC\ \sqrt{(x-h)^2+(y-k)^2}$$

$$=\ell nC\ \sqrt{x^2+y^2+h^2+k^2-2xh-2yk}$$

Thus, $\tan^{-1}\left(\frac{2y+1}{2x+1}\right)=\ell nC\ \sqrt{x+y^2+\frac{1}{2}+x+y}$ is the required solution of given differential equation.

TEXTUAL EXERCISE–5: (SUBJECTIVE)

1. Solve the following differential equation:

(a) $(x^2+y^2)\dfrac{dy}{dx}=xy$

(b) $2\dfrac{dy}{dx}=\dfrac{x}{y}-1$

(c) $\dfrac{dy}{dx}=\dfrac{y}{x}+\tan\dfrac{y}{x}$

(d) $\dfrac{dy}{dx}=\dfrac{x-2y+5}{2x+y-1}$

(e) $\dfrac{dy}{dx}=\dfrac{ax+by-a}{bx+ay-b}$

(f) $\dfrac{dy}{dx}+\dfrac{x-2y}{2x-y}=0$

(g) $x\dfrac{dy}{dx}=y-\sqrt{x^2+y^2}$

(h) $x\sin\dfrac{y}{x}dy=\left(y\sin\dfrac{y}{x}-x\right)dx$

(i) $\dfrac{dy}{dx}=\dfrac{x+y+1}{2x+2y+3}$

2. Solve the following differential equation:

(a) $\dfrac{dy}{dx}=\dfrac{x^2+xy}{x^2+y^2}$

(b) $(x^3-3xy^2)dx=(y^3-3x^2y)dy$

3. Solve the following differential equation:

(a) $y^2+x^2\dfrac{dy}{dx}=xy\dfrac{dy}{dx}$

(b) $(2x+y+1)dx+(4x+2y-1)dy=0$

(c) $(3y-7x-3)dx+(7y-3x-7)dy=0$

4. Use the substitution $y^2=ax^3-x$ to reduce the equation $y^3.\dfrac{dy}{dx}+x+y^2=0$ to homogeneous form, and hence solve it.

5. Solve the differential equation $\left[x\cos\dfrac{y}{x}+y\sin\dfrac{y}{x}\right]y=\left[y\sin\dfrac{y}{x}-x\cos\dfrac{y}{x}\right]x\dfrac{dy}{dx}$

Answer Keys

1. (a) $y=ce^{\frac{x^2}{2y^2}}$ (b) $\dfrac{\left(\frac{y}{x}-2\right)/\left(\frac{y}{x}+4\right)}{\dfrac{1}{\left(2.\frac{y^2}{x^2}+\frac{y}{x}-1\right)^3}}$ (c) $\dfrac{y}{x}=\sin^{-1}(kx)$

(d) $x^2-y^2-4xy+10x+2y=c$ (e) $(y-x+1)^{a+b}(y+x-1)^{a-b}=c$ (f) $(x+y)^3=c(y-x)$

(g) $c-y=\sqrt{x^2+y^2}$ (h) $\log x=\cos\left(\dfrac{y}{x}\right)+c$ (i) $x+y+\dfrac{4}{3}=c'e^{3(x-2y)}$

2. (a) $\dfrac{1}{\sqrt{3}}\tan^{-1}\left(\dfrac{2y+x}{\sqrt{3}x}\right)=\ln\left|C(x-y)^{2/3}(x^2+xy+y^2)^{1/6}\right|$ (b) $y^2-x^2=c(y^2+x^2)^2$

3. (a) $\dfrac{y}{x}=c+\log y$ (b) $\log(2x+y-1)+x+2y=c$

(c) $c(y-x-1)^2(y+x-1)^5=1$

4. $ax^4+y^4=c'$ 5. $xy\cos\dfrac{y}{x}=c'$

TEXTUAL EXERCISE–5: (OBJECTIVE)

1. The solution of the differential equation $y' = \frac{y}{x} + \frac{\phi(y/x)}{\phi'(y/x)}$ is

(a) $x\,\phi(y/x) = k$ (b) $\phi(y/x) = kx$
(c) $y\,\phi(y/x) = k$ (d) $\phi(y/x) = ky$

2. The solution of $(y + x + 5)dy = (y - x + 1)dx$ is

(a) $\log[(y+3)^2 + (x+2)^2] + \tan^{-1}\frac{y+3}{x+2} = C$

(b) $\log[(y+3)^2 + (x-2)^2] + \tan^{-1}\frac{y-3}{x-2} = C$

(c) $\log[(y+3)^2 + (x+2)^2] + 2\tan^{-1}\frac{y+3}{x+2} = C$

(d) $\log[(y+3)^2 + (x-2)^2] + 2\tan^{-1}\frac{y+3}{x+2} = C$

3. The curve satisfying the equation $y_1 = \frac{y^2 - 2xy - x^2}{y^2 + 2xy - x^2}$ passing through $(1, -1)$ is a

(a) straight line (b) circle
(c) ellipse (d) None of these

4. The solution of $x\sin\left(\frac{y}{x}\right)dy = \left\{y\sin\left(\frac{y}{x}\right) - x\right\}dx$, is given by

(a) $\log x - \cos\left(\frac{y}{x}\right) = \log C$

(b) $\log x - \sin\left(\frac{y}{x}\right) = C$

(c) $\log\left(\frac{x}{y}\right) - \cos\left(\frac{y}{x}\right) = \log C$

(d) None of these

5. The solution of $\left(1 + e^{\frac{x}{y}}\right)dx + e^{\frac{x}{y}}\left(1 - \frac{x}{y}\right)dy = 0$, is given by

(a) $x - ye^{x/y} = C$ (b) $x + ye^{x/y} = C$

(c) $y - \frac{x}{y}e^{x/y} = C$ (d) None of these

6. The solution of $x^2\frac{dy}{dx} = x^2 + xy + y^2$ is

(a) $\tan^{-1}\frac{y}{x} = \log x + C$

(b) $\tan^{-1}\frac{x}{y} = \log x + C$

(c) $\tan^{-1}\frac{x}{y} = \log y + C$

(d) $\tan^{-1}\frac{y}{x} = \log y + C$

7. The solution of the differential equation $(x^2 + y^2)dx = 2xydy$ is

(a) $x = c(x^2 + y^2)$ (b) $x = c(x^2 - y^2)$
(c) $x + c(x^2 - y^2) = 0$ (d) None of these

8. Solution of differential equation $\frac{dy}{dx} = \frac{y-x}{y+x}$ is

(a) $\log_e(x^2 + y^2) + 2\tan^{-1}\frac{y}{x} + c = 0$

(b) $\frac{y^2}{2} + xy = xy - \frac{x^2}{2} + c$

(c) $\left(1 + \frac{x}{y}\right)y = \left(1 - \frac{x}{y}\right)x + c$

(d) $y = x - 2\log_e y + c$

9. If $(x^2 + y^2)\,dy = xydx$ and $y(x_0) = e$, $y(1) = 1$, then the value of x_0 may be

(a) $\sqrt{3}e$ (b) $\sqrt{e^2 - \frac{1}{2}}$

(c) $\sqrt{\frac{e^2 - 1}{2}}$ (d) $\sqrt{\frac{e^2 + 1}{2}}$

10. If $(y^3 - 2x^2y)dx + (2xy^2 - x^3)\,dy = 0$, then the value of $xy\sqrt{|y^2 - x^2|}$, is

(a) $y^2 + x$ (b) xy^2
(c) any constant (d) None of these

Answer Keys

1. (b) 2. (c) 3. (a) 4. (a) 5. (b) 6. (a) 7. (b) 8. (a) 9. (a) 10. (c)

■ EXACT EQUATION AND NON-EXACT DIFFERENTIAL EQUATION

A differential equation is called exact iff it can be written as complete differential of some function of x, y without any rearrangement. That is, without any further operation of elimination or reduction by multiplying with any function of x and y

Theorem: $Mdx + Ndy = 0$, where M and N are function of x and y is exact iff $\frac{\partial M}{\partial y} = \frac{\partial N}{\partial x}$.

Analytical Proof: Let $Mdx + Ndy = d(f(x, y))$, where f is some function of x and y.

$$\Rightarrow \quad Mdx + Ndy = \frac{\partial f}{\partial x}dx + \frac{\partial f}{\partial y}dy$$

$$\Rightarrow \quad M = \frac{\partial f}{\partial x} \text{ and } N = \frac{\partial f}{\partial y}$$

$$\Rightarrow \quad \frac{\partial M}{\partial y} = \frac{\partial^2 f}{\partial x \partial y}, \frac{\partial N}{\partial x} = \frac{\partial^2 f}{\partial x \partial y}$$

$$\Rightarrow \quad \frac{\partial M}{\partial y} = \frac{\partial N}{\partial x}$$

Geometrical Proof:

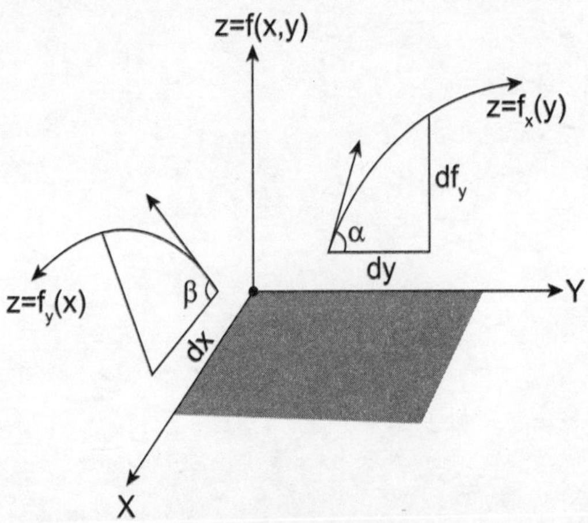

FIGURE 4.40

$$\because \quad \tan\alpha = \frac{\partial f}{\partial y} \quad \Rightarrow \quad df_y = \frac{\partial f}{\partial y}.dy$$

$$\because \quad \tan\beta = \frac{\partial f}{\partial x} \quad \Rightarrow \quad df_x = \frac{\partial f}{\partial x}.dx$$

Total change in $f(x, y)$ due to change dx in x and dy in y is given by

$$d\left(f(x,y)\right) = \frac{\partial f}{\partial x}.dx + \frac{\partial f}{\partial y}.dy \equiv Mdx + Ndy \text{ (say)}$$

Now, $M = \frac{\partial f}{\partial x}$

$$\Rightarrow \quad \frac{\partial M}{\partial y} = \frac{\partial^2 f}{\partial y \partial x} \text{ and } N = \frac{\partial f}{\partial y}$$

$$\Rightarrow \quad \frac{\partial N}{\partial x} = \frac{\partial^2 f}{\partial x \partial y}$$

$\therefore$ Condition of exactness is $\frac{\partial M}{\partial y} = \frac{\partial N}{\partial x}$

Solving Exact Differential Equation

Conversely, let $\frac{\partial M}{\partial y} = \frac{\partial N}{\partial x}$

Let $\int\limits_{y-const.} Mdx = f$

$$\Rightarrow \quad M = \frac{\partial}{\partial x}\left(\int\limits_{y-const.} Mdx\right) = \frac{\partial f}{\partial x}$$

$$\Rightarrow \quad M = \frac{\partial f}{\partial x}$$

$$\Rightarrow \quad \frac{\partial M}{\partial y} = \frac{\partial^2 f}{\partial x \partial y}$$

Similarly $\frac{\partial N}{\partial x} = \frac{\partial^2 f}{\partial x \partial y}$

$$\Rightarrow \quad N = \frac{\partial f}{\partial y} + f(y)$$

$$\Rightarrow \quad Mdx + Ndy = \frac{\partial f}{\partial x}dx + \left(\frac{\partial f}{\partial y} + f(y)\right)dy$$

$$= \frac{\partial f}{\partial x}dx + \frac{\partial f}{\partial y}dy + f(y)dy = df + f(y)dy$$

$$\Rightarrow \quad Mdx + Ndy = d\left(f + \int f(y)\,.\,dy\right).$$

Which is an exact differential.

$\therefore$ If $Mdx + Ndy = 0$ and

$$\text{Mdx} + \text{Ndy} = \text{d}\left(\text{f} + \int f(y)dy\right)$$

$$\Rightarrow \quad d\left(f + \int f(y)dy\right) = 0$$

$$\Rightarrow \quad f + \int f(y)dy = c; \text{ where } f = \int\limits_{y-constt} M.dx$$

$\therefore$ Solution of $Mdx + Ndy = 0$ is

$$\int\limits_{y-constt} M.dx + \int(\text{terms of } N \text{ not containing } x)dy = c$$

Method of Solving an Exact Differential Equation

(A) General Method

Step I: Integrate M with respect to x regarding y as a constant.

Step II: Then integrate with respect to y those terms in N which do not involve x.

Step III: The sum of the two expressions, thus obtained equated to a constant is the required solution

ILLUSTRATION 63: Solve $(x^2 - ay)dx + (y^2 - ax)dy = 0$

SOLUTION: Let $(x^2 - ay)dx + (y^2 - ax)dy = 0$

Here we have $M = x^2 - ay$ and $N = y^2 - ax$

$$\therefore \quad \frac{\partial M}{\partial y} = -a = \frac{\partial N}{\partial x}$$

Thus, the equation is exact, the solution is

$$\Rightarrow \quad \int_{y\text{ constant}} (x^2 - ay)dx + \int y^2 dy = c$$

$$\Rightarrow \quad \frac{x^3}{3} - axy + \frac{y^3}{3} = c$$

ILLUSTRATION 64: Solve $(2x\log y)dx + \left(\frac{x^2}{y} + 3y^2\right)dy = 0$

SOLUTION: Here we have $M = 2x \log y$ and $N = \frac{x^2}{y} + 3y^2$

$\therefore \quad \frac{\partial M}{\partial y} = \frac{2x}{y}; \frac{\partial N}{\partial x} = \frac{2x}{y}$, and hence, the equation is exact.

The solution is $\int_{y\text{-constant}} (2x\log y)dx + \int 3y^2 dy = c$

$\Rightarrow x^2 \log y + y^3 = c$

ILLUSTRATION 65: Solve $\frac{dy}{dx} = \frac{x - 2y + 5}{2x + y - 1}$

SOLUTION: Cross multiplying, $2xdy + y\,dy - dy = xdx - 2ydx + 5dx$

$2\,(xdy + y\,dx) + ydy - dy = xdx + 5\,dx$

$2\,d(xy) + y\,dy - dy = xdx + 5dx$; On integrating,

$$2xy + \frac{y^2}{2} - y = \frac{x^2}{2} + 5x + C$$

$\Rightarrow x^2 - 4xy - y^2 + 10x + 2y = C'$; where $C' = 2C$

ILLUSTRATION 66: Solve $y\,dx + x\,dy = \frac{xdy - ydx}{x^2 + y^2}$

SOLUTION: $d(xy) = d\,(\tan^{-1} y/x)$

Integrating both sides, we get

$xy = \tan^{-1}(y/x) + C$

(B) By Method of Inspection:

To solve the exact differential equations we use the knowledge of standard complete differential expression.

- ❑ $dx \pm dy = d(x \pm y)$
- ❑ $xdy + ydx = d(xy)$.
- ❑ $xdx \pm ydy = \frac{1}{2}d(x^2 \pm y^2)$
- ❑ $\frac{ydx - xdy}{y^2} = d\left(\frac{x}{y}\right)$
- ❑ $\frac{xdy - ydx}{x^2} = d\left(\frac{y}{x}\right)$
- ❑ $d\left(-\frac{1}{xy}\right) = \frac{x\,dy + y\,dx}{x^2y^2}$
- ❑ $d\left(\frac{x^2}{y}\right) = \frac{2xy\,dx - x^2dy}{y^2}$
- ❑ $d\left(\frac{y^2}{x}\right) = \frac{2xy\,dy - y^2dx}{x^2}$
- ❑ $d\left(\frac{x^2}{y^2}\right) = \frac{2xy^2dx - 2x^2ydy}{y^4}$
- ❑ $d\left(\frac{y^2}{x^2}\right) = \frac{2yx^2dy - 2y^2xdx}{x^4}$
- ❑ $d\left(\tan^{-1}\frac{x}{y}\right) = \frac{ydx - xdy}{x^2 + y^2}$
- ❑ $\frac{xdy - ydx}{x^2 + y^2} = d\left(\tan^{-1}\frac{y}{x}\right)$
- ❑ $d(\ln(xy)) = \frac{x\,dy + y\,dx}{xy}$
- ❑ $d\left(\frac{1}{2}\ln(x^2 + y^2)\right) = \frac{xdx + ydy}{x^2 + y^2}$
- ❑ $d\left(\ln\left(\frac{x}{y}\right)\right) = \frac{y\,dx - x\,dy}{xy}$
- ❑ $d\left(\ln\left(\frac{y}{x}\right)\right) = \frac{x\,dy - y\,dx}{xy}$
- ❑ $d\left(\frac{e^x}{y}\right) = \frac{ye^x dx - e^x dy}{y^2}$
- ❑ $d\left(\frac{e^y}{x}\right) = \frac{xe^y dy - e^y dx}{x^2}$
- ❑ $d\left(\frac{1}{2}\log\left(\frac{x+y}{x-y}\right)\right) = \frac{xdy - ydx}{x^2 - y^2}$
- ❑ $d\left(\sqrt{x^2 + y^2}\right) = \frac{x\,dx + y\,dy}{\sqrt{x^2 + y^2}}$
- ❑ $\frac{d[f(x,y)]^{1-n}}{1-n} = \frac{f'(x,y)}{(f(x,y))^n}$

ILLUSTRATION 67: $\frac{xdy - ydx}{x^2 + y^2} + \tan^{-1}\left(\frac{y}{x}\right)(xdy + ydx) = 0$

SOLUTION: $d\left[\tan^{-1}\left(\frac{y}{x}\right)\right] + \tan^{-1}\left(\frac{y}{x}\right)(xdy + ydx) = 0$

$\Rightarrow \frac{d\left[\tan^{-1}(y/x)\right]}{\tan^{-1}(y/x)} + d(xy) = 0$ $\qquad \Rightarrow \ell n\left|\tan^{-1}\left(\frac{y}{x}\right)\right| = -xy + c$

$\Rightarrow \tan^{-1}\frac{y}{x} = ke^{-xy}$ $\qquad \therefore\ y = x\tan(ke^{-xy})$

ILLUSTRATION 68: Solve the equation $y\,dx - (1 + e - xy^2)\,dy = 0$

SOLUTION: Rearranging, we get $y\,dx - dy = e^{-x}y^2\,dy$

$\Rightarrow e^x(y\,dx - dy) = y^2\,dy$ $\qquad \Rightarrow e^x(y\,dx - dy) = y^2\,dy$

$\Rightarrow \frac{e^x\ y\,dx - e^x dy}{y^2} = dy$ $\qquad \Rightarrow d\left(\frac{e^x}{y}\right) = dy$

Integrating both sides, we get

$\Rightarrow e^x = y^2 + Cy$ $\qquad \Rightarrow \frac{e^x}{y} = y + C$

ILLUSTRATION 69: Solve the differential equation $y(2x^2y + e^x)dx - (e^x + y^3)dy = 0$.

SOLUTION: Let $y(2x^2y + e^x)dx - (e^x + y^3)dy = 0$

$\Rightarrow e^x(y\,dx - dy) + 2x^2 y^2dx - y^3\,dy = 0$

Dividing by y^2, we get

$\Rightarrow \dfrac{e^x(y\,dx - dy)}{y^2} + 2x^2dx - y\,dy = 0 \qquad \Rightarrow d\left(\dfrac{e^x}{y}\right) = y\,dy - 2x^2dx$

Integrating both sides, we get

$\Rightarrow \int d\left(\dfrac{e^x}{y}\right) = \int y\,dy - \int 2x^2dx \qquad \Rightarrow \dfrac{e^x}{y} = \dfrac{y^2}{2} - \dfrac{2}{3}x^3 + C$ is the required solution.

ILLUSTRATION 70: Solve the differential equation $(x^2 + y^2 + x)dx - (2x^2 + 2y^2 - y)dy = 0$

SOLUTION: Let $(x^2 + y^2 + x)dx - (2x^2 + 2y^2 - y)dy = 0$

$\Rightarrow (x^2 + y^2)dx - 2(x^2 + y^2)dy + (xdx + ydy) = 0$

$\Rightarrow dx - 2\,dy + \left(\dfrac{x\,dx + y\,dy}{x^2 + y^2}\right) = 0 \qquad \Rightarrow dx - 2dy + d\left[\dfrac{1}{2}\ln(x^2 + y^2)\right] = 0$

$\Rightarrow \int dx - 2\int dy + \dfrac{1}{2}\int d(x^2 + y^2) = C \qquad \Rightarrow x - 2y + \dfrac{1}{2}\ln(x^2 + y^2) = C$

ILLUSTRATION 71: Solve the differential equation $\dfrac{x + y\dfrac{dy}{dx}}{y - x\dfrac{dy}{dx}} = x^2 + 2y^2 + \dfrac{y^4}{x^2}$

SOLUTION: Let the given equation $\dfrac{x + y\dfrac{dy}{dx}}{y - x\dfrac{dy}{dx}} = x^2 + 2y^2 + \dfrac{y^4}{x^2} = \dfrac{x^4 + y^4 + 2x^2y^2}{x^2} = \dfrac{(x^2 + y^2)^2}{x^2}$

$\Rightarrow \dfrac{xdx + ydy}{(x^2 + y^2)^2} = \dfrac{y\,dx - x\,dy}{y^2}\left(\dfrac{y^2}{x^2}\right) \qquad \Rightarrow 2\int \dfrac{1}{(x^2/y^2)}d\left(\dfrac{x}{y}\right)$

$\Rightarrow -\dfrac{1}{2}\int d\left(\dfrac{1}{(x^2 + y^2)}\right) = -\int d\left(\dfrac{1}{x/y}\right)$

$\Rightarrow \int d\left(\dfrac{1}{(x^2 + y^2)}\right) = 2\int d\left(\dfrac{y}{x}\right) \qquad \Rightarrow \dfrac{1}{x^2 + y^2} = 2\left(\dfrac{y}{x}\right) + C$

$\Rightarrow \dfrac{1}{(x^2 + y^2)} = -\dfrac{1}{x/y} + C \qquad \Rightarrow \dfrac{y}{x} - \dfrac{1}{(x^2 + y^2)} = C$

NON-EXACT EQUATIONS: (INTEGRATING FACTORS)

If $Mdx + Ndy = 0$ is a non-exact equation if $Mdx + Ndy$ is not a complete differential of a function $f(x, y)$ and that is only when $\dfrac{\partial M}{\partial y} \neq \dfrac{\partial N}{\partial x}$; e.g., $ydx - x\,dy = 0$ is non-exact equation.

Integrating Factor

If a non-exact equation is multiplied by a function of x, y and the equation becomes exact (i.e., differential), then such function is known as integrating factor.

ILLUSTRATION 72: Verify whether the differential equation $ydx - xdy = 0$ is exact or not. If non-exact, then find the integrating factor, and hence integrate it to obtain its primitive.

SOLUTION: Given equation is $ydx - x\,dy = 0$. Comparing with $Mdx + Ndy = 0$

$\Rightarrow M = y$ and $N = -x$ $\qquad \Rightarrow \dfrac{\partial M}{\partial y} = 1$ and $\dfrac{\partial N}{\partial x} = -1$

So, it is non-exact equation $1/y^2$ is one of its integrating factor because when multiplied by $1/y^2$ the equation becomes $\dfrac{y\,dx - x\,dy}{y^2} = 0$

$\Rightarrow d(x/y) = 0$ $\qquad \Rightarrow x = cy$

Similarly, if multiplied by $1/xy$

$\Rightarrow \dfrac{dx}{x} - \dfrac{dy}{y} = 0; \ln(x/y) = c$

Therefore, a non-exact equation can have more than one integrating factors.

ILLUSTRATION 73: Find the solution of $(xy^4 + y)\,dx - xdy = 0$.

(a) $\dfrac{x^4}{4} + \left(\dfrac{x}{y}\right)^3 = c$ $\qquad$ (b) $\dfrac{x^4}{4} + \dfrac{1}{3}\left(\dfrac{x}{y}\right)^2 = c$

(c) $\dfrac{x^4}{4} + 3\left(\dfrac{x}{y}\right)^2 = c$ $\qquad$ (d) None of these

SOLUTION: (a) Given differential equation can be written as $Mdx + Ndy = 0$

Where $M = xy^4 + y$ and $N = -x$

$\Rightarrow \dfrac{\partial M}{\partial y} = 4xy^3 + 1$ and $\dfrac{\partial N}{\partial x} = -1$ $\qquad \therefore \dfrac{\partial M}{\partial y} \neq \dfrac{\partial N}{\partial x}$

$\Rightarrow$ The given differential equation is non-exact.

Rearrange the diff. equation $xdx + \dfrac{ydx - xdy}{y^4} = 0$

Multiplying both side by x^2 (I.F.), we get $x^3dx + \dfrac{x^2}{y^2}\cdot\dfrac{ydx - xdy}{y^2} = 0$

$\Rightarrow x^3dx + \left(\dfrac{x}{y}\right)^2 \dfrac{d}{dx}\left(\dfrac{x}{y}\right) = 0$

Integrating, $\dfrac{x^4}{4} + \dfrac{1}{3}\left(\dfrac{x}{y}\right)^3 = c$

TEXTUAL EXERCISE–6: (SUBJECTIVE)

1. Check the following equation are exact or not, and hence solve them accordingly:
   (a) $(ax + hy + g)dx + (hx + by + f)dy = 0$
   (b) $x\,dy + (x + y)\,dx = 0$
   (c) $(e^y + 1)\cos x dx + e^y \sin x dy = 0$
   (d) $(x^2 - ay)dx + (y^2 - ax)dy = 0$
   (e) $[y(1 + x^{-1}) + \sin y]\,dx + (x + \log x + x\cos y)dy = 0$

2. Show that $(y - 2x^3)dx - x(1 - xy)dy = 0$ becomes exact on multiplication by $1/x^2$, and hence solve it .

3. Solve the differential equation, $ydx - xdy + \log x dx = 0$ by making it exact.

4. Solve $(x^2 - 4xy - 2y^2)\,dx + (y^2 - 4xy - 2x^2)\,dy = 0$

5. Solve $xdx + ydy + \dfrac{xdy - ydx}{x^2 + y^2} = 0$

Answer Keys

1. (a) $ax^2 + 2hxy + by^2 + 2gx + 2fy + c = 0$ (b) $xy+\frac{1}{2}x^2 = c$ (c) $(e^y + 1)\sin x = c$
 (d) $x^3 + y^3 - 3axy = c$ (e) $xy + y \log x + x \sin y = c$
2. $xy^2 = cx + 2y + 2x^3$
3. $cx + y + \log x + 1 = 0$ 4. $y^3 - 6xy^2 - 6yx^2 + x^3 = C$ 5. $\frac{x^2+y^2}{2}+\tan^{-1}\left(\frac{y}{x}\right)=C$

TEXTUAL EXERCISE-6: (OBJECTIVE)

1. The curve satisfying $ydx - x\,dy + \log x dx = 0$ $(x > 0)$ passing through $(1, -1)$ is
 (a) $y + \log x + 1 = 0$
 (b) $-y^2 + \log x + 1 = 0$
 (c) $y^3 + (\log x)^2 + 1 = 0$
 (d) None of these
2. The solution of $\frac{x^3dx+yx^2dy}{\sqrt{x^2+y^2}} = ydx - xdy$ is
 (a) $\sqrt{x^2+y^2} = Cx$ (b) $\sqrt{x^2+y^2}+\frac{y}{x}=C$
 (c) $\sqrt{x^2+y^2}+\frac{y}{x^2}=C$ (d) $(x^2 + y^2)^2 + xy^2 = C$
3. The solution of the differential equation $ydx - xdy + xy^2dx = 0$, is
 (a) $\frac{x}{y}+x^2=\lambda$ (b) $\frac{x}{y}+\frac{x^2}{2}=\lambda$
 (c) $\frac{x}{2y^2}+\frac{x^2}{2}=\lambda$ (d) None of these
4. The solution of $xdy + ydx + 2x^3dx = 0$, is
 (a) $xy + x^4 = c$ (b) $xy+\frac{1}{2}x^4=c$
 (c) $\frac{x^2}{y}+\frac{x^4}{4}=c$ (d) None of these
5. The solution of, $ydx - xdy + (1 + x^2)dx + x^2 \sin ydy = 0$, is given by
 (a) $x + 1 - y^2 + \cos y + c = 0$
 (b) $y + 1 - x^2 + x \cos y + c = 0$
 (c) $\frac{x}{y}+\frac{1}{y}-y+\cos y+c=0$
 (d) $\frac{y}{x}+\frac{1}{x}-x+\cos y+c=0$
6. The solution of $ydx - xdy + 3x^2y^2e^{x^3}dx = 0$ is
 (a) $\frac{x}{y}+e^{x^3}=C$ (b) $\frac{x}{y}-e^{x^3}=C$
 (c) $\frac{-x}{y}+e^{x^3}=C$ (d) None of these
7. If $xdy = y(dx + ydy)$, $y > 0$ and $y(1) = 1$, then $y(-3) =$
 (a) 1 (b) 3
 (c) 5 (d) –1
8. The solution of $(1 + xy)ydx + (1 - xy)\,xdy = 0$ is
 (a) $\frac{x}{y}+\frac{1}{xy}=k$ (b) $\log\left(\frac{x}{y}\right)=\frac{1}{xy}+k$
 (c) $\frac{x}{y}=e^{xy}+k$ (d) $\log\left(\frac{x}{y}\right)=xy+k$
9. The solution of the differential equation, $ydx + (x + x^2y)dy = 0$
 (a) $\log y = cx$ (b) $-\frac{1}{xy}-\log y=c$
 (c) $-\frac{1}{xy}+\log y=c$ (d) None of these
10. The solution of $\frac{x+y\,dy/dx}{y-x\,dy/dx}=\frac{x\sin^2(x^2+y^2)}{y^3}$, is given by
 (a) $-\cot(x^2+y^2)=\left(\frac{x}{y}\right)^2+c$
 (b) $\tan(x^2 + y^2) = x^2y^2 + c$
 (c) $\cot(x^2+y^2)=\frac{x}{y}+c$
 (d) None of these

Answer Keys

1. (a) 2. (b) 3. (b) 4. (b) 5. (d) 6. (a) 7. (b) 8. (b) 9. (c) 10. (a)

LEIBNITZ LINEAR DIFFERENTIAL EQUATION

A differential equation in which the dependent variable and its differential coefficients occur only in first degree and are not multiplied together is called a linear differential equation. Linear equation of nth order is given as

$$a_0(x)\frac{d^n y}{dx^n}+a_1(x)+\frac{d^{n-1}y}{dx^{n-1}}+.....+a_{n-1}(x)\frac{dy}{dx}+a_n(y)+\varphi(x)=0$$

Where $a_0, a_1,...,a_n$ are functions of only x is n^{th} order linear differential equation (i.e., no term contains product of powers of y and derivatives or higher power of derivatives). Those which are not linear are termed as non-linear differential equations.

ILLUSTRATION 74: Find whether the following differential equation is linear or not.

(a) $\left(\frac{d^3y}{dx^3}\right)^3-6\left(\frac{d^2y}{dx^2}\right)-4y=0$

(b) $\frac{d^2y}{dx^2}-5\frac{dy}{dx}+6y=\sin x$

(c) $\frac{d^3y}{dx^3}-5x\frac{dy}{dx}+6y=0$

SOLUTION: (a) It is not a linear differential equation because its degree is 3.

(b) It is linear differential equation.

(c) It is linear differential equation.

REMARK:

A linear differential equation is always of the first degree but every differential equation of the first degree need not be linear. e.g., the differential equation $\frac{d^2y}{dx^2}+2\left(\frac{dy}{dx}\right)^3+5y^3=0$ *is not linear, though its degree is 1.*

1st Order Linear Differential Equation

The differential equation of the form $\frac{dy}{dx}+P(x).y=Q(x)$; where $P(x)$ and $Q(x)$ are functions of only x is called a first order linear differential equation. It is non-exact equation. The integrating factor (I.F.) for such equation is $e^{\int P(x)dx}$. By multiplying the above equation with this factor the equation becomes an exact equation as shown below: Multiplying both sides of given equation by $e^{\int Pdx}$, we get

$$e^{\int P(x)dx}\frac{dy}{dx}+P(x)\,e^{\int P(x)dx}.\,y=Q(x).e^{\int P(x)dx}$$

$$\Rightarrow \frac{d}{dx}\left(y.e^{\int P(x)dx}\right)=Q(x)e^{\int P(x)dx}$$

$$\Rightarrow d\left(y.e^{\int P(x)dx}\right)=Q(x)e^{\int P(x)dx}dx$$

Integrating both sides, we get

$$\int d\left(y.e^{\int P(x)dx}\right)=\int Q(x)e^{\int P(x)dx}dx$$

$$\Rightarrow y.e^{\int P(x)dx}=\int Q(x)\,e^{\int P(x)dx}dx + c$$

$\therefore$ the G.S. of above equation is

$$y.(I.F.)=\int Q(x).(I.F.)\,dx+c$$

e.g. solve the differential equation $x\frac{dy}{dx}+y=x^3$

The standard form of the equation is $\frac{dy}{dx}+\frac{y}{x}=x^2$

Hence, $p=\frac{1}{x}$

$$\Rightarrow I.F.=e^{\int p\,dx}=e^{\int\frac{dx}{x}}=e^{\ln x}=x$$

Multiplying the equation by x, we get $x\frac{dy}{dx}+y=x^3$

$$\Rightarrow \frac{d}{dx}(xy)=x^3$$

$\Rightarrow xy=\frac{x^4}{4}+C$ which is the required solution.

Proof: Let us analyze the above technique by solving linear differential equation by using integrating factor. We represent the given function y as a product of two functions of x, $u(x)$ and $v(x)$

i.e., $y = uv$

$$\Rightarrow \frac{dy}{dx} = u\frac{dv}{dx} + v\frac{du}{dx} \quad ...(1)$$

Using (1) in linear differential equation $\frac{dy}{dx} + Py = Q$, we have $u\frac{dv}{dx} + v\frac{du}{dx} + Pu.v = Q$

$$\text{or} \quad v\frac{du}{dx} + u\left[\frac{dv}{dx} + Pv\right] = Q \quad ...(2)$$

One of the two functions $u(x)$ and $v(x)$ can be choosen arbitrarily and the other function is obtained so that the product of two function satisfy the given differential equation.

$$\text{Let us set } \frac{dv}{dx} + Pv = 0 \quad ...(3)$$

$$\Rightarrow \frac{dv}{v} = -Pdx \qquad \Rightarrow \ln(v) = -\int P\,dx$$

$$\Rightarrow v = e^{-\int P(x)dx} \quad ...(4)$$

Now using (3) in (2) we obtain $v\frac{du}{dx} = Q$

$$\Rightarrow \frac{du}{dx} = \frac{Q}{v} = e^{\int P(x)dx}$$

$$\Rightarrow u = \int Qe^{\int P(x)dx}dx + C$$

$$\therefore y = uv \Rightarrow y = e^{-\int Pdx}\cdot\left(\int Qe^{\int P(x)dx}dx + C\right)$$

$$\Rightarrow ye^{\int Pdx} = \int Q.e^{\int P(x)dx}dx + C$$

The above equation expresses the general solution of given linear differential equation.

Since on multiplying the both sides of given differential equation by $e^{\int P\,dx}$ reduces the differential equation integrable form $e^{\int Pdx}$ is called integrating factor denoted by I.F.

Thus, the complete general solution of linear differential equation $\frac{dy}{dx} + Py = Q$; where P and Q are functions of x is given by $y(I.F.) = \int Q.(I.F.)dx + C$

Let us solve the linear differential equation, $\frac{dy}{dx} + 2xy = x$. Comparing it with $\frac{dy}{dx} + Py = Q$, we get $P = 2x$, $Q = x$

$$\therefore \quad I.F. = e^{\int Pdx} = e^{\int 2xdx} = e^{x^2}$$

$\therefore$ Solution of above linear differential equation will be given by

$$y(I.F.) = \int Q.(I.F.)dx + C \text{ or } ye^{x^2} = \int xe^{x^2}dx + C$$

$$\text{or} \quad ye^{x^2} = \frac{1}{2}\int 2x.e^{x^2}dx + C$$

$$\text{or} \quad ye^{x^2} = \frac{1}{2}\left[e^{x^2}\right] + C \text{ or } y = \frac{1}{2} + Ce^{-x^2}$$

REMARK:

Some times a given differential equation becomes linear if we take y as the independent variable and x as the dependent variable.

ILLUSTRATION 75: Solve the equation $(x + 2y^3)\frac{dy}{dx} = y$

SOLUTION: The above equation can be written as $\frac{dx}{dy} = \frac{x + 2y^3}{y} = \frac{1}{y}x + 2y^2$ which is the a linear differential equation in x and $\frac{dx}{dy}$.

Comparing the given equation with $\frac{dx}{dy} + Px = Q$; where P and Q are functions of y, we have

$$P = -\frac{1}{y}, Q = 2y^2$$

$$I.F. = e^{\int Pdy} = e^{\int -\frac{1}{y}dy} = e^{-\ln y} = \frac{1}{y}$$

$\therefore$ Solution of differential equation is given by $x.(I.F.) = \int Q.(I.F.)dy + C$

$$\Rightarrow x.\frac{1}{y} = \int 2y^2.\frac{1}{y}dy + C$$

$\Rightarrow \dfrac{x}{y}=\dfrac{2y^2}{2}+C$

$\Rightarrow \dfrac{x}{y}=y^2+C \qquad \Rightarrow x=y^3+Cy$

ILLUSTRATION 76: Solve the equation $\dfrac{dy}{dx}+x^2y=x^5$

SOLUTION: Given $\dfrac{dy}{dx}+x^2y=x^5$, Since $P = x^2$ and $Q = x^5$

$I.F.=e^{\int x^2 dx}=e^{x^3/3}$

$\Rightarrow$ The solution is given by $y\left(e^{x^3/3}\right)=\int x^5.e^{x^3/3}\,dx+C$

For RHS, put $\dfrac{x^3}{3}=z$

$\Rightarrow x^2\,dx = dz$

$\Rightarrow y.e^{\frac{x^3}{3}}=\int(3z)e^z\,dz = 3\int z\,e^z\,dz=3\left[z\,e^z-\int e^z\,dz\right]=3[(z-1)e^z]+C$

$\Rightarrow y\,e^{x^3/3}=3\left(\dfrac{x^3}{3}-1\right)e^{x^3/3}+C \qquad \Rightarrow y=x^3-3+C.e^{-x^3/3}$

ILLUSTRATION 77: Solve the differential equation $x\log x\dfrac{dy}{dx}+y=2\log x$.

SOLUTION: Let $x\log x\dfrac{dy}{dx}+y=2\log x$

$\Rightarrow \dfrac{dy}{dx}+\dfrac{1}{x\log x}y=\dfrac{2}{x}$

This is linear differential equation with

$I.F=\exp.\int\dfrac{dx}{x\log x}=\exp.(\log.\log x)=\log x$

$\therefore$ The required solution is, $y\log x=\int\dfrac{2}{x}\log x\,dx+C$

$\Rightarrow y\log x=(\log x)^2+C$

ILLUSTRATION 78: Solve the differential equation $x\dfrac{dy}{dx}=y-\cos\left(\dfrac{1}{x}\right)$.

SOLUTION: Here, $x\dfrac{dy}{dx}-y=-\cos\left(\dfrac{1}{x}\right)$

$\therefore \dfrac{dy}{dx}-\dfrac{1}{x}.y=-\dfrac{1}{x}\cos\left(\dfrac{1}{x}\right)$; this is in the linear form.

$\Rightarrow P=-\dfrac{1}{x};\ Q=-\dfrac{1}{x}\cos\left(\dfrac{1}{x}\right)$

And integrating factor $=e^{\int -\frac{1}{x}dx}=e^{-\log x}=e^{\log x^{-1}}=x^{-1}$

Multiplying it by the integrating factor $\dfrac{1}{x}$, we get $\dfrac{dy}{dx}-\dfrac{1}{x^2}y=-\dfrac{1}{x^2}\cos\left(\dfrac{1}{x}\right)$

or $\dfrac{d}{dx}\cdot\left\{\dfrac{1}{x}.y\right\}=-\dfrac{1}{x^2}\cos\left(\dfrac{1}{x}\right)$ or $d\left(\dfrac{y}{x}\right)=-\dfrac{1}{x^2}\cos\left(\dfrac{1}{x}\right)dx$

or $\int d\left(\dfrac{y}{x}\right)=\int-\dfrac{1}{x^2}\cos\left(\dfrac{1}{x}\right)dx$ $\therefore$ $\dfrac{y}{x}=\int\cos\left(\dfrac{1}{x}\right)d\left(\dfrac{1}{x}\right)$

or $\dfrac{y}{x}=\sin\left(\dfrac{1}{x}\right)+C$ $\Rightarrow$ $y-x\sin\left(\dfrac{1}{x}\right)=Cx$

ILLUSTRATION 79: If the gradient of a curve at any point (x, y) is $2y + x$ and it passes through the origin, then find its equation.

SOLUTION: Given equation is $\dfrac{dy}{dx}=2y+x$ or $\dfrac{dy}{dx}-2y=x$ which is the linear differential equation.

Its $I.F.=e^{\int-2dx}=e^{-2x}$

$\therefore$ Its solution is $ye^{-2x}=\int xe^{-2x}\,dx+C=\dfrac{xe^{-2x}}{-2}+\dfrac{1}{2}\int e^{-2x}dx+C=-\dfrac{1}{2}xe^{-2x}-\dfrac{1}{4}e^{-2x}+C$

$\Rightarrow$ $y=-\dfrac{1}{2}x-\dfrac{1}{4}+Ce^{2x}$ ...(i)

$\because$ It passes through origin (0, 0)

$\Rightarrow$ $0 = C - 1/4$ $\Rightarrow$ $C = 1/4$ ...(ii)

From (i) and (ii), we have $y=\dfrac{1}{4}e^{2x}-\dfrac{1}{2}x-\dfrac{1}{4}$ or $4y = e^{2x} - 2x - 1$

which is the required equation of the curve.

Method 2

A linear differential equations of the first order can be written in the form

$y' = f(x)y + g(x)$ ...(1)

If $g(x) \equiv 0$, then the linear differential equation (1) is called homogenous.

It has the form $y' = f(x)y$ ...(2)

Equation (2) is an equation with variable separable. It can be shown that all solutions of this equation are given b the formula $y = Ce^{F(x)}$. ...(3)

Where $F(x)$ is a certain primitive of the function $f(x)$, and C is an arbitrary constant. In particular, if the function $f(x)$ is constant, say $f(x) = k$ for any x, then the equation $y' = ky$ has the general solution $y = Ce^{kx}$.

If $f(x) \equiv 0$, then equation (1) takes the form $y' = g(x)$.

As is known, the general solution of this equation will be $y = G(x) + C$; where $G(x)$ is a certain primitive of function $g(x)$ and C is an arbitrary constant (the constant of integral)

Theorem: If $y = \phi(x)$ is a certain solution of equation (1), then all solutions of this equation are given by the formula $y = Ce^{F(x)} + \phi(x)$ ...(4)

Where $Ce^{F(x)}$ is the general solution of homogeneous equation (2)

Proof: First of all we check whether for any value of the constant C, function (4) is a solution of equation (1).

Indeed $y' = Ce^{F(x)}F'(x) + \phi(x) = Ce^{F(x)}f(x) + f(x)\phi(x) + g(x)$

$= f(x)\,(Ce^{F(x)} + \phi(x)) + g(x) = f(x)y + g(x)$

Let now $\psi(x)$ be a certain solution of equation (1). We are going to show that the function

$y = \psi(x) - \phi(x)$ is a solution of homogeneous equation (2).

$y' = \psi'(x) - \phi'(x) = f(x)\,\psi(x) + g(x) - f(x)\phi(x) - g(x) = f(x)\,(\psi(x) - \phi(x)) = f(x)y.$

Therefore, there exist a constant C such that $\psi(x) - \phi(x) = Ce^{F(x)}$

And consequently, $\psi(x) = Ce^{F(x)} + \phi(x)$.

Thus, any solution of equation (1) is obtained by formula (4) for a certain value of constant C.

The theorem has been proved

It follows from this theorem that in order to find the general solution of equation (1), it is sufficient to find at least one of its particular solutions.

ILLUSTRATION 80: Find the general solution of the differential equation $y' + xy = 4x$.

SOLUTION: By trial and error we find that the function y 4 is the solution of the given non-homogeneous equation. Let us now find the general solution of the corresponding homogeneous equation $y' + xy = 0$

By formula (4) the general solution of this equation has the form $y = Ce^{-\frac{1}{2}x^2}$

According to the above proved theorem, the general solution of the given non-homogeneous linear equation is given by the formula $y = Ce^{-\frac{1}{2}x^2} + 4$; where C is an arbitrary constant.

Now we are going to indicate the method for finding the particular solution of the non-homogeneous equation $Y' = f(x)y + g(x)$ ...(1)

Let $y = Ce^{F(x)}$ ...(2)

Be the general solution of the homogeneous linear equation

$y' = u(x)\, e^{F(x)}$. ...(3)

then we shall find the particular solution of equation (1) in the following form:

$y = u(x)e^{F(x)}$ ...(4)

where $u(x)$ is an unknown function. Substituting function (4) into equation (1), we get

$u'e^F + ue^F f = fue^F + g$ and finally $u' = g(x)\, e^{-F(x)}$.

Consequently, the function $u(x)$ is certain primitive of the function $g(x)\, e^{-F(x)}$.

Thus, in order to find the particular solution of non-homogenous equation (1), we have to replace the constant C by a certain primitive for the function $g(x)\, e^{-F(x)}$ in the general solution (2) of the corresponding homogeneous equation (3).

This way of finding the particular solution is called the method of variation of the constant.

ILLUSTRATION 81: Find a bounded solution of the differential equation $y' = y + (\cos x - \sin x)$.

SOLUTION: The given differential equation is $y' - 1y = (\cos x - \sin x)$

$\Rightarrow \quad I.F. = e^{\int -dx} = e^{-x}$

$\therefore$ General solution is given by $y.e^{-x} = \int (\cos x - \sin x)e^{-x}dx + C$

or $ye^{-x} = \sin xe^{-x} + C$ or $y = \sin x + Ce^x$

Any solution of the equation obtained from the general solution when $C \neq 0$ will be unbounded since when $x \to \infty$, the function $\sin x$ is bounded and $e^x \to \infty$. It follows that the given equation has a unique bounded solution $y = \sin x$, which is obtained from the general solution when $C = 0$.

ILLUSTRATION 82: If u and v are two solutions of the differential equation $\frac{dy}{dx} + P(x).y = Q(x)$, then prove that $y = u + c(u - v)$ is the general solution of the equation, where c is any constant. Find the relation between α and β such that $y = \alpha u + \beta v$ is a solution of given differential equation.

SOLUTION: As u, v are the solutions of the differential equation

$$\frac{dy}{dx} + P(x).y = Q(x) \qquad ...(1)$$

$$\Rightarrow \quad \frac{du}{dx} + P(x).u = Q(x) \qquad ...(2)$$

$$\text{And} \quad \frac{dv}{dx} + P(x).v = Q(x) \qquad ...(3)$$

From (1) and (2), we have $\left(\frac{dy}{dx}-\frac{du}{dx}\right)+P(x)(y-u)=0$

$\frac{d}{dx}(y-u)+P(x)(y-u)=0$ ...(4)

Parallely $\frac{d}{dx}(u-v)+P(x).(u-v)=0$ ...(5)

From (4) and (5), $\frac{\frac{d}{dx}(y-u)}{\frac{d}{dx}(u-v)}=\frac{y-u}{u-v}$

$\Rightarrow \frac{d(y-u)}{y-u}=\frac{d(u-v)}{(u-v)}$

Integrating both sides, we get $\ln(y-u)=\ln(u-v)$

$\therefore$ $y=u+c(u-v)$

Now, $y=\alpha u+\beta v$ will be a solution if

$\frac{d}{dx}(\alpha u+\beta v)+P(x)(\alpha u+\beta v)=Q(x)$ or $\alpha\left(\frac{du}{dx}+P(x)u\right)+\beta\left(\frac{dv}{dx}+P(x)v\right)=Q(x)$

or $\alpha Q(x)+\beta Q(x)=Q(x)$ (using (2) and (3))

$\Rightarrow$ $(\alpha+\beta)\,Q(x)=Q(x)$

$\Rightarrow$ $\alpha+\beta=1$ is the required relation between α and β.

ILLUSTRATION 83: Solve the differential equation $\left(x^2-1\right)\frac{dy}{dx}+2xy=\frac{1}{x^2-1}$

SOLUTION: The given differential equation is $(x^2-1)\frac{dy}{dx}+2xy=\frac{1}{x^2-1}$

$\Rightarrow \frac{dy}{dx}+\frac{2x}{x^2-1}y=\frac{1}{(x^2-1)^2}$ ...(i)

This is a linear differential equation of the form $\frac{dy}{dx}+Py=Q$, where $P=\frac{2x}{x^2-1}$ and $Q=\frac{1}{(x^2-1)^2}$

$\therefore$ I.F. $=e^{\int Pdx}=e^{\int 2x/(x^2-1)dx}=e^{\log(x^2-1)}=\left(x^2-1\right)$

Multiplying both sides of (i) by $I.F.=(x^2-1)$, we get $\left(x^2-1\right)\frac{dy}{dx}+2xy=\frac{1}{x^2-1}$

Integrating both sides, we get $y\left(x^2-1\right)=\int\frac{1}{x^2-1}dx+C$

[Using: $y(I.F.)=\int Q.(I.F.)dx+C$]

$\Rightarrow$ $y\left(x^2-1\right)=\frac{1}{2}\log\left|\frac{x-1}{x+1}\right|+C$. This is the required solution.

ILLUSTRATION 84: Solve $(1+x^2)\frac{dy}{dx}+2xy-4x^2=0$ subject to the initial condition $y(0)=0$.

SOLUTION: The given differential equation can be written as $\frac{dy}{dx}+\frac{2x}{1+x^2}y=\frac{4x^2}{1+x^2}$ ...(i)

This is a linear differential equation of the form $\frac{dy}{dx}+Py=Q$, where $P=\frac{2x}{1+x^2}$ and $Q=\frac{4x^2}{1+x^2}$

We have I.F. $= e^{\int P dx} = e^{\int 2x/(1+x^2)dx} = e^{\log(1+x^2)} = (1+x^2)$

Multiplying both sides of (i) by I.F. = $(1+x^2)$, we get $y(1+x^2) = \int 4x^2 dx + C$

$\Rightarrow \quad (1+x^2)\dfrac{dy}{dx} + 2xy = 4x^2$

Integrating both sides w.r.t. x, we get $y(1+x^2) = \int 4x^2 dx + C$

$\Rightarrow \quad y(1+x^2) = \dfrac{4x^3}{3} + C$

It is given that $y = 0$ when $x = 0$. So, $0 + 0 + C$

$\Rightarrow \quad C = 0$

Hence, $y(1+x^2) = \dfrac{4x^3}{3}$ is the required solution

ILLUSTRATION 85: Solve the equation $(1-x^2)\dfrac{dy}{dx} + 2xy = x(1-x^2)^{1/2}$

SOLUTION: Given differential equation $(1-x^2)\dfrac{dy}{dx} + 2xy = x(1-x^2)^{1/2}$ ...(i)

$\Rightarrow \quad \dfrac{dy}{dx} + \left(\dfrac{2x}{1-x^2}\right)y = \dfrac{x}{\sqrt{1-x^2}} \qquad \Rightarrow \quad P = \dfrac{2x}{1-x^2}$ and $Q = \dfrac{x}{\sqrt{1-x^2}}$

Now, I.F. $= e^{\int \frac{2x}{1-x^2}dx} = \dfrac{1}{1-x^2}$

$\therefore$ Solution of given differential equation (i) is given by

$y.\left(\dfrac{1}{1-x^2}\right) = \int \dfrac{1}{1-x^2}.\dfrac{x}{\sqrt{1-x^2}}dx + C$

$\Rightarrow \quad y.\dfrac{1}{(1-x^2)} = \int \dfrac{xdx}{(1-x^2)^{3/2}} + C$ ...(ii)

put $1 - x^2 = t^2$

and $xdx = -\,tdt$ in (ii), we get $\dfrac{y}{1-x^2} = \int -\dfrac{tdt}{t^3}$

$\Rightarrow \quad y.\dfrac{1}{(1-x^2)} = \dfrac{1}{t} + C$

$\Rightarrow \quad y.\dfrac{1}{(1-x^2)} = \dfrac{1}{\sqrt{1-x^2}} + C \qquad \Rightarrow \quad y = c(1-x^2) + \sqrt{1-x^2}$

ILLUSTRATION 86: Solve the differential equation $x(x-1)\dfrac{dy}{dx} - (x-2)y = x^3(2x-1)$

SOLUTION: Given differential equation is $x(x-1)\dfrac{dy}{dx} - (x-2)y = x^3(2x-1)$ ...(i)

$\Rightarrow \quad \dfrac{dy}{dx} - \dfrac{(x-2)}{x(x-1)}y = \dfrac{x^2(2x-1)}{x-1}$

$\therefore$ I.F. $= e^{-\int \frac{x-2}{x(x-1)}dx} = \dfrac{x-1}{x^2}$

$\therefore$ Solution of (i) is given by $y.\left(\frac{x-1}{x^2}\right)=\int\frac{x^2(2x-1)}{x-1}.\frac{x-1}{x^2}$

$\Rightarrow\ y.\left(\frac{x-1}{x^2}\right)=x^2-x+C$

$\Rightarrow\ y(x-1)=x^2(x^2-x+c)$

ILLUSTRATION 87: If solution of differential equation $\frac{dy}{dx}-y=1-e^{-x}$; $y(0)=y_0$ and y has a finite value when $x\to\infty$, then find y_0.

SOLUTION: Given differential equation is $\frac{dy}{dx}-y=1-e^{-x}$ ...(i)

$\Rightarrow\ P=-1$ and $Q=1-e^{-x}$

$\Rightarrow\ I.F.=e^{\int Pdx}=e^{\int -1dx}=e^{-x}$

$\therefore$ Solution of differential equation (i) is given by $y.e^{-x}=\int e^{-x}(1-e^{-x})dx+C$

$\Rightarrow\ ye^{-x}=-e^{-x}+\frac{1}{2}e^{-2x}+C$ $\qquad\Rightarrow\ y=-1+\frac{1}{2}e^{-x}+Ce^{x}$

Now at $x=0$ and $y=y_0$

$\Rightarrow\ C=y_0+\frac{1}{2}$ $\qquad\Rightarrow\ y=-1+\frac{1}{2}e^{-x}+\left(y_0+\frac{1}{2}\right)^{e^x}$

Now, as $x\to\infty$, $e^{-x}\to 0$

$\Rightarrow\ y=-1+\left(y_0+\frac{1}{2}\right)^{e^x}$

$\Rightarrow$ given that as $x\to\infty$, y is finite

$\Rightarrow\ y_0+\frac{1}{2}=0$ $\qquad\Rightarrow\ y_0=-\frac{1}{2}$

EQUATION REDUCIBLE TO LINEAR FORM (BERNOULLI'S DIFFERENTIAL EQUATION)

An equation of the form $\frac{dy}{dx}+P(x).y=Q(x).y^n$ (where P and Q are either functions of x or constants and n is a constant other than 0 or 1) is called Bernoulli's differential equation.

Given differential equation can be written as

$$\frac{1}{y^n}\frac{dy}{dx}+\frac{1}{y^{n-1}}P(x)=Q(x) \qquad \text{...(i)}$$

To reduce (i) to linear form, substitute $\frac{1}{y^{n-1}}=u$ ...(ii)

$$\Rightarrow\ \frac{-(n-1)}{y^n}\frac{dy}{dx}=\frac{du}{dx} \qquad \text{...(iii)}$$

Using (ii) and (iii) in (i), we get

$$-\frac{1}{(n-1)}\frac{du}{dx}+P(x)u=Q(x)$$

$$\Rightarrow\ \frac{du}{dx}+(1-n)P(x)u=(1-n)Q(x)$$

Which is a linear differential equation in u and hence can be solved for u. Resubstituting $u=\frac{1}{y^{n-1}}$, we get solution to original differential equation.

ILLUSTRATION 88: Solve the differential equation $\frac{x^2 dy}{dx}+xy=y^2$

SOLUTION: Standard form of equation is $\frac{dy}{dx}+\frac{y}{x}=\frac{y^2}{x^2}$

Dividing the equation by y^2, $\frac{1}{y^2}\frac{dy}{dx}+\frac{1}{xy}=\frac{1}{x^2}$

Now putting $y^{1-2}=y^{-1}=t$ and $\frac{-1}{y^2}\frac{dy}{dx}=\frac{dt}{dx}$; we have

$\Rightarrow \quad -\frac{dt}{dx}+\frac{t}{x}=\frac{1}{x^2}$ $\qquad \Rightarrow \quad \frac{dt}{x}-\frac{t}{x}=-\frac{1}{x^2}$

Here, $P=-\frac{1}{x}$ $\qquad \Rightarrow \quad I.F.=e^{\int pdx}=e^{\int -\frac{dx}{x}}=e^{-\ln x=}\frac{1}{x}$

Multiplying the equation by $\frac{1}{x}$, we get $\frac{1}{x}\frac{dt}{dx}-\frac{t}{x^2}=-\frac{1}{x^3}$

$\Rightarrow \quad \frac{d}{dx}\left(\frac{t}{x}\right)=-\frac{1}{x^3}$ $\qquad \Rightarrow \quad \frac{t}{x}=\frac{1}{2x^2}+C$

Resubstituting $t=\frac{1}{y}$, we have $\frac{1}{xy}=\frac{1}{2x^2}+C$, which is the required equation

ILLUSTRATION 89: Solve the differential equation $2\frac{dy}{dx}-y\sec x=y^3\tan x$

SOLUTION: Given differential equation is $2\frac{dy}{dx}-y\sec x=y^3\tan x$ ...(i)

$\Rightarrow \quad \frac{2}{y^3}\frac{dy}{dx}+\left(\frac{-1}{y^2}\right)\sec x=\tan x$ ...(ii)

Putting $\frac{-1}{y^2}=v$

And $\frac{2}{y^3}\frac{dy}{dx}=\frac{dv}{dx}$ in (ii), we get $\frac{dv}{dx}+(\sec x)v=\tan x$ ...(iii)

$\Rightarrow \quad P=\sec x,\ Q=\tan x$

$\therefore \quad$ I.F. $=e^{\int \sec x\,dx}=e^{\ln(\sec x+\tan x)}=\sec x+\tan x$

$\therefore \quad$ Solution of differential equation (iii) will be given by

$v(\sec x+\tan x)=\int(\sec x+\tan x)\tan x dx+C$

$\Rightarrow \quad v(\sec x+\tan x)=\sec x+\int(\sec^2 x-1)dx+C$

$\Rightarrow \quad v(\sec x+\tan x)=\sec x+\tan x-x+C$

$\Rightarrow \quad -\frac{1}{y^2}(\sec x+\tan x)=\sec x+\tan x-x+C$

ILLUSTRATION 90: Solve the differential equation $y(2xy + e^x)\,dx - e^x\,dy = 0$

SOLUTION: Given differential equation is $y(2xy + e^x)dx - e^x dy = 0$ ...(i)

$\Rightarrow y(2xy + e^x) = e^x \dfrac{dy}{dx}$ $\qquad \Rightarrow \dfrac{dy}{dx} - y = \dfrac{2xy^2}{e^x}$

$\Rightarrow \dfrac{1}{y^2}\dfrac{dy}{dx} - \dfrac{1}{y} = \dfrac{2x}{e^x}$ ...(ii)

Putting $\dfrac{1}{y} = v$ and $\dfrac{1}{y^2}\dfrac{dy}{dx} = -\dfrac{dv}{dx}$ in (ii) we have $-\dfrac{dv}{dx} - v = \dfrac{2x}{e^x}$

$\Rightarrow \dfrac{dv}{dx} + v = -\dfrac{2x}{e^x}$ ...(iii)

$\Rightarrow P = 1, Q = -\dfrac{2x}{e^x}$ $\qquad \therefore\ I.F. = e^{\int 1dx} = e^x$

$\therefore$ Solution of (iii) will be given by $v.e^x = \int \dfrac{-2x}{e^x} e^x dx + C$

$\Rightarrow \dfrac{e^x}{y} = -x^2 + C$

$\Rightarrow y^{-1} e^x = c - x^2$ which is the required solution of given differential equation.

■ DIFFERENTIAL EQUATION REDUCIBLE TO LINEAR DIFFERENTIAL EQUATION BY SUBSTITUTION

$f'(y)\dfrac{dy}{dx} + Pf(y) = Q$; Where P and Q are functions of x or constants can be reduce to linear differential equation if we put $f(y) = v$ so that $f'(y)\dfrac{dy}{dx} = \dfrac{dv}{dx}$

$\therefore$ The equation becomes $\dfrac{dv}{dx} + Pv = Q$, which is a linear equation in v and x.

NOTE

In each of these equations, single out Q (function on the right) and then make suitable substitution to reduce the equation in linear form.

ILLUSTRATION 91: Solve the differential equation $\sin y \dfrac{dy}{dx} = \cos y(1 - x\cos y)$

SOLUTION: Given differential equation is $\sin y \dfrac{dy}{dx} = \cos y(1 - x\cos y)$

or $\sin y \dfrac{dy}{dx} - \cos y = -x\cos^2 y$

Dividing by $\cos^2 y$, we get $\tan y \sec y \dfrac{dy}{dx} - \sec y = -x$ ...(i)

Substituting sec $y = v$ and $\sec y \tan y \dfrac{dy}{dx} = \dfrac{dv}{dx}$ in (i),

we get $\dfrac{dv}{dx} - v = -x$ ...(ii)

(ii) is linear differential equation with $P = -1, Q = -x$

$\Rightarrow$ $I.F. = e^{\int Pdx} = e^{\int -1dx} = e^{-x}$

$\therefore$ Its solution is given by

$v.e^{-x} = \int -xe^{-x}dx = xe^{-x} + e^{-x} + c = e^{-x}(x+1) + c$

or $v = (1 + x) + ce^x$ or $\sec y = (1 + x) + ce^x$

ILLUSTRATION 92: Solve the differential equation $x\dfrac{dy}{dx} + y\ \ell ny = xye^x$

SOLUTION: Given differential equation is $\dfrac{dy}{dx} + \dfrac{y\ \ell ny}{x} = \dfrac{xye^x}{x}$

$\Rightarrow$ $\dfrac{1}{y}\dfrac{dy}{dx} + \dfrac{\log y}{x} = e^x$ ...(i)

Which is of the form $f'(y)\dfrac{dy}{dx} + P(x)f(y) = Q(x)$

$\therefore$ putting $\log y = v$ in (i), we get $\dfrac{1}{y}\dfrac{dy}{dx} = \dfrac{dv}{dx}$

$\Rightarrow$ $\dfrac{dv}{dx} + \left(\dfrac{1}{x}\right)v = e^x$ ...(ii)

$\Rightarrow$ $P = \dfrac{1}{x}, Q = e^x$ $\qquad\therefore$ $I.F. = e^{\int \frac{1}{x}dx} = x$

$\therefore$ Solution of given differential equation (ii) is given by $v.x = \int e^x.x\,dx + c$

$\Rightarrow$ $vx = xe^x - ex + C$

$\Rightarrow$ $x \log y = e^x(x - 1) + C$ is the required solution of (i).

ILLUSTRATION 93: Solve the differential equation $\dfrac{dy}{dx} - \dfrac{\tan y}{1+x} = (1+x)e^x \sec y$

SOLUTION: Given differential equation is $\dfrac{dy}{dx} - \dfrac{\tan y}{1+x} = (1+x)e^x \sec y$ ...(i)

$\Rightarrow$ $\cos y\dfrac{dy}{dx} + (-\sin y)\dfrac{1}{(1+x)} = e^x(1+x)$ ...(ii)

putting $\sin y = v$ and $\cos y\dfrac{dy}{dx} = \dfrac{dv}{dx}$ in (ii), we get $\dfrac{dv}{dx} + \left(\dfrac{-1}{1+x}\right)v = e^x(1+x)$ ...(ii)

$\Rightarrow$ $P = -\dfrac{1}{1+x}, Q = e^x(1+x)$ $\qquad\Rightarrow$ $I.F. = e^{-\int \frac{1}{1+x}dx} = \dfrac{1}{1+x}$

$\therefore$ Solution of differential equation (iii) is given by $v.\dfrac{1}{(x+1)} = \int \dfrac{1}{(x+1)}e^x(1+x)dx + C$

$\Rightarrow$ $\dfrac{\sin y}{x+1} = e^x + C$

$\Rightarrow$ $\sin y = (e^x + C)(x + 1)$, which is the required solution of given differential equation(i)

ILLUSTRATION 94: Solve the differential equation $\frac{dy}{dx}=\frac{e^y}{x^2}-\frac{1}{x}$

SOLUTION: Given differential equation $\frac{dy}{dx}=\frac{e^y}{x^2}-\frac{1}{x}$

$\Rightarrow \frac{1}{e^y}\frac{dy}{dx}+\frac{1}{xe^y}=\frac{1}{x^2}$

$\Rightarrow e^{-y}\frac{dy}{dx}+\frac{1}{x}e^{-y}=\frac{1}{x^2}$ ...(i)

Putting $e^{-y}=v$ and $e^{-y}\frac{dy}{dx}=-\frac{dv}{dx}$ in (i)

$\Rightarrow -\frac{dv}{dx}+\frac{1}{x}v=\frac{1}{x^2}$

$\Rightarrow \frac{dv}{dx}+\left(-\frac{1}{x}\right)v=-\frac{1}{x^2}$ ...(ii)

$\Rightarrow I.F.=e^{-\int\frac{1}{x}dx}=\frac{1}{x}$

$\therefore$ Solution of linear differential equation (ii) is given by $v.\frac{1}{x}=-\int\frac{1}{x}.\frac{1}{x^2}dx+C$

$\Rightarrow e^{-y}.\frac{1}{x}=\frac{1}{2x^2}+C$

$\Rightarrow 2xe^{-y}=1+kx^2$; where $k=2c$, which is the required solution of given differential equation.

ILLUSTRATION 95: Solve the differential equation $\frac{dy}{dx}=e^{x-y}(e^x-e^y)$

SOLUTION: Given differential equation is $\frac{dy}{dx}=e^{x-y}(e^x-e^y)$ ...(i)

$\Rightarrow \frac{dy}{dx}=\frac{e^{2x}}{e^y}-e^x$

$\Rightarrow e^y\frac{dy}{dx}+e^xe^y=e^{2x}$ ...(ii)

Substituting $e^y=v$ and $e^y\frac{dy}{dx}=\frac{dv}{dx}$ in (ii), we have $\frac{dv}{dx}+e^x.v=e^{2x}$

$\Rightarrow I.F.=e^{\int e^x dx}=e^{e^x}$

$\therefore$ Solution of linear deferential equation (ii) is $v.e^{e^x}=\int e^{e^x}e^x.e^x dx+C$

putting $e^x=t$, we have $v.e^{e^x}=\int e^t t dt+C=te^t-e^t+C=e^xe^{e^x}-e^{e^x}+C$

$\Rightarrow e^y.e^{e^x}=e^{e^x}(e^x-1)+C$

$\Rightarrow e^y=(e^x-1)+Ce^{-e^x}$, which is the required solution of given differential equation.

ILLUSTRATION 96: Solve $y\sin x\frac{dy}{dx}=\cos x(\sin x-y^2)$

SOLUTION: The given differential equation can be reduced to linear form by change of variable by a suitable substitution.

Substituting $y^2=z$; $2y\frac{dy}{dx}=\frac{dz}{dx}$ differential equation becomes, $\frac{\sin x}{2}\frac{dz}{dx}+\cos x.z=\sin x\cos x$

$\Rightarrow \quad \dfrac{dz}{dx} + 2\cot x.z = 2\cos x$ which is linear in $\dfrac{dz}{dx}$

$\Rightarrow \quad I.F. = e^{\int 2\cot dx} = e^{2\ell n \sin x} = \sin^2 x$

$\therefore$ General solutions is given by $z.\sin^2 x = \int 2\cos x.\sin^2 x.dx + C$

$\Rightarrow \quad y^2 \sin^2 x = \dfrac{2}{3}\sin^3 x + C$

ILLUSTRATION 97: Show that the tangent to all integral curves of the differential equation $y' + y \tan x + 1$ at the point of intersection with y-axis are parallel. Determine the angle at which the integral curve cut the y-axis.

SOLUTION: Given differential equation $\dfrac{dy}{dx} + y\tan x = (x\tan x + 1)$ ...(1)

Comparing with $\dfrac{dy}{dx} + py = \theta$, we have $p = \tan x$; $Q = x \tan x + 1$

I.F. $= e^{\int p\,dx} = e^{\int \tan x\,dx} = e^{\ln|\sec x + \tan x|} = |\sec x + \tan x|$

$\therefore$ Solution of (1) is given by y(I.F.) $= \int Q$ (I.F.) $dx + C_1$.

$y(\sec x + \tan x) = \int (x\tan x + 1)(\sec x + \tan x)dx + C_1$

$\Rightarrow \quad y(\sec x + \tan x) = \int (x\sec x\tan x + x\tan^2 x + \sec x + \tan x)\,dx + C_1$

$y(\sec x + \tan x) = \left[x\sec x - \int 1.\sec x\,dx + \int x(\sec^2 x - 1)dx + \int \sec x\,dx + \int \tan x\,dx\right] + C_1$

$= \left[x\sec x + x\tan x - \int 1.\tan x\,dx + \int 1.\tan x\;dx + \int \tan x\,dx - \dfrac{x^2}{2}\right] + C_1$

$= \left[x\sec x + x\tan x - \dfrac{x^2}{2}\right] + C_1$

$\therefore \quad y(\sec x + \tan x) = \left(x\sec x + x\tan x - \dfrac{x^2}{2}\right) + C_1$

At the point where curve (2) cut y-axis, $x = 0$

$\Rightarrow \quad y(1 + 0) = (0) + C_1$

$\Rightarrow \quad C_1 = y$

$\therefore$ Curve (2) intersect y-axis at $(0, C_1)$

Now from (1) tangents to curves (2) have slopes given by

$\dfrac{dy}{dx} = x\tan x + 1 - y\tan x$

$\therefore \quad \left(\dfrac{dy}{dx}\right)_{(0, C_1)} = 1$

That is, all the curves given by (2) have tangents parallel at the point $(0, C_1)$.

That is, the point where they intersect y-axis.

Clearly the angle at which the integral curves (2) cut y-axis is $\pi/4$

$(\therefore \tan\theta = 1 \Rightarrow \theta = \pi/4)$

ILLUSTRATION 98: Find the curve passing through points (1, 1) and (2, 0) and possessing the property that the intercept, the tangent at any point of a curve cuts off on the y-axis is equal to the square of the abscissa of the point of tangency.

SOLUTION: Let $P(x, y)$ be any point on the given curve $y = f(x)$.

Thus, equation of tangent at $P(x, y)$ is given by

$$(Y - y) = \frac{dy}{d}(X - x) \quad \ldots(\text{i})$$

It intersect y-axis, where $X = 0$

$$\Rightarrow \; Y - y = \frac{dy}{dx}(-x)$$

$$\Rightarrow \; Y = y - x\frac{dy}{dx} \quad \ldots(\text{ii})$$

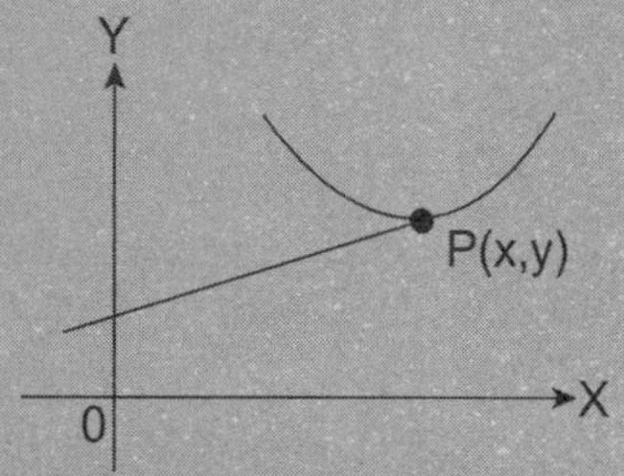

FIGURE 4.41

Now, according to question, Y^2 = (abscissa of point P)

$$\Rightarrow \; \left(y - x\frac{dy}{dx}\right)^2 = x^2 \qquad \Rightarrow \; y - x\frac{dy}{dx} = \pm x$$

$$\Rightarrow \; x\frac{dy}{dx} - y = \pm x \qquad \Rightarrow \; \frac{dy}{dx} + \left(-\frac{1}{x}\right)y = \pm 1$$

$$\Rightarrow \; P = -\frac{1}{x}, Q = \pm x\text{; Here I.F.} = e^{\int -\frac{1}{x}dx} = e^{\ln x^{-1}} = \frac{1}{x}$$

$\therefore$ Solution of given differential equation is given by $y.\frac{1}{x} = \int (\pm x).\frac{1}{x}\,dx + C$

$$\Rightarrow \; \frac{y}{x} = \pm x + C$$

$\Rightarrow \; \pm x^2 + Cx$ or $y = Cx \pm x^2$

Now, the curve is passing through point (1, 1)

$\Rightarrow \; 1 = C + 1$ or $1 = C - 1 \qquad \Rightarrow \; C = 0$ or $C = 2$

$\therefore \; y = x^2$ or $y = 2x - x^2$; Also the curve passes through the point (2, 0)

$\therefore \; y = 2x - x^2$ is such a curve

ILLUSTRATION 99: Find the curve such that the area of the rectangle constructed on the abscissa of any point and the initial ordinate of the tangent at this point is a constant.

SOLUTION: Let $P(x, y)$ be any point on the curve $y = f(x)$

Equation of tangent to curve at point $P(x, y)$ is

$(Y - y) = \frac{dy}{dx}(X - x)$ on y-axis $X = 0$

$$\Rightarrow \; Y - y = \frac{dy}{dx}(-x)$$

$$\Rightarrow \; Y = y - x\frac{dy}{dx}$$

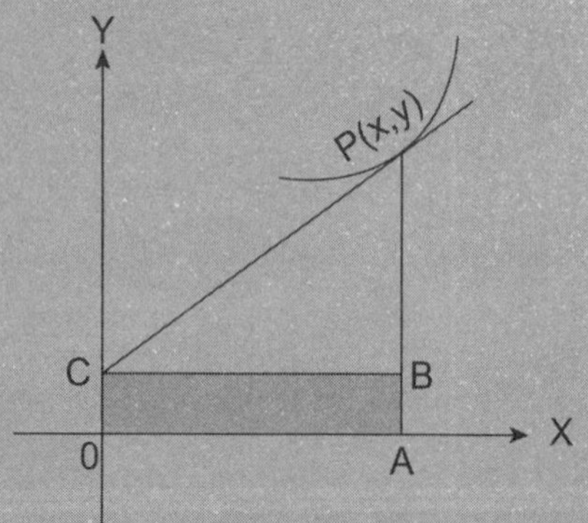

FIGURE 4.42

$\therefore$ Area of rectangle $= |xY| = k$ (constant given)

$$\Rightarrow \; \left|x\left(y - x\frac{dy}{dx}\right)\right| = k$$

$$\Rightarrow \; xy - x^2\frac{dy}{dx} = \pm k$$

$\Rightarrow x\dfrac{dy}{dx} - xy = \pm k \qquad \Rightarrow \dfrac{dy}{dx} - \dfrac{1}{x}y = \pm\dfrac{k}{x^2}$ ...(1)

which a linear differential equation with $I.F. = e^{\int p dx} = e^{\int -\frac{1}{x}dx} = e^{\ln x^{-1}} = \dfrac{1}{x}$

solution of (1) is given by $y\left(\dfrac{1}{x}\right) = \int \pm\dfrac{k}{x^2}.\dfrac{1}{x}dx + C$

$\Rightarrow \dfrac{y}{x} = \pm k\dfrac{x^{-2}}{-2} + C \qquad \Rightarrow \dfrac{y}{x} = \pm\dfrac{k}{2x^2} + C$

$\Rightarrow y = \pm\dfrac{k}{2x} + Cx$

ILLUSTRATION 100: A tank with a capacity of 1000 litres originally contains 100 gms of salt dissolved in 400 litres of water. Beginning at time $t = 0$ and ending water containing 1 gm of salt per litre enters the tank at the rate of 4 litres per minute, and the well mixed solution is drained from the tank at a rate of 2 litre/minute. Find the differential equation for the amount of salt y in the tank at time t, Also find the amount of salt in take at any instant t.

SOLUTION: Let y be the amount of salt in the tank at any time (t). Intially amount of salt = 100gms and amount of water = 400 lt.

Now, 4 liters of water is entering the tank per minute and each litre of water contains 1 gm of salt.

$\therefore$ Amount of salt entering the tank per minutes = 4gm

Net amount of water entering tank at time $t = 400 + (4t - 2t) = (400 + 2t)$

$\therefore$ Amount of salt leaving out the tank per minute = $\left(\dfrac{y}{400+2t}\right) \times 2$

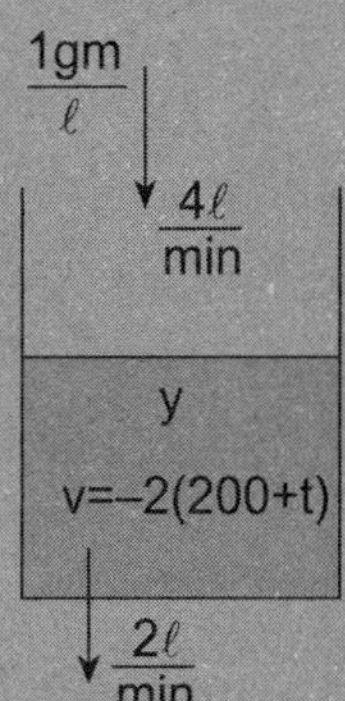

FIGURE 4.43

$\therefore$ Rate of change of salt = salt inflow – salt outflow

$= 4 - \left(\dfrac{2y}{400+2t}\right) = \dfrac{dy}{dt}$

$\Rightarrow \dfrac{dy}{dt} = 4 - \dfrac{y}{200+t}$

$\Rightarrow \dfrac{dy}{dt} + \dfrac{1}{(200+t)}y = 4$ ...(i)

$\Rightarrow I.F. = e^{\int \frac{1}{200+t}dt} = e^{\ln(200+t)} = (200+t)$

$\therefore$ Solution of differential equation (i) is $y(200+t) = \int 4(200+t)dt + C$

$\Rightarrow y(200 + t) = 800t + 2t^2 + C$

Now, when $t = 0, y = 100$

$\Rightarrow 100(200) = C$

$\Rightarrow y = \dfrac{800 + 2t^2}{(200+t)} + \dfrac{20000}{200+t}$

NEWTON'S LAW OF COOLING

Newton's law of cooling is related with the rate of change of temperature of a body when put in surrounding having temperature different from that body. The law states that the time rate of change of the temperature of a body is proportional to the temperature difference between the body and its surrounding medium.

Let T denotes the temperature of the body and let T' denotes the temperature of the surrounding medium. Then the time rate of change of temperature of the body is $\frac{dT}{dt}$. If $T > T'$, then cooling of body take place and if $T < T'$, then heating of body takes place.

Newton's law of cooling can be formulated as $\frac{dT}{dt} = -k(T - T')$; Here since $T > T'$, cooling takes place, and hence, the rate of change of temperature is negative. Hence, k is a positive constant of proportionality. When T' is greater than T heating process takes place, thus, $\frac{dT}{dt}$ is positive, and hence, k is positive.

ILLUSTRATION 101: A body whose temperature T is initially 300°C is immersed in a liquid having constant temperature 150°C. If the temperature of the body is 200°C at $t = 1$ minute, what is its temperature at $t = 2$ minutes.

SOLUTION: We have $\frac{dT}{dt} = -k(T - 150)$

$\Rightarrow \frac{dT}{dt} + kT = 150k$

Here $I.F. = e^{\int k dt} = e^{kt}$

$\therefore$ Solution of differential equation (1) is given by $Te^{kt} = \int 150ke^{kt}dt + C$

$\Rightarrow Te^{kt} = 150k\frac{e^{kt}}{k} + C$

$\Rightarrow T = 150 + Ce^{-kt}$ ...(ii)

Now, it is given that initially when $t = 0$, $T = 300$

$\Rightarrow 300 = 150 + C$

$\Rightarrow C = 150$

$\therefore$ From (ii), $T = 150 + 150e^{-kt}$

Also, we are given $T = 200$ when $t = 1$

$\Rightarrow 200 = 150 + 150e^{-k}$

$\Rightarrow \frac{1}{3} = e^{-k}$

$\Rightarrow -k = -\ln 3$

$\Rightarrow k = \ln 3$

$\therefore T = 150 + 150e^{-t\ln 3}$

$\therefore$ When $t = 2$, $T = 150 + 150e^{-2\ln 3}$

$\Rightarrow 150 + 150\left(\frac{1}{9}\right) = \frac{500^\circ}{3}C$

ILLUSTRATION 102: A body at an unknown temperature is placed in a room which is held at a constant temperature of 40°F. If after 10 minutes the temperature of the body is 10°F and after 20 minutes the temperature 20°F, find the unknown initial temperature.

SOLUTION: We have $\frac{dT}{dt} = -k(T-40)$

$\Rightarrow \frac{dT}{dt} + kT = 40k$ ...(i)

$\Rightarrow$ I.F. $= e^{kt}$

$\therefore$ Solution of differential equation (i) is given by $Te^{kt} = \int 40ke^{kt}dt + C$

$\Rightarrow T = 40 + Ce^{-kt}$ ...(ii)

Initially when $t = 0$, let $T = T_0$ $\therefore$ from (ii), $T_o = 40 + C$ ...(iii)

Now it is given that $T = 10$, when $t = 10$

$\therefore$ from (ii), $10 = 40 + C.e^{-10k}$ $\Rightarrow Ce^{-10k} = -30$ ...(iv)

Also $T = 20$, $t = 20$

$\therefore$ from (ii), $20 = 40 + C^{-20k}$ ...(v)

From 4, $e^{-10k} = -\frac{30}{C}$

$\Rightarrow e^{-20k} = -\frac{900}{C^2}$ ...(vi)

Using (vi) in (v), we get $-20 = C\left(\frac{900}{C^2}\right)$

$\Rightarrow C = -45$ $\therefore$ $T_o = 40 + (-45) = -5$°F

Initial temperature of body was –5°F

TEXTUAL EXERCISE–7: (SUBJECTIVE)

1. Solve the following differential equations:

(a) $\sin x\left(\frac{dy}{dx}\right) + 3y = \cos x$

(b) $x(x^2+1)\left(\frac{dy}{dx}\right) = y(1-x^2) + x^3 \log x$

(c) $\frac{dy}{dx} + 2xy = e^{-x^2}$

(d) $(1+x^2)\frac{dy}{dx} + y = \tan^{-1} x$

(e) $\frac{dy}{dx}(x \log x) + y = 2 \log x$

(f) $\frac{dy}{dx} + \frac{x}{1+x^2}y = \frac{1}{2x(1+x^2)}$

2. Solve $(xy^2 - e^{1/x^3})dx - x^2 y\, dy = 0$

3. Solve $(1 + y^2)dx = (\tan^{-1}y - x)dy$

4. Solve $3\frac{dy}{dx} + \frac{2}{1+x}y = \frac{x^3}{y^2}$

5. A curve is such that the intercept cut off from ordinate axis by tangent is half of the sum of the coordinates of the point of tangency. Find the equation of the curve if it passes through the point (4, 2).

6. A curve passes through (2, 0) and the slope of the tangent at $P(x, y)$ equals $\frac{(x+1)^2 + (y-3)}{x+1}$, then find the equation of curve.

7. Solve the differential equation $(x^2 + y)\frac{dy}{dx} = 6x$

8. Solve the differential equation $x\frac{dy}{dx} + y = x^3 y^6$

9. Solve the differential equation $(y\ln x - 1)ydx = xdy$

10. Solve the differential equation $x^2 y - x^3 \frac{dy}{dx} = y^4 \cos x$

11. A body at a temperature of 50° F is placed outdoors where the temperature is 100°F. If after 5 minutes the temperature of the body is 60°F, find the temperature of the body after 20 minutes.

Answer Keys

1. (a) $\left(y+\frac{1}{3}\right)\tan^3\frac{x}{2}=2\tan\frac{x}{2}-x+C$ (b) $4(x^2+1)y+x^3(1-2\ln x)=Cx$

(c) $y.e^{x^2}=x+C$ (d) $e^{\tan^{-1}x}=\left(\tan^{-1}x-1\right)e^{\tan^{-1}x}+c$

(e) $y\ln x=(\ln x)^2+C$ (f) $y\sqrt{1+x^2}=\frac{1}{2}\ln\left[\frac{\sqrt{1+x^2}-1}{x}\right]+C$

2. $3y=2x^2e^{1/x^3}+cx^2$
3. $x=\tan^{-1}y-1+C.e^{-\tan^{-1}y}$
4. $60y^3(x+1)^2=10x^6+24x^5+15x^4+C$
5. $y=3\sqrt{x}-x$
6. $y=x^2-2x$
7. $y=3\ln(x^2+y+3)+k$
8. $y^{-5}x^{-5}=\frac{5}{2}x^{-2}+C$
9. $1=y(cx+\ln ex)$
10. $x^3y^{-3}=3\sin x+C$
11. $100-50\left(\frac{4}{5}\right)^4$

TEXTUAL EXERCISE–7: (OBJECTIVE)

1. Equation of the curve through the origin satisfying $dy=(\sec x+y\tan x)\,dx$ is
(a) $y\sin x=x$ (b) $y\cos x=x$
(c) $y\tan x=x$ (d) None of these

2. The general solution of the equation $\frac{dy}{dx}=x+xy$ is:
(a) $y=ce^{-\frac{x^2}{2}}$ (b) $y=ce^{\frac{x^2}{2}}$
(c) $y=(x+c).e^{-\frac{x^2}{2}}$ (d) None of these

3. Integrating factor of the differential equation $\cos x\frac{dy}{dx}+y\sin x=1$ is:
(a) $\cos x$ (b) $\tan x$
(c) $\sec x$ (d) $\sin x$

4. Integrating factor of $\frac{dy}{dx}+\frac{y}{x}=x^3-3;\ (x>0)$ is
(a) x (b) $\log x$
(c) $-x$ (d) e^x

5. The integrating factor of $x(1-x^2)\,dy+(2x^2y-y-ax^3)\,dx=0$ is $e^{\int Pdx}$, then P is
(a) $\frac{2x^2-a^3}{x(1-x^2)}$ (b) $2x^3-1$
(c) $\frac{2x^2-1}{ax^3}$ (d) $\frac{2x^2-1}{x(1-x^2)}$

6. The solution of $y'-y=1$, $y(0)=1$ is given by $y(x)=$
(a) $-\exp.(x)$ (b) $-\exp.(-x)$
(c) -1 (d) $2\exp.(x)-1$

7. Which of the following equation is non-linear:
(a) $\frac{dy}{dx}+\frac{y}{x}=\log x$ (b) $y\frac{dy}{dx}+4x=0$
(c) $dx+dy=0$ (d) $\frac{dy}{dx}=\cos x$

8. Which of the following equation is linear:
(a) $\left(\frac{d^2y}{dx^2}\right)^2+x^2\left(\frac{dy}{dx}\right)^2=0$
(b) $y=\frac{dy}{dx}+\sqrt{1+\left(\frac{dy}{dx}\right)^2}$
(c) $\frac{dy}{dx}+\frac{y}{x}=\log x$
(d) $y\frac{dy}{dx}-4=x$

9. An integrating factor for the differential equation $(1+y^2)dx-(\tan^{-1}y-x)\,dy=0$
(a) $\tan^{-1}y$ (b) $e^{\tan^{-1}y}$
(c) $\frac{1}{1+y^2}$ (d) $\frac{1}{x(1+y^2)}$

10. The equation of the curve passing through the origin and satisfying the equation $(1+x^2)\frac{dy}{dx}+2xy=4x^2$ is
(a) $3(1+x^2)y = 4x^3$
(b) $3(1-x^2)y = 4x^3$
(c) $3(1+x^2) = x^3$
(d) None of these

11. Which of the following equation is linear?
(a) $\frac{dy}{dx}+xy^2=1$ (b) $x^2\frac{dy}{dx}+y=e^x$
(c) $\frac{dy}{dx}+3y=xy^2$ (d) $x\frac{dy}{dx}+y^2=\sin x$

12. Solution of differential equation $\frac{dy}{dx}+ay=e^{mx}$ is
(a) $(a+m)y = e^{mx}+c$
(b) $ye^{ax}+me^{mx}+c$
(c) $y = e^{mx}+ce^{-ax}$
(d) $(a+m)y = e^{mx}+ce^{-ax}(a+m)$

13. Solution of differential equation $x\frac{dy}{dx}=y+x^2$ is
(a) $y=\log_e x+\frac{x^2}{2}+a$
(b) $y=\frac{x^3}{3}+\frac{a}{x}$
(c) $y = x^2+ax$
(d) None of these

14. Integrating factor of equation $(x^2+1)\frac{dy}{dx}+2xy=x^2-1$ is
(a) x^2+1 (b) $\frac{2x}{x^2+1}$
(c) $\frac{x^2-1}{x^2+1}$ (d) None of these

15. To reduce the differential equation $\frac{dy}{dx}+P(x)y = Q(x).y^n$ to the linear form, the substitution is
(a) $v=\frac{1}{y^n}$ (b) $v=\frac{1}{y^{n-1}}$
(c) $v=y^n$ (d) $v=y^{n-1}$

16. The solution of $(1+x^2)\frac{dy}{dx}+y=e^{\tan^{-1}x}$, is given by
(a) $2y.e^{\tan^{-1}x} = e^{2\tan^{-1}x}+c$
(b) $y.e^{\tan^{-1}y} = e^{2\tan^{-1}x}+c$
(c) $2ye^{\tan^{-1}y} = e^{2\tan^{-1}y}+c$
(d) None of these

Answer Keys

1. (b)	**2.** (d)	**3.** (c)	**4.** (a)	**5.** (d)	**6.** (d)	**7.** (b)	**8.** (c)	**9.** (b)	**10.** (a)
11. (b)	**12.** (d)	**13.** (c)	**14.** (a)	**15.** (b)	**16.** (a)				

■ DIFFERENTIAL EQUATION OF FIRST ORDER AND HIGHER DEGREE

Type (A): Equation solvable for *p*

If $(p-f_1(x, y))\,(p-f_2(x, y)) .. (p-f_n(x, y)) = 0$, then $p_k = f_k(x, y)$ each of these is of Ist order. Let $g_k(x,y, C_k) = 0$; where $k = 1, 2, ...,n$ are solution, then general solution is $\prod_{k=1}^{n} g_k(x,y,C_k)=0$. It contains n arbitrary constants but being an equation of 1st order it must contain only one arbitrary constant, so, without loss of generality we can take $C_1 = C_2 = ... = C_n = C$. Hence, general solution is $\prod_{k=1}^{n} g_k(x,y,C)=0$

ILLUSTRATION 103: Solve the differential equation $p(p+x) - y(x+y) = 0$.

SOLUTION: Let $p(p+x) - y(x+y) = 0$

$\Rightarrow p^2+px-xy-y^2=0$

$\Rightarrow x(p-y)+(p-y)(p+y)=0$

$\Rightarrow (p-y)(p+y+x)=0$

$\Rightarrow \frac{dy}{dx}=y$ or $\frac{dy}{dx}+y=-x$

Now, $\frac{dy}{y} = dx$

$\Rightarrow$ $\ln y = x + C$ ...(i)

$\Rightarrow$ $y = e^{x+C}$

And for linear differential equation $\frac{dy}{dx} + y = -x$; I.F. $= e^{\int 1dx} = e^x$ and the solution of differential equation is given by $y.e^x = \int -xe^x dx + C$

$\Rightarrow$ $y.e^x = -[xe^x - e^x] + C$ $\Rightarrow$ $y = -x + 1 + Ce^{-x}$

or $y = 1 - x + Ce^{-x}$

Thus, $y = ke^x$ and $y = 1 - x + Ce^{-x}$ are the required solution.

By keeping both the constant same and combining both the solutions $(y - ce^x)(y + x - 1 - ce^{-x}) = 0$ is the complete general solution.

ILLUSTRATION 104: Solve the differential equation $p^2 + 2py \cot x = y^2$

SOLUTION: Given differential equation is $p^2 + 2py \cot x = y^2$

Solving for p, we obtain $p = \frac{-2y\cot x \pm \sqrt{4y^2 \cot^2 x + 4y^2}}{2}$

$= -y \cot x \pm y \operatorname{cosec} x = y(-\cot x \pm y \operatorname{cosec} x)$

Thus, we have $\frac{dy}{dx} = y(-\cot x + \operatorname{cosec} x)$ ...(i)

and $\frac{dy}{dx} = -y(\cot x + \operatorname{cosec} x)$ ...(ii)

In (i) and (ii) the variables are separable.

Now, (i) gives $\frac{dy}{y} = (-\cot x + \operatorname{cosec} x)\, dx$

$\Rightarrow$ $\log y = -\log \sin x + \log \tan\frac{x}{2} + \log c = \log\frac{c\tan\frac{x}{2}}{\sin x}$

$\Rightarrow$ $y = \frac{c\tan\frac{x}{2}}{\sin x} = \frac{c}{2\cos^2\frac{x}{2}} = \frac{c}{1+\cos x}$ ...(iii)

Again (ii) gives, $\frac{dy}{y} = -(\cot x + \operatorname{cosec} x)dx$

$\Rightarrow$ $\log y = -\left(\log \sin x + \log\tan\frac{x}{2}\right) + \log c = \log\frac{c}{\left(\sin x \tan\frac{x}{2}\right)}$

$\Rightarrow$ $y = \frac{c}{\sin x \tan\frac{x}{2}} = \frac{c}{2\sin^2\frac{x}{2}} = \frac{c}{1-\cos x}$ ...(iv)

Thus, the solutions of (i) and (ii) are $y - \frac{c}{1+\cos x} = 0$, $y - \frac{c}{1-\cos x} = 0$

The composite solution of the given differential equation, Therefore, is

$$\left(y - \frac{c}{1+\cos x}\right)\left(y - \frac{c}{1-\cos x}\right) = 0$$

ILLUSTRATION 105: Solve the differential equation $\left(\frac{dy}{dx}\right)^2-(x+y)\frac{dy}{dx}+xy=0$

SOLUTION: Given differential equation is $\left(\frac{dy}{dx}\right)^2-(x+y)\frac{dy}{dx}+xy=0$

$\Rightarrow \left(\frac{dy}{dx}-x\right)\left(\frac{dy}{dx}-y\right)=0$ $\qquad \Rightarrow \frac{dy}{dx}=x$ or $\frac{dy}{dx}=y$

$\Rightarrow dy = xdx$ or $\frac{dy}{y}=dx$ $\qquad \Rightarrow y=\frac{x^2}{2}+C_1$ or $\ln y = x + C_2$

$\Rightarrow y=\frac{x^2}{2}+C$ or $y = ce^x$ are the required possible solutions

$\Rightarrow \left(y-\frac{x^2}{2}+C\right)\left(y-Ce^x\right)=0$ is the complete solution.

ILLUSTRATION 106: Solve the differential equation $\left(\frac{dy}{dx}\right)^2-5\left(\frac{dy}{dx}\right)+6=0$

SOLUTION: Given differential equation is $\left(\frac{dy}{dx}\right)^2-5\left(\frac{dy}{dx}\right)+6=0$ ...(i)

Let $\left(\frac{dy}{dx}\right)=p$

Equation (i) becomes $p^2-5p+6=0$

$\Rightarrow p^2-3p-2p+6=0$ $\qquad \Rightarrow p(p-3)-2(p-3)=0$

$\Rightarrow (p-2)(p-3)=0$

Thus, either $p-2=0$

or $p-3=0$

Therefore, we get $p=2$ ...(ii)

or $p=3$ ...(iii)

(ii) Gives $\frac{dy}{dx}=2$. Integrating, we get $y=2x+C_1$

(iii) Gives $\frac{dy}{dx}=3$. Integrating, we get $y=3x+C_2$

Where c_1 and c_2 are arbitrary constants.

$\therefore$ $(y-2x+C)(y-3x+C)=0$ is the composite solution.

Type (B): Equation solvable for *y*

Equation can be expressed $y=f(x,p)$ ...(i)

Differentiating both sides with respect to x,

$\frac{dy}{dx}=h\left(x,\ p,\ \frac{dp}{dx}\right)$ ...(ii)

Let the solution of (ii) be $g(x,p,c)=0$ ...(iii)

Eliminating p between (i) and (iii), we get relation between x, y and c and is general solution.

ILLUSTRATION 107: Solve the differential equation $y + px = p^2x^4$.

SOLUTION: Differentiating with respect to x, we have $\frac{dy}{dx}+p+x\frac{dp}{dx}=4x^3p^2+2x^4p\frac{dp}{dx}$

$\Rightarrow 2p-4x^3p^2-2x^4p\frac{dp}{dx}+x\frac{dp}{dx}=0$ $\Rightarrow 2p(1-2x^3p)+x(1-2x^3p)\frac{dp}{dx}=0$

$\Rightarrow (1-2x^3p)+\left(2p+x\frac{dp}{dx}\right)=0$ $\Rightarrow 2p+x\frac{dp}{dx}=0$

$\Rightarrow \frac{dp}{p}+\frac{2dx}{x}=0$ $\Rightarrow \log p + 2\log x = \text{constant} = \log c$

$\Rightarrow px^2=c$ $\Rightarrow p=\frac{c}{x^2}$

Substituting this value of p in the given differential equation so as to eliminate p, zwe obtain $y=-\frac{c}{x}+c^2$

$\Rightarrow xy = c^2x - c$, is the required solution

ILLUSTRATION 108: Solve $x - yp = ap^2$

SOLUTION: Here $y=\frac{x-ap^2}{p}$

Differentiating and clearing of fractions, $(ap^2+x)\frac{dp}{dx}=p(1-p^2)$

This can be put in the linear form $\frac{dx}{dp}-\frac{1}{p(1-p^2)}x=\frac{ap}{1-p^2}$

Solving, $x=\frac{p}{\sqrt{1-p^2}}(c+a\sin^{-1}p)$

Substituting in the value for y above, $y=-ap+\frac{1}{\sqrt{1-p^2}}(c+a\sin^{-1}p)$

Clairaut's Equation

It is equation of first degree in x and y of the form
$y = px + f(p)$ ...(i)

where $p=\frac{dy}{dx}$.

Differenting both sides w.r.t. x, we get

$\frac{dy}{dx}=p+(x+f'(p))\frac{dp}{dx}$

$\Rightarrow p=p+(x+f'(p))\frac{dp}{dx}$

$\Rightarrow (x+f'(p))\frac{dp}{dx}=0$

$\Rightarrow$ either $(x + f'(p)) = 0$ or $\frac{dp}{dx}=0$

If $\frac{dp}{dx}=0$

$\Rightarrow p = c$ (constant) ...(ii)

Eliminating p from (i) and (ii) we have $y = Cx + f(c)$ as a solution.

If $x + f'(p) = 0$, then by eliminating p, again we obtain another solution.

REMARKS

1. *Some given differential equation can be reduced to Clairauts form by suitable substitution.*
2. *To obtain general solution of differential equation in Clairauts form simply replace p by (c) in the given equation y = px + f(p)*

ILLUSTRATION 109: Solve the differential equation $y = xf_1(p) + f_2(p)$

SOLUTION: Given differential equation is $y = xf_1(p) + f_2(p)$

While this equation is not clairout's it will be seen that the method adopted for solving Clairout's equations will deliver the goods. Differentiating with respect to x, we obtain

$$p = f_1(p) + x\, f_1'(p)\frac{dp}{dx} + f_2'(p)\frac{dp}{dx}$$

$$\Rightarrow \quad \frac{dx}{dp} = \frac{f_1'(p)}{p - f_1(p)}x + \frac{f_2'(p)}{p - f_1(p)}$$

Which is linear with p as independent and x, as dependent variable.

Suppose that on solving this linear equation, we obtain $\phi(x, p, c) = 0$

then, eliminating p between this solution and the given equation, we obtain the required solution.

ILLUSTRATION 110: Solve $y = px + p - p^3$ where, $p = \dfrac{dy}{dx}$

SOLUTION: Given equation is $y = px + p - p^3$ ...(i)

The given equation is in clairaut's form

Now, differentiating w.r.t, x, we get $\dfrac{dy}{dx} = p + x\dfrac{dp}{dx} + \dfrac{dp}{dx} - 3p^2\dfrac{dp}{dx}$

$$\Rightarrow \quad p = p + x\frac{dp}{dx} + \frac{dp}{dx} - 3p^2\frac{dp}{dx}$$

$$\Rightarrow \quad \frac{dp}{dx}(x + 1 - 3p^2) = 0$$

$$\Rightarrow \quad \frac{dp}{dx} = 0 \Rightarrow p = c \qquad \text{...(ii)}$$

Or $x + 1 - 3p^2$ $\qquad \Rightarrow p^2 = \dfrac{x+1}{3}$ ...(iii)

Eliminating 'p' between (i) and (ii), we get general solution of the given equation. i.e., $y = cx + c - c^3$; where 'c' is an arbitrary constant. Again, eliminating 'p' between (i) and (iii), we get singular solution of the given equation. i.e., $y = \left(\dfrac{x+1}{3}\right)^{1/2}\left(x + 1 - \dfrac{x+1}{3}\right)$

$$\Rightarrow \quad y = \left(\frac{x+1}{3}\right)^{1/2} \times \frac{2}{3}(x+1) \qquad \Rightarrow \quad y = 2\left(\frac{x+1}{3}\right)^{3/2}$$

$$\Rightarrow \quad y^2 = \frac{4}{27}(x+1)^3 \qquad \Rightarrow \quad 27y^2 = 4(x+1)^3$$

ILLUSTRATION 111: Solve $y = (1 + p)x + p^2$

SOLUTION: Given differential equation is $y = (1 + p)x + p^2$

Differentiating, we get $p = 1 + p + (x + 2p)\dfrac{dp}{dx}$

$$\Rightarrow \quad -1 = (x + 2p)\frac{dp}{dx} \qquad \Rightarrow \quad -\frac{dx}{dp} = x + 2p$$

$\therefore \quad \dfrac{dx}{dp}+x=-2p$ which is linear with dependent variable x and independent variable p.

$\Rightarrow$ I.F. $= e^{\int 1dp} = e^p$

$\Rightarrow$ General solution is given by $xe^p = \int -2pe^p dp + C$

$\Rightarrow x = 2(1-p) + ce^{-p}$

Hence, $y = 2 - p^2 + (1+p)ce^{-p}$

ILLUSTRATION 112: Solve $x^2(y - px) = yp^2$

SOLUTION: Given differential equation is $x^2(y - px) = yp^2$

On putting $x^2 = u$ and $y^2 = v$, the equation becomes $v = u\dfrac{dv}{du}+\left(\dfrac{dv}{du}\right)^2$, which is in Clairaut's form

$\therefore \quad v = cu + c^2$ is the general solution.

$\Rightarrow y^2 = cx^2 + c^2$ is the general solution

Type (C): Equation solvable for *x*

Let the given differential equation be of the form $x = f(y, p)$ ...(i)

Differentiating with respect to y, we get $\dfrac{dx}{dy}=\dfrac{1}{p}=h\left(y, p, \dfrac{dp}{dy}\right)$ ...(ii)

(Linear is in y and p so solve to get solution $g(y, p, c) = 0$ ..(iii)

Eliminate p from (i) and (iii) to get relation set x, y and c.

If it is difficult to eliminate then eliminate of (i) and (iii) will the required general solution.

ILLUSTRATION 113: Solve the differential equation $y = 2px + y^2p^3$

SOLUTION: Solving it for x, we obtain $x = \dfrac{y - y^2p^3}{2p} = \dfrac{y}{2p} - \dfrac{y^2p^2}{2}$

Differentiating with respect to y, we obtain $\dfrac{1}{p}=\dfrac{dx}{dy}=\dfrac{1}{2p}-\dfrac{y}{2p^2}\dfrac{dp}{dy}-yp^2-py^2\dfrac{dp}{dy}$

$\Rightarrow \quad \dfrac{1}{2p}+p^2y+\left(\dfrac{y}{2p^2}+py^2\right)\dfrac{dp}{dy}=0 \qquad \Rightarrow \quad \dfrac{1+2p^3y}{2p}+\dfrac{y(1+2p^3y)}{2p^2}\dfrac{dp}{dy}=0$

$\Rightarrow \quad \dfrac{(1+2p^3y)}{2p}\left(1+\dfrac{y}{p}\dfrac{dp}{dy}\right)=0$

$\Rightarrow \quad 1+\dfrac{y}{p}\dfrac{dp}{dy}=0 \qquad \Rightarrow \quad \dfrac{dp}{p}+\dfrac{dy}{y}=0$

$\Rightarrow \log y + \log p = \text{constant} = \log c$

$\Rightarrow py = c \qquad \Rightarrow p = \dfrac{c}{y}$

Substituting this value of p in the given equation, we obtain

$$y = \frac{2cx}{y} + y^2 . \frac{c^3}{y^3}$$

$\Rightarrow y^2 = 2cx + c^3$ which is the required solution

ILLUSTRATION 114: Solve $p^2 + px - x = 0$ where $p = \frac{dy}{dx}$

SOLUTION: The given differential equation can be written as $x = py + p^2$

Differentiating (i) w.r.t., y, we get $\frac{dx}{dy} = \frac{1}{p} = p + y\frac{dp}{dy} + 2p\frac{dp}{dy}$

or $\frac{(1-p^2)}{p} = y\frac{dp}{dy} + 2p\frac{dp}{dy}$ or $\frac{dy}{dp} + \frac{p}{(p^2-1)}y = -\frac{2p^2}{(p^2-1)}$. ...(ii)

which is linear differential equation.

$$\Rightarrow I.F. = e^{\int \frac{p}{(p^2-1)}dp} = e^{\frac{1}{2}\ln(p^2-1)} = \sqrt{(p^2-1)}$$

$\therefore$ Solution of (2) is $y\sqrt{(p^2-1)} = \int -\frac{2p^2}{(p^2-1)}\sqrt{(p^2-1)}dp + C$

$$= -2\int \frac{p^2}{\sqrt{(p^2-1)}}dp + C = -2\int \frac{(p^2-1)+1}{\sqrt{(p^2-1)}}dp + C$$

$$= -2\int \left(\sqrt{(p^2-1)} + \frac{1}{\sqrt{(p^2-1)}}\right)dp + C$$

$$= -2\left\{\frac{p}{2}\sqrt{(p^2-1)} - \frac{1}{2}\ln\left(p + \sqrt{(p^2-1)}\right) + \ln\left(p + \sqrt{(p^2-1)}\right)\right\} + C$$

$$= -p\sqrt{(p^2-1)} - \ln(p + \sqrt{(p^2-1)} + C)$$

$$\therefore \quad y = \frac{C - \ln\left(p + \sqrt{(p^2-1)}\right)}{\sqrt{(p^2-1)}} - p \qquad \text{...(iii)}$$

Substituting y in (i), we get $x = \frac{p\left\{C - \ln\left(p + \sqrt{(p^2-1)}\right)\right\}}{\sqrt{(p^2-1)}}$ ...(iv)

Hence, (iii) and (iv) gives the solution of (i).

TEXTUAL EXERCISE–8: (SUBJECTIVE)

1. Solve the following differential equations:

(a) $x\left(\frac{dy}{dx}\right)^2 + (y-x)\frac{dy}{dx} - y = 0$

(b) $y^2 + xyp - x^2p^2 = 0$

(c) $xyp^2 - (x^2 + y^2)p + xy = 0$

(d) $p^2y - (x - y)p - x = 0$

2. Solve the following differential equations:

(a) $p^2y + 2px - y = 0$

(b) $\left(\frac{dy}{dx}\right)^3 - 4xy\frac{dy}{dx} + 8y^2 = 0$

(c) $\left(\frac{dy}{dx}\right)^3 y^2 - 2x\frac{dy}{dx} + y = 0$

3. Solve the following equations:

(a) $(y - px)(p - 1) = p$

(b) $y = x\frac{dy}{dx} + \left(\frac{dy}{dx}\right)^2$

(c) $y = x\frac{dy}{dx} + e^{dy/dx}$

(d) $(px - y)(py + x) = a^2p$

4. Solve $p^2 - 7p + 12 = 0$; $p = \frac{dy}{dx}$

5. Solve $y = 2px - p^2$; $p = \frac{dy}{dx}$

6. Solve $y = 2px + y^2p^3$; $p = \frac{dy}{dx}$

7. Solve $(2x - b)p = y - aypb$; where $p = \frac{dy}{dx}$ and a, b are constant.

Answer Keys

1. (a) $(y - c - x)(xy - c) = 0$ (b) $(y^2 - cx^{1+\sqrt{5}})(y^2 - cx^{1-\sqrt{5}}) = 0$
(c) $(y - cx)(x^2 - y^2 - c) = 0$ (d) $(x^2 - y^2 - c)(y + x - c) = 0$

2. (a) $x = \frac{c(1-p^2)}{p^2}$, $y = \frac{2c}{p}$ (b) $64y = c(4x - c)^2$ (c) $2cx = c^3 + y^2$

3. (a) $(y - cx)(c - 1) = c$ (b) $y = cx + c^2$
(c) $y = cx + e^c$ (d) $y^2 = cx^2 - \frac{a^2c}{1+c}$

4. $(y - 3x - C)(y - 4x - C) = 0$ 5. $p^2x = \frac{2p^3}{3} + C$ 6. $y^2 = 2Cx + C$

7. $x = \frac{b}{2} + \frac{y(y-abx)}{2C} - \frac{aby}{2}$

TEXTUAL EXERCISE–8: (OBJECTIVE)

1. Solutions of the differential equation $\left(\frac{dy}{dx}\right)^2 - \frac{dy}{dx}(e^x + e^{-x}) + 1 = 0$ are given by

(a) $y + e^{-x} = C$ (b) $y - e^{-x} = C$
(c) $y + e^x = C$ (d) $y - e^x = C$

2. The solution of $y = x\frac{dy}{dx} + \frac{dy}{dx} - \left(\frac{dy}{dx}\right)^2$, is

(a) $y = (x - 1)^2 + C$ (b) $4y = (x + 1)^2 + C$
(c) $(y - 1)^2 = 4x + C$ (d) None of these

3. The solution of $\left(\frac{dy}{dx}\right)^2 + (2x + y)\frac{dy}{dx} + 2xy = 0$, is

(a) $(y + x^2 - c)(x + \log y + y^2 + c) = 0$
(b) $(y + x^2 - c)(x - \log y - c) = 0$
(c) $(y + x^2 - c)(x + \log y - c) = 0$
(d) None of these

4. General solution of the differential equation $y = x\frac{dy}{dx} + \frac{dx}{dy}$ represents

(a) a straight line or a hyperbola
(b) a straight line or a parabola
(c) a parabola or a parabola
(d) circles

5. Solutions of the differential equation $y = p(x - b) + \frac{a}{p}$ is equal to

(a) $y = c(x - b) + \frac{a}{c}$ (b) $y = c(x + b) + \frac{a}{c}$
(c) $y = c(x - a) + \frac{b}{c}$ (d) None of these

6. The solution of $p^2 - 9p + 18 = 0$, is
   (a) $(y - 6x + c)(y - 3x + c) = 0$
   (b) $(y + 6x + c)(y - 3x + c) = 0$
   (c) $(y - 6x + c)(y + 3x + c) = 0$
   (d) None of these

7. The solution of differential equation $y^2(1 - p^2) = b$, is equal to
   (a) $y^2 - b = (x + c)^2$ (b) $y^2 + b = (x + c)^2$
   (c) $y^2 + b = (x - c)^2$ (d) None of these

8. The solution of differential equation $x + \frac{p}{\sqrt{1+p^2}} = a$ is equal to
   (a) $(y + c)^2 + (x + a)^2 = 1$
   (b) $(y + c) + (x - a) = 1$
   (c) $(y + c)^2 + (x - a)^2 = 1$
   (d) None o these

9. The solution of differential equation $y - (1+p^2)^{-\frac{1}{2}} = b$ is equal to
   (a) $(x + c)^2 + (y - b)^2 = 1$
   (b) $(x + c)^2 + (y + b)^2 = 1$
   (c) $(x + c)^2 + (x - b)^2 = 1$
   (d) None of these

10. The solution of differential equation $y = px + \frac{m}{p}$ is equal to
    (a) $y = cx + \frac{m}{c}$ (b) $y = cx - \frac{m}{c}$
    (c) $y = cx + \frac{m^2}{c}$ (d) None of these

11. The solution of differential equation $y = -xp + x^4p^2$ is equal to
    (a) $xy = c + cx^2$
    (b) $xy = c + cx$
    (c) $xy = c - cx$
    (d) None of these

12. A solution of the differential equation $\left(\frac{dy}{dx}\right)^2 - x\frac{dy}{dx} + y = 0$ is
    (a) $y = 2$ (b) $y = 2x$
    (c) $y = 2x - 4$ (d) $y = 2x^2 - 4$

Answer Keys

1. (a,d) **2.** (b) **3.** (c) **4.** (b) **5.** (a) **6.** (a) **7.** (a) **8.** (c) **9.** (a) **10.** (a)
11. (b) **12.** (b), (c)

HIGHER ORDER DIFFERENTIAL EQUATION

Equation of Type: $\frac{d^2y}{dx^2} = f(x)$

This requires merely ordinary integrations w.r.t. x,

Thus, $\frac{dy}{dx} = \int f(x)dx + C$

$y = \int\left\{\int f(x)dx\right\}dx + Cx + D$; where C, D are arbitrary constants.

ILLUSTRATION 115: Solve the differential equations:

(a) $\frac{d^2y}{dx^2} = xe^x + \cos x$ (b) $\frac{d^2y}{dx^2} + \sin x = x$

SOLUTION: (a) $\frac{d^2y}{dx^2} = xe^x + \cos x$

$\Rightarrow \int d\left(\frac{dy}{dx}\right) = \int\left(xe^x + \cos x\right)dx$

$$\Rightarrow \frac{dy}{dx} = e^x(x-1) + \sin x + C_1$$

$$\Rightarrow \int dy = \int e^x(x-1)dx + \int \sin x\,dx + \int C_1\,dx$$

$$\Rightarrow y = e^x(x-2) - \cos x + C_1x + C_2$$

(b) $\dfrac{d^2y}{dx^2} + \sin x = x$

$$\Rightarrow \int d\left(\frac{dy}{dx}\right) = \int (x - \sin x)dx$$

$$\Rightarrow \frac{dy}{dx} = \frac{x^2}{2} + \cos x + C_1$$

$$\Rightarrow \int dy = \int\left(\frac{x^2}{2} + \cos x + C_1\right)dx$$

$$\Rightarrow y = \frac{x^3}{6} + \sin x + C_1x + C_2$$

❑ **Equation of Type:** $\dfrac{d^2y}{dx^2} = f(y)$ ...(1)

Method 1: Multiply both sides by $\dfrac{dy}{dx}$,

$$\Rightarrow \frac{dy}{dx}\frac{d^2y}{dx^2} = f(y)\frac{dy}{dx}$$

$\Rightarrow \dfrac{dy}{dx}.\dfrac{d^2y}{dx^2}dx = f(y)dy$ and then integrating both sides,

$$\Rightarrow \int \frac{dy}{dx} d\left(\frac{dy}{dx}\right) = \int f(y)dy$$

$$\Rightarrow \frac{1}{2}\left(\frac{dy}{dx}\right)^2 = \int f(y)dy + C \quad ...(2)$$

Method 2: Given $\dfrac{d^2y}{dx^2} = f(y)$ ...(1)

Let symbol p denote $\dfrac{dy}{dx}$

$$\Rightarrow \frac{d^2y}{dx^2} = \frac{dp}{dx} = \frac{dp}{dy}\frac{dy}{dx} = p\frac{dp}{dy},$$

Therefore, equation (1) becomes, $p\left(\dfrac{dp}{dy}\right) = f(y)$

Consider it as first order differential equation, with p as dependent, and y as independent variable.

$$\Rightarrow \int p\,dp = \int f(y)\,dy$$

$\Rightarrow \left(\dfrac{1}{2}\right)p^2 = \int f(y)\,dy + A$, which is equivalent to equation (2)

$$\Rightarrow \frac{dy}{\sqrt{2\int f(y)\,dy + 2A}} = \pm dx$$

Now solve as the variable are separated.

ILLUSTRATION 116: Solve the differential equations:

(a) $\frac{d^2y}{dx^2} - 2y = 0;\ y' = 1$ at $(0, 0)$ (b) $\frac{d^2y}{dx^2} - a^2y = 0$

SOLUTION: (a) $\frac{d^2y}{dx^2} - 2y = 0$

$$\Rightarrow \frac{d}{dx}\left(\frac{dy}{dx}\right) = 2y \qquad \Rightarrow \frac{d}{dy}\left(\frac{dy}{dx}\right).\frac{dy}{dx} = 2y$$

$$\Rightarrow p\frac{dp}{dy} = 2y \qquad \Rightarrow \int p\,dp = \int 2y\,dy$$

$$\Rightarrow \frac{p^2}{2} = y^2 + C \qquad \ldots\text{(i)}$$

Given $p = 1$ at $x = 0$, $y = 0$

$$\Rightarrow \frac{1}{2} = 0 + C$$

$$\Rightarrow C = \frac{1}{2}$$

$$\Rightarrow \frac{p^2}{2} = y^2 + \frac{1}{2}$$

$$\Rightarrow \frac{dy}{dx} = \pm\sqrt{2y^2 + 1}, \text{ but } \frac{dy}{dx} = 1 \text{ at } y = 0$$

$$\Rightarrow \frac{dy}{dx} = \sqrt{2y^2 + 1}$$

$$\Rightarrow \int \frac{dy}{\sqrt{2y^2 + 1}} = \int dx$$

$$\Rightarrow \frac{1}{\sqrt{2}}\int \frac{dy}{\sqrt{y^2 + \frac{1}{2}}} = \int dx$$

$$\Rightarrow \frac{1}{\sqrt{2}}\ln\left|y + \sqrt{y^2 + \frac{1}{2}}\right| = x + C_0$$

At $x = 0$, $y = 0$

$$\Rightarrow \frac{1}{\sqrt{2}}\ln\left|\frac{1}{\sqrt{2}}\right| = C_0$$

$$\Rightarrow \frac{1}{\sqrt{2}}\times\left(-\frac{1}{2}\right)\ln 2 = C_0$$

$$\Rightarrow C_0 = -\frac{1}{2\sqrt{2}}\ln 2$$

$$\Rightarrow \frac{1}{\sqrt{2}}\ln\left|y+\sqrt{y^2+\frac{1}{2}}\right| = x-\frac{1}{2\sqrt{2}}\ln 2$$

$$\Rightarrow \ln\left(y+\sqrt{\left(y^2+\frac{1}{2}\right)}\right)^2 = 2\sqrt{2}x-\ln 2$$

$$\Rightarrow \ln\left(\sqrt{2}y+\sqrt{2y^2+1}\right)^2 = 2\sqrt{2}x$$

(b) Let $\frac{dy}{dx} = p$

$$\Rightarrow \frac{d^2y}{dx^2} = \frac{d}{dx}\left(\frac{dy}{dx}\right) = \frac{d}{dy}\left(\frac{dy}{dx}\right).\frac{dy}{dx} = p.\frac{dp}{dy}$$

$\Rightarrow$ Equation reduces to $p\frac{dp}{dy} = a^2y$

$$\Rightarrow \int pdp = \int a^2ydy \qquad \Rightarrow \frac{p^2}{2} = \frac{a^2y^2}{2}+\frac{C_0}{2}$$

$$\Rightarrow p^2 = a^2y^2 + C_0$$

$$\Rightarrow \frac{dy}{dx} = \pm\sqrt{a^2y^2+C_0}$$

$$\Rightarrow \int\frac{dy}{\sqrt{a^2y^2+C_0}} = \pm\int dx \qquad \Rightarrow \frac{\ln\left|ay+\sqrt{a^2y^2+C_0}\right|}{a} = \pm x + C_1$$

$$\Rightarrow x = \frac{1}{2}\ln\left|y+\sqrt{y^2+\frac{C_0}{a^2}}\right| + C$$

■ INTEGRAL EQUATIONS AND THEIR SOLVING METHOD

Some equations involve the unknown function $f(x)$ under integral sign and are called integral equations. To solve such equations differentiate the equation and form a differential equation. And thereafter solve the obtained equation.

ILLUSTRATION 117: Given a differentiable function $f : \mathbb{R}^+ \to \mathbb{R}$; where $f(x) = (x-1)(\ln x - 1) + \int_1^x f(x)dx$. Find $f(x)$.

SOLUTION: Given integral equation is $y = (x-1)(\ln x - 1) + \int_1^x f(x)dx$. ...(i)

Differentiating both sides w.r.t. x, we get $\frac{dy}{dx} = (x-1)\left[\frac{1}{x}\right] + (\ln x - 1) + f(x)$

$$\Rightarrow \frac{dy}{dx} = 1 - \frac{1}{x} + \ln x - 1 + y$$

$$\Rightarrow \quad \frac{dy}{dx} - y = \left(\ln x - \frac{1}{x}\right) \qquad \text{...(ii)}$$

Which is a linear differential equation with I.F. $= e^{\int(-1)dx} = e^{-x}$

$\therefore$ Solution of (ii) is given by $y.e^{-x} = -\int e^{-x}\left(\frac{1}{x} - \ln x\right)dx$

Let $-x = t$

$\Rightarrow -dx = dt$

$\Rightarrow \quad ye^{t} = \int e^{t}\left(\ln(-t) + \frac{1}{t}\right)dt = ye^{t} = e^{t}\ln(-t)$

$\Rightarrow y = \ln(-t) + Ce^{-t}$

$y = \ln c + Ce^{x}$.

ILLUSTRATION 118: Solve the differential equation $\frac{dy}{dx} = y + \int_0^1 ydx$, given $y = 1$, when $x = 0$

SOLUTION: Let $y = f(x)$

$\therefore \quad \frac{dy}{dx} = f'(x)$ then given equation can be written as

$$f'(x) = f(x) + \int_0^1 f(x)dx \qquad \text{...(i)}$$

Differentiating both sides w.r.t. x then $f''(x) = f'(x) + 0$

or $\frac{f''(x)}{f'(x)} = 1$ integrating both sides w.r.t. x then

$\ln f'(x) = x + \ln c$

or $\ln\left(\frac{f'(x)}{c}\right) = c$ or $\frac{f'(x)}{c} = e^{x}$

$\Rightarrow f'(x) = ce^{x}$

$\therefore \quad f(x) = ce^{x} + D$

given $y = f(x) = 1$ when $x = 0$

$\therefore \quad 1 = ce^{0} + D$

$\Rightarrow c + D = 1$

$$\text{then } f(x) = ce^{x} + 1 - c \qquad \text{...(ii)}$$

Now from (i), $ce^{x} = ce^{x} + 1 - c + \int_0^1 (ce^{x} + 1 - c)dx$

or $c - 1 = \{ce^{x} + (1-c)x\}_0^1$

$c - 1$ or $ce + 1 - c - c$

$\therefore \quad c = \frac{2}{3-e}$

Hence, from (ii), $f(x) = \frac{2e^{x}}{(3-e)} + 1 - \frac{2}{(3-e)} = \frac{(2e^{x} - e + 1)}{(3-e)}$

ILLUSTRATION 119: Solve the differential equation $\frac{dy}{dx} = 2y + \int_0^1 y\,dx, y(0) = e^2 - 1$

SOLUTION: Let $\int_0^1 y\,dx = c$

$\therefore \quad \frac{dy}{dx} = 2y + c \qquad \Rightarrow \frac{dy}{dx} - 2y = c$

$\therefore \quad I.F. = e^{\int -2dx} = e^{-2x}$

then solution is given by $y(e^{-2x}) = \int c.e^{-2x}dx + d$ ...(i)

$\Rightarrow \quad ye^{-2x} = -\frac{c}{2}e^{-2x} + d$

given $y(0) = e^2 - 1$

$\Rightarrow (e^2 - 1)e^{-0} = -\frac{c}{2}e^{-0} + d$

$e^2 - 1 = -\frac{c}{2} + d$ ...(ii)

From (i) and (ii), we get $ye^{-2x} = -\frac{c}{2}e^{-2x} + e^2 - 1 + \frac{c}{2}$

$\Rightarrow x\int_0^x (1-t) - f(t)dt = \int_0^x tf(1)dt; f(t) = 1$ ..(iii)

But $c = \int_0^1 ydx = \int_0^1 \left\{-\frac{c}{2} + (e^2 - 1 + c/2)e^{2x}\right\}dx$

$c = \left[-\frac{c}{2}x + (e^2 - 1 + c/2)\frac{e^{2x}}{2}\right]_0^1$

$\Rightarrow \quad c = -\frac{c}{2} + \left(e^2 - 1 + \frac{c}{2}\right)\frac{e^2}{2} + 0 - \frac{1}{2}(e^2 - 1 + c/2)$

$\Rightarrow \quad c\left(\frac{3}{2} - \frac{e^2}{4} + \frac{1}{4}\right) = \frac{e^2}{2}(e^2 - 1) - \frac{1}{2}(e^2 - 1)$

$\Rightarrow \quad c\left(\frac{7 - e^2}{4}\right) = \frac{(e^2 - 1)^2}{2} \Rightarrow c = \frac{2(e^2 - 1)^2}{(7 - e^2)}$

from (iii), $y = (e^2 - 1)e^{2x} + \frac{1}{2}c(e^{2x} - 1)$

$= \left(e^2 - 1\right)e^{2x} + \frac{(e^2 - 1)^2(e^{2x} - 1)}{(7 - e^2)}$

$= \frac{(e^2 - 1)}{(7 - e^2)}\{(7 - e^2) + e^{2x} + (e^2 - 1)(e^{2x} - 1)\}$

$= \frac{(e^2 - 1)}{(7 - e^2)}\{6e^{2x} - e^2 + 1\}$

TEXTUAL EXERCISE–9: (SUBJECTIVE)

1. Solve the differential equations:
   (a) $\frac{d^2y}{dx^2} - 2y^3 = 0$; given $y(0) = 1 = y'(0)$
   (b) $\frac{d^2y}{dx^2} + \frac{1}{y^3} = 0$; given $y(0) = 1 = y'(0)$
2. Solve the differential equations:
   (a) $\frac{d^2y}{dx^2} - a^2x = b^2x^2$
   (b) $3\frac{dx}{dt} + 2\frac{dy}{dt} = e^x$ and $\frac{dx}{dt} - \frac{dy}{dt} = 1$
   (c) $ydx - xdy + y^2 \cos x\, dx = 0$
3. The equations of motion of a particle in a plane are given by $\frac{dx}{dt} = t(t+1)$ and $(1+t)\frac{dy}{dt} = 1$; where the particle is at the point (x, y) at time t. If the particle is at the origin at the time $t = 0$, then obtain the cartesian equation of the path of the particle.
4. Population of a country doubles in 50 years, in how many years it will triple under the assumption that the rate of increase of population at any instant is directly proportional to number of inhabitant in the country?
5. Prove that the general solution of the first order non-homogeneous linear equation $\frac{dy}{dx} + P(x).y = Q(x)$ if two particular integrals of the equation $y_1(x)$ and $y_2(x)$ are known is given by $y = y_1(x) + C[y_2(x) - y_1(x)]$.
6. Substituting $y = v(x).e^x$ solve the differential equation $\frac{d^2y}{dx^2} - 2\frac{dy}{dx} + y = xe^x$, and hence, find the solution if $y(1) = 1$ and $y'(1) = 0$.
7. Solve the differential equations $\left(xy^2 - \frac{e}{x^3}\right)dx - x^2y\,dy = 0$. Given that $y = 0$; where $x = 1$.
8. Solve the integral equation $\int_0^x t\,y(t)dt = x^2 + y(x)$
9. Solve the integral equation $x\int_0^x y(t)dt = (x+1)\int_0^x t\,y(t)dt$; where $x > 0$.
10. Tangent at any point P of a curve meets the y-axis at A and the line parallel to y-axis through P meets x-axis at B. If area of ΔOAB is constant (O being origin). Form the differential equation of curve and show that it is a hyperbola.
11. (a) Find the general solution y_h of the homogeneous differential equation $\frac{dy}{dx} + 2xy = 0$
    (b) Show that the general solution of the non-homogeneous equation $\frac{dy}{dx} + 2xy = 3e^{-x^2}$ is equal to the solution y_h in part (a) plus a particular solution of the non-homogeneous equation.
12. Show that a linear equation remains linear whatever replacements of the independent variable $x = \varphi(t)$, where $\varphi(t)$ is a differentiable function, are made.

Answer Keys

1. (a) $xy - y + 1 = 0$ (b) $y = \sqrt{2x+1}$
2. (a) $y = \frac{a^2}{6}x^3 + \frac{b^2}{12}x^4 + c_1x + c_2$; where c_1 and c_2 is an arbitrary constant.
   (b) $y = 5\ln(e^x + 2) - 4x + c$ (c) $x + y \sin x = cy$
3. $x = \frac{(e^y - 1)^3}{3} + \frac{(e^y - 1)^2}{2}$
4. $t_1 = 50\frac{\ln 3}{\ln 2}$
6. $y = e^x\left(\frac{x^3}{6} + Ax + B\right)$
7. $\frac{y^2}{x^2} = \frac{e}{3}\left(\frac{1}{x^6} - 1\right)$
8. $y = 2 + C.e^{\frac{x^2}{2}}$
9. $y = \frac{C}{x^3}e^{-1/x}$
10. $xy = Cx^2 + k$
11. (a) $y_h = Ce^{-x^2}$

TEXTUAL EXERCISE–9: (OBJECTIVE)

1. The solution of the differential equation $\frac{d^2y}{dx^2} = \sin 3x + e^x + x^2$; when $y_1(0) = 1$ and $y(0) = 0$ is

(a) $\frac{-\sin 3x}{9} + e^x + \frac{x^4}{12} + \frac{1}{3}x - 1$

(b) $\frac{-\sin 3x}{9} + e^x + \frac{x^4}{12} - \frac{1}{3}x + 1$

(c) $\frac{-\cos 3x}{3} + e^x + \frac{x^4}{12} + \frac{1}{3}x + 1$

(d) None of these

2. A function $y = f(x)$ has second order derivative $f''(x) = 6(x - 1)$. If its graph passes through the point (2, 1) and at that point the tangent to the graph is $y = 3x - 5$ then the function is

(a) $(x + 1)^3$ (b) $(x - 1)^3$
(c) $(x + 1)^2$ (d) $(x - 1)^2$

3. If $f(x)$ is a function such that $x\int_0^x \{(1-t) - f(t)\}dt = \int_0^x tf(t)dt; f(1) = 1$, then

(a) $f(x)$ can be solved by reducing into linear differential equation

(b) $f(x) = x^2e^{1-1/x}$

(c) $f(x) = \frac{2}{3} - \frac{3}{5}x + \frac{14}{15}x^{-3/2}$

(d) None of these

4. The function $f(t) = \frac{d}{dt}\int_0^t \frac{dx}{1 - \cos t \cos x}$ satisfies the differential equation

(a) $\frac{df}{dt} + 2f(t)\cot t = 0$ (b) $\frac{df}{dt} - 2f(t)\cot t = 0$

(c) $\frac{df}{dt} + 2f(t) = 0$ (d) $\frac{df}{dt} - 2f(t) = 0$

5. If $\phi(x) = \int \{\phi(x)\}^{-2} dx$ and $\phi(1) = 0$ then $\phi(x)$ is equal to

(a) $\{2(x - 1)\}^{1/4}$ (b) $\{5(x - 2)\}^{1/5}$
(c) $\{3(x - 1)\}^{1/3}$ (d) None of these

Answer Keys

1. (a) **2.** (b) **3.** (a,c) **4.** (a) **5.** (c)

■ ORTHOGONAL TRAJECTORY OF A GIVEN CURVE

Trajectory

A curve of family or curves $\phi(x, y, c) = 0$ which cuts every member of a given family of curves $f(x, y, c) = 0$ according to a fixed rule is called a trajector of the family of curves.

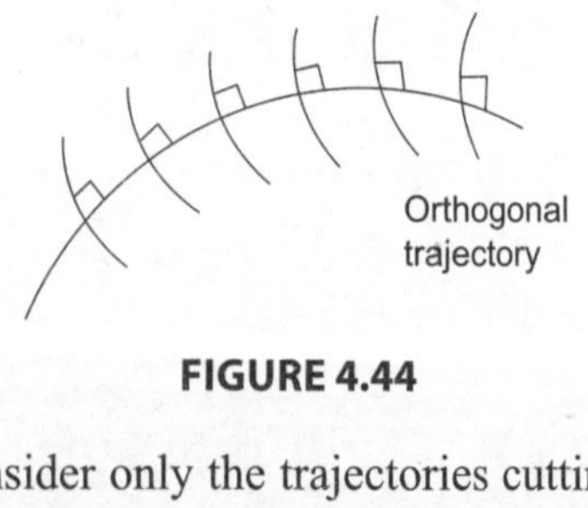

FIGURE 4.44

If we consider only the trajectories cutting each member of family of curves $f(x, y, c) = 0$ at a constant angle, then the curve which cuts every member of a given family of curves at right angle, is called an orthogonal trajectory of the family.

In order to find out the orthogonal trajectories the following steps are taken.

Step 1: Let $f(x, y, c) = 0$ be the equation where c is an arbitrary parameter.

Step 2: Differentiate the given equation w.r.t x and eliminate c.

Step 3: Substitute $-\frac{dx}{dy}$ for $\frac{dy}{dx}$ in the equation obtained in step 2.

Step 4: Solve the differential equation obtained from step 3.

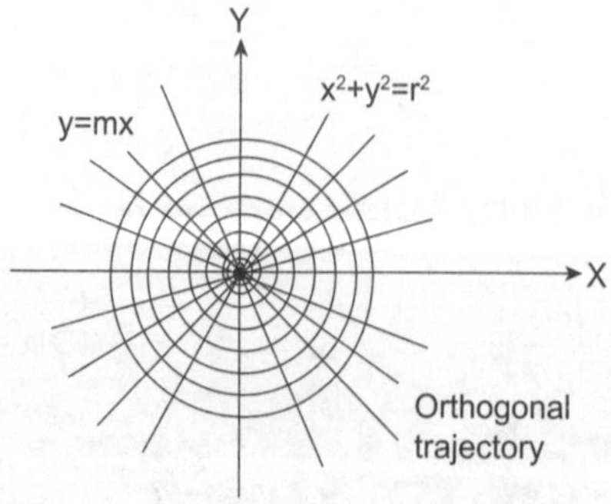

FIGURE 4.45

ILLUSTRATION 120: Find the orthogonal trajectory of family of straight lines passing through the origin.

SOLUTION: Family of straight lines passing through the origin is $y = mx$ .....(i)

where 'm' is an arbitrary constant.

Differentiating w.r.t. x, we get $\frac{dy}{dx} = m$ ...(ii)

Eliminating 'm' from (i) and (ii), we get $y = \frac{dy}{dx}x$

Replacing $\frac{dy}{dx}$ by $-\frac{dx}{dy}$, we get $y = -\frac{dx}{dy}x$ $x\,dx + y\,dy = 0$

Integrating both sides, we get $\frac{x^2}{2} + \frac{y^2}{2} = c$

$\Rightarrow$ $x^2 + y^2 = 2c$

Which is the required orthogonal trajectory

ILLUSTRATION 121: Find the orthogonal trajectories of the curve $y = ax^2$.

SOLUTION: Let $y = ax^2$ ...(i)

Differentiating equation (i), we get $\frac{dy}{dx} = 2ax$ ...(ii)

Eliminating a from equations (i) and (ii), we get $\frac{dy}{dx} = \frac{2y}{x^2}x$ ...(iii)

Putting $-\frac{dx}{dy}$ in equation (iii) in the place of $\frac{dy}{dx}$, we get $-\frac{dx}{dy} = \frac{2y}{x}$

$\Rightarrow$ $-xdx = 2y\,dy$ $\qquad\Rightarrow$ $-\frac{x^2}{2} = \frac{2y^2}{2}$

$\Rightarrow$ $2y^2 + x^2 = 0$

This is the family of required orthogonal trajectories.

ILLUSTRATION 122: Find the orthogonal trajecories of the hyperbola $xy = c$.

SOLUTION: The equation of the given family of curves is $xy = c$ ...(i)

Differentiating (i) w.r.t. x, we get $x\frac{dy}{dx} + y = 0$ ...(ii)

Substituting $-\frac{dx}{dy}$ for $\frac{dy}{dx}$ in (ii), we get $-x\frac{dx}{dy} + y = 0$ ...(iii)

This is the differential equation of the orthogonal trajectories of given family of hyperbolas. (iii) can be rewritten as $xdx = ydy$, which on integration given $x^2 - y^2 = c$.

This is the required family of orthogonal trajectories.

ILLUSTRATION 123: Find the orthogonal trajectories of the curves $\frac{x^2}{a^2+\lambda} + \frac{y^2}{b^2+\lambda} = 1$, λ being the parameter of the family

SOLUTION: Let $\frac{x^2}{a^2+\lambda} + \frac{y^2}{b^2+\lambda} = 1$ ...(i)

Differentiating (i) w.r.t. x, we have $\frac{x}{a^2+\lambda} + \frac{y}{b^2+\lambda}\frac{dy}{dx} = 0$ ...(ii)

From (i) and (ii) we have to eliminate λ.

Now (ii) gives, $\lambda = -\left(\dfrac{b^2x + a^2y\dfrac{dy}{dx}}{x + y\dfrac{dy}{dx}}\right)$

$\Rightarrow\ a^2 + \lambda = \dfrac{(a^2 - b^2)x}{x + y\dfrac{dy}{dx}}$; $b^2 + \lambda = -\dfrac{(a^2 - b^2)y\dfrac{dy}{dx}}{x + y\dfrac{dy}{dx}}$

Substituting these values in (i), we get $\left(x - y\dfrac{dx}{dy}\right)\left(x + y\dfrac{dy}{dx}\right) = a^2 - b^2$ ...(iii)

is the differential equation of the given family of curves.

Replacing $\dfrac{dy}{dx}$ to $-\dfrac{dx}{dy}$ in (iii), we obtain $\left(x + y\dfrac{dy}{dx}\right)\left(x - y\dfrac{dx}{dy}\right) = a^2 - b^2$ ...(iv)

which is the same as (iii). Thus, we see that the family (i) is self orthogonal. That is, every member of the family (i) cuts every other member of the same family orthogonally.

ILLUSTRATION 124: Find the orthogonal trajectories of the circles $x^2 + y^2 - ay = 0$ where 'a' is a parameter.

SOLUTION: Here, $x^2 + y^2 - ay = 0$. Differentiating w.r.t. x, we get $2x + 2y\dfrac{dy}{dx} - a\dfrac{dy}{dx} = 0$

$\Rightarrow\ 2x + 2y\dfrac{dy}{dx} - \dfrac{x^2 + y^2}{y}\dfrac{dy}{dx} = 0$ $\left(\because\ x^2 + y^2 - ay = 0\ \Rightarrow\ a = \dfrac{x^2 + y^2}{y}\right)$

$\Rightarrow\ 2x + \dfrac{y^2 - x^2}{y}\dfrac{dy}{dx} = 0$. This is the differential equation of the given circles.

∴ The equation of orthogonal trajectories is $2x + \dfrac{y^2 - x^2}{y}.\left(-\dfrac{dx}{dy}\right) = 0$

$\left(\text{putting } \dfrac{-dx}{dy} \text{ in place of } \dfrac{dy}{dx}\right)$

$\Rightarrow\ 2xydy + (x^2 - y^2)\,dx = 0$

It is a homogeneous equation.

Put $y = \upsilon x$, then $\dfrac{dy}{dx} = \upsilon + x\dfrac{d\upsilon}{dx}$

$\Rightarrow\ 2x.\upsilon x.\left(\upsilon + x\dfrac{d\upsilon}{dx}\right) + x^2 - \upsilon^2x^2 = 0$

or $2\upsilon\left(\upsilon + x\dfrac{d\upsilon}{dx}\right) + 1 - \upsilon^2 = 0$ $\Rightarrow\ 1 + \upsilon^2 + 2\upsilon x\dfrac{d\upsilon}{dx} = 0$

$\Rightarrow\ \dfrac{dx}{x} + \dfrac{2\upsilon}{1 + \upsilon^2}d\upsilon = 0;$

Integrating, we get $\ln x + \ln(1 + \upsilon^2) = \ln c$

$\Rightarrow\ x(1 + \upsilon^2) = c$ $\Rightarrow\ x\left(1 + \dfrac{y^2}{x^2}\right) = c$, i.e., $x^2 + y^2 = cx$

Which is the required family of orthogonal trajectories.

TEXTUAL EXERCISE–10: (SUBJECTIVE)

1. Find the orthogonal trajectories of the family of semi cubical parabolas $ay^2 = x^3$; where a is the variable parameter.
2. Find the orthogonal trajectories of the family of parabolas $y = ax^2$.
3. Find the orthogonal trajectories of $\frac{x^2}{a^2}+\frac{y^2}{a^2+\lambda}=1$; where λ is an arbitrary parameter.
4. Find the orthogonal trajectory of $y^2 = 4ax$ (a being the parameter).
5. Find the orthogonal trajectories for the given family of curves when 'a' is the parameter.
   (i) $\cos y = a\,e^{-x}$ (ii) $x^k + y^k = a^k$
6. Find the trajectories orthogonal to ellipse having a common major axis equal to $2a$, along x-axis and centre at origin.

Answer Keys

1. $3y^2 + 2x^2 = c^2$
2. $x^2 + 2y^2 = c$
3. $x^2 + y^2 + c = 2a^2 \log x$
4. $2x^2 + y^2 = c$
5. (i) $\sin y = ce^{-x}$, (ii) $y = cx$ if $k = 2$ and $\frac{1}{x^{k-2}}-\frac{1}{y^{k-2}} = c$ if $k \neq 2$ and $y = cx$ if $k = 2$
6. $x^2 + y^2 = 2a^2\ln|cx|$

TEXTUAL EXERCISE–10: (OBJECTIVE)

1. The orthogonal trajectories of the family of curve $y = c\,x^k$ are given by
   (a) $x^2 + cy^2 =$ const. (b) $x^2 + k\,y^2 =$ const.
   (c) $k\,x^2 + y^2 =$ const. (d) $x^2 - k\,y^2 =$ const.
2. The trajectories orthogonal to $(2a - x)\,y^2 = x^3$ is
   (a) $(x^2 + y^2)^2 = C(y^2 + 2x^2)$
   (b) $(y^2 + 2x^2)^2 = Cxy$
   (c) $(y^2 + 2x^2)^2 = C(y^2 + x^2)$
   (d) $(y^2 + 2x^2) = x^3 + xy^2$
3. The orthogonal trajectories of the family of curves $xy = k^2$ are
   (a) rectangular hyperbola
   (b) $y^2 = 4a\,(x + a)$
   (c) $x^2 - y^2 = a^2$
   (d) system of circles with centre on x-axis
4. Equation of a curve cutting $x^2 + y^2 - 2x - 4y - 15 = 0$ orthogonally can be
   (a) $(y - 2) = \lambda(x - 1)$ (b) $(y - 2) = \lambda(x - 2)$
   (c) $(y + 2) = \lambda(x + 1)$ (d) $(y + 1) = \lambda(x + 2)$
5. Orthogonal trajectories of family of the curve $x^{2/3} + y^{2/3} = a^{2/3}$, where '$a$' is any arbitrary constant, is
   (a) $x^{2/3} - y^{2/3} = c$ (b) $x^{4/3} - y^{4/3} = c$
   (c) $x^{4/3} + y^{4/3} = c$ (d) $x^{1/3} - y^{1/3} = c$
6. The orthogonal trajectories of the system of curves $\left(\frac{dy}{dx}\right)^2 = a/x$ are
   (a) $9a(y + c) = 4x^3$ (b) $y+C=\frac{-2}{3\sqrt{a}}x^{3/2}$
   (c) $y+C=\frac{2}{3\sqrt{a}}x^{3/2}$ (d) None of these
7. Orthogonal trajectories of the family of curves represented by $x^2 + 2y^2 - y + C = 0$, is
   (a) $y^2 = a(4x - 1)$ (b) $y^2 = a(4x^2 - 1)$
   (c) $x^2 = a(4y - 1)$ (d) $x^2 = a(4y^2 - 1)$
8. Orthogonal trajectories of family of parabolas $y^2 = 4a(x + a)$ here 'a' is an arbitrary constant is
   (a) $ax^2 = 4cy$
   (b) $x^2 + y^2 = a^2$
   (c) $y^2 = 2x/k + 2k$
   (d) $axy = c^2$ (where c is arbitrary constant)

Answer Keys

1. (b) 2. (a) 3. (a, c) 4. (a) 5. (b) 6. (a,b, c) 7. (c) 8. (c)

APPLICATION OF DIFFERENTIAL EQUATION

Now a days differential equations are used in modeling almost all natural phenomena related to physics, natural sciences, chemistry, biology, social sciences, geology even in economics. In-depth study of differential equation has become compulsory due to its importance in all modern scientific investigation because the mathematical model of any natural phenomena applies the formation and solution of differential equation.

Covering up the complete domain of its application is not possible, so, let us make an effort to learn some of its specific applications.

Some Physical Problems Involving Applications of Differential Equation

1. ***Radioactive Decay:*** If $f(t) = 0$ is the amount present at a time t, then $f'(t)$ represents the rate of change of amount at time t, then law of decay states that $\frac{df(t)}{dt} = -K.f(t)$
2. ***Falling body in a resisting medium:*** If a body of weights m falling in a resisting medium, then according to Newton's law, we get the following equation $ma = mg - kv$
   $\Rightarrow \frac{dv}{dt} + \frac{k}{m}v = g$. It represents a linear different equation.
3. ***Cooling problem:*** If $f(t)$ is the temperature of the body at time t and if $M(t)$ denotes the (known) temperature of the surrounding medium, then according to Newton's law of cooling $\frac{df(t)}{dt} = -k[f(t) - M(t)]$
4. ***Dilution problem:*** If $f(t)$ denote the number of points of salt in the tank at time t minutes after mixing begins. Then according to dilution problem two factors which cause $f(t)$ to change, the incoming mixture per minute (k) and outgoing mixture which removes salt $R.f(t)$.

   Then $\frac{df(t)}{dt} = k - R\,f(t)$
5. ***Electric circuit:*** If voltage is denoted by $v(t)$ and current by $I(t)$, then according to kirchhoff's law (here L and R are constants) $\frac{L.dI(t)}{dt} + RI(t) = v(t)$.
   It represents a linear differential equation.

ILLUSTRATION 125: Application of differential equation in the field of kinematics. An object moves along the x-axis in such a way that its position at time $t > 0$ is governed by the differential equation $\frac{dx}{dt} + (t - t^{-1})x = t^2$. If the object was at position $x = 2$ at time $t = 1$, where will it be at time $t = 3$?

SOLUTION: Let $\frac{dx}{dt} + (t - t^{-1})x = t^2$ is a linear differential equation

$\therefore\ I.F = e^{\int (t-1/t)dt} = e^{\frac{t^2}{2} - \ln t} = \frac{e^{t^2/2}}{t}$

Thus, the solution of differential equation is given by

$$x\frac{e^{\frac{t^2}{2}}}{t} = \int t^2 \frac{e^{t^2/2}}{t}\,dt + c$$

$$\Rightarrow\ x = te^{-\frac{t^2}{2}}\left(\int t\,e^{t^2/2}\,dt + c\right)$$

put $t^2/2 = u$ $\qquad \Rightarrow tdt = du$

$$\Rightarrow\ x = te^{\frac{-t^2}{2}}\int e^u du + C \qquad \Rightarrow\ x = te^{-\frac{t^2}{2}}(e^{t^2/2} + c)$$

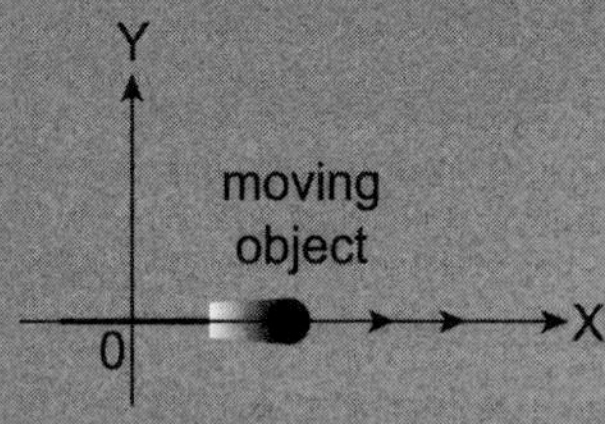

FIGURE 4.46

$\Rightarrow\ x = t(1 + ce^{-\frac{t^2}{2}})$ ...(i)

Given that $x = 2$ at $t = 1$

$\Rightarrow\ 2 = \left(1 + Ce^{\frac{-1}{2}}\right)$ $\Rightarrow\ 1 = Ce^{\frac{-1}{2}}$

$\Rightarrow\ C = e^{\frac{1}{2}}$

$\therefore$ (i) becomes $x = t\left(1 + e^{\left(\frac{1-t^2}{2}\right)}\right)$

$\therefore$ when $t = 3$ $x = 3[1 + e^{-4}]$

ILLUSTRATION 126: Problem involving application of differential equation in the field of Economics. It is known that, if the interest is compounded continuously, the principal changes at the rate equal to the product of the rate of bank interest per annum and the principal. If the interest is compounded continuously at 5% per annum, in how many years will 100 double itself?

SOLUTION: If A denotes the principal at any instant t, according to the law given in the problem,

we have $\frac{dA}{dt} = (0.05)A$ ...(i)

On integrating (i), we get $A = Ce^{(0.05)t}$ ...(ii)

As 100 was invested initially, we have

$A = 100$ when $t = 0$

So, from (ii), we get, $C = 100$

$\Rightarrow\ A = 100e^{(0.05)t}$ ...(iii)

If T years is the time necessary for doubling 100, we have from (iii); $200 = 100e^{(0.05)T}$

$\Rightarrow\ 2 = 100e^{(0.05)T}$

$\Rightarrow\ \ln 2 = (0.05)T$

Hence, $T = (20 \ln 2)$ years.

ILLUSTRATION 127: Problems involving application of differential equation in the field of Medical Science. The doctor took the temperature of a dead body at 11: 30 pm which was 94.6°F. He took the temperature of the body again after one hour, which was 93.4° F. If the temperature of the room was 70°F, estimate the time of death. Taking normal temperature of human body = 98.6°F.

SOLUTION: The Newton's law of cooling states that the temperature of body changes at a rate which is proportional to the difference in temperature between that of the surrounding medium and that of the body itself. If T denotes the temperature of the body at time t, following the Newton's law of cooling we have (with k as the constant of proportionality)

$\frac{dT}{dt} = k(T - 70); k < 0$ ...(i)

which is a first order differential equation with variable separable

On integrating (i), we obtain $T = 70 + Ce^{kt}$ (C : parameter) ...(ii)

As at $t = 0$ we had $T = 94.6$, it follows that $C = 24.6$

$\Rightarrow T = 70 + (24.6)e^{kt}$

Again $T = 93.4$ at $t = 1$ hrs; so, $k = \ln\frac{117}{123} < 0$

Hence, the time t_1 that has elasped after the death at 11.30 is given by

$98.6 = 70 + (24.6).\, e^{kt_1}$

$\Rightarrow \frac{28.6}{24.6} = e^{kt_1}$ $\Rightarrow \ln\left[\frac{143}{123}\right] = kt_1$

This implies $t_1 = \frac{1}{k}\ln\frac{143}{123} = \frac{\ln\left(\frac{143}{123}\right)}{\ln\left(\frac{117}{123}\right)} = -3.01$ hrs.

So, the estimated time of death is 11:30 – 3.01 = 8.30 pm (approx)

ILLUSTRATION 128: Problems involving application of differential equation in the field of Bio-Science. The number of bacteria in a yeast culture grows at a rate, which is proportional to the number present. If the population of a colony of yeast bacteria triples in 1 hour, find the number of bacteria, which will be present at the end of 5 hours.

SOLUTION: Suppose that the number of bacteria is x_0 when $t = 0$ and it is x at time t (in hours)

Then given that $\frac{dx}{dt} \propto x$

$\Rightarrow \frac{dx}{dt} = kx$

$\Rightarrow \frac{dx}{x} = k\,dt$ ...(i)

Where k is the constant of proportionality. Solution of (i) is given by $\ln x - \ln c = kt$ (c is an arbitrary constant)

$\Rightarrow \ln\frac{x}{c} = kt$

$\Rightarrow x = ce^{kt}$; when $t = 0$; $x = x_0$

$\therefore c = x_0$

$\therefore$ we have $x = x_0e^{kt}$; given $x = 3x_0$; when $t = 1$

$\therefore 3x_0 = x_0\, e^k$ i.e., $e^k = 3$

We have to find x_5 when $t = 5$.

$\therefore x_5 = x_0\, e^{5k} = x_0\,(e^k)^5 = 3^5x_0$

$\Rightarrow x_5 = 243x_0$, i.e., 243 times the number of bacteria initially.

ILLUSTRATION 129: The rate of cooling of a substance in moving air is proportional to the difference of temperatures of the substance and the air. A substance cools from 36°C to 34°C in 15 minutes. Find when the substance will have the temperature 32°C, it being known that the constant temperature of air is 30°C.

SOLUTION: Let the temperature of the substance at time t minutes be T.

The rate of cooling of the substance

$= k(T-30)$°C per minute (from the question).

But the rate of cooling = rate of decrease of temperature $= -\dfrac{dT}{dt}$

from the question, we get $-\dfrac{dT}{dt} = k(T-30); k > 0$

$$\Rightarrow \quad -\frac{dT}{T-30} = kdt$$

$$\Rightarrow \quad \int_{36}^{34} -\frac{dT}{T-30} = \int_0^{15} kdt$$

$$\Rightarrow \quad [-\ln(T-30)]_{36}^{34} = k[t]_0^{15} \qquad \Rightarrow \quad \ln\frac{6}{4} = k.(15)$$

$$\Rightarrow \quad k = \frac{1}{15}\ln\frac{3}{2}$$

Again, $\displaystyle\int_{36}^{32} -\frac{dT}{T-30} = \int_0^t kdt$; where t minutes is the required time.

$$\Rightarrow \quad [-\ln(T-30)]_{36}^{32} = \frac{1}{15}\ln\frac{3}{2}.[t]_0^t \qquad \Rightarrow \quad \ln 3 = \frac{1}{15}\ln\frac{3}{2}.t$$

$$\Rightarrow \quad t = \frac{15\ln 3}{\ln(3/2)} \text{ minutes.}$$

ILLUSTRATION 130: Problem involving application of differential equation in the field of Geometry. A normal is drawn at a point $P(x, y)$ of a curve. It meets the x-axis and y-axis in the points A and B, respectively, such that $\dfrac{1}{OA} + \dfrac{1}{OB} = 1$; where O is the origin. Find the equation of such a curve passing through (5, 4).

SOLUTION: The equation of the normal at (x, y) is $(X-x)+(Y-y)\dfrac{dy}{dx} = 0$

$$\Rightarrow \quad \frac{X}{x+y\frac{dy}{dx}} + \frac{Y}{\left(x+y\frac{dy}{dx}\right)\Big/\frac{dy}{dx}} = 1$$

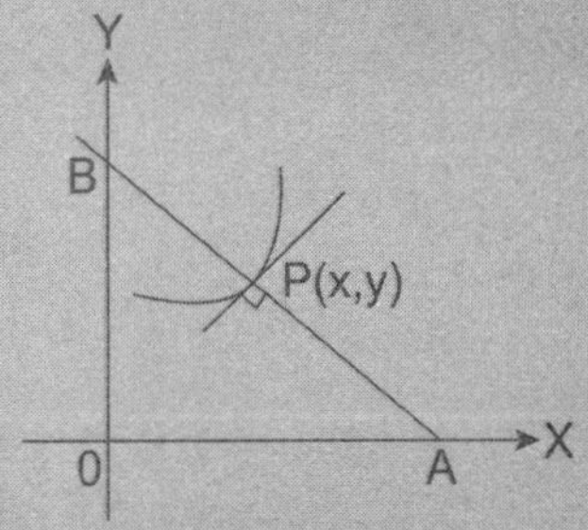

FIGURE 4.47

Put $OA = x+y\dfrac{dy}{dx}$, and $OB = \dfrac{x+y\frac{dy}{dx}}{\frac{dy}{dx}}$

$$\Rightarrow \quad \frac{1}{OA} + \frac{1}{OB} = 1$$

$$\Rightarrow \quad 1+\frac{dy}{dx} = x+y\frac{dy}{dx}$$

$$\Rightarrow \quad (y-1)\frac{dy}{dx} + (x-1) = 0$$

Integrating, we get $(y-1)^2 + (x-1)^2 = C$. Since the curve passes through (5, 4), $C = 25$

Hence the curve is $(x-1)^2 + (y-1)^2 = 25$. That is, a circle with centre at (1, 1) and radius 5.

TEXTUAL EXERCISE–11: (SUBJECTIVE)

1. It is given that the rate at which some bacteria multiply is proportional to the instantaneous number present. If the original number of bacteria doubles in two hours, in how many hours will it be five times?
2. It is given that radium decomposes at a rate proportional to the amount present. If p percent of the original amount of radium disappears in l years, what percentage of it will remain after $2l$ years?
3. A and B are two separate reservoirs of water. Capacity of reservoir A is double the capacity of reservoir B. Both the reservoirs are filled completely with water, their inlets are closed and then the water is released simultaneously from both the reservoirs. The rate of flow of water out of each reservoir at any instant of time is proportional to the quantity of water in the reservoir at that time. One hour after the water is released the quantity of water in reservoir A is 1.5 times the quantity of water in reservoir B. After how many hours do both the reservoirs have the same quantity of water ?
4. A curve $y = f(x)$ passes through the point $P(1, 1)$. The normal to the curve at P is; a $(y - 1) + (x - 1) = 0$. If the slope of the tangent at any point on the curve is proportional to the ordinate of the point, determine the equation of the curve. Also obtain the area bounded by the y-axis, the curve and the normal to the curve at P.
5. A curve passing through the point (1, 1) has the property that the perpendicular distance of the origin from the normal at any point P of the curve is equal to the distance of P from the x-axis. Determine the equation of the curve.
6. An inverted cone of height H and radius R is pointed at bottom. It is filled with a volatile liquid completely. If the rate of evaporation is directly proportional to the surface area of the liquid in contact with air (constant of proportionality $k > 0$), find the time in which whole liquid evaporates.
7. Find the curve for which the sum of the lengths of the tangent and subtangent at any of its point is proportional to the product of the co-ordinates of the point of tangency, the proportionality factor is equal to k.

Answer Keys

1. $2\dfrac{\ln 5}{\ln 2}$ hours 2. $\left(10-\dfrac{p}{10}\right)^2 \%$ 3. $t=\dfrac{\ln 2}{\ln(4/3)}$

4. $y=e^{a(x-1)};\left|\dfrac{1}{a}\left(a-\dfrac{1}{2}+e^{-a}\right)\right|$ sq. unit 5. $x^2 + y^2 - 2x = 0$ 6. $t = H/k$

7. $y=\dfrac{1}{k}\,\ell n\left|c\left(k^2x^2-1\right)\right|$

TEXTUAL EXERCISE–11: (OBJECTIVE)

1. A curve C has the property that if the tangent drawn at any point P on C meets the coordinate axes at A and B, then P is the mid-point of AB. The curve passes through the point (1, 1). Then the equation of the curve is given by

   (a) $xy = 1$ (b) $x^2y = 1$
   (c) $2xy = x + y$ (d) None of these

2. The curve such that the area of the trapezium formed by the coordinate axes. Ordinate of an arbitrary point and the tangent at this point equals half the square of its abscissa is given by

   (a) $y = cx^2 + x$ (b) $y^2 = cx^2 + x$
   (c) $y = cx^2 - x$ (d) None of these

3. A wet porous substance in the open air loses its moisture at a rate proportional to the moisture content. If a sheet hung in the wind lose half its moisture during the first hour, then the time after which will it have lost 99% (weather conditions remaining the same) is

(a) $t = \dfrac{\ln 100}{\ln 2}$ hrs. (b) $t = \dfrac{\ln 150}{\ln 2}$ hrs.

(c) $t = \dfrac{\ln 120}{\ln 2}$ hrs. (d) None of these

4. A tank consists of 50 litres of fresh water. Two litres of brine each litre containing 5 gms of dissolved salt are run into tank per minute; the mixture is kept uniform by stirring, and runs out at the rate of one litre per minute. If '*m*' grams of salt are present in the tank after t minute, express 'm' in terms of *t*, then the amount of salt present after 10 minutes is

(a) $91\frac{2}{3}$ gram (b) $27\frac{5}{9}$ gram

(c) $27\frac{1}{9}$ gram (d) None of these

5. A flu type virus has spread over a city. The population of that city is 50,000. The rate of spreading that virus is proportion to the affected and unaffected people. If in the very beginning there are 100 affected people and 550 people are those who get affected after 10 days, then the function expressing the effected people is given by

(a) $\dfrac{P}{1-ce^{-kpt}}; c = 499, p = 50000,\ k = -\dfrac{1}{P}\ln\left(\dfrac{99}{499}\right)$

(b) $\dfrac{P}{1+ce^{kpt}}; c = 499,\ p = 50000,\ k = -\dfrac{1}{P}\ln\left(\dfrac{99}{499}\right)$

(c) $\dfrac{p}{1+ce^{-kpt}}; c = 499,\ p = 50000,\ k = -\dfrac{1}{10p}\ln\left(\dfrac{989}{5489}\right)$

(d) None of these

Answer Keys

1. (a) **2.** (a, c) **3.** (a) **4.** (a) **5.** (c)

MULTIPLE CHOICE QUESTIONS

SECTION–I

OBJECTIVE-TYPE SOLVED EXAMPLES

1. The degree of the differential equation satisfying $\sqrt{1-x^2}+\sqrt{1-y^2}=a(x-y)$ is

(a) 3 (b) 1

(c) 2 (d) None of these

Solution: (b) Given family of curve is $\sqrt{1-x^2}+\sqrt{1-y^2}=a(x-y)$ in order to simplify the expression to remove radicals

Put $x = \sin\theta$, $y = \sin\phi$, so that given equation is reduced to $\cos\theta + \cos\phi = a(\sin\theta - \sin\phi)$

$\Rightarrow\ 2\cos\frac{\theta+\phi}{2}\cos\frac{\theta-\phi}{2} = 2a\cos\frac{\theta+\phi}{2}\sin\frac{\theta-\phi}{2}$

$\Rightarrow\ \cot\frac{\theta-\phi}{2}=a$

$\Rightarrow\ \theta-\phi = 2\cot^{-1}a \quad \Rightarrow\ \sin^{-1}x - \sin^{-1}y = 2\cot^{-1}a$

Now differentiating w.r.t. x we, get

$\frac{1}{\sqrt{1-x^2}}-\frac{1}{\sqrt{1-y^2}}\frac{dy}{dx}=0$. Of course the degree of differential equation is one.

2. If the solution of $\left(1+2e^{\frac{x}{y}}\right)dx+2e^{\frac{x}{y}}\left(1-\frac{x}{y}\right)dy=0$ is $\left(x+\lambda ye^{\frac{x}{y}}\right)=c$;(c is an arbitrary constant), then λ is

(a) 1 (b) 2

(c) 3 (d) None of these

Solution: (b) The appearance of $\frac{x}{y}$ in the given equation suggests the substitution $\frac{x}{y}=u$

$\Rightarrow\ dx = udy + y\,du$

So, the given equation can be written as $(1 + 2e^u)(udy + ydu) + 2e^u(1 - u)\,dy = 0$, which is a variable separable form.

$\Rightarrow\ \frac{(1+2e^u)}{u+2e^u}du+\frac{dy}{y}=0$

$\Rightarrow\ \int\left(\frac{1+2e^u}{u+2e^u}\right)du+\int\frac{dy}{y}=0$

$\Rightarrow\ \log|u + 2e^u| + \log|y| = \log|c|$

$\Rightarrow\ (u + 2e^u)y = c$

$\Rightarrow\ (x + 2ye^{x/y}) = c$; comparing with given general solution, we get $\lambda = 2$.

3. The solution of $y(xy + e^{xy})\,dx + x(xy - e^{xy})\,dy = 0$ is

(a) $\frac{1}{2}(\ln|xy|+xy)=\ln|y|+c$

(b) $\frac{1}{2}(\ln|xy|-xy)=\ln|y|+c$

(c) $(\ln|xy|+xy)=\ln|y|+c$

(d) None of these

Solution: (a) The given equation can be expressed as $xy^2dx + x^2ydy + y.e^{xy}dx - xe^{xy}dy = 0$

The symmetric presence of xy in the equation inspires the substitution $xy = u$

$\Rightarrow\ x\,dy + y\,dx = du$

$\Rightarrow\ xy(dyx + xdy) + e^{xy}(ydx - xdy) = 0$

$\Rightarrow\ xy(ydx + xdy) + e^{xy}(ydx + xdy - 2xdy) = 0$

$\Rightarrow\ u\,du+e^u\left(du-2.\frac{u}{y}dy\right)=0$

$\Rightarrow\ u\,du+e^u du-\frac{2u.e^u}{y}.dy=0$

Which is indeed a variable separable case. Integrating both side, we get

$\frac{1}{2}\int\left(\frac{u+e^u}{u-e^u}\right)du-\int\frac{dy}{y}=0$

$\Rightarrow\ \frac{1}{2}(\ln|u|+\ln|e^u|)=\ln|y|-c$

$\Rightarrow\ \frac{1}{2}(\ln|xy|+xy)=\ln|y|+c$; where $c = c'$

4. The solution of the differential equation $\frac{y+\sin x.\cos^2(xy)}{\cos^2(xy)}dx+\left(\frac{x}{\cos^2(xy)}+\sin y\right)dy=0$ is

(a) $\tan xy + \cos x + \cos y = C$

(b) $\tan xy - \cos x - \cos y = C$

(c) $\tan xy + \cos x - \cos y = C$

(d) None of these

Solution: (b) Rearranging the terms wisely the differential equation can be written as

$\frac{ydx+xdy}{\cos^2 xy}+\sin x\,dx+\sin y\,dy=0$

$\Rightarrow \quad \dfrac{d(xy)}{\cos^2 xy} + \sin x\,dx + \sin y\,dy = 0$

(observing $xdy + ydx = d(xy)$]

$\Rightarrow$ $\sec^2(xy)\, d(xy) + \sin x\, dx + \sin y\, dy = 0$

$\Rightarrow$ $\tan xy - \cos x - \cos y = C$.

5. The solution of the differential equation, $\dfrac{dy}{dx} = \dfrac{(1+y)^2}{x(1+y) - x^2}$ is given as $\ln(1+y) =$

(a) $\dfrac{1+y}{x} + c$ (b) $\dfrac{1-y}{x} + c$

(c) $\dfrac{-1-y}{x} + c$ (d) None of these

Solution: (a) Consider $\dfrac{dx}{dy} = \dfrac{x}{1+y} - \dfrac{x^2}{(1+y)^2}$

$\Rightarrow \quad -\dfrac{1}{x^2}\dfrac{dy}{dx} + \dfrac{1}{x(1+y)} = \dfrac{1}{(1+y)^2}$

Substituting $\dfrac{1}{x} = t$, we get $\dfrac{dt}{dy} + \dfrac{t}{1+y} = \dfrac{1}{(1+y)^2}$;

which is linear $I.F. = e^{\int \frac{1}{1+y} dy} = (1+y)$

$\Rightarrow$ Solution of differential equation is

$t(1+y) = \int \dfrac{1}{1+y} dy = c \Rightarrow \quad c + \dfrac{1+y}{x} = \ln(1+y)$

6. The solution of the differential equation $xdy + ydx + y^2(xdy - ydx) = 0$ is

(a) $-\dfrac{1}{xy} + \dfrac{y}{x} = c$ (b) $\dfrac{1}{xy} + \dfrac{y}{x} = c$

(c) $-\dfrac{1}{xy} - \dfrac{y}{x} = c$ (d) None of these

Solution: (a) Let $xdy + ydx + y^2(xdy - ydx) = 0$

Rearranging the expression

$\Rightarrow \quad xdy + ydx + x^2y^2\left(\dfrac{x\,dy - y\,dx}{x^2}\right) = 0$

observing the complete derivative using inspection, we get

$\Rightarrow \quad d(x.y) + x^2y^2 d\left(\dfrac{y}{x}\right) = 0$

$\Rightarrow \quad \dfrac{d(x.y)}{x^2y^2} + d\left(\dfrac{y}{x}\right) = 0$ integrating both side

$\Rightarrow$ $(y^2 - 1) = c\,xy$

$\Rightarrow \quad -\dfrac{1}{xy} + \dfrac{y}{x} = c$ is the required solution.

7. The foci of the curve which satisfies the differential equation $(1 + y^2)dx - xydy = 0$ and passes through the point (1, 0) are

(a) $(\sqrt{2}, 0)$ (b) $(0, \sqrt{2})$

(c) $(0, -\sqrt{2})$ (d) $(-\sqrt{2}, 0)$

Solution: (a, d) The given differential equation is reduced to variable separable form as $\dfrac{dx}{x} = \dfrac{ydy}{1+y^2}$

$\Rightarrow$ $\ell n\, x^2 = \ell n\,(1 + y^2) + C$

$\because$ the curve passes through (1, 0), therefore $C = 0$

$\Rightarrow$ $x^2 - y^2 = 1$ is the required particular integral which is a rectangular hyperbola with eccentricity $e = \sqrt{2}$; $a = 1$, thus, foci are $(\pm\, ae, 0)$

$\Rightarrow$ foci are given as $(-\sqrt{2}, 0)$ and $(\sqrt{2}, 0)$

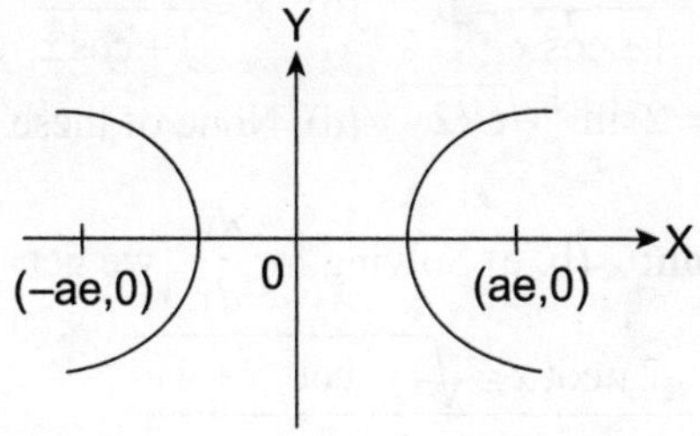

8. Solutions of the differential equation $\left(\dfrac{dy}{dx}\right)^2 - \dfrac{dy}{dx}(e^x + e^{-x}) + 1 = 0$ are given by

(a) $y + e^{-x} = C$ (b) $y - e^{-x} = C$

(c) $y + e^x = C$ (d) $y - e^x = C$

Solution: (*a, d*) Solving the equation as quadratic in $\dfrac{dy}{dx}$, the given equation can be written as $\left(\dfrac{dy}{dx} - e^{-x}\right)$ $\left(\dfrac{dy}{dx} - e^x\right) = 0$

$\Rightarrow \quad \dfrac{dy}{dx} - e^{-x} = 0 \quad$ or $\quad \dfrac{dy}{dx} - e^x = 0$

$\Rightarrow$ $dy - e^{-x}dx = 0$ or $dy - e^x dx = 0$

Now integrating, we get $y + e^{-x} = C$ or $y - e^x = C$

General solution of equation is given as $(y + e^{-x} - C)(y - e^x - C) = 0$

9. Which of the following differential equations has solution as the function represented parametrically by the equations $x = \dfrac{1 + \ell nt}{t^2}$; $y = \dfrac{3 + 2\ell nt}{t}$?

(a) $y''(x - 2xy') = y$ (b) $yy' = 2x(y')^2 + 1$

(c) $xy' = 2y(y')^2 + 2$ (d) $y''(y - 4xy') = (y')^2$

Solution: (*b, d*) Clearly

$\dfrac{dy}{dy} = \dfrac{t\left(\dfrac{2}{t}\right) - (3 + 2\ln t)}{t^2} = \dfrac{-1 - 2\ln t}{t^2}$

$$\frac{dx}{dt} = \frac{t^2\left(\frac{1}{t}\right) - (1+\ln t)2t}{t^4} = \frac{-1-2\ln t}{t^4} = \frac{-1-2\ln t}{t^3}$$

$$y' = \frac{dy}{dx} = \frac{dy}{dt}\Big/\frac{dx}{dt} = t,$$

$$\frac{d^2y}{dx^2} = y'' = \frac{d}{dt}\left(\frac{dy}{dx}\right) = -\frac{2\ln t + 1}{t^3}$$

10. The solution of $\left(\frac{dy}{dx}\right)^2 + 2y\cot x\frac{dy}{dx} = y^2$ is

(a) $y - \frac{C}{1+\cos x} = 0$ (b) $y = \frac{C}{1+\cos x}$

(c) $x = 2\sin^{-1}\sqrt{C/2y}$ (d) None of these

Solution: (b, c) Solving for $\frac{dy}{dx}$, we get

$$\frac{dy}{dx} = \frac{-2y\cot x \pm \sqrt{4y^2\cot^2 x + 4y^2}}{2}$$

$= y(-\cot x \pm \text{cosec } x)$

Thus, we have $\frac{dy}{y} = (-\cot x + \text{cosec } x)dx$

(considering positive sign)

$\Rightarrow \log y = -\log\sin x + \log\tan\frac{x}{2} + \log C$

$\Rightarrow y = \frac{C\tan x/2}{\sin x} = \frac{C}{2\cos^2 x/2} = \frac{C}{1+\cos x}$

Now considering the equation with negative sign and solving $\frac{dy}{y} = -(\cot x + \text{cosec } x)dx$,

we get $y = \frac{C}{1-\cos x}$

$\Rightarrow x = 2\sin^{-1}\sqrt{C/2y}$

11. A solution of the differential equation $yx^{y-1}\,dx + x^y\,\ell nx\,dy = 0$ is

(a) $y^x = 1$ (b) $x^y - 1 = 0$

(c) $\frac{1}{y} = \log_2 x$ (d) $x = \log_2 y$

Solution: (b, c) $yx^{y-1}\,dx + xy\,\ell nx\,dy = 0$

By method of inspection, observing the complete differential we get $d(x^y) = 0$

$\Rightarrow x^y = C$

taking $C = 1$, one of the solution is $x^y - 1 = 0$

taking $C = 2$, are more solution is $x^y - 2 = 0$

or $y\ell nx = \ell n2$ $\Rightarrow$ $\frac{1}{y} = \log_2 x$

Thus, $y\,\ell nx = 0$ or $y = \ell n\,x^2$ are two particular integrals of the equation.

12. Solution of equation $x\cos x\left(\frac{dy}{dx}\right) + y(-x\sin x + \cos x) = 1$ is

(a) $xy = (x + C)\sec x$

(b) $y = \frac{x+C}{x\cos x}$

(c) $xy + \sin x + C\cos x = 0$

(d) None of these

Solution: (a, b) $\frac{dy}{dx} + y\left(\frac{-x\sin x + \cos x}{x\cos x}\right) = \frac{1}{x\cos x}$

which is a linear equation.

I.F.$= e^{\int\frac{-x\sin x + \cos x}{x\cos x}dx} = e^{\int\frac{\cos x - x\sin x}{x\cos x}dx} = e^{\ln(x\cos x)} = x\cos x$

Therefore, solution of differential equation is

$yx\cos x = \int 1dx + C$

$\Rightarrow xy\cos x = x + C \Rightarrow xy = x\sec x + C\sec x.$

13. Solution of differential equation $(2x\cos y + y^2 \cdot \cos x)dx + (2y\cdot\sin x - x^2\cdot\sin y)dy = 0$ is

(a) $x^2\cdot\cos y + y^2\cdot\sin x = C$

(b) $x\cdot\cos y - y\cdot\sin x = C$

(c) $x^2\cdot\cos^2 y + y^2\cdot\sin^2 x = C$

(d) $x\cos y + y\sin x = C$

Solution: (a) Rearranging the terms of given differential equation, we get, $2x\cos y\,dx + y^2\cos x\,dx + 2y\sin x\,dy - x^2\sin y\,dy = 0$

$\Rightarrow (2x\cos y\,dx - x^2\sin y\,dy) + (y^2\cos x\,dx + 2y\sin x\,dy) = 0$

By method of inspection, we get $d(x^2\cos y) + d(y^2\sin x) = 0$

$\Rightarrow d(x^2\cos y + y^2\sin x) = 0$

$\Rightarrow x^2\cos y + y^2\sin x = C$

14. The real value of m for which the substitution $y = u^m$ will transform the differential equation $2x^4y\frac{dy}{dx} + y^4 = 4x^6$ into a homogeneous equation is

(a) $m = 0$ (b) $m = 1$

(c) $m = 3/2$ (d) $m = 2/3$

Solution: (c) Let $y = u^m$

$\Rightarrow \frac{dy}{dx} = mu^{m-1}\frac{du}{dx}$

The given differential equation becomes

$$2x^4\cdot u^m\cdot mu^{m-1}\frac{du}{dx} + u^{4m} = 4x^6$$

$$\Rightarrow \frac{du}{dx} = \frac{4x^6 - u^{4m}}{2mx^4x^{2m-1}}$$

For homogeneous equation degree should be same in numerator and denominator
Therefore, $6 = 4m = 4 + 2m - 1 \Rightarrow m = 3/2$

15. The solution of $\frac{d^3y}{dx^3} - 8\frac{d^2y}{dx^2} = 0$ satisfying $y(0) = 1/8$, $y_1(0) = 0$ and $y_2(0) = 1$ is

(a) $y = \frac{1}{8}\left(\frac{e^{8x}}{8} - x + \frac{7}{8}\right)$

(b) $y = \frac{1}{8}\left(\frac{e^{8x}}{8} + x + \frac{7}{8}\right)$

(c) $y = \frac{1}{8}\left(\frac{e^{8x}}{8} + x - \frac{7}{8}\right)$

(d) None of these

Solution: (a) We have $\frac{y_3}{y_2} = 8 \int \frac{d(y_2)}{y_2} = \int 8\, dx$

$\Rightarrow \ell n\, y_2 = 8x + C_1$. Now since $y_2(0) = 1$, therefore
Putting $x = 0$, we have $C_1 = \log y_2(0) = \log 1 = 0$

$\therefore \log y_2 = 8x$ or $y_2 = e^{8x}$

$\Rightarrow \int dy_1 = \int e^{8x} dx$

i.e., $y_1 = \frac{e^{8x}}{8} + C_2$ $\quad (\because$ given $y_1(0) = 0)$

Substituting $x = 0$, we have $C_2 = -\frac{1}{8}$

So, $y_1 = \frac{1}{8}(e^{8x} - 1)\ \int dy = \frac{1}{8}\int (e^{8x} - 1) dx$

$\Rightarrow y = \frac{1}{8}\left(\frac{e^{8x}}{8} - x\right) + C_3$

Putting $x = 0$, we have $C_3 = \frac{1}{8} - \frac{1}{64} = \frac{7}{64}$ $\quad (y(0) = 1/8)$

Thus, $y = \frac{1}{8}\left(\frac{e^{8x}}{8} - x + \frac{7}{8}\right)$ is the required particular solution.

16. The differential equation of the family of hyperbolas with asymptotes as the line $x + y = 1$ and $x - y = 1$ is:

(a) $yy' + x = 0$ (b) $yy' = (x - 1)$
(c) $yy'' + y' = 0$ (d) $y' + xy = 0$

Solution: (b) Clearly asymptotes are perpendicular, thus family of hyperbola is rectangular ($e = \sqrt{2}$ and $a = b$)
Solving the equations of the asymptotes the centre is $x = 1$ and $y = 0$. Since $e = \sqrt{2}$, the equation of the family of the hyperbola is $\frac{(x-1)^2}{a^2} - \frac{(y)^2}{a^2} = 1$
Now differentiating w.r.t. x, we get

$\Rightarrow 2(x-1) - 2y\frac{dy}{dx} = 0$

$\Rightarrow (x - 1) = yy'$ is the required differential equation.

17. If $f(x)$ and $g(x)$ are two solutions of the differential equation $ay'' + x^2y' + y = e^x$ then $f(x) - g(x)$ is solution of

(a) $a^2y'' + y' + y = e^x$ (b) $ay'' + y = e^x$
(c) $ay'' + x^2y' + y = 0$ (d) $y'' + x^2y' + y = 0$

Solution: (c) Since $f(x)$ and $g(x)$ are solution of given differential equation

$af''(x) + x^2 f'(x) + f(x) = e^x$ ...(1)

and $ag''(x) + x^2 g'(x) + g(x) = e^x$ ...(2)

(1) – (2) given $a[f''(x) - g''(x)] + x^2 [f'(x) - g'(x)] + [f(x) - g(x)] = 0$

Thus, $f(x) - g(x)$ is solution of $dy'' + x^2y' + y = 0$

18. If $\phi(x)$ is a differentiable function then the solution of the equation $dy + [y\phi'(x) - \phi(x)\,\phi'(x)]\, dx = 0$ is

(a) $y = (\phi(x) - 1) + ce^{-\phi(x)}$
(b) $y\phi(x) = (\phi(x))^2 + c$
(c) $ye^{\phi(x)} = \phi(x)\, e^{\phi(x)} + c$
(d) $(y - \phi(x)) = \phi(x)\, e^{-\phi(x)}$

Solution: (a) Rearranging the differential equation

$\frac{dy}{dx} = -[y - \phi(x)]\phi'(x)$ ...(1)

Put $y - \phi(x) = z$

$\Rightarrow \frac{dy}{dx} - \phi'(x) = \frac{dz}{dx}$ replacing in equation (1), we get

$\phi'(x) + \frac{dz}{dx} = -z\phi'(x) \quad \Rightarrow \quad \frac{dz}{1+z} = -\phi'(x)dx$

Integrating both sides, we get

$\Rightarrow \log(1 + z) = -\phi(x) + k$

$\Rightarrow 1 + z = e^{-\phi(x) + k} \quad \Rightarrow 1 + y - \phi(x) = ce^{-\phi(x)}$

$\Rightarrow y = \phi(x) - 1 + ce^{-\phi(x)}$ in the general solution.

19. Solution of the differential equation $\left\{\frac{1}{x} - \frac{y^2}{(x-y)^2}\right\}dx + \left\{\frac{x^2}{(x-y)^2} - \frac{1}{y}\right\}dy = 0$ is

(a) $\ln\left|\frac{x}{y}\right| + \frac{xy}{x-y} = C$ (b) $\frac{xy}{x-y} = Ce^{x/y}$

(c) $\ln|xy| = C + \frac{xy}{x-y}$ (d) None of these

Solution: (a) Rearranging the terms of differential equation, we get $\left(\frac{dx}{x} - \frac{dy}{y}\right) + \left(\frac{x^2dy - y^2dx}{(x-y)^2}\right) = 0$

$\Rightarrow \left(\frac{dx}{x} - \frac{dy}{y}\right) + \frac{\left(\frac{dy}{y^2} - \frac{dx}{x^2}\right)}{\left(\frac{1}{y} - \frac{1}{x}\right)^2} = 0$

Observing the complete differentials by method of inspection

$$\Rightarrow \left(\frac{dx}{x}-\frac{dy}{y}\right)+\left[\frac{\frac{dy}{y^2}-\frac{dx}{x^2}}{\left(\frac{1}{x}-\frac{1}{y}\right)^2}\right]=0$$

$$\Rightarrow \ln|x|-\ln|y|-\frac{1}{\left(\frac{1}{x}-\frac{1}{y}\right)}=C$$

$$\Rightarrow \ln\left|\frac{x}{y}\right|+\frac{xy}{x-y}=C \text{ is the general solution.}$$

20. The equation of the curve passing through the point $\left(a,-\frac{1}{a}\right)$ and satisfying the differential equation $y-x\frac{dy}{dx}=a\left(y^2+\frac{dy}{dx}\right)$ is

(a) $(x + a)(1 + ay) = -4a^2y$
(b) $(x + a)(1 - ay) = 4a^2y$
(c) $(x + a)(1 - ay) = -4a^2y$
(d) None of these

Solution: (c) We have, $y-x\frac{dy}{dx}=a\left(y^2+\frac{dy}{dx}\right)$

$\Rightarrow y\,dx - x\,dy = ay^2\,dx + a\,dy$, converting to variable separable form, we get

$\Rightarrow y(1 - ay)\,dx = (x + a)\,dy$

$\Rightarrow \frac{dx}{x+a}-\frac{dy}{y(1-ay)}=0$ Integrating, we get

$\log(x + a) - \log y + \log(1 - ay) = \log c$

$\Rightarrow \log\frac{(a+x)(1-ay)}{y}=\log c$

$\Rightarrow (x + a)(1 - ay) = cy.$

Since the curve passes through $\left(a,-\frac{1}{a}\right)$,

$\therefore\ c = -4a^2.$

Consequently, the equation of curve is obtained as $(x + a)(1 - ay) = -4a^2y.$

21. Solution of the equation $xdy=\left(y+x\frac{f(y/x)}{f'(y/x)}\right)dx$ is

(a) $f\left(\frac{x}{y}\right)=cy$ (b) $f\left(\frac{y}{x}\right)=cx$

(c) $f\left(\frac{y}{x}\right)=cxy$ (d) None of these

Solution: (b) We have, $xdy=\left(y+x\frac{f(y/x)}{f'(y/x)}\right)dx$

$\Rightarrow \frac{dy}{dx}=\frac{y}{x}+\frac{f(y/x)}{f'(y/x)}$ which is homogeneous.

Put $y = Vx$

$\Rightarrow \frac{dy}{dx}=V+x\frac{dV}{dx}$,

Replacing in the above equation, we obtain

$$V+x\frac{dV}{dx}=V+\frac{f(V)}{f'(V)}dV$$

$\Rightarrow \frac{f'(V)}{f(V)}dV=\frac{dx}{x}$. Integrating both sides, we get

$\log(f(V)) = \log cx$

$\Rightarrow f\left(\frac{y}{x}\right)=cx.$

22. Solution of the equation $xdx+ydy+\frac{xdy-ydx}{x^2+y^2}=0$ is

(a) $y=x\tan\left(\frac{c+x^2+y^2}{2}\right)$

(b) $x=y\tan\left(\frac{c+x^2+y^2}{2}\right)$

(c) $y=x\tan\left(\frac{c-x^2-y^2}{2}\right)$

(d) None of these

Solution: (c) Given differential equation is $xdx+ydy+\frac{x\,dy-y\,dx}{x^2+y^2}=0$;

observing the complete differentials by inspection, the equation reduces to $\frac{1}{2}d(x^2+y^2)+d\tan^{-1}\left(\frac{y}{x}\right)=0$

Therefore integrating, we get

$$\frac{1}{2}(x^2+y^2)+\tan^{-1}\frac{y}{x}=\frac{c}{2}$$

$$\Rightarrow x^2+y^2+2\tan^{-1}\frac{y}{x}=c$$

$\therefore\ y=x\tan\left(\frac{c-x^2-y^2}{2}\right)$ is the required solution.

23. If the solution of the differential equation $\frac{dy}{dx}=\frac{ax+3}{2y+f}$ represents a real circle with non-zero radius, then

(a) $a = 2$ and $4f^2 - 4c + 9 > 0$
(b) $a = 2$ and $4f^2 - 4c + 9 \geq 0$
(c) $a = -2$ and $4f^2 - 4c + 9 > 0$
(d) $a = -4;\ f, c \in \mathbb{R}$

Solution: (c) We have the equation, $\frac{dy}{dx}=\frac{ax+3}{2y+f}$ which is clearly variable separable case

$\Rightarrow (ax + 3)\,dx = (2y + f)\,dy$

On integrating, we obtain $a\frac{x^2}{2}+3x=y^2+fy+c$

$\Rightarrow\ -\frac{a}{2}x^2 + y^2 - 3x + fy + c = 0$

This will represent a circle, if $-\frac{a}{2} = 1$

[∵ coefficient of x^2 = coefficient of y^2]

and $9/4 + f^2 - c > 0$

[Using $g^2 + f^2 - c > 0$]

$\Rightarrow a = -2$ and $9 + 4f^2 - 4c > 0$.

24. A solution of the differential equation $\frac{dy}{dx} = \frac{1}{xy[x^2 \sin y^2 + 1]}$ is given by

(a) $x^2(\cos y^2 - \sin y^2 - 2Ce^{-y^2}) = 2$

(b) $y^2(\cos x^2 - (\sin y^2 - 2Ce^{-y^2})) = 2$

(c) $x^2(\cos y^2 - \sin y^2 - e^{-y^2}) = 4$

(d) None of these

Solution: (a) The given differential equation can be written as $\frac{dx}{dy} = xy\,[x^2 \sin y^2 + 1]$

$\Rightarrow\ \frac{1}{x^3}\frac{dx}{dy} - \frac{1}{x^2}y = y\sin y^2$.

(since it is in reducible to linear equation)

So, putting $-1/x^2 = u$, the last equation can be written as $\frac{du}{dy} + 2uy = 2y\sin y^2$

The integrating factor of this equation is e^{y^2}.

Therefore the required solution is given by

$ue^{y^2} = \int 2y\sin y^2 . e^{y^2}\,dy + C$

$= \int (\sin t)e^t\,dt + C; (t = y^2)$

$= (1/2)e^{y^2}(\sin y^2 - \cos y^2) + C$

$\Rightarrow\ 2u = (\sin y^2 - \cos y^2) + Ce^{-y^2}$

$\Rightarrow\ 2 = x^2[\cos y^2 - \sin y^2 - 2Ce^{-y^2}]$

25. The curves satisfying the differential equation $(1 - x^2)\,y' + xy = ax$ are

(a) ellipses and hyperbolas

(b) ellipses and parabola

(c) ellipses and straight lines

(d) circles and ellipses

Solution: (a) The given equation is linear in y and can be written as $\frac{dy}{dx} + \frac{x}{1-x^2}y = \frac{ax}{1-x^2}$ (clearly a linear differential equation)

Its integrating factor is $e^{\int \frac{x}{1-x^2}dx} = e^{-(1/2)\log(1-x^2)}$

$= \frac{1}{\sqrt{1-x^2}}$ if $-1 < x < 1$

and if $x^2 > 1$, then $I.F. = \frac{1}{\sqrt{x^2-1}}$

$\frac{d}{dx}\left(y\frac{1}{\sqrt{1-x^2}}\right) = \frac{ax}{(1-x^2)^{3/2}} = -\frac{1}{2}a\frac{-2x}{(1-x^2)^{3/2}}$

$\Rightarrow\ y\frac{1}{\sqrt{1-x^2}} = \frac{a}{\sqrt{1-x^2}} + C$

$\Rightarrow\ y = a + C\sqrt{1-x^2} \quad \Rightarrow (y - a)^2 = C^2(1 - x^2)$

$\Rightarrow (y - a)^2 + C^2x^2 = C^2$

Thus, if $-1 < x < 1$, the given equation represents an ellipse. If $x^2 > 1$, then the solution is of the form $-(y - a)^2 - C^2x^2 = C^2$ which represents a hyperbola.

26. The equation of a curve passing through (0, 1) and having gradient $\frac{-(y+y^3)}{1+x+xy^2}$ at (x, y) is

(a) $xy + \tan^{-1} y = \pi/2$ (b) $xy + \tan^{-1} y = \pi/4$

(c) $xy - \tan^{-1} y = \pi/2$ (d) $xy - \tan^{-1} y = \pi/4$

Solution: (b) We have, $\frac{dy}{dx} = \frac{-(y+y^3)}{1+x(1+y^2)}$

or $\frac{dx}{dy} = -\frac{1+x(1+y^2)}{y+y^3} = -\left[\frac{1}{y(y^2+1)} + \frac{x(1+y^2)}{y(1+y^2)}\right]$

$\Rightarrow\ \frac{dx}{dy} + \frac{x}{y} = \frac{-1}{y(1+y^2)}$, which is a linear differential equation with $I.F. = e^{\int\frac{dy}{y}} = e^{\log y} = y$.

Hence, the solution is, $x.y = -\int \frac{1}{y(1+y^2)}.y\,dy + C$

$= -\int \frac{dy}{1+y^2} + C = -\tan^{-1} y + C$

or $xy + \tan^{-1} y = C$.

This passes through (0, 1), therefore, $\tan^{-1} 1 = C$ i.e., $C = \pi/4$.

Thus, the equation of the curve is

$xy + \tan^{-1} y = \pi/4$.

27. Solution of the equation $xdy - [y + xy^3(1 + \log x)]\,dx = 0$ is

(a) $\frac{-x^2}{y^2} = \frac{2x^3}{3}\left(\frac{2}{3} + \log x\right) + C$

(b) $\frac{x^2}{y^2} = \frac{2x^3}{3}\left(\frac{2}{3} + \log x\right) + C$

(c) $\frac{-x^2}{y^2} = \frac{x^3}{3}\left(\frac{2}{3} + \log x\right) + C$

(d) None of these

Solution: (a) We have,

$xdy - ydx = xy^3 (1 + \log x)\, dx$

$\Rightarrow -\left(\frac{ydx - xdy}{y^2}\right) = xy(1+\log x)dx$

Observing the complete differentials, we get

$-d\left(\frac{x}{y}\right) = xy(1+\log x)dx$

$\Rightarrow -\frac{x}{y}d\left(\frac{x}{y}\right) = x^2(1+\log x)dx$

$-\frac{\left(\frac{x}{y}\right)^2}{2} = (1+\log x)\frac{x^3}{3} - \int \frac{x^3}{3}.\frac{1}{x}dx$

$\Rightarrow -\frac{x^2}{2y^2} = \frac{x^3}{3}(1+\log x) - \frac{x^3}{9} + \frac{C}{2}$

$\Rightarrow -\frac{x^2}{y^2} = \frac{2x^3}{3}\left(\frac{2}{3}+\log x\right) + C.$

28. Find the time required for a cylindrical tank of radius 'r' and height 'H' to empty through a circular orifice of area 'a' at the bottom. The flow through the orifice is according to the law $v(t) = k\sqrt{2g\,h(t)}$; where $v(t)$ and $h(t)$ are respectively the velocity of flow through the orifice and the height of the water level above the bottom at time 't' and 'g' is the acceleration due to gravity

(a) $\frac{\pi r^2}{ak}\sqrt{\left(\frac{H}{g}\right)}$ (b) $\frac{\pi r^2}{ak}\sqrt{\left(\frac{2H}{g}\right)}$

(c) $\frac{\pi r^3}{ak}\sqrt{\left(\frac{2H}{g}\right)}$ (d) None of these

Solution: (b) Let at time t the depth of water is h and radius of water surface is r. If in time 'dt' the decrease of water level is 'dh' then

$-\pi r^2 dh = ak\sqrt{(2g\,h)}\, dt$

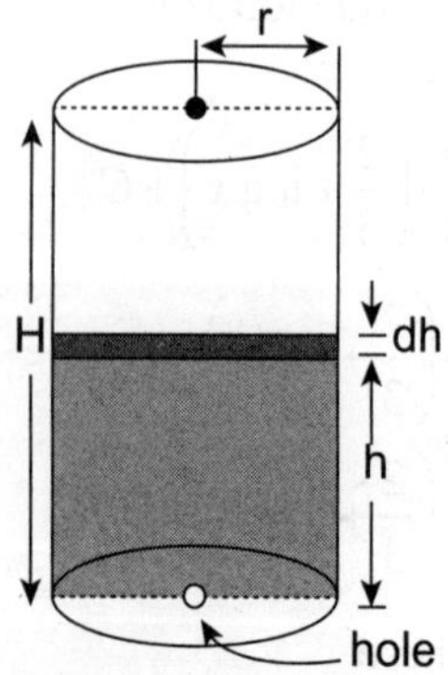

$\Rightarrow \frac{-\pi r^2}{ak\sqrt{2g}\sqrt{h}}dh = dt \Rightarrow -\frac{\pi r^2}{ak\sqrt{2g}}\frac{dh}{\sqrt{h}} = dt$

Now when $t = 0$, $h = H$ and when $t = t$, $h = 0$

$\Rightarrow \frac{-\pi r^2}{ak\sqrt{2g}}\int_H^0 \frac{dh}{\sqrt{h}} = \int_0^t dt \Rightarrow \frac{-\pi r^2}{ak\sqrt{2g}}\left\{2\sqrt{h}\right\}_H^0 = t$

$\Rightarrow t = \frac{\pi r^2 .2\sqrt{H}}{ak\sqrt{2g}} = \frac{\pi r^2}{ak}\sqrt{\left(\frac{2H}{g}\right)}.$

29. Solve $xy^2 (p^2 + 2) = 2py^3 + x^3$; where $p = \frac{dy}{dx}$

(a) $(y^2 + x^2 - c)(y^2 - x^2 - cx^4) = 0$

(b) $(y^2 - x^2 - c)(y^2 - x^2 - cx^4) = 0$

(c) $(y^2 - x^2 - c)(y^2 - x^2 + cx^4) = 0$

(d) None of these

Solution: (b) The given equation can be written as;
$(xy^2p^2 - x^3) + 2(xy^2 - py^3) = 0$

$\Rightarrow x(y^2p^2 - x^2) + 2y^2(x - py) = 0$. Factorizing and solving for p, we get

$\Rightarrow (py - x)[x(py + x) - 2y^2] = 0$

If $py - x = 0$ then $y\,dy - x\,dx = 0$

$\Rightarrow y^2 - x^2 = c_1$ whereas

If $x\,yp + x^2 - 2y^2 = 0$, then, $2y\frac{dy}{dx} - \frac{4y^2}{x} = -2x$.

Substituting $y^2 = t$ the equation reduces to linear

$\frac{dt}{dx} - \frac{4}{x}t = -2x$ with $I.F. = e^{-\int\frac{4}{x}dx} = e^{-4\ln x} = \frac{1}{x^4}$

$\therefore$ Its solution is $t\left(\frac{1}{x^4}\right) = \int -2x.\frac{1}{x^4}dx$

$\Rightarrow \frac{t}{x^4} = \frac{1}{x^2} + c_2$, i.e., $y^2 = x^2 + c_2 x^4$

Hence, the required solutions is; $(y^2 - x^2 - c)(y^2 - x^2 - cx^4) = 0$.

30. Solve the differential equation

$x\left(\frac{dy}{dx}\right)^2 - 2y\frac{dy}{dx} + ax = 0$

(a) $y^2 = 3cx + c^2$ (b) $y^2 = cx + c^2$

(c) $2y = cx^2 + a/c$ (d) None of these

Solution: (c) Let $\frac{dy}{dx} = p$

The given equation can be written as;

$y = \frac{xp}{2} + \frac{ax}{2p}$ ...(i)

Differentiating with respect to x both sides treating p as function of x, we get

$$=\frac{dy}{dx}=\frac{p}{2}+\frac{x}{2}\cdot\frac{dp}{dx}+\frac{a}{2p}-\frac{ax}{2p^2}\cdot\frac{dp}{dx}$$

$$\Rightarrow p(p^2-a)=x(p^2-a)\cdot\frac{dp}{dx}\Rightarrow\frac{dp}{dx}=\frac{p}{x}\Rightarrow p=cx.$$

(The equation $p^2 - a = 0$ gives us singular general solution in which we are not interested).

Now substituting $p = cx$ in equation (i), we get the required general solution; $2y = cx^2 + a/c$.

31. Solution of differential equation

$$\frac{dt}{dx}=\frac{t\left(\frac{d}{dx}(g(x))\right)-t^2}{g(x)} \text{ is}$$

(a) $t=\frac{g(x)}{x}+c$ (b) $t=\frac{g(x)}{x^2}+c$

(c) $t=\frac{g(x)}{x+c}$ (d) $t = g(x) + x + c$

Solution: (c) Rearranging the terms of equation,

we get $\frac{dt}{dx}-t\frac{g'(x)}{g(x)}=-\frac{t^2}{g(x)}$

$$\Rightarrow -\frac{1}{t^2}\frac{dt}{dx}+\frac{1}{t}\frac{g'(x)}{g(x)}=\frac{1}{g(x)} \quad ...(1)$$

Let $z=\frac{1}{t}$ $\Rightarrow$ $-\frac{1}{t^2}\frac{dt}{dx}=\frac{dz}{dx}$

Thus, from (i) we obtain $\frac{dz}{dx}+\frac{g'(x)}{g(x)}z=\frac{1}{g(x)}$

which is clearly linear in z and $\frac{dz}{dx}$ with

$$I.F.=e^{\int\frac{g'(x)}{g(x)}dx}=e^{\log[g(x)]}=g(x)$$

$\Rightarrow$ Thus, complete solution is

$$z\cdot g(x)=\int g(x).\frac{1}{g(x)}dx+C$$

$$\Rightarrow \frac{1}{t}g(x)=x+c \quad\Rightarrow\quad \frac{g(x)}{x+c}=t$$

32. Solution of differential equation $(1 + y^2)dx = (\tan^{-1} y - x)\, dy$ is given as

(a) $xe^{\tan^{-1}y}=e^{\tan^{-1}y}\left(\tan^{-1}y-1\right)+c$

(b) $xe^{\tan^{-1}y}=e^{\tan^{-1}y}\left(\tan^{1}y+1\right)+c$

(c) $xe^{\tan^{-1}y}=e^{\tan^{-1}y}\left(\tan^{-1}y-2\right)+c$

(d) None of These

Solution: (a) Given differential equation is

$$\frac{dy}{dx}=\frac{1+y^2}{\tan^{-1}y-x}$$

Rearranging the expression, we get a linear differential equation in x and $\frac{dx}{dy}$; $\frac{dx}{dy}=\frac{\tan^{-1}y}{1+y^2}-\frac{x}{1+y^2}$

$$\Rightarrow \frac{dx}{dy}+\frac{1}{1+y^2}x=\frac{\tan^{-1}y}{1+y^2}$$

Now, $I.F.=e^{\int\frac{1}{1+y^2}dy}=e^{\tan^{-1}y}$

Therefore, general solution is given by,

$$xe^{\tan^{-1}y}=\int e^{\tan-1\,y}\,\frac{\tan^{-1}y}{1+y^2}\,dy+c$$

$= \int te^t\,dt + c$ (here $t - \tan^{-1}y$) $= te^t - e^t + c$

$$=(\tan^{-1}y)\,e^{\tan^{-1}y}-e^{\tan^{-1}y}+c$$

$$\Rightarrow xe^{\tan^{-1}y}=e^{\tan^{-1}y}\left(\tan^{-1}y-1\right)+c$$

is the required general solution

33. Solution of differential equation

$$\frac{dz}{dx}+\frac{z}{x}\log z=\frac{z}{x^2}(\log z)^2 \text{ is}$$

(a) $\frac{x}{\log z}=\frac{1}{2}+Cx^2$ (b) $\frac{x}{\log z}=\frac{1}{2}-Cx^2$

(c) $\frac{x}{\log z}=\frac{1}{3}+Cx^2$ (d) None of These

Solution: (a) Dividing the complete equation by $z(\log z)^2$ the transformed equation obtained is $\frac{1}{z(\log z)^2}\frac{dz}{dx}+\frac{1}{x\log z}=\frac{1}{x^2}$; Now substituting

$$\frac{1}{\log z}=y \Rightarrow -\frac{1}{z(\log z)^2}\frac{dz}{dx}=\frac{dy}{dx} \quad ...(i)$$

Then (i) reduced to linear differential equation as below $-\frac{dy}{dx}+\frac{1}{x}y=\frac{1}{x^2}$

$$\Rightarrow \frac{dy}{dx}-\frac{1}{x}y=-\frac{1}{x^2} \text{ and } I.F.=e^{-\int\frac{1}{x}dx}=\frac{1}{x}$$

Its solution is given by $\frac{y}{x}=-\int\frac{1}{x^3}dx+C$

$$\Rightarrow \frac{y}{x}=\frac{1}{2x^2}+C \quad\Rightarrow\quad \frac{y}{x}=\frac{1}{2x^2}+C$$

$$\Rightarrow \frac{x}{\log z}=\frac{1}{2}+Cx^2 \text{ is the required general solution.}$$

34. Solution of $\frac{xdy}{x^2+y^2}=\left(\frac{y}{x^2+y^2}-1\right)dx$ is

(a) $x-\tan^{-1}\frac{y}{x}$ (b) $\tan^{-1}\frac{y}{x}=c$

(c) $x\tan^{-1}\frac{y}{x}=c$ (d) None of these

Solution: (d)

$$\frac{dy}{dx}=\left(\frac{y}{x^2+y^2}-1\right)\left(\frac{x^2+y^2}{x}\right)=\left(\frac{y}{x}-\frac{x^2+y^2}{x}\right)$$

Substituting $y = vx$ and $\frac{dy}{dx}=v+x\cdot\frac{dv}{dx}$ in the above equation, we have $v+x\cdot\frac{dv}{dx}=\left(v-\frac{x^2+v^2x^2}{x}\right)$

$\Rightarrow v+x\cdot\frac{dv}{dx}=v-x\left(1+v^2\right)$ which reduces to variable seperable form as:

$\frac{dv}{1+v^2}=-dx$, integrating both sides is

$\Rightarrow \int\frac{dv}{1+v^2}=-\int dx+c \quad \Rightarrow \tan^{-1}v=-x+c$

$\Rightarrow \tan^{-1}\left(\frac{y}{x}\right)=-x+c$ is desired complete primitive.

35. The length of latus rectum of the conic passing through the origin and having the property that normal at each point (x, y) intersects the x-axis at $((x + 1), 0)$ is:

(a) 1 (b) 2

(c) 4 (d) None of these

Solution: (b) Let $P(x, y)$ be any point on the conic.

$\therefore$ slope of normal $= -\frac{dx}{dy}$

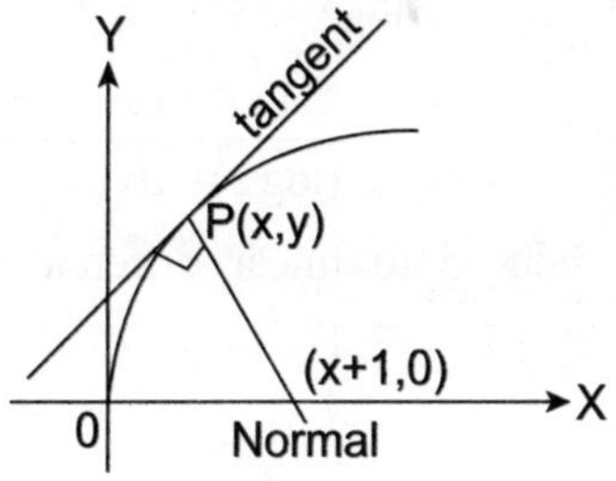

Equation of normal to conic at $P(x, y)$ is

$(Y-y)=-\frac{dx}{dy}(X-x)$ on x-axis $Y = 0$

$\Rightarrow -y=-\frac{dx}{dy}(X-x)$

$\Rightarrow X=x+y\frac{dx}{dy}$

Given $X=y\frac{dy}{dx}+x=x+1 \quad \Rightarrow ydy = dx$

$\Rightarrow \frac{y^2}{2}=x+C \quad \ldots$(i)

Since the conic passes through origin, $x = 0$, $y = 0$ in (i), we get $C = 0$

$\therefore$ From (i) $y^2 = 2x$

Which is parabola having length of latus rectum $= 4a = 2$ units.

36. The slope of the tangent to a curve $y = f(x)$ at $(x, f(x))$ is $2x + 1$. If the curve passes through the point (1, 2), then the area of the region bounded by the curve, the x-axis and the line $x = 1$ is

(a) $\frac{5}{6}$ (b) $\frac{6}{5}$

(c) $\frac{1}{6}$ (d) 6

Solution: (a) Given slope of tangent to curve at arbitrary point $(x, f(x)) = 2x + 1$

$\Rightarrow f'(x) = 2x + 1$; integrating both sides, we get

$\Rightarrow f(x)=x^2+x+C$ passes through (1, 2)

$\Rightarrow 2 = 1 + 1 + C \quad \Rightarrow C = 0$

$\Rightarrow f(x)=x^2+x$; graphically shown below:

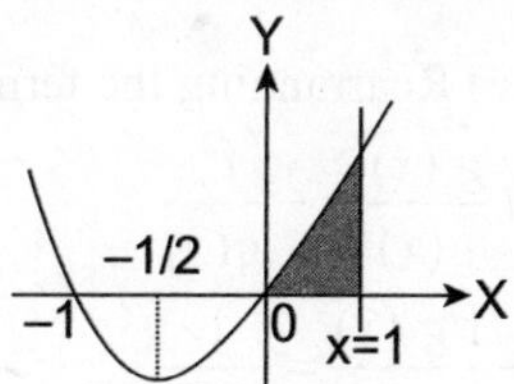

$\therefore$ Required area $=\int_0^1\left(x^2+x\right)dx=\left.\frac{x^3}{3}+\frac{x^2}{2}\right|_0^1$

$=\frac{1}{3}+\frac{1}{2}=\frac{5}{6}$ square units

37. The area bounded by $y = f(x)$, x-axis and the line $y = 1$; where $f(x)=1+\frac{1}{x}\int_1^x f(t)dt$ is

(a) $2(e + 1)$ (b) $2\left(1-\frac{1}{e}\right)$

(c) $2(e - 1)$ (d) None of these

Solution: (b) Given $xf(x)=x+\int_1^x f(t)dt$

on differentiating both sides, we get

$f(x) + xf'(x) = 1 + f(x) \Rightarrow f(x) = \ln|x| + C$

Now, $f(1) = 1$ (from the given equation $f(x)=1+\frac{1}{x}\int_1^x f(t)dt$)

$\Rightarrow C = 1 \quad \Rightarrow f(x) = \ln|x| + 1$

$\therefore$ Required area $=2\int_0^1 e^{y-1}dy=2\left(1-\frac{1}{e}\right)$

SECTION–II

SUBJECTIVE-TYPE SOLVED EXAMPLES

1. Solve the differential equation $\frac{dy}{dx}=\frac{y^2-x}{2y(x+1)}$

Solution: Given differential equation is

$$\frac{dy}{dx}=\frac{y^2-x}{2y(x+1)} \Rightarrow 2y\frac{dy}{dx}-\frac{y^2}{x+1}=-\frac{x}{x+1} \quad \text{...(i)}$$

Substituting $y^2 = v$ and $2y\frac{dy}{dx}=\frac{dv}{dx}$ in (i),

we have $\frac{dv}{dx}+\left(\frac{-1}{x+1}\right)v=-\frac{x}{x+1}$,

which becomes a linear differential equation,

having $I.F. = e^{-\int\frac{1}{x+1}dx}=\frac{1}{x+1}$

∴ Solution of differential equation is given by

$$v.\frac{1}{x+1}=-\int\frac{1}{x+1}\frac{x}{x+1}dx+c$$

$$\Rightarrow y^2.\frac{1}{x+1}=-\int\frac{x+1-1}{(x+1)^2}dx+c$$

$$\Rightarrow y^2.\frac{1}{x+1}=-\ln(x+1)-\frac{1}{(x+1)}+\ln C$$

$$\Rightarrow y^2=(x+1)\ln\left(\frac{C}{x+1}\right)-1$$

2. Solve the differential equation $(1 - xy + x^2y^2) dx = x^2 dy$

Solution: Given differential equation is

$(1 - xy + x^2y^2)\, dx = x^2\, dy$ ...(i)

$\Rightarrow (1 - (xy) + (xy)^2)dx = x^2\, dy$

Substituting $xy = v$

$$\Rightarrow y=\frac{v}{x} \text{ and } \frac{dy}{dx}=\frac{\left(x\frac{dv}{dx}-v\right)}{x^2}$$

i.e., $x^2dy = xdv - v\,dx$ in (i), we have

$(1 - v + v^2)\, dx = xdv - vdx$

$$\Rightarrow (1 + v^2)dx = xdv \Rightarrow \int\frac{dv}{1+v^2}=\int\frac{dx}{x}$$

$\Rightarrow \tan^{-1}v = \ln|x| + \ln C$

$\Rightarrow \tan^{-1} v = \ln |Cx| \quad \Rightarrow v = \tan \ln |Cx|$

$$\Rightarrow xy = \tan \ln |Cx| \quad \Rightarrow y=\frac{1}{x}\tan(\ln|Cx|)$$

3. Solve the differential equation $\frac{dy}{dx}=\frac{2(y+2)^2}{(x+y-1)^2}$

Solution: Given differential equation is

$$\frac{dy}{dx}=\frac{2(y+2)^2}{(x+y-1)^2} \quad \text{...(i)}$$

Putting $y + 2 = 0 \quad \Rightarrow y = -2$

and $x + y - 1 = 0 \quad \Rightarrow x - 2 - 1 = 0$

$\Rightarrow x = 3$; Putting $y = -2 + v$ and $\frac{dy}{dv}=1$; $x = 3 + u$

and $\frac{dx}{du}=1$ Now, $\frac{dy}{dx}=\frac{dy}{dv}\times\frac{du}{dx}\times\frac{dv}{du}=(1)(1)\left(\frac{dv}{du}\right)$

∴ $\frac{dy}{dx}=\frac{dv}{du}$; Thus, from equation (i), we get

$$\frac{dv}{du}=\frac{2(-2+v+2)^2}{(3+u-2+v-1)^2} \Rightarrow \frac{dv}{du}=\frac{2\times v^2}{(u+v)^2} \quad \text{...(ii)}$$

Putting $v = ut$ and $\frac{dv}{du}=t+\frac{udt}{du}$ in (ii)

we have $t+\frac{udt}{du}=\frac{2u^2t^2}{(u+ut)^2}=\frac{2t^2}{(1+t)^2}$

$$\Rightarrow \frac{udt}{du}=\frac{2t^2}{(1+t)^2}-t \Rightarrow \frac{udt}{du}=\frac{2t^2-t(t^2+2t+1)}{(1+t)^2}$$

$$\Rightarrow \int\frac{(1+t)^2}{t(2t-t^2-2t-1)}dt=\int\frac{du}{u}$$

$$\Rightarrow -\int\frac{(t+1)^2}{t(t^2+1)}dt=\int\frac{du}{u} \quad \text{...(iii)}$$

Let $\frac{(t+1)^2}{t(t^2+1)}=\frac{A}{t}+\frac{Bt+C}{(t^2+1)}$ and solving by partial fraction, we get $A = 1, B = 0, C = 2$

$$\therefore \frac{(t+1)^2}{t(t^2+1)}=\frac{1}{t}+\frac{2}{(t^2+1)}$$

∴ From equation (iii); $\int\frac{1}{t}+\frac{2}{(t^2+1)}dt=-\int\frac{du}{u}$

$\Rightarrow (\ln t + 2\tan^{-1} t) = -\ln u + \ln C$

$\Rightarrow \ln ut + 2\tan^{-1} t = \ln C$

$$\Rightarrow \log(ute^{2\tan^{-1}t})=\ln C \Rightarrow ute^{2\tan^{-1}t}=C$$

$$\Rightarrow vte^{2\tan^{-1}t}=C \Rightarrow ve^{2\tan^{-1}\left(\frac{v}{u}\right)}=C$$

$$\Rightarrow (y+2)e^{2\tan^{-1}\left(\frac{y+2}{x-3}\right)}=C \Rightarrow (y+2)=Ce^{-2\tan^{-1}\left(\frac{y+2}{x-3}\right)}$$

$$\Rightarrow (y+2)=Ce^{-2\tan^{-1}\left(\frac{y+2}{x-3}\right)} \Rightarrow e^{-2\tan^{-1}\left(\frac{y+2}{x-3}\right)}=c'(y+2)$$

4. Solve the differential equation
$$\frac{dy}{dx}+\frac{\cos x(3\cos y-7\sin x-3)}{\sin y(3\sin x-7\cos y+7)}=0$$

Solution: $\frac{dy}{dx}=-\frac{\cos x[3(\cos y-1)-7\sin x]}{\sin y[3\sin x-7\cos y+7]}=0$ ...(i)

Putting $\cos y - 1 = Y$; $\sin x = X$

and $-\sin y\, dy = dY$; $\cos x\, dx = dX$, in (i), we get

$$\frac{dY}{dX}=\frac{3Y-7X}{3X-7Y} \quad ...(ii)$$

Putting $Y = vX$ and $\frac{dY}{dX}=v+X\frac{dv}{dX}$ in (ii), we get

$$v+X\frac{dv}{dX}=\frac{3v-7}{3-7v}$$

$$\Rightarrow X\frac{dv}{dX}=\frac{3v-7}{3-7v}-v=\frac{3v-7-3v+7v^2}{3-7v}=\frac{7(v^2-1)}{3-7v}$$

$$\Rightarrow \frac{(3-7v)}{7(v^2-1)}dv=\frac{dX}{X}$$

$$\Rightarrow \frac{3}{7}\int\frac{dv}{(v^2-1)}-\int\frac{v}{v^2-1}dv=\int\frac{dX}{X}$$

$$\Rightarrow \frac{3}{7}\times\frac{1}{2}\ln\left|\frac{v-1}{v+1}\right|-\frac{1}{2}\ln\left|v^2-1\right|=\ln X+\ln C_1$$

$$\Rightarrow \frac{3}{14}\ln\left|\frac{v-1}{v+1}\right|-\frac{1}{2}\ln\left|v^2-1\right|=\ln C_1X$$

$$\Rightarrow \ln\left|\frac{v-1}{v+1}\right|^{3/14}.\left|v^2-1\right|^{-1/2}=\ln C_1X$$

$$\Rightarrow \left|\frac{v-1}{v+1}\right|^{3/14}.\frac{1}{\left|v^2-1\right|^{1/2}}=C_1X$$

$$\Rightarrow \frac{|v-1|^{\frac{3}{14}-\frac{1}{2}}}{|v+1|^{\frac{3}{14}+\frac{1}{2}}}=C_1X \Rightarrow \frac{|v-1|^{-\frac{2}{7}}}{|v+1|^{\frac{5}{7}}}=C_1X$$

$$\Rightarrow 1=C_1X|v+1|^{\frac{5}{7}}.|v-1|^{\frac{2}{7}}$$

$$\Rightarrow 1=C_1X\left|\frac{Y}{X}+1\right|^{\frac{5}{7}}.\left|\frac{Y}{X}-1\right|^{\frac{2}{7}}$$

$$\Rightarrow 1=C_1|Y+X|^{\frac{5}{7}}.|Y-X|^{\frac{2}{7}}$$

$$\Rightarrow 1=C_1|\cos y-1+\sin x|^{\frac{5}{7}}.|\cos y-1-\sin x|^{\frac{2}{7}}$$

$$\Rightarrow (\cos y+\sin x-1)^5(\cos y-\sin x-1)^2=C$$

5. Solve the differential equation $\frac{dy}{dx}-y\ln 2=2^{\sin x}$. $(\cos x - 1)\, \ell n2$, y being bounded when $x \to +\infty$.

Solution: Given differential equation is

$$\frac{dy}{dx}-y\ln 2=2^{\sin x}\cdot(\cos x-1)\,\ell n2 \quad ...(i)$$

Which is linear differential equation with I.F. $=e^{\int -\ell n 2 dx}=e^{-(\ln 2)x}=2^{-x}$

Multiplying (i) with 2^{-x} we have

$$2^{-x}\frac{dy}{dx}-y.2^{-x}\ln 2=2^{-x}\cdot 2^{\sin x}(\cos x-1)\ell n2$$

$$\Rightarrow \frac{d}{dx}(y.2^{-x})=2^{\sin x-x}(\cos x-1)\ln 2$$

$$\Rightarrow d(y.2^{-x})=2^{\sin x-x}(\cos x-1)\,\ell n2\,dx$$

$$\Rightarrow \int d(y.2^{-x})=\ln 2\int 2^{\sin x-x}.(\cos x-1)\,dx$$

$$\Rightarrow y.2^{-x}=\ln 2\frac{2^{\sin x-x}}{\ln 2}+c \Rightarrow y=2^{\sin x}+c2^x$$

Now, we are given $\lim_{x\to\infty} y$ = finite (it's possible only when $c = 0$)

$\therefore$ $y = 2^{\sin x}$ will be the solution of given differential equation.

6. Solve the differential equation $3x^2y^2 + \cos(xy) - xy\sin(xy) + \frac{dy}{dx}\{2x^3y - x^2\sin(xy)\} = 0$.

Solution: Given differential equation $3x^2y^2 + \cos(xy) - xy\sin(xy) + \frac{dy}{dx}\{2x^3y - x^2\sin(xy)\} = 0$

Let $xy = t$ $\Rightarrow x\frac{dy}{dx}+y=\frac{dt}{dx}$

$\Rightarrow y\log_e x + x\log_e y = c$

$\therefore$ $3x^2y^2 + \cos(xy) - xy\sin(xy) + x^2\frac{dy}{dx}(2xy - \sin(xy)) = 0$

$$\Rightarrow 3t^2+\cos t-t\sin t+x^2\left(\frac{1}{x}\frac{dt}{dx}-\frac{t}{x^2}\right)(2t-\sin t)=0$$

$$\Rightarrow 3t^2+\cos t-t\sin t+\left(x\frac{dt}{dx}-t\right)(2t-\sin t)=0$$

$$\Rightarrow x\frac{dt}{dx}-t+\frac{t^2+\cos t+2t^2-t\sin t}{2t-\sin t}=0$$

$$\Rightarrow x\frac{dt}{dx}-t+\frac{t^2+\cos t}{2t-\sin t}+t=0$$

$$\Rightarrow x\frac{dt}{dx}+\frac{t^2+\cos t}{2t-\sin t}=0 \Rightarrow \int\frac{(2t-\sin t)}{t^2+\cos t}dt+\int\frac{dx}{x}=0$$

$\Rightarrow \ell n(t^2 + \cos t) + \ell n x = k \Rightarrow x(t^2 + \cos t) = k$

$\Rightarrow x(x^2y^2 + \cos(xy)) = k$; $k \in \mathbb{R}$ is required solution.

7. Show that the differential equation $y^3dy + (x + y^2)dx = 0$ can be reduced to a homogenous equation. Hence, solve it.

Solution: Put $x = X$, $y^2 = Y$. Then $dx = dX$, $2y\,dy = dY$

$\therefore$ $2y\frac{dy}{dx}=\frac{dY}{dX}$. Using this in the given equation,

we get $y^3\frac{dy}{dx}+x+y^2=0$; or $\frac{1}{2}Y\frac{dY}{dX}+X+Y=0$

which is a homogenous equation. So, in order to solve the equation put $Y = vx$ or $y^2 = vx$; and hence, $2y\frac{dy}{dx} = v + x\frac{dv}{dx}$.

$\therefore$ The equation becomes $y^3 \frac{dy}{dx} + x + y^2 = 0$

$$\text{or}\quad y^2 \cdot \frac{1}{2}\left(v + x\frac{dv}{dx}\right) + (x + y^2) = 0$$

$$\text{or}\quad vx \cdot \frac{1}{2}\left(v + x\frac{dv}{dx}\right) + x + vx = 0$$

$$\text{or}\quad \frac{v}{2}\left(v + x\frac{dv}{dx}\right) + 1 + v = 0$$

$$\Rightarrow 1 + v + \frac{v^2}{2} + \frac{vx}{2}\frac{dv}{dx} = 0$$

$$\Rightarrow \frac{dx}{x} + \frac{vdv}{2\left(1 + v + \frac{v^2}{2}\right)} = 0$$

$$\Rightarrow \frac{dx}{x} + \frac{vdv}{v^2 + 2v + 2} = 0$$

$$\Rightarrow \int\frac{dx}{x} + \frac{1}{2}\int\frac{(2v+2) - 2}{v^2 + 2v + 2}dv = 0$$

$$\Rightarrow \ln x + \frac{1}{2}\int\frac{2v + 2}{v^2 + 2v + 2}dv - \int\frac{dv}{(v+1)^2 + 1} = 0$$

$$\Rightarrow \ln x + \frac{1}{2}\ln(v^2 + 2v + 2) - \tan^{-1}(v+1) = C$$

$$\Rightarrow \ln x + \frac{1}{2}\ln\left(\frac{y^4}{x^2} + 2\frac{y^2}{x} + 2\right) - \tan^{-1}\left(\frac{y^2}{x} + 1\right) = C$$

$$\Rightarrow \frac{1}{2}\ln(y^4 + 2y^2x + 2x^2) - \tan^{-1}\frac{y^2 + x}{x} = C$$

8. Solve $\left[\frac{1}{x} - \frac{y^2}{(x-y)^2}\right]dx + \left[\frac{x^2}{(x-y)^2} - \frac{1}{y}\right]dy = 0$

Solution:

Given $\left[\frac{1}{x} - \frac{y^2}{(x-y)^2}\right]dx + \left[\frac{x^2}{(x-y)^2} - \frac{1}{y}\right]dy = 0$

$$\Rightarrow \frac{dx}{x} - \frac{dy}{y} + \frac{x^2\,dy - y^2\,dx}{(x-y)^2} = 0$$

$$\Rightarrow \frac{dx}{x} - \frac{dy}{y} + \frac{x^2\,dy - y^2\,dx}{x^2y^2\left(\frac{1}{y} - \frac{1}{x}\right)^2} = 0$$

$$\Rightarrow \frac{dx}{x} - \frac{dy}{y} + \frac{\frac{dy}{y^2} - \frac{dx}{x^2}}{\left(\frac{1}{y} - \frac{1}{x}\right)^2} = 0$$

$$\Rightarrow \frac{dx}{x} - \frac{dy}{y} + d\left[\frac{1}{\left(\frac{1}{y} - \frac{1}{y}\right)}\right] = 0$$

$$\Rightarrow \ln|x| - \ln|y| + \left[\frac{xy}{x-y}\right] = C$$

9. Solve the differential equation

$$2y\frac{dy}{dx} = e^{\frac{x^2+y^2}{x}} + \frac{x^2 + y^2}{x} - 2x$$

Solution: Substituting $x^2 + y^2 = z$, and hence, $\frac{dz}{dx} = 2x + 2y\frac{dy}{dx}$, we get $\frac{dz}{dx} = e^{z/x} + \frac{z}{x}$, which is a homogeneous equation.

So, let $z = t\,x$, and hence, $\frac{dz}{dx} = t + x\frac{dt}{dx}$

$$\Rightarrow t + x\frac{dt}{dx} = e^t + t \quad \Rightarrow \frac{dt}{e^t} = \frac{dx}{x}$$

$$\Rightarrow -e^{-t} = \ln|x| + c \quad \Rightarrow -e^{-\frac{x^2+y^2}{x}} = \ln|x| + C$$

$$\Rightarrow \ln|cx| = -e^{-\frac{x^2+y^2}{x}}$$

10. Obtain the differential equation associated with the primitive $y = C_1e^{3x} + C_2e^{2x} + C_3e^x$.

Solution: Given equation is $y = C_1e^{3x} + C_2e^{2x} + C_3e^x$

$$\Rightarrow \frac{dy}{dx} = 3C_1e^{3x} + 2C_2e^{2x} + C_3e^x$$

$$\Rightarrow \frac{d\,y}{dx} = 9C_1e^{3x} + 4C_2e^{2x} + C_3e^x$$

$$\Rightarrow \frac{d^3y}{dx^3} = 27C_1e^{3x} + 8C_2e^{2x} + C_3e^x$$

To eliminate the constant finding C_1, C_2, C_3 from first three and putting to forth using determinant method, determinant can be written in following form (known as eliminante)

$$\begin{vmatrix} e^{3x} & e^{2x} & e^x & y \\ 3e^{3x} & 2e^{2x} & e^x & y' \\ 9e^{3x} & 4e^{2x} & e^x & y'' \\ 27e^{3x} & 8e^{2x} & e^x & y''' \end{vmatrix} = e^{6x}\begin{vmatrix} 1 & 1 & 1 & y \\ 3 & 2 & 1 & y' \\ 9 & 4 & 1 & y'' \\ 27 & 8 & 1 & y''' \end{vmatrix} = 0$$

$\therefore\ e^{6x} > 0 \Rightarrow (-2y''' + 12y'' - 22y' + 12y) = 0$

$\Rightarrow \frac{d^3y}{dx^3} - 6\frac{d^2y}{dx^2} + 11\frac{dy}{dx} - 6y = 0$ is the required differential equation.

11. Solve the differential equation $(x \cos y - y \sin y)\, dy + (x \sin y + y \cos y)\, dx = 0$.

Solution: Put $x \sin y + y \cos y = t$

$\Rightarrow (x\cos y - y\sin y)\frac{dy}{dx} + \sin y + \cos y\frac{dy}{dx} = \frac{dt}{dx}$ ...(i)

$\Rightarrow \frac{dt}{dx} - \left(\sin y + \cos y\frac{dy}{dx}\right) + t = 0$

(from (i) and given differential equation)

Substituting $\sin y = z$

$\Rightarrow \cos y\frac{dy}{dx} = \frac{dz}{dx} \quad \Rightarrow \quad \frac{dt}{dx} - \frac{dz}{dx} + t - z = 0$

$\Rightarrow d(t - z) = -(t - z)dx$

$\Rightarrow \int \frac{d(t-z)}{t-z} = -\int dx \quad \Rightarrow \quad \ln(t - z) = -x + C$

$\Rightarrow \ln(x \sin y + y \cos y - \sin y) = -x + C$

$\Rightarrow e^x (x \sin y + y \cos y - \sin y) = C$

12. Make the substitution $x = r \cos \theta$ and $y = r\sin \theta$ to convert the differential equation $(x^2 + y^2 + y)\, dx = xdy$ into a linear differential equation with θ as independent and r as a dependent variable and solve it. Verify the solution by the substitution $y = tx$.

Solution: Given differential equation is $(x^2 + y^2)\, dx = xdy - ydx$; Put $x = r \cos \theta$; $y = r \sin \theta$

$\Rightarrow \tan\theta = \frac{y}{x} \quad \Rightarrow \quad r^2[-r \sin\theta\, d\theta + \cos\theta\, dr] = r^2 d\theta$

$\Rightarrow \frac{dr}{d\theta} - r\tan\theta = \sec\theta$

Which is linear differential equation in r and θ having I.F. $= e^{-\int \tan\theta\, d\theta} = \cos\theta$

The solution is given by $r\cos\theta = \int d\theta = \theta + C$

$\Rightarrow x = \tan^{-1}\frac{y}{x} + C \quad \Rightarrow \quad \tan^{-1}\frac{y}{x} = x - C$

$\Rightarrow \frac{y}{x} = \tan(x - C) \quad \Rightarrow y = x \tan(x + C_1)$ ...(i)

Now, for $y = tx$; $\frac{dy}{dx} = t + x\frac{dt}{dx}$; then given differential equation becomes

$\Rightarrow (x^2 + t^2x^2 + tx) = x\left[t + x\frac{dt}{dx}\right] = tx + x^2\frac{dt}{dx}$

$\Rightarrow \frac{dt}{dx} = 1 + t^2$

$\Rightarrow \tan^{-1}t = x + C$

$\Rightarrow \tan^{-1}\left(\frac{y}{x}\right) = x + C$

$\Rightarrow y = x \tan(x + C)$; which is same as (i)

13. Solve the differential equation, $(2y + xy^3)\, dx + (x + x^2y^2)\, dy = 0$.

Solution: $(2y\, dx + x\, dy) + (xy^3\, dx + x^2y^2\, dy) = 0$

Multiplying by x, we get $(2xy\, dx + x^2\, dy) + x^2y^2(y\, dx + x\, dy) = 0$

$\Rightarrow d(x^2y) + x^2y^2\, d(xy) = C$

$\Rightarrow d(x^2y) + t^2\, dt = C$; where $xy = t$

$\Rightarrow x^2y + \frac{t^3}{3} = C \quad \Rightarrow \quad x^2y + \frac{x^3y^3}{3} = C$

Alternative Method: Taking $xy = t$, and hence,

$x\frac{dy}{dx} + y = \frac{dt}{dx}$

We get $\left(2\frac{t}{x} + t\,.\frac{t^2}{x^2}\right) + \frac{1}{x}(x + t^2)\left(\frac{dt}{dx} - y\right) = 0$

$\Rightarrow \frac{2t}{x} + \frac{t^3}{x^2} + \frac{dt}{dx} - \frac{t}{x} + \frac{t^2}{x}\frac{dt}{dx} - \frac{t^3}{x^2} = 0$

$\Rightarrow \frac{t}{x} + \frac{dt}{dx}\left(\frac{t^2}{x} + 1\right) = 0 \quad \Rightarrow \quad (t^2 + x)\frac{dt}{dx} + t = 0$

$\Rightarrow \frac{dt}{dx} = \frac{-t}{t^2 + x} \quad \Rightarrow \quad \frac{dx}{dt} = \frac{t^2 + x}{-t}$

$\Rightarrow \frac{dx}{dt} + \frac{x}{t} = -t$, which is linear in x and t having

I.F. $= e^{\int \frac{1}{t}dx} = t$

$\therefore$ Its solution is given by $xt = \int(-t)t\,dt + C$

$\Rightarrow xt = -\frac{t^3}{3} + C$; where $t = xy$.

14. Find the equation of the curve passing through (1, 2) whose differential equation is $y(x + y^3)\, dx = x(y^3 - x)\, dy$.

Solution: Here, $(xy + y^4)\, dx = (xy^3 - x^2)dy$

$\Rightarrow y^3(dyx - xdy) + x(ydx + xdy) = 0$

$\Rightarrow -x^2y^3.\frac{xdy - ydx}{x^2} + xd(xy) = 0$

$\Rightarrow -\frac{y}{x}d\left(\frac{y}{x}\right) + \frac{d(xy)}{x^2y^2} = 0$ (dividing by x^3y^2)

$\Rightarrow -\int\frac{y}{x}d\left(\frac{y}{x}\right) + \int\frac{d(xy)}{(xy)^2} = C$

$\Rightarrow -\frac{\left(\frac{y}{x}\right)^2}{2} + \frac{(xy)^{-1}}{-1} = C \quad \Rightarrow \quad \frac{1}{2}.\frac{y^2}{x^2} + \frac{1}{xy} + C = 0$

$\Rightarrow\ y^3 + 2x + 2cx^2y = 0$

It passes through (1, 2), so, $2^3 + 2 + 2c.2 = 0$

$\Rightarrow\ c = \frac{-10}{4} = \frac{-5}{2}$

$\therefore$ The curve is $y^3 + 2x - 5x^2y = 0$

15. Find the one-to-one, twice differentiable solutions to the equation $\frac{d^2y}{dx^2} + \frac{d^2x}{dy^2} = 0$

Solution: $\frac{d^2x}{dy^2} = \frac{d}{dy}\left(\frac{dx}{dy}\right) = \frac{d}{dy}\left(\frac{1}{\frac{dy}{dx}}\right)$

$= \frac{d}{dx}\left[\left(\frac{dy}{dx}\right)^{-1}\right].\frac{dx}{dy} = -\left(\frac{dy}{dx}\right)^{-2}.\frac{d^2y}{dx^2}\left(\frac{dx}{dy}\right)$

$= -\left(\frac{dx}{dy}\right)^3.\frac{d^2y}{dx^2} \quad \therefore \quad \frac{d^2y}{dx^2} + \frac{d^2x}{dy^2} = 0$

$\Rightarrow\ \frac{d^2y}{dx^2} - \left(\frac{dx}{dy}\right)^3\frac{d^2y}{dx^2} = 0 \Rightarrow \frac{d^2y}{dx^2}\left\{1 - \left(\frac{dx}{dy}\right)^3\right\} = 0$

$\Rightarrow$ Either $\frac{d^2y}{dx^2} = 0$ or $\left(\frac{dx}{dy}\right)^3 = 1$, i.e., $\left(\frac{dy}{dx}\right)^3 = 1$

$\Rightarrow\ y = ax + b$ or $\frac{dy}{dx} = 1 \quad \Rightarrow \quad y = x + c$

$\therefore$ The solution is $y = ax + b$; $a \neq 0$, i.e., all non-constant linear functions

16. Find the integral curve of the differential equation, $x(1 - x\ln y).\frac{dy}{dx} + y = 0$ which passes through $\left(1, \frac{1}{e}\right)$.

Solution: Given differential equation is $x(1 - x\ln y)\frac{dy}{dx} + y = 0$

$\Rightarrow\ \frac{dy}{dx}(x - x^2\ln y) + y = 0 \Rightarrow x - x^2\ln y + \frac{dx}{dy}y = 0$

$\Rightarrow\ y\frac{dx}{dy} + x = x^2\ln y \qquad \ldots(i)$

Putting $xy = t$ and $y\frac{dx}{dy} + x = \frac{dt}{dy}$ in (i),

we get $\frac{dt}{dy} = \frac{t^2}{y^2}\ell n\, y \quad \Rightarrow \quad \int\frac{dt}{t^2} = \int\frac{\ell n y}{y^2}dy \quad \ldots(ii)$

Now, consider $I = \int\frac{\ell n\, y}{y^2}dy$ and put $u = \ell n y$

$\Rightarrow\ du = \frac{dy}{y} \qquad \Rightarrow\ I = \int\frac{u}{e^u}du$

$= \int ue^{-u}du = \frac{ue^{-u}}{-1} + \int e^{-u}du = -ue^{-u} - e^{-u} \qquad \ldots(iii)$

$\therefore$ From (ii) and (iii), we have

$-\frac{1}{t} = -e^{-\ln y}(\ln y + 1) = -\frac{1}{y}(\ln y + 1)$

$\Rightarrow\ -\frac{1}{t} = -\frac{1}{y}(\ln y + 1) + k_1 \Rightarrow -\frac{1}{xy} = -\frac{1}{y}(\ln y + 1) + k_1$

$\Rightarrow\ \frac{1}{x} = (\ln y + 1) + k_1 \qquad \ldots(iv)$

$\Rightarrow$ Above curve passes through $(1, 1/e)$ (given)

$1 = (\ln e^{-1} + 1) + k_1 \Rightarrow k_1 = 1$

$\therefore$ (iv) Becomes $\frac{1}{x} = (\ln y + 1) + 1$

$\Rightarrow\ (2 + \ln y)x = 1$

17. Let the function $\ell n\, f(x)$ is defined where $f(x)$ exists for $x \geq 2$ and k is fixed positive real number, prove that if $\frac{d(xf(x))}{dx} \leq -k\, f(x)$, then $f(x) \leq A\, x^{-1-k}$; where A is independent of x.

Solution: Given $\frac{d}{dx}(xf(x)) \leq -kf(x)$

$\Rightarrow\ x\frac{d}{dx}f(x) + f(x) \leq -kf(x)$

$\Rightarrow\ x\frac{dy}{dx} + y(1 + k) \leq 0$

($\because$ $\ln f(x) \Rightarrow f(x) = y > 0$ and $x \geq 0$)

$\Rightarrow\ \frac{dy}{y} \leq -\frac{(1+k)}{x}dx$, on integrating, we have ln

$\ln y \leq -(1 + k)\ln x + C$

$\Rightarrow\ y \leq A\, x^{-1-k}$; where $A = e^c$

18. Let f: $[0, \infty) \to \mathbb{R}$ be a twice differentiable function satisfying $f(0) \geq 0$ and $f'(x) > f(x)$ for all $x > 0$. Prove that $f(x) > 0$ for all $x > 0$

Solution: Given $f'(x) - f(x) > 0$

Multiplying by the integrating factor e^{-x} on both sides, we get

$\Rightarrow\ e^{-x}f'(x) - e^{-x}f(x) > 0$

$\Rightarrow\ \frac{d}{dx}\{e^{-x}f(x)\} > 0$

$\Rightarrow\ e^{-x}f(x)$ is strictly increasing on $[0, \infty)$

$\Rightarrow$ For $x > 0$, we have $e^{-x}f(x) > e^{-0}f(x)$

$\Rightarrow\ e^{-x}f(x) > f(0) \geq 0$ ($\because$ $f(0) \geq 0$)

$\Rightarrow\ e^{-x}f(x) > 0\ \forall\ x \in (0, \infty)$

$\Rightarrow\ f(x) > 0\ \forall\ x > 0$

19. An uncommon mistake is to believe that the product rule for derivatives, say that $(f.g)' = f'g'$. If $f(x) = e^{x^2}$, determine whether there exists an open interval (a, b) and a non-zero function f defined on (a, b) such that this wrong product rule is true for f and g on (a, b).

Solution: We are required to determine a function f such that $f'.g + f.g' = f'.g'$

$\Rightarrow f(x) = e^{x^2}$ has non-trivial solutions

Now, $f'.g + f.g' = f'.g'$

$$\Rightarrow 2xe^{x^2}.g + e^{x^2}.g' = 2xe^{x^2}.g'$$

$$\Rightarrow g'(1-2x) = -2x.g$$

$$\Rightarrow \frac{g'}{g} = \frac{2x}{2x-1} = 1 + \frac{1}{(2x-1)}$$

Integrating, we get $\ln g(x) = x + \frac{1}{2}\ln|2x-1| + C$

$\Rightarrow g(x) = Ae^x\sqrt{|2x-1|}$, $A \in \mathbb{R}$ and it is defined on any interval which does not contain 1/2.

20. Let f and g be differentiable functions on the real line satisfying the equation $(f^2 + g^2).f' + (fg).g' = 0$. Prove that f has minima.

Solution: Multiplying by f, we get

$$(f^3 + g^2f).f' + (f^2g).g' = 0$$

$$\Rightarrow f^3f' + g^2ff' + f^2gg' = 0$$

$$\Rightarrow \frac{d}{dx}\left\{\frac{1}{4}f^4\right\} + \frac{1}{2}\frac{d}{dx}\{f^2g^2\} = 0$$

$$\Rightarrow f^4 + 2f^2g^2 = c$$

The equation being an even degree polynomial in f and coefficient of f^4 being positive proves that f would attain minimum value.

21. Find the equation of the curve passing through the origin if the middle point of the segment of its normal from any point of the curve to the x-axis lies on the parabola $2y^2 = x$.

Solution: Equation of normal to curve at point $P(x_1, y_1)$ is $y - y_1 = \frac{-1}{\left(\frac{dy}{dx}\right)_{(x_1,y_1)}}(x - x_1)$ and it intersect x-axis, where $y = 0$

i.e., where $x = y_1\left(\frac{dy}{dx}\right)_{(x_1,y_1)} + x_1$

$$\Rightarrow Q\left(\frac{dy}{dx}.y_1 + x_1, 0\right)$$

$\because$ Middle point (R) of segment PQ, lies on curve $2y^2 = x$

$$\Rightarrow R \equiv \left(\frac{x_1 + \left(\frac{dy}{dx}\right)_{(x_1+y_1)} y_1 + x_1}{2}, \frac{y_1}{2}\right)$$ lies on curve

$2y^2 = x$

$$\Rightarrow 2\left(\frac{y_1}{2}\right)^2 = \frac{2x_1 + \left(\frac{dy}{dx}\right)_{(x_1,y_1)} y_1}{2}$$

$$\Rightarrow y_1^2 = 2x_1 + \left(\frac{dy}{dx}\right)_{(x_1,y_1)} y_1$$

$$\Rightarrow \left(\frac{dy}{dx}\right)_{(x_1,y_1)}.y_1 = y_1^2 - 2x_1 \Rightarrow \frac{dy}{dx}_{(x_1,y_1)}.y_1 = y_1^2 - 2x_1$$

$$\Rightarrow \left(\frac{dy}{dx}\right)y = y^2 - 2x \qquad \text{...(i)}$$

(replacing (x_1, y_1) by (x, y))

Substituting $y^2 = t \Rightarrow 2y\frac{dy}{dx} = \frac{dt}{dx}$

$$\Rightarrow y\frac{dy}{dx} = \frac{1}{2}\frac{dt}{dx} \qquad \text{...(ii)}$$

$\therefore$ From (i) and (ii) we have $\frac{1}{2}\frac{dt}{dx} = t - 2x$

$\Rightarrow \frac{dt}{dx} - 2t + 4x = 0$; which is a linear differential equation with I.F. $= e^{\int -2dx} = e^{-2x}$

$\therefore$ The solution of differential equation is given by

$$t.e^{-2x} = \int(-4x)e^{-2x}dx + C$$

$$\Rightarrow t.e^{-2x} = -4\left[\frac{x.e^{-2x}}{-2} - \int\frac{1.e^{-2x}}{-2}dx\right]$$

$\Rightarrow 2xe^{-2x} + e^{-2x} + C \Rightarrow y^2 = 2x + 1 + Ce^{2x}$

$\therefore$ The curve passes through origin (0, 0)

$\Rightarrow C = -1$

$\therefore$ $y^2 = 2x - e^{2x} + 1$ is the required equation of curve.

22. A perpendicular drawn from any point P of the curve on the x-axis meets the x-axis at A. Length of the perpendicular from A on the tangent line at P is equal to 'a'. If this curve cuts the y-axis orthogonally, find the equation to all possible curves, expressing the answer explicitly.

Solution: Let $P(x_1, y_1)$ be a point on the given curve and PA and AQ are perpendicular drawn from P on x-axis and from A on the tangent at P, as shown below:

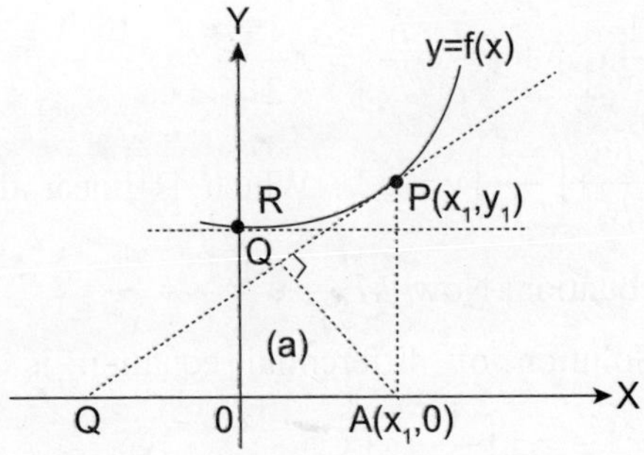

Equation of tangent at point $P(x_1, y_1)$ is

$$y - y_1 = \left.\frac{dy}{dx}\right|_{(x_1,y_1)} (x - x_1)$$

$\Rightarrow y - y_1 = f'(x_1)(x - x_1)$; Now, $AQ = a$ (given)

$$\Rightarrow \frac{|f'(x_1)(x_1 - x_1) - 0 + y_1|}{\sqrt{(f'(x_1))^2 + 1}} = a$$

$$\Rightarrow y_1 = a\sqrt{(f'(x_1))^2 + 1} \Rightarrow y_1^2 = a^2\left[\left(\frac{dy}{dx}\right)^2 + 1\right]$$

On generalizing, we have $\frac{y^2}{a^2} = \left(\frac{dy}{dx}\right)^2 + 1$

$$\Rightarrow \frac{dy}{dx} = \pm\sqrt{\frac{y^2 - a^2}{a^2}} \quad \Rightarrow \int \frac{a\,dy}{\sqrt{y^2 - a^2}} = \pm\int dx$$

$$\Rightarrow a \ln(y + \sqrt{y^2 - a^2}) = \pm x$$

$$\Rightarrow y + \sqrt{y^2 - a^2} = e^{\pm x/a} \quad \Rightarrow y - e^{\pm x/a} = -\sqrt{y^2 - a^2}$$

$$\Rightarrow y^2 - 2e^{\pm x/a}y + e^{\pm 2x/a} = y^2 - a^2$$

$$\Rightarrow 2e^{\pm x/a}y = e^{\pm 2x/a} + a^2 \quad \Rightarrow y = \frac{e^{\pm x/a} + a^2 e^{\mp x/a}}{2}$$

Considering tangent at point R

$y = \pm a$ ($\because$ since distance from origin is a)

$$\Rightarrow y = \pm a, x = 0 \quad \Rightarrow \pm a = \frac{1 + a^2}{2}$$

$$\Rightarrow a^2 + 1 = \pm 2a \Rightarrow (a \pm 1)^2 = 0 \Rightarrow a = \pm 1$$

$\therefore$ Equation of curve will be $y = e^x + e^{-x} = \cos bx$

23. Show that the equation of the curve intersecting with the x-axis at the point $x = 1$ and for which the length of the subnormal at any point of the curve is equal to the arithmetic mean of the co-ordinates of this point is $(y - x)^2 (x + 2y) = 1$.

Solution: Length of subnormal at any point $P(x, y)$ on the curve $y = f(x)$ is given by $y\frac{dy}{dx}$. It is given that the length of subnormal is equal to the mean of coordinates of P.

$$\Rightarrow y\frac{dy}{dx} = \frac{x + y}{2}$$

$\Rightarrow \frac{dy}{dx} = \frac{x + y}{2y}$, which is a homogeneous differential equation

$\therefore$ put $y = vx$ and $\frac{dy}{dx} = v + x\frac{dv}{dx}$

$$\Rightarrow v + x\frac{dv}{dx} = \frac{1 + v}{2v} \quad \Rightarrow x\frac{dv}{dx} = \frac{1 + v - 2v^2}{2v}$$

$$\Rightarrow \frac{2v}{2v^2 - v - 1}dv = -\frac{dx}{x}$$

$$\Rightarrow \int \frac{2v\,dv}{2v^2 - 2v + v - 1} = -\ln x + \ln c$$

$$\Rightarrow \int \frac{2v}{(2v + 1)(v - 1)}dv = \ln\left(\frac{c}{x}\right)$$

$$\Rightarrow \int\left(\frac{2}{3(2v + 1)} + \frac{2}{3(v - 1)}\right)dv = \ln\left(\frac{c}{x}\right)$$

$$\Rightarrow \frac{2}{3}\frac{\ln(2v + 1)}{2} + \frac{2}{3}\ln(v - 1) = \ln\frac{c}{x}$$

$$\Rightarrow \ln\{(2v + 1)^{1/3}(v - 1)^{2/3}\} = \ln\frac{c}{x}$$

$$\Rightarrow (2v + 1)^{1/3}(v - 1)^{2/3} = \frac{c}{x} \Rightarrow (2v + 1)(v - 1)^2 = \frac{c^3}{x^3}$$

$$\Rightarrow \left(\frac{2y + x}{x}\right)\left(\frac{(y - x)^2}{x^2}\right) = \frac{C}{x^3}$$

$$\Rightarrow (y - x)^2 (x + 2y) = C$$

It passes through the point $(1, 0) \Rightarrow C = 1$

$\Rightarrow (y - x)^2 (x + 2y) = 1$ is the required curve.

24. A curve passing through $(1, 0)$ such that the ratio of the square of the intercept cut by any tangent off the y-axis to the subnormal is equal to the ratio of the product of the co-ordinates of the point of tangency to the product of square of the slope of the tangent and the subtangent at the same point. Determine all such possible curves.

Solution: Equation of tangent at point $P(x_1, y_1)$ is

$y - y_1 = \left.\frac{dy}{dx}\right|_{(x_1,y_1)} (x - x_1)$, it meets y–axis.

Where $x = 0$, i.e., where $y = y_1 - x_1\left(\frac{dy}{dx}\right)_{(x_1,y_1)}$

i.e., at $Q\left(0, y_1 - x_1\left(\frac{dy}{dx}\right)_{(x_1,y_1)}\right)$

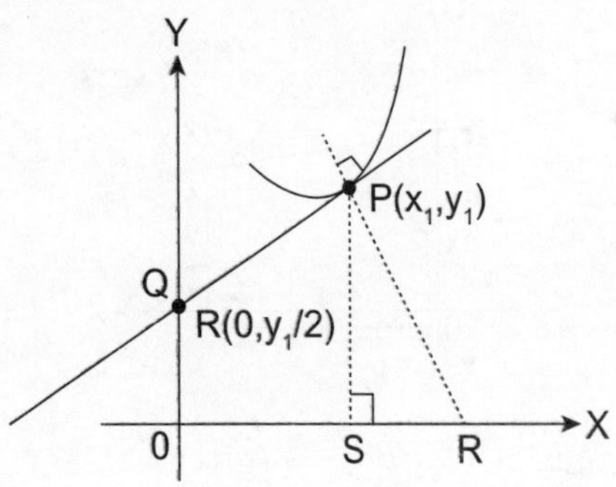

Let the normal at point P meets x-axis at R then,

SR = length of sub normal = $y\left(\frac{dy}{dx}\right)_{(x_1,y_1)}$

TS = sub tangent = $\frac{y_1}{\left(\frac{dy}{dx}\right)_{(x_1,y_1)}} = \frac{y_1}{f'(x_1)}$

Now, according to question

$$\frac{\left(y_1 - x_1\frac{dy}{dx}\right)^2}{y_1\frac{dy}{dx}} = \frac{x_1y_1}{[f'(x_1)]^2 \cdot \frac{y_1}{f'(x_1)}}$$

On generalizing, $\frac{(y-x\,f'(x))^2}{y\,f'(x)} = \frac{x.f'(x)}{(f'(x_1))^2} = \frac{x}{f'(x)}$

$\Rightarrow (y-x\,f'(x))^2 = xy \Rightarrow y - xf'(x) = \pm\sqrt{xy}$

$\Rightarrow x\frac{dy}{dx} - y = \pm\sqrt{xy} \Rightarrow \frac{xdy - ydx}{dx} = \pm\sqrt{xy}$

$\Rightarrow \frac{xdy - ydx}{y^2} = \pm\sqrt{xy}\frac{dx}{y^2}$

$\Rightarrow d\left(\frac{x}{y}\right) = \pm\sqrt{\frac{x}{y}}.\frac{dx}{y} = \pm\sqrt{\frac{x}{y}}.\frac{x}{y}\frac{dx}{x}$

$\Rightarrow \int\frac{d\left(\frac{x}{y}\right)}{\left(\frac{x}{y}\right)^{3/2}} = \pm\int\frac{dx}{x} \Rightarrow \frac{\left(\frac{x}{y}\right)^{1-3/2}}{1-\frac{3}{2}} = \pm\ln x$

$\Rightarrow \left(\frac{y}{x}\right)^{1/2} = \pm\frac{1}{2}\ell n\,x \Rightarrow \ln x = \pm 2\left(\frac{y}{x}\right)^{1/2}$

$\therefore\ x = e^{\pm 2(y/x)^{1/2}}$

25. Find the curve such that the area of the trapezium formed by the co-ordinate axes, ordinate of an arbitrary point and the tangent at this point equals half the square of its abscissa.

Solution: Let $P(x, y)$ be any arbitrary point on the curve $y = f(x)$, such that tangent at P intersects y-axis at B and let the ordinate at P has foot at point A on x-axis as shown below:

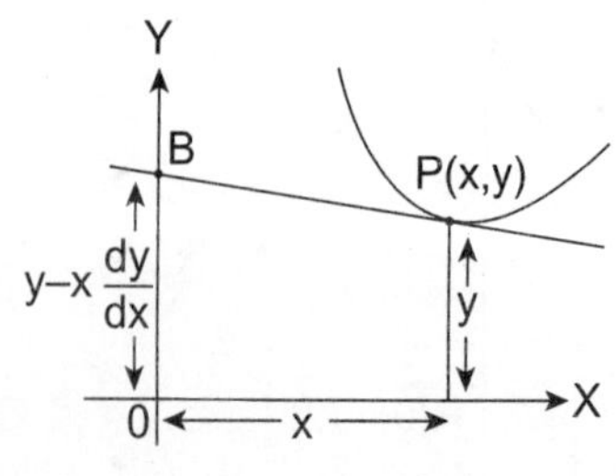

Now, area of $OAPB = \frac{x^2}{2}$ (given)

$\Rightarrow \frac{1}{2}x\left[y + y - x\frac{dy}{dx}\right] = \pm\frac{1}{2}x^2$

$\Rightarrow \frac{dy}{dx} + \left(\frac{-2}{x}\right)y = \pm 1$, Which is linear differential equation; Now, $I.F. = e^{-\int\frac{2}{x}dx} = \frac{1}{x^2}$

$\therefore$ Solution of differential equation is given by

$y.\frac{1}{x^2} = \pm\int\frac{1}{x^2}dx + C$

$\Rightarrow \frac{y}{x^2} = \pm\frac{1}{x} + C \qquad \Rightarrow y = Cx^2 \pm x$

26. The perpendicular length from the origin to the tangent at any point on a curve is equal to the abscissa of the point of contact. Find the equation of the curve satisfying the above condition and passesing through (1, 1).

Solution: Let $P(x, y)$ be any point on the curve $y = f(x)$.

Then the equation of tangent to curve at $P(x, y)$ is given by $(Y - y) = \frac{dy}{dx}(X - x)$ ...(i)

$\therefore$ Length of tangent drawn from origin to tangent (i)

will be $(p) = \frac{\left|0 - y + x\frac{dy}{dx}\right|}{\sqrt{(1)^2 + \left(\frac{dy}{dx}\right)^2}} = x$ (Given)

$\Rightarrow \left(x\frac{dy}{dx} - y\right)^2 = x^2\left(1 + \left(\frac{dy}{dx}\right)^2\right)$

$\Rightarrow x^2\left(\frac{dy}{dx}\right)^2 + y^2 - 2xy\frac{dy}{dx} = x^2 + x^2\left(\frac{dy}{dx}\right)^2$

$\Rightarrow \frac{y^2 - x^2}{2xy} = \frac{dy}{dx}$ ...(ii)

Equation (ii) is a homogeneous differential equation.

Thus, put $y = vx$ in (ii) and $\frac{dy}{dx} = v + x\frac{dv}{dx}$

$\Rightarrow v + x\frac{dv}{dx} = \frac{v^2 - 1}{2v}$

$\Rightarrow x\frac{dv}{dx} = \frac{v^2 - 1 - 2v^2}{2v} = -\left(\frac{1 + v^2}{2v}\right)$

$\Rightarrow \int\frac{2v}{v^2 + 1}dv = -\int\frac{dx}{x} \Rightarrow \ell n(v^2 + 1) = -\ell nx + \ell nc$

$\Rightarrow v^2 + 1 = \frac{c}{x} \qquad \Rightarrow \frac{y^2 + x^2}{x^2} = \frac{c}{x}$

$\Rightarrow y^2 + x^2 = cx$; It passes through (1, 1) (given)

$\Rightarrow c = 2$

$\Rightarrow x^2 + y^2 - 2x = 0$ is the required equation of curve.

27. Show that the curve such that the distance between the origin and the tangent at an arbitrary points is equal to the distance between the origin and the normal at the same point is $\sqrt{x^2+y^2} = ce^{\pm\tan^{-1}\frac{y}{x}}$

Solution: Let $P(x_1, y_1)$ be an arbitrary point on the curve $y = f(x)$

$\therefore$ Equation of tangent at (x_1, y_1) is $\frac{y-y_1}{x-x_1} = \left.\frac{dy}{dx}\right|_{(x_1,y_1)}$

$$\Rightarrow y - y_1 = x\left(\frac{dy}{dx}\right)_{(x_1,y_1)} - x_1\left(\frac{dy}{dx}\right)_{(x_1,y_1)}$$

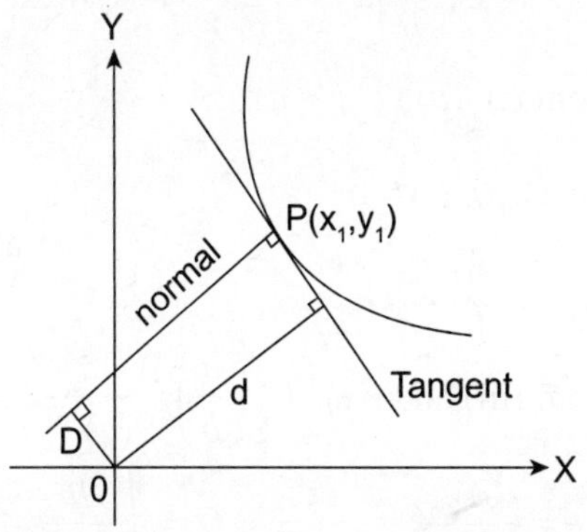

$$\text{Distance from origin} = d = \frac{\left|y_1 - x_1\left(\frac{dy}{dx}\right)_{(x_1,y_1)}\right|}{\sqrt{\left(\frac{dy}{dx}\right)^2_{(x_1,y_1)}+1}}$$

Equation of normal at (x_1, y_1) is

$$y - y_1 = \frac{(-1)}{\left(\frac{dy}{dx}\right)_{(x_1,y_1)}}(x - x_1)$$

$$\Rightarrow -x - y\left(\frac{dy}{dx}\right)_{(x_1,y_1)} + y_1\left(\frac{dy}{dx}\right)_{(x_1,y_1)} + x_1 = 0$$

$$\text{Distance from origin} = D = \frac{\left|y_1\left(\frac{dy}{dx}\right)_{(x_1,y_1)} + x_1\right|}{\sqrt{1+\left(\frac{dy}{dx}\right)^2_{(x_1,y_1)}}}$$

Now given $d = D$

$$\Rightarrow \frac{\left|y_1 - x_1\left(\frac{dy}{dx}\right)_{x_1,y_1}\right|}{\sqrt{1+\left(\frac{dy}{dx}\right)^2_{(x_1,y_1)}}} = \frac{\left|y_1\left(\frac{dy}{dx}\right)_{(x_1,y_1)} + x_1\right|}{\sqrt{1+\left(\frac{dy}{dx}\right)^2_{(x_1,y_1)}}}$$

$$\Rightarrow \left(y_1 - x_1\left(\frac{dy}{dx}\right)_{(x_1,y_1)}\right) = \pm\left(y_1\left(\frac{dy}{dx}\right)_{(x_1,y_1)} + x_1\right)$$

Renewing (x_1, y_1) by (x, y), we have

$$y - x\left(\frac{dy}{dx}\right) = \pm\left(y\left(\frac{dy}{dx}\right) + x\right)$$

$$y - x\frac{dy}{dx} = \pm y\frac{dy}{dx} \pm x$$

Case I: Taking +ve sign, we have

$$y - x\frac{dy}{dx} = +y\frac{dy}{dx} + x$$

$$\Rightarrow y - x = \frac{dy}{dx}(y+x) \Rightarrow \frac{dy}{dx} = \frac{y-x}{y+x} \quad \text{...(i)}$$

Substituting $y = xv$ and $\frac{dy}{dx} = x\frac{dv}{dx} + v$ in (i),

we get $v + x\frac{dv}{dx} = \frac{v-1}{v+1} \Rightarrow x\frac{dv}{dx} = \frac{v-1-v^2-v}{(v+1)}$

$$\Rightarrow x\frac{dv}{dx} = -\frac{(v^2+1)}{(v+1)} \Rightarrow \int\frac{v+1}{v^2+1}dv = -\int\frac{dx}{x}$$

$$\Rightarrow \int\left\{\frac{1}{2}\left(\frac{2v}{v^2+1}\right) + \frac{1}{v^2+1}\right\}dv = -\log x$$

$$\Rightarrow \frac{1}{2}\ln(v^2+1) + \tan^{-1}v = -\ln|x| + \ln C$$

$$\Rightarrow \ln\sqrt{v^2+1} + \tan^{-1}v = \ln\left(\frac{C}{|x|}\right)$$

$$\Rightarrow \ln\sqrt{v^2+1} + \ln e^{\tan^{-1}v} = \ln\left(\frac{C}{|x|}\right)$$

$$\Rightarrow \sqrt{v^2+1}.e^{\tan^{-1}v} = \left(\frac{C}{|x|}\right) \Rightarrow |x|\sqrt{v^2+1}.e^{\tan^{-1}v} = C$$

$$\Rightarrow \frac{|x|\sqrt{y^2+x^2}}{|x|}.e^{\tan^{-1}v} = C \Rightarrow \sqrt{y^2+x^2}.e^{\tan^{-1}v} = C$$

$$\Rightarrow \sqrt{y^2+x^2} = C.e^{-\tan^{-1}(y/x)} = C \quad \text{........(ii)}$$

Case II: Taking –ve sign, we have

$$y - x\frac{dy}{dx} = -y\frac{dy}{dx} - x$$

$$\Rightarrow (y-x)\frac{dy}{dx} = -(x+y) \Rightarrow \frac{dy}{dx} = -\frac{(x+y)}{(y-x)} \quad \text{..(iii)}$$

Putting $y = vx$ and $\frac{dy}{dx} = v + x\frac{dv}{dx}$ in (iii),

we have $v + x\frac{dv}{dx} = -\frac{(1+v)}{(v-1)}$

$$\Rightarrow \frac{xdv}{dx} = \frac{-1-v-v^2+v}{(v-1)} \Rightarrow \int\frac{v-1}{v^2+1}dv = -\int\frac{dx}{x}$$

$\Rightarrow \frac{1}{2}\ln(v^2+1)-\tan^{-1}v=-\ln|x|+\ln C$

$\Rightarrow |x|.\sqrt{v^2+1}\,e^{-\tan^{-1}v}=C$

$\Rightarrow \sqrt{x^2+y^2}=Ce^{\tan^{-1}(y/x)}$ ...(iv)

Combining (iii) and (iv), we have $\sqrt{x^2+y^2}=Ce^{\pm\tan^{-1}(y/x)}$ is the equation of required curve.

28. Find the differentiable function which satisfies the equation $f(x)=-\int_0^x f(t)\tan t\,dt+\int_0^x \tan(t-x)dt$; where $x\in(-\pi/2,\pi/2)$

Solution: Given differential equation is $f(x)=-\int_0^x f(t)\tan t dt+\int_0^x \tan(t-x)\,dt$ +

Differentiating w.r.t. x, we have

$f'(x)=-f(x)\tan x-\int_0^x \sec^2(t-x)dt$

$=-f(x)\tan x-[\tan(t-x)]_0^x$

$\Rightarrow \frac{dy}{dx}=-(\tan x)y-\tan x$

$\Rightarrow \frac{dy}{dx}+(\tan x)y=-\tan x$

Which is a linear differential equation having I.F. $=e^{\int\tan x\,dx}=e^{\ln\sec x}=\sec x$

$\therefore$ Solution of given differential equation is given by $y.\sec x=-\int\sec x\tan x+C$

$\Rightarrow y\sec x=-\sec x+C$

$\Rightarrow y=C\cos x-1$ is the general solution.

29. Find the differentiable function $f(0,\infty)\to(0,\infty)$ for which there is a positive number 'a' such that $f'\left(\frac{a}{x}\right)=\frac{x}{f(x)}$ for all $x>0$.

Solution: Let $g(x)=f(x).f\left(\frac{a}{x}\right)$

where $f(x)f'\left(\frac{a}{x}\right)=x$ ...(i)

Replacing x by a/x in the given condition, we have

$f\left(\frac{a}{x}\right)f'(x)=\frac{a}{x}$ ...(ii)

Now $g'(x)=f'(x)f\left(\frac{a}{x}\right)+f(x)f'\left(\frac{a}{x}\right)\left(-\frac{a}{x^2}\right)$

$=f'(x)f\left(\frac{a}{x}\right)-\frac{a}{x^2}f'\left(\frac{a}{x}\right).f(x)$

$=f'(x)f\left(\frac{a}{x}\right)-\frac{a}{x^2}.x$ ($\because$ by (i))

$=\frac{a}{x}-\frac{a}{x}$ (By (ii)) $=0$

$\Rightarrow g(x)=b$ (Constant) $\Rightarrow f(x)f\left(\frac{a}{x}\right)=b$

$\Rightarrow f(x).\frac{a}{x}\frac{1}{f'(x)}=b \Rightarrow \frac{f'(x)}{f(x)}=\frac{a}{bx}$

Integrating both sides, we get

$\ln f(x)=\frac{a}{b}\ln x+\ln C=\ln C.x^{\frac{a}{b}}$

$\Rightarrow f(x)=Cx^{\frac{a}{b}}$ for all $x>0$

$\Rightarrow f'(x)=C.\left(\frac{a}{b}\right)x^{\frac{a}{b}-1} \Rightarrow f'(1)=C.\left(\frac{a}{b}\right)$ ...(iii)

From (i) $f(a).f'(1)=a$

$\Rightarrow C.(a)^{\frac{a}{b}}.f'(1)=a$

$\Rightarrow f'(1)=a^{\left(1-\frac{a}{b}\right)}/C$ ...(iv)

$\therefore$ From (iii) and (iv); $C^2\left(\frac{a}{b}\right)=\frac{a}{(a)^{a/b}}$

$\Rightarrow \frac{C^2}{b}=\frac{1}{(a)^{a/b}} \Rightarrow C=\sqrt{\frac{b}{(a)^{a/b}}}$

$\therefore$ By eliminating C, we get the family of solutions as $f(x)=\sqrt{b}\left(\frac{x}{\sqrt{a}}\right)^{a/b}$; where $b>0$.

30. Solve the integral equation $\frac{dy}{dx}=y+\int_0^1 y\,dx$; given $y=1$, where $x=0$

Solution: Given differential equation is

$\frac{dy}{dx}=y+\int_0^1 ydx$ ...(i)

$\Rightarrow \frac{dy}{dx}=y+k_1$; where $k_1=\int_0^1 y\,dx$

$\Rightarrow \int\frac{dy}{y+k_1}=\int dx$

$\Rightarrow \ell n(y+k_1)=x+c$

$\Rightarrow y+k_1=k_2e^x=k_2=e^C$. ...(ii)

Now, it is given, $y=1$ for $x=0$

$\Rightarrow 1+k_1=k_2$ ...(iii)

Putting the value of y (from equation (ii) in equation (i)), we have

$$\frac{dy}{dx}=(k_2e^x-k_1)+\int_0^1(k_2e^x-k_1)dx$$

$$\Rightarrow \frac{dy}{dx}=(k_2e^x-k_1)+[k_2e^x-k_1x]_0^1$$

$$\Rightarrow \frac{dy}{dx}=k_2e^x-k_1+k_2e-k_1-k_2$$

$\Rightarrow dy = (k_2e^x + k_2e - 2k_1 - k_2)dx$

$$\Rightarrow \int_1^y dy=\int_0^x(k_2e^x+k_2e-2k_1-k_2)dx$$

$$\Rightarrow y-1=[k_2e^x+(k_2e-2k_1-k_2)x]_0^x$$

$\Rightarrow y - 1 = k_2e^x + (k_2 e - 2k_1 - k_2)x - k_2$ ...(iv)

Since equation (ii) and (iv) are similar

$\therefore$ $k_2e - 2k_1 - k_2 = 0$ and $1 - k_2 = - k_1$

$\Rightarrow k_2e - k_2 = 2k_1$ ...(v)

Solving equation (iii) and (v), we get

$$k_2=\frac{2}{3-e},\ k_1=\frac{e-1}{3-e}$$

$\therefore$ From equation (ii), $y + k_1 = k_2e^x$

$$\Rightarrow y=\frac{2}{3-e}e^x-\frac{e-1}{3-e}$$

$$\therefore\ y=\frac{1}{3-e}(2e^x-e+1)$$

31. Find the continuous function which satisfies the relation, $\int_0^x tf(x-t)dt=\int_0^x f(t)dt$ + sin x + cos x – x – 1, for all real number x.

Solution: Given equation is $\int_0^x t\,f(x-t)dt$

$$=\int_0^x f(t)dt+\sin x+\cos x-x-1$$

Apply Leibnitz's rule of differentiation, we have

$$\int_0^x tf'(x-t)dt + xf(x-x) = f(x) + \cos x - \sin x - 1$$

$$\Rightarrow \int_0^x t\,f'(x-t)dt+xf(0) = f(x) + \cos x - \sin x - 1$$

$$\left[\begin{aligned}&\because \int t\,f'(x-t)dt\\&=t\int f'(x-t)dt-\int\left(\frac{dt}{dt}\int f'(x-t)\right)\\&=t\,f(x-t)-\int f(x-t)dt\end{aligned}\right]$$

$$\Rightarrow [t\,f(x-t)]_0^x-\int_0^x f(x-t)\,dt+xf(0)$$

$= f(x) + \cos x - \sin x - 1$

$$\Rightarrow xf(0)-\int_0^x f(x-t)\,dt+xf(0)$$

$= f(x) + \cos x - \sin x - 1$

$$\Rightarrow 2xf(0)-\int_0^x f(x-t)\,dt = f(x) + \cos x - \sin x - 1$$

Again applying Leibnitz rule.

$\Rightarrow 2f(0) - f(0) = f'(x) - \sin x - \cos x$

$$\Rightarrow \frac{dy}{dx}=\sin x+\cos x+f(0)$$

$\Rightarrow y = -\cos x + \sin x + f(0)\cdot x$

$\Rightarrow f(x) = \sin x - \cos x + kx$; where $k = f(0)$.

32. Find all continuous functions $f:\mathbb{R}\to\mathbb{R}$ satisfying the equation $f(x)=\lambda(1+x^2)\left[1+\int_0^x\frac{f(t)}{1+t^2}dt\right]$ for all $x\in\mathbb{R}$, where λ is a fixed given real number

Solution: Because f is continuous, the right hand side of the functional equation is a differentiable function; and f itself is differentiable. Now,

$$\frac{f(x)}{1+x^2}=\lambda\left[1+\int_0^x\frac{f(t)}{1+t^2}dt\right]$$

Differentiating w.r.t. x, we get

$$\frac{f'(x)(1+x^2)-f(x)(2x)}{(1+x^2)^2}=\frac{\lambda f(x)}{1+x^2}$$

$$\Rightarrow \frac{f'(x)}{1+x^2}=f(x)\left[\frac{2x}{(1+x^2)^2}+\frac{\lambda}{1+x^2}\right]$$

$$\Rightarrow \frac{f'(x)}{f(x)}=\lambda+\frac{2x}{1+x^2}$$

Integrating, we get $\ln f(x) = \lambda x + \ln(1+x^2) + C$

Hence, $f(x) = A(1+x^2)e^{\lambda x}$.

Substituting in original equation, we get $A = \lambda$

$\therefore$ $f(x) = \lambda(1+x^2)\cdot e^{\lambda x}$.

33. Let $u(x)$ and $v(x)$ satisfy the differential equations $\frac{dy}{dx}+p(x)y=f(x)$ and $\frac{dy}{dx}+p(x)y=g(x)$ respectively; where $p(x)$, $f(x)$ and $g(x)$ are continuous functions. If $u(x_1) > v(x_1)$ for some x_1 and $f(x) > g(x)$ for all $x > x_1$. Prove that any point (x, y); where $x > x_1$, does not satisfy the equations $y = u(x)$ and $y = v(x)$.

Solution: Here, $\frac{du(x)}{dx}+p(x)\,u(x)=f(x)$

and $\frac{d\upsilon(x)}{dx}+p(x)\upsilon(x)=g(x)$

$$\Rightarrow \frac{d\{u(x)-\upsilon(x)\}}{dx}+p(x)\{u(x)-\upsilon(x)\}$$

$= \{f(x) - g(x)\}$.

Which is a linear differential equation having I.F. $= e^{\int p(x)dx}$

$$\Rightarrow \frac{d}{dx}\left[\{u(x)-\upsilon(x)\}.e^{\int P(x)dx}\right] = \{f(x)-g(x)\}e^{\int P(x)dx}$$

$$\Rightarrow \left[\{u(x)-\upsilon(x)\}e^{\int p(x)dx}\right]_{x_1}^{x}$$

$$= \int_{x_1}^{x}\{f(x)-g(x)\}e^{\int p(x)dx}dx \quad \ldots(i)$$

Let $\left(e^{\int p(x)dx}\right)_x = \lambda; \left(e^{\int p(x)dx}\right)_{x_1} = \mu$

Clearly λ, μ are positive and R.H.S. of (i) is positive

$[\because f(x) > g(x)$ for $x > x_1$ and $e^{\int p(x)dx} > 0]$

$\Rightarrow \{u(x)-\upsilon(x)\}\lambda - \{u(x_1)-\upsilon(x_1)\}\mu > 0$

$\Rightarrow \{u(x)-\upsilon(x)\}\lambda > \{u(x_1)-\upsilon(x_1)\}\mu > 0$ because $u(x_1) > \upsilon(x_1)$

$\Rightarrow u(x) - \upsilon(x) > 0$ for $x > x_1$

$\Rightarrow u(x) > \upsilon(x)$ when $x > x_1$

$\Rightarrow y = u(x)$ and $y = v(x)$ can-not be satisfied by any point (x, y) for which $x > x_1$.

Aliter: Given differential equations are

$$\frac{du}{dx} + P(x)u = f(x) \quad \ldots(i)$$

And $\dfrac{dv}{dx} + P(x)v = g(x) \quad \ldots(ii)$

On subtracting the two differential equations, we get

$$\frac{d}{dx}(u-v) + P(x)(u-v) = \{f(x)-g(x)\}$$

For $x > x_1$; $f(x) > g(x)$ (given)

$$\Rightarrow \frac{d}{dx}(u-v) + P(x)(u-v) > 0$$

$$\Rightarrow \frac{d(u-v)}{u-v} > -P(x)dx$$

Integrating both sides, we get

$$\ln(u-v) + C > \int -P(x)dx$$

$$\Rightarrow \ln(u-v) > -C - \int P(x)dx$$

$$\Rightarrow u - v > e^{-\int P(x)dx - C}$$

As RHS > 0, for all x, $u > v$ for all $x > x_1$

$\Rightarrow y = u(x)$ and $y = v(x)$ have no common solution (x, y); $x > x_1$.

(i.e., no point of intersection as one curve lies above the other)

34. Consider the differential equation, $\dfrac{dy}{dx} + P(x)y = Q(x)$

(i) If two particular solutions of given equation $u(x)$ and $v(x)$ are known, find the general solution of the same equation in terms of $u(x)$ and $v(x)$

(ii) If α and β are constants such that the linear combinations $\alpha.u(x) + \beta.v(x)$ is a solution of the given equation, find the relation between α and β.

(iii) If $w(x)$ is the third particular solution different from $u(x)$ and $v(x)$, then find the ratio $\dfrac{v(x)-u(x)}{w(x)-u(x)}$

Solution: Given differential equation is

$$\frac{dy}{dx} + P(x)y = Q(x) \quad \ldots(i)$$

(i) ∵ $y = u(x)$ and $y = v(x)$ are solutions of above equation

$$\Rightarrow \frac{d\,u(x)}{dx} + P(x)u(x) = Q(x) \quad \ldots(ii)$$

And $\dfrac{d(v(x))}{dx} + P(x)v(x) = Q(x) \quad \ldots(iii)$

Thus, (i) – (ii) gives

$$\frac{d}{dx}(y-u(x)) + (y-u(x))P(x) = 0 \quad \ldots(iv)$$

And [(ii) – (iii)] gives

$$\frac{d}{dx}(u(x)-v(x)) + (u(x)-v(x))P(x) = 0 \quad \ldots(v)$$

Now, from equation (iv) and (v) , we have

$$\frac{\frac{d}{dx}(y-u(x))}{\frac{d}{dx}(u(x)-v(x))} = \frac{y-u(x)}{u(x)-v(x)}$$

$$\Rightarrow \int\frac{d(y-u(x))}{y-u(x)} = \int\frac{d(u(x)-v(x))}{u(x)-v(x)}$$

$\Rightarrow \ell n\,|y - u(x)| = \ell n\,|u(x) - v(x)| + \ln C$

$|y - u(x)| = C|u(x) - v(x)|$

$y - u(x) = \pm\, C(u(x) - v(x))$

$y = u(x) + (\pm C)(u(x) - v(x))$

∴ $y = u(x) + k(u(x) - v(x))$; $k \in \mathbb{R}$ is general solution

(ii) ∵ $y = \alpha\, u(x) + \beta\, v(x)$ is a solution of differential equation $\dfrac{dy}{dx} + P(x)y = Q(x)$

∴ $\alpha u(x) + \beta v(x) = u(x) + k(u(x) - v(x))$ for some $k \in \mathbb{R}$

∴ Comparing coefficient of $u(x)$ and $v(x)$, we have $\alpha = 1 + k$, $\beta = -k$

∴ $\alpha + \beta = 1$

(iii) Again $y = w(x)$ is also a solution of above equation

$\therefore$ $w(x) = u(x) + k(u(x) - v(x))$ for some $k \in \mathbb{R}$

$\Rightarrow$ $w(x) - u(x) = k[u(x) - v(x)]$

$$\Rightarrow \frac{u(x)-v(x)}{w(x)-u(x)} = \frac{1}{k}$$

$$\therefore \frac{v(x)-u(x)}{w(x)-u(x)} = -\frac{1}{k} \text{ which is a constant number}$$

35. Tangent is drawn at the point (x_i, y_i) on the curve $y = f(x)$, which intersects the x-axis at $(x_{i+1}, 0)$. Now again at tangent is drawn at (x_{i+1}, y_{i+1}) on the curve which intersects the x-axis at $(x_{i+2}, 0)$ and the process is repeated n times, i.e., $i = 1, 2, 3, \ldots, n$.

(a) If $x_1, x_2, x_3, \ldots, x_n$ form an arithmetic progression with common difference equal to $\log_2 e$ and curve passes through (0, 2), then find the equation of the curve.

(b) If $x_1, x_2, x_3, \ldots, x_n$ form a geometric progression with common ratio equal to 2 and the curve passes through (1, 2), then find the equation of the curve.

Solution: (a) Equation of Tangent at $P(x_1, y_1)$ of $y = f(x)$ is given by $y - y_1 = \left[\frac{dy}{dx}\right]_{(x_1, y_1)} .(x - x_1)$ ...(1)

This tangent cuts the x-axis at

$$x_2 = x_1 - \frac{y_1}{\left(\frac{dy}{dx}\right)_{(x_1,y_1)}} \quad \ldots(2)$$

$\because$ $x_1, x_2, x_3 \ldots\ldots x_n$ are in *A.P.* with common difference $\log_2 e$; $x_2 - x_1 = -\frac{y_1}{\left(\frac{dy}{dx}\right)_{(x_1,y_1)}} = \log_2 e$

$$\Rightarrow -y = \log_2 e \frac{dy}{dx}$$

$$\Rightarrow \frac{dy}{y}\log_2 e = -dx \text{; Integrating both sides, we get}$$

$\ln y = -x \ln 2 + C$

$$\Rightarrow y = ke^{-x\ln 2} = k_2^{-x}$$

Now, $y = f(x)$ passes through (0, 2)

$\Rightarrow 2 = ke^0 \qquad \Rightarrow k = 2$

$$\Rightarrow y = 2.2^{-x} = 2^{1-x}$$

Thus, $y = 2^{1-x}$ is the required equation of the curve.

(b) $\because$ $x_1\, x_2\, x_3 \ldots\ldots x_n$ are in G.P. with common ratio 2

$$\Rightarrow \text{From (2); } x_2 = x_1 - \frac{y_1}{\left(\frac{dy}{dx}\right)(x_1, y_1)}$$

$$\Rightarrow \frac{x_2}{x_1} = 1 - \frac{y_1}{x_1\left(\frac{dy}{dx}\right)} \qquad \Rightarrow 1 - \frac{y\,dx}{x\,dy} = 2$$

$$\Rightarrow -\frac{y\,dx}{x\,dy} = 1 \qquad \Rightarrow \frac{dx}{x} = -\frac{dy}{y}$$

$\ln x = -\ln y + \ln c$ (integrating)

$\Rightarrow xy = c$

Since the curve passes through the point (1, 2), it is implies $C = 2$.

$\therefore$ The equation of curve will be $xy = 2$.

36. Given two curves $y = f(x)$ passing through the points (0, 1) and $y = \int_0^x f(t)\,dt$ passing through the points (0, 0). The tangents drawn to both curves at the points with equal abscissas intersect on the x-axis. Find the curve $f(x)$.

Solution: Let $P(x_1, y_1)$ and $Q(x_1, y_2)$ be points on given curves having same abscissa as shown below

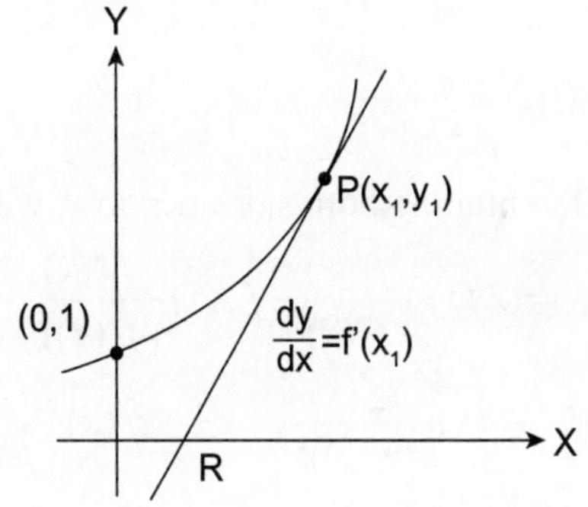

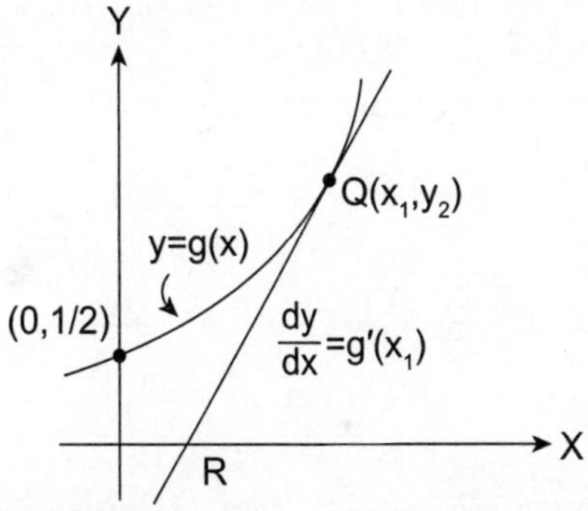

Now, Equation of tangent at point $P(x_1, y_1)$ is given by

$$y - y_1 = \left(\frac{dy}{dx}\right)_{(x_1,y_1)} (x - x_1)$$

$\Rightarrow$ $y - y_1 = f'(x_1)(x - x_1)$ which intersects x-axis,

where $y = 0$, i.e., $x = x_1 - \frac{y_1}{f'(x_1)}$

i.e., at $R \equiv \left(x_1 - \frac{y_1}{f'(x_1)}, 0\right)$

Now, Equation of tangent at Q is

$$y - y_2 = \left(\frac{dy}{dx}\right)_{(x_1, y_2)} (x - x_1)$$

$\Rightarrow y - y_2 = g'(x_1)\,(x - x_1)$, which intersect x-axis, where $y = 0$. i.e., $x = x_1 - \dfrac{y_2}{f'(x_1)}$

i.e., at $S \equiv R \equiv \left(x_1 - \dfrac{y_2}{g'(x_1)}, 0\right)$

Now according to question

$$\Rightarrow x_1 - \frac{y_1}{f'(x_1)} = x_1 - \frac{y_2}{g'(x_1)}$$

$$\Rightarrow \frac{f'(x_1)}{g'(x_1)} = \frac{y_1}{y_2} \quad \Rightarrow \quad \frac{f'(x_1)}{f(x_1)} = \frac{f(x_1)}{\int_0^{x_1} f(t)dt}$$

$$\left\{\because\ y_1 = f(x_1); y_2 = \int_0^{x_1} f(t)dt\ \&\ g'(x_1) = f(x_1)\right\}$$

$$\Rightarrow \int_0^{x_1} f(t)dt = \frac{f^2(x_1)}{f'(x_1)}; \text{ on generalization, we get}$$

$$\int_0^{x} f(t)dt = \frac{f^2(x)}{f'(x)}$$

Differentiating both sides w.r. to x, we get

$$f(x) = 2f(x)\frac{f'(x)}{f'(x)} - f^2(x)\frac{f''(x)}{(f'(x))^2}$$

$$\Rightarrow 1 = 2 - f(x)\frac{f''(x)}{(f'(x))^2} \quad \Rightarrow \quad f(x)\frac{f''(x)}{(f'(x))^2} = 1$$

$$\Rightarrow \int \frac{f''(x)}{f'(x)}dx = \int \frac{f'(x)}{f(x)}dx \Rightarrow \ell n\, f'(x) = \ell n\, f(x) + k_1$$

$\Rightarrow f'(x) = k_2 f(x)$, where $k_2 = e^{k_1}$

$$\Rightarrow \frac{f'(x)}{f(x)} = k_2 \quad \Rightarrow \quad \int \frac{f'(x)}{f(x)}dx = \int k_2 dx$$

$\Rightarrow \ell n\, f(x) = k_2 x + k_3$

$\Rightarrow f(x) = k_4 . e^{k_2 x}$; where $k_4 = e^{k_3}$

Now, for 2nd curve, $y = \int_0^x f(t)dt = \int_0^x k_4 e^{k_2 x} dx$

$$= \left[\frac{k_4 e^{k_2 x}}{k_2}\right]_0^x = \frac{k_4}{k_2}\left[e^{k_2 x} - 1\right]$$

$$\Rightarrow y = \frac{k_4}{k_2}\left(e^{k_2 x} - 1\right)$$

$\therefore$ 1st curve is $y = k_4 e^{k_2 x}$ and 2nd curve is $y = \dfrac{k_4}{k_2}\left(e^{k_2 x} - 1\right)$

Now, curves first and second pass through points (0, 1) and (0, 0) respectively.

$\Rightarrow 1 = k_4 e^0 \quad \Rightarrow k_4 = 1$ and $0 = \dfrac{1}{k_2}\left(e^0 - 1\right)$

$\Rightarrow 0 = \dfrac{1}{k_2}(0) \quad \Rightarrow k_2 \in \mathbb{R} \sim \{0\}$

Hence, equation of 1st curve is $y = e^{k_2 x}$ and that of second curve is $y = \dfrac{1}{k^2}\left(e^{k_2 x} - 1\right)$

or $y = e^{kx}$ and $y = \dfrac{1}{k}\left(e^{kx} - 1\right)$ respectively.

37. In a college hostel accommodating 1000 students, one of them came in carrying a flu virus, then the hostel was isolated. If the rate at which the virus spreads is assumed to be proportional not only to the number N_i of infected students, but also to the number of non-infected students, and if the number of infected students is 50 after 4 days, then show that more than 95% of the students will be infected after 10 days.

Solution: According to the assumptions of the problems, we have

$$\frac{dN_i}{dt} = kN_i(1000 - N_i),\ \ N_i(0) = 1 \qquad \text{...(i)}$$

where k is constant of proportionality. (i) is a different equation with variables separable, we write

$$k\,dt = \frac{dN_i}{N_i(1000 - N_i)} = \frac{1}{1000}\left[\frac{1}{N_i} + \frac{1}{1000 - N_i}\right]dN_i$$

$$\Rightarrow kt = \frac{1}{1000}(\ell n\, N_i - \ell n(1000 - N_i)) + C$$

$$\Rightarrow 1000(kt - C) = \ell n\left[\frac{N_i}{1000 - N_i}\right]$$

From here, we get $\dfrac{N_i}{(1000 - N_i)} = Ae^{1000kt}$;

(A is a parameter) ...(ii)

Using the fact the $N_i(0) = 1$, we find that $A = \dfrac{1}{999}$

$$\Rightarrow \frac{N_i}{1000 - N_i} = \frac{1}{999}e^{1000kt}$$

$$\Rightarrow 999N_i e^{-1000kt} + N_i = 1000$$

$$\Rightarrow N_i(1 + 999e^{-1000kt}) = 1000 \qquad \text{...(iii)}$$

Now, we use $N_i(4) = 50$ to determine k, this gives

$$50(1 + 999e^{-4000k}) = 1000$$

$$\Rightarrow 1 + 999e^{-4000k} = 20 \Rightarrow 999e^{-4000k} = 19$$

$\Rightarrow\ e^{-4000k} = \dfrac{19}{999} \qquad \Rightarrow\ e^{4000k} = \dfrac{999}{19}$

Hence, $k = \dfrac{1}{4000}\ln\dfrac{999}{19} = 0.0009906$ (approx)

Substituting the value of k in (iii) and then putting $t = 10$, we get $N_i(10) = \dfrac{1000}{1+999e^{-\frac{10}{4}\ln\frac{999}{19}}}$

$= \dfrac{1000}{1+(19)^{\frac{5}{2}}999^{-\frac{3}{2}}} = 952$ (approx)

So, more than 95% of the students will be infected after 10 days.

38. A tank contains 20 lb of salt dissolved in 50 gallon of water. Suppose 3 gallon of brine containing 2 lb of dissolved salt per gallon run into the tank every minute and that the mixture (kept uniform by stirring) runs out of the tank at the rate of 2 gal/min. Find the amount of salt in the tank at any time t. How much salt is in the tank at the end of one hour?

Solution: Let $S(t)$ denotes the amount of salt in the tank at the end of t minutes. Because 3 gallon of brine flows into the tank each minute and each gallon contains 2 lb of salt, it follows that (3) (2) = 6 lb of salt flow into the tank each minute as shown in figure given below. This is the inflow rate

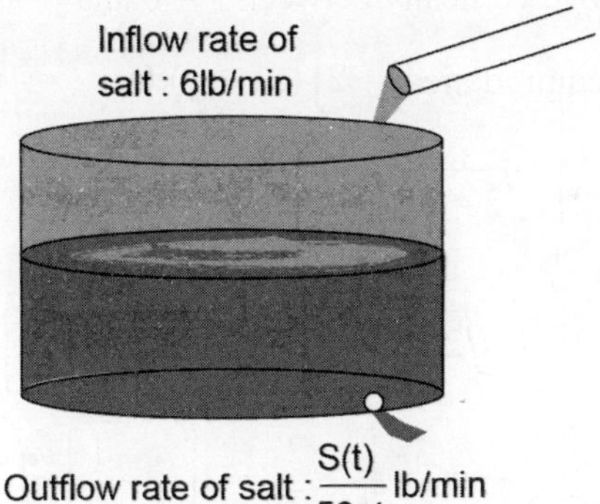

For the outflow, note that at time t, there are S(t) lb of salt and 50 + (3 – 2)t gallons of solution (because solution flows in at 3 gal/min and out at 2 gal/min). Thus, the concentration of salt in the solution at time t is $\dfrac{S(t)}{50+t} lb/gal$ and the outflow rate of salt is

$\left[\dfrac{S(t)}{50+t}\text{lb/gal}\right]\times[2\text{gal/min}] = \dfrac{2S(t)}{50+t}\text{lb/min}$

Combining these observations, we see that the net rate of change of salt $\dfrac{dS}{dt}$ is given by $\dfrac{dS}{dt} = \underbrace{6}_{\text{inflow}} - \underbrace{\dfrac{2S}{50+t}}_{\text{outflow}}$

$\Rightarrow\ \dfrac{dS}{dt}+\dfrac{2S}{50+t} = 6$, Which we recognize as a first order linear differential equation with $P(t) = \dfrac{2}{50+t}$ and $Q(t) = 6$.

$\therefore$ The $I.F. = e^{\int P(t)\,dt} = e^{\int (2)/(50+t)dt} = e^{2\ln|50+t|} = (50+t)^2$

and the general solution is given by

$S(t) = \dfrac{1}{(50+t)^2}\left[\int 6(50+t)^2\,dt + C\right]$

$= \dfrac{1}{(50+t)^2}\left[2(50+t)^3 + C\right]$

$= 2(50+t) + \dfrac{C}{(50+t)^2}$

To evaluate C, we recall that there are 20 lb of salt initially in the solution. This means $S(0) = 20$, so that $S(0) = 2(50+0)+\dfrac{C}{(50+0)^2}$

$\Rightarrow\ 20 = 100+\dfrac{C}{50^2} \qquad \Rightarrow\ -80(50)^2 = C$

$\Rightarrow\ C = -2\times10^5$

Thus, the solution to given differential equation, subject to the initial condition $S(0) = 20$ is

$S(t) = 2(50+t) - \dfrac{2\times10^5}{(50+t)^2}$

Now, at the end of 1 hour (60 min), the tank contains $= S(60) = 2(50+60) - \dfrac{2\times10^5}{(50+60)^2}$

$= 220 - \dfrac{2\times10^5}{121\times10^2} = 220 - \dfrac{2\times10^3}{121} \simeq 203.4$ lbs

39. Let $f(x)$ be a real valued function satisfying $f\left(\dfrac{x}{y}\right) = f(x) - f(y)$ for all $x, y \in \mathbb{R}, y \neq 0$ and $\lim\limits_{x\to0}\dfrac{f(1+x)}{x} = 3$. Find the area bounded by the curve $y = f(x)$, the y-axis and the line $y = 3$.

Solution: We have, $f\left(\dfrac{x}{y}\right) = f(x) - f(y)$ for all x, $y \in \mathbb{R}, y \neq 0$ ...(i)

and, $\lim\limits_{x\to0}\dfrac{f(1+x)}{x} = 3$ ...(ii)

Now, $f'(x) = \lim\limits_{x\to0}\dfrac{f(x+h)-f(x)}{h}$

$= \lim\limits_{x\to0}\dfrac{f\left(\dfrac{x+h}{h}\right)}{h} \quad \left[\because f(x)-f(y) = f\left(\dfrac{x}{y}\right)\right]$

$= \lim\limits_{x\to0}\dfrac{f\left(1+\dfrac{h}{x}\right)}{\dfrac{h}{x}\times x} = \dfrac{3}{x} \quad \left[\because \lim\limits_{x\to0}\dfrac{f(1+x)}{x} = 3\right]$

$\Rightarrow f(x) = 3 \ln x + \ln C$ ...(iii)

[On integrating]

Putting $x = y = 1$ in (i), we get $f(1) = 0$

Putting $x = 1$ in (iii), we get $f(1) = 3 \ln 1 + \ln C$

$\Rightarrow \ln C = 0$

Putting $\ln C = 0$ in (iii), we obtain

$f(x) = 3 \ln x$ for all $x \in \mathbb{R} - \{0\}$; we are to find the area bounded by $y = f(x) = 3\ln|x|$, $x = 0$ and $y = 3$. That is, in figure, we have to find the area of the shaded region. Let us slice this region into horizontal strips. For the approximating rectangle shown in figure we have

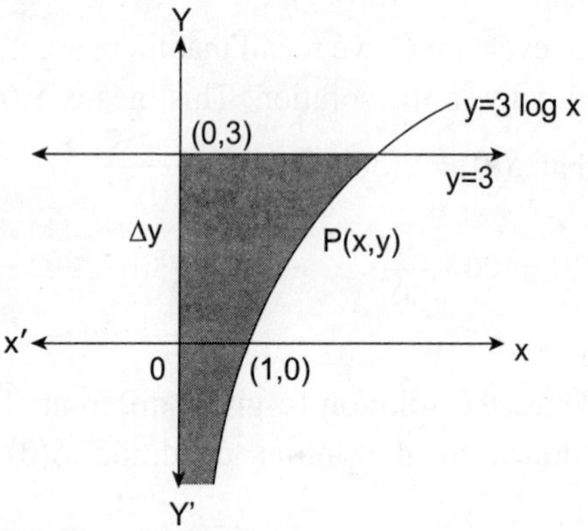

Length = x, Width = Δy and it can move from $y = -\infty$ to $y = 3$.

So, required area = $\int_{-\infty}^{3} e^{y/3} dy$

$= \left[\frac{e^{y/3}}{1/3}\right]_{-\infty}^{3} = 3\left[e^{1} - e^{-\infty}\right]$

$= 3(e - 0) = 3e$ square units.

40. Let f be a differentiable function satisfying the condition: $f\left(\frac{x}{y}\right) = \frac{f(x)}{f(y)}$, where $y \neq 0$, $f(y) \neq 0$ for all $x, y \in \mathbb{R}$ and $f'(1) = 2$, then find out the area enclosed by $y = f(x)$, $x^2 + y^2 = 2$ and x-axis.

Solution: We have, $f\left(\frac{x}{y}\right) = \frac{f(x)}{f(y)}$ for all $x, y \in \mathbb{R}$ such that $y \neq 0$ and $f(y) \neq 0$

$\therefore f(1) = \frac{f(1)}{f(1)} \quad \Rightarrow \{f(1)\}^2 - f(1) = 0$

$\Rightarrow f(1) = 1$ $[\because f(1) \neq 0]$

Now, $f'(x) = \lim_{h \to 0} \frac{f(x+h) - f(x)}{h}$

$= \lim_{h \to 0} \frac{f(x)\left[\frac{f(x+h)}{f(x)} - 1\right]}{h}$

$= f(x) \cdot \lim_{h \to 0} \frac{f\left(\frac{x+h}{x}\right) - 1}{h}$ $\left[\because \frac{f(x)}{f(x)} = f\left(\frac{x}{y}\right)\right]$

$= \frac{f(x)}{x} \cdot \left\{\lim_{h \to 0} \frac{f\left(1 + \frac{h}{x}\right) - f(1)}{\left(1 + \frac{h}{x}\right) - 1}\right\}$ $[\because f(1) = 1]$

$= \frac{f(x)}{x} f'(1)$

$\Rightarrow \frac{d(f(x))}{dx} = \frac{2f(x)}{x}$ $[\because f'(1) = 2]$

$\Rightarrow \frac{df(x)}{f(x)} = \frac{2}{x} dx$

Integrating both sides, we get $\ln f(x) = 2 \ln x + \ln C$

$\Rightarrow f(x) = Cx^2$ ...(i)

But, $f(1) = 1$ Therefore, $C = 1$, Putting $C = 1$ in (i), we obtain $f(x) = x^2$

Thus, we have to find the area enclosed by the curves $y = x^2$, $x^2 + y^2 = 2$ and x-axis. Graphs of these curves and region enclosed are shown in fig. Clearly, $y = x^2$ and $x^2 + y^2 = 2$ intersect at (1, 1) and (–1, 1). The shaded region in fig. is sliced into horizontal strips. The approximating rectangle shown in fig. is of length = $(x_2 - x_1)$, width = Δy and it can move vertically between $y = 0$ and $y = 1$. So,

Required area = $2\int_0^1 (x_2 - x_1) dy$

$= 2\int_0^1 (\sqrt{2 - y^2} - \sqrt{y}) dy$

$= 2\left[\frac{1}{2} y\sqrt{2 - y^2} + \frac{2}{2}\sin^{-1}\frac{y}{\sqrt{2}} - \frac{2}{3} y^{3/2}\right]_0^1$

$= 2\left[\frac{1}{2} + \sin^{-1}\frac{1}{\sqrt{2}} - \frac{2}{3}\right] = 2\left[\frac{\pi}{4} - \frac{1}{6}\right] = \left(\frac{\pi}{2} - \frac{1}{3}\right)$

square units

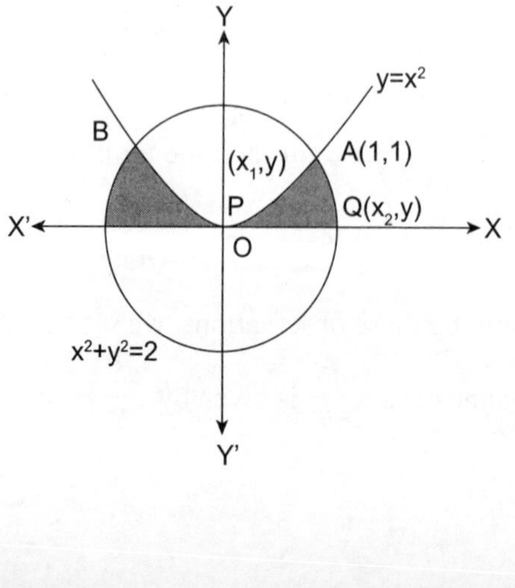

Assertion and Reasion

(a) A is true, R is a correct explanation for A

(b) A is true, R is true R is not a correct explanation for A

(c) A is true, R is false

(d) A is false, R is true

41. Let a solution $y = y(x)$ of the differential equation $x\sqrt{x^2-1}dy = y\sqrt{y^2-1}dx$ satisfies $y(2) = 2/\sqrt{3}$

A: $y(x) = \sec\left(\sec^{-1}x - \frac{\pi}{6}\right)$

R: $y(x)$ is given by $\frac{1}{y} = \frac{2\sqrt{3}}{x} - \sqrt{1-\frac{1}{x^2}}$.

Solution: (c) Given differential equation is $x\sqrt{x^2-1}dy = y\sqrt{y^2-1}dx$

Separating the variables, we have

$$\frac{dx}{x\sqrt{x^2-1}} = \frac{dy}{y\sqrt{y^2-1}}$$

$$\Rightarrow \int\frac{dy}{y\sqrt{y^2-1}} = \int\frac{dx}{x\sqrt{x^2-1}}$$

$$\Rightarrow \sec^{-1}y = \sec^{-1}x + C \qquad ...(1)$$

Given at $x = 2, y = 2/\sqrt{3}$

$$\Rightarrow C = -\frac{\pi}{6}$$

$\therefore$ from (1), $y = \sec\left[\sec^{-1}x - \frac{\pi}{6}\right]$

$\therefore$ Assertion is true.

Now again $y = \dfrac{1}{\cos\left[\cos^{-1}\left(\frac{1}{x}\right) - \frac{\pi}{6}\right]}$

$$= \frac{1}{\frac{1}{x}\cdot\frac{\sqrt{3}}{2} + \sqrt{1-\frac{1}{x^2}}\cdot\left(\frac{1}{2}\right)} \qquad = \frac{1}{y} = \frac{\sqrt{3}}{2x} + \frac{\sqrt{1-1/x^2}}{2}$$

Reason is false.

42. A: The solution of $ydx - xdy + y^2dx = 0$ is $\frac{x}{y} + x = c$

R: $d\left(\frac{x}{y}\right) = \frac{(ydx - x.\,dy)}{y^2}$

Solution: (a) Given differential equation is $ydx - xdy + y^2\,dx = 0$

$$\Rightarrow \frac{ydx - xdy}{y^2} = -1dx \Rightarrow ydx - xdy = -y^2dx$$

$$\Rightarrow \int d\left(\frac{x}{y}\right) = \int -dx + c$$

$$\Rightarrow \frac{x}{y} = -x + c \qquad \Rightarrow \frac{x}{y} + x = c$$

Thus, both assertion and reason are correct and reason is the correct explanation of assertion.

43. A: The differential equation $x(x^2 + y^2 + 1)dx + y(x^2 - y^2 + 1)dy = 0$ becomes homogeneous by putting $x^2 = u, y^2 = v$

R: Differential equation $\frac{dv}{du} = \frac{u+v+1}{u-v+1}$ is reducible to homogeneous differential equation.

Solution: (d) By putting $x^2 = u$ and $y^2 = v$, we get $(u + v + 1)du + (u - v + 1)dv = 0$

Or $\frac{dv}{du} = -\frac{u+v+1}{u-v+1}$, which is not homogeneous but is reducible to homogeneous by change of origin (put $u = U + \alpha$, $v = V + \beta$ and choose α and β such that $\alpha + \beta + 1 = 0$, $\alpha - \beta + 1 = 0$). Thus, A is false and R is true.

44. A: The differential equation of all parabolas in a plane must be of order 4.

R: The equation $(ax + by)^2 + 2gx + 2fy + 1 = 0$ may represent a parabola.

Solution: (a) R is correct since second degree terms are forming a perfect square. The number of arbitrary constants in the equation

$(ax + by)^2 + 2gx + 2fy + 1 = 0$ ...(i)

$\Rightarrow$ The order of the differential equation obtained from (i) must be four.

45. A: Let $f(x)$ be a differential on the interval $(0, \infty)$ such that $f(1) = 1$ and $\lim_{t\to x}\frac{t^2f(x) - x^2f(t)}{t-x} = 1$ for each $x > 0$. Then $f(x) = \frac{1}{3x} + \frac{2x^2}{3}$

R: Differential equation of $f(x)$ is linear.

Solution: (a) $\lim_{t\to x}\frac{t^2f(x) - x^2f(t)}{t-x} = 1$,

$\lim_{t\to x}\frac{2tf(x) - x^2f'(t)}{1} = 1$ (By L.H. Rule)

$2xf(x) - x^2f'(x) = 1$

$f'(x) - \frac{2}{x}f(x) = -\frac{1}{x^2}$, which is linear

Reason is true

$$\text{I.F.} = e^{\int -\frac{2}{x}dx} = e^{-2\log x} = \frac{1}{x^2}$$

Solution is $\frac{y}{x^2} = -\int \frac{1}{x^4}dx + c$

$\Rightarrow \frac{y}{x^2} = \frac{x^{-3}}{3} + c \qquad \Rightarrow \frac{y}{x^2} = \frac{1}{3x^3} + c$

$\Rightarrow \frac{y}{x^2} - \frac{1}{3x^3} = c \qquad \Rightarrow 1 - \frac{1}{3} = c\ (\because f(1) = 1)$

$\Rightarrow c = \frac{2}{3} \qquad \Rightarrow \frac{y}{x^2} = \frac{2}{3} + \frac{1}{3x^3}$

$\Rightarrow y = \frac{2x^2}{3} + \frac{1}{3x}$

Assertion is also true and is correctly explained by reason.

Passage Type

A: If in a certain process one substance turns into another, and the rate of generation of the product is proportional to the available quantity of the original substance, then such a phenomenon is called a process (or reaction) of first order. A substance whose initial quantity is m_0 turns into another substance and from the product, thus obtained a second product begins to generate immediately. Both reactions are of first order; the proportionality factors are known; k_1 for the first process and k_2 for the second reaction. If x is the quantity of the first product generated during time t units y is the quantity of the second product.

46. y at $t = 2$ is given by

(a) $m_0 + \frac{m_0}{k_1 - k_2}(2k_2e^{-k_1} - 2k_1e^{-k_2})$

(b) $m_0 + \frac{2m_0}{k_2 - k_1}(k_2e^{-k_1} - k_1e^{-k_2})$

(c) $m_0 + \frac{m_0}{k_1 - k_2}(k_1e^{-2k_1} - k_2e^{-2k_2})$

(d) $m_0 + \frac{m_0}{k_1 - k_2}(k_2e^{-2k_1} - k_1e^{-2k_2})$

47. $\lim\limits_{t\to\infty} y$ is equal to

(a) m_0 (b) $m_0 + \frac{m_0}{k_1 - k_2}$

(c) $m_0 + \frac{2m_0}{k_1 - k_2}$ (d) $k_1m_0 + k_2$

48. $\int_0^1 y\,dt$ is equal to

(a) $m_0 + \frac{m_0}{k_1 - k_2}[e^{-2k_2} - e^{-k_1}]$

(b) $m_0 + \frac{m_0}{(k_1 - k_2)}\left[\frac{k_1}{k_2}(e^{-k_2} - 1) - \frac{k_2}{k_1}(e^{-k_1} - 1)\right]$

(c) $m_0 + \frac{m_0}{k_1 - k_2}[e^{-k_1} - e^{-k_2}]$

(d) $m_0 + \frac{m_0}{k_1 - k_2}k_2[e^{-k_2} - e^{-k_1}]$

Solutions: $\frac{dx}{dt} = k_1(m_0 - x)$ ...(i)

and $\frac{dy}{dt} = k_2(x - y)$ ...(ii)

From the first equation $\frac{dx}{dt} + k_1x = k_1m_0$. This is a linear equation with integrating factor e^{k_1t}. So, the solution is given by $xe^{k_1t} = k_1m_0\frac{e^{k_1t}}{k_1} + \text{C}$. But for t = 0, x = 0 so constant = $-m_0$. Hence, $x = m_0(1 - e^{-k_1t})$. The equation (ii) reduces to $\frac{dy}{dt} + k_2y = k_2x = k_2m_0 1 - e^{k_1t}$

Which is again a linear equation with $I.F. = e^{\int k_2dt = k_2t}$ Hence, its solution is given by

$$y^{k_2t} = k_2m_0\left[\frac{e^{k_2t}}{k_2} - \frac{e^{(k_2-k_1)t}}{k_2 - k_1}\right] + \text{C}$$

But y = 0 at t = 0, so, $C = -m_0 + \frac{k_2m_0}{k_2 - k_1}$.

Hence, $y = m_0 + \frac{m_0}{k_2 - k_1}(k_1e^{-k_2t} - k_2e^{-k_1t})$ ...(i)

46. (d) by equation (i)

At $t = 2$, $y = m_0 + \frac{m_0}{k_2 - k_1}(k_1e^{-2k_2} - k_2e^{-2k_1})$

47. (a) by equation (i) $\lim\limits_{t\to\infty} y = m_0$.

48. (b) by equation (i)

$$\int_0^1 y\,dt = m_0 + \frac{m_0}{k_1 - k_2}\left(\frac{-k_2e^{-k_1t}}{k_1} + \frac{k_1e^{-k_2t}}{k_2}\right)\Bigg|_0^1$$

$$= m_0 + \frac{m_0}{k_1 - k_2}\left[-\frac{k_2}{k_1}(e^{-k_1} - 1) + \frac{k_1}{k_2}(e^{-k_2} - 1)\right]$$

B: Consider the differential equation $e^x (ydx - dy) = e^{-x} (ydx + dy)$. Let $y = f(x)$ be a particular solution to this differential equation which passes through the point (0, 2). Let $C \equiv y = \log_{1/4}\left(x - \frac{1}{4}\right) + \frac{1}{2}\log_4(16x^2 - 8x + 1)$, be another curve

49. The range of the function $g(x) = \log_2 (f(x))$ is
(a) $[1, \infty)$
(b) $[2, \infty)$
(c) $[0, \infty)$
(d) None of these

50. The area bounded by the curve C, $y = f(x)$ and the line $x = 1/4$ and $x = 1$ is; $\left(\sinh x = \frac{e^x - e^{-x}}{2}\right)$

(a) $\left(\sin 1 - \sin\frac{1}{4}\right)$ (b) $2\left(\sin 1 - \sin\frac{1}{4}\right)$

(c) $2\left[\sin 1 - \sin\frac{1}{4}\right] - \frac{3}{4}$ (d) None of these

51. If the area bounded by the curve $y = f(x)$, curve C, ordinate $x = 1/4$ and the ordinate $x = a$ is $4 - \ln 4 + \frac{1}{e^{1/4}} - e^{1/4}$, then value of a is
(a) $\ell n\ 6$ (b) $\ell n\ 4$
(c) 4 (d) $\ell n\ 12$

Solutions:

49. (b) $ydx\ (e^x - e^{-x}) = (e^x + e^{-x})\ dy \Rightarrow \frac{dy}{y} = \frac{e^x - e^{-x}}{e^x + e^{-x}} dx$

$\Rightarrow \ell n\ (e^x + e^{-x}) = \ell n\ (ky)$, where k is a constant

$\Rightarrow e^x + e^{-x} = ky$

Now, $y = f(x)$ passes through (0, 2) (Given)

$\Rightarrow k = 1$

$\Rightarrow f(x) = e^x + e^{-x}$

Now, $g(x) = (f(x)) \log_2 (e^x + e^{-x})$

$\therefore\ 1 \le g(x) < \infty$ as $e^x + e^{-x} \in [2, \infty)$

50. (c) $y = \log_{1/4}(x - 1/4) + \frac{1}{2}\log_4(16(x - 1/4)^2)$

$= \log_{1/4}(x - 1/4) + 1 - \log_{1/4}(x - 1/4)$

$\therefore\ y = 1 \forall x > \frac{1}{4}$, Also $y = f(x) = e^x + e^{-x}$

Thus, the required area is as shown below and is given by

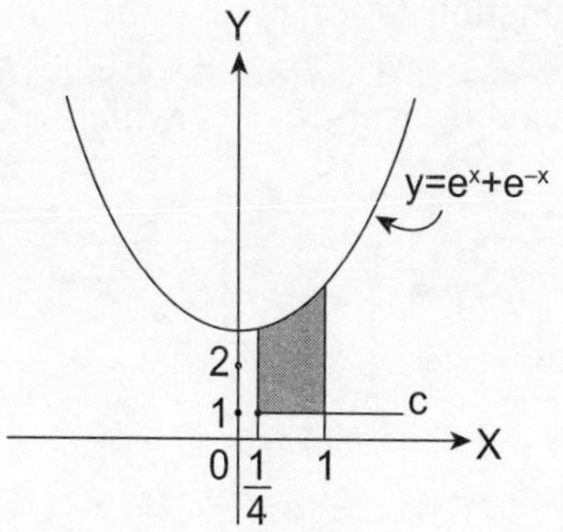

$$A = \int_{1/4}^{1} (e^x + e^{-x} - 1)dx = \left|e^x + e^{-x} - x\right|_{1/4}^{1}$$

$$= \left[\left(e - e^{-1} - 1\right) - e^{1/4} + e^{-1/4} + \frac{1}{4}\right]$$

$$= \left[\left(e - e^{-1}\right) - \left(e^{1/4} - e^{-1/4}\right) - \frac{3}{4}\right] \text{ square units}$$

$$= 2\sin h1 - 2\sin h\left(\frac{1}{4}\right) - \frac{3}{4}; \text{ where } \sin hx = \frac{e^x - e^{-x}}{2}$$

51. (b) Given $\int_{1/4}^{a} (e^x + e^{-x} - 1)dx$

$= 4 - \ln 4 + \frac{1}{e^{1/4}} - e^{1/4}$

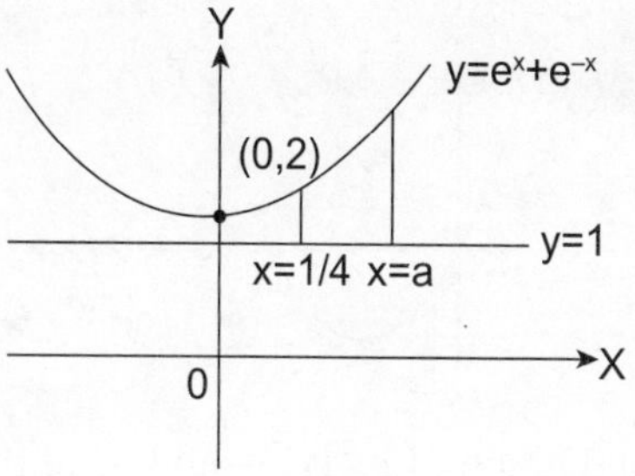

$\Rightarrow (e^x - e^{-x} - x)_{1/4}^{a} = 4 - \ln 4 + \frac{1}{e^{1/4}} - e^{1/4}$

$\Rightarrow e^a - e^{-a} - a - e^{1/4} + \frac{1}{e^{1/4}} + \frac{1}{4} = 4 - \ln 4 + \frac{1}{e^{1/4}} - e^{1/4}$

$\Rightarrow e^a - e^{-a} - a + \frac{1}{4} = 4 - \ln 4 \quad \Rightarrow \quad a = \ell n\ 4$

C: let f: $[0,1] \to \mathbb{R}$ (the set of all real numbers) be a function. Suppose the function f is twice differentiable, $f(0) = f(1) = 0$ and satisfies $f''(x) - 2f'(x) + f(x) \ge e^x, x \in [0,1]$.

52. Which of the following is true for $0 < x < 1$?

(a) $0 < f(x) < \infty$ (b) $-\frac{1}{2} < f(x) < \frac{1}{2}$

(c) $-\frac{1}{4} < f(x) < 1$ (d) $-\infty < f(x) < 0$

53. If the function $e^{-x} f(x)$ assumes its minimum in the interval [0,1] at $x = \frac{1}{4}$, which of the following is true?

(a) $f'(x) < f(x), \frac{1}{4} < x < \frac{3}{4}$

(b) $f'(x) > f(x), 0 < x < \frac{1}{4}$

(c) $f'(x) < f(x), 0 < x < \frac{1}{4}$

(d) $f'(x) < f(x), \frac{3}{4} < x < 1$

Solutions:

52. (d) $f''(x) - 2f'(x) + f(x) \geq e^x; x \in [0, 1]$
Multiplying both sides by e^{-x}, we get $e^{-x}f''(x) - 2e^{-x} f'(x) + e^{-x} f(x) \geq 1$

$\Rightarrow \frac{d^2}{dx^2}\left(e^{-x} f(x)\right) \geq 1 \Rightarrow \frac{d^2}{dx^2}\left(e^{-x} f(x)\right) > 0$

$\Rightarrow e^{-x}f(x)$ has its graph concave upwards

Also $f(0) = f(1) = 0$

If $g(x) = e^{-x}f(x)$, then $g(0) = g(1) = 0$

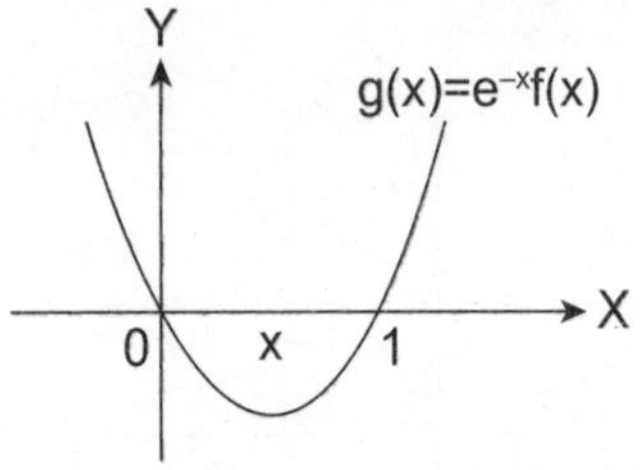

$\Rightarrow$ Rough graph of $e^{-x}f(x)$ would be of the form

$\Rightarrow e^{-x}f(x) < 0 \ \forall\ x \in (0, 1) \Rightarrow f(x) < 0 \ \forall\ x \in (0, 1)$

$\Rightarrow -\infty < f(x) < 0 \ \forall\ x \in (0, 1)$

53. (c) It is given that $g(x) = e^{-x} f(x)$ has minimum at $x = 1/4$

$\Rightarrow g'(x) < 0$ for $x \in \left(0, \frac{1}{4}\right)$ and $g'(x) > 0$ for $x \in \left(\frac{1}{4}, 1\right)$

$\Rightarrow e^{-x}f'(x) - e^{-x}f(x) < 0$ for $x \in \left(0, \frac{1}{4}\right)$

And $e^{-x}f'(x) - e^{-x}f(x) > 0$ for $x \in \left(\frac{1}{4}, 1\right)$

$\Rightarrow f'(x) < f(x)$ for $x \in \left(0, \frac{1}{4}\right)$

And $f'(x) > f(x)$ for $x \in \left(\frac{1}{4}, 1\right)$

Column Matching

54. **Column I Diff. equation**

(i) $(1 + xy)\, xdy + (1 - xy)\, ydx = 0$

(ii) $(x^2 - 4xy - 2y^2)dx + (y^2 - 4xy - 2x^2)dy = 0$

(iii) $e^y.dx + (xe^y - 2y)\, dy = 0$

(iv) $\frac{xdx + ydy}{\sqrt{x^2 + y^2}} = \frac{ydx - xdy}{y^2}$

Column II Solution curve

(a) $\frac{x^3}{3} + \frac{y^3}{3} - 2x^2y - 2xy^2 = C$

(b) $\frac{-1}{xy} + \left(\frac{y}{x}\right)\ln = C$

(c) $\sqrt{x^2 + y^2} - x/y = C$

(d) $xe^y - y^2 = C$

Ans: (i) → b, (ii) → a, (iii) → d, (iv) → c,

Solution: (i) Given differential equation is $(1 + xy)\, xdy + (1 - xy)\, ydx = 0$

$\Rightarrow (xdy + ydx) + xy\,(xdy - ydx) = 0$

$\Rightarrow \frac{(xdy + ydx)}{(xy)^2} + \frac{xdy - ydx}{xy} = 0$

$\Rightarrow \frac{d(xy)}{(xy)^2} + \frac{1}{y}dy - \frac{1}{x}dx = 0$

$\Rightarrow \frac{d(xy)}{(xy)^2} + d\ln\left(\frac{y}{x}\right) = 0$

Integrating, we get $\frac{-1}{xy} + \log\left(\frac{y}{x}\right) = C$

(ii) Given differential equation is $x^2dx + y^2dy - 4xy\, dx - 2y^2\, dx - 4xydy - 2x^2dy = 0$

$\Rightarrow x^2dx + y^2dy - 2\,(2xy\, dx + x^2dy) - 2\,(2xydy + y^2dx) = 0$

$\Rightarrow x^2dx + y^2dy - 2d\,(x^2y) - 2d(xy^2) = 0$

Integrating, we get $\frac{x^3}{3} + \frac{y^3}{3} - 2x^2y - 2xy^2 = C$

(iii) Given differential equation is $e^ydx + (xe^y - 2y)\, dy = 0$

$\Rightarrow e^y\, dx + xe^ydy - 2ydy = 0 \Rightarrow d(xe^y) - d(y^2) = 0$

Integrating, we get $xe^y - y^2 = C$

(iv) Given differential equation is

$\frac{xdx + ydy}{\sqrt{x^2 + y^2}} = \frac{ydx - xdy}{y^2}$

$\Rightarrow \frac{1}{2}\frac{d(x^2 + y^2)}{\sqrt{x^2 + y^2}} = d\left(\frac{x}{y}\right) \Rightarrow \frac{1}{2}\frac{d(x^2 + y^2)}{\sqrt{x^2 + y^2}} = d\left(\frac{x}{y}\right)$

$\Rightarrow \sqrt{x^2+y^2}-\frac{x}{y}=C$

55. **Column I:**

(i) If $xdy = y(dx + ydy)$, $y > 0$; $y(1) = 1$ and $y(x_0) = -3$, then $x_0 =$

(ii) If $y(t)$ is solution of $(t+1)\frac{dy}{dt}-ty=1$, $y(0) = -1$, then $y(1) =$

(iii) $(x^2 + y^2)\, dy = xydx$ and $y(1) = 1$ and $y(x_0) = e$, then $x_0 =$

(iv) $\frac{dy}{dx}+\frac{2y}{x}=0$, $y(1) = 1$, then $y(2) =$

Column II:

(a) $\frac{1}{4}$

(b) -15

(c) $-\frac{1}{2}$

(d) 16

(e) $\sqrt{3}e$

Ans. (i) → (b), (ii) → (c), (iii) → (e), (iv) → (a)

Solution: (i) $xdy = ydx + y^2\, dy$

$\Rightarrow \frac{xdy-ydx}{y^2}=dy \quad \Rightarrow -d\left(\frac{x}{y}\right)=dy$

$-\frac{x}{y}=y+c$ put $x = 1, y = 1$

$\Rightarrow c = -2 \quad \Rightarrow -\frac{x}{y}=y-2$

Now $\frac{x_0}{3}=-5 \quad \Rightarrow x_0 = -15$

(ii) $\frac{dy}{dt}-\frac{t}{t+1}y=\frac{1}{t+1}$

$I.F.=e^{-\int\frac{t+1-1}{t+1}dt} = e^{-t+\ell n(t+1)}=(t+1)e^{-t}$

∴ Solution is $(t + 1)\, e^{-t}\, y = -e^{-t} + c$

put $t = 0$ and $y = -1$

$\Rightarrow c = 0 \quad \Rightarrow (t + 1)e^{-t}y = -e^{-t}$

Now at $t = 1 \quad \therefore\ 2e^{-1}\, y = -e^{-1}$

$\Rightarrow y=-\frac{1}{2}$

(iii) $(x^2 + y^2)\, dy = xy\, dx$ ....(i)

$\frac{dy}{dx}=\frac{xy}{x^2+y^2}$; put $y = vx$ and $\frac{dy}{dx}=v+x\frac{dv}{dx}$ in (i)

$\Rightarrow \frac{v}{1+v^2}=v+x\frac{dv}{dx} \quad \Rightarrow \frac{v}{1+v^2}-v=x\frac{dv}{dx}$

$\Rightarrow \frac{-v^3}{1+v^2}=x\frac{dv}{dx} \quad \Rightarrow \frac{(1+v^2)}{v^2}dv=-\frac{dx}{x}$

$\Rightarrow \int\left(v^{-3}+\frac{1}{v}\right)dv=-\int\frac{dx}{x}$

$\Rightarrow \ln v-\frac{1}{2v^2}=-\ln x+c$

put $x = 1, y = 1, v = 1$, then $c=-\frac{1}{2}$

$\Rightarrow \ln\frac{y}{x}-\frac{1}{2}\frac{x^2}{y^2}=-\ln x-\frac{1}{2}$; put $y = e$ and $x = x_0$

$\Rightarrow x_0=\sqrt{3}e$

(iv) $\frac{dy}{dx}+2\frac{y}{x}=0$; Separating the variables, we get

$\frac{dy}{y}=-\frac{2}{x}dx$

$\Rightarrow \ln y + 2\ln x = \ln C$

$x^2 y = C$; putting $x = 1, y = 1$, we get $C = 1$; $x^2y = 1$

Now, putting $x = 2$, we get $y=\frac{1}{4}$

56. Match the equations given in column I with their corresponding differential equation given in Column II.

Column I

(i) $y = cx + c^2$

(ii) $y = ae^{2x} + be^{3x}$

(iii) $y^2 = 4a(x + a)$

(iv) $xy = ae^x + be^{-x} + x^2$

Column II

(a) $1-\left(\frac{dy}{dx}\right)^2=2\frac{x}{y}\left(\frac{dy}{dx}\right)$

(b) $x\frac{d^2y}{dx^2}+\frac{2dy}{dx}-xy+x^2-2=0$

(c) $\frac{d^2y}{dx^2}-\frac{5dy}{dx}+6y=0$

(d) $y=\frac{xdy}{dx}+\left(\frac{dy}{dx}\right)^2$

Ans. (i) → (d) (ii) → (c) (iii) → (a) (iv) → (b)

Solution: (i) $y = cx + c^2$

$\Rightarrow \frac{dy}{dx}=c \quad \Rightarrow y=\frac{xdy}{dx}+\left(\frac{dy}{dx}\right)^2$

(ii) $y = ae^{2x} + be^{3x}$ $\Rightarrow \frac{dy}{dx} = 2ae^{2x} + 3be^{3x}$

$\Rightarrow \frac{d^2y}{dx^2} = 4ae^{2x} + 9be^{3x}$; For consistent system,

we must have $\begin{vmatrix} a & b & y \\ 2a & 3b & y' \\ 4a & 9b & y'' \end{vmatrix} = 0$

$\Rightarrow \begin{vmatrix} 1 & 1 & y \\ 2 & 3 & y' \\ 4 & 9 & y'' \end{vmatrix} = 0$

$\Rightarrow y'' - 5y' + 6y = 0 \Rightarrow \frac{d^2y}{dx^2} - \frac{5dy}{dx} + 6y = 0$

(iii) $y^2 = 4a(x + a)$ $\Rightarrow 2yy' = 4a$

$\Rightarrow a = \frac{1}{2}yy'$ $\therefore y^2 = 4\left(\frac{1}{2}yy'\right)\left(x + \frac{1}{2}yy'\right)$

$\Rightarrow y = 2y'x + y(y')^2$

$\Rightarrow y - y(y')^2 = 2x\left(\frac{dy}{dx}\right) \Rightarrow 1 - \left(\frac{dy}{dx}\right)^2 = 2\frac{x}{y}\left(\frac{dy}{dx}\right)$

(iv) $xy = ae^x + be^{-x} + x^2$

$\Rightarrow x\frac{dy}{dx} + y = ae^x + be^{-x}(-1) + 2x$

$\Rightarrow x\frac{d^2y}{dx^2} + \frac{2dy}{dx} = ae^x + be^{-x} + 2$

$\Rightarrow x\frac{d^2y}{dx^2} + \frac{2dy}{dx} = xy - x^2 + 2$

$\Rightarrow x\frac{d^2y}{dx^2} + \frac{2dy}{dx} - xy + x^2 - 2 = 0$

Integer Type

57. Let $y = f(x)$ is a polynomial function satisfying $x^2 f'(x) f\left(\frac{1}{x}\right) - f(x) f'\left(\frac{1}{x}\right) = x^2 f'(x) - f'\left(\frac{1}{x}\right)$. If $f(1) = 2$ and $f(5) = 26$, then find $f(6)$.

Solution: Given

$$x^2 f'(x) f\left(\frac{1}{x}\right) - f(x) f'\left(\frac{1}{x}\right) = x^2 f'(x) - f'\left(\frac{1}{x}\right)$$

$$\Rightarrow x^2 f'(x)\left[f\left(\frac{1}{x}\right) - 1\right] = f'\left(\frac{1}{x}\right)[f(x) - 1]$$

$$\Rightarrow f'(x)\left\{f\left(\frac{1}{x}\right) - 1\right\} = \frac{1}{x^2} f'\left(\frac{1}{x}\right)\{f(x) - 1\}$$

$$\Rightarrow \frac{f'(x)}{f(x) - 1} + \frac{f'\left(\frac{1}{x}\right)\left(-\frac{1}{x^2}\right)}{f\left(\frac{1}{x}\right) - 1} = 0$$

Integrating, we get $\ln|f(x) - 1| + \ln\left|f\left(\frac{1}{x}\right) - 1\right| = c$

$\Rightarrow (f(x) - 1)\left(f\left(\frac{1}{x}\right) - 1\right) = e^c = k$

$\Rightarrow f(x) f\left(\frac{1}{x}\right) - f(x) - f\left(\frac{1}{x}\right) + 1 = k$

$\Rightarrow (f(1))^2 - f(1) - f(1) + 1 = k$ (substituting $x = 1$)

$\Rightarrow k = 1$ ($\because f(1) = 2$, given)

$\Rightarrow f(x) f\left(\frac{1}{x}\right) = f(x) + f\left(\frac{1}{x}\right)$

$\Rightarrow f(x) = 1 \pm x^n$ (From functional equation)

Since $f(1) = 2$, we must have $f(x) = 1 + x^n$

Since $f(5) = 26$, $26 = 1 + 5^n \Rightarrow n = 2$

$\therefore f(x) = 1 + x^2$ $\therefore f(6) = 1 + (6)^2 = 37$

58. If the solution of differential equation $x^2\frac{d^2y}{dx^2} + 2x\frac{dy}{dx} = 12y$ is $y = Ax^m + Bx^{-n}$, then find the value of $m + n$, if m and $n \in \mathbb{N}$.

Solution: $y = Ax^m + Bx^{-n}$

$\Rightarrow \frac{dy}{dx} = Amx^{m-1} - nBx^{-n-1}$

$\Rightarrow \frac{d^2y}{dx^2} = Am(m-1)x^{m-2} + n(n+1)Bx^{-n-2}$

Putting these values in $x^2\frac{d^2y}{dx^2} + 2x\frac{dy}{dx} = 12y$

We have, $m(m + 1)Ax^m + n(n - 1)Bx^{-n}$
$= 12(Ax^m + Bx^{-n})$

$\Rightarrow m(m + 1) = 12$ and $n(n - 1) = 12$ (By comparing the coefficient)

$\Rightarrow m = 3, -4$ or $n = 4, -3$; But $m, n \in \mathbb{N}$

$\Rightarrow m = 3, n = 4$ $\Rightarrow m + n = 7$

59. The rate at which a substance cools in moving air is proportional to the difference between the temperatures of the substance and that of the air. If the temperature of the air is 290° K and the substance cools from 370° K to 330°K in 10 minutes, after how much time (in minutes), the temperature will be 295° K.

Solution: Let T be the temperature of the substance at a time t, then $\frac{dT}{dt} \propto (T - 290)$

$\Rightarrow \frac{dT}{dt} = -k(T - 290); k > 0$

Where k is constant of proportionality and negative sign denotes rate of cooling.

$\Rightarrow \dfrac{dT}{(T-290)} = -kdt$

Integrating, we get $\int \dfrac{dT}{(T-290)} = -\int dt$

$\Rightarrow \ln(T-290) = -kt + \ln c$

$\Rightarrow \left(\dfrac{T-290}{c}\right) = e^{-kt} \quad \Rightarrow (T-290) = ce^{-kt}$

If initially, i.e., when $t = 0$; $T = 370° K$

Then, $(370 - 290) = c$

$\Rightarrow c = 80 \qquad \therefore \; T - 290 = 80e^{-kt}$ ...(1)

Now, given for $t = 10$, $T = 330° K$

$\Rightarrow 330 - 290 = 80e^{-10k} \Rightarrow (40) = 80e^{-10k}$.

$\Rightarrow 2 = e^{10k} \qquad \Rightarrow \ln 2 = 10k$ ...(2)

Now, we are to find t, when $T = 295$

$\therefore$ from (1), $295 - 290 = 80e^{-kt}$

$\Rightarrow \dfrac{5}{80} = e^{-kt}$

$\Rightarrow \ln 16 = kt \qquad$ or $\quad 4 \ln 2 = kt$ ...(3)

Dividing (3) by (2), we get $4 = \dfrac{t}{10}$

$\Rightarrow t = 40$ minutes.

60. For a certain curve $y = f(x)$ satisfying $\dfrac{d^2y}{dx^2} = 6x - 4$, $f(x)$ has a local minimum value 5 when $x = 1$. Find the product of the global maximum and global minimum values of $f(x)$; given that $0 \le x \le 2$.

Solution: Let $\dfrac{d^2y}{dx^2} = 6x - 4$

Integrating again, we get $\dfrac{dy}{dx} = 3x^2 - 4x + A$

When $x = 1$, $\dfrac{dy}{dx} = 0$, so that $A = 1$.

$\Rightarrow \dfrac{dy}{dx} = 3x^2 - 4x + 1$ ...(1)

Integrating, we get $y = x^3 - 2x^2 + x + B$

When $x = 1$, $y = 5$, so that $B = 5$.

Thus, we have $y = x^3 - 2x^2 + x + 5$.

From (1), we get the critical points $x = \dfrac{1}{3}, x = 1$

At the critical point $x = \dfrac{1}{3}$, $\dfrac{d^2y}{dx^2}$ is –ve.

Therefore at $x = \dfrac{1}{3}$, y has local maximum.

At $x = 1$, $\dfrac{d^2y}{dx^2}$ is +ve

Therefore at $x = 1$, y has local minimum value and $f(1) = 5$

$\Rightarrow y\left(\dfrac{1}{3}\right) = \dfrac{139}{27}$ and $f(0) = 5, f(2) = 7$

Hence, global maximum value = 7, global minimum value = 5

$\Rightarrow$ Product of global maximum and global minimum values = 35

61. Given $y(0) = 2000$ and $\dfrac{dy}{dx} = 32000 - 20y^2$, then find the value of $\lim\limits_{x\to\infty} y(x)$

Solution: Given equation is $\dfrac{dy}{dx} = 32000 - 20y^2$

$\Rightarrow \int \dfrac{dy}{32000 - 20y^2} = \int dx$

$\Rightarrow \dfrac{1}{20}\int \dfrac{dy}{1600 - y^2} = \int dx \Rightarrow \dfrac{1}{20}\int \dfrac{dy}{(40)^2 - y^2} = \int dx$

$\Rightarrow \dfrac{1}{20} \cdot \dfrac{1}{2\times 40} \ln\left|\dfrac{y+40}{y-40}\right| = x + c$

$\Rightarrow \ln\left|\dfrac{y+40}{y-40}\right| = 1600x + c \Rightarrow \dfrac{y+40}{y-40} = ke^{1600x}$ ...(1)

Now, according to question, $y(0) = 2000$

$\Rightarrow \dfrac{2000+40}{2000-40} = k \qquad \Rightarrow k = \dfrac{2040}{1960}$ ...(2)

$\therefore \dfrac{y+40}{y-40} = ke^{1600x}$

$\Rightarrow y + 40 = (y - 40)\,ke^{1600x}$

$\Rightarrow y + 40 = y\,ke^{1600x} - 40\,ke^{1600x}$

$\Rightarrow y\,ke^{1600x} - y = 40\,ke^{1600x} + 40$

$\Rightarrow y\,(ke^{1600x} - 1) = 40ke^{1600x} + 40$

$\therefore y(x) = \dfrac{40ke^{1600x} + 40}{ke^{1600x} - 1}$

$\therefore \lim\limits_{x\to\infty} y(x) = \lim\limits_{x\to\infty} \dfrac{40ke^{1600x} + 40}{ke^{1600x} - 1}$

$= \lim\limits_{x\to\infty} \dfrac{40k + \dfrac{40}{e^{1600x}}}{k - \dfrac{1}{e^{1600x}}} = \dfrac{40k}{k} = 40$

TUTORIAL EXERCISE

SECTION–III

ONLY ONE CORRECT ANSWER

1. The degree and order of the differential equation of all parabolas whose axis is x-axis are
   (a) 2, 1 (b) 1, 2
   (c) 3, 2 (d) None of these

2. The degree of the differential equation $y(x)=1+\frac{dy}{dx}+\frac{1}{1.2}\left(\frac{dy}{dx}\right)^2+\frac{1}{1.2.3}\left(\frac{dy}{dx}\right)^3+....$ is
   (a) 2 (b) 3
   (c) 1 (d) None of these

3. If m and n are order and degree of the equation $\left(\frac{d^2y}{dx^2}\right)^5+4.\frac{\left(\frac{d^2y}{dx^2}\right)^3}{\frac{d^3y}{dx^3}}+\frac{d^3y}{dx^3}=x^2-1$, then
   (a) $m = 3, n = 3$ (b) $m = 3, n = 2$
   (c) $m = 3, n = 5$ (d) $m = 3, n = 1$

4. The order of the differential equation of all circles having centre on y-axis and passing through the origin is
   (a) 1 (b) 2
   (c) 3 (d) 4

5. The differential equation of all circles in the first quadrant which touch the coordinate axes is of order
   (a) 1 (b) 2
   (c) 3 (d) None of these

6. The order and degree of the differential equation $\frac{d^2y}{dx^2}+\left(\frac{dy}{dx}\right)^{\frac{1}{3}}+x^{\frac{1}{4}}=0$ are respectively
   (a) 2, 3 (b) 3, 3
   (c) 2, 6 (d) 2, 4

7. The differential equation of all parabolas with axis parallel to the axis of y is
   (a) $yy_2+(y_1)^2=0$ (b) $y_3=2y_1$
   (c) $y_3^2=y_1$ (d) None of these

8. If $y = e^{-x}(A\cos x + B\sin x)$, then y satisfies:
   (a) $\frac{d^2y}{dx^2}+2\frac{dy}{dx}=0$ (b) $\frac{d^2y}{dx^2}-2\frac{dy}{dx}+2y=0$
   (c) $\frac{d^2y}{dx^2}+2\frac{dy}{dx}+2y=0$ (d) $\frac{d^2y}{dx^2}+2y=0$

9. The differential equation of all non-vertical lines in a plane is given by
   (a) $\frac{d^2y}{dx^2}=0$ (b) $\frac{d^2x}{dy^2}=0$
   (c) $\frac{d^2x}{dy^2}=0$ & $\frac{d^2y}{dx^2}=0$ (d) All of these

10. Family $y = Ax + A^3$ of curve is represented by the differential equation of degree
    (a) Three (b) Two
    (c) one (d) None of these

11. The differential equation for all the straight lines which are at a unit distance from the origin is
    (a) $\left(y-x\frac{dy}{dx}\right)^2=1-\left(\frac{dy}{dx}\right)^2$
    (b) $\left(y+x\frac{dy}{dx}\right)^2=1+\left(\frac{dy}{dx}\right)^2$
    (c) $\left(y-x\frac{dy}{dx}\right)^2=1+\left(\frac{dy}{dx}\right)^2$
    (d) None of these

12. The elimination of the arbitrary constants A, B and C from $y = A + Bx + Ce^{-x}$ leads to the differential equation
    (a) $y'''-y'=0$ (b) $y'''-y''+y'=0$
    (c) $y'''+y''=0$ (d) $y'''+y''-y'=0$

13. $y = ae^{mx} + be^{-mx}$ satisfies which of the following differential equations
    (a) $\frac{dy}{dx}-my=0$ (b) $\frac{dy}{dx}+my=0$
    (c) $\frac{d^2y}{dx^2}+m^2y=0$ (d) $\frac{d^2y}{dx^2}-m^2y=0$

14. The differential equations of all circles touching the x-axis at origin is

(a) $(y^2 - x^2) = 2xy\left(\dfrac{dy}{dx}\right)$

(b) $(x^2 - y^2)\dfrac{dy}{dx} = 2xy$

(c) $(x^2 - y^2) = 2xy\left(\dfrac{dy}{dx}\right)$

(d) None of these

15. The differential equation of all conics whose centre lies at origin, is given by

(a) $(3xy_2 + x^2y_3)(y - xy_1) = 3xy_2(y - xy_1 - x^2y_2)$

(b) $(3xy_1 + x^2y_2)(y_1 - xy_3) = 3xy_1(y - xy_2 - x^2y_3)$

(c) $(3xy_2 + x^2y_3)(y_1 - xy) = 3xy_1(y - xy_1 - x^2y_2)$

(d) None of these

16. The differential equation of all conics whose axes coincide with the coordinate axes, is

(a) $xyy_2 + xy_1^{\,2} - yy_1 = 0$

(b) $yy_2 + y_1^{\,2} = 0$

(c) $xyy_2 + (x - y)y_1 = 0$

(d) None of these

17. The differential equation of circles passing through the points of intersection of unit circle with centre at the origin and the line bisecting the first quadrant, is

(a) $y_1(x^2 + y^2 - 1) + (x + yy_1) = 0$

(b) $(y_1 - 1)(x^2 + y^2 - 1) + 2(y - x)(x + yy') = 0$

(c) $(x^2 + y^2 - 1) + yy_2 = 0$

(d) None of these

18. The equation to the curve which is such that portion of the axis of x cut off between the origin and the tangent at any point is proportional to the ordinate of that point is

(a) $x = y(C + K\log y)$

(b) $\log x = Ky^2 + C$

(c) $x^2 = y(C - K\log y)$

(d) None of these

19. Which of the following statement is true for general solution of a differential equation?

(a) It contains as many parameters as the degree of differential equation

(b) It contains as many parameters as the order of differential equation

(c) Number of parameters may not depend on order/degree of differential equation

(d) all of the above

20. If degree of a differential equation is 2, then which of the following is true for such differential equation?

(a) It has two direction of motions at each point on solution

(b) It can have more than two direction

(c) It has at most two directions

(d) None of these

21. The solution of the equation $\dfrac{dy}{dx} = \dfrac{3x - 4y - 2}{3x - 4y - 3}$ is

(a) $(x - y)^2 + C = \log(3x - 4y + 1)$

(b) $x - y + C = \log(3x - 4y + 4)$

(c) $x - y + C = \log(3x - 4y - 3)$

(d) $x - y + C = \log(3x - 4y + 1)$

22. The equation of the curve satisfying the differential equation $y^2(x^2 + 1) = 2x\dfrac{dy}{dx}$ passing through the point (0,1) is

(a) $y = \dfrac{4}{5 + x + \ln x}$ (b) $y = \dfrac{4}{5 - x + 2\ln x}$

(c) $y = \dfrac{4}{5 - x^2 + 2\ln x}$ (d) None of these

23. The solution of the differential equation $y' = \dfrac{y}{x} + \dfrac{\phi(y/x)}{\phi'(y/x)}$ is

(a) $x\,\phi(y/x) = k$ (b) $\phi(y/x) = kx$

(c) $y\,\phi(y/x) = k$ (d) $\phi(y/x) = ky$

24. The solution of $x\sin\left(\dfrac{y}{x}\right)dy = \left\{y\sin\left(\dfrac{y}{x}\right) - x\right\}dx$, is given by

(a) $\log x - \cos\left(\dfrac{y}{x}\right) = \log c$

(b) $\log x - \sin\left(\dfrac{y}{x}\right) = c$

(c) $\log\left(\dfrac{x}{y}\right) - \cos\left(\dfrac{y}{x}\right) = \log c$

(d) None of these

25. The solution of $(1 + e^{x/y})\,dx + e^{x/y}\left(1 - \dfrac{x}{y}\right)dy = 0$, is given by

(a) $x - ye^{x/y} = c$ (b) $x + ye^{x/y} = c$

(c) $y - \dfrac{x}{y}e^{x/y} = c$ (d) None of these

26. The number of solutions of $y' = \dfrac{y+1}{x-1}$, $y(1) = 2$ is

(a) 0 (b) 1

(c) 2 (d) infinite

27. The solution of the equation $\frac{dy}{dx} = e^{x-y} + x^2 e^{-y}$ is

(a) $e^y = e^x + \frac{x^3}{3} + c$ (b) $e^y = e^x + 2x + c$

(c) $e^y = e^x + x^3 + c$ (d) $y = e^x + c$

28. The solution of the differential equation $(\sin x + \cos x)\, dy + (\cos x - \sin x)dx = 0$ is

(a) $e^x(\sin x + \cos x) + c = 0$

(b) $e^y(\sin x + \cos x) = c$

(c) $e^y(\cos x - \sin x) = c$

(d) $e^x(\sin x - \cos x) = c$

29. If $\frac{dy}{dx} = \frac{xy + y}{xy + x}$, then the solution of the differential equation is

(a) $y = xe^x + c$ (b) $y = e^x + c$

(c) $y = Axe^{x-y}$ (d) $y = x + A$

30. The solution of the equation $\sin^{-1}\left(\frac{dy}{dx}\right) = x + y$ is

(a) $\tan(x + y) + \sec(x + y) = x + c$

(b) $\tan(x + y) - \sec(x + y) = x + c$

(c) $\tan(x + y) + \sec(x + y) + x + c = 0$

(d) None of these

31. The slope of a curve at any point is the reciprocal of twice the ordinate at the point and it passes through the point (4, 3). The equation of the curve is

(a) $x^2 = y + 5$ (b) $y^2 = x - 5$

(c) $y^2 = x + 5$ (d) $x^2 = y - 5$

32. A function $y = f(x)$ has second order derivative $f''(x) = 6(x - 1)$. If its graph passes through the point (2, 1) and at that point the tangent to the graph is $y = 3x - 5$, then the function is

(a) $(x + 1)^3$ (b) $(x - 1)^3$

(c) $(x + 1)^2$ (d) $(x - 1)^2$

33. The solution of $\frac{dy}{dx} = (x + y - 1) + \frac{x + y}{\log(x + y)}$ is given by

(a) $\{1 + \log(x + y)\} - \log\{1 + \log(x + y)\} = x + c$

(b) $\{1 + \log(x + y)\} - \log\{1 - \log(x + y)\} = x + c$

(c) $\{1 + \log(x + y)\}^2 - \log\{1 + \log(x + y)\} = x + c$

(d) None of the above

34. The complete solution of the differential equation $y = x\frac{dy}{dx} + \frac{dx}{dy}$ represents

(a) a family of straight line or a hyperbola

(b) a family of straight line or a parabola

(c) a parabola or a circle

(d) circles

35. Solution of the differential equation $(x - y)^2 \frac{dy}{dx} = a^2$ is

(a) $y = \frac{a}{2}\log\left|\frac{x - y - a}{x - y + a}\right| + c$

(b) $y = \frac{a}{2}\log\left|\frac{x - y + a}{x - y - a}\right| + c$

(c) $y^2 = a\log\left|\frac{x - y + a}{x - y - a}\right| + c$

(d) None of these

36. The solution of $\frac{x^3 dx + yx^2 dy}{\sqrt{x^2 + y^2}} = ydx - xdy$ is

(a) $\sqrt{x^2 + y^2} = Cx$

(b) $\sqrt{x^2 + y^2} + y/x = C$

(c) $\sqrt{x^2 + y^2} + y/x^2 = C$

(d) $(x^2 + y^2)^2 + xy^2 = C$

37. The solution of differential equation $xdy(y^2e^{xy} + e^{x/y}) = ydx(e^{x/y} - y^2e^{xy})$, is

(a) $xy = \log(e^x + \lambda)$ (b) $x^2/y = \log(e^{x/y} + \lambda)$

(c) $xy = \log(e^{x/y} + \lambda)$ (d) $xy^2 = \log(e^{x/y} + \lambda)$

38. The solution of $ydx - xdy + (1 + x^2)dx + x^2 \sin ydy = 0$, is given by:

(a) $x + 1 - y^2 + \cos y + c = 0$

(b) $y + 1 - x^2 + x\cos y + c = 0$

(c) $\frac{x}{y} + \frac{1}{y} - y + \cos y + c = 0$

(d) $\frac{y}{x} + \frac{1}{x} - x + \cos y + c = 0$

39. Integrating factor of the differential equation $\cos x\frac{dy}{dx} + y\sin x = 1$ is:

(a) $\cos x$ (b) $\tan x$

(c) $\sec x$ (d) $\sin x$

40. The integrating factor of $x(1 - x^2)\, dy + (2x^2y - y - ax^3)\, dx = 0$ is $e^{\int pdx}$, then P is

(a) $\dfrac{2x^2 - a^3}{x(1-x^2)}$ (b) $2x^3 - 1$

(c) $\dfrac{2x^2 - 1}{ax^3}$ (d) $\dfrac{2x^2 - 1}{x(1-x^2)}$

41. The solution of $ydx - xdy + 3x^2y^2e^{x^3}dx = 0$ is

(a) $\dfrac{x}{y} + e^{x^3} = C$ (b) $\dfrac{-x}{y} - e^{x^3} = 0$

(c) $\dfrac{-x}{y} + e^{x^3} = 0$ (d) None of these

42. If $xdy = y(dx + ydy)$, $y > 0$ and $y(1) = 1$, then $y(-3) =$

(a) 1 (b) 3

(c) 5 (d) –1

43. The solution of $(1 + xy)ydx + (1 - xy)x\,dy = 0$ is

(a) $\dfrac{x}{y} = k$ (b) $\log\left(\dfrac{x}{y}\right) = \dfrac{1}{xy} + k$

(c) $\dfrac{-x}{y} = e^{xy} + k$ (d) $\log\left(\dfrac{x}{y}\right) = xy + k$

44. The solution of the differential equation, $y\,dx + (x + x^2y)dy = 0$ is

(a) $\log y = cx$ (b) $\dfrac{1}{xy} + \log y = c$

(c) $-\dfrac{1}{xy} + \log y = c$ (d) $-\dfrac{1}{xy} + \log x = c$

45. An integrating factor for the differential equation $(1+ y^2)dx - (\tan^{-1} y - x)\,dy = 0$ is

(a) $\tan^{-1}y$ (b) $e^{\tan^{-1}y}$

(c) $\dfrac{1}{1+y^2}$ (d) $\dfrac{1}{x(1+y^2)}$

46. Solution of differential equation $\dfrac{dy}{dx} + ay = e^{mx}$ is

(a) $(a + m)y = e^{mx} + c$ (b) $ye^{ax} + me^{mx} + c = 0$

(c) $y = e^{mx} + ce^{-ax}$ (d) $(a+m)y = e^{mx} + ce^{-ax}(a+m)$

47. Equation of curve through point (1, 0) which satisfies the differential equation $(1 + y^2)dx - xydy = 0$ is

(a) $x^2 + y^2 = 1$ (b) $x^2 - y^2 = 1$

(c) $2x^2 + y^2 = 2$ (d) None of these

48. The solution of $(1+x^2)\dfrac{dy}{dx} + y = e^{\tan^{-1}x}$, is given by

(a) $3y.e^{\tan^{-1}x} = e^{3\tan^{-1}x} + C$

(b) $y.e^{2\tan^{-1}y} = e^{2\tan^{-1}x} + c$

(c) $2ye^{\tan^{-1}y} = e^{2\tan^{-1}y} + c$

(d) None of these

49. The solution of $y = x\dfrac{dy}{dx} + \dfrac{dy}{dx} - \left(\dfrac{dy}{dx}\right)^2$, is

(a) $y = (x - 1)^2$ (b) $4y = (x + 1)^2$

(c) $(y - 1)^2 = 4x$ (d) None of these

50. The solution of $\left(\dfrac{dy}{dx}\right)^2 + (2x+y)\dfrac{dy}{dx} + 2xy = 0$, is

(a) $(y + x^2 - c_1)(x + \log y + y^2 + c_2) = 0$

(b) $(y + x^2 - c_1)(x - \log y - c_2) = 0$

(c) $(y + x^2 - c_1)(x + \log y - c) = 0$

(d) None of these

51. The orthogonal trajectories of the family of curves $y = c\,x^k$ are given by

(a) $x^2 + c\,y^2 = C$ (b) $x^2 + k\,y^2 = C$

(c) $k\,x^2 + y^2 = C$ (d) $x^2 - k\,y^2 = C$

52. The degree of the differential equation $\dfrac{d^2y}{dx^2} + 3\left(\dfrac{dy}{dx}\right)^2 = x\log\dfrac{d^2y}{dx^2}$ is

(a) 1 (b) 2

(c) 3 (d) None of these

53. The equation of the curve whose subnormal is equal to a constant a is

(a) $y = a\,x + b$ (b) $y^2 = 2ax + 2b$

(c) $ay^2 - x^3 = a$ (d) None of these

where b is an arbitrary constant.

54. The solution of the equation $dy/dx = \cos(x - y)$ is

(a) $y + \cot\left(\dfrac{x-y}{2}\right) = C$

(b) $x + \cot\left(\dfrac{x-y}{2}\right) = C$

(c) $x + \tan\left(\dfrac{x-y}{2}\right) = C$

(d) None of these

55. If the differential equation whose solution represents the family $y = ae^{3x} + be^x$ is $a\dfrac{d^2y}{dx^2} + b\dfrac{dy}{dx} + cy = 0$, then a, b, c are respectively

(a) 1, –4, 3 (b) 1, 3, 4

(c) 3, 3, 4, (d) None of these

56. The orthogonal trajectory of the curve $a^{n-1}y = x^n$ is

(a) $nx^2 + y^2 = 0$ (b) $ny^2 + x^2 =$ constant

(c) $y^2 - x^2 =$ constant (d) None of these

57. If the solution of $(1 + 2e^{x/y})dx + 2e^{x/y}(1 - x/y)\,dy = 0$ is $(x + \ell ye^{x/y}) = c$ (c is an arbitrary constant), then ℓ is
(a) 1 (b) 2
(c) 3 (d) None of these

58. The solution of the differential equation $\dfrac{xdy}{dx} - 2y = x^4$ is
(a) $\dfrac{y}{x^2} = \dfrac{x^2}{2} + c$ (b) $\dfrac{y}{x^2} = -\dfrac{x^2}{2} + c$
(c) $\dfrac{y}{x^2} = \dfrac{x^4}{2} + c$ (d) None of these

59. The solution of the differential equation $\dfrac{x\,dy}{dx} + y = x^3y^6$ is
(a) $y^{-5}x^{-5} = \dfrac{5}{2}x^{-2} + c$ (b) $y^5x^5 = \dfrac{5}{2}x^{-2} + c$
(c) $y^{-5}x^{-5} = \dfrac{5}{2}x^2 + c$ (d) None of these

60. The solution of the differential equation $\dfrac{y + \sin x.\cos^2(xy)}{\cos^2(xy)}dx + \left(\dfrac{x}{\cos^2(xy)} + \sin y\right)dy = 0$ is
(a) $\tan xy + \cos x + \cos y = c$
(b) $\tan xy - \cos x - \cos y = c$
(c) $\tan xy + \cos x - \cos y = c$
(d) None of these

61. The solution of differential equation $y\cos\dfrac{y}{x}(xdy - ydx) + x\sin\dfrac{y}{x}(xdy + ydx) = 0$ is
(a) $xy\sin\dfrac{x}{y} = k$ (b) $xy\sin\dfrac{y}{x} = k$
(c) $xy \sin xy = k$ (d) None of these

62. The equation of curve whose sub-tangent is n times the abscissa of the point of contact , is given by
(a) $y = cx^n$ (b) $y^n = cx$
(c) $y^n = cx^2$ (d) $y = cx^{2n}$

63. The differential equation of the family of circles passing through the fixed points $(a, 0)$ and $(-a, 0)$ is.
(a) $y_1(y^2 - x^2) + 2xy + a^2 = 0$
(b) $y_1(y^2 + xy + a^2x^2) = 0$
(c) $y_1(y^2 - x^2 + a^2) + 2xy = 0$
(d) None of these

64. Equation of the curve through the origin satisfying $dy = (\sec x + y \tan x)$ dx is
(a) $y \sin x = x$ (b) $y \cos x = x$
(c) $y \tan x = x$ (d) None of these

65. If $y = f(x)$ passing through (1, 2) satisfies the differential equation $y(1 + xy)\,dx - xdy = 0$, then $f(x)$ is
(a) $\dfrac{2x}{2-x^2}$ (b) $\dfrac{x+1}{x^2+1}$
(c) $\dfrac{x-1}{4-x^2}$ (d) $\dfrac{4x}{1-2x^2}$

66. Let a and b be respectively the degree and order of the differential equation of the family of circles touching the lines $y^2 - x^2 = 0$ and lying in the first and second quadrant, then
(a) $a = 1, b = 2$ (b) $a = 1, b = 1$
(c) $a = 2, b = 1$ (d) $a = 2, b = 2$

67. The equation $f(t) = \dfrac{d}{dt}\int_0^{-1}\dfrac{dx}{1-\cos t\cos x}$ satisfies the differential equation
(a) $\dfrac{df}{dt} + 2f(t)\cot t = 0$
(b) $\dfrac{df}{dt} - 2f(t)\cot t = 0$
(c) $\dfrac{df}{dt} + 2f(t) = 0$
(d) $\dfrac{df}{dt} - 2f(t) = 0$

68. The curves for which the square of the normal is equal to the square of the length of radius vector, are
(a) only circles
(b) only rectangular hyperbolas
(c) either circles or rectangular hyperbola
(d) None of these

69. The largest value of c such that there exists a differentiable function $h(x)$ for $-c < x < c$ that is a solution of $y_1 = 1 + y^2$ with $h(0) = 0$ is
(a) 2π (b) π
(c) $\dfrac{\pi}{2}$ (d) $\dfrac{\pi}{4}$

70. Which of the following transformation reduce the differential equation $\dfrac{dz}{dx} + \dfrac{z}{x}\log z = \dfrac{z}{x^2}(\log z)^2$ into the form $\dfrac{du}{dx} + P(x)u = Q(x)$?
(a) $u = \log z.$ (b) $u = e^z$
(c) $u = (\log z)^{-1}$ (d) $u = (\log z)^2$

71. A spherical raindrop evaporates at a rate proportional to its surface area at any instant t. The differential equation giving the rate of change of the radius of the raindrop is

(a) $\frac{d^2r}{dt^2}+2r=0$ (b) $\frac{d^2r}{dt^2}-3r=0$

(c) $\frac{d^2r}{dt^2}=0$ (d) None of these

72. If $\phi(x)=\int\{\phi(x)\}^{-2}\,dx$ and $\phi(1)=0$, then $\phi(x)$ is equal to

(a) $\{2(x-1)\}^{1/4}$ (b) $\{5(x-2)\}^{1/5}$

(c) $\{3(x-1)\}^{1/3}$ (d) None of these

73. Solution of differential equation $(2x\cos y+y^2\cos x)dx+(2y\sin x-x^2\sin y)dy=0$ is

(a) $x^2\cos y+y^2\sin x=c$

(b) $x\cos y-y\sin x=c$

(c) $x^2\cos^2 y+y^2\sin^2 x=c$

(d) None of these

74. The family of curves represented by $\frac{dy}{dx}=\frac{x^2+x+1}{y^2+y+1}$ and the family represented by $\frac{dy}{dx}+\frac{y^2+y+1}{x^2+x+1}=0$

(a) touch each other (b) are orthogonal

(c) are one & the same (d) None of these

75. The solution of $\cot\left(\frac{x}{y}\right)(y\,dx-x\,dy)=ny^2dx$ is equal to

(a) $\log\sin\left(\frac{x}{y}\right)=nx+c$

(b) $\log\sin(xy)=ny+c$

(c) $\log\cos\left(\frac{x}{y}\right)=ny+c$

(d) None of these

76. The solution of $\sin\left(\frac{x}{y}\right)(ydx-xdy)=xy^3(xdy+ydx)$ is

(a) $\frac{xy}{2}+\sin\left(\frac{x}{y}\right)+c=0$

(b) $\frac{(xy)^2}{2}+\sin\left(\frac{x}{y}\right)+c=0$

(c) $\frac{(xy)^2}{2}+\cos\left(\frac{x}{y}\right)+c=0$

(d) $xy+\tan\left(\frac{x}{y}\right)+c=0$

77. The curve satisfying the equation $\frac{dy}{dx}=\frac{y(x+y^3)}{x(y^3-x)}$ and passing through the point (4, –2) is

(a) $y^2=-2x$ (b) $y=-x$

(c) $y^3=-2x$ (d) None of these

78. Solution of $y(xy+1)dx+x(1+xy+x^2y^2)\,dy=0$ is

(a) $\log y=\frac{1}{xy}+c$

(b) $\log y=\frac{1}{2x^2y^2}+c$

(c) $\log y=\frac{1}{xy}+\frac{1}{2x^2y^2}+c$

(d) None of these

79. If $y=y(x)$ and $\left(\frac{2+\sin x}{y+1}\right)\left(\frac{dy}{dx}\right)=-\cos x,\ y(0)=1$, then $y(\pi/2)$ equals

(a) 1/3 (b) 2/3

(c) –1/3 (d) 1

80. Tangent to a curve intersects the y-axis at a point P. A line perpendicular to this tangent through P passes through another point (1, 0). The differential equation of the curve is

(a) $y\frac{dy}{dx}-x\left(\frac{dy}{dx}\right)^2=1$ (b) $\frac{xd^2y}{dx^2}-\left(\frac{dy}{dx}\right)^2=1$

(c) $y\frac{dx}{dy}+x=1$ (d) None of these

81. Solution to the differential equation $\frac{x+\frac{x^3}{3!}+\frac{x^5}{5!}+\ldots\ldots}{1+\frac{x^2}{2!}+\frac{x^4}{4!}}=\frac{dx-dy}{dx+dy}$ is

(a) $2y\,e^{2x}=C.e^{2x}+1$ (b) $2y\,e^{2x}=C.e^{2x}-1$

(c) $y\,e^{2x}=C.e^{2x}+2$ (d) None of these

82. A curve is such that the mid point of the portion of the tangent intercepted between the point where the tangent is drawn and the point where the tangent meets y-axis, lies on the line $y=x$. If the curve passes through (1, 0), then the curve is

(a) $2y=x^2-x$ (b) $y=x^2-x$

(c) $y=x-x^2$ (d) $y=2(x-x^2)$

83. The solution of the differential equation $dx(x^2-t)=dt$ is

(a) $t=(x-1)^2e^x+c$

(b) $t=(x+1)^2e^x+c$

(c) $t=(x^2-2x+2)+ce^{-x}$

(d) None of these

84. The equation of the curve, passing through (2, 5) and having the area of triangle formed by the x-axis, the ordinate of a point on the curve and the tangent at the point is 5 sq units

(a) $xy=10$ (b) $x^2=10y$

(c) $y^2=10x$ (d) $xy^{1/2}=10$

85. The equation of the curve satisfying the differential equation $y_2(x^2 + 1) = 2xy_1$ passing through the point (0, 1) and having slope of tangent at $x = 0$ as 3 is

(a) $y = x^2 + 3x + 2$ (b) $y^2 = x^2 + 3x + 1$

(c) $y = x^3 + 3x + 1$ (d) None of these

86. Differential equation of the family of circles touching the line $y = 2$ at (0, 2) is

(a) $x^2 + (y-2)^2 + \frac{dy}{dx}(y-2) = 0$

(b) $x^2 + (y-2)\left(2 - 2x\frac{dx}{dy} - y\right) = 0$

(c) $x^2 + (y-2)^2 + \left(\frac{dx}{dy} + y - 2\right)(y-2) = 0$

(d) None of these

87. Solution of $\left(\frac{xdy}{x^2+y^2}\right) = \left(\frac{y}{x^2+y^2} - 1\right)dx$ is

(a) $x + \tan^{-1}\left(\frac{y}{x}\right) = c$ (b) $\tan^{-1}\left(\frac{y}{x}\right) = c$

(c) $x\tan^{-1}\left(\frac{y}{x}\right) = c$ (d) None of these

88. If each $a_i > 0$, then the shortest distance between the point (0, –3) and the curve $y = 1 + a_1x^2 + a_2x^4 + ... + a_nx^{2n}$ is

(a) 1 (b) 2

(c) 3 (d) 4

89. Solution of differential equation $x^2 = 1 + \left(\frac{x}{y}\right)^{-1}\frac{dy}{dx} + \frac{\left(\frac{x}{y}\right)^{-2}\left(\frac{dy}{dx}\right)^2}{2!} + \frac{\left(\frac{x}{y}\right)^{-3}\left(\frac{dy}{dx}\right)^3}{3!} + ...$ is

(a) $y^2 = x^2(\ln x^2 - 1) + c$

(b) $y = x^2(\ln x - 1) + c$

(c) $y^2 = x(\ln x - 1) + c$

(d) $y = e^{x^2} + c$

90. Solution of differential equation

$$\frac{x^2}{\left(\frac{1}{x^2} + y^2\right)}(xdy + ydx) + y^2(xdy - ydx) = 0 \text{ is}$$

(a) $\tan^{-1}xy - \frac{1}{2}\left(\frac{y}{x}\right)^2 = c$

(a) $\tan^{-1}xy + \frac{1}{2}\left(\frac{y}{x}\right)^2 = c$

(a) $\tan^{-1}xy + \frac{1}{2}\left(\frac{y}{x}\right)^3 = c$

(a) None of these

91. Solution of the differential equation $\frac{y}{x} + \frac{dy}{dx} = \frac{\sqrt{xy}}{dx}$

(a) $2\sqrt{xy} = \frac{x^2}{2} + c$ (b) $2\sqrt{xy} + \frac{x^2}{2} = c$

(c) $2\sqrt{\frac{y}{x}} = \frac{x^2}{2} + c$ (d) $2\sqrt{\frac{y}{x}} + \frac{x^2}{2} = c$

92. The differential equation satisfying the curve $\frac{x^2}{a^2+\lambda} + \frac{y^2}{b^2+\lambda} = 1$, is

(a) $(x + yy_1)(xy_1 - y) = (a^2 - b^2)y_1$

(b) $(x + yy_1)(x - yy_1) = y_1$

(c) $(x - yy_1)(xy_1 + y) = (a^2 - b^2)y_1$

(d) None of these

93. The equation of curve for which the normal at every point passes through a fixed point, is

(a) a circle (b) an ellipse

(c) a hyperbola (d) None of these

94. If the tangent at any point P of a curve meets the axis of x in T. Then the curve for which $OP = PT$, O being the origin is

(a) $x = cy^2$ (b) $x = cy^2$ or $x = c/y^2$

(c) $x = cy$ or $x = c/y$ (d) None of these

95. The general solution of the differential equation $\frac{dy}{dx} = \frac{1-x}{y}$ is a family of curves which looks most like which of the following?

(a) 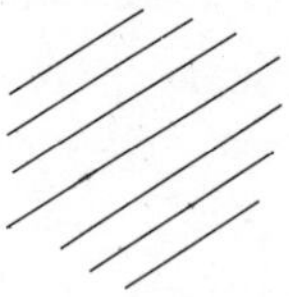

(b) 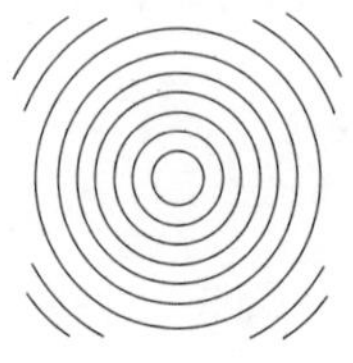

(c) 

(d) 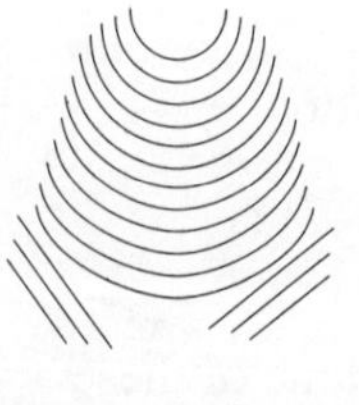

SECTION–IV

MORE THAN ONE COREECT ANSWER

1. Which of the following is true for singular solution?
   (a) It has no parameter
   (b) it cannot be derived from general solution
   (c) It is the envelope of the general solution
   (d) All of the above

2. The orthogonal trajectories of the family of curves $xy = k^2$ are
   (a) rectangular hyperbola
   (b) $y^2 = 4a(x + a)$
   (c) $x^2 - y^2 = a^2$
   (d) system of circles with centre on x-axis

3. The solution of $y = x\left(\frac{dy}{dx} + \left(\frac{dy}{dx}\right)^3\right)$ are given by
   (a) The constant function $y = 0$
   (b) $y = p^{-3}e^{\frac{1}{2}p^2}(p + p^3)$
   (c) $y = p^3e^{-\frac{1}{2p^2}}(p + p^3)$
   (d) $y = ye^{-\frac{1}{2}p^2} = p^{-2} + 1$

4. The differential equation of the curve such that the initial ordinate of any tangent is equal to the corresponding subnormal is
   (a) a linear equation
   (b) a homogeneous equation
   (c) an equation with separable variables
   (d) None of these

5. A tangent drawn to the curve $y = f(x)$ at $P(x, y)$cuts the x-axis and y-axis at A and B respectively such that $BP : AP = 3 : 1$, given that $f(1) = 1$, then
   (a) differential equation of curve is $x\frac{dy}{dx} - 3y = 0$
   (b) normal at (1,1) is $x + 3y = 4$
   (c) curve passes through (2,1/8)
   (d) differential equation of curve is $x\frac{dy}{dx} + 3y = 0$

6. For the differential equation $x\frac{dy}{dx} + y = xy^3$
   (a) solution can be obtained by substituting $\frac{1}{y^2} = t$
   (b) on solving the differential equation reduces to linear form
   (c) equation reduces to $\frac{1}{x^3y^3}d(xy) = \frac{dx}{x^2}$.
   (d) solution is $\frac{1}{2x^2y^2} - \frac{1}{x} = c$.

7. A spherical rain drop evaporates at a rate proportional to its surface area at that instant. The radius of the drop initially is 3 mm and after one hour it is found to be 2 mm. If $r(t)$ represents radius of the drop at time 't', then
   (a) differential equation representing the rate of change of volume w.r.t. time is $\frac{dV}{dt} = -k4\pi r^2; k > 0$
   (b) $r(t) = 3 - t$
   (c) $r(t) = 3 + t^2 - 2t$
   (d) $r(t) = 3 - t^2$

8. If y_1, y_2 are the solutions of the differential equation $\frac{dy}{dx} + p(x)y = Q(x)$, then
   (a) $y = y_1 + C(y_1 - y_2)$ is the general solution of equation
   (b) $y = y_1 + C(y_1 + y_2)$ is the general solution of equation
   (c) $\alpha y_1 + \beta y_2$ is a solution if $\alpha + \beta = 1$
   (d) $\alpha y_1 + \beta y_2$ is a solution if $\alpha - \beta = 1$

9. A right circular cylinder with radius R and height H contains a liquid which evaporates at a rate proportional to its surface area in contact with air (proportionality constant $= k > 0$). If T is time after which cylinder will be empty, then
   (a) T is dependent on R (b) T is independent of R
   (c) T is dependent on H (d) T is dependent on K

10. The normal to the curve $y = f(x)$ passing through the point (1, 1) is $a(y - 1) + (x - 1) = 0$. If the slope of tangent at any point on the curve is proportional to the ordinate of that point, then
    (a) Equation of curve is $y = e^{a(x-1)}$
    (b) Equation of curve is $y = e^{ax-1}$
    (c) Area bounded by the y-axis, the curve and the normal to the curve at P is $\left|\frac{1}{a}\left(a - \frac{1}{2} + e^{-a}\right)\right|$
    (d) None of these

11. Let $S_1 \equiv x^2 + y^2 - kx = 0$ and $S_2 \equiv x^2 - y^2 - cx = 0$
 (a) S_1 and S_2 intersect at an angle of $\pi/4$
 (b) S_1 and S_2 intersect orthogonally
 (c) abscissas of the point of intersection of S_1 and S_2 is *A.M.* of c and k
 (d) point of intersection of S_1 and S_2 is origin

SECTION–V

ASSERTION AND REASON TYPE QUESTIONS

1. **A:** The degree of differential equation $\frac{d^2y}{dx^2} + \frac{dy}{dx} = ln\left(\frac{d^2y}{dx^2}\right)$ is 2.
 R: The degree of differential equation which can be written as a polynomial in the derivatives is the degree of the derivative of the highest order occurring in it.
2. **A:** The differential equation of the form $y\phi(xy)\,dx + x\psi(xy)dy = 0$ can be converted into homogeneous forms by substitution of $xy = v$.
 R: All differential equations of first order and first degree do not become homogeneous if we substitute $y = vx$.
3. **A:** The equation of the curve through the point (1,0) which satisfies the differential equation $(1 + y^2)\,dx - xy\,dy = 0$ is $x^2 - y^2 = 1$
 R: Differential equation $\frac{dy}{dx} = f(x).g(y)$ can be solved by separating variables $\frac{dy}{g(y)} = f(x)dx$.
4. **A:** The differential equation of all circles in a plane must be of order 3.
 R: There is only one circle passing through three non-collinear points.
5. **A:** The differential equation $y^3dy + (x + y^2)dx = 0$ becomes homogeneous if we put $y^2 = t$
 R: All differential equation of first order first degree becomes homogeneous if we put $y = tx$

SECTION–VI

COMPREHENSION-TYPE QUESTIONS

A: If any differential equation in the form $f(f_1(x, y))\,d(f_1(x, y)) + \phi(f_2(x, y))\,d(f_2(x, y)) + ... = 0$, then each term can be integrated separately. For e.g.,

$$\int \sin xy d(xy) + \int\left(\frac{x}{y}\right)d\left(\frac{x}{y}\right) = -\cos xy + \frac{1}{2}\left(\frac{x}{y}\right)^2 + c$$

1. The solution of the differential equation $xdy - ydx = \sqrt{x^2 - y^2}\,dx$ is
 (a) $cx = e^{\sin^{-1}\left(\frac{y}{x}\right)}$ (b) $xe^{\sin^{-1}\left(\frac{y}{x}\right)} = c$
 (c) $x + e^{\sin^{-1}\frac{y}{x}} = c$ (d) None of these
2. The solution of the differential equation $(xy^4 + y)\,dx - xdy = 0$ is
 (a) $\frac{x^3}{4} + \frac{1}{2}\left(\frac{x}{y}\right)^2 = c$ (b) $\frac{x^4}{4} + \frac{1}{3}\left(\frac{x}{y}\right)^3 = c$
 (c) $\frac{x^4}{4} - \frac{1}{2}\left(\frac{x}{y}\right)^2 = c$ (d) $\frac{x^3}{4} - \frac{1}{2}\left(\frac{x}{y}\right)^2 = c$
3. Solution of differential equation $(2x \cos y + y^2 \cos x)\,dx + (2y \sin x - x^2 \sin y)\,dy = 0$ is
 (a) $x^2 \cos y + y^2 \sin x = c$
 (b) $x \cos y - y \sin x = c$
 (c) $x^2 \cos^2 y + y^2 \sin^2 x = c$
 (d) None of these

B: One of the important applications of the differential equation is to find out the family of curves for which some conditions involving the derivatives are given. For this one can proceed by making use of the following facts. Equation of the tangent at a point (x, y) to the curve $y = f(x)$ is given by $Y - y = \frac{dy}{dx}(X - x)$.

At the x-axis, $Y = 0$, and $X = x - \frac{y}{dy/dx}$. At the y-axis, $X = 0$ and $Y = y - x\frac{dy}{dx}$. Similar things, can be obtained for normal by writing its equation as $(Y - y)\frac{dy}{dx} + X - x = 0$.

4. If $y = f(x)$ be a curve such length of x intercept of tangent is equal to the distance of the point of tangency from x-axis, then $f(x)$ is given by

(a) $c = ye^{x/y}$ (b) $c = ye^{x^2/y}$

(c) $c = y^2e^{x/y}$ (d) $c = y^2e^{y/x}$

5. The equation of curve $y = f(x)$, such that length of sub normal is equal to the abscissa of tangency is

(a) $y^2 = 4ax$ (b) $x^2 + y^2 = c$

(c) $x^2 - y^2 = c$ (d) (b) and (c)

6. The slope of the curve at any point is the reciprocal of twice the ordinate at the point. If the curve passes through the point (4, 3), then its equation is

(a) $y^2 = x + 1$ (b) $y^2 = x + 5$

(c) $y^2 = 4x + 5$ (d) $y^2 = 4x - 5$

7. The equation of curve passing through the point (5, 3) such that the product of slope of tangent at any point (x, y) and the ordinate is equal to its abscissa is

(a) $x^2 + y^2 = 16$ (b) $x^2 - y^2 = 9$

(c) $x^2 - y^2 = 16$ (d) $x^2 + y^2 = 9$

8. The equation of curve passing through the point (1, 0) and the slope of whose tangent at (x, y) is $\frac{x^2+y^2}{2xy}$, is

(a) $x^2 - y^2 = x$ (b) $x^2 - y^2 = 4$

(c) $x^2 + y^2 = x$ (d) $x^2 + y^2 = y$

C: Differential equations are solved by reducing them to the exact differential of an expression in x and y, i.e., they are reduced to the form $d(f(x, y)) = 0$.

E.g. $\frac{xdx+ydy}{\sqrt{x^2+y^2}} = \frac{ydx-xdy}{x^2}$

$\Rightarrow \frac{1}{2}\frac{2xdx+2ydy}{\sqrt{x^2+y^2}} = -\frac{xdy-ydx}{x^2}$

$\Rightarrow \frac{d(x^2+y^2)}{2\sqrt{x^2+y^2}} = -d\left(\frac{y}{x}\right)$

$\Rightarrow d\left(\sqrt{x^2+y^2}\right) = -d\left(\frac{y}{x}\right)$

$\Rightarrow d\left(\sqrt{x^2+y^2}+\frac{y}{x}\right) = 0$

$\therefore$ solution is $\sqrt{x^2+y^2}+\frac{y}{x} = C$

Use the above method to answer the following questions.

9. The general solution of $(2x^3 - xy^2)\,dx + (2y^3 - x^2y)dy = 0$ is

(a) $x^4 + x^2y^2 - y^4 = c$ (b) $x^4 - x^2y^2 + y^4 = c$

(c) $x^4 - x^2y^2 - y^4 = c$ (d) $x^4 + x^2y^2 + y^4 = c$

10. General solution of the differential equation $\frac{xdy}{x^2+y^2} + \left(1 - \frac{y}{x^2+y^2}\right)dx = 0$ is

(a) $x + \tan^{-1}\left(\frac{y}{x}\right) = c$ (b) $x + \tan^{-1}\frac{x}{y} = c$

(c) $x - \tan^{-1}\left(\frac{y}{x}\right) = c$ (d) None of these

11. General solution of the differential equation $e^y dx + (xe^y - 2y)\,dy = 0$

(a) $xe^y - y^2 = c$ (b) $ye^x - x^2 = c$

(c) $xe^y - x = c$ (d) $xe^y - 1 = cy^2$

D: A differential equation of the form $\frac{d^2y}{dx^2} + a_1\frac{dy}{dx} + a_2y = 0$ is called linear differential equation; where a_1 and a_2 are function of x only. In case a_1 and a_2 are constants, the solution of the linear differential equation can be easily written by following facts.

(i) $y = 0$ is a solution of differential equation

(ii) If $y = f(x)$ is a solution, then $y = c\,f(x)$ is also a solution

(iii) If $y = f_1(x)$ and $y = f_2(x)$ are two solutions then $y = f_1(x) + f_2(x)$ will also be a solution

(iv) If distinct roots of quadratic equation $m^2 + a_1m + a_2 = 0$ are m_1 and m_2 (real or imaginary), then solution of differential equation is $y = c_1e^{m_1x} + c_2e^{m_2x}$. In case roots are complex the solution can be transformed to the form $y = e^{ax}(c_1 \cos bx + c_2 \sin bx)$ by using Euler's theorem.

(v) In case roots of $m^2 + a_1m + a_2 = 0$ are equal (say m_1) the differential equation can be made linear by putting $\frac{dy}{dx} - m_1y = v$ can also be satisfied by some other functions which are not of the above type such functions are called particular integrals

12. $y = e^x$ is solution of differential equation $\frac{d^2y}{dx^2} - y = 0$, then which of the following is not a solution

(a) e^{-x} (b) e^{-2x}

(c) $ae^x + be^{-x}$ (d) $e^x + e^{-x}$

13. Which of the following is solution of the equation $\frac{d^2y}{dx^2} - 6\frac{dy}{dx} + 9y = 0$

(a) $c_1 + c_2x$ (b) $(c_1 + c_2x)e^{3x}$

(c) $c_1 \cos 3x + c_2 \sin 3x$ (d) None of these

E: A country has a food deficit of 10%. Its population grow continuously at a rate of 3% per year. It's annual food production every year is 4% more than that of the last year. Assume that the average food requirement per person remains constant. Let the country will become self sufficient in food after n years.

14. The growth of population is

(a) Exponential (b) Logarithmic

(c) Linear (d) None of these

15. The food production after 2 years becomes _____ times more than that of the initial production

(a) 1.04 (b) 1.08

(c) $(1.04)^2$ (d) 0.16

16. The population after 100 years becomes _____times more than that of the initial population–

(a) 1.03 (b) e^3

(c) 103 (d) $(1.03)^{100}$

17. If $n = (m)$; where (m) is smallest integer greater than or equal to m ,then m is

(a) $\dfrac{\ln 10 - \ln 9}{\ln 1.04 - 0.03}$ (b) $\dfrac{\ln(10/9)}{\ln(1.04/1.03)}$

(c) $\dfrac{\ln 10 - 9}{\ln 1.04 - 0.03}$ (d) $\dfrac{10 - \ln 9}{\ln(1.04/1.03)}$

18. Rather than continuous growth, if population becomes 3% more than that of last year and $n = (m)$; where (m) is smallest integer $\leq m$, then m is

(a) $\dfrac{\ln 10 - \ln 9}{\ln 1.04 - 0.03}$ (b) $\dfrac{\ln(10/9)}{\ln(1.04/1.03)}$

(c) $\dfrac{\ln 10 - 9}{\ln 1.04 - 0.03}$ (d) $\dfrac{10 - \ln 9}{\ln(1.04/1.03)}$

G: The average birth rate and average death rate of mosquito in a certain part of India is given by $B(t) = 2t^2 - t + 1$, $D(t) = -t^2 + 3t + 4$ respectively; where t = time in years. It is given that the population is $p_0 = 100$ at $t = 0$ (starting point from where the measurement is taken up) and population at any time t is given by, $P(t) = \int_0^t \{B(t) - D(t)\}\,dt + P_0$ and total population at any time t is divided into three groups as group of larva $A(t)$, group of youngs $B(t)$, group of olds $C(t)$; where $A(t) = t^3 - 9t + 10$, $B(t) = -t^2 + 2t + 40$, $C(t) = -t^2 + 4t + 50$, at any time t. Negative population means absence of population. All population functions attain integer values at any time t. If at any time population is non-integer then it takes the nearest integer value and mid-value takes higher integer (example: 7.5 is equal to 8). Calculation should be based on single digit after decimal.

19. What is the total population when population of group of young's is maxima?

(a) 104 (b) 101

(c) 98 (d) 96

20. What is the population of Larva when population is minimum?

(a) 10 (b) 5

(c) 3 (d) disappear

21. What is the population of 'Group of old' at the time when the population of 'Group of young's' started disappearing?

(a) 32 (b) 25

(c) 34 (d) 43

22. After how long the group of larva started recovering their population? Choose appropriate option

(a) In one year (approximate)

(b) two year (approximate)

(c) In half year (approximate)

(d) 1/4 year (approximate)

23. At the moment group of olds started disappearing, what is the percentage of Larva in total population?.

(a) 0% (b) 45%

(c) 79% (d) 100%

SECTION–VII

MATRIX MATCH TYPE

1. **Column I**

(i) If the curve satisfy the equation $(e^x + 1)\,y\,dy = (y + 1)e^x\,dx$, passes through (0, 0) and $(k, 1)$, then k is

(ii) If the curve satisfy the equation $x\dfrac{dy}{dx} + y = xy^3$ passes through (1, 1) and $(3/2, p)$, then p is

(iii) If $\dfrac{dy}{dx} = \dfrac{xy + y}{xy + x}$, then the solution of the differential

(iv) The solution of the equation $\frac{dy}{dx}=\frac{3x-4y-2}{3x-4y-3}$ passes through origin, is

Column II

(a) $x - y = \ln(3x - 4y + 1)$

(b) Not defined

(c) $\ln(e - 1)$ equation always passes through the origin and point $(k, 1)$ then k is

(d) $\pm\frac{2}{\sqrt{3}}$

2. **Column I**

(i) Order of differential equation whose general solution is given by $y = (c_1 + c_2)\cos(x + c_3) - c_4e^{x+c_5} + c_5 \sin x$, where c_1, c_2, c_3, c_4, c_5 are arbitrary constants , is

(ii) Order of differential equation formed by eliminating the constants from $y = a \sin^2 x + b \cos^2 x + c \sin^2 x + d \cos 2x + e \sin x$, where a,b,c,d are arbitrary constants, is

(iii) The degree of equation $\frac{d^2y}{dx^2}+\left[1+\left(\frac{dy}{dx}\right)^2\right]^{3/2}=0$ is

(iv) Order of differential equation whose solution is $y = cx + c^2 - 3c^{3/2} + 2$, where c is a parameter is

Column II

(a) 1

(b) 2

(c) 3

(d) 4

3. Match the properties of the curves given in Column I with the corresponding curve(s) given the column II

Column I

(i) A curve passing through (2, 3) having the property that the length of the radius vector of any of its point P is equal to the length of the tangent drawn at this point, can be

(ii) A curve passing through (1, 1) having the property that any tangent intersects the y-axis at the point which is equidistant from the point of tangency and the origin, can be

(iii) A curve passing thorugh (1, 0) for which the length of normal is equal to the radius vector, can be

(iv) A curve passes through the point (2, 1) and having the property that the segment of any of its tangent between the point of tangency and the x-axis is bisected by the y-axis, can be

Column II

(a) Straight line

(b) Circle

(c) Parabola

(d) Hyperbola

SECTION–VIII

INTEGER-TYPE QUESTIONS

1. Find the order of the differential equation whose general solution is given by $y=(C_1+C_2)\cos(x+C_3)-C_4e^{x+C_5}$

2. A curve C has the property that if the tangent drawn at any point P on C meets the co-ordinates axes at A and B, then P is the mid-point of AB. The curve passes through the point (1, 1). Determining the equation of the curve, find $f\left(\frac{1}{5}\right)$.

3. A solution of the differential equation $\left(\frac{dy}{dx}\right)^2-x\frac{dy}{dx}+y=0$ is $y = kx - \lambda$, then find the greatest value of $-24(k + \lambda)$.

4. The differential equation representing the family of curves $y^2 = 2c(x+\sqrt{c})$, where c is a positive parameter, has its order and degre respectively (n) and (m), then find $(n + m)$.

5. If $y(t)$ is a solution of $(1+t)\frac{dy}{dt}-ty=1$ and $y(0) = -1$, then find $|2y(1)|$.

6. A right circular cone with radius R and height H contains a liquid which evaporates at a rate proportional to its surfce area in contact with air (proportionality constan$t = k > 0$). Find the time after which the cone is empty, when $H = 16k$.

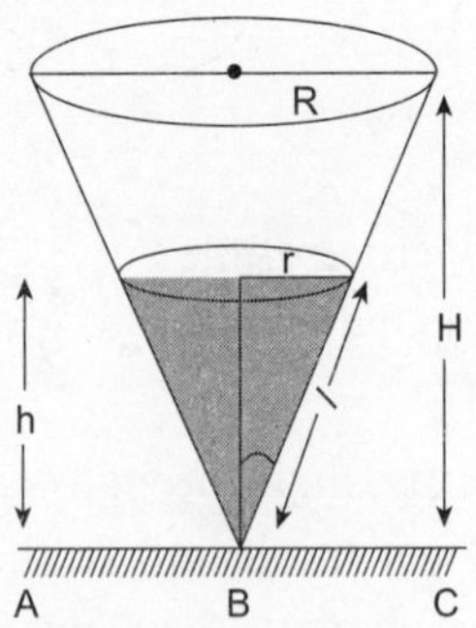

7. If $y = y(z)$ and $\frac{2+\sin x}{y+1}\left(\frac{dy}{dx}\right) = -\cos x$, $y(0) = 1$, then find $y\left(-\frac{\pi}{2}\right)$.

8. If $xdy = ydx + y^2dy$ and $y(1) = 1$, then find the algebraic sum of possible values of $y(-3)$.

9. If $(x^2 + y^2)dy = xydx$ and $y(1) = 1$. If $f(x_0) = e$, then x_0 is equal to $e\sqrt{k}$, then find k.

10. A cuve passes through (1, 1) and any tangent at a point P on the curve is such that it intersect x and y-axis at A and B respectively. If $PA : PB = 3:1$, then finding the differential equation of the curve and solving, it is found that curve passes through the point $\left(\frac{1}{8}, \lambda\right)$; then find λ.

Answer Keys

SECTION–III

1. (b) 2. (c) 3. (b) 4. (a) 5. (a) 6. (a) 7. (d) 8. (c) 9. (a) 10. (a)
11. (c) 12. (c) 13. (d) 14. (b) 15. (b) 16. (a) 17. (b) 18. (a) 19. (b) 20. (c)
21. (d) 22. (c) 23. (b) 24. (a) 25. (b) 26. (a) 27. (a) 28. (b) 29. (c) 30. (b)
31. (c) 32. (b) 33. (a) 34. (b) 35. (a) 36. (b) 37. (c) 38. (d) 39. (c) 40. (d)
41. (a) 42. (b) 43. (b) 44. (c) 45. (b) 46. (d) 47. (b) 48. (a) 49. (b) 50. (c)
51. (b) 52. (d) 53. (b) 54. (b) 55. (a) 56. (b) 57. (b) 58. (a) 59. (a) 60. (b)
61. (b) 62. (b) 63. (c) 64. (b) 65. (a) 66. (c) 67. (a) 68. (c) 69. (c) 70. (c)
71. (c) 72. (c) 73. (a) 74. (b) 75. (a) 76. (c) 77. (c) 78. (c) 79. (a) 80. (a)
81. (b) 82. (c) 83. (c) 84. (a) 85. (c) 86. (b) 87. (a) 88. (d) 89. (a) 90. (c)
91. (a) 92. (a) 93. (a) 94. (c) 95. (b)

SECTION–IV

1. (a,b,c,d) 2. (a,c) 3. (a,c) 4. (a,b) 5. (c,d) 6. (a,b,c,d) 7. (a,b) 8. (a,c)
9. (b,c,d) 10. (a,c) 11. (c,d)

SECTION–V

1. (d) 2. (d) 3. (a) 4. (b) 5. (c)

SECTION–VI

1. (a) 2. (b) 3. (a) 4. (a) 5. (d) 6. (b) 7. (c) 8. (a) 9. (b) 10. (a)
11. (a) 12. (b) 13. (b) 14. (a) 15. (c) 16. (b) 17. (a) 18. (b) 19. (d) 20. (d)
21. (b) 22. (b) 23. (d)

SECTION–VII

1. (i) → (c) (ii) → (d) (iii) → (b) (iv) → (a)
2. (i) → (c) (ii) → (c) (iii) → (b) (iv) → (a)
3. (i) → (a,d) (ii) → (b) (iii) → (b,d) (iv) → (c)

SECTION–VIII

1. 3 2. 5 3. 6 4. 4 5. 1 6. 16 7. 3 8. 2 9. 3 10. 2

HINTS AND SOLUTIONS

TEXTUAL EXERCISE-1: (SUBJECTIVE)

1. (a) $(x^2+y^2)dx - 2x\,dy = 0$

$\Rightarrow \dfrac{(x^2+y^2)}{2x} = \dfrac{dy}{dx}$

$\Rightarrow$ It is of first order and degree 1

(b) $\sqrt{1+\left(\dfrac{dy}{dx}\right)^2} = x^3$

$\Rightarrow \left(\dfrac{dy}{dx}\right)^2 = x^6 - 1$

$\Rightarrow$ It is of order 1 and degree 2.

(c) $\dfrac{dy}{dx} = \cos x$

$\Rightarrow$ It is of order 1 and degree 1

(d) $\sqrt{\dfrac{d^3y}{dx^3}} = \sqrt[4]{\left(\dfrac{dy}{dx}\right)+5}$

$\Rightarrow \left(\dfrac{d^3y}{dx^3}\right)^2 = \left(\dfrac{dy}{dx}\right)+5$

which is of order 3 and degree 2

(e) $y = x\left(\dfrac{dy}{dx}\right) + r\sqrt{1+\left(\dfrac{dy}{dx}\right)^2}$

$\Rightarrow y - x\dfrac{dy}{dx} = r\sqrt{1+\left(\dfrac{dy}{dx}\right)^2}$

$\Rightarrow y^2 + x^2\left(\dfrac{dy}{dx}\right)^2 - 2xy\dfrac{dy}{dx} = r^2\left(1+\left(\dfrac{dy}{dx}\right)^2\right)$

$\Rightarrow (x^2-r^2)\left(\dfrac{dy}{dx}\right)^2 - 2xy\dfrac{dy}{dx} + (y^2-r^2) = 0$

It is of order 1 and degree 2

(f) $\dfrac{d^2y}{dx^2} = 0$

It is of order 2 and degree 1

(g) $\left\{1+\left(\dfrac{dy}{dx}\right)^2\right\}^{3/2} = r\dfrac{dy^2}{dx^2}$

$\Rightarrow \left\{1+\left(\dfrac{dy}{dx}\right)^2\right\}^3 = r^2\left(\dfrac{d^2y}{dx^2}\right)^2$

It is of order 2 and degree 2

(h) $y = x\dfrac{dy}{dx} + \dfrac{a}{(dy/dx)}$

$\Rightarrow y\dfrac{dy}{dx} = x\left(\dfrac{dy}{dx}\right)^2 + a$

$\Rightarrow$ It is of order 1 and degree 2

(i) $(y+C)^2\dfrac{dx}{dz} + z\dfrac{dy}{dz} - (y+a) = 0$

$\Rightarrow (y+C)^2\dfrac{dx}{dy}.\dfrac{dy}{dz} + z\dfrac{dy}{dx}.\dfrac{dx}{dz} - (y+a) = 0$

$\Rightarrow (y+C)^2\dfrac{dy/dz}{dy/dx} + z\dfrac{dy}{dx}.\dfrac{dx}{dz} - (y+a) = 0$

$\Rightarrow (y+C)^2\dfrac{dy}{dz} + z\left(\dfrac{dy}{dx}\right)^2.\dfrac{dx}{dz} - (y+a)\dfrac{dy}{dx} = 0$

$\Rightarrow z\left(\dfrac{dx}{dz}\right)\left(\dfrac{dy}{dx}\right)^2 - (y+a)\dfrac{dy}{dx} + (y+C)^2\dfrac{dy}{dx} = 0$

which is of order 1 and degree 2.

2. (a) $y = \dfrac{dy}{dx}.x + \sqrt{a^2\left(\dfrac{dy}{dx}\right)^2 + b^2}$

$\Rightarrow \left(y - \dfrac{dy}{dx}.x\right)^2 + a^2\left(\dfrac{dy}{dx}\right)^2 + b^2$

$\Rightarrow y^2 + x^2\left(\dfrac{dy}{dx}\right)^2 - 2xy\dfrac{dy}{dx} = a^2\left(\dfrac{dy}{dx}\right)^2 + b^2$

$\Rightarrow (x^2-a^2)\left(\dfrac{dy}{dx}\right)^2 - 2xy\dfrac{dy}{dx} + y^2 - b^2 = 0$

which is of order 1 and degree 2

(b) $x^2\left(\dfrac{d^2y}{dx^2}\right)^3 + y\left(\dfrac{dy}{dx}\right)^4 + y^4 = 0$

which is of order 2 and 3

(c) $x\dfrac{\partial z}{\partial x} + y\dfrac{\partial z}{\partial y} = nz$ ...(1)

Here $z = f(x, y)$ and partial differential equation (1) consists of first order partial differential coefficients.

$\dfrac{\partial z}{\partial x}$ and $\dfrac{\partial z}{\partial y}$, if is of order 1 and degree 1

(d) $\dfrac{\partial^2 z}{\partial x^2} - a^2\dfrac{\partial^2 z}{\partial y^2} = 0$ ...(1)

Here $z = f(x, y)$ and (1) consists of second order partial differential coefficients,

$\dfrac{\partial^2 z}{\partial x^2}$ and $\dfrac{\partial^2 z}{\partial y^2} = 0$. It is of order 2 and degree 1

3. $y = 1 + \left(\dfrac{dy}{dx}\right) + \dfrac{1}{2!}\left(\dfrac{dy}{dx}\right)^2 + \dfrac{1}{3!}\left(\dfrac{dy}{dx}\right)^3 + ...$

$\Rightarrow y = e^{(dy/dx)}$ $\Rightarrow \ln y = dy/dx$

which is of order 1 and degree 1

4. $\dfrac{d^2y}{dx^2} = 3\left(\dfrac{dy}{dx}\right)^2 = x\log\left(\dfrac{d^2y}{dx^2}\right)$

Above differential equation is of order 2, but degree is not defined as the above differential equation can't be expressed as a polynomial equation in differential coefficient.

5. (a) $y' + \sin y' = 0$

$\Rightarrow \dfrac{dy}{dx} + \sin\left(\dfrac{dy}{dx}\right) = 0$

Which is of order 1 and degree is not defined

(b) $y'' + 2y' + \sin y = 0$

which is of order 2 and degree 1

TEXTUAL EXERCISE–1: (OBJECTIVE)

1. (a) Given parabola is $y = x^2$ ...(i)

equations of tangent lines to (1) is $y = mx + \dfrac{1}{m}$ ...(ii)

$\Rightarrow y' = m$ ...(iii)

$\therefore$ From (ii) and (iii), we get $y = y'x + \dfrac{1}{y'}$ or $x(y')^2 - yy' + 1 = 0$, which is of order 1 and degree 2.

2. (b) Equation of parabolas having their axes as x-axis is given by $y^2 = 4a(x - h)$ ...(i)

$\Rightarrow 2yy' = 4a$ ...(ii)

$\Rightarrow 2yy'' + 2(y')^2 = 0$ or $yy'' + (y')^2 = 0$, which is of order 2 and degree 1

3. (b) Given differential equation is $y_3^{2/3} + 2 + 3y_2 + y_1 = 0$ or

$\left(\dfrac{d^3y}{dx^3}\right)^{2/3} = -(3y_2 + y_1 + 2)$

$\Rightarrow \left(\dfrac{d^3y}{dx^3}\right)^2 = -(3y_2 + y_1 + 2)^3$, which is of order 3 and degree 2.

4. (c) $y(x) = 1 + \dfrac{dy}{dx} + \left(\dfrac{dy}{dx}\right)\dfrac{2}{12} + \dfrac{1}{1.2.3}\left(\dfrac{dy}{dx}\right)^3 + ...$

$\Rightarrow y = e^{dy/dx}$

$\Rightarrow \dfrac{dy}{dx} = \ln y$

$\Rightarrow$ Degree 1

5. (b) Given differential equation can be written as

$$\left(\frac{d^3y}{dx^3}\right)^2 + \left(\frac{d^2y}{dx^2}\right)^5\left(\frac{d^3y}{dx^3}\right) + 4\left(\frac{d^2y}{dx^2}\right)^3 + (1 - x^2)\frac{d^3y}{dx^3} = 0$$

$\Rightarrow$ Order = 3 and degree = 2

$\Rightarrow m = 3$ and $n = 2$

6. (b) The order of differential equation is same as the number of effective arbitrary constants present in the family of curves

$\Rightarrow$ Order = 4

7. (c) $dy + dx = 0$

$\Rightarrow \dfrac{dy}{dx} = 1$

It is an equation of first order and first degree

8. (a) Equation of family of circles is $x^2 + (y \pm r)^2 = r^2$

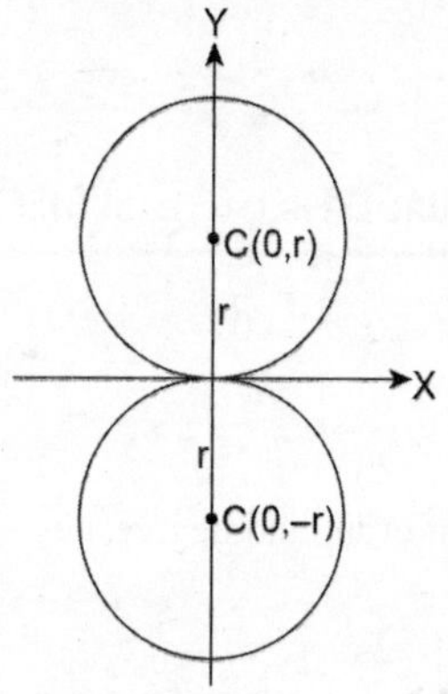

$\Rightarrow x^2 + y^2 \pm 2ry = 0$

$\Rightarrow$ Order = 1 (As there is only one parameter r)

9. (a) Equation of such a circle is the first quadrant is $(x - r)^2 + (y - r)^2 = r^2$

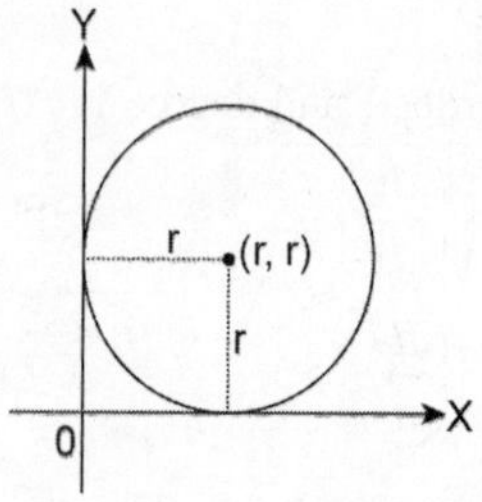

Since these is one arbitrary constant, i.e., one order

10. (d) $\dfrac{d^2y}{dx^2} = \left\{y + \left(\dfrac{dy}{dx}\right)^2\right\}^{1/4}$

which can be written as $\left(\dfrac{d^2y}{dx^2}\right)^4 = y + \left(\dfrac{dy}{dx}\right)^2$

$\Rightarrow$ order = 2 and degree = 4

11. (a) $\dfrac{d^2y}{dx^2} + \left(\dfrac{dy}{dx}\right)^{1/3} + x^{1/4} = 0$

which can be written as $\dfrac{d^2y}{dx^2} + x^{1/4} = -\left(\dfrac{dy}{dx}\right)^{1/3}$

$\Rightarrow \left(\dfrac{d^2y}{dx^2} + x^{1/4}\right)^3 = -\dfrac{dy}{dx}$

$\Rightarrow$ Order = 2 and degree = 3

12. (b) $\left[1 + \left(\dfrac{dy}{dx}\right)^2\right]^{3/4} = \left(\dfrac{d^2y}{dx^2}\right)^{1/3}$

$\Rightarrow \left(1 + \left(\dfrac{dy}{dx}\right)^2\right)^9 = \left(\dfrac{d^2y}{dx^2}\right)^4$

$\Rightarrow$ Order = 2 and degree = 4

TEXTUAL EXERCISE–2: (SUBJECTIVE)

1. $Ax^2 + By^2 = 1$, differentiating, we get

$A(2x) + (B)\ 2y\dfrac{dy}{dx} = 0$ ...(1)

Differentiating again, $2A+2By\frac{d^2y}{dx^2}+2B\left(\frac{dy}{dx}\right)^2=0$ ...(2)

By equation (i), $y\frac{dy}{dx}=-2\frac{Ax}{2B}=-\frac{Ax}{B}$

By equation (2), $2A+2B\left(y\frac{d^2y}{dx^2}+\left(\frac{dy}{dx}\right)^2\right)=0$

$\Rightarrow \left(y\frac{d^2y}{dx^2}+\left(\frac{dy}{dx}\right)^2\right)=\frac{-A}{B}$

$\Rightarrow x\left(y\frac{d^2y}{dx^2}+\left(\frac{dy}{dx}\right)^2\right)-y\frac{dy}{dx}=0$ (by (3))

2. $(x-h)^2+(y-k)^2=a^2$ ...(1), h, k are arbitrary constants.

Differentiating twice, we get $1+\left(\frac{dy}{dx}\right)^2+(y-k)\frac{d^2y}{dx^2}=0$

and $(x-h)+(y-k)\frac{dy}{dx}=0$

$\Rightarrow (y-k)=-\frac{\left\{1+\left(\frac{dy}{dx}\right)^2\right\}}{\frac{d^2y}{dx^2}}$ ...(2) and $(x-h)=-(y-k)\frac{dy}{dx}$

$=\frac{\left\{1+\left(\frac{dy}{dx}\right)^2\right\}\frac{dy}{dx}}{\frac{d^2y}{dx^2}}$ ...(3)

On substituting from (2) and (3) in (1), we get

$\left[1+\left(\frac{dy}{dx}\right)^2\right]^3=a^2\left(\frac{d^2y}{dx^2}\right)^2$

which is the required differential equation of (1)

3. $xy=ce^x+be^{-x}+x^2$ ...(1)

$\Rightarrow \frac{xdy}{dx}+y=ce^x-be^{-x}+2x$ ...(2)

$\Rightarrow \frac{xd^2y}{dx^2}+\frac{dy}{dx}+\frac{dy}{dx}=Ce^x+be^{-x}+2$ ...(3)

By (1) and (3), we get $x\frac{d^2y}{dx^2}+2\frac{dy}{dx}=xy-x^2+2$

$\Rightarrow x\frac{d^2y}{dx^2}+2\frac{dy}{dx}-xy+x^2-2=0$ which is the required differential equation

4. $y^2=4a(x+a)=4ax+4a^2$ ...(1)

Differentiating, we get $2y.\frac{dy}{dx}=4a$ ...(2)

and $a=\frac{y}{2}.\frac{dy}{dx}$ ...(3)

Using (2) and (3) in (1), we get $y^2=2y\left(\frac{dy}{dx}\right)\left(x+\frac{y}{2}\frac{dy}{dx}\right)$

$\Rightarrow y=2\frac{dy}{dx}\left(x+\frac{ydy}{2dx}\right)$

$\Rightarrow y=\frac{2xdy}{dx}+y\left(\frac{dy}{dx}\right)^2$

$\Rightarrow y\left(1-\left(\frac{dy}{dx}\right)^2\right)=\frac{2xdy}{dx}$ which is the required differential equation

5. Let $(0, k)$ be the centre.
Since r is the radius, the equation of the family of circles is given by $(x-0)^2+(y-k)^2=r^2$.
$\Rightarrow x+(y-k)^2=r^2$ ...(1)
Differentiating, we get $2x+2(y-k)\frac{dy}{dx}=0$

$\Rightarrow (y-k)=\frac{-x}{dy/dx}$

$\Rightarrow (y-k)^2=\frac{x^2}{(dy/dx)^2}$ ...(2)

$\therefore$ From (1) and (2), we get $x^2\left(\frac{dy}{dx}\right)^2+x^2=r^2\left(\frac{dy}{dx}\right)^2$ or $\left(\frac{dy}{dx}\right)^2(x^2-r^2)+x^2=0$ which is the differential equation of (1)

6. **(a)** $y=C_1\tan^2x+C_2\sec^2x+C_3$
Since we can re-write the equation as $y=C_2+(C_1+C_2)\tan^2x+C_3$
$=(C_2+C_3)+(C_1+C_2)\tan^2x=k_1+k_2\tan^2x$
$\therefore$ k_1, k_2 are two effective arbitrary constants.
$\Rightarrow$ Order is 2

(b) Let the equation of ellipse having fixed directions be
$\frac{(x-h)^2}{a^2}+\frac{(y-k)^2}{b^2}=1$ ...(1)
Let for above ellipses D_1 and D_2 be the fixed directrices at constant distances from their centre. i.e., $\frac{a}{e}=\lambda$ (constant)

$\Rightarrow \frac{(x-h)^2}{(a^2/e^2)}+\frac{(y-k)^2}{\frac{a^2}{e^2}(1-e^2)}=e^2$

$\Rightarrow \frac{(x-h)^2}{\lambda^2}+\frac{(y-k)^2}{\lambda^2(1-e^2)}=e^2$ ...(2)

Clearly (2) has exactly 3 effective arbitrary constants h, k, e but λ is constant.
Thus, order of differential equation (2) will be 3.

(c) $xy=C_1e^x-C_2e^{-x}+x^2$
$\because$ C_1 and C_2 are two arbitrary constant
$\Rightarrow$ Order is 2

(d) $y=C_1x+C_2x^2$
$\because$ C_1, C_2 are two arbitrary constants.
$\Rightarrow$ Order = 2

(e) $y=C_1x+\frac{C_2}{x}+C_3$
It has 3 arbitrary constants, hence is of order 3.

(f) $y=C_1e^{3x}+C_2e^{2x}+C_3e^x$
It has 3 arbitrary constants, and hence is of order 3.

(g) $y = (\sin^{-1}x)^2 + A\sin^{-1}x + B$

It has 2 arbitrary constant, and hence is of order 2.

7. $y = (C_1 + C_2)\sin(x + C_3) - C_4 e^{x+C_2}$

Or $y = k_1 \sin(x + C_3) - e^{C_2}C_4e^x$ or $y = k_1\sin(x + C_3) - k_2e^x$

$\Rightarrow$ There are 3 effective arbitrary constant, K_1, C_3 and K_2

$\Rightarrow$ Order = 3

8. $y = e^x(A\cos x + B\sin x)$

Differentiating, we get $\frac{dy}{dx} = e^x(-A\sin x + B\cos x) + e^x$ $(A\cos x + B\sin x)$

$$\Rightarrow \frac{dy}{dx} = e^x(-A\sin x + B\cos x) + y \quad \ldots(1)$$

$$\Rightarrow \frac{d^2y}{dx^2} = e^x(-A\cos x - B\sin x) + e^x(-A\sin x + B\cos x) + \frac{dy}{dx} = -y + \left(\frac{dy}{dx} - y\right) + \frac{dy}{dx} \text{ (using (1))}$$

9. Let the voltage of battery = $E(t)$ at any instant t.

Voltage drop across capacitor = q/C

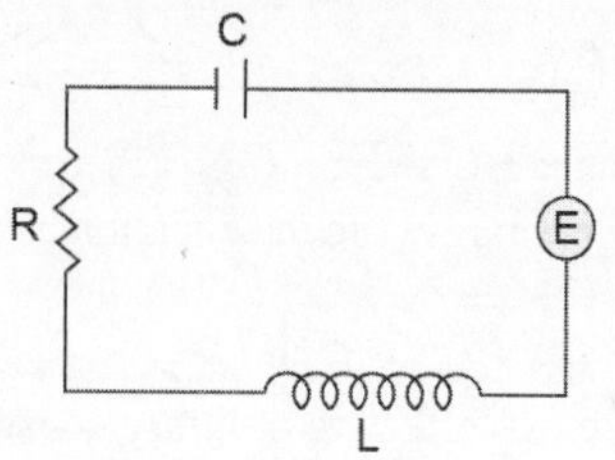

Voltage drop across resistor = $RI = R\frac{dq}{dt}$ and voltage across inductance L = $L\frac{dI}{dt} = L\frac{d^2q}{dt^2}$

$$\therefore \quad E(t) = L\frac{d^2q}{dt^2} + R\frac{dq}{dt} + \frac{q}{C}$$

10. Slope of $OP = \tan(\phi + \theta) = y/x$ ...(1)

Also slope of normal PN at P to curve $y = f(x)$ is given by

$$\tan\left(\frac{\pi}{2} + \theta\right) = -\frac{dx}{dy}$$

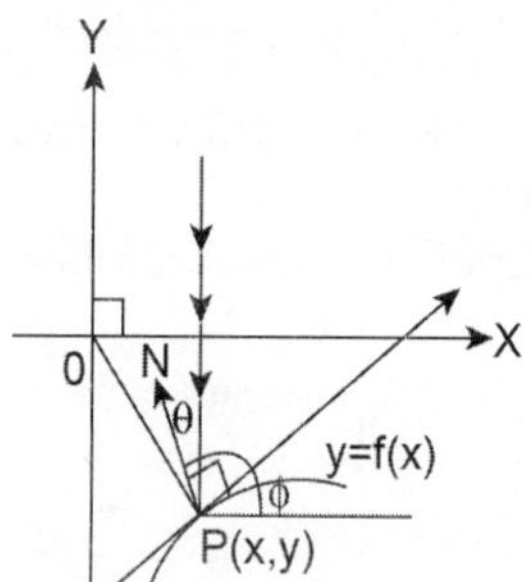

$$\Rightarrow -\cot\theta = -\frac{dx}{dy}$$

$$\Rightarrow \cot\theta = \frac{dx}{dy} \quad \ldots(2)$$

Also, $\phi - \theta = \pi/2$

$$\Rightarrow \phi = \pi/2 + \theta \quad \ldots(3)$$

Using (3) in (1), we get $\tan\left(\frac{\pi}{2} + 2\theta\right) = \frac{y}{x}$

$$\Rightarrow -\cot 2\theta = \frac{y}{x}$$

$$\Rightarrow \tan 2\theta = \frac{-x}{y}$$

$$\Rightarrow \frac{2\tan\theta}{1-\tan^2\theta} = \frac{-x}{y} \text{ or } \frac{2\cot\theta}{\cot^2\theta - 1} = \frac{-x}{y}$$

$$\Rightarrow \frac{2\left(\frac{dx}{dy}\right)}{\left(\frac{dx}{dy}\right)^2 - 1} = \frac{-x}{y}$$

$$\Rightarrow 2y\frac{dx}{dy} = x - x\left(\frac{dx}{dy}\right)^2$$

$$\Rightarrow x\left(\frac{dx}{dy}\right)^2 + 2y\left(\frac{dx}{dy}\right) = x$$

which is the required differential equation of curve.

11. Let a = acceleration in body of mass 'm'

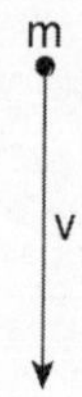

$\Rightarrow$ $ma = mg - k(v)^2$; k = constant of proportionality

$$\Rightarrow m\frac{dv}{dt} = g - \frac{k}{m}v^2$$

$$\Rightarrow \frac{dv}{dt} = g - \frac{k}{m}v^2$$

Which is the required differential equation of velocity v of body.

TEXTUAL EXERCISE–2: (OBJECTIVE)

1. (b) Length of sub normal is given by $y\frac{dy}{dx} = a$ (constant)

$\Rightarrow yy' = a$

$\Rightarrow y\,dy = a\,dx$

$\Rightarrow \int y\,dy = a\int dx$

$\Rightarrow \frac{y^2}{2} = ax + b$

$\Rightarrow y^2 = 2ax + 2b$

2. (d) Equation of parabolas with their axis parallel to y-axis are given by $(x - h)^2 = 4a(y - k)$ ...(1)

where h, k, a are arbitrary constant

$\Rightarrow 2(x - h) = 4ay'$ ...(2)

$\Rightarrow 2 = 4ay''$

$\Rightarrow 4a = \frac{2}{y''}$ ...(3)

Using equations (3) in (2), we get $2(x-h) = \frac{2}{y''}.y'$

$\Rightarrow (x-h) = y'/y''$ ...(4)

$\Rightarrow 1 = \frac{(y'')^2 - y'.y'''}{(y'')^2}$

$\Rightarrow (y'')^2 = (y'')^2 - y'y''' = 0$ or $y'.y''' = 0$

3. (b) Equation of ellipses having their centres at origin is $ax^2 + by^2 + 2hxy + c = 0$ or $\frac{a}{c}x^2 + \frac{b}{c}y^2 + 2\frac{h}{c}xy + 1 = 0$ or

$a'x^2 + b'y^2 + 2h'xy + 1 = 0$ which has 3 arbitrary effective parameters a', b' and h'

$\Rightarrow$ Differential equation would have order 3.

4. (b) $y = Ae^{3x} + Be^{5x}$ ...(1)

$\Rightarrow y' = A(3)e^{3x} + B(5)e^{5x}$ ...(2)

$\Rightarrow y'' = 9Ae^{3x} + 25B\,e^{5x}$ ...(3)

Using (3) – 3(2) gives,

$\Rightarrow y'' - 3y' = 10\,Be^{5x}$

$\Rightarrow Be^{5x} = \frac{y'' - 3y'}{10}$ ...(4)

Now, (3) – 5(2) gives $y'' - 5y' = -6Ae^{3x}$

$\Rightarrow Ae^{3x} = \frac{5y' - y''}{6}$ ...(6)

Using (4) and (5) in (1), we get $y = \frac{5y' - y''}{6} + \frac{y'' - 3y'}{10}$

$\Rightarrow y = \frac{25y' - 5y'' + 3y'' - 9y'}{30}$

$\Rightarrow 30y = 16y' - 2y''$ or $15y = 8y' - y''$

$\Rightarrow y'' - 8y' + 15y = 0$

5. (c) $y = e^{-x}(A\cos x + B\sin x)$

$\Rightarrow y' = e^{-x}(-A\sin x + B\cos x) - e^{-x}(A\cos x + B\sin x)$

$\Rightarrow y' = e^{-x}(-A\sin x + B\cos x) - y$ ...(1)

$\Rightarrow y'' = e^{-x}(-A\sin x - B\sin x) - e^{-x}(-A\sin x + B\cos x) - y'$

$\Rightarrow y'' = -y - (y' + y) - y'$ (using (1))

$\Rightarrow y'' = -2y' - 2y$ *or* $y'' + 2y' + 2y = 0$

6. (a) Equation of non-vertical lines are given by, $y = ax + b$; $a, b \in \mathbb{R}$

$\Rightarrow y' = A$

$\Rightarrow y'' = 0$

7. (a) $y = Ax + A^3$

$\Rightarrow y' = A$

$\Rightarrow y = xy' + (y')^3$

$\Rightarrow$ degree is 3

8. (c) Let the equation of family of straight lines having their distances from origin = p be $y = ax + b$

$\Rightarrow \frac{|a(0) - (0) + b|}{\sqrt{a^2+1}} = p$

$\Rightarrow \frac{|b|}{\sqrt{a^2+1}} = p$

$\Rightarrow b = \pm p\sqrt{a^2+1}$

$\therefore\ y = ax \pm p\sqrt{y'^2+1} \Rightarrow y' = a$

$\therefore\ y = xy' \pm p\sqrt{y'^2+1}$

$\Rightarrow (y - xy')^2 = p^2(y'^2 + 1)$ or $\left(y - x\frac{dy}{dx}\right)^2 = p^2\left(1 + \left(\frac{dy}{dx}\right)^2\right)$

9. (b) $y = C_1\cos ax + C_2\sin ax$ ...(1)

$\Rightarrow y' = -C_1\,a\sin ax + C_2 a\cos ax$

$\Rightarrow y' = -C_1a^2\cos ax - C_2\,a^2\sin ax$

$\Rightarrow y'' = -a^2(y)$ ...(2)

$\Rightarrow y'' + a^2y = 0$ or $\frac{d^2y}{dx^2} + a^2y = 0$

10. (b) $y = Cx + C - C^3$

$\Rightarrow y' = C$

$\Rightarrow y = xy' + y' - (y')^3$ or $y = x\frac{dy}{dx} + \frac{dy}{dx} - \left(\frac{dy}{dx}\right)^3$

11. (c) $y = A + Bx + Ce^{-x}$

$\Rightarrow y' = B - Ce^{-x}$

$\Rightarrow y'' = Ce^{-x}$

$\Rightarrow y''' = -Ce^{-x}$

$\Rightarrow y''' = -y''$ or $y''' + y'' = 0$

12. (d) $y = ae^{mx} + be^{-mx}$

$\Rightarrow y' = ame^{mx} - bme^{-mx}$

$\Rightarrow y'' = am^2e^{mx} + bm^2e^{-mx}$

$\Rightarrow y'' = m^2y$ or $\frac{d^2y}{dx^2} - m^2y = 0$

13. (b) $x^2 + y^2 = 1$

$\Rightarrow 2x + 2yy' = 0$

$\Rightarrow x + yy' = 0$

$\Rightarrow 1 + yy'' + (y')^2 = 0$ or $yy'' + (y')^2 + 1 = 0$

14. (c) $y = \sec(\tan^{-1}x)$

$\Rightarrow y' = \sec(\tan^{-1}x).\tan(\tan^{-1}x) \times \frac{1}{1+x^2}$

$\Rightarrow (1 + x^2)y' = y.x$ or $(1+x^2)\frac{dy}{dx} = xy$

15. (c) Equation of family of circle having radius 'r' is given by

$(x-h)^2 + (y-k)^2 = r^2$ ...(1)

$\Rightarrow 2(x-h) + 2(y-k).y' = 0$

$\Rightarrow y' = \frac{-(x-h)}{(y-k)}$ ...(2)

$\Rightarrow y'' = -\left[\frac{(y-k) - (x-h).y'}{(y-k)^2}\right]$

$\Rightarrow y'' = -\left[\frac{(y-k)^2 + (x-h)^2}{(y-k)^3}\right]$

$\Rightarrow y'' = -\left[\frac{r^2}{(y-k)^3}\right]$ ...(3)

From (3), $(y-k)^3 = -r^2/y''$

$\Rightarrow (y-k) = -\frac{r^{2/3}}{(y'')^{1/3}}$ ......(4)

From (2), $-y'(y-k) = (x-h)$ ...(5)

Using (4) and (5) in (1), we get $y'^2(y-k)^2 + (y-k)^2 = r^2$

$\Rightarrow (1 + y'^2)(y-k)^2 = r^2$

$\Rightarrow (1+y'^2)\left(\frac{r^{4/3}}{(y'')^{2/3}}\right) = r^2$ or $\frac{(1+y'^2)}{(y'')^{2/3}} = r^{2-\frac{4}{3}} = r^{2/3}$

or $(1 + y'^2) = r^{2/3}\,(y'')^{2/3}$

$\Rightarrow (1 + y'^2)^3 = r^2(y'')^2$.

16. (b) Equation of family of circle is $x^2 + (y - r)^2 = r^2$ ...(1)

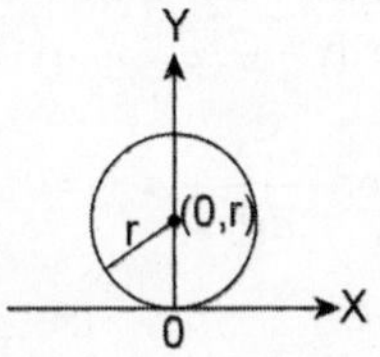

$\Rightarrow 2x + 2(y - r)y' = 0$

$\Rightarrow (y-r) = \frac{-x}{y'}$ ...(2)

Using (2) in (1), we get

$x^2 + \frac{x^2}{y'^2} = r^2$ or $x^2y'^2 + x^2 = r^2y'^2$ ...(3)

Again from (2), $r = y + \frac{x}{y'}$ ...(4)

From equation (3), (4), we get $x^2y'^2 + x^2 = \left(y + \frac{x}{y'}\right)^2 . y'^2$

or $x^2y'^2 + x^2 = (yy' + x)^2$ or $(x^2 - y^2)y'^2 - 2xyy' = 0$

or $(x^2 - y^2)\frac{dy}{dx} = 2xy$

17. (a) Equation of family of circles is

$(x - r)^2 + (y - r)^2 = r^2$ ...(1)

$\Rightarrow x^2 + y^2 - 2xr - 2yr + r^2 = 0$

$\Rightarrow 2x + 2yy' - 2r - 2ry' = 0$

$\Rightarrow r = \frac{x + yy'}{(1 + y')}$ ...(2)

Using (2) in (1), we get $\left(x - \frac{x+yy'}{(1+y')}\right)^2 + \left(y - \frac{x+yy'}{(1+y')}\right)^2$

$= \left(\frac{x+yy'}{1+y'}\right)^2$

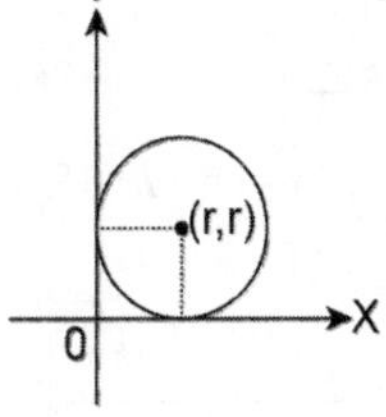

or $(x + xy' - x - yy')^2 + (y + yy' - x - yy')^2 = (x - yy')^2$ or $(xy' + xy')^2 + (y - x)^2 = (x + yy')^2$

or $(x-y)^2\left(\frac{dy}{dx}\right)^2 + (y-x)^2 = (x+yy')^2$ or $(x - y)^2 (1 + y'^2)$

$= (x + yy')^2$.

18. (a) Equation of family of circles is $(x - r)^2 + y^2 = r^2$ ...(1)

$\Rightarrow 2(x - r) + 2yy' = 0$

$\Rightarrow (x - r) = -yy'$ ...(2)

And $r = x + yy'$ ...(3)

Using (2) and (3) in (1), we get $y^2y'^2 + y^2 = (x + yy')^2$ or $y^2(1 + y'^2) = (x + yy')^2$

or $y^2 + y^2y'^2 = x^2 + y^2y'^2 + 2xyy'$ or $y^2 - x^2 = 2xyy'$

19. (b) Equation of parabolas having their axis coincident with x-axis is $(y - 0)^2 = 4a(x - h)$ or $y^2 = 4a(x - h)$

$\Rightarrow 2yy' = 4a$

$\Rightarrow yy' = 2a$

$\Rightarrow yy'' + (y')^2 = 0$

TEXTUAL EXERCISE–3: (SUBJECTIVE)

1. (i) $y = x - 1/x;\ xy' + xy = 2x$

$\Rightarrow y' = 1 + 1/x^2$

$\Rightarrow xy' = x + 1/x$

$\Rightarrow xy' + y = \left(x + \frac{1}{x}\right) + \left(x - \frac{1}{x}\right)$

$\Rightarrow xy' + y = 2x$, yes satisfies.

(ii) $y = 2x^2 + C$

$\Rightarrow y' = 4x$

Now, $y'^2 - 2xy' - 8x^2 = 16x^2 - 2x(4x) - 8x^2 = 0$, yes satisfies

(iii) $y = -x^2/4$

$\Rightarrow y' = \frac{-1}{4}(2x) = \frac{-x}{2}$

$\therefore xy' + y'^2 = \frac{-x^2}{2} + \frac{x^2}{4} = -\frac{x^2}{4} = y$

$\therefore xy' + y'^2 = y'$ yes satisfies.

2. (a) $x + yy' = 0;\ x \in \mathbb{R}, y \neq 0;\ y = \pm\sqrt{A^2 - x^2}\ ; x \in (-A, A)$

$\Rightarrow y' = \pm\left(\frac{1}{2\sqrt{A^2-x^2}}(-2x)\right)$

$\Rightarrow y' = \mp\frac{x}{\sqrt{A^2-x^2}}$

$\Rightarrow y' = -x\left(\frac{1}{\pm\sqrt{A^2-x^2}}\right)$

$\Rightarrow y' = -\frac{x}{y}$

$\Rightarrow x + yy' = 0$

(b) $xy' + y = y^2;\ (x \in \mathbb{R} - \{0\})$

$\Rightarrow y = \frac{A}{x+A};\ (x \in \mathbb{R} - \{A\})$

$\Rightarrow y' = \frac{-A}{(x+A)^2}$

$\Rightarrow xy' + y = \frac{-Ax}{(x+A)^2} + \frac{A}{(x+A)}$

$= \frac{-Ax + A(x+A)}{(x+A)^2} = \frac{A^2}{(x+A)^2} = y^2$

(c) $x^3y'' = 1;\ (x \in \mathbb{R} - \{0\})$

$\Rightarrow y = 1/2x + Ax + B;\ x \in \mathbb{R} - \{0\}$

$\Rightarrow y' = \frac{1}{x^3}$ $\Rightarrow x^3y'' = 1$, hence verified.

3. **(i)** $y^2 - 4x^2 = 0$

$\Rightarrow\ 2yy' - 8x = 0$

$\Rightarrow\ y' = \dfrac{4x}{y}$

$\therefore$ LHS $= 2yy' = 8x$

RHS $= x(y'^2 + 4) = x\left(\dfrac{16x^2}{y^2} + 4\right) = x\left(\dfrac{16x^2}{4x^2} + 4\right) = 8x$,

yes it is a solution.

(ii) $y = (x^2 - x)e^x$

$\Rightarrow\ y' = (x^2 - x)e^x + e^x(2x - 1)$

$\Rightarrow\ y' = y + e^x(2x - 1)$

Now, LHS $= 2yy' = 2y(y + e^x(2x - 1)) = 2y^2 + 2ye^x(2x - 1)$

RHS $= x(y'^2 + 4) = x(y^2 + e^{2x}(2x - 1)^2 + 2y(2x - 1)e^x + 4)$

$= xy^2 + xe^{2x}(2x - 1)^2 + 2yxe^x(2x - 1) + 4x$

Clearly LHS $\neq$ RHS

$\therefore$ It is not a solution.

(iii) $y = 3x^2 + 1/3$

$\Rightarrow\ y' = 6x$

$\therefore\ 2yy' = 2\left(3x^2 + \dfrac{1}{3}\right)(6x) = 2\left(\dfrac{9x^2 + 1}{3}\right)(6x) = 4x(9x^2 + 1)$

And RHS $= x(y'^2 + 4) = x(36x^2 + 4) = 4x(9x^2 + 1)$

It is a solution.

4. **(a)** $\phi(x) = e^{-x} + 2;\ y' + y = 2,\ y(0) = 3$

Here $y = e^{-x} + 2 \qquad \Rightarrow\ y' = -e^{-x} = -y + 2$

$\Rightarrow\ y + y' = 2,$

Clearly $y(0) = 3$ holds. Hence, verified

(b) $y = x^2 + 2x + 1$

$\Rightarrow\ y(0) = 1$

$\Rightarrow\ y' = 2x + 2$

$\Rightarrow\ y'(0) = 2$

$\Rightarrow\ y'' = 2$

$\Rightarrow\ y''(0) = 2$

$\Rightarrow\ y''' = 0$

5. Yes, $\left(\dfrac{dy}{dx}\right)^2 + a^2 = 0$ has no solution for $a \in \mathbb{R}$ and $a \neq 0$

6. Yes, $\left(\dfrac{dy}{dx}\right)^2 + y^2 = 0$ has the only particular solution $y = 0$ (i.e., x-axis)

7. $A = p\tan^{-1}\left(\dfrac{A + l}{p}\right) + C$

$\Rightarrow\ \dfrac{A - C}{p} = \tan^{-1}\left(\dfrac{A + l}{p}\right)$

$\Rightarrow\ \dfrac{1}{p}\left(\dfrac{dA}{dl}\right) = \dfrac{1}{1 + \left(\dfrac{A + l}{p}\right)^2}\left(\dfrac{1}{p}\left(\dfrac{dA}{dl} + 1\right)\right)$

$\Rightarrow\ \dfrac{dA}{dl} = \dfrac{\dfrac{dA}{dl} + 1}{1 + \left(\dfrac{A + l}{p}\right)^2}$

$\Rightarrow\ \dfrac{dA}{dl} + \dfrac{dA}{dl}\left(\dfrac{A + l}{p}\right)^2 = \dfrac{dA}{dl} + 1$

$\Rightarrow\ \left(\dfrac{dA}{dl}\right)\left(\dfrac{A + l}{p}\right)^2 = 1$

$\Rightarrow\ (A + l)^2\dfrac{dA}{dl} = p^2$

8. Let $y = ke^x$,

$\Rightarrow\ y' = ke^x \qquad \Rightarrow\ y'' = ke^x$

$\Rightarrow\ y'' = y \qquad \Rightarrow\ y'' - y = 0$ and for $y = ke^{-x}$

$\Rightarrow\ y' = -ke^{-x} \qquad \Rightarrow\ y'' = ke^{-x}$

$\Rightarrow\ y'' = y \qquad \Rightarrow\ y'' - y = 0$

Thus, above area also true for $k = 1$

$\therefore\ y = y''$ for $y = e^x, e^{-x}, k_1e^x$ and k_2e^{-x}.

9. Given function is $y = ax^2$

$\Rightarrow\ y' = 2ax \qquad \Rightarrow\ y'^2 - 4xy' + 2y + 2x^2 = 0$

$\Rightarrow\ (4a^2x^2) - 8ax^2 + 2ax^2 + 2x^2 = 0$

$\Rightarrow\ 4a^2 - 6a + 2 = 0 \qquad \Rightarrow\ 2a^2 - 3a + 1 = 0$

$\Rightarrow\ 2a^2 - 2a - a + 1 = 0 \ \Rightarrow\ 2a(a - 1) - (a - 1) = 0$

$\Rightarrow\ a = \dfrac{1}{2}$ or $a = 1$

10. $y'' = -\dfrac{1}{y^3}$ ...(1)

Given equation is $(C_1x + C_2)^2 - C_1y^2 = 1$ ...(2)

Differentiability both sides,

we get $2(C_1)(C_1x + C_2) - 2C_1yy' = 0$ ...(3)

$\Rightarrow\ 2C_1^2 - 2C_1yy'' - 2C_1(y')^2 = 0$

$\Rightarrow\ C_1^2 - C_1y'^2 = C_1yy''$

$\Rightarrow\ C_1 - y'^2 = yy''$

$\Rightarrow\ y'' = \dfrac{C_1 - y'^2}{y}$ ...(4)

From (3); $y' = \dfrac{C_1x + C_2}{y}$ ...(5)

Again from (5) and (2), $(y')^2 = \dfrac{1 + C_1y^2}{y^2} = C_1 + \dfrac{1}{y^2}$ ...(6)

$\therefore$ From (4) and (6), $y'' = -1/y^3$

Hence, (2) is a solution of (1).

Since $y'' = \dfrac{-1}{y^3}$

$\Rightarrow\ y''(x) \neq 0$

$\Rightarrow\ y(1) = 0$ and $y''(0) = 0$

Are not sufficient conditions to eliminate C_1 and C_2

Also for $y(1) = 0$, we get $(C_1 + C_2)^2 = 1$ ...(7)

Now from (3), $(C_1x + C_2) - yy' = 0$

$\Rightarrow\ (C_1x + C_2) - yy' = 0$

$\Rightarrow\ C_1 + C_2 = 0\ (\because y(1) = 0)$ ...(8)

$\therefore$ From (7) and (8), we have a contradiction that $0 = 1$

If we have conditions, that $y(1) = 1$ and $y'(1) = 2$,

then from (2), $(C_1 + C_2)^2 = 1 + C_1$ ...(9)

From (3), $(C_1x + C_2) = yy'$

At $x = 1$, $C_1 + C_2 = y(1) \cdot y'(1)$

$\Rightarrow\ C_1 + C_2 = (1)(2) = 2$ ...(10)

$\therefore$ From (9) and (10), $4 = 1 + C_1$

$\Rightarrow\ C_1 = 3$ and $C_2 = -1$

$\therefore$ $(3x-1)^2 - 3y^2 = 1$ is a particular solution for $y(1) = 1$ and $y'(1) = 2$

11. **(i)** $y' = x^2$

$\Rightarrow \ y = \frac{x^3}{3} + C$

Which can't be the function represented by the graph as $y' = x^2 \geq 0 \ \forall \ x \in \mathbb{R}$

$\Rightarrow$ $f(x)$ is strictly increasing function $\forall \ x \in \mathbb{R}$

(ii) $y' = e^x > 0 \ \forall \ x \in \mathbb{R}$ and

(iii) $y' = \sqrt{x} \geq 0 \ \forall \ x \in \mathbb{R}$

None of the above can be the function representing the given graph.

Clearly $f'(x) < 0 \ \forall \ x \in \mathbb{R}$ as its (graph) represents a decreasing function

$f''(x) > 0$ for $x \in (-\infty, 0)$ and for $x \in (a, \infty)$; where $f(a) = 0$, $f(0) = b > 0$ and $f''(x) < 0$ for $x \in (0, a)$; $f''(x) = 0$ at $x = 0$ and $x = a$

$\Rightarrow$ $f''(x) = k^2x(x-a)$; where $k \in \mathbb{R}$

$\Rightarrow \ f'(x) = k^2\left(\frac{x^3}{3} - \frac{ax^2}{2}\right) + C_1$

$\Rightarrow \ f(x) = k^2\left(\frac{x^4}{12} - \frac{ax^3}{6}\right) + C_1x + C_2$

Now $f(a) = 0$

$\Rightarrow \ 0 = k^2\left(\frac{a^4}{12} - \frac{a^4}{6}\right) + C_1a + C_2$

$\Rightarrow \ k^2\left(\frac{-a^4}{12}\right) + C_1a + C_2 = 0$

Also $f(0) = b > 0$

$\Rightarrow b = C_2$ ...(2)

$\therefore \ k^2\left(\frac{-a^4}{12}\right) + C_1a + b = 0$

$\Rightarrow \ \frac{k^2a^4}{12} = C_1a + b$

$\Rightarrow \ C_1 > -b/a$

$\Rightarrow \ k^2 = \frac{12(C_1a+b)}{a^4}$ ...(3)

$\therefore \ f(x) = \frac{12(C_1a+b)}{a^4}\left(\frac{x^4}{12} - \frac{ax^3}{6}\right) + C_1x + b$

$\Rightarrow \ f(x) = \frac{(C_1a+b)}{a^4}(x^4 - 2ax^3) + C_1x + b$; where $a > 0$, $b > 0$, $C_1 > -b/a$

12. Given differential equation is $y' = ax^2 + bx + C$; $(a \geq 0)$

$\Rightarrow \ y = \frac{a}{3}x^3 + \frac{b}{2}x^2 + Cx + d$

Which is a cubic polynomial, and hence is a continuous function on $\mathbb{R}$. But the given graph is discontinuous on $\mathbb{R}$.

Thus, given graph can't be the differential equation $y' = ax^2 + bx + c$ $(a \geq 0)$

13. $y' = 1 - \sin x \geq 0 \ \forall \ x \in \mathbb{R}$ ...(1)

$\Rightarrow \ y = x - \cos x + C$

If $y(0) = 0$

$\Rightarrow \ 0 = -1 + C$

$\Rightarrow \ C = 1$

$\therefore \ y = x - \cos x + 1$ or $y = x + (1 - \cos x)$ or $y = x + 2\sin^2(x/2)$ ...(2)

In view of (1), $y' \geq 0 \ \forall \ x \in \mathbb{R}$

$\Rightarrow$ $f(x)$ is strictly increasing $\forall \ x \in \mathbb{R}$

$\Rightarrow$ None of (2), (3) and (4) can be the correct option.

Also $y'' = -\cos x < 0$ for $x \in \left(0, \frac{\pi}{2}\right)$; and $y'' > 0$ for $x \in \left(\frac{\pi}{2}, \frac{3\pi}{2}\right)$

$\therefore$ Option (1) is correct

14. Clearly $y' = \left|e^x + \sin e^{-x} + \sqrt{1-x^2}\right|$

$\Rightarrow \ y' \geq 0 \ \forall \ x \in [-1, 1]$

That is, y' is defined at most only for $x \in [-1, 1]$ and $f(x)$ is strictly increasing in $[-1, 1]$

$\Rightarrow$ The given graph can't be the solution for given differential equation.

TEXTUAL EXERCISE–3: (OBJECTIVE)

1. **(b)** Since the order of a differential equation is same as the number of effective parameters involved in the general solution

2. **(c)** The directions of motion at any point on the curve having its differential equation of degree 2 can be at most 2. e.g., If the differential equation is of order 1 and degree 2, then at any point on the curve at most two directions of motions are possible (i) for instance,

$$\left(\frac{dy}{dx}\right)^2 + x^2 = 0$$

$\Rightarrow \ \left(\frac{dy}{dx}\right)^2 = -x^2$ having no direction of motion at any point (x, y).

(ii) If $\left(\frac{dy}{dx}\right)^2 - x^2 = 0$

$\Rightarrow \ \frac{dy}{dx} = \pm x$

$\Rightarrow \ y = \pm\frac{x^2}{2} + C$, i.e., two directions of motion are possible.

(iii) If the order is 2 .e.g., $\left(\frac{d^2y}{dx^2}\right)^2 - x^2 = 0$

$\Rightarrow \ \left(\frac{d^2y}{dx^2}\right) = \pm x = \frac{dy}{dx} = \pm\frac{x^2}{2} + C$, i.e., two directions of motion.

3. **(d)** Since singular solutions are the solutions which can't be obtained from general solution by giving any value to parameter, and form envelope to the family of solution curves, statements given in options (a), (b) and (c) are true, i.e., option (d) is false.

4. **(a, b)** Since each point $P(x', y')$ on solution curve is such that x', y' and d at P satisfy the differential equation, option (a) is true. Also solutions of differential equations are of three types particular solution, general solutions and singular solutions, so, option (b) is also true. Further singular solutions are the solutions, which are not among the parametric family of curves, so, option (c) is not true.

5. **(a,b,c)** $y = x\dfrac{dy}{dx} + \left(\dfrac{dy}{dx}\right)^2$ ...(1)

$\Rightarrow\ y = mx + m^2$ ...(2)

(2) is a family of straight lines since the envelope also satisfy the given differential equation, non-linear curve will also satisfy the given differential equation. Now (1) being a quadratic in (dy/dx), shows that at each point of general solution there can be atmost two directions of motion.

6. **(b, c)** $2y + 3Ax - A^2$ ...(1)

$\Rightarrow\ 2\dfrac{dy}{dx} + 3A = 0$

$\Rightarrow\ A = \dfrac{-2}{3}\dfrac{dy}{dx}$ ...(2)

Using (2) in (1), we get $2y + \left(-2\dfrac{dy}{dx}\right)x - \left(\dfrac{4}{9}\right)\left(\dfrac{dy}{dx}\right)^2 = 0$

or $y - x\dfrac{dy}{dx} - \dfrac{2}{9}\left(\dfrac{dy}{dx}\right)^2 = 0$

It has order 1 and degree 2.

7. **(b)** $\dfrac{dy}{dx} = \dfrac{2x}{1+x^2}$

$\Rightarrow\ dy = \dfrac{2x}{1+x^2}dx$

$\Rightarrow\ \int dy = \int \dfrac{2x}{1+x^2}dx$

$\Rightarrow\ y = \ln(1 + x^2) + C$

In each graph $f(0) = 0$

$\Rightarrow\ C = 0$

$\Rightarrow\ y = \ln(1 + x^2)$ ...(1)

(1) is symmetric about y-axis

Also $\dfrac{dy}{dx} = \dfrac{2x}{1+x^2}$

$\Rightarrow\ \dfrac{dy}{dx} < 0$ for $x < 0$ and > 0 for $x > 0$

Also $\left(\dfrac{dy}{dx}\right) = 0$ at $x = 0$

Now, $\dfrac{d^2y}{dx^2} = \dfrac{(1+x^2)(2) - 2x(2x)}{(1+x^2)^2} = \dfrac{1-2x^2}{(1+x^2)^2} = 0$ at $x = \pm\dfrac{1}{\sqrt{2}}$ and is concave upwards for $x \in \left(-\dfrac{1}{\sqrt{2}}, \dfrac{1}{\sqrt{2}}\right)$

and concave downwards for $x \in \left(-\infty, -\dfrac{1}{\sqrt{2}}\right) \cup \left(\dfrac{1}{\sqrt{2}}, \infty\right)$.

TEXTUAL EXERCISE–4: (SUBJECTIVE)

1. **(a)** $\dfrac{dy}{dx} = (x+y)^2$ ...(1)

Let $x + y = z$

$\Rightarrow\ 1 + \dfrac{dy}{dx} = \dfrac{dz}{dx}$ $\Rightarrow\ \dfrac{dz}{dx} - 1 = z^2$

$\Rightarrow\ \dfrac{dz}{1+z^2} = dx$ $\Rightarrow\ \int \dfrac{dz}{1+z^2} = \int dx$

$\Rightarrow\ \tan^{-1}(z) = x + C$ $\Rightarrow\ \tan^{-1}(x + y) = x + C$

(b) $\dfrac{dy}{dx} = e^{x-y} + x^2e^{-y}$

$\Rightarrow\ \dfrac{dy}{dx} = e^{-y}(e^x + x^2)$ $\Rightarrow\ \int e^y dy = \int (e^x + x^2)dx$

$\Rightarrow\ e^y = e^x + \dfrac{x^3}{3} + C$ $\Rightarrow\ e^y - e^x = \dfrac{x^3}{3} + C$

(c) $\sin^{-1}\left(\dfrac{dy}{dx}\right) = x + y$

$\Rightarrow\ \dfrac{dy}{dx} = \sin(x + y)$ ...(1)

Put $x + y = z$

$\Rightarrow\ 1 + \dfrac{dy}{dx} = \dfrac{dz}{dx}$ $\Rightarrow\ \dfrac{dz}{dx} - 1 = \sin z$

$\Rightarrow\ \dfrac{dz}{1+\sin z} = dx$ $\Rightarrow\ \int \dfrac{dz}{1+\sin z} = \int dx$

$\Rightarrow\ \int(\sec^2 z - \sec z\tan z)dz = \int dx$

$\Rightarrow\ (\tan z - \sec ^z) = x + C$

$\Rightarrow\ \tan(x + y) - \sec(x + y) = x + C$

2. **(a)** $(xy^2 + x)dx + (yx^2 + y)dy = 0$

$\Rightarrow\ x(y^2 + 1)dx + y(x^2 + 1)dy = 0$

$\Rightarrow\ x(y^2 + 1)dx = -y(x^2 + 1)dy = 0$

$\Rightarrow\ \int \dfrac{-y}{y^2+1}dy = \int \dfrac{x}{x^2+1}dy$

$\Rightarrow\ -\dfrac{1}{2}\ln(y^2 + 1) = \dfrac{1}{2}\ln(x^2 + 1) - \ln C$

$\Rightarrow\ \dfrac{1}{2}\ln(x^2 + 1)(y^2 + 1) = \ln C$

$\Rightarrow\ \sqrt{(x^2+1)(y^2+1)} = C$ or $(x^2 + 1)(y^2 + 1) = C$

(b) $y\sqrt{(1+x^2)}dx + x\sqrt{(1+y^2)}dy = 0$

$\Rightarrow\ y\sqrt{1+x^2}dx = -x\sqrt{1+y^2}dy$

$\Rightarrow\ \int \dfrac{\sqrt{1+x^2}}{x}dx = -\int \dfrac{\sqrt{1+y^2}}{y}dy$

Put $x = \tan\theta$, $y = \tan\phi$

$\Rightarrow\ \int \dfrac{\sec\theta}{\tan\theta}.\sec^2\theta d\theta = -\int \dfrac{\sec\phi}{\tan\phi}.\sec^2\phi d\phi$

$\Rightarrow\ \int \dfrac{1}{\cos^3\theta\sin\theta}\cos\theta\, d\theta = -\int \dfrac{1.\cos\theta}{\cos^3\phi\sin\phi}d\phi$

$\Rightarrow\ \int \dfrac{\sin^2\theta + \cos^2\theta}{\sin\theta\cos^2\theta}d\theta = -\int \dfrac{\sin^2\phi + \cos^2\phi}{\sin\phi\cos^2\phi}d\phi$

$\Rightarrow \int(\sec\theta\tan\theta+\text{cosec}\theta)d\theta$

$= -\int(\sec\phi\tan\phi+\text{cosec}\phi)d\phi$

$\Rightarrow$ secθ + ln |cosecθ – cotθ| = –secϕ – ln |cosec ϕ – cotϕ| + C

$\Rightarrow$ secθ + secϕ = –{ln |cosecϕ – cotϕ| . |cosecθ – cotθ|} + C

$\Rightarrow \sqrt{1+x^2}+\sqrt{1+y^2}$

$= -\left\{\ln\left|\sqrt{1+\frac{1}{y^2}}-\frac{1}{y}\right|\left|\sqrt{1+\frac{1}{x^2}}-\frac{1}{x}\right|+C\right\}$

$\Rightarrow \sqrt{1+x^2}+\sqrt{1+y^2} =$

$-\left\{\ln\left|\frac{\sqrt{y^2+1}}{y}-\frac{1}{y}\right|\left|\frac{\sqrt{x^2+1}}{x}-\frac{1}{x}\right|\right\}+C$ or

$\sqrt{1+x^2}+\sqrt{1+y^2}+\ln\frac{\left(\sqrt{y^2+1}-1\right)\left(\sqrt{x^2+1}-1\right)}{|xy|}=C$

(c) $\frac{dy}{dx}=\frac{\sin x+x\cos x}{y(2\log y+1)}$

$\Rightarrow$ $(2y\log y + y)dy = (\sin x + x\cos x)\,dx$

$\Rightarrow \int(2y\log y+y)dy = \int(\sin x+x\cos x)dx$

$\Rightarrow 2\left[\log y.\frac{y^2}{2}-\int\frac{1}{y}.\frac{y^2}{2}dy\right]+\frac{y^2}{2}$

$= -\cos x + \left[x\sin x-\int(1.(\sin x))dx\right]$

$\Rightarrow y^2\log y-\left[\frac{y^2}{2}\right]+\frac{y^2}{2} = -\cos x + x\sin x + \cos x + C$

$\Rightarrow y^2\log y = x\sin x + C$

(d) $\frac{dy}{dx}=e^{x+y}+x^2.e^y$

$\Rightarrow \frac{dy}{dx}=e^y(e^x+x^2) \quad \Rightarrow \frac{1}{e^y}dy=(e^x+x^2)dx$

$\Rightarrow \int e^{-y}dy=\int(e^x+x^2)dx \Rightarrow \frac{e^{-y}}{-1}=e^x+\frac{x^3}{3}+C$

$\Rightarrow e^x+e^{-y}=-\frac{x^3}{3}+C$

3. $\cos y\log(\sec x+\tan x)dx = \cos x\log(\sec y+\tan y)\,dy$

$\Rightarrow \int\frac{\log(\sec x+\tan x)}{\cos x}dx = \int\frac{\log(\sec y+\tan y)}{\cos y}dy$

$\Rightarrow \int\sec x.\log(\sec x+\tan x)dx$

$\Rightarrow \int\sec y.\log(\sec y+\tan y)dy$

$\Rightarrow \frac{[\log(\sec x+\tan x)]^2}{2}=\frac{[\log(\sec y+\tan y)]^2}{2}$

or $[\log(\sec x + \tan x)]^2 - [\log(\sec y + \tan y)]^2 = C$

4. (a) $\frac{dy}{dx}=\frac{6x^2}{2y+\cos y}$; $y(1) = \pi$

$\Rightarrow (2y + \cos y)dy = 6x^2\,dx$

$\Rightarrow y^2 + \sin y = 2x^3 + C$

$\Rightarrow C = \pi^2 - 2$

$\Rightarrow y^2 + \sin y = 2x^3 + p^2 - 2$

(b) $\sec^2x\tan y\,dx + \sec^2y\tan x\,dy = 0$

$\Rightarrow \int\frac{\sec^2 x\,dx}{\tan x}+\int\frac{\sec^2 y\,dy}{\tan y}=0$

$\Rightarrow \ln|\tan x| + \ln|\tan y| = \ln C$

$\Rightarrow \ln|\tan x\tan y| = \ln C$

$\Rightarrow \tan x\tan y = C$

(c) $\frac{dy}{dx}=\cos(x+y)+\sin(x+y)$ ...(1)

Put $(x + y) = z$

$\Rightarrow 1+\frac{dy}{dx}=\frac{dz}{dx}$ ...(2)

$\therefore$ from (1) and (2), $\frac{dz}{dx}-1=\cos z+\sin z$

$\Rightarrow \int\frac{dz}{\sin z+1+\cos z}=\int dx$

$\Rightarrow \int\frac{dz}{\left(2\sin\frac{z}{2}\cos\frac{z}{2}+2\cos^2\frac{z}{2}\right)}=\int dx$

$\Rightarrow \int\frac{1}{2\cos\frac{z}{2}}\frac{1}{\left(\sin\frac{z}{2}+\cos\frac{z}{2}\right)}dz=\int dx$

$\Rightarrow \frac{1}{2}\int\frac{\sec\frac{z}{2}}{\left(\sin\frac{z}{2}+\cos\frac{z}{2}\right)}dz=\int dx$

$\Rightarrow \ln\left|1+\tan\frac{z}{2}\right|=x+C$

$\Rightarrow \ln\left|1+\tan\left(\frac{x+y}{2}\right)\right|=x+C$

5. Length of sub tangent $= y\frac{dx}{dy}\propto\frac{1}{(x)^2}$

$\Rightarrow y\frac{dx}{dy}=\frac{k}{x^2}$

$\Rightarrow x^2dx=k\frac{dy}{y}$

$\Rightarrow \frac{x^3}{3}=k\ln y+\ln C_1$

$\Rightarrow \frac{x^3}{3}=\ln C_1y^k$

$\Rightarrow C_1y^k=e^{\frac{x^3}{3}}$

$\Rightarrow y^k=\frac{1}{C_1}e^{\frac{x^3}{3}}$

$\Rightarrow y=\left(\frac{1}{C_1}\right)^{1/k}.e^{\frac{x^3}{3k}}$

$\Rightarrow y=C.e^{\frac{x^3}{3k}}$

6. (a) $\sin x\cos y\,dx + \cos x\cos y\,dy = 0$; $y(0) = \pi/4$

$\Rightarrow \frac{\sin x\,dx}{\cos x}+\frac{\sin y\,dy}{\cos y}$

$\Rightarrow \int \tan x\, dx + \int \tan y\, dy = 0$

$\Rightarrow \ln|\sec x| + \ln|\sec y| = \ln c$

$\Rightarrow \sec x . \sec y = C$

$\Rightarrow \dfrac{1}{\cos x . \cos y} = C$

$\Rightarrow \cos y = \left(\dfrac{1}{C\cos x}\right)$

$\Rightarrow y = \cos^{-1}\left(\dfrac{1}{C\cos x}\right)$; Given, $y(0) = \pi/4$

$\Rightarrow \dfrac{\pi}{4} = \cos^{-1}\left(\dfrac{1}{C}\right)$

$\Rightarrow \dfrac{1}{C} = \cos\dfrac{\pi}{4} = \dfrac{1}{\sqrt{2}}$

$\Rightarrow C = \sqrt{2}$

$\therefore y = \cos^{-1}\left(\dfrac{1}{\sqrt{2}\cos x}\right)$

$\Rightarrow y = \cos^{-1}\left(\dfrac{\sec x}{\sqrt{2}}\right); x \in \left[-\dfrac{\pi}{4}, \dfrac{\pi}{4}\right]$

(b) $xdy + ydx = xy\, dx$, $y(-1) = 0$

$\Rightarrow \dfrac{dy}{y} + \dfrac{dx}{x} = dx$

$\Rightarrow \int \dfrac{dy}{y} = \int\left(1 - \dfrac{1}{x}\right)dx$

$\Rightarrow \ln y = x - \ln x + \ln C$

$\Rightarrow \ln\left(\dfrac{xy}{C}\right) = x$

$\Rightarrow \dfrac{xy}{C} = e^x$

$\Rightarrow y = \dfrac{1}{x}C.e^x$

Now $y(-1) = -e^{-2} = -e^{-2} = -C.e^{-1}$

$\Rightarrow C = e^{-1}$

$\Rightarrow y = \dfrac{1}{x}e^{-1}.e^x$

$\Rightarrow y = \dfrac{1}{x}.e^{x-1}$; $x \in \mathbb{R} - \{0\}$

(c) $x(dy - y\, dx) = y\, dx$

$\Rightarrow xdy = ydx + xy\, dx$

$\Rightarrow xdy = (1 + x)y\, dx$

$\Rightarrow \int \dfrac{dy}{y} = \int \dfrac{1+x}{x}dx$

$\Rightarrow \ln y = x + \ln x + \ln C$

$\Rightarrow \ln\left(\dfrac{y}{Cx}\right) = x$

$\Rightarrow \dfrac{y}{Cx} = e^x$

$\Rightarrow y = Cxex$ $\quad\Rightarrow -e^{-2} = C(-1)e^{-1}$

$\Rightarrow C = -e^{-1}$ $\quad\Rightarrow y = xex^{-1}; x > 0$

TEXTUAL EXERCISE–4: (OBJECTIVE)

1. (d) $\dfrac{dy}{dx} = \dfrac{3x - 4y - 2}{3x - 4y - 3}$ ...(1)

Put $3x - 4y = z$

$\Rightarrow 3 - 4\dfrac{dy}{dx} = \dfrac{dz}{dx}$

$\Rightarrow \dfrac{1}{4}\left(3 - \dfrac{dz}{dx}\right) = \dfrac{dy}{dx}$ ...(2)

$\therefore$ From (1) and (2), $\dfrac{1}{4}\left(3 - \dfrac{dz}{dx}\right) = \dfrac{z-2}{z-3}$

$\Rightarrow \dfrac{dz}{dx} = 3 - \dfrac{4z - 8}{z - 3}$

$\Rightarrow \dfrac{dz}{dx} = \dfrac{3z - 9 - 4z + 8}{z - 3}$

$\Rightarrow \dfrac{dz}{dx} = \dfrac{-z - 1}{z - 3}$

$\Rightarrow \dfrac{3 - z}{z + 1}dz = dx$

$\Rightarrow \int \dfrac{z-3}{z+1}dz + \int dx = 0$

$\Rightarrow z - 4\ln|z + 1| + x = C_1$

$\Rightarrow (3x - 4y) - 4\ln(3x - 4y + 1) + x = C_1$

$\Rightarrow 4(x - y) - 4\ln(3x - 4y + 1) = C_1$

$\Rightarrow (x - y) - \ln(3x - 4y + 1) = C$ or $x - y + C' = \ln(3x - 4y + 1)$

2. (b) $\dfrac{dy}{dx} = \cos(x - y)$

Put $(x - y) = z$

$\Rightarrow 1 - \dfrac{dy}{dx} = \dfrac{dz}{dx}$ $\quad\Rightarrow 1 - \dfrac{dz}{dx} = \cos z$

$\Rightarrow \dfrac{dz}{1 - \cos z} = dx$ $\quad\Rightarrow \dfrac{dz}{2\sin^2\dfrac{z}{2}} = dx$

$\Rightarrow \dfrac{1}{2}\int \text{cosec}^2\dfrac{z}{2}dz = \int dx \Rightarrow \dfrac{1}{2}\left(\dfrac{-\cot z/2}{1/2}\right) = x + C$

$\Rightarrow -\cot\left(\dfrac{z}{2}\right) = x + C$

$\Rightarrow -\cot\left(\dfrac{x-y}{2}\right) = x + C$ or $x + \cot\left(\dfrac{x-y}{2}\right) = C'$

3. (a), (b) $y = ae^{-1/x} + b$ ...(1)

$\Rightarrow \dfrac{dy}{dx} = ae^{-1/x}\left(\dfrac{1}{x^2}\right)$

$\Rightarrow \dfrac{dy}{dx} = (y - b)\dfrac{1}{x^2}$

$\Rightarrow \dfrac{dy}{dx} = \dfrac{y}{x^2} - \dfrac{b}{x^2}$

$\Rightarrow b = 0$ ($\because \dfrac{dy}{dx} = \dfrac{y}{x^2}$ is the differential equation) and $a \in \mathbb{R} - \{0\}$

4. (d) $\frac{dy}{dx} = e^{y+x} + e^{y-x}$

$\Rightarrow \frac{dy}{dx} = e^y\left(e^x + e^{-x}\right)$

$\Rightarrow \int e^{-y}dy = \int\left(e^x + e^{-x}\right)dx$

$\Rightarrow \frac{e^{-y}}{-1} = e^x - e^{-x} + C_1 \quad \Rightarrow \quad -e^{-y} = e^x - e^{-x} + C_1$

$\Rightarrow e^{-y} = e^{-x} - e^x + C$

5. (c) $2x\frac{dy}{dx} - y = 3$

$\Rightarrow 2x\frac{dy}{dx} = y + 3$

$\Rightarrow \int \frac{1}{y+3}dy = \int \frac{dx}{2x}$

$\Rightarrow \ln|y + 3| = (1/2)\ln|x| + \ln|C|$

$\Rightarrow \ln|y + 3| = \ln|x|^{1/2} + \ln|C|$

$\Rightarrow |y + 3| = |C\,|x|^{1/2}|$

$\Rightarrow (y+3) = \pm C\sqrt{|x|}$

$\Rightarrow y^2 + 6y + 9 = \pm C^2x$ or $(y + 3)^2 = \pm C^2x$

$\therefore$ Its represents a parabola

6. (a) $y' = \frac{y+1}{x-1}$, $y(1) = 2$

$\Rightarrow \frac{dy}{dx} = \frac{y+1}{x-1}$

$\Rightarrow \frac{1}{y+1}dy = \frac{1}{x-1}dx$

$\Rightarrow \int \frac{dy}{y+1} = \int \frac{1}{x-1}dx$

$\Rightarrow \ln|y + 1| = \ln|x - 1| + \ln|C|$

$\Rightarrow |y + 1| = |C(x - 1)|$

$\Rightarrow (y + 1) = \pm C(x - 1)$ at $x = 1, y = 2$

$\Rightarrow 3 = \pm C(0)$

Which is impossible, hence, there no solution.

7. (a) $y' = 1 + y^2$

$\Rightarrow \int \frac{dy}{1+y^2} = \int dx$

$\Rightarrow \tan^{-1}(y) = x + C$

$\Rightarrow y = \tan(x + C)$

Given $y(0) = 0 = y(\pi)$

$\Rightarrow C = 0$

$\Rightarrow y = \tan x$

8. (a) $\frac{dy}{dx} = e^{x-y} + x^2e^{-y}$

$\Rightarrow \frac{dy}{dx} = e^{-y}(e^x + x^2)$

$\Rightarrow \int e^y = \int (e^x + x^2)dx$

$\Rightarrow e^y = e^x + \frac{x^3}{3} + C$

9. (b) $(\sin x + \cos x)\,dy + (\cos x - \sin x)dx = 0$

$\Rightarrow dy = \frac{(\sin x - \cos x)dx}{(\sin x + \cos x)}$

$\Rightarrow -\int dy = \int \frac{(\cos x - \sin x)dx}{(\sin x + \cos x)}$

$\Rightarrow -y = \ln|\sin x + \cos x| + \ln|C_1|$

$\Rightarrow y = -\ln|C_1(\sin x + \cos x)|$

$\Rightarrow e^{-y} = |C_1(\sin x + \cos x)|$

$\Rightarrow (\sin x + \cos x) = Ce^{-y}$ or $e^y(\sin x + \cos x) = C$

10. (d) $\frac{dy}{dx} = (1+x)(1+y^2)$

$\Rightarrow \int \frac{dy}{1+y^2} = \int (1+x)dx \Rightarrow \tan^{-1}y = x + x^2/2 + C$

$\Rightarrow y = \tan\left(\frac{x^2}{2} + x + C\right)$

11. (a) $\frac{dy}{dx} = 1 + x + y + xy$

$\Rightarrow \frac{dy}{dx} = (1+x)(1+y)$

$\Rightarrow \frac{dy}{1+y} = (1+x)dx$

$\Rightarrow \ln|1 + y| = x + \frac{x^2}{2} + C$

12. (c) $x\frac{dy}{dx} + y = y^2$

$\Rightarrow \frac{dy}{y^2 - y} = \frac{dx}{x}$

$\Rightarrow \int \frac{dy}{y(y-1)} = \int \frac{dx}{x}$

$\Rightarrow \int\left(\frac{-1}{y} + \frac{1}{y-1}\right)dy - \int \frac{dx}{x}$

$\Rightarrow \ln\left|\frac{y-1}{y}\right| = \ln|x| + \ln|C|$

$\Rightarrow \ln\left|\frac{y-1}{y}\right| = \ln|Cx|$

$\Rightarrow (y - 1) = \pm\, Cya$

13. (c) $\frac{dy}{dx} = \frac{xy+y}{xy+x}$

$\Rightarrow \frac{dy}{dx} = \frac{(x+1)y}{x(y+1)}$

$\Rightarrow \left(\frac{y+1}{y}\right)dy = \frac{x+1}{x}dx$

$\Rightarrow \int\left(1 + \frac{1}{y}\right)dy = \int\left(1 + \frac{1}{x}\right)dx$

$\Rightarrow y + \ln|y| = x + \ln|x| + \ln|C|$

$\Rightarrow \ln\left|\frac{y}{Cx}\right| = x - y$

$\Rightarrow \dfrac{y}{Cx} = e^{x-y}$

$\Rightarrow y = Cx.e^{x-y}$ or $y = Axe^{x-y}$.

14. (c) $\dfrac{(y-1)dy}{y} = \dfrac{x+1}{x}dx$

$\Rightarrow \dfrac{(y-1)}{y}dy = \dfrac{x+1}{x}dx$

$\Rightarrow \int\left(1-\dfrac{1}{y}\right)dy = \int\left(1+\dfrac{1}{x}\right)dx$

$\Rightarrow y - \ln|y| = x + \ln|x| + \ln|C|$

$\Rightarrow y - x = \ln|xyC|$ or $\ln|xy| + x - y = C$

15. (c) $\dfrac{dy}{dx} = \dfrac{(x-y)+3}{2(x-y)+5}$

Put $(x - y) = z$

$\Rightarrow 1-\dfrac{dz}{dx} = \dfrac{z+3}{2z+5}$

$\Rightarrow \dfrac{dz}{dx} = 1-\dfrac{z+3}{2z+5}$

$\Rightarrow \dfrac{dz}{dx} = \dfrac{2z+5-z-3}{2z+5}$

$\Rightarrow \dfrac{dz}{dx} = \dfrac{z+2}{2z+5}$

$\Rightarrow \dfrac{2z+5}{z+2}dz = dx$

$\Rightarrow \int\left(\dfrac{2(z+2)+1}{z+2}\right)dz = \int dx$

$\Rightarrow 2z + \ln|z + 2| = x + C$ or $2(x - y) + \ln|x - y + 2| = x + C$

16. (c) $(1 + x^2)(1 + y)dy + (1 + x)(1 + y^2)dx = 0$

$\Rightarrow \dfrac{-(1+x)}{1+x^2}dx = \dfrac{(1+y)}{1+y^2}dy$

$\Rightarrow -\tan^{-1}x - (1/2)\ln(1 + x^2) = \tan^{-1}y + (1/2)\ln(1 + y^2) + C$

$\Rightarrow \tan^{-1}y + \tan^{-1}x + (1/2)\ln(1 + x^2)(1 + y^2) + C = 0$

17. (b) $\sin\left(\dfrac{dy}{dx}\right) = a \Rightarrow \dfrac{dy}{dx} = \sin^{-1}(a)$

$\Rightarrow \int dy = \int \sin^{-1}(a)\,dx$

$\Rightarrow y = x\sin^{-1}(a) + C$

$\because y(0) = 1$

$\Rightarrow 1 = C$

$\Rightarrow y = x\sin^{-1}(a) + 1$

$\Rightarrow \dfrac{y-1}{x} = \sin^{-1}(a)$

$\Rightarrow \sin\left(\dfrac{y-1}{x}\right) = a$

18. (c) $\left(\dfrac{2+\sin x}{1+y}\right)\dfrac{dy}{dx} = \cos x$, $y(0) = 1$

$\Rightarrow \dfrac{1}{1+y}dy = \dfrac{\cos x}{2+\sin x}dx$

$\Rightarrow \int\dfrac{1}{1+y}dy = \int\dfrac{\cos x}{2+\sin x}dx$

$\Rightarrow \ln|1 + y| = \ln|2 + \sin x| + \ln|C_1|$

$\Rightarrow \ln|1 + y| = \ln|C_1(2 + \sin x)|$

$\Rightarrow (1 + y) = C(2 + \sin x)$

$\therefore y(0) = 1$

$\Rightarrow 2 = C(2 + 0)$

$\Rightarrow C = 1$

$\Rightarrow y + 1 = 2 + \sin x$

$\Rightarrow y = 1 + \sin x$

$\Rightarrow y(\pi/2) = 2$

19. (b) $e^{dy/dx} = (x + 1)$, $y(0) = 3$

$\Rightarrow \dfrac{dy}{dx} = \ln(x+1)$

$\Rightarrow \int dy = \int \ln(x+1)\,dx$

$\Rightarrow y = \ln(x + 1).x - \int\dfrac{1}{x+1}x\,dx$

$\Rightarrow y = x\ln(x + 1) - \int\left(1-\dfrac{1}{x+1}\right)dx$

$\Rightarrow y = x\ln|(x + 1)| - x + \ln|x + 1| + C$

$\Rightarrow y = (x + 1)\ln|x + 1| - x + C$

Also, $y(0) = 3$

$\Rightarrow C = 3$

$\therefore y = (x + 1)\ln|x + 1| - x + 3$

20. (b) $\dfrac{dy}{dx} = 1-\dfrac{1}{x^2}$

$\Rightarrow dy = \left(1-\dfrac{1}{x^2}\right)dx$

$\Rightarrow y = x-\left(-\dfrac{1}{x}\right)+C$

$\Rightarrow y = x+\dfrac{1}{x}+C$

Since, the curve passes through (2, 7/2)

$\Rightarrow \dfrac{7}{2} = 2+\dfrac{1}{2}+C$

$\Rightarrow C = 1$

$\Rightarrow y = x + 1/x + 1$ or $xy = x^2 + x + 1$

21. (a) $\dfrac{dy}{dx} = \dfrac{y-1}{x^2+x}$

$\Rightarrow \dfrac{dy}{y-1} = \dfrac{dx}{x(x+1)}$

$\Rightarrow \int\dfrac{dy}{y-1} = \int\left(\dfrac{1}{x}-\dfrac{1}{x+1}\right)dx$

$\Rightarrow \ln|(y - 1)| = \ln\left|\dfrac{x}{x+1}\right| + \ln|C_1|$

$\Rightarrow |y - 1| = \left|\dfrac{C_1x}{x+1}\right|$

$\Rightarrow (y - 1) = \pm\dfrac{C_1x}{x+1}$

$\Rightarrow\ y-1=\dfrac{Cx}{x+1}$

$\Rightarrow\ y=1+\dfrac{Cx}{x+1}$

$\Rightarrow\ y(1)=0$

$\Rightarrow\ 0=1+C/2$

$\Rightarrow\ C=-2$

$\Rightarrow\ y=1-\dfrac{2x}{x+1}$ or $\dfrac{2x}{x+1}=1-y$ or $(1-y)(x+1)=2x$ or $(y-1)(x+1)+2x=0$

22. (c) $\dfrac{dy}{dx}=\dfrac{1}{2y}$

$\Rightarrow\ 2y\,dy=dx$

$\Rightarrow\ y^2=x+C$

It passes through (4, 3)

$\Rightarrow\ 9=4+C$

$\Rightarrow\ C=5$

$\Rightarrow\ y^2=x+5$

23. (b) $x\,dy-y\,dx=0$

$\Rightarrow\ x\,dy=y\,dx$

$\Rightarrow\ \int\dfrac{dy}{y}=\int\dfrac{dx}{x}$

$\Rightarrow\ \ln|y|=\ln|x|+\ln|C|\quad\Rightarrow\ y=Cx$

Which is a straight line through origin

24. (a) $\dfrac{dy}{dx}=(x+y-1)+\dfrac{x+y}{\log(x+y)}$ ...(1)

Put $x+y=z$ in (1)

$\Rightarrow\ 1+\dfrac{dy}{dx}=\dfrac{dz}{dx}$

$\Rightarrow\ \dfrac{dy}{dx}=\dfrac{dz}{dx}-1$ ...(2)

$\therefore$ From (1) and (2), $\dfrac{dz}{dx}-1=(z-1)+\dfrac{z}{\log(z)}$

$\Rightarrow\ \dfrac{dz}{dx}=z+\dfrac{z}{\log z}$

$\Rightarrow\ \dfrac{\log z}{z(\log z+1)}dz=dx$

$\Rightarrow\ \int\dfrac{(\log z+1-1)}{z(\log z+1)}dz=\int dx$

$\Rightarrow\ \int\left(\dfrac{1}{z}-\dfrac{1}{z(\log z+1)}\right)dz=\int dx$

$\Rightarrow\ [\ln z-\ln(\ln z+1)]=x+C'$

$\Rightarrow\ \ln(x+y)-\ln(1+\ln(x+y))=x+C'$

$\Rightarrow\ \{1+\ln(x+y)\}-\ln\{1+\ln(x+y)\}=x+(C'+1)$ or $\{1+\ln(x+y)\}-\ln\{1+\ln(x+y)\}=(x+C)$

25. (a) $(x-y)^2\dfrac{dy}{dx}=a^2$ ...(1)

Put $(x-y)=z$

$\Rightarrow\ 1-\dfrac{dy}{dx}=\dfrac{dz}{dx}$ ...(2)

From (1) and (2), $z^2\left(1-\dfrac{dz}{dx}\right)=a^2$

$\Rightarrow\ 1-\dfrac{dz}{dx}=\dfrac{a^2}{z^2}\qquad\Rightarrow\ \dfrac{dz}{dx}=1-\dfrac{a^2}{z^2}$

$\Rightarrow\ \dfrac{dz}{dx}=\dfrac{z^2-a^2}{z^2}\qquad\Rightarrow\ \dfrac{z^2-a^2+a^2}{z^2-a^2}dz=dx$

$\Rightarrow\ \int\left(1+\dfrac{a^2}{z^2-a^2}\right)dz=\int dx$

$\Rightarrow\ z+a^2\dfrac{1}{2a}\ln\left|\dfrac{z-a}{z+a}\right|=x+C'$

$\Rightarrow\ z+\dfrac{a}{2}\ln\left|\dfrac{x-y-a}{x-y+a}\right|=x+C'$

$\Rightarrow\ x-y+\dfrac{a}{2}\ln\left|\dfrac{x-y-a}{x-y+a}\right|=x+C'$

$\Rightarrow\ y=\dfrac{a}{2}\ln\left|\dfrac{x-y-a}{x-y+a}\right|+C$

26. (b) $x\,dy-y\,dx=0$

$\Rightarrow\ x\,dy=y\,dx$

$\Rightarrow\ \dfrac{dy}{y}=\dfrac{dx}{x}$

$\Rightarrow\ \ln y=\ln x+\ln C$

$\Rightarrow\ y=Cx$ which represents a straight line.

27. (b) $(1+y^2)dx=xy\,dy$

$\Rightarrow\ \dfrac{dx}{x}=\dfrac{y\,dy}{y^2+1}$

$\Rightarrow\ \int\dfrac{dx}{x}=\dfrac{1}{2}\int\dfrac{2y}{y^2+1}dy$

$\Rightarrow\ \ln|x|=(1/2)\ln(y^2+1)+\ln C$

$\Rightarrow\ |x|=C\sqrt{y^2+1}$

$\Rightarrow\ x=C\sqrt{y^2+1}$

Since, curve passes through (1, 0)

$\Rightarrow\ 1=C\sqrt{1}$

$\Rightarrow\ C=1$

$\Rightarrow\ x=\sqrt{y^2+1}$

$\Rightarrow\ x^2-y^2=1$

28. (b) $y\dfrac{dy}{dx}+x=a$

$\Rightarrow\ y\dfrac{dy}{dx}=a-x$

$\Rightarrow\ \int y\,dy=\int(a-x)dx$

$\Rightarrow\ \dfrac{y^2}{2}=ax-\dfrac{x^2}{2}+C$ or $y^2=2ax-x^2+2C$

or $x^2+y^2-2ax-2C=0$

which represents a circle with centre at $(a, 0)$ and radius $=\sqrt{a^2+2C}$ i.e., circle having its centre on x-axis.

TEXTUAL EXERCISE–5: (SUBJECTIVE)

1. (a) $(x^2+y^2)\dfrac{dy}{dx}=xy$

$\Rightarrow \dfrac{dy}{dx}=\dfrac{xy}{x^2+y^2}$ ...(1)

Put $y = vx$

$\Rightarrow \dfrac{dy}{dx}=v+x\dfrac{dv}{dx}$

$\Rightarrow \dfrac{dy}{dx}=x\dfrac{dv}{dx}+v$ ...(2)

$\therefore$ From (1) and (2), $x^2(1+v^2)\left(x\dfrac{dv}{dx}+v\right)=x(vx)$

$\Rightarrow (1+v^2)\left(x\dfrac{dv}{dx}+v\right)=v$

$\Rightarrow (1+v^2)x\dfrac{dv}{dx}=v(1-1-v^2)$

$\Rightarrow \dfrac{(1+v^2)}{v^3}dv=\dfrac{-dx}{x}$

$\Rightarrow \dfrac{v^{-2}}{-2}+\ln|v|=-\ln|x|+\ln|C'|$

$\Rightarrow \dfrac{-1}{2v^2}=\ln\left|\dfrac{C'}{vx}\right|$

$\Rightarrow \left|\dfrac{C'}{vx}\right|=e^{-1/2v^2}$

$\Rightarrow \dfrac{C'}{vx}=\pm e^{-\frac{x^2}{2y^2}}$

$\Rightarrow \dfrac{C'}{y}=\pm e^{-\frac{x^2}{2y^2}}$

$\Rightarrow y=\pm\dfrac{C'}{e^{-\frac{x^2}{2y^2}}}$

$\Rightarrow y=\pm C'e^{\frac{x^2}{2y^2}}$

$\Rightarrow y=Ce^{\frac{x^2}{2y^2}}$

(b) $2\dfrac{dy}{dx}=\dfrac{x}{y}-1$ ...(1)

Put $y = vx$

$\Rightarrow \dfrac{dy}{dx}=v+x\dfrac{dv}{dx}$ ...(2)

$\therefore$ From (1) and (2), we get $2\left(v+x\dfrac{dv}{dx}\right)=\dfrac{1}{v}-1$

$\Rightarrow 2x\dfrac{dv}{dx}=\dfrac{1}{v}-1-2v$

$\Rightarrow \displaystyle\int\frac{2v}{1-v-2v^2}dv=\int\frac{dx}{x}$

$\Rightarrow -\dfrac{1}{2}\displaystyle\int\frac{(-4v-1+1)}{1-v-2v^2}dv=\int\frac{dx}{x}$

$\Rightarrow -\dfrac{1}{2}\displaystyle\int\frac{-4v-1}{1-v-2v^2}dv+\frac{1}{2}\int\frac{dv}{2v^2+v-1}=\int\frac{dx}{x}$

$\Rightarrow -\dfrac{1}{2}\ln|1-v-2v^2|+\dfrac{1}{4}\displaystyle\int\frac{dv}{\left(v^2+\frac{v}{2}-\frac{1}{2}\right)}=\int\frac{dx}{x}$

$\Rightarrow -\dfrac{1}{2}\ln\left|1-\dfrac{y}{x}-\dfrac{2y^2}{x^2}\right|+\dfrac{1}{4}\displaystyle\int\frac{dv}{\left(v+\frac{1}{4}\right)^2-\left(\frac{3}{4}\right)^2}=\int\frac{dx}{x}$

$\Rightarrow -\dfrac{1}{2}\ln\left|\dfrac{x^2-xy-2y^2}{x^2}\right|+\dfrac{1}{4}\times\dfrac{1}{2\left(\frac{3}{4}\right)}\ln\left|\dfrac{\left(v+\frac{1}{4}\right)-\frac{3}{4}}{\left(v+\frac{1}{4}\right)+\frac{3}{4}}\right|$

$=\ln|x|+\ln|C|$

$\Rightarrow -\dfrac{1}{2}\ln\left|\dfrac{x^2-xy-2y^2}{x^2}\right|+\dfrac{1}{6}\ln\left|\dfrac{y-2}{y+4}\right|=\ln|Cx|$

$\Rightarrow \ln\left|\dfrac{y-2x}{y+4x}\times\dfrac{x^6}{(x^2-xy-2y^2)^3}\right|=|Cx|^6$

$\Rightarrow \dfrac{y-2x}{y+4x}\times\dfrac{x^6}{(x^2-xy-2y^2)^3}=C'x^6$

$\Rightarrow \dfrac{y-2x}{(y+4x)}\times\dfrac{1}{(x^2-xy-2y^2)^3}=C'$

$\Rightarrow \dfrac{y-2x}{(y+4x)}\times\dfrac{1}{-x^6\left(-1+\frac{y}{x}+\frac{2y^2}{x^2}\right)^3}=C'$

$\Rightarrow \dfrac{\left(\frac{(y/x)-2}{(y/x)+4}\right)}{\dfrac{1}{\left(2.\frac{y^2}{x^2}+\frac{y}{x}-1\right)^3}}=-C'x^6$ or $Cx^6=\dfrac{\left(\frac{y}{x}-2\right)/\left(\frac{y}{x}+4\right)}{\dfrac{1}{\left(2.\frac{y^2}{x^2}+\frac{y}{x}-1\right)^3}}$

(c) $\dfrac{dy}{dx}=\dfrac{y}{x}+\tan\left(\dfrac{y}{x}\right)$ ...(1)

Put $y = vx$ ...(2)

$\Rightarrow \dfrac{dy}{dx}=v+x\dfrac{dv}{dx}$ ...(3)

$\therefore$ From (1), (2) and (3), we get $v+x\dfrac{dv}{dx}=v+\tan v$

$\Rightarrow \displaystyle\int\frac{dv}{\tan v}=\int\frac{dx}{x}$

$\Rightarrow \ln|\sin v|=\ln|x|+\ln|C'|$

$\Rightarrow |\sin v|=|C'x|$

$\Rightarrow \sin v=\pm C'x$

$\Rightarrow \sin\left(\dfrac{y}{x}\right)=kx$

$\Rightarrow \dfrac{y}{x}=\sin^{-1}(kx)$

(d) $\dfrac{dy}{dx}=\dfrac{x-2y+5}{2x+y-1}=\dfrac{ax+by+c}{a_1x+b_1y+c_1}$ ...(1)

$\Rightarrow \dfrac{a}{a_1}=\dfrac{1}{2};\ \dfrac{b}{b_1}=\dfrac{-2}{1}$

$\Rightarrow \quad \frac{a}{a_1} \neq \frac{b}{b_1}$

Let $x = X + h$ and $y = Y + k$

$\Rightarrow \quad \frac{dy}{dx} = \frac{dY}{dX}$ ...(2)

$\therefore$ From (1) and (2), $\frac{dY}{dX} = \frac{(X+h)-2(Y+k)+5}{2(X+h)+(Y+k)-1}$

$= \frac{X-2Y}{2X+Y}$ ...(3)

Choosing h and k, such that $h - 2k + 5 = 0$ and $2h + k - 1 = 0$

$\Rightarrow \quad h = -\frac{3}{5}, k = \frac{11}{5}$ ...(4)

$\Rightarrow \quad \frac{dY}{dX} = \frac{X-2Y}{2X+Y}$; Put $Y = vX$

$\Rightarrow \quad \frac{dY}{dX} = v + X\frac{dv}{dX}$

$\Rightarrow \quad V + X\frac{dv}{dX} = \frac{X(1+2v)}{x(2+v)}$

$\Rightarrow \quad X\frac{dv}{dX} = \frac{1-2v}{2+v} - v$

$\Rightarrow \quad \frac{2+v}{-v^2-4v+1}dv = \frac{dX}{X}$

$\Rightarrow \quad -\frac{1}{2}\int \frac{-2v-4}{-v^2-4v+1}dv = \int \frac{dX}{X}$

$\Rightarrow \quad -\frac{1}{2}\ln|-v^2-4v+1| = \ln|X| + \ln|C'|$

$\Rightarrow \quad \ln\left(\sqrt{|-v^2-4v+1|}\right)^{-1} = \ln|C'X|$

$\Rightarrow \quad \sqrt{|-v^2-4v+1|} = (C'X)^{-1}$

$\Rightarrow \quad \frac{-Y^2}{-X^2} - \frac{4Y}{X} + 1 = \frac{1}{C'^2}$

$\Rightarrow \quad 1.\frac{-Y^2}{X^2} - \frac{4Y}{X} = \frac{1}{C'^2 X^2}$

$\Rightarrow \quad X^2 - Y^2 - 4XY = \frac{1}{C'^2}$

$\Rightarrow \quad \left(x+\frac{3}{5}\right)^2 - \left(y-\frac{11}{5}\right)^2 - 4\left(x+\frac{3}{5}\right)\left(y-\frac{11}{5}\right) = \frac{1}{C'^2}$

$\Rightarrow \quad x^2 - y^2 + \left(\frac{6}{5}+\frac{44}{5}\right)x + \left(\frac{22}{5}-\frac{12}{5}\right)y - 4xy + C = 0$

$\Rightarrow \quad x^2 - y^2 + 10x + 2y - 4xy + C = 0$

(e) $\frac{dy}{dx} = \frac{ax+by-a}{bx+ay-b}$ ...(1)

Put $x = X + h$; $y = Y + k$ ...(2)

$\Rightarrow \quad \frac{dy}{dx} = \frac{dY}{dX}$ ...(3)

$\therefore$ From (1), (2) and (3), we get

$\frac{dY}{dX} = \frac{a(X+h)+b(Y+k)-a}{b(X+h)+a(Y+k)-b}$

$\Rightarrow \quad \frac{dY}{dX} = \frac{aX+bY+(ah+bk-a)}{bX+aY+(bh+ak-b)}$ ...(4)

$\Rightarrow \quad \frac{dY}{dx} = \frac{aX+bY}{bX+aY}$; where $ah + kb - a = 0$ and $bh + ak - b = 0$

$\Rightarrow \quad h = 1, k = 0$

Put $Y = vX$

$\Rightarrow \quad \frac{dY}{dX} = v + X\frac{dv}{dX}$ ...(5)

$\therefore$ From (4) and (5), we get $v + X\frac{dv}{dX} = \frac{X(a+bv)}{X(b+av)}$

$\Rightarrow \quad X\frac{dv}{dx} = \frac{a+bv}{b+av} - v$

$\Rightarrow \quad X\frac{dv}{dx} = \frac{a+bv-bv-av^2}{b+av}$

$\Rightarrow \quad X\frac{dv}{dX} = \frac{a-av^2}{b+av}$

$\Rightarrow \quad \int \frac{b+av}{a-av^2} = \int \frac{dx}{x}$

$\Rightarrow \quad \frac{b}{a}\int \frac{1}{1-v^2}dv + \frac{1}{-2}\int \frac{-2v}{1-v^2}dv = \int \frac{dX}{X}$

$\Rightarrow \quad \frac{b}{a}.\frac{1}{2}\ln\left|\frac{1+v}{1-v}\right| - \frac{1}{2}\ln|1-v^2| = \ln|x| + \ln|C|$

$\Rightarrow \quad \frac{b}{2a}\ln\left|\frac{1+v}{1-v}\right| - \frac{1}{2}\ln|1-v^2| = \ln|CX|$

$\Rightarrow \quad \ln\left|\frac{\left(\frac{1+v}{1-v}\right)^{b/2a}}{\sqrt{1-v^2}}\right| = \ln|CX|$

$\Rightarrow \quad \left(\frac{1+v}{1-v}\right)^{b/2a} . \frac{1}{\sqrt{1-v^2}} = \pm Cx$

$\Rightarrow \quad \left(\frac{1+\frac{Y}{X}}{1-\frac{Y}{X}}\right)^{b/2a} . \frac{1}{\sqrt{1-\frac{Y^2}{X^2}}} = \pm CX$

$\Rightarrow \quad \left(\frac{X+Y}{X-Y}\right)^{b/2a} . \frac{|X|}{\sqrt{X^2-Y^2}} = \pm CX$

$\Rightarrow \quad \left(\frac{x-1+y}{x-1-y}\right)^{b/2a} . \frac{|x-1|}{\sqrt{(x-1)^2-y^2}} = \pm C(x-1)'$

$\Rightarrow \quad \frac{(x-1+y)^{\frac{b}{2a}-\frac{1}{2}}}{(x-1-y)^{\frac{b}{2a}+\frac{1}{2}}}(x-1) = \pm C(x-1)'$

$\Rightarrow \quad \frac{(x-1+y)^{\frac{b}{2a}-\frac{1}{2}}}{(x-1-y)^{\frac{b}{2a}+\frac{1}{2}}}(x-1) = \pm C(x-1)$

$\Rightarrow \quad \frac{(x+y-1)^{\frac{b-a}{2a}}}{(x-y-1)^{\frac{b+a}{2a}}} = \pm C$

$\Rightarrow \quad (x-y-1)^{\frac{b+a}{2a}}.(x+y-1)^{\frac{a-b}{2a}} = \pm\frac{1}{C}$

$\Rightarrow \quad (x-y-1)^{a+b}.(x+y-1)^{a-b} = \left(\frac{1}{C}\right)^{2a}$ or

$(y-x-1)^{a+b}.(x+y-1)^{a-b} = C$

(f) $\dfrac{dy}{dx} = \dfrac{+2y-x}{2x-y}$ ...(1)

Put $y = vx$ ...(2)

$\Rightarrow \quad \dfrac{dy}{dx} = v + x\dfrac{dv}{dx}$ ...(3)

$\therefore$ From (1), (2) and (3), we have $v + x\dfrac{dv}{dx} = +\dfrac{2vx-x}{2x-vx}$

$\Rightarrow \quad v + x\dfrac{dv}{dx} = \dfrac{2v-1}{2-v}$

$\Rightarrow \quad x\dfrac{dv}{dx} = \dfrac{2v-1}{2-v} - v$

$\Rightarrow \quad x\dfrac{dv}{dx} = \dfrac{2v-1-2v+v^2}{2-v}$

$\Rightarrow \quad x\dfrac{dv}{dx} = \dfrac{v^2-1}{2-v}$

$\Rightarrow \quad \int\dfrac{2-v}{v^2-1}dv = \int\dfrac{dx}{x}$

$\Rightarrow \quad 2\int\dfrac{1}{v^2-1}dv - \dfrac{1}{2}\int\dfrac{2v}{v^2-1}dv = \int\dfrac{dx}{x}$

$\Rightarrow \quad 2\times\dfrac{1}{2}\ln\left|\dfrac{v-1}{v+1}\right| - \dfrac{1}{2}\ln|v^2-1| = \ln|Cx|$

$\Rightarrow \quad \ln\left|\dfrac{v-1}{v+1}\times\dfrac{1}{\sqrt{v^2-1}}\right| = \ln|Cx|$

$\Rightarrow \quad \dfrac{(v-1)^{1/2}}{(v+1)^{3/2}} = \pm Cx$

$\Rightarrow \quad \dfrac{(y-x)^{1/2}}{(y+x)^{3/2}}.x = \pm Cx$ or $(y-x) = C^2(y+x)^3$ or $(x+y)^3 = C'(y-x)$

(g) $x\dfrac{dy}{dx} = y - \sqrt{x^2+y^2}$

$\Rightarrow \quad \dfrac{dy}{dx} = \dfrac{y}{x} - \sqrt{1+\dfrac{y^2}{x^2}}$ ...(1)

Put $y = vx$ ...(2)

$\Rightarrow \quad \dfrac{dy}{dx} = v + x\dfrac{dv}{dx}$ ...(3)

$\therefore$ From (1), (2) and (3), we get $v + x\dfrac{dv}{dx} = v - \sqrt{1+v^2}$

$\Rightarrow \quad x\dfrac{dv}{dx} = -\sqrt{1+v^2}$

$\Rightarrow \quad x\dfrac{dv}{dx} = -\sqrt{1+v^2}$

$\Rightarrow \quad \int\dfrac{dv}{\sqrt{1+v^2}} = -\int\dfrac{dx}{x}$

$\Rightarrow \quad \ln|v+\sqrt{1+v^2}| + \ln|x| = \ln|C|$

$\Rightarrow \quad \ln\left|\left(v+\sqrt{1+v^2}\right).x\right| = \ln|C|$

$\Rightarrow \quad \left(y+\sqrt{x^2+y^2}\right) = C$ or $C - y = \sqrt{x^2+y^2}$

(h) $x\sin\dfrac{y}{x}dy = \left(y\sin\dfrac{y}{x} - x\right)dx$

$\Rightarrow \quad \dfrac{dy}{dx} = \dfrac{y\sin\dfrac{y}{x} - x}{\left(x\sin\dfrac{y}{x}\right)}$

$\Rightarrow \quad \dfrac{dy}{dx} = \dfrac{\dfrac{y}{x}\sin\dfrac{y}{x} - 1}{\left(\sin\dfrac{y}{x}\right)}$ ...(1)

Put $y = vx$ ...(2)

$\Rightarrow \quad \dfrac{dy}{dx} = v + x\dfrac{dv}{dx}$ ...(3)

$\therefore$ From (1), (2) and (3), we get $v + x\dfrac{dv}{dx} = \dfrac{v\sin v - 1}{\sin v}$

$\Rightarrow \quad x\dfrac{dv}{dx} = \dfrac{-1}{\sin v}$

$\Rightarrow \quad \int\sin v\,dv + \int\dfrac{dx}{x} = 0$

$\Rightarrow \quad -\cos v + \ln|x| = C$

$\Rightarrow \quad \ln|x| = \cos\left(\dfrac{y}{x}\right) + C$

(i) $\dfrac{dy}{dx} = \dfrac{x+y+1}{2x+2y+3}$

$\Rightarrow \quad \dfrac{dy}{dx} = \dfrac{(x+y)+1}{2(x+y)+3}$ ...(1)

Put $x + y = z$

$\Rightarrow \quad 1 + \dfrac{dy}{dx} = \dfrac{dz}{dx}$

$\Rightarrow \quad \dfrac{dz}{dx} - 1 = \dfrac{z+1}{2z+3}$

$\Rightarrow \quad \dfrac{dz}{dx} = \dfrac{z+1+2z+3}{2z+3}$

$\Rightarrow \quad \dfrac{dz}{dx} = \dfrac{3z+4}{2z+3}$

$\Rightarrow \quad \int\dfrac{2z+3}{3z+4}dz = \int dx$

$\Rightarrow \quad 2\int\dfrac{z+\dfrac{3}{2}}{3z+4}dz = \int dx$

$\Rightarrow \quad \dfrac{2}{3}\int\dfrac{3z+\dfrac{9}{2}}{3z+4}dz = \int dx$

$\Rightarrow \quad \dfrac{2}{3}\int\dfrac{3z+4+\dfrac{1}{2}}{3z+4}dz = \int dx$

$$\Rightarrow \frac{2}{3}\int\left(1+\frac{1}{2(3z+4)}\right)dz = \int dx$$

$$\Rightarrow \frac{2}{3}\left[z+\frac{1}{2}\frac{\ln|3z+4|}{3}\right] = x$$

$$\Rightarrow \frac{2}{3}\left[(x+y)+\frac{1}{6}\ln|3x+3y+4|\right] = x$$

$$\Rightarrow \frac{1}{3}x-\frac{2}{3}y=\frac{1}{9}\ln|3x+3y+4|$$

$$\Rightarrow 3(x-2y)=\ln|3x+3y+4|$$

$$\Rightarrow 3x+3y+4 = e^{3(x-2y)} \Rightarrow x+y+4/3 = ce^{3(x-2y)}$$

2. (a) $\dfrac{dy}{dx}=\dfrac{x^2+xy}{x^2+y^2}$ ...(1)

Put $y = vx$ ...(2)

$$\Rightarrow \frac{dy}{dx}=v+x\frac{dv}{dx} \quad ...(3)$$

$\therefore$ From (1), (2) and (3) we have, $v+x\dfrac{dv}{dx}=\dfrac{x^2+x^2v}{x^2+v^2x^2}$

$$\Rightarrow v+x\frac{dv}{dx}=\frac{1+v}{1+v^2} \Rightarrow x\frac{dv}{dx}=\frac{1+v}{1+v^2}-v$$

$$\Rightarrow x\frac{dv}{dx}=\frac{1+v-v-v^3}{1+v^2} \Rightarrow x\frac{dv}{dx}=\frac{1-v^3}{1+v^2}$$

$$\Rightarrow \frac{1+v^2}{1-v^3}dv=\frac{dx}{x}$$

$$\Rightarrow \int\frac{1}{1-v^3}dv+\int\frac{v^2}{1-v^3}dv=\int\frac{dx}{x}$$

$$\Rightarrow \int\frac{1}{(1-v)(1+v^2+v)}dv-\frac{1}{3}\int\frac{-3v^2}{1-v^3}=\int\frac{dx}{x}$$

$$\Rightarrow \int\frac{A}{1-v}dv+\int\frac{Bv+C}{v^2+v+1}dv-\frac{1}{3}\ln|1-v^3|=\ln|x| \quad ...(1)$$

Here $\dfrac{A}{1-v}+\dfrac{Bv+C}{v^2+v+1}=\dfrac{1}{(1-v)(v^2+v+1)}$

$\Rightarrow A(v^2+v+1)+(Bv+C)(1-v)=1$

$\Rightarrow (A-B)v^2+(A+B-C)v+(A+C)=1$

$\Rightarrow A=B;\ A+C=1;\ A+B-C=0$

$\Rightarrow 2A-C=0,\ A+C=1$

$\Rightarrow A=1/3,\ B=1/3,\ C=2/3$

$$\therefore \frac{1}{3}\int\frac{1}{1-v}dv+\int\frac{\frac{1}{3}(v+2)}{v^2+v+1}dv-\frac{1}{3}\ln|1-v^3| = \ln|x|$$

$$\Rightarrow -\frac{1}{3}\ln|1-v|+\frac{1}{2\times3}\int\frac{2v+4}{v^2+v+1}dv$$

$$= \ln|x|+\frac{1}{3}\ln|1-v^3|$$

$$\Rightarrow \frac{1}{6}\int\frac{2v+1}{v^2+v+1}dv+\frac{1}{2}\int\frac{1}{v^2+v+1}dv$$

$$= \ln|x|+\frac{1}{3}\ln\left(|1-v^3||-v|\right)$$

$$\Rightarrow \frac{1}{6}\ln\left(v^2+v+1\right)+\frac{1}{2}\int\frac{1}{\left(v+\frac{1}{2}\right)^2+\left(\frac{\sqrt{3}}{2}\right)^2}dv$$

$$= \ln|x(1-v^3)^{1/3}(1-v)^{1/3}|$$

$$\Rightarrow \frac{1}{6}\ln\left(v^2+v+1\right)+\frac{1}{2}\times\frac{2}{\sqrt{3}}\tan^{-1}\left(\frac{v+\frac{1}{2}}{\sqrt{3}/2}\right)$$

$$= \ln|x(1-v^3)^{1/3}(1-v)^{1/3}|+\ln C$$

$$\Rightarrow \frac{1}{\sqrt{3}}\tan^{-1}\left(\frac{2v+1}{\sqrt{3}}\right) = \ln\left|C\frac{x(1-v^3)^{1/3}(1-v)^{1/3}}{(v^2+v+1)^{1/6}}\right|$$

$$\Rightarrow \frac{1}{\sqrt{3}}\tan^{-1}\left(\frac{2y+x}{\sqrt{3}x}\right) = \ln\left|C\frac{x\left(\frac{x^3-y^3}{x^3}\right)^{1/3}\left(\frac{x-y}{x}\right)^{1/3}}{\left(\frac{y^2+yx+x^2}{x^2}\right)^{1/6}}\right|$$

$$\Rightarrow \frac{1}{\sqrt{3}}\tan^{-1}\left(\frac{2y+x}{\sqrt{3}x}\right) = \ln\left|\frac{C\left(x^3-y^3\right)^{1/3}\left(x-y\right)^{1/3}}{\left(x^2+xy+y^2\right)^{1/6}}\right|$$

$$\Rightarrow \frac{1}{\sqrt{3}}\tan^{-1}\left(\frac{2y+x}{\sqrt{3}x}\right) = \ln\left|C(x-y)^{2/3}(x^2+xy+y^2)^{1/6}\right|$$

(b) $(x^3-3xy^2)dx=(y^3-3x^2y)dy$

$\dfrac{dy}{dx}=\dfrac{x^3-3xy^2}{y^3-3x^2y}$ ...(1)

Put $y = vx$ ...(2)

$\Rightarrow \dfrac{dy}{dx}=v+x\dfrac{dv}{dx}$ ...(3)

From (1), (2) and (3), $v+x\dfrac{dv}{dx}=\dfrac{x^3-3v^2x^3}{v^3x^3-3x^3v}$

$$\Rightarrow v+x\frac{dv}{dx}=\frac{1-3v^2}{v^3-3v}$$

$$\Rightarrow x\frac{dv}{dx}=\frac{1-3v^2-v^4+3v^2}{v^3-3v}$$

$$\Rightarrow dv=\frac{1-v^4}{v^3-3v}.\frac{dx}{x}$$

$$\Rightarrow \int\left(\frac{v^3-3v}{1-v^4}\right)dv=\int\frac{dx}{x}$$

$$\Rightarrow \int\left(\frac{v^3-3v}{1-v^4}\right)dv=\int\frac{dx}{x}$$

$$\Rightarrow \int\frac{v^3}{1-v^4}dv+3\int\frac{v}{(v^2-1)(v^2+1)}=\int\frac{dx}{x}$$

$$\Rightarrow -\int\frac{v^3}{v^4-1}dv+3\int\left(\frac{Av+B}{v^2-1}+\frac{Cv+B}{v^2+1}\right)dv=\int\frac{dx}{x} \quad ...(1)$$

where $\dfrac{Av+B}{v^2-1}+\dfrac{Cv+D}{v^2+1}=\dfrac{v}{(v^2-1)(v^2+1)}$

$\Rightarrow (Av+B)(v^2+1)+(Cv+D)(v^2-1)=v$

$\Rightarrow v^3(A+C)+v^2(B+D)+v(A-C)+(B-D)=v$

$\Rightarrow A+C=0;\ B+D=0;\ A-C=1;\ B-D=0$

$\Rightarrow \quad A = \frac{1}{2}, C = \frac{-1}{2}; B = 0, D = 0$

$\Rightarrow \quad -\int \frac{v^3}{v^4-1} dv + 3\int \frac{\frac{1}{2}v}{v^2-1} dv + 3\int \frac{-\frac{1}{2}v}{v^2+1} dv = \int \frac{dx}{x} dv$

$\Rightarrow \quad -\frac{1}{4}\int \frac{4v^3}{v^4-1} dv + \frac{3}{4}\int \frac{2v}{v^2-1} dv - \frac{3}{4}\int \frac{2v}{v^2+1} dv = \int \frac{dx}{x}$

$\Rightarrow \quad \frac{-1}{4}\ln|v^4-1| + \frac{3}{4}\ln|v^2-1|$

$-\frac{3}{4}\ln|v^2+1| = \ln|x| + \ln|C|$

$\Rightarrow \quad \frac{-1}{4}\ln|v^4-1| + \frac{3}{4}\ln\left|\frac{v^2-1}{v^2+1}\right| = \ln|Cx|$

$\Rightarrow \quad \frac{1}{4}\ln\left|\left(\frac{v^2-1}{v^2+1}\right)^3 \times \frac{1}{v^4-1}\right| = \ln|Cx|$

$\Rightarrow \quad \left|\frac{(v^2-1)^3}{(v^2+1)^3(v^2-1)(v^2+1)}\right| = |Cx|^4$

$\Rightarrow \quad \frac{(v^2-1)^2}{(v^2+1)^4} = C^4x^4$

$\Rightarrow \quad \frac{\left(\frac{y^2-x^2}{x^2}\right)^2}{\left(\frac{y^2+x^2}{x^2}\right)^4} = C^4x^4$

$\Rightarrow \quad \frac{(y^2-x^2)^2}{x^4} \times \frac{x^8}{(y^2+x^2)^4} = C^4x^4$

$\Rightarrow \quad \frac{(y^2-x^2)^2.x^4}{(y^2+x^2)^4} = C^4x^4$

$\Rightarrow$ $(y^2 - x^2)^2 = C^4 (y^2 + x^2)^4$ or $(y^2 - x^2) = k(y^2 + x^2)^2$.

3. (a) $y^2 + x^2\frac{dy}{dx} = xy\frac{dy}{dx}$

$\Rightarrow \quad \frac{dy}{dx}(x^2 - xy) = -y^2$

$\Rightarrow \quad \frac{dy}{dx} = \frac{y^2}{xy - x^2}$ ...(1)

Put $y = vx$ ...(2)

$\Rightarrow \quad \frac{dy}{dx} = v + x\frac{dv}{dx}$ ...(3)

Using (2) and (3) in (1), we get $v + x\frac{dv}{dx} = \frac{v^2x^2}{vx^2 - x^2}$

$\Rightarrow \quad v + x\frac{dv}{dx} = \frac{v^2}{v-1}$

$\Rightarrow \quad x\frac{dv}{dx} = \frac{v^2 - v^2 + 1}{(v-1)}$

$\Rightarrow \quad x\frac{dv}{dx} = \frac{v}{(v-1)}$

$\Rightarrow \quad \int \frac{v-1}{v} = \int \frac{dx}{x}$

$\Rightarrow$ $v - \ln|v| = \ln|x| + \ln|C|$

$\Rightarrow$ $v = \ln|Cvx|$

$\Rightarrow$ $y/x = \ln|c.y|$ or $\frac{y}{x} = c + \ln|y|$

(b) $(2x + y + 1)dx + (4x + 2y - 1)dy = 0$

$\Rightarrow \quad \frac{dy}{dx} = -\frac{(2x+y+1)}{(4x+2y-1)}$

$\Rightarrow \quad \frac{dy}{dx} = -\frac{[(2x+y)+1]}{[2(2x+y)-1]}$

Put $2x + y = z$

$\Rightarrow \quad 2 + \frac{dy}{dx} = \frac{dz}{dx}$

$\Rightarrow \quad \frac{dz}{dx} - 2 = \frac{-[z+1]}{(2z-1)}$

$\Rightarrow \quad \frac{dz}{dx} = \frac{-(z+1)+4z-2}{2z-1}$

$\Rightarrow \quad \frac{dz}{dx} = \frac{3z-3}{2z-1}$

$\Rightarrow \quad \int \frac{2z-1}{3z-3} dz = \int dx$

$\Rightarrow \quad 2\int \frac{z-1/2}{3z-3} dz = \int dx$

$\Rightarrow \quad \frac{2}{3}\int \frac{3z-3/2}{3z-3} dz = \int dx$

$\Rightarrow \quad \frac{2}{3}\int \frac{3z-3+3/2}{3z-3} dz = \int dx$

$\Rightarrow \quad \frac{2}{3}\int \left[1 + \frac{1}{2(z-1)}\right] dz = \int dx$

$\Rightarrow \quad \frac{2}{3}z + \frac{1}{3}\ln|z-1| = x + C$

$\Rightarrow \quad \frac{2}{3}z + \frac{1}{3}\ln|z-1| = x + C$

$\Rightarrow \quad \frac{2}{3}(2x+y) + \frac{1}{3}\ln|(2x+y)-1| = x + C$

$\Rightarrow \quad \frac{4}{3}x + \frac{2y}{3} + \frac{1}{3}\ln|2x+y-1| = x + C$

$\Rightarrow \quad \frac{1}{3}x + \frac{2y}{3} + \frac{1}{3}\ln|2x+y-1| = C$

$\Rightarrow$ $(x + 2y) + \ln|2x + y - 1| = C$

(c) $(3y - 7x - 3)dx + (7y - 3x - 7) = 0$

$\Rightarrow$ $(7y - 3x - 7)dy = -(3y - 7x - 3)dx$

$\Rightarrow \quad \frac{dy}{dx} = -\frac{(3y-7x-3)}{(7y-3x-7)}$ ...(1)

Put $x = X + h, y = Y + k$

$\Rightarrow \quad \frac{dy}{dx} = \frac{dY}{dX}$

$\Rightarrow \quad \frac{dY}{dX} = -\frac{[3(Y+k)-7(X+h)-3]}{[7(Y+k)-3(X+h)-7]}$

$\Rightarrow \dfrac{dY}{dX}=\dfrac{7X-3Y}{-3X+7Y}$; where $7h-3k+3=0$ and $-3h+7k-7=0$

$\Rightarrow h=0, k=1$

Put $Y=VX$

$\Rightarrow \dfrac{dY}{dX}=V+X\dfrac{dV}{dX}$

$\Rightarrow V+X\dfrac{dV}{dX}=\dfrac{7X-3(VX)}{-3X+7VX}$

$\Rightarrow V+X\dfrac{dV}{dX}=\dfrac{-V}{-3+7V}$

$\Rightarrow X\dfrac{dV}{dX}=\dfrac{7-3V+3V-7V^2}{-3+7V}$

$\Rightarrow X\dfrac{dV}{dX}=\dfrac{7-7V^2}{-3+7V}$

$\Rightarrow \dfrac{-3+7V}{7-7V^2}dV=\dfrac{dX}{X}$

$\Rightarrow \dfrac{-3}{7}\int\dfrac{1}{1-V^2}dV+\int\dfrac{V}{1-V^2}dV=\int\dfrac{dX}{X}$

$\Rightarrow \dfrac{-3}{7}\times\dfrac{1}{2}\ln\left|\dfrac{1+V}{1-V}\right|+\left(\dfrac{-1}{2}\right)\int\dfrac{-2V}{1-V^2}dV=\ln|x|+\ln|C|$

$\Rightarrow \dfrac{-3}{14}\ln\left|\dfrac{1+Y/X}{1-Y/X}\right|-\dfrac{1}{2}\ln|1-V^2|=\ln|Cx|$

$\Rightarrow \dfrac{-3}{14}\ln\left|\dfrac{X+Y}{X-Y}\right|-\dfrac{1}{2}\ln|1-V^2|=\ln|CX|$

$\Rightarrow \dfrac{-3}{14}\ln\left|\dfrac{x+y-1}{x-y+1}\right|-\dfrac{1}{2}\ln\left|1-\dfrac{Y^2}{X^2}\right|=\ln|C(X)|$

$\Rightarrow \dfrac{-3}{14}\ln\left|\dfrac{x+y-1}{x-y+1}\right|-\dfrac{1}{2}\ln\left|\dfrac{x^2-(y-1)^2}{x^2}\right|=\ln|C(x)|$

$\Rightarrow \left|\dfrac{x-y+1}{x+y-1}\right|^{3/14}\cdot\left|\dfrac{x^2}{x^2-(y-1)^2}\right|^{1/2}=|Cx|$

$\Rightarrow \left|\dfrac{x(x-y+1)^{\frac{3}{14}-\frac{1}{2}}}{(x+y-1)^{\frac{3}{14}+\frac{1}{2}}}\right|=|Cx|$

$\Rightarrow \dfrac{x(x-y+1)^{-\frac{4}{14}}}{(x+y-1)^{\frac{10}{14}}}=|Cx|$

$\Rightarrow \dfrac{(x-y+1)^{-\frac{2}{7}}}{(x+y-1)^{\frac{5}{7}}}=\pm C^7$

$\Rightarrow (x+y-1)^5(x-y+1)^2=\pm 1/C^7$

$\Rightarrow C'(y-x-1)^2(y+x-1)^5=1$ or $C(y-x-1)^2(y+x-1)^5=1$

4. $y^3\dfrac{dy}{dx}+x+y^2=0$

$\Rightarrow \dfrac{dy}{dx}=\dfrac{-y^2-x}{y^3}$

Put $y^2=ax^3-x \quad \Rightarrow x+y^2=ax^3$

$\Rightarrow \dfrac{dy}{dx}=-\dfrac{ax^3}{y^3}$ ...(1)

Put $y=vx$

$\Rightarrow \dfrac{dy}{dx}=v+x\dfrac{dv}{dx}$ ...(2)

$\therefore$ From (1) and (2), $v+x\dfrac{dv}{dx}=-\dfrac{ax^3}{v^3x^3}$

$\Rightarrow x\dfrac{dv}{dx}=-\dfrac{a}{v^3}-v$

$\Rightarrow \dfrac{v^3}{a+v^4}dv=-\dfrac{dx}{x}$

$\Rightarrow \dfrac{1}{4}\int\dfrac{4v^3}{a+v^4}dv+\int\dfrac{dx}{x}=0$

$\Rightarrow \dfrac{1}{4}\ln|a+v^4|+\ln|x|=\ln|C|$

$\Rightarrow |(a+v^4)^{1/4}x|=|C| \quad \Rightarrow (a+v^4)^{1/4}.x=\pm C$

$\Rightarrow [a+v^4].x^4=C^4$

$\Rightarrow \left(a+\dfrac{y^4}{x^4}\right).x^4=C^4$

$\Rightarrow (ax^4+y^4)=C^4$

$\Rightarrow ax^4+y^4=C'$

5. $\left(x\cos\dfrac{y}{x}+y\sin\dfrac{y}{x}\right)y=\left(y\sin\dfrac{y}{x}-x\cos\dfrac{y}{x}\right)x\dfrac{dy}{dx}$

$\Rightarrow \left(\cos\dfrac{y}{x}+\dfrac{y}{x}\sin\dfrac{y}{x}\right)\dfrac{y}{x}=\left(\dfrac{y}{x}\sin\dfrac{y}{x}-\cos\dfrac{y}{x}\right).\dfrac{dy}{dx}$ ...(1)

Put $y=vx$ ...(2)

From (1), (2) and (3), we get $(\cos v+v\sin v)v$

$=(v\sin v-\cos v)\left(v+x\dfrac{dv}{dx}\right)$

$\Rightarrow \dfrac{(\cos v+v\sin v)v}{(v\sin v-\cos v)}-v=x\dfrac{dv}{dx}$

$\Rightarrow \dfrac{v\cos v+v^2\sin v-v^2\sin v+v\cos v}{(v\sin v-\cos v)}=x\dfrac{dv}{dx}$

$\Rightarrow \dfrac{2v\cos v}{v\sin v-\cos v}=x\dfrac{dv}{dx}$

$\Rightarrow \dfrac{v\sin v-\cos v}{2v\cos v}dv=\dfrac{dx}{x}$

$\Rightarrow \int\left(\dfrac{1}{2}\tan v-\dfrac{1}{2v}\right)dv=\int\dfrac{dx}{x}$

$\Rightarrow \dfrac{1}{2}\ln|\sec v|-\dfrac{1}{2}(\ln|v|)=\ln|x|+C'$

$\Rightarrow \ln\left|\left(\dfrac{\sec v}{v}\right)^{1/2}.\dfrac{1}{x}\right|=C'$

$\Rightarrow \left(\dfrac{\sec v}{v}\right)=C_1x^2$

$\Rightarrow \sec v=C_1vx^2$

$\Rightarrow \sec(y/x)=C_1(xy)$

$\Rightarrow \quad xy\cos\left(\frac{y}{x}\right) = \frac{1}{C_1}$

$\Rightarrow \quad xy\cos\left(\frac{y}{x}\right) = C'$

TEXTUAL EXERCISE–5: (OBJECTIVE)

1. (b) $y' = \frac{y}{x} + \frac{\phi(y/x)}{\phi'(y/x)}$

Put $y = vx$

$\Rightarrow \quad y' = v + x\frac{dv}{dx}$

$\Rightarrow \quad v + x\frac{dv}{dx} = v + \frac{\phi(v)}{\phi'(v)}$

$\Rightarrow \quad x\frac{dv}{dx} = \frac{\phi(v)}{\phi'(v)}$

$\Rightarrow \quad \int \frac{\phi'(v)}{\phi(v)}dv = \int \frac{dv}{dx}$

$\Rightarrow \quad \ln|\phi(v)| = \ln|x| + \ln|C|$

$\Rightarrow \quad \phi(v) = \pm Cx$

$\Rightarrow \quad \phi(v) = C'x$

$\Rightarrow \quad \phi(y/x) = C'x$

2. (c) $(y + x + 5)dy = (y - x + 1)dx$

$\Rightarrow \quad \frac{dy}{dx} = \frac{y-x+1}{y+x+5}$ ...(1)

Put $y = Y + k, x = X + h$ ...(2)

$\Rightarrow \quad \frac{dy}{dx} = \frac{dY}{dX}$ ...(3)

$\Rightarrow \quad \frac{dY}{dX} = \frac{(Y+k)-(X+h)+1}{(Y+k)+(X+h)+5}$

$\Rightarrow \quad \frac{dY}{dX} = \frac{-X+Y-h+k+1}{X+Y+h+k+5}$

$\Rightarrow \quad \frac{dY}{dX} = \frac{-X+Y}{X+Y}$ ...(4)

Choosing h and k such that $-h + k + 1 = 0$ and $h + k + 5 = 0$

$\Rightarrow \quad k = -3$ and $h = -2$ ...(5)

Let $Y = VX$ ...(6)

$\Rightarrow \quad \frac{dY}{dX} = V + X\frac{dV}{dX}$ ...(7)

Using (6) and (7) in (4), we get $V + X\frac{dV}{dX} = \frac{-X+VX}{X+VX}$

$\Rightarrow \quad V + X\frac{dV}{dX} = \frac{-1+V}{1+V}$

$\Rightarrow \quad X\frac{dV}{dX} = \frac{-1+V}{1+V} - V$

$\Rightarrow \quad X\frac{dV}{dX} = \frac{-1+V-V-V^2}{1+V}$

$\Rightarrow \quad X\frac{dV}{dX} = \frac{-1-V^2}{1+V}$

$\Rightarrow \quad \int \frac{1+V}{1+V^2}dV = -\int \frac{dX}{X}$

$\Rightarrow \quad \int \frac{1}{1+V^2}dV + \frac{1}{2}\int \frac{2V}{1+V^2}dV = -\int \frac{dX}{X}$

$\Rightarrow \quad \tan^{-1}(V) + \frac{1}{2}\ln|1+V^2| = -\ln|X| + \ln|C|$

$\Rightarrow \quad \tan^{-1}(V) + \frac{1}{2}\ln\left|\frac{X^2+Y^2}{X^2}\right| = \ln|C/X|$

$\Rightarrow \quad \tan^{-1}\left(\frac{Y}{X}\right) + \ln\left|\frac{\sqrt{X^2+Y^2}}{X}\right| = \ln|C/X|$

$\Rightarrow \quad \tan^{-1}\left(\frac{Y}{X}\right) = \ln\left|\frac{C/X.X}{\sqrt{X^2+Y^2}}\right|$

$\Rightarrow \quad \tan^{-1}\left(\frac{Y}{X}\right) = \ln|C| - \frac{1}{2}\ln(X^2+Y^2)$

$\Rightarrow \quad \tan^{-1}\left(\frac{y+3}{x+2}\right) + \frac{1}{2}\ln\left((x+2)^2+(y+3)^2\right) = \ln|C|$

$\Rightarrow \quad 2\tan^{-1}\left(\frac{y+3}{x+2}\right) + \ln\left((x+2)^2+(y+3)^2\right) = 2\ln|C|$ or

$2\tan^{-1}\left(\frac{y+3}{x+2}\right) + \ln\left[(y+3)^2+(x+2)^2\right] = C$

3. (a) $y_1 = \frac{y^2-2xy-x^2}{y^2+2xy-x^2}$ ...(1)

Put $y = vx$ ...(2)

$\Rightarrow \quad y_1 = v + x\frac{dv}{dx}$ ...(3)

$\therefore$ from (1), (2) and (3), we get $v + x\frac{dv}{dx} = \frac{v^2x^2-2vx^2-x^2}{v^2x^2+2vx^2-x^2}$

$\Rightarrow \quad v + x\frac{dv}{dx} = \frac{+v^2-2v-1}{v^2+2v-1}$

$\Rightarrow \quad x\frac{dv}{dx} = \frac{v^2-2v-1-v^3-2v^2+v}{v^2+2v-1}$

$\Rightarrow \quad \frac{v^2+2v-1dv}{-v^3-v^2-v-1} = \frac{dx}{x}$

$\Rightarrow \quad \frac{v^2+2v+1-2}{-v^2(v+1)-1(v+1)}dv = \frac{dx}{x}$

$\Rightarrow \quad \frac{(v+1)^2-2dv}{-(v+1)(v^2+1)} = \frac{dx}{x}$

$\Rightarrow \quad \int \frac{2-(v+1)^2}{(v+1)(v^2+1)}dv = \int \frac{dx}{x}$

$\Rightarrow \quad \int \frac{2}{(v+1)(v^2+1)}dv - \frac{1}{2}\int \frac{2v}{v^2+1}dv - \int \frac{1}{v^2+1}dv = \int \frac{dx}{x}$ ...(1)

Let $\frac{1}{(v+1)(v^2+1)} = \frac{A}{v+1} + \frac{Bv+C}{v^2+1}$

$\Rightarrow \quad 1 = A(v^2+1) + (Bv+C)(v+1)$

$\Rightarrow \quad 1 = (A+B)v^2 + (B+C)v + (A+C)$

$\Rightarrow \quad A + B = 0; B + C = 0; A + C = 1$

$\Rightarrow\ A - C = 0$

$A + C = 1$

$\Rightarrow\ A = 1/2;\ B = -1/2;\ C = 1/2$

$\therefore$ From equation (1), we get $2\int\left[\dfrac{1/2}{v+1}+\dfrac{\frac{1}{2}(-v+1)}{v^2+1}\right]dv$

$-\dfrac{1}{2}\ln(v^2+1)-\tan^{-1}v=\ln|Cx|$

$\Rightarrow\ \ln|v+1|-\dfrac{1}{2}\ln(v^2+1)+\tan^{-1}(v)$

$-\dfrac{1}{2}\ln(v^2+1)-\tan^{-1}v=\ln|Cx|$

$\Rightarrow\ \ln\left|\dfrac{v+1}{v^2+1}\right|=\ln|Cx|$

$\Rightarrow\ \dfrac{v+1}{v^2+1}=\pm Cx$

$\Rightarrow\ \dfrac{(y+x)}{(y^2+x^2)}.x=\pm Cx$

$\Rightarrow\ (y+x)=\pm C(x^2+y^2)$

$\Rightarrow\ k(x^2+y^2)-x-y=0$

$\because$ It passes through $(1, -1)$

$\Rightarrow\ k(2)-1+1=0$

$\Rightarrow\ k=0$

$\Rightarrow\ -x-y=0$ or $y=-x$

$\therefore$ It represents a straight line.

4. (a) $x\sin\left(\dfrac{y}{x}\right)dy=\left\{y\sin\left(\dfrac{y}{x}\right)-x\right\}dx$

$\Rightarrow\ \dfrac{dy}{dx}=\left[\dfrac{\frac{y}{x}\sin\left(\frac{y}{x}\right)-1}{\sin\left(\frac{y}{x}\right)}\right]$

Put $y = vx$

$\Rightarrow\ \dfrac{dy}{dx}=v+x\dfrac{dv}{dx}$

$\Rightarrow\ v+x\dfrac{dv}{dx}=\dfrac{v\sin v-1}{\sin v}$

$\Rightarrow\ x\dfrac{dv}{dx}=-\text{cosec}v \quad \Rightarrow\ \int\sin v\,dv+\int\dfrac{dx}{x}=0$

$\Rightarrow\ -\cos v+\ln|x|=\ln|C|$

$\Rightarrow\ -\cos\left(\dfrac{y}{x}\right)+\ln|x|=\ln|C|$ or $\ln|x|-\cos\left(\dfrac{y}{x}\right)=\ln|C|$

5. (b) $\left(1+e^{x/y}\right)dx+e^{x/y}\left(1-\dfrac{x}{y}\right)dy=0$

$\Rightarrow\ \dfrac{dx}{dy}=\dfrac{-e^{x/y}\left(1-\frac{x}{y}\right)}{\left(1+e^{x/y}\right)}$

$\Rightarrow\ \dfrac{dx}{dy}=\dfrac{e^{x/y}\left(\frac{x}{y}-1\right)}{\left(1+e^{x/y}\right)}$

Put $x = vy$

$\Rightarrow\ \dfrac{dx}{y}=v+y\dfrac{dv}{dy} \quad \Rightarrow\ v+y\dfrac{dv}{dy}=\dfrac{e^v(v-1)}{(1+e^v)}$

$\Rightarrow\ y\dfrac{dv}{dy}=\dfrac{ve^v-e^v-v-ve^v}{(1+e^v)}$

$\Rightarrow\ y\dfrac{dv}{dy}=\dfrac{-(v+e^v)}{1+e^v} \quad \Rightarrow\ \int\left(\dfrac{1+e^v}{v+e^v}\right)dv+\int\dfrac{dv}{y}=0$

$\Rightarrow\ \ln|v+e^v|+\ln|y|=\ln|C|$

$\Rightarrow\ (v+e^v)y=\pm C \quad \Rightarrow\ \left(\dfrac{x}{y}+e^{x/y}\right)y=\pm C$

$\Rightarrow\ x+y\,e^{x/y}=\pm C$ or $x+y\,e^{x/y}=C$

6. (a) $x^2\dfrac{dy}{dx}=x^2+xy+y^2$

$\Rightarrow\ \dfrac{dy}{dx}=\dfrac{x^2+xy+y^2}{x^2}$ ...(1)

Put $y = vx$

$\Rightarrow\ \dfrac{dy}{dx}=v+x\dfrac{dv}{dx}$

$\Rightarrow\ v+x\dfrac{dv}{dx}=\dfrac{x^2+x^2v+v^2x^2}{x^2}$

$\Rightarrow\ v+x\dfrac{dv}{dx}=1+v+v^2 \quad \Rightarrow\ x\dfrac{dv}{dx}=1+v^2$

$\Rightarrow\ \int\dfrac{dv}{1+v^2}=\int\dfrac{dx}{x} \quad \Rightarrow\ \tan^{-1}v=\ln|x|+C$

$\Rightarrow\ \tan^{-1}\left(\dfrac{y}{x}\right)=\ln|x|+C$

7. (b) $(x^2+y^2)dx=2xy\,dy$

$\Rightarrow\ \dfrac{dy}{dx}=\dfrac{x^2+y^2}{2xy}$ ...(1)

Put $y = vx$

$\Rightarrow\ \dfrac{dy}{dx}=v+x\dfrac{dv}{dx} \quad \Rightarrow\ v+x\dfrac{dv}{dx}=\dfrac{x^2+v^2x^2}{2x^2v}$

$\Rightarrow\ v+x\dfrac{dv}{dx}=\dfrac{1+v^2}{2v} \quad \Rightarrow\ x\dfrac{dv}{dx}=\dfrac{1+v^2}{2v}-v$

$\Rightarrow\ x\dfrac{dv}{dx}=\dfrac{1-v^2}{2v} \quad \Rightarrow\ \int\dfrac{2v}{1-v^2}dv=\int\dfrac{dx}{x}$

$\Rightarrow\ \ln|v^2-1|+\ln|x|=\ln|C|$

$\Rightarrow\ |(v^2-1)x|=|C| \quad \Rightarrow\ \left(\dfrac{y^2-x^2}{x}\right)=\pm C$

$\Rightarrow\ (y^2-x^2)=C'x$ or $x=\dfrac{1}{C'}(y^2-x^2)$ or $x=-\dfrac{1}{C'}(x^2-y^2)$

or $x=C(x^2-y^2)$

8. (a) $\dfrac{dy}{dx}=\dfrac{y-x}{y+x}$ ...(1)

Put $y = vx$

$\Rightarrow\ \dfrac{dy}{dx}=v+x\dfrac{dv}{dx}$

$\Rightarrow \quad v + x\dfrac{dv}{dx} = \dfrac{v-1}{v+1}$

$\Rightarrow \quad x\dfrac{dv}{dx} = \dfrac{v-1-v^2-v}{v+1}$

$\Rightarrow \quad x\dfrac{dv}{dx} = \dfrac{-(v^2+1)}{(v+1)}$

$\Rightarrow \quad \dfrac{(v+1)}{(v^2+1)}dv + \int\dfrac{dx}{x} = 0$

$\Rightarrow \quad \dfrac{1}{2}\int\dfrac{2v}{v^2+1}dv + \int\dfrac{1}{v^2+1}dv + \int\dfrac{dx}{x} = 0$

$\Rightarrow \quad \dfrac{1}{2}\ln(v^2+1) + \tan^{-1}v + \ln|x| = C'$

$\Rightarrow \quad \dfrac{1}{2}\ln\left(\dfrac{y^2+x^2}{x^2}\right) + \tan^{-1}\left(\dfrac{y}{x}\right) + \ln|x| = C'$

$\Rightarrow \quad \ln\left(\dfrac{x^2+y^2}{x^2}\right) + 2\tan^{-1}\left(\dfrac{y}{x}\right) + \ln x^2 = 2C'$

$\Rightarrow \quad \ln\left(x^2+y^2\right) + 2\tan^{-1}\left(\dfrac{y}{x}\right) + C = 0$

9. (a) $(x^2 + y^2)\, dy = xy\, dx$

$\Rightarrow \quad \dfrac{dy}{dx} = \dfrac{xy}{x^2+y^2}$

Put $y = vx$

$\Rightarrow \quad \dfrac{dy}{dx} = v + x\dfrac{dv}{dx}$

$\Rightarrow \quad v + x\dfrac{dv}{dx} = \dfrac{vx^2}{x^2+v^2x^2}$

$\Rightarrow \quad v + x\dfrac{dv}{dx} = \dfrac{v}{1+v^2}$

$\Rightarrow \quad x\dfrac{dv}{dx} = \dfrac{v-v-v^3}{1+v^2}$

$\Rightarrow \quad \int\dfrac{1+v^2dv}{v^3} + \int\dfrac{dv}{x} = 0$

$\Rightarrow \quad \dfrac{v^{-2}}{-2} + \ln|v| + \ln|x| = C$

$\Rightarrow \quad \ln|y| - \dfrac{1}{2}\left(\dfrac{x^2}{y^2}\right) = C \quad \ldots(1)$

Given, $y(1) = 1$

$\Rightarrow \quad 0 - \dfrac{1}{2}(1) = C$

$\Rightarrow \quad C = -1/2$

$\Rightarrow \quad \ln|y| - \dfrac{1}{2}\left(\dfrac{x^2}{y^2}\right) = \dfrac{-1}{2} \quad \ldots(2)$

Now, $y(x_0) = e$ (given)

$\Rightarrow \quad 1 - \dfrac{1}{2}\left(\dfrac{x_0^2}{e^2}\right) = -\dfrac{1}{2} \quad \Rightarrow \quad \dfrac{3}{2} = \dfrac{1}{2}\left(\dfrac{x_0^2}{e^2}\right)$

$\Rightarrow \quad x_0^2 = 3e^2 \quad \Rightarrow \quad x_0 = \pm\sqrt{3}\, e$

10. (c) $(y^3 - 2x^2y)dx + (2xy^2 - x^3)dy = 0$

$\Rightarrow \quad \dfrac{dy}{dx} = \dfrac{2x^2y - y^3}{2xy^2 - x^3}$

Put $y = vx$

$\Rightarrow \quad \dfrac{dy}{dx} = v + x\dfrac{dv}{dx}$

$\Rightarrow \quad v + x\dfrac{dv}{dx} = \dfrac{2vx^3 - v^3x^3}{2x^3v^2 - x^3}$

$\Rightarrow \quad x\dfrac{dv}{dx} = \dfrac{2v - v^3}{2v^2-1} - v$

$\Rightarrow \quad x\dfrac{dv}{dx} = \dfrac{2v - v^3 - 2v^3 + v}{2v^2-1}$

$\Rightarrow \quad x\dfrac{dv}{dx} = \dfrac{3v - 3v^3}{2v^2-1}$

$\Rightarrow \quad \dfrac{(2v^2-1)}{3v(1-v^2)}dv = \dfrac{dx}{x}$

$\Rightarrow \quad \int\dfrac{v^2-1+v^2}{3v(1-v^2)}dv = \int\dfrac{dx}{x}$

$\Rightarrow \quad \dfrac{-1}{3}\int\dfrac{1}{v}dv + \dfrac{1}{3}\int\dfrac{v}{1-v^2}dv = \int\dfrac{dx}{x}$

$\Rightarrow \quad \dfrac{-1}{3}\ln|v| - \dfrac{1}{(2\times3)}\int\dfrac{-2v}{1-v^2}dv = \int\dfrac{dx}{x}$

$\Rightarrow \quad \dfrac{-1}{3}\ln|v| - \dfrac{1}{6}\ln|1-v^2| = \ln|x| + \ln|C|$

$\Rightarrow \quad \ln|Cx| + \ln|v|^{1/3} + \ln|1 - v^2|^{1/6} = 0$

$\Rightarrow \quad \ln(|Cx|.|v|^{1/3}.|1 - v^2|^{1/6}) = 0$

$\Rightarrow \quad |Cx|.|v|^{1/3}.|1 - v^2|^{1/6} = 1$

$\Rightarrow \quad |C.x|\left|\dfrac{y}{x}\right|^{1/3}.\left|1-\dfrac{y^2}{x^2}\right|^{1/6} = 1$

$\Rightarrow \quad \dfrac{|C||x||y|^{1/3}}{x^{1/3}}.\dfrac{|x^2-y^2|^{1/6}}{|x^2|^{1/6}} = 1$

$\Rightarrow \quad \dfrac{|C||x|^{2/3}.|y|^{1/3}.|x^2-y^2|^{1/6}}{x^{1/3}} = 1$

Cubing gives, $|C|^3\, |x|^2\, |y|.|x^2 - y^2|^{1/2} = x$

$\Rightarrow \quad |C|^3\, x^2\, (|y|)\, .\, \sqrt{|x^2-y^2|} = x$

$\Rightarrow \quad x|y|.\sqrt{|x^2-y^2|} = \dfrac{1}{|C|^3}$

$\Rightarrow \quad xy\sqrt{|x^2-y^2|} = \pm\dfrac{1}{|C|^3}$

$\Rightarrow \quad xy\sqrt{|x^2-y^2|} = \pm\dfrac{1}{|C|^3}$ constant

TEXTUAL EXERCISE–6: (SUBJECTIVE)

1. (a) Given differential equation is

$(ax + by + g)dx + (hx + by + f)\, dy = 0 \quad \ldots(1)$

Comparing with $Mdx + Ndy = 0 \quad \ldots(2)$

We get, $M = ax + hy + g$ and $N = hx + by + f$

$\Rightarrow \quad \frac{\partial M}{\partial y} = h; \frac{\partial N}{\partial x} = h \quad \Rightarrow \quad \frac{\partial M}{\partial y} = \frac{\partial N}{\partial x}$

⇒ (1) is exact differential equation solution of (1) is given by

$\Rightarrow \int\limits_{y-\text{constant}} M\,dx + \int (\text{terms of } N \text{ not containing } x)dy = C$

$\Rightarrow \int\limits_{y-\text{constant}} (ax + hy + g)dx + \int (by + f)dy = C$ or $ax^2 + 2hgx + 2gx + by^2 + 2fy - 2C = 0$

or $ax^2 + 2hxy + by^2 + 2gx + 2fy + C' = 0$

(b) $x\,dy + (x + y)dx = 0$ ...(1)

$\Rightarrow M = (x + y); N = x$

$\Rightarrow \frac{\partial M}{\partial y} = 1; \frac{\partial N}{\partial x} = 1$

$\Rightarrow \frac{\partial M}{\partial y} = \frac{\partial N}{\partial x}$

⇒ (1) is exact

⇒ Solution of (1) is given by

$\int\limits_{y-\text{constant}} M\,dx + \int (\text{terms of } N \text{ not containing } x)dy = C$

$\Rightarrow \int (x + y)dx = C \quad \Rightarrow \quad \frac{x^2}{2} + xy = C$

(c) $(e^y + 1)\cos x\,dx + e^y \sin x\,dy = 0$ ...(1)

$\Rightarrow M = (e^y + 1)\cos x, N = e^y \sin x$

$\Rightarrow \frac{\partial M}{\partial y} = e^y \cos x$

$\Rightarrow \frac{\partial N}{\partial x} = e^y \cos x$

$\Rightarrow \frac{\partial M}{\partial y} = \frac{\partial N}{\partial x}$

⇒ (1) is exact differential equation

⇒ Solution of (1) is given by

$\int\limits_{y=\text{constant}} M\,dx + \int (\text{terms of } N \text{ not containing } x)dy = C$

$\Rightarrow \int (e^y + 1)\cos x\,dx = C$

$\Rightarrow (e^y + 1)\sin x = C$

(d) $(x^2 - ay)dx + (y^2 - ax)dy = 0$ ...(1)

Comparing (1) with $Mdx + Ndy = 0$, we get $M = x^2 - ay$, $N = y^2 - ax$

$\Rightarrow \frac{\partial M}{\partial y} = -a, \frac{\partial N}{\partial x} = -a$

$\Rightarrow \frac{\partial M}{\partial y} = \frac{\partial N}{\partial x}$

⇒ equation (1) is exact differential equation

⇒ Solution of (1) is given by

$\int\limits_{y=\text{constant}} M\,dx + \int (\text{terms of } N \text{ not containing } x)dy = C$

$\Rightarrow \int (x^2 - ay)dx + \int y^2\,dy = C$

$\Rightarrow \frac{x^3}{3} - axy + \frac{y^3}{3} = C$

$\Rightarrow x^3 - 3axy + y^3 = C'$

(e) Given differential equations is $[y(1 + x^{-1}) + \sin y]dx + (x + \ln x + x\cos y)\,dy = 0$ ...(1)

$\Rightarrow M = y(1 + x^{-1}) + \sin y$ and $N = x + \ln x + x\cos y$

$\Rightarrow \frac{\partial M}{\partial y} = (1 + x^{-1}) + \cos y$ and $\frac{\partial N}{\partial x} = (1 + x^{-1}) + \cos y$

$\Rightarrow \frac{\partial M}{\partial y} = \frac{\partial N}{\partial x}$

⇒ (1) is exactly differential equation

∴ solution of (1) is given by

$\int\limits_{y=\text{constant}} M\,dx + \int (\text{terms of } N \text{ not containing } x)dy = C$

$\Rightarrow \int\limits_{y=\text{constant}} \{y(1 + x^{-1}) + \sin y\}dx = C$

$\Rightarrow yx + y\ln|x| + x\sin y = C$

2. Given differential equation is $(y - 2x^3)dx - x(1 - xy)dy = 0$ ...(1)

$\Rightarrow M = (y - 2x^3), N = -x(1 - xy).$

$\Rightarrow \frac{\partial M}{\partial y} = 1, \frac{\partial N}{\partial x} = -1 + 2xy$

⇒ (1) is not exact. On multiplying (1) by $(1/x^2)$, we get

$\left(\frac{y}{x^2} - 2x\right)dx - \frac{(1 - xy)}{x}dy = 0$ ...(2)

Now, $M = \frac{y}{x^2} - 2x, \quad N = \frac{-1 + xy}{x}$

$\Rightarrow \frac{\partial M}{\partial y} = \frac{1}{x^2}, \frac{\partial N}{\partial x} = \frac{x(y) - (-1 + xy).1}{x^2} = \frac{1}{x^2}$

⇒ (2) becomes exact differential equation

∴ Solution of (2) is given by

$\int\limits_{y=\text{constant}} M\,dx + \int (\text{terms of } N \text{ not containing } x)dy = C$

$\Rightarrow \int\limits_{y-\text{constant}} \left(\frac{y}{x^2} - 2x\right)dx + \int y\,dy = C$

$\Rightarrow y\left(\frac{x^{-1}}{-1}\right) - x^2 + \frac{y^2}{2} + C$

$\Rightarrow -\frac{y}{x} - x^2 + \frac{y^2}{2} = C$ or $-2y - 2x^3 + xy^2 = 2Cx$ or $xy^2 = C'x + 2y + 2x^3$.

3. $ydx - xdy + \ln x\,dx = 0$

$\Rightarrow \ln x\,dx = xdy - ydx$

$\Rightarrow \frac{\ln x}{x^2}dx = \frac{xdy - ydx}{x^2}$

$\Rightarrow \int \frac{\ln x}{x^2}dx = \int d\left(\frac{y}{x}\right)$

$\Rightarrow (\ln x)\left(\frac{x^{-1}}{-1}\right) - \int \frac{1}{x}\left(\frac{x^{-1}}{-1}\right)dx = \int d\left(\frac{y}{x}\right)$

$\Rightarrow\ -\frac{\ln x}{x}+\left[\frac{x^{-1}}{-1}\right]=\frac{y}{x}$

$\Rightarrow\ \frac{-\ln x}{x}-\frac{1}{x}=\frac{y}{x}+C$

$\Rightarrow\ Cx + y + \ln x + 1 = 0$

4. $(x^2 - 4xy - 2y^2)dx + (y^2 - 4xy - 2x^2)dy = 0$

$\Rightarrow\ \frac{dy}{dx}=\frac{-(x^2-4xy-2y^2)}{(y^2-4xy-2x^2)}$

Put $y = vx$

$\Rightarrow\ \frac{dy}{dx}=v+x\frac{dv}{dx}$

$\Rightarrow\ v+x\frac{dv}{dx}=\frac{-x^2+4vx^2+2v^2x^2}{v^2x^2-4vx^2-2x^2}$

$\Rightarrow\ v+x\frac{dv}{dx}=\frac{-1+4v+2v^2}{v^2-4v-2}$

$\Rightarrow\ x\frac{dv}{dx}=\frac{-1+4v+2v^2-v^3+4v^2+2v}{(v^2-4v-2)}$

$\Rightarrow\ x\frac{dv}{dx}=\frac{-v^3+6v^2+6v-1}{(v^2-4v-2)}$

$\Rightarrow\ \frac{v^2-4v-2}{-v^3+6v^2+6v-1}dv=\frac{dx}{x}$

$\Rightarrow\ -\frac{1}{3}\int\frac{-3v^2+12v+6}{-v^3+6v^2+6v-1}dv=\int\frac{dx}{x}$

$\Rightarrow\ -\frac{1}{3}\ln|-v^3+6v^2+6v-1|=\ln|x|+\ln|C|$

$\Rightarrow\ |-v^3+6v^2+6v-1|=|Cx|^{-3}$

$\Rightarrow\ (-v^3+6v^2+6v-1)=\pm\frac{C}{x^3}$

$\Rightarrow\ \left(-\frac{y^3}{x^3}+\frac{6y^2}{x^2}+\frac{6y}{x}-1\right)=\pm\frac{C^{-3}}{x^3}$

$\Rightarrow\ -y^3 + 6xy^2 + 6yx^2 - x^3 = \pm C^{-3}$ or $y^3 - 6xy^2 - 6yx^2 + x^3 = C$

5. $xdx + ydy + \frac{xdy-ydx}{x^2+y^2}=0$

$\Rightarrow\ \frac{1}{2}d(x^2+y^2)+d\left(\tan^{-1}\left(\frac{y}{x}\right)\right)=0$

$\Rightarrow\ \frac{1}{2}(x^2+y^2)+\tan^{-1}\left(\frac{y}{x}\right)=C$

TEXTUAL EXERCISE-6: (OBJECTIVE)

1. (a) $ydx - xdy + \ln x\, dx = 0\ (x > 0)$

$\Rightarrow\ \frac{\ln x}{x^2}dx=\frac{xdy-ydx}{x^2}$

$\Rightarrow\ \int\frac{\ln x}{x^2}dx=\int d\left(\frac{y}{x}\right)$

Put $\ln x = t$

$\Rightarrow\ \frac{1}{x}dx=dt$

$\Rightarrow\ \int\frac{t}{e^t}dt=\int d\left(\frac{y}{x}\right)$

$\Rightarrow\ \left[t.\frac{e^{-t}}{-1}\right]-\int 1.\frac{e^{-t}}{-1}dt=\int d\left(\frac{y}{x}\right)$

$\Rightarrow\ -te^{-t}+\frac{e^{-t}}{-1}=\frac{y}{x}$

$\Rightarrow\ -(\ln x).\frac{1}{x}-\frac{1}{x}=\frac{y}{x}+C$

$\Rightarrow\ y + \ln x + 1 + C = 0$

$\therefore$ It passes through $(1, -1)$

$\Rightarrow\ -1 + 1 + C = 0$

$\Rightarrow\ C = 0$

$\Rightarrow$ Curve is $y + \ln x + 1 = 0$

2. (b) $\frac{x^3dx+yx^2dy}{\sqrt{x^2+y^2}}=ydx-xdy$

$\Rightarrow\ \frac{x^2(xdx+ydy)}{\sqrt{x^2+y^2}}=ydx-xdy$

$\Rightarrow\ \frac{xdx+ydy}{\sqrt{x^2+y^2}}=\frac{ydx-xdy}{x^2}$

$\Rightarrow\ \left(\frac{xdx+ydy}{\sqrt{x^2+y^2}}\right)=\frac{ydx-xdy}{x^2}$

$\Rightarrow\ d\left(\sqrt{x^2+y^2}\right)=-\left(d\left(\frac{y}{x}\right)\right)$

$\Rightarrow\ \sqrt{x^2+y^2}+\frac{y}{x}=C$

3. (b) $ydx - xdy + xy^2dx = 0$

$\Rightarrow\ \int\frac{ydx-xdy}{y^2}+\int xdx=\int d(c)$

$\Rightarrow\ \int d\left(\frac{x}{y}\right)+\frac{1}{2}\int d(x^2)=\int dc$

$\Rightarrow\ \frac{x}{y}+\frac{x^2}{2}=C$

4. (b) $xdy + ydx + 2x^3\, dx = 0$

$\Rightarrow\ \int d(xy)+\frac{2}{4}\int d(x^4)=\int d(c)$

$\Rightarrow\ xy+\frac{1}{2}x^4=C$

5. (d) $ydx - xdy + (1 + x^2)dx + x^2 \sin y\, dy = 0$

$\Rightarrow\ \left(\frac{ydx-xdy}{x^2}\right)+\left(1+\frac{1}{x^2}\right)dx+\sin y\,dy$

$\Rightarrow\ -\left(\frac{xdy-ydx}{x^2}\right)+\left(1+\frac{1}{x^2}\right)dx+\sin y\,dy$

$\Rightarrow\ \left\{\int d\left(-\left(\frac{y}{x}\right)\right)+\int dx+d\left(\frac{-1}{x}\right)\right\}+\int d(-\cos y)=\int d(c)$

$\Rightarrow \quad -\frac{y}{x}+x-\frac{1}{x}-\cos y=C$

$\Rightarrow \quad \frac{y}{x}+\frac{1}{x}-x+\cos y+C=0$

6. (a) $ydx-xdy+3x^2y^2e^{x^3}dx=0$

$\Rightarrow \quad \frac{ydx-xdy}{y^2}+3x^2e^{x^3}dx=0$

$\Rightarrow \quad \int d\left(\frac{x}{y}\right)+\int d\left(e^{x^3}\right)=\int d(c)$

$\Rightarrow \quad \frac{x}{y}+e^{x^3}=C$

7. (b) $xdy=y(dx+ydy),\ y<0$

$\Rightarrow x\,dy-y\,dx=y^2dy$

$\Rightarrow \quad \frac{ydx-xdy}{y^2}+dy=0$

$\Rightarrow \quad d\left(\frac{x}{y}\right)+dy=0 \quad \Rightarrow \quad \frac{x}{y}+y=C$

Given $y(1)=1$

$\Rightarrow \ 1+1=C$

$\Rightarrow \ C=2$

$\Rightarrow \quad \frac{x}{y}+y=2$ is the curve

$\therefore$ At $x=-3$

$\Rightarrow \quad \frac{-3}{y}+y=2$

$\Rightarrow \ y^2-2y-3=0$

$\Rightarrow \ (y-3)(y+1)=0$

$\Rightarrow \ y=-1$ or 3 but $y>0$ (given)

$\Rightarrow \ y=3$

8. (b) $(1+xy)y\,dx+(1-xy)x\,dy=0$

$\Rightarrow ydx+xdy+xy^2dx-x^2ydy=0$

$\Rightarrow \quad \frac{ydx+xdy}{xy}+ydx-xdy=0$

$\Rightarrow \quad \frac{ydx+xdy}{x^2y^2}+\frac{ydx-xdy}{xy}=0$

$\Rightarrow \quad d\left(\frac{-1}{xy}\right)+\frac{dx}{x}-\frac{dy}{y}=0$

$\Rightarrow \quad \frac{-1}{xy}+\ln|x|-\ln|y|=C$

$\Rightarrow \quad \ln\left|\frac{x}{y}\right|=\frac{1}{xy}+C$

9. (c) $y\,dx+(x+x^2y)dy=0$

$\Rightarrow (xdy+ydx)+x^2y\,dy=0$

$\Rightarrow \quad \frac{xdy+ydx}{x^2y^2}+\frac{dy}{y}=0$

$\Rightarrow \quad d\left(\frac{-1}{xy}\right)+\frac{dy}{y}=0 \quad \Rightarrow \quad -\frac{1}{xy}+\ln|y|=C$

10. (a) $\dfrac{x+y\frac{dy}{dx}}{y-x\frac{dy}{dx}}=\frac{x\sin^2(x^2+y^2)}{y^3}=\frac{xdx+ydy}{ydx-xdy}$

$=\frac{x\sin^2(x^2+y^2)}{y^3}=\frac{xdx+ydy}{\sin^2(x^2+y^2)}=\frac{x(ydx-xdy)}{y^3}$

$\Rightarrow \quad d\left(-\frac{\cot(x^2+y^2)}{2}\right)=\frac{xydx-x^2dy}{y^3}=\frac{x}{y}\left[\frac{ydx-xdy}{y^2}\right]$

$\Rightarrow \quad d\left(-\cot(x^2+y^2)\right)=2\frac{x}{y}\left[\frac{ydx-xdy}{y^2}\right]$

$\Rightarrow \quad d\left(-\cot(x^2+y^2)\right)=d\left(\frac{x}{y}\right)^2$

$\Rightarrow \quad -\cot(x^2+y^2)=\left(\frac{x}{y}\right)^2+C$

TEXTUAL EXERCISE–7: (SUBJECTIVE)

1. (a) $\sin x\left(\frac{dy}{dx}\right)+3y=\cos x$

$\Rightarrow \quad \frac{dy}{dx}+\frac{3}{\sin x}y=\cot x \qquad \ldots(1)$

Comparing (1) with $\frac{dy}{dx}+Py=Q$, we have $P=3\text{cosec}\ x$, $Q=\cot x$

$I.F.=e^{\int Pdx}=e^{3\int \text{cosec}\,x\,dx}$

$=e^{3\ln|\text{cosec}\,x-\cot x|}=|\text{cosec}\,x-\cot x|^3 \qquad \ldots(2)$

$\therefore$ Solution of (1) is given by $y(\text{I.F.})=\int Q.(I.F.)dx+C$

$\Rightarrow \ y|\text{cosec}x-\cot x|^3=\int \cot x\,|\text{cosec}x-\cot x|^3\,dx+C$

$\Rightarrow \ y(\text{cosec}\,x-\cot x)^3=\int \cot x\left(\frac{1-\cos x}{\sin x}\right)^3dx+C$

$\Rightarrow \ y(\text{cosec}\,x-\cot x)^3=\int\left(\frac{2\sin^2\frac{x}{2}}{2\sin\frac{x}{2}\cos\frac{x}{2}}\right)^3\cot x\,dx+C$

$\Rightarrow \ y(\text{coscec}\,x-\cot x)^3=\int \tan^3\frac{x}{2}\left(\frac{1-\tan^2\frac{x}{2}}{2\tan\frac{x}{2}}\right)dx+C$

$\Rightarrow \ y(\text{cosec}\,x-\cot x)^3=\int\frac{1}{2}\left(\tan^2\frac{x}{2}\right)\left(1-\tan^2\frac{x}{2}\right)dx+C$

$=\int\frac{1}{2}\left(\tan^2\frac{x}{2}\right)\left(1-\left(\sec^2\frac{x}{2}-1\right)\right)dx+C$

$=\int\frac{1}{2}\left(\tan^2\frac{x}{2}\right)\left(2-\sec^2\frac{x}{2}\right)dx+C$

$=\int\tan^2\frac{x}{2}dx-\int\frac{1}{2}\tan^2\frac{x}{2}\sec^2\frac{x}{2}dx$

$= \int\left(\sec^2\frac{x}{2}-1\right)dx - \int\frac{1}{2}\tan^2\frac{x}{2}\sec^2\frac{x}{2}+C$

$= 2\tan\frac{x}{2}-x-\dfrac{\tan^3\frac{x}{2}}{3}+C$

$\Rightarrow \left(\tan^3\frac{x}{2}\right)\left(y+\frac{1}{3}\right) = 2\tan\frac{x}{2}-x+C$

(b) $x(x^2+1)\left(\frac{dy}{dx}\right) = y(1-x^2)+x^3\log x$

$\Rightarrow \frac{dy}{dx}+\frac{(x^2-1)}{x(x^2+1)}y = \frac{x^3\log x}{x(x^2+1)} = \frac{x^2\log x}{(x^2+1)}$

$\Rightarrow P = \frac{x^2-1}{x(x^2+1)},\ Q = x^2\log\frac{x}{(x^2+1)}$

$\therefore\ I.E. = e^{\int Pdx} = e^{\int\frac{x^2-1}{x(x^2+1)}dx}$

$= e^{\frac{1}{3}\int\frac{3x^2+1-1-3}{(x^3+x)}dx} = e^{\frac{1}{3}\int\frac{(3x^2+1)}{x^3+x}dx}.e^{-\frac{4}{3}\int\frac{dx}{x(x^2+1)}dx}$

$= e^{\frac{1}{3}\ln(x^3+x)}.e^{-\frac{4}{3}\left\{\frac{1}{x}+\left(\frac{-x}{x^2+1}\right)\right\}dx}$

$= (x^3+x)^{1/3}\ .\ (x)^{-4/3}\ .\ (x^2+1)^{2/3} = x^{1/3}(x^2+1)^{1/3}.x^{-4/3}$.

$(x^2+1)^{2/3} = \frac{(x^2+1)}{x}$

$\therefore$ Solution of given equation is given by

$y\left(\frac{x^2+1}{x}\right) = \int\left(\frac{x^2\log x}{(x^2+1)}\right)\left(\frac{x^2+1}{x}\right)dx+C$

$\Rightarrow \frac{y(x^2+1)}{x} = \int x\ln x\,dx+C$

$\Rightarrow \frac{y(x^2+1)}{x} = \frac{x^2}{2}(\ln x)-\int\frac{1}{x}.\frac{x^2}{2}dx+C$

$\Rightarrow \frac{y(x^2+1)}{x} = \frac{x^2}{2}\ln x-\frac{1}{2}\left(\frac{x^2}{2}\right)+C$

$\Rightarrow y(x^2+1) = \frac{x^3}{2}\ln x-\frac{1}{4}x^3+Cx$

$\Rightarrow 4y(x^2+1) = x^3(2\ln x-1)+Cx$ *or* $4(x^2+1)y+x^3(1-2\ln x) = Cx$

(c) $\frac{dy}{dx}+2xy = e^{-x^2}$

$\Rightarrow P = 2x,\ Q = e^{-x^2}$

$\Rightarrow I.F. = e^{\int Pdx} = e^{\int 2x} = ex^2$

$\therefore$ Solution is given by $y(I.F.) = \int Q(I.F.)dx+C$

$\Rightarrow ye^{x^2} = \int e^{-x^2}.e^{x^2}dx+C = \int 1dx+C = x+C$

i.e., $y.e^{x^2} = x+C$

(d) $(1+x^2)\frac{dy}{dx}+y = \tan^{-1}x$

$\Rightarrow \frac{dy}{dx}+\frac{1}{1+x^2}y = \frac{\tan^{-1}x}{1+x^2}$ ...(1)

$\Rightarrow P = \frac{1}{1+x^2},\ Q = \frac{\tan^{-1}x}{1+x^2}$

$\Rightarrow I.F. = e^{\int Pdx} = e^{\int\frac{1}{1+x^2}dx} = e^{\tan^{-1}x}$

$\therefore$ Solution is given by $y.e^{\tan^{-1}x} = \int\frac{\tan^{-1}x}{x^2+1}.e^{\tan^{-1}x}dx+C$

$= \int e^t.t\,dt+C = te^t-\int e^t\,dt = te^t-e^t+C$

$\Rightarrow ye^{\tan^{-1}x} = (\tan^{-1}x-1)e^{\tan^{-1}x}+C$

(e) $\frac{dy}{dx}(x\log x)+y = 2\log x$

$\Rightarrow \frac{dy}{dx}+\frac{1}{x\log x}\frac{y}{x} = \frac{2}{x}\ \Rightarrow\ P = \frac{1}{x\log x},\ Q = \frac{2}{x}$

$\therefore\ I.F. = e^{\int Pdx} = e^{\int\frac{1}{x\log x}dx} = \ln(x)$

$\therefore$ Solution is given by $y(\ln x) = \int\frac{2}{x}\ln x\,dx+C$

$\Rightarrow y\ln x = \frac{2(\ln x)^2}{2}+C\ \Rightarrow\ y\ln x = (\ln x)^2+C$

(f) $\frac{dy}{dx}+\frac{x}{1+x^2}y = \frac{1}{2x(1+x^2)}$

$\Rightarrow P = \frac{x}{1+x^2},\ Q = \frac{1}{2x(1+x^2)}$

$\Rightarrow I.F. = e^{\int Pdx} = e^{\int\frac{x}{x^2+1}dx} = e^{\ln(x^2+1)^{1/2}} = (x^2+1)^{1/2}$.

$\Rightarrow$ Solution is given by,

$y(x^2+1)^{1/2} = \int\frac{1}{2x(x^2+1)}.(x^2+1)^{1/2}dx+C$

$\Rightarrow y.\sqrt{x^2+1} = \frac{1}{2}\int\frac{1}{x\sqrt{x^2+1}}dx+C$

$\Rightarrow y.\sqrt{x^2+1} = \frac{1}{2}\int\frac{1}{x\sqrt{x^2+1}}dx+C$

Put $x = \tan q$ on R.H.S.

$\Rightarrow dx = \sec^2\theta\ d\theta$

$\Rightarrow y\sqrt{x^2+1} = \frac{1}{2}\int\frac{1}{\tan\theta.\sec\theta}.\sec^2\theta d\theta$

$= \frac{1}{2}\int\frac{\cos\theta}{\sin\theta}.\sec\theta d\theta = \frac{1}{2}\int\text{cosec}\,\theta d\theta$

$\Rightarrow y\sqrt{x^2+1} = \frac{1}{2}\ln|\text{cosec}\,\theta-\cot\theta|+C$

$= \frac{1}{2}\ln\left|\frac{1-\cos\theta}{\sin\theta}\right|+C = \frac{1}{2}\ln\left|\frac{\sec\theta-1}{\tan\theta}\right|+C$

$= \frac{1}{2}\ln\left|\frac{\sqrt{1+x^2}-1}{x}\right|+C$

2. $\left(xy^2 - e^{x^{-3}}\right)dx = x^2y\,dy \;=\; x^2y\dfrac{dy}{dx} = xy^2 - e^{x^{-3}}$

$\Rightarrow \dfrac{dy}{dx} = \dfrac{y}{x} - \dfrac{e^{x^{-3}}}{x^2y} \;=\; \dfrac{1}{y}\dfrac{dy}{dx} = \dfrac{1}{x} - \dfrac{e^{x^{-3}}}{y^2x^2}$

$\Rightarrow y\dfrac{dy}{dx} = \dfrac{1}{x}y^2 - \dfrac{e^{x^{-3}}}{x^2}$

Put $y^2 = z$

$\Rightarrow y\dfrac{dy}{dx} = \dfrac{1}{2} - \dfrac{dz}{dx}$

$\Rightarrow \dfrac{1}{2}\dfrac{dz}{dx} = \dfrac{1}{x}z - \dfrac{e^{x^{-3}}}{x^2}$

$\Rightarrow \dfrac{dz}{dx} - \dfrac{2}{x}z = -\dfrac{2e^{x^{-3}}}{x^2}$

$\Rightarrow P = \dfrac{-2}{x},\ Q = \dfrac{-2e^{x^{-3}}}{x^2}$

$\Rightarrow I.F. = e^{\int P\,dx} = e^{\int \frac{-2}{x}dx} = e^{-2\ln x} = \dfrac{1}{x^2}$

$\therefore$ Solution is given by $y.\dfrac{1}{x^2} = \int -2e^{x^{-3}}.\dfrac{1}{x^4}dx$

Put $e^{x^{-3}} = t$

$\Rightarrow e^{x^{-3}}.(-3x^{-4})dx = dt$

$\Rightarrow \dfrac{e^{x^{-3}}}{x^4}dx = \dfrac{-dt}{3}$

$\Rightarrow y.\dfrac{1}{x^2} = -2\int\left(-\dfrac{dt}{3}\right) + C$

$\Rightarrow \dfrac{y}{x^2} = \dfrac{2}{3}t + C$

$\Rightarrow \dfrac{y}{x^2} = \dfrac{2}{3}e^{x^{-3}} + C$

$\Rightarrow 3y = 2x^2e^{x^{-3}} + 3Cx^2$

$\Rightarrow 3y = 2x^2e^{x^{-3}} + C'x^2$

$\Rightarrow 3y = 2x^2e^{1/x^3} + C'x^2$

3. $(1 + y^2)dx = (\tan^{-1}y - x)dy$

$\Rightarrow \dfrac{dx}{dy} = \dfrac{\tan^{-1}y}{1+y^2} - \dfrac{x}{1+y^2}$

$\Rightarrow \dfrac{dx}{dy} + \dfrac{1}{1+y^2}x = \dfrac{\tan^{-1}y}{1+y^2}$

$\Rightarrow P = \dfrac{1}{1+y^2}\quad Q = \dfrac{\tan}{1+y^2}$

$\Rightarrow I.F. = e^{\int\frac{1}{1+y^2}dy} = e^{\tan^{-1}y}$

$\Rightarrow$ Solution is given by $x.e^{\tan^{-1}y} = \int \dfrac{\tan^{-1}y}{1+y^2}.e^{\tan^{-1}y}dy$

Put $\tan^{-1}y = t$

$\Rightarrow \dfrac{1}{1+y^2}dy = dt$

$\Rightarrow x.e^{\tan^{-1}y} = \int t.e^t dt$

$\Rightarrow x.e^{\tan^{-1}y} = \left[t.e^t - \int 1.e^t dt\right] + C$

$\Rightarrow x.e^{\tan^{-1}y} = te^t - e^t + C$

$\Rightarrow x.e^{\tan^{-1}y} = \tan^{-1}y.e^{\tan^{-1}y} - e^{\tan^{-1}y} + C$

$\Rightarrow x = \tan^{-1}y - 1 + C.e^{-\tan^{-1}y}$

4. $3\dfrac{dy}{dx} + \dfrac{2}{1+x}y = \dfrac{x^3}{y^2}$

$\Rightarrow \dfrac{dy}{dx} + \dfrac{2}{3(1+x)}y = \dfrac{x^3}{3y^2}$

$\Rightarrow 3y^2\dfrac{dy}{dx} + \dfrac{2y^3}{(1+x)} = x^3$

Put $y^3 = z$

$\Rightarrow 3y^2\dfrac{dy}{dx} = \dfrac{dz}{dx}$

$\Rightarrow \dfrac{dz}{dx} + \dfrac{2}{(1+x)}z = x^3$

$\Rightarrow P = \dfrac{2}{1+x},\ Q = x^3$

$\Rightarrow I.F. = e^{\int P dx} = e^{2\ln|1+x|} = (1+x)^2$

$\Rightarrow$ Solution is given by $z(1+x)^2 = \int x^3(1+x)^2dx + C$

$\Rightarrow z(x+1)^2 = \int(x^5 + 2x^4 + x^3)dx + C$

$\Rightarrow z(x+1)^2 = \dfrac{x^6}{6} + \dfrac{2x^5}{5} + \dfrac{x^4}{4} + C$

$\Rightarrow 60y^3(x+1)^2 = 10x^6 + 24x^5 + 15x^4 + C'$

5. Equation of tangent to curve at $P(x, y)$ is $(Y - y) = \dfrac{dy}{dx}(X - x)$

On ordinate axis, $X = 0$

$\Rightarrow (Y - y) = -x\dfrac{dy}{dx}$

$\Rightarrow Y = y - x\dfrac{dy}{dx}$ ...(1)

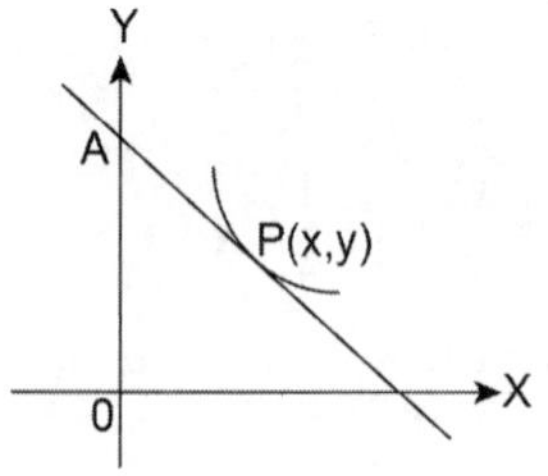

A.T.Q., $Y = 1/2\ (x + y)$

$\Rightarrow y - x\dfrac{dy}{dx} = \dfrac{1}{2}(x+y)$

$\Rightarrow 2y - 2x\dfrac{dy}{dx} = x + y$

$\Rightarrow y = x + 2x\dfrac{dy}{dx}$

$\Rightarrow 2x\dfrac{dy}{dx} - y = -x \qquad \Rightarrow \dfrac{dy}{dx} - \dfrac{1}{2x}y = -\dfrac{1}{2}$

$\Rightarrow \quad P = -\frac{1}{2x}, Q = -\frac{1}{2} \quad \Rightarrow \quad I.F. = e^{\int P dx} = e^{\int \frac{-1}{2x} dx}$

$\Rightarrow \quad e^{-\frac{1}{2}\ln|x|} = |x|^{-1/2}$

$\Rightarrow \quad y.|x|^{-1/2} = \int \frac{-1}{2} |x|^{-1/2}\, dx + C$

$\Rightarrow \quad \frac{y}{\sqrt{|x|}} = -\frac{1}{2}\int \frac{1}{\sqrt{|x|}} dx + C$

Let $x > 0$

$\Rightarrow \quad \frac{y}{\sqrt{|x|}} = -\frac{1}{2}\int (x)^{-1/2} dx + C$

$\Rightarrow \quad \frac{y}{\sqrt{x}} = -\frac{1}{2}\frac{(x)^{1/2}}{1/2} + C \quad \Rightarrow \quad \frac{y}{\sqrt{x}} = -\sqrt{x} + C$

$\Rightarrow \quad y = -x + C\sqrt{x}$ ...(1)

It passes through (4, 2)

$\Rightarrow \quad 2 = -4 + 2C$

$\Rightarrow \quad C = 3$

$\Rightarrow \quad y = -x + 3\sqrt{x}$

6. $\frac{dy}{dx} = \frac{(x+1)^2(y-3)}{(x+1)}$

$\Rightarrow \quad \frac{dy}{dx} = (x+1) + \frac{y}{x+1} - \frac{3}{x+1}$

$\Rightarrow \quad \frac{dy}{dx} - \frac{1}{(x+1)}y = \frac{(x+1)^2 - 3}{x+1}$

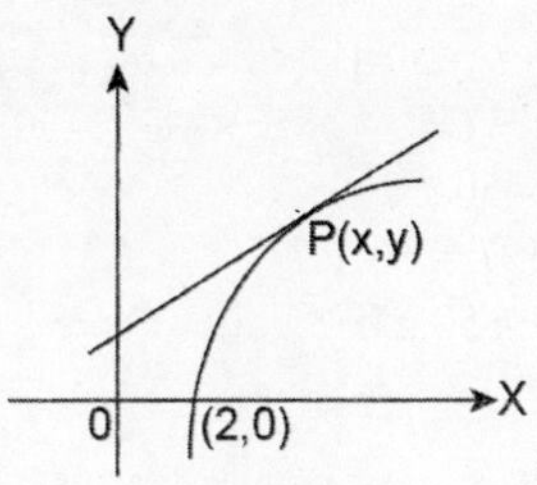

$\Rightarrow \quad P = -\frac{1}{(x+1)}, Q = \frac{x^2+2x-2}{(x+1)}$

$\therefore \quad I.F. = e^{\int P dx} = e^{\int \frac{-1}{x+1} dx} = e^{-\ln|x+1|} = \frac{1}{|x+1|}$

$\therefore$ Solution is given by $y.\frac{1}{|x+1|} = \int \frac{x^2+2x-2}{(x+1)|x+1|} dx$

Let $x + 1 > 0$

$\Rightarrow \quad \frac{y}{(x+1)} = \int \frac{x^2+2x-2}{x^2+2x+1} dx$

$\Rightarrow \quad \frac{y}{(x+1)} = \int \left\{1 - \frac{3}{(x+1)^2}\right\} dx$

$\Rightarrow \quad \frac{y}{(x+1)} = x - 3\frac{(x+1)^{-1}}{-1} + C$

$\Rightarrow \quad y = x(x+1) + 3 + C(x+1)$

It passes through (2, 0)

$\Rightarrow \quad 0 = 6 + 3 + 3C$

$\Rightarrow \quad C = -3$

Curve is $y = x(x+1) + 3 - 3(x+1)$

$\Rightarrow \quad y = x^2 - 2x.$

7. $(x^2 + y)\frac{dy}{dx} = 6x$

$\Rightarrow \quad (x^2 + y) = 6x.\frac{dx}{dy}$

$\Rightarrow \quad \frac{x}{6} + \frac{1}{6x}.y = \frac{dx}{dy}$

$\Rightarrow \quad \frac{dx}{dy} - \frac{1}{6}x = \frac{y}{6x}$

$\Rightarrow \quad x\frac{dx}{dy} - \frac{1}{6}x^2 = \frac{y}{6}$

Put $x^2 = z$

$\Rightarrow \quad 2x\frac{dx}{dy} = \frac{dz}{dy}$

$\Rightarrow \quad x\frac{dx}{dy} = \frac{1}{2}\frac{dz}{dy}$

$\Rightarrow \quad \frac{1}{2}\frac{dz}{dy} - \frac{1}{6}z = \frac{y}{6}$

$\Rightarrow \quad \frac{dz}{dy} - \frac{1}{3}z = \frac{1}{3}y$

$\Rightarrow \quad P = \frac{-1}{3}, Q = \frac{1}{3}y$

$\Rightarrow \quad I.F. = e^{\int P dy} = e^{-\frac{1}{3}\int dy} = e^{-\frac{1}{3}y}$

$\therefore$ Solution is given by $z\left(e^{-\frac{1}{3}y}\right) = \int \frac{1}{3}y.e^{-y/3} dy$

Put $y/3 = u$ on R.H.S.

$\Rightarrow \quad dy = 3du$

$\Rightarrow \quad z.e^{-y/3} = \int u.e^{-u}(3du) = 3\left[\frac{u.e^{-u}}{-1} - \int \frac{1.e^{-u}}{-1} du\right] + C$

$= ze^{-y/3} = -3ue^{-u} - 3e^{-u} + C$

$\Rightarrow \quad z = -3\,(y/3) - 3 + Ce^{y/3}$

$= z = -y - 3 + Ce^{y/3}$

$\Rightarrow \quad x^2 = -y - 3 + Ce^{y/3}$

$\Rightarrow \quad x^2 + y + 3 = Ce^{y/3}$

$\Rightarrow \quad \frac{x^2+y+3}{C} = e^{y/3}$

$\Rightarrow \quad \frac{y}{3} = \ln\left|\frac{x^2+y+3}{C}\right|$

$\Rightarrow \quad y = 3\ln|x^2 + y + 3|$

8. $x\frac{dy}{dx} + y = x^3y^6$

Put $xy = t$

$\Rightarrow \quad x\frac{dy}{dx} + y = \frac{dt}{dx}$

$\Rightarrow \quad \frac{dt}{dx} = t^3y^3 \quad \Rightarrow \quad \frac{dt}{dx} = t^3\left(\frac{t^3}{x^3}\right)$

$\Rightarrow \dfrac{dt}{t^6} = x^{-3}dx$

$\Rightarrow \int \dfrac{dt}{t^6} = \int x^{-3}dx$

$\Rightarrow \dfrac{t^{-5}}{-5} = \dfrac{x^{-2}}{-2} + C$

$\Rightarrow -\dfrac{1}{5}.t^{-5} = \dfrac{-1}{2}x^{-2} + C$

$\Rightarrow -\dfrac{1}{5}(x^{-5}y^{-5}) = \dfrac{-1}{2}x^{-2} + C$

$\Rightarrow x^{-5}y^{-5} = \dfrac{5}{2}x^{-2} + C'$

9. $(y \ln x - 1)y\, dx = xdy$ ...(1)

$\Rightarrow \dfrac{y^2 \ln x - y}{x} = \dfrac{dy}{dx}$

$\Rightarrow \dfrac{\ln x}{x} - \dfrac{1}{xy} = y^{-2}\dfrac{dy}{dx}$

Put $y^{-1} = t$

$\Rightarrow -y^{-2}\dfrac{dy}{dx} = \dfrac{dt}{dx}$

$\Rightarrow -\dfrac{dt}{dx} = \dfrac{\ln x}{x} - \dfrac{1}{xy}$

$\Rightarrow \dfrac{dt}{dx} = \dfrac{1}{x}t - \dfrac{\ln x}{x}$

$\Rightarrow \dfrac{dt}{dx} + \left(-\dfrac{1}{x}\right)t = \dfrac{-\ln x}{x}$

$\Rightarrow I.F. = e^{\int -\frac{1}{x}dx} = e^{\int -\ln x} = \dfrac{1}{x}$

$\Rightarrow$ Solution of (1) is given by $(t)\left(\dfrac{1}{x}\right) = \int \dfrac{-\ln x}{x}.\dfrac{1}{x}dx + C$

$\Rightarrow \dfrac{1}{xy} = -\int x^{-2}\ln x\, dx + C$

$\Rightarrow \dfrac{1}{xy} = -\left[(\ln x)\dfrac{x^{-1}}{-1} - \int \dfrac{1}{x}.\dfrac{x^{-1}}{-1}dx\right]$

$\Rightarrow \dfrac{1}{xy} = \dfrac{\ln x}{x} - \left[\dfrac{x^{-1}}{-1}\right] + C$

$\Rightarrow \dfrac{1}{xy} = \dfrac{\ln x}{x} + \dfrac{1}{x} + C$

$\Rightarrow 1 = y(\ln x + 1) + Cxy$

$\Rightarrow 1 = y(Cx + \ln ex)$

10. Given differential equation is $x^2y - x^3\dfrac{dy}{dx} = y^4\cos x$ ...(1)

$\Rightarrow \dfrac{y}{x} - \dfrac{dy}{dx} = \dfrac{y^4}{x^3}.\cos x$

$\Rightarrow \dfrac{dy}{dx} - \dfrac{y}{x} = -y^4.\dfrac{\cos x}{x^3}$

$\Rightarrow y^{-4}\dfrac{dy}{dx} - y^{-3}.\dfrac{1}{x} = -\dfrac{\cos x}{x^3}$

Put $y^{-3} = t$

$\Rightarrow -3y^{-4}\dfrac{dy}{dx} = \dfrac{dt}{dx}$ $\Rightarrow -\dfrac{1}{3}\dfrac{dt}{dx} + \left(-\dfrac{1}{x}\right)t = \dfrac{-\cos x}{x^3}$

$\Rightarrow \dfrac{dt}{dx} + \dfrac{3}{x}t = \dfrac{3\cos x}{x^3}$ ...(2)

$\Rightarrow I.F. = e^{\int \frac{3}{x}dx} = e^{3\ln x} = x^3$

$\therefore$ Solution of (2) is given by $t(I.F.) = \int (Q).(I.F.)dx + C$

$\Rightarrow \dfrac{1}{y^3}.x^3 = \int 3\cos x\, dx + C$

$\Rightarrow \dfrac{x^3}{y^3} = 3\cos x + C$

$\Rightarrow x^3y^{-3} = 3\sin x + C$

11. By Newton's law of cooling, $\dfrac{dT}{dt} = -k(T - T')$

Here T' = out door temperature = 100°F

$\Rightarrow \dfrac{dT}{dt} = -k(T - 100)$

$\Rightarrow \dfrac{dT}{dt} + kT = 100k$ ...(1)

$\Rightarrow I.F. = e^{\int k\,dt} = e^{kt}$

Solution of (1) is given by $T(e^{kt}) = \int (100k)e^{kt}dt + C$

$\Rightarrow Te^{kt} = \dfrac{(100k)e^{kt}}{k} + C$

$\Rightarrow T = 100 + Ce^{-kt}$

At, $t = 0$, $T = 50$°F

$\Rightarrow 50 = 100 + C$ $\Rightarrow C = -50$

$\Rightarrow T = 100 - 50e^{-kt}$.

Also At, $t = 5$, $T = 60$°F

$\Rightarrow 60 = 100 - 50\, e^{-5k}$

$\Rightarrow e^{-5k} = \dfrac{4}{5}$

$\Rightarrow e^{-k} = \left(\dfrac{4}{5}\right)^{1/5}$

$\Rightarrow T = 100 - 50\left[\left(\dfrac{4}{5}\right)^{1/5}\right]^t$

$\Rightarrow$ After t = 20 minutes

$\Rightarrow T = 100 - 50\left[\left(\dfrac{4}{5}\right)^{1/5}\right]^{20}$

$\Rightarrow T = 100 - 50\left(\dfrac{4}{5}\right)^4 °F$

TEXTUAL EXERCISE–7: (OBJECTIVE)

1. (b) $\dfrac{dy}{dx} = \sec x + y\tan x$

$\Rightarrow \dfrac{dy}{dx} = -(\tan x)y = \sec x$ ...(1)

$\Rightarrow I.F. = e^{\int Pdx} = e^{\int -\tan x\, dx} = e^{-\ln(\sec x)} = \cos x$

$\therefore$ Solution of (1) is given by $y.\cos x = \int \sec x.\cos x\, dx + C$

$\Rightarrow$ y.cosx = x + C.

It passes through origin (0, 0)

$\Rightarrow C = 0$

$\Rightarrow$ y cos$x$ = x is the required curve.

2. (d) Given differential equation is $\frac{dy}{dx} - xy = x$ ...(1)

$\Rightarrow I.F. = e^{\int P dx} = e^{\int -x\, dx} = e^{(-x^2/2)}$

$\therefore$ Solution of (1) is given by $y.e^{-x^2/2} \int x.e^{-x^2/2} dx + C$

Put $e^{-x^2/2} = t$

$\Rightarrow e^{-x^2/2}(-x)dx = dt$

$\Rightarrow xe^{-x^2/2}dx = -dt$

$\Rightarrow y.e^{-x^2/2} = -t + C$

$\Rightarrow y.e^{-x^2/2} = -e^{-x^2/2} + C$

$\Rightarrow y = -1 + Ce^{x^2/2}$

3. (c) Given differential equation is $(\cos x)\frac{dy}{dx} + y \sin x = 1$

$\Rightarrow \frac{dy}{dx} + (\tan x)y = \sec x$

$\Rightarrow I.F. = e^{\int P dx} = e^{\tan x\, dx}$

$\Rightarrow$ eln(sec$x$) = sec$x$

4. (a) $\frac{dy}{dx} + \frac{y}{x} = x^3 - 3$; (x > 0)

$\Rightarrow I.F. = e^{\int \frac{1}{x} dx} = e^{\ln x} = x$

5. (d) $x(1 - x^2)dy + (2x^2y - y - ax^3)dx = 0$

$\Rightarrow \frac{dy}{dx} + \frac{(2x^2 - 1)}{x(1 - x^2)}y = \frac{ax^3}{x(1 - x^2)}$

$\Rightarrow I.F. = e^{\int P dx}$ $\Rightarrow P = \frac{(2x^2 - 1)}{x(1 - x^2)}$

6. (d) $\frac{dy}{dx} - y = 1$

$\Rightarrow y(0) = 1$

$\Rightarrow I.F. = e^{\int P dx} = e^{\int -dx} = e^{-x}$

$\Rightarrow$ Solution is given by, $y.(I.F.) = \int Q(I.F.)dx + C$

$\Rightarrow ye^{-x} = \int e^{-x}dx + C$

$\Rightarrow ye^{-x} = \frac{e^{-x}}{-1} + C$

$\Rightarrow y = -1 + Ce^x$ but $y(0) = 1$

$\Rightarrow 1 = -1 + C$

$\Rightarrow C = 2$

$\Rightarrow y = -1 + 2e^x$

7. (b) $\because\ y\frac{dy}{dx} + 4x = 0$ ...(1)

Can be written as $\frac{dy}{dx} + 4xy^{-1} = 0$ ...(2)

or $y + 4x\frac{dx}{dy} = 0$ or $\frac{dx}{dy} + \frac{y}{4}x^{-1} = 0$ ...(3)

From (2) and (3) we found that there are not linear differential equation ($\because$ of y^{-1} and x^{-1})

8. (c) (a) $\left(\frac{d^2y}{dx^2}\right)^2 + x^2\left(\frac{dy}{dx}\right)^2 = 0$ is of degree 2, and hence is not linear.

(b) $\left(y - \frac{dy}{dx}\right)^2 = 1 + \left(\frac{dy}{dx}\right)^2 = y^2 - 2y\frac{dy}{dx} = 1$

$= \frac{dy}{dx} - \frac{y}{2} + \frac{1}{2}y^{-1} = 0$, which is not linear because of y^{-1}

(c) $\frac{dy}{dx} + \frac{1}{x}(y) = \log x$ is linear

(d) $\frac{dy}{dx} - 4y^{-1} = xy^{-1}$ which is not linear

9. (b) Given differential equation is $(1 + y^2)dx - (\tan^{-1}y - x)dy = 0$

$\Rightarrow (\tan^{-1} y - x)dy = (1 + y^2)dx$

$\Rightarrow \frac{dy}{dx} = \frac{1 + y^2}{\tan^{-1} y - x}$

$\Rightarrow \frac{1}{1 + y^2}.\frac{dy}{dx} = \frac{1}{\tan^{-1} y - x}$

Put $\tan^{-1}y = z$

$\Rightarrow \frac{1}{1 + y^2}.\frac{dy}{dx} = \frac{dz}{dx}$ $\Rightarrow \frac{dz}{dx} = \frac{1}{z - x}$

$\Rightarrow \frac{dx}{dz} = z - x$ $\Rightarrow \frac{dx}{dz} + x = z$

$\Rightarrow I.F. = e^{\int 1 dz} = e^z = e^{\tan^{-1} y}$

10. (a) $(1 + x^2)\frac{dy}{dx} + 2xy = 4x^2$

$\Rightarrow \frac{dy}{dx} + \frac{2x}{1 + x^2}y = \frac{4x^2}{1 + x^2}$ ...(1)

$\Rightarrow I.F. = e^{\int \frac{2x}{1+x} dx} = \frac{4x^2}{1 + x^2} = (1 + x^2)$

$\therefore$ Solution of (1) is given by $y(1 + x^2) = \int 4x^2 dx + C$ or $y(1 + x^2) = \frac{4x^3}{3} + C$

$\therefore$ It passes through origin $y(0) = 0$

$\Rightarrow C = 0$

$\Rightarrow$ The required curve will be $3y(1 + x^2) = 4x^3$.

11. (b) (a) $\frac{dy}{dx} + xy^2 = 1$ is not linear as y^2 has degree 2

(b) $\frac{dy}{dx} + \frac{1}{x^2}y = \frac{e^x}{x^2}$ is nto linear.

(c) $\frac{dy}{dx} + 3y = xy^2$ is not linear as y^2 has degree 2

(d) $x\frac{dy}{dx} + y^2 = \sin x$ is not linear as y^2 is involved.

12. (d) $\frac{dy}{dx}+ay=e^{mx}$

$\Rightarrow$ $I.F.=e^{\int P\,dx}=e^{\int a\,dx}=e^{ax}$

$\Rightarrow$ Solution of (1) is given by $y.(e^{ax})=\int e^{mx}.e^{ax}dx+C$

$\Rightarrow$ $y.(e^{ax})=\frac{e^{(a+m)x}}{a+m}+C$

$\Rightarrow$ $(a+m)y=e^{mx}+Ce^{-ax}(a+m)$

13. (c) Given differential equation is $x\frac{dy}{dx}=y+x^2$

$\Rightarrow$ $\frac{dy}{dx}-\frac{1}{x}y=x$ ...(1)

$\Rightarrow$ $I.F.=e^{\int -\frac{1}{x}dx}=e^{-\ln x}=\frac{1}{x}$

Solution of (1) is given by $y\left(\frac{1}{x}\right)=\int x.\frac{1}{x}dx+C$

$\Rightarrow$ $\frac{y}{x}=x+C$

$\Rightarrow$ $y=x^2+Cx$

14. (a) Given differential equation is $(x^2+1)\frac{dy}{dx}+2xy=x^2-1$

$\Rightarrow$ $\frac{dy}{dx}+\frac{2x}{x^2+1}y=\frac{x^2-1}{x^2+1}$

$\Rightarrow$ $I.F.=e^{\int\frac{2x}{x^2+1}dx}=e^{\ln(x^2+1)}=(x^2+1)$

15. (b) $\frac{dy}{dx}+P(x).y=Q(x).y^n$

$\Rightarrow$ $y^{-n}\frac{dy}{dx}+P(x).y^{-n+1}=Q(x)$ ...(1)

Is Bernoulli's differential equation and is reducible to linear differential equation by the substitution

$y^{-n+1}=t$ or $t=\frac{1}{y^{n-1}}$

$\Rightarrow$ $(-n+1)y\frac{dy}{dx}=\frac{dt}{dx}$

$\Rightarrow$ (1) be curve, $\frac{1}{(-n+1)}.\frac{dt}{dx}+P(x).t=Q(x)$ or

$\frac{dt}{dx}+(1-n)P(x)t=(1-n)Q(x)$ or $\frac{dt}{dx}+P_1(x)t=Q_1(x)$

which is linear with dependent variable t and independent variable x.

16. (a) Given differential equation is $(1+x^2)\frac{dy}{dx}+y=e^{\tan^{-1}x}$ or

$\frac{dy}{dx}=\frac{e^{\tan^{-1}x}-y}{1+x^2}$

$\Rightarrow$ $\frac{1}{(1+x^2)}.\frac{dy}{dx}=\frac{1}{(e^{\tan^{-1}x}-y)}$

Put $\tan^{-1}x=t$

$\Rightarrow$ $\frac{1}{1+x^2}.\frac{dx}{dy}=\frac{dt}{dy}$

$\Rightarrow$ $\frac{dt}{dy}=\frac{1}{e^t-y}$

$\Rightarrow$ $\frac{dy}{dt}=e^t-y$

$\Rightarrow$ $\frac{dy}{dt}+y=e^t$ ...(1)

$\Rightarrow$ $I.F.=e^{\int 1dt}=e^t$

$\Rightarrow$ Solution of (1) is given by $y.e^t=\int e^t.e^t\,dt+C$

$\Rightarrow$ $y.e^t=\frac{e^{2t}}{2}+C$

$\Rightarrow$ $y=\frac{1}{2}e^t+Ce^{-t}$

$\Rightarrow$ $y=\frac{1}{2}e^{\tan^{-1}x}+Ce^{-\tan^{-1}x}$

$\Rightarrow$ $2y=e^{\tan^{-1}x}+2Ce^{-\tan^{-1}x}$

$\Rightarrow$ $2y.e^{\tan^{-1}x}=e^{2\tan^{-1}x}+C$ or $2y.e^{\tan^{-1}x}=e^{2\tan^{-1}x}+C'$

TEXTUAL EXERCISE-8: (SUBJECTIVE)

1. (b) $xp^2+(y-x)p-y=0$ ...(1)

$\Rightarrow$ $xp^2-xp+py-y=0$

$\Rightarrow$ $xp(p-1)+y(p-1)=0$

$\Rightarrow$ $(xp+y)(p-1)=0$

$\Rightarrow$ $p=\frac{-y}{x}$ or p = 1

$\Rightarrow$ $\frac{dy}{dx}=\frac{-y}{x}$ or $\frac{dy}{dx}=1$

$\Rightarrow$ $\frac{dy}{y}=-\frac{dx}{x}$ or $dy=dx$

$\Rightarrow$ $\ln y=-\ln x$ or $y=x+C_2+\ln C_1$

$\Rightarrow$ $xy=C_1$ or $y=x+C_2$

$\Rightarrow$ Solution of (1) is given by $(xy-c)(y-x-c)=0$

(b) $y^2+xyp-x^2p^2=0$ or $x^2p^2-xyp-y^2=0$ ...(1)

$\Rightarrow$ $p=\frac{xy\pm\sqrt{x^2y^2+4x^2y^2}}{2x^2}$

$\Rightarrow$ $p=\frac{xy\pm\sqrt{5}xy}{2x^2}$

$\Rightarrow$ $p=\frac{y\pm\sqrt{5}y}{2x}$

$\Rightarrow$ $\frac{dy}{dx}=\frac{(1\pm\sqrt{5})y}{2x}$

$\Rightarrow$ $\frac{dy}{y}=\frac{(1\pm\sqrt{5})dx}{2x}$

$\Rightarrow$ $\ln y=\frac{(1\pm\sqrt{5})}{2}\ln x+\ln C$

$\Rightarrow$ $y=C.(x)^{\left(\frac{(1\pm\sqrt{5})}{2}\right)}$

$\Rightarrow$ $y^2=C^2.(x)^{(1\pm\sqrt{5})}$

$\Rightarrow$ $y^2=C^2.x^{(1\pm\sqrt{5})}$ and $y^2=C^2.e^{1-\sqrt{5}}$ or $y^2-kx^{1+\sqrt{5}}=0$ and $y^2-k\,x^{1-\sqrt{5}}=0$

$\therefore$ Solution of (1) is given by $(y^2-kx^{1+\sqrt{5}})(y^2-kx^{1-\sqrt{5}})=0$

(c) $xyp^2 - (x^2 + y^2)p + xy = 0$

$\Rightarrow xyp^2 - x^2p - y^2p + xy = 0$

$\Rightarrow xp(yp - x) - y(yp - x) = 0$

$\Rightarrow (xp - y)(yp - x) = 0$

$\Rightarrow P = y/x \text{ or } p = x/y$

$\Rightarrow \frac{dy}{dx} = \frac{y}{x} \text{ or } \frac{x}{y}$

$\Rightarrow \frac{dy}{y} = \frac{dx}{x} \text{ or } ydy = xdx$

$\Rightarrow \ln y = \ln x + \ln C \text{ or } \frac{y^2}{2} = \frac{x^2}{2} + C$

$\Rightarrow y = Cx \text{ or } y^2 = x^2 + C$

$\Rightarrow$ Solution is given by $(y - Cx)(y^2 - x^2 - C) = 0$

(d) $p^2y - (x - y)p - x = 0$ ...(1)

$\Rightarrow p^2y - xp + py - x = 0$

$\Rightarrow p(py - x) + 1(py - x) = 0$

$\Rightarrow (py - x)(p + 1) = 0$

$\Rightarrow p = \frac{x}{y} \text{ or } p = -1$

$\Rightarrow \frac{dy}{dx} = \frac{x}{y} \text{ or } \frac{dy}{dx} = -1 \Rightarrow ydy = xdx \text{ or } dy = -dx$

$\Rightarrow \frac{y^2}{2} = \frac{x^2}{2} + C_1 \text{ or } y = -x + C_2$

$\Rightarrow y^2 = x^2 + 2C_1 \text{ or } y + x - C_2 = 0 \text{ or } y^2 - x^2 - 2C = 0 \text{ or } y + x - C = 0$

$\therefore$ Solution of (1) is given by $(y^2 - x^2 - C)(y + x - C) = 0$

2. (a) $p^2y + 2px - y = 0$ ...(1)

$\Rightarrow x = \frac{y - p^2x}{2p}$ ...(2)

$\Rightarrow x = f(y, p)$

$\Rightarrow$ Solvable for x, differential both side w.r.t., y

$$\Rightarrow \frac{dx}{dy} = \frac{1}{2}\left[\frac{p.\left(1 - p^2 - y.(2p)\frac{dp}{dy}\right) - (y - p^2y).\frac{dp}{dy}}{p^2}\right]$$

$$\Rightarrow \frac{1}{p} = \frac{1}{2}\left[\frac{p - p^3 - 2yp^2\frac{dp}{dy} - y\frac{dp}{dy} + p^2y\frac{dp}{dy}}{p^2}\right]$$

$\Rightarrow 2p = p - p^3 - p^2y\frac{dp}{dy} - y\frac{dp}{dy}$

$\Rightarrow p = -p^3 - p^2y\frac{dp}{dy} - y\frac{dp}{dy}$

$\Rightarrow (p^2y + y)\frac{dp}{dy} = -p - p^3$

$\Rightarrow y(p^2 + 1)\frac{dp}{dy} = -p(1 + p^2)$

$\Rightarrow y\frac{dp}{dy} = -p$

$\Rightarrow \frac{dp}{p} = -\frac{dy}{y}$

$\Rightarrow \ln p = -\ln y + \ln C$

$\Rightarrow p = \frac{C}{y} \text{ or } y = \frac{C}{p}$

$\Rightarrow$ From (1) $p^2.\frac{C}{p} + 2px - \frac{C}{p} = 0$

$\Rightarrow 2px = \frac{Cp}{p} - Cp$

$\Rightarrow x = \frac{C}{2p}\left(\frac{1}{p} - p\right) = \frac{C(1 - p^2)}{2p^2}$

(b) $\left(\frac{dy}{dx}\right)^3 - 4xy\frac{dy}{dx} + 8y^2 = 0$

$\Rightarrow p^3 - 4xyp + 8y^2 = 0$

$\Rightarrow 4xyp = p^3 + 8y^2$

$\Rightarrow x = \frac{p^3 + 8y^2}{4yp} = \frac{p^2}{4y} + \frac{2y}{p}$

$\Rightarrow x = f(p, y)$

Solvable for x, differentiate both sides w.r.t., y

$$\Rightarrow \frac{dx}{dy} = \frac{1}{4}\left[\frac{y.2p\frac{dp}{dy} - p^2.1}{y^2}\right] + 2\left[\frac{p(1) - y\frac{dp}{dy}}{p^2}\right]$$

$$\Rightarrow \frac{1}{p} = \frac{1}{4}\left[\frac{2p\frac{dp}{dy}}{y} - \frac{p^2}{y^2}\right] + \frac{2}{p} - \frac{2y}{p^2}\frac{dp}{dy}$$

$\Rightarrow \frac{-1}{p} = \frac{p}{2y}\frac{dp}{dy} - \frac{p^2}{4y^2} - \frac{2y}{p^2}\frac{dp}{dy}$

$\Rightarrow \frac{p^2}{4y^2} - \frac{1}{p} = \left(\frac{p}{2y} - \frac{2y}{p^2}\right)\frac{dp}{dy}$

$\Rightarrow \frac{p^3 - 4y^2}{4y^2p} = \left(\frac{p^3 - 4y^2}{2yp^2}\right)\frac{dp}{dy}$

$\Rightarrow (p^3 - 4y^2)\left[\frac{1}{2yp^2}\frac{dp}{dy} - \frac{1}{4y^2p}\right] = 0$

$\Rightarrow p^3 = 4y^2 \text{ or } 2y\frac{dp}{dy} = p$

$\Rightarrow 2\frac{dp}{p} = \frac{dy}{y}$

$\Rightarrow 2\ln p = \ln Cy \text{ or } y = p^2/C$ ...(2)

$\therefore$ From given equation $4yxp = p^3 + 8y^2$

$\Rightarrow \frac{4p^2}{C}xp = p^3 + \frac{8p^4}{C^2}$

$\Rightarrow x = \frac{p^3.C}{4p^3} + \frac{8p^4}{C^2}.\frac{C}{4p^3}$

$\Rightarrow x = \frac{C}{4} + \frac{2p}{C}$

$\Rightarrow\ x = \left(\dfrac{C^2+8p}{4C}\right)$

$\Rightarrow\ 4Cx - C^2 = 8p$

$\Rightarrow\ C(4x - C) = 8p$

$\Rightarrow\ C^2(4x - C)^2 = 64p^2$

$\Rightarrow\ C^2(4x - C)^2 = 64cy$ (using (2))

$\Rightarrow\ C(4x - C)^2 = 64y$

(c) $\left(\dfrac{dy}{dx}\right)^3 y^2 - 2x\dfrac{dy}{dx} + y = 0$

$\Rightarrow\ p^3y^2 - 2xp + y = 0$ ...(*i*)

$\Rightarrow\ 2xp = p^3y^2 + y$

$\Rightarrow\ x = \dfrac{p^3y^2+y}{2p} \quad \Rightarrow\ x = \dfrac{p^2y^2}{2} + \dfrac{y}{2p}$

$\Rightarrow$ Solvable of x

$\Rightarrow\ \dfrac{dx}{dy} = \dfrac{1}{2}p^2(2y) + \dfrac{1}{2}y^2\left(2p\dfrac{dp}{dy}\right) + \dfrac{1}{2}\left[\dfrac{p - y.\dfrac{dp}{dy}}{p^2}\right]$

$\Rightarrow\ \dfrac{1}{p} = p^2y + py^2\dfrac{dp}{dy} + \dfrac{1}{2p} - \dfrac{y}{2p^2}\dfrac{dp}{dy}$

$\Rightarrow\ \dfrac{1}{2p} = p^2y + \left(py^2 - \dfrac{y}{2p^2}\right)\dfrac{dp}{dy}$

$\Rightarrow\ \dfrac{1}{2p} - p^2y = \left(py^2 - \dfrac{y}{2p^2}\right)\dfrac{dp}{dy}$

$\Rightarrow\ \dfrac{(1-2p^3y)}{2p} = \left(\dfrac{2p^3y^2-y}{2p^2}\right)\dfrac{dp}{dy} = \dfrac{-y(1-2p^3y)}{2p^2}\dfrac{dp}{dy}$

$\Rightarrow\ \dfrac{(1-2p^3y)}{2p}\left[1 + \dfrac{y}{p}\dfrac{dp}{dy}\right] = 0$

$\Rightarrow\ \dfrac{y}{p}\dfrac{dp}{dy} = -1$

$\Rightarrow\ \dfrac{dp}{p} = -\dfrac{dy}{y}$

$\Rightarrow\ \ln p + \ln y = \ln C$

$\Rightarrow\ py = C$

$\Rightarrow\ y = C/p$ ...(2)

$\therefore$ From (1) and (2), we get $p^3.\dfrac{C^2}{p^2} - 2xp + \dfrac{C}{p} = 0$

$\Rightarrow\ C^2p + \dfrac{C}{p} = 2xp$

$\Rightarrow\ x = \dfrac{C^2p}{2p} + \dfrac{C}{2p^2}$

$\Rightarrow\ x = \dfrac{C}{2p^2}(Cp^2 + 1)$

$\Rightarrow\ 2Cx = \dfrac{C^2}{p^2}(Cp^2 + 1)$

$\Rightarrow\ 2Cx = y^2(Cp^2 + 1)$

$\Rightarrow\ 2Cx = y^2\left(\dfrac{C.C^2}{y^2} + 1\right)$

$\Rightarrow\ 2Cx = C^3 + y^2.$

3. (a) $(y - px)(p - 1) = p$

$\Rightarrow\ (y - px) = \dfrac{p}{p-1}$

$\Rightarrow\ y = px + \dfrac{p}{p-1}$

$\Rightarrow\ y = px + f(p)$ ...(1)

It is Clairaut's equation, differenting both side w.r.t., x,

we get $\dfrac{dy}{dx} = p + x\dfrac{dp}{dx} + \left(\dfrac{(p-1).\dfrac{dp}{dx} - p\dfrac{dp}{dx}}{(p-1)^2}\right)$

$\Rightarrow\ x\left(\dfrac{dp}{dx}\right) - \dfrac{1}{(p-1)^2}\dfrac{dp}{dx}$

$\Rightarrow\ \left(\dfrac{dy}{dx}\right)\left(x - \dfrac{1}{(p-1)^2}\right) = 0$

$\Rightarrow\ \dfrac{dp}{dx} = 0$

$\Rightarrow\ p = C$

$\Rightarrow$ General solution is given by $(y - Cx)(C - 1) = C$

(b) $y = x\dfrac{dy}{dx} + \left(\dfrac{dy}{dx}\right)^2$

$\Rightarrow\ y = px + p2$ (Clairaut's equation)

Differenting both side w.r.t. x, we get

$\dfrac{dy}{dx} = p + x\dfrac{dp}{dx} + 2p\dfrac{dp}{dx}$

$\Rightarrow\ (x + 2p)\dfrac{dp}{dx} = 0$

$\Rightarrow\ \dfrac{dp}{dx} = 0$

$\Rightarrow\ p = C$

$\therefore$ General solution is given by $y = Cx + C^2$

(c) $y = x\dfrac{dy}{dx} + e^{dy/dx}$ *or* $y = px + e^p$ ...(1)

Differenting both side w.r.t. x, we get

$\dfrac{dy}{dx} = p + x\dfrac{dp}{dx} + e^p\dfrac{dp}{dx}$

$\Rightarrow\ \dfrac{dp}{dx}(x + e^p) = 0$

$\Rightarrow\ \dfrac{dp}{dx} = 0$

$\Rightarrow\ p = C$

$\therefore$ General solution is given by $y = Cx + e^C$.

(d) $(px - y)(py + x) = a^2p$ ...(1)

$p^2xy + px^2 - py^2 - xy - a^2p = 0$

$p^2xy + p(x^2 - y^2 - a^2) = xy$

$p^2\sqrt{uv} + p\left(u - v - a^2\right) = \sqrt{uv}$

$\Rightarrow\ \dfrac{u}{v}\sqrt{uv}.\left(\dfrac{dv}{du}\right)^2 + (u - v - a^2)\dfrac{\sqrt{u}}{\sqrt{v}}\left(\dfrac{dv}{du}\right) = \sqrt{uv}$

$\Rightarrow\ (py + x) = \dfrac{a^2p}{px - y}$

$\Rightarrow$ $(xdy - ydx)(y\,dy + xdx) = a^2dy$

Put $xy = u$; $y/x = v$

$\Rightarrow$ $xdy + ydx = du$

$\Rightarrow$ $x\dfrac{dy}{dx} + y = \dfrac{du}{dx}$

$\Rightarrow$ p

Put $x^2 + y^2 = u$; $x^2 - y^2 = v$

$\Rightarrow$ $x + py = \dfrac{1}{2}\dfrac{du}{dx}$

Put $x^2 = u$; $y^2 = v$

$\Rightarrow$ $2x\,dx = du$; $2y\,dy = dv$

$\Rightarrow$ $\dfrac{y}{x}p = \dfrac{dv}{du}$

$\Rightarrow$ $\dfrac{y^2}{x^2}p^2 = \left(\dfrac{dv}{du}\right)^2$

$\Rightarrow$ $\dfrac{v}{u}p^2 = \left(\dfrac{dv}{du}\right)^2$

$\Rightarrow$ $p^2xy + p(x^2 - y^2 - a^2) = xy$

Put $x^2 = u$, $y^2 = v$ $\quad\Rightarrow\quad x^2y^2 = uv$

$\Rightarrow$ $p^2\sqrt{uv} + p(u - v - a^2) = \sqrt{uv}$

$\Rightarrow$ $p^2 + p\left(\sqrt{\dfrac{u}{v}} - \sqrt{\dfrac{u}{v}} - \dfrac{a^2}{\sqrt{uv}}\right) = 1$

4. $p^2 - 7p + 12 = 0$

$\Rightarrow$ $(p - 4)(p - 3) = 0$

$\Rightarrow$ $p = 4$ *or* $p = 3$

$\Rightarrow$ $\dfrac{dy}{dx} = 4$ or $\dfrac{dy}{dx} = 3$

$\Rightarrow$ $y = 4x + C_1$ and $y = 3x + C_2$

$\because$ $(y - 4x + C)(y - 3x + C) = 0$ is complete solution

5. $y = 2px - p^2$

$\Rightarrow$ $\dfrac{dy}{dx} = 2p + 2x\dfrac{dp}{dx} - 2p\dfrac{dp}{dx}$

$\Rightarrow$ $-p = (2x - 2p)\dfrac{dp}{dx}$

$\Rightarrow$ $-\dfrac{dx}{dp} = \dfrac{2x}{p} - 2$

$\Rightarrow$ $\dfrac{dx}{dp} + \dfrac{2x}{p} = 2$, Which is a linear differential equation of first degree

$\Rightarrow$ $I.F. = e^{\int\frac{2}{p}dp} = 2^{2\ln p} = p^2$

$\therefore$ Solution is given by x (I.F.) = $\int 2(I.F.)dp + C$

$\Rightarrow$ $xp^2 = \int 2p^2dp + C$

$\Rightarrow$ $xp^2 = \dfrac{2}{3}p^3 + C$

6. $y = 2px + y^2p^3$ ...(1)

$\Rightarrow$ $2px = y - y^2p^3$

$\Rightarrow$ $x = \dfrac{y}{2p} - \dfrac{y^2p^2}{2}$

$\Rightarrow$ $\dfrac{dx}{dy} = \dfrac{1}{2}\left[\dfrac{p - y\dfrac{dp}{dy}}{p^2}\right] - \dfrac{y^2}{2}\left(2p.\dfrac{dp}{dy}\right) - \dfrac{p^2}{2}(2y)$

$\Rightarrow$ $\dfrac{1}{p} = \dfrac{1}{2p} - \dfrac{y}{2p^2}\dfrac{dp}{dy} - py^2\dfrac{dp}{dy} - p^2y$

$\Rightarrow$ $\dfrac{1}{2p} = -p^2y - \dfrac{dp}{dy}\left(\dfrac{y}{2p^2} + py^2\right)$

$\Rightarrow$ $\dfrac{dp}{dy}\left(\dfrac{y}{2p^2} + py^2\right) + \dfrac{1}{2p} + p^2y = 0$

$\Rightarrow$ $\dfrac{dp}{dy}\left(y + 2p^3y^2\right) + p + 2p^4y + C$

$\Rightarrow$ $\dfrac{dp}{dy}y\left(1 + 2p^3y\right) + p(1 + 2p^3y) = 0$

$\Rightarrow$ $y\dfrac{dp}{dy} + p = 0$ or $\dfrac{dp}{dy} = \dfrac{-p}{y}$

$\Rightarrow$ $\dfrac{dp}{p} + \dfrac{dy}{y} = C$

$\Rightarrow$ $\ln p + \ln y = \ln C$

$\Rightarrow$ $\ln(py) = \ln C$

$\Rightarrow$ $py = C$ ...(1)

Eliminating p from (1) and (2), we get $y = 2\left(\dfrac{C}{y}\right)x + y^2\left(\dfrac{C^3}{y^3}\right)$

$\Rightarrow$ $y = \dfrac{2Cx}{y} + \dfrac{C^3}{y}$

$\Rightarrow$ $y2 = 2Cx + C^3$ or $y^2 = 2Cx + C$

7. $(2x - b)p = y - ay\,pb$ ...(1)

$\Rightarrow$ $2x - b = \dfrac{y}{p} - ayb$

$\Rightarrow$ $2x = \dfrac{y}{p} + b - ayb$ ...(2)

$\Rightarrow$ $x = \dfrac{y}{2p} + \dfrac{b}{2} - \dfrac{ayb}{2}$ $\quad\Rightarrow\quad$ $\dfrac{dx}{y} = \dfrac{1}{2}\left[\dfrac{p - y\dfrac{dp}{dy}}{p^2}\right] - \dfrac{ab}{2}$

$\Rightarrow$ $\dfrac{1}{p} = \dfrac{1}{2p} - \dfrac{y}{2p^2}\dfrac{dp}{dy} - \dfrac{ab}{2}$

$\Rightarrow$ $\dfrac{1}{2p} = -\dfrac{y}{2p^2}\dfrac{dp}{dy} - \dfrac{ab}{2}$

$\Rightarrow$ $\dfrac{y}{2p^2}\dfrac{dp}{dy} + \dfrac{1}{2p} + \dfrac{ab}{2} = 0$

$\Rightarrow$ $\dfrac{y}{2p^2} + \left(\dfrac{1 + abp}{2p}\right)\dfrac{dy}{dp} = 0$ or $\dfrac{2p}{(1 + abp)}.\dfrac{y}{2p^2} + \dfrac{dy}{dp} = 0$

$\Rightarrow$ $\dfrac{dy}{dp} + \dfrac{1}{p(1 + abp)}y = 0$ or $\dfrac{dy}{y} = -\dfrac{dp}{p(1 + abp)}$

$= \dfrac{-[(1 + abp) - abp]dp}{p(1 + abp)} = \left(-\dfrac{1}{p} + \dfrac{ab}{1 + abp}\right)dp$

$\Rightarrow \ln y = \ln(1 + abp) - \ln p + \ln C$

$\Rightarrow y = \dfrac{C(1+abp)}{p}$ ...(3)

$\therefore$ We have $y = \dfrac{C(1+abp)}{p}$ and $x = \dfrac{y}{2p} + \dfrac{b}{2} - \dfrac{ayb}{2}$

$\Rightarrow x = \dfrac{y}{2}\left(\dfrac{y - Cab}{C}\right) + \dfrac{b}{2} - \dfrac{aby}{2}$

$\Rightarrow x = \dfrac{b}{2} + \dfrac{y(y-Cab)}{2C} - \dfrac{aby}{2}$

TEXTUAL EXERCISE–8: (OBJECTIVE)

1. (a), (d) $p^2 - p(e^x + e^{-x}) + 1 = 0$

Differentiating both sides w.r.t. x, we get

$2p\dfrac{dp}{dx} - p(e^x - e^{-x}) - \dfrac{dp}{dx}(e^x - e^{-x}) = 0$

$\Rightarrow [2p - (e^x - e^{-x})]\dfrac{dp}{dx} = p(e^x - e^{-x})$

$\Rightarrow \left(\dfrac{dy}{dx}\right)^2 - \dfrac{dy}{dx}\left(\dfrac{e^{2x}+1}{e^x}\right) + 1 = 0$

$\Rightarrow e^x\left(\dfrac{dy}{dx}\right)^2 - \dfrac{dy}{dx}(e^{2x}+1) + e^x = 0$

$\Rightarrow p^2 - p\left(e^x + \dfrac{1}{e^x}\right) + 1 = 0$

Put $e^x = t$

$\Rightarrow e^x.\dfrac{dx}{dy} = \dfrac{dt}{dy}$ $\qquad \Rightarrow e^x.\dfrac{1}{p} = \dfrac{dt}{dy}$

$\Rightarrow \dfrac{t}{p} = \dfrac{dt}{dy}$ $\qquad \Rightarrow p = t\dfrac{dy}{dt}$

$\Rightarrow t^2\left(\dfrac{dy}{dt}\right)^2 - t\left(\dfrac{dy}{dt}\right)\left(t + \dfrac{1}{t}\right) + 1 = 0$

$\Rightarrow t^2\left(\dfrac{dy}{dt}\right)^2 - t^2\dfrac{dy}{dt} - \dfrac{dy}{dt} + 1 = 0$

$\Rightarrow t^2\dfrac{dy}{dt}\left(\dfrac{dy}{dt} - 1\right) - \left(\dfrac{dy}{dt} - 1\right) = 0$

$\Rightarrow \left(t^2\dfrac{dy}{dt} - 1\right)\left(\dfrac{dy}{dt} - 1\right) = 0$

$\Rightarrow \dfrac{dy}{dt} = \dfrac{1}{t^2}$ or $\dfrac{dy}{dt} = 1$

$\Rightarrow t^{-2}dt = dy$ or $dy = dt$

$\Rightarrow \dfrac{t^{-1}}{-1} = y + C_1$ or $y = t + C_2$

$\Rightarrow -\dfrac{1}{t} = y + C_1$ or $y = t + C_2$

$\Rightarrow y = -e^{-x} + C_1$ and $y = e^x + C_2$ or $y + e^{-x} = C_1$ or $y - e^x = C_2$

2. (b) $y = x\dfrac{dy}{dx} + \dfrac{dy}{dx} - \left(\dfrac{dy}{dx}\right)^{21}$

$\Rightarrow y = px + (p - p^2)$

$\Rightarrow$ It is a Claurit's Equation

$\therefore$ Its solution is given by $y = Cx + (C - C^2)$

Differentiating both side w.r.t. x, we get

$\dfrac{dy}{dx} = x.\dfrac{dp}{dx} + p + \dfrac{dp}{dx} - 2p\dfrac{dp}{dx}$

$\Rightarrow 0 = (x + 1 - 2p)\dfrac{dp}{dx}$

$\Rightarrow x + 1 - 2p = 0$

$\Rightarrow p = \dfrac{x+1}{2}$

$\Rightarrow \dfrac{dy}{dx} = \dfrac{1}{2}(x+1)$

$\Rightarrow 2dy = (x + 1)dx = 2y = \dfrac{(x+1)^2}{2} + C$

$\Rightarrow 2y = \dfrac{(x+1)^2}{2} + \dfrac{C}{2}$

$\Rightarrow 4y = (x + 1)^2 + C$

3. (c) $p^2 + (2x + y)p + 2xy = 0$

$\Rightarrow p(p + 2x) + y(p + 2x) = 0$

$\Rightarrow (p + y)(p + 2x) = 0$

$\Rightarrow \dfrac{dy}{dx} = -y$ or $\dfrac{dy}{dx} = -2x$

$\Rightarrow \dfrac{dy}{y} = -dx$ or $dy = -2x\,dx$

$\Rightarrow \ln y = -x + C_1$ or $y = -x^2 + C_2$

$\Rightarrow (x + \ln y - C) = 0$ or $(x^2 + y - C) = 0$

$\therefore$ Complete solution is $(x + \ln y - C)(x^2 + y - C) = 0$

4. (b) $y = xp + \dfrac{1}{p}$

Differentiating both sides w.r.t. x, we get

$\dfrac{dy}{dx} = p + x\dfrac{dp}{dx} + \left(-\dfrac{1}{p^2}\right)\dfrac{dp}{dx}$

$\Rightarrow \dfrac{dp}{dx}\left(x - \dfrac{1}{p^2}\right) = 0$

$\Rightarrow \dfrac{dp}{dx} = 0$ or $p^2 = \dfrac{1}{x}$

$\Rightarrow P = C_1$ or $p = \pm\dfrac{1}{\sqrt{x}}$

$\Rightarrow \dfrac{dy}{dx} = C_1$ or $\dfrac{dy}{dx} = \pm\dfrac{1}{\sqrt{x}}$

$\Rightarrow y = C_1dx$ or $dy = \pm(x)^{-1/2}\,dx$

$\Rightarrow y = C_1x + C_2$ or $y = \pm\dfrac{(x)^{1/2}}{1/2} + C_3$

$\Rightarrow y = C_1x + C_2$ or $y = \pm2\sqrt{x} + C_3$

$\Rightarrow$ Curve is either is straight line or parabola

5. (a) $y = p(x-b) + \frac{a}{p} \Rightarrow y = px + \left(\frac{a}{p} - bp\right)$

$\Rightarrow y = px + f(p)$

Which is a Claurit's equation having its solution $y = Cx + f(c)$

i.e., $y = Cx + \left(\frac{a}{C} - Cb\right)$ or $y = C(x-b)\frac{a}{C}$

6. (a) $p^2 - 9p + 18 = 0$

$\Rightarrow (p-6)(p-3) = 0$

$\Rightarrow \frac{dy}{dx} = 6$ or $\frac{dy}{dx} = 3$

$\Rightarrow y = 6x + C$ *or* $y = 3x + C$

$\Rightarrow$ Complete solution is $(y - 6x + C')(y - 3x + C') = 0$

7. (a) $y^2(1-p^2) = b$

$\Rightarrow (1-p^2) = \frac{b}{y^2}$

$\Rightarrow p^2 = 1 - \frac{b}{y^2} = \frac{y^2-b}{y^2}$

$\Rightarrow p = \pm\frac{\sqrt{y^2-b}}{y}$

$\Rightarrow \frac{dy}{dx} = \pm\frac{\sqrt{y^2-b}}{y}$

$\Rightarrow \frac{y}{\sqrt{y^2-b}}dy = \pm dx$

$\Rightarrow \frac{1}{2}\int 2y(y^2-b)^{-1/2}dy = \pm\int dx$

$\Rightarrow \frac{1}{2}\frac{(y^2-b)^{1/2}}{1/2} = \pm x + C_1$

$\Rightarrow (y^2-b)^{1/2} = \pm x + C_1 \Rightarrow (y^2-b) = (x+C)^2$ or $(x-C)^2$

$\Rightarrow y^2 - b = (x+C)^2$

8. (c) $x + \frac{p}{\sqrt{1+p^2}} = a$

$\Rightarrow \frac{p}{\sqrt{1+p^2}} = a - x \Rightarrow \frac{p^2}{(1+p^2)} = (a-x)^2$

$\Rightarrow p^2 = (a-x)^2(1+p^2)$

$\Rightarrow p^2(1-(a-x)^2) = (a-x)^2$

$\Rightarrow p = \pm\sqrt{\frac{(a-x)^2}{1-(a-x)^2}}$

$\Rightarrow \frac{dy}{dx} = \pm\sqrt{\frac{(a-x)^2}{1-(a-x)^2}}$

$\Rightarrow y = \pm\int\sqrt{\frac{(a-x)^2}{1-(a-x)^2}}dx$

Put $(a-x) = t$

$\Rightarrow dx = -dt$

$\therefore y = \pm\int\sqrt{\frac{t^2}{1-t^2}}(-dt)$

$\Rightarrow y = \pm\frac{1}{2}\int\frac{-2t}{\sqrt{1-t^2}}dt$

$\Rightarrow y = \pm\frac{1}{2}\frac{(1-t^2)^{1/2}}{1/2} + C_1$

$\Rightarrow y = \pm\sqrt{1-t^2} + C_1$

$\Rightarrow y = \pm\sqrt{1-(a-x)^2} + C_1$

$\Rightarrow y - C_1 = \pm\sqrt{1-(a-x)^2}$

$\Rightarrow (y-C_1)^2 = 1-(a-x)^2$

$\Rightarrow (y+C)^2 + (x-a)^2 = 1$

9. (a) $y - (1+p^2)^{-1/2} = b$

$\Rightarrow y - b = \frac{1}{\sqrt{1+p^2}}$

Square $(y-b)^2$

$\Rightarrow 1 + p^2 = \frac{1}{(y-b)^2}$

$\Rightarrow p^2 = \frac{1-(y-b)^2}{(y-b)^2}$

$\Rightarrow p^2 = \pm\frac{\sqrt{1-(y-b)^2}}{(y-b)}$

$\Rightarrow \frac{dy}{dx} = \pm\frac{\sqrt{1-(y-b)^2}}{(y-b)}$

$\Rightarrow \int\frac{(y-b)}{\sqrt{1-(y-b)^2}}dx = \pm\int dx$

Put $y - b = t$

$\Rightarrow \frac{1}{2}\int\frac{-2t}{\sqrt{1-t^2}}dt = \mp\int dx$

$\Rightarrow \frac{1}{2}\frac{(1-t^2)^{1/2}}{1/2} = \pm x + C_1$

$\Rightarrow \sqrt{1-t^2} = \pm(x \pm C_1)$

$\Rightarrow (1-t^2) = (x \pm C_1)^2$

$\Rightarrow (x+C)^2 + t^2 = 1$

$\Rightarrow (x+C)^2 + (y-b)^2 = 1$

10. (a) $y = px + \frac{m}{p}$; which is a Claurit's equation having its solution $y = Cx + \frac{m}{C}$

11. (b) $y = -px + x^4p^2$

Differentiating both side w.r.t. x, we get

$\frac{dy}{dx} = -p - x\frac{dp}{dx} + x^4\left(2p\frac{dp}{dx}\right) + p^2(4x^3)$

$\Rightarrow 2p = -x\frac{dp}{dx} + 2x^4p\frac{dp}{dx} + 4p^2x^3$

$\Rightarrow \frac{dp}{dx}(x - 2x^4 p) = 4p^2x^3 - 2p$

$\Rightarrow \frac{dp}{dx}.x(1 - 2x^3p) = -2p(1 - 2px^3)$

$\Rightarrow (1 - 2x^3p)\left(x\frac{dp}{dx} + 2p\right) = 0$

$\Rightarrow x\frac{dp}{dx} = -2p$

$\Rightarrow \frac{dp}{p} = \frac{-2dx}{x}$

$\Rightarrow \ln p = -2\ln x + \ln C_1$

$\Rightarrow p = C_1x^{-2}$

$\Rightarrow \frac{dy}{dx} = C_1x^{-2}$

$\Rightarrow dy = C_1x^{-2}dx$

$\Rightarrow y = C_1(-1/x) + C_2$

$\Rightarrow xy = -C_1 + C_2x$

$\Rightarrow xy = C + Cx$

12. (b), (c) $p^2 - xp + y = 0$

Differentiating both sides w.r.t. x, we get

$2p\frac{dp}{dx} - x\frac{dp}{dx} - p + p = 0$

$\Rightarrow (2p - x)\frac{dp}{dx} = 0$

$\Rightarrow 2p = x$ or $\frac{dp}{dx} = 0$

$\Rightarrow 2\frac{dy}{dx} = x$ or $p = C_1$

$\Rightarrow y = \frac{1}{2}\frac{x^2}{2} + C_2$ or $y = C_1x + C_3$

$\Rightarrow y = \frac{1}{4}x^2 + C_2$ or $y = C_1x + C_3$

$\therefore$ $y = C_1x + C_3$ will be a solution for $C_1 = 2$ and $C_3 = -4$ and also for $C_1 = 2$ and $C_3 = 0$, i.e., $y = 2x$ and $y = 2x - 4$.

TEXTUAL EXERCISE–9: (SUBJECTIVE)

1. (a) $\frac{d^2y}{dx^2} = 2y^3$

$\Rightarrow \frac{d}{dx}\left(\frac{dy}{dx}\right) = 2y^3$

$\Rightarrow \frac{d}{dy}\left(\frac{dy}{dx}\right).\frac{dy}{dx} = 2y^3$

$\Rightarrow \frac{dp}{dy}p = 2y^3$

$\Rightarrow p\,dp = 2y^3\,dy$

$\Rightarrow \frac{p^2}{2} = \frac{2y^4}{4} + C$

$\Rightarrow p^2 = y^4 + 2C$ ...(1)

Given $p = 1$ at $x = 0$ and $y = 1$ at $x = 0$

$\Rightarrow 1 = 1 + 2C$

$\Rightarrow C = 0$

$\Rightarrow p^2 = y^4$

$\Rightarrow \frac{dy}{dx} = \pm y^2$

But $\frac{dy}{dx} = 1$ and $y = 1$ at $x = 0$

$\Rightarrow \frac{dy}{dx} = y^2$ $\Rightarrow y^{-2}dy = dx$

$\Rightarrow -y^{-1} = x + C_1$ $\Rightarrow 1/y + x + C = 0$

Also given at $x = 0$, $y = 1$

$\Rightarrow 1 + C = 0$

$\Rightarrow C = -1$

$\Rightarrow 1/y + x - 1 = 0$ or $xy - y + 1 = 0$

(b) $\frac{d^2y}{dx^2} + \frac{1}{y^3} = 0$

$\Rightarrow \frac{d}{dx}\left(\frac{dy}{dx}\right) + \frac{1}{y^3} = 0$

$\Rightarrow \frac{d}{dy}\left(\frac{dy}{dx}\right).\frac{dy}{dx} + y^{-3} = 0 \Rightarrow \frac{dp}{dy}.p = -y^{-3}$

$\Rightarrow pdp = -y^{-3}dy$

$\Rightarrow \frac{p^2}{2} = -\frac{(y)^{-2}}{-2} + C$

$\Rightarrow p^2 = \frac{1}{y^2} + 2C$

Given $y(0) = 1 = y'(0)$

$\Rightarrow C = 0$

$\Rightarrow p^2 = 1/y^2$

$\Rightarrow p = \pm 1/y$

But at $x = 0$, $p = y = 1$

$\Rightarrow p = 1/y$

$\Rightarrow \frac{dy}{dx} = \frac{1}{y}$

$\Rightarrow ydy = dx$

$\Rightarrow \frac{y^2}{2} = x + C_1$

For $x = 0$, $y = 1$

$\Rightarrow C_1 = 1/2$

$\Rightarrow \frac{y^2}{2} = x + \frac{1}{2}$

$\Rightarrow y^2 = 2x + 1$

$\Rightarrow y = \sqrt{2x+1}$ as $y = 1$ at $x = 0$

$\therefore y = \sqrt{2x+1}$

2. (a) $\frac{d^2y}{dx^2} - a^2x = b^2x^2$

$\Rightarrow \frac{d^2y}{dx^2} = a^2x + b^2x^2$

$\Rightarrow \frac{dy}{dx} = \left(\frac{a^2x^2}{2} + \frac{b^2x^3}{3}\right) + C_1$

$\Rightarrow\ y=\frac{a^2x^3}{6}+\frac{b^2x^4}{12}+C_1x+C_2$; where C_1 and C_2 are arbitrary constant.

(b) $3\frac{dx}{dt}+2\frac{dy}{dt}=e^x$ and $\frac{dx}{dt}-\frac{dy}{dx}=1$

$\Rightarrow\ \frac{dx}{dt}=\frac{e^x+2}{5}$ ...(1)

and $\frac{dy}{dt}=\frac{e^x-3}{5}$ ...(2)

Now, from (1), we get $\int\frac{dx}{e^x+2}=\frac{1}{5}\int dt$

$=\int\frac{e^x dx}{e^x(e^x+2)}=\frac{1}{5}\int dt=\int\frac{du}{u(u+2)}=\frac{1}{5}\int dt$

$\Rightarrow\ \int\frac{(u+2)-u}{u(u+2)}du=\frac{1}{5}\int dt$

$\Rightarrow\ \int\left(\frac{1}{u}-\frac{1}{u+2}\right)du=\frac{1}{5}\int dt$

$\Rightarrow\ \ln\left|\frac{u}{u+2}\right|=\frac{1}{5}t+C_1$

$\Rightarrow\ \ln\left|\frac{e^x}{e^x+2}\right|=\frac{1}{5}t+C_1$

$\Rightarrow\ x-\ln(e^x+2)=\frac{1}{5}t+C_1$

$\Rightarrow\ 5x-5\ln(e^x+2)=t+5C_1$ ...(3)

Now $dx-dy=dt$

$\Rightarrow\ d(x-y)=dt$

$\Rightarrow\ (x-y)=t+C_2$ ...(4)

$\therefore$ From (3) and (4), we get $5x-5\ln(e^x+2)=(x-y)-C_2+5C_1$

$\Rightarrow\ y=-4x+5\ln(e^x+2)+C$ or $y=5\ln(e^x+2)-4x+C$

(c) $ydx-xdy+y^2\cos x\,dx=0$

$\Rightarrow\ \frac{ydx-xdy}{y^2}=-\cos x dx$

$\Rightarrow\ d\left(\frac{x}{y}\right)=-\cos x dx$

$\Rightarrow\ \frac{x}{y}=-\sin x+C$ or $x+y\sin x=Cy$

3. $\frac{dx}{dt}=t(t+1)$ ...(1)

and $(1+t)\frac{dy}{dt}=1$ ...(2)

$x(t=0)$ and $y(t=0)$

$\Rightarrow\ dx=(t^2+t)dt;\ dy=(t+1)dt$

$\Rightarrow\ x=\frac{t^3}{3}+\frac{t^2}{2}+C_1;\ y=\frac{t^2}{2}+t+C_2$

At $t=0, x=0, y=0$

$\Rightarrow\ C_1=0, C_2=0$

$\Rightarrow\ x=\frac{t^3}{3}+\frac{t^2}{2};\ y=\frac{t^2}{3}+t$ ...(3)

Also from (2), $dy=\frac{dt}{1+t}$

$\Rightarrow\ y=\ln(1+t)+C_3$

At $t=0, y=0$

$\Rightarrow\ C_3=0$

$\Rightarrow\ y=\ln(1+t)$

$\Rightarrow\ t=e^y-1$

$\Rightarrow\ x=\frac{t^3}{3}+\frac{t^2}{2}$

$\Rightarrow\ x=\frac{(e^y-1)^3}{3}+\frac{(e^y-1)^2}{2}$

4. Let the population of country at any time t be $y(t)$, given that rate of increase of population

$=\frac{dy}{dt}=ky(t); k>0$ and is constant of proportionally

$\Rightarrow\ \frac{dy}{y}=kdt$; Let $y(t=0)=P_0$

$\Rightarrow\ \ln y=kt+C$ $\Rightarrow\ \ln\left(\frac{y}{P_0}\right)=kt$

$\Rightarrow\ \frac{y}{P_0}=e^{kt}$ $\Rightarrow\ y=P_0e^{kt}$

It is given that population becomes double in 50 years.

$\Rightarrow\ 2P_0=P_0.\ e^{50k}$

$\Rightarrow\ e^{50k}=2$

$\Rightarrow\ 50k=\ln 2$

$\Rightarrow\ k=1/50\ \ln 2$

$\therefore\ y=P_0e^{\left(\frac{1}{50}\ln 2\right)t}$

$\Rightarrow\ y=P_0.e^{\left(\ln(2)^{1/50}\right)t}$

$\Rightarrow\ y=P_0(2)^{t/50}$.

Now $y=3P_0$

$\Rightarrow\ 3P_0=P_0(2)^{t/50}$

$\Rightarrow\ 3=(2)^{t/50}$

$\Rightarrow\ \ln_2 3=t/50$

$\Rightarrow\ t=50\log_2 3$

$\Rightarrow\ t=50\frac{\ln 3}{\ln 2}$

5. Since $y_1(x)$ and $y_2(x)$ are particular integrals of the given differential eqution

$\Rightarrow\ \frac{dy_1}{dx}+Py_1=Q$ ...(1)

and $\frac{dy_2}{dx}+Py_2=Q$ ...(2)

Now, let $y=y_1(x)+C[y_2(x)-y_1(x)]$

$\Rightarrow\ \frac{dy}{dx}=\frac{dy_1}{dx}+C\left[\frac{dy_2}{dx}-\frac{dy_1}{dx}\right]$

$\therefore\ \frac{dy}{dx}+Py=\frac{dy_1}{dx}+C\left[\frac{dy_2}{dx}-\frac{dy_1}{dx}\right]+P(y_1+C[y_2-y_1])$

$\Rightarrow \frac{dy}{dx}+Py=$

$\left(\frac{dy_1}{dx}+Py_1\right)+C\left[\frac{dy_2}{dx}+Py_2\right]-C\left[\frac{dy_1}{dx}+Py_1\right]$

$\Rightarrow \frac{dy}{dx}+Py=Q+CQ-CQ$ (using (1) and (2))

$\Rightarrow \frac{dy}{dx}+Py=Q$

$\Rightarrow y=y_1(x)+C[y_2(x)-y_1(x)]$ is a general solution of given differential equation

6. $y=v(x).e^x$ ...(1)

$\Rightarrow \frac{dy}{dx}=v(x).e^x+e^x.v'(x)$ ...(2)

$\Rightarrow \frac{dy}{dx}=y+e^x.v'(x)$

$\Rightarrow \frac{d^2y}{dx^2}=\frac{dy}{dx}+e^xv''(x)+v'(x)e^x$

$\Rightarrow \frac{d^2y}{dx^2}=\frac{dy}{dx}+e^xv''(x)+\frac{dy}{dx}-y=0$

$\Rightarrow \frac{d^2y}{dx^2}-2\frac{dy}{dx}+y=e^xv''(x)$ ...(3)

Given differential equation is $\frac{d^2y}{dx}-2\frac{dy}{dx}+y=xe^x$ ...(4)

$\therefore$ From (3) and (4), we get $e^x\,v''(x)=xe^x$

$\Rightarrow v''(x)=x$

$\Rightarrow v'(x)=\frac{x^2}{2}+C_1$

$\Rightarrow v(x)=\frac{1}{6}x^3+C_1x+C_2$

$\Rightarrow y=\left(\frac{1}{6}x^3+C_1x+C_2\right).e^x$ or $y=e^x\left(\frac{x^3}{6}+Ax+B\right)$

7. Given differential equation is $\left(xy^2-\frac{e}{x^3}\right)dx-x^2ydy=0$

$\Rightarrow (x^4y^2-e)dx-x^5ydy=0$

$\Rightarrow \frac{dy}{dx}=\frac{x^4y^2-e}{x^5y}$

$\Rightarrow \frac{dy}{dx}=\frac{y}{x}-\frac{e}{x^5y}$

$\Rightarrow \frac{1}{x}\frac{dy}{dx}-\frac{y}{x^2}=\frac{-e}{x^6y}$

Put $\frac{y}{x}=t$

$\Rightarrow \frac{1}{x}.\frac{dy}{dx}-\frac{y}{x^2}=\frac{dt}{dx}$

$\Rightarrow \frac{dt}{dx}=\frac{-e}{x^7t}$

$\Rightarrow tdt=-ex^{-7}\,dx$

$\Rightarrow \frac{t^2}{2}=-\frac{ex^{-6}}{-6}+C_1$

$\Rightarrow \frac{t^2}{2}=\frac{e}{6x^6}+C_1$

$\Rightarrow \frac{1}{2}\left(\frac{y^2}{x^2}\right)=\frac{e}{6x^6}+C_1$

It passes through (1, 0)

$\Rightarrow -e/6=C_1$

$\Rightarrow \frac{y^2}{x^2}=\frac{-e}{3}+\frac{e}{3x^6}$

$\Rightarrow \frac{y^2}{x^2}=\frac{e}{3}\left(\frac{1}{x^6}-1\right)$

8. Given integral equation is $\int_0^x t\,y(t)\,dt=x^2+y(x)$

Differentiating both sides, w.r.t. x, we get $xy(x)=2x+y'(x)$

$\Rightarrow \frac{dy}{dx}-xy=-2x$ ...(1)

Which is a linear differential equation of first order, having $I.F.=e^{\int -x\,dx}=e^{-x^2/2}$

$\therefore$ Solution of (1) is given by $y.e^{-x^2/2}=\int(-2x)e^{-x^2/2}dx+C$

$\Rightarrow y.e^{-x^2/2}=2\int(-x)e^{-x^2/2}dx+C=2\left[e^{-x^2/2}\right]+C$

$\Rightarrow y=2+Ce^{x^2/2}$

9. Given integral equation is $x\int_0^x y(t)\,dt=(x+1)\int_0^x ty(t)\,dt; x>0$

Differentiating w.r.t. x, gives $\int_0^x y(t)\,dt+x.y(x)=(x+1)$ $xy(x)+\int_0^x ty(t)\,dt$

Differenting again w.r.t. x, gives $y(x)=x^2y'(x)+2x.y(x)+xy(x)$

$\Rightarrow x^2y'(x)+(3x-1)y(x)=0$

$\Rightarrow \frac{dy}{dx}+\frac{(3x-1)}{x^2}y=0$

$\Rightarrow \frac{dy}{y}=\frac{(1-3x)}{x^2}dx$

$\Rightarrow \ln y=\frac{-1}{x}-3\ln x+C_1$

$\Rightarrow \ln x^3y=C_1-\frac{1}{x}$

$\Rightarrow x^3y=e^{C_1-\frac{1}{x}}=e^{C_1}.e^{-\frac{1}{x}}$

$\Rightarrow y=\frac{C}{x^3}.e^{-1/x}$

10. Equation of tangent to curve $y=f(x)$ at $P(x, y)$ is given by

$Y-y=\left(\frac{dy}{dx}\right)(X-x)$

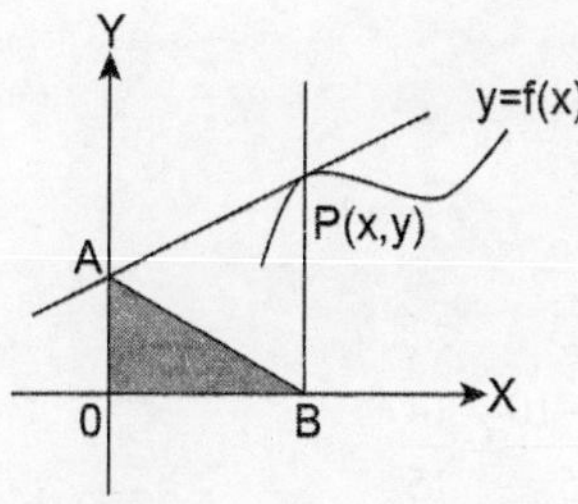

It intersects, y-axis, where $X = 0$

$\Rightarrow\ Y - y = -x\left(\frac{dy}{dx}\right) \quad \Rightarrow\ Y = y - x\left(\frac{dy}{dx}\right)$

Area of $\Delta OAB = \frac{1}{2}(OB)(OA) = \frac{1}{2}x\left(y - x\frac{dy}{dx}\right) = k$ (say) (constant)

$\Rightarrow\ xy - x^2\frac{dy}{dx} = 2k \quad \Rightarrow\ x^2\frac{dy}{dx} - xy = -2k$

$\Rightarrow\ \frac{dy}{dx} - \frac{1}{x}y = \frac{-2k}{x^2}$ ...(1)

which is a linear differential equation of first order, having $I.F. = e^{\int -\frac{1}{x}dx} = e^{-\ln x} = \frac{1}{x}$

$\therefore$ Solution of (1) is given by $y.\frac{1}{x} = \int \frac{1}{x}\left(\frac{-2k}{x^2}\right)dx$

$\Rightarrow\ \frac{y}{x} = -2k\int x^{-3}dx$

$\Rightarrow\ \frac{y}{x} = -2k\left(\frac{x^{-2}}{-2}\right) + C$

$\Rightarrow\ \frac{y}{x} = \frac{k}{x^2} + C$

$\Rightarrow\ xy = k + Cx^2$ (2)

$\Rightarrow\ Cx^2 - xy + 0.y^2 + 0.x + 0.y + K = 0$

$\Rightarrow\ h^2 - ab = \left(\frac{-1}{2}\right)^2 - (C)(0) = \frac{1}{4} > 0$ and

$$\Delta = \begin{vmatrix} a & h & g \\ h & b & f \\ g & f & c \end{vmatrix} = \begin{vmatrix} c & -\frac{1}{2} & 0 \\ -\frac{1}{2} & 0 & 0 \\ 0 & 0 & k \end{vmatrix}$$

$= \ k\left(0 - \frac{1}{4}\right) = \frac{-1}{4}k \neq 0$

$\Rightarrow$ represents a hyperbola.

11. (a) $\frac{dy}{dx} + 2xy = 0$

$\Rightarrow\ \frac{dy}{y} = -2x\,dx \quad \Rightarrow\ \ln y = -x^2 + C_1$

$\Rightarrow\ y = e^{-x^2 + C_1} \quad \Rightarrow\ y = e^{C_1}.e^{-x^2}$

$\Rightarrow\ y_n = C.e^{-x^2}$

(b) Let y_1 be a particular solution of non-homogeneous $\frac{dy}{dx} + 2xy = 3e^{-x^2}$ ...(1)

$\Rightarrow\ \frac{dy_1}{dx} + 2xy_1 = 3e^{-x^2}$ ...(2)

Consider $y = y_n + y_1$

$\Rightarrow\ \frac{dy_0}{dx} = \frac{dy_n}{dx} + \frac{dy_1}{dx} = \frac{d}{dx}(C.e^{-x^2}) + \frac{dy_1}{dx}$

$= \ C(-2x)e^{-x^2} + \frac{dy_1}{dx}$

$\therefore\ \frac{dy_0}{dx} + 2xy_0 = -2Cxe^{-x^2} + 3e^{-x^2} - 2xy_1 + 2x(C.e^{-x^2} + y_1)$

$\Rightarrow\ \frac{dy_0}{dx} = 2xy_0 = 3x^{-x^2}$

$\Rightarrow\ y_0 = y_n + y_1$ is a general solution of non-homogeneous equation $\frac{dy}{dx} + 2xy = 3e^{-x^2}$

12. Let us consider the nth order linear differential equation

$a_0(x)\frac{d^n y}{dx^n} + a_1(x)\frac{d^{n-1}y}{dx^{n-1}} + a_2(x)\frac{d^{n-2}y}{dx^{n-2}} + \ldots.. + a_n(x)y + \psi(x) = 0$ ...(1)

where $a_i(x)$ are functions of x only.

Let us substitute x = $\phi(t)$, a differentiable function

$\frac{dx}{dt} = \phi'(t)$

$\Rightarrow\ y = f(x) = f(\phi(t))$

$\Rightarrow\ \frac{dy}{dx} = f'(\phi(t)) = \phi'(t)\frac{dt}{dx} = f(\phi(t))$

$(\because \phi'(t) = dx/dt)$

$\therefore\ \frac{dy}{dx} = f'(\phi(t))$

$\Rightarrow\ \frac{d^2y}{dx^2} = \frac{d}{dx}(f'(\phi(t))) = f''(\phi(t)) . \phi'(t). \frac{dt}{dx} = f''(\phi(t))$

$\left[\because \phi'(t) = \frac{dx}{dt}\right]$

Similally $\frac{d^n y}{dx^n} = f^n(\phi(t))$

$\therefore$ (1) becomes, $a_0(\phi(t)) . f^n(\phi(t)) + a_1(\phi(t)) . f^{n-1}(\phi(t)) + \ldots.. + a_n(\phi(t))\, f(\phi(t)) + y(\phi(t)) = 0$

$\Rightarrow\ A_0(t)\, g^n(t) + A_1(t)\, g^{n-1}(t) + \ldots\ldots + A_n(t).g(t) + h(t) = 0$

which is a linear with independent variable t.

TEXTUAL EXERCISE–9: (OBJECTIVE)

1. (a) $\frac{d^2y}{dx^2} = \sin 3x + e^x + x^2$ ...(1)

$y_1(0) = 1$ and $y(0) = 0$ (given)

From (1), $\frac{dy}{dx} = \frac{-\cos 3x}{3} + e^x + \frac{x^3}{3} + C_1$

$\Rightarrow \quad y = -\frac{1}{9}\sin 3x + e^x + \frac{x^4}{12} + C_1x + C_2$

Given $y(0) = 0$

$\Rightarrow \quad 0 = 1 + C_2$

$\Rightarrow \quad C_2 = -1$ and $y_1(0) = 1$

$\Rightarrow \quad 1 = -\frac{1}{3} + 1 + C_1$

$\Rightarrow \quad C_1 = \frac{1}{3}$

$\Rightarrow \quad y = -\frac{1}{9}\sin 3x + e^x + \frac{x^4}{12} + \frac{x}{3} - 1$

2. (b) $\frac{d^2y}{dx^2} = 6(x-1)$ ...(1)

$f(2) = 1, f'(2) = 3$ ...(2)

From (1), $\frac{dy}{dx} = 6\left(\frac{x^2}{2} - x\right) + C_1$ ...(3)

$\Rightarrow \quad 3 = 6[2 - 2] + C_1$

$\Rightarrow \quad C_1 = 3$

$\therefore$ From (3) $\frac{dy}{dx} = 3x^2 - 6x + 3$

$\Rightarrow \quad y = x^3 - 3x^2 + 3x + C_2$

$\Rightarrow \quad 1 = 8 - 12 + 6 + C_2$

$\Rightarrow \quad C_2 = -1$

$\Rightarrow \quad y = x^3 - 3x^2 + 3x - 1$

$\Rightarrow \quad y = (x-1)^3$

3. (a), (c) Given $x\int_0^x \{(1-t) - f(t)\}dt = \int_0^x t f(t)dt$ and $f(1) = 1$

Differentiating both side w.r.t. x, we get $x[(1-x) - f(x)]$

$+ \int_0^x \{(1-t) - f(t)\}dt = xf(x)$

$\Rightarrow \quad \int_0^x \{(1-t) - f(t)\}dt = 2x f(x) + x^2 - x$

Differentiating by again w.r.t. x, we get $(1-x) - f(x) = 2xf'(x) + 2f(x) + 2x - 1$

$\Rightarrow \quad 2xf'(x) + 3f(x) + 3x - 2 = 0$

or $\frac{dy}{dx} + \frac{3}{2x}y = \frac{2-3x}{2x}$ ...(2)

Which is a L.D.E. of first order, having $I.F. = e^{\int \frac{2}{3x}dx} = e^{\frac{3}{2}\ln x} = (x)^{\frac{3}{2}}$, and hence, solution is given by $yx^{3/2} = \int\left(\frac{2-3x}{2x}\right)(x^{3/2})dx + C$

$\Rightarrow \quad y.x^{3/2} = \frac{1}{2}\int\left(2x^{1/2} - 3x^{3/2}\right)dx + C$

$\Rightarrow \quad y.x^{3/2} = \frac{2}{3}x^{3/2} - \frac{3}{2}\left(\frac{2}{5}\right)x^{5/2} + C$

$\Rightarrow \quad y.x^{3/2} = \frac{2}{3}x^{3/2} - \frac{3}{5}x^{5/2} + C$

$\therefore \quad f(1) = 1$

$\Rightarrow \quad 1 = \frac{2}{3} - \frac{3}{5} + C$

$\Rightarrow \quad C = \frac{8}{5} - \frac{2}{3}$

$\Rightarrow \quad C = \frac{24-10}{15} = \frac{14}{15}$

$\Rightarrow \quad y.x^{3/2} = \frac{2}{3}x^{3/2} - \frac{3}{5}x^{5/2} + \frac{14}{15}$

$\Rightarrow \quad y = \frac{2}{3} - \frac{3}{5}x + \frac{14}{15}x^{-3/2}$

4. (a) $f(t) = \frac{d}{dt}\int_0^t \frac{dx}{1 - \cos t \cos x}$

$\Rightarrow \quad f(t) = \frac{1}{1 - \cos^2 t} = \text{cosec}^2 t$

$\Rightarrow \quad \frac{df}{dt} = -2\text{cosec}^2 t \cot t$

$\Rightarrow \quad \frac{df}{dt} + 2f(t)\cot t = 0$

5. (c) Given $\phi(x) = \int \{\phi(x)\}^{-2}dx$.

Differentiating both side w.r.t. x, we get $\phi'(x) = \{\phi(x)\}^{-2}$

$\Rightarrow \quad \frac{dy}{dx} = \frac{1}{y^2}$; where $y = \phi(x)$ (say)

$\Rightarrow \quad y^2dy = dx$

$\Rightarrow \quad \frac{y^3}{3} = x + C$

But given $\phi(1) = 0$, i.e., $y = 0$ at $x = 1$

$\Rightarrow \quad C = -1$

$\Rightarrow \quad y^3 = 3(x-1)$

$\Rightarrow \quad y = \{3(x-1)\}^{1/3}$

TEXTUAL EXERCISE–10: (SUBJECTIVE)

1. $ay^2 = x^3$ ...(1)

$\Rightarrow \quad 2ay\frac{dy}{dx} = 3x^2$

$\Rightarrow \quad a = \frac{3x^2}{2y\frac{dy}{dx}}$ ...(2)

Using (2) in (1), we get $\frac{3x^2}{2y\frac{dy}{dx}}.y^2 = x^3$

$\Rightarrow \quad 3y = 2x\frac{dy}{dx}$

Replacing $\frac{dy}{dx}$ by $-\frac{dx}{dy}$, we get $3y = 2x\left(\frac{-dx}{dy}\right)$

$\Rightarrow \quad 3y\,dy = -2x\,dx$

$\Rightarrow \quad \frac{3y^2}{2} = -x^2 + C_1$ or $3y^2 + 2x^2 = 0$

2. Given family of curves is $y = ax^2$ ...(1)

$\Rightarrow \dfrac{dy}{dx} = 2ax$

$\Rightarrow a = \dfrac{dy/dx}{2x}$ ...(2)

Using (2) in (1), we get $y = \dfrac{x}{2}.\dfrac{dy}{dx}$

Replacing $\dfrac{dy}{dx}$ by $-\dfrac{dx}{dy}$, we get $y = \dfrac{x}{2}\left(\dfrac{-dx}{dy}\right)$

$\Rightarrow 2y\,dy - x\,dx = 0$

$\Rightarrow y^2 + \dfrac{x^2}{2} = C_1$

$\Rightarrow 2y^2 + x^2 = C$

3. Given family of curves is $\dfrac{x^2}{a^2} + \dfrac{y^2}{a^2+\lambda} = 1$ ...(1)

λ = Parameter

Differentiating (1) w.r.t. x, we get $\dfrac{2x}{a^2} + \dfrac{1}{(a^2+\lambda)}(2y)\dfrac{dy}{dx} = 0$

$\Rightarrow \dfrac{2y}{(a^2+\lambda)}.\dfrac{dy}{dx} = -\dfrac{2x}{(a^2)}$

$\Rightarrow (a^2+\lambda) = -\dfrac{a^2 y}{x}\left(\dfrac{dy}{dx}\right)$ ...(2)

Using (2) in (1), we get $\dfrac{x^2}{a^2} - \dfrac{y^2}{a^2 y}\left(x\dfrac{dx}{dy}\right) = 1$

$\Rightarrow x^2 - xy\dfrac{dx}{dy} = a^2$

Replacing, $\dfrac{dy}{dx}$ by $-\dfrac{dx}{dy}$, we get $x^2 - xy\left(-\dfrac{dy}{dx}\right) = a^2$

$\Rightarrow xy\dfrac{dy}{dx} = a^2 - x^2$

$\Rightarrow ydy = \dfrac{a^2 - x^2}{x}dx$

$\Rightarrow ydy = \left(\dfrac{a^2}{x} - x\right)dx$

$\Rightarrow \dfrac{y}{2} = a^2 \ln|x| - \dfrac{x^2}{2} + C_1$ or $x^2 + y^2 + C = 2a^2 \ln|x|$

4. Given equation of family of curves is $y^2 = 4ax$ ...(1)

$\Rightarrow 2y\dfrac{dy}{dx} = 4a$ ...(2)

Eliminating (1) and (2) from (1) and (2), we get $y^2 = 2yx\dfrac{dy}{dx}$

Replacing $\dfrac{dy}{dx}$ by $-\dfrac{dx}{dy}$, we get $y^2 = 2xy\left(\dfrac{-dx}{dy}\right)$

$\Rightarrow y\,dy + 2x\,dy = 0$

$\Rightarrow \dfrac{y^2}{2} + x^2 = C_1$ or $y^2 + 2x^2 = C$

5. **(i)** $\cos y = a.e^{-x}$ ...(1)

$\Rightarrow -\sin y\dfrac{dy}{dx} = -a.e^{-x}$

$\Rightarrow a = \sin y\dfrac{dy}{dx}.e^{x}$ ...(2)

Using (2) in (1), we get $\cos y = \sin y\dfrac{dy}{dx}$

Replacing $\dfrac{dy}{dx}$ by $-\dfrac{dx}{dy}$, we get $\cos y = \sin y\left(\dfrac{-dx}{dy}\right)$

$\Rightarrow \cot y\,dy + dx = 0$

$\Rightarrow \ln|\sin y| + x = C_1$

$\Rightarrow \ln|\sin y| = C_1 - x$

$\Rightarrow |\sin y| = e^{C_1 - x}$

$\Rightarrow \sin y = \pm e^{C_1}.e^{-x}$ or $\sin y = Ce^{-x}$.

(ii) $x^k + y^k = a^k$

Differentiating w.r.t. x, we get $kx^{k-1} + k.y^{k-1}\dfrac{dy}{dx} = 0$

$\Rightarrow x^{k-1} + y^{k-1}\left(\dfrac{dy}{dx}\right) = 0$

Replacing $\dfrac{dy}{dx}$ by $-\dfrac{dx}{dy}$, we get $x^{k-1} + y^{k-1}\left(\dfrac{-dx}{dy}\right) = 0$

$\Rightarrow x^{k-1} = y^{k-1}.\dfrac{dx}{dy}$

$\Rightarrow \dfrac{dx}{x^{k-1}} = \dfrac{dy}{y^{k-1}}$

$\Rightarrow \dfrac{x^{-k+2}}{-k+2} = \dfrac{y^{-k+2}}{-k+2} + C_1$

$\Rightarrow$ if $k \neq 2$ and $\ln x = \ln y + \ln C_2$ if $k = 2$

$\Rightarrow \dfrac{1}{x^{k-2}} - \dfrac{1}{y^{k-2}} = C$ if $k \neq 2$ and $y = Cx$ if $k = 2$

6. Family of curve is given by $\dfrac{x^2}{a^2} + \dfrac{y^2}{b^2} = 1$; b = parameter

Differentiating both sides w.r.t. x, we get

$\dfrac{1}{a^2(2x)} = \dfrac{1}{b^2}\left(2y\dfrac{dy}{dx}\right) = 0$

$\Rightarrow \dfrac{x}{a^2} = -\dfrac{y}{b^2}\dfrac{dy}{dx}$

$\Rightarrow b^2 = -\dfrac{a^2 y}{x}\dfrac{dy}{dx}$ ...(2)

Using (2) in (1), we get $\dfrac{x^2}{a^2} + y^2\left(-\dfrac{x}{a^2 y}\right)\left(\dfrac{dx}{dy}\right) = 1$

$\Rightarrow \dfrac{x^2}{a^2} - \dfrac{xy}{a^2}\left(\dfrac{dx}{dy}\right) = 1$

$\Rightarrow \dfrac{x^2}{a^2} - 1 = \dfrac{xy}{a^2}.\dfrac{dx}{dy}$

$\Rightarrow x^2 - a^2 = (xy)\left(\dfrac{dx}{dy}\right)$

Replacing $\left(\dfrac{dy}{dx}\right)$ by $-\left(\dfrac{dy}{dx}\right)$, we get $(x^2 - a^2) = (xy)\left(\dfrac{-dy}{dx}\right)$

$$\Rightarrow \frac{x^2-a^2}{x} = -y\frac{dy}{dx}$$

$$\Rightarrow \left(x-\frac{a^2}{x}\right)dx + ydy = 0$$

$$\Rightarrow \frac{x^2}{2} - a^2 \ln|x| \frac{y^2}{2} = \ln C_1$$

$\Rightarrow x^2 + y^2 = 2a^2 \ln|x| + 2\ln C_1$

$\Rightarrow x^2 + y^2 = \ln\left(|x|^{2a^2}.C_1^2\right)$

$\Rightarrow x^2 + y^2 = \ln|xC|^{2a^2}$ (say)

$\Rightarrow x^2 + y^2 = 2a^2 \ln|Cx|$

TEXTUAL EXERCISE–10: (OBJECTIVE)

1. **(b)** Given family of curve is $y = Cx^k$

$$\Rightarrow \frac{dy}{dx} = C(k)x^{k-1}$$

$$\Rightarrow \frac{dy}{dx} = \frac{y}{x^k}.k.x^{k-1} \text{ (Eliminating C)}$$

$$\Rightarrow \frac{dy}{dx} = k\left(\frac{y}{x}\right)$$

Replacing $\frac{dy}{dx}$ by $-\frac{dx}{dt}$, we get $\frac{-dx}{dt} = k\frac{y}{x}$

$\Rightarrow -x\,dx = ky\,dy$

$$\Rightarrow -\frac{x^2}{2} = \frac{ky^2}{2} - C_1 \quad \Rightarrow \quad \frac{x^2}{2} + \frac{ky^2}{2} = C_1$$

$\Rightarrow x^2 + ky^2 = 2C_1$

2. **(a)** Given family of curve is $(2a - x)y^2 = x^3$

$\Rightarrow 2ay^2 - xy^2 = x^3$ ...(1)

Differentiate both sides w.r.t. x, we get

$$2a\left(2y\frac{dy}{dx}\right) - x\left(2y\frac{dy}{dx}\right) - y^2 = 3x^2$$

Eliminating $2a$ from (1) and (2), we get

$$\left(\frac{x^3+xy^2}{y^2}\right)\left(2y\frac{dy}{dx}\right) - 2xy\frac{dy}{dx} = 3x^2 + y^2$$

$$\Rightarrow \left[\frac{2(x^3+xy^2)}{y} - 2xy\right]\frac{dy}{dx} = 3x^2 + y^2$$

$$\Rightarrow \left[\frac{2x^3}{y}\frac{dy}{dx}\right] = 3x^2 + y^2$$

Replacing $\frac{dy}{dx}$ by $-\frac{dx}{dy}$, we get $\frac{2x^3}{y}\left(-\frac{dx}{dy}\right) = 3x^2 + y^2$

$$\Rightarrow -\frac{dx}{dy} = \frac{3x^2y + y^3}{2x^3}$$

$$\Rightarrow \frac{dx}{dy} = -\frac{(3x^2y + y^3)}{2x^3}$$

Put $y = vx$ $\Rightarrow$ $\frac{dy}{dx} = v + x\frac{dv}{dx}$

$$\Rightarrow v + x\frac{dv}{dx} = \frac{-2x^3}{3x^2y + y^3}$$

$$\Rightarrow v + x\frac{dv}{dx} = \frac{-2x^3}{3vx^3 + v^3x^3}$$

$$\Rightarrow x\frac{dv}{dx} = \frac{-2}{3v+v^3} - v$$

$$\Rightarrow x\frac{dv}{dx} = \frac{-2-3v^2-v^4}{3v+v^3} \quad \Rightarrow \quad \frac{v^3+3v}{v^4+3v^2+2}dv + \frac{dx}{x} = 0$$

$$\Rightarrow \int\frac{v(v^2+3)}{(v^2+2)(v^2+1)}dv + \int\frac{dx}{x} = 0$$

$$\Rightarrow \frac{1}{2}\int\frac{(t+3)}{(t+1)(t+2)}dt + \int\frac{1}{x}dx = 0$$

$$\Rightarrow \frac{1}{2}\int\left(\frac{2}{t+1} - \frac{1}{t+2}\right)dt + \int\frac{1}{x}dx = 0$$

$$\Rightarrow \ln|t+1| - \frac{1}{2}\ln|t+2| + \ln|x| = \ln|C_1|$$

$$\Rightarrow \ln\left|\frac{(t+1)}{\sqrt{|t+2|}}\right| = \ln\left|\frac{C_1}{x}\right|$$

$$\Rightarrow \frac{t+1}{\sqrt{|t+2|}} = \pm\frac{C_1}{x} \quad \Rightarrow \quad \frac{\frac{y^2}{x^2}+1}{\sqrt{\frac{y^2}{x^2}+2}} = \pm\frac{C_1}{x}$$

$$\Rightarrow \frac{y^2+x^2}{x^2}.\frac{x}{\sqrt{y^2+2x^2}} = \pm\frac{C_1}{x}$$

$$\Rightarrow \frac{y^2+x^2}{\sqrt{y^2+2x^2}} = \pm C_1 \quad \Rightarrow \quad (x^2+y^2)^2 = C_1^2(2x^2+y^2)$$

$\Rightarrow (x^2 + y^2)^2 = C(y^2 + 2x^2)$

3. **(a), (c)** Given family of curve is $xy + k^2$ ...(1)

Differentiate w.r.t. x, we get $x\frac{dy}{dx} + y = 0$

Replacing $\frac{dy}{dx}$ by $-\left(\frac{dx}{dy}\right)$, we get $-x\frac{dx}{dy} + y = 0$

$$\Rightarrow x\frac{dx}{dy} = y$$

$\Rightarrow x\,dx = y\,dy$

$$\Rightarrow \frac{x^2}{2} = \frac{y^2}{2} + C \text{ or } x^2 - y^2 = 2C$$

Clearly, it represents a rectangular hyperbola

4. **(a)** Equation of curve is $x^2 + y^2 - 2x - 4y - 15 = 0$

$$\Rightarrow 2x + 2y\frac{dy}{dx} - 2 - 4\frac{dy}{dx} = 0$$

$$\Rightarrow (2y-4)\frac{dy}{dx} = 2 - 2x$$

Replacing $\frac{dy}{dx}$ by $-\frac{dx}{dy}$, we get $(2y-4)\left(-\frac{dy}{dx}\right) = 2 - 2x$

$$\Rightarrow (2y-4)\frac{dx}{dy} = (1-x) \quad \Rightarrow \quad \frac{dx}{1-x} = \frac{dy}{2-y}$$

$$\Rightarrow \frac{\ln|1-x|}{(-1)} = \frac{\ln|2-y|}{-1} + \ln C_1$$

$\Rightarrow \ln\left|\frac{2-y}{1-x}\right| = \ln C_1$

$\Rightarrow \left|\frac{2-y}{1-x}\right| = C_1 \quad \Rightarrow (2-y) = \pm C_1(1-x)$

$\Rightarrow (y-2) = \pm C_1(x-1) \Rightarrow (y-2) = \lambda(x-1)$

5. **(b)** Given family of curve is $x^{2/3} + y^{2/3} + a^{2/3}$ ...(1)

$\Rightarrow \frac{2}{3}x^{-1/3} + \frac{2}{3}y^{-1/3}.\frac{dy}{dx} = 0$

$\Rightarrow x^{-1/3} + y^{-1/3}.\frac{dy}{dx} = 0$

Replacing $\frac{dy}{dx}$ by $-\frac{dx}{dy}$, we get $x^{-1/3} + y^{-1/3}\left(-\frac{dx}{dy}\right) = 0$

$\Rightarrow x^{-1/3} = y^{-1/3}\frac{dx}{dy} \Rightarrow \frac{dx}{x^{-1/3}} = -\frac{y}{y^{-1/3}}$

$\Rightarrow \int x^{1/3}dx = \int y^{1/3}dy$

$\Rightarrow \frac{3}{4}x^{4/3} = \frac{3}{4}y^{4/3} + C_1$

$\Rightarrow x^{4/3} = y^{4/3} + \frac{4}{3}C_1$

$\Rightarrow x^{4/3} - y^{4/3} = C$

6. **(a), (b), (c)**

Given family of curve is $\left(\frac{dy}{dx}\right)^2 = \frac{a}{x}$ ...(1)

Replacing $\frac{dy}{dx}$ by $-\frac{dx}{dy}$, we get $\left(\frac{dx}{dy}\right)^2 = \frac{a}{x}$

$\Rightarrow \frac{dx}{dy} = \pm\frac{\sqrt{a}}{\sqrt{x}}$

$\Rightarrow \sqrt{x}dx = \pm\sqrt{a}dy$

$\Rightarrow \frac{2}{3}(x)^{3/2} = \pm\sqrt{a}y + C_1$

$\Rightarrow \frac{2}{3\sqrt{a}}(x)^{3/2} = \pm y + \frac{C_1}{\sqrt{a}}$

$\Rightarrow y = \frac{2}{3\sqrt{a}}x^{3/2} - \frac{C_1}{\sqrt{a}}$ or $y = \frac{-2}{3\sqrt{a}}x^{3/2} + \frac{C_1}{\sqrt{a}}$

$\Rightarrow y + C = \pm\frac{2}{3\sqrt{a}}x^{3/2}$

$\Rightarrow (y+C)^2 = \frac{4}{9a}x^3$

$\Rightarrow 9a(y + C) = 4x^3$

7. **(c)** Given family of curve $x^2 + 2y^2 - y + C = 0$ ...(1)

$\Rightarrow 2x + 4y\frac{dy}{dx} - \frac{dy}{dx} = 0$

$\Rightarrow (4y-1)\frac{dy}{dx} = -2x$

Replacing $\frac{dy}{dx}$ by $-\frac{dx}{dy}$, we get $(4y-1)\left(-\frac{dx}{dy}\right) = -2x$

$\Rightarrow \frac{dx}{2x} = \frac{dy}{4y-1}$

$\Rightarrow \frac{1}{2}\ln|x| = \frac{1}{4}\ln|4y-1| + \ln|C|$

$\Rightarrow \ln|x|^{1/2} = \ln(|C|.|4y-1|^{1/4})$

$\Rightarrow |x|^{1/2} = |C| . |4y-1|^{1/4}$

$\Rightarrow x^2 = |C|^4 . |4y-1|$

$\Rightarrow x^2 = \pm C^4(4y-1)$

$\Rightarrow x^2 = a(4y-1)$

8. **(c)** Equation of family of curve is $y^2 = 4a(x + a)$ ...(1)

Differentiating both sides w.r.t. x, we get $2y\frac{dy}{dx} = 4a$

$\Rightarrow a = \frac{y\frac{dy}{dx}}{2}$ ...(2)

$\therefore$ From (1), $y^2 = \left(2y\frac{dy}{dx}\right)\left(x + \frac{y\frac{dy}{dx}}{2}\right)$

$\Rightarrow y^2 = \left(y\frac{dy}{dx}\right)\left(2x + y\frac{dy}{dx}\right)$

$\Rightarrow y^2 = 2xy\frac{dy}{dx} + y^2\left(\frac{dy}{dx}\right)^2$

$\Rightarrow y = 2x\frac{dy}{dx} + y\left(\frac{dy}{dx}\right)^2$

Replacing $\frac{dy}{dx}$ by $-\frac{dx}{dy}$, we get $y = 2x\left(-\frac{dx}{dy}\right) + y\left(-\frac{dx}{dy}\right)^2$

$\Rightarrow y = -2x\frac{dx}{dy} + y\left(\frac{dx}{dy}\right)^2$

$\Rightarrow \left(\frac{dx}{dy}\right)^2 - \frac{2x}{y}\left(\frac{dx}{dy}\right) - 1 = 0$

$\Rightarrow \frac{1}{p^2} - 2\frac{x}{y}.\frac{1}{p} - 1 = 0$

$\Rightarrow 1 - 2\frac{x}{y}p - p^2 = 0$ or $y - 2xp - p^2y = 0$

$\Rightarrow 2xp = y - p^2y$

$\Rightarrow x = \frac{1}{2}\left[\frac{y - p^2y}{p}\right]$

$\Rightarrow \frac{dx}{dy} = \frac{1}{2}\left[\frac{p - y.\frac{dp}{dy}}{p^2}\right] - \frac{1}{2}\left[p + y.\frac{dp}{dy}\right]$

$\Rightarrow \frac{1}{p} = \frac{1}{2}.\frac{1}{p} - \frac{1}{2}.\frac{y}{p^2}.\frac{dp}{dy} - \frac{1}{2}p - \frac{1}{2}y.\frac{dp}{dy}$

$\Rightarrow \frac{1}{2p} + \frac{1}{2}p = -\frac{y}{2}\left[\frac{1}{p^2} + 1\right]\frac{dp}{dy}$

$$\Rightarrow \frac{1}{2p}(1+p^2) = -\frac{y}{2}\left[\frac{1+p^2}{p^2}\right]\frac{dp}{dy}$$

$$\Rightarrow 1 = \left(\frac{-y}{p}\right)\frac{dp}{dy} \qquad \Rightarrow -\frac{dy}{y} = \frac{dp}{p}$$

$$\Rightarrow -\ln y = \ln p + \ln C_1$$

$$\Rightarrow \frac{1}{y} = C_1 p \qquad \Rightarrow \frac{1}{y} = C_1 . \frac{dy}{dx}$$

$$\Rightarrow \frac{y^2}{2} = \frac{1}{C_1}x + C_1 \qquad \Rightarrow y^2 = \frac{2}{C_1}x + 2C_1$$

$$\Rightarrow y^2 = \frac{2}{C_1}x + 2k$$

TEXTUAL EXERCISE-11: (SUBJECTIVE)

1. Let the present number of bacteria = P_0 and let at any instant 't' number of bacteria be $P(t)$

$\therefore \quad \frac{dP(t)}{dt} = k\,P(t)$; k = constant of proportionality

$$\Rightarrow \frac{dP}{P} = kdt \qquad \Rightarrow \ln P = kt + C_1$$

$$\Rightarrow P = C_2 e^{kt} \qquad \text{...(A)}$$

Given that after $t = 2$ hours, $P(2) = 2P_0$

$$\Rightarrow 2P_0 = C_2 e^{2k} \qquad \text{...(1)}$$

Also, at $t = 0$, $P = P_0$

$$\Rightarrow P_0 = C_2 \qquad \text{...(2)}$$

$\therefore$ From (1) and (2), $2P_0 = P_0 \cdot e^{2k}$

$$\Rightarrow e^{2k} = 2$$

$$\Rightarrow e^k = \sqrt{2} \qquad \text{...(3)}$$

$\therefore$ From (A), $P = P_0(\sqrt{2})^t$

$$\Rightarrow P = 5P_0 \qquad \Rightarrow 5P_0 = P_0(\sqrt{2})^t$$

$$\Rightarrow 5 = (\sqrt{2})^t \qquad \Rightarrow \log_{\sqrt{2}}^{5} = t$$

$$\Rightarrow \frac{\log 5}{\frac{1}{2}\log 2} = t \qquad \Rightarrow t = 2\left(\frac{\ln 5}{\ln 2}\right) \text{ hours.}$$

2. Let the amount of radium present initially = P_0

Let $P(t)$ be the amount of radium present at any time 't'

$\therefore$ A.T.Q., $\frac{dP}{dt} = kp$; where k = constant of proportionality

$$\Rightarrow \frac{dP}{P} = kdt$$

$$\Rightarrow \ln P = kt + C_1 \qquad \text{...(1)}$$

After l years, amount of radium $P_0\left(1 - \frac{p}{100}\right)$

$$\Rightarrow \ln\left[P_0\left(1 - \frac{p}{100}\right)\right] = kl + C_1$$

At $t = 0$, $P = P_0$ ...(2)

$$\Rightarrow C_1 = \ln P_0 \text{ (using (1))}$$

$\therefore$ From (2), $\ln\left[P_0\left(1 - \frac{p}{100}\right)\right] = kl + \ln P_0$

$$\Rightarrow \frac{1}{l}\ln\left(1 - \frac{p}{100}\right) = k \qquad \text{...(3)}$$

$\therefore$ From (1), $\ln P = \frac{t}{l}\ln\left(1 - \frac{p}{100}\right) + \ln P_0$

$\therefore$ After $2l$ years, $\ln P = \frac{2l\ln}{l}\left(1 - \frac{p}{100}\right) + \ln P_0$

$$\Rightarrow \ln P = 2\ln P_0\left(1 - \frac{p}{100}\right)$$

$$\Rightarrow P = P_0\left(1 - \frac{p}{100}\right)^2$$

$\therefore$ % age of radium remind after $2l$ years.

$$\Rightarrow \frac{P_0\left(1 - \frac{p}{100}\right)^2}{P_0} \times 100$$

$$\Rightarrow 100\left(1 - \frac{p}{100}\right)^2 \% \qquad \Rightarrow \left(10 - \frac{p}{10}\right)^2 \%$$

3.

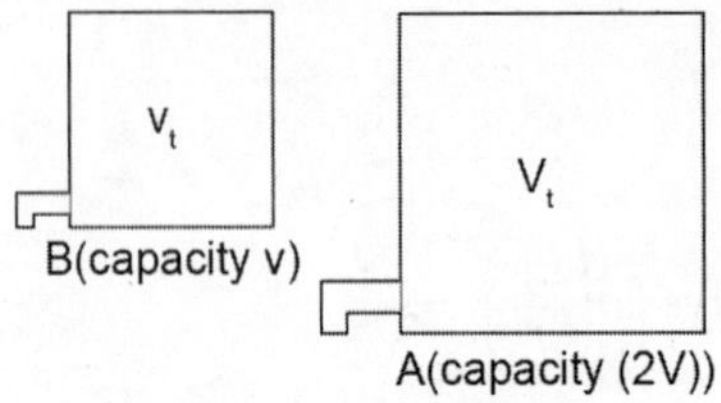

$$\frac{d(V_t)}{dt} = k_1 V_t \text{ and } \frac{d(v_t)}{dt} = k_2 v_t$$

$$\Rightarrow \frac{dV_t}{V_t} = k_1 dt \text{ and } \frac{dv_t}{v_t} = k_2 dt$$

$$\Rightarrow \int\frac{dV_t}{V_t} = \int k_1\,dt \text{ and } \int\frac{dv_t}{v_t} = \int k_2\,dt$$

$\Rightarrow \ln V_t = k_1 t + C_1$ and $\ln v_t = k_2 t + C_2$

At $t = 0$, $V_t = 2vt$

$\Rightarrow \ln(2vt) = C_1$ and $\ln vt = C_2$

$\Rightarrow \ln 2 + \ln vt = C_1$

$\Rightarrow \ln 2 + C_2 = C_1$

$\Rightarrow \ln Vt = k_1 t + C_1$ ...(1)

And $\ln vt = k_2 t + C_1 - \ln 2$ ...(2)

After 1 hour, $V_t = 1.5\,v_t$.

$\Rightarrow \ln(1.5)\,v_t = k_1 + C_1$ and $\ln V_t = k_2 + C_1 - \ln 2$

$\Rightarrow \ln(1.5) + k_2 + C_1 - \ln 2 = k_1 + C_1$

$\Rightarrow \ln(0.75) = k_1 - k_2$ ...(3)

Let after time, t, $Vt = v_t$

$\Rightarrow \ln Vt = \ln v_t \qquad \Rightarrow k_1 t + C_1 = k_2 t + C_1 - \ln 2$

$\Rightarrow (k_1 - k_2)t = -\ln 2 \qquad \Rightarrow \ln(0.75)t = -\ln 2$

$$\Rightarrow t = \frac{-\ln 2}{\ln 0.75} = \frac{\ln 1/2}{\ln 0.75} = \frac{\ln 1/2}{\ln 3/4} = \frac{\ln 2}{\ln(4/3)} \text{ hours}$$

4. 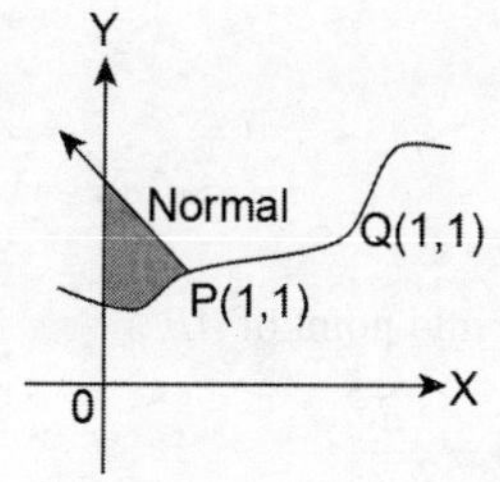

According to question $\frac{dy}{dx} = ky$ ...(1)

k = constant of proportionality

$\Rightarrow \frac{dy}{y} = kdx$ ...(2)

$\Rightarrow \ln y = kx + C_1$ ...(3)

From (1), slope of normal at $P(1, 1) = \left(\frac{-dx}{dy}\right)_{(1,1)} = -\frac{1}{k}$ ...(4)

But equation of normal to curve at $P(1, 1)$ is given to be $a(y - 1) + (x - 1) = 0$

$\Rightarrow$ Slope of normal to curve at $P(1, 1) = -1/a$ ...(5)

$\therefore$ From (4) and (5), $k = a$

$\therefore$ From (3) $\ln y = ax + C_1$ ...(6)

$\therefore$ Curve passes through (1, 1)

$\Rightarrow$ from (6)

$\ln 1 = a + C_1$

$\Rightarrow C_1 = -a$

$\therefore$ Equation of curve is $\ln y = ax - a$

$\Rightarrow y = e^{a(x-1)}$

Now area bounded by y-axis, normal and the curve is given by

$$\int_0^1 \left|e^{a(x-1)} - \left\{1 - \frac{1}{a}(x-1)\right\}\right| dx = \left|\int_0^1 \left\{e^{a(x-1)} - 1 + \frac{1}{a}(x-1)\right\} dx\right|$$

$$= \left|\left[\frac{e^{a(x-1)}}{a} - x + \frac{x^2}{2a} - \frac{x}{a}\right]_0^1\right| = \left|\left\{\left(\frac{1}{a} - 1 + \frac{1}{2a} - \frac{1}{a}\right) - \left(\frac{e^{-a}}{a}\right)\right\}\right|$$

$$= \left|\left(\frac{1}{2a} - 1\right) - \left(\frac{e^{-a}}{a}\right)\right| = \left|\frac{1}{a}\left(\frac{1}{2} - a - e^{-a}\right)\right| = \left|\frac{1}{a}\left(a - \frac{1}{2} + e^{-a}\right)\right|$$

square units

5. 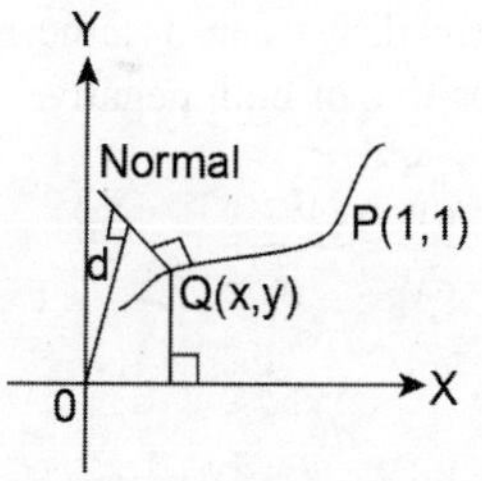

Equation of normal to curve at point $Q(x, y)$ is given by

$(Y - y) = -\frac{dx}{dy}(X - x)$ ...(1)

Distance of normal from origin (0, 0) is $d = \frac{\left|-y - x\frac{dx}{dy}\right|}{\sqrt{1 + \left(\frac{dx}{dy}\right)^2}} = y$

$\Rightarrow \left|y + x\frac{dx}{dy}\right| = y\sqrt{1 + \left(\frac{dx}{dy}\right)^2}$

$\Rightarrow y^2 + x^2\left(\frac{dx}{dy}\right)^2 + 2xy\frac{dx}{dy}$

$\Rightarrow y^2 + y^2\left(\frac{dx}{dy}\right)^2$

$\Rightarrow x^2\left(\frac{dx}{dy}\right) + 2xy = y^2\left(\frac{dx}{dy}\right)$

$\Rightarrow (x^2 - y^2)\frac{dx}{dy} = -2xy \Rightarrow \frac{dy}{dx} = \frac{x^2 - y^2}{-2xy} = \frac{y^2 - x^2}{2xy}$

Put $y = vx$

$\Rightarrow \frac{dy}{dx} = v + x\frac{dv}{dx}$

$\Rightarrow v + x\frac{dv}{dx} = \frac{v^2x^2 - x^2}{2vx^2} = \frac{v^2 - 1}{2v}$

$\Rightarrow x\frac{dv}{dx} = \frac{v^2 - 1 - 2v^2}{2v} = \frac{-1 - v^2}{2v}$

$\Rightarrow \frac{2v}{v^2 + 1}dv = -\frac{dx}{x} \Rightarrow \ln(v^2 + 1) = -\ln|x| + \ln C_1$

$\Rightarrow \ln|x(v_2 + 1)| = \ln C_1 \Rightarrow \left|x\left(\frac{y^2}{x^2} + 1\right)\right| = C_1$

$\Rightarrow y^2 + x^2 = Cx$

If passes through (1, 1)

$\Rightarrow C = 0$

$\Rightarrow$ Equation curve is $x^2 + y^2 - 2x = 0$

6. 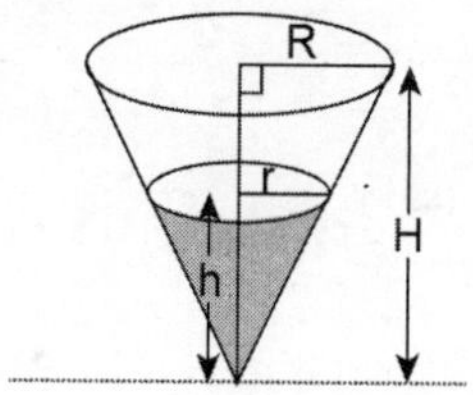

Let at any instant 't' volume of liquid in cone = $V(t)$

A.T.Q., $\frac{dV(t)}{dt} = -k(\pi r^2)$; $k > 0$

$\Rightarrow \frac{d}{dt}\left(\frac{1}{3}\pi r^2 h\right) = -k\pi r^2$

$\Rightarrow \frac{1}{3}\pi.\frac{d}{dt}(r^2h) = -k\pi r^2$ ...(1)

Here $\frac{R}{r} = \frac{H}{h}$

$\Rightarrow h = \frac{rH}{R}$ ...(2)

Using (2) in (1), we get $\frac{1}{3}.\frac{d}{dt}\left(r^2.\frac{r+1}{R}\right) = -kr^2$

$\Rightarrow \frac{1}{3}.\frac{H}{R}\left(3r^2\frac{dr}{dt}\right) = -k \Rightarrow \frac{H}{R}\frac{dr}{dt} = -k$

$\Rightarrow \; dr = -\frac{kR}{H}dt$

$\Rightarrow \; r = -\frac{kR}{H}t + C_1$ ...(3)

Initially, $t = 0, r = R$

$\Rightarrow \; R = C_1 \qquad \Rightarrow \; r = R - \frac{kR}{H}t$

$\therefore$ Whole liquid will disappear when $r = 0$

$\Rightarrow \; R = \frac{kR}{H}t \qquad \Rightarrow \; t = \frac{H}{k}$

7. Length of tangent and sub tangent at any point $P(x, y)$ to any curve $y = f(x)$ are given by $y\sqrt{1+\left(\frac{dx}{dy}\right)^2}$ and $y\frac{dx}{dy}$ respectively.

A.T.Q., $y\frac{dx}{dy} + y\sqrt{1+\left(\frac{dx}{dy}\right)^2} = kxy$

$\Rightarrow \; kx - \frac{dx}{dy} = \sqrt{1+\left(\frac{dx}{dy}\right)^2}$

On squaring, we get $k^2x^2 + \left(\frac{dx}{dy}\right)^2 - 2kx\frac{dx}{dy}$

$= 1+\left(\frac{dx}{dy}\right)^2$

$\Rightarrow \; k^2x^2 - 2kx\frac{dx}{dy} = 1 = 2kx\frac{dx}{dy} = k^2x^2 - 1$

$= \frac{2kx}{k^2x^2-1}dx = dy$

$\Rightarrow \; k\int\frac{2xdx}{k^2x^2-1} = \int dy \qquad \Rightarrow \; \frac{1}{k}\int\frac{2kx^2\,dx}{(k^2x^2-1)} = \int dy$

$\Rightarrow \; \frac{1}{k}\ln|k^2x^2-1| = y + C_1$

$\Rightarrow \; \frac{1}{k}\ln|k^2x^2-1| = y - \ln C^{1/k}$ (say)

$\Rightarrow \; \frac{1}{k}\ln|C(k^2x^2-1)| = y$

TEXTUAL EXERCISE–11: (OBJECTIVE)

1. (a) Equation of tangent to curve at $P(x, y)$ is given by $(Y - y) = \frac{dy}{dx}(X - x)$ on x-axis, $Y = 0$

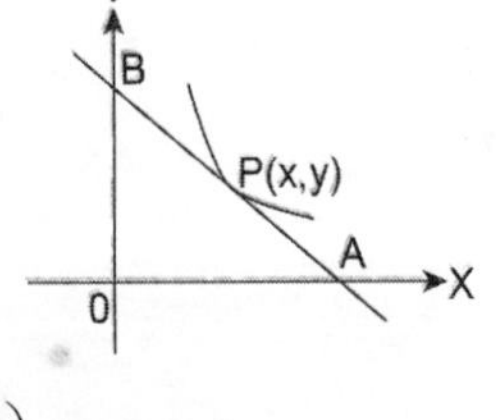

$\Rightarrow \; -y = \left(\frac{dy}{dx}\right)(X - x)$

$\Rightarrow \; A \equiv \left(\left(x - y\frac{dx}{dy}\right), 0\right)$ on y-axis, $X = 0$

$\Rightarrow \; Y - y = -x\frac{dy}{dx}$

$\Rightarrow \; B \equiv \left(0, y - x\frac{dy}{dx}\right)$

Now, by question P is the mid point of AB

$\Rightarrow \; 2x = x - y\frac{dx}{dy}$ and $2y = y - x\frac{dy}{dx}$

$\Rightarrow \; \frac{xdy}{dx} = -y$ and $y = -\frac{xdy}{dx}$

$\Rightarrow \; \frac{dy}{y} = -\frac{dx}{x}$

$\Rightarrow \; \ln y + \ln x = \ln C$

$\Rightarrow \; xy = C$

2. Area of trapezium OLPT = $\frac{1}{2}(x)^2$

$\Rightarrow \; \frac{1}{2}[(OT) + (PL)] \times (OL) = \frac{x^2}{2}$

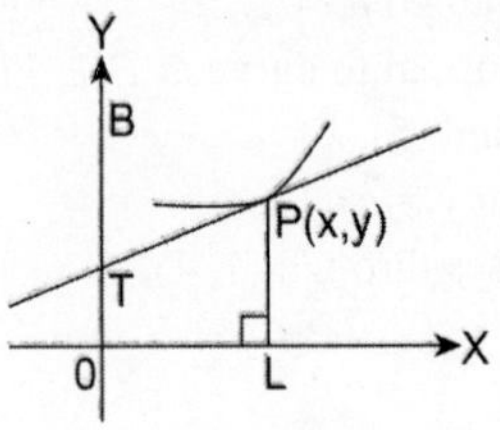

$\Rightarrow \; [|OT| + |y|]\,|x| = x^2$

$\Rightarrow \; (|OT| + |y|) = |x|$ ...(1)

Equation of tangent at $P(x, y)$ is $(Y - y) = \frac{dy}{dx}(X - x)$, it intersects y-axis, at $X = 0$

$\Rightarrow \; Y - y = \frac{dy}{dx}(-x)$

$\Rightarrow \; OT = y - x\frac{dy}{dx}$ ...(2)

Using (2) in (1), we get $\left(\left|y - x\frac{dy}{dx}\right| + |y|\right) = |x|$

$\Rightarrow \; y - x\frac{dy}{dx} + y = \pm x$

Since trapezium is formed, we can assume either both OT and PL are positive or both negative

$\Rightarrow \; x\frac{dy}{dx} \pm x = 2y \qquad \Rightarrow \; \frac{dy}{dx} = \frac{2y \mp x}{x}$

Put $y = vx$

$\Rightarrow \; \frac{dy}{dx} = v + x\frac{dv}{dx} \qquad \Rightarrow \; v + x\frac{dv}{dx} = 2v \mp 1$

$\Rightarrow \; x\frac{dv}{dx} = v \mp 1 \qquad \Rightarrow \; \frac{dv}{v \mp 1} = \frac{dx}{x}$

$\Rightarrow \; \ln|v \pm 1| = \ln|x| + \ln C \Rightarrow \; |v + 1| = |Cx|$

$\Rightarrow \; |y \pm x| = |Cx^2| \qquad \Rightarrow \; y \pm x = \pm Cx^2$

$\Rightarrow \; y = \pm Cx^2 \mp x$

$\Rightarrow \; y = kx^2 + x$ or $y \; kx^2 - x$

3. Let M_0 be the moisture present originally and let M be that at an instant 't'.

A.T.Q. $\frac{dM}{dt} = -kM$; $k > 0$

$\Rightarrow \frac{dM}{M} = -k\,dt \qquad \Rightarrow \ln M = -kt + C_1$

At $t = 0$, $M = M_0$

$\Rightarrow \ln M = -kt + \ln M_0 \qquad \Rightarrow \ln\left(\frac{M}{M_0}\right) = -kt$

$\Rightarrow M = M_0.e^{-kt}$

Given that, $M = \frac{M_0}{2}$ when $t = 1$

$\Rightarrow \frac{M_0}{2} = M_0.e^{-k} \qquad \Rightarrow e^{-k} = \frac{1}{2}$

$\therefore$ From (1), $M = M_0\left(\frac{1}{2}\right)^t$

$\therefore$ When M becomes 1% of M_0, i.e., $M = \frac{M_0}{100}$

$\Rightarrow \frac{M_0}{100} = M_0\left(\frac{1}{2}\right)^t \qquad \Rightarrow \frac{1}{100} = \frac{1}{2^t}$

$\Rightarrow 2^t = 100 \qquad \Rightarrow t = \log_2 100 = \frac{\ln 100}{\ln 2}$ hours

4. Let $f(t)$ be the concentration of salt at any time t, (i.e., $f(t)$ grams of salt present)

$\therefore \frac{d}{dt}(f(t)) = 10 - \left[\frac{f}{50+2t-t}\right]$

$\Rightarrow \frac{d}{dt}f = 10 - \frac{f}{(50+t)} \qquad \Rightarrow \frac{df}{dt} + \frac{1}{50+t}f = 10$

$\Rightarrow I.F. = e^{\int \frac{1}{50+t}dt} = (50+t)$

$\therefore$ Solution is given by $f(t)\,(50+t) = \int 10(50+t)dt + C$

$= f(t)\,(50+t) = 500\,t + 5t^2 + C_1$

Initially, $t = 0$, $f(t) = 0$

$\Rightarrow C_1 = 0 \qquad \Rightarrow f(t) = \frac{500t + 5t^2}{50+t}$

Given $f(t) = m$

$\Rightarrow m = \left(\frac{500t+5t^2}{50+t}\right)$

Now amount of salt present after 10 minutes is given by

$m = \frac{500\times 10 + 5\times 100}{5+10}$

$\Rightarrow m = \frac{5500}{60} = \frac{550}{6} = \frac{275}{3} = 91\frac{2}{3}$ gram.

5. Let P_0 denotes the present population of city and $P(t)$ denotes the affected people at any instant t.

Thus, $P_0 = 50{,}000$

$\therefore$ A.T.Q. $\frac{dP(t)}{dt} = kP(t)\,(50{,}000 - P(t))$

$\Rightarrow \frac{dP}{P(50000-P)} = k\,dt$

$\Rightarrow \frac{1}{(50000)}\int \frac{P + (50000-P)dp}{P(50000-P)} = \int k\,dt$

$\Rightarrow \frac{1}{50000}\int \frac{1}{50000-P}dP + \frac{1}{50000}\int \frac{1}{P}dP = \int k\,dt$

$\Rightarrow \frac{-1}{50000}\ln|50000-P| + \frac{1}{50000}\ln|P| = kt + C_1$

$\Rightarrow \frac{1}{50000}\ln\left|\frac{P}{50000-P}\right| = kt + C_1$

$\Rightarrow \frac{P}{50000-P} = e^{(50000)(kt+C_1)} = e^{C_1(50000)}.e^{50000\,kt}$

$\Rightarrow \frac{P}{50000-P} = \pm e^{C_1(50000)}.e^{50000kt}$

$\Rightarrow \frac{P}{50000-P} = C.e^{(50000)}$

Let 50,000 = p

$\Rightarrow \frac{P}{p-P} = C.e^{Pkt} \qquad \Rightarrow P = p\,Ce^{Pkt} - PC.e^{Pkt}$

$\Rightarrow P = \frac{PCe^{Pkt}}{1+Ce^{Pkt}}$ ...(1)

Now at $t = 0$, $P = 100$ and at $t = 10$, $P = 550$

$\Rightarrow 100 = \frac{P.C}{1+C} \qquad \Rightarrow 100 = 50000\,C - 100\,C$

$\Rightarrow 100 = 49{,}5900C$

$\Rightarrow C = \frac{1}{499}$ ...(2)

$\Rightarrow k = \frac{1}{5\times 10}\ln\left(\frac{11\times 499}{989}\right) = \frac{-1}{5\times 10^5}\ln\left(\frac{989}{11\times 499}\right)$

From (1), we get $P = \frac{p}{1+\frac{1}{C}e^{-Pkt}}$ or $P = \frac{p}{1+Ce^{-Pkt}}$

where $C = 499$

$\therefore 550 = \frac{50000}{1+499.e^{-Pkt}}$

$\Rightarrow 550 + 550 \times 550 \times 499\, e^{-Pkt} = 50000$

$\Rightarrow 550 \times 499\, e^{-Pkt} = 49450$

$\Rightarrow e^{-Pkt} = \ln\left(\frac{49450}{550\times 499}\right)$

$\Rightarrow -Pk(10) = \ln\left(\frac{989}{11\times 499}\right)$

$\Rightarrow k = -\frac{1}{10P}\ln\left(\frac{989}{5489}\right)$

SECTION–III: (TUTORIAL EXERCISE)

1. (b) Equation of all parabolas with axis as x-axis is $y^2 = 4a(x-\lambda)$

$\Rightarrow 2yy' = 4a$

$\Rightarrow yy'' + (y')^2 = 0$

is the required differential equation having order 2 and degree 1.

2. **(c)** $y=1+\frac{y'}{1!}+\frac{(y')^2}{2!}+\frac{(y')^3}{3!}+..........\infty$

$\Rightarrow\ y=e^{y'}\Rightarrow \ln y=\frac{dy}{dx}$ an equation of order 1 and degree 1.

3. **(b)** Given $(y'')^5+\frac{4(y'')^3}{y'''}+y'''=x^2-1$

$\Rightarrow\ (y''')^2+(y'')^5.y'''+4(y'')^3-(x^2-1)y'''=0$

(m) order = 3 and degree(n) = 2

4. **(a)** Equation of circles with radius 'r' and centre on y-axis and passing through origin is $x^2+(y-r)^2=r^2$

$\Rightarrow\ x^2+y^2-2ry=0$ ...(i)

when r is parameter difference w.r.t, x

$\Rightarrow\ 2x+2y\frac{dy}{dx}-2r\frac{dy}{dx}=0$ ...(ii)

Replacing value of r from equation (i) to (ii), we get

$$2x+2y\frac{dy}{dx}-\left(\frac{x^2+y^2}{y}\right)\frac{dy}{dx}=0$$

$$\Rightarrow\ 2x+\frac{dy}{dx}\left(\frac{y^2-x^2}{y}\right)=0$$

5. **(a)** Equation of family of circle is $(x-r)^2+(y-r)^2=r^2$

$\Rightarrow\ x^2+y^2-2rx-2ry+r^2=0$ ...(i)

$\Rightarrow\ 2x+2y\frac{dy}{dx}-2r-2r\frac{dy}{dx}=0$ (On differentiate w.r.t. x)

$\Rightarrow\ \dfrac{x+y\frac{dy}{dx}}{1+\frac{dy}{dx}}=r$ ...(ii)

Replacing in (i), $x^2+y^2+\dfrac{\left(x+y\frac{dy}{dx}\right)^2}{\left(1+\frac{dy}{dx}\right)^2}$

$$-2(x+y)\left(\frac{x+y\frac{dy}{dx}}{1+\frac{dy}{dx}}\right)=0$$

$$\Rightarrow\ (x^2+y^2)\left(1+\frac{dy}{dx}\right)^2+\left(x+y\frac{dy}{dx}\right)^2$$

$$-2(x+y)\left(x+y\frac{dy}{dx}\right)\left(1+\frac{dy}{dx}\right)=0$$

Clearly order = 1 and degree – 2

6. **(a)** $\left(\frac{d^2y}{dx^2}\right)+\left(\frac{dy}{dx}\right)^{1/3}+x^{1/4}=0$

To make derivatives free from all radicals

$\left(\frac{d^2y}{dx^2}+x^{1/4}\right)^3=\frac{dy}{dx}$. Thus, clearly order = 2 and degree is 3.

7. **(d)** equation of parabolas with axis parallel to y axis is $y=ax^2+bx+c$

$\Rightarrow\ \frac{dy}{dx}=2ax+b \qquad \Rightarrow\ \frac{d^2y}{dx^2}=2a$

$\Rightarrow\ \frac{d^3y}{dx^3}=0$

8. **(c)** $y=e^{-x}(A\cos x+B\sin x)$ ...(i)

$\Rightarrow\ y'=e^{-x}(-A\sin x+B\cos x-A\cos x-B\sin x)$

$\Rightarrow\ y'=e^{-x}(B\cos x-A\sin x)\ -e^{-x}(A\cos x+B\sin x)$

$\Rightarrow\ y'=e^{-x}(B\cos x-A\sin x)-y$ ...(ii)

Differentiating again, we get

$y''=e^{-x}(-B\sin x-A\cos x-B\cos x+A\sin x)-y''$

$\Rightarrow\ y''=-y'-e^{-x}(A\cos x+B\sin x)-e^{-x}(B\cos x-A\sin x)$

$\Rightarrow\ y''=-y'-y-(y+y')$ for equation ...(ii)

$\Rightarrow\ y''+2(y'+y)=0$

9. **(a)** Equation of all non-vertical lines in a plane is $ax+by+c=0$; where $b\neq 0$

$\Rightarrow\ a+b\frac{dy}{dx}=0 \qquad \Rightarrow\ b\frac{d^2y}{dx^2}=0$; But $b\neq 0$

$\Rightarrow\ \frac{d^2y}{dx^2}=0$

10. **(a)** $y=Ax+A^3$ has single parameter A and degree in A =3. thus degree of its deferential equation is (3)

Aliter: $y'=A$ Replacing in (i), we get $y=xy'+(y')^3$. Clearly degree =3 and order is 1.

11. **(c)** Equation of family of straight line at unit distance for origin is $x\cos\alpha+y\sin\alpha=1$ ...(i)

$\Rightarrow\ \cos\alpha+y'\sin\alpha=0$

$\Rightarrow\ y'=-\frac{\cos\alpha}{\sin\alpha}$

From (i), $x\cot\alpha+y=\operatorname{cosec}\alpha$

$\Rightarrow\ -xy'+y=\sqrt{1+(y')^2}$ (using (ii))

$\Rightarrow\ (y-xy')^2=1+(y')^2$

12. **(c)** $y=A+Bx+Ce^{-x}$ ...(i)

has 3 effective arbitrary parameters

$y'=B-ce^{-x}$ ...(ii)

$y''=Ce^{-x}$

$y'''=-Ce^{-x}=-y''$

$\Rightarrow\ y'''+y''=0$

13. **(d)** $y=ae^{mx}+be^{-mx}$

$\Rightarrow\ \frac{dy}{dx}=mae^{mx}-mbe^{-mx}$

$\Rightarrow\ \frac{d^2y}{dx^2}=m^2ae^{mx}+m^2be^{-mx}$

$\Rightarrow\ \frac{d^2y}{dx^2}=m^2(ae^{mx}+be^{-mx})$

$\Rightarrow\ \frac{d^2y}{dx^2}=m^2y \qquad \Rightarrow\ \frac{d^2y}{dx^2}-m^2y=0$

14. (b) Equation of circles touching x-axis at origin is

$x^2 + y^2 - 2ry = 0$ ...(i)

Differentiating w.r.t., x, we get

$2x + 2yy' - 2ry' = 0$ ...(ii)

From (i) and (ii), we get $2x + 2yy' - \left(\frac{x^2 + y^2}{y}\right)y' = 0$

$\Rightarrow 2xy + 2y^2y' - x^2y' - y^2y' = 0$

$\Rightarrow 2xy + (y^2 - x^2)y' = 0$

$\Rightarrow (x^2 - y^2)\frac{dy}{dx} = 2xy$

15. (b) Equation of ellipse centered at origin and axes as co-ordinate axes is $\frac{x^2}{a^2} + \frac{y^2}{b^2} = 1$

$\Rightarrow \frac{2x}{a^2} + \frac{2yy'}{b^2} = 0$, i.e., $\frac{b^2}{a^2} = -\frac{yy'}{x}$

Differentiating again, $\frac{1}{a^2} + \frac{yy'' + (y')^2}{b^2} = 0$

$\Rightarrow yy'' + (y')^2 = -\frac{b^2}{a^2} = \frac{yy'}{x}$

$\Rightarrow xyy'' + xy'^2 - yy' = 0$

16. (a) $ax^2 + by^2 = 1 \Rightarrow 2ax + 2byy' = 0$

$\Rightarrow -\frac{a}{b} = \frac{yy'}{x}$

Differentiating w.r.t. 'x', $2a + 2b\,(y'^2 + yy'') = 0$

$\Rightarrow \frac{a}{b} + (y')^2 + yy'' = 0 \Rightarrow -\frac{yy'}{x} + (y')^2 + yy'' = 0$

$\Rightarrow xyy'' + x(y')^2 - yy' = 0$

17. (b) $x^2 + y^2 - 1 + \lambda(x - y) = 0$

Differentiating w.r.t. 'x', $2x + 2yy' + \lambda(1 - y') = 0$

Dividing (i) and (ii), we get $\left(\frac{x^2 + y^2 - 1}{2(x + yy')}\right) = \left(\frac{y - x}{y' - 1}\right)$

$\Rightarrow (x^2 + y^2 - 1)(y' - 1) = 2(y - x)(x + yy')$

18. (a) Equation of tangent to curve at $P(x, y)$ is

$Y - y = \frac{dy}{dx}(X - x)$

$\Rightarrow OA = x - y\frac{dx}{dy} \Rightarrow PM = y$

$\because OA \propto PM$

$\Rightarrow x - y\frac{dx}{dy} = ky \Rightarrow xdy - ydx = kydy$

$\Rightarrow \frac{ydx - xdy}{y^2} = -k\frac{dy}{y}$

$\Rightarrow d\left(\frac{x}{y}\right) = -k\frac{dy}{y}$

Integrating, we get $\int d\left(\frac{x}{y}\right) = -k\int\frac{dy}{y}$

$\Rightarrow \frac{x}{y} = -k\ln y + c \Rightarrow x = yc - ky\ln y$

19. (b) Clearly the number of effective parameter in the general solution is equal to order of differential equation.

20. (c) Degree represents maximum possible directions at a point on the family of curves represented by differential equation.

21. (d) $\frac{dy}{dx} = \frac{3x - 4y - 2}{3x - 4y - 3}$

Let $3x - 4y - 3 = t \Rightarrow 3 - 4\frac{dy}{dx} = \frac{dt}{dx}$

Replacing in equation (i), $\frac{1}{4}\left(3 - \frac{dt}{dx}\right) = \frac{t+1}{t}$

$\Rightarrow \frac{dt}{dx} = -\frac{t+4}{t} \Rightarrow \int\frac{t}{t+4}dt = \int -dx$

$\Rightarrow t - 4\ln(t + 4) = -x + C_0$

$\Rightarrow 4x - 4y - 3 = 4\ln(3x - 4y + 1) + C_0$

$\Rightarrow x - y - \frac{3}{4} - C_0 = \ln(3x - 4y + 1)$

$\Rightarrow x - y + c = \ln(3x - 4y + 1)$ is the general solution

22. (c) Given differential equation after rearranging the terms is $\int\frac{x^2+1}{2x}dx = \int\frac{dy}{y^2}$

$\Rightarrow \frac{1}{2}\left(\ln x + \frac{x^2}{2}\right) = -\frac{1}{y} + C$

$\because$ It Passes through (1, 1)

$\Rightarrow \frac{1}{4} = -1 + C \Rightarrow C = \frac{5}{4} \Rightarrow \frac{1}{y} = \frac{5}{4} - \left(\frac{x^2 + 2\ln x}{4}\right)$

$\Rightarrow y = \frac{4}{5 - x^2 - 2\ln x}$

23. (b) $\frac{dy}{dx} = \frac{y}{x} + \frac{\phi(y/x)}{\phi'(y/x)}$

Let $y = vx$

$\Rightarrow \frac{dy}{dx} = v + x\frac{dv}{dx}$

$\Rightarrow v + x\frac{dv}{dx} = u + \frac{\phi(v)}{\phi'(v)} \Rightarrow \int\frac{\phi'(v)}{\phi(v)}du = \int\frac{dx}{x}$

$\Rightarrow \ln\phi(v) = \ln cx \Rightarrow \phi(v) = Cx$

$\Rightarrow \phi\left(\frac{y}{x}\right) = cx$

24. (a) $x\sin\left(\frac{y}{x}\right)dy = \left(y\sin\frac{y}{x} - x\right)dx$

$\Rightarrow \sin\frac{y}{x}\frac{dy}{dx} = \frac{y}{x}\sin\frac{y}{x} - 1$

$\Rightarrow \frac{dy}{dx} = \frac{y}{x} - \text{cosec}\frac{y}{x}$

Let $y = vx$

$\Rightarrow v + x\frac{dv}{dx} = v - \text{cosec}\, v$

$\Rightarrow \int \sin v dv = -\int \frac{dx}{x}$ $\Rightarrow$ $-\cos v = -\ln x - \ln c$

$\Rightarrow \cos\frac{y}{x} = \ln cx$

25. (b) $x = yt \Rightarrow \frac{dx}{dy} = y\frac{dt}{dy} + t$

Replacing in the given equation,

$(1+e^t)\left(y\frac{dt}{dy}+t\right)+e^t(1-t)=0$

$\Rightarrow y(1+e^t)\frac{dt}{dy}+t+te^t+e^t-te^t=0$

$\Rightarrow \int\frac{(1+e^t)}{t+e^t}dt=-\int\frac{dy}{y}$

$\Rightarrow \ln(t+e^t) = -\ln y + \ln c$

$\Rightarrow t+e^t=\frac{c}{y}$

$\Rightarrow \frac{x}{y}+e^{x/y}=\frac{c}{y} \Rightarrow x+ye^{x/y}=c$

26. (a) $\frac{dy}{dx}=\frac{y+1}{x-1}$ is variable separable form

$\Rightarrow \int\frac{dy}{y+1}=\int\frac{dx}{x-1}$ $\Rightarrow \ln(y+1)=\log c(x-1)$

$\Rightarrow y+1=c(x-1)$ ...(i)

$\because (y)_{x=1}=2$

Which clearly does not satisfies the solution .....(i)

Thus, no curve belonging to general solution passes through point (1, 2)

27. (a) $\frac{dy}{dx}=e^{x-y}+x^2e^{-y}$

$\Rightarrow \int e^y dy=\int(e^x+x^2)dx$

$\Rightarrow e^y=e^x+\frac{x^3}{3}+c$

28. (b) $(\sin x+\cos x)\,dy+(\cos x-\sin x)\,dx=0$

$\Rightarrow \int dy=\int\frac{\sin x-\cos x}{\sin x+\cos x}dx$

Put $\cos x+\sin x=t$ $\Rightarrow y=-\int\frac{dt}{t}$

$\Rightarrow y=-\ln t+\ln c$

$\Rightarrow y=\ln\left(\frac{c}{\sin x+\cos x}\right)$

$\Rightarrow e^y=\frac{c}{\sin x+\cos x}\Rightarrow e^y(\sin x+\cos x)=c$

29. (c) $\because \frac{dy}{dx}=\frac{y(x+1)}{x(y+1)}$

$\Rightarrow \int\frac{y+1}{y}dy=\int\frac{x+1}{x}dx$ $\Rightarrow y+\ln y=x+\ln x$

$\Rightarrow \ln\left(\frac{y}{x}\right)=x-y+c$ $\Rightarrow \frac{y}{x}=e^{x-y+c}$

$\Rightarrow y=(xe^{x-y})e^c$ $\Rightarrow y=Axe^{x-y}$

30. (b) $\sin^{-1}\left(\frac{dy}{dx}\right)=x+y$

$\Rightarrow \frac{dy}{dx}=\sin(x+y)$ ...(i)

Put $x+y=t$, we get $1+\frac{dy}{dx}=\frac{dt}{dx}$

Substituting in (i), we get $\frac{dt}{dx}-1=\sin t$

$\Rightarrow \int\frac{dt}{1+\sin t}=\int dx$

$\Rightarrow \int\frac{1-\sin t}{\cos^2 t}dt=\int dx$

$\Rightarrow \tan t-\sec t=x+c$

$\Rightarrow \tan(x+y)-\sec(x+y)=x+c$

31. (c) $\frac{dy}{dx}=\frac{1}{2y}$

$\Rightarrow \int 2y dy=\int dx$ $\Rightarrow y^2=x+c$

It passes through (4, 3)

$\Rightarrow 9=4+c$ $\Rightarrow c=5$

$\Rightarrow y^2=x+5$ is the equation of curve.

32. (b) $f''(x)=6(x-1)$

$\Rightarrow \int df'(x)=\int 6(x-1)dx$

$\Rightarrow f'(x)=6\left(\frac{x^2}{2}-x\right)+c$

$\because$ Slope of tangent at (2, 1) is 3

$\Rightarrow f'(2)=3$ $\Rightarrow 6(2-2)+c=3$

$\Rightarrow c=3$ $\Rightarrow \frac{dy}{dx}=3x^2-6x+3$

$\Rightarrow \int dy=\int(3x^2-6x+3)dx$

$\Rightarrow y=x^3-3x^2+3x+c$

$\because$ Point (2,1) lies on the curve, so, $1=8-12+6+C$

Thus, $y=x^3-3x^2+3x-1$ i.e., $y=(x-1)^3$ is equation.

33. (a) $\frac{dy}{dx}=(x+y-1)+\frac{x+y}{\ln(x+y)}$

Let $x+y=z$

$\Rightarrow 1+\frac{dy}{dx}=\frac{dz}{dx}$ $\Rightarrow \frac{dz}{dx}-1=z-1+\frac{z}{\log z}$

$\Rightarrow \frac{dz}{dx}=\frac{z}{\log z}+z=z\left(\frac{1+\log z}{\log z}\right)$

$\Rightarrow \int\frac{\log z dz}{z(1+\log z)}=\int dx$

Let $\log z = t$

$\Rightarrow \int \frac{t}{1+t}dt = \int dx$

$\Rightarrow t - \ln(1+t) = x + c_0$

$\Rightarrow \log(x+y) - \log(1+\log(x+y)) = x + C_0$

Rearranging the expression by adding 1 both side, we get $1 + \log(x+y) - \log(1+\log(x+y)) = x + c$

34. (a) $y = x\frac{dy}{dx} + \frac{dx}{dy}$, Let $\frac{dy}{dx} = p$

$\Rightarrow y = xp + \frac{1}{p}$

Differentiating w.r.t., x, we get $\frac{dp}{dx}\left(x - \frac{1}{p^2}\right) = 0$

$\Rightarrow \frac{dp}{dx} = 0$ or $x = \frac{1}{p^2}$ $\Rightarrow p = c$ or $\frac{1}{p} = \sqrt{x}$

$\Rightarrow y = cx + \frac{1}{c}$ or $y = 2\sqrt{x}$, i.e., $y^2 - 4x$

Complete solution of family of tangents is $y = mx + \frac{1}{m}$ for parabola $y^2 = 4x$

35. (a) $\frac{dy}{dx} = \frac{a^2}{(x-y)^2}$

Let $x - y = t$ $\Rightarrow 1 - \frac{dt}{dx} = \frac{a^2}{t^2}$

$\Rightarrow \int dx = \int \frac{t^2 dt}{t^2 - a^2}$ $\Rightarrow \int dx = \int \frac{t^2 - a^2 + a^2}{t^2 - a^2}dt$

$\Rightarrow x = t + \frac{a^2}{2a}\ln\left|\frac{t-a}{t+a}\right| + c$

$\Rightarrow x = x - y + \frac{a}{2}\ln\left|\frac{x-y-a}{x-y+a}\right| + C$

$\Rightarrow y = \frac{a}{2\ln}\left|\frac{x-y-a}{x-y+a}\right| + C$

36. (b) $\frac{x^3dx + yx^2dy}{\sqrt{x^2+y^2}} = ydx - xdy$

$\Rightarrow \frac{xdx + ydy}{\sqrt{x^2+y^2}} = \frac{ydx - xdy}{x^2}$

$\Rightarrow \frac{\frac{1}{2}d(x^2+y^2)}{\sqrt{x^2+y^2}} = -d\left(\frac{y}{x}\right)$

$\Rightarrow \int \frac{d(x^2+y^2)}{2\sqrt{x^2+y^2}} = -\int d\left(\frac{y}{x}\right)$

$\Rightarrow \sqrt{x^2+y^2} = \frac{-y}{x} + C$ $\Rightarrow \sqrt{x^2+y^2} + \frac{y}{x} = C$

37. (c) $xdy(y^2e^{xy} + e^{\frac{x}{y}}) = ydx(e^{\frac{x}{y}} - y^2e^{xy})$

$\Rightarrow e^{\frac{x}{y}}(xdy - ydx) = -e^{xy}(xdy + ydx)y^2$

$\Rightarrow e^{\frac{x}{y}}\left(\frac{ydx - xdy}{y^2}\right) = e^{xy}(xdy + ydx)$

$\Rightarrow \int e^{\frac{x}{y}}d\left(\frac{x}{y}\right) = \int e^{xy}d(xy)$

$\Rightarrow e^{\frac{x}{y}} + c = e^{xy}$ $\Rightarrow xy = \log\left(e^{\frac{x}{y}} + c\right)$

38. (d) $ydx - xdy + (1+x^2)dx + x^2\sin ydy = 0$

$\Rightarrow \frac{xdy - ydx}{x^2} - \frac{1+x^2}{x^2}dx - \sin ydy = 0$

$\Rightarrow \int d\left(\frac{y}{x}\right) = \int\left(1 + \frac{1}{x^2}\right)dx + \int \sin ydy$

$\Rightarrow \frac{y}{x} = x - \frac{1}{x} - \cos y + C$

39. (c) $\cos x\frac{dy}{dx} + y\sin x = 1$

$\Rightarrow \frac{dy}{dx} + y\tan x = \sec x$

Linear in y and $\frac{dy}{dx}$

If $e^{\int \tan xdx} = e^{\ln\sec x} = \sec x$

40. (d) Given differential equation is

$x(1-x^2)dy + (2x^2y - y - ax^3)dx = 0$

$\Rightarrow \frac{dy}{dx} + \frac{(2x^2-1)}{x(1-x^2)}y = \frac{ax^2}{(1-x^2)}$

$\Rightarrow p = \frac{2x^2-1}{x(1-x^2)}$

41. (a) Given differential equation is

$ydx - xdy + 3x^2y^2e^{x^3}dx = 0$

$\Rightarrow ydx - xdy = -3x^2y^2e^{x^3}dx$

$\Rightarrow \frac{ydx - xdy}{y^2} = -3x^2y^2e^{x^3}dx$

$\Rightarrow d\left(\frac{x}{y}\right) = -d(e^{x^3})$ $\Rightarrow \frac{x}{y} = -e^{x^3} + c$

$\Rightarrow \frac{x}{y} + e^{x^3} = c$

42. (b) Given differential equation is $xdy = y(dx + ydy), y > 0$

$\Rightarrow xdy - ydx = y^2dy$ $\Rightarrow \frac{ydx - xdy}{y^2} = -dy$

$\Rightarrow d\left(\frac{x}{y}\right) = -dy$ $\Rightarrow \frac{x}{y} = -y + c$

Given that y(1)=1

$\Rightarrow 1 = -1 + C$ $\Rightarrow C = 2$

$\Rightarrow \frac{x}{y} = -y + 2$

At $x = -3$

$\Rightarrow -3 = -y^2 + 2y$

$\Rightarrow y^2 - 2y - 3 = 0$

$\Rightarrow (y-3)(y+1) = 0$

$\Rightarrow y = 3 \, or \, y = -1$

But $y > 0 \Rightarrow y = 3$

43. (b) Given differential equation is

$$(1+xy)ydx + (1-xy)xdy = 0$$

$$\Rightarrow ydx + xdy + xy^2dx - x^2ydy = 0$$

$$\Rightarrow \frac{1}{x^2y^2}(ydx + xdy) = \frac{x^2ydy - xy^2dx}{x^2y^2} = \frac{dy}{y} - \frac{dx}{x}$$

$$= \frac{xdy - ydx}{xy} = \frac{x^2}{xy}\left(\frac{xdy - ydx}{x^2}\right)$$

$$\Rightarrow \frac{1}{x^2y^2}(ydx + xdy) = \frac{x}{y}.d\left(\frac{y}{x}\right) = d\left(\ln\left(\frac{y}{x}\right)\right)$$

$$\Rightarrow \frac{1}{(xy)^2}.d(xy) = d\left(\ln\left(\frac{y}{x}\right)\right) \quad \Rightarrow d\left(-(xy)^{-1}\right) = d\left(\ln\left(\frac{y}{x}\right)\right)$$

$$\Rightarrow -\frac{1}{xy} = \ln\left(\frac{y}{x}\right) + c \quad \Rightarrow \ln\left(\frac{x}{y}\right) = \frac{1}{xy} + c$$

44. (c) Given differential equation is

$$ydx + (x + x^2y)dy = 0 \text{ or } ydx + xdy + x^2ydy = 0$$

$$\Rightarrow \frac{ydx + xdy}{x^2y} + dy = 0$$

$$\Rightarrow \frac{ydx + xdy}{x^2y^2} + dy = 0$$

$$\Rightarrow \frac{dy}{y} = -(xy)^{-2}.d(xy)$$

$$\Rightarrow d(\ln y) = d\left((xy)^{-1}\right)$$

$$\Rightarrow \ln y = \frac{1}{xy} + c$$

45. (b) Given differential equation is

$$(1+y^2)dx - (\tan^{-1}y - x)dy = 0 \text{ or } \frac{dx}{dy} - \left(\frac{\tan^{-1}y - x}{1+y^2}\right) = 0$$

$$\text{or } \frac{dy}{dx} + \left(\frac{1}{1+y^2}\right)x = \frac{\tan^{-1}y}{1+y^2}$$

$$\Rightarrow \text{Integrating factor} = e^{\int pdy} = e^{\int \frac{1}{1+y^2}dy} = e^{\tan^{-1}y}$$

46. (d) Given differential equation is

$$\frac{dy}{dx} + ay = e^{mx}$$

$$\Rightarrow I.F. = e^{\int adx} = e^{ax}$$

$\therefore$ Solution is given by $y.e^{ax} = \int e^{(a+m)x}dx + c$

$$\Rightarrow y.e^{ax} = \frac{e^{(a+m)x}}{a+m} + c \text{ or } (a+m)y = e^{mx} + c(a+m)e^{-ax}$$

47. (b) Given differential equation is

$$(1+y^2)dx - xydy = 0$$

$$\Rightarrow \frac{dx}{x} - \frac{y}{1+y^2}dy = 0 \qquad \Rightarrow \ln x - \frac{1}{2}\ln(1+y^2) = \ln c$$

$$\Rightarrow \frac{x}{\sqrt{1+y^2}} = c \qquad \Rightarrow x^2 = c^2(1+y^2)$$

As it passes through (1, 0)

$$\Rightarrow 1 = c^2 \qquad \Rightarrow x^2 - y^2 = 1$$

48. (a) Given differential equation is $(1+x^2)\frac{dy}{dx} + y = e^{\tan^{-1}x}$

$$\Rightarrow \frac{dy}{dx} + \frac{1}{(1+x^2)}y = \frac{e^{\tan^{-1}x}}{1+x^2}$$

$$\Rightarrow \text{I.F.} = e^{\int \frac{1}{1+x^2}dx} = e^{\tan^{-1}x}$$

Solution is given by $y.e^{\tan^{-1}x} = \int \frac{(e^{\tan^{-1}x})^2}{1+x^2}dx$

$$\Rightarrow \quad y.e^{\tan^{-1}x} = \frac{\left(e^{\tan^{-1}x}\right)^3}{3} + C_1$$

$$\Rightarrow 3ye^{\tan^{-1}x} = (e^{\tan^{-1}x}) + c$$

$$\Rightarrow 3ye^{\tan^{-1}x} = e^{3\tan^{-1}x} + c$$

49. (b) Given differential equation is $y = x\frac{dy}{dx} + \frac{dy}{dx} - \left(\frac{dy}{dx}\right)^2$

$$\Rightarrow y = px + (p - p^2)$$

$$\Rightarrow \frac{dy}{dx} = p + x\frac{dp}{dx} + \frac{dp}{dx} - 2p\frac{dp}{dx}$$

$$\Rightarrow 0 = x\frac{dp}{dx} + \frac{dp}{dx} - 2p\frac{dp}{dx}$$

$$\Rightarrow \frac{dp}{dx} = 0 \, or \, x + 1 - 2p = 0$$

$$\Rightarrow p = c_1 \, or \, 2\frac{dy}{dx} = x + 1$$

$$\Rightarrow y = c_1x + c_2 \, or \, 2dy = (x+1)dx$$

$$\Rightarrow y = c_1x + c_2 \text{ or } 2y = \frac{x^2}{2} + x + c_3$$

$$\Rightarrow y = c_1x + c_2 \, or \, 4y = x^2 + 2x + 2c_3$$

$\therefore 4y = x^2 + 2x + 1$ is a particular salution for $2c_3 = 1$

i.e., $4y = (x+1)^2$ is a solution

50. (c) Given differential equation is

$$\left(\frac{dy}{dx}\right)^2 + (2x+y)\frac{dy}{dx} + 2xy = 0$$

$$\Rightarrow \left(\frac{dy}{dx}\right)\left(\frac{dy}{dx} + y\right) + 2x\left(\frac{dy}{dx} + y\right) = 0$$

$$\Rightarrow \left(\frac{dy}{dx} + 2x\right)\left(\frac{dy}{dx} + y\right) = 0$$

$$\Rightarrow dy = -2xdx \, or \, \frac{dy}{y} = -dx$$

$\Rightarrow y=-x^2+c_1$

or $\ln y=-x+c_2$

$\Rightarrow y+x^2-c_1=0$

or $\ln y+x-c_2=0$

$(y+x^2-c_1)(x+\ln y-c_2)=0$

51. (b) Given family of curves is $y=cx^k \Rightarrow c=y/x^k$

$\Rightarrow \frac{dy}{dx}=ck.x^{k-1}$

$\Rightarrow \frac{dy}{dx}=\frac{y}{x^k}.k.x^{k-1}$

$\Rightarrow \frac{dy}{dx}=\frac{ky}{x}$

Replacing $\frac{dy}{dx}$ by $-\left(\frac{dx}{dy}\right)$, we get $-\frac{dx}{dy}=\frac{ky}{x}$

$\Rightarrow -xdx=kydy$

$\Rightarrow -\frac{x^2}{2}=\frac{ky^2}{2}+c_1$

$\Rightarrow ky^2+x^2+2c_1=0$

$\Rightarrow x^2+ky^2=$ constant which is the required equation of orthogonal trajectories

52. (d) Given differential equation is

$$\frac{d^2y}{dx^2}+3\left(\frac{dy}{dx}\right)^2=x\log\left(\frac{d^2y}{dx^2}\right)$$

The above differential equations is not a polynomial in differential coefficient, hence its degree is not defined, no doubt order is 2.

53. (b) length of subnormal at $p(x,y)=y\frac{dy}{dx}=a(\text{constant})$

$\Rightarrow ydy=adx$

$\Rightarrow \frac{y^2}{2}=ax+c$

$\Rightarrow y^2=2ax+2c$

$\Rightarrow y^2=2ax+2b$ is the equation of required curve .

54. (b) Given equation is $\frac{dy}{dx}=\cos(x-y)$

Put $(x-y)=z \Rightarrow 1-\frac{dy}{dx}=\frac{dz}{dx}$

$\Rightarrow 1-\frac{dz}{dx}=\cos z \Rightarrow \frac{dz}{dx}=1-\cos z$

$\Rightarrow \frac{dz}{1-\cos z}=dx$

$\Rightarrow \frac{1}{2}\int \text{cosec}^2\left(\frac{z}{2}\right)dz=\int dx$

$\Rightarrow -\cot\left(\frac{z}{2}\right)=x+c_1$

$\Rightarrow \cot\left(\frac{x-y}{2}\right)=x+c_1$

$\Rightarrow x+\cot\left(\frac{x-y}{2}\right)=c$

55. (a) Given family of curve is $y=ae^{3x}+be^x$ (i)

$\Rightarrow \frac{dy}{dx}=3ae^{3x}+be^x$ ...(ii)

$\Rightarrow \frac{d^2y}{dx^2}=9ae^{3x}+be^x$ ...(iii)

(iii) – (ii) gives,

$\Rightarrow \frac{d^2y}{dx^2}-\frac{dy}{dx}=6ae^{3x}$ ...(iv)

Also, $3\times(2)-(3)$ gives $3\frac{dy}{dx}-\frac{d^2y}{dx^2}=2be^x$ ...(v)

Using (iv) and (v) in (i), we get

$$y=\frac{1}{6}\left(\frac{d^2y}{dx^2}-\frac{dy}{dx}\right)+\frac{1}{2}\left(3\frac{dy}{dx}-\frac{d^2y}{dx^2}\right)$$

$\Rightarrow 6y=\frac{d^2y}{dx^2}-\frac{dy}{dx}+9\frac{dy}{dx}-3\frac{d^2y}{dx^2}$

$\Rightarrow 6y=-2\frac{d^2y}{dx^2}+8\frac{dy}{dx}$ $\Rightarrow 2\frac{d^2y}{dx^2}-8\frac{dy}{dx}+6y=0$

$\Rightarrow \frac{d^2y}{dx^2}-4\frac{dy}{dx}+3y=0$ $\Rightarrow a=1,\ b=-4,\ c=3$

56. (b) Given family of curves is $a^{n-1}y=x^n$

$\Rightarrow y=\frac{1}{a^{n-1}}x^n \Rightarrow \frac{1}{a^{n-1}}=\frac{y}{x^n}$

$\Rightarrow \frac{dy}{dx}=\frac{1}{a^{n-1}}n.x^{n-1}$ $\Rightarrow \frac{dy}{dx}=\frac{ny}{x^n}x^{n-1}$

$\Rightarrow \frac{dy}{dx}=\frac{ny}{x}$ ...(i)

Replacing $\frac{dy}{dx}$ by $-\frac{dx}{dy}$ in (i),

We get $-\frac{dx}{dy}=\frac{ny}{x}$

$\Rightarrow nydy=-xdx$ $\Rightarrow \frac{ny^2}{2}=-\frac{x^2}{2}+c_1$

$\Rightarrow ny^2+x^2=$ constant, orthnogonal trajectory

57. (b) Given differential equation is

$$(1+2e^{\frac{x}{y}})dx+2e^{\frac{x}{y}}(1-\frac{x}{y})dy=0$$

$\Rightarrow \frac{dy}{dx}=-\frac{(1+2e^{\frac{x}{y}})}{2e^{\frac{x}{y}}(1-\frac{x}{y})}$ ...(i)

Put $x=vy$ ...(ii)

$$\Rightarrow \frac{dx}{dy} = v + y\frac{dv}{dy} \quad \ldots\text{(iii)}$$

From (i), (ii) and (iii), we get $\dfrac{1}{v + y\dfrac{dv}{dy}} = \dfrac{-(1+2e^v)}{2e^v(1-v)}$

$$\Rightarrow v + y\frac{dv}{dy} = \frac{2e^v(1-v)}{-(1+2e^v)}$$

$$\Rightarrow y\frac{dv}{dy} = \frac{2ve^v - 2e^v - v - 2ve^v}{(1+2e^v)}$$

$$\Rightarrow \frac{(1+2e^v)dv}{(2e^v+v)} = -\frac{dy}{y} \qquad \Rightarrow \ln(2e^v + v) = -\ln y + \ln c_1$$

$$\Rightarrow y(2e^v + v) = c_1 \qquad \Rightarrow y(2e^{\frac{x}{y}} + \frac{x}{y}) = c_1$$

$$\Rightarrow x + 2ye^{\frac{x}{y}} = c_1 \qquad \Rightarrow \; 1 = 2$$

58. **(a)** Given differential equation is $x\dfrac{dy}{dx} - 2y = x^4$

$$\Rightarrow \quad \frac{dy}{dx} - \frac{2}{x}y = x^3$$

It's a L.D.E of 1st degree.

$$\text{I.F.} = e^{\int -\frac{2}{x}dx} = x^{-2}$$

$\therefore$ solution of (i) is given by $y.x^{-2} = \int x^3.x^{-2}dx + c$

$$\Rightarrow \frac{y}{x^2} = \frac{x^2}{2} + c$$

59. **(a)** Given differential equation is $x\dfrac{dy}{dx} + y = x^3y^6$

$$\Rightarrow xdy + ydx = x^3y^6dx \qquad \Rightarrow xdy + ydx = \frac{x^6y^6}{x^3}dx$$

$$\Rightarrow \frac{1}{x^6y^6}(xdy + ydx) = x^{-3}dx$$

$$\Rightarrow d\left(-\frac{(xy)^{-5}}{5}\right) = d\left(\frac{x^{-2}}{-2}\right)$$

$$\Rightarrow \; -\frac{1}{5}(xy)^{-5} = -\frac{x^{-2}}{2} + C_1$$

$$\Rightarrow y^{-5}x^{-5} = \frac{5}{2}x^{-2} - 5c_1 \qquad \Rightarrow y^{-5}x^{-5} = \frac{5}{2}x^{-2} + c$$

60. **(b)** Given differential equation is

$$\frac{y + \sin x.\cos^2(xy)}{\cos^2(xy)}dx + \left(\frac{x}{\cos^2(xy)} + \sin y\right)dy = 0$$

$$\Rightarrow (y\sec^2(xy) + \sin x)dx + (x\sec^2(xy) + \sin y)dy = 0$$

$$\Rightarrow \sec^2(xy).(xdy + ydx) + \sin xdx + \sin ydy = 0$$

$$\Rightarrow d(\tan xy) + d(-\cos x) + d(-\cos y) = 0$$

$$\Rightarrow \tan(xy) = \cos x + \cos y + C$$

61. **(b)** Given differential equation is

$$y\cos\left(\frac{y}{x}\right)(xdy - ydx) + x\sin\left(\frac{y}{x}\right)(xdy + ydx) = 0$$

$$\Rightarrow y\cot\left(\frac{y}{x}\right)(xdy - ydx) + x(xdy + ydx) = 0$$

$$\Rightarrow \frac{y}{x}\cot\left(\frac{y}{x}\right)(xdy - ydx) + (xdy + ydx) = 0$$

$$\Rightarrow xy\cot\left(\frac{y}{x}\right)\left(\frac{xdy - ydx}{x^2}\right) = -[xdy + ydx]$$

$$\Rightarrow \cot\left(\frac{y}{x}\right)\left(\frac{xdy - ydx}{x^2}\right) = -\frac{1}{xy}(xdy + ydx) = -d(\ln xy)$$

$$\Rightarrow d\left(\ln\sin\left(\frac{y}{x}\right)\right) = d(-\ln(xy))$$

$$\Rightarrow (xy)\sin\left(\frac{y}{x}\right) = c$$

62. **(b)** A.T.Q, length of subtangent at any point $P(x, y)$

$$= y\frac{dx}{dy} = n(x) \qquad \Rightarrow \frac{dx}{x} = n\frac{dy}{y}$$

$$\Rightarrow \ln x = n\ln y + \ln c$$

$$\Rightarrow x = c_1y^n \text{ or } y^n = \frac{1}{c_1}x \text{ or } y^n = cx$$

63. **(c)** Equation of circles passing through $(a, 0)$ and $(-a, 0)$ is

$$(x-0)^2 + (y-k)^2 = (a^2 + k^2)$$

$$\Rightarrow x^2 + y^2 - 2ky = a^2 \quad \ldots\text{(i)}$$

Differentiating w.r.t.x , we get $2x + 2y\dfrac{dy}{dx} - 2k\dfrac{dy}{dx} = 0$

$$\Rightarrow k\frac{dy}{dx} = x + y\frac{dy}{dx}$$

$$\Rightarrow k = y + x\frac{dx}{dy} \quad \ldots\text{(ii)}$$

Using (ii) in (i), we get $x^2 + y^2 - 2\left(y + x\dfrac{dx}{dy}\right)y = a^2$

or $x^2 - y^2 - 2xy\dfrac{dx}{dy} = a^2$ or $x^2 - y^2 - a^2 = 2xy\dfrac{dx}{dy}$

or $y_1(x^2 - y^2 - a^2) = 2xy$ or $y_1(y^2 - x^2 + a^2) + 2xy = 0$

64. **(b)** Given differential equation is

$$dy = (\sec x + y\tan x)dx$$

$$\Rightarrow \frac{dy}{dx} - (\tan x)y = \sec x$$

which is a L.D.E of 1st degree having

$$\text{I.F.} = e^{\int -\tan x dx} = e^{\ln\cos x} = \cos x$$

Hence, solution is given by $y.\cos x = \int \sec x.\cos x dx + c$

or $y\cos x + C$

As it passes through origin (0, 0)

$\Rightarrow \; C = 0$

$\Rightarrow$ Equation of curve is $y \cos x = x$

65. **(a)** Given differential equation is

$$y(1 + xy)dx - xdy = 0$$

$$\Rightarrow \; ydx - xdy + xy^2dx = 0 \text{ or } \frac{ydx - xdy}{y^2} + xdx = 0$$

$$\text{or } d\left(\frac{x}{y}\right)+d\left(\frac{x^2}{2}\right)=d(c_1)$$

$$\Rightarrow \frac{x}{y}+\frac{x^2}{2}=c_1$$

It passes through (1, 2)

$$\Rightarrow \frac{1}{2}+\frac{1}{2}=c_1 \Rightarrow c_1=1 \qquad \Rightarrow \frac{x}{y}+\frac{x^2}{2}=1$$

$$\Rightarrow \frac{x}{y}=\frac{2-x^2}{2} \qquad \Rightarrow y=\frac{2x}{2-x^2}$$

66. (c) The given lines are $y^2-x^2=0$

$\Rightarrow y=\pm x$

Here $2r^2=k^2$

⇒ Equation of family of cicles toching the lines $y=x$ and $y=-x$ is given by $(x-0)^2+(y-k)^2=\frac{k^2}{2}$

$$\text{or } x^2+y^2-2ky+\frac{k^2}{2}=0$$

$$\text{or } 2x^2+2y^2-4ky+k^2=0 \qquad \ldots(i)$$

Differentiating, we get $4x+4y\frac{dy}{dx}-4k\frac{dy}{dx}=0$

$$\Rightarrow x+y\frac{dy}{dx}=k\frac{dy}{dx}$$

$$\Rightarrow k=\frac{x+y\frac{dy}{dx}}{\left(\frac{dy}{dx}\right)}$$

Using (ii) in (i), we get

$$2x^2+2y^2-4y\left(\frac{x+y\frac{dy}{dx}}{\frac{dy}{dx}}\right)+\left(\frac{x+y\frac{dy}{dx}}{\frac{dy}{dx}}\right)^2=0$$

$$\Rightarrow (2x^2+2y^2)\left(\frac{dy}{dx}\right)^2+\left(x+y\frac{dy}{dx}\right)^2$$

$$-4y\left(x+y\frac{dy}{dx}\right)\left(\frac{dy}{dx}\right)=0$$

$$\Rightarrow \left(\frac{dy}{dx}\right)^2(2x^2+2y^2+y^2-4y^2)$$

$$+\left(\frac{dy}{dx}\right)(2xy-4xy)+(x)^2=0$$

$$\text{or } (2x^2-y^2)(y')^2-2xyy'+x^2=0$$

⇒ Order 1, degree 2

67. (a) $f(t)=\frac{d}{dt}\int_0^t \frac{dx}{1-\cos t\cos x}$

$$\Rightarrow f(t)=\frac{1}{1-\cos^2 t} \qquad \Rightarrow f(t)=\frac{1}{\sin^2 t}=\operatorname{cosec}^2 t$$

$$\Rightarrow \frac{df}{dt}=-2\operatorname{cosec} t(\operatorname{cosec} t\cot t)$$

$$\Rightarrow \frac{df}{dt}=-2\operatorname{cosec}^2 t+\cot t \Rightarrow \frac{df}{dt}=-2f(t)\cot t$$

$$\Rightarrow \frac{df}{dt}+2f(t).\cot t=0$$

68. (c) Length of normal to curve at any point $p(x, y)$ is given by $y\sqrt{1+\left(\frac{dy}{dx}\right)^2}$

$$\text{A.T.Q., } y^2\left(1+\left(\frac{dy}{dx}\right)^2\right)=x^2+y^2$$

$$\Rightarrow y^2\left(\frac{dy}{dx}\right)^2=x^2 \qquad \Rightarrow \left(\frac{dy}{dx}\right)=\pm\frac{x}{y}$$

$$\Rightarrow ydy=\pm xdx \qquad \Rightarrow \frac{y^2}{2}=\pm\frac{x^2}{2}+c$$

$$\Rightarrow y^2\mp x^2=2c$$

⇒ Either circles or rectangular hyperbolas

69. (c) Given differential equation is $\frac{dy}{dx}=1+y^2$

$$\Rightarrow \frac{dy}{1+y^2}=dx \qquad \Rightarrow \tan^{-1}y=x+c_1$$

Given that $h(0)=0$

$$\Rightarrow c_1=0 \qquad \Rightarrow \tan^{-1}y=x$$

$$\Rightarrow y=\tan x$$

∴ $h(x)=\tan x$, which is differential for $x \in \left(\frac{-\pi}{2},\frac{\pi}{2}\right)$

∴ Largest value of $c=\frac{\pi}{2}$

70. (c) Given differential equation is $\frac{dz}{dx}+\frac{z}{x}\log z=\frac{z}{x^2}(\log z)^2$

$$\text{or} \frac{1}{z}\frac{dz}{dx}+\frac{\log z}{x}=\frac{(\log z)^2}{(x)^2}$$

$$\frac{1}{(\log z)^2}.\frac{1}{z}\frac{dz}{dx}+\frac{1}{(\log z)}.\frac{1}{x}=\frac{1}{x^2}$$

Put $(\log z)^{-1}=u$

$$\Rightarrow \frac{-1}{(\log z)^2}.\frac{1}{z}\frac{dz}{dx}=\frac{du}{dx} \qquad \Rightarrow -\frac{du}{dx}+\frac{u}{x}=\frac{1}{x^2}$$

$$\Rightarrow \frac{du}{dx}+\left(-\frac{1}{x}\right)u=-\frac{1}{x^2}$$

Which is L.D.E of the form $\frac{du}{dx}+P(x).u=Q(x)$

∴ $u=(\log z)^{-1}$ is the required substitution.

71. (c) $\frac{dv}{dt}=-k(4\pi r^2), k>0$

$$\Rightarrow \frac{d}{dt}\left(\frac{4}{3}\pi r^3\right)=-4k\pi r^2 \qquad \Rightarrow -\pi(3r^2).\frac{dr}{dt}=-4k\pi r^2$$

$$\Rightarrow \frac{dr}{dt}=-k \Rightarrow \frac{d^2r}{dt^2}=0$$

72. **(c)** $\phi(x)=\sqrt{\{\phi(x)\}^{-2}dx};\phi(1)=0$

$\Rightarrow\phi'(x)=(\phi(x))^{-2}\Rightarrow\phi'(x)=\dfrac{1}{(\phi(x))^2}\Rightarrow y^2\dfrac{dy}{dx}=1$

$\Rightarrow y^2dy=dx\Rightarrow\dfrac{y^3}{3}=x+c_1$

As $y(1)=0$

$\Rightarrow 0=1+c_1\Rightarrow c_1=-1$

$\Rightarrow\dfrac{y^3}{3}=x-1\Rightarrow y^3=3(x-1)\Rightarrow y=[3(x-1)]^{\frac{1}{3}}$

73. **(a)** Given differential equation is

$(2x\cos y+y^2\cos x)dx+(2y\sin x-x^2\sin y)dy=0$

$\Rightarrow(\cos y)(2x)dx+x^2(-\sin y)dy+y^2\cos x dx+2y\sin x dy=0$

$\Rightarrow d(x^2\cos y)+d(y^2\sin x)=dc_1$

Where c_1= constant

$\Rightarrow x^2\cos y+y^2\sin x=c_1$

74. **(b)** Given differential equation is $\dfrac{dy}{dx}=\dfrac{x^2+x+1}{y^2+y+1}$ ...(i)

Replacing $\dfrac{dy}{dx}$ by $-\dfrac{dx}{dy}$, we get $-\dfrac{dx}{dy}=\dfrac{x^2+x+1}{y^2+y+1}$

or $\dfrac{dy}{dx}=-\dfrac{y^2+y+1}{x^2+x+1}$

$\Rightarrow\dfrac{dy}{dx}+\dfrac{y^2+y+1}{x^2+x+1}=0$ ...(ii)

$\therefore$ (i) and (ii) represent ortnogonal family of curves.

75. **(a)** Given differential equation is $\cot\left(\dfrac{x}{y}\right)\left(\dfrac{ydx-xdy}{y^2}\right)=ndx$

$\Rightarrow\ d\left(\ln\sin\left(\dfrac{x}{y}\right)\right)=ndx$

$\Rightarrow\ \ln\sin\left(\dfrac{x}{y}\right)=nx+c$

76. **(c)** Given differential equation is

$\sin\left(\dfrac{x}{y}\right)(ydx-xdy)=xy^3(xdy+ydx)$

$\Rightarrow\sin\left(\dfrac{x}{y}\right)\left(\dfrac{ydx-xdy}{y^2}\right)=xy(xdy+ydx)$

$\Rightarrow d\left(-\cos\left(\dfrac{x}{y}\right)\right)=\dfrac{1}{2}d(xy)^2$

$\Rightarrow-\cos\left(\dfrac{x}{y}\right)=\dfrac{1}{2}(xy)^2+c$

$\Rightarrow\dfrac{(xy)^2}{2}+\cos\left(\dfrac{x}{y}\right)+c=0$

77. **(c)** Given differential equation is

$\dfrac{dy}{dx}=\dfrac{y(x+y^3)}{x(y^3-x)}$

$\Rightarrow(xy^3-x^2)dy=(xy+y^4)dx$

$xy^3dy-y^4dx=xydx+x^2dy=x(ydx+xdy)$

$\dfrac{xy^3dy-y^4dx}{x}=(ydx+xdy)$

$\Rightarrow x\left(\dfrac{xy^3dy-y^4dx}{x^2}\right)=d(xy)\Rightarrow xy^3\left(\dfrac{xdy-ydx}{x^2}\right)=d(xy)$

$\Rightarrow xy^3\left(d\left(\dfrac{y}{x}\right)\right)=d(xy)$

$(x^2y^2).\left(\dfrac{y}{x}\right)d\left(\dfrac{y}{x}\right)=d(xy)$

$\Rightarrow\left(\dfrac{y}{x}\right)d\left(\dfrac{y}{x}\right)=\dfrac{1}{(xy)^2}d(xy)\Rightarrow\dfrac{1}{2}d\left(\dfrac{y}{x}\right)^2=-d\left((xy)^{-1}\right)$

$\Rightarrow\dfrac{1}{2}\left(\dfrac{y}{x}\right)^2=-\dfrac{1}{xy}+c$

As it passes through (4, –2)

$\Rightarrow\dfrac{1}{2}\left(\dfrac{-2}{4}\right)^2=\dfrac{-1}{4(-2)}+c\Rightarrow\dfrac{1}{2}\left(\dfrac{1}{4}\right)=\dfrac{1}{8}+c\Rightarrow c=0$

$\therefore\dfrac{1}{2}\left(\dfrac{y^2}{x^2}\right)=-\dfrac{1}{-xy}\Rightarrow y^2=-\dfrac{2x^2}{xy}\Rightarrow y^2=\dfrac{-2x}{y}\Rightarrow y^3=-2x$

78. **(c)** Given differential equation is

$y(xy+1)dx+x(1+xy+x^2y^2)dy=0$

$\Rightarrow xy^2dx+x^2ydy+x^3y^2dy+ydx+xdy=0$

$\Rightarrow xy(ydx+xdy)+x^3y^2dy+(ydx+xdy)=0$

$xyd(xy)+x^3y^2dy+(ydx+xdy)=0$

$\Rightarrow\dfrac{xy}{x^3y^3}d(xy)+\dfrac{x^3y^2}{x^3y^3}dy+\dfrac{1}{x^3y^3}d(xy)=0$

$\Rightarrow\dfrac{1}{(xy)^2}d(xy)+\dfrac{1}{y}dy+\dfrac{1}{(xy)^3}d(xy)=0$

$\Rightarrow(xy)^{-2}d(xy)+d(\ln y)+(xy)^{-3}.d(xy)=0$

$d\left[-(xy)^{-1}\right]+d(\ln y)+\left[-\dfrac{1}{2}d(xy)^{-2}\right]=0$

$\Rightarrow-\dfrac{1}{xy}+\ln y-\dfrac{1}{2}.\dfrac{1}{x^2y^2}=c$ or $\ln y=\dfrac{1}{xy}+\dfrac{1}{2x^2y^2}+c$

79. **(a)** Given $y=y(x)$ and $\left(\dfrac{2+\sin x}{y+1}\right)\left(\dfrac{dy}{dx}\right)=-\cos x, y(0)=1$

$\Rightarrow\dfrac{1}{(y+1)}dy=\dfrac{-\cos x}{2+\sin x}dx$

$\Rightarrow\ln(y+1)=-\ln(2+\sin x)+\ln c$

$\Rightarrow(y+1)(2+\sin x)=c$

As $y(0)=1 \Rightarrow 4=c$

$(y+1)(2+\sin x)=4$

$\therefore \left[y\left(\frac{\pi}{2}\right)+1\right][3]=4 \qquad \Rightarrow y\left(\frac{\pi}{2}\right)=\frac{4}{3}-1=\frac{1}{3}$

80. (a) Equation of tangent to curve at $Q(x, y)$ is given by $(Y-y)\frac{dy}{dx}(X-x)$

If Intersecr is y-axis at $X=0$

$\Rightarrow Y-y=-x\frac{dy}{dx}$

$\Rightarrow Y=y-x\frac{dy}{dx}$, i.e., at $P\left(0, y-x\frac{dy}{dx}\right)$

Equation of perpendicular line through P is given by $\left[Y-\left(y-x\frac{dy}{dx}\right)\right]=\left(-\frac{dx}{dy}\right)(X-0)$

It passes through (1, 0)

$\Rightarrow 0=y-x\frac{dy}{dx}-\frac{dx}{dy} \qquad \Rightarrow 0=y\frac{dy}{dx}-x\left(\frac{dy}{dx}\right)^2-1$

$\Rightarrow y\left(\frac{dy}{dx}\right)-x\left(\frac{dy}{dx}\right)^2=1$

81. (b) Given differential equation is

$$\frac{x+\frac{x^3}{3!}+\frac{x^5}{5!}+.......}{1+\frac{x^2}{2!}+\frac{x^4}{4!}.......}=\frac{dx-dy}{dx+dy}$$

$$\Rightarrow \frac{\left(x+\frac{x^3}{3!}+\frac{x^5}{5!}+.....\right)}{\left(1+\frac{x^2}{2!}+\frac{x^4}{4!}+.....\right)}=\frac{1-\frac{dy}{dx}}{1+\frac{dy}{dx}}$$

$$\Rightarrow \frac{1+\frac{x^2}{2!}+\frac{x^4}{4!}+.....}{x+\frac{x^3}{3!}+\frac{x^5}{5!}+.....}=\frac{1+\frac{dy}{dx}}{1-\frac{dy}{dx}}$$

By C and D, $\dfrac{1+x+\frac{x^2}{2!}+\frac{x^3}{3!}+\frac{x^4}{4!}+\frac{x^5}{5!}+.....}{1-x+\frac{x^2}{2!}-\frac{x^3}{3!}+\frac{x^4}{4!}-\frac{x^5}{5!}}=\dfrac{2}{2\frac{dy}{dx}}$

$$\Rightarrow \frac{dy}{dx}=\frac{1-x+\frac{x^2}{2!}-\frac{x^3}{3!}+\frac{x^4}{4!}-\frac{x^5}{5!}+.....}{1+x+\frac{x^2}{2!}+\frac{x^3}{3!}+\frac{x^4}{4!}+\frac{x^5}{5!}+.....}$$

$=\frac{e^{-x}}{e^x}=e^{-2x} \Rightarrow dy=e^{-2x}dx$

$\Rightarrow \quad y=\frac{-1}{2}e^{-2x}+C$ or $2ye^{2x}=ce^{2x}-1$

82. (c) Equation of tangent to curve at $P(x, y)$ is

$(Y-y)=\frac{dy}{dx}(X-x)$

If intersects y-axis where $X=0$

$\Rightarrow (Y-y)=\frac{dy}{dx}(0-x)$

$\Rightarrow Y=y-x\frac{dy}{dx}$, i.e., at $a\left(0, y-x\frac{dy}{dx}\right)$

$\therefore$ Mid-point of AP is $M \equiv \left(\frac{x}{2}, \frac{2y-x\frac{dy}{dx}}{2}\right)$

A.T.Q., M lies on $y=x$

$\Rightarrow x=2y-x\frac{dy}{dx} \qquad \Rightarrow x\frac{dy}{dx}+x=2y$

$\Rightarrow \frac{dy}{dx}-\frac{2}{x}y=-1$, which is a L.D.E, with I.F., $=e^{\int -\frac{2}{x}dx}$

$=e^{-2\ln x}=\frac{1}{x^2}$

$\therefore$ Solution is given by $y.\left(\frac{1}{x^2}\right)=\int(-1)\frac{1}{x^2}dx+c$

or $\frac{y}{x^2}=-\left(\frac{x^{-1}}{-1}\right)+c$

$\Rightarrow \frac{y}{x^2}=\frac{1}{x}+c \qquad \Rightarrow y=x+cx^2$

It passes through (1, 0)

$\Rightarrow 0=1+c \Rightarrow c=-1 \qquad \Rightarrow y=x-x^2$

83. (c) Given differential equation is $dx(x^2-t)=dt$

$\Rightarrow x^2-t=\frac{dt}{dx}$

$\Rightarrow \frac{dt}{dx}+t=x^2$, Which is a L.D.E. having $I.F.$

$=e^{\int 1dx}=e^x$, and its solution is given by,

$\Rightarrow \quad te^x=\int x^2e^x dx+c$

$\Rightarrow te^x=x^2e^x-\int 2xe^x dx+c$

$\Rightarrow te^x=x^2e^x-2\left[xe^x-\int e^x dx\right]+c$

$\Rightarrow te^x=x^2e^x-2xe^x+2e^x+c$ or $t=(x^2-2x+2)+ce^{-x}$

84. (a) A.T.Q. area of $\Delta ATP=5$ sq.units.

Equation of tangent to curve at $P(x, y)$ is given by

$(Y-y)=\frac{dy}{dx}(X-x)$

If intersect x-axis at $Y=0$

$\Rightarrow -y=\frac{dy}{dx}(X-x)$

$\Rightarrow X = x - y\dfrac{dy}{dx}$, i.e., at $T\left(x - y\dfrac{dx}{dy}, 0\right)$

Area of ΔAPT = 5sq.units.

$\Rightarrow \dfrac{1}{2}\left(y\dfrac{dx}{dy}\right)(y) = \pm 5$

$\Rightarrow \dfrac{dx}{dy} = \pm\dfrac{10}{y^2}$

$\Rightarrow dx = \pm 10 y^{-2dy}$

$\Rightarrow x = \pm 10\left(\dfrac{y^{-1}}{-1}\right) + c$

$\Rightarrow x = \mp\left(\dfrac{10}{y}\right) + c$

If Passes through (2, 5)

$\Rightarrow 2 = \pm\left(\dfrac{10}{5}\right) + c$

$\Rightarrow 2 = \pm 2 + c$

$\Rightarrow c = 0$ or 4

$\therefore x = \left(\dfrac{10}{y}\right) + 0$ or $x = \dfrac{-10}{y} + 4$

$\Rightarrow xy = 10$ or $xy = 4y - 10$

85. (c) Given differential equation is $y_2(x^2+1) = 2xy_1$

$\Rightarrow \dfrac{d^2y}{dx^2}(x^2+1) = 2x\dfrac{dy}{dx}$

$\Rightarrow \dfrac{dp}{dx}(x^2+1) = 2xp$

$\Rightarrow \dfrac{dp}{p} = \dfrac{2x}{x^2+1}dx$

$\Rightarrow \int\dfrac{dp}{p} = \int\dfrac{2x}{x^2+1}dx$

$\Rightarrow \ln p = \ln(x^2+1) + \ln c$

$\Rightarrow p = c(x^2+1)$

$\Rightarrow \dfrac{dy}{dx} = c(x^2+1)$

$\Rightarrow \int dy = \int c(x^2+1)dx$

$\Rightarrow y = c\left(\dfrac{x^3}{3} + x\right) + c_1$ ...(ii)

As it passes through (0,1) and $p(0) = 3$

$\Rightarrow 3 = c$ and $1 = c_1$

$\therefore$ From (*ii*), we get $y = x^3 + 3x + 1$

86. (b) Clearly centre of family of circles lie on *y*-axis, i.e., having centre at (0, *k*) and radius *r* and each member is passing through (0, 2).
Let the equation of family of circles be
$(x-0)^2 + (y-k)^2 = r^2$

As it passes through (0, 2)
$\Rightarrow 0 + (2-k)^2 = r^2$

i.e., $x^2 + (y-k)^2 = (2-k)^2$

Differentiating, we get $2x + 2(y-k).\dfrac{dy}{dx} = 0$

$\Rightarrow (y-k) = -x\dfrac{dx}{dy}$ ...(i)

$\Rightarrow x^2 + \left(x^2\left(\dfrac{dx}{dy}\right)^2\right) = \left(2 - y - x\dfrac{dx}{dy}\right)^2$

$\Rightarrow x^2 + x^2\left(\dfrac{dx}{dy}\right)^2 = (2-y)^2 + x^2\left(\dfrac{dx}{dy}\right)^2 - 2(2-y)x\dfrac{dx}{dy}$

$\Rightarrow x^2 = (2-y)^2 - 2(2-y)x\dfrac{dx}{dy}$

or $x^2 = (y-2)\left[(y-2) + 2x\dfrac{dx}{dy}\right]$

$\Rightarrow \quad x^2 + (y-2)\left[2 - 2x\dfrac{dx}{dy} - y\right] = 0$

87. (a) Given differential equation is

$$\left(\frac{xdy}{x^2+y^2}\right) = \left(\frac{y}{x^2+y^2} - 1\right)dx$$

$\Rightarrow \dfrac{xdy - ydx}{x^2+y^2} = -dx \Rightarrow \dfrac{1}{1+\left(\dfrac{y}{x}\right)^2}.\left(\dfrac{xdy - ydx}{x^2}\right) = -dx$

$\Rightarrow d\left(\tan^{-1}\left(\dfrac{y}{x}\right)\right) = -dx$

$\Rightarrow \tan^{-1}\left(\dfrac{y}{x}\right) = -x + c$ or $x + \tan^{-1}\left(\dfrac{y}{x}\right) = c$

88. (d) Clearly, $y = 1 + a_1x^2 + a_2x^4 + ... + a_nx^{2n}$.,
Where $a_i > 0 \forall i \Rightarrow y > 0 \; \forall x \in \mathbb{R}$

At $(x = 0, y = 1)$ and $(y')_0 = 0$ and $(y'')_{x=0} = 2a_1 > 0$

$\Rightarrow$ *A*(0, 1) is the point of local minima on the curve, and here line segment joining *p*(0, –3)and *A*(0, 1) is normal, and hence, shortest distance of point *P*(0,-3) from curve is

$\Rightarrow$ *PA* = 4 units

89. (a) Given differential equation is

$$x^2 = 1 + \left(\frac{x}{y}\right)^{-1}\frac{dy}{dx} + \frac{\left(\frac{x}{y}\right)^{-2}\left(\frac{dy}{dx}\right)^2}{2!} + \frac{\left(\frac{x}{y}\right)^{-3}\left(\frac{dy}{dx}\right)^3}{3!} + ...$$

$\Rightarrow x^2 = e^{\left(\frac{y}{x}.\frac{dy}{dx}\right)}$

$\Rightarrow \ln x^2 = \dfrac{y}{x}.\dfrac{dy}{dx}$

$\Rightarrow 2\ln x = \dfrac{y}{x}.\dfrac{dy}{dx}$

$\Rightarrow 2x\ln x\,dx = y\,dy$

$\Rightarrow 2\int x\ln x\,dx = \int y\,dy$

$\Rightarrow 2\left[(\ln x).\frac{x^2}{2} - \int \frac{1}{x}.\frac{x^2}{2}dx\right] = \frac{y^2}{2} + c$

$\Rightarrow 2x^2\ln x - x^2 = y^2 + 2c_1$ or $y^2 = x^2(2\ln x - 1) + c$

or $y^2 = x^2(\ln x^2 - 1) + c$

90. **(c)** Given differential equation is

$$\frac{x^2}{\left(\frac{1}{x^2} + y^2\right)}(xdy + ydx) + y^2(xdy - ydx) = 0$$

$$\Rightarrow \frac{x^4}{(1 + x^2y^2)}(xdy + ydx) + y^2(xdy - ydx) = 0$$

$$\Rightarrow \frac{1}{1 + x^2y^2}(xdy + ydx) + \frac{y^2}{x^2}\left(\frac{xdy - ydx}{x^2}\right) = 0$$

$$\Rightarrow d\left(\tan^{-1}xy\right) + \frac{1}{3}d\left(\frac{y}{x}\right)^3 = 0$$

$$\Rightarrow \tan^{-1}(xy) + \frac{1}{3}\left(\frac{y}{x}\right)^3 = c$$

91. **(a)** Given differenetial equation is $\frac{y}{x} + \frac{dy}{dx} = \frac{\sqrt{xy}}{dx}$

$$\Rightarrow ydx + xdy = x\sqrt{xy} \Rightarrow \frac{ydx + xdy}{\sqrt{xy}} = x$$

$$\Rightarrow \frac{1}{\sqrt{xy}}(ydx + xdy) = x \Rightarrow d\left(2\sqrt{xy}\right) = \frac{1}{2}d\left(x^2\right)$$

$$\Rightarrow 2\sqrt{xy} = \frac{x^2}{2} + c$$

92. **(a)** Given differential equation is

$$\frac{x^2}{a^2 + \lambda} + \frac{y^2}{b^2 + \lambda} = 1 \quad \ldots\text{(i)}$$

$\Rightarrow$ Here λ is a Parameter and a^2, b^2 are constants. Hence, (i) represent a single parameter family, hence, its differential equation will be of 1st degree.

From (i) $x^2(b^2 + \lambda) + y^2(a^2 + \lambda) = (a^2 + \lambda)(b^2 + \lambda)$

$$\Rightarrow 2x(b^2 + \lambda) + 2yy_1(a^2 + \lambda) = 0$$

$$\Rightarrow x(b^2 + \lambda) + yy_1(a^2 + \lambda) = 0$$

$$\Rightarrow \lambda(x + yy_1) = -(b^2x + a^2yy_1)$$

$$\Rightarrow \lambda = -\frac{(a^2yy_1 + b^2x)}{(x + yy_1)}$$

$$\Rightarrow a^2 + \lambda = \frac{(a^2 - b^2)x}{(x + yy_1)} \text{ and } b^2 + \lambda = \frac{(b^2 - a^2)yy_1}{(x + yy_1)}$$

$$\Rightarrow \frac{1}{a^2 + \lambda} = \frac{x + yy_1}{(a^2 - b^2)x}, \frac{1}{b^2 + \lambda} = \frac{x + yy_1}{(b^2 - a^2)yy_1}$$

$\Rightarrow$ From (i) and (ii), we get $\frac{x(x + yy_1)}{(a^2 - b^2)} + \frac{y(x + yy_1)}{-(a^2 - b^2)y_1} = 1$

$$\Rightarrow xy_1(x + yy_1) - y(x + yy_1) = (a^2 - b^2)y_1$$

$$\Rightarrow (xy_1 - y)(x + yy_1) = (a^2 - b^2)y_1$$

93. **(a)** Equation of normal to a curve $y = f(x)$ at $P(x, y)$ is

$$(Y - y) = -\frac{dx}{dy}(X - x) \quad \ldots\text{(i)}$$

Let it passes through fixed point (h, k)

$$\Rightarrow (k - y) = -\frac{dx}{dy}(h - x) \Rightarrow (k - y)dy = (x - h)dx$$

$$\Rightarrow ky - \frac{y^2}{2} = \frac{x^2}{2} - hx + c \Rightarrow \frac{x^2}{2} + \frac{y^2}{2} - hx - ky + c = 0$$

$$\Rightarrow x^2 + y^2 - 2hx - 2ky + 2c = 0$$

$$(x^2 - 2hx + h^2) + (y^2 - 2ky + k^2) = h^2 + k^2 - 2c$$

$$\Rightarrow (x - h)^2 + (y - k)^2 = h^2 + k^2 - 2c$$

which represent a circle with centre at (h, k) and radius $= \sqrt{h^2 + k^2 - 2c}$

94. **(c)** Equation of tangent at $P(x, y)$ is given by

$$(Y - y) = \frac{dy}{dx}(X - x)$$

It meets x-axis, where $Y = 0$

$$\Rightarrow -y = \frac{dy}{dx}(X - x)$$

$\Rightarrow x - y\frac{dx}{dy} = X$, i.e., at $T(X, 0) \equiv \left(x - y\frac{dx}{dy}, 0\right)$

$$\therefore PT = OP \Rightarrow (PT)^2 = (OP)^2$$

$$\Rightarrow \left(-y\frac{dx}{dy}\right)^2 + (-y)^2 = x^2 + y^2$$

$\Rightarrow y^2\left(\frac{dx}{dy}\right)^2 = x^2 \qquad \Rightarrow \frac{dx}{dy} = \pm\frac{x}{y}$

$\Rightarrow \frac{dx}{x} = \pm\frac{dy}{y} \qquad \Rightarrow \ln x = \pm\ln y + \ln c$

$$\Rightarrow x = cy \text{ or } x = \frac{c}{y}$$

95. **(b)** Given differential equation is $\frac{dy}{dx} = \frac{1 - x}{y}$

$$\Rightarrow ydy = (1 - x)dx$$

$$\Rightarrow \frac{y^2}{2} = x - \frac{x^2}{2} + c$$

$$\Rightarrow \frac{x^2}{2} + \frac{y^2}{2} - x = c$$

$$\Rightarrow x^2 + y^2 - 2x = 2c$$

$$\Rightarrow x^2 - 2x + 1 + y^2 = 2c + 1$$

$$\Rightarrow (x - 1)^2 + y^2 = (2c + 1)$$

Which represent a family of circles with centre at (1,0) and radius $= \sqrt{|2c + 1|}$

SECTION–IV: (MORE THAN ONE CORRECT)

1. (a), (b), (c), (d)
Singular solution is the envelope of general solution and has no parameter, i.e., it can not be derived from general solution, hence, all the given options are correct

2. (a), (c) Given family of curve is $xy = k^2$

$$\Rightarrow x\frac{dy}{dx} + y = 0$$

Replacing $\frac{dy}{dx}$ by $-\frac{dx}{dy}$, we get $x\left(\frac{-dx}{dy}\right) + y = 0$

$$\Rightarrow x\frac{dx}{dy} = y \Rightarrow xdx = ydy \Rightarrow \frac{x^2}{2} = \frac{y^2}{2} + c \Rightarrow x^2 = y^2 + 2c$$

or $x^2 - y^2 = a^2$, where $2c = a^2$.
Which is the required equation of orthogonal trajectory and is a rectangular hyperbola.

3. (a), (c) $y = x\frac{dy}{dx} + x\left(\frac{dy}{dx}\right)^3 \Rightarrow y = px + p^3x$

Differentiating both sided w.r.t x, we get

$$\frac{dy}{dx} = p + x\frac{dp}{dx} + p^3 + x.3p^2\frac{dp}{dx}$$

$$\Rightarrow 0 = x\frac{dp}{dx} + p^3 + 3p^2x\frac{dp}{dx}$$

$$\Rightarrow \frac{dp}{dx}(1+3p^2)x = -p^3$$

$$\Rightarrow \frac{(1+3p^2)}{p^3}dp = \frac{-dx}{x} \quad \int\frac{1+3p^2}{p^3}dp = \int\frac{dx}{x}$$

$$\Rightarrow \int p^{-3}dp + \int\frac{3p^2}{p^3}dp = \int\frac{dx}{x}$$

$$\Rightarrow \frac{p^{-2}}{-2} + \ln|p^3| = \ln|x| + \ln|c_1|$$

$$\Rightarrow -\frac{1}{2p^2} = \ln\left|\frac{c_1x}{p^3}\right|$$

$$\Rightarrow e^{-\frac{1}{2p^2}} = \left|\frac{c_1x}{p^3}\right| \qquad \Rightarrow \frac{c_1x}{p^3} = \pm e^{-\frac{1}{2p^2}}$$

$$\Rightarrow c_1x = \pm p^3e^{-\frac{1}{2p^2}} \qquad \Rightarrow x = cp^3e^{-\frac{1}{2p^2}}$$

Also, $y = x(p+p^3)$

$$\Rightarrow x = \frac{y}{p+p^3}$$

From (i), we get $y = cp^3e^{-\frac{1}{2p^2}}(p+p^3)$

or $y = p^3e^{-\frac{1}{2p^2}}(p+p^3)$ for $c = 1$

Also $y = 0$ also satisfies the given equation

4. (a), (b) $y = y\frac{dy}{dx}$

$$\Rightarrow \frac{dy}{dx} = 1 \qquad \text{...(i)}$$

$$\Rightarrow y = x + c$$

Clearly (i) is linear equation and is a homogeneous equation

5. (c), (d) Equation tangent to curve at $p(x, y)$ is

$$(Y - y) = \frac{dy}{dx}(X - x)$$

$$\Rightarrow A \equiv \left(\left(-y/\frac{dy}{dx}\right) + x, 0\right) \text{ and } B \equiv \left(0, y - x\frac{dy}{dx}\right)$$

A.T.Q. $x = \dfrac{3\left[\frac{-ydx}{dy} + x\right] + 1(0)}{4}$ and

$$y = \frac{3(0) + 1\left(y - x\frac{dy}{dx}\right)}{4}$$

$$x = \frac{-3}{4}y\frac{dx}{dy} \text{ and } \frac{3x}{4} \text{ and } y = \frac{y}{4} - \frac{x}{4}\frac{dy}{dx}$$

$$\Rightarrow \frac{x}{4} = \frac{-3}{4}y\frac{dx}{dy} \text{ and } \frac{3}{4}y = \frac{-x}{4}\frac{dy}{dx}$$

$$\Rightarrow x = -3y\frac{dx}{dy} \Rightarrow x\frac{dy}{dx} + 3y = 0$$

$$\Rightarrow \frac{dx}{x} = -\frac{dy}{3y} \Rightarrow \ln|x| + \frac{1}{3}\ln|y| = \ln|c|$$

$$\Rightarrow \ln\left|xy^{\frac{1}{3}}\right| = \ln|c_1| \qquad \Rightarrow xy^{\frac{1}{3}} = c$$

Given, $f(1) = 1 \Rightarrow c = 1$

$$\Rightarrow xy^{\frac{1}{3}} = 1$$

Clearly, curve passes through $\left(2, \frac{1}{8}\right)$.

Equation of normal at (1, 1) is given by

$$(y-1) = -\frac{1}{\left(\frac{dy}{dx}\right)_{(1,1)}}(x-1)$$

$$\Rightarrow (y-1) = \frac{-1}{(-3x^{-4})_{(1,1)}}(x-1)$$

$$\Rightarrow y - 1 = \frac{1}{3}(x-1) \qquad \Rightarrow 3y - 3 = x - 1$$

$$\Rightarrow x - 3y = -2$$

6. (a), (b), (c), (d),

Given differential equation is $x\frac{dy}{dx} + y = xy^3$

or $\frac{dy}{dx} + \frac{1}{x}y = y^3$ or $y^{-3}\frac{dy}{dx} + \frac{1}{x}y^{-2} = 1$ ...(i)

Put $y^{-2} = u$

$$\Rightarrow -2y^{-3}\frac{dy}{dx} = \frac{du}{dx} \qquad \Rightarrow y^{-3}\frac{dy}{dx} = -\frac{1}{2}\frac{du}{dx} \qquad \text{...(ii)}$$

$$\Rightarrow \frac{-1}{2}\frac{du}{dx} + \frac{1}{x}u = 1 \qquad \Rightarrow \frac{du}{dx} + \left(\frac{-2}{x}\right)u = -2$$

Also equation (ii) can be written as $\frac{1}{y^3}\frac{dy}{dx}+\frac{1}{xy^2}=1$
or $x^3dy + x^2ydx = x^2y^3dx$

$\Rightarrow x^2(xdy+ydx)=x^3y^3dx$

$\Rightarrow x^2d(xy)=x^3y^2dx$

$\Rightarrow \frac{1}{x^3y^3}d(xy)=\frac{dx}{x^2}$ $\quad \Rightarrow \int\frac{d(xy)}{(xy)^3}=\int\frac{dx}{x^2}$

$\Rightarrow \frac{(xy)^{-2}}{-2}=\frac{x^{-1}}{-1}+c_1$ $\quad \frac{-1}{2x^2y^2}=\frac{-1}{x}+C_1$

7. (a),(b) Volume of spherical rain drop $=V=\frac{4}{3}\pi r^3$

$\Rightarrow \frac{dV}{dt}=-k(4\pi r^2);k>0 \Rightarrow \frac{d}{dt}\left(\frac{4}{3}\pi r^3\right)=-4k\pi r^2$

$\Rightarrow \frac{4}{3}\pi(3r^2)\frac{dr}{dt}=-4k\pi r^2 \quad \Rightarrow \frac{dr}{dt}=-k$

$\Rightarrow r=-kt+C_1$ ...(i) when, $t=0, r=3$

$\Rightarrow 3=c_1$ $\quad \Rightarrow r=-kt+3$

At $t=1hr., r=2$ $\quad \Rightarrow 2=-k+3\Rightarrow k=+1$

$\Rightarrow r=3-t$ $\quad \therefore r(t)=3-t$

8. (a),(c) $\frac{dy_1}{dx}+P(x)y_1=Q(x)$ ...(i)

and $\frac{dy_2}{dx}+P(x)y_2=Q(x)$ ...(ii)

$\Rightarrow$ y_1-y_2 is a solution of $\frac{dy}{dx}+P(x)y=0(c.f.)$

$\Rightarrow$ $y=y_1+c(y_1-y_2)$ is the general solution of equation

Now if $\alpha y_1+\beta y_2$ is a solution,

$\frac{d}{dx}(\alpha y_1+\beta y_2)+P(x)(\alpha y_1+\beta y_2)=Q(x)$

$\Rightarrow \alpha\left(\frac{dy_1}{dx}+P(x)y_1\right)+\beta\left(\frac{dy_2}{dx}+P(x)y_2\right)=Q(x)$

$\Rightarrow \alpha Q(x)+\beta Q(x)=Q(x)$

$\Rightarrow \alpha+\beta=1$

(General sol. = *P.S.* + *k*(*C.F.*))

9. (b), (c), (d)

$V=\pi R^2h$

$\frac{dV}{dt}=-k(\pi R^2);k>0$

$\Rightarrow \frac{d}{dt}(\pi R^2h)=-k\pi R^2$ $\quad \Rightarrow \pi R^2\frac{dh}{dt}=-k\pi R^2$

$\Rightarrow \frac{dh}{dt}=-k$ $\quad \Rightarrow dh=-kdt$

$h=-kt+c$

When $t=0, h=H$

$\Rightarrow H=C$ $\quad \Rightarrow h=-kt+H$

when, $h=0, t=\frac{H}{K}$ $\quad \Rightarrow T=\frac{H}{K}$

$\Rightarrow$ *T* is independent of *R*, only depends on *H* and *K*.

10. (a),(c) Normal to curve at *P*(1,1)is $(y-1)=\left(\frac{-dx}{dy}\right)(x-1)$

$\Rightarrow a=\left(\frac{dy}{dx}\right)_{(1,1)}$

$\frac{dy}{dx}=ky$; constant of Proportionality

$\Rightarrow \frac{dy}{y}=kdx \Rightarrow \ln|y|=kx+c$ at, (1,1),

$0=k+c\Rightarrow c=-k$

$\therefore \ln|y|=kx-k$

now, $\frac{1}{y}y'=k\Rightarrow y'=ky$

$\therefore$ at (1,1), $a=k(1)\Rightarrow k=a$

$\therefore \ln|y|=(ax-a)$

$\Rightarrow |y|=e^{a(x-1)}$ $\quad \Rightarrow y=\pm e^{a(x-1)}$

Normal intersects *y*-axis at $x=0\Rightarrow y=\frac{1}{a}+1$

i.e., *at* $\left(0,\frac{1+a}{a}\right)$

$\therefore$ Area bounded $=\left|\int_0^1\left[e^{a(x-1)}-\left[\left(\frac{1-x}{a}\right)+1\right]\right]dx\right|$

$=\left|\frac{e^{a(x-1)}}{a}-\frac{1}{a}x+\frac{1}{a}.\frac{x^2}{2}-x\right|_0^1$

$=\left|\frac{1}{a}(1-e^{-a})-\frac{1}{a}(a)+\frac{1}{2a}-1\right|$

$=\left|-1+\frac{1}{2a}-\frac{e^{-a}}{a}\right|=\left|\frac{1}{a}\left(a-\frac{1}{2}+e^{-a}\right)\right|$ sq. unit.

11. (c),(d) $S_1\equiv x^2+y^2-kx=0$ ...(i)

$S_2\equiv x^2-y^2-cx=0$ ...(ii)

$2x+2yy'-k=0$ ...(iii)

and $2x-2yy'-c=0$ ...(iv)

$\therefore$ From (iii), $y'=\frac{k-2x}{2y}=m_1$ (say)

and from (iv), $y'=\frac{2x-c}{2y}=m_2$ (say)

At the point of intersection, $\tan\theta=\left|\frac{m_1-m_2}{1+m_1m_2}\right|$

$=\left|\frac{\left(\frac{k-2x}{2y}\right)-\left(\frac{2x-c}{2y}\right)}{1+\left(\frac{k-2x}{2y}\right)\left(\frac{2x-c}{2y}\right)}\right|$ ...(iv)

At the point of intersection, $2x^2-(k+c)x=0$

$\Rightarrow x=0\ or\ 2x=k+c$

$\Rightarrow x=0;\ x=\dfrac{k+c}{2}$

$\Rightarrow (0,0)$ and $\left(\dfrac{k+c}{2},\pm\dfrac{\sqrt{k^2-c^2}}{2}\right)$

SECTION–V: (ASSERTION AND REASON)

1. **(d)** Degree of differential equation $\dfrac{d^2y}{dx^2}+\dfrac{dy}{dx}=\ln\left(\dfrac{d^2y}{dx^2}\right)$ is not defined as the differential equation can not be expressed as a
polynomial in derivatives. Reason is correct

2. **(d)** Given differential equation is $y\phi(xy)dx+x\psi(xy)dy=0$

$\Rightarrow \dfrac{dy}{dx}=\dfrac{-y\phi(xy)}{x\psi(xy)}$

Put $xy=v$

$\Rightarrow y=\dfrac{v}{x}$ and $x\dfrac{dy}{dx}+y=\dfrac{dv}{dx}$

$\Rightarrow \dfrac{dy}{dx}=\dfrac{1}{x}\dfrac{dv}{dx}-\dfrac{y}{x}$ $\qquad \Rightarrow \dfrac{1}{x}\dfrac{dv}{dx}-\dfrac{y}{x}=\dfrac{-v}{x^2}\dfrac{\phi(v)}{\psi(v)}$

$\Rightarrow \dfrac{dv}{dx}=y-\dfrac{v}{x}\dfrac{\phi(v)}{\psi(v)}$

$\Rightarrow \dfrac{dv}{dx}=\dfrac{xy\psi(v)-v\phi(v)}{x\psi(v)}$, which is not homogeneous, rather variable equation of first order and first degree.

Put $y=vx$

$\Rightarrow \dfrac{-dy}{dx}=v+x\dfrac{dv}{dx}$ ...(ii)

From (i), (ii), we get $v+x\dfrac{dv}{dx}+f_1(x).vx=f_2(x)$

$\Rightarrow \dfrac{dv}{dx}=\dfrac{f_2(x)-f_1(x)vx-v}{x}$, which is not homogenous,

Thus, assertion is false but reason is correct

3. **(a)** Given differential equation is $(1+y^2)dx-xydy=0$

$\Rightarrow (1+y^2)dx=xydy$ $\qquad \Rightarrow \dfrac{(dx)}{x}=\dfrac{ydy}{1+y^2}$

$\Rightarrow \ln|x|=\dfrac{1}{2}\ln|1+y^2|+\ln c_1$

$\Rightarrow |x|=c_1\sqrt{1+y^2}$ $\qquad \Rightarrow x^2=c_1^2(1+y^2)$

It passes through (1, 0)

$\Rightarrow 1=c_1^2 \Rightarrow x^2=(1+y^2)\Rightarrow x^2-y^2=1$

Hence, assertion is correct, obviously the reason is correct. Also reason correctly explains the assertion.

4. **(b)** Equation of family of circles on given plane is given by $(x-h)^2+(y-k)^2=r^2$ which has 3 parameters h,k,r, hence, the differential equation of family of circles on a given plane must be of order 3.
Clearly, reason is correct, but does not explain the assertion correctly.

5. **(c)** Given differential equation is $ydy+(x+y^2)dx=0$,

Put $y^2=t\Rightarrow 2y\dfrac{dy}{dx}=\dfrac{dt}{dx}$

$\Rightarrow \dfrac{1}{2}\dfrac{dt}{dx}=-(x+t)$ or $\dfrac{dt}{dx}=-x\left(1+\dfrac{t}{x}\right)$, which is a homogeneous equation of degree 1.

$\Rightarrow$ Assertion is correct, obviously reason is incorrect

SECTION–VI: (COMPREHENSION TYPE)

Passage A:

1. **(a)** $xdy-ydx=\sqrt{x^2-y^2dx}$

$\Rightarrow \dfrac{xdy-ydx}{x^2}=\dfrac{\sqrt{x^2-y^2}}{x^2}dx=x\dfrac{\sqrt{1-\left(\dfrac{y}{x}\right)^2}dx}{x^2}$

$\Rightarrow \dfrac{xdy-ydx}{x^2}.\dfrac{1}{\sqrt{1-\left(\dfrac{y}{x}\right)^2}}=\dfrac{dx}{x}$

$\Rightarrow d\left(\sin^{-1}\left(\dfrac{y}{x}\right)\right)=d(\ln x)$

$\Rightarrow \int d\left(\sin^{-1}\left(\dfrac{y}{x}\right)\right)=\int d(\ln x)$

$\Rightarrow \sin^{-1}\left(\dfrac{y}{x}\right)=\ln x+\ln c$

$\Rightarrow \sin^{-1}\left(\dfrac{y}{x}\right)=\ln cx$ $\qquad \Rightarrow cx=e^{\sin^{-1}\left(\frac{y}{x}\right)}$

2. **(b)** $(xy^4+y)dx-xdy=0$

$\Rightarrow xy^4dx=xdy-ydx \Rightarrow \dfrac{xy^4}{x^2}dx=\dfrac{xdy-ydx}{x^2}$

$dx=\dfrac{x}{y^4}.\left(\dfrac{xdy-ydx}{x^2}\right)=-\dfrac{1}{xy^2}\left(\dfrac{ydx-xdy}{y^2}\right)$

$=-\dfrac{1}{x^3}.\dfrac{x^2}{y^2}\left(\dfrac{ydx-xdy}{y^2}\right)$

$\Rightarrow x^3dx=-\left(\dfrac{x}{y}\right)^2d\left(\dfrac{x}{y}\right)$ $\qquad \Rightarrow -3x^3dx=3\left(\dfrac{x}{y}\right)^2d\left(\dfrac{x}{y}\right)$

$\Rightarrow -\int 3x^3dx=\int d\left(\dfrac{x}{y}\right)^3$ $\qquad \Rightarrow -\dfrac{3x^4}{4}+C_1=\left(\dfrac{x}{y}\right)^3$

$\Rightarrow \dfrac{x^4}{4}+\dfrac{1}{3}\left(\dfrac{x}{y}\right)^3=\dfrac{C_1}{3}$ or $\dfrac{x^4}{4}+\dfrac{1}{3}\left(\dfrac{x}{y}\right)^3=C$

3. (a) $\left(2x\cos y + y^2\cos x\right)dx + \left(2y\sin x - x^2\sin y\right)dy = 0$

$\Rightarrow \left(2x\cos y dx - x^2\sin y dy\right) + \left(y^2\cos x dx + 2y\sin x dy\right) = 0$

$\Rightarrow d\left(x^2\cos y\right) + d\left(y^2\sin x\right) = 0$

$\Rightarrow \int d\left(x^2\cos y\right) + \int d\left(y^2\sin x\right) = 0$

$\Rightarrow x^2\cos y + y^2\sin x = C$

Passage-B

4. (a) Equation of tangent at P(x, y) is $(Y - y) = \frac{dy}{dx}(X - x)$ on $x - axis, Y = 0$

$\Rightarrow -y = \frac{dy}{dx}(X - x)$

$\Rightarrow |X| = \left|x - y\frac{dx}{dy}\right| = x -$ intercept of tangent $= |y| (A.T.Q)$

$\Rightarrow \; x - y\frac{dx}{dy} = \pm y \qquad \Rightarrow -y\frac{dx}{dy} = \pm y - x$

$\Rightarrow \frac{dx}{dy} = \frac{x \mp y}{y}$

Put, $x = vy \Rightarrow \frac{dx}{dy} = v + y\frac{dv}{dy}$

$\Rightarrow v + y\frac{dv}{dy} = \frac{vy \mp y}{y} \qquad \Rightarrow v + y\frac{dv}{dy} = v \mp 1$

$\Rightarrow y\frac{dv}{dy} = \pm 1 \qquad \Rightarrow dv = \pm\frac{dy}{y} \Rightarrow v = \pm\ln y + \ln C_1$

$\Rightarrow v = \ln C_1 \pm \ln y \qquad \Rightarrow v = \ln\left(C_1 y\right)$ or $\ln\left(\frac{C_1}{y}\right)$

$\Rightarrow C_1 y = e^v$ or $\frac{C_1}{y} = e^v \Rightarrow C_1 = \frac{1}{y}e^{x/y}$ or $C_1 = ye^{x/y}$

5. (d) Length of subnormal at a point $P(x, y)$ on the curve $y = f(x)$ is given by $\left|y\frac{dy}{dx}\right| = x$

$\Rightarrow y\frac{dy}{dx} = \pm x \qquad \Rightarrow ydy = \pm xdx$

$\Rightarrow \frac{y^2}{2} = \frac{\pm x^2}{2} + C_1 \qquad \Rightarrow \frac{\pm x^2}{2} - \frac{y^2}{2} = -C_1$

$\Rightarrow \frac{x^2}{2} - \frac{y^2}{2} = -C_1$ or $\frac{x^2}{2} + \frac{y^2}{2} = C_1$

$x^2 - y^2 = C$ or $x^2 + y^2 = C$

6. (b) A.T.Q., $\frac{dy}{dx} = \frac{1}{2y}$

$\Rightarrow \int 2ydy = \int dx \qquad \Rightarrow y^2 = x + c$

As it passes through (4, 3)

$\Rightarrow 9 = 4 + c \Rightarrow c = 5$

$\therefore$ The equation of curve is $y^2 = x + 5$

7. (c) A.T.Q., $y.\left(\frac{dy}{dx}\right) = x$

$\Rightarrow ydy = xdx \qquad \Rightarrow \frac{y^2}{2} = \frac{x^2}{2} + c$

$\Rightarrow$ As it passes through (5, 3)

$\Rightarrow \frac{9}{2} = \frac{25}{2} + c \Rightarrow c = -8 \quad \Rightarrow x^2 - y^2 = 16$

8. (a) $\frac{dy}{dx} = \frac{x^2 + y^2}{2xy}$ ...(i)

Put $y = vx \Rightarrow \frac{dy}{dx} = v + x\frac{dv}{dx}$

$\Rightarrow v + x\frac{dv}{dx} = \frac{x^2 + v^2x^2}{2vx^2} = \frac{1 + v^2}{2v} \Rightarrow x\frac{dv}{dx} = \frac{1 + v^2 - 2v^2}{2v}$

$\Rightarrow x\frac{dv}{dx} = \frac{1 - v^2}{2v} \Rightarrow \frac{2v}{1 - v^2}dv = \frac{dx}{x}$

$\Rightarrow -\ln\left|1 - v^2\right| = \ln|x| + \ln|C_1| \quad \Rightarrow \ln\left|C_1 x\left(1 - v^2\right)\right| = 0$

$C_1 x\left(1 - \frac{y^2}{x^2}\right) = \pm 1$

$\therefore$ It Passes through (1, 0) $\Rightarrow C_1(1 - 0) = \pm 1 \Rightarrow C_1 = \pm 1$

$\Rightarrow$ Equation of the curve will be $\pm x\left(1 - \frac{y^2}{x^2}\right) = 1$

$\Rightarrow x^2 - y^2 = \pm x$

Passage C:

9. (b) Given differential equation is

$\left(2x^3 - xy^2\right)dx + \left(2y^3 - x^2y\right)dy = 0$

$\Rightarrow 4x^3dx - y^2(2x)dx + 4y^3dy - x^2(2y)dy = 0$

$\Rightarrow d\left(x^4\right) - y^2 d\left(x^2\right) + d\left(y^4\right) - x^2 d\left(y^2\right) = 0$

$\Rightarrow d\left(x^4 + y^4 - \left(x^2y^2\right)\right) = 0$

$\Rightarrow x^4 + y^4 - x^2y^2 = C$

10. (a) Given differential equation is

$\frac{xdy}{x^2 + y^2} + \left(1 - \frac{y}{x^2 + y^2}\right)dx = 0$

$\Rightarrow \; \frac{xdy - ydx}{x^2 + y^2} + dx = 0$

$\Rightarrow \; \frac{xdy - ydx}{x^2}.\frac{1}{\left(1 + \frac{y^2}{x^2}\right)} + dx = 0$

$\Rightarrow d\left(\tan^{-1}\left(\frac{y}{x}\right)\right) + dx = 0$

$\Rightarrow d\left(\tan^{-1}\left(\frac{y}{x}\right) + x\right) = 0 \quad \Rightarrow \tan^{-1}\left(\frac{y}{x}\right) + x = c$

11. (a) Given differential equation is $e^y dx + \left(xe^y - 2y\right)dy = 0$

$d\left(xe^y\right) - d\left(y^2\right) = 0$

$\Rightarrow d\left(xe^y - y^2\right) = 0 \qquad \Rightarrow xe^y - y^2 = c$

Passage – D

12. (b) Given differential equation is $\frac{d^2y}{dx^2} - y = 0$ ...(i)

Corresponding quadratic equation is
$m^2 - 1 = 0 \Rightarrow m = \pm 1$

$\Rightarrow y = c_1e^x + c_2e^{-x}$ will be a solution for arbitrary constants C_1, C_2

$\therefore$ For $C_1 = 0, C_2 = 1 \Rightarrow y = e^{-x}$ is solution

For $C_1 = a$, $C_2 = b \Rightarrow y = ae^x + be^{-x}$ is a Solution and for $C_1 = 1$, $C_2 = 1$, $y = e^x + e^{-x}$ will be a Solution

Solution given in option (b) is incorrect

13. (b) Given differential equation is $m^2 - 6m + 9 = 0$

$\Rightarrow (m-3)^2 = 0$ having 2 roots, $m = 3, 3$

Solution is given by $y = (C_1 + C_2x)e^{3x}$

Passage: E

14. (a) $\frac{dp}{dt} = 0.03P \quad \Rightarrow \frac{dp}{p} = 0.03dt$

$\Rightarrow \ln P = 0.03t + C' \Rightarrow P = e^{c'}.e^{0.03t}$

$\Rightarrow P = e^{0.03t}(C_1)$

At $t = 0$, let $P = P_0$

$\Rightarrow P_0 = C_1 \Rightarrow C_1 = P_0$

$\therefore P = P_0e^{0.03t}$ ...(i)

$\Rightarrow$ Population groups exponentially

15. (c) Let the food requirement for instant population P_0 be F_0

$\therefore$ Food requirement for per person $= \frac{F_0}{P_0}$.

(Initial) Present ford production $= \frac{90}{100} \times F_0 = \frac{9}{10}(F_0)$

Food production after n-years $= F(n) = \frac{9}{10}(F_0)\left(1 + \frac{4}{100}\right)^n$

$\therefore F(2) = \frac{9}{10}F_0(1.04)^2$

$= (1.04)^2$ times the initial food production

16. (b) $P(t) = P_0e^{0.03t}$

$P(100) = P_0e^{0.03(100)}.e^3.P_0$

$= e^3$ times the initial population.

17. (a) Given that the country be comes self sufficient in food after n-year.

$\Rightarrow F(n) \geq \frac{F_0}{P_0}(P(n))$

$\Rightarrow \frac{9}{10}(F_0)(1.04)^n \geq \frac{F_0}{P_0}.P_0.e^{0.03n}$

$\Rightarrow \frac{9}{10}(1.04)^n \geq e^{0.03n} \qquad \Rightarrow \frac{9}{10} \geq \left(\frac{e^{0.03}}{1.04}\right)^n$

$\Rightarrow \left(\frac{e^{0.03}}{1.04}\right)^n \leq \frac{9}{10}$ ...(i)

$\Rightarrow \frac{e^{0.03}}{1.04} < 1$ as otherwise (i) is impossible

$\Rightarrow n\ln\left(\frac{e^{0.03}}{1.04}\right) \geq \ln\left(\frac{9}{10}\right)$

$\Rightarrow n \geq \frac{\ln 9 - \ln 10}{0.03 - \ln 1.04} \qquad \Rightarrow n \geq \frac{\ln 10 - \ln 9}{\ln 1.04 - 0.03}$

18. (b) $P(n) = p_0\left(1 + \frac{3}{100}\right)^n$

$\therefore$ For self sufficient in food after n-year

$\Rightarrow P(n).\frac{F_0}{P_0} \geq F(n)$

$\Rightarrow P_0\left(1 + \frac{3}{100}\right)^n.\frac{F_0}{P_0} \geq \frac{9}{10}F_0(1.04)^n$

$\Rightarrow (1.03)^n \geq \frac{9}{10}(1.04)^n \qquad \Rightarrow \left(\frac{1.03}{1.04}\right)^n \geq \frac{9}{10}$

$\Rightarrow n\ln\left(\frac{1.03}{1.04}\right) \geq \ln\left(\frac{9}{10}\right) \quad \left(\because 0 < \frac{1.03}{1.04} < 1\right)$

$\Rightarrow n \leq \frac{\ln 9 - \ln 10}{\ln(1.03) - \ln(1.04)}$

$\Rightarrow n = (m); m = \frac{\ln 9 - \ln 10}{\ln(1.03) - \ln(1.04)} = \frac{\ln 10 - \ln 9}{\ln 1.04 - \ln 1.03}$

$= \ln\left(\frac{10/9}{1.04/1.03}\right)$

Passage – G

$B(t) = 2t^2 - t + 1,$
$D(t) = -t^2 + 3t + 4,$

Population at time t is given by $P(t) = \int_0^t (B(t) - D(t))dt + P_0$

$= \int_0^t (3t^2 - 4t - 3)dt + P_0 = \left[t^3 - 2t^2 - 3t\right]_0^t + P_0$

$= t^3 - 2t^2 - 3t + P_0 = t^3 - 2t^2 - 3t + 100 = A(t) + B(t) + C(t)$

19. (d) Solution maximum of

$B(t) = -t^2 + 2t + 40 = -\left[\frac{4 - 4(-1)(40)}{4(-1)}\right] = -\left[\frac{164}{-4}\right] = 41$

at $t = \frac{-2}{2(-1)} = 1$

$\therefore$ Total population at $t = 1$

$= (1)^3 - 2(1)^2 - 3(1) + 100 = 96$

20. **(d)** $P(t)=t^3-2t^2-3t+100$

$P'(t)=3t^2-4t-3=0$

$t=\frac{4\pm\sqrt{16-4(3)(-3)}}{2(3)}$

$\Rightarrow t=\frac{4\pm\sqrt{16+36}}{6}\qquad \Rightarrow t=\frac{4\pm\sqrt{52}}{6}$

$\Rightarrow t=\frac{2\pm\sqrt{13}}{3}\Rightarrow t=\frac{2+\sqrt{13}}{3}$

$p''(t)=6t-4$

$\Rightarrow\ 4+2\sqrt{13}-4=2\sqrt{13}>0$

$\Rightarrow$ $P(t)$ will be minimum at $t=\frac{2+\sqrt{13}}{3}$

It this time population of Larva = $A(t)=t^3-9t+10$

$=t(t^2-9)+10=\frac{1}{3}t(3t^2-27)+10$

$=\frac{t}{3}(4t+3-27)+10=\frac{t}{3}(4t-24)+10$

$=\left(\frac{2+\sqrt{13}}{3}\right)\left(\frac{8+4\sqrt{13}}{3}-24\right)+10$

$=\left(\frac{2+\sqrt{13}}{9}\right)\left(\frac{4\sqrt{13}-64}{3}\right)+10$

$=\frac{4}{27}(2+\sqrt{13})(\sqrt{13}-16)+10$

$=\frac{4}{27}(2\sqrt{13}-32+13-16\sqrt{13})+10$

$=\frac{4}{27}(-19-14\sqrt{13})+10=\frac{270-76-56\sqrt{13}}{27}$

$=\frac{194-56(3.6)}{27}=\frac{194-201.6}{27}<0$

$\Rightarrow$ Larwa will disappear.

21. **(b)** When the population of group of young's started disappearing , $-t^2+2t+40\le 0$

$\Rightarrow t^2-2t-40\ge 0\qquad \Rightarrow t^2-2t+1\ge 41$

$\Rightarrow (t-1)^2\ge 41\qquad \Rightarrow t-1\le -\sqrt{41}$ or $\ge\sqrt{41}$

$\Rightarrow t\le 1-\sqrt{41}$ or $t\ge 1+\sqrt{41}$

When t=1 + $\sqrt{41}$, the young's start disappearing,

at that time group of old = $C(1+\sqrt{41})$

$=(-t^2+4t+50)=(-t^2+2t)+2t+50=(-40)+2t+50$

$=2t+10=2(1+\sqrt{41})+10=2\sqrt{41}+12$

$=2(6.4)+12=12.8+12=24.8$, i.e., 25

22. $A(t)=t^3-9t+10$, $A(2)=0$

$A'(t)=3t^2-9=3(t^2-3)$

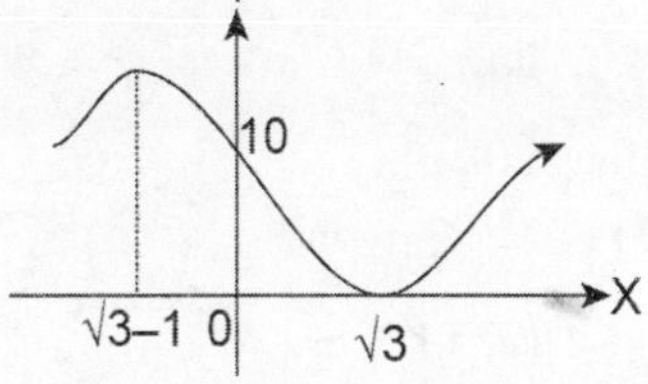

$A''(t)=6t>0$ for $t>0$ and <0 for $t<0$

and $A'(t)>0$ for $t<-\sqrt{3}$ or $t>\sqrt{3}$

and $A'(t)<0$ for $t\in-(-\sqrt{3},\sqrt{3})$

Clearly at $t=2$, $A(t)=0$ and for $t\ge 2, A(t)\ge 0$

and $A(t)$ increases $\forall t[2,\infty]$

$\Rightarrow$ Larva will again population after 2 Years.

23. **(d)** Groups of old starts disappearing $\Rightarrow C(t)\le 0$

$\Rightarrow -t^2+4t+50\le 0$

$\Rightarrow t^2-4t-50\ge 0$

Corresponding roots are $t=\frac{4\pm\sqrt{16+200}}{2}$

$t=2\pm 3\sqrt{2}\Rightarrow t\ge 2+3\sqrt{2}$

$\therefore$ When olds starts disappearing $t=2+3\sqrt{2}$, At that instant, % age of Larva in total population

$=\frac{\text{Population Larva}}{\text{Total population}}\times 100=\frac{A(t)}{t^3-2t^2-3t+100}\times 100$

$=\frac{t^3-9t+10}{t^3-2t^2-3t+100}\times 100$

$=\frac{(t^3-9t+10)}{(t^3-9t+10)+(-2t^2+6t+90)}\times 100$

$=\frac{(t^3-9t+10)\times 100}{(t^3-9t+10)-2(t^2-4t-50)-2t-10}$

$=\frac{(t^3-9t+10)}{(t^3-9t+10)-2(t+5)}\times 100\ \left[\because \text{At } t=2+3\sqrt{2},\ t^2-4t-50=0\right]$

$=\frac{x}{y}\times 100$

Clearly $x>y>0\Rightarrow\frac{x}{y}>1$

$\Rightarrow$ %age of larva will be 100%

SECTION–VII: (MATRIX MATCH TYPE)

1. **(i)→(c), (ii)→(d), (iii)→(b), (iv)→(a)**

(i) $(e^x+1)y\,dy=(y+1)e^x dx$

$\frac{y}{y+1}dy=\frac{e^x}{e^x+1}dx$

$\Rightarrow\left(1-\frac{1}{y+1}\right)dy=\left(\frac{e^x}{e^x+1}\right)dx$

$\Rightarrow y-\ln(y+1)=\ln(e^x+1)+C$

$\Rightarrow y=\ln(e^x+1)(y+1)+C$

It Passes through (0, 0)

$\Rightarrow 0=\ln(2)+C\Rightarrow C=-\ln 2$

$\Rightarrow y=\ln(y+1)(e^x+1)-\ln 2$

$\Rightarrow y=\ln\left(\frac{(y+1)(e^x+1)}{2}\right)$

At $y=1$

$\Rightarrow 1=\ln(e^x+1)$ $\qquad \Rightarrow e=e^x+1\Rightarrow e^x=e-1$

$\Rightarrow x=\ln(e-1)$

∴ (i)→(c)

(ii) Given differential equation is

$x\frac{dy}{dx}+y=xy^3$

$\Rightarrow\frac{dy}{dx}+\frac{y}{x}=y^3$ $\qquad \Rightarrow\frac{1}{y^3}\frac{dy}{dx}+\frac{1}{y^2}.\frac{1}{x}=1$

$\Rightarrow y^{-3}\frac{dy}{dx}+\frac{1}{x}.y^{-2}=1$ $\qquad$ Put $y^{-2}=t\Rightarrow -2y^{-3}\frac{dy}{dx}=\frac{dt}{dx}$

$\Rightarrow\frac{-1}{2}\frac{dt}{dx}+\frac{1}{x}t=1$

$\Rightarrow\frac{dt}{dx}-\frac{2}{x}t=-2$ ...(i)

It is a L.D.E of first degree

$\Rightarrow$ $I.F.=e^{\int\frac{-2}{x}dx}=e^{-2\ln x}=x^{-2}$

∴ Solution of (i) is given by, $t.x^{-2}=\int(-2)x^{-2}dx+C$

$\Rightarrow t.x^{-2}=-2\left[\frac{x^{-1}}{-1}\right]+c$

$\Rightarrow\frac{t}{x^2}=\frac{2}{x}+c$ $\qquad \Rightarrow\frac{1}{x^2y^2}=\frac{2}{x}+c$

It Passes through(1, 1)

$\Rightarrow 1=2+c\Rightarrow\boxed{C=-1}$ $\qquad \Rightarrow\frac{1}{x^2y^2}=\frac{2}{x}-1$

If it passes through $\left(\frac{3}{2},P\right)$

$\Rightarrow\frac{4}{9p^2}=\frac{4}{3}-1\Rightarrow\frac{1}{p^2}=\frac{9}{4}\left(\frac{1}{3}\right)=\frac{3}{4}$

$\Rightarrow p=\pm\frac{2}{\sqrt{3}}$

∴ (ii) → (d)

(iii) Given, $\frac{dy}{dx}=\frac{xy+y}{xy+x}$

$\frac{dy}{dx}=\frac{(x+1)y}{x(y+1)}$

$\Rightarrow\frac{y+1}{y}dy=\frac{x+1}{x}dx$ $\qquad \Rightarrow\int\left(1+\frac{1}{y}\right)dy=\int\left(1+\frac{1}{x}\right)dx$

$\Rightarrow y+\ln y=x+\ln x+c$

As it passes through (0, 0), It is impossible, i.e., solution is not defined

∴ (iii) → (b)

(iv) Given differential equation is $\frac{dy}{dx}=\frac{3x-4y-2}{3x-4y-3}$

Put $3x-4y=z$

$\Rightarrow 3-4\frac{dy}{dx}=\frac{dz}{dx}$ $\qquad \Rightarrow 4\frac{dy}{dx}=3-\frac{dz}{dx}$

$\Rightarrow\frac{dy}{dx}=\frac{3}{4}-\frac{1}{4}\frac{dz}{dx}$ $\qquad \therefore\frac{3}{4}-\frac{1}{4}\frac{dz}{dx}=\frac{z-2}{z-3}$

$\Rightarrow\frac{1}{4}\frac{dz}{dx}=\frac{3}{4}-\left(\frac{z-2}{z-3}\right)$ $\qquad \Rightarrow\frac{dz}{dx}=4\left[\frac{3(z-3)-4(z-2)}{4(z-3)}\right]$

$\Rightarrow\frac{dz}{dx}=\frac{-z-1}{z-3}$ $\qquad \Rightarrow\frac{z-3}{z+1}dz=-dx$

$\Rightarrow\int\frac{z+1-4}{z+1}dz=-\int dx$ $\qquad \Rightarrow z-4\ln(z+1)=-x+c$

$\Rightarrow(3x-4y)-4\ln(3x-4y+1)=-x+C$

As it passes through (origin)

$\Rightarrow 0-4(0)=-0+C\Rightarrow C=0$

$\Rightarrow(3x-4y)-4\ln(3x-4y+1)=-x$

$\Rightarrow 4(x-y)=4\ln(3x-4y+1)$

$\Rightarrow x-y=\ln(3x-4y+1)$

∴ (iv) → (a)

2. (i)→(c), (ii)→(c), (iii)→(b), (iv)→(a)

(i) Given differential equation is

$y=(c_1+c_2)\cos(x+c_3)-c_4e^{x+c_5}+c_5\sin x$

Let $c_1+c_2=A$ and $c_4e^{c_5}=B$

$\Rightarrow y=A\cos(x+c_3)-Be^x+c_5\sin x$

$\Rightarrow y=A\cos x\cos c_3-A\sin x\sin c_3-Be^x+c_5\sin x$

$\Rightarrow y=A\cos c_3\cos x+(c_5-A\sin c_3)\sin x-Be^x$

$\Rightarrow y=A_1\cos x+A_2\sin x+A_3e^x$

∴ There are exactly 3 Effective parameters

∴ order = 3

∴ (i)→(c)

(ii) $y=a\sin^2x+b\cos^2x+c\sin^2x+d\cos 2x+e\sin x$

$y=(a+c)\left[\frac{1-\cos 2x}{2}\right]+b\left[\frac{1-\cos 2x}{2}\right]+d\cos 2x+e\sin x$

$\Rightarrow y=\left(-\left(\frac{a+c}{2}\right)+\frac{b}{2}+d\right)\cos 2x+e\sin x+\left(\frac{a+c}{2}+\frac{b}{2}\right)$

$\Rightarrow y=A\cos 2x+B\sin x+c$

It has 3 effective arbitrary constants

⇒ order = 3

∴ (ii)→(c),

(iii) Given differential equation is $\dfrac{d^2y}{dx^2}+\left[1+\left(\dfrac{dy}{dx}\right)^2\right]^{3/2}=0$

$$\Rightarrow \frac{d^2y}{dx^2}=-\left(1+\left(\frac{dy}{dx}\right)^2\right)^{3/2} \qquad \Rightarrow \left(\frac{d^2y}{dx^2}\right)^2=\left[1+\left(\frac{dy}{dx}\right)^2\right]^3$$

⇒ Degree=2

∴ (iii)→(b)

(iv) $y=cx+c^2-3c^{3/2}+2$

It has only one effective parameter *'c'*

⇒ Order = 1

∴ (iv)→(a)

3. (i)→(a,d), (ii)→(b), (iii)→(b,d), (iv)→(c)

(i) $\sqrt{x^2+y^2}=y\sqrt{1+\left(\dfrac{dx}{dy}\right)^2}$

$$\Rightarrow x^2+y^2=y^2\left(1+\left(\frac{dx}{dy}\right)^2\right) \Rightarrow \frac{x^2}{y^2}+1=1+\left(\frac{dx}{dy}\right)^2$$

$$\Rightarrow \left(\frac{dx}{dy}\right)^2=\frac{x^2}{y^2} \Rightarrow \frac{dx}{dy}=\pm\frac{x}{y} \qquad \Rightarrow \frac{dx}{x}=\pm\frac{dy}{y}$$

$$\Rightarrow \ln x=\pm\ln y+\ln c$$

$$\Rightarrow \ln x=\ln(yc)\text{ or }\ln\left(\frac{c}{y}\right) \qquad \Rightarrow x=yc \text{ or } xy=c$$

As it passes through (2, 3)

$\Rightarrow 2=3c$ or $(2)(3)=c$

$\Rightarrow x=\dfrac{2}{3}y$ or $xy=6$

⇒ Straight line or hyperbola

∴ (i)→(a), (d)

(ii) Let $P(x, y)$ be any point on the curve, then equation of tangent at $P(x, y)$ to the curve will be $(Y-y)=\dfrac{dy}{dx}(X-x)$

It intersect y-axis, where $X=0$

$$\Rightarrow Y-y=\frac{dy}{dx}(-x) \qquad \Rightarrow Y=y-x\frac{dy}{dx}$$

∴ Tangent at P intersects y-axis at $A\left(0, y-x\dfrac{dy}{dx}\right)$

∴ *A.T.Q.*, $OA=OP$

$$\Rightarrow \left|y-x\frac{dy}{dx}\right|=\sqrt{(x-0)^2+\left(x\frac{dy}{dx}\right)^2}$$

$$\Rightarrow \left(y-x\frac{dy}{dx}\right)^2=x^2+x^2\left(\frac{dy}{dx}\right)^2$$

$$\Rightarrow y^2+x^2\left(\frac{dy}{dx}\right)^2-2xy\frac{dy}{dx} \qquad \Rightarrow x^2+x^2\left(\frac{dy}{dx}\right)^2$$

$$\Rightarrow y^2-2xy\frac{dy}{dx}=x^2 \qquad \Rightarrow 2xy\frac{dy}{dx}=y^2-x^2$$

$$\Rightarrow \frac{dy}{dx}=\frac{y^2-x^2}{2xy} \qquad ...(1)$$

Put $y=vx$

$$\Rightarrow \frac{dy}{dx}=v+x\frac{dv}{dx}$$

$$\Rightarrow v+x\frac{dv}{dx}=\frac{v^2x^2-x^2}{2vx^2} \qquad \Rightarrow v+x\frac{dv}{dx}=\frac{v^2-1}{2v}$$

$$\Rightarrow x\frac{dv}{dx}=\frac{v^2-1-2v^2}{2v} \qquad \Rightarrow x\frac{dv}{dx}=\frac{-1-2v^2}{2v}$$

$$\Rightarrow \frac{2v}{2v^2+1}=\frac{-dx}{x} \qquad \Rightarrow \frac{1}{2}\ln(2v^2+1)=-\ln x+\ln C$$

$$\Rightarrow \sqrt{2v^2+1}=\frac{C}{x} \qquad \Rightarrow 2\left(\frac{y^2}{x^2}+1\right)=\frac{C^2}{x^2}$$

$\Rightarrow 2(x^2+y^2)=C^2$

As it passes through (1, 1)

$\Rightarrow 4=C^2$ ∴ $x^2+y^2=2$

∴ (ii)→(b)

(iii) Length of normal is $y\sqrt{1+\left(\dfrac{dy}{dx}\right)^2}=\sqrt{x^2+y^2}$

$$\Rightarrow y^2\left(1+\frac{dy}{dx}\right)^2=x^2+y^2 \Rightarrow y^2+y^2\left(\frac{dy}{dx}\right)^2=x^2+y^2$$

$$\Rightarrow y^2\left(\frac{dy}{dx}\right)^2=x^2 \qquad \Rightarrow \frac{dy}{dx}=\pm\frac{x}{y}$$

$$\Rightarrow y\,dy=\pm x\,dx \qquad \Rightarrow \frac{y^2}{2}=\pm\frac{x^2}{2}+C$$

$\Rightarrow y^2=\pm x^2+2C$

As it passes through (1, 0)

$\Rightarrow 0=\pm1+2C \qquad \Rightarrow 2C=\mp1$

∴ $y^2=\pm x^2\mp1$

$\Rightarrow y^2-x^2=-1$ or $y^2+x^2=1$ or $x^2-y^2=1$ or $x^2+y^2=1$

⇒ Circle or hyperbola

∴ (iii)→(b), (d)

(iv) Tangent to curve at $P(x, y)$ insects x-axis at $A\left(x-y\dfrac{dx}{dy}, 0\right)$ and insects y-axis at $B\left(0, y-x\dfrac{dy}{dx}\right)$

A.T.Q., B is mid point of AP

$$\Rightarrow 0=\frac{x+\left(x-y\dfrac{dx}{dy}\right)}{2} \text{ and } y-x\frac{dy}{dx}=\frac{0+y}{2}$$

$$\Rightarrow 0=2x-y\frac{dx}{dy} \text{ and } y-2x\frac{dy}{dx}=0$$

$$\Rightarrow 2x=y\frac{dx}{dy} \qquad \Rightarrow \frac{dy}{y}=\frac{dx}{2x}$$

$\Rightarrow \ln y=\ln\sqrt{x}+\ln C \qquad \Rightarrow y=C\sqrt{x}$

As it passes through (2, 1)

$\Rightarrow 1=\sqrt{2}\,C \qquad \Rightarrow C=1/\sqrt{2}$

$$\Rightarrow y=\frac{\sqrt{x}}{\sqrt{2}} \qquad \Rightarrow y^2=\frac{x}{2}$$

⇒ Parabola

∴ (iv)→(c)

SECTION–VIII: (INTEGER TYPE)

1. $y = (C_1 + C_2)\cos(x + C_3) - C_4e^{x+C_5}$

$\Rightarrow y = A[\cos x \cos C_3 - \sin x \sin C_3] - C_4e^{C_5}.e^x$

$\Rightarrow y = (A\cos C_3)\cos x - (A\sin C_3)\sin x - (C_4.e^{C_5}).e^x$

$\Rightarrow y = A_1\cos x + A_2\sin x + A_3 e^x$ which has 3 effective parameters

$\Rightarrow$ Order of corresponding differential equation will be 3.

2. Equation of tangent at $P(x, y)$ to the curve is given by $(Y - y) = \frac{dy}{dx}(X - x)$ ...(1)

It intersects x-axis at $A\left(x - y\frac{dx}{dy}, 0\right)$ and y-axis at $B\left(0, y - x\frac{dy}{dx}\right)$

A.T.Q., P is mid-point of AB

$\Rightarrow 2x = x - y\frac{dx}{dy}$ and $2y = y - x\frac{dy}{dx}$

$\Rightarrow x = -y\frac{dx}{dy}$ $\qquad \Rightarrow \frac{dx}{x} = \frac{-dy}{y}$

$\Rightarrow \ln xy = \ln C$ $\qquad \Rightarrow xy = C$

As it passes through (1, 1)

$\Rightarrow C = 1$ $\qquad \Rightarrow xy = 1$

$\Rightarrow f(1/5) = 5$

3. $\left(\frac{dy}{dx}\right)^2 - x\frac{dy}{dx} + y = 0$

$\Rightarrow y = px - p^2$ ...(1)

If is Clairault's from having solution $y = Cx - C^2$

It is given to be $y = kx - \lambda$

$\Rightarrow y = kx - \lambda$ $\qquad \Rightarrow k = C, \lambda = C^2$

$\Rightarrow k + \lambda = k^2 + k$ $\qquad \Rightarrow$ Least value of $k + \lambda = \frac{-[1]}{4}$

$\Rightarrow k + \lambda \geq (-1/4)$

$\Rightarrow$ Greatest value of $-24(k + \lambda) = 6$

4. $y^2 = 2cx + 2c\sqrt{c}$

$\Rightarrow 2y\frac{dy}{dx} = 2c$

$\Rightarrow c = y\frac{dy}{dx}$

$\therefore \quad y^2 = 2xy\frac{dy}{dx} + 2\left(y\frac{dy}{dx}\right)^{3/2}$

$\Rightarrow y^2 - 2xy\frac{dy}{dx} = 2\left(y\frac{dy}{dx}\right)^{3/2}$

$\Rightarrow \left(y^2 - 2xy\frac{dy}{dx}\right)^2 = 4\left(y\frac{dy}{dx}\right)^3$

$\Rightarrow \left(y - 2x\frac{dy}{dx}\right)^2 = 4y\left(\frac{dy}{dx}\right)^3$

$\Rightarrow$ Order = 1, degree = 3

$\Rightarrow n = 1, m = 3$

$\Rightarrow n + m = 4$

5. $(1+t)\frac{dy}{dt} - ty = 1$

$\Rightarrow \frac{dy}{dt} - \frac{t}{1+t}y = \frac{1}{(1+t)}$ ...(1)

It is a L.D.E., having $I.F. = e^{\int -\frac{t}{1+t}dt} = e^{-\int\left(1-\frac{1}{1+t}\right)dt} = e^{-t + \ln(1+t)}$ $= (1 + t).e^{-t}$

$\therefore$ Solution of (1) is given by $y(1+t).e^{-t} = \int 1\frac{(1+t).e^{-t}}{(1+t)}dt$

or $y(1+t).e^{-t} = \frac{e^{-t}}{-1}$ or $y = \frac{-1}{(1+t)}$

$\Rightarrow y(1) = \frac{-1}{2}$

$\Rightarrow |2y(1)| = 1$

6. At any instant 't' volume of liquid in case $= \frac{1}{3}\pi r^2 h$ surface area in contact $= \pi r^2$

$\therefore$ A.T.Q. $\frac{dv}{dt} = -k\pi r^2;\ k > 0$

$\Rightarrow \frac{d}{dt}\left(\frac{1}{3}\pi r^2 h\right) = -k\pi r^2$

$\Rightarrow \frac{1}{3}\pi\frac{d}{dt}(r^2 h) = -k\pi r^2$ ...(1)

Also, $\frac{R}{r} = \frac{H}{h}$

$\Rightarrow h = \frac{Hr}{R}$

$\therefore$ from (1), $\frac{1}{3}\pi\frac{d}{dt}\left(\frac{Hr^3}{R}\right) = -k\pi r^2$

$\Rightarrow \frac{1}{3}H\frac{\pi}{R}(3r^2)\frac{dr}{dt} = -k\pi r^2$

$\Rightarrow \frac{H}{R}\frac{dr}{dt} = -k$ $\qquad \Rightarrow dr = -\frac{KR}{H}dt$

$\Rightarrow r = \frac{-K}{H}Rt + C$

When $t = 0$, $r = R$

$\Rightarrow R = C$ $\qquad \Rightarrow r = \frac{-K}{H}Rt + R$

Where $r = 0$ (when the vessel is empty)

$\Rightarrow \frac{KRt}{H} = R$ $\qquad \Rightarrow t = \frac{H}{K} = 16$

($\because$ H = 16 k given)

7. $y = y(z)$ and $\frac{2+\sin x}{y+1}\left(\frac{dy}{dx}\right) = -\cos x$

$\Rightarrow \frac{dy}{y+1} = \frac{-\cos x}{2+\sin x}dx$

$\Rightarrow \ln(y + 1) = -\ln(2 + \sin x) + \ln C$

$\Rightarrow (y + 1)(2 + \sin x) = C$

$\Rightarrow y(0) = 1$ $\qquad \Rightarrow (2)(2) = C$

$\Rightarrow C = 4 \qquad \Rightarrow (y + 1)(2 + \sin x) = 4$

$\therefore \left(y\left(-\frac{\pi}{2}\right)+1\right)(2-1) = 4$

$\Rightarrow y\left(-\frac{\pi}{2}\right) = 3$

8. $x\,dy = y\,dx + y^2\,dy$

$\Rightarrow \frac{xdy - ydx}{y^2} = dy \qquad \Rightarrow \frac{ydx - xdy}{y^2} = -dy$

$\Rightarrow d\left(\frac{x}{y}\right) = -dy \qquad \Rightarrow \frac{x}{y} = -y + C$

Given $y(1) = 1$

$\Rightarrow 1 = -1 + C \qquad \Rightarrow C = 2$

$\Rightarrow x/y = 2 - y$

At $x = -3$, $-3 = 2y - y^2$

$\Rightarrow y^2 - 2y - 3 = 0 \qquad \Rightarrow$ Sum of roots = 2

9. $(x^2 + y^2)dy = xy\,dx$

$\Rightarrow \frac{dy}{dx} = \frac{xy}{x^2 + y^2}$

Put $y = vx$

$\Rightarrow \frac{dy}{dx} = v + x\frac{dv}{dx} \qquad \Rightarrow v + x\frac{dv}{dx} = \frac{v}{1+v^2}$

$\Rightarrow x\frac{dv}{dx} = \frac{v - v - v^3}{1+v^2} \qquad \Rightarrow x\frac{dv}{dx} = \frac{-v^3}{1+v^2}$

$\Rightarrow \frac{1+v^2}{v^3}dv = \frac{-dx}{x} \qquad \Rightarrow \frac{v^{-2}}{-2} + \ln v = -\ln x + C$

$\Rightarrow -\frac{1}{2v^2} + \ln vx = C \qquad \Rightarrow -\frac{1}{2y^2}.x^2 + \ln y = C$

Given $y(1) = 1$

$\Rightarrow 0 = 1/2 + C \qquad \Rightarrow C = -1/2$

$\therefore \ln y = \frac{x^2}{2y^2} - \frac{1}{2}$

$\Rightarrow \ln e = \frac{x_{(0)}^{\;2}}{2e^2} - \frac{1}{2} \qquad (\because f(x_0) = e)$

$\Rightarrow 1 = \frac{x_0^2}{2e^2} - \frac{1}{2} \qquad \Rightarrow x_0^2 = 2e^2\left(\frac{3}{2}\right)$

$\Rightarrow x_0^{\;2} = 3e^2 \qquad \Rightarrow x_0 = \sqrt{3}\,e$

$\Rightarrow k = 3$

10. Equation of any tangent to curve at $P(x, y)$ is given by $(Y - y) = \frac{dy}{dx}(X - x)$

It intersects x-axis at $A\left(x - y\frac{dx}{dy}, 0\right)$ and y-axis at $B\left(0, y - x\frac{dy}{dx}\right)$

$$\Rightarrow (x, y) = \left(\frac{3(0) + \left(x - y\frac{dx}{dy}\right)}{4}, \frac{3\left(y - x\frac{dy}{dx}\right)}{4}\right)$$

$$\Rightarrow (x, y) = \left(\frac{x - y\frac{dx}{dy}}{4}, \frac{3\left(y - x\frac{dy}{dx}\right)}{4}\right)$$

$\Rightarrow 4x = x - y\frac{dy}{dx},\; 4y = 3y - 3x\frac{dy}{dx}$

$\Rightarrow 3x = -y\frac{dx}{dy},\; y = -3x\frac{dy}{dx}$

$\Rightarrow \frac{dy}{y} = -\frac{1}{3}\frac{dx}{x} \qquad \Rightarrow \ln y = -\frac{1}{3}\ln x + C$

$\Rightarrow \ln xy^3 = C$

It passes through (1, 1)

$\Rightarrow C = 0$

$\therefore \ln xy^3 = 0$

$\Rightarrow xy^3 = 1$

It passes through $\left(\frac{1}{8}, \lambda\right)$

$\Rightarrow \frac{1}{8}(\lambda)^3 = 1 \qquad \Rightarrow \lambda^3 = 8$

$\Rightarrow \lambda = (8)^{1/3} = 2$